W9-AYR-745

STANDARD CATALOG SERIES

JULIETTE YAAKOV, GENERAL EDITOR

CHILDREN'S CATALOG

FICTION CATALOG

MIDDLE AND JUNIOR HIGH SCHOOL

  LIBRARY CATALOG

PUBLIC LIBRARY CATALOG

SENIOR HIGH SCHOOL LIBRARY CATALOG

CHILDREN'S CATALOG

SEVENTEENTH EDITION

CHILDREN'S CATALOG

SEVENTEENTH EDITION

EDITED BY

ANNE PRICE

AND

JULIETTE YAAKOV

NEW YORK AND DUBLIN
THE H. W. WILSON COMPANY
1996

12420030

Copyright © 1996 by The H. W. Wilson Company. All rights reserved. No
part of this work may be reproduced or copied in any form or by any means,
including but not restricted to graphic, electronic, or mechanical—for example,
photocopying, recording, taping, or information storage and retrieval systems—
without the express written permission of the Publisher.

Printed in the United States of America

Library of Congress Cataloging-in-Publication Data

Children's catalog / edited by Anne Price and Juliette
Yaakov. — 17th ed.

p.   cm. — (Standard catalog series)

Includes index.

ISBN 0-8242-0893-5 (lib. bdg.)

1. Children's literature—Bibliography.   2. Cataloging of children's
literature—Specimens.   3. Children's literature—Book lists.   4. School
libraries—Book lists.   I. Price, Anne, 1946- .   II. Yaakov, Juliette.   III. Series.

Z1037.C5443   1996
[PN1009.A1]
011.62—dc20

96-34846
CIP

PREFACE

Children's Catalog is a comprehensive list of fiction and nonfiction books and magazines for children from preschool through grade six, along with review sources and other professional aids for children's librarians and school media specialists. It includes analytical entries for parts of books and a select list of recommended electronic resources. Annual supplements to this volume will be published in 1997, 1998, 1999 and 2000.

Preparation. In preparing this edition The H.W. Wilson Company has benefited from the work of two groups of experts in library service to children. An advisory committee of distinguished librarians reevaluated the previous edition of the Catalog and its supplements and proposed many new titles. The list that resulted from the committee's deliberations was then submitted to a group of experienced librarians familiar with the needs of children. This group, representing diverse geographical areas, elected the titles included. In most cases their vote represents the composite judgment of a number of their colleagues.

Scope and Purpose. The Catalog lists books and magazines for children from preschool through sixth grade. With this edition a separate section listing essential reference works published on CD-ROM has been added. The availability of a CD-ROM version of a print equivalent continues to be indicated in the entry for the print version. Sources for the librarian or school media specialist include works on the history and development of children's literature; literary criticism; bibliographies; selection aids; guides to the operation of media centers; and periodicals relating to library science, reviewing, and education.

The seventeenth edition includes 6,971 titles and 6,732 analytical entries. Four annual supplements are intended for use with this volume. Libraries and media centers serving large systems or users with special needs will undoubtedly wish to augment this list. To accommodate the precocious child the reader is referred to *Middle and Junior High School Library Catalog.*

Books listed were published in the United States, or published in Canada or the United Kingdom and distributed in the United States. A small number of out-of-print titles that were considered essential to a well-rounded collection have been retained at the suggestion of the advisory committee. They are noted as o.p. All other titles were in print at the time of listing. Paperbacks are included when the hardcover edition has gone out of print or if a work was originally published in paper. Those concerned about the durability of paperbound editions may wish to utilize a commercial rebinding service.

The advisory committee found that monographs covering the history and geography of some countries were outdated, inaccurate or unavailable. The committee recommends the use of electronic media, current reference tools and periodical articles for such information. The folklore section has been greatly expanded to reflect the prominence of folk tales in multicultural education. Access under publishers' series has been added to the Index. The convention of citing the first book in a fiction series in full with brief listings for other works in the series has been retained. In cases where more than one edition of a title illustrated by a notable artist is available, a listing of editions is provided with complete ordering information. Notes specify prizes or medals won, indicate the availability of large print editions, and identify sequels or companion volumes.

The catalog excludes the following: textbooks; nonprint materials, with the exception of CD-ROMs; board books, pop-up and similar novelty items; and non-English-language materials, except for dictionaries and bilingual works. A non-English version of an English-language work is cited in the main entry for the work and is also listed in the Index under an appropriate heading such as "Spanish-language editions."

Organization. The Catalog consists of four parts. Part 1, the Classified Catalog, is arranged according to the Dewey Decimal Classification. Items have been classified according to the twelfth abridged edition. Fiction, story collections, and easy books follow the nonfiction classes. Within classes, arrangement is by main entry, with complete bibliographical information supplied for each book. Prices have been obtained from publishers and are as current as possible. Grade level designation, suggested subject headings based on *Sears List of Subject Headings,* a descriptive annotation, and an evaluation, frequently from a quoted source, are also included.

Part 2, the Author, Title, Subject, and Analytical Index, serves as a comprehensive key to the classified list. With this edition, entries under publishers' series have been added. Analytical entries, which provide indexing for parts of works, are an important feature of the Catalog. Subject analytics afford access to parts of books not covered by the subject headings for the whole, while author and title analytics provide an approach to anthologies and collections, especially of stories and tales. In a time of restricted funding they aid in maximizing use of the library's holdings.

Part 3, Select List of Recommended CD-ROM Reference Works, is new to the Catalog. It consists chiefly of interactive multimedia resources of high quality and reference value.

Part 4, Directory of Publishers and Distributors, includes fuller information about the publishers of the books listed.

The section that follows, How to Use Children's Catalog, contains more detailed information about the uses, content and arrangement of the Catalog.

Acknowledgments. The H.W. Wilson Company is indebted to the publishers who supplied copies of their books and information about editions and prices. The Company is grateful to Suzanne W. Hawley, media specialist at Laurel Oak Elementary School, Naples, Florida, for assistance in the selection of electronic resources. This Catalog could not have been published without the efforts of the advisory committee and the consultants who gave so generously of their time and expertise. Their names appear below.

The advisory committee comprised:

Amy Kellman, Chair
    Program Specialist
    Children's Services
    Carnegie Library of Pittsburgh
        Pittsburgh, Pa.

Joan L. Atkinson, Associate Professor
    University of Alabama School of Library
        & Information Studies
    Tuscaloosa, Ala.

Suzanne W. Hawley, Media Specialist
    Laurel Oak Elementary School
    Naples, Fla.

Sara L. Miller, Library Director
    Rye Country Day School
    Rye, N.Y.

Kathleen F. Odean, Librarian
    Moses Brown School
    Providence, R.I.

Connie C. Rockman, Children's
        Literature Consultant
    Stratford, Conn.

Lucinda Frances Ware, Branch Manager
    Catonsville Library
    Baltimore County Public Library System
    Catonsville, Md.

The following consultants participated in the voting:

Barbara Barstow, Children's
    Services Manager
  Cuyahoga County Public Library
  Parma, Ohio

Jane Botham, Coordinator of
    Children's Services
  Milwaukee Public Library
  Milwaukee, Wis.

Julie Cummins, Coordinator
  Children's Services
  New York Public Library
  New York, N.Y.

Eileen Dunne, Coordinator of
    Library Services
  Abilene Independent School District
  Abilene, Tex.

Barbara Feldstein, Coordinator of
    Library Services
  Newton Public Schools
  Newton, Mass.

Helma Hawkins, Director
  Children's Services
  Kansas City Public Library
  Kansas City, Mo.

Barbara Howell, Librarian
  Increase Miller Elementary School
  Goldens Bridge, N.Y.

Marilyn Kaye, Associate Professor
  Division of Library & Information Science
  St. John's University
  Jamaica, N.Y.

Linda Perkins, Library Services
    Manager
  Children's Services
  Berkeley Public Library
  Berkeley, Calif.

Connie C. Rockman, Children's
    Literature Consultant
  Stratford, Conn.

Maria B. Salvadore, Coordinator
  Children's Services
  District of Columbia Public Library
  Washington, D.C.

Frances V. Sedney, Coordinator
  Children's Services
  Harford County Library
  Belcamp, Md.

HOW TO USE CHILDREN'S CATALOG

Children's Catalog is arranged in four parts: Part 1. Classified Catalog; Part 2. Author, Title, Subject, and Analytical Index; Part 3. Select List of Recommended CD-ROM Reference Works; Part 4. Directory of Publishers and Distributors.

USES OF THE CATALOG

Children's Catalog is designed to serve these purposes:

As an aid in purchasing. The annotations and grade level designation provided for each work in the Classified Catalog, along with information concerning publisher, ISBN, price, and availability, are intended to assist in the selection and ordering of titles. Arrangement of the Classified Catalog according to the Dewey Decimal Classification expedites the process of identifying elements of the collection that should be strengthened or updated. A separate section lists recommended reference works published in CD-ROM format. Evaluation of the suitability of a particular work will always take into account the special character of the children, the school, and the community that the library or media center serves. It is inadvisable, of course, to depend upon a single source for materials selection.

As an aid in user service. Reference work and user service are furthered by information about grade level, sequels, companion volumes and by the descriptive and critical annotations in the Classified Catalog, as well as the series and subject approach in the Index. In addition, the Index includes entries under names of illustrators, form headings such as "Large print books," and headings for Newbery and Caldecott medal winners. Analytical entries augment the local catalog by providing access to parts of composite works.

As an aid in verification of information. Full bibliographical data, recommended subject headings based upon *Sears List of Subject Headings*, a suggested classification derived from the *Abridged Dewey Decimal Classification and Relative Index*, and notes that describe editions available, awards, and publication history are provided for this purpose.

As an aid in curriculum support. The classified approach, subject indexing, annotations, and grade level designations are helpful in identifying materials appropriate for classroom use.

As an aid in collection maintenance. Items elected to this edition of the Catalog comprise newly published works along with works listed in the previous edition or its supplements that have retained their usefulness. Information about the range of titles available in a field facilitates decisions to rebind, replace, or discard materials in the library's collection.

As an instructional aid. The Catalog is useful in courses that deal with children's literature and book selection, particularly on the preschool and elementary level.

DESCRIPTION OF THE CATALOG
Part 1. Classified Catalog

The Classified Catalog is arranged with the nonfiction books first, classified by the Dewey Decimal Classification in numerical order from 000 to 999. Individual biographies are classed in 92 and follow the 920's (collective biography). Three sections follow the nonfiction: Fiction, denoted by the symbol "Fic";

Story Collections, denoted by "S C"; and Easy Books, consisting chiefly of picture books of interest to children from preschool to grade three, denoted by "E."

An Outline of Classification, which serves as a table of contents to the Classified Catalog, is reproduced on page 2. Many books may properly be classified in more than one discipline. If a particular title is not found where it might be expected, the Index should be consulted to determine if the work is classified elsewhere.

Within classes, works are arranged alphabetically under main entry, usually the author. An exception is made for works of individual biography, classed in 92, which are arranged alphabetically under the name of the person written about.

Following is a sample entry and a description of the components of a typical entry:

> **Pringle, Laurence P.**
> Vanishing ozone; protecting earth from ultra-violet radiation; [by] Laurence Pringle. Morrow Junior Bks. 1995 64p il $16; lib bdg $15.93 (4 and up)   **363.7**
> 1. Ozone layer
> ISBN 0-688-04157-4; 0-688-04158-2 (lib bdg)
>   LC 94-25928
>
> "A Save-the-earth book"
> This is an "introduction to the science and politics of the ozone layer. A history of the scientific study of ozone includes names of major scientists and the titles of their published articles. The political side of the debate includes reactions of elected officials and members of the chemical industry." Horn Book Guide
> "The organization is excellent. . . . Technical terms are well balanced. . . . Crisp black-and-white photographs, diagrams, and maps illustrate the text. Concluding chapters offer suggestions for taking action and include addresses for government agencies and environmental groups." SLJ
>
> Includes glossary and bibliography

The name of the author, which is inverted and printed in bold face type, is given in conformity with *Anglo-American Cataloguing Rules,* 2nd edition, 1988 revision, with 1993 Amendments. It is followed by the title, subtitle, responsibility statement, edition, and publisher. For further information about the publisher, refer to the Directory of Publishers and Distributors. Next are the date of publication, pagination, illustration note, series note, price, binding and grade level. Prices given were current when the Catalog went to press. As time passes they should be confirmed with the publisher.

The figure printed in bold face on the last line of type in the body of the entry is the classification number derived from the *Abridged Dewey Decimal Classification.* A numbered term is a recommended subject heading for this book. In some instances subject headings assigned to the entire book will not show that portions of the book deal with more specific topics. In such cases subject analytic entries are made. All subject headings are based on *Sears List of Subject Headings.*

The ISBN (International Standard Book Number) or ISSN (International Standard Serial Number) is included to facilitate ordering. The Library of Congress control (card) number is provided when available.

Notes supply additional information about the book. Most entries include both a note describing the book's content and a critical note, which is useful in evaluating books for selection and in determining which of several books on the same subject is best suited for the individual reader. Other notes list special features or describe sequels and companion volumes, editions available, awards, and publication history.

Part 2. Author, Title, Subject, and Analytical Index

This is an alphabetical index of all the books entered in the Catalog. Each book is entered under author; title, if distinctive; and subject, with added entries for joint author, illustrator, editor, and publisher's series as necessary. Also included are subject, author, and title analytics for parts of composite works. The classification number in bold face type is the key to the location of the main entry of the book in the Classified Catalog. Works classed in 92, individual biography, will be found under the name of the person written about.

Entries are also made under headings that indicate form or publication characteristics such as "Large print books," "American Library Association publications," "Caldecott medal titles," and "Spanish language editions." Books that are also published in a CD-ROM version are listed under "CD-ROM." The user interested in electronic resources should also consult Part 3, Select List of Recommended CD-ROM Reference Works.

"See" references are made from forms of names or subjects not used as headings. "See also" references are made to related or more specific headings. The suggested grade level of a book is repeated in the Index.

Examples of entries for the book cited above:

Author	**Pringle, Laurence P.** Vanishing ozone (4 and up)	**363.7**
Title	**Vanishing** ozone. Pringle, L. P.	**363.7**
Subject	**Ozone layer** Pringle, L. P. Vanishing ozone (4 and up)	**363.7**
Publisher's series	**Save-the-earth book [series]** Pringle, L. P. Vanishing ozone	**363.7**

Examples of other types of entries:

Joint author	**McKissack, Fredrick, 1939-** (jt. auth) McKissack, P. C. African-American inventors	**920**
Illustrator	**Pinkney, Brian** (il) Pinkney, A. D. Seven candles for Kwanzaa	**394.2**
Editor	**Opie, Iona Archibald** (ed) I saw Esau. See I saw Esau	**398.8**
Author analytic	**Godden, Rumer, 1907-** The story of Holly and Ivy (2-4) *also in* Godden, R. Four dolls p68-106	**Fic** **S C**
Title analytic	The **story** of Holly and Ivy. Godden, R. *also in* Godden, R. Four dolls p68-106	**Fic** **S C**
Subject analytic	**Aaron, Hank, 1934-** *See/See also pages in the following book(s):* Kramer, S. Baseball's greatest hitters p38-45 (2-4)	**920**

Part 3. Select List of Recommended CD-ROM Reference Works

The resources on this list are largely interactive multimedia. The list is highly selective and is limited to items of superior quality and reference value.

Entries in the Classified Catalog for books that are also available in a CD-ROM version contain a note to that effect.

Bibliographic information includes the title, edition, publisher's name and address, date, an indication that the work has sound capability and is in color, and price. A system requirements note and descriptive annotation follow. Versions, prices and system requirements of electronic media are subject to frequent change and should be checked with the publisher.

Part 4. Directory of Publishers and Distributors

This Directory provides the full name, address, telephone number, and other pertinent information about the publisher or distributor of the books listed.

TABLE OF CONTENTS

PART 1

CLASSIFIED CATALOG

Outline of Classification

Reproduced below is the Second Summary of the Dewey Decimal Classification.* Part 1 of the Catalog is arranged according to the Dewey schedules and the outline thus serves as a table of contents. Fiction (Fic), Story collections (S C), and Easy books (E) have been added at the end of the summary since these sections are included in the Catalog following the nonfiction classes.

* Reproduced from the Dewey Decimal Classification Abridged Edition 12, published in 1990, by permission of Forest Press, a division of OCLC Online Computer Library Center, owner of copyright.

CHILDREN'S CATALOG

SEVENTEENTH EDITION

CLASSIFIED CATALOG

000 GENERALITIES

001.9 Controversial knowledge

Graham, Ian, 1953-
Fakes and forgeries. Raintree Steck-Vaughn
Pubs. 1995 46p il (Science spotlight) $22.80 (5
and up) **001.9**
1. Fraud 2. Science
ISBN 0-8114-3843-0 LC 94-13834
This book "presents information on scandals throughout
history that have resulted from forgery. Chapters on false
sightings of flying saucers, the Loch Ness monster, counter-
feit money, and the discovery of the forged Hitler Diaries
are included." SLJ
"The fundamental skepticism inherent in scientific inquiry is deftly illustrated in this slim volume. The young reader is challenged to seek further data on unresolved puzzles.
The topics presented are wide ranging." Sci Books Films
Includes glossary and bibliography

Landau, Elaine
The Loch Ness monster. Millbrook Press
1993 48p il (Mysteries of science) lib bdg
$14.90 (3-5) **001.9**
1. Loch Ness monster
ISBN 1-56294-347-2 LC 92-35145
Introduces the folklore and reported sightings of the unidentified creature known as the Loch Ness Monster and
evaluates the evidence for and against its existence
This book is "of value in a library of science. . . . Photographs and illustrations are all very good." Appraisal
Includes glossary and bibliography

Sasquatch; wild man of the woods.
Millbrook Press 1993 47p il (Mysteries of
science) lib bdg $14.90 (3-5) **001.9**
1. Sasquatch
ISBN 1-56294-348-0 LC 92-35144
Introduces the unidentified apelike Sasquatch said to
dwell in the Pacific Northwest, recounts sightings throughout history, and discusses the evidence and theories advanced about its existence
"Balancing disproved evidence with possible valid reports, the text . . . fosters an open mind about the subject."
SLJ
Includes glossary and bibliography

Yeti; abominable snowman of the
Himalayas. Millbrook Press 1993 47p il
(Mysteries of science) lib bdg $14.90 (3-5)
001.9
1. Yeti
ISBN 1-56294-349-9 LC 92-35147

Introduces the Yeti or Abominable Snowman of the Himalayas, recounts sightings throughout history, and considers the reliability of the evidence advanced as proof of its
existence
"Landau has done a good job of factually treating these
mysterious beings . . . reporting the folklore, claimed sightings and scientific findings in an interesting way that does
not sensationalize." Appraisal
Includes glossary and bibliography

Randles, Jenny
World's best "true" UFO stories; [by] Jenny
Randles & Peter A. Hough; illustrated by
Jason Hurst. Sterling 1994 96p il $13.95; pa
$4.95 (5 and up) **001.9**
1. Unidentified flying objects
ISBN 0-8069-1258-8; 0-8069-1259-6 (pa)
LC 94-19807
This book includes "20 accounts of UFO sightings and
human encounters with presumably alien life. . . . In the
preface, the authors urge open-mindedness on the parts of
believers and skeptics alike. One-third of the well-detailed
stories are the de rigueur standards found in similar collections. . . . One of this title's most notable features is a finely
detailed name, place, and subject index." SLJ

Walker, Paul Robert
Bigfoot and other legendary creatures;
illustrated by William Noonan. Harcourt
Brace Jovanovich 1991 56p il map $15.95
(4-6) **001.9**
1. Monsters
ISBN 0-15-207147-4 LC 90-45856
Explores the myths and scientific inquiries surrounding
repeated sightings of such legendary creatures as the Loch
Ness monster, Bigfoot, and the Yeti

004 Data processing. Computer science

Miller, Elizabeth B.
The Internet resource directory for K-12
teachers and librarians. Libraries Unlimited pa
$29.75 **004**
1. Internet (Computer network) 2. Information
systems—Directories
Annual. First published 1994 for 1994-1995
This directory "provides details on accessing more than
400 discussion groups, electronic books and newspapers,
lesson plans, and a variety of other teaching resources by E-
mail, gopher, telnet, and FTP. . . . The directory proper is
arranged under broad curricular areas plus resources for educators, reference, and school library media applications.
Each of these is further divided by narrower disciplines. . .

Miller, Elizabeth B.—*Continued*
. Recommended for all school library media centers." Booklist

Simpson, Carol Mann, 1949-
Internet for library media specialists. Linworth Pub. 1995 144p il (Professional growth series) $23.95   **004**

1. Internet (Computer network)
ISBN 0-938865-39-0   LC 94-45791
This book "opens with an explanation of the nature and history of the Internet. Sample screens accompany clear explanations of diverse features and utilities. . . . With growing concerns about children accessing inappropriate material on the Internet, the section on acceptable use policies will be helpful to librarians." SLJ
Includes bibliographical references

Spencer, Donald D., 1931-
Illustrated computer dictionary for young people. Camelot 1995 117p il pa $16.95
    004

1. Computers—Dictionaries   2. Electronic data processing—Dictionaries
ISBN 0-89218-245-8   LC 94-44181
This dictionary contains some 700 entries covering all areas of computer science, including artificial intelligence, computer graphics, computer networks and desktop publishing

Webster's New World dictionary of computer terms; compiled by Donald Spencer. Macmillan pa $9.95   **004**

1. Computers—Dictionaries   2. Electronic data processing—Dictionaries
First edition compiled by Laura Darcy and Louise Boston published 1983 by Simon & Schuster. (5th edition 1994) Frequently revised
This dictionary defines "more than 5,000 of the most frequently used computer terms. Headwords range from 'A: drive' to 'zooming,' with almost any conceivable computer-related term in between. . . . A useful desk reference for all levels of readers." Choice [review of 1992 edition]

011   General bibliographies

Encyclopedias, atlases & dictionaries; Marion Sader, Amy Lewis, editors; Charles A. Bunge [et al.], consultants. Bowker 1995 495p il maps (Bowker buying guide series) $85   **011**

1. Encyclopedias and dictionaries—Bibliography 2. Atlases—Bibliography
ISBN 0-8352-3669-2   LC 95-6195
An updated, combined edition of Reference books for young readers and General reference books for adults, both published 1988
This guide offers evaluations of some 200 general encyclopedias, world atlases, and general dictionaries, in print and electronic formats, for children and adults. Topical reference works are not included

011.6   General bibliographies of works for specific kinds of users

Adventuring with books; a booklist for pre-K—grade 6; edited by Julie M. Jensen, Nancy L. Roser. 10th ed. National Council of Teachers of English 1993 603p il (NCTE bibliography series) pa $19.95   **011.6**

1. Children's literature—Bibliography 2. Books and reading—Best books
ISBN 0-8141-0079-1   LC 93-30112
New edition in preparation
First published 1950. Editors vary
This work contains "summaries of nearly 1,800 children's books published between 1988 and 1992. . . . These summaries contain brief synopses of each book's plot or contents, full bibliographic information, the ISBN number for each book, the total page count, and, when appropriate, information on illustrations, applications in the classroom, and book awards." Publisher's note
For a review see: Booklist, April 15, 1994

American Library Association best of the best for children; books, magazines, videos, audio, software, toys, travel; Denise Perry Donavin, editor. Random House 1992 366p il hardcover o.p. paperback available $20
    011.6

1. Children's literature—Bibliography 2. Audiovisual materials—Bibliography 3. Books and reading—Best books
ISBN 0-679-74250-6 (pa)   LC 92-24234
The book recommends "around 1500 items. Recent books, magazines, videos, music and storytelling audio cassettes, software, toys, games, and travel activities are included for children from infancy through early teens." Publisher's note

Barstow, Barbara
Beyond picture books; a guide to first readers; [by] Barbara Barstow, Judith Riggle. 2nd ed. Bowker 1995 501p $52.25   **011.6**

1. Children's literature—Bibliography 2. Books and reading—Best books
ISBN 0-8352-3519-X   LC 94-49731
First published 1989
This "annotated bibliography, arranged by author's last name, provides full bibliographic information (except price) as well as series note, subjects, and reading category. If a title is out of print, it is so noted. The annotations are brief, ranging from 20 to 50 words. They give a brief summary of contents, note illustrations, and occasionally have a critical comment." Booklist

Best books for children: preschool through grade 6; John T. Gillespie and Corinne J. Naden, editors. 5th ed. Bowker 1994 1411p $58   **011.6**

1. Children's literature—Bibliography 2. Books and reading—Best books
ISBN 0-8352-3455-X   LC 94-12278
First published 1978

Best books for children: preschool through grade 6—*Continued*

"Aims 'to provide a list of books, gathered from a number of sources, that are highly recommended to satisfy both a child's recreational reading needs and the demands of a typical school curriculum.'—*Pref.* Classed arrangement with author/illustrator, title, and subject indexes, plus a list of biographical subjects." Guide to Ref Books. 11th edition

Books for children. Library of Congress pa $1
011.6

1. Children's literature—Bibliography 2. Books and reading—Best books

ISSN 0882-5343

Annual. First published 1964 with title: Children's books

Compiled by the Children's Literature Center of the Library of Congress

This annotated list of recommended books for preschool through junior high school age children is arranged by categories such as: picture books and picture stories; stories for the middle group; fiction for older readers; folklore; poetry, rhymes, songs and plays; art and hobbies; biography; history, people, and places; nature and science. Reading levels are indicated

Dreyer, Sharon Spredemann

The best of Bookfinder; a guide to children's literature about interests and concerns of youth aged 2-18. American Guidance Service 1992 xxi, 451p $89.95; pa $19.95
011.6

1. Children's literature—Bibliography

ISBN 0-88671-440-0; 0-88671-439-7 (pa)

LC 91-76898

"This volume describes 676 children's books selected from volumes 1-3 [of the Bookfinder, entered below] that are still useful. . . . Libraries and media centers having the original volumes will want to have *The Best of Bookfinder*, since outdated material has been dropped. Those who do not have the original volumes will certainly want this selected volume." Booklist

The bookfinder; a guide to children's literature about the needs and problems of youth aged 2-15. American Guidance Service 1977-1989 4v v1-3 o.p.; v4-5 ea $89.95, pa $49.95
011.6

1. Children's literature—Bibliography

LC 78-105919

Volumes 1-2, 4 issued in a split-page format

Volume 5 has subtitle: A guide to children's literature about the needs and problems of youth aged 2-18

Contents: [v1 Annotations of books published through 1974]; v2 Annotations of books published 1975-1978; v3 Annotations of books published 1979 through 1982; v4 Annotations of books published 1983 through 1986 (ISBN 0-913476-50-1; 0-913476-51-X); v5 Annotations of books published 1987 through 1990 (ISBN 0-88671-168-1; 0-88671-169-X)

Each volume contains an annotated section, arranged alphabetically by author, and a subject section which arranges the titles under 450 psychological, behavioral, and developmental topics important to children and young people

"This set is invaluable for teachers, librarians, parents, and for students themselves." Peterson. Ref Books for Child. 4th edition

The **Elementary** school library collection; a guide to books and other media, phases 1-2-3. Brodart $139.95
011.6

1. Classified catalogs 2. Children's literature—Bibliography 3. Audiovisual materials—Catalogs 4. School libraries—Catalogs

Also available CD-ROM version

First published 1965. Revised biennially

This is "a core collection of currently available books, nonprint media, magazines, and professional reference materials for elementary schools (K-6). The classified (DDC plus fiction and easy) arrangement, fully cataloged entries, and indexes make ESLC a media catalog as well as a selection tool. . . . Entries give full cataloging data, prices, Fry readability level and interest level codes, acquisition phase, concise annotations, and subject headings. Author, title, and subject indexes are appended." Wynar. Guide to Ref Books for Sch Media Cent. 3d edition

Fiction, folklore, fantasy & poetry for children, 1876-1985. Bowker 1986 2v o.p.
011.6

1. Children's literature—Bibliography

LC 84-20474

Contents: v 1 Authors; illustrators; v2 Titles; awards

This "is a comprehensive listing of children's literature published over the last century. The 133,000 entries, taken from the *Publisher's Trade List Annual* and verified in other sources, are listed by author, title, and illustrator. A fourth section lists the year-by-year winners of 20 major children's-book awards. Entries, in a format similar to Bowker's *Books in Print*, give the title, author or editor, illustrator, their birth and death dates, series, pagination, publication date, LC card number, ISBN, publisher, and other information when available." Am Libr

For younger readers: braille and talking books. Library of Congress. Natl. Lib. Service for the Blind & Physically Handicapped pa gratis
011.6

1. Blind—Books and reading—Bibliography 2. Talking books—Bibliography 3. Children's literature—Bibliography

ISSN 0093-2825

Biennial. First published 1964

"Arranged by the broad topics Nonfiction, Fiction, Very Young Readers, and Young Adults, the bibliography is further broken down by subject with separate listings for Cassettes, Braille, and Handcopied Braille. Entries give title, author, date, order number, and a paragraph-long annotation." Peterson. Ref Books for Child. 4th edition

Freeman, Judy

Books kids will sit still for; the complete read-aloud guide. 2nd ed. Bowker 1990 660p il $45
011.6

1. Children's literature—Bibliography 2. Books and reading—Best books

ISBN 0-8352-3010-4

LC 90-2373

First published 1984 by Alleyside Press

"This work offers inventive ways to introduce children to books. There are chapters on storytelling, using nonfiction and biography; booktalks; creative dramatics, pantomime, and readers' theater; and ways to celebrate books, such as debates, awards, and workshops. The main body of the guide recommends 2,100 read-aloud books. . . . Each entry includes a brief plot summary, numerous suggested activities, related titles, and a subject designation." Nichols. Guide to Ref Books for Sch Media Cent. 4th edition

Freeman, Judy—*Continued*

More books kids will sit still for; a read-aloud guide. Bowker 1995 869p il $45; pa $29.95   **011.6**

1. Children's literature—Bibliography 2. Books and reading—Best books
ISBN 0-8352-3520-3; 0-8352-3731-1 (pa)
LC 95-36760

Beginning with a manual on reading aloud, booktalking, storytelling and other ways to use books with children, this book goes on to list more than 1,400 titles, mostly from 1990-1995

"This annotated compilation is an excellent stand-alone acquisition. . . . What distinguishes this volume and its previous companion work from other similar compilations are the refreshing, enticing annotations." Am Ref Books Annu, 1996

Kaleidoscope; a multicultural booklist for grades K-8; Rudine Sims Bishop, editor, and the Multicultural Booklist Committee of the National Council of Teachers of English. National Council of Teachers of English 1994 169p il pa $14.95   **011.6**

1. Multiculturalism—Bibliography   2. Children's literature—Bibliography 3. Books and reading—Best books 4. Minorities—Bibliography
ISBN 0-8141-2543-3   LC 94-22268

A select annotated bibliography of titles published in 1990-1992 "about or related to African Americans, Asian Americans, Hispanic Americans/Latinos, and Native Americans. It also lists books involving people and countries in Africa, Asia, South and Central America, and the Caribbean, as well as relevant books set in Mexico, Canada, or England. In addition, it includes works that focus on interracial and intercultural topics, issues, and relationships." Introduction

For a review see: Booklist, March 1, 1995

Lima, Carolyn W.

A to zoo; subject access to children's picture books; [by] Carolyn W. Lima, John A. Lima. 4th ed. Bowker 1993 xxvii, 1158p $57.50   **011.6**

1. Picture books for children—Bibliography
ISBN 0-8352-3201-8   LC 93-6224
First published 1982

This work provides subject accessibility to nearly 15,000 picture books. Arranged under more than 700 subject headings, entries list only authors and titles. Complete bibliographic information is given in a separate bibliographic section arranged alphabetically by author, and there are title and illustrator indexes

For a review see: Booklist, March 15, 1994

Magazines for kids and teens; a resource for parents, teachers, librarians, and kids! Donald R. Stoll, editor. Educational Press Association of Am. 1994 101p pa $10   **011.6**

1. Periodicals—Bibliography
ISBN 0-87207-397-1

First published 1990 with title: Magazines for children

This work "includes more than 250 periodicals. . . . Each periodical entry includes a brief paragraph describing the magazine, as well as a column of facts about its subject, editor, publisher, circulation, the cost of a subscription or a sample issue, and editorial and ordering addresses. In the appended lists, the titles are grouped by age level and subject. . . . Librarians will find the book a well-designed, practical selection tool." Booklist

Magazines for young people; [edited] by Bill Katz and Linda Sternberg Katz. 2nd ed. Bowker 1991 361p $38   **011.6**

1. Periodicals—Bibliography
ISBN 0-8352-3009-0

First published 1987 with title: Magazines for school libraries

"This guide evaluates over 1,100 magazines appropriate for preschool through high school levels. The titles include curriculum-related periodicals, others of general interest, and professional journals directed toward educators. An introduction and core list of titles preface each of the 60 subject areas. Entries contain the beginning year of publication; frequency; cost; address; presence of illustrations, advertising, and an index; circulation; availability in other formats; indexing elsewhere; inclusion of book reviews; and suggested library level. The evaluations indicate strengths, weaknesses, and political bias." Nichols. Guide to Ref Books for Sch Media Cent. 4th edition

Middle and junior high school library catalog; edited by Anne Price and Juliette Yaakov; editorial staff: John Greenfieldt [et al.] 7th ed. Wilson, H.W. 1995 988p lib bdg $175   **011.6**

1. Classified catalogs 2. School libraries—Catalogs
ISBN 0-8242-0880-3

"Standard catalog series"

First published 1965 with title: Junior high school library catalog

Kept up to date by annual supplements which are included in price of main volume

Expanding its coverage to include material for the middle grades, the seventh edition of the catalog includes 4,224 titles and nearly 5,000 analytical entries of books for the middle school grades through grade nine. Entries contain full bibliographic information, Dewey Decimal Classification number, subject headings, descriptive, and when available, critical annotations

Miller-Lachmann, Lyn, 1956-

Our family, our friends, our world; an annotated guide to significant multicultural books for children and teenagers. Bowker 1992 710p il $51.25   **011.6**

1. Children's literature—Bibliography 2. Young adults' literature—Bibliography 3. Minorities—Bibliography
ISBN 0-8352-3025-2   LC 91-24549

This is an annotated guide to some 1,000 books for children and teens, published between 1970 and 1990, "that focus on cultures, identities, and histories of minority groups in the U.S. and Canada as well as cultures from the rest of the world." Booklist

"With its clear and informative background information, convenient format, and extensive scope, this book is a valuable tool—a must for every professional collection that supports a collection of literature for young people." Voice Youth Advocates

Nichols, Margaret Irby

Guide to reference books for school media centers. 4th ed. Libraries Unlimited 1992 463p $38.50   011.6

1. Reference books—Bibliography
ISBN 0-87287-833-3   LC 91-45242
First edition by Christine Gehrt Wynar published 1973

This guide to reference sources for elementary, middle, and high schools contains 2,280 annotated entries for titles published between 1985 and early 1991 as well as some significant older titles

Peterson, Carolyn Sue, 1938-

Reference books for children; by Carolyn Sue Peterson and Ann D. Fenton. 4th ed. Scarecrow Press 1992 399p $39.50   011.6

1. Reference books—Bibliography
ISBN 0-8108-2543-0   LC 92-14234
First published 1970 with title: Reference books for elementary and junior high school libraries

"The authors list over a thousand books published before mid-1990 and recommended by use or reviews for children's reference collections. Each receives a full citation, including price . . . as of Spring '92, and a 50-to-100-word descriptive annotation that highlights strengths, as well as indicating intended and potential audiences." SLJ

Pilla, Marianne Laino, 1955-

The best high/low books for reluctant readers. Libraries Unlimited 1990 100p pa $11.50   011.6

1. High interest-low vocabulary books—Bibliography
2. Slow learning children—Books and reading
ISBN 0-87287-532-6   LC 90-5756
"A Libraries Unlimited data book"

"This list of high interest-low vocabulary books for grades 3-12, selected for their literary quality, assists school media specialists in collection development and making recommendations to reluctant readers. For each of the carefully selected titles, it provides complete bibliographic data, a brief annotation, suggested subject headings, and reading/interest levels. Indexed by reading level and subject. Recommended. The disk version, which may be customized to fit the library's collection and used to produce printed reading lists by subject or reading level, is available in three formats." Nichols. Guide to Ref Books for Sch Media Cent. 4th edition

Richardson, Selma K., 1931-

Magazines for children; a guide for parents, teachers, and librarians. 2nd ed. American Lib. Assn. 1991 xxxv, 139p pa $25   011.6

1. Periodicals—Bibliography
ISBN 0-8389-0552-8   LC 90-45152
First published 1983

"An annotated list of periodicals published primarily for children ages two through fourteen. . . . Each entry includes subscription information, frequency, a descriptive annotation and evaluation. Age and grade levels, circulation figures, additional young adult and adult magazines often found in children's collections, and a subject index are appended." Ref Sources for Small & Medium-Sized Libr. 5th edition

Richey, Virginia H.

Wordless/almost wordless picture books; a guide; [by] Virginia H. Richey, Katharyn E. Puckett. Libraries Unlimited 1992 223p $27.50   011.6

1. Picture books for children—Bibliography
2. Children's literature—Bibliography
ISBN 0-87287-878-3   LC 91-29364

"The guide covers almost 700 books in which the illustrations provide the complete story: alphabet and number books, concept books, adult novels, and board books for babies. Books with minimal text are also included. Each entry contains a brief annotation and lists themes linked to the story." Publisher's note
For a review see: Booklist, July 1992

Rochman, Hazel

Against borders; promoting books for a multicultural world. American Lib. Assn. 1993 288p il pa $25   011.6

1. Young adults' literature—Bibliography 2. Books and reading 3. Minorities—Bibliography
ISBN 0-8389-0601-X   LC 93-17840

"Starting with her personal immigrant's journey from South Africa to the U.S., Rochman's essays focus on using books across cultures. The second part of the book is made up of bibliographies—many of them updated and expanded from *Booklist*—on specific ethnic groups and cultural issues." Booklist
"The subject access by ethnic group and nationality will prove useful for doing reader's advisory work as well as developing units on ethnic and cultural identity." SLJ

Schon, Isabel

Books in Spanish for children and young adults: an annotated guide [series I-VI]. Scarecrow Press 1978-1993 6v v1 o.p.; v2, 3 $22.50 ea; v4 $29.50; v5 $20, v6 $35
011.6

1. Latin American literature—Bibliography 2. Spanish literature—Bibliography 3. Children's literature—Bibliography
ISBN 0-8108-1620-2 (v2); 0-8108-1807-8 (v3); 0-8108-2004-8 (v4); 0-8108-2238-5 (v5); 0-8108-2622-4 (v6)

A selection guide for books in Spanish written by Hispanic authors for children of preschool through high school age originating mostly from Latin American countries and Spain. Each volume covers roughly a three-year period. Arranged by country and by topic

"This series is a useful selection tool for librarians who need to build their collection of Spanish-language materials." Nichols. Guide to Ref Books for Sch Media Cent. 4th edition

Totten, Herman L., 1938-

Culturally diverse library collections for children; [by] Herman L. Totten, Risa W. Brown. Neal-Schuman 1994 299p pa $35
011.6

1. Minorities—Bibliography 2. Children's literature—Bibliography
ISBN 1-55570-140-X   LC 94-25712

This volume "lists 1,300 books about Native, Asian, Hispanic, and African Americans. The chapters about each ethnic group are divided into sections listing biographies,

Totten, Herman L., 1938-—*Continued*
folklore, fiction, nonfiction, and reference works. Entries note appropriate grade level and brief annotations describe content." Am Libr

Venture into cultures; a resource book of multicultural materials and programs; edited by Carla D. Hayden. American Lib. Assn. 1992 165p il pa $25   **011.6**

1. Children's   literature—Bibliography
2. Multiculturalism—Bibliography   3. Minorities—Bibliography
ISBN 0-8389-0579-X   LC 91-43373

"African American, Arabic, Asian, Hispanic, Jewish, Native American, Persian: these are the groups covered in this handy, enlightening guide to multicultural materials and programming at the elementary and middle school levels. . . . A selected bibliography of materials for adults, notes on the authors, and an index by culture round out the presentation." Booklist

Your reading; an annotated booklist for middle school and junior high. National Council of Teachers of English (NCTE bibliography series) pa $21.95   **011.6**

1. Children's literature—Bibliography 2. Young adults' literature—Bibliography 3. Books and reading—Best books
ISSN 1051-4740

First published 1954. (1995-96 edition) Periodically revised

This work annotates approximately 1,100 recent fiction and nonfiction titles appropriate for middle school and junior high readers. Entries are arranged in topical categories and are indexed by author, title and subject

015.73   Bibliographies and catalogs of works issued or printed in the United States

Children's books in print. Bowker $149.95   **015.73**

1. Children's literature—Bibliography
ISSN 0069-3480
Also available CD-ROM version
Annual. First published 1969

"Gives current publisher's information for juvenile titles listed in their catalogs as 'in print.' Useful, but not complete." N Y Public Libr. Ref Books for Child Collect. 2d edition

Subject guide to Children's books in print. Bowker $149.95   **015.73**

1. Children's literature—Bibliography 2. Subject catalogs
ISSN 0000-0167
Also available CD-ROM version
Annual. First published 1970

This publication provides a subject approach to its companion work: Children's books in print. The headings used are based on the Sears list of subject headings supplemented by headings from LC. Entries include author, title, publisher, year of publication, binding, price, ISBN, and, in some cases, grade level. A directory of publishers and distributors is included

016   Bibliographies and catalogs of works on specific subjects or in specific disciplines

Friedberg, Joan Brest, 1927-

Portraying persons with disabilities: an annotated bibliography of nonfiction for children and teenagers; [by] Joan Brest Friedberg, June B. Mullins, Adelaide Weir Sukiennik. 2nd ed. Bowker 1992 385p (Serving special needs series) $39.95   **016**

1. Handicapped—Bibliography 2. Children's literature—Bibliography 3. Young adults' literature—Bibliography
ISBN 0-8352-3022-8   LC 92-15047

Continues the authors' Accept me as I am, published 1985 and still available $36 (ISBN 0-8352-1974-7)

This "bibliotherapeutic guide provides access to more than 300 titles published between 1980 and 1991 that are suitable for preschool through high school readers. . . . Each entry contains a standard citation, a suggested reading level, citations to previous reviews, the specific disability, one to three pages of plot summary, an objective analysis . . . and suggested uses. Author, title, and subject analysis round out the work. The authors have succeeded admirably in their goal to present interesting, informative, and well-written nonfiction books that promote positive attitudes toward differences." Am Ref Books Annu, 1993

Gallivan, Marion F.

Fun for kids II; an index to children's craft books. Scarecrow Press 1992 472p $42.50   **016**

1. Handicraft—Indexes
ISBN 0-8108-2546-5   LC 92-16667

Companion volume to Fun for kids (1981)

This volume indexes craft books for children prekindergarten through eighth grade published from 1981 to 1990

Kister, Kenneth F., 1935-

Kister's best encyclopedias; a comparative guide to general and specialized encyclopedias. 2nd ed. Oryx Press 1994 506p $42.50   **016**

1. Encyclopedias and dictionaries—Bibliography
ISBN 0-89774-744-5   LC 94-11282

First published 1986 with title: Best encyclopedias

"An excellent source that surveys and evaluates more than 1,000 encyclopedias, both print and electronic. While the emphasis is on works in English, major foreign-language encyclopedias are covered as well. Includes a title/topic index and a directory of publishers and distributors." Guide to Ref Books. 11th edition

Includes bibliographical references

Marantz, Sylvia S.

Multicultural picture books; art for understanding others; by Sylvia and Kenneth Marantz. Linworth Pub. 1994 150p il (Professional growth series) $28.95 **016**

1. Books and reading 2. Children's literature—Bibliography 3. Picture books for children—Bibliography 4. Multiculturalism—Bibliography

ISBN 0-938865-22-6 LC 93-50811

"A publication of Book report and Library talk"
The authors describe "how the illustrations in picture books can transmit information about a culture and an authentic sense of its spirit   For each title, there is a brief summary and an excellent description of the illustrations, along with explanations of the artist's medium and technique, references to the characteristics of artistic styles from various cultures, and comparisons with other books by the illustrators." SLJ

016.02 Bibliographies of library science

Van Orden, Phyllis J.

Library service to children; a guide to the research, planning, and policy literature; [by] Phyllis Van Orden. American Lib. Assn. 1992 141p pa $27 **016.02**

1. Children's libraries—Bibliography 2. Books and reading 3. Library science—Bibliography

ISBN 0-8389-0584-6 LC 92-3823

"This valuable though specialized bibliography is designed 'to facilitate the location of English language materials about public library service to children and children's librarianship.' . . . The entries include books, journal articles, doctoral dissertations, nationally and regionally published standards and guidelines for children's services, annual reports, and pamphlet material. Arranged alphabetically by title, the 298 entries have complete bibliographic information and a succinct summary of the content." J Youth Serv Libr

016.3 Bibliographies of the social sciences

Notable children's trade books in the field of social studies. Children's Bk. Council pa $2 **016.3**

1. Social sciences—Bibliography 2. Books and reading—Best books

An annual annotated list, reprinted from an issue of the periodical Social Education, of the preceding year's best trade books in the field of social studies of interest to children in grades K-8. Prepared by the Book Review Panel of the National Council for the Social Studies—Children's Book Council Joint Committee. Titles are selected for emphasis on human relations, originality, readability and, when appropriate, illustrations. General reading levels (primary, intermediate, advanced) are indicated

016.3058 Bibliographies of racial, ethnic, national groups

The **Black** experience in children's books; selected by the New York Public Library, Black Experience in Children's Books Committee. New York Public Lib. pa $5 **016.3058**

1. African Americans—Bibliography 2. Blacks—Bibliography

First published 1957. (1994 edition) periodically revised
This "bibliography has over 500 titles portraying African-American life in the United States and the Black Experience in Africa and the Caribbean. Arranged geographically with brief descriptive annotations of fiction, folklore, poetry, history and other nonfiction books for children from preschool through junior high school." N Y Public Libr. Ref Books for Child Collect. 2d edition

Williams, Helen Elizabeth, 1933-
Books by African-American authors and illustrators for children and young adults. American Lib. Assn. 1991 270p $43 **016.3058**

1. Children's literature—Bibliography 2. Young adults' literature—Bibliography 3. African American authors 4. Illustrators

ISBN 0-8389-0570-6 LC 91-13931

"Annotated descriptive bibliography containing over 1250 books written and illustrated by African-Americans and published between 1900 and 1990. The titles are divided into three sections by reading/interest level (preK-gr 4; gr 5-8; gr 9+), with the majority for senior high school level and above. A final chapter highlights 53 black illustators and their work." SLJ
"The amount of information given is impressive and is well-organized and usable by students and teachers." Voice Youth Advocates

016.3627 Bibliographies of problems of and services to young people

Rudman, Masha Kabakow
Books to help children cope with separation and loss; an annotated bibliography; [by] Masha Kabakow Rudman, Kathleen Dunne Gagne, Joanne E. Bernstein. 4th ed. Bowker 1993 514p (Serving special needs series) $51.25 **016.3627**

1. Children's literature—Bibliography 2. Bereavement—Bibliography

ISBN 0-8352-3412-6 LC 93-32768

First published 1977 under the authorship of Joanne E. Bernstein
This "is an annotated bibliography of more than 740 books arranged in thematic categories such as death, divorce, and serious illness. Each entry includes a descriptive, evaluative annotation noting the book's strengths and weaknesses, data, and interest level. . . . The emphasis in selection was on books published between 1985 and 1993, although some books appearing prior to 1985 were included." Am Ref Books Annu, 1995

016.3713 Bibliographies of instructional materials

Educators guide to free films, filmstrips and slides. Educators Progress Service $32.95
016.3713

1. Free material

Also available are guides to free computer materials, videotapes, health, physical education and recreation materials, science materials, social studies materials, teaching aids, and guidance materials

Annual. First published 1941

This guide annotates film "titles available for free loan from a variety of sponsors and agencies. Material is screened for availability and educational value. The arrangement is under curriculum-related subject areas, and indexing is by title, subject and source." Nichols. Guide to Ref Books for Sch Media Cent. 4th edition

016.5 Bibliographies of science

Appraisal; science books for young people. Children's Science Bk. Review Com. $44 per year
016.5

1. Science—Bibliography—Periodicals 2. Books—Reviews

ISSN 0003-7052

Quarterly. First published 1967

This periodical "reviews almost all science and math books published each year that are written for children and young adults. . . . Some 70 trade books and series are reviewed in each quarterly issue; two signed reviews, 100-200 words each, by two reviewers, a librarian and a subject specialist; complete bibliographic and order information and grade level; five rating codes." Nichols. Guide to Ref Books for Sch Media Cent. 4th edition

Kennedy, DayAnn M.

Science & technology in fact and fiction: a guide to children's books; [by] DayAnn M. Kennedy, Stella S. Spangler, Mary Ann Vanderwerf. Bowker 1990 319p $38 **016.5**

1. Science—Bibliography 2. Technology—Bibliography 3. Children's literature—Bibliography 4. Books and reading—Best books

ISBN 0-8352-2708-1 LC 89-27374

"An annotated guide to children's literature for ages up to 11 years that arranges entries for some 500 recommended works of fiction and nonfiction under the two broad categories of science and technology. Each entry includes a complete bibliographic description, a summary of the work, and evaluative comments on the literary and scientific qualities of the book. Indexed by author, title, illustrator, subject, and reading level." Guide to Ref Books. 11th edition

Outstanding science trade books for children. Children's Bk. Council pa $2 **016.5**

1. Science—Bibliography 2. Books and reading—Best books

An annual annotated list, reprinted from an issue of the periodical Science and Children, of the preceding year's best trade books in the field of science of interest to children in grades K-8. Prepared by a Book Review Committee appointed by the National Science Teachers Association in cooperation with the Children's Book Council. Titles are selected for accuracy, readability and pleasing format. General reading levels (primary, intermediate, advanced) are indicated

Science Books & Films. American Assn. for the Advancement of Science $40 per year
016.5

1. Science—Bibliography—Periodicals 2. Books—Reviews 3. Audiovisual materials—Reviews

ISSN 0098-342X

Nine issues a year. First published 1965 with title: Science Books, a quarterly review

"This magazine is an indispensable tool for librarians in all types of libraries who wish to make informed collection development decisions in the area of science. . . . Arranged by Dewey decimal class numbers, the reviews cover books, audiovisual (AV) materials, and even software." Katz. Mag for Libr. 8th edition

Science books & films' Best books for children, 1992-1995; edited by Tracy Gath and Maria Sosa. American Assn. for the Advancement of Science 1996 286p pa $24
016.5

1. Science—Bibliography 2. Books and reading—Best books

ISBN 0-87168-586-8

An annotated bibliography of recommended or highly recommended titles from Science books & films reviewed during the calendar years 1992-1995. Each entry contains bibliographic and ordering information, including appropriate reading/interest level (kindergarten through grade 9)

016.79143 Bibliographies of motion pictures

From page to screen; children's and young adult books on film and video; Joyce Moss and George Wilson, editors. Gale Res. 1992 443p $40 **016.79143**

1. Motion pictures—Catalogs 2. Videotapes—Catalogs

ISBN 0-8103-7893-0 LC 92-9781

This "is a guide to 1,400 film, video, and laser disc adaptations of 750 literary works for children ages five through high school. Materials treated range from fairy tales and Shakespeare to the more contemporary works of Alex Haley and Dr. Seuss. . . . This work is highly recommended for the public and school library where it will help parents, teachers, and librarians find the best films and videos that transform the printed page to the screen." Booklist

016.8 Bibliographies of literature

Adamson, Lynda G.

Recreating the past; a guide to American and world historical fiction for children and young adults. Greenwood Press 1994 xxii, 494p $55 **016.8**

1. Children's literature—Bibliography 2. Young adults' literature—Bibliography 3. Historical fiction—Bibliography

ISBN 0-313-29008-3 LC 94-14435

This work consists of 20 separate annotated bibliographies of historical fiction. Coverage is international. Each section is arranged alphabetically by author and includes

Adamson, Lynda G.—*Continued*
publication information, a summary and reading and interest levels

This "will be especially useful for teachers and media specialists in interdisciplinary and whole language settings." SLJ

Anderson, Vicki, 1928-
Cultures outside the United States in fiction; a guide to 2,875 books for librarians and teachers, K-9. McFarland & Co. 1994 414p lib bdg $35   **016.8**

1. Young adults' literature—Bibliography 2. Children's literature—Bibliography

ISBN 0-89950-905-3   LC 94-6272

This publication lists "works of fiction, from more than 150 countries, that emphasize daily life and cultural diversity. Titles were published between 1960 and 1993, but some earlier classic works are also included (e.g., those of Rudyard Kipling). Titles are arranged alphabetically by entry number. . . . Listings include standard bibliographical information as well as grade level, short descriptive annotations, and suggested subject headings. Author, title, and subject indexes round out the work." Recomm Ref Books for Small & Medium-sized Libr & Media Cent, 1995

Native Americans in fiction; a guide to 765 books for librarians and teachers, K-9. McFarland & Co. 1994 166p lib bdg $24.95   **016.8**

1. Children's literature—Bibliography 2. Young adults' literature—Bibliography 3. Indians of North America—Fiction—Bibliography

ISBN 0-89950-907-X   LC 94-6271

"This bibliography lists 765 fiction books dealing with 116 tribes. They are listed alphabetically by tribe and geographical area. . . . The books were published between 1960 and 1993, with some older classics included. The chronological ages represented range from 1700 to the present. Each annotation lists author, title, publisher, date of publication, grade level, and subject, along with a brief summary of the book." Recomm Ref Books for Small & Medium-sized Libr & Media Cent, 1995

Baskin, Barbara Holland, 1929-
More notes from a different drummer; a guide to juvenile fiction portraying the disabled; by Barbara H. Baskin and Karen H. Harris. Bowker 1984 495p (Serving special populations series) $39.95   **016.8**

1. Handicapped—Fiction—Bibliography 2. Children's literature—Bibliography

ISBN 0-8352-1871-6   LC 84-12283

"This extends the author's earlier edition [entered below] to include 450 new fiction titles published between 1976 and 1981 concerning the disabled. Lengthy annotations remain thoughtful and informative. Earlier work should be retained." N Y Public Libr. Ref Books for Child Collect. 2d edition

Notes from a different drummer; a guide to juvenile fiction portraying the handicapped; by Barbara H. Baskin and Karen H. Harris. Bowker 1978 c1977 375p il $34.95   **016.8**

1. Handicapped—Fiction—Bibliography 2. Children's literature—Bibliography

ISBN 0-8352-0978-4   LC 77-15067

"Comprehensive guide to juvenile fiction written between 1940 and 1975 that depicts mentally and physically disabled characters. Critical and descriptive annotations, reading level and analysis of depiction of the disabled are included." N Y Public Libr. Ref Books for Child Collect. 2d edition

Colborn, Candy, 1942-
What do children read next? a reader's guide to fiction for children. Gale Res. 1994 1135p $55   **016.8**

1. Books and reading—Best books 2. Children's literature—Bibliography

ISBN 0-8103-8886-3   LC 93-49685

"Includes almost 2000 annotations, arranged alphabetically by author, for fiction for children in grades one through eight. . . . Each annotation includes basic bibliographic information, suggested age range, subject(s) and genre, names and descriptions of major characters, time period, locale(s), plot summary, citations of selected reviews [and] awards received." Bull Cent Child Books

"All who love children and literature will find in this volume exciting choices for early readers, reluctant readers, dedicated readers, readers looking for a topic or genre, and those with inquisitive minds." SLJ

Hall, Susan, 1940-
Using picture storybooks to teach literary devices; recommended books for children and young adults. 2nd ed. Oryx Press 1994 239p pa $24.95   **016.8**

1. Children's literature—Bibliography 2. Picture books for children—Bibliography 3. Literature—Study and teaching

ISBN 0-89774-849-2   LC 89-8574

Original volume published 1990 available $29.95 (ISBN 0-89774-582-5)

This edition, designated volume 2, contains 300 titles which expand the coverage of the original volume. The author advocates the use of picture books in language arts programs at all grade levels. Entries are listed alphabetically under the literary device they illustrate

"This is a well conceived and functional bibliography. . . . It will encourage one to take a longer look at the picture storybook genre and its application to older youth. An excellent addition to the reference collection of any school or public library." Voice Youth Advocates [review of 1990 edition]

Helbig, Alethea
This land is our land; a guide to multicultural literature for children and young adults; [by] Alethea K. Helbig and Agnes Regan Perkins. Greenwood Press 1994 401p $55.50   **016.8**

1. Children's literature—Bibliography 2. Young adults' literature—Bibliography 3. Minorities—Bibliography

ISBN 0-313-28742-2   LC 94-16124

An annotated bibliography of 570 books published from 1985 through 1993 focusing on the fiction, poetry and oral traditions of African, Asian, Hispanic and Native Americans

"Libraries and curriculum resource centers will want to consider *This Land is Our Land* for its currency and comprehensive coverage of quality multicultural literature for children." Booklist

Lynn, Ruth Nadelman, 1948-

Fantasy literature for children and young adults; an annotated bibliography. 4th ed. Bowker 1995 lxxix, 1092p $54.25   **016.8**

1. Fantasy fiction—Bibliography 2. Fairy tales—Bibliography

ISBN 0-8352-3456-8   LC 94-42529

First published 1979 with title: Fantasy for children

This volume is divided into two parts. Part One is an annotated bibliography of 4,800 fantasy novels and story collections, published between 1900 and 1994, for children and young adults in grades 3-12. Part Two is a research guide to some 10,500 articles, books and dissertations about the authors who write fantasy literature for children and young adults

Robertson, Debra

Portraying persons with disabilities: an annotated bibliography of fiction for children and teenagers; [by] Debra E. J. Robertson. 3rd ed. Bowker 1992 482p (Serving special needs series) $39.95   **016.8**

1. Handicapped—Fiction—Bibliography 2. Children's literature—Bibliography 3. Young adults' literature—Bibliography

ISBN 0-8352-3023-6   LC 91-39177

Continues Baskin and Harris' Notes from a different drummer and More notes from a different drummer, both entered above

This "presents annotated bibliographies of fiction books with characters that have physical, mental or emotional impairments. This particular volume extends the coverage of books for infants to adolescents from 1982-1992. . . . The annotated books are grouped into four major categories: physical problems; sensory problems; cognitive and behavior problems; and multiple/severe and various disabilities. Each annotation gives a reading level; a broad disability category; a summary; and, an analysis of the book and its appeal. . . . This volume is a must for any professional dealing with children and young adults." Voice Youth Advocates

Wilkin, Binnie Tate, 1933-

Survival themes in fiction for children and young people; foreword by Virginia A. Walter. 2nd ed. Scarecrow Press 1993 200p $27.50
    016.8

1. Fiction—Bibliography 2. Fiction—History and criticism 3. Children's literature—Bibliography 4. Children's literature—History and criticism

ISBN 0-8108-2676-3   LC 93-26421

First published 1978

In this bibliography, "Wilkin examines 'contemporary, realistic, children's fiction to explore . . . issues of human existence and survival.' . . . The entry for each book lists title, author, illustrator (if applicable), publisher, city and date of publication, and age group. Annotations range from one sentence to several paragraphs and are both descriptive and evaluative." Booklist

016.9 Bibliographies of geography and history

Khorana, Meena

Africa in literature for children and young adults; an annotated bibliography of English-language books. Greenwood Press 1994 l, 313p (Bibliographies and indexes in world literature) $59.95   **016.9**

1. Children's literature—Bibliography 2. Young adults' literature—Bibliography 3. Africa in literature—Bibliography

ISBN 0-313-25488-5   LC 94-34223

"Lists and critically annotates 700 titles about Africa by Western and African authors, published in or translated into English, 1873-1994. The evaluations include a plot or theme summary but also point out any bias found. The volume has six chapters by region: general books, North Africa, West Africa, East Africa, Central Africa, and Southern Africa, each chapter further subdivided by genre." Choice

For a fuller review see: Booklist, April 15, 1995

016.973 Bibliographies of United States history

Exploring the United States through literature series. Oryx Press 1994 7v pa ea $24.95
    016.973

1. United States—Bibliography

Contents: Exploring the Great Lakes States through literature; Exploring the Mountain States through literature; Exploring the Northeast States through literature; Exploring the Pacific States through literature; Exploring the Plains States through literature; Exploring the Southeast States through literature; Exploring the Southwest States through literature

Each book in this series of annotated bibliographies of print and nonprint materials for grades K-8 "is divided alphabetically into states sections, each of which is further subdivided into nonfiction, biography, fiction, periodicals, and professional materials. All entries contain complete standard bibliographic data as well as cost, running time, and format specifications for nonprint items. . . . Comprehensive and well-organized, this is a treasure trove of curriculum planning help for teachers as well as a user-friendly resource for students working on state reports." SLJ

VanMeter, Vandelia

American history for children and young adults: an annotated bibliographic index. Libraries Unlimited 1990 324p $32.50
    016.973

1. United States—History—Bibliography

ISBN 0-87287-731-0   LC 90-5815

"A Libraries Unlimited data book"

"Each of the 2,901 entries is placed in its historical period and then listed under a Sears subject heading. Information includes title, author/editor, series, publisher/distributor, publication date, cost, physical description, grade level, and brief annotation. Indexed by grade level." Nichols. Guide to Ref Books for Sch Media Cent. 4th edition

025.1   Library administration

Youth services librarians as managers; a how-to guide from budgeting to personnel; [by] Association for Library Service to Children; compiled and edited by Kathleen Staerkel, Mary Fellows, and Sue McCleaf Nespeca. American Lib. Assn. 1995 171p pa $30   **025.1**

1. Children's libraries 2. Libraries—Administration
ISBN 0-8389-3446-3   LC 94-43721

"Specific and practical information on a variety of topics, including planning, budgeting, developing policies and procedures, evaluating programs and services, job descriptions, recruitment, conducting meetings, and continuing education, will be of value to both the new and the experienced practitioner." Booklist
Includes bibliographical references

025.2   Collection development and acquisitions

Berger, Pam
CD-ROM for schools; a directory and practical handbook for media specialists; [by] Pam Berger, Susan Kinnell. Eight Bit Bks. 1994 272p il pa $29.95   **025.2**

1. CD-ROM—Reviews   2. School   libraries
3. Instructional materials centers
ISBN 0-910965-13-7   LC 95-121192

This introduction to CD-ROM technology presents reviews of more than 300 titles, including a core collection of 100 titles; provides information on hardware requirements and networking needs; and covers planning, managing, evaluation, and selection of CD-ROMs

"If library media specialists are looking for the definitive book on CD-ROM, this is it. . . . What is best about this book is the authors' obvious commitment to CD-ROM as an information format that supports the overall goals and objectives of the library media program and the curriculum." SLJ

025.3   Bibliographic analysis and control

ALA filing rules; [prepared by the] Filing Committee, Resources and Technical Services Division, American Library Association. American Lib. Assn. 1980 50p pa $15   **025.3**

1. Files and filing 2. Library catalogs
ISBN 0-8389-3255-X   LC 80-22186

Successor to ALA Rules for filing catalog cards, second edition

"The rules set forth in *ALA Filing Rules*, which apply to the arrangement of bibliographic records of library materials in card, book, or online format, are based on the 'file-as-is' principle." Nichols. Guide to Ref Books for Sch Media Cent. 4th edition

According to a 1981 announcement of the American Library Association, this may be considered as an alternative to, rather than a definite replacement for, the 1968 edition of ALA Rules for filing catalog cards. Libraries may choose to continue using the earlier publication

Cataloging correctly for kids; an introduction to the tools; edited by Sharon Zuiderveld. rev ed. American Lib. Assn. 1991 78p il pa $16   **025.3**

1. Cataloging
ISBN 0-8389-3395-5   LC 91-8675

First edition by the Cataloging of Children's Materials Committee published 1989

"Focusing on such questons as the annotated card program, cataloging nonbook materials, and vendors of cataloging for children's materials, this slim work is an invaluable source for the elementary level. The editor has compiled articles that recognize that users of children's materials have unique characteristics and requirements." Nichols. Guide to Ref Books for Sch Media Cent. 4th edition
Includes bibliographical references

Gorman, Michael, 1941-
The concise AACR2, 1988 revision. American Lib. Assn. 1989 161p pa $28   **025.3**

1. Anglo-American cataloguing rules 2. Cataloging
ISBN 0-8389-3362-9   LC 89-15110

Based on Anglo-American cataloguing rules, 2nd edition, 1988 revision, available for $55 (ISBN 0-8389-3346-7); pa $45 (ISBN 0-8389-3360-2). Amendments published 1993 available in loose-leaf format $15 (ISBN 0-8389-3431-5)

"Many smaller libraries will find this volume more helpful than the complete *AACR2*, although some may eventually progress to the full set of rules. . . . Capitalization rules, glossary and comparative table of *AACR2* and *Concise AACR2* rules appended." Booklist

McCroskey, Marilyn J.
Cataloging nonbook materials with AACR2 and MARC; a guide for the school library media specialist; by Marilyn McCroskey, for the American Association of School Librarians. American Lib. Assn. 1994 77p pa $20   **025.3**

1. Cataloging—Audiovisual materials
ISBN 0-8389-7736-7

"The author has attempted to summarize and simplify the cataloging process for the various formats as much as possible without sacrificing important information needed in the school library media center. . . . General guidelines for cataloging and for creating MARC records for AV items are first in this booklet, followed by separate sections on the various formats along with examples for each format. Cataloging terminology is from AACR2." Preface

Miller, Rosalind E.
Commonsense cataloging; a cataloger's manual; [by] Rosalind E. Miller & Jane C. Terwillegar. 4th ed rev. Wilson, H.W. 1990 180p pa $29   **025.3**

1. Cataloging
ISBN 0-8242-0789-0   LC 89-70716

First edition by Esther J. Piercy published 1965; this is a revision of the fourth edition published 1989

Miller, Rosalind E.—*Continued*
This practical manual for the beginning cataloger discusses such topics as: applications of AACR2; subject organization; Dewey classification; subject access; cataloging with copy; mechanical preparation and maintenance; special problems posed by serials, maps, kits and electronic software; computers and cataloging
Includes glossary and bibliography

025.4 Subject analysis and control

Dewey, Melvil, 1851-1931
Abridged Dewey decimal classification and relative index; devised by Melvil Dewey. ed 12, edited by John P. Comaromi [et al.] Forest Press (Albany) 1990 857p $88   **025.4**

1. Dewey Decimal Classification
ISBN 0-910608-42-3   LC 90-31428

First abridged edition published 1894
The 12th Abridged Edition is an abridgement of the four-volume 20th Edition. Adapted to the needs of small and growing libraries, the 12th Abridged Edition is designed primarily for school and public libraries with collections of up to 20,000 titles

Sears list of subject headings. 15th ed, edited by Joseph Miller. Wilson, H.W. 1994 lvi, 758p $49   **025.4**

1. Subject headings
ISBN 0-8242-0858-7   LC 94-16705

Also available Canadian companion $24 (ISBN 0-8242-0879-X)
First published 1923 with title: List of subject headings for small libraries, by Minnie Earl Sears
This edition presents several new features: all inverted headings have been changed to the uninverted form; references are labeled BT, NT, RT, SA, and UF (to conform with the NISO standards for thesauri); a list of cancelled and replacement headings is included; and there is a new emphasis on the expandable nature of the List

Subject headings for children; a list of subject headings used by the Library of Congress with Dewey numbers added; edited by Lois Winkel. Forest Press (Albany) 1994 2v pa set $70   **025.4**

1. Subject headings 2. Classification—Books 3. Dewey Decimal Classification
ISBN 0-910608-46-6   LC 94-29295

Contents: v1 List of headings; v2 Keyword index
"In this compilation of children's subject headings used by the Library of Congress, Winkel has transformed a convoluted and difficult source, *Library of Congress Subject Headings*, into a highly useful tool. The result is a boon to catalogers and customers alike. Because LC uses its own classification system while most libraries serving children use Dewey, Winkel has added Dewey numbers to further simplify categorizing children's materials." SLJ

025.7 Physical preparation for storage of library materials

Greenfield, Jane
Books: their care and repair. Wilson, H.W. 1984 204p il $42   **025.7**

1. Books—Conservation and restoration
ISBN 0-8242-0695-9   LC 83-25926

"Geared to librarians, this useful handbook explains in clear, precise language how major and minor book repairs can be performed in-house without costly materials. . . . [The author] also furnishes basic background material on the structure of books and how proper care prevents deterioration. Simple line drawings supplement the text." Booklist
Includes glossary and bibliography

027 General libraries, information centers

Gibbons, Gail
Check it out! the book about libraries. Harcourt Brace Jovanovich 1985 unp il lib bdg $13.95; pa $4.95 (k-3)   **027**

1. Libraries
ISBN 0-15-216400-6 (lib bdg); 0-15-216401-4 (pa)
                                     LC 85-5414

The author explains what is found in a library and how different libraries serve their communities
"Gibbons provides a solid base for spinoff discussions, making the book useful as an introduction to library skills and for discussion in story hours." SLJ

027.4 Public libraries

Jaspersohn, William
My hometown library. Houghton Mifflin 1994 47p il $14.95 (3-5)   **027.4**

1. Public libraries
ISBN 0-395-55723-2   LC 92-17372

The author describes the resources and services at his hometown library and how they have changed over the years
"The clear, concise view of a library and its functions is useful for acquainting children with its resources. . . . Color photographs depict the warm atmosphere of this integral part of the community." Horn Book Guide

027.62 Libraries for children and young adults

Bauer, Caroline Feller, 1935-
Read for the fun of it; active programming with books for children; drawings by Lynn Gates Bredeson. Wilson, H.W. 1992 xx, 372p il $45   **027.62**

1. Children—Books and reading 2. Children's literature 3. Children's libraries
ISBN 0-8242-0824-2   LC 91-31450

Bauer, Caroline Feller, 1935——*Continued*

"Among the topics covered are reading aloud, reaching parents, author visits, storytelling with visual aids, teaching children to present stories and poetry, and using puppetry and magic tricks in storytelling." Booklist

"Diagrams artwork, and word games are . . . scattered appropriately throughout the book. All are reproducible and available for reader use. . . . *Read for the Fun of It* emphasizes Bauer's obvious passion for reading, making this book a delightful addition to the professional collection." J Youth Serv Libr

Includes bibliographical references

Benne, Mae, 1924-

Principles of children's services in public libraries. American Lib. Assn. 1991 332p $45
027.62

1. Children's libraries 2. Public libraries 3. Children—Books and reading

ISBN 0-8389-0555-2   LC 90-47427

The author's discussion of public library services to children "falls into four major areas: organizational patterns, design of services, collection development, and facilities. Appendices include examples of budgeting and program forms, and annotated bibliographies of aids for selection, reference services, and programming services to special audiences." Publisher's note

DeSalvo, Nancy

Beginning with books; library programming for infants, toddlers, and preschoolers; [by] Nancy N. DeSalvo; foreword by Faith Hektoen. Library Professional Publs. 1993 186p pa $27.50
027.62

1. Children's libraries 2. Books and reading

ISBN 0-208-02318-6   LC 92-14858

This is a "presentation of the professional philosophy and practical logistics of library programming for children from infancy through the age of five. . . . [This is] a solid, eminently practical book filled with programming ideas that can be easily adapted to any library setting or budget. A variety of useful information is appended." Booklist

Fasick, Adele M., 1930-

Managing children's services in the public library. Libraries Unlimited 1991 182p il pa $25
027.62

1. Children's libraries 2. Public libraries 3. Children—Books and reading

ISBN 0-87287-643-8   LC 90-28689

The material in this volume is organized "under three broad categories: working within the department, working within the system, and working within the community. . . . It will provide solid background reading for library school students as well as serve as a working manual for practicing librarians." J Youth Serv Libr

Includes bibliography

Feinberg, Sandra, 1946-

Running a parent/child workshop; a how-to-do-it manual for librarians; [by] Sandra Feinberg, Kathleen Deere; with special assistance from the staff of the Middle Country Public Library. Neal-Schuman 1995 166p il (How-to-do-it manuals for libraries) pa $32.50
027.62

1. Children's libraries

ISBN 1-55570-189-2   LC 94-46345

"The goals of the workshop, Feinberg says, are to increase parents' awareness of library services and materials, to tell them about child development and community agencies, and to provide a comfortable place for parent-child interaction. The authors provide bibliographies of materials for both children and parents. . . . Also included are sample program forms, publicity ideas, suggestions for workshop content, floor plans for workshop space, a list of references, and an index." SLJ

Greene, Ellin, 1927-

Books, babies, and libraries; serving infants, toddlers, their parents & caregivers. American Lib. Assn. 1991 187p il pa $28
027.62

1. Children's libraries 2. Children—Books and reading

ISBN 0-8389-0572-2   LC 91-17050

The author "begins with a look at some model early childhood centers in libraries, an overview of major theories of early child development, and a discussion of the roles of parents and librarians in fostering literacy. Subsequent chapters cover the development of collections (both for toddlers themselves and for their parents), program planning, networking and outreach, and the overall planning, implementation, and evaluation of library service to early childhood." SLJ

Includes bibliographies

Kladder, Jeri, 1947-

Story hour; 55 preschool programs for public libraries. McFarland & Co. 1995 219p $38.50
027.62

1. Storytelling 2. Children's libraries 3. Books and reading

ISBN 0-7864-0065-X   LC 94-42093

In this guidebook, "Kladder has included ideas for name tags, picture books, poems, films, filmstrips, videos, songs, and activities, as well as helpful annotated bibliography of professional resources." Booklist

MacDonald, Margaret Read

Booksharing: 101 programs to use with preschoolers; with illustrations by Julie Liana MacDonald. Library Professional Publs. 1988 236p il $32.50; pa $19.50
027.62

1. Children's libraries 2. Library services 3. Books and reading

ISBN 0-208-02159-0; 0-208-02314-3 (pa)

LC 87-35777

The author "provides 101 complete, 45-minute programs to use with children ages 2½ to 6; each of the thematic sessions lists several books, followed by songs, films, poems, creative dramatics, science experiments, and art and craft experiences. . . . A complete alphabetical bibliography, an index of films, and musical notations are appended." Booklist

Marino, Jane

Mother Goose time; library programs for babies and their caregivers; by Jane Marino and Dorothy F. Houlihan; music arrangements by Jane Marino; photographs by Susan G. Drinker. Wilson, H.W. 1992 172p il music $30 **027.62**

1. Children's libraries 2. Nursery rhymes

ISBN 0-8242-0850-1 LC 91-46986

"The book was inspired by a program designed by the authors, librarians . . . who conducted 'Mother Goose Time' sessions for more than five years at the White Plains, New York, Public Library. These interactive sessions involved sharing songs and rhymes with babies and adults. . . . There are musical arrangements for the songs; bibliographies of picture books, display books, and resource books; an evaluation of form; and various indexes categorizing the rhymes and songs by title, first line, and developmental level." J Youth Serv Libr

Nespeca, Sue McCleaf

Library programming for families with young children. Neal-Schuman 1994 180p il (How-to-do-it manuals for libraries) $39.95 **027.62**

1. Children's libraries

ISBN 1-55570-181-7 LC 94-37894

The author "outlines the developmental characteristics of young children, providing book-sharing ideas for different age groups, sample family programs, current bibliographies of suggested titles, and places to write for additional information. Multicultural, intergenerational, institutional, and outreach programs are discussed separately, with suggestions for their implementation." SLJ

Includes bibliographical references

Rollock, Barbara T., 1924-1992

Public library services for children; with a foreword by Augusta Baker. Library Professional Publs. 1988 228p $35 **027.62**

1. Children's libraries 2. Children—Books and reading

ISBN 0-208-02016-0 LC 88-12863

"After a historical perspective on library service to children and an analysis of the impact of four studies on services, Rollock deals with management concerns. . . . The second part of the book explores the multidimensional services and programs of the children's department." Booklist

Includes bibliography

Walter, Virginia A.

Output measures for public library service to children; a manual of standardized procedures. American Lib. Assn. 1992 129p pa $22 **027.62**

1. Children's libraries 2. Public libraries

ISBN 0-8389-3404-8 LC 91-44354

"This manual has been designed as a tool for quantifying and measuring the results of public library service to children. . . . Among the many topics covered are material use measures, in-library use of children's materials, and children's library visits. Other management techniques, such as focus groups and user surveys, add an extra dimension." Booklist

Includes bibliographical references

027.6205 Libraries for children and young adults—Serial publications

Emergency Librarian. Ken Haycock & Assocs., P.O. Box C34069, Dept. 284, Seattle, WA 98124-1069 $49 per year **027.6205**

1. Children's libraries—Periodicals 2. School libraries—Periodicals 3. Books—Reviews

ISSN 0315-8888

Five issues a year. First published 1973

"A truly outstanding journal from Canada for teachers and librarians working with children and young adults. Issues include feature articles, reviews of professional reading, and materials for children and young adults in various formats. This journal takes an active view of library service to young people and is highly recommended for school library professional collections." Katz. Mag for Libr. 8th edition

Journal of Youth Services in Libraries. American Lib. Assn. $30 per year **027.6205**

1. Young adults' library services—Periodicals 2. Children's libraries—Periodicals 3. Books—Reviews

ISSN 0894-2498

Quarterly. Formerly Top of the News

"As a source for ideas and critical thinking on issues of concern to librarians serving children and young adults, this journal is excellent. . . . The articles are written for the most part by practicing librarians and reflect the reality of library work with young people." Katz. Mag for Sch Libr

027.8 School libraries

American Association of School Librarians

Information power; guidelines for school library media programs; prepared by the American Association of School Librarians and Association for Educational Communications and Technology. American Lib. Assn.; Association for Educ. Communications & Technology 1988 171p il pa $15 **027.8**

1. School libraries 2. Instructional materials centers

ISBN 0-8389-3352-1 LC 88-3480

Replaces Media programs: district and school, published 1975

"The book begins with the mission statement—to ensure that students and staff are effective users of ideas and information—and lists five challenges that library media specialists face. Following are individual chapters, complete with helpful bibliographies, that discuss programs; roles and responsibilities; leadership, planning, and management; personnel; resources and equipment; facilities; and district, regional and state leadership." Booklist

Assessment and the school library media center; editor, Carol Collier Kuhlthau; associate editors, M. Elspeth Goodin and Mary Jane McNally. Libraries Unlimited 1994 152p pa $20 **027.8**

1. Bibliographic instruction 2. Instructional materials centers

ISBN 1-56308-211-X LC 94-27290

Assessment and the school library media center—*Continued*

This book is a compilation of articles addressing the impact of school library media programs on student learning. Among the topics discussed are new methods of assessment, and the instructional role of the library media specialist

Includes bibliographical references

Automation for school libraries; how to do it from those who have done it; edited by Teresa Thurman Day, Bruce Flanders, Gregory Zuck. American Lib. Assn. 1994 138p il pa $20   **027.8**

1. School libraries—Automation
ISBN 0-8389-0637-0   LC 94-15406

This book addresses "the areas of automation systems, peripheral equipment and, most important, funding. Also included are practical advice, case experiences, model procedures and basic facts. . . . Whether you are a computer hacker or brand new at the game, this title will fill a void on your professional shelf." Book Rep

Includes glossary and bibliography

Bucher, Katherine Toth, 1947-
Computers & technology in school library media centers. Linworth Pub. 1994 238p il (Professional growth series) loose-leaf $34.95   **027.8**

1. School libraries 2. Instructional materials centers
ISBN 0-938865-36-6   LC 94-21890

Devoting one "chapter to each topic, the author handles instructional technology, computer basics, library management using a computer, multimedia CD-ROM, videodiscs, local area networks, computer telecommunications, video and computers, television and distance learning, and multimedia presentations. . . . Each chapter offers a satisfactory overview of technology and its utilization in school libraries and includes good diagrams, sample record-keeping forms, and instructions for using equipment." Booklist

Includes bibliographical references

Cook, Sybilla Avery, 1930-
Books, battles, and bees; a reader's competition resource for intermediate grades; [by] Sybilla Avery Cook, Cheryl A. Page. American Lib. Assn. 1994 166p il pa $20   **027.8**

1. Children's libraries 2. School libraries—Activity projects 3. Books and reading
ISBN 0-8389-0626-5   LC 93-29756

"A hands-on guide to book quiz programs for teachers and librarians working with grades three through eight, this provides all kinds of practical advice on choosing the books and organizing and promoting the programs. Most of the book is made up of sample quiz questions, five questions each for 250 titles commonly read in the middle grades." Booklist

Includes bibliographical references

Craver, Kathleen W.
School library media centers in the 21st century; changes and challenges. Greenwood Press 1994 xxxi, 179p $35   **027.8**

1. School libraries 2. Instructional materials centers
ISBN 0-313-29100-4   LC 94-5146

The author has compiled "statistics, studies, and examples in this discussion of school library media centers (SLMCs) of the future. She devotes chapters to technological, economic, employment, educational, social/behavioral, instructional, and organizational/managerial trends; she presents eight challenges for the media specialist. The emphasis here is . . . on technology." Voice Youth Advocates

"This is a 'must-read' for practicing and potential school library media specialists." SLJ

Includes bibliographical references

Skaggs, Gayle, 1952-
Off the wall! school year bulletin boards and displays for the library. McFarland & Co. 1995 142p il pa $24.50   **027.8**

1. School libraries 2. Libraries—Exhibitions 3. Bulletin boards
ISBN 0-7864-0116-8   LC 95-5693

"Arranged to 'correlate with the school year, September through May' this . . . guide contains more than 100 bulletin board and display ideas. . . . Skaggs has concentrated on ideas that can be inexpensively made and assembled fairly quickly." Booklist

"This is a handy aid for quick displays and to stimulate further creative ideas." Voice Youth Advocates

Van Orden, Phyllis J.
The collection program in schools; concepts, practices, and information sources. 2nd ed. Libraries Unlimited 1995 376p il $42.50; pa $32.50   **027.8**

1. School libraries
ISBN 1-56308-120-2; 1-56308-334-5 (pa)
     LC 94-32233

First published 1988

This "book is divided into three parts. The first section covers the librarian's role within the school and the community, aspects of the collection program, and concerns with censorship and intellectual freedom. . . . Part Two lists types of materials available and selection criteria specific to format. . . . Part Three identifies selection tools and offers suggestions for collection maintenance and evaluation." Book Rep

027.805   School libraries—Serial publications

Library Talk; the magazine for elementary school libraries. Linworth Pub. $39 per year   **027.805**

1. School libraries—Periodicals
Bimonthly. First published 1988

Provides articles, tips and ideas for day-to-day school library management. Each issue highlights a particular concern of the school librarian

"The articles are practical and full of useful ideas that school librarians can try. The book and media reviews are numerous and of good quality." Katz. Mag for Libr. 8th edition

School Library Journal; the magazine of children's, young adult, and school libraries. Bowker $59 per year   **027.805**

1. School libraries—Periodicals 2. Books—Reviews
ISSN 0362-8930

Monthly. First published 1954 with title: Junior Libraries

School Library Journal—*Continued*

"This is the leading magazine for childrens' and young adult public librarians and school librarians. The articles are timely, well edited, and full of information. Besides the feature articles, the journal includes a calendar, news, notes on people, a checklist of inexpensive pamphlets, posters, and the like, and lots of reviews, concisely written and evaluative. . . . Besides reviews of books, SLJ provides reviews of micro software and audiovisuals. This is an absolutely essential purchase for all libraries serving children and/or young adults." Katz. Mag for Libr. 6th edition

School Library Media Annual. Libraries Unlimited lib bdg $45   **027.805**

1. School libraries—Periodicals 2. Instructional materials centers—Periodicals

ISSN 0739-7712

Annual. First published 1983

This annual "is designed to keep practitioners abreast of new developments in the school media area. It is an essential source for school media specialists. Part 1 contains articles of current interest. . . . Part 2 has reports from professional organizations and governing bodies; a list of institutions that offer degree programs in library and information science, school library media services, and educational media; and award recipients. The final part lists the best books and software and award-winning books for the previous year." Nichols. Guide to Ref Books for Sch Media Cent. 4th edition

School Library Media Quarterly. American Lib. Assn. $40 per year   **027.805**

1. School libraries—Periodicals 2. Instructional materials centers—Periodicals

ISSN 0278-4823

Quarterly. First published 1972 with title: School Media Quarterly, as a successor to School Libraries

"Journal of the American Association of School Librarians"

This journal provides "feature articles that are well edited and timely; news of the association and of school library related legislation; reviews of professional reading, software, and audiovisuals; and annual AASL conference coverage. This is essential for school library professional collections." Katz. Mag for Libr. 8th edition

028   Reading and use of other information media

Booktalk! 2-5. Wilson, H.W. 1985-1993 4v ea pa $32   **028**

1. Books and reading

ISBN 0-8242-0716-5 (v2); 0-8242-0764-5 (v3); 0-8242-0835-8 (v4); 0-8242-0836-6 (v5)

Original Booktalk! published 1980 o.p.

Edited by Joni Bodart-Talbot

Volume 2 explains what booktalks are and contains 250 examples; volume 3 offers 500 booktalks and has a combined index to booktalks in volumes 2-3; volume 4 is a collection of 350 booktalks and 5 articles which appeared in the Booktalker section of Wilson Library Bulletin between September 1989 and May 1992; volume 5 adds 320 more talks and 4 articles on booktalking

Rochman, Hazel

Tales of love and terror; booktalking the classics, old and new. American Lib. Assn. 1987 120p pa $22   **028**

1. Books and reading 2. Literature—Stories, plots, etc.

ISBN 0-8389-0463-7   LC 86-32285

"Rochman's booktalks begin with themes of nearly universal interest, such as love and terror, to provide a framework for brief descriptions of a dozen or more titles. . . . Later chapters . . . demonstrate how a single book may relate to many different themes, and describe the range of books which might be used." Publisher's note

"Both experienced and new booktalkers will find a wealth of ideas in *Tales of Love and Terror*. . . . [It] should be a part of every young adult librarian's professional collection." SLJ

Thomas, Rebecca L.

Primaryplots; a book talk guide for use with readers ages 4-8. Bowker 1989 392p $41

    028

1. Children's literature—Bibliography 2. Books and reading 3. Literature—Stories, plots, etc.

ISBN 0-8352-2514-3   LC 88-34054

This is "essentially a book talk guide for use with children in grades K-3. It includes brief summaries of the books featured, information on the authors, materials and activities for book talks, lists of similar and/or related titles, audiovisuals and thematic materials." Libr J

Primaryplots 2; a book talk guide for use with readers ages 4-8. Bowker 1993 431p $43.75   **028**

1. Children's literature—Bibliography 2. Books and reading 3. Literature—Stories, plots, etc.

ISBN 0-8352-3411-8   LC 93-21138

This volume contains 150 titles published between 1988 and 1992

028.1   Reviews of books and other media

The **Best** in children's books; the University of Chicago guide to children's literature, 1966-1972—1985-1990; written and edited by Zena Sutherland. University of Chicago Press 1973-1991 4v   **028.1**

1. Children's literature—Bibliography 2. Books and reading—Best books 3. Books—Reviews

Successor to Good books for children; a selection of outstanding children's books published 1950-65, compiled by Mary K. Eakin

1985-1990 volume written by Zena Sutherland, Betsy Hearne, and Roger Sutton

Volumes available are: 1966-1972 $28 (ISBN 0-226-78057-0); 1973-1978 $28 (ISBN 0-226-78059-7); 1979-1984 $36.50 (ISBN 0-226-78060-0); 1985-1990 $39.25 (ISBN 0-226-78064-3)

These volumes bring together reviews originally published in The Bulletin of the Center for Children's Books. Some 1400 recommended titles from each period are covered in each volume. The listings are arranged alphabetically by author, with title, developmental values, curricular use, reading level, subject, and type of literature indexes

Booklist. American Lib. Assn. $65 per year

028.1

1. Books—Reviews 2. Books and reading—Best books
ISSN 0006-7385

Semimonthly September through June; monthly July and August. First published 1905 with title: A.L.A. Booklist. Merged with Subscription Books Bulletin in 1956

The Reference Books Bulletin section is also available separately in an annual cumulation for $26

"Intended chiefly as a guide for librarians in public and school libraries, each issue covers titles in five major areas: forthcoming titles, adult books, books for youth, audiovisual media, and reference books. . . . Because of its selectivity, its early reviews, and its broad coverage of popular non-print media, *Booklist* is essential reading for public, school, and many academic libraries." Katz. Mag for Libr. 8th edition

Bulletin of the Center for Children's Books. University of Ill. Press $35 per year

028.1

1. Books—Reviews 2. Children's literature—Reviews—Periodicals
ISSN 0008-9036

Monthly except August. First published 1945 for the University of Chicago, Graduate Library School

"This highly regarded reviewing source covers selected titles from the thousands of children's books published each year. In addition to complete bibliographic information, the critical annotations are supplemented by an indication of suitable age and/or grade level, a shorthand code noting a range of quality, from 'books of special distinction' to 'NR' for not recommended. . . . Librarians in schools, public libraries, and academic libraries with children's literature collections will find this an indispensable guide." Katz. Mag for Libr. 8th edition

Children's book review index. Gale Res. $114

028.1

1. Books—Reviews—Indexes 2. Children's literature—Reviews—Indexes
ISSN 0147-5681

A four volume master cumulation, 1985-1994 (ISBN 0-8103-5457-8) is available for $400

Annual. First published 1975

"Each annual cites more than 17,700 reviews of more than 10,000 children's books, preschool through grade 10. The same citations also appear in *Book Review Index*, of which this is a spinoff. Reviews cited can be found in the 470 periodicals indexed in *BRI*. It is arranged in a single alphabet by author." Nichols. Guide to Ref Books for Sch Media Cent. 4th edtion

Parents' Choice: a review of children's media. Parents' Choice Foundation $18 per year

028.1

1. Children's literature—Reviews—Periodicals 2. Audiovisual materials—Reviews

Quarterly. First published 1979

"The most important feature of *Parent's Choice* is the well-balanced reviews of children's media. Selection guidance is provided for parents and librarians on books, TV programs, movies, videos, computer software, music, toys, and games. . . . Annotated bibliographies provide an opportunity for further research. Articles are entertaining and often provide helpful hints on how to contribute informally to a child's education. The advisory board is comprised of eminent professors, authors, poets, and publishers." Katz. Mag for Sch Libr

Thomas, James L., 1945-
Play, learn, and grow; an annotated guide to the best books and materials for very young children. Bowker 1992 xxxv, 439p $31.25

028.1

1. Books and reading—Best books 2. Children's literature—Bibliography 3. Audiovisual materials—Catalogs
ISBN 0-8352-3019-8   LC 92-15458

This is an "extensive guide to the selection of print and nonprint materials for infants, toddlers, preschoolers, and kindergarteners. More than 1,000 titles were chosen, graded, and ranked as to purchase priority by an impressive panel of 64 librarians and early childhood education specialists." Booklist

The **Web**. Ohio State Univ. $10 per year

028.1

1. Books—Reviews 2. Children's literature—Reviews—Periodicals

Three issues a year. First published 1976

"This excellent reviewing tool 'is a publication devoted to reviewing books and suggesting ways that they can be used in the classroom.' . . . No fancy printing or glossy paper here, just a compilation of photocopied pages filled with interesting and personal reviews by teachers, often accompanied by very lively accounts of how these books 'worked' in their classrooms. There are also bibliographies around themes, with lesson plans suggested." Katz. Mag for Libr. 8th edition

028.5 Reading and use of other information media by children and young adults

The **Arbuthnot** lectures, 1970-1979/1980-1989; [by] Association for Library Service to Children, American Library Association. American Lib. Assn. 1980-1990 2v

028.5

1. Children's literature—History and criticism

Analyzed in Essay and general literature index

1970-1979 volume o.p.; 1980-1989 pa $6 (ISBN 0-8389-3388-2)

These volumes contain lectures presented in honor of May Hill Arbuthnot by distinguished international authorities on children's literature. Among the lecturers are John Rowe Townsend, Jean Fritz, Sheila Egoff, Virginia Betancourt, Fritz Eichenberg, and Aidan Chambers

Battling dragons; issues and controversy in children's literature; edited by Susan Lehr. Heinemann (Portsmouth) 1995 288p $22.50

028.5

1. Children's literature—History and criticism
ISBN 0-435-08828-9   LC 94-31973

"Lehr presents essays on children's literature within a loose framework of thematic divisions, including censorship, heroes, family values and the roles of children. . . . The essays, varied and generally quite readable, offer such a wide range of viewpoints that any reader with an interest in children's books can find both something to applaud and something to disagree with. A lively, provocative book." Booklist

Includes bibliographical references

Bauer, Caroline Feller, 1935-

This way to books; drawings by Lynn Gates. Wilson, H.W. 1983 363p il $45   **028.5**

1. Books and reading 2. Children's literature

ISBN 0-8242-0678-9   LC 82-19985

"Designed to involve children in books, this compendium is chock-full of ideas for programs, booktalks, games, crafts, and exhibits. Bauer's upbeat tone lends enthusiasm, and her numerous suggestions, which include easy-to-implement activities, short poems, directions for crafts, recipes, and unusual but effective bibliographies, will inspire readers with new ideas. . . . Teachers, librarians, and other adults working with children will find the collection worthwhile and helpful as a springboard to their own variations." Booklist

Booktalking the award winners; edited by Joni Richards Bodart. Wilson, H.W. pa ea $32   **028.5**

1. Books and reading—Best books 2. Children's literature—Stories, plots, etc. 3. Young adults' literature—Stories, plots, etc.

Retrospective volume in preparation

Annual. First published 1994 for 1992-1993

Each volume of this series is composed of 200-300 booktalks on children's and young adult titles which have won national-level awards during the previous year. Among the awards represented are the Caldecott, Carnegie and Newbery medals, the Coretta Scott King Book Award and the Scott O'Dell Award for Historical Fiction. Bibliographies by author, by age level, and by theme and genre are included

Caldecott Medal books, 1938-1957; with the artist's acceptance papers & related material chiefly from The Horn Book Magazine; edited by Bertha Mahony Miller and Elinor Whitney Field. Horn Bk. 1957 329p il o.p.   **028.5**

1. Children's literature—History and criticism 2. Illustrators

Companion volume to Newbery Medal books, 1922-1955

"Horn Book papers"

"A short study of Randolph Caldecott, for whom the award is named, prefaces the chronological listing of the award books. With this listing are given the acceptance speech of each artist and a biographical sketch of each." Booklist

Followed by Newbery and Caldecott Medal books, 1956-1965 (o.p.)

Cameron, Eleanor, 1912-

The seed and the vision; on the writing and appreciation of children's books. Dutton Children's Bks. 1993 xx, 362p $24.99   **028.5**

1. Children's literature—History and criticism 2. Books and reading

ISBN 0-525-44949-3   LC 92-8220

Also available in paperback from New Am. Lib.

A series of essays examining the writing, themes, influence, range, and critical appreciation of children's books

"Thoughtful and probing, Cameron's critiques bring a broad range of reading and a rigorous intellect to bear on children's books." Booklist

Carpenter, Humphrey

The Oxford companion to children's literature; [by] Humphrey Carpenter and Mari Prichard. Oxford Univ. Press 1984 586p il $52.25   **028.5**

1. Children's literature—Dictionaries

ISBN 0-19-211582-0   LC 83-15130

"One volume work with brief critiques of authors, illustrators, books, characters, and radio and television programs. Largely British in coverage of materials but does include most Newbery winners as well as well-known American, Australian and Canadian authors. Contemporary and historical subjects related to children's literature are examined." N Y Public Libr. Ref Books for Child Collect. 2d edition

Cart, Michael

What's so funny? wit and humor in American children's literature. HarperCollins Pubs. 1995 223p $25   **028.5**

1. Children's literature—History and criticism 2. American wit and humor—History and criticism

ISBN 0-06-024453-4   LC 94-15583

"Cart begins by presenting the history of humor and its evolution in children's literature. He then discusses the various types of humor and focuses on three: hyperbole and tall-tale humor, domestic or family comedy, and universal humor, specifically talking-animals. There is an analysis of the Dr. Doolittle stories, Walter R. Brooks' *Freddy the Pig*, Robert Lawson's works, Arnold Lobel's *Frog and Toad* titles, and Sid Fleischman's publications. Cart also intersperses biographical information about many of the writers." Book Rep

Includes bibliographical references

Children and their books; a celebration of the work of Iona and Peter Opie; edited by Gillian Avery and Julia Briggs; with a foreword by Iona Opie. Oxford Univ. Press 1989 424p hardcover o.p. paperback available $19.75   **028.5**

1. Opie, Iona Archibald 2. Opie, Peter, 1918-1982 3. Children's literature—History and criticism

ISBN 0-19-812253-5 (pa)   LC 88-27005

"The editors have gathered twenty essays into a substantial volume; they pay tribute to the Opies' remarkable achievement in amassing a vast collection of books to support their research into the lore and literature of childhood. . . . The pieces, in general, reflect not only children's literature but the Opies' concern with the evolution of society's attitudes toward children." Horn Book

Children's books and their creators; Anita Silvey, editor. Houghton Mifflin 1995 800p il $40   **028.5**

1. Children's literature—Bio-bibliography 2. Children's literature—History and criticism

ISBN 0-395-65380-0   LC 95-19049

This volume "compiles, in alphabetical order, 823 articles, most of them essays on contemporary creators of children's books. Writers as early as Aesop and as varied as Anna Sewell and Mark Twain are also included. . . . Each essay focuses on the subject's importance to the field of children's books and notes major contributions. . . . Silvey's editorial judgment is sound, and the entries, although varying in quality and depth, are usually well done." SLJ

Children's books: awards & prizes; includes prizes and awards for young adult books; compiled & edited by the Children's Book Council. Children's Bk. Council $85; pa $57.50 **028.5**

1. Literary prizes—Bibliography 2. Children's literature—Bibliography 3. Young adults' literature—Bibliography

ISSN 0069-3472

First published 1969. (1992 edition published 1993) Periodically revised

This publication lists 190 awards divided as follows: Part I: United States awards selected by adults; Part II: United States awards selected by young readers; Part III: Australian, Canadian, New Zealand, and United Kingdom (UK) awards; Part IV: Selected international and multinational awards; Part V: Awards classified; Part VI: Publications and lists for selecting U. S. children's and young adult books. A brief history of each award precedes the list of winners

Children's literature review; excerpts from reviews, criticism, and commentary on books for children. Gale Res. il ea $120 **028.5**

1. Children's literature—History and criticism 2. Books—Reviews

Started publication 1976. Frequency varies

"Each volume [of this ongoing series] offers excerpts from reviews and criticism (from both books and periodicals) of some 20-40 authors. International in scope. Cumulative indexes to authors and titles in successive volumes." Guide to Ref Books. 11th edition

Cook, Elizabeth
The ordinary and the fabulous; an introduction to myths, legends and fairy tales. 2nd ed. Cambridge Univ. Press 1976 xx, 182p o.p. **028.5**

1. Children's literature—History and criticism 2. Books and reading 3. Storytelling LC 75-7213

First published 1962

The author's "discussions include the significance and values found in myths and fairy tales; suggest various myths for different age groups with comments on children's responses; deal with practical problems of the storyteller, and reproduce and dissect parallel passages from children's book versions and their original sources. The annotated selective bibliography, though excellent, is British oriented." Booklist

The **Coretta** Scott King Awards book; from vision to reality; Henrietta M. Smith, editor; [by] Coretta Scott King Task Force, Social Responsibilities Round Table. American Lib. Assn. 1994 115p il pa $25 **028.5**

1. Literary prizes 2. Children's literature—History and criticism 3. American literature—African American authors 4. African Americans in literature

ISBN 0-8389-3441-2

"Commemorating the twenty-fifth anniversary of the establishment of the Coretta Scott King Awards, Smith has compiled a comprehensive survey of the award winning titles. . . . Useful as a retrospective selection tool, the book is also a browsable overview of the best of the last twenty-five years of African-American literature for children." Bull Cent Child Books

Crosscurrents of criticism; Horn book essays, 1968-1977; selected and edited by Paul Heins. Horn Bk. 1977 359p $14.95 **028.5**

1. Children's literature—History and criticism

ISBN 0-87675-034-X LC 77-24256

Analyzed in Essay and general literature index

Companion volume to A Horn Book Sampler on children's books and reading and Horn Book Reflections on children's books and reading, both entered below

A collection of 45 essays selected from The Horn Book Magazine. "Articles grouped around topics such as status of children's literature, classification, standards, current trends, fantasy, humor, the historical scene, internationalism, translation concerns, and books and authors offer a wide diversification of thought and opinion in the field of criticism. Index to authors and titles appended." Booklist

Egoff, Sheila A.
Worlds within; children's fantasy from the Middle Ages to today. American Lib. Assn. 1988 339p $9 **028.5**

1. Children's literature—History and criticism 2. Fantasy fiction—History and criticism

ISBN 0-8389-0494-7 LC 88-10058

"Following an opening chapter on the roots, substance, types, and value of fantasy for children [Egoff] examines the genre chronologically. The fluid text, for the most part, is divided by decade, starting with the Middle Ages and continuing into the 1980s. In her discussion, Egoff reflects on more than 375 novels, often comparing and contrasting them with other books of merit and commenting on the book's contribution, uniqueness, and role as trendsetter." Booklist

Gillespie, John Thomas, 1928-
Juniorplots; a book talk manual for teachers and librarians; by John Gillespie and Diana Lembo. Bowker 1967 222p $29.95 **028.5**

1. Books—Reviews 2. Literature—Stories, plots, etc. 3. Books and reading

ISBN 0-3352-0063-9 LC 67-18146

Contains plot summaries of eighty books to be used in book talk with young people ages 9 to 16

More juniorplots; a guide for teachers and librarians; by John T. Gillespie. Bowker 1977 xxv, 253p $29.95 **028.5**

1. Books—Reviews 2. Literature—Stories, plots, etc. 3. Books and reading

ISBN 0-8352-1002-2 LC 77-8786

This volume analyzes seventy-two titles organized under nine developmental goals associated with adolescence

Juniorplots 3; a book talk guide for use with readers ages 12-16; by John T. Gillespie with Corinne J. Naden. Bowker 1987 352p $34 **028.5**

1. Books—Reviews 2. Literature—Stories, plots, etc. 3. Books and reading

ISBN 0-8352-2367-1 LC 87-27305

Presents summaries of eighty fiction and nonfiction titles divided by eight basic behavioral themes

Gillespie, John Thomas, 1928-—_Continued_

Juniorplots 4; a book talk guide for use with readers ages 12-16; by John T. Gillespie and Corinne J. Naden. Bowker 1993 450p $35.50

028.5

1. Books—Reviews 2. Literature—Stories, plots, etc. 3. Books and reading
ISBN 0-8352-3167-4   LC 92-35670

Continues the series of Juniorplots entered in main catalog

This volume provides entries for 80 contemporary fiction and nonfiction titles arranged by genre. Cumulative author, title and subject indexes for the earlier Juniorplots volumes are included in this volume

Middleplots 4; a book talk guide for use with readers ages 8-12; by John T. Gillespie and Corinne J. Naden. Bowker 1994 434p $42

028.5

1. Books—Reviews 2. Young adults' literature—Stories, plots, etc. 3. Books and reading
ISBN 0-8352-3446-0   LC 93-21146

Continues Gillespie's Introducing books (1970), Introducing more books, by D. L. Spirt (1978), and Introducing bookplots 3, by D. L. Spirt (1988). All three titles currently available

"The selections are organized thematically in eight interest categories such as 'Adventure and Mystery' and 'Other Lands and Times.' Each selection is organized under six sections: plot summary, thematic material, booktalk suggestions, similar books, review citations, and books and articles about the author. . . . Author, title, and subject indexes for this volume are followed by cumulative author, title, and subject indexes to the series." Booklist

Includes bibliographical references

Hazard, Paul, 1878-1944

Books, children, and men; translated by Marguerite Mitchell, with an introduction by Sheila A. Egoff. 5th ed. Horn Bk. 1983 196p pa $11.95

028.5

1. Children's literature—History and criticism 2. Books and reading
ISBN 0-87675-059-5   LC 82-25851

Original French edition, 1932. First United States edition, 1944

A series of essays in which the author discusses children's books in terms of the cultures of various peoples
Includes bibliography

Hey! listen to this; stories to read aloud; edited by Jim Trelease. Viking 1992 414p hardcover o.p. paperback available $11.95

028.5

1. Children—Books and reading 2. Literature—Collections 3. Authors
ISBN 0-14-014653-9 (pa)   LC 91-37668

"Divided into categories such as 'Animal Tales,' 'Children of Courage,' or 'Classic Tales,' the forty-eight selections cover a wide spectrum from folktales to fantasy, classics to contemporary stories. More than half are complete stories, while the remainder are one or two chapters from longer books. Trelease skillfully weaves his choices into a cohesive whole. Beyond merely categorizing them, he refers to other authors or stories in the discussions that precede and follow each story." J Youth Serv Libr

Includes bibliographies

Horn Book reflections on children's books and reading; selected from eighteen years of The Horn Book Magazine, 1949-1966; edited by Elinor Whitney Field. Horn Bk. 1969 367p pa $6.95

028.5

1. Children's literature—History and criticism
ISBN 0-87675-979-3

Companion volume to A Horn Book sampler on children's books and reading, entered below, and Crosscurrents of criticism: Horn Book essays, 1968-1977, entered above

This collection of "articles and essays relating to various aspects of children's reading and literature includes material by authors, illustrators, parents, teachers, and librarians." Booklist

A **Horn** Book sampler on children's books and reading; selected from twenty-five years of The Horn Book Magazine, 1924-1948; edited by Norma R. Fryatt; introduction by Bertha Mahony Miller. Horn Bk. 1959 261p hardcover o.p. paperback available $6.95

028.5

1. Children's literature—History and criticism
ISBN 0-87675-032-3 (pa)

Analyzed in Essay and general literature index

"Articles, editorials, book reviews, and a few poems reprinted from the 'Horn Book' from its founding in 1924 to 1948. The sampler includes essays by authors on how certain of their stories came to be written, evaluations of the work of such illustrators as Kate Greenaway, Arthur Rackham, and Leslie Brooke, criticisms of single books and of trends in children's literature, discussions of fairy tales and books for small children, and a group of papers addressed to parents." Booklist

Huck, Charlotte S.

Children's literature in the elementary school; [by] Charlotte S. Huck, Susan Hepler, Janet Hickman. Harcourt Brace College Pubs. $46

028.5

1. Children's literature—History and criticism

First published 1961. (5th edition 1993) Periodically revised

This resource "provides criteria for evaluation of various kinds of genres and discusses favorite books of children at various developmental levels as well as children's responses to literature. It also suggests ideas on how to plan and extend the literature program in the classroom. Lists Book Awards and Book Selection Aids and includes subject and author/illustrator/title indexes." N Y Public Libr. Ref Books for Child Collect. 2d edition

Kobrin, Beverly

Eyeopeners II; children's books to answer children's questions about the world around them. Scholastic 1995 305p il pa $6.95

028.5

1. Children's literature—History and criticism 2. Books and reading
ISBN 0-590-48402-8   LC 95-36183

Original Eyeopeners published 1988 by Viking o.p.

This work "describes more than 800 nonfiction titles for preschool through middle school. The books are arranged by topic. . . . Most titles were published from 1990 to 1995. The brief annotations not only describe what the books are about, but also offer stimulating ideas for their use. . . . An

Kobrin, Beverly—*Continued*
easy-to-use reference for adults working with children."
Booklist

Konigsburg, E. L.

TalkTalk; a children's book author speaks to grown-ups. Atheneum Pubs. 1995 198p il $29.95 **028.5**

1. Children's literature—History and criticism

ISBN 0-689-31993-2   LC 94-32341

"A Jean Karl book"

"Nine entertaining and provocative speeches, ranging from the author's 1968 Newbery acceptance to a reassuring rationale for the continuing significance of children's books in the multimedia nineties." J Youth Serv Libr

Many faces, many voices; multicultural literary experiences for youth: the Virginia Hamilton Conference; edited by Anthony L. Manna and Carolyn S. Brodie. Highsmith Press 1992 xxiii, 183p il pa $29 **028.5**

1. Children's literature—History and criticism 2. Books and reading 3. Minorities—Bibliography

ISBN 0-917846-12-5   LC 92-31119

A collection of papers presented at the Virginia Hamilton Conference on multicultural literature for young people. Appendixes list recommended titles and identify sources of multicultural materials

McElmeel, Sharron L.

Great new nonfiction reads. Libraries Unlimited 1995 225p il pa $21 **028.5**

1. Children—Books and reading

ISBN 1-56308-228-4   LC 94-20258

"A bibliography of recent nonfiction recommended for reading aloud or sharing with elementary students. For each of the 120 main titles, the author includes a comprehensive annotation and complete bibliographic information, including the book's Dewey number, its target audience, and suggestions for connecting the book to other readings, family activities, and curriculum topics. . . . This volume will be helpful not only to children's librarians and teachers but also to parents who want to provide their children with recommended books that cover a wide spectrum of subjects." SLJ

The **Newbery** and Caldecott awards; a guide to the medal and honor books; [by] Association for Library Service to Children. American Lib. Assn. il pa $15 **028.5**

1. Newbery Medal 2. Caldecott Medal

ISSN 1070-4493

Annual

"An annotated listing of winning titles since the inception of the awards (1922 and 1938 respectively). . . . Annotations serve as a reliable guide for collection development, reader's advisory, curriculum development, and a host of other programs." Publisher's note

Newbery and Caldecott Medal books, 1966-1975; with acceptance papers, biographies, and related material chiefly from The Horn Book magazine; edited by Lee Kingman. Horn Bk. 1975 xx, 321p il $22.95 **028.5**

1. Newbery Medal 2. Caldecott Medal 3. Children's literature—History and criticism 4. Authors 5. Illustrators

ISBN 0-87675-003-X

Continues Newbery Medal books, 1922-1955, Caldecott Medal books, 1938-1957, and Newbery and Caldecott Medal books, 1956-1965 (o.p.)

"Gives for each Newbery or Caldecott award winner his acceptance speech, a biographical note, and a book note. An excerpt from each Newbery book gives an example of the writer's style; a sample illustration from each Caldecott book is supplemented by notes on size, medium, printing process, number of illustrations and type used." Choice

Newbery and Caldecott Medal books, 1976-1985; with acceptance papers, biographies, and related material chiefly from The Horn Book magazine; edited by Lee Kingman. Horn Bk. 1986 358p il $24.95 **028.5**

1. Newbery Medal 2. Caldecott Medal 3. Children's literature—History and criticism 4. Authors 5. Illustrators

ISBN 0-87675-004-8   LC 86-15223

This volume "compiles the winning speeches, biographies and book notes for the 1976 through 1985 awards. It includes essays by Barbara Bader, Ethel Heins and Zena Sutherland." Bookbird

Newbery Medal books, 1922-1955; with their authors' acceptance papers & related material chiefly from The Horn Book magazine; edited by Bertha Mahony Miller and Elinor Whitney Field. Horn Bk. 1955 458p il $22.95 **028.5**

1. Newbery Medal 2. Children's literature—History and criticism 3. Authors

ISBN 0-87675-000-5

Companion volume to Caldecott Medal books, 1938-1957

"Largely biographical notes about award recipients and the acceptance papers." Ref Sources for Small & Medium-sized Libr. 5th edition

Only connect: readings on children's literature; edited by Sheila Egoff [et al.] 3rd ed. Oxford Univ. Press 1996 416p il pa $19.95 **028.5**

1. Children's literature—History and criticism

ISBN 0-19-541024-6

First published 1969 and analyzed in Essay and general literature index

This volume "presents a completely new selection of more than 40 essays and brief studies on history and criticism, literary standards, changing tastes, science fiction, young adult literature, fantasy, the problem novel, racism, and sexism. Among the essayists are Joan Aiken, Margaret Mahy, P.L. Travers, Perry Nodelman, Brian Attebery, John Rowe Townsend, Myra Cohn Livingston, Peter Hunt, and Jane Yolen." Publisher's note

Pauses; autobiographical reflections of 101 creators of children's books; [compiled by] Lee Bennett Hopkins. HarperCollins Pubs. 1995 233p $23　　　　**028.5**

1. Children's literature—History and criticism 2. Authors 3. Illustrators
ISBN 0-06-024748-7　　　　LC 94-14641

"This is a compilation of Hopkins' interviews with authors and illustrators, conducted primarily in the '60s and '70s. Each figure gets a paragraph of updated biography and a two or three-page edited version of the interviews; while topics addressed vary, the interviews all tend to describe growing up, beginnings as a children's author or illustrator, and the creative process." Bull Cent Child Books

Sendak, Maurice
Caldecott & Co.: notes on books and pictures. Farrar, Straus & Giroux 1988 216p il hardcover o.p. paperback available $8.95　　　　**028.5**

1. Children's literature—History and criticism 2. Illustrators
ISBN 0-374-52218-9 (pa)　　　　LC 87-19772

"Michael di Capua books"

A collection of 32 essays, speeches and reviews culled from the author/illustrator's critical work of the past 33 years

The author offers a "remarkably clear and consistent vision of excellence in both children's picture books and popular culture." N Y Times Book Rev

Smith, Lillian H., 1887-1983
The unreluctant years; a critical approach to children's literature; with a new introduction by Kay E. Vandergrift. American Lib. Assn. 1991 xxxii, 183p $25　　　　**028.5**

1. Children's literature—History and criticism
ISBN 0-8389-0557-9　　　　LC 90-23850

A reissue of the title first published 1953

"Analysis of the qualities of selected established children's classics as a basis for judging new books in terms of literary, ethical, and aesthetic values. Smith applies critical standards to identify high literary quality in literature of interest to children. As valuable now as when originally published." Ref Sources for Small & Medium-sized Libr. 5th edition

Sutherland, Zena, 1915-
Children and books; [by] Zena Sutherland, May Hill Arbuthnot; chapters contributed by Dianne L. Monson. HarperCollins Pubs. il $57　　　　**028.5**

1. Children's literature—History and criticism
First edition by May Hill Arbuthnot published 1947 by Scott, Foresman. (8th edition 1991) Periodically revised

"This standard textbook for courses in children's literature also serves as a handbook and selection aid for the field. Arranged in five major sections, it provides extensive information on all aspects of children's literature. . . . Indexed by subject and by author-title-illustrator. An essential holding for elementary and junior high school libraries.DD Nichols. Guide to Ref Books for Sch Media Cent. 4th edition

Trelease, Jim
The read-aloud handbook. 4th ed. Penguin Bks. 1995 xxvi, 387p pa $12.95　　　　**028.5**

1. Books and reading 2. Children's literature—Bibliography
ISBN 0-14-046971-0　　　　LC 95-2269

First published 1982

"Trelease shares his firm belief in books. A pep talk, with new research on the value of reading aloud and new methods for its encouragement, is followed by the 'Treasury of Read-Alouds,' featuring 300 children's books . . . all nicely annotated and with notes leading to even more titles. An essential library book, of value to parents and professionals." Booklist [review of 1989 edition]

Includes bibliographical references

Yolen, Jane
Touch magic; fantasy, faerie and folklore in the literature of childhood. Philomel Bks. 1981 96p il hardcover o.p. paperback available $10.95　　　　**028.5**

1. Children's literature—History and criticism 2. Folklore
ISBN 0-399-21897-1 (pa)　　　　LC 81-10578

Contents: How basic is shazam?; The lively fossil; Once upon a time; The eye and the ear; Touch magic; The mask on the lapel; Tough magic; Here there be dragons; The gift of tongues; An inlet for apple pie

"This should be required reading for teachers, librarians, and parents especially. The historical background of folk literature is absorbing reading." Child Book Rev Serv

Includes bibliography

028.505　Children's reading—Serial publications

Book Links. American Lib. Assn. $20　　　　**028.505**

1. Children's literature—Periodicals 2. Books and reading—Best books
ISSN 1055-4742

Bimonthly. First issued as an insert in Booklist, Nov. 15, 1990

This periodical "offers feature articles on children's books (e.g., best books of the year, a Newbery/Caldecott retrospective) and regular columns that suggest ways to incorporate fine children's literature into the curriculum. Background information on a topic . . . is accompanied by an annotated bibliography, complete with citation and appropriate grade level. Columns devoted to specific children's books and interviews with authors and illustrators review the subject for the adult who wants to read to or select books for children." Katz. Mag for Libr. 8th edition

Bookbird; world of children's books. $40 per year　　　　**028.505**

1. Children's literature—Periodicals 2. Books—Reviews 3. Books and reading—Best books
ISSN 0006-7377

Quarterly. First published 1962

Issued by the International Board on Books for Young People. For subscriptions write to P.O. Box 3156, West Lafayette, IN 47906

"This English-language journal provides news and literary essays on the most pertinent activities of the 16 countries that contribute to this worldwide effort. Articles, criticism, and occasional brief book reviews survey the best of children's literature." Katz. Mag for Sch Libr

Five Owls; a publication for readers personally and professionally involved in children's literature. 2004 Sheridan Ave. S., Minneapolis, MN 55405 $20 per year

028.505

1. Children's literature—Periodicals 2. Books—Reviews
ISSN 0892-6735
Bimonthly. First published 1986
Contains articles on children's literature, bibliographies, and reviews of recent books

The **Horn** Book Guide to Children's and Young Adult Books. Horn Bk. $50 per year

028.505

1. Children's literature—Periodicals 2. Books—Reviews
ISSN 1044-405X
Biannual. First published 1990
"This offshoot of *The Horn Book Magazine* provides critical annotations on all hardcover trade children's and young adult books published in the United States during the previous six months. Fiction is arranged by grade level and genre (picture books, readers), nonfiction by the ten broad Dewey classes and then narrower topics. . . . Numerous indexes (author, title, series, subject, new editions, and reissues) help the librarian track down particular titles." Katz. Mag for Libr. 8th edition

The **Horn** Book Magazine. Horn Bk. $42 per year

028.505

1. Children's literature—Periodicals 2. Books and reading—Best books 3. Books—Reviews
ISSN 0018-5078
Bimonthly. First published 1924 with title. The Horn Book
"One of the first magazines to treat children's literature as serious material for discussion and review. . . . The book reviews, most of which are for recommended titles, are grouped by age level and/or format (picture books, folklore, etc.). Other sections of the magazine include lists of new paperbacks, reissues, books in Spanish, and the occasional audio or video." Katz. Mag for Libr. 8th edition

The **New** Advocate. Christopher-Gordon Pubs., 480 Washington St., Norwood, MA 02062 $45

028.505

1. Children's literature—Periodicals 2. Books—Reviews
ISSN 0895-1381
Four issues a year. First published 1981 with title: Advocate
This professional journal features articles on using children's literature in the classroom, and includes book reviews

031 American general encyclopedic works

Children's Britannica. Encyclopaedia Britannica 20v il maps apply to publisher for price

031

1. Encyclopedias and dictionaries
First published 1960 in the United Kingdom. First United States edition published 1988 as successor to Britannica junior encyclopedia for boys and girls. Frequently revised
"Approximately 4,000 articles provide information on some 35,000 topics. . . . The set is suitable for a slightly younger age group than *World book* and comparable children's encyclopedias." Guide to Ref Books. 11th edition

Compton's encyclopedia and fact-index. Compton's Learning, for sale by SoftKey International, One Atheneum St., Cambridge, MA 02142 26v il maps apply to distributor for price

031

1. Encyclopedias and dictionaries
Also available CD-ROM version
First published 1922 with title: Compton's pictured encyclopedia. Frequently revised
Supplemented by: Compton yearbook
"An encyclopedia for young adults, ages nine through eighteen, for home and school use, with emphasis on practical and curriculum-related information. Among the . . . contributors are scholars, writers, and notable librarians. Arrangement is letter by letter and each volume . . . is divided into two parts. The illustrated 'Fact Index' at the back refers the readers to text and illustrations in the volume at hand and to information contained elsewhere in the set." A L A. Ref Sources for Small & Medium-sized Libr. 5th edition

Merit students encyclopedia. Macmillan Educ. Co. 20v il maps apply to publisher for price

031

1. Encyclopedias and dictionaries
First published 1967 by Crowell-Collier Educational Corporation. Frequently revised
"This set, designed for grades 5 through high school, is curriculum-oriented. . . . *Merit* maintains a good subject balance in its . . . entries. . . . The articles are accurate, objective, and clearly written. The balanced treatment of controversial topics is commendable." Nichols. Guide to Ref Books for Sch Media Cent. 4th edition

The **New** book of knowledge; the children's encyclopedia. Grolier 21v il maps apply to publisher for price

031

1. Encyclopedias and dictionaries
First published 1966 as successor to The Book of knowledge. Frequently revised
Supplemented by The New book of knowledge annual
"Intended to interest a wide range of readers from those in early childhood to students nearly ready to use an adult encyclopedia; thus, articles are written at various levels of understanding, with the main emphasis being for children in grades three to six. Longer articles are signed by contributors or consultants. Suggested activities or projects are incorporated into some articles to further the educational value." Guide to Ref Books. 11th edition

The **New** Grolier student encyclopedia. Grolier 23v il maps apply to publisher for price

031

1. Encyclopedias and dictionaries
Also available CD-ROM version
First published 1972 by American Educ. Publs. with title: Young students encyclopedia. Frequently revised
"The articles are designed for elementary and some junior high school children. As in many similar works, the entries start simply and grow more complex. The range of topics is wide and occasionally eclectic. . . . *The New Grolier Student Encyclopedia* will attract users with its abundant and interesting pictures and then hold them with its well-written text." Am Ref Books Annu, 1993

The **World** Book encyclopedia. World Bk. 22v il maps apply to publisher for price

031

1. Encyclopedias and dictionaries
Also available CD-ROM version
First published 1917-1918 by Field Enterprises. Frequently revised
Supplemented by The World Book year book; another available supplement is Science year
"A good juvenile encyclopedia, one of the leading American works in the field; approximates the form and treatment of the standard works for adults, so is especially good for the older child nearly ready to use adult material. . . . Children's librarians generally agree that *World book* continues to be the most popular general encyclopedia for readers 10 years of age and older." Guide to Ref Books. 11th edition

031.02   American books of miscellaneous facts

Information please almanac, atlas & yearbook. Houghton Mifflin $21.95; pa $8.95

031.02

1. Almanacs 2. Statistics 3. United States—Statistics
ISSN 0073-7860
Annual. First published 1947 by Doubleday. Publisher varies
"Statistical and factual material organized by subject area; contains special articles by experts. Illustrated, with a color map section and detailed index." N Y Public Libr. Book of How & Where to Look It Up

Kane, Joseph Nathan, 1899-
Famous first facts: a record of first happenings, discoveries, and inventions in American history. 4th ed expanded & rev. Wilson, H.W. 1981 1350p $80   **031.02**
1. Encyclopedias and dictionaries 2. United States—History—Dictionaries
ISBN 0-8242-0661-4   LC 81-3395
First published 1933
"This unusual work focuses on 'firsts' on the North American continent (1,007 to date) that concern a wide range of subjects (e.g., events, inventions, discoveries)— 9,000 in all. Arrangement is by subject with appropriate cross-references and concise explanations for each entry. Indexing is by year and month/date of occurrence, names of persons directly and indirectly involved, and location of the event." Nichols. Guide to Ref Books for Sch Media Cent. 4th edition

The **World** almanac and book of facts. World Almanac il maps pa $9.95   **031.02**
1. Almanacs 2. Statistics 3. United States—Statistics
ISSN 0084-1382
Also available large print edition and CD-ROM version
Annual. First published 1868. Publisher varies
"This is the most comprehensive and well-known of almanacs. . . . Contains a chronology of the year's events, consumer information, historical anniversaries, annual climatological data, and forecasts. Color section has flags and maps. Includes detailed index." N Y Public Libr. Book of How & Where to Look It Up

032   English general encyclopedic works

Oxford children's encyclopedia. Oxford Univ. Press 7v il maps apply to publisher for price

032

1. Encyclopedias and dictionaries
First published 1991 as successor to Oxford junior encyclopedia. Frequently revised
These volumes examine "2,000 topics for the 8- to 13-year-old child. The set is appealing for browsing, study, or research. . . . The encyclopedia is arranged in one alphabet with the exception of volume 6, *Biography,* and the writing is appropriate for its intended audience. . . . The only problem with it in the hands of American children will be some word usage and topic selection, but the *Oxford Children's Encyclopedia* does give more of a world view than traditional American sources." Booklist

032.02   English books of miscellaneous facts

The **Guinness** book of answers; the complete reference handbook. Facts on File il $21.95

032.02

1. Encyclopedias and dictionaries
First published 1978 by Guinness Bks. (9th edition 1993) Periodically revised
"This compendium contains useful information for junior and senior high school students. . . . [It] focuses on 31 areas of knowledge, such as astronomy, plants and animals, the arts, sports, computers, and nations. An index provides easy access to the entries." Nichols. Guide to Ref Books for Sch Media Cent. 4th edition [review of 1991 edition]

Guinness book of records. Facts on File il $24.95   **032.02**
1. Curiosities and wonders
ISSN 1057-4557
Also available CD-ROM version
Annual. First published 1955 in the United Kingdom; in the United States 1962. Variant title: Guinness book of world records
"A compendium of information concerning the longest, shortest, tallest, deepest, fastest, etc., in relation to natural features, manmade structures, people, events and achievements (in sports, politics, arts and entertainment), etc., grouped in topical sections." Guide to Ref Books. 11th edition

051   American general serial publications and their indexes

Abridged Readers' guide to periodical literature. Wilson, H.W. $100 per year

051

1. Periodicals—Indexes
ISSN 0001-334X
First published July 1935. Monthly except June, July, and August (The indexing for these months is included in the September issue). Permanent bound annual cumulations
An index to 82 periodicals of general interest which have been chosen by the subscribers to the index from the approximately 190 periodicals covered by the unabridged Readers' Guide to Periodical Literature. The form of index-

Abridged Readers' guide to periodical litera-ture—*Continued*
ing is the same as that used in the unabridged Readers' Guide
"Designed especially for school and small public libraries unable to afford the regular Readers' guide." Sheehy. Guide to Ref Books. 10th edition

Children's Magazine Guide; subject index to children's magazines. Bowker $48 per year **051**

1. Periodicals—Indexes
ISSN 0743-9873
Nine issues a year. First published 1949 with title: Subject index to Children's Magazines. Publisher and frequency vary
This publication "indexes 45 magazines for children and 11 professional journals published for librarians and teachers. . . . Entries are arranged under subject headings in alphabetical order by the title of the article. Bibliographic information includes article and journal titles, author's name (when available), issue month and year, and page numbers." Katz. Mag for Libr. 8th edition

Cricket; the magazine for children. Carus Corp. $29.97 **051**

1. Children's literature—Periodicals
ISSN 0090-6034
Monthly. First published 1973 by Open Court Publishing
Intended for ages 9 to 14, "*Cricket* is a general-interest magazine for children, with a variety of stories, poems, and articles. The stories come from various cultures and should entertain as well as broaden children's interests. Lovely drawings enhance the stories and articles." Katz. Mag for Libr. 8th edition

Highlights for Children. P.O. Box 182346, Columbus, OH 43272-2167 $26.04 per year **051**

1. Children's literature—Periodicals
ISSN 0018-165X
Monthly. First published 1946
This magazine "is intended for children of all ages . . . and carries stories, articles, and regular items appropriate to various reading and interest levels. The diversity of subject matter places this magazine among the few general-interest ones available for children. . . . [Included in each issue are] crafts and projects; puzzles, hidden pictures, and word games; and contributions from children." Richardson. Mag for Child. 2d edition

Ladybug; the magazine for young children. Carus Corp. $29.97 **051**

1. Children's literature—Periodicals
ISSN 1051-4961
Monthly. Started publication 1990
Aimed at ages 2 to 6, "*Ladybug* is a companion magazine to *Cricket* and *Spider*. It features stories, articles, poems, songs, and games. Issues also feature 'Ladybug for Parents,' with ideas for parents that relate to the articles in the issue. The illustrations are beautiful, depict a diverse population, and will appeal to children." Katz. Mag for Libr. 8th edition

Spider; the magazine for children. Carus Corp. $29.97 **051**

1. Children's literature—Periodicals
ISSN 1070-2911
Monthly. Started publication 1994

"*Spider* is a general-interest magazine for children [ages 6 to 9], with a variety of stories, poems, and articles. Like other magazines by this publisher (*Ladybug* and *Cricket*), *Spider* provides content that will both entertain and broaden children's interests. The drawings are beautiful and enhance the stories. The high quality of this magazine makes it an excellent choice for schools, libraries, and individuals." Katz. Mag for Libr. 8th edition

060.4 General rules of order (Parliamentary procedure)

Robert, Henry Martyn, 1837-1923
The Scott, Foresman Robert's Rules of order newly revised. a new and enl ed, by Sarah Corbin Robert, with the assistance of Henry M. Robert III, William J. Evans. Scott, Foresman $18.95; pa $9.95 **060.4**

1. Parliamentary practice
A simplified paperback version with title: The new Robert's Rules of order, by Mary A. De Vries, is available from New Am. Lib.
First published 1876 as: Pocket manual of rules of order for deliberate assemblies. Later editions have title: Robert's Rules of order
"Long the standard compendium of parliamentary law, explaining methods of organizing and conducting the business of societies, conventions, and other assemblies. Includes convenient charts and tables." Ref Sources for Small & Medium-sized Libr. 5th edition

Sturgis, Alice
Standard code of parliamentary procedure. 3rd ed new and rev. McGraw-Hill 1988 xxiv, 275p hardcover o.p. paperback available $12.95 **060.4**

1. Parliamentary practice
ISBN 0-07-062522-0 (pa)   LC 88-460194
First published 1950
"A somewhat simpler and clearer presentation of the rules of parliamentary procedure, supported by explanations of the underlying purpose of the rules and examples of their use. Revised with the assistance of the Revision Committee, American Institute of Parliamentarians." Ref Sources for Small & Medium-sized Libr. 5th edition
Includes bibliography

070.5 Publishing

Brookfield, Karen
Book; written by Karen Brookfield; photographed by Laurence Pordes. Knopf 1993 63p il (Eyewitness books) $19; lib bdg $18.99 (4 and up) **070.5**

1. Books
ISBN 0-679-84012-5; 0-679-94012-X (lib bdg)
                                    LC 93-18833
"A Dorling Kindersley book"
Text and photographs trace the evolution of the written word, how the alphabet grew out of pictures, the development of papermaking, bookbinding, children's books, and more
"The text is augmented heavily with numerous high-

Brookfield, Karen—*Continued*
quality photographs, which are, perhaps, the crowning
touch. They make the text come alive." Sci Books Films

070.5025 Publishing—Directories

Children's media market place. Neal-Schuman
pa $49.95   **070.5025**

1. Publishers and publishing—Directories 2. Audiovisual
materials—Directories
First published 1978 by Gaylord Professional Publs. (4th
edition 1995) Frequently revised. Editors vary
This tool provides directory information about children's
book publishers, software producers and distributors, AV
producers and distributors, periodicals for children, book
clubs, networking resources and other media services for
children

070.505 Publishing—Serial publications

Publisher's Weekly; the international news
magazine of book publishing. Cahners $149
per year   **070.505**

1. Publishers and publishing—Periodicals 2. Books—
Reviews
ISSN 0000-0019
Weekly. First published 1872
"Chock-full of news on publishers and publishing, with
an emphasis on the American scene, PW talks with and
about the editors, designers, and marketers of books. For
[librarians] . . . its most useful feature is the 'Forecasts' section, which reviews new titles, with notes on special promo-
tions or ad campaigns.The regular issues in specific subject
areas (children's books, religion) are useful checklists."
Katz. Mag for Libr. 8th edition

071 Journalism and newspapers—North America

Fleming, Thomas J., 1927-
Behind the headlines; the story of American
newspapers. Walker & Co. 1989 154p
(Walker's American history series for young
people) $14.95; lib bdg $15.85 (5 and up)
                                                071

1. American newspapers 2. Reporters and reporting
ISBN 0-8027-6890-3; 0-8027-6891-1 (lib bdg)
                                          LC 89-5690
Surveys the history of American newspapers and how reporting techniques and perceptions have changed over the
years
"There are no slow news days in this view of the fourth
estate, but along with all the fireworks, Fleming provides
solid information on how the American newspaper industry
flourished in the nineteenth century, illustrating in the process how a high literacy rate can actually change the course
of history." Booklist
Includes bibliography

Granfield, Linda
Extra! Extra! the who, what, where, when
and why of newspapers; written by Linda
Granfield; illustrated by Bill Slavin. Orchard
Bks. 1994 72p il lib bdg $16.99; pa $7.95 (4-6)
                                                071

1. Newspapers
ISBN 0-531-08683-6 (lib bdg); 0-531-07049-2 (pa)
                                          LC 93-11807
The author "analyzes the different departments and components of a typical paper. Next, she takes readers behind
the scenes to catch cameo glimpses of reporters, editors, designers, fact checkers, press workers, and delivery kids at
work. The third section shows readers how to publish their
own papers. . . . In the final chapter, she offers a series of
crafts and other new uses for old newspapers. . . . Cartoonlike drawings enliven every page. This volume packs a lot
of newspaper facts and lore into an appealing, though busy,
format." Booklist

100 PHILOSOPHY AND PSYCHOLOGY

133.1 Apparitions

Cohen, Daniel, 1936-
Ghost in the house; illustrated by John Paul
Caponigro. Cobblehill Bks. 1993 60p il $13.99
(4 and up)   **133.1**

1. Ghosts
ISBN 0-525-65131-4   LC 92-37858
Includes nine stories about some of the best known
haunted houses in the world, including the Octagon in
Washington, D.C., and the Weir house in Edinburgh, Scotland
"The stories are very simply told in very simple language
and will serve to whet the appetite for additional information." Booklist

Ghosts of the deep. Putnam 1993 103p
$14.95 (4 and up)   **133.1**

1. Ghosts
ISBN 0-399-22435-1   LC 92-34669
Also available in paperback from Simon & Schuster
"These accounts of ocean-going specters—from sailing
ship days to World War II—are dramatically written, and
many include corroborating historical detail, heightening the
impression of authenticity. . . . The book reflects Cohen's
open-minded attitude toward the uncanny—neither credulous nor scornful." SLJ

The ghosts of war. Putnam 1990 95p $13.95
(4 and up)   **133.1**

1. Ghosts 2. War
ISBN 0-399-22200-6   LC 89-27789
Recounts supposedly true stories about ghosts connected
in some way with war, from haunted battlefields to soldiers'
premonitions of death
These are "well-chosen tales, based on historic accounts.
. . . The eerie cover, an apparition wandering on a battlefield, will attract readers; once drawn in, they won't be disappointed." Booklist

Cohen, Daniel, 1936——*Continued*
Great ghosts; illustrated by David Linn.
Cobblehill Bks. 1990 48p il $13.99 (4 and up)

133.1

1. Ghosts
ISBN 0-525-65039-3   LC 90-34333
"Nine retellings of encounters with ghosts—six English,
one Dutch, one Greek, and one Middle Eastern. Each succinct, concisely told story is from three to four pages long,
and sports an illustration. While most of the tales can be
found in other sources, here they are lively and easily read,
without clutter." SLJ

133.4   Demonology and witchcraft

Jackson, Shirley, 1919-1965
The witchcraft of Salem Village. Random
House 1987 c1956 146p lib bdg $9.99; pa
$4.99 (4 and up)   **133.4**

1. Witchcraft 2. Salem (Mass.)—History
ISBN 0-394-90369-2 (lib bdg); 0-394-89176-7 (pa)
LC 87-4543

"Landmark books"
A reissue of the title first published 1956
"A simple, chilling account of the witchcraft trials of
1692 and '93 when, because of testimony given by a group
of little girls, twenty persons were executed as witches and
others died in jail. There is good introductory background
and though the story's subject is by nature horrifying the
book does not play on the emotions. . . It presents a difficult theme lucidly and without condescension." Horn Book

Krensky, Stephen, 1953-
Witch hunt; it happened in Salem Village;
illustrated by James Watling. Random House
1989 48p il lib bdg $7.99; pa $3.99 (2-4)

133.4

1. Witchcraft 2. Salem (Mass.)—History
ISBN 0-394-91923-8 (lib bdg); 0-394-81923-3 (pa)
LC 88-42865

"Step into reading. A step 4 book"
A retelling of the madness that overtook Salem Village,
Massachusetts, when several young girls accused a number
of adults in the community of being witches
This account possesses a "smooth, storytelling style that
admits the dramatic without spilling into the sensational. .
. While some of the watercolor illustrations seem content
to evoke a generic colonialism, many, including the cover,
have the requisite dark drama." Bull Cent Child Books

152.1   Sensory perception

Cobb, Vicki, 1938-
How to really fool yourself; illusions for all
your senses; illustrated by Leslie Morrill.
Lippincott 1981 145p il lib bdg $14.89 (5 and
up)   **152.1**

1. Senses and sensation 2. Perception 3. Optical
illusions
ISBN 0-397-31907-X   LC 79-9620
"The book begins with an explanation of perception and
explores many different sensory aspects of it through experiments, definitions of important terms (italicized), back-

ground information and how illusions affect us in everyday
life. It concludes with how some great misconceptions such
as the earth being flat were disproved. . . . All the senses
are covered here, even the 'sense' of imagination. The book
is easy to read, and directions are clear and accurate, viewing illusions from a scientific viewpoint. . . . Interesting, informative, and fun both for kids to use on their own and
for science classes." SLJ

McMillan, Bruce
Sense suspense; a guessing game for the five
senses; written and illustrated with
photographs and graphics by Bruce McMillan.
Scholastic 1994 unp il maps $15.95 (k-2)

152.1

1. Senses and sensation
ISBN 0-590-47904-0   LC 93-30272
"Bright photographs taken on the Caribbean island of
Culebra depict objects for readers to identify. The five
senses are represented by color-coded symbols, allowing
readers to choose what senses can be used with the objects,
which include a palm tree, parrot, flower, pineapple, conch,
and steel drum. Possible answers to the guessing game are
presented in both Spanish and English at the back." Horn
Book Guide

152.14   Visual perception

O'Neill, Catherine, 1950-
You won't believe your eyes! National
Geographic Soc. 1987 104p il $12.50 (4 and
up)   **152.14**

1. Optical illusions 2. Perception
ISBN 0-87044-611-8   LC 87-7637
"Books for world explorers"
"Introduces the world of visual illusion, describing the
workings of the eye-brain system and how different types of
illusions in nature, in art, and in architecture occur." Publisher's note
This book "is filled with exciting full-color photographs
and drawings. The captions are excellent, and the five chapters of prose are well-crafted. . . . As is appropriate for the
intended audience, primary attention is given to demonstrating clearly many familiar illusions. This book is not an
introduction to brain function, projective geometry, or laser
optics. Nevertheless, it should stimulate many young people
to do further reading into the mathematics and science of
visual perception and illusions." Appraisal
Includes bibliography

Westray, Kathleen
Picture puzzler. Ticknor & Fields Bks. for
Young Readers 1994 unp il $13.95 (2-4)

152.14

1. Optical illusions
ISBN 0-395-70130-9   LC 94-4066
This "explanation of assorted optical illusions employs .
. . gouache sketches in the style of American folk art to
demonstrate the visual phenomena—afterimages, blind
spots, incomplete pictures, the arrangement of lines and
shapes to alter perspective, color deceptions, and reversible
drawings." Horn Book
"The layout and ample white space will snare reluctant
readers; explanations of the illusions and how they work are
adequate, although not detailed. A fresh presentation for
young puzzlers." SLJ

152.3   Movements and motor functions

McMillan, Bruce
Beach ball—left, right; conceived and photo-illustrated by Bruce McMillan. Holiday House 1992 unp il lib bdg $14.95 (k-2)

152.3

1. Left and right
ISBN 0-8234-0946-5   LC 91-32802
Introduces the concept of "left" and "right" as the reader follows the airborne travels of a colorful beach ball

152.4   Emotions and feelings

Aliki
Feelings. Greenwillow Bks. 1984 32p il $16; lib bdg $15.93; pa $4.95 (k-3)   **152.4**
1. Emotions
ISBN 0-688-03831-X; 0-688-03832-8 (lib bdg); 0-688-06518-X (pa)   LC 84-4098
"Small pen-and-ink cartoons with vivid coloring depict boys and girls interacting and experiencing the full range of feelings which evolve in everyday settings. This creative, unique book would be ideal for parent/child interaction or use by elementary teachers in language arts classes. Children will enjoy the comic book 'frame' format." Child Book Rev Serv

153.4   Knowledge (Cognition)

Burns, Marilyn
The book of think; or, How to solve a problem twice your size; written by Marilyn Burns; illustrated by Martha Weston. Little, Brown 1976 125p il hardcover o.p. paperback available $10.95 (4 and up)   **153.4**
1. Thought and thinking 2. Problem solving
ISBN 0-316-11743-9 (pa)   LC 76-17848
"A Brown paper school book"
"A provocative text invites the reader to solve problems by looking for alternatives, sharpening the senses, studying people, and expressing ideas in words. Brain-teasers, riddles, and suggested projects are interpolated and represented by black-and-white line drawings." Child Books, 1976

Nozaki, Akihiro
Anno's hat tricks; text by Akihiro Nozaki; pictures by Mitsumasa Anno. Philomel Bks. 1985 41p il $15.95 (1-4)   **153.4**
1. Problem solving 2. Logic 3. Mathematics
ISBN 0-399-21212-4   LC 84-18900
Three children, Tom, Hannah, and Shadowchild, who represents the reader, are made to guess, using the concept of binary logic, the color of the hats on their heads. An introduction to logical thinking and mathematical problem-solving
"An introduction to 'if . . ., then . . .' thinking for those who enjoy intellectual puzzles, enlivened by Anno's charming illustrations. The early puzzles are fairly easy; succeed-

ing ones grow in difficulty. Along the way, the author helps the reader cultivate a method for attacking logical puzzles. There is a note for parents and older readers to help them use the book with children." Sci Child

154.6   Sleep phenomena

Silverstein, Alvin
The mystery of sleep; by Alvin and Virginia Silverstein; illustrated by Nelle Davis. Little, Brown 1987 43p il lib bdg $12.95 (4-6)

154.6

1. Sleep 2. Dreams
ISBN 0-316-79117-2   LC 86-20104
Discusses the subject of sleep, including animal sleep, dreams, nightmares, and sleep problems
"Satisfyingly information packed, the book links research findings with readers' experiences while being neither oversimplified nor patronizing. . . . Davis' upbeat drawings are a great addition and set a cozy mood. This is a fine book for readers curious about an aspect of themselves that they can't observe directly." SLJ

Stafford, Patricia
Dreaming and dreams; illustrated with photographs and with diagrams by the author. Atheneum Pubs. 1992 53p il $13.95 (5 and up)

154.6

1. Dreams
ISBN 0-689-31658-5   LC 91-22898
Areas discussed include "animal dreams, the importance of dreams, dream themes, and the meaning of dreams. The chapter on dream themes discusses dreams where content is especially relevant to children." Sci Books Films
Includes bibliographical references

155.2   Individual psychology

LeShan, Eda J.
What makes you so special? [by] Eda LeShan. Dial Bks. for Young Readers 1992 145p $15 (5 and up)   **155.2**
1. Individuality 2. Psychology
ISBN 0-8037-1155-7   LC 91-16925
Discusses the many different factors that make each one of us a unique human being
The author "treats her audience with considerable respect in discussing mature subjects without resorting to psychological jargon. . . . Many of her examples of children's backgrounds are engrossing and extraordinary: separated twins, a Southeast Asian refugee, children living in cars. . . . LeShan's compassion is evident as she encourages children to find their way to friendship with themselves." Publ Wkly
Includes bibliography

155.4   Child psychology

Rogers, Fred
Making friends; photographs by Jim Judkis. Putnam 1987 unp il $12.95; pa $6.95 (k-1)
155.4

1. Friendship
ISBN 0-399-21382-1; 0-399-21385-6 (pa)
LC 86-12353

"From its opening lines ('When people like each other and like to do things together, they're friends. Can you think of someone who's your friend?'), Rogers's inimitable voice reaches out to his small readers with understanding and reassurance. He describes the pleasures of friendship as well as potential problem areas. . . . Judkis's large color photos capture the range of emotions Rogers writes about." Publ Wkly

Moving; photographs by Jim Judkis. Putnam 1987 unp il o.p. (k-1)   **155.4**

1. Moving
LC 86-9426
"Following a little boy and his parents from their old house to their new one, full-color photographs and simple text express both the adventure and travail of a family's relocation. . . . If Mr. Rogers 'levels' with children rather than writing down to them, Judkis provides comparable illustrations by taking most of the photographs from a child's-eye view rather than shooting down from an adult's perspective. Using people who look like neighbors rather than actors or models gives the clear, colorful photos an appealing visual counterpoint to the carefully worded but informal text." Booklist

Rosenberg, Maxine B., 1939-
Being a twin, having a twin; photographs by George Ancona. Lothrop, Lee & Shepard Bks. 1985 unp il lib bdg $14.93 (2-4)   **155.4**

1. Twins
ISBN 0-688-04329-1
LC 84-17159
Describes the experiences of several different sets of twins, both identical and fraternal
"The author presents a warm and very personal look at twins. . . . Ancona's photographs . . . show a variety of action and subjects. Common situations that any child can relate to form the background for the photographs, and the text points out what would be special about the situation for a twin." Horn Book

155.9   Environmental psychology

Bernstein, Joanne E.
Loss and how to cope with it. Seabury Press 1977 151p il o.p. (5 and up)   **155.9**

1. Death 2. Bereavement
LC 76-50027
"A Clarion book"
"The author relates death to losses of other kinds, from the infant's temporary loss as a parent leaves the room to the adult's permanent loss of a favorite necklace or a job. She explains that, from childhood, experiencing inevitable losses helps prepare us to handle death. She then alerts the reader to the succession of feelings that accompanies mourning and provides sound advice about coping." Kobrin Letter
Includes bibliography

Fry, Virginia Lynn
Part of me died, too; stories of creative survival among bereaved children and teenagers; illustrated with the children's own artwork, with a foreword by Katherine Paterson. Dutton Children's Bks. 1995 xx, 218p il $16.99 (5 and up)   **155.9**

1. Death 2. Bereavement
ISBN 0-525-45068-8
LC 94-36536
The author "tells stories of children and teenagers who have lost a loved one and how they coped. The types of death experienced are on all levels from that of a beloved pet to the death of parents, siblings and friends. Suicide, murder and AIDs-related deaths are included. Each story is resolved through therapy involving people close to the youngsters and art activities that help them cope with the pain." Book Rep
"Highly compelling, compassionate and comforting, this powerful book should be part of libraries, counseling centers and anywhere else where adults help those who deal with death." Child Book Rev Serv

Hyde, Margaret Oldroyd, 1917-
Meeting death; [by] Margaret O. Hyde and Lawrence E. Hyde. Walker & Co. 1989 129p il $14.95; lib bdg $15.85 (4 and up)
155.9

1. Death 2. Bereavement
ISBN 0-8027-6873-3; 0-8027-6874-1 (lib bdg)
LC 88-27933
Provides information to promote the acceptance of the concept of death, discussing such aspects as the terminally ill, suicide, grief and mourning, and the treatment of death in various cultures
"This offers thought-provoking material that will be useful to students or those simply interested in a topic that's often tough to talk about." Booklist
Includes bibliography

The **Kids'** book about death and dying; by and for kids; [by] the Unit at Fayerweather Street School; edited and coordinated by Eric E. Rofes. Little, Brown 1985 119p $16.95 (5 and up)   **155.9**

1. Death
ISBN 0-316-75390-4
LC 85-180
This book contains "the thoughts, perceptions and feelings of 14 students, ages 11-14, who spent a year studying and sharing various aspects of death. . . . Chapter topics include funeral customs; death of pets; death of family members; violent death; and life after death." Voice Youth Advocates
"The best aspects of student authorship, case histories, handbooks, cultural anthropology, bibliographies, advice books and almanacs are all blended together. Although it is written in a readable and almost casual manner, the content is far from casual. . . . Quotes, footnotes and specific references to data sources are sprinkled liberally within and around lists, charts, etc. . . . A unique and valuable book." SLJ

Krementz, Jill
How it feels when a parent dies. Knopf 1981 110p il hardcover o.p. paperback available $7.95 (4 and up)   **155.9**

1. Death 2. Bereavement
ISBN 0-394-75854-4 (pa)
LC 80-8808

Krementz, Jill—*Continued*
Also available in hardcover from P. Smith

This book is "a hopeful tribute to the healing power sustained by young survivors, who are competently interviewed and photographed in their widely varied reactions and situations. The subjects range in age from 7 to 16 and cope with a variety of deaths by suicide, accident, and illness. Adults helping children through a hard time will better understand their charges' problems through the honest opinions expressed here, and young readers might feel less alone." Booklist

LeShan, Eda J.
Learning to say good-by; when a parent dies; illustrated by Paul Giovanopoulos. Macmillan 1976 85p il $15 (4 and up)
                                       155.9

1. Death 2. Bereavement
ISBN 0-02-756360-X
Also available in paperback from Avon Bks.

The author "puts the bereaved children in touch with their grief. She then proceeds to explain the universality and validity of these feelings and how to cope with them healthfully. Actual examples illustrate many of her points." SLJ

Includes bibliography

Stein, Sara Bonnett
About dying; an open family book for parents and children together; by Sara Bonnett Stein, in cooperation with Gilbert W. Kliman [et al.]; photography by Dick Frank; graphic design, Michel Goldberg. Walker & Co. 1977 47p il $10.95; pa $8.95 (k-3)
                                       155.9

1. Death
ISBN 0-8027-6170-0; 0-8027-7223-4 (pa)

"A book with two running texts, one addressed to parents and the other to be read aloud to small children, is illustrated with photographs. The text for adults discusses children's needs and fears, the ways in which a parent can describe death, help a child grow in understanding, and the behavior patterns that can show a child's fears or confusion in reacting to the death of a pet or a person. The attitude stressed is that of being open and natural." Bull Cent Child Books

179   Other ethical norms

Pringle, Laurence P.
The animal rights controversy; [by] Laurence Pringle. Harcourt Brace Jovanovich 1989 103p $16.95 (6 and up)
                                       179

1. Animal welfare
ISBN 0-15-203559-1   LC 89-11095

Presents viewpoints of both scientists and animal rights advocates on the use of animals for scientific research, for food, and for human enjoyment

"Whether describing the procedures of 'factory farming' or Draize testing, Pringle is never sensational, making this book both a sensible witness and an effective counterpoint to overheated propaganda. . . . Black-and-white photographs illustrate the points without sensationalizing them." Bull Cent Child Books

Includes bibliography

200   RELIGION

Gellman, Marc
How do you spell God? answers to the big questions from around the world; [by] Marc Gellman & Thomas Hartman; illustrated by Jos. A. Smith; with a foreword by his Holiness the Dalai Lama. Morrow Junior Bks. 1995 206p il $15 (5 and up)
                                       200

1. Religions
ISBN 0-688-13041-0   LC 94-28770

The authors "show how the various religions—Judaism, Christianity, Islam, Buddhism, and Hinduism—deal with the soul-searching questions central to all people. . . . There is also information on each religion's teachers, holy days and places, sanctuaries, and prayers, among other topics." Booklist

This book "is warm, friendly and, most of all, respectful of the importance and variety of belief." Book Rep

Keats, Ezra Jack, 1916-1983
God is in the mountain; selected and illustrated by Ezra Jack Keats. Holt & Co. 1994 c1966 unp il $15.95
                                       200

1. Religion—Quotations
ISBN 0-8050-3168-5   LC 93-29721
A reissue of the title first published 1966

"Twenty-four quotations from the religious literature of the world—from Taoism to Judaism, Islam to Aztec—reflect, as Keats's note says, 'the awareness of a dimension without which life is indeed meaningless.' This exploration of spirituality is simply and elegantly illustrated in varying techniques and moods." Horn Book Guide

220.5   Bible—Modern versions

Bible
The Holy Bible; containing the Old and New Testaments; translated out of the original tongues; and with the former translations diligently compared and revised by King James's special command, 1611. Oxford Univ. Press prices vary
                                       220.5

Available in various bindings and editions

The authorized or King James Version originally published 1611

The Holy Bible: new revised standard version; containing the Old and New Testaments with the Apocryphal/Deuterocanonical books. Nelson, T. maps prices vary
                                       220.5

Available in various bindings and editions including a large print edition

This version first published 1989

"Intended for public reading, congregational worship, private study, instruction, and meditation, it attempts to be as literal as possible while following standard American English usage, avoids colloquialism, and prefers simple, direct terms and phrases." Sheehy. Guide to Ref Books. 10th edition. suppl

220.8 Nonreligious subjects treated in Bible

Bible. Selections

Animals of the Bible; a picture book by Dorothy P. Lathrop; with text selected by Helen Dean Fish from the King James Bible. Harper & Row 1987 65p il $16; lib bdg $15.89 (1-4) **220.8**

1. Bible—Natural history 2. Animals
ISBN 0-397-31536-8; 0-397-30047-6 (lib bdg)

Awarded the Caldecott Medal, 1938

A reissue of the title first published 1937 by Lippincott
"Dorothy Lathrop's love and understanding of animals, the sensitiveness and joy with which she draws them, make her the ideal artist for such a volume. It is more than a beautiful picture book, for she has studied the fauna and flora of Bible lands until each animal and bird, each flower and tree, is true to natural history." N Y Times Book Rev

Paterson, John Barstow

Consider the lilies; plants of the Bible; [by] John and Katherine Paterson; paintings by Anne Ophelia Dowden. Crowell 1986 96p il $14.95; lib bdg $14.89 (5 and up) **220.8**

1. Bible—Natural history 2. Plants
ISBN 0-690-04461-5; 0-690-04463-1 (lib bdg)
LC 85-43603

This book gives information "on forty-five shrubs, crops, trees, weeds, fruits and flowers mentioned in the Old and New Testaments with emphasis on the . . . symbolic values of each. Divided into three groups—plants of Revelation, Necessity, and Celebration—each plant is cited in a Bible story or passage (quoted from the King James, New English, or Revised Standard versions of the Bible or paraphrased)." SLJ

"The quality of the art and intelligent explanations coupled with carefully selected examples from both Old and New Testaments will make the book prime read-aloud material for family sharing, Sunday School classes, and religious reports." Bull Cent Child Books

220.9 Bible—Geography, history, biography, stories

Bible. Selections

Tomie dePaola's book of Bible stories. Putnam 1989 127p il $21.95 **220.9**

1. Bible stories
ISBN 0-399-21690-1
LC 88-26468

"A collection of 17 stories from the Old Testament, 15 from the New Testament, and 4 psalms. The text is from the New International Version. . . . De Paola uses the text as written with some abridgement to make the stories an appropriate length. Done in his typical style, the illustrations feature stylized people and objects. . . . There are several illustrations for each story, many of which are full page, and most make dramatic use of color. The large format enhances the impact of the pictures." SLJ

Stoddard, Sandol, 1927-

A child's first Bible; pictures by Tony Chen. Dial Bks. for Young Readers 1991 96p il $17.99 (k-2) **220.9**

1. Bible stories
ISBN 0-8037-0941-2
LC 90-40102

An illustrated retelling of twenty-two stories from the Old Testament and seventeen from the New Testament. Also includes the story of the Maccabees

"Each story is reduced to a single page; facing is one of Chen's handsome full-page watercolors incorporating a number of aspects (dress, tools, weapons, adornments) of biblical life. Though the stories are naturally greatly simplified, the language is dignified yet accessible." Booklist

The Doubleday illustrated children's Bible; paintings by Tony Chen. Doubleday 1983 384p il $25; pa $14.95 (4-6) **220.9**

1. Bible stories
ISBN 0-385-18541-3; 0-385-18521-9 (pa)
LC 82-45340

An illustrated retelling of more than 100 stories from the Old and New Testaments

"There are many pluses here: inviting format, easy reading, plentiful illustrations, large clear type and an appealing cover featuring Noah's ark. This is an excellent selection, particularly for libraries lacking a basic collection of Bible stories." SLJ

221.9 Bible. Old Testament— Geography, history, biography, stories

Chaikin, Miriam, 1928-

Children's Bible stories from Genesis to Daniel; retold by Miriam Chaikin; pictures by Yvonne Gilbert. Dial Bks. for Young Readers 1993 92p il $17.99; lib bdg $17.89 (4 and up) **221.9**

1. Bible stories
ISBN 0-8037-0956-0; 0-8037-0990-0 (lib bdg)
LC 90-42588

"This features 26 stories from the Old Testament . . . that are made readily accessible to young readers and listeners, thanks to Chaikin's clear, uncluttered text. Illustrating the tales are Gilbert's dramatic color-pencil artwork." Booklist

Day, Malcolm

The ancient world of the Bible. Viking 1994 78p il maps $19.99 (4 and up) **221.9**

1. Bible—History of Biblical events
ISBN 0-670-85607-X
LC 94-60486

"Beginning with the story of Adam and Eve and ending with the return of the Jews to Jerusalem, this source takes the reader through the history of biblical times. Readers can explore famous events, structures, customs, and the daily lives of many people during this time. . . . [This] is an enjoyable and easy to use guide to biblical history." Voice Youth Advocates

Fisher, Leonard Everett, 1924-
The Wailing Wall. Macmillan 1989 unp il
map $15.95 (4 and up)   **221.9**

1. Jews—History 2. Western Wall (Jerusalem) 3. Bible
stories
ISBN 0-02-735310-9   LC 88-27192
"Fisher recounts the history of the Western (Wailing)
Wall of the Second Temple in Jerusalem. Briefly, beginning
in Abraham's time, he chronicles the building and destruction of the First and Second Temples, Palestine's occupation by various cultures, and the history of the Jewish
people in the Holy Land to the present. A chronology and
a well-defined map of the area further clarify the information. Dramatic, two-page paintings in black-and-white acrylics showing architecture, costumes, and weapons of various
periods enliven the text." SLJ

Gellman, Marc
Does God have a big toe? stories about
stories in the Bible; paintings by Oscar de
Mejo. Harper & Row 1989 88p il $16; pa
$7.95 (4-6)   **221.9**

1. Bible stories
ISBN 0-06-022432-0; 0-06-440453-6 (pa)
     LC 89-1893
This is a collection of twenty "tales that use familiar
characters and situations from the Bible, but which imagine
events and feelings and consequences the Bible never
recorded. . . . Oscar de Mejo's primitive-style paintings suit
the text exactly. Adam and Eve, for example, pop up behind the bushes in the Garden of Eden, just as a child
might imagine them. These tales have the ring of genuine
folk-fables and the wit of a single, affectionate heart." N Y
Times Book Rev

Waddell, Martin
Stories from the Bible; Old Testament
stories; retold by Martin Waddell; illustrated
by Geoffrey Patterson. Ticknor & Fields 1993
69p il $17.95   **221.9**

1. Bible stories
ISBN 0-395-66902-2   LC 92-36114
Waddell "offers here his interpretation of 17 stories from
the Old Testament. Many familiar heroes of the Scriptures
appear . . . in these simplified, light-toned tales designed to
be easily grasped by children. . . . Patterson's bright, flowing, acrylic paintings are of varying sizes, and each is individually framed with colored borders." Publ Wkly

222   Historical books of Old Testament

Bible. O.T. Genesis
The story of the creation; words from
Genesis; [pictures by] Jane Ray. Dutton
Children's Bks. 1993 c1992 unp il $16 (k-3)
     222

1. Creation 2. Bible stories
ISBN 0-525-44946-9   LC 92-20862
Also available Spanish language edition $16 (ISBN 0-
525-45055-6)
First published 1992 in the United Kingdom
Illustrates the story of creation, from the book of Genesis
of the King James version of the Bible

"Folk-art exuberance, sapphire and emerald hues, and
decorative detail mark Ray's style and reflect Creation's
rich abundance." SLJ

Brent, Isabelle
Noah's ark; illuminated by Isabelle Brent.
Little, Brown 1992 unp il $12.95 (k-3)
     222

1. Noah's ark 2. Bible stories
ISBN 0-316-10837-5   LC 91-35673
This is an illustrated retelling of the biblical story in
which Noah builds an ark and saves specimens of the
world's animal species from the flood
"Using as inspiration excerpts from the Revised English
Bible, this particular version should prove popular with religious education classes and for family reading as well as
serving as an example of modern bookmaking inspired by
the art of the medieval monasteries. . . . The artist has used
a palette as rich and brilliant as a fabled cache of jewels but
has further enhanced its innate luminosity with gold leaf."
Horn Book

Chaikin, Miriam, 1928-
Exodus; adapted from the Bible by Miriam
Chaikin; illustrated by Charles Mikolaycak.
Holiday House 1987 unp il $15.95 (2-4)
     222

1. Moses (Biblical figure) 2. Bible stories
ISBN 0-8234-0607-5   LC 85-27361
"Oversize pages, lavishly illustrated, provide a visual interpretation of the Biblical story of the plagues in Egypt that
led to a pharaoh's reluctant permission for the departure of
the Hebrew slaves and of their journey to the promised
land. Chaikin has done a good job of adapting the story so
that it is simplified and coherent yet preserves the flow of
Biblical language. Mikolaycak's paintings, in his distinctively bold and flowing style, are carefully integrated with textual references; they extend the story and add excitement to
its inherent drama." Bull Cent Child Books

Joshua in the Promised Land; woodcuts by
David Frampton. Clarion Bks. 1982 83p il
hardcover o.p. paperback available $6.95 (4
and up)   **222**

1. Joshua (Biblical figure) 2. Bible stories
ISBN 0-395-54797-0 (pa)   LC 82-4131
"Except for a bit of condensing, dialogue, and some extra
characters (Mrs. Joshua and household), Chaikin sticks to
the biblical story in which Joshua, successor to Moses, is
commanded by God to lead the Israelites into Canaan and
capture the Promised Land. Those familiar with more sani-
tized versions of Bible stories may be surprised at the jealous and vengeful God of the Old Testament. . . . This is
written at a level children can understand, and it would certainly make a good starting point for a discussion of the Bible and biblical times." Booklist

Cohen, Barbara, 1932-1992
David. Clarion Bks. 1995 108p $15.95 (5
and up)   **222**

1. David, King of Israel 2. Bible stories
ISBN 0-395-58702-6   LC 91-8255

Cohen, Barbara, 1932-1992—*Continued*

A retelling of the story of David, going beyond what is in the Bible to include today's knowledge of archaeology, history, politics, psychology, etc., to present the ruler of Israel as he must have been in 1000 B.C.

This "biography is, like its subject, inspiring, cautionary, and memorable." SLJ

Includes bibliographical references

Fisher, Leonard Everett, 1924-

David and Goliath; adapted from the Bible and illustrated by Leonard Everett Fisher. Holiday House 1993 unp il $15.95 (k-3)

222

1. David, King of Israel 2. Goliath (Biblical figure) 3. Bible stories
ISBN 0-8234-0997-X   LC 92-24063

Retells the Bible story in which a Hebrew shepherd boy kills the giant Philistine warrior Goliath with a slingshot

"Fisher has created majestic images that reflect the grandeur of the story in all its mythic proportions. The concise telling works in counterpoint to the thickly painted images, which Fisher has chosen carefully." Booklist

Moses; retold from the Bible and illustrated by Leonard Everett Fisher. Holiday House 1995 unp il $15.95 (k-3)   222

1. Moses (Biblical figure) 2. Bible stories
ISBN 0-8234-1149-4   LC 94-12131

"Fisher's version of the biblical story of Moses and the Exodus from Egypt suggests a great staged pageant. . . Each double-page spread captures a mythic drama, with the Old Testament figures bold against mountain, desert, and sky, from the hiding of the baby in the bulrushes to the coming of the plagues, the parting of the waters, the wandering in the desert, and the receiving of the Ten Commandments." Booklist

The seven days of creation; adapted from the Bible and illustrated by Leonard Everett Fisher. Holiday House 1981 unp il lib bdg $12.95 (k-3)   222

1. Creation 2. Bible stories
ISBN 0-8234-0398-X   LC 81-2952

The author "remains true to the creation account found in Genesis while simplifying the language for his intended audience. Despite the fact that he condenses the account, he maintains the essential story. Rich full-color illustrations reinforce the majestic quality of Fisher's adaptation. . . . The book's large pictures and sparse text make it ideal for reading aloud to a group." SLJ

Geisert, Arthur

The ark. Houghton Mifflin 1988 48p il lib bdg $17.95 (k-3)   222

1. Noah's ark 2. Bible stories
ISBN 0-395-43078-X   LC 88-15889

"Beginning with God's decision to destroy his creation—except for Noah and his family—Geisert details the story on buff-colored pages. The illustrator employs intricate cross hatching and unusual perspectives to show Noah building the ark and housing all the creatures of the earth. . . . As a result of its astonishing illustrations, as well as its compact text, this book can be used with a wide range of audiences, all of whom will no doubt want to look closely at the meticulous detail that abounds on every spread." Booklist

Hutton, Warwick

Adam and Eve; the Bible story; adapted and illustrated by Warwick Hutton. Margaret K. McElderry Bks. 1987 unp il $14.95 (k-3)

222

1. Adam (Biblical figure) 2. Eve (Biblical figure) 3. Creation 4. Bible stories
ISBN 0-689-50433-0   LC 86-27690

"Using the first three chapters of Genesis in the King James version, Hutton retells the familiar story from the first day of Creation to Adam and Eve's expulsion from the garden of Eden." Horn Book

"Until they share the fruit of knowledge, Adam and Eve are sketched in matter-of-fact nudity amid Eden's floral profusion. After eating the apple, they either cover themselves or are observed from discreet distances or in rear views. Hutton's streaks of light pierce the shadowy garden overgrowth like knowledge penetrating innocence in this evocative interpretation." Booklist

Moses in the bulrushes; retold and illustrated by Warwick Hutton. Atheneum Pubs. 1986 unp il lib bdg $14.95; pa $4.95 (k-3)   222

1. Moses (Biblical figure) 2. Bible stories
ISBN 0-689-50393-8 (lib bdg); 0-689-71553-6 (pa)
LC 85-72261

"A Margaret K. McElderry book"

Retells the Old Testament story of how the baby Moses was saved from death by the Pharaoh's daughter

"Using some twenty delicate and expressive watercolor drawings, Mr. Hutton has told the ancient story with a degree of tenderness not often seen in contemporary work." NY Times Book Rev

Segal, Lore Groszmann

The book of Adam to Moses; [by] Lore Segal and Leonard Baskin. Knopf 1987 115p il lib bdg $14.99 (4-6)   222

1. Bible stories
ISBN 0-394-96757-7   LC 87-2581

A modern English version of the stories of the five books of Moses

"What Segal has done is simplify the language and give cohesion to the narrative without sacrificing sonority, sequence, or flow. The tone is reverent, the language comprehensible. Baskin's black-and-white illustrations are handsome in their dramatic sweep and strength." Bull Cent Child Books

Spier, Peter, 1927-

Noah's ark; illustrated by Peter Spier. Doubleday 1977 unp il lib bdg $15.95; pa $5.99 (k-2)   222

1. Noah's ark 2. Bible stories
ISBN 0-385-09473-6 (lib bdg); 0-440-40693-5 (pa)
LC 76-43630

Also available Spanish language edition

Awarded the Caldecott Medal, 1978

"A seventeenth-century Dutch poem, 'The Flood' by Jacobus Revius, opens the otherwise almost wordless book. Skillfully translated by the artist and set in a readable, appropriately archaic type, the artlessly reverent verses add an unexpected dimension to the full-color pictures. Peter Spier's characteristic panoramas are marvels of minute detail, activity, vitality, and humor." Horn Book

223   Poetic books of Old Testament

Eisler, Colin T.
David's songs; his Psalms and their story; selected, edited, and with an introduction by Colin Eisler; illustrations by Jerry Pinkney. Dial Bks. for Young Readers 1992 57p il $17; lib bdg $16.89 (4 and up)   **223**

1. David, King of Israel 2. Bible. O.T. Psalms
ISBN 0-8037-1058-5; 0-8037-1059-3 (lib bdg)
                           LC 90-25459

Eisler presents forty-six versions of passages from the Book of Psalms that he believes reflect King David's "life and faith. They are presented to re-create a self-portrait in poetry." Preface

"The excerpts are slightly 'retold,' but the results are close to (and often better than) the New English Bible." SLJ

224   Prophetic books of Old Testament

Patterson, Geoffrey, 1943-
Jonah and the whale. Lothrop, Lee & Shepard Bks. 1992 unp il $14; lib bdg $13.93 (1-3)   **224**

1. Jonah (Biblical figure) 2. Bible stories
ISBN 0-688-11238-2; 0-688-11239-0 (lib bdg)
                           LC 91-53021

Retells the Biblical story of Jonah, who failed to obey the commands of the Lord

"Patterson's illustrations are dramatic, bold, deeply hued, and even exhibit flashes of humor." Booklist

232.9   Family and life of Jesus

Bible. N.T. Selections
The Christmas story; from the King James version; illuminated by Isabelle Brent. Dial Bks. for Young Readers 1989 unp il $13.95 (k-3)   **232.9**

1. Jesus Christ—Nativity
ISBN 0-8037-0730-4   LC 89-1149

"The text, extracted from the King James Version of the Bible, is a seamless interweaving of selections from the Gospels of Luke and Matthew. The exquisite illustrations are rendered in the style of medieval manuscript and glow with a lovely light." Horn Book Guide

The Christmas story: told through paintings; with commentary by Richard Mühlberger. Metropolitan Mus. of Art; Harcourt Brace Jovanovich 1990 39p il $16.95 (4 and up)
                           232.9

1. Jesus Christ—Nativity 2. Renaissance art
ISBN 0-15-200426-2   LC 90-4774
"Gulliver books"

"The events surrounding the birth of Christ are depicted through masterworks—shown both in their entirety and in detail—from New York City's Metropolitan Museum of Art. Accompanying the illustrations are excerpts from the King James Version of the Bible, along with interpretations of the works and discussion of technique and historical context." Publ Wkly

"The commentaries—conversational, thoughtful, comprehensible, and thorough—incorporate an amazing amount of information in carefully honed paragraphs which range from historical and technical references to explanations of the iconography." Horn Book

The first Christmas; illustrated with paintings from the National Gallery, London. Simon & Schuster Bks. for Young Readers 1992 29p il $16 (4 and up)   **232.9**

1. Jesus Christ—Nativity
ISBN 0-671-79364-0   LC 92-11580

The story of the birth of Jesus is illustrated with paintings from the National Gallery in London

"A showcase of ornately beautiful art from 13th, 14th, and 15th century Italy, France, and the Netherlands. . . . The paintings are an apt match for the classic words of the King James Version of the Bible. This book starts with the Annunciation by the Angel Gabriel and ends with the Holy Family returning home by way of Egypt. This is a handsome book in terms of layout, quality of reproduction, and selection of paintings." SLJ

Brown, Margaret Wise, 1910-1952
Christmas in the barn; pictures by Barbara Cooney. Crowell 1952 unp il $14.89; pa $5.95 (k-2)   **232.9**

1. Jesus Christ—Nativity 2. Bible stories
ISBN 0-690-19272-X; 0-06-443082-0 (pa)

A retelling of the Nativity story in simple rhyme. The illustrations are large and detailed

There is "use of modern dress in the pictures instead of the traditional Biblical costume, but this does not detract from the spirit of Barbara Cooney's illustrations. They are lovely." Libr J

De Paola, Tomie, 1934-
The miracles of Jesus; retold from the Bible and illustrated by Tomie dePaola. Holiday House 1987 unp il $15.95 (k-3)   **232.9**

1. Jesus Christ 2. Bible stories
ISBN 0-8234-0635-0   LC 86-18297

"Thirteen miracles, with the Biblical texts only slightly shortened and simplified, are retold with the beauty and dignity of the original. The artist's typical stylized, flat, highly decorative illustrations of sturdy, pensive figures, their faces often expressing awe, in soft, warm tones, have a still, timeless quality particularly appropriate to the spirituality and eternity of the subject." SLJ

Kurelek, William, 1927-1977
A northern nativity; Christmas dreams of a prairie boy. Tundra Bks. 1976 unp il $16.95 (4 and up)   **232.9**

1. Jesus Christ—Nativity 2. Canada—Social life and customs
ISBN 0-88776-071-6

Each of "20 anecdotal accounts is accompanied by a painting and recalls [the author/artist's] personal dreams of watching the Holy Family as they seek shelter and succor from farmers, fishermen, lumbermen, truckers, skiers and rod riders; from Eskimos, blacks, Indians and Mennonites." N Y Times Book Rev

"The familiar events are revitalized and given added di-

Kurelek, William, 1927-1977—*Continued*
mension when relocated in Canada during the Depression years. . . . The magnificent representational paintings, in combination with a nonsentimental but moving text, place religious experience in the context of daily life." Horn Book

Wildsmith, Brian, 1930-
The Easter story. Knopf 1994 c1993 unp il $18 (k-3)   **232.9**
1. Jesus Christ 2. Bible stories
ISBN 0-679-84727-8   LC 93-25097
First published 1993 in the United Kingdom
The story of the last days of Jesus' life, the crucifixion, and the resurrection, as seen through the eyes of a small donkey
"Employing a rich palette of jewel tones and metallic golds, Wildsmith offers an opulent and symbol-laden visual re-creation of Jesus' last days. The actual retelling . . . is simplified, yet faithful to the biblical account." Booklist

Winthrop, Elizabeth
A child is born: the Christmas story; adapted from the New Testament by Elizabeth Winthrop; illustrated by Charles Mikolaycak. Holiday House 1983 unp il lib bdg $15.95 (k-3)   **232.9**
1. Jesus Christ —Nativity 2. Bible stories
ISBN 0-8234-0472-2   LC 82-11728
"A deftly simplified story of the Nativity is based on the Books of St. Luke and St. Matthew, King James version. There are some omissions, but none of import, and Winthrop has kept the beauty of the Biblical language, deleting only for the sake of easy comprehension. Mikolaycak's paintings are stunning; they are bold in composition but reverent in mood, colorful, and dramatic." Bull Cent Child Books

He is risen: the Easter story; adapted from the New Testament by Elizabeth Winthrop; illustrated by Charles Mikolaycak. Holiday House 1985 unp il lib bdg $15.95 (k-3)   **232.9**
1. Jesus Christ 2. Easter 3. Bible stories
ISBN 0-8234-0547-8   LC 84-15869
"The Easter story, adapted from the King James Version of the Gospels of John and Matthew, has been slightly altered and some of the obscure passages omitted for the benefit of young readers." Child Book Rev Serv
"Mikolaycak's potent, yet emotionally controlled compositions are enclosed along with the text in narrow, rust-colored borders that echo the earthy tones of the pictures themselves. . . . The text is lengthy, and adults may want to paraphrase the story in parts to hold youngsters' attention, but older listeners will be moved by the timelessness of the language and the reverent beauty of Mikolaycak's spellbinding interpretation." Booklist

242 Devotional literature

Beckett, Wendy
A child's book of prayer in art. Dorling Kindersley 1995 32p il $12.95 (3-6)   **242**
1. Prayers 2. Art appreciation
ISBN 1-56458-875-0   LC 94-40362

"Linking the work of 15 different artists, from Michelangelo to Millet, to a spiritual value such as respect or forgiveness, Sister Wendy Beckett introduces children to art as a means of discovering faith. . . . With appeal to older as well as middle readers, this is a remarkable book, not only for its innate spirituality and wisdom, but also for its harmonious partnership of great art and astute interpretation." Booklist

Field, Rachel, 1894-1942
Prayer for a child; pictures by Elizabeth Orton Jones. Macmillan 1944 unp il $13; pa $3.95 (k-3)   **242**
1. Prayers
ISBN 0-02-735190-4; 0-02-043070-1 (pa)
Awarded the Caldecott Medal, 1945
One of Rachel Field's "greatest legacies to [children] has been this [brief] prayer. It was written for her own daughter, but now belongs to all boys and girls everywhere. It is a prayer, beautifully written and . . . bespeaking the faith, love, hopes, and the trust of little children." Libr J
"The pictures have a freshness and childlikeness which match the text perfectly." Boston Globe

Goble, Paul
I sing for the animals. Bradbury Press 1991 unp il $9.95   **242**
1. Creation
ISBN 0-02-737725-3   LC 90-19812
Reflects on how we are all connected to everything in nature and how all things in nature relate to their Creator
The author's "hallmark artistic technique, bold outlines and clean colors, are used to good effect, and the random thoughts are expressed in a careful and sensitive way." SLJ

Le Tord, Bijou, 1945-
Peace on earth; a book of prayers from around the world; collected and illustrated by Bijou Le Tord. Delacorte Press 1992 79p il $18   **242**
1. Prayers
ISBN 0-385-30692-X   LC 91-39913
A collection of prayers from around the world, in such categories as Children, Animals, The Sea, and Songs & Celebrations
"Simplicity and dignity characterize this perceptively edited anthology. . . . Le Tord gracefully suggests the universality of religious experience without drawing attention to particular denominations or creeds. . . . The artist's apparently effortless, delicately hued watercolors blend an appreciation of the everyday world with an intimation of the mystical—here, spirituality is both lightly worn and spontaneous." Publ Wkly

Prayers, praises, and thanksgivings; compiled by Sandol Stoddard; pictures by Rachel Isadora. Dial Bks. for Young Readers 1992 152p il $18.50 (3-6)   **242**
1. Prayers 2. Religious poetry
ISBN 0-8037-0421-6   LC 86-32822
An anthology of prayers and religious poetry from many different religions and from different races and nationalities throughout the world
"Watercolor paintings, mainly landscapes and scenes with children, brighten the pages of the attractive anthology. While not a book to read in one sitting, it's a refreshing

Prayers, praises, and thanksgivings—*Continued*

source of brief, unsentimental prayers and devotional poems for children." Booklist

289 Other denominations and sects

Bial, Raymond
Shaker home. Houghton Mifflin 1994 37p il $15.95 (3-5)   **289**

1. Shakers
ISBN 0-395-64047-4   LC 93-17917
Text and photographs depict the way of life of the Shakers

"Bial's color photographs are well composed, and his writing is crisp, yet thoughtful. Readers finish the book with a clear understanding of how the Shakers and their idealistic belief in a utopian society have enriched our lives." Horn Book Guide.
Includes bibliography

Bolick, Nancy O'Keefe
Shaker inventions; [by] Nancy O'Keefe Bolick and Sallie G. Randolph; illustrated by Melissa Francisco. Walker & Co. 1990 96p il map $12.95; lib bdg $13.85 (5 and up)
                                      289

1. Shakers 2. Inventions
ISBN 0-8027-6933-0; 0-8027-6934-9 (lib bdg)
                                  LC 89-70618
Among the Shaker labor-saving inventions explored in this book are the circular saw, metal pen nibs, the manufactured broom, and washing machine
This book about "Shaker inventions, also gives an overview of Shaker society. . . . Clearly written prose makes this both a useful research tool and fascinating browsing." BAYA Book Rev

289.7 Mennonite churches

Ammon, Richard
Growing up Amish. Atheneum Pubs. 1989 102p il $13.95 (5 and up)   **289.7**

1. Amish 2. Pennsylvania Dutch
ISBN 0-689-31387-X   LC 88-27493
"This account of the daily life of a girl named Anna and her Amish family on a farm in Pennsylvania addresses both the myths and the realities of the Anabaptist sect." N Y Times Book Rev
"The attractive format includes rather wide pages, photographs that are good but dark in tone, occasional insets of added information, verses and music." Horn Book
Includes bibliography

Bial, Raymond
Amish home. Houghton Mifflin 1993 40p il $14.95 (3-5)   **289.7**

1. Amish
ISBN 0-395-59504-5   LC 92-4406

Text and photographs depict the way of life of the Amish
The full-color photos depict "cozy kitchens, lovingly tended gardens, prized horses, and rolling landscapes. As well as being informative, these photographs create a mood through which readers enter another lifestyle." SLJ
Includes bibliography

291 Comparative religion and religious mythology

Bulfinch, Thomas, 1796-1867
Bulfinch's mythology (6 and up)   **291**

1. Mythology 2. Folklore—Europe 3. Chivalry
Hardcover and paperback editions available from various publishers
First combined edition published 1913 by Crowell. First published in three separate volumes 1855, 1858 and 1862 respectively
Contents: The age of fable; The age of chivalry; Legends of Charlemagne
"The basic work on classical mythology. Includes information on Greek, Roman, Norse, Egyptian, Asian, Germanic myths, as well as the Arthurian cycle and other heroic epics." N Y Public Libr. Ref Books for Child Collect

Hamilton, Virginia, 1936-
In the beginning; creation stories from around the world; told by Virginia Hamilton; illustrated by Barry Moser. Harcourt Brace Jovanovich 1988 161p il lib bdg $22.95; pa $14.95 (5 and up)   **291**

1. Creation 2. Mythology
ISBN 0-15-238740-4 (lib bdg); 0-15-238742-0 (pa)
                                  LC 88-6211
A Newbery Medal honor book, 1989
"Hamilton has gathered 25 creation myths from various cultures and retold them in language true to the original. Images from the tales are captured in Moser's 42 full-page illustrations, tantalizing oil paintings that are rich with somber colors and striking compositions. Included in the collection are the familiar stories (biblical creation stories, Greek and Roman myths), and some that are not so familiar (tales from the Australian aborigines, various African and native American tribes, as well as from countries like Russia, China, and Iceland). At the end of each tale, Hamilton provides a brief commentary on the story's origin and originators." Booklist
Includes bibliography

291.4 Religious experience, life, practice

Baylor, Byrd, 1924-
The way to start a day; by Byrd Baylor; illustrated by Peter Parnall. Scribner 1978 unp il lib bdg $14.95; pa $3.95 (1-4)   **291.4**

1. Worship 2. Sun worship
ISBN 0-684-15651-2 (lib bdg); 0-689-71054-2 (pa)
                                  LC 78-113
A Caldecott Medal honor book, 1979
Text and illustrations describe how people all over the world celebrate the sunrise

Baylor, Byrd, 1924—*Continued*

"While the format is that of a picture book, the concepts in the poetic text of this handsome volume are more appropriate for independent readers who can grasp the historic and ritual values of Baylor's thoughts." Bull Cent Child Books

292 Classical religion and religious mythology

Aliki

The gods and goddesses of Olympus; written and illustrated by Aliki. HarperCollins Pubs. 1994 48p il $16; lib bdg $15.89 (2-5)   292

1. Classical mythology

ISBN 0-06-023530-6; 0-06-023531-4 (lib bdg)
LC 93-17834

"After the Uranus-Gaea, Cronus-Rhea background is sketched, the occupants of the 12 golden thrones are each described, along with Hades (underground), Hestia (hearthbound) and Eros (hovering). The author outlines the deities' characters and attributes, sometimes including a brief incident from their lives." SLJ

"This large-format book provides a quick, brightly illustrated introduction to the ancient Greek gods and goddesses." Booklist

Asimov, Isaac, 1920-1992

Words from the myths; decorations by William Barss. Houghton Mifflin 1961 225p il $14.95 (6 and up)   292

1. Classical mythology 2. English language—Etymology

ISBN 0-395-06568-2

Also available in paperback from New Am. Lib.

The author's "informal retelling and discussion of the myths to point out the scores of words rooted in mythology and to explain their usage in the English language provide a fresh look at the myths and a better understanding of the words and expressions derived from them." Booklist

Climo, Shirley, 1928-

Atalanta's race; a Greek myth; retold by Shirley Climo; illustrated by Alexander Koshkin. Clarion Bks. 1995 31p il $15.95 (3-5)   292

1. Atalanta (Greek mythology)

ISBN 0-395-67322-4   LC 93-26734

Retells the myth of the Greek princess, rejected by her father, raised by bears, won in marriage in a race by Melanion, and then changed into a lioness by an angry Aphrodite

"Climo's well-told tale raises issues of female worth and inclusion in male-dominated activities. . . . Koshkin's striking, deep-toned, classically inspired paintings amplify the drama; framing each painting with architectural motifs, he matches Climo in her sensitivity to detail and ambience." Publ Wkly

Colum, Padraic, 1881-1972

The Golden Fleece and the heroes who lived before Achilles; illustrated by Willy Pogany. Macmillan 1962 c1921 316p il $15.95; pa $9.95 (5 and up)   292

1. Argonauts (Greek mythology) 2. Classical mythology

ISBN 0-02-723620-X; 0-02-042260-1 (pa)

A reissue of the title first published 1921

Contents: The voyage to Colchis; The return to Greece; The heroes of the quest

"Mr. Colum preserves the spirit of the Greek tales and weaves them into a magic whole. In this he is aided by the spirited drawings." Booklist

Daly, Kathleen N.

Greek and Roman mythology A to Z; a young reader's companion. Facts on File 1992 132p il map lib bdg $19.95 (5 and up)   292

1. Classical mythology—Dictionaries

ISBN 0-8160-2151-1   LC 91-43037

Presents the gods, goddesses, heroes, places, and other aspects of Greek and Roman mythology in alphabetically arranged entries

"The format is accessible, making the book useful for school assignments, as well as enjoyable for general reading. . . . The broad coverage, ample cross-references, and extensive index enable readers to recognize the many connections and interrelationships between characters and myths." SLJ

Includes bibliography

Evslin, Bernard, 1922-1993

Hercules; illustrated by Jos. A. Smith. Morrow 1984 144p il lib bdg $16 (5 and up)   292

1. Hercules (Legendary character)

ISBN 0-688-02748-2   LC 83-23834

Retells the adventures of the demi-god Hercules as he struggles to accomplish seemingly impossible tasks

"Evslin mixes Greek names of gods and goddesses with the more common Roman variant of the hero's name, rather than the Greek 'Heracles.' The tale is softened to some extent and certain of the 12 labors are omitted entirely. . . . Evslin invests the story with easy dialogue and razor-sharp wit. . . . A zesty recounting that can stand alone or lead readers to fuller tellings of the Hercules story." Booklist

Jason and the Argonauts; illustrated by Bert Dodson. Morrow 1986 165p il lib bdg $16 (5 and up)   292

1. Jason (Greek mythology) 2. Argonauts (Greek mythology)

ISBN 0-688-06245-8   LC 85-32114

Ekion, the son of Hermes, relates how he came to be one of Jason's Argonauts and the adventures they shared in search of the Golden Fleece

The author "has sifted through the multitude of legends that make up the Argosy and has written a unique version of Jason's adventures. . . . Evslin uses contemporary language and a generous amount of dialogue but never loses the grandeur of the Greek epic. Bert Dodson's creative illustrations enhance the tale." Best Sellers

Fisher, Leonard Everett, 1924-

Cyclops; written and illustrated by Leonard Everett Fisher. Holiday House 1991 unp il map lib bdg $15.95; pa $5.95 (3-5)   292

1. Cyclopes (Greek mythology) 2. Odysseus (Greek mythology) 3. Classical mythology
ISBN 0-8234-0891-4 (lib bdg); 0-8234-1062-5 (pa)
     LC 90-29317

Describes the encounter between the Cyclops Polyphemus and Odysseus and his men after the end of the Trojan War

"Fisher's narrative is compressed and direct; the illustrations, in rich, saturated oils complement its simplified and dramatic qualities." SLJ

Includes bibliographical references

Jason and the golden fleece; written and illustrated by Leonard Everett Fisher. Holiday House 1990 unp il map lib bdg $14.95 (3-5)   292

1. Jason (Greek mythology) 2. Argonauts (Greek mythology)
ISBN 0-8234-0794-2   LC 89-20074

This is a retelling of the Greek legend. . . . "Jason sails forth to capture the Golden Fleece from distant Colchis. Four impossible tasks prescribed by the King of Colchis are accomplished with the help of Medea, the king's daughter, and the two escape with the Golden Fleece. Jason, Medea, and their two sons are happy, until Jason falls in love with Glauce." SLJ

"The book is well-paced, all of the story's major elements are included and readers will certainly be carried along by the episodic flow. Fisher's vivid art makes masterful use of each spread to advance the narrative and expand the text." Publ Wkly

Includes bibliography

The Olympians; great gods and goddesses of ancient Greece. Holiday House 1984 unp il lib bdg $15.95; pa $6.95 (3-5)   292

1. Classical mythology
ISBN 0-8234-0522-2 (lib bdg); 0-8234-0740-3 (pa)
     LC 84-516

Offers brief biographical sketches of the twelve gods and goddesses that reside on Mount Olympus including such information as their Roman names, their parents, and the symbols that represent them

"Each portrait has a massive, almost sculptured look despite the fact that the paintings are in full color. . . . This is a handsome book, and it's an excellent introduction to the Greek/Roman pantheon." Bull Cent Child Books

Includes bibliography

Theseus and the Minotaur; written and illustrated by Leonard Everett Fisher. Holiday House 1988 unp il map lib bdg $14.95; pa $5.95 (3-5)   292

1. Theseus (Greek mythology) 2. Minotaur (Greek mythology)
ISBN 0-8234-0703-9 (lib bdg); 0-8234-0954-6 (pa)
     LC 88-1970

Retells the Greek myth of the hero Theseus and his battle with the bull-headed monster called the Minotaur

"Fisher's paintings, styled in monumental proportions, somber colors, and simple compositions, are well suited to a Greek tale of heroic deeds and death. . . . Fisher has also done a careful job of selecting and consolidating various versions, for which he cites sources in the beginning. An impressive meeting of myth and picture book." Bull Cent Child Books

Hamilton, Edith, 1867-1963

Mythology; illustrated by Steele Savage. Little, Brown 1942 497p il $24.95 (6 and up)   292

1. Classical mythology 2. Norse mythology
ISBN 0-316-34114-2

Also available in paperback from New Am. Lib.

Contents: The gods, the creation and the earliest heroes; Stories of love and adventure; Great heroes before the Trojan War; Heroes of the Trojan War; Great families of mythology; Less important myths; Mythology of the Norsemen; Genealogical tables

Hodges, Margaret

The arrow and the lamp; the story of Psyche; retold by Margaret Hodges; illustrated by Donna Diamond. Little, Brown 1989 unp il $14.95 (2-4)   292

1. Psyche (Greek deity) 2. Eros (Greek deity) 3. Aphrodite (Greek deity) 4. Classical mythology
ISBN 0-316-36790-7   LC 86-2728

Based on an original story by Lucius Apuleius

Relates how Psyche married the god of love, Eros, how she lost him, and had to overcome many obstacles before she became an immortal and could join him on Mount Olympus

Hutton, Warwick

Persephone; retold and illustrated by Warwick Hutton. Margaret K. McElderry Bks. 1994 unp il $14.95 (3-5)   292

1. Persephone (Greek deity)
ISBN 0-689-50600-7   LC 93-20590

Retells the Greek myth in which Persephone must spend six months out of every year below the Earth in Hades

"The story of Persephone is given an accessible interpretation in a simplified, but not simplistic, retelling. Hutton's spare, yet evocative, prose is extended in shimmering watercolors that are charged with meaning and that echo motifs found in classical Greek sculpture." Horn Book Guide

Perseus; retold and illustrated by Warwick Hutton. Margaret K. McElderry Bks. 1993 unp il $14.95 (3-5)   292

1. Perseus (Greek mythology) 2. Medusa (Greek mythology) 3. Classical mythology
ISBN 0-689-50565-5   LC 92-7639

Retells the Greek myth in which the hero Perseus beheads Medusa, the most horrible of the Gorgons

"Children will be caught up in the action-packed adventure. The watercolor art is as typically graceful as that on a Greek vase—blue, green, and gold with touches of russet." SLJ

Theseus and the Minotaur; retold and illustrated by Warwick Hutton. Margaret K. McElderry Bks. 1989 unp il $14.95 (3-5)   292

1. Theseus (Greek mythology) 2. Minotaur (Greek mythology)
ISBN 0-689-50473-X   LC 88-26875

Recounts how Theseus killed the monster, Minotaur, with the help of Ariadne

Hutton "makes specific use of patterns and designs of Minoan artifacts, architecture, and costume. And whether he depicts action viewed from daring perspectives or in

Hutton, Warwick—*Continued*

broad panoramas or whether he reveals character in close-ups, his narrative paintings carry emotional intensity and are imbued with personal as well as with universal meanings." Horn Book

Low, Alice, 1926-

The Macmillan book of Greek gods and heroes; illustrated by Arvis Stewart. Macmillan 1985 184p il $15.95; pa $12.95 (3-6)   **292**

1. Classical mythology

ISBN 0-02-761390-9; 0-689-71874-8 (pa)

LC 85-7170

This collection "tells of the Olympians and of the grand drama, both tragic and comic, that they played out in the heavens and on the earth. It tells, too, of the many mortals with whom they became entangled, both simple people like Pandora and Pygmalion and great heroes like Heracles and Perseus. Included are the popular myths and the legend of Odysseus." Publisher's note

"The tales are clearly told, without embroidery. A useful index not only refers the reader to a page or pages, but briefly identifies the character or subject as well. Watercolors in glowing earth tones with touches of blue and decorative pen-and-ink drawings enhance the book's appeal." Booklist

McCaughrean, Geraldine, 1951-

Greek myths; retold by Geraldine McCaughrean; illustrated by Emma Chichester Clark. Margaret K. McElderry Bks. 1993 c1992 96p il $19.95 (4-6)   **292**

1. Classical mythology

ISBN 0-689-50583-3   LC 92-61748

First published 1992 in the United Kingdom

Retells sixteen tales from Greek mythology, including Pandora's box, King Midas, The twelve labors of Heracles, and Orpheus and Eurydice

"McCaughrean's style is fresh and lively, dynamic and direct. She is faithful in essentials, but not afraid to edit. . . . The text is matched by clear, rainbow-bright illustrations. Clark's watercolors are lighthearted and engaging, and a picture or decoration enlivens every page." SLJ

Osborne, Mary Pope, 1949-

Favorite Greek myths; retold by Mary Pope Osborne; illustrated by Troy Howell. Scholastic 1989 81p il lib bdg $16.95 (3-6)
292

1. Classical mythology

ISBN 0-590-41338-4   LC 87-32332

Retells twelve tales from Greek mythology, including the stories of King Midas, Echo and Narcissus, the Golden Apples, and Cupid and Psyche

"Osborne's retellings are both lively and descriptive, while Howell's full-color, often iridescent illustrations set the scene and mood at the start of each tale." Publ Wkly

Includes glossary and bibliography

Rockwell, Anne F., 1934-

The robber baby; stories from the Greek myths. Greenwillow Bks. 1994 79p il $18; lib bdg $17.93 (3-5)   **292**

1. Classical mythology

ISBN 0-688-09740-5; 0-688-09741-3 (lib bdg)

LC 90-39560

Retells fifteen tales from Greek mythology, including the stories of Hermes, Demeter and Kore, Daedalus, Atalanta, and Pandora

These stories "are appealingly and accurately retold. Rockwell's colorful, flat, schematic illustrations are an interesting blend of the archaic, the modern, and the cute. Although the book seems designed for a young audience, the harsher aspects of the myths are not deleted." SLJ

293   Germanic religion and religious mythology

Climo, Shirley, 1928-

Stolen thunder; a Norse myth; retold by Shirley Climo; illustrated by Alexander Koshkin. Clarion Bks. 1994 32p il lib bdg $15.95 (3-5)   **293**

1. Norse mythology

ISBN 0-395-64368-6   LC 93-24627

"In order to retrieve Thor's powerful hammer, which has been stolen by the giant Thrym, Thor - the thunder god - and the trickster Loki disguise themselves as bride and handmaiden and travel to the land of the blue-skinned frost giants." Horn Book Guide

Climo's "dramatic text, jammed with snappy dialogue and colorful emotions, is framed in gold. The lovely full- and half-page paintings, also neatly framed, heighten both the distinctive characters and the fast-moving plot." Booklist

Colum, Padraic, 1881-1972

The children of Odin; the book of northern myths; illustrated by Willy Pogány. Macmillan 1984 c1920 271p il $15.95; pa $9.95 (5 and up)   **293**

1. Norse mythology

ISBN 0-02-722890-8; 0-02-042100-1 (pa)

LC 83-20367

A reissue of the title first published 1920

Contents: Dwellers in Asgard; Odin the wanderer; Witch's heart; Sword of the Volsungs and Twilight of the gods

"The stories of the Norse sagas, from the Twilight of the gods to the destruction of Asgard, are told in a connected narrative that flows in a simple rhythmic prose sometimes poetic." Booklist

296.1   Judaism—Sources

Jaffe, Nina

While standing on one foot; puzzle stories and wisdom tales from the Jewish tradition; [by] Nina Jaffe and Steve Zeitlin; pictures by John Segal. Holt & Co. 1993 120p il $14.95 (4 and up)   **296.1**

1. Jewish legends
ISBN 0-8050-2594-4   LC 93-13750

"Each of seventeen tales is divided into two sections: the first poses a dilemma for the main character; the second describes the clever solution. . . . The entire collection is of general interest because of the solve-it-yourself aspect . . . and the suspense or humor of the difficulties. . . . Wash drawings in black and white are whimsically stylized with figures that have a humorous, paper-doll quality." Bull Cent Child Books

Includes glossary and bibliography

Patterson, José

Angels, prophets, rabbis & kings from the stories of the Jewish people; text by José Patterson; colour illustrations by Claire Bushe. Bedrick Bks. 1991 144p il (World mythology series) $22.50 (4-6)   **296.1**

1. Jewish legends 2. Bible stories
ISBN 0-87226-912-4   LC 90-23469

Spine title: Stories of the Jewish people

A collection of traditional Jewish legends from the earliest times, stories of the rabbis, and tales from the communities of medieval Europe

"Written in a conversational tone with sufficient dialogue for children to identify with the characters. . . . Very little, if any, adaptation is needed for storytelling use. The book is magnificently illustrated in both full color and black and white." SLJ

296.4   Judaism—Traditions, rites, public services

Burns, Marilyn

The Hanukkah book; illustrated by Martha Weston. Four Winds Press 1981 120p il $15 (4 and up)   **296.4**

1. Hanukkah
ISBN 0-02-716140-4   LC 80-27935

Also available in paperback from Avon Bks.

Beginning with the historical background, "this book offers a thoughtful, sensitive, broad approach to the Jewish holiday. It explores the past, and gives a number of new ways to enrich Hanukkah, plus recipes, craft projects, and games. Included is a section on how Jewish children might feel about celebrating Hanukkah instead of Christmas and lots of advice on creative living as a minority." Child Book Rev Serv

Chaikin, Miriam, 1928-

Hanukkah; illustrated by Ellen Weiss. Holiday House 1990 unp il lib bdg $15.95 (k-2)   **296.4**

1. Hanukkah
ISBN 0-8234-0816-7   LC 89-77512

"The first three-quarters of this informational book is a synopsis in simple prose of the wicked acts of King Antiochus, the uprising of the Jews under Mattathias, and the miracle of the holy oil. The last quarter shows families celebrating Hanukkah today." SLJ

"Pen-and-ink drawings accompany a simple yet graceful text. . . . Weiss' brightly colored drawings effectively reinforce the story's message. A useful introduction to Hanukkah and its traditions." Booklist

Light another candle; the story and meaning of Hanukkah; illustrated by Demi. Clarion Bks. 1981 80p il hardcover o.p. paperback available $6.95 (3-6)   **296.4**

1. Hanukkah
ISBN 0-89919-057-X (pa)   LC 80-28137

"Delicate pen-and-ink drawings accented in bright red add a festive note to the study of the Hanukkah festival. Emphasis is placed throughout not only on the relationship between holiday traditions and historical events but also on the religious aspects of the celebration. . . . Chapters on Jewish law; the types and significance of Hanukkah foods, games, and gifts; local variations on the festival theme; and anecdotes from the Holocaust era documenting the holiday's role in Jewish life round out the presentation." Horn Book

Includes glossary and bibliography

Make noise, make merry; the story and meaning of Purim; illustrated by Demi. Clarion Bks. 1983 90p il $11.95; pa $6.95 (3-6)   **296.4**

1. Purim
ISBN 0-89919-140-1; 0-89919-424-9 (pa)

    LC 82-12926

"Providing a first section on the historical background for the period in which the Persian king Ahasweros (Xerxes) reigned, Chaikin then tells—in a smooth fictionalization—the story of his queen, Esther, who saved the lives of her people, the Persian Jews. The last sections of the book focus on how the holiday grew in importance and on how it is celebrated. . . . The format is handsome, with wide margins and with deep purple illustrations, delicate in detail and strong in composition, often incorporating traditional designs or motifs of Mid-Eastern art." Bull Cent Child Books

Includes glossary and bibliography

Menorahs, mezuzas, and other Jewish symbols; illustrated by Erika Weihs. Clarion Bks. 1990 102p il $15.95 (5 and up)   **296.4**

1. Jewish art and symbolism 2. Judaism—Customs and practices
ISBN 0-89919-856-2   LC 89-77719

Explains the history and significance of many Jewish symbols, such as the Shield of David, the menorah, and the mezuza, and discusses holiday symbols and rituals

"Embellished with bibliographical references as well as Weihs' simple yet elegant and wonderfully dramatic scratchboard illustrations, this smoothly woven patchwork of history and culture is a fine introduction that will attract browsers and be useful for children investigating the subject of symbolism in school." Booklist

Edwards, Michelle

Blessed are you; traditional everyday Hebrew prayers. Lothrop, Lee & Shepard Bks. 1993 unp il $15; lib bdg $14.93 (k-3)

296.4

1. Prayers 2. Judaism
ISBN 0-688-10759-1; 0-688-10760-5 (lib bdg)

LC 92-1666

"Edwards has taken 13 traditional Hebrew prayers, and shown how they can be incorporated into daily life. Each selection is short and laid out on a full page with the Hebrew on top, a transliteration at the bottom, and an English translation filling up the middle. Lush, full-color borders surround the text. . . . The language is accessible to young children, but maintains the spirit and integrity of the original Hebrew." SLJ

Ehrlich, Amy, 1942-

The story of Hanukkah; told by Amy Ehrlich; paintings by Ori Sherman. Dial Bks. 1989 unp il $14.95; lib bdg $14.89; pa $5.99 (1-3)

296.4

1. Hanukkah
ISBN 0-8037-0615-4; 0-8037-0616-2 (lib bdg); 0-14-055285-5 (pa)

LC 88-31109

"The story of how the single lamp kept burning is told in straightforward text and set off by stunning, folkloric illustrations." N Y Times Book Rev

Goldin, Barbara Diamond

The Passover journey; a Seder companion; illustrated by Neil Waldman. Viking 1994 56p il $15.99 (4 and up)

296.4

1. Passover
ISBN 0-670-82421-6

LC 93-5133

Retells the story of the Israelites' fight for liberation from slavery in Egypt and explains the traditions of the Passover Seder

"Goldin speaks simply, warmly, and directly throughout the book and lets her own love of the holiday shine through. . . . The many illustrations are an attractive mix of bold graphics and soft colors. The geometric borders and pastels characteristic of Waldman's work are . . . combined with stylized, classic Egyptian hieroglyphic figures and set against softly tinted pages that actually glow." Booklist

Includes glossary and bibliographical references

Hirsh, Marilyn, 1944-1988

I love Hanukkah; written and illustrated by Marilyn Hirsh. Holiday House 1984 unp il $13.95; pa $5.95 (k-3)

296.4

1. Hanukkah
ISBN 0-8234-0525-7; 0-8234-0622-9 (pa)

LC 84-497

"At Hanukkah, a small boy, who remembers only the candles from the previous year, is told the Hanukkah story by his grandfather, and then describes the eight-day celebration." SLJ

"The color artwork features large, sturdy drawings of the family, while the scenes of the ancient Hanukkah story are drawn on a smaller scale. A welcome picture-book edition that will prove handy to have on the shelves during the Holiday season." Booklist

Jaffe, Nina

The uninvited guest and other Jewish holiday tales; illustrated by Elivia. Scholastic 1993 72p il $16.95 (4-6)

296.4

1. Jewish holidays 2. Jewish legends
ISBN 0-590-44653-3

LC 92-36308

Includes background information and retellings of traditional tales from Jewish folklore and legend related to major holidays, such as Yom Kippur, Sukkot, Hanukkah, and Purim

"Elivia's bright, flowing artwork, in a rainbow of colors, reflects both the magic and the joy of the seven splendid Jewish holiday tales simply and beautifully retold here." Booklist

Includes glossary and bibliography

Kimmel, Eric A.

Bar mitzvah; a Jewish boy's coming of age; illustrated by Erika Weihs. Viking 1995 143p il $15 (5 and up)

296.4

1. Bar mitzvah
ISBN 0-670-85540-5

LC 94-34956

"Kimmel imparts basic information about Judaism, including some comparisons between Judaism and Catholicism and Islam, and discusses ritual objects, important texts, the Shabbat service, and the actual responsibilities of the bar mitzvah child. The vivid impact traditionally left by the ceremony is made clear through several short interviews." Booklist

"Children with no previous exposure to Jewish beliefs and rituals will find the explanations here both clear and enticing, respectful of different religious traditions. . . . Kimmel also accommodates Jewish readers from a variety of backgrounds, from Reform to Orthodox." Publ Wkly

Days of Awe; stories for Rosh Hashanah and Yom Kippur; adapted from traditional sources by Eric A. Kimmel; illustrated by Erika Weihs. Viking 1991 47p il $13.95; pa $4.99 (3-6)

296.4

1. Rosh ha-Shanah 2. Yom Kippur
ISBN 0-670-82772-X; 0-14-050271-8 (pa)

LC 91-50198

"The three themes central to the Jewish High Holidays of Rosh Hashanah and Yom Kippur are charity, prayer, and repentance. Eric Kimmel uses three stories from very old sources and, adding some of his own touches as a storyteller, beautifully illustrates the essence of each of these concepts. . . . Erika Weihs's paintings add warmth and quiet dignity to the moving tales." Horn Book

Koralek, Jenny

Hanukkah, the festival of lights; written by Jenny Koralek; illustrated by Juan Wijngaard. Lothrop, Lee & Shepard Bks. 1990 29p il $15; lib bdg $14.93 (k-3)

296.4

1. Hanukkah
ISBN 0-688-09329-9; 0-688-09330-2 (lib bdg)

LC 89-8064

This book relates the events commemorated by the Jewish festival of Hanukkah, including the desecration of the Temple by Antiochus, the revolt of the Maccabees against foreign domination, and the rededication of the Temple

"The tone of this simplified text is almost folklore. . . . Facing each page of text is a formal, full-page illustration (framed, ironically, between marbled Corinthian columns) depicting a scene from the story with distant elegance." Bull Cent Child Books

Kuskin, Karla
A great miracle happened there; a Chanukah story; illustrated by Robert Andrew Parker. Perlman Bks. 1993 unp il $15; lib bdg $14.89; pa $5.95 (k-3) **296.4**

1. Hanukkah
ISBN 0-06-023617-5; 0-06-023618-3 (lib bdg); 0-06-443426-5 (pa) LC 92-17909
On the first night of Hanukkah, a mother tells her family and a young guest the story of the holiday's origin
"The illustrations pulse with energy, reinforcing the action of Kuskin's well-paced story-within-a-story." Horn Book

Schwartz, Lynne Sharon
The four questions; text by Lynne Sharon Schwartz; paintings by Ori Sherman. Dial Bks. 1989 unp il $15.99; lib bdg $15.89 (k-3) **296.4**

1. Passover
ISBN 0-8037-0600-6; 0-8037-0601-4 (lib bdg) LC 88-18881
This book explores the meaning of Passover by explicating the symbolism of the seder and the four questions
"Framed by the rituals of a Seder, an excellent text gives brief background on the celebration of Passover. . . . The stunningly stylized illustrations facing each page of text are a sophisticated carnival of animals that reflect a kind of Chagallian surrealism grounded by strongly outlined shapes, deep colors, and dense compositions." Bull Cent Child Books

297 Islam and religions originating in it

Macdonald, Fiona
A 16th century mosque; [by] Fiona Macdonald, Mark Bergin. Bedrick Bks. 1994 48p il (Inside story) $17.95 (5 and up) **297**

1. Mosques 2. Islam
ISBN 0-87226-310-X LC 94-20008
The author describes "the construction of the great Süleymaniye Mosque in Istanbul, built in the mid-16th century by the Ottoman Turkish imperial architect Sinan. . . . The text is much enhanced by numerous attractive and informative illustrations." Sci Books Films
Includes glossary

Macmillan, Dianne
Ramadan and Id al-Fitr; [by] Dianne M. Macmillan; reading consultant, Michael P. French. Enslow Pubs. 1994 48p il (Best holiday books) lib bdg $14.95 (2-4) **297**

1. Islam
ISBN 0-89490-502-3 LC 93-46185
The author describes the Islamic month of Ramadan and the festival of Id-al-Fitr and discusses other aspects of the religion such as the prophet Muhammad, mosques, minarets, and the Koran
Includes glossary

Oppenheim, Shulamith Levey
Iblis; retold by Shulamith Levey Oppenheim; illustrated by Ed Young. Harcourt Brace Jovanovich 1994 unp il $15.95 (2-4) **297**

1. Adam (Biblical figure) 2. Eve (Biblical figure)
ISBN 0-15-238016-7 LC 92-15060
An Islamic version of the story of Adam and Eve and the fall from Paradise
"Young's dramatic pastels and watercolor artwork juxtaposes the dark shadows of evil with neon-bright swaths and splotches of electric color. . . . Based on a 9th century scholarly version, the text is charged with the tension, while Young's rich paintings bridge our temporal and cultural distance from the source to bring its message powerfully home." SLJ

300 SOCIAL SCIENCES

302 Social interaction

Hoose, Phillip M., 1947-
It's our world, too! stories of young people who are making a difference; by Phillip Hoose. Little, Brown 1993 166p il $22.95; pa $12.95 (5 and up) **302**

1. Voluntarism 2. Social action 3. Community development
ISBN 0-316-37241-2; 0-316-37245-5 (pa) LC 92-24873

"Joy Street books"
"Hoose tells fourteen stories of children and young adolescents who have stood up to gangs, pitted their wits against corporate interests, performed volunteer service, or organized for ecological causes. This fine, large handbook includes a background chapter on the history of 'young activists who went before you' and a substantial concluding section on techniques of organizing for social activism." Horn Book

302.2 Communication

Adkins, Jan
Symbols, a silent language; written, designed, and illustrated by Jan Adkins. Walker & Co. 1978 31p il hardcover o.p. paperback available $4.95 (4-6) **302.2**

1. Signs and symbols
ISBN 0-8027-7216-1 (pa)
Text and illustrations explore the uses and meaning of the various families of symbols including traffic signs, map symbols, trademarks, and many others

Aliki
Communication. Greenwillow Bks. 1993 unp il $14; lib bdg $13.93 (k-3) **302.2**

1. Communication
ISBN 0-688-10529-7; 0-688-11248-X (lib bdg) LC 91-48156

Also available Spanish language edition

Aliki—*Continued*

"The text considers not only the telling and listening aspects of person-to-person exchange, but also the importance of responding. Aliki relies on various combinations of handwritten and typeset text, large drawings, and cartoon strips to introduce some of the ways communication is accomplished—writing, speaking, braille—and to offer a glimpse of the subtle, emotional aspects of interchange." Booklist

Fisher, Leonard Everett, 1924-

Symbol art; thirteen [square]s, [circle]s, [triangle]s from around the world; written and illustrated by Leonard Everett Fisher. Four Winds Press 1985 61p il $16.95 (4 and up) **302.2**

1. Signs and symbols
ISBN 0-387-15203-2   LC 85-42805

In this volume the author "covers the meanings of symbols and their importance in business, religion, music, astrology, magic, and sciences. Each of the descriptive sections examines the history of the symbols and their uses." SLJ

Fisher "provides, on a large, double-page spread, easily discernible, key symbols connected with that field. Juxtaposed with the text are evocative, scratchboard drawings done in deep rustic browns against a stark white field. Language and history students will profit from this intriguing look at universal, nonverbal communication devices." Booklist

Gibbons, Gail

Puff—flash—bang! a book about signals. Morrow Junior Bks. 1993 unp il $15; lib bdg $14.93 (k-3) **302.2**

1. Signs and symbols
ISBN 0-688-07377-8; 0-688-07378-6 (lib bdg)
                                      LC 92-13170

Describes ways people say things to each other without using spoken or written words such as beacon fires, hand signals, alarms, and flags

"Above the boxed text, brightly colored drawings clearly illustrate the meaning that a signal is communicating. Color bars at the top and bottom of each page add to the crisp, clean format. This handsome volume will be a strong addition to communication units." Booklist

Ventura, Piero

Communication; means and technologies for exchanging information; with the collaboration of Max Casalini [et al.] Houghton Mifflin 1994 64p il $16.95 (4 and up) **302.2**

1. Communication—History
ISBN 0-395-66789-5   LC 94-4521

Original Italian edition, 1993

"A panoramic view of the history of communication from hieroglyphics to satellites. Along the way, Ventura discusses oral traditions, such as Greek theater, minstrels, and balladeers; visual communication such as religious symbols and art . . . as well as inventions like the printing press, radio, television, and computers. The information-packed volume achieves a good balance of text and minutely detailed drawings." SLJ

Includes glossary

304.2 Human ecology

Jeffers, Susan

Brother eagle, sister sky; a message from Chief Seattle; paintings by Susan Jeffers. Dial Bks. 1991 unp il $16.99; lib bdg $14.89
                                              304.2

1. Human ecology 2. Indians of North America—Claims 3. Environmental protection
ISBN 0-8037-0969-2; 0-8037-0963-3 (lib bdg)
                                      LC 90-27713

Also available Spanish language edition

A Suquamish Indian chief describes his people's respect and love for the earth, and concern for its destruction

"Jeffers's delicate yet strong illustrations offer a combination of sadness and hope. Glorious, almost spiritual, pictures of Native Americans living at peace with animals, flowers, and streams are followed by desolate depictions of endless fields of tree stumps. But even as we see the destruction of the forests, we see a family with children replanting seedlings. Although the text has been heavily adapted, the combination of message and illustration is potent and timely." Horn Book

305.23 Young people

Burns, Marilyn

I am not a short adult! getting good at being a kid; illustrated by Martha Weston. Little, Brown 1977 125p il hardcover o p. paperback available $10.95 (4 and up) **305.23**

1. Children 2. Human behavior
ISBN 0-316-11746-3 (pa)   LC 77-24486

"A Brown paper school book"

"A scatter gun approach, but nonetheless one of the few available, to discussing the state of childhood with children. There are some opening nudges to help find out 'what kind of kid you are' with lists and games; a brief social history of children's treatment by adults; an examination of children's legal status; a look at the influences and institutions that most affect children (the family, school, television); facts about work, finances and protection from child abuse; and suggestions about communication with adults." Booklist

Kindersley, Barnabas

Children just like me; by Barnabas & Anabel Kindersley. Dorling Kindersley 1995 79p il maps $16.95 (3-6) **305.23**

1. Children—Pictorial works
ISBN 0-7894-0201-7   LC 95-10199

Also available Spanish language edition

At head of title: In association with United Nations Children's Fund

This is a "compilation of facts, photographs, and interviews with thirty-seven children from thirty-two countries, including the U.S. Each child gets a full-page or double spread built around a large color photograph of the child and, often, his or her siblings; smaller photos show other family members, home and school, favorite foods and toys, homework or schoolbooks, and file photos of famous sights." Bull Cent Child Books

"A delightful, attractive look at children from around the world. . . . This book is factual, respectful, and insightful. It provides just the right balance of information and visual interest for the intended audience." SLJ

305.4 Women

Ash, Maureen
The story of the women's movement.
Childrens Press 1989 30p il (Cornerstones of
freedom) lib bdg $14.60; pa $3.95 (4-6)
305.4

1. Feminism 2. Women's movement
ISBN 0-516-04724-8 (lib bdg); 0-516-44724-6 (pa)
LC 89-17325
This title discusses the history of the women's movement
in England and the United States
This "book gives a broad treatment of historical events
and [is] illustrated with numerous photographs, reproduc-
tions, and drawings." SLJ

Blumberg, Rhoda, 1917-
Bloomers! illustrated by Mary Morgan.
Bradbury Press 1993 unp il $14.95; pa $4.95
(k-3)
305.4

1. Women's rights 2. Costume
ISBN 0-02-711684-0; 0-689-80455-5 (pa)
LC 92-27154
Explains how the new-fashioned outfit, bloomers, helped
Amelia Bloomer, Elizabeth Cady Stanton, and Susan B. Anthony spread the word about women's rights
"Young audiences will get a full sense of what life and
attitudes were like in the mid-19th century, as Blumberg
makes these historical characters real. Morgan's bright,
cheerful, watercolor paintings convey a sense of time and
place while they carry the narrative along." SLJ

305.8 Racial, ethnic, national groups

Ashabranner, Brent K., 1921-
An ancient heritage; the Arab-American
minority; [by] Brent Ashabranner; photographs
by Paul S. Conklin. HarperCollins Pubs. 1991
148p il lib bdg $14.89 (5 and up) **305.8**

1. Arab Americans
ISBN 0-06-020049-9
LC 90-30641
Discusses the cultural experience of Arab Americans and
the history of Arab immigration to the United States
"The book's strength lies in the personal stories told by
Arab Americans of all ages and all walks of life. Black-and-
white photographs of the storytellers deepen the impact of
their tales and help readers to relate to them as fellow
Americans." SLJ
Includes bibliography

The **Black** Americans: a history in their own
words, 1619-1983; edited by Milton Meltzer.
Crowell 1984 306p il lib bdg $15.89; pa
$9.95 (6 and up) **305.8**

1. African Americans—History—Sources
ISBN 0-690-04418-6 (lib bdg); 0-06-446055-X (pa)
LC 83-46160
This is a revised and updated edition of In their own
words: a history of the American Negro, edited by Milton
Meltzer and published in three volumes, 1964-1967
A history of black people in the United States, as told
through letters, speeches, articles, eyewitness accounts, and
other documents

Brown, Tricia
Konnichiwa! I am a Japanese-American girl;
photographs by Kazuyoshi Arai. Holt & Co.
1995 unp il $15.95 (1-4) **305.8**

1. Japanese Americans 2. San Francisco (Calif.)—Social
life and customs
ISBN 0-8050-2353-4
LC 94-36107
The author provides an "introduction to the Japanese
American experience told from the point of view of a child
named Lauren Seiko Kamiya. Lauren guides readers
through San Francisco's Japantown and shows how her
family takes part in the annual Cherry Blossom Festival."
Booklist
"While the most obvious audience for this title is children of Japanese extraction or teachers needing multicultural materials, this book has great visual appeal and will be
readily picked up by browsers." SLJ
Includes glossary and bibliography

Cavan, Seamus
The Irish-American experience. Millbrook
Press 1993 64p il (Coming to America) lib bdg
$15.90 (4 and up) **305.8**

1. Irish Americans
ISBN 1-56294-218-2
LC 92-7512
Traces the history of Irish immigration to the United
States, discussing why the Irish emigrated, their problems in
a new land, and their contributions to American culture
Includes bibliographical references

Gordon, Ginger
My two worlds; photographs by Martha
Cooper. Clarion Bks. 1993 unp il $14.95 (k-3)
305.8

1. Dominican Americans
ISBN 0-395-58704-2
LC 92-39271
Contrasts the two worlds of eight-year-old Kirsy Rod-
riquez, a Dominican American girl who lives in New York
and frequently returns to her island home
"The strong contrasts between the snow-covered streets
of New York and the heat of her hometown, with its barefoot children and house lizards, are captured in bright and
active color photographs. . . . 'My Two Worlds' is an optimistic and energetic view of a life of two interwoven cultures." N Y Times Book Rev

Graff, Nancy Price, 1953-
Where the river runs; a portrait of a refugee
family; photographs: Richard Howard. Little,
Brown 1993 71p il $16.95 (4-6) **305.8**

1. Cambodian Americans
ISBN 0-316-32287-3
LC 92-24184
Describes the experiences of a family of Cambodian refugees as they learn to adjust to a different way of life in the
United States while holding on to their ethnic heritage
"This in-depth photo-essay is candid about the difficulties as well as the hopes of a family who fled the civil war
in Cambodia and came to Boston six years ago, penniless
and homeless. Informal black-and-white photographs and a
graceful text weave together the past and present lives of
three generations." Booklist

Halliburton, Warren J.

The West Indian-American experience. Millbrook Press 1994 64p il (Coming to America) lib bdg $15.90 (4 and up)   **305.8**

1. West Indian Americans

ISBN 1-56294-340-5   LC 93-19233

Traces the history of West Indian immigration to the United States, discussing why they emigrated, their problems in a new land, and their contributions to American culture

Includes bibliographical references

Hamanaka, Sheila

The journey; Japanese Americans, racism and renewal; painting and text by Sheila Hamanaka; book design by Steve Frederick. Orchard Bks. 1990 39p il $19.95; lib bdg $19.99; pa $8.95 (5 and up)   **305.8**

1. World War, 1939-1945—United States 2. Japanese Americans—Evacuation and relocation, 1942-1945

ISBN 0-531-05849-2; 0-531-08449-3 (lib bdg); 0-531-07060-3 (pa)   LC 89-22877

"A Richard Jackson book"

"Hamanaka has created a five-panel mural depicting the Japanese-American experience with particular emphasis on the watershed of that experience, the concentration camps. Here the mural is reproduced detail by detail with amplifying text. . . . There are other books on this subject . . . but none with the punch and universality of this one." SLJ

Hispanic American almanac; Bryan Ryan and Nicolás Kanellos, editors. U.X.L 1995 213p il maps $29 (5 and up)   **305.8**

1. Hispanic Americans

ISBN 0-8103-9823-0   LC 95-196496

Also available adult version with same title published 1993 by Gale Res.

This volume "provides information about 'the heritage, the communities and the growing influence of hispanics on U.S. culture.'. . . Fourteen chapters cover Spanish exploration, immigration to the U.S. from Mexico, Puerto Rico, and Cuba; family structure and the role of religion; the workplace and education; and contributions in the arts and sports." Booklist

Hoobler, Dorothy

The African American family album; [by] Dorothy and Thomas Hoobler; introduction by Phylicia Rashad. Oxford Univ. Press 1995 127p il (American family albums) $19.95; lib bdg $22.95 (5 and up)   **305.8**

1. African Americans

ISBN 0-19-509460-3; 0-19-508128-5 (lib bdg)

LC 94-34697

This work "traces the history of African Americans from their homeland in West Africa at least 2,500 years ago to the achievements of contemporary African Americans such as Nobel Prize-winning novelist Toni Morrison. This book is an 'album' in the sense that the story is told in a unique collection of photographs as well as in first-hand accounts." Voice Youth Advocates

Includes bibliography

The Chinese American family album; [by] Dorothy and Thomas Hoobler; introduction by Bette Bao Lord. Oxford Univ. Press 1994 128p il map (American family albums) $19.95; lib bdg $22.95 (5 and up)   **305.8**

1. Chinese Americans

ISBN 0-19-509123-X; 0-19-508130-7 (lib bdg)

LC 93-11873

"This sourcebook on the Chinese immigrant experience is divided into six topics: the homeland, the voyage to America, arrival in America, first-generation life, the integration of successive generations, and Chinese Americans today. The authors introduce each chapter with a summary essay, then let the immigrants and their descendents speak for themselves in excerpts from oral reminiscences, written histories, and fiction spanning the years from the Gold Rush to the 1980s. Period photographs and drawings, maps, and sidebars enhance the text. The result resembles a well-organized, handsomely designed scrapbook. . . . A valuable resource." SLJ

Includes bibliography

The Irish American family album; [by] Dorothy and Thomas Hoobler; introduction by Joseph P. Kennedy II. Oxford Univ. Press 1995 128p il (American family albums) $19.95; lib bdg $22.95 (5 and up)   **305.8**

1. Irish Americans

ISBN 0-19-509461-1; 0-19-508127-7 (lib bdg)

LC 94-19569

"Selections from diaries, letters, interviews, newspaper and magazine articles, and books provide an arresting picture of what it has meant to be of Irish heritage in America. . . . Topics such as prejudice, working conditions and labor unions, politics, and the importance of family, friends, and the Catholic Church are touched upon." SLJ

Includes bibliography

The Italian American family album; [by] Dorothy and Thomas Hoobler; introduction by Governor Mario M. Cuomo. Oxford Univ. Press 1994 127p il map (American family albums) $19.95; lib bdg $22.95 (5 and up)   **305.8**

1. Italian Americans

ISBN 0-19-509124-8; 0-19-508126-9 (lib bdg)

LC 93-46918

This volume includes selections from "diaries, letters, and oral histories. . . . Each of the six chapters begins with background information and then goes on to discuss life in the old country, coming to America, first impressions, working, forming a new life, and becoming a part of America." SLJ

Includes bibliography

The Jewish American family album; [by] Dorothy and Thomas Hoobler; introduction by Mandy Patinkin. Oxford Univ. Press 1995 127p il (American family albums) $19.95; lib bdg $22.95 (5 and up)   **305.8**

1. Jews—United States

ISBN 0-19-509935-4; 0-19-508135-8 (lib bdg)

LC 94-43460

Hoobler, Dorothy—*Continued*

This volume "begins with a five-page thumbnail sketch of Jewish history from Abraham to the rise of the State of Israel. Successive chapters detail Jewish life in 'the old country', immigration to America, and the contributions Jews have made to their new homeland." Book Rep

"What makes this title unique is the high quality of the carefully researched and varied historical information and the Hooblers' judicious selection of primary-source excerpts, many of which are by well-known writers, politicians, and celebrities." SLJ

Includes bibliography

The Mexican American family album; [by] Dorothy and Thomas Hoobler; introduction by Henry G. Cisneros. Oxford Univ. Press 1994 127p il (American family albums) $19.95; lib bdg $25.50 (5 and up)   **305.8**

1. Mexican Americans
ISBN 0-19-509459-X; 0-19-508129-3 (lib bdg)
                          LC 94-7785

"Using almost exclusively first-person accounts, the Hooblers present vignettes of history, culture, and experience from the first Mexican American settlers to the Chicano Movement. . . . Gathered together, these accounts present a powerful portrait of a strong people, rich in history and culture. A must for multicultural studies." Book Rep

Includes bibliography

Hoyt-Goldsmith, Diane

Hoang Anh; a Vietnamese-American boy; photographs by Lawrence Migdale. Holiday House 1992 30p il map $14.95 (3-5)
                         305.8

1. Vietnamese Americans
ISBN 0-8234-0948-1   LC 91-28880

A Vietnamese American boy describes the daily activities of his family in San Rafael, California, and the traditional culture and customs that shape their lives

"Color photographs of good quality are carefully placed in relation to a text that is direct, informative, and convincing." Bull Cent Child Books

Includes glossary

The **In** America series. Lerner Publs. 1987-1995 19v il ea lib bdg $17.50; pa $5.95 (5 and up)   **305.8**

1. Ethnic groups 2. Minorities

Some newly revised and recently published titles in this series are: Africans in America, by A. Hart and E. Spangler; The American Indians in America v2, by J. C. Jones; Cubans in America, by A. Mendez; The Danes in America, by P. L. Petersen; The Filipinos in America, by F. H. Winter; The French in America, by V. B. Kunz; Germans in America, by T. Schouweiler; The Greeks in America, by J. C. Jones; Irish in America, by J. E. Johnson; Italians in America, by R. P. Grossman; The Japanese in America, by N. L. Leathers; The Jews in America, by F. Butwin; Koreans in America, by W. Patterson and H. Kim; The Lebanese in America, by E. M. Harik; The Mexicans in America, by J. Pinchot; Norwegians in America, by P. V. Hillbrand; The Puerto Ricans in America, by R. J. Larsen; The Scots and Scotch-Irish in America, by J. E. Johnson; Ukrainians in America, by M. B. Kuropas

This series of books deals with the background, social life, problems and achievements of various ethnic and minority groups in the United States, including their immigrant experiences and subsequent life in America. Illustrated with photographs

The **Jewish** Americans: a history in their own words, 1650-1950; edited by Milton Meltzer. Crowell 1982 174p il lib bdg $14.89 (6 and up)   **305.8**

1. Jews—United States—History—Sources
ISBN 0-690-04228-0   LC 81-43886

"Excerpts from letters, journals, books, documents, and assorted other sources provide a varied, firsthand look at Jewish experience in America from colonial times to 1950 when Holocaust survivors made their way to the U.S. . . . [The author] offers commentary before each [selection] helping to clarify context or define perspective by illuminating the times contemporary to the writing." Booklist

"The book has multiple curriculum uses and will be a welcome addition to any library. Interesting historical photographs and a comprehensive index add to [its] usefulness." SLJ

Includes bibliography

Krull, Kathleen, 1952-

City within a city; how kids live in New York's Chinatown; photographs by David Hautzig. Lodestar Bks. 1994 48p il maps (World of my own) $15.99 (4 and up)
                         305.8

1. Chinese Americans 2. Chinatown (New York, N.Y.)—Social life and customs
ISBN 0-525-67437-3   LC 93-15846

Describes the lives of two young Chinese Americans and their customs and conditions at home in New York City's Chinatown

The author "writes here with an informal, chatty style. . . . The warm, intimate photos show what's special about the kids and their neighborhood and what is universal." Booklist

Includes bibliography

The other side; how kids live in a California Latino neighborhood; photographs by David Hautzig. Lodestar Bks. 1994 48p il maps (World of my own) $15.99 (4 and up)
                         305.8

1. Mexican Americans 2. San Diego (Calif.)—Social life and customs
ISBN 0-525-67438-1   LC 93-15845

Depicts the life of two Mexican American boys in San Diego and their enjoyment of a bilingual culture

"In a straightforward and readable style [the author] shows three children who have successfully adapted to a new culture and language, while maintaining close ties to their extended families in Tijuana. . . . With many glowing full-color photographs and simply stated social commentary, this is a useful and valuable addition to library collections." SLJ

Includes bibliography

Kuklin, Susan

How my family lives in America. Bradbury Press 1992 unp il $13.95 (k-3)   **305.8**

1. African Americans 2. Chinese Americans 3. Puerto Ricans—United States
ISBN 0-02-751239-8   LC 91-22949

"Sanu's father was born in Senegal, Eric's father came from Puerto Rico, and both of April's parents were born in Taiwan. Each section provides special words, foods, games, clothes, music and other ways in which families transmit their heritages and integrate them with the life-styles of the

Kuklin, Susan—*Continued*
United States. The photographs provide insights as to how cultures are cherished and continued." Child Book Rev Serv

"Each child's first-person narration is simple and uncomplicated, with occasional humorous touches. . . . The full-color photographs are well composed and serviceable." SLJ

Martinez, Elizabeth Coonrod, 1954-
The Mexican-American experience. Millbrook Press 1995 59p il (Coming to America) lib bdg $15.90 (4 and up)   **305.8**
1. Mexican Americans
ISBN 1-56294-515-7   LC 94-19625
Traces the dual heritage of Mexican Americans as early settlers before the formation of the United States and as more recent immigrants who came to escape political and economic turmoil in their homeland
Includes bibliographical references

Medearis, Angela Shelf, 1956-
Our people; illustrated by Michael Bryant. Atheneum Pubs. 1994 unp il $15 (k-2)
305.8
1. African Americans
ISBN 0-689-31826-X   LC 92-44499
This book "features an African American father and daughter sharing important moments in black history." Booklist
"Bryant's watercolor illustrations emphasize the inspirational aspects of the text, alternating dramatic historical scenes with cozy interiors in which the narrator acts out her fantasies." Bull Cent Child Books

Myers, Walter Dean, 1937-
Now is your time! the African-American struggle for freedom. HarperCollins Pubs. 1991 292p il lib bdg $17.89; pa $10.95 (6 and up)   **305.8**
1. African Americans—History
ISBN 0-06-024371-6 (lib bdg); 0-06-446120-3 (pa)
LC 91-314
Coretta Scott King Award for text, 1992
A history of the African-American struggle for freedom and equality, beginning with the capture of Africans in 1619, continuing through the American Revolution, the Civil War, and into contemporary times
"Myers's unique episodic approach makes this history a compelling exploration of the African-American experience. . . . This fascinating book will engender pride in heritage for young African Americans and provide insight into American history for all of us." Horn Book
Includes bibliography

Stanley, Jerry, 1941-
I am an American; a true story of Japanese internment. Crown 1994 102p il $15; lib bdg $15.99; pa $9.99 (5 and up)   **305.8**
1. Japanese Americans—Evacuation and relocation, 1942-1945 2. World War, 1939-1945—United States
ISBN 0-517-59786-1; 0-517-59787-X (lib bdg); 0-517-88551-4 (pa)   LC 93-41330
The author discusses "the internment of Japanese-Americans during World War II. He has spun a cogent nar-

rative of the shameful events, focusing them through the experiences of Shi Nomura, a high school student sent with his family to Manzanar in 1942. . . . This is a first-rate, readable introduction to this particular part of history, and it's complemented by a spacious page design, numerous black-and-white photos, an exemplary bibliographic note, and an index." Bull Cent Child Books

Wu, Dana Ying-hui, 1969-
The Chinese-American experience; by Dana Ying-hui Wu and Jeffrey Dao-sheng Tung. Millbrook Press 1993 61p il (Coming to America) lib bdg $15.90 (4 and up)   **305.8**
1. Chinese Americans
ISBN 1-56294-271-9   LC 92-15649
Traces the history of Chinese immigration to the United States, discussing why they emigrated, their problems in a new land, and their contributions to American culture
Includes bibliographical references

306.05   Culture and institutions— Serial publications

Faces; the magazine about people. Cobblestone Pub. $23.95 per year
306.05
1. Anthropology—Periodicals
ISSN 0749-1387
Nine issues a year. First published 1984
Published with the cooperation of the American Museum of Natural History
A magazine for young people designed to introduce them "to the fascination of natural history and anthropology. There are some 8 to 10 articles in each well-illustrated number. Some issues concentrate on a particular subject. . . . Numerous projects for children are scattered throughout the magazine." Katz. Mag for Sch Libr

306.8   Marriage and family

Jenness, Aylette
Families; a celebration of diversity, commitment, and love; photographs by the author. Houghton Mifflin 1989 47p il $13.95; pa $4.95 (4 and up)   **306.8**
1. Family
ISBN 0-395-47038-2; 0-395-66952-9 (pa)
LC 89-7507
Photographs and text depict the lives of seventeen families from around the country, some with step relationships, divorce, gay parents, foster siblings, and other diverse components. The material was originally a traveling exhibition, begun at the Children's Museum in Boston
"Individual and familial black-and-white photos accompany each single-page textual family portrait; they are relayed with candid sensitivity that will elicit thoughtful and emotional responses from readers and will encourage comparisons to their own family units." SLJ
Includes bibliography

LeShan, Eda J.

Grandparents: a special kind of love; illustrated by Tricia Taggart. Macmillan 1984 119p il $13.95 (4 and up)   **306.8**

1. Grandparents 2. Conflict of generations

ISBN 0-02-756380-4   LC 84-5673

The author "presents matter-of-factly such issues as why grandparents and parents sometimes differ in attitudes; multigenerational living situations; learning about getting old (Alzheimer's disease and strokes); and multiple sets of grandparents. . . . The soft black-and-white illustrations add to the feeling of affection which permeates the work. . . . Invaluable for parents and children to share." Horn Book

When grownups drive you crazy. Macmillan 1988 121p $13.95 (4 and up)   **306.8**

1. Parent and child 2. Conflict of generations

ISBN 0-02-756340-5   LC 87-22005

Explores the conflicts and misunderstandings that occur between adults and children and offers advice to youngsters on understanding and dealing with the things adults do that distress them

"Understanding is the key here; LeShan's warm, supportive world will go a long way toward bringing her young readers to a more mature view of themselves and the grown-ups in their lives." Booklist

Rosenberg, Maxine B., 1939-

Brothers and sisters; photographs by George Ancona. Clarion Bks. 1991 32p il lib bdg $14.95 (k-2)   **306.8**

1. Brothers and sisters

ISBN 0-395-51121-6   LC 90-48547

Follows the ever-changing and growing relationships of brothers and sisters in three different families

"This is very simply written so that, read aloud, it will be comprehensible to young children. . . . This should be a useful book to clarify advantages and disadvantages of each position in a family constellation. . . . Ancona's photographs are, as usual, very good in quality." Bull Cent Child Books

Living with a single parent. Bradbury Press 1992 113p il $14.95 (4 and up)   **306.8**

1. Single parent family

ISBN 0-02-777915-7   LC 92-3883

Seventeen children from single-parent families describe how they cope with their circumstances

"Ranging in age from 8 to 13, the young people who speak out are not just from homes of divorce. One lives with an unwed mother, another has a homosexual parent, and at least one has had a parent die. . . . These kids are 'copers,' not 'moaners,' and their stories, filled with the stuff of everyday life, depict positive adjustments as well as the different ways kids handle their feelings. . . . Rosenberg's suggestions for coping, included in a final chapter, are rooted in common sense and pivot on opening lines of communication." Booklist

Includes bibliography

Talking about stepfamilies; afterword by Emily Visher. Bradbury Press 1990 145p il $14.95 (4 and up)   **306.8**

1. Stepfamily

ISBN 0-02-777913-0   LC 90-33540

Children and adults who have become part of stepfamilies describe their experiences in coping with new stepparents and stepsiblings

"This is an excellent resource for teachers and other adults who work with youngsters, as well as for children who live in stepfamilies." Booklist

Includes bibliographical references

306.89   Separation and divorce

Brown, Laurene Krasny

Dinosaurs divorce; a guide for changing families; [by] Laurene Krasny Brown and Marc Brown. Atlantic Monthly Press 1986 31p il $15.95; pa $6.95 (k-3)   **306.89**

1. Divorce

ISBN 0-316-11248-8; 0-316-10996-7 (pa)

LC 86-1079

"After a table of contents and glossary of relevant terms (readers are challenged to find the starred ones in the book) come 11 sections on some reasons why parents divorce, on likely repercussions and reactions, and on ways to deal with visitations, living in two homes, dealing with holidays, and adjusting to new developments such as parent dating, remarriage, and step-siblings." Bull Cent Child Books

"The picture-book, almost comic-book, format, the touches of humor, and the distancing effect of the dinosaurs as surrogate humans may make the book accessible to young or extremely anxious children. A thoughtful, useful book." Horn Book

Krementz, Jill

How it feels when parents divorce. Knopf 1984 115p il hardcover o.p. paperback available $14 (4 and up)   **306.89**

1. Divorce

ISBN 0-394-75855-2 (pa)   LC 83-48856

In a personal interview format "19 boys and girls, ranging in age from 7 to 16 years, tell of their parents' divorces and of the effects the divorce has had on them and their families." SLJ

"The full-page portraits that precede each piece are exceptionally expressive. While the accounts have many similarities, experiences and personalities are unique; Krementz' ear for language ensures that the children project their own individuality." Horn Book

Stein, Sara Bonnett

On divorce; an open family book for parents and children together; Thomas R. Holman, consultant; photographs by Erika Stone. Walker & Co. 1979 47p il $10.95; pa $4.95 (k-3)   **306.89**

1. Divorce

ISBN 0-8027-6344-8; 0-8027-7226-9 (pa)

LC 78-19687

Two separate texts appear on each page. One, in large type, is written on a child's level. The other, intended for adults, presents psychological explanations of the family's behavior

"The scope of 'On Divorce,' makes it a perceptive book to share with children whose own families are intact." SLJ

307.7 Specific kinds of communities

Provensen, Alice, 1918-
Town & country; [by] Alice and Martin Provensen. Browndeer Press 1994 unp il $16.95 (k-2)   **307.7**
1. City life 2. Farm life 3. Villages
ISBN 0-15-200182-4   LC 93-44749
A reissue of the title first published 1984 in the United Kingdom; first United States edition, 1985
"Describes life in a big city and on a farm near a village"
"Oversize pages filled with colorful drawings, details that fill but do not seem to crowd the pages, interesting urban perspectives and rural landscapes are combined in a book that should make children feel that both city and country are nice places to live. The authors point out differences, but their accent is always positive." Bull Cent Child Books

Von Tscharner, Renata
New Providence; a changing cityscape; conceived by Renata von Tscharner and Ronald Lee Fleming (the Townscape Institute); illustrations by Denis Orloff. Harcourt Brace Jovanovich 1987 unp il o.p. (3-6)   **307.7**
1. Cities and towns—Pictorial works 2. Urban renewal—Pictorial works   LC 86-46225
"Gulliver books"
"The changing view over the years of the main street in the fictional town of New Providence is the focus of this . . . study of cityscapes in picture-book format. . . . Alternating pages contain commentary, pointing out specific happenings and briefly explaining socioeconomic effects on New Providence. The pages containing text have partial reproductions in black and white of the large illustrations, which zero in on specific points." Booklist
"A thoughtful and imaginative visualization. . . . All details . . . are accounted for and help make readers more fully understand the changes in the buildings and streets. Seasonal changes also add visual texture." SLJ

323.1 Civil and political rights of nondominant aggregates

Duncan, Alice Faye
The National Civil Rights Museum celebrates everyday people; photos by J. Gerard Smith. BridgeWater Bks. 1995 63p il $16.95; pa $6.95 (3-6)   **323.1**
1. National Civil Rights Museum (Memphis, Tenn.) 2. African Americans—Civil rights 3. United States—Race relations
ISBN 0-8167-3502-6; 0-8167-3503-4 (pa)
LC 94-15831
"Once the site of Dr. King's assassination, the Lorraine Motel is now the National Civil Rights Museum. This instructive and inspirational book takes readers through an exhibit on the civil rights movement from 1954 to 1968. Photos featuring students visiting the museum are included." Soc Educ
Includes bibliography

Haskins, James, 1941-
Freedom Rides; journey for justice. Hyperion Bks. for Children 1995 99p il $14.95; lib bdg $14.89 (5 and up)   **323.1**
1. African Americans—Civil rights 2. Southern States—Race relations
ISBN 0-7868-0048-8; 0-7868-2037-3 (lib bdg)
LC 94-7996
The author discusses the efforts of the people who tested the series of court decisions aimed at desegregating buses and trains in the United States. The story begins in the 1850's with a New York City incident and trial, but the focus is mainly on the events of the 1940's, 1950's and 1960's and the freedom riders of those years
"Good-quality black-and-white photographs are scattered throughout. Haskins has . . . given YAs an important source of information on African American history with this well-researched, well-documented book." SLJ
Includes bibliographical references

Levine, Ellen
Freedom's children; young civil rights activists tell their own stories. Putnam 1993 167p il $16.95 (6 and up)   **323.1**
1. African Americans—Civil rights 2. United States—Race relations
ISBN 0-399-21893-9   LC 92-1358
Also available Thorndike Press large print edition and in paperback from Avon Bks.
Southern blacks who were young and involved in the civil rights movement during the 1950s and 1960s describe their experiences
"Freedom's Children belongs in every school library and should quickly take its place as an invaluable resource for teachers planning thematic units on prejudice or American minorities. Powerful, readable, authentic." ALAN
Includes bibliography

McKissack, Patricia C., 1944-
The Civil Rights Movement in America from 1865 to the present; by Patricia and Fredrick McKissack. 2nd ed. Childrens Press 1991 351p il $31.88 (5 and up)   **323.1**
1. African Americans—Civil rights 2. African Americans—History
ISBN 0-516-00579-0   LC 91-4103
First published 1987
From the beginning of Reconstruction to the present, this book traces the struggle of blacks to gain their civil rights in America, with a brief comparison of their problems to those of other minorities
"The biographical sketches of civil rights personalities and short explanations of particular events make this an effective ready reference tool." SLJ
Includes bibliographical references

323.44 Freedom of action (Liberty)

Intellectual freedom manual; compiled by the Office for Intellectual Freedom of the American Library Association. American Lib. Assn. il pa $35   **323.44**
1. Intellectual freedom 2. Libraries—Censorship
First published 1974 (5th edition 1996). Periodically revised

Intellectual freedom manual—*Continued*

This guide to preserving intellectual freedom includes: ALA interpretations to the Library Bill of Rights; recommendations for special libraries and specific situations; information about legal decisions affecting school and public libraries; a section on the ALA's Intellectual Freedom Action Network

Includes bibliographical references

Newsletter on Intellectual Freedom. American Lib. Assn. $40 per year   **323.44**

1. Intellectual freedom—Periodicals 2. Censorship—Periodicals

ISSN 0028-9485

Bimonthly. First published 1952

"The articles in this ALA publication focus on issues related to First Amendment rights. The news reports cover stories on censorship in American cities and towns, schools, and libraries. Articles deal with religious expression in school and restrictions of access to reading and viewing materials, as well as to restrictions of other types. This newsletter is informative and easy to read." Katz. Mag for Libr. 8th edition

Weiss, Ann E., 1943-

Who's to know? information, the media, and public awareness. Houghton Mifflin 1990 182p $14.95 (5 and up)   **323.44**

1. Freedom of information 2. Freedom of the press 3. Right of privacy

ISBN 0-395-49702-7   LC 89-26901

A discussion of the issue of the public's right to know and the various factors that may interfere with that right. In addition to historical background, the author "looks at the issue from a number of different angles, discussing the importance of accessing information and even pointing out where the media has perhaps given the public more information than might be necessary." Booklist

Includes bibliographical references

325.73   Immigration to the United States

Ashabranner, Brent K., 1921-

Still a nation of immigrants; [by] Brent Ashabranner; photographs by Jennifer Ashabranner. Cobblehill Bks. 1993 131p il $15.99 (5 and up)   **325.73**

1. United States—Immigration and emigration

ISBN 0-525-65130-6   LC 92-44335

Identifies who today's immigrants to the United States are, describes their experiences, contributions, and impact on society, and discusses how an immigrant becomes a citizen

"Engaging contemporary photographs, in addition to archival prints from the Library of Congress . . . personalize the commentary and add to the book's appeal. A carefully thought-out presentation." SLJ

Includes bibliography

Fisher, Leonard Everett, 1924-

Ellis Island; gateway to the New World. Holiday House 1986 64p il map lib bdg $14.95 (4 and up)   **325.73**

1. Ellis Island Immigration Station 2. United States—Immigration and emigration

ISBN 0-8234-0612-1   LC 86-2286

Companion volume to The Statue of Liberty, entered in class 974.7

"This is a detailed history of the island in Upper New York Bay that eventually came to be called Ellis Island. It served for many years as the entry point for immigrants, and it is this aspect that Fisher stresses, describing the laws that affected immigrants and the procedures that were used to screen and process them." Bull Cent Child Books

"Fisher relates the experiences of the immigrants in a straightforward manner, but his . . . [illustrations] often show the callousness with which these people were treated. . . . The black-and-white reproductions and Fisher's scratchboard drawings are excellent and enhance understanding of the clear, descriptive text." SLJ

Freedman, Russell

Immigrant kids. Dutton 1980 72p il hardcover o.p. paperback available $5.99 (4 and up)   **325.73**

1. Children of immigrants 2. United States—Immigration and emigration 3. City life

ISBN 0-14-037594-5 (pa)   LC 79-20060

The author has "assembled an interesting collection of old photographs for a book that gives a broad view of the experiences of immigrant children in an urban environment. The text is divided into such areas as the journey to America, schools, play, work (much of it illegal), and home life. Photographs are carefully placed in relation to textual references, and the text itself is enlivened by quotations from the reminiscences of several people about their first days in the United States as child immigrants. Large, clear print and an index add to the book's usefulness." Horn Book

I was dreaming to come to America; memories from the Ellis Island Oral History Project; selected and illustrated by Veronica Lawlor; foreword by Rudolph W. Giuliani. Viking 1995 38p il $14.99 (4 and up)   **325.73**

1. Ellis Island Immigration Station 2. United States—Immigration and emigration

ISBN 0-670-86164-2   LC 95-1281

In their own words, coupled with hand-painted collage illustrations, immigrants recall their arrival in the United States. Includes brief biographies and facts about the Ellis Island Oral History Project

"There is a flavor of Chagall in the peasant figures dancing above the ship or hopping ashore near the turreted towers of the huge building on Ellis Island. The elegant rendering offers a timeless view of this significant journey that is at once personal and universal." Horn Book

Jacobs, William Jay

Ellis Island; new hope in a new land. Scribner 1990 34p il lib bdg $14.95 (3-5)   **325.73**

1. Ellis Island Immigration Station 2. United States—Immigration and emigration

ISBN 0-684-19171-7   LC 89-38075

Jacobs, William Jay—*Continued*

Traces the history of Ellis Island and immigration to America and describes the experiences of immigrants arriving in 1907

"A book that is lavishly illustrated with photographs. . . . It will give children a realistic look at how children like themselves came to this country, the hardships they underwent during their voyages, and the anxieties and uncertainties they faced in their new country." SLJ

Levine, Ellen

. . . if your name was changed at Ellis Island; illustrated by Wayne Parmenter. Scholastic 1993 80p $15.95 (3-5)   **325.73**

1. Ellis Island Immigration Station 2. United States—Immigration and emigration

ISBN 0-590-46134-6   LC 92-27940

Describes, in question and answer format, the great migration of immigrants to New York's Ellis Island, from the 1880s to 1914. Features quotes from children and adults who passed through the station

The author "writes in a clear, direct style that's packed with information and lively case histories. . . . There are many illustrations, sometimes full-page, sometimes small, in acrylic earth colors . . . they are an attractive part of a clear and accessible design." Booklist

Rosenberg, Maxine B., 1939-

Making a new home in America; illustrated with photographs by George Ancona. Lothrop, Lee & Shepard Bks. 1986 unp il $11.95; lib bdg $11.88 (4-6)   **325.73**

1. United States—Immigration and emigration

ISBN 0-688-05824-8; 0-688-05825-6 (lib bdg)
          LC 85-11642

"This is a photo essay . . . about contemporary immigration, looking at the lives of children who have recently come from Japan, Guyana, India, Cuba and Vietnam in a wide range of social circumstances." N Y Times Book Rev

"The simple text describes the anticipation of new lives, the homesickness, and the difficulties with new language and customs as well as the sharing of native foods and traditions with American classmates and neighbors. Handsome in appearance and thoughtfully constructed as a vehicle to promote personal understanding, the book comes at a time of great need to develop multicultural awareness among children." Horn Book

326   Slavery and emancipation

Bial, Raymond

The Underground Railroad. Houghton Mifflin 1995 48p il map $14.95 (4 and up)
          326

1. Underground railroad 2. Slavery—United States
ISBN 0-395-69937-1   LC 94-19614

Using first-person accounts, historical documents, and his own photographs, the author "focuses on the history of the Underground Railroad, building on the experiences of both riders and conductors as he outlines the political climate and the moral beliefs that allowed slavery to thrive and those that helped bring about its downfall." Publ Wkly

"Although the text covers ground often trodden by other works on this popular subject, Bial's shots of places and things which now appear tidy and innocent conjure spirits of desperate freedom-seekers as handily as do more detailed narratives." Bull Cent Child Books

Includes bibliographical references

Hamilton, Virginia, 1936-

Many thousand gone; African Americans from slavery to freedom; illustrated by Leo and Diane Dillon. Knopf 1993 151p il $18; lib bdg $18.99; pa $12 (5 and up)   **326**

1. Underground railroad 2. Slavery—United States

ISBN 0-394-82873-9; 0-394-92873-3 (lib bdg); 0-679-87936-6 (pa)   LC 89-19988

In this book the author tells "the story of slavery through a series of dramatic biographical vignettes. . . . Her book includes such famous historical figures as Frederick Douglass, Sojourner Truth and Harriet Tubman. She also presents some more obscure individuals. . . . All of these profiles drive home the sickening realities of slavery in a personal way. . . . These are powerful stories eloquently told." N Y Times Book Rev

Includes bibliography

Haskins, James, 1941-

Get on board: the story of the Underground Railroad. Scholastic 1993 152p il map $13.95; pa $3.50 (5 and up)   **326**

1. Underground railroad 2. Slavery—United States

ISBN 0-590-45418-8; 0-590-45419-6 (pa)
          LC 92-13247

The author "relates the history of the Underground Railroad in the U.S., and introduces those who made it a success." SLJ

"Weaving together poignant personal stories and carefully researched historical data, Haskins has produced a stirring account of the founding and the workings of the Underground Railroad." Publ Wkly

Includes bibliography

Lester, Julius

To be a slave; illustrated by Tom Feelings. Dial Bks. for Young Readers 1968 160p il $15.99 (6 and up)   **326**

1. Slavery—United States
ISBN 0-8037-8955-6

Also available in paperback from Scholastic

"Through the words of the slave, interwoven with strongly sympathetic commentary, the reader learns what it is to be another man's property; how the slave feels about himself; and how he feels about others. Every aspect of slavery, regardless of how grim, has been painfully and unrelentingly described." Read Ladders for Hum Relat. 6th edition

Includes bibliography

Meltzer, Milton, 1915-

All times, all peoples: a world history of slavery; illustrated by Leonard Everett Fisher. Harper & Row 1980 65p il lib bdg $15.89 (4 and up)   **326**

1. Slavery—History
ISBN 0-06-024187-X

The author "discusses slavery as a part of world history, showing how it developed from economic situations and desire for power. Using examples from Egypt, Rome, China, and other cultures, as well as the United States, he explains how slavery affected society and the life of the individual slave." SLJ

Meltzer "has dipped into his deep knowledge of the subject to write a brief, but not superficial, account in clear, trenchant terms." Horn Book

Includes bibliography

Our song, our toil; the story of American slavery as told by slaves; edited by Michele Stepto. Millbrook Press 1994 95p il lib bdg $17.90 (4 and up)   **326**

1. Slavery—United States
ISBN 1-56294-401-0   LC 93-8323

Recounts the story of American slavery from African captivity to emancipation, through excerpts from slave autobiographies and slavery documents

"By making heavy use of carefully selected excerpts from the narratives of enslaved persons and setting these quotations in a compassionate, sensitive, yet unflinching description of the historical circumstances and conditions of slavery in America, Stepto has created a deeply moving and accurate account of its painful and horrifying history. . . . The well-reproduced illustrations, including photographs, reproductions, and written documents, add to the impact." SLJ

Includes bibliography

Rappaport, Doreen

Escape from slavery; five journeys to freedom; illustrated by Charles Lilly. HarperCollins Pubs. 1991 117p il $13.95; lib bdg $13.89 (4 and up)   **326**

1. Underground railroad 2. Slavery—United States
ISBN 0-06-021631-X; 0-06-021632-8 (lib bdg)
     LC 90-38170

Five accounts of black slaves who managed to escape to freedom during the period preceding the Civil War

"These accounts of a courageous and daring people deserve a wide readership. Readable, clear and precise, the book shows evidence of careful research and is an excellent addition to books on Black History." Child Book Rev Serv

Includes bibliography

328.73   The legislative process in the United States

Stein, R. Conrad, 1937-

The powers of Congress. Childrens Press 1995 30p il (Cornerstones of freedom) lib bdg $12.98 (4-6)   **328.73**

1. United States. Congress 2. Separation of powers—United States
ISBN 0-516-06696-X   LC 94-36913

First published 1985 with title: The story of the powers of Congress

"Stein uses the Marbury decision, the impeachment of Andrew Johnson, the resignation of Richard Nixon, and the struggle between Congress's ability to declare war versus the President's authority as Commander-in-Chief to illustrate the shifting balance among the three branches of government and the roots of the doctrine of separation of powers." SLJ

Includes glossary

331.3   Workers of specific age groups

Freedman, Russell

Kids at work; Lewis Hine and the crusade against child labor; with photographs by Lewis Hine. Clarion Bks. 1994 104p il $16.95 (5 and up)   **331.3**

1. Hine, Lewis Wickes, 1874-1940 2. Children—Employment
ISBN 0-395-58703-4   LC 93-5989

"Using the photographer's work throughout, Freedman provides a documentary account of child labor in America during the early 1900s and the role Lewis Hine played in the crusade against it. He offers a look at the man behind the camera, his involvement with the National Child Labor Committee, and the dangers he faced trying to document unjust labor conditions." SLJ

Freedman "does an outstanding job of integrating historical photographs with meticulously researched and highly readable prose." Publ Wkly

Includes bibliography

331.4   Women workers

Colman, Penny

Rosie the riveter; women working on the home front in World War II. Crown 1995 120p il $16; lib bdg $16.99 (5 and up)
     331.4

1. Women—Employment 2. World War, 1939-1945—United States
ISBN 0-517-59790-X; 0-517-59791-8 (lib bdg)
     LC 94-3614

This is an account of women's employment in wartime industry during the Second World War. "Colman looks at the jobs women took, the impact women had on the workplace, and what happened to working women at war's end. . . . [She also discusses] the public relations campaign that not only 'wooed' women into the workplace, but also sought to change firmly entrenched attitudes about women's role in society." Booklist

"A thoughtfully prepared look at women's history and wartime society, this dynamic book is characterized by extensive research." Horn Book

Includes bibliography

331.5 Special categories of workers other than by age or sex

Atkin, S. Beth

Voices from the fields; children of migrant farmworkers tell their stories; interviews and photographs by S. Beth Atkin. Little, Brown 1993 96p il $16.95 (5 and up)   **331.5**

1. Migrant labor 2. Agricultural laborers 3. Mexican Americans 4. Children's writings

ISBN 0-316-05633-2   LC 92-32248

"Joy Street books"

Photographs, poems in Spanish and English, and interviews with children reveal the hardships and hopes of Mexican American migrant farm workers and their families

"The Spanish is accurate, the English expressive, and the whole is a thoughtful tribute to the migrant experience. The black-and-white photographs are crisp and clear, frequently transcending the representational to achieve art." SLJ

Includes bibliography

331.7 Labor by industry and occupation

Sinnott, Susan

Chinese railroad workers. Watts 1994 63p il lib bdg $13.51 (4 and up)   **331.7**

1. Central Pacific Railroad 2. Railroads—History 3. Chinese Americans

ISBN 0-531-20169-4   LC 94-50

"A First book"

The author depicts the role played by Chinese immigrant laborers in the construction of the Central Pacific Railroad

"The clear and lively text make this a good source for reports or pleasure reading. It is illustrated throughout with black-and-white archival photographs and full-color reproductions." SLJ

Includes bibliographical references

331.8 Labor unions and labor-management relations

Altman, Linda Jacobs, 1943-

The Pullman strike of 1894; turning point for American labor. Millbrook Press 1994 63p il (Spotlight on American history) lib bdg $15.40 (5 and up)   **331.8**

1. Chicago Strike, 1894 2. Railroads—History

ISBN 1-56294-346-4   LC 93-10880

Discusses the people and events involved in the unsuccessful but influential strike by railroad workers at the Pullman Company in Chicago in 1894

"This slim volume leaves as moving an impression and understanding of the importance of the happenings as a far weightier book might." SLJ

Includes bibliography

McKissack, Patricia C., 1944-

A long hard journey; the story of the Pullman porter; by Patricia and Frederick McKissack. Walker & Co. 1989 144p il (Walker's American history series for young people) $17.95; lib bdg $18.85; pa $9.95 (5 and up)   **331.8**

1. Brotherhood of Sleeping Car Porters 2. Railroads—Employees

ISBN 0-8027-6884-9; 0-8027-6885-7 (lib bdg); 0-8027-7437-7 (pa)   LC 89-9139

Coretta Scott King Award for text, 1990

"Covering a 150-year period, this sympathetic account successfully focuses on the efforts of a small group who sought to gain recognition for the Brotherhood of Sleeping Car Porters, the first black American-controlled union. Led by Asa Philip Randolph, better known to recent generations as the organizer of the 1963 march on Washington, this revolt is profiled in an approach that emphasizes the men's commitment and sacrifices during their intensive 12-year stuggle." Booklist

Includes bibliography

332.024 Personal finance

Wilkinson, Elizabeth, 1926-

Making cents; every kid's guide to money, how to make it, what to do with it; drawings by Martha Weston. Little, Brown 1989 128p il hardcover o.p. paperback available $10.95 (4 and up)   **332.024**

1. Moneymaking projects for children 2. Personal finance

ISBN 0-316-94102-6 (pa)   LC 88-34634

"A Brown paper school book"

The author presents advice on making money through a variety of activities such as garage sales, dog walking, making Halloween costumes and beach sitting. This is an adaptation of Good Cents, by the Amazing Life Games Company

"Ideas are accompanied by a wealth of whimsical pencil drawings, most of which offer detailed instructions . . . or suggest creative activities." SLJ

332.4 Money

Cribb, Joe

Money. Knopf 1990 63p il (Eyewitness books) $19; lib bdg $18.99 (4 and up)   **332.4**

1. Money

ISBN 0-679-80438-2; 0-679-90438-7 (lib bdg)   LC 89-15589

Examines, in text and photographs, the symbolic and material meaning of money, from shekels, shells, and beads to gold, silver, checks, and credit cards. Also discusses how coins and banknotes are made, the value of money during wartime, and how to collect coins

Maestro, Betsy, 1944-

The story of money; illustrated by Giulio Maestro. Clarion Bks. 1993 43p il maps $15.95 (3-5) **332.4**

1. Money
ISBN 0-395-56242-2 LC 91-24997

Also available in paperback from Mulberry Bks.

A history of money, beginning with the barter system in ancient times, to the first use of coins and paper money, to the development of modern monetary systems

"A successful, readable presentation of a complicated subject. . . . Guilio Maestro's meticulously drawn watercolor illustrations brighten each page." SLJ

333.91 Water

Ancona, George, 1929-

Riverkeeper; photographs and text by George Ancona. Macmillan 1990 unp il $14.95 (3-6) **333.91**

1. Cronin, John 2. Hudson River (N.Y. and N.J.) 3. Water—Pollution 4. Nature conservation
ISBN 0-02-700911-4 LC 89-36777

"A photo-essay about the environmentalist, hired by the Hudson River Fishermen's Association as caretaker of one of New York's most important waterways, describes his work as a boatman, wildlife monitor, pollution detective, political activist, and public speaker." Sci Child

"A balanced, rational presentation, the book speaks directly to our times in a manner as informative as it is appealing." Horn Book

333.95 Biological resources

Patent, Dorothy Hinshaw

Places of refuge; our national wildlife refuge system; photographs by William Muñoz. Clarion Bks. 1992 80p il map $15.95 (4 and up) **333.95**

1. Wildlife refuges 2. National parks and reserves
ISBN 0-89919-846-5 LC 91-29273

Examines some of the popular wildlife refuges, in such states as Texas, North Dakota, and California, and focuses on the different methods used to help maintain a natural balance there

"The tight organization, clear writing, handsome format and handy map, list of addresses for more information, and index add up to a book that will be useful for reports and can serve as background for less generalized coverage." Bull Cent Child Books

Pringle, Laurence P.

Living treasure; saving earth's threatened biodiversity; [by] Laurence Pringle; illustrated by Irene Brady. Morrow Junior Bks. 1991 64p il maps $13.95; lib bdg $13.88 (4 and up) **333.95**

1. Wildlife conservation 2. Plant conservation
ISBN 0-688-07709-9; 0-688-07710-2 (lib bdg)
LC 90-21463

Discusses the rich variety of life on earth, the origins of such diversity, its rapid loss, and how to save organisms from extinction

"The text is both well written and informative and is must reading for young people who need to know what is happening and how they can get involved to solve some of the problems that are described." Sci Books Films

Includes glossary and bibliography

341.23 United Nations

Brenner, Barbara

The United Nations 50th anniversary book. Atheneum Bks. for Young Readers 1995 90p il $19.95 (4-6) **341.23**

1. United Nations
ISBN 0-689-31912-6 LC 94-12784

"A Byron Preiss book"

Brenner "analyzes the international organization founded to promote world peace and economic development. In addition to the text, numerous color photographs, a time line of key historical events and primary quotes facilitate discussion about the organizational structure and mission of the General Assembly, Security Council, and subsidiary groups such as UNICEF and the World Bank." Horn Book Guide

The author "has taken a very complicated organization and written about it in a clear, meaningful and understandable manner." Child Book Rev Serv

342 Constitutional and administrative law

Commager, Henry Steele, 1902-

The great Constitution; a book for young Americans. Macmillan 1961 128p il o.p. (5 and up) **342**

1. United States—Constitutional history

First published by Bobbs-Merrill

This description of the Constitution tells of the work and ideals of George Washington, James Madison, Alexander Hamilton, and the others who were a part of its creation. It describes the many difficulties of preparing a document that would provide a better government than the Articles of Confederation had, and indicates the attitudes of the states to the new Constitution

Fritz, Jean

Shhh! we're writing the Constitution; illustrated by Tomie dePaola. Putnam 1987 64p il $14.95; pa $8.95 (2-4) **342**

1. United States—Constitutional history
ISBN 0-399-21403-8; 0-399-21404-6 (pa)
LC 86-22528

"This book discusses how the Constitution came to be written and ratified. It includes the full text of the document produced by the Constitutional Convention of 1787." Bull Cent Child Books

"Jean Fritz gives a vivid, vibrant picture of the 1787 Constitutional Convention. The wonderful, full-color illustrations are a perfect match for the captivating text." Child Book Rev Serv

Hauptly, Denis J., 1945-

"A convention of delegates"; the creation of the Constitution. Atheneum Pubs. 1987 148p il $14.95 (5 and up) **342**

1. United States—Constitutional history

ISBN 0-689-31148-6 LC 86-17260

The author "presents the background, personalities, and events of the Constitutional Convention of 1787, where the American form of government was hammered out. His straightforward approach to the facts will be useful to students researching the topic, and he brings the historical tableaux to life through excellent portrayals of key figures such as George Washington, James Madison, Edmund Randolph, William Peterson, Roger Sherman, Benjamin Franklin, Alexander Hamilton, and John Jay. . . . A list of delegates, the text of the Constitution with the amendments, and a bibliography are appended. An intriguing introduction to a potentially dry subject." Booklist

Maestro, Betsy, 1944-

A more perfect union; the story of our Constitution; illustrated by Giulio Maestro. Lothrop, Lee & Shepard Bks. 1987 48p il $15.95; lib bdg $15.88; pa $7.95 (2-4) **342**

1. United States—Constitutional history

ISBN 0-688-06839-1; 0-688-06840-5 (lib bdg); 0-688-10192-5 (pa) LC 87-4083

Also available Spanish language edition

The Maestros "cover the birth of the Constitution from the initial decision to hold the convention, through the summer meetings in Philadelphia, the ratification struggle, the first election, and the adoption of the Bill of Rights." SLJ

"A simple, straightforward account using an oversize format with full-color illustration throughout. There is an excellent, fact-filled addenda that also includes the Preamble, chronologies and summaries of the Articles of the Constitution, the Bill of Rights, the Amendments and the Connecticut Compromise. This fine book places important events in historical context." Publ Wkly

Rappaport, Doreen

Tinker vs. Des Moines; student rights on trial. HarperCollins Pubs. 1993 153p il (Be the judge/Be the jury) lib bdg $14.89; pa $4.95 (5 and up) **342**

1. Tinker, John Frederick 2. Freedom of speech 3. Students—Law and legislation 4. Vietnam War, 1961-1975—Protests, demonstrations, etc.

ISBN 0-06-025118-2 (lib bdg); 0-06-446114-9 (pa) LC 92-25019

Using edited transcripts of testimony, this book recreates the trial of John Tinker and two other students who were suspended from school for protesting the Vietnam War, and invites the reader to act as judge and jury

"As an examination of a recent period in history, the book is an intriguing account that conscientiously presents both sides of the issue; as an exercise in how the U.S. legal system operates, it is even more effective." Booklist

Includes bibliographical references

Spier, Peter, 1927-

We the people; the Constitution of the United States of America. Doubleday 1987 unp il hardcover o.p. paperback available $7.95 (2-4) **342**

1. United States—Constitutional history

ISBN 0-385-41903-1 (pa) LC 86-24205

This "book opens with a basic textbook background describing the historical facts that resulted in the Constitution. The opening Preamble is richly illustrated to convey the wonderful diversity of America. The basic rights which the Constitution guarantees are expressed in cartoon-like drawings which can be easily comprehended by the reader. The complete text of the Constitution and its amendments are provided in the back. A good resource for Social Studies classes." Child Book Rev Serv

347 Civil procedure and courts

Stein, R. Conrad, 1937-

The powers of the Supreme Court. Childrens Press 1995 30p il (Cornerstones of freedom) lib bdg $12.98 (4-6) **347**

1. United States. Supreme Court

ISBN 0-516-06697-8 LC 94-38266

First published 1989 with title: The story of the powers of the Supreme Court

Stein "cites several landmark cases, such as Marbury v. Madison, Plessy v. Ferguson, Brown v. Board of Education of Topeka, Roe v. Wade, and Miranda v. Arizona, to illustrate the evolution of the Court's powers. He also explains how cases get their names and the impact of some of these decisions." SLJ

Includes glossary

353.04 The cabinet

Parker, Nancy Winslow

The president's cabinet and how it grew; with an introduction by Dean Rusk. new ed. HarperCollins Pubs. 1991 40p il maps lib bdg $14.89 (3-5) **353.04**

1. Cabinet officers

ISBN 0-06-021618-2 LC 89-70851

First published 1978 by Parents Magazine Press

Outlines the purpose and historical development of the President's cabinet, and explains the functions of each cabinet post

355.1 Military life and customs

The **Visual** dictionary of military uniforms. Dorling Kindersley 1992 64p il (Eyewitness visual dictionaries) $16.95; lib bdg $15.99 (4 and up) **355.1**

1. Military uniforms

ISBN 1-56458-010-5; 1-56458-011-3 (lib bdg) LC 91-58206

Labeled illustrations with explanatory text show the parts of various military uniforms that have been used from ancient Roman times to the twentieth century

"The book uses beautiful color photographs of actual or

The Visual dictionary of military uniforms—
Continued
reproduced military uniforms. Each uniform has been taken
apart in minute detail, and all relevant parts are labeled
clearly and accurately." Sci Books Films

355.3 Organization and personnel of military forces

Cosner, Shaaron, 1940-
War nurses. Walker & Co. 1988 106p il
$16.95; lib bdg $17.85 (6 and up)   **355.3**
1. Nurses 2. Military hospitals
ISBN 0-8027-6826-1; 0-8027-6828-8 (lib bdg)
    LC 88-14245
Traces the history of organized military nursing during
wartime, from its beginnings during the Civil War to the
conflict in Vietnam
"The text is factual but not dry; the black-and-white photographs, many historical, are revealing. Background information is livened by quotes from letters (no sources cited)
and occasionally fictionalized stories about individuals who
pioneered the field, from Clara Barton and Florence Nightingale to contemporary women who have crusaded for recognition of nurses' status as veterans." Bull Cent Child
Books

355.7 Military installations and reservations

Macdonald, Fiona
A Roman fort; illustrated by Gerald Wood.
Bedrick Bks. 1993 48p il maps (Inside story)
$17.95; pa $8.95 (5 and up)   **355.7**
1. Fortification 2. Rome—Antiquities
ISBN 0-87226-370-3; 0-87226-259-6 (pa)
    LC 93-16397
Text and illustrations describe the construction of an ancient Roman fort and the lives of the soldiers who manned
it in defense of the Empire
"Full-color, detailed drawings and diagrams are an integral part of the presentation. A wealth of information can
be obtained from the blocks of text and numerous cutaways
showing the inside and outside of buildings." SLJ
Includes glossary

355.8 Military equipment and supplies

Byam, Michèle
Arms & armor. Knopf 1988 63p il
(Eyewitness books) $16; lib bdg $16.99 (4 and
up)   **355.8**
1. Armor
ISBN 0-394-89622-X; 0-394-99622-4 (lib bdg)
    LC 87-26449
A photo essay examining the design, construction, and
uses of hand weapons and armor from a Stone Age axe to
the revolvers and rifles of the Wild West
"The brilliantly colored photos have a luminous sheen,
imparting an almost three-dimensional quality." Booklist

Gravett, Christopher
Arms and armor; written by Chris Gravett;
illustrated by Richard Hook, Chris Rothero,
and Peter Sarson. Raintree Steck-Vaughn
Pubs. 1995 32p il (Pointers) lib bdg $19.97 (4
and up)   **355.8**
1. Weapons—History 2. Armor—History
ISBN 0-8114-6190-4   LC 94-7938
This is a brief illustrated history of weapons and armor
from ancient Egypt to the present
"The art is precise, and the descriptions are brief and accurate." Sci Books Films
Includes glossary

Yue, Charlotte
Armor; [by] Charlotte and David Yue.
Houghton Mifflin 1994 92p il $14.95 (4 and
up)   **355.8**
1. Armor 2. Knights and knighthood
ISBN 0-395-68101-4   LC 93-50601
The authors "discuss European knighthood, the historical
development of armor as new weapons called for new defenses, the armorer's craft, the complicated task of dressing
a knight, armor for horses, jousts, and the end of knighthood. . . . The text makes the distinction between what historians know from evidence and what they surmise. Black-
and-white drawings illustrate the text." Booklist
Includes bibliography

359.1 Naval life and customs

Biesty, Stephen
Stephen Biesty's cross-sections: Man-of-war;
illustrated by Stephen Biesty; written by
Richard Platt. Dorling Kindersley 1993 27p il
$16.95 (4 and up)   **359.1**
1. Great Britain. Royal Navy 2. Seafaring life 3. Ships
ISBN 1-56458-321-X   LC 92-21227
Text and cutaway illustrations depict life aboard a British warship of the Napoleonic era, covering such topics as
work, leisure, discipline, navigating, and fighting
"The intriguing text, presented in brief, anecdotal notes,
is accompanied by smaller drawings, making this meticulously presented book a treasure of factual content and visual imagery." Booklist
Includes glossary

359.9 Specialized combat forces

Warner, J. F. (John F.), 1929-
The U.S. Marine Corps. Lerner Publs. 1991
88p il (Lerner's armed services series) lib bdg
$22.95 (5 and up)   **359.9**
1. United States. Marine Corps
ISBN 0-8225-1432-X   LC 90-19327
Reviews the history, modern day life, and equipment of
the Marine Corps, and details the enlistment and promotion procedures
"The smoothly written, fast-reading text . . . has wide
margins, and is printed on high quality nonglare paper.
Black-and-white photos appear on virtually every page;
many of the older ones are of vintage quality. Some full-
color photographs are also included." SLJ

361.2 Social action

Lewis, Barbara A., 1943-
The kid's guide to social action; how to solve the social problems you choose—and turn creative thinking into positive action; edited by Pamela Espeland. Free Spirit 1991 185p il pa $14.95 (4 and up) **361.2**

1. Social action
ISBN 0-915793-29-6 LC 90-44297
"A Do something! book"
Resource guide for young people for learning political action skills that can help them make a difference in solving social problems at the community, state, and national levels
"Clearly but informally written, the book is packed with well-organized, practical information and includes plenty of inspiring quotes and anecdotes. . . . This is an exemplary reference and curricular resource that works as enlightening browsing material as well." Bull Cent Child Books
Includes bibliography

362.1 Physical illness. Medical care

Howe, James, 1946-
The hospital book; text by James Howe; photographs by Mal Warshaw. Morrow Junior Bks. 1994 94p il $16; pa $7.95 (2-4) **362.1**

1. Hospitals 2. Medical care
ISBN 0-688-12731-2; 0-688-12734-7 (pa)
LC 93-15701
First published 1981 by Crown
A guide to a stay in the hospital discussing what happens there, the people one meets, what will hurt and how one gets better and goes home
This "is accessible, helpful, reassuring, and direct. . . . An invaluable resource." Horn Book Guide

Rockwell, Anne F., 1934-
The emergency room; [by] Anne & Harlow Rockwell. Macmillan 1985 unp il $13.95 (k-2) **362.1**

1. Hospitals 2. Medical care
ISBN 0-02-777300-0 LC 84-20161
This book explores the equipment and procedures of a hospital emergency room by describing what one patient sees while being treated for a sprained ankle
"Large, rounded letters and short lines of print encourage the child to read the book. Although the hospital personnel are depicted, the clean-lined illustrations emphasize the sophisticated emergency room apparatus. The drawings show enough detail to interest reluctant older readers. Light, bright color imparts a reassuring warmth to the surroundings." Horn Book

Rogers, Fred
Going to the hospital; photographs by Jim Judkis. Putnam 1988 unp il hardcover o.p. paperback available $6.95 (k-2) **362.1**
1. Hospitals 2. Medical care
ISBN 0-399-21530-1 (pa) LC 87-19170

Describes what happens during a stay in the hospital, including some of the common forms of medical treatment
"The author's style is just right for this level of information book: reassuring yet candid, matter-of-fact about those aspects of hospitalization that may be frightening or painful, yet not in itself alarming." Bull Cent Child Books

362.2 Mental and emotional illnesses and disturbances

Dinner, Sherry H.
Nothing to be ashamed of: growing up with mental illness in your family. Lothrop, Lee & Shepard Bks. 1989 212p lib bdg $13; pa $8 (5 and up) **362.2**

1. Mental illness
ISBN 0-688-08482-6 (lib bdg); 0-688-08493-1 (pa)
LC 88-13244
"The intent of this book is to inform family members, particularly adolescents, about the nature, causes, and treatments of selected emotional and mental disorders, such as schizophrenia, mood, anxiety, eating disorders, and Alzheimer's disease." Sci Books Films
"One of the valuable points in this book is that young adults do not have to feel alone in their emotions towards this family crisis, and can cope sucessfully as well as advance their own lives." Voice Youth Advocates
Includes glossary and bibliography

362.29 Substance abuse

O'Neill, Catherine, 1950-
Focus on alcohol; illustrated by David Neuhaus. 21st Cent. Bks. (NY) 1990 56p il (Drug-alert book) lib bdg $14.95 (3-6) **362.29**

1. Alcohol 2. Alcoholism
ISBN 0-941477-96-7 LC 89-20410
The author discusses the history, use, and dangers of alcohol, the problems of alcoholism, and coping with the pressures to drink
"This book does not presuppose any other introduction to the subject, and the detail and reading level make it very suitable for the intended age group." Sci Child

Rosenberg, Maxine B., 1939-
Not my family: sharing the truth about alcoholism. Bradbury Press 1988 97p $14.95 (4 and up) **362.29**

1. Alcoholics 2. Parent and child 3. Children of alcoholics
ISBN 0-02-777911-4 LC 88-10468
The author of this book "interviewed eight youngsters referred to her through treatment centers and six adult children of alcoholics about their family experiences. The bibliography is addressed to adults as well as children, and there is also a list of seven national organizations that can be contacted for help." N Y Times Book Rev

Shulman, Jeffrey, 1951-

Focus on cocaine and crack; illustrated by David Neuhaus. 21st Cent. Bks. (NY) 1990 56p il (Drug-alert book) lib bdg $14.95 (3-6)

362.29

1. Cocaine 2. Crack (Drug) 3. Drug abuse
ISBN 0-941477-98-3   LC 89-20446

Discusses how cocaine and crack affect the mind and body and presents a brief history of cocaine use

"A truthful, factual . . . book about drugs for elementary school children. . . . The facts are all here, simplified, but complete enough to relay the message—drugs are dangerous. The information is sufficient for reports, even on a middle-school level. Analogies are in the realm of children's experience without making the activity appear desirable." SLJ

Includes glossary and bibliographical references

Zeller, Paula Klevan

Focus on marijuana; illustrated by David Neuhaus. 21st Cent. Bks. (NY) 1990 56p il (Drug-alert book) lib bdg $14.95 (3-6)

362.29

1. Marijuana
ISBN 0-941477-97-5   LC 89-20430

Describes the history, effects, social aspects, and physical dangers of using marihuana

The book points "out new findings on the dangers of this drug and includes a good section on using dogs to detect this substance. . . . [The volume] includes an index and glossary, and is illustrated with pastel-shaded black-line drawings." Booklist

362.4 Problems of and services to people with physical disabilities

Alexander, Sally Hobart

Mom can't see me; photograhs by George Ancona. Macmillan 1990 unp il $14.95 (3-5)

362.4

1. Blind 2. Mothers and daughters
ISBN 0-02-700401-5   LC 89-13241

Blind author Alexander gives "readers a picture of her life, told from the vantage point of her nine-year-old daughter. . . . Alexander participates in all the family activities: cooking, cleaning, taking the children to lessons, and volunteering at school. She includes some of the frustrations of blindness as well, such as the fear children express of 'catching' blindness and the sadness that Alexander feels in not seeing what her children are seeing. Ancona's clear black-and-white photographs greatly amplify the text, showing the family at work and play. This is one of the best books available on blindness." SLJ

Mom's best friend; photographs by George Ancona. Macmillan 1992 unp il $14.95 (3-5)

362.4

1. Guide dogs 2. Blind 3. Mothers and daughters
ISBN 0-02-700393-0   LC 91-43809

"Sally Alexander's story, first told in *Mom Can't See Me* continues when Marit, Sally's first guide dog, dies, and Sally decides to get another dog. Sally's daughter Leslie describes the family's grief over losing Marit, their trials during Sally's extended absence to get a new dog from the Seeing Eye Institute, and the carefully executed adjustment period during which the family and the new dog get to know and care for each other. . . . Exceptionally clear black-and-white photographs show scenes of family life as well as activities at the Seeing Eye. A touching, real-life photo-essay with broad appeal." Booklist

Arnold, Caroline, 1944-

A guide dog puppy grows up; written by Caroline Arnold; photographs by Richard Hewett. Harcourt Brace Jovanovich 1991 unp il $16.95 (3-5)

362.4

1. Guide dogs 2. Blind
ISBN 0-15-232657-X   LC 90-5154

Follows the career of a guide dog named Honey from her raising as a puppy, through the training process, and placement with a blind person

"Clear full-color photographs show the transition from puppy to working canine. The text is lucid and brief." SLJ

Bergman, Thomas

Finding a common language; children living with deafness. Gareth Stevens Children's Bks. 1989 48p il (Don't turn away) lib bdg $18.60 (1-3)

362.4

1. Deaf
ISBN 1-55532-916-0   LC 88-42969

Original Swedish edition, 1987

Follows the activities of a six-year-old Swedish girl as she attends a nursery school for the deaf

Includes glossary and bibliography

Going places; children living with cerebral palsy. Gareth Stevens Children's Bks. 1991 48p il (Don't turn away) lib bdg $18.60 (1-3)

362.4

1. Cerebral palsy
ISBN 0-8368-0199-7   LC 90-48266

Original Swedish edition, 1990

"Mathias, six-years-old, was born with cerebral palsy and subsequently diagnosed as almost totally deaf. . . . Readers follow him through examinations, various therapies, riding horseback, ice-skating, etc.; mostly they will witness a busy, good-natured child adjusting to his limitations. The simply written, clear text augments and expands the large black-and-white photographs that help readers enter this young boy's world." SLJ

Includes glossary and bibliography

Meeting the challenge; children living with diabetes. Stevens, G. 1992 48p il (Don't turn away) lib bdg $18.60 (1-3)

362.4

1. Diabetes
ISBN 0-8368-0738-3   LC 91-50334

Describes the medical problems and daily routine of a ten-year-old Swedish boy with diabetes and discusses the two main types of this chronic disease

"Bergman presents a realistic portrait, focusing on the ways having this disease changes one's life, but also showing that one can cope and adapt to have a good childhood. . . . The photography is superb." Appraisal

Includes glossary and bibliography

Moments that disappear; children living with epilepsy. Stevens, G. 1992 48p il (Don't turn away) lib bdg $18.60 (1-3)

362.4

1. Epilepsy
ISBN 0-8368-0739-1   LC 91-50335

Bergman, Thomas—*Continued*

The author "chronicles the daily successes and struggles of his own twelve year old son who is coping with this disease. Bergman's photography is clear and eye-catching. His text explains the types of epilepsy, how epilepsy is diagnosed and treated, and how his son, Joakim, adapts to this condition." Appraisal

Includes glossary and bibliography

On our own terms; children living with physical disabilities. Gareth Stevens Children's Bks. 1989 48p il (Don't turn away) lib bdg $18.60 (1-3) **362.4**

1. Physically handicapped children
ISBN 1-55532-942-X   LC 88-42973

Original Swedish edition, 1981
Describes the activities at the Caroline Hospital in Stockholm where children with congenital handicaps receive training and physiotherapy
Includes glossary and bibliography

Butler, Dorothy, 1925-

Cushla and her books. Horn Bk. 1980 c1979 128p il o.p. **362.4**

1. Yeoman, Cushla, 1971- 2. Handicapped children 3. Books and reading   LC 79-25695

First published 1979 in the United Kingdom
"Cushla was born with multiple birth defects . . . and almost died at least twice before her first birthday. Her development lagged behind that of normal peers except in the area of speech and cognition, and her poor coordination and motor skills narrowed her ability to experience the world around her. Yet she also had an astounding grasp of concepts and an insatiable appetite for learning. The most successful therapeutic medium for Cushla turned out to be books, which her family began reading aloud to her when she was only four months old. . . . Butler, who originally wrote this work as a Ph.D. thesis, includes plenty of backup material to document Cushla's problems and treatment. Invaluable for libraries serving parents of handicapped children, and primary education teachers, and children's and school librarians." Libr J

Haldane, Suzanne

Helping hands; how monkeys assist people who are disabled; text and photographs by Suzanne Haldane. Dutton Children's Bks. 1991 unp il $14.95 (4 and up) **362.4**

1. Physically handicapped 2. Monkeys
ISBN 0-525-44723-7   LC 90-27382

A photo-essay focusing on Greg, a teenager with quadriplegia and his capuchin monkey named Willie, illustrating how capuchins are trained by the Helping Hands program to provide help and companionship to people who are disabled

"Haldane's candid black-and-white photographs are fascinating. . . . In combination with the informative text, the pictures capture the functional aspects of the unusual relationship as well as the affection that underlies it." Booklist

Krementz, Jill

How it feels to live with a physical disability. Simon & Schuster 1992 176p il $18 (4 and up) **362.4**

1. Physically handicapped children
ISBN 0-671-72371-5   LC 91-43335

This "book introduces readers to 12 young people, ages 6 to 16, who have been challenged by physical disabilities, including dwarfism, paralysis, blindness, missing limbs, and the effects of cerebral palsy. Krementz devotes a chapter to each story, writing in first person from the child's point of view. While the tone of the text is even throughout, individual voices of the young people come through, and the many good black-and-white photographs also give readers a sense of identity with particular children. . . . Krementz offers insight as well as information on a seldom discussed topic." Booklist

Peterson, Jeanne Whitehouse

I have a sister—my sister is deaf; pictures by Deborah Ray. Harper & Row 1977 unp il lib bdg $16.75; pa $4.95 (k-3) **362.4**

1. Deaf 2. Sisters
ISBN 0-06-024702-9 (lib bdg); 0-06-443059-6 (pa)
    LC 76-24306

"Being deaf has some assets as well as liabilities. This book helps to point out some ways a deaf child compensates and some ways that other senses are developed more fully. It has an appreciation for accomplishments and strengths. It gives a picture of a warm relationship between a girl and her younger deaf sister." Child Book Rev Serv

"A lovely, tender story, with a sense of poetry that is quite captivating. The pencil sketch illustrations by Deborah Ray aptly evoke the mood of the text." Babbling Bookworm

Rosenberg, Maxine B., 1939-

Finding a way; living with exceptional brothers and sisters; photographs by George Ancona. Lothrop, Lee & Shepard Bks. 1988 48p il $12.95; lib bdg $12.88 (2-4) **362.4**

1. Physically handicapped children 2. Brothers and sisters
ISBN 0-688-06873-1; 0-688-06874-X (lib bdg)
    LC 88-6776

"Rosenberg writes about what it is like to be the brother or sister of a child who has a special physical problem; covered here are diabetes, asthma, and spina bifida. What is most valuable in her writing is the objectivity with which she approaches the fact that the sibling who is not disabled also has problems of acceptance and adjustment; a second strength is the recurrent emphasis on the positive, both in the coverage of sibling relationships and in the demonstration of the fact that, disabled or not, children have similar needs and interests." Bull Cent Child Books

My friend Leslie; the story of a handicapped child; photographs by George Ancona. Lothrop, Lee & Shepard Bks. 1983 48p il $16; lib bdg $15.93 (1-3) **362.4**

1. Physically handicapped children
ISBN 0-688-01690-1; 0-688-01691-X (lib bdg)
    LC 82-12734

"In a photodocumentary about a child with multiple handicaps, the text is narrated by Leslie's best friend and kindergarten classmate Karin. Leslie is legally blind, has some hearing loss, a cleft palate, muscular disability, and ptosis of the eyelids. She's needed surgery several times, and she's a merry, friendly child whose classmates help her when help is needed, accept her as she is, and enjoy her company." Bull Cent Child Books

"This title shows a positive, practical approach to having handicapped children in an ordinary classroom setting. It is a good, realistic explanation that children will be able to comprehend." Child Book Rev Serv

Rosenberg, Maxine B., 1939-—*Continued*

"The black-and-white photographs by Ancona go well with the text and enhace the message of the book." SLJ

Roy, Ron, 1940-

Move over, wheelchairs coming through! seven young people in wheelchairs talk about their lives; photographs by Rosmarie Hausherr. Clarion Bks. 1985 83p il $15.95 (3 and up)   **362.4**

1. Physically handicapped children

ISBN 0-89919-249-1   LC 84-14314

"Brief studies of seven disabled children, aged 8 to 19. Each short chapter describes the handicap and how the young person copes with it from a wheelchair. The text stresses what the children can do and how they face barriers in the world as they go to school, to restaurants and around their home towns. Both text and well-placed, high-quality photographs emphasize the daily activities of these children, showing that they like to do the things their friends and family do. The children all take part in sports and other physical activities." SLJ

Includes bibliography

Smith, Elizabeth Simpson

A guide dog goes to school; the story of a dog trained to lead the blind; illustrated by Bert Dodson. Morrow 1987 51p il $12.95; lib bdg $12.88 (3-5)   **362.4**

1. Guide dogs

ISBN 0-688-06844-8; 0-688-06846-4 (lib bdg)
                                      LC 87-11056

"The author describes the life, selection, and training of a golden retriever puppy from birth until it graduates with its master and begins a new life as a guide dog. Sixteen full-page drawings complement the text. A brief introduction describes the history of guide dog use and a postscript cautions against disturbing a guide dog when it is working. This book accurately and sensitively portrays the concern, effort, and nurturing that are required to select and train any guide dog." Sci Child

362.5 Problems of and services to the poor

Nichelason, Margery G.

Homeless or hopeless? Lerner Publs. 1994 112p il (Pro/Con) lib bdg $17.50 (5 and up)
                                      362.5

1. Homeless persons

ISBN 0-8225-2606-9   LC 92-19675

Examines the problem of homelessness in the United States, including its causes and effects, society's responsibilities, and government and private assistance programs

"This well-written and appealing book is an excellent homework resource for students, but it will also attract those whose reading preference is nonfiction." Booklist

Includes glossary and bibliography

Wolf, Bernard, 1930-

Homeless; written and photographed by Bernard Wolf. Orchard Bks. 1995 unp il $16.95; lib bdg $16.99 (2-4)   **362.5**

1. Henry Street Settlement (New York, N.Y.) 2. Homeless persons 3. New York (N.Y.)—Social conditions

ISBN 0-531-06886-2; 0-531-08736-0 (lib bdg)
                                      LC 94-27293

This photoessay "focuses on a New York City family that faces difficulties in finding affordable housing. The book begins as eight-year-old Mikey and his family . . . receive assistance in the form of a temporary rent-free apartment in the Henry Street Settlement Urban Family Center, one of the United States' first transitional housing projects for the homeless." Horn Book

"Crisp color photos of the threadbare but 'squeaky clean' apartment, long lines for the check-cashing office, and expectant young faces at the charity Christmas party will speak as eloquently as the narration does to an audience of kids more fortunate than Mikey." Bull Cent Child Books

362.7 Problems of and services to young people

Banish, Roslyn, 1942-

A forever family; story and pictures by Roslyn Banish with Jennifer Jordan-Wong. HarperCollins Pubs. 1992 44p il $14; lib bdg $13.89; pa $5.95 (k-3)   **362.7**

1. Adoption 2. Foster home care

ISBN 0-06-021673-5; 0-06-021674-3 (lib bdg); 0-06-446116-5 (pa)   LC 90-28725

Eight-year-old Jennifer Jordan-Wong describes her adoption by a family after four years of living as a foster child with many different families

"The matter-of-fact tone of the text is one of the book's strengths; another is the excellent photography. Details of fostering and the adoption process emerge through a thoughtful combination of pictures and a simple, declarative text." Horn Book

Includes glossary

Berck, Judith, 1960-

No place to be; voices of homeless children; foreword by Robert Coles. Houghton Mifflin 1991 148p il $14.95 (5 and up)   **362.7**

1. Homeless persons

ISBN 0-395-53350-3   LC 91-11432

"An exploration of homelessness in America, specifically New York City, this incorporates quotes from 30 children from ages 9 to 18. Statistics relating to homelessness and poverty levels are incorporated into the text along with background information." BAYA Book Rev

"Rigorously documented. . . . Helped by a selection of black-and-white photographs, the book's balance between information and anecdote is excellent, avoiding both fact-packing and sentimentality." Bull Cent Child Books

Includes bibliography

Krementz, Jill

How it feels to be adopted. Knopf 1982
107p il hardcover o.p. paperback available $13
(4 and up) **362.7**

1. Adoption

ISBN 0-394-75853-6 (pa) LC 82-48011

"Nineteen youngsters ranging in age from 8 to 16 voice
their feelings about being adopted. . . . Several of the accounts are by youngsters who 'have' found their birth mothers and are in the process of getting to know them. Single-
parent adoptees are included, too." Booklist

This "is an important contribution to literature on adoption and the question of searching for biological parents."
SLJ

Includes bibliography

Rogers, Fred

Adoption; photographs by Jim Judkis.
Putnam 1994 unp il (Let's talk about it)
$15.95; pa $6.95 (k-2) **362.7**

1. Adoption

ISBN 0-399-22432-7; 0-399-22525-0 (pa)

LC 92-15607

Discusses what it means to be part of a family and examines some feelings that adopted children may have

"This is a gentle, matter-of-fact, and reassuring approach
to the topic of adoption. The text addresses the young listener directly. . . . The illustrations are sharp, clear color
photographs following the daily tasks of three different families." Bull Cent Child Books

Rosenberg, Maxine D., 1939-

Being adopted; photographs by George
Ancona. Lothrop, Lee & Shepard Bks. 1984
unp il $16; lib bdg $15.93 (2-4) **362.7**

1. Interracial adoption

ISBN 0-688-02672-9; 0-688-02673-7 (lib bdg)

LC 83-17522

"The author stresses the problems adoptive children—
especially those from other countries or those who look
markedly different from other members of their families—
have in ajusting to their new homes." Bull Cent Child
Books

"Although most of the crisp black-and-white photographs
appearing on every page are purposely posed to go along
with the narrative, they are relaxed and informal in style,
successfully capturing the warmth of these special family relationships. This exceptional photo-documentary look at an
increasingly common type of adoption will be reassuring for
children who are adopted and enlightening for those who
aren't." Booklist

Terkel, Susan Neiburg, 1948-

Feeling safe, feeling strong; how to avoid
sexual abuse and what to do if it happens to
you; [by] Susan N. Terkel & Janice E. Rench.
Lerner Publs. 1984 68p il lib bdg $18.95 (4
and up) **362.7**

1. Child sexual abuse

ISBN 0-8225-0021-3 LC 84-9664

This book presents "six stories, each about a young person faced with a particular type of abuse, from obscene
phone calls to incest. In every case the young person either
gets control of the situation alone or goes to an adult who
helps. All six stories are followed by facts about the type of
abuse and information on how to avoid it or seek help."

Child Book Rev Serv

"This polished, professional presentation offers a wealth
of sound information and advice. The tone is supportive
and straight-forward; it's useful for both the independent
reader and the teacher or parent who wishes to educate
young audiences on the topic." Booklist

363 Other social problems and services

Pringle, Laurence P.

Living in a risky world; [by] Laurence
Pringle. Morrow Junior Bks. 1989 105p il
$12.95 (6 and up) **363**

1. Environmental health 2. Safety education

ISBN 0-688-04326-7 LC 88-31686

In this study the author attempts to explore "the scientific and social factors in risk assessment and risk management. The problems associated with acid rain, carcinogens,
and other hazardous results of human activity and counter-
measures, such as animal testing and the science of toxicol-
ogy, are cited, and the study of risk as a distinct field of
specialization is [considered]." Horn Book

Includes glossary and bibliography

363.3 Other aspects of public safety

Gibbons, Gail

Emergency! Holiday House 1994 unp il
$15.95; pa $6.95 (k-3) **363.3**

1. Vehicles

ISBN 0-8234-1128-1; 0-8234-1201-6 (pa)

LC 94-2109

The author "covers emergency vehicles, from ambu-
lances and fire engines to helicopters, boats and planes, distinguishing . . . between the different types of fire trucks
and including utility trucks sent out after storms." Bull Cent
Child Books

"Gibbons's stylistic, flat, colorful illustrations accurately
depict the events described in the text and add more for observant readers to interpret." SLJ

Fire! Fire! Crowell 1984 unp il lib bdg
$14.89; pa $5 (k-3) **363.3**

1. Fire fighting

ISBN 0-690-04416-X (lib bdg); 0-06-446058-4 (pa)

LC 83-46162

This book "depicts fire fighting in the city, country, forest, and on the water, and integrates some points on fire
safety." Child Book Rev Serv

The author/illustrator "uses bright colors and simplified
diagrams to convey the excitement and teamwork necessary
in firefighting. There are details for children to pore over
and the equipment in the illustrations is clearly labeled."
SLJ

363.5   Housing

Shachtman, Tom, 1942-

The president builds a house; photographs by Margaret Miller; introduction by Jimmy Carter. Simon & Schuster Bks. for Young Readers 1989 unp il $14.95 (3-5)   **363.5**

1. Habitat for Humanity Inc. 2. Housing
ISBN 0-671-67705-5   LC 88-33267

"A well-organized photo essay shows how volunteers from the Habitat for Humanity organization, including former President Jimmy Carter and his wife, built 20 houses in Atlanta in one week during the summer of 1988. The short text gives the history of the group and its goals." NY Times Book Rev

363.7   Environmental problems and services

50 simple things kids can do to recycle; [by] The Earth Works Group; illustrations by Michele Montez. Earthworks Press 1994 144p il pa $6.95 (4 and up)   **363.7**

1. Recycling
ISBN 1-879682-00-1

This "urges children to do their share to save the Earth's resources by following the 'Three R's'—reducing, reusing, recycling—and makes commonsense suggestions that are fairly easy to follow. Readers learn what garbage can be recycled, how to reuse things around the house, how to be a wise shopper, and more. Black-and-white sketches illustrate the text. A valuable resource for both reports and classroom discussion." SLJ

Includes bibliography

50 simple things kids can do to save the earth; [by] the Earth Works Group; illustrations by Michele Montez (and a few kids). Andrews & McMeel 1990 156p il pa $6.95 (4 and up)   **363.7**

1. Environmental protection
ISBN 0-8362-2301-2   LC 90-34753

This book explains how specific things in a child's environment are connected to the rest of the world, how using them affects the planet, and how the individual can develop habits and projects that are environmentally sound

"A practical and upbeat guide to saving resources and protecting the environment. . . . Parents and teachers will find this to be a useful guide for increasing awareness of environmental problems and a superb teaching tool." SLJ

Anderson, Joan

Earth keepers; text by Joan Anderson; photographs by George Ancona. Harcourt Brace & Co. 1993 unp il $17.95 (4-6)   **363.7**

1. Environmental protection
ISBN 0-15-242199-8   LC 92-38627

"A Gulliver Green book"

Discusses the work of three environmental protection groups: the Clearwater on the Hudson River, gardeners in New York City, and Lynn Rogers studying black bears in Minnesota

This features "attractive photographs and a smoothly developed narrative." Horn Book

Anderson, Madelyn Klein

Oil spills. Watts 1990 63p il lib bdg $13.93 (4 and up)   **363.7**

1. Oil spills
ISBN 0-531-10872-4   LC 90-32896

"A First book"

Describes the problem of oil spills, their effect on the environment, and what must be done to clean up after them

"The final two chapters, which describe the types of spills, the variety of methods used to deal with them, and the specialists involved are clear and adequately treated, providing current technological information that is not readily available to young readers. Excellent full-color photographs enhance and explain the text." SLJ

Includes glossary and bibliography

Asimov, Isaac, 1920-1992

Pollution in space; with revisions and updating by Greg Walz-Chojnacki. rev & updated ed. Stevens, G. 1995 32p il (Isaac Asimov's new library of the universe) lib bdg $18.60 (3-5)   **363.7**

1. Space debris
ISBN 0-8368-1196-8   LC 94-32485

First published 1989 with title: Space garbage

The author contends that our "40 year presence in outer space has already led to the accumulation of an impressive amount of space debris. Tracking satellites, alive and dead, remnants of manned launches, and other trash has become an essential element of all launches." Publisher's note

Baines, John D. (John David), 1943-

Acid rain; [by] John Baines. Steck-Vaughn 1990 48p il (Conserving our world) lib bdg $22.13; pa $5.95 (5 and up)   **363.7**

1. Acid rain
ISBN 0-8114-2385-9 (lib bdg); 0-8114-3450-8 (pa)
         LC 89-21656

Discusses the vast contamination of forests and lakes throughout the world by the acidity in the rainfall

"Acid Rain is highly recommended for supplementary reading and study in a classroom situation. It is also an excellent introductory resource text in summary form." Sci Books Films

Includes glossary and bibliography

Berger, Melvin, 1927-

Oil spill! illustrated by Paul Mirocha. HarperCollins Pubs. 1994 31p il (Let's-read-and-find-out science books) $15; lib bdg $14.89; pa $4.95 (k-3)   **363.7**

1. Oil spills
ISBN 0-06-022909-8; 0-06-022912-8 (lib bdg); 0-06-445121-6 (pa)   LC 92-34779

Explains why oil spills occur and how they are cleaned up and suggests strategies for preventing them in the future

"The text is simple and clear. . . . Subtle in texture and deep in tone, the colorful artwork effectively illustrates marine animals and oil tankers. . . . A good introduction to the subject." Booklist

Brown, Laurene Krasny

Dinosaurs to the rescue! a guide to protecting our planet; [by] Laurie Krasny Brown and Marc Brown. Little, Brown 1992 unp il $14.95; pa $5.95 (k-3) **363.7**

1. Environmental protection
ISBN 0-316-11087-6; 0-316-11397-2 (pa)

LC 91-27177

"Joy Street books"

Text and illustrations of dinosaur characters introduce the earth's major environmental problems and suggest ways children can help

"Information is presented in a straightforward way, enlivened by energetic, brightly colored, cartoon-style illustrations. Irreverent and often humorous comments . . . appear in conversational balloons and help to lighten the decidedly earnest tone of the narrative. With plenty of practical suggestions and projects . . . this book is an ideal and upbeat way to introduce the problems in our environment and to inspire children to make a difference in the health of our planet." Horn Book

Carr, Terry

Spill!: the story of the Exxon Valdez. Watts 1991 64p il maps lib bdg $18.90 (4 and up) **363.7**

1. Exxon Valdez (Ship) 2. Oil spills
ISBN 0-531-10998-4

LC 90-13104

"This photodocumentary addresses, in full color, the Prince William Sound ecological crisis following the 1989 *Exxon Valdez* oil spill." Bull Cent Child Books

"The numerous photographs that illustrate the book are of high quality and add to the story. . . . This book will be good informational reading for the intended grade levels and can be the basis for a discussion of other environmental issues and problems." Sci Books Films

Includes bibliography

Foster, Joanna

Cartons, cans, and orange peels; where does your garbage go? Clarion Bks. 1991 64p il $15.95; pa $7.95 (4-6) **363.7**

1. Refuse and refuse disposal 2. Recycling
ISBN 0-395-56436-0; 0-395-66504-3 (pa)

LC 90-2616

Outlines the composition of garbage and trash and discusses the various methods of disposing of it with an emphasis on recycling

"Basic problems involved with solid waste disposal are presented in the text and in the informative full-color photographs. . . . Not only is the writing lively and descriptive, but also the seriousness of the subject comes through without sensationalism." SLJ

Includes glossary and bibliography

Gibbons, Gail

Recycle! a handbook for kids. Little, Brown 1992 unp il $15.95; pa $4.95 (k-3) **363.7**

1. Recycling
ISBN 0-316-30971-0; 0-316-30943-5 (pa)

LC 91-4317

Explains the process of recycling from start to finish and discusses what happens to paper, glass, aluminum cans, and plastic when they are recycled into new products

"An eminently readable and well-organized offering that's filled with information. . . . The top two-thirds of each page is devoted to illustrations that perfectly complement the brief text below." SLJ

Going green; a kid's handbook to saving the planet; [by] John Elkington [et al.]; illustrated by Tony Ross. Viking 1990 111p il hardcover o.p. paperback available $9.99 (4 and up) **363.7**

1. Environmental protection
ISBN 0-14-034597-3 (pa)

LC 90-12682

"A Tilden Press book"

A guide to saving the environment, including explanations of ecological issues and projects

"Tony Ross' colorful cartoons and ironic humor add to the consistently sober message that the Earth is in very big trouble, and that we must all make lifestyle changes. Informative, attractive, and timely, this offers a multitude of uses in classrooms and at home." Appraisal

Includes bibliography

Hadingham, Evan

Garbage! where it comes from, where it goes; [by] Evan & Janet Hadingham. Simon & Schuster Bks. for Young Readers 1990 48p il maps $14.95 (4 and up) **363.7**

1. Refuse and refuse disposal
ISBN 0-671-69424-3

LC 89-26205

"A Novabook"

Published in association with WGBH, Boston

Documents the ever-increasing problem of what can be done to dispose of our garbage

"A realistic presentation of the enormity of a current problem, emphasizing the difficulties of finding answers, but encouraging personal and political alternatives. Each page is lavishly illustrated with high-quality color photographs; inserts enhance the basic text with 'Amazing Garbage Facts' and similar material." SLJ

Johnson, Rebecca L.

Investigating the ozone hole. Lerner Publs. 1993 112p il maps lib bdg $23.95 (5 and up) **363.7**

1. Ozone layer
ISBN 0-8225-1574-1

LC 93-15225

A "comprehensive and clearly written book about ozone research in Antarctica. Describes destructive chlorofluorocarbon (CFC) use and long-range ultra-violet problems that will result. Unusually good profiles of scientists at work. Excellent color photographs, maps, and charts." Sci Child

Lampton, Christopher

Oil spill. Millbrook Press 1992 48p il map lib bdg $13.40; pa $5.95 (4-6) **363.7**

1. Oil spills
ISBN 1-56294-071-6 (lib bdg); 1-56294-783-4 (pa)

LC 91-43565

"A Disaster! book"

Describes how and why oil spills happen, the damage such accidents can do to the environment, and methods used to clean up spills

"Interesting and informative. . . . [This volume is] illustrated with good-quality full-color photographs and charts." SLJ

Includes glossary and bibliography

Langone, John, 1929-

Our endangered earth; what we can do to save it. Little, Brown 1992 197p $16.95 (6 and up)   **363.7**

1. Pollution 2. Environmental protection

ISBN 0-316-51415-2   LC 91-13763

Discusses the environmental crisis, focusing on such problems as overpopulation, the pollution of water, air and land, ozone depletion, global warming, and disappearing wildlife. Suggests ways to improve life in the twenty-first century

"A well-documented problem-solving discussion of earth's major environmental concerns. Very invitingly written in clear, concise language." BAYA Book Rev

Includes glossary and bibliographical references

Miles, Betty, 1928-

Save the earth; an action handbook for kids; with drawings by Nelle Davis and photographs. rev ed. Knopf 1991 118p il hardcover o.p. paperback available $6.95 (4-6)   **363.7**

1. Pollution 2. Environmental protection

ISBN 0-679-81731-X (pa)   LC 90-46514

First published 1974

An overview of the environmental problems of land, atmosphere, water, energy, plants, animals, and people. Includes projects and a section on becoming an environmental activist

"This book is an excellent introduction to the Earth's environmental problems. The text is clearly written and easy to understand." Appraisal

Includes glossary and bibliography

Pringle, Laurence P.

Global warming; [by] Laurence Pringle. Arcade Pub. 1990 46p il maps $15.95 (3-5)   **363.7**

1. Greenhouse effect

ISBN 1-55970-012-2   LC 89-82204

"An assessment of the greenhouse threat in an appealing format with . . . information on the causes and effects of temperature changes around the world. Includes a discussion of reducing greenhouse gases." Sci Child

Includes glossary

Oil spills; damage, recovery, and prevention; [by] Laurence Pringle. Morrow Junior Bks. 1993 56p il maps $15; lib bdg $14.93 (4 and up)   **363.7**

1. Oil spills 2. Petroleum

ISBN 0-688-09860-6; 0-688-09861-4 (lib bdg)
      LC 92-30348

"A Save-the-earth book"

Describes petroleum and its uses, examines the harmful effects of oil spills, and discusses how such environmental disasters can be cleaned up or prevented

"Photographs of the areas and animals affected by spills reinforce the written descriptions. This small book contains a wealth of well-organized and clearly stated information." Booklist

Includes glossary and bibliography

Vanishing ozone; protecting earth from ultraviolet radiation; [by] Laurence Pringle. Morrow Junior Bks. 1995 64p il $16; lib bdg $15.93 (4 and up)   **363.7**

1. Ozone layer

ISBN 0-688-04157-4; 0-688-04158-2 (lib bdg)
      LC 94-25928

"A Save-the-earth book"

This is an "introduction to the science and politics of the ozone layer. A history of the scientific study of ozone includes names of major scientists and the titles of their published articles. The political side of the debate includes reactions of elected officials and members of the chemical industry." Horn Book Guide

"The organization is excellent. . . . Technical terms are well balanced. . . . Crisp black-and-white photographs, diagrams, and maps illustrate the text. Concluding chapters offer suggestions for taking action and include addresses for government agencies and environmental groups." SLJ

Includes glossary and bibliography

Showers, Paul, 1910-

Where does the garbage go? illustrated by Randy Chewning. rev ed. HarperCollins Pubs. 1994 32p il (Let's-read-and-find-out science books) $15; lib bdg $14.89; pa $4.95 (k-3)   **363.7**

1. Refuse and refuse disposal 2. Recycling

ISBN 0-06-021054-0; 0-06-021057-5 (lib bdg); 0-06-445114-3 (pa)   LC 91-46115

First published 1974 by Crowell

"A class of grade-school students learns about waste disposal and recycling in a simple, accessible text. The clear, color illustrations are particularly effective in showing the recycling process for paper, aluminum, and glass." Horn Book Guide

Simon, Seymour, 1931-

Earth words; a dictionary of the environment; illustrated by Mark Kaplan. HarperCollins Pubs. 1995 48p il maps $16; lib bdg $15.89 (3-5)   **363.7**

1. Pollution—Dictionaries 2. Ecology—Dictionaries

ISBN 0-06-020233-5; 0-06-020234-3 (lib bdg)
      LC 92-34005

Simon defines "66 essential environmental terms: words that explain how the Earth works and describe the forces that threaten to upset the delicate balance of our global ecosystem." Publisher's note

"Less space is devoted to text than to the unusual and sometimes striking illustrations, which vary from the diagrammatic to the impressionistic to the hyperrealistic." Booklist

369.463 Girl Scouts and Girl Guides

World Association of Girl Guides and Girl Scouts

Trefoil round the world; girl guiding and girl scouting in many lands. World Assn. of Girl Guides & Girl Scouts il pa $9.25 **369.463**

1. Girl Scouts

First published 1950. (9th edition 1992) Periodically revised

This history of girl scouting tells how the World Association of Girl Guides and Girl Scouts began, and includes words of promise and law, mottos, and programs of the member countries

370.19 Education—Social aspects

Coles, Robert

The story of Ruby Bridges; illustrated by George Ford. Scholastic 1995 unp il $13.95 (1-3) **370.19**

1. Bridges, Ruby 2. School integration 3. New Orleans (La.)—Race relations

ISBN 0-590-43967-7 LC 92-33674

"Ruby Bridges was the first African American child to attend an all-white elementary school in New Orleans in 1960. Coles tells the brief story of her daily walk past . . . white adults, her time alone with her teacher in an otherwise empty classroom because white parents kept their children home, and the . . . moment when she prays in front of the . . . crowd for God to forgive them." SLJ

Coles "tells one girl's heroic story, part of the history of ordinary people who have changed the world. . . . Ford's moving watercolor paintings mixed with acrylic ink are predominantly in sepia shades of brown and red. They capture the physical warmth of Ruby's family and community, the immense powers against her, and her shining inner strength." Booklist

O'Neill, Laurie, 1949-

Little Rock; the desegregation of Central High. Millbrook Press 1994 64p il (Spotlight on American history) lib bdg $15.40 (5 and up) **370.19**

1. Central High School (Little Rock, Ark.) 2. School integration 3. African Americans—Civil rights 4. Arkansas—Race relations

ISBN 1-56294-354-5 LC 93-29057

This is an "account of a year in the life of the group of nine brave African-American teenagers who integrated Central High School in Little Rock, Arkansas, in 1957. O'Neill's well-written narrative documents human nature at its best and worst." SLJ

Includes bibliography

370.9 Education—Historical and geographic treatment

Loeper, John J.

Going to school in 1776. Atheneum Pubs. 1973 79p il $14.95 (4 and up) **370.9**

1. Education—United States—History 2. Schools—United States—History 3. United States—Social life and customs—1600-1775, Colonial period

ISBN 0-689-30089-1 LC 72-86940

The author tells what it was like to be a child and to go to school in America in 1776. He describes children's dress, schools, teachers, school books, lessons, discipline and after-school recreation

Includes bibliography

Going to school in 1876. Atheneum Pubs. 1984 83p il $15 (4 and up) **370.9**

1. Education—United States—History 2. Schools—United States—History 3. United States—Social life and customs

ISBN 0-689-31015-3 LC 83-15669

Describes the life of school children in 1876: their dress, teachers, schoolhouses, books, lessons, discipline, and pastimes

"Punctuated with excerpts from diaries, correspondence, newspaper advertisements and contemporary textbooks, as well as black-and-white prints highlighting various aspects of the society in 1876, the book breathes life into history." SLJ

Includes bibliography

371.3 Methods of instruction and study

Ellsworth, Jill H., 1949-

Education on the Internet; [by] Jill Ellsworth. Sams 1994 xxvi, 591p $25 **371.3**

1. Internet (Computer network) 2. Computer assisted instruction

ISBN 0-672-30595-X LC 94-67097

"Designed as a resource for educators using the Internet, this book is divided into three main areas: elementary and secondary education, higher education, and life-long learning. . . . This is one of the few Internet books devoted entirely to education. It's easy to use and covers a lot of ground." Book Rep

James, Elizabeth

How to be school smart; secrets of successful schoolwork; [by] Elizabeth James & Carol Barkin; pictures by Roy Doty; with an introduction by M. Jean Greenlaw. Lothrop, Lee & Shepard Bks. 1988 94p il lib bdg $12.93; pa $6.95 (5 and up) **371.3**

1. Study skills

ISBN 0-688-06799-9 (lib bdg); 0-688-06798-0 (pa) LC 87-2899

"The authors discuss home study areas, time management, learning styles, homework, test taking, and attitude. . . . The book is full of practical hints such as using a tape recorder for note taking and studying, making flash cards,

James, Elizabeth—*Continued*

etc. The chapter on test taking includes many helpful strategies. This positive book will help students interested in improving their schoolwork." Voice Youth Advocates

371.3025　Audio and visual materials—Directories

AV market place; the complete business directory of: audio, audiovisual, computer systems, film, video, programming, with industry yellow pages. Bowker il pa $145
371.3025

1. Audiovisual materials—Directories
ISSN 1044-0445
Annual. First published 1969 with title: Audiovisual market place

This volume identifies more than "6,300 companies that create, supply, or distribute an extraordinary range of audiovisual equipment and services. An index of . . . products and services is cross-referenced to companies in the main body. The products, services, and company index identifies all firms geographically. . . . Companies are also indexed by name." Nichols. Guide to Ref Books for Sch Media Cent. 4th edition

371.9　Special education

Stanley, Jerry, 1941-

Children of the Dust Bowl; the true story of the school at Weedpatch Camp. Crown 1992 85p il maps $15; lib bdg $15.99; pa $7.99 (5 and up)
371.9

1. Migrant labor　2. Economic depressions 3. Education—Social aspects
ISBN 0-517-58781-5; 0-517-58782-3 (lib bdg); 0-517-88094-6 (pa)　　　　LC 92-393

Describes the plight of the migrant workers who traveled from the Dust Bowl to California during the Depression and were forced to live in a federal labor camp and discusses the school that was built for their children

"Stanley's text is a compelling document. . . . The story is inspiring and disturbing, and Stanley has recorded the details with passion and dignity." Booklist

Includes bibliographical references

Walker, Lou Ann

Hand, heart, & mind; the story of the education of America's deaf people. Dial Bks. 1994 136p il $14.99 (5 and up)　　　**371.9**

1. Deaf—Education
ISBN 0-8037-1225-1　　　　LC 92-45631

This book "covers education of the deaf from ancient Greece to the present, with particular attention paid to the raging debate between Alexander Graham Bell and Edward Miner Gallaudet over the proper method of communication. . . . The text is well organized, interest-holding, and thoughtfully presented." SLJ

Includes bibliography

372.05　Elementary education— Serial publications

Childhood Education. Association for Childhood Educ. Int. $78 per year
372.05

1. Elementary education—Periodicals
ISSN 0009-4056
Five issues a year. First published 1924

"A journal for teachers, teachers-in-training, teacher educators, parents, day care workers, librarians, pediatricians and other child caregivers."

This "is a valuable journal for all individuals concerned with the well-being and education of children of all ages. The language is easily accessible and the content diverse and practical. . . . Departments include 'For Parents Particularly,' reviews of books and films for both children and professionals, and summaries of research in periodicals and ERIC." Katz. Mag for Libr. 8th edition

Instructor. Scholastic $19.95 per year
372.05

1. Elementary education—Periodicals
ISSN 1049-5851
Eight issues a year. First published 1891. Title and publisher vary

This magazine "aims to provide teachers with nuts-and-bolts ideas for everyday classroom life. Each issue has a wide range of quick and easy tips for teaching, as well as suggestions for networking, lists of free or inexpensive teaching aids, book reviews, short interviews with authors, etc." Katz. Mag for Libr. 8th edition

Teaching K-8; the professional magazine for teachers. Early Years, 40 Richards Ave., Norwalk, CT 06854-2309 $19.77　　**372.05**

1. Elementary education—Periodicals
ISSN 0891-4508
Eight issues a year. Continues Early Years (ceased publication 1987)

Also known as Teaching Pre-K-8

This magazine "offers a wealth of information and should be a basic title for libraries serving elementary and middle schools and teacher preparation programs." Katz. Mag for Libr. 8th edition

372.1　Generalities of elementary schools

Cole, Ann

I saw a purple cow, and 100 other recipes for learning; [by] Ann Cole [et al.]; illustrated by True Kelley. Little, Brown 1972 96p il hardcover o.p. paperback available $8.95
372.1

1. Preschool education 2. Amusements
ISBN 0-316-15175-0 (pa)

"Based on research done in Project Headstart, this book serves as a guide to the effective use of throw-away objects found in the house and environs as creative learning devices for young children. It is geared to the important first six years of children's lives and attempts to help the untrained mother during this period." Libr J

372.2 Levels of elementary education

Howe, James, 1946-
When you go to kindergarten; text by James Howe; photographs by Betsy Imershein. rev & updated ed. Morrow Junior Bks. 1994 unp il $15; lib bdg $14.93; pa $5.95 (k-1)   **372.2**

1. Kindergarten
ISBN 0-688-12912-9; 0-688-12913-7 (lib bdg); 0-688-14387-3 (pa)   LC 93-48152
First published 1986 by Knopf
"The author tells youngsters what school might look like and how they might get there, and describes some of the possible activities. . . . Multicultural children are welcomed and taught by both male and female teachers. Smiling, busy kids engaged in many activities portray school as an exciting, interesting, and happy place." SLJ

Kuklin, Susan
Going to my nursery school. Bradbury Press 1990 unp il $13.95 (k-1)   **372.2**

1. Nursery schools
ISBN 0-02-751237-1   LC 89-37077
Pre-school photo essay about the First Presbyterian Church Nursery School in New York City
A little boy describes, in text and photographs, what he does in his nursery school class. Includes information for parents on how to select a nursery school for their children
"The color pictures are of an excellent quality. . . . Informative and cheerful, this maintains the child's voice in a way that increases the accessibility of the recorded experiences. An unusually good introduction to the great mystery of what goes on at a nursery school." Bull Cent Child Books

372.4 Reading

Herb, Steven
Using children's books in preschool settings; a how-to-do-it manual; [by] Steven Herb and Sara Willoughby-Herb. Neal-Schuman 1994 181p (How-to-do-it manuals for school and public librarians) pa $32.50   **372.4**

1. Reading 2. Books and reading
ISBN 1-55570-156-6   LC 94-8238
Includes sections on child and language development, literary genres and setting up a storybook corner. Problems posed by restless listeners, disliked books, and language barriers are addressed
"The treatment is a nice mixture of the theoretical and the pragmatic." Bull Cent Child Books
Includes bibliographical references

Kaye, Peggy, 1948-
Games for reading; playful ways to help your child read; written by Peggy Kaye; with illustrations by the author. Pantheon Bks. 1984 213p il hardcover o.p. paperback available $14.95   **372.4**

1. Reading 2. Games
ISBN 0-394-72149-7 (pa)   LC 83-19403

"This guide suggests a whole new way for parents and teachers to encourage reading as a delightful activity. Besides the reading-aloud concept, suggestions include 70 clear-cut games and activities that contribute to reading development. The author suggests a bingo game to learn vocabulary. A rhyming game helps children hear letter sounds more accurately. There are mazes and puzzles, games that train the ear so a child can sound out words, games that awaken a child's imagination and creativity, and games that encourage motivation for reading." Read Teach
Includes bibliography

Miles, Betty, 1928-
Hey! I'm reading! illustrated by Sylvie Wickstrom. Knopf 1995 59p il lib bdg $16.99; pa $12 (k-2)   **372.4**

1. Reading
ISBN 0-679-95644-1 (lib bdg); 0-679-85644-7 (pa)   LC 93-25884
A "book about learning to read. The opening two sections are about the process. The last section gives 19 brief selections to read such as poems, knock-knock jokes, an alphabet of names, and a double-page spread of a school scene with labels, dialogue balloons, and a chalkboard message. Wickstrom's pictures are delightful." SLJ

372.405 Reading—Serial publications

The **Reading** Teacher. International Reading Assn. $38 per year   **372.405**

1. Reading—Periodicals
ISSN 0034-0561
Eight issues a year. First published 1947
This journal "explores reading and literacy education in an intelligent and professional way. . . . Elementary teachers' and students' voices are clearly heard in articles, adding a personal and authentic note. This journal is important for reading and literacy teachers." Katz. Mag for Libr. 8th edition

372.6 Language arts. Storytelling

Baker, Augusta, 1911-
Storytelling: art and technique; by Augusta Baker and Ellin Greene. 2nd ed. Bowker 1987 182p il $35   **372.6**

1. Storytelling
ISBN 0-8352-2336-1   LC 87-26539
First published 1977
This book examines the history, purpose, and value of storytelling as practiced in the United States. The preparation, presentation, and administration of story hour programs is discussed and an overview of available materials is provided
Includes bibliography

Bauer, Caroline Feller, 1935-

Caroline Feller Bauer's new handbook for storytellers; with stories, poems, magic, and more; illustrations by Lynn Gates Bredeson. American Lib. Assn. 1993 550p il music $45; pa $30   **372.6**

1. Storytelling
ISBN 0-8389-0613-3; 0-8389-0664-8 (pa)
                      LC 93-14959
First published 1977 with title: Handbook for storytellers
Bauer's introduction "incorporates a broad variety of media and props into the storytelling process. . . . Beginners and veterans alike can benefit from this practical approach to program planning and promotion, story selection and preparation, and activities extending various themes or occasions." Bull Cent Child Books
Includes bibliographical references

The poetry break; an annotated anthology with ideas for introducing children to poetry; illustrations by Edith Bingham. Wilson, H.W. 1995 xxv, 347p il $45   **372.6**

1. Poetry—Study and teaching
ISBN 0-8242-0852-8   LC 93-42069
This book serves as a "do-it-yourself poetry-break packet, including ideas for presentation, settings, and general poetry activities; she includes a good 250 pages of poems, suggesting a poem-specific project or topic-extending book after most of the verses." Bull Cent Child Books
Includes bibliographical references

Dailey, Sheila, 1947-

Putting the world in a nutshell; the art of the formula tale. Wilson, H.W. 1994 118p $35   **372.6**

1. Storytelling
ISBN 0-8242-0860-9   LC 94-829
Dailey "introduces nine variations of formula tales that are easy to learn because of their rhythm and repetition. Two introductory chapters define what storytelling is, explain why stories need to be shared with children, and provide tips for selecting and learning stories by using the ROVER (Read, Organize, Visualize, Energize, and Rehearse) technique. Subsequent chapters introduce each type of formula tale, illustrating with several examples." Book Rep
"The author's writing style is deft and knowledgeable, never slipping into condescension or scholarly jargon. The book has an encouraging tone and easily incorporates wisdom from some of the great early scholars of folklore as well as from current American storytellers." J Youth Serv Libr
Includes bibliographical references

Goforth, Frances S., 1932-

Using folk literature in the classroom; encouraging children to read and write; by Frances S. Goforth and Carolyn V. Spillman. Oryx Press 1994 225p il pa $24.95   **372.6**

1. Folklore 2. Reading 3. English language—Study and teaching
ISBN 0-89774-747-X   LC 94-18808

This volume "covers the range of popular folk literature, from nursery rhymes and ballads to fables and tall tales. Story summaries and source descriptions are arranged by theme (such as magical animals, overcoming odds, epic heroes, etc.), followed by instructional strategies, such as shared reading, readers' theater, and writers' workshops." Publisher's note
Includes bibliographical references

Hopkins, Lee Bennett, 1938-

Pass the poetry, please! rev enl & updated ed. Harper & Row 1987 262p hardcover o.p. paperback available $10.95   **372.6**

1. Poetry—Study and teaching
ISBN 0-06-446062-2 (pa)   LC 86-45758
First published 1972
"Following his introductory comments on what poetry is and the reasons for exposing children to it, Hopkins introduces 20 contemporary poets . . . and suggests specific works from their repertoires. In a third section, the author gives ways to rouse children's interest in writing poetry and then rounds out his presentation with ideas to help children appreciate verse in the home, library, and classroom. Hopkins' excitement about his topic overflows the pages and will be an inspirational source for the novice and the experienced adult working at bringing children and poetry together." Booklist
Includes bibliographies

Juba this and Juba that; selected by Virginia Tashjian; illustrated by Nadine Bernard Westcott. 2nd ed. Little, Brown 1995 106p il $15.95   **372.6**

1. Storytelling 2. Literature—Collections
ISBN 0-316-83234-0   LC 94-27143
A revised and newly illustrated edition of the title first published 1969
"A useful source of chants, poetry and rhyme, stories, finger plays, riddles, songs, tongue twisters, and jokes. The selections accompanied by lively orange and black illustrations, are all suitably silly. They require and inspire audience participation." SLJ [review of 1969 edition]

Livingston, Myra Cohn

Poem-making; ways to begin writing poetry. HarperCollins Pubs. 1991 162p $16; lib bdg $15.89 (4 and up)   **372.6**

1. Poetry—Study and teaching 2. Creative writing
ISBN 0-06-024019-9; 0-06-024020-2 (lib bdg)
                      LC 90-5012
"A Charlotte Zolotow book"
Introduces the different kinds of poetry and the mechanics of writing poetry, providing an opportunity for the reader to experience the joy of making a poem
"As a writing guide, this book will be most useful in creative writing groups with a teacher or leader. . . . What Livingston does communicate on every page is the excitement of poetry and its strange power to 'arrest our senses' and help us see the world in a new way." Booklist
Includes bibliographical references

MacDonald, Margaret Read

Celebrate the world; twenty tellable folktales for multicultural festivals; illustrations by Roxane Murphy Smith. Wilson, H.W. 1994 225p il $40 **372.6**

1. Storytelling 2. Folklore 3. Festivals
ISBN 0-8242-0862-5 LC 94-6682

In this collection of twenty folktales the author "has interwoven the stories with holidays and festivals from various countries and presented tips on how to present both the story and the holiday in a storytelling program. . . . *Celebrate the World* is a thorough and wide-ranging work that will prove valuable to most collections." J Youth Serv Libr

Includes bibliography

Look back and see; twenty lively tales for gentle tellers; illustrations by Roxane Murphy. Wilson, H.W. 1991 178p il $35 **372.6**

1. Storytelling 2. Folklore
ISBN 0-8242-0810-2 LC 91-2539

The author presents twenty non-violent folktales from around the world, with background notes and suggestions for storytelling uses

"Delightfully varied in mood, the tales range from silly and rowdy to contemplative and touching. . . . MacDonald's useful, informative, and entertaining notes follow each story. . . . The notes alone are worth the price of the book." J Youth Serv Libr

Includes bibliography

The storyteller's start-up book; finding, learning, performing, and using folktales including twelve tellable tales. August House 1993 215p $23.95; pa $13.95 **372.6**

1. Storytelling 2. Folklore
ISBN 0-87483-304-3; 0-87483-305-1 (pa)
LC 93-1580

The author's advice on storytelling "covers the practical ground, from selection, learning (in one hour!), performance, and setting to classroom applications. . . . A dozen texts of proven success follow, with performance tips and source notes. Equally valuable are the selected and annotated bibliographies appended to every chapter." Libr J

Twenty tellable tales; audience participation folktales for the beginning storyteller; drawings by Roxane Murphy. Wilson, H.W. 1986 220p il $35; pa $20 **372.6**

1. Storytelling 2. Folklore 3. Fairy tales
ISBN 0-8242-0719-X; 0-8242-0822-6 (pa)
LC 85-26565

"Dividing her book into three sections—tales, notes, and sources—MacDonald gives instructions for selecting, shaping, learning, and telling each tale and includes notes on their origin as well as comments on audience participation and performance style in other cultures. All the tales are short and include repetitive verses, making them highly suitable for telling aloud." Booklist

Includes bibliography

When the lights go out; twenty scary tales to tell; illustrations by Roxane Murphy. Wilson, H.W. 1988 176p il $35; pa $20 **372.6**

1. Storytelling 2. Horror fiction 3. Folklore
ISBN 0-8242-0770-X; 0-8242-0823-4 (pa)
LC 88-14197

"Divided into six sections—Not Too Scary, Scary in the Dark, Gross Stuff, Jump Tales, Tales to Act Out, and Tales to Draw or Stir Up—the selections will be especially useful around Halloween, although, as the author points out, the book can be used year round. Following each inclusion are helpful notes on telling the stories and a section that gives sources on origins and variants. Murphy's decorative drawings introduce chapters and are scattered throughout the text. Several concluding chapters list bibliographies and provide other helpful information." Booklist

Pellowski, Anne

The family storytelling handbook; how to use stories, anecdotes, rhymes, handkerchiefs, paper, and other objects to enrich your family traditions; illustrated by Lynn Sweat. Macmillan 1987 150p il $16.95 **372.6**

1. Storytelling
ISBN 0-02-770610-9 LC 87-7981

"In brief chapters divided into the why, when, what, and how of telling stories, this renowned storyteller gives all the basics along with amusing anecdotes. She also includes stories to tell using a variety of methods." Child Book Rev Serv

"The author's encouraging, easy style will motivate parents and other adults, but this will also serve beginning librarians who need support as well as the simple storytelling basics. A bibliography, compilation of sources, and a list of storytelling events around the world are appended." Booklist

The story vine; a source book of unusual and easy-to-tell stories from around the world; illustrated by Lynn Sweat. Macmillan 1984 116p il $15.95; pa $9.95 **372.6**

1. Storytelling 2. Folklore
ISBN 0-02-770590-0; 0-02-044690-X (pa)
LC 83-27307

"The two dozen folk stories in this book use aids; string or braided yarn, picture-drawing, dolls, a traditional musical instrument, or the storyteller's fingers. Step by step directions with drawings make this a practical book for the storyteller, and there's a bibliography at the end of each section, helpful in building an extensive aided-story collection. Ingenious are the 'sand stories' from Australia. These and others can inspire children to tell aided stories of their own." Read Teach

The storytelling handbook; a young people's collection of unusual tales and helpful hints on how to tell them; illustrated by Martha Stoberock. Simon & Schuster 1995 129p il $15 **372.6**

1. Storytelling
ISBN 0-689-80311-7 LC 95-2991

This work "addresses the young person who wants to tell stories in a public setting. It is similar in format to many adult books on storytelling how-tos, with sections on getting started and selecting and preparing stories, as well as a selection of sample tales. Pellowski's notes are extensive and will be very useful to novices looking for ways to research stories." Booklist

Includes bibliographical references

The world of storytelling. expanded and rev ed. Wilson, H.W. 1990 xxi, 311p il $40 **372.6**

1. Storytelling
ISBN 0-8242-0788-2 LC 90-31151

First published 1977

Pellowski, Anne—*Continued*

This guide "reviews the oral traditions from which literature for children grew, addresses the controversy between storytellers and folklorists, and offers a modern-day definition for storytelling. *The world of storytelling* also includes chapters on: types of storytelling—bardic, folk, religious, theatrical, library and institutional, campground and playground, hygienic and therapeutic storytelling; format and style of storytelling—opening and closing of a story session; language, voice, and audience response; musical accompaniment; pictures and objects used; training of storytellers—history and survey of training methods; visuality, orality, and literacy; storytelling festivals." Publisher's note

"This is an important work for collections serving adult students of storytelling and the oral tradition." J Youth Serv Libr

Includes bibliography

Sawyer, Ruth, 1880-1970

The way of the storyteller. Viking 1962 360p il o.p.; Penguin Bks. paperback available $12   **372.6**

1. Storytelling 2. Literature—Collections
ISBN 0-14-004436-1 (pa)

First published 1942

"This is not primarily a book on how to tell stories; it is rather the whole philosophy of story telling as a creative art. From her own rich experience the author writes inspiringly of the background, experience, creative imagination, technique and selection essential to this art. A part of the book is devoted to a few well-loved stories with suggestions and comments." Booklist

Includes bibliography

Shedlock, Marie L., 1854-1935

The art of the story-teller; foreword by Anne Carroll Moore. 3d ed rev, with a new bibliography by Eulalie Steinmetz. Dover Publs. 1951 xxi, 290p pa $7.95   **372.6**

1. Storytelling 2. Literature—Collections
ISBN 0-486-20635-1

First published 1915

"This has long been considered one of the . . . standard books on storytelling. . . . Suggestions for selecting and for telling stories are included as well as eighteen of Miss Shedlock's own favorites." Horn Book

Includes bibliography

372.605   Language arts—Serial publications

Language Arts. National Council of Teachers of English $40 per year   **372.605**

1. English language—Study and teaching—Periodicals
ISSN 0360-9170

Eight issues a year. First published 1924 with title: Elementary English Review. Also published previously with title: Elementary English

This journal "explores language issues in a thematically arranged format. . . . Also included are 30 to 35 reviews of books for young students in the 'Bookalogue' section. *LA* is an intelligent journal that gives press to thoughtful issues related to the teaching of language arts." Katz. Mag for Libr. 8th edition

372.8   Other studies

Pérez-Stable, María A.

Understanding American history through children's literature: instructional units and activities for grades k-8; by María A. Pérez-Stable and Mary Hurlbut Cordier. Oryx Press 1994 312p il pa $24.95   **372.8**

1. Children's literature—Study and teaching 2. United States—History—Study and teaching

ISBN 0-89774-795-X   LC 94-2636

"The text is divided first by grade level . . . and then chronologically into units. . . . The readings include both nonfiction and fiction titles; the bibliographies are extensive, the annotations thoughtful. The innovative activities are multidisciplinary and just plain fun. Written from a deeply felt and clearly articulated humanist standpoint, this is a rich treasure chest of creative ideas that will enrich history classes for teachers as well as students." SLJ

385.09   Railroad transportation— Historical and geographic treatment

Fisher, Leonard Everett, 1924-

Tracks across America; the story of the American railroad, 1825-1900. Holiday House 1992 192p il maps $17.95 (5 and up)   **385.09**

1. Railroads—History

ISBN 0-8234-0945-7   LC 91-28244

Examines the development of the railroad in the United States from its nineteenth-century beginnings to the end of that century

"Visually impressive, with its profusion of photographs and drawings, its clear print and wide margins, this tour de train is just as effective textually. Fisher covers an enormous amount of material in a book that is balanced, logically organized, and capably written." Bull Cent Child Books

Includes bibliography

Murphy, Jim, 1947-

Across America on an emigrant train. Clarion Bks. 1993 150p il $16.95 (5 and up)   **385.09**

1. Stevenson, Robert Louis, 1850-1894 2. Railroads—History 3. United States—Description

ISBN 0-395-63390-7   LC 92-38650

"Murphy presents a forthright and thoroughly engrossing history of the transcontinental railway, with entries from Robert Louis Stevenson's 1879 journal as he rode cross country. It's also an inviting introduction to Stevenson, with a romance in the bargain." SLJ

Includes bibliography

386 Inland waterway and ferry transportation

Gibbons, Gail

The great St. Lawrence Seaway. Morrow Junior Bks. 1992 unp il maps $15; lib bdg $14.93 (k-3) **386**

1. Saint Lawrence Seaway
ISBN 0-688-06984-3; 0-688-06985-1 (lib bdg)
LC 91-9851

Tells the story of this inland waterway from the earliest explorers' dream of an Orient passage to today's vast computer-operated system of canals, locks, and gates, and the ships that traverse them
"Gibbons's crisp, detailed pictures and explicit yet animated text enable readers to absorb her well-researched facts with ease. . . . Concise definitions and clearly labeled maps and illustrations make this journey informative as well as entertaining." Publ Wkly

Harness, Cheryl

The amazing impossible Erie Canal. Macmillan Bks. for Young Readers 1995 unp il maps $16 (3-5) **386**

1. Erie Canal (N.Y.)
ISBN 0-02-742641-6
LC 94-11114

"Focusing on the celebration that marked the completion of the Erie Canal in 1825, Harness uses words, maps, and pictures to explain the history and commerce of the canal. The book discusses the need for the canal, the politics of its planning and building, the workings of the locks and canals, the pleasure and pride people took in the accomplishment of this engineering feat, and the reasons for its demise." Booklist
"Harness has done a wonderful job of making the history and construction of the Erie Canal come alive. . . . The narrative is matched with illustrations that cover each page." SLJ

Includes bibliographical references

Nirgiotis, Nicholas

Erie Canal; gateway to the West. Watts 1993 64p il maps lib bdg $13.93 (4 and up) **386**

1. Erie Canal (N.Y.)
ISBN 0-531-20146-5
LC 92-24547
"A First book"
Describes the building of the Erie Canal and discusses its historical, political, economic, and sociological impact on the country
"A superior addition to history shelves. Although the information is standard, it is complemented by attractive prints and clear, full-color photographs." SLJ

Includes glossary and bibliography

387.1 Ports. Lighthouses

Gibbons, Gail

Beacons of light: lighthouses. Morrow Junior Bks. 1990 unp il $16; lib bdg $15.93 (k-3) **387.1**

1. Lighthouses
ISBN 0-688-07379-4; 0-688-07380-8 (lib bdg)
LC 89-33884

The author traces the development of lighthouses "from hilltop bonfires to the electronically controlled beacons that flash warnings to today's passing ships. Drawings of specific lighthouses grace every page. . . . Readers are told of lighthouse keepers' duties, the changing technology of lighthouses, and their status today as high-tech markers." Booklist
"The history of lighthouses is told in a picture book format for independent readers. Although the narrative is simple, the vocabulary and some of the concepts are more difficult than is typical in picture books. . . . However, each difficult concept is clarified with supplementary illustrations or text." Bull Cent Child Books

387.2 Ships

Barton, Byron

Boats. Crowell 1986 unp il lib bdg $14.89 (k-1) **387.2**

1. Boats and boating 2. Ships
ISBN 0-690-04536-0
LC 85-47900

Depicts a variety of boats and a cruise ship docking and unloading passengers
"Thick black outlines contain vivid colors . . . clean lines, bright hues, and undemanding text." Booklist

Gibbons, Gail

Boat book. Holiday House 1983 unp il lib bdg $14.95; pa $5.95 (k-3) **387.2**

1. Boats and boating 2. Ships
ISBN 0-8234-0478-1 (lib bdg); 0-8234-0709-8 (pa)
LC 82-15851

An introduction to "all sorts of seafaring craft . . . [including] speedboats, sailboats, canoes, cruise ships, police and fire boats, and commercial and military vessels. Various means of propulsion (wind, oars and paddles, engine power) are explained, as are the uses of each type of boat." Publ Wkly
"The text, though stilted, is logically presented in a noncondescending manner. Bright color illustrations throughout show an array of boats moving through the water. . . . Most of the illustrations are full page, and all of them are playfully bordered with a scalloped edge that resembles an ocean wave." SLJ

Kentley, Eric

Boat; written by Eric Kentley. Knopf 1992 63p il (Eyewitness books) $16; lib bdg $16.99 (4 and up) **387.2**

1. Ships 2. Boats and boating
ISBN 0-679-81678-X; 0-679-91678-4 (lib bdg)
LC 91-53136

Also available Spanish language edition
"A Dorling Kindersley book"
A history of the development and uses of boats, ships, and rafts, from birch-bark canoes to luxury liners

Macaulay, David, 1946-
Ship. Houghton Mifflin 1993 96p il $19.95;
pa $8.95 (4 and up)   **387.2**
1. Shipwrecks 2. Underwater exploration 3. Caribbean
region—Antiquities
ISBN 0-395-52439-3; 0-395-74518-7 (pa)
    LC 92-1346
This book "opens with an underwater find in the Caribbean and, in story and illustration, follows the work of marine archeologists in studying the wreck. As part of the
background research in Spain, one of the team finds a diary
recording the building of a caravel in 1504. The rest of the
book contains a 'translation' of the diary with accompanying illustrations. Though a fictional account, the narrative
gives a good feel for the maritime technology of the early
16th century." Sci Books Films

Rockwell, Anne F., 1934-
Boats; by Anne Rockwell. Dutton 1982 unp
il hardcover o.p. paperback available $4.99
(k-1)   **387.2**
1. Boats and boating 2. Ships
ISBN 0-14-054988-9 (pa)   LC 82-2420
The author describes "boats that float on quiet ponds,
rivers 'and the wide, blue sea.' The craft, ranging from tiny
sailboats that children maneuver in a park pool to great liners, are all manned by bears who will gain the affection of
tykes and also introduce them to boats that are for work,
for play; boats that go fast or slow, that float, are pushed
and/or pulled by motors, etc." Publ Wkly
"The cheerful line drawings filled with rich, limpid watercolors show the boats on water of varied shades of blue.
Of certain appeal to the young, unsophisticated viewer, the
book is an outstanding example of an informational picture
book." Horn Book

The **Visual** dictionary of ships and sailing.
Dorling Kindersley 1991 64p il (Eyewitness
visual dictionaries) $15.95; lib bdg $15.99 (4
and up)   **387.2**
1. Boats and boating 2. Ships
ISBN 1-879431-20-3; 1-879431-35-1 (lib bdg)
    LC 91-60900
This is a visual guide to nautical terminology with brief
text describing ships and boats from ancient times to the
present
"*Ships and Sailing* is intriguing. The pages proceed from
the ships of Greece, Rome, and the Vikings through wood-
en and iron ships of all kinds to knots, signals, flags, and
gear used and worn by sailors. The detailed cutaways are
works of art." Booklist

387.7   Air transportation

Barton, Byron
Airplanes. Crowell 1986 unp il lib bdg
$11.89 (k-1)   **387.7**
1. Airplanes
ISBN 0-690-04532-8   LC 85-47899
Brief text and illustrations present a variety of airplanes
and what they do, "as well as some of the usual scenes surrounding each (e.g., workers checking a passenger plane).
Brightly colored illustrations outlined in heavy black convey
a bold and simple first impression, yet they portray a good
number of accurate details that preschoolers find so fascinating." SLJ

Airport. Crowell 1982 unp il $15; lib bdg
$14.89; pa $4.95 (k-1)   **387.7**
1. Airports 2. Airplanes
ISBN 0-690-04168-3; 0-690-04169-1 (lib bdg);
0-06-443145-2 (pa)   LC 79-7816
"In a brightly illustrated book, the author/artist captures
the hustle and bustle of passenger traffic from arrival at the
terminal to take off." Kobrin Letter

Sullivan, George
How an airport really works. Lodestar Bks.
1993 122p il $15.99 (4 and up)   **387.7**
1. Airports
ISBN 0-525-67378-4   LC 92-20154
Examines all aspects of what goes on behind the scenes
at an airport, exploring such topics as how metal detectors
work and how airplane meals are planned
"Black-and-white photographs complement the text and
capture the complexity of airport operations. A straightforward look at what goes on in a high-energy segment of the
transportation world." Booklist
Includes glossary

388.1   Roads and highways

Gibbons, Gail
From path to highway: the story of the
Boston Post Road. Crowell 1986 32p il lib bdg
$14.89 (k-3)   **388.1**
1. Roads—History 2. New England—Description
ISBN 0-690-04514-X   LC 85-47897
"The author goes back 500 years to trace the develop-
ment of the Boston Post Road (connecting Boston and New
York City), as it changed from a narrow path into a mod-
ern, four-lane highway. In doing so, Gibbons touches upon
important stages of the nation's history." Publ Wkly
"The clear, factual, and deliberate text is matched by
completely charming illustrations. . . . A wonderful introduction to roads, transportation, history, progress." Bull
Cent Child Books

388.3   Vehicular transportation

Tunis, Edwin, 1897-1973
Wheels: a pictorial history; written and
illustrated by Edwin Tunis. Crowell 1977
c1955 96p il o.p. (5 and up)   **388.3**
1. Carriages and carts 2. Transportation—History
    LC 76-25809
A reissue of the title first published 1955 by World Publishing Company
Beginning with the first primitive roller this history of
land transportation, exclusive of railroads, progresses to the
earliest known wheeled vehicle, the Elamite chariot,
through Egyptian, Greek, Roman, Oriental chariots, and
carts, through the development of the road coaches of Europe and on to automobiles and buses

391 Costume and personal appearance

Barkin, Carol, 1944-

The scary Halloween costume book; by Carol Barkin and Elizabeth James; illustrated by Katherine Coville. Lothrop, Lee & Shepard Bks. 1983 94p il $12.95; lib bdg $12.88 (3-6)   **391**

1. Costume 2. Halloween
ISBN 0-688-00956-5; 0-688-00957-3 (lib bdg)
LC 81-14249

A book of instructions for making a variety of easy and scary outfits and creating ghoulish faces for Halloween

"The directions for each costume and facial design are clear; charcoal illustrations show the delightfully creepy finished products. A thorough index provides an easy way to discover how to blacken teeth, act like a witch and more." SLJ

Chernoff, Goldie Taub

Easy costumes you don't have to sew; costumes designed and illustrated by Margaret A. Hartelius. Four Winds Press 1975 41p il $15.50 (3-5)   **391**

1. Costume 2. Paper crafts
ISBN 0-02-718230-4

"Garbage bags, cartons, cardboard, paper bags, and old white sheets provide the basis for a variety of easy-to-make costumes. At-hand materials (newspaper, milk cartons, string) and clear directions result in simply constructed snowmen, mice, shaggy dogs, turtles, ladybugs, bats, skeletons, robots, totem poles, and even a group dragon. Each two-page spread is devoted to one costume, with careful diagrams, lists of necessary materials, precise instructions for each part, and guidelines for putting on the costume." Booklist

Christian, Mary Blount

Hats are for watering horses; why the cowboys dressed that way; illustrated by Lyle Miller. Hendrick-Long 1993 64p il $14.95 (3-5)   **391**

1. Cowhands
ISBN 0-937460-89-3   LC 93-35748

"From the ten gallon hat to the pointed-toe Western boot, everything that the cowboy wore is described and explained in simple sentences. The resulting portrait of the cowboy's working life pays tribute to this unique figure in the American West. Casually composed pencil sketches help make the cowboy look at home 'on the range.'" Horn Book Guide

"The text is informative enough to go back to, and go back yet again for another delightful read." SLJ

Hofsinde, Robert, 1902-1973

Indian costumes; written and illustrated by Robert Hofsinde (Gray-Wolf). Morrow 1968 94p il lib bdg $12.93 (3-6)   **391**

1. Indians of North America—Costume
ISBN 0-688-31614-X

"The distinctive costumes of ten different North American Indian tribal groups are here illustrated, showing their ceremonial, warring or everyday apparel. Black and white drawings help in explaining how they were made." Bruno. Books for Sch Libr, 1968

The tribes represented are the Apache, Blackfoot, Crow, Iroquois, Navaho, Northwest Coast Indians, Ojibwa, Pueblo, Seminole and Sioux Indians

Kalman, Bobbie, 1947-

18th century clothing. Crabtree 1993 32p il (Historic communities) lib bdg $15.95; pa $7.95 (3-6)   **391**

1. Costume 2. United States—Social life and customs—1600-1775, Colonial period
ISBN 0-86505-492-4 (lib bdg); 0-86505-512-2 (pa)
LC 93-30701

This guide to clothing worn in the United States in the 18th century describes fashions and accessories for men, women, and children, hats and hairstyles, personal hygiene habits, underclothing, wigs, and footwear and offers suggestions for making your own costumes

The book is "well organized and [makes] lavish use of full-color drawings, reproductions, and photographs." SLJ
Includes glossary

19th century clothing. Crabtree 1993 32p il (Historic communities) lib bdg $15.95; pa $7.95 (3-6)   **391**

1. Costume 2. Frontier and pioneer life 3. United States—Social life and customs
ISBN 0-86505-493-2 (lib bdg); 0-86505-513-0 (pa)
LC 93-6209

This volume focuses on 19th century dress and follows the format of the above title
Includes glossary

Morris, Ann

Hats, hats, hats; photographs by Ken Heyman. Lothrop, Lee & Shepard Bks. 1989 unp il $16; lib bdg $15.93; pa $4.95 (k-3)   **391**

1. Hats
ISBN 0-688-06338-1; 0-688-06339-X (lib bdg); 0-688-12274-4 (pa)   LC 88-26676

This book introduces a variety of hats worn around the world

"The vivid color photographs, one or two per page, show people engaged in lively activities while . . . wearing their hats. Each picture offers a strong ethnic identity or a thought-provoking human interaction, with captions of only a few words in large print. An unusual index . . . gives background information about the pictures, citing the countries of origin and a few facts about each . . . kind of hat." SLJ

Perl, Lila

From top hats to baseball caps, from bustles to blue jeans; why we dress the way we do; drawings by Leslie Evans. Clarion Bks. 1990 118p il $14.95 (4 and up)   **391**

1. Costume 2. Clothing and dress
ISBN 0-89919-872-4   LC 89-77717

Perl, Lila—*Continued*

Discusses the types of clothing people have worn throughout history, why they dressed the way they did, and how clothing reflects and even influences history

"The interesting, storylike format leads readers through periods of history in western Europe and the United States, and will be easily understood by those with no background knowledge in this area." SLJ

Includes bibliography

Rowland-Warne, L.

Costume; written by L. Rowland-Warne. Knopf 1992 63p il (Eyewitness books) $16; lib bdg $16.99 (4 and up) **391**

1. Costume 2. Clothing and dress
ISBN 0-679-81680-1; 0-679-91680-6 (lib bdg)
LC 91-53135

Also available Spanish language edition
"A Dorling Kindersley book"

Photographs and text document the history and meaning of clothing, from loincloths to modern children's clothes

This "fascinating historical overview . . . blends close-up, full-color photographs of period clothing and accessories with brief snippets of text that explain the item's significance and purpose." SLJ

392 Customs of life cycle and domestic life

Knight, Margy Burns

Welcoming babies; illustrated by Anne Sibley O'Brien. Tilbury House 1994 unp il $14.95 (k-2) **392**

1. Manners and customs 2. Infants
ISBN 0-88448-123-9 LC 94-6854

"A discussion of the various ceremonies used to greet newborns: Muslim, Jewish, Christian, and Hopi; Korean, Greek, Nigerian, and Latin American. . . . Boldly painted, strongly colored double-page pictures in a combination of realism in the foreground and sketchiness in the background show the babies being cherished in special ways by family and friends. The text describes each occasion simply, with helpful amplification given in the notes at the end that identify the cultures and geographic settings represented." Libr J

393 Death customs

Bendick, Jeanne, 1919-

Tombs of the ancient Americas; written and illustrated by Jeanne Bendick. Watts 1993 64p il maps lib bdg $13.93 (4 and up) **393**

1. Funeral rites and ceremonies 2. Indians 3. America—Antiquities 4. Tombs
ISBN 0-531-20148-1 LC 92-24546
"A First book"

"Bendick introduces the reader to a number of archeological questions based on the mysteries surrounding the tombs discovered throughout the Americas. The material is divided geographically into South American, Mesoamerican, and North American tombs." Sci Books Films

This is an "attractive volume, written in a style that will appeal to browsers more than information seekers. . . . Illustrating the book is a combination of color photos and color pencil drawings executed in an appealing folk-art style." Booklist

Includes glossary and bibliography

Berrill, Margaret

Mummies, masks, & mourners; illustrated by Chris Molan and with photographs. Lodestar Bks. 1990 c1989 48p il (Time detectives) $14.95 (4-6) **393**

1. Funeral rites and ceremonies 2. Mummies
ISBN 0-525-67282-6 LC 89-31822
First published 1989 in the United Kingdom

"This book examines funeral rites and burial customs discovered by archeology and discusses what the excavations of ancient graves can teach scientists about the lives and belief systems of past societies. Among the peoples covered are the Stone Age inhabitants of Çatal Hüyük (Turkey), the ancient Egyptians, the Sumerians, the Siberians, the Celts of Lindow (England), and the Basket Makers of the American Southwest." SLJ

"The topic is far-reaching, but manageable, the writing is consistently lively, the graphics and layout are pleasing." Child Book Rev Serv

Includes glossary

Perl, Lila

Mummies, tombs, and treasure; secrets of ancient Egypt; drawings by Erika Weihs. Clarion Bks. 1987 120p il lib bdg $15.95; pa $5.95 (4 and up) **393**

1. Mummies 2. Funeral rites and ceremonies 3. Egypt—Antiquities
ISBN 0-89919-407-9 (lib bdg); 0-395-54796-2 (pa)
LC 86-17646

The author incorporates "information on burial customs, religious beliefs, and historical background along with specifics of the mummification process and the archeological finds that have kept the study of the dead a dynamic one." Bull Cent Child Books

This "book is attractive, readable, plentifully illustrated with drawings and black-and-white photographs. There are sufficient grisly details to keep the pages turning, and readers will come away with a healthy understanding of Egyptian religion, scientific accomplishments, and architectural skills. Phonetic pronunciations throughout make this easily accessible." Appraisal

Includes bibliography

Putnam, James

Mummy; written by James Putnam; photographed by Peter Hayman. Knopf 1993 c1992 63p il (Eyewitness books) $15; lib bdg $15.99 (4 and up) **393**

1. Mummies 2. Funeral rites and ceremonies
ISBN 0-679-83881-3; 0-679-93881-8 (lib bdg)
LC 92-1591

Also available Spanish language edition
"A Dorling Kindersley book"
First published 1992 in the United Kingdom

Putnam, James—*Continued*

Documents the history and significance of mummies, both natural and man-made, and describes the principles and ceremonies associated with them

"A great collection of mummy information and specimens. . . . The full-color photographs and illustrations are well lit, and captions add additional information." SLJ

Wilcox, Charlotte

Mummies & their mysteries. Carolrhoda Bks. 1993 64p il lib bdg $22.95; pa $7.95 (4-6)

393

1. Mummies 2. Antiquities

ISBN 0-87614-767-8; 0-87614-643-4 (pa)

LC 92-32160

Discusses mummies found around the world, including Peru, Denmark, and the Italian Alps, and explains how studying them provides clues to past ways of life

The author's "tone is respectful, and she addresses the controversial issue of educational display and scientific research on bodies of persons who have been revered in life and death by their own peoples. . . . Captioned, full-color photographs on every page inject rich personality into the discussion, while an open format, arresting cover, and large print will encourage browsers to pick this up for more than reports." Bull Cent Child Books

Includes glossary

394 General customs

Lasker, Joe

A tournament of knights; written and illustrated by Joe Lasker. Crowell 1986 unp il lib bdg $14.89; pa $5.95 (1-3) **394**

1. Knights and knighthood 2. Medieval civilization

ISBN 0-690-04542-5 (lib bdg); 0-06-443192-4 (pa)

LC 85-48075

The author "describes a medieval tournament, from the pronouncement and tent raisings, to the gathering of knights and testing of noble-born in melee and joust. Lasker makes it clear that these duels were violent and costly—often the loser became a prisoner who had to ransom his horse, arms, and armor, perhaps even land. The story here is of a young lord who must defend his father's barony against an experienced knight errant." Bull Cent Child Books

"We are lucky to have Mr. Lasker's beautifully illustrated account of how a tournament took place, how the horses were prepared, how the knights were armored. . . . This is exactly the kind of specific information that young readers treasure." N Y Times Book Rev

Includes glossary

394.1 Customs—Eating, drinking

Aliki

A medieval feast; written and illustrated by Aliki. Crowell 1983 unp il $14.95; lib bdg $14.89; pa $5.95 (2-5) **394.1**

1. Dining—History 2. Courts and courtiers 3. Medieval civilization 4. Festivals—History

ISBN 0-690-04245-0; 0-690-04246-9 (lib bdg); 0-06-446050-9 (pa)

LC 82-45923

Also available Spanish language edition

"In pictures of minute, charming detail and vibrant, translucent colors, Aliki takes us through the ritual of preparation and the enthusiastic consumption of a medieval feast served to a king and his retinue when they stop for a few days at Camdenton Manor. Not to be outdone by the art, the text has its own various facets. There is the fictional story set in type outside the art and there is within the paintings a collection of delightful historical, gastronomical, agricultural, and zoological facts printed by hand. And throughout the spendid whole are border decorations worthy of the great illuminated manuscripts." Child Book Rev Serv

Cobb, Vicki, 1938-

Feeding yourself; pictures by Marylin Hafner. Lippincott 1989 32p il lib bdg $12.89 (1-3) **394.1**

1. Tableware

ISBN 0-397-32325-5

LC 88-14192

Describes how knives, forks, spoons, and chopsticks came to be invented and how they are used today in eating

The utensils' "origins and uses in many cultures are interpreted through Hafner's lively watercolor iluustrations, which are true to the text, yet humorous. Detailed instructions using chopsticks will intrigue readers of all ages." SLJ

Giblin, James, 1933-

From hand to mouth; or, How we invented knives, forks, spoons, and chopsticks & the table manners to go with them; [by] James Cross Giblin. Crowell 1987 86p il lib bdg $14.89 (4 and up) **394.1**

1. Tableware 2. Table etiquette

ISBN 0-690-04662-6

LC 86-29341

The author "traces the history of eating utensils and customs from the ancient world to the present. Beginning with the use of small spears to pick meat out of the fire and spoons made of curved goat horns, he follows the development to the controversial introduction of forks, the invention of stainless steel, and the return to casual eating practices with the popularity of fast foods. Readers will be especially interested in the information on eating customs and table manners in different eras and cultures." SLJ

Includes bibliography

Penner, Lucille Recht

Eating the plates; a pilgrim book of food and manners; with illustrations selected by the author. Macmillan 1991 117p il $14.95 (4 and up) **394.1**

1. Eating customs 2. Pilgrims (New England colonists)

ISBN 0-02-770901-9

LC 90-5918

Discusses the eating habits, customs, and manners of the Pilgrims in the colony of New Plymouth

"A pilgrim menu—from corn soup to hot nuts—complete with recipes adapted for modern kitchens, concludes the easy-to-read text. While food is the focus, the author also includes more general information about living conditions and social customs, some details of which will engross young readers. . . . Period prints add atmosphere." Bull Cent Child Books

Includes glossary and bibliography

Penner, Lucille Recht—*Continued*

A Native American feast; with illustrations selected by the author. Macmillan 1994 xxv, 99p il $14.95 (4 and up)   **394.1**

1. Eating customs 2. Indians of North America—Social life and customs 3. Cooking
ISBN 0-02-770902-7   LC 94-10336

"Penner looks at the plant and animal life used as food-stuffs by the Indians of North America. . . . This overview discusses the various Native peoples' concepts of food and the social obligations and meanings that traditionally accompanied them. . . . The text describes traditional, pre-Columbian foods eaten by various peoples and the changes that resulted with the introduction of European plants and animals." SLJ

"Big print and a variety of illustrations—photographs, old engravings, sketches—increase the volume's accessibility. . . . Food is a great medium for an entree into cultural understanding, and this will sharpen many young readers' appetite for both snacks and lore." Bull Cent Child Books

Includes bibliography

394.2 Customs—Special occasions

The **American** book of days; compiled and edited by Jane M. Hatch. 3d ed. Wilson, H.W. 1978 xxvi, 1214p $87   **394.2**

1. Holidays 2. Festivals—United States
ISBN 0-8242-0593-6   LC 78-16239

First edition, by George W. Douglas, published 1937

"Emphasis is on historical events relating to the founding and development of the U.S. and major religious and public holidays; descriptive articles; chronological order with detailed index by topic, key people and events." N Y Public Libr. Ref Books for Child Collect. 2d edition

Ancona, George, 1929-

Pablo remembers; the fiesta of the Day of the Dead. Lothrop, Lee & Shepard Bks. 1993 42p il $15; lib bdg $14.93 (k-3)   **394.2**

1. All Souls' Day 2. Mexico—Social life and customs
ISBN 0-688-11249-8; 0-688-11250-1 (lib bdg)
LC 92-22819

Also available Spanish language edition

During the three-day celebration of the Day of the Dead, a young Mexican boy and his family make elaborate preparations to honor the spirits of the dead

"The photography has the intimacy of high-quality family snapshots, and the tone of the text is clear and natural." Bull Cent Child Books

Includes glossary

Barkin, Carol, 1944-

Happy Thanksgiving! by Carol Barkin & Elizabeth James; pictures by Giora Carmi. Lothrop, Lee & Shepard Bks. 1987 80p il $15; lib bdg $14.93 (4-6)   **394.2**

1. Thanksgiving Day
ISBN 0-688-06800-6; 0-688-06801-4 (lib bdg)
LC 86-33734

The authors "have compiled a variety of suggestions for projects and activities, recipes, jokes, and decorations. The meaning and history of Thanksgiving are expounded and made relevant for today's children." Child Book Rev Serv

"Teachers will certainly find this worthwhile for class projects, and children who locate the book on their own will be enthusiastic about the many ideas." Booklist

Happy Valentine's Day! by Carol Barkin & Elizabeth James; pictures by Martha Weston. Lothrop, Lee & Shepard Bks. 1988 96p il $15 (4-6)   **394.2**

1. Valentine's Day
ISBN 0-688-06796-4   LC 87-35812

Presents a short history of Valentine's Day and includes recipes for appropriate foods and desserts and instructions for making Valentines and other decorations

Barth, Edna

Hearts, cupids, and red roses; the story of the Valentine symbols; illustrations by Ursula Arndt. Clarion Bks. 1974 64p il hardcover o.p. paperback available $7.95 (3-6)   **394.2**

1. Valentine's Day 2. Signs and symbols
ISBN 0-89919-036-7 (pa)

First published by Seabury Press

The author explores the "symbols and legends associated with Valentine's Day in various countries." Publisher's note

Includes an annotated list of children's Valentine's Day stories and poems, and a list of sources

Includes bibliography

Holly, reindeer, and colored lights; the story of the Christmas symbols; illustrated by Ursula Arndt. Clarion Bks. 1971 96p il $15.95; pa $5.95 (3-6)   **394.2**

1. Christmas 2. Signs and symbols
ISBN 0-395-28842-8; 0-89919-037-5 (pa)

First published by Seabury Press

The author tells the story behind such Christmas symbols as the star, the tree, the Yule log, Santa Claus, Christmas colors, etc. She stresses the similarities between Christmas and earlier pagan festivals that celebrated the winter solstice and describes some of the varying practices in different countries

"The well-written text is concise and interesting and the two-colored marginal drawings are festive. A selected list of books containing Christmas stories and poems is appended." Booklist

Lilies, rabbits, and painted eggs; the story of the Easter symbols; illustrations by Ursula Arndt. Clarion Bks. 1970 63p il hardcover o.p. paperback available $5.95 (3-6)   **394.2**

1. Easter 2. Signs and symbols
ISBN 0-395-30550-0 (pa)

First published by Seabury Press

Traces the history of Easter symbols from their Christian and pagan origins to such present-day additions as rabbits and new clothes

"The small pen drawings which illustrate the symbols and the celebrations will please the children, and an index and a bibliography of other Easter books will please the librarian." Horn Book

Shamrocks, harps, and shillelaghs; the story of the St. Patrick's Day symbols; illustrations by Ursula Arndt. Clarion Bks. 1977 95p il $15.95; pa $5.95 (3-6)   **394.2**

1. Saint Patrick's Day 2. Signs and symbols
ISBN 0-395-28845-2; 0-89919-038-3 (pa)
LC 77-369

Barth, Edna—*Continued*

First published by Seabury Press

"Irish history, lore, and legend are part of a wealth of information provided about Patrick the real missionary, St. Patrick's Day, and its celebration. Includes lists of stories for St. Patrick's Day and sources." LC. Child Books, 1977

Turkeys, Pilgrims, and Indian corn; the story of the Thanksgiving symbols; illustrations by Ursula Arndt. Clarion Bks. 1975 96p il hardcover o.p. paperback available $5.95 (3-6)   **394.2**

1. Thanksgiving Day 2. Pilgrims (New England colonists) 3. Signs and symbols

ISBN 0-89919-039-1 (pa)

First published by Seabury Press

This book provides "information about the Pilgrims' voyage to and life in America and their dealings with the Indians. (The point is made, but not belabored, that the settled land was taken from the Indians.) Interesting sidelights are included about prominent men and women, myths such as Plymouth Rock, and harvest feasts in cultures around the world." SLJ

Witches, pumpkins, and grinning ghosts; the story of the Halloween symbols; illustrations by Ursula Arndt. Clarion Bks. 1972 95p il hardcover o.p. paperback available $5.95 (3-6)   **394.2**

1. Halloween 2. Signs and symbols

ISBN 0-89919-040-X (pa)

First published by Seabury Press

"This discusses the origins of Halloween and the way it is celebrated today in different countries. Witches (male and female), bats, toads, ghosts, traditional foods, and other customs and symbols related to All Saint's Day are covered. Barth also touches on the incorporation of pagan beliefs into Christianity." SLJ

"A diverting as well as useful account appropriately illustrated with drawings in black and orange." Booklist

Brown, Tricia

Chinese New Year; photographs by Fran Ortiz. Holt & Co. 1987 unp il $14.95 (1-4)   **394.2**

1. Chinese New Year 2. Chinese Americans—Social life and customs

ISBN 0-8050-0497-1   LC 87-8532

Text and photographs depict the celebration of Chinese New Year by Chinese Americans living in San Francisco's Chinatown

"The photographs are excellent and well-matched to the text. Intimate and charming scenes of family life are contrasted with public shopping and parade shots." SLJ

Chase's calendar of events; the day-by-day directory to special days, weeks and months. Contemporary Bks. $49.95   **394.2**

1. Calendars 2. Almanacs 3. Holidays

ISSN 0740-5286

Annual. First published 1958

Arranged chronologically this reference work "includes significant historical events the editor chose from the past five decades and special days of other countries. The inclusion of presidential proclamations shows its national focus, but many local events are listed as well. Many unusual sponsored events are listed with the name and address of the sponsor. *Chases's* has an excellent index, which includes the names of events, locations, and broad subject areas." Booklist

Chocolate, Deborah M. Newton

Kwanzaa; illustrations by Melodye Rosales. Childrens Press 1990 31p il lib bdg $12.38; pa $4.95 (3-5)   **394.2**

1. Kwanzaa 2. African Americans—Social life and customs

ISBN 0-516-03991-1 (lib bdg); 0-516-43991-X (pa)

LC 89-25418

Discusses the holiday in which Afro-Americans celebrate their roots and cultural heritage from Africa

"Using clear and direct language, Chocolate provides a wealth of detail as she shares her family's Kwanzaa festival. . . . Rosales's brightly colored paintings in a realistic style draw readers into the warmth and joy of this celebration." SLJ

My first Kwanzaa book; illustrated by Cal Massey. Scholastic 1992 unp il $10.95 (k-2)   **394.2**

1. Kwanzaa 2. African Americans—Social life and customs

ISBN 0-590-45762-4   LC 92-1200

"Cartwheel books"

Introduces Kwanzaa, the holiday in which Afro-Americans celebrate their cultural heritage

"The book effectively conveys the spirit of the holiday through the text and the acrylic paint and colored-pencil illustrations, all outlined in a thin line of earthy brown." SLJ

Includes glossary

Christmas gif'; an anthology of Christmas poems, songs, and stories, written by and about African-Americans; compiled by Charlemae Rollins; illustrated by Ashley Bryan; a new introduction by Augusta Baker. Morrow Junior Bks. 1993 xxii, 106p $14 (3-6)   **394.2**

1. Christmas 2. American literature—African American authors—Collections 3. African Americans in literature

ISBN 0-688-11667-1   LC 92-18976

A newly illustrated edition of the title first published 1963 by Follett

A collection of Christmas poems, songs, stories and recipes. Langston Hughes, Frederick Douglass, Gwendolyn Brooks and Countee Cullen are among the authors included

"Bryan's black-and-white woodcuts are a fitting complement to this classic anthology." Horn Book

The **Folklore** of world holidays; Margaret Read MacDonald, editor. Gale Res. 1992 xxix, 739p $95   **394.2**

1. Holidays 2. Festivals 3. Folklore

ISBN 0-8103-7577-X   LC 91-38032

"This compilation explains the folklore surrounding 340 holidays in over 150 countries, excluding the United States. The contents section lists holidays in chronological order, and countries are arranged below each holiday." Libr J

Includes bibliographical references

Gibbons, Gail

Easter. Holiday House 1989 unp il lib bdg $15.95; pa $6.95 (k-3)   **394.2**

1. Easter
ISBN 0-8234-0737-3 (lib bdg); 0-8234-0866-3 (pa)
LC 88-23292

Examines the background, significance, symbols, and traditions of Easter

Gibbons "simplifies complex beliefs and traditions in a straightforward way, though transitions are occasionally abrupt. Pleasing watercolors outlined in black ink illustrate the text." Booklist

Halloween. Holiday House 1984 unp il lib bdg $15.95; pa $5.95 (k-3)   **394.2**

1. Halloween
ISBN 0-8234-0524-9 (lib bdg); 0-8234-0577-X (pa)
LC 84-519

The author "describes the origins of Halloween beliefs and observances, and discusses the many ways it is celebrated today: the costumes, parties, carved pumpkins, trick-or-treat visiting, games, visits to 'haunted' houses, and costume contests. The text is terse, the subject one in which most children will be interested. . . . The illustrations are bright and bold, with filled pages but no fussy details." Bull Cent Child Books

Happy birthday! Holiday House 1986 unp il $15.95 (k-3)   **394.2**

1. Birthdays
ISBN 0-8234-0614-8   LC 86-297

Examines the historical beliefs, traditions, and celebrations associated with birthdays

"Simple text explains that everybody has one and tells why the traditional cake is round, why there's a candle for each year, why the candles are blown out and other historical birthday customs. . . . The story is accompanied by brightly colored artwork, complete with ribbons, confetti, party hats and decorations, making this book as festive and fun as the day it describes." Publ Wkly

St. Patrick's Day. Holiday House 1994 unp il lib bdg $15.95 (k-3)   **394.2**

1. Saint Patrick's Day
ISBN 0-8234-1119-2   LC 93-29570

"A basic introduction to the holiday—how it began, the life and works of St. Patrick, and the various ways in which the day is celebrated. The text is clear and concise, and the pages are full of information. Gibbons's simple, clean, full-page watercolor-and-ink illustrations flow logically from one to the next." SLJ

Thanksgiving Day. Holiday House 1983 unp il lib bdg $15.95; pa $5.95 (k-3)   **394.2**

1. Thanksgiving Day
ISBN 0-8234-0489-7 (lib bdg); 0-8234-0576-1 (pa)
LC 83-175

This book presents information about the first Thanksgiving and the way that holiday is celebrated today

"Cheery shades of gold and orange and other hues animate the scenes illustrating Gibbon's incisive history of the American holiday." Publ Wkly

Valentine's Day. Holiday House 1986 unp il $15.95; pa $6.95 (k-3)   **394.2**

1. Valentine's Day
ISBN 0-8234-0572-9; 0-8234-0764-0 (pa)
LC 85-916

The author "briefly describes the history, meaning, and customs of Valentine's Day in picture-book format. Simple line drawings are brightened with the bright, crisp colors that are the artist's hallmark. . . . On the last two pages she shows how to make valentines and a valentine box. A useful addition to a holiday collection for young children and a serviceable read-aloud choice for classrooms where Valentine's Day is celebrated." Booklist

Giblin, James, 1933-

Fireworks, picnics, and flags; [by] James Cross Giblin; illustrated by Ursula Arndt. Clarion Bks. 1983 90p il $14.95; pa $7.95 (3-6)   **394.2**

1. Fourth of July
ISBN 0-89919-146-0; 0-89919-174-6 (pa)
LC 82-9612

Traces the social history behind America's celebration of Independence Day and explains the background of such national symbols as the flag, the bald eagle, the Liberty Bell, and Uncle Sam

"Giblin was the editor of Edna Barth's books on holiday symbols; according to his author's note, he knew that Barth intended to write about the Fourth of July and took on the project himself after her death. The result is consistent in both format and spirit with the well-known Barth series, complete with Arndt's unpretentious two-color drawings." Booklist

The truth about Santa Claus. Crowell 1985 86p il lib bdg $15.89 (4 and up)   **394.2**

1. Santa Claus 2. Christmas
ISBN 0-690-04484-4   LC 85-47541

"Historical discussion of the religious, mythological, folk and commercial traditions that have become the contemporary image of Santa Claus." Soc Educ

"Reproductions of paintings and cartoons, as well as photographs, illustrate the diverse European legends and the contemporary Santa Claus figure. . . . An interesting picture of the ways in which customs arise, fuse, change, are diffused only to change again." Bull Cent Child Books

Includes bibliography

Gregory, Ruth W. (Ruth Wilhelme), 1910-

Anniversaries and holidays. 4th ed. American Lib. Assn. 1983 262p $40   **394.2**

1. Holidays 2. Calendars 3. Birthdays
ISBN 0-8389-0389-4   LC 83-3784

First edition by Mary Emogene Hazeltine published 1928

"Covers, in calendar form, the names of important people, holidays, religious festivals and special events for nearly 200 countries. Annotated bibliographies about holidays, etc." N Y Public Libr. Ref Books for Child Collect. 2d edition

Hoyt-Goldsmith, Diane

Celebrating Kwanzaa; photographs by Lawrence Migdale. Holiday House 1993 32p il $15.95; pa $6.95 (3-5)   **394.2**

1. Kwanzaa 2. African Americans—Social life and customs
ISBN 0-8234-1048-X; 0-8234-1130-3 (pa)
LC 93-16799

Hoyt-Goldsmith, Diane—*Continued*

Text and photographs depict how a Chicago family celebrates the African American holiday, Kwanzaa

"The rituals of Kwanzaa are clearly presented and handsomely photographed in this well-designed photo-documentary." Booklist

Includes glossary

Day of the Dead; a Mexican-American celebration; photographs by Lawrence Migdale. Holiday House 1994 30p il $15.95; pa $6.95 (3-5)   **394.2**

1. All Souls' Day 2. Mexican Americans—Social life and customs

ISBN 0-8234-1094-3; 0-8234-1200-8 (pa)

LC 93-42106

"Ten-year-old twins from Sacramento, California, tell the story of their family's Day of the Dead celebration. . . . Aztec beliefs and their intermingling with Catholic rituals are explained, and descriptions of dancing, art, and prayer repeatedly illustrate the unity of past and present during festival days." Booklist

"The excellent-quality, full-color photographs, drawings, and cut-paper illustrations are well placed and appealing. . . . Hoyt-Goldsmith provides a good deal of background, making *Day of the Dead* a solid report source." SLJ

Includes glossary

Lasky, Kathryn

Days of the Dead; photographs by Christopher G. Knight. Hyperion Bks. for Children 1994 48p il $15.95; lib bdg $15.89 (4-6)   **394.2**

1. All Souls' Day 2. Mexico—Social life and customs

ISBN 0-7868-0022-4; 0-7868-2018-7 (lib bdg)

LC 93-47957

The author "details the history and customs associated with this traditional Mexican celebration, briefly tells how it is linked to practices in ancient cultures, and describes a contemporary rural family's preparations and observances. . . . Large, bold, and often dramatic full-color photographs fill the pages, amplifying and extending the text." SLJ

Macmillan, Dianne

Chinese New Year; [by] Dianne M. MacMillan; reading consultant: Michael P. French. Enslow Pubs. 1994 48p il (Best holiday books) lib bdg $14.95 (2-4)   **394.2**

1. Chinese New Year 2. Chinese Americans—Social life and customs

ISBN 0-89490-500-7

LC 93-46183

This explains how the Chinese New Year is celebrated in the United States and is illustrated with both black and white and color photographs

Includes glossary

McKissack, Patricia C., 1944-

Christmas in the big house, Christmas in the quarters; by Patricia C. McKissack and Fredrick L. McKissack; illustrated by John Thompson. Scholastic 1994 68p il $15.95 (4-6)   **394.2**

1. Plantation life 2. Christmas 3. Slavery—United States

ISBN 0-590-43027-0

LC 92-33831

Coretta Scott King award for text, 1995

"The authors view the holiday from the perspectives of both slaveholder and his household in the 'Big House' and the slaves in the 'Quarters.' Rich descriptions of preparations fill the text—recipes and menus from both groups are provided—and colorful paintings reflect the antebellum period. Sprinkled throughout the book are lyrics of traditional spirituals, carols, and poetry. . . . Use of authentic language of the time helps the narrative flow, and carefully documented notes illuminate the interesting text." Horn Book

Includes bibliography

Perl, Lila

Piñatas and paper flowers; holidays of the Americas in English and Spanish, illustrated by Victoria de Larrea. Clarion Bks. 1983 91p il hardcover o.p. paperback available $6.95 (4 and up)   **394.2**

1. Holidays 2. Folklore—Latin America 3. Bilingual books—English-Spanish

ISBN 0-89919-155-X (pa)

LC 82-1211

Text and title page in English and Spanish; Spanish version by Alma Flor Ada

A brief overview of eight holidays and their customs as celebrated in the Americas. Holidays covered include: The New Year, Three Kings' Day; Carnival and Easter; St. John the Baptist Day; Columbus Day; Halloween; The Festival of the Sun; and Christmas

Pinkney, Andrea Davis

Seven candles for Kwanzaa; pictures by Brian Pinkney. Dial Bks. for Young Readers 1993 unp il $14.99; lib bdg $14.89 (k-3)   **394.2**

1. Kwanzaa 2. African Americans—Social life and customs

ISBN 0-8037-1292-8; 0-8037-1293-6 (lib bdg)

LC 92-3698

Describes the origins and practices of Kwanzaa, the seven-day festival during which people of African descent rejoice in their ancestral values

The "joyful text is accompanied by equally joyful scratchboard illustrations, set within colorful textilelike borders, depicting a family preparing for and celebrating the holiday." Booklist

Includes bibliography

Presilla, Maricel E.

Feliz Nochebuena, Feliz Navidad; Christmas feasts of the Hispanic Caribbean; pictures by Ismael Espinosa Ferrer. Holt & Co. 1994 unp il $15.95 (k-3)   **394.2**

1. Christmas 2. Caribbean region—Social life and customs 3. Cooking

ISBN 0-8050-2512-X

LC 93-43009

In a "first-person account, Presilla describes the festivities in her native Cuba and its surrounding Hispanic islands. . . . Readers learn the origin of marzipan and how the first pigs arrived on these islands. They are given a glimpse into the lives of the Tainos, who inhabited the region before the arrival of the Europeans. The influence of the Africans, who were brought to the Caribbean as slaves, is also discussed. . . . Four recipes are included." SLJ

"The watercolor and ink illustrations complement the beautifully descriptive writing perfectly and provide a gorgeous Hispanic Caribbean setting." Child Book Rev Serv

Includes glossary and bibliography

Take joy! The Tasha Tudor Christmas book; selected, edited and illustrated by Tasha Tudor. Philomel Bks. 1980 c1966 157p il music $18.95   **394.2**

1. Christmas
ISBN 0-399-20766-X

First published 1966 by World Publishing Company

"A collection of Christmas stories, poems, customs, and carols and their music, celebrating both the religious and the secular aspects of the holiday. Included are the particular traditions and recipes of the Tudor family." Adventuring with Books. 2d edition

"Generously illustrated with tenderness and reverence in full-color and black-and-white pictures." Booklist

Waters, Kate

Lion dancer: Ernie Wan's Chinese New Year; by Kate Waters and Madeline Slovenz-Low; photographs by Martha Cooper. Scholastic 1990 unp il $15.95; pa $3.95 (k-3)   **394.2**

1. Chinese New Year 2. Chinese Americans—Social life and customs
ISBN 0-590-43046-7; 0-590-43047-5 (pa)
    LC 89-6423

Describes six-year-old Ernie Wan's preparations, at home and in school, for the Chinese New Year celebrations and his first public performance of the lion dance

"While some of the pictures look posed, the marvelously colorful photographs successfully capture Ernie's pride and anticipation as he is dressed in his gorgeous costume and the excitement and swirling movement of the subsequent parade. Illustrations of a Chinese lunar calendar and a Chinese horoscope are extra dividends in a useful and appealing book." Horn Book

395   Etiquette (Manners)

Aliki

Manners. Greenwillow Bks. 1990 unp il $16; lib bdg $15.93 (k-3)   **395**

1. Etiquette
ISBN 0-688-09198-9; 0-688-09199-7 (lib bdg)
    LC 89-34622

Also available Spanish language edition

The author discusses etiquette and good manners

"Aliki makes manners accessible to children through colorful cartoon-style illustrations. . . . Her lively primer sparkles with examples of the proper and the poor." Booklist

Buehner, Caralyn

It's a spoon, not a shovel; pictures by Mark Buehner. Dial Bks. for Young Readers 1995 unp il $14.99; lib bdg $14.89 (k-3)   **395**

1. Etiquette 2. Questions and answers
ISBN 0-8037-1494-7; 0-8037-1495-5 (lib bdg)
    LC 93-36293

This book shows "various animals and insects in 14 manners-related dilemmas. On one page, three possible scenarios are offered, and readers must choose the correct behavior. Two of them are always obviously wrong, but for those who can't figure the answer out, the letter (a, b, or c) of the correct choice is hidden in the picture." SLJ

"A handsome combination of humor, puzzles, and lessons in elementary good behavior." Horn Book

Joslin, Sesyle

What do you do, dear? pictures by Maurice Sendak. Harper & Row 1985 c1961 unp il lib bdg $13.89; pa $4.95 (k-2)   **395**

1. Etiquette
ISBN 0-06-023075-4 (lib bdg); 0-06-443113-4 (pa)
    LC 84-43139

First published 1961 by Addison-Wesley

A "handbook of etiquette for young ladies and gentlemen to be used as a guide for everyday social behavior." The Author

"The propriety of what the well-mannered child will do is related to extraordinary situations, as for example: The Sheriff of Nottingham interrupts you while you are reading, to take you to jail; you will, naturally, 'Find a bookmark to save your place.' Sendak's pictures account for a great share of the fun." Horn Book

A "wonderful spoof on manners in a hilarious picture-book made for laughing aloud." Child Study Assoc of Am

What do you say, dear? pictures by Maurice Sendak. Harper & Row 1986 c1958 unp il lib bdg $14.89; pa $4.95 (k-2)   **395**

1. Etiquette
ISBN 0-06-023074-6 (lib bdg); 0-06-443112-6 (pa)
    LC 84-43140

A Caldecott Medal honor book, 1959

First published 1958 by Addison-Wesley

A "handbook of etiquette for young ladies and gentlemen to be used as a guide for everyday social behavior." The Author

"A rollicking introduction to manners for the very young. A series of delightfully absurd situations—being introduced to a baby elephant, bumping into a crocodile, being rescued from a dragon—are posed and appropriately answered. The illustrations are among Sendak's best—and funniest." Bull Cent Child Books

This "funny and imaginative picture book . . . may stimulate children to invent situations of their own." Booklist

398   Folklore

Giblin, James, 1933-

The truth about unicorns; [by] James Cross Giblin ; illustrated with drawings by Michael McDermott. HarperCollins Pubs. 1991 113p il $15; lib bdg $14.89; pa $5.95 (4 and up)   **398**

1. Unicorns
ISBN 0-06-022478-9; 0-06-022479-7 (lib bdg); 0-06-446147-5 (pa)   LC 90-47233

Describes the origins of the unicorn, including the real-life animals that inspired it, and the various myths told about unicorns throughout the world

"Giblin's perspective is multicultural, his research scholarly, and his style casual and open, with vivid examples in story and pictures. McDermott's full-page, shaded drawings capture some of the romance and energy of the legendary creatures." Booklist

Includes bibliography

MacDonald, Margaret Read

The storyteller's sourcebook; a subject, title, and motif index to folklore collections for children. Neal-Schuman; Gale Res. 1982 818p o.p. **398**

    1. Folklore—Indexes   LC 82-954

"Locates tales by subject, ethnic or geographical area; includes variants and specific titles in collections and gives tale synopsis. Also indexes picture books. Confined to folktales. Epics, romances, tall tales and literary fairy tales are omitted. Current through 1980. Does not supplant Ireland's 'Index to Fairy Tales' [entered in class 398.2]." N Y Public Libr. Ref Books for Child Collect

Opie, Iona Archibald

The lore and language of schoolchildren; by Iona and Peter Opie. Oxford Univ. Press 1960 c1959 417p il maps hardcover o.p. paperback available $10.95 **398**

    1. Folklore—Great Britain
    ISBN 0-19-282059-1 (pa)

A collection of the "rhymes, riddles, incantations, jeers, torments, parodies, nicknames, holiday customs, and other types of lore that is . . . transmitted orally, some of it over a period of hundreds of years. The basic study was made in Great Britain and detailed analysis of geographic usage is made for Great Britain but some usage in other countries is also noted. Chiefly of interest to folklorists, teachers, librarians, and others who work with children but nostalgic appeal for the general reader." Booklist

Perl, Lila

Don't sing before breakfast, don't sleep in the moonlight; everyday superstitions and how they began; illustrated by Erika Weihs. Clarion Bks. 1988 90p il $14.95 (4-6) **398**

    1. Superstition
    ISBN 0-89919-504-0   LC 87-24295

Examines common superstitions associated with the events of a typical day, how these superstitions developed, and how they influence our behavior today

"Writing conversationally and informatively, Perl considers the meaning of well-known expressions, such as 'not worth his salt,' as she weaves ancient rhymes into her fascinating analyses of individual superstitions. Adding to the mystery are Weihs' finely executed woodcuts, which provide appropriate flavor." Booklist

Includes bibliography

Schwartz, Alvin, 1927-1992

Cross your fingers, spit in your hat: superstitions and other beliefs; collected by Alvin Schwartz; illustrated by Glen Rounds. Lippincott 1974 161p il lib bdg $13.89; pa $4.95 (4 and up) **398**

    1. Superstition
    ISBN 0-397-32436-7 (lib bdg); 0-06-446138-6 (pa)

This is a compilation of superstitions about such subjects as love and marriage, food and drink, witches, travel, the human body, ailments and curses, plants and animals, and death

"This delightful book reveals the sometimes humorous but always interesting ideas people have about what's happening. . . . Comically illustrated by Glen Rounds, this book will give hours of fun and fascinating information about people and their beliefs." Child Book Rev Serv

Includes bibliography

Flapdoodle: pure nonsense from American folklore; collected by Alvin Schwartz; illustrated by John O'Brien. Lippincott 1980 125p il lib bdg $14.89 (4 and up) **398**

    1. American wit and humor 2. Riddles
    ISBN 0-397-31920-7   LC 79-9618

"Included are samples of spoonerisms, double-talk, visual jokes, tricks, silly rhymes, and shaggy dog stories. The introduction states that some of the folklore is old, and some of it new; children may be surprised to find several of the jokes and rhymes currently very much alive in the schoolyard. Nearly every page of the entertaining book is decorated with a suitably absurd line drawing. Notes, sources, and bibliography." Horn Book

Tomfoolery: trickery and foolery with words; collected from American folklore by Alvin Schwartz; illustrated by Glen Rounds. Lippincott 1973 127p il lib bdg $14.89; pa $4.95 (4 and up) **398**

    1. American wit and humor 2. Riddles
    ISBN 0-397-32437-5 (lib bdg); 0-06-446154-8 (pa)

"This is a sampling of verbal trickery garnered not only from folklore archives, publications, and folklorists but also from Schwartz's childhood, his children, and other children. Rounds' amusing line drawings add visual interest to the collection which includes wisecracks, riddles, practical jokes, double talk, endless tales, and anecdotes with trick endings. Appended are notes, sources, and a bibliography." Booklist

Witcracks: jokes and jests from American folklore; illustrated by Glen Rounds. Lippincott 1973 128p il $14.89; pa $4.95 (4 and up) **398**

    1. American wit and humor 2. Jokes
    ISBN 0-397-31475-2; 0-06-446146-7 (pa)

A collection of American humor including "riddles, shaggy dog stories, Tom Swifties, hate jokes, noodle-head humor, ethnic humor, and knock-knock jokes." Bull Cent Child Books

"Short explanations about when and why such jokes are told precede each section; copious notes give the origins of jokes and stories; and black-and-white line drawings add to the humor. It is unfortunate, however, that hate or ethnic jokes as well as sick jokes popular in the '50's have been included." SLJ

Includes bibliography

398.03   Folklore—Encyclopedias and dictionaries

Briggs, Katharine Mary

An encyclopedia of fairies; hobgoblins, brownies, bogies, and other supernatural creatures; [by] Katherine Briggs. Pantheon Bks. 1977 c1976 481p il $12.95; pa $19

                             398.03

1. Fairies—Dictionaries 2. Folklore—Great Britain—Dictionaries

ISBN 0-394-40918-3; 0-394-73467-X (pa)

First published 1976 in the United Kingdom with title: A dictionary of fairies

"This eclectic encyclopedia covers British fairy lore, broadly constituted as 'that whole area of the supernatural which is not claimed by angels, devils or ghosts.' Entries are alphabetically arranged and terms are capitalized in the text to indicate that they have separate entries. . . . Supplementary material includes a selected reading list and indexes of tale types and motifs mentioned in the text." Libr J

398.2   Folk literature

Sagas, romances, legends, ballads, and fables in prose form, and fairy tales, folk tales, and tall tales are included here, instead of with the literature of the country of origin, to keep the traditional material together and to make it more readily accessible. Modern fairy tales are classified with Fiction, Story collections (SC), or Easy books (E)

Aardema, Verna

Anansi finds a fool; an Ashanti tale; pictures by Bryna Waldman. Dial Bks. for Young Readers 1992 unp il $14.99; lib bdg $13.89 (k-3)   **398.2**

1. Ashanti (African people)—Folklore 2. Anansi (Legendary character)

ISBN 0-8037-1164-6; 0-8037-1165-4 (lib bdg)

                           LC 91-21127

In this Ashanti folktale, Lazy Anansi seeks to trick someone into doing the heavy work of laying his fish trap, but instead he is fooled into doing the job himself

"The watercolor illustrations glow with a clear, warm light. An amusing tale of a trickster outtricked." SLJ

Includes bibliographical references

Bimwili & the Zimwi; a tale from Zanzibar; retold by Verna Aardema; pictures by Susan Meddaugh. Dial Bks. for Young Readers 1985 unp il $14.99; lib bdg $12.89; pa $4.95 (k-3)

                             398.2

1. Folklore—Zanzibar

ISBN 0-8037-0212-4; 0-8037-0213-2 (lib bdg); 0-8037-0553-0 (pa)   LC 85-4449

Text adapted from Little sister and the Zimwi, published 1969 in Tales for the third ear. Another version: The children and the Zimwi, published 1896 in Swahili stories

A Swahili girl is abducted by Zimwi, an ugly ogre, and told to be the voice inside his singing drum

"Making the most of each dramatic situation, the bright watercolor and pencil illustrations are well suited to sharing with a group of children. . . . A tightly written, slightly scary story with a heroine who uses her wits and courage to overcome a powerful enemy, this could become a favorite for reading aloud to children in the primary grades." Booklist

Borreguita and the coyote; a tale from Ayutla, Mexico; retold by Verna Aardema; illustrated by Petra Mathers. Knopf 1991 unp il $15; lib bdg $15.99 (k-3)   **398.2**

1. Folklore—Mexico 2. Coyote (Legendary character) 3. Sheep—Fiction

ISBN 0-679-80921-X; 0-679-90921-4 (lib bdg)

                           LC 90-33302

A little lamb uses her clever wiles to keep a coyote from eating her up

This folk tale "is energetically told and comfortably packed with many recognizable motifs. Mathers enlarges upon the humorous elements of the story in her boldly colored paintings. . . . Aardema and Mathers are felicitously paired in a tale of trickery rewarded that begs to be read aloud." Horn Book

Includes glossary

Bringing the rain to Kapiti Plain; a Nandi tale; retold by Verna Aardema; pictures by Beatriz Vidal. Dial Bks. for Young Readers 1981 unp il $15.99; lib bdg $22.25; pa $3.95 (k-3)   **398.2**

1. Folklore—Africa 2. Stories in rhyme 3. Droughts—Fiction

ISBN 0-8037-0809-2; 0-8037-0807-6 (lib bdg); 0-8037-0904-8 (pa)   LC 80-25886

"Retold from an African folk tale, this is a cumulative rhyming tale with the rhythm and repetition of 'The House that Jack Built.' It tells of how Ki-pat, the herdsman, works out a clever method to save the plain from a long drought." SLJ

"Effective both in the rhythm of its metered storytelling and in the brilliance of its stylized paintings, the panoramic picture book quickly engages both eye and ear." Horn Book

Misoso; once upon a time tales from Africa; retold by Verna Aardema; illustrated by Reynold Ruffins. Knopf 1994 87p il $18; lib bdg $18.99 (3-5)   **398.2**

1. Folklore—Africa

ISBN 0-679-83430-3; 0-679-93430-8 (lib bdg)

                           LC 92-43288

"An Apple Soup book"

A collection of twelve folktales from different parts of Africa

"Aardema's usual attention to detail and the rhythm and structure of the oral folk style make the stories a particular pleasure to read aloud. Vibrant illustrations in pencil and acrylic paints, notes about each story, a map of Africa, and a glossary for each tale complete this exceptional collection." Horn Book Guide

Includes bibliography

Oh, Kojo! How could you! an Ashanti tale; retold by Verna Aardema; pictures by Marc Brown. Dial Bks. for Young Readers 1984 unp il $14; lib bdg $12.89; pa $4.99 (k-3)

                             398.2

1. Ashanti (African people)—Folklore 2. Anansi (Legendary character)

ISBN 0-8037-0006-7; 0-8037-0007-5 (lib bdg); 0-8037-0449-6 (pa)   LC 84-1710

"An adaptation of the author's earlier book, 'The Na of Wa' [1960]." Horn Book

"An Ananse story that explains why cats are favored over dogs in Ashantiland. The text and full-color illustrations combine to make a fun book that is sure to be enjoyed by many." Child Book Rev Serv

Aardema, Verna—*Continued*

Rabbit makes a monkey of lion; a Swahili tale; retold by Verna Aardema; pictures by Jerry Pinkney. Dial Bks. for Young Readers 1989 unp il $11.95; lib bdg $11.89 (k-3)

398.2

1. Folklore—Zanzibar 2. Animals—Fiction
ISBN 0-8037-0297-3; 0-8037-0298-1 (lib bdg)

LC 86-11523

Also available in paperback from Puffin Bks.

Text adapted from The hare and the lion, published 1901 in Zanzibar tales

With the help of his friends Bush-rat and Turtle, smart and nimble Rabbit makes a fool of the mighty but slow-witted king of the forest

"Aardema's version of the tale reinforces the amusing trickster qualities of rascally Rabbit, making it a sure-fire choice for sharing with groups of children, who will instantly root for her success. Pinkney's lovely watercolor and pencil paintings in hues of green, brown, and gold fill the pages with lush scenes which evoke the East African setting." Horn Book

Traveling to Tondo; a tale of the Nkundo of Zaire; retold by Verna Aardema; illustrated by Will Hillenbrand. Knopf 1991 unp il lib bdg $14.99; pa $5.99 (k-3)   **398.2**

1. Folklore—Africa 2. Animals—Fiction
ISBN 0-679-90081-0 (lib bdg); 0-679-85309-X (pa)

LC 90-39419

On his way to his wedding, with his friends as attendants, a civet cat meets with extraordinary and unexpected delays

"This satisfying tale owes its success to a clean, straightforward telling and beautiful illustrations in blues, browns, greens, and gold. . . . Told with a steady ryhthm that's perfect for reading aloud, this is a traveling tale for all collections." SLJ

Includes glossary

What's so funny, Ketu? a Nuer tale; retold by Verna Aardema; pictures by Marc Brown. Dial Bks. for Young Readers 1982 unp il hardcover o.p. paperback available $4.95 (k-3)

398.2

1. Folklore—Sudan
ISBN 0-8037-0646-4 (pa)

LC 81-68776

Also available in paperback from Puffin Bks.

Earlier version of this story by the author published 1960 by Coward-McCann with title: Otwe

"Retelling of 'The man and the snake' in Neur customs and folklore, by Ray Huffman." Verso of title page

For saving the life of a snake, Ketu is rewarded by being allowed to hear animals think

"Brown's full-page pencil and ink drawings with black, brown, yellow and red halftones are often composed to contrast Ketu's delight with the anger and disruption around him. The large figures, with their exaggerated expressions and gestures, reinforce and enhance this funny story which demands reading aloud." SLJ

Who's in Rabbit's house? a Masai tale; retold by Verna Aardema; pictures by Leo and Diane Dillon. Dial Bks. for Young Readers 1977 unp il hardcover o.p. paperback available $4.95 (k-3)   **398.2**

1. Masai (African people)—Folklore 2. Animals—Fiction
3. Folklore—East Africa
ISBN 0-8037-9549-1 (pa)

LC 77-71514

This "tale relates the attempts of Rabbit to regain possession of her house after it is taken over by an intruder. Rabbit's friends offer suggestions on how to solve the problem, but the solution comes from 'an unexpected source.' The story, adapted from the Masai tale 'The Long One,' uses repetition of key phrases to produce a rhythmic read-aloud text. The Dillons skillfully present their artistry in a vivid, colorful and impressive manner which contributes to the story and sets the tone." Child Book Rev Serv

Why mosquitoes buzz in people's ears; a West African tale retold; pictures by Leo and Diane Dillon. Dial Bks. for Young Readers 1975 unp il $15.99; lib bdg $15.89; pa $4.95 (k-3)   **398.2**

1. Folklore—West Africa 2. Mosquitoes—Fiction
3. Animals—Fiction
ISBN 0-8037-6089-2; 0-8037-6087-6 (lib bdg); 0-8037-6088-4 (pa)

Awarded the Caldecott Medal, 1976

This tale relates "how a mosquito's silly lie to an iguana sets in motion a cumulative series of events that finally causes Mother Owl not to call up the sun. The resulting hardship ends only after King Lion traces the problem back to its source." Booklist

"Stunning full-color illustrations—watercolor sprayed with air gun, overlayed with pastel, cut out and repasted—give an eye-catching abstract effect and tell the story with humor and power." SLJ

Ada, Alma Flor, 1938-

The rooster who went to his uncle's wedding; a Latin American folktale; retold by Alma Flor Ada; illustrated by Kathleen Kuchera. Putnam 1993 unp il $14.95 (k-3)

398.2

1. Folklore—Latin America
ISBN 0-399-22412-2

LC 92-14087

"A Whitebird book"

In this cumulative folktale from Latin America, the sun sets off a chain of events which results in the cleaning of Rooster's beak in time for his uncle's wedding

"The story . . . will delight young children with the sheer joy of its repetitive rhythms, and it is particularly appropriate to be told aloud. The illustrations, bright with tropical colors, depict a Latin American setting." Booklist

Aesop

Aesop's fables; illustrated by Heidi Holder. Viking 1981 25p il $16; pa $4.99   **398.2**

1. Fables
ISBN 0-670-10643-7; 0-14-054872-6 (pa)

LC 80-26265

Contents: The dove and the snake; The country mouse and the city mouse; The bat, the bramblebush, and the cormorant; A laden ass and a horse; The fox and the grapes; The marriage of the sun; The cock and the jewel; The hare and the tortoise; The stag and the hounds

"It would be difficult to imagine an 'Aesop's Fables' more beautifully illustrated or lovingly designed than this edition. The pictures, first drawn in pencil, then traced in pen and ink, were finished in watercolor. The results are Rackham-style illustrations filled with intricate detail. . . . The fables and their morals are retold in clear but sophisticated language, so despite the picture-book format, this is not appropriate for young children; others will be captivated." Booklist

Aesop—*Continued*

Aesop's fables; illustrated by Lisbeth Zwerger. Picture Bk. Studio 1989 unp il $16; pa $4.95   **398.2**

1. Fables

ISBN 0-88708-108-8; 0-88708-179-7 (pa)

      LC 89-31370

Also available Spanish language edition

"A Michael Neugebauer book"

Contents: Town mouse & country mouse; The milkmaid & her pail; The man & the satyr; The shepherd's boy & the wolf; The hares & the frogs; The monkey & the camel; The fox & the grapes; The hare & the tortoise; The fox & the crow; The dog & the sow; The moon & her mother; The ass & the lap dog

"The characters—both animal and human—are executed in a fairly realistic manner which accommodates Zwerger's impish sense of humor. The balance between each page of text and its accompanying illustration is pleasing, with the book's overall effect being one of a leisurely journey through the reasons for human behavior." SLJ

Afanas´ev, A. N. (Aleksandr Nikolaevich), 1826-1871

Russian fairy tales; translated by Norbert Guterman from the collections of Aleksandr Afanas´ev; illustrated by Alexander Alexeieff; folkloristic commentary by Roman Jakobson. Pantheon Bks. 1975 c1945 661p il hardcover o.p. paperback available $18 (4 and up)   **398.2**

1. Folklore—Russia 2. Fairy tales

ISBN 0-394-73090-9 (pa)

A reprint of the title first published 1945

Afanas´ev's "tales carry the reader to faraway Russian villages, long winter nights, deep snow, thatched huts, forests teeming with wild animals and muzhiks (peasants), who have never progressed beyond the very beginnings of human civilization. . . . [This is a] beautiful book. I recommend it to all readers, young and old who are interested in the folktale and its unique qualities." N Y Times Book Rev

Includes bibliographical references

Aladdin and other tales from the Arabian nights; with illustrations by W. Heath Robinson and others. Knopf 1993 346p il $12.95   **398.2**

1. Fairy tales 2. Arabs—Folklore

ISBN 0-679-42533-0   LC 92-55071

"Everyman's library children's classics"

A reissue of the title first published 1907

Contents: The story of Aladdin; The King of Persia and the Princess of the Sea; Prince Camaralzaman and the Princess of China; The loss of the talisman; The first voyage of Sinbad the sailor; The second voyage of Sinbad the sailor; The third voyage of Sinbad the sailor; The fourth voyage of Sinbad the sailor; The fifth voyage of Sinbad the sailor; The sixth voyage of Sinbad the sailor; The seventh and last voyage of Sinbad the sailor; The story of Ali Baba and the forty thieves; The story of the enchanted horse; The story of the fisherman and the genie

A collection of tales told by Scheherazade to amuse the cruel sultan and stop him from executing her as he had his other daily wives

Alexander, Ellen

Llama and the great flood; a folktale from Peru. Crowell 1989 39p il lib bdg $14.89 (1-3)   **398.2**

1. Folklore—Peru

ISBN 0-690-04729-0   LC 88-1194

In this Peruvian myth about the great flood, a llama warns his master of the coming destruction and suggests taking refuge on a high peak in the Andes

"A note explains the background of the story and some of the artist's graphic motifs, which she attributes to 'several pre-Inca cultures such as the Wari and the Moche.' The full-color wash drawings are vivid . . . and the rocky landscapes are expressive." Bull Cent Child Books

Anno, Mitsumasa, 1926-

Anno's twice told tales; The fisherman and his wife & The four clever brothers; by the Brothers Grimm & Mr. Fox; [retold and] illustrated by Mitsumasa Anno. Philomel Bks. 1993 unp il $17.95 (3-5)   **398.2**

1. Fairy tales 2. Folklore—Germany

ISBN 0-399-22005-4   LC 92-25307

Original Japanese edition, 1991

"In the framework story carried at the bottom of each page, little Freddy Fox finds an illustrated book with two of the Grimms' fairy tales and runs home to ask his father to read to him. With considerably more imagination than decoding skills, Mr. Fox puzzles over the illustrations and fashions his own stories to fit the pictures provided, rather than telling Freddy that he can't read. Meanwhile, at the top of each page, a book within a book appears page by page, telling the Grimms' tales of 'The Fisherman and His Wife' and 'The Four Clever Brothers.' . . . Anno's clean, spare, ink-and-watercolor artwork makes a pleasing jumping-off point for both literal and imaginative interpretations." Booklist

The **Arabian** nights entertainments; selected and edited by Andrew Lang; with numerous illustrations by H. J. Ford. Dover Publs. 1969 424p il pa $7.95 (5 and up)   **398.2**

1. Arabs—Folklore 2. Fairy tales

ISBN 0-486-22289-6

Also available in hardcover from Amereon and P. Smith

First published 1898 in the United Kingdom

"A collection of popular tales assembled over many centuries, and well known in Europe from the 18th cent. It contains the stories of 'Aladdin, Alibaba, and Sindbad the sailor'. . . . The framing story in which the tales are set concerns Scheherazade, who is determined to delay her royal husband's plan of killing her—he has taken to murdering his wives because the first was unfaithful to him—by telling him a story every evening. She leaves each evening's tale incomplete until the next day, so that he has to spare her life in order to hear its conclusion. He is so entertained that he finally abandons his murderous plan." Oxford Companion to Child Lit

Asbjornsen, Peter Christen, 1812-1885

East o' the sun and west o' the moon; illustrated by P.J. Lynch; translated by George Webb Dasent; with an introduction by Naomi Lewis. Candlewick Press 1992 c1991 unp il $15.95 (3-6)   **398.2**

1. Fairy tales 2. Folklore—Norway

ISBN 1-56402-049-5   LC 91-58727

Asbjornsen, Peter Christen, 1812-1885—Continued

This illustrated edition first published 1991 in the United Kingdom is one story from the collection of the same title

"When a poor girl becomes the reluctant guest of a white bear, she discovers he's actually a prince under a spell. But her discovery has dire consequences—now he must marry a troll princess. It is only through the girl's love and persistence that he is saved from this disastrous marriage. With its language both economic and evocative, Dasent's translation is the ideal text for Lynch's sumptuous watercolor illustrations. Using layer upon layer of transparent washes, he has produced highly detailed, realistic illustrations that complement but never overwhelm the story. . . . An introduction by the respected historian and critic Naomi Lewis provides a fascinating background to the story." SLJ

East of the sun and west of the moon: old tales from the North; illustrated by Kay Nielsen. Doubleday 1977 c1976 108p il o.p. (3-6)   **398.2**

1. Folklore—Norway 2. Fairy tales   LC 77-74791

This edition first published 1976 in the United Kingdom

The six Norwegian folktales included in this volume were originally part of a larger collection of the same title published in 1914

Bang, Molly, 1943-

Wiley and the Hairy Man; adapted from an American folk tale. Macmillan 1976 64p il $9.95; pa $3.95 (1-4)   **398.2**

1. African Americans—Folklore 2. Folklore—Southern States

ISBN 0-02-708370-5; 0-689-71162-X (pa)

"A Ready-to-read book"

In this adaptation of an Alabama folk yarn "the swamp-dwelling Hairy Man must be tricked three times before a person is safe from being caught and carried off by him. Wiley, a Black boy, twice meets the Hairy Man in the swamp, and both times quick thinking and his hound dogs save him. On the critical third time, Wiley's mother traps the conjure man into taking a piglet instead of her son." SLJ

Barton, Byron

The little red hen. HarperCollins Pubs. 1993 unp il $12.95; lib bdg $14.89 (k-2)   **398.2**

1. Folklore 2. Chickens—Fiction

ISBN 0-06-021675-1; 0-06-021676-X (lib bdg)

LC 91-4051

The little red hen finds none of her lazy friends willing to help her plant, harvest, or grind wheat into flour, but all are eager to eat the bread she makes from it

"Barton here skillfully pares down a well-known tale for the youngest readers and listeners. Vibrant hues abound in his full-page, collage-like illustrations." Publ Wkly

The three bears. HarperCollins Pubs. 1991 unp il $15; lib bdg $14.89 (k-1)   **398.2**

1. Folklore 2. Bears—Fiction

ISBN 0-06-020423-0; 0-06-020424-9 (lib bdg)

LC 90-43151

"Here's the familiar tale of the three bears and their blond gal pal drawn for the very youngest. Byron uses large simple shapes, bright colors, and a spare text to tell his story. . . . The size of the art makes this a good choice for mother-toddler story hours." Booklist

Baylor, Byrd, 1924-

Moon song; illustrations by Ronald Himler. Scribner 1982 unp il $13.95 (1-4)   **398.2**

1. Pima Indians—Legends 2. Coyote (Legendary character) 3. Moon—Fiction

ISBN 0-684-17463-4   LC 81-18427

After giving birth to Coyote "the Moon has work to do; she can't stay with her child. But when Coyote sees her; he rushes to the top of a hill, howling for his mother. . . . That is how the Pimas tell about nights when Coyote and his descendants gather on the hills and sing their longing song to the Moon, and she fills them with mysterious power." Publ Wkly

This book "pairs Baylor's graceful language with heavily shaded black-and-white illustrations by Ronald Himler. Many of these are impressively stark and dramatic." SLJ

Begay, Shonto

Ma'ii and cousin Horned Toad; a traditional Navajo story. Scholastic 1992 unp il $14.95 (k-3)   **398.2**

1. Navajo Indians—Legends 2. Coyote (Legendary character) 3. Toads—Fiction

ISBN 0-590-45391-2   LC 91-34888

A lazy, conniving coyote takes advantage of all his animal cousins until a horned toad teaches him a lesson he never forgets

Begay "seasons his forceful language with spontaneous songs and Navajo phrases. Faintly drawn lines pull the eye to the focal points of his boldly colored, dynamic full-spread illustrations, which, like the text, pay equal tribute to the charming rogue Coyote and his earnest but resourceful cousin." Publ Wkly

Includes glossary

Belting, Natalia Maree, 1915-

Moon was tired of walking on air; [by] Natalia M. Belting; art by Will Hillenbrand. Houghton Mifflin 1992 41p il map $16.95 (4 and up)   **398.2**

1. Indians of South America—Legends

ISBN 0-395-53806-8   LC 91-20946

A collection of myths of various South American Indian tribes, explaining the natural world

"Belting's lean prose has a staccato tempo aptly suited to the oral nature of these tales, and Hillenbrand's illustrations are appropriately dark and mysterious." Publ Wkly

Bernier-Grand, Carmen T.

Juan Bobo; four folktales from Puerto Rico; retold by Carmen T. Bernier-Grand; pictures by Ernesto Ramos Nieves. HarperCollins Pubs. 1994 58p il $14; lib bdg $13.89; pa $3.75 (k-2)   **398.2**

1. Folklore—Puerto Rico

ISBN 0-06-023389-3; 0-06-023390-7 (lib bdg); 0-06-444185-7 (pa)   LC 93-12936

"An I can read book"

Four folktales from rural Puerto Rico about the comical Juan Bobo's nonsensical shenanigans

The tales "are told with immediacy and spirit. The exuberant folk-style illustrations in bright tropical colors reflect the island setting and the scenes of comic confrontation. . . . A Spanish translation is provided in small print at the back." Booklist

Berry, James

Spiderman Anancy; written by James Berry; illustrated by Joseph Olubo. Holt & Co. 1989 c1988 119p il $13.95 (5 and up)   **398.2**

1. Folklore—West Indies 2. Anansi (Legendary character)
ISBN 0-8050-1207-9   LC 89-33418

First published 1988 in the United Kingdom with title: Anancy-Spiderman

"This collection of 20 Anancy stories springs from Africa by way of the West Indies. . . . Just as in the African tales, the clever trickster uses cunning and spunk, but the colloquial speech patterns used in Berry's stories add distinctive spice. Olubo's evocative black-and-white ink drawings successfully combine the human/animal facets of the characters. A lively resource." Booklist

Bierhorst, John

Doctor Coyote; a native American Aesop's fables; retold by John Bierhorst; pictures by Wendy Watson. Macmillan 1987 unp il $15.95 (1-4)   **398.2**

1. Aztecs—Legends 2. Coyote (Legendary character) 3. Fables
ISBN 0-02-709780-3   LC 86-8669

"These stories, printed for the first time in English, are taken from an early copy of Aesop found in Mexico where the fables were translated into Aztec by a 16th century scribe. Coyote, a perpetual trickster who appears in various North American Indian tales, becomes the main character in the fables." Child Book Rev Serv

"Elaborate cartoons . . . take such vast liberties with lore (a modern gas station, a chicken in a sleeping bag, everyone decked out in squash blossom necklaces) that you're back in a secret garden of delight. Don't miss this unique, perfectly turned-out book." Read Teach

The woman who fell from the sky; the Iroquois story of creation; retold by John Bierhorst; pictures by Robert Andrew Parker. Morrow Junior Bks. 1993 unp il $15; lib bdg $14.93 (k-3)   **398.2**

1. Iroquois Indians—Legends 2. Creation—Fiction
ISBN 0-688-10680-3; 0-688-10681-1 (lib bdg)
        LC 92-5591

Describes how the creation of the world was begun by a woman who fell down to earth from the sky country, and how it was finished by her two sons Sapling and Flint

"Bierhorst's text has a dignified simplicity well matched by Parker's impressionistic watercolors. . . . Bierhorst's source note . . . is exemplary, with exact citations of all the published and unpublished sources on which he drew to adapt the tale." Bull Cent Child Books

Birdseye, Tom

A song of stars; an Asian legend; adapted by Tom Birdseye; illustrated by Ju-hong Chen. Holiday House 1990 unp il $14.95 (3-5)
    398.2

1. Folklore—China 2. Milky Way—Fiction
ISBN 0-8234-0790-X   LC 89-20066

"When Princess Chauchau, who weaves the shimmering threads of the firmament, and Newlang, the herdsman, fall in love, they neglect their important duties. As punishment, the Emperor of the Heavens banishes them to opposite sides of the Milky Way and decrees that they will be allowed to meet only once a year. When the seventh night of

the seventh month finally comes, Newlang attempts to reach his wife but is forced back by the turbulent river of stars. The merciful emperor then sends the magpies to create a bridge that enables Chauchau to join her husband." Booklist

"The lush illustrations, which at times are reminiscent of Brian Wildsmith's early work, complement the romantic quality of the retelling." Horn Book

The **Blue** fairy book; edited by Andrew Lang; with numerous illustrations by H. J. Ford and G. P. Jacomb Hood. Dover Publs. 1965 390p il pa $6.95 (4-6)   **398.2**

1. Folklore 2. Fairy tales
ISBN 0-486-21437-0

Also available in hardcover from P. Smith

Companion volume to The Green fairy book, The Red fairy book, and The Yellow fairy book, each entered separately; also available: The Pink fairy book pa $6.95 (ISBN 0-486-21792-2) and in hardcover from P. Smith

A reprint of the title first published 1889 by Longmans

A collection of thirty-seven fairy tales from various countries, consisting largely of old favorites from such sources as Perrault, the Brothers Grimm, Madame D'Aulnoy, Asbjörnsen and Möe, the Arabian Nights and Swift's Gulliver's travels

Bowden, Joan Chase, 1925-

Why the tides ebb and flow; illustrated by Marc Brown. Houghton Mifflin 1979 unp il $14.95; pa $5.95 (k-2)   **398.2**

1. Folklore 2. Tides—Fiction
ISBN 0-395-28378-7; 0-395-54952-3 (pa)
        LC 79-12359

In this folktale explaining why the sea has tides, an old woman threatens to pull the rock from the hole in the ocean floor if Sky Spirit does not honor his promise to give her shelter

"The lyrical text, perfect for reading aloud, is touched with humor and lightly seasoned with onomatopoeic expressions. The elegant illustrations sweep in broad strokes across buff-colored pages." Horn Book

Brett, Jan, 1949-

Beauty and the beast; retold and illustrated by Jan Brett. Clarion Bks. 1989 unp il lib bdg $15.95; pa $5.95 (1-3)   **398.2**

1. Folklore—France 2. Fairy tales
ISBN 0-89919-497-4 (lib bdg); 0-395-55702-X (pa)
        LC 88-16965

Through her great capacity to love, a kind and beautiful maid releases a handsome prince from the spell which has made him an ugly beast

"A Beauty of distinguished appearance, a delightful set of animal servants, and a suitably hideous Beast are presented in Jan Brett's distinctive, decorative style. Small details, such as tapestries mirroring the action of the tale, add to the effect of the simply written story." Horn Book Guide

The mitten; a Ukrainian folktale; adapted and illustrated by Jan Brett. Putnam 1989 unp il $15.95 (k-2)   **398.2**

1. Folklore—Ukraine 2. Animals—Fiction
ISBN 0-399-21920-X   LC 88-32198

"Grandmother knits snow-white mittens that Nikki takes on an adventure. Readers will enjoy the charm and humor in the portrayal of the animals as they make room for each newcomer in the mitten and sprawl in the snow after the big sneeze." Horn Book Guide

Brett, Jan, 1949-—*Continued*

Town mouse, country mouse. Putnam 1994
unp il $15.95 (k-3)   **398.2**
1. Fables 2. Mice—Fiction
ISBN 0-399-22622-2   LC 93-41227
A retelling of the Aesop fable. After trading houses, the
country mice and the town mice discover there's no place
like home
"In Brett's version, the town mice are as charming and
naive as their country cousins. . . . Brett's narrative alternates the parallel mishaps of the two sets of mice with lively, smooth writing and a deft touch of humor. . . . The
illustrations are rich with meticulous detail." SLJ

Brooke, Leonard Leslie, 1862-1940

The golden goose book; a fairy tale picture
book; illustrated by L. Leslie Brooke; with an
afterword by Neil Philip. Clarion Bks. 1992
96p il $16.95 (k-3)   **398.2**
1. Folklore
ISBN 0-395-61303-5   LC 91-26584
"An Albion book"
A reissue of the title first published 1906 by Warne
"This volume contains four stories—'The Golden
Goose,' 'The Three Bears,' 'The Three Little Pigs,' and
'Tom Thumb.' Brooke's retellings follow the classic versions
of these tales, and only an occasional archaic word or
phrase betrays their nearly century-old origins. The illustrations, which include both black line drawings and full-color
paintings, are a highlight. . . . Brooke's realistic animals and
expressive faces seem to fairly jump off the page, and children will pore over the details of the art long after the stories are finished." Booklist

Brown, Marcia, 1918-

Once a mouse; a fable cut in wood.
Atheneum Pubs. 1961 unp il $14.95; pa $3.95
(k-3)   **398.2**
1. Folklore—India 2. Fables
ISBN 0-684-12662-1; 0-689-71343-6 (pa)
Awarded the Caldecott Medal, 1962
At head of title: From ancient India
A "fable from the Indian 'Hitopadesa.' There is lively action in spreads showing how a hermit 'thinking about big
and little' suddenly saves a mouse from a crow and then
from larger enemies by turning the little creature into the
forms of bigger and bigger animals—until as a royal tiger it
has to be humbled." Horn Book
"The illustrations are remarkably beautiful. The emotional elements of the story . . . are conveyed with just as much
intensity as the purely visual ones." New Yorker

Stone soup; an old tale; told and pictured by
Marcia Brown. Scribner 1947 unp il $14; pa
$4.95 (k-3)   **398.2**
1. Folklore—France
ISBN 0-684-92296-7; 0-689-71103-4 (pa)
Also available Spanish language edition
A Caldecott Medal honor book, 1948
"When the people in a French village heard that three
soldiers were coming, they hid all their food for they knew
what soldiers are. However, when the soldiers began to
make soup with water and stones the pot gradually filled
with all the vegetables which had been hidden away. The
simple language and quiet humour of this folktale are amplified and enriched by gay and witty drawings of clever

light-hearted soldiers, and the gullible 'light-witted' peasants." Ont Libr Rev

Bruchac, Joseph, 1942-

The boy who lived with the bears and other
Iroquois stories; told by Joseph Bruchac;
illustrated by Murv Jacob. HarperCollins
Pubs. 1995 63p il $15.95; lib bdg $15.89 (3-5)
                                                      398.2
1. Iroquois Indians—Legends
ISBN 0-06-021287-X; 0-06-021288-8 (lib bdg)
                                      LC 94-9829
Presents a collection of traditional Iroquois tales in
which animals learn about the importance of caring and responsibility and the dangers of selfishness and pride
"The reteller's introduction is instructive and sets the
mood for these humorous, moral—but never didactic—
tales. Each one is carefully crafted with precise language and
striking images. . . . Jacob's stunning, brilliantly colored
paintings, one for each selection, capture the moods clearly
and gracefully." SLJ

The first strawberries; a Cherokee story;
retold by Joseph Bruchac; pictures by Anna
Vojtech. Dial Bks. for Young Readers 1993
unp il $14.99; lib bdg $14.89 (k-3)   **398.2**
1. Cherokee Indians—Legends 2. Strawberries—Fiction
ISBN 0-8037-1331-2; 0-8037-1332-0 (lib bdg)
                                      LC 91-31058
A quarrel between the first man and the first woman is
reconciled when the Sun causes strawberries to grow out of
the earth
"This retelling . . . is simply and clearly written, and as
sweet as the berries the woman stops to taste. The attractive watercolors and colored-pencil illustrations show an
idealized pastoral world." SLJ

Flying with the eagle, racing the great bear;
stories from Native North America; told by
Joseph Bruchac. BridgeWater Bks. 1993 128p
il $13.95; pa $5.95 (5 and up)   **398.2**
1. Indians of North America—Legends
ISBN 0-8167-3026-1; 0-8167-3027-X (pa)
                                     LC 93-21966
"This collection of Native American folktales revolves
around the central theme of journeying from boyhood to
manhood. . . . The stories are excellent and could be used
for independent reading or as read-alouds." Book Rep
Includes bibliography

The girl who married the Moon; tales from
Native North America; told by Joseph
Bruchac and Gayle Ross. BridgeWater Bks.
1994 127p il $13.95 (5 and up)   **398.2**
1. Indians of North America—Legends
ISBN 0-8167-3480-1   LC 93-43824
"This anthology focuses on the role of women in traditional Indian cultures. The 16 stories, collected from tribes
representing all areas of North America, range from female
rites of passage to cautionary and *pourquoi* tales. . . . Striking black-and-white stylized drawings as well as background
information about the region and the stories introduce each
section. . . . An excellent addition for storytelling collections." Booklist
Includes bibliography

Bruchac, Joseph, 1942---*Continued*

Gluskabe and the four wishes; retold by Joseph Bruchac; illustrated by Christine Nyburg Shrader. Cobblehill Bks. 1995 unp il $14.99 (k-3)   **398.2**

1. Abnaki Indians—Legends
ISBN 0-525-65164-0   LC 93-26924

"Four Abenaki men paddle to the fog-enshrouded island of the reclusive god-hero Gluskabe to make wishes. Impressed by their determination, Gluskabe hands each a bag of his granted wishes inside, but warns them not to open the bags until they reach home." Bull Cent Child Books

"The impeccably sourced, well-told tale . . . is illustrated with dramatic, atmospheric oil paintings that aptly suggest an inchoate new world." Horn Book

The great ball game; a Muskogee story; retold by Joseph Bruchac; illustrated by Susan L. Roth. Dial Bks. for Young Readers 1994 unp il $14.99; lib bdg $14.89 (k-3)   **398.2**

1. Creek Indians—Legends 2. Animals—Fiction
ISBN 0-8037-1539-0; 0-8037-1540-4 (lib bdg)
LC 93-6269

Bat, who has both wings and teeth, plays an important part in a game between the Birds and the Animals to decide which group is better

"Roth's dynamic collages combine cut papers of varied textures and hues to create a series of effective illustrations. Short and well told, this appealing *pourquoi* tale lends itself to reading aloud." Booklist

Brusca, María Cristina

When jaguars ate the moon and other stories about animals and plants of the Americas; retold by María Cristina Brusca and Tona Wilson; illustrated by María Cristina Brusca. Holt & Co. 1995 unp il $16.95 (2-4)   **398.2**

1. Indians—Legends 2. Animals—Fiction
ISBN 0-8050-2797-1   LC 93-50197

Also available Spanish language edition

"This alphabetically arranged anthology features stories based on the folklore of North and South American native cultures. A typical page has a wide, horizontal border with a letter in large type and several small pictures of animals and plants whose names begin with that letter." Booklist

"The watercolor and ink paintings are charming and interesting, and are a perfect match for the tales. The retellings are short, but each makes a complete story, and any of them would be enjoyed by listeners." SLJ

Includes bibliography

Bryan, Ashley, 1923-

Beat the story-drum, pum-pum; retold and illustrated by Ashley Bryan. Atheneum Pubs. 1980 68p il $15.95; pa $8.95 (1-4)   **398.2**

1. Folklore—Nigeria
ISBN 0-689-31356-X; 0-689-71107-7 (pa)
LC 80-12045

Coretta Scott King Award for illustration, 1981

"Five African folk tales for storytelling, humorous, informal and direct, with the rhythm and idiom of the African oral tradition. Integrated into the text are the appropriate actions, beats and chants and changing voices (even animal noises) for each character. . . . Beautifully illustrated with bold stylized woodcuts, some in black and white, some also with brick red and mustard yellow." SLJ

The cat's purr; written & illustrated by Ashley Bryan. Atheneum Pubs. 1985 42p il lib bdg $12.95 (k-2)   **398.2**

1. Folklore—West Indies 2. Cats—Fiction
ISBN 0-689-31086-2   LC 84-21534

Cat and Rat are friends, but when Rat tricks Cat and plays the cat drum, which only cats may play, Cat ends up swallowing the drum, and that is how he got his purr

"Sketchy reddish-brown drawings follow the action but lack the excitement and subtle humor of the text. However, this is a story that begs to be learned and told aloud rather than read, and it should not be negated because of the bland illustrations. The complete text of a version of the tale published in 1936 appears at the conclusion." SLJ

The ox of the wonderful horns and other African folktales; retold and illustrated by Ashley Bryan. Atheneum Pubs. 1993 c1971 42p il $14.95 (4-6)   **398.2**

1. Folklore—Africa
ISBN 0-689-31799-9

A reissue of the title first published 1971

"From Africa, five diverting folktales retold with spirit and handsomely illustrated in three colors. . . . The stories tell how Spider Ananse makes a fool of himself while seeking to make a fool of another, trouble comes to Frog when he marries two wives, Tortoise outwits trickster Hare, Frog makes good his claim that Elephant is his horse, and a boy makes his fortune with nothing but a pair of ox horns." Booklist

The story of Lightning & Thunder. Atheneum Pubs. 1993 unp il $14.95 (3-5)   **398.2**

1. Folklore—Africa
ISBN 0-689-31836-7   LC 92-40509

"A Jean Karl book"

In this retelling of a West African tale, Ma Sheep Thunder and her impetuous son Ram Lightning are forced to leave their home on Earth because of the trouble Ram causes

"Bryan tells the story . . . with playful, rhythmic prose that rhymes intermittently and begs to be read aloud. . . . Bryan's vibrant watercolors are delightful." SLJ

Caduto, Michael J.

Keepers of the night; Native American stories and nocturnal activities for children; [by] Michael J. Caduto and Joseph Bruchac; story illustrations by David Kanietakeron Fadden; chapter illustrations by Jo Levasseur and Carol Wood; foreword by Merlin D. Tuttle. Fulcrum 1994 146p il pa $14.95
398.2

1. Indians of North America—Legends 2. Nature study 3. Night—Fiction
ISBN 1-55591-177-3   LC 94-2602

Also available Keepers of the Earth (1988); Keepers of the animals (1991) and Keepers of life (1994)

Caduto, Michael J.—*Continued*
"Caduto and Bruchac use stories from various American Indian tribes as the basis for activities and lessons about the nighttime world. Written as a guide for teachers, outdoor education leaders, and other adults working with children in a nature setting, the guide gives detailed instructions for preparing, conducting, and evaluating a variety of activities that focus on the nocturnal habits of animals, on astronomy and nighttime weather, and on campfire activities, such as storytelling, dances, and games." Booklist
"The well-written chapters include discussions with illuminating scientific information." Sci Books Films
Includes glossary and bibliographical references

Carpenter, Frances
Tales of a Chinese grandmother; illustrated by Malthé Hasselriis. Tuttle 1973 261p pa $8.95 (4 and up)   398.2
1. Folklore—China 2. Fairy tales
ISBN 0-8048-1042-7
Also available in hardcover from Amereon and Buccaneer Bks.
"Tut books"
First published 1937 by Doubleday
"Thirty Chinese folk stories and legends from various sources are retold with the full flavor of the Orient. . . . They are told to a boy and girl by their grandmother on occasions in their daily life which suggest a story. Useful for storytelling." Booklist
"Phrased with grace and charm, the stories are revelatory of Chinese beliefs in years past, and of customs and home life. Drawings in color and black and white." N Y Libr

Clark, Margaret
The best of Aesop's fables; retold by Margaret Clark; illustrated by Charlotte Voake. Little, Brown 1990 61p il $16.95 (k-3)   398.2
1. Fables
ISBN 0-316-14499-1   LC 90-52642
"Joy Street books"
"This variation on the standard Aesop contains a selection of tales, simply told, with the moral omitted. . . . Voake's cool blue-green countryside and expressive animals appear ideal accompaniments to the timeless tales. A delightful, readable version of Aesop." Horn Book

The **Classic** fairy tales; [edited by] Iona and Peter Opie. Oxford Univ. Press 1974 336p il $30; pa $11.95   398.2
1. Fairy tales
ISBN 0-19-211559-6; 0-19-520219-8 (pa)
This book "contains the earliest published English texts of the tales selected, together with notes on the history and analogues of the stories." Oxford Companion to Child Lit
"Helpful indexing, bibliography, list of sources of illustrations." Choice

Climo, Shirley, 1928-
The Egyptian Cinderella; illustrated by Ruth Heller. Crowell 1989 unp il $15; lib bdg $14.89; pa $4.95 (k-3)   398.2
1. Folklore—Egypt 2. Fairy tales
ISBN 0-690-04822-X; 0-690-04824-6 (lib bdg); 0-06-443279-3 (pa)   LC 88-37547

In this version of Cinderella set in Egypt in the sixth century B.C., Rhodopes, a slave girl, eventually comes to be chosen by the Pharaoh to be his queen
"The beauty of the language is set off to perfection by Heller's arresting full-color illustrations." SLJ

The Korean Cinderella; illustrated by Ruth Heller. HarperCollins Pubs. 1993 unp il $15; lib bdg $14.89; pa $4.95 (k-3)   398.2
1. Folklore—Korea 2. Fairy tales
ISBN 0-06-020432-X; 0-06-020433-8 (lib bdg); 0-06-443397-8 (pa)   LC 91-23268
In this version of Cinderella set in ancient Korea, Pear Blossom, a stepchild, eventually comes to be chosen by the magistrate to be his wife
"Heller's paintings are exotically lush and colorful as well as engaging. Climo includes an explanatory note about Cinderella variants (the Korean version in particular), and Heller explains the decorations, costumes, and settings she used in the illustrations. An agreeable retelling of the Cinderella story." Booklist

Someone saw a spider; spider facts and folktales; illustrated by Dirk Zimmer. Crowell 1985 133p il lib bdg $14.89 (4 and up)   398.2
1. Spiders—Fiction 2. Folklore
ISBN 0-690-04436-4   LC 84-45340
"Climo retells tales from Japan, Africa, America, Scotland, and Russia, showing the spider's wise, crafty, and magical sides. There are facts about spiders—body parts, web spinning, and mating practices—as well as spider folklore. . . . Zimmer's black-and-white line drawings are humorous and, in places, as delicate as a spider's web." Booklist
Includes bibliographical references

Cohen, Barbara, 1932-1992
Yussel's prayer; a Yom Kippur story; retold by Barbara Cohen; illustrated by Michael J. Deraney. Lothrop, Lee & Shepard Bks. 1981 unp il lib bdg $12.88; pa $4.95 (3-5)   398.2
1. Jews—Folklore 2. Prayers—Fiction 3. Yom Kippur—Fiction
ISBN 0-688-00461-X (lib bdg); 0-688-04581-2 (pa)
                                                   LC 80-25377
A cowherd's simple but sincere Yom Kippur prayer is instrumental in ending the day's fast
"The legend is masterfully interpreted in soft-focus sepia drawings full of fine textures, careful shadowing, and understated detail. They're deep and rich, with a slightly mystical aura that suits the story's religious core." Booklist

Cohen, Caron Lee
The mud pony; a traditional Skidi Pawnee tale retold by Caron Lee Cohen; illustrated by Shonto Begay. Scholastic 1988 unp il $14.95; pa $4.95 (k-3)   398.2
1. Pawnee Indians—Legends 2. Horses—Fiction
ISBN 0-590-41525-5; 0-590-41526-3 (pa)
                                                   LC 87-23451
A poor boy becomes a powerful leader when Mother Earth turns his mud pony into a real one, but after the pony turns back to mud, he must find his own strength
"The text is powerful because it is spare and unadorned. It is extended well by the softly toned, full-color, impressionistic pictures." Helbig. This land is our land

Cole, Joanna

Bony-Legs; pictures by Dirk Zimmer. Four Winds Press 1983 unp il $15 (k-3)　　**398.2**

1. Folklore—Russia 2. Fairy tales
ISBN 0-02-722970-X　　　　　　LC 82-7424

Also available in paperback from Scholastic

"Based on the tale 'Baba-Yaga' in Russian fairy tales by Aleksandr Afanas'ev." Verso of title page

When a terrible witch vows to eat her for supper, a little girl escapes with the help of a mirror and comb given to her by the witch's cat and dog

"The rich text leaves out some of the grisly details of the original without castrating the story, and it is matched by clear yet densely lined drawings that borrow some from Ivan Bilibin's earlier illustrations, yet add amusing detail and fine design and layout of their own." SLJ

Compton, Joanne

Ashpet; an Appalachian tale; retold by Joanne Compton; illustrated by Kenn Compton. Holiday House 1994 unp il $15.95 (k-3)　　**398.2**

1. Folklore—Appalachian Mountains
ISBN 0-8234-1106-0　　　　　LC 93-16034

In this Appalachian variant of the Cinderella tale, old Granny helps Ashpet attend the church picnic where she charms Doc Ellison's son but loses one of her fancy red shoes

"The basic outline of the tale is clear enough and the frisky dialogue . . . adds zip to the familiar story. Compton's line-and-watercolor illustrations set amiably doltish cartooned figures against a gentle landscape." Bull Cent Child Books

Sody Sallyratus; retold by Joanne Compton; illustrated by Kenn Compton. Holiday House 1995 unp il $15.95 (k-3)　　**398.2**

1. Folklore—Appalachian Mountains
ISBN 0-8234-1165-6　　　　　LC 94-28261

When Ma runs out of baking soda for her biscuits, two of her sons and Ma herself disappear on the way to the store, leaving her son Jack to solve the mystery

"Compton's lively pen-and-ink cartoons . . . extend the text with lots of humorous details. The author's language is colorful and has lots of child appeal." SLJ

Compton, Patricia A., 1936-

The terrible eek; a Japanese tale; retold by Patricia A. Compton; illustrated by Sheila Hamanaka. Simon & Schuster Bks. for Young Readers 1991 unp il $14.95; pa $5.95 (k-3)　　**398.2**

1. Folklore—Japan
ISBN 0-671-73737-6; 0-671-87169-2 (pa)
　　　　　　　　　　　　　　LC 91-6421

"In a small house in the mountains of Japan, a boy asks his father if he is ever afraid. The father says he fears a thief in the night, and the thief lurking on the roof feels proud. The father says he fears the wolf, and a wolf skulking outside feels proud. But when the father says he fears a terrible leak, the wolf does not know what that is, and the thief hears 'terrible eek.' . . . Hamanaka's oil paintings, full of exaggerated expressions and movements, are a perfect slapstick accompaniment to the wild antics in this Japanese folktale." Booklist

Conover, Chris, 1950-

Mother Goose and the sly fox; retold and with pictures by Chris Conover. Farrar, Straus & Giroux 1989 unp il $15; pa $4.95 (k-2)　　**398.2**

1. Folklore
ISBN 0-374-35072-8; 0-374-45397-7 (pa)
　　　　　　　　　　　　　　LC 89-45502

"Mother Goose, who watches over her seven goslings and one do-nothing mouse, goes to market one day. The goslings innocently open the door to a hungry fox, who needs food for his own young cubs. Six of the goslings are bagged and carted off, but Mother Goose saves her children when the lazy fox takes a nap." Publ Wkly

"Conover's glowing watercolors outlined in ink are full of charming detail; the fully realized animals, dressed in seventeenth-century garb, star in evocative double- and single-page spreads." Booklist

Cooper, Susan, 1935-

The selkie girl; retold by Susan Cooper; illustrated by Warwick Hutton. Margaret K. McElderry Bks. 1986 unp il $14.95; pa $4.95 (1-4)　　**398.2**

1. Folklore—Great Britain 2. Seals (Animals)—Fiction
ISBN 0-689-50390-3; 0-689-71467-4 (pa)
　　　　　　　　　　　　　　LC 86-70147

A retelling of the legend from British coasts and islands in which a man falls in love with a beautiful seal girl and forces her to live on land and be his bride

"The prose is rhythmic, the pictures cool and blue-hued, with loose shapes and pages bled to give a sense of boundlessness. The selkie appears naked with her sisters in the first spread, but discreetly so, all the better to contrast with her primly confined form as she stares longingly to sea with her first child. The seascapes and shore scenes are light-filled, vintage Hutton." Bull Cent Child Books

The silver cow: a Welsh tale; retold by Susan Cooper; illustrated by Warwick Hutton. Atheneum Pubs. 1983 unp il lib bdg $14.95; pa $4.95 (1-4)　　**398.2**

1. Folklore—Wales 2. Cattle—Fiction
ISBN 0-689-50236-2 (lib bdg); 0-689-71512-9 (pa)
　　　　　　　　　　　　　　LC 82-13928

"A Margaret K. McElderry book"

A young Welsh boy is rewarded for his beautiful harp playing with a silver cow, the gift of the magic people living in the lake. The cow makes his family rich but when his father becomes greedy the magic people take their revenge

"A lilting text, complemented by luminous watercolor illustrations, captures the enchantment inherent in a traditional tale explaining the genesis of the water lilies fringing Llyn Barfog, 'the bearded lake,' set high in the Welsh hills." Horn Book

Tam Lin; retold by Susan Cooper; illustrated by Warwick Hutton. Margaret K. McElderry Bks. 1991 unp il $14.95 (1-4)　　**398.2**

1. Folklore—Scotland 2. Fairy tales
ISBN 0-689-50505-1　　　　　LC 90-5571

A retelling of the old Scottish ballad in which a young girl rescues the human knight Tam Lin from his bondage to the Elfin Queen

"Susan Cooper's prose rendering, based on several versions, is a beautifully paced literary fairy tale, told and pictured with precision and restraint. . . . Warwick Hutton is a masterful watercolorist, and his paintings literally and fig-

Cooper, Susan, 1935- — *Continued*
uratively illuminate the story of faithfulness, heroism, and love. Close-ups lend immediacy to the dramatic action, and panoramic scenes, often with the use of chiaroscuro, convey emotion and establish atmosphere—idyllic, eerie, fearful, and ultimately triumphant." Horn Book

Courlander, Harold, 1908-1996
The cow-tail switch, and other West African stories; by Harold Courlander and George Herzog; drawings by Madye Lee Chastain. Holt & Co. 1987 143p il $13.95; pa $7.95 (4-6)
398.2
1. Folklore—West Africa 2. Ashanti (African people)—Folklore
ISBN 0-8050-0288-X; 0-8050-0298-7 (pa)
LC 86-46267
A Newbery Medal honor book, 1948
A reissue of the title first published 1947
"The seventeen stories mostly gathered in the Ashanti country, are fresh to collections and are told with humor and originality. Their themes, chosen with discrimination, are frequently primitive explanations of the origin of folk sayings and customs, or show examples of animal trickery and ingenuity." Horn Book
Includes glossary and bibliography

Craig, Helen
The town mouse and the country mouse; retold and illustrated by Helen Craig. Candlewick Press 1992 unp il $13.95; pa $5.99 (k-3)
398.2
1. Fables 2. Mice—Fiction
ISBN 1-56402-102-5; 1-56402-467-9 (pa)
LC 91-58761
A retelling of the Aesop fable in which a town mouse and a country mouse exchange visits and they find that they prefer very different ways of life
"Craig has personalized her characters, naming them Charlie and Tyler, and she adds embellishments to the story. . . . There's plenty of visual detail to enjoy in Craig's watercolor art, and the text is full of fun." Booklist

Crespo, George, 1962-
How the sea began; a Taino myth; retold and illustrated by George Crespo. Clarion Bks. 1993 unp il $14.95 (2-4)
398.2
1. Taino Indians—Legends 2. Folklore—Puerto Rico
ISBN 0-395-63033-9
LC 91-39651
"This simple retelling of a Taino myth explains how the sea was formed when salt-water and ocean creatures poured from the burial gourd of the best hunter in the village, creating the island of Puerto Rico. Crespo's primitive oil paintings reflect the harmonious colors of nature. . . . This unusual Puerto Rican Indian legend provides an interesting read-aloud as well as a cultural lesson. Source notes and a pronunciation guide are appended." SLJ

Creswick, Paul, 1866-1947
Robin Hood; illustrated by N.C. Wyeth. Scribner 1984 362p il $24.95 (5 and up)
398.2
1. Robin Hood (Legendary character)
ISBN 0-684-18162-2
LC 84-10662

A reissue of a title first published 1917 by McKay
Recounts the life and adventures of Robin Hood, who, with his band of followers, lived as an outlaw in Sherwood Forest dedicated to fight against tyranny

Crossley-Holland, Kevin
British folk tales; new versions. Orchard Bks. 1987 383p $22.95 (4 and up)
398.2
1. Folklore—Great Britain
ISBN 0-531-05733-X
LC 87-9918
This collection includes "ghost stories, hero tales, tales of trials and conflict, brave princes, tricksters, fairies, and goblins. . . . Familiar old favorites such as 'Jack and the Beanstalk' and 'The Three Bears' rub elbows with lesser known versions of old favorites such as 'Mossycoat,' a version of Cinderella, and 'Hughbo,' a version of 'The Shoemaker and the Elves.' . . . A pronunciation guide (although it is not comprehensive) and an appendix giving scholarly sources and author's comments adds to the value of this highly recommended collection." SLJ

Cruz, Alejandro
The woman who outshone the sun; the legend of Lucia Zenteno; from a poem by Alejandro Cruz Martinez; pictures by Fernando Olivera; story by Rosalma Zubizarreta, Harriet Rohmer, David Schecter. Children's Bk. Press 1991 30p $14.95; pa $6.95 (k-3)
398.2
1. Zapotec Indians—Legends 2. Bilingual books—English-Spanish
ISBN 0-89239-101-4; 0-89239-126-X (pa)
LC 91-16646
Title page and text in English and Spanish
Retells the Zapotec legend of Lucia Zenteno, a beautiful woman with magical powers who is exiled from a mountain village and takes its water away in punishment
This "Hispanic folktale is skillfully told, and is solid and colorfully steeped with imagery of the earth and sky. Both the Spanish and English read gracefully, and the poetic use of language suits the story well for telling. The illustrations have a sense of volume that is reminiscent of Orozco." SLJ

Curry, Jane Louise, 1932-
Back in the beforetime; tales of the California Indians; retold by Jane Louise Curry; illustrated by James Watts. Margaret K. McElderry Bks. 1987 134p il $14 (4-6)
398.2
1. Indians of North America—Legends 2. Coyote (Legendary character)
ISBN 0-689-50410-1
LC 86-21339
A retelling of twenty-two legends about the creation of the world from a variety of California Indian tribes
"The predominantly humorous tone of the stories is highlighted by the black-and-white illustrations, each with its geometrically patterned border. Curry's rhythmic prose lends itself well to storytelling or reading aloud." SLJ

Robin Hood and his Merry Men; retold by Jane Louise Curry; illustrated by John Lytle. Margaret K. McElderry Bks. 1994 42p il $13.95 (3-5)
398.2
1. Robin Hood (Legendary character)
ISBN 0-689-50609-0
LC 94-14023

Curry, Jane Louise, 1932- — *Continued*

Recounts the life and adventures of Robin Hood, who, with his band of followers, lived in Sherwood Forest as an outlaw dedicated to fighting tyranny

"Curry provides a short, fluid retelling of the Robin Hood legends based on a fifteenth-century poem. . . . Thirteen nicely executed ink-and-wash drawings illustrate the book. Short and simple enough for children new to chapter books, this episodic volume will reward readers with its appealing subject, attractive design, and well-told tales." Booklist

Czernecki, Stefan

The singing snake; story by Stefan Czernecki and Timothy Rhodes; illustrated by Stefan Czernecki. Hyperion Bks. for Children 1993 40p il $14.95; lib bdg $14.89; pa $4.95 (k-3) **398.2**

1. Folklore—Australia 2. Snakes—Fiction

ISBN 1-56282-399-X; 1-56282-400-7 (lib bdg); 0-7868-1036-X (pa) LC 92-85515

A retelling of the Australian aboriginal tale about a snake that swallows a lark in an effort to win a singing contest

"Formal in composition, Czernecki's distinctive illustrations—in which the stylized forms of animals and plants are outlined and stippled with contrasting colors—reflect the artist's research into Australian aboriginal painting. This eye-catching picture book will find use as a read-aloud in the classroom or library." Booklist

Daly, Niki, 1946-

Why the Sun & Moon live in the sky. Lothrop, Lee & Shepard Bks. 1995 unp il $15; lib bdg $14.93 (k-3) **398.2**

1. Folklore—Nigeria 2. Sun—Fiction 3. Moon—Fiction

ISBN 0-688-13331-2; 0-688-13332-0 (lib bdg) LC 93-47304

"Sun, an adventurous roamer, lives on earth with Moon, a domestic homebody. Sun invites Sea and all her children to visit, but Sea floods the house, causing great distress for Moon. The flooding forces Sun and Moon into the sky, where they have been to this day." Booklist

"Daly's witty illustrations immerse this Nigerian tale in offbeat charm. His sophisticated watercolors showcase sketchy images borrowed from Renaissance motifs." Publ Wkly

Day, Nancy Raines

The lion's whiskers; an Ethiopian folktale; illustrated by Ann Grifalconi. Scholastic 1995 unp il $14.95 (k-3) **398.2**

1. Folklore—Ethiopia 2. Stepmothers—Fiction

ISBN 0-590-45803-5 LC 94-14453

In this tale from the Amhara people of Ethiopia, a patient woman uses her experience with a wild lion to win the love of her new stepson

"Grifalconi's striking illustrations are constructed from textured papers, photographs, cloth and other materials to great three-dimensional effect. This provides an excellent counterpoint to tales of wicked stepmothers, with its African setting providing additional interest." Bull Cent Child Books

De Paola, Tomie, 1934-

Christopher, the holy giant. Holiday House 1994 unp il $15.95; pa $6.95 (k-3) **398.2**

1. Christopher, Saint, 3rd cent.?

ISBN 0-8234-0862-0; 0-8234-1169-9 (pa) LC 90-49926

As Reprobus carries a child across a river one stormy night, the boy gets heavier and heavier until Reprobus feels he is carrying the world on his shoulders—thus goes the legend of the name Christ-bearer, or Christopher

"DePaola's prose is simple and eloquent, and his expressive folk art style, here rendered in the intense but muted shades of the desert, is perfectly attuned to the legend's reverent tone." Publ Wkly

The clown of God; an old story; told and illustrated by Tomie de Paola. Harcourt Brace Jovanovich 1978 unp il $13.95; pa $6 (k-3) **398.2**

1. Legends 2. Miracles—Fiction 3. Christmas—Fiction

ISBN 0-15-219175-5; 0-15-618192-4 (pa) LC 78-3845

"An orphan whose juggling skill led him to a career as a traveling entertainer has grown old and clumsy and returns as a hungry beggar to his birthplace. On Christmas Eve in the monastery church a miracle occurs as he summons his last strength to make his only possible offering

"Mr. de Paola has written the tale with love, tenderness, and joy. He has executed authentic Renaissance illustrations that are magnificent in design and beauty." Child Book Rev Serv

Jamie O'Rourke and the big potato; an Irish folktale; retold and illustrated by Tomie dePaola. Putnam 1992 unp il $14.95 (k-3) **398.2**

1. Folklore—Ireland

ISBN 0-399-22257-X LC 91-10626

The laziest man in all of Ireland catches a leprechaun, who offers a potato seed instead of a pot of gold for his freedom

"Illustrated in dePaola's signature style, this has an inviting look. Buoyant watercolors are framed by thin orange borders, but the potato simply can't be contained and bulges beyond the boundaries, graphic proof of its enormous size, an engaging read-aloud choice for Saint Patrick's Day." Booklist

The legend of Old Befana; an Italian Christmas story; retold and illustrated by Tomie de Paola. Harcourt Brace Jovanovich 1980 unp il lib bdg $14.95; pa $4.95 (k-3) **398.2**

1. Befana (Legendary character) 2. Folklore—Italy 3. Christmas—Fiction

ISBN 0-15-243816-5 (lib bdg); 0-15-243817-3 (pa) LC 80-12293

Because Befana's household chores kept her from finding the Baby King, she searches to this day, leaving gifts for children on the Feast of the Three Kings

This version of the Italian legend "is attractively designed with rich colors and decorative detail. The tale is told in simple but effective language." SLJ

De Paola, Tomie, 1934-—*Continued*

The legend of the Indian paintbrush; retold and illustrated by Tomie dePaola. Putnam 1988 unp il lib bdg $14.95; pa $5.95 (k-3)
398.2

1. Indians of North America—Legends

ISBN 0-399-21534-4 (lib bdg); 0-399-21777-0 (pa)
LC 87-20160

Also available Spanish language edition

A "folktale of the Plains Indians that reveals how the Indian Paintbrush, the state flower of Wyoming, first bloomed. An Indian boy's dream to recreate the colors of the sunset comes true when he discovers paintbrushes filled with the colors he needs. A voice in the night had promised him this because he had shared his artistic talent with his people." Child Book Rev Serv

"The native American motifs are rendered simply and authentically; the night sky and glorious sunset spreads are truly beautiful with line, color, and form perfectly balanced to capture the text." Horn Book

The legend of the Persian carpet; retold by Tomie DePaola; illustrated by Claire Ewart. Putnam 1993 unp il $14.95 (k-3)   **398.2**

1. Folklore—Iran

ISBN 0-399-22415-7   LC 91-45816

"A Whitebird book"

Tells how the first Persian carpet was created to replace King Balash's lost treasure
The story is told "in simple, direct prose. . . . The atmospheric jewel-tone watercolors have a strong sense of color and light and shadow." Booklist

The legend of the poinsettia; retold and illustrated by Tomie de Paola. Putnam 1994 unp il $15.95 (k-3)   **398.2**

1. Folklore—Mexico   2. Flowers—Fiction
3. Christmas—Fiction

ISBN 0-399-21692-8   LC 92-20459

Also available Spanish language edition

When Lucida is unable to finish her gift for the Baby Jesus in time for the Christmas procession, a miracle enables her to offer the beautiful flower we now call the poinsettia
"dePaola establishes a sense of place in his use of glowing colors and architectural details as he retells another legend of miraculous transcendence." Horn Book

Tony's bread: an Italian folktale. Putnam 1989 unp il $14.95 (k-3)   **398.2**

1. Folklore—Italy

ISBN 0-399-21693-6   LC 88-7687

"A Whitebird book"

"This tale captures the flavor of an Italian folk tale with both textual and visual humor. The story of Angelo—a rich, young nobleman from Milan who attempts to win the hand of his true love, the beautiful daughter of Tony the baker—explains the origin of *panettone,* the delicious Milanese Christmas bread made with eggs, raisins, and candied fruit. . . . The pictures and story combine to make a delectable Christmas treat." Horn Book

De Regniers, Beatrice Schenk

Little Sister and the Month Brothers; retold by Beatrice Schenk de Regniers; pictures by Margot Tomes. Lothrop, Lee & Shepard Bks. 1994 unp il lib bdg $13.93; pa $4.95 (k-3)
398.2

1. Slavs—Folklore 2. Fairy tales

ISBN 0-688-05293-2 (lib bdg); 0-688-13633-8 (pa)
LC 93-44053

A reissue of the title first published 1976 by Seabury Press

A retelling of the Slavic fairy tale in which the Month Brothers' magic helps Little Sister fulfill seemingly impossible tasks which prove the undoing of her greedy stepmother and stepsister

"Tomes's intimate, unpretentious illustrations extend the text brilliantly. A timeless treasure." Horn Book Guide

Dee, Ruby

Tower to heaven; retold by Ruby Dee; illustrated by Jennifer Bent. Holt & Co. 1991 unp il $14.95 (k-3)   **398.2**

1. Folklore—Africa

ISBN 0-8050-1460-8   LC 90-34131

When Yaa, who loves to talk while she works, hits the sky god one too many times with her pestle he disappears high up into the heavens and the villagers decide to build a tower to heaven to find him

"Youngsters will warm to the story's sly humor enlivened by boldly defined and vividly colored primitive art." Publ Wkly

DeFelice, Cynthia C.

The dancing skeleton; illustrated by Robert Andrew Parker. Macmillan 1989 unp il $13.95 (k-3)   **398.2**

1. Folklore—United States

ISBN 0-02-726452-1   LC 88-30245

"Aaron Kelly got up out of his grave, went home and sat down in his chair by the fire. Here's the story of how the fiddler who wanted to court Aaron's widow got rid of the skeleton. The elegant watercolor illustrations capture the way the skeleton dances himself to bits, as well as the mood of night in the graveyard." N Y Times Book Rev

Three perfect peaches; a French folktale; retold by the Wild Washerwomen Storytellers, Cynthia DeFelice & Mary DeMarsh; pictures by Irene Trivas. Orchard Bks. 1995 unp il $15.95; lib bdg $16.99 (k-3)   **398.2**

1. Folklore—France 2. Fairy tales

ISBN 0-531-06872-2; 0-531-08722-0 (lib bdg)
LC 94-24872

"A Richard Jackson book"

"The youngest of three brothers cures a princess's illness with three perfect peaches and wins her hand in marriage through courtesy, craft, and the help of a magic whistle. . . . The rhythm and pace of DeFelice and DeMarsh's narrative make it ideal for reading aloud, and it is embellished in a way that invites participation. Trivas's vibrant, fluid, cheery illustrations round out the text perfectly—they are done in glowing, jewel-like colors and are full of nifty humorous touches." SLJ

Demi, 1942-

The empty pot. Holt & Co. 1990 unp il $15.95 (k-3)   **398.2**

1. Folklore—China

ISBN 0-8050-1217-6   LC 89-39062

"Ping is a Chinese boy with an emerald green thumb; he can make anything grow 'as if by magic.' One day the Emperor announces that he needs a successor. . . . He gives each child one seed, and the one who grows the best flower will take over after him. . . . On the day of the competition, [Ping] is the only child with an empty pot; all the others bring lush plants. But the Emperor has tricked everyone by distributing cooked seeds, unable to grow; and Ping, with his empty pot, is the only honest gardener—and the winner." Publ Wkly

"This simple story with its clear moral is illustrated with beautiful paintings. . . . A beautifully crafted book that will be enjoyed as much for the richness of its illustrations as for the simplicity of its story." SLJ

The Firebird. Holt & Co. 1994 unp il $16.95 (k-3)   **398.2**

1. Folklore—Russia

ISBN 0-8050-3244-4   LC 94-4376

"Dimitri's Horse of Power helps him bring home the marvelous Firebird, do away with the terrible Tsar Ivan, and marry the fairy princess Vassilissa, who also has a hand in Dimitri's success. Demi's illustrations, with their intricate patterns and liberal use of gold, are well suited to her retelling of the Russian tale." Horn Book Guide

The magic tapestry; a Chinese folktale; retold and illustrated by Demi. Holt & Co. 1994 unp il $17.95 (k-3)   **398.2**

1. Folklore—China

ISBN 0-8050-2810-2   LC 93-11426

The youngest of three sons must overcome frightening obstacles to win back his mother's heavenly tapestry, stolen by the fairies of Sun Mountain

"The grandeur of the story is enhanced by the liberal use of shimmering gold in the art. Set against white backgrounds and surrounded by narrow borders, the delicate paintings, with their small figures, vibrant colors, and stippled textures, resemble the hanging scrolls of ancient China." Booklist

The stonecutter. Crown 1995 unp il $15; lib bdg $15.99 (k-3)   **398.2**

1. Folklore—China

ISBN 0-517-59864-7; 0-517-59865-5 (lib bdg)
     LC 93-42413

"A humble stonecutter, dissatisfied with his lot, longs for wealth and power. A helpful angel grants him a series of escalating wishes, but in the end he becomes a stonecutter again—a happy one this time." SLJ

"The moral is simple enough for youngsters to grasp, and Demi's delicate pen-and-ink drawings, painted in vibrant hues and placed against gold backgrounds, have plenty of intricate details." Booklist

The **Diane** Goode book of American folk tales and songs; collected by Ann Durell. Dutton 1989 63p il music lib bdg $15.95 (2-5)
     398.2

1. Folklore—United States 2. Folk songs—United States

ISBN 0-525-44458-0   LC 89-1097

"Ann Durell has selected nine stories and seven songs from various regions and ethnic groups, and Diane Goode's wonderfully expressive illustrations grace every page. . . . The folk songs . . . will be familiar to most schoolchildren, and because the simple melodic lines are included, they will be accessible for singing and playing." Horn Book

Diane Goode's book of scary stories & songs. Dutton Children's Bks. 1994 64p il music $15.99 (2-5)   **398.2**

1. Ghost stories 2. Folklore 3. Folk songs

ISBN 0-525-45175-7   LC 93-32610

Selections collected by Lucia Monfried

This "anthology of mildly scary stories, songs, and verse includes folktales from English and American (including Native American and African American) sources. Varied in tone and subject, the selections are consistently entertaining. Appealing, full-color illustrations, from the weird to the wonderful, appear throughout the book, lending more of a sense of humor than a sense of menace." Booklist

Includes bibliographical references

Diane Goode's book of silly stories & songs. Dutton Children's Bks. 1992 64p il music $15 (2-5)   **398.2**

1. Folklore 2. Folk songs

ISBN 0-525-44967-1   LC 91-38192

This is a collection of folktales and songs from around the world

"The retellings are bare-bones versions of the stories that retain the flavor and authenticity of the originals, while being accessible to young children. . . . Goode's illustrations are crisp, playful line-and-wash paintings that clearly celebrate the comic tone of the text." SLJ

Includes bibliographical references

Dixon, Ann, 1954-

How Raven brought light to people; retold by Ann Dixon; illustrated by James Watts. Margaret K. McElderry Bks. 1992 unp il $13.95 (k-3)   **398.2**

1. Tlingit Indians—Legends 2. Ravens—Fiction

ISBN 0-689-50536-1   LC 90-28948

This "adaptation of an Alaskan Tlingit Indian legend explains how Raven gave the sun, moon, and stars back to man and how he got his feathers sooty in the process. . . . The story is fast moving with its magical transformations, and the language is simple and direct. The illustrations are dramatically shaded watercolor and acrylic drawings full of Native American detail and design." SLJ

Dupré, Judith

The mouse bride; a Mayan folk tale; illustrated by Fabricio Vanden Broeck. Knopf 1993 unp il $8.99; lib bdg $9.99 (k-3)
     398.2

1. Mayas—Legends

ISBN 0-679-83273-4; 0-679-93273-9 (lib bdg)
     LC 92-15275

Also available Spanish language edition

"Two mice set out to find a perfect husband for their perfect daughter. They first ask the Moon's advice and are directed to the Sun then to the Cloud, the Wind and the Wall. They learn that the Wall considers the mouse more powerful than he so the mice return home to find a perfect mouse groom waiting." Child Book Rev Serv

"The detailed, muted blue, green, and brown drawings match the gentle prose." Booklist

Early, Margaret, 1951-
William Tell; retold and illustrated by Margaret Early. Abrams 1991 unp il $17.95
398.2

1. Tell, William 2. Legends—Switzerland
ISBN 0-8109-3854-5

This is a retelling of the legend of the Swiss archer who saved his country from the oppressive Austrian emperor Gessler
"Early's illustrations, lavishly embellished with gold, reflect the medieval period in which the events took place. A unique border decorates each page, framing the elaborate paintings with elegant repetitive designs, lending a fittingly mannered feeling to the art. Even the skies, the water, and the trees are made up of minutely executed patterns. A welcome new retelling that makes this inspiring story of freedom accessible to a new generation of young people." Horn Book

Ehlert, Lois, 1934-
Moon rope. Un lazo a la luna; a Peruvian folktale; translated into Spanish by Amy Prince. Harcourt Brace Jovanovich 1992 unp il $14.95 (k-3)
398.2

1. Folklore—Peru 2. Moon—Fiction 3. Bilingual books—English-Spanish
ISBN 0-15-255343-6 LC 91-36438

An adaptation of the Peruvian folktale in which Fox and Mole try to climb to the moon on a rope woven of grass
"Designed as a bilingual book from title page to the concluding double-page spread, this handsome addition to material for multicultural education impels young audiences to try reading the story in both languages. . . . The text moves smoothly, just right for reading aloud; the pictures are dramatic abstractions that glow like jewels against richly toned, calendared pages." Horn Book

Emberley, Rebecca
Three cool kids. Little, Brown 1995 unp il lib bdg $15.95 (k-3)
398.2

1. Folklore 2. Goats—Fiction
ISBN 0-316-23666-7 LC 93-40113

"In this modernized urban version of the 'Three Billy Goats Gruff,' Big, Little and Middle Kid want to move to 'greener pastures' in a different vacant lot, but must first cross a sewer grating where a ferocious rat lives." Child Book Rev Serv
"Large, crisp collages made from paper, corrugated cardboard, and natural objects bring the goats to vibrant life and create the perfect backdrop for the action. . . . The text is witty, the illustrations whimsical, and the combination utterly charming." SLJ

Esbensen, Barbara Juster
The great buffalo race; how the buffalo got his hump: a Seneca tale; retold by Barbara Juster Esbensen; illustrated by Helen K. Davie. Little, Brown 1994 unp il $14.95 (k-3)
398.2

1. Seneca Indians—Legends 2. Bison—Fiction
ISBN 0-316-24982-3 LC 92-23410

A retelling of the Seneca legend in which the buffalo receives its hump from the Great Spirit

Ladder to the sky; how the gift of healing came to the Ojibway nation: a legend; retold by Barbara Juster Esbensen; illustrated by Helen K. Davie. Little, Brown 1989 unp il $15.95 (k-3)
398.2

1. Ojibwa Indians—Legends
ISBN 0-316-24952-1 LC 87-22729

"A retelling of the Ojibway or Chippewa legend that explains why healing powers were given to Indian medicine men. Elegant, luminous illustrations are set within borders or entwined leaves and herbs. A substantial addition to folklore collections about native Americans." Horn Book Guide

The star maiden: an Ojibway tale; retold by Barbara Juster Esbensen; illustrated by Helen K. Davie. Little, Brown 1988 unp il lib bdg $15.95; pa $5.95 (k-3)
398.2

1. Ojibwa Indians—Legends
ISBN 0-316-24951-3 (lib bdg); 0-316-24955-6 (pa)
LC 87-3247

"Based on an Ojibway or Chippewa Native American legend, this tells why there are water lilies. It is a lovely retelling which keeps the dignity and wonder associated with Native American attitudes towards nature. The watercolor illustrations are remarkable for their authentic details and the borders which are based on Ojibway pattern. This is a must for units on American Indians." Child Book Rev Serv

Fang, Linda
The Ch'i-lin purse; a collection of ancient Chinese stories; retold by Linda Fang; pictures by Jeanne M. Lee. Farrar, Straus & Giroux 1994 127p il $16 (5 and up)
398.2

1. Folklore—China
ISBN 0-374-31241-9 LC 94-9909

A collection of "Chinese stories derived from the history of the Warring States Period (770-221 B.C.E.) and from operatic versions of popular tales. Retellings are vivid, lively, and read aloud well. Many have a moral, and all are entertaining. . . . The black-and-white illustrations—one per selection—are graceful, depicting widely different epochs with amazing accuracy." SLJ
Includes glossary and bibliographical references

Faulkner, William J.
Brer Tiger and the big wind; illustrated by Roberta Wilson. Morrow Junior Bks. 1995 unp il $15; lib bdg $14.93 (k-3)
398.2

1. African Americans—Folklore 2. Folklore—United States
ISBN 0-688-12985-4; 0-688-12986-2 (lib bdg)
LC 94-15408

"Brer Tiger guards the only source of water on a parched earth, preventing other animals from relieving their thirst. Along comes Brer Rabbit, and . . . he convinces Brer Tiger that a big wind is going to blow everyone off the earth. After the thoroughly tricked tiger is secured to a tree, the animals get all the water they need. . . . With attractive, full-page, egg tempera paintings in gold and sienna tones, this picture book will be a solid addition to comparative folklore and multicultural collections." Booklist

Forest, Heather

The baker's dozen; a colonial American tale; retold by Heather Forest; illustrated by Susan Gaber. Harcourt Brace Jovanovich 1988 unp il hardcover o.p. paperback available $4.95 (k-3)   **398.2**

1. Folklore—United States

ISBN 0-15-205687-4 (pa)   LC 87-17103

"Gulliver books"

"A seventeenth-century legend describes the rise and fall of a prosperous baker whose famous St. Nicholas cookies bring him a booming business until he begins to cheat his customers. . . . A mysterious old woman curses him for his greed, and thereafter everything goes wrong. Only on her return visit, when he adds an extra cookie to her dozen, does good fortune return." Bull Cent Child Books

"Gaber's elegant watercolors are vivid and stylized, showing a dusted palette of burgundies with charcoal and burnished oranges. This is a fine explanation of a long-standing custom, and Forest backs it up with an author's note on the facts." Publ Wkly

The woman who flummoxed the fairies; an old tale from Scotland; retold by Heather Forest; illustrated by Susan Gaber. Harcourt Brace Jovanovich 1990 unp il $14.95 (k-3)   **398.2**

1. Folklore—Scotland 2. Cake—Fiction

ISBN 0-15-200648-6   LC 88-28448

"Gulliver books"

Asked to make a cake for the fairies, a clever bakerwoman must figure out a way to prevent the fairies from wanting to keep her with them always to bake her delicious cakes

"While depicting a strong, resourceful heroine, Forest's graceful retelling perfectly captures the story's fairy-tale flavor. Using deep tones of violet, blue and green, Gaber's haunting paintings range from the wonderfully eerie to the comfortably reassuring." Publ Wkly

Fox, Paula

Amzat and his brothers: three Italian tales; remembered by Floriano Vecchi and retold by Paula Fox; illustrations by Emily McCully. Orchard Bks. 1993 67p il $15.95; lib bdg $15.99 (3-5)   **398.2**

1. Folklore—Italy

ISBN 0-531-05462-4; 0-531-08612-7 (lib bdg)
LC 92-19494

Also available in paperback from Dell

"In the first tale, clever Amzat and his wife foil his greedy brothers' schemes to cheat him out of his property. The second story is a variation of 'The Bremen Town Musicians.' . . . And in the final story, this one in the noodlehead tradition, the author introduces Olimpia and her simpleton son Cucol. . . . Paula Fox has retained the darker elements that are as much a part of folktales in their original forms as the humor. . . . Emily McCully's drawings, with their heavy deep brown lines and animated characters, pick up both aspects of these intriguing tales." Horn Book

Freedman, Florence B. (Florence Bernstein)

Brothers: a Hebrew legend; retold by Florence B. Freedman; with illustrations by Robert Andrew Parker. Harper & Row 1985 unp il o.p. (k-3)   **398.2**

1. Jews—Folklore 2. Brothers—Fiction

LC 85-42616

"Simple retelling of an ancient Hebrew legend about the loving relationship between Dan and Joel. When hard times strike, each brother displays his concern for the other's wellbeing" Soc Educ

"Parker echoes the simplicity in his striking full-page watercolor illustrations with pen-and-ink detail. The use of shadows and subtle shadings gives a feeling of warmth to the golden-toned afternoons and the brilliant blueness of night. The religious aspect of this Hebrew legend has been played down here, giving it universal appeal." SLJ

Fritz, Jean

Brendan the Navigator; a history mystery about the discovery of America; illustrated by Enrico Arno. Coward, McCann & Geoghegan 1979 31p il $14.95 (3-5)   **398.2**

1. Brendan, Saint, the Voyager, ca. 483-577 2. America—Exploration

ISBN 0-698-20473-5   LC 78-13247

Recounts St. Brendan's life and voyage to North America long before the Vikings arrived

"Jean Fritz's narrative is beautifully cadenced, lively and wry. Her historical postscript is all right, too, and the two-color illustrations are appropriately convoluted and Celtic." N Y Times Book Rev

Galdone, Joanna

The tailypo; a ghost story; told by Joanna Galdone; illustrated by Paul Galdone. Clarion Bks. 1984 unp il hardcover o.p. paperback available $6.95 (k-3)   **398.2**

1. Folklore—United States

ISBN 0-395-30084-3 (pa)   LC 77-23289

First published by Seabury Press

"An old man lives in the Tennessee backwoods with his three hunting dogs, Uno, Ino and Cumptico-Calico. . . . The old man sees an odd animal squeezing through a crack in his cabin and grabs it. All he gets is its tail but he makes a snack of that and gets into bed with a satisfied appetite. But the dismembered [creature] wants its tail back. When he haunts the old man with his keening, 'Tailypo, tailypo, all I want is my tailypo' in vain, he settles for vengeance instead." Publ Wkly

"The energetic postures of the old man and his dogs form a strong accompaniment to the clean, vigorous storytelling, and the subtly underplayed color in the paintings not only suggests the ghostliness of the story but is pleasing in itself." Horn Book

Galdone, Paul, 1914-1986

The elves and the shoemaker; retold and illustrated by Paul Galdone. Clarion Bks. 1984 unp il $14.95; pa $5.95 (k-2)   **398.2**

1. Folklore—Germany 2. Fairy tales

ISBN 0-89919-226-2; 0-89919-422-2 (pa)

LC 83-14979

"Based on Lucy Crane's translation from the German of the Brothers Grimm." Title page

Galdone, Paul, 1914-1986—*Continued*

A pair of elves help a poor shoemaker become successful, and the shoemaker and his wife reward them with elegant outfits

"The pictures in flashing hues emphasize the secret helpers' impishness; they seem to be performing the service more for a lark than in the name of sweet charity." Publ Wkly

The gingerbread boy. Clarion Bks. 1975 unp il $14.95; pa $5.95 (k-2)   398.2

1. Folklore 2. Fairy tales
ISBN 0-395-28799-5; 0-89919-163-0 (pa)
First published by Seabury Press

"A lively version of the tale of the gingerbread boy who sprang into action as soon as he was baked and gleefully eluded all would-be captors until he was finally outwitted by a fox. The artist's gingerbread boy is a strong-legged, cocky individual, who sets out on a merry race through the countryside. The action of the tale is well-paced; large, humorous illustrations with stone fences, a covered bridge, and hearty rural folk suggest a New England background, while the triumphant fox is the epitome of all slyness." Horn Book

Henny Penny; retold and illustrated by Paul Galdone. Clarion Bks. 1968 unp il $14.95; pa $5.95 (k-2)   398.2

1. Folklore 2. Animals—Fiction
ISBN 0-395-28800-2; 0-89919-225-4 (pa)
First published by Seabury Press

A folktale also popularly known as Chicken Little. "The simple retelling has a different ending which makes the fox seem somewhat less villainous—when Henny Penny and her credulous friends follow Foxy Loxy into the cave they are never seen again and the king is never told that the sky is falling, but Foxy Loxy, his wife, and seven little foxes (appealingly portrayed in a picture as a family group) still remember the fine feast they had that day." Booklist

King of the Cats; a ghost story; by Joseph Jacobs retold and illustrated by Paul Galdone. Clarion Bks. 1980 unp il $14.95; pa $4.95 (k-2)   398.2

1. Folklore—Great Britain 2. Fairy tales 3. Cats—Fiction
ISBN 0-395-29030-9; 0-89919-400-1 (pa)

LC 79-16659

"In this retelling of a century-old English tale, a woman and her cat wait long into the evening for the return of the gravedigger husband. Finally he bursts into the cottage wild-eyed and demands, 'Who is Tom Tildrum?' As he goes on to recount a funeral procession of black cats that he witnessed, his own cat, Old Tom, is much affected by the description." SLJ

"Galdone follows closely, in his adaptation, the version by Joseph Jacobs on which this tale is based . . . but has simplified the exposition and removed the dialect from the dialogue. A smooth retelling, the story is handsomely illustrated by large-scale pictures that fill, but do not crowd, the pages; Galdone's draughtsmanship is at its best here." Bull Cent Child Books

The little red hen. Clarion Bks. 1973 unp il $14.95; pa $5.95 (k-2)   398.2

1. Folklore 2. Chickens—Fiction
ISBN 0-395-28803-7; 0-89919-349-8 (pa)
First published by Seabury Press

"In a light-hearted interpretation of the old tale, a domesticated little hen, complete with mobcap and apron, busies herself in a picturesquely shabby cottage while her three house mates—a cat, a dog, and a mouse—doze blissfully. The industry of the little hen produces a cake; and only when 'a delicious smell filled the cozy little house,' do her lazy companions come to life." Horn Book

"The large, clear, colorful pictures perfectly suit the book for pre-school story hours; the simple text, with one or two lines per page, will make it a success with beginning readers." SLJ

The monkey and the crocodile; a Jataka tale from India. Clarion Bks. 1969 unp il $14.95; pa $5.95 (k-2)   398.2

1. Folklore—India 2. Fables 3. Animals—Fiction 4. Jataka stories
ISBN 0-395-28806-1; 0-89919-524-5 (pa)
First published by Seabury Press

Illustrated by Galdone, this is a retelling of one of the Jataka fables about Buddha in his animal incarnations. "The crocodile wants a meal of monkey, but the intended prey is far wilier than his antagonist." SLJ

The story "has the humor, plot, and movement to make it a good book for any young child, even one unused to stories: the brilliant colors, clear pictures, and brief text should make it very successful for sharing with groups of children." Horn Book

Puss in boots. Clarion Bks. 1976 unp il hardcover o.p. paperback available $6.95 (k-2)   398.2

1. Folklore—France 2. Fairy tales
ISBN 0-89919-192-4 (pa)
First published by Seabury Press

"Galdone follows Perrault's story line faithfully, as Puss works mischief to obtain a fortune for his master. The writing, fluid and readable, makes even this familiar tale sound fresh—no mean feat. Galdone's large, humorous caricatures—easily seen for story hour—have great gusto, and Puss is the embodiment of cleverness and knavery." SLJ

The teeny-tiny woman; a ghost story. Clarion Bks. 1984 unp il $14.95; pa $5.95 (k-2)   398.2

1. Folklore—Great Britain 2. Ghost stories
ISBN 0-89919-270-X; 0-89919-463-X (pa)

LC 84-4311

Retold and illustrated by Galdone, this is an English folk tale about a "teeny-tiny woman who lives in a teeny-tiny house in a teeny-tiny village goes for a teeny-tiny walk, etc. Opening the gates to a churchyard, she finds a bone that will add flavor to the soup she plans for supper. Back home, she goes to bed but is alarmed by a voice . . . demanding, 'Give me back my bone!'" Publ Wkly

"Quarter-inch type will attract reticent readers, and the comfortable, cozy country and cottage scenes defuse whatever scariness young readers might conjure up. Fences, trees, balustrades and cupboards in murky, inky tones are designed to suggest watchful faces and add to the atmospheric tension of the narrative." SLJ

Three Aesop fox fables. Clarion Bks. 1971 unp il $13.95 (k-3)   398.2

1. Fables 2. Foxes—Fiction
ISBN 0-395-28810-X
First published by Seabury Press

A retelling of The fox and the grapes, The fox and the stork, and The fox and the crow

"Paul Galdone's bright-eyed fox is the quintessence of merry cunning. . . . The pictures, full of movement and humor, are especially good for showing to a group because of the large animal figures and simple composition." Saturday Rev

Galdone, Paul, 1914-1986—*Continued*

The three bears. Clarion Bks. 1972 unp il
$14.95; pa $5.95 (k-2)   **398.2**

1. Folklore 2. Bears—Fiction
ISBN 0-395-28811-8; 0-590-11820-X (pa)
Also available Spanish language edition
First published by Seabury Press

In Galdone's illustrations for his retelling of the tale of
Goldilocks, "his three bears are beautifully groomed, civi-
lized creatures, living a life of rustic contentment in an astonishingly verdant forest, while his Goldilocks is a horrid,
be-ringletted, overdressed child who rampages wantonly
through the bears' tidy home." Times Lit Suppl

The three Billy Goats Gruff. Clarion Bks.
1973 unp il $14.95; pa $5.95 (k-2)   **398.2**

1. Folklore—Norway 2. Goats—Fiction
ISBN 0-395-28812-6; 0-89919-035-9 (pa)
Also available Spanish language edition
First published by Seabury Press

In this retelling of the old Norwegian folk tale, "the goats
flummox the wicked troll and send him over the rickety
bridge to a watery grave." Publ Wkly

"Galdone's illustrations are in his usual bold, clear style.
The three Billy Goats Gruff are expressively drawn, and the
troll looks appropriately ferocious and ugly. The large, lively, double-page spreads are sure to win a responsive audience at story hour." SLJ

What's in fox's sack? an old English tale;
retold and illustrated by Paul Galdone.
Clarion Bks. 1982 unp il $13.95; pa $6.95
(k-2)   **398.2**

1. Folklore—Great Britain 2. Foxes—Fiction
ISBN 0-89919-062-6; 0-89919-491-5 (pa)
      LC 81-10251

"This is the story of a trickster who is tricked, a sly fox
who leaves his sack at a series of homes, each time warning
the occupant not to peek; each time she does, and he takes
better booty for his sack." Bull Cent Child Books

"Galdone's version of an old English tale rolls onward as
it discloses ever more absurdities, repeating the key phrases,
the kind of story little ones like best. The full-color pictures
are dazzlingly dressy and very funny." Publ Wkly

Garland, Sherry, 1948-
Why ducks sleep on one leg; illustrated by
Jean and Mou-sien Tseng. Scholastic 1993 unp
il $14.95 (k-3)   **398.2**

1. Folklore—Vietnam 2. Ducks—Fiction
ISBN 0-590-45697-0   LC 92-9709

A Vietnamese folktale about the life of three one-legged
ducks who seek replacements for their missing limbs

"This is a sparkling *pourquoi* tale, smoothly retold. The
perky, colorful paintings capture the characters and dilemmas of the ducks in a refreshing fashion." Booklist

Gerson, Mary-Joan
Why the sky is far away; a Nigerian folktale;
retold by Mary-Joan Gerson; pictures by Carla
Golembe. Little, Brown 1992 unp il lib bdg
$15.95; pa $4.95 (k-3)   **398.2**

1. Folklore—Nigeria
ISBN 0-316-30852-8 (lib bdg); 0-316-30874-9 (pa)
      LC 91-24949

"Joy Street books"
A revised and newly illustrated edition of the title first
published 1974 by Harcourt

The sky was once so close to the Earth that people cut
parts of it to eat, but their waste and greed caused the sky
to move far away

"Golembe's simple, theatrical illustrations combine
monotype prints and collages in brilliant colors. . . . With
its playfulness and drama, this is a fine book for story hour,
especially in an ecology program." Booklist

Ginsburg, Mirra
The Chinese mirror; adapted from a Korean
folktale by Mirra Ginsburg; illustrated by
Margot Zemach. Harcourt Brace Jovanovich
1988 unp il lib bdg $15.95; pa $5 (k-3)
      398.2

1. Folklore—Korea
ISBN 0-15-200420-3 (lib bdg); 0-15-217508-3 (pa)
      LC 86-22940

"Gulliver books"
"A man brings a mirror—an object unknown to his fellow villagers—home from a trip to China. He secretes it in
a chest, but when his curious family each indulge in a peek
and see a different image (his or her own face, of course),
each has a different reaction." Booklist

"This elegantly simple little story is a seamless blend of
folk-tale adaptation with illustrations that were inspired by
Korean genre paintings of the eighteenth century." Horn
Book

Merry-go-round; four stories; pictures by
Jose Aruego and Ariane Dewey. Greenwillow
Bks. 1992 48p il $15; lib bdg $13.93 (k-2)
      398.2

1. Fables 2. Folklore 3. Animals—Fiction
ISBN 0-688-09256-X; 0-688-09257-8 (lib bdg)
      LC 90-30439

"A collection of four of Ginsburg's previously published
animal fables—'The Strongest One of All,' 'What Kind of
Bird Is That?' 'Where Does the Sun Go at Night?' [entered
in E section] and 'The Fox and the Hare'—newly illustrated. . . . The simple, spare stories are well served by the
bouncy, bright illustrations. The artists' characterizations of
the animals are amusing. . . . The compilation will make a
cheery addition to the folktale collection for preschoolers."
Booklist

Goble, Paul
Adopted by the eagles; a Plains Indian story
of friendship and treachery; told & illustrated
by Paul Goble. Bradbury Press 1994 unp il
$15.95 (2-4)   **398.2**

1. Dakota Indians—Legends
ISBN 0-02-736575-1   LC 93-24047

"Two young warriors swear friendship, but when they
become rivals for the same maiden, one abandons the other
on a rocky ledge. Saved by eagles, the abandoned warrior
returns to his village and shames his former friend into
leaving, then marries the girl. The illustrations are vintage
Goble—stylized figures in historically accurate clothing,
outlined in white and set against landscapes of vast sky or
dark, slanting rock." Booklist

Includes bibliographical references

Goble, Paul—*Continued*

Buffalo woman; story and illustrations by Paul Goble. Bradbury Press 1984 unp il $14.95; pa $4.95 (2-4)   **398.2**

1. Indians of North America—Legends 2. Bison—Fiction
ISBN 0-02-737720-2; 0-689-71109-3 (pa)

LC 83-15704

A young hunter marries a female buffalo in the form of a beautiful maiden, but when his people reject her he must pass several tests before being allowed to join the buffalo nation

"Each page sparkles with the lupins and yuccas of the Southwest and teems with native birds, butterflies, and small animals, the richness of detail never detracting from the overall design of the handsome illustrations. The author-artist successfully combines a compelling version of an old legend with his own imaginative and striking visual interpretation." Horn Book

Includes bibliography

Crow chief; a Plains Indian story; told and illustrated by Paul Goble. Orchard Bks. 1992 unp il $15.95; lib bdg $15.99; pa $5.95 (2-4)   **398.2**

1. Indians of North America—Legends
ISBN 0-531-05947-2; 0-531-08547-3 (lib bdg); 0-531-07064-6 (pa)   LC 90-28457

"A Richard Jackson book"

Crow Chief always warns the buffalo that hunters are coming, until Falling Star, a savior, comes to camp, tricks Crow Chief, and teaches him that all must share and live like relatives together

"Stylized, stylish, and strongly decorative, Goble's distinctive paintings use symbol, design, and repetition to illustrate a retelling of a Plains Indians myth that is both a pourquoi story and a hero tale. . . . Goble discusses the legend of Falling Star, 'the Savior,' in a prefatory note that should be of special interest to storytellers." Bull Cent Child Books

The gift of the sacred dog; story and illustrations by Paul Goble. Bradbury Press 1980 unp il $14.95; pa $4.95 (2-4)   **398.2**

1. Indians of North America—Legends 2. Horses—Fiction
ISBN 0-02-736560-3; 0-02-043280-1 (pa)

LC 80-15843

The author "presents one of the common myths of how the Plains Indians got horses. In this case, a boy from a tribe whose members are starving because they cannot find buffalo goes to a high mountain to talk to the Great Spirit. From heaven the boy gets sacred dogs (horses) for hunting the buffalo." Child Book Rev Serv

"Goble's handsome paintings, vigorous in composition and often delicate in style, often stylized, always reflect his identification with the Native American way of life and his empathy with their respect for natural things. . . . The text, which can be read aloud to younger children, ends with Sioux songs about horses and buffalo." Bull Cent Child Books

The great race of the birds and animals; story and illustrations by Paul Goble. Bradbury Press 1985 unp il $14.95; pa $4.95 (2-4)   **398.2**

1. Indians of North America—Legends
ISBN 0-02-736950-1; 0-689-71452-1 (pa)

LC 85-4202

A retelling of the Cheyenne and Sioux myth about the Great Race, a contest called by the Creator to settle the question whether man or buffalo should have supremacy and thus become the guardians of Creation

"With variety in color, pattern, and page design, the brilliant illustrations strengthen the drama and powerfully depict the animals—their massed effects and their individual characteristics." Horn Book

Her seven brothers; story and illustrations by Paul Goble. Bradbury Press 1988 unp il $14.95; pa $4.95 (2-4)   **398.2**

1. Cheyenne Indians—Legends 2. Stars—Fiction
ISBN 0-02-737960-4; 0-689-71730-X (pa)

LC 86-31776

Retells the Cheyenne legend in which a girl and her seven chosen brothers become the Big Dipper

"The story is lovely, the retelling echoes its delicate and gentle charm. The illustrations . . . emphasize the flora and fauna associated with hope and spring. The pages are filled with detail. . . . The author's note not only gives the sources for his art and for his retelling but also describes the particular techniques employed for the illustrations." Horn Book

Iktomi and the boulder; a Plains Indian story; retold and illustrated by Paul Goble. Orchard Bks. 1988 unp il $15.95; lib bdg $15.99; pa $5.95 (k-3)   **398.2**

1. Dakota Indians—Legends
ISBN 0-531-05760-7; 0-531-08360-8 (lib bdg); 0-531-07023-9 (pa)   LC 87-35789

"A Richard Jackson book"

Iktomi, a Plains Indian trickster, attempts to defeat a boulder with the assistance of some bats, in this story which explains why the Great Plains are covered with small stones

"Goble has adapted his usually formal narrative style to suit this boisterous trickster tale. The type is large, the narrative voice is informal, offering numerous asides from Iktomi and the storyteller. Goble's signature ink and vivid watercolor illustrations contain more movement than usual, and fewer stylized symbols are in evidence. . . . A deft blending of text and illustration which will appeal to a wide audience." SLJ

Other available titles about Iktomi are:
Iktomi and the berries (1989)
Iktomi and the buffalo skull (1991)
Iktomi and the buzzard (1994)
Iktomi and the ducks (1990)

The lost children; the boys who were neglected; story and illustrations by Paul Goble. Bradbury Press 1993 unp il $14.95 (k-3)   **398.2**

1. Siksika Indians—Legends 2. Stars—Fiction
ISBN 0-02-736555-7   LC 91-44283

A Blackfoot Indian legend in which six neglected orphaned brothers decide to go to the Above World where they become the constellation of the "Lost Children," or Pleiades

"Goble's retelling is smooth, respectful, and carefully documented. Many of his stylistic trademarks—the use of bright color; impeccable attention to illustrating authentic regalia; minutely detailed portraits of animals and insects—are evident in the artwork." Horn Book Guide

Love flute; story and illustrations by Paul Goble. Bradbury Press 1992 unp il $14.95 (2-4)   **398.2**

1. Indians of North America—Legends
ISBN 0-02-736261-2   LC 91-19716

Goble, Paul—*Continued*
A gift to a shy young man from the birds and animals
helps him to express his love to a beautiful girl
"Goble's measured prose brings this Santee Dakota myth
to life. The lyricism of the romantic story is highlighted by
the restraint and dignity of his writing. His familiar painting
style is both rich and formal as befits the telling of a myth.
. . . A note on sources and historical information on courtship rituals is a welcome plus." SLJ

Star Boy; retold and illustrated by Paul
Goble. Bradbury Press 1983 unp il $14.95; pa
$4.95 (2-4)   **398.2**
1. Siksika Indians—Legends
ISBN 0-02-722660-3; 0-689-71499-8 (pa)
           LC 82-20599
This is a retelling of the Blackfeet Indian "legend of Star
Child, called Scarface by his people after the Sun marks
him as a reminder of his mother's disobedience. Ugly and
poor, Star Boy loses hopes of wedding the girl he loves,
daughter of a chief. She gives him the courage, however, to
persevere in finding the torturous way to Sky World where
Sun rewards the youth with beauty and riches. The Sun also
gives Star Boy the secret of the Sun Dance, the gift he
brings to the Blackfeet, and it is this benison that the tribe
celebrates each year." Publ Wkly
"This strong sense of design, the restrained and effective
use of color, and the stylized use of Native American motifs
in bold composition contribute to the distinctive work that
won Goble the Caldecott Medal." Bull Cent Child Books

Grandfather tales; American-English folk tales;
selected and edited by Richard Chase;
illustrated by Berkeley Williams, Jr.
Houghton Mifflin 1948 239p il $17.95; pa
$6.95 (4 and up)   **398.2**
1. Folklore—Southern States
ISBN 0-395-06692-1; 0-395-56150-7 (pa)
Folklore gathered in Alabama, "North Carolina, Virginia
and Kentucky. Written down only after many tellings, these
[twenty-four] humorous tales are told in the vernacular of
the region with added touches of local color provided by
the storytellers as they meet together to keep Old-Christmas
Eve. . . . Of special interest to storytellers." Booklist

Green, Roger Lancelyn, 1918-1987
King Arthur and his Knights of the Round
Table; retold out of the old romances; with
illustrations by Aubrey Beardsley. Knopf 1993
355p il $13.95 (5 and up)   **398.2**
1. Arthur, King 2. Arthurian romances
ISBN 0-679-42311-7   LC 92-55073
Also available in paperback from Puffin Bks.
"Everyman's library children's classics"
A newly illustrated edition of the title first published
1953 in the United Kingdom
Relates the exploits of King Arthur and his knights from
the birth of Arthur to the destruction of Camelot

The **Green** fairy book; edited by Andrew Lang;
with numerous illustrations by H. J. Ford.
Dover Publs. 1965 366p il pa $7.95 (4-6)
           398.2
1. Folklore 2. Fairy tales
ISBN 0-486-21439-7
Also available in hardcover from P. Smith
A reprint of the title first published 1892 by Longmans

This collection of forty-two fairy tales from various
countries includes many from the Brothers Grimm and several by the Comte de Caylus. Other sources include Madame D'Aulnoy, Paul Sebillot, Charles Deulin, Fénelon, and
traditional tales from Spain and China

Greene, Ellin, 1927-
Billy Beg and his bull; an Irish tale; retold
by Ellin Greene; illustrated by Kimberly
Bulcken Root. Holiday House 1994 unp il
$15.95 (2-4)   **398.2**
1. Folklore—Ireland
ISBN 0-8234-1100-1   LC 93-7730
With magical gifts from the bull his mother had given
him, the son of an Irish king manages to prove his bravery
and win a princess as his wife
"The text is good for reading aloud, while the lively illustrations, dominated by shades of green, effectively portray
the multiheaded giants and the snaky, twelve-headed dragon
that Billy overcomes with the aid of gifts from his bull."
Horn Book Guide

The legend of the Christmas rose; [by]
Selma Lagerlöf; retold by Ellin Greene; with
illustrations by Charles Mikolaycak. Holiday
House 1990 unp il lib bdg $15.95 (2-4)
           398.2
1. Folklore—Sweden 2. Christmas—Fiction
ISBN 0-8234-0821-3   LC 89-77511
In hope of getting her husband pardoned, an exiled out-
law's wife agrees to reveal to an old monk the miracle in
Goïnge Forest, where every Christmas Eve a beautiful gar-
den blooms in remembrance of the birth of the Christ Child
"Greene's prose is crisp and elegant, and Mikolaycak's
lightly brooding illustrations—in somber browns and
greys—tie in well with the story's myth-like elements." Publ
Wkly

Grifalconi, Ann
The village of round and square houses.
Little, Brown 1986 unp il lib bdg $16.95 (k-3)
           398.2
1. Folklore—Africa
ISBN 0-316-32862-6   LC 85-24150
A Caldecott Medal honor book, 1987
A grandmother explains to her listeners why in their village on the side of a volcano the men live in square houses
and the women in round ones
The author "illustrates her own tale, told to her by a
young girl who grew up in Tos. The resting purple volcano,
suddenly erupting into orange; the eerie orange sun; the villagers covered with ash; the fiery colored skies; the dense,
lush jungles—all are captured beautifully by Grifalconi's
art." Publ Wkly

Grimm, Jacob, 1785-1863
About wise men and simpletons; twelve
tales from Grimm; translated by Elizabeth
Shub; etchings by Nonny Hogrogian.
Macmillan 1986 c1971 118p il $14.95 (3-6)
           398.2
1. Folklore—Germany 2. Fairy tales
ISBN 0-02-737450-5   LC 85-15330
A reissue of the title first published 1971

Grimm, Jacob, 1785-1863—*Continued*

"This collection includes such favorites as 'Hansel and Gretel,' 'The Bremen Town Musicians,' and 'Rumpelstiltskin.' The versions are brief, less ornamented than they are in familiar versions, and chosen because, Elizabeth Shub says in her preface, 'here, even more than in later editions, the storyteller's voice is omnipresent.'" Sutherland. The Best in Child Books

"Nonny Hogrogian's etchings, spare and deft, are beautifully appropriate for the ingenuous simplicity of the writing." Saturday Rev

The complete Grimm's fairy tales; introduction by Padraic Colum; folkloristic commentary by Joseph Campbell; 212 illustrations by Josef Scharl. Pantheon Bks. 1974 c1972 836p il hardcover o.p. paperback available $18 (4 and up)   398.2

1. Folklore—Germany 2. Fairy tales
ISBN 0-394-70930-6 (pa)

A reissue of the edition first published 1944 with title: Grimm's fairy tales. Copyright renewed 1972

"The text of this edition is based on the translation of Margaret Hunt. It has been thoroughly revised, corrected and completed by James Stern." Verso of title page

"A standard edition of the collected household tales. A discussion of folk literature, with examples from the Grimm's stories, adds to the value of the book." Bull Cent Child Books

The fisherman and his wife; a tale from the brothers Grimm; translated by Randall Jarrell; pictures by Margot Zemach. Farrar, Straus & Giroux 1980 unp il hardcover o.p. paperback available $4.95 (k-3)   398.2

1. Folklore—Germany 2. Fairy tales
ISBN 0-374-42326-1 (pa)   LC 79-3248

The fisherman's greedy wife is never satisfied with the wishes granted to them by an enchanted fish

"The hilarious tale of greed and retribution is handsomely illustrated in an oversize format that is used to full advantage by Zemach, whose paintings are imaginative, comic, and effective in composition and color. Jarrell's translation of the story is flowing and colloquial, as nice to use for storytelling as it is to read aloud." Bull Cent Child Books

Hansel and Gretel; [by] the Brothers Grimm; pictures by Susan Jeffers. Dial Bks. 1980 unp il $16; lib bdg $14.89; pa $4.95 (k-3)   398.2

1. Folklore—Germany 2. Fairy tales
ISBN 0-8037-3492-1; 0-8037-3491-3 (lib bdg); 0-8037-0318-X (pa)   LC 80-15079

Also available Spanish language edition

"A simple, crisply stated translation tells this timeless story of innocence pitted against evil. . . . Jeffers's stunning full-color illustrations expand both the children's purity and the malevolence of the stepmother/witch in an atmosphere that is flawlessly and beautifully executed." Booklist

Hansel and Gretel; by the Brothers Grimm; illustrated by Lisbeth Zwerger; translated by Elizabeth D. Crawford. Picture Bk. Studio 1988 unp il $16 (k-3)   398.2

1. Folklore—Germany 2. Fairy tales
ISBN 0-88708-068-5   LC 87-32833

"A Michael Neugebauer book"

First published 1979 by Morrow

When they are left in the woods by their parents, two children find their way home despite an encounter with a wicked witch

"Working from a faithful translation of the original text, Zwerger has created rosy-cheeked, appealing children who look as if they have just descended the Alps. The witch, by contrast, is a shapeless, fiery-eyed ghoul with real scare potential." Publ Wkly

Little Red Cap; [by] the Brothers Grimm; illustrated by Lisbeth Zwerger; translated from the German by Elizabeth D. Crawford. North-South Bks. 1995 c1983 unp il $14.95; pa $5.95 (k-3)   398.2

1. Folklore—Germany 2. Wolves—Fiction
ISBN 1-55858-382-3; 1-55858-430-7 (pa)

LC 94-32154

"A Michael Neugebauer book"

A reissue of the title first published 1983 by Morrow

In this translation of Little Red Riding Hood "Little Red Cap strays from the path while taking wine and cake to grandmother. The wolf then gobbles up grandmother and Red Cap. Justice ultimately prevails when the hunter cuts open the wolf, frees the child and grandmother and finishes off the wolf." SLJ

This translation "gives the text a smooth pace and natural-sounding dialogue. . . . Washes in muted earth tones provide suggestions of backgrounds against which expressively drawn figures play out their familiar roles." Horn Book

The seven ravens; [by] the Brothers Grimm; illustrated by Lisbeth Zwerger; translation from the German by Elizabeth D. Crawford. Picture Bk. Studio 1989 unp il $14.95; pa $5.95 (k-3)   398.2

1. Folklore—Germany 2. Fairy tales
ISBN 0-88708-092-8; 0-685-24951-4 (pa)

First published 1981 by Morrow

"Here seven brothers are changed into 'seven coal-black ravens' after they fail to return from fetching water for their sister's christening quickly enough to satisfy their father. Their sister, feeling herself responsible, sets out to undo the terrible magic. . . . Miss Zwerger is a lyrically witty artist; there is smooth movement in her warmly hued pictures, as well as visual sophistication. . . . The translation, by Elizabeth D. Crawford, is felicitous and true to the original." NY Times Book Rev

Snow White & Rose Red; by Jakob and Wilhelm Grimm; illustrated by Gennady Spirin. Philomel Bks. 1992 31p il $14.95 (1-4)   398.2

1. Folklore—Germany 2. Fairy tales
ISBN 0-399-21873-4   LC 91-29414

A newly illustrated version of the classic tale about two kind sisters' experiences with an enchanted bear and an ungrateful gnome

"Spirin's romantic watercolor-and-pencil illustrations recall books of hours with their medieval setting, their delightful interpretations of flowers, trees, and forest animals, and their arched borders that contain the text and main illustrations on every page. . . . This Russian illustrator's distinctive style lends an other-worldly quality that is well suited to the 'long ago and far away' spirit of fairy tales." Booklist

Guy, Rosa

Mother Crocodile; Maman-Caïman; by Birago Diop; translated and adapted by Rosa Guy; illustrated by John Steptoe. Delacorte Press 1981 unp il $10.42; pa $4.99 (k-3)

398.2

1. Folklore—Senegal 2. Crocodiles—Fiction
ISBN 0-440-06406-6; 0-440-41006-1 (pa)

LC 80-393

Coretta Scott King Award for illustration, 1982

In this folk tale from Senegal, the old storyteller Uncle Amadou says that "Mother Crocodile probably had the best memory on earth. . . . But her children . . . ignored her when she warned that they should learn from past experience. Then, warring men returned to the land, and the conquerors sought crocodile skins from which to make purses for their wives. Only through recalling Mother Crocodile's stories were the young ones able—literally—to save their skins." Horn Book

"Artist Steptoe's characteristic style is softened here by lighter colors, spatter-brush effects, and stencilike patterning for his framed scenes of the crocodiles' world." Booklist

Haley, Gail E.

Mountain Jack tales; as told and illustrated by Gail E. Haley. Dutton Children's Bks. 1992 131p il $15.99 (4 and up)

398.2

1. Folklore—United States
ISBN 0-525-44974-4

LC 92-6432

Companion volume Jack and the bean tree (1986)

These stories featuring the hero Jack are set in the mountains of North Carolina, but have their roots in old world folklore

"Haley's use of metaphor, hyperbole and dialect captures the playful spirit of mountain lore. Her emotive, elaborate wood engravings—as well as her afterwords about the stories, the art and the language itself—enrich this buoyant anthology." Publ Wkly

Includes glossary and bibliography

A story, a story; an African tale retold and illustrated by Gail E. Haley. Atheneum Pubs. 1970 unp il lib bdg $15.95; pa $4.95 (k-3)

398.2

1. Folklore—Africa 2. Anansi (Legendary character)
ISBN 0-689-20511-2 (lib bdg); 0-689-71201-4 (pa)

Awarded the Caldecott Medal, 1971

"The story explains the origin of that favorite African folk material, the spider tale. Here Ananse, the old spider man, wanting to buy the Sky God's stories, completes by his cleverness three seemingly impossible tasks set as the price for the golden box of stories which he takes back to earth." Sutherland. The Best in Child Books

Hamanaka, Sheila

Screen of frogs; an old tale; retold and illustrated by Sheila Hamanaka. Orchard Bks. 1993 unp il $15.95; lib bdg $15.99 (k-3)

398.2

1. Folklore—Japan
ISBN 0-531-05464-0; 0-531-08614-3 (lib bdg)

LC 92-24172

"A Richard Jackson book"

A giant frog convinces rich lazy Koji not to sell his estate because of the harm it would do to the land and animals

"Hamanaka's fluid retelling guides readers smoothly through the detailed proceedings, providing an air of antici-

pation and occasional humor. . . . Collage and acrylic illustrations, rendered on handmade paper, are liberally adorned with Asian motifs, while the figures' stark black outlines suggest the strokes of Japanese lettering." Publ Wkly

Hamilton, Virginia, 1936-

The dark way; stories from the spirit world; told by Virginia Hamilton; illustrated by Lambert Davis. Harcourt Brace Jovanovich 1990 154p il $19.95 (4 and up)

398.2

1. Supernatural—Fiction
ISBN 0-15-222340-1

LC 90-36251

A collection of folk tales, legends, and myths involving the supernatural, from cultures around the world

"Hamilton breathes life into the tales with her highly personal and intelligent brand of storytelling, and Lambert Davis's grisly monsters are appropriately horrific." Horn Book Guide

Includes bibliography

Her stories; African American folktales, fairy tales, and true tales; told by Virginia Hamilton; illustrated by Leo & Diane Dillon. Blue Sky Press (NY) 1995 112p il $19.95 (4 and up)

398.2

1. African American women—Folklore
ISBN 0-590-47370-0

LC 94-33055

Coretta Scott King award for text, 1996

"Nineteen African-American fairy tales, animal stories, supernatural tales, legends and true narratives of a female kind are presented in this single volume." Child Book Rev Serv

"Retold from a variety of sources, the stories flow smoothly in Hamilton's expertly measured prose. The full-color illustrations, one per story, are lush and detailed. . . . These are tales to be read over and over again." Publ Wkly

Includes bibliographical references

The people could fly: American black folktales; told by Virginia Hamilton; illustrated by Leo and Diane Dillon. Knopf 1985 178p il $18; lib bdg $18.99; pa $12 (4 and up)

398.2

1. African Americans—Folklore
ISBN 0-394-86925-7; 0-394-96925-1 (lib bdg); 0-679-84336-1 (pa)

LC 84-25020

Coretta Scott King Award for text, 1986

"Hamilton retells 24 representative black folktales. . . . The stories are organized into four sections: tales of animals; the supernatural; the real, extravagant, and fanciful; and freedom tales." Booklist

The author "has been successful in her efforts to write these tales in the Black English of the slave storytellers. Her scholarship is unobtrusive and intelligible. She has provided a glossary and notes concerning the origins of the tales and the different versions in other cultures. Handsomely illustrated." N Y Times Book Rev

Han, Suzanne Crowder, 1953-

The rabbit's escape; illustrated by Yumi Heo. Holt & Co. 1995 unp il $15.95 (k-3)

398.2

1. Folklore—Korea 2. Bilingual books—English-Korean
ISBN 0-8050-2675-4

LC 94-36516

"This adaptation of a Korean folktale is bilingual, with text appearing in both Korean and English. When the Drag-

Han, Suzanne Crowder, 1953—*Continued*
on King of the East Sea falls ill, the court physician declares the only cure to be the liver of a rabbit. . . . The tale is illustrated with large, whimsical paintings in pencil and oil. Characters are drawn in a two-dimensional, naive style against backgrounds of swirling sea creatures." Booklist

Hancock, Sibyl
Esteban and the ghost; adapted by Sibyl Hancock; pictures by Dirk Zimmer. Dial Bks. for Young Readers 1983 unp il lib bdg $10.89 (k-3) **398.2**
1. Folklore—Spain 2. Ghost stories 3. Halloween—Fiction
ISBN 0-8037-2411-X   LC 82-22125
Esteban, a merry Spanish tinker, spends All Hallows' Eve in a haunted castle and helps a ghost win his way into heaven
"This adaptation of a Spanish folktale . . . is well told, with a rich vocabulary and some wonderful sound effects for story hours. The black line drawings with full color washes are dusty but not dull, and complement the story." Child Book Rev Serv

Harper, Wilhelmina
The Gunniwolf; retold by Wilhelmina Harper; illustrated by William Wiesner. Dutton 1967 unp il $13.99 (k-1)   **398.2**
1. Folklore—Southern States
ISBN 0-525-31139-4
Text, adapted from a Southern nonsense tale, first published 1918 in the author's collection: Story hour favorites
A retelling of the folktale about Little Girl who ignores her mother's warnings, wanders into the jungle searching for pretty flowers, and encounters the fierce Gunniwolf
"Pictures are green and orange with numerous black lines." Bruno. Books for Sch Libr, 1968

Haskins, James, 1941-
The headless haunt and other African-American ghost stories; collected and retold by James Haskins; illustrated by Ben Otero. HarperCollins Pubs. 1994 116p il $14; lib bdg $13.89; pa $3.95 (4 and up)   **398.2**
1. African Americans—Folklore 2. Ghost stories
ISBN 0-06-022994-2; 0-06-022997-7 (lib bdg); 0-06-440602-4 (pa)   LC 93-26223
A collection of ghost stories and anecdotes that are part of the folklore of African Americans
"These selections have chilled the blood and scared the living daylights out of many a listener. . . . Readers can almost hear the storytellers voices. . . . A fascinating book to expand or build a collection on African American culture." SLJ
Includes bibliographical references

Hastings, Selina
The firebird; retold by Selina Hastings; illustrated by Reg Cartwright. Candlewick Press 1993 c1992 unp il $15.95 (1-4)
                                                     398.2
1. Folklore—Russia
ISBN 1-56402-096-7   LC 92-52997
First published 1992 in the United Kingdom

A retelling of the Russian folktale in which a young huntsman and his wise and magical horse are ordered by the king to undertake a series of increasingly difficult tasks
This "is aptly told and illustrated with stylized, flat paintings in shades of brown, green, and gold." Horn Book

Sir Gawain and the Green Knight; words by Selina Hastings; illustrations by Juan Wijngaard. Lothrop, Lee & Shepard Bks. 1981 unp il $12.95 (3 and up)   **398.2**
1. Arthurian romances 2. Gawain (Legendary character)
ISBN 0-688-00592-6   LC 80-85379
An Arthurian "tale of young Gawain's proving at the hands of the Green Knight. His adventures during a winter's search for the Green Chapel and his tests of purity in Sir Bercilak's castle serve as an archetypal example of Round Table fare." Booklist
"Hastings reduces the poem's 2530 long lines to 23 pages of simple prose. . . . The colored paintings illustrating the text are simply ravishing, capturing the awestruck court, the wild landscape and the forceful characters. A handsome book worth the price for the pictures alone." SLJ

Sir Gawain and the loathly lady; retold by Selina Hastings; illustrated by Juan Wijngaard. Lothrop, Lee & Shepard Bks. 1985 unp il $15; pa $4.95 (3 and up)   **398.2**
1. Arthurian romances 2. Gawain (Legendary character)
ISBN 0-688-05823-X; 0-688-07046-9 (pa)
                                              LC 85-63
Also available Spanish language edition
After a horrible hag saves King Arthur's life by answering a riddle, Sir Gawain agrees to marry her to save the King's honor and thus releases her from an evil enchantment
"This version of the old romance . . . is charmingly retold and gloriously illustrated. . . . Wijngaard combines the illuminator's precision with a modern miniaturist's detailed perspective; each page of text is framed with manuscript-inspired designs of lacy leaves in scarlet, blue and gold, inset with wonderful, naturalistic paintings. These are full of details for readers to discover." SLJ

Hausman, Gerald
Coyote walks on two legs; a book of Navajo myths and legends; collected and retold by Gerald Hausman; illustrated by Floyd Cooper. Philomel Bks. 1995 unp il $15.95 (2-4)
                                                     398.2
1. Navajo Indians—Legends 2. Coyote (Legendary character)
ISBN 0-399-22018-6   LC 92-25115
"In these five short tales based on Navajo myths, Coyote becomes a victim of his own greed and vanity and often causes considerable trouble for those around him." Booklist
These selections are "told in lyrical, free-flowing prose. . . . Cooper's fittingly muted, sepia and gold-toned watercolor illustrations have a dreamlike quality." SLJ

Heins, Ethel L., 1918-
The cat and the cook and other fables of Krylov; retold by Ethel Heins; pictures by Anita Lobel. Greenwillow Bks. 1995 32p il $15; lib bdg $14.93 (1-4)   **398.2**
1. Fables
ISBN 0-688-12310-4; 0-688-12311-2 (lib bdg)
                                              LC 94-4116

Heins, Ethel L., 1918-—*Continued*

In this "collection, 12 Russian fables warn against pride, show the importance of cooperation and counsel moderation. Includes notes about the fabulist Krylov (1768-1844) and sources for this volume." Publ Wkly

Lobel "outdoes herself with watercolor-and-gouache paintings that are brilliantly colored and wonderfully composed. . . . Heins' prose retellings . . . are elegant. Based on scholarly sources in translation, these brief morality tales are more subtle and complex than the more familiar ones attributed to Aesop." Booklist

Heyer, Marilee, 1942-

The weaving of a dream; a Chinese folktale; retold and illustrated by Marilee Heyer. Viking Kestrel 1986 unp il $15.99; pa $4.99 (3-5)   **398.2**

1. Folklore—China
ISBN 0-670-80555-6; 0-14-050528-8 (pa)
LC 85-20187

When the beautiful tapestry woven by a poor woman is stolen by fairies, her three sons set out on a magical journey to retrieve it. A retelling of a traditional Chinese tale

The story "is faithfully retold in a volume of exquisite beauty. . . . Heyer's 15 illustrations show a masterful artistic technique. . . . Each painting offers an experience of sensuous delight." SLJ

Ho, Minfong

The two brothers; by Minfong Ho & Saphan Ros; illustrated by Jean & Mou-sien Tseng. Lothrop, Lee & Shepard Bks. 1995 unp il $15; lib bdg $14.93 (1-4)   **398.2**

1. Folklore—Cambodia
ISBN 0-688-12550-6; 0-688-12551-4 (lib bdg)
LC 94-14516

"Raised in a monastery, orphaned brothers Kem and Sem ask the abbot's permission to leave and see the world outside. The abbot offers them some sage advice, and Kem, who takes the abbot's words to heart, becomes a merchant and prospers. Sem, who neglects the words of wisdom, falls upon hard times until he remembers the abbot's advice and finds the path to his destiny. . . . Lively, colorful paintings highlight the drama, humor, and beauty of the tale." Booklist

Hodges, Margaret

The hero of Bremen; retold by Margaret Hodges; with illustrations by Charles Mikolaycak. Holiday House 1993 unp il $15.95 (3-5)   **398.2**

1. Folklore—Germany
ISBN 0-8234-0934-1
LC 91-22357

Retells the German legend in which a shoemaker who cannot walk helps the town of Bremen, aided by the spirit of the great hero Roland

"Mikolaycak's realistic watercolor and colored pencil drawings have powerful lines, sculptural forms, and a strong narrative quality. . . . This eloquent retelling of a gentle, little-known tale honoring the chivalric virtues of service and sacrifice is all the more beautiful for its understated quality; the documentation is detailed and scholarly." Booklist

The kitchen knight; a tale of King Arthur; retold by Margaret Hodges and illustrated by Trina Schart Hyman. Holiday House 1990 unp il $15.95; pa $5.95 (3 and up)   **398.2**

1. Gareth (Legendary character) 2. Arthurian romances
ISBN 0-8234-0787-X; 0-8234-1063-3 (pa)
LC 89-11215

A retelling of the Arthurian legend of how Sir Gareth becomes a knight and rescues the lady imprisoned by the fearsome Red Knight of the Red Plain

"Hyman's richly romantic illustrations are lush watercolors, framed and broken with framed insets for closeups and framed text inside the panoramic picture. The format is horizontal, capturing the sweep of the story. While not a tale of King Arthur, it's a wonderful taste of Arthurian legend, hopefully whetting young appetites for more." SLJ

Of swords and sorcerers; the adventures of King Arthur and his knights; by Margaret Hodges and Margery Evernden; woodcuts by David Frampton. Scribner 1993 96p il $14.95 (4-6)   **398.2**

1. Arthur, King 2. Arthurian romances
ISBN 0-684-19437-6
LC 91-40811

Nine episodes in the Arthurian cycle, from the placing of the boy Arthur in Merlin's care to Arthur's departure for Avalon

"The stories . . . move along at a good pace in more readable, speakable language than in Howard Pyle's classic version without losing the sense of time and place. Dramatic black-and-white woodcuts, well placed, reinforce the action. This storyteller's edition, organized excellently for performance, is for anyone who would like to present the cycle for children and avoid the darker sexual passages that presage the destruction of Camelot." SLJ

Saint George and the dragon; a golden legend; adapted by Margaret Hodges from Edmund Spenser's Faerie Queene; illustrated by Trina Schart Hyman. Little, Brown 1984 32p il $16.95; pa $6.95 (2-5)   **398.2**

1. George, Saint, d. 303 2. Knights and knighthood—Fiction 3. Dragons—Fiction
ISBN 0-316-36789-3; 0-316-36795-8 (pa)
LC 83-19980

Awarded the Caldecott Medal, 1985

Retells the segment from Spenser's The Faerie Queene, in which George, the Red Cross Knight, slays the dreadful dragon that has been terrorizing the countryside for years and brings peace and joy to the land

"Hyman's illustrations are uniquely suited to this outrageously romantic and appealing legend. . . . The paintings are richly colored, lush, detailed and dramatic. . . . This is a beautifully crafted book, a fine combination of author and illustrator." SLJ

Saint Patrick and the peddler; story by Margaret Hodges; paintings by Paul Brett Johnson. Orchard Bks. 1993 unp il $15.95; lib bdg $15.99 (k-3)   **398.2**

1. Patrick, Saint, 373?-463? 2. Folklore—Ireland
ISBN 0-531-05489-6; 0-531-08639-9 (lib bdg)
LC 92-44522

"A Richard Jackson book"

When a poor Irish peddler follows the instructions given to him by Saint Patrick in a dream, his life is greatly changed. Includes background on Saint Patrick and on the origin of the story

"Johnson's lovely acrylic paintings display the Irish countryside and the city of Dublin with a strong sense of

Hodges, Margaret—*Continued*

place. The muted colors match the overall tone of the story, and the eerie ghost of Saint Patrick adds a dramatic touch." Booklist

Hogrogian, Nonny

The contest; adapted and illustrated by Nonny Hogrogian. Greenwillow Bks. 1976 unp il $16; lib bdg $15.93 (k-3)   **398.2**

1. Folklore—Armenia
ISBN 0-688-80042-4; 0-688-84042-6 (lib bdg)

A Caldecott Medal honor book, 1977

A "gently humorous retelling of an Armenian folk tale about two robbers who not only share the same occupation but are engaged to the same girl." SLJ

"The symmetrical elements of the tale, which create arabesques of humor, are well-served by the full-color, full-page illustrations and by the pencil drawings scattered through the text. Some of the colored illustrations are bordered by oriental rug patterns, and all of the paintings and drawings are strong in their depiction of Armenian physiognomy." Horn Book

The devil with the three golden hairs; a tale from the Brothers Grimm; retold and illustrated by Nonny Hogrogian. Knopf 1983 unp il lib bdg $10.99 (k-3)   **398.2**

1. Folklore—Germany 2. Fairy tales
ISBN 0-394-95560-9   LC 82-12735

This adaptation of the German folk tale relates "the trials of a youth destined to marry a princess. Because the young man is poor, the king sends him on missions that would kill an ordinary mortal, if they could be accomplished. One is to snatch three golden hairs from the devil's head. Every step of the brave lad's perilous journey, leading to his triumph, comes alive in this saga of good and evil." Publ Wkly

"The accompanying pictures are accomplished and absorbing. Hogrogian's soft touch and her preference for rich, mellow color that shines against drab backgrounds make the art glow from within." Booklist

One fine day. Macmillan 1971 unp il $14.95; pa $4.95 (k-3)   **398.2**

1. Folklore—Armenia 2. Foxes—Fiction
ISBN 0-02-744000-1; 0-02-043620-3 (pa)

Awarded the Caldecott Medal, 1972

When a fox drinks the milk in an old woman's jug, she chops off his tail and refuses to sew it back on unless he gives her milk back. The author-illustrator's cumulative tale, based on an Armenian folktale, tells of the many transactions the fox must go through before his tail is restored

"A charming picture book that is just right for reading aloud to small children, the scale of the pictures also appropriate for group use." Sutherland. The Best in Child Books

Hong, Lily Toy, 1958-

How the ox star fell from heaven; retold and illustrated by Lilly Toy Hong. Whitman, A. 1991 unp il $14.95; pa $6.95 (k-3)

398.2

1. Folklore—China
ISBN 0-8075-3428-5; 0-8075-3429-3 (pa)

LC 90-38978

A Chinese folk tale which explains why the ox was banished from heaven to become the farmer's beast of burden

"Hong's clear, simple text is strongly illustrated in airbrushed acrylics and gouache. The images are formed by large and small blocks of deep color, joined rather like tiles with thick defining lines of contrasting colors between them. The resulting pictures are intriguingly variegated yet clean and fresh." Booklist

Two of everything; a Chinese folktale; retold and illustrated by Lily Toy Hong. Whitman, A. 1993 unp il $15.95 (k-3)   **398.2**

1. Folklore—China
ISBN 0-8075-8157-7   LC 92-29880

A poor old Chinese farmer finds a magic brass pot that doubles or duplicates whatever is placed inside it, but his efforts to make himself wealthy lead to unexpected complications

The author "here paints with muted colors, defining rounded forms with broad outlines. Retold with verve and gentle humor, this Chinese folktale could become a read-aloud favorite." Booklist

Hooks, William H.

Moss gown; illustrations by Donald Carrick. Clarion Bks. 1987 48p il $13.95; pa $5.95 (k-3)

398.2

1. Fairy tales
ISBN 0-89919-460-5; 0-395-54793-8 (pa)

LC 86-17199

After failing to flatter her father as much as her two evil sisters, Candace is banished from his plantation and only after much time and meeting her Prince Charming, is her father able to appreciate her love

"Many children and most adults will recognize in 'Moss Gown' the Cinderella story, while the most astute may note its resemblance to 'King Lear.' But everyone will enjoy this beautifully told North Carolina tale from the oral tradition. Carrick, a master of the dark and mysterious, has created haunting illustrations that are a wonderful complement to the story." Child Book Rev Serv

The three little pigs and the fox; illustrated by S.D. Schindler. Macmillan 1989 unp il $14.95 (k-3)   **398.2**

1. Folklore—United States 2. Pigs—Folklore
ISBN 0-02-744431-7   LC 88-29296

In this Appalachian version of the classic tale, Hamlet, the youngest pig, rescues her two greedy brothers from the clutches of the mean, tricky old drooly-mouth fox

"With an ear for colloquial wit and an eye on the family dynamic that sends these characters on their journey of maturation, Hooks has found a perfect fit in Schindler's watercolor scenes. Drafted with ease of proportion, colored with rural blends, and elegantly underplayed in expression, the animals are fresh and funny without being self-conscious." Bull Cent Child Books

Huck, Charlotte S.

Princess Furball; retold by Charlotte Huck; illustrated by Anita Lobel. Greenwillow Bks. 1989 unp il $16; lib bdg $15.93; pa $4.95 (1-3)

398.2

1. Fairy tales
ISBN 0-688-07837-0; 0-688-07838-9 (lib bdg); 0-688-13107-7 (pa)   LC 88-18780

This book is about a "princess who rebels against her tyrannical father and makes the most of her gifts to survive in another kingdom and win the hand of the king. This narrative focuses on the ingenuity of a girl who plots her own destiny." N Y Times Book Rev

"The paintings glimmer with intense colors—Lobel's flair

Huck, Charlotte S.—*Continued*
for both historical and humorous detail has never been more apparent, nor more luxuriously bold." SLJ

Hunter, Mollie, 1922-
Gilly Martin the Fox; retold by Mollie Hunter; illustrated by Dennis McDermott. Hyperion Bks. for Children 1994 36p il $15.95; lib bdg $15.89 (k-3)   **398.2**

1. Folklore—Scotland
ISBN 1-56282-517-8; 1-56282-518-6 (lib bdg)
                 LC 93-24112
With the help of a shape-shifting fox, the Prince of Alban goes on a series of quests, among such enemies as the Giant With Five Heads and the Seven Big Women of Jura
"Mollie Hunter's retelling of this old Highland story displays her sure touch, combining fidelity to the oral tradition with phrasing and structure that flow easily for contemporary readers. . . . The illustrations are as satisfying as the story—full of action, variety, and colour, with many details to enrich the narrative." Quill Quire

Hutton, Warwick
Beauty and the beast; retold and illustrated by Warwick Hutton. Atheneum Pubs. 1985 unp il $14.95 (1-4)   **398.2**

1. Folklore—France 2. Fairy tales
ISBN 0-689-50316-4   LC 84-48441
"A Margaret K. McElderry book"
"Hutton retells the story of the beast whose true form (a young and handsome prince) reappears when Beauty declares her love, engendered by his kindness and patience and love. The watercolor illustrations are rich and imaginative, with settings that have a Moorish influence and a beast who is like a giant cat, ugly of face, walking like a man. Hutton is particularly good at using light and shadow to establish mood." Bull Cent Child Books

Hyman, Trina Schart, 1939-
Little Red Riding Hood; by the Brothers Grimm retold and illustrated by Trina Schart Hyman. Holiday House 1983 unp il lib bdg $15.95; pa $5.95 (k-2)   **398.2**

1. Folklore—Germany 2. Wolves—Fiction
ISBN 0-8234-0470-6 (lib bdg); 0-8234-0653-9 (pa)
                 LC 82-7700
This retelling "basically follows the Grimm story, although the text has been fleshed out with some extraneous details (for instance, the little girl is called Elisabeth). . . . The illustrations seem to be a labor of love; richly colored paintings of the forest teem with exquisitely detailed plant and animal life, and the interior scenes, awash with atmospheric light, are beautifully composed and executed." Horn Book

Index to fairy tales; including folklore, legends, and myths in collections. Scarecrow Press 1985-1994 4v   **398.2**

1. Folklore—Indexes   2. Fairy tales—Indexes
3. Legends—Indexes 4. Mythology—Indexes
Volumes covering 1949-1972 and 1973-1977 first published by Faxon 1973 and 1979 respectively
A continuation of Index to fairy tales, myths and legends and its two supplements, compiled by Mary Huse Eastman, published 1926-1952 by Faxon (o.p.)

Volume covering 1949-1972 compiled by Norma Olin Ireland $45 (ISBN 0-8108-2011-0); volume covering 1973-1977 compiled by Norma Olin Ireland $29.50 (ISBN 0-8108-1855-8); volume covering 1978-1986 compiled by Norma Olin Ireland and Joseph W. Sprug $49.50 (ISBN 0-8108-2194-X); volume covering 1987-1992 compiled by Joseph W. Sprug $59.50 (ISBN 0-8108-2750-6)
"An invaluable reference source for locating specific tales in collections." Peterson. Ref Books for Child. 4th edition

Isadora, Rachel
Firebird; adapted and illustrated by Rachel Isadora. Putnam 1994 unp il $15.95 (1-4)   **398.2**

1. Folklore—Russia
ISBN 0-399-22510-2   LC 93-1253
A simple retelling of the Russian tale in which Prince Ivan encounters the magical Firebird who helps him defeat the evil Kotschei and rescue a princess
"This fine picture book was inspired by the Balanchine version of the Stravinsky ballet. . . . The text is clear and simple but strongly evokes the magical atmosphere of *The Firebird*. The illustrations are outstanding—strongly romantic, impressionistic paintings that are alive with movement, drama, and the bold use of color." SLJ

The princess and the frog; adapted from the Frog King and Iron Heinrich by the Brothers Grimm. Greenwillow Bks. 1989 unp il $12.95; lib bdg $12.88 (k-2)   **398.2**

1. Folklore—Germany 2. Fairy tales
ISBN 0-688-06373-X; 0-688-06374-8 (lib bdg)
                 LC 88-61
As payment for retrieving the princess's ball, the frog exacts a promise which the princess is reluctant to fulfill
"Isadora freely adapts—and illustrates with lush paintings—the Grimm tale. . . . Isadora provides a smooth retelling and rich watercolor art that fills the pages. Her impressionist portraits, whether of a princess or a frog, catch the eye and hold attention. Verdant backgrounds and shafts of sunlight illuminate the scenes and extend the book's luxuriant feel, while silhouetted characters on the ribbon-bordered pages of text add a piquant note." Booklist

Ishii, Momoko, 1907-
The tongue-cut sparrow; retold by Momoko Ishii; illustrated by Suekichi Akaba; translated from the Japanese by Katherine Paterson. Lodestar Bks. 1987 unp il $13.95 (k-3)   **398.2**

1. Folklore—Japan
ISBN 0-525-67199-4   LC 86-29314
A "traditional Japanese folk tale about a kind old man who befriends a sparrow and is richly rewarded, and his greedy wife who is taught her lesson." N Y Times Book Rev
"The free-flowing, graceful yet lively translation retains several Japanese onomatopoeic words, which are explained at the end of the book. . . . Traditional black brush drawings in a free and animated style mirror the spirited tale and establish—despite the occasional addition of color—a connection with classic Japanese scroll work." Horn Book

The **Jack** tales; with an appendix compiled by Herbert Halpert; and illustrations by Berkeley Williams, Jr. Houghton Mifflin 1943 201p il $13.95; pa $5.95 (4-6)

398.2

1. Folklore—Southern States
ISBN 0-395-06694-8; 0-395-66951-0 (pa)

"Told by R. M. Ward and his kindred in the Beech Mountain section of Western North Carolina and by other descendants of Council Harmon (1803-1896) elsewhere in the Southern mountains; with three tales from Wise County, Virginia. Set down from these sources and edited by Richard Chase." Title page

"Humor, freshness, colorful American background, and the use of one character as a central figure in the cycle mark these 18 folk tales, told here in the dialect of the mountain country of North Carolina. A scholarly appendix by Herbert Halpert, giving sources and parallels, increases the book's value as a contribution to American folklore. Black-and-white illustrations in the spirit of the text." Booklist

Jacobs, Joseph, 1854-1916

English fairy tales; with illustrations by John Batten. Knopf 1993 428p il $13.95 (4-6)

398.2

1. Fairy tales 2. Folklore—Great Britain
ISBN 0-679-42809-7   LC 93-13878

Also available in paperback from Dover Publs. and in hardcover from Amereon and P. Smith

"Everyman's library children's classics"

A reissue in one volume of the author's English fairy tales (1891) and More English fairy tales (1894)

A collection of more than eighty traditional stories that recount the adventures of giants, witches, princes, princesses, and animals

Johnston, Tony

The badger and the magic fan; a Japanese folktale; adapted by Tony Johnston; illustrated by Tomie dePaola. Putnam 1990 unp il $13.95 (k-3)

398.2

1. Folklore—Japan
ISBN 0-399-21945-5   LC 89-4027

"A Whitehead book"

"The *tengu*, goblins of Japan, relish the magic fan that allows them to make their long noses even longer and short again. A greedy badger, after changing himself into a girl, steals the fan, elongates the nose of a beautiful princess, and then agrees to reduce the ugly appendage for half her father's kingdom." Booklist

"Bright oranges, purples, peaches, pinks, and reds flamboyantly illustrate a funny Japanese folk tale. . . . The combined humor of the illustrations and fast-paced narrative guarantee a wide appeal for kids." Bull Cent Child Books

The tale of Rabbit and Coyote; illustrated by Tomie de Paola. Putnam 1994 unp il $14.95 (k-3)

398.2

1. Zapotec Indians—Legends 2. Rabbit (Legendary character) 3. Coyote (Legendary character)
ISBN 0-399-22258-8   LC 92-43652

Rabbit outwits Coyote in this Zapotec tale which explains why coyotes howl at the moon

"DePaola's vivid, spicy palette of gold, red, and turquoise tones and his use of folk-art borders evoke the desert setting and complement the broad humor of Johnston's text. A glossary of the Spanish phrases that pepper the illustrations is appended." Booklist

Joseph, Lynn

The mermaid's twin sister: more stories from Trinidad; illustrated by Donna Perrone. Clarion Bks. 1994 63p il $13.95 (4 and up)

398.2

1. Folklore—Trinidad and Tobago
ISBN 0-395-64365-1   LC 93-28436

"Tantie, Amber's great-aunt, passes the traditions and values of their Trinidad culture to the many children in the extended family. She has chosen Amber to be her successor, and it is Amber who faithfully records these stories, giving them the flavor of the Trinidad patois but keeping them completely intelligible to the American reader." Booklist

"Accompanied by striking black-and-white illustrations in chalk pastel. . . . The authentic folklore is told with flair, and a fine afterword sets each story in context." Horn Book Guide

A wave in her pocket; stories from Trinidad; illustrated by Brian Pinkney. Clarion Bks. 1991 51p il $14.95 (4 and up)   **398.2**

1. Folklore—Trinidad and Tobago
ISBN 0-395-54432-7   LC 90-39359

On the island of Trinidad, Tantie tells the children six stories, some originating in the countries of West Africa, some in Trinidad, and some in her own imagination

"Fresh and warm as an island breeze, these six stories combine Trinidad's traditional folklore with a child's view of island life. . . . Pinkney's distinctive drawings in white crosshatch on a black background echo the mysterious side of island life. This wonderful addition to the folklore shelf is spiced with magic and suspense." Booklist

Includes glossary

Karlin, Barbara

Cinderella; retold by Barbara Karlin; illustrated by James Marshall. Little, Brown 1989 unp il hardcover o.p. paperback available $4.95 (k-2)   **398.2**

1. Fairy tales
ISBN 0-316-48303-6 (pa)   LC 88-25913

"Those seeking a condensed version of the classic fairy tale will find just what they want in Karlin's brief retelling; without compromising the original, she has pared the story down to the essential action by eliminating much of the descriptive material. . . . James Marshall's witty, warts-and-all illustrations add the sparkle that brings out the best in Karlin's straightforward retelling." Horn Book

Keats, Ezra Jack, 1916-1983

John Henry; an American legend; story and pictures by Ezra Jack Keats. Knopf 1987 unp il lib bdg $12.99; pa $5 (k-3)   **398.2**

1. John Henry (Legendary character)
ISBN 0-394-99052-8 (lib bdg); 0-394-89052-3 (pa)
     LC 86-27453

First published 1965 by Pantheon

This is a picture book retelling of the legend of the Black American folk hero who drove spikes for the railroads

"The dynamic power with which John Henry wields his hammer is matched by the strong illustrations: brilliant oranges and reds contrast with grays and blacks that are often silhouettes; unusual backgrounds produce startling effects. A good picture-story to show to a group." Horn Book

Kellogg, Steven, 1941-

Chicken Little; retold & illustrated by Steven Kellogg. Morrow 1985 unp il lib bdg $15.93; pa $4.95 (k-3)   **398.2**

1. Folklore 2. Animals—Fiction
ISBN 0-688-05691-1 (lib bdg); 0-688-07045-0 (pa)
LC 84-25519

Also available Spanish language edition

Chicken Little and his feathered friends, alarmed that the sky seems to be falling, are easy prey to hungry Foxy Loxy when he poses as a police officer in hopes of tricking them into his truck

"Kellogg has enlivened the text [by] giving it some modern touches (Turkey Lurkey carries golf clubs, Foxy Loxy is caught when a 'hippoliceman' tumbles out of a patrol helicopter to land him). Children have always enjoyed the repetition and cumulation of the story, as well as the silliness of the fowls who believe the sky is falling; here there's added fun." Bull Cent Child Books

Jack and the beanstalk; retold and illustrated by Steven Kellogg. Morrow Junior Bks. 1991 unp il $16; lib bdg $15.93 (k-3)   **398.2**

1. Fairy tales 2. Folklore—Great Britain 3. Giants—Fiction
ISBN 0-688-10250-6; 0-688-10251-4 (lib bdg)
LC 90-45990

A boy climbs to the top of a giant beanstalk, where he uses his quick wits to outsmart a giant and make his and his mother's fortune

"Seldom has the ogre at the top of the beanstalk been depicted with such gusto! The warty, fanged, pug-nosed lout dressed in animal skins and a necklace of teeth is a wonder to behold. Steven Kellogg's humorous detail provides witty embellishment for savoring. His story line is quite faithful to the Joseph Jacobs version of the story, the sturdy text offering a strong framework for the energetic illustrations." Horn Book

Mike Fink; a tall tale; retold and illustrated by Steven Kellogg. Morrow Junior Bks. 1992 unp il $15; lib bdg $14.93 (k-3)   **398.2**

1. Fink, Mike, 1770-1823?—Fiction 2. Tall tales
ISBN 0-688-07003-5; 0-688-07004-3 (lib bdg)
LC 91-46014

Relates the extraordinary deeds of the frontiersman who became King of the Keelboatmen on the Mississippi River

"Steven Kellogg's ebullient retelling of Mike's tall-tale feats—illustrated with large, glowing scenes suffused with blue and yellow and with smaller vignettes emphasizing comic detail—follows Mike's prodigious childhood exploits, his teenage wrestling practice with Rocky Mountain grizzlies, and his years as King of the Keelboatmen, and closes with a final showdown with enormous steamboats taking over the river trade." Horn Book

Paul Bunyan; a tall tale; retold and illustrated by Steven Kellogg. Morrow 1984 unp il $16; lib bdg $15.88; pa $5.95 (k-3)   **398.2**

1. Bunyan, Paul (Legendary character) 2. Tall tales
ISBN 0-688-03849-2; 0-688-03850-6 (lib bdg); 0-688-05800-0 (pa)
LC 83-26684

Also available Spanish language edition

"Numerous events from the legendary north woodsman's life have been linked together as Bunyan and Babe, his big blue ox, traverse the U.S." Booklist

"Kellogg uses oversize pages for busy, detail-crowded illustrations that have vitality and humor, echoing the exaggeration and ebullience of the story." Bull Cent Child Books

Pecos Bill; a tall tale; retold and illustrated by Steven Kellogg. Morrow 1986 unp il $16; lib bdg $15.93; pa $4.95 (k-3)   **398.2**

1. Pecos Bill (Legendary character) 2. Tall tales
ISBN 0-688-05871-X; 0-688-05872-8 (lib bdg); 0-688-09924-6 (pa)
LC 86-784

Also available Spanish language edition

Incidents from the life of Pecos Bill, from his childhood among the coyotes to his unusual wedding day

"Although there's a lot going on in these pictures, they're not cluttered; both the gradations of color and the page design smooth the lines of continuous action and tumult of humorous detail. Kellogg's portrayal of Pecos Bill as a perpetual boy will appeal to children. The retelling is a smooth adaptation for introducing young listeners to longer versions or to accompany storytelling sessions centered around tall-tale heroes." Bull Cent Child Books

Kendall, Carol

The wedding of the rat family; retold by Carol Kendall; illustrated by James Watts. Margaret K. McElderry Bks. 1988 unp il $13.95 (k-3)   **398.2**

1. Folklore—China
ISBN 0-689-50450-0
LC 88-2197

"In this traditional Chinese story, a family of lordly rats want to marry their daughter to the most exalted suitor. . . . The rat mother decides perhaps the best plan is to marry her daughter to their most ferocious enemy, the cat." Booklist

"A cautionary tale enlivened with considerable wit is illustrated with delicately small-scale paintings of the rats in opulent dress." Bull Cent Child Books

Kherdian, David, 1931-

Feathers and tails; animal fables from around the world; retold by David Kherdian; illustrated by Nonny Hogrogian. Philomel Bks. 1992 95p il $19.95 (2-5)   **398.2**

1. Fables 2. Animals—Fiction
ISBN 0-399-21876-9
LC 91-31270

A collection of animal fables and folklore from such sources as the Bidpai fables, Aesop, Panchatantra, Grimm, and Wu Cheng-en

"A stellar blend of story and illustration that will appeal to storytellers, readers, and listeners of many ages. . . . Like the fables they illustrate, Hogrogian's pen-and-ink-and-watercolor drawings are spare, uncluttered, and engaging. Her beautifully drawn animals remain animals despite their human activities and foibles. Brief descriptions of the sources are appended." SLJ

Kimmel, Eric A.

Anansi and the talking melon; retold by Eric A. Kimmel; illustrated by Janet Stevens. Holiday House 1994 unp il $15.95; pa $6.95 (k-3)   **398.2**

1. Folklore—Africa 2. Anansi (Legendary character)
ISBN 0-8234-1104-4; 0-8234-1167-2 (pa)
LC 93-4239

Anansi the Spider tricks Elephant and some other animals into thinking the melon in which he is hiding can talk

"The snappy narration is well suited for individual reading or group sharing. The colorful line-and-wash illustrations are filled with movement and playful energy." SLJ

Kimmel, Eric A.—*Continued*

Anansi goes fishing; retold by Eric A. Kimmel; illustrated by Janet Stevens. Holiday House 1992 unp il $15.95; pa $5.95 (k-3)

398.2

1. Folklore—Africa 2. Anansi (Legendary character)
ISBN 0-8234-0918-X; 0-8234-1022-6 (pa)

LC 91-17813

Anansi the spider plans to trick Turtle into catching a fish for his dinner, but Turtle proves to be smarter and ends up with a free meal. Explains the origin of spider webs

"Children able to comprehend the wordplay will be delighted when the lazy but lovable trickster figure is outwitted by the clever turtle, and Stevens' colorful, comical illustrations are perfect for this contemporary rendition of the tale." Booklist

Bearhead; a Russian folktale; adapted by Eric A. Kimmel with illustrations by Charles Mikolaycak. Holiday House 1991 unp il $15.95 (k-3)

398.2

1. Folklore—Russia 2. Fairy tales
ISBN 0-8234-0902-3

LC 91-55026

Bearhead succeeds in outwitting the witch Madame Hexaba and a frog-headed goblin

"Kimmel's lively text plays up the broad, almost slapstick humor of the story. Mikolaycak's watercolor-and-colored-pencil illustrations are deftly drawn." SLJ

Boots and his brothers; a Norwegian tale; retold by Eric A. Kimmel; illustrated by Kimberly Bulcken Root. Holiday House 1992 unp il $14.95 (k-3)

398.2

1. Folklore—Norway
ISBN 0-8234-0886-8

LC 90-23659

A young man's kindness to an old beggar woman earns him his weight in gold and half a kingdom

"With a combination of plainness and magic, the story is well paced and dramatic, told in simple rhythmic prose. . . . The line and wash illustrations, loosely framed by a gold string, are in different shapes and sizes, like wall hangings and banners." Booklist

The gingerbread man; retold by Eric A. Kimmel; illustrated by Megan Lloyd. Holiday House 1993 unp il $15.95; pa $5.95 (k-2)

398.2

1. Folklore
ISBN 0-8234-0824-8; 0-8234-1137-0 (pa)

LC 90-33202

A freshly baked gingerbread man escapes when he is taken out of the oven and eludes a number of animals until he meets a clever fox

"This version softens the ending with a final page of fresh, recently baked gingerbread men. This is a story that calls for energetic art, and Lloyd provides just that in warm-toned watercolors that feature the gingerbread man zipping across the pages. A compact text and suitably large pictures make this just right for groups." Booklist

I-know-not-what, I-know-not-where; a Russian tale; adapted by Eric A. Kimmel; illustrated by Robert Sauber. Holiday House 1994 63p il $16.95 (4-6)

398.2

1. Folklore—Russia
ISBN 0-8234-1020-X

LC 92-32692

"The life of Frol changes completely when he shoots a magical white dove. He treats her wound, and when the czar sets him impossible and perilous tasks, Frol successful-ly completes each feat with the dove's advice. Colorful, figurative language, edge-of-the-seat excitement, and rich and romantic illustrations characterize this retelling of an old Russian tale." Horn Book Guide

Iron John; adapted from the Brothers Grimm by Eric A. Kimmel; illustrated by Trina Schart Hyman. Holiday House 1994 unp il $15.95 (2-5)

398.2

1. Fairy tales 2. Folklore—Germany
ISBN 0-8234-1073-0

LC 93-7534

With help of Iron John, the wild man of the forest who is under a curse, a young prince makes his way in the world and finds his true love

"Abridged and, as the afterword explains, somewhat changed from the Grimms' tale, Kimmel's dramatic narrative flows from scene to scene with a clear sense of adventure and romance and an underlying sense of mystery. Hyman's beautifully composed illustrations . . . are notable for their rich colors and subtle interplay of light and darkness." Booklist

The spotted pony: a collection of Hanukkah stories; retold by Eric A. Kimmel; illustrated by Leonard Everett Fisher. Holiday House 1992 70p il $14.95 (3-6)

398.2

1. Jews—Folklore 2. Hanukkah—Fiction
ISBN 0-8234-0936-8

LC 91-24214

This is a collection of "stories for Hanukkah. There are eight tales, one for each night, and each has a *shammes* or 'servant' story preceding it. All of the selections are rich in plot, character, and tradition. . . . Perfect for any occasion, this collection will truly shine when its selections are told or read aloud." SLJ

The three princes; a tale from the Middle East; retold by Eric A. Kimmel; illustrated by Leonard Everett Fisher. Holiday House 1994 unp il $15.95 (k-3)

398.2

1. Folklore—Middle East
ISBN 0-8234-1115-X

LC 93-25862

A princess promises to marry the prince who finds the most precious treasure

"Sly humor and high spirits buoy Kimmel's text. . . . Fisher . . . suggests the exotic Arabian setting with a rich palette of striking tones—pink desert skies, violet vistas—and by incorporating unexpected closeups and unusual angles in his compositions. The play of light and shadow is spectacular." Publ Wkly

Three sacks of truth; a story from France; adapted by Eric A. Kimmel; illustrated by Robert Rayevsky. Holiday House 1993 unp il $15.95 (2-4)

398.2

1. Fairy tales 2. Folklore—France
ISBN 0-8234-0921-X

LC 91-19265

With the aid of a perfect peach, a silver fife, and his own resources, Petit Jean outwits a dishonest king and wins the hand of a princess

"In this crisp and sprightly interpretation, storyteller Kimmel takes full advantage of the plot's sly humor, which he accentuates through many colorful, deft turns of phrase. . . . Rayevsky adds rich, predominantly earth-toned illustrations that emphasize character and expression with a slight ironic bite." Publ Wkly

Knutson, Barbara

How the guinea fowl got her spots; a Swahili tale of friendship; retold and illustrated by Barbara Knutson. Carolrhoda Bks. 1990 unp il lib bdg $18.95; pa $6.95 (k-3)
398.2

1. Folklore—Africa 2. Guinea fowl—Fiction
ISBN 0-87614-416-4 (lib bdg); 0-87614-537-3 (pa)
LC 89-25191

"In this traditional Swahili folktale, Guinea Fowl twice saves her friend Cow from Lion. In return, Cow sprinkles milk over the formerly all-black guinea fowl, disguising her from the lion and allowing her to easily hide in the grasses. . . . Knutson's scratchboard illustrations . . . perfectly match the content and tone of the story. . . . The placement of the drawings and the exquisite design create a harmony that makes this a strikingly handsome addition to folktale collections." SLJ

Sungura and Leopard; a Swahili trickster tale. Little, Brown 1993 unp il lib bdg $15.95 (k-3)
398.2

1. Folklore—Africa 2. Rabbits—Fiction 3. Leopards—Fiction
ISBN 0-316-50010-0
LC 92-31905

A small but clever hare and a fierce leopard agree to share a house, but as the hare's family grows, he realizes that he must find a way to get rid of his bad-tempered neighbor

"Knutson's rhythm, pacing and presence make this an excellent read-aloud selection. Scratchboard and watercolor renderings evoke traditional African design, while vivid earthy hues enhance the strong sense of place. An author's note preceding the tale explains the traditions of the trickster tale and of honoring ancestors in stories." Publ Wkly

Kurtz, Jane

Fire on the mountain; illustrated by E. B. Lewis. Simon & Schuster Bks. for Young Readers 1994 unp il $15 (1-4)
398.2

1. Folklore—Ethiopia
ISBN 0-671-88268-6
LC 93-11477

A clever young shepherd boy uses his wits to gain a fortune for himself and his sister from a haughty rich man

"Lewis uses color to achieve intriguing contrast and articulates characters' faces with expression and power. Kurtz, who heard the story as a child in Ethiopia, retells it in a strong narrative voice: her language is simple and spare yet evocative." Booklist

Lattimore, Deborah Nourse

Why there is no arguing in heaven; a Mayan myth. Harper & Row 1989 unp il lib bdg $14.89 (3-6)
398.2

1. Mayas—Legends
ISBN 0-06-023718-X
LC 87-35045

Hunab Ku, the first Creator God of the Mayas, challenges the Moon Goddess and Lizard House to create a being to worship him, but the Maize God succeeds where the others fail

"Based on research into ancient documents . . . this lively retelling of the Mayan creation myth combines several versions into a straightforward plot line with a smoothly flowing text suitable for independent reading or oral interpretation. . . . The accompanying illustrations . . . depict the setting as a lush, tropical paradise; the characters are suggestive of reliefs and statues from the pre-Columbian period." SLJ

Bold and dynamic, the paintings capture the earthy humor of the tale, enhancing its impact." Horn Book

Lee, Jeanne M.

Legend of the Milky Way; retold and illustrated by Jeanne M. Lee. Holt & Co. 1982 unp il hardcover o.p. paperback available $5.95 (k-3)
398.2

1. Folklore—China 2. Milky Way—Fiction
ISBN 0-8050-1361-X (pa)
LC 81-6906

Retells the Chinese legend of the Weaver Princess who came down from heaven to marry a mortal, a love story represented in the stars of the Milky Way

"The cool colors and serene lines of Lee's artwork capture the subtle emotions in this retelling." Booklist

Toad is the uncle of heaven; a Vietnamese folk tale; retold and illustrated by Jeanne M. Lee. Holt & Co. 1985 unp il hardcover o.p. paperback available $5.95 (k-3)
398.2

1. Folklore—Vietnam 2. Toads—Fiction
ISBN 0-8050-1147-1 (pa)
LC 85-5639

Toad leads a group of animals to ask the King of Heaven to send rain to the parched earth

"The story is simple and reminiscent of motifs common to many cultures. . . . The author's simple prose and beautiful page design, far from being static or stilted, are fluid and convey movement and earthy humor. Her tale of courage born of common sense and perseverance will satisfy a wide audience." Horn Book

Lent, Blair, 1930-

Baba Yaga; by Ernest Small; illustrated by Blair Lent. Houghton Mifflin 1966 48p il hardcover o.p. paperback available $5.95 (k-3)
398.2

1. Folklore—Russia
ISBN 0-395-63037-1 (pa)

"Little Marusia searching for turnips in the forest comes on the house of a wicked witch. . . . Baba Yaga takes little Marusia captive, but Marusia shows herself more than a match for the witch's evil . . . ways. The story is a composite of many of the Baba Yaga stories told to Russian children." Christ Sci Monit

"While rather cursory this tale is redeemed by illustrations that sweep, tumble and soar through the environs of Baba Yaga's haunted forest." N Y Times Book Rev

Lesser, Rika

Hansel and Gretel; retold by Rika Lesser; illustrated by Paul O. Zelinsky. Putnam 1989 c1984 unp il $15.95; pa $7.95 (1-3)
398.2

1. Folklore—Germany 2. Fairy tales
ISBN 0-399-21733-9; 0-399-21725-8 (pa)
LC 88-30615

A Caldecott Medal honor book, 1985
First published 1984 by Dodd, Mead

"Lesser's telling reflects the earliest, clean-lined versions and leaves out the psychological embellishments frequently included in other settings. . . . Zelinsky has chosen a painterly style that suggests the naturalistic genre works of the 17th-Century Dutch or German. The paintings are rich in detail of forest and architecture and consistent in the costuming." SLJ

Lester, Julius

Further tales of Uncle Remus; the misadventures of Brer Rabbit, Brer Fox, Brer Wolf, the Doodang, and other creatures; as told by Julius Lester; illustrated by Jerry Pinkney. Dial Bks. 1990 148p il $17.99; lib bdg $14.89 (4-6) **398.2**

1. African Americans—Folklore 2. Animals—Fiction
ISBN 0-8037-0610-3; 0-8037-0611-1 (lib bdg)
LC 88-20223
A retelling of thirty-two African American tales

How many spots does a leopard have? and other tales; illustrated by David Shannon. Scholastic 1989 72p il $15.95; pa $5.95 (2-5) **398.2**

1. Folklore—Africa
ISBN 0-590-41973-0; 0-590-41972-2 (pa)
LC 88-33647
An illustrated collection of twelve folk tales, ten African and two Jewish
"The combination of the two cultures works well; each story in this eclectic collection begs to be read aloud. . . . Lester's retellings are beguiling and graceful, his language attuned to each story's nuances. Shannon's striking paintings, in rich browns and greens, are as full of depth as the stories themselves." Publ Wkly

John Henry; pictures by Jerry Pinkney. Dial Bks. for Young Readers 1994 unp il $16.99; lib bdg $16.89 (k-3) **398.2**

1. John Henry (Legendary character) 2. African Americans—Folklore 3. Folklore—United States
ISBN 0-8037-1606-0; 0-8037-1607-9 (lib bdg)
LC 93-34583
A Caldecott Medal honor book, 1995
"The original legend of John Henry and how he beat the steam drill with his sledgehammer has been enhanced and enriched, in Lester's retelling, with wonderful contemporary details and poetic similes that add humor, beauty, and strength. Pinkney's evocative illustrations—especially the landscapes, splotchy and impressionistic, yet very solid and vigorous—are little short of magnificent." Horn Book Guide

The knee-high man, and other tales; pictures by Ralph Pinto. Dial Bks. 1972 28p il hardcover o.p. paperback available $3.95 (k-3) **398.2**

1. African Americans—Folklore 2. Animals—Fiction
ISBN 0-8037-0234-5 (pa)
The author retells six animal stories from black folklore
"These are excellent for story telling and should be so presented for the greatest impact." N Y Times Book Rev

The last tales of Uncle Remus; as told by Julius Lester; illustrated by Jerry Pinkney. Dial Bks. 1994 156p il $18.99; lib bdg $17.89 (4-6) **398.2**

1. African Americans—Folklore 2. Animals—Fiction
ISBN 0-8037-1303-7; 0-8037-1304-5 (lib bdg)
LC 93-7531
A retelling of thirty-nine African American tales

The man who knew too much; a moral tale from the Baila of Zambia; retold by Julius Lester; illustrated by Leonard Jenkins. Clarion Bks. 1994 32p il $14.95 (2-4) **398.2**

1. Folklore—Zambia
ISBN 0-395-60521-0
LC 93-40810
"Twice a giant eagle lands on a crying baby, calming the child with the soft beating of its wings as the mother works in the nearby field. The woman chases the bird with her hoe. Awed by the spectacle, and amazed that her baby is unhurt by the bird's great talons, she describes the scene to her unbelieving husband, who shoots an arrow at the eagle, killing his own child instead." SLJ
"Despite its picture-book format and spare text, this poetic version of an African story will appeal to older readers, who may want to think about all that it means. . . . Jenkins' sunlit oil paintings evoke the wide southern African bushveld, against which the heartrending mystery is acted out." Booklist

More tales of Uncle Remus; further adventures of Brer Rabbit, his friends, enemies, and others; as told by Julius Lester; illustrated by Jerry Pinkney. Dial Bks. 1988 143p il $16.99; lib bdg $15.89 (4-6) **398.2**

1. African Americans—Folklore 2. Animals—Fiction
ISBN 0-8037-0419-4; 0-8037-0420-8 (lib bdg)
LC 86-32890
A retelling of thirty-seven classic African American tales

The tales of Uncle Remus; the adventures of Brer Rabbit; as told by Julius Lester; illustrated by Jerry Pinkney. Dial Bks. 1987 151p il $18.99; lib bdg $16.89 (4-6) **398.2**

1. African Americans—Folklore 2. Animals—Fiction
ISBN 0-8037-0271-X; 0-8037-0272-8 (lib bdg)
LC 85-20449
This adaptation of 48 Brer Rabbit stories "is the work of a writer familiar with the methodology of folkloristic and historical research but also with the techniques of flavoring fiction. Lester himself makes wry narrative asides that punctuate but don't intrude on the stories the way the 'Uncle Remus' framework did. . . . Pinkney's illustrations—black-and-white drawings with occasional double-page spreads in full color—are well drafted, fresh, and funny." Bull Cent Child Books

Levine, Arthur A., 1962-

The boy who drew cats; a Japanese folktale; retold by Arthur A. Levine; pictures by Frédéric Clément. Dial Bks. for Young Readers 1994 unp il $16; lib bdg $15.89 (k-3) **398.2**

1. Folklore—Japan 2. Cats—Fiction
ISBN 0-8037-1172-7; 0-8037-1173-5 (lib bdg)
LC 91-46232
An artistic young boy's love for drawing cats gets him into trouble and leads him to a mysterious experience
"The unembellished, smooth narrative nicely complements Clément's elegant acrylics. A source note is included, as well as a chart giving the pronunciation and meanings of the Japanese characters that appear at the top of each page of text." Horn Book Guide

Lewis, J. Patrick

The frog princess; a Russian folktale; retold by J. Patrick Lewis; paintings by Gennady Spirin. Dial Bks. for Young Readers 1994 32p il $15.99; lib bdg $15.89 (1-4) **398.2**

1. Fairy tales 2. Folklore—Russia
ISBN 0-8037-1623-0; 0-8037-1624-9 (lib bdg)
LC 93-10827

Forced to marry an ugly frog, the youngest son of the Tsar is astounded to learn that the frog is really the beautiful princess Vasilisa the Wise

"Spirin's elegant watercolor illustrations complement the stately tone of the text, and the decorative borders framing most of the paintings add to the book's appeal." Booklist

Lewis, Richard

All of you was singing; art by Ed Young. Atheneum Pubs. 1991 unp il $13.95; pa $4.95 **398.2**

1. Aztecs—Legends
ISBN 0-689-31596-1; 0-689-71853-5 (pa)
LC 89-18263

"A retelling of an Aztec myth about how music came to earth. In controlled, sometimes lyric prose, Lewis recounts the creation of earth and sky from the remains of the earth-monster, torn in two by serpents. . . . Young's multimedia illustrations (cut-paper collage, watercolor, colored pencil and chalk on colored paper) are arresting and have a certain grandeur in spite of their apparent simplicity. . . . Highly sophisticated and with limited child appeal, it will, nonetheless, reward those bold enough to make the endeavor." SLJ

Littledale, Freya, 1929-1992

The elves and the shoemaker; retold by Freya Littledale; pictures by Brinton Turkle. Four Winds Press 1975 unp il o.p.; Scholastic paperback available $4.95 (k-3) **398.2**

1. Folklore—Germany 2. Fairy tales
ISBN 0-590-44855-2 (pa)

This is "a picture-book version of the famous tale about the destitute shoemaker who is rescued from poverty by the aid of two energetic elves, who appear at midnight to make shoes." SLJ

"Few illustrators could infuse the familiar fairy-tale with so much charm as Brinton Turkle has. His pictures dance with life and color in an authentic 19th century setting. And Ms. Littledale's retelling is equally compelling." Publ Wkly

Lottridge, Celia Barker

The name of the tree; a Bantu folktale; retold by Celia Barker Lottridge; and illustrated by Ian Wallace. Margaret K. McElderry Bks. 1989 unp il $14.95 (k-3) **398.2**

1. Folklore—Africa
ISBN 0-689-50490-X
LC 89-2430

"When in time of drought the animals leave the land of the short grass in search of food, they find a tree that will give up its fruit only to someone who knows its name. The story moves quickly in an easy, conversational style, and the grainy illustrations capture the parched, cracked countryside." Horn Book Guide

Louie, Ai-Ling, 1949-

Yeh-Shen; a Cinderella story from China; retold by Ai-Ling Louie; illustrated by Ed Young. Philomel Bks. 1982 unp il $15.95 (2-4) **398.2**

1. Folklore—China 2. Fairy tales
ISBN 0-399-20900-X
LC 80-11745

This version of the Cinderella story, in which a young girl overcomes the wickedness of her stepsister and stepmother to become the bride of a prince, is based on ancient Chinese manuscripts written 1000 years before the earliest European version

"The reteller has cast the tale in well-cadenced prose, fleshing out the spare account with elegance and grace. In a manner reminiscent of Chinese scrolls and of decorated folding screens, the text is chiefly set within vertical panels, while the luminescent illustrations—less narrative than emotional—often increase their impact by overspreading the narrow framework or appearing on pages of their own." Horn Book

The **Magic** orange tree, and other Haitian folktales; collected by Diane Wolkstein; drawings by Elsa Henriquez. Knopf 1978 212p il music o.p.; Schocken Bks. paperback available $16 (5 and up) **398.2**

1. Folklore—Haiti
ISBN 0-8052-0650-7 (pa)
LC 77-15003

"A rare collection of folktales and songs is presented in this volume. Miss Wolkstein travelled throughout Haiti listening to the many storytellers in all areas. Each of the twenty-eight tales is preceded by an introduction which details the circumstances surrounding the collection of each story. The blend of cultures found in Haiti is well-depicted in her selections. The introduction in itself is as spellbinding as are the stories. . . . An added delight is the inclusion of music and words in both English and Creole." Bibliophile

Mahy, Margaret

The seven Chinese brothers; illustrated by Jean and Mou-Sien Tseng. Scholastic 1990 unp $14.95; pa $3.95 (1-3) **398.2**

1. Folklore—China 2. Fairy tales
ISBN 0-590-42055-0; 0-590-42057-7 (pa)
LC 88-33668

Also available Spanish language edition

A story about "seven brothers, each of whom was blessed with an extraordinary power. Together, they use their amazing talents to avoid death at the hands of Emperor Ch'in Shih Huang, while trying to help the exhausted conscripted laborers working on the Great Wall." Child Book Rev Serv

"The handsome watercolor illustrations show a sensitivity to landscape and character portrayal . . . a hint of humor, and a flair for the dramatic. Written with Mahy's accustomed storytelling skill, this book will find an eager audience as a read-aloud for elementary school children." Booklist

Marshak, S. (Samuil), 1887-1964

The Month-Brothers; a Slavic tale; retold by Samuil Marshak; translation from the Russian by Thomas P. Whitney; illustrated by Diane Stanley. Morrow 1983 unp il lib bdg $15.93 (1-3) **398.2**

1. Slavs—Folklore 2. Fairy tales
ISBN 0-688-01510-7
LC 82-7927

Marshak, S. (Samuil), 1887-1964—*Continued*

A retelling of the Slavic folktale in which a young girl outwits her greedy stepmother and stepsister with the help of the Month Brothers who use their magic to enable her to fulfill seemingly impossible tasks

"Here is a beautiful book sure to delight a wide audience. . . . The language of the translation is readable, idiomatic English, neither archaic nor too informal. Stanley's watercolors are beautifully executed with intricate details of pattern and full color." Child Book Rev Serv

Marshall, James, 1942-1992

Goldilocks and the three bears; retold and illustrated by James Marshall. Dial Bks. for Young Readers 1988 unp il $14.99; lib bdg $13.89 (k-2)   398.2

1. Folklore 2. Bears—Fiction
ISBN 0-8037-0542-5; 0-8037-0543-3 (lib bdg)
LC 87-32983

Also available Spanish language edition
A Caldecott Medal honor book, 1989

"Marshall's Goldilocks, the naughty little girl who disrupts a placid bear household, is no adorable blond moppet led more by curiosity than by mischievous intent. Instead, she is a sturdy, brazen, mini-hussy who stomps over the doorsill with a determined set to her mouth and a confident bounce in her step. . . . The big cartoonlike pictures depict a cozy modern setting for the respectable, suburban bears with snug rooms cluttered with books, bulbous upholstered furniture and a messy little bear's room. . . . The story contains a genuine enjoyment of Goldilock's adventures as they are reflected in Marshall's usual slapdash and rollicking illustrations." Horn Book

Hansel and Gretel; retold and illustrated by James Marshall. Dial Bks. for Young Readers 1990 unp il $12.95; lib bdg $12.89 (k-2)   398.2

1. Folklore—Germany 2. Fairy tales
ISBN 0-8037-0827-0; 0-8037-0828-9 (lib bdg)
LC 89-26011

Also available in paperback from Puffin Bks.
A poor woodcutter's children, lost in the forest, come upon a house made of cookies, cakes, and candy, occupied by a wicked witch who likes to have children for dinner

"Marshall's trademark wit and slyness mark every page of this effervescent interpretation. Never has there been a more horribly magnificent witch than his—an overstuffed, cackling harridan resplendent in scarlet costume, lipstick and rouge, her hair bedecked with incongruously delicate bows." Publ Wkly

Red Riding Hood; retold and illustrated by James Marshall. Dial Bks. for Young Readers 1987 unp il $14.99; lib bdg $10.89 (k-2)   398.2

1. Folklore—Germany 2. Wolves—Fiction
ISBN 0-8037-0344-9; 0-8037-0345-7 (lib bdg)
LC 86-16722

Also available in paperback from Puffin Bks.
A "retelling of the familiar tale . . . maintaining the integrity of the Grimm Brothers' version, with both Grandma and Red Riding Hood eaten and later rescued by a hunter." SLJ

This version "will have both children and their parents gripped with the drama and amused by the up-to-date dialogue. . . . The humorous, slightly sinister illustrations display Marshall's wacky style to its best advantage. Funny and wonderful for reading aloud." Horn Book

The three little pigs; retold and illustrated by James Marshall. Dial Bks. for Young Readers 1989 unp il $13.99; lib bdg $12.89 (k-2)   398.2

1. Folklore—Great Britain 2. Pigs—Fiction 3. Wolves—Fiction
ISBN 0-8037-0591-3; 0-8037-0594-8 (lib bdg)
LC 88-33411

"In his spiffed-up version of the story, the three porkers follow the traditional course of straw, sticks, and bricks with the traditional results, but the players and accoutrements have a bit more zip than those in other versions. . . . The large, exuberant, cartoonlike illustrations provide much additional entertainment, jouncing readers along delightfully from one amusing scene to the next." Horn Book

Martin, Claire

Boots & the glass mountain; retold by Claire Martin; pictures by Gennady Spirin. Dial Bks. for Young Readers 1992 unp il $15; lib bdg $14.89 (2-4)   398.2

1. Folklore—Norway 2. Fairy tales
ISBN 0-8037-1110-7; 0-8037-1111-5 (lib bdg)
LC 91-9724

Boots saves his father's fields from the ravages of the trolls' wild stallions, and with their help, he rides up the glass mountain and wins the princess's hand

"The tradition of the romantic fairy tale is richly upheld in this version of a Norwegian story. . . . Spirin's elaborate illustrations, like medieval tapestries, sparkle with jewellike colors and are arranged within bordered pages decorated in the style of illuminated manuscripts." SLJ

Martin, Rafe, 1946-

The boy who lived with the seals; illustrated by David Shannon. Putnam 1993 unp il $15.95 (1-4)   398.2

1. Chinook Indians—Legends 2. Seals (Animals)—Fiction
ISBN 0-399-22413-0
LC 91-46023

In this Chinook legend, a lost boy who has grown up in the sea with seals returns to his tribe but is strangely changed

"Shannon's dark, romantic paintings are dramatically stylized. . . . Martin's retelling employs lyrical language while carefully retaining a clarity appropriate for the intended audience." Publ Wkly

Mayer, Marianna, 1945-

Baba Yaga and Vasilisa the brave; as told by Marianna Mayer; illustrated by K. Y. Craft. Morrow Junior Bks. 1994 unp il $16; lib bdg $15.93 (3-5)   398.2

1. Fairy tales 2. Folklore—Russia
ISBN 0-688-08500-8; 0-688-08501-6 (lib bdg)
LC 90-38514

A retelling of the old Russian fairy tale in which beautiful Vasilisa uses the help of her doll to escape from the clutches of the witch Baba Yaga, who in turn sets in motion the events which lead to the once ill-treated girl's marrying the tzar

"Mayer's graceful prose conveys both the wonder and power of the tale. Complementing the text are Craft's illustrations done in a mixture of watercolor, gouache, and oils. The palette of red and gold set against a dark background resembles Russian folk-art paintings on black-lacquered wood." SLJ

Mayer, Marianna, 1945-—*Continued*

Beauty and the beast; retold by Marianna Mayer; illustrated by Mercer Mayer. Four Winds Press 1978 unp il $15.95; pa $5.95 (1-4)
398.2

1. Folklore—France 2. Fairy tales
ISBN 0-02-765270-X; 0-689-71151-4 (pa)
LC 78-54679

Through her great capacity to love, a kind and beautiful maid releases a handsome prince from the spell which has made him an ugly beast

"This fresh, new version of the classic French tale is a valid condensation of its lengthier ancestors. Ms. Mayer's clear, crisp style perfectly complements the book's visual qualities. Mercer Mayer's illustrations are, quite simply, superb. They are dramatic and evocative, rich in warm, earth tones and exotic detail." Child Book Rev Serv

Mayo, Gretchen

That tricky Coyote! retold and illustrated by Gretchen Will Mayo. Walker & Co. 1993 35p il $12.95; lib bdg $13.85 (k-3) **398.2**

1. Coyote (Legendary character) 2. Indians of North America—Legends
ISBN 0-8027-8200-0; 0-8027-8201-9 (lib bdg)
LC 92-12440

This collection "presents traditional Native American stories about Coyote, a mischievous figure present in the fables of several tribes." Child Book Rev Serv

"Filled with dialogue and action, these entertaining tales will delight young readers and listeners. The soft colors and subtle expressions of the characters perfectly reflect the tone of each tale and add greatly to the reader's enjoyment." Booklist

Another available title about tricky Coyote is:
Meet tricky Coyote! (1993)

Includes bibliography

Mayo, Margaret, 1935-

Magical tales from many lands; retold by Margaret Mayo; illustrated by Jane Ray. Dutton Children's Bks. 1993 126p il $19.99 (3-6) **398.2**

1. Folklore
ISBN 0-525-45017-3
LC 93-12164

"Mayo presents 14 traditional tales from around the world. . . . As retold by Mayo, the stories read aloud well, and that makes them a pleasure to read silently as well. Ray's striking, full-color artwork appears on every page, illustrating the tales with richly patterned, well-composed illustrations that will draw readers to the book." Booklist

Includes bibliographical references

McClintock, Barbara, 1955-

Animal fables from Aesop; adapted and illustrated by Barbara McClintock. Godine 1991 unp il $18.95 (1-4) **398.2**

1. Fables 2. Animals—Fiction
ISBN 0-87923-913-1
LC 91-55368

The fables "are framed at the beginning and end by scenes from a stage set, with the actors posing as animals introducing themselves to us on the opening page and bowing at our expected applause on the last. The graceful full-color illustrations are both delicate and theatrical, as the limited cast reappears in various tales . . . dressed as 18th-

or 19th-century townspeople, with the dramatic gestures and facial expressions of humans. . . . The whole feel of this book is in the tradition of La Fontaine: gay, witty, full of charm and foible." N Y Times Book Rev

McDermott, Gerald

Anansi the spider; a tale from the Ashanti; adapted and illustrated by Gerald McDermott. Holt & Co. 1972 unp il $15.95; pa $5.95 (k-3)
398.2

1. Folklore—Ghana 2. Ashanti (African people)—Folklore 3. Anansi (Legendary character)
ISBN 0-8050-0310-X; 0-8050-0311-8 (pa)
A Caldecott Medal honor book, 1973

The adaptation of this traditional tale of Ghana is based on an animated film by McDermott. It tells of Anansi, a spider, who is saved from terrible fates by his six sons and is unable to decide which of them to reward. The solution to his predicament is also an explanation for how the moon was put into the sky

"This folk tale is illustrated with strikingly stylized, boldly colored designs based on the traditional geometrical forms of Ashanti art." Saturday Rev

"The simplicity of the writing style makes this a good adaptation for reading aloud to young children or as a source for storytelling." Bull Cent Child Books

Arrow to the sun; a Pueblo Indian tale; adapted and illustrated by Gerald McDermott. Viking 1974 unp il $15.99; pa $4.99 (k-3)
398.2

1. Pueblo Indians—Legends
ISBN 0-670-13369-8; 0-14-050211-4 (pa)
Also available Spanish language edition
Awarded the Caldecott Medal, 1975

This myth tells how Boy searches for his immortal father, the Lord of the Sun, in order to substantiate his paternal heritage. Shot as an arrow to the sun, Boy passes through the four chambers of ceremony to prove himself. Accepted by his father, he returns to earth to bring the Lord of the Sun's spirit to the world of men

"The simple, brief text—which suggests similar stories in religion and folklore—is amply illustrated in full-page and doublespread pictures. . . . The strong colors and the bold angular forms powerfully accompany the text." Horn Book

Coyote: a trickster tale from the American Southwest; told and illustrated by Gerald McDermott. Harcourt Brace & Co. 1994 unp il $14.95; pa $5 (k-3) **398.2**

1. Indians of North America—Legends 2. Coyote (Legendary character)
ISBN 0-15-220724-4; 0-15-200032-1 (pa)
LC 92-32979

Also available Spanish language edition

"Coyote persuades the crows to help him fly, but he becomes so obnoxious and boastful that they abandon him in midair, so he falls back to earth. Told with playful illustrations against the glowing orange of a desert sky, the humorous Zuni tale explains how Coyote, who once had blue fur, got his dust-colored coat and black-tippped tail." Horn Book Guide

The magic tree; a tale from the Congo; adapted and illustrated by Gerald McDermott. Holt & Co. 1994 unp il $15.95 (k-3)
398.2

1. Folklore—Zaire
ISBN 0-8050-3080-8
LC 93-35588

McDermott, Gerald—*Continued*

A reissue of the title first published 1973

"When Mavungu, an ill-favored, ignored twin, discovers a magic tree in the jungle, a princess endows him with beauty and riches and becomes his wife. But when he can't resist divulging to his family the source of all his glory, he loses everything. . . . The simplicity and starkness of the shapes and colors, resembling those found in Central African art, fit the Congolese tale perfectly." Horn Book Guide

Raven; a trickster tale from the Pacific Northwest; told and illustrated by Gerald McDermott. Harcourt Brace Jovanovich 1993 unp il $14.95 (k-3)   **398.2**

1. Indians of North America—Legends

ISBN 0-15-265661-8   LC 91-14563

A Caldecott Medal honor book, 1994

Raven, a Pacific Coast Indian trickster, sets out to find the sun

"Raven, whether he appears as a bird or child, is always marked with a distinctive design of clear-cut red, green, and blue on black, sharply contrasting with the softer hues and forms of the backgrounds and the other characters. In this way, Raven is always recognizable, even when he shifts his shape to human form. . . . Read this picture book aloud for the full effect of its simple, rhythmic text and striking artwork." Booklist

Zomo the Rabbit; a trickster tale from West Africa; told and illustrated by Gerald McDermott. Harcourt Brace Jovanovich 1992 unp il $14.95; pa $5 (k-3)   **398.2**

1. Folklore—Africa 2. Rabbits—Fiction

ISBN 0-15-299967-1; 0-15-201010-6 (pa)

LC 91-14558

"Zomo the Rabbit, an African trickster . . . goes to Sky God and requests wisdom. Sky God informs him that he must earn it and assigns him three impossible tasks." Child Book Rev Serv

"Like the spare text, the shapes here are boldly controlled—ideal for sharing with a group of very young children. Because of their rich patterns and sharp color contrasts, the images in the gouache paintings, although simple, never become simplistic." Bull Cent Child Books

McGovern, Ann

Too much noise; illustrated by Simms Taback. Houghton Mifflin 1967 44p il $14.95; pa $5.95 (k-3)   **398.2**

1. Folklore

ISBN 0-395-18110-0; 0-395-62985-3 (pa)

"The too crowded house of a familiar old tale becomes a too noisy house in this entertaining picture-book story. Bothered by the noises in his house, an old man follows the advice of the village wise man by first acquiring and then getting rid of a cow, donkey, sheep, hen, dog, and cat. Only then can he appreciate how quiet his house is. The simplicity and straightforwardness of the folktale are evident in both the telling of the cumulative story and in the amusing colored illustrations." Booklist

Medicine Story

The Children of the Morning Light: Wampanoag tales; as told by Manitonquat (Medicine Story); illustrated by Mary F. Arquette. Macmillan 1994 72p il $16.95 (4-6)   **398.2**

1. Wampanoag Indians—Legends 2. Creation—Folklore

ISBN 0-02-765905-4   LC 92-32328

A collection of traditional stories that describe the creation of the world and the early history of the Wampanoag Indians in southeastern Massachusetts

"Engagingly told with clarity and humor, the stories are particularly good for reading aloud. Each one has a full-color, full-page illustration by Arquette, a Mohawk artist. This warm collection deserves a place in most libraries." SLJ

Mikolaycak, Charles, 1937-1993

Babushka; an old Russian folktale; retold and illustrated by Charles Mikolaycak. Holiday House 1984 unp il lib bdg $15.95; pa $5.95 (k-3)   **398.2**

1. Folklore—Russia

ISBN 0-8234-0520-6 (lib bdg); 0-8234-0712-8 (pa)

LC 84-500

Retells the traditional tale of the old lady who, having missed her chance to take gifts to the newborn Christ Child, still wanders leaving gifts for all children in hopes that, one day, she will come upon Him

"Exquisitely detailed pencil drawings are richly hued by shading of watercolors and pencils. . . . A fine book, one that will serve children well." SLJ

Mollel, Tololwa M. (Tololwa Marti)

The orphan boy; a Maasai story; illustrated by Paul Morin. Clarion Bks. 1990 unp il $15.95; pa $5.95 (k-3)   **398.2**

1. Masai (African people)—Folklore 2. Folklore—Africa

ISBN 0-89919-985-2; 0-395-72079-6 (pa)

LC 90-2358

"A solitary old man on the wide plains welcomes into his compound an orphan boy, Kileken, who helps with the work and the cattle and brings prosperity even in times of drought. But when the old man insists on knowing the boy's secret, Kileken returns to his place in the sky. He is the steadily shining star . . . that is the planet Venus." Booklist

"Infused with an aura of mystery, Mollel's compelling story is told skillfully and dramatically. Morin's richly textured paintings, evoking in bold colors an Africa of both parched desert and lush vegetation, are worthy companions." Publ Wkly

The **Monkey's** haircut, and other stories told by the Maya; edited by John Bierhorst; illustrated by Robert Andrew Parker. Morrow 1986 152p il $15 (5 and up)   **398.2**

1. Mayas—Legends

ISBN 0-688-04269-4   LC 85-28471

The Monkey's haircut, and other stories told by the Maya—*Continued*

"A collection of 22 stories told by the Maya people of Mexico, some of which are from ancient traditions and some of which reflect the influence of Western European traditions on Mexican folk tales. Bierhorst has included a lengthy introduction to help teachers and librarians to see the connections between these tales and those of the West and to point out how the tales reflect the life style and beliefs of the Maya people. . . . Each story is illustrated by a simple black-and-white drawing which highlights a special moment in the tale. . . . Bierhorst's book provides a valuable addition to folklore collections." SLJ

Includes bibliography

Morgan, Pierr

The turnip; an old Russian folktale; retold and illustrated by Pierr Morgan. Philomel Bks. 1990 unp il lib bdg $14.95 (k-2)   **398.2**

1. Folklore—Russia
ISBN 0-399-22229-4   LC 89-34023

One of Dedoushka's turnips grows to such an enormous size that the whole family, including the dog, cat, and mouse, is needed to pull it up

This "picture book version of a popular Russian folktale . . . uses the lively retelling found in Katherine Milhous and Alice Dalgliesh's *Once on a Time* (1938). . . . The paintings, done in the Slavic tradition, make use of bold colors and rough textures and are complemented by a crisp, pleasing design." Booklist

Morimoto, Junko

The inch boy; illustrated by Junko Morimoto. Viking Kestrel 1986 unp il o.p.; Penguin Bks. paperback available $4.99 (k-3)   **398.2**

1. Folklore—Japan
ISBN 0-14-050677-2 (pa)   LC 85-40592

In this Japanese folktale, an inch-high boy proves himself a warrior by vanquishing the dreaded giant red demon with his cunning and bravery

"Morimoto's illustrations are large and bold. Striking colors splash across the pages, and a full-page Buddha appears dramatically luminescent. The perspective—often from the view of a small figure looking up—will delight young sensibilities. The action and humor of the harmonious pictures and text make this an excellent choice for group presentation." SLJ

Moroney, Lynn

Baby rattlesnake; told by Te Ata; adapted by Lynn Moroney; illustrated by Veg Reisberg. Children's Bk. Press 1989 30p il $14.95; pa $6.95 (k-2)   **398.2**

1. Chickasaw Indians—Legends 2. Rattlesnakes—Fiction
ISBN 0-89239-049-2; 0-89239-111-1 (pa)
         LC 89-9892

Also available Spanish language edition

"Baby Rattlesnake wants a rattle that's just like his big brother and sister's in this native American cautionary tale. The young snake makes such a ruckus that the elders decide to give in to him, even though he is still too young to use his rattle wisely. As the elders predict, Baby Rattlesnake creates mischief with his new power. He meets his match, however, when he tries to scare the chief's daughter." SLJ

"The short sentences, onomatopoeia, and repetition will hold the attention of the youngest listeners as will the bold-ly colored, stylized gouache and cut-paper illustrations that depict the endearing Rattlesnake family." Booklist

Mosel, Arlene

The funny little woman; retold by Arlene Mosel; pictures by Blair Lent. Dutton 1972 unp il $16; pa $4.95 (k-2)   **398.2**

1. Folklore—Japan
ISBN 0-525-30265-4; 0-525-45036-X (pa)
Awarded the Caldecott Medal, 1973
Based on Lafcadio Hearn's The old woman and her dumpling

While chasing a dumpling, a little lady is captured by wicked creatures from whom she escapes with the means of becoming the richest woman in Japan

"The tale unfolds in a simple tellable style. . . . Using elements of traditional Japanese art, the illustrator has made marvelously imaginative pictures. . . . All the inherent drama and humor of the story are manifest in the illustrations." Horn Book

Tikki Tikki Tembo; retold by Arlene Mosel; illustrated by Blair Lent. Holt & Co. 1968 unp il $14.95; pa $5.95 (k-2)   **398.2**

1. Folklore—China 2. Personal names—Fiction
ISBN 0-8050-0662-1; 0-8050-1166-8 (pa)
Also available Spanish language edition

A "Chinese folk tale about a first son with a very long name. When Tikki Tikki Tembo-No Sa Rembo-Chari Bari Ruchi-Pip Peri Pembo fell into the well, it took his little brother so long to say his name and get help that Tikki almost drowned." Hodges. Books for Elem Sch Libr

"In this polished version of a story hour favorite, beautifully stylized wash drawings of serene Oriental landscapes are in comic contrast to amusingly visualized folk and the active disasters accruing to the possessor of a 21-syllable, irresistibly chantable name." Best Books of the Year, 1968

Mwalimu

Awful aardvark; by Mwalimu and Adrienne Kennaway. Little, Brown 1989 unp il $14.95 (k-2)   **398.2**

1. Folklore—Africa 2. Aardvark—Fiction
ISBN 0-316-59218-8   LC 89-80028

Published in the United Kingdom with title: Awkward aardvark

"In folktale style, Mongoose conspires with other jungle animals to stop Aardvark's loud snoring, but the monkeys, lion, and rhinoceros only manage to rouse him briefly. It is the lowly termites that topple his tree." Bull Cent Child Books

"The double-page spreads seem to linger on the rounded shapes and rough textures of the animals as they move across the pages amid the hot greens, yellows, and browns of the background. The well-paced story reads aloud well, and Kennaway's illustrations make even swarming nests of crawling termites into splendidly decorative and eye-catching arrangements." Horn Book

The **Naked** bear; folktales of the Iroquois; edited by John Bierhorst; illustrated by Dirk Zimmer. Morrow 1987 xx, 123p il $15 (4 and up)   **398.2**

1. Iroquois Indians—Legends 2. Indians of North America—Legends
ISBN 0-688-06422-1   LC 86-21836

The Naked bear—*Continued*

"Following a brief introduction on the storytelling and culture of the Six Nations of the Iroquois are sixteen folktales with some haunting themes and images. Consistently woven through them all is the close relationship of human and animal, as well as ubiquitous magic powers upon which mortals often call to combat extraordinary forces. . . . These tales are easy to read and taut enough to tell, each sustained with the suspense of life and death situations." Bull Cent Child Books

Includes bibliography

Norman, Howard

How Glooskap outwits the Ice Giants, and other tales of the Maritime Indians; retold by Howard Norman; wood engravings by Michael McCurdy. Little, Brown 1989 60p il lib bdg $14.95 (3-6)   **398.2**
1. Indians of North America—Legends
ISBN 0-316-61181-6   LC 89-2379
"Joy Street books"

Six tales featuring the mythical giant who roamed the coast to New England and Canada, created the Indian peoples to keep him company, and fought battles to protect them ever after

These tales "are witty, fresh, and stylish. . . . Executed with technical virtuosity, the handsome black-and-white wood engravings engage the eye with dramatic perspectives, expressive characterizations, and intricate detailing. A field-tested delight for reading aloud and storytelling." Booklist

Oodgeroo, 1920-1993

Dreamtime; aboriginal stories; illustrated by Bronwyn Bancroft. Lothrop, Lee & Shepard Bks. 1994 c1972 95p il $16 (4 and up)   **398.2**
1. Australian aborigines—Folklore 2. Folklore—Australia
ISBN 0-688-13296-0   LC 93-79375
First published 1972 in Australia with title: Stradbroke dreamtime

"A combination of traditional and autobiographical tales, this title is divided into two sections. 'Stories from Stradbroke' comprises family stories from the author's life on Stradbroke Island off the Queensland coast and reflects the hardships and joys of Aboriginal living under encroaching white civilization. The second section is called 'Stories from the Old and New Dreamtime' and includes traditional stories recalled by the author from her youth as well as some new stories written in the traditional format." Booklist

"This generous collection provides a fascinating and personal introduction to Aboriginal culture." Publ Wkly

Ormerod, Jan

The frog prince; retold by Jan Ormerod and David Lloyd; illustrated by Jan Ormerod. Lothrop, Lee & Shepard Bks. 1990 unp il $15; lib bdg $12.95 (k-3)   **398.2**
1. Folklore—Germany 2. Fairy tales
ISBN 0-688-09568-2; 0-688-09569-0 (lib bdg)
LC 89-12977
In this version of the fairy tale, "it is the princess' growing fondness for the frog and the fact that she allows him to sleep on her pillow three times that breaks the enchantment, transforming him into a handsome prince." SLJ

"Although textually straightforward, this is a visually so-phisticated treatment of Grimm's tale. . . . Ormerod paints a somber world dominated by grays and greens, with only an occasional splash of gold or orange for relief. Not until the final spread, when the princess and her prince are married, does a fuller, lighter palette emerge." Publ Wkly

The story of Chicken Licken. Lothrop, Lee & Shepard Bks. 1986 c1985 unp il $13 (k-2)   **398.2**
1. Folklore
ISBN 0-688-06058-7   LC 85-7911
First published 1985 in the United Kingdom

"Here the story of the gullible chicken is being acted out by a group of schoolchildren in an auditorium. One by one, the actors appear—everyone from Henny Penny to Drake Lake—much to the appreciation of the silhouetted parental audience that sits in the foreground. But the action is not only on stage. Careful observers will notice a baby in the audience who climbs out of his carryall basket and unobtrusively, page by page, makes his way up a short flight of steps until he is center stage. The contrast of shiny bright colors and the black silhouettes gives an interesting effect resulting in a warm and personal book that extends the appeal of the original story." Booklist

Osborne, Mary Pope, 1949-

American tall tales; wood engravings by Michael McCurdy. Knopf 1991 115p il map $18; lib bdg $18.99 (3-6)   **398.2**
1. Tall tales 2. Folklore—United States
ISBN 0-679-90089-1; 0-679-90089-6 (lib bdg)
LC 89-37236
A collection of tall tales about such American folk heroes as Sally Ann Thunder Ann Whirlwind, Pecos Bill, John Henry, and Paul Bunyan

"As tantalizing as Osborne's storytelling are McCurdy's . . . elaborate, full-color wood engravings, which in their robust stylization dramatically render the grandeur of these engrossing yarns." Publ Wkly

Includes bibliography

Mermaid tales from around the world; retold by Mary Pope Osborne; illustrated by Troy Howell. Scholastic 1993 84p il $16.95 (4-6)   **398.2**
1. Mermaids and mermen 2. Folklore
ISBN 0-590-44377-1   LC 92-30527
A collection of twelve mermaid tales from around the world, featuring such sources as France, Greece, and North Africa

"Howell's noteworthy illustrations render each painting in a style reflective of the traditional artwork from the tale's place of origin. . . . Both author and illustrator provide extensive source notes for their work. A great choice for primary read-alouds and a welcome compilation for folk-tale units." Booklist

Parks, Van Dyke

Jump! the adventures of Brer Rabbit; by Joel Chandler Harris; adapted by Van Dyke Parks and Malcolm Jones; illustrated by Barry Moser. Harcourt Brace Jovanovich 1986 40p il $15.95 (1-4)   **398.2**
1. African Americans—Folklore 2. Animals—Fiction
ISBN 0-15-241350-2   LC 86-7654

Parks, Van Dyke—*Continued*

Jump again! more adventures of Brer Rabbit; by Joel Chandler Harris; adapted by Van Dyke Parks; illustrated by Barry Moser. Harcourt Brace Jovanovich 1987 39p il $16.95 (1-4)   **398.2**

1. African Americans—Folklore 2. Animals—Fiction

ISBN 0-15-241352-9   LC 86-33622

Jump on over! the adventures of Brer Rabbit and his family; by Joel Chandler Harris; adapted by Van Dyke Parks; illustrated by Barry Moser. Harcourt Brace Jovanovich 1989 39p il $15.95 (1-4)   **398.2**

1. African Americans—Folklore 2. Animals—Fiction

ISBN 0-15-241354-5   LC 89-7417

These volumes contain retellings of folktales in which crafty Brer Rabbit tries to outsmart all the other creatures in the animal community

"Handsome watercolors by artist Barry Moser depict the animal characters as distinctive personalities. . . . The combination of elegance and humor is perfectly suited to the diction and tone of the text." Horn Book

Paterson, Katherine

The tale of the mandarin ducks; illustrated by Leo & Diane Dillon. Lodestar Bks. 1989 unp il $15.99 (1-3)   **398.2**

1. Folklore—Japan 2. Ducks—Fiction

ISBN 0-525-67283-4   LC 88-30484

Also available in paperback from Puffin Bks.

"A Japanese fairy tale, in picture-book format, about a Mandarin duck caught and caged at the whim of a wealthy Japanese lord. Separated from his mate, the bird languishes in captivity until a compassionate servant girl sets him free. The lord sentences the girl and her beloved to death, but they in turn are freed and rewarded with happiness." Booklist

"Paterson's story is rich with magic, compassion and love. The Dillons' elegantly detailed watercolor and pastel drawings, in the style of 18th-century Japanese woodcuts, are exquisite." Publ Wkly

Paxton, Tom, 1937-

Aesop's fables; retold in verse by Tom Paxton; illustrated by Robert Rayevsky. Morrow Junior Bks. 1988 unp il $16; lib bdg $15.93 (3-5)   **398.2**

1. Fables

ISBN 0-688-07360-3; 0-688-07361-1 (lib bdg)

LC 88-1652

A collection of fables from Aesop retold in verse, including The fox and the grapes, The tortoise and the hare, The boy who cried wolf, The grasshopper and the ants

"These ten well-known fables by Aesop have been given a new twist with songwriter Paxton's bouncy verse retellings. . . . Rayevsky's expressive pen-and-ink with color wash illustrations are a perfect complement to Aesop's wry observations of human nature." SLJ

Androcles and the lion and other Aesop's fables; retold in verse by Tom Paxton; illustrated by Robert Rayevsky. Morrow Junior Bks. 1991 unp il $13.95; lib bdg $13.88 (3-5)   **398.2**

1. Fables

ISBN 0-688-09682-4; 0-688-09683-2 (lib bdg)

LC 90-19173

A collection of Aesop's fables, retold in verse, including The wolf in sheep's clothing, The man, the boy, and the donkey, and The wolf and the crane

"Paxton's ditties are energetic, humorous . . . and perfectly suited to Aesop's tidy morals. Rayevsky's weird and wonderful visual style . . . runs the gamut from the sublimely ridiculous . . . to the deliciously macabre." Publ Wkly

Belling the cat and other Aesop's fables; retold in verse by Tom Paxton; illustrated by Robert Rayevsky. Morrow Junior Bks. 1990 unp il $13.95; lib bdg $13.88 (3-5)   **398.2**

1. Fables

ISBN 0-688-08158-4; 0-688-08159-2 (lib bdg)

LC 89-39851

Selected fables from Aesop include The night singer, Honesty is the best policy, and The milkmaid and her pail

"The fables are retold in Paxton's sprightly, often contagious verse. . . . The ink-wash and watercolor illustrations utilize an earth-tone palette of beiges, blues, and golds. The characters and settings are executed in a stylized but highly detailed manner with an overall page layout that is attractive and balanced. A lively and invigorating interpretation of Aesop." SLJ

Birds of a feather and other Aesop's fables; retold in verse by Tom Paxton; illustrated by Robert Rayevsky. Morrow Junior Bks. 1993 unp il $15; lib bdg $14.93 (3-5)   **398.2**

1. Fables

ISBN 0-688-10400-2; 0-688-10401-0 (lib bdg)

LC 92-2909

An illustrated retelling in verse of ten fables by Aesop, including The laborer and the nightingale, The frogs choose a king, and The horse and the donkey

"Paxton's rhymed verse tells the tales succinctly and sometimes wittily, making even the morals palatable in context. Rayevsky's full-color illustrations use graceful, elongated figures to play out the little dramas." Booklist

Perrault, Charles, 1628-1703

Cinderella; or, The little glass slipper; a free translation from the French of Charles Perrault; with pictures by Marcia Brown. Scribner 1954 unp il $14 (k-3)   **398.2**

1. Folklore—France 2. Fairy tales

ISBN 0-684-12676-1

Also available in paperback from Puffin Bks.

Awarded the Caldecott Medal, 1955

This is the classic story of the poor, good-natured girl who works for her selfish step-sisters until a fairy godmother transforms her into a beautiful 'princess' for just one night

"With soft, delicate colors and lines that subtly suggest, Miss Brown creates a thoroughly fairyland atmosphere, at the same time recreating the sophistication of the French Court with its golden coach, canopied bed, dazzling chandeliers, liveried footmen, curled and pompadoured ladies, and peruked (bewigged) courtiers." Libr J

Perrault, Charles, 1628-1703—*Continued*

The complete fairy tales of Charles Perrault; illustrated by Sally Holmes; newly translated by Neil Philip and Nicoletta Simborowski; with an introduction and notes on the stories by Neil Philip. Clarion Bks. 1993 156p il $18.95 (4-6)   **398.2**

1. Folklore—France 2. Fairy tales
ISBN 0-395-57002-6   LC 92-17781

An illustrated collection of eleven tales including such familiar titles as "Cinderella" and "Sleeping Beauty" and less familiar ones such as "Tufty Ricky" and "The Fairies"

"This new edition, with its simple, unembroidered language; attractive illustrations; terse, informative commentary; and extensive bibliography deserves to be among the first books considered for a core collection." SLJ

Puss in boots; illustrated by Fred Marcellino; translated by Malcolm Arthur. Farrar, Straus & Giroux 1990 unp il $16 (k-3)   **398.2**

1. Folklore—France 2. Fairy tales
ISBN 0-374-36160-6   LC 90-82136
Also available Spanish language edition
A Caldecott Medal honor book, 1991

"Opulently designed and handsomely illustrated, this picture book provides a fitting showcase for Perrault's artful tale of deceit and resourcefulness. Unsullied by type, the striking front of the book features a close-up portrait of the cat's face. Befitting a fairy tale, the artwork inside is suffused with a golden light that proclaims the story to be from a sunnier, more dreamlike world." Booklist

Philip, Neil

The Arabian nights; retold by Neil Philip; illustrated by Sheila Moxley. Orchard Bks. 1994 157p il $19.95 (4 and up)   **398.2**

1. Arabs—Folklore 2. Fairy tales
ISBN 0-531-06868-4   LC 94-9137

"Sixteen of the classic stories are retold, each accompanied by one full-page and several smaller illustrations rendered in jewel-toned acrylics. A worthy addition to any collection, the volume includes a helpful explanation of the origins of the tales." Horn Book Guide

Plume, Ilse

The Bremen town musicians; retold and illustrated by Ilse Plume. Doubleday 1980 unp il o.p.; HarperCollins Pubs. paperback available $5.95 (k-3)   **398.2**

1. Folklore—Germany 2. Animals—Fiction
ISBN 0-06-443141-X (pa)   LC 79-6622
A Caldecott Medal honor book, 1981

A retelling of an old Grimm's tale in which "a donkey, cat, dog, and rooster find that their usefulness to their masters has gone, and they set out to make new lives for themselves. When their 'music' frightens away some robbers, they find a quiet, peaceful world and live happily ever after." Child Book Rev Serv

The author/illustrator's "realistic illustrations have . . . mild and unpretentious charm; the animal principals are too conventionally bland, but the human bit players individualized and appealing. The style of the crayon-like paintings is pleasantly naive." SLJ

Pyle, Howard, 1853-1911

The merry adventures of Robin Hood of great renown in Nottinghamshire; as written and illustrated by Howard Pyle. Scribner 1976 288p il $50 (5 and up)   **398.2**

1. Robin Hood (Legendary character)
ISBN 0-684-14838-2
Also available in paperback from Dover Publs. and NAL/Dutton and in hardcover from Amereon and P. Smith
First published 1883

Twenty-two stories of Robin Hood and his adventures with the King's foresters in Sherwood Forest

"Of all the books of Robin Hood this is best for literary style, adherence to the spirit and events of the old ballads and wealth of historical background." Toronto Public Libr

The wonder clock; or, Four & twenty marvelous tales, being one for each hour of the day; written & illustrated by Howard Pyle; embellished with verses by Katharine Pyle. Dover Publs. 1965 318p il pa $8.95 (4-6)   **398.2**

1. Folklore 2. Fairy tales
ISBN 0-486-21446-X
Also available in hardcover from P. Smith
A reprint of the title first published 1887 by Harper

"Tales told by the puppet figures of an old clock found in Time's garret." Hodges. Books for Elem Sch Libr

"Pyle adapted tales from Grimm and other legends in his own lively and humorous way." Adventuring with Books. 3d edition

Quayle, Eric

The shining princess, and other Japanese legends; illustrated by Michael Foreman. Arcade Pub. 1989 111p il $15.95 (5 and up)   **398.2**

1. Folklore—Japan
ISBN 1-55970-039-4   LC 89-84076

A "collection of Japanese legends drawn from the two earliest-known English translations." Publisher's note

This "collection of ten exciting tales is surely destined to become a standard source of Japanese folktales. . . . Each tale is sure to enthrall read-aloud audiences as well as independent readers. Foreman's remarkable watercolors, perfectly suited to each text, complete the package." SLJ

The **Rainbow** fairy book; edited by Andrew Lang; selected and illustrated by Michael Hague. Books of Wonder 1993 288p il $20 (4-6)   **398.2**

1. Folklore 2. Fairy tales
ISBN 0-688-10878-4   LC 92-33449

"These 31 folktales and fairy tales were selected by artist Hague from Lang's Colored Fairy Books. Included are many of the more traditional tales from Andersen, the Brothers Grimm, and Perrault. . . . Hague also gives a nod toward cultural inclusiveness, incorporating such tales as 'The Snake Prince' from India, 'The Hero Makóma' from Zimbabwe, and 'Hok Lee and the Dwarfs' from China. . . . Hague . . . surpasses himself here with 23 full-color plates and 41 black-and-white pencil drawings. . . . A strong anthology that will have a multitude of uses." Booklist

Ransome, Arthur, 1884-1967

The Fool of the World and the flying ship; a Russian tale retold by Arthur Ransome; pictures by Uri Shulevitz. Farrar, Straus & Giroux 1968 unp il $16; pa $6.95 (k-3)

398.2

1. Folklore—Russia
ISBN 0-374-32442-5; 0-374-42438-1 (pa)
Also available Spanish language edition
Awarded the Caldecott Medal, 1969
"An Ariel book"
Text first published 1916 in Ransome's Old Peter's Russian tales

The Fool of the World, was the third and youngest son whose parents thought little of him. When the Czar announced that his daughter would marry the hero who could bring him a flying ship, Fool of the World went looking and found one. Aided in surprising ways by eight peasants with magical powers, he then had to outwit the treacherous Czar

This "is a fascinating tale, told with humor and grace and brought vividly to life by Uri Shulevitz's illustrations." N Y Times Book Rev

Rappaport, Doreen

The new king; pictures by E.B. Lewis. Dial Bks. for Young Readers 1995 unp il $14.99; lib bdg $14.89 (k-3)

398.2

1. Folklore—Madagascar
ISBN 0-8037-1460-2; 0-8037-1461-0 (lib bdg)

LC 93-28561

"Young Prince Rakoto becomes king when his father is killed while hunting. In his grief, the boy commands the Royal Doctor and the Royal Magician to bring the man back to life, and when they say they cannot, he commands the High Councilor to punish them. At the councilor's refusal to do so, the child turns to the Wise Woman. Rappaport uses a Malagasy folktale as the centerpiece for her lovely and moving text. . . . Lewis's watercolor paintings exhibit graceful simplicity while paying close attention to detail." SLJ

Raw Head, bloody bones; African-American tales of the supernatural; selected by Mary E. Lyons. Scribner 1991 88p il $14; pa $3.95 (4-6)

398.2

1. African Americans—Folklore 2. Folklore—United States 3. Folklore—Caribbean region
ISBN 0-684-19333-7; 0-689-80306-0 (pa)

LC 91-10690

Fifteen black and African-American tales of the supernatural from various states and several Caribbean countries. Includes commentary on black folklore in the New World

"In retelling these delightfully eerie and gruesome stories, Lyons has preserved the richness and immediacy of the African and African-American oral traditions. Vigorously told in rhythmic and colorful language, the stories demand to be read aloud." SLJ

Includes bibliography

The **Red** fairy book; edited by Andrew Lang; with numerous illustrations by H. J. Ford and Lancelot Speed. Dover Publs. 1966 367p il pa $6.95 (4-6)

398.2

1. Folklore 2. Fairy tales
ISBN 0-486-21673-X
Also available in hardcover from Amereon, Buccaneer Bks. and P. Smith
A reprint of the title first published 1890 by Longmans

"This book includes a wide assortment of fairy tales from French, Scandinavian, German, and Rumanian folklore sources, including tales of the Brothers Grimm and Madame d'Aulnoy. Accompanying the 37 stories are 100 line drawings." Adventuring with Books

Reeves, James, 1909-1978

English fables and fairy stories; retold by James Reeves; illustrated by Joan Kiddell-Monroe. Oxford Univ. Press 1954 234p il (Oxford myths and legends) hardcover o.p. paperback available $10.95 (4-6)

398.2

1. Folklore—Great Britain 2. Fairy tales
ISBN 0-19-274137-3 (pa)
Also available in hardcover from P. Smith

A "collection of nineteen English tales, told in language beautiful for either reading or telling. Several familiar tales are included with old favorites such as 'Molly Whipple,' 'Dick Whittington', and 'Jack and the Beanstalk.'" Second Educ Board

Renberg, Dalia Hardof

King Solomon and the bee; adapted by Dalia Hardof Renberg; illustrated by Ruth Heller. HarperCollins Pubs. 1994 unp il $15; lib bdg $14.89 (k-3)

398.2

1. Solomon, King of Israel—Fiction 2. Jews—Folklore
ISBN 0-06-022899-7; 0-06-022902-0 (lib bdg)

LC 92-30411

In this "adaptation of a tale recorded by folklorist and storyteller Hayyam Nahman Bialik (1873-1934), a bee mistakes King Solomon's nose . . . for a flower and accidentally stings the royal schnoz. . . . The bee eventually repays the king's mercy by helping him answer the Queen of Sheba's greatest riddle." Publ Wkly

"This simple story is fresh and appealing. The brightly colored pictures, accented with masses of flowers on every page, are occasionally stiff, but they do have child appeal." Booklist

Reyher, Rebecca Hourwich, 1897-1987

My mother is the most beautiful woman in the world; a Russian folktale retold by Becky Reyher; pictures by Ruth Gannett. Lothrop, Lee & Shepard Bks. 1962 c1945 39p il lib bdg $14.93 (1-4)

398.2

1. Folklore—Russia
ISBN 0-688-51251-8
A Caldecott Medal honor book, 1946
First published 1945 by Howell, Soskin

A Russian folktale about a little peasant girl, lost in the wheat fields, who tried to describe her mother as the "most beautiful woman in the world." When an exceptionally ugly woman claimed the little girl, they remembered the proverb: "We do not love people because they are beautiful, but they seem beautiful to us because we love them"

"Though its people are Russian peasants a long time ago and though Ruth Gannett has brought them to us in brilliant, convincing pictures, there is not a little listening child to whom it is read that will not claim it for his own. These are just the right pictures for a story told in just the right way." N Y Her Trib Books

Rhee, Nami

Magic spring; a Korean folktale; retold and illustrated by Nami Rhee. Putnam 1993 unp il $15.95 (k-3)   **398.2**

1. Folklore—Korea
ISBN 0-399-22420-3   LC 92-7728
"A Whitebird book"

An old man and his wife discover a fountain of youth and benefit from its magic, but the water has a different effect on their greedy neighbor

"The soft-toned artwork was created on handmade rice paper with Korean ink and watercolor. The Korean characters positioned next to the English text are excerpts from the story. These details add beautifully to the authenticity of the enchanting tale." Child Book Rev Serv

Robbins, Ruth

Baboushka and the three kings; illustrated by Nicolas Sidjakov; adapted from a Russian folk tale. Houghton Mifflin 1960 unp il $14.95; pa $5.95 (1-4)   **398.2**

1. Folklore—Russia 2. Christmas—Fiction
ISBN 0-395-27673-X; 0-395-42647-2 (pa)
Awarded the Caldecott Medal, 1961
First published by Parnassus Press

A retelling of the Christmas legend about the old woman who declined to accompany the three kings on their search for the Christ Child and has ever since then searched for the Child on her own. Each year as she renews her search she leaves gifts at the homes she visits, acting, in this respect, as a Russian equivalent to Santa Claus

"Mystery and dignity are in the retelling. . . . At the end of the book is the story in verse set to original music." Horn Book

Rockwell, Anne F., 1934-

Puss in boots, and other stories; told and illustrated by Anne Rockwell. Macmillan 1988 88p il $16.95 (2-4)   **398.2**

1. Folklore 2. Fairy tales
ISBN 0-02-777781-2   LC 87-14976

"Rockwell retells 12 fairy tales and fables remembered from her childhood. Although some elements of these stories differ from most familiar versions, their timelessness will cast a spell once more. Among the book's pleasing physical features are its fine, heavy pages; its wide margins; and the full-color illustrations on each double-page spread. The simple line drawings with their bright, clear colors have a childlike innocence and charm." Booklist

Rogasky, Barbara

Rapunzel; from the Brothers Grimm; retold by Barbara Rogasky; with illustrations by Trina Schart Hyman. Holiday House 1982 unp il lib bdg $15.95; pa $5.95 (1-3)
                              398.2

1. Folklore—Germany 2. Fairy tales
ISBN 0-8234-0454-4 (lib bdg); 0-8234-0652-0 (pa)
                              LC 81-6419

A retelling of the folktale "about the beautiful girl whose lover climbs her rope of golden hair and whose cruel treatment by a possessive witch ends when Rapunzel, her prince, and their infant twins are united." Bull Cent Child Books

"Some of Hyman's familiar specialities . . . appear again to advantage. . . . Most engaging of all are the lovely borders and vignettes on every page, filled with fruits, flowers, small landscapes and decorative patterns. The highly organized layout and borders, attractive in themselves, enhance Hyman's art by imposing a kind of discipline on her romantic style." SLJ

The water of life; a tale from the Brothers Grimm; retold by Barbara Rogasky; illustrated by Trina Schart Hyman. Holiday House 1986 unp il $15.95; pa $5.95 (1-3)   **398.2**

1. Folklore—Germany 2. Fairy tales
ISBN 0-8234-0552-4; 0-8234-0907-4 (pa)
                              LC 84-19226

A prince searching for the Water of Life to cure his dying father finds an enchanted castle, a lovely princess, and treachery from his older brothers

"This traditional tale with all the trappings of magical elements, romance, and underlying psychological truth, is brought to life by Rogasky's spirited telling and Hyman's lush illustrations." SLJ

Rohmer, Harriet

Brother Anansi and the cattle ranch; told by James de Sauza; adapted by Harriet Rohmer; illustrations by Stephen Von Mason; version in Spanish, Rosalma Zubizarretta. Children's Bk. Press 1989 32p il $14.95   **398.2**

1. Folklore 2. Bilingual books—English-Spanish 3. Anansi (Legendary character)
ISBN 0-89239-044-1   LC 88-37091

"Anansi, the traditional West African trickster, also made his way into Caribbean, Central American, and North American folklore. In this modern bilingual version Brother Anansi is a man living on the Nicaraguan coast. When Brother Tiger wins the lottery, Anansi devises a way to acquire all of Tiger's money." Horn Book

This tale is "recently collected, imaginatively illustrated, and solidly translated. . . . [It is] retold in simple, colloquial language. . . . The full-page artwork . . . is represented in a primitive and naturalistic style; the Central American tale [has] bold, flat, stylized figures that are intensely colored with acrylics." Booklist

The invisible hunters; a legend from the Miskito Indians of Nicaragua; [by] Harriet Rohmer, Octavio Chow, Morris Vidaure; illustrations, Joe Sam; version in Spanish Rosalma Zubizarreta & Alma Flor Ada. Children's Bk. Press 1987 32p il (Stories from Central America) $13.95; pa $6.95 (2-4)
                              398.2

1. Mosquito Indians—Legends 2. Bilingual books—English-Spanish
ISBN 0-89239-031-X; 0-89239-109-X (pa)
                              LC 86-32658
Title page and text in English and Spanish

This Miskito Indian legend set in seventeenth-century Nicaragua concerns the impact of the first European traders on traditional life. "Three hunters eat a vine of invisibility, the Dar, which they use initially to bag more wari to feed their tribe but eventually to betray their hungry people and become rich off traders' money. . . . The hunters are punished by wandering forever invisible." Bull Cent Child Books

"The lavish collage-style illustrations evoke a sense of movement and are in perfect step with the rhythm of the text." Horn Book

Rohmer, Harriet—*Continued*

Mother Scorpion country; a legend from the Miskito Indians of Nicaragua; [by] Harriet Rohmer, Dorminster Newton Wilson; illustrations, Virginia Stearns; version in Spanish [by] Rosalma Zubizarreta & Alma Flor Ada. Children's Bk. Press 1987 32p il (Stories from Central America) $14.95 (2-4)
398.2

1. Mosquito Indians—Legends 2. Bilingual books—English-Spanish

ISBN 0-89239-032-8   LC 86-32649

Title page and text in English and Spanish

A brave young Miskito Indian follows his wife from the land of the living to the spirit world

"This lovely and tender retelling is appropriate and enticing for young children. . . . The bold and vibrant illustrations will help children clearly visualize the people and culture of the Atlantic coast of Nicaragua." Horn Book

Uncle Nacho's hat; adapted by Harriet Rohmer; illustrations by Veg Reisberg; Spanish version, Rosalma Zubizarreta. Children's Bk. Press 1989 31p il $14.95; pa $6.95 (k-3)
398.2

1. Folklore—Nicaragua 2. Bilingual books—English-Spanish

ISBN 0-89239-043-3; 0-89239-112-X (pa)
     LC 88-37090

Title page and text in English and Spanish

"Adaptation of a Nicaraguan folktale. . . . When his niece, Ambrosia, gives Uncle Nacho a new hat, he tries unsuccessfully several times to get rid of the old, holey one. Seeing him dejected because his hat keeps coming back, Ambrosia suggests he put his mind on the new one instead. Flattened primitive paintings in brilliant, clear tropical colors and motifs enhance the fun of this comedy of errors." Helbig. This land is our land

Rosen, Michael, 1946-

How the animals got their colors; animal myths from around the world; illustrated by John Clementson. Harcourt Brace Jovanovich 1992 48p il $14.95 (3-5)
398.2

1. Folklore 2. Animals—Fiction

ISBN 0-15-236783-7   LC 91-30113

First published 1991 in the United Kingdom

"From the Zuni, New Guineans, Greeks, Chinese, aborigines, Loma of Liberia, Khasi of India, Ugandans, and Ayoreo Indians of South America, these nine myths explain animal characteristics from the time of creation. . . . Short and sweet, these will fit neatly into brief bedtime sessions or story hour niches between longer tales. The angular, collage-effect art leans on designer patterns that leap off the page in technicolor." Bull Cent Child Books

Includes bibliographical references

Ross, Gayle

How Rabbit tricked Otter and other Cherokee trickster stories; told by Gayle Ross; illustrated by Murv Jacob; with a foreword by Wilma Mankiller. HarperCollins Pubs. 1994 79p il $17; lib bdg $16.89 (4-6)
398.2

1. Cherokee Indians—Legends 2. Rabbit (Legendary character)

ISBN 0-06-021285-3; 0-06-021286-1 (lib bdg)
     LC 93-3637

Fifteen traditional tales follow the adventures of Rabbit, the Cherokee trickster

"The drama of the stories is enhanced by the direct, unadorned writing style and the detailed, full-page illustrations with elaborate borders, which resemble tapestries." Horn Book Guide

How Turtle's back was cracked; a traditional Cherokee tale; retold by Gayle Ross; illustrated by Murv Jacob. Dial Bks. for Young Readers 1995 unp il $14.99; lib bdg $14.89 (k-3)
398.2

1. Cherokee Indians—Legends

ISBN 0-8037-1728-8; 0-8037-1729-6 (lib bdg)
     LC 93-40657

"When Turtle's friend Possum kills a greedy wolf, Turtle not only takes all the credit for the deed, but boasts and flaunts his trophies. The wolves take revenge on him, but they are stupid and quarrelsome, and Turtle tricks them into throwing him into the river instead of a fire. Although he escapes death, he hits a rock and his shell is cracked into pieces." SLJ

"Ross, a storyteller of Cherokee descent, retains a sense of the oral tradition through the language and rhythm of the text. . . . Jacob . . . illustrates the tale with warm paintings full of pattern and texture, echoing the patterns on the clothing and jewelry that the animals wear." Horn Book

Roth, Susan L.

The story of light. Morrow Junior Bks. 1990 unp il $12.95; lib bdg $12.88 (k-3)
398.2

1. Indians of North America—Legends 2. Animals—Fiction

ISBN 0-688-08676-4; 0-688-08677-2 (lib bdg)
     LC 90-5654

"The sun is alive on one side of the world; however, the animals on the other side are in darkness. Spider successfully carries a tiny spark of light back to the animal people in a little clay pot. Inspired by a Cherokee tale, this simply told *pourquoi* story, a natural for reading aloud, is stunningly illustrated with black, white, and yellow woodcuts which satisfyingly convey the worlds of dark and light." Horn Book Guide

Rothenberg, Joan

Yettele's feathers. Hyperion Bks. for Children 1995 31p il $14.95; lib bdg $14.89 (k-3)
398.2

1. Jews—Folklore

ISBN 0-7868-0097-6; 0-7868-2081-0 (lib bdg)
     LC 94-26623

"Yettele Babbelonski loves to gossip. . . . When the neighbors complain about her tall tales, she shrugs them off. After all, she says, her stories are only words, and words are no more hurtful than feathers. It takes a wise rabbi with a clever ruse to change her mind. . . . Rothenberg's moral tale has a warm, comic quality. The gouache

Rothenberg, Joan—*Continued*
illustrations feature candylike tones of green, purple, and blue. Characters are drawn with broad, humorous strokes, and the town is a happy jumble of people, buildings, trees and sky." Booklist

Rounds, Glen, 1906-
Ol' Paul, the mighty logger. Holiday House 1976 93p il $12.95; pa $5.95 (3-6) **398.2**
1. Bunyan, Paul (Legendary character)
ISBN 0-8234-0269-X; 0-8234-0713-6 (pa)
First published 1936
"Being a truc account of the seemingly incredible exploits and inventions of the great Paul Bunyan, profusely illustrated by drawings made at the scene by the author, Glen Rounds, and now republished in this special fortieth anniversary edition." Subtitle

Three billy goats Gruff; retold and illustrated by Glen Rounds. Holiday House 1993 unp il $15.95; pa $5.95 (k-3) **398.2**
1. Folklore—Norway 2. Goats—Fiction
ISBN 0-8234-1015-3; 0-8234-1136-2 (pa)
LC 92-23951
Retells the folktale about three billy goats who trick a troll that lives under a bridge
"Spare and straightforward in text and illustrations, this interpretation of the old tale has an energy lacking in more elaborate versions. . . . Shaded, mottled crayon markings color the scenes here and there with good effect, and the broad white pages make a bright, clean background for the action." Booklist

Three little pigs and the big bad wolf; written and illustrated by Glen Rounds. Holiday House 1992 unp il $14.95 (k-3) **398.2**
1. Folklore 2. Pigs—Fiction 3. Wolves—Fiction
ISBN 0-8234-0923-6
LC 91-18173
"A straightforward, stripped-down retelling of a traditional tale is set in a poverty-stricken, trash-strewn rural area and depicts three lean hogs and a scrawny wolf. The typeface in three sizes—large, larger, and largest—and the matter-of-fact, homely illustrations, in Rounds's familiar bristly, spiky style, perfectly convey this no-frills, unadorned, and very tellable version." Horn Book

San Souci, Robert, 1946-
Cut from the same cloth; American women of myth, legend, and tall tale; collected and told by Robert D. San Souci; illustrated by Brian Pinkney; introduction by Jane Yolen. Philomel Bks. 1993 140p il $18.95 (4-6) **398.2**
1. Folklore—United States 2. Tall tales 3. Women—Folklore
ISBN 0-399-21987-0
LC 92-5233
A collection of fifteen stories about legendary American women from Anglo-American, African American, and Native American folklore
"San Souci's language is vigorous and action verbs abound; Pinkney's black-and-white block prints match the strength of the telling. The inclusion of notes on the sources and a general bibliography make this an academic resource as well as a good collection of rolicking stories." Child Book Rev Serv

The enchanted tapestry; a Chinese folktale; retold by Robert D. San Souci; pictures by László Gál. Dial Bks. for Young Readers 1987 unp il hardcover o.p. paperback available $4.95 (k-3) **398.2**
1. Folklore—China
ISBN 0-8037-0862-9 (pa)
LC 85-29283
"This story, based on a Chinese legend, is a variation on the testing of a faithful child. A widow weaves exquisite silk tapestries to support her three sons. One day the wind tears her masterwork out of its frame. The two older sons, both greedy cowards, search for it. They encounter a sorceress and fail to meet her challenges. The youngest son succeeds." N Y Times Book Rev
"The soft-hued, delicately detailed illustrations capture the beauty of the tapestry. The suspense builds, and young listeners caught up in the story are rewarded with a happy ending." Child Book Rev Serv

The faithful friend; [by] Robert D. San Souci; illustrated by Brian Pinkney. Simon & Schuster Bks. for Young Readers 1995 unp il $16 (2-4) **398.2**
1. Folklore—Martinique
ISBN 0-02-786131-7
LC 93-40672
A Caldecott Medal honor book, 1996
"A West Indian folktale from Martinique. . . . When Clement seeks the lovely Pauline as his wife, it is Hippolyte who protects the couple from the zombies and her vengeful uncle." Child Book Rev Serv
"Pinkney's scratchboard and oil artwork switches from bright daytime hues for most of the book to purples and grays for scenes with the zombies and snakes, which are very effective. . . . This excellent title contains all the elements of a well-researched folktale, and convincingly conveys the richness of the West Indian culture." SLJ
Includes bibliographical references

The Hobyahs; [by] Robert D. San Souci; illustrated by Alexi Natchev. Doubleday Bks. for Young Readers 1994 unp il $14.95 (k-3) **398.2**
1. Fairy tales 2. Folklore—Great Britain
ISBN 0-385-30934-1
LC 92-28655
A version of the folktale about five faithful dogs who rescue their mistress from the goblinlike Hobyahs
"The addition of rhyming quatrains at key moments in the plot turns the book into a storytelling treat, and Natchev's just-a-little-scary illustrations are great for showing to groups during reading aloud." Booklist

Larger than life; the adventures of American legendary heroes; by Robert D. San Souci; illustrated by Andrew Glass. Doubleday 1991 59p il hardcover o.p. paperback available $10.95 (4-6) **398.2**
1. Tall tales 2. Folklore—United States
ISBN 0-385-32180-5 (pa)
LC 89-35692
"The five stories—'John Henry,' 'Old Stormalong,' 'Slue-Foot Sue and Pecos Bill,' 'Strap Buckner,' and 'Paul Bunyan and Babe the Blue Ox'—are related in language that captures the flavor of frontier America while remaining accessible to children. Text and illustrations are exuberant; the robust heroes and heroines are bold but gentle souls who all come to a peaceful or appropriate end." SLJ

San Souci, Robert, 1946-—*Continued*

More short & shivery; thirty terrifying tales; retold by Robert D. San Souci; illustrated by Katherine Coville and Jacqueline Rogers. Delacorte Press 1994 163p il $13.95 (4 and up)　　　　　　　　　　　　　　**398.2**

1. Folklore 2. Ghost stories
ISBN 0-385-32102-3　　　　　　　　LC 94-479

A collection of scary folktales from the United States, China, England, Italy, Russia, and other countries around the world

Includes bibliographical references

The samurai's daughter; a Japanese legend retold by Robert D. San Souci; pictures by Stephen T. Johnson. Dial Bks. for Young Readers 1992 unp il $15.99; lib bdg $15.89 (1-4)　　　　　　　　　　　　　**398.2**

1. Folklore—Japan
ISBN 0-8037-1135-2; 0-8037-1136-0 (lib bdg)
　　　　　　　　　　　　　　　LC 91-15585

A Japanese folk tale about the brave daughter of a samurai warrior and her journey to be reunited with her exiled father

"San Souci's retelling of this Kamakura Period folktale is smooth, lively, and makes a resonant read-aloud. Johnson's pastel and ink illustrations capture authentic small details yet remain dreamily impressionistic." SLJ

Short & shivery; thirty chilling tales; retold by Robert D. San Souci; illustrated by Katherine Coville. Doubleday 1987 175p il hardcover o.p. paperback available $6.95 (4 and up)　　　　　　　　　　　　　**398.2**

1. Folklore
ISBN 0-385-26426-7 (pa)　　　　　LC 86-29067

"A collection of spooky stories, competently adapted and retold (sometimes quite freely) from world folklore, including Japan, Africa, and Latin America, as well as Europe and the U.S. . . . The stories drawn from collections of regional American folklore are not only the freshest, but often the scariest. Sources are fully documented. . . . There are some delicious shivers here, with plenty of fodder for an active imagination, as well as excitement." SLJ

The snow wife; [by] Robert D. San Souci; pictures by Stephen T. Johnson. Dial Bks. for Young Readers 1993 unp il $14.99; lib bdg $14.89 (2-4)　　　　　　　　　　**398.2**

1. Folklore—Japan
ISBN 0-8037-1409-2; 0-8037-1410-6 (lib bdg)
　　　　　　　　　　　　　　　LC 92-28966

When a Japanese woodcutter breaks his promise and describes his encounter with a terrifying snow woman, he loses his wife and must make a dangerous journey to win her back

"The hero's quest to reclaim his wife, told with lilting language and evocative images, involves various supernatural obstacles. . . . Johnson's full-page, watercolor-and-pastel illustrations in misty violets and burnished golds impart an appropriately delicate and faraway quality to the tale." Publ Wkly

Sootface; an Ojibwa Cinderella story; retold by Robert D. San Souci; illustrated by Daniel San Souci. Doubleday Bks. for Young Readers 1994 unp il $15.95 (1-4)　　　　　　　**398.2**

1. Ojibwa Indians—Legends
ISBN 0-385-31202-4　　　　　　　LC 93-10553

Although she is mocked and mistreated by her two older sisters, Sootface, an Ojibwa Indian maiden, wins a mighty invisible warrior for her husband with her kind and honest heart

"The San Souci version reads aloud well, and the watercolor artwork illustrates the story with quiet grace." Booklist

Sukey and the mermaid; [by] Robert D. San Souci; illustrated by Brian Pinkney. Four Winds Press 1992 unp il $15; pa $5.95 (1-4)
　　　　　　　　　　　　　　　398.2

1. Mermaids and mermen 2. African Americans—Fiction
ISBN 0-02-778141-0; 0-689-80718-X (pa)
　　　　　　　　　　　　　　　LC 90-24559

Unhappy with her life at home, Sukey receives kindness and wealth from Mama Jo the mermaid

"In a magnificent marriage of word and image, San Souci and Pinkney serve up an atmospheric folktale with Afro-Caribbean roots featuring a most unusual protagonist. . . . San Souci, a seasoned teller of folktales, outdoes himself here with pungent, lyrical prose that reverberates with the cadences of the South Carolina islands. In vivid testament to a mature talent, the supple lines of Pinkney's fluid scratchboard technique capture the grace and spirit of this magical tale and serve as the perfect foil to its darker undertones." Publ Wkly

The talking eggs; a folktale from the American South; retold by Robert D. San Souci; pictures by Jerry Pinkney. Dial Bks. for Young Readers 1989 unp il $15; lib bdg $14.89 (k-3)　　　　　　　　　　　　　**398.2**

1. Folklore—Southern States
ISBN 0-8037-0619-7; 0-8037-0620-0 (lib bdg)
　　　　　　　　　　　　　　　LC 88-33469

Also available Spanish language edition

A Caldecott Medal honor book, 1990

A Southern folktale in which kind Blanche, following the instructions of an old witch, gains riches, while her greedy sister makes fun of the old woman and is duly rewarded

"Adapted from a Creole folk tale originally included in a collection of Louisiana stories by folklorist Alcee Fortier, this tale captures the flavor of the nineteenth-century South in its language and story line. . . . Jerry Pinkney's watercolors are chiefly responsible for the excellence of the book; his characters convey their moods with vivid facial expressions." Horn Book

The white cat; an Old French fairy tale; retold by Robert D. San Souci; illustrated by Gennady Spirin. Orchard Bks. 1989 unp il $16.99; lib bdg $15.99 (2-4)　　　　　　**398.2**

1. Folklore—France 2. Fairy tales
ISBN 0-531-05809-3; 0-531-08409-4 (lib bdg)
　　　　　　　　　　　　　　　LC 88-19698

"Based on Madame D'Aulnoy's 1698 literary tale, which in turn draws on a folktale in which a king sends his three sons on three tests to decide their inheritance. The youngest son produces, at the end of the first year, the tiniest dog and, at the end of the second year, the finest linen—both with the help of a magical white cat who becomes his human bride when he breaks a spell bewitching her." Bull Cent Child Books

"San Souci's retelling is suitably magical and mysterious, and his words flow like music. Spirin's sumptuous paintings, each abounding with meticulous detail from foreground to furthest distance, glow with light and expression." Publ Wkly

San Souci, Robert, 1946-—*Continued*

Young Merlin; illustrated by Daniel Horne. Doubleday 1990 unp il $14.95 (2-5) **398.2**

1. Merlin (Legendary character) 2. Folklore—Great Britain
ISBN 0-385-24800-8   LC 88-30916

Presents the life of Merlin the magician from his miraculous birth through the age of seventeen, before he met King Arthur

This book "is handsomely designed, offering intriguing perspectives, subtle lines, and warm, deep colors. . . . Text and pictures are well balanced. . . . A good choice for reading aloud or for individual enjoyment." SLJ

Sanfield, Steve

The adventures of High John the Conqueror; illustrated by John Ward. Orchard Bks. 1988 113p il o.p.; Dell paperback available $3.50 (4 and up) **398.2**

1. African Americans—Folklore
ISBN 0-440-40556-4 (pa)   LC 88-17946

"A Richard Jackson book"

"A competent retelling of 16 African-American folktales about the black trickster hero who always manages to outwit others, particularly his white master. Simply told in language comprehensible to very young readers, these tales are short, funny, and entertaining. . . . Fourteen full-page black-and-white pencil drawings illustrate some of the more dramatic moments in the stories." SLJ

Includes bibliography

Bit by bit; illustrated by Susan Gaber. Philomel Bks. 1995 unp il $15.95 (k-3) **398.2**

1. Jews—Folklore
ISBN 0-399-22736-9   LC 94-8752

"When his old winter coat wears out, Zundel the tailor makes himself a replacement out of a beautiful piece of cloth with red, gold, blue, and green threads. He loves the coat so much that he wears it morning and night until it, too, wears out. The cloth is subsequently made into a jacket, a vest, a cap, a pocket, and a button. Finally, when there seems to be nothing left of Zundel's favorite fabric, it becomes the threads of a story, this story." SLJ

"Based on a Yiddish song that Sanfield's grandmother brought with her from Russia, this is a kind of cumulative story, told with a joyful rhythm and repetition, and illustrated with bright, clear, large figures that make it great for group sharing." Booklist

The feather merchants & other tales of the fools of Chelm; illustrated by Mikhail Magaril. Orchard Bks. 1991 102p il $15.95; lib bdg $15.99 (4-6) **398.2**

1. Jews—Folklore 2. Folklore—Poland
ISBN 0-531-05958-8; 0-531-08558-9 (lib bdg)
          LC 90-29273

Also available in paperback from Morrow

"A Richard Jackson book"

Thirteen traditional Eastern European Jewish tales of the town of Chelm and its silly citizens

"The 13 selections, many well known, will raise broad smiles and deep chuckles. . . . Sanfield's apt choices of words are strung together in lyrical prose that easily takes the reader to the Eastern European countryside. . . . Deftly made woodcuts, often simple yet poignant, add to the volume's flair. Perfect for reading aloud to all ages." Booklist

Includes glossary and bibliography

Strudel, strudel, strudel; paintings by Emily Lisker. Orchard Bks. 1995 unp il $14.95; lib bdg $14.99 (k-3) **398.2**

1. Jews—Folklore
ISBN 0-531-06879-X; 0-531-08729-8 (lib bdg)
          LC 94-24858

"A Richard Jackson book"

"Zaynul the school teacher and his wife Zeitel are poor but happy Chelmites—until they develop an uncontrollable craving for strudel. . . . If they each save just one *zloty* a week, hiding the coins in an old trunk with wheels, they will be able to afford the ingredients. After the first week, both husband and wife secretly decide to let their spouse do the saving. The trunk is finally opened in the spring, revealing only the two original coins. In the argument that follows, they fall into the trunk, which rolls down the street and wreaks havoc in the marketplace. In response, the town leaders use their best Chelm logic to make some new rules: teachers may not live on a hill, own a trunk with wheels, or eat strudel." SLJ

"The lively retelling of a traditional Jewish tale from Poland is handily partnered by robust watercolors, bright with hardy yellows and oranges, deep forest greens, and primary reds and blues." Booklist

Sawyer, Ruth, 1880-1970

The remarkable Christmas of the cobbler's sons; told by Ruth Sawyer; pictures by Barbara Cooney. Viking 1994 unp il $14.99 (k-3) **398.2**

1. Folklore—Austria 2. Christmas—Fiction
ISBN 0-670-84922-7   LC 94-10934

Originally appeared under title Schnitzle, Schnotzle, and Schnootzle, in Sawyer's The long Christmas, collection of seasonal poems and stories published 1941

A poor cobbler and his three sons worry about having food for their Christmas feast, until a playful goblin king pays them a visit

"A handsome picture book adorned with full-color illustrations that combine the earthy quality of peasant lore with luminous evocations of Alpine landscapes." Horn Book

Schwartz, Alvin, 1927-1992

All of our noses are here, and other noodle tales; retold by Alvin Schwartz; pictures by Karen Ann Weinhaus. Harper & Row 1985 64p il lib bdg $14.89 (k-2) **398.2**

1. Folklore 2. Wit and humor
ISBN 0-06-025288-X (lib bdg)   LC 84-48330

"An I can read book"

This companion volume to There is a carrot in my ear, and other noodle tales, entered below, contains additional stories about members of the Brown family

"The illustrations show them looking very much like mice and always smiling and cheerful. Cousins, no doubt, to the Stupids, the family is bound to be as appealing to young readers. With a list of sources." Horn Book

And the green grass grew all around; folk poetry from everyone; illustrations by Sue Truesdell. HarperCollins Pubs. 1992 195p il music $15; lib bdg $14.89 **398.2**

1. Folklore
ISBN 0-06-022757-5; 0-06-022758-3 (lib bdg)
          LC 89-26722

Schwartz, Alvin, 1927-1992—*Continued*

This collection includes "chants and teases, wishes and warnings, jokes and riddles, skip-rope rhymes and stories, fun and games." Booklist

"Full of vigorous, swinging rhythms and funny, often nasty, sentiments, the pages are filled with well-known rhymes as well as new discoveries. . . . Sue Truesdell's cartoon drawings dance and tumble across the pages as a perfect accompaniment to the rhymes they illustrate. . . . A wonderful collection for reading, singing, and laughing out loud, this book is strongly recommended for sharing in groups." Horn Book

Includes bibliography

Ghosts! ghostly tales from folklore; retold by Alvin Schwartz; illustrated by Victoria Chess. HarperCollins Pubs. 1991 63p il $14.95; lib bdg $14.89; pa $3.75 (k-2)   **398.2**

1. Ghost stories 2. Folklore
ISBN 0-06-021796-0; 0-06-021797-9 (lib bdg); 0-06-444170-9 (pa)   LC 90-21746

"An I can read book"

Presents seven, easy-to-read ghost stories based on traditional folk tales and legends from various countries

"All of the pen-and-watercolor illustrations are tidy and cheery and creepy. . . . Retold in a style that is simple but not choppy . . . and accompanied by a page of brief notes, all the tales will lend themselves to elaboration and innovation." Bull Cent Child Books

I saw you in the bathtub, and other folk rhymes; collected by Alvin Schwartz; pictures by Syd Hoff. Harper & Row 1989 64p il $14.95; lib bdg $14.89; pa $3.50 (k-2)   **398.2**

1. Folklore
ISBN 0-06-025298-7; 0-06-025299-5 (lib bdg); 0-06-444151-2 (pa)   LC 88-16111

"An I can read book"

Presents an illustrated collection of traditional folk rhymes, some composed by children

"Kids may be surprised to see their recess yells on the printed page but will relish the confirmation of significance. Hoff's full-color cartoons interpret the rhymes literally, an approach that leads to some pretty surreal results." Bull Cent Child Books

In a dark, dark room, and other scary stories; retold by Alvin Schwartz; illustrated by Dirk Zimmer. Harper & Row 1984 63p il $14.95; lib bdg $14.89; pa $3.50 (k-2)   **398.2**

1. Folklore 2. Ghost stories 3. Horror fiction
ISBN 0-06-025271-5; 0-06-025274-X (lib bdg); 0-06-444090-7 (pa)   LC 83-47699

"An I can read book"

This is a collection of "seven traditional tales from around the world retold in simple yet effective language. . . The chill here springs from suspense, an eerie setting or a ghostly surprise, rather than from blood and gore. Though pared down somewhat from longer versions, the stories retain their genuine creepiness. . . . The colorfully dark illustrations are sinister without being gruesome and add a comic touch." SLJ

More scary stories to tell in the dark; collected & retold from folklore by Alvin Schwartz; drawings by Stephen Gammell. Lippincott 1984 100p il $14.95; lib bdg $14.89; pa $3.95 (4 and up)   **398.2**

1. Ghost stories 2. Horror fiction 3. Folklore—United States
ISBN 0-397-32081-7; 0-397-32082-5 (lib bdg); 0-06-440177-4 (pa)   LC 83-49494

This volume contains stories of ghosts, murders, graveyards and other horrors

"The stories are all short and lively, very tellable, and greatly enhanced by the gray, ghoulish, horrifying illustrations of dismembered bodies, hideous creatures, and mysterious lights. A fine compendium by a well-known collector, easily accessible to young readers." Horn Book

Includes bibliography

Scary stories 3; more tales to chill your bones; collected from folklore and retold by Alvin Schwartz; drawings by Stephen Gammell. HarperCollins Pubs. 1991 115p il music $14.95; lib bdg $14.89; pa $3.95 (4 and up)   **398.2**

1. Ghost stories 2. Horror fiction 3. Folklore—United States
ISBN 0-06-021794-4; 0-06-021795-2 (lib bdg); 0-06-440418-8 (pa)   LC 90-47474

Traditional and modern-day stories of ghosts, haunts, superstitions, monsters, and horrible scary things

"The book is well paced and continually captivates, surprises, and entices audiences into reading just one more page. Gammell's gauzy, cobwebby, black-and-white pen-and-ink drawings help to sustain the overall creepy mood." SLJ

Includes bibliography

Scary stories to tell in the dark; collected from American folklore by Alvin Schwartz; with drawings by Stephen Gammell. Lippincott 1981 111p il $14.95; lib bdg $14.89; pa $3.95 (4 and up)   **398.2**

1. Ghost stories 2. Horror fiction 3. Folklore—United States
ISBN 0-397-31926-6; 0-397-31927-4 (lib bdg); 0-06-440170-7 (pa)   LC 80-8728

Also available in paperback boxed set with the two titles listed above for $11.95 (ISBN 0-06-440465-4)

"A collection of scary, semi-scary, and humorous stories about ghosts and witches collected from American folklore. Most of the stories (poems and songs also) are very short and range from the traditional to the modern. The author includes suggestions on how to tell scary stories effectively." Bull Cent Child Books

"The scholarship in the source notes and bibliography will be useful to serious literature students." SLJ

There is a carrot in my ear, and other noodle tales; retold by Alvin Schwartz; pictures by Karen Ann Weinhaus. Harper & Row 1982 64p il lib bdg $14.89; pa $3.75 (k-2)   **398.2**

1. Folklore 2. Wit and humor
ISBN 0-06-025234-0 (lib bdg); 0-06-444103-2 (pa)   LC 80-8442

"An I can read book"

This "is a collection of six stories from sources . . . as diverse as American 'Little Moron' stories, ancient Greek tales and vaudeville pieces. Explaining in his foreword that

Schwartz, Alvin, 1927-1992—_Continued_
a 'noodle is a silly person,' reteller Alvin Schwartz goes on
to introduce the noodly Brown family and reveal their various foibles. . . . Most of the stories don't appear in other
beginning noodle collections and will provide laughs for
readers who catch the puns and absurdities the stories hinge
on. The drawings by Karen Ann Weinhaus . . . show funny,
pointy-proboscised folk blissfully unaware of their own
goofiness." SLJ

Schwartz, Howard, 1945-
The diamond tree; Jewish tales from around
the world; selected and retold by Howard
Schwartz and Barbara Rush; illustrated by Uri
Shulevitz. HarperCollins Pubs. 1991 120p il
$17; lib bdg $16.89 (3-5)   **398.2**
   1. Jews—Folklore
   ISBN 0-06-025239-1; 0-06-025243-X (lib bdg)
                                     LC 90-32420
This collection "comprises fifteen Jewish tales that span
many centuries and come for the most part from countries
of the Middle East, Africa, and eastern Europe." Horn Book
  "Schwartz and Rush weave a rich tapestry that shows the
diversity of Jewish culture. . . . The language is simple and
vivid, and the narrative moves along at a good pace. . . .
Ten tales are accompanied by Shulevitz's bright, dramatic
watercolor paintings." SLJ
Includes bibliographical references

Shannon, George, 1952-
More stories to solve; fifteen folktales from
around the world; told by George Shannon;
illustrated by Peter Sis. Greenwillow Bks. 1991
64p il $14; pa $4.95 (3 and up)   **398.2**
   1. Folklore 2. Riddles
   ISBN 0-688-09161-X; 0-688-12947-1 (pa)
  "Shannon combines the folktale and the riddle in a brief
collection that brings together 15 international stories."
Booklist
Includes bibliographical references

Still more stories to solve; fourteen folktales
from around the world; told by George
Shannon; pictures by Peter Sis. Greenwillow
Bks. 1994 64p il $15 (3 and up)   **398.2**
   1. Folklore 2. Riddles
   ISBN 0-688-04619-3   LC 93-26529
This volume contains folktales in which there is a mystery or problem that the reader is invited to solve before
the resolution is presented

Stories to solve; folktales from around the
world; told by George Shannon; illustrated by
Peter Sis. Greenwillow Bks. 1985 55p il $15;
lib bdg $14.93; pa $4.95 (3 and up)   **398.2**
   1. Folklore 2. Riddles
   ISBN 0-688-04303-8; 0-688-04304-6 (lib bdg);
   0-688-10496-7 (pa)   LC 84-18656
  "Each of these 14 delightful folktales is a short puzzle to
be solved through cleverness, common sense or careful observations of details in the text. . . . Sis' pointillistic pen-
and-ink drawings illustrate each puzzle, and sometimes clarify the solutions." SLJ
Includes bibliographical references

Shepard, Aaron
The gifts of Wali Dad; a tale of India and
Pakistan; retold by Aaron Shepard; pictures by
Daniel San Souci. Atheneum Bks. for Young
Readers 1995 unp il $16 (2-4)   **398.2**
   1. Fairy tales 2. Folklore—India 3. Folklore—Pakistan
   ISBN 0-684-19445-7   LC 94-14175
  "Wali Dad is an elderly grass-cutter with simple tastes.
. . . When he gives a golden bracelet to a merchant with in-
structions for it to be taken to the 'noblest lady,' he has no
idea that he'll end up bringing together a princess and a
prince and being wealthier than he could have imagined.
However, he is happiest only when he gets his best wish—
to become a simple grasscutter again. . . . In addition to introducing some figures of Indian and Pakistani folklore, the
illustrations convey an atmosphere of radiating generosity."
Booklist

Sherlock, Sir Philip Manderson, 1902-
West Indian folk-tales; retold by Philip
Sherlock; illustrated by Joan Kiddell-Monroe.
Oxford Univ. Press 1966 151p il (Oxford
myths and legends) hardcover o.p. paperback
available $10.95 (4-6)   **398.2**
   1. Folklore—West Indies
   ISBN 0-19-274127-6 (pa)   LC 66-701268
  "Twenty-one tales of the ancient peoples, the Caribs and
the Arawaks, are intertwined here with the folklore of the
African slaves. Simply structured and ably retold, the collection includes the familiar 'pourquoi' (why) stories, several
tales of Anansi, the spiderman, and other legends that recount the trials and successes of the West Indian birds and
animals." SLJ

Shub, Elizabeth
Seeing is believing; pictures by Rachel
Isadora. Greenwillow Bks. 1994 c1979 63p il
$14 (1-3)   **398.2**
   1. Fairy tales 2. Folklore
   ISBN 0-688-13647-8
  A reissue of the title first published 1979
  "From Irish and Cornish folklore Shub has created two
stories about Tom and his encounters with a leprechaun
('The Leprechaun's Trick') and elves ('Pisky Mischief')."
SLJ
  "Both stories, while spare, succeed in entertaining as well
as in revealing the strong, sometimes dangerous power of
the Wee Folk. . . . Between her fine straight-lined pen-and-
ink forms of the solid, real world, Isadora hides wild, curl-
ing berry vines that house hundreds of ethereal faces and
figures—some mocking, some musing—all beyond any lasting grasp of humans." Booklist

Shulevitz, Uri, 1935-
The secret room. Farrar, Straus & Giroux
1993 unp il $15 (k-3)   **398.2**
   1. Folklore
   ISBN 0-374-34131-1   LC 93-10094
  The king's clever treasurer tries to clear his name when
the chief minister accuses the treasurer of stealing
  "There's an exotic, modern, almost cubist feel to
Shulevitz's art, which relies less on movement and embellishment than on angular shapes and blocks of bright, often
flat color to draw the eye. The dramatic simplicity that results makes the pictures great for group sharing while the
uncomplicated narrative will be easy to read aloud." Booklist

Shulevitz, Uri, 1935— *Continued*

The treasure. Farrar, Straus & Giroux 1978
unp il $16; pa $5.95 (k-3)   **398.2**

1. Folklore
ISBN 0-374-37740-5; 0-374-47955-0 (pa)

Also available Spanish language edition

A Caldecott Medal honor book, 1980

This is the "tale of a poor man, here named Isaac, who
three times dreams of a voice telling him to go to the capital and look for a treasure under the bridge by the palace.
When he gets to the capital, the captain of the guard tells
him of his dream: a treasure is buried under the stove of a
man named Isaac back in Isaac's home city. So Isaac returns home, finds the treasure under his own stove, and
lives happily ever after." SLJ

"Although the story is known in many cultures the retelling suggests the Hassidic tradition. . . . The eastern European influence is extended in the illustrations." Horn Book

Singer, Isaac Bashevis, 1904-1991

Mazel and Shlimazel; or, The milk of a
lioness; pictures by Margot Zemach; translated
from the Yiddish by the author and Elizabeth
Shub. Farrar, Straus & Giroux 1967 42p il
$17; pa $6.95 (2-5)   **398.2**

1. Jews—Folklore
ISBN 0-374-34884-7; 0-374-44786-1 (pa)

Also available Spanish language edition

"An Ariel book"

The happiness of Tam, a poor peasant lad, and lovely
Crown Princess Nesika depends upon the outcome of a battle of wits between Mazel, the spirit of good luck, and Shlimazel, the spirit of bad luck

This story "is based on a Jewish folk tale. . . . The way
Shlimazel contrives to win the wager is a witty surprise, and
how, moreover, the story-teller arranges to have the story
end happily after all is also ingenious and satisfying. The
colored illustrations . . . have the flavor of folk art but, like
the text, are anything but artless." New Yorker

When Shlemiel went to Warsaw & other
stories; pictures by Margot Zemach; translated
by the author and Elizabeth Shub. Farrar,
Straus & Giroux 1968 115p il $16; pa $4.95 (4
and up)   **398.2**

1. Jews—Folklore
ISBN 0-374-38316-2; 0-374-48365-5 (pa)

A Newbery Award honor book, 1969

"An Ariel book"

"A fine collection of five retold traditional Yiddish folk
tales and three original stories. . . . The original stories—
'Tsirtsur and Peziza,' 'Rabbi Leib and the Witch
Cunegunde,' and 'Menasheh's Dream'—blend well with the
reworked tales, and Margot Zemach's delightful black-and-
white illustrations fittingly capture moods and protagonists." SLJ

Zlateh the goat, and other stories; pictures
by Maurice Sendak; translated from the
Yiddish by the author and Elizabeth Shub.
Harper & Row 1966 90p il $15.89; lib bdg
$16; pa $5.95 (4 and up)   **398.2**

1. Jews—Folklore
ISBN 0-06-025698-2; 0-06-025699-0 (lib bdg);
0-06-440147-2 (pa)

Also available Spanish language edition

A Newbery Award honor book, 1967

"Seven tales drawn from middle-European Jewish village
life, with illustrations which extend the humor and subtlety
of the situations." Hodges. Books for Elem Sch Libr

Snyder, Dianne

The boy of the three-year nap; illustrated by
Allen Say. Houghton Mifflin 1988 32p il
$16.95; pa $4.95 (1-3)   **398.2**

1. Folklore—Japan
ISBN 0-395-44090-4; 0-395-66957-X (pa)

      LC 87-30674

Also available Spanish language edition

A Caldecott Medal honor book, 1989

"Japan's contribution to the trickster folktale, in which a
lazy son cons a rich man, only to be outsmarted by his
own, even trickier mother. Lilting prose and shimmering illustrations combine in perfect harmony." SLJ

Spagnoli, Cathy, 1950-

Nine-in-one, Grr! Grr! a folktale from the
Hmong people of Laos; told by Blia Xiong;
adapted by Cathy Spagnoli; illustrated by
Nancy Hom. Children's Bk. Press 1989 30p il
$13.95; pa $6.95 (k-2)   **398.2**

1. Folklore—Laos 2. Tigers—Fiction
ISBN 0-89239-048-4; 0-89239-110-3 (pa)

      LC 89-9891

Also available Spanish language edition

When the great god Shao promises Tiger nine cubs each
year, Bird comes up with a clever trick to prevent the land
from being overrun by tigers

"Simply and eloquently told, this *pourquoi* tale from a
minority Laotian culture is boldly illustrated in a style
adapted from the multi-imaged embroidered story cloths of
the Hmong people. Its rhythmic text and appealing, brightly
colored pictures make it a good choice for preschool story
hours." Booklist

Spariosu, Mihai

Ghosts, vampires, and werewolves; eerie
tales from Transylvania; [retold] by Mihai
Spariosu and Dezsö Benedek; illustrated by
Laszlo Kubinyi. Orchard Bks. 1994 104p il
$16.95; lib bdg $16.99 (5 and up)   **398.2**

1. Folklore—Romania 2. Supernatural—Fiction
ISBN 0-531-06860-9; 0-531-08710-7 (lib bdg)

      LC 93-48837

Includes sixteen tales from Transylvanian folklore, arranged in three sections: Ghosts, Vampires, and Werewolves; Haunted Treasures; and Eerie Fairy Tales

"Scary, sometimes gruesome, with dark humor and dramatic immediacy, these stories are great for storytelling and
reading aloud." Booklist

Includes bibliography

Stamm, Claus

Three strong women; a tall tale from Japan;
pictures by Jean and Mou-sien Tseng. Viking
1990 unp il $12.95; pa $4.99 (k-3)   **398.2**

1. Folklore—Japan 2. Tall tales
ISBN 0-670-83323-1; 0-14-054530-1 (pa)

      LC 89-48758

A newly illustrated edition of the title first published
1962

Stamm, Claus—_Continued_

"Forever-Mountain is a famous wrestler, smug and rather conceited—until he meets Maru-me. Along with her mother and grandmother, she shows him what real strength is. Under their tutelage, he gains not only physical prowess, but the humility of the truly strong. This version of the Japanese tall tale is filled with sly humor and witty exaggeration. The Tsengs' illustrations match the text perfectly; the glowing watercolors evoke a rural Japan of long ago." SLJ

Stanley, Diane, 1943-

Petrosinella; a Neapolitan Rapunzel; retold and illustrated by Diane Stanley. Dial Bks. for Young Readers 1995 unp il $14.99; lib bdg $14.89 (3-5) **398.2**

1. Fairy tales 2. Folklore—Italy

ISBN 0-8037-1712-1; 0-8037-1714-8 (lib bdg)

LC 94-17456

Also available Spanish language edition

"The illustrations in this book first appeared in an edition of Petrosinella published by Frederick Warne & Co. Inc. in 1981." Verso of title page

In this version of Rapunzel, the heroine breaks the enchantment put on her by the ogress who keeps her prisoner with the aid of three acorns

This version of the fairy tale "predates the Grimms by 200 years. . . . Here the women play a more active part in the plot. . . . Stanley's watercolors and colored inks are rendered in royal blues and verdant greens—a fitting backdrop for the young woman and the prince with whom she falls in love, and an effective contrast to the ugly hag." SLJ

Steptoe, John, 1950-1989

Mufaro's beautiful daughters; an African tale. Lothrop, Lee & Shepard Bks. 1987 unp il $16; lib bdg $15.93 (k-3) **398.2**

1. Folklore—Africa

ISBN 0-688-04045-4; 0-688-04046-2 (lib bdg)

LC 84-7158

A Caldecott Medal honor book, 1988; Coretta Scott King award for illustration, 1988

Mufaro's two beautiful daughters, one bad-tempered, one kind and sweet, go before the king, who is choosing a wife

"The pace of the text matches the rhythm of the illustrations—both move in dramatic unity to the climax. By changing perspective the artist not only captures the lush, rich background but also the personalities of the characters with revealing studies of their faces." Horn Book

The story of Jumping Mouse; a native American legend; retold and illustrated by John Steptoe. Lothrop, Lee & Shepard Bks. 1984 unp il $16; lib bdg $15.93; pa $4.95 (1-3) **398.2**

1. Indians of North America—Legends

ISBN 0-688-01902-1; 0-688-01903-X (lib bdg); 0-688-08740-X (pa) LC 82-14848

A Caldecott Medal honor book, 1985

"By keeping hope alive within himself, a mouse is successful in his quest for the far-off land. Steptoe's retelling of an unattributed tribal legend is exquisite in its use of language and in its expansive drawings which employ dazzling subtleties of light and shadow." SLJ

Stevens, Janet

Coyote steals the blanket; an Ute tale; retold and illustrated by Janet Stevens. Holiday House 1993 unp il $15.95; pa $5.95 (k-3) **398.2**

1. Ute Indians—Legends 2. Coyote (Legendary character)

ISBN 0-8234-0996-1; 0-8234-1129-X (pa)

LC 92-54415

"When Coyote swipes a blanket, thus angering the spirit of the desert, he is pursued by a rock on a rampage. This traditional trickster tale features a scraggly, scruffy yet lovable character, a narrative that will roll right off storytellers' tongues, and hilarious pictures of boastful animals trying to halt the furious boulder." SLJ

Tops and bottoms; adapted and illustrated by Janet Stevens. Harcourt Brace & Co. 1995 unp il $15 (k-3) **398.2**

1. African Americans—Folklore 2. Rabbits—Fiction 3. Bears—Fiction

ISBN 0-15-292851-0 LC 93-19154

A Caldecott Medal honor book, 1996

"Bear agrees to enter into a farming partnership with Hare, but first Hare makes Bear choose which half he will receive at harvest time: tops or bottoms. Because Bear picks tops, Hare sows all root vegetables. For the second crop, Bear chooses bottoms; this time Hare grows lettuce, broccoli, and celery. Finally, the frustrated Bear demands tops and bottoms from the final season's crop. But Hare is still the winner: he grows corn [and] keeps the ears 'in the middle' for his family. . . . Steven's bold, well-composed watercolor, pencil, and gesso illustrations cover every inch of each vertically oriented double-page spread. . . . The story contains enough sly humor and reassuring predictability to captivate listeners." Horn Book

The town mouse and the country mouse; an Aesop fable; adapted and illustrated by Janet Stevens. Holiday House 1987 unp il $15.95; pa $5.95 (k-2) **398.2**

1. Mice—Fiction 2. Fables

ISBN 0-8234-0633-4; 0-8234-0733-0 (pa)

LC 86-14276

A town mouse and a country mouse exchange visits and discover each is suited to his or her own home

"In her usual sassy fashion, Stevens takes a classic tale . . . and turns it into a comic romp. . . . The cheerful watercolors showcase not only Stevens' humor, but also her strong sense of color and composition. . . . Text and graphics are in harmony, and the large-scale drawings will make this tale a welcome read-aloud in story hours." Booklist

Sutcliff, Rosemary, 1920-1992

The light beyond the forest; the quest for the Holy Grail; decorations by Shirley Felts. Dutton 1980 143p o.p.; Viking paperback available $3.99 (4 and up) **398.2**

1. Arthur, King 2. Grail—Fiction 3. Arthurian romances

ISBN 0-14-037150-8 (pa) LC 79-23396

First published 1979 in the United Kingdom

This is a retelling of the adventures of King Arthur's knights as they search for the Holy Grail. "After a vision of the Cup from the Last Supper appears, Sir Lancelot, Sir Galahad, Sir Bors, and Sir Percival quit Camelot to look for the Grail, knowing that only the world's most perfect knight will succeed. The individual adventures, which take on a loftier meaning as the journeys also become the knights' personal searches for God, will be most appreciated by spe-

Sutcliff, Rosemary, 1920-1992—*Continued*
cial readers interested in King Arthur and his time." Booklist

Followed by The sword and the circle

The road to Camlann; decorations by Shirley Felts. Dutton 1982 142p o.p.; Viking paperback available $3.99 (4 and up)
398.2

1. Arthur, King 2. Arthurian romances
ISBN 0-14-037147-8 (pa)   LC 82-9481
First published 1981 in the United Kingdom

"This book completes Rosemary Sutcliff's Arthurian trilogy, begun with 'The Light Beyond the Forest' and 'The Sword and the Circle'. Here Sutcliff describes the events from the coming of Mordred to the death of Lancelot. The title refers to The Last Battle, in which Arthur and his civilization perish. Sutcliff writes with her usual economy and rich prose, with a touch of archaic diction in the speeches. . . . Other than Malory, I can think of no better introduction to the whole sweep of Arthurian stories and values." SLJ

The sword and the circle; King Arthur and the Knights of the Round Table. Dutton 1981 260p $14.99 (4 and up)   **398.2**

1. Arthur, King 2. Arthurian romances
ISBN 0-525-40585-2   LC 81-9759
Also available in paperback from Penguin Bks.

The second volume in the author's Arthurian trilogy, begun with: The light beyond the forest. The events in this volume precede those in the earlier volume

"The author has brought together thirteen stories associated with the Arthurian cycle, beginning with 'The Coming of Arthur' and concluding not with the passing of Arthur but with 'The Coming of Perceval.' Although she has relied on Malory's 'Morte d'Arthur' for most of her material, she has drawn upon other medieval sources for some of her best storytelling: For example 'Sir Gawain and the Green Knight' comes from a Middle English poem, and the twenty-nine-page 'Tristan and Iseult' is indebted to Godfrey of Strasburg's version." Horn Book

Followed by The road to Camlann

The **Tall** book of nursery tales; pictures by Feodor Rojankovsky. Artists & Writers Guild 1944 120p il $9.95 (k-2)   **398.2**

1. Folklore 2. Fairy tales
ISBN 0-06-025065-8

A collection of 24 well-known traditional tales such as Little Red Riding Hood, The three bears, The gingerbread boy, The ugly duckling, etc.

"The many, many illustrations—both colored and black and white—are delightful and the stories themselves are the best-known versions." Libr J

Taylor, Harriet Peck

Coyote and the laughing butterflies; retold and illustrated by Harriet Peck Taylor. Macmillan Bks. for Young Readers 1995 unp il $15 (k-3)   **398.2**

1. Pueblo Indians—Legends 2. Coyote (Legendary character)
ISBN 0-02-788846-0   LC 94-15278

"After a long journey to get salt for his wife, Coyote takes a nap. While he sleeps, mischievous butterflies carry him home. Coyote can't explain the trip—or the two that follow—but he is grateful that a sack of salt, finally, travels

too. This tale explains that butterflies flutter because they are laughing too hard to fly straight." Publisher's note

"A delightful retelling of a Tewa legend. . . . The softly textured batik illustrations add feeling and depth. . . . Dusty oranges, blues, tans, and greens capture the New Mexican landscape and bring to life the vibrant scenes of the mesa and the animals' expressions and antics." SLJ

Coyote places the stars; retold and illustrated by Harriet Peck Taylor. Bradbury Press 1993 unp il $15 (k-3)   **398.2**

1. Chinook Indians—Legends 2. Coyote (Legendary character) 3. Stars—Fiction

ISBN 0-02-788845-2   LC 92-46431

"Based on a Wasco Native American legend, this . . . pourquoi tale explains the designs of the constellations. It is the curious coyote who decides to discover the secrets of the heavens by creating a ladder of arrows he shoots into the sky. Once in the heavens, he moves the stars around forming the shapes of his animal friends." SLJ

"Taylor's batik-and-dye paintings are a good match for the casual, playful rhythm of her retelling." Booklist

Te Kanawa, Kiri

Land of the long white cloud; Maori myths, tales and legends; illustrated by Michael Foreman. Arcade Pub. 1990 118p il $16.95 (3-6)   **398.2**

1. Maoris—Folklore

ISBN 1-55970-046-7   LC 89-45534

"Opera singer Dame Kiri Te Kanawa retells the Maori folktales she remembers from her childhood in New Zealand." Booklist

"Lively and full of action, adventure, and magic, the collection is well balanced with myths, hero legends, fairy tales, and *pourquoi* stories. . . . Jewel-toned watercolor illustrations capture the vibrant quality of the stories and convey the changing moods of sea and sky. This book is a rich source of Pacific island material." SLJ

Temple, Frances, 1945-1995

Tiger soup; an Anansi story from Jamaica; retold and illustrated by Frances Temple. Orchard Bks. 1994 unp il $15.95; lib bdg $15.99 (k-3)   **398.2**

1. Folklore—Jamaica 2. Anansi (Legendary character)

ISBN 0-531-06859-5; 0-531-08709-3 (lib bdg)
LC 93-48834

"A Richard Jackson book"

After tricking Tiger into leaving the soup he has been cooking, Anansi the spider eats the soup himself and manages to put the blame on the monkeys

"Temple's retelling is filled with the easy rhythm of the Jamaican dialect and begs to be read—even partly sung— aloud. The story moves along at a pleasant pace and provides opportunities for participation. . . . The torn-and-painted paper collages convey the warmth and color of the tropical setting and suggests a real sense of movement." SLJ

Terada, Alice M.

Under the starfruit tree; folktales from Vietnam; told by Alice M. Terada; illustrations by Janet Larsen; introduction and notes by Mary C. Austin. University of Hawaii Press 1989 136p il hardcover o.p. paperback available $11.95 (4-6) **398.2**

1. Folklore—Vietnam

ISBN 0-8248-1553-X (pa) LC 89-5123

"A Kolowalu book"

"Twenty-seven tales culled from North and South Vietnam and translated by native speakers are grouped in four sections: foibles and quirks; tales from the lowlands and the highlands; the spirit world; and food, love and laughter. . . . Each narration is followed by an afterword that . . . reveals customs, beliefs and values." Publ Wkly

"Although the book's format is not particularly attractive, these 27 stories from Vietnam will certainly find a place on library shelves. . . . Occasional black-and-white drawings add some visual interest." Booklist

Includes bibliography

Tomie dePaola's Favorite nursery tales. Putnam 1986 127p il $21.95 (k-3) **398.2**

1. Folklore 2. Fables

ISBN 0-399-21319-8 LC 85-28302

"The book begins, appropriately enough, with a verse about reading picture books from Stevenson's *Child's Garden of Verses*, followed by Longfellow's 'Children's Hour.' The story selections—'Johnny Cake,' 'The Little Red Hen,' Rumpelstiltskin,' 'The Princess and the Pea,' 'The Tortoise and the Hare,' 'The House on the Hill,' and 22 more." Booklist

"DePaola's droll, witty, and very funny illustrations capture the essence of each story from a child's point of view. . . . The beautiful layout of these pages, in which the print and pictures are perfectly at ease with one another, invites confident new readers as well as adults for reading aloud." SLJ

Tompert, Ann, 1918-

Bamboo hats and a rice cake; a tale adapted from Japanese folklore; illustrated by Demi. Crown 1993 unp il $13; lib bdg $13.99 (k-3) **398.2**

1. Folklore—Japan

ISBN 0-517-59272-X; 0-517-59273-8 (lib bdg) LC 92-26849

Wishing to have good fortune in the new year, an old man tries to trade his wife's kimono for rice cakes

"The story is simply and gracefully told, with seven Japanese characters interspersed throughout the text. These are quickly learned since they also appear on the left- and right-hand margins of each double-page spread. The illustrator's distinctive miniaturistic style is well-suited to the story, controlled and elegant. . . . Author's and illustrator's notes on the last page add pertinent background information." Horn Book

Tresselt, Alvin R., 1916-

The mitten; an old Ukrainian folktale; retold by Alvin Tresselt; illustrated by Yaroslava; adapted from the version by E. Rachev. Lothrop, Lee & Shepard Bks. 1964 unp il lib bdg $14.93; pa $4.95 (k-2) **398.2**

1. Folklore—Ukraine 2. Animals—Fiction

ISBN 0-688-51053-1 (lib bdg); 0-688-09238-1 (pa)

"On the coldest day of the year a little Ukrainian boy loses his fur-lined mitten, which becomes so overcrowded with animals seeking a snug shelter that it finally bursts. Brightly colored pictures show the animals dressed in typical Ukrainian costumes." Hodges. Books for Elem Sch Libr

Uchida, Yoshiko, 1921-1992

The magic purse; retold by Yoshiko Uchida; illustrated by Keiko Narahashi. Margaret K. McElderry Bks. 1993 unp il $15.95 (k-3) **398.2**

1. Folklore—Japan

ISBN 0-689-50559-0 LC 92-30132

After facing danger and demons to help a young woman, a poor farmer receives a magic purse that always refills itself with gold

"The author's elegant retelling is well paced and dotted with lyrical imagery. . . . Narahashi clearly evokes Japanese scroll paintings through her boldly outlined, seemingly spontaneous watercolors. Her luminous art sets the mood perfectly for Uchida's magical tale." Publ Wkly

The wise old woman; retold by Yoshiko Uchida; illustrated by Martin Springett. Margaret K. McElderry Bks. 1994 unp il $14.95 (k-3) **398.2**

1. Folklore—Japan 2. Old age—Fiction

ISBN 0-689-50582-5 LC 92-46048

"The cruel, young village lord decrees that people over 70 are useless and must be taken to the mountains to die. A young farmer cannot bear to abandon his mother, so he hides her deep in a cave beneath the kitchen. One day when the village is threatened by a mighty conqueror, the wisdom of the hidden old woman saves the people; then respect and honor are restored for all of the aged. The stylized airbrush-and-ink illustrations in strong shades of purple, brown, and blue have the elegance and fluidity of traditional Japanese prints." Booklist

Van Laan, Nancy

Buffalo dance; a Blackfoot legend; retold by Nancy Van Laan; illustrated by Beatriz Vidal. Little, Brown 1993 unp il $15.95 (2-4) **398.2**

1. Siksika Indians—Legends

ISBN 0-316-89728-0 LC 92-15444

A retelling of the Blackfoot legend about the ritual performed before the buffalo hunt

"Vidal's glowing, stylistic paintings have strength and dignity and appear to reflect the originating culture. Van Laan lists four books as sources for her story, and Vidal incorporates Blackfoot patterns and designs and symbols from Native American tradition in her paintings. A story of courage and faith, this makes effective storytelling material and a good read aloud for older groups." Booklist

Van Laan, Nancy—*Continued*

In a circle long ago; a treasury of native lore from North America; illustrated by Lisa Desimini. Apple Soup Bks. 1995 128p il $20; lib bdg $21.99 (3-5) **398.2**

1. Indians of North America—Legends
ISBN 0-679-85807-5; 0-679-95807-X (lib bdg)
LC 94-37975

"Twenty-five creation stories, *pourquoi* tales, and poems from North American tribes explore the natural world. The selections are divided into the eight major cultural groups, and Van Laan introduces each section with a brief description of the people. . . . Inviting, colorful illustrations in an assortment of styles enliven the works and will add to youngsters' enjoyment." Booklist

Includes bibliographical references

The legend of El Dorado; a Latin American tale; story and illustrations by Beatriz Vidal; adapted by Nancy Van Laan. Knopf 1991 unp il $16 (k-3) **398.2**

1. Chibcha Indians—Legends
ISBN 0-679-80136-7
LC 89-7998

A retelling of the Chibcha Indian legend about how the treasure of El Dorado came to be

"The splendid pairing of Van Laan's suave retelling and Vidal's richly colored illustrations—meticulously executed and imbued with a primitive charm—capture all the beauty and mysticism of a culture from long ago and far away." Publ Wkly

The tiny, tiny boy and the big, big cow; a Scottish folk tale; pictures by Marjorie Priceman. Knopf 1993 unp il $8.99; lib bdg $9.99 (k-3) **398.2**

1. Folklore—Scotland 2. Cattle—Fiction
ISBN 0-679-82078-7; 0-679-92078-1 (lib bdg)
LC 91-33738

"An Umbrella book"

A cumulative story in which a tiny, tiny boy tries to milk a big, big cow who will not stand still

"Hilarious full-page pen-and-ink and watercolor illustrations in warm, rosy tones are delightfully detailed and rush the exuberant action forward to its sensible, satisfying conclusion." SLJ

Vuong, Lynette Dyer, 1938-

The brocaded slipper and other Vietnamese tales; illustrations by Vo-Dinh Mai. HarperCollins Pubs. 1982 111p il hardcover o.p. paperback available $3.95 (4-6) **398.2**

1. Folklore—Vietnam 2. Fairy tales
ISBN 0-06-440440-4 (pa)
LC 81-19139

First published by Addison-Wesley

"These five Vietnamese fairy tales have motifs that will be familiar to Western readers. The title story is a 'Cinderella' variant. 'Little Finger of the Watermelon Patch' is similar to 'Thumbelina.' 'The Fairy Grotto,' in which a man enters fairyland and then comes back to a world that is 300 years older, has a protagonist not unlike Rip van Winkle. In 'Master Frog' the frog heroine must survive in cruel and humble circumstances before she is reunited with her true love." Booklist

"The stories . . . are often more satisfyingly complex than their Western counterparts. . . . The simple, fluid ink-wash illustrations are captioned in both English and Vietnamese. An excellent and unusual addition to folklore collections." SLJ

The golden carp and other tales from Vietnam; [retold by] Lynette Dyer Vuong; [illustrated by] Manabu Saito. Lothrop, Lee & Shepard Bks. 1993 128p il $15 (4-6) **398.2**

1. Folklore—Vietnam
ISBN 0-688-12514-X
LC 92-38208

"Six traditional tales from Vietnam have been retold and illustrated with striking paintings to create a lovely and accessible volume. The stories of love, loyalty, and heroism are engrossing. . . . Each story is accompanied by a full page illustration, painted in vivid colors, including many hues of red, green, and black." Horn Book

Sky legends of Vietnam; illustrated by Vo-Dinh Mai. HarperCollins Pubs. 1993 103p il $14; lib bdg $13.89 (4-6) **398.2**

1. Folklore—Vietnam
ISBN 0-06-023000-2; 0-06-023001-0 (lib bdg)
LC 92-38345

"This collection of six Vietnamese tales opens with two simple *pourquoi* stories explaining how the sun and moon got their respective jobs in the sky. Following are four affecting, unusual stories, three of which concern sky fairies and their doomed relationships with humans. . . . Vuong includes notes on common motifs in Vietnamese and Chinese folklore, sources her tales in the original Vietnamese texts, and incorporates a pronunciation guide to Vietnamese names and phrases. Nicely illustrated with pen-and-ink drawings." Booklist

Walker, Barbara K.

A treasury of Turkish folktales for children; retold by Barbara K. Walker. Linnet Bks. 1988 155p $18.50 (4 and up) **398.2**

1. Folklore—Turkey
ISBN 0-208-02206-6
LC 88-6859

"The 34 stories are organized into sections on animals, fables, Keloglan tales, Nasreddin Hoca tales, witch/giant/jinn/dragon tales, trickster tales, tales of fate, and stories of wish fulfillment. The tonal range offers great variety for storytelling, reading aloud, or just plain entertainment among children fond of folktales, though the format is formidable for young readers." Bull Cent Child Books

Includes glossary

Walker, Paul Robert

Big men, big country; a collection of American tall tales; written by Paul Robert Walker; illustrated by James Bernardin. Harcourt Brace Jovanovich 1993 79p il $16.95 (4-6) **398.2**

1. Tall tales 2. Folklore—United States
ISBN 0-15-207136-9
LC 91-45126

A collection of American tall tales featuring such legendary characters as Davy Crockett, Paul Bunyan, and Pecos Bill

"Walker's informal style and easygoing humor make a natural fit for these nine stories of larger-than-life heroes, and he's done a thorough job of researching the background for them and telling us about it. . . . Bernardin has captured this cast with strong black-and-white drawings, plus full-color pictures with a kind of muscular Frederic Remington energy." Bull Cent Child Books

Includes bibliography

Wang, Rosalind C.

The fourth question; a Chinese tale; retold by Rosalind C. Wang; illustrated by Ju-Hong Chen. Holiday House 1991 unp il $14.95 (k-3)
398.2

1. Folklore—China
ISBN 0-8234-0855-8   LC 90-43536

A young man named Yee-Lee goes on a journey to the Wise Man of Kun-lun Mountain to discover the reason for his poverty

"The story is an interesting variation on an old folklore motif, and the illustrations have a luminous quality with strong line and muted colors." SLJ

The treasure chest; a Chinese tale; retold by Rosalind C. Wang; illustrated by Will Hillenbrand. Holiday House 1995 unp il $15.95 (2-4)
398.2

1. Folklore—China
ISBN 0-8234-1114-1   LC 93-20744

"Laifu, a poor widow's son, rescues a beautiful, rainbow-colored fish and earns the gratitude of the Ocean King, whose gift of three bamboo sticks helps the young man save the woman he loves." SLJ

"Wang's retelling of a Chinese folktale that was told often during her Taiwanese childhood merits a larger audience. . . . Hillenbrand, basing his mottled, magical illustration style on the southern Sung paintings (circa A.D. 1200), lends welcome authenticity to this entertaining slice of oral history." Booklist

Watkins, Yoko Kawashima

Tales from the bamboo grove; illustrated by Jean and Mou-sien Tseng. Bradbury Press 1992 49p il $14.95 (4-6)
398.2

1. Folklore—Japan
ISBN 0-02-792525-0   LC 91-38218

The author "retells six Japanese folktales that she had heard as a child from her parents while they were living in Korea, far from home. The stories are of sadness and parting, of virtue rewarded, bullies subverted, meekness triumphant, with the wishes, transformations, and journeys common to folklore everywhere. . . . The fine full-page brush-and-ink illustrations with each tale are both individualized and formal, and small calligraphy panels reinforce the traditional frame of the telling." Booklist

Watson, Richard Jesse, 1951-

Tom Thumb; retold and illustrated by Richard Jesse Watson. Harcourt Brace Jovanovich 1989 unp il $12.95; pa $5.95 (k-3)
398.2

1. Folklore 2. Fairy tales
ISBN 0-15-289280-X; 0-15-289281-8 (pa)
                                 LC 87-12045

After many adventures, a tiny boy, no bigger than his father's thumb, earns a place as the smallest Knight of the Round Table

"Although it is not stated, this is a loose adaptation of an English variant of the tale. . . . However, Watson's heroic ending, in which Tom Thumb replaces the giant's beloved broken shell, is not mentioned in other variants available. The writing borders on the flowery, but is quite readable. The realistic, microscopically detailed tempera and watercolor illustrations are particularly suitable for this tale." SLJ

Werner, Vivian L.

Petrouchka; the story of the ballet; illustrated by John Collier; retold by Vivian Werner. Viking 1992 30p il $16 (4-6)
398.2

1. Petrouchka (Ballet) 2. Folklore—Russia
ISBN 0-670-83607-9   LC 91-46309

"A Byron Preiss book"

Werner "tells the story of Stravinsky's ballet about Petrouchka, the clown-puppet with a heart, who yearns for his freedom from the Old Magician so that he can both dance freely and love the beautiful Ballerina." Adventuring with books

"Collier's paintings in pastel and gouache do a fine job of capturing Petrouchka's inner torment as well as the ballet's Russian peasant setting. This book will find an audience among young dancers and lovers of the dance." Booklist

Wildsmith, Brian, 1930-

The hare and the tortoise; based on the fable by La Fontaine. Oxford Univ. Press 1966 unp il $16.75; pa $7.50 (k-2)
398.2

1. Fables 2. Rabbits—Fiction 3. Turtles—Fiction
ISBN 0-19-279625-9; 0-19-272126-7 (pa)

"Wildsmith tells, simply and eloquently, his version of the La Fontaine fable about the slow and steady tortoise who wins the race from the quick and careless hare. The paintings are astonishing creations in all the colors of the spectrum. The vistas of a countryside bursting with blooms, birds soaring overhead as interested observers like the animals gathered along the route; every one of the scenes is a wonder." Publ Wkly

The miller, the boy and the donkey. Oxford Univ. Press 1969 unp il $16.75; pa $7.50 (k-2)
398.2

1. Fables
ISBN 0-19-279652-6; 0-19-272114-3 (pa)

Adapted and illustrated by Brian Wildsmith

The miller and his son take their donkey to market to sell him. To keep him clean they decide to carry him, but a passing farmer laughs at them and they ride the donkey instead. Thus begins a series of suggestions from other people they meet as to who should ride the donkey. The poor miller is utterly confused trying to please everyone and in the end decides that next time he will only please himself

"A spirited and attractive picture book." Child Books, 1970

Willard, Nancy

Beauty and the beast; wood engravings by Barry Moser. Harcourt Brace Jovanovich 1992 67p il $19.95 (5 and up)
398.2

1. Folklore—France 2. Fairy tales
ISBN 0-15-206052-9   LC 91-28398

Through her great capacity to love, a kind and beautiful young woman releases a handsome young man from the spell which has made him into an ugly beast

"This elegant, handsomely packaged retelling, set in turn-of-the-century New York, is graced by Moser's quietly dramatic woodcuts and Willard's sure command of language." Publ Wkly

Williams, Carol
Tsubu, the little snail; by Carol Ann
Williams; illustrated by Tatsuro Kiuchi.
Simon & Schuster Bks. for Young Readers
1995 unp il $15 (2-4)   **398.2**
1. Folklore—Japan
ISBN 0-671-87167-6   LC 93-49344
"In a retelling of a classic Japanese folktale, the Water
God answers the prayers of a rice farmer and his wife for
a baby, not with a child but with a *tsuba,* a 'little snail.' .
. . Tsubu takes the yearly rice tax to the powerful landowner and winds up marrying his daughter, whose unconditional love frees him from his shell and transforms him into a
handsome young man. . . . An author's note describes how
the message of the tale grew out of the beliefs of the Shinto
religion, and Kiuchi's handsome oil paintings, depicting
beautiful landscape scenes of the Japanese countryside, effectively transport us to an ancient Japanese village." Booklist

Winthrop, Elizabeth
Vasilissa the beautiful; a Russian folktale;
adapted by Elizabeth Winthrop; illustrated by
Alexander Koshkin. HarperCollins Pubs. 1991
36p il lib bdg $15.89; pa $5.95 (2-5)
           398.2
1. Folklore—Russia
ISBN 0-06-021663-8 (lib bdg); 0-06-443345-5 (pa)
         LC 89-26903
A retelling of the old Russian fairy tale in which beautiful Vasilissa uses the help of her doll to escape from the
clutches of the witch Baba Yaga
"Elizabeth Winthrop's adaptation of the tale is very readable and is beautifully illustrated in the deep colors and
richly elaborate costumes of seventeenth-century Russia."
Horn Book

Wolkstein, Diane
The banza; a Haitian story; pictures by
Marc Brown. Dial Bks. for Young Readers
1981 unp il $15.99; pa $4.95 (k-3)   **398.2**
1. Folklore—Haiti
ISBN 0-8037-0428-3; 0-8037-0058-X (pa)
"Cabree the goat becomes friends with a young tiger
named Teegra. . . . Teegra gives Cabree a 'banza' (an old
African instrument something like a banjo), which belonged
to his uncle, for protection. When Cabree is surrounded by
ten hungry tigers, she plays the banza, mobilizing her own
resources to frighten the tigers away." Interracial Books
Child Bull
"Told with rich economy, this brief tale is laced with action and humor; . . . Brown's solid, textured drawings in
bright Caribbean colors are a fine extension of the text, and
their size and clarity make the book excellent for sharing
with groups." SLJ

The magic wings; a tale from China;
illustrated by Robert Andrew Parker. Dutton
1983 unp il hardcover o.p. paperback
available $4.95 (2-4)   **398.2**
1. Folklore—China
ISBN 0-525-44275-8 (pa)   LC 83-1611
"A Unicorn book"
A strange event occurs across the land when a little Chinese goose girl sprinkles her shoulders with water and begins to wave her arms, believing that she will sprout wings,
fly, and enjoy all the beautiful flowers of spring

"Parker's distinctive line work is so appropriate for this
tale. . . . The use of color matches the use of line. The different hues have a life of their own, overlapping the object
lines and building a gentle movement of color that often
suggests light and shadow and at other times just animates
the surface. Parker includes rich architectural detail to draw
attention to the Chinese locale." Wilson Libr Bull

Oom Razoom; or, Go I know not where,
bring back I know not what: a Russian tale;
retold by Diane Wolkstein; illustrated by
Dennis McDermott. Morrow Junior Bks. 1991
unp il $14.95; lib bdg $14.88 (2-5)   **398.2**
1. Folklore—Russia
ISBN 0-688-09416-3; 0-688-09417-1 (lib bdg)
         LC 91-6308
A retelling of an old Russian tale of Alexis the king's archer, his beautiful and magical wife Olga, and their adventures
"Wolkstein brings uncommon warmth, playfulness, and
immediacy to her narrative. . . . McDermott's glowing
paintings in oil glaze are equally skilled. Rich colors, elaborate detail, and ornate framing recall Russian icons and lac-
quer boxes." Booklist

Womenfolk and fairy tales; edited by
Rosemary Minard; illustrated by Suzanna
Klein. Houghton Mifflin 1975 163p il
$16.95 (3-6)   **398.2**
1. Folklore 2. Fairy tales
ISBN 0-395-20276-0
This collection features stories by the Brothers Grimm,
Lafcadio Hearn, Andrew Lang, Joseph Jacobs, and others
"Although the tales are available in a multitude of collec-
tions, this handsomely illustrated volume brings them to-
gether in a convenient form for those searching for feminist
folklore." Horn Book

Yacowitz, Caryn
The jade stone; a Chinese folktale; adapted
by Caryn Yacowitz; illustrated by Ju-hong
Chen. Holiday House 1992 unp il $15.95 (k-3)
           398.2
1. Folklore—China
ISBN 0-8234-0919-8   LC 91-17934
When the Great Emperor of All China commands him
to carve a Dragon of Wind and Fire in a piece of perfect
jade, Chan Lo discovers the stone wants to be something
else
"The book's simple statement about artistic integrity and
courage is expanded in scope by the energetic, soft-tone watercolors executed on rice paper. Crowded with comical representations of busybody aids and courtly hangers-on, the
bustling scenes are models of expressive wit." Horn Book

Yagawa, Sumiko
The crane wife; retold by Sumiko Yagawa;
translation from the Japanese by Katherine
Paterson; illustrated by Suekichi Akaba.
Morrow 1981 unp il hardcover o.p. paperback
available $4.95 (1-3)   **398.2**
1. Folklore—Japan
ISBN 0-688-07048-5 (pa)   LC 80-29278
Also available in hardcover from P. Smith
Original Japanese edition, 1979
After Yohei tends a wounded crane, a beautiful young
woman begs to become his wife and three times weaves for

Yagawa, Sumiko—*Continued*

him an exquisite silken fabric on her loom

"One of Japan's best-loved folktales is given a treatment worthy of its popularity. . . . Katherine Paterson has done a fine job of translation, keeping in a few Japanese words to good effect. But it is Suekichi Akaba's illustrations that will be remembered. The muted line-and-wash drawings done on textured paper make use of traditional Japanese techniques." Booklist

The **Yellow** fairy book; edited by Andrew Lang; with numerous illustrations by H. J. Ford. Dover Publs. 1966 321p il pa $7.95 (4-6) 398.2

1. Folklore 2. Fairy tales

ISBN 0-486-21674-8

Also available in hardcover from P. Smith

A reprint of the title first published 1894 by Longmans

A collection of more than 40 tales, including many by Andersen and the Brothers Grimm, and others from the folklore of Hungary, Russia, Poland, Iceland, Germany, France, England, and the American Indians

Yeoman, John

The singing tortoise and other animal folktales; pictures by Quentin Blake. Tambourine Bks. 1994 c1993 95p il $18 (4-6) 398.2

1. Folklore 2. Animals—Fiction

ISBN 0-688-13366-5 LC 93-31208

First published 1993 in the United Kingdom

"Eleven folktales spanning the globe portray animals pitted against problems natural and self-made. Variety in theme and style—from humorous trickster tales to tragic stories of sacrifice and loss—make the collection appropriate for many age groups. Blake's trademark sketchy illustrations enhance the text." Horn Book Guide

Yep, Laurence

The man who tricked a ghost; pictures by Isadore Seltzer. BridgeWater Bks. 1993 unp il $15.95; pa $4.95 (k-3) 398.2

1. Folklore—China 2. Ghost stories

ISBN 0-8167-3030-X; 0-8167-3031-8 (pa)

LC 93-22202

"Set in medieval China, the story has as its hero the brave Sung, who isn't scared of otherworldly creatures. . . . When he meets a ghost, Sung says he's a ghost, too. . . . Sung sharpens his wits, tricking the ghost every step of the way—first getting the ghost to show him his many disguises, then persuading his companion to tell him the secret of what frightens a ghost most. When Sung learns it is human spit, the ghost's fate is sealed." Booklist

The text is "zesty and exuberant. . . . Seltzer's illustrations are as robust as the telling. . . . His strong compositions and rich, vibrant palette command the eye and create a sense of drama and dimension." SLJ

The rainbow people; [retold by] Lawrence Yep; illustrated by David Wiesner. Harper & Row 1989 194p il $16; lib bdg $15.89; pa $3.95 (4 and up) 398.2

1. Folklore—China

ISBN 0-06-026760-7; 0-06-026761-5 (lib bdg); 0-06-440441-2 (pa) LC 88-21203

"Twenty Chinese folktales, selected and retold by Yep from those collected in the 1930s in the Oakland China-

town as part of a WPA project. . . . The tales, while drawn from and depicting Chinese culture, present a variety of familiar motifs and types: wizards and saints, shape changing and magical objects, pourquoi tales and lessons. An 'Afterword' provides suggestions for further reading on Chinese folktales. This is an excellent introduction to Chinese and Chinese-American folklore." SLJ

The shell woman & the king; a Chinese folktale; retold by Laurence Yep; paintings by Yang Ming-yi. Dial Bks. for Young Readers 1993 unp il $13.99; lib bdg $13.89 (2-4) 398.2

1. Folklore—China

ISBN 0-8037-1394-0; 0-8037-1395-9 (lib bdg)

LC 92-9583

To save herself and her husband from an evil king, Shell, who can change into a seashell, agrees to bring the king three wonders

"Yep's evocative yet gentle retelling emphasizes the story's romantic aspects as well as its supernatural qualities. . . Yang's exquisite pen-and-watercolor scenes have the simultaneous delicacy and strength of traditional Chinese art." Publ Wkly

Tongues of jade; illustrated by David Wiesner. HarperCollins Pubs. 1991 194p il $14.95; lib bdg $14.89 (4 and up) 398.2

1. Folklore—China

ISBN 0-06-022470-3; 0-06-022471-1 (lib bdg)

LC 91-2119

A retelling of seventeen Chinese American folktales from a variety of Chinese communities in the United States

"The writing is replete with Irish descriptions, witty asides, and crackling dialogue. . . . All open with an attractive ink and wash illustration." SLJ

Includes bibliography

The tree of dreams; ten tales from the garden of night; pictures by Isadore Seltzer. BridgeWater Bks. 1995 93p il $13.95 (4 and up) 398.2

1. Folklore 2. Dreams—Fiction

ISBN 0-8167-3498-4 LC 94-11250

"Yep retells 10 stories from Japan, India, China, Greece, Brazil, and Senegal in lively prose, shaping plot and point of view to emphasize each tale's dream aspect. . . . Seltzer offers one illustration per tale in a brash, deliberately roughhewn style emphasizing the tales' strangeness." SLJ

Includes bibliographical references

Yolen, Jane

The sleeping beauty; retold by Jane Yolen; illustrated by Ruth Sanderson. Knopf 1986 unp il $12.95 (k-2) 398.2

1. Fairy tales

ISBN 0-394-55433-7 LC 86-45374

"An Ariel book"

Enraged at not being invited to the princess's christening, the wicked fairy casts a spell that dooms the princess to sleep for 100 years

"Yolen's graceful retelling of the Sleeping Beauty story suits the painterly yet lifelike feel of the illustrations. . . . The pictures are solemn and formal, with a brooding quality that suits the story's magical happenings. . . . This ambitious, meticulous presentation invites close inspection." Booklist

Yolen, Jane—_Continued_

Tam Lin; an old ballad; retold by Jane Yolen and illustrated by Charles Mikolaycak. Harcourt Brace Jovanovich 1990 unp $14.95 (3-6) **398.2**

1. Folklore—Scotland 2. Fairy tales
ISBN 0-15-284261-6   LC 88-2280

In this retelling of an old Scottish ballad, a Scottish lass, on the Halloween after her sixteenth birthday, reclaims her family home which has been held for years by the fairies and at the same time effects the release of Tam Lin, a human held captive by the Queen of the Fey

"Yolen's prose is both vivid and economical—it reads aloud very well, and Mikolaycak's brooding pictures swirl with motion, drama, and a compelling play of pattern and color." Booklist

Young, Ed

Little Plum. Philomel Bks. 1994 unp il $15.95 (k-3) **398.2**

1. Folklore—China
ISBN 0-399-22683-4   LC 93-11526

An old Chinese couple has a son who never grows any larger than a plum seed, but his size does not prevent him from saving his village from a cruel lord

"Young's spare, action-filled text will hold listeners' attention, while his artwork adds emotional resonance, rhythm, and unity to the tale. He fills each page with pastel paintings in a rich, dark palette. . . . Unusual angles and inventive use of scale dramatize Little Plum's unique perspective." SLJ

Lon Po Po; a Red-Riding Hood story from China; translated and illustrated by Ed Young. Philomel Bks. 1989 unp il $15.95 (1-3) **398.2**

1. Folklore—China 2. Wolves—Fiction
ISBN 0-399-21619-7   LC 88-15222

Awarded the Caldecott Medal, 1990

Three sisters staying home alone are endangered by a hungry wolf who is disguised as their grandmother

"The text possesses that matter-of-fact veracity that characterizes the best fairy tales. The watercolor and pastel pictures are remarkable: mystically beautiful in their depiction of the Chinese countryside, menacing in the exchanges with the wolf, and positively chilling in the scenes inside the house." SLJ

Moon mother; a native American creation tale; adapted and illustrated by Ed Young. HarperCollins Pubs. 1993 unp il $15; lib bdg $14.89 (2-4) **398.2**

1. Indians of North America—Legends 2. Moon—Fiction
ISBN 0-06-021301-9; 0-06-021302-7 (lib bdg)
                                      LC 92-14981

"Willa Perlman books"

A retelling of a traditional Native American tale in which the Spirit that made animals and people falls in love with a Woman Spirit who becomes the moon he carries through the sky every night

"Ed Young's pastel illustrations have a soothing clarity that lends itself nicely to this retelling. Images within images add visual layers of meaning to the complex creation myth, which Young tells with deceptive simplicity." Booklist

Red thread. Philomel Bks. 1993 unp il $14.95 (2-4) **398.2**

1. Folklore—China
ISBN 0-399-21969-2   LC 91-45442

"Proud young Wei Gu learns from a matchmaker that he will some day marry the ugly baby being carried on the back of an old, blind market woman. Aghast, Wei hires a servant to kill the child, but years later he learns he has married the girl whose feet the old man said were bound to his by the mystical red thread of destiny." Child Book Rev Serv

"Young's pastel and watercolor illustrations alternate panoramic overviews of a busy Chinese village with impressionistic personal close-ups. . . . Dramatic and haunting." Publ Wkly

Seven blind mice. Philomel Bks. 1992 unp il $16.95 (k-3) **398.2**

1. Fables 2. Elephants—Fiction 3. Folklore—India 4. Mice—Fiction
ISBN 0-399-22261-8   LC 90-35396

A Caldecott Medal honor book, 1993

"In Young's version of the familiar Indian folktale of the blind men and the elephant, seven blind _mice_ approach an elephant, ask what it is, explore various parts of the beast, and arrive at different conclusions. . . . Many preschool and primary grade teachers will find that the book reinforces their students' learning of colors, days of the week, and ordinal numbers, while heeding the story's admonition not to lose sight of the whole in their enthusiasm for identifying the parts. Graphically, this picture book is stunning, with the cut-paper figures of the eight characters dramatically silhouetted against black backgrounds. . . . At once profound and simple, intelligent and playful." Booklist

Zelinsky, Paul O.

Rumpelstiltskin; from the German of the Brothers Grimm; retold & illustrated by Paul O. Zelinsky. Dutton 1986 unp il lib bdg $15.99 (k-4) **398.2**

1. Folklore—Germany 2. Fairy tales
ISBN 0-525-44265-0   LC 86-4482

Also available Spanish language edition

A Caldecott Medal honor book, 1987

"The paintings feature a realistic miller's daughter who gets unexpected help in turning her bunches of hay into shimmering gold thread from a gnomelike little man outfitted in medieval garb. Zelinsky makes thoughtful use of composition and provides strong interplay between light and shadow. . . . Zelinsky's story uses an . . . ending in which the little man runs off rather than tearing himself in half when his name is discovered. . . . A lush and substantial offering." Booklist

Zemach, Harve

A penny a look; an old story retold by Harve Zemach; pictures by Margot Zemach. Farrar, Straus & Giroux 1971 unp il $16; pa $4.95 (k-3) **398.2**

1. Folklore
ISBN 0-374-35793-5; 0-374-45758-1 (pa)

"A redheaded rascal persuades his reluctant brother, a lazy good-for-nothing, to go with him to capture a one-eyed man to exhibit in the marketplace for a penny a look. The scheme backfires: the brothers are captured and the redheaded rascal is put in a cage while the lazy good-for-nothing is made to collect the pennies paid to see a two-eyed man with red hair." Booklist

Zemach, Harve—*Continued*
"Delightfully droll, fancifully detailed pen-and-ink and watercolor illustrations add enormously to the wry, sly proceedings." SLJ

Zemach, Margot
The little red hen; an old story. Farrar, Straus & Giroux 1983 unp il $14; pa $4.95 (k-2)   **398.2**
1. Folklore 2. Chickens—Fiction
ISBN 0-374-34621-6; 0-374-44511-7 (pa)
LC 83-14159
Also available Spanish language edition
A retelling of the traditional tale about the little red hen whose lazy friends are unwilling to help her plant, harvest, or grind the wheat into flour, but all are willing to help her eat the bread that she makes from it
"The pleasingly retold, rhythmical text is appropriately extended by scrappy, cartoonish, softly glowing color illustrations. The animals are anthropomorphized just enough, and their characters perfectly caught." Child Book Rev Serv

The three little pigs; an old story. Farrar, Straus & Giroux 1989 unp il $14; pa $3.95 (k-2)   **398.2**
1. Folklore—Great Britain 2. Pigs—Fiction 3. Wolves—Fiction
ISBN 0-374-37527-5; 0-374-47717-5 (pa)
LC 87-73488
"Michael di Capua books"
Zemach "has brought a familiar, often-told tale to life with marvelous ink-and-watercolor illustrations. Her wolf, wearing a dapper green hat and radiating slyness with every inch of his furry self, cuts a spendidly sinister figure as he attempts to wile his way to three pork chop dinners. With simple, lively sentences Zemach has related the complete story, including the apple-picking and country fair episodes." Horn Book

The three wishes; an old story. Farrar, Straus & Giroux 1986 unp il $16 (k-2)
                                                      398.2
1. Folklore 2. Wishes—Fiction
ISBN 0-374-37529-1   LC 86-80956
Also available Spanish language edition
In this "version of the familiar folk tale, a woodcutter and his wife rescue an imp in the forest. He gives them three wishes, which they foolishly manage to squander on a long chain of sausages." N Y Times Book Rev
This "is a natural for the picture-book format, and Zemach has taken full advantage of the humor with her watercolor illustrations. . . . The characters are homely and affectionate, their dog an amusing echo of their own lively expressions." Bull Cent Child Books

398.6 Riddles

Schwartz, Alvin, 1927-1992
Unriddling: all sorts of riddles to puzzle your guessery; collected from American folklore by Alvin Schwartz; drawings by Sue Truesdell. Lippincott 1983 118p il lib bdg $14.89; pa $4.95 (4 and up)   **398.6**
1. American wit and humor 2. Riddles
ISBN 0-397-32030-2 (lib bdg); 0-06-446057-6 (pa)
LC 82-48778

"Schwartz has made this volume useful as well as entertaining by dividing his puzzles into categories, some of which depend on visual interpretation, many of which are based on traditional American humor. The quality is high, and the compiler provides answers to the riddle jokes, punctuation riddles, rebus riddles, etc., as well as information about sources, notes on the puzzles, and a fairly extensive divided bibliography." Bull Cent Child Books

398.8 Rhymes and rhyming games

Anna Banana: 101 jump-rope rhymes; compiled by Joanna Cole; illustrated by Alan Tiegreen. Morrow Junior Bks. 1989 64p il $15; pa $6.95 (2-4)   **398.8**
1. Jump rope rhymes 2. Games
ISBN 0-688-07788-9; 0-688-08809-0 (pa)
LC 88-29108
An illustrated collection of jump rope rhymes arranged according to the type of jumping they are meant to accompany
"Heavily inked drawings provide cartoon-style humor; sources for jump-rope rhymes and an index of first lines are appended." Booklist

Aylesworth, Jim, 1943-
The completed hickory dickory dock; illustrated by Eileen Christelow. Atheneum Pubs. 1990 unp il $13.95; pa $4.95 (k-2)
                                                      398.8
1. Nursery rhymes
ISBN 0-689-31606-2; 0-689-71862-4 (pa)
LC 89-38484
"This extended version of the familiar nursery rhyme successfully combines simple counting concepts, the numbers one through 12 and a gentle introduction to telling time. Laced with phonetic harmonies, the additional verses have a nonsensical, bouncing quality that offer a fun-filled challenge for little ones to master. . . . The endearingly chubby mouse and his family are humorously portrayed in Christelow's colorful, frantic cartoons." Publ Wkly

The **Baby's** lap book; [compiled and illustrated by] Kay Chorao. rev ed. Dutton 1990 58p il lib bdg $14.99 (k-1)   **398.8**
1. Nursery rhymes
ISBN 0-525-44604-4   LC 89-23273
First published 1977
A collection of more than fifty traditional nursery rhymes accompanied by "Chorao's soft, eminently careful pencil drawings of the characters and their situations. Innocence is all pervasive, in the alternating pastel pink and yellow pages that nicely counter the light grays of the framed drawings; in the young faces, both animal and human; and in the fullness of cozy interiors and bucolic outdoor field and forest scenes. The artist's light hand is right for her interpretation, unabashedly, uncloyingly sweet, and admirably suited to its purpose." Booklist [review of 1977 edition]

Baker, Keith, 1953-
Big fat hen; illustrated by Keith Baker. Harcourt Brace & Co. 1994 unp il $13.95 (k-1)
                                                      398.8
1. Nursery rhymes 2. Counting 3. Chickens—Fiction
ISBN 0-15-292869-3   LC 93-19160

Baker, Keith, 1953-—*Continued*

"The text is the old rhyme, 'One, two, buckle my shoe,' and the double-page spreads show the hen and her chicks (first appearing as eggs) enacting the words. . . . Children who want to skip the counting altogether can just enjoy the singsong text and the pictures executed in acrylic paints. The big fat hen is very large and quite beautiful, with iridescent green feathers accented with purple and red; her friends are just as lovely, all colors, some with delicate patterns in their feathers." Booklist

Chorao, Kay, 1936-

Mother Goose magic. Dutton Children's Bks. 1994 64p il $15.99 (k-1)   **398.8**

1. Nursery rhymes

ISBN 0-525-45064-5   LC 92-37160

"Eight of the more obscure nursery rhymes—including 'Dickory, Dickory, Dare,' 'Sam, Sam, the Butcher Man,' and 'I like Little Pussy'—are linked by Chorao's illustrations, which construe them as a play being put on in a flowery meadow by Mother Goose, a little boy, and his animal friends." Horn Book Guide

"Cheerful watercolor interpretations . . . leap off the pages and immediately engage readers' eyes, ears, and imaginations. The rhythm and tempo of the verses lend themselves to pat-a-caking, toe-tapping, knee-bouncing, and other romping activities." SLJ

The **Comic** adventures of Old Mother Hubbard and her dog; illustrated by Tomie de Paola. Harcourt Brace Jovanovich 1981 unp il $13.95; pa $6 (k-3)   **398.8**

1. Nursery rhymes

ISBN 0-15-219541-6; 0-15-219542-4 (pa)

    LC 80-19270

This "version of the popular, early-nineteenth-century nursery rhyme places two familiar and beloved characters in a theatrical setting lavish with magnificent costumes and props. Spectators in box seats attending to the trials of the solicitous, beribboned dame and her mischievous poodle include Humpty Dumpty, the King and Queen of Hearts, and Little Bo Peep, while the stage curtains are decorated with scenes from the stories of still other well-known Mother Goose characters. The fun and action of the story are captured perfectly in a series of large, framed illustrations." Child Book Rev Serv

Craig, Helen

I see the moon, and the moon sees me. . . .; Helen Craig's book of nursery rhymes. Perlman Bks. 1993 c1992 49p il $16; lib bdg $15.89 (k-2)   **398.8**

1. Nursery rhymes

ISBN 0-06-021453-8; 0-06-021454-6 (lib bdg)

    LC 92-18996

First published 1992 in the United Kingdom

An illustrated collection of fifty-four nursery rhymes

"Many of the selections will be familiar to children, but a few . . . may be brand new. All will both amuse and strengthen language development. The delightful watercolors add humor (Old King Cole calls for his bubble pipe!); variety; and a strong sense of movement, rhythm, and playfulness." SLJ

Dabcovich, Lydia, 1935-

The keys to my kingdom; a poem in three languages. Lothrop, Lee & Shepard Bks. 1992 unp il $14; lib bdg $13.93 (k-2)   **398.8**

1. Nursery rhymes 2. Polyglot materials

ISBN 0-688-09774-X; 0-688-09775-8 (lib bdg)

    LC 90-40402

Retells the traditional nursery rhyme which takes the reader through the kingdom and through the day. The text appears in English, French, and Spanish

"Dabcovich's colored pencil and crayon illustrations have a sense of volume and life, as well as an endearingly childlike character imparted by the rounded forms she uses to such good effect. Her colors are bright, pure, unmixed, with shapes clearly outlined in black marker. The minimal text of this traditional nursery rhyme is clearly translated into literal French and Spanish, giving this added mileage potential in ESL classes or language programs." SLJ

Demi, 1942-

Dragon kites and dragonflies; a collection of Chinese nursery rhymes; adapted and illustrated by Demi. Harcourt Brace Jovanovich 1986 unp il lib bdg $14.95 (k-2)

    398.8

1. Nursery rhymes

ISBN 0-15-224199-X   LC 86-7637

An illustrated collection of twenty-two traditional Chinese nursery rhymes

"Sumptuously handsome illustrations in the vivid, jewel-bright colors of Chinese folk art are the setting for [these verses]. . . . Most of the poems are characterized by humor, energy, and strong rhythms. . . . With a wealth of visual details and a seamless blend of words and art, Demi has created a book to be enjoyed and treasured." Horn Book

Emberley, Barbara

Drummer Hoff; adapted by Barbara Emberley; illustrated by Ed Emberley. Simon & Schuster 1987 c1967 unp il lib bdg $14; pa $5.95 (k-3)   **398.8**

1. Nursery rhymes

ISBN 0-671-66682-7 (lib bdg); 0-671-66745-9 (pa)

    LC 87-35755

Awarded the Caldecott Medal, 1968

First published 1967 by Prentice-Hall

"A cumulative folk rhyme is adapted in spirited style and illustrated with arresting black woodcuts accented with brilliant color. The characters who participate in the building and firing of a cannon—'Sergeant Crowder brought the powder, Corporal Farrell brought the barrel,' etc.—are hilariously rugged characters, while 'Drummer Hoff who fired it off stands by, deadpan, waiting to touch off the marvelously satisfying explosion." Hodges. Books for Elem Sch Libr

Galdone, Paul, 1914-1986

The cat goes fiddle-i-fee; adapted and illustrated by Paul Galdone. Clarion Bks. 1985 unp il lib bdg $14.95; pa $6.95 (k-1)

    398.8

1. Nursery rhymes

ISBN 0-89919-336-6 (lib bdg); 0-89919-705-1 (pa)

    LC 85-2686

An old English rhyme names all the animals a farm boy feeds on his daily rounds

Galdone, Paul, 1914-1986—*Continued*

"Galdone's line-and-watercolor illustrations have all the verve and accessible good humor associated with his work, and the varied and irresistible rhythm of the verses carries the nonsense along at a good pace, enhancing its appeal to the very young. Whether told or sung, this is a diverting selection for preschool story times." Booklist

Three little kittens. Clarion Bks. 1986 unp il $14.95; pa $5.95 (k-1)   398.8
1. Nursery rhymes 2. Cats—Poetry
ISBN 0-89919-426-5; 0-89919-796-5 (pa)
LC 86-2655

Three little kittens lose, find, soil, and wash their mittens
"Galdone's characteristically exuberant pen-and-wash drawings fill these pages with feline faces, first rueful then joyful, then repentant, and finally excited about the prospects of catching 'a rat close by.' This is one of those sustained nursery rhymes that initiates youngest listeners into the concentration required for stories, and there's enough dramatic movement and color contrast in the art to hold toddlers' attention." Bull Cent Child Books

The **Glorious** Mother Goose; selected by Cooper Edens; with illustrations by the best artists from the past. Atheneum Pubs. 1988 88p il $18; lib bdg $18 (k-2)   398.8
1. Nursery rhymes
ISBN 0-689-31434-5; 0-689-31434-5 (lib bdg)
LC 87-35491

"The 42 rhymes collected here are the tried and true; what distinguishes this compilation are the wisely chosen, diverse graphics that grace the pages. For the most part, two illustrations varying between full color and black and white—by artists working in the late-nineteenth and early-twentieth centuries have been chosen for each rhyme, usually with the intention of depicting different interpretations. . . . The work of artists such as Randolph Caldecott, Walter Crane, Arthur Rackham, L. Leslie Brooke, E. Boyd Smith, Margaret Tarrant, William Donahey, Charles Robinson, and Fern Bisel Peat contribute to the overall fine effect." Booklist

Granfa' Grig had a pig, and other rhymes without reason from Mother Goose; compiled and illustrated by Wallace Tripp. Little, Brown 1976 96p il hardcover o.p. paperback available $10.95 (k-3)   398.8
1. Nursery rhymes
ISBN 0-316-85284-8 (pa)

"Children of all ages and their parents will have fun exploring the jolly scrap-bag of nursery rhymes. The illustrations are full of detail; there are caricatures of famous people (Toscanini as the conductor of Old King Cole's band); contemporary allusions (the picture with 'The fox gives warning,/It's a cold frosty morning' shows the fox as a TV weatherman); and surprising interpretations (the grand old Duke of York's ten thousand men are depicted as toy soldiers). . . . The characters are frequently charming and expressive animals, and the action is portrayed vigorously. A lively, colorful book, sometimes far from traditional but always exuding an air of high good humor." Horn Book

I saw Esau; the schoolchild's pocket book; edited by Iona and Peter Opie; illustrated by Maurice Sendak. Candlewick Press 1992 160p il $19.95   398.8
1. Folklore—Great Britain 2. English poetry—Collections
ISBN 1-56402-046-0
LC 91-71845

A revised and newly illustrated edition of the title first published 1947 in the United Kingdom
A collection of rhymes and riddles traditionally passed on orally from child to child
"From lamentation, pun, and insult to rebuttal, tongue-twister, and comic complaint, these schoolyard folk rhymes are vulgar, absurd, fierce, and utterly compelling. . . . [The book features] Sendak's wicked, joyful illustrations. Blending the factual and the surreal, the pictures (most in color, some in sepia or in black and white) extend the rhymes with characters and scenarios that are gross and tender. Sendak knows kids' ferocity and their fear." Booklist

James Marshall's Mother Goose. Farrar, Straus & Giroux 1979 unp il $15; pa $6.95 (k-3)   398.8
1. Nursery rhymes
ISBN 0-374-33653-9; 0-374-43723-8 (pa)
LC 79-2574

"Clean, translucent pastel colors and jolly cartoon figures give this limited collection [of thirty-five rhymes] a cheerful countenance. . . . Several of the old favorites are here, plus a number of lesser known rhymes such as little Poll Parrot and Little Tommy Tittlemouse. The illustrations depict the action in a literal way, with a breezy, occasionally offbeat humor." Booklist

Jeffers, Susan

Three jovial huntsmen; adapted and illustrated by Susan Jeffers. Bradbury Press 1973 unp il o.p.; Aladdin Bks. (NY) paperback available $3.95 (k-2)   398.8
ISBN 0-689-71309-6 (pa)

A Caldecott Medal honor book, 1974
Title on cover: Mother Goose—Three jovial huntsmen
"The story involves three dimwits who hunt through a forest full of game without ever seeing any. However, viewers will have the pleasure of spotting all the nearly hidden animals the huntsmen either fail to see or mistake for something else." SLJ

The **Little** dog laughed; [illustrated by] Lucy Cousins. Dutton 1990 c1989 64p il lib bdg $14.95 (k-2)   398.8
1. Nursery rhymes
ISBN 0-525-44573-0
LC 89-34517

Also available in paperback from Puffin Bks.
First published 1989 in the United Kingdom
A collection of sixty-four nursery rhymes
"This vibrant, joyous collection of familiar and beloved nursery rhymes is certain to be solid competition for the many fine books of this genre. . . . The childlike tempra artwork is irresistible in its bright boldness and immediately captures attention. Each cleanly formatted page contains at least one rhyme. . . . The end product is creativeness at its best." SLJ

Mother Goose; seventy-seven verses; with pictures by Tasha Tudor. Random House 1989 87p il $14 (k-2)   398.8
1. Nursery rhymes
ISBN 0-394-84407-6
LC 88-30674

A Caldecott Medal honor book, 1945
A reissue of the title first published 1944 by Oxford University Press
A lovely "Mother Goose, fresh in its interpretation both as to selection and illustration. . . . The pictures in soft colors and in black and white are quaint and charming." Booklist

Mother Goose; nursery rhymes; illustrated by Brian Wildsmith. Oxford Univ. Press 1964 80p il $16; pa $10 (k-2)   **398.8**

1. Nursery rhymes

ISBN 0-19-279611-9; 0-19-272180-1 (pa)

Has also been published with title: Brian Wildsmith's Mother Goose

These eighty-six verses "are well selected and include many quaint and lesser-known verses." Book Week

"The artist's wholly original, sophisticated yet childlike interpretation of long-familiar material is revealed in his clever composition, unconventional humor, and characteristic watercolor technique with its use of geometric patterns and brilliant chromatic modulations." Horn Book

A **Nursery** companion; provided by Iona and Peter Opie. Oxford Univ. Press 1980 128p il $31.25   **398.8**

1. Nursery rhymes 2. Picture books for children

ISBN 0-19-212213-4   LC 82-460507

"Reproduced with their original pictures and with slightly edited texts are about two dozen 'pretty books,' publications that were extremely popular with children and adults in the early nineteenth century. Included are alphabet books like 'The History of an apple pie,' old favorites like 'The House that Jack built,' such less familiar comic adventures as 'The History of the sixteen wonderful old women,' and the cumulative rhyme 'The Gaping, wide-mouthed, waddling frog.' These booklets are so scarce today the Opies were over thirty years assembling the ones for this volume." Child Book Rev Serv

Includes bibliographical references

Old Mother Hubbard and her wonderful dog; illustrated by James Marshall. Farrar, Straus & Giroux 1991 unp il $13.95; pa $4.95 (k-2)   **398.8**

1. Nursery rhymes

ISBN 0-374-35621-1; 0-374-45611-9 (pa)

     LC 90-56145

"This adaptation of a favorite nursery rhyme is a romp of rhythm and will bring on the smiles because of the inimitable style of Marshall's cartoons and tongue-in-cheek humor." SLJ

The **Orchard** book of nursery rhymes; rhymes chosen by Zena Sutherland; pictures by Faith Jaques. Orchard Bks. 1990 88p il $22.95 (k-2)   **398.8**

1. Nursery rhymes

ISBN 0-531-05903-0   LC 89-71002

"A collection of familiar short verses, including Mother Goose rhymes, tongue twisters, and nonsense poems, with illustrations set in 18th-century England and France." SLJ

"Sutherland's collection is a particularly fresh and satisfying entry in a crowded field. The selections are sequenced with care. . . . Sprinkled throughout the verses, Jaques's bustling illustrations brim with pleasingly old-fashioned details." Publ Wkly

Includes bibliographical references

The **Oxford** dictionary of nursery rhymes; edited by Iona and Peter Opie. Oxford Univ. Press 1951 xxvii, 1467p il $47.50   **398.8**

1. Nursery rhymes—Dictionaries

ISBN 0-19-869111-4

"A collection of 550 rhymes, songs and riddles which, through the years, have come to be associated with child-hood. While some are printed here with variations, notes on all of them list approximate age, first appearance in print, literary and historical associations, and parallels in other languages. . . . Arrangement is alphabetical according to the most important word. Nearly 100 reproductions scattered through the text show the changes in illustration of nursery literature during the past two centuries. An index of notable figures and an index of first lines make for easy reference. A comprehensive and authoritative study of the subject, this is an essential tool for all who are engaged in the study or teaching of children's literature." Wilson Libr Bull

The **Oxford** Nursery rhyme book; assembled by Iona and Peter Opie; with additional illustrations by Joan Hassall. Oxford Univ. Press 1955 223p il $31.25   **398.8**

1. Nursery rhymes

ISBN 0-19-869112-2

This collection "begins with the simplest ditties and progresses to more mature riddles, songs, and ballads. Almost every verse has a picture—small and black only, but amazingly effective. Many of the illustrations are taken from the old chapbooks and toy books. The work of Thomas and John Bewick is well represented, and the distinguished drawings of contemporary artist Joan Hassall are in keeping with their style." Sutherland. Child & Books. 6th edition

Pat-a-cake and other play rhymes; compiled by Joanna Cole and Stephanie Calmenson; illustrated by Alan Tiegreen. Morrow Junior Bks. 1992 48p il $14; lib bdg $13.93; pa $6.95   **398.8**

1. Nursery rhymes 2. Finger play

ISBN 0-688-11038-X; 0-688-11039-8 (lib bdg); 0-688-11533-0 (pa)   LC 91-32264

A collection of nursery rhymes and action rhymes, in such categories as finger and hand rhymes, tickling rhymes, and knee-and-foot-riding rhymes

"A charming source of bounce-and-tickle rhymes, this book features a good choice of games, an inviting format, and illustrations that make the most of the fun. . . . The simple line drawings, one to four on a page, combine an appealing informality of line with the delicacy of watercolor washes." Booklist

Includes bibliography

Patz, Nancy

Moses supposes his toeses are roses and 7 other silly old rhymes; retold and illustrated by Nancy Patz. Harcourt Brace Jovanovich 1983 unp il $13.95; pa $4.95 (k-2)   **398.8**

1. Nursery rhymes

ISBN 0-15-255690-7; 0-15-255691-5 (pa)

     LC 82-3099

"Eight English and American nonsense rhymes have lilt, nonsense, and humor. On each page, the ebullient paintings erupt from their tidy frames with vigorous and at times grotesque people and animals painted in the style of eighteenth and nineteenth century Pennsylvania Dutch pictures." Bull Cent Child Books

The **Random** House book of Mother Goose; selected and illustrated by Arnold Lobel. Random House 1986 176p il $17; lib bdg $16.99 (k-2)   **398.8**

1. Nursery rhymes

ISBN 0-394-86799-8; 0-394-96799-2 (lib bdg)

     LC 86-47532

The Random House book of Mother Goose—
Continued

"Arnold Lobel has included over 300 nursery rhymes in this Mother Goose collection. Some are known, while others are less familiar. Lobel's colorful, bright, lively illustrations will, for the most part, delight young children. However, the pictures are overpowering at times and, in contrast, the print is quite small. A helpful addition is an index of first lines. A worthwhile addition to every library's Mother Goose section." Child Book Rev Serv

The Real Mother Goose; illustrated by Blanche Fisher Wright. Checkerboard Press 1987 c1944 128p il $12.95 (k-2)   398.8
1. Nursery rhymes
ISBN 1-56288-041-1   LC 87-13778
First published 1916 by Rand McNally
A comprehensive collection of over three-hundred traditional nursery rhymes

Ring o' roses; a nursery rhyme picture book; illustrated by L. Leslie Brooke; with an afterword by Neil Philip. Clarion Bks. 1992 96p il $16.95 (k-2)   398.8
1. Nursery rhymes
ISBN 0-395-61304-3   LC 91-27028
"An Albion book"
A reissue of the title first published 1922 by Warne
An illustrated collection of twenty-one Mother Goose nursery rhymes, including "Hickety Pickety My Black Hen," "The Three Wise Men of Gotham," and "The Lion and the Unicorn"
"The pictures have a charm and vitality that span the years, and the handsome volume will delight a whole new generation of children." Booklist

Sendak, Maurice
Hector Protector, and As I went over the water; two nursery rhymes with pictures. Harper & Row 1965 unp il $16; lib bdg $15.89; pa $5.95 (k-1)   **398.8**
1. Nursery rhymes
ISBN 0-06-025485-8; 0-06-025486-6 (lib bdg); 0-06-443237-8 (pa)
"The fun the artist must have had in illustrating these two nursery rhymes will surely carry over to the reader and viewer of this diverting picture book. With originality and imaginativeness . . . Sendak not only interprets but extends the rhymes in his delightful pictures." Booklist

To market! To market!; illustrated by Peter Spier. Doubleday 1967 unp il hardcover o.p. paperback available $3.99 (k-2)   398.8
1. Nursery rhymes
ISBN 0-440-40713-3 (pa)
"Nineteen traditional rhymes and proverbs have been woven into a charming tapestry of 19th century American rural life. . . . Most of the rhymes date back to English sources, but they seem quite at home in the New England setting." SLJ

Tomie dePaola's Mother Goose. Putnam 1985 127p il $21.95 (k-2)   398.8
1. Nursery rhymes
ISBN 0-399-21258-2   LC 84-26314
This "is a large, ample, unfussy edition of every child's first staple of literature. . . . The neat, flat illustrations are

darkly outlined and colored generally in the illustrator's favorite palette of clear pinks, blues, and violets and surrounded with a lot of white space. Each verse is pictured in a simple and unmistakable interpretation. . . . A perfectly basic and lovely Mother Goose, lavish yet simple, and a splendid beginning for the youngest listener." Horn Book

Tortillitas para mamá and other nursery rhymes; Spanish and English; selected and translated by Margot C. Griego [et al.]; illustrated by Barbara Cooney. Holt & Co. 1981 unp il $14.95; pa $5.95 (k-2)   398.8
1. Nursery rhymes 2. Folklore—Latin America 3. Bilingual books—English-Spanish
ISBN 0-8050-0285-5; 0-8050-0317-7 (pa)
                                               LC 81-4823
A bilingual collection of 13 popular Latin American nursery rhymes
The purpose of this book "is to preserve a unique aspect of Hispanic culture which deserves to be passed down to all children. . . . The illustrations are strikingly beautiful, capturing the rich color and texture of some parts of South America. . . . [But their] homogenized view of Latin Americans can easily lead to the perpetuation of some familiar stereotypes." Interracial Books Child Bull

Trot, trot to Boston: play rhymes for baby; compiled by Carol F. Ra; pictures by Catherine Stock. Lothrop, Lee & Shepard Bks. 1987 unp il $12.95; lib bdg $14.93   398.8
1. Nursery rhymes 2. Finger play
ISBN 0-688-06100-7; 0-688-06101-5 (lib bdg)
                                               LC 86-7354
"This book presents twenty-two traditional nursery rhymes with illustrations and instructions for accompanying finger plays." Bull Cent Child Books
"Stock's watercolors seem to shimmer with a light of their own, defined by free-flowing lines. An exuberant abundance of color and pattern alternately excites and overwhelms the eye. . . . A sparkling collection to charm children and parents." Booklist

Wendy Watson's Mother Goose. Lothrop, Lee & Shepard Bks. 1989 160p il $19.95 (k-2)   398.8
1. Nursery rhymes
ISBN 0-688-05708-X   LC 88-37913
This book "will appeal to many for its lively but gentle illustrations with their combination of child-like simplicity and often intricate details. Soft blue-grays and greens with touches of orange, pink, and gold predominate in these delicately robust pictures of round-faced human characters and humorous, if not always identifiable, animals." SLJ

400 LANGUAGE

413 Dictionaries

Feder, Jane
Table, chair, bear; a book in many languages. Ticknor & Fields Bks. for Young Readers 1995 unp $13.95 (k-2)   **413**
1. Polyglot materials 2. Vocabulary
ISBN 0-395-65938-8   LC 92-40529

Feder, Jane—*Continued*

Presents illustrations of objects found in a child's room, labeled in thirteen different languages, including Spanish, Vietnamese, Japanese, and French

"Adults and children will find many ways to explore this deceptively simple concept book, from trying to pronounce the unfamiliar words to investigating the many lettering styles. Feder's clear acrylic illustrations, done in vivid primary colors, and the book's clean design make this a particularly handsome contribution to picture-book shelves." Horn Book

419   Verbal language not spoken and written

Ancona, George, 1929-

Handtalk zoo; [by] George Ancona & Mary Beth. Four Winds Press 1989 unp il $14.95 (k-3)   **419**

1. Sign language 2. Animals
ISBN 0-02-700801-0   LC 88-36861

"Readers learn to sign the names of animals as they tour the zoo with five special children. Full-color photographs and minimal text chronicle a day of visiting animals, eating lunch, and going home tired. Signs are repeated, and numbers and the finger alphabet appear in black-and-white boxes." Sci Child

"George Ancona's brilliantly colored photographs with close-ups of the children and the animals will be appealing to readers. Although some of the signed words are blurs of motion that might be confusing to children trying to imitate them, other photos of signs capture very clearly the essence of the animal, like the elephant's trunk or the zebra's stripes." Horn Book

Baker, Pamela J., 1947-

My first book of sign; illustrations by Patricia Bellan Gillen. Gallaudet Univ. Press 1986 76p il o.p.; Forest House reprint available $16.95 (k-3)   **419**

1. Sign language
ISBN 0-878363-92-1 (lib bdg)   LC 86-14937

"A Kendall Green publication"

Pictures of children demonstrate the forming in sign language of 150 basic alphabetically arranged words, accompanied by illustrations of the words themselves. Includes a discussion of fingerspelling and general rules for signing

"Looking like an ABC book, this is both appealing and useful. . . . Illustrations are brightly colored and have an even mixture of boys and girls of various racial backgrounds, some with hearing aids, some without. Some are a bit confusing because the chubby fingers are not always clearly distinguished from the thumb, but the descriptions in back help with clarification. Printed on glossy paper in a large format, this book is a good addition to most sign language collections for children." SLJ

Charlip, Remy

Handtalk; an ABC of finger spelling & sign language; [by] Remy Charlip, Mary Beth [and] George Ancona. Four Winds Press 1980 unp il lib bdg $15.95 (k-3)   **419**

1. Sign language
ISBN 0-02-718130-8
Also available in paperback from Aladdin Bks. (NY)

First published 1974 by Parents Magazine Press

This book provides an "introduction to the two modes of manual communication used primarily by the deaf: signs (gestures which represent words) and fingerspelling (the process by which words are spelled using the letters of the manual alphabet). . . . The format includes full-page scenes of persons making various signs, with insets at the bottom of each page which illustrate the fingerspelling of the word represented by the sign." Sci Books

Handtalk birthday; a number & story book in sign language; [by] Remy Charlip, Mary Beth [and] George Ancona. Four Winds Press 1987 unp il $15.95 (k-3)   **419**

1. Sign language 2. Birthdays
ISBN 0-02-718080-8   LC 86-22755

Also available in paperback from Aladdin Bks. (NY)

This picture book "finds Mary Beth celebrating a birthday. Guessing what's in her birthday packages provides a perfect opportunity to introduce sign language vocabulary. . . . Fingerspelling and signing combine with the action of the double-page spread photographs [by George Ancona] to tell the story." SLJ

"While the book can be used in picture-book story hours for the hearing impaired, it is not restricted to a particular group. . . . The photographs are as dynamic as the concept. Brilliantly composed, they range in perspective from close-up shots of Mary Beth's expressive face to joyous group portraits and from full-page spreads to sequences of small candids." Horn Book

Greene, Laura, 1935-

Sign-me-fine; experiencing American sign language; [by] Laura Greene, Eva Barash Dicker. Green, K. 1990 110p il pa $6.95 (5 and up)   **419**

1. Sign language
ISBN 0-930323-76-9   LC 90-5148

First published 1989 by Watts with title: Sign language talk

This introduction to American Sign Language emphasizes how its structure differs from English. Includes ASL sentences, sign games, poetry, and music

Hofsinde, Robert, 1902-1973

Indian sign language; written and illustrated by Robert Hofsinde (Gray-Wolf). Morrow 1956 96p il lib bdg $13.93 (3-6)   **419**

1. Indians of North America—Sign language
ISBN 0-688-31610-7

"This book shows how to form the gestures representing about five hundred words [in Indian sign language] ranging from familiar terms, such as 'man,' 'beaver,' and 'rapids,' to modern additions like 'motion picture' and 'coffee.' The key words are printed in heavy type, and are accompanied by concise directions and explanatory sketches. Words related in meaning are arranged in groups, and there is an alphabetical index." Ont Libr Rev

Mary Beth

Handtalk school; [by] Mary Beth Miller & George Ancona. Four Winds Press 1991 unp il $14.95 (k-3)   **419**

1. Sign language
ISBN 0-02-700912-2   LC 90-24030

Mary Beth—*Continued*

Words and sign language depict a group of students involved in putting on a Thanksgiving play at a school for deaf children

"Color photographs of good quality show the smiling faces of an interracial group of children using American Sign Language." Bull Cent Child Books

Rankin, Laura

The handmade alphabet. Dial Bks. 1991 unp il $14.99; lib bdg $14.89 **419**

1. Sign language 2. Alphabet

ISBN 0-8037-0974-9; 0-8037-0975-7 (lib bdg)

LC 90-24593

Presents the handshape for each letter of the American manual alphabet accompanied by an object whose name begins with that letter

"This [is] an excellent introduction to American sign, as well as an engaging ABC book. The art work is multiethnic, visually appealing, anatomically correct, and full of life. Clever use of props, light, and reflections add to the enjoyment." SLJ

422 Etymology of standard English

McMillan, Bruce

Super, super, superwords. Lothrop, Lee & Shepard Bks. 1989 unp il $12.95; lib bdg $12.88 (k-2) **422**

1. Vocabulary 2. English language—Comparison

ISBN 0-688-08098-7; 0-688-08099-5 (lib bdg)

LC 88-9342

Adjectives are used visually and grammatically to demonstrate the three degrees of comparison: positive, comparative, and superlative

"Each trio of words is accompanied by a double-page spread of three cheerful photographs of kids at play. . . . Because the words are confined to -er and-est comparatives (a limitation the afterword acknowledges) be prepared for a rash of good, gooder, goodest, but for what it does, this is one of the bestest language concept books around." Bull Cent Child Books

Sarnoff, Jane

Words: a book about the origins of everyday words and phrases; by Jane Sarnoff and Reynold Ruffins. Scribner 1981 64p il $13.95 (4 and up) **422**

1. English language—Etymology

ISBN 0-684-16958-4

LC 81-8943

"Following a discussion of the language sources that have contributed to contemporary English, the authors describe the origins of individual words (occasionally groups of words or variants of words) within certain categories. . . . A section that discusses (very briefly) suffixes, prefixes, word roots, etc. is appended." Bull Cent Child Books

423 English language— Dictionaries

The **American** heritage children's dictionary; by the editors of the American heritage dictionaries. Houghton Mifflin 1994 842p il $14.95 (3-6) **423**

1. English language—Dictionaries

ISBN 0-395-69191-5

LC 93-24531

Also available CD-ROM version

First published 1986

This dictionary "includes a section on how to use the dictionary, syllabication, pronunciation, word histories and ways to build vocabulary using homophones, plurals, verb forms, prefixes, suffixes etc. Most illustrations are in color and there are color bars on the edges of the pages to indicate the beginning, middle and end of the word list." Appraisal

The **American** heritage first dictionary; by the editors of the American heritage dictionaries. Houghton Mifflin 1994 362p $13.95 (1-3) **423**

1. English language—Dictionaries

ISBN 0-395-67289-9

LC 93-24530

First published 1986

This dictionary "is designed to meet the needs of children too old for a 'baby' dictionary and too young to handle the sometimes confusing wealth of information found in standard children's dictionaries. Bright and colorful, this volume is lavishly illustrated with full-color photographs and drawings that feature real children and adults wherever appropriate. It is written at a primary-grade reading level and contains an introduction that teaches its use." Am Ref Books Annu, 1995

The **American** heritage picture dictionary; by the editors of the American heritage dictionaries. Houghton Mifflin $11.95 (k-1) **423**

1. English language—Dictionaries 2. Picture dictionaries

First published 1986 (1994 printing)

A dictionary for preschool and early elementary grades, with each of the approximately 900 words defined by a sentence using the word to describe the object or activity portrayed in the accompanying illustration

"The almost 650 illustrations are in bright, clear colors. There are several family groupings of different races whose members and pets appear frequently in the illustrations and example sentences. The illustrations are nonsexist." Booklist

Bunting, Jane

The children's visual dictionary; illustrated by Dave Hopkins. Dorling Kindersley 1995 64p il $14.95 (k-3) **423**

1. Picture dictionaries 2. English language—Dictionaries

ISBN 1-56458-881-5

LC 94-29950

"This attractive, visual dictionary for children ages 6 and up includes more than 700 high-quality color photographs and illustrations and more than 2,500 nouns, verbs, and adjectives to help enrich children's vocabularies. The individual pages, as well as the cover, are visually stimulating. Material is broken down by themes such as prehistoric life, school, and farm life. . . . There is an obvious attempt to be multicultural in the illustrations and in the selection of terms." Am Ref Books Annu, 1996

The **Cat** in the Hat beginner book dictionary; by the Cat himself and P. D. Eastman. Beginner Bks. 1964 133p il $12.99; lib bdg $9.99 (k-3) **423**

1. Picture dictionaries 2. English language—Dictionaries
ISBN 0-394-81009-0; 0-394-91009-5 (lib bdg)

Also available French-English edition and Spanish-English edition

"This alphabetically arranged dictionary, illustrated with rollicking funny drawings, explains word meanings with sentences and pictures. It intends to help pre-schoolers 'recognize, remember, and really enjoy a basic vocabulary of 1,350 words.' Despite its age, this book will still appeal to young children." Peterson. Ref Books for Child. 4th edition

Grisewood, John

The Doubleday children's dictionary. Doubleday 1989 319p il $14.95 (4 and up) **423**

1. English language—Dictionaries
ISBN 0-385-26356-2   LC 89-30106

This dictionary "offers definitions for more than 8,000 words. . . . The word is emphasized in boldface print, followed by an abbreviation for part of speech and one or more definitions. Sample phrases and sentences printed in italics put the words in context. Pronunciation is given for a minority of words, often in terms of 'rhymes with.' While compiled in Great Britain, American spelling is used. . . . Colorful illustrations appear on almost every page. An italicized sentence is placed next to the picture so the reader can easily relate the picture with the appropriate word." Booklist

The **Harcourt** Brace student dictionary. 2nd ed. Harcourt Brace & Co. 1994 901p il $17.95 (4 and up) **423**

1. English language—Dictionaries
ISBN 0-15-200187-5   LC 94-27633

Replaces The Lincoln writing dictionary for children, published 1988

This dictionary includes "about 35,000 entries. . . . Many of the definitions are exemplified by quotations from over 500 writers of the past and present, from Judy Blume to the Wolfes, Tom and Thomas, and interspersed are some 600 short, lively topical essays on the craft of writing. . . . Reasonably spacious layout and small, clear, full-color photos or paintings give this title an appealing look, and its stress on literary usage will help young writers in ways that more conventional dictionaries cannot." SLJ

The **Harcourt** Brace student thesaurus. 2nd ed. Harcourt Brace & Co. 1994 312p il $14.95 (4 and up) **423**

1. English language—Synonyms and antonyms
ISBN 0-15-200186-7   LC 94-15603

Replaces The HBJ student thesaurus, published 1991
Editor, Christopher Morris

"The 800 main entries are all given part-of-speech, one-line definitions, and four to six synonyms, each of which is used in a sentence. Full-color illustrations in a variety of cartoon styles appear with about 150 of the entries." SLJ

For a fuller review see: Booklist, March 1, 1995

Macmillan dictionary for children; Judith S. Levey, editor-in-chief. Macmillan il $14.95 (3 and up) **423**

1. English language—Dictionaries
Also available CD-ROM version

First published 1975. (1989 edition) Periodically revised

"A good choice for elementary school libraries. Clear definitions for 35,000 words include frequent color pictures to assist in clarifying meaning. Syllabication, pronunciation, parts of speech, and different word forms are provided. Pronunciation guides are clear and well placed, and highlighted guidewords assist the reader in finding the proper page. There are also a 10-page section on how to use a dictionary and a reference section that consists of U.S. and world history timelines, pictures of the presidents, national flags, world maps, and tables of weights and measures." Nichols. Guide to Ref Books for Sch Media Cent. 4th edition

Macmillan first dictionary; Judith S. Levey, editor in chief. Macmillan 1990 402p il $12.95 (1-3) **423**

1. English language—Dictionaries
ISBN 0-02-761731-9   LC 90-6062

Replaces Macmillan very first dictionary, published 1983

"This work focuses on the most common words in the English language. An introduction outlines the development of words and explains how to use a dictionary. Simple definitions for each of the 2,200 words are often supported by illustrative sentences. Nearly 550 pictures in color explain concepts and abstract words." Nichols. Guide to Ref Books for Sch Media Cent. 4th edition

McIllwain, John

The Dorling Kindersley children's illustrated dictionary. Dorling Kindersley 1994 256p il $19.95 (k-3) **423**

1. English language—Dictionaries 2. Picture dictionaries
ISBN 1-56458-625-1   LC 94-9561

"Presented in a four-column arrangement bursting with boxed entries, font variations for each letter, bright photographs, drawings, and diagrams in Crayola colors, the dictionary clarifies an alphabetic list of over 5,000 words. Presentation is attractive enough to invite browsing. . . . A nonviolent, nonsexist, multicultural reference source at a reasonable price." Am Ref Books Annu, 1995

Merriam-Webster's elementary dictionary. Merriam-Webster 1994 20a, 587p il $14.95 (4-6) **423**

1. English language—Dictionaries
ISBN 0-87779-575-4   LC 93-41502

Replaces Webster's elementary dictionary, published 1986

This illustrated dictionary for grades four to six includes some 32,000 entries; a color-keyed guide to using the dictionary; word history and synonym paragraphs; abbreviations; signs and symbols; U.S. presidents and vice-presidents; and geographical names

Merriam-Webster's intermediate dictionary. Merriam-Webster 1994 14, 943p il $14.95 (5 and up) **423**

1. English language—Dictionaries
ISBN 0-87779-379-4   LC 93-30427

Replaces Webster's intermediate dictionary, published 1986

"Written for junior high school and middle school students, this dictionary contains more than 70,000 definitions and 1,000 pictorial illustrations." Publisher's note

Roget's children's thesaurus. rev ed. HarperCollins Pubs. 1994 240p il $14 (3-5) **423**

1. English language—Synonyms and antonyms
ISBN 0-06-275013-5

Replaces the edition published 1991 under the authorship of Andrew Schiller and William A. Jenkins

Published also under titles: In other words, a beginning thesaurus and Scott Foresman beginning thesaurus

Under alphabetically arranged entries are more than a thousand words with illustrative sentences to help the middle grader in choosing the exact word from several synonyms

Roget's student thesaurus. rev ed. HarperCollins Pubs. 1994 536p il $15 (5 and up) **423**

1. English language—Synonyms and antonyms
ISBN 0-06-275012-7

Replaces the edition published 1991 under the authorship of Andrew Schiller and William A. Jenkins

"This book also appears under the titles In Other Words, a Junior thesaurus and Scott Foresman Junior thesaurus." Verso of title page

An illustrated alphabetical list of words, their synonyms, antonyms, and the shades of meaning between them. Entries include such features as idioms, words at play, word stories, and writing tips

Root, Betty

My first dictionary; written by Betty Root; illustrated by Jonathan Langley. Dorling Kindersley 1993 96p il $16.99 (k-2)   **423**

1. English language—Dictionaries 2. Picture dictionaries
ISBN 1-56458-277-9   LC 93-20145

Also available CD-ROM version

This picture dictionary includes definitions and illustrations for 1000 words often used by young children

This "is highly recommended for public and school library preschool and primary collections. Its format and outstanding illustrations will make it appealing to young children and a valuable learning tool for the pre- and beginning reader." Booklist

Thorndike-Barnhart children's dictionary; by E. L. Thorndike, Clarence L. Barnhart. Scott, Foresman il $14.95 (3-5)   **423**

1. English language—Dictionaries

Same as Scott, Foresman beginning dictionary. First published 1945 by Scott, Foresman with title: Thorndike century beginning dictionary. Title and publishers vary. Frequently revised

A beginning dictionary which includes illustrations, examples of usage in most definitions, and self-teaching lessons for developing skills in using the dictionary

Webster's New World children's dictionary; Victoria Neufeldt, editor in chief; Fernando de Mello Vianna, project editor. Webster's New World 1991 896p il $15.95 (3-5) **423**

1. English language—Dictionaries
ISBN 0-13-945726-7   LC 90-25279

This dictionary provides definitions for an alphabetical listing of general vocabulary words, biographical and geographical names, and abbreviations. Includes word histories, synonyms, lists of words with prefixes or suffixes, and spelling tips

Webster's third new international dictionary of the English language, unabridged. Merriam-Webster il   **423**

1. English language—Dictionaries

Prices vary according to binding

Original edition by Noah Webster published 1828 with title: An American dictionary of the English language. Has also appeared under various other titles. First published with present title 1961. (1993 edition) Frequently reprinted with additions and changes to keep it up to date

"First choice unabridged dictionary." N Y Public Libr. Ref Books for Child Collect. 2d edition

Words for new readers. Scott, Foresman 1990 312p il $12 (k-1)   **423**

1. Picture dictionaries 2. English language—Dictionaries
ISBN 0-06-275008-9   LC 91-129575

Also available from HarperCollins Pubs. is another picture dictionary for preschool through first grade: Good morning, words! for $11 (ISBN 0-06-275000-3)

Also published with title: My first picture dictionary

"Fifteen hundred words, chosen from textbooks and everyday life, are included. Most entries have a definition, an example sentence, and a picture. . . . Illustrations are in varied media: photographs, drawings, and cartoons; each is labeled with the entry word. . . . *Words for New Readers* is an attractive book that combines an understanding of young children with dictionary conventions." Booklist

The World Book dictionary; edited by Robert K. Barnhart. World Bk. 2v il apply to publisher for price (5 and up)   **423**

1. English language—Dictionaries

"A Thorndike-Barnhart dictionary"

First published 1963 under the editorship of Clarence L. Barnhart with title: The World Book Encyclopedia dictionary. Revised annually

Entries give "syllabication, pronunciation, part of speech, definition (most common meaning first), usage notes, etymologies, illustrative sentences and phrases, inflected forms, and slang expressions. Since it is designed to complement 'World Book Encyclopedia' [entered in class 031], all encyclopedic information, including biographical and geographic names, has been omitted. . . . Clearly written and easy to use, this dictionary should be a first purchase for libraries serving children in elementary and middle school." Peterson. Ref Books for Child. 4th edition

The World Book student dictionary. World Bk. il apply to publisher for price (3-5)   **423**

1. English language—Dictionaries

First published 1989. Also published, without student exercises, under the title: Childcraft dictionary

This dictionary emphasizes vocabulary development and includes exercises intended to help the student master language skills. More than 30,000 entries and 1,000 color illustrations are included

427   English language variations

Juster, Norton, 1929-

As: a surfeit of similes; pictures by David Small. Morrow Junior Bks. 1989 unp il $15; lib bdg $9.88 (3-5)   **427**

1. English language—Terms and phrases
ISBN 0-688-08139-8; 0-688-08140-1 (lib bdg)

LC 88-8449

Juster, Norton, 1929-—*Continued*

"Clever drawings that are scratchy, often cross-hatched, animated and amusing, illustrate a series of similes-in-verse that are interrupted a few times by dialogue.... The repetitive form produces deja vu reading, but the book should indelibly imprint the simile in readers' minds; it is more often funny than forced, and the appeals of rhyme and metric lilt make it easy to remember verses and likely that they will be quoted." Bull Cent Child Books

Terban, Marvin

Mad as a wet hen! and other funny idioms; illustrated by Giulio Maestro. Clarion Bks. 1987 64p il hardcover o.p. paperback available $6.95 (3-5)   427

1. English language—Idioms 2. English language—Terms and phrases

ISBN 0-89919-479-6 (pa)   LC 86-17575

Illustrates and explains over 100 common English idioms, in categories including animals, body parts, and colors

"Maestro's two-color cartoonlike illustrations are amusing and informative themselves, providing visual clues that support the textual explanations.... Although some of the expressions included are dated, the alphabetical index enables teachers and librarians to pick and choose. This book might be particularly beneficial in schools having a large ESL program, especially for older, more advanced students." SLJ

Superdupers! really funny real words; illustrated by Giulio Maestro. Clarion Bks. 1989 63p il hardcover o.p. paperback available $4.95 (3-5)   427

1. Vocabulary 2. English language—Etymology

ISBN 0-395-51123-2 (pa)   LC 88-38325

Explains the meaning and origins of over 100 nonsense words that make the English language more colorful including such examples as "flip-flop," "fuzzy-wuzzy," "cancan," and "tutti frutti"

Includes bibliography

428   Standard English usage

Heller, Ruth

A cache of jewels and other collective nouns; written and illustrated by Ruth Heller. Grosset & Dunlap 1987 unp il $14.95; pa $6.95 (2-4)   428

1. English language—Terms and phrases

ISBN 0-448-19211-X; 0-448-40451-6 (pa)

LC 87-80254

"In light verse and brightly colored pictures, Heller provides an introduction to a specialized part of speech, the collective noun. She lists and depicts more than 25, including such familiar terms as 'batch of bread' and 'bunch of bananas,' as well as more unusual phrases.... The concept will stimulate the curiosity and imaginations of children with an ear for language. The illustrations, containing large, bold objects in simple yet striking compositions, ensure a visually inspiring exploration as well." Publ Wkly

Kites sail high: a book about verbs; written and illustrated by Ruth Heller. Grosset & Dunlap 1988 unp il $14.95; pa $6.95 (k-2)

428

1. English language—Grammar

ISBN 0-448-10480-6; 0-448-40452-4 (pa)

LC 87-82718

This "book explicates and celebrates verbs of all kinds, in ebullient verses which themselves sail and soar.... The verses are accompanied by bold, gaily colored graphics that are especially striking for their skillful use of pattern and design." Publ Wkly

Many luscious lollipops: a book about adjectives; written and illustrated by Ruth Heller. Grosset & Dunlap 1989 unp il lib bdg $15.95; pa $6.95 (k-2)   428

1. English language—Grammar

ISBN 0-448-03151-5 (lib bdg); 0-448-40316-1 (pa)

LC 88-83045

"The text begins: 'An adjective's terrific/when you want to be specific/It easily identifies/by number, color or by size/TWELVE LARGE, BLUE, GORGEOUS butterflies.' And there they are, blue and yellow, filling a double-page spread.... There is great diversity and technical brilliance in the art work, and the text has rhyme, rhythm, humor, and a very clear presentation of the concepts of different kinds of adjectives and what they do." Bull Cent Child Books

Merry-go-round; a book about nouns; written and illustrated by Ruth Heller. Grosset & Dunlap 1990 unp il $14.95; pa $7.95 (k-2)

428

1. English language—Terms and phrases

ISBN 0-448-40085-5; 0-448-40315-3 (pa)

LC 90-80645

Rhyming text and illustrations present explanations of various types of nouns and rules for their usage

"While the text will be helpful to children struggling with noun usage, the large, bountiful illustrations will appeal to everyone." Horn Book Guide

Up, up and away; a book about adverbs; written and illustrated by Ruth Heller. Grosset & Dunlap 1991 unp il $15.95; pa $7.95 (k-2)

428

1. English language—Grammar

ISBN 0-448-40249-1; 0-448-40159-2 (pa)

LC 91-70668

"Here the author explains concisely how adverbs answer precisely the questions of How? How often? When? and Where? The adverbs, in capital letters, stand out boldly and cannot be missed.... In the large, appealing illustrations, her penguins stand proudly, her pandas eat daintily, and her cat stares piercingly.... The cheerful volume ... offers a clever introduction to kinds of words." Booklist

Maestro, Betsy, 1944-

All aboard overnight; a book of compound words; [by] Betsy and Giulio Maestro. Clarion Bks. 1992 32p il $14.95 (k-3)   428

1. English language—Terms and phrases

ISBN 0-395-51120-8   LC 90-23987

Introduces a number of compound words, such as suitcase, railroad, and tablecloth, through the story of a family taking a train trip

"A concept book with a story that blends perfectly into

Maestro, Betsy, 1944— *Continued*

the language arts and social studies curricula. . . . The text, one or two sentences per page with the compound words in bold, is easy enough for beginning readers. The pen-and ink and watercolor illustrations further the story with Maestro's attention to detail both within the train and the passing scenery of city and countryside." SLJ

McMillan, Bruce

Becca backward, Becca frontward; a book of concept pairs. Lothrop, Lee & Shepard Bks. 1986 unp il $16; lib bdg $15.93 (k-2)   **428**

1. English language—Synonyms and antonyms
ISBN 0-688-06282-2; 0-688-06283-0 (lib bdg)
LC 86-7221

"A dozen pairs of opposites illustrated with full color photographs of a young girl. This is a well-designed book, with large, clear photographs to illustrate each of the pairs printed on facing pages and with the concept word printed in bold letters below each photograph. Becca is charming, the photographs are beautiful, and, in most instances, the concepts are very clear." SLJ

438   Standard German usage

Cooper, Lee Pelham

Fun with German; [by] Lee Cooper; illustrated by Elizabeth M. Githens. Little, Brown 1965 119p il lib bdg $15.95 (4 and up)   **438**

1. German language
ISBN 0-316-15588-8

"Using a circus motif [the author] begins with phrases and sentence sequences to introduce vowel and consonant sounds and a few essentials of grammar, and then presents stories, games, songs, and ideas and activities for a German club. Includes a guide to pronunciation symbols and a German-English vocabulary." Booklist

"A delightful introduction to the German language. . . . The phonetic symbols are excellent, especially for those sounds which do not have exact English equivalents. Elizabeth Githens has contributed lively and amusing illustrations." SLJ

443   French language— Dictionaries

The **Cat** in the Hat beginner book dictionary in French. Beginner Bks. 1965 133p il $15.95 (k-3)   **443**

1. Picture dictionaries 2. French language—Dictionaries 3. Bilingual books—English-French
ISBN 0-394-81063-5

This bilingual picture dictionary is based on The Cat in the Hat beginner book dictionary

463   Spanish language— Dictionaries

The **Cat** in the Hat beginner book dictionary in Spanish. Beginner Bks. 1966 133p il $16 (k-3)   **463**

1. Picture dictionaries 2. Spanish language—Dictionaries 3. Bilingual books—English-Spanish
ISBN 0-394-81542-4

This bilingual picture dictionary is based on The Cat in the Hat beginner book dictionary

Emberley, Rebecca

Let's go/Vamos; a book in two languages. Little, Brown 1993 unp il lib bdg $16.95 (k-3)   **463**

1. Picture dictionaries 2. Bilingual books—English-Spanish 3. Spanish language
ISBN 0-316-23454-0   LC 92-37278

Captioned illustrations and text in English and Spanish describe the four seasons, trips to the zoo and aquarium, camping, skiing, and a trip to the fair

"The bright colors and unusual compositions of [the author's] cut-paper collages combine to produce an attractive celebratory effect." Booklist

My day/Mi día; a book in two languages. Little, Brown 1993 unp il lib bdg $15.95 (k-3)   **463**

1. Picture dictionaries 2. Bilingual books—English-Spanish 3. Spanish language
ISBN 0-316-23450-8   LC 92-37277

Captioned illustrations and text in English and Spanish describe activities in a child's daily routine

My house/Mi casa: a book in two languages. Little, Brown 1990 unp il lib bdg $15.95; pa $5.95 (k-3)   **463**

1. Picture dictionaries 2. Bilingual books—English-Spanish 3. Spanish language
ISBN 0-316-23637-3 (lib bdg); 0-316-23448-6 (pa)
LC 89-12893

"Lively, brilliantly colored collages are used to illustrate various objects in English and Spanish. Young readers will find it little trouble to learn the words for such an appealing house and its furnishings, pets, toys, and surroundings." Horn Book Guide

Taking a walk/Caminando: a book in two languages. Little, Brown 1990 unp il hardcover o.p. paperback available $5.95 (k-3)   **463**

1. Picture dictionaries 2. Bilingual books—English-Spanish 3. Spanish language
ISBN 0-316-23471-0 (pa)   LC 89-12923

Labeled illustrations and Spanish and English text introduce the things a child sees while on a walk

The "book uses brightly patterned collages to illustrate the sights a child would see in a walk around his neighborhood. The definitions in Spanish and English are clear, and the subjects, such as blue jeans and swings, are interesting to a child. A fine example of a bilingual book." Horn Book Guide

492.4   Hebrew language

Edwards, Michelle
Alef-bet; a Hebrew alphabet book. Lothrop,
Lee & Shepard Bks. 1992 unp il $15; lib bdg
$14.93 (k-3)   **492.4**

1. Hebrew language 2. Alphabet
ISBN 0-688-09724-3; 0-688-09725-1 (lib bdg)
      LC 91-31011

This Hebrew alphabet book features three siblings and
their parents in their everyday family life at home
"A helpful introductory note gives some background on
the Hebrew language, introduces the fictional family, and
features the full alphabet with a pronunciation guide. . . .
Clear, artful, and involving, this is a model of what foreign-
language alphabets should be." Bull Cent Child Books

493   Non-Semitic Afro-Asiatic languages

Giblin, James, 1933-
The riddle of the Rosetta Stone; key to
ancient Egypt; [by] James Cross Giblin.
Crowell 1990 85p il $15; lib bdg $14.89; pa
$5.95 (5 and up)   **493**

1. Rosetta stone 2. Egyptian language 3. Hieroglyphics
ISBN 0-690-04797-5; 0-690-04799-1 (lib bdg);
0-06-446137-8 (pa)   LC 89-29289

Describes how the discovery and deciphering of the Rosetta Stone unlocked the secret of Egyptian hieroglyphics
"Suspense keeps the reader glued to this fine piece of
nonfiction as the mystery of hieroglyphs is slowly unrav-
eled. . . . The author has done a masterful job of distilling
information, citing the highlights, and fitting it all together
in an interesting and enlightening look at a puzzling subject." Horn Book

Includes bibliography

Katan, Norma Jean
Hieroglyphs, the writing of ancient Egypt;
by Norma Jean Katan with Barbara Mintz.
Atheneum Pubs. 1981 96p il map $14.95 (4
and up)   **493**

1. Egyptian language 2. Hieroglyphics
ISBN 0-689-50176-5   LC 80-13576

"A Margaret K. McElderry book"

Explains the origins of hieroglyphics and what they
mean, tells how this ancient form of writing was decoded,
and describes the training and importance of scribes
"A clear, concise, and animated text has been handsomely designed and illustrated. . . . An excellent appetite ar-
ouser for more books on ancient Egypt." Child Book Rev
Serv

495.1   Chinese language

Lee, Huy Voun
At the beach; written and illustrated by Huy
Voun Lee. Holt & Co. 1994 unp il $14.95
(k-3)   **495.1**

1. Chinese language
ISBN 0-8050-2768-8   LC 93-25462

A mother amuses her young son at the beach by drawing
in the sand Chinese characters, many of which resemble the
objects they stand for
"The intricate, visually captivating cut-paper collages
have borders with sea motifs. Useful for beginning language
study and interesting due to its artistic innovation, the book
includes a pronunciation guide." Horn Book Guide

495.6   Japanese language

Wells, Ruth
A to Zen; a book of Japanese culture; [by]
Ruth Wells; illustrated by Yoshi. Picture Bk.
Studio 1992 unp il map $15.95 (3-5)
      495.6

1. Japanese language 2. Alphabet 3. Japan—Social life
and customs 4. Bilingual books—English-Japanese
ISBN 0-88708-175-4   LC 91-14183

"The format of the alphabet book is used here to introduce young readers to aspects of Japanese life. Each page
contains a Japanese term (printed both in English letters
and in Japanese characters), a defining paragraph, and a
richly colored painting. . . . Among the topics covered are
aikido, the bunraku puppet theater, Japanese writing systems, and the tea ceremony." Booklist
"The selections are meaningfully described in lively
prose and will add pleasant detail to a child's knowledge of
Japan. Readers studying the language will be pleased at the
vocabulary enrichment offered. The illustrations in ink and
watercolors are bright, vibrant, and culturally accurate." SLJ

500   NATURAL SCIENCES AND MATHEMATICS

Cobb, Vicki, 1938-
Natural wonders; stories science photos tell.
Lothrop, Lee & Shepard Bks. 1990 31p il
$14.95; lib bdg $14.88 (4 and up)   **500**

1. Science—Pictorial works 2. Photography—Scientific
applications
ISBN 0-688-09317-5; 0-688-09318-3 (lib bdg)
      LC 90-30914

"The author has assembled 14 single or group photos
that extend our normal vision and reveal underlying scientific principles at work in the natural world. . . . Each full-
color photo is accompanied by an explanation of how the
photo was taken and what interesting thing the photo tells
us about nature. . . . The volume will appeal not only to the
scientifically curious, but to photographers as well, looking
to expand their subject matter. There are abundant ideas
here for students and teachers searching for science projects;
many scientific principles can be illustrated without specialized photographic equipment." Sci Books Films

Includes glossary

Simon, Seymour, 1931-
The dinosaur is the biggest animal that ever
lived, and other wrong ideas you thought were
true; illustrated by Giulio Maestro. Lippincott
1984 64p il lib bdg $14.89; pa $5.95 (3-6)
      500

1. Science
ISBN 0-397-32076-0 (lib bdg); 0-06-446053-3 (pa)
      LC 83-48960

Simon, Seymour, 1931-—*Continued*
Explains why many commonly accepted scientific "facts"—lightning never strikes twice, the sky is blue, snakes are slimy, etc.—are untrue

"If you think that dinosaurs were the biggest animals that ever lived, or that the sun is farthest from the earth in winter, or that a compass needle points to the North Pole—you're wrong. Simon debunks these and 26 other myths in a breezy, eclectic science lesson that sets the facts straight. Many of the mistaken notions are familiar ones; each merits a double-page explanation bolstered with humorous cartoons and occasional diagrams. This should have lots of popular appeal." Booklist

Hidden worlds; pictures of the invisible. Morrow 1983 48p il $15; lib bdg $13.93 (5 and up) **500**
1. Science—Pictorial works 2. Photography—Scientific applications 3. Microscopes
ISBN 0-688-02464-5; 0-688-02465-3 (lib bdg)
LC 83-5407
This book "introduces young readers to worlds which are too small, too far away or too fast to see. Large, outstanding photographs convey the incredible variety in these unseen worlds. Included in the book are photographs of the eye of an ant, a bullet slicing a playing card and the surface of a star. Accompanying the photographs are careful explanations of the methodologies that were used to produce the pictures. . . . Simon's explanations of these techniques are concise and easy to understand. The book is divided into five sections: those dealing with hidden worlds in general, in the body, of time, of the earth and of space." SLJ

500.5 Space sciences

Simon, Seymour, 1931-
Space words; a dictionary; illustrated by Randy Chewning. HarperCollins Pubs. 1991 48p il lib bdg $14.89 (3-5) **500.5**
1. Outer space—Dictionaries 2. Astronomy—Dictionaries 3. Astronautics—Dictionaries
ISBN 0-06-022533-5
LC 90-37402
This illustrated dictionary serves as a compendium of "core information about people, planets, programs, and space-related devices and phenomena, explained in a simple, clearly stated sentence or two." Booklist

502.8 Science—Auxiliary techniques and procedures; apparatus, equipment, materials

Selsam, Millicent Ellis, 1912-
Greg's microscope; pictures by Arnold Lobel. Harper & Row 1963 64p il hardcover o.p. paperback available $3.50 (k-2) **502.8**
1. Microscopes
ISBN 0-06-444144-X (pa)
"A Harper I can read book"
"The acquisition of a microscope entices Greg into looking at anything tiny, so he prepares his own slides of salt and sugar, water and flour, and bits of many other household things. Eventually he isolates some amoebae from his fish tank, but finds himself third in the microscope line—Mother and Dad are in front." NY Times Book Rev

503 Science—Encyclopedias and dictionaries

The **Dorling** Kindersley science encyclopedia. Dorling Kindersley 1993 448p il maps $39.95 (5 and up) **503**
1. Science—Dictionaries
ISBN 1-56458-328-7
LC 93-18541
This work "is organized in 12 thematic sections, not alphabetically. There are 400 major entries, such as *Kinetic Theory*, *Polymers* and *Tornadoes*. Most entries cover one to two pages. They often include biographical sketches of scientists and inventors. A 'Find Out More' box in the bottom corner of each right-hand page lists cross-references." Booklist

"The text is appropriate for older children and young adults; it is simple without being condescending and explains things very clearly." Am Ref Books Annu, 1994

The **New** book of popular science. Grolier 6v il maps apply to publisher for price **503**
1. Science—Dictionaries 2. Technology—Dictionaries 3. Natural history—Dictionaries
First published 1924 with title: The Book of popular science. Changed to present title 1978. Annually revised
The information in this set is classified under such broad categories as astronomy & space science, computers & mathematics, earth sciences, energy, environmental sciences, physical sciences, general biology, plant life, animal life, mammals, human sciences and technology

Simon, Seymour, 1931-
Science dictionary; illustrations by Oxford Illustrators Ltd. HarperCollins Pubs. 1994 256p il maps $29.95; lib bdg $29.89 (4 and up) **503**
1. Science—Dictionaries
ISBN 0-06-025629-X; 0-06-025630-3 (lib bdg)
LC 94-9962
More than 2,000 "entries cover all branches of science, from astronomy to zoology. For words that have both a scientific and an everyday meaning, only the scientific meaning is included. . . . Also included are brief biographies of about 85 important scientists. The 250 simple line drawings that illustrate the volume are either in black and white or highlighted with blue. A final section includes classification of living things, maps of constellations, common weights and measures, weather-map symbols, a geological time scale, the periodic table, and eight other charts and tables." Booklist

505 Science—Serial publications

3-2-1 Contact. Children's Television Workshop $17.97 per year **505**
1. Science—Periodicals 2. Technology—Periodicals
ISSN 0195-4105
Monthly except February and August. First published 1979
This "is a science magazine from the Children's Television Workshop. Issues run about 40 full-color pages, each focusing on a particular theme. . . . Each issue includes factual articles and activities for elementary school children to carry out. The magazine has enough flash to appeal to children while presenting enough substance to make it educationally worthwhile." Mag for Libr. 8th edition

Chickadee. Young Naturalist Foundation
$14.95 per year   **505**

1. Natural history—Periodicals

ISSN 0707-4611

Monthly except July and August. First published 1979

This "is a nature-oriented magazine for young children. Through articles, stories, colorful photos and drawings, puzzles, and activities, children build an appreciation for nature, science, and the environment around them. Each issue includes a colorful poster. This is an attractive magazine that will appeal to children; the reading level is low so that children can read it independently or with an adult." Katz. Mag for Libr. 8th edition

Owl; the discovery magazine for children. Young Naturalist Foundation $15.95 per year   **505**

1. Natural history—Periodicals

ISSN 0382-6627

Monthly except July and August. First published 1976 as successor to The Young Naturalist

This is a "nature- and environment-oriented magazine for children. It is a companion to *Chickadee* a title aimed at younger readers. The well-written articles teach about science and nature while entertaining readers. *Owl* includes a variety of puzzles, activities, and contests, as well as color photos and drawings that are appealing to its intended audience." Katz. Mag for Libr. 8th edition

Ranger Rick. National Wildlife Federation $15 per year   **505**

1. Natural history—Periodicals

ISSN 0738-6656

Monthly. First published 1967 with title: Ranger Rick's Nature Magazine

This magazine "for elementary school children, uses color photos, stories, games, and activities to teach children about animals and the environment. Regular features include letters to the editor, 'Adventures of Ranger Rick,' and a question-and-answer column about animals. This is a visually appealing magazine with beautiful photographs." Katz. Mag for Libr. 8th edition

Your Big Backyard. National Wildlife Federation $12 per year   **505**

1. Natural history—Periodicals

ISSN 0886-5299

Monthly. First published 1979

This is a nature magazine "for preschool children. Each 20-page issue is full of color pictures of animals that children should find appealing, along with stories and activities designed to teach word and number recognition. Most of the text is written at a low reading level; one story in each issue is designed to be read to the child. The magazine is wrapped by four pages of information for parents or teachers relating to the issue." Katz. Mag for Libr. 8th edition

507 Science—Education and related topics

Kramer, Stephen
How to think like a scientist; answering questions by the scientific method; [by] Stephen P. Kramer; illustrated by Felicia Bond. Crowell 1987 44p il lib bdg $14.89 (3-5)   **507**

1. Science—Methodology
ISBN 0-690-04565-4   LC 85-43604

An "exploration of the ways questions are asked and how scientists try to make sure that the questions are answered correctly. Relying on concrete story examples, Kramer shows how observed information can result in different or incorrect conclusions. Examples are also used to explain the principles of the scientific method." Booklist

"This is a pleasant book with an open format; an amusing halftone cartoon on almost every page illustrates the child oriented experiments and supports the light tone of the book." SLJ

507.05 Science—Education and related topics—Serial publications

Science and Children. National Science Teachers Assn. $52 per year   **507.05**

1. Science—Study and teaching—Periodicals
ISSN 0036-8148

Eight issues a year, September through May. First published 1963 as successor to: Elementary School Science Bulletin

This journal "is 'devoted to preschool through middle school science teaching.' It combines a very appealing mixture of classroom lesson plans, teaching tidbits, and longer informational articles. . . . Regular departments include 'Geography and Weather,' 'Solid Waste Science,' software reviews, and 'Helpful Hints.' A useful, high-quality magazine." Katz. Mag for Libr. 8th edition

507.8 Science—Use of apparatus and equipment in study and teaching

Allison, Linda, 1948-
Gee, Wiz! how to mix art and science or the art of thinking scientifically; illustrated by Linda Allison. Little, Brown 1983 128p il hardcover o.p. paperback available $10.95 (4 and up)   **507.8**

1. Science—Experiments
ISBN 0-316-03445-2 (pa)   LC 83-9834

"A Brown paper school book"

"There are activites with color, soap bubbles, capillarity, surface tension, immiscible liquids, vision, magnification, symmetry, center of mass, and falling bodies. All are safe to do, and the required materials are easily available." Appraisal

"The authors have endeavored to make science fun by presenting a cartoon strip format in addition to chapter introductions and a clear scientific method of approach." Child Book Rev Serv

Amato, Carol

Super science fair projects; by Carol J. Amato; illustrated by Kerry Manwaring; cover photography by Chuck Potter. Lowell House Juvenile 1994 80p il pa $5.95 (4 and up)

507.8

1. Science projects 2. Science—Experiments
ISBN 1-56565-141-3   LC 94-5358

The author "outlines how to develop and enrich an activity to produce a high-quality science fair project. . . . The author's project suggestions are enhanced by clear, creative illustrations. . . . [This book] contains sample problems, which will help even the most timid student or teacher to feel comfortable." Sci Child

Ardley, Neil, 1937-

The science book of air. Harcourt Brace Jovanovich 1991 29p il $9.95 (3-5)   **507.8**

1. Air—Experiments 2. Flight—Experiments
ISBN 0-15-200578-1   LC 90-36103

"Gulliver books"

Simple experiments demonstrate basic principles of air and flight

"Although most of these activities have appeared in other publications, it is the visual execution of the information which makes this an outstanding and highly recommended purchase. The directions are easy to follow and children (both black and white) are shown engaged in the experiments giving a message of success." Appraisal

Cobb, Vicki, 1938-

More science experiments you can eat; illustrated by Giulio Maestro. Lippincott 1979 126p il lib bdg $14.89; pa $4.95 (5 and up)

507.8

1. Science—Experiments 2. Cooking
ISBN 0-397-31878-2 (lib bdg); 0-06-446003-7 (pa)
LC 78-12732

This book utilizes some basic principles of science and applies them to typical foodstuffs so that the reader might learn about the nature of these foods. Among the simple scientific processes introduced are: heating, cooling, freezing, thawing, dehydration, distillation, mixing, infusing, and of course, tasting

Science experiments you can eat; illustrated by David Cain. rev & updated. HarperCollins Pubs. 1994 214p il $15; lib bdg $14.89; pa $4.95 (5 and up)   **507.8**

1. Science—Experiments 2. Cooking
ISBN 0-06-023534-9; 0-06-023551-9 (lib bdg); 0-06-446002-9 (pa)   LC 93-13679

First published 1972

Experiments with food demonstrate various scientific principles and produce an eatable result. Includes rock candy, grape jelly, cupcakes, and popcorn

Includes glossary

Diehn, Gwen, 1943-

Science crafts for kids; 50 fantastic things to invent & create; [by] Gwen Diehn & Terry Krautwurst. Sterling 1994 144p il $21.95 (5 and up)   **507.8**

1. Science projects 2. Handicraft
ISBN 0-8069-0283-3   LC 93-39112

"A Sterling/Lark book"

This "hands-on guide introduces a number of different branches of science. The projects range from the fairly simple (clay pot wind chimes, pinwheel helicopter) to the complex (model grist mill, powered model boats, xylophone). The detailed instructions include a list of materials needed and explanatory line drawings." SLJ

"The book is laid out quite well, with lots of excellent color photographs and easy-to-read and -follow directions. This book offers an excellent opportunity for youngsters to do independent work and is a resource for teachers, parents, and children." Sci Books Films

Gardner, Robert, 1929-

Robert Gardner's favorite science experiments. Watts 1992 128p il lib bdg $13.72; pa $6.95 (5 and up)   **507.8**

1. Science—Experiments
ISBN 0-531-11038-9 (lib bdg); 0-531-15255-3 (pa)
LC 92-17579

Science experiments, mostly using materials found in the home, demonstrating principles of chemistry, mechanics, biology, light, astronomy, heat, and electricity

"The experiments in the book are simple and interesting. . . . The illustrations are clear." Sci Books Films

Includes bibliography

Hands-on science [series]; step-by-step science activity projects from the Smithsonian Institution. Stevens, G. 1993 6v il ea $18.60 (4-6)   **507.8**

1. Science—Experiments

Contents: Color and light (ISBN 0 8368 0954 8); Food and the kitchen (ISBN 0-8368-0955-6); Fun machines (ISBN 0-8368-0956-4); Games, puzzles, and toys (ISBN 0-8368-0957-2); Mystery and magic (ISBN 0-8368-0958-0); Things that grow (ISBN 0-8368-0959-9)

Each volume "is illustrated with eye-appealing drawings that clarify some component of the investigations. . . . Each investigation in the series has a catchy title that fits its nature and sense of fun generated." Sci Books Films

Includes glossary and bibliography

Hann, Judith, 1942-

How science works. Reader's Digest Assn. 1991 192p il $24 (4 and up)   **507.8**

1. Science—Experiments 2. Scientific recreations
ISBN 0-89577-382-1   LC 90-26457

This volume offers an exploration "of scientific principles through hands-on experimentation. . . . Each of the six sections—matter, energy, force, and motion; light and sound; air and water; electricity and magnetism; and electronics and computers—combines . . . text with a number of activities and projects that illustrate the topic." SLJ

This "is a useful source of interesting experiments. It is a positive attempt to convey the pleasures of scientific activity." New Sci

Includes glossary

Katz, Phyllis, 1946-

Great science fair projects; [by] Phyllis Katz and Janet Frekko; illustrations by Paul Harvey. Watts 1992 79p il lib bdg $13.23; pa $6.95 (3-6)   **507.8**

1. Science projects 2. Science—Exhibitions
ISBN 0-531-11015-X (lib bdg); 0-531-15628-1 (pa)
LC 91-17299

Katz, Phyllis, 1946-—*Continued*

Suggestions for science fair projects, with information on collecting data and displaying the final result

"This book suggests a number of simple but interesting activities. . . . The book is intriguing and should appeal to children. Best of all, the suggested projects should stimulate problem solving and critical thinking." Sci Books Films

Includes bibliography

Markle, Sandra, 1946-

Science to the rescue. Atheneum Pubs. 1994 48p il $15.95 (4 and up)   507.8

1. Science

ISBN 0-689-31783-2   LC 92-41096

Presents ways science is being used today to meet problems such as the necessity for precision surgery, atmospheric pollution, and overpopulation of coastal cities. Provides hands-on projects for the reader and stresses the importance of the scientific method

This offers a "concise, conversational prose that is lively enough to read aloud. The book has an attractive cover and high-quality, full-color photographs." SLJ

The young scientist's guide to successful science projects; illustrations by Marti Shohet. Lothrop, Lee & Shepard Bks. 1990 112p il lib bdg $12.88; pa $6.95 (5 and up)   507.8

1. Science projects

ISBN 0-688-07217-8 (lib bdg); 0-688-09137-7 (pa)
LC 89-45290

"Markle offers a step-by-step explanation of what an experiment is and how to design, perform, interpret, and display the finished product. She covers issues from choosing the topic to controlling variables to answering a science fair judge's questions, as she gradually nudges readers into understanding the how and why of the scientific method. . . . Effectively illustrated with line drawings, this book is pleasingly simple and direct in both design and writing." Booklist

Richards, Roy

101 science tricks; fun experiments with everyday materials; illustrated by Alex Pang. Sterling 1991 104p il $16.95; pa $9.95 (4 and up)   507.8

1. Science—Experiments 2. Scientific recreations

ISBN 0-8069-8388-4; 0-8069-8389-2 (pa)
LC 91-13263

First published 1990 in the United Kingdom

Presents 101 experiments and activities involving such scientific principles as aerodynamics, light and color perception, and optical illusion

"While learning how to make paper boats, mathematical magic squares, or curves from circles, children are able to discover the fun in science. . . . Full-page color illustrations and clear instructions assist children in completing these harmless experiments independently." Adventuring with Books. 10th edition

Science experiments on file; experiments, demonstrations, and projects for school and home. Facts on File 1988 various paging il loose-leaf $155 (6 and up)   507.8

1. Science—Experiments

ISBN 0-8160-1888-X   LC 88-3883

"Eighty-four inexpensive, innovative, reproducible experiments in the categories of earth science, biology, physi-

cal science/chemistry, and physics are included. . . . Each experiment includes introductions, time and materials needed, safety precautions, procedures, and analysis. . . . Experiments are aimed at students in grades six through twelve and were prepared by a group of science teachers who have received awards from the National Science Foundation." Am Libr

Science fair project index, 1973-1980/1985-1989. Scarecrow Press 1983-1992 3v   507.8

1. Science—Experiments—Indexes 2. Science projects

Volume covering 1960-1972, published 1975, o.p.; volume covering 1973-1980 $52.50 (ISBN 0-8108-1605-9); volume covering 1981-1984 $47.50 (ISBN 0-8108-1892-2); volume covering 1985-1989 $47.50 (ISBN 0-8108-2555-4)

Prepared by the Science and Technology staff of the Akron-Summit County Public Library

"An index, based on Library of Congress subject headings, to books and general science periodicals that describe projects, experiments, and display techniques useful for teachers and secondary school students. References are alphabetical by article titles, or by authors when an entire book is cited. A bibliography provides complete citation for monographs." Guide to Ref Books. 11th edition

VanCleave, Janice Pratt

Janice VanCleave's 201 awesome, magical, bizarre & incredible experiments. Wiley 1994 118p il pa $12.95 (4-6)   507.8

1. Science—Experiments

ISBN 0-471-31011-5   LC 93-29807

The experiments in this book "are organized by field: astronomy, biology, chemistry, earth science, and physics; the purpose, materials needed, procedure, results, and an explanation are included for each demonstration. The author writes in a clear, easy-to-understand style. . . . The book will be especially useful to teachers looking for ideas that can be adapted as hands-on activities." SLJ

Includes glossary

White, Laurence B.

Air; simple experiments for young scientists; [by] Larry White; illustrated by Laurie Hamilton. Millbrook Press 1995 48p il (Gateway science) lib bdg $13.90 (2-4)
507.8

1. Air—Experiments 2. Experiments

ISBN 1-56294-471-1   LC 94-9837

These experiments demonstrate how to "use 'windcasting' to predict the weather, be an atmosphere watcher, [and] build the world's best paper glider." Publisher's note

Includes glossary and bibliography

Energy; simple experiments for young scientists; [by] Larry White; illustrated by Laurie Hamilton. Millbrook Press 1995 48p il (Gateway science) lib bdg $13.90 (2-4)
507.8

1. Force and energy—Experiments 2. Experiments

ISBN 1-56294-473-8   LC 94-9836

This book discusses common forms of energy and includes experiments to "create sound energy, make a kitchen 'volcano,' [and] catch rays in a solar collector." Publisher's note

Includes glossary and bibliography

White, Laurence B.—*Continued*
Gravity; simple experiments for young scientists; [by] Larry White; illustrated by Laurie Hamilton. Millbrook Press 1995 48p il (Gateway science) lib bdg $13.90 (2-4)

507.8

1. Gravitation—Experiments 2. Experiments
ISBN 1-56294-470-3   LC 94-9838
These experiments provide answers to questions such as "Why does the moon go around the earth? What is weightlessness? Why don't buildings fall down? What is artificial gravity?" Publisher's note
Includes glossary and bibliography

Water; simple experiments for young scientists; [by] Larry White; illustrated by Laurie Hamilton. Millbrook Press 1995 48p il (Gateway science) lib bdg $13.90 (2-4)

507.8

1. Water—Experiments
ISBN 1-56294-472-X   LC 94-10818
These experiments demonstrate how to "turn salt water into fresh water, make waves in a bottle, [and] build a bird's-eye view of what rain does." Publisher's note
Includes glossary and bibliography

Wood, Robert W., 1933-
What? experiments for the young scientist; illustrated by Steve Hoeft. TAB Bks. 1994 143p il pa $10.95 (4 and up)   **507.8**

1. Science—Experiments
ISBN 0-07-051636-7   LC 94-3086
The experiments "are divided into six disciplines: engineering, astronomy, chemistry, meteorology, biology and physiology. . . . Each project starts as a basic, but thought-provoking question that is then addressed by the scientific method: identifying the problem, materials and procedure to execute the experiment and how to interpret the obtained results. . . . Adult supervision is required for most of the experiments." Appraisal

When? experiments for the young scientist; illustrated by Steve Hoeft. TAB Bks. 1995 133p il pa $10.95 (4 and up)   **507.8**

1. Science—Experiments
ISBN 0-07-051640-5   LC 94-10825
"The activities are thematically divided into six categories: engineering, astronomy, chemistry, meteorology, biology and physics. . . . Each activity begins with a list of materials, is followed by step-by-step procedure, and concludes with a paragraph explaining the results, suggestions for further studies and several related science trivia facts. . . . This excellent book is filled with information and activities that can enlighten, entertain and encourage young scientists to learn more." Appraisal

Where? experiments for the young scientist; illustrated by Steve Hoeft. TAB Bks. 1995 133p il maps pa $10.95 (4 and up)   **507.8**

1. Science—Experiments
ISBN 0-07-051638-3   LC 94-37670
The author "introduces engineering, astronomy, chemistry, meteorology, biology and physiology through five or six projects in each area. . . . Each project begins with a materials list followed by the sequenced procedure, diagrams, expected results, suggestions for further projects and a 'did you know' section of scientific anecdotes. The black-line diagrams are well labeled and easy to understand." Appraisal

508 Natural history

An **Adventure** in the Amazon; [by] the Cousteau Society. Simon & Schuster Bks. for Young Readers 1992 45p il map $15 (3-6)   **508**

1. Natural history—South America 2. Indians of South America 3. Amazon River valley
ISBN 0-671-77071-3   LC 91-34167
Follows Jacques Cousteau on an expedition along the Amazon River as he observes the native people and wildlife of the region
"The numerous, high-quality photos are intriguing and well matched to the narrative. The book will attract browsers and also serve as an effective introduction to the area." Booklist

Baker, Jeannie
The story of rosy dock. Greenwillow Bks. 1995 unp il $15; lib bdg $14.93 (k-3)   **508**

1. Natural history—Australia 2. Plant introduction
ISBN 0-688-11491-1; 0-688-11493-8 (lib bdg)
LC 94-4677
"Baker examines the consequences of introducing non-native flora and fauna into the environment. An unthinking gardener cultivates rosy dock in the central desert of Australia and the seeds spread over a wide area during a flash flood. Now, when precious rain falls, the imported plant thrives at the expense of native species." SLJ
"Intricately constructed collage paintings illustrate this gentle ecological lesson about rosy dock . . . With their organic materials and stunning dioramic effects, the collage landscapes never assume the distant, glassy look of photographed realia, and viewers will find something new—a branch that is actually a snake, birds that look like leaves—each time they look." Bull Cent Child Books

Björk, Christina
Linnea's almanac; text [by] Christina Björk; drawings [by] Lena Anderson. R & S Bks. 1989 61p il $13 (2-5)   **508**

1. Nature study
ISBN 91-29-59176-7   LC 89-83540
Original Swedish edition, 1982
Linnea, featured in Linnea in Monet's garden and Linnea's windowsill garden (entered in Fiction section and class 635 respectively), "is inspired by the *Old Farmer's Almanac* to track the growing things in her city world. Month by month, the round-faced girl with stick-straight hair never lacks for activities, whether making flower garlands, identifying birds or creating a Christmas-present collage out of beach debris." Publ Wkly
"The book is unusually fresh and charming in its approach; the many facts are presented agreeably and lightened by the child's pleasure in activities which young readers could copy." Grow Point

Burnie, David
How nature works. Reader's Digest Assn. 1991 192p il $24 (4 and up)   **508**

1. Natural history 2. Nature study 3. Science—Experiments
ISBN 0-89577-391-0   LC 91-12432

Burnie, David—*Continued*

"This illustrated text introduces the study of the natural world. Topics covered include the classification of living things, life on the seashore, and the anatomy of the mammalian body. Projects, tests, and experiments accompany the scientific explanations." SLJ

"The quantity, explicitness, and clarity of the presentatons make this book a welcome resource for both children and parents who want to share in the fun and learning." Booklist

Includes glossary

Fleischman, Paul

Townsend's warbler. HarperCollins Pubs. 1992 52p il maps lib bdg $12.89 (4 and up)
508

1. Townsend, John Kirk, 1809-1851 2. Nuttall, Thomas, 1786-1859 3. Natural history 4. Overland journeys to the Pacific
ISBN 0-06-021875-4　　　　　　　　LC 91-26836

"A Charlotte Zolotow book"

"Naturalists John Kirk Townsend and Thomas Nuttall traveled west on the Oregon trail in 1834 to examine, record, and preserve plants, birds, flowers, and insects in the area. Townsend's journal details their experiences. This book includes pictures and maps highlighting their journey. The maps include the route of the bird named for Townsend." Soc Educ

Frasier, Debra, 1953-

On the day you were born. Harcourt Brace Jovanovich 1991 unp il $15 (k-3)　　**508**

1. Earth 2. Childbirth
ISBN 0-15-257995-8　　　　　　　　LC 90-36816

This combination of text and paper-collage graphics depicts the earth's preparation for, and celebration of, the birth of a newborn baby

"The text reads like unrhymed poetry, and both parents and educators will find themselves wanting to share this book over and over with individuals and with groups. A three-page appendix that includes miniature versions of each spread elaborates on natural phenomena for older readers—migrating animals, spinning Earth, rising tide, falling rain, growing trees, and more." SLJ

Gates, Phillip

Nature got there first. Kingfisher (NY) 1995 80p il $17.95 (4 and up)　　**508**

1. Nature 2. Technology 3. Inventions
ISBN 1-85697-587-8　　　　　　　　LC 94-42784

"Inventions from eight categories of technology, including building materials and building designs, and the shape of tools, are presented and contrasted with nature's designs." Sci Child

"The color pictures, a mix of original artwork and photographs, will intrigue kids, who may want to pursue in more depth elsewhere the connections Gates introduces." Booklist

Includes glossary

Hirschi, Ron

Fall; photographs by Thomas D. Mangelsen. Cobblehill Bks. 1991 unp il $14.99 (k-2)
508

1. Autumn
ISBN 0-525-65053-9　　　　　　　　LC 90-19595

Spring; photographs by Thomas D. Mangelsen. Cobblehill Bks. 1990 unp il $14.99 (k-2)
508

1. Spring
ISBN 0-525-65037-7　　　　　　　　LC 89-49039

Summer; photographs by Thomas D. Mangelsen. Cobblehill Bks. 1991 unp il $14.99 (k-2)
508

1. Summer
ISBN 0-525-65054-7　　　　　　　　LC 90-19596

Winter; photographs by Thomas D. Mangelsen. Cobblehill Bks. 1990 unp il $14.99 (k-2)
508

1. Winter
ISBN 0-525-65026-1　　　　　　　　LC 89-23935

"A Wildlife seasons book"

Simple text and color photographs introduce each season by focusing on animal behavior and the changing scenery

Jordan, Martin, 1944-

Angel Falls; a South American journey; [by] Martin and Tanis Jordan. Kingfisher (NY) 1995 34p il $15.95 (2-4)　　**508**

1. Natural history—Venezuela 2. Venezuela
ISBN 1-85697-541-X　　　　　　　　LC 94-30243

"While traveling to the base of Angel Falls, in the wilderness of the Venezuelan highlands, Martin and Tanis Jordan had the good fortune to observe many exotic animals. . . . The natural history of the creatures they saw, ranging from fireflies, frogs, and falcons to bird-eating spiders, jaguarundis, and capybaras, is balanced by the well-evoked atmosphere and physical challenges provided by the jungle trek." Sci Books Films

"Brilliant text and stunning oil paintings capture the beauty of the Venezuelan Highlands." Sci Child

Includes glossary

Lang, Susan S.

Nature in your backyard; simple activities for children; by Susan Lang with the staff of Cayuga Nature Center; illustrated by Sharon Lane Holm. Millbrook Press 1995 47p il lib bdg $16.90; pa $6.95 (2-4)　　**508**

1. Nature study 2. Science projects
ISBN 1-56294-451-7 (lib bdg); 1-56294-893-8 (pa)
LC 94-9278

"This book presents simple science-related projects that children will have fun duplicating. Six sections explore insects, worms, birds, other creatures, seeds, plants, soil, air, and water. Each activity is deftly and attractively designed, including a list of materials needed, procedures, full-color illustrations, results, explanations, and further comments." SLJ

Includes bibliographical references

Lasky, Kathryn
Surtsey; the newest place on earth; photographs by Christopher G. Knight. Hyperion Bks. for Children 1992 64p il $15.95; lib bdg $15.89; pa $6.95 (4 and up) **508**

1. Surtsey (Iceland) 2. Natural history
ISBN 1-56282-300-0; 1-56282-301-9 (lib bdg); 0-7868-1004-1 (pa)   LC 92-52990
This book relates the natural history of the island which was formed in 1963 off the coast of Iceland from a volcanic eruption
"Here in a sometimes lyrical text, accompanied by dramatic full-color photographs and apt quotations from Snorri Sturluson's *Prose Edda* (A.D. 1220-1230), readers are introduced to the brief history of this harsh, bitter land. . . . Well-organized, finely tooled, and beautifully designed—a treat for inquiring minds and eyes." SLJ

Litteral, Linda Lambert, 1949-
Boobies, iguanas & other critters; nature's story in the Galápagos. American Kestrel Press 1994 71p il maps (Biosphere reserve series) $23 (5 and up) **508**

1. Natural history—Galapagos Islands 2. Galapagos Islands
ISBN 1-883966-01-9   LC 93-5745
The author "covers the flora, fauna, and geology of the Galápagos Islands, with special attention to those features that Charles Darwin found so intriguing." Bull Cent Child Books
This volume "packs a lot of information into an appealing, well-organized format that will grab the attention of the student doing a science report, as well as the student just browsing for an interesting book. Both will be in for a rewarding experience." Appraisal
Includes bibliographical references

Maass, Robert
When spring comes. Holt & Co. 1994 unp il $14.95; pa $6.95 (k-2) **508**

1. Spring
ISBN 0-8050-2085-3; 0-8050-4705-0 (pa)
                  LC 93-29816
Companion volumes: When autumn comes (1990), When summer comes (1993), When winter comes (1993)
Color photographs and brief text introduce activities of the spring season
"The spirit of hope and renewal unfolds in the uncomplicated text, which is accompanied by large and small photographs warmly expressing the feelings of this special time of year." Booklist

Markle, Sandra, 1946-
Exploring autumn; a season of science activities, puzzlers, and games. Atheneum Pubs. 1991 152p il $16 (4 and up) **508**

1. Autumn
ISBN 0-689-31620-8   LC 90-24209

Exploring spring; a season of science activities, puzzles and games. Atheneum Pubs. 1990 122p il $14.95 (4 and up) **508**

1. Spring
ISBN 0-689-31341-1   LC 89-394

Exploring summer; illustrated with drawings and computer graphics by the author. Atheneum Pubs. 1987 170p il $14.95 (4 and up) **508**

1. Summer
ISBN 0-689-31212-1   LC 86-17322

Exploring winter; written and illustrated by Sandra Markle. Atheneum Pubs. 1984 154p il $14.95 (4 and up) **508**

1. Winter
ISBN 0-689-31065-X   LC 84-3049
Titles also available in paperback from Avon Bks.
Each illustrated volume contains science facts, history, crafts, games, riddles and lore related to the season
"Remarkable in its variety, this collection . . . is both entertaining and informative." SLJ

McGovern, Ann
Swimming with sea lions; and other adventures in the Galapagos Islands. Scholastic 1992 48p il map $13.95 (3-5) **508**

1. Natural history—Galapagos Islands 2. Galapagos Islands
ISBN 0-590-45282-7   LC 91-13130
In a series of diary entries, a young child describes a trip to the Galapagos Islands, focusing on the exotic animal life
"The appealing diary format of this book is an excellent model for journal writing. The author integrates the facts and feelings of a young boy and his grandmother on the adventure of their lifetimes. Includes information about animals native to the Islands and gentle reminders about animal rights and their welfare. Photographs complement the text and help initiate questions." Sci Child

McMillan, Bruce
Summer ice; life along the Antarctic peninsula; written and photo-illustrated by Bruce McMillan. Houghton Mifflin 1995 48p il maps $15.95 (3-6) **508**

1. Natural history—Antarctic regions 2. Antarctic regions
ISBN 0-395-66561-2   LC 93-38831
"This photo-essay introduces readers to the animals and plants of the Antarctic Peninsula. . . . After showing the landforms and glacial iceforms there, McMillan turns to the unexpected wealth of summer wildlife: algae and moss, plankton and krill, humpback whales and orcas, skuas and shags, seals and (of course) penguins." Booklist
"The full-color photography is brilliant in its beauty and attention to detail. However, the text is lively and knowledgeable, and could stand alone and still catch readers' interest." SLJ
Includes glossary and bibliography

Pandell, Karen
Land of dark, land of light; the Arctic National Wildlife Refuge; photographs by Fred Bruemmer. Dutton Children's Bks. 1993 unp il $14.99 (k-3) **508**

1. Natural history—Arctic regions 2. Arctic regions
ISBN 0-525-45094-7   LC 92-40405
Text and photographs present the animals and plants of the Arctic throughout a year

Pandell, Karen—*Continued*
"Outstanding photography provides a close-up view of the ever-changing landscape in the land of dark and light." Sci Child

Potter, Jean, 1947-
Nature in a nutshell for kids; over 100 activities you can do in ten minutes or less. Wiley 1995 136p il pa $10.95 (2-4)   **508**
1. Nature study
ISBN 0-471-04444-X   LC 94-28953
"Each of the 102 experiments is easy, uses safe and mostly readily available household supplies, and is fun at the same time. Divided into seasonal sections, the activities have catchy titles, state hypotheses, list materials, lay out procedures, and finish with clear explanations. Among the noteworthy investigations are: how duck feathers react to water, how mountains are formed, what keeps a seal from freezing in icy weather, whether ants prefer sugar or aspertame, and more." SLJ
Includes glossary and bibliography

Quinlan, Susan E.
The case of the mummified pigs and other mysteries in nature; illustrated by Jennifer Owings Dewey. Boyds Mills Press 1995 128p il $15.95 (4 and up)   **508**
1. Natural history 2. Ecology
ISBN 1-878093-82-7   LC 94-71027
"A wildlife biologist describes 14 real-life science adventures, all of which start with puzzling observations. Readers follow the steps of scientists as they track down the clues and discover some of the amazing ways that nature works." Sci Child
"Real mysteries are as popular as the fictional variety, and this compilation will be a welcome addition to any natural-science collection." Horn Book

Rights, Mollie
Beastly neighbors; all about wild things in the city, or why earwigs make good mothers; written by Mollie Rights; illustrations by Kim Solga. Little, Brown 1981 125p il hardcover o.p. paperback available $9.95 (4 and up)   **508**
1. Nature study
ISBN 0-316-74577-4 (pa)   LC 80-21556
"A Brown paper school book"
Describes some of the animals that live in the soil, under leaves, bricks, or boards, and around the roots of plants and suggests ways the reader may study their characteristics and behavior more closely
"The author provides clear and often deep explanations of scientific questions; in addition, she poses some provocative questions of her own. . . . The monochromatic drawings are instructive and often whimsical. There is no index, but a comprehensive table of contents makes individual topics easy to locate." SLJ

Rotner, Shelley
Nature spy; written by Shelley Rotner and Ken Kreisler; photographs by Shelley Rotner. Macmillan 1992 unp il $14.95 (k-2)   **508**
1. Nature
ISBN 0-02-777885-1   LC 91-38430

A child takes a close-up look at such aspects of nature as an acorn, the golden eye of a frog, and an empty hornet's nest
"This is a very good book for teaching children how to observe carefully objects around them." Sci Child

Simon, Seymour, 1931-
Autumn across America. Hyperion Bks. for Children 1993 unp il $14.95; lib bdg $14.89 (3-5)   **508**
1. Autumn 2. Natural history—North America
ISBN 1-56282-467-8; 1-56282-468-6 (lib bdg)
          LC 92-55043
Describes the signs of autumn that are seen in different parts of the United States, such as leaves changing color, migration of birds and insects, harvesting of crops, and changes in weather
"Simon's first book in a series about the changing seasons introduces autumn as a 'season of memory and change.'. . . Throughout this tribute, each double-page spead contains at least one, sometimes two, four-color photographs of a typical fall scene opposite two or three paragraphs of Simon's information-packed text, all appearing on a brilliant background color." Booklist

Smith, Alison, 1932-
The kids' nature almanac; great outdoor discoveries and activities for parents and children; illustrated by Jennifer Harper. Crown Trade Paperbacks 1995 214p il pa $13   **508**
1. Nature study 2. Science projects
ISBN 0-517-88293-0   LC 94-25410
This sourcebook includes 68 outdoor nature activities for the year. Each family oriented project is designed to encourage learning and inquisitiveness in children
Includes bibliographical references

Thomson, Peggy, 1922-
Auks, rocks and the odd dinosaur; inside stories from the Smithsonian's Museum of Natural History. Crowell 1985 120p il lib bdg $14.89 (5 and up)   **508**
1. National Museum of Natural History (U.S.)
ISBN 0-690-04492-5   LC 85-47744
The author describes "the fascinating oddities assembled in the Smithsonian's Museum of Natural History. Revealed are the difficulties in reconstructing life forms and the remarkable ingenuity employed to create exhibits in a believable and realistic format. Black-and-white photos include several rare finds from the 1880s. . . . Illustrations and text complement the overall format." SLJ

Wilkes, Angela
My first nature book. Knopf 1990 48p il lib bdg $13.99 (1-4)   **508**
1. Nature study
ISBN 0-394-96610-4   LC 89-8019
Provides an introduction to nature through a variety of simple indoor and outdoor activities including collecting seeds, feeding birds, watching a butterfly grow, and others
This "is an attractive and appealing activity book. It is quite a large book, and this format allows the illustrations to be life size. This results in a work that has dramatic visual impact. The design of each page is well planned, relying on photographs as well as text." Appraisal

509 Science—Historical and geographic treatment

Beshore, George W.
Science in ancient China; [by] George Beshore. Watts 1988 95p il map lib bdg $11.62 (4 and up) **509**
1. Science—China—History 2. Science and civilization
ISBN 0-531-10485-0 LC 87-23748
"A First book"
Surveys the achievements of the ancient Chinese in science, medicine, astronomy, and cosmology, and describes such innovations as rockets, wells, the compass, water wheels, and movable type
"Attractive black-and-white photographs and historical illustrations appear on almost every page." Booklist
Includes glossary and bibliography

Gay, Kathlyn
Science in ancient Greece. Watts 1988 95p il map lib bdg $11.62 (4 and up) **509**
1. Science—Greece—History 2. Science and civilization
ISBN 0-531-10487-7 LC 87-23747
"A First book"
Discusses the theories of ancient Greek philosopher-scientists such as Ptolemy, Pythagoras, Hippocrates, and Aristotle, and describes scientific discoveries and their applications in ancient Greece
Includes glossary and bibliography

510 Mathematics

Allison, Linda, 1948-
Eenie meenie miney math! math play for you and your preschooler; by Linda Allison and Martha Weston. Little, Brown 1993 48p il pa $8.95 **510**
1. Mathematics 2. Counting
ISBN 0-316-03464-9 LC 92-37497
"A Brown paper preschool book"
This "suggests simple games to help children grasp concepts; the book includes short chapters on exploring numbers, counting, matching, sorting, patterns, measuring, and 'parts and wholes.' Presenting excellent ideas with clear text written in a down-to-earth tone, the only puzzling thing about the book is its format. The bright, cartoonlike illustrations appearing in full color on each page make this look like a book for six-year-olds, rather than for parents." Booklist

Markle, Sandra, 1946-
Math mini-mysteries. Atheneum Pubs. 1993 58p il maps $14.95 (4 and up) **510**
1. Mathematics 2. Problem solving
ISBN 0-689-31700-X LC 92-11217
"This book provides some easy-to-follow examples of problem solving using mathematics. The examples place the greatest emphasis on the application of mathematical ideas, such as estimation, prediction, and simple computations, rather than on scientific concepts. The first section presents a list of problem solving suggestions to be used throughout the text. Almost every problem has an illustration or photograph to help understand the problems." Sci Books Films

Merriam, Eve, 1916-1992
12 ways to get to 11; written by Eve Merriam; illustrated by Bernie Karlin. Simon & Schuster Bks. for Young Readers 1993 unp il $14; pa $5.99 (k-3) **510**
1. Mathematics 2. Counting
ISBN 0-671-75544-7; 0-689-80892-5 (pa)
LC 91-25810
Uses ordinary experiences to present twelve combinations of numbers that add up to eleven. Example: At the circus, six peanut shells and five pieces of popcorn
"Some of the double-page spreads are simpler to solve than others, which allows children to progress as they learn more about counting. The huge, vibrant cut-paper and colored-pencil pictures make the book fun, lively, and painlessly educational." Horn Book Guide

510.7 Mathematics—Education and related topics

Teaching Children Mathematics. National Council of Teachers of Mathematics $45
510.7
1. Arithmetic—Study and teaching—Periodicals
ISSN 1073-5836
Monthly September through May. Supersedes Arithmetic Teacher (ceased publication May 1994)
This journal, focusing on pre-kindergarten through grade six, features "articles by teachers for teachers, highlighting math lessons and methods that work in real classroom situations, research and curriculum updates, clip-out calendars and minilessons, reviews of new resources, and tips on networking, summer institutes, and bibliographies. The emphasis . . . is on practical teaching skills." Katz. Mag for Libr. 8th edition

512 Algebra and number theory

Anno, Masaichiro
Anno's mysterious multiplying jar; [by] Masaichiro and Mitsumasa Anno; illustrated by Mitsumasa Anno. Philomel Bks. 1983 unp il $17.95 (2-5) **512**
1. Factorials 2. Mathematics
ISBN 0-399-20951-4 LC 82-22413
Simple text and pictures introduce the mathematical concept of factorials
This book "begins with a painting of a handsome blue and white lidded jar, moves into fantasy with pictures of the water in the jar becoming a sea on which an old sailing ship is moving, transfers to an island on the sea, and goes on to describe the rooms in the houses in the kingdoms on the mountains in the countries on the island. Each time the number grows: one island, two countries, three mountains, etc. How many jars, then, were in the boxes that were in the cupboards in the rooms? . . . The explanation is in itself clear, and is expanded by other examples of factorials." Bull Cent Child Books

513 Arithmetic

Adler, David A., 1947-
Roman numerals; illustrated by Byron Barton. Crowell 1977 33p il lib bdg $14.89 (2-4) 513

1. Numerals
ISBN 0-690-01302-7 LC 77-2270

"Adler provides exercises on how to write Roman numerals and handle the subscription principle involved in writing the symbols representing four and nine. He also explains the historical origins of the symbols for five and ten plus the uses and development of Roman numerals." SLJ

"A simple demonstration with labeled cards clearly explains how the symbols are ordered; another practice lesson tests readers' comprehension of when to use subtraction symbols. . . . A jaunty cartoon figure acts out textual descriptions against an orange-and-brown backdrop. It's a light, lucid, good-humored lesson." Booklist

Anno, Mitsumasa, 1926-
Anno's magic seeds; written and illustrated by Mitsumasa Anno. Philomel Bks. 1995 unp il $15.95 (k-3) 513

1. Mathematics
ISBN 0-399-22538-2 LC 92-39309

The reader is asked to perform a series of mathematical operations integrated into the story of a lazy man who plants magic seeds and reaps an increasingly abundant harvest

"Anno has succeeded in combining both the moral issue of conservation of resources and arithmetical games in a charming story for young readers. A tour de force from a most original author-illustrator." Horn Book

Anno's math games. Philomel Bks. 1987 104p il $21.95 (k-3) 513

1. Mathematics
ISBN 0-399-21151-9 LC 86-30513

"From extremely simple 'what is different?' pictures, Anno quickly builds in complexity to tables, mapping, bar graphs, and visual presentations of proportions." SLJ

Anno leads "the reader into an enchanting world full of interesting observations of things that are different and the same, that combine and come apart, and turn out to be an introduction to mathematics so sophisticated it is absolutely simple and clear. The watercolor illustrations are cheery." NY Times Book Rev

Anno's math games II. Philomel Bks. 1989 103p il $19.95 (k-3) 513

1. Mathematics
ISBN 0-399-21615-4 LC 86-30513

"The book presents mathematics and a great deal more with many pictures and very little to read. There are sections on counting, numeration, and measurement as well as left-right orientation, conservation, block building, comparing and contrasting, and other types of picture puzzles." Sci Child

"In an excellent afterword to parents and teachers, Anno discusses his ideas and approach to each section. Best used one-on-one, the book stimulates children to develop their thinking, creativity, and organizational skills." Booklist

Anno's math games III. Philomel Bks. 1991 103p il $19.95 (k-3) 513

1. Mathematics
ISBN 0-399-22274-X LC 90-35398

Picture puzzles, games, and simple activities introduce the mathematical concepts of abstract thinking, circuitry, geometry, and topology

"The humor, brightness, and simplicity of the illustrations make these math games irresistible." Booklist

Burns, Marilyn
The I hate mathematics! book; illustrated by Martha Hairston. Little, Brown 1975 127p il $17.95; pa $11.95 (4 and up) 513

1. Mathematics
ISBN 0-316-11740-4; 0-316-11741-2 (pa)

"A Brown paper school book"

"This lively collection of puzzles, riddles, magic tricks, and brain teasers provides a painless introduction to mathematical concepts and terms through the process of experimentation and discovery. The cartoon-like illustration and breezy titles . . . should appeal to the not-so-mathematically inclined as well as to puzzle devotees. Required materials are readily available and inexpensive; the techniques described are educationally sound and exciting. An excellent resource for parents, teachers, and children." Horn Book

Math for smarty pants; illustrated by Martha Weston. Little, Brown 1982 128p il $17.95; pa $11.95 (4 and up) 513

1. Mathematics
ISBN 0-316-11738-2; 0-316-11739-0 (pa)
LC 81-19314

"A Brown paper school book"

Text, illustrations, and suggested activities offer a common-sense approach to mathematic fundamentals for those who are slightly terrified of numbers

This book "is a step up for those readers who have mastered the concepts in the author's 'I Hate Mathematics! Book'." Booklist

Fisher, Leonard Everett, 1924-
Number art: thirteen 1 2 3s from around the world; written and illustrated by Leonard Everett Fisher. Four Winds Press 1982 61p il $16.95 (4 and up) 513

1. Numerals
ISBN 0-02-735240-4 LC 82-5050

"Traces the history and design of 13 systems of numerical notation—Arabic, Armenian, Brahmi, Chinese, Egyptian, Gothic, Greek, Mayan, Roman, Runes, Sanskrit, Thai and Tibetan. Beautifully designed, this book will be useful as an introduction to the different number systems." N Y Public Libr. Ref Books for Child Collect. 2d edition

Leedy, Loreen, 1959-
Fraction action; written and illustrated by Loreen Leedy. Holiday House 1994 31p il $15.95 (k-3) 513

1. Fractions
ISBN 0-8234-1109-5 LC 93-22800

Miss Prime and her animal students explore fractions by finding many examples in the world around them

"Thickly pigmented paintings loaded with sporty animal figures add to the humorous presentation, which should make fractions not only more understandable, but also more fun for young children." Bull Cent Child Books

McMillan, Bruce

Eating fractions; cooked, written, drafted, and photo-illustrated by Bruce McMillan. Scholastic 1991 unp il $15.95 (k-2)   **513**

1. Fractions 2. Cooking
ISBN 0-590-43770-4   LC 90-9139

Food is cut into halves, quarters, and thirds to illustrate how parts make a whole. Simple recipes included

"A mouth-watering introduction to fractions is served up by McMillan in this concept book. . . . The excellent photographs owe their appeal not only to their bright colors, clear focus, and good framing, but also to their winsome subjects, two infectiously happy children and a strawberry-pie eating shaggy dog." SLJ

516 Geometry

Sharman, Lydia

The amazing book of shapes. Dorling Kindersley 1994 37p il $14.95 (3 5)   **516**

1. Size and shape 2. Patterns (Mathematics)
ISBN 1-56458-514-X   LC 93-34260

"In a large and colorful format and through a great variety of creative activities and art projects, children are introduced to basic concepts of shape and pattern. For each concept (shapes, patterns, symmetry, polygons, etc.), clear step-by-step instructions for craft activities are described and extended suggested activities involving the world of nature are included. Attached to the book is a flexible mirror that students can use to make observations about symmetry; included are stencils of several geometric shapes, as well as square and triangular grids that can be used to draw a variety of patterns." Appraisal

VanCleave, Janice Pratt

Janice VanCleave's geometry for every kid; easy activities that make learning geometry fun; [by] Janice VanCleave. Wiley 1994 221p il $24; pa $10.95 (3-5)   **516**

1. Geometry
ISBN 0-471-31142-1; 0-471-31141-3 (pa)
                                          LC 93-43049

This "introductory text covers many topics in geometry, from lines, optical illusions, and art-related activities to applications with protractors and the construction of basic solids. Terms are presented in a simplified fashion and are easily understood. Graphics are clear. The hands-on activities encourage learning, creativity, and excitement." Sci Books Films

Includes glossary

520 Astronomy and allied sciences

Asimov, Isaac, 1920-1992

Astronomy in ancient times; with revisions and updating by Francis Reddy. rev and updated ed. Stevens, G. 1995 32p il (Isaac Asimov's new library of the universe) lib bdg $18.60 (3-5)   **520**

1. Astronomy
ISBN 0-8368-1191-7   LC 94-31253

First published 1988 with title: Ancient astronomy

This volume covers "worldwide prehistoric evidence of celestial observation and developments in the field from the ancient Greeks to Galileo." SLJ

Bonnet, Robert L.

Space and astronomy: 49 science fair projects; [by] Robert L. Bonnet, G. Daniel Keen. TAB Bks. 1992 128p il (Science fair projects) $16.95; pa $10.95 (6 and up)   **520**

1. Astronomy 2. Science projects
ISBN 0-8306-3939-X; 0-8306-3938-1 (pa)
                                          LC 91-34394

Suggests a variety of astronomy projects suitable for science fairs

This "is a well-written and exciting presentation of suggested projects. . . . For many experiments, the required materials are available in the average household, and equipment can be constructed very inexpensively. The topics covered can give a child a good foundation in fields as broad as observational astronomy, the history and construction of calendars, optics, and many other sciences." Sci Books Films

Includes glossary

Hirst, Robin

My place in space; by Robin and Sally Hirst; illustrated by Roland Harvey with Joe Levine. Orchard Bks. 1990 unp il $15.95; lib bdg $15.99; pa $5.95 (2-4)   **520**

1. Astronomy
ISBN 0-531-05859-X; 0-531-08459-0 (lib bdg); 0-531-07030-1 (pa)   LC 89-37893
First published 1988 in Australia

"Little drawings of a small Australian town serve as foreground for dramatic paintings of the universe—all illustrating exactly where Henry Wilson and his sister Rosie live. The science is sound, presented in enough detail to be interesting but with enough simplicity to be recalled and repeated aloud." Bull Cent Child Books

Lippincott, Kristen, 1954-

Astronomy; written by Kristen Lippincott. Dorling Kindersley 1994 64p il (Eyewitness science) $15.95 (4 and up)   **520**

1. Astronomy
ISBN 1-56458-680-4   LC 94-18479

The author "defines basic terms and concepts of astronomy. . . . Information ranges from ancient discoveries and scientists to the most modern equipment and advances. Many colorful photographs and diagrams are scattered throughout the book." Appraisal

Stott, Carole

Night sky; written by Carole Stott. Dorling Kindersley 1993 61p il (Eyewitness explorers) $9.95 (3-5)   **520**

1. Astronomy
ISBN 1-56458-393-7   LC 93-644

Describes and illustrates the astronomical aspects of the sky, including constellations, planets, moons, and the astronomer's role in observing these

This book "does an excellent job of conveying the fact

Stott, Carole—*Continued*

that there is still so much to be learned about the Universe and encourages the reader to join in the search for knowledge." Appraisal

The **Visual** dictionary of the universe. Dorling Kindersley 1993 64p il (Eyewitness visual dictionaries) $16.95 (4 and up)   **520**

1. Astronomy

ISBN 1-56458-336-8   LC 93-22419

Also available Spanish language edition

"Thousands of astronomy terms are defined with full-color photographs and illustrations in logical groups, easy to understand with related information. A great book for browsing or for reference if the comprehensive index is used." Sci Child

520.5   Astronomy—Serial publications

Odyssey; science that's out of this world. Cobblestone Pub. $24.95   **520.5**

1. Astronomy—Periodicals

ISSN 0163-0946

Monthly September through May. First published 1979 by AstroMedia Corp.

This "is a magazine that focuses on astronomy and outer space for upper elementary and junior high school readers. Each issue focuses on a particular theme, such as women in astronomy or the mathematics of astronomy. The 48 color pages look at each topic from a variety of angles. Regular features include sky charts, 'mind bogglers,' a question-and-answer column about astronomy, and 'Future Forum,' where readers send their responses to questions." Katz. Mag for Libr. 8th edition

522   Techniques, equipment, materials of astronomy

Scott, Elaine, 1940-

Adventure in space; the flight to fix the Hubble; [by] Elaine Scott; [photographs by] Margaret Miller. Hyperion Bks. for Children 1995 64p il $16.95; lib bdg $16.89 (4 and up)   **522**

1. Hubble Space Telescope 2. Outer space—Exploration

ISBN 0-7868-0038-0; 0-7868-2031-4 (lib bdg)

       LC 94-7756

This "book tells the story of the space shuttle *Endeavor's* 1993 mission to repair the Hubble telescope. After explaining 'Hubble's troubles' and scientists' plans to repair the telescope, the book introduces the astronauts and shows them at home with their families as well as at work, practicing every movement of their tasks and anticipating anything that could go wrong." Booklist

"The astronauts are portrayed as three-dimensional people, which helps readers identify with them. There are many full-color photographs throughout; those taken from the shuttle are breathtaking, showing closeups of the astronauts with the Earth featuring prominently in the background." SLJ

523   Specific celestial bodies and phenomena

Branley, Franklyn Mansfield, 1915-

Sun dogs and shooting stars; a skywatcher's calendar; by Franklyn M. Branley; illustrated by True Kelley. Houghton Mifflin 1980 115p il o.p.; Avon Bks. paperback available $3.50 (5 and up)   **523**

1. Astronomy 2. Meteorology

ISBN 0-380-71848-0 (pa)   LC 80-17430

"After an introduction to the calendar is a brief summary of the seasonal night skies and information on solstices or equinoxes, etc.; then, in a month-by-month arrangement within each season, there is information on the names of the months, what sky events occur that month and anecdotal material on important events or persons connected to the month. . . . The style is chatty and encouraging; the solid information clearly presented." SLJ

Includes bibliography

Cole, Joanna

The magic school bus, lost in the solar system; illustrated by Bruce Degen. Scholastic 1990 unp il $14.95; pa $4.95 (2-4)   **523**

1. Astronomy 2. Outer space—Exploration 3. Planets

ISBN 0-590-41428-3; 0-590-41429-1 (pa)

       LC 89-10185

Also available Spanish language edition
Also available CD-ROM version

"The planetarium is closed for repairs, so the Magic School Bus blasts off on a real tour of the solar system. After their previous field trips, the children in Ms. Frizzle's class are all blasé about such things; as they land on the Moon, Venus, and Mars, and fly by the other planets and the Sun, they comment on what they see, generate a blizzard of one- or two-sentence reports on special topics and—even while Ms. Frizzle is temporarily left behind in the asteroid belt—crack terrible jokes." SLJ

Jobb, Jamie

The night sky book; an everyday guide to every night; illustrated by Linda Bennett. Little, Brown 1977 127p il hardcover o.p. paperback available $10.95 (4 and up)

    523

1. Astronomy

ISBN 0-316-46552-6 (pa)   LC 77-24602

"A Brown paper school book"

An introductory stargazing manual including information and projects on the zodiac, moon, time, solar system, and finding directions and location using the stars

523.1 The universe; space, galaxies, quasars

Apfel, Necia H., 1930-
Nebulae; the birth and death of stars.
Lothrop, Lee & Shepard Bks. 1988 48p il $17;
lib bdg $16.93 (4 and up)   **523.1**

1. Galaxies 2. Stars
ISBN 0-688-07228-3; 0-688-07229-1 (lib bdg)
LC 86-33765

Describes how nebulae or clouds of dust particles and
gases in space form from the residue of dying stars and how
some nebulae contain matter from which stars are born
"The photographs of nebulae and other formations are
stunning. Apfel's text is straightforward and informative
without overwhelming readers; each paragraph is a small,
comprehensible essay beautifully matched with a clear, captioned, full-color photograph. This picture book is a delightful, accessible introduction to an appealing topic." Publ
Wkly
Includes bibliography

Simon, Seymour, 1931-
Galaxies. Morrow Junior Bks. 1988 unp il
$16; lib bdg $15.93; pa $5.95 (2-5)   **523.1**

1. Galaxies
ISBN   0-688-08002-2;   0-688-08004-9 (lib   bdg);
0-688-10992-6 (pa)   LC 87-23967
"This is a step-by-step introduction to and description of
the many galaxies in the universe. . . . He includes discussions of the ways in which astronomers classify galaxies,
black holes, smaller satellite galaxies such as the Magellanic
Clouds and supernovas. The terms are explained within the
text." Publ Wkly
"This fine introduction to an awe-inspiring subject will
surely stimulate interest in stargazing, further reading, and
investigation." Horn Book

523.2 Solar system

Leedy, Loreen, 1959-
Postcards from Pluto; a tour of the solar
system; written and illustrated by Loreen
Leedy. Holiday House 1993 unp il $15.95
(k-3)   **523.2**

1. Planets 2. Solar system
ISBN 0-8234-1000-5   LC 92-32658
A robot named Dr. Quasar gives a group of children a
tour of the solar system, describing each of the planets from
Mercury to Pluto
"What's different about this celestial excursion is that
Earth-bound postcards are allowed. It's through these hand-
printed missives that most of the information is conveyed,
with more delivered through balloon dialogues between
Quasar and his eager passengers." Booklist

Simon, Seymour, 1931-
Our solar system. Morrow Junior Bks. 1992
64p il $20; lib bdg $19.93 (3-6)   **523.2**

1. Solar system
ISBN 0-688-09992-0; 0-688-09993-9 (lib bdg)
LC 91-36665

"With a variety of full-color photographs, the solar system and its characteristics are described, including the sun,
asteroids, meteoroids, and comets. This book is a wonderful
introduction into the mysteries surrounding the solar system." Sci Child

523.3 Moon

Branley, Franklyn Mansfield, 1915-
The moon seems to change; by Franklyn M.
Branley; illustrations by Barbara and Ed
Emberley. rev ed. Crowell 1987 29p il
(Let's-read-and-find-out   science   books)
hardcover o.p. paperback available $4.95 (k-3)
523.3

1. Moon
ISBN 0-06-445065-1 (pa)   LC 86-47747
A revised and newly illustrated edition of the title first
published 1960
The author "explains the waxing and waning of the
moon and compares the length of a day on earth and on
the moon. Each page has colorful explanatory illustrations.
. . . Branley's brief-easy-to-read text and the Emberleys' diagrams make this book a welcome addition to science collections for young children or the picture book section." SLJ

What the moon is like; [by] Franklyn M.
Branley; illustrated by True Kelley. rev ed.
Crowell 1986 31p il (Let's-read-and-find-out
science books) lib bdg $14.89 (k-3)   **523.3**

1. Moon
ISBN 0-690-04512-3   LC 85-45400
A revised and newly illustrated edition of the title first
published 1963
"NASA photographs and information gathered by the
Apollo space missions are incorporated into [this book]
along with a comparative description of how the moon's
composition, terrain, and atmosphere differ from the
earth's." Booklist
"This is a good first introduction to the subject, neither
too technical nor diluted to blandness. The illustrations
combine a few unimpressive photos . . . with a new set of
simple, clear, uncluttered drawings, including a map showing the Apollo landing sites." SLJ

Simon, Seymour, 1931-
The moon. Four Winds Press 1984 unp il
$14.95 (1-4)   **523.3**

1. Moon
ISBN 0-02-782840-9   LC 83-11707
"This book provides [an] . . . introduction to the Moon's
composition, the lunar environment, and the information
gathered by the 'Apollo' space expeditions." Sci Child
"A large, square book with large, clear print and a text
that is lucid, continuous, accurate, and clearly written." Bull
Cent Child Books

523.4 Planets

Apfel, Necia H., 1930-

Voyager to the planets. Clarion Bks. 1990 48p il $15.95; pa $6.95 (4 and up)   **523.4**

1. Project Voyager 2. Planets 3. Outer space—Exploration

ISBN 0-395-55209-5; 0-395-69622-4 (pa)

LC 90-45057

Examines the development and travels of the space probes Voyager I and Voyager II and the information they have provided since the first launch in 1977

"Handsome color photographs of Jupiter, Saturn, Uranus, and Neptune and their rings and satellites illustrate a text that is continuous, clear, and carefully organized." Bull Cent Child Books

Includes bibliography

Branley, Franklyn Mansfield, 1915-

Neptune; Voyager's final target; by Franklyn M. Branley. HarperCollins Pubs. 1992 56p il (Voyage into space book) $15; lib bdg $14.89 (3-6)   **523.4**

1. Neptune (Planet) 2. Project Voyager

ISBN 0-06-022519-X; 0-06-022520-3 (lib bdg)

LC 91-2469

Details the activities of the American Voyager 2 space probe as it made its 1989 flyby of Neptune and its moons. Discusses the eighth planet's orbit, atmosphere, rings, and geology

"Branley shows a keen sense of what to leave out and what his audience wants to know. The inclusion of up-to-date information and full-color photographs, as well as clear writing, good organization, and an attractive format, make this a solid choice for astronomy shelves." Booklist

Includes bibliography

Uranus; the seventh planet; [by] Franklyn M. Branley; illustrations by Yvonne Buchanan. Crowell 1988 53p il (Voyage into space book) lib bdg $13.89 (3-6)   **523.4**

1. Uranus (Planet) 2. Project Voyager

ISBN 0-690-04687-1

LC 87-35046

Describes the physical characteristics, movements, satellites, and other features of Uranus, with an emphasis on recent discoveries from Project Voyager

"Black-and-white Voyager II photographs show details of the surfaces of Uranus and her satellites. Black-and-white line drawings are used to illustrate explanations, and a color photo insert is also included." SLJ

Includes bibliography

Venus; Magellan explores our twin planet; by Franklyn M. Branley. HarperCollins Pubs. 1994 56p il (Voyage into space book) $16; lib bdg $15.89 (3-6)   **523.4**

1. Magellan (Spacecraft) 2. Venus (Planet)

ISBN 0-06-020298-X; 0-06-020384-6 (lib bdg)

LC 92-32990

Describes the topography and motions of the planet Venus, explains theories about its origin and evolution, and presents recent discoveries made by the Magellan spacecraft

"Branley has written a fine introductory account of the exploration of our nearest neighbor in space. He has utilized the latest results, including spectacular images of the planet's unusual topography. . . . Middle-and upper-elementary age audiences will enjoy this book and its high-quality illustrations." Sci Books Films

Includes bibliography

Daily, Robert

Pluto. Watts 1994 63p il lib bdg $13.93 (4 and up)   **523.4**

1. Pluto (Planet)

ISBN 0-531-20166-X

LC 94-58

"A First book"

This book "features an account of the discovery of the planet, current speculation on its physical attributes and a discussion of the 'double planet' theory. The proposed 'Pluto Fast Flyby' is also mentioned." Appraisal

Includes glossary and bibliography

Gibbons, Gail

The planets. Holiday House 1993 unp il $15.95; pa $5.95 (k-3)   **523.4**

1. Planets

ISBN 0-8234-1040-4; 0-8234-1138-8 (pa)

LC 92-44429

Discusses the movements, location, and characteristics of the nine known planets of our solar system

"Well designed and laid out, the pages feature appealing full-color illustrations." Booklist

Harris, Alan, 1944-

The great Voyager adventure; a guided tour through the solar system; [by] Alan Harris and Paul Weissman. Messner 1990 79p il $14.95; lib bdg $16.98 (5 and up)   **523.4**

1. Planets 2. Outer space—Exploration 3. Project Voyager

ISBN 0-671-72539-4; 0-671-72538-6 (lib bdg)

LC 90-6423

Discusses the Voyager space probes and the information they have brought back about Jupiter, Saturn, Uranus, and Neptune

"The authors write with clarity and enthusiasm, imparting plenty of information without bogging down in technical detail. Their tale of discovery is enhanced by arrays of sharp, well-chosen photographs, mostly in color, plus a running timeline and plenty of tables and diagrams." SLJ

Includes glossary

Lauber, Patricia, 1924-

Journey to the planets. 4th ed. Crown 1993 90p il $20 (4 and up)   **523.4**

1. Planets

ISBN 0-517-59029-8

LC 92-16094

First published 1982

Explores the planets of our solar system, highlighting the prominent features of each. Includes photographs and information gathered by the Voyager and Magellan explorations

Moore, Patrick
The planets; illustrated by Paul Doherty. Copper Beech Bks. 1995 24p il (Starry sky) lib bdg $11.90 (k-3)   **523.4**
1. Planets
ISBN 1-56294-624-2   LC 94-43928
First published 1994 in the United Kingdom
This volume "discusses the sizes and makeup of the *planets* of our solar system, and addresses the possibility of interplanetary travel." SLJ

Ride, Sally K.
Voyager; an adventure to the edge of the solar system; [by] Sally Ride, Tam O'Shaughnessy. Crown 1992 36p il (Face to face with science) $14; lib bdg $14.99 (3-5)
523.4
1. Planets 2. Outer space—Exploration 3. Project Voyager
ISBN 0-517-58157-4; 0-517-58158-2 (lib bdg)
LC 91-32495
Describes the twelve-year Voyager missions to Jupiter, Saturn, Uranus, and Neptune, including details of the spacecraft and their discoveries about the planets and their moons
"The smartly produced photo essay provides a compelling text that makes astronomical facts immediate and accessible. Involving discussions . . . offer astronomical data perfectly geared to the intended audience. Another definite plus is the book's effective design, which features well-formed page layouts coupled with extraordinary color photos transmitted from Voyager and enhanced by informative paintings." Publ Wkly

Simon, Seymour, 1931-
Jupiter. Morrow 1985 unp il $16; lib bdg $15.93; pa $4.95 (3-6)   **523.4**
1. Jupiter (Planet)
ISBN 0-688-05796-9; 0-688-05797-7 (lib bdg); 0-688-08403-6 (pa)   LC 85-2922
Describes the characteristics of the planet Jupiter and its moons as revealed by photographs sent back by two unmanned Voyager spaceships which took one-and-one half years to reach this distant giant
"Large color (and black-and-white) photographs taken by the two Voyager spacecraft are the primary focus and will attract even resolute non-science readers." Appraisal

Mars. Morrow 1987 unp il $16; lib bdg $15.93; pa $5.95 (3-6)   **523.4**
1. Mars (Planet)
ISBN 0-688-06584-8; 0-688-06585-6 (lib bdg); 0-688-09928-9 (pa)   LC 86-31106
"There is no life on Mars. And there are no 'canals' on its surface. Scientists have ascertained this information from the Viking spacecraft landing in 1975. Astonishing pictures of the red planet are some of the highlights of this book that illuminate the way we think about Mars and about space. Simon has combined these vivid resources, with his characteristic spare, smooth prose." Publ Wkly

Mercury. Morrow Junior Bks. 1992 unp il $14; lib bdg $13.93 (3-6)   **523.4**
1. Mercury (Planet) 2. Project Mariner
ISBN 0-688-10544-0; 0-688-10545-9 (lib bdg)
LC 91-17404

Describes what is known about Mercury from the photographs taken by Project Mariner
"The *Mariner 10* photographs of Mercury and the other illustrations are of high quality and enhance the written exposition. *Mercury* is a very good and timely resource for elementary school science studies." Sci Books Films

Neptune. Morrow Junior Bks. 1991 unp il $13.95; lib bdg $13.88 (3-6)   **523.4**
1. Neptune (Planet)
ISBN 0-688-09631-X; 0-688-09632-8 (lib bdg)
LC 90-13213
Discusses the physical features and moons of the planet Neptune and how we have gained our knowledge of this giant world
This book "is reliable, well written, and largely illustrated with the pictures sent back to Earth by Voyager 2." Appraisal

Saturn. Morrow 1985 unp il $16; lib bdg $15.93; pa $5.95 (3-6)   **523.4**
1. Saturn (Planet)
ISBN 0-688-05798-5; 0-688-05799-3 (lib bdg); 0-688-08404-4 (pa)   LC 85-2995
"Features large NASA photographs in color and several illustrations of the spectacular ringed planet. Concise, up-to-date information gathered by Voyager I about Saturn's surface, rings, and the 9 largest of its 20 (so far) moons. A beautiful first planet book for young readers." Sci Child

Uranus. Morrow 1987 unp il $15; lib bdg $14.93; pa $5.95 (3-6)   **523.4**
1. Uranus (Planet)
ISBN 0-688-06582-1; 0-688-06583-X (lib bdg); 0-688-09929-7 (pa)   LC 86-31223
This introduction to the seventh planet in the solar system incorporates data results from a 1986 pass by Voyager 2
"The photographs are mostly from those sent back by the spacecraft and show amazing detail which is clearly explained in the text." Horn Book

Venus. Morrow Junior Bks. 1992 unp il maps $15; lib bdg $14.93 (3-6)   **523.4**
1. Venus (Planet)
ISBN 0-688-10542-4; 0-688-10543-2 (lib bdg)
LC 91-12171
Describes the movements and physical features of the planet Venus and recent findings about its climate and surface
"Striking photographs and attractive, accessible pages. . . . Remarkable for the clear, readable text and attention to accuracy. Simon carefully distinguishes between known facts and scientific hypotheses." Horn Book

Vogt, Gregory
Jupiter. Millbrook Press 1993 31p il (Gateway solar system) lib bdg $14.40; pa $6.95 (2-4)   **523.4**
1. Jupiter (Planet)
ISBN 1-56294-329-4 (lib bdg); 1-56294-799-0 (pa)
LC 92-30187
Presents information about the largest planet in our solar system and its moons
Includes glossary and bibliography

Vogt, Gregory—*Continued*

Mars. Millbrook Press 1994 32p il (Gateway solar system) lib bdg $14.40; pa $6.95 (2-4)
   523.4

1. Mars (Planet) 2. Project Mariner

ISBN 1-56294-392-8 (lib bdg); 0-7613-0156-9 (pa)
   LC 93-11219

Presents information on Mars, the reddish orange planet, and its exploration by the U.S. spacecraft, Mariner and Viking

Includes glossary and bibliography

Mercury. Millbrook Press 1994 31p il (Gateway solar system) lib bdg $14.40; pa $6.95 (2-4)
   523.4

1. Mercury (Planet) 2. Project Mariner

ISBN 1-56294-390-1 (lib bdg); 0-7613-0157-7 (pa)
   LC 93-11218

Presents information on Mercury, the planet closest to the sun, as it was photographed by the U.S. spacecraft, Mariner 10

Includes glossary and bibliography

Neptune. Millbrook Press 1993 32p il (Gateway solar system) lib bdg $14.40; pa $6.95 (2-4)
   523.4

1. Neptune (Planet)

ISBN 1-56294-331-6 (lib bdg); 1-56294-800-8 (pa)
   LC 92-30183

An introduction to Neptune, eighth planet from the sun
Includes glossary and bibliography

Pluto. Millbrook Press 1994 31p il (Gateway solar system) lib bdg $14.40; pa $6.95 (2-4)
   523.4

1. Pluto (Planet) 2. Project Mariner

ISBN 1-56294-393-6 (lib bdg); 0-7613-0158-5 (pa)
   LC 93-11224

Presents information on Pluto, the farthest known planet, and its moon, Charon
Includes glossary and bibliography

Saturn. Millbrook Press 1993 31p il (Gateway solar system) lib bdg $14.40; pa $6.95 (2-4)
   523.4

1. Saturn (Planet)

ISBN 1-56294-332-4 (lib bdg); 1-56294-801-6 (pa)
   LC 92-30188

Presents information known about Saturn, its rings, and moons
Includes glossary and bibliography

The search for the killer asteroid. Millbrook Press 1994 71p il lib bdg $16.90 (4-6)
   523.4

1. Asteroids 2. Catastrophes (Geology)

ISBN 1-56294-448-7
   LC 93-47328

"This book begins with a recreation of possible events on the day, 65 million years ago, that an asteroid slammed into the surface of a Cretaceous period Earth, initiating the series of occurrences leading to the extinction of the dinosaurs. It then moves into a fascinating discussion of how the asteroid-extinction hypothesis was formulated and how research and exploration unearthed the site of the impact." Appraisal

"The presentation is clear, organized, and illustrated with realistic paintings and large, full-color photographs. A brief but wide-ranging book that deserves a place in both large and small collections." SLJ

Includes glossary and bibliography

Uranus. Millbrook Press 1993 31p il (Gateway solar system) lib bdg $14.40; pa $6.95 (2-4)
   523.4

1. Uranus (Planet)

ISBN 1-56294-330-8 (lib bdg); 1-56294-802-4 (pa)
   LC 92-30184

An introduction to the bluish-green planet, discovered in 1718 by Frederich Herschel

Includes glossary and bibliography

Venus. Millbrook Press 1994 31p il (Gateway solar system) lib bdg $14.40; pa $6.95 (2-4)
   523.4

1. Venus (Planet)

ISBN 1-56294-391-X (lib bdg); 0-7613-0159-3 (pa)
   LC 93-11217

Presents information on Venus, including its volcanoes, arachnoids, and pancake domes, as studied by U.S. and Soviet spacecraft

Includes glossary and bibliography

523.5   Meteoroids, solar wind, zodiacal light

Lauber, Patricia, 1924-

Voyagers from space; meteors and meteorites; illustrated with photographs, and with drawings by Mike Eagle. Crowell 1989 74p il lib bdg $15.89 (4 and up)
   523.5

1. Meteors 2. Asteroids 3. Comets

ISBN 0-690-04634-0
   LC 86-47745

Discusses asteroids, comets, and meteorites, explaining where they come from, how they were formed, and what effect these voyagers from space have when they streak past the Earth or plummet to its surface

"The design of the book is crisp and clean, with excellent photographs and drawings well chosen to illustrate the various phases of meteorites." Horn Book

Includes bibliography

523.6   Comets

Branley, Franklyn Mansfield, 1915-

Shooting stars; by Franklyn M. Branley; illustrated by Holly Keller. Crowell 1989 32p il (Let's-read-and-find-out science books) $14.95; lib bdg $14.89; pa $4.50 (k-1)
   523.6

1. Meteors

ISBN 0-690-04701-0; 0-690-04703-7 (lib bdg); 0-06-445103-8 (pa)
   LC 88-14190

Branley, Franklyn Mansfield, 1915-—*Continued*

Explains what shooting stars are, what they are made of, and what happens to them when they land on Earth

"At times, the text is almost lyrical, while brightly colored, cartoon-style graphics (plus a few photos) catch the eye." Booklist

Moore, Patrick

Comets and shooting stars; illustrated by Paul Doherty. Copper Beech Bks. 1995 24p il (Starry sky) lib bdg $11.90 (k-3)   **523.6**

1. Comets 2. Meteors

ISBN 1-56294-625-0   LC 94-43938

First published 1994 in the United Kingdom

The author "describes the composition and orbits of *Comets and Shooting Stars,* including the annual August meteor showers and Halley's Comet." SLJ

"The information is presented in an easy-to-understand text with pertinent questions being answered." Child Book Rev Serv

Simon, Seymour, 1931-

Comets, meteors, and asteroids. Morrow Junior Bks. 1994 unp il $15; lib bdg $14.93 (3-6)   **523.6**

1. Comets 2. Meteors 3. Asteroids

ISBN 0-688-12709-6; 0-688-12710-X (lib bdg)
                                     LC 93-51251

"Simon presents basic information about comets, meteors, and asteroids in an attractive oversize book. . . . Blocks of text appear in fairly large type, usually facing a full-page illustration. . . . Simon writes in plain language, without talking down to his audience. The intriguing photographs include shots of comets and meteor showers in the sky, a meteorite in Antarctica, and an enormous impact crater in Arizona." Booklist

523.7 Sun

Asimov, Isaac, 1920-1992

How did we find out about sunshine? illustrated by David Wool. Walker & Co. 1987 63p il $10.95; lib bdg $12.85 (5 and up)
                                            523.7

1. Force and energy 2. Sun

ISBN 0-8027-6697-8; 0-8027-6698-6 (lib bdg)
                                     LC 86-32581

"A historical overview of the importance of the Sun and humans' attempts to understand it. Discoveries by Galileo, Copernicus, Cassini, Newton, and Helmholtz, among others, and the discovery of nuclear energy are explained in a clear, easy-to-follow text. Readers readily understand how one discovery leads to new questions and that the process continues today." Sci Child

Branley, Franklyn Mansfield, 1915-

Eclipse: darkness in daytime; by Franklyn M. Branley; illustrated by Donald Crews. rev ed.   Crowell   1988   32p   il (Let's-read-and-find-out science books) lib bdg $14.89; pa $4.95 (k-3)   **523.7**

1. Solar eclipses

ISBN 0-690-04619-7 (lib bdg); 0-06-445081-3 (pa)
                                     LC 87-45276

A revised and newly illustrated edition of the title first published 1973

This "book describes a total solar eclipse and how living things react to this daytime darkness. Mentioned also are myths of old. Partial eclipse and annular eclipse are also described." Sci Books Films

"Crews' illustrations offer a rich tapestry of pastels. The images are often impressionistic and soft, but sometimes Crews will call attention to some detail by the use of color or placing an object at an unusual angle. The results are striking and make an effective complement to this wonderful book." SLJ

The sun; our nearest star; [by] Franklyn M. Branley; illustrated by Don Madden. rev ed. Crowell 1988 31p il (Let's-read-and-find-out science books) lib bdg $14.89 (k-3)   **523.7**

1. Sun

ISBN 0-690-04678-2   LC 87-45678

A revised and newly illustrated edition of the title first published 1961

Describes the sun and how it provides the light and energy which allow plant and animal life to exist on the earth

Daily, Robert

The sun. Watts 1994 63p il lib bdg $13.93 (4 and up)   **523.7**

1. Sun

ISBN 0-531-20105-8   LC 94-2241

"A First book"

This book "discusses stars in general and the history of astronomy and fusion. Another chapter highlights the parts of the sun with clear explanations and great photographs." Appraisal

Includes glossary and bibliography

Gibbons, Gail

Sun up, sun down; written and illustrated by Gail Gibbons. Harcourt Brace Jovanovich 1983 unp il $14.95; pa $4.95 (k-3)   **523.7**

1. Sun

ISBN 0-15-282781-1; 0-15-282782-X (pa)
                                     LC 82-23420

The author explains "the sun and its effect on the earth. Narrated by a little girl who notices the sun shining when she wakes up one morning, this . . . [book covers] what the sun does, what makes shadows, how the sun helps form rain clouds, and how it keeps the planet warm." Booklist

"The illustrations clarify the text with bold, clear drawings in full color." SLJ

Moore, Patrick

The sun and moon; illustrated by Paul Doherty. Copper Beech Bks. 1995 24p col il (Starry sky) lib bdg $11.90 (k-3)   **523.7**

1. Sun 2. Moon

ISBN 1-56294-622-6   LC 94-43932

Moore, Patrick—*Continued*
First published 1994 in the United Kingdom
This book "describes the features of *The Sun and Moon*, and explains how they move and how eclipses occur. . . . The brightly colored paintings and photographs serve to clarify the already lucid texts." SLJ

Simon, Seymour, 1931-
The sun. Morrow 1986 unp il $17; lib bdg $16.93; pa $5.95 (3-6)   **523.7**
1. Sun
ISBN 0-688-05857-4; 0-688-05858-2 (lib bdg); 0-688-09236-5 (pa)   LC 85-32018
Describes the nature of the sun, its origin, source of energy, layers, atmosphere, sunspots, and activity
"Stunning full-color photographs show the turbulent surface of the sun, and clear illustrations clarify the cause and effect of such phenomena as gigantic prominences (geysers of flaming gas) and flares (fiery explosions with the power of ten million hydrogen bombs that last but a few minutes)." Publ Wkly

523.8   Stars

Apfel, Necia H., 1930-
Orion, the Hunter. Clarion Bks. 1995 48p il $16.95 (4 and up)   **523.8**
1. Stars
ISBN 0-395-68962-7   LC 94-44268
"Color photographs from the Hubble Space Telescope portray the splendor of the constellation Orion, its nebula, and other nearby constellations. Origins of stars such as blue-white giants and red supergiants are explained in easy-to-understand terms." Sci Child
"Large pages allow the spectacular photographs, which are supplemented by diagrams, to be fully appreciated." Booklist

Branley, Franklyn Mansfield, 1915-
The Big Dipper; by Franklyn M. Branley; illustrated by Molly Coxe. rev ed. HarperCollins Pubs. 1991 32p il (Let's-read-and-find-out science books) hardcover o.p. paperback available $4.95 (k-1)   **523.8**
1. Ursa Major
ISBN 0-06-445100-3 (pa)   LC 90-31199
A revised and newly illustrated edition of the title first published 1962
Explains basic facts about the Big Dipper, including which stars make up the constellation, how its position changes in the sky, and how it points to the North Star

Journey into a black hole; by Franklyn M. Branley; illustrated by Marc Simont. Crowell 1986 32p il (Let's-read-and-find-out science books) lib bdg $14.89 (k-3)   **523.8**
1. Black holes (Astronomy)
ISBN 0-690-04544-1   LC 85-48249
The author attempts "to explain how a black hole arises, what happens in its vicinity, and how astronomers might recognize one." Sci Books Films
"Simont's paintings effectively convey the mystery and magnitude of the unimaginable, the space and distance and density of a black hole. They are deft in interpreting Branley's lucid text, which skillfully streamlines the explanation of a complicated astronomical phenomenon so that it will be comprehensible to primary grades readers." Bull Cent Child Books

The sky is full of stars; illustrated by Felicia Bond. Crowell 1981 34p il (Let's-read-and-find-out science books) lib bdg $14.89; pa $4.95 (k-3)   **523.8**
1. Stars
ISBN 0-690-04123-3 (lib bdg); 0-06-445002-3 (pa)   LC 81-43037
"This picture-book introduction to stargazing explains what constellations are and helps youngsters find them in seasonal skies. Brief background information calls attention to star colors and differing brightness; it also notes star movement. . . . A unique feature is the use of real photographs to picture some of the constellations. These appear twice, once unmarked, as you would really see them, and again with the constellation outlined. This gives youngsters a realistic idea of how obscure some figures can seem, yet how simple they are once one knows where to look. With cheery cartoon drawings in black and white or blue and yellow." Booklist

Star guide; [by] Franklyn M. Branley; illustrated by Ellen Eagle. Crowell 1987 51p il (Voyage into space book) lib bdg $13.89 (3-6)   **523.8**
1. Stars
ISBN 0-690-04351-1   LC 82-45928
Describes the composition and behavior of stars and notes which ones can be seen at different times of the year
"Illustrated with a mix of soft charcoal drawings, astronomy photographs, and clear diagrams." Booklist

Gallant, Roy A.
The constellations, how they came to be. rev ed. Four Winds Press 1991 203p il maps $15.95 (5 and up)   **523.8**
1. Stars 2. Mythology
ISBN 0-02-735776-7   LC 91-223330
First published 1979
This book "divides the skies into seasons, explaining what the viewer will see at each time during the year. With each of these primers, the author has added background about the constellations—in relation to the myths behind each. Each constellation is carefully drawn and/or 'photographed,' giving the reader the opportunity to see 'how' the ancients arrived at their creations." Voice Youth Advocates
Includes glossary

Gustafson, John
Stars, clusters, and galaxies; the young stargazer's guide to the galaxy. Messner 1993 64p il maps $12.98; pa $6.95 (4 and up)   **523.8**
1. Stars 2. Galaxies
ISBN 0-671-72536-X; 0-671-72537-8 (pa)
     LC 92-11228
"This is a basic introduction to stars and their observation, including double stars, star clusters, nebulae and galaxies. . . . Color photographs of various constellations and phenomena are included as well as information on using star maps, measuring distances in the sky, and experiments on the effects of light pollution." Voice Youth Advocates

Gustafson, John—*Continued*
"This is an excellent book for the amateur scientist." Sci Child

Moore, Patrick

The stars; illustrated by Paul Doherty. Copper Beech Bks. 1995 24p il (Starry sky) lib bdg $11.90 (k-3) **523.8**

1. Stars

ISBN 1-56294-623-4   LC 94-43937

First published 1994 in the United Kingdom

This book "looks at the birth and death of *Stars*, and examines the different types and colors found in the Milky Way and other galaxies. . . . White print on black pages sets off the illustrations and gives the appearance of looking into the night sky." SLJ

Rey, H. A. (Hans Augusto), 1898-1977

Find the constellations. rev ed. Houghton Mifflin 1976 72p il $17.95; pa $8.95 **523.8**

1. Stars

ISBN 0-395-24509-5; 0-395-24418-8 (pa)

First published 1954

"Constellation diagrams are presented with and without connecting lines and are drawn for 40° N. Latitude to cover the continental United States. The use of color in these diagrams is a refreshing change from the black-and-white usually used. . . . Scientific accuracy is stressed, stellar magnitudes are indicated on the diagrams, and the concept of light year is discussed. Some of the myths surrounding the names of the constellations are given." Sci Books Films

"This is unquestionably a readable, enjoyable, and informative guide." SLJ

523.9 Satellites and rings; eclipses, transits, occultations

Kelch, Joseph W., 1958-

Small worlds: exploring the 60 moons of our solar system. Messner 1990 157p il $13.95; lib bdg $16.98 (6 and up) **523.9**

1. Satellites 2. Outer space—Exploration

ISBN 0-671-70014-6; 0-671-70013-8 (lib bdg)

LC 87-2424

Discusses the origin and characteristics of each of the moons circling the planets of the solar system and presents information on both manned and unmanned space exploration

"An exciting book that clearly differentiates fact from theory. . . . A 20-page 'Checklist of Moons,' a tabular summary of each satellite's characteristics, is a valuable feature. The index is inclusive and accurate. The illustrations are mostly black-and-white photographs scattered throughout the book and color photographs grouped in the center. All are cited in the text and are well-chosen to illustrate Kelch's verbal descriptions. A must purchase because it brings together so much information." SLJ

525 Earth (Astronomical geography)

Branley, Franklyn Mansfield, 1915-

Sunshine makes the seasons; by Franklyn M. Branley; illustrated by Giulio Maestro. rev ed. Crowell 1986 32p il (Let's-read-and-find-out science books) lib bdg $14.89; pa $4.95 (k-3) **525**

1. Seasons

ISBN 0-690-04482-8 (lib bdg); 0-06-445019-8 (pa)

LC 85-42750

A revised and newly illustrated edition of the title first published 1974

"The narrative and illustrations describe the real and apparent motions of the sun and the earth relative to one another and their relationships to changes of season. . . . Although there is nothing earth-shaking about the quality of the illustrations, it is appropriate for the topics covered, and it should be attractive to those for whom the book seems designed." Sci Books Films

What makes day and night; [by] Franklyn M. Branley; illustrated by Arthur Dorros. rev ed. Crowell 1986 32p il (Let's-read-and-find-out science books) lib bdg $14.89; pa $4.95 (k-3) **525**

1. Earth 2. Day 3. Night

ISBN 0-690-04524-7 (lib bdg); 0-06-445050-3 (pa)

LC 85-47903

A revised and newly illustrated edition of the title first published 1961

A simple explanation of how the rotation of the earth causes night and day

The illustrations feature "clear, colorful and sometimes mildly silly scenes that add some playfulness." SLJ

Fradin, Dennis B.

Earth. Childrens Press 1989 45p il lib bdg $13.50; pa $4.95 (2-4) **525**

1. Earth

ISBN 0-516-01172-3 (lib bdg); 0-516-41172-1 (pa)

LC 89-9982

"New true book"

Discusses the Earth as a planet and describes its temperatures, movements in space, and other characteristics

"Illustrated with helpful full-color photographs and diagrams. Glossaries and brief fact lists appended." Booklist

Gibbons, Gail

The reasons for seasons. Holiday House 1995 unp il $15.95 (k-3) **525**

1. Seasons

ISBN 0-8234-1174-5   LC 94-32904

"Gibbons uses simple words and clear, colorful pictures to explain the seasons, the solstices, and the equinoxes. Besides discussing the earth's tilt and orbit, she also comments on what people and animals do in each season of the year." Booklist

Lauber, Patricia, 1924-

How we learned the earth is round; illustrated by Megan Lloyd. Crowell 1990 32p il maps (Let's-read-and-find-out science books) lib bdg $14.89; pa $4.95 (k-3)   **525**

1. Earth
ISBN 0-690-04862-9 (lib bdg); 0-06-445109-7 (pa)
      LC 89-49650

Explains various changes in humanity's beliefs about the shape of the earth, from the flat earth theories of the ancients to the round earth theories which were proven true by the voyages of Columbus and Magellan

"Colorful, cartoonlike illustrations appear on almost every page, and two-color NASA photos of the earth are appended. Purists may quibble about the use of the term *round* instead of *spherical*, but children will understand exactly what Lauber means, and teachers will welcome the simple explanation of a rather complex idea." Booklist

Seeing Earth from space. Orchard Bks. 1990 80p il maps $19.95; lib bdg $19.99; pa $9.95 (4 and up)   **525**

1. Earth sciences 2. Earth
ISBN 0-531-05902-2; 0-531-08502-3 (lib bdg); 0-531-07057-3 (pa)   LC 89-77523

"This book uses photographs taken in space by astronauts and man-made satellites to describe Earth. It also discusses remote sensors and how they are used to study our planet." Voice Youth Advocates

"Well researched, clearly written, and beautifully made, this eye-opening book represents non-fiction at its best." Booklist

Includes bibliography

Ride, Sally K.

The third planet; exploring the earth from space; [by] Sally Ride & Tam O'Shaughnessy. Crown 1994 46p il $15; lib bdg $15.99 (4 and up)   **525**

1. Astronautics 2. Earth
ISBN 0-517-59361-0; 0-517-59362-9 (lib bdg)
      LC 92-40609

Astronaut Sally Ride examines how the earth is studied from space, its critical relationship with the other planets in the solar system, and some of the earth's features, including climate, orbits, atmosphere, and light

"Clear text and spectacular photographs make this book enjoyable to read or to flip through just to admire the beauty of earth from orbit." Sci Books Films

Simon, Seymour, 1931-

Earth, our planet in space. Four Winds Press 1984 unp il $14.95 (1-4)   **525**

1. Earth
ISBN 0-02-782830-1   LC 83-11706

"The author discusses our world's unique position in space and how our days, seasons, and topography are affected by our position there." Booklist

"Black and white photographs of good quality are carefully combined with textual references to achieve a maximum level of conveyance of information. . . . This . . . title should be welcome because of the clean layout of pages, the careful and accurate marshalling of facts, the directness of style, and the combination of good coverage and controlled scope." Bull Cent Child Books

529 Chronology

Anno, Mitsumasa, 1926-

Anno's sundial. Philomel Bks. 1987 28p il map o.p. (4 and up)   **529**

1. Sundials 2. Time   LC 86-91447

The author explains how the earth's movements around the sun and the resulting movement of shadows have been used to tell time, using illustrations that pop up or fold out to demonstrate how sundials work

"The pop-up features of the book, like the text, require attentive study of the diagrams and the explanations of principles involved. . . . Anno's treatment of this very basic set of scientific principles is informative and demanding; his multidimensional figures invite reader involvement and seem very likely to stimulate further exploration of the ideas by older children and adolescents with a penchant for science." Horn Book

Branley, Franklyn Mansfield, 1915-

Keeping time; from the beginning and into the 21st century; [by] Franklyn M. Branley; illustrated by Jill Weber. Houghton Mifflin 1993 105p il $13.95 (4-6)   **529**

1. Time 2. Clocks and watches 3. Calendars
ISBN 0-395-47777-8   LC 92-6783

"From the history of timekeeping and calendars to the theory of relativity to the reasons we divide time as we do, Branley challenges readers with difficult, abstract concepts and offers simple, concrete projects. . . . Weber's cartoonlike ink drawings appear on nearly every page . . . providing an upbeat counterpoint to the text." Booklist

Includes bibliography

Burns, Marilyn

This book is about time; illustrated by Martha Weston. Little, Brown 1978 127p il $15.95; pa $11.95 (4 and up)   **529**

1. Time
ISBN 0-316-11752-8; 0-316-11750-1 (pa)
      LC 78-6614

"A Brown paper school book"

Burns describes when, why, and how people started to measure time and discusses such topics as time zones, biorhythms, and jet lag. Also includes instructions for a variety of related projects

Fisher, Leonard Everett, 1924-

Calendar art; thirteen days, weeks, months, and years from around the world; written and illustrated by Leonard Everett Fisher. Four Winds Press 1987 61p il $15.95 (4 and up)   **529**

1. Calendars
ISBN 0-02-735350-8   LC 86-25835

"Fisher explains the origins of the calendar and the human need to divide the solar year into months, weeks, and days. He describes 13 such calendars, ranging through history from the Aztecs, Babylonians, and Egyptians to . . . those in more recent history, including the one formed during the French Revolution and the 1930 World Calendar." SLJ

"The information is clear, concise, and fascinating. . . . Whether used for browsing, curriculum enhancement, reference, or study of graphics, the book illuminates the subject instead of merely conveying information." Horn Book

530 Physics

Cooper, Chris
Matter; written by Christopher Cooper. Dorling Kindersley 1992 64p il (Eyewitness science) $15.95 (4 and up)   **530**

1. Matter 2. Atoms 3. Molecules
ISBN 1-87943-188-2   LC 92-6928

Examines the elements that make up the physical world and the properties and behavior of different kinds of matter

This book features "lavish full-color photographs and drawings. . . . Many are of items rarely seen in science books—historic equipment from museum collections. . . . Because the art dominates, the text is limited." SLJ

Wellnitz, William R., 1949-
Be a kid physicist. TAB Bks. 1993 114p il $17.95; pa $9.95 (5 and up)   **530**

1. Physics—Experiments
ISBN 0-8306-4091-6; 0-8306-4092-4 (pa)
                LC 92-40506

Presents experiments that use materials found around the home and explore the principles of light, electricity, magnetism, motion, heat, and sound

This is a "delightful book for parents, teachers, and children. . . . [It] is attractively illustrated with line drawings and black-and-white photographs. Commendably, the illustrations are neutral in terms of gender—many of the drawings show hands doing the works, and, when children are shown, boys and girls are represented equally." Sci Child

Includes glossary

530.8 Testing and measurement

Wells, Robert E.
Is a blue whale the biggest thing there is? Whitman, A. 1993 unp il $13.95; pa $6.95 (1-3)   **530.8**

1. Size and shape 2. Measurement
ISBN 0-8075-3655-5; 0-8075-3656-3 (pa)
                LC 93-2703

Illustrates the concept of big, bigger, and biggest by comparing the physical measurements of such large things as a blue whale, a mountain, a star, and the universe

"With its bright primary colors; cartoon illustrations; and readable, conversational text, this picture book will find a niche in most collections. . . . Librarians and teachers could use this book to introduce units on size, measuring, or relativity. And it would be useful to demonstrate how to make beginning graphs in a fun, accessible way." SLJ

531 Mechanics. Solid mechanics

Ardley, Neil, 1937-
The science book of gravity. Harcourt Brace Jovanovich 1992 29p il $9.95 (3-5)   **531**

1. Gravitation—Experiments
ISBN 0-15-200621-4   LC 92-3413
"Gulliver books"
Simple experiments demonstrate the laws of gravity

"The experiments presented . . . are simple enough for most fourth graders to do on their own and interesting enough to intrigue them. Although not complex, they do demonstrate important basic scientific principles. . . . Full-color photographs set against a white background are both attractive and useful." SLJ

The science book of motion. Harcourt Brace Jovanovich 1992 29p il $9.95 (3-5)   **531**

1. Motion—Experiments
ISBN 0-15-200622-2   LC 92-3412
"Gulliver books"
Simple experiments demonstrate the laws of motion

"Most experiments include a small captioned photograph that ties the activity involved to real-life examples, thus broadening readers' understanding of the principle demonstrated. The best science project books include appealing experiments and clear instructions, while successfully teaching scientific concepts. Ardley's books meet all of these standards." SLJ

Branley, Franklyn Mansfield, 1915-
Gravity is a mystery; by Franklyn M. Branley; illustrated by Don Madden. rev ed. Crowell 1986 32p il (Let's-read-and-find-out science books) lib bdg $14.89 (k-3)   **531**

1. Gravitation
ISBN 0-690-04527-1   LC 85-48247
First published 1970

"Branley talks about the gravitational forces exerted by the earth, moon, sun, and planets on objects in or on them." Booklist

"Madden's cartoon-like illustrations are specifically wedded to the scientific information presented by Branley." Libr J

Cobb, Vicki, 1938-
Why doesn't the earth fall up? and other not such dumb questions about motion; illustrated by Ted Enik. Lodestar Bks. 1988 40p il $14.99 (3-5)   **531**

1. Motion
ISBN 0-525-67253-2   LC 88-11108

"Four cartoon kids and an omniscient narrator explore nine questions about motion: motions which children can cause and watch, how they can detect motions that they cannot feel, Newton's laws, center of gravity, orbits, and pendula. Along the way, there are simple experiments and brief mention of Newton, Galileo, and Copernicus. It's all very short and simple, in an open, appealing format, and for the most part the science does not suffer from the simplification." SLJ

Lafferty, Peter
Force & motion; written by Peter Lafferty. Dorling Kindersley 1992 64p il (Eyewitness science) $15.95 (4 and up)   **531**

1. Force and energy 2. Motion
ISBN 1-87943-185-8   LC 92-6927

Illustrated with full-color photographs and drawings, this book explores the principles of force and motion, describing how they have been applied from ancient to modern times

Skurzynski, Gloria
Zero gravity. Bradbury Press 1994 32p il
$14.95 (2-4)   **531**
1. Gravitation 2. Weightlessness 3. Astronautics
ISBN 0-02-782925-1   LC 93-46735
"Skurzynski discusses the sensation of zero gravity in orbiting space shuttles, explaining it in terms of physical
forces, and then describes astronauts' experiences of weightlessness while orbiting the earth. . . . Full-color illustrations
appear throughout the book, including many intriguing photographs of astronauts sleeping, working, and playing with
food aboard the space shuttles. A brief but intriguing book
combining the science of space travel with human experience." Booklist
Includes glossary

Zubrowski, Bernie, 1939-
Mobiles; building and experimenting with
balancing toys; illustrated by Roy Doty.
Morrow Junior Bks. 1993 104p il lib bdg
$13.93; pa $6.95 (4 and up)   **531**
1. Balance 2. Science—Experiments 3. Mobiles
(Sculpture)
ISBN 0-688-10590-4 (lib bdg); 0-688-10589-0 (pa)
                                        LC 92-28408
"A Boston Children's Museum activity book"
"Zubrowski presents simple activities to demonstrate
various concepts of balance. Clear instructions and easy-to-
find materials (cardboard, coat hangers, and paper clips are
typical) ensure that most children will be able to complete
the projects on their own. Doty's line drawings are cartoonlike, but useful and precise. . . . The title is slightly misleading, since the book focuses on balance in general, not just
mobiles." SLJ

532 Fluid mechanics

Zubrowski, Bernie, 1939-
Making waves; finding out about rhythmic
motion; illustrated by Roy Doty. Morrow
Junior Bks. 1994 96p il $13.93; pa $6.95 (4
and up)   **532**
1. Waves 2. Science projects
ISBN 0-688-11787-2; 0-688-11788-0 (pa)
                                        LC 93-35455
"A Boston Children's Museum activity book"
"Zubrowski shows readers how to build equipment and
observe waves in water, soap film, plastic and cloth materials, string, and a 'wave machine' constructed with dowels,
nails, masking tape, and rubber bands. The step-by-step directions and the use of everyday objects for apparatus make
this book useful for students preparing for science fairs as
well as for teachers who want to demonstrate waves in their
classrooms. Illustrated with cartoonlike line drawings, the
experiments look enjoyable as well as useful." Booklist

533 Gas mechanics (Pneumatics)

Devonshire, Hilary
Air. Watts 1992 32p il (Science through art)
lib bdg $13.23 (3-5)   **533**
1. Air 2. Art and science
ISBN 0-531-14134-9   LC 91-10947

Explores fundamental principles of air through art techniques and explains how they can be used in art
"Devonshire looks at such principles as the weight and
pressure of *Air*, its movement and wind measurement, and
suggests activities that illustrate these concepts. Projects include: bubble paints, paper spirals, wind socks, and weather
vanes." SLJ
Includes glossary

535 Light and related radiations

Bulla, Clyde Robert, 1914-
What makes a shadow? illustrated by June
Otani. rev ed. HarperCollins Pubs. 1994 32p il
(Let's-read-and-find-out science books) $15; lib
bdg $14.89; pa $4.95 (k-1)   **535**
1. Shades and shadows
ISBN 0-06-022915-2; 0-06-022916-0 (lib bdg);
0-06-445118-6 (pa)   LC 92-36350
A revised and newly illustrated edition of the title first
published 1962 by Crowell
"Using short sentences and developmentally appropriate
language, the author explains how shadows are formed,
gives numerous examples of shadows, and describes how to
make shadow pictures on the wall. Each page is illustrated
with bright, colorful drawings, and the gender and cultural
representation is excellent." Sci Books Films

Burnie, David
Light. Dorling Kindersley 1992 64p il
(Eyewitness science) lib bdg $15.95 (4 and up)
                                        535
1. Light
ISBN 1-879431-79-3   LC 92-7661
A guide to the origins, principles, and historical study of
light
"Each double-page spread is lavishly illustrated with full-
color photographs and diagrams, and each contains a
wealth of information." Booklist

Cobb, Vicki, 1938-
Light action! amazing experiments with
optics; [by] Vicki Cobb and Josh Cobb;
illustrated by Theo Cobb. HarperCollins Pubs.
1993 198p il $15; lib bdg $14.89 (5 and up)
                                        535
1. Optics 2. Light
ISBN 0-06-021436-8; 0-06-021437-6 (lib bdg)
                                        LC 92-25528
Explains what light is and explores the basic principles of
optics through experiments
"The activities are simple and well designed and will
give students basic knowledge. Cheerful line drawings and
diagrams illustrate the text." Booklist

Devonshire, Hilary
Light. Watts 1991 32p il (Science through
art) lib bdg $13.23 (3-5)   **535**
1. Light 2. Art and science
ISBN 0-531-14126-8   LC 91-8401

Devonshire, Hilary—Continued

Examines the various properties of light and offers a number of art projects demonstrating these principles

"The science principles are stated clearly and concisely, so the reader knows exactly what the art activity is demonstrating. . . . The directions are stated clearly and are well illustrated. . . . A child with little or no knowledge of science would have no trouble understanding the principles or completing the activities on their own." Sci Books Films

Includes glossary

Goor, Ron, 1940-

Shadows; here, there, and everywhere; [by] Ron & Nancy Goor. Crowell 1981 47p il lib bdg $14.89 (k-3)   **535**

1. Shades and shadows
ISBN 0-690-04133-0   LC 81-43036

Presents information about shadows, including how they are formed, why they can be of various lengths, and how they reveal the shape and texture of things

"The well-placed, striking photographs effectively illustrate the strange and often beautiful shapes of shadows." Horn Book

Lauber, Patricia, 1924-

What do you see? exploring light, color, and vision; photographs by Leonard Lessin. Crown 1994 48p il $17; lib bdg $17.99 (4 and up)
535

1. Light 2. Color 3. Vision
ISBN 0-517-59390-4; 0-517-59391-2 (lib bdg)
LC 93-2388

This book discusses "the way that light travels, how it is reflected and bent, and how the absorption and reflection of light determines colors. Two chapters cover the way that we see and how the eye works. There is also a chapter on wavelengths that are not visible to human eyes: infrared and ultraviolet rays. . . . The photographs add a great deal to the information presented in the book and are very good examples of the subjects discussed." Appraisal

Murata, Michinori, 1924-

Water and light; looking through lenses; photographs by Isamu Sekido. Lerner Publs. 1993 24p il (Science all around you) lib bdg $18.95 (1-3)   **535**

1. Light 2. Lenses
ISBN 0-8225-2904-1   LC 92-19969

Original Japanese edition, 1984

Explains how such things as a goldfish bowl, a drop of water, or a magnifying glass act as lenses and describes the appearance of objects viewed through them

"Readers will find that material interesting, well-developed, and appropriately sequenced. The Japanese children pictured add a multicultural dimension as do some of the objects shown in the photographs." Appraisal

Includes glossary

Simon, Seymour, 1931-

Mirror magic; illustrated by Anni Matsick. Bell Bks. (Honesdale) 1991 47p il $9.95 (k-3)
535

1. Mirrors
ISBN 1-878093-07-X

A reissue of the title first published 1980 by Lothrop, Lee & Shepard Bks.

Explains how mirrors work and presents activities to illustrate the scientific principles involved

"The clear, concise text and simple experiments and activities in this unique book give young readers a basic understanding of how mirrors work." SLJ

Shadow magic; illustrated by Stella Ormai. Lothrop, Lee & Shepard Bks. 1985 48p il lib bdg $13.88 (k-3)   **535**

1. Shades and shadows
ISBN 0-688-02682-6   LC 84-4433

"A look at shadows: what they are, how they are created, how they are used. Simon's clear, direct text explains, among other things, that night is caused by the Earth's shadow. A consideration of sundials includes directions for making one from readily available materials, and suggestions are given for a hand-shadow show." SLJ

"Illustrated with pencil-and-wash drawings that are uneven but largely effective in backing up the text." Booklist

Zubrowski, Bernie, 1939-

Mirrors; finding out about the properties of light; illustrated by Roy Doty. Morrow Junior Bks. 1992 96p il $13.93; pa $6.95 (4 and up)
535

1. Mirrors 2. Light 3. Science—Experiments
ISBN 0-688-10592-0; 0-688-10591-2 (pa)
LC 91-29142

"A Boston Children's Museum activity book"

Suggested activities explore how mirrors work and how they demonstrate the properties of light

"The activities, many of which use household materials, range in scope from forming funny reflections to making a stage illusion of a ghost. The clear and well-drawn illustrations are done in cartoon form. . . . The best thing about this book is that it makes learning science fun." Sci Books Films

535.6   Color

Devonshire, Hilary

Color. Watts 1992 32p il (Science through art) lib bdg $13.23 (3-5)   **535.6**

1. Color 2. Art and science
ISBN 0-531-14221-3   LC 91-11871

Presents basic principles of color, demonstrating their use in art

"Directions are provided for making color spinners and other projects that explain the characteristics of watercolors, acrylics, and oil paint, and the effect of color on feelings. Making a leaf collage and homemade dyes provide opportunities to learn about colors in nature." SLJ

Includes glossary

Dewey, Ariane

Naming colors. HarperCollins Pubs. 1995 48p il maps $16; lib bdg $15.89 (4-6)

535.6

1. Color 2. English language—Etymology
ISBN 0-06-021291-8; 0-06-021292-6 (lib bdg)

LC 93-2635

"Beginning with a history of the first words used to describe black, white, and the primary colors, Dewey goes on to trace the history of the English names for hues as varied as puce, sepia, and electric pink. While the language of color is the focus here, much multicultural and geographical information is included." SLJ

"Entertaining as well as informative, the text is organized by thematic categories. . . . The useful index includes a strip of each color with its name." Horn Book Guide

Westray, Kathleen

A color sampler. Ticknor & Fields 1993 unp il $14.95 (2-4)

535.6

1. Color
ISBN 0-395-65940-X

LC 93-19967

The author "uses patchwork-quilt patterns to present primary, secondary, intermediate, and complementary colors. She demonstrates how the color wheel is formed, how adding black or white changes colors, and how they are affected by placement in a design or by the hues surrounding them." SLJ

"The simple clarity of the text and illustrations is lent flair by the inventive format." Bull Cent Child Books

536 Heat

Ardley, Neil, 1937-

The science book of hot & cold. Harcourt Brace Jovanovich 1992 29p il $9.95 (3-5)

536

1. Heat 2. Cold 3. Science—Experiments
ISBN 0-15-200612-5   LC 91-21792
"Gulliver books"

Explores and explains different properties of temperature through simple experiments

"Bright, colorful, sharp photographs are interspersed among blocks of large-type text. . . . The supplies needed for the experiments are inexpensive and readily available household and school items. Children will be fascinated and entertained by what they can learn by using familiar objects." Sci Books Films

537 Electricity and electronics

Ardley, Neil, 1937-

The science book of electricity. Harcourt Brace Jovanovich 1991 29p il $9.95 (3-5)

537

1. Electricity—Experiments
ISBN 0-15-200583-8   LC 90-48030
"Gulliver books"

Simple experiments demonstrate basic principles of electricity

Berger, Melvin, 1927-

Switch on, switch off; illustrated by Carolyn Croll. Crowell 1989 32p il (Let's-read-and-find-out science books) lib bdg $14.89; pa $4.95 (k-3)

537

1. Electricity
ISBN 0-690-04786-X (lib bdg); 0-06-445097-X (pa)

LC 88-17638

"This book presents rudimentary exploration of electricity and how electrical current flows to the light switch in a child's room. Follow the current from the generator to a power plant to the switch on the wall. Includes instructions for a simple generator. A good, first look at a topic that mystifies young scientists." Sci Child

Markle, Sandra, 1946-

Power up; experiments, puzzles, and games exploring electricity. Atheneum Pubs. 1989 40p il $14.95 (3-5)

537

1. Electricity—Experiments
ISBN 0-689-31442-6   LC 88-7772

The author "focuses principally on circuits, conductors, and bulbs as conveyors of electricity in an informative, extended science lesson that is a model of clarity and simplicity. At the outset she lists easily obtained supplies for demonstrating the principles discussed." Horn Book

Parker, Steve

Electricity; written by Steve Parker. Dorling Kindersley 1992 64p il (Eyewitness science) $15.95 (4 and up)

537

1. Electricity
ISBN 1-87943-182-3   LC 92-6926

Discusses the properties of electricity and describes how it is made and used

"Pictures and text work together to offer a lucid chronicle of pertinent experiments, discoveries and inventions from ancient times to the present." Publ Wkly

VanCleave, Janice Pratt

Janice VanCleave's electricity; mind-boggling experiments you can turn into science fair projects; [by] Janice VanCleave. Wiley 1994 89p il $9.95 (5 and up)

537

1. Electricity—Experiments 2. Science projects
ISBN 0-471-31010-7   LC 93-40913

"The experiments move from the simple, which do not require the use of batteries, to those that require small batteries, sizes AA, AAA, C, or D. An appendix shows how to make strips of aluminum foil that can be used to form the electrical circuits that are part of some of the experiments. By encouraging students to move beyond the basic problems (with adult supervision), the author encourages them to be creative in designing science fair projects." Booklist

Includes glossary

538 Magnetism

Souza, D. M. (Dorothy M.)

Northern lights. Carolrhoda Bks. 1994 48p il (Nature in action) lib bdg $19.95; pa $7.95 (4-6)   **538**

1. Auroras

ISBN 0-87614-799-6 (lib bdg); 0-87614-629-9 (pa)

LC 93-3027

Discusses the origins, characteristics, and lore of the Northern and Southern Lights known as auroras

This "is written in a clear, concise style and is illustrated with magnificent color photographs and accurate paintings." Sci Books Films

Includes glossary

539 Modern physics

Wells, Robert E.

What's smaller than a pygmy shrew? Whitman, A. 1995 unp il $13.95; pa $6.95 (1-3)   **539**

1. Atoms 2. Size and shape

ISBN 0-8075-8837-7; 0-8075-8838-5 (pa)

LC 94-27150

"Wells compares the size of a tiny animal (a pygmy shrew) to an insect (a ladybug), which is in turn contrasted with one-celled animals, bacteria, molecules, atoms, and sub-atomic particles." SLJ

"Using humorous illustrations, this volume facilitates readers' understanding of the relative term 'small.'" Sci Child

Includes glossary

540 Chemistry and allied sciences

Newmark, Ann

Chemistry; written by Ann Newmark. Dorling Kindersley 1993 64p il (Eyewitness science) $15.95 (4 and up)   **540**

1. Chemistry

ISBN 1-56458-231-0   LC 92-54480

Explores the world of chemical reactions and shows the role that chemistry plays in our world

"The book is an inspiration for demonstrations or experiments. The brightly colored illustrations are appealing, and . . . the snippets of information are a useful way to introduce many topics or examples relating to the themes under discussion." Sci Books Films

540.7 Chemistry—Education and related topics

Gardner, Robert, 1929-

Kitchen chemistry: science experiments to do at home. [rev ed] Messner 1989 128p il lib bdg $13.98; pa $5.95 (4 and up)   **540.7**

1. Chemistry—Experiments

ISBN 0-671-67776-4 (lib bdg); 0-671-67576-1 (pa)

LC 88-23128

First published 1982

This book contains instructions for conducting sixty one chemical experiments using the stove, refrigerator, counter, sink, and materials commonly found in the kitchen

"Safety is the key word in this easy-to-use book. . . . The experiments are well-designed, leading young scientists logically through basic chemical principles without a heavy dose of discussion." Appraisal

Kramer, Alan

How to make a chemical volcano and other mysterious experiments. Watts 1989 111p il lib bdg $13.72; pa $6.95 (4-6)   **540.7**

1. Chemistry—Experiments

ISBN 0-531-10771-X (lib bdg); 0-531-15610-9 (pa)

LC 89-8994

The author presents various experiments, using household chemicals or materials, in order to demonstrate chemical principles

"The easy-to-follow, clearly illustrated instructions include 'Caution' warnings for steps which suggest adult supervision. . . . Kramer's low-key enthusiasm makes this ideal for the reluctant scientist." Bull Cent Child Books

Includes bibliography

547 Organic chemistry

Cobb, Vicki, 1938-

Gobs of goo; illustrated by Brian Schatell. Lippincott 1983 38p il lib bdg $14.89 (2-4)   **547**

1. Chemistry 2. Science—Experiments

ISBN 0-397-32022-1   LC 82-48457

This book describes various types of sticky substances and shows how they are made and used in everyday life

"This book is excellent for stimulating curiosity in youngsters. The materials are common household items, and the experiments are short and diverse. The scientific explanations are well integrated and will be highly informative." Sci Books Films

548 Crystallography

Maki, Chū, 1929-

Snowflakes, sugar, and salt; crystals up close; photographs by Isamu Sekido. Lerner Publs. 1993 24p il (Science all around you) lib bdg $18.95 (1-3)   **548**

1. Crystallography

ISBN 0-8225-2903-3   LC 92-18538

Original Japanese edition, 1988

Maki, Chū, 1929-—*Continued*

This volume "describes crystals, such as snow, salt, baking soda, and alum." Sci Child

"Beautiful photographs illustrate the crystalline forms; clear photos of children document the methods of making solutions from which crystals can be grown." Sci Books Films

Includes glossary

Stangl, Jean, 1928-

Crystals and crystal gardens you can grow. Watts 1990 64p il lib bdg $13.93 (4 and up)
548

1. Crystallography 2. Science—Experiments
ISBN 0-531-10889-9   LC 89-38999

"A First book"

The author discusses the nature and structure of crystals and presents experiments in crystal formation

With "clear explanatory background on crystal formations, and easy directions for experiments, this will meet a real need in every classroom and public library collection." Bull Cent Child Books

Includes bibliography

Symes, R. F.

Crystal & gem; written by R.F. Symes and R.R. Harding. Knopf 1991 63p il (Eyewitness books) $19; lib bdg $18.99 (4 and up)
548

1. Crystallography 2. Precious stones
ISBN 0-679-80781-0; 0-679-90781-5 (lib bdg)
LC 90-4930

Also available Spanish language edition

Describes how crystals form in nature, how crystals are grown artificially, and how crystals are used in industry. Numerous color photos with text identify the various gemstones

"The color photographs and drawings are dazzling and show care in selection and positioning. . . . The text is lucid, readable, and informative." Appraisal

549 Mineralogy

Podendorf, Illa, 1903-1983

Rocks and minerals. Childrens Press 1982 45p il lib bdg $13.50; pa $5.50 (2-4)   **549**

1. Rocks 2. Mineralogy
ISBN 0-516-01648-2 (lib bdg); 0-516-41648-0 (pa)
LC 81-38494

"A New true book"

First published 1958 with title: The true book of rocks and minerals

Simple introduction to formation and identification of a variety of rocks and minerals. Illustrated with photographs including some in full color

Includes glossary

Symes, R. F.

Rocks & minerals; written by R.F. Symes and the staff of the Natural History Museum, London. Knopf 1988 63p il (Eyewitness books) $19; lib bdg $18.99 (4 and up)
549

1. Mineralogy 2. Rocks
ISBN 0-394-89621-1; 0-394-99621-6 (lib bdg)
LC 87-26514

Also available Spanish language edition

Text and photographs examine the creation, importance, erosion, mining, and uses of rocks and minerals

"The material presented is technically sound and well and appropriately condensed. This book is not a textbook, nor is it a field manual. As a general reference for the lay person, it provides, through the use of visual aids and associated text, useful information for individuals with no formal training in geology." Sci Books Films

Zim, Herbert S.

Rocks and minerals; a guide to familiar minerals, gems, ores and rocks; by Herbert S. Zim and Paul R. Shaffer; illustrated by Raymond Perlman. Golden Bks. 1957 160p il maps hardcover o.p. paperback available $5.95 (4 and up)   **549**

1. Mineralogy 2. Rocks
ISBN 0-307-24499-7 (pa)

"A Golden guide"

"Introductory material on the earth and its rocks gives basic geological information, and activities for amateurs are suggested in identifying, collecting and studying rocks and minerals. Colored diagrams and pictures of specimens aid in identification. Descriptions [of over 400 specimens] include information on formation, structure, use and importance." Bull Cent Child Books

550 Earth sciences

Markle, Sandra, 1946-

Earth alive! Lothrop, Lee & Shepard Bks. 1991 38p il $14.95; lib bdg $14.88 (4-6)
550

1. Geology
ISBN 0-688-09360-4; 0-688-09361-2 (lib bdg)
LC 90-5803

Describes the ways in which the earth is constantly changing and examines the reasons for and the effects of these changes. Also includes instructions for a variety of related experiments

"Handsome color photographs from diverse sources. . . . The causes of natural wonders or disasters are clearly explained. . . . Informative and handsome, the book may encourage readers to look for more material on the geological drama of our world." Bull Cent Child Books

Pope, Joyce

The children's atlas of natural wonders. Millbrook Press 1995 94p il maps lib bdg $19.40; pa $12.95 (4 and up)   **550**

1. Physical geography 2. Geology
ISBN 1-56294-564-5 (lib bdg); 1-56294-886-5 (pa)
LC 95-11778

Pope, Joyce—*Continued*

This volume "covers all the major land masses and describes 36 natural 'wonders' in terms of their geological evolution. It provides an excellent overview and can be used to initiate an in-depth study of how the Earth evolved." Sci Child

Includes glossary

Robbins, Ken

Earth; the elements. Holt & Co. 1995 unp il (Elements) $16.95 (4-6)   **550**

1. Earth sciences
ISBN 0-8050-2294-5   LC 94-28049

The author "presents his view of the many ways the solids of Earth affect us and are used for our benefit, from plate tectonics to the fertility of soil to the creation of coal under heat and pressure." SLJ

"Robbins' signature illustration technique—hand coloring his own 35-mm photographs—has a way of helping us revisualize the familiar. . . . Sedimentary rocks seem full of stories, and sand dunes seem mysterious. Robbins' text is fluid, not dry." Booklist

Van Rose, Susanna

Earth; written by Susanna Van Rose. Dorling Kindersley 1994 64p il maps (Eyewitness science) $15.95 (4 and up)

550

1. Earth sciences
ISBN 1-56458-476-3   LC 93-33102

This "opens with ideas on the composition and formation of the planet; discusses properties of water and minerals (including the basic types of rock); covers oceanography, seismology, and the forces that build and destroy mountains; and ends with a mention of paleontology." SLJ

"Clear color photographs, maps, satellite images, and historical artwork are an integral part of a well-designed book." Horn Book Guide

The earth atlas; illustrated by Richard Bonson. Dorling Kindersley 1994 63p il maps $19.95 (5 and up)   **550**

1. Geology
ISBN 1-56458-626-X   LC 94-8765

"This very oversize volume looks at the geography of the earth, including the earth's crust, the ocean floor, and various kinds of rocks as well as the history of the earth." Booklist

"What is unique and fascinating about this book is its format: Each topic appears on a double page and consists of a brief introduction to major ideas, photographs, illustrations, maps, charts, and captions. The one-paragraph captions are crisp and informative. The full-color illustrations . . . are outstanding, and most portray geologic features in three-dimensional blocks." Sci Books Films

VanCleave, Janice Pratt

Janice VanCleave's earth science for every kid; 101 easy experiments that really work. Wiley 1991 231p il $24.95; pa $11.95 (3-5)

550

1. Earth sciences—Experiments
ISBN 0-471-54389-6; 0-471-53010-7 (pa)

LC 90-42724

Instructions for experiments, each introducing a different earth science concept

"An entertaining, educational, and nonthreatening aid to understanding earth science. The easy experiments are carefully organized." SLJ

The **Visual** dictionary of the earth. Dorling Kindersley 1993 64p il maps (Eyewitness visual dictionaries) $15.95 (4 and up)

550

1. Earth sciences
ISBN 1-56458-335-X   LC 93-18571

Also available Spanish language edition

This volume provides an "overview of the Earth and all its systems. Included among its 25 two-page topical sections are coverage of geological time; the rock cycle; mineral resources; and processes such as faulting and folding, mountain building, and weathering and erosion. In addition, the Earth's waters (rivers, lakes and groundwater, coastlines, oceans, and seas) are addressed, as well as the atmosphere and weather." Am Ref Books Annu, 1994

Includes glossary

551.1 Gross structure and properties of the earth

Cole, Joanna

The magic school bus inside the Earth; illustrated by Bruce Degen. Scholastic 1987 40p il $14.95; pa $4.95 (2-4)   **551.1**

1. Earth—Internal structure 2. Geology
ISBN 0-590-40759-7; 0-590-40760-0 (pa)

LC 87-4563

Also available Spanish language edition
Also available CD-ROM version

In this book Ms. Frizzle teaches "geology via a field trip through the center of the earth. As her class learns about fossils, rocks, and volcanoes, so will readers, absorbing information painlessly as they vicariously travel through the caves, tunnels, and up through the cone of a volcanic island shortly before it erupts. . . . Degen's bright, colorful artwork includes many witty details to delight observant children. Carried in cartoonlike balloons, the schoolmates' thoughts, banter, and asides add spice to the geology lesson. Bright, sassy, and savvy, the magic school bus books rate high in child appeal." Booklist

McNulty, Faith

How to dig a hole to the other side of the world; pictures by Marc Simont. Harper & Row 1979 32p il lib bdg $14.89; pa $4.95 (2-4)

551.1

1. Earth—Internal structure 2. Geology
ISBN 0-06-024148-9 (lib bdg); 0-06-443218-1 (pa)

LC 78-22479

A child takes an imaginary 8,000-mile journey through the earth and discovers what's inside

"The material will be useful collateral reading for students studying the internal structure of our planet." Sci Books Films

Sattler, Helen Roney

Our patchwork planet; the story of plate tectonics; illustrated by Giulio Maestro, and with photographs. Lothrop, Lee & Shepard Bks. 1995 48p il maps $16; lib bdg $15.93 (5 and up)   **551.1**

1. Plate tectonics 2. Continental drift 3. Geology
ISBN 0-688-09312-4; 0-688-09313-2 (lib bdg)
     LC 90-32623

"Sattler discusses the formation of the Earth's plates, their locations, and how their movements affect what happens on our planet's surface. She explains how earthquakes and volcanoes occur, and gives detailed descriptions of 'hot spots' in the world." SLJ

"Report writers and students seeking material to supplement textbook lessons will particularly appreciate Maestro's comprehensible diagrams and maps. . . . This title will claim a place even in basic science collections and will be useful to readers well into junior high." Bull Cent Child Books

Includes bibliographical references

551.2 Volcanoes, earthquakes, thermal waters and gases

Bramwell, Martyn

Volcanoes and earthquakes. updated ed. Watts 1994 32p il (Earth science library) lib bdg $12.60 (4-6)   **551.2**

1. Volcanoes 2. Earthquakes
ISBN 0-531-14337-6   LC 93-42018
First published 1986

Describes the causes, characteristics, and effects of volcanoes and earthquakes and examines how they can be measured and predicted

Includes glossary

Branley, Franklyn Mansfield, 1915-

Earthquakes; by Franklyn M. Branley; illustrated by Richard Rosenblum. Crowell 1990 32p il (Let's-read-and-find-out science books) $15; lib bdg $14.89; pa $4.95 (k-3)   **551.2**

1. Earthquakes
ISBN 0-690-04661-8; 0-690-04663-4 (lib bdg); 0-06-445135-6 (pa)   LC 89-35424

The author "explains what earthquakes are, where they occur, and how they change the earth. He also describes some famous quakes of the past and the efforts of scientists to predict and measure earthquakes today. On every page, line drawings, bright with watercolor washes, illustrate scenes such as shaking cityscapes, concepts such as waves emanating from the epicenter of a quake, and practical advice on what to do when the house begins to jiggle." Booklist

Volcanoes; by Franklyn M. Branley; illustrated by Marc Simont. Crowell 1985 32p il (Let's-read-and-find-out science books) lib bdg $13.89; pa $4.95 (k-3)   **551.2**

1. Volcanoes
ISBN 0-690-04431-3 (lib bdg); 0-06-445059-7 (pa)
     LC 84-45344

Explains how volcanoes are formed and how they affect the earth when they erupt

"Incorporating details sparingly, the book provides clear, easily understandable descriptions of technical points. . . . Effective also are the illustrations, for not only do they beautifully portray in vivid color the geological phenomena, but they also depict an assortment of human figures—including a plump, bespectacled geologist—with a bit more humor than might ordinarily be found in a book on this subject." Horn Book

Elting, Mary, 1909-

Volcanoes and earthquakes; [by] Mary Elting with Rachel Folsom and Robert Moll; illustrated by Courtney. Simon & Schuster Bks. for Young Readers 1990 unp il maps $9.95 (4-6)   **551.2**

1. Volcanoes 2. Earthquakes
ISBN 0-671-67217-7   LC 89-37107

Discusses how earthquakes and volcanic eruptions occur and how they can be predicted

"The information in the book is accurate and portrayed in an interesting manner, and the action shown in the illustrations further adds to the drama." Appraisal

Lauber, Patricia, 1924-

Volcano: the eruption and healing of Mount St. Helens. Bradbury Press 1986 60p il $16.95; pa $6.95 (4 and up)   **551.2**

1. Mount Saint Helens (Wash.) 2. Volcanoes
ISBN 0-02-754500-8; 0-689-71679-6 (pa)
     LC 85-22442

A Newbery Medal honor book, 1987

"A clearly written account of the volcano's 1980 eruption in Washington State, with handsome color photographs of every phase of the eruption and its aftermath. Perhaps most interesting is the detailed description of the healing process—what flora and fauna survived and how." N Y Times Book Rev

Simon, Seymour, 1931-

Earthquakes. Morrow Junior Bks. 1991 unp il maps $14.95; lib bdg $14.88; pa $5.95 (3-6)   **551.2**

1. Earthquakes
ISBN 0-688-09633-6; 0-688-09634-4 (lib bdg); 0-688-14022-X (pa)   LC 90-19328

Examines the phenomenon of earthquakes, describing how and where they occur, how they can be predicted, and how much damage they can inflict

"This makes a lasting impression with its combination of direct text and sharp color photos and drawings. . . . This informational treasure will draw science enthusiasts and browsers alike." Booklist

Volcanoes. Morrow Junior Bks. 1988 unp il $15.95; lib bdg $15.88; pa $5.95 (3-6)   **551.2**

1. Volcanoes
ISBN 0-688-07411-1; 0-688-07412-X (lib bdg); 0-688-14029-7 (pa)   LC 87-33316

"Using examples like St. Helens and the volcanoes of Iceland and Hawaii, the author is able to address all aspects of his subject: the history, nature and causes of volcanoes." Publ Wkly

"The photographs are large, informative, and spectacular,

Simon, Seymour, 1931-——*Continued*
reproduced in brilliant color. Aside from one confusing map of the earth's tectonic plates, this is a solid introduction." Bull Cent Child Books

Van Rose, Susanna
Volcano & earthquake; written by Susanna van Rose. Knopf 1992 61p il maps (Eyewitness books) $19; lib bdg $18.99 (4 and up) **551.2**
1. Volcanoes 2. Earthquakes
ISBN 0-679-81685-2; 0-679-91685-7 (lib bdg)
LC 92-4710
Also available Spanish language edition
"A Dorling Kindersley book"
Photographs and text explain the causes and effects of volcanoes and earthquakes and examine specific occurrences throughout history
"Gorgeous graphics and outstanding design. . . . Coverage is primarily visual, with brief introductory text and informative captions. . . . This book will attract readers to an already popular topic, and will provide one of the most effective introductions available." SLJ

Walker, Sally M.
Volcanoes: earth's inner fire. Carolrhoda Bks. 1994 56p il maps (Carolrhoda earth watch book) lib bdg $14.96 (3-6) **551.2**
1. Volcanoes
ISBN 0-87614-812-7
LC 93-23172
Describes volcanoes, where they form, the kinds of lava and landforms they create, and how volcanologists are learning to predict eruptions
Includes glossary

551.3 Surface and exogenous processes and their agents

Bannan, Jan Gumprecht
Sand dunes. Carolrhoda Bks. 1989 47p il (Carolrhoda earth watch book) hardcover o.p. paperback available $6.95 (3-6) **551.3**
1. Sand dunes
ISBN 0-87614-513-6 (pa)
LC 87-27978
"A look at the birth, formation, and movement of sand dunes along the Oregon coast line. Beautiful, full-color photographs and lucid text explain how the forces of sand, wind, water, and plant life determine the life cycles of sand dunes. A well-organized text assures reader understanding of the more difficult concepts." Sci Child
Includes glossary

Bramwell, Martyn
Glaciers and ice caps. updated ed. Watts 1994 32p il (Earth science library) lib bdg $12.60 (4-6) **551.3**
1. Glaciers 2. Polar regions
ISBN 0-531-14302-3
LC 93-42017
First published 1986
This volume discusses the formation of glaciers and ice caps, life in the Arctic region, and scientific exploration in Antarctica
Includes glossary

Simon, Seymour, 1931-
Icebergs and glaciers. Morrow 1987 unp il $15; lib bdg $14.95 (3-5) **551.3**
1. Glaciers 2. Icebergs
ISBN 0-688-06186-9; 0-688-06187-7 (lib bdg)
LC 86-18142
"After an explanation of the consistency of snowflakes, packed snow, and ice fields, the text describes the movement of glaciers by sliding or creeping, various processes of measurement, landscape alteration, geological effects of glacial movement, and the formation of icebergs." Bull Cent Child Books
The author "chronicles the development of glaciers and icebergs with a wonderfully clear, almost Spartan text that receives all of the support necessary from the magnificent color photographs which accompany it. . . . This book would be an excellent addition to any elementary school library or any personal juvenile collection." Appraisal

Walker, Sally M.
Glaciers; ice on the move. Carolrhoda Bks. 1990 47p il (Carolrhoda earth watch book) lib bdg $19.95 (3-6) **551.3**
1. Glaciers
ISBN 0-87614-373-7
LC 89-22102
This volume examines "how glaciers are formed, how they move, how they terminate, and how they have changed the surface and shape of the terrain over which they have moved. Walker discusses the possibilites of tapping glaciers as possible sources of clean water and of energy." Bull Cent Child Books
"The author manages to pack a significant amount of information into a slim volume. . . . The prose is clear, and, with minor exceptions, the illustrations are extraordinarily good." Sci Books Films

551.4 Geomorphology and hydrosphere

Bramwell, Martyn
Mountains. updated ed. Watts 1994 31p il (Earth science library) lib bdg $12.60 (4 and up) **551.4**
1. Mountains
ISBN 0-531-14303-1
LC 93-40313
First published 1986
Describes the characteristics, formation and ecology of mountains
Includes glossary

Henderson, Kathy
The Great Lakes. Childrens Press 1989 45p il lib bdg $13.50; pa $4.95 (2-4) **551.4**
1. Great Lakes
ISBN 0-516-01163-4 (lib bdg); 0-516-41163-2 (pa)
LC 88-34670
"A New true book"
An introduction to the five fresh-water lakes that contain one-fifth of the earth's standing fresh water
"Captioned, mostly full-color photographs on nearly every page provide visual interest, while short sentences and a simple writing style allows easy access for beginning readers without sacrificing substance." Booklist

Kramer, Stephen

Caves; photographs by Kenrick L. Day. Carolrhoda Bks. 1995 48p il (Nature in action) lib bdg $14.21; pa $7.95 (4-6)   **551.4**

1. Caves
ISBN 0-87614-447-4 (lib bdg); 0-87614-896-8 (pa)
LC 93-42136

The author "explains many aspects of speleology. He discusses various kinds of caves but focuses on limestone caves, describing the creation of stalactites, stalagmites, and other speleothems, giving an overview of cave flora and fauna, and offering guidelines for those interested in exploring caves themselves." Bull Cent Child Books

"Through an enticing introduction, full-color photographs of spectacular sites and features, and a generally accurate and useful text, this book provides readers with a glimpse of the alluring world of caving." SLJ

Includes glossary

Peters, Lisa Westberg

The sun, the wind and the rain; illustrated by Ted Rand. Holt & Co. 1988 unp il $13.95; pa $5.95 (k-2)   **551.4**

1. Mountains 2. Nature
ISBN 0-8050-0699-0; 0-8050-1481-0 (pa)
LC 87-23808

"This colorfully illustrated book presents geology concepts to young children. Pictures of a young girl making a mountain of sand and of a regular mountain are paired to introduce children to the ideas of mountain building, weathering, and erosion. . . . This book is a good addition to a classroom library for children who can read or for younger nonreaders who can follow the pictures." Sci Child

Simon, Seymour, 1931-

Mountains. Morrow Junior Bks. 1994 unp il $15; lib bdg $14.93 (3-6)   **551.4**

1. Mountains
ISBN 0-688-11040-1; 0-688-11041-X (lib bdg)
LC 93-11398

Introduces various mountain ranges, how they are formed and shaped, and how they affect vegetation and animals, including humans

"The striking color photographs work well with the clear text to illustrate key points and highlight the diversity among the Earth's mountain ranges." Horn Book Guide

Zoehfeld, Kathleen Weidner

How mountains are made; illustrated by James Graham Hale. HarperCollins Pubs. 1995 29p il maps (Let's-read-and-find-out science books) $14.95; lib bdg $14.89; pa $4.95 (k-3)   **551.4**

1. Mountains 2. Geology
ISBN 0-06-024509-3; 0-06-024510-7 (lib bdg); 0-06-445128-3 (pa)   LC 93-45436

"Four children and a dog climbing a forest trail provide the framework for this discussion of mountains. Along the way, the knowledgeable characters explain the earth's structure and tectonic plates as well as the different types of mountains and how they are formed." Booklist

"The text and illustrations work together well in this sequential, well-organized book. Much credit goes to Hale's engaging watercolor illustrations done in cheery colors; they are simply drawn but add effective examples and diagrams." SLJ

551.46 Hydrosphere. Oceanography

Bramwell, Martyn

The oceans. updated ed. Watts 1994 32p il maps (Earth science library) lib bdg $12.90 (4-6)   **551.46**

1. Ocean 2. Marine biology
ISBN 0-531-14304-X   LC 93-40312
First published 1987

This book contains 13 illustrated chapters on such topics as: ocean currents; explorers and traders; the surging tides; and life in the oceans

Includes glossary

Ganeri, Anita, 1961-

The oceans atlas; illustrated by Luciano Corbella. Dorling Kindersley 1994 63p il maps $19.95 (5 and up)   **551.46**

1. Ocean
ISBN 1-56458-475-5   LC 93-28724
Also available Spanish language edition

"More a broad introduction to facts about the Earth's oceans than an atlas, the lavishly illustrated, oversized book briefly explains many relevant topics, including plate tectonics, the vertical food chain, the continental shelf, and hydrothermal vents." Horn Book Guide

This volume "offers an amazing amount of well-written, accurate information, complemented by wonderful photographs and clear, easy-to-understand illustrations." Sci Child

Johnson, Rebecca L.

Diving into darkness: a submersible explores the sea. Lerner Publs. 1989 72p il lib bdg $22.95 (4 and up)   **551.46**

1. Submersibles 2. Underwater exploration
ISBN 0-8225-1587-3   LC 88-27154

"A brief, straightforward history of undersea explorations, followed by a discussion of the work of Edwin Link. The equipment used during the course of a dive is effectively described. Photographs are vivid and well chosen; the environmental aspect is mentioned." Horn Book

Includes glossary

Kraske, Robert

The voyager's stone; the adventures of a message-carrying bottle adrift on the ocean sea; illustrated by Brian Floca. Orchard Bks. 1995 unp il maps $15.95; lib bdg $15.99 (4 and up)   **551.46**

1. Oceanography
ISBN 0-531-06890-0; 0-531-08740-9 (lib bdg)
LC 94-21049

"A Richard Jackson book"

"Although written as a fictional account of a message-carrying bottle, this book really explores oceanography—currents, animals, and the variety of life found at the margins of the world's oceans. While on a Caribbean vacation, a boy from Minnesota puts a message in a bottle. His note is eventually retrieved by a girl living on Australia's north coast." Booklist

"Illustrator Floca's plentiful maps will keep readers firmly afloat and his cross-hatched pen illustrations add drama." Bull Cent Child Books

Markle, Sandra, 1946-

Pioneering ocean depths. Atheneum Bks. for Young Readers 1995 48p il $17 (4-6)

551.46

1. Underwater exploration 2. Oceanography

ISBN 0-689-31823-5   LC 93-33555

This book describes how scientists explore the ocean and includes simple home experiments that resemble those that scientists perform

"Each page is illustrated with one or more nondistinctive full-color photograph of scientists at work, ships and underwater vessels, and the animal and plant life found at various depths. The experiments are performed by the same three children throughout, two girls and one boy, and their pleasure at learning is shown on their faces." SLJ

Peters, Lisa Westberg

Water's way; illustrated by Ted Rand. Arcade Pub. 1991 unp il $14.95 (k-2)

551.46

1. Water

ISBN 1-55970-062-9   LC 90-55648

This is "an attempt to show the many forms that H$_2$O takes in the atmosphere and on Earth, contrasting the weather conditions on a winter day with the changing water forms inside a boy's home." SLJ

"Ted Rand's background as a landscape painter always tells in his picture books, and never better than in his clean pictures of the moods of sky and weather. . . . [The] brief text gracefully parallels, on facing pages, the actions of weather inside and out." Bull Cent Child Books

Simon, Seymour, 1931-

How to be an ocean scientist in your own home; illustrated by David A. Carter. Lippincott 1988 136p il lib bdg $14.89 (4 and up)

551.46

1. Oceanography—Experiments

ISBN 0-397-32292-5   LC 87-45988

"Twenty-four easy-to-understand experiments with readily available materials that can be done safely at home are described clearly and provocatively. Labeled line drawings illustrate activities that range from investigating seawater to making waves to hatching and studying brine shrimp. Includes suppliers for aquarium materials." Sci Child

Includes bibliography

Oceans. Morrow Junior Bks. 1990 unp il $13.95; lib bdg $13.88 (3-6)   **551.46**

1. Ocean

ISBN 0-688-09453-8; 0-688-09454-6 (lib bdg)

LC 89-28452

This book "covers the geography of the ocean floor, major currents, and El Nino (a shift in the prevailing currents that causes severe climactic changes). Tides, tsunami, waves, coastal erosion, and marine life are also touched upon." Booklist

"Simon presents clear, simplified explanations of natural phenomena with well-chosen full-color photographs that go beyond decoration. He includes good black-and-white diagrams of how tides work and how waves form and transfer energy. The endpapers are maps of the world showing how and where the major currents flow." SLJ

Waters, John F.

Deep-sea vents; living worlds without sun. Cobblehill Bks. 1994 48p il $14.99 (4 and up)

551.46

1. Ocean bottom 2. Marine biology

ISBN 0-525-65145-4   LC 92-41111

Describes the discovery and investigation of openings in the ocean floor where heated water escapes and examines the new life forms and other phenomena that have been found there

"This is a satisfying introduction. . . . Fine photographs illustrate fauna, ships, gear, and the people involved in this world-wide deep-ocean study and of the physical and chemical properties of the ocean at those vents." Sci Books Films

551.47 Tides, ocean currents, ocean waves

Souza, D. M. (Dorothy M.)

Powerful waves. Carolrhoda Bks. 1992 48p il maps (Nature in action) lib bdg $19.95 (4-6)

551.47

1. Ocean waves 2. Tsunamis

ISBN 0-87614-661-2   LC 91-885

Facts about ordinary waves precede information about the causes of the huge waves known as tsunamis and the destruction they bring

"Several examples of the horrible damage caused by tsunamis are included, along with many excellent photographs and drawings of places that tsunamis have actually struck. This would be an excellent reference book to use when studying oceanography in the middle school." Sci Books Films

Includes glossary

551.48 Hydrology

Bramwell, Martyn

Rivers and lakes. updated ed. Watts 1994 31p il maps (Earth science library) lib bdg $12.60 (4-6)   **551.48**

1. Rivers 2. Lakes

ISBN 0-531-14305-8   LC 93-40311

First published 1986 in the United Kingdom; first United States edition, 1987

This book "explains the origins of these water sources and their development. Specific habitats and wildlife associated with each water body are described. The remarkable properties of water and its function as 'nature's bloodstream' are apprised. Bramwell details drought, underground rivers, water at work, and pollution. . . . Could be used for both research and teacher-guided explorations." SLJ

Includes glossary

Cole, Joanna

The magic school bus at the waterworks; illustrated by Bruce Degen. Scholastic 1986 39p il $14.95; pa $4.95 (2-4)   **551.48**

1. Water 2. Water supply

ISBN 0-590-43739-9; 0-590-40360-5 (pa)

LC 86-6672

Also available Spanish language edition
Also available CD-ROM version

Cole, Joanna—*Continued*

The author presents "specific facts about water and a memorable image of the water cycle process. The story involves a 'strange' teacher who takes her class on a magical trip: up to the clouds—down to earth in raindrops—down a stream into a reservoir where the water is purified—finally into the underground pipes leading back to school. The illustrations both enhance the humor and provide visual presentation of the water cycle." Appraisal

Dorros, Arthur

Follow the water from brook to ocean; written and illustrated by Arthur Dorros. HarperCollins Pubs. 1991 32p il (Let's-read-and-find-out science books) lib bdg $14.89; pa $4.95 (k-3)   **551.48**

1. Water

ISBN 0-06-021599-2 (lib bdg); 0-06-445115-1 (pa)
     LC 90-1438

Explains how water flows from brooks, to streams, to rivers, over waterfalls, through canyons and dams, to eventually reach the ocean

"An excellent presentation of introductory material about water. . . . The illustrations are simple, almost childlike, in soft colors." SLJ

Rauzon, Mark J.

Water, water everywhere; [by] Mark J. Rauzon and Cynthia Overbeck Bix. Sierra Club Bks. for Children 1994 32p il $14.95; pa $5.95 (k-3)   **551.48**

1. Water

ISBN 0-87156-598-6; 0-87156-383-5 (pa)
     LC 92-34521

Describes the forms water takes, how it has shaped Earth, and its importance to life

"Water's vital role in the life of our planet is vividly portrayed in a crisp, economical text that cultivates respect for the environment. . . . Striking, often full-page, color photographs will engage the imagination of young readers." Horn Book Guide

Robbins, Ken

Water; the elements. Holt & Co. 1994 unp il $16.95 (4-6)   **551.48**

1. Water

ISBN 0-8050-2257-0   LC 93-44632

The author "begins with the water cycle—clouds forming, fog, and various types of precipitation. Next the reader views a variety of water bodies and learns how each is unique. Finally he finishes the book with ways in which man uses water—drinking, washing, irrigation, power, boating, fishing, swimming, fountains and rituals." Appraisal

"Hand-colored photographs illustrate the multitude of wondrous forms that water can take, while a poetic text describes the continuous interplay of water within its various reservoirs, including the atmosphere, oceans, glaciers, and springs. . . . Without preaching, Robbins quietly instills in the reader a sense of respect for this precious commodity." Horn Book

551.5   Meteorology

Bramwell, Martyn

Weather. updated ed. Watts 1994 32p il maps (Earth science library) lib bdg $12.60 (4-6)   **551.5**

1. Weather

ISBN 0-531-14306-6   LC 93-42016

First published 1987 in the United Kingdom; first United States edition, 1988

"This introduction to the science of meteorology, explains the forces that cause clouds, winds, and weather. Also discusses weather observing and forecasting." SLJ

Includes glossary

Branley, Franklyn Mansfield, 1915-

Air is all around you; by Franklyn M. Branley; illustrated by Holly Keller. rev ed. Crowell 1986 31p il (Let's-read-and-find-out science books) lib bdg $14.89; pa $4.95 (k-1)   **551.5**

1. Air

ISBN 0-690-04503-4 (lib bdg); 0-06-445048-1 (pa)
     LC 85-45405

A revised and newly illustrated edition of the title first published 1962

Describes the various properties of air and shows how to prove that air takes up space and that there is air dissolved in water

"Illustrations in both bold and pastel colors are coordinated with the easy-to-read text and make this an eye-pleasing and informative book." SLJ

Flash, crash, rumble, and roll; by Franklyn M. Branley; pictures by Barbara and Ed Emberley. rev ed. Crowell 1985 31p il (Let's-read-and-find-out science books) lib bdg $14.89; pa $4.95 (k-3)   **551.5**

1. Thunderstorms 2. Lightning 3. Rain

ISBN 0-690-04425-9 (lib bdg); 0-06-445012-0 (pa)
     LC 84-45333

First published 1964

The author "explains how thunderclouds form, why lightning occurs, and why thunder sometimes sounds so loud. He discusses the dangers of lightning and describes the best ways to stay safe." Publisher's note

It's raining cats and dogs; all kinds of weather, and why we have it; by Franklyn M. Branley; illustrated by True Kelley. Houghton Mifflin 1987 112p il $14.95 (3-6)   **551.5**

1. Rain 2. Weather

ISBN 0-395-33070-X   LC 86-27546

Also available in paperback from Avon Bks.

"Human hailstones, pink and green snow, St. Elmo's Fire, dancing devils, horse latitudes, and contrails and distrails are among the curiosities explained in this anecdotal . . . discussion of weather phenomena. . . . There are . . . lists of precautions to follow during lightning and tornadoes as well as . . . instructions for measuring rainfall, wind velocity, and air pollution." Horn Book

The author "intersperses factual information about clouds, precipitation, and winds with interesting anecdotes and easy experiments. The amusing black-and-gray wash illustrations are helpful in setting up the experiments." SLJ

Includes bibliography

Dorros, Arthur

Feel the wind; written and illustrated by Arthur Dorros. Crowell 1989 32p il (Let's-read-and-find-out science books) lib bdg $14.89; pa $4.95 (k-3) **551.5**

1. Winds

ISBN 0-690-04741-X (lib bdg); 0-06-445095-3 (pa)

LC 88-18961

"The motion of air in the form of wind is discernible in many ways. Simple text accompanied by bright illustrations explains the causes, power, effects, and uses of wind. Encourages outdoor experimentation." Sci Child

Gallant, Roy A.

Rainbows, mirages and sundogs; the sky as a source of wonder. Macmillan 1987 94p il $14.95 (4 and up) **551.5**

1. Meteorology 2. Optics

ISBN 0-02-737010-0

LC 86-23728

Discusses and explains visual phenomena seen in the sky, primarily interactions of light and atmosphere such as rainbows, mirages, the twinkling of stars, the blue color of the sky, and the Northern Lights

"The lucid, thorough text raises questions, provides considerable scientific detail, and includes instructions for conducting intriguing and relatively simple demonstrations. . . . There are captioned diagrams to illustrate many of the explanations, and several of the photographs have an almost surreal look as they capture instances of light that are indeed unearthly." Horn Book

Kahl, Jonathan D.

Thunderbolt; learning about lightning. Lerner Publs. 1994 56p il (How's the weather?) lib bdg $19.95 (4-6) **551.5**

1. Lightning 2. Thunderstorms

ISBN 0-8225-2528-3

LC 92-45177

"Kahl describes the conditions under which thunderstorms develop, how lightning travels through the sky, what happens when it strikes, and how scientists study it. He provides interesting examples of damage caused by lightning to property and people and gives safety tips. . . . Instructions for photographing lightning are included." SLJ

Includes glossary

Kramer, Stephen

Lightning; photographs by Warren Faidley. Carolrhoda Bks. 1992 48p il (Nature in action) lib bdg $18.95; pa $7.95 (4-6) **551.5**

1. Lightning

ISBN 0-87614-422-9 (lib bdg); 0-87614-617-5 (pa)

LC 91-21793

This introduction to lightning "explains how a thunderhead develops, how lightning results from negatively and positively charged electrons, kinds of lightning, and [includes] safety information." Bull Cent Child Books

"Diagrams supplement the well-written narrative in describing scientific concepts. Exceptionally fine, full-color photographs—each a work of art—perfectly illustrate the text, powerfully and spectacularly showing the majesty and might of this phenomenon." SLJ

Includes glossary

McVey, Vicki

The Sierra Club book of weatherwisdom; illustrated by Martha Weston. Sierra Club Bks. 1991 104p il maps $16.95 (4-6) **551.5**

1. Weather

ISBN 0-316-56341-2

LC 90-20501

Discusses climates and seasons, wind and rain, warm and cold fronts, atmospheric pressure, and weather prediction. Features activities, games, and experiments

"Written in a bright, conversational style and illustrated with effective pencil drawings on nearly every page, this eminently readable book offers solid information in an informal way that should suit its intended audience." Booklist

Includes glossary

Robbins, Ken

Air. Holt & Co. 1995 unp il (Elements) $16.95 (4-6) **551.5**

1. Air

ISBN 0-8050-2292-9

LC 95-6692

In this photo essay "topics range from oxygen to oxidation, airplanes to seed dispersion." N Y Times Book Rev

"Robbins's carefully chosen palettes emphasize what he wishes readers to see in his writing, and complement his brief text page by page." SLJ

Simon, Seymour, 1931-

Weather. Morrow Junior Bks. 1993 unp il $15; lib bdg $14.93 (3-6) **551.5**

1. Weather 2. Meteorology

ISBN 0-688-10546-7; 0-688-10547-5 (lib bdg)

LC 92-31069

Explores the causes, changing patterns, and forecasting of weather

"Gorgeous full-page color photos, helped by a few cogent diagrams, illustrate Simon's outline of how weather works. . . . The organization is clear and logical." Bull Cent Child Books

551.55 Atmospheric disturbances and formations

Erlbach, Arlene

Hurricanes. Childrens Press 1993 45p il lib bdg $13.50; pa $5.50 (2-4) **551.55**

1. Hurricanes

ISBN 0-516-01333-5 (lib bdg); 0-516-41333-3 (pa)

LC 92-37811

"A New true book"

Describes the movements and destructive power of hurricanes and explains how they are predicted and monitored

"Included is an explanation of how hurricanes are classified by their wind speed, with Category 5 being the most destructive. Informative charts illustrate the five categories. The system used to name hurricanes is also discussed briefly. This is a very interesting and well-written book." Sci Books Films

Tornadoes. Childrens Press 1994 45p il lib bdg $13.50; pa $5.50 (2-4) **551.55**

1. Tornadoes

ISBN 0-516-01071-9 (lib bdg); 0-516-41071-7 (pa)

LC 94-10472

"A New true book"

Erlbach, Arlene—*Continued*

"*Tornadoes* describes this weather phenomena, and how weathermen track their path so they can issue warnings." Appraisal

"The remarkably clear full-color photos show examples of these destructive windstorms and their aftereffects. . . . An excellent addition to any weather section." SLJ

Includes glossary

Hiscock, Bruce, 1940-

The big storm; written and illustrated by Bruce Hiscock. Atheneum Pubs. 1993 unp il maps $14.95 (k-3)   **551.55**

1. Storms 2. Weather
ISBN 0-689-31770-0   LC 92-13973

This presents information on basic weather phenomena while describing a particularly devastating storm that moved across the United States in March-April 1982

"Excellent maps, charts, and diagrams enhance the easily read text." Sci Child

Kahl, Jonathan D.

Storm warning; tornadoes and hurricanes. Lerner Publs. 1993 64p il maps (How's the weather?) lib bdg $19.95 (4-6)   **551.55**

1. Tornadoes 2. Hurricanes
ISBN 0-8225-2527-5   LC 92-13627

"The development of thunderstorms, necessary precursors to tornadoes, is explained with a discussion of water vapor, condensation, latent heat, and mechanisms that create upward air currents. The formation of hurricanes, which depends on some of the same physics, but on a different scale, follows logically. A brief survey of some severe tornadoes and hurricanes provides a view of the destruction they can wreak." Sci Books Films

Kahl "uses clear, uncomplicated terms to describe and explain complex phenomena. Sharp, full-color photographs appropriately illustrate the text." SLJ

Includes glossary

Kramer, Stephen

Tornado. Carolrhoda Bks. 1992 48p il maps (Nature in action) lib bdg $18.95 (4-6)   **551.55**

1. Tornadoes
ISBN 0-87614-660-4   LC 91-42520

Describes the formation, different types, and study of tornadoes

"Kramer explains in an easy-to-read, straightforward style what tornadoes are. . . . Excellent colorful photographs and illustrations in an uncluttered layout add to the attractiveness of this book." Appraisal

Includes glossary

Simon, Seymour, 1931-

Storms. Morrow Junior Bks. 1989 unp il $16; lib bdg $15.93; pa $4.95 (3-6)

     551.55

1. Storms
ISBN 0-688-07413-8; 0-688-07414-6 (lib bdg); 0-688-11708-2 (pa)   LC 88-22045

This book describes the atmospheric conditions which create thunderstorms, hailstorms, lightning, tornadoes, and hurricanes and how violent weather affects the environment and people

"The half- to full-page glossy color photographs are sure to attract young readers as will the subject. *Storms* is an excellent way to introduce the science of meteorology to children." Sci Books Films

551.57   Hydrometeorology

Branley, Franklyn Mansfield, 1915-

Rain & hail; illustrated by Harriett Barton. rev ed. Crowell 1983 39p il (Let's-read-and-find-out science books) lib bdg $14.89 (k-3)   **551.57**

1. Rain 2. Hail
ISBN 0-690-04353-8   LC 83-45058

A newly illustrated edition of the title first published 1963

A "clear, simple explanation of where rain and hail come from, tracing the cycle from water vapor to raindrops and hail. . . . Whereas the original illustrations were merely decorative and are now dated, Barton's new watercolors are good-humored pictures that add extra information as well as diagrams that simply detail the text." SLJ

Snow is falling; by Franklyn M. Branley; illustrated by Holly Keller. rev ed. Crowell 1986 32p il (Let's-read-and-find-out science books) lib bdg $14.89; pa $4.95 (k-1)

     551.57

1. Snow
ISBN 0-690-04548-4 (lib bdg); 0-06-445058-9 (pa)
     LC 85-48256

A newly illustrated edition of the title first published 1963

Describes the characteristics of snow, its usefulness to plants and animals, and the hazards it can cause

"The vocabulary level allows beginning readers to manage the material with little help, with the advantage of the child having the chance to experience firsthand the idea that books don't always have to have a story; books filled with facts also can be interesting. The illustrations are colorful and childlike. They provide not only visual satisfaction but visual information." Sci Books Films

De Paola, Tomie, 1934-

The cloud book; words and pictures by Tomie de Paola. Holiday House 1975 30p il lib bdg $15.95; pa $5.95 (k-3)   **551.57**

1. Clouds
ISBN 0-8234-0259-2 (lib bdg); 0-8234-0531-1 (pa)

Also available Spanish language edition

The author instructs "young readers about the ten most common types of clouds, how they were named, and what they mean in terms of changing weather. Actually a very good text to use for early science instruction. Includes a scattering of traditional myths that have clouds as a basis." Adventuring with Books

Kahl, Jonathan D.

Wet weather; rain showers and snowfall. Lerner Publs. 1992 64p il map (How's the weather?) lib bdg $19.95 (4-6)   **551.57**

1. Rain 2. Snow
ISBN 0-8225-2526-7   LC 91-26065

Kahl, Jonathan D.—*Continued*

Explains the water cycle: where water comes from, how clouds are formed, weather patterns that bring rain or snow, and more

"Fifty-four pages of well-edited text, with 34 color photos and 6 graphics, comprise an attractive introduction to meterology for elementary school children." Sci Books Films

Includes glossary

Lampton, Christopher

Drought. Millbrook Press 1992 63p il lib bdg $13.40; pa $5.95 (4-6)   **551.57**

1. Droughts

ISBN 1-56294-125-9 (lib bdg); 1-878841-91-2 (pa)

LC 91-18053

"A Disaster! book"

Investigates the causes and disastrous effects of drought, giving the history of some of the severest droughts on record in the United States and elsewhere

This is "delightful. . . . The photographs and illustrations are excellent and to the point. The hydrologic cycle is particularly well done." Sci Books Films

Includes glossary and bibliography

Markle, Sandra, 1946-

A rainy day; illustrated by Cathy Johnson. Orchard Bks. 1993 unp il $14.95; lib bdg $14.99 (k-2)   **551.57**

1. Rain

ISBN 0-531-05976-6; 0-531-08576-7 (lib bdg)

LC 91-17059

Examines simple scientific concepts by observing the effect of raindrops on puddles, the sky, animals, and the surrounding landscape on a rainy day

"The text is straightforward and friendly, associating scientific concepts with familiar objects and examples. The visual narrative is supplied by watercolors that picture a young girl in a yellow slicker exploring her environment before, during, and after the rain." Booklist

McMillan, Bruce

The weather sky; photographed, illustrated, and written by Bruce McMillan. Farrar, Straus & Giroux 1991 40p il maps $16.95 (4 and up)   **551.57**

1. Weather 2. Clouds

ISBN 0-374-38261-1   LC 90-56151

A study of weather patterns and clouds that occur in the Earth's temperate zones

"The well-chosen black-and-white and color photographs . . . are as important in conveying the information as the text. . . . A clear and coherent introduction to meteorology that will certainly encourage readers to do some forecasting of their own." SLJ

Includes glossary

551.6 Climatology and weather

DeWitt, Lynda

What will the weather be? illustrated by Carolyn Croll. HarperCollins Pubs. 1991 32p il (Let's-read-and-find-out science books) lib bdg $14.89; pa $4.95 (k-3)   **551.6**

1. Weather forecasting

ISBN 0-06-021597-6 (lib bdg); 0-06-445113-5 (pa)

LC 90-1446

Explains the basic characteristics of weather—temperature, humidity, wind speed and direction, air pressure—and how meteorologists gather data for their forecasts

Gibbons, Gail

Weather forecasting. Four Winds Press 1987 unp il $13.95; pa $4.95 (k-3)   **551.6**

1. Weather forecasting

ISBN 0-02-737250-2; 0-689-71683-4 (pa)

LC 86-7602

"The book is divided into four sections, one per season, which treat different kinds of weather as they're observed, recorded, and reported at a weather station." Bull Cent Child Books

"Any child can learn the basic concepts from the text at the bottom of each page, while the precocious can garner an impressive weather vocabulary by absorbing the terms la beled and defined within the artwork. Brightly illustrated with the artist's usual bold, flat colors, this book will serve as an appealing introduction to weather forecasting for young children." Booklist

Weather words and what they mean. Holiday House 1990 unp il $15.95; pa $5.95 (k-3)   **551.6**

1. Weather

ISBN 0-8234-0805-1; 0-8234-0952-X (pa)

LC 89-39515

The author discusses the meaning of meteorological terms such as temperature, air pressure, thunderstorm and moisture

"Gibbons' easily identifiable artistic style works well with her explanations of sometimes misunderstood weather-related terms. Drawings are appealing, attractively arranged, and closely matched to the textual information. . . . An attractive introduction for weather units in the primary grades." SLJ

Kahl, Jonathan D.

Weatherwise; learning about the weather. Lerner Publs. 1992 64p il maps (How's the weather?) lib bdg $19.95 (4-6)   **551.6**

1. Weather

ISBN 0-8225-2525-9   LC 91-2015

Discusses many aspects of weather, including climate and the seasons, wind, humidity, clouds, rain, and weather forecasting

Includes glossary

552   Petrology

De Paola, Tomie, 1934-
The quicksand book. Holiday House 1977 unp il lib bdg $15.95; pa $5.95 (k-3)   **552**

1. Quicksand
ISBN 0-8234-0291-6 (lib bdg); 0-8234-0532-X (pa)
LC 76-28762

Also available Spanish language edition
"Jungle Girl, swinging on a vine from her treehouse, falls into a patch of . . . [quicksand] but, fortunately, is observed by Jungle Boy. As she slowly sinks, her scholarly bespectacled young Tarzan delivers a long but interesting lecture on the properties of and useful means of rescue from quicksand." Horn Book
"De Paola "uses a picture-book format to present basic science information in an utterly appealing, humorous way. . . . Very funny and very sensible." SLJ

Gans, Roma, 1894-
Rock collecting; illustrated by Holly Keller. Crowell 1984 28p il (Let's-read-and-find-out science books) lib bdg $14.89; pa $4.95 (k-3)   **552**

1. Rocks—Collectors and collecting
ISBN 0-690-04266-3 (lib bdg); 0-06-445063-5 (pa)
LC 83-46170

The author includes some "hints on how to start and organize a rock collection, but the major emphasis of the book is on the history, types and uses of rocks. She refers to the use of concrete for sidewalks and chalk for blackboards, and also some historical applications, such as the pyramids in Egypt. The three main kinds of rocks—igneous, metamorphic and sedimentary—are also explained with examples." SLJ
"The text is considerably enlivened by Keller's three-color, cartoon-style pictures and clearly labeled diagrams. Actual small photographs of rocks are also inserted into the art." Booklist

Selsam, Millicent Ellis, 1912-
A first look at rocks; by Millicent E. Selsam and Joyce Hunt; illustrated by Harriett Springer. Walker & Co. 1984 32p il lib bdg $12.85 (1-3)   **552**

1. Rocks 2. Petrology
ISBN 0-8027-6531-9
LC 83-40394

This book describes the three main types of rocks: sedimentary, metamorphic, and igneous
"There are frequent references in the text to the large, carefully-detailed black-and-white drawings which clearly show distinguishing characteristics." SLJ

553.4   Metals and semimetals

Meltzer, Milton, 1915-
Gold; the true story of why people search for it, mine it, trade it, steal it, mint it, hoard it, shape it, wear it, fight and kill for it. HarperCollins Pubs. 1993 167p il $15; lib bdg $14.89 (4 and up)   **553.4**

1. Gold
ISBN 0-06-022983-7; 0-06-022984-5 (lib bdg)
LC 92-44497

"Meltzer explores the history, economics, and sociology connected with the precious metal. The clear and interesting view of world history through a very specific lens has sure-fire appeal, and the intriguing material, illustrated with black-and-white photographs, is carefully written and researched." Horn Book Guide
Includes bibliography

553.7   Water

Devonshire, Hilary
Water. Watts 1991 32p il (Science through art) lib bdg $13.23 (3-5)   **553.7**

1. Water 2. Art and science
ISBN 0-531-14125-X
LC 91-8378

Defines and demonstrates the properties of water through artistic experiments and projects
This is a "valuable asset to teachers and youth leaders for adapting art to their science curricula. What an exciting and creative method of study!" Sci Books Films
Includes glossary

Seixas, Judith S.
Water: what it is, what it does; illustrated by Tom Huffman. Greenwillow Bks. 1987 56p il $13; lib bdg $12.93 (1-3)   **553.7**

1. Water
ISBN 0-688-06607-0; 0-688-06608-9 (lib bdg)
LC 86-14926

"A Greenwillow read-alone book"
A simple introduction to water, describing its properties, uses, and interaction with people and the environment. Includes five basic experiments
"Readers should gain from *Water* a scientific understanding and appreciation of water's importance to all life forms and the need to protect and conserve it as a natural resource. The format is clear, the illustrations add to the text, and the sequence is logical." SLJ

560   Paleontology. Paleozoology

Aliki
Fossils tell of long ago. rev ed. Crowell 1990 32p il (Let's-read-and-find-out science books) lib bdg $14.89; pa $4.95 (k-3)   **560**

1. Fossils
ISBN 0-690-31379-9 (lib bdg); 0-06-445093-7 (pa)
LC 89-17247

Also available Spanish language edition
First published 1972
"Information about how fossils are formed and discovered is presented in simple text and an appealing variety of colorful illustrations. Includes directions for creating a fossil." Sci Child

Arnold, Caroline, 1944-
Trapped in tar; fossils from the Ice Age; photographs by Richard Hewett. Clarion Bks. 1987 57p il hardcover o.p. paperback available $5.95 (3-5)   **560**

1. Fossil mammals
ISBN 0-395-54783-0 (pa)
LC 86-17614

Arnold, Caroline, 1944-—*Continued*
"California's Rancho La Brea tar pits are the subject of this photo essay, which explains what the tar pits are and why they are important for scientists studying Ice Age life. . . . Arnold describes how the remains are excavated and briefly surveys the kinds of large and small animals that have been discovered." Booklist
"In addition to the inherent child appeal of the subject and the clear explanations, the book has a lively format, with pictures dramatically featuring young museum visitors in involved inspection or even hands-on experience of the displays." Bull Cent Child Books

Gibbons, Gail
Prehistoric animals. Holiday House 1988 unp il lib bdg $15.95 (k-3)   **560**
1. Prehistoric animals 2. Fossils
ISBN 0-8234-0707-1   LC 88-4661
Introduces, in text and illustrations, a variety of prehistoric animals whose fossilized remains have provided scientists with clues about their physical characteristics and the environment in which they lived
"A prehistoric animal 'timeline,' covering a period from 65 million to 10 thousand years ago, is helpful. Color illustrations of the animals set against simple stylized backgrounds offer a suggestion of scale." Booklist

Henderson, Douglas
Dinosaur tree. Bradbury Press 1994 31p il $15.95 (2-4)   **560**
1. Fossil plants 2. Dinosaurs
ISBN 0-02-743547-4   LC 93-34204
This book traces the hypothetical life cycle of a conifer tree not fossilized in the Petrified Forest National Park in Arizona. "Each full-page painting faces a page of text that explains the surrounding atmospheric, plant, and animal conditions as [the] tree grows in a Triassic forest. The tree's story starts 225 million years ago, and readers see it at 4 years, 50 years, 200 years, 300 years, 400 years, 500 years, and then . . . fossilization. Dinosaurs that lived at the time are pictured in their natural surroundings." SLJ
Includes glossary

Lauber, Patricia, 1924-
Dinosaurs walked here, and other stories fossils tell. Bradbury Press 1987 56p il maps $16.95; pa $5.95 (3-5)   **560**
1. Fossils 2. Geology 3. Dinosaurs
ISBN 0-02-754510-5; 0-689-71603-6 (pa)
          LC 86-8239
Discusses how fossilized remains of plants and animals reveal the characteristics of the prehistoric world
"A marvelous introduction to fossils, those fascinating windows to ancient landscapes and seascapes of Earth's prehistoric past. The polished, lucid text is accompanied by superb, full-color photographs, paintings, and maps in an appealing volume." Sci Child

Lindsay, William
Prehistoric life; photographed by Harry Taylor. Knopf 1994 63p il maps (Eyewitness books) $16; lib bdg $16.99 (4 and up)
          560
1. Fossils 2. Evolution
ISBN 0-679-86001-0; 0-679-96001-5 (lib bdg)
          LC 93-32076

Also available Spanish language edition
"A Dorling Kindersley book"
The author discusses "the fossil record and its evolutionary implications. . . . The information presented with the excellent photos of fossils and reconstructions is fact focused and generally accurate. In addition to presentations on various early life forms, there are pages devoted to the ice ages, fossil hunting, and extinctions." Sci Books Films

Rand McNally picture atlas of prehistoric life; illustrated by Tim Hayward; written by Robert Muir Wood. Rand McNally 1992 64p il maps $16.95 (4 and up)   **560**
1. Prehistoric animals 2. Fossils
ISBN 0-528-83525-4   LC 92-5761
Provides a picture of what life was like on Earth in prehistoric times, how it evolved, and what can be learned from fossils
"The profuse illustratons, text arrangement, and clarity of scientific explanations make the *Picture Atlas of Prehistoric Life* usable at many levels of interest and reading ability. This reasonably priced *Picture Atlas* is recommended for the circulating collections of all elementary school libraries and public libraries needing additional material on the subject." Booklist
Includes glossary

Taylor, Paul D., 1953-
Fossil. Knopf 1990 63p il (Eyewitness books) $16; lib bdg $16.99 (4 and up)
          560
1. Fossils
ISBN 0-679-80440-4, 0-679-90440-9 (lib bdg)
          LC 89-36444
Also available Spanish language edition
This book "details how fossils are formed and what man has learned about life on Earth from discovering them. The sections on early paleontology, fossil folklore, and the tools of paleontology are particularly well done." SLJ

Thompson, Sharon Elaine, 1952-
Death trap; the story of the La Brea Tar Pits. Lerner Publs. 1995 72p il lib bdg $21.50 (4 and up)   **560**
1. Fossils 2. California—Antiquities
ISBN 0-8225-2851-7   LC 93-39583
Thompson "begins at Hancock Park in Los Angeles, California, the site of the La Brea Tar Pits. She describes the unique conditions 25 million years ago that caused the formation of the asphalt pools where thousands of Ice Age animals were trapped, their bones preserved in the oily asphalt. . . . [She also] discusses how scientists use the fossil findings to learn more about Ice Age animal populations, migration patterns, climate, vegetarian and animal extinctions." Appraisal
"Excellent artist's re-creations of the prehistoric bring extra life to a fascinating story." Booklist
Includes glossary

The **Visual** dictionary of prehistoric life. Dorling Kindersley 1995 64p il (Eyewitness visual dictionaries) $15.95 (4 and up)
          560
1. Prehistoric man 2. Fossils 3. Dinosaurs
ISBN 1-56458-859-9   LC 94-30705
This volume presents a "history of the development of life on earth through skillful integration of text, diagrams,

The Visual dictionary of prehistoric life—*Continued*

and color photographs of fossils. Representations of biological development are divided into sections on plants and animals, introduced by text that sets the time frame and evolutionary frame. Useful charts allow readers to compare population growth and extinction over time." Horn Book Guide

567.9 Fossil reptiles. Dinosaurs

Aliki

Digging up dinosaurs. rev ed. Crowell 1988 32p il (Let's-read-and-find-out science books) lib bdg $14.89; pa $4.95 (k-3)   567.9

1. Dinosaurs
ISBN 0-690-04716-9 (lib bdg); 0-06-445078-3 (pa)
LC 87-29949

A revised and newly illustrated edition of the title first published 1981

Briefly introduces various types of dinosaurs, explaining how scientists find, preserve, and reassemble the giant dinosaur skeletons seen in museums

Dinosaur bones. Crowell 1988 32p il (Let's-read-and-find-out science books) lib bdg $14.89; pa $4.95 (k-3)   567.9

1. Dinosaurs 2. Fossils
ISBN 0-690-04550-6 (lib bdg); 0-06-445077-5 (pa)
LC 85-48246

"An easy-to-read look at the development of dinosaur paleontology from first finds and early skeptics to the study of the fossilization process and a quick overview of the dinosaur age. Informative text is paired with clever drawings that include fascinating insights and witty asides. Includes an indexed glossary of dinosaurs mentioned in the book." Sci Child

Dinosaurs are different. Crowell 1985 32p il (Let's-read-and-find-out science books) $15; lib bdg $14.89; pa $4.95 (k-3)   567.9

1. Dinosaurs
ISBN 0-690-04456-9; 0-690-04458-5 (lib bdg); 0-06-445056-2 (pa)
LC 84-45332

Also available Spanish language edition

This work discusses how the various orders and suborders of dinosaurs were similar and different in structure and appearance

"This book is excellent in its organization and treatment of the material. The illustrations are fairly good and do a reasonable job of supplementing the text." Sci Books Films

Arnold, Caroline, 1944-

Dinosaur mountain; graveyard of the past; photographs by Richard Hewett. Clarion Bks. 1989 48p il $15.95; pa $6.95 (4 and up)   567.9

1. Dinosaurs 2. Dinosaur National Monument (Colo. and Utah)
ISBN 0-89919-693-4; 0-395-66503-5 (pa)
LC 88-30218

This book describes the work of paleontologists in learning about dinosaurs, especially the discoveries made at Dinosaur National Monument

"Arnold seamlessly blends general information about paleontology with facts about specific finds near the Monu-

ment and additionally offers intriguing descriptions of ongoing work. . . . Lively writing, a dramtic subject, and a sure-fire hit with young readers." Horn Book

Dinosaurs all around; an artist's view of the prehistoric world; photographs by Richard Hewett. Clarion Bks. 1993 48p il $14.95 (4 and up)   567.9

1. Dinosaurs
ISBN 0-395-62363-4
LC 92-5726

On a visit to the workshop of Stephen and Sylvia Czerkas where a life-size dinosaur model is being constructed, the reader learns much information about dinosaurs and how conclusions are made from fossil remains

"The meticulous work involved in creating the sculptures is pictured and described in clear photographs and a direct, concise text." Horn Book

Dinosaurs down under and other fossils from Australia; photographs by Richard Hewett. Clarion Bks. 1990 48p il maps $15.95; pa $6.95 (4 and up)   567.9

1. Dinosaurs 2. Fossils 3. Museums—Technique
ISBN 0-89919-814-7; 0-395-69119-2 (pa)
LC 89-32783

"Describes how a museum mounts an exhibit and gives specifics about fossils unique to Australia, with focus on the exhibit 'Kadimakara: Fossils of the Australian Dreamtime,' Los Angeles, 1988. Excellent photographs give readers a you-are-there feeling for a museum. Maps illustrate plate tectonics." Sci Child

Benton, M. J. (Michael J.), 1956-

How do we know dinosaurs existed? [by] Mike Benton. Raintree Steck-Vaughn Pubs. 1995 41p il maps lib bdg $15.98 (4 and up)   567.9

1. Dinosaurs
ISBN 0-8114-3878-3
LC 94-16252

First published 1993 in the United Kingdom

"Detailed illustrations and graphs enhance the fact-filled text in a question-and-answer format. Numerous theories and unanswered questions are interspersed with a few activities. For the dinosaur buff and a good resource book for elementary students." Sci Child

Includes glossary

Booth, Jerry

The big beast book; dinosaurs and how they got that way; drawings by Martha Weston. Little, Brown 1988 128p il hardcover o.p. paperback available $10.95 (4 and up)   567.9

1. Dinosaurs
ISBN 0-316-10266-0 (pa)
LC 87-36206

"A Brown paper school book"

An introduction to dinosaurs with instructions for related projects

"Teachers, parents, and students looking for science and other school or personal projects will find this book a marvelous resource. The line drawings are detailed, and, at times, humorous." Appraisal

Includes glossary and bibliography

Cohen, Daniel, 1936-
Where to find dinosaurs today; [by] Daniel and Susan Cohen. Cobblehill Bks. 1992 209p il $15 (5 and up) **567.9**
1. Dinosaurs—Collections 2. Museums
ISBN 0-525-65098-9   LC 91-32084
Also available in paperback from Puffin Bks.
This "guidebook for travelers or researchers annotates dinosaur museums and sites in the U.S. and Canada. Organized geographically, entries include interesting facts plus location, hours, admission fees, phone numbers, and a description of what to see." Sci Child
"This is an indispensable guide for any serious dinophile and a kick for the mildly curious. All of the obvious places to visit are here, of course . . . and so are the little-known and downright weird, for instance, a store that sells replicas of dinosaur skulls." Booklist

Cole, Joanna
The magic school bus: in the time of the dinosaurs; illustrated by Bruce Degen. Scholastic 1994 unp il $14.95; pa $4.95 (2-4) **567.9**
1. Dinosaurs
ISBN 0-590-44688-6; 0-590-44639-4 (pa)
          LC 93-5753
Also available Spanish language edition
Also available CD-ROM version
"The fashionable Ms. Frizzle warps her students back to the late Triassic period, where they begin a journey forward through time in search of Maiasaura eggs for Jeff, the Friz's paleontologist friend from high school." Bull Cent Child Books
"An eye-catching, humorous book with bright, busy illustrations . . . packed with information." Sci Books Films

Dixon, Dougal, 1947-
Dougal Dixon's dinosaurs. Boyds Mills Press 1993 160p il maps $17.95 (4 and up) **567.9**
1. Dinosaurs
ISBN 1-56397-261-1
"Twenty-six dinosaurs from the Triassic through the Cretaceous period are illustrated in full-color in complement to a spirited text that describes fact and theory." Booklist
Includes glossary

Dodson, Peter
An alphabet of dinosaurs; paintings by Wayne D. Barlowe; black-and-white illustrations by Michael Meaker. Scholastic 1995 unp il $14.95 (k-3) **567.9**
1. Dinosaurs
ISBN 0-590-46486-8   LC 94-15522
"A Byron Preiss book"
"Using the alphabet as an arbitrary device, this book introduces 26 dinosaurs through brief informative text and two kinds of artwork. . . . Each right-hand page displays a full-color painting. On the left, a precise black-and-white ink drawing shows a full skeleton or a detail of bones, along with a few lines of text commenting on the dinosaur's physical features and habits." Booklist
"Barlowe's original artwork, more than the text . . . is what makes this alphabet book extraordinary. It shows how well illustration can work, by capturing a fine balance of realism, drama, and imagination." SLJ

Funston, Sylvia
The dinosaur question and answer book; from OWL magazine and the Dinosaur Project; written by Sylvia Funston. Little, Brown 1992 64p il $16.95 (4-6) **567.9**
1. Dinosaurs
ISBN 0-316-67736-1   LC 91-59004
"Joy Street books"
This is a compilation of some one hundred questions about dinosaurs submitted by readers of OWL and Chickadee magazines. Answers are supplied by members of the Dinosaur Project, a group of Canadian and Chinese paleontologists
"Nicely executed photographs, lifelike drawings, and cartoons are arranged for eye appeal. . . . Quick quizzes throughout the book are an added bonus (answers appear at the end). These exciting discoveries should be of interest to a wide audience." Booklist
Includes glossary

Gillette, J. Lynett
The search for Seismosaurus; the world's longest dinosaur; paintings by Mark Hallett. Dial Bks. for Young Readers 1993 40p il $14.99; lib bdg $14.89 (4-6) **567.9**
1. Dinosaurs 2. Fossils
ISBN 0-8037-1358-4; 0-8037-1359-2 (lib bdg)
          LC 92-28199
A "look at the ongoing excavation of the longest dinosaur ever found begins in 1979, when hikers found large bones in the desert near Albuquerque, New Mexico. Color photographs and conceptual paintings work with the text to show young readers the long and arduous, but thrilling, work of uncovering a dinosaur skeleton." Horn Book Guide

Horner, John R.
Digging up Tyrannosaurus rex; [by] John R. Horner & Don Lessem. Crown 1992 36p il (Face to face with science) $15; lib bdg $15.99; pa $6.99 (3-5) **567.9**
1. Dinosaurs 2. Fossils
ISBN 0-517-58783-1; 0-517-58784-X (lib bdg); 0-517-88336-8 (pa)   LC 92-2204
Describes the discovery and excavation of the world's only complete Tyrannosaurus fossil in Montana, and what was learned from it
"Clear photographs and concise text provide an intimate view of the painstaking procedures involved in digging up a dinosaur." Sci Child
Includes bibliography

Lasky, Kathryn
Dinosaur dig; photographs by Christopher G. Knight. Morrow Junior Bks. 1990 unp il $13.95; lib bdg $13.88 (3-6) **567.9**
1. Dinosaurs 2. Fossil reptiles
ISBN 0-688-08574-1; 0-688-08575-X (lib bdg)
          LC 89-13212
"An informative text combines geological history, field methodology, and human emotions in a colorful photoessay that features families participating in an expedition to discover dinosaur fossils. Young and old sift dirt and risk blisters unearthing finds under a paleontologist's guidance in the Montana Badlands." Sci Child

Lauber, Patricia, 1924-

Living with dinosaurs; illustrated by Douglas Henderson. Bradbury Press 1991 46p il maps $16.95 (3-6) **567.9**

1. Dinosaurs

ISBN 0-02-754521-0 LC 90-43265

This book "describes a stretch of sea and land in what is now Montana about 75 million years ago and depicts the dinosaurs, pterosaurs, mosasaurs, ammonites, and land and sea plants that lived in the area." Sci Books Films

The news about dinosaurs. Bradbury Press 1989 48p il $16.95; pa $6.95 (3-6) **567.9**

1. Dinosaurs

ISBN 0-02-754520-2; 0-689-71870-5 (pa)

LC 88-24140

The author "describes current ideas about dinosaurs' herding instincts, their coloration, and the way in which they raised their young. She also explains why dinosaurs are now thought to be related to birds and some of the conflicting opinions of dinosaur extinction." SLJ

"This is one of the most attractively illustrated children's books on dinosaurs ever produced. The colorful artwork, drawn from a number of contemporary sources, is dynamic, dramatic, and set in naturalistic backgrounds but executed with a high degree of attention to scientific detail." Sci Books Films

Lindsay, William

Barosaurus. Dorling Kindersley 1993 c1992 29p il $12.95 (4 and up) **567.9**

1. Dinosaurs 2. Fossil reptiles

ISBN 1-56458-123-3 LC 92-52819

Corythosaurus. Dorling Kindersley 1993 29p il maps $12.95 (4 and up) **567.9**

1. Dinosaurs 2. Fossil reptiles

ISBN 1-56458-225-6 LC 92-54309

Triceratops. Dorling Kindersley 1993 29p il maps $12.95 (4 and up) **567.9**

1. Dinosaurs 2. Fossil reptiles

ISBN 1-56458-226-4 LC 92-54308

Tyrannosaurus. Dorling Kindersley 1993 29p il map $12.95 (4 and up) **567.9**

1. Dinosaurs 2. Fossil reptiles

ISBN 1-56458-124-1 LC 92-52820

First published in the United Kingdom

At head of title: American Museum of Natural History

Each of these four books "concentrates on a single, well-known fossil skeleton in the American Museum of Natural History. . . . The colorful, large-format books are profusely illustrated with cartoons of fossil preservation, archival photos, photos of whole skeletons and of anatomical details, and reconstructions of muscles, whole bodies, the environment in which the dinosaur lived, and modern animals that provide anatomical or ecological analogies." Sci Books Films

Most, Bernard, 1937-

How big were the dinosaurs. Harcourt Brace & Co. 1994 unp il $15; pa $5 (k-2) **567.9**

1. Dinosaurs

ISBN 0-15-236800-0; 0-15-200852-7 (pa)

LC 93-19152

Describes the size of different dinosaurs by comparing them to more familiar objects, such as a school bus, a trombone, or a bowling alley

"The colorful drawings, of children interacting with dinosaurs, will be attractive to children. The text is easy to read. This book will delight young dinosaur lovers." Sci Books Films

The littlest dinosaurs. Harcourt Brace Jovanovich 1989 unp il $13.95; pa $5.95 (k-2) **567.9**

1. Dinosaurs

ISBN 0-15-248125-7; 0-15-248126-5 (pa)

LC 88-30063

Describes some of the smaller dinosaurs, all measuring fourteen feet or under, in terms of fact and fancy

This book is "a bright, fresh addition to the shelves and shelves of children's titles about those prehistoric beasts that fascinate the very young. . . . The illustrations are imaginative and the dinosaurs themselves eminently traceable, another passion of young dinosaur lovers." N Y Times Book Rev

Where to look for a dinosaur. Harcourt Brace Jovanovich 1993 unp il $12.95 (k-2) **567.9**

1. Dinosaurs

ISBN 0-15-295616-6 LC 92-19443

"Various dinosaurs are described in relation to where their fossils have been found. . . . Two or three sentence descriptions tell location, what the reptile's name means, and give a brief comment or joke on the animal's size, appearance, feeding habits, etc. The cartoon illustrations are in color marker, and show smiling walruses and dinosaurs. A listing of museums that have dinosaurs is included." SLJ

"The idea is great, and the pictures, which show plenty of evidence of Most's usual good humor, are lots of fun." Booklist

Mullins, Patricia

Dinosaur encore. HarperCollins Pubs. 1993 unp il hardcover o.p. paperback available $6.95 (k-3) **567.9**

1. Dinosaurs

ISBN 0-06-443465-6 (pa) LC 92-19848

"Willa Perlman books"

Fold-out flaps reveal comparisons between various dinosaurs and familiar animals living today

"Scrumptious collages. . . . Factual notes on the final page round out a fresh, inviting view of the all-time favorite subject." Horn Book Guide

Norman, David

Dinosaur; written by David Norman and Angela Milner. Knopf 1989 unp il (Eyewitness books) $16; lib bdg $16.99 (4 and up) **567.9**

1. Dinosaurs

ISBN 0-394-82253-6; 0-394-92253-0 (lib bdg)

LC 88-27167

Also available Spanish language edition

Text and photographs explore the world of the dinosaurs, focusing on such aspects as their teeth, feet, eggs, and fossils

"*Dinosaur* is complete, authoritative, exact, and imaginative. It is sure to survive when many other dinosaur books become extinct." Sci Books Films

Pringle, Laurence P.
Dinosaurs! strange and wonderful; illustrated by Carol Heyer. Boyds Mills Press 1995 unp il $14.95 (k-3)   **567.9**
1. Dinosaurs
ISBN 1-878093-16-9   LC 92-71273
The author "introduces topics ranging from where the dinosaurs lived, what they ate, fossils, paleontologists, to how new discoveries lead to updated theories about dinosaurs' appearance, behavior and evolution." Appraisal
"Clearly written and well-suited to a younger audience, the book is meaty enough for slightly older readers too. Heyer's detailed acrylics, alternately realistic and stylized, offer an up-to-date representation of what the 'terrible lizards' may well have looked like." Publ Wkly

Sattler, Helen Roney
Baby dinosaurs; illustrated by Jean Zallinger. Lothrop, Lee & Shepard Bks. 1984 32p il $14; lib bdg $13.93 (1-4)   **567.9**
1. Dinosaurs
ISBN 0-688-03817-4; 0-688-03818-2 (lib bdg)
LC 83-25631
"This book presents theories about the early life of dinosaurs based on the discoveries of fossilized baby dinosaurs." Sci Child
"Zallinger's color pictures recreate the great creatures and their world of 225 million years ago with convincing realism. Closing the book, a time chart and pronunciation guide describe the periods in the Mesozoic Era and list the dinosaurs alive in each." Publ Wkly

Dinosaurs of North America; illustrated by Anthony Rao; with an introduction by John H. Ostrom. Lothrop, Lee & Shepard Bks. 1981 151p il $18 (5 and up)   **567.9**
1. Dinosaurs
ISBN 0-688-51952-0   LC 80-27411
"Arranged by broad geologic time periods (Triassic, Jurassic, Cretaceous), this carefully researched book features more than 80 different types of dinosaurs native to North America. Each category, introduced with descriptions of the period, explains the creatures' various physical characteristics, eating habits, habitats, and other pertinent details. A final chapter explores the mystery of dinosaur extinction." Booklist
Includes bibliography

The new illustrated dinosaur dictionary; with a foreword by John H. Ostrom; illustrated by Joyce Powzyk. rev ed. Lothrop, Lee & Shepard Bks. 1990 363p il maps $24.95; pa $17.95 (5 and up)   **567.9**
1. Dinosaurs—Dictionaries
ISBN 0-688-08462-1; 0-688-10043-0 (pa)
LC 90-3313
First published 1983 with title: The illustrated dinosaur dictionary
Sattler "has assembled brief descriptions of more than 350 dinosaurs . . . plus general information under such headings as Food, Size, Teeth, and Parental Care. Each entry includes the Greek or Latin derivation of the dinosaur's name, scientific classification, physical characteristics, and the geologic period and geographic area in which the dinosaur lived. . . . Black-and-white line drawings are scattered throughout the text, and there is a 12-page color gallery." Booklist
Includes bibliography

Stegosaurs; the solar-powered dinosaurs; illustrated by Turi MacCombie. Lothrop, Lee & Shepard Bks. 1992 32p il map $15; lib bdg $14.93 (3-6)   **567.9**
1. Dinosaurs
ISBN 0-688-10055-4; 0-688-10056-2 (lib bdg)
LC 90-49733
Discusses the armor-plated dinosaur called Stegosaurus and some of its lesser-known relatives
"It's everything anyone could want in a dinosaur book. The author presents intriguing, up-to-date information. . . . Provides plenty of well-indexed information for report writers. The attractive watercolor illustrations are helpful and clear. . . . Superior science writing." SLJ
Includes bibliography

Tyrannosaurus rex and its kin: the Mesozoic monsters; illustrated by Joyce Powzyk. Lothrop, Lee & Shepard Bks. 1989 48p il $14.95; lib bdg $13.88 (3-6)   **567.9**
1. Dinosaurs
ISBN 0-688-07747-1; 0-688-07748-X (lib bdg)
LC 88-1577
Discusses the fossil remains, probable appearance, and possible behavior of the gigantic flesh-eating dinosaurs of the Mesozoic, including Tyrannosaurus rex, Allosaurus, and such lesser known relatives as Acrocanthosaurus and Baryonyx walkeri
"Generously scaled, labelled watercolor illustrations will attract young browsers. . . . A helpful map and a time chart augment the catalogue-style text." Bull Cent Child Books
Includes bibliography

Simon, Seymour, 1931-
The largest dinosaurs; illustrated by Pamela Carroll. Macmillan 1986 32p il $13.95 (1-3)
567.9
1. Dinosaurs
ISBN 0-02-782910-3   LC 85-24088
Surveys findings on Brachiosaurus, Diplodocus, and four other examples of the largest dinosaurs, including the locations of the discoveries and explanations of their names
"Against an imposing array of black-and-white line-and-wash drawings, Simon explores the latest theories on what these animals looked like, how and where they lived, and what they ate. . . . Illustrations include both overall views of the species as well as conceptions of what physical details such as heads, feet, or tails may have looked like. An explanation of mystery surrounding dinosaurs' extinction rounds out the presentation. Useful for students and browsers, this may also be read aloud to children unable to read it on their own." Booklist
Includes glossary

New questions and answers about dinosaurs; illustrated by Jennifer Dewey. Morrow Junior Bks. 1990 45p il $16; lib bdg $15.93; pa $4.95 (3-6)   **567.9**
1. Dinosaurs
ISBN 0-688-08195-9; 0-688-08196-7 (lib bdg); 0-688-12271-X (pa)   LC 88-36226
"The book answers twenty-two questions, including 'which was the biggest dinosaur,' 'which dinosaur had the most teeth,' and 'what color were the dinosaurs.' One paragraph of text is used per double-page spread with illustrations filling the remaining space. The subjects are portrayed in soft crayon drawings." Horn Book

The **Visual** dictionary of dinosaurs. Dorling Kindersley 1993 64p il (Eyewitness visual dictionaries) $14.99 (4 and up)   **567.9**

1. Dinosaurs
ISBN 1-56458-188-8   LC 92-53446

Also available Spanish language edition

Text and labeled illustrations present the different types of dinosaurs, their anatomy, behavior, and the physical environments in which they lived

"A remarkable resource for the study of these creatures and, in fact, for the study of the entire Mesozoic era (the 'Age of the Reptiles'). It is well written, authoritative, and superbly illustrated." Sci Books Films

For a fuller review see: Booklist, Dec. 1, 1993

Whitfield, Philip J.

Macmillan children's guide to dinosaurs and other prehistoric animals. Macmillan 1992 96p il maps $16.95 (3-6)   **567.9**

1. Dinosaurs 2. Prehistoric animals
ISBN 0-02-762362-9   LC 91-45562

Describes the dinosaurs and other prehistoric animals that lived in various areas of the world during the different geological periods, from the Triassic through the Cretaceous

"What distinguishes this from the run-of-the-mill catalog is the striking two-page spreads introducing each time period, overviews of the eras, and focus articles on selected dinosaurs or animal groups. Appropriate for browsing and research." Booklist

Includes bibliography

568   Fossil birds

Witmer, Lawrence M.

The search for the origin of birds; illustrated by Kit Mather. Watts 1995 63p il (Prehistoric life) lib bdg $15.33 (4 and up)   **568**

1. Birds 2. Prehistoric animals
ISBN 0-531-11232-2   LC 95-14635

This volume "looks at how scientists have searched for clues about the beginnings of birds, and are now building a body of evidence suggesting that birds descended from—and, in fact, are—carnivorous dinosaurs." Publisher's note

Includes glossary and bibliography

569   Fossil mammals

Aliki

Wild and woolly mammoths; written and illustrated by Aliki. rev ed. HarperCollins Pubs. 1996 32p il $14.95; lib bdg $14.89 (k-3)   **569**

1. Mammoths
ISBN 0-06-026276-1; 0-06-026277-X (lib bdg)
    LC 94-48217

A revised and newly illustrated edition of the title first published 1977

An easy-to-read account of the woolly mammoth, a giant land mammal which has been extinct for over 11,000 years

"With concise text and informative art, Aliki illuminates the timeless appeal of these long-gone animals—and drops a gentle warning about the possible fate of tusked decendants." Publ Wkly

573   Physical anthropology

Intrater, Roberta Grobel

Two eyes, a nose, and a mouth. Cartwheel Bks. 1995 unp il $12.95 (k-2)   **573**

1. Physical anthropology 2. Face
ISBN 0-590-48247-5   LC 94-18390

"Using numerous color photographs portraying a variety of faces and facial features, Intrater discusses eyes, eyebrows, noses, mouths, and lips. The simple, rhyming text reassures young listeners that differences in appearance are both interesting and desirable." Booklist

"Outstanding photography and design add greatly to the text and make this a must for sharing with children." Child Book Rev Serv

573.2   Evolution and genetics of humankind

Cole, Joanna

The human body: how we evolved; illustrated by Walter Gaffney-Kessell and Juan Carlos Barberis. Morrow 1987 63p il $12.95; lib bdg $12.88 (4 and up)   **573.2**

1. Human origins 2. Prehistoric man 3. Evolution
ISBN 0-688-06719-0; 0-688-06720-4 (lib bdg)
    LC 86-23679

"The interesting story of human evolution is punctuated by fascinating explanations of the development of specific parts of the human body. Not only are descriptions of development of the brain, foot, hair, eyes, hands, opposable thumb, skull and jaw clear and simple, but the reasons behind the development of these body parts are rivetingly imparted. Ideas are also portrayed through many beautiful sketches. . . . This is a must-read book that will not only inform but encourage the reader's creative thinking process." Sci Books Films

Lasky, Kathryn

Traces of life; the origins of humankind; illustrated by Whitney Powell. Morrow Junior Bks. 1989 144p il maps $16.95 (5 and up)   **573.2**

1. Human origins 2. Prehistoric man
ISBN 0-688-07237-2   LC 89-12092

"The history of hominid research and the work of scientists involved are accurately and pleasantly described in an easy-to-read chronology. A comprehensible guide to how various finds and reconstructions explain the evolution of *Homo sapiens*." Sci Child

Includes bibliography

573.3   Prehistoric humankind

Sattler, Helen Roney

Hominids: a look back at our ancestors; illustrated by Christopher Santoro. Lothrop, Lee & Shepard Bks. 1988 125p il lib bdg $15.95 (5 and up)   **573.3**

1. Prehistoric man
ISBN 0-688-06061-7   LC 86-10624

Sattler, Helen Roney—*Continued*
A "chronological examination of the ancestry of the human family in which the fossil record is the link that helps describe changes in human form and behavior through the millennia. Special emphasis is given to the changes in brain size, tooth size and function, the onset of bipedalism, and the importance of toolmaking." Sci Child
"The text provides a sensible summary of the generally accepted knowledge in this area as well as the lack of knowledge about many details and the abundance of controversial knowledge, though, happily, it avoids creation science and evolutionary biology. This book is a significant accomplishment." Sci Books Films
Includes bibliography

574 Biology

Tomb, Howard, 1959-
Microaliens; dazzling journeys with an electron microscope; [by] Howard Tomb and Dennis Kunkel; with drawings by Tracy Dockray. Farrar, Straus & Giroux 1993 79p il $16 (5 and up)   **574**
1. Electron microscopes 2. Science—Pictorial works
ISBN 0-374-34960-6   LC 93-1403
Text and photographs taken with an electron microscope examine such items as bird feathers, fleas, skin, mold, and blood
"Tomb's short introduction is a good overview of the history of the electron microscope and how it works. . . . [This is] a fascinating look at a relatively unknown world." Booklist
Includes bibliography

574.3 Development and maturation

Kuhn, Dwight
My first book of nature. Scholastic 1993 61p il (Cartwheel learning bookshelf) $11.95 (k-2)
574.3
1. Growth
ISBN 0-590-45502-8   LC 92-14329
"Cartwheel books"
Provides an introduction to growth, explaining how it occurs in such everyday things as guppies, apples, dogs, trees, and humans
"A spacious format features concise text and sharply focused, full-color photographs that effectively illustrate the various stages." SLJ

Martin, Linda
Watch them grow; written by Linda Martin. Dorling Kindersley 1994 45p il $14.95 (k-2)
574.3
1. Growth
ISBN 1-56458-458-5   LC 93-25426
Explores the different stages in the life cycles of a variety of living things, including rabbits, frogs, puppies, and mushrooms
"Clearly numbered boxes contain uncluttered, full-color photographs and a simple sentence or two describing the specific changes that take place. . . . A visual treat for

youngsters that teachers and parents will appreciate for its realistic presentation." SLJ

574.5 Ecology

Baylor, Byrd, 1924-
The desert is theirs; illustrated by Peter Parnall. Scribner 1975 unp il lib bdg $14.95; pa $4.95 (1-4)   **574.5**
1. Desert ecology 2. Papago Indians
ISBN 0-684-14266-X (lib bdg); 0-689-71105-X (pa)
LC 74-24417
"Poetic interpretations of Papago Indians' ecological and spiritual relationships with desert resources. . . . Illustrations add to the usefulness of this mood piece for sensitizing children to respect for nature, reading aloud, studying Indian cultures and techniques of using line, space and color." Read Teach

Brandenburg, Jim
An American safari; adventures on the North American prairie; edited by JoAnn Bren Guernsey. Walker & Co. 1995 44p il $16.95; lib bdg $17.85 (4 and up)   **574.5**
1. Prairie ecology 2. Prairie animals
ISBN 0-8027-8319-8; 0-8027-8320-1 (lib bdg)
LC 94-24654
"Mingling facts with personal reflections, Brandenburg acquaints readers with the habitat that inspired him to become a nature photographer: the American prairie. Besides describing the experiences that led him to hunt with his camera rather than with traps and guns, he introduces various types of prairies, the animals that live there, what threatens their habitat, and how it can be saved." Booklist
"Exquisite photographs of the animals and the terrain, along with some astonishing figures, tell a dramatic story." Horn Book

Cobb, Vicki, 1938-
This place is wet; illustrated by Barbara Lavallee. Walker & Co. 1989 unp il (Imagine living here) $12.95; lib bdg $13.85; pa $6.95 (2-4)   **574.5**
1. Rain forest ecology 2. Amazon River valley
ISBN 0-8027-6880-6; 0-8027-6881-4 (lib bdg); 0-8027-7399-0 (pa)   LC 89-32445
Focuses on the land, ecology, people, and animals of the Amazon rain forest in Brazil, presenting it as an example of a place where there is so much water that some houses need to be built on stilts

Dewey, Jennifer
A night and day in the desert; [by] Jennifer Owings Dewey. Little, Brown 1991 unp il lib bdg $15.95 (2-4)   **574.5**
1. Desert ecology
ISBN 0-316-18210-9   LC 89-13697
Depicts the unique environment of the desert, with its plant and animal life and special climatic conditions
"The illustrations provide an enriching presentation of the desert and its life forms. . . . The words, phrases, and sophisticated statements in the text are woven together in such a way that images of the desert appear clear and near." Sci Books Films

Dorros, Arthur
Rain forest secrets; written and illustrated by Arthur Dorros. Scholastic 1990 unp il map $14.95 (k-3) **574.5**

1. Rain forest ecology
ISBN 0-590-43369-5 LC 89-49069

Describes the characteristics, various forms of plant and animal life, and destruction of the world's rain forests

"Interesting facts stud the general descriptions. . . . The accompanying pen-and-wash drawings are extensive and effective in suggesting the lush greenery. . . . The format and conversational tone will make this accessible to a wide audience." Booklist

Dunphy, Madeleine
Here is the southwestern desert; illustrated by Anne Coe. Hyperion Bks. for Children 1995 unp il $14.95; lib bdg $14.89 (k-3)
574.5

1. Desert ecology 2. Sonoran Desert
ISBN 0-7868-0049-6; 0-7868-2038-1 (lib bdg)
LC 94-9375

"Dunphy's cumulative poem explores the interrelationships between the living and nonliving elements of the Sonoran Desert. Coming full circle, she begins and ends with the cactus." Booklist

"The book is beautifully designed. On each double-page spread, text appears in a narrow section on the left against a glowing earth-pink background; remaining space is filled with an acrylic painting saturated with dazzling desert light." SLJ

Here is the tropical rainforest; illustrated by Michael Rothman. Hyperion Bks. for Children 1994 unp il $14.95; lib bdg $14.89 (k-3)
574.5

1. Rain forest ecology
ISBN 1-56282-636-0; 1-56282-637-9 (lib bdg)
LC 93-24850

Cumulative text presents the animals and plants of the tropical rain forest and their relationship with one another and their environment

"Rothman's lovely illustrations, done in the lush greens of the wet tropics, accompany the sing-song verses that mimic 'The House that Jack Built.'. . . The last page names some of the animals shown in the text and suggests that the National Wildlife Federation be contacted in order to help save these threatened lands." SLJ

Ekey, Robert
Fire! in Yellowstone; story by Robert Ekey. Gareth Stevens Children's Bks. 1990 32p il map lib bdg $17.27 (2-4) **574.5**

1. Forest fires 2. Yellowstone National Park 3. Forest ecology
ISBN 0-8368-0226-8 LC 89-43156

"A True adventure"

Adapted from an adult book: Yellowstone on fire, published 1989 by The Billings Gazette

Discusses the fire that ravaged nearly one million acres of Yellowstone National Park during several months in 1988, and explains the two sides to the controversy over letting nature take its course

A "Well-written and excellently photographed book. . . . Good thought-provoking questions stimulate class discussions." Sci Child

Includes glossary and bibliography

Facklam, Howard
Parasites; [by] Howard and Margery Facklam. 21st Cent. Bks. (NY) 1994 64p il (Invaders) lib bdg $15.95 (5 and up)
574.5

1. Parasites
ISBN 0-8050-2858-7 LC 94-25431

The authors provide an "introduction to parasitology. . . . The five chapters in the book are entitled 'Eating for Two,' 'The Bloodsuckers,' 'Flatworms and Roundworms,' 'Microscopic Parasites,' and 'Strangers in the Nest.'" Sci Books Films

"The information is well researched and generally very up to date. . . . The photographs and illustrations are excellent and complement the text material." Appraisal

Includes glossaary and bibliography

Gallant, Roy A.
Earth's vanishing forests. Macmillan 1991 162p il maps $15.95 (6 and up) **574.5**

1. Rain forest ecology
ISBN 0-02-735774-0 LC 91-2624

This book discusses the ecology of rain forests, the problem posed by the present danger to rain forests, and possibilities for the future

"The author has created a very readable text. . . . He skillfully educates his audience about the value of the tropical rain forests. . . . The beauty of the rain forests is captured in rapturous prose." Voice Youth Advocates

Includes glossary and bibliography

George, Jean Craighead, 1919-
One day in the alpine tundra; illustrations by Walter Gaffney-Kessell. Crowell 1984 44p il lib bdg $14.89; pa $3.95 (4-6) **574.5**

1. Mountain ecology 2. Tundra ecology
ISBN 0-690-04326-0 (lib bdg); 0-06-442027-2 (pa)
LC 82-45590

"What's life like above the tree line? This is the story—partly fictional—of how plants and animals have adapted to the harsh conditions of the tops of mountains." Sci Child

Includes bibliography

One day in the desert; illustrated by Fred Brenner. Crowell 1983 48p il lib bdg $14.89 (4-6) **574.5**

1. Desert ecology 2. Sonoran Desert 3. Papago Indians
ISBN 0-690-04341-4 LC 82-45924

Explains how the animal and human inhabitants of the Sonoran Desert of Arizona, including a mountain lion, a roadrunner, a coyote, a tortoise, and members of the Papago Indian tribe, adapt to and survive the desert's merciless heat

"With a measured, yet vivid, style, this simplified introduction to desert ecology makes a memorable impact that goes beyond ready reference facts. Delicate black-and-white sketches, well placed on each page, break up the text and illustrate the plants and animals discussed." SLJ

Includes bibliography

One day in the prairie; illustrated by Bob Marstall. Crowell 1986 42p il lib bdg $14.89 (4-6) **574.5**

1. Prairie ecology 2. Tornadoes
ISBN 0-690-04566-2 LC 85-48254

George, Jean Craighead, 1919- —*Continued*
The animals on a prairie wildlife refuge sense an approaching tornado and seek protection before it touches down and destroys everything in its path
"Black-and-white pencil drawings expand the text and bring out the threat of the coming tornado. . . . George provides a brief but intense and detailed look at the North American prairie, equally suitable for a homework assignment or for browsing." SLJ
Includes bibliography

One day in the tropical rain forest; illustrated by Gary Allen. Crowell 1990 56p il $14.95; lib bdg $14.89; pa $3.95 (4-6)
574.5
1. Rain forest ecology 2. Natural history—Venezuela
ISBN 0-690-04767-3; 0-690-04769-X (lib bdg); 0-06-442016-7 (pa)
LC 89-36583
"The final day of a struggle between developers and conservationists over the Tropical Rain Forest of the Macaw as seen by a young Indian boy. A beautifully written story details the complexity, majesty, and interdependence of flora and fauna and teaches about indigenous people and scientists who inhabit a small part of Venezuela's rain forest." Sci Child
Includes bibliography

One day in the woods; illustrated by Gary Allen. Crowell 1988 42p il lib bdg $14.89; pa $3.95 (4-6)
574.5
1. Forest ecology 2. Birds
ISBN 0-690-04724-X (lib bdg); 0-06-442017-5 (pa)
LC 87-21712
Rebecca discovers many things about plant and animal life when she spends the day in Teatown Woods in the Hudson Highlands of New York looking for the ovenbird
"Through naturalist George's precise descriptions, readers follow Rebecca's progress through the day discovering the secrets of the spring foliage and learning much about the temperate forest and its inhabitants. Allen's refined pencil drawings of the skunk, wood ducks, flying squirrel, gypsy moth caterpillar, and other creatures that Rebecca encounters on her quest beautifully transcribe George's textual details." Booklist
Includes bibliography

George, Michael, 1964-
Tundra; written by Michael George. Creative Educ. 1994 39p il (Images) lib bdg $17.95 (3-5)
574.5
1. Tundra ecology 2. Arctic regions
ISBN 0-88682-601-2
LC 93-18275
Describes the location, climate, and plant and animal life of the tundras in the Arctic regions
"Breathtaking panoramas of the polar regions' unique land and captivating closeups of their plants and animal inhabitants fill full- and double-page spreads, creating a visually powerful resource." SLJ

Gibbons, Gail
Nature's green umbrella; tropical rain forests. Morrow Junior Bks. 1994 unp il maps $15; lib bdg $14.93 (k-3)
574.5
1. Rain forest ecology
ISBN 0-688-12353-8; 0-688-12354-6 (lib bdg)
LC 93-17569

Describes the climatic conditions of the rain forest as well as the different layers of plants and animals that comprise the ecosystem
The language is "simple, yet poetic and evocative. . . . Colorful maps pinpoint the locations of these global resources. Green vines entwine around the borders of each page and enclose the text and bright illustrations." Sci Books Films

Godkin, Celia, 1948-
Wolf island. Scientific Am. Bks. for Young Readers 1993 c1989 36p il $15.95 (k-3)
574.5
1. Ecology 2. Food chains (Ecology)
ISBN 0-7167-6513-6
LC 93-15498
First published 1989 in Canada
When a family of wolves is removed from the food chain on a small island, the impact on the island's ecology is felt by the other animals living there
This features "beautiful language and illustrations." Sci Child

Goodman, Susan, 1952-
Bats, bugs, and biodiversity; adventures in the Amazonian rain forest; photographs by Michael J. Doolittle. Atheneum Bks. for Young Readers 1995 45p il $16 (4 and up)
574.5
1. Rain forest ecology 2. Amazon River valley
ISBN 0-689-31943-6
LC 94-35029
This book provides a "description of the Peruvian rain forest as told through the eyes of seventh and eighth graders from Michigan. . . . The 74 middle school students spent one week living lives similar to those of the inhabitants of the region. . . . They explored the jungle's canopy, climbed trees, walked on rope bridges, and identified many of the plants and animals they had studied in the classroom." Sci Books Films
"There is enough factual material to tie in with more thorough studies of rain forests, but the real value of this book is the opportunity it offers children to relate to an exotic environment by seeing it through the eyes of their peers. A real plus to any collection." SLJ
Includes glossary and bibliography

Greenaway, Frank
Desert life; photographed by Frank Greenaway; written by Barbara Taylor. Dorling Kindersley 1992 unp il (Look closer) $9.95 (3-6)
574.5
1. Desert ecology
ISBN 1-87943-193-9
LC 91-58195
Also available Spanish language edition
Examines the variety of life found in the desert, including the Greek tortoise, desert scorpion, and jewel wasp
"The double-page spreads feature at least one striking, high-quality, full-color photograph. . . . The text is very readable and generally accurate." SLJ
Includes glossary

Rain forest; photographed by Frank Greenaway; written by Barbara Taylor. Dorling Kindersley 1992 unp il (Look closer) $9.95 (3-6)
574.5
1. Rain forest ecology
ISBN 1-87943-191-2
LC 91-58197

Greenaway, Frank—*Continued*

Also available Spanish language edition

Examines the variety of life found in a rain forest, including the flying gecko, poison dart frog, and curly-haired tarantula

"While the information is engagingly presented, it is the clearly focused, bright photographs that will captivate readers. . . . Carefully placed labels contribute to the usefulness of the information." Horn Book

Includes glossary

Greenaway, Theresa, 1947-

Jungle; written by Theresa Greenaway; photographed by Geoff Dann. Knopf 1994 63p il (Eyewitness books) $16; lib bdg $16.99 (4 and up)   **574.5**

1. Rain forest ecology
ISBN 0-679-86168-8; 0-679-96168-2 (lib bdg)
                  LC 94-7948

"A Dorling Kindersley book"

Color photographs, drawings, and brief text describe the animals, plants, and ecology of tropical forests of the world

The author "presents a clear understanding of the composition, similarities and differences among rain forests around the world. A good addition to the book lies in the explanation of the value of this type of ecosystem and, sadly, how jungles are being destroyed at a rapid rate on a daily basis." Appraisal

Jaspersohn, William

How the forest grew; illustrated by Chuck Eckart. Greenwillow Bks. 1989 55p il $13.95; pa $5.95 (1-3)   **574.5**

1. Forest ecology
ISBN 0-688-80232-X; 0-688-11508-X (pa)
                  LC 79-16286

"A Greenwillow read-alone book"

A reissue of the title first published 1980

This "book traces the growth of a Massachusetts hardwood forest. . . . The book recounts each stage of the forest's growth and explains the reasons for the succession of diffrent types of plant and animal life." Horn Book

"Many beautifully detailed black-and-white sketches thoroughly capture the atmosphere of the developing forest." Appraisal

Jenike, David

A walk through a rain forest; life in the Ituri Forest of Zaire; [by] David Jenike, Mark Jenike. Watts 1994 63p il lib bdg $14.91; pa $9.95 (4-6)   **574.5**

1. Rain forest ecology 2. Ituri Forest (Zaire)
ISBN 0-531-11168-7 (lib bdg); 0-531-15721-0 (pa)
                  LC 94-29389

"A Cincinnati Zoo book"

A walk through the Ituri Forest "with local farmers and foragers introduces readers to its sights, sounds, and smells. Lush, full-color photographs as well as profiles of the various animals found in this very fragile ecosystem give a realistic impression of the region. Hunting, gathering, and fishing methods of native peoples are explained, as are some of the medicinal uses of the abundant plant life, and the successful coexistence of the people and the natural environment is described." SLJ

Includes glossary and bibliography

Jordan, Martin, 1944-

Jungle days, jungle nights; [by] Martin and Tanis Jordan. Kingfisher (NY) 1993 unp il $14.95 (1-3)   **574.5**

1. Rain forest ecology 2. Amazon River valley
ISBN 1-85697-885-0   LC 92-40366

This book examines some of the mammals, reptiles, and insects that live in the jungles of South America

"Shimmering with brilliant colors set against the exotic shadows of the rain forest, rich oil paintings capture the animal and plant life unique to this environment. These dramatic visions are given deeper resonance and immediacy by an elegant and informative narrative that weaves them together into a seasonal sequence." Booklist

Lauber, Patricia, 1924-

Summer of fire; Yellowstone 1988. Orchard Bks. 1991 64p il map $19.95 (4 and up)
                  574.5

1. Forest fires 2. Yellowstone National Park 3. Forest ecology
ISBN 0-531-05943-X   LC 90-23032

Describes the season of fire that struck Yellowstone in 1988, and examines the complex ecology that returns plant and animal life to a seemingly barren, ash-covered expanse

"Interesting, action-filled writing plus a very detailed description of the fire and how it spread make for exciting reading. . . . The new, clear full-color photographs are outstanding." SLJ

Includes glossary and bibliography

Who eats what? food chains and food webs; illustrated by Holly Keller. HarperCollins Pubs. 1995 32p il (Let's-read-and-find-out science books) $15; lib bdg $14.89; pa $4.95 (k-3)   **574.5**

1. Food chains (Ecology)
ISBN 0-06-022981-0; 0-06-022982-9 (lib bdg); 0-06-445130-5 (pa)   LC 93-10609

The author "demonstrates the interconnectedness of nature by showing how creatures form chains through the foods they eat. . . . Lauber gives several examples, from short chains (apple to child) to the web of connections between sea creatures. She uses sea otters to show how the disappearance of one link in the chain can disrupt the flow of food both up and down." Bull Cent Child Books

"Clear, simple ink-and-watercolor drawings illustrate the clear, simple text. Informative and intriguing, this basic science book leads children to think about the complex and interdependent web of life on Earth." Booklist

Lavies, Bianca

Mangrove wilderness; nature's nursery; text & photographs by Bianca Lavies. Dutton Children's Bks. 1994 unp il $15.99 (4-6)
                  574.5

1. Wetlands 2. Ecology
ISBN 0-525-45186-2   LC 93-33956

"Florida's red mangrove trees are home to a thriving plant and animal community. This book describes the interdependence of living things and the ways in which these trees provide a safe and nurturing environment for a variety of animals. Beautiful, close-up photographs accompany a well-written text." Sci Child

Lerner, Carol, 1927-

A desert year. Morrow Junior Bks. 1991 48p
il $13.95; lib bdg $13.88 (3-5)   **574.5**

1. Desert ecology 2. Seasons
ISBN 0-688-09382-5; 0-688-09383-3 (lib bdg)
                                    LC 90-44643

The author "follows seasonal changes in the desert from
winter to winter, describing the behavior of animals and alterations in plants throughout the year. Lovely illustrations
provide enough detail to identify the creatures, and descriptions provide interesting details about each of the animals."
Sci Books Films

Includes glossary and bibliography

A forest year. Morrow 1987 48p il $12.95;
lib bdg $12.88 (3-5)   **574.5**

1. Forest ecology 2. Seasons
ISBN 0-688-06413-2; 0-688-06414-0 (lib bdg)
                                    LC 86-9741

"Arranged by season, this book provides 16 glimpses of
the plants and animals that might live in a typical forest in
the eastern half of the United States. For every season there
are four full-page water-color illustrations, each facing a
page of descriptive text and each highlighting a set of wildlife: mammals, birds, reptiles and amphibians, or insects."
Booklist

Luenn, Nancy, 1954-

Squish! a wetland walk; illustrated by
Ronald Himler. Atheneum Pubs. 1994 unp il
$14.95 (k-2)   **574.5**

1. Wetlands 2. Ecology
ISBN 0-689-31842-1   LC 93-22628

This is "an introduction to the sights, sounds, and smells
of a wetland as experienced by a young boy. . . . Luenn uses
simple language to explain some of the many ways wetlands
are beneficial, and Himler's quiet watercolors beautifully
capture the unusual, wondrous atmosphere." Booklist

Macquitty, Miranda

Desert; photographed by Alan Hills and
Frank Greenway. Knopf 1994 63p il map
(Eyewitness books) $19; lib bdg $18.99 (4 and
up)   **574.5**

1. Deserts 2. Human influence on nature
ISBN 0-679-86003-7; 0-679-96003-1 (lib bdg)
                                    LC 93-21068

Also available Spanish language edition
"A Dorling Kindersley book"
This book "features photographs and drawings of flora
and fauna, mainly of the deserts of northern Africa and the
Middle East. Examples from the American Southwest and
Australia are included, but not Arctic, Antarctic, or high-
elevation regions. Brief explanatory paragraphs accompany
the illustrations. . . . A browser's delight." SLJ

Mallory, Kenneth

Water hole; life in a rescued tropical forest.
Watts 1992 57p il maps $15.95; lib bdg $16.87
(5 and up)   **574.5**

1. Forest ecology 2. Natural history—Costa Rica
ISBN 0-531-15250-2; 0-531-11154-7 (lib bdg)
                                    LC 92-14360

"A New England Aquarium book"

Examines the world of a tropical dry forest in Santa
Rosa National Park in Costa Rica and the work being done
to preserve it
"Curious coatis are our surrogate eyes and ears as they
poke their inquisitive noses into the diverse nature of a
Costa Rican dry tropical forest. . . . With dazzling photos
and crisp narrative, we follow the adventures of one small,
seven-member band of coatis as they scamper about on a
daylong foray during the dry season. . . . The volume is
ideal for elementary-level ecology and conservation studies
and would be useful to speakers and teachers at any level."
Sci Books Films

Includes glossary and bibliography

Mutel, Cornelia Fleischer, 1947-

Tropical rain forests; [by] Cornelia F. Mutel
and Mary M. Rodgers. Lerner Publs. 1991 64p
il map (Our endangered planet) lib bdg $21.50;
pa $8.95 (4 and up)   **574.5**

1. Rain forest ecology 2. Nature conservation
ISBN 0-8225-2503-8 (lib bdg); 0-8225-9629-6 (pa)
                                    LC 90-44354

Studies the ecology of tropical rain forests and the vital
role of their water, air, plant, and animal resources in preserving the global environmental balance. Also describes
how easily man's activities can endanger or upset this fragile environment
"The photographs are striking; the diagrams are generally
excellent; and the text is clear, factual, and logical. Suggested activities are included." Horn Book Guide

Includes glossary

Norsgaard, E. Jaediker (Ernestine Jaediker)

Nature's great balancing act; in our own
backyard; photographs by Campbell
Norsgaard. Cobblehill Bks. 1990 63p il $14.95
(4-6)   **574.5**

1. Ecology
ISBN 0-525-65028-8   LC 89-38589

"The interrelationships of plants, animals, insects, and
birds are explored in a semi-wild New England backyard.
Excellent photographs complement a lively text." Sci Child

Includes glossary

Orr, Richard

Nature cross-sections; illustrated by Richard
Orr; written by Moira Butterfield. Dorling
Kindersley 1995 30p il $17.95 (4 and up)
                                    574.5

1. Habitat (Ecology) 2. Ecology
ISBN 0-7894-0147-9   LC 94-44798

"Orr's colorful paintings show cutaway views of ecosystems such as a rain forest, a tidal pool, and an American
desert, as well as structures such as a beaver lodge and a
beehive. . . . In addition to the brief introduction to each
subject, short paragraphs identify and discuss portions of
the illustrations." Booklist
"The large pages will captivate readers of all ages, kin-
dling a long-lasting interest in the natural world." Sci Child

Patent, Dorothy Hinshaw

Yellowstone fires; flames and rebirth; photos by William Muñoz and others. Holiday House 1990 40p il $14.95 (2-4)   **574.5**

1. Forest fires 2. Yellowstone National Park 3. Forest ecology

ISBN 0-8234-0807-8   LC 89-24544

An account of the 1988 forest fire in Yellowstone National Park

"This is the only book which covers some financial issues, the media depiction of the fire, and the animals and birds disturbed or killed by firefighters. . . . Clear, colorful photos illustrate points covered in the text." SLJ

Pollock, Steve

Ecology; written by Steve Pollock. Dorling Kindersley 1993 64p il (Eyewitness science) $15.95 (4 and up)   **574.5**

1. Ecology

ISBN 1-56458-326-0   LC 93-10064

Illustrations and text provide information about ecology in general, specific ecosystems, and our changing understanding of life around us

"An appealing format, coupled with striking visual representations, provides an excellent view of ecosystems." Voice Youth Advocates

Pringle, Laurence P.

Fire in the forest; a cycle of growth and renewal; by Laurence Pringle; paintings by Bob Marstall. Atheneum Pubs. 1995 32p il $16 (4-6)   **574.5**

1. Forest fires 2. Forest ecology 3. Yellowstone National Park

ISBN 0-689-80394-X   LC 92-32257

"This book presents fire as a natural phenomenon necessary for the health of the forest. Pringle urges readers to look beyond the media presentation of fire as a destroyer, using the northern Rocky Mountain landscape to show the forest ecosystem before, during, and after a fire, and regrowth over two centuries. Small, labeled pictures identify plants and animals in the side margins." Sci Child

Includes bibliographical references

Rood, Ronald N.

Wetlands; by Ronald Rood; illustrated by Marlene Hill Donnelly. HarperCollins Pubs. 1994 48p il (HarperCollins nature study book) $15; lib bdg $14.89 (3-5)   **574.5**

1. Wetlands

ISBN 0-06-023010-X; 0-06-023011-8 (lib bdg)
       LC 92-47140

Introduces the many kinds of plants and animals found in freshwater wetlands, including flycatchers, whirligig beetles, and tiny water fleas and worms

"Each species described is accompanied by a clear, realistic illustration in color. The text is likewise clear and compact, capable of firing young imaginations by lively descriptions." Sci Books Films

Includes bibliography

Sayre, April Pulley

Desert. 21st Cent. Bks. (NY) 1994 64p il maps (Exploring Earth's biomes) lib bdg $15.95 (5 and up)   **574.5**

1. Desert ecology

ISBN 0-8050-2825-0   LC 94-21427

Grassland. 21st Cent. Bks. (NY) 1994 64p il maps (Exploring Earth's biomes) lib bdg $15.95 (5 and up)   **574.5**

1. Grassland ecology 2. Prairie ecology

ISBN 0-8050-2827-7   LC 94-19389

Taiga. 21st Cent. Bks. (NY) 1994 64p il maps (Exploring Earth's biomes) lib bdg $15.95 (5 and up)   **574.5**

1. Forest ecology

ISBN 0-8050-2830-7   LC 94-19388

Temperate deciduous forest. 21st Cent. Bks. (NY) 1994 64p il maps (Exploring Earth's biomes) lib bdg $15.95 (5 and up)   **574.5**

1. Forest ecology

ISBN 0-8050-2828-5   LC 94-25425

Tropical rain forest. 21st Cent. Bks. (NY) 1994 64p il maps (Exploring Earth's biomes) lib bdg $15.95 (5 and up)   **574.5**

1. Rain forest ecology

ISBN 0-8050-2826-9   LC 94-25427

Tundra. 21st Cent. Bks. (NY) 1994 64p il maps (Exploring Earth's biomes) lib bdg $15.95 (5 and up)   **574.5**

1. Tundra ecology 2. Arctic regions

ISBN 0-8050-2829-3   LC 94-19385

"After a standard introduction, each book locates a particular geographic biome, giving an overall description and treating the plants, animals, and people found there. Individual chapters, which are broken into small units, are brief and well illustrated and include suggestions for experiments using easily obtainable materials. . . . Each book concludes with a glossary and a resource list." Booklist

Silver, Donald M., 1947-

African savanna; illustrated by Patricia J. Wynne and Dianne Ettl. Scientific Am. Bks. for Young Readers 1994 48p il (One small square) $14.95 (3-5)   **574.5**

1. Grassland ecology 2. Natural history—Africa

ISBN 0-7167-6516-0   LC 93-41285

Arctic tundra; illustrated by Patricia J. Wynne. Scientific Am. Bks. for Young Readers 1994 48p il (One small square) $14.95 (3-5)   **574.5**

1. Tundra ecology

ISBN 0-7167-6517-9   LC 94-4143

Backyard; illustrated by Patricia J. Wynne. Scientific Am. Bks. for Young Readers 1993 47p il (One small square) $14.95 (3-5)

    574.5

1. Nature study 2. Ecology

ISBN 0-7167-6510-1   LC 93-18353

Silver, Donald M., 1947-—*Continued*

Cactus desert; illustrated by Patricia J. Wynne. Scientific Am. Bks. for Young Readers 1995 48p il (One small square) $14.95 (3-5)
574.5

1. Desert ecology
ISBN 0-7167-6573-X
LC 95-7096

Cave; illustrated by Patricia J. Wynne. Scientific Am. Bks. for Young Readers 1993 48p il (One small square) $14.95 (3-5)
574.5

1. Caves
ISBN 0-7167-6514-4
LC 93-36570

Pond; illustrated by Patricia J. Wynne. Scientific Am. Bks. for Young Readers 1994 48p il (One small square) $14.95 (3-5)
574.5

1. Pond ecology
ISBN 0-7167-6518-7
LC 94-18044

Seashore; illustrated by Patricia J. Wynne. Scientific Am. Bks. for Young Readers 1993 48p il (One small square) $14.95 (3-5)
574.5

1. Seashore ecology
ISBN 0-7167-6511-X
LC 93-18354

Woods; illustrated by Patricia J. Wynne. Scientific Am. Bks. for Young Readers 1995 48p il (One small square) $14.95 (3-5)
574.5

1. Forest ecology
ISBN 0-7167-6610-8
LC 95-30815

Each volume in this series examines a small part of a specific ecosystem, revealing the plant and animal life within that environment through text, instructions for activities, and full-color illustrations

"The combination of humorous, scientifically grounded text with detailed, realistic drawings will pique the interest of armchair naturalists and active explorers alike." Publ Wkly

Simon, Seymour, 1931-

Deserts. Morrow Junior Bks. 1990 unp il maps $13.95; lib bdg $13.88 (3-6)
574.5

1. Desert ecology
ISBN 0-688-07415-4; 0-688-07416-2 (lib bdg)
LC 89-39738

Describes the nature and characteristics of deserts, where they are located, and how they are formed

"Spectacular photos of the deserts of the American southwest are used to show the various features from rippling sand, to wind-eroded rock formations, to the sparse vegetation characteristic of the area. There is a little information on how both plant and animal life have adapted to the harsh climate, and on the wonderful public lands such as Monument Valley, The Grand Canyon, etc." SLJ

Staub, Frank J.

America's prairies; written and photographed by Frank Staub. Carolrhoda Bks. 1994 47p il maps (Carolrhoda earth watch book) lib bdg $19.95 (3-6)
574.5

1. Prairie ecology
ISBN 0-87614-781-3
LC 93-7841

Describes the ecology and biology of the three different types of North American prairie—tallgrass, mixed-grass, and shortgrass

"A fact-filled trip from Indiana through the tallgrass prairie and the Great Plains to eastern Colorado. Discover ongoing changes through colorful photographs and informative text, and learn about plants that made travel difficult for previous generations." Sci Child

Includes glossary

America's wetlands; written and photographed by Frank Staub. Carolrhoda Bks. 1995 47p il (Carolrhoda earth watch book) lib bdg $19.95 (3-6)
574.5

1. Wetlands
ISBN 0-87614-827-5
LC 94-3872

The author "describes types of North American wetlands and discusses their importance in the ecosystem. . . . On every page, clear colorful photographs illustrate the many kinds of wetlands in the U.S. and the plants and animals that thrive in these habitats. . . . An effective introduction to an important subject." Booklist

Includes glossary

Yellowstone's cycle of fire; by Frank Staub. Carolrhoda Bks. 1993 47p il (Carolrhoda earth watch book) lib bdg $19.95 (3-6)
574.5

1. Forest fires 2. Forest ecology 3. Yellowstone National Park
ISBN 0-87614-778-3
LC 92-29631

Describes the dramatic forest fires in Yellowstone National Park during the summer of 1988 and the subsequent renewal of the land

This book offers "informative text, amplified with color photographs." Horn Book Guide

Includes glossary

Tresselt, Alvin R., 1916-

The gift of the tree; illustrated by Henri Sorensen. Lothrop, Lee & Shepard Bks. 1992 unp il $16; lib bdg $15.93 (k-3)
574.5

1. Forest ecology 2. Oak
ISBN 0-688-10684-6; 0-688-10685-4 (lib bdg)
LC 90-20846

A revised and newly illustrated edition of The dead tree, first published 1972 by Parents Mag. Press

Traces the life cycle of an oak tree and describes the animals that depend on it for shelter and food

"While changes to the text are minor, the revitalized book features a more upbeat title as well as beautiful woodland paintings stretching across its large, double-page spreads. With ecological studies part of the curriculum in many schools, this would be a good choice to read aloud as part of a science unit in the primary grades." Booklist

Vogel, Carole Garbuny

The great Yellowstone fire; [by] Carole Garbuny Vogel and Kathryn Allen Goldner. Sierra Club Bks.; Little, Brown 1990 30p il $15.95; pa $6.95 (3-6)   **574.5**

1. Forest fires 2. Forest ecology 3. Yellowstone National Park

ISBN 0-316-90522-4; 0-316-90249-7 (pa)

LC 89-29318

Describes the 1988 Yellowstone National Park forest fires and their effects on the ecology

"Well-chosen photographs . . . include many full-page scenes and are particularly effective in conveying the power of the fires, the human involvement, and the park as a habitat for animals. The descriptive prose in this book clearly and vividly conveys events and their significance as history." Horn Book

574.87 Cytology (Cell biology)

Balkwill, Frances R.

DNA is here to stay; by Fran Balkwill; illustrated by Mic Rolph. Carolrhoda Bks. 1993 32p il lib bdg $13.13; pa $8.95 (3-6)   **574.87**

1. DNA

ISBN 0-87614-763-5 (lib bdg); 0-87614-638-8 (pa)

LC 92-4802

First published 1992 in the United Kingdom

A simple explanation of what DNA is and what it does in the body

This "is a great introduction to a very complex and intriguing subject that today's students will no doubt encounter again and again as they progress through school." Appraisal

574.92 Aquatic biology. Marine biology

Arnold, Caroline, 1944-

A walk on the Great Barrier Reef; photographs by Arthur Arnold; with additional photographs by Marty Snyderman [et al.] Carolrhoda Bks. 1988 47p il (Carolrhoda nature watch book) lib bdg $19.95; pa $6.95 (3-5)   **574.92**

1. Coral reefs and islands 2. Marine animals 3. Great Barrier Reef (Australia)

ISBN 0-87614-285-4 (lib bdg); 0-87614-501-2 (pa)

LC 87-27746

The author leads "the reader on a tour of discovery that explores the structure of the reef and the life cycles and habits of its various inhabitants. Following a discussion of how the reef was formed, the book includes diagrams of the three types of coral reef formations (fringing, barrier, and atoll)." Sci Child

"The fascinating plants and animals of Australia's Great Barrier Reef are described in a straightforward way and illustrated with stunning, clear full-color photographs." SLJ

Includes glossary

Bellamy, David, 1933-

The rock pool; with illustrations by Jill Dow. Potter 1988 unp il (Our changing world) $9.95 (1-4)   **574.92**

1. Marine ecology

ISBN 0-517-56977-9   LC 88-4167

"The author begins his tour of the pool with the small creatures and seaweeds then moves to the larger fish. Everything seems to be ideal and in balance in this habitat. A storm occurs that causes an ocean tanker to spill oil thus the tidal pool is damaged so severely it seems its inhabitants will be unable to survive. As time passes the tides do cleanse the pool, and within a year the pool has begun to be a community again." Appraisal

Bendick, Jeanne, 1919-

Exploring an ocean tide pool; illustrated by Todd Telander. Holt & Co. 1992 56p il $14.95; pa $4.95 (3-5)   **574.92**

1. Marine ecology

ISBN 0-8050-2043-8; 0-8050-3273-8 (pa)

LC 91-34572

"A Redfeather book"

"Bendick presents basic information about the plants and animals of the tide pool, describing them and discussing their food web as well as their adaptations to this unique ecosystem. With full-color photographs and excellent black-and-white drawings and diagrams, this small-format book is attractive. . . . Libraries needing materials on tide pools will find the book a useful selection." Booklist

Burnie, David

Seashore; written by David Burnie. Dorling Kindersley 1994 61p il (Eyewitness explorers) $9.95 (3-5)   **574.92**

1. Seashore 2. Marine animals 3. Marine plants

ISBN 1-56458-323-6   LC 93-31075

"*Seashore* shows how the seashore is formed and changed by waves and tides. Animal and plant life are shown in color and discussed in detail. The author explains in simple terms different types of shores, marshes, dunes, swamps, and harbors." Sci Child

"Small and attractively printed in color. . . . Young people will be delighted with the pictures, as well as the copy, which is both easily accessible and authoritative." Sci Books Films

Burton, Jane, 1933-

Coral reef; photographed by Jane Burton; written by Barbara Taylor. Dorling Kindersley 1992 29p il (Look closer) $9.95 (3-6)   **574.92**

1. Coral reefs and islands

ISBN 1-87943-192-0   LC 91-58198

Also available Spanish language edition

Examines the variety of life found on coral reefs, including the seahorse, hermit crab, and sea slug

"The material is accurate and well balanced and demonstrates many important concepts in biology. The production is superb, the high-resolution photos are presented well." Sci Books Films

Includes glossary

Downer, Ann, 1960-
Spring pool; a guide to the ecology of temporary ponds. Watts 1992 57p il maps (Endangered habitats) $15.95; lib bdg $16.87 (5 and up)   **574.92**

1. Pond ecology
ISBN 0-531-15251-0; 0-531-11150-4 (lib bdg)
LC 92-19269
"A New England Aquarium book"
The author "follows the formation of ponds by rain and melting snow and documents the subsequent growth of plant and animal life in and around the water. She also explains the effects of environmental hazards, such as acid rain and land development. . . . Physical descriptions, diet, life cycle, and photos of specific plants and animals are appended." SLJ
"Readers are encouraged to 'adopt' a pond and to record their investigations in a useful and precise manner. Safety and the ethics of collecting specimens are stressed. . . . The photos are all excellent." Sci Books Films
includes glossary and bibliography

Johnson, Rebecca L.
The Great Barrier Reef; a living laboratory. Lerner Publs. 1991 96p il lib bdg $23.95 (5 and up)   **574.92**

1. Coral reefs and islands 2. Marine biology 3. Great Barrier Reef (Australia)
ISBN 0-8225-1596-2   LC 91-10096
An account of various research projects involving the animal and plant life of Australia's Great Barrier Reef
"The author captures the excitement and commitment of the scientists as they work to ensure the survival of the threatened ecosystems. . . . Clear, full-color photos show the wildlife and the scientists at work." Booklist
Includes glossary

Johnson, Sylvia A.
Coral reefs; photographs by Shohei Shirai. Lerner Publs. 1984 55p il (Lerner natural science book) lib bdg $19.95; pa $5.95 (4 and up)   **574.92**

1. Coral reefs and islands 2. Marine animals
ISBN 0-8225-1451-6 (lib bdg); 0-8225-1451-6 (pa)
LC 84-816
Adapted from a work by Shohei Shirai published 1975 in Japan
"Beginning with a description of a coral polyp itself, through some of the varied members of that unusual group, to the types of coral reefs and a brief look at some of the fish, crabs, starfish and other animals that call the reef home, this is a colorful introduction to the strange and beautiful world of the coral reef. Unusual terms that are defined in the glossary are in bold type; a two-page note on scientific classification is also included." SLJ

Kricher, John C.
Peterson first guide to seashores; [by] John Kricher; illustrated by Gordon Morrison. Houghton Mifflin 1992 128p il pa $4.95 (6 and up)   **574.92**

1. Seashore 2. Marine biology
ISBN 0-395-61901-7   LC 91-38829
This is a guide to identification of plants and animals found at the seashore

This is "sure to satisfy the curiosity of novices and inspire a deeper interest in nature. . . . The selections, grouped geographically and by habitat, are limited to those most commonly discovered by hikers or beachcombers. The clear, full-color pictures are simply labeled for easy identification." SLJ

Lampton, Christopher
Coral reefs in danger. Millbrook Press 1992 63p il lib bdg $15.90 (4 and up)   **574.92**

1. Coral reefs and islands 2. Marine ecology
ISBN 1-56294-091-0   LC 91-41441
Describes the formation of a coral reef, its ecosystem, and the current problem of dying reefs—possibly caused by global warming
"To the author's credit, some controversial issues within the scientific disciplines are mentioned. . . . The book is illustrated with interesting and colorful photographs." Appraisal
Includes glossary and bibliography

Lavies, Bianca
Lily pad pond; text and photographs by Bianca Lavies. Dutton 1989 unp il $14 (k-2)   **574.92**

1. Pond ecology
ISBN 0-525-44483-1   LC 88-31697
Also available in paperback from Puffin Bks.
"Details of life in a woodland pond, with particular emphasis on a tadpole turned bullfrog. Different animals in the food chain are brilliantly photographed as they search for food in a competitive world." Sci Child

McGovern, Ann
Down under, down under; diving adventures on the Great Barrier Reef; photographs by Jim and Martin Scheiner and the author. Macmillan 1989 48p il $14.95 (3-6)   **574.92**

1. Marine biology 2. Scuba diving 3. Great Barrier Reef (Australia)
ISBN 0-02-765770-1   LC 88-30530
A twelve-year-old girl recounts her experiences on the Great Barrier Reef, encountering sharks, sea snakes, and giant clams, exploring the wreck of a ghost ship, observing shore life, and exploring the reef from a dive boat as well as a helicopter
"The first person narrative is a wonderful way for young people to learn about underwater life. This experience is enhanced by the outstanding color photographs. Technically reliable, competently photographed, and engagingly written, here is one of the best books of its kind." Appraisal

Parker, Steve
Pond & river; written by Steve Parker. Knopf 1988 63p il (Eyewitness books) $16; lib bdg $16.99 (4 and up)   **574.92**

1. Pond ecology 2. River ecology
ISBN 0-394-89615-7; 0-394-99615-1 (lib bdg)
LC 88-1575
Also available Spanish language edition
An "introduction to the plants and animals found in various aquatic habitats. . . . This is first and foremost a picture book; each section consists of an introductory paragraph and several pages full of labeled and captioned

Parker, Steve—*Continued*

photographs and illustrations of plants and animals. The photographs are excellent and are a first-rate way for youngsters to identify the more common organisms found in aquatic habitats." Sci Books Films

Seashore; written by Steve Parker. Knopf 1989 63p il (Eyewitness books) $19; lib bdg $18.99 (4 and up)   **574.92**

1. Seashore 2. Marine animals 3. Marine plants
ISBN 0-394-82254-4; 0-394-92254-9 (lib bdg)
                   LC 88-27173

Also available Spanish language edition

A photo essay introduces the animal inhabitants of the seashore, including fish, crustaceans, snails, and shorebirds

This book "contains . . . exquisite, three dimensional photographs and a myriad of easily digested facts about life where land and sea meet. . . . Better for browsing than indepth research." BAYA Book Rev

Reid, George K.

Pond life; a guide to common plants and animals of North America ponds and lakes; by George K. Reid, under the editorship of Herbert S. Zim and George S. Fichter; illustrated by Sally D. Kaicher and Tom Dolan. Golden Bks. 1967 160p il pa $5.95 (4 and up)   **574.92**

1. Pond ecology
ISBN 0-307-24017-7

"A Golden guide"

The book "explains the dynamics of a pond or lake, shows some of the plants, animals, insects, and fishes likely to be found in or near it, and tells how to collect specimens." Publ Wkly

Includes bibliography

Sargent, William, 1946-

Night reef; dusk to dawn on a coral reef. Watts 1991 41p il maps lib bdg $15.82 (5 and up)   **574.92**

1. Coral reefs and islands
ISBN 0-531-11073-7   LC 91-18526

"A New England Aquarium book"

"The life of nocturnal coral reef animals found in the Pacific, Caribbean, and Indian oceans is described beautifully and illustrated vividly in this book. *Night Reef* treats us to beautiful underwater photographs. . . . The information is presented in an accurate, clear, and well-organized manner." Sci Books Films

Includes glossary and bibliography

Schwartz, David M., 1951-

The hidden life of the pond; photographs by Dwight Kuhn. Crown 1988 unp il lib bdg $15 (3-5)   **574.92**

1. Pond ecology
ISBN 0-517-57060-2   LC 88-11863

This book "presents the wide and complex variety of life in an American pond. . . . Plant, insect, bird, and mammal life are described, accompanied by excellent clear, crisp color photographs." SLJ

Silverstein, Alvin

Life in a tidal pool; [by] Alvin and Virginia Silverstein; illustrated by Pamela and Walter Carroll. Little, Brown 1990 60p il $14.95 (4-6)   **574.92**

1. Marine ecology
ISBN 0-316-79120-2   LC 89-12676

Describes the varied forms of shore life found in and around tidal pools and discusses their struggle for survival

Information is "presented in a lively style to interest both landlocked readers and coastal inhabitants." SLJ

Includes glossary

Stolz, Mary, 1920-

Night of ghosts and hermits; nocturnal life on the seashore; illustrated by Susan Gallagher. Harcourt Brace Jovanovich 1985 47p il $12.95 (3-5)   **574.92**

1. Marine animals 2. Seashore
ISBN 0-15-257333-X   LC 84-15665

"A blending of fiction and science. On a beach on the Gulf of Mexico, three brothers reluctantly leave their sandcastle. That night the seemingly peaceful shore comes to life as a ghost crab escapes a heron's notice, a whelk and a horse conch battle, a loggerhead turtle lays her eggs, and a hermit crab finds a new home. Soft, luminous illustrations capture the drama and beauty of the seashore after dark." Sci Child

Includes glossary and bibliography

Swanson, Diane, 1944-

Safari beneath the sea; the wonder world of the North Pacific coast; photographs by the Royal British Columbia Museum. Sierra Club Bks. for Children 1994 58p il $16.95; pa $7.95 (4 and up)   **574.92**

1. Marine biology 2. Northwest Coast of North America
ISBN 0-87156-415-7; 0-87156-860-8 (pa)
                   LC 94-1465

This is a "study of the inhabitants of the North Pacific coastal waters. Remarkable oddities of ocean life are featured in text and picture. The author sets the geographic scene by describing wind currents, temperatures, and terrain. . . . The family life, eating habits, and preservation techniques of the creatures are explored."

"A lively, informative text, brilliant photographs, and a crisp, attractive layout make this a 'must' resource for up-to-date research projects concerning the sea and its significance to our lives." Child Book Rev Serv

Zim, Herbert S.

Seashores; a guide to animals and plants along the beaches; by Herbert S. Zim and Lester Ingle; illustrated by Dorothea and Sy Barlowe; sponsored by the Wildlife Management Institute. Golden Bks. 1955 160p il pa $5.95 (4 and up)   **574.92**

1. Marine biology
ISBN 0-307-24496-2

"A Golden guide"

"A comprehensive pocket guide for identifying 'plant and animal life found in North American tidal waters.' Algae, sponges, corals, shellfish, birds, flowering plants, etc. are included with brief descriptive text and illustrations in full color. Index." Horn Book

574.999 Astrobiology

Branley, Franklyn Mansfield, 1915-
Is there life in outer space? Franklyn M.
Branley; illustrated by Don Madden. Crowell
1984 32p il (Let's-read-and-find-out science
books) lib bdg $14.89; pa $4.95 (k-3)
574.999

1. Life on other planets 2. Outer space—Exploration
ISBN 0-690-04375-9 (lib bdg); 0-06-445049-X (pa)
LC 83-45057

This book describes what "investigations have shown
about the moon and Mars, what is known about other planets in the solar system that makes it unlikely that they sustain life, and what probably exists of life on planets in other
galaxies. . . . Branlcy makes it clear that his opinions on the
last topic are conjectural." Bull Cent Child Books

575 Evolution and genetics

Cole, Joanna
Evolution; illustrated by Aliki. Crowell 1987
31p il (Let's-read-and-find-out science books)
lib bdg $14.89; pa $4.50 (k-3)
575

1. Evolution 2. Fossils
ISBN 0-690-04598-0 (lib bdg); 0-06-445086-4 (pa)
LC 87-638

Describes, using evidence found in fossil layers, how
one-cell organisms evolved into complex plants and animals
"The text is lucid, simple, and sequential; the drawings
are carefully labelled and are nicely integrated with the text,
and the format is spacious, with broad margins and good-
sized print." Bull Cent Child Books

Gallant, Roy A.
Before the sun dies; the story of evolution.
Macmillan 1989 190p il $15.95 (6 and up)
575

1. Evolution
ISBN 0-02-735771-6
LC 88-8284

"An outline of the history of evolution, relying heavily
on fossil evidence for the depictions of life in earlier ages.
Beginning with a . . . description of the scientific definition
of living processes, Gallant proceeds to cover the formation
and evolution of the universe, the galaxies, and the physical
Earth, and presents early and current ideas of how life began here." SLJ

"The book has an exceptionally nice format; the slightly
wide page size is pleasant as is the design of the chapter
headings. The captioned pictures and diagrams are useful
adjuncts rather than dominant features of the book, and
there is a good bibliography including both children's books
and more advanced sources." Horn Book

Includes glossary

Gamblin, Linda
Evolution; written by Linda Gamblin.
Dorling Kindersley 1993 64p il map
(Eyewitness science) $15.95 (4 and up)
575

1. Evolution
ISBN 1-56458-233-7
LC 92-54478

Text about and photography of experiments, animals,
plants, bones, and fossils reveal the ideas and discoveries
that have changed our understanding of the natural world
and how life began

This offers "a wealth of outstanding color photographs
and drawings and interesting information in a format that
is particularly attractive for browsing." SLJ

Sandak, Cass R., 1950-
Living fossils. Watts 1992 64p il lib bdg
$13.93 (4 and up)
575

1. Evolution
ISBN 0 531 20048-5
LC 91-34423
"A First book"

Describes plants and animals that developed in ancient
times and remain relatively unchanged today, including the
cockroach, opossum, and ginkgo tree

"The book is illustrated beautifully. . . . The text is clear
and understandable. . . . The author presents a good summary of Darwin's theory of how plants and animals evolve
and of his mechanism of natural selection." Sci Books
Films

Includes glossary and bibliography

575.1 Genetics

Aronson, Billy
They came from DNA; illustrated by Danny
O'Leary. Scientific Am. Bks. for Young
Readers 1993 80p il (Scientific American
mysteries of science) $19.95; pa $13.95 (5 and
up)
575.1

1. Genetics 2. DNA
ISBN 0-7167-9006-8; 0-7167-6526-8 (pa)
LC 93-1038

Explains genetics and how DNA works through imaginary newspaper columns, letters from parent to child, and
other scenarios

"A fictional alien ferreting through a town dump seeking
genetic grounds for human diversity furnishes the framework for a lighthearted romp with serious factual foundations. A sparkling approach to the scientific method as
well." Sci Child

Includes glossary and bibliography

576 Microbiology

Facklam, Howard
Viruses; [by] Howard and Margery Facklam.
21st Cent. Bks. (NY) 1994 64p il (Invaders) lib
bdg $15.95 (5 and up)
576

1. Viruses
ISBN 0-8050-2856-0
LC 94-25429

"In the first two chapters, the authors describe the nature
of viruses and trace the work of scientists that went into the
final identification of the organisms. . . . The next three
chapters describe some specific diseases for which vaccines
were made and take the reader through the history of small-
pox, rabies, yellow fever, polio, HIV, and other flu viruses.
The last two chapters touch upon the impact of viruses on
plants and upon emerging viruses." Sci Books Films

Includes glossary and bibliography

579 Collection and preservation of biological specimens

Cutchins, Judy
Are those animals real? how museums prepare wildlife exhibits; [by] Judy Cutchins and Ginny Johnston. rev & updated ed. Morrow Junior Bks. 1995 40p il $15; lib bdg $14.93 (3-5)   **579**

1. Taxidermy 2. Zoological specimens—Collection and preservation 3. Museums—Technique
ISBN 0-688-12854-8; 0-688-12855-6 (lib bdg)
     LC 94-23891
First published 1984
The authors cover "a variety of museum display projects and practices. In a brief introduction, readers learn why taxidermy is useful and, in each of the six chapters that follow, see how different creatures (lions, pelicans, praying mantises) are prepared for public display. The simple text explains the major steps or unique aspects of each preparation; dramatic, well-captioned, full-color photographs highlight the descriptions." SLJ
Includes glossary

581 Botany

Ardley, Neil, 1937-
The science book of things that grow. Harcourt Brace Jovanovich 1991 29p il $9.95 (3-5)   **581**

1. Plants—Experiments
ISBN 0-15-200586-2   LC 90-48097
"Gulliver books"
Simple experiments explain plant growth
"This is a valuable resource for elementary teachers, home schoolers, and other parents who want to extend their child's appreciation and understanding of plant biology." Sci Books Films

Burnie, David
Plant; written by David Burnie. Knopf 1989 63p il (Eyewitness books) $16; lib bdg $16.99 (4 and up)   **581**

1. Plants
ISBN 0-394-82252-8; 0-394-92252-2 (lib bdg)
     LC 88-27172
Also available Spanish language edition
A photo essay introduces the world of plants, including the germination of seeds, plant defenses, and uses of plants
"Probably the most impressive feature of this book is the quality of the carefully composed images, such as the parts of a plant, the time-lapse aging of a blossom, and the photographs shot through a microscope. Each superbly designed two-page spread contains a complete topic. . . . Everything from the history of botany to plant lore gets its due." Sci Books Films

Gibbons, Gail
From seed to plant. Holiday House 1991 unp il $15.95; pa $6.95 (k-3)   **581**

1. Seeds 2. Plants
ISBN 0-8234-0872-8; 0-8234-1025-0 (pa)
     LC 90-47037

"Tracing the cycle of how seeds grow into plants and how flowering plants produce seeds, Gibbons creates a brightly illustrated picture book that includes a simple project . . . as well as information on the subject. . . . The basic facts are there, enhanced by illustrations that young children will find not only attractive, but also informative." Booklist

Landau, Elaine
Endangered plants. Watts 1992 60p il lib bdg $13.93; pa $5.95 (4 and up)   **581**

1. Rare plants 2. Plant conservation
ISBN 0-531-20134-1 (lib bdg); 0-531-15645-1 (pa)
     LC 91-34926
"A First book"
Describes plants, such as the Catalina mahogany, dwarf ilianus, and Okeechobee gourd, that are at risk of becoming extinct and efforts to save them
This book is "clearly written, well designed, and carefully detailed. Landau introduces 16 plants, each with a full-page, full-color photograph and a page or two of description." SLJ
Includes glossary and bibliography

Lewin, Betsy, 1937-
Walk a green path. Lothrop, Lee & Shepard Bks. 1995 unp il $15 (2-5)   **581**

1. Plants 2. Natural history 3. Gardens
ISBN 0-688-13425-4   LC 94-14824
In this "collection of short poems and paintings, Betsy Lewin takes the reader on a worldwide nature jaunt to fascinating wilderness and exotic sites including the Florida Everglades, the Brazilian rain forest and the Brooklyn (NY) Botanic Garden." Child Book Rev Serv
"The paintings are the most memorable part of the book, beautifully conveying a sense of Lewin's affection for growing things, both backyard and exotic." Booklist

Selsam, Millicent Ellis, 1912-
A first look at the world of plants; by Millicent E. Selsam and Joyce Hunt; illustrated by Harriett Springer. Walker & Co. 1978 32p il lib bdg $9.85 (1-3)   **581**

1. Plants
ISBN 0-8027-6299-9   LC 77-78088
This introduction to plant study includes illustrated pages on bacteria, algae, bryophytes, fungi, ferns, gymnosperms, and angiosperms. The author shows how each class differs from the others, and provides games where the reader is invited to match names and pictures
"Just enough material, just enough classification in the plant world is included in an excellent book for the primary-grades reader. . . . The text and illustrations are nicely coordinated." Bull Cent Child Books

The Visual dictionary of plants. Dorling Kindersley 1992 64p il (Eyewitness visual dictionaries) $16.95 (4 and up)   **581**

1. Plants
ISBN 1-56458-016-4   LC 91-58208
Also available Spanish language edition
Text and labeled illustrations depict a variety of plants and their parts, including woody, flowering, desert, and tropical plants
"Excellent photographs and clear illustrations depict a large sampling of plants. The text includes both scientific and common names and is filled with detailed labels and a brief, informative introduction for each ecosystem. This is

The Visual dictionary of plants—*Continued*
an important reference for the classroom library or for the plant enthusiast." Sci Child

581.1 Physiology of plants

Asimov, Isaac, 1920-1992
How did we find out about photosynthesis? illustrated by Erika Kors. Walker & Co. 1989 64p il $11.95; lib bdg $12.85 (5 and up)
581.1
1 Photosynthesis
ISBN 0-8027-6899-7; 0-8027-6886-5 (lib bdg)
LC 89-5832
Traces the scientific discoveries that led to our understanding of photosynthesis and how this process relates to the food supply, changing ecological balance, and threats to the Earth's atmosphere
"A complicated book, but certainly a worthwhile purchase for school libraries." Appraisal

581.6 Economic botany

Dowden, Anne Ophelia Todd, 1907-
Poisons in our path; plants that harm and heal; [by] Anne Ophelia Dowden. HarperCollins Pubs. 1994 61p il $17; lib bdg $16.89 (5 and up)
581.6
1. Poisonous plants 2. Medical botany
ISBN 0-06-020861-9; 0-06-020862-7 (lib bdg)
LC 92-9518
Describes the physical characteristics and natural habitats of several varieties of plants, as well as their poisonous, medical, and magical properties
This "is a useful reference book of poisonous plants, with all plants indexed and pictured, but it is also a captivating narrative on the influence of poisonous plants in history and medicine. Beautiful color drawings and detailed black-and-white halftones on nearly every page are a great help and are critical to being able to identify in nature the plants described in the text." Sci Books Films

Lerner, Carol, 1927-
Dumb cane and daffodils; poisonous plants in the house and garden. Morrow Junior Bks. 1990 32p il lib bdg $13.88 (4-6)
581.6
1. Poisonous plants
ISBN 0-688-08796-5
LC 89-33622
Describes the physical characteristics, natural habitats, and harmful effects of several varieties of plants grown in North America
"Lerner's detailed botanical drawings and paintings are the real highlight of the book, though descriptions of the plants and explanations of their effects on humans, especially children and house pets, are capably written." Bull Cent Child Books

Moonseed and mistletoe; a book of poisonous wild plants. Morrow Junior Bks. 1988 32p il $12.95; lib bdg $12.88 (4-6)
581.6
1. Poisonous plants
ISBN 0-688-07307-7; 0-688-07308-5 (lib bdg)
LC 87-13989

Beginning with "poison ivy and poison oak and other species that irritate the skin, five groups of plants are considered. . . . Varieties of berries, wildflowers, bushes, and trees that are poisonous if eaten are discussed, and the final chapter, 'Deck the Halls,' is devoted to holly, mistletoe, and bittersweet. One full-page color painting in each chapter groups the plants discussed, and small sketches of some leaves, fruit, or roots are set into the text." Horn Book
"An accessible beginning book on an eternally popular topic." SLJ

Sekido, Isamu, 1946-
Fruits, roots, and fungi; plants we eat; text and photos by Isamu Sekido. Lerner Publs. 1993 24p il (Science all around you) lib bdg $18.95 (1-3)
581.6
1. Edible plants 2. Vegetables
ISBN 0-8225-2902-5
LC 92-19958
Original Japanese edition, 1984
This book "purports to examine the parts of fungi and flowering plants that are eaten. Fruits and seeds (melon, squash, cucumber, strawberry, bell pepper, beans) leaves (onion bulbs, cabbage), and fungus (mushrooms) are . . . photographed to illustrate these parts of plants." Sci Books Films
"Distinguishing fruits from vegetables based upon their botanical and therefore, natural classification will help children with the normally held misconceptions based upon culinary uses." Appraisal
Includes glossary

582 Seed-bearing plants

Dowden, Anne Ophelia Todd, 1907-
The clover and the bee; a book of pollination; [by] Anne Ophelia Dowden; illustrated by the author. Crowell 1989 90p il $18; lib bdg $17.89 (5 and up)
582
1. Flowers 2. Fertilization of plants
ISBN 0-690-04677-4; 0-690-04679-0 (lib bdg)
LC 87-30116
Explains the process of pollination, describing the reproductive parts of a flower and the role that insects, birds, mammals, wind, and water play in the process
"Impeccable detail in both text and illustrations makes this the most beautiful as well as the most comprehensive work on pollination available to children." Horn Book

From flower to fruit. Ticknor & Fields Bks. for Young Readers 1994 56p il $15.95; pa $8.95 (5 and up)
582
1. Flowers 2. Fruit 3. Seeds 4. Fertilization of plants
ISBN 0-395-68376-9; 0-395-68943-0 (pa)
LC 93-24972
A reissue of the title first published 1984 by Crowell
Illustrated with numerous full-color watercolors and black-and-white drawings, the author describes the structure of flowers, plant reproduction, and fruits and seeds, including technical botanical terms and concepts

Jordan, Helene J.

How a seed grows; illustrated by Loretta Krupinski. rev ed. HarperCollins Pubs. 1992 unp il (Let's-read-and-find-out science books) lib bdg $14.89; pa $4.50 (k-1)   **582**

1. Seeds

ISBN 0-06-020185-1 (lib bdg); 0-06-445107-0 (pa)

LC 91-10165

Also available Spanish language edition

A revised and newly illustrated edition of the title first published 1960

This "introduction to science leads young readers through a series of steps that result in bean plants as well as a basic understanding of how seeds work. Children are encouraged to follow each aspect of the botanical process, from sowing bean seeds, to the growth of tiny root hairs, to transplanting the plant in the garden." SLJ

"The pleasant multicultural illustrations permit even young children with limited reading ability to identify with the process and perform the experiment." Appraisal

Lauber, Patricia, 1924-

Seeds pop, stick, glide; text by Patricia Lauber; photographs by Jerome Wexler. Crown 1991 c1981 57p il lib bdg $14.99 (2-4)   **582**

1. Seeds

ISBN 0-517-58554-5   LC 80-14553

First published 1981

Text and photographs describe the many different ways that seeds travel and disperse

"Well-balanced, this book includes all the important aspects needed for a general understanding of the methods of seed dispersal. The simple language is clear, flowing, and at the same time, scientifically precise. The black-and-white photographs are superb. . . Even more outstanding is the coordination between text and illustrations." Sci Books Films

Lerner, Carol, 1927-

Plant families. Morrow Junior Bks. 1989 32p il $15; lib bdg $14.93 (4 and up)   **582**

1. Plants 2. Botany

ISBN 0-688-07881-8; 0-688-07882-6 (lib bdg)

LC 88-26653

This book "provides a concise introduction to taxonomic principles of plant identification through examination of 12 of the largest and most common plant families: buttercup, mustard, pink, mint, pea, rose, parsley, composite, lily, arum, grass, and orchid. Each group is discussed in simplified, accurate terms, complete with pronunciation keys within the text and a brief, appended glossary." Sci Books Films

Overbeck, Cynthia

How seeds travel; photographs by Shabo Hani. Lerner Pubs. 1982 48p il (Lerner natural science book) lib bdg $19.95; pa $5.95 (4 and up)   **582**

1. Seeds

ISBN 0-8225-1474-5 (lib bdg); 0-8225-9569-9 (pa)

LC 81-17217

Adapted from a work by Shabo Hani published 1978 in Japan

This book "explores the ways seeds leave their parent plants to establish themselves in appropriate terrain." Book-list

"New and difficult concept words are listed in bold type as they appear in the text. All color graphics are excellent; the close-up photographs are stunning." SLJ

582.13   Herbaceous flowering plants

Burnie, David

Flowers; written by David Burnie. Dorling Kindersley 1992 61p il (Eyewitness explorers) $9.95; lib bdg $10.99 (3-5)   **582.13**

1. Flowers

ISBN 1-56458-023-7; 1-56458-024-5 (lib bdg)

LC 91-58209

Describes the physical characteristics and life cycles of flowers and examines kinds of garden flowers, woodland flowers, desert flowers, and others

"Full of bright, colorful photos and illustrations, this book provides an apt, anecdotal snapshot of the variety and function of flowers. A handbook-sized volume with topical organization, it will entice and invite youngsters to see the beauty around them." SLJ

Dowden, Anne Ophelia Todd, 1907-

State flowers; illustrated by the author. Crowell 1978 86p il lib bdg $14.89 (5 and up)   **582.13**

1. State flowers

ISBN 0-690-03884-4   LC 78-51927

The author/illustrator has "etched the leaves, stems, petals, and stamens, capturing the intricate individuality of each flower in its natural shades and colors. Statutes enacting the state flower laws are given verbatim along with historical and other background information appearing in the brief text juxtaposed with the paintings. Except in a few cases where two states have the same flower and thus are placed together, an alphabetical order by state is observed." Booklist

Johnson, Sylvia A.

Roses red, violets blue; why flowers have colors; photographs by Yuko Sato. Lerner Pubs. 1991 64p il lib bdg $23.95 (4 and up)   **582.13**

1. Flowers

ISBN 0-8225-1594-6   LC 90-27643

Adapted from a work by Yuko Sato published 1988 in Japan

Examines the nature and function of flower colors and explains their role in attracting animal pollinators to help the plants reproduce

"The brilliant photographs are the book's most dazzling and distinctive feature, and they are appropriately matched with the text." SLJ

Includes glossary

Kelly, M. A.

A child's book of wildflowers; illustrated by Joyce Powzyk. Four Winds Press 1992 32p il $15.95 (4-6)   **582.13**

1. Wild flowers

ISBN 0-02-750142-6   LC 91-30368

Kelly, M. A.—*Continued*

"Introducing 24 North American wildflowers . . . this book devotes a page or two to each plant. Powzyk's pencil-and-watercolor artwork lights up the pages with its graceful interpretations of the plants in late summer and early fall. . . . The text gives each plant's various common names as well as its botanical name, and describes its flowers, stems, berries, and other features. A paragraph or two describes the plant's history, qualities, and uses, followed by suggestions of things children can do with it. . . . A most attractive introduction to wildflowers." Booklist

Samson, Suzanne M.

Fairy dusters and blazing stars; exploring wildflowers with children; illustrated by Preston Neel. Roberts Rinehart Pubs. 1994 unp il pa $9.95   **582.13**

1. Wild flowers

ISBN 1-879373-81-5   LC 94-65089

Samson and Neel provide "an introduction to wildflowers and a clever way for chidren (and adults) to remember the names of thirty common and unusual ones. In Neel's . . . crayon drawings (each scene is devoted to a particular wild flower) the shape of the flower is associated with an animal (real or mythical), an object or an action." Appraisal

"The illustrations, bold and inventive, sing with color. . . . Some may find the transformations of these plants to fairies, Indians, or animals to be misleading, but it is all in fun and will serve to give children a way to personalize their knowledge of nature." SLJ

Includes glossary and bibliography

Zim, Herbert S.

Flowers; a guide to familiar American wildflowers; by Herbert S. Zim and Alexander C. Martin; illustrated by Rudolf Freund. Golden Bks. 1987 159p il maps pa $5.95 (4 and up)   **582.13**

1. Wild flowers

ISBN 0-307-24054-1   LC 88-109647

"A Golden guide"

A reissue of the title first published 1950 by Simon & Schuster

"To facilitate identification the flowers are arranged in four groups according to color. Each flower is pictured in color with a range map. . . . Brief descriptive text gives characteristics, habitat, growing season and family." Booklist

582.16 Trees

Arnosky, Jim

Crinkleroot's guide to knowing the trees. Bradbury Press 1992 unp il $14.95 (k-3)
                                      582.16

1. Trees 2. Forest ecology

ISBN 0-02-705855-7   LC 91-18651

Crinkleroot "invites young readers to join him on a walk through the woods, where . . . [he] describes the differences between hardwoods and conifers. . . . How seedlings and saplings grow and factors affecting their development are also discussed." SLJ

"Arnosky's book is the most attractive botany book for children. . . . Its age appeal is broad: The illustrations will

engage tots, while the scientific information, which is very compact, will attract older students." Sci Books Films

Brenner, Barbara

The tremendous tree book; by Barbara Brenner and May Garelick; illustrated by Fred Brenner. Caroline House (Honesdale) 1992 unp il $14.95 (k-3)   **582.16**

1. Trees

ISBN 1-878093-56-8   LC 91-73753

A reissue of the title first published 1979 by Four Winds Press

This introduction to trees "includes information about photosynthesis, unusual trees, the importance of trees to animals, and how to identify a tree by its leaves." Publisher's note

Burnie, David

Tree; written by David Burnie. Knopf 1988 63p il (Eyewitness books) $16; lib bdg $16.99 (4 and up)   **582.16**

1. Trees

ISBN 0-394-89617-3; 0-394-99617-8 (lib bdg)
                                      LC 88-1572

Also available Spanish language edition

"Every imaginable aspect of the life of a tree is examined in a series of 2-page poster-format chapters, from 'The Birth of a Tree' to 'The Death of a Tree.' Anatomy, physiology, reproduction, growth and development are described using the best photographs I have seen in botanical literature and succinct, lively captions. Each page is a delight to the eye . . . Of particular note is the coverage of tree diseases and pollution including acid rain, and the practical, amateur study of trees." Sci Books Films

Ehlert, Lois, 1934-

Red leaf, yellow leaf. Harcourt Brace Jovanovich 1991 unp il $14.95 (k-3)
                                      582.16

1. Trees

ISBN 0-15-266197-2   LC 90-21195

"In a quiet, first-person narrative, a young child details the life cycle of a sugar maple tree. . . . The story is quite brief, and the choice of a very large typeface makes the main portion of the book accessible to beginning readers. The concluding section offers more detailed and concrete botanical information and provides hints on selecting and planting one's own tree. . . . Ehlert has combined many media to create the book's dazzling illustrations." Horn Book

Gackenbach, Dick, 1927-

Mighty tree; story and pictures by Dick Gackenbach. Harcourt Brace Jovanovich 1992 unp il $13.95; pa $5 (k-2)   **582.16**

1. Trees

ISBN 0-15-200519-6; 0-15-201013-0 (pa)
                                      LC 91-12904

"Gulliver books"

"Three seeds float to the ground and take root. . . . The first tree turns into paper products such as birthday party hats, books, and cardboard boxes. The second becomes a city Christmas tree. . . . The third—and most important—still stands in the woods, providing a place of shelter and shadow for birds, insects, and animals, as well as seeds for the next generation. Gackenbach's pen-and-ink and water-

Gackenbach, Dick, 1927-—*Continued*
color drawings gloriously capture this life cycle. . . . Gackenbach's sense of detail is lovely. His pictures glow with warmth." Booklist

Hiscock, Bruce, 1940-
The big tree; written and illustrated by Bruce Hiscock. Atheneum Pubs. 1991 unp il $14.95; pa $4.95 (k-3)   **582.16**
1. Trees
ISBN 0-689-31598-8; 0-689-71803-9 (pa)
                            LC 89-18286
Follows the development of a large old maple tree from its growth from a seed during the American Revolution to its maturity in the late twentieth century
"Bright, warm paintings . . . reflect the subtle partnership between humankind and nature. . . . Hiscock exhibits a sense of awe at the majesty of the big tree and provides a storylike narrative, making this a comfortable initiation into some of the mysteries of the natural world." Booklist

Lauber, Patricia, 1924-
Be a friend to trees; illustrated by Holly Keller. HarperCollins Pubs. 1994 32p il (Let's-read-and-find-out science books) $15; lib bdg $14.89; pa $4.95 (k-3)   **582.16**
1. Trees
ISBN 0-06-021528-3; 0-06-021529-1 (lib. bdg.); 0-06-445120-8 (pa)   LC 92-24082
In this book "photosynthesis is explained, as well as the beauty and usefulness of trees. Easy conservation suggestions are also offered." Horn Book Guide
"This conveys a lot of information in a simple text with clear line-and-watercolor illustrations." Booklist

Locker, Thomas, 1937-
Sky tree; seeing science through art; by Thomas Locker with Candace Christiansen. HarperCollins Pubs. 1995 unp il $15.95; lib bdg $15.89 (1-3)   **582.16**
1. Trees 2. Seasons
ISBN 0-06-024883-1; 0-06-024884-X (lib bdg)
                            LC 94-38342
"This treasure combines the seasonal changes of a tree perched atop a hill near a riverbank with lyrical text and delicately muted color drawings. A must volume for integrating science and the arts." Sci Child

Maestro, Betsy, 1944-
Why do leaves change color? illustrated by Loretta Krupinski. HarperCollins Pubs. 1994 32p il (Let's-read-and-find-out science books) $15; lib bdg $14.89; pa $4.95 (k-3)
                            582.16
1. Leaves 2. Autumn
ISBN 0-06-022873-3; 0-06-022874-1 (lib bdg); 0-06-445126-7 (pa)   LC 93-9611
Explains how leaves change their colors in autumn and then separate from the tree as the tree prepares for winter
"This is an informative concept book. . . . Krupinski's bright gouache-and-colored pencil illustrations show a boy and a girl playing in a country landscape that changes with weather and light. There are also detailed pictures of leaves in different sizes, shapes, and colors. Maestro includes simple instructions for making a leaf rubbing and for pressing leaves, as well as suggestions for places to visit where the fall foliage is special." Booklist

Markle, Sandra, 1946-
Outside and inside trees. Bradbury Press 1993 39p il $15.95 (2-4)   **582.16**
1. Trees
ISBN 0-02-762313-0   LC 92-5145
Discusses various parts of trees and their functions, including the bark, sapwood tubes, roots, and leaves
"The scientifically precise vocabulary is explained in a glossary that also serves as an index. . . . An excellent visual guide, this book will be useful for projects and offers a smorgasbord of facts for both researchers and browsers." SLJ

Pine, Jonathan
Trees; illustrated by Ken Joudrey. HarperCollins Pubs. 1995 48p il (HarperCollins nature study book) $15; lib bdg $14.89 (3-5)   **582.16**
1. Trees
ISBN 0-06-021468-6; 0-06-021469-4 (lib bdg)
                            LC 93-3136
This book discusses "roots, leaves, cones, nuts, seeds, and photosynthesis. Individual chapters focus on seven species: the ginkgo, maple, oak, ailanthus, willow, sycamore, and pine. Attractive oil paintings illustrate the text. . . . A good complement for traditional field guides." Booklist

Romanova, N. (Natal'īā)
Once there was a tree; by Natalia Romanova; pictures by Gennady Spirin. Dial Bks. for Young Readers 1985 unp il hardcover o.p. paperback available $4.99 (2-4)
                            582.16
1. Trees 2. Forest ecology
ISBN 0-8037-0705-3 (pa)   LC 85-6730
Also available in paperback from Penguin Bks.
Original Russian edition, 1983
An old stump attracts many living creatures, even man, and when it is gone, a new tree attracts the same creatures, who need it for a variety of reasons
"The illustrations make up for what may be translation errors, and the writing is more poetic than didactic. The paintings, too, are lyrical both in landscape vistas and in close botanical detail." Bull Cent Child Books

Zim, Herbert S.
Trees; a guide to familiar American trees; by Herbert S. Zim and Alexander C. Martin; illustrated by Dorothea and Sy Barlowe. rev ed. Golden Bks. 1956 160p il maps pa $5.95 (4 and up)   **582.16**
1. Trees—United States
ISBN 0-307-24056-8
"A Golden guide"
First published 1952 by Simon & Schuster
"A beginner's pocket-size guidebook . . . illustrates in color and describes . . . American trees, pointing up the features important in identification—form and height of tree, leaves, bark, fruit, flowers, buds—and including, in most cases, a range map." Booklist

583 Dicotyledons

Bash, Barbara
Desert giant; the world of the saguaro cactus. Sierra Club Bks.; Little, Brown 1989 unp il $15.95; pa $5.95 (3-5)   **583**

1. Cactus 2. Desert ecology
ISBN 0-316-08301-1; 0-316-08307-0 (pa)
LC 88-4706
"Animals find food and shelter in the towering plant of the Sonoran desert, and the local Tohono O'odom Indians have multiple uses for it. The cactus's 200-year life cycle is depicted as part of the ecosystem with colorful illustrations and clear text." Sci Child

Tree of life: the world of the African baobab. Sierra Club Bks. 1990 c1989 unp il (Tree tales) $15.95; pa $5.95 (3-5)   **583**

1. Baobab
ISBN 0-316-08305-4; 0-316-08322-4 (pa)
LC 89-6028
This book examines the life cycle and ecosystem of the Baobab. The author describes the "wildlife that the tree supports and discusses the varied uses Africans find for its bark, fruit, roots, and leaves." Booklist

Cowcher, Helen
Whistling thorn. Scholastic 1993 unp il $14.95 (k-3)   **583**

1. Acacia 2. Natural history—Africa
ISBN 0-590-47299-2
LC 92-39533
"Cowcher explains the natural phenomenon of the whistling thorns of Africa's grassland acacia bushes. . . . Cowcher's watercolors are done with a warm palette and an eye for close-up details that will fascinate children. The adroit combination of narrative appeal with natural history makes this an effective piece of nonfiction for the pre- and just-reading sets." Booklist

Guiberson, Brenda Z.
Cactus hotel; illustrated by Megan Lloyd. Holt & Co. 1991 unp il $15.95; pa $4.95 (k-3)   **583**

1. Cactus 2. Desert ecology
ISBN 0-8050-1333-4; 0-8050-2960-5 (pa)
LC 90-41748
Describes the life cycle of the giant saguaro cactus, with an emphasis on its role as a home for other desert dwellers
"Guiberson's simple, understandable text gives an enjoyable lesson in desert ecology. Crisply attractive illustrations in color pencil and watercolor show the beauty of the desert landscape and its variety of wildlife." Booklist

Lerner, Carol, 1927-
Cactus. Morrow Junior Bks. 1992 32p il $15; lib bdg $14.93 (4 and up)   **583**

1. Cactus
ISBN 0-688-09636-0; 0-688-09637-9 (lib bdg)
LC 91-35678

Discusses the physical characteristics, growth patterns, habitats, and varieties of cacti
"Lerner's clear prose and precise botanical drawings in color and black and white enhance this presentation of a plant family that is inherently interesting for its adaptation to arid conditions." Bull Cent Child Books
Includes glossary

Lucht, Irmgard, 1937-
The red poppy. Hyperion Bks. for Children 1995 27p il $13.95; lib bdg $13.89 (k-3)   **583**

1. Poppies
ISBN 0-7868-0055-0; 0-7868-2043-8 (lib bdg)
LC 94-15057
Original German edition, 1994
This "picture book begins by describing a field of rye in summer, but a particular poppy growing at the edge of the field soon becomes the focus. . . . During its one day in the sun, the flower is visited by a variety of insects bringing pollen from the stamens of other poppies to its pistil. The petals fall, days pass, and poppy seeds form and fall to the ground, ready to grow next summer." Booklist
"The star attraction of the book is its enormous, intensely colored flower paintings." Bull Cent Child Books

Nielsen, Nancy J.
Carnivorous plants. Watts 1992 63p il lib bdg $13.93; pa $5.95 (4 and up)   **583**

1. Carnivorous plants
ISBN 0-531-20056-6 (lib bdg); 0-531-15644-3 (pa)
LC 91-34422
"A First book"
Describes various plants that prey on animals, including the Venus Fly Trap, bladderwort, and pitcher plant
"Full-page, close-up pictures are interspersed well between the interesting text. . . . This is a high-quality book, from the feel of the paper to the print size and style, the art package, and the writing. It is an excellent book for student reports or as a library reference." Sci Books Films
Includes bibliography

Wexler, Jerome
Sundew stranglers; plants that eat insects. Dutton Children's Bks. 1995 unp il $15.99 (3-5)   **583**

1. Carnivorous plants
ISBN 0-525-45208-7
LC 94-24188
The author "first gives a brief overview of insect-eating plants in general. . . . He then zeroes in on the sundew, discussing its range, size, carnivorous method, and suitability for home cultivation." Bull Cent Child Books
"Fascinating photographs, dramatic book design, and a straightforward text combine to produce an excellent book." Horn Book

Wonderful pussy willows. Dutton Children's Bks. 1992 unp il $14.99 (3-5)   **583**

1. Pussy willow
ISBN 0-525-44867-5
LC 91-32262
Describes the appearance, growth, and pollination of the soft white plant that is a relative of the weeping willow
"The author's superlative photographs illustrate the text clearly and accurately. . . . This is the kind of book that helps convert young nature lovers into budding biologists." Sci Books Films

584 Monocotyledons

Wexler, Jerome
Jack-in-the-pulpit. Dutton Children's Bks.
1993 unp il $14.99 (3-5)   **584**

1. Jack-in-the-pulpit
ISBN 0-525-45073-4   LC 92-44375
Describes the structure and life cycle of the wildflower
known as the jack-in-the-pulpit
"One of nature's true surprises is pictured in gorgeous
color photographs and described in crisp, clear text." Horn
Book Guide

585 Gymnosperms (Naked-seed plants)

Bash, Barbara
Ancient ones; the world of the old-growth
Douglas fir. Sierra Club Bks. for Children
1994 unp il (Tree tales) $16.95 (3-5)   **585**

1. Douglas fir 2. Forest ecology
ISBN 0-87156-561-7   LC 93-45251
"Boxes of text set into double-page paintings sketch the
activities of animals occupying a Pacific Northwest forest of
mixed trees. Striking scenes of the skyward view, the lush
canopy, dead and fallen trees, night and winter, and even a
forest ablaze offer a broad view of life in this ecosystem,
with special focus on the 'mighty Douglas fir.'" Horn Book
Guide

589.2 Fungi

Selsam, Millicent Ellis, 1912-
Mushrooms; [by] Millicent E. Selsam;
photographs by Jerome Wexler. Morrow 1986
48p il $12.95 (2-4)   **589.2**

1. Mushrooms
ISBN 0-688-06248-2   LC 85-18953
"Concentrating on a variety of mushroom commonly
sold in grocery stores, the book provides a historical overview of the plant, details the process of commercially growing mushrooms in compost, and—with the use of some fine
close-up photography—describes the physical components
of the plant itself." Horn Book

589.9 Prokaryotes. Bacteria

Facklam, Howard
Bacteria; [by] Howard and Margery
Facklam. 21st Cent. Bks. (NY) 1994 64p il
(Invaders) lib bdg $15.95 (5 and up)

589.9

1. Bacteria 2. Microbiology
ISBN 0-8050-2857-9   LC 94-25430

This book "consists of six chapters that tell the reader
where bacteria are located, who first discovered bacteria,
ways to kill bacteria, how bacteria interact with the environment, how scientists have changed bacteria so the bacteria do things the scientists want them to do, and how
scientists are using bacteria to introduce genetic materials
into other organisms. The illustrations and the examples
used in the text complement each other well." Sci Books
Films
Includes glossary and bibliography

590.74 Zoological museums, collections, exhibits

Gibbons, Gail
Zoo. Crowell 1987 unp il lib bdg $14.89; pa
$4.95 (k-3)   **590.74**

1. Zoos
ISBN 0-690-04633-2 (lib bdg); 0-06-446096-7 (pa)
                    LC 87-582
Provides a behind-the-scenes look at a working day at
the zoo, from the moment the workers arrive until the night
guard locks the gate
"The writing is crisp, clear, and informative. This interesting and authoritative look behind the zoo scenes is illustrated in Gibbons' usual flat, simple, clearly-defined style in
the very bright colors so appealing to young children." SLJ

Johnston, Ginny, 1946-
Windows on wildlife; [by] Ginny Johnston
and Judy Cutchins. Morrow Junior Bks. 1990
48p il $13.95; lib bdg $13.88 (3-6)   **590.74**

1. Zoos 2. Aquariums
ISBN 0-688-07872-9; 0-688-07873-7 (lib bdg)
                    LC 89-34487
"From gavials lazing in a jungle river to kelp swaying in
a sunlit sea, two bright photo-essays provide an enticing
glimpse of six natural habitat exhibits around the country—
Zoo Atlanta in Georgia; Sea World's Penguin Encounter in
Orlando, Florida; the Bronx Zoo's Jungle World in New
York; the Hippoquarium in the Toledo Zoo in Ohio; the
Zoological Park's Forest Aviary in North Carolina; and the
Monterey Bay Aquarium in California." Sci Child
Includes glossary

Machotka, Hana
What do you do at a petting zoo? Morrow
Junior Bks. 1990 unp il lib bdg $13.88 (k-2)
                    590.74

1. Zoos 2. Animals
ISBN 0-688-08738-8   LC 89-34478
"Seven animals—a goat, hen, donkey, pig, duck, sheep,
and llama—are individually introduced in photographs that
picture only part of the animal, encouraging children to join
a game to guess its identity. A large photograph of each animal follows, accompanied by a page describing habits and
characteristics that a child would be likely to observe at
close range. The text is brief, including just enough information to pique interest and spark discussion. A unique
and engaging subject presented in an eye-catching format
seemingly designed with large groups of listeners in mind."
Horn Book

McMillan, Bruce

The baby zoo; written and photo-illustrated by Bruce McMillan. Scholastic 1992 40p il maps $13.95; pa $3.95   590.74

1. Zoos 2. Animal babies
ISBN 0-590-44634-7; 0-590-44635-5 (pa)

LC 91-17267

"This survey of 16 baby animals found in two American zoos boasts exceptionally well-composed full-color photographs opposite paragraphs of text that describe each animal's habitat, eating habits, and growth patterns. A map accompanies each entry. . . . McMillan also indicates whether each species is threatened, endangered, or survives only in captivity. The usefulness of the book is further enhanced by a chart that lists most of the English names for animal young, as well as by the inclusion of a clearly reasoned discussion of the mission of modern zoos. The book will appeal to a wide range of ages: younger children will enjoy the eye-catching photos and the very large labels; older readers will appreciate the many details included." SLJ

Ormerod, Jan

When we went to the zoo. Lothrop, Lee & Shepard Bks. 1991 c1990 unp il $13.95; lib bdg $13.88 (k-2)   590.74

1. Zoos
ISBN 0-688-09878-9; 0-688-09879-7 (lib bdg)

LC 90-6283

Touring the zoo, two children pet, ride, and observe a variety of animals

"Ormerod has taken a common childhood experience and turned it into a celebration. . . . As usual it's her illustrations that lift the book above the ordinary. Colorful line-and-wash pictures show the animals with realism and dignity." SLJ

Smith, Roland, 1951-

Inside the zoo nursery; photographs by William Muñoz. Cobblehill Bks. 1993 57p il $15.99 (4 and up)   590.74

1. Zoos 2. Animal babies
ISBN 0-525-65084-9

LC 92-3344

Explains the different reasons why some zoo animal babies are raised in the zoo nursery and examines what happens to them when they get there and after they leave

"This very readable and enjoyable book is well illustrated with excellent color photographs and even contains a one-page, reasonably complete index." Sci Books Films

Thomson, Peggy, 1922-

Keepers and creatures at the National Zoo; photographs by Paul S. Conklin. Crowell 1988 198p il $13.95 (5 and up)   590.74

1. National Zoological Park (U.S.)
ISBN 0-690-04710-X

LC 87-47697

Describes, in text and illustrations, the many different tasks performed by keepers at the National Zoo and the interrelationship between them and the animals they care for

"Plenty of photographs with informative, often witty captions enliven the text and tone. A realistic, yet optimistic book for young people interested in a career working with animals, this gives insight into numerous species as well as the humans responsible for preserving them." Bull Cent Child Books

591 Zoology

Amazing animals of the world. Grolier 1995 24v il maps set $279 (2-5)   591

1. Animals
ISBN 0-7172-7396-2

This "set covers more than 900 animals arranged from *Aardwolf* to *Zebrafish*. . . . Coverage includes simple animals, such as sponges and corals, and extinct ones, such as dinosaurs. Each one-page-per-animal entry includes a sidebar listing the animal's common and scientific names and classification; data such as length, weight, diet, number of young, and home; a map showing the animal's range; and symbols indicating natural biome, class, and endangered or extinct status. A color photograph and a 250-word profile highlighting how the animal lives and reproduces fill the rest of the page." Booklist

Arnosky, Jim

Crinkleroot's 25 more animals every child should know. Bradbury Press 1994 unp il $12.95 (k-3)   591

1. Animals
ISBN 0-02-705846-8

LC 93-7584

The jovial woodsman Crinkleroot introduces twenty-five realistically drawn animals, including the frog, starfish, and grasshopper

"The presentation is simple. . . . Arnosky's lively watercolors are both precise and informal." Booklist

Heberman, Ethan

The city kid's field guide. Simon & Schuster Bks. for Young Readers 1989 48p il $14.95; pa $5.95 (4 and up)   591

1. Animals
ISBN 0-671-67749-7; 0-671-67746-2 (pa)

LC 89-30062

"A Novabook"
Published in association with WGBH Boston

"Clear, full-color photographs, interesting diagrams, and an engaging text describe a wide array of plants and animals available for observation in urban neighborhoods. Readers find that vacant lots are never vacant, parks are always populated, and a city home harbors more denizens than just the family." Sci Child

Jenkins, Steve

Biggest, strongest, fastest. Ticknor & Fields Bks. for Young Readers 1995 unp il $14.95 (k-2)   591

1. Animals
ISBN 0-395-69701-8

LC 94-21804

"Here are 14 creatures of distinction, including elephants, ants, jellyfish, cheetahs and fleas. The collage illustrations show them at work, and silhouette graphics with captions provide scientific information about comparative achievement." N Y Times Book Rev

"A helpful chart at the end contains further information about each creature, such as diet and habitat. An all-round superlative effort." SLJ

Marshall Cavendish international wildlife encyclopedia. Reference ed. Marshall Cavendish 1989 24v il maps set $499.95

591

1. Zoology—Dictionaries
ISBN 0-86307-734-X   LC 88-5375

First published 1969-70 in 20 volumes with title: The international wildlife encyclopedia

General editors: Maurice Burton and Robert Burton

This reference work "covers the world's fish, birds, reptiles, and mammals, as well as lower orders such as crustaceans and insects. Domestic animals are addressed by groups (e.g., dogs, cats) and by breed (e.g., Great Dane, Siamese). The arrangement is alphabetical, aardvark to zebra fish. Some 1,000 readable articles, 2 to 3 pages in length, provide a brief description of the animal or group; details about its biology, feeding, reproduction, appearance, and special features; and a brief tabular list of scientific terminology, with 2 or 3 levels of classification. An abundance of outstanding full-page (and smaller) pictures in color and thematic maps illustrate the volume." Nichols. Guide to Ref Books for Sch Media Cent. 4th edition

Parker, Steve

Eyewitness natural world; written by Steve Parker. Dorling Kindersley 1994 192p il $29.95 (4 and up)   **591**

1. Animals
ISBN 1-56458-719-3   LC 94-18467

"An informative resource on animal life. With modern photographic techniques and careful drawings, this encyclopedic book presents such topics as form and function, life cycles, and natural survival in vivid terms. Children of all ages will appreciate this opportunity to study animals in amazing detail." Sci Child

Includes glossary

Rand McNally children's atlas of world wildlife. Rand McNally 1990 93p il maps $14.95 (4 and up)   **591**

1. Animals
ISBN 0-528-83409-6

"Presents geographic information about selected animal species, many of which are endangered or vulnerable. . . . The book is divided into continental areas and further subdivided into regions or environmental habitats. Given for each region are a brief physical description of the region and its available food sources and the impact of societal or environmental changes. A locator map, captioned photographs, and colorful drawings of about seven animals complete the two facing pages on each environment." Booklist

"Excellent! *The Atlas of World Wildlife* could serve in both science and social studies. The maps and descriptions are well made and easy to understand. The regional information is brief but accurate." Appraisal

Includes glossary

Small animals. Dorling Kindersley 1991 17p il (What's inside?) $8.95 (k-3)   **591**

1. Animals
ISBN 1-879431-09-2   LC 91-60533

Text and illustrations present the internal and external anatomy of mice, spiders, chickens, goldfish, snakes, frogs, and lizards

"Attractive, informative. . . . Set against a clean, white background, each double-page spread contrasts a crisply detailed photograph of an animal's external anatomy with a clear, colorful 'peeled-back' diagram that reveals its internal parts. Simple, straightforward captions point out intriguing

features . . . that will engage young children and satisfy their curiosity." Booklist

591.05   Zoology—Serial publications

International Wildlife. National Wildlife Federation $16 per year   **591.05**

1. Wildlife conservation—Periodicals
ISSN 0020-9112

Bimonthly. First published 1971

This magazine "focuses on international topics. Many articles are about wildlife, but broader topics are included. Beautiful photos and informative articles make it a good educational source for wildlife lovers. A standard for libraries at a reasonable price." Katz. Mag for Libr. 8th edition

Zoonooz. Zoological Soc. of San Diego $10 per year   **591.05**

1. Zoos—Periodicals
ISSN 0044-5282

Monthly. First published 1926

This magazine describes the activities and exhibits of the San Diego Zoo. It includes illustrated articles written by members of the Zoo's staff

591.1   Physiology of animals

Heller, Ruth

Chickens aren't the only ones. Grosset & Dunlap 1981 unp il $11.95; pa $6.95 (k-1)   **591.1**

1. Reproduction 2. Animal babies
ISBN 0-448-01872-1; 0-448-40454-0 (pa)
    LC 80-85257

Also available Spanish language edition

A pictorial introduction to the animals that lay eggs, including chickens as well as other birds, reptiles, amphibians, fishes, insects, and even a few mammals

The animals "are displayed in buoyant but realistic full-color drawings that sing out from the page. It's unusual to see a science lesson so festively done for such a young audience; in fact this has the fun of pure fiction, though it is straight fact." Booklist

Presnall, Judith Janda

Animals that glow. Watts 1993 64p il lib bdg $13.93; pa $5.95 (4 and up)   **591.1**

1. Bioluminescence
ISBN 0-531-20071-X (lib bdg); 0-531-15672-9 (pa)
    LC 92-25529

"A First book"

A study of insects and other animals that are bioluminescent, including fireflies, glowworms, and squids

"Full-color realistic photographs accompany each well-written explanation." Sci Child

Includes glossary and bibliography

591.3 Development and maturation of animals

Burton, Robert, 1941-
Egg; photographed by Jane Burton and Kim Taylor; written by Robert Burton. Dorling Kindersley 1994 45p il $13.95 (3-5)   **591.3**
1. Embryology 2. Eggs
ISBN 1-56458-460-7   LC 93-28365
In this photographic story of hatching "introductory pages define an egg, name groups of animals that lay them, and show diagrams of one developing in a hen. Most examples presented are from the bird family, but amphibians, insects, snakes, and even a slug are represented. . . . Burton's book is one that children and teachers will reach for to further their understanding of the fascinating emergence of new life." SLJ
Includes glossary

591.4 Anatomy and morphology of animals

Legg, Gerald
The X-ray picture book of amazing animals; written by Gerald Legg; created and designed by David Salariya. Watts 1994 48p il lib bdg $14.98; pa $8.95 (4 and up)   **591.4**
1. Animals
ISBN 0-531-14285-X (lib bdg); 0-531-15708-3 (pa)
                                                LC 93-36703
This volume "presents snails, frogs, fish, snakes, birds, rats, tigers, elephants, and whales. The cutaway sections show not only the various systems in an animal's body, but also how they relate to one another in their positioning." Booklist
"Schools and libraries should put this book on their 'must have' list." Sci Books Films
Includes glossary

Llamas Ruiz, Andrés
Animals on the inside; a book of discovery & learning. Sterling 1994 91p il $17.95; pa $10.95 (4 and up)   **591.4**
1. Anatomy 2. Animals
ISBN 0-8069-0830-0; 0-8069-0831-9 (pa)
                                                LC 94-17467
This volume explores "the anatomy of 31 animals, including insects, marine creatures, amphibians, reptiles, birds, mammals, and dinosaurs. Clear, colorful cross-section diagrams with explanatory labels along with brief text that provides scientific classification and other facts reveal nature's complex machinery. . . . A welcome addition for reports as well as for browsing." SLJ
Includes glossary

The **Visual** dictionary of animals. Dorling Kindersley 1991 64p il (Eyewitness visual dictionaries) $16.95 (4 and up)   **591.4**
1. Animals
ISBN 1-878431-19-X   LC 91-60901
Also available Spanish language edition
This is a visual guide to animal anatomy and classification with brief text

This book includes "upwards of 200 color photographs and up to 100 full-color drawings. . . . The colors of the illustrations are vibrant and seem true to life." Booklist

The **Visual** dictionary of the skeleton. Dorling Kindersley 1995 64p il (Eyewitness visual dictionaries) $16.95 (4 and up)   **591.4**
1. Skeleton 2. Bones
ISBN 0-7894-0135-5   LC 95-11936
"This comprehensive and exquisitely illustrated treasure trove of anatomical terms provides clear and instant access to the skeletons of humans, trees, amphibians, sea mammals, and others." Sci Child

Zoehfeld, Kathleen Weidner
What lives in a shell? illustrated by Helen K. Davie. HarperCollins Pubs. 1994 32p il (Let's-read-and-find-out science books) $15; lib bdg $14.89; pa $4.95 (k-1)   **591.4**
1. Shells 2. Animal defenses
ISBN 0-06-022998-5; 0-06-022999-3 (lib bdg); 0-06-445124-0 (pa)   LC 93-12428
Describes such animals as snails, turtles, and crabs, which live in shells and use these coverings as protection
This book uses "interesting and accurate illustrations and just the right words. . . . The science here is good, and the explanations should cause young readers to want to learn more." Sci Books Films

591.5 Ecology of animals

Arnosky, Jim
Crinkleroot's book of animal tracking. Bradbury Press 1989 48p il $14.95 (k-3)
                                                591.5
1. Animal tracks
ISBN 0-02-705851-4   LC 88-15353
First published 1979 by Putnam with title: Crinkleroot's book of animal tracks and wildlife signs
"Crinkleroot—a curious old codger with a long white beard and hiking stick—provides young readers with clear, accurate information on some habits of wildlife common to the northeastern United States. His short discourses are accompanied by precisely-drawn illustrations showing the tracks of each animal or bird. Each creature's habitats and unusual habits are included, as well." SLJ

I see animals hiding. Scholastic 1995 unp il $12.95 (k-2)   **591.5**
1. Camouflage (Biology)
ISBN 0-590-48143-6   LC 94-10422
The author "describes the ways animals in nature camouflage themselves to escape danger. He explains how protective coloration helps woodcocks, owls, and moths stay hidden; how seasonal changes in the fur of weasels and snowshoe hares aid in concealment; and how the body shapes of speckled trout, snakes, and bittern assist them in blending in with their environments. Arnosky's distinctive watercolor paintings help clarify the text, and several invite listener participation." Booklist

Arnosky, Jim—*Continued*

Secrets of a wildlife watcher; written and illustrated by Jim Arnosky. Lothrop, Lee & Shepard Bks. 1983 64p il $16; lib bdg $15.93; pa $7.95 (4 and up) **591.5**

1. Nature study 2. Animal behavior
ISBN 0-688-02079-8; 0-688-02081-X (lib bdg); 0-688-10531-9 (pa) LC 82-24920

"Explains techniques for finding, stalking, and watching such wildlife as owls, deer, squirrels, and rabbits. Over 100 full-color and black-and-white drawings depicting animal tracks, signs, feeding habits, and the like." Sci Child

"Arnosky's delight in wildlife, and the effectiveness with which he conveys it, conspire to lure the young naturalist, book in hand, out into the wild. The book's attention to detail and straightforward manner make it a fine choice for a beginner watcher of any age." Appraisal

Brooks, Bruce, 1950-

Nature by design. Farrar, Straus & Giroux 1991 74p il (Knowing nature) $13.95; pa $8.95 (5 and up) **591.5**

1. Animals—Habitations
ISBN 0-374-30334-7; 0-374-35495-2 (pa) LC 91-15445

Describes functional structures built by such animals as the beaver, termite, and tailorbird

"Numerous high-quality color photographs of animal architects at work superbly complement the text. The scientific concepts are thoroughly explained in terms understandable to elementary school students. . . . I highly recommend this book to budding scientists at the elementary school level as an excellent introduction to animal ecology." Sci Books Films

Includes glossary

Predator! Farrar, Straus & Giroux 1991 74p il (Knowing nature) $13.95; pa $8.95 (5 and up) **591.5**

1. Food chains (Ecology) 2. Animal behavior
ISBN 0-374-36111-8; 0-374-36112-6 (pa) LC 91-3369

The author examines the ways in which animals hunt and protect themselves, food chains, and the role of humans as predators

This is "informative, well researched, and thoroughly entertaining. Browsers will be attracted by the outstanding dust [jacket] and color photographs and be drawn quickly into the text by Brooks' witty, conversational style." Booklist

Includes glossary

Craighead, Charles

The eagle and the river; photographs by Tom Mangelsen. Macmillan 1994 unp il $14.95 (3-5) **591.5**

1. Stream animals 2. Bald eagle
ISBN 0-02-762265-7 LC 92-23240

"Craighead and Mangelsen provide a bald eagle's view of Wyoming's Snake River and its wintry surroundings. . . . Craighead's clearly written text tells the story of an eagle's search for food and conveys much natural history without anthropomorphizing. Mangelsen's crisp photos further clarify the text, providing detailed closeups of the animals. An excellent addition to units on ecology or winter animals." Booklist

Cutchins, Judy

Parenting papas; unusual animal fathers; [by] Judy Cutchins and Ginny Johnston. Morrow Junior Bks. 1994 40p il $15; lib bdg $14.93 (3-5) **591.5**

1. Animal behavior
ISBN 0-688-12255-8; 0-688-12256-6 (lib bdg) LC 93-27014

This book "focuses on the important roles that seven male animals play in the lives of their offspring. These animals are dwarf seahorses, three-spined stickleback fish, giant water bugs, hip-pocket frogs, Chilean flamingoes, red foxes and cotton-top tamarins. . . . A summary chapter explains why the evolutionary process has sometimes included greater degrees of father-care." Appraisal

"Close-up photos and micrographic enlargements captivatingly focus on these intriguing animals, while the brief, informative, and highly readable chapters invite leisure reading and reward young researchers." Booklist

Includes glossary

Dewey, Jennifer

Animal architecture; by Jennifer Owings Dewey. Orchard Bks. 1991 72p il $16.95; lib bdg $16.99 (4-6) **591.5**

1. Animals—Habitations
ISBN 0-531-05930-8; 0-531-08530-9 (lib bdg) LC 90-43010

This book describes how various animals build shelters, food-catching traps and storage rooms. It includes chapters on spiders, bees, termites, birds, tent-making bats, harvest mice, prairie dogs and beavers

"Dewey combines information with occasional personal asides, giving her text a congenial, conversational quality. Her many pencil illustrations possess a simple charm as well as being accurate and detailed." Booklist

Dorros, Arthur

Animal tracks; written and illustrated by Arthur Dorros. Scholastic 1991 unp il $14.95 (k-3) **591.5**

1. Animal tracks
ISBN 0-590-43367-9 LC 90-21269

Also available Spanish language edition

Introduces the tracks and signs left by various animals, including the raccoon, duck, frog, black bear, and human

"Simple text in clear typeface, accompanied by attractive watercolor-and-ink paintings, introduces beginning naturalists to animal tracks. . . . A good addition to nature study collections." SLJ

Emory, Jerry

Nightprowlers; written by Jerry Emory; illustrated by Annie Cannon; with additional drawings by Renée Menge. Harcourt Brace & Co. 1994 48p il pa $14.95 (3-6) **591.5**

1. Animal behavior 2. Night
ISBN 0-15-200694-X LC 93-27547

"A Greenpatch book"

Emory, Jerry—*Continued*

This volume provides an "introduction to the wonders of nocturnal animals and the night sky they live under. The habits of spiders, fireflies, cockroaches, frogs, armadillos, bats, opossums, owls, skunks, frogs, deer, and many more animals are covered. . . . The book encourages a hands-on approach to learning about the night. It is full of explicit directions for enjoyable and educational activities." Sci Books Films

"Cannon adds beautiful and realistic watercolor illustrations of animals and people of all races and genders. The combination of accurate, appealing textual content and artwork makes this large book . . . a worthwhile part of every school or teacher's library." Sci Child

Includes glossary and bibliography

Evans, Lisa Gollin, 1956-

An elephant never forgets its snorkel; how animals survive without tools and gadgets; illustrated by Diane de Groat. Crown 1992 unp il $10; lib bdg $10.99 (3-5)   **591.5**

1. Animal behavior

ISBN 0-517-58401-8; 0-517-58404-2 (lib bdg)

LC 91-31828

Contains eighteen analogies between human and animal behavior, showing how animals use their bodies in place of the tools, gadgets, and equipment on which humans depend

"Text and artwork are good-humored and to the point. An entertaining look at a variety of animal structures and behaviors." Booklist

Facklam, Margery, 1927-

And then there was one; the mysteries of extinction; illustrations by Pamela Johnson. Little, Brown 1990 56p il lib bdg $15.95; pa $7.95 (3-6)   **591.5**

1. Extinct animals 2. Rare animals 3. Wildlife conservation

ISBN 0-316-25984-5 (lib bdg); 0-316-25982-9 (pa)

LC 89-70133

"A Lucas-Evans book"

Examines the many reasons for the extinction and near-extinction of animal species. Discusses how some near-extinctions have been reversed through special breeding programs and legislation to save endangered species

"The book is a tour de force in arguing for ecological balance. The fine-honed pencil drawings, spacious format, and creamy paper contribute to a handsomely designed volume." Bull Cent Child Books

Bees dance and whales sing; the mysteries of animal communication; illustrations by Pamela Johnson. Sierra Club Bks. for Children 1992 48p il $14.95 (3-6)   **591.5**

1. Animal communication

ISBN 0-87156-573-0

LC 91-40556

"A Lucas Evans book"

Explores the mysteries of how and why animals send messages to one another and to humans

"A volume loaded with interesting facts. . . . Remarkable, also, is Facklam's inclusion of the latest scientific information, from robot bees to elephants' infrasonic communication. The pen-and-ink illustrations quietly complement the lively text." SLJ

Do not disturb; the mysteries of animal hibernation and sleep; illustrations by Pamela Johnson. Sierra Club Bks.; Little, Brown 1989 47p il lib bdg $15.95 (3-6)   **591.5**

1. Hibernation 2. Sleep

ISBN 0-316-27379-1

LC 88-10921

"A Lucas-Evans book"

This book discusses "hibernation; estivation (summertime hibernation); and sleep in mammals, birds, and fish." SLJ

"Exquisite pencil drawings of animals in their assorted habitats support the text. A handsomely designed, informative book." Booklist

Partners for life; the mysteries of animal symbiosis; illustrations by Pamela Johnson. Sierra Club Bks. 1989 48p il lib bdg $15.95 (3-6)   **591.5**

1. Animal behavior 2. Ecology

ISBN 0-316-25983-7

LC 88-35929

"A Lucas-Evans book"

"Ants, cleaner fish, hungry mosquitoes, and cowbirds have their symbiotic relationships with other creatures in common. Delicate, black-and-white drawings and a clear text explain the unique pairings in an especially pleasing format." Sci Child

What does the crow know? the mysteries of animal intelligence; illustrations by Pamela Johnson. Sierra Club Bks. for Children 1994 48p il $15.95 (3-6)   **591.5**

1. Animal intelligence

ISBN 0-87156-544-7

LC 93-17811

Raises the issue of whether or not animals are capable of thought, learning, remembering, and creativity, with examples of animal behavior that appears to be truly intelligent

"Fascinating stories are presented about parrots, chimps, elephants, and dolphins. . . . Fine black-and-white drawings add interest and appeal. This book is an excellent choice for leisure reading and a high-quality supplement for research." SLJ

Few, Roger

Macmillan children's guide to endangered animals. Macmillan 1993 96p il maps $17.95 (4 and up)   **591.5**

1. Endangered species 2. Wildlife conservation

ISBN 0-02-734545-9

LC 92-41433

"A Marshall edition"

"Few organizes his material according to habitats, describing the endangered animals in one or two paragraphs that are always accompanied by a colorful photograph or painting. Maps pinpoint places where the animals can still be found in the wild, and statistical data list location, main threats, scientific name, and size." Booklist

"Libraries needing material on global wildlife in danger will be well served by this fine volume." SLJ

The **Grolier** student encyclopedia of endangered species. Grolier 1995 10v il maps set $279 (4 and up)   **591.5**

1. Endangered species—Dictionaries 2. Wildlife conservation

ISBN 0-7172-7385-7

"The 400 entries are organized alphabetically by common name. . . . Each begins with a colorful graphic that serves as a summary of the animal's vital statistics: common name, Latin name, endangerment code, a small map

The Grolier student encyclopedia of endangered species—*Continued*

with the animal's habitat marked in red, and a color code that identifies the animal as a mammal, bird, reptile, or amphibian. The entry contains a description of the animal, its size, habitat, diet, breeding habits, young, and interesting facts. It also notes the estimated remaining populations, the reasons for endangerment, and whether any conservation measures are being employed." Booklist

Guiberson, Brenda Z.

Spoonbill swamp; illustrated by Megan Lloyd. Holt & Co. 1992 unp il $14.95; pa $4.95 (k-3)   **591.5**

1. Swamp animals 2. Spoonbills 3. Alligators
ISBN 0-8050-1583-3; 0-8050-3385-8 (pa)

                  LC 91-8555

Depicts a swamp and the creatures that inhabit it, focusing on the day-to-day activities of spoonbills and alligators

"Interesting facts about the natural history of both species, as well as suspense and drama, are carefully woven into the story line and portrayed in the accompanying meticulously textured watercolors." SLJ

Harrar, George

Signs of the apes, songs of the whales; adventures in human-animal communication; [by] George & Linda Harrar. Simon & Schuster Bks. for Young Readers 1989 48p il maps $14.95; pa $5.95 (4 and up)   **591.5**

1. Animal intelligence
ISBN 0-671-67748-9; 0-671-67745-4 (pa)

                  LC 89-30061

"A Novabook"

Published in association with WGBH Boston

"An engaging report of what researchers have been able to discover about the capacity for intelligence in gorillas, chimpanzees, humpback whales, and dolphins. The pleasing format describes what scientists have learned about animal communication and experiments in teaching animals human communication." Sci Child

Hirschi, Ron

Loon lake; photographs by Daniel J. Cox. Cobblehill Bks. 1991 unp il $13.95 (k-2)   **591.5**

1. Lake ecology
ISBN 0-525-65046-6   LC 90-34396

Text and photographs explore a northern lake and its wildlife

"The clear, sometimes striking nature shots show the animals in their natural setting as well as in framed close-ups. An afterword includes some information on pollution threats to the loon, which 'has come to symbolize wilderness for many people.' An inviting pictorial accompaniment for environmental discussions with children at home or in school." Bull Cent Child Books

A time for babies; photographs by Thomas D. Mangelsen. Cobblehill Bks. 1993 unp il (How animals live book) $13.99 (k-2)   **591.5**

1. Animal babies
ISBN 0-525-65095-4   LC 92-21409

Text and photographs depict the raising of their young by various animals, including the grizzly bear, eagle, and fox

This features "brilliant photographs accompanied by interesting descriptions." Sci Child

A time for playing; photographs by Thomas D. Mangelsen. Cobblehill Bks. 1994 unp il (How animals live book) $13.99 (k-2)   **591.5**

1. Animal behavior
ISBN 0-525-65159-4   LC 93-36773

Hirschi "gives insight into the ways in which various types of play prepare animal babies for survival. Most species discussed can be seen in North America, but there is an abrupt jump to the African plains to show lions, baboons, and a zebra." SLJ

This volume offers "spectacular color photographs of birds and animals in many environments. The flowing text, centered neatly on each page, offers details in simple, almost poetic language." Booklist

A time for singing; photographs by Thomas D. Mangelsen. Cobblehill Bks. 1994 unp il (How animals live book) $13.99 (k-2)   **591.5**

1. Animal communication
ISBN 0-525-65096-2   LC 93-36772

The author "explores how and why birds, animals, and even fish sing. Animals communicate for many of the same reasons humans do—to find a friend or mate, to warn of danger, to examine a new home, and just to keep in touch." Booklist

"The photographs . . . are excellent—most of them illustrate clearly the behavior discussed, and the common name of each species is given in small print at the corner of each picture. . . . The text avoids anthropomorphic statements, which are too often found in books written for children." Sci Books Films

Hirschland, Roger B.

How animals care for their babies. National Geographic Soc. 1987 28p il pa $4.95 (k-3)   **591.5**

1. Animals 2. Animal babies
ISBN 0-7922-3407-3; 0-87044-683-5   LC 87-12411

"Books for young explorers"

This illustrated text "covers nesting, feeding, educating, protecting, and playing behaviors. Examples used vary from insects like the wolf spiders carrying their young on their backs to salamanders protecting their eggs." Sci Child

Includes bibliography

Johnson, Rebecca L.

The secret language: pheromones in the animal world. Lerner Publs. 1989 64p il lib bdg $21.50 (5 and up)   **591.5**

1. Animal communication
ISBN 0-8225-1586-5   LC 88-19175

Johnson, Rebecca L.—*Continued*

"After describing how pheromones are used to bring about behavioral changes, the author focuses on the honey bee, a species which uses pheromones to regulate almost all activities. . . . The author concludes with ways in which knowledge of pheromones can benefit humans: attracting helpful insects, fighting insect pests, and learning more about animal and human behavior. A useful and attractive title." Appraisal

"Forty excellent photographs (38 in color and 2 in black and white) and 4 excellent line drawings (all from the one bee chapter) are included." Sci Books Films

Includes bibliography

Kitchen, Bert

Somewhere today. Candlewick Press 1992 unp il $15.95; pa $5.99 (k-3) **591.5**

1. Animal behavior
ISBN 1-56402-074-6; 1-56402-377-X (pa)

LC 91-58754

Describes unusual animal rituals of work, play, courtship, and survival

"Precise, dramatic paintings illustrate the informative text. . . . There are many examples of strange behaviors described and illustrated in this extraordinarily beautiful book." Sci Child

Lauber, Patricia, 1924-

Fur, feathers, and flippers; how animals live where they do. Scholastic 1994 48p il maps $16.95 (4 and up) **591.5**

1. Habitat (Ecology) 2. Biogeography
ISBN 0-590-45071-9

LC 93-40915

The author "looks at five widely differing habitats: the seas of Antarctica, the grasslands of East Africa, the forests of New England, the desert of the southwestern U.S., and the tundra of the Far North. In each case, she shows with vivid examples how the plants and animals 'fit together' to help each other survive through the day and through the seasons. . . . Each chapter includes a small map and splendid color photographs from a variety of sources." Booklist

Lavies, Bianca

Compost critters; text and photographs by Bianca Lavies. Dutton Children's Bks. 1993 unp il $14.99 (4 and up) **591.5**

1. Compost 2. Soil ecology
ISBN 0-525-44763-6

LC 92-35651

Examines how creatures, from bacteria and mites to millipedes and earthworms, aid in the process of turning compost into humus

"The author is to be commended for her excellent use of basic taxonomy in reference to animals. . . . The writing is very well done, and almost every page has a beautiful full-color photograph." Sci Books Films

Tree trunk traffic; text and photographs by Bianca Lavies. Dutton 1989 unp il o.p.; Penguin Bks. paperback available $4.99 (k-2) **591.5**

1. Animals 2. Ecology 3. Trees
ISBN 0-14-054837-8 (pa)

LC 88-30001

This book "gives young readers a glimpse of the wildlife activities on and around a 70-year-old maple tree. Color photographs by the author provide close-up views of squirrels, a cicada, baby crab spiders, a skipper, and assassin bugs, among other animals." Sci Books Films

"While the full-color photos are superior to the text, which is a tinge anthropomorphic, Lavies' facility with a lens presents readers with valuable visual insights for their nature studies." Booklist

Martin, James, 1950-

Hiding out; camouflage in the wild; photographs by Art Wolfe. Crown 1993 32p il $13; lib bdg $13.99 **591.5**

1. Camouflage (Biology)
ISBN 0-517-59392-0; 0-517-59393-9 (lib bdg)

LC 92-38211

"The author and a nature photographer . . . draw on vertebrates and insects from around the world to demonstrate that both predators and prey need to conceal their presence and that they do so through protective coloration, body shape, and mimicry. Tropical frogs and insects, reef fish, chameleons, various hares, polar bears, and big cats all appear in full color photographs, closely tracked by well-written and helpful text." Sci Books Films

McGrath, Susan, 1955-

How animals talk. National Geographic Soc. 1987 32p il pa $4.95 (k-3) **591.5**

1. Animal communication
ISBN 0-7922-3406-5

LC 87-14173

"Books for young explorers"

This book "shows the body posture, smells, sounds, and touches used by animals to communicate. Described and beautifully pictured are manatees 'kissing' in greeting and monkeys grooming each other." Sci Child

Includes bibliography

Powzyk, Joyce Ann

Animal camouflage; a closer look. Bradbury Press 1990 40p il $15.95 (3-6) **591.5**

1. Camouflage (Biology)
ISBN 0-02-774980-0

LC 89-9848

"Concealing coloration, disruptive coloration, disguise, mimicry, and masking are methods of animal camouflage exemplified in 13 double-page-spread case studies. Additional information about featured animals and further examples of animals that hide their presence are included." Sci Child

Includes glossary and bibliography

Riley, Linda Capus

Elephants swim; illustrated by Steve Jenkins. Houghton Mifflin 1995 unp il $14.95 (k-2) **591.5**

1. Animal behavior
ISBN 0-395-73654-4

LC 94-42185

"Elephants swim gracefully, holding their trunks out of the water as snorkels. But what do other animals do? Sixteen wonderfully diverse animals, each with its own way of dealing with water, plunge, paddle, and propel themselves across the double-page spreads." SLJ

"Notes at the end of the book repeat the line of text from each spread and provide additional information about the animal and its water habits. Natural science engenders a fine picture book experience in this handsome, intriguing presentation." Horn Book

Selsam, Millicent Ellis, 1912-

How to be a nature detective; by Millicent E. Selsam; illustrated by Marlene Hill Donnelly. HarperCollins Pubs. 1995 32p il (Let's-read-and-find-out science books) $14.95; lib bdg $14.89; pa $4.95 (k-1)   **591.5**

1. Animal tracks 2. Nature study
ISBN 0-06-023447-4; 0-06-023448-2 (lib bdg); 0-06-445134-8 (pa)   LC 93-28523

A newly illustrated edition of the title published 1966

"The text was first published in a different form under the title Nature detective." Verso of title page

This book "shows children how to interpret, through observation, the tracks and movements of birds and animals living, but seldom seen, in their neighborhoods." Sci Books Films

"The essence of science writing for the youngest children is clear, sequential explanation, and Selsam accomplishes this expertly. . . . Donnelly adds interest to her watercolor washes with delicate pen-and-ink lines. Her animals are softly realistic, their tracks are easily distinguished, and at the end there is a guessing game of tracks, with answers on the last page." Bull Cent Child Books

591.9 Geographic treatment of animals

Powzyk, Joyce Ann

Wallaby Creek; [by] Joyce Powzyk. Lothrop, Lee & Shepard Bks. 1985 unp il map lib bdg $12.88 (3-6)   **591.9**

1. Animals—Australia
ISBN 0-688-05693-8   LC 84-29757

The author describes the unique and varied assortment of animals she observed during a stay at Wallaby Creek, Australia. Her own watercolor paintings of goannas, cockatoos, kookaburras, platypuses, wallabies, kangaroos, koalas, dingoes, and other animals accompany her descriptions

"Physical characteristics, eating habits, and distinctive traits get casual but accurate mention in a first-person narrative that aligns science with wild-life adventure." Bull Cent Child Books

591.92 Marine zoology

Cole, Joanna

The magic school bus on the ocean floor; illustrated by Bruce Degen. Scholastic 1992 unp il $14.95; pa $4.95 (2-4)   **591.92**

1. Ocean 2. Marine animals
ISBN 0-590-41430-5; 0-590-41431-5 (pa)
     LC 91-17695

Also available Spanish language edition
Also available CD-ROM version

On another special field trip on the magic school bus, Ms. Frizzle's class learns about the ocean and the different creatures that live there

"Cole's straightforward text explains the main action while energetic (but never hectic), colorful doublespread pictures supply a wealth of detail. . . . A perfect match of text and art, this is another first-class entry in a stellar series that makes science fascinating and fun." Booklist

Oppenheim, Joanne

Oceanarium; the museum that explores the wonders of our world's oceans; illustrated by Alan Gutierrez; with an introduction by Ellen Fries and Merryl Kafka, science consultants. Bantam Bks. 1994 47p il maps (Bank Street museum book) $15.95 (3-5)   **591.92**

1. Marine animals 2. Marine aquariums
ISBN 0-553-09361-4   LC 93-3157

"A Byron Preiss book"

This introduces "children to the diversity of marine life by taking them on a simulated deep-sea dive. Vivid color illustrations portray the species of fish that live within the sunlit upper water, the dim midwater, and the sunless depths of the sea. . . . The authors interweave throughout the text a message of responsible stewardship toward marine animals." Sci Child

593.4 Parazoa. Sponges

Esbensen, Barbara Juster

Sponges are skeletons; illustrated by Holly Keller. HarperCollins Pubs. 1993 32p il (Let's-read-and-find-out science books) $15; lib bdg $14.89 (k-3)   **593.4**

1. Sponges
ISBN 0-06-021034-6; 0-06-021037-0 (lib bdg)
     LC 92-9740

Explains how sponges are animals that live in the ocean and how they are harvested and used by humans

"The presentation is both lively and informative. . . . The text is simple and thought provoking, and the illustrations are bright and animated." Booklist

593.7 Hydrozoa and scyphozoa

Gowell, Elizabeth Tayntor

Sea jellies; rainbows in the sea. Watts 1993 57p il $15.95; lib bdg $16.87 (5 and up)   **593.7**

1. Jellyfishes
ISBN 0-531-15259-6; 0-531-11152-0 (lib bdg)
     LC 92-38515

"A New England Aquarium book"

Introduces the anatomy, feeding, reproduction, and environment of various sea jellies throughout the world

"This book features an outstanding range of color photographs and fascinating information" Sci Books Films

Includes glossary and bibliography

594 Mollusks and mollusk-like animals

Abbott, R. Tucker (Robert Tucker), 1919-1995

Seashells of the world; a guide to the better-known species; under the editorship of Herbert S. Zim; illustrated by George and Marita Sandström. rev ed. Golden Bks. 1985 160p il maps pa $5.95 (5 and up)   **594**

1. Shells
ISBN 0-307-24410-5   LC 86-162343

Abbott, R. Tucker (Robert Tucker), 1919-1995—*Continued*
"A Golden guide"
First published 1962
This guide identifies over 500 sea shells of the world. Locations of shell regions and tips on collecting are included. Illustrated with colored drawings

Arthur, Alex
Shell; written by Alex Arthur. Knopf 1989 62p il (Eyewitness books) $19; lib bdg $18.99 (4 and up)   **594**
1. Shells
ISBN 0-394-82256-0; 0-394-92256-5 (lib bdg)
LC 88-13449
"Arthur showcases varieties of shelled mollusks, echinoderms, crustaceans, turtles, tortoises, and terrapins, illustrating how shells and pearls form and comparing species that inhabit such different environments as freshwater bodies and coral reefs." Booklist

Buholzer, Theres
Life of the snail. Carolrhoda Bks. 1987 c1985 47p il (Carolrhoda nature watch book) lib bdg $19.95 (3-6)   **594**
1. Snails
ISBN 0-87614-246-3   LC 86-21544
Original German edition published 1984 in Switzerland; this translation first published 1985 in the United Kingdom
Describes the physical characteristics, habits, and natural environment of the snail
This "is a detailed, informative and very attractive work. . . . The colored photographs are outstanding. They show in detail exactly what the text is describing, and they also provide a source of information that supplements the text." Appraisal
Includes glossary

Carrick, Carol
Octopus; illustrated by Donald Carrick. Clarion Bks. 1978 unp il hardcover o.p. paperback available $5.95 (2-4)   **594**
1. Octopuses
ISBN 0-395-59759-5 (pa)   LC 77-12769
First published by Seabury Press
"Carrick follows a female octopus as she skims along the ocean floor, finding meals of lobster and crab and encountering her enemy, the moray eel. A male octopus comes to her, they mate, and she moves away to find and prepare a place tp lay her eggs. As she waits for her young to hatch, she rarely stirs, slowing starving to death. The thoughtfully written text is complemented by expressive pen-and-wash drawings in cool sea colors." SLJ

Coldrey, Jennifer
Shells; written by Jennifer Coldrey. Dorling Kindersley 1993 61p il (Eyewitness explorers) $9.95 (3-5)   **594**
1. Shells
ISBN 1-56458-229-9   LC 92-54311
This volume provides "information such as how and when shells grow, the development of the layers of a shell, what is a bivalve (two shells) and single shells. The author describes how to determine whether a crab is a male or female and includes beautiful pictures along with the interesting discussions. In addition, the center of the book provides a project for collecting shells and making a display box to keep the shells in." Appraisal

Florian, Douglas, 1950-
Discovering seashells. Scribner 1986 unp il $15 (1-3)   **594**
1. Shells
ISBN 0-684-18740-X   LC 86-11903
"In addition to some really beautiful illustrations of shells, *Discovering Seashells* includes information on the two types of mollusks—univalve and bivalve—and describes the various habitats of mollusks whose shells are commonly found on both the East and West coasts of the United States, plus a few from foreign waters. Suggestions are given for starting a shell collection." Horn Book

Kite, L. Patricia, 1940-
Down in the sea, The sea slug; [by] Patricia Kite. Whitman, A. 1994 unp il lib bdg $14.95 (2-4)   **594**
1. Sea slugs
ISBN 0-8075-1717-8   LC 93-3765
Describes some of the more than three thousand types of sea slugs, their habitats, eating habits, how they reproduce, and how they protect themselves from enemies
"Because sea slugs are difficult to maintain in aquariums, this will be an especially valuable resource for young eyes and minds." Booklist

Lauber, Patricia, 1924-
An octopus is amazing; illustrated by Holly Keller. Crowell 1990 32p il (Let's-read-and-find-out science books) $15; lib bdg $14.89; pa $4.95 (k-3)   **594**
1. Octopuses
ISBN 0-690-04801-7; 0-690-04803-3 (lib bdg); 0-06-445157-7 (pa)   LC 89-29300
An introduction to one of the curiosities of the sea—the multi-tentacled, highly intelligent octopus
"Lauber's chatty, fact-filled text makes the book a good read-aloud, and Keller's amusing and colorful drawings enhance it by depicting exactly what is described on each page—a perfect match of text and illustration." SLJ

Martin, James, 1950-
Tentacles; the amazing world of octopus, squid, and their relatives. Crown 1993 32p il $14; lib bdg $14.99 (4-6)   **594**
1. Cephalopods
ISBN 0-517-59149-9; 0-517-59150-2 (lib bdg)
LC 92-22234
Introduces the defense mechanisms, reproduction, and other characteristics of such cephalopods as the octopus, squid, nautilus, and cuttlefish
"The book is well written, the photographs and artwork are striking, and the combination of text and illustrations should hold the interest of a wide range of readers." Sci Books Films
Includes glossary

Selsam, Millicent Ellis, 1912-
A first look at seashells; by Millicent E.
Selsam and Joyce Hunt; illustrated by Harriett
Springer. Walker & Co. 1983 32p il lib bdg
$12.85 (1-3)   **594**
1. Shells 2. Mollusks
ISBN 0-8027-6503-3   LC 83-5876
The authors teach "that shellfish are divided into two
main groups, univalves and bivalves, and then proceed to
illustrate both. The real effectiveness of the book lies in its
direct question and answer approach; the text poses questions that readers answer with the help of the illustrations.
The black-and-white drawings are skillfully done and in
each case precisely illustrate the authors' points." SLJ

595.1   Worms and related animals

Lauber, Patricia, 1924-
Earthworms: underground farmers;
illustrated by Todd Telander. Holt & Co. 1994
55p il $14.95 (3-5)   **595.1**
1. Worms
ISBN 0-8050-1910-3   LC 93-79784
"A Redfeather book"
Based in part on the author's earlier work of the same title, published 1976 by Garrard
"Lauber introduces the anatomy, physiology, and life cycle of these easily recognizable invertebrates, exploring their
preferred habitat (dark, cool, moist ground) and the role
they play in aerating the soil and decomposing waste. Several chapters describe commercial worm production. . . .
Short chapters, large print, and several full-color photos
make for an attractive layout that will appeal to young
readers." Booklist

595.3   Crustaceans and chelicerates

Cerullo, Mary M.
Lobsters; gangsters of the sea; text by Mary
M. Cerullo; photographs by Jeffrey L.
Rotman. Cobblehill Bks. 1994 56p il $15.99
(4-6)   **595.3**
1. Lobsters
ISBN 0-525-65153-5   LC 93-1288
Describes the physical aspects, habits, and life cycle of
the Maine lobster as well as the activities of New England
lobstermen
"Cerullo develops a thought-provoking theme of interde-
pendence between humans and the lobster. Fine color pho-
tographs round out a first-rate presentation." Horn Book
Guide
Includes bibliography

Johnson, Sylvia A.
Hermit crabs; photographs by Kazunari
Kawashima. Lerner Publs. 1989 47p il (Lerner
natural science book) lib bdg $19.95; pa $5.95
(4 and up)   **595.3**
1. Crabs
ISBN 0-8225-1488-5 (lib bdg); 0-8225-9577-X (pa)
LC 89-8221

This adaptation of Kazunari Kawashima's Hermit Crabs
discusses "physical and behavior characteristics common to
all crabs, the special characteristics of hermit crabs, and the
way they differ from true crabs." SLJ
"Any classroom that contains a hermit crab, any person
who owns one as a pet, or any science teachers who include
marine education in their curricula should have a copy of
this book. It is lavishly illustrated with color photographs
and drawings. The text is clearly written, with new terms
printed in bold face type when they are first introduced.
The book also contains a glossary and index so readers
should be able to easily locate information." Sci Teach

Kite, L. Patricia, 1940-
Down in the sea, The crab; [by] Patricia
Kite. Whitman, A. 1994 unp il lib bdg $14.95
(2-4)   **595.3**
1. Crabs
ISBN 0-8075-1709-7   LC 93-21494
Presents the life cycle and habits of crabs
"The format of this book is an attractive combination of
photographs and easy-to-read text, with a concluding page
of information. . . . The book wisely concludes with a warning against picking up crabs." Booklist

McDonald, Megan, 1959-
Is this a house for Hermit Crab? pictures by
S.D. Schindler. Orchard Bks. 1990 unp il
$15.95; lib bdg $15.99; pa $5.95 (k-2)
     595.3
1. Crabs
ISBN 0-531-05855-7; 0-531-08455-8 (lib bdg);
0-531-07041-7 (pa)   LC 89-35653
"A Richard Jackson book"
"Hermit Crab has outgrown his house once again and
prowls the beach looking for the right new domicile. Along
the way he tries out a tin can, a bucket and a log, before
he finds the right fit. The text has a read-aloud cadence and
the illustrations are spacious and charming." N Y Times
Book Rev

595.4   Arachnids

Markle, Sandra, 1946-
Outside and inside spiders. Bradbury Press
1994 40p il $15.95 (2-4)   **595.4**
1. Spiders
ISBN 0-02-762314-9   LC 93-22643
"Magnified color photographs that provide remarkable
views of spider bodies accompany a particularly intelligent
essay. Both text and captions are informative and well spun
with clear explanations and analogies." Horn Book Guide
Includes glossary

Parsons, Alexandra
Amazing spiders; written by Alexandra
Parsons; photographed by Jerry Young. Knopf
1990 29p il (Eyewitness juniors) lib bdg $9.99;
pa $7.99 (2-4)   **595.4**
1. Spiders
ISBN 0-679-90226-0 (lib bdg); 0-679-80226-6 (pa)
LC 89-38833
Also available Spanish language edition

Parsons, Alexandra—*Continued*

Text and photographs introduce some of the most amazing members of the spider family, such as bird-eating spiders, spitting spiders, and banana spiders

"The tone is lively and friendly, and each page is sprinkled with snappy subheads that catch the eye and imagination." Publ Wkly

Schnieper, Claudia

Amazing spiders; photographs by Max Meier. Carolrhoda Bks. 1989 48p il (Carolrhoda nature watch book) lib bdg $19.95; pa $6.95 (3-6) **595.4**

1. Spiders

ISBN 0-87614-342-7 (lib bdg); 0-87614-518-7 (pa)

LC 88-39199

Introduces the varieties, appearance, behavior, and life cycles of spiders

"The text is clearly written, well organized, and lavishly illustrated; the excellent photographs reveal careful composition." SLJ

Includes glossary

595.7 Insects

Bernhard, Emery

Dragonfly; written by Emery Bernhard; illustrated by Durga Bernhard. Holiday House 1993 unp il $15.95 (k-3) **595.7**

1. Dragonflies

ISBN 0-8234-1033-1

LC 92-39930

An introduction to the physical characteristics, life cycle, natural environment, and relationship to humans of the dragonfly

"The clear description of the natural history of the insect is complemented by excellent illustrations." Sci Books Films

Includes glossary

Ladybug; written by Emery Bernhard; illustrated by Durga Bernhard. Holiday House 1992 unp il $14.95 (k-3) **595.7**

1. Ladybugs

ISBN 0-8234-0986-4

LC 92-52714

This book "describes the life cycle of the ladybug, adding some interesting facts about its agricultural use, some bits of folklore, and history." SLJ

"The illustrations are simple, clear, and colorful; and the text is readable with a good match of print and pictures. The large, bold labels provide clarification of some difficult concepts for the young reader. The format is appealing—large white borders on which a whimsical ladybug creeps and flies, carrying the text from page to page." Sci Child

Includes glossary

Brenner, Barbara

Where's that insect? by Barbara Brenner and Bernice Chardiet; illustrated by Carol Schwartz. Scholastic 1993 unp il (Hide & seek science) hardcover o.p. paperback available $4.95 (k-3) **595.7**

1. Insects 2. Puzzles

ISBN 0-590-45211-8 (pa)

LC 92-20906

"Cartwheel books"

Presents information about different kinds of insects. The reader is invited to find insects hidden in the illustrations

"Schwartz captures the minute detail of the insect world in bright bold colors that are a definite invitation for browsing. . . . A good jumping-off place for curious children." SLJ

Cole, Joanna

An insect's body; photographs by Jerome Wexler and Raymond A. Mendez. Morrow 1984 48p il $15; lib bdg $14.93 **595.7**

1. Crickets

ISBN 0-688-02771-7; 0-688-02772-5 (lib bdg)

LC 83-22027

The author "explains the anatomy of the cricket, its compound eyes, efficient digestive system, and unique mating habits, to name but a few of the areas. The lucid text is dramatized by stunning black-and-white photos that give children a very special look at how these insects live, reproduce, and function, while clearly labeled diagrams provide additional information. While this is particularly suitable for middle-graders, anyone whose curiosity is intact cannot help but be captivated by this fascinating work." Booklist

Demuth, Patricia, 1948-

Those amazing ants; by Patricia Brennan Demuth; illustrated by S.D. Schindler. Macmillan 1994 unp il $14.95 (k-2) **595.7**

1. Ants

ISBN 0-02-728467-0

LC 93-1769

This describes the life cycle, job differentiation, and habitat of ants

"An excellent resource for young readers. . . . The language is simple, yet the portrayal of the complex life of these insects is accurate and informative." Sci Child

Dorros, Arthur

Ant cities; written and illustrated by Arthur Dorros. Crowell 1987 28p il (Let's-read-and-find-out science books) lib bdg $14.89; pa $4.95 (k-3) **595.7**

1. Ants

ISBN 0-690-04570-0 (lib bdg); 0-06-445079-1 (pa)

LC 85-48244

Also available Spanish language edition

"Using harvester ants as a basic example, Dorros shows how the insects build tunnels with rooms for different functions and how workers, queens, and males have distinct roles in the ant hill. Along the way, she works in details of food and reproduction, ending with descriptions of other kinds of ants and suggestions for ways to observe them (including instructions for making an ant farm). The text is simple without becoming choppy, the full-color illustrations are inviting as well as informative." Bull Cent Child Books

Facklam, Howard

Insects; [by] Howard and Margery Facklam. 21st Cent. Bks. (NY) 1994 64p il (Invaders) lib bdg $15.95 (5 and up) **595.7**

1. Insects 2. Arthropoda

ISBN 0-8050-2859-5

LC 94-25428

Facklam, Howard—*Continued*

This book provides "a broad overview of the science of entomology and illustrates the enormous impact that insects have on our daily life. [It] is well organized, nicely illustrated, and clearly written. Particularly good is the balance between practical information, such as how to avoid bee stings and spider bites, and more esoteric tidbits." Sci Books Films

Includes glossary and bibliography

Facklam, Margery, 1927-

The big bug book; illustrated in actual size by Paul Facklam. Little, Brown 1994 32p il $15.95 (3-6)   **595.7**

1. Insects
ISBN 0-316-27389-9   LC 92-24517

Describes thirteen of the world's largest insects, including the birdwing butterfly and the Goliath beetle

"The full-color, airbrushed paintings are quite amazing. Their realistic, close-up views are certain to intrigue young audiences." Booklist

Includes glossary

Feltwell, John

Butterflies and moths; written by John Feltwell. Dorling Kindersley 1993 61p il (Eyewitness explorers) $9.95 (3-5)   **595.7**

1. Butterflies 2. Moths
ISBN 1-56458-227-2   LC 92-54313

This guide "describes how butterflies fly, and how they see and smell. Also discussed is mating and laying eggs, and the birth of a caterpillar. Butterflies of the rain forest, the woodlands, the mountains, the desert and even the arctic are shown." Appraisal

Fischer-Nagel, Heiderose, 1956-

An ant colony; by Heiderose and Andreas Fischer-Nagel. Carolrhoda Bks. 1989 47p il (Carolrhoda nature watch book) lib bdg $19.95 (3-6)   **595.7**

1. Ants
ISBN 0-87614-333-8   LC 88-31564

Original German edition published 1985 in Switzerland
Describes the life cycle and community life of ants

"The reading level is appropriate for the elementary age group, and several features, such as highlighted vocabulary terms, will aid students and teachers. Although the text is not divided into chapters, it flows well and contains a good index." Sci Child

Includes glossary

The housefly; by Heiderose and Andreas Fischer-Nagel. Carolrhoda Bks. 1990 48p il (Carolrhoda nature watch book) lib bdg $19.95 (3-6)   **595.7**

1. Flies
ISBN 0-87614-374-5   LC 89-32365

Original German edition published 1988 in Switzerland

Describes, in text and illustrations, the physical characteristics, habits, natural environment, and relationship with humans of the housefly

"Large, closeup and magnified color pictures match with paragraphs which are like lengthened captions. They are sure to motivate young readers without much emphasis on terminology. . . . The text is easy to read and interesting." Appraisal

Includes glossary

Life of the butterfly; by Heiderose and Andreas Fischer-Nagel. Carolrhoda Bks. 1987 47p il (Carolrhoda nature watch book) hardcover o.p. paperback available $6.95 (3-6)   **595.7**

1. Butterflies
ISBN 0-87614-484-9 (pa)   LC 86-23217

Original German edition published 1983 in Switzerland

"The authors describe the insect's mating and egg-laying activities; the physical and behavioral characteristics of each of the four stages of development; diet; habitat; protective coloration; natural enemies; and function in the pollination of flowers." SLJ

"The reader is drawn in by the magnificent photographs; close-up shots of butterflies on brilliantly colored blossoms highlight the beauty of these creatures. The text is well organized and, in clear language, explains the metamorphosis and other aspects of the butterfly's existence." Sci Books Films

Includes glossary

Life of the honeybee; by Heiderose and Andreas Fischer-Nagel. Carolrhoda Bks. 1986 48p il (Carolrhoda nature watch book) hardcover o.p. paperback available $6.95 (3-6)   **595.7**

1. Bees
ISBN 0-87614-470-9 (pa)   LC 85-13960

Original German edition published 1983 in Switzerland

"Greatly magnified pictures . . . depict the tasks of the three kinds of bees and help explain metamorphosis, pollination, and hive formation." Booklist

Includes glossary

Life of the ladybug; by Heiderose and Andreas Fischer-Nagel. Carolrhoda Bks. 1986 48p il (Carolrhoda nature watch book) lib bdg $19.95 (3-6)   **595.7**

1. Ladybugs
ISBN 0-87614-240-4   LC 85-25467

Original German edition published 1981 in Switzerland

The text "describes the insects' physical and behavioral characteristics, metamorphosis and diet; it also explains their benefits to humankind. The book concentrates on the seven-spot variety, but a few other species of ladybugs are also mentioned and illustrated." SLJ

Includes glossary

George, Jean Craighead, 1919-

The moon of the monarch butterflies; illustrated by Kam Mak. new ed. HarperCollins Pubs. 1993 48p il (Thirteen moons) $15; lib bdg $14.89 (3-6)   **595.7**

1. Butterflies
ISBN 0-06-020816-3; 0-06-020817-1 (lib bdg)
       LC 91-33152

A revised and newly illustrated edition of the title first published 1968 by Crowell

George, Jean Craighead, 1919-—*Continued*

Describes a female Monarch butterfly's solitary flight from Arkansas to Michigan as she lays the eggs that will hatch and repeat her life cycle

The "full-color illustrations are large and attractive and add to the enjoyment of this informational book for transitional readers." SLJ

Includes bibliography

Gibbons, Gail

Monarch butterfly. Holiday House 1989 unp il $15.95; pa $6.95 (k-3)   **595.7**

1. Butterflies
ISBN 0-8234-0773-X; 0-8234-0909-0 (pa)

LC 89-1880

"Large-scale paintings, clearly detailed, and a simply written, sequential text describe the life cycle of the monarch butterfly and its migratory patterns. This is Gibbons at her best, providing information in a text that is cohesive and comprehensible." Bull Cent Child Books

Godkin, Celia, 1948-

What about ladybugs? Sierra Club Bks. for Children 1995 unp il $14.95 (k-3)   **595.7**

1. Garden ecology 2. Insect pests 3. Ladybugs
ISBN 0-87156-549-8   LC 93-4202

This book is about "a gardener and his attempt to rid his garden of pests. . . . He sprays with a chemical pesticide, which destroys both the good and bad insects. The garden falters, becomes infested with aphids and ants, and begins to die. The gardener realizes his mistake and turns to the natural way of doing things, allowing the ladybugs to keep the aphids in check." Appraisal

"A plea to children to value organic gardening, and a useful book for classes studying and protecting the environment." SLJ

Goor, Ron, 1940-

Insect metamorphosis; from egg to adult; [by] Ron and Nancy Goor. Atheneum Pubs. 1990 26p il $14.95 (2-6)   **595.7**

1. Insects
ISBN 0-689-31445-0   LC 89-15144

Explains how insects grow, describing the various stages of incomplete and complete metamorphosis

"Outstanding, closeup photography and intriguing text carefully illustrate each stage of insect development. Numerous examples of interesting species help readers become skillful observers of insects in their natural habitats." Sci Child

Hariton, Anca, 1955-

Butterfly story. Dutton Children's Bks. 1995 unp il $14.99 (k-3)   **595.7**

1. Butterflies
ISBN 0-525-45212-5   LC 94-19377

"This introduction focuses on the life cycle of the common red admiral butterfly. Brief text describes each stage in its metamorphosis. One or more attractive watercolors illustrate each page. . . . [An appendix] introduces and defines some scientific terms not employed in the main text, outlines the species' geographic range, and describes major physical characteristics in more detail." SLJ

Hawes, Judy

Fireflies in the night; illustrated by Ellen Alexander. rev ed. HarperCollins Pubs. 1991 32p il (Let's-read-and-find-out science books) lib bdg $14.89; pa $4.95 (k-1)   **595.7**

1. Fireflies
ISBN 0-06-022485-1; 0-06-445101-1 (pa)

LC 90-1587

A revised and newly illustrated edition of the title first published 1963

Describes how fireflies make their light, tells how to catch and handle them, and notes several uses for firefly light

"Alexander uses richly hued pastels for her illustrations of a young girl, her grandparents' farm, and the creatures of a summer night. . . . The colorful drawings and appealing cover represent the major changes in the book. . . . The brief, clearly written text is thorough enough to satisfy its intended audience." SLJ

Hunt, Joni Phelps, 1956-

Insects; writer, Joni Phelps Hunt; principal photographers, Robert and Linda Mitchell; photographers, Frank Balthis [et al.] Silver Burdett Press 1995 43p il (Close up: a focus on nature) lib bdg $14.95; pa $7.95 (5 and up)   **595.7**

1. Insects
ISBN 0-382-24878-3 (lib bdg); 0-382-24879-1 (pa)

LC 94-3046

"Close-up photographs and detailed text unlock the mysteries of the behaviors, body parts, and life cycles of many kinds of insects. Ants, grasshoppers, and termites are just a few of the insects discussed. Includes list of insect exhibits." Sci Child

Includes glossary and bibliography

Johnson, Sylvia A.

Beetles; photographs by Isao Kishida. Lerner Publs. 1982 48p il (Lerner natural science book) lib bdg $19.95 (4 and up)   **595.7**

1. Beetles
ISBN 0-8225-1476-1   LC 82-7230

Adapted from a work by Isao Kishida published 1971 in Japan

"Remarkable color photographs . . . allow readers to see the insects in various stages of development. [The book] features the scarab beetle, but other species are pictured and discussed." Booklist

Includes glossary

Chirping insects; photographs by Yuko Sato. Lerner Publs. 1986 47p il (Lerner natural science book) lib bdg $19.95; pa $5.95 (4 and up)   **595.7**

1. Insects
ISBN 0-8225-1486-9 (lib bdg); 0-8225-1486-9 (pa)

LC 86-15380

Adapted from: The world of chirping insects by Hidetomo Oda, published 1976 in Japan

Johnson, Sylvia A.—*Continued*

This book "highlights the biology and taxonomy of the sound-making insects and how they produce their distinctive 'chirps'; it addresses primarily the order Orthoptera—'straight-winged' insects—which includes the short- and long-horned grasshoppers and the crickets, but it also considers the order Homoptera, which includes the cicadas." Sci Books Films

"Scientific names and proper terminology for body parts and processes are adhered to, and crystal-clear, captioned color photographs support the explanations." Booklist

Includes glossary

Fireflies; photographs by Satoshi Kuribayashi. Lerner Publs. 1986 47p il (Lerner natural science book) lib bdg $19.95 (4 and up)   **595.7**

1. Fireflies
ISBN 0-8225-1485-0   LC 86-26

Describes the physical characteristics, habits, and natural environment of the soft-bodied member of the beetle family that uses its light to attract a mate

The text is accompanied by "striking full-color photographs with concise, well-stated captions." Booklist

Includes glossary

Ladybugs; photographs by Yuko Sato. Lerner Publs. 1983 48p il (Lerner natural science book) lib bdg $19.95 (4 and up)   **595.7**

1. Ladybugs
ISBN 0-8225-1481-8   LC 83-18777

Adapted from a work by Yuko Sato published 1978 in Japan

"Examines the metamorphosis of the ladybug, its behavior, and its usefulness in controlling harmful insects in fields and gardens." Sci Child

This is "a prodigious pictorial book. . . . The sharp illustrations will hold the young readers' interest and at the same time expose them to explicit entomological educational material." Appraisal

Includes glossary

Wasps; photographs by Hiroshi Ogawa. Lerner Publs. 1984 48p il (Lerner natural science book) lib bdg $19.95 (4 and up)   **595.7**

1. Wasps
ISBN 0-8225-1460-5   LC 83-23847

Adapted from a work by Hiroshi Ogawa published 1975 in Japan

This book "tells the detailed life story of the wasp, beginning with the foundress of the colony who emerges from hibernation in the spring to the reproductive wasps who emerge and mate in late summer to the death of the males and the hibernation of the females over the winter." Sci Books Films

"The diagrams and outstanding color photos detailing the life stages and behavior of wasps clarify many concepts that might be difficult to visualize." Booklist

Includes glossary

Water insects; photographs by Modoki Masuda. Lerner Publs. 1989 48p il (Lerner natural science book) lib bdg $19.95 (4 and up)   **595.7**

1. Insects
ISBN 0-8225-1489-3   LC 89-12372

Adapted from a work by Modoki Masuda published 1987 in Japan

Describes the physical characteristics, behavior, and life cycles of some insects that spend most of their lives in the water

"Colorful, informative, and interesting, this will fascinate children looking for report materials as well as casual browsers. . . . Habitats, reproduction, and hibernation are all discussed in detail and clarified with many fine, full-color, captioned photographs." SLJ

Includes glossary

Kerby, Mona

Cockroaches; [illustrations by Anne Canevari Green] Watts 1989 64p il lib bdg $13.93 (4 and up)   **595.7**

1. Cockroaches
ISBN 0-531-10689-6   LC 88-37857

"A First book"

Examines the body parts, behavior, and likes and dislikes of one of the oldest creatures in the world

"Diagrams, drawings, full-color photographs, and a well-organized text describe the structure and behavior of various species of cockroaches. Includes suggestions for experimentation and observation, and a list of cockroach suppliers." Sci Child

Includes glossary

Lasky, Kathryn

Monarchs; photographs by Christopher G. Knight. Harcourt Brace & Co. 1993 63p il $16.95; pa $8.95 (4 and up)   **595.7**

1. Butterflies 2. Wildlife conservation
ISBN 0-15-255296-0; 0-15-255297-9 (pa)
    LC 92-33972

"A Gulliver Green book"

Describes the life cycle and winter migrations of the eastern and western monarch butterflies and towns that protect their winter habitats including Pacific Grove, California and El Rosario, Mexico

"Vibrant description melds with fascinating full-color photographs in a book that strikes a perfect balance between science and humanity." SLJ

Lavies, Bianca

Backyard hunter: the praying mantis; text and photographs by Bianca Lavies. Dutton 1990 unp il o.p.; Penguin Bks. paperback available $4.99 (2-4)   **595.7**

1. Praying mantis
ISBN 0-14-055494-7 (pa)   LC 89-37485

"Outstanding photographs document a thorough discussion of the behavior, life cycle, and development of an impressive insect that eats other insects alive. Insect observers will find the account stimulating and informative." Sci Child

Killer bees; text and photographs by Bianca Lavies. Dutton Children's Bks. 1994 unp il maps $15.99 (4 and up)   **595.7**

1. Bees
ISBN 0-525-45243-5   LC 94-18581

"Drawing on conversations with honey hunters, beekeepers, and scientists, this book explores life in the nests of killer bees, how climate has shaped their behavior, and the current breeding experiments to create a milder but equally productive bee." Publisher's note

"The many outstanding photographs help make this

Lavies, Bianca—*Continued*
book feel very personal, as we get to see photographs of the scientist and people who work with or have been attacked by the bees." Sci Books Films

Monarch butterflies; mysterious travelers; text and photographs by Bianca Lavies. Dutton Children's Bks. 1992 unp il $15.99 (4 and up)   595.7

1. Butterflies 2. Natural history—Mexico
ISBN 0-525-44905-1   LC 92-28337

Text and photographs describe the physical characteristics, life cycle, migration, and study of monarch butterflies
"How butterflies are tagged and scientific data gathered leads to many interesting facts about their survival during dormancy. . . . The photo-documentary style with its open format and direct, clearly written text makes information accessible." SLJ

Wasps at home; text and photographs by Bianca Lavies. Dutton Children's Bks. 1991 unp il $13.95 (4 and up)   595.7

1. Wasps
ISBN 0-525-44704-0   LC 90-27338

Reveals the hidden world of social wasps at home in their nests, focusing on the activities of paper wasps and baldfaced hornets
"Explanations of wasp behavior are clear and scientific . . . providing a level-headed complement to the bug-eyed photographs and making them all the more marvelous in their reality." Bull Cent Child Books

McLaughlin, Molly
Dragonflies. Walker & Co. 1989 28p il $14.95; lib bdg $15.85 (3-5)   595.7

1. Dragonflies
ISBN 0-8027-6846-6; 0-8027-6847-4 (lib bdg)
LC 88-20632

The "text introduces a variety of types [of dragonflies] and describes the life cycle of the jewel-like insect." Sci Child
"Excellent color photographs (with varying degrees of magnification) are well-placed in relation to the text and are adequately provided with full captions, adding to the visual appeal and the accessibility of a fine science book." Bull Cent Child Books

Meyers, Susan
Insect zoo; photographs by Richard Hewett. Lodestar Bks. 1991 48p il $16.95 (4-6)
595.7

1. San Francisco Insect Zoo 2. Insects
ISBN 0-525-67325-3   LC 90-35177

Describes, in text and photographs, the San Francisco Insect Zoo and the many insects that are kept there
"There are 41 large, color photographs of insects, other arthropods, and zoo facilities. Most of the photographs are of good quality, although several are out of focus. The biological information is accurate and presented in an interesting manner by relating it to the zoo's operation." Sci Books Films

Micucci, Charles
The life and times of the honeybee. Ticknor & Fields Bks. for Young Readers 1995 32p il $13.95 (2-4)   595.7

1. Bees 2. Honey
ISBN 0-395-65968-X   LC 93-8135

The author "covers everything from distribution, reproduction, behavior, and honey manufacture to the honeybee's niche in history." Booklist
"The multitude of original watercolors bring the subject to life, provide a sense of scale and amplify the text. . . . A must acquisition for a library." Appraisal

Mitchell, Robert T.
Butterflies and moths; a guide to the more common American species; by Robert T. Mitchell and Herbert S. Zim; illustrated by Andre Durenceau. rev ed. Golden Bks. 1987 160p il pa $5.95 (4 and up)   595.7

1. Butterflies 2. Moths
ISBN 0-307-24052-5   LC 87-171378
First published 1964

Text and photographs provide information and description of butterflies and moths commonly found in the United States

Mound, L. A. (Laurence Alfred), 1934-
Amazing insects; written by Laurence Mound; photographed by Frank Greenaway. Knopf 1993 29p il (Eyewitness juniors) lib bdg $11.99; pa $9.99 (2-4)   595.7

1. Insects
ISBN 0-679-93925-3 (lib bdg); 0-679-83925-9 (pa)
LC 92-26735

"Two-page sections briefly introduce insect anatomy, diet, communication, development of young, defense mechanisms, relationship to humans, etc. . . . A wide variety of insects are included." SLJ
"This beautifully illustrated book . . . provides . . . a tremendous amount of well articulated, concise information on insects." Sci Books Films

Insect; written by Laurence Mound. Knopf 1990 63p il (Eyewitness books) $19; lib bdg $18.99 (4 and up)   595.7

1. Insects
ISBN 0-679-80441-2; 0-679-90441-7 (lib bdg)
LC 89-15603

Also available Spanish language edition
This volume covers "insect anatomy, particular insect species, and how insects survive and relate to other living things in an appealing, thorough presentation suitable for browsing or close study." Sci Child

Overbeck, Cynthia
Ants; by Cynthia Overbeck; photographs by Satoshi Kuribayashi. Lerner Publs. 1982 48p il (Lerner natural science book) lib bdg $19.95; pa $5.95 (4 and up)   595.7

1. Ants
ISBN 0-8225-1468-0 (lib bdg); 0-8225-9525-7 (pa)
LC 81-17216

Adapted from a work by Satoshi Kuribayashi published 1971 in Japan

Overbeck, Cynthia—_Continued_

Text and color photographs depict the characteristics and behavior of ants

"New and difficult concept words are listed in bold type as they appear in the text. All color graphics are excellent; the close-up photographs are stunning." SLJ

Includes glossary

Parker, Nancy Winslow

Bugs; [by] Nancy Winslow Parker and Joan Richards Wright; illustrations by Nancy Winslow Parker. Greenwillow Bks. 1987 40p il $15; lib bdg $14.93; pa $4.95 (1-3)　　**595.7**

1. Insects
ISBN 0-688-06623-2; 0-688-06624-0 (lib bdg); 0-688-08296-3 (pa)　　LC 86-29387

Insects are depicted in drawings accompanied by short alliterative verses identifying them. The animal's common and scientific names, physical or behavioral characteristics, and habitat and geographical range are provided

"The authors use the word _bug_ as children use it and present insects that children may know, such as flies, ants, fleas, cicadas, roaches, head lice, and fireflies. The text may not answer all their questions, but it's an excellent starting place. The thoughtfully planned layout and Parker's appealing, full-color illustrations of the children, pets, and bugs lend this book a certain charm that might be unexpected, given its subject matter." Booklist

Includes bibliography

Parker, Steve

Insects; written by Steve Parker. Dorling Kindersley 1992 61p il (Eyewitness explorers) $9.95 (3-5)　　**595.7**

1. Insects
ISBN 1-56458-025-3　　LC 91-58212

Describes the physical characteristics, behavior, and metamorphosis of insects and examines kinds of garden insects, woodland insects, insects in the home, and others

"The full-color pictures are of high quality and the text clear and readable." SLJ

Patent, Dorothy Hinshaw

Looking at ants. Holiday House 1989 48p il $12.95 (3-5)　　**595.7**

1. Ants
ISBN 0-8234-0771-3　　LC 89-1943

"Patent offers students brief chapters on ants' physical characteristics, hierarchical social structure, work roles within colonies, communication capabilities, and mutually beneficial host-tenant relationship with plants (for example, the whistling thorn acacia of Africa). She also stresses the worldwide ecological significance of these creatures." Booklist

Mosquitoes. Holiday House 1986 40p il $12.95 (4 and up)　　**595.7**

1. Mosquitoes
ISBN 0-8234-0627-X　　LC 86-45387

Discusses the mosquito's habits, development, and diseases it carries, as well as ways to control these creatures

"The layout is clean, and the first-class text is made even stronger by the pictures, some of which are scanning electron micrographs—their clarity will surely intrigue readers." Booklist

Ryder, Joanne

Where butterflies grow; pictures by Lynne Cherry. Lodestar Bks. 1989 unp il lib bdg $14.99 (k-2)　　**595.7**

1. Butterflies
ISBN 0-525-67284-2　　LC 88-37989

Describes what it feels like to change from a caterpillar into a butterfly. Includes gardening tips to attract butterflies

"The book is packed with good information presented in an imaginative way. Cherry's illustrations span the full page, using boxes in sequence to magnify details or follow action. Another special feature of her lush watercolors is the many small creatures hidden among the plant life, inviting readers to sharpen their powers of observation." SLJ

Souza, D. M. (Dorothy M.)

Insects around the house. Carolrhoda Bks. 1991 40p il (Creatures all around us) lib bdg $18.95 (4-6)　　**595.7**

1. Insects 2. Household pests
ISBN 0-87614-438-5　　LC 90-38290

Describes the life cycles and habits of various insects found in the house, including the termite, housefly, and cockroach

"Sharp full-color photographs appear on almost every page, many of which are dramatic close-ups. The text [is] clearly written and well organized." SLJ

Includes glossary

Insects in the garden. Carolrhoda Bks. 1991 40p il (Creatures all around us) lib bdg $18.95 (4-6)　　**595.7**

1. Insects
ISBN 0-87614-439-3　　LC 90-38292

This volume discusses "the special characteristics, diet, and life cycles of . . . grasshoppers, mantises, dragonflies, and wasps." SLJ

This is a "solid and valuable offering for children. In tandem with an excellent collection of photographs runs a text that gives a clear and straightforward introduction to insects and arachnids." Appraisal

Includes glossary

Still, John

Amazing beetles; written by John Still. Knopf 1991 29p il (Eyewitness juniors) lib bdg $9.99; pa $6.95 (2-4)　　**595.7**

1. Beetles
ISBN 0-679-91519-2 (lib bdg); 0-679-81519-8 (pa)　　LC 91-6516

Also available Spanish language edition

Text and photographs introduce amazing members of the beetle world, including scarabs and weevils

"This brief book is an ideal way to introduce children to the diversity of beetles. . . . The book is profusely illustrated with color photographs and drawings." Sci Books Films

Amazing butterflies & moths; written by John Still; photographed by Jerry Young. Knopf 1991 29p il (Eyewitness juniors) lib bdg $9.99; pa $7.99 (2-4)　　**595.7**

1. Butterflies 2. Moths
ISBN 0-679-91515-X (lib bdg); 0-679-81515-5 (pa)　　LC 90-19234

Also available Spanish language edition

Still, John—*Continued*
Photographic guide illustrates the life cycles and characteristics of various kinds of moths, butterflies, and caterpillars

Watts, Barrie
Honeybee. Silver Burdett Press 1990 c1989 24p il $6.95; lib bdg $9.98 (k-3)   **595.7**
1. Bees
ISBN 0-382-24013-8; 0-382-24011-1 (lib bdg)
LC 89-38981
"A Stopwatch book"
First published 1989 in the United Kingdom
Describes the life cycle and behavior of the honeybee
"Immaculately reproduced photographic enlargements transport readers into a hive to observe the life cycle of these small creatures. The striking camerawork focuses on newly laid eggs in their honeycomb, reveals pupae developing in their cells; and shows a queen and her workers leaving for a new home." Booklist

Whalley, Paul Ernest Sutton
Butterfly & moth; written by Paul Whalley. Knopf 1988 63p il (Eyewitness books) $16; lib bdg $16.99 (4 and up)   **595.7**
1. Butterflies 2. Moths
ISBN 0-394-89618-1; 0-394-99618-6 (lib bdg)
LC 88-1574
Also available Spanish language edition
This book "explores the changes that occur at each stage of the life cycles of these insects. Temperate, mountain, and exotic species are described as are shapes, camouflage, and mimicry." Sci Teach
"This is an impressive, informative, and high-quality book." Sci Books Films

Zim, Herbert S.
Insects; a guide to familiar American insects; by Herbert S. Zim and Clarence Cottam; illustrated by James Gordon Irving. Golden Bks. il pa $5.95 (4 and up)   **595.7**
1. Insects
"A Golden guide"
First published 1951 by Simon & Schuster. Periodically revised
This guide to familiar American insects describes their life cycles, feeding, habits and ranges, with color illustrations
Includes bibliography

596 Vertebrates

Bischhoff-Miersch, Andrea
Do you know the difference? text by Andrea and Michael Bischhoff-Miersch; paintings by Christine Faltermayr. North-South Bks. 1995 unp $14.95; lib bdg $14.88 (2-4)   **596**
1. Animals
ISBN 1-55858-371-8; 1-55858-372-6 (lib bdg)
LC 94-40035
"A Michael Neugebauer book"

"Twelve of nature's 'confusables'—animals with similar physical characteristics . . .—are presented on facing, softly shaded, pastel pages. Each lifelike illustration, done in natural tones, depicts an animal with its name in bold type, a simple caption, and text that explains why it is often misidentified." SLJ
"Although the coverage is too sketchy for report writers, browsers will find the book inviting and informative. It will also be useful for classrooms planning a trip to the zoo." Booklist

Parker, Steve
Skeleton; written by Steve Parker. Knopf 1988 63p il (Eyewitness books) $19; lib bdg $18.99 (4 and up)   **596**
1. Skeleton 2. Bones
ISBN 0-394-89620-3; 0-394-99620-8 (lib bdg)
LC 87-26314
Also available Spanish language edition
"An introduction to the structure and evolution of human and animal skeletal systems. Photographs of actual bones are used with some drawings to illustrate the book. There is a brief text, but the bulk of the book is the illustrations and their captions." BAYA Book Rev

597 Cold-blooded vertebrates. Fishes

Arnosky, Jim
Crinkleroot's 25 fish every child should know. Bradbury Press 1993 unp il $12.95 (k-3)   **597**
1. Fishes
ISBN 0-02-705844-1   LC 92-39381
Presents paintings of twelve freshwater fish, including the carp, bass, and trout, and thirteen saltwater fish, including the flounder, tuna, swordfish and seahorse
"Arnosky's choice of a sunlit palette against an expansive white background pleases the eye while helping to train it to particulars." Publ Wkly

The **Audubon** Society field guide to North American fishes, whales, and dolphins; [by] Herbert T. Boschung, Jr. [et al.]; visual key by Carol Nehring and Jordan Verner. Knopf 1983 848p il maps flexible bdg $19 (5 and up)   **597**
1. Fishes—North America 2. Whales 3. Dolphins
ISBN 0-394-53405-0   LC 83-47962
"A Chanticleer Press edition. The Audubon Society field guide series"
This guide has "a first section containing excellent photographs of 529 marine and freshwater fishes and 45 cetacean species found in or near North America north of Mexico, and a second section giving brief descriptions of each species. . . . The well-organized and well-written text includes descriptions of physical features, habitat, range (generally with a small map), and related or similar species." Choice
Includes glossary

Berman, Ruth

Sharks; photographs by Jeffrey L. Rotman. Carolrhoda Bks. 1995 47p il (Carolrhoda nature watch book) lib bdg $14.96; pa $7.95 (3-6) **597**

1. Sharks

ISBN 0-87614-870-4 (lib bdg); 0-87614-897-6 (pa)
LC 94-21468

The author introduces shark physiology "through brief but detailed descriptions. Full-color photographs show the variety of sharks, and colorful diagrams amplify the easy-to-understand explanations of their behavior and anatomy. Unfamiliar terms are highlighted in bold print and defined in context; a photograph and caption further explicate them." SLJ

Includes glossary

Cerullo, Mary M.

Sharks; challengers of the deep; text by Mary M. Cerullo; photographs by Jeffrey L. Rotman. Cobblehill Bks. 1993 57p il $15.99 (4 and up) **597**

1. Sharks

ISBN 0-525-65100-4   LC 92-14206

Describes the physical characteristics, behavior, and varieties of sharks and dispels common myths about them

"This is an attractively designed volume, with clear type, quality paper, and outstanding full-color photographs. . . . The combination of excitement and straightforward fact is what makes this book compelling." Booklist

Includes bibliography

Coupe, Sheena M.

Sharks; [written by Sheena and Robert Coupe] Facts on File 1990 68p il maps (Great creatures of the world) $17.95 (5 and up) **597**

1. Sharks

ISBN 0-8160-2270-4   LC 89-34671

Describes the physical; characteristics, habits, and natural environment of sharks and discusses their evolution and relationship with human beings

"The many orders of sharks and their unique physiology are described, including an excellent section on reproduction. A series of incredible photographs shows the birth of shark pups. Much of the text is devoted to the issue of shark attacks with interesting observations and statistics. . . . Illustrated with a stunning collection of color photographs, charts, tables, and maps." SLJ

Do fishes get thirsty?; questions answered by Les Kaufman and the staff of the New England Aquarium. Watts 1991 40p il lib bdg $15.82 (5 and up) **597**

1. Fishes

ISBN 0-531-10992-5   LC 90-46871

"A New England Aquarium book"

Explains, using a question-and-answer format, the differences between several fish and other aquatic species

"Basic, but thoughtful, questions . . . provide a mechanism for presenting some solidly scientific answers, in large type, that are fit for the youngest reader but appealing to the oldest and any age in between. . . . Each page is rich with color photographs and diagrams pertinent to the text." Sci Books Films

Includes glossary and bibliography

Freedman, Russell

Sharks. Holiday House 1985 40p il lib bdg $13.95 (3-5) **597**

1. Sharks

ISBN 0-8234-0582-6   LC 85-42881

A physical description of sharks and a discussion of their methods of hunting, details of birth, and their usefulness to humans

"The numerous black-and-white photographs are well coordinated with the text. The writing is lucid and succinct; most unfamiliar terms are explained. Freedman uses some interesting analogies to better illustrate facts about sharks." SLJ

Gibbons, Gail

Sharks. Holiday House 1992 unp il $15.95; pa $6.95 (k-3) **597**

1. Sharks

ISBN 0-8234-0960-0; 0-8234-1068-4 (pa)
LC 91-31524

Describes shark behavior and different kinds of sharks

The author's "bold, appealing illustrations (many of them labeled and explained) are the strength of the presentation. An excellent choice for even the youngest shark fan, this will be useful for simple reports as well." Booklist

Guiberson, Brenda Z.

Salmon story; with illustrations by the author. Holt & Co. 1993 71p il $14.95; pa $5.95 (3-5) **597**

1. Salmon 2. Endangered species

ISBN 0-8050-2754-8; 0-8050-4254-7 (pa)
LC 93-1360

"A Redfeather book"

Describes the salmon's life journey to the sea and back, and the threat posed by pollution, commercial fishing, and other factors

"The matter-of-fact discussion is hopeful despite the arresting facts; children will understand from this account that the salmon is in serious trouble but will also be aware that environmentalists and many others are using science and common sense to find ways to save the species. Neat, labeled drawings and effective photos in color and black-and-white illustrate the text." Bull Cent Child Books

Lavies, Bianca

The Atlantic salmon; text and photographs by Bianca Lavies. Dutton Children's Bks. 1992 unp il $14.50 (3-5) **597**

1. Salmon

ISBN 0-525-44860-8   LC 91-27990

The author "describes the young salmon's first several years of life in fresh water, the preparation for the seaward migration, and the eventual return to the original stream for nest building and egg laying." Horn Book

"Breathtaking underwater photographs and a lucid text describe the arduous journey made by this hearty fish. Nature photography at its finest; factual description at its best." SLJ

Ling, Mary

Amazing fish; written by Mary Ling; photographed by Jerry Young. Knopf 1991 29p il (Eyewitness juniors) lib bdg $9.99; pa $7.99 (2-4) **597**

1. Fishes

ISBN 0-679-91516-8 (lib bdg); 0-679-81516-3 (pa)

LC 90-49651

Also available Spanish language edition

Introduces memorable members of the fish world, explains what makes them unique, and describes important characteristics of the entire group

Macquitty, Miranda

Shark; written by Miranda MacQuitty. Knopf 1992 62p il maps (Eyewitness books) $19; lib bdg $18.99 (4 and up) **597**

1. Sharks

ISBN 0-679-81683-6; 0-679-91683-0 (lib bdg)

LC 92-4712

Also available Spanish language edition

"A Dorling Kindersley book"

Describes, in text and photographs, the physical characteristics, behavior, and life cycle of various types of sharks

This "concentrates on the unusual, the strange, the odd, and the frightening with minimal text and clear, bright illustrations. . . . This is clearly a book for dipping in and out of, and not for reference." SLJ

Parker, Steve

Fish; written by Steve Parker. Knopf 1990 63p il (Eyewitness books) $19; lib bdg $20.99 (4 and up) **597**

1. Fishes

ISBN 0-679-80439-0; 0-679-80439-5 (lib bdg)

LC 89-36445

Also available Spanish language edition

This illustrated guide to fish life discusses "color as camouflage, types of early fishes, oddities in the fish world, and fish physiology (feeding, breathing, reproducing, and defending themselves)." Booklist

Sattler, Helen Roney

Sharks, the super fish; illustrated by Jean Zallinger. Lothrop, Lee & Shepard Bks. 1986 96p il $15.95 (4 and up) **597**

1. Sharks

ISBN 0-688-03993-6

LC 84-4381

This work provides "general information about sharks—their body structure, their feeding habits, their life cycles, their enemies and their interactions with humans." Appraisal

"The copious shaded drawings include numerous detailed diagrams and some pleasant full-page scenes." Horn Book

Includes glossary and bibliography

Simon, Seymour, 1931-

Sharks. HarperCollins Pubs. 1995 unp il $15.95; lib bdg $15.89; pa $5.95 (2-4) **597**

1. Sharks

ISBN 0-06-023029-0; 0-06-023032-0 (lib bdg); 0-06-446187-4 (pa)

LC 95-1593

The author "explores the fascinating undersea life of sharks, examining the truths and myths about these amazing creatures. Astounding close-up photographs enhance the informative and exciting text." Sci Child

Wallace, Karen

Think of an eel; illustrated by Mike Bostock. Candlewick Press 1993 unp il $14.95; pa $5.99 (k-3) **597**

1. Eels

ISBN 1-56402-180-7; 1-56402-465-2 (pa)

LC 92-53131

"Read and wonder"

"Wallace conveys a sense of the life cycle of the eel, as well as its more unusual habits. Bostock's illustrations are graceful, slithery watercolors, perfectly suited to the eel's underwater world." Horn Book Guide

Zim, Herbert S.

Fishes, a guide to fresh- and salt-water species; by Herbert S. Zim and Hurst H. Shoemaker; illustrated by James Gordon Irving. Golden Bks. il pa $5.95 (4 and up) **597**

1. Fishes

"A Golden guide"

First published 1956 by Simon & Schuster. Periodically revised

"A pocket identification guide with suggestions for collecting, classifying, and photographing fishes." Hodges Books for Elem Sch Libr

Includes bibliography

597.6 Amphibians

Bernhard, Emery

Salamanders; pictures by Durga Bernhard. Holiday House 1995 unp il $15.95 (k-3) **597.6**

1. Salamanders

ISBN 0-8234-1148-6

LC 94-15306

"The author explains habitats, respiration, life cycles, food-gathering techniques, and defense mechanisms. He also describes individual species of the major families of salamanders found in North America, including mole salamanders, newts, giant salamanders, sirens, lungless salamanders, mud puppies, and water dogs. A final section covers their importance in the ecosystem, their uncertain future, and related myths and legends." Booklist

"The large print, simple but informative narrative, and appealing illustrations will attract both browsers and report writers." SLJ

Clarke, Barry

Amphibian; written by Barry Clarke; photographed by Geoff Brightling and Frank Greenaway. Knopf 1993 63p il (Eyewitness books) $16; lib bdg $16.99 (4 and up) **597.6**

1. Amphibians

ISBN 0-679-83879-1; 0-679-93879-6 (lib bdg)

LC 92-1589

Clarke, Barry—_Continued_
Also available Spanish language edition
"A Dorling Kindersley book"
Photographs and text examine the evolution, behavior, physical characteristics, and life cycle of all kinds of amphibians

Conant, Roger, 1909-
Peterson first guide to reptiles and amphibians; [by] Roger Conant, Robert C. Stebbins, Joseph T. Collins. Houghton Mifflin 1992 128p il pa $4.95 (6 and up)   **597.6**
1. Reptiles 2. Amphibians
ISBN 0-395-62232-8   LC 91-33016
This is a guide to identification of reptile and amphibian species
This is "easy to use. The information is accurate and easy to understand. . . . Useful for browsing as well as for identification in the field." Voice Youth Advocates

George, Jean Craighead, 1919-
The moon of the salamanders; illustrated by Marlene Hill Werner. new ed. HarperCollins Pubs. 1992 47p il (Thirteen moons) lib bdg $14.89 (3-6)   **597.6**
1. Salamanders
ISBN 0-06-022694-3   LC 90-25591
A revised and newly illustrated edition of the title first published 1967 by Crowell
"On the night of the first spring rain, a male salamander journeys to a breeding pond, encountering various plants and animals that share his habitat along the way." SLJ
Includes bibliography

Johnston, Ginny, 1946-
Slippery babies; young frogs, toads, and salamanders; [by] Ginny Johnston, Judy Cutchins. Morrow Junior Bks. 1991 40p il $15; lib bdg $14.93 (3-5)   **597.6**
1. Amphibians 2. Animal babies
ISBN 0-688-09605-0; 0-688-09606-9 (lib bdg)
                                      LC 90-49665
Describes the physical characteristics and behavior of a variety of baby amphibians as they struggle to survive and grow to maturity
"Rather than superficially list many variations within each group, the book wisely selects single species as examples. The result is a rather thorough understanding of the species selected. There are no serious errors in the book, and the photographs are excellent." Sci Books Films
Includes glossary

Parker, Nancy Winslow
Frogs, toads, lizards, and salamanders; [by] Nancy Winslow Parker and Joan Richards Wright; illustrations by Nancy Winslow Parker. Greenwillow Bks. 1990 48p il maps $15; lib bdg $14.93 (k-3)   **597.6**
1. Frogs 2. Toads 3. Lizards 4. Salamanders
ISBN 0-688-08680-2; 0-688-08681-0 (lib bdg)
                                      LC 89-11686
The authors "introduce 16 species of amphibian and reptile via a deft balance of comic rhyming couplet and illus-

tration on each left-hand page and carefully labeled scientific drawing on the right. The collaborators indicate each animal's maximum size, genus, species and subspecies, whether it is diurnal or nocturnal, and describe the anatomy of each in the picture glossary that precedes a glossary of terms." Kobrin Letter

Snedden, Robert
What is an amphibian? photographs by Oxford Scientific Films; illustrated by Adrian Lascom. Sierra Club Bks. for Children 1994 32p il $14.95 (3-6)   **597.6**
1. Amphibians
ISBN 0-87156-469-6   LC 93-11619
Defines amphibians and describes their lives, including their maturation, mating, sense perception, and feeding
"With stunning photographs and illustrations on each page [this book] can not help but be appealing to youngsters. In addition, the text is well written and simple without being condescending or cute." Appraisal
Includes glossary

Souza, D. M. (Dorothy M.)
Shy salamanders. Carolrhoda Bks. 1995 40p il (Creatures all around us) lib bdg $14.21 (4-6)   **597.6**
1. Salamanders
ISBN 0-87614-826-7   LC 94-9108
"There are many similarities and differences among the various families of salamanders found in the world. _Shy Salamanders_ examines these traits, along with the life cycles and habits of these elusive creatures." Publisher's note
Includes glossary

Stebbins, Robert C. (Robert Cyril), 1915-
A field guide to western reptiles and amphibians; text and illustrations by Robert C. Stebbins. 2nd ed rev. Houghton Mifflin 1985 336p il $24.95; pa $16.95   **597.6**
1. Reptiles 2. Amphibians
ISBN 0-395-38254-8; 0-395-38253-X (pa)
                                      LC 84-25125
"The Peterson field guide series"
First published 1966
Sponsored by the National Audubon Society and National Wildlife Federation
"Field marks of all species in western North America, including Baja California." Title page
This field guide features over 240 species, most accompanied by illustration and distribution map. Coverage includes Baja California and information on reptile reproduction
Includes bibliography

Winner, Cherie
Salamanders. Carolrhoda Bks. 1993 48p il (Carolrhoda nature watch book) lib bdg $19.95; pa $6.95 (3-6)   **597.6**
1. Salamanders
ISBN 0-87614-757-0 (lib bdg); 0-87614-614-0 (pa)
                                      LC 92-10430
"An informational presentation of interesting facts and descriptions about salamanders in a variety of settings. Great photographs accompany the text." Sci Child
Includes glossary

597.8 Anura (Salientia)

Clarke, Barry

Amazing frogs & toads; written by Barry Clarke; photographed by Jerry Young. Knopf 1990 29p il (Eyewitness juniors) lib bdg $9.99; pa $7.99 (2-4) **597.8**

1. Frogs 2. Toads

ISBN 0-679-90688-6 (lib bdg); 0-679-80688-1 (pa)
LC 90-31882

Also available Spanish language edition

Text and photographs introduce members of the frog and toad world and describe their unique characteristics

"Starting with a general statement . . . 11 intriguing topics are presented, with each double-spread dominated by a spectacular color photo." SLJ

Cole, Joanna

A frog's body; with photographs by Jerome Wexler. Morrow 1980 47p il lib bdg $15.93
597.8

1. Frogs

ISBN 0-688-32228-X   LC 80-10705

"Cole and Wexler have constructed a superb introduction to the life processes and anatomy of the adult bullfrog. The author is exceptionally skillful at selecting interesting bits of information   and deftly combining explanations of fact and concepts in a simple, lucid text. Wexler's photographs, in color and black-and-white, include almost uncanny shots of the frog in motion. . . . The photographs are complemented by clear drawings of the frog's internal organs." SLJ

Gibbons, Gail

Frogs. Holiday House 1993 unp il $15.95; pa $5.95 (k-3) **597.8**

1. Frogs

ISBN 0-8234-1052-8; 0-8234-1134-6 (pa)
LC 93-269

An introduction to frogs, discussing their tadpole beginnings, noises they make, their hibernation, body parts, and how they differ from toads

"Gibbons' distinctive, labeled drawings identify the features described in the text, and her subjects float, swim, jump, and dive in colorful, lifelike illustrations. . . . This attractive book will appeal to prereaders, beginning readers, and the adults who read to those groups." Booklist

Lacey, Elizabeth A.

The complete frog; a guide for the very young naturalist; illustrated by Christopher Santoro. Lothrop, Lee & Shepard Bks. 1989 72p il $12.95; lib bdg $12.88 (4-6) **597.8**

1. Frogs

ISBN 0-688-08017-0; 0-688-08018-9 (lib bdg)
LC 88-9343

The author examines "the differences between frogs and toads, describes why frogs are well adapted to their particular habitats, and looks at reproductive cycles, feeding habits, and the transformation from tadpole to frog. An album of some [unusual] species (illustrated in color) follows, and the book ends with a look at frogs in the lore and literature of assorted cultures." Booklist

Santoro's "illustrations in color featured in the chapter 'The Odd Fellows' steal the show as they detail the truly startling and uncommon members of the frog family. Without resorting to overstatement or attention-getting exclamation points, Lacey conveys her awe and admiration for the successful survival of these small creatures." Horn Book

Includes bibliography

Pfeffer, Wendy, 1929-

From tadpole to frog; illustrated by Holly Keller. HarperCollins Pubs. 1994 32p il (Let's-read-and-find-out science books) $15; lib bdg $14.89; pa $4.95 (k-1) **597.8**

1. Frogs

ISBN 0-06-023044-4; 0-06-023117-3 (lib bdg); 0-06-445123-2 (pa)   LC 93-3135

This "introduction sketches the most basic aspects of frog life - the laying and hatching of eggs, the stages of growth, eating and the danger of being eaten, and hibernation." Horn Book Guide

"The illustrations are simple, interesting, and just right for young children. The science is accurate and presented in a way to excite young readers to get outside and look for some frogs and tadpoles." Sci Books Films

Souza, D. M. (Dorothy M.)

Frogs, frogs everywhere. Carolrhoda Bks. 1995 40p il (Creatures all around us) lib bdg $14.21 (4-6) **597.8**

1. Frogs

ISBN 0-87614-825-9   LC 94-6897

This book contains seven "chapters, each of which introduces readers to important aspects of the biology of the Anura. The last chapter, 'Disappearing,' emphasizes ecologists' current concerns regarding the decrease in numbers of amphibians in their natural habitats." Appraisal

"Excellent full-color photographs on nearly every page imbue the glistening subjects with a kind of slimy charm. . . . A chart near the end of each volume gives the scientific names of the major families." SLJ

Includes glossary

597.9 Reptiles

Ancona, George, 1929-

Turtle watch; photographs and text by George Ancona. Macmillan 1987 unp il $14.95 (2-4) **597.9**

1. Sea turtles 2. Endangered species 3. Wildlife conservation

ISBN 0-02-700910-6   LC 87-9316

Ancona, George, 1929-—*Continued*

An illustrated look at a project in Brazil designed to save sea turtles on the verge of extinction

"The details of the turtles' egg-laying, of the project's operation, and of two local children's participation are vividly projected in both pictures and text. The ending seems abrupt—one wishes for more information on the habits and characteristics of the sea turtle, but the book is successful within its defined focus; it will serve as a springboard to further exploration." Bull Cent Child Books

Includes bibliography

Arnold, Caroline, 1944-

Snake; photographs by Richard Hewett. Morrow Junior Bks. 1991 48p il $13.95; lib bdg $13.88 (3-5)   **597.9**

1. Snakes

ISBN 0-688-09409-0; 0-688-09410-4 (lib bdg)

LC 90-22591

Describes the physical characteristics, behavior, and life cycle of several kinds of snakes, especially the boas and pythons

"An enticing blend of concise text and outstanding full-color photographs." SLJ

Arnosky, Jim

All about alligators. Scholastic 1994 unp il map $14.95 (1-3)   **597.9**

1. Alligators

ISBN 0-590-46788-3   LC 93-41045

This look at the life cycle and habitat of the alligator discusses "physical characteristics, behavior, comparisons with other animals sharing its wetland habitat, and its place within that ecosystem." SLJ

"Arnosky's clear text and handsome watercolors convey a sense of wonder." Booklist

Berger, Melvin, 1927-

Look out for turtles! illustrated by Megan Lloyd. HarperCollins Pubs. 1992 32p il (Let's-read-and-find-out science books) $15; lib bdg $14.89; pa $4.95 (k-3)   **597.9**

1. Turtles

ISBN 0-06-022539-4; 0-06-022540-8 (lib bdg); 0-06-445156-9 (pa)   LC 90-36894

"This simple introductory resource provides an overview of the different types of turtles and their characteristics and habits. It is a good resource for young children to use independently." Sci Child

Brenner, Barbara

A snake-lover's diary. Addison-Wesley 1970 90p il lib bdg $15.89 (5 and up)   **597.9**

1. Snakes

ISBN 0-06-020697-7

A young boy keeps a diary recording the physical characteristics and habits of the reptiles he catches during a spring and summer

Includes glossary

Broekel, Ray, 1923-

Snakes. Childrens Press 1982 45p il $13.50; pa $5.50 (2-4)   **597.9**

1. Snakes

ISBN 0-516-01649-0; 0-516-41649-9 (pa)

LC 81-38487

"A New true book"

Describes the physiology, habits, and behavior of snakes

Cole, Joanna

A snake's body; photographs by Jerome Wexler. Morrow 1981 48p il $15; lib bdg $14.93   **597.9**

1. Snakes 2. Pythons

ISBN 0-688-00702-3; 0-688-00703-1 (lib bdg)

LC 81-9443

Examines the unique anatomical features of an Indian python that enable it and other snakes to survive without legs

"Wexler's photographs, stills or action shots, are of the high quality his fans have come to expect. . . . This has a well-organized continuous text, careful integration of illustrative and textual material, and a direct style for the accurate information provided." Bull Cent Child Books

Freedman, Russell

Killer snakes. Holiday House 1982 40p il $13.95 (2-5)   **597.9**

1. Snakes

ISBN 0-8234-0460-9   LC 82-80821

The author describes "over thirty of the world's deadliest snakes, discussing their habits and habitats, why and how they kill." Bull Cent Child Books

"Several pages of clear, concise text are devoted to each snake group while excellent black-and-white photos of the particular species will capture the reader's attention immediately. A well-thought-out book in every respect, this lives up to its rather sensational title." Booklist

George, Jean Craighead, 1919-

The moon of the alligators; illustrated by Michael Rothman. new ed. HarperCollins Pubs. 1991 48p il (Thirteen moons) $15; lib bdg $14.89 (3-6)   **597.9**

1. Alligators

ISBN 0-06-022427-4; 0-06-022428-2 (lib bdg)

LC 90-38169

A revised and newly illustrated edition of the title first published 1969 by Crowell

Describes an alligator's desperate search for food in the Florida Everglades during the month of October

This book "features lush, full-color illustrations. . . . George's flowing, carefully nonanthropomorphic text evokes the dense green seeping ecosystem illustrated in Rothman's realistic gouache paintings." SLJ

Includes bibliography

Gibbons, Gail

Sea turtles. Holiday House 1995 unp il $15.95 (k-3)   **597.9**

1. Sea turtles

ISBN 0-8234-1191-5   LC 94-48579

This book examines "the size, habitat, and diet of the eight kinds of sea turtles and efforts environmentalists are

Gibbons, Gail—*Continued*
making to protect them." Sci Child

This is "a very appealing book. . . . The illustrations are lovely paintings, highlighted with black outlines and clear labels. Children should find the diagram that shows differences between sea turtles and other turtles fascinating because they are often familiar only with the latter." Sci Books Films

Gove, Doris
A water snake's year; illustrated by Beverly Duncan. Atheneum Pubs. 1991 31p il $19.50 (3-5)   597.9

1. Snakes
ISBN 0-689-31597-X   LC 90-673
Presents a year in the life of a female water snake, resident of Great Smoky Mountains National Park

"Gore's elegant language and Duncan's handsome, naturalistic paintings make this a sure bet for group sharing and nature units." Booklist

Grace, Eric S.
Snakes. Sierra Club Bks. for Children 1994 64p il (Sierra Club wildlife library) $15.95 (4-6)   597.9

1. Snakes
ISBN 0-87156-490-4   LC 93-45407
The "text begins with a clear, precise definition of the term *cold-blooded*. It then moves on to anatomy, classification, hunting, and reproduction, and concludes with a look at the role these 'slithering serpents' play in their ecosystems. The 40 attractive color photographs illustrate the diversity of which Grace . . . speaks. Engaging nonfiction." Booklist

Gross, Ruth Belov, 1929-
Snakes. rev ed. Four Winds Press 1990 63p il $14.95 (3-5)   597.9

1. Snakes
ISBN 0-02-737022-4   LC 89-38254
First published 1973

This book "covers basic information about all snakes: baby snakes, shedding, . . . food, methods of getting food, enemies and methods of movement. This section of the book is illustrated with black and white photographs. . . . The second section of the book contains information about specific poisonous and nonpoisonous snakes in the United States, as well as the boa, python, anaconda and cobra." Appraisal

Hirschi, Ron
Turtle's day; photographs by Dwight Kuhn; text by Ron Hirschi. Cobblehill Bks. 1994 unp il $11.99 (k-2)   597.9

1. Turtles
ISBN 0-525-65172-1   LC 93-9006
A simple text and color photos follow an eastern box turtle through her day

"Hirschi conveys basic facts in a direct, lively manner that provides immediacy. . . . Kuhn's full-color photographs are exceptionally clear and display a wide range of this gentle creature's physical characteristics and behavior." SLJ

Johnston, Ginny, 1946-
Scaly babies; reptiles growing up; [by] Ginny Johnston and Judy Cutchins. Morrow Junior Bks. 1988 40p il $15; lib bdg $14.93; pa $4.95 (3-5)   597.9

1. Reptiles
ISBN 0-688-07305-0; 0-688-07306-9 (lib bdg); 0-688-09998-X (pa)   LC 87-18559
This book offers a look at young snakes, lizards, crocodilians, and turtles during their first year of life

"In this outstanding book, text, design, graphics, and photographs work beautifully to provide basic information. . . . The quality and choice of photographs are particularly noteworthy." Horn Book

Includes glossary

Lauber, Patricia, 1924-
Alligators: a success story; illustrated by Lou Silva. Holt & Co. 1993 64p il $14.95, pa $6.95 (3-5)   597.9

1. Alligators
ISBN 0-8050-1909-X; 0-8050-4258-X (pa)   LC 93-3302
"A Redfeather book"
Based in part on the author's Who need's alligators! published 1974 by Garrard

Examines the life cycle of the alligator from egg to adult and analyzes its significance in the ecological balance of nature

"This title is written with grace and excitement. The design . . . is inviting, with large type, dramatic color photographs, and clear black-and-white drawings." Booklist

Snakes are hunters; illustrated by Holly Keller. Crowell 1988 32p il (Let's-read-and-find-out science books) lib bdg $14.89; pa $4.95 (k-3)   597.9

1. Snakes
ISBN 0-690-04630-8 (lib bdg); 0-06-445091-0 (pa)   LC 87-47695
Describes the physical characteristics of a variety of snakes and how they hunt, catch, and eat their prey

"Holly Keller's bright and cheerful drawings make a potentially frightening subject more approachable and add just enough detail to enhance the brief text. An upbeat, simple, and readable presentation of an inherently interesting subject." Horn Book

Lavies, Bianca
A gathering of garter snakes; text and photographs by Bianca Lavies. Dutton Children's Bks. 1993 unp il $15.99 (3-6)   597.9

1. Snakes
ISBN 0-525-45099-8   LC 93-18932
Text and photographs depict the physical characteristics, behavior, and life cycle of the red-sided garter snake

"Lavies brings new vitality to a perennially popular subject with superb action color photographs and a clear, fact-filled text that is dramatic without being in any way sensationalist." Booklist

Lavies, Bianca—*Continued*

The secretive timber rattlesnake; text and photographs by Bianca Lavies. Dutton Children's Bks. 1990 unp il $13.95 (3-6)

597.9

1. Rattlesnakes
ISBN 0-525-44572-2 LC 90-31964

"An informative, handsome photo-essay documents the behaviors of the timber rattlesnake and demonstrates how the impressive reptile contributes to the balance of nature." Sci Child

Leedy, Loreen, 1959-

Tracks in the sand; written and illustrated by Loreen Leedy. Doubleday Bks. for Young Readers 1993 unp il $15.95 (k-3) **597.9**

1. Sea turtles
ISBN 0-385-30658-X LC 92-3405

Eggs laid in the sand by a female sea turtle hatch into tiny turtles, which eventually grow large enough to lay their own eggs

This features "lyrical prose and soft colored-pencil illustrations." Sci Child

Ling, Mary

Amazing crocodiles & reptiles; written by Mary Ling; photographed by Jerry Young. Knopf 1991 29p il (Eyewitness juniors) lib bdg $9.99; pa $7.99 (2-4) **597.9**

1. Reptiles
ISBN 0-679-90689-4 (lib bdg); 0-679-80689-X (pa)
LC 90-19239

Also available Spanish language edition

Photographs and text depict the habits, diet, and characteristics of several kinds of crocodiles, alligators, turtles, snakes, and lizards

This book includes "fascinating tidbits and vibrant color photographs." Horn Book Guide

Maestro, Betsy, 1944-

Take a look at snakes; written by Betsy Maestro; illustrated by Giulio Maestro. Scholastic 1992 40p il $14.95 (k-3) **597.9**

1. Snakes
ISBN 0-590-44935-4 LC 91-37780

Describes the varieties, habitats, behavior, and physical characteristics of snakes

"Provides a great deal of information that is clearly detailed in the watercolor and pencil drawings and in the fine diagrams. . . . Text and illustrations work perfectly together to extend the child's understanding." Horn Book

Markle, Sandra, 1946-

Outside and inside snakes. Macmillan Bks. for Young Readers 1995 40p il $16 (2-4)

597.9

1. Snakes
ISBN 0-02-762315-7 LC 94-20647

This volume "discusses how snakes capture their food, how they move, and how their sensory, digestive, musculo-skeletal, and reproductive systems function. The text is conversational, leading the young reader to each important question and its answer." Sci Books Films

"The photographs are particularly strong in this title, depicting unfamiliar snakes and showing close-ups of amazing snake activity. A fine addition to reptile collections." Horn Book

Includes glossary

Martin, James, 1950-

Chameleons; dragons in the trees; photographs by Art Wolfe. Crown 1991 36p il map $13; lib bdg $13.99 (3-5) **597.9**

1. Chameleons
ISBN 0-517-58388-7; 0-517-58389-5 (lib bdg)
LC 91-8736

Text and photographs introducing the behavior, African habitat, physical adaptations, endangered status, and other aspects of several species of chameleon

"Though the text is concise, Martin covers his subject with clarity and wit. . . . Wolfe's photographs are truly remarkable; large and vividly colored, they show the chameleon engaged in activities from warning and courting to eating and shedding its skin." Booklist

McCarthy, Colin, 1951-

Reptile; written by Colin McCarthy. Knopf 1991 63p il (Eyewitness books) $16; lib bdg $16.99 (4 and up) **597.9**

1. Reptiles
ISBN 0-679-80783-7; 0-679-90783-1 (lib bdg)
LC 90-4890

Photographs and text depict the many different kinds of reptiles, their similarities and differences, habitats, and behavior

This book "stands out because of the fascinating photographs, which are brilliantly lifelike and well-chosen to demonstrate concepts discussed. . . . The text is nicely balanced between straightforward factual data and intriguing bits of trivia." SLJ

Parsons, Alexandra

Amazing snakes; written by Alexandra Parsons; photographed by Jerry Young. Knopf 1990 29p il (Eyewitness juniors) lib bdg $9.99; pa $7.99 (2-4) **597.9**

1. Snakes
ISBN 0-679-90225-2 (lib bdg); 0-679-80225-8 (pa)
LC 89-38944

Also available Spanish language edition

Text and photographs introduce amazing members of the snake world, including the sunbeam snake, milk snake, and reticulated python

This book is distinguished by its "attractive graphic layout. . . . The text includes a variety of trivia, folklore, and world-record-type information." Booklist

Patent, Dorothy Hinshaw

The American alligator; photographs by William Muñoz. Clarion Bks. 1994 77p il $15.95 (4 and up) **597.9**

1. Alligators
ISBN 0-395-63392-3 LC 93-37704

Patent, Dorothy Hinshaw—*Continued*

This "book offers an overview of the facts and folklore surrounding alligators and their family, the crocodilians. The informative text, which discusses the habits and life cycle of the cold-blooded animals, is complemented by the well-chosen full-color photographs that appear on almost every page." Booklist

Includes bibliography

Ryder, Joanne

Lizard in the sun; illustrated by Michael Rothman. Morrow Junior Bks. 1990 unp il $13.95; lib bdg $13.88; pa $4.95 (k-2)

597.9

1. Lizards
ISBN 0-688-07172-4; 0-688-07173-2 (lib bdg); 0-688-13031-X (pa)   LC 89-33886
"A Just for a day book"

A child is transformed into an anole for a day and discovers what it is like to be a tiny lizard changing colors in a sunny, leafy world

"The essence of the anole is caught through a subtle blending of clear, lyrical text and vibrant illustrations. . . . Although the text is relatively sparse, much information is imparted about the behavior of the anole." SLJ

Schafer, Susan

The Galápagos tortoise. Dillon Press 1992 64p il (Remarkable animals) $13.95; pa $5.95 (3-5)

597.9

1. Turtles
ISBN 0-87518-544-4; 0-382-39232-9 (pa)
                                          LC 92-7396
"The story of the Galápagos tortoise describes the animal's habitat; characteristics; behaviors, such as competing for dominance within the hierarchy; mating and egg-laying; endangerment; and other interesting facts. The text and color photographs weave an intriguing narrative about this remarkable hard-shelled vertebrate." Sci Child

Includes glossary

Schnieper, Claudia

Chameleons; photographs by Max Meier. Carolrhoda Bks. 1989 47p il (Carolrhoda nature watch book) lib bdg $19.95 (3-6)

597.9

1. Chameleons
ISBN 0-87614-341-9   LC 88-37646
Original German edition published 1986 in Switzerland

Discusses the physical characteristics, behavior, and life cycle of the lizard known for its ability to change its color

"The book has many outstanding features—good quality paper and typography, excellent photography, a fine index, and much current information on the subject. Students, with the help of the teacher, will find this book an important supplement in reptile study." Sci Child

Lizards; photographs by Max Meier. Carolrhoda Bks. 1990 47p il (Carolrhoda nature watch book) lib bdg $19.95 (3-6)

597.9

1. Lizards
ISBN 0-87614-405-9   LC 89-22158
Original German edition published 1988 in Switzerland

"Schnieper handily describes the unique features of the lizard's body, its breeding habits, and its broad distribution across the globe. Meier's vivid, full-color, captioned photographs clarify and extend the information presented." SLJ

Includes glossary

Simon, Seymour, 1931-

Snakes. HarperCollins Pubs. 1992 unp il $16; lib bdg $15.89; pa $5.95 (4-6)   597.9

1. Snakes
ISBN 0-06-022529-7; 0-06-022530-0 (lib bdg); 0-06-446165-3 (pa)   LC 91-15948
Describes, in text and photographs, the physical characteristics, habits, and natural environment of various species of snakes

"Once again Simon demonstrates his skill in molding a lucid discussion and striking photographs into a compelling, informative overview." Horn Book

Smith, Trevor

Amazing lizards; written by Trevor Smith; photographed by Jerry Young. Knopf 1990 29p il (Eyewitness juniors) lib bdg $9.99; pa $7.99 (2-4)   597.9

1. Lizards
ISBN 0-679-90819-6 (lib bdg); 0-679-80819-1 (pa)
                                          LC 90-31884
Also available Spanish language edition

Features some of the remarkable members of the lizard world, including the chameleon, flying gecko, and blue tongue skink, and describes important characteristics of the whole group

"This very attractive little book should delight younger readers with excellent color photographs of and interesting facts about selected lizards." Sci Books Films

Snedden, Robert

What is a reptile? photographs by Oxford Scientific Films; illustrated by Adrian Lascom. Sierra Club Bks. for Children 1995 32p il $14.95 (3-6)   597.9

1. Reptiles
ISBN 0-87156-493-9   LC 94-14422
"What do turtles, snakes, crocodiles, and tuataras have in common? Color photographs on double-page spreads compare these reptiles, describing their physical characteristics, movement, senses, defenses, and eating habits." Sci Child

"This attractively formatted title is a good, solid introduction to a remarkably diverse class of animals." SLJ

Includes glossary

Staub, Frank J.

Alligators; written and photographed by Frank Staub. Lerner Publs. 1995 47p il maps (Early bird nature books) lib bdg $14.21 (2-4)

597.9

1. Alligators
ISBN 0-8225-3007-4   LC 94-39112

Staub, Frank J.—*Continued*

"A distribution map, plus key words to anticipate, introduces short chapters outlining the appearance, behavior, and habitat of the alligator. Much information is conveyed, for example, on relatives, group behavior, nesting, sex determination, rearing of young, ecto- and endothermy diets, catching prey, eyes, teeth, etc. . . . The text is clear and well illustrated with mostly excellent color photographs." Sci Books Films

Includes glossary

Sea turtles; written and photographed by Frank Staub. Lerner Publs. 1995 48p il (Early bird nature books) lib bdg $14.21 (2-4)

597.9

1. Sea turtles
ISBN 0-8225-3005-8   LC 94-4630

"Staub looks at the life cycles of the five types of sea turtles. Full-color photographs depict the animals in the ocean waters surrounding the U.S. and on the beaches where they lay their eggs. . . . Environmental dangers and attempts at protection are thoughtfully treated in a separate chapter." SLJ

Includes glossary

Stone, Lynn M.

Alligators and crocodiles. Childrens Press 1989 45p il lib bdg $13.50; pa $5.50 (2-4)

597.9

1. Alligators 2. Crocodiles
ISBN 0-516-01170-7 (lib bdg); 0-516-41170-5 (pa)
LC 89-9985

"A New true book"

Describes the physical characteristics, behavior, habitats, and different species of alligators and crocodiles

"Captioned, mostly full-color photographs on nearly every page provide visual interest, while short sentences and a simple writing style allows easy access for beginning readers without sacrificing substance." Booklist

Includes glossary

Stoops, Erik D., 1966-

Snakes; [by] Erik D. Stoops & Annette T. Wright. Sterling 1992 80p il hardcover o.p. paperback available $9.95 (3-5)   **597.9**

1. Snakes
ISBN 0-8069-8483-X (pa)   LC 92-16995

Questions and answers explore the world of snakes, their physical characteristics, behavior, and interaction with people

This book "successfully reaches the targeted audience through the beautifully presented color photographs, which are sure to draw the eye of the young readers. Most of the questions and answers are thought-provoking, and are succinctly stated." Appraisal

Turtles; [by] the Cousteau Society. Little Simon 1992 unp il pa $3.95 (k-2)   **597.9**

1. Sea turtles
ISBN 0-671-77059-4   LC 91-32184

Original French edition, 1991

Describes the physical characteristics, behavior, and life cycle of the sea turtle

"The photographs are full color and more than pretty. . . . A sparkling and informative view for the very youngest." Sci Books Films

598 Birds

Arnold, Caroline, 1944-

Flamingo; photographs by Richard Hewett. Morrow Junior Bks. 1991 48p il $13.95; lib bdg $13.88 (3-5)   **598**

1. Flamingos
ISBN 0-688-09411-2; 0-688-09412-0 (lib bdg)
LC 90-19186

Examines the different kinds of flamingos, their physical characteristics, natural habitat, and behavior

"The book is accurate and well written, with outstanding photography." Sci Books Films

House sparrows everywhere; photographs by Richard R. Hewett. Carolrhoda Bks. 1992 47p il (Carolrhoda nature watch book) lib bdg $19.95 (3-5)   **598**

1. Sparrows
ISBN 0-87614-696-5   LC 91-26310

Describes the physical characteristics, habitat, and life cycle of the house sparrow

"The benefits and consequences of tampering with the balance of nature are interestingly and technically—but simply—discussed, as is the house sparrow's life, including its home, communication, and reproduction and parenting." Horn Book Guide

Includes glossary

On the brink of extinction; the California condor; photographs by Michael Wallace. Harcourt Brace Jovanovich 1993 48p il $17.95; pa $8.95 (4 and up)   **598**

1. Condors 2. Endangered species 3. Wildlife conservation
ISBN 0-15-257990-7; 0-15-257991-5 (pa)
LC 92-14914

"A Gulliver Green book"

Describes the history of the condor in North America and the efforts to capture and breed the few remaining California condors to save them from extinction

"Author and photographer have collaborated to describe, with a clearly written text and outstanding, informative photographs, the efforts to save the condor." Sci Books Films

Ostriches and other flightless birds; photographs by Richard R. Hewett. Carolrhoda Bks. 1990 47p il map (Carolrhoda nature watch book) lib bdg $12.95 (3-5)

598

1. Ostriches 2. Birds
ISBN 0-87614-377-X   LC 89-820

An introduction to the physical characteristics, habits, and natural environment of ostriches and a variety of other birds that do not fly including the rhea, emu, cassowary, kiwi, and tinamou

"The photographs dramatically enhance the text. Feathers of ostriches and other birds are compared. An egg is held in a hand, effectively demonstrating its size. Bones of these flightless birds are different. Photographs and text combine to make these concepts clear, as well as others related to their speed, eye size, and preening." Appraisal

Includes glossary

Arnold, Caroline, 1944-—_Continued_
Penguin; photographs by Richard Hewett.
Morrow Junior Bks. 1988 48p il $12.95; lib
bdg $12.88 (3-5)   **598**
1. Penguins
ISBN 0-688-07706-4; 0-688-07707-2 (lib bdg)
                                        LC 87-31458
Discusses the physical characteristics, habits, and life cy-
cle of the Magellanic penguin, a native of South America.
Focuses on the lives of Humberto and Domino, a pair of
Magellanics at the San Francisco Zoo, as they prepare a
nest and care for their baby chick, Uno
"The author and photographer provide an interesting account. . . . Excellent nonfiction for both students and
browsers." Booklist

Saving the peregrine falcon; photographs by
Richard R. Hewett. Carolrhoda Bks. 1985 48p
il (Carolrhoda nature watch book) lib bdg
$19.95; pa $7.95 (3-5)   **598**
1. Falcons 2. Birds—Protection
ISBN 0-87614-225-0 (lib bdg); 0-87614-523-3 (pa)
                                        LC 84-15576
Describes the efforts of scientists who are trying to save
the peregrine falcon from extinction by taking the fragile
eggs that would not survive in the wild, hatching them,
raising the chicks, and then releasing the birds back into the
wild
"An outstanding account of scientists' ingenious efforts
to increase the population of the endangered peregrine falcon. The peregrine falcon's strength and beauty are conveyed through striking color photographs and clearly
written text." Sci Child
Includes glossary

Arnosky, Jim
All about owls. Scholastic 1995 unp il
$14.95 (1-3)   **598**
1. Owls
ISBN 0-590-46790-5   LC 94-44859
Text and illustrations show "where owls live, what they
eat, how they care for their young, and how they see so well
at night." Sci Child
"Arnosky writes with clarity and a sure sense of what
will interest young children. With its well-composed watercolor paintings, this volume will appeal to science-book
browsers as well as young students researching the topic."
Booklist

Crinkleroot's 25 birds every child should
know. Bradbury Press 1993 unp il $12.95 (k-3)
                                             598
1. Birds
ISBN 0-02-705859-X   LC 92-36059
The author "presents paintings of 25 feathered creatures,
from the familiar robin to the exotic ostrich." SLJ
"Arnosky's watercolors are his usual high quality, and
Crinkleroot is an engaging guide." Booklist

Crinkleroot's guide to knowing the birds.
Bradbury Press 1992 32p il $14.95 (k-3)
                                             598
1. Birds
ISBN 0-02-705857-3   LC 91-38234
An introduction to birds one might see in the woods
"Arnosky has created another wonderful nature guide
featuring his lovable woodsman, Crinkleroot. . . . Arnosky's
bright watercolors and precise renderings of different species

make this an especially attractive book, and one that parents will enjoy using with their children. Teachers preparing
nature units for primary grade students will also find this a
useful resource." Booklist

Bailey, Jill
Birds; written by Jill Bailey and David
Burnie. Dorling Kindersley 1992 61p il
(Eyewitness explorers) $9.95; lib bdg $10.99
(3-5)   **598**
1. Birds
ISBN 1-56458-021-0; 1-56458-022-9 (lib bdg)
                                        LC 91-58211
Describes the physical characteristics, habitats, and behavior of birds and examines kinds of seashore birds,
woodland birds, birds of prey, and others
"Beautifully illustrated with clear, full-color photographs.
. . . The text appears as captions to the photos, providing
chunks of information short enough for a child to assimilate
quickly. The information is interesting, accurate, and informally but clearly written." Sci Books Films

Bash, Barbara
Urban roosts: where birds nest in the city.
Sierra Club Bks.; Little, Brown 1990 unp il
hardcover o.p. paperback available $5.95 (1-4)
                                             598
1. Birds—Eggs and nests
ISBN 0-316-08312-7 (pa)   LC 89-70187
"Excellent treatment of an unusual subject reveals that
human-made places of steel, stone, and concrete are home
to a variety of birds. Includes information on sparrows,
finches, barn and snowy owls, swallows, swifts, nighthawks,
killdeers, pigeons, wrens, crows, starlings, and falcons that
have successfully adapted to city life." Sci Child

Bernhard, Emery
Eagles; lions of the sky; written by Emery
Bernhard; illustrated by Durga Bernhard.
Holiday House 1994 unp il $15.95 (k-3)
                                             598
1. Eagles
ISBN 0-8234-1105-2   LC 93-1833
This "describes eagles' flying and hunting behavior; the
physical characteristics of the four main groups of eagles;
courtship, mating, and rearing of the young; their ecological
value; and conservation problems." Horn Book Guide
"This dramatic picture book introduces a wealth of factual information. . . . The direct text is smoothly integrated
with clear color illustrations that provide detail and connection." Booklist
Includes glossary

Brown, Mary Barrett
Wings along the waterway. Orchard Bks.
1992 80p il $18.95; lib bdg $18.99 (4-6)
                                             598
1. Water birds
ISBN 0-531-05981-2; 0-531-08581-3 (lib bdg)
                                        LC 91-18559

Brown, Mary Barrett—*Continued*

Discusses the habitat, lifecycle, appearance and habits of twenty-one water birds and examines the risks posed to them by technological civilization

"The heart of this book . . . consists of boldly executed double-page and full-page paintings and smaller colored sketches of each of the 21 species covered. These illustrations portray the birds and their habitats faithfully and contain a wealth of visual information. . . . The accompanying short, well-written text is as tantalizing as the illustrations." Sci Books Films

Includes bibliography

Burnie, David

Bird; written by David Burnie. Knopf 1988 63p il (Eyewitness books) $16; lib bdg $16.99 (4 and up) **598**

1. Birds

ISBN 0-394-89619-X; 0-394-99619-4 (lib bdg)
LC 87-26441

Also available Spanish language edition

A photo essay on the world of birds examining such topics as body construction, feathers and flight, the adaptation of beaks and feet, feeding habits, courtship, nests and eggs, and bird watching

"From first impression to final reading, this photographic encyclopedia on the world of birds is an inviting pleasure. . . . *Bird* has a distinctly British tone, and many of the illustrative species are not native to the United States, but since they are each selected as examples of various adaptations, this should cause no problems." Sci Books Films

Burton, Maurice, 1898-

Birds. Facts on File 1985 64p il (World of science) $15.95 (5 and up) **598**

1. Birds

ISBN 0-8160-1063-3

This book "begins with definitions and general characteristics, including special sections on feathers, evolution, flight, sense organs, feeding, songs, and nest-building. . . . Many different species are discussed, each in a one- or two-page spread, emphasizing special adaptations, physical features, and behavior." Booklist

Includes glossary

Cole, Joanna

A bird's body; photographs by Jerome Wexler. Morrow 1982 48p il $12.95; lib bdg $12.88 **598**

1. Birds

ISBN 0-688-01470-4; 0-688-01471-2 (lib bdg)
LC 82-6446

"A bird's body is designed primarily for flight, and expectedly, Cole spends a significant part of her examination explaining both how a bird flies and how its anatomy makes that possible. A parakeet and a cockatiel are her subjects, and Wexler's able photographs include numerous close-ups of body parts, flight, and some behavior traits. There are also descriptions of birds' digestive systems, vision, breathing, and hearing." Booklist

Demuth, Patricia, 1948-

Cradles in the trees; the story of bird nests; by Patricia Brennan Demuth; illustrated by Suzanne Barnes. Macmillan 1994 unp il $14.95 (1-3) **598**

1. Birds—Eggs and nests

ISBN 0-02-728466-2
LC 93-9114

Describes the methods and materials used by various birds to build their nests

"The watercolor-and-pencil artwork makes an already clear text clearer, and the pages are well designed, with the illustrations close to the descriptions. Demuth also gives careful and correct advice on nest collecting. The book will inspire specific projects as well as a sense of wonder." Booklist

DeWitt, Lynda

Eagles, hawks, and other birds of prey. Watts 1989 63p il lib bdg $13.93 (4 and up) **598**

1. Birds of prey

ISBN 0-531-19570-9
LC 88-31371

"A First book"

"Illustrated with superb color photographs, the text discusses the characteristics and ecology of vultures, eagles, kites, hawks, falcons, and owls. . . . A good index and a glossary add to the overall superior quality of the book." Sci Books Films

Epple, Wolfgang

Barn owls; photographs by Manfred Rogl. Carolrhoda Bks. 1992 48p il (Carolrhoda nature watch book) lib bdg $19.95 (3-6) **598**

1. Owls

ISBN 0-87614-742-2
LC 91-36818

Describes the physical characteristics, habitat, and life cycle of the barn owl

"The direct text and open format will encourage young readers, but the spectacular full-color photographs will attract nature enthusiasts of all ages. The clarity and detail are amazing. . . . More of a photo-essay than an inclusive text, this is one of the best entries in this series." SLJ

Includes glossary

Esbensen, Barbara Juster

Tiger with wings; the great horned owl; illustrated by Mary Barrett Brown. Orchard Bks. 1991 unp il $16.95; lib bdg $17.99; pa $5.95 (2-4) **598**

1. Owls

ISBN 0-531-05940-5; 0-531-08540-6 (lib bdg); 0-531-07071-9 (pa)
LC 90-23034

Describes the hunting technique, physical characteristics, mating ritual, and nesting and child-rearing practices of the great horned owl

"The watercolor paintings in mainly grays, brown, and blues beautifully convey information, mood, and sometimes humor. . . . The writing is clean and clear, with an occasional colorful simile or metaphor." SLJ

George, Jean Craighead, 1919-

The moon of the owls; illustrated by Wendell Minor. new ed. HarperCollins Pubs. 1993 47p il (Thirteen moons) $15; lib bdg $14.89 (3-6)   598

1. Owls

ISBN 0-06-020192-4; 0-06-020193-2 (lib bdg)

LC 91-2735

A revised and newly illustrated edition of the title first published 1967 by Crowell

A great horned owl's stirrings to mate carry him across a forest in January in the Catskill Mountains, where he observes the nocturnal activities of other animals

This is a "solid work of nonfiction that offers information about the behavior of many of the animals that share the owl's habitat and special insight into the instinctual forces that drive him towards his mate." SLJ

Includes bibliography

The moon of the winter bird; illustrated by Vincent Nasta. new ed. HarperCollins Pubs. 1992 48p il (Thirteen moons) lib bdg $14.89 (3-6)   598

1. Sparrows

ISBN 0-06-020268-8   LC 91-15237

A revised and newly illustrated edition of the title first published 1970 by Crowell

During a cold spell in December, a song sparrow that has not migrated south must adapt to the changes that winter brings

The author "conveys the immediacy and fragility of a birds's life without dependency on anthropomorphism. . . . Full-page illustrations in natural tones true to the seasons complement the story." SLJ

Includes bibliography

Gibbons, Gail

The puffins are back! HarperCollins Pubs. 1991 unp il $15; lib bdg $14.89 (k-3)   598

1. Puffins

ISBN 0-06-021603-4; 0-06-021604-2 (lib bdg)

LC 90-30525

A simple introduction to the physical characteristics, life cycle, and natural environment of the puffins living off the coast of Maine

"Gail Gibbons tells the story of the endangered puffin colony in a clear, direct text, weaving facts about puffin characteristics and behavior throughout her dramatic narrative. Her rich palette of blues and greens gives life and depth to the island setting and contrasts with the clean black and white of the puffins." Horn Book

Guiberson, Brenda Z.

Spotted owl; bird of the ancient forest; with illustrations by the author. Holt & Co. 1994 69p il $14.95 (3-5)   598

1. Owls 2. Forest ecology

ISBN 0-8050-3171-5   LC 94-13888

"A Redfeather book"

The author "describes the delicate balance of nature necessary for the spotted owl and other creatures to survive, while explaining human economic dependence on the old-growth forests." Publisher's note

"Illustrations in this appealingly designed volume include black-and-white drawings of animals, early-twentieth-century photographs of loggers, and beautiful, full-color photos of the spotted owl and its habitat. A simple yet many-faceted introduction to an endangered species and the complex issues raised by its protection." Booklist

Includes bibliography

Jenkins, Priscilla Belz

A nest full of eggs; illustrated by Lizzy Rockwell. HarperCollins Pubs. 1995 32p il (Let's-read-and-find-out science books) $14.95; lib bdg $14.89; pa $4.95 (k-1)   598

1. Robins 2. Birds—Eggs and nests

ISBN 0-06-023441-5; 0-06-023442-3 (lib bdg); 0-06-445127-5 (pa)   LC 93-43804

This story features "a pair of robins that arrives in the spring, raises a family, and departs in the fall before winter arrives. . . . In addition to the robin family, several examples of the diversity of feathers and nests of other birds are included." Sci Books Films

This book "will catch children's interest, and the author's suggestions for materials to leave out to help robins build their nests are ones many children will want to follow." Bull Cent Child Books

Johnson, Sylvia A.

Inside an egg; photographs by Kiyoshi Shimizu. Lerner Publs. 1982 48p il (Lerner natural science book) lib bdg $19.95; pa $5.95 (4 and up)   598

1. Eggs 2. Chickens

ISBN 0-8225-1472-9 (lib bdg); 0-8225-9522-2 (pa)

LC 81-17235

Adapted from a work by Kiyoshi Shimizu published 1975 in Japan

Text and photographs trace the development of a chicken egg from the time it is laid until it is hatched

"New and difficult concept words are listed in bold type as they appear in the text. All color graphics are excellent; the close-up photographs are stunning. The format and general layout of text to photograph is without confusion and the [book is] loaded with facts." SLJ

Includes glossary

Lang, Aubrey

Eagles; photographs by Wayne Lynch; general editor, R.D. Lawrence. Sierra Club Bks. 1990 62p il maps (Sierra Club wildlife library) hardcover o.p. paperback available $7.95 (4-6)   598

1. Eagles

ISBN 0-316-51383-0 (pa)   LC 90-8729

"Discussion of physical characteristics focuses on body features crucial to the eagle's life as a hunter: eyes, feet, beak, ears, and wings. . . . Hunting, eating, nest building, and rearing of the young are described in other short segments. . . . Along with the numerous handsome photographs there are pen drawings in framed insets which feature body parts, comparative silhouettes, sky dancing, use of air currents, distribution maps, and the progression of pesticides through the food chain. The inherent appeal of the eagles is beautifully conveyed." Horn Book

Lavies, Bianca

Tundra swans; text & photographs by Bianca Lavies. Dutton Children's Bks. 1994 unp il $15.99 (4-6)   **598**

1. Swans

ISBN 0-525-45273-7   LC 94-26898

The author "explores the migration of the tundra swans. The first half of the book describes the swans themselves; the second part concerns the efforts of a scientific team to band the birds and track their migratory route from Chesapeake Bay to the arctic tundra." Booklist

Lavies "weaves factural information with stunning color photos, each of which not only is artistic, but also demonstrates some aspect of the science in a fashion that is both interesting and sure to elicit wonder from the reader." Sci Books Films

Legg, Gerald

Amazing tropical birds; written by Gerald Legg; photographed by Jerry Young. Knopf 1991 29p il (Eyewitness juniors) lib bdg $9.99; pa $6.95 (2-4)   **598**

1. Birds

ISBN 0-679-91520-6 (lib bdg); 0-679-81520-1 (pa)
                                      LC 91-6515

Also available Spanish language edition

Text and photographs introduce amazing tropical birds, including the Gouldian finch, Lady Amherst's pheasant, and the sulphur-crested cockatoo

"The photographs and illustrations in *Amazing Tropical Birds* are superb. . . . The book is really a collection of illustrated sidebars that should excite youngsters to think about interesting facts associated with the lives of tropical birds. . . . The material covered is accurate." Sci Books Films

Lerner, Carol, 1927-

Backyard birds of winter. Morrow Junior Bks. 1994 48p il maps $16; lib bdg $15.93 (3-6)   **598**

1. Birds

ISBN 0-688-12819-X; 0-688-12820-3 (lib bdg)
                                      LC 94-3036

This "introduction to birds in winter begins with a discussion of how their anatomy and behavior help them survive the cold weather in northern climates. The heart of the book presents the physical features, diets, habits, and ranges of more than two dozen relatively common species. Precise watercolor paintings of birds, usually shown as three-quarters life size, appear on nearly every page, making this a beautiful as well as a practical way to learn about wildlife that even city children can observe." Booklist

Includes bibliography

Markle, Sandra, 1946-

Outside and inside birds. Bradbury Press 1994 40p il $15.95 (2-4)   **598**

1. Birds

ISBN 0-02-762312-2   LC 93-38910

"Among the topics Markle tackles are feathers, flying, anatomy, eating habits, senses, birth, and growth. Other pictures examine in close detail the outsides of the winged wonders: their feathers, feet, preen glands, wings, beaks, and much more." SLJ

"Markle writes with verve, easily engaging her audience with questions, simple analogies, and comparisons. . . . The selection and display of photographs is masterful in demonstrating both the design features of bird bodies and the internal organs." Horn Book

Includes glossary

McMillan, Bruce

A beach for the birds; written and photo-illustrated by Bruce McMillan. Houghton Mifflin 1993 32p il $15.95 (2-4)
                                      598

1. Terns 2. Seashore ecology 3. Wildlife conservation 4. Endangered species

ISBN 0-395-64050-4   LC 92-10920

Discusses the physical characteristics and habits of the endangered Least Terns and describes the Maine beach where they spend the summer and raise their young, alongside their human neighbors

"The text is clear and full of information. . . . The brilliant action shots are enough to lure kids into a nature watch of their own." Bull Cent Child Books

Includes glossary and bibliography

Nights of the pufflings; written and photo-illustrated by Bruce McMillan. Houghton Mifflin 1995 32p il $14.95 (2-4)
                                      598

1. Puffins

ISBN 0-395-70810-9   LC 94-14808

"For two weeks every year, the children of Heimaey Island, Iceland, stay out late rescuing hundreds of stranded pufflings. Many of the birds are confused by the village lights and need help flying toward the sea." Sci Child

"Young readers have a natural affinity for the young of other species, and this fascinating story, combined with gorgeous color photographs, a simple, clear text, and handsome book design, makes an appealing package. McMillan includes the pronunciation of unfamiliar Icelandic names and words within the text and follows his story with an afterwood about the North Atlantic puffins." Horn Book

Includes bibliography

Penguins at home; gentoos of Antarctica; written and photo-illustrated by Bruce McMillan. Houghton Mifflin 1993 32p il $15.95 (2-4)   **598**

1. Penguins

ISBN 0-395-66560-4   LC 92-34769

Describes the physical characteristics, behavior, and life cycle of the timid gentoo penguin

"First-rate photographs illustrate a text that supplies interesting information. . . . Large captions summarize important facts and detailed descriptions are provided to enrich the volume." Sci Child

Includes bibliography

Puffins climb, penguins rhyme; written and photo-illustrated by Bruce McMillan. Harcourt Brace & Co. 1995 unp il maps $14 (k-2)
                                      598

1. Puffins 2. Penguins

ISBN 0-15-200362-2   LC 94-27225

McMillan, Bruce—*Continued*
"Gulliver books"

"Antarctic penguins and Icelandic puffins are pictured in photographs on alternating double-page spreads, with simple, rhyming text in very large black letters set below each picture." Booklist

Puffins and penguins "share an endearing gawkiness, and McMillan's unadorned, crystalline photographs capture surprising humor and personality in the simplest of situations." Publ Wkly

Paladino, Catherine
Pomona: the birth of a penguin. Watts 1991
33p il lib bdg $13.72 (2-4)   **598**
1. Penguins
ISBN 0-531-10988-7 (lib bdg)   LC 90-13062
"A New England Aquarium book"
Using one blackfooted penguin as an example, this book describes the birth, growth, and nurture of the species
"Beautiful color pictures supplement the text. . . . The book is interesting and good reading for young learners." Sci Books Films
Includes glossary and bibliography

Parry-Jones, Jemima
Amazing birds of prey; written by Jemima Parry-Jones; photographed by Mike Dunning. Knopf 1992 29p il (Eyewitness juniors) lib bdg $9.99; pa $7.99 (2-4)   **598**
1. Birds of prey
ISBN 0-679-82771-9 (lib bdg); 0-679-82771-4 (pa)
                                            LC 92-909
Also available Spanish language edition
Introduces the physical characteristics and habits of birds of prey, including falcons, eagles, vultures, owls, and hawks

Parsons, Alexandra
Amazing birds; written by Alexandra Parsons; photographed by Jerry Young. Knopf 1990 29p (Eyewitness juniors) lib bdg $11.99; pa $7.95 (2-4)   **598**
1. Birds
ISBN 0-679-90223-6 (lib bdg); 0-679-80223-1 (pa)
                                            LC 89-38943
Also available Spanish language edition
Text and photographs describe amazing members of the bird world, including the vulture, flamingo, and hummingbird
"The text is informal and full of interesting facts. . . . The photography is well done." Appraisal

Patent, Dorothy Hinshaw
Eagles of America; photographs by William Muñoz. Holiday House 1995 40p il $15.95 (4 and up)   **598**
1. Eagles
ISBN 0-8234-1198-2   LC 95-6083
"The only two native species of North American eagles, the bald and golden, are treated in this comparative presentation. Patent describes how their numbers declined dramatically during the 19th and 20th centuries. . . . She also discusses the work of wildlife rehabilitators and conservation efforts. Splendid full-color photographs illustrate the lively text and clarify descriptions." SLJ

Feathers; photographs by William Muñoz. Cobblehill Bks. 1992 64p il $15 (4 and up)
                                            598
1. Birds
ISBN 0-525-65081-4   LC 91-20465
Describes, in text and photographs, birds' feathers—from structure, type, and color to various uses
"This captivating volume, with its fact-filled pages (almost encyclopedic in nature) and exceedingly clear color photos is a nonfiction bonanza." Booklist

Looking at penguins; photographs by Graham Robertson. Holiday House 1993 40p il $15.95 (3-5)   **598**
1. Penguins
ISBN 0-8234-1037-4   LC 92-37673
Describes the different kinds of penguins, their habitat, behavior, and status as an endangered species
This features "good, clear photographs. . . . Intriguing information is scattered through the text." Booklist

Ospreys; photographs by William Muñoz. Clarion Bks. 1993 63p il $15.95 (4 and up)
                                            598
1. Ospreys 2. Wildlife conservation
ISBN 0-395-63391-5   LC 92-30103
Describes the physical characteristics and habits of ospreys, or fish hawks, as well as threats to their survival and efforts to protect them
"Clearly presented information and an attractive format (large print with numerous color photographs) will attract young readers." Booklist
Includes bibliography

Pelicans; photographs by William Muñoz. Clarion Bks. 1992 64p il $14.95 (4 and up)
                                            598
1. Pelicans
ISBN 0-395-57224-X   LC 92-1221
Describes the physical characteristics, habits, and natural habitats of the various species of pelicans, as well as the threats to their survival
"Excellent full-color photos. . . . Patent packs in the facts, delivering them quickly, concisely, and straight on. . . . A nicely designed book, useful for student research." Booklist
Includes bibliography

Where the bald eagles gather; photographs by William Muñoz. Clarion Bks. 1984 56p il map $15.95; pa $5.95 (4 and up)   **598**
1. Bald eagle 2. Glacier National Park (Mont.)
ISBN 0-89919-230-0; 0-395-52598-5 (pa)
                                            LC 83-20852
Describes the annual autumn gathering of bald eagles in Glacier National Park and examines the work of the wildlife research project that bands the birds for later tracking that will provide information on the habits and life cycle of our national bird
"Exceptional photographs set the mood for this informative book. . . . The text contains interesting well-organized information as well as a fine description of how scientists work." Appraisal

Wild turkey, tame turkey; photographs by William Muñoz. Clarion Bks. 1989 57p il $14.95; pa $5.95 (4 and up)   **598**
1. Turkeys
ISBN 0-89919-704-3; 0-395-55275-3 (pa)
                                            LC 89-613

Patent, Dorothy Hinshaw—*Continued*

"A well-written text enhanced by full-color photographs explains the similarities and differences between the native American wild turkey and the domesticated variety. Discusses the importance of maintaining the wild turkey population. Raises concern for the welfare of domesticated turkeys and other farm animals." Sci Child

Peters, Lisa Westberg

This way home; illustrated by Normand Chartier. Holt & Co. 1994 unp il $14.95 (k-3)   **598**

1. Birds—Migration
ISBN 0-8050-1368-7   LC 93-45751

"This picture book details the migratory trip of the Savannah sparrow, a song bird that is born on the Minnesota prairie, travels to Georgia for the winter, and goes back North when the warm April breezes blow. This is a poetic account, beautifully illustrated with double-page watercolors." SLJ

Peterson, Roger Tory, 1908-1996

A field guide to the birds; a completely new guide to all the birds of eastern and central North America; text and illustrations by Roger Tory Peterson; maps by Virginia Marie Peterson. 4th ed, completely rev and enl. Houghton Mifflin 1980 384p il maps $24.95; pa $15.95   **598**

1. Birds—North America
ISBN 0-395-26621-1; 0-395-26619-X (pa)
     LC 80-14304

Also available CD-ROM version that covers birds throughout North America

"The Peterson field guide series"

First published 1934

Sponsored by the National Audubon Society and National Wildlife Federation

This guide to birds found east of the Rocky Mountains contains colored illustrations painted by the author, with description of each species on the facing page. Views of young birds and seasonal variations in plumage are included. Birds are arranged in eight major groups of body shape. There are also 390 colored maps showing summer and winter range

A field guide to western birds; text and illustrations by Roger Tory Peterson; maps by Virginia Marie Peterson. 3rd ed, completely rev and enl. Houghton Mifflin 1989 432p il maps $22.95; pa $16.95   **598**

1. Birds—West (U.S.)
ISBN 0-395-51749-4; 0-395-51424-X (pa)
     LC 89-31517

"The Peterson field guide series"

First published 1941

"A completely new guide to field marks of all species found in North America west of the 100th meridian and north of Mexico." Title page

Sponsored by the National Audubon Society, the National Wildlife Federation, and the Roger Tory Peterson Institute

This guide illustrates over 1,000 birds (700 species) on 165 color plates. In addition, over 400 distribution maps are included

Pine, Jonathan

Backyard birds; illustrated by Julie Zickefoose. HarperCollins Pubs. 1993 48p il (HarperCollins nature study book) hardcover o.p. paperback available $7.95 (3-5)   **598**

1. Birds 2. Bird watching
ISBN 0-06-446150-5 (pa)   LC 91-45184

Provides information on the habits and behavior of house sparrows, starlings, robins, wrens, hummingbirds, and nighthawks, with clues for easy identification

The "narrative flows in a conversational tone that concentrates on the birds' habitats and behavior. Soft watercolor illustrations show the backyard settings described in the text, and most species are realistically painted and readily recognizable." SLJ

Includes bibliography

Robbins, Chandler S.

Birds of North America; a guide to field identification; by Chandler S. Robbins, Bertel Bruun, and Herbert S. Zim; illustrated by Arthur Singer. expanded rev ed. Golden Bks. 1983 360p il maps $13.95; pa $11.95 (4 and up)   **598**

1. Birds—North America
ISBN 0-307-37002-X; 0-307-33656-5 (pa)
     LC 83-60422

"Golden field guide"

First published 1966

"Water birds are presented first, followed by land birds; within each of these two main divisions, arrangement is by related groups of species. Featured are carefully made, full-color illustrations, clear textual descriptions, and detailed range maps." Booklist

Rockwell, Anne F., 1934-

Our yard is full of birds; by Anne Rockwell; illustrated by Lizzy Rockwell. Macmillan 1992 unp il $13.95 (k-2)   **598**

1. Birds
ISBN 0-02-777273-X   LC 90-30436

Describes the variety of birds visiting a yard, from the phoebe and wren to the crows and blue jays

"Lovely and accurate color drawings of birds common to most yards enhance a simple story of what a child sees near home. The lively format encourages bird identification and nature observation for the very young reader." Sci Child

Sattler, Helen Roney

The book of eagles; illustrated by Jean Day Zallinger. Lothrop, Lee & Shepard Bks. 1989 64p il maps lib bdg $15.93 (4 and up)   **598**

1. Eagles
ISBN 0-688-07022-1   LC 88-38806

"Comprehensive treatment of different species of eagles found in many parts of the world. Numerous full-color paintings on almost every page illustrate various eagle behaviors." Sci Child

Includes glossary and bibliography

Sattler, Helen Roney—*Continued*

The book of North American owls; illustrated by Jean Day Zallinger. Clarion Bks. 1995 64p il maps $15.95 (4 and up)   **598**

1. Owls

ISBN 0-395-60524-5   LC 91-43626

This volume "includes owl classification and history, hunting and habitat, courtship and nesting, and the complex relationship between owls and humans. The comprehensive glossary includes all of the 21 North American species." Sci Child

This "is a superb ornithological primer. . . . The book is lavishly illustrated." Appraisal

Includes bibliography

Schafer, Susan

The vulture. Dillon Press 1994 60p il map (Dillon remarkable animals book) $13.95 (3-5)   **598**

1. Vultures

ISBN 0-87518-604-1   LC 93-44534

Describes the physical characteristics, habits, and life cycle of the turkey vulture, an important scavenger, as well as its related species in the Americas

"The text is not only factual, but readable and interesting. . . . All but two of the two-page spreads include a brilliant, colorful captioned photograph that enhances the text." Appraisal

Includes glossary and bibliography

Selsam, Millicent Ellis, 1912-

A first look at bird nests; by Millicent E. Selsam and Joyce Hunt; illustrated by Harriett Springer. Walker & Co. 1984 32p il lib bdg $9.85 (1-3)   **598**

1. Birds—Eggs and nests

ISBN 0-8027-6565-3   LC 84-15238

An introduction to the many places birds make their nests, such as chimneys, cliffs, bushes, traffic lights, and window ledges, and the unusual things that might be built into the nests

"A text geared to spur careful observation and critical thinking is paired with black-and-white pencil drawings of various birds and their nests." Booklist

A first look at owls, eagles, and other hunters of the sky; by Millicent E. Selsam and Joyce Hunt; illustrated by Harriett Springer. Walker & Co. 1986 32p il $10.95; lib bdg $10.85 (1-3)   **598**

1. Birds of prey

ISBN 0-8027-6625-0; 0-8027-6642-0 (lib bdg)
                                         LC 86-7738

The authors "introduce birds of prey—owls, hawks, eagles, falcons, and vultures—to young children, encouraging them to notice differences in shapes and sizes and to identify some of the species. Springer's precise black-and-white drawings serve the text well; the distinctions the authors address are clear, and youngsters should have no trouble observing them." Booklist

Silverstein, Alvin

The peregrine falcon; [by] Alvin, Virginia, and Robert Silverstein. Millbrook Press 1995 64p il (Endangered in America) lib bdg $15.40 (4 and up)   **598**

1. Falcons 2. Endangered species

ISBN 1-56294-417-7   LC 94-17991

"The authors begin with an explanation of how pesticides and overhunting have jeopardized this bird of prey. They also provide detailed lifecycle information and recount the various techniques being employed to ensure the falcon's continued survival." Booklist

This book "is recommended for use in classrooms, for general awareness, and as a reference." Sci Books Films

Includes bibliography

The spotted owl; [by] Alvin, Virginia, and Robert Silverstein. Millbrook Press 1994 63p il map (Endangered in America) lib bdg $15.40 (4 and up)   **598**

1. Owls 2. Endangered species 3. Birds—Protection

ISBN 1-56294-415-0   LC 93-42624

The authors examine the controversial government programs designed to protect the spotted owl. This illustrated work explores how timber industry jobs are threatened by efforts to conserve the owl's extensive breeding habitat in old-growth forests

"This book gives an exceptionally balanced treatment of both sides of the disagreement." Sci Books Films

Includes bibliography

Stone, Lynn M.

Vultures. Carolrhoda Bks. 1993 48p il (Carolrhoda nature watch book) lib bdg $19.95 (3-6)   **598**

1. Vultures

ISBN 0-87614-768-6   LC 92-26721

The author "describes the lives of raptors in general and specifically vultures. Often connected with death, these birds suffer from a negative image that Stone . . . disputes, discussing the important role of scavengers in cleaning up carrion and preventing the spread of disease. She also examines the different breeds, their nesting habits, modern-day threats to their existence, and the successful captive breeding program of the California Condor." SLJ

This book features "a readable text, accompanied by clear color photographs." Sci Child

Includes glossary and bibliography

Taylor, Barbara, 1954-

The bird atlas; illustrated by Richard Orr; written by Barbara Taylor. Dorling Kindersley 1993 64p il maps $19.95 (5 and up)   **598**

1. Birds

ISBN 1-56458-327-9   LC 93-18225

Describes the physical characteristics and habitats of birds around the world

"This excellent atlas has fantastically well-developed drawings combined with photographs and inset boxes containing information about the various groups of birds it presents. . . . The text is easy to read, yet is highly informative." Sci Books Films

Tyrrell, Esther Quesada

Hummingbirds; jewels in the sky; photographs by Robert A. Tyrrell. Crown 1992 36p il $14; lib bdg $14.99 (3-6)   **598**

1. Hummingbirds
ISBN 0-517-58390-9; 0-517-58391-7 (lib bdg)
                 LC 91-40857

Text and photographs introduce the physical characteristics and behavior of several species of hummingbirds

"The vivid stop-action photographs are striking. . . . This excellent introduction to the world of birds may very well spark an early interest in science and nature." Booklist

Zim, Herbert S.

Birds; a guide to the most familiar American birds; by Herbert S. Zim and Ira N. Gabrielson; revised and updated by Chandler S. Robbins; illustrated by James Gordon Irving. rev ed. Golden Bks. il maps pa $5.95 (4 and up)   **598**

1. Birds
"A Golden guide"
First published 1949 by Simon & Schuster. Periodically revised

This book contains full color pictures of the most familiar American birds. The text describes additional related and similar species

Includes bibliography

599 Mammals

Arnosky, Jim

Crinkleroot's 25 mammals every child should know. Bradbury Press 1994 unp il $12.95 (k-3)   **599**

1. Mammals
ISBN 0-02-705845-X   LC 93-7585

The jovial woodsman Crinkleroot introduces twenty-five realistically drawn mammals, including the dog, beaver, and elephant

"The softly toned watercolors often place the subjects in their natural habitats, and the endpapers are inviting and dreamlike." SLJ

Bramwell, Martyn

Mammals: the small plant-eaters; [by] Martyn Bramwell and Steve Parker, with contributions by Jill Bailey and Linda Losito. Facts on File 1988 96p il (Encyclopedia of the animal world) $17.95 (4 and up)   **599**

1. Herbivores
ISBN 0-8160-1958-4   LC 88-16934

Examines those mammals which are herbivores, including koalas, marmots, hamsters, and squirrels

"Outstanding action photographs and drawings of animals at work and play in their habitats complement an easy-to-read text." SLJ

Includes glossary and bibliography

Kerrod, Robin, 1938-

Mammals: primates, insect eaters, and baleen whales. Facts on File 1988 96p il (Encyclopedia of the animal world) $17.95 (4 and up)   **599**

1. Mammals
ISBN 0-8160-1961-4   LC 88-16931

Introduces a number of mammals, including the bat, baboon, and gray whale

"This is not a treatise on taxonomy but an informative survey of the life styles of animals. Young nature lovers will be fascinated by the brief essays that highlight the characteristics unique to each animal group. . . . The strongest point of this book is the spectacular photography, which includes sensitive close-up portraits of animals in natural positions." Sci Books Films

Includes glossary and bibliography

Lilly, Kenneth

Kenneth Lilly's animals; text by Joyce Pope. Lothrop, Lee & Shepard Bks. 1988 93p il maps o.p.; Candlewick Press paperback available $12.99 (3 and up)   **599**

1. Animals
ISBN 1-56402-513-6 (pa)   LC 87-31147

"Each beautiful, full-color illustration is accompanied by one page of descriptive text which provides valuable information on how a variety of animals are adapted to their particular habitats. Animals are grouped according to habitat: hot forests, cool forests, seas and rivers, grasslands, deserts, and mountains." Sci Child

O'Toole, Christopher

Mammals: the hunters; [by] Christopher O'Toole and John Stidworthy. Facts on File 1988 96p il (Encyclopedia of the animal world) $17.95 (4 and up)   **599**

1. Mammals
ISBN 0-8160-1959-2   LC 88-16933

"This book introduces mammals who are carnivores. A chapter on each mammal includes habitat, physical features, and lifestyles. A fact panel with color-coded symbols shows distribution of the mammal on a world map, diet, habitat, size, color, and lifespan. There are outstanding full-color photographs. . . . An excellent resource for any age reader." Okla State Dept of Educ

Includes glossary and bibliography

Parker, Steve

Mammal; written by Steve Parker. Knopf 1989 63p il (Eyewitness books) $19; lib bdg $18.99 (4 and up)   **599**

1. Mammals
ISBN 0-394-82258-7; 0-394-92258-1 (lib bdg)
                 LC 88-22656

Also available Spanish language edition

Photographs and text examine the world of mammals, depicting their development, feeding habits, courtship rituals, protective behavior, and physical adaptation to their various ways of life

This book takes a "comprehensive yet detailed look at members of the class that includes humans. Filled with color photographs keyed to the text, the book provides ample illustrations of a variety of mammals and their unique traits." Sci Books Films

Parsons, Alexandra

Amazing mammals; written by Alexandra Parsons; photographed by Jerry Young. Knopf 1990 29p il (Eyewitness juniors) lib bdg $11.99; pa $9.99 (2-4)   **599**

1. Mammals
ISBN 0-679-90224-4 (lib bdg); 0-679-80224-X (pa)
LC 89-38831

Also available Spanish language edition

Introduces such notable mammals as the elephant, sloth, koala, and porcupine, explains what makes them unique, and describes the important characteristics of the entire group

This book is distinguished by "spectacular photographs and absolute clarity of text." Publ Wkly

Patent, Dorothy Hinshaw

Why mammals have fur; photographs by William Muñoz. Cobblehill Bks. 1995 26p il $14.99 (4 and up)   **599**

1. Mammals 2. Fur 3. Hair
ISBN 0-525-65141-1   LC 94-28064

Patent "discusses the many forms of fur and their contributions to the success of mammals, whether for warmth, camouflage, or weaponry." Booklist

"An appealing assortment of color photographs, generally small in size, illustrate points about such disparate types of hair as a kitten's whiskers, the quills of a porcupine, the compressed hair that makes up a rhinoceros horn, the soft fur of a sea otter, and the ragged coat of a molting Bactrian camel." Horn Book

The **Sierra** Club book of great mammals. Sierra Club Bks. for Children 1992 68p il $16.95 (4 and up)   **599**

1. Mammals
ISBN 0-87156-507-2   LC 92-11373

Text and pictures introduce a gallery of mammals

"The photos are compelling—from a yawning hippo to a brooding orangutan—and for those who want to read closely there's more technical detail. . . . A great deal of factual information is presented here with informality and enthusiasm." Booklist

Includes glossary

Snedden, Robert

What is a mammal? photographs by Oxford Scientific Films; illustrated by Adrian Lascom. Sierra Club Bks. for Children 1994 32p il $14.95 (3-6)   **599**

1. Mammals
ISBN 0-87156-468-8   LC 93-26145

This book begins with a discussion of mammalian "characteristics, followed by sections describing fur and hair, temperature control, life cycles, locomotion, teeth and jaws, and the senses." Booklist

This book "provides an excellent balance of written and visual information for young readers." Appraisal

Includes glossary

Stidworthy, John

Mammals: the large plant-eaters. Facts on File 1988 96p il (Encyclopedia of the animal world) $17.95 (4 and up)   **599**

1. Herbivores
ISBN 0-8160-1960-6   LC 88-16935

Introduces mammals which live and feed on the plains and savannahs, such as gazelles, tapirs, and kangaroos

"This is tantalizing fare for researchers and browsers. . . . Attractive animal portraits on glossy, paper-covered boards invite heavy-duty use." SLJ

Includes glossary and bibliography

Yamashita, Keiko, 1949-

Paws, wings, and hooves; mammals on the move; photographs by Isamu Sekido. Lerner Publs. 1993 24p il (Science all around you) lib bdg $17.50 (1-3)   **599**

1. Animal locomotion 2. Mammals
ISBN 0-8225-2901-7   LC 92-18506

Original Japanese edition, 1986

This book "examines mammalian locomotion by looking at 11 animals and their adaptations to the task. . . . Bat, bear, cat, chimp, cow, dog, elephant, horse, mole, rhino, and seal are used to document how mammals are adapted to their environments for walking, burrowing, swimming, or flying." Sci Books Films

This volume "uses excellent photographs of the bottoms of those structures to capture the reader's attention and make connections with the correct animal." Appraisal

Includes glossary

Zim, Herbert S.

Mammals; a guide to familiar American species; 218 animals in full color; by Herbert S. Zim and Donald F. Hoffmeister; illustrated by James Gordon Irving. rev ed Golden Bks. il pa $5.95 (4 and up)   **599**

1. Mammals
"A Golden guide"

First published 1955 by Simon & Schuster. Periodically revised

This guide presents general and specific information about mammals commonly found in North America

Includes bibliography

599.2   Marsupials

Arnold, Caroline, 1944-

Kangaroo; photographs by Richard Hewett. Morrow 1987 48p il $13; lib bdg $12.93; pa $5.95 (3-5)   **599.2**

1. Kangaroos
ISBN 0-688-06480-9; 0-688-06481-7 (lib bdg); 0-688-11502-0 (pa)   LC 86-18103

Discusses the kangaroo family, their characteristics and behavior, and, in particular, the experiences of an Australian couple with an orphaned baby kangaroo during his first year in which they prepared him to be on his own

"Vivid descriptions . . . enhance the writing, as do the copious photographs. They range from action shots of leaping kangaroos to an impressive close-up of a tiny, glistening joey newly arrived in its mother's pouch." Horn Book

Koala; photographs by Richard Hewett. Morrow 1987 48p il $13.95; lib bdg $13.88; pa $5.95 (3-5)   **599.2**

1. Koalas
ISBN 0-688-06478-7; 0-688-06479-5 (lib bdg); 0-688-11503-9 (pa)   LC 86-18092

Arnold, Caroline, 1944-—*Continued*
This "account provides standard information on physical characteristics, behavior, care of the young, related species, and efforts at conservation. . . . Interwoven into *Koalas* is the rearing of one youngster until in early maturity she is selected, along with three other young females, for shipment to the San Francisco Zoo." SLJ

Darling, Kathy
Kangaroos on location; photographs by Tara Darling. Lothrop, Lee & Shepard Bks. 1993 40p il $14; lib bdg $13.93 (3-5)   **599.2**
1. Kangaroos
ISBN 0-688-09728-6; 0-688-09729-4 (lib bdg)
     LC 92-38418
"The Darlings visit diverse sites in Australia and Tasmania to track down examples of the 60 species of the kangaroo family. . . . The authors map locations and show the fascinating variety of nocturnal marsupial herbivores. . . . Their diets, means of locomotion, and gestation periods are explained in an interesting text and through good-quality, full-color photos." SLJ

Tasmanian devil on location; photographs by Tara Darling. Lothrop, Lee & Shepard Bks. 1992 40p il $16; lib bdg $15.93 (3-5)
     599.2
1. Tasmanian devils
ISBN 0-688-09726-X; 0-688-09727-8 (lib bdg)
     LC 91-27561
Describes the physical characteristics, behavior, and eating habits of the tasmanian devil
"Superb full-color photographs (many taken at night) on nearly every page portray these creatures engaging in a variety of activities. . . . An excellent book about a species not frequently covered, this will be useful for report writers and popular with some browsers." Booklist

Lepthien, Emilie U. (Emilie Utteg)
Opossums. Childrens Press 1994 45p il lib bdg $13.50; pa $5.50 (2-4)   **599.2**
1. Opossums
ISBN 0-516-01055-7 (lib bdg); 0-516-41055-5 (pa)
     LC 93-33516
"A New true book"
In this introduction to opossums "special sections on appearance, feet, tails, homes, birth, and babies are all covered, with copious color photographs to illustrate. The final quarter of the book discusses marsupials on continents other than North America, including the mouse-like murine opossums of Central and South America and the gliding opossum of Australia." Sci Books Films
Includes glossary

Triggs, Barbara
Wombats. Houghton Mifflin 1991 c1990 unp il maps $14.95 (4-6)   **599.2**
1. Wombats
ISBN 0-395-55993-6   LC 90-34042
First published 1990 in Australia
Presents, in text and photographs, the habits, life cycle, and natural environment of the Australian wombat, one of the world's largest burrowing animals
"The curious nature of the Australian wombat . . . is expertly delineated in this introduction. Sharp full-color photos appear on almost every page." SLJ

599.3   Unguiculata

Lavies, Bianca
It's an armadillo; text and photographs by Bianca Lavies. Dutton 1989 unp il $13.95 (1-3)   **599.3**
1. Armadillos
ISBN 0-525-44523-4   LC 89-31821
Also available in paperback from Penguin Bks.
Text and photographs describe the physical characteristics, eating habits, reproduction, and infancy of the nine-banded armadillo
"The text correlates perfectly with the full-color photographs and offers a mix of basic life-cycle information and interesting behavioral sidelights. Moreover, the text flows well; here is a nonfiction title that will be right at home in a story hour." Booklist

Stuart, Dee
The astonishing armadillo. Carolrhoda Bks. 1993 48p il maps (Carolrhoda nature watch book) lib bdg $19.95; pa $6.95 (3-6)
     599.3
1. Armadillos
ISBN 0-87614-769-4 (lib bdg); 0-87614-630-2 (pa)
     LC 92-25970
Describes the physical characteristics, habitat, and life cycle of the armadillo
"The book is well written and has excellent photographs." Appraisal
Includes glossary

599.32   Lagomorphs and rodents

Arnosky, Jim
Come out, muskrats. Lothrop, Lee & Shepard Bks. 1989 unp il $12.95; lib bdg $12.88; pa $3.95 (k-2)   **599.32**
1. Muskrats
ISBN 0-688-05457-9; 0-688-05458-7 (lib bdg); 0-688-10490-8 (pa)   LC 88-26611
"Clearly emphasizing the crepuscular and nocturnal nature of muskrats, the text's colorful two-page drawings captivate the senses. One experiences the behavior of the animals as well as the water, air, scenery, and sounds around them. This is an excellent 'read-to' book, and the large-print format is ideal for the novice reader." Sci Child

Fischer-Nagel, Heiderose, 1956-
A look through the mouse hole; by Heiderose and Andreas Fischer-Nagel. Carolrhoda Bks. 1989 47p il (Carolrhoda nature watch book) lib bdg $19.95 (3-6)
     599.32
1. Mice
ISBN 0-87614-326-5   LC 88-39639
Original German edition published 1986 in Switzerland

Fischer-Nagel, Heiderose, 1956—_Continued_
Photographs and text observe the behavior of a family of mice living in a basement, comparing their habits to those of outdoor mice. Includes information on the care of pet mice
"The narrative is clearly written and flows smoothly except for rare occasions in which it is interrupted by personal observations. Large print, an open format, and striking photographs will hold readers' attention." SLJ
Includes glossary

George, Jean Craighead, 1919-
The moon of the chickarees; illustrated by Don Rodell. new ed. HarperCollins Pubs. 1992 48p il (Thirteen moons) lib bdg $14.89 (3-6)   **599.32**
1. Squirrels
ISBN 0-06-022508-4   LC 90-22409
A revised and newly illustrated edition of the title first published 1968 by Crowell
Describes the activities of a mother red squirrel during the month of April as she nurtures her newborn babies in the Bitterroot Valley of Montana

Lepthien, Emilie U. (Emilie Utteg)
Rabbits and hares. Childrens Press 1994 45p il lib bdg $13.50; pa $5.50 (2-4)   **599.32**
1. Rabbits
ISBN 0-516-01058-1 (lib bdg); 0-516-41058-X (Pa)
                                        LC 93-33514
"A New true book"
"This volume provides the facts and figure to assist any early elementary report on rabbits and hares. High-quality color photographs accompany nearly every page." Sci Books Films
Includes glossary

McNulty, Faith
Orphan; the story of a baby woodchuck; illustrated by Darby Morrell. Scholastic 1992 40p il $11.95 (2-4)   **599.32**
1. Marmots
ISBN 0-590-43838-7   LC 91-25333
The author describes finding an orphaned baby woodchuck and caring for it until it was able to fend for itself in the wild again
"An appealing offering that will serve well as an introduction to a common wild creature." SLJ

Patent, Dorothy Hinshaw
Prairie dogs; photographs by William Muñoz. Clarion Bks. 1993 63p il lib bdg $15.95 (4 and up)   **599.32**
1. Prairie dogs 2. Prairie ecology
ISBN 0-395-56572-3   LC 92-34724
Discusses the habits and life cycle of prairie dogs and examines their place in the ecology of their grassland environment
"The text and illustrations work together, each enlarging the other and both enlightening the reader. Appearing on nearly every page, the full-color photographs take readers out to the prairie to see its plants and animals clearly." Booklist
Includes bibliography

Powell, E. Sandy
Rats; photographs by Jerry Boucher. Lerner Publs. 1994 48p il (Early bird nature books) lib bdg $18.95 (2-4)   **599.32**
1. Rats
ISBN 0-8225-3003-1   LC 93-40925
This book contains "information about rat habits and habitats, different types of rats, their foods and burrows, and baby rats and their growing up." Sci Books Films
"Rats is a delightful book that gives a great boost to the reputation of these creatures. . . . It is loaded with beautiful color photographs." Sci Child
Includes glossary

Ring, Elizabeth, 1920-
Lucky mouse; photographs by Dwight Kuhn. Millbrook Press 1995 unp il lib bdg $15.40 (k-3)   **599.32**
1. Mice
ISBN 1-56294-344-8   LC 94-46948
"The life cycle of an orphaned deer mouse unfolds as a group of children place it with a white-footed mouse family. Relevant facts on mice are included in a question-and-answer section." Sci Child
"The readable text is accompanied by engaging, well-suited full-color photographs. . . . Young children, especially those who like small furry animals, will enjoy this and find it useful for assignments." Booklist

Ryden, Hope
The beaver. Putnam 1986 62p il o.p.; Lyons & Burford paperback available $9.95 (3-5)
                                        599.32
1. Beavers
ISBN 1-55821-142-X (pa)   LC 86-9425
Text and photographs describe the physical characteristics and habits of the beaver and illustrate the beneficial effects of his work on the environment that he inhabits

599.4 Bats

Bash, Barbara
Shadows of night; the hidden world of the little brown bat. Sierra Club Bks. for Children 1993 unp il $16.95; pa $6.95 (1-3)   **599.4**
1. Bats
ISBN 0-87156-562-5; 0-87156-440-8 (pa)
                                        LC 92-22713
Describes the life cycle, physical characteristics, and habits of the little brown bat
"The author's fascination with and unabashed affection for these nocturnal insect catchers comes through in her informative text and outstanding watercolors." SLJ

Maestro, Betsy, 1944-
Bats; night fliers; illustrated by Giulio Maestro. Scholastic 1994 32p il map $14.95 (k-3)   **599.4**
1. Bats
ISBN 0-590-46150-8   LC 93-26153
Describes the varieties, habitats, behavior, and physical characteristics of bats

Maestro, Betsy, 1944-—*Continued*

"Basic information is given in language that will prove both interesting and readily understandable to young children. An effort is made to stress the wonder, beauty, and usefulness of the animals while downplaying the idea that they are weird or ugly. Pencil and watercolor illustrations are informative and appealing." SLJ

Pringle, Laurence P.

Batman; exploring the world of bats; [by] Laurence Pringle; photographs by Merlin D. Tuttle. Scribner 1991 42p il $16 (4 and up)
599.4

1. Tuttle, Merlin D. 2. Bats

ISBN 0-684-19232-2   LC 90-8679

Describes Merlin Tuttle's interest in bats, his study of them in their natural habitat, and his work to protect them through such efforts as the organization he founded, Bat Conservation International

"This is an excellent review for junior scientists of the role of bats in nature. . . . Tuttle's photographic artistry is quite evident from the series of superb photographs that accompany the text." Sci Books Films

Includes bibliography

Selsam, Millicent Ellis, 1912-

A first look at bats; [by] Millicent E. Selsam and Joyce Hunt; illustrations by Harriett Springer. Walker & Co. 1991 32p il $11.95; lib bdg $12.85 (1-3)   **599.4**

1. Bats

ISBN 0-8027-8135-7; 0-8027-8136-5 (lib bdg)
LC 91-2862

This book examines the distinctive characteristics of bats and views several different species

"Selsam gives basic information on feeding habits, dwelling places, and identifying features in clear, lively prose. . . . The author and illustrator collaborate to explain echolocation simply. . . . This is a useful, informative introduction to our only flying mammals." Booklist

Stuart, Dee

Bats; mysterious flyers of the night. Carolrhoda Bks. 1994 47p il (Carolrhoda nature watch book) lib bdg $19.95; pa $6.95 (3-6)   **599.4**

1. Bats

ISBN 0-87614-814-3 (lib bdg); 0-87614-631-0 (pa)
LC 93-34304

"The volume includes a general discussion on bats: where they live, how they fly in the dark, their food, hibernation, migration, raising young, their place and usefulness in the scheme of nature, and the urgent need for their protection and conservation." Sci Books Films

Includes glossary

599.5 Cetaceans and sirenians

Arnold, Caroline, 1944-

Killer whale; photographs by Richard Hewett. Morrow Junior Bks. 1994 48p il $15; lib bdg $14.93 (3-5)   **599.5**

1. Whales

ISBN 0-688-12029-6; 0-688-12030-X (lib bdg)
LC 93-33668

"*Killer Whale* introduces Takara, who was born in captivity at Sea World in San Diego, and to the other killer whales that live there." SLJ

"The handsome photographs and text show extensive human interaction with the killer whales. . . . Caroline Arnold and Richard Hewett achieve a very high standard of nonfiction." Horn Book

Clark, Margaret Goff

The vanishing manatee. Cobblehill Bks. 1990 64p il $14.99 (4 and up)   **599.5**

1. Manatees

ISBN 0-525-65024-5   LC 89-38676

"Facts, anecdotes, and details describe the physical characteristics and behaviors of the friendly and curious manatee, Florida's largest mammal. Includes a discussion of research efforts to ensure manatee survival in their aquatic environment and sources for more information. A charming, instructive study." Sci Child

Darling, Kathy

Manatee on location; photographs by Tara Darling. Lothrop, Lee & Shepard Bks. 1990 48p il $14.95; lib bdg $14.88 (3-5)   **599.5**

1. Manatees

ISBN 0-688-09030-3; 0-688-09031-1 (lib bdg)
LC 89-45904

Text and photographs describe the life history, physical characteristics, behavior, and underwater activities of the Florida manatee and how scientists and others are trying to save this endangered sea mammal

"Illustrated with full-color underwater photographs, Darling's text of simple sentences and clear descriptions evokes the environment of the Crystal River Refuge in Florida, where her manatee research took place." Booklist

Dow, Lesley

Whales. Facts on File 1990 68p il (Great creatures of the world) $17.95 (5 and up)
599.5

1. Whales

ISBN 0-8160-2271-2   LC 89-34670

Describes the physical characteristics, habits, and natural environment of whales and discusses their evolution and relationship with human beings

This book is "filled with amazing photographs, some of which actually make me gasp with delight. Graceful and anatomically accurate renderings round out its visual appeal." Appraisal

Esbensen, Barbara Juster

Baby whales drink milk; illustrated by Lambert Davis. HarperCollins Pubs. 1994 32p il (Let's-read-and-find-out science books) $15; lib bdg $14.89; pa $4.95 (k-1)   **599.5**

1. Whales 2. Mammals
ISBN 0-06-021551-8; 0-06-021552-6 (lib bdg); 0-06-445119-4 (pa)   LC 92-30375

Describes the behavior of the humpback whale, with an emphasis on the fact that it is a mammal and shares the characteristics of other mammals

"Full-color paintings, mainly in watery greens and blues, show the animals in their habitat, along with a scene of a whale model in a museum and a map of migration. The book's strong point, though, is Esbensen's simple, informative text, which keeps its young audience clearly in view." Booklist

Gibbons, Gail

Whales. Holiday House 1991 unp il $15.95; pa $5.95 (k-3)   **599.5**

1. Whales
ISBN 0-8234-0900-7; 0-8234-1030-7 (pa)   LC 91-4507

"Information on the lives of different kinds of whales, including how they swim, breathe . . . eat, use sonar, and bear young." Publisher's note

"The simple, straightforward, though choppy text is enhanced by nicely balanced, captioned paintings that emphasize clean, clear figures against aqueous backgrounds in watercolor." Booklist

Grover, Wayne, 1934-

Dolphin adventure; a true story; illustrated by Jim Fowler. Greenwillow Bks. 1990 47p il $14; pa $3.95 (3-5)   **599.5**

1. Dolphins
ISBN 0-688-09442-2; 0-688-12277-9 (pa)   LC 89-27226

"While scuba diving off the Florida coast, the author was approached by two adult dolphins and their baby, who had a fishhook in its back. After the dolphins circled and clicked at him, Grover realized that he was being asked for help. He patiently soothed the baby dolphin and removed the embedded hook with his diving knife while the parent dolphins drove off sharks." Booklist

"This a fascinating story, nicely illustrated with drawings in shades of gray, black, and white." SLJ

Kraus, Scott D.

The search for the right whale; [by] Scott Kraus & Kenneth Mallory. Crown 1993 36p il maps $14; lib bdg $14.99 (5 and up)   **599.5**

1. Whales 2. Endangered species 3. Wildlife conservation
ISBN 0-517-57844-1; 0-517-57845-X (lib bdg)   LC 92-18091

"A New England Aquarium book"

Follows a team of New England Aquarium scientists as they follow and study migrating North Atlantic right whales and speculates about the future survival of this endangered species

"Illustrations include informative photographs, historical drawings, and maps that add new whale information to the basic story line. . . . This is a fine effort to personalize scientists for young readers, while maintaining a high standard of science reporting." Appraisal

McMillan, Bruce

Going on a whale watch; written and illustrated with photographs and drawings by Bruce McMillan. Scholastic 1992 39p il map $14.95 (k-3)   **599.5**

1. Whales
ISBN 0-590-45768-3   LC 91-39728

Two six-year-olds on a whale-watching expedition see different kinds of whales engaging in such activities as headstanding and lunge-feeding. Includes facts about each kind of whale

"While clear, full-color photographs document whale anatomy and behavior as seen above the water's surface, smaller diagrams show what is happening underwater at the same time. Two-word captions, such as 'Humpback spout' and 'paired blowholes,' appear in large type below photos on facing pages forming a single concept on each spread . . . An excellent choice for young children curious about whales." Booklist

Includes glossary and bibliography

Milton, Joyce

Whales; the gentle giants; illustrated by Alton Langford. Random House 1989 48p il lib bdg $7.99; pa $3.99 (1-3)   **599.5**

1. Whales
ISBN 0-394-99809-X (lib bdg); 0-394-89809-5 (pa)   LC 88-15616

"Step into reading. A step 2 book"

This book discusses different types of whales and "how they care for their young and defend each other against predators, how they migrate, how they sleep in the water, and how and what they eat." SLJ

"Illustrated with appropriately scaled dramatic portraits that dive across double-page spreads, this easy-reader treatment of a popular subject leaps with appeal. Milton understands what kids like about whales . . . and packs a considerable amount of information into the constraints of the format." Bull Cent Child Books

Patent, Dorothy Hinshaw

Dolphins and porpoises. Holiday House 1987 89p il $15.95 (5 and up)   **599.5**

1. Dolphins 2. Porpoises
ISBN 0-8234-0663-6   LC 87-45332

"A fascinating book about dolphins and porpoises that holds the reader spellbound as the anatomy, feeding habits, complex sonar system, social organization, and reproduction of these friendly mammals are discussed. Beautiful, black-and-white photographs enhance the text. Includes cetacean classifications." Sci Child

Humpback whales; photographs by Deborah A. Glockner-Ferrari and Mark J. Ferrari. Holiday House 1989 32p il $15.95 (2-4)   **599.5**

1. Whales
ISBN 0-8234-0779-9   LC 89-2026

Describes the physical characteristics, habitat, and behavior of the humpback whale

Patent, Dorothy Hinshaw—*Continued*

Killer whales; photographs by John K.B. Ford. Holiday House 1993 31p il $15.95 (2-4)
599.5

1. Whales
ISBN 0-8234-0999-6   LC 92-23949

Describes the physical characteristics, behavior, and habitats of killer whales

The author's "choice of intriguing facts and her straightforward writing style make the book accessible to browsers and suitable for beginning research. Stunning full-color photographs add an important dimension to the information." Horn Book

Looking at dolphins and porpoises. Holiday House 1989 48p il $13.95 (3-5)   **599.5**

1. Dolphins 2. Porpoises
ISBN 0-8234-0748-1   LC 88-39985

Discusses the characteristics and habits, the family life and intelligence of dolphins and porpoises

"A good introduction to a topic most children find interesting, this has a combination of spacious format, good black and white photographs, clear writing, accuracy, and capable organization of material (logical, sequential) that should appeal to readers in the middle grades or to younger children to whom the text may be read aloud." Bull Cent Child Books

Whales, giants of the deep. Holiday House 1984 90p il map lib bdg $15.95 (5 and up)
599.5

1. Whales
ISBN 0-8234-0530-3   LC 84-729

"This study of whales is distinguished in content, illustration, and format. It contains . . . scientific data on bearing and rearing the young, migratory patterns, feeding habits, and the whale's complex sonar system. A brief history of whaling and a discussion of [the] save-the-whale movement are also included." Sci Child

Schomp, Virginia

The bottlenose dolphin. Dillon Press 1994 60p il (Dillon remarkable animals book) lib bdg $13.95; pa $5.95 (3-5)   **599.5**

1. Dolphins 2. Endangered species
ISBN 0-87518-605-X (lib bdg); 0-382-24729-8 (pa)
LC 93-37927

In this "account of the life cycle of the bottlenose dolphin, Schomp conveys the grace and intelligence of this fascinating animal. . . . In addition to the usual descriptions of physical characteristics, reproduction, and habitats, she includes a detailed explanation of echolocation and presents interesting stories, dating back to ancient Greece and Rome, that tell of the unusual bond between dolphins and human beings." Booklist

Sibbald, Jean H.

The manatee. Dillon Press 1990 59p il (Dillon remarkable animals book) lib bdg $13.99; pa $5.95 (3-5)   **599.5**

1. Manatees
ISBN 0-87518-429-4 (lib bdg); 0-382-39233-7 (pa)
LC 89-26048

"A general introduction to the manatee (or sea cow) and its relatives around the world. The primary emphasis is on the Florida manatee—where it lives, what it eats, and how the increasing development of its habitat is endangering its chances for survival. A slightly fictionalized account of one manatee's life dramatizes the manmade dangers the animals face." SLJ

"The writing style is clear and direct. . . . The photographs . . . are excellent. They are plentiful, colorful and well labeled." Appraisal

Includes glossary

Simon, Seymour, 1931-

Whales. Crowell 1989 unp il $17; lib bdg $16.89; pa $6.95 (3-5)   **599.5**

1. Whales
ISBN 0-690-04756-8; 0-690-04758-4 (lib bdg); 0-06-446095-9 (pa)   LC 87-45285

"Whales in their natural habitat, the sea and the sky, are lavishly illustrated in this introduction to their physical characteristics and biology. The full-color photographs are lush, the text is succinct, and the oversized format sets off the large scale of these huge, magnificent creatures. Unusual close-ups show body angles not often seen. . . . A beautiful and factual addition for all collections." SLJ

599.6   Paenungulata

Arnold, Caroline, 1944-

Elephant; photographs by Richard Hewett. Morrow Junior Bks. 1993 48p il $15; lib bdg $14.93 (3-5)   **599.6**

1. Elephants
ISBN 0-688-11344-3; 0-688-11345-1 (lib bdg)
LC 92-31094

Provides information about the physical characteristics and habits of African and Asian elephants in the wild and in captivity

This features "an attractive layout that includes both succinct, clear text and striking color photographs." Booklist

Dorros, Arthur

Elephant families. HarperCollins Pubs. 1994 32p il (Let's-read-and-find-out science books) $15; lib bdg $14.89; pa $4.95 (k-3)   **599.6**

1. Elephants
ISBN 0-06-022948-9; 0-06-022949-7 (lib bdg); 0-06-445122-4 (pa)   LC 92-38972

Describes the unique qualities, status as an endangered species, and familial behavior of elephants

"This is an excellent book for the preschool or primary school child. The story is clear and conveys much of the life and behavior of elephants. . . . The illustrations are clever, are simple, and fit the story." Sci Books Films

Grace, Eric S.

Elephants. Sierra Club Bks. for Children 1993 62p il (Sierra Club wildlife library) $15.95 (4-6)   **599.6**

1. Elephants
ISBN 0-87156-538-2   LC 92-32835

Describes the physical characteristics of the elephant, how it searches for food and behaves in its natural environment, and how it interacts with people

Grace, Eric S.—*Continued*
"Beautiful full-color photographs illustrate a text that describes interesting aspects of elephant life in the wild." Sci Child

Macmillan, Dianne
Elephants; our last land giants; by Dianne M. MacMillan. Carolrhoda Bks. 1993 48p il (Carolrhoda nature watch book) lib bdg $19.95 (3-6) **599.6**
1. Elephants
ISBN 0-87614-770-8 LC 92-35268
Text and photos describe the physical characteristics, life cycle, behavior, habitats, and survival problems of the African and Asiatic elephants
"The text reads smoothly and easily, and provides as much information as an encyclopedia without sounding like one." Appraisal
Includes glossary

McClung, Robert M.
America's first elephant; illustrated by Marilyn Janovitz. Morrow Junior Bks. 1991 unp il lib bdg $14.88 (k-3) **599.6**
1. Elephants
ISBN 0-688-08359-5 LC 89-13764
"Based on historical facts, this tells of the arrival of the gentle elephant to our shores in 1796. Young children are introduced to America's early history as actual events are combined with the story of Kandi's long voyage from Bengal." Child Book Rev Serv
This is a "lively story. . . . Janovitz's brightly colored, folksy drawings have sturdy, slightly disproportionate figures that draw their inspiration from early American portrait art and visually lead youngsters on Kandi's international journey." Booklist

Patent, Dorothy Hinshaw
African elephants; giants of the land; photographs by Oria Douglas-Hamilton. Holiday House 1991 40p il $14.95 (3-5) **599.6**
1. Elephants
ISBN 0-8234-0911-2 LC 91-55028
Describes the physical characteristics, behavior, feeding, family life, and habitat of the African elephant
"Text and photographs successfully meld to create an informative book about the African elephant and its threatened survival in the wild." Booklist

Payne, Katharine
Elephants calling. Crown 1992 36p il (Face to face with science) $14; lib bdg $14.99 (3-5) **599.6**
1. Elephants 2. Animal communication
ISBN 0-517-58175-2; 0-517-58176-0 (lib bdg)
LC 91-34547
"Two female research scientists on location in Africa report on their observation studies of a family of elephants. Interesting text accompanied by great photographs illustrate each elephant's activities." Sci Child

599.72 Odd-toed ungulates

Arnold, Caroline, 1944-
Rhino; photographs by Richard Hewett, with additional photographs by Arthur P. Arnold. Morrow Junior Bks. 1995 48p il $16; lib bdg $15.93 (3-5) **599.72**
1. Rhinoceros
ISBN 0-688-12694-4; 0-688-12695-2 (lib bdg)
LC 94-23904
This volume "covers the life cycle, daily habits, problems, and efforts to save the five species of rhinoceroses in captivity and the wild." Sci Child
"The opening photos of Shimba, a three-week-old white rhino from the Edinburgh Zoo, quickly lure browsers into the accompanying text." SLJ

Zebra; photographs by Richard Hewett. Morrow 1987 48p il $13.95; lib bdg $13.88; pa $5.95 (3 5) **599.72**
1. Zebras
ISBN 0-688-07067-1; 0-688-07068-X (lib bdg); 0-688-12273-6 (pa) LC 87-1503
The author gives basic information on the behavior patterns, physical characteristics, reproduction, species and subspecies of zebras, using as a focal point a newborn zebra living at New Jersey's wildlife park
"Excellent full-color photographs demonstrate [the] creature's unique appearance and habits. Often capturing the animals in striking poses, the pictures illustrate well the information offered in text." Booklist

599.73 Even-toed ungulates

Arnold, Caroline, 1944-
Camel; photographs by Richard Hewett. Morrow Junior Bks. 1992 48p il $15; lib bdg $14.93 (3-5) **599.73**
1. Camels
ISBN 0-688-09498-8; 0-688-09499-6 (lib bdg)
LC 91-26805
Discusses the habitats, physical characteristics, and behavior of the two kinds of camels
"Once again Caroline Arnold and Richard Hewett display mastery at collaboration as they mold striking photographs and informative text into [a] seamless, interesting [presentation]." Horn Book

Giraffe; photographs by Richard Hewett. Morrow 1987 48p il $12.95; lib bdg $12.88; pa $5.95 (3-5) **599.73**
1. Giraffes
ISBN 0-688-07069-8; 0-688-07070-1 (lib bdg); 0-688-12272-8 (pa) LC 87-1502
The author describes the characteristics and habitats of giraffes and discusses life for these animals at a large open-air wildlife park in New Jersey
"Hewett has a good eye for detail and composition and provides a fine variety of shots of individual animals and groups resting, eating, moving, and occasionally interacting with humans. . . . The care given to both the writing and photography is also demonstrated in the attractive layout of the pages." Horn Book

Arnold, Caroline, 1944-—*Continued*

Hippo; photographs by Richard Hewett.
Morrow Junior Bks. 1989 48p il $12.95; lib
bdg $12.88; pa $5.95 (3-5)   **599.73**

1. Hippopotamus

ISBN 0-688-08145-2; 0-688-08146-0 (lib bdg);
0-688-11697-3 (pa)   LC 88-39794

Presents the characteristics and habits of hippopotamuses
in the wild and of a family at the San Francisco Zoo

"Hewett's charming full-color photographs succeed in
making this admittedly odd-looking animal . . . engaging. .
. . A well-rounded look at the hippopotamus for unsophisticated readers." SLJ

Llama; photographs by Richard Hewett.
Morrow Junior Bks. 1988 48p il $12.95; lib
bdg $12.88 (3-5)   **599.73**

1. Llamas

ISBN 0-688-07540-1; 0-688-07541-X (lib bdg)
                                        LC 87-27130

Describes the characteristics and behavior of llamas and
their usefulness to man, discusses other members of the la-
moid family, and reports on the growing number of llamas
now being bred in the United States

Tule elk; photographs by Richard R.
Hewett. Carolrhoda Bks. 1989 47p il
(Carolrhoda nature watch book) lib bdg $19.95
(3-5)   **599.73**

1. Elk

ISBN 0-87614-343-5   LC 88-31565

"Tule elk—a smaller California subspecies, less familiar
than the Rocky Mountain variety—were practically extinct
in the early twentieth century. Efforts to restore the species
are reported along with characteristics of the breed." Horn
Book

Includes bibliography

Berman, Ruth

American bison; photographs by Cheryl
Walsh Bellville. Carolrhoda Bks. 1992 48p il
map (Carolrhoda nature watch book) lib bdg
$19.95 (3-6)   **599.73**

1. Bison

ISBN 0-87614-697-3   LC 91-25852

Discusses the life cycle of the bison, its role in the settlement of the American West, and its near extinction

"Readers will learn many interesting facts about this, the
largest native American mammal. The book is replete with
excellent color photos." Sci Books Films

Includes glossary

Lepthien, Emilie U. (Emilie Utteg)

Buffalo. Childrens Press 1989 45p il lib bdg
$16.60; pa $5.50 (2-4)   **599.73**

1. Bison

ISBN 0-516-01161-8 (lib bdg); 0-516-41161-6 (pa)
                                        LC 89-457

"A New true book"

This book presents a "chronology and natural history of
the near demise and eventual rise of North American bison.
The heaviest emphasis is on the necessary exploitation of
them by American Indians and the wanton destruction by
early Western settlers and sport hunters. Conservation laws,
advocate groups, and programs to restore sizeable, natural
herds are recounted. The eventual success from hundreds of
the animals in the late 1800's to nearly 100,000 today is
strong support for educating youngsters to value natural resources." Appraisal

Includes glossary

Reindeer. Childrens Press 1994 45p il lib
bdg $13.50; pa $5.50 (2-4)   **599.73**

1. Reindeer 2. Caribou

ISBN 0-516-01059-X (lib bdg); 0-516-41059-8 (pa)
                                        LC 93-33513

"A New true book"

The author discusses "reindeer's diet, mating, calving,
migrations, their place in history and legend— particularly
in the legend of Santa Claus, and their great importance,
even today, to the natives of Lapland. The book is well illustrated with informative color photographs, the text is accurate and interesting." Sci Books Films

Includes glossary

Lindblad, Lisa

The Serengeti migration; Africa's animals on
the move; photography by Sven-Olof
Lindblad. Hyperion Bks. for Children 1994
40p il maps $15.95; lib bdg $15.89 (3-6)
                                        599.73

1. Gnus 2. Zebras 3. Serengeti National Park (Tanzania)
4. Animals—Migration

ISBN 1-56282-668-9; 1-56282-669-7 (lib bdg)
                                        LC 93-26338

"As the seasons change and food supplies dwindle, vast
herds of wildebeests and zebras cross seven hundred miles
of the Serengeti National Park to find food. Their journey,
along with many other animals, across the varied and
changing landscape is beautifully illustrated with dramatic
color photographs. The narrative and photographs evoke
the drama of the age-old migration." Horn Book Guide

Includes glossary

Miller, Debbie S.

A caribou journey; illustrated by Jon Van
Zyle. Little, Brown 1994 unp il $15.95 (2-4)
                                        599.73

1. Caribou 2. Animals—Migration 3. Natural history—
Alaska

ISBN 0-316-57380-9   LC 93-9777

Surveys the migrations, habits, and habitat of a herd of
caribou in Alaska

"Van Zyle's dramatic paintings that flow across each
double-page spread are created with acrylics painted on un-
tempered masonite panels, and vividly portray seasonal
changes in the land and life cycle of the caribou. Both the
words and pictures breathe life into the images of a cold
and windy Arctic winter." SLJ

Nicholson, Darrel

Wild boars; photographs by Craig Blacklock. Carolrhoda Bks. 1987 47p il (Carolrhoda nature watch book) lib bdg $19.95 (3-6)
599.73

1. Boars

ISBN 0-87614-308-7   LC 87-677

"Straightforward, informative text and fine, full-color photographs introduce the Eurasian wild boar, brought to North America for hunting and studied at a Minnesota farm. An excellent book about a hardy, adaptable animal." Sci Child

Patent, Dorothy Hinshaw

Buffalo; the American bison today; photographs by William Muñoz. Clarion Bks. 1986 73p il hardcover o.p. paperback available $6.95 (4 and up)   **599.73**

1. Bison

ISBN 0-395-55278-8 (pa)   LC 85-25483

The author "discusses both the habits and behavior of this historically important animal and the careful management needed to maintain it in its current artificial environment." SLJ

This "is a captivating account of the contemporary bison. The author's portrayal of this imposing creature is forthright, realistic and creative. William Munoz' marvelous photos add greatly to describing the rutting rituals of summer, the population management in the fall, the bison's struggles for food in the winter and the birth and care of its newborn in the spring." Appraisal

Deer and elk; photographs by William Muñoz. Clarion Bks. 1994 77p il maps $15.95 (4 and up)   **599.73**

1. Deer 2. Elk

ISBN 0-395-52003-7   LC 93-25894

"The text describes in detail the lives, enemies, and survival of North American whitetail deer, mule deer, and elk, among others. The color photographs of the shy, gentle creatures are effective, crisp, and clear." Horn Book Guide

"Numerous full-color photographs enhance the presentation; each includes a caption. A great addition to the animal science section of any library." SLJ

Includes bibliography

Sattler, Helen Roney

Giraffes; the sentinels of the Savannas; illustrated by Christopher Santoro. Lothrop, Lee & Shepard Bks. 1990 80p il $15.95 (5 and up)   **599.73**

1. Giraffes

ISBN 0-688-08284-X   LC 89-2287

"A comprehensive examination of Giraffidae, from fossil remains to the benign giants of today, in an elegant format enhanced by rich sepia illustrations and cream-colored paper. Includes a glossary, geological timeline, and scientific classifications. Bibliography." Sci Child

Staub, Frank J.

Mountain goats; written and photographed by Frank Staub. Lerner Publs. 1994 48p il (Early bird nature books) lib bdg $18.95 (2-4)
599.73

1. Goats

ISBN 0-8225-3000-7   LC 93-32491

"The adaptations that enable mountain goats to survive in their cold, rocky habitat are described in this introduction to the animal. Every page contains crisp color photographs. . . . The writing is clear, and the narrative flows in short, well-organized chapters." Horn Book Guide

Includes glossary

599.74   Carnivores

Arnold, Caroline, 1944-

Cats: in from the wild; photographs by Richard R. Hewett. Carolrhoda Bks. 1993 48p il lib bdg $19.95 (3-5)   **599.74**

1. Cats 2. Wild cats

ISBN 0-87614-692-2   LC 92-32986

"Arnold sets domestic cats next to their wilderness cousins to explore feline behaviors and the physical characteristics that allow cats to climb, hunt, and prowl so successfully. . . . Hewett . . . supplies an excellent variety of good-quality photographs." Booklist

Includes glossary

Cheetah; photographs by Richard Hewett. Morrow Junior Bks. 1989 48p il $16; lib bdg $15.93; pa $5.95 (3-5)   **599.74**

1. Cheetahs

ISBN 0-688-08143-6; 0-688-08144-4 (lib bdg); 0-688-11696-5 (pa)   LC 88-39940

"A full-color photo essay about the daily activities of cheetahs in the wild and in captivity. Includes information about the scientific community's efforts to save cheetahs from extinction and a portrait of Damara, a tame cheetah from the Wildlife Safari in Winston, Oregon." Sci Child

Panda; photographs by Richard Hewett. Morrow Junior Bks. 1992 46p il $15; lib bdg $14.93 (3-5)   **599.74**

1. Giant panda

ISBN 0-688-09496-1; 0-688-09497-X (lib bdg)
LC 91-33251

A discussion of pandas with an introduction to those at the Chapultepec Zoo in Mexico City, which features the largest giant panda exhibit outside of China

"Lively text, accompanied by full-color, on-location photos." SLJ

Sea lion; photographs by Richard Hewett. Morrow Junior Bks. 1994 48p il $15; lib bdg $14.93 (3-5)   **599.74**

1. Seals (Animals) 2. Wildlife conservation

ISBN 0-688-12027-X; 0-688-12028-8 (lib bdg)
LC 93-27007

"*Sea Lion* begins with Pumpkin and Piper, two sea lions who were brought to a marine mammal rescue center, but broadens out to consider other sea lions, their characteristics, habits, food, and natural enemies. The book ends with the release of Pumpkin and Piper a few months after their rescue. . . . The clear, full-color photography provides a good visual counterpoint to the lucid, well-organized text." Booklist

Arnosky, Jim

Otters under water. Putnam 1992 unp il
$14.95; pa $5.95 (k-2)   **599.74**

1. Otters

ISBN 0-399-22339-8; 0-399-22842-X (pa)

      LC 91-36792

This book offers a "glimpse of two young otters swimming, playing, and feeding in a sunlit pond under the watchful gaze of their mother. As always, this naturalist author/artist has enhanced the basic lesson through his inclusion of plants, creatures, and rock formations that form a part of the animals' natural habitat. His carefully executed colored-pencil and watercolor illustrations . . . reflect his keen observations of nature and his fine artistic talent. . . . The short, simple, oversized text, one sentence or phrase to a page, succinctly describes the pictured activity without detracting from the eye-catching view." SLJ

Watching foxes. Lothrop, Lee & Shepard
Bks. 1985 unp il $12.95; lib bdg $12.88 (k-2)
      599.74

1. Foxes

ISBN 0-688-04259-7; 0-688-04260-0 (lib bdg)

      LC 84-20157

"Arnosky shares his observations of four fox pups at play while mother fox is hunting. Their antics unfold in a series of double-page spreads. One or two brief sentences in large type accompany each pair of pages. . . . The illustrations, in color pencil and watercolor wash, are clear and attractive; they will be readily interpreted by the very young audience for whom they are intended." SLJ

Bonners, Susan, 1947-

Hunter in the snow: the lynx. Little, Brown
1994 unp il $14.95 (2-4)   **599.74**

1. Lynx

ISBN 0-316-10201-6   LC 93-24975

Focuses on a year in the life of a female lynx, describing hunting practices, courtship and mating, denning, and the birth and care of the young

This book conveys "a wealth of information. . . . Bonners doesn't flinch here. We see the limp bunny and the bloody snow; however, the soft pencil drawings—detailed with gently blurred photo-realism—take off the edge. Mating is handled with similar frankness, though tastefully enough to minimize snickering. . . . The book's lively tone and its specific focus on one lynx make this as good for personal reading as it is for curriculum support." Booklist

Brandenburg, Jim

To the top of the world; adventures with Arctic wolves; edited by JoAnn Bren Guernsey. Walker & Co. 1993 44p il $16.95; lib bdg $17.85; pa $6.95 (4 and up)

      599.74

1. Wolves

ISBN 0-8027-8219-1; 0-8027-8220-5 (lib bdg); 0-8027-7462-8 (pa)   LC 93-12105

A wildlife photographer records in text and photographs two visits to Ellesmere Island, Northwest Territories, where he filmed a pack of Arctic wolves over several months

"Captivating pictures combine with an informal narrative to create a topnotch, firsthand view of a much-maligned animal." SLJ

Clark, Margaret Goff

The endangered Florida panther. Cobblehill
Bks. 1993 54p il $14.99 (4 and up)

      599.74

1. Pumas 2. Wildlife conservation

ISBN 0-525-65114-4   LC 92-14816

Examines the physical characteristics, habits, and natural environment of the endangered Florida panther and what is being done to save it from extinction

This features "engaging writing and good color photographs." Sci Child

The threatened Florida black bear.
Cobblehill Bks. 1995 64p il $15.99 (4 and up)
      599.74

1. Bears 2. Endangered species

ISBN 0-525-65196-9   LC 94-48532

This volume provides "information about how biologists and government agencies are working to keep the Florida black bear from becoming an endangered animal. Includes a section of black bear statistics and Florida black bear milestones." Sci Child

"Attractive photos and a clear, conversational text mark this volume on a threatened species. . . . Descriptions of real-life encounters between bears and commission biologists enliven the text and illuminate the work of wildlife research." Booklist

Clutton-Brock, Juliet

Cat; written by Juliet Clutton-Brock. Knopf
1991 63p il (Eyewitness books) $19; lib bdg
$18.99 (4 and up)   **599.74**

1. Wild cats 2. Cats

ISBN 0-679-81458-2; 0-679-91458-7 (lib bdg)

      LC 91-9399

Also available Spanish language edition

Text and photographs present the anatomy, behavior, habitats, and other aspects of wild and domestic cats

"The information is generally well written and well presented. . . . This is a browser's delight that will also appeal to the serious reader seeking facts about cats." Sci Books Films

Cossi, Olga

Harp seals. Carolrhoda Bks. 1991 47p il
map (Carolrhoda nature watch book) lib bdg
$19.95; pa $6.95 (3-6)   **599.74**

1. Seals (Animals)

ISBN 0-87614-437-7 (lib bdg); 0-87614-567-5 (pa)

      LC 90-2481

Describes the life cycle, migratory patterns, behavior, and habitat of the harp seal

"The combination of text and photographs does a magnificent job of depicting the harp seal's world." Sci Books Films

Includes glossary

Esbensen, Barbara Juster

Playful slider; the North American river otter; illustrated by Mary Barrett Brown. Little, Brown 1993 unp il lib bdg $15.95 (2-4)
      599.74

1. Otters

ISBN 0-316-24977-7   LC 92-13783

Esbensen, Barbara Juster—*Continued*
"The book describes the life of the otter as the seasons change—its home, feeding habits and reproductive cycle. The picture-book format works well. The large pages share a balance between text and color illustrations that capture the essence of these animals." Booklist

George, Jean Craighead, 1919-
The moon of the bears; illustrated by Ron Parker. new ed. HarperCollins Pubs. 1993 48p il (Thirteen moons) lib bdg $14.89 (3-6)
599.74
1. Bears
ISBN 0-06-022792-3   LC 91-22557
A revised and newly illustrated edition of the title first published 1967 by Crowell
Chronicles a year in a black bear's life, beginning with her emerging from hibernation in Tennessee's Smoky Mountains during the spring thaw in February
"Luminous, realistic color paintings, including a double-page spread and some compelling closeups of the bear's face perfectly enhance the text." SLJ
Includes bibliography

The moon of the fox pups; illustrated by Norman Adams. new ed. HarperCollins Pubs. 1992 48p il (Thirteen moons) lib bdg $14.89 (3-6)
599.74
1. Foxes
ISBN 0-06-022860-1   LC 90-22386
A revised and newly illustrated edition of the title first published 1968 by Crowell
Describes the experiences of five fox pups during the month of June in the farmland of Pennsylvania
Includes bibliography

The moon of the gray wolves; illustrated by Sal Catalano. new ed. HarperCollins Pubs. 1991 48p il (Thirteen moons) $14.95; lib bdg $14.89 (3-6)
599.74
1. Wolves
ISBN 0-06-022442-8; 0-06-022443-6 (lib bdg)
LC 90-38166
A revised and newly illustrated edition of the title first published 1969 by Crowell
Describes the experiences of a wolf pack in the Toklat Pass of Alaska during the November moon
This is "a readable, inviting book. Catalano's impressive illustrations, executed in acrylics, tempera, and pastels, greatly enhance the story of the wolf pack's November hunt for caribou." SLJ

The moon of the mountain lions; illustrated by Ron Parker. new ed. HarperCollins Pubs. 1991 48p il (Thirteen moons) $14.95; lib bdg $14.89 (3-6)
599.74
1. Pumas
ISBN 0-06-022429-0; 0-06-022438-X (lib bdg)
LC 90-39451
A revised and newly illustrated edition of the title first published 1968 by Crowell
Describes the experiences of a young mountain lion during the month of August in his natural habitat on the side of Mount Olympus, in Washington State
"As always, [George's] settings are ecologically accurate. . . . [This book includes] ten full-color, full-page paintings by wildlife artist Parker." SLJ
Includes bibliography

Gibbons, Gail
Wolves. Holiday House 1994 unp il $15.95; pa $6.95 (k-3)
599.74
1. Wolves
ISBN 0-8234-1127-3; 0-8234-1202-4 (pa)
LC 94-2108
"A simply written introduction that focuses on the gray, or timber, wolf. . . . Material covered includes physical characteristics, behavior within a pack, and communication by howling and body language. . . . The format is open and spacious, the print is large, and the realistic, watercolor illustrations are set against backgrounds of white and deep blues." SLJ

Greenaway, Theresa, 1947-
Amazing bears; written by Theresa Greenaway; photographed by Dave King. Knopf 1992 29p il (Eyewitness juniors) lib bdg $9.99; pa $7.99 (2-4)
599.74
1. Bears 2. Giant panda
ISBN 0-679-92769-7 (lib bdg); 0-679-82769-2 (pa)
LC 92-910
Also available Spanish language edition
Introduces the physical characteristics and habits of bears and pandas

Hewett, Joan
Tiger, tiger, growing up; photographs by Richard Hewett. Clarion Bks. 1993 32p il $13.95 (1-4)
599.74
1. Tigers 2. Zoos
ISBN 0-395-61583-6   LC 92-9741
Describes the special care and training of a tiger cub at Marine World/Africa USA in Vallejo, California through her first nine months of life
This features "brilliant, full-color photos and an easy, narrative text. . . . The photography is full of texture, color, and life." SLJ

Johnson, Sylvia A.
Elephant seals; photographs by Frans Lanting. Lerner Publs. 1989 48p il (Lerner natural science book) lib bdg $19.95 (4 and up)
599.74
1. Seals (Animals)
ISBN 0-8225-1487-7   LC 88-12924
"Many full-color photographs supplement a clear text explaining the life cycle, physical characteristics, habits, and natural environment of the unusual looking sea mammal." Sci Child
Includes glossary

Wolf pack; tracking wolves in the wild; [by] Sylvia A. Johnson & Alice Aamodt. Lerner Publs. 1985 96p il map lib bdg $23.95; pa $6.95 (4 and up)
599.74
1. Wolves
ISBN 0-8225-1577-6 (lib bdg); 0-8225-9526-5 (pa)
LC 85-37
"This book traces the development of wolves from pups. Discusses social development and communication within a family group and includes chapters on tracking wolves and myths surrounding wolves. A well-written, interesting, and informative account with excellent photographs and illustrations." Sci Child
Includes glossary

Lawrence, R. D., 1921-

Wolves. Sierra Club Bks. 1990 62p il maps (Sierra Club wildlife library) $16.95 (4-6)
599.74

1. Wolves

ISBN 0-316-51676-7   LC 90-8730

"A sympathetic, up-to-date treatment of wolves with special emphasis on the social nature of wild wolves. Includes a wealth of information about the growth and development of pups from a variety of species." Sci Child

Lewin, Ted, 1935-

Tiger trek; written and illustrated by Ted Lewin. Macmillan 1990 unp il $14.95 (2-4)
599.74

1. Tigers

ISBN 0-02-757381-8   LC 89-12710

"A simple story and beautiful watercolors describe a tiger as she hunts to feed herself and her cubs. Includes a visit to wildlife preserves in India, where a variety of indigenous animal and plant life can be seen." Sci Child

McClung, Robert M.

Lili: a giant panda of Sichuan; illustrated by Irene Brady. Morrow Junior Bks. 1988 85p il $15; lib bdg $14.93 (3-6)   **599.74**

1. Giant panda

ISBN 0-688-06942-8; 0-688-06943-6 (lib bdg)
         LC 87-28271

"A well-written story that follows the first several years of a female panda's life in the only remaining natural habitat for the panda, China's Sichuan Province. Text includes a discussion of threats to the survival of the less than one thousand pandas alive today as well as current preservation efforts." Sci Child

Includes bibliography

North, Sterling, 1906-1974

Rascal; illustrated by John Schoenherr. Dutton 1984 c1963 189p il $14.99 (5 and up)
599.74

1. Raccoons

ISBN 0-525-18839-8   LC 84-10292

Also available in hardcover from P. Smith and in paperback from Penguin Bks.; Spanish language edition also available

A Newbery Award honor book, 1964

First published 1963 with subtitle: A memoir of a better era

A book about Rascal "a young raccoon, Sterling North's pet the year he was eleven, in rural Wisconsin. . . . The book calls up a series of marvelous pictures; boy fishing in peaceful company of raccoon, boy riding on bike with raccoon (a demon for speed) standing up in the bike basket, raccoon with friend, a prize trotting horse, raccoon helping boy to win a pie-eating contest. A central episode is about an idyllic camping trip." Publ Wkly

Parsons, Alexandra

Amazing cats; written by Alexandra Parsons; photographed by Jerry Young. Knopf 1990 29p il (Eyewitness juniors) lib bdg $11.99; pa $9.99 (2-4)   **599.74**

1. Cats

ISBN 0-679-90690-8 (lib bdg); 0-679-80690-3 (pa)
         LC 90-31885

Also available Spanish language edition

Features unusual members of the cat world, including the Turkish swimming cat, Scottish wildcat, and ocelot, and describes important characteristics of the whole group

"The text is generally interesting and accurate; the facts are presented in clear, simple language. The illustrations are detailed and engaging." Sci Books Films

Patent, Dorothy Hinshaw

Dogs: the wolf within; photographs by William Muñoz. Carolrhoda Bks. 1993 48p il lib bdg $19.95; pa $7.95 (3-6)   **599.74**

1. Dogs 2. Wolves

ISBN 0-87614-691-4 (lib bdg); 0-87614-604-3 (pa)
         LC 92-12334

Compares the physical characteristics and behavior of wolves and dogs and describes how dogs evolved from their wild relatives

"The writing is clear and interesting, and excellent photographs with good captions accompany the text." Sci Books Films

Includes glossary and bibliography

Gray wolf, red wolf; photographs by William Muñoz. Clarion Bks. 1990 64p il $15.95; pa $6.95 (4 and up)   **599.74**

1. Wolves

ISBN 0-89919-863-5; 0-395-69627-5 (pa)
         LC 89-77718

Describes the physical characteristics, life cycle, and behavior of the two species of wolves found in North America and discusses efforts to save them from extinction by reintroducing them to wilderness areas

"Excellent photographs of wolves in the wild, and in the care of those seeking to repatriate them, accompany a lively, clear text." Appraisal

Looking at bears; photographs by William Muñoz. Holiday House 1994 40p il $15.95 (3-5)   **599.74**

1. Bears

ISBN 0-8234-1139-7   LC 94-1834

This introduction to bears of the world includes "the ancestry, physical characteristics, eating habits, intelligence, hibernation, senses, birth and growth, and interesting facts on each species of bear. What sets the book apart from others of its kind is Patent's elegant writing style as well as her small dazzling details. . . . Fine full-color photographs complement the text nicely." SLJ

The way of the grizzly; photographs by William Muñoz. Clarion Bks. 1987 65p il $13.95; pa $5.95 (4 and up)   **599.74**

1. Grizzly bear

ISBN 0-89919-383-8; 0-395-58112-5 (pa)
         LC 86-17562

Describes, in text and illustrations, the physical characteristics, habits, and natural environment of the grizzly bear and discusses the threats that humans pose to their survival

"Clear black-and-white photos appear on almost every

Patent, Dorothy Hinshaw—*Continued*
page and show grizzlies in their daily life and being examined by environmentalists. This will certainly be useful to report writers." SLJ

Pringle, Laurence P.
Bearman: exploring the world of black bears; photographs by Lynn Rogers. Scribner 1989 42p il $13.95 (4 and up)   **599.74**
1. Rogers, Lynn L. 2. Bears
ISBN 0-684-19094-X   LC 89-5890
Pringle's study of biologist Lynn Rogers "concentrates on Rogers's work tracking and observing black bears in Minnesota. Traveling by small plane or snowmobile or on snowshoes, Rogers has tagged and attached collars to hundreds of bears, often entering winter dens to do so." Horn Book
"Sharp, full-color photographs taken by Rogers himself (with photographic credits provided for pictures of Rogers) accompany the thoughtful, informative text." Sci Child
Includes bibliography

Jackal woman; exploring the world of jackals; [by] Laurence Pringle; photographs by Patricia D. Moehlman. Scribner 1993 42p il $14.95 (4 and up)   **599.74**
1. Moehlman, Patricia Des Roses, 1943- 2. Jackals
ISBN 0-684-19435-X   LC 92-28207
A photographic account of the work of Patricia Moehlman, a wildlife biologist who specializes in the study of jackals
"Pringle captures the zoologist's excitement in her work and the respect and admiration she feels for her subjects. . . Students doing their own research for reports on African wildlife will find a wealth of information about the habits and characteristics of two species of jackal, the golden and the silver-backed. Many of Moehlman's own beautiful color photographs illustrate the text." Booklist
Includes bibliography

Ryden, Hope
Your cat's wild cousins; photographs and text by Hope Ryden. Lodestar Bks. 1991 48p il $16 (4-6)   **599.74**
1. Wild cats 2. Cats
ISBN 0-525-67354-7   LC 90-28992
The author "explains some of the similarities and differences between a domestic cat and its wild relatives, following up with a closer look at 18 different feline species. Each species is presented in lively text and beautiful full-color photographs on a double-page spread. . . . Ryden incorporates a great deal of information without sacrificing the storylike quality of the text." Booklist

Your dog's wild cousins; photographs and text by Hope Ryden. Lodestar Bks. 1994 36p il $16.99 (4-6)   **599.74**
1. Wild dogs 2. Dogs
ISBN 0-525-67482-9   LC 93-26855
In this book "information is provided on 15 wild cousins of the family dog. Each section is two pages in length and is accompanied by two large color photos that illustrate the facts set forth in the text. A particular insightful technique is the addition of a third photo that illustrates the same trait or behavior in the domestic dog. . . . Students will enjoy it for its readability rather than its research value." Sci Books Films
Includes glossary

Ryder, Joanne
White bear, ice bear; illustrated by Michael Rothman. Morrow Junior Bks. 1989 unp il $15; lib bdg $14.93; pa $4.95 (k-2)   **599.74**
1. Polar bear
ISBN 0-688-07174-0; 0-688-07175-9 (lib bdg); 0-688-13111-5 (pa)   LC 87-36781
"A Just for a day book"
Describes the awakening, feeding, and wandering of a polar bear, from its own viewpoint
"Neither the polar bear nor the Arctic are named, but the poetic text set within the full double-page illustrations draws the reader into the cold and ice." Sci Books Films

Schlein, Miriam
Project panda watch; illustrated by Robert Shetterly. Atheneum Pubs. 1984 87p il $15 (4 and up)   **599.74**
1. Giant panda 2. Wildlife conservation
ISBN 0-689-31071-4   LC 84-2914
This book focuses partly on efforts to save the giant panda from extinction by providing food during shortages in the supply of its usual bamboo diet. It is "an account of the work of Chinese and American scientists studying pandas in the Wolong Nature Preserve in China, with chapters on zoo pandas as well." N Y Times Book Rev
Includes glossary and bibliography

Schwartz, Alvin, 1927-1992
Fat man in a fur coat, and other bear stories; collected and retold by Alvin Schwartz; pictures by David Christiana. Farrar, Straus & Giroux 1984 167p il $14; pa $3.50 (4 and up)   **599.74**
1. Bears
ISBN 0-374-32291-0; 0-374-42273-7 (pa)
          LC 84-4161
A "portrayal of bears as truly extraordinary, intelligent, sometimes humorous animals who have been misunderstood and abused by most yet revered and respected by many. Schwartz includes 50 stories—old and recent, true and tall—and intermingles straight factual material on the animals." SLJ
"Softly textured, dramatically effective pencil drawings illustrates a nicely varied anthology." Bull Cent Child Books
Includes bibliography

Selsam, Millicent Ellis, 1912-
A first look at seals, sea lions, and walruses; by Millicent E. Selsam and Joyce Hunt; illustrated by Harriett Springer. Walker & Co. 1988 36p il maps $10.95; lib bdg $11.85 (1-3)   **599.74**
1. Seals (Animals) 2. Walruses
ISBN 0-8027-6787-7; 0-8027-6788-5 (lib bdg)
          LC 87-29491
This "introduction teaches scientific classification by high-lighting the physical differences among true seals, eared seals, and walruses: flippers, ears, markings, size, tusks, whiskers, and others. . . . Except for the map, coverage is confined to the animals' physical characteristics, without facts on habitat, food, life cycle, etc." SLJ

Silverstein, Alvin

The red wolf; [by] Alvin, Virginia, and Robert Silverstein. Millbrook Press 1994 64p il map (Endangered in America) lib bdg $13.40 (4 and up)   **599.74**

1. Wolves 2. Endangered species

ISBN 1-56294-416-9   LC 93-42480

A look at the pros and cons of reintroducing the red wolf, thought to be threatened with extinction, to two sites in North Carolina

"The book is equally fair in discussing the opposition to the reintroduction of wolves to the wild by ranchers or other property owners adjacent to the release sites. Rarely has a book so dispassionately presented these areas of controversy. The illustrations are well chosen to complement the text." Sci Books Films

Includes bibliography

The sea otter; [by] Alvin, Virginia, and Robert Silverstein. Millbrook Press 1995 64p il map (Endangered in America) lib bdg $15.40 (4 and up)   **599.74**

1. Otters 2. Endangered species

ISBN 1-56294-418-5   LC 94-17998

"The sea otter's behavior is described, including swimming, hunting, feeding, reproducing, and growing. Its main physical features are detailed, including those especially important to its lifestyle. . . . With color photographs, readng and organizations lists, a factual summary, and an index, this book is very suitable for use as a reference, in classrooms, and for general awareness." Sci Books Films

Includes bibliography

Simon, Seymour, 1931-

Big cats. HarperCollins Pubs. 1991 unp il $17; lib bdg $16.89; pa $5.95 (3-6)

    599.74

1. Wild cats

ISBN   0-06-021646-8;   0-06-021647-6   (lib   bdg); 0-06-446119-X (pa)   LC 90-36374

Simon "begins with a general overview of the big cats, and then presents details on the tiger, lion, leopard, jaguar, puma, cheetah and snow leopard. . . . The author also discusses concerns about wildlife conservation." Appraisal

The author "offers a clear, succinct text illuminated with stunning, large color photographs." Booklist

Wolves. HarperCollins Pubs. 1993 unp il $16; lib bdg $15.89; pa $5.95 (3-6)

    599.74

1. Wolves

ISBN   0-06-022531-9;   0-06-022534-3   (lib   bdg); 0-06-446176-9 (pa)   LC 92-25924

Text and photographs present the physical characteristics, habits, and natural environment of various species of wolves

"The text is well suited to the emerging naturalist—almost chatty in tone. The carefully credited photographs combine the beauty of the animal with action and the natural beauty of its habitat to effect a dramatic backdrop for the text." Horn Book

Sobol, Richard

Seal journey; by Richard and Jonah Sobol; photographs by Richard Sobol. Cobblehill Bks. 1993 unp il $14.99 (3-5)   **599.74**

1. Seals (Animals) 2. Animal babies

ISBN 0-525-65126-8   LC 92-25974

The author/photographer and his eight-year-old son journey to the ice floes of eastern Canada to observe the thousands of harp seal pups born there each year

This features "stunning photographs and an articulate text." Sci Child

Stirling, Ian

Bears; text by Ian Sterling; photographs by Aubrey Lang. Sierra Club Bks. for Children 1992 64p il maps (Sierra Club wildlife library) $14.95; pa $7.95 (4-6)   **599.74**

1. Bears

ISBN 0-87156-574-9; 0-87156-441-6 (pa)

      LC 91-35808

Text and photographs introduce the origins, evolution, habitats, behavior, and life cycles of the eight present-day species of bears

"An attractive volume. . . . Photographs and drawings are clear and informative with the exception of a murky color map that shows where bears live. . . . This a good choice for reports." SLJ

Winner, Cherie

Coyotes. Carolrhoda Bks. 1995 48p il (Carolrhoda nature watch book) lib bdg $14.96; pa $7.95 (3-6)   **599.74**

1. Coyotes

ISBN 0-87614-938-7 (lib bdg); 0-87614-957-3 (pa)

      LC 94-45585

"This book describes the coyote from pack life to courtship and mating behavior. Beautiful photographs, accompanied by clear, concise text, provide readers with accurate information about an often misunderstood animal. . . . Text throughout the book focuses on distinguishing characteristics, social behavior, and preferred environment. A final chapter touches on primate conservation." Sci Child

Includes glossary

Yoshida, Toshi, 1911-

Young lions; written and illustrated by Toshi Yoshida. Philomel Bks. 1989 unp il $14.95 (1-3)   **599.74**

1. Lions

ISBN 0-399-21546-8   LC 87-29162

Original Japanese edition, 1982

"Three young lions leave the pride to attempt their first hunt. They encounter a variety of African plains animals depicted in panoramic, full-color pages. The descriptive text details their return home without success and a happy reunion with their mother." Sci Child

599.8 Primates

Arnold, Caroline, 1944-
Monkey; photographs by Richard Hewett. Morrow Junior Bks. 1993 48p il $15; lib bdg $14.93 (3-5)   **599.8**

1. Monkeys
ISBN 0-688-11342-7; 0-688-11343-5 (lib bdg)
LC 92-31095
Describes the physical characteristics, habits, behavior, natural environment, and zoo life of the red-crowned mangabey monkey
This "is a delightful introduction. . . . [The text is] accompanied by one or two superb, full-color photos per page, including many fascinating closeups." SLJ

Maynard, Thane
Primates, apes, monkeys, and prosimians. Watts 1994 63p il map lib bdg $14.91 (4-6)
599.8

1. Primates
ISBN 0-531-11169-5   LC 94-19596
"A Cinicinnati Zoo book"
"Three groups of primates are considered: apes, monkeys, and their more primitive cousins, prosimians. A distribution map locates the species around the world, and brief, factual discussion of each species is accompanied by a color photo. . . . Text throughout the book focuses on distinguishing characteristics, social behavior, and preferred environment. A final chapter touches on primate conservation." Booklist
Includes glossary and bibliography

Selsam, Millicent Ellis, 1912-
A first look at monkeys and apes; by Millicent E. Selsam and Joyce Hunt; illustrated by Harriett Springer. Walker & Co. 1979 32p il maps lib bdg $9.85 (1-3)
599.8

1. Monkeys 2. Apes
ISBN 0-8027-6359-6   LC 79-4701
"The authors describe characteristics which separate different monkeys by dividing them into two groups, New and Old World monkeys. Further separations and their characteristics follow." Sci Child

Steedman, Scott
Amazing monkeys; written by Scott Steedman; photographed by Jerry Young. Knopf 1991 29p il (Eyewitness juniors) lib bdg $9.99; pa $6.95 (2-4)   **599.8**

1. Monkeys
ISBN 0-679-91517-6 (lib bdg); 0-679-81517-1 (pa)
LC 90-19238
Also available Spanish language edition
Text and photographs focus on some of the more interesting members of the monkey world

599.88 Apes

Arnold, Caroline, 1944-
Orangutan; photographs by Richard Hewett. Morrow Junior Bks. 1990 48p il $13.95; lib bdg $13.88 (3-5)   **599.88**

1. Orangutan
ISBN 0-688-08826-0; 0-688-08827-9 (lib bdg)
LC 89-38957
Depicts the physical characteristics and behavior of the orangutan and discusses the possible future of the species
"In addition to the stunning photographs, this text is very well written." Appraisal

DaVolls, Andy, 1967-
Tano & Binti; two chimpanzees return to the wild; [by] Andy and Linda DaVolls. Clarion Bks. 1994 unp il $14.95 (k-3)
599.88

1. Chimpanzees 2. Wildlife conservation
ISBN 0-395-68701-2   LC 93-25403
Describes the experiences of two young chimpanzees that were raised in the London Zoo and then released in Gambia, where an older chimpanzee helped them learn to survive in the wild
"The simple nature narrative is well paced to its picture-book format, with a personable tone and natural ease of style. Even more distinguished is the spacious pastel art, drafted with fluid grace against earthtone backgrounds. The animals are expressive without becoming cute, their dignity reflected in adeptly varied postures of exploration, social dynamics, foraging, and nesting." Bull Cent Child Books

Goodall, Jane, 1934-
The chimpanzee family book; with photographs by Michael Neugebauer. Picture Bk. Studio 1989 unp il $17.95 (3-5)
599.88

1. Chimpanzees
ISBN 0-88708-090-1   LC 88-33359
The primatologist describes a day in the life of a chimpanzee family, noting the animals' "behavior, relationships, and interactions with other animals and with their environment." Booklist
The photographs "are both appropriate and inviting. The writing is informative and comfortable to read. Goodall combines factual events with personal reminiscence and observations." SLJ

Grace, Eric S.
Apes. Sierra Club Bks. for Children 1995 64p il maps (Sierra Club wildlife library) $15.95 (4-6)   **599.88**

1. Apes
ISBN 0-87156-365-7   LC 95-2167
"This book explores the evolution of apes and examines their similarities to humans. Readers will discover differences among the primates' parenting communication, social bonding, dexterity, and eating habits." Sci Child

Lemmon, Tess

Apes; written by Tess Lemmon; illustrated by John Butler. Ticknor & Fields 1993 30p il map $15.95 (2-4)   **599.88**

1. Apes

ISBN 0-395-66901-4   LC 92-37692

Describes the physical characteristics, habits, and behavior of the members of the ape family: gorillas, chimpanzees, orangutans, and gibbons

"The pictures greatly enhance the text and provide supportive information." Sci Child

McNulty, Faith

With love from Koko; illustrated by Annie Cannon. Scholastic 1990 unp il $12.95 (1-4)   **599.88**

1. Gorillas 2. Animal communication

ISBN 0-590-42774-1   LC 89-6183

The author records her visit with Koko, a young gorilla in California who uses sign language and who experiences many of the same feelings a child feels

"McNulty does an exceptionally find job of capturing the anticipation, fear, and excitement of her visit with Koko, and of conveying her respect for this unique creature. . . . Cannon's watercolor drawings help to capture the gentle side of Koko's personality." SLJ

Patterson, Francine

Koko's kitten; photographs by Ronald H. Cohn. Scholastic 1985 unp il $14.95; pa $4.95 (1-4)   **599.88**

1. Gorillas 2. Cats 3. Animal communication

ISBN 0-590-40952-2; 0-590-44425-5 (pa)

    LC 85-2311

The real life experience of Koko, a gorilla in California who uses sign language, with a young kitten whom she loved and grieved over when it died

"Children will empathize with Koko's feelings of love and later grief when her kitten All Ball is killed. And like Koko, they will experience a sense of well-being when, over the mourning, Koko establishes a new and loving relationship with Lipstick, her new kitten." Read Teach

Koko's story; photographs by Ronald H. Cohn. Scholastic 1987 unp il hardcover o.p. paperback available $5.95 (1-4)   **599.88**

1. Gorillas 2. Animal communication

ISBN 0-590-41364-3 (pa)   LC 86-17717

"The author begins by describing how she first saw Koko when the gorilla was three months old; a year later, Patterson began teaching Koko sign language. Soon the gorilla was signing requests for food, and gradually her vocabulary expanded to 500 words. Also introduced is Michael, Koko's playmate and potential breeding partner. Patterson describes the gorillas' daily lives, relates amusing anecdotes, and speculates on what the future will hold for Koko and Michael. The oversize volume is profusely illustrated with color photographs." Booklist

600 TECHNOLOGY (APPLIED SCIENCES)

Biesty, Stephen

Stephen Biesty's incredible cross-sections; illustrated by Stephen Biesty; written by Richard Platt. Knopf 1992 48p il $22 (4 and up)   **600**

1. Technology 2. Architecture

ISBN 0-679-81411-6   LC 91-27439

"A Dorling Kindersley book"

Cross-sectional illustrations present an inside view of such structures as a medieval castle, factory, subway station, coal mine, and oil rig

"Readers will be mesmerized by these intricately drawn illustrations. . . . The detailed drawings are fascinatingly realistic. But while the visuals can steal the show, the well-researched text should not be overlooked. . . . A sense of humor flavors both art and text in the striking oversize volume guaranteed to intrigue browsers and serious researchers alike." Booklist

Bridgman, Roger Francis, 1940-

Technology; by Roger Bridgman. Dorling Kindersley 1995 64p il (Eyewitness science) $15.95 (4 and up)   **600**

1. Technology

ISBN 1-56458-883-1   LC 94-34859

This volume "deals with how the development of machines and materials has affected the areas of communication, farming, medicine, and more. Endoscopes, food mixers, fax machines, and robots are presented, as well as everyday items like the Bic pen and the hollow tennis racquet." SLJ

Macaulay, David, 1946-

The way things work. Houghton Mifflin 1988 384p il $29.95 (4 and up)   **600**

1. Technology 2. Machinery 3. Inventions

ISBN 0-395-42857-2   LC 88-11270

Also available CD-ROM version

This is a "visual and textual guide to the world of how machines work. There are four parts to the book: The Mechanics of Movement, Harnessing the Elements, Working with Waves, and Electricity and Automation with each part broken into subparts based on specific principles. Also included is a guide to the invention of major machines through history. . . . Each machine is explained by drawing and text on one or two pages." Voice Youth Advocates

"This is a work of mammoth imagination, energy, and humor. It justifies every critic's belief that information and entertainment are not mutually exclusive—good nonfiction is storytelling at its best." Bull Cent Child Books

Includes glossary

Parker, Steve

The Random House book of how things work. Random House 1991 c1990 157p il lib bdg $19.99; pa $18 (4 and up)   **600**

1. Technology

ISBN 0-679-90908-7 (lib bdg); 0-679-80908-2 (pa)

    LC 90-9137

First published 1990 in the United Kingdom

Parker, Steve—*Continued*
A comprehensive, illustrated guide showing how more than 300 machines, mechanisms, and processes that affect our everyday lives work
This "is a well-illustrated, clearly written book. . . . Simple explanation and very clear figures make this book a delight to peruse or to use as a quick reference. . . . Scientific details are correct and succinctly but clearly stated." Appraisal
Includes glossary

608   Inventions and patents

Konigsburg, E. L.
Samuel Todd's book of great inventions; written and illustrated by E.L. Konigsburg. Atheneum Pubs. 1991 unp il $13.95 (k-2)
608
1. Inventions
ISBN 0-689-31680-1   LC 90-23688
Companion volume to Samuel Todd's book of great colors (1990)
"A Jean Karl book"
Samuel Todd shows readers some inventions that make his day easier and better, including velcro, a thermos bottle, training wheels, backpacks, and mittens
"Wonderfully illustrated with colorful paintings. . . . This is a simple yet elegant book about wonder; hence, an important book about science." Sci Child

609   Technology—Historical and geographic treatment

Aaseng, Nathan, 1953-
The inventors: Nobel prizes in chemistry, physics, and medicine. Lerner Publs. 1988 79p il (Nobel Prize winners) lib bdg $17.50 (5 and up)
609
1. Inventors 2. Inventions 3. Nobel Prizes
ISBN 0-8225-0651-3   LC 87-3979
Discusses eight inventions or discoveries (X ray, radio, EKG, phase contrast microscope, transistor, radiocarbon dating, laser, and CT scan) which brought the Nobel prize to their developers
In this "book the narrative style carries the reader into a series of dramatic stories linked by common themes." Booklist
Includes glossary

Bender, Lionel
Invention; written by Lionel Bender. Knopf 1991 63p il (Eyewitness books) $19; lib bdg $18.99 (4 and up)
609
1. Inventions
ISBN 0-679-80782-9; 0-679-90782-3 (lib bdg)
LC 90-4888
Also available Spanish language edition
Photographs and text explore such inventions as the wheel, gears, levers, clocks, telephones, and rocket engines
"The photographs are . . . stunning, the information served up in tiny but fascinating bites." BAYA Book Rev

Jones, Charlotte Foltz, 1945-
Mistakes that worked; illustrated by John O'Brien. Doubleday 1991 78p il hardcover o.p. paperback available $10.95 (4-6)
609
1. Inventions
ISBN 0-385-32024-4 (pa)   LC 89-37408
This book presents the stories behind forty things that were invented or named by accident, including aspirin, X-rays, frisbees, silly putty, and velcro
This is "a splendid book that is as informative as it is entertaining. . . . [O'Brien] contributes a wonderful assortment of quirky, colorful cartoons that add just the right touch of levity." Booklist
Includes bibliography

Murphy, Jim, 1947-
Guess again: more weird & wacky inventions. Bradbury Press 1986 91p il $13.95 (4 and up)
609
1. Inventions
ISBN 0-02-767720-6   LC 85-24320
Companion volume to Weird and wacky inventions (1978)
"Murphy presents a number of unusual inventions and invites readers, through the descriptions and drawings, to guess their purpose. . . . Each of the 45 inventions is illustrated with patent drawings or magazine illustrations. Easy-to-understand explanations describe how the inventions worked (or didn't)." Booklist
Includes bibliography

Tucker, Tom, 1944-
Brainstorm! the stories of twenty American kid inventors; with drawings by Richard Loehle. Farrar, Straus & Giroux 1995 148p il $15 (5 and up)
609
1. Inventors 2. Inventions
ISBN 0-374-30944-2   LC 94-38780
The author looks at inventions devised by children since the 18th century. Ear muffs, water skis, the popsicle, colored car wax and the electronic television are among the products discussed. Includes a discussion of how the Patent Office works
Includes glossary and bibliographical references

610   Medical sciences. Medicine

Parker, Steve
Medicine; written by Steve Parker. Dorling Kindersley 1995 64p il (Eyewitness science) $15.95 (4 and up)
610
1. Medicine
ISBN 1-56458-882-3   LC 94-34860
This book "travels from ancient times to the future, addressing alternative treatments, modern drugs, fads in health care, diagnostic techniques, etc. What really stands out are the numerous examples of tools of the trade, like the 18th-century brass enema syringe and the 20th-century electronic hand." SLJ
"Many readers will enjoy just browsing through the volume, looking at the numerous excellent illustrations and reading the text more closely if they are interested. The author makes a concerted effort to avoid controversial questions." Sci Books Films

610.69 Medical personnel

Kuklin, Susan
When I see my doctor. Bradbury Press 1988
unp il $15 (k-3)   **610.69**
1. Medical care
ISBN 0-02-751232-0   LC 87-25621
Four-year-old Thomas describes his trip to the doctor for
a physical checkup
"No painful procedures are included, although Thomas
does have a blood test and an oral vaccination. The outstanding feature of [this book] is the photographs, which are
clear, colorful, natural, and unposed." SLJ

Rockwell, Harlow, 1910-1988
My doctor. Macmillan 1973 unp il lib bdg
$14; pa $3.95 (k-1)   **610.69**
1. Physicians 2. Medicine
ISBN 0-02-777480-5 (lib bdg); 0-689-71606-0 (pa)
The author describes a child's routine examination in a
doctor's office, pointing out the familiar instruments and
materials used for checkups
"Satisfying and reassuring in its explicit, calm presentation of standard medical office equipment, the book is also
noteworthy for avoiding stereotyped roles without blatantly
advertising the fact. 'My doctor' is depicted as a woman."
Horn Book

611 Human anatomy, cytology, histology

Balestrino, Philip
The skeleton inside you; illustrated by True
Kelley. rev ed. Crowell 1989 32p il
(Let's-read-and-find-out science books) lib bdg
$14.89; pa $4.95 (k-3)   **611**
1. Skeleton 2. Bones
ISBN 0-690-04733-9 (lib bdg); 0-08-445087-2 (pa)
                                              LC 88-23672
Also available Spanish language edition
A revised and newly illustrated edition of the title first
published 1971
Balestrino seeks to "explain the human skeleton: what it
is and what it does for us. He tells how the 206 different
bones of the skeleton are joined together, how they grow,
and how they help make blood for your whole body. He
also describes what happens when bones break, and how
they mend." Publisher's note
"Colorful, entertaining illustrations provide an excellent
supplement to the clearly written text. . . . [This] is highly
recommended as an introductory science book for young
children." Sci Books Films

Balkwill, Frances R.
Cells are us; by Fran Balkwill; illustrated by
Mic Rolph. Carolrhoda Bks. 1993 32p il
$18.95; pa $8.95 (3-6)   **611**
1. Cells
ISBN 0-87614-762-7; 0-87614-636-1 (pa)
                                              LC 92-8867
First published 1990 in the United Kingdom

This book examines the functions of cells in the human
body
"The book is packed with vibrant illustrations and fun
facts, making it a nice supplement to the science curriculum." Sci Books Films
Includes glossary

Parker, Steve
The body atlas; illustrated by Giuliano
Fornari. Dorling Kindersley 1993 63p il
$19.95 (5 and up)   **611**
1. Human anatomy
ISBN 1-56458-224-8   LC 92-54307
"The human body is mapped here in detail from head to
toe, and in that order. Sections entitled 'Head and Neck,'
'Upper Torso,' 'Arm and Hand,' 'Lower Torso,' and 'Leg
and Foot' neatly group a huge amount of information into
meaningful, manageable units. Throughout, various organs
are illustrated from both the outside and the inside. . . . In
all sections, scientific photographs have been included to
supplement Fornari's interesting medical illustrations."
Booklist

Rowan, Peter
Some body! illustrations by John
Temperton. Knopf 1995 44p il $20 (4 and up)
                                                   611
1. Human anatomy
ISBN 0-679-87043-1   LC 94-20402
"Covering the brain; sense organs; circulatory and immune systems; and skeletal, muscular, digestive, urinary,
and reproductive systems, the book serves as an introduction to the basic makeup of the human body." Sci Books
Films
"Temperton's meticulous, lifelike renderings range from
elaborate cross-sections to detailed spot art, while complete
or partial fold-outs on 10 pages afford a more realistic scale
and show precisely what lies beneath specific body parts."
Publ Wkly

The **Visual** dictionary of the human body.
Dorling Kindersley 1991 64p il (Eyewitness
visual dictionaries) $15.95; lib bdg $15.99 (4
and up)   **611**
1. Human anatomy
ISBN 1-87943-118-1; 1-87943-133-5 (lib bdg)
                                              LC 91-60899
Also available Spanish language edition
This dictionary portrays and labels parts and systems of
the human body, illustrated with hundreds of color photographs and drawings
"The colors of the illustrations are vibrant and seem true
to life. . . . [This book] will provide enhancement and excitement to study activities." Booklist

612 Human physiology

Aliki
My feet. Crowell 1990 31p il
(Let's-read-and-find-out science books) lib bdg
$14.89; pa $4.50 (k-1)   **612**
1. Foot
ISBN 0-690-04815-7 (lib bdg); 0-06-445106-2 (pa)
                                              LC 89-49357

Aliki—*Continued*
"An extensive discussion of feet, through simple text and playful illustration, demonstrates their parts, relative sizes, what they do, and what they wear in different seasons. Includes a handicapped child whose crutches supplement feet." Sci Child

My hands. rev ed. Crowell 1990 32p il (Let's-read-and-find-out science books) $14.95; lib bdg $14.89; pa $4.95 (k-1)   **612**
1. Hand
ISBN 0-690-04878-5; 0-690-04880-7 (lib bdg); 0-06-445096-1 (pa)   LC 89-49158
First published 1962
The author "calls attention to hand structure—fingers, nails, an opposable thumb—and the special ways we use our hands to carry on everyday activities. . . . The jaunty illustrations and simple but efficient text combine for a fresh take on some very basic information." Booklist

Cole, Joanna
Cuts, breaks, bruises, and burns; how your body heals; illustrated by True Kelley. Crowell 1985 47p il lib bdg $14.89 (2-4)   **612**
1. Wounds and injuries 2. Blood 3. Physiology
ISBN 0-690-04438-0   LC 84-45335
Explains how specialized cells in the body function to heal simple wounds and injuries
"Cole has taken a complex subject and successfully rendered it in simple language for young readers. The excellent illustrations are fun, informative, self-explanatory, and a useful adjunct to the text. This book will be a useful addition to primary school libraries." Sci Books Films

The magic school bus inside the human body; illustrated by Bruce Degen. Scholastic 1989 unp il lib bdg $14.95; pa $4.95 (2-4)
                    612
1. Physiology 2. Human anatomy
ISBN 0-590-41426-7 (lib bdg); 0-590-41427-5 (pa)
                    LC 88-3070
Also available Spanish language edition
Also available CD-ROM version
"Ms. Frizzle's class leaves on a trip to the science museum, but stops for a snack along the way. Arnold is left behind when his classmates reboard the bus. Meanwhile, Ms. Frizzle has miniaturized the bus and its riders. Unwittingly, Arnold swallows it. Traveling through Arnold's insides, the class visits his digestive system, arteries, lungs, heart, brain, and muscles, finally departing through his nostrils when he sneezes." Booklist
"This is an enjoyable look at factual material painlessly packaged with the ribbons and balloons of jokes and asides meant to appeal to kids. Degen's zany, busy, full-color drawings fill the pages with action and information far beyond the text." SLJ

Your insides; illustrated by Paul Meisel. Putnam 1992 unp il $14.95 (k-2)   **612**
1. Human anatomy 2. Physiology
ISBN 0-399-22123-9   LC 91-61236
Examines the different parts of the body and how they work, including the muscles, digestive organs, and lungs
"Cole here employs everyday metaphors such as peeling carrots, blowing up balloons and swinging doors to provide instruction on the stomach, lungs and joints. With a playful approach, Meisel's jaunty light-toned illustrations demonstrate a sensitivity to child life that enhances Cole's lively approach to these body basics." Publ Wkly

Markle, Sandra, 1946-
Outside and inside you. Bradbury Press 1991 39p il $15.95; pa $4.95 (2-4)   **612**
1. Physiology 2. Human anatomy
ISBN 0-02-762311-4; 0-689-71896-9 (pa)
                    LC 90-37791
Discusses the various parts of the body and their functions
"An excellent introduction to anatomy and physiology for the young reader. The book strikes an appropriate balance between scientific complexity and a young child's ability to grasp technical concepts. . . . The real strength of the book rests with its illustrations. . . . The combination of radiographics and gross dissections with microscopic techniques is an excellent mechanism for introducing the material. The quality of the macrophotography is exceptional." Sci Books Films
Includes glossary

Miller, Jonathan, 1934-
The human body; with three-dimensional, movable illustrations showing the workings of the human body designed by David Pelham. Viking 1983 unp il $22.95; pa $22.50 (4 and up)   **612**
1. Human anatomy 2. Physiology
ISBN 0-670-85570-7; 0-670-38605-7 (pa)
                    LC 83-80311
"This book's six 'pop-up' semidiagrammatic representations of the skull and facial muscles, the inner ear, the torso (chest, abdomen, and muscles), the rib cage and lungs, the heart, and the upper torso (including the muscles of the arms in detail) dramatically illustrate how these parts of the body are put together and, in a limited way, how they function. The pop-ups are surrounded by explanatory text." Sci Books Films

Parker, Steve
Human body; written by Steve Parker. Dorling Kindersley 1994 61p il (Eyewitness explorers) $9.95 (3-5)   **612**
1. Human anatomy 2. Physiology
ISBN 1-56458-322-8   LC 93-31076
This work "begins by taking a general look at the body's functions and exploring what constitutes a healthy body. The author then proceeds to examine body parts in more detail, looking at skin, hair, nails, muscles, bones, the heart, the digestive system, teeth, the brain, the nervous system, and glands and hormone development. *Human Body* also includes well-developed sections on each of the five senses, germ fighting, and conception." Sci Child

VanCleave, Janice Pratt
Janice VanCleave's the human body for every kid; easy activities that make learning science fun. Wiley 1995 223p il $24.95; pa $10.95 (5 and up)   **612**
1. Physiology 2. Human anatomy 3. Science—Experiments
ISBN 0-471-02413-9; 0-471-02408-2 (pa)
                    LC 94-20862
"The book's 23 chapters cover cells, skin, the brain, the senses, lungs, blood and the heart, the digestive system, bones, muscles, and genetics. Each chapter includes . . . background information, problem-solving strategies, and simple activities." Sci Child

VanCleave, Janice Pratt—*Continued*
"The activities described are easy to follow, are inexpensive, use readily obtainable supplies, and, most importantly, make the learning of human anatomy and physiology fun and exciting. Moreover, the material is presented in an organized, clear, and accurate manner." Sci Books Films

612.1   Blood and circulation

Parker, Steve

The heart and blood. rev ed. Watts 1989 48p il (Human body) lib bdg $19; pa $6.95 (4 and up)   **612.1**

1. Heart 2. Blood—Circulation
ISBN 0-531-10711-6 (lib bdg); 0-531-24604-3 (pa)
                                              LC 88-51610
First published 1982 under the authorship of Brian R. Ward
Discusses the heart, arteries, veins, blood, and other parts of the body's circulatory system and the causes and prevention of coronary heart disease
Includes glossary

Showers, Paul, 1910-

A drop of blood; illustrated by Don Madden. rev ed. Crowell 1989 30p il (Let's-read-and-find-out science books) lib bdg $13.89; pa $4.95 (k-3)   **612.1**

1. Blood
ISBN 0-690-04717-7 (lib bdg); 0-06-445090-2 (pa)
                                              LC 88-3623
First published 1967
"A simple, entertaining introduction to blood and its function. The information is basic but lively and highly readable, peppered with rhymes that reinforce the text. Simple activities are included. What really makes this book special are Madden's energetic, full-color illustrations, which are mostly depictions of a young boy and his highly expressive dog engaged in some activity related to the text. A couple of drawings of blood components are included, but the style is fully in keeping with the rest of the illustrations, light and interpretive rather than precisely detailed." SLJ

Silverstein, Alvin

The circulatory system; [by] Alvin, Virginia and Robert Silverstein. 21st Cent. Bks. (NY) 1994 96p il (Human body systems) lib bdg $16.98 (5 and up)   **612.1**

1. Heart 2. Blood—Circulation
ISBN 0-8050-2833-1   LC 94-21426
This illustrated introduction to the circulatory system "briefly discusses related systems in plants and animals and the history of our knowledge of the human heart and blood vessels, then focuses on the various parts of the human circulatory system." Booklist
Includes glossary

612.2   Respiration

Ganeri, Anita, 1961-

Breathing. Raintree Steck-Vaughn Pubs. 1995 32p il (First starts) lib bdg $19.97 (k-2)
                                              612.2

1. Respiration
ISBN 0-8114-5520-3   LC 94-14387
This illustrated introduction to the respiratory system also includes "brief discussions of speaking and singing, coughing and sneezing, and breathing underwater and at high altitudes." SLJ
Includes glossary

Sandeman, Anna

Breathing; illustrated by Ian Thompson. Copper Beech Bks. 1995 30p il (Body books) lib bdg $12.90 (k-3)   **612.2**

1. Respiration
ISBN 1-56294-620-X   LC 94-44382
This is a guide to the anatomy and physiology of human respiration
This provides "basic information, simple experiments, and interesting facts, and the attractive graphics combine full-color photographs and illustrations." SLJ

Silverstein, Alvin

The respiratory system; [by] Alvin, Virginia and Robert Silverstein. 21st Cent. Bks. (NY) 1994 96p il (Human body systems) lib bdg $16.98 (5 and up)   **612.2**

1. Respiration
ISBN 0-8050-2831-5   LC 94-21422
This illustrated introduction to the morphology and physiology of the respiratory system also discusses respiratory diseases and their treatments
Includes glossary

612.3   Digestion

Ganeri, Anita, 1961-

Eating. Raintree Steck-Vaughn Pubs. 1995 32p il (First starts) $19.97 (k-2)   **612.3**

1. Digestion
ISBN 0-8114-5522-X   LC 94-14375
This "outlines the digestive and excretory systems, with added information on food, calories, and exercise." SLJ
"Illustrated with full color photographs and some of the clearest diagrams I have ever seen. Simple readable text and a logical sequence and organization." Appraisal
Includes glossary

Parker, Steve

Eating a meal; how you eat, drink, and digest. Watts 1991 32p il (Body in action) lib bdg $12.25 (3-5)   **612.3**

1. Digestion 2. Nutrition
ISBN 0-531-14086-5   LC 89-77856

Parker, Steve—*Continued*

A brief look at the digestive system, explaining why it is important to maintain proper eating habits

"The writing . . . is clear, concise, and interesting." SLJ

Includes glossary

Food and digestion. rev ed. Watts 1990 48p il (Human body) lib bdg $13.93; pa $6.95 (4 and up)   **612.3**

1. Digestion

ISBN 0-531-14027-X (lib bdg); 0-531-24603-5 (pa)

LC 89-36399

First published 1982 under the authorship of Brian R. Ward

An introduction to the digestive system, discussing each stage of digestion, the organs which aid in the digestive process, and the assimilation of nutrients into the body's structure

Includes glossary

Patent, Dorothy Hinshaw

Nutrition; what's in the food we eat; photos by William Muñoz. Holiday House 1992 40p il $15.95 (3-6)   **612.3**

1. Nutrition

ISBN 0-8234-0968-6

LC 92-3665

The author "explains the purpose of food (providing the body with energy and nutrients), discusses the major food categories (carbohydrates, proteins, and fats), and briefly introduces the concept of vitamins and minerals. She also compares several healthy food choices with junk foods. . . . Muñoz's numerous full-color photographs present mouthwatering examples of the foods mentioned in the text and feature an appealing mix of children enjoying the fare." Booklist

Includes glossary

Showers, Paul, 1910-

How many teeth? illustrated by True Kelley. rev ed. HarperCollins Pubs. 1991 32p il (Let's-read-and-find-out science books) $15; lib bdg $14.89; pa $4.95 (k-1)   **612.3**

1. Teeth

ISBN 0-06-021633-6; 0-06-021634-4 (lib bdg); 0-06-445098-8 (pa)

LC 89-13995

A revised and newly illustrated edition of the title first published 1962 by Crowell

This introduction to teeth describes how many we have at various stages of life, why they fall out, and what they do

"Kelley's exuberant . . . pictures show a multiracial classroom and nonsexist family roles. . . . This text is unsurpassed in the clarity and wit with which it treats a subject of obsessive interest to young children." Booklist

What happens to a hamburger; illustrated by Anne Rockwell. rev ed. Crowell 1985 32p il (Let's-read-and-find-out science books) lib bdg $14.89; pa $4.95 (k-3)   **612.3**

1. Digestion

ISBN 0-690-04427-5 (lib bdg); 0-06-445013-9 (pa)

LC 84-45343

First published 1970

A "step-by-step explanation of digestion. . . . Pastel illustrations enliven the text. . . . Easy 'kitchen' experiments demonstrate physical and chemical changes in the food which has been eaten, and simple diagrams illustrate what happens to food in each area of the system, emphasizing

that food is the source of our bodies' energy and it makes bones and muscles strong." SLJ

Silverstein, Alvin

Carbohydrates; by Alvin Silverstein, Virginia Silverstein, and Robert Silverstein; illustrations by Anne Canevari Green. Millbrook Press 1992 48p il (Food power!) lib bdg $15.40 (3-6)   **612.3**

1. Carbohydrates 2. Nutrition

ISBN 1-56294-207-7

LC 91-41245

Examines the different kinds of carbohydrates, their sources, and their role in nutrition

This book is "crammed with logically and concisely presented information. Helpful boxed inserts contain additional facts, and there are loads of easy-to-read charts as well as humorous, full-color illustrations." Booklist

Includes glossary and bibliography

The digestive system; [by] Alvin, Virginia & Robert Silverstein. 21st Cent. Bks. (NY) 1994 96p il (Human body systems) lib bdg $16.98 (5 and up)   **612.3**

1. Digestion

ISBN 0-8050-2832-3

LC 94-19384

This illustrated overview of the physiology and anatomy of the digestive system also includes chapters on diet, eating habits and food poisoning

"The book has a clear, simple flow and primarily conversational style that make it easy to read." Sci Books Films

Includes glossary

Fats; by Alvin Silverstein, Virginia Silverstein, and Robert Silverstein; illustrations by Anne Canevari Green. Millbrook Press 1992 48p il (Food power!) lib bdg $15.40 (3-6)   **612.3**

1. Oils and fats 2. Nutrition

ISBN 1-56294-208-5

LC 91-42169

Describes fats and their function in our diet. Includes a gram-calorie chart and experiments

Includes glossary and bibliography

Proteins; by Alvin Silverstein, Virginia Silverstein, and Robert Silverstein; illustrations by Anne Canevari Green. Millbrook Press 1992 48p il (Food power!) lib bdg $15.40 (3-6)   **612.3**

1. Proteins 2. Nutrition

ISBN 1-56294-209-3

LC 91-41230

Explains the function of proteins in our body, how we can get protein, and what amino acids are

"The explanation of complete versus incomplete proteins is well presented; likewise for essential and nonessential amino acids. Translating these ideas to diet, Proteins gives many examples of simple, often meatless, combinations of foods that provide proper groupings of proteins." Sci Books Films

Includes glossary and bibliography

Vitamins and minerals; by Alvin Silverstein, Virginia Silverstein, and Robert Silverstein; illustrations by Anne Canevari Green. Millbrook Press 1992 48p il (Food power!) lib bdg $15.40 (3-6)   **612.3**

1. Vitamins 2. Nutrition

ISBN 1-56294-206-9

LC 91-41231

Silverstein, Alvin—*Continued*

Examines the major vitamins and minerals, their functions, sources, proper daily dosages, and deficiency symptoms

"*Vitamins and Minerals* does a nice job of putting the micro size of vitamins into perspective. The text and the cartoon illustrations show the relative proportions of these materials in the food we eat and why vitamins are so important to ingest. . . . Sidebars contain extra bits of information or simple experiments that are suitable for young readers." Sci Books Films

Includes glossary and bibliography

612.4 Secretion, excretion, related functions

Silverstein, Alvin

The excretory system; [by] Alvin, Virginia and Robert Silverstein. 21st Cent. Bks. (NY) 1994 94p il (Human body systems) lib bdg $16.98 (5 and up)   612.4

1. Excretion
ISBN 0-8050-2834-X   LC 94-21425

This begins with a description of "excretion in animals, how wastes are formed, and a brief history. The urinary system and excretion through the skin, lungs, and digestive tract are all described, followed by sections on kidney dialysis, transplants, etc. [The text is] lucid, to the point, and highly readable. Photographs and simple diagrams are all in full color." SLJ

Includes glossary

612.6 Reproduction, development, maturation

Aliki

I'm growing! HarperCollins Pubs. 1992 31p il (Let's-read-and-find-out science books) $14; lib bdg $14.89; pa $4.95 (k-1)   612.6

1. Growth
ISBN 0-06-020244-0; 0-06-020245-9 (lib bdg); 0-06-445116-X (pa)   LC 91-14087

"A brief examination of the human growth process, detailed by a young boy who has outgrown his clothing." SLJ

"Aliki's bright, clear, realistic illustrations show a smiling child who's delighted that he's growing bigger. . . . Some basic concepts of physiology are explained in a straightforward, simple text with playful pictures of the Hispanic boy, his extended family, and his friends. . . . This entertaining concept book celebrates individual differences while it acknowledges every child's longing to be big and strong." Booklist

Bourgeois, Paulette

Changes in you and me: a book about puberty, mostly for boys; by Paulette Bourgeois and Martin Wolfish; illustrated by Louise Phillips and Kam Yu. Andrews & McMeel 1994 64p il $14.95 (4 and up)   612.6

1. Adolescence 2. Hygiene 3. Sex education
ISBN 0-8362-2814-6   LC 94-1162

"A Somerville House book"

This introductory text for boys discusses the general physical and emotional changes of adolescence and defines terms and topics related to sexual matters

Changes in you and me: a book about puberty, mostly for girls; by Paulette Bourgeois and Martin Wolfish; sexual health consultant, Kim Martyn; illustrated by Louise Phillips and Kam Yu. Andrews & McMeel 1994 64p il $14.95 (4 and up)   612.6

1. Adolescence 2. Hygiene 3. Sex education
ISBN 0-8362-2815-4   LC 94-1161

"A Somerville House book"

This is a guide to puberty and sex education for girls

"The scope of the information is exemplary, including, for instance, information on toxic-shock syndrome, douching and pelvic examinations that most girls need to know and may not find elsewhere." N Y Times Book Rev

Cole, Joanna

How you were born; photographs by Margaret Miller. rev & expanded ed. Morrow Junior Bks. 1993 48p il $15; lib bdg $14.93; pa $4.95 (k-2)   612.6

1. Pregnancy 2. Childbirth 3. Infants
ISBN 0-688-12059-8; 0-688-12060-1 (lib bdg); 0-688-12061-X (pa)   LC 92-23970

A revised and newly illustrated edition of the title first published 1984

"Illustrated with photographs of culturally diverse families, Cole's text explains conception, the development of the fetus, and the birth process. A note to parents and a suggested reading list are included." J Youth Serv Libr

Ganeri, Anita, 1961-

Birth and growth. Raintree Steck-Vaughn Pubs. 1995 32p il (First starts) $19.97 (k-2)   612.6

1. Growth 2. Childbirth
ISBN 0-8114-5519-X   LC 94-14373

This "traces human life from fertilization to old age. . . . The writing is clear and informative. New terminology appears in bold type and is defined both within the text and in the glossary. . . . The pictures are pertinent." SLJ

Kitzinger, Sheila, 1929-

Being born; photography by Lennart Nilsson. Grosset & Dunlap 1986 64p il hardcover o.p. paperback available $12.95 (3-5)   612.6

1. Pregnancy 2. Fetus 3. Childbirth
ISBN 0-399-22225-1 (pa)   LC 86-80513

Photographs and text describe the baby's nine-month journey from conception to birth

"An astounding photo-essay on fetal development. Microphotography shows sperm entering the ovum, then, via a fiber optic lens, the growth of the fetus from a few weeks until the infant's birth. Tiny white silhouettes of the actual size of the fetus at 30 and 37 days are juxtaposed against the enlarged fetal photographs. Subsequent stages are represented lifesize on the page, brilliant color against the glossy black page. Kitzinger's second-person text matches the pictures in wonder and delight." SLJ

Marzollo, Jean

Getting your period; a book about menstruation; illustrated by Kent Williams; introduction by Marcia Storch. Dial Bks. for Young Readers 1988 99p il $13.95; pa $6.95 (5 and up) **612.6**

1. Menstruation
ISBN 0-8037-0355-4; 0-8037-0356-2 (pa)
LC 88-3986

The author "combines information on menstruation with quotations that show a reassuring range of reactions from girls who tell about their own concerns and experiences. . . . Common physical and emotional symptoms are the emphasis here, but there are brief factual references to PMS, toxic shock syndrome, and sexually transmitted diseases (including AIDS)." Bull Cent Child Books

Silverstein, Alvin

The reproductive system; [by] Alvin, Virginia, and Robert Silverstein. 21st Cent. Bks. (NY) 1994 96p il (Human body systems) lib bdg $16.98 (5 and up) **612.6**

1. Sex education
ISBN 0-8050-2838-2
LC 94-25912

This "describes male and female systems, hormones, fertilization, stages of pregnancy, STDs, and birth control. . . . Informative full-color photos, clear illustrations, and fact boxes appear throughout." SLJ
Includes glossary

612.7 Motor functions and skin (integument), hair, nails

Ganeri, Anita, 1961-

Moving. Raintree Steck-Vaughn Pubs. 1995 32p il (First starts) lib bdg $19.97 (k-2) **612.7**

1. Skeleton 2. Muscles
ISBN 0-8114-5521-1
LC 94-14378

This illustrated guide to human locomotion describes the skeleton, vertebrae, joints and muscles
Includes glossary

Parker, Steve

Singing a song; how you sing, speak and make sounds. Watts 1991 32p il (Body in action) lib bdg $12.25 (3-5) **612.7**

1. Voice 2. Singing
ISBN 0-531-14212-4
LC 91-17018

"The book includes sections on making sounds, structures of the respiratory system involved in the production of sound, the characteristics of sound, breathing, hearing, nervous system control of speech, and other air movements in the respiratory system. It has lots of colorful pictures and diagrams demonstrating appropriate ethnic diversity. There are plenty of hands-on activities for children to try. The activities use simple things that most children would have available to them." Sci Books Films
Includes glossary and bibliography

The skeleton and movement. rev ed. Watts 1989 48p il (Human body) lib bdg $25.75; pa $6.95 (4 and up) **612.7**

1. Skeleton 2. Muscles
ISBN 0-531-10709-4 (lib bdg); 0-531-24606-X (pa)
LC 88-51608

First published 1981 under the authorship of Brian R. Ward
This book discusses "the structure of bones and muscles; cartilage, ligaments, and tendons; the skull, the backbone, and the rib cage; and other related topics." Publisher's note
Includes glossary

Sandeman, Anna

Bones; illustrated by Ian Thompson. Copper Beech Bks. 1995 30p il (Body books) lib bdg $12.90 (k-3) **612.7**

1. Skeleton 2. Bones
ISBN 1-56294-621-8
LC 94-42182

The "text explains how bones hold up our bodies and how muscles, joints, and ligaments work together to facilitate movement. . . . The color photos of energetic kids are overlaid with skeletal drawings, and the effect is slyly amusing and lively. . . . This ia an animated and satisfying introduction." Bull Cent Child Books

Showers, Paul, 1910-

Your skin and mine; illustrated by Kathleen Kuchera. rev ed. HarperCollins Pubs. 1991 32p il (Let's-read and find out science books) lib bdg $14.89; pa $4.50 (k-3) **612.7**

1. Skin
ISBN 0-06-022523-8 (lib bdg); 0-06-445102-X (pa)
LC 90-37430

A revised and newly illustrated edition of the title first published 1965 by Crowell
Explains the basic properties of skin, how it protects the body, and how it can vary in color
"This book proves far superior to its predecessor. . . . Ink-and-watercolor illustrations are lively and vibrant." SLJ

Silverstein, Alvin

The muscular system; [by] Alvin, Virginia, and Robert Silverstein. 21st Cent. Bks. (NY) 1994 96p il (Human body systems) lib bdg $16.98 (5 and up) **612.7**

1. Muscles
ISBN 0-8050-2836-6
LC 94-21424

"The authors begin with a brief discussion of how animals move on land, in water, or in the air and go on to point out that plants also move, although they do not have muscles. The remainder of the book discusses the human muscular system, how muscles work, disorders and diseases and the importance of exercises in maintaining the health of muscles." Appraisal
Includes glossary

The skeletal system; [by] Alvin, Virginia, and Robert Silverstein. 21st Cent. Bks. (NY) 1994 96p il (Human body systems) lib bdg $16.98 (5 and up) **612.7**

1. Skeleton 2. Bones
ISBN 0-8050-2837-4
LC 94-21421

Silverstein, Alvin—Continued

This volume "includes descriptions of bones, ligaments, tendons, skeletal deformities, artificial limbs, and how to keep bones healthy. . . . Written in a lively, readable manner. All of the material is presented objectively and scientifically. Informative full-color photos, clear illustrations." SLJ

Includes glossary

612.8   Nervous functions. Sensory functions

Aliki

My five senses. rev ed. Crowell 1989 31p il (Let's-read-and-find-out science books) $14.89; lib bdg $15; pa $4.95 (k-1)   **612.8**

1. Senses and sensation

ISBN 0-690-04794-0; 0-690-04792-4 (lib bdg); 0-06-445083-X (pa)   LC 88-35350

Also available Spanish language edition

First published 1962

The faculties of touch, hearing, sight, smelling and taste are introduced in relation to everyday experiences

"Each sense is used independently to observe common phenomena. Next, the author demonstrates more than one sense being used. . . . The book effectively introduced the five senses to young people." Appraisal

Ardley, Neil, 1937-

The science book of the senses. Harcourt Brace Jovanovich 1992 29p il $9.95 (3-5)   **612.8**

1. Senses and sensation 2. Science—Experiments

ISBN 0-15-200614-1   LC 91-20587

"Gulliver books"

Gives instructions for a variety of simple experiments that explain how the body's five senses operate

"The layout . . . is extremely appealing—bright, colorful, sharp photographs are interspersed among blocks of large-type text. . . . Each experiment is accurate, well designed, and easy to perform. . . . The supplies needed for the experiments are inexpensive and readily available household and school items. . . . The children in the photographs are girls and boys of different nationalities and races enjoying their projects." Sci Books Films

Berger, Melvin, 1927-

Why I cough, sneeze, shiver, hiccup, & yawn; illustrated by Holly Keller. Crowell 1983 34p il (Let's-read-and-find-out science books) lib bdg $14.89 (k-3)   **612.8**

1. Reflexes 2. Nervous system

ISBN 0-690-04254-X   LC 82-45587

An introduction to reflex acts that explains why we cough, sneeze, shiver, hiccup, yawn, and blink

"This book would be an excellent way to introduce children to a study of the human body, since [these] are questions that children really do ask. In finding out the answers . . . they will gain a very basic understanding of the nervous system, and can also have fun trying out such reflexes as the knee jerk or the painter reflex. The alternating black and white and colored drawings are appealing as well as informative." Appraisal

Bruun, Ruth Dowling

The brain—what it is, what it does; by Ruth Dowling Bruun and Bertel Bruun; illustrated by Peter Bruun. Greenwillow Bks. 1989 63p il $12.95; lib bdg $12.88 (1-3)   **612.8**

1. Brain

ISBN 0-688-08453-2; 0-688-08454-0 (lib bdg)

     LC 88-21182

"A Greenwillow read-alone book"

The authors "cover what the brain is made of, how people think and learn, what constitutes intelligence and feelings, and why people sleep. The authors also warn about the effects of drugs and alcohol on the brain. The subject matter necessitates a number of difficult words, which are explained in context as well as in the glossary; however, there is no pronunciation guide. Simple line drawings dotted with orange break up the text and are surprisingly informative considering their simplicity." Booklist

Bryan, Jenny

Sound and vision; the sensory systems. Dillon Press 1994 c1993 48p il (Body talk) lib bdg $13.95 (4-6)   **612.8**

1. Hearing 2. Vision

ISBN 0-87518-591-6   LC 93-37306

First published 1993 in the United Kingdom

This book discusses "how ears and eyes work, the importance of taking care of them, and some ailments (along with solutions) that may arise. In this volume, the photographs and diagrams augment and enhance the material being presented." SLJ

Includes glossary and bibliography

Funston, Sylvia

It's all in your brain; [by] Sylvia Funston, Jay Ingram; illustrated by Gary Clement. Grosset & Dunlap 1994 64p il $13.99; pa $9.95 (4 and up)   **612.8**

1. Brain

ISBN 0-448-40940-2; 0-448-40939-9 (pa)

     LC 94-22507

Published in Canada with title: A kid's guide to the brain

"Senses, emotions, memory, and thinking are the major categories featured in this interactive tour through the brain. The activities in each category are an excellent introduction to concepts not often discussed in the classroom." Sci Child

Otto, Carolyn

I can tell by touching; illustrated by Nadine Bernard Westcott. HarperCollins Pubs. 1994 32p il (Let's-read-and-find-out science books) $15; lib bdg $14.89; pa $4.95 (k-1)   **612.8**

1. Touch

ISBN 0-06-023324-9; 0-06-023325-7 (lib bdg); 0-06-445125-9 (pa)   LC 93-18630

Explains how the sense of touch helps to identify everyday objects and familiar surroundings

"Science writing for preschoolers doesn't get much better than this. Otto evokes the physicality of the child's experience as she gives precise, factual information about the sense of touch. Bright, clear illustrations in pen and ink, acrylic, and watercolor." Booklist

Parker, Steve

The brain and nervous system. rev ed. Watts 1990 48p il (Human body) lib bdg $18.43; pa $6.95 (4 and up)   **612.8**

1. Brain 2. Nervous system
ISBN 0-531-14026-1 (lib bdg); 0-531-24600-0 (pa)
LC 89-36486

First published 1981 under the authorship of Brian R. Ward

"Parker describes the control system of the body: its structure and function, sleep mechanism, reflexes and autonomic nervous system, and the two brain hemispheres. He also touches on memory, mental health, and aging." SLJ

Includes glossary

The ear and hearing. rev ed. Watts 1989 40p il (Human body) lib bdg $19; pa $6.95 (4 and up)   **612.8**

1. Ear 2. Hearing
ISBN 0-531-10712-4 (lib bdg); 0-531-24601-9 (pa)
LC 88-51611

First published 1981 under the authorship of Brain R. Ward

Examines the anatomy of the ear, how the ear receives sounds and transfers them to the brain, how to protect our hearing, and current developments in hearing aids and surgery

Includes glossary

The eye and seeing. rev ed. Watts 1989 48p il (Human body) lib bdg $19; pa $6.95 (4 and up)   **612.8**

1. Eye 2. Vision
ISBN 0-531-10654-3 (lib bdg); 0-531-24602-7 (pa)
LC 88-51606

First published 1982 under the authorship of Brain R. Ward

The author discusses the structure of the eye and how we see; how the lens provides an image on the retina; the functions of rods and cones; and defects of vision, eyeglasses, contact lens, colorblindness, etc.

Includes glossary

Touch, taste and smell. rev ed. Watts 1989 40p il (Human body) lib bdg $18.43; pa $6.95 (4 and up)   **612.8**

1. Touch 2. Taste 3. Smell
ISBN 0-531-10655-1 (lib bdg); 0-531-24607-8 (pa)
LC 88-51607

First published 1982 under the authorship of Brian R. Ward

The book "explains the physiological process at work in each of these sensations, including identification of the organs involved and descriptions of how they transmit their vital information to the brain." Booklist

Includes glossary

Showers, Paul, 1910-

Ears are for hearing; illustrated by Holly Keller. Crowell 1990 32p il (Let's-read-and-find-out science books) lib bdg $14.89; pa $4.50 (k-3)   **612.8**

1. Hearing 2. Ear
ISBN 0-690-04720-7 (lib bdg); 0-06-445112-7 (pa)
LC 89-17479

This book covers "the anatomy and function of the ear . . . detailing the mechanics of hearing, the role of the inner ear in balance, and cause of hearing loss." SLJ

"The illustrator has supplied good diagrams and peopled the book with perky characters to help the reader understand how sound travels through the ear to send messages to the brain." Horn Book

Look at your eyes; illustrated by True Kelley. rev ed. HarperCollins Pubs. 1992 32p il (Let's-read-and-find-out science books) lib bdg $13.89; pa $4.50 (k-1)   **612.8**

1. Eye
ISBN 0-06-020189-4 (lib bdg); 0-06-445108-9 (pa)
LC 91-10167

A revised and newly illustrated edition of the title first published 1962 by Crowell

Using a little boy's daily activities as a focal point, the author introduces some basic facts about the eyes

Silverstein, Alvin

The nervous system; [by] Alvin, Virginia, and Robert Silverstein. 21st Cent. Bks. (NY) 1994 96p il (Human body systems) lib bdg $16.98 (5 and up)   **612.8**

1. Nervous system
ISBN 0-8050-2835-8
LC 94-25917

This "title covers the specialization of each cell and explains the parts of the brain and what they control. Memory, intelligence, and how drugs affect the mind are also discussed." SLJ

Includes glossary

Smell, the subtle sense; [by] Alvin, Virginia, and Robert Silverstein; illustrated by Ann Neumann. Morrow Junior Bks. 1992 90p il $14; lib bdg $13.93 (5 and up)   **612.8**

1. Smell
ISBN 0-688-09396-5; 0-688-09397-3 (lib bdg)
LC 91-21745

Discusses the complex nature of the sense of smell and the importance of the nose. Also discusses how odors are produced, how they help in identifying specific diseases, and their psychological and physical effects

"This has the Silversteins' usual painstakingly detailed coverage of many aspects of their chosen subject, and the material is logically arranged, so that . . . it can both answer questions and stimulate further interest." Bull Cent Child Books

Includes bibliography

Stafford, Patricia

Your two brains; illustrated by Linda Tunney. Atheneum Pubs. 1986 75p il $13.95 (5 and up)   **612.8**

1. Brain
ISBN 0-689-31142-7
LC 85-28575

A simple explanation of the separate function of each half of the brain describing what each half does, how they work together, and how one can achieve whole brain thinking

"There are discussions of right- and left-handedness and genius, and well-known but accurately presented descriptions of highly creative, famous individuals add to the usefulness of this little gem." Sci Books Films

Includes glossary and bibliography

Wright, Lillian

Hearing. Raintree Steck-Vaughn Pubs. 1995 32p il (First starts) lib bdg $19.97 (k-2)

612.8

1. Hearing

ISBN 0-8114-5516-5   LC 94-10719

This describes the anatomy and physiology of hearing and briefly covers ear care, hearing loss, and noise pollution

This is "written simply enough to be accessible to children in the early grades and in enough detail to be interesting. The pictures and diagrams are clear and colorful. . . . Children using these books can develop solid understanding of the topics covered." Appraisal

Includes glossary

Seeing. Raintree Steck-Vaughn Pubs. 1995 32p il (First starts) lib bdg $19.97 (k-2)

612.8

1. Vision

ISBN 0-8114-5515-7   LC 94-10720

This describes the anatomy and physiology of vision and briefly covers eye care, eyeglasses, blindness, seeing color, and optical illusions

Includes glossary

Smelling and tasting. Raintree Steck-Vaughn Pubs. 1995 32p il (First starts) lib bdg $19.97 (k-2)

612.8

1. Smell 2. Taste

ISBN 0-8114-5518-1   LC 94-21454

This briefly describes the anatomy and physiology of taste and smell and how these senses are used

Includes glossary

Touching. Raintree Steck-Vaughn Pubs. 1995 32p il (First starts) lib bdg $19.97 (k-2)

612.8

1. Touch

ISBN 0-8114-5517-3   LC 94-12939

This briefly describes the anatomy and physiology of touch, reflex actions, sensation of hot and cold, pain, itching and tickles, balance, and numbness

Includes glossary

613   Promotion of health

Brown, Laurene Krasny

Dinosaurs alive and well!: a guide to good health; [by] Laurie Krasny Brown, Marc Brown. Little, Brown 1990 32p il $15.95; pa $5.95 (k-3)   **613**

1. Health

ISBN 0-316-10998-3; 0-316-11009-4 (pa)

LC 89-37182

The authors present advice on nutrition, hygiene, exercise, first aid, and ways of handling stress

"A liberal mix of humorous dinosaurs and lively text create a unique treatment in health education. . . . Frequent exposure to this book will help children realize the ultimate goal—that of staying healthy and feeling good about themselves. An upbeat mood pervades this nonpatronizing treatment of an otherwise 'doesn't-everybody-know-that' subject. The exuberant watercolor illustrations make the book a complete success." SLJ

613.2   Dietetics

Leedy, Loreen, 1959-

The edible pyramid; good eating every day; written & illustrated by Loreen Leedy. Holiday House 1994 unp il $15.95 (k-3)

613.2

1. Nutrition 2. Diet

ISBN 0-8234-1126-5   LC 94-2122

"Ushering a group of elegantly clothed animals into the grand opening of the Edible Pyramid restaurant, the suave waiter introduces the selections on the U.S. Department of Agriculture food pyramid, explaining the choices in each category, the number of daily servings recommended for each group, and what a 'serving' means." Booklist

"Children will get a good basic overview of the food groups and how to apply the knowledge to their own diets." Bull Cent Child Books

Reef, Catherine

Eat the right stuff; food facts. 21st Cent. Bks. (NY) 1993 64p il (Good health guidelines) lib bdg $15.95 (4 and up)

613.2

1. Nutrition

ISBN 0-8050-2442-5   LC 93-1370

This "covers nutrition and digestion, including ways to improve diet and control weight safely. A detailed explanation of the USDA food pyramid is included. Roles of various vitamins are discussed in table form. . . . Reef takes a friendly, helpful approach. . . . Attractive full-color photographs introduce each chapter, and students' viewpoints and experiences are included." SLJ

Includes bibliography

613.6   Promotion of health—Special topics

Brown, Marc Tolon

Dinosaurs, beware! a safety guide; [by] Marc Brown and Stephen Krensky. Little, Brown 1982 30p il $15.95; pa $6.95 (k-3)   **613.6**

1. Accidents—Prevention

ISBN 0-316-11228-3; 0-316-11219-4 (pa)

LC 82-15207

"An Atlantic Monthly Press book"

Illustrated by Marc Brown

Approximately sixty safety tips are demonstrated by dinosaurs in situations at home, during meals, camping, in the car, and in other familiar places

"Bright colors and the expressive antics of your average, residential dinosaur effectively illustrate a multitude of common-sense safety tips. . . . The text is clear and to the point. The presentation is non-threatening and in a more or less do's-and-don'ts style. All tips are appropriate for the intended age group." SLJ

613.7 Physical fitness

Reef, Catherine

Stay fit; build a strong body. 21st Cent. Bks. (NY) 1993 64p il (Good health guidelines) lib bdg $15.95 (4 and up)   **613.7**

1. Physical fitness 2. Exercise

ISBN 0-8050-2441-7   LC 93-19349

This book discusses "the importance of fitness; information about the body; stretching and strength-building exercises; how to develop a safe, individualized physical activity program; and how to live a healthy life. The accurate text and lively writing style convey the idea that fitness is a total concept. Full-page, full-color photographs add interest." SLJ

Includes bibliography

613.9 Birth control and sex hygiene

Harris, Robie H.

It's perfectly normal; a book about changing bodies, growing up, sex, and sexual health; illustrated by Michael Emberley. Candlewick Press 1994 89p il $19.95; pa $9.99 (4 and up)   **613.9**

1. Sex education

ISBN 1-56402-199-8; 1-56402-159-9 (pa)

LC 93-48365

The author "explains the physical, psychological, emotional and social changes that occur during puberty—and the implications of these changes." Publ Wkly

"This caring, conscientious, and well-crafted book will be a fine library resource as well as a marvelous adjunct to the middle-school sex-education curriculum. . . . The bold color cartoon drawings are very candid: a double-page spread of nudes, which beautifully demonstrates the varied shapes and sizes humans come in; a picture of a couple making love; one of a boy masturbating as he sits on his bed; another of a girl examining her genitals with a mirror. . . . Harris' text, as forthright as Emberley's art, encompasses . . . (the structure of the reproductive system and puberty) . . . intercourse, birth, abortion, sexual health, abuse, and issues of responsibility and respect." Booklist

Madaras, Lynda

The what's happening to my body? book for boys: a growing up guide for parents and sons; [by] Lynda Madaras with Dane Saavedra; drawings by Jackie Aher. new ed. Newmarket Press 1987 251p il $18.95; pa $11.95 (4 and up)   **613.9**

1. Adolescence 2. Hygiene 3. Sex education

ISBN 1-55704-002-8; 0-937858-99-4 (pa)

LC 87-28116

Also available: My body, my self: the what's happening workbook for boys (ISBN 1-55704-230-6) $11.95

First published 1984

Discusses the changes that take place in a boy's body during puberty, including information on the body's changing size and shape, the growth spurt, reproductive organs, pubic hair, beards, pimples, voice changes, wet dreams, and puberty in girls

"A good addition to a library's health or sex education collection." Voice Youth Advocates

Includes bibliography

The what's happening to my body? book for girls: a growing up guide for parents and daughters; [by] Lynda Madaras with Area Madaras; drawings by Claudia Ziroli and Jackie Aher. new ed. Newmarket Press 1987 269p il $18.95; pa $11.95 (4 and up)   **613.9**

1. Adolescence 2. Hygiene 3. Sex education

ISBN 1-55704-001-X; 0-937858-98-6 (pa)

LC 87-28117

Also available: My body, my self: the what's happening workbook for girls (ISBN 1-55704-150-4) $11.95

First published 1983 with title: What's happening to my body? A growing up guide for mothers and daughters

This is a "beginning book to help girls going through puberty understand their bodies and how they are changing and realize what they are going through is normal and part of growing up. The book is geared for girls between the ages of nine and 15 and is really one of those books that should be read by both parents and daughters and then discussed. It does give factual information and tries to present both sides of an issue making it a good addition to any school library's sex education collection." Voice Youth Advocates

Includes bibliography

Westheimer, Ruth

Dr. Ruth talks to kids; where you came from, how your body changes, and what sex is all about; illustrated by Diane deGroat. Macmillan 1993 96p il $13.95 (5 and up)   **613.9**

1. Sex education

ISBN 0-02-792532-3   LC 92-11397

The author "discusses body development and sexuality." Bull Cent Child Books

"Her casual, yet authoritative, reassuring tone spills onto every page. . . . Westheimer ranges widely over common preteen and teen concerns, and most of the basics about puberty, sex, contraception, and birth are presented practically and frankly." Booklist

Includes bibliography

616 Diseases

Nourse, Alan Edward, 1928-

Lumps, bumps, and rashes; by Alan E. Nourse. rev ed. Watts 1990 64p il lib bdg $13.93 (4-6)   **616**

1. Communicable diseases

ISBN 0-531-10865-1   LC 90-32785

"A First book"

First published 1976

Nourse, Alan Edward, 1928-—*Continued*
Examines rashes, infections, and other common childhood diseases and describes methods of curing them or vaccinations to prevent them

"The pictures are clear and useful, and the way the subject is presented should make the book easy to read. . . . This is one of the best books of its kind." Sci Books Films

Includes glossary and bibliography

616.2 Diseases of the respiratory system

Hyde, Margaret Oldroyd, 1917-

Living with asthma; [by] Margaret O. Hyde and Elizabeth H. Forsyth. Walker & Co. 1995 86p il $14.95; lib bdg $15.85 (4 and up) 616.2

1. Asthma
ISBN 0-8027-8286-8; 0-8027-8287-6 (lib bdg)
LC 94-41884

"Questions are answered and myths dispelled as children learn what asthma is and what life is like for the six million people in the United States living with this disease. Readers will gain insight and empathy." Sci Child

Includes glossary and bibliography

Lerner, Carol, 1927-

Plants that make you sniffle and sneeze. Morrow Junior Bks. 1993 32p il $15; lib bdg $14.93 (4 and up) 616.2

1. Hay fever 2. Plants
ISBN 0-688-11489-X; 0-688-11490-3 (lib bdg)
LC 92-21561

Discusses hay fever and describes the various plants whose pollen triggers hay fever allergies with information on where they grow, how their pollen is dispersed, and what can be done to avoid exposure to these irritants

This is "an intelligent, simply written volume. . . . Botanical illustrations notable for their clarity and grace appear throughout the book, some in full color and others in black and white." Booklist

Includes bibliography

Ostrow, William

All about asthma; [by] William Ostrow and Vivian Ostrow; illustrated by Blanche Sims. Whitman, A. 1989 39p il lib bdg $12.95; pa $5.95 (3-5) 616.2

1. Asthma
ISBN 0-8075-0276-6 (lib bdg); 0-8075-0275-8 (pa)
LC 89-5254

"Young William Ostrow, who has written this book with his mother, has asthma, and in a first-person narrative he tells about when he first developed the disease and how he has learned to live with it." Booklist

"A clear and thorough picture of living with asthma. The text is well organized. . . . The emphasis is upbeat and positive. . . . Sims' cheery turquoise and gray watercolors add humorous touches throughout." SLJ

Parker, Steve

Catching a cold; how you get ill, suffer and recover. Watts 1991 32p il (Body in action) lib bdg $12.25 (3-5) 616.2

1. Cold (Disease)
ISBN 0-531-14146-2
LC 91-747

This "briefly outlines the workings of the immune system; the body's physical reactions to a cold; the role of bone marrow, the spleen, and lymph nodes; and provides tips for disease prevention." SLJ

"There are a large number of colorful pictures and diagrams and several hands-on activities that children could perform with simple household items. . . . The book should be of interest to children over a wide age range and could be a useful resource for elementary science units." Sci Books Films

Includes glossary and bibliography

Weiss, Jonathan H.

Breathe easy; young people's guide to asthma; illustrated by Michael Chesworth. Magination Press 1994 64p il pa $9.95 (4 and up) 616.2

1. Asthma
ISBN 0-945354-62-2
LC 94-21581

This describes what an asthma attack is like and how to control it with medicines and relaxation, how to identify and control triggers, how to recognize early warning signs, and how to talk to your doctor

"Comprehensive without being overloaded with detail and casual in tone without being flip or losing focus, this is one of the most accessible self-help approaches to asthma." Booklist

616.4 Diabetes

Pirner, Connie White

Even little kids get diabetes; pictures by Nadine Bernard Westcott. Whitman, A. 1991 unp il $10.95; pa $4.95 (k-1) 616.4

1. Diabetes
ISBN 0-8075-2158-2; 0-8075-2159-0 (pa)
LC 90-12738

A young girl who has had diabetes since she was two years old describes her adjustments to the disease

"Language is simple, age appropriate, and effectively gets the point across. The ink-and-watercolor drawings are lively and often upbeat. . . . Perhaps the most valuable part of the book is the 'note for parents,' which relates Pirner's personal experience over the last three years in caring for a diabetic child." SLJ

Tiger, Steven

Diabetes; illustrated by Michael Reingold. Messner 1987 63p il (Understanding disease series) lib bdg $13.98 (5 and up) 616.4

1. Diabetes
ISBN 0-671-63273-6
LC 86-23498

This book discusses "diabetes, its history, victims, treatment, and current developments in research. Diabetes Types I and II are examined as aberrations of the metabolic process, . . . followed by mention of the lesser types, including diabetes during pregnancy, hyperglycemia, and hypoglycemia. Symptoms and diagnosis, current treatment, and the outlook for the disease conclude the text." SLJ

Includes glossary

616.86 Substance abuse (Drug abuse)

Friedman, David P.

Focus on drugs and the brain; illustrated by David Neuhaus. 21st Cent. Bks. (NY) 1990 64p il (Drug-alert book) $14.95 (3-6)

616.86

1. Drugs 2. Drug abuse 3. Psychotropic drugs
ISBN 0-941477-95-9 LC 89-28417
The author begins "by defining psychoactive drugs—those that change the way people think, feel, or behave and explaining why people use them. He then describes the function of the brain and nervous system and delineates how these drugs affect the body. The author also provides information on addiction and drug treatment." Booklist
This book "provides a fine introduction to the topic of licit and illicit drugs. It explains enough about brain function so that young people will understand why psychoactive drugs are so pleasureable and potentially dangerous." Appraisal
Includes glossary

Hyde, Margaret Oldroyd, 1917-

Alcohol: uses and abuses; [by] Margaret O. Hyde. Enslow Pubs. 1988 96p il lib bdg $16.95 (4 and up)

616.86

1. Alcohol 2. Alcoholism
ISBN 0-89490-155-9 LC 87-12161
The author "describes the medical and social problems that alcohol causes alcoholics and the community in which they live. . . . Using hypothetical cases and simulated situations, she equips readers with information on how to get help for the alcoholic, how to get help for themselves as children of alcoholics, and how to act in social situations, emphasizing that sometimes there are no right answers and that not all stories have a happy ending." SLJ
"It is factual, yet interesting, due to its many vignettes of young peoples' experiences with alcohol." BAYA Book Rev
Includes glossary and bibliography

Know about smoking; [by] Margaret O. Hyde. 3rd ed. Walker & Co. 1995 100p il $13.95; lib bdg $14.85 (4 and up) **616.86**

1. Smoking
ISBN 0-8027-8399-6; 0-8027-8400-3 (lib bdg)
LC 94-45287
First published 1983
"Hyde discusses the history of nicotine and tobacco, effects on the body, public perceptions, and prevention, paying particular attention to advertising." SLJ
Includes glossary and bibliography

Perry, Robert Louis, 1950-

Focus on nicotine and caffeine; [by] Robert Perry; illustrated by David Neuhaus. 21st Cent. Bks. (NY) 1990 64p il (Drug-alert book) $14.95 (3-6)

616.86

1. Smoking 2. Caffeine
ISBN 0-941477-99-1 LC 89-20409
The author discusses the history, effects, social aspects, and physical dangers of using tobacco and caffeine products
"An excellent resource for teachers in the elementary grades." Sci Books Films

Seixas, Judith S.

Drugs—what they are, what they do; illustrated by Tom Huffman. Greenwillow Bks. 1987 47p il $15; lib bdg $11.88 (1-3)

616.86

1. Drugs 2. Drug abuse
ISBN 0-688-07399-9; 0-688-07400-6 (lib bdg)
LC 86-33624
"A Greenwillow read-alone book"
This book "begins with a definition of drugs and [seeks to] explain such topics as drug tolerance, and what factors can influence the effect of a drug on a person. The test focuses on psychoactive drugs like stimulants and hallucinogens." Appraisal
"The book's organization helps take the reader on a journey through readable text and clever illustrations about the different kinds of psychoactive drugs, how they are used, how they make one feel, and what their effects are. There is also an important chapter on 'How to Say No,' giving the reader many appropriate responses if asked to try drugs. It is important that young children be educated through excellent books of this type on the hazards and consequences of drug use." Sci Books Films

Tobacco; what it is, what it does; illustrated by Tom Huffman. Greenwillow Bks. 1981 55p il $13.95 (1-3) **616.86**

1. Smoking
ISBN 0-688-00769-4 LC 81-837
"A Greenwillow read-alone book"
The text begins with "a brief geographical history of tobacco, then concentrates on cigarette smoking in particular; its social history, consequences for health and the psychological factors involved in starting and stopping. The anti-smoking case, is well-documented with many physiological explanations, and though the cartoonlike line drawings and diagrams are not detailed . . . this emerges as a well-reasoned argument and a useful source of information." SLJ

616.9 Other diseases

Balkwill, Frances R.

Cell wars; by Fran Balkwill; illustrated by Mic Rolph. Carolrhoda Bks. 1993 28p il lib bdg $18.95; pa $8.95 (3-6) **616.9**

1. Immunity 2. Viruses 3. Bacteria
ISBN 0-87614-761-9 (lib bdg); 0-87614-637-X (pa)
LC 92-6377
First published 1990 in the United Kingdom
This "focuses on the human immune system, particularly on how specialized cells in the body help to contain and destroy viral and bacterial infections and repair damage to healthy cells and tissue." Appraisal
"Ideas are presented clearly and concisely in an appropriately conversational tone, often with splashes of humor. Difficult concepts are easily understood, while vibrant colors and cartoonlike characters of both sexes and various ethnicities add to the appeal." SLJ

Berger, Melvin, 1927-

Germs make me sick! illustrated by Marylin Hafner. rev ed. HarperCollins Pubs. 1995 32p il (Let's-read-and-find-out science books) $14.95; lib bdg $14.89; pa $4.95 (k-3)

616.9

1. Bacteria 2. Viruses

ISBN 0-06-024249-3; 0-06-024250-7 (lib bdg); 0-06-445154-2 (pa)   LC 93-27059

First published 1985

Explains how bacteria and viruses affect the human body and how the body fights them

This features "Hafner's lively color cartoon illustrations. . . . [It offers a] lively combination of fact and narrative that has made this a great title for easy reading and for sharing aloud." Booklist

Hyde, Margaret Oldroyd, 1917-

Know about tuberculosis; [by] Margaret O. Hyde. Walker & Co. 1994 106p il $13.95; lib bdg $14.85 (4 and up)   **616.9**

1. Tuberculosis

ISBN 0-8027-8338-4; 0-8027-8339-2 (lib bdg)   LC 94-26288

This is an "account of the history of tuberculosis and various methods of treating it over the centuries. . . . The link between TB and AIDS, and poverty and homelessness is also discussed and personal narratives detail the spread of TB within these groups." Voice Youth Advocates

"There is an interesting selection of black-and-white illustrations and graphs." SLJ

Includes glossary

Landau, Elaine

Lyme disease. Watts 1990 63p il lib bdg $13.93 (4 and up)   **616.9**

1. Lyme disease

ISBN 0-531-10931-3   LC 89-70514

"A First book"

The author examines topics such as "the tick that causes the disease, its life cycle, and the ways in which it infects and affects human beings and other life forms; she discusses symptoms, progress of Lyme disease, and treatment, and . . . current measures of prevention and of diagnosis." Bull Cent Child Books

"Plentiful photographs support the text and the book's design is handsome." Booklist

Includes glossary and bibliography

Rabies. Lodestar Bks. 1993 52p il $14.99 (4 and up)   **616.9**

1. Rabies

ISBN 0-525-67403-9   LC 92-26117

Discusses rabies and its effects, how it is spread, how to protect animals and humans, and scientific advances in its control

"The informative text and photographs make this book outstanding." Sci Child

Includes glossary and bibliography

Silverstein, Alvin

Lyme disease, the great imitator; how to prevent and cure it; by Alvin Silverstein, Virginia Silverstein & Robert Silverstein; with a foreword by Leonard H. Sigal. AVSTAR Pub. Corp. 1990 126p il hardcover o.p. paperback available $5.95 (6 and up)

616.9

1. Lyme disease

ISBN 0-9623653-9-4 (pa)   LC 90-81250

Discusses the scope and history of this growing health problem, its medical and ecological background, symptoms, diagnosis, treatment, practical methods for avoiding infection, and current research into possible cures

This "is a well organized and thorough account, taking complex topics and making them understandable without oversimplification." Appraisal

Includes glossary and bibliography

616.97   Diseases of the immune system

Greenberg, Lorna

AIDS; how it works in the body. Watts 1992 64p il lib bdg $12.90 (4 and up)

616.97

1. AIDS (Disease)

ISBN 0-531-20074-4   LC 91-28620

"A First book"

The author "reviews the current knowledge about HIV and AIDS within an overall historical, generic context. The reader learns about basic science, the pathogenesis of a 'new' virus, AIDS-associated infectious diseases, and the treatment and prevention of cancer in an easy-to-read, interesting style. The young reader is enticed further by superb color illustrations throughout the text." Sci Books Films

Includes glossary and bibliography

Hausherr, Rosmarie

Children and the AIDS virus; a book for children, parents, & teachers. Clarion Bks. 1989 48p il lib bdg $15.95; pa $6.95 (1-3)

616.97

1. AIDS (Disease)

ISBN 0-89919-834-1 (lib bdg); 0-395-51167-4 (pa)   LC 88-39196

In this book the author seeks to explain what a virus is, how the AIDS virus affects the body, and how it is contracted. She examines the lives of two children who have AIDS

"With thoughtfully composed black-and-white photos attractively placed throughout, Hausherr's text forthrightly and nonthreateningly fosters schoolchildren's understanding of AIDS." Booklist

Includes bibliography

Seixas, Judith S.
Allergies; what they are, what they do; illustrated by Tom Huffman. Greenwillow Bks. 1991 55p il $12.95; lib bdg $12.88 (1-3)
616.97

1. Allergy
ISBN 0-688-09638-7; 0-688-08877-5 (lib bdg)
LC 90-30753
"A Greenwillow read-alone book"
Outlines various types of allergy symptoms and describes diagnostic and treatment procedures
"Well written, clear, and readable, the text avoids condescension. . . . Two-color cartoon-style drawings are amusing and add interest." SLJ

Terkel, Susan Neiburg, 1948-
All about allergies; illustrated by Paul Harvey. Lodestar Bks. 1993 57p il $13.99 (2-4)
616.97

1. Allergy
ISBN 0-525-67410-1
LC 92-17770
Provides information about different kinds of allergies, and their symptoms, diagnoses, and treatments
This is a "good-humored yet straightforward introduction to a problem that affects many youngsters. . . . A welcome addition to the shelves. The crisp line drawings are nicely executed and sometimes humorous." Booklist
Includes glossary and bibliography

616.99 Tumors and cancers

Bergman, Thomas
One day at a time; children living with leukemia. Gareth Stevens Children's Bks. 1989 56p il (Don't turn away) lib bdg $18.60 (1-3)
616.99

1. Leukemia
ISBN 1-55532-913-6
LC 88-42972
This book records in photographs and text, some of the experiences of leukemia patients Hanna and Frederick, ages 2 and three. Appended are a question and answer section
"Noted Swedish photographer, Bergman . . . looks unflinchingly at children who have had to cope with difficulties most people can only imagine; yet there's not a trace of condescension—only a sense of caring and an affirmation of life. . . . Uniquely informative and will push readers to reexamine their own feelings about seriously disabled individuals." Booklist
Includes glossary and bibliography

Landau, Elaine
Cancer. 21st Cent. Bks. (NY) 1994 64p il (Understanding illness) lib bdg $15.95 (6 and up)
616.99

1. Cancer
ISBN 0-8050-2990-7
LC 94-13844
This volume explains the symptoms, diagnosis, and treatment of cancer and addresses preventive measures and how to live with the disease
This work is "clearly written and well documented. . . . Average-quality, full-color photographs make the [discussion] accessible and understandable." SLJ
Includes glossary and bibliography

Terkel, Susan Neiburg, 1948-
Understanding cancer; by Susan Neiburg Terkel and Marlene Lupiloff-Brazz; illustrated by Annette Shaw. Watts 1993 54p il lib bdg $18.90 (3-5)
616.99

1. Cancer
ISBN 0-531-11085-0
LC 92-38715
An introduction to cancer, its types and treatments, and the common emotions associated with cancer
"This book fills a need, both in terms of information in an easily accessible format for children and in terms of emotional support for those with a family member or friend suffering from the disease." Booklist
Includes glossary and bibliography

617.6 Dentistry

Kuklin, Susan
When I see my dentist. Bradbury Press 1988 unp il $13.95 (k-3)
617.6

1. Dentistry
ISBN 0-02-751231-2
LC 87-25695
"Erica's trip to the dentist includes visiting his assistant for teeth cleaning, a brushing lesson, and an explanation of how sugar harms teeth. As Dr. Steve examines and x-rays her teeth, he explains every procedure to Erica." Booklist
"Kuklin has included rather serious-looking pictures with less formal moments; this accounts for her reassuring tone, which neither white washes the truth nor makes the visit sound too scary." Publ Wkly

Rockwell, Harlow, 1910-1988
My dentist. Greenwillow Bks. 1975 unp il $15; lib bdg $15.93; pa $4.95 (k-1)
617.6

1. Dentistry
ISBN 0-688-80011-4; 0-688-84004-3 (lib bdg); 0-688-07040-X (pa)
This is a "straightforward run-through of a routine trip to the dentist. A young patient describes each of the pieces of standard dental equipment she sees on her visit and explains how her dentist uses them." SLJ
"Because of the simple, restrained format, and because of the precise, detailed illustrations, the author-illustrator has been able to turn what can be a frightening experience for a child into an understandable, necessary event." Horn Book

Rogers, Fred
Going to the dentist; photographs by Jim Judkis. Putnam 1989 unp il hardcover o.p. paperback available $6.95 (k-2)
617.6

1. Dentistry
ISBN 0-399-21634-0 (pa)
LC 88-15045
This work describes a visit to the dentist and the procedures and equipment which will be encountered during a dental examination
"The attractively photographed volume features young patients and dentists in a happy mix of races and genders, and timely inclusion of the now standard gloves and masks worn by staff sets this book apart." Horn Book

617.8   Otology and audiology

Levine, Edna Simon, 1910-1992

Lisa and her soundless world; by Edna S. Levine; illustrated by Gloria Kamen. Human Sciences Press 1974 unp il $18.95; pa $10.95 (1-3)   **617.8**

1. Deafness 2. Deaf
ISBN 0-87705-104-6; 0-89885-204-8 (pa)

This book follows the progress of a little girl with impaired hearing who gains some hearing by using a hearing aid and learns to lip read and use speech

"The book accomplishes several things: it makes the deaf child's plight explicit, it makes clear the difficulty a deaf child has in learning to speak, it explains why a child so handicapped may feel angry and unloved, and it stresses the fact that the halting speech of the deaf may be governed by physical limitations, that it is not due to a lack of intelligence." Bull Cent Child Books

620   Engineering and allied operations

Bortz, Alfred B.

Catastrophe! great engineering failure—and success; by Fred Bortz; illustrations by Gary Tong. Scientific Am. Bks. for Young Readers 1995 80p il maps (Scientific American mysteries of science) $19.95; pa $13.95 (5 and up)   **620**

1. Engineering 2. Disasters 3. Accidents
ISBN 0-7167-6538-1; 0-7167-6539-X (pa)
         LC 94-37774

"Beginning with the origin, meaning, and usefulness of Murphy's law, Bortz looks at catastrophic events involving a skywalk at a Kansas City hotel, the Tacoma Narrows Bridge, DC-10 airplanes, the space shuttle *Challenger*, nuclear power plants, and the northeastern U.S. power grid. Throughout the book, Bortz focuses on the avoidance of problems through anticipation of unusual situations." Booklist

"The lively text and the high-quality black-and-white photographs vividly set the scene and report the details. The clear explanations of the science behind each event is enhanced by diagrams." SLJ

Skurzynski, Gloria

Almost the real thing; simulation in your high-tech world; with photographs chosen and arranged by the author. Bradbury Press 1991 64p il $16.95 (5 and up)   **620**

1. Simulation methods
ISBN 0-02-778072-4   LC 91-238

An introduction to physical and computer simulations, focusing on the use of wind tunnels, air and automotive safety testing, astronaut training, and current and future uses of images created by computer simulation

"High-quality, full-color photographs and computer-generated graphics illustrate the six chapters. An excellent and lively book on an offbeat topic." SLJ

Includes glossary

621   Applied physics

Challoner, Jack

Energy. Dorling Kindersley 1993 64p il (Eyewitness science) $15.95 (4 and up)
         621

1. Energy resources 2. Force and energy
ISBN 1-56458-232-9   LC 92-54479

Surveys various sources of energy and the ways in which they have been harnessed

This "serves well as a first exploration of its topic, emphasizing historical connections but also considering technological and societal aspects. [This book's] striking visual impact will draw in even the most casual readers." SLJ

621.381   Electronics

Asimov, Isaac, 1920-1992

How did we find out about microwaves? illustrated by Erika Kors. Walker & Co. 1989 63p il $11.95; lib bdg $12.85 (5 and up)
         621.381

1. Microwaves
ISBN 0-8027-6837-7; 0-8027-6838-5 (lib bdg)
         LC 88-20470

Describes the discovery of microwaves and explains how they function and their many uses

"An excellent summary of how scientists gradually made discoveries about microwaves and how this knowledge has been used in many different ways. . . . The information is presented in a concise and fast-paced manner, yet the book is always readable, and gives young people a clear understanding of how scientific discoveries are built upon the discoveries that proceeded them." SLJ

621.382   Communications engineering

Skurzynski, Gloria

Get the message; telecommunications in your high-tech world. Bradbury Press 1993 64p il $16.95 (5 and up)   **621.382**

1. Telephone 2. Telecommunication
ISBN 0-02-778071-6   LC 92-14892

Explains the scientific principles and technology involved in telephone calls and facsimile transmissions and discusses future possibilities in telecommunications

"The writing is lively, clear, and follows a logical sequence. Explanations are basic and thorough. The mostly full-color photographs and illustrations are captioned and provide relevant information." SLJ

Includes glossary

621.43 Internal-combustion engines and propulsion

Maurer, Richard, 1950-

Rocket! how a toy launched the space age. Crown 1995 64p il $17; lib bdg $17.99 (5 and up)   **621.43**

1. Goddard, Robert Hutchings, 1882-1945 2. Rocketry
ISBN 0-517-59628-8; 0-517-59629-6 (lib bdg)
LC 94-19243

"Maurer guides readers from early science fiction speculations of rocket travel to the scientific trials and errors of three important scientists—Robert Goddard, Hermann Oberth, and Konstantin Tsiolkovsky—and to the U.S.-Soviet space race." Booklist

"An interesting and informative introduction to the history of modern rocketry." SLJ

Includes bibliography

621.44 Geothermal engineering

Jacobs, Linda

Letting off steam; the story of geothermal energy. Carolrhoda Bks. 1989 47p il (Carolrhoda earth watch book) lib bdg $19.95; pa $6.95 (3-6)   **621.44**

1. Geothermal resources 2. Steam
ISBN 0-87614-300-1 (lib bdg); 0-87614-510-1 (pa)
LC 88-6147

The author examines how geothermal energy, the force underlying hot springs, geysters, and mudpots, is being used as an alternative energy source in various parts of the world

This "is an extremely interesting book. . . . Linda Jacobs has taken a relatively advanced scientific topic and made it accessible for young readers. Her format combines well-explained vocabulary with excellent photographs, diagrams, and boxed topic highlights." Appraisal

621.48 Nuclear engineering

Pringle, Laurence P.

Nuclear energy: troubled past, uncertain future. Macmillan 1989 124p il $14.95 (5 and up)   **621.48**

1. Nuclear energy
ISBN 0-02-775391-3
LC 88-28664

First published 1979 with title: Nuclear power

The author looks "at nuclear energy, examining the history, development, and current status of nuclear technology—from the basic physics of splitting the atom to the search for an ultrasafe reactory—and the many changes in nuclear economics, politics, and safety that have occured in the 1980s." Publisher's note

"The information is current, in depth, and clearly presented. The physics behind nuclear reactors is explained without writing down to readers or losing them in technical jargon. Highly recommended." Voice Youth Advocates

Includes glossary and bibliography

621.8 Machine engineering

Burnie, David

Machines and how they work; written by David Burnie. Dorling Kindersley 1991 64p il (See & explore library) $12.95; lib bdg $12.99 (5 and up)   **621.8**

1. Machinery
ISBN 1-879431-15-7; 1-879431-30-0 (lib bdg)
LC 91-060147

This volume "traces the evolution and use of the earliest muscle-powered machines, such as the fiddle borer and the shaduf, to modern robots used on automobile assembly lines. Each facing page spread describes related equipment. Some unusual offerings are offshore-oil rigs, roller coasters, tunnel-making machines, fire-fighting equipment, and large construction machines. [It features] two-page topic treatments with full-color illustrations and diagrams with labels and accompanying captions." SLJ

Hoban, Tana

Dig, drill, dump, fill. Greenwillow Bks. 1975 unp il $14.93; pa $3.95   **621.8**

1. Machinery
ISBN 0-688-84016-7; 0-688-11703-1 (pa)

"This all-photographic presentation shows loaders, rollers, dump trucks, and other heavy construction machines at work. What they are and what they do are explained simply and concisely in a three-page picture glossary." Publisher's note

Robbins, Ken

Power machines. Holt & Co. 1993 unp il $15.95 (k-3)   **621.8**

1. Machinery
ISBN 0-8050-1410-1
LC 92-30649

"Using his hallmark hand-tinted photographs, Robbins presents 13 different power machines." SLJ

"Each double-spread display includes at least two photos as well as a catchy header ('Crush and Grind' for the concrete crusher; 'Scoop and Dump' for the payloader). Robbins distills the essence of each of the big machines into a single paragraph, minimal but meaty enough to satisfy even the most demanding truck aficionado." Publ Wkly

Rockwell, Anne F., 1934-

Machines; by Anne & Harlow Rockwell. Macmillan 1972 unp il lib bdg $13.95 (k-1)   **621.8**

1. Machinery
ISBN 0-02-777520-8

This book describes machines and machine parts: pulley, block and tackle, gear, jackscrew, sprocket

"One of the highlights of the book is the use of full-color watercolor paintings as illustrations of the types of machines. Large primary print is used describing the simple machines such as the wheel or gears." Sci Books

Zubrowski, Bernie, 1939-
Wheels at work; building and experimenting with models of machines; illustrated by Roy Doty. Morrow 1986 112p il lib bdg $16.75 (4 and up)   **621.8**
1. Machinery 2. Wheels 3. Science—Experiments
ISBN 0-688-06348-9   LC 86-12500
"A Boston Children's Museum activity book"
Instructions for using readily available materials to make models of machines such as pulleys, windlasses, and water wheels, with suggested experiments to demonstrate their capabilities
"Since most models have more than one easily adjusted variation, this book is great vacation-time fun for mechanically minded young people. An adult might need to help with hammering a hole in one model and puncturing holes (in soft materials) in others, giving parents and children an opportunity to explore simple physics together. An invaluable resource book." SLJ

621.9   Tools and fabricating equipment

Gibbons, Gail
Tool book. Holiday House 1982 unp il lib bdg $15.95; pa $5.95 (k-3)   **621.9**
1. Tools
ISBN 0-8234-0444-7 (lib bdg); 0-8234-0694-6 (pa)
                                        LC 81-13386
This book depicts a number of different tools used in building and the kinds of work they are used for
"Gibbons's pictures are clear, colorful, accurate, and detailed. It is simple enough to use with a toddler who has just discovered tools yet sophisticated enough for a first grader to learn about tools and their use." Child Book Rev Serv

Rockwell, Anne F., 1934-
The toolbox; by Anne & Harlow Rockwell. Macmillan 1971 unp il $13.95; pa $3.95 (k-1)
                                        621.9
1. Tools
ISBN 0-02-777540-2; 0-689-71382-7 (pa)
Illustrated by Harlow Rockwell, this book describes the contents of a toolbox and explains the uses of each tool
"A picture book celebrates with unadorned economy of words and illustrations the simple beauty of useful tools. The brief text is printed in clear, handsome type; very little boys—and undoubtedly some girls as well—will pore over the appreciative portraits of common implements, which make ingenious use of watercolor to show textures and surfaces of wood and metal." Horn Book

623.8   Nautical engineering and seamanship

Butterfield, Moira
Ships; illustrated by Jonathan Potter; written by Moira Butterfield. Dorling Kindersley 1994 32p il (Look inside cross-sections) pa $5.95 (4 and up)   **623.8**
1. Ships 2. Seafaring life
ISBN 1-56458-521-2   LC 93-46382

"Ten ships are presented, each in a two-page spread (except for the *USS Lexington,* which gets four) that contains on average six sentences of facts and a box entitled 'Technical Data,' which lists length, beam, and other details. Children will probably be more interested in the clear, detailed, well-labeled drawings." SLJ
Includes glossary

Weiss, Harvey, 1922-
Submarines and other underwater craft. Crowell 1990 64p il lib bdg $13.89 (4 and up)
                                        623.8
1. Submarines 2. Submersibles
ISBN 0-690-04761-4   LC 89-37614
The author examines "the principles on which submersibles work . . . [and their] history. Subsequent discussion covers war uses and antisubmarine tactics, disasters, life aboard submarines, movement underwater, and the design and uses of . . . different machines." Horn Book

624   Civil engineering

Doherty, Craig A.
The Golden Gate Bridge; [by] Craig A. Doherty and Katherine M. Doherty. Blackbirch Press 1995 48p il map (Building America) lib bdg $14.95 (4-6)   **624**
1. Golden Gate Bridge (San Francisco, Calif.) 2. Bridges
ISBN 1-56711-106-8   LC 94-29996
Black-and-white and full-color photographs complement an examination of the architectural and engineering aspects of the construction of San Francisco's celebrated bridge
Includes glossary and bibliography

Oxlade, Chris
Bridges and tunnels; illustrated by Raymond Turvey; photography by Martyn Chillmaid. Watts 1994 32p il (Technology craft topics) lib bdg $12.60 (4-6)   **624**
1. Bridges 2. Tunnels 3. Handicraft
ISBN 0-531-14328-7   LC 93-41962
This "book explores the technological principles underlying the construction of various types of bridges and tunnels. . . . Seven two-page chapters describe the value of bridges and tunnels for commerce and transportation, the distinguishing structural characteristics of various types of bridges (e.g., suspension bridges, beams and cantilevers, arch bridges), and methods of tunneling (e.g., through mountains, under water). Each of the first six chapters is followed by instructions on how to construct a model that relates to the topic described in the chapter." Sci Books Films
Includes glossary and bibliography

Robbins, Ken
Bridges. Dial Bks. 1991 30p il $13.95; lib bdg $13.89 (k-3)   **624**
1. Bridges
ISBN 0-8037-0929-3; 0-8037-0930-7 (lib bdg)
                                        LC 90-35776
Hand-colored photographs illustrate bridges of many different types, with descriptions of their design and use
"The magical quality of bridges spanning space is captured in text and illustrations. . . . The hand-tinted photo-

Robbins, Ken—*Continued*
graphs poetically capture vistas of sky and water and portray the spider-web-like fragility as well as the great strength of bridges." Horn Book

624.1 Structural engineering and underground construction

Gibbons, Gail
Tunnels. Holiday House 1984 unp il lib bdg $15.95; pa $5.95 (k-3)   **624.1**

1. Tunnels

ISBN 0-8234-0507-9 (lib bdg); 0-8234-0670-9 (pa)
LC 83-18589
After "noting the underground passages animals build for homes and food storage, the book emphasizes the tunnels humans build to gain access to raw materials, such as ore and coal, and to gain passage under cities, under water, and through mountains. Tunnel shapes and types are discussed." Horn Book
The author "describes the different kinds of tunnels and illustrates their structures in cutaway diagrams. Most children find the subject appealing, and this introduces it very simply." Bull Cent Child Books

Macaulay, David, 1946-
Underground. Houghton Mifflin 1976 109p il $16.95; pa $8.95 (4 and up)   **624.1**

1. Civil engineering 2. Building 3. Public utilities

ISBN 0-395-24739-X; 0-395-34065-9 (pa)
In this "examination of the intricate support systems that lie beneath the street levels of our cities, Macaulay explains the ways in which foundations for buildings are laid or reinforced, and how the various utilities or transportation services are constructed." Bull Cent Child Books
"Introduced by a visual index—a bird's eye view of a busy, hypothetical intersection with colored indicators marking the specific locations analyzed in subsequent pages—detailed illustrations are combined with a clear, precise narrative to make the subject comprehensible and fascinating." Horn Book
Includes glossary

625.1 Railroads

Barton, Byron
Trains. Crowell 1986 unp il $6.95; lib bdg $13.89; pa $2.95 (k-1)   **625.1**

1. Railroads

ISBN 0-694-00061-2; 0-690-04534-4 (lib bdg); 0-694-00601-7 (pa)   LC 85-47898
Brief text and illustrations present a variety of trains and what they do
"The concepts are simple and Barton's illustrations are just enough, and no more." Publ Wkly

Bowler, Michael
Trains; written by Mike Bowler; illustrated by Steve Herridge, Paul Higgens, and Martin Woodward. Raintree Steck-Vaughn Pubs. 1995 32p il (Pointers) lib bdg $19.97 (4 and up)
625.1

1. Railroads

ISBN 0-8114-6192-0   LC 94-9029
This book "uses a historical approach, from the first steam-powered locomotive to the electrical and diesel trains of today. Each stage of development occupies a two-page spread. The information is accurate, and the art is colorful and precise." Sci Books Films
Includes glossary

Coiley, John
Train; written by John Coiley. Knopf 1992 63p il (Eyewitness books) $19; lib bdg $20.99 (4 and up)   **625.1**

1. Railroads

ISBN 0-679-81684-4; 0-679-91684-9 (lib bdg)
LC 92-4711
"A Dorling Kindersley book"
Traces the development of railways from the first Babylonian rutways to the electromagnetic, driverless trains of today and describes how trains are built and operated
"This book will appeal to those who enjoy trains and like to read about and look at a rich visual display of engines, cars, and other artifacts." Sci Books Films

Gibbons, Gail
Trains. Holiday House 1987 unp il lib bdg $15.95; pa $6.95 (k-3)   **625.1**

1. Railroads

ISBN 0-8234-0640-7 (lib bdg); 0-8234-0699-7 (pa)
LC 86-19595
Gibbons illustrates different kinds of trains, past and present, and describes their features and functions

Rockwell, Anne F., 1934-
Trains. Dutton 1988 unp il $13.99 (k-1)
625.1

1. Railroads

ISBN 0-525-44377-0   LC 87-22180
Also available in paperback from Puffin Bks.
"A delightful introduction to a variety of trains that includes steam engines, modern diesel and electric locomotives, subways and monorails. Simple text and bright, full-color drawings that include anthropomorphic foxes." Sci Child

625.4 Rapid transit systems

Hewett, Joan
Tunnels, tracks, and trains; building a subway; photographs by Richard Hewett. Lodestar Bks. 1995 48p il $15.99 (4-6)
625.4

1. Subways

ISBN 0-525-67466-7   LC 94-9037
The authors explore "different aspects of the building of a segment of Los Angeles' subway. The how-to of construct-

Hewett, Joan—*Continued*

ing tunnels, tracks, and stations is covered in interesting detail and documented in photographs that record almost every step of the process, from site preparation to the final readying of the track. . . . Middle-graders will come away not only with an idea of how subways are constructed, but also with a notion of some very interesting jobs." Booklist

625.7 Roads

Gibbons, Gail

New road! Crowell 1983 unp il lib bdg $14.89; pa $4.95 (k-3) **625.7**

1. Roads

ISBN 0-690-04343-0 (lib bdg); 0-06-446059-2 (pa)

LC 82-45917

This "book describes how roads are constructed, focusing on the variety of people with differing skills who participate in the planning and construction of the road and the kinds of equipment used in the actual construction. . . . The final pages of the book consist of a brief pictorial history of roads from Roman times to the concrete and asphalt roads of the present day." SLJ

"The crisp lines and bright poster colors of this road-building exposition are inviting. Gibbons shows the process, scene by scene, from start to finish." Booklist

Hennessy, B. G. (Barbara G.)

Road builders; pictures by Simms Taback. Viking 1994 unp il $14.99 (k-2) **625.7**

1. Roads 2. Trucks

ISBN 0-670-83390-8 LC 93-42248

This book introduces "children to the process of building a road. The focus is on the vehicles involved, depicting them all together and then individually or in pairs as the project unfolds. Taback's cartoon illustration show the multiethnic crew at work and a flatbed truck carrying them to the next job when the highway is completed. This book is a good choice for both beginning readers and preschool construction buffs." SLJ

627 Hydraulic engineering

Doherty, Craig A.

Hoover Dam; [by] Craig A. Doherty and Katherine M. Doherty. Blackbirch Press 1995 48p il (Building America) lib bdg $14.95 (4-6) **627**

1. Hoover Dam (Ariz. and Nev.) 2. Colorado River (Colo.-Mexico)

ISBN 1-56711-107-6 LC 94-23267

This book on the building of Hoover Dam on the Colorado River "details the project, the people involved, and what it took to bring the task to completion. Illustrated with excellent-quality historical photographs, reproductions, and current pictures." SLJ

Includes glossary and bibliography

628.3 Sewage treatment and disposal

Coombs, Karen Mueller, 1947-

Flush! treating wastewater; photographs by Jerry Boucher. Carolrhoda Bks. 1995 56p il lib bdg $16.13 (3-6) **628.3**

1. Sewage disposal

ISBN 0-87614-879-8 LC 94-37676

"Ever wonder what happens to water you flush down the toilet? A step-by-step trip through the process of cleaning wastewater gives a behind-the-scenes look using excellent, full-color photographs. A unique book concerning our most valuable natural resource—water." Sci Child

Includes glossary

628.9 Fire-fighting technology

Bingham, Caroline

Fire truck. Dorling Kindersley 1995 21p il (Mighty machines) $9.95 (k-3) **628.9**

1. Fire engines

ISBN 0-7894-0212-2 LC 95-12442

This "book features brief descriptions and full-color photos of fire-fighting equipment, from aerial ladder trucks to airport crash rescue and support vehicles. Numerous labels and captions, as well as 'Amazing Facts,' add interest." SLJ

Kuklin, Susan

Fighting fires. Bradbury Press 1993 unp il $14.95 (k-3) **628.9**

1. Fire fighters

ISBN 0-02-751238-X LC 92-38678

Text and photographs present the vehicles, equipment, and procedures used by fire fighters

The "full-color photographs vary in size from quarter to full page. Most of the action shots look a little staged, but are not stiff. Kuklin's prose reads easily and smoothly. . . . An excellent title to use with a community social-studies unit and during fire prevention week." SLJ

Maass, Robert

Fire fighters. Scholastic 1989 unp il hardcover o.p. paperback available $3.95 (k-3) **628.9**

1. Fire fighters

ISBN 0-590-41460-7 (pa) LC 88-18340

This describes what it means to be a firefighter, including life at the firehouse, practice drills, service to the community, and fire emergencies

"Many full-color photographs, some of excellent artistic quality, illustrate this behind-the-scenes look at the life of a big-city fire fighter. The brief text is clearly written. . . . Although most young aspiring fire fighters might seek the excitement of danger, Maass' book, in its realistic look at the other activities of fire fighters, provides a reasonable balance." SLJ

Rockwell, Anne F., 1934-

Fire engines; by Anne Rockwell. Dutton 1986 unp il $13.99 (k-1) **628.9**

1. Fire engines
ISBN 0-525-44259-6   LC 86-4464
Also available in paperback from Puffin Bks.

Describes the parts of a fire engine and how fire fighters use them to fight fires

This book provides "crisp, bright illustrations in a spectrum of primary colors; a direct, simple text that is personalized by the use of the first person to heighten the appeal to very young children; and solid information conveyed in a picture book format." SLJ

629.04 Transportation engineering

Baer, Edith, 1924-

This is the way we go to school; a book about children around the world; illustrated by Steven Björkman. Scholastic 1990 unp il map hardcover o.p. paperback available $3.95 (k-2) **629.04**

1. Vehicles 2. Transportation
ISBN 0-590-43162-5 (pa)   LC 89-48511
Also available Spanish language edition

Describes, in rhymed text and illustrations, the many different modes of transportation children all over the world use to get to school

"The various vehicles . . . are informative and interesting, and the multicultural lesson is deftly understated. Pen-and-watercolor illustrations are fresh and optimistic." Bull Cent Child Books

Rockwell, Anne F., 1934-

Things that go; [by] Anne Rockwell. Dutton 1986 23p il hardcover o.p. paperback available $3.95 (k-1) **629.04**

1. Transportation 2. Vehicles
ISBN 0-525-44703-2 (pa)   LC 86-6199

Trains, tow trucks, sailboats, buses, sleds, jeeps, bicycles, and other things that go can be seen in the city, in the country, on the water, in the park, and many other places

"Rockwell's familiar animals briskly propel the vehicles, toys and tools; each confetti-colored spread is crammed with action. An amiable compendium of information for young readers." Publ Wkly

Somerville, Louisa

Rescue vehicles; illustrated by Hans Jenssen; written by Louisa Somerville. Dorling Kindersley 1995 32p il (Look inside cross-sections) pa $5.95 (4 and up) **629.04**

1. Vehicles
ISBN 1-56458-879-3   LC 94-23756

This volume includes labeled cross-section drawings of 12 rescue vehicles, including a police car, fire engine, lifeboat, ambulance, and helicopter, with brief text

Includes glossary

629.13 Aeronautics

Berliner, Don, 1930-

Before the Wright brothers. Lerner Publs. 1990 72p il lib bdg $19.95 (5 and up) **629.13**

1. Aeronautics—History 2. Flight—History
ISBN 0-8225-1588-1   LC 89-31837

The author "tracks the evolution of successful human-controlled flight through a series of short vignettes of experimenters, beginning with George Cayley in the early 1800s. Unfamiliar names, such as William Henson and John Stringfellow, are intermixed with more familiar ones, such as Hiram Maxim, Otto Lilienthal, Octave Chanute, and Samuel Langley." Sci Books Films

"Berliner writes clear, declarative sentences filled with the facts needed for reports. Every page has a well-drawn sketch or a clearly reproduced archival photograph, giving a period atmosphere to the book." SLJ

Includes bibliography

Boyne, Walter J., 1929-

The Smithsonian book of flight for young people. Atheneum Pubs. 1988 128p il $16.95 (4 and up) **629.13**

1. Aeronautics—History 2. Flight—History
ISBN 0-689-31422-1   LC 87-35912

The author "uses clear, concise text and nearly one hundred color and black-and-white photographs to present the history of aviation and explore the triumphs and failures of those who dared to soar like a bird." Sci Child

Includes bibliography

Brown, Don, 1949-

Ruth Law thrills a nation; story and pictures by Don Brown. Ticknor & Fields 1993 unp il $13.95 (k-3) **629.13**

1. Law, Ruth, b. 1887 2. Women air pilots
ISBN 0-395-66404-7   LC 92-45701

Describes the record-breaking flight of a daring woman pilot, Ruth Law, from Chicago to New York in 1916

"Using a simple text and effective watercolors, Brown successfully re-creates the historical flying feat. He sets Law in her historical context with humor and precision." Booklist

Gibbons, Gail

Flying. Holiday House 1986 unp il lib bdg $15.95; pa $5.95 (k-3) **629.13**

1. Aeronautics—History 2. Flight—History
ISBN 0-8234-0599-0 (lib bdg); 0-8234-0977-5 (pa)
     LC 85-22027

Presents a brief history of flight, from balloons evolving into more sophisticated means of air transportation such as helicopters, jet planes, and shuttles

"In primary-color gaiety, Gibbons envisions the history of flight. From the first balloon launch of small barnyard animals to a rocket's stunning ascent, a variety of flying machines race across the pages. Both their development and purposes are covered: cameras aboard a blimp peer into athletic stadiums, propeller planes fight fires and dust crops, and helicopters aid in traffic reporting and rescues at sea. Flying into and out of stylized clouds, Gibbons' vehicles lend vigor to her concise, clear text as she briefly tracks aeronautical highlights." Booklist

Hart, Philip S.
Flying free; America's first black aviators; foreword by Reeve Lindbergh. Lerner Publs. 1992 64p il lib bdg $19.95 (4 and up)
　　　　　　　　　　　　　　　　629.13

1. African American pilots
ISBN 0-8225-1598-9　　　　　　LC 91-21433
Surveys the history of black aviators, from the early black aviation community in Chicago in the 1920s through World War II to modern times
"Hart eloquently documents the lives of America's pioneer black aviators. . . . This well-written account, with quotes from personal and newspaper interviews and historic photographs, brings these inspiring stories to life." SLJ
Includes bibliography

Haskins, James, 1941-
Black eagles; African Americans in aviation. Scholastic 1995 196p il $14.95 (5 and up)
　　　　　　　　　　　　　　　　629.13

1. African American pilots
ISBN 0-590-45912-0　　　　　　LC 94-18623
"Haskins presents the . . . achievements of African-American aviators from the beginning of the twentieth century to the present." Horn Book Guide
"In addition to introducing the people involved, Haskins ably sets the background scene, revealing a social context of discrimination. . . . An excellent job of dealing with the particular and the more general aspects of 'what it was like.'" Booklist
Includes bibliography

Moser, Barry
Fly! a brief history of flight illustrated. Perlman Bks. 1993 unp il lib bdg $15.89 (3-6)
　　　　　　　　　　　　　　　　629.13

1. Flight—History
ISBN 0-06-022894-6　　　　　　LC 92-30960
Highlights sixteen episodes in the development of aviation ranging from balloons to the space shuttle. Also iincludes a time line and historical notes
"The impressive paintings are evocative rather than intricately detailed, but they show the beauty and variety of the aircraft. . . . Moser's text, though brief, contains enough to pique curiosity, and his pictures are certain to attract browsers. His notes, written for an older reader than his main text, are a lively elaboration of the history presented in each spread." Booklist
Includes bibliography

Taylor, Richard L., 1933-
The first unrefueled flight around the world; the story of Dick Rutan and Jeana Yeager and their airplane, Voyager. Watts 1994 63p il lib bdg $13.93 (4 and up)
　　　　　　　　　　　　　　　　629.13

1. Rutan, Dick 2. Yeager, Jeana 3. Voyager (Airplane) 4. Aeronautics—Flights
ISBN 0-531-20176-7　　　　　　LC 94-2596
"A First book"
"A brief description of the design, testing, and record-setting flight of the *Voyager* in December, 1986." SLJ
"The tale of the actual flight is written with suspense and an appropriate amount of detail. Numerous color photos inject reality into this incredible story, which is enhanced by a short listing of facts, figures, and dates." Booklist
Includes bibliography

629.132　Principles of aerial flight

Aaseng, Nathan, 1953-
Breaking the sound barrier. Messner 1992 c1991 107p il hardcover o.p. paperback available $7.95 (6 and up)　　　629.132

1. High speed aeronautics 2. Supersonic transport planes
ISBN 0-671-74213-2 (pa)　　　　LC 91-23693
Chronicles the events leading up to the breaking of the sound barrier, focusing on the test pilots who risked their lives to achieve supersonic flight
"Aaseng's account of the events that led to Chuck Yeager's breaking the sound barrier on October 14, 1947, is fascinating. . . . Along the way, students are treated to a highly readable history of aviation." Booklist
Includes glossary and bibliography

Taylor, Richard L., 1933-
The first supersonic flight; Captain Charles E. Yeager breaks the sound barrier. Watts 1994 63p il lib bdg $13.93 (4 and up)
　　　　　　　　　　　　　　　629.132

1. Yeager, Chuck, 1923- 2. High speed aeronautics
ISBN 0-531-20177-5　　　　　　LC 94-57
"A First book"
This history of high speed flight focuses on Charles Yeager, his plane Glamourous Glennis, and their record-breaking flights over the California desert in 1947
Includes bibliography

629.133　Aircraft types

Johnstone, Michael
Planes; illustrated by Hans Jenssen; written by Michael Johnstone. Dorling Kindersley 1994 32p il (Look inside cross-sections) pa $5.95 (4 and up)　　　　　629.133

1. Airplanes
ISBN 1-56458-520-4　　　　　　LC 93-46373
"Each of the 10 planes featured in this book is drawn in colorful cross sections. Clear labels and narrative texts, coupled with authentic figures, heighten interest and provide information." Sci Books Films
Includes bibliography

Magee, Doug, 1947-
Let's fly from A to Z; [by] Doug Magee and Robert Newman. Cobblehill Bks. 1992 unp il $14 (k-2)　　　　　　　　　　629.133

1. Airplanes 2. Alphabet
ISBN 0-525-65105-5　　　　　　LC 91-39774
"This alphabet book explores the world of airplanes for the beginning reader. The people, places, and things specific to airplanes are clearly described in text and photographs. The young reader is introduced to a host of relevant airplane concepts with accompanying vocabulary. The author includes a page of airplane radio talk that young airplane buffs will find intriguing." Sci Child

Munro, Roxie, 1945-
Blimps. Dutton 1988 unp il $12.95 (2-4)
629.133

1. Airships
ISBN 0-525-44441-6 LC 88-18138
Also available in paperback from Puffin Bks.
A "description of blimps, their history, manufacture, and historical as well as current use. Munro also delineates the launching and piloting of the large airship. Her watercolor illustrations are attractive in their simplicity, although there are no diagrams to aid understanding. The text, however, is concise and easy to understand." SLJ

Nahum, Andrew
Flying machine; written by Andrew Nahum. Knopf 1990 62p il (Eyewitness books) $19; lib bdg $18.99 (4 and up) **629.133**

1. Aeronautics—History
ISBN 0-679-80744-6; 0-679-90744-0 (lib bdg)
LC 90-4007
Also available Spanish language edition
A photo essay tracing the history and development of aircraft from hot-air balloons to jetliners. Includes information on the principles of flight and the inner workings of various flying machines
"Strikingly clear images leap from a white background; numerous captions and brief text encourage browsing over methodical exploration. The whole effect is made orderly by careful layout and unobtrusive black outlines around each spread." SLJ

Parker, Steve
What's inside airplanes? Bedrick Bks. 1995 c1993 45p il lib bdg $16.95 **629.133**

1. Airplanes
ISBN 0-87226-394-0 LC 94-48544
First published 1993 in the United Kingdom
This volume includes labeled cross section drawings of various types of aircraft and their parts including gliders, early airplanes, blimps, aircraft engines, wings, steering controls, fuel systems, navigation and landing gear
Includes glossary

Rockwell, Anne F., 1934-
Planes; by Anne Rockwell. Dutton 1985 unp il lib bdg $13.99 (k-1) **629.133**

1. Airplanes
ISBN 0-525-44159-X LC 84-13732
Also available in paperback from Puffin Bks.
"With simple text and clear, cheerful watercolors, Rockwell introduces preschoolers to airplanes. Her brightly colored illustrations depict seaplanes and helicopters, jets and model planes as they fly over mountains, seas, cities and farms, propelled by engines, propellers or (in the case of hang gliders) the wind. . . . This is a fine primary presentation of a popular, often requested subject." SLJ

Tanaka, Shelley
The disaster of the Hindenburg. Scholastic 1993 64p il (Time quest book) $16.95 (4 and up) **629.133**

1. Hindenburg (Airship) 2. Airships
ISBN 0-590-45750-0 LC 92-39434
"A Scholastic/Madison Press book"

Describes the last voyage of the zeppelin, or airship, Hindenburg, which crashed in flames on a New Jersey airfield in 1937, and examines some possible causes for the disaster
"Numerous black-and-white photos of the ship, crew, and passengers give the text life. Full-color pictures of posters and drawings help create a complete understanding of the excitement, complexity, and comfort of traveling on the *Hindenburg*." SLJ
Includes glossary and bibliography

The **Visual** dictionary of flight. Dorling Kindersley 1992 64p il (Eyewitness visual dictionaries) $16.95 (4 and up) **629.133**

1. Airplanes 2. Aeronautics
ISBN 1-56458-101-2 LC 92-7670
Also available Spanish language edition
Text and labeled illustrations depict a variety of historic and modern aircraft and their components, as well as aviation-related equipment
This "offers strikingly visual and comprehensively informative material to provide instant access to the specialized vocabulary of its topic. . . . While simple in presentation [it is] rich in visual splendor." Booklist

629.136 Airports

Maynard, Christopher
Airplane. Dorling Kindersley 1995 21p il (Mighty machines) $9.95 (k-3) **629.136**

1. Airports 2. Airplanes 3. Machinery
ISBN 0-7894-0211-4 LC 95-19035
Explains how the airplanes and major pieces of equipment in an airport work and interact
"Each double-page spread focuses on one very large, clear, close-up photograph of a machine, with lots of visual and textual details all around it, including amazing facts of power and scale." Booklist

629.222 Passenger automobiles

Cole, Joanna
Cars and how they go; illustrated by Gail Gibbons. Crowell 1983 unp il lib bdg $14.89; pa $4.95 (k-3) **629.222**

1. Automobiles
ISBN 0-690-04262-0 (lib bdg); 0-06-446052-5 (pa)
LC 82-45575
"The author explains that wheels make cars go, and describes the several procedures that turn the wheels and the moving or stationary parts that are involved." Bull Cent Child Books
"This picture-book explanation of how a car works is an interesting example of how a complicated topic can be rendered in basic terms without sacrificing key concepts. . . . Gibbons' crisp, pure, sunny illustrations do a good deal of explaining." Booklist

Johnstone, Michael
Cars; illustrated by Alan Austin. Dorling Kindersley 1994 32p il (Look inside cross-sections) pa $5.95 (4 and up)
629.222

1. Automobiles
ISBN 1-56458-681-2 LC 94-18481

Johnstone, Michael—*Continued*
This volume includes labeled cross section drawings of 11 automobiles with brief text
Includes glossary

Rockwell, Anne F., 1934-
Cars; by Anne Rockwell. Dutton 1984 unp il $13.99; pa $3.95 (k-1)   **629.222**
1. Automobiles
ISBN 0-525-44079-8; 0-525-44241-3 (pa)
                                                  LC 83-14080
Also available in paperback from Puffin Bks.
"Rockwell's bright watercolor paintings depict a world in which all sorts of cars are driven to a variety of places by a cast of canine characters." Booklist
"Humor and universality are introduced through the canine characters who operate, service, or travel in the engaging vehicles. Despite their generic similarities, each dog is given an expression suited to the occasion." Horn Book

Sutton, Richard
Car; written by Richard Sutton. Knopf 1990 63p il (Eyewitness books) $19 (4 and up)
                                                  629.222
1. Automobiles
ISBN 0-679-80743-8   LC 90-4025
Also available Spanish language edition
A photo essay about the history, development, and impact of automobiles from horseless carriages and Model T Fords to today's high performance racing cars; detailed cutaway photos show how the moving parts of a car work
This book's "highly detailed, crisp photographs are a delight. . . . Its dynamic presentation and technical detail will truly entertain and inform anyone interested in automobiles." SLJ

The **Visual** dictionary of cars. Dorling Kindersley 1992 64p il (Eyewitness visual dictionaries) $16.95; lib bdg $15.99 (4 and up)   **629.222**
1. Automobiles
ISBN 1-56458-007-5; 1-56458-008-3 (lib bdg)
                                                  LC 91-58205
Text and labeled illustrations depict a variety of historical, classic, and contemporary automobiles and their components
This "is comprehensive in its scope. . . . [This features] excellent-quality, full-color photographs and clearly written [text]." SLJ

629.223 Light trucks

Sullivan, George
Here come the monster trucks. Cobblehill Bks. 1989 64p il $15; pa $4.99 (3-6)
                                                  629.223
1. Trucks
ISBN 0-525-65005-9; 0-525-65085-7 (pa)
                                                  LC 88-38464
Narrates the short history of monster trucks—ordinary pickup trucks on four enormous tires—describing some of the outstanding examples of these unusual vehicles, which can be used to crush cars, race, jump cars, and engage in mud bog competition
"Color photographs show action shots; the material is clearly presented; an index and a glossary of 'Monster Words and Terms' are included." Bull Cent Child Books

629.224 Trucks

Barton, Byron
Trucks. Crowell 1986 unp il $6.95; lib bdg $13.89; pa $2.95 (k-1)   **629.224**
1. Trucks
ISBN 0-694-00062-0; 0-690-04530-1 (lib bdg); 0-694-00602-5 (pa)   LC 85-47901
Brief text and illustrations present a variety of trucks from cement trucks to ice-cream trucks, and what they do
"A tightly focused (book) . . . featuring Barton's trademark bright, blocky graphics and spare text." Publ Wkly

Llewellyn, Claire
Truck. Dorling Kindersley 1995 21p il (Mighty machines) $9.95 (k-3)   **629.224**
1. Trucks 2. Machinery
ISBN 1-56458-516-6   LC 94-38034
Brief text accompanies labeled photographs and drawings describing large trucks and machinery used in construction including a giant dump truck, bulldozer, wheel loader, mass excavator, forklift, and paver

Marston, Hope Irvin, 1935-
Big rigs. rev & updated ed. Cobblehill Bks. 1993 unp il $14.99 (1-3)   **629.224**
1. Trucks
ISBN 0-525-65123-3   LC 92-39881
First published 1979 by Dodd Mead
Describes various kinds of tractor-trailer combinations, the biggest trucks on the highway
"This color photo-essay celebrates in words and crisp photos the insides and outsides of these mammoth vehicles. . . . Glossary of CB radio talk appended." Booklist

Rockwell, Anne F., 1934-
Trucks; by Anne Rockwell. Dutton 1984 unp il hardcover o.p. paperback available $3.95 (k-1)   **629.224**
1. Trucks
ISBN 0-525-44432-7 (pa)   LC 84-1556
Also available in paperback from Viking
In this volume "Rockwell introduces the very young to the world of trucks—a world 'peopled' with fully-clothed cats. Illustrated with her usual clear, amusing watercolors, the book begins and ends with toy trucks and in between touches upon such common favorites as ice cream trucks, firetrucks and garbage trucks. The text is simple, sometimes overly so. . . . The appeal to very young children is heightened by the stylistic use of the first person plural." SLJ

Salter, Andrew, 1969-
Trucks; written by Andrew Salter; illustrated by Ian Moores, Mike Saunders, and Gerald Witcomb. Raintree Steck-Vaughn Pubs. 1995 32p il (Pointers) $19.97 (4 and up)
                                                  629.224
1. Trucks
ISBN 0-8114-6189-0   LC 93-49568

Salter, Andrew, 1969-—*Continued*

This work "shows the kinds of trucks in use throughout the world today. The title, however, should probably have been *Large Trucks,* since they are the only type described. There are 12 categories of large trucks, from the straight truck to the tank and low-boy truck. . . . Technical details are accurately included in the fine illustrations." Sci Books Films

Includes glossary

629.225   Work vehicles

Butterfield, Moira

Bulldozers; illustrated by Chris Lyon and Gary Biggin; written by Moira Butterfield. Dorling Kindersley 1995 32p il (Look inside cross-sections) pa $5.95 (4 and up)   **629.225**

1. Vehicles 2. Machinery

ISBN 0-7894-0012-X   LC 94-41309

This volume includes labeled drawings of 12 construction machines, including a dump truck, mining shovel, track paver, and cement mixer

Includes glossary

Llewellyn, Claire

Tractor. Dorling Kindersley 1995 21p il (Mighty machines) $9.95 (k-3)   **629.225**

1. Agricultural machinery

ISBN 1-56458-515-8   LC 94-24403

Labeled photographs and drawings and brief text describe tractors, manure spreaders, plows, combine and forage harvesters, balers, and other agricultural machines

629.227   Cycles

Rockwell, Anne F., 1934-

Bikes; [by] Anne Rockwell. Dutton 1987 unp il hardcover o.p. paperback available $3.95 (k-1)   **629.227**

1. Bicycles

ISBN 0-525-44736-9 (pa)   LC 86-19923

This "picture book shows tigers in a wide variety of locales riding an even greater variety of bikes. . . . Unicycles, tandems, high-speed racers and slower, clumsier delivery bikes are all introduced. Even the more unusual types join the collection: the stationary exercise bike, a trick motorcycle, a motor scooter, trail bikes and mopeds." Publ Wkly

This "is vintage Rockwell: bright, amusing watercolors that convey a comforting tone and illustrate a very simple text." SLJ

629.28   Motor land vehicles and cycles—Tests, driving, maintenance, repairs

Florian, Douglas, 1950-

An auto mechanic. Greenwillow Bks. 1991 unp il (How we work) $13.95; lib bdg $13.88; pa $4.95 (k-1)   **629.28**

1. Automobiles—Maintenance and repair

ISBN 0-688-10635-8; 0-688-10636-6 (lib bdg); 0-688-13104-2 (pa)   LC 90-48809

"Florian uses extra large type and a very simple narrative to make an aspect of the workday world accessible to young children. Nicely sequenced, splashy watercolor washes, bright with yellows, rusts, and blues, follow a red-haired mechanic through the day as he accomplishes the many tasks his job requires." Booklist

Gibbons, Gail

Fill it up! all about service stations. Crowell 1985 unp il lib bdg $14.89 (k-3)   **629.28**

1. Service stations

ISBN 0-690-04440-2   LC 84-45345

"Gibbons records an array of typical activities carried on by men and women on the day shift at John and Peggy's Service Station: not only do the attendants pump gas, but the mechanics replace worn parts, adjust brakes, check wheels, fix flat tires, change oil, and so forth." Booklist

"The concise text is well integrated with bright, cheerful illustration in which equipment described in the text is labeled with the correct terminology. A final page features names and pictures of common service station tools. Accurate and appealing." SLJ

629.4   Astronautics

Graham, Ian, 1953-

Spacecraft; written by Ian Graham; illustrated by Roger Stewart. Raintree Steck-Vaughn Pubs. 1995 32p il (Pointers) lib bdg $19.97 (4 and up)   **629.4**

1. Space vehicles

ISBN 0-8114-6193-9   LC 94-2875

In this book "the reader will find 12 two-page descriptions of rocket-launched spacecraft, from the first Sputnik to the Hubble telescope and the space station *Mir.* Technical details and descriptions are nicely done. Cutaways help to show the internal workings of the American Apollo craft and the Russian Soyuz." Sci Books Films

Includes glossary

Kettelkamp, Larry, 1933-

Living in space. Morrow Junior Bks. 1993 104p il $14 (5 and up)   **629.4**

1. Space stations 2. Space shuttles 3. Space biology

ISBN 0-688-10018-X   LC 92-35118

The author "provides a brief history of U.S. space exploration before explaining how astronauts currently live and work in space and describing existing plans for manned and unmanned space exploration in the near future. . . . The book is a good introduction to the topic of living in space, and it is certain to inspire further reading on the subject. .

Kettelkamp, Larry, 1933— *Continued*
. . The volume is illustrated with black-and-white photographs." Booklist

Smith, Howard Everett, 1927-
Daring the unknown: a history of NASA; [by] Howard E. Smith. Harcourt Brace Jovanovich 1987 178p il $16.95 (5 and up)
629.4

1. United States. National Aeronautics and Space Administration 2. Astronautics—History
ISBN 0-15-200435-1 LC 86-33617
"Gulliver books"
"Lucid text and excellent, black-and-white and color photographs convey the history of the American Space Program from the challenge of Sputnik, to the dramatic Apollo Moon landing, to the shocking Challenger disaster, and plans for future exploration." Sci Child
Includes bibliography

629.45 Manned space flight

Baird, Anne
Space Camp; the great adventure for NASA hopefuls; photographs by Robert Koropp; foreword by Alan B. Shepard, Jr.; introduction by Edward O. Buckbee. Morrow Junior Bks. 1992 48p il $14; lib bdg $13.93; pa $6.95 (4 and up)
629.45

1. Astronautics
ISBN 0-688-10227-1; 0-688-10228-X (lib bdg); 0-688-14423-3 (pa) LC 91-21587
Text and photographs follow young campers as they experience NASA-style astronaut training at the Space Camp in Huntsville, Alabama
The book includes "a plethora of candid, full-color photographs. . . . The kids' own words add drama and immediacy to Baird's colorful narrative." Booklist

Barton, Byron
I want to be an astronaut. Crowell 1988 unp il $14; lib bdg $14.89; pa $4.95 (k-1)
629.45

1. Astronautics
ISBN 0-694-00261-5; 0-690-04744-4 (lib bdg); 0-06-443280-7 (pa) LC 87-24311
"First-person text describes the experiences the speaker might have on a space mission. Simple text and bold, full-color illustrations are a delightful introduction to an astronaut's activities." Sci Child

Long, Kim
The astronaut training book for kids. Lodestar Bks. 1990 116p il $15.95 (5 and up)
629.45

1. Astronautics—Vocational guidance
ISBN 0-525-67296-6 LC 89-34668
"A practical guide intended to give a head start to those interested in pursuing an aerospace career. The author is clearly excited about the potential for today's child in the space industry and conveys the feeling in a readable and interesting text." Horn Book Guide
Includes glossary and bibliographies

Mullane, Richard M.
Liftoff! an astronaut's dream; [by] R. Mike Mullane. Silver Burdett Press 1995 96p il $13.95; pa $4.95 (4 and up)
629.45

1. Atlantis (Spacecraft) 2. Space flight
ISBN 0-382-24663-2; 0-382-24664-0 (pa)
LC 94-18122
This is an "autobiographical account of Mike Mullane, an astronaut, which examines his successes and setbacks in achieving his dream." Sci Child
"This book offers honest insights into the preparation, drama, and teamwork necessary for spaceflight." Sci Books Films

Ride, Sally K.
To space & back; by Sally Ride with Susan Okie. Lothrop, Lee & Shepard Bks. 1986 96p il $19; pa $12.95 (4 and up)
629.45

1. Space flight 2. Space shuttles
ISBN 0-688-06159-1; 0-688-09211-1 (pa)
LC 85-23757
This "account of a space journey, from blastoff to landing, gives intimate, you-are-there details of adjusting to weightlessness, preparing and eating meals, going to the bathroom, sleeping, washing, dressing, and working on scientific projects or up-keep technology on board the shuttle. Ride gives plenty of examples from her own experience but keeps the focus generalized enough to be broadly informative." Bull Cent Child Books
Includes glossary

Sullivan, George
The day we walked on the moon; a photo history of space exploration. Scholastic 1990 72p il hardcover o.p. paperback available $5.95 (4 and up)
629.45

1. Outer space—Exploration
ISBN 0-590-45587-7 (pa) LC 89-24234
"Sullivan documents the history of U.S. space exploration, providing newspaper clippings and news and NASA photographs. . . . Using the U.S. moon landing to introduce this story of human and technological achievement, Sullivan considers such successes as the first woman in space and the first spacewalk . . . Skylab, and the space shuttles. . . . Sections on astronaut training and future projects round out the treatment." Booklist
"Writing in his usual clear, concise way, this reliable author focuses special attention on the achievements of the *Appollo* and Space Shuttle programs rather than on the personal lives of astronauts." SLJ
Includes bibliography

629.47 Astronautical engineering

Butterfield, Moira
Space; illustrated by Nick Lipscombe and Gary Biggin. Dorling Kindersley 1994 32p il (Look inside cross-sections) pa $5.95 (4 and up)
629.47

1. Astronautics
ISBN 1-56458-682-0 LC 94-18480
This volume includes labeled cross-section drawings of 12 spacecraft, including a Mercury capsule and the Hubble telescope, with brief text
Includes glossary

629.8 Automatic control engineering

Berger, Fredericka
Robots; what they are, what they do; illustrated by Tom Huffman. Greenwillow Bks. 1992 47p il $14; lib bdg $13.93 (1-3)

629.8

1. Robots 2. Robotics
ISBN 0-688-09863-0; 0-688-09864-9 (lib bdg)

LC 91-14128

"A Greenwillow read-alone book"
Examines different kinds of robots, what they do, and how they work
"Clearly written and crisply illustrated with line drawings printed in two colors, the text will engage readers' interest. . . . A good choice to get students interested in technology." SLJ

Includes glossary

Skurzynski, Gloria
Robots: your high-tech world. Bradbury Press 1990 64p il $16.95 (5 and up)

629.8

1. Robots 2. Robotics
ISBN 0-02-782917-0

LC 89-70805

The author presents a "comprehensive look at the history, development, and future of robotics in industry, medicine, and space exploration, she explains how robots work and what they can do as she explores the connection between computers and robots. In an inviting format, information is presented both in text and captions. The well-chosen photographs are attractively arranged to add pace, variety, and excitement to the book." Horn Book

630.1 Agriculture—Philosophy and theory. Country and farm life

Allen, Thomas B., 1928-
On Granddaddy's farm. Knopf 1989 unp il $13.95; lib bdg $14.99 (1-3)   **630.1**

1. Farm life 2. Grandparents 3. Tennessee—Description
ISBN 0-394-89613-0; 0-394-99613-5 (lib bdg)

LC 88-23374

The author relates the events from the 1930s when he and his cousins spent summers on their grandparents's farm in the hills of Tennessee
"Straightforward, unadorned prose and stunning muted colored paintings. Scenes of farmyard creatures, chores, and playtime effectively capture one's interest as they bring to life a less technological era. The book is a gem that should not be missed." Child Book Rev Serv

Ancona, George, 1929-
The American family farm; a photo essay by George Ancona; text by Joan Anderson. Harcourt Brace Jovanovich 1989 unp il $25 (5 and up)   **630.1**

1. Farm life 2. Agriculture
ISBN 0-15-203025-5

LC 88-30068

"George Ancona and Joan Anderson reflect on both the adversities of farm life and its benefits in this photo essay, which is divided into three segments devoted to a dairy farm in Massachusetts, a poultry farm in Georgia, and a hog, cattle, and grain farm in Iowa. . . . The exceptional collaboration of photographer and author results in both an integrated flow of uncaptioned, black-and-white photographs and text and a discerning view into the lives of real people." Horn Book

Gibbons, Gail
Farming. Holiday House 1988 unp il lib bdg $15.95; pa $5.95 (k-3)   **630.1**

1. Farm life 2. Agriculture
ISBN 0-8234-0682-2 (lib bdg); 0-8234-0797-7 (pa)

LC 87-21254

"Simple text and full-color illustrations describe the many indoor and outdoor chores that are performed on a family farm each season. Fields are plowed and planted; animals are born, fed and cared for; and crops are harvested. Includes brief explanations of different kinds of specialized farms." Sci Child

Graff, Nancy Price, 1953-
The strength of the hills; a portrait of a family farm; photographs by Richard Howard. Little, Brown 1989 80p il $14.95 (4 and up)

630.1

1. Farm life
ISBN 0-316-32277-6

LC 89-7950

This "photo-essay follows the daily routines of Bill and Jenny Nelson and their four children on a Vermont dairy farm." Bull Cent Child Books
"With evocative prose and dominant, well-executed, black-and-white photographs, the book . . . details the real work of each family member. . . . It is a natural, unglamorous portrayal of a single day, and captures the determination, luck, and labor it takes to keep a farm going." SLJ

633.1 Cereal grains

Aliki
Corn is maize; the gift of the Indians; written and illustrated by Aliki. Crowell 1976 33p il (Let's-read-and-find-out science books) lib bdg $14.89; pa $4.95 (k-3)   **633.1**

1. Corn
ISBN 0-690-00975-5 (lib bdg); 0-06-445026-0 (pa)

In this book, the author provides a history of corn, or maize, and "also the life cycle of the plant itself, its growth and reproductive patterns, and its many uses. Excellent illustrations by the author help convey both cultural aspects and technological uses of corn." Sci Child

Johnson, Sylvia A.
Wheat; photographs by Masaharu Suzuki. Lerner Publs. 1990 48p il (Lerner natural science book) lib bdg $19.95 (4 and up)

633.1

1. Wheat
ISBN 0-8225-1490-7

LC 89-13237

Johnson, Sylvia A.—*Continued*

Explains the life cycle of wheat, its varieties, its cultivation, its harvesting, and its importance in feeding millions of people all over the world

"Scientific terms are used when necessary. Maps are used to show the locations of major grain producting areas of the world. . . . This is a good choice for scientific study of the wheat kernal and how it grows." SLJ

Includes glossary

633.5 Fiber crops

Selsam, Millicent Ellis, 1912-

Cotton; [by] Millicent E. Selsam; photographs by Jerome Wexler. Morrow 1982 48p il $12.95; lib bdg $14.88 (3-5)   **633.5**

1. Cotton

ISBN 0-688-01499-2; 0-688-01500-X (lib bdg)

LC 82-6496

Surveys the history, growth cycle, processing, and varied uses of one of the world's most important fiber plants

"The book is well written and can be easily understood by mid- to upper-elementary school children. . . . Wexler's photographs and the diagrams do much to enhance the text." Sci Books Films

633.6 Sugar, syrup, starch crops

Lasky, Kathryn

Sugaring time; photographs by Christopher G. Knight. Macmillan 1983 unp il $11.95; pa $4.95 (5 and up)   **633.6**

1. Maple sugar

ISBN 0-02-751680-6; 0-689-71081-X (pa)

LC 82-23928

A Newbery Medal honor book, 1984

"The author explains the steps involved in making maple syrup, from 'breaking out' the sugar trails to grading the final product. The book chronicles the activities of the Lacey family during the March sugaring time on their Vermont farm." Horn Book

"Laskey's text is informative and contains a down-home charm. Knight's photos portray not only the sugaring process but also the warmth and love of the Lacey clan." Publ Wkly

634 Orchards, fruit, forestry

Burns, Diane L.

Cranberries: fruit of the bogs; photographs by Cheryl Walsh Bellville. Carolrhoda Bks. 1994 48p il (Photo books) lib bdg $19.95; pa $7.95 (3-5)   **634**

1. Cranberries

ISBN 0-87614-822-4 (lib bg); 0-87614-964-6 (pa)

LC 93-29620

"After a brief history of the cranberry in North America, the photo-essay focuses on the planting, growing, harvesting, and processing of the fruit known as the 'bog ruby.' An interesting account of a fruit with historical importance is accompanied by color photographs as clear as the autumn days needed for harvesting the cranberries." Horn Book Guide

Includes glossary

Jaspersohn, William

Cranberries. Houghton Mifflin 1991 32p il $14.95 (3-5)   **634**

1. Cranberries

ISBN 0-395-52098-3   LC 90-41989

Depicts the history of cranberries, the stages of cultivation and harvest, and the processing and packaging of this native American fruit

"With sharp color photos and a concise but meaty text, this is a first-rate examination of cranberries from blossoms to packing plant." Booklist

Johnson, Sylvia A.

Apple trees; photographs by Hiroo Koike. Lerner Publs. 1983 48p il (Lerner natural science book) $19.95 (4 and up)   **634**

1. Apple

ISBN 0-8225-1479-6   LC 83-16230

Adapted from a work by Hiroo Koike published 1976 in Japan

The book "offers botanical descriptions of how these trees produce their fruits. Seasonal changes in the tree and a thorough explanation of fertilization and seed-formation processes are central. The use of insecticides is mentioned (they 'have to be used carefully, or they can kill helpful insects as well as harmful ones'), and harvesting patterns are briefly described." Booklist

Includes glossary

Maestro, Betsy, 1944-

How do apples grow? illustrated by Giulio Maestro. HarperCollins Pubs. 1992 32p il (Let's-read-and-find-out science books) $15; lib bdg $14.89; pa $4.95 (k-3)   **634**

1. Apple

ISBN 0-06-020055-3; 0-06-020056-1 (lib bdg); 0-06-445117-8 (pa)   LC 91-9468

Describes the life cycle of an apple from its initial appearance as a spring bud to that point in time when it becomes a fully ripe fruit

"Clear, complete. . . . Inquisitive children will find simple yet scientifically accurate answers to their questions about apple trees and their fruit. Large illustrations and limited text facilitate group-reading. The endearing, soft-toned drawings are clearly labelled, providing an excellent teaching tool or reference point for the science teacher." Sci Child

Micucci, Charles

The life and times of the apple. Orchard Bks. 1992 32p il $15.95; lib bdg $15.99; pa $5.95 (2-4)   **634**

1. Apple

ISBN 0-531-05939-1; 0-531-08539-2 (lib bdg); 0-531-07067-0 (pa)   LC 90-22779

Presents a variety of facts about apples, including how they grow, crossbreeding and grafting techniques, harvesting practices, and the uses, varieties, and history of this popular fruit

"In covering so many aspects of the subject, the book stretches across the curriculum, incorporating science, history, geography, and math. The format provides for interplay between the text and the many full-color illustrations, creating a most effective and attractive presentation of the subject." Booklist

Schnieper, Claudia

An apple tree through the year; photographs by Othmar Baumli. Carolrhoda Bks. 1987 48p il (Carolrhoda nature watch book) lib bdg $19.95; pa $6.95 (3-6) **634**

1. Apple

ISBN 0-87614-248-X (lib bdg); 0-87614-483-0 (pa)

LC 87-7997

Original German edition published 1982 in Switzerland

"While tracing the development of an apple tree from bud to fruit, Schnieper also follows the progress of an apple tree through the four seasons. Although the book focuses on a single tree's progress, information about other creatures is also presented, thus providing an overview of life in an orchard. Beautiful full-color photos and black-and-white line drawings highlight and elucidate the text. An excellent explanation of grafting is also included." SLJ

Includes glossary

634.9 Forestry

Appelbaum, Diana Karter

Giants in the land; [by] Diana Appelbaum; illustrated by Michael McCurdy. Houghton Mifflin 1993 unp il $14.95 (2-4) **634.9**

1. Trees 2. Lumber and lumbering 3. Shipbuilding—History

ISBN 0-395-64720-7

LC 92-26526

Describes how giant pine trees in New England were cut down during the colonial days to make massive wooden ships for the King's Navy

"The prose is restrained and lyrical. . . . McCurdy's dramatic black-and-white scratchboard drawings, many spread across two pages, capture the sweep and detail of the landscape." Booklist

Kurelek, William, 1927-1977

Lumberjack; paintings and story by William Kurelek. Houghton Mifflin 1974 unp il o.p.; Tundra Bks. reprint available $17.95 (3-5) **634.9**

1. Lumber and lumbering

ISBN 0-88776-052-X

Twenty-five color paintings portray life in a lumber camp and the lumberjack at work. The accompanying text tells of the author's experiences in Canadian lumber camps just after World War II

Lampton, Christopher

Forest fire. Millbrook Press 1991 64p il (Disaster!) hardcover o.p. paperback available $5.95 (4-6) **634.9**

1. Forest ecology 2. Forest fires

ISBN 1-56294-779-6 (pa)

LC 93-188324

The author describes what causes forest fires, how they are detected, techniques used to put them out, and the damage that is done. Lampton also explores some of the beneficial effects of forest fires

Includes glossary and bibliography

635 Garden crops (Horticulture)

Björk, Christina

Linnea's windowsill garden; by Christina Björk and Lena Anderson; translated by Joan Sandin. R & S Bks. 1988 59p il $13 (3-6) **635**

1. Gardening 2. Plants

ISBN 91-29-59064-7

LC 87-15016

Original Swedish edition, 1978

A "young plant lover gives information about every aspect of indoor gardening: choosing, planting, pruning, fertilizing, spraying, adjusting light and water." Bull Cent Child Books

Linnea's "zeal is infectious; readers will be looking around the house for seeds they can press into soil or coax into germination. Anderson's two-color illustrations explicate the projects cleanly and clearly, giving gardeners an excellent idea of when to look for shoots and when to run for the insecticide." Publ Wkly

Brown, Marc Tolon

Your first garden book; [by] Marc Brown. Little, Brown 1981 48p il $12.45; pa $6.95 (1-3) **635**

1. Gardening

ISBN 0-316-11217-8; 0-316-11215-1 (pa)

LC 81-3681

"An Atlantic Monthly Press book"

Suggested projects outline for beginning gardeners how to sprout seeds, turn soil, plant, and care for the results

"Reading this book will be fun. Sound gardening advice shares the pages with jokes, riddles and assorted tidbits of information. Brown's industrious animals make each page attractive and humorous. . . . Brown also shows a variety of easily made birdhouses and feeders and other garden-related crafts." Child Book Rev Serv

Creasy, Rosalind

Blue potatoes, orange tomatoes; illustrations by Ruth Heller. Sierra Club Bks. for Children 1994 40p il $15.95 (3-5) **635**

1. Vegetable gardening 2. Vegetables

ISBN 0-87156-576-5

LC 92-38800

Describes how to plant and grow a variety of colorful vegetables, including red corn, yellow watermelons, and multicolored radishes, and includes recipes

"With interesting and authentic information about gardening accompanied by brilliant, life-like illustrations, this book will not only promote the delight in growing plants but enhance the wonder in the natural world right in your own backyard." Appraisal

Huff, Barbara A.

Greening the city streets; the story of community gardens; photographs by Peter Ziebel. Clarion Bks. 1990 61p il $15.95 (4-6) **635**

1. Gardening 2. Community life 3. New York (N.Y.)—Description

ISBN 0-89919-741-8

LC 89-22193

Huff, Barbara A.—*Continued*

"The depiction of successful community gardens organized and maintained by amateurs of all ages demonstrates that urban life need not be colorless. Manhattan's Sixth Street and Avenue B Garden is highlighted. Includes a list of gardening organizations." Sci Child

Includes bibliography

King, Elizabeth, 1953-

The pumpkin patch; story and photographs by Elizabeth King. Dutton Children's Bks. 1990 unp il $14.99 (k-3)   **635**

1. Pumpkin

ISBN 0-525-44640-0   LC 89-25938

Text and photographs describe the activities in a pumpkin patch, as pink-colored seeds become fat pumpkins, ready to be carved into jack-o'-lanterns

"The book is informative, has wonderful photographs, and teaches accurately the development of a plant from the seed to the fruit stage. . . . The book is an excellent starting point for developing an interest in and awareness of plants." Appraisal

Kuhn, Dwight

More than just a vegetable garden; photos and text by Dwight Kuhn. Silver Press 1990 40p il $12.95; lib bdg $12.95 (2-4)   **635**

1. Vegetable gardening 2. Ecology

ISBN 0-671-69645-9; 0-671-69643-3 (lib bdg)
                                 LC 89-39504

Companion volume to More than just a flower garden, entered in class 635.9

"A beautifully photographed look at the changing world of a vegetable garden and the many creatures that inhabit it is enhanced with clear, informative text. Includes simple instructions for starting a garden." Sci Child

Includes glossary

Meltzer, Milton, 1915-

The amazing potato; a story in which the Incas, conquistadors, Marie Antoinette, Thomas Jefferson, wars, famines, immigrants, and french fries all play a part. HarperCollins Pubs. 1992 116p il $15; lib bdg $14.89 (4 and up)   **635**

1. Potatoes

ISBN 0-06-020806-6; 0-06-020807-4 (lib bdg)
                                 LC 91-29610

Introduces the history, effects, and current uses of the potato in the world marketplace

This "is a wonderful example of nonfiction writing at its best: it's interesting . . . amusing, fact-filled . . . and carefully sourced. The title provides a good idea of the history Meltzer traces, which stretches from the potato's domestication by the Incas through its introduction to Europe, the Irish potato famine, and the tuber's effect on U.S. immigration, to the processing of potatoes for the fast-food trade and today's consumers. Meltzer also discusses modern efforts to preserve the genetic diversity of the potato and the food's potential for alleviating world hunger. Photographs and boxed inserts provide additional useful information." Booklist

Includes bibliography

Rhoades, Diane, 1952-

Garden crafts for kids; 50 great reasons to get your hands dirty. Sterling 1995 144p il $19.95 (4-6)   **635**

1. Gardening 2. Nature craft

ISBN 0-8069-0998-6   LC 94-37108

"A Sterling/Lark book"

In this introduction to gardening and nature crafts the author "suggests selecting plants based on what readers like to eat, smell, and look at, and clearly describes every step in planting from soil to compost and worms. . . . The author describes how to make tools, includes easy crafts and experiments, and provides a pictorial index of easy-to-grow vegetables and flowers. Full-color photographs are clear and well placed to illustrate the text." SLJ

Watts, Barrie

Tomato. Silver Burdett Press 1990 c1989 24p il $6.95; lib bdg $9.98; pa $3.95 (k-3)
                                          635

1. Tomatoes

ISBN 0-382-24010-3; 0-382-24008-1 (lib bdg); 0-382-24344-7 (pa)   LC 89-38982

"A Stopwatch book"

First published 1989 in the United Kingdom

Follows, in text and illustrations, the development of a tomato from seedling to full maturity

"The photos, many in close-up, are so clear and well lit that every tiny hair glistens. History, gardening tips, and recipes are not included here: the scope of this book is strictly the growth of a tomato plant, and is presented exceptionally well." SLJ

Wilkes, Angela

My first garden book. Knopf 1992 48p il $13 (3-6)   **635**

1. Gardening

ISBN 0-679-81412-4   LC 90-40332

"A Dorling Kindersley book"

Features simple gardening projects from collecting seeds to growing a miniature desert garden

"Superb color photos against white backgrounds, explicit step-by-step illustrated directions, and age-appropriate activities combine to fashion a choice bouquet. . . . Not only do youngsters learn a bit of botany and proper methods for successful gardening, but they also discover the amazing potential for beauty and nourishment plants provide. Perfect for home use or school experiments." Booklist

635.9 Flowers and ornamental plants

Holmes, Anita, 1937-

Flowers for you; blooms for every month; illustrated by Virginia Wright-Frierson. Bradbury Press 1993 48p il $16.95 (4 and up)
                                       635.9

1. House plants

ISBN 0-02-744280-2   LC 91-9482

Describes twelve flowering plants and what it takes to grow them successfully indoors

"Beautiful color drawings enhance a book to be used all year." Sci Child

Includes glossary

Jordan, Sandra
Christmas tree farm. Orchard Bks. 1993 unp il $14.95; lib bdg $14.99 (k-3) **635.9**
1. Christmas trees 2. Tree planting 3. Farms
ISBN 0-531-05499-3; 0-531-08649-6 (lib bdg)
LC 93-20142
"Chronicling the operation of a Christmas tree farm from seed to sale and beyond, this book shares information, as well as an appreciation for the memories a family-run tree farm offers. Clear explanations, hand-colored sepia-toned photographs and an invitation for children to consider what happens to the trees after Christmas are some of the interesting aspects of this very readable story." Child Book Rev Serv

King, Elizabeth, 1953-
Backyard sunflower; story and photographs by Elizabeth King. Dutton Children's Bks. 1993 unp il $13.99 (k-3) **635.9**
1. Sunflowers
ISBN 0-525-45082-3
LC 92-31002
Text and photographs follow the life cycle of a sunflower, from the time that Samantha plants a seed in her garden to the maturity of the sunflower and the harvest of its own seeds
"One is immediately impressed by the lucid style of the text and the stunningly beautiful photographs." Sci Books Films

Kuhn, Dwight
More than just a flower garden; photos and text by Dwight Kuhn. Silver Press 1990 40p il $12.95; lib bdg $15.98 (2-4) **635.9**
1. Flower gardening 2. Ecology
ISBN 0-671-69644-0; 0-671-69642-4 (lib bdg)
LC 89-39511
Companion volume to More than just a vegetable garden, entered in class 635
Describes the living things in a flower garden, focusing on the dynamic variety of plants and the creatures that depend on them. Includes tips for starting your own flower garden
"The text is not technical in [this] . . . stunningly photographed book. . . . Each enlargement of a part of a plant is the last word in clarity and beauty. In addition to gorgeous flowers . . . pictures are included of birds, worms, insects and other familiar garden visitors." Child Book Rev Serv
Includes glossary

Laird, Elizabeth
Rosy's garden: a child's keepsake of flowers; text by Elizabeth Laird, [illustrations by] Satomi Ichikawa. Philomel Bks. 1990 48p il $16.95 (3-5) **635.9**
1. Flowers
ISBN 0-399-21881-5
LC 89-22955
Visiting her grandmother in the country, Rosy learns facts and folklore about flowers as she presses flowers, gathers seeds, and makes potpourri
"One of the things Rosy learns is how to make potpourri, and that word best describes this book. Grandmother's reminiscences, flower poems, some history and legends of individual flowers, the meanings of their names, and a few recipes are scattered randomly throughout, seemingly as a vehicle for Ichikawa's beautiful, botanically correct watercolors." SLJ

Patent, Dorothy Hinshaw
Flowers for everyone; photographs by William Muñoz. Cobblehill Bks. 1990 64p il $14.95 (4 and up) **635.9**
1. Flowers
ISBN 0-525-65025-3
LC 89-23937
The author discusses "the social significance of flowers, . . . how today's varieties are produced and distributed, . . . how flowers produce seeds or bulbs, . . . [and] the companies that make up the flower industry, including seed businesses, whose sole purpose is to provide seed; 'flower farmers,' who cultivate blossoms for florists; and nurseries, which grow starter plants for home gardeners." Booklist
"Profusely illustrated with large, often dazzling, color photographs. . . . Patent discusses the patient gamble of individual gardeners and large nurseries in developing new varieties and gives some interesting facts about plants of special interest to many hobbists—orchids, for example. The writing is crisp and direct; a glossary [is included]." Bull Cent Child Books

636 Animal husbandry

Epstein, Sam, 1909-
You call that a farm? raising otters, leeches, weeds, and other unusual things; [by] Sam and Beryl Epstein. Farrar, Straus & Giroux 1991 63p il $13.95 (4-6) **636**
1. Farms
ISBN 0-374-38705-2
LC 90-56157
Describes the activities at several farms where unusual plants or animals are raised
"The smoothly flowing text is enhanced by black-and-white photographs. The title and eye-catching cover add to the book's appeal." SLJ

Facklam, Margery, 1927-
Who harnessed the horse? the story of animal domestication; illustrated by Steven Parton. Little, Brown 1992 160p il $15.95 (3-6) **636**
1. Domestic animals
ISBN 0-316-27381-3
LC 91-13079
Illustrates the ways in which humans and animals have worked together throughout history, from the dogs that helped Stone Age people hunt to bacteria that gobble up oil spills
"Science and history students will find information for reports in this volume. . . . The narrative presents history, lore, and breeds, including many unusual facts." SLJ
Includes glossary

Ryden, Hope
Out of the wild; the story of domesticated animals; photographs and text by Hope Ryden. Lodestar Bks. 1995 56p il $15.99 (4 and up) **636**
1. Domestic animals
ISBN 0-525-67485-3
LC 94-20763
This "book traces the domestication of a variety of animals from different cultures, describing and comparing them to their wild ancestors. How their domestication relates to a particular stage of human development is also discussed. . . . This well-written look at the contributions that

Ryden, Hope—*Continued*
animals have made to humankind is further enhanced by
Ryden's fine-quality full-color photographs." SLJ

636.088   Animals for specific purposes

Arnold, Caroline, 1944-
Pets without homes; photographs by
Richard Hewett. Clarion Bks. 1983 46p il lib
bdg $15.95 (k-3)   **636.088**
1. Pets 2. Animal welfare
ISBN 0-89919-191-6   LC 83-2106
"The book focuses on one puppy picked up by a police
officer whose job includes work for the city's animal shelter,
enforcement of municipal laws about animals, and giving
talks at schools." Bull Cent Child Books
"Hewett's photographs are engaging, expressive and well
composed. The clean, varied, well-chosen layout complements the emotional points of the text. Throughout, the
text and illustrations form a harmonious unity of compassion and care beyond the lucid, informative focus of the
book." SLJ

Bare, Colleen Stanley
Guinea pigs don't read books; photographs
by the author. Dodd, Mead 1985 unp il o.p.;
Puffin Bks. paperback available $3.99 (k-2)
            636.088
1. Guinea pigs
ISBN 0-14-054995-1 (pa)   LC 84-18707
"Color photographs of good quality illustrate a text that
is simply written, an excellent first book on the subject for
young children. The text points out what guinea pigs do
and what they cannot do; it shows some of the varieties of
the species, and it points out that guinea pigs make good
pets, being calm and gentle animals that like to be held and
cuddled." Bull Cent Child Books

Chrystie, Frances N., 1904-1986
Pets; a comprehensive handbook for kids.
4th rev ed, revised and updated by Margery
Facklam; illustrations by Gillett Good Griffin.
Little, Brown 1995 xxii, 279p il pa $7.95 (4
and up)   **636.088**
1. Pets
ISBN 0-316-14281-6   LC 94-41229
First published 1953
This "handbook covers the care, understanding, and ap-
preciation of dogs, cats, rabbits, guinea pigs, numerous va-
rieties of birds and fish, reptiles, wild animals, farm
animals, and many more." Publisher's note
Includes bibliography

Hansen, Elvig
Guinea pigs. Carolrhoda Bks. 1992 48p il
(Carolrhoda nature watch book) lib bdg
$14.95; pa $6.95 (3-6)   **636.088**
1. Guinea pigs
ISBN 0-87614-681-7; 0-87614-613-2 (pa)
             LC 91-30694
Original German edition published 1988 in Switzerland

Describes the physical characteristics, habitat, and life
cycle of the guinea pig
"Though uncaptioned, the pictures (featuring Hansen's
own animals) are marvelous. . . . But the photos are more
than simply bright, clear shots. They're informative and
carefully keyed to the text. . . . It supplies plenty for both
student researchers and prospective pet owners, all of whom
will join browsers in eagerly thumbing through the wonderful pictures." Booklist
Includes glossary

King-Smith, Dick, 1922-
I love guinea pigs; illustrated by Anita
Jeram. Candlewick Press 1995 c1994 unp il
$14.95 (k-3)   **636.088**
1. Guinea pigs
ISBN 1-56402-389-3   LC 94-4880
"Read and wonder"
First published 1994 in the United Kingdom
"King-Smith provides a bit of history and some general
information about physical characteristics, concentrating
most fully on the care of these responsive animals as pets.
He mentions the rudiments of handling, housing, feeding,
and watering, explaining that guinea pigs can live for sever-
al years and describing their repertoire of sounds. King-
Smith's advice is interspersed with anecdotes about favorite
guinea pigs he has owned." Horn Book
"Jeram's line-and-watercolor illustrations transform fuzzy
lumps into curious, cuddly, thoroughly engaging creatures."
SLJ

Silverstein, Alvin
Hamsters: all about them; [by] Alvin &
Virginia Silverstein; with photographs by
Frederick Breda. Lothrop, Lee & Shepard Bks.
1974 126p il lib bdg $14.93 (5 and up)
            636.088
1. Hamsters
ISBN 0-688-50056-0
This book is a manual for the hamster owner, with information on the care, feeding, housing, and breeding of these
pets. Types of hamsters and their use in laboratory research
is also discussed

Wexler, Jerome
Pet mice; text and photos by Jerome
Wexler. Whitman, A. 1989 48p il $15.95 (3-5)
            636.088
1. Mice
ISBN 0-8075-6524-5
Text and color photographs describe how to house, feed,
and handle a pair of pet mice and the families they produce
"A wealth of information on the selection, care, breeding,
and training of pet mice. Attractive color photographs highlight and supplement the text. Wexler's writing is clear and
his advice practical. . . . This is an excellent resource for
both new and experienced pet mice owners." SLJ

Ziefert, Harriet
Let's get a pet; pictures by Mavis Smith.
Viking 1993 32p il $13.50; pa $4.99 (k-3)
            636.088
1. Pets
ISBN 0-670-84550-7; 0-14-054808-4 (pa)
             LC 91-48458

Ziefert, Harriet—*Continued*
Discusses all the things involved in choosing a pet
"Sensible ideas are shared, practical questions are posed, and young children are presented with an authentic decision-making situation. Easy-to-read text and colorful illustrations are coordinated in an almost comic-strip fashion." Sci Child

636.1   Horses and related animals

Ancona, George, 1929-
Man and mustang; photographs and text by George Ancona. Macmillan 1992 unp il $15.95 (3-6)   636.1
1. Horses
ISBN 0-02-700802-9   LC 91-29513
This "photo essay describes the rescue of a wild mustang from capture to adoption. Inmates from the New Mexico State Penitentiary serve as horse trainers. The succinct text and action photographs combine to produce an informative and interesting book." Horn Book

Clutton-Brock, Juliet
Horse; written by Juliet Clutton-Brock. Knopf 1992 63p il (Eyewitness books) $19; lib bdg $20.99 (4 and up)   636.1
1. Horses
ISBN 0-679-81681-X; 0-679-91681-4 (lib bdg)
LC 91-33132
Also available Spanish language edition
"A Dorling Kindersley book"
A photo essay introducing members of the horse family, their evolution, behavior, importance, history, breeding, and training. Includes major international breeds of domestic horses
"Browsers will find this smorgasbord of equine facts fascinating." SLJ

Cole, Joanna
A horse's body; photographs by Jerome Wexler. Morrow 1981 45p il $15; lib bdg $13.88   636.1
1. Horses
ISBN 0-688-00362-1; 0-688-00363-X (lib bdg)
LC 80-28147
An introduction to the horse, its habits, anatomy, physiology, and evolution
"A sensible, straightforward, and comprehensive introduction to the anatomy of the horse, neatly packaged in a simple format." Horn Book

Henry, Marguerite, 1902-
Album of horses; illustrated by Wesley Dennis. Rand McNally 1951 112p il o.p.; Aladdin Bks. (NY) paperback available $9.95 (4 and up)   636.1
1. Horses
ISBN 0-689-71709-1 (pa)
"A handsomely illustrated volume describing 20 breeds of horses, from the Shetland pony to the thoroughbred race horse, anecdotal in style and including many little-known facts." Hodges. Books for Elem Sch Libr

Isenbart, Hans-Heinrich, 1923-
Birth of a foal; photographs by Thomas David. Carolrhoda Bks. 1986 48p il (Carolrhoda nature watch book) lib bdg $19.95 (3-6)   636.1
1. Horses
ISBN 0-87614-239-0   LC 85-17406
Original German edition published 1983 in Switzerland
This book describes the birth and first few hours of a foal's life
"The text is quite detailed, containing many facts and figures about the developing fetus, how long it takes to be born, size and weight at birth, etc. . . . The illustrations are color photographs, varying somewhat in quality. Although most of the photographs are sharp and clear, a few are fuzzy or grainy. . . . All of the photographs are appropriate for even very young readers." Appraisal
Includes glossary

Jurmain, Suzanne
Once upon a horse; a history of horses—and how they shaped our history. Lothrop, Lee & Shepard Bks. 1989 176p il $15.95 (6 and up)   636.1
1. Horses
ISBN 0-688-05550-8   LC 88-17522
"To describe the horse's contribution to history, Jurmain includes myths, legends, art, and fact in a readable narrative. The subject is divided by chapters that cover each type of interaction between horses and people (e.g. 'The War-Horse,' 'The Messenger,' 'The Racehorse'). The result is a special-interest book for the combination horse lover/history buff. The photographs of period artwork have been carefully selected." Bull Cent Child Books
Includes bibliography

LaBonte, Gail
The miniature horse. Dillon Press 1990 59p il (Dillon remarkable animals book) $13.95 (3-5)   636.1
1. Horses
ISBN 0-87518-424-3   LC 89-26046
The author describes the appearance, behavior, and rearing of the miniature horse and discusses its development, uses, and growing popularity in North America
"Excellent full-color action photographs, including those matching a miniature ear-to-ear with a child and nose-to-nose with a dog to establish its relative size, make the book as appealing as its subject. The glossary of bold-type words, index, and list of places that welcome visits expand the book's information potential." SLJ

McFarland, Cynthia
Hoofbeats; the story of a thoroughbred. Atheneum Pubs. 1993 unp il $14.95 (3-5)   636.1
1. Horses
ISBN 0-689-31757-3   LC 92-14255
Text and photographs describe the life of a thoroughbred race horse, from birth through training to its first race as a two-year-old
"Bright and informative full-color photographs are sure to appeal to horse lovers of all ages. This is a fascinating story." Sci Child
Includes glossary

Patent, Dorothy Hinshaw

Appaloosa horses; photographs by William
Muñoz. Holiday House 1988 74p il $15.95 (4
and up)   **636.1**

1. Horses
ISBN 0-8234-0706-3   LC 88-4470

"Following a discussion of the Nez Perce and Palouse
tribes' development of the horses and the subsequent dis-
banding of the animals by white settlers are chapters on Appaloosa traits and on organizations sponsoring activities for
riders. Black-and-white photographs show common markings, including blankets and spots, roans, and combinations.
A natural for browsers in 'the horse stage' or students seeking information for reports." Bull Cent Child Books

Includes glossary and bibliography

Baby horses; photographs by William
Muñoz. Carolrhoda Bks. 1991 56p il $17.50
(3-6)   **636.1**

1. Horses 2. Animal babies
ISBN 0-87614-690-6   LC 91-14662

A revised edition of the title first published 1985 by
Dodd, Mead. Muñoz' name appeared first in earlier edition

Full-color photographs accompany a description of the
activities of foals in their first months of life

Horses; photos by William Muñoz.
Carolrhoda Bks. 1994 48p il (Understanding
animals) lib bdg $19.95 (3-6)   **636.1**

1. Horses
ISBN 0-87614-766-X   LC 93-12329

Discusses the physical characteristics and behavior of
horses and describes how domestic horses evolved from
their wild relatives

This book features "accurate, accessible narrative, complemented by clear color photographs." Horn Book Guide

Includes glossary

Horses of America. Holiday House 1981
80p il lib bdg $15.95 (4 and up)   **636.1**

1. Horses
ISBN 0-8234-0399-8   LC 81-4165

Discusses the evolution and characteristics of various
breeds of horses and identifies breeds for work, sports, and
pleasure, and those that are "all-around" horses

"Striking photographs supplement the concise text, making a volume less detailed than some books on horses but
one that is nevertheless a valuable and attractive reference
work." Horn Book

Includes glossary and bibliography

Rodenas, Paula

The Random House book of horses and
horsemanship; with a foreword by Walter
Farley; drawings by Jean Cassels. Random
House 1991 180p il $17.50 (4 and up)
     636.1

1. Horses 2. Horsemanship
ISBN 0-394-88705-0   LC 86-42934

"This book is a comprehensive examination of the world
of horses. Breeds, care, anatomy, behavior, and training are
but a selection of the topics discussed." Sci Child

"Rodenas' well-balanced manual features a text accessible to middle-grade readers and a scope that will satisfy
both the novice and the expert. . . . Sharp, full-color photographs, diagrams, and line drawings are well placed to enhance the text." Booklist

Includes bibliography

The **Visual** dictionary of the horse. Dorling
Kindersley 1994 64p il (Eyewitness visual
dictionaries) $16.95 (4 and up)   **636.1**

1. Horses
ISBN 1-56458-504-2   LC 93-20819

"Along with spreads detailing the animal's anatomy,
there are two double-page spreads illustrated with full-color
photographs of the various breeds, divided into light and
heavy horses. Following this overview, the guide briefly focuses on the care and activities of equines today, including
grooming, shoeing, racing, jumping, and equipment." SLJ

"In this visually spectacular introduction to horses and
equine and equestrian terms, the information is complete
and concise; color photographs and diagrams extend the
text. The anatomical drawings, with detailed labeling, are
particularly instructive and useful." Horn Book Guide

Includes glossary

636.2   Ruminants. Bovines. Cattle

McFarland, Cynthia

Cows in the parlor; a visit to a dairy farm.
Atheneum Pubs. 1990 unp il $14.95 (1-3)
     636.2

1. Dairying
ISBN 0-689-31584-8   LC 89-14972

The author discusses the daily routine of Clear Creek
Farm and its herd of fifty dairy cows

This book "clearly shows the basic workings of a dairy
farm, including haymaking, silaging, feeding, and automatic
milking. The color photos are sometimes dark . . . but the
commonsensical tone informing both text and pictures is
forthrightly informative." Bull Cent Child Books

636.3   Sheep and goats

Paladino, Catherine

Spring fleece; a day of sheepshearing. Little,
Brown 1990 48p il lib bdg $14.95 (3-6)
     636.3

1. Sheep 2. Wool
ISBN 0-316-68890-8   LC 89-12820

"Joy Street books"

"A handsome photo-essay describes the work of sheep-
shearers as they travel to two New England farms. A
comprehensive look at an ancient craft told with warmth
and drama." Sci Child

636.4   Swine

King-Smith, Dick, 1922-

All pigs are beautiful; illustrated by Anita
Jeram. Candlewick Press 1993 unp il $14.95;
pa $5.99 (k-3)   **636.4**

1. Pigs
ISBN 1-56402-148-3; 1-56402-431-8 (pa)

     LC 92-53136

"Read and wonder"

King-Smith, Dick, 1922-—_Continued_
The author "interlards fond reminiscences of porkers he has known with interesting facts about them that are sure to keep children absorbed. His tone is affectionate, amusing, and informative. Jeram's pen-and-ink and watercolor illustrations, done in soft, earthy colors, are a warm match for the text." SLJ

636.5 Poultry. Chickens

Burton, Jane, 1933-
Chick; photographed by Jane Burton. Lodestar Bks. 1992 c1991 21p il (See how they grow) $6.95 (k-2)   **636.5**
1. Chickens
ISBN 0-525-67355-5   LC 91-96
First published 1991 in the United Kingdom
Photographs and text depict the development of a chick from the egg stage to the eighth week
"Crisp, clean, full-color photographs on snow-white pages. . . . The first-person text lets readers know just how and when the simple learning processes unfold. . . . Watercolor borders soften the artificial tidiness of the page layout." SLJ

Cole, Joanna
A chick hatches; photographs by Jerome Wexler. Morrow 1976 46p il lib bdg $14.93 (k-3)   **636.5**
1. Chickens 2. Reproduction 3. Eggs
ISBN 0-688-32087-2   LC 76-29017
"A simply written account of the development from egg to embryo to fetus to chick is made more meaningful by the accompanying photographs, some in color and almost all enlarged. The writing is matter-of-fact, but the pictures of the developing fetus make the recurrent miracle of reproduction vividly clear." Bull Cent Child Books

Hariton, Anca, 1955-
Egg story. Dutton Children's Bks. 1992 unp il $12 (k-3)   **636.5**
1. Chickens 2. Eggs
ISBN 0-525-44861-6   LC 91-34588
Follows an egg from the time it is laid, through its incubation under the hen's body, to the chick's birth after twenty-one days
"Hariton's approach and her watercolor illustrations in springlike hues not only give the volume the narrative appeal of a picture book, but also provide a new view of a familiar science lesson." Booklist

Selsam, Millicent Ellis, 1912-
Egg to chick; by Millicent E. Selsam; pictures by Barbara Wolff. rev ed. Harper & Row 1970 63p il (Science I can read book) $14.89; pa $3.50 (k-3)   **636.5**
1. Chickens 2. Eggs
ISBN 0-06-025290-1; 0-06-444113-X (pa)
First published 1946
Easy-to-read science text traces the fertilization of the egg and the growth and hatching out of the chick

636.6 Birds other than poultry

Mowat, Farley
Owls in the family; illustrated by Robert Frankenberg. Little, Brown 1961 103p il o.p.; Bantam Bks. paperback available $3.50 (4 and up)   **636.6**
1. Owls
ISBN 0-553-15585-7 (pa)
Also available in hardcover from Amereon
"An Atlantic Monthly Press book"
"Two owls, Wol and Weeps, who are found as babies at the beginning of this account, were the author's own pets during his boyhood in Saskatoon. The description of the owls' endearing and humorous traits, their intelligence and mischief in upsetting household and neighbors, is continuously absorbing and provocative of hearty laughter. Their personalities are vividly different. . . . Outstanding for reading aloud." Horn Book

636.7 Dogs

American Kennel Club
The complete dog book. Howell Bk. House il $27.50   **636.7**
1. Dogs
First published 1935. (18th edition 1992) Frequently revised
"The official guide to 124 AKC registered breeds and their history, appearance, selection, training, care and feeding, and first aid. Some color plates." N Y Public Libr. Ref Books for Child Collect

Ancona, George, 1929-
Sheep dog; words and photographs by George Ancona. Lothrop, Lee & Shepard Bks. 1985 unp il $12.95; lib bdg $12.88 (4 and up)   **636.7**
1. Sheep dogs 2. Working animals
ISBN 0-688-04118-3; 0-688-04119-1 (lib bdg)
LC 84-20100
Describes the various breeds of dogs used to guard and herd sheep, explains how they work, and discusses the importance of these dogs to the sheep industry
Black-and-white photographs depict the "natural setting for the dogs at work and play. The text is concise, interesting and highly informative for research for both dogs and the sheep industry. George Ancona is a professional photographer, but it is his special affinity for children that contributes to the appeal of this book. It is a must for the ever popular book section about dogs." Okla State Dept of Educ
Includes bibliography

Calmenson, Stephanie
Rosie; a visiting dog's story; photographs by Justin Sutcliffe. Clarion Bks. 1994 47p il $15.95 (k-3)   **636.7**
1. Dogs
ISBN 0-395-65477-7   LC 93-21243
"Rosie is the true story of an endearing Tibetan terrier who works as a therapy dog with Delta Society's Pet Partners Program of New York City. Rosie's tenderness and en-

Calmenson, Stephanie—*Continued*
thusiasm come through in Sutcliffe's fantastic photos that chronicle Rosie's training and first visit to a children's hospital and a nursing home." Child Book Rev Serv

Cohen, Susan, 1938-
What kind of dog is that? rare & unusual breeds of dogs; [by] Susan and Daniel Cohen. Cobblehill Bks. 1989 131p il $12.95 (4 and up)
636.7

1. Dogs
ISBN 0-525-65011-3   LC 89-34462
Discusses the history, physical characteristics, and behavior of twenty-five unusual dog breeds including the Fila Brasileiro, the Peruvian Inca Orchid, the Jack Russell Terrier, and the Chinese Crested
Written with "humor and a lively style. . . . A wonderful picture of each breed emerges, reinforced by expressive black-and-white photographs."
Includes bibliography

Cole, Joanna
A dog's body; photographs by Jim and Ann Monteith. Morrow 1986 48p il $12.95; lib bdg $14.93
636.7
1. Dogs
ISBN 0-688-04153-1; 0-688-04154-X (lib bdg)
LC 85-25885
"Cole discusses dogs' lupine ancestry, how different breeds were developed, why certain senses are more important than others." Bull Cent Child Books
"A clear and simple account of how a dog's body is suited for his lifestyle. . . . Black-and-white photographs and line drawings enhance the text. This book will be helpful to 3rd and 4th graders writing reports and will be enjoyed by younger children and parents who want to know more about their favorite pet." Appraisal

My puppy is born; photographs by Margaret Miller. rev and expanded ed. Morrow Junior Bks. 1991 unp il $15; lib bdg $14.93; pa $5.95 (k-3)
636.7
1. Dogs 2. Reproduction
ISBN 0-688-09770-7; 0-688-09771-5 (lib bdg); 0-688-10198-4 (pa)   LC 90-42011
A revised and newly illustrated edition of the title first published 1973
"As a little girl anxiously awaits the birth of puppies by the Norfolk terrier next door, a story unfolds. The puppies' arrival and first few weeks of life and development are shown and described in a simple narrative." SLJ
Exquisitely sharp, well-designed color photos capture the events, stage by stage. . . . As the puppy grows, the reader watches its first halting steps, messy eating habits, and snoozing poses. A gem for preschoolers and a sure bet for older youngsters." Booklist

Hausherr, Rosmarie
My first puppy. Four Winds Press 1986 64p il $14.95 (1-3)
636.7
1. Dogs
ISBN 0-02-743410-9   LC 86-14979
Photographs and text follow a girl as she selects her first puppy and learns about its feeding, grooming, training, and medical care. A section for parents discusses where and how to acquire a dog, spaying and neutering, various aspects of home care, and suggested rules for children

Jones, Robert F., 1934-
Jake; a Labrador puppy at work and play; photographs by Bill Eppridge. Farrar, Straus & Giroux 1992 unp il $15; pa $5.95 (3-5)
636.7

1. Dogs—Training
ISBN 0-374-33655-5; 0-374-43713-0 (pa)
LC 92-8105
The author describes his new Labrador puppy's first year and how he trained the dog to sit, heel, fetch, and more
"An adorable puppy and a writer who understands dogs as deeply as he loves them are the subjects of this splendid photo essay. . . . Eppridge's photographs . . . cleanly capture Jake's brand of animal magnetism." Publ Wkly

Kuklin, Susan
Taking my dog to the vet. Bradbury Press 1988 unp il $13.95 (k-3)   **636.7**

1. Dogs 2. Veterinary medicine
ISBN 0-02-751234-7   LC 88-5047
"A little girl takes her Cairn Terrier to the veterinarian for his annual check-up. The vet is gentle and explains to Minal what he is doing to her dog and why. . . . Color photographs illustrate the text well and add a warm touch to the story." SLJ

Patent, Dorothy Hinshaw
Hugger to the rescue; photographs by William Muñoz. Cobblehill Bks. 1994 31p il $13.99 (2-4)   **636.7**

1. Dogs 2. Rescue work
ISBN 0-525-65161-6   LC 93-32031
The author and illustrator "introduce the Black Paws Search, Rescue & Avalanche Dogs team of Bigfork, Montana. Patent describes the training and special equipment used by these Newfoundlands, whose keen sense of smell helps them locate people—whether they are buried under an avalanche submerged in water, or simply lost in the woods. . . . Muñoz's crisp, clear photos capture the consummate skill and loving devotion of these gentle giants." Booklist

Petersen-Fleming, Judy
Puppy care and critters, too! [by] Judy Petersen-Fleming and Bill Fleming; photographs by Debra Reingold-Reiss. Tambourine Bks. 1994 36p il $15; lib bdg $14.93 (k-3)   **636.7**

1. Dogs 2. Pets 3. Animals
ISBN 0-688-12563-8; 0-688-12564-6 (lib bdg)
LC 93-23129
Photographs and text describe how to choose and care for a pet puppy. Comparisons are made with the care and behavior of wild animals in zoos and wild animal parks
"Excellent-quality, full-color photographs bring the words to life. . . . [This features] charming photographs . . . brief yet solid advice and interesting tidbits on wildlife." SLJ

Pinkwater, Jill

Superpuppy: how to choose, raise, and train the best possible dog for you; by Jill and D. Manus Pinkwater; line drawings by Jill Pinkwater. Clarion Bks. 1977 206p il hardcover o.p. paperback available $7.95 (5 and up)   **636.7**

1. Dogs

ISBN 0-89919-084-7 (pa)   LC 76-8825

First published by Seabury Press

"The authors begin by suggesting that you examine your reasons for owning a dog. The rest of the book details all the problems and rewards of caring for a dog." Publ Wkly

Includes bibliography

Silverstein, Alvin

Dogs: all about them; by Alvin and Virginia Silverstein; with an introduction by John C. McLoughlin. Lothrop, Lee & Shepard Bks. 1986 256p il lib bdg $16 (5 and up)

636.7

1. Dogs

ISBN 0-688-04805-6   LC 84-29723

Discusses the evolution of dogs and their uses throughout history and includes information on different breeds, training, care as pets, relationship with people, and other relevant topics

"This book is superb; its informative; its readable, and most of all its enjoyable." Appraisal

Includes bibliography

Smith, Elizabeth Simpson

A service dog goes to school; the story of a dog trained to help the disabled; illustrated by Steven Petruccio. Morrow Junior Bks. 1988 65p il $12.95; lib bdg $12.88 (3-5)   **636.7**

1. Dogs—Training 2. Animals and the handicapped

ISBN 0-688-07648-3; 0-688-07649-1 (lib bdg)

LC 88-17598

Follows the selection, raising, training, and placement with a young disabled boy of a service dog named Licorice. Includes a list of service dog schools and organizations

"A photoessay might have had more immediacy than Smith's fictionalized account, which features many pencil illustrations, but format notwithstanding, this volume has both drama and heartfelt emotion, along with useful information." Booklist

636.8 Cats

Cole, Joanna

A cat's body; photographs by Jerome Wexler. Morrow 1982 48p il lib bdg $12.88

636.8

1. Cats

ISBN 0-688-01054-7   LC 81-22386

The authors "show how well designed and programmed a cat is to catch small rodents (but not birds) and how its abilities, instincts and ways of socializing with other cats fit into the domestic cat's life with humans. The brief, substantive text, clear, informative photos and open, welcoming layout will attract preschoolers." SLJ

My new kitten; photographs by Margaret Miller. Morrow Junior Bks. 1995 unp il $15; lib bdg $14.93 (k-2)   **636.8**

1. Cats

ISBN 0-688-12901-3; 0-688-12902-1 (lib bdg)

LC 94-20295

"A brief, first-person text and full-page photographs follow the birth and growth of a litter of kittens in this simple, appealing documentary. A little girl watches her aunt's cat, Cleo, as she gives birth and cares for her kittens; eventually, the girl is allowed to choose a kitten for herself. The fine photographs of the luxuriant gray kittens have an inherent narrative." Horn Book

De Paola, Tomie, 1934-

The kids' cat book; written and illustrated by Tomie de Paola. Holiday House 1979 unp il lib bdg $14.95; pa $5.95 (2-4)   **636.8**

1. Cats

ISBN 0-8234-0365-3 (lib bdg); 0-8234-0534-6 (pa)

LC 79-2090

Patrick goes to Granny Twinkle's for a free kitten and learns everything there is to know about cats—their different breeds, care, place in art and literature, and history

"The illustrations add great touches of humor and show cats being cats everywhere. All those who have new kittens will find useful information." Child Book Rev Serv

Hausherr, Rosmarie

My first kitten. Four Winds Press 1985 48p il $13.95 (1-3)   **636.8**

1. Cats

ISBN 0-02-743420-6   LC 85-42804

Seven-year-old Adam has a summer full of new experiences and responsibilities when he receives a kitten for a pet

"Quite a bit of information on cats works its way into the story, including safety tips, health needs, and feline habits both funny and annoying. A last page addressed to parents summarizes tips on pet care. The black-and-white photographs are large, clear, and well-composed, with no posturing on the part of the people or cutesiness in the presentation of the animal. An attractive introduction to responsible pet ownership." Bull Cent Child Books

Jessel, Camilla, 1937-

The kitten book. Candlewick Press 1992 c1991 unp il $14.95; pa $4.99 (k-3)   **636.8**

1. Cats

ISBN 1-56402-020-7; 1-56402-278-1 (pa)

LC 91-71841

First published 1991 in the United Kingdom

Text and photographs follow the birth and development of seven Burmese kittens

"What fascinating photographs! . . . Jessel's accompanying narrative [is] forthright and very informative. . . . Her photos reflect her sensitivity toward the children-pet bond." Booklist

Kuklin, Susan

Taking my cat to the vet. Bradbury Press 1988 unp il $13.95 (k-3)   **636.8**

1. Cats 2. Veterinary medicine

ISBN 0-02-751233-9   LC 88-5052

Kuklin, Susan—*Continued*

"Young Ben tells readers about taking his cat Willa, adopted as a kitten from the A.S.P.C.A., to the veterinarian for a standard checkup. The vet . . . explains her way through the examination, testing Willa's eyes and ears, taking her temperature, trimming her nails, and giving her shots. The dialogue rarely strains to be informative, and the large color photographs are well composed and business-like." Bull Cent Child Books

Petersen-Fleming, Judy

Kitten care and critters, too! [by] Judy Petersen-Fleming and Bill Fleming; photographs by Debra Reingold-Reiss. Tambourine Bks. 1994 40p il $15; lib bdg $14.93 (k-3)			**636.8**

1. Pets 2. Cats
ISBN 0-688-12565-4; 0-688-12566-2 (lib bdg)
			LC 93-24200

Explains how to choose, train, and care for a kitten, with comparisons to other animals

"Excellent-quality, full-color photographs bring the words to life." SLJ

637 Processing dairy and related products

Aliki

Milk from cow to carton. rev ed. HarperCollins Pubs. 1992 31p il (Let's-read-and-find-out science books) $14; lib bdg $13.89; pa $4.95 (k-3)			**637**

1. Dairying 2. Milk 3. Cattle
ISBN 0-06-020434-6; 0-06-020435-4 (lib bdg); 0-06-445111-9 (pa)			LC 91-23807
Also available Spanish language edition
First published 1974 by Crowell with title: Green grass and white milk

Briefly describes how a cow produces milk, how the milk is processed in a dairy, and how various other dairy products are made from milk

This features "full-color artwork. . . . An excellent primary-level introduction to dairy science." Booklist

Carrick, Donald

Milk. Greenwillow Bks. 1985 unp il lib bdg $13.93 (k-1)			**637**

1. Milk 2. Dairying
ISBN 0-688-04823-4			LC 84-25879

"This beautifully illustrated book follows milk from the farm to the grocer's shelf. The large, clear print and carefully detailed full-page illustrations make this an excellent read-aloud book for young children. A delightful vicarious experience that can set the stage for a field trip to a dairy farm." Sci Child

Gibbons, Gail

The milk makers. Macmillan 1985 unp il $14.95; pa $3.95 (k-3)			**637**

1. Dairying 2. Milk 3. Cattle
ISBN 0-02-736640-5; 0-689-71116-6 (pa)
			LC 84-20081

Explains how cows produce milk and how it is processed before being delivered to stores

"Starting with dairy cows grazing at pasture, nothing is overlooked in the procedure, from the role of the calf to winter feed and shelter, the function of four stomachs, milking, milk handling, and the operation of a dairy. Diagrams of the cow stomachs as well as the machines used at farm and dairy leave no question unanswered, although city children will be unfamiliar with what it means to breed a cow. Finally, there is a pictorial list of the many other dairy products found in most homes." Sci Books Films

Giblin, James, 1933-

Milk: the fight for purity; [by] James Cross Giblin; illustrated with photographs and prints. Crowell 1986 106p il lib bdg $12.89 (5 and up)			**637**

1. Milk 2. Dairying
ISBN 0-690-04574-3			LC 85-48252

The author "discusses the history of milk as a central source of nutrition, from ancient times to the present, and as a carrier of disease due to ignorance and careless handling. Given high profile here are the people responsible for creating standards—from Louis Pasteur to Nathan Straus, a man who understood the importance of pure milk early on and provided it to poor families and orphans. Also covered are more than recent problems that have plagued the industry, from radiation poisoning . . . to salmonella poisoning." Publ Wkly

"Clearly written and well illustrated . . . this book also contains an index and a bibliography documenting the thorough research that went into its writing." Appraisal

Jaspersohn, William

Ice cream; written and photographed by William Jaspersohn. Macmillan 1988 43p il $14.95 (3-5)			**637**

1. Ben & Jerry's Homemade Inc. 2. Ice cream, ices, etc.
ISBN 0-02-747821-1			LC 87-38331

"Looking at a small Vermont manufacturer, Ben & Jerry's, Jaspersohn describes in text and black-and-white photographs how ice cream is made, from cow to cone. The photos are clear and precise and in most cases add detail to the text rather than just mirroring it. Informative diagrams provide more information. Jaspersohn's text is well written and full of interesting details that will fascinate youngsters." SLJ

Peterson, Cris, 1952-

Extra cheese, please! mozzarella's journey from cow to pizza; photographs by Alvis Upitis. Boyds Mills Press 1994 unp il $14.95 (k-3)			**637**

1. Dairying 2. Cheese
ISBN 1-56397-177-1			LC 93-70876

In photographs and text, this book introduces "dairying and cheese making. Using her own farm as an example, Peterson describes the care and feeding of dairy cattle, the milking process, and the steps involved in producing mozzarella cheese." Booklist

"Nicely balanced pages contain brief blocks of clearly written text and many full-color photographs." SLJ

Includes glossary and bibliography

638 Insect culture

Johnson, Sylvia A.
A beekeeper's year; photographs by Nick Von Ohlen. Little, Brown 1994 32p il lib bdg $16.95 (4 and up)   **638**

1. Bees 2. Honey
ISBN 0-316-46745-6   LC 93-10199
Follows a beekeeper through the four seasons, showing how bees and humans work together to make honey
"This is a most intriguing book. . . . Johnson's conversational text is wonderfully informative, clearly explaining every aspect of the beekeeper's responsibilities, and Von Ohlen's many clear and engaging photos, all in full color, show the work in progress, often taking us right inside the hive." Booklist
Includes glossary

639 Hunting, fishing, conservation, related technologies

Koch, Frances King
Mariculture; farming the fruits of the sea. Watts 1992 57p il lib bdg $22.71 (5 and up)   **639**

1. Aquaculture
ISBN 0-531-11116-4   LC 91-35172
"A New England Aquarium book"
Examines mariculture, some of its problems, and its possible future
"This is an excellent first book, for both students and their teachers. . . . The high-quality color photographs add significantly to its value. Along with the easily readable and accurate text, the author makes use of photographs with sidebars." Sci Books Films
Includes glossary and bibliography

Simon, Seymour, 1931-
Pets in a jar; collecting and caring for small wild animals; illustrated by Betty Fraser. Viking 1975 95p il hardcover o.p. paperback available $5.95 (4 and up)   **639**

1. Invertebrates 2. Pets
ISBN 0-14-049186-4 (pa)
The author "offers valuable information not readily found elsewhere on collecting and maintaining hydras, planaria, several water insects, crickets, ants, saltwater brine shrimp, hermit crabs, and starfish. Moreover, he suggests experiments such as causing a planarian to generate two heads." Horn Book

639.2 Commercial fishing, whaling, sealing

Carrick, Carol
Whaling days; woodcuts by David Frampton. Clarion Bks. 1993 40p il $15.95; pa $6.95 (3-6)   **639.2**

1. Whaling 2. Whales
ISBN 0-395-50948-3; 0-395-76480-7 (pa)
LC 91-22483

Surveys the whaling industry, ranging from hunting in colonial America to modern whaling regulations and conservation efforts
"Frampton's strong woodcuts, tinted with muted tones of tan and blue, give the book a period look and a sense of drama. An informative and visually striking picture book for older children." Booklist
Includes glossary and bibliography

Florian, Douglas, 1950-
A fisher. Greenwillow Bks. 1994 unp il (How we work) $15; lib bdg $14.93 (k-1)   **639.2**

1. Fishing
ISBN 0-688-13129-8; 0-688-13130-1 (lib bdg)
LC 93-26515

This book follows a fisherman "from early in the morning to late at night. The boat shown in the watercolor-and-pencil drawings is a small one with a lone man aboard. Later, a dockworker is added to the illustrations. The simple story depicts the physical strength and know-how as well as the special equipment and clothing needed to fish." Booklist

639.3 Fish culture

Aliki
My visit to the aquarium. HarperCollins Pubs. 1993 unp il $15; lib bdg $14.89 (k-3)   **639.3**

1. Marine aquariums 2. Marine animals 3. Freshwater animals
ISBN 0-06-021458-9; 0-06-021459-7 (lib bdg)
LC 92-18678

During his visit to an aquarium, a boy finds out about the characteristics and environments of many different marine and freshwater creatures
"Fish facts, selected for their child-appeal and delivered in a brisk, conversational tone, are neatly organized by marine environment. . . . The dominant blues and greens of Aliki's watercolors are not only cool and inviting; they also provide visual continuity amid the riot of brightly colored fish." Booklist

Ancona, George, 1929-
The aquarium book; written and photographed by George Ancona. Clarion Bks. 1991 47p il lib bdg $15.95; pa $6.95 (3-5)   **639.3**

1. Marine aquariums
ISBN 0-89919-655-1 (lib bdg); 0-395-69940-1 (pa)
LC 90-33328

Text and photographs depict four major aquariums, describing how they are able to recreate various aquatic environments for many species of life
"Sharp color photography (spectacular underwater shots and engrossing displays of contemporary architecture and designs from unusual perspectives) enhances the information-packed text." Booklist

Cone, Molly

Come back, salmon; how a group of dedicated kids adopted Pigeon Creek and brought it back to life; photographs by Sidnee Wheelwright. Sierra Club Bks. for Children 1992 48p il $16.95; pa $6.95 (3-6) **639.3**

1. Salmon 2. Wildlife conservation

ISBN 0-87156-572-2; 0-87156-489-0 (pa)

LC 91-29023

Describes the efforts of the Jackson Elementary School in Everett, Washington, to clean up a nearby stream, stock it with salmon, and preserve it as an unpolluted place where the salmon could return to spawn

"The photographs are superb. . . . Personal and inspiring, the text alternates between descriptions of the project, background information about pollution and renewal, and dialogue of the students recorded; additional scientific information is displayed in panels set off from the main text." Horn Book

Includes glossary

Evans, Mark, 1962-

Fish. Dorling Kindersley 1993 45p il (ASPCA pet care guides for kids) $9.95 (2-5) **639.3**

1. Aquariums 2. Fishes

ISBN 1-56458-222-1

LC 92-53476

Describes how to set up and maintain an aquarium and how to care for fish as household pets

"Attractive, informative. . . . The bright full-color photos show multiethnic children caring for their animals. Lots of white space in the background make the step-by-step text easy to follow." SLJ

639.9 Conservation of biological resources

Ancona, George, 1929-

The golden lion tamarin comes home. Macmillan 1994 unp il $15.95 (3-5) **639.9**

1. Golden Lion Tamarin Conservation Program 2. Tamarins 3. Wildlife conservation

ISBN 0-02-700905-X

LC 93-23705

"An account of the remarkable efforts of people and governments to save one endangered species from extinction. Through unprecedented U.S. breeding programs, golden lion tamarins are being released into the jungles of Brazil." Sci Child

Dewey, Jennifer

Wildlife rescue; the work of Dr. Kathleen Ramsay; by Jennifer Owings Dewey; photographs by Don MacCarter. Boyds Mills Press 1994 63p il $16.95 (4-6) **639.9**

1. Ramsay, Kathleen 2. Wildlife Center (Española, N.M.) 3. Wildlife conservation

ISBN 1-56397-045-7

LC 93-71478

This is an account of the work of Dr. Kathleen Ramsay and the Wildlife Center in Española New Mexico which treats injured animals and returns them to the wild

"This well-written book, illustrated with many clear, full-color photographs, will prove interesting to anyone curious about this timely subject." SLJ

Fraser, Mary Ann

Sanctuary; the story of Three Arch Rocks; written and illustrated by Mary Ann Fraser. Holt & Co. 1994 unp il $15.95 (3-5)

639.9

1. Finley, William L. (William Lovell), 1876-1953 2. Bohlman, Herman 3. Wildlife conservation

ISBN 0-8050-2920-6

LC 93-41362

"Fraser recounts the story of William Finley and Herman Bohlman, two early-twentieth-century naturalists who helped save the wildlife of Three Arch Rocks, a group of small islands off the Oregon coast. . . . Numerous full-color acrylic paintings and labeled diagrams supplement the text and add visual appeal. Reproductions of four original photographs from the expedition have also been included. A very readable account that will be of interest to browsers as well as classes studying endangered species." Booklist

Includes glossary

Friedman, Judi, 1935-

Operation Siberian crane; the story behind the international effort to save an amazing bird. Dillon Press 1992 96p il map $13.95 (5 and up) **639.9**

1. Cranes (Birds) 2. Birds—Protection 3. Wildlife conservation

ISBN 0-87518-515-0

LC 92-13775

Describes the cooperative effort by scientists in the Soviet Union and the United States to save the Siberian crane, with the support and aid of conservationists from other nations

"This book is packed with information, emotion, and possibilities, and it is encouraging for conservationists." Sci Child

Includes glossary and bibliography

Johnson, Sylvia A.

Raptor rescue! an eagle flies free; photographs by Ron Winch. Dutton Children's Bks. 1995 32p il $15.99 (4 and up) **639.9**

1. Gabbert Raptor Center 2. Birds of prey 3. Bald eagle

ISBN 0-525-45301-6

LC 94-41483

"A behind-the-scenes tour of Gabbert Raptor Center at the University of Minnesota explores what happens when eagles and other birds of prey are injured. Readers will be intrigued by the dedicated staff and volunteers who care for these remarkable raptors." Sci Child

Kessler, Cristina

All the king's animals; the return of endangered wildlife to Swaziland; written and photographed by Cristina Kessler; with a foreword by Mswati III. Boyds Mills Press 1995 64p il $17.95 (4-6) **639.9**

1. Swaziland 2. Wildlife conservation

ISBN 1-56397-364-2

LC 94-79621

Factual account of how Swaziland, with the effort of native conservationist Ted Reilly and the approval of the king, restored its native wildlife, which was once lost due to poaching and disease

"Kessler infuses this story with drama, while her closeup shots of sometimes ferocious, but always fascinating, beasts will captivate readers." SLJ

Mallory, Kenneth

Rescue of the stranded whales; [by] Kenneth Mallory and Andrea Conley. Simon & Schuster Bks. for Young Readers 1989 63p il $14.95 (5 and up) **639.9**

1. New England Aquarium Corporation 2. Whales 3. Wildlife conservation
ISBN 0-671-67122-7   LC 88-26408
"A New England Aquarium book"
Published in association with the New England Aquarium

"Three pilot whales saved in a 1986 Cape Cod beaching are restored at the New England Aquarium and returned to the sea. A true ecological drama told in a moving narrative with numerous clear, full-color photographs." Sci Child

Maynard, Thane

Saving endangered mammals; a field guide to some of the earth's rarest animals. Watts 1992 57p il $15.95; lib bdg $15.47 (4-6) **639.9**

1. Rare animals 2. Mammals 3. Wildlife conservation
ISBN 0-531-15253-7; 0-531-11076-1 (lib bdg)
                         LC 92-14439
"A Cincinnati Zoo book"
"Following a brief description of why certain mammals are endangered and what is being done to save them, the author presents a two-page spread on each of more than 20 mammals. Every spread includes a full-page color photograph, a map highlighting the mammal's range, a table of vital facts, and text that describes interesting characteristics and what is and needs to be done in order to save them. The book also includes a list of conservation organizations." Sci Child
Includes glossary and bibliography

Patent, Dorothy Hinshaw

Where the wild horses roam; photographs by William Muñoz. Clarion Bks. 1989 72p il lib bdg $15.95 (4 and up) **639.9**

1. Horses 2. Wildlife conservation
ISBN 0-89919-507-5   LC 88-20360
Also available in paperback from Houghton Mifflin
This book describes the history of wild horses in the United States, protective legislation, the horses' life in the wild, problems caused by overpopulation, and possible solutions, including refuges, the Adopt-A-Horse program; and birth control. A list of wild horse protection associations is appended
"The handsome color photographs, including stunning western landscapes, will hook horse lovers, and the indexed text provides students with smoothly written information for reports." Bull Cent Child Books

The whooping crane; a comeback story; photographs by William Muñoz. Clarion Bks. 1988 88p il $14.95; pa $6.95 (4 and up) **639.9**

1. Cranes (Birds) 2. Birds—Protection 3. Wildlife conservation
ISBN 0-89919-455-9; 0-395-66505-1 (pa)
                         LC 88-2871
Traces the forty-year-old and ongoing attempt to save the endangered whooping crane from extinction, focusing on efforts at wildlife refuges and the captive breeding program

Smith, Roland, 1951-

Sea otter rescue; the aftermath of an oil spill; photographs by the author. Cobblehill Bks. 1990 64p il $14.99 (5 and up) **639.9**

1. Otters 2. Wildlife conservation 3. Oil spills
ISBN 0-525-65041-5   LC 89-49446
"Focusing on a single species, Smith illustrates the damage the Exxon *Valdez* oil spill caused to all species in Alaska's Prince William Sound in the spring of 1989. . . . Although the writing is sometimes dry, this information-packed book not only introduces the sea otter but also describes what was involved in setting up an animal-rescue operation in a small, remote town. Almost every page has an excellent quality, full-color photograph of a different phase of the rescue." SLJ

640.73 Consumer education

Schmitt, Lois

Smart spending; a young consumer's guide. Scribner 1989 102p $13.95 (5 and up) **640.73**

1. Consumer education
ISBN 0-684-19035-4   LC 88-29524
The author offers advice on how to recognize and avoid consumer traps. Case studies discuss misleading advertising, consumer fraud, mail order problems, refund policies, product safety, food poisoning, fad diets, money management, and effective complaining
"Schmitt's integration of teen-oriented case studies into his brisk, no-nonsense text is an engaging approach. Money is a mesmerizing topic and youngsters are bound to keep reading. . . . Clearly delineated chapters make this a handy resource for assignments." Booklist

Zillions. Consumers Union of U.S. $16 per year **640.73**

1. Consumer education—Periodicals
ISSN 1050-8163
Bimonthly. First published 1980 with title: Penny Power
This "is *Consumer Reports* for kids. Just as the adult version of the magazine informs consumers about what to look for in automobiles or electronic gear, this version helps preteens evaluate products they might purchase, such as board games, sweatshirts, and cookies. The evaluations are generally made by panels of preteen consumers. The magazine also covers topics like homework, selecting gifts, and spending money wisely. This magazine is flashy, colorful, and visually appealing. Regular features include letters, book reviews, reports of what bothers readers about advertising, and questions and answers about family life and growing up." Katz. Mag for Libr. 8th edition

641.3 Food

Ancona, George, 1929-

Bananas; from Manolo to Margie. Clarion Bks. 1982 unp il hardcover o.p. paperback available $5.95 (3-5) **641.3**

1. Banana
ISBN 0-395-54787-3 (pa)   LC 82-1247

Ancona, George, 1929——*Continued*

"From Manolo, who lives on a Honduran banana plantation with his family, to Margie, who shops for fruit with her mother in an American grocery store, the book relates the banana's story. Included are a brief history of the fruit, a description of its growth and harvest, and a travelogue of the two-week journey the banana takes by train, boat, and truck to wholesale markets." Horn Book

"Juxtaposition of photos and text is excellent, as is the design." SLJ

Includes glossary

D'Amico, Joan, 1957-

The science chef; 100 fun food experiments and recipes for kids; [by] Joan D'Amico, Karen Eich Drummond; illustrations by Tina Cash-Walsh. Wiley 1995 180p il $12.95 (5 and up)   **641.3**

1. Food 2. Cooking 3. Science—Experiments

ISBN 0-471-31045-X   LC 94-9045

This includes facts about food, recipes, and experiments with food

"Attractively illustrated with black-and-white line drawings, easy and interesting to read, and filled with tidbits of information." SLJ

Includes glossary

De Paola, Tomie, 1934-

The popcorn book. Holiday House 1978 unp il lib bdg $15.95; pa $6.95 (k-3)

641.3

1. Popcorn

ISBN 0-8234-0314-9 (lib bdg); 0-8234-0533-8 (pa)
LC 77-21456

Also available Spanish language edition

"While one twin prepares the treat, the other stays closeby and reads aloud what popcorn is, how it's cooked, stored, and made, how the Indians of the Americas discovered it, and who eats the most. . . . The best thing about popcorn, the twins decide, is eating it. Two recipes are included." Babbling Bookworm

The author-artist's "amusing soft-color pictures—each bordered with a lavender frame—show action in the past or the present while a few lines of text or balloon speeches describe what is happening." Horn Book

Foodworks; over 100 science activities and fascinating facts that explore the magic of food; from the Ontario Science Centre; illustrated by Linda Hendry. Addison-Wesley 1987 90p il pa $9.95 (4-6)

641.3

1. Food 2. Nutrition 3. Science—Experiments

ISBN 0-201-11470-4   LC 87-1796

"One- or two-page sections on many aspects of food, nutrition, health, plants, and animals each include facts and statistics . . . plus 'try this' activities and questions." SLJ

"The writing style and drawings are up-beat and lively, making this an appealing book for browsing and science projects alike. Teachers will also appreciate this guide to active learning." Appraisal

Hausherr, Rosmarie

What food is this? Scholastic 1994 40p il $14.95; pa $4.95 (k-3)   **641.3**

1. Food 2. Nutrition

ISBN 0-590-46583-X; 0-590-46584-8 (pa)
LC 93-17328

Discusses, in question-and-answer format, eighteen different foods representing the four food groups and provides additional information on nutrition, healthy eating habits, and meal preparation with kids in mind

"The real draw here is the attractive format and the delightful multiethnic array of child food-presenters. . . . This is a cheerful and appealing introduction to the serious topic of food." Bull Cent Child Books

Includes glossary

King, Elizabeth, 1953-

Chile fever; a celebration of peppers; story and photographs by Elizabeth King. Dutton Children's Bks. 1995 unp il $14.99 (3-5)

641.3

1. Peppers

ISBN 0-525-45255-9   LC 94-31279

King takes readers on a "visual tour of the New Mexico chile fields. . . . Amply illustrated, the book provides a brisk discussion of the plants, their historical background, and how they are grown and marketed, concluding with a description of the autumn harvest festival in the town of Hatch. An appendix gives notes on the chile heat index, a pronunciation guide, and a recipe." SLJ

Patent, Dorothy Hinshaw

Where food comes from; photographs by William Muñoz. Holiday House 1991 40p il $14.95 (k-3)   **641.3**

1. Food

ISBN 0-8234-0877-9   LC 90-49833

Shows how all food—grains, vegetables, fruits, and dairy and meat products—begins on the farm as sun, earth, air, and water combine to grow plants

"This book presents a clear, matter-of-fact text accompanied by excellent color photographs." Sci Child

Seixas, Judith S.

Junk food—what it is, what it does; illustrated by Tom Huffman. Greenwillow Bks. 1984 47p il $12.95 (1-3)   **641.3**

1. Food 2. Nutrition

ISBN 0-688-02559-5   LC 83-14135

"A Greenwillow read-alone book"

An introduction to facts about junk food—what it is, where it is found, and how it affects the body—with suggestions for snacking more nutritionally

"The text is straightforward, logical, easily understood and mildly admonishing. . . . Though the anti-junk position is clearly stated, it's never a diatribe that would turn kids off. A clearly rational exposition on an increasingly important subject." SLJ

641.5 Cooking

American Heart Association kids' cookbook; edited by Mary Winston; with a special message from James H. Moller; illustrated by Joan Holub. Times Bks. 1993 127p il $15 (3-6) **641.5**

1. Cooking
ISBN 0-8129-1930-0 LC 91-50596

"Targeted at the taste buds of 8- to 12-year-olds, this exceptional cookbook presents health-conscious recipes for such favorites as pizza, pasta, chips, and cookies. Necessary ingredients and equipment are listed clearly at the beginning of each recipe and are followed by step-by-step instructions. The attractive, well-organized format is enhanced by bright watercolor illustrations that depict some of the procedures." Booklist

Includes glossary

Better Homes and Gardens step-by-step kids' cook book. Meredith Corp. 1984 96p il $9.95 (4 and up) **641.5**

1. Cooking
ISBN 0-696-01325-8 LC 83-61317

"After some basic cooking tips, the book continues with simple recipes that require no cooking . . . and quickly moves on to more complicated dishes. . . . Most ambitious are the meal-menu recipes, such as crispy oven chicken. Instructions are divided into blocks with appealing color photographs . . . across from each step. . . . Large, clear type and an especially attractive layout are the frosting on the cake." Booklist

Brady, April A.

Kwanzaa karamu; cooking and crafts for a Kwanzaa feast; illustrations by Barbara Knutson; photographs by Robert L. and Diane Wolfe; additional recipes by Cheryl Davidson Kaufman [et al.] Carolrhoda Bks. 1995 64p il lib bdg $19.95; pa $6.95 (4-6) **641.5**

1. Cooking 2. Kwanzaa 3. African Americans—Social life and customs
ISBN 0-87614-842-9 (lib bdg); 0-87614-633-7 (pa) LC 94-20871

This "introduction to the African American holiday of Kwanzaa not only clearly explains the origin and rituals of the holiday, but also introduces traditional foods and crafts. The 18 recipes included range from simple side and main dishes to salads and desserts. A 'Cooking Smart' section contains helpful hints and safety tips about handling raw food, hot pans, and knives." Booklist

Easy menu ethnic cookbooks. Lerner Publs. 1982-1995 29v il maps lib bdg ea $17.50 (5 and up) **641.5**

1. Cooking
Some titles also available in paperback

Available volumes in this series are: Cooking the African way, by C. R. Nabwire and B. V. Montgomery; Cooking the Australian way, by E. Germaine and A. Burckhardt; Cooking the Austrian way, by H. Hughes; Cooking the Caribbean way, by C. D. Kaufman; Cooking the Chinese way, by L. Yu; Cooking the English way, by B. W. Hill; Cooking the French way, by L. M. Waldee; Cooking the German way, by H. Parnell; Cooking the Greek way; by L. W. Villios; Cooking the Hungarian way, by M. Hargittai; Cooking the Indian way, by V. Madavan; Cooking the Israeli way, by J. Bacon; Cooking the Italian way, by A. Bisignano; Cooking the Japanese way, by R. Weston; Cooking the Korean way, by O. Chung and J. Monroe; Cooking the Lebanese way, by S. Amari; Cooking the Mexican way, by R. Coronado; Cooking the Polish way, by D. Zanojska-Hutchins; Cooking the Russian way, by G. Plotkin and R. Plotkin; Cooking the South American way, by H. Parnell; Cooking the Spanish way, by R. Christian; Cooking the Swiss way, by H. Hughes; Cooking the Thai way, by S. Harrison and J. Monroe; Cooking the Vietnamese way, by C. T. Nguyen and J. Monroe; Desserts around the world; Ethnic cooking the microwave way, by N. Cappelloni; Holiday cooking around the world; How to cook a gooseberry fool, by M. Vaughan; Vegetarian cooking around the world

"Each of these attractive little cookbooks features workable and fairly authentic recipes that use readily available ingredients. Some basic facts about the geography, customs, and eating habits are given for each country. Cooking safety rules are included." Child Book Rev Serv

Hautzig, Esther Rudomin, 1930-

Holiday treats; illustrated by Yaroslava. Macmillan 1983 86p il $13.95 (3-6) **641.5**

1. Cooking
ISBN 0-02-743350-1 LC 83-9347

A collection of recipes, which can be prepared for the most part without adult help, for sixteen holidays throughout the year, including Purim, Halloween, Mother's Day, and Christmas

Linde, Polly van der

Around the world in 80 dishes; by Polly and Tasha Van der Linde; pictures by Horst Lemke. Scroll Press 1971 85p il $10.95 (3-6) **641.5**

1. Cooking
ISBN 0-87592-007-1

"Easy-to-follow recipes for 53 dishes from many different countries which utilize common or readily obtainable ingredients, are presented in a cookbook written by two sisters, ages ten and eight. The cheerfully illustrated book is divided into sections of side dishes, soups, eggs, fish, meats, vegetables and salad, sauces and dressings, desserts, and drinks." Booklist

Osseo-Asare, Fran

A good soup attracts chairs; a first African cookbook for American kids; [by] Fran Osseo-Asare with help from Abena, Masi, and D.K. Pelican 1993 159p il map $18.95 (4 and up) **641.5**

1. African cooking
ISBN 0-88289-816-7 LC 92-42982

Presents over thirty-five easy-to-follow recipes from the kitchens of West Africa and Ghana and instructions on how to throw an African party

"A nice addition to multicultural collections." Booklist

Includes glossary and bibliography

Perl, Lila

Hunter's stew and hangtown fry: what pioneer America ate and why; pictures by Richard Cuffari. Clarion Bks. 1977 156p il map $13.95 (4 and up) **641.5**

1. Cooking 2. United States—Social life and customs
ISBN 0-395-28922-X LC 77-5366

Perl, Lila—*Continued*

First published by Seabury Press

"This is a culinary cultural history of the growing United States during the 19th Century. The author divides the country into five sections and, in a readable style, describes the people, the food, and the ambience of the times. There are 20 choice and representative recipes, a few at the end of each chapter." SLJ

"Illustrated with atmospheric gray wash over black line drawings. Worthwhile for social history studies." Booklist

Includes bibliography

Slumps, grunts, and snickerdoodles: what Colonial America ate and why; drawings by Richard Cuffari. Clarion Bks. 1975 125p il map $14.95 (4 and up)   **641.5**

1. Cooking 2. United States—Social life and customs—1600-1775, Colonial period

ISBN 0-395-28923-8

First published by Seabury Press

"In three major chapters dividing the pre-Revolutionary colonies into regions—New England, Middle Atlantic, Southern—the author explains ' . . . not only "what" the colonists ate and "why," but . . . the geographical and historical background as well as the intimate domestic surroundings.' . . . Emphasis is on foods grown in different areas and how traditional recipes developed from the materials available, but local manners and mores are also skillfully woven into the narrative." SLJ

Scobey, Joan

The Fannie Farmer junior cook book; illustrated by Patience Brewster. new & rev ed. Little, Brown 1993 280p il $19.95 (6 and up)   **641.5**

1. Cooking

ISBN 0-316-77624-6   LC 92-42632

First published 1942 under the authorship of Wilma Lord Perkins

Introduces the basic ingredients, utensils and equipment, and safety aspects of cooking and provides recipes for soups, main dishes, vegetables, and other foods

"Scobey has adapted one of the bibles of basic good cooking to reflect today's busy lifestyles and time-saving techniques. . . . The attractively designed pages are laced with delicate drawings of herbs, flowers, fruits, and other foods, a tantalizing enhancement to a promising cookbook." Booklist

Walker, Barbara Muhs, 1928-

The Little House cookbook; frontier foods from Laura Ingalls Wilder's classic stories; by Barbara M. Walker; illustrated by Garth Williams. Harper & Row 1979 240p il $15.95; lib bdg $15.89; pa $6.95 (5 and up)   **641.5**

1. Wilder, Laura Ingalls, 1867-1957 2. Cooking 3. Frontier and pioneer life

ISBN 0-06-026418-7; 0-06-026419-5 (lib bdg); 0-06-446090-8 (pa)   LC 76-58733

Recipes based on the pioneer food written about in the "Little House" books of Laura Ingalls Wilder, along with quotes from the books and descriptions of the food and cooking of pioneer times

"Illustrated by Williams's familiar warm drawings, the adaptations of menus from pioneer days include paragaphs describing the Wilder and Ingalls families working together, preparing holiday meals, individual foods, special treats and staple fare." Publ Wkly

Includes bibliographical references

Wilkes, Angela

The children's step by step cookbook. Dorling Kindersley 1994 128p il $18.95 (4-6)   **641.5**

1. Cooking

ISBN 1-56458-474-7   LC 93-28860

"The book starts with an explanation of its symbols and arrangement, a list of kitchen rules . . . and a picture of all the kitchen equipment needed for the book's recipes. The recipes themselves are divided into sections: Snacks; Eggs and Cheese; Pasta, Rice, and Pizza; Vegetables; Meat and Fish; Cookies, Breads, and Cakes; and Desserts and Treats." Bull Cent Child Books

"Detailed, delectable color photographs accompany over fifty tantalizing, easy-to-follow recipes." Horn Book Guide

Includes glossary

641.8   Cooking specific kinds of composite dishes

Morris, Ann

Bread, bread, bread; photographs by Ken Heyman. Lothrop, Lee & Shepard Bks. 1989 unp il $15.93; lib bdg $16; pa $4.95 (k-3)   **641.8**

1. Bread

ISBN 0-688-06335-7; 0-688-06334-9 (lib bdg); 0-688-12275-2 (pa)   LC 88-26677

This photo essay shows different kinds of bread around the world from baguettes to challah

"Each picture offers a strong ethnic identity or a thought-provoking human interaction, with captions of only a few words in large print. An unusual index . . . gives background information about the pictures, citing the countries of origin and a few facts about each type of bread." SLJ

Paulsen, Gary

The tortilla factory; paintings by Ruth Wright Paulsen. Harcourt Brace & Co. 1995 unp il $14 (k-3)   **641.8**

1. Tortillas

ISBN 0-15-292876-6   LC 93-48590

Also available Spanish language edition

"Paulsen traces the journey of the corn, from harvest and grinding, to the tortilla factory, where people turn the corn flour into tortillas that, filled with beans, 'give strength to the brown hands that work the black earth to plant yellow seeds . . . '. Replete with the lush greens of healthy plants, the rich browns of adobe buildings and fertile soil, and the vibrant gold of ears of corn, the highly satisfying illustrations reinforce the reverential mood established by the spare poetic narrative." Horn Book

643 Housing and household equipment

Colman, Penny

Toilets, bathtubs, sinks, and sewers; a history of the bathroom. Atheneum Pubs. 1994 70p il $14.95 (5 and up)   **643**

1. Bathrooms—History 2. Sanitation—History

ISBN 0-689-31894-4   LC 93-48413

"The author relates the history of our efforts to deal with human waste. . . . The book is packed with facts succinctly delivered in a crisp writing style with sufficient explanation to clearly place the material in historic context. Neatly inserted asides are used to lighten the tone. The author has chosen appropriate vintage prints and photographs to illustrate the evolution of fixtures." Horn Book

Includes bibliography

646.2 Sewing and related operations

Hoffman, Christine

Sewing by hand; pictures by Harriett Barton. HarperCollins Pubs. 1994 29p il $14; lib bdg $13.89 (2-4)   **646.2**

1. Sewing

ISBN 0-06-021146-6; 0-06-021147-4 (lib bdg)

LC 92-9516

"The tools and techniques to create a round pillow, beanbag cat, and stuffed doll are clearly illustrated and explained in this full-color craft book. Simple patterns are well designed for tracing onto paper. . . . The projects offer challenges to beginners without overwhelming them." SLJ

649 Child rearing

Brown, Laurene Krasny

Toddler time; a book to share with your toddler; pictures by Marc Brown. Little, Brown 1990 40p il $14.95   **649**

1. Child rearing

ISBN 0-316-11263-1   LC 90-32342

"Joy Street books"

This book "is a discussion of the primary stages, pleasures, and problems of the toddler years. . . . Topics include everyday routines, feelings and values, play, learning new concepts, excursions, and staying well and happy." SLJ

"Sensible advice and playful scenes abound in this enjoyable handbook for parents of young children. . . . Marc Brown illuminates the mundane moments of daily life with humor and an astute eye for the endearing and exasperating ways of children." Horn Book

650.1 Personal success in business

Barkin, Carol, 1944-

Jobs for kids; the guide to having fun and making money; [by] Carol Barkin & Elizabeth James; illustrated by Roy Doty. Lothrop, Lee & Shepard Bks. 1990 113p il lib bdg $11.93; pa $6.95 (5 and up)   **650.1**

1. Moneymaking projects for children 2. Children—Employment 3. Personal finance

ISBN 0-688-09324-8 (lib bdg); 0-688-09323-X (pa)

LC 89-45900

Discusses the advantages of working and offers tips on assessing your talents and abilities, finding a job, acting responsibly, handling disasters, and setting prices

"The friendly tone is appealing, and even kids who aren't looking for work are likely to tuck away some of this counsel for future reference. Occasional cartoon drawings break up the text." Booklist

652 Processes of written communication

Huckle, Helen

The secret code book. Dial Bks. 1995 57p il $14.99 (4 and up)   **652**

1. Cryptography 2. Ciphers

ISBN 0-8037-1725-3   LC 94-30019

This "book features one-to four-page sections explaining 19 codes, many of them significant in history, as well as methods for encoding and deciphering messages using the codes. Full-color photographs, diagrams, and reproductions of period artwork and documents illustrate the text. . . . The codes will intrigue and challenge readers. Tipped into the back endcovers is a heavy paper sheet with press-out pieces for making two cipher disks." Booklist

Includes glossary

Janeczko, Paul B., 1945-

Loads of codes and secret ciphers. Macmillan 1984 108p il $15 (5 and up)   **652**

1. Cryptography 2. Ciphers

ISBN 0-02-747810-6   LC 84-5791

"Information on breaking codes as well as on building simple coding devices to transmit secret messages is interspersed with historical background notes on the ciphers used, for instance, by the 1920s hobos, cowboys of the Old West, and the U.S. naval navigators. Practice codes are given with handy answers for beginners to check out their expertise." Booklist

Mango, Karin N., 1936-

Codes, ciphers, and other secrets. Watts 1988 93p il lib bdg $15.57 (4 and up)   **652**

1. Cryptography 2. Ciphers

ISBN 0-531-10575-X   LC 88-5638

"A First book"

Mango, Karin N., 1936—_Continued_

Describes the many ways of hiding the real meaning of what someone is trying to say by using a code or replacing the message with a cipher

"Enciphered and encoded sentences from a Sherlock Holmes story form a thread through the book's numerous examples, which are pleasingly combined with Mango's anecdotal history of the subject. Diagrams illuminate the construction of a St. Cyr's slide, a cipher wheel, and other devices." Booklist

Includes bibliography

Schwartz, Alvin, 1927-1992

The cat's elbow, and other secret languages; collected by Alvin Schwartz; pictures by Margot Zemach. Farrar, Straus & Giroux 1982 82p il $15; pa $3.95 (4 and up)   **652**

1. Ciphers 2. Cryptography
ISBN 0-374-31224-9; 0-374-41054-2 (pa)

                           LC 81-5513

Beginning with Pig Latin "Schwartz progresses to more arcane explanations of twisting languages, for fun and sometimes practical purposes. The folklorist gives examples of codes used by kids in Africa, China, Germany and, most notably, by the entire town, adults and children, in Boonville, Calif. From the 1880s onward, the citizens have been frustrating outsiders with their private communications in Boontling." Publ Wkly

"Funny, exuberant Alvin Schwartz is a lucid teacher, clearly describing 13 secret languages and codes . . . and demonstrating them with riddles and jokes. . . . The proverbial children of all ages will find the book irresistible." SLJ

Includes bibliography

659.13   Signs and signboards

Hoban, Tana

I read signs. Greenwillow Bks. 1983 unp il $16; lib bdg $15.93; pa $4.95 (k-2)

                           659.13

1. Signs and signboards
ISBN 0-688-02317-7; 0-688-02318-5 (lib bdg); 0-688-07331-X (pa)   LC 83-1482

In this book "30 verbal and 27 symbolic street signs have been caught on location in close-ups with a minimum of background to give just a soupçon of milieu (city, sky or apple tree) or hint of meaning ('Beware of dog' on chain link fence). Design is bold; primary colors are emphasized. The familiar predominates; more unusual signs . . . add interest." SLJ

I read symbols. Greenwillow Bks. 1983 unp il $14.95; lib bdg $15.93 (k-2)   **659.13**

1. Signs and signboards 2. Signs and symbols
ISBN 0-688-02331-2; 0-688-02332-0 (lib bdg)

                           LC 83-1481

This picture book "shows sharp, full-color close-up photographs of common signs . . . displaying some 27 road, street, and building symbols that youngsters will find it worthwhile to know." Booklist

"The only words in Hoban's new book appear on the last two pages, explaining what the symbols in her photos say. She has, however, photographed so impressively in color virtually all the instantly informative messages that even little children will not need the postscript except to confirm their findings. . . . The pictures in this book can teach one to really see and comprehend the meanings in everyday things most of us ignore." Publ Wkly

I walk and read. Greenwillow Bks. 1984 unp il lib bdg $16.93 (k-2)   **659.13**

1. Signs and signboards
ISBN 0-688-02576-5   LC 83-14215

"In this book of brightly-colored photographs, Hoban invites children to experience the diversity of signs, including restaurant, traffic and emergency signs. A tool for perceptual learning, this book will help children experience the colors, shapes and textures of signs without leaving their seats. Symbols often accompany or are integrated within the sign itself, and children will be able to interpret meaning without being able to read." SLJ

664   Food technology

Busenberg, Bonnie

Vanilla, chocolate, & strawberry; the story of your favorite flavors. Lerner Publs. 1994 112p il maps lib bdg $22.95 (5 and up)

                           664

1. Flavoring essences
ISBN 0-8225-1573-3   LC 93-15101

Describes how vanilla, chocolate, and strawberry came to become popular flavorings, how they were originally used, how they're used today, and what makes them taste the way they do. Includes recipes

"This book truly has something for everyone. It is genuinely fun to read, fascinating, and well illustrated." Sci Books Films

Includes glossary

Jaspersohn, William

Cookies; written and photographed by William Jaspersohn. Macmillan 1993 unp il $14.95 (3-5)   **664**

1. Famous Amos Chocolate Chip Cookie Corp. 2. Cookies
ISBN 0-02-747822-X   LC 91-45023

A behind-the-scenes look at how chocolate chip cookies are made at a Famous Amos cookie factory

"There are plenty of helpful black-and-white photographs. . . . Although a visit to the factory would be preferable, this book is the second best thing." SLJ

Machotka, Hana

Pasta factory. Houghton Mifflin 1992 32p il $14.95 (3-5)   **664**

1. Pasta products
ISBN 0-395-60197-5   LC 92-4333

"A photographic journey through a local pasta factory in New Jersey, _Pasta Factory_ shows the reader how pasta is made and packaged to be sold. How the different shapes are formed and colors are made is discussed in a straightforward manner." Sci Books Films

668 Technology of other organic products

Cobb, Vicki, 1938-

The secret life of cosmetics: a science experiment book; illustrated by Theo Cobb. Lippincott 1985 111p il lib bdg $14.89 (5 and up) **668**

1. Cosmetics 2. Science—Experiments

ISBN 0-397-32122-8   LC 85-40097

The author "examines cosmetics: soaps, lotions, perfumes, shampoos, conditioners, and makeup. She often provides a brief historical perspective of each substance . . . as well as information on the scientific principles that underlie it. . . . There are some good opportunities here for science experiments or classroom demonstrations, and the subject is sure to interest many who would not otherwise think in scientific terms. Illustrated with pen-and-ink cartoon drawings." Booklist

670 Manufacturing

Rose, Sharon

CD's, super glue, and salsa; how everyday products are made; [by Sharon Rose & Neil Schlager] U.X.L 1995 2v il set $34.95 (5 and up) **670**

1. Manufactures

ISBN 0-8103-9791-9   LC 94-35243

This work examines the "manufacture of thirty familiar items. The entries represent progress and fashion trends that influence industry (optical fiber), transportation (helicopter), music (trumpet), diet (chocolate), entertainment (baseball), and lifestyle (lipstick). Unhurried, step-by-step descriptions of processes, explanations of technical terms, and clear drawings and photographs accompany each entry." Voice Youth Advocates

For a fuller review see: Booklist, Apr. 15, 1995

Tunis, Edwin, 1897-1973

Colonial craftsmen and the beginnings of American industry; written and illustrated by Edwin Tunis. Crowell 1976 c1965 159p il o.p. (5 and up) **670**

1. Decorative arts 2. United States—Social life and customs—1600-1775, Colonial period 3. Handicraft

A reprint of the title first published 1965 by World Publishing Company

"Superb illustrations and comprehensive text describe the working methods, products, houses, shops and trades of the New World." N Y Public Libr. Ref Books for Child Collect

674 Lumber processing, wood products, cork

Miller, Cameron

Woodlore; [by] Cameron Miller and Dominique Falla. Ticknor & Fields Bks. for Young Readers 1995 c1994 unp il $14.95 (3-5) **674**

1. Woodwork 2. Wood

ISBN 0-395-72034-6   LC 94-27987

First published 1994 in Australia

"Verses describe the craft of woodworking and each wood for each use. . . . Appended notes further elucidate why particular woods are best for particular purposes. . . . Each homely scene, most set in the eighteenth and nineteenth centuries, shows woodworkers at their painstaking tasks, enclosed by inventive wood frames that use the wood described on the page. . . . The variety of grains and shades relieves the basic brown, and the trompe l'oeil effects will keep kids looking." Bull Cent Child Books

676 Pulp and paper technology

Perrins, Lesley, 1953-

How paper is made; design, Arthur Lockwood. Facts on File 1985 32p il (How it is made) $12.95 (4 and up) **676**

1. Paper

ISBN 0-8160-0036-0   LC 84-18638

The author discusses "the history, development of production techniques, varied uses and the environmental effects of the manufacturing process of paper." SLJ

677 Textiles

Keeler, Patricia A.

Unraveling fibers; [by] Patricia A. Keeler and Francis X. McCall, Jr. Atheneum Bks. for Young Readers 1995 35p il $16 (3-5) **677**

1. Fibers 2. Fabrics

ISBN 0-689-31777-8   LC 93-13906

This book "looks at the sources of plant, animal, and synthetic fibers; describes the processes used to extract them from their natural states; and provides examples of finished products." SLJ

"The authors combine thoughtful explanations with liberal sprinklings of photographs silhouetted against white space in an attractive page design. . . . A useful and inviting overview." Horn Book

681 Precision instruments and other devices

Cobb, Vicki, 1938-

Writing it down; pictures by Marylin Hafner. Lippincott 1989 32p il lib bdg $12.89 (1-3) **681**

1. Writing—Materials and instruments

ISBN 0-397-32327-1   LC 88-14191

Cobb, Vicki, 1938-—*Continued*

Simple descriptions of paper, pencils, pens, and crayons explain how they work and how they were invented

The "behind-the-scenes stories of things children use daily are just right for primary-grade readers who can easily understand the concepts. [This] excellent addition to nonfiction collections will be fun to booktalk, and may be used as [a] model of effective writing and illustration for children." SLJ

681.1   Instruments for measuring time

Zubrowski, Bernie, 1939-

Clocks; building and experimenting with model timepieces; illustrated by Roy Doty. Morrow 1988 112p il lib bdg $12.88 (4 and up)   **681.1**

1. Clocks and watches

ISBN 0-688-06926-6   LC 87-18467

"A Boston Children's Museum activity book"

"From simple sundials and hourglasses to more complex water and mechanical timepieces, this guide to clock building has clear, step-by-step instructions, includes good diagrams, and requires only easily obtainable materials like pop bottles, sand, and string (and, for the more complicated projects, plastic tubing and pulleys). Occasionally the focus seems to shift from how to tell time to principles of mechanics and physics." Bull Cent Child Books

684   Furnishings and home workshops

Adkins, Jan

Toolchest; written, designed, and illustrated by Jan Adkins; carpenter in residence, Joseph Karson. Walker & Co. 1973 48p il hardcover o.p. paperback available $4.95 (5 and up)   **684**

1. Carpentry tools 2. Woodwork

ISBN 0-8027-7218-8 (pa)   LC 72-81374

"Meticulously illustrated with drawings that show exact details of tools, hardware, wood grains, and techniques, this is a superb first book for the amateur carpenter. Adkins explains the uses of each tool, the ways in which each variety of saw or chisel is fitted for a particular task, such procedures as dowelling, gluing, or cutting a tenon and mortise, and he describes the uses for each kind of nail and screw. This most useful book concludes with advice on the care of tools." Bull Cent Child Books

686   Printing and related activities. Book arts

Aliki

How a book is made; written and illustrated by Aliki. Crowell 1986 32p il $14.95; lib bdg $14.89; pa $5.95 (2-5)   **686**

1. Books 2. Book industries 3. Publishers and publishing 4. Printing

ISBN   0-690-04496-8;   0-690-04498-4   (lib   bdg); 0-06-446085-1 (pa)   LC 85-48156

Also available Spanish language edition

Describes the stages in making a book, starting with the writing of the manuscript and the drawing of the pictures, and explaining all the technical processes leading to printed and bound copies

"With charm and whimsy, and using a cartoon format, Aliki delightfully shares the agonies and ecstasies of being an author/artist. . . . Her fictional characters are all adorable cats, which makes Goodbooks Publishing Company a very caring, helpful, happy 'cat house'." Child Book Rev Serv

690   Buildings

Barton, Byron

Building a house. Greenwillow Bks. 1981 unp il lib bdg $16.93; pa $4.95 (k-1)   **690**

1. Building 2. Houses

ISBN 0-688-84291-7 (lib bdg); 0-688-09356-6 (pa)

"In the simplest possible book on building a house, a step-by-step, one-line description is given of the major factors in construction. Such workers as bricklayers, carpenters, plumbers, electricians, and painters do their own jobs until the small, bright red-and-green house is completed and a family moves in. Flat drawings in brilliant primary colors enable the very young to visualize the methods of house-building." Horn Book

Machines at work. Crowell 1987 unp il $15; lib bdg $14.89 (k-1)   **690**

1. Building

ISBN 0-694-00190-2; 0-690-04573-5 (lib bdg)

     LC 86-24221

"Double-page illustrations depict a busy day at a construction site as workers (with the positive inclusion of women) knock down a building and start a new one." SLJ

"The short, punchy narrative reinforces the dynamics of the illustrations. . . . This should be a popular read-aloud for preschoolers and satisfying read-alone for beginners." Publ Wkly

Gibbons, Gail

How a house is built. Holiday House 1990 unp il $15.95 (k-3)   **690**

1. Building 2. Houses

ISBN 0-8234-0841-8   LC 90-55107

This book describes how the surveyor, heavy machinery operators, carpenter crew, plumbers, and other workers build a house

"With her customary bright illustrations, Gibbons gives a fine introduction to the construction of a wood-frame house. . . . Construction machines and materials as well as parts of the house are identified, and each stage of construction logically follows the others. Workers are drawn in both sexes and several skin tones." Booklist

Up goes the skyscraper! Four Winds Press 1986 unp il $14.95; pa $5.95 (k-3)   **690**

1. Skyscrapers 2. Building

ISBN 0-02-736780-0; 0-689-71411-4 (pa)

     LC 85-16245

"Without oversimplification, the author traces in straightforward text and brightly colored pictures the construction of a skyscraper from the clearing of the site to tenant move-in." SLJ

Macaulay, David, 1946-
Mill. Houghton Mifflin 1983 128p il $16.95; pa $7.95 (4 and up) **690**
1. Mills 2. Textile industry—History
ISBN 0-395-34830-7; 0-395-52019-3 (pa)
LC 83-10652
This is an "account of the development of four fictional 19th-Century Rhode Island cotton mills. In explaining the construction and operation of a simple water-wheel powered wooden mill, as well as the more complex stone, turbine and steam mills to follow, the author also describes the rise and decline of New England's textile industry." SLJ
Includes glossary

Unbuilding. Houghton Mifflin 1980 78p il $16.95; pa $7.95 (4 and up) **690**
1. Empire State Building (New York, N.Y.) 2. Building 3. Skyscrapers
ISBN 0-395-29457-6; 0-395-45425-5 (pa)
LC 80-15491
This fictional account of the dismantling and removal of the Empire State Building describes the structure of a skyscraper and explains how such an edifice would be demolished
"Save for the fact that one particularly stunning double-page spread is marred by tight binding, the book is a joy: accurate, informative, handsome, and eminently readable." Bull Cent Child Books

Oxlade, Chris
Houses and homes, illustrated by Raymond Turvey; photography by Martyn Chillmaid. Watts 1994 32p il (Technology craft topics) lib bdg $12.60 (4-6) **690**
1. House construction 2. Handicraft
ISBN 0-531-14330-9
LC 94-15514
"Besides providing factual information on ancient, medieval, and modern houses and homes, [this book] gives instructions for making models of five different dwellings and a solar heater. The projects include easy-to-understand directions, easy-to-find materials, outstanding full-color illustrations and photographs, and enough information to motivate readers." SLJ
Includes glossary and bibliography

Walker, Lester
Housebuilding for children; written, photographed, and illustrated by Les Walker; preface by Nonny Hogrogian. Overlook Press 1977 174p il hardcover o.p. paperback available $13.95 **690**
1. Building 2. Houses
ISBN 0-87951-332-2 (pa)
LC 76-47220
"This book is written for young people who want to build houses just as older people do. I designed six small houses that would educate children in the different 'real-life' ways of building houses." Introduction
"An enthusiastically written and clearly illustrated guide. Preparatory projects are included to help children learn the use of basic tools and methods. The six houses—including a tree house—were all built by children from seven to nine, supervised by an adult. Full-page photographs of the young builders and of houses under construction appear on nearly every other page, adjacent to drawings of materials and the step-by-step procedures." Horn Book

Wilkinson, Philip, 1955-
Building; written by Philip Wilkinson; photographed by Dave King & Geoff Dann. Knopf 1995 61p il (Eyewitness books) $19; lib bdg $20.99 (4 and up) **690**
1. Structural engineering 2. House construction 3. Building materials
ISBN 0-679-87256-6; 0-679-97256-0 (lib bdg)
LC 94-37733
"A Dorling Kindersley book"
Fist published 1994 in the United Kingdom
This covers "the history of building techniques, materials, and philosophy from earth-and-thatch houses to cathedrals and skyscrapers." SLJ
An "extremely handsome volume. . . . This is an informative book, fascinating for study or browsing." Sci Books Films

693 Construction in specific types of materials and for specific purposes

Ancona, George, 1929-
Cutters, carvers & the cathedral. Lothrop, Lee & Shepard Bks. 1995 unp il $15; lib bdg $14.93 (3-5) **693**
1. Cathedral of St. John the Divine (New York, N.Y.) 2. Stonecutting 3. Cathedrals
ISBN 0-688-12056-3, 0-688-12057-1 (lib bdg)
LC 94-10549
"The story of the Cathedral of Saint John the Divine in Manhattan—from the limestone used to build it to the people who mold it—emerges in fine prose and exquisite photographs. . . . Not only beautiful to behold, but useful in so many areas of the curriculum, this book is an outstanding photo essay." Horn Book
Includes glossary

Rounds, Glen, 1906-
Sod houses on the Great Plains; written and illustrated by Glen Rounds. Holiday House 1995 unp il $15.95 (k-3) **693**
1. Houses 2. Frontier and pioneer life
ISBN 0-8234-1162-1
LC 94-27390
"The author explains plainly and clearly just how the homesteaders built their warm, dry, fireproof, ecologically sound sod dwellings on the prairies more than a century ago. His spare but evocative crayon illustrations detail the text and add sly wit." N Y Times Book Rev

694 Wood construction. Carpentry

Florian, Douglas, 1950-
A carpenter. Greenwillow Bks. 1991 unp il $13.95; lib bdg $13.88 (k-1) **694**
1. Carpentry
ISBN 0-688-09760-X; 0-688-09761-8 (lib bdg)
LC 90-30752
A simple description of what a carpenter does in his daily work

Florian, Douglas, 1950-—*Continued*

"The full-page illustrations, predominantly brown, orange, and tan, suggest the enticing surfaces of fresh-cut, aromatic wood. . . . [This is a] charming concept book." SLJ

Walker, Lester

Carpentry for children; preface by David Macaulay. Overlook Press 1982 208p il hardcover o.p. paperback available $12.95 (4 and up)   **694**

1. Carpentry 2. Handicraft

ISBN 0-87951-990-8 (pa)   LC 82-3469

A step-by-step guide to carrying out such carpentry projects as a birdhouse, candle chandelier, doll cradle, puppet theater, and coaster car

697 Heating, ventilating, air-conditioning engineering

Giblin, James, 1933-

Chimney sweeps: yesterday and today; by James Cross Giblin; illustrated by Margot Tomes. Crowell 1982 56p il hardcover o.p. paperback available $5.95 (4 and up)   **697**

1. Chimneys

ISBN 0-06-446061-4 (pa)   LC 81-43878

The author "explores the history, folklore and romance of the chimney sweep in this introduction to an old and colorful profession. Following the sweep from his European beginnings to his present-day operation in America, the author details changes and developments in practice. . . . Giblin's relaxed, affable manner belies the amount of information he offers in this highly accessible, enjoyable history of the chimney sweep. Fine illustrations by Margot Tomes complement the text." SLJ

Includes bibliography

700 THE ARTS

Isaacson, Philip M., 1924-

A short walk around the pyramids & through the world of art. Knopf 1993 120p il $22; lib bdg $20.99 (5 and up)   **700**

1. Art

ISBN 0-679-81523-6; 0-679-91523-0 (lib bdg)
                                          LC 91-8854

Introduces tangible and abstract components of art, and the many forms art can take including sculpture, pottery, painting, photographs, and even furniture and cities

"A handsomely designed book with spacious margins and brilliantly clear full-color photographs. . . . Isaacson conducts his tour with a gentle, conversational style, surprising readers with fascinating juxtapositions." SLJ

701 Philosophy and theory

Davidson, Rosemary

Take a look; an introduction to the experience of art. Viking 1994 c1993 128p il $18.99 (5 and up)   **701**

1. Art

ISBN 0-670-84478-0   LC 92-1180

First published 1993 in the United Kingdom

An introductory look at artists, media, concepts, styles and art periods

"This comprehensive volume addresses not only the more traditional aspects of art appreciation but also social and cultural forces that introduction-to-art books rarely discuss. . . . The language is straightforward, simple, and engaging . . . and sections often end with thought-provoking, clearly open-ended questions to the reader." Bull Cent Child Books

Includes glossary and bibliography

Micklethwait, Lucy

A child's book of art; great pictures, first words; selected by Lucy Micklethwait. Dorling Kindersley 1993 64p il $16.95 (k-3)   **701**

1. Art appreciation 2. Vocabulary

ISBN 1-56458-203-5   LC 92-54320

An introduction to art that uses well-known works of art to illustrate familiar words

"Micklethwait wisely includes an abundance of paintings featuring children, action scenes and vibrant colors—all elements guaranteed to snare a youngster's attention. The thematic arrangement of the works of art places them in contexts familiar to kids." Publ Wkly

708 Art—Galleries, museums private collections

Brown, Laurene Krasny

Visiting the art museum; [by] Laurene Krasny Brown and Marc Brown. Dutton 1986 32p il lib bdg $14.99 (k-3)   **708**

1. Art museums 2. Art appreciation

ISBN 0-525-44233-2   LC 85-32552

Also available in paperback from Puffin Bks.

As a family wanders through an art museum, they see examples of various art styles from primitive through twentieth-century pop art

"A lively, fact-filled introduction to the art museum for the whole family, with animated drawings and full-color reproductions of art from all over the world. . . . All of the paintings are identified, both in the text and in the back, and all possible periods of art—from primitive to modern—are shown." Publ Wkly

709.01 Arts of nonliterate peoples, and earliest times to 499

La Pierre, Yvette

Native American rock art; messages from the past; illustrated by Lois Sloan. Thomasson-Grant 1994 48p il $16.95 (4 and up) **709.01**

1. Indians of North America—Antiquities 2. Rock drawings, paintings, and engravings
ISBN 1-56566-064-1 LC 94-13659
This is an introduction to "petroglyphs and pictographs, images carved into and painted onto stone surfaces by early Native Americans. La Pierre explains how paints were made and used, identifies common symbols found in rock art and demonstrates the importance of art to native American culture." Publ Wkly
"While this book will supplement titles on Native American culture that only mention rock art, it also stands on its own as an outstanding study of a fascinating art form and means of communication." SLJ
Includes glossary

711 Area planning

Macaulay, David, 1946-

City: a story of Roman planning and construction. Houghton Mifflin 1974 112p il $16.95; pa $7.95 (4 and up) **711**

1. City planning—Rome 2. Civil engineering 3. Roman architecture
ISBN 0-395-19492-X; 0-395-34922-2 (pa)
"By following the inception, construction, and development of an imaginary Roman city, the account traces the evolution of Verbonia from the selection of its site under religious auspices in 26 B.C. to its completion in 100 A.D." Horn Book
Includes glossary

720 Architecture

Brown, David J., 1946-

The Random House book of how things were built. Random House 1992 140p il lib bdg $19.99; pa $15 (4 and up) **720**

1. Architecture
ISBN 0-679-92044-7 (lib bdg); 0-679-82044-2 (pa)
LC 91-27638
First published 1991 in the United Kingdom with title: The Kingfisher book of how they were built
An illustrated history of more than sixty notable structures of the ancient and modern world. Includes detailed diagrams and a glossary of architectural terms
"Large, colorful double-spread illustrations and frequent inset diagrams, depicting stages of building as well as the finished product, make the volume a browser's delight. Although the text is brief, consisting mostly of captions, it conveys a great deal of information." Booklist

Isaacson, Philip M., 1924-

Round buildings, square buildings, & buildings that wiggle like a fish; with photographs by the author. Knopf 1988 121p il $22; pa $13 (4 and up) **720**

1. Architecture
ISBN 0-394-89382-4; 0-679-80649-0 (pa)
LC 87-16967
This discussion of architecture presents ninety-three buildings and structures from various times and places, including Stonehenge, Chartres, the Taj Mahal, the Great Mosque in Córdoba, the Parthenon, and the Brooklyn Bridge
"Beautifully composed and reproduced color photographs are numbered for reference in the text, which describes almost poetically the effects of contrasting architectural elements, styles, shapes, materials, and functions. . . . The writing is lyrical without abandoning fact, and the photographic perspectives are arresting." Bull Cent Child Books

The **Visual** dictionary of buildings. Dorling Kindersley 1992 64p il (Eyewitness visual dictionaries) $15.95 (4 and up) **720**

1. Architecture
ISBN 1-56458-102-0 LC 92-7673
Also available Spanish language edition
Labeled illustrations with explanatory text depict historical and contemporary structures, architectural elements, and building components from ancient times to the present
"This visual dictionary easily stands tall as an art history source as well as a reference for the structures, forms, and components of buildings." Booklist

725 Public structures

Doherty, Craig A.

The Sears Tower; [by] Craig A. Doherty and Katherine M. Doherty. Blackbirch Press 1995 48p il (Building America) lib bdg $14.95 (4-6) **725**

1. Sears Tower (Chicago, Ill.)
ISBN 1-56711-109-2 LC 94-40642
This book "describes the design and construction of the world's tallest building, and includes information on the Calder sculpture, the 'hidden floors,' and window washing. Photographs, color or black-and white, appear on nearly every page." Booklist
Includes glossary and bibliographical references

726 Buildings for religious and related purposes

Macaulay, David, 1946-

Cathedral: the story of its construction. Houghton Mifflin 1973 77p il $16.95; pa $7.95 (4 and up) **726**

1. Cathedrals 2. Gothic architecture
ISBN 0-395-17513-5; 0-395-31668-5 (pa)
A Caldecott Medal honor book, 1974

Macaulay, David, 1946— *Continued*
This is a description, illustrated with black-and-white line drawings, of the construction of an imagined representative Gothic cathedral "in southern France from its conception in 1252 to its completion in 1338. The spirit that motivated the people, the tools and materials they used, the steps and methods of constructions, all receive . . . attention." Booklist
Includes glossary

Pyramid. Houghton Mifflin 1975 80p il $16.95; pa $7.95 (4 and up)   **726**
1. Pyramids 2. Egypt—Civilization
ISBN 0-395-21407-6; 0-395-32121-2 (pa)
The construction of a pyramid in 25th century B.C. Egypt is described. "Information about selection of the site, drawing of the plans, calculating compass directions, clearing and leveling the ground, and quarrying and hauling the tremendous blocks of granite and limestone is conveyed as much by pictures as by text." Horn Book
Includes glossary

728 Residential and related buildings

Dorros, Arthur
This is my house; written and illustrated by Arthur Dorros. Scholastic 1992 unp il $14.95; pa $3.95 (k-3)   **728**
1. Domestic architecture
ISBN 0-590-45302-5; 0-590-49444-9 (pa)
LC 91-34273
Also available Spanish language edition
"Each page has a full-page, colorful illustration of a house from around the world with an accompanying text that reads 'this is my house' in the language of that country." Soc Educ

Morris, Ann
Houses and homes; photographs by Ken Heyman. Lothrop, Lee & Shepard Bks. 1992 32p il map $14; lib bdg $13.93; pa $4.95 (k-3)   **728**
1. Houses
ISBN 0-688-10168-2; 0-688-10169-0 (lib bdg); 0-688-13578-1 (pa)   LC 92-1365
A simple discussion of different kinds of houses and what makes them homes
"A striking photographic survey of housing around the world that will be a real eyeopener for many children. The lush, full-color photos, one to two per page, tell the real story, conveying nearly as much about those who live in these homes as they do about the dwellings themselves. . . . This is a solid addition for collections that support social studies or multicultural units, but would be equally fascinating to browsers throughout the age group." SLJ

Ventura, Piero
Houses; structures, methods, and ways of living; [by] Piero Ventura with the collaboration of Max Casalini, Pierluigi Longo, Marisa Murgo Ventura. Houghton Mifflin 1993 64p il $16.95 (4 and up)   **728**
1. Domestic architecture 2. Houses
ISBN 0-395-66792-5   LC 93-108

Original Italian edition, 1992
"A brief history of houses, illustrated with . . . ink-outlined watercolors. Starting with cave dwellings, each double-page spread offers several paragraphs of basic descriptions of homes from ancient Egypt through Greece, Rome, the Vikings, the Middle Ages, on through to modern apartments. All are enlivened by Ventura's illustrations that show exteriors, cut-away views of interiors, details of physical construction." SLJ
Includes glossary

Yue, Charlotte
The igloo; [by] Charlotte and David Yue. Houghton Mifflin 1988 117p il $13.95; pa $4.95 (3-6)   **728**
1. Igloos 2. Inuit
ISBN 0-395-44613-9; 0-395-62986-1 (pa)
LC 88-6154
Describes how an igloo is constructed and the role it plays in the lives of the Eskimo people. Also discusses many other aspects of Eskimo culture that have helped them adapt to life in the Arctic
"This book is a tidy source of reference information, curriculum support, and just plain compelling reading." SLJ
Includes bibliography

728.8 Large and elaborate private dwellings

Adkins, Jan
The art and industry of sandcastles; being an illustrated guide to basic constructions along with divers information devised by one Jan Adkins, a wily fellow. Walker & Co. 1971 xxixp il maps hardcover o.p. paperback available $9.95 (4 and up)   **728.8**
1. Castles
ISBN 0-8027-7205-6 (pa)
"Designed with an unobtrusive mastery of form and line the text and illustrations together serve both as a sophisticated guide to making sandcastles and as a record of the evolution of castle building in Europe. The explanation of various processes used to make sand structures and to build various kinds of actual castles is given in a pleasing, skillfully presented book for all ages, with information included on the duties of major personnel in the traditional castle." Booklist

Gravett, Christopher
Castle; written by Christopher Gravett; photographed by Geoff Dann. Knopf 1994 63p il (Eyewitness books) $19; lib bdg $18.99 (4 and up)   **728.8**
1. Castles 2. Fortification
ISBN 0-679-86000-2; 0-679-96000-7 (lib bdg)
LC 93-32594
"A Dorling Kindersley book"
"*Castle* looks at European fortifications, Byzantine and Muslim-influenced constructions of the Crusades, and Japanese strongholds and defense strategies through photographs of architectural features, designs, and weapons. Everyday life is also documented with pictures of artifacts and people in period costumes." SLJ
"This book offers page after page of excellent photo-

Gravett, Christopher—*Continued*

graphs. . . . Each photo is clearly described in language concise enough that the reader understands the functioning of obscure implements and features of castles. The information presented is generally accurate." Sci Books Films

Macaulay, David, 1946-

Castle. Houghton Mifflin 1977 74p il $16; pa $7.95 (4 and up) **728.8**

1. Castles 2. Fortification

ISBN 0-395-25784-0; 0-395-32920-5 (pa)

LC 77-7159

A Caldecott Medal honor book, 1978

Macaulay depicts "the history of an imaginary thirteenth-century castle—built to subdue the Welsh hordes—from the age of construction to the age of neglect, when the town of Aberwyfern no longer needs a fortified stronghold." Economist

"The line drawings are meticulous in detail, lucidly illustrating architectural features described in the text and injected with a refreshing humor. . . . The writing is clear, crisp, and informative, with a smooth narrative flow." Bull Cent Child Books

Includes glossary

Steele, Philip

Castles. Kingfisher (NY) 1995 63p il $14.95 (4 and up) **728.8**

1. Castles

ISBN 1-85697-547-9

LC 94-29366

An "overview of medieval European (and a few Near Eastern) castles. The book's strengths are its well-organized format and careful balance of text and illustrations. Steele touches on almost every facet of castle construction, inhabitants, celebrations, and rituals, as well as more mundane topics such as sanitation and the kitchen." SLJ

Includes glossary

730.9 Sculpture—Historical and geographic treatment

Doherty, Craig A.

Mount Rushmore; [by] Craig A. Doherty and Katherine M. Doherty. Blackbirch Press 1995 48p il map (Building America) lib bdg $14.95 (4-6) **730.9**

1. Borglum, Gutzon, 1867-1941 2. Mount Rushmore National Memorial (S.D.)

ISBN 1-56711-108-4

LC 94-24757

This book "discusses the planning, funding, sculpting, maintenance, and popularity of the enormous carvings of four presidents, as well as the original and continuing controversy concerning the taking of the Black Hills from the Sioux and the use of Mount Rushmore for the monument. . . . Useful for school reports." Booklist

Includes glossary and bibliographical references

Greenberg, Jan, 1942-

The sculptor's eye; looking at contemporary American art; [by] Jan Greenberg and Sandra Jordan. Delacorte Press 1993 128p il $19.95 (6 and up) **730.9**

1. American sculpture 2. Modern sculpture—1900-1999 (20th century) 3. Art appreciation

ISBN 0-385-30902-3

LC 92-16323

Discusses the nature, subject matter, and techniques of modern American sculpture and presents such contemporary artists as Red Grooms, Viola Frey, and George Segal

"Every bit as informative and beautifully produced as *The Painter's Eye* [entered in class 759.13]. . . . The sculptures are presented in glorious, full color, but the artists are pictured in candid black-and-white shots." Booklist

Includes glossary and bibliography

736 Carving and carvings. Paper cutting and folding

Irvine, Joan, 1951-

How to make super pop-ups; illustrated by Linda Hendry. Morrow Junior Bks. 1992 96p il $14; lib bdg $13.93; pa $6.95 (3-6) **736**

1. Paper crafts 2. Handicraft

ISBN 0-688-10690-0; 0-688-10691-9 (lib bdg); 0-688-11521-7 (pa)

LC 92-2637

Companion volume to the author's How to make pop-ups (1988)

Provides instructions for making a variety of paper pop-ups, including animals, boats, robots, and enormous pop-ups for the stage

"Explicit, step-by-step instructions, accompanied by helpful black-and-white line drawings, are easy to follow. Each project includes suggestions for variation that will encourage children to think creatively." SLJ

Sarasas, Claude

The ABC's of origami; paper folding for children; illustrated by the author. Tuttle 1964 55p il $14.95 (4-6) **736**

1. Origami 2. Alphabet

ISBN 0-8048-0000-6

First published 1951 in Japan

Here are "diagramed directions for folding 26 objects from Albatross to Zebra with each heading [first in English and then] translated into French and transliterated Japanese. Color illustrations show finished object against an oriental background." SLJ

737.4 Coins

Hughes, Roderick P.

Fell's United States coin book. Lifetime Bks. (Hollywood) il pa $12.95 **737.4**

1. Coins

First edition published 1949 by Fell. (12th edition 1995) Periodically revised

Current edition by Roderick P. Hughes

Hughes, Roderick P.—*Continued*

This guide contains complete tables showing today's value of every coin minted in the United States. Along with illustrations is information on the history of coins, speculation and investment, how to start a collection, how to sell coins and recognize worthless coins

738.1 Ceramic arts—Techniques, equipment, materials

Florian, Douglas, 1950-

A potter. Greenwillow Bks. 1991 unp il $13.95; lib bdg $13.88 (k-1)   **738.1**

1. Pottery
ISBN 0-688-10100-3; 0-688-10101-1 (lib bdg)

LC 90-33940

This book illustrates what a potter does with clay

The "actions are described in just a few clear words per page, set in large type against plenty of white space. . . . The naïf artwork is accessible and warmly attractive, drawn and painted with a combination of crayons, felt pen, and watercolors in sunny tones of orange and yellow. . . . [This is a] cheerful, welcoming treatment that not only informs the young about [its] subject, but also makes [it] quite appealing." Booklist

741.2 Drawing—Techniques, equipment, materials

Emberley, Ed

Ed Emberley's big green drawing book. Little, Brown 1979 91p il $15.95 (2-5)

    741.2

1. Drawing
ISBN 0-316-23595-4   LC 79-16247

The author "combines basic shapes (circles, triangles, lines, squiggles) to create a variety of cartoon people and animals. The crisp green-and-black illustrations on a white background are large and well spaced. . . . As in his other drawing books, Emberley's wordless step-by-step method is easy to follow; even very young children can successfully reproduce the simple but appealing figures." SLJ

Ed Emberley's big red drawing book. Little, Brown 1987 unp il $14.95; pa $9.95 (2-5)

    741.2

1. Drawing
ISBN 0-316-23434-6; 0-316-23435-4 (pa)

LC 87-3091

The author explains "how to create objects and figures by building up a series of simple lines and squiggles into a more complicated and complete whole. The color red suggests most of the subjects, among them a U.S. flag, a fire engine, and assorted red-and-green Christmas items." Booklist

Ed Emberley's drawing book: make a world. Little, Brown 1972 unp il hardcover o.p. paperback available $6.95 (2-5)   **741.2**

1. Drawing
ISBN 0-316-23644-6 (pa)

"Emberley gives directions for drawing, among a myriad of other things, 10 different kinds of cars, 16 varieties of trucks, and animals of all species including anteaters and dinosaurs." Book World

"The final three pages, which supply suggestions for making comic strips, posters, mobiles and games, help make the volume particularly appealing. For all developing artists and even plain scribblers." Horn Book

Ed Emberley's picture pie: a circle drawing book. Little, Brown 1984 unp il $15.95; pa $8.95 (2-5)   **741.2**

1. Drawing 2. Paper crafts
ISBN 0-316-23425-7; 0-316-23426-5 (pa)

LC 84-9666

"Shows how to make myriad designs based on circle cutouts. Whole circles, halves, quarters, and eighths are layered and arranged to form gloriously colorful geometric collages, borders, patterns, and—with the addition of a few dots and lines—processions of birds, flowers, fish, plants, and much more. The array of spectacular sample designs is followed by suggestions for putting the artwork to use and adding further embellishments." Booklist

741.5 Cartoons, caricatures, comics

Benjamin, Carol Lea

Cartooning for kids. Crowell 1982 71p il lib bdg $14.89 (4-6)   **741.5**

1. Cartoons and caricatures 2. Drawing
ISBN 0-690-04208-6   LC 81-43876

Outlines how to draw simple cartoons from circles, dots, lines, and curves and how to add professional touches such as shading, decorative detail, or color

"Written in a cheerful, humorous tone and full of line drawings, the book encourages the budding cartoonist to use his imagination to create his own successful cartoon." Horn Book

Hoff, Syd, 1912-

The young cartoonist; the ABC's of cartooning. Stravon Educ. Press 1983 192p il $19.95 (4 and up)   **741.5**

1. Cartoons and caricatures
ISBN 0-87396-094-7   LC 82-5980

"A Rainbow book"

This book covers such aspects of cartooning as "how to draw faces, figures, and expressions and how to block out a composition." Horn Book

"This is less a book of useful instructions than a series of examples of the cartoonist's work: pages of figures based on a particular line, pages in which features are added, one by one. . . . There's a chapter on how to make up jokes and choose captions. This could be used for imitation, but ideas that might act as a catalyst for creativity are sparse." Bull Cent Child Books

Jenkins, Patrick

Animation; how to draw your own flipbooks, and other fun ways to make cartoons move. Addison-Wesley 1991 96p il pa $9.95   **741.5**

1. Animation (Cinematography) 2. Drawing
ISBN 0-201-56757-1   LC 91-26233

First published in Canada with title: Flipbook animation

Jenkins, Patrick—*Continued*
Includes instructions for creating drawings that give the illusion of various kinds of movement and special effects. Also describes several early motion picture devices

"The activities are aptly demonstrated with step-by-step instructions, tools needed, and multiple charming graphics. . . . This book is chock-full of activities for energetic individuals. It shouldn't sit on the shelf for long." SLJ

Weiss, Harvey, 1922-
Cartoons and cartooning. Houghton Mifflin 1990 64p il $13.95 (4 and up)   **741.5**
1. Cartoons and caricatures
ISBN 0-395-49217-3   LC 89-39596
"Weiss describes cartoons from the past as well as what the art of cartooning has become. Comic strips, gag panels, story cartoons, political or editorial cartoons, and the art of caricature, as well as the business of cartooning, comic books, and animated cartoons are all included. The last chapter gives some hints about doing your own cartoons." SLJ

"This entire book has the instant appeal and immediate impact typical of good comic books: brief but interesting text and well executed, eye-catching illustrations." Voice Youth Advocates

Includes bibliography

741.6 Graphic design, illustration and commercial art

The **Illustrator's** notebook; edited by Lee Kingman. Horn Bk. 1978 153p il $28.95
          741.6
1. Illustration of books 2. Illustrators 3. Children's literature—History and criticism
ISBN 0-87675-013-7   LC 77-20028
This is a collection of excerpts from articles originally published in "Horn Book Magazine." The artists discuss their feelings about book illustration in terms of its history and its significance as an art form and as a means of communication. They also discuss various illustration techniques, including woodcut, lithography, collage and color separation. The book contains over a hundred illustrations, many in color, that provide examples of the illustrator's craft

Includes bibliography

Illustrators of children's books. Horn Bk. 1947-1978 4v il v1, 3 o.p.; v2 $28.95; v4 $35.95   **741.6**
1. Illustration of books 2. Illustrators 3. Children's literature—History and criticism
Contents: v 1 1744-1945, compiled by Bertha E. Mahony, Louise Payson Latimer and Beulah Folmsbee (o.p.); v2 1946-1956, compiled by Ruth Hill Viguers, Marcia Dalphin and Bertha Mahony Miller (ISBN 0-87675-016-1); v3 1957-1966, compiled by Lee Kingman, Joanne Foster and Ruth Giles Lontoft (o.p.); v4 1967-1976, compiled by Lee Kingman, Grace Allen Hogarth and Harriet Quimby (ISBN 0-87675-018-8)

"This standard series contains biographies and bibliographies of outstanding illustrators of children's books. Each book also includes essays on the history and evolution of the art of illustrating children's books. The 1967-1976 volume contains a cumulative index for the series." Nichols. Guide to Ref Books for Sch Media Cent. 4th edition

Lanes, Selma G.
The art of Maurice Sendak. Abrams 1980 278p il $34.95   **741.6**
1. Sendak, Maurice
ISBN 0-8109-8063-0   LC 80-10796
The author "tells the story of Sendak's career as an illustrator of his own and others' books. . . . Ninety-four full-color illustrations and 165 black and white ones (including many sketches and preliminary drawings) sample the career from 1950 to 1981. The reader will learn a great deal about the planning and execution of children's books along the way." Best Sellers

Stevens, Janet
From pictures to words; a book about making a book; written and illustrated by Janet Stevens. Holiday House 1995 unp il $15.95 (k-3)   **741.6**
1. Picture books for children 2. Authorship
ISBN 0-8234-1154-0   LC 94-18976
"Stevens, appearing as herself sketched in black-and-white, is the main character in her story. She's surrounded by . . . animal characters who encourage her to write a book starring them. With help from Cat, Koala Bear, and Rhino, she does, explaining as she goes along the basic elements of writing and illustrating—setting, plot, tension, and characterization." Booklist

"The straightforward text carefully presents information while maintaining the narrative flow. Dialogue balloons and funny asides from the characters keep the presentation lively." SLJ

Stewig, John W.
Looking at picture books; by John Warren Stewig. Highsmith Press 1995 269p il $49
          741.6
1. Picture books for children 2. Illustration of books 3. Children's literature—History and criticism
ISBN 0-917846-29-X   LC 94-35026
This overview includes chapters on "pictorial elements, such as shape, line, color, or proportion, and on composition. . . . The chapter on book design considers such things as the book's shape, type of paper chosen, typefaces, and page layout. There is also information here about the various media used in picture books." J Youth Serv Libr

Includes bibliographical references

Talking with artists [I]-II; compiled and edited by Pat Cummings. Bradbury Press 1992-1995 2v il $18.95; $19.95 (4 and up)
          741.6
1. Illustrators 2. Illustration of books
ISBN 0-02-724245-5 (v1); 0-689-80310-9 (v2 Simon & Schuster)
Volume two published by Simon & Schuster Bks. for Young Readers

Each volume presents interviews with illustrators, who discuss their lives and works. Among the 14 artists in the first volume are Victoria Chess, Leo and Diane Dillon, Amy Schwartz, Tom Feelings, and Steven Kellogg. The 13 artists represented in the second volume include Brian Pinkney, Denise Fleming, Floyd Cooper, Maira Kalman, and David Wisniewski. Samples of each illustrator's work are included

741.9   Collections of drawings

—I never saw another butterfly—; children's drawings and poems from Terezin concentration camp, 1942-1944; edited by Hana Volavková; foreword by Chaim Potok; afterword by Vaclav Havel. expanded 2nd ed, by U.S. Holocaust Memorial Mus. Schocken Bks. 1993 xxii, 106p il $25; pa $14   **741.9**

1. Child artists 2. Child authors 3. Terezin (Czechoslovakia: Concentration camp)
ISBN 0-8052-4115-9; 0-8052-1015-6 (pa)

                          LC 92-50477

Original Czech edition, 1959; first American edition published 1964 by McGraw-Hill

"Of the 15,000 children who passed through Terezin before going to Auschwitz, only 100 lived. This book is a collection of poems and drawings by some of them. . . . This touching book adds another facet to library collections on the Holocaust." SLJ

743   Drawing and drawings by subject

Ames, Lee J., 1921-
[Draw 50 series] Doubleday 1974-1995 22v prices vary (4 and up)   **743**

1. Drawing

Most titles available only in paperback

Available titles are: Draw 50 animals (1974); Draw 50 boats, ships, trucks, & trains (1976); Draw 50 airplanes, aircraft, & spacecraft (1977); Draw 50 dinosaurs and other prehistoric animals (1977); Draw 50 famous faces (1978); Draw 50 vehicles (1978); Draw 50 famous cartoons (1979); Draw 50 buildings and other structures (1980); Draw 50 dogs (1981); Draw 50 monsters, creeps, superheroes, demons, dragons, nerds, dirts, ghouls, giants, vampires, zombies, and other curiosa (1983); Draw 50 horses (1984); Draw 50 athletes (1985); Draw 50 cats (1986); Draw 50 cars, trucks, and motorcycles (1986); Draw 50 holiday decorations (1987); Draw 50 beasties and yugglies and turnover uglies and things that go bump in the night (1988); Draw 50 sharks, whales, and other sea creatures (1989); Draw 50 creepy crawlies (1991); Draw 50 endangered animals (1992); Draw 50 people (1993); Draw 50 flowers, trees, and other plants (1994); Draw 50 people of the Bible (1995)

Each volume presents step-by-step instructions for drawing a variety of animals, people, or objects

Arnosky, Jim
Drawing from nature. Lothrop, Lee & Shepard Bks. 1982 unp il $15; pa $8.95 (4 and up)   **743**

1. Drawing 2. Animal painting and illustration
ISBN 0-688-01295-7; 0-688-07075-2 (pa)

                          LC 82-15327

The author "shows how to draw land and water—both above and below the surface—how to draw snow, animal tracks in it and in mud, how to draw animals still and in motion, birds in flight and landing. . . . Arnosky's goal seems to be to teach young readers how to see as an artist would, and observe as a naturalist would. He succeeds beautifully." SLJ

Drawing life in motion. Lothrop, Lee & Shepard Bks. 1984 unp il $16; pa $8.95 (4 and up)   **743**

1. Drawing 2. Animal painting and illustration
ISBN 0-688-03803-4; 0-688-07076-0 (pa)

                          LC 83-25129

The author/artist provides tips on how to illustrate motion in both plants and animals

"Intended for artists with some experience, the book is not a step-by-step manual for beginners but, at all times, encourages young people to rely on their own observations." Horn Book

Bolognese, Don
The way to draw and color monsters; [by] Don Bolognese, Elaine Raphael; calligraphy by Jeanne Greco. Random House 1991 unp il hardcover o.p. paperback available $5.99 (4 and up)   **743**

1. Monsters in art 2. Drawing
ISBN 0-679-80478-1 (pa)   LC 90-8637

Provides basic techniques for drawing such monstrous and mythical creatures as vampires, dragons, and Frankenstein-type characters

Emberley, Ed
Ed Emberley's drawing book of faces. Little, Brown 1975 32p il hardcover o.p. paperback available $5.95 (2-5)   **743**

1. Drawing 2. Face in art
ISBN 0-316-23655-1 (pa)

Provides step-by-step instructions for drawing a wide variety of faces reflecting various emotions and professions

Ed Emberley's great thumbprint drawing book. Little, Brown 1977 37p il lib bdg $14.95 (2-5)   **743**

1. Drawing
ISBN 0-316-23613-6   LC 76-57346

"The artist shows how to combine thumbprints and simple lines to create a multitude of animals, people, birds, and flowers." Booklist

"There is little text; most of the book consists of illustrations, step-by-step, of making pictures out of thumbprints. A few Emberley embellishments and a page that suggests other ways of making prints (carrot or potato) are included." Bull Cent Child Books

Frame, Paul, 1913-1994
Drawing cats and kittens. Watts 1979 71p il (How-to-draw book) hardcover o.p. paperback available $3.95 (4 and up)   **743**

1. Drawing 2. Cats in art 3. Animal painting and illustration
ISBN 0-531-15198-0 (pa)   LC 79-11935

"This is for serious beginners, ones willing to put in the practice time Frame stresses is necessary to develop drawing skills. The overall emphasis is on studied observations of form, with exercises that allow work on problems such as perspective changes or distribution of light and shadow. . . . Sketches are plentiful and helpful as practice ideals. The parade of completed cats that finishes the presentation gives readers a standard to aim for." Booklist

745.5 Handicrafts

Haldane, Suzanne
Painting faces. Dutton 1988 32p il lib bdg
$13.95 (4-6)   **745.5**
1. Decoration and ornament 2. Face
ISBN 0-525-44408-4   LC 88-3706
Also available in paperback from Puffin Bks.

Text and photographs introduce painted faces from various cultures and countries. The book includes directions that children can follow for painting some of them
"Many young readers will be content to browse through the pictures rather than spend time on the text. Even so, the book will open up connections to other times and societies as well as stimulate a popular activity. Warnings about skin allergies are included." Bull Cent Child Books

Hauser, Jill Frankel
Kids' crazy concoctions; 50 mysterious mixtures for art & craft fun; illustrated by Loretta Trezzo Braren. Williamson 1995 156p il pa $12.95 (3-6)   **745.5**
1. Handicraft
ISBN 0-913589-81-0   LC 94-4633
"A Williamson kids can! book"

"Hauser includes recipes for homemade papers, glues, paints, molding doughs and clay; they are followed by directions for making decorator boxes, stationery, books, bookmarks, gift tags, mobiles, sand paintings, ornaments, toys, stained-glass art, and jewelry. Illustrated with pen-and-ink sketches, each project begins with a 'What You Need' list and numbered steps of 'What You Do.'. . . An outstanding practical resource for classrooms." SLJ

Kerina, Jane
African crafts; illustrated by Tom Feelings, with diagrams by Marylyn Katzman. Lion Bks. 1970 64p il lib bdg $13.95 (4 and up)
                                                745.5
1. Handicraft
ISBN 0-87460-084-1

This book includes "directions for making a variety of useful and decorative objects in the tradition of African craftsmen, including pottery, jewelry, wood carvings, calabash kitchen-ware, Akuaba dolls, tie-dyed cloth, a musical instrument, and simple danshiki and other articles of clothing. The objects, which utilize easily obtainable materials, are identified as to their use, history, and region of origin. Clear drawings show the finished objects and some of the steps in their creation. Since the directions are frequently sketchy, children may require adult help in making many of the projects." Books for Child, 1970-1971

McGraw, Sheila
Gifts kids can make. Firefly Bks. (Willowdale) 1994 96p il lib bdg $19.95; pa $10.65 (4 and up)   **745.5**
1. Handicraft 2. Gifts
ISBN 1-895565-36-7 (lib bdg); 1-895565-35-9 (pa)

"McGraw provides directions for 14 inexpensive gifts that children can make from easily obtainable materials. A bunny made from a facecloth, a cotton sock doll, homemade dog biscuits, and a hobby horse are among the projects included." SLJ

"The step-by-step instructions simply couldn't be any clearer. . . . The projects themselves result in interesting gifts." Quill Quire

Press, Judy, 1944-
The little hands art book; illustrated by Loretta Trezzo Braren. Williamson 1994 156p il pa $12.95   **745.5**
1. Handicraft
ISBN 0-913589-86-1   LC 94-13910
"A Williamson kids can! book"
Exploring arts & crafts with 2- to 6- year-olds on cover

The author "begins her book of project ideas with introductory advice to adults on creativity and safety. . . . Although written for librarians, teachers, and parents, some six-year-olds may be able to read the directions themselves, aided visually by corresponding black-and-white illustrations. Appendices provide 11 recipes for supplies like paste, clay, and paint as well as a list of art materials children can easily find around the house. There are a multitude of ideas here." SLJ

Ross, Kathy, 1948-
Crafts for Kwanzaa; illustrated by Sharon Lane Holm. Millbrook Press 1994 47p il (Holiday crafts for kids) lib bdg $15.40; pa $6.95 (1-3)   **745.5**
1. Kwanzaa 2. Handicraft
ISBN 1-56294-412-6 (lib bdg); 1-56294-740-0 (pa)
                                        LC 93-36690
This introduction to the African American celebration explains holiday history and includes ideas for gifts as well as decorations

Crafts for Valentine's Day; illustrated by Sharon Lane Holm. Millbrook Press 1995 47p il (Holiday crafts for kids) lib bdg $15.40; pa $5.95 (1-3)   **745.5**
1. Handicraft 2. Valentines
ISBN 1-56294-489-4 (lib bdg); 1-56294-887-3 (pa)
                                        LC 94-9834
"Each of 20 simple projects appears on a two-page spread; materials are pictured and named in a sidebar on the left-hand side. Step-by-step directions include full color illustrations of the process and of the completed item. Materials are readily available. . . . The activities are presented in a readable format so that youngsters will be able to do them with minimal adult supervision." SLJ

Sattler, Helen Roney
Recipes for art and craft materials; with new illustrations by Marti Shohet. rev ed. Lothrop, Lee & Shepard Bks. 1987 144p il $15 (4 and up)   **745.5**
1. Handicraft—Equipment and supplies 2. Artists' materials
ISBN 0-688-07374-3   LC 86-34271
Also available in paperback from Beech Tree Bks.
First published 1973

The author explains "how to make pastes and glues, modeling compounds, papier-mâché, casting compounds, paints, inks, flower preservatives, recycled paper, and more. Activities are studies in applied science that can provoke questions that invite investigations, encourage careful observation, and celebrate the cleverness of hands as well as brain." Sci Child

Thomson, Ruth
Get set—go! [Arts & crafts series]. Childrens
Press 1994 4v il ea lib bdg $14.90; pa $4.95
(k-3)　　　　　　　　　　　　　　**745.5**
1. Handicraft
Contents: Collage; Drawing; Painting; Printing
This series describes and illustrates projects that explore
a variety of techniques using readily available materials

Tofts, Hannah
The paint book; written and edited by
Diane James; photography by Jon Barnes.
Simon & Schuster Bks. for Young Readers
1990 unp il $11.95 (k-3)　　　　　**745.5**
1. Handicraft
ISBN 0-671-70364-1　　　　　　LC 89-21893
Describes and illustrates a variety of painting techniques,
including wax and paint, stencilling, glass painting, and face
painting

Wilkes, Angela
My first activity book. Knopf 1990 c1989
48p il $13; lib bdg $13.99 (1-4)　　**745.5**
1. Handicraft
ISBN 0-394-86583-9; 0-394-96583-3 (lib bdg)
　　　　　　　　　　　　　　　LC 89-2640
Also available Spanish language edition
First published 1989 in the United Kingdom
Instructions for making masks, jewelry, Christmas tree
decorations, and other objects from materials readily avail-
able in the home
"This large-sized volume contains a treasure trove of in-
viting and imaginative things to make. Concise directions
are amplified by bright, step-by-step photographs." Publ
Wkly

745.54　Paper handicrafts

Corwin, Judith Hoffman
Papercrafts; origami, papier-mâché, and
collage. Watts 1988 72p il lib bdg $18.50 (3
and up)　　　　　　　　　　　　**745.54**
1. Paper crafts 2. Handicraft
ISBN 0-531-10465-6　　　　　　LC 87-21611
This book includes "24 activities involving origami, papier-mâché, and collage. Origami projects include several
animals, a mask, and some flowers. The papier-mâché section gives a recipe for paste followed by directions for making beads, a ladybug, and several other items. Collage
offerings are the most diverse and plentiful: birds, a cat,
bunnies, circus performers, and other amply decorated figures." Booklist
"Illustrations in two colors are plentiful, instructions are
clear and specific, and materials lists are complete." SLJ

Irvine, Joan, 1951-
Build it with boxes; illustrated by Linda
Hendry. Morrow Junior Bks. 1993 96p il $14;
lib bdg $13.93; pa $6.95 (3-6)　　　**745.54**
1. Boxes 2. Handicraft
ISBN　0-688-12081-4;　0-688-11524-1　(lib bdg);
0-688-11525-X (pa)　　　　　　LC 91-45589

First published 1991 in Canada with title: Make it with
boxes
Explains how to make boxes and box creations, including a fish, dragon, camera, airplane, and tropical rain forest
"The cheerful line drawings provide step-by-step demonstrations of projects as well as inviting illustrations of kids
having fun with their box toys. Throughout the book, Irvine encourages safety and recycling as well as creativity. A
good addition to crafts collections." Booklist

Renfro, Nancy
Bags are big! a paper bag craft book; written
and illustrated by Nancy Renfro. Nancy
Renfro Studios 1986 63p il pa $14.95
　　　　　　　　　　　　　　　745.54
1. Paper crafts 2. Handicraft
ISBN 0-931044-10-3　　　　　　LC 88-141246
"This book shows how even the lowly paper bag can be
transformed by the wizardry of our imaginations into something marvelous or magical. . . . It features animated and
colorful illustrations and photos, and will make a good addition to any classroom, recreational or library how-to corner." Sch Arts

Tofts, Hannah
The 3-D paper book; written and edited by
Diane James; photography by Jon Barnes.
Simon & Schuster Bks. for Young Readers
1990 32p il $11.95; pa $4.95 (k-3)　**745.54**
1. Paper crafts 2. Models and model making
ISBN 0-671-70370-6; 0-671-70371-4 (pa)
　　　　　　　　　　　　　　　LC 89-27416
Provides illustrated instructions for a variety of paper
modelling activities

West, Robin
Dinosaur discoveries; how to create your
own prehistoric world; photographs by Bob
and Diane Wolfe; drawings by Mindy Rabin.
Carolrhoda Bks. 1989 71p il lib bdg $19.95
(3-5)　　　　　　　　　　　　　**745.54**
1. Paper crafts 2. Dinosaurs
ISBN 0-87614-351-6　　　　　　LC 88-32513
"This attractive book gives directions for making three-
dimensional paper models of nine prehistoric creatures and
three prehistoric plants. Included are dinosaurs, a mammoth, and a giant dragonfly. . . . Directions are given in
clearly worded, numbered paragraphs supplemented by an
informative color photograph of each project and a sequence of illustrative diagrams." SLJ

745.58　Handicrafts from beads, found and other objects

Ross, Kathy, 1948-
Every day is Earth Day; a craft book;
illustrated by Sharon Lane Holm. Millbrook
Press 1995 47p il (Holiday crafts for kids) lib
bdg $15.40; pa $5.95 (1-3)　　　　**745.58**
1. Handicraft 2. Recycling 3. Earth Day
ISBN 1-56294-490-8 (lib bdg); 1-56294-888-1 (pa)
　　　　　　　　　　　　　　　LC 94-9835

Ross, Kathy, 1948-—*Continued*

Following an explanation of Earth Day, this book provides "instructions for 20 crafts that reflect an interest in recycling and/or using everyday materials. . . . Materials are clearly listed and include such recyclable items as old puzzle pieces, plastic bottles, and used socks, as well as standard art items such as scissors, glue, and paint. The instructions are numbered and illustrated in bright, attractive colors." SLJ

745.59 Making specific objects

Wright, Lyndie

Masks; photography: Chris Fairclough. Watts 1990 48p il (Fresh start) lib bdg $12.95 (4 and up)   **745.59**

1. Masks (Facial) 2. Handicraft

ISBN 0-531-10856-2   LC 89-36533

Provides step-by-step illustrated instructions for making a variety of masks, including painted masks, balloon masks, cardboard robot masks, and shadow masks

"Clear instructions and crisp, full-color photographs create an attractive and logical format." SLJ

Includes bibliography

745.592 Toys, models, miniatures, related objects

Churchill, E. Richard (Elmer Richard)

Fast & funny paper toys you can make; illustrated by James Michaels. Sterling 1989 128p il $14.95 (3-5)   **745.592**

1. Toys 2. Handicraft

ISBN 0-8069-5770-0   LC 89-32411

This book provides directions for making paper toys from household articles. Includes boats, noisemakers, puppets, mobiles, and more

"Milk cartons, cereal boxes, notebook paper, rubber bands, and tape are among the easily accessible materials used, making this an ideal resource where budgets are tight. Numbered illustrations on every page augment the clear step-by-step instructions." Booklist

Instant paper airplanes; illustrated by James Michaels. Sterling 1988 128p il hardcover o.p. paperback available $8.95 (3-5)   **745.592**

1. Airplanes—Models 2. Paper crafts

ISBN 0-8069-6797-8 (pa)   LC 88-12325

"Churchill gives directions for no less than 28 different folded paper gliders, divided into six groups ranging from the very easiest to fold and fly to experimental designs. He intersperses the definitions of many aeronautical terms in boxes with the step-by-step directions for each plane. He then incorporates these terms into the directions so that thoughtful readers can gain 'hands-on' knowledge of them. All directions are concise and clear. Diagrams show step-by-step procedures and are well marked and easily referred to in the narrative." SLJ

Kuklin, Susan

From head to toe; how a doll is made. Hyperion Bks. for Children 1994 unp il $15.95; lib bdg $15.89 (k-3)   **745.592**

1. Dolls

ISBN 1-56282-666-2; 1-56282-667-0 (lib bdg)

LC 93-23332

"The intricate process of doll manufacturing is conveyed effectively through a readable text and excellent color photographs that are further enhanced by an especially attractive format. Creative as well as technical aspects are mentioned in a survey made more vivid by detailing the work of actual employees, named and pictured." Horn Book Guide

Simon, Seymour, 1931-

The paper airplane book; illustrated by Byron Barton. Viking 1971 48p il lib bdg $11.95; pa $4.99 (3 5)   **745.592**

1. Airplanes—Models 2. Paper crafts

ISBN 0-670-53797-7 (lib bdg); 0-14-030925-X (pa)

Step-by-step instructions for making paper airplanes with suggestions for experimenting with them

745.594 Decorative objects

Ancona, George, 1929-

The piñatamaker: El piñatero. Harcourt Brace & Co. 1994 unp il $16.95; pa $8.95 (k-3)   **745.594**

1. Paper crafts 2. Bilingual books—English-Spanish 3. Mexico—Social life and customs

ISBN 0-15-261875-9; 0-15-200060-7 (pa)

LC 93-2389

Describes how Don Ricardo, a craftsman from Ejutla de Crespo in southern Mexico, makes piñatas for all the village birthday parties and other fiestas

"Ancona tells his story in both English and Spanish, with both languages on every page. His clear, bright, full-color photographs complement the detailed text, giving the reader much additional information." Horn Book

Elliot, Marion

My party book; [by] Marion Elliot, Cheryl Owen. Little, Brown 1995 c1994 96p il $14.95 (3-5)   **745.594**

1. Parties 2. Handicraft

ISBN 0-316-77114-7   LC 94-76968

First published 1994 in the United Kingdom

An "assortment of party crafts for birthdays, Christmas, Halloween, and general occasions. Projects range from favors and decorations to sandwiches and 'witch's brew.' Each one is presented in a well-designed two-page spread. A list of supplies and step-by-step written and illustrated instructions accompany each activity." SLJ

745.6   Calligraphy, illumination, heraldic design

Fisher, Leonard Everett, 1924-
Alphabet art: thirteen ABCs from around the world; written and illustrated by Leonard Everett Fisher. Four Winds Press c1978 61p il lib bdg $16.95 (4 and up)   **745.6**
1. Alphabets 2. Lettering
ISBN 0-02-735230-7   LC 84-28752
A reissue of the title first published 1978
"Well written and beautifully designed book. Provides brief information on the people and background for each of the following alphabets in use around the world today—Arabic, Cherokee, Chinese, Cyrillic, Eskimo, Gaelic, German, Greek, Hebrew, Japanese, Sanskrit, Thai and Tibetan." N Y Public Libr. Ref Books for Child Collect. 2d edition

Lattimore, Deborah Nourse
The sailor who captured the sea; a story of the Book of Kells. HarperCollins Pubs. 1991 unp il lib bdg $15.89; pa $5.95 (2-5)
   745.6
1. Book of Kells 2. Illumination of books and manuscripts
ISBN 0-06-023711-2 (lib bdg); 0-06-443342-0 (pa)
     LC 89-26937
A sailor continues the work of others in creating the illuminated Book of Kells
"The fine detail that is the wonder of the Book of Kells is beautifully recalled in a lavish style that retains the spirit and the beauty of the genuine article. . . . Lattimore is in her element when retelling legends, using rich and stylized artwork to surround and accompany her words." SLJ

745.7   Decorative coloring

Butterfield, Moira
Fun with paint. Random House 1994 47p il (Creative crafts) lib bdg $9.99; pa $6.99 (4 and up)   **745.7**
1. Painting—Technique 2. Handicraft
ISBN 0-679-93492-8 (lib bdg); 0-679-83492-3 (pa)
     LC 92-18650
This illustrated how-to manual includes instructions for a variety of painting projects, such as straw and splatter painting, stenciling, marbling, and wet paper painting

746.42   Nonloom weaving and related techniques

Gryski, Camilla, 1948-
Friendship bracelets. Morrow Junior Bks. 1993 48p il $14; lib bdg $13.93; pa $6.95 (4 and up)   **746.42**
1. Macramé 2. Jewelry
ISBN 0-688-12435-6; 0-688-12436-4 (lib bdg); 0-688-12437-2 (pa)   LC 92-31097

Provides step-by-step instructions for creating bracelets in a variety of patterns using embroidery thread
"Color diagrams seem clear and easy to follow, and the color photographs will get kids excited about the projects." Booklist

Lanyard; having fun with plastic lace; illustrated by Linda Hendry. Morrow Junior Bks. 1994 c1993 32p il $15; lib bdg $14.93; pa $6.95 (4 and up)   **746.42**
1. Plastics craft
ISBN 0-688-13324-X; 0-688-13325-8 (lib bdg); 0-688-13684-2 (pa)   LC 93-35992
First published 1993 in Canada with title: Boondoggle
"Lanyards are woven strips of brightly colored plastic (or other materials) that can become bracelets, keychains, and earrings. This attractive book provides a number of designs and easy-to-follow instructions that are clearly illustrated." Booklist

746.46   Patchwork and quilting

Cobb, Mary
The quilt-block history of pioneer days; with projects kids can make; illustrated by Jan Davey Ellis. Millbrook Press 1995 64p il lib bdg $17.40; pa $7.95 (2-5)   **746.46**
1. Quilts 2. Frontier and pioneer life 3. Handicraft
ISBN 1-56294-485-1 (lib bdg); 1-56294-692-7 (pa)
     LC 94-9279
"Presenting the history of American pioneers through the quilts they made, this appealing book links common experiences of the period with various quilt patterns." Booklist
Includes bibliographical references

749   Furniture and accessories

Giblin, James, 1933-
Be seated: a book about chairs; [by] James Cross Giblin. HarperCollins Pubs. 1993 136p il lib bdg $14.89 (4 and up)   **749**
1. Chairs
ISBN 0-06-021538-0   LC 92-25073
Chronicles the history, technological development, and social significance of chairs, in Europe, Africa, Asia, and the United States, from prehistory to the present
"Details are judiciously chosen to give young readers a careful history without overwhelming them, and the black-and-white photographs are expertly selected to amplify descriptions." Bull Cent Child Books
Includes bibliography

750   Painting and paintings

Roalf, Peggy
Looking at paintings. Hyperion Bks. for Children 1992-1993 12v il lib bdg ea $14.89; pa ea $6.95 (5 and up)   **750**
1. Painting 2. Art appreciation
Some titles available only in paperback
Contents: Cats; Children; Circus; Dancers; Dogs; Families; Flowers; Horses; Landscapes; Musicians; Seascapes; Self-portraits

Roalf, Peggy—*Continued*

Each volume explores the history of painting by focusing on paintings of a common subject by various artists

This "encompasses all the elements that make art come alive. . . . Roalf's lucid prose fluidly weaves social, political and historical information into vivid descriptions of each artist's life and techniques. The layouts are marvels of simplicity and grace, creating the feeling of a leisurely stroll through a small but exquisitely chosen exhibit." Publ Wkly

752   Color in painting

Heller, Ruth

Color color color color. Putnam & Grosset Group 1995 unp il $18.95 (1-4)   **752**

1. Color

ISBN 0-399-22815-2   LC 94-29097

"A rhyming text gives some general information about color, but is mostly geared to explaining the concept of commercial color printing—dots of yellow, magenta, cyan blue, and black blend to create the illusion of a full spectrum." SLJ

"Transparent multihued overlays and an entertainingly playful sensibility enhance the book's appeal as well as help it make its points." Bull Cent Child Books

758   Other subjects in painting

Arnosky, Jim

In the forest; a portfolio of paintings. Lothrop, Lee & Shepard Bks. 1989 28p il lib bdg $13.88 (4 and up)   **758**

1. Forest ecology—Pictorial works

ISBN 0-688-09138-5   LC 89-2341

"Evocative oil paintings are accompanied by intelligent commentary on particular aspects of the forest—from the growth cycle that reclaims abandoned farmlands to the various kinds of wildlife one might see. Spanning two seasons, the book's illustrations are alight with the rich colors of autumn and the muted shades of winter." Publ Wkly

Near the sea; a portfolio of paintings. Lothrop, Lee & Shepard Bks. 1990 28p il $13.95; lib bdg $13.88 (4 and up)   **758**

1. Seashore in art

ISBN 0-688-08164-9; 0-688-09327-2 (lib bdg)
LC 90-5722

"On textured canvas, Arnosky's oil paintings chronicle his stay on a small island off the rocky coast of Maine. . . . Accompanying each painting are a few paragraphs of information that form a word picture of his experience." Horn Book

"Arnosky's love of nature and his sharp eye for both natural and artistic details are very clearly displayed here." Booklist

759   Painting—Historical and geographic treatment

Mühlberger, Richard

What makes a Bruegel a Bruegel? Viking 1993 48p il pa $9.95 (5 and up)   **759**

1. Brueghel, Pieter, the Elder, 1522?-1569

ISBN 0-670-85203-1   LC 93-7578

What makes a Cassatt a Cassatt? Viking 1994 48p il pa $11.99 (5 and up)   **759**

1. Cassatt, Mary, 1844-1926

ISBN 0-670-85742-4   LC 94-18109

What makes a Degas a Degas? Viking 1993 48p il pa $9.95 (5 and up)   **759**

1. Degas, Edgar, 1834-1917

ISBN 0-670-85205-8   LC 93-7580

What makes a Goya a Goya? Viking 1994 48p il pa $11.99 (5 and up)   **759**

1. Goya, Francisco, 1746-1828

ISBN 0-670-85743-2   LC 94-18108

What makes a Leonardo a Leonardo? Viking 1994 48p il pa $11.99 (5 and up)
759

1. Leonardo, da Vinci, 1452-1519

ISBN 0-670-85744-0   LC 94-18106

What makes a Monet a Monet? Viking 1993 48p il pa $9.95 (5 and up)   **759**

1. Monet, Claude, 1840-1926

ISBN 0-670-85200-7   LC 93-7583

What makes a Picasso a Picasso? Viking 1994 48p il pa $11.99 (5 and up)   **759**

1. Picasso, Pablo, 1881-1973

ISBN 0-670-85741-6   LC 94-18107

What makes a Raphael a Raphael? Viking 1993 48p il pa $9.95 (5 and up)   **759**

1. Raphael, 1483-1520

ISBN 0-670-85204-X   LC 93-7579

What makes a Rembrandt a Rembrandt? Viking 1993 48p il pa $9.95 (5 and up)
759

1. Rembrandt Harmenszoon van Rijn, 1606-1669

ISBN 0-670-85199-X   LC 93-7581

What makes a Van Gogh a Van Gogh? Viking 1993 48p il pa $9.95 (5 and up)
759

1. Gogh, Vincent van, 1853-1890

ISBN 0-670-85198-1   LC 93-7582

Produced by the Metropolitan Museum of Art

This "series provides a brief biography of each artist, followed by discussions of 12 significant paintings. Each book ends with a summary of the distinctive qualities that define or suggest the artist's style. . . . These handsome volumes will be useful to students researching artists." Booklist

759.13 American painting

Greenberg, Jan, 1942-

The painter's eye; learning to look at contemporary American art; [by] Jan Greenberg and Sandra Jordan. Delacorte Press 1991 96p il $20; pa $9.95 (6 and up)
759.13

1. American painting 2. Modern painting—1900-1999 (20th century) 3. Art appreciation
ISBN 0-385-30319-X; 0-385-32040-X (pa)
LC 90-44877

This book introduces ways of seeing, experiencing, and appreciating art through the examination of contemporary American works
"A well-designed example of the bookmaking art, with handsome art reproductions and a thoughtful and useful text." SLJ
Includes glossary and bibliography

Lawrence, Jacob

The great migration; an American story; paintings by Jacob Lawrence; with a poem in appreciation by Walter Dean Myers. HarperCollins Pubs. 1993 unp il $23.50; lib bdg $23.89; pa $6.95
759.13

1. African Americans in art
ISBN 0-06-023037-1; 0-06-023038-X (lib bdg); 0-06-443428-1 (pa)
LC 93-16788

Published by The Museum of Modern Art, The Phillips Collection, and HarperCollins Pubs.
"A noted African-American artist chronicles the 1916-1919 migration of blacks from the South through a sequence of 60 paintings and accompanying narrative captions." SLJ
"Lawrence is a storyteller with words as well as pictures: his captions and his own 1992 introduction to this book are the best commentary on his work." Booklist

759.3 German painting

Raboff, Ernest

Albrecht Dürer. Lippincott 1988 unp il (Art for children) o.p.; HarperCollins Pubs. paperback available $5.95 (5 and up)
759.3

1. Dürer, Albrecht, 1471-1528
ISBN 0-06-446071-1 (pa)
LC 87-16863

First published 1970 by Doubleday
A brief biography of the German painter and printmaker accompanies fifteen color reproductions and critical interpretations of his works

760 Graphic arts. Printmaking and prints

Fleischman, Paul

Copier creations; using copy machines to make decals, silhouettes, flip books, films, and much more! illustrated by David Cain. HarperCollins Pubs. 1993 122p il hardcover o.p. paperback available $8.95 (4 and up)
760

1. Copy art
ISBN 0-06-446152-1 (pa)
LC 91-45413

This "tells how to use copiers to create original, personalized artwork. . . . Directions are easy to follow and are clearly illustrated with black-and-white drawings, many of which look as if they were copied." SLJ
Includes bibliography

Tofts, Hannah

The print book; written and edited by Diane James; photography by Jon Barnes. Simon & Schuster Bks. for Young Readers 1990 unp il $11.95; pa $4.95 (k-3)
760

1. Prints
ISBN 0-671-70368-4; 0-671-70369-2 (pa)
LC 89-21960

Describes and illustrates a variety of simple printing activities

769.5 Forms of prints

Parker, Nancy Winslow

Money, money, money; the meaning of the art and symbols on United States paper currency. HarperCollins Pubs. 1995 32p il map $14.95; lib bdg $14.89 (3-5)
769.5

1. Paper money 2. Signs and symbols
ISBN 0-06-023411-3; 0-06-023412-1 (lib bdg)
LC 93-43534

"The text provides information regarding the graphics of our money. Brief snippets about the various U.S. presidents, the decorations, and other related facts are supplied. The illustrations of the bills in question are small and blurred, but pertinent details on the bills are shown enlarged." Horn Book Guide

770 Photography and photographs

Morgan, Terri

Photography; take your best shot; [by] Terri Morgan & Shmuel Thaler. Lerner Publs. 1991 72p il (Media workshop) lib bdg $19.95; pa $8.95 (5 and up)
770

1. Photography
ISBN 0-8225-2302-7 (lib bdg); 0-8225-9605-9 (pa)
LC 90-27054

Morgan, Terri—*Continued*

A practical guide to photographic technique, providing information on composition, lighting, special effects, color and black-and-white photographs, equipment, darkroom skills, and careers in photography

This is "a well-crafted, comprehensive guide to photography. . . . The inclusion of chapters detailing how to display photographs and identifying career opportunities makes this a solid work for beginning or advanced photographers." Booklist

Includes glossary

771 Photography—Techniques, equipment, materials

Ancona, George, 1929-

My camera. Crown 1992 47p il lib bdg $15.99; pa $8.99 (3-6)   **771**

1. Photography 2. Cameras
ISBN 0-517-58280-5 (lib bdg); 0-517-58279-1 (pa)
LC 91-2288

Describes the use of a simple 35mm camera, and gives advice and projects on composition, lighting, action, etc.

"This is an empowering book that proves children make great artists and should be encouraged to use their creativity." Booklist

King, Dave

My first photography book. Dorling Kindersley 1994 48p il $12.95 (4 and up)   **771**

1. Photography
ISBN 1-56458-673-1   LC 94-7359

This "handbook . . . offers advice and creative projects for beginning photographers. . . . Materials and equipment are inexpensive and readily available, e.g, colored, transparent candy wrappers are used as filters, and magnifying glasses are used as close-up lenses. . . . Vivid, well-labeled illustrations in primary colors are attractive and informative." SLJ

Includes glossary

778.5 Motion picture and television photography

Andersen, Yvonne

Make your own animated movies and videotapes; film and video techniques from the Yellow Ball Workshop. Little, Brown 1991 176p il $22.95 (5 and up)   **778.5**

1. Animation (Cinematography)
ISBN 0-316-03941-1   LC 90-33756

First published 1970 with title: Make your own animated movies

This book provides instructions for making animated movies including drawing the cartoon, operating the camera, and synchronizing the sound. Also discusses the equipment needed for the projects

"The structure makes this how-to book appropriate for beginners as well as for those with advanced levels of expertise. It has basic information for individual projects and is also sophisticated enough for group instruction. Dynamic, readable, and highly informative." SLJ

778.7 Photography under specific conditions

Zubrowski, Bernie, 1939-

Shadow play; making pictures with light and lenses; illustrated by Roy Doty. Morrow Junior Bks. 1995 112p il $15.93; pa $7.95 (4 and up)   **778.7**

1. Shades and shadows—Experiments
ISBN 0-688-13210-3; 0-688-13211-1 (pa)
LC 94-27425

"A Boston Children's Museum activity book"

The author explains "the basic properties of light and how the study of shadows led to the invention of the camera. The more than 50 experiments are grouped into three general sections: the first shows how shadows are made in natural and artificial light; the second describes how a shadow box is constructed and used in further activities; and the third tells how a box camera is made." SLJ

"Most of the experiments, illustrated with simple line drawings, are best accomplished by pairs or small groups. Zubrowski knows his audience: these are exactly the activities children will enjoy doing and demonstrating to family, friends, and classmates." Horn Book

778.9 Photography of specific subjects

Lasky, Kathryn

Think like an eagle; at work with a wildlife photographer; photographs by Christopher G. Knight and Jack Swedberg. Little, Brown 1992 48p il $15.95 (4 and up)   **778.9**

1. Photography of animals
ISBN 0-316-51519-1   LC 91-26448

"Joy Street books"

Follows photographer Jack Swedberg through a cycle of seasons as he tracks wildlife in three very different regions of the United States

"Lasky's text details the various natural settings and behaviors of the subjects photographed, but she does not discuss any camera specifics or techniques. Numerous full-color photographs, taken by both Knight and Swedberg, appear on nearly every page, making this volume a visual delight." Booklist

779 Photographs

Tucker, Jean S.

Come look with me: discovering photographs with children. Thomasson-Grant 1994 32p il $13.95 (4 and up)   **779**

1. Artistic photography 2. Art appreciation
ISBN 1-56566-062-5   LC 94-10835

In this book "all the photographs included are of children, and the text is designed to help adults talk with young people about what photos reveal. The majority of the pictures are twentieth-century shots with a contemporary feel; some are color, but most are black-and-white. . . . Accompanying each picture is a page of text pointing out interesting design and thematic points in an open-ended way that allows for discussion." Booklist

Includes bibliographical references

780 Music

Ardley, Neil, 1937-
A young person's guide to music; with music by Poul Ruders. Dorling Kindersley 1995 80p il $24.95 (5 and up) **780**

1. Music 2. Orchestra
ISBN 0-7894-0313-7   LC 95-19595

"In association with the BBC Symphony Orchestra conducted by Andrew Davis." Title page

This "interactive guide to the orchestra is a combination of book and compact disk. The CD features a new work by the Dutch composer Poul Ruder. . . . The text itself has facts on the orchestra as a whole, the conductor, composer, and each instrument. . . . A history section features a timeline, names of musicians and composers, definitions of musical forms with examples, and a glossary." SLJ

"A rich resource for young people who want to understand orchestral music." Booklist

McLeish, Kenneth, 1940-
The Oxford first companion to music; [by] Kenneth and Valerie McLeish. Oxford Univ. Press 1982 various paging il $29.95 (5 and up) **780**

1. Music
ISBN 0-19-314303-8   LC 82-223971

"Contains entries about people, places, musical styles, instruments, and terminology for classical, jazz, and popular music worldwide. . . . Recommended." Nichols. Guide to Ref Books for Sch Media Cent. 4th edition

Spence, Keith
The young people's book of music; consultant, Hugo Cole. Millbrook Press 1995 144p il lib bdg $19.90; pa $14.95 (6 and up) **780**

1. Music
ISBN 1-56294-605-6 (lib bdg); 1-56294-784-2 (pa)
                                      LC 94-36699

First published 1993 in the United Kingdom with title: Watts book of music

The "author attempts to present the types of music, families of instruments, the history of music and a few major composers, all in two-page spreads which are packed with text and boxed photos and diagrams. It is truly a concise encyclopedia of music and musicians. The reading level of the text is demanding, although the captions of the photos and diagrams are easier. A useful reference tool for music studies of all kinds." Child Book Rev Serv

Includes glossary and bibliographical references

780.9 Music—Historical and geographical treatment

Ventura, Piero
Great composers. Putnam 1989 124p il $25.95 (4 and up) **780.9**

1. Composers 2. Music—History and criticism
ISBN 0-399-21746-0   LC 89-32861

"Early segments are devoted to the Chinese, Indians, Egyptians, and Greeks and Romans, but the majority of the book focuses on individual figures, from Vivaldi, Handel, Beethoven, Chopin, and Debussy, to Gershwin, Louis Armstrong, and Duke Ellington. Ventura stresses their artistic personalities and talks about their talents in the context of the time in which they lived. . . . A highly pleasurable invitation to the world of music." Booklist

782.25 Sacred songs

All night, all day; a child's first book of African-American spirituals; selected and illustrated by Ashley Bryan; musical arrangements by David Manning Thomas. Atheneum Pubs. 1991 48p il music $14.95 **782.25**

1. Spirituals (Songs)
ISBN 0-689-31662-3   LC 90-753145

This is a "selection of 20 well-known spirituals." SLJ

"An exuberance of warm color and great variety in pattern and design distinguish the illustrations. . . . Excellent piano accompaniments and guitar chords further enrich the beautiful, wholly gratifying book." Horn Book

Climbing Jacob's ladder; heroes of the Bible in African-American spirituals; selected and edited by John Langstaff; illustrated by Ashley Bryan; piano arrangements by John Andrew Ross. Margaret K. McElderry Bks. 1991 unp il music $14.95 **782.25**

1. Spirituals (Songs)
ISBN 0-689-50494-2   LC 90-27297

This is a collection of nine African-American spirituals which feature Biblical figures from the Old Testament

This "is a vibrant celebration for the senses that works well both as a testimony to the musical heritage of black Americans and as a practical resource for music teachers and their students. . . . Bryan uses distinctive primitive-toned paintings with swirling bands of color." Booklist

What a morning!; the Christmas story in black spirituals; selected and edited by John Langstaff; illustrated by Ashley Bryan; arrangements for singing and piano by John Andrew Ross. Margaret K. McElderry Bks. 1987 unp il music $14.95 **782.25**

1. Spirituals (Songs)
ISBN 0-689-50422-5   LC 87-750130

This "volume presents five black spirituals that celebrate the Christmas story. Langstaff has chosen 'Mary Had a Baby,' 'My Lord, What a Morning,' 'Go Tell it on the Mountain,' 'Sister Mary Had One Child,' and 'Behold That Star.'" Booklist

"Bryan's illustrations tie into the African-American theme, showing a black Holy family and multiracial wise men and shepherds. Bold brush strokes line each landscape and every garment. . . . This collection of songs exhibits an intimacy and compassion that give these spirituals a stunning universality." Publ Wkly

782.28 Carols

Hark! the herald angels sing; music arranged by Barrie Carson Turner; illustrated with paintings from the National Gallery, London. Simon & Schuster Bks. for Young Readers 1993 45p il music $17   **782.28**

1. Carols 2. Medieval art 3. Renaissance art
ISBN 0-671-87146-3   LC 93-9144

"An art-lover's collection of Christmas carols, this handsome volume reproduces sacred and secular paintings from the National Gallery, London. Well-chosen details, taken from such sources as 14th-century altarpieces and 17th-century devotional works, illustrate each of 18 traditional carols." Publ Wkly

Joy to the world!; carols selected by Maureen Forrester; illustrated by Frances Tyrrell. Dutton Children's Bks. 1993 c1992 31p il music $14.99   **782.28**

1. Carols
ISBN 0-525-45169-2   LC 93-2894

First published 1992 in Canada

Forrester "chooses 12 carols from a range of different countries and, in endnotes, adds colorful details about each. . . . Tyrrell's illustrations—contemporary vignettes set into decorative borders—present a multicultural cast." Publ Wkly

Mohr, Joseph, 1792-1848

Silent night; verses by Joseph Mohr; illustrated by Susan Jeffers. Dutton 1984 unp il music $14.95; pa $4.95 (k-2)   **782.28**

1. Carols
ISBN 0-525-44144-1; 0-8037-4443-9 (pa)
LC 84-8113

An illustrated version of the well-known German Christmas hymn celebrating the birth of Christ

"The book has a sumptuous appearance. . . . Elegant and ambitious, this will be a strong visual draw in any Christmas book display." Booklist

Tomie dePaola's book of Christmas carols. Putnam 1987 81p il music $19.95

782.28

1. Carols
ISBN 0-399-21432-1   LC 86-755157

This collection contains "more than 30 well-known traditional carols. . . . Music is rendered in singable and playable keys . . . but no chords are given." SLJ

"The carols are lovingly placed among pictures with varied settings: Victorian and biblical, some on gatefold pages. DePaola's intense hues—slate blues, rich burgundies and mossy greens—reflect the way colors show up in a wintry background. His Christmas spirit, here of subdued joy, is infectious." Publ Wkly

The **Twelve** days of Christmas   **782.28**

1. Carols
Some editions are:
Boyds Mills Press $14.95 Illustrated by John O'Brien (ISBN 1-56397-142-9)
Putnam $15.95; pa $3.95 Illustrated by Jan Brett (ISBN 0-399-22037-2; 0-399-22197-2)
Simon & Schuster $15 Illustrated by Linnea Asplind Riley (ISBN 0-689-80275-7)

Illustrated versions of The Christmas carol in which a young woman's true love sends her extravagant gifts on each of the twelve days of Christmas

We wish you a merry Christmas; a traditional Christmas carol; pictures by Tracey Campbell Pearson. Dial Bks. for Young Readers 1983 unp il music hardcover o.p. paperback available $3.95   **782.28**

1. Carols
ISBN 0-8037-0310-4 (pa)   LC 82-22224

"A group of young carollers, trudging about in the snow, is welcomed indoors by an elderly, hospitable couple." Bull Cent Child Books

"Using as her text nothing more than the four stanzas of the familiar carol, the illustrator has concocted a thoroughly captivating picture book. . . . Washed with clear vibrant color, the lively ink drawings are full of hilarious detail, extrapolating the carol's inherent humor. Words and music are appended." Horn Book

782.42 Songs

Arroz con leche; popular songs and rhymes from Latin America; selected and illustrated by Lulu Delacre; English lyrics by Elena Paz; musical arrangements by Ana-María Rosado. Scholastic 1989 32p il music $14.95; pa $4.95 (k-3)   **782.42**

1. Folk songs 2. Folklore—Latin America 3. Bilingual books—English-Spanish
ISBN 0-590-41887-4; 0-590-41886-6 (pa)

This is a bilingual collection of twelve folk songs and rhymes from Puerto Rico, Mexico and Argentina. Instructions for fingerplays and games accompany some of the songs. Musical arrangements for nine of the entries are included at the end of the book

"Delacre has selected lilting verses that are pleasing to the ear—ones likely to encourage non-Spanish-speakers to join in the fun. . . . Fresh, springlike colors brighten the pictures, though some faces look more Anglo than expected. An author's note explains that many of the scenes depict real places." Booklist

Bangs, Edward, 1756-1818

Steven Kellogg's Yankee Doodle; written by Edward Bangs. Simon & Schuster Bks. for Young Readers 1996 c1976 unp il music $16; pa $5.99 (k-3)   **782.42**

1. National songs—United States
ISBN 0-689-80158-0; 0-689-80726-0 (pa)
LC 94-23603

A reissue of the edition first published 1976 by Parents' Magazine Press

An illustrated version of the popular Revolutionary War song, originally penned in 1775 by Harvard student Edward Bangs. "A commentary about the history of the song and its variations precedes the text; the eight measures of the familiar melody are given at the end of the book." Horn Book

"The color illustrations are zesty and action filled." Publ Wkly

Bullock, Kathleen, 1946-

She'll be comin' round the mountain. Simon & Schuster Bks. for Young Readers 1993 unp il music $14 (k-3)   **782.42**

1. Folk songs—United States
ISBN 0-671-79153-2   LC 92-17340

A family welcomes a young visitor in this illustrated version of the familiar American folk song

Bullock's "watercolors are brimming with humorous delights and chaotic details. . . . With the music score included at the end, the book is simply loads of fun." Booklist

Burgie, Irving

Caribbean carnival; songs of the West Indies; pictures by Frané Lessac; afterword by Rosa Guy. Tambourine Bks. 1992 unp il music $15; lib bdg $14.93 (k-3)   **782.42**

1. Songs 2. Caribbean region—Social life and customs
ISBN 0-688-10779-6; 0-688-10780-X (lib bdg)
       LC 91-760838

This is a collection of thirteen original and traditional songs of the West Indies

This is "a vibrant and vigorous collection. . . . An eloquent and informative commentary . . . places these lilting, highly syncopated work songs, spirituals, ballads, and children's songs in an appropriate social, historical, and cultural context. . . . The boldly colored, naive-style gouache paintings have intricate details and flat figures that capture the color and character of everyday life on the islands." Booklist

Carle, Eric

Today is Monday; pictures by Eric Carle. Philomel Bks. 1993 unp il music $14.95 (k-3)   **782.42**

1. Songs
ISBN 0-399-21966-8   LC 91-45866

Each day of the week brings a new food, until on Sunday all the world's children can come and eat it up

This song "gets new life in a picture book bursting with food, animals, and lots of energy. Beginning with the grinning cat on the cover . . . a zooful of animals act out the lyrics: snakes get tangled in spaghetti, elephants use their trunks to slurp 'Zoooop,' and pelicans catch fish on Friday. With text at a minimum, Carle's always innovative artwork steps center stage in an oversize format that allows gloriously colored collages to spread over two pages." Booklist

De colores and other Latin-American folk songs for children; selected, arranged, and translated by José-Luis Orozco; illustrated by Elisa Kleven. Dutton Children's Bks. 1994 56p il music $16.99 (k-3)   **782.42**

1. Folk songs 2. Bilingual books—English-Spanish
ISBN 0-525-45260-5

"Each of the 27 songs is presented with background notes; lyrics in both Spanish and English; simple arrangements for the voice, piano, and guitar; and suggestions for group sing-alongs and musical games. . . . The book is a delight for the eyes as well as the ear. . . . Kleven provides bountiful illustrations—the endpapers are sunshine bright with a crisp quilt of yellow flowers, and playful borders that ripple with colorful patterns and miniature pictures line the edge of every page." Booklist

The Fox went out on a chilly night
    782.42

1. Folk songs—United States
Some editions are:
Dell pa $5.99 Illustrated by Peter Spier (ISBN 0-440-40829-6)
Lothrop, Lee & Shepard Bks. $16; lib bdg $15.95 Illustrated by Wendy Watson (ISBN 0-688-10765-6; 0-688-10766-4)

Set in New England, this old song tells about the trip the fox father made to town to get some of the farmer's plump geese for his family's dinner, and how he manages to evade the farmer who tries to shoot him. Both versions include music

Spier's version is "a true picture book in the Caldecott-Brooke tradition. Fine drawings, lovely colors, and pictures so full of amusing details that young viewers will make fresh discoveries every time they . . . scrutinize these beautiful, action-filled pages." Horn Book

"Watson's timeless illustrations offer abundant particulars to pore over. Her audience will chuckle at the comic antics of Fox's energetic offspring." Publ Wkly

Gilbert, W. S. (William Schwenck), 1836-1911

"I have a song to sing, O!"; an introduction to the songs of Gilbert and Sullivan; selected and edited by John Langstaff; illustrated by Emma Chichester Clark; piano arrangements by Brian Holmes. Margaret K. McElderry Bks. 1994 74p il music $17.95 (4 and up)
    782.42

1. Songs 2. Operetta
ISBN 0-689-50591-4   LC 93-10215

"Sixteen songs from eight operettas by Gilbert and Sullivan are given the deluxe treatment in this well-constructed volume. Black-and-white and color illustrations on heavy, glossy pages, which give the book strong middle-grade appeal, accompany crisp musical notation for both piano and guitar." Booklist

Glazer, Tom

Tom Glazer's Treasury of songs for children; illustrated by John O'Brien. Doubleday 1988 256p il music spiral binding $12.95 (3-5)   **782.42**

1. Songs
ISBN 0-385-23693-X

A newly illustrated version of Tom Glazer's Treasury of folk songs, published 1964

"Words and sheet music for 130 of America's favorite songs are presented with pertinent, historical annotations." Soc Educ

Go in and out the window; an illustrated songbook for young people; music arranged and edited by Dan Fox; commentary by Claude Marks. Metropolitan Mus. of Art; Holt & Co. 1987 144p il music $24.95
    782.42

1. Metropolitan Museum of Art (New York, N.Y.) 2. Songs
ISBN 0-8050-0628-1 (Holt)

"Sixty-one favorite songs . . . are presented alphabetically and illustrated with treasures from the Metropolitan Museum of Art. . . . The songs . . . are traditional rather than contemporary and come primarily from America and England, while the pictures, jewelry, sculpture, photographs,

Go in and out the window—*Continued*
and so forth span 5,000 years of worldwide art." Booklist

"Imaginative and luxurious, the volume should stimulate and challenge the adult to deepen the awareness and broaden the aesthetic horizons of the young." Horn Book

Gonna sing my head off!; American folk songs for children; collected and arranged by Kathleen Krull; illustrated by Allen Garns; introductory note by Arlo Guthrie. Knopf 1992 145p il music $20; pa $12   **782.42**

1. Folk songs—United States

ISBN 0-394-81991-8; 0-679-87232-9 (pa)

                LC 89-49562

"Work songs, love songs, ballads and blues, lullabies, spirituals, protest songs, and sheer nonsense make up this entertaining collection of 62 traditional and contemporary favorites. For each song, Krull provides the simplest piano and guitar arrangements in a clear double-page spread design that includes the words to all the verses. . . . The exuberant illustrations, mostly in bright pastels, manage to be both familiar and dramatic. . . . Informal notes at the head of each song give something about history, origin, performance, and possibilities for variation." Booklist

Guthrie, Woody, 1912-1967

Woody's 20 grow big songs; [by] Woody Guthrie, with Marjorie Mazia Guthrie; pictures by Woody Guthrie. HarperCollins Pubs. 1992 unp il music lib bdg $15.89

                782.42

1. Songs

ISBN 0-06-020283-1

"This book is a 'replication of an unpublished songbook' and features hand-lettered lyrics, music, and pen-and-ink sketches with watercolor washes done by Guthrie himself. Despite the volume's antique flavor, the songs are truly timeless and so singable. They're written with much repetition and with a lot of action—just the ticket for preschool children! . . . Preschool teachers, care givers, music teachers, and family, all will appreciate this versatile collection of one of America's finest folksingers and song writers." SLJ

I know an old lady who swallowed a fly

                782.42

1. Folk songs

Some editions are:

Holiday House lib bdg $15.95 Illustrated by Glen Rounds (ISBN 0-8234-0814-0)

Scholastic $14.95 Illustrated by G. Brian Karas (ISBN 0-590-46575-9) Has title: I know an old lady. This version is by Rose Bonne and Alan Mills

Illustrated versions of the cumulative folk song in which an old lady swallows a variety of progressively larger animals

Rounds' "old lady who swallowed a fly encounters a slew of oddball animals who are as distinctly unappetizing as they're supposed to be in order to gross out the primary audience. . . . These humorously head-on images are all contained within heavy black lines filled with colored chalk, set against plenty of white space, and accompanied by large black print." Bull Cent Child Books

"Karas' exaggerated cartoon-style pictures in gouache, acrylic, and pencil revel in the slapstick action and laconic absurdity. . . . It's crazy and, yes, deliciously funny."

Jane Yolen's Mother Goose songbook; selected, edited, and introduced by Jane Yolen; musical arrangements by Adam Stemple; illustrations by Rosekrans Hoffman. Caroline House (Honesdale) 1992 95p il music $16.95   **782.42**

1. Songs 2. Nursery rhymes

ISBN 1-878093-52-5   LC 91-77616

This is a "collection of 49 rhymes set to music. . . . With a brief, informative foreword and short notes, Yolen places the rhymes within a historical context that will add to the understanding as well as the enjoyment of each. The two-handed piano arrangements are accessible and fun to play with music that varies from high drama . . . to soothing familiarity. . . . Hoffman's wonderful pen-and-ink and watercolor illustrations enhance the verses." SLJ

Johnson, James Weldon, 1871-1938

Lift every voice and sing   **782.42**

1. African American music 2. Songs

Some editions are:

Scholastic $14.95 Illustrated by Jan Spivey Gilchrist (ISBN 0-590-46982-7) Has title: Lift ev'ry voice and sing

Walker & Co. $14.95; lib bdg $15.85; pa $6.95 Illustrated by Elizabeth Catlett (ISBN 0-8027-8250-7; 0-8027-8251-5; 0-8027-7442-3)

Illustrated versions of the song that has come to be considered the African American national anthem

Gilchrist "seamlessly blends scenes of Africa with those of black America. With colored pencil, gouache, and watercolors, she brings the words to life." SLJ

"Ms Catlett's woodcuts, done in the 1940's, are a perfect complement to the text and help make this a book to be treasured for generations to come." Child Book Rev Serv

Key, Francis Scott, 1779-1843

The Star-Spangled Banner; illustrated by Peter Spier. Doubleday 1973 unp il map music hardcover o.p. paperback available $8

                782.42

1. National songs—United States

ISBN 0-385-23401-5

An illustrated version of Francis Scott Key's text for our national anthem. It includes an historical note on the writing of the song, a reproduction of the original manuscript, and a musical arrangement

Kovalski, Maryann, 1951-

The wheels on the bus. Little, Brown 1987 unp il music $14.95; pa $4.95 (k-2)

                782.42

1. Songs

ISBN 0-316-50256-1; 0-316-50259-6 (pa)

                LC 87-3441

"Joy Street books"

In this adaptation of a traditional children's song, "a long wait at the bus stop precipitates a suggestion from a grandmother that she and her two grandchildren pass the time by singing 'The Wheels on the Bus.' . . . Kovalski expertly conveys the spirit with which people sing this song. . . . The action of the song is followed through in detail, flowing from page to page with a cast of assorted characters depicted in watercolor with pencil illustrations." SLJ

Kroll, Steven

By the dawn's early light; the story of the Star spangled banner; illustrated by Dan Andreasen. Scholastic 1994 40p il maps music $14.95 (3-5)   **782.42**

1. Key, Francis Scott, 1779-1843 2. Star spangled banner (Song) 3. United States—History—1812-1815, War of 1812

ISBN 0-590-45054-9   LC 92-27101

This is an account of the events that led Francis Scott Key to compose the United States national anthem, during the War of 1812

"Handsome full-page oil paintings in warm golden tones blend nineteenth-century romance with twentieth-century realism. . . . Kroll's details of this dramatic story match those told at Fort McHenry today; judicious use of dialogue moves the story along while remaining true to the facts." Bull Cent Child Books

Includes bibliographical references

Langstaff, John M., 1920-

Frog went a-courtin'; retold by John Langstaff; with pictures by Feodor Rojankovsky. Harcourt Brace Jovanovich 1955 unp il music $14.95; pa $4.95 (k-3)   **782.42**

1. Folk songs

ISBN 0-15-230214-X; 0-15-633900-5 (pa)

"Retelling of a merry old Scottish ballad with many-colored illustrations about the marriage between Mr. Frog and Miss Mouse. A composite American version set to Appalachian mountain music." Chicago Public Libr

Oh, a-hunting we will go; [by] John Langstaff; pictures by Nancy Winslow Parker. Atheneum Pubs. 1974 unp il music $14.95; pa $4.95 (k-2)   **782.42**

1. Folk songs

ISBN 0-689-50007-6; 0-689-71503-X (pa)

"A Margaret K. McElderry book"

The nonsense verses of this folk song trace the hunt for such animals as an armadillo, a fox, and a snake, and describe the imagined treatment of each animal once it is caught

"The 12 stanzas are complemented by Parker's droll crayon illustrations (the fox caught in the box is watching TV), and a score for guitar and piano is appended. An amusing addition to 'song' picture books." SLJ

Over in the meadow; with pictures by Feodor Rojankovsky. Harcourt Brace Jovanovich 1957 unp il music $14.95; pa $3.95 (k-2)   **782.42**

1. Folk songs 2. Counting

ISBN 0-15-258854-X; 0-15-670500-1 (pa)

"This old counting rhyme tells of ten meadow families whose mothers advise them to dig, run, sing, play, hum, build, swim, wink, spin and hop. The illustrations, half in full color, show the combination of realism and imagination which little children like best. The tune, arranged simply, is on the last page, and children will have fun acting the whole thing out." Horn Book

The **Lap-time** song and play book; edited by Jane Yolen; with musical arrangements by Adam Stemple; pictures by Margot Tomes. Harcourt Brace Jovanovich 1989 32p il music $15.95   **782.42**

1. Songs 2. Singing games 3. Nursery rhymes 4. Finger play

ISBN 0-15-243588-3   LC 88-752289

"Tomes's dancing mice and well-dressed pigs are beguiling additions to a collection of sixteen familiar nursery games and rhymes for small children. Each game is accompanied by a brief paragraph on its origin and instructions on how it may be played; a simple musical notation is included when appropriate. An author's note about lap songs is appended." Horn Book

The **Laura** Ingalls Wilder songbook; favorite songs from the Little house books; compiled and edited by Eugenia Garson; illustrated by Garth Williams; arranged for piano and guitar by Herbert Haufrecht. HarperCollins Pubs. 1996 160p il music $23.95   **782.42**

1. American songs 2. Folk songs

ISBN 0-06-027036-5

A newly repackaged edition of the title first published 1968

At head of title: Little house, Laura Ingalls Wilder

This songbook contains 62 songs that appear in Wilder's "Little House" books. The songs range from folk songs and hymns to dance songs and ballads, and contain music arranged for piano and guitar

Leodhas, Sorche Nic, 1898-1968

Always room for one more; illustrated by Nonny Hogrogian. Holt & Co. 1965 unp il music $14.95; pa $5.95 (k-3)   **782.42**

1. Folk songs

ISBN 0-8050-0331-2; 0-8050-0330-4 (pa)

Awarded the Caldecott Medal, 1966

"A picture book based on an old Scottish folk song about hospitable Lachie MacLachlan, who invited in so many guests that his little house finally burst. Rhymed text . . . a glossary of Scottish words, and music for the tune are combined into an effective whole." Hodges. Books for Elem Sch Libr

London Bridge is falling down!; illustrated by Peter Spier. Doubleday 1967 unp il music o.p.; Dell paperback available $3.99 (k-2)   **782.42**

1. Folk songs 2. Nursery rhymes

ISBN 0-440-40710-9 (pa)

This picture book illustrated with scenes of eighteenth-century London presents the traditional verses of the Mother Goose nursery rhyme. The musical score is included, as well as a three-page historical sketch of London Bridge through the centuries

Lullabies and night songs; [edited by] William Engvick; music by Alec Wilder; pictures by Maurice Sendak. Harper & Row 1965 77p il music $25.95 (k-3)   **782.42**

1. Lullabies 2. Songs

ISBN 0-06-021820-7

"The editor has selected verses, in addition to some of his own, from poets as notable and varied as Eleanor Farjeon, Tennyson, Thurber, Stevenson, Kipling, Walter de la Mare, and William Blake, as well as many anonymous, traditional poems like 'Sleep, Baby, Sleep,' 'Wee Willie Winkie,' 'Now the Day is Over.'" Horn Book

The **Lullaby** songbook; edited by Jane Yolen; with musical arrangements by Adam Stemple; pictures by Charles Mikolaycak. Harcourt Brace Jovanovich 1986 31p il music $13.95 (1-3)   **782.42**

1. Lullabies 2. Songs

ISBN 0-15-249903-2   LC 85-752855

"Fifteen mostly familiar lullabies are presented with musical accompaniment in this lusciously designed book. Full-color pictures and frames edge the large white spreads that contain the music and brief notes on the songs' origins. Mikolaycak's rich, full-bodied scenes receive their drama from intense color and vigorous composition." Booklist

Mallett, David

Inch by inch; the garden song; pictures by Ora Eitan. HarperCollins Pubs. 1995 unp il music $13.95; lib bdg $13.89 (k-2)   **782.42**

1. Songs 2. Gardens

ISBN 0-06-024303-1; 0-06-024304-X (lib bdg)

LC 93-38352

"In this picture-book version of the song first published in 1975 . . . a young child plants seeds . . . weeds and tends them, and finally, gleans a bountiful harvest. . . . Employing a variety of media including cut paper, Eitan uses color and space to create a striking effect." SLJ

Medearis, Angela Shelf, 1956-

The zebra-riding cowboy; a folk song from the Old West; collected by Angela Shelf Medearis; illustrated by María Cristina Brusca. Holt & Co. 1992 unp il music $14.95 (k-3)
782.42

1. Cowhands—Songs

ISBN 0-8050-1712-7   LC 91-27941

In this Western folk song, an educated fellow mistaken for a greenhorn proves his cowboy ability by riding a wild horse. Includes a discussion of Afro-American and Hispanic cowboys in the nineteenth century

"Brusca's color drawings burst with energy as she portrays the tough cowboys—whites, Hispanics, and African Americans—in the Wild West setting. The angular quality of the drawings communicates the harsh life of these hardworking men." Booklist

Las Navidades; popular Christmas songs from Latin America; selected and illustrated by Lulu Delacre; English lyrics by Elena Paz; musical arrangements by Ana-Maria Rosado. Scholastic 1990 32p il music $13.95; pa $3.95 (k-3)   **782.42**

1. Folk songs 2. Folklore—Latin America 3. Bilingual books—English-Spanish 4. Carols

ISBN 0-590-43548-5; 0-590-43549-3 (pa)

LC 89-28375

"Twelve Christmas songs from Central and South American tradition [are] arranged chronologically from Christmas Eve to Epiphany, with Spanish and English texts. Melody lines and guitar chords are appended." SLJ

"The illustrations are varied in both composition and mood, their bright pastels and soft shading providing unity. . . . Happily, the translations are not forced into English rhyme. . . . A festive addition to holiday music collections." Booklist

Includes bibliography

Old MacDonald had a farm   **782.42**

1. Folk songs—United States

Some editions are:

Holiday House lib bdg $15.95; pa $5.95 Illustrated by Glen Rounds (ISBN 0-8234-0739-X; 0-8234-0846-9)

Lothrop, Lee & Shepard Bks. $14 Illustrated by Gus Clarke (ISBN 0-688-12215-9) Has title: E I E I O: the story of Old MacDonald, who had a farm

North-South Bks. $14.95; lib bdg $14.88 Illustrated by Holly Berry (ISBN 1-55858-281-9; 1-55858-282-7)

"Rounds drafts portraits of some very expressive and feisty animals. . . . The large type and larger than life-size animals—each displayed on its own page—will keep children turning the pages and singing along." Horn Book

In Clarke's "new twist on the classic rhyme, the poor man can no longer take the barking, quacking, and other noises, so he sells the animals and starts over with a whole new business venture. Clarke's cartoon illustrations and the text are raucously fun pairing." SLJ

Berry's rendition "stars old MacDonald as a kindly, musically inclined father-figure to his animals. The familiar tune is energized by Berry's bordered pencil-and-watercolor compositions." Publ Wkly

Paxton, Tom, 1937-

The animals' lullaby; illustrated by Erick Ingraham. Morrow Junior Bks. 1993 unp il music $15; lib bdg $14.93 (k-2)   **782.42**

1. Lullabies 2. Songs

ISBN 0-688-10468-1; 0-688-10469-X (lib bdg)

LC 92-18841

"Paxton offers a soothing lullaby. . . . Verse by verse, the animals prepare themselves for sleep. . . . Ingraham's vibrant acrylic artwork portrays lifelike animals in their natural settings. . . . The music has been included on the mauve end papers, making this a perfect pick for a bedtime performance." Booklist

Peterson, Carolyn Sue, 1938-

Index to children's songs; a title, first line, and subject index; compiled by Carolyn Sue Peterson and Ann D. Fenton. Wilson, H.W. 1979 318p $38   **782.42**

1. Songs—Indexes

ISBN 0-8242-0638-X   LC 79-14265

"A numbered indexed list of 298 children's song books published between 1909 and 1977, identifying more than

Peterson, Carolyn Sue, 1938-—*Continued*

5000 songs (both American and foreign) and variations, arranged alphabetically by author. There are also a title and first line index and a subject index, using more than 1000 subject headings. The titles are likely to be held in schools and public libraries." Ref Sources for Small & Medium-sized Libr. 5th edition

Raffi

Baby Beluga; illustrated by Ashley Wolff. Crown 1990 unp il music (Raffi songs to read) $16; pa $4.99 (k-2)   **782.42**

1. Songs

ISBN 0-517-57839-5; 0-517-58362-3 (pa)

LC 89-49367

Presents the illustrated text to the song about the little white whale who swims wild and free

"Wolff's striking double-page spreads show the young whale among its fellow Arctic Sea inhabitants. Diversifying her views, the illustrator eyes Baby Beluga and mother swimming together underwater; takes an aerial angle, looking down on the whales from a puffin's perspective; and observes the icy yet welcoming formations where seals, polar bears, and an Eskimo find shelter. . . . An inviting approach to reading encouragement." Booklist

Down by the bay; illustrated by Nadine Bernard Westcott. Crown 1987 unp il music (Raffi songs to read) lib bdg $14; pa $4.99 (k-2)   **782.42**

1. Songs

ISBN 0-517-56644-3 (lib bdg); 0-517-56645-1 (pa)

LC 87-750291

This illustrated version of one of Raffi's songs depicts a variety of unusual sights to be seen "down by the bay"

The "cheerful nonsense verses are illustrated with equal cheer. Westcott's scraggly lines and bright, clear colors humorously portray the busy children, jolly animals, and frantic mothers that populate the song." SLJ

Five little ducks; illustrated by Jose Aruego and Ariane Dewey. Crown 1989 unp il music (Raffi songs to read) $12; pa $4.99 (k-2)   **782.42**

1. Songs

ISBN 0-517-56945-0; 0-517-58360-7 (pa)

LC 88-3752

"In bold colors and uncluttered spreads, Aruego and Dewey present Mother Duck and her five ducklings waddling 'over the hills and far away'. . . . But after each outing, one less duckling returns until all have left the nest. Come spring, however, Mother is greeted by all five youngsters returning with their own quacking broods." Booklist

One light, one sun; illustrated by Eugenie Fernandes. Crown 1988 unp il music (Raffi songs to read) $9.95; pa $4.99 (k-2)   **782.42**

1. Songs

ISBN 0-517-56785-7; 0-517-57644-9 (pa)

LC 87-22256

This book "describes how some things are shared by everyone in the world. The illustrations capture this theme by showing three different families engaged in similar daily activities (playing, mealtime, bedtime, etc.). Brightly colored illustrations depict a single parent family, a handicapped child, and an extended family living under one roof. The words of the song are set apart from the pictures, making it easy to read or sing along as the pages are turned." SLJ

The Raffi Christmas treasury; fourteen illustrated songs and musical arrangements; illustrated by Nadine Bernard Westcott. Crown 1988 84p il music lib bdg $17.95   **782.42**

1. Carols 2. Songs

ISBN 0-517-56806-3   LC 88-750620

"The fourteen songs, taken from 'Raffi's Christmas Album,' include both traditional carols and original melodies. . . . Although the buoyant, cheerful spirit of Raffi's collection could easily defy accurate visual interpretation, Nadine Westcott should take a bow. Brimming with cheer, warmth, and humor, her watercolor illustrations play their role to perfection." Horn Book

Rayner, Mary, 1933-

One by one; Garth Pig's rain song. Dutton Children's Bks. 1994 unp il music $5.99 (k-3)   **782.42**

1. Songs 2. Counting 3. Pigs

ISBN 0-525-45240-0   LC 93-42225

Ten pink piglets; Garth Pig's wall song. Dutton Children's Bks. 1994 unp il music $5.99 (k-3)   **782.42**

1. Songs 2. Counting 3. Pigs

ISBN 0-525-45241-9   LC 93-42226

"Marching and dancing their way through simple counting songs, Rayner's beloved, bouncy pigs outwit a hungry wolf in *Ten Pink Piglets* and narrowly outrun a rainstorm in *One by One*. The engaging watercolors contain plenty of humorous detail. Music included." Horn Book Guide

Seeger, Ruth Crawford, 1901-1953

American folk songs for children in home, school and nursery school; a book for children, parents and teachers; illustrated by Barbara Cooney. Doubleday 1948 190p il music hardcover o.p. paperback available $12   **782.42**

1. Folk songs—United States 2. Singing games

ISBN 0-385-15788-6 (pa)

A big book of 90 folk songs from all parts of the country that may be sung and acted out with many variations. The tunes and piano accompaniments are simple enough for most adults to play. It is a source book for family fun

Animal folk songs for children; traditional American songs; illustrated by Barbara Cooney. Linnet Bks. 1993 80p il music lib bdg $22.50; pa $13.95   **782.42**

1. Folk songs—United States 2. Animals

ISBN 0-208-02364-X (lib bdg); 0-208-02365-8 (pa)

LC 92-767692

A reissue of the title first published 1950 by Doubleday

Illustrated with black and white drawings, this is a collection of forty-three traditional songs arranged for piano

Silverman, Jerry
Songs and stories from the American Revolution. Millbrook Press 1994 71p il music lib bdg $18.90 (6 and up) **782.42**

1. United States—History—1775-1783, Revolution—Songs
ISBN 1-56294-429-0   LC 94-10658
"This book presents 10 broadside ballads of the 1770s and 1780s, with piano and chord notations and the story behind each song. . . . An interesting combination of music and history." Booklist

Singing bee!; a collection of favorite children's songs; compiled by Jane Hart; pictures by Anita Lobel. Lothrop, Lee & Shepard Bks. 1989 160p il music $22.95; pa $11.95 **782.42**

1. Songs
ISBN 0-688-41975-5; 0-688-09113-X (pa)
     LC 82-15296
This is "a fine collection of songs for young children, arranged primarily by origin (English traditional) but partly by form (rounds) or by season (Christmas, Hanukkah) or by function (singing games). Subject and title indexes give access to the selections, and both simple guitar chords and simple piano accompaniments are provided." Bull Cent Child Books
"The glory of the book is its illustrations, which provide an imaginative, lively, often witty visual commentary. Because much of the material is traditional, the artist used historical settings; and her 'interest in all things theatrical' and her 'love of eighteenth-century garb' is visible in the profusion of pictures in black and white and in warm, luminous color." Horn Book

Songs of Chanukah; compiled by Jeanne Modesitt; illustrated by Robin Spowart; musical arrangements by Uri Ophir. Little, Brown 1992 32p il music lib bdg $15.95 **782.42**

1. Hanukkah 2. Songs
ISBN 0-316-57739-1   LC 90-27455
"This book assembles more than a dozen songs, including the blessings that are sung over the candles, and presents them all in both English and transliterated Hebrew, with music for voice, piano, and guitar. The comments that introduce each song give explanations of the holiday, including detailed instructions for playing the dreidel game and a recipe for the obligatory potato pancakes. The collection will be a boon for teachers and parents. . . . A welcome addition to holiday books." Horn Book

Songs of the Wild West; commentary by Alan Axelrod; arrangements by Dan Fox. Metropolitan Mus. of Art; Simon & Schuster Bks. for Young Readers 1991 128p il music $19.95 **782.42**

1. Cowhands—Songs 2. Folk songs—United States
ISBN 0-671-74775-4 (Simon & Schuster)
At head of title: The Metropolitan Museum of Art, in association with the Buffalo Bill Historical Center
"Axelrod combines 45 songs of the Old West with works of art from the Metropolitan Museum of Art and the Buffalo Bill Historical Center to create a nostalgic picture of cowboys and western settlers. . . . Each score is lavishly illustrated with memorable western art and introduced by a brief essay linking the song with art and history. A beautifully designed book that will appeal to armchair browsers as well as students researching the westward movement through its music and art." Booklist

Staines, Bill
All God's critters got a place in the choir; words and music by Bill Staines; pictures by Margot Zemach. Dutton 1989 unp il music $14.99 (k-2) **782.42**

1. Songs 2. Animals
ISBN 0-525-44469-6   LC 88-31696
Also available in paperback from Puffin Bks.
This is an illustrated version of the children's song about musical animals. The score is included at the end of the volume
"While the noise of the animals' brays, moos, and quacks will be more fun when led and encouraged by a skilled folk singer, the rollicking, good-natured illustrations provide plenty of amusement for those who just want to look." Horn Book

Sweet, Melissa
Fiddle-i-fee; a farmyard song for the very young; adapted and illustrated by Melissa Sweet. Little, Brown 1992 unp il music $15.95; pa $5.95 (k-2) **782.42**

1. Folk songs—United States
ISBN 0-316-82516-6; 0-316-82522-0 (pa)
     LC 90-40884
"Joy Street books"
In this cumulative folk song, a parade forms when several farm animals join a boy and his apple wagon
"The cumulative nature of the rhyme lends itself to singing along or chiming in on the chorus, and a series of animal noises grows a little longer with each verse. Simple line drawings with bright watercolor washes show the characters larking about on the farm. Piano music (with words and guitar chords) is appended." Booklist

There's a hole in the bucket; [by] Nadine Bernard Westcott. Harper & Row 1990 unp il music lib bdg $14.89; pa $4.95 (k-2) **782.42**

1. Folk songs
ISBN 0-06-026423-3 (lib bdg); 0-06-443195-9 (pa)
     LC 89-34538
As Liza instructs Henry how to fix a hole in the bucket, Henry gives her all the reasons why he can't. An illustrated version of a humorous old folk song
"Westcott's characterizations are right on target, and children will enjoy the song's repetition. . . . A musical score is included. Sprightly illustrations accompany this humorous adaptation of the familiar folksong." SLJ

Watson, Clyde, 1947-
Father Fox's feast of songs; words and music by Clyde Watson; pictures by Wendy Watson. Philomel Bks. 1983 31p il music o.p.; Wordsong reprint available $14.95 (k-3) **782.42**

1. Songs
ISBN 1-878093-84-3
"From the sisters' previous books, 'Father Fox's Pennyrhymes . . . and 'Catch Me & Kiss Me & Say It Again' the author has selected twenty-one bouncy, rhythmic verses and has set them to simple, singable tunes for young children. And for the older children or the adults who may be assisting, guitar chords and uncomplicated piano accompaniments are included." Horn Book

Weiss, Nicki, 1954-

If you're happy and you know it; eighteen story songs set to pictures by Nicki Weiss; music arranged by John Krumich. Greenwillow Bks. 1987 40p il music $16 (k-2)
782.42

1. Songs

ISBN 0-688-06444-2

"The lettering and the scores are all hand-done, perfectly clear for humming alone, but not as easy for simple piano accompaniment—some of the bars aren't presented conventionally, as on a sheet of music, and are sometimes even upside down. This whimsical touch doesn't hamper the exuberance of Weiss's characters, who dance, prance, stomp, clap and all but samba to the tunes herein." Publ Wkly

What shall we do when we all go out?; a traditional song; illustrated by Shari Halpern. North-South Bks. 1995 unp il music $14.95; lib bdg $14.88 (k-1)
782.42

1. Songs

ISBN 1-55858-424-2; 1-55858-425-0 (lib bdg)

LC 94-38573

"Text adapted by Philip H. Bailey." Verso of title page

Words and illustrations depict the activities of the day as children go out to play

"Bold and blazingly bright illustrations capture the action in this traditional song. . . . The declarative lyrics use repetition and an emphatic, bouncy rhythm to energize the vigorous activities. Double-page spreads of unusual collages . . . dazzle the eye with their multiple shapes, blocks of pure color, elaborate patterns, and lines that convey motion." SLJ

784.19 Musical instruments

Ardley, Neil, 1937-

Music. Knopf 1989 63p il (Eyewitness books) $19; lib bdg $18.99 (4 and up)
784.19

1. Musical instruments

ISBN 0-394-82259-5; 0-394-92259-X (lib bdg)

LC 88-13394

Also available Spanish language edition

Text and pictures introduce musical instruments from early times to the present—from pipes and flutes to electronic synthesizers

"Interesting historical asides and highlights about famous musicians contrast with the precisely labeled parts of the numerous illustrated instruments." Booklist

Hayes, Ann

Meet the Marching Smithereens; written by Ann Hayes; illustrated by Karmen Thompson. Harcourt Brace & Co. 1995 unp il $15 (k-3)
784.19

1. Bands (Music) 2. Musical instruments

ISBN 0-15-253158-0 LC 94-11896

This "picture book explains the brass, woodwind and percussion instruments as each, played by a comical assortment of animals, marches by. You can almost hear the sounds from the text as the colorful group parades by the cheering animal on-lookers." Child Book Rev Serv

Meet the orchestra; written by Ann Hayes; illustrated by Karmen Thompson. Harcourt Brace Jovanovich 1990 unp il $13.95; pa $5 (k-3)
784.19

1. Orchestra 2. Musical instruments

ISBN 0-15-200526-9; 0-15-200222-7 (pa)

LC 89-32959

Also available Spanish language edition

"Gulliver books"

Describes the features, sounds, and role of each musical instrument in the orchestra

"Spacious watercolors depicting animal musicians in formal evening dress enhance this charming introduction to the orchestra. . . . The descriptive writing has immediacy . . . while the artwork has a subtle sense of color and humor that increases the fun." Booklist

Hewitt, Sally

Get set—go! [Music & sound series]; photography by Peter Millard. Childrens Press 1994 4v il ea lib bdg $14.90; pa $4.95 (k-3)
784.19

1. Musical instruments

Contents: Bang and rattle; Pluck and scrape; Puff and blow; Squeak and roar

Each book presents directions for using such materials as bottles, boxes, cans, string, spoons, buttons and rubber bands to construct objects for producing sounds, musical and otherwise

Oates, Eddie Herschel

Making music; 6 instruments you can create; illustrated by Michael Koelsch. HarperCollins Pubs. 1995 32p il $15; lib bdg $15.75 (3-5)
784.19

1. Musical instruments 2. Handicraft

ISBN 0-06-021478-3; 0-06-021479-1 (lib bdg)

LC 92-20060

"After a brief, simple introduction to percussion, wind and string instruments, there are very clear instructions on how to make six instruments. The materials truly can be found in most homes and alternatives are given in many cases. Middle elementary students should be able to read and construct the instruments by themselves." Child Book Rev Serv

Walther, Tom, 1950-

Make mine music! written and illustrated by Tom Walther. Little, Brown 1981 126p il hardcover o.p. paperback available $10.95 (4 and up)
784.19

1. Musical instruments 2. Handicraft

ISBN 0-316-92112-2 (pa) LC 80-23600

"A Brown paper school book"

"The author discusses a variety of musical instruments and includes directions for making and playing them. The instructions for making the instruments are relatively easy for children to understand; however, it should be noted that some jobs require tools such as drills and saws that should be used under adult supervision. The format makes a distinction between the discussion of the instruments . . . and the directions for making them. . . . The book is illustrated with attractive line drawings. A brief list of books about musical instruments has been included." SLJ

Wiseman, Ann Sayre, 1926-
Making musical things; improvised instruments; [by] Ann Wiseman. Scribner 1979 63p il $14.95 (3-6)   **784.19**
1. Musical instruments 2. Handicraft
ISBN 0-684-16114-1   LC 79-4474
Wiseman's "clever black-and-white drawings and short, clear directions show how to make over fifty basic but ingenious musical instruments. Many of the supplies needed can be found around the house, particularly in the kitchen." Babbling Bookworm
Includes bibliography

787.2 Violin

Fleisher, Paul
The master violinmaker; photographs by David Saunders. Houghton Mifflin 1993 31p il $14.95 (3-5)   **787.2**
1. Larrimore, John 2. Violins
ISBN 0-395-65365-7   LC 92-28050
Photographs and text document the creation of a violin by master violinmaker John Larrimore
This "is readable, understandable, and precise. Excellent color photographs clearly show each step in the production process." Horn Book Guide

788 Wind instruments and their music

Krementz, Jill
A very young musician; written and photographed by Jill Krementz. Simon & Schuster Bks. for Young Readers 1991 unp il hardcover o.p. paperback available $5.95 (3-6)   **788**
1. Music—Study and teaching
ISBN 0-671-79251-2 (pa)   LC 90-10017
This photo-essay is about "fifth grader Josh Broder, a trumpet player. . . . In addition to describing his musical life, Josh discusses all of the instruments in the school band." Bull Cent Child Books
"Sprinkled throughout Josh's first-person narrative are nuggets of information that aspiring musicians will appreciate." Publ Wkly

790.1 Recreational activities

Drake, Jane
The kids' summer handbook; by Jane Drake & Ann Love; illustrated by Heather Collins. Ticknor & Fields Bks. for Young Readers 1994 c1993 207p il $15.95; pa $10.95 (4 and up)   **790.1**
1. Recreation 2. Handicraft 3. Nature craft
ISBN 0-395-68711-X; 0-395-68709-8 (pa)
          LC 93-2524
First published 1993 in Canada with title: The kids cottage book

"Beach games, water safety, hiking and camping, wild-animal watching, snacks, and crafts are among the many outdoor and indoor activities covered in the thick volume. Most topics are introduced in two-page entries, with detailed directions and plentiful, homely drawings. The practical volume will interest children, parents, and teachers." Horn Book Guide

Tricks of the trade for kids; edited by Jerry Dunn. Houghton Mifflin 1994 218p il pa $8.95 (5 and up)   **790.1**
1. Amusements 2. Hobbies
ISBN 0-395-65027-5   LC 94-22264
In this book, readers can "learn the art of performing magic tricks from Harry Blackstone, Jr.; how to build muscles like Arnold Schwarzenegger's; get advice on coping with the death of their pet from Mister Rogers; learn to draw an animated flip book from Disney's Tom Sito; and find out how to master Monopoly from the inventors of the game. The book is illustrated with more than 100 black-and-white diagrams and whimsical line drawings and is both humorous and informative." SLJ

791.3 Circuses

Cushman, Kathleen
Circus dreams; the making of a circus artist; by Kathleen Cushman and Montana Miller; photographs by Michael Carroll. Little, Brown 1990 90p il $15.95 (5 and up)   **791.3**
1. Circus
ISBN 0-316-16561-1   LC 90-36285
"Joy Street books"
Text and photographs follow eighteen-year-old Montana Miller's move to France to study with the circus in hopes of becoming a trapeze artist
This book is a "must-read for youngsters who dream of a profession in the performing arts, whatever the medium. The coauthors honestly describe not only the pleasure but, more importantly, the frustration, disappointment, doubt, and other inevitable stumbling blocks." Kobrin Letter

Johnson, Neil, 1954-
Big-top circus. Dial Bks. for Young Readers 1995 unp il $14.99; lib bdg $14.89 (1-4)   **791.3**
1. Clyde Beatty-Cole Bros. Circus 2. Circus
ISBN 0-8037-1602-8; 0-8037-1603-6 (lib bdg)
          LC 93-40274
"A brief history of the circus from its 18th-century British origins to the present day precedes this . . . narrative that covers all aspects of this unique form of entertainment." SLJ
"The pictures will attract young children, but the book is actually most distinctive because it introduces and explains the technical names for circus events and people. . . . Johnson's attention to how circus animals are treated is another feature that will interest children of the 1990s." Booklist

Machotka, Hana
The magic ring; a year with the Big Apple Circus; introduction by Paul Binder. Morrow 1988 72p il $13.95; pa $8.95 (3-6)   **791.3**
1. Big Apple Circus 2. Circus
ISBN 0-688-07449-9; 0-688-08222-X (pa)
          LC 87-28230

Machotka, Hana—*Continued*

Briefly surveys the history of circuses and describes the growth, rehearsals, performances, and personnel of the successful one-ring circus known as the Big Apple Circus

"Author/photographer Machotka masterfully captures the personalities, warmth and spirit of this unique nonprofit endeavor. . . . Vivid, full-color photos enhance and expand the text. In sum, *The Magic Ring* masterfully communicates the excitement that this small gem of a circus inspires in its audiences." Publ Wkly

791.43 Motion pictures

Gibbons, Gail

Lights! Camera! Action! how a movie is made. Crowell 1985 unp il lib bdg $14.89 (k-3)
    791.43

1. Motion pictures—Production and direction

ISBN 0-690-04477-1   LC 85-47536

A step-by-step description of how a movie is made, including writing the script, casting, rehearsing, creating the scenery and costumes, editing the film, and attending the premiere

"Characteristically graphic writing explains the processes involved in bringing a major movie from idea through its glittering premiere. Boldly colored, detailed cartoons show men and women handling their responsibilities (scriptwriter, producer, art director, casting director, editors: a myriad of specialists). Like all Gibbons's primers on facets of modern life, the movie book stands out as attractive and useful." Publ Wkly

Scott, Elaine, 1940-

Look alive; behind the scenes of an animated film; written by Elaine Scott; photographs by Richard Hewett. Morrow Junior Bks. 1992 68p il $14; lib bdg $13.93 (4 and up)
    791.43

1. Ralph S. Mouse (Motion picture) 2. Motion pictures—Production and direction

ISBN 0-688-09936-X; 0-688-09937-8 (lib bdg)
     LC 91-36220

Provides an insider's view of the making of the animated movie "Ralph S. Mouse," in which stop-action animation and other special effects are used to bring a puppet to life as the character from three popular Beverly Cleary books

"Although puppet animation is a complicated topic, the process is explained very clearly in this narrative. There is even a physical example of animation, a juggling flip-book mouse located in the lower corner of every righthand page. Terms like 'pre-production,' 'budgets,' and 'pixilate' are defined and then described in detail. . . . The black-and-white photos supplement the text nicely. . . . This book is detailed enough for the technically-minded and clear enough for the neophyte." Bull Cent Child Books

791.45 Television

Scott, Elaine, 1940-

Ramona: behind the scenes of a television show; written by Elaine Scott; photographs by Margaret Miller. Morrow Junior Bks. 1988 88p il $14.95; lib bdg $14.88 (4 and up)
    791.45

1. Ramona (Television program) 2. Television—Production and direction

ISBN 0-688-06818-9; 0-688-06819-7 (lib bdg)
     LC 87-33313

"This book gives readers an insider's view of a television show from conception to broadcast. . . . Each step is explained as it took place during the filming of *Ramona*, a 10-part television series based on Beverly Cleary's . . . books about Ramona Quimby." Booklist

"The text, liberally illustrated with photographs of people and procedures, is direct, clear, sequential, and informative." Bull Cent Child Books

791.5 Puppetry and toy theaters

Renfro, Nancy

Puppet show made easy! photographs by Nancy Scanlan; illustrated by Ellen Scott Turner and Nany Renfro. Nancy Renfro Studios 1984 80p il (Puppetry in education) pa $14.95 (3-6)
    791.5

1. Puppets and puppet plays

ISBN 0-931044-13-8

Contents: On with the show; A story; From story to script; Building the show; Staging the show; Show time!

The emphasis is on creating one's own scenario, hand puppets of different types, and stagecraft, with how-to directions throughout

792.3 Pantomime

Straub, Cindie

Mime: basics for beginners; [by] Cindie and Matthew Straub; photography by Jeff Blanton. Plays 1984 152p il $13.95 (6 and up)
    792.3

1. Mime

ISBN 0-8238-0263-9   LC 84-11694

Drawings and photographs accompany a discussion of the physical and technical aspects of mime

Includes glossary

792.5 Opera

Price, Leontyne

Aïda; as told by Leontyne Price; illustrated by Leo and Diane Dillon. Harcourt Brace Jovanovich 1990 unp il $17; pa $5 (4 and up)
    792.5

1. Opera—Stories, plots, etc.

ISBN 0-15-200405-X; 0-15-200987-6 (pa)
     LC 89-36481

Price, Leontyne—*Continued*

Coretta Scott King Award for illustration, 1990

"Gulliver books"

"Based on the opera by Giuseppi Verdi"

Tragedy results when an enslaved Ethiopian princess falls in love with an Egyptian general

"The text appears on the left surmounted by a friezelike series of figures which interpret the action; on the right, a full-page illustration focuses on a particular character or grouping. A worthy introduction to the opera for a varied audience." Horn Book Guide

Rosenberg, Jane, 1949-

Sing me a story; the Metropolitan Opera's book of opera stories for children; introduction by Luciano Pavarotti. Thames & Hudson 1989 158p il $24.95 (4-6)   **792.5**

1. Opera—Stories, plots, etc.

ISBN 0-500-01467-1   LC 88-51929

"Alongside the so-called ABC's—*Aida, La Boheme* and *Carmen*—are less often performed works such as *L'Enfant et les Sortileges, Porgy and Bess* and *The Love for Three Oranges*. The author skillfully refers to specific musical passages and uses dialogue drawn from the libretto to link each story to an actual performance. . . . Although brief accounts in general cannot do justice to the deep emotion and psychological insight of *Pagliacci* or *The Magic Flute*, these failings are more than redeemed by Rosenberg's handsomely detailed watercolors, which convey the opulent sensuality of opera at its most sublime." Publ Wkly

792.7 Variety shows

Fradon, Dana

The king's fool; a book about Medieval and Renaissance fools; words and pictures by Dana Fradon. Dutton Children's Bks. 1993 unp il $14.99 (3-5)   **792.7**

1. Fools and jesters 2. Renaissance

ISBN 0-525-45074-2   LC 92-43836

Examines the role of fools or jesters in medieval and Renaissance society and describes such individuals as Will Sommers of sixteenth-century England and Querno of sixteenth-century Italy

"In his humorous illustrations and well-conceived text . . . Fradon . . . displays a wit that would do honor to any sharp medieval or renaissance fool." Publ Wkly

792.8 Ballet and modern dance

Anderson, Joan

Twins on toes; a ballet debut; photographs by George Ancona. Lodestar Bks. 1993 unp il $14.99 (4 and up)   **792.8**

1. Ballet 2. Twins

ISBN 0-525-67415-2   LC 92-35104

Describes the experiences of twins Amy and Laurel Foster, who trained for ten years to become professional ballerinas and studied at the School of American Ballet

"An absorbing look at two girls, professionals consecrated to their art, and at the hard work of endless classes and endless hopes. The photographs are splendid and varied." Bull Cent Child Books

Bussell, Darcey

The young dancer; [by] Darcey Bussell with Patricia Linton. Dorling Kindersley 1994 64p il $15.95 (4 and up)   **792.8**

1. Ballet

ISBN 1-56458-468-2   LC 93-36790

Published in association with Royal Ballet School

This "book introduces children to the positions, movements, traditions, and history of ballet. Both the text and the illustrations are unusually clear and precise. . . . Dorling Kindersley's signature visual style works quite effectively here, with full-color photographs throughout. . . . Appendixes include an address list of American dance companies and a glossary of ballet terms." Booklist

Fonteyn, Dame Margot, 1919-1991

Swan lake; as told by Margot Fonteyn and illustrated by Trina Schart Hyman. Harcourt Brace Jovanovich 1988 unp il $15.95; pa $6.95 (3-5)   **792.8**

1. Swan lake (Ballet) 2. Fairy tales

ISBN 0-15-200600-1; 0-15-283352-8 (pa)

          LC 87-7573

"Gulliver books"

"In the story, Prince Siegfried has fallen in love with Odette, a queen turned swan by an evil owl-magician. When the owl-magician's daughter appears at a ball disguised as Odette, Siegfried pledges his troth, only to discover the deception too late." Bull Cent Child Books

"Both prose and paintings are haunting in their elegant evocation of this sad, mysterious tale. An uncommonly fine ballet book for children, this communicates not only the story but a touch of the magic as well." Booklist

Isadora, Rachel

My ballet class. Greenwillow Bks. 1980 unp il $15 (1-3)   **792.8**

1. Ballet

ISBN 0-688-80253-2   LC 79-16297

"This is a short look at a young girl's experience in ballet class. The large, close-up line drawings show male and female students changing, doing warm-up exercises, doing the five basic positions, and practicing leaps with their male instructor." Child Book Rev Serv

"The book is excellent: simply written, nicely illustrated, and introducing ballet basics not only in a way that is clear but also in a tone that suggests ballet lessons are enjoyable." Bull Cent Child Books

Kuklin, Susan

Going to my ballet class. Bradbury Press 1989 unp il $15 (k-3)   **792.8**

1. Ballet

ISBN 0-02-751235-5   LC 88-37556

"Color photographs show young boys and girls in a ballet class for beginners; the pictures are technically good and visually appealing as well as informative. The text is simply written in first person, so that facts about lessons and positions and steps are always from a child's viewpoint. The book concludes with a section (in smaller print) addressed to adults, giving some useful advice on choosing a ballet class and on researching what's available and has a good professional reputation." Bull Cent Child Books

McCaughrean, Geraldine, 1951-

The Random House book of stories from the ballet; retold by Geraldine McCaughrean; illustrated by Angela Barrett. Random House 1995 c1994 112p il $18; lib bdg $19.99 (4 and up)   **792.8**

1. Ballet—Stories, plots, etc.
ISBN 0-679-87125-X; 0-679-97125-4 (lib bdg)
LC 94-22640
First published 1994 in the United Kingdom with title: The Orchard book of stories from the ballet

Contents: Swan Lake; Coppelia; Giselle; Cinderella; La Sylphide; The nutcracker; Romeo and Juliet; The firebird; Petrouchka; The sleeping beauty

"Dramatic plots, unusual characters, and magical spells are interwoven into each of the well-written retellings. The essence of a ballet production is successfully captured by the full-color illustrations." Booklist

Morris, Ann

On their toes; a Russian ballet school; photographs by Ken Heyman. Atheneum Pubs. 1991 unp il $14.95 (3-5)   **792.8**

1. Vaganova Choreographic Institute (Saint Petersburg, Russia) 2. Ballet
ISBN 0-689-31660-7
LC 91-11903
A behind-the-scenes look at the Kirov Ballet Academy, a training school for young dancers in Russia

"Full-color photographs concentrate on students from the second-year class, showing them at work and at play, in the studio and at home. . . . The text is straightforward and informative, but the spirit is in the visual images." SLJ

Switzer, Ellen Eichenwald, 1923-

The nutcracker; a story & a ballet; photographs by Steven Caras and Costas. Atheneum Pubs. 1985 101p il $16.95 (4 and up)   **792.8**

1. New York City Ballet 2. Nutcracker (Ballet) 3. Ballet
ISBN 0-689-31061-7
LC 85-7463
Describes the Tchaikovsky ballet, the Hoffman story on which it was based, and the version staged by Balanchine for the New York City Ballet, as shown through photographs and interviews with some of the dancers

"The next best thing to watching the New York City Ballet perform *The Nutcracker* is to read this book. . . . A short bibliography that includes titles for adults as well as younger readers closes the book and invites us to experience 'The Nutcracker' again and again." SLJ

Verdy, Violette, 1933-

Of swans, sugarplums, and satin slippers; ballet stories for children; illustrated by Marcia Brown. Scholastic 1991 90p il $17.95 (4-6)   **792.8**

1. Ballet—Stories, plots, etc.
ISBN 0-590-43484-5
LC 91-98
The author "retells the stories of six familiar ballets, *The Firebird, Coppelia, Swan Lake, The Nutcracker, Giselle, and Sleeping Beauty*." Booklist

"The accounts here are fresh, dramatic and lush with detail, and the prose is as graceful as a pas de deux. . . . Brown's dreamy, ethereal illustrations sustain the entrancing mood." Publ Wkly

793   Indoor games and amusements

Cole, Joanna

Pin the tail on the donkey and other party games; compiled by Joanna Cole and Stephanie Calmenson; illustrated by Alan Tiegreen. Morrow Junior Bks. 1993 48p il $15; lib bdg $14.93; pa $6.95 (k-2)   **793**

1. Games 2. Parties
ISBN 0-688-11891-7; 0-688-11892-5 (lib bdg); 0-688-12521-2 (pa)
LC 92-29786
Provides instructions for 20 simple party games for young children such as Musical Chairs, Giant Steps, and Peanut Hunt

"The step-by-step directions and parenthetical advice will please older kids, teachers, and parents, while young children looking for birthday party games will find the appealing ink-and-watercolor illustrations a big help in choosing their personal favorites." Booklist

Includes bibliography

Rockwell, Anne F., 1934-

Things to play with; [by] Anne Rockwell. Dutton 1988 24p il o.p.; Puffin Bks. paperback available $3.99 (k-1)   **793**

1. Amusements 2. Play
ISBN 0-14-050308-0 (pa)
LC 87-33399
Introduces a variety of situations and objects that may be used for play, including things to play with in the yard, at school, on snow and ice, and at a party

"Each category merits a double-page spread of boxed scenes featuring an animal child and toy. The pages are visually full, laid out in comic-book style, with no intervening space between frames. Rockwell's neat line work and cheery colors create a lighthearted mood that perfectly suits the parent-child sharing for which this is designed." Booklist

793.7   Games not characterized by action

Blum, Raymond

Math tricks, puzzles & games; illustrated by Jeff Sinclair. Sterling 1994 127p il $13.95; pa $4.95 (4 and up)   **793.7**

1. Mathematical recreations
ISBN 0-8069-0582-4; 0-8069-0583-2 (pa)
LC 93-46750
"The book is divided into various chapters, such as 'Card Tricks,' 'Brain Teasers,' and 'Calculator Riddles.' . . . With more than 120 different entries (some with variations), the book provides a good variety of puzzle types, with varying degrees of difficulty. Hints and answers are provided, as is a glossary of mathematical terms. None of the puzzles require elaborate materials . . . and the illustrations and examples are clearly written." Appraisal

Math for the very young; a handbook of activities for parents and teachers; [by] Lydia Plonsky [et al.]; illustrated by Marcia Miller. Wiley 1995 210p il $24.95; pa $12.95

793.7

1. Mathematical recreations
ISBN 0-471-01671-3; 0-471-01647-0 (pa)

LC 94-20861

"This guide suggests ways to introduce math to children through everyday activities. Sections include making a record book about the child and the family as well as activities for each month of the year, geometric crafts, math games, counting rhymes and stories, and ways to use math in the home and on the road." Booklist

Includes bibliographical references

793.73 Puzzles and puzzle games

Adler, David A., 1947-

The carsick zebra and other animal riddles; illustrated by Tomie de Paola. Holiday House 1983 unp il $11.95 (1-3)

793.73

1. Riddles
ISBN 0-8234-0479-X

LC 82-48750

In this collection of riddles "the questions appear at the top of the page, Tomie dePaola's simple yet witty black-and-white drawings fill the middle, and the answer appears at the bottom." Booklist

A teacher on roller skates and other school riddles; illustrated by John Wallner. Holiday House 1989 unp il $12.95 (1-3)

793.73

1. Riddles
ISBN 0-8234-0775-6

LC 89-1929

A collection of jokes and riddles about school. Each page features one riddle, accompanied by a cartoon-style drawing

The twisted witch, and other spooky riddles; illustrated by Victoria Chess. Holiday House 1985 unp il $12.95 (1-3)

793.73

1. Riddles
ISBN 0-8234-0571-0

LC 85-909

"An irresistible cauldron of 60 riddles for the witching season. On each page, a pithy riddle is paired with a playful black-and-white drawing, and the result is more often hilarious than horrifying. In fact, it is the illustrations, detailed down to witches' warts and monsters' toenails, that revive the deader punch lines." SLJ

Agee, Jon

Go hang a salami! I'm a lasagna hog! and other palindromes. Farrar, Straus & Giroux 1992 unp il $12.21; pa $5.95

793.73

1. Word games
ISBN 0-374-33473-0; 0-374-44473-0 (pa)

LC 91-31319

A collection of palindromes, sentences that read the same forward and backward

"Agee offers a humorous look at the concept, using more than 50 wacky alphabetical examples. . . . Cartoon sketches extend and often clarify the meaning of the crazy phrases." Booklist

So many dynamos! and other palindromes. Farrar, Straus & Giroux 1994 80p il $12.21

793.73

1. Word games
ISBN 0-374-22473-0

LC 94-73749

"This book features one palindromic phrase per page or spread. . . . Even children who have never heard of a palindrome will be drawn to the cartoons, while readers fascinated by concept may want to try writing (and illustrating) their own." Booklist

Beisner, Monika

Catch that cat! a picture book of rhymes and puzzles. Farrar, Straus & Giroux 1990 unp il $15

793.73

1. Puzzles 2. Riddles 3. Cats—Poetry
ISBN 0-374-31226-5

LC 90-55144

Also available Spanish language edition

Illustrations and rhyming text present picture puzzles and riddles featuring cats

"Whether searching for the solution to a riddle or simply appreciating the luxurious color and intricate detail of Beisner's sublime illustrations, readers will be entranced by these pages." Publ Wkly

Calmenson, Stephanie

What am I? very first riddles; pictures by Karen Gundersheimer. Harper & Row 1989 unp il lib bdg $12.89; pa $4.95 (k-2)

793.73

1. Riddles
ISBN 0-06-020998-4 (lib bdg); 0-06-443291-2 (pa)

LC 87-22959

A collection of easy-to-read riddles in verse about everyday objects

"Never tricky and always toddler-tested (keys, flowers, a swing), the riddles provide the appeal of rhyming as well as pride in the accomplishment of figuring out the answer. And, of course, the fun of shouting it out. Tidy drawings on the riddle page provide visual nudges; illustrations of the mystery of objects are generic enough to be readily identified while maintaining interest through color (a yellow telephone) and detail (a terrific toy train)." Bull Cent Child Books

Cerf, Bennett, 1898-1971

Bennett Cerf's book of riddles; illustrated by Roy McKie. Beginner Bks. 1960 62p il $7.99; lib bdg $7.99 (k-3)

793.73

1. Riddles
ISBN 0-394-80015-X; 0-394-90015-4 (lib bdg)

These thirty-one riddles are arranged with the riddles being asked on one page and answered on the next, to keep the element of surprise

"Simple cartoonlike drawings use strong colour for their effect." Ont Libr Rev

Cole, Joanna

Why did the chicken cross the road? and other riddles, old and new; compiled by Joanna Cole and Stephanie Calmenson; illustrated by Alan Tiegreen. Morrow Junior Bks. 1994 64p il $15; lib bdg $14.93; pa $6.95 (3-5)   **793.73**

1. Riddles
ISBN 0-688-12202-7; 0-688-12203-5 (lib bdg); 0-688-12204-3 (pa)   LC 94-2582

The authors "begin with a brief explanation about the origin of riddles and proceed with a collection of over two hundred, classic and new. Though many of the riddles appear in other collections, the book, illustrated with black-and-white line drawings, will be useful for its short bibliography and subject index." Horn Book Guide

Hall, Katy, 1947-

Snakey riddles; by Katy Hall and Lisa Eisenberg; pictures by Simms Taback. Dial Bks. for Young Readers 1990 48p il o.p.; Puffin Bks. paperback available $3.99 (k-2)   **793.73**

1. Riddles
ISBN 0-14-054588-3 (pa)   LC 88-23687
"Dial easy-to-read"

An illustrated collection of riddles about snakes
"Riddle lovers will groan with delight at some of these riddles. . . . The best thing about the book is the cleverly drawn, lively cartoon illustrations. Long, colorful snakes form borders framing the text and picture for each riddle." SLJ

Keller, Charles, 1942-

Belly laughs; food jokes & riddles; illustrated by Ron Fritz. Simon & Schuster Bks. for Young Readers 1990 unp il $13.95; pa $5.95 (k-3)   **793.73**

1. Riddles 2. Jokes
ISBN 0-671-70068-5; 0-671-70069-3 (pa)
    LC 89-28201

An illustrated collection of jokes and riddles with an emphasis on food
"Lavishly illustrated in full color. . . . Many of these are fresh and funny, and most are within the understanding of younger, less sophisticated readers. Witty illustrations illustrate this outstanding joke book." SLJ

Kessler, Leonard P., 1920-

Old Turtle's 90 knock-knocks, jokes, and riddles; [by] Leonard Kessler. Greenwillow Bks. 1991 48p il $13.95; lib bdg $13.88; pa $4.95 (1-3)   **793.73**

1. Jokes 2. Riddles
ISBN 0-688-09585-2; 0-688-09586-0 (lib bdg); 0-688-04586-3 (pa)   LC 89-77505

An illustrated collection of animal jokes and riddles
This book includes "a string of jokes and riddles silly enough to please kids this age and usually simple enough not to baffle them. . . . Kessler's cartoonlike drawings, bright with watercolor washes, give the book a fresh, funny look that makes the verbal humor twice as effective." Booklist

Old Turtle's riddle and joke book; [by] Leonard Kessler. Greenwillow Bks. 1986 47p il $14; lib bdg $19.50 (1-3)   **793.73**

1. Riddles
ISBN 0-688-05953-8; 0-688-05954-6 (lib bdg)
    LC 85-12565
"A Greenwillow read-alone book"

"Old Turtle is compiling a riddle book, which serves as a convenient excuse for all of his friends to tell him their favorites. . . . The jokes veer from being integrated into the story to appearing as abrupt block sections of riddles from each animal friend. The slight pretext for the joke sessions won't bother young readers; they'll devour the wordplay, enjoy the riddle-followed-by-a-box-with-the-upside-down-answer-and-a-cartoon-illustration format, and snort over the additional cracks made by a pair of birds at the bottom of each page." SLJ

Maestro, Giulio, 1942-

Halloween howls; riddles that are a scream. Dutton 1983 unp il $10.95 (2-4)   **793.73**

1. Riddles
ISBN 0-525-44059-3   LC 83-1419
Also available in paperback from Puffin Bks.

"Maestro's cornucopia of riddles stars ghosts, monsters, skeletons, ghouls and witches all cavorting in funny, violently colored pictures. Since kids dearly love this brand of humor, the book should be very popular among boys and girls planning Halloween festivities." Publ Wkly

Macho nacho and other rhyming riddles. Dutton Children's Bks. 1994 unp il $12.99 (2-4)   **793.73**

1. Riddles
ISBN 0-525-45261-3   LC 93-47137

A "collection of riddles based on the traditional word game known as Inky Pinky, Stinky Pinky, or Hinky Pinky, in which the two-word answers rhyme. . . . Full-color, humorous, and brightly colored illustrations complement each riddle and give visual clues to help answer them." Booklist

More Halloween howls; riddles that come back to haunt you. Dutton Children's Bks. 1992 unp il $12 (2-4)   **793.73**

1. Riddles
ISBN 0-525-44899-3   LC 91-23505

A collection of riddles about witches, vampires, skeletons, and other scary Halloween creatures
"Kids will groan and laugh at the garish illustrations, which are both mad and literal, from the haunted house whose scared windows get the shudders to the vampire with bat breath." Booklist

Riddle roundup. Clarion Bks. 1989 64p il hardcover o.p. paperback available $6.95 (2-4)   **793.73**

1. Riddles 2. Word games
ISBN 0-89919-537-7 (pa)   LC 86-33403

A collection of sixty-one riddles based on different kinds of word play such as puns, homonyms, and homographs

What's a frank frank? tasty homograph riddles. Clarion Bks. 1984 64p il hardcover o.p. paperback available $4.95 (2-4)   **793.73**

1. Riddles 2. Word games
ISBN 0-89919-317-X (pa)   LC 84-5021

Maestro, Giulio, 1942-—*Continued*

"Homographs are the inspiration for this collection of riddles that will set youngsters to thinking about the idiosyncrasies of their language. 'What's a spare spare? A skinny extra tire.' Is an example of the sort of wordplay that passes for good, pedantic humor. . . . Maestro's accompanying cartoons are adequate but not especially fresh; still, they do help liven up the atmosphere and give some of the more esoteric jokes a concrete base." Booklist

Peterson, Scott K.

Plugged in; electric riddles; pictures by Susan Slattery Burke. Lerner Publs. 1995 unp il (You must be joking!) lib bdg $10.13; pa $3.95 (2-4) **793.73**

1. Riddles
ISBN 0-8225-2344-2 (lib bdg); 0-8225-9700-4 (pa)
LC 94-24871

The jokes in this book are based on common household appliances

Phillips, Louis, 1942-

Haunted house jokes; illustrated by James Marshall. Viking Kestrel 1987 57p il hardcover o.p. paperback available $3.95 (3-5) **793.73**

1. Jokes 2. Riddles
ISBN 0-14-032062-8 (pa)
LC 87-8336

A "collection of riddles, jokes, knock-knocks, and puns, gathered into chapters by creatures (ghosts, werewolves, skeletons, etc.) and profusely illustrated with Marshall's goofy, unthreatening figures." SLJ

Sloat, Teri

Rib-ticklers; a book of punny animals; [by] Teri & Robert Sloat. Lothrop, Lee & Shepard Bks. 1995 unp il $15 (2-5) **793.73**

1. Riddles
ISBN 0-688-12519-0
LC 93-48619

"Each two-page spread in this book features 15-20 theme-related riddles, asked and answered by various creatures. . . . The Sloats' full-color illustrations are subtly humorous rather than cartoonishly wacky, and kids will enjoy perusing the pages. The riddles and answers are scattered about in well-placed word balloons." SLJ

Steig, William, 1907-

C D C? Farrar, Straus & Giroux 1984 unp il hardcover o.p. paperback available $3.95 (3-6) **793.73**

1. Word games
ISBN 0-374-41024-0 (pa)
LC 84-48515

Companion volume C D B! available in paperback from Simon & Schuster

"Steig has devised letter and number sequences, with a few figures like $ and ¢ thrown in for good measure, which, when pronounced aloud, translate roughly into captions for the accompanying cartoon drawings. The cartoons also contain helpful clues to the words' meanings, as in the title phrase, which is matched with a drawing of a man and boy looking out at sea. Some of these quips contain references that children will have difficulty interpreting. . . . Also the vocabulary is often demanding." Booklist

"Flawlessly executed, purely pleasurable, the book is definitely 'D Q-R' for doldrums at any season." Horn Book

Terban, Marvin

The dove dove; funny homograph riddles; illustrated by Tom Huffman. Clarion Bks. 1988 64p il lib bdg $12.95; pa $6.95 (3-5) **793.73**

1. Riddles 2. Word games
ISBN 0-89919-723-X (lib bdg); 0-89919-810-4 (pa)
LC 88-2611

"An introduction to the sometimes confusing world of homographs—words that are spelled alike, but are pronounced differently and have different meanings. Using the general pattern of riddle and accompanying illustration, Terban leads readers through a variety of homographs. . . . The format of the book appears to be designed for readers in grades three and four. However . . . some homographs may prove much too difficult for that age group, and the format seems too young for older students. The book will prove of interest to those students who enjoy the challenge of, and appreciate, word play." SLJ

Funny you should ask; how to make up jokes and riddles with wordplay; illustrated by John O'Brien. Clarion Bks. 1992 64p il $14.95; pa $5.95 (3-5) **793.73**

1. Riddles 2. English language—Homonyms 3. Puns and punning
ISBN 0-395-60556-3; 0-395-58113-3 (pa)
LC 91-19509

The author "introduces four kinds of wordplay— homonyms, 'almost-sound-alike words,' homographs, and idioms. In a laid-back fashion that won't put off readers, he shows clearly how each type of wordplay works, provides numerous examples to illustrate . . . and suggests some words to use when making up jokes and riddles of one's own. O'Brien's black-and-white cartoon sketches, liberally scattered throughout, add the perfect visual touch. Great for classroom use and for aspiring comedians—of any age." Booklist

Includes bibliography

Hey, hay! a wagonful of funny homonym riddles; illustrated by Kevin Hawkes. Clarion Bks. 1991 64p il $14.95 (3-5) **793.73**

1. English language—Homonyms 2. Riddles
ISBN 0-395-54431-9
LC 90-39432

A collection of riddles based on homonyms, arranged according to construction and level of difficulty

"Combine puns, riddles, and wild cartoons, and you get ridiculous wordplay that leaps between sound and sense. . . . The wry juxtapositions . . . will keep kids laughing while they look up the answers to the riddles." Booklist

Includes bibliography

Wick, Walter

I spy; a book of picture riddles; photographs by Walter Wick; riddles by Jean Marzollo; design by Carol Devine Carson. Scholastic 1992 33p il $12.95 **793.73**

1. Puzzles
ISBN 0-590-45087-5
LC 91-28268

Also available Spanish language edition

I spy Christmas; a book of picture riddles; photographs by Walter Wick; riddles by Jean Marzollo. Scholastic 1992 33p il $12.95 **793.73**

1. Puzzles
ISBN 0-590-45846-9
LC 91-45732

Also available Spanish language edition

Wick, Walter—*Continued*

I spy fantasy; a book of picture riddles; photographs by Walter Wick; riddles by Jean Marzollo. Scholastic 1994 37p il $12.95

793.73

1. Puzzles
ISBN 0-590-46295-4   LC 93-44814

I spy fun house; a book of picture riddles; photographs by Walter Wick; riddles by Jean Marzollo. Scholastic 1993 33p il $12.95

793.73

1. Puzzles
ISBN 0-590-46293-8   LC 92-16425

I spy mystery; a book of picture riddles; photographs by Walter Wick; riddles by Jean Marzollo. Scholastic 1993 37p il $12.95

793.73

1. Puzzles
ISBN 0-590-46294-6   LC 92-40863

I spy school days; a book of picture riddles; photographs by Walter Wick; riddles by Jean Marzollo. Scholastic 1995 33p il $12.95

793.73

1. Puzzles
ISBN 0-590-48135-5   LC 94-43629
"Cartwheel books"
"On oversize pages, brightly colored photographs are crammed with small objects; each double-page spread is organized by theme. . . . The rhyming captions at the foot of each page suggest objects to be found. . . . While the pages are very busy, it's the sort of crowding many young children enjoy, and it certainly fosters observation of detail." Bull Cent Child Books

793.8 Magic and related activities

Besmehn, Bobby

Juggling step-by-step. Sterling 1995 79p $17.95; pa $7.95 (4 and up)   **793.8**

1. Juggling
ISBN 0-8069-0814-9; 0-8069-0815-7 (pa)
                                 LC 94-12873
"A Sterling/Chapelle book"
"A basic introduction to juggling. Beginning with a tossing move using one scarf, the tricks progress to two-person passes with several balls. Other routines include juggling rings and clubs, a special 'neck catch' trick, and an 'eat-an-apple-while-juggling' move." SLJ
"Each exceptionally clear, full-color photograph features a close-up of a young person juggling. The simple clothes and black backgrounds in the photos allow readers to focus on the jugglers' action." Booklist
Includes glossary

Broekel, Ray, 1923-

Hocus pocus: magic you can do; [by] Ray Broekel and Laurence B. White, Jr; illustrated by Mary Thelen. Whitman, A. 1984 48p il $12.95 (3-5)   **793.8**

1. Magic tricks
ISBN 0-8075-3350-5   LC 83-26096
Step-by-step instructions for twenty simple magic tricks, together with tips on patter, timing, slight-of-hand, and misdirection for the beginning magician
"Most children, if they read carefully, will be able to figure out the tricks. The black-and-white illustrations dabbed with purple are clearly marked, and the jokes that accompany them add a spot of humor." Booklist

Brown, Dave

Amazing magic tricks; [by] Dave Brown & Paul Reeve. Dorling Kindersley 1995 47p il $12.95 (4-6)   **793.8**

1. Magic tricks
ISBN 1-56458-877-7   LC 94-34863
"Directions for how to do each trick include the patter magicians use as they perform and any special instructions that will make the trick work. There is quite a bit of preparation required to make the props—they are lovely, but may prove difficult for any but the most determined youngsters to complete on their own." SLJ

Cobb, Vicki, 1938-

Bet you can! science possibilities to fool you; [by] Vicki Cobb and Kathy Darling; illustrated by Stella Ormai. Lothrop, Lee & Shepard Bks. 1990 112p il $12.95 (4 and up)   **793.8**

1. Scientific recreations 2. Magic tricks
ISBN 0-688-09865-7   LC 90-6690
Original Avon Bks. paperback, published 1983, still available
Provides instructions for more than sixty tricks based on scientific experiments described in the text

Bet you can't! science impossibilities to fool you; by Vicki Cobb and Kathy Darling; illustrated by Martha Weston. Lothrop, Lee & Shepard Bks. 1980 128p il $15; lib bdg $14.93 (4 and up)   **793.8**

1. Scientific recreations 2. Magic tricks
ISBN 0-688-41905-4; 0-688-51905-9 (lib bdg)
                                 LC 79-9254
Also available in paperback from Avon Bks.
More than 60 tricks are contained in this book. "Explanations of the scientific principles that make the trick impossible to accomplish are included. Some explanations contain an example from a child's everyday life in which the same scientific principles apply." Sci Books Films

Magic—naturally! science entertainments & amusements; illustrated by Lionel Kalish. rev ed. HarperCollins Pubs. 1993 150p il $15; lib bdg $14.89; pa $4.95 (4 and up)   **793.8**

1. Scientific recreations 2. Magic tricks
ISBN 0-06-022474-6; 0-06-022475-4 (lib bdg); 0-06-446031-2 (pa)   LC 90-21829
First published 1976 by Lippincott

Cobb, Vicki, 1938-—*Continued*
"Each of the 30 tricks/experiments . . . begins with a list of easy-to-find materials and is followed by a description of the set up. Cobb . . . clearly explains the scientific principles behind the demonstrations. She emphasizes proper cautions when using fire or poisonous substances. Kalish's pen-and-ink illustrations are simple, but attractive and detailed enough to enhance the text. Performance tips enable young magicians to select just the right activities for their acts." SLJ

Wanna bet! science challenges to fool you; [by] Vicki Cobb and Kathy Darling; illustrated by Meredith Johnson. Lothrop, Lee & Shepard Bks. 1993 128p il $13 (4 and up)   **793.8**
1. Scientific recreations 2. Magic tricks
ISBN 0-688-11213-7   LC 92-8962
Also available in paperback from Avon Bks.

Provides instructions for a variety of scientific tricks or challenges, such as slicing an apple in midair with a hammer or tying a knot in a chicken bone
"The text is lively, and Johnson's black-and-white sketches are humorous and abundant." Booklist

Friedhoffer, Robert
The magic show; a guide for young magicians; [by] Bob Friedhoffer; illustrated by Linda Eisenberg. Millbrook Press 1994 80p il lib bdg $14.40 (4 and up)   **793.8**
1. Magic tricks
ISBN 1-56294-355-3   LC 93-42272
This offers "youngsters the insight into how to plan an entire show. Friedhoffer explains exactly what makes a strong performance; offers suggestions for opening, middle, and closing tricks; and even reveals how to construct a servante, the table magicians use. The tricks themselves are organized by level of difficulty. . . . Blue-and-white illustrations scattered throughout further explicate the detailed instructions. Notes about famous magicians and advice about protecting your tricks are included. An excellent, frankly fascinating, resource." Booklist
Includes glossary and bibliography

Magic tricks, science facts; illustrated by Richard Kaufman; photographs by Timothy White. Watts 1990 126p il lib bdg $19.60; pa $6.95 (5 and up)   **793.8**
1. Scientific recreations 2. Magic tricks
ISBN 0-531-10902-X (lib bdg); 0-531-15186-7 (pa)
                                     LC 89-28487
This "book contains almost two dozen magic tricks. The tricks are based on either math or science principles. . . . Most of the chemistry and physiology tricks are more suitable for older children and should be performed with adult supervision, especially when chemicals must be handled." Sci Books Films
Includes bibliography

Kettelkamp, Larry, 1933-
Magic made easy; drawings by Loring Eutemey; photographs by Donovan Klotzbeacher. Newly rev ed. Morrow 1981 96p il $16; lib bdg $15.93 (4 and up)
                                          793.8
1. Magic tricks
ISBN 0 688 00458 X; 0 688 00377 X (lib bdg)
                                     LC 80-22947

First published 1954
Describes twenty-one tricks illustrated with diagrams, drawings, and photographs and suggests the accompanying line of patter

Leyton, Lawrence
My first magic book. Dorling Kindersley 1993 48p il $12.95 (3-5)   **793.8**
1. Magic tricks
ISBN 1-56458-319-8   LC 93-22104
Presents instructions for performing magic tricks and putting on a magic show
"An appealing presentation. Full-color photographs show multiethnic children making life-sized props and doing tricks, with explanations of how they are done and bits of appropriate patter." SLJ

Magic fun; by the editors of Owl and Chickadee magazines; edited by Marilyn Baillie. Little, Brown 1992 32p il $14.95 (3-5)   **793.8**
1. Magic tricks 2. Puzzles
ISBN 0-316-67741-8   LC 91-75546
"Joy Street books"
Magic tricks, puzzles, and treats requiring few items and little practice
"This large, thin volume is heavy on child appeal. Brightly colored, close-up photographs illustrate the magic tricks, all performed by kids. Occasionally, line drawings rather than photos are combined with the easily followed, step-by-step directions. . . . Along the way, readers can pick up incidental facts from history and science or try to solve scattered math and logic puzzlers, which are answered on the back page." Booklist

Oxlade, Chris
Science magic with light. Barron's Educ. Ser. 1994 30p il $9.95; pa $4.95 (4-6)   **793.8**
1. Magic tricks 2. Light 3. Scientific recreations
ISBN 0-8120-6445-3; 0-8120-1984-9 (pa)
                                     LC 94-5549
"This book presents 10 'magic' tricks with descriptions of what props to prepare for them and what kind of presentation is needed to put them over. . . . Each of the tricks contains a brief scientific explanation of what optical principle makes it effective." Sci Books Films
Includes glossary

Science magic with sound. Barron's Educ. Ser. 1994 30p il $9.95; pa $4.95 (4-6)
                                          793.8
1. Magic tricks 2. Sound 3. Scientific recreations
ISBN 0-8120-6446-1; 0-8120-1985-7 (pa)
                                     LC 94-5550
"This book demonstrates 10 magic tricks that rely on the basic properties of sound. Each one is alloted a double-page spread that includes a list of materials, preparations, . . . easy-to-follow instructions, and a brief outline of the science involved. . . . An introductory section on being an expert magician and a concluding section on making costumes and backdrops round out the volume. . . . The science here definitely takes a backseat to magic, but the book is an entertaining way to introduce the physics of sound." SLJ
Includes glossary

Simon, Seymour, 1931-

Soap bubble magic; illustrated by Stella Ormai. Lothrop, Lee & Shepard Bks. 1985 48p il lib bdg $13.88 (1-3)   **793.8**

1. Scientific recreations

ISBN 0-688-02685-0   LC 84-4432

Explains what soap bubbles are, how they are formed, and what can be done with them

"Interracial, nonsexist illustrations accompany a text designed to encourage children to think for themselves. . . . The experiments use simple, inexpensive home or schoolroom materials, some of them made by the child." Sci Books Films

Thomson, David

Visual magic. Dial Bks. for Young Readers 1991 57p il $14.95 (5 and up)   **793.8**

1. Tricks 2. Optical illusions

ISBN 0-8037-1118-2   LC 91-10425

A collection of over thirty visual tricks and illusions involving colors, shapes, patterns, and perspective. Includes 3-D glasses and an answer key

White, Laurence B.

Math-a-magic: number tricks for magicians; [by] Laurence B. White, Jr. and Ray Broekel; illustrated by Meyer Seltzer. Whitman, A. 1989 48p il $12.95; pa $4.95 (3-6)   **793.8**

1. Mathematical recreations 2. Magic tricks

ISBN 0-8075-4994-0; 0-8075-4995-9 (pa)

     LC 89-35395

"Each of the 21 tricks is presented in three sections: 'The Trick,' 'How to do it,' and 'The Math-A-Magic Secret' of why the trick works. . . . The showmanship and production of the trick as magic is stressed, with the math in the background as the key to making the tricks work." SLJ

Shazam! simple science magic; [by] Laurence B. White, Jr., & Ray Broekel; illustrated by Meyer Seltzer. Whitman, A. 1990 48p il $11.95; pa $4.95 (3-6)   **793.8**

1. Scientific recreations 2. Magic tricks

ISBN 0-8075-7332-9; 0-8075-7333-7 (pa)

     LC 90-42441

"Section titles such as 'How to Hypnotize a Potato' or 'The Uncanny Can That Can' will entice young readers to investigate nineteen simple science 'tricks.' Humorous illustrations in simple black line, highlighted with orange, add appeal and clarity. Directions are given in short paragraphs rather than prescriptive 'steps,' and each bit of magic is explained scientifically in a highly readable style." Adventuring with Books

Wyler, Rose

Magic secrets; by Rose Wyler and Gerald Ames; pictures by Arthur Dorros. rev ed. Harper & Row 1990 63p il $14.95; lib bdg $14.89; pa $3.50 (k-2)   **793.8**

1. Magic tricks

ISBN 0-06-026646-5; 0-06-026647-3 (lib bdg); 0-06-444153-9 (pa)   LC 89-35841

"An I can read book"

A revised and newly illustrated edition of the title first published 1967

Easy magic tricks for the aspiring young magician

Spooky tricks; by Rose Wyler and Gerald Ames; pictures by S. D. Schindler. rev & newly il ed. HarperCollins Pubs. 1994 63p il $14; lib bdg $13.89; pa $3.50 (k-2)   **793.8**

1. Magic tricks

ISBN 0-06-023025-8; 0-06-023026-6 (lib bdg); 0-06-444172-5 (pa)   LC 92-47501

"An I can read book"

First published 1967

Describes how to write invisible messages, make ghosts appear on walls, and many other tricks

793.9   Other indoor diversions

Gryski, Camilla, 1948-

Cat's cradle, owl's eyes; a book of string games; illustrated by Tom Sankey. Morrow 1984 c1983 78p il lib bdg $15.93; pa $6.95 (4-6)   **793.9**

1. String figures

ISBN 0-688-03940-5 (lib bdg); 0-688-03941-3 (pa)

     LC 84-9075

First published 1983 in Canada

This "book contains readily grasped directions for tricky, entertaining play. Sankey illustrates cat's cradle and its variations with expert, well-defined drawings of each step in the games. Children should enjoy practising manual dexterity as they master the feats described by themselves or in groups." Publ Wkly

"Brief notes on the ethnic and historical background accompany each figure, adding to the pleasure of achievement." Horn Book

Many stars & more string games; illustrated by Tom Sankey. Morrow 1985 80p il lib bdg $13.93; pa $7.95 (4-6)   **793.9**

1. String figures

ISBN 0-688-05793-4 (lib bdg); 0-688-05792-6 (pa)

     LC 85-4875

A collection of string games culled from various cultures. "The figures proceed in order of difficulty; directions are clear, with blue arrow lines that clarify complicated maneuvers. Several stories to tell with string figures are also included. Straightforward, clearly illustrated, and marked by an infectious enthusiasm, this should be a fine resource for performing storytellers as well as dabbling readers." Booklist

Super string games; illustrated by Tom Sankey. Morrow Junior Bks. 1988 c1987 80p il lib bdg $11.88; pa $6.95 (4-6)   **793.9**

1. String figures

ISBN 0-688-07685-8 (lib bdg); 0-688-07684-X (pa)

     LC 87-18365

First published 1987 in Canada

"This collection of 25 string figures from around the world is for the nimble-fingered of all ages who have mastered simple string figures like cat's cradle and are ready to move on to something more complicated. The directions and illustrations are clear, including a suggestion for how to turn the pages when your hands are all tied up." Child Book Rev Serv

794.8 Electronic games. Computer games

Skurzynski, Gloria
Know the score; video games in your high-tech world. Bradbury Press 1994 64p il (Your high-tech world) $16.95 (4-6) **794.8**
1. Video games
ISBN 0-02-782922-7 LC 93-19470
"This book introduces video games, their history, design, hardware, presentation, and state-of-the-art technology." Booklist
"Full-color photographs, featuring a balance of girls and boys, are sharp and effectively advance the text. . . . The technical information is accurate and clearly presented; there is enough of it to educate, without overwhelming, the intended audience." SLJ
Includes glossary

795.4 Card games

Cole, Joanna
Crazy eights and other card games; by Joanna Cole and Stephanie Calmenson; illustrated by Alan Tiegreen. Morrow Junior Bks. 1994 76p il $15; lib bdg $14.93; pa $6.95 (3-5) **795.4**
1. Card games
ISBN 0-688-12199-3; 0-688-12200-0 (lib bdg); 0-688-12201-9 (pa) LC 93-5427
Introduces the different suits and face cards in a deck of cards, explains how to hold, shuffle, and deal them, and provides instructions for such games as Aces Up, Go Fish, and Spit
"A good introduction to cards and card playing. . . . The text is clear, with big print and lots of white space. Black, white, and red line drawings are often funny and complement the text well." SLJ
Includes bibliography

796 Athletic and outdoor sports and games

Gibbons, Gail
Playgrounds. Holiday House 1985 unp il $15.95 (k-3) **796**
1. Playgrounds
ISBN 0-8234-0553-2 LC 84-19285
"Gibbons' text offers opportunities for children to extend their vocabularies and compare differences in swings, slides, climbing apparatus and sandbox tools. . . . A colorful treatment of a subject familiar to young children but seldom discussed in picture book format." SLJ

The **Guinness** book of sports records. Facts on File il $21.95; pa $13.95 **796**
1. Sports
ISSN 1054-4178
Annual. First published 1972 with title: Guinness sports record book. Variant title: Guinness book of sports records, winners & champions
Taken in part from the Guinness book of records, entered in class 032.02

This compilation presents records set in over seventy sports, from archery to yachting. Entries are arranged alphabetically by sport and include a brief history of the sport

Sports Illustrated for Kids. Time $23.95 per year **796**
1. Sports—Periodicals
ISSN 1042-394X
Monthly. First published 1989
This magazine features articles about young people in sports, biographies of pros, playing tips, stories and puzzles
"The excitement and tension of sports are captured in the action-filled full-color photographs and brisk writing. . . . The focus of the . . . magazine is on fun, but stories 'emphasize the importance of values such as hard work, teamwork, practice, fair play, and a positive attitude.'" Richardson. Mag for Child. 2d edition

Sportworks; more than fifty fun games and activities that explore the science of sports; from the Ontario Science Centre; illustrated by Pat Cupples. Addison-Wesley 1989 96p il $9.95 (4 and up) **796**
1. Games 2. Sports
ISBN 0-201-15296-7 LC 88-34317
The authors outline various experiments and activities with which they seek to illustrate the scientific aspects of sports
"Students interested in trivia and information on the human body, sports, and sports activities will find Sportworks entertaining and informative. . . . The suggested activities permit active involvement and experimentation with the concepts. Each spread has black-and-white sketches that entertain or visually explain the subject. . . . Topics range from checking the heart rate to parachuting and proteins." SLJ

796.1 Miscellaneous games

Brown, Marc Tolon
Finger rhymes; collected and illustrated by Marc Brown. Dutton 1980 32p il $14.99 **796.1**
1. Finger play 2. Nursery rhymes
ISBN 0-525-29732-4 LC 80-11492
Also available in paperback from Puffin Bks.
"A Unicorn book"
Presents 14 rhymes with instructions for accompanying finger plays

Hand rhymes; collected and illustrated by Marc Brown. Dutton 1985 31p il lib bdg $14.99 **796.1**
1. Finger play 2. Nursery rhymes
ISBN 0-525-44201-4 LC 84-25918
Also available in paperback from Puffin Bks.
This collection "contains several adaptations, some new and lively material, and a few old favorites. . . . Each double-page spread contains the rhyme, with small but carefully detailed diagrams of the accompanying finger action and warmly colorful, amusing illustrations of fat kittens, bemused ducks, and happy children. Cozy, useful, and a pleasure to look at, the book is for those who deal with a lapsitter as well as for the storyteller." Horn Book

Brown, Marc Tolon—*Continued*

Play rhymes; collected and illustrated by Marc Brown. Dutton 1987 32p il music lib bdg $12.95 **796.1**

1. Finger play 2. Nursery rhymes

ISBN 0-525-44336-3 LC 87-13537

Also available in paperback from Puffin Bks.

A collection of twelve play rhymes with illustrations to demonstrate the accompanying finger plays or physical activities. Includes music for the six rhymes which are also songs

"The illustrations are full-color pastels with many small details and humorous elements to appeal to children. This is a good choice for program planning or for a rainy afternoon with a favorite child." SLJ

Clap your hands; finger rhymes; chosen by Sarah Hayes; illustrated by Toni Goffe. Lothrop, Lee & Shepard Bks. 1988 29p il $13; lib bdg $12.88 **796.1**

1. Finger play 2. Nursery rhymes

ISBN 0-688-07692-0; 0-688-07693-9 (lib bdg) LC 87-16958

"This bouncy collection of 23 finger games includes old favorites as well as lesser-known selections. The charming cartoon-like ink and watercolor illustrations are well placed, with many single rhymes placed on double-page spreads. Children and animals are shown enacting the finger rhymes instead of using written instructions." SLJ

Defty, Jeff

Creative fingerplays & action rhymes; an index and guide to their use; illustrations by Ellen Kae Hester. Oryx Press 1992 255p il pa $29.50 **796.1**

1. Finger play 2. Nursery rhymes

ISBN 0-89774-709-7 LC 92-9655

"Part one includes the definition and history of action verses along with specific developmental guides for selecting and evaluating them. . . . Part two of the book contains subject and first-line indexes to ninety-five fingerplay and action rhyme collections. The subject index includes more than 600 headings and 550 cross-references." J Youth Serv Libr

Includes bibliographies

Eden, Maxwell

Kiteworks: explorations in kite building & flying. Sterling 1989 287p il hardcover o.p. paperback available $19.95 (5 and up) **796.1**

1. Kites

ISBN 0-8069-6713-7 (pa) LC 89-11372

Color illustrations accompany specific instructions for making a variety of kites. Includes practical advice on materials, repairs, safety, and clubs and events

Includes bibliography

The **Eentsy,** weentsy spider; fingerplays and action rhymes; compiled by Joanna Cole and Stephanie Calmenson; illustrated by Alan Tiegreen. Morrow Junior Bks. 1991 64p il music $13.95; lib bdg $13.88; pa $6.95 **796.1**

1. Finger play 2. Songs

ISBN 0-688-09438-4; 0-688-09439-2 (lib bdg); 0-688-10805-9 (pa) LC 90-44594

"This collection of 38 fingerplays and action rhymes ranges from the familiar 'I'm a Little Teapot,' to the older 'Two Fat Gentlemen.' Simple musical arrangements are included where appropriate." SLJ

"Tiegreen uses a few simple lines to create a cast of multicultural characters whose enthusiasm is infectious. . . . An attractive, upbeat addition to the finger-play collection." Booklist

Includes bibliography

Gibbons, Gail

Catch the wind! all about kites. Little, Brown 1989 unp il $15.95; pa $4.95 (k-3) **796.1**

1. Kites

ISBN 0-316-30955-9; 0-316-30996-6 (pa) LC 88-28820

"Two children visit Ike's Kite Shop, where proprietor Ike is happy to tell the children about his myriad models and how to fly them. The information he dispenses includes brief bits of kite history and a description of such items as box, bowed, and compound kites. The artist's trademark pen lines and bright colors back her text, and instructions for making and flying a simple flat kite are included at the end. (Safety precautions appear here, too.)" Booklist

Grayson, Marion F., 1906-1976

Let's do fingerplays; illustrated by Nancy Weyl. Luce, R.B. 1962 109p il $14.95 **796.1**

1. Finger play

ISBN 0-88331-003-1

"Approximately 200 rhymes and songs, with directions for accompanying finger plays, are organized under such headings as Animal Antics, Counting and Counting Out, and Holidays and Special Occasions." Hodges. Books for Elem Sch Libr

Miss Mary Mack and other children's street rhymes; compiled by Joanna Cole and Stephanie Calmenson; illustrated by Alan Tiegreen. Morrow Junior Bks. 1990 64p lib bdg $11.88; pa $6.95 **796.1**

1. Games 2. Nursery rhymes

ISBN 0-688-08330-7 (lib bdg); 0-688-09749-9 (pa) LC 89-37266

This is a collection of over 100 traditional childhood hand-clapping and street rhymes

"Tiegreen's lighthearted pen-and-ink illustrations are sure to tickle the fancy of young readers. . . . A book that's sure to produce smiles in any story hour or program." SLJ

Opie, Iona Archibald

Children's games in street and playground; by Iona and Peter Opie. Oxford Univ. Press 1969 xxvi, 371p il maps hardcover o.p. paperback available $10.95   796.1

1. Games 2. Folklore
ISBN 0-19-281489-3 (pa)

"Chasing, catching; seeking; hunting; racing; duelling; exerting; daring; guessing; acting; pretending." Title page

"Illustrated with game diagrams and photographs. . . . This volume concerns the 'games that children, aged about 6-12, play of their own accord when out of doors, and usually out of sight.' Compared and documented both geographically and in relation to earlier lore are hundreds of examples of starting-out or counting-out rhymes, ritualistic folk dialogues, chants of chasing and catching games, and the many other categories named in the subtitle. These are helpfully indexed to make the book a useful reference work as well as fascinating reading." Horn Book

Stamp your feet, action rhymes, chosen by Sarah Hayes; illustrated by Toni Goffe. Lothrop, Lee & Shepard Bks. 1988 29p il $13; lib bdg $12.88   796.1

1. Nursery rhymes 2. Games
ISBN 0-688-07694-7; 0-688-07695-5 (lib bdg)
LC 87-29779

"Twenty action rhymes that are suitable for use in preschool storyhours. Pen-and-ink and watercolor drawings demonstrate possible actions to accompany the rhymes. . . . The poems are ebullient." SLJ

796.2 Active games requiring equipment

Brimner, Larry Dane

Rolling—in-line! Watts 1994 63p il lib bdg $19.90; pa $5.95 (4 and up)   796.2

1. In-line skating
ISBN 0-531-20171-6 (lib bdg); 0-531-15739-3 (pa)
LC 93-51255

"A First book"

"Brimner looks briefly at in-line skating history before concentrating on the mechanics of the popular pastime. . . . The discussion of skate selection, which considers such factors as flexibility, wheel hardness, and liner size, will be useful. There's also strong emphasis on protective equipment." Booklist

Includes bibliographical references

Lankford, Mary D., 1932-

Hopscotch around the world; illustrated by Karen Milone. Morrow Junior Bks. 1992 47p il map $16; lib bdg $15.93 (3-5)   796.2

1. Hopscotch
ISBN 0-688-08419-2; 0-688-08420-6 (lib bdg)
LC 91-17152

The author "presents 19 variations of hopscotch played in 16 countries around the world. Each double-page spread contains a diagram of the pattern to be scratched or chalked on the ground, a description of the game, step-by-step directions, and a large illustration showing how it is played. Lankford's research, briefly described in the text, brings in history as well as geography, language, and cultural differences. . . . A handsomely designed book on an unusual topic." Booklist

Includes bibliography

Sullivan, George

In-line skating; a complete guide for beginners. Cobblehill Bks. 1993 48p il $14.99; pa $5.99 (4 and up)   796.2

1. In-line skating
ISBN 0-525-65124-1; 0-14-054987-0 (pa)
LC 92-25896

Ways to use and enjoy in-line skates, the kind with wheels in a row instead of side-by-side

"The clear, concise text emphasizes safety and conditioning while enthusiastically detailing the pleasures of the exercise. Ample full-color photographs." Booklist

Includes glossary

796.323 Basketball

Anderson, Dave

The story of basketball; foreword by Julius Erving. Morrow 1988 182p il hardcover o.p. paperback available $10.95 (5 and up)
796.323

1. Basketball
ISBN 0-688-06749-2 (pa)   LC 88-6842

"Divided into two sections, the book first views basketball historically. . . . The second part of the discussion gives the important elements of the game: shooting, passing, rebounding, defensive moves, and coaching. Rather than simply explaining these fundamentals, Anderson illustrates them by citing the careers of various athletes." Booklist

Sullivan, George

All about basketball. Putnam 1991 160p il hardcover o.p. paperback available $8.95 (4 and up)   796.323

1. Basketball
ISBN 0-399-21793-2 (pa)   LC 91-10141

Gives an overview of the history and the rules of the game of basketball, along with discussion of various plays and profiles of famous players

"This is an ideal book for readers who know little about the game. . . . Fans and players will also find the book interesting. . . . The text is liberally illustrated with action photos, portrait shots, line drawings, and diagrams. . . . A glossary of basketball words and terms and a good index give this work value as a reference book as well as for general reading." Booklist

796.325   Volleyball

Jensen, Julie, 1957-
Beginning volleyball; adapted from Fundamental volleyball; photographs by Andy King. Lerner Publs. 1995 63p il (Beginning sports) lib bdg $19.95 (3-5)   **796.325**

1. Volleyball
ISBN 0-8225-3502-5   LC 94-29509
Using large print and simple language, this adapted work explains the basics of playing volleyball
Includes glossary and bibliography

Fundamental volleyball; photographs by Andy King. Lerner Publs. 1995 63p il (Fundamental sports) lib bdg $19.95 (5 and up)   **796.325**

1. Volleyball
ISBN 0-8225-3452-5   LC 94-5743
This book begins with a brief history of the sport. The following chapters describe how to play the game; the importance of conditioning and practicing; advanced moves; and variations on the game
Includes glossary and bibliography

796.332   American football

Sullivan, George
All about football. Dodd, Mead 1987 128p il hardcover o.p. paperback available $8.95 (4 and up)   **796.332**

1. Football
ISBN 0-399-21907-2 (pa)   LC 87-17383
The author explains the game of football: "how it is played, the various playing positions, basic offensive and defensive strategy. There is a bit of football history, a close-up look at the field and equipment, and an explanation of competition at the different levels, with various conferences, leagues, and ruling bodies defined." Publisher's note
Includes glossary

796.334   Soccer

Coleman, Lori
Fundamental soccer; photographs by Andy King. Lerner Publs. 1995 64p il (Fundamental sports) lib bdg $19.95 (5 and up)   **796.334**

1. Soccer
ISBN 0-8225-3451-7   LC 94-11907
This "book covers the history of the sport, positions, equipment, basic and more advanced moves, rules, the merits of practice, and variations in the game. . . . King's colorful, clear, informative photographs enhance the text." SLJ
Includes glossary and bibliography

Jensen, Julie, 1957-
Beginning soccer; adapted from Lori Coleman's Fundamental soccer; photographs by Andy King. Lerner Publs. 1995 64p il (Beginning sports) lib bdg $19.95 (3-5)   **796.334**

1. Soccer
ISBN 0-8225-3501-7   LC 94-37742
Using large print and simple language, this adapted work explains the basics of playing soccer
Includes glossary and bibliography

796.342   Tennis

Jensen, Julie, 1957-
Beginning tennis; adapted from Marc Miller's Fundamental tennis; photographs by Andy King. Lerner Publs. 1995 64p il (Beginning sports) lib bdg $19.95 (3-5)   **796.342**

1. Tennis
ISBN 0-8225-3500-9   LC 93-48385
Using large print and simple language, this adapted work explains the basics of playing tennis
Includes glossary and bibliography

Miller, Marc, 1957-
Fundamental tennis; photographs by Andy King. Lerner Publs. 1995 64p il (Fundamental sports) lib bdg $19.95 (5 and up)   **796.342**

1. Tennis
ISBN 0-8225-3450-9   LC 94-21107
This book presents a brief history of the game, the basics (including rackets, clothes, strokes, grips, serves, and stance), rules for singles play and rules for doubles, practice drills, and advanced shots. Color photographs show young tennis players in action
Includes glossary and bibliography

796.35   Games with ball driven by club, mallet, bat

Gutman, Bill
Field hockey; start right and play well; with illustrations by Ben Brown. Marshall Cavendish 1990 64p il (Go for it! series) lib bdg $9.95 (4-6)   **796.35**

1. Field hockey
ISBN 0-942545-93-1   LC 89-7587
Describes the history and current teams, leagues, and championships of field hockey and provides instruction on how to play the game

796.352 Golf

Jensen, Julie, 1957-
Beginning golf; adapted from Peter Krause's Fundamental golf; photographs by Andy King. Lerner Publs. 1995 64p il (Beginning sports) lib bdg $19.95 (3-5)   **796.352**

1. Golf
ISBN 0-8225-3504-1   LC 94-37101
Using large print and simple language, this adapted work explains the basics of playing golf
Includes glossary and bibliography

Krause, Peter, 1954-
Fundamental golf; photographs by Andy King. Lerner Publs. 1995 64p il (Fundamental sports) lib bdg $19.95 (5 and up)   **796.352**

1. Golf
ISBN 0-8225-3454-1   LC 94-23166
This book presents a brief history of the game; the basics, including the function of each type of golf club; rules and etiquette; and skill shots. Photographs of young golfers illustrate proper stance and swing motion
Includes glossary and bibliography

796.357 Baseball

Brashler, William
The story of Negro league baseball. Ticknor & Fields 1994 166p il $15.95; pa $10.95 (5 and up)   **796.357**

1. Baseball 2. African American athletes
ISBN 0-395-67169-8; 0-395-69721-2 (pa)
                    LC 93-36547
"This book intersperses chapters on such black stars as Satchel Paige, Josh Gibson, and Jackie Robinson among the accounts of the various Negro Leagues. Archival and scrapbook black-and-white photographs . . . appear throughout. A list of Negro League all-star teams chosen by a variety of groups and individuals is appended." SLJ
"The author brings to life some of the finest players and most interesting men who ever chose the career of baseball." Horn Book
Includes bibliography

Cooper, Michael L., 1950-
Playing America's game; the story of Negro league baseball. Lodestar Bks. 1993 96p il $15.99 (5 and up)   **796.357**

1. Baseball 2. African American athletes
ISBN 0-525-67407-1   LC 92-2927
A photo essay presents the history of the Negro Baseball League
"With a spacious format and many black-and-white photographs, this attractive book looks reader friendly. Appended are a list of museums and organizations to contact for more information." Booklist
Includes bibliography

Egan, Terry, 1957-
The Macmillan book of baseball stories; by Terry Egan, Stan Friedmann, and Mike Levine. Macmillan 1992 127p il $15.95 (4 and up)   **796.357**

1. Baseball
ISBN 0-02-733280-2   LC 92-6447
"The successes and trials of major stars, average players, and even baseball fans are detailed in the 19 chapters, which vary from 2-to-5 pages in length. The subjects range from Bruce Nelson, an average baseball fan . . . [to] Oakland Athletics pitcher Dave Stewart, whose diligent efforts on helping earthquake victims during the 1989 World Series is chronicled. The most appealing aspect of this title is that major baseball stars are not put on pedestals." SLJ

Galt, Margot Fortunato
Up to the plate; the All American Girls Professional Baseball League. Lerner Publs. 1995 96p il lib bdg $17.21 (5 and up)
                    796.357

1. All-American Girls Professional Baseball League
2. Baseball 3. Women athletes
ISBN 0-8225-3326-X   LC 94-10636
"This book chronicles the league from its start—as a substitute for men's baseball during World War II—through 12 successful seasons of play. News reports from the period, . . . photographs from the players' own scrapbooks, and interviews with former players [are included]." Publisher's note

Gardner, Robert, 1929-
The forgotten players; the story of black baseball in America; [by] Robert Gardner and Dennis Shortelle. Walker & Co. 1993 120p il $12.95; lib bdg $13.85 (5 and up)
                    796.357

1. Baseball 2. African American athletes
ISBN 0-8027-8248-5; 0-8027-8249-3 (lib bdg)
                    LC 92-29618
Traces the history of the Negro leagues from the late nineteenth through the early twentieth century
"Sports fans who are used to being fed statistics, game accounts, and biographical information will get some of this, but more significantly will be exposed to an insightful look at social history. Both the black-and-white photographs and the text are fully documented with the inclusion of over 125 endnotes." SLJ

Healy, Dennis, 1927-
The illustrated rules of baseball; illustrated by Patrick T. McRae. Ideals Children's Bks. 1995 32p il (Illustrated sports series) pa $6.95 (3-4)   **796.357**

1. Baseball
ISBN 1-57102-017-9   LC 94-32773
This "book provides an overview of the game, an explanation of 20 of its rules, details about equipment, basic positions of play, umpire signals, an explanation of sportsmanship, and a one-page summary. The information is presented in easy-to-read sentences and accompanied by appealing watercolor-and-pencil illustrations that clarify the material." SLJ

Hughes, Dean, 1943-
Baseball tips; by Dean Hughes and Tom Hughes; illustrated by Dennis Lyall. Random House 1993 91p il lib bdg $9.99; pa $6.99 (3-5)   **796.357**
1. Baseball
ISBN 0-679-93642-4 (lib bdg); 0-679-83642-X (pa)
    LC 92-13406
A beginner's guide to baseball basics with tips on how to hit, run bases, field, throw, and sharpen skills through practice
"The authors' uncomplicated style, the open format, and the lively tone make the book pleasant as well as easy to read, and the illustrations . . . are generally excellent." Booklist
Includes glossary

Kreutzer, Peter
Little League's official how-to-play baseball book; [by] Peter Kreutzer and Ted Kerley; illustrated by Alexander Verbitsky. Doubleday 1990 210p il hardcover o.p. paperback available $10.95 (4 and up)   **796.357**
1. Little League Baseball, Inc. 2. Baseball
ISBN 0-385-24700-1 (pa)   LC 89-28097
The "contents include gripping, throwing, and catching the ball; hitting; bunting; base running; sliding; pitching; defensive positioning; fitness; and warm-ups. . . . An added bonus is the inclusion of the Official Little League playing rules." Voice Youth Advocates

McKissack, Patricia C., 1944-
Black diamond; the story of the Negro baseball leagues; [by] Patricia C. McKissack and Fredrick McKissack, Jr. Scholastic 1994 184p il $13.95; pa $3.99 (6 and up)
    796.357
1. Baseball 2. African American athletes
ISBN 0-590-45809-4; 0-590-45810-8 (pa)
    LC 93-22691
Traces the history of baseball in the Negro Leagues and its great heroes, including Monte Irwin, Buck Leonard, and Cool Papa Bell
This is "an engaging account. . . . It includes a chronology, player profiles and wonderful photographs from the Negro Leagues." N Y Times Book Rev
Includes bibliography

Ritter, Lawrence S.
Leagues apart; the men and times of the Negro baseball leagues; illustrations by Richard Merkin. Morrow Junior Bks. 1995 unp il $15; lib bdg $14.93 (2-4)   **796.357**
1. Baseball 2. African American athletes
ISBN 0-688-13316-9; 0-688-13317-7 (lib bdg)
    LC 94-17512
"Beginning with a brief history of the Negro Leagues, the text provides short biographies of twenty-two baseball players of color, interspersed with information about segregation and the racism of the 1920s through the 1940s. . . . Most of the players' biographies are accompanied by large stylized portraits in oil pastel." Horn Book
This "is a fine melding of text and illustration that makes accessible an important part of baseball history." SLJ

Ward, Geoffrey C.
25 great moments; by Geoffrey C. Ward and Ken Burns, with S.A. Kramer. Knopf 1994 61p il (Baseball, the American epic) $15; lib bdg $16.99 (4 and up)   **796.357**
1. Baseball
ISBN 0-679-86751-1; 0-679-96751-6 (lib bdg)
    LC 94-1674
"Based on the Public Television series." Title page
"25 Great Moments provides one or two page synopses of some of the most legendary events and moments from baseball's past, ranging from the first game in Hoboken, New Jersey, in 1846 to Joe Carter's Series-winning home run in 1993." SLJ
"Lays out a feast of story and illustration for fans who savor baseball history." Booklist

Shadow ball; the history of the Negro leagues; by Geoffrey C. Ward and Ken Burns, with Jim O'Connor. Knopf 1994 79p il (Baseball, the American epic) $15; lib bdg $16.99 (4 and up)   **796.357**
1. Baseball 2. African American athletes
ISBN 0-679-86749-X; 0-679-96749-4 (lib bdg)
    LC 94-5552
"Based on the Public Television series." Title page
"Shadow Ball focuses on the Negro leagues, from their formation after a 'gentleman's' agreement effectively barred black players from professional baseball through the breakthrough of players to the major leagues. . . . It tells the story well, and the excellent photos and quotations help make the players memorable." Booklist

Who invented the game? by Geoffrey C. Ward and Ken Burns, with Paul Robert Walker. Knopf 1994 79p il (Baseball, the American epic) $15; lib bdg $16.99 (4 and up)
    796.357
1. Baseball
ISBN 0-679-86750-3; 0-679-96750-8 (lib bdg)
    LC 94-9166
"Based on the Public Television series." Title page
"Who invented the Game? has a misleading title since it deals with far more than merely the origins of baseball. In fact, each chapter of this book is a summary of an episode of the television series. Thus, it provides a condensed history of the game. . . . The layout and photographs are excellent and the index is comprehensive." SLJ

796.42 Track and field

Parker, Steve
Running a race. Watts 1991 32p il (Body in action) lib bdg $17.50 (3-5)   **796.42**
1. Running
ISBN 0-531-14096-2   LC 90-31110
Describes what happens to the human body while running a race and provides tips for technique in such areas as warming up, breathing, and recovering from the race
The author "makes it clear how various bodily systems work together and how they are influenced by outside circumstances in our daily lives. A series of simple experiments . . . reinforce the informational content and help make learning more fun." Booklist
Includes glossary and bibliography

796.44 Sports gymnastics

Jackman, Joan
The young gymnast; foreword by Shannon Miller. Dorling Kindersley 1995 45p il $15.95 (4 and up) **796.44**
1. Gymnastics
ISBN 1-56458-677-4   LC 94-36256
"The author differentiates between events such as vaulting, the balance beam, rhythmic gymnastics, sports acrobatics, and tumbling. The many full-color photographs reflect the descriptive text as well as add information." SLJ

796.47 Acrobatics, tumbling, trampolining, contortion

Schmidt, Diane
I am a Jesse White tumbler; text and photographs by Diane Schmidt. Whitman, A. 1990 unp il lib bdg $14.95 (3-6) **796.47**
1. Conner, Kenyon 2. Jesse White Tumbling Team 3. Acrobats and acrobatics
ISBN 0-8075-3444-7   LC 89-16590
Kenyon Conner, an eighth-grader from Chicago, tells of his life with the Jesse White Tumbling Team, a program designed to help inner city young people complete school and avoid drugs and crime. Text and photographs describe the team's acrobatic performances
This is "an honest and unaffected narrative. . . . Unlike many glamorous photodocumentaries, this does not gloss over the discipline of performing on the hot streets during a street fair or a freezing field during the intermission of a football game." Bull Cent Child Books

796.48 Olympic games

Glubok, Shirley, 1933-
Olympic games in ancient Greece; by Shirley Glubok and Alfred Tamarin. Harper & Row 1976 116p il lib bdg $15.89 (5 and up) **796.48**
1. Olympic games 2. Greek civilization
ISBN 0-06-022048-1
"The authors take a systematic look at the ancient Greek Olympics around 400 B.C. . . . The subsequent narrative describes the pageantry and the competitions, many of which have come down to us in modern form while others, such as chariot races and the race in armor, have passed out of existence. Bits of Greek history influencing the games, recorded anecdotes, and legends add color to the account." Booklist

796.5 Outdoor life

Arnosky, Jim
Crinkleroot's guide to walking in wild places. Bradbury Press 1990 unp il $14.95 (k-3) **796.5**
1. Walking 2. Wilderness areas 3. Nature study
ISBN 0-02-705842-5   LC 89-38427

Also available in paperback from Aladdin Bks. (NY)
Crinkleroot the forest dweller provides tips for walking in wild places and avoiding such hazards as ticks, poisonous plants, and wild animals
"Arnosky's text is a felicitous blending of spare, elegant description and homey conversation. . . . Coupled with the ebullient, comic drawings, the text conveys a grand invitation to enjoy the natural world." Horn Book

796.54 Camping

Carlson, Laurie M., 1952-
Kids camp! activities for the backyard or wilderness; [by] Laurie Carlson and Judith Dammel. Chicago Review Press 1995 171p il pa $12.95 (3-6) **796.54**
1. Camping 2. Outdoor recreation
ISBN 1-55652-237-1   LC 94-41030
"The chapters feature directions for making inexpensive equipment and projects while exploring nature; crafts; outdoor games; and recipes for snacks and meals. The large pages are illustrated with black-line drawings and diagrams placed alongside detailed instructions and, often, special boxes with helpful 'stay safe' and 'nature note' tips." SLJ
Includes bibliographical references

796.6 Cycling and related activities

Hautzig, David
1,000 miles in 12 days; pro cyclists on tour. Orchard Bks. 1995 unp il map $15.95; lib bdg $16.99 (4-6) **796.6**
1. Bicycle racing
ISBN 0-531-06896-X; 0-531-08746-8 (lib bdg)   LC 94-33809
"Using the 1994 Tour De Pont (held in the eastern United States) as an example, Hautzig describes a professional-cycling stage race. . . . Although not a history of the sport or its personalities, nor an in-depth look at life on the professional racing circuit, this book will help spectators understand just what goes on in this type of race. A brief list for further reading mentions books and magazines that can update readers on current events." SLJ

Stine, Megan
Wheels! the kids' bike book. Little, Brown 1990 83p il hardcover o.p. paperback available $9.95 (4 and up) **796.6**
1. Bicycles
ISBN 0-316-81624-8 (pa)   LC 89-29661
"A Sports Illustrated for kids book"
This book discusses choosing a bike, equipment, accessories, instructions for riding, and customizing
"A bright, fast-paced survey of bicycling. . . . The glossy look and numerous colorful sidebars make this appealing to browsers as well as information seekers." Horn Book Guide
Includes glossary and bibliography

796.7　Driving motor vehicles

Sullivan, George

Racing Indy cars. Cobblehill Bks. 1992 64p il $15 (5 and up) **796.7**

1. Automobile racing
ISBN 0-525-65082-2　　　　　　LC 91-19439

"Sullivan focuses on the Team Shierson vehicle driven by Arie Luyendyk to victory in the 1990 Indianapolis 500 race. The clear text reveals many of the nitty gritty facts of the sport, including an eye-opening breakdown of the costs. . . . Dramatic photographs." SLJ

Includes glossary

796.8　Combat sports

Bailey, Donna

Judo. Steck-Vaughn 1991 32p il (Sports world) lib bdg $19.97; pa $3.95 (1-4) **796.8**

1. Judo
ISBN 0-8114-2900-8 (lib bdg); 0-8114-4714-6 (pa)
　　　　　　　　　　　　　　LC 90-23058

Beginning judo students learn the skills, techniques, and exercises that help them master this art of unarmed self-defense

Brimner, Larry Dane

Karate. Watts 1988 71p il lib bdg $11.62 (4 and up) **796.8**

1. Karate
ISBN 0-531-10480-X　　　　　　LC 87-25341
"A First book"

"Briefly surveying the development of karate styles, the author stresses developing disciplined, controlled power by progressive mastery of moves from white- to black-belt level. Mixed quality black-and-white photographs accompany the descriptions of stances, kicks, punches, and combinations, but the text provides a clear, concise survey of the sport and guidance in preparing for formal instruction." Booklist

Includes bibliography

Goedecke, Christopher J., 1951-

The wind warrior; the training of a karate champion; [by] Christopher J. Goedecke, Rosmarie Hausherr. Four Winds Press 1992 64p il $15.95 (4 and up) **796.8**

1. Karate
ISBN 0-02-736262-0　　　　　　LC 91-6405

Describes, in text and black-and-white photographs, the training of a thirteen-year-old boy for a karate competition

This "is what every karate book should be. It is interesting, enlightening, and educational. Black and white photographs cover every page and add greatly to the text. . . . This book is very well done. A definite must for all school and public libraries." Voice Youth Advocates

Gutman, Bill

Wrestling; start right and wrestle well; with illustrations by Ben Brown. Marshall Cavendish 1990 63p il (Go for it! series) lib bdg $9.95 (4-6) **796.8**

1. Wrestling
ISBN 0-942545-94-X　　　　　　LC 89-7596

Describes the history, current organizations, including teams, leagues, and championships, and techniques of wrestling

Queen, J. Allen

Karate for kids. Sterling 1994 96p il $13.95; pa $5.95 (4 and up) **796.8**

1. Karate
ISBN 0-8069-0614-6; 0-8069-0615-4 (pa)
　　　　　　　　　　　　　　LC 93-45837

The author describes "blocks, kicks, and stances along with other karate protocol without overwhelming readers. Clear black-and-white photos, a rarity in martial-arts books, will help children put the text into action. Models shown in the photos include both boys and girls of various races." SLJ

797.1　Boating

Kalman, Bobbie, 1947-

A canoe trip. Crabtree 1995 32p il (Crabapples) lib bdg $15.95; pa $5.95 (2-4) **797.1**

1. Canoes and canoeing
ISBN 0-86505-619-6 (lib bdg); 0-86505-719-2 (pa)
　　　　　　　　　　　　　　LC 94-44937

This book "covers the parts of the boat, safety, and some basic strokes. Then it follows a typical outing, showing a group of young campers as they pack, pitch their tents, and cook outdoors. A nice blend of full-color photographs and small drawings extend the text and add interesting details." SLJ

797.5　Air sports

Johnson, Neil, 1954-

Fire & silk: flying in a hot air balloon. Little, Brown 1991 unp il $15.95 (1-4) **797.5**

1. Balloons
ISBN 0-316-46959-9　　　　　　LC 90-43215
"Joy Street books"

This book depicts what it is like to ride in a hot air balloon and discusses how it was invented and how it works

"With the excitement and eccentricity of true-adventure stories, this photo-essay in brilliant color gives the facts and the feel of ballooning. . . . With dramatic photos from every perspective . . . the text weaves information about weather and physics." Booklist

798 Equestrian sports and animal racing

Dolan, Ellen M.
Susan Butcher and the Iditarod Trail. Walker & Co. 1993 103p il $14.95; lib bdg $15.85 (5 and up) **798**
1. Butcher, Susan 2. Iditarod Trail Sled Dog Race, Alaska
ISBN 0-8027-8211-6; 0-8027-8212-4 (lib bdg)
LC 92-36837
Describes the annual dog sled race from Anchorage to Nome, Alaska, and the life of the woman who was the first person to win it for three consecutive years

798.2 Horsemanship

Green, Lucinda
The young rider. Dorling Kindersley 1993 64p il $15.95 (4 and up) **798.2**
1. Horsemanship
ISBN 1-56458-320-1
LC 93-22103
Covers how to choose, care for, and train a pony, basic and more advanced riding skills, and necessary equipment
"Green's style is breezy and encouraging, and the text is concise and easy to read, all of which should make the book popular with young readers." Booklist
Includes glossary

799.1 Fishing

Arnosky, Jim
Fish in a flash! a personal guide to spin-fishing. Bradbury Press 1991 63p il $14.95 (4 and up) **799.1**
1. Fishing
ISBN 0-02-705854-9
LC 90-45832
An introduction to the techniques and joys of fishing with spinning lures
"Arnosky combines personal anecdotes about his own fishing successes and failures along with information written in an appealing and conversational tone. . . . The illustrations of fish and fishing tackle are lovely and delicate, some done in black pencil and others in pencil and color wash." Booklist

Flies in the water, fish in the air; a personal introduction to fly fishing. Lothrop, Lee & Shepard Bks. 1986 96p il $12.95 (5 and up) **799.1**
1. Fly casting
ISBN 0-688-05834-5
LC 84-29684
An anecdotal account of the pleasures of fly fishing, discussing the choice and use of tackle, kinds of flies, walking in water, and watching for fish
"This book is a hybrid. Coupled with a how-to manual on fly fishing is a naturalist's exploration of freshwater streams and ponds and their inhabitants. . . . The author's delightful, intricately detailed black-and-white drawings complement the clear, informative prose." Appraisal

Freshwater fish & fishing; illustrated by the author. Four Winds Press 1982 63p il $15 (4 and up) **799.1**
1. Fishing 2. Fishes
ISBN 0-02-705850-6
LC 81-12520
"This beginners' guide focuses on trout, sunfish, perch and pike, catfish and carp—both descriptions of the fish and their habitat and sound, practical fishing advice, including easy step-by-step instructions for making your own flies, cork popping bugs, and rubber tails for spoon lures." SLJ

799.2 Hunting

Patent, Dorothy Hinshaw
A family goes hunting; photographs by William Muñoz. Clarion Bks. 1991 64p il $14.95; pa $6.95 (4 and up) **799.2**
1. Hunting
ISBN 0-395-52004-5; 0-395-66507-8 (pa)
LC 90-28301
This book relates, in text and photographs, the experiences of twelve-year-old Leif as he goes on his first hunting trip with his family in Montana
"By incorporating many quotations into the account, Patent achieves an intimate tone that expresses both the appreciation of nature shared by responsible hunters and the controversial aspects associated with the sport. . . . Muñoz's black-and-white photographs mix candid with composed shots to instruct, illustrate, or add intimacy to the narrative." Booklist

800 LITERATURE AND RHETORIC

803 Literature—Encyclopedias and dictionaries

Brewer's dictionary of phrase and fable. Harper & Row $35; pa $20 **803**
1. Literature—Dictionaries 2. Allusions
First published 1870. (14th edition 1989) Periodically revised
Current edition edited by Ivor H. Evans
"Over 15,000 brief entries give the meanings and origins of a broad range of terms, expressions, and names of real, fictitious and mythical characters from world history, science, the arts and literature." N Y Public Libr. Ref Books for Child Collect. 2d edition

808 Rhetoric

Asher, Sandy, 1942-
Where do you get your ideas? helping young writers begin; illustrated by Susan Hellard. Walker & Co. 1987 88p il $12.95; lib bdg $13.85; pa $6.95 (5 and up) **808**
1. Authorship
ISBN 0-8027-6690-0; 0-8027-6691-9 (lib bdg); 0-8027-7421-0 (pa)
LC 86-28258

Asher, Sandy, 1942——*Continued*

In this manual featuring quotes from well-known children's authors, "Asher makes many of the usual suggestions—keep a journal, listen in on conversations—but she also includes much more: exercises . . ., ideas on ways to structure a written piece, and a bibliography." Booklist
"Amusing black-and-white drawings accompany the light but informative text. . . . Teachers and librarians who wish to promote creative writing will find this a useful tool." SLJ

Wild words! how to train them to tell stories; illustrated by Dennis Kendrick. Walker & Co. 1989 110p il $13.95; lib bdg $14.85 (5 and up) **808**

1. Authorship
ISBN 0-8027-6887-3; 0-8027-6888-1 (lib bdg)
LC 89-5692

Presents advice for budding writers on how to put ideas down on paper in language that is expressive and literate, how to bring characters to life, how to line up a plot, and how to polish the final product
"Pen-and-ink cartoon sketches enliven the book, which will be of most use when introduced by an enthusiastic teacher." Booklist
Includes bibliography

James, Elizabeth

Sincerely yours; how to write great letters; by Elizabeth James & Carol Barkin. Clarion Bks. 1993 166p $14.95; pa $6.95 (4 and up) **808**

1. Letter writing
ISBN 0-395-58831-6; 0-395-58832-4 (pa)
LC 91-42374

Discusses the general purposes of writing letters and outlines the elements of different types of personal and business letters. Includes information on state abbreviations, forms of address, and pen pals

Leedy, Loreen, 1959-

Messages in the mailbox; how to write a letter; written and illustrated by Loreen Leedy. Holiday House 1991 unp il $15.95; pa $5.95 (k-3) **808**

1. Letter writing
ISBN 0-8234-0889-2; 0-8234-1079-X (pa)
LC 91-8718

Discusses the different kinds of letters, the parts of a letter, and who can be a potential correspondent, and provides examples
"Leedy's softly colored realistic illustrations feature both animal characters and people from a variety of cultures. The partnership of text and illustration gives a lively and interesting perspective to an otherwise dull topic. . . . A superb book that shouldn't be missed." SLJ

Stevens, Carla

A book of your own; keeping a diary or journal. Clarion Bks. 1993 100p $14.95; pa $7.95 (5 and up) **808**

1. Authorship 2. Diaries
ISBN 0-89919-256-4; 0-395-67887-0 (pa)
LC 92-33818

"The author offers advice on getting started, selecting tools to use, maintaining privacy, and overcoming writer's block. . . . Stevens includes excerpts from the diaries of personal friends and historical figures. Among the famous diarists quoted are Anne Frank, Anais Nin, Theodore Roosevelt, Beatrix Potter, and Louisa May Alcott." Voice Youth Advocates
"A very useful book; libraries where journal writing is in the curriculum may want more than one copy." Booklist
Includes bibliography

808.06 Writing children's literature

75 years of Children's Book Week posters; celebrating great illustrators of American children's books; sponsored by the Children's Book Council; with introduction and text by Leonard S. Marcus. Knopf 1994 xxii, 74p il $30 **808.06**

1. Children—Books and reading 2. Children's literature—History and criticism 3. Posters 4. Illustration of books
ISBN 0-679-85106-2
LC 93-3692

"This book is both a handsome catalogue of . . . [Book Week] posters and a veritable who's who of children's book illustration in the United States in the greater part of the 20th century." N Y Times Book Rev
"Not only is this tribute to Book Week a visual feast, it is also a fascinating piece of social history, thanks in large measure to Leonard Marcus's penetrating introduction and perceptive commentaries." Horn Book

808.1 Rhetoric of poetry

Poetry from A to Z; a guide for young writers; compiled by Paul B. Janeczko; illustrated by Cathy Bobak. Bradbury Press 1994 131p il $15.95 **808.1**

1. Poetics 2. American poetry—Collections
ISBN 0-02-747672-3
LC 94-10528

"In his guide, Janeczko gives many examples and ideas to get young writers started writing poetry. The book is organized alphabetically with seventy-two poems on almost any topic you could imagine. In addition, fourteen exercises labeled 'Try This' explain how to write different types of poems and help a young writer get started." Voice Youth Advocates
Includes bibliographical references

808.3 Rhetoric of fiction

Bauer, Marion Dane, 1938-

What's your story? a young person's guide to writing fiction. Clarion Bks. 1992 134p $14.95; pa $6.95 (5 and up) **808.3**

1. Authorship 2. Creative writing
ISBN 0-395-57781-0; 0-395-57780-2 (pa)
LC 91-3816

Discusses how to write fiction, exploring such aspects as character, plot, point of view, dialogue, endings, and revising
"Bauer reveals the somber reality that writing can be hard work, though worth the effort for those who persevere.

Bauer, Marion Dane, 1938-—*Continued*
What follows is a clear, concise elucidation on the elements of fiction. . . . Bauer has taken a thorough, clear, and functional approach to this topic." Horn Book

808.8 Literature—Collections

Bauer, Caroline Feller, 1935-
Celebrations; read-aloud holiday and theme book programs; drawings by Lynn Gates Bredeson. Wilson, H.W. 1985 301p il $45
808.8
1. Holidays 2. Literature—Collections 3. Books and reading 4. Children's libraries
ISBN 0-8242-0708-4   LC 85-714
"Aimed at librarians and other adults who work with middle-grade children, this book offers a potpourri of ideas and suggestions for planning holiday programs. Each chapter focuses on a holiday—some well known, some concocted by Bauer—and includes prose [and poetry] selections, activities, and a booklist." Booklist

The **Family** read-aloud Christmas treasury; selected by Alice Low; illustrated by Marc Brown. Little, Brown 1989 136p il $17.95
808.8
1. Christmas 2. Literature—Collections
ISBN 0-316-53371-8   LC 89-83826
"Joy Street books"
"Over 50 excerpts or abridgments from well-known children's books by such authors as Beverly Cleary, Carolyn Haywood, Russell Hoban, and Jane Thayer; poetry old and new; plus words to a few holiday carols grace this collection with humor and heart. The book is indespensible for librarians and teachers searching for holiday pieces of various lengths and weights to read aloud to a variety of ages. Brown's exuberant watercolors add warmth and good spirits for laptime and story hour listeners." SLJ

The **Family** read-aloud holiday treasury; selected by Alice Low; illustrated by Marc Brown. Little, Brown 1991 154p il $19.95
808.8
1. Holidays 2. Literature—Collections
ISBN 0-316-53368-8   LC 91-53174
"Joy Street books"
"With over 60 poems, songs, and story excerpts, this compilation celebrates 30 of our best known holidays along with other less sanctioned reasons for joy such as friendship and summer vacation. . . . There is good variety to the collection, ranging from Jean Fritz's *George Washington's Breakfast* to selections by John Ciardi, Nikki Giovanni, Beverly Cleary, and Laura Ingalls Wilder. Great care has been taken to maintain cultural diversity. Using pastels and watercolor, Brown's distinctive cartoons bring life, humor, and energy to every page." SLJ

Halloween: stories and poems; edited by Caroline Feller Bauer; illustrated by Peter Sis. Lippincott 1989 78p il $15; lib bdg $14.89; pa $4.95 (2-4)
808.8
1. Halloween 2. Literature—Collections
ISBN 0-397-32300-X; 0-397-32301-8 (lib bdg);
0-06-446111-4 (pa)   LC 88-2675

"Most of the stories and poems in [this] . . . anthology concern spooky happenings suitable for reading on Halloween though not directly related to the holiday. . . . While many of the selections are readily available elsewhere, this anthology is a good choice for libraries needing more books of spooky stories and poems." Booklist
Includes bibliography

Herds of thunder, manes of gold; a collection of horse stories and poems; compiled and edited by Bruce Coville; illustrated by Ted Lewin. Doubleday 1989 176p il $15.95 (4 and up)
808.8
1. Horses—Fiction 2. Literature—Collections
ISBN 0-385-24642-0   LC 88-34651
A collection of seventeen stories, poems, and excerpts from books about horses, by well-known authors over several centuries
"Although the contents can be found elsewhere, this collection is exceptionally well chosen and illustrated beautifully with paintings in full color that celebrate the horse. A very nice compilation, attractively illustrated and designed." Horn Book

The **Laugh** book; a new treasury of humor for children; compiled by Joanna Cole and Stephanie Calmenson; drawings by Marylin Hafner. Doubleday 1986 302p il $17 (4-6)
808.8
1. Literature—Collections 2. Wit and humor
ISBN 0-385-18559-6   LC 85-13113
"Jokes, riddles, tongue twisters, knock knocks, limericks, puzzles, and games. Also included are nonsense poems by . . . Shel Silverstein, Lewis Carroll, Edward Lear, and Ogden Nash." Publisher's note

Mahy, Margaret
Bubble trouble & other poems and stories; written and illustrated by Margaret Mahy. Margaret K. McElderry Bks. 1992 c1991 66p il $13.95 (3-5)
808.8
1. Literature—Collections 2. Humorous poetry
ISBN 0-689-50557-4   LC 92-3540
First published 1991 in the United Kingdom
A collection of humorous stories and poems featuring a baby flying in a bubble, a lovestruck crocodile, and a grandmother who is tired of winter
"This is a lighthearted collection of silly stories and bouncy narrative poems in the Learian spirit. . . . They're good for quick entertainment at bedtime or for mood brightening in a classroom." Bull Cent Child Books

The **Oxford** book of scary tales; [edited by] Dennis Pepper. Oxford Univ. Press 1992 155p il $20 (5 and up)
808.8
1. Literature—Collections 2. Supernatural—Fiction
ISBN 0-19-278131-6
"The 35 stories and poems (half of them written for this book) vary in scariness, eschew the gruesome, and some—like that of the gravedigging great-grandfather—share a laugh. Although mostly British, there are retellings from Africa, India, Japan, and the United States." SLJ
"The poems here are as good as the tales, direct in voice and domestic in detail. The whole collection is clearly meant for reading aloud and sharing." Booklist

Pooley, Sarah

It's raining, it's pouring; a book for rainy days; compiled and illustrated by Sarah Pooley. Greenwillow Bks. 1993 76p il $18

808.8

1. Literature—Collections
ISBN 0-688-11803-8   LC 92-16859

A collection of stories, poems, and story-based activities including art, craft, and cooking projects

"Children at different developmental levels can participate in the themed activities. . . . [Pooley's] spot illustrations on white backgrounds lend an uncluttered look to the pages." Booklist

Rainy day: stories and poems; edited by Caroline Feller Bauer; illustrated by Michele Chessare. Lippincott 1986 74p il lib bdg $14.89 (2-4)

808.8

1. Literature—Collections
ISBN 0-397-32105-8   LC 85-45170

"Three tall tales—'Cloudy with a Chance of Meatballs' (contemporary), 'The Jolly Tailor' (Polish), and 'When the Rain Came Up from China' (Paul Bunyan) are bolstered with 23 short poems, a double-page spread of sayings, one of 'rainy day facts,' and a few suggested activities. Black-and-white wash drawings (sometimes monotonous) illustrate almost every page in a young format suitable for a picture-book audience as well as good primary readers." Bull Cent Child Books

Includes bibliography

The **Read-aloud** treasury; compiled by Joanna Cole and Stephanie Calmenson; illustrated by Ann Schweninger. Doubleday 1988 255p il $18.95

808.8

1. Literature—Collections
ISBN 0-385-18560-X   LC 86-24138

An illustrated collection of classic and modern nursery rhymes, poems, stories, and activity games

"A lively and surprisingly inclusive treasury. . . . Some of the most valuable items include five stories reprinted with their original illustrations: 'Little Bear Goes to the Moon' from *Little Bear, Sylvester and the Magic Pebble, Angus and the Cat, Corduroy* and 'The Very Tall Mouse and the Very Short Mouse' from *Mouse Tales*. . . . Schweninger's full-color illustrations complement and enhance the positive and inviting tone of this collection." Publ Wkly

Snowy day: stories and poems; edited by Caroline Feller Bauer; illustrated by Margot Tomes. Lippincott 1986 68p il lib bdg $14.89; pa $5.95 (2-4)

808.8

1. Literature—Collections
ISBN 0-397-32177-5 (lib bdg); 0-06-446123-8 (pa)
          LC 85-45858

This collection "features three short stories—Uchida's Japanese 'New Year's Hats for the Statues,' Singer's Jewish 'The Snow in Chelm,' and Bauer's adaptation of the Russian 'Marika the Snowmaiden.' The 28 poems include selections by X. J. Kennedy, Gwendolyn Brooks, David McCord, Lilian Moore, Dennis Lee, Kaye Starbird, John Ciardi, Myra Cohn Livingston, Karla Kuskin, and others." Bull Cent Child Books

"Margot Tomes's charming, evocative, black-and-white illustrations of snowflakes and leafless trees, sleds, and snowballs add the perfect touch to a wintry treat." Horn Book

Includes bibliography

Windy day: stories and poems; edited by Caroline Feller Bauer; illustrated by Dirk Zimmer. Lippincott 1988 74p il lib bdg $13.89 (2-4)

808.8

1. Literature—Collections
ISBN 0-397-32208-9   LC 86-42994

"Twenty-nine poems, three stories, two fact pages, and a page of craft ideas pretty much cover the subject. . . . Familiar children's poets such as Jack Prelutsky, Lillian Moore, and Felice Holman are included, as well as poets such as William Carlos Williams, usually only accessible via adult poetry collections. The stories include a Chinese folk tale, an original tale by Christian Garrison, and a rollicking story by Ruth Park. Dirk Zimmer's black-and-white drawings have depth, detail, and humor and add much to the collection." SLJ

Includes bibliography

Yolen, Jane

Hark! a Christmas sampler; illustrations and decorations by Tomie dePaola; original music and arrangements by Adam Stemple. Putnam 1991 128p il music $19.95

808.8

1. Christmas 2. Literature—Collections
ISBN 0-399-21853-X   LC 90-42865

A collection of stories, poems, legends, folktales, and carols relating to Christmas

"This book contains tempting morsels of delectable fact and fancy about Christmas. . . . Carefully selected, skillfully adapted, beautifully written and charmingly illustrated." SLJ

808.81 Poetry—Collections

A. Nonny Mouse writes again!; poems selected by Jack Prelutsky; illustrated by Marjorie Priceman. Knopf 1993 unp il $13; $13.99 (1-3)

808.81

1. Poetry—Collections
ISBN 0-679-83715-9; 0-679-93715-3   LC 92-5214

An illustrated collection of primarily traditional or anonymous verses, in such categories as "Wordplay," "Food," "Impossible Doings," and "Bad Kids"

"There's something here for every taste—all enlivened by Marjorie Priceman's fluid, inviting watercolors." Horn Book

Animal, vegetable, mineral; poems about small things; selected by Myra Cohn Livingston. HarperCollins Pubs. 1994 69p il $14; lib bdg $13.89

808.81

1. Poetry—Collections
ISBN 0-06-023008-8; 0-06-023009-6 (lib bdg)
          LC 93-43712

A collection of poems about some things that usually go unnoticed, but are worth looking for, by such authors as Arnold Adoff, Karla Kuskin, John Ciardi, and Charlotte Zolotow

"A well-balanced collection that will often catch readers off guard with its next little insight." SLJ

The **Baby's** bedtime book; [compiled and illustrated by] Kay Chorao. Dutton 1984 64p il $15.99

808.81

1. Poetry—Collections 2. Nursery rhymes 3. Lullabies
ISBN 0-525-44149-2   LC 84-6067

Also available in paperback from Puffin Bks.

The Baby's bedtime book—*Continued*

This collection includes traditional rhymes, lullabies and prayers ("Now I lay me down to sleep") and poems by authors including Blake, Kipling, Tennyson, Rossetti and Robert Louis Stevenson

"Luminous cross-hatched illustrations create magic for the 27 poems collected here. Each poem is adorned with Chorao's softly-colored full-page illustrations, bordered in tranquil blue. The poems include a few selections that well deserve a place in childhood, such as 'Hush, Little Baby' and 'Rock-a-bye Baby'; the majority are less familiar, including a few very special selections, such as Naidu's 'Cradle Song.'" SLJ

The **Baby's** good morning book; [compiled and illustrated by] Kay Chorao. Dutton 1986 64p il $13.95 **808.81**

1. Poetry—Collections 2. Nursery rhymes
ISBN 0-525-44257-X   LC 86-6415

This volume offers a "group of verses evocative of morning. Some of the poems are presented in full; others are excerpted from longer works. The moods vary from sassy to somnambulant. . . . There are 26 poems in all, set off by Chorao's warm, sunny pictures rich with fresh, morning hues and tender children's faces." Booklist

Carle, Eric

Eric Carle's animals, animals; poems compiled by Laura Whipple. Philomel Bks. 1989 82p il $18.95 **808.81**

1. Animals—Poetry 2. Poetry—Collections
ISBN 0-399-21744-4   LC 88-31646

"Illustrations take center stage in *Eric Carle's Animals Animals* . . . compiled by Laura Whipple. The well-chosen poems are from a variety of sources—the Bible, Shakespeare, Japanese Haiku, Pawnee Indian, weather sayings and contemporary poets like Judith Viorst, Ogden Nash, and Jack Prelutsky. On many pages the poem may be only two or three lines but the pictures are full-page spreads in Mr. Carle's familiar vividly colored, collage style." Kobrin Letter

Eric Carle's dragons dragons and other creatures that never were; compiled by Laura Whipple. Philomel Bks. 1991 69p il $18.95 **808.81**

1. Mythical animals—Poetry 2. Poetry—Collections
ISBN 0-399-22105-0   LC 91-11986

An illustrated collection of poems about dragons and other fantastic creatures by a variety of authors

"The collection offers a sumptuous viewing of Carle's rich blend of tissue-paper and paint collages and a grand introduction to the imaginary beasts. Laura Whipple concludes this adroit compilation with a brief commentary on the fabulous animals as 'a magical part of our human heritage.'" Horn Book
Includes glossary

Cat poems; selected by Myra Cohn Livingston; illustrated by Trina Schart Hyman. Holiday House 1987 32p il lib bdg $14.95 **808.81**

1. Cats—Poetry 2. Poetry—Collections
ISBN 0-8234-0631-8   LC 86-14810

"A collection of 19 poems about cats—some old and familiar, some relatively new and surprising—by, among other writers, Eve Merriam, Karla Kuskin, William Jay Smith and X. J. Kennedy." N Y Times Book Rev

"Livingston's eclectic collection of cat-inspired poetry does a nice job of reflecting the many moods and modes of felines, as well as the human fascination with these sometimes inscrutable animal companions. . . . Hyman's drawings top off the offering with some knowing evocations of cat behavior. Pleasingly designed and well chosen, this collection should suit feline fanciers nicely." Booklist

Cats are cats; poems compiled by Nancy Larrick; drawings by Ed Young. Philomel Bks. 1988 80p il lib bdg $17.95 **808.81**

1. Cats—Poetry 2. Poetry—Collections
ISBN 0-399-21517-4   LC 87-16728

A collection of thirty-six poems about all kinds of cats, from old grumbling cats to proud cats who sit tall, by poets including Eve Merriam, Jane Yolen, John Ciardi, and T. S. Eliot

"This is a solid selection with striking art, the latter especially notable for varied textures and perspectives that catch the reader by surprise as often as do the verbal nuances." Bull Cent Child Books

Christmas poems; selected by Myra Cohn Livingston; illustrated by Trina Schart Hyman. Holiday House 1984 32p il lib bdg $14.95 **808.81**

1. Christmas—Poetry 2. Poetry—Collections
ISBN 0-8234-0508-7   LC 83-18559

The selections "range from the Nativity to John Ciardi's speculations about how Santa gets down to Key West to a nice limerick applauding Mrs. S. Claus. The collection gets its unity from Trina Schart Hyman's drawings, placing all the figures in the vicinity of a Christmas tree supervised by the family cat." Read Teach

Classic poems to read aloud; selected by James Berry; with line drawings by James Mayhew. Kingfisher (NY) 1995 256p il $16.95 (4 and up) **808.81**

1. Poetry—Collections
ISBN 1-85697-987-3   LC 94-26815

"Berry has selected 138 poems that represent a wide variety of voices and organized them by subject. Poets range from Shakespeare to Wordsworth and from Anne Sexton to Shel Silverstein. He includes Native American poems as well as selections from Africa, India, and his native Jamaica. . . . Small line drawings and 16 full-color paintings by various artists are interspersed throughout." SLJ

The **Columbia** Granger's index to poetry; indexing anthologies published through June 30, 1993. 10th ed, completely rev, edited by Edith P. Hazen. Columbia Univ. Press 1994 2150p $199 **808.81**

1. Poetry—Indexes
ISBN 0-231-08408-0   LC 93-38761

Also available as part of Columbia Granger's world of poetry on CD-ROM

First edition, edited by Edith Granger, published 1904 by A. C. McClurg with title: Index to poetry and recitations. Fifth through eighth editions have title Granger's index to poetry

This work is organized into title and first line index, author index, subject index and a list of anthologies with their symbols. Coverage includes poetry translated into English

A **Cup** of starshine; poems and pictures for young children; selected by Jill Bennett; illustrated by Graham Percy. Harcourt Brace Jovanovich 1991 57p il $16.95 (k-2)

808.81

1. Poetry—Collections
ISBN 0-15-220982-4   LC 90-47978

"Bennett has compiled 71 short poems about ordinary, everyday experiences as well as imaginative adventures all geared to the preschool and primary sensibility. Well-known poets such as Eve Merriam, Margaret Wise Brown, William Jay Smith, Jack Prelutsky are among those included, along with traditional nursery verses. The rhyme, rhythm, repetition, and humor make the selections especially appealing to this audience. Percy's whimsical illustrations in soft-colored chalk and pencil capture the lighthearted, joyous mood of this eye-catching anthology." SLJ

Dilly dilly piccalilli; poems for the very young; chosen by Myra Cohn Livingston; illustrated by Eileen Christelow. Margaret K. McElderry Bks. 1989 68p il $12.95

808.81

1. American poetry—Collections 2. English poetry—Collections
ISBN 0-689-50466-7   LC 88-23005

A collection of poems about such topics as bugs, weather, food, and the sea, by poets ranging from Robert Louis Stevenson and Walter de la Mare to Gwendolyn Brooks and Arnold Lobel

"Livingston's ordering and placement of selections is astute; subjects seem to flow effortlessly from one page to the next. . . . Christelow's pleasant pencil drawings are interspersed sparingly throughout; they overwhelm neither the poetry nor a child's imagination by offering an overly literal interpretation." Horn Book

Dog poems; selected by Myra Cohn Livingston; illustrated by Leslie Morrill. Holiday House 1990 32p il lib bdg $12.95

808.81

1. Dogs—Poetry 2. Poetry—Collections
ISBN 0-8234-0776-4   LC 89-2061

A collection of poems by a variety of authors celebrating the joys of canines, from puppies to old hounds, from Chihuahuas to mongrels

"Surprisingly varied in form, mood, and subject, the poems not only portray the idiosyncrasies of individual hounds, but also show many facets of the complex relationships between children and their dogs. . . . Morrill contributes lively pencil drawings, which appear on every double-page spread, with verve and sensitivity. Read individually or to a group, this collection will tap into many children's experiences." Booklist

The **Earth** is painted green; a garden of poems about our planet; edited by Barbara Brenner; illustrated by S. D. Schindler. Scholastic 1994 81p il $15.95 (4-6)

808.81

1. Nature—Poetry 2. Poetry—Collections 3. Earth—Poetry
ISBN 0-590-45134-0   LC 93-21466

"A Byron Preiss book"

"Nearly one hundred poems from around the world extol the various aspects of our great, green Earth and all of its botanical beauty. The tone of the poems ranges from playful to thought provoking; profuse illustrations rendered in precise watercolor add visual lushness to a rich, poetic experience." Horn Book Guide

Easter buds are springing; poems for Easter; selected by Lee Bennett Hopkins; illustrated by Tomie de Paola. Wordsong 1993 30p il $9.95 (1-3)

808.81

1. Easter—Poetry 2. American poetry—Collections
ISBN 0-878093-58-4   LC 92-81073

A reissue of the title first published 1979 by Harcourt Brace Jovanovich

The poems "move through Easter morning greetings, speculations about the Easter rabbit, celebrations of Christ risen, flowers, colors, and egg hunts. Drawings are gay enough in jelly bean purple, but aside from one March Hare in mask, cape, and 'Try and Egg Me On' shirt, they are expected de Paola, and demure. The 19 poems are pleasant, useful to satisfy school assignments and build some anticipation for the season." SLJ

Easter poems; selected by Myra Cohn Livingston; illustrated by John Wallner. Holiday House 1985 32p il lib bdg $13.95

808.81

1. Easter—Poetry 2. Poetry—Collections
ISBN 0-8234-0546-X   LC 84-15866

A collection of poems on Easter themes by John Ciardi, William Jay Smith, Joan Aiken, and other authors, including poems translated from Russian and German

"Notable for their composition and textural qualities, Wallner's black and white illustrations are each touched with the purple or green of traditional Easter coloring. Livingston, a distinguished anthologist and poet, uses none of her own work here. . . . [This is a] fresh, verdant, and varied Easter anthology." Bull Cent Child Books

Flit, flutter, fly!; poems about bugs and other crawly creatures; selected by Lee Bennett Hopkins; illustrated by Peter Palagonia. Doubleday 1992 32p il $14 (1-4)

808.81

1. Insects—Poetry 2. Poetry—Collections
ISBN 0-385-41468-4   LC 91-12441

A collection of poems about bugs and other creatures that crawl by a variety of authors

"A charming assortment of 20 easy-to-read creature features crawling with vitality and humor. Youngsters will find the book a dance for the senses, lending itself to a roll of the tongue or a perk of the ears. . . . Palagonia's colored pencil illustrations leap from the page, weaving a larger-than-life-size web of bright hues and friendly insects. His playful use of perspectives creates a rich, lush tapestry." Booklist

Good morning to you, Valentine; poems for Valentine's day; selected by Lee Bennett Hopkins; illustrated by Tomie de Paola. Wordsong 1993 32p il $9.95 (2-4)

808.81

1. Valentine's Day—Poetry 2. Poetry—Collections
ISBN 1-878093-59-2   LC 91-70412

A reissue of the title first published 1976 by Harcourt Brace Jovanovich

"Aileen Fisher, Shel Silverstein, and John Updike are among the contributors. Tomie de Paola's cheery red-and-white drawings give the book an appropriate candy-box look." Booklist

Halloween poems; selected by Myra Cohn Livingston; illustrated by Stephen Gammell. Holiday House 1989 30p il lib bdg $13.95
808.81

1. Halloween—Poetry 2. Poetry—Collections
ISBN 0-8234-0762-4   LC 89-1741

Eighteen poems celebrate the holiday of pumpkins, black cats, witches, and ghosts

"This is a wise selection and has considerable variety of mood, style, and form. The selections are interpreted with relish in Gammell's black and white illustrations." Bull Cent Child Books

If the owl calls again; a collection of owl poems; selected by Myra Cohn Livingston; woodcuts by Antonio Frasconi. Margaret K. McElderry Bks. 1990 114p il $13.95 (6 and up)
808.81

1. Owls—Poetry 2. Poetry—Collections
ISBN 0-689-50501-9   LC 89-27659

"From reverent Indian chants to jaunty nursery rhymes, from William Wordsworth to Jack Prelutsky, Livingston has collected owl poems written in many styles and moods." Booklist

"Frasconi's arresting black-and-white woodcuts further the total effect of an elegant piece of bookmaking. However, it is the poems themselves that lure one on." Bull Cent Child Books

Index to children's poetry; a title, subject, author, and first line index to poetry in collections for children and youth; compiled by John E. and Sara W. Brewton. Wilson, H.W. 1942-1965 3v
808.81

1. Poetry—Indexes
Basic volume published 1942 $63 (ISBN 0-8242-0021-7); first supplement published 1954 $40 (ISBN 0-8242-0022-5); second supplement published 1965 $90 (ISBN 0-8242-0023-3)

The main volume indexes 15,000 poems by 2,500 authors in 130 collections. The two supplements analyze another 15,000 poems by 2700 authors in 151 collections

"This tool is an invaluable reference source." Peterson. Ref Books for Child

Index to poetry for children and young people; a title, subject, author, and first line index to poetry in collections for children and young people. Wilson, H.W. 1972-1994 5v
808.81

1. Poetry—Indexes
A continuation of: Index to children's poetry, entered above. The volume published 1972 covering 1964-1969 compiled by John E. and Sara W. Brewton and G. Meredith Blackburn III $53 (ISBN 0-8242-0435-2); 1970-1975 published 1978 compiled by John E. Brewton, G. Meredith Blackburn III and Lorraine A. Blackburn $53 (ISBN 0-8242-0621-5); 1976-1981 published 1984 compiled by John E. Brewton, G. Meredith Blackburn III and Lorraine A. Blackburn $53 (ISBN 0-8242-0681-9); 1982-1987 published 1989 compiled by G. Meredith Blackburn III and Lorraine A. Blackburn $58 (ISBN 0-8242-0773-4); 1988-1992 published 1994 compiled by G. Meredith Blackburn III $58 (ISBN 0-8242-0861-7)

Each volume analyzes approximately 10,000 poems by some 2,000 authors in more than 110 collections. Over 2,000 subject headings are used in each volume

Mice are nice; poems compiled by Nancy Larrick; art by Ed Young. Philomel Bks. 1990 45p il $15.95
808.81

1. Mice—Poetry 2. Poetry—Collections
ISBN 0-399-21495-X   LC 87-11159

A collection of poems about mice by David McCord, A. A. Milne, John Ciardi, Ian Serraillier, and others

"For the most part the verses are lighthearted, humorous, and affectionate, with quick, brisk rhythms and sporadic flashes of surprise. Although the individual poems can be found elsewhere, the book is well worth purchasing for the sake of Ed Young's exemplary art. Charcoal and pastel illustrations portray tiny, bright-eyed mice—frequently drawn to scale against full-page renderings of cats or human hands and faces—with their long tails trailing gracefully behind." Horn Book

My song is beautiful; poems and pictures in many voices; selected by Mary Ann Hoberman. Little, Brown 1994 32p il lib bdg $15.95 (k-3)
808.81

1. Poetry—Collections
ISBN 0-316-36738-9   LC 93-24976

"This small anthology of 14 poems celebrates diversity, not only in culture, but also in mood and genre (from invocation to nonsense verse) and in illustrator, artistic medium, and style. . . . There are fine poems by Nikki Giovanni, Jack Prelutsky, A. A. Milne, and others, including a Brooklyn seventh-grader; and there are translations from Central Eskimo, ancient Mexico, Korea, and Chippewa Indian. Each poem is illustrated by a different artist, among them, Ashley Bryan, David Diaz, and Keiko Narahashi." Booklist

New Year's poems; selected by Myra Cohn Livingston; illustrated by Margot Tomes. Holiday House 1987 32p il lib bdg $12.95
808.81

1. New Year—Poetry 2. Poetry—Collections
ISBN 0-8234-0641-5   LC 86-22885

"Livingston has commissioned 13 New Years poems from contemporary poets for children, added 2 new poems of her own, and 2 others which have been previously published. . . . The poems describe a range of feelings about the new year from hopefulness to merriment and celebration." SLJ

"This diverse and engaging collection of poems for the New Year is . . . annotated with explanations of regional customs. . . . Tomes' three-color illustrations are as spare and elegant as winter itself." Publ Wkly

The Night of the whippoorwill; poems selected by Nancy Larrick; illustrated by David Ray. Philomel Bks. 1992 71p il $19.95
808.81

1. Night—Poetry 2. Poetry—Collections
ISBN 0-399-21874-2   LC 91-28374

"Thirty-four poems that convey the special mystery of the night. Federico Garcia Lorca, Estonian folklore, and tales from the Hopi share space with Langston Hughes, Eve Merriam and others. Some poems are familiar . . . but the collection still remains fresh and exciting. . . . The quiet atmosphere is echoed in the illustrations; soft, misty paintings in the blues and muted colors of night are occasionally lit by the bright oranges of fire or artificial light." SLJ

The **Oxford** book of Christmas poems; edited by Michael Harrison and Christopher Stuart-Clark. Oxford Univ. Press 1983 160p il hardcover o.p. paperback available $10.95 (4 and up)   **808.81**

1. Christmas—Poetry 2. Poetry—Collections
ISBN 0-19-276080-7 (pa)   LC 85-120897

This "collection of 120 British and American poems is organized into four sections around the season of winter, the coming of Advent, the Nativity and celebration of Christmas, and the anticipation of a new year. The poets are both well and lesser known, carefully chosen for a balance of old and new." Booklist

Piping down the valleys wild; poetry for the young of all ages; edited with a new introduction by Nancy Larrick; illustrated by Ellen Raskin. Delacorte Press 1985 xxiv, 253p il hardcover o.p. paperback available $4.99   **808.81**

1. Poetry—Collections
ISBN 0-440-46952-X (pa)

A reissue with new introduction of the title first published 1968

Dylan Thomas, Eve Merriam, Carl Sandburg, and Gwendolyn Brooks are among the authors included

"A pleasant, quite comprehensive collection that includes little unfamiliar material; the selections range widely in source, somewhat less widely in mood. . . . An index of first lines and an author-title index [are] appended. The compiler's introduction is addressed to adults and discusses reading aloud to the young." Sutherland. The Best in Child Books

Poems for brothers, poems for sisters; selected by Myra Cohn Livingston; illustrated by Jean Zallinger. Holiday House 1991 32p il $12.95   **808.81**

1. Brothers and sisters—Poetry 2. Poetry—Collections
ISBN 0-8234-0861-2   LC 90-44463

A collection of poems exploring the relationship between brothers and sisters, by authors including X. J. Kennedy, Lewis Carroll, and Ted Hughes

"The prominence of the soft, realistic pencil drawings and the book's design make it attractive to primary-grade children." SLJ

Poems of A. Nonny Mouse; selected by Jack Prelutsky; illustrated by Henrik Drescher. Knopf 1989 unp il $12.95; lib bdg $13.99 (1-3)   **808.81**

1. Poetry—Collections
ISBN 0-394-88711-5; 0-394-98711-X (lib bdg)
     LC 89-31672

"With tongue firmly in cheek, Prelutsky prefaces this comical collection of traditional and anonymous verses by elucidating the trials and tribulations of A. Nonny Mouse. Ms. Mouse—obviously 'no ordinary rodent'—claims that a typographical error caused all her 'little verses' to be printed under the wrong name, a mistake Prelutsky rectifies with the publication of this book. . . . Children will enjoy spotting Ms. Mouse on every page as she exhorts Drescher's droll characters in their wacky pursuits and smiles serenely at a world where boots have sharp teeth and a dog's tail turns into a snake." Publ Wkly

Ring out, wild bells; poems about holidays and seasons; selected by Lee Bennett Hopkins; illustrated by Karen Baumann. Harcourt Brace Jovanovich 1992 80p il $17.95   **808.81**

1. Holidays—Poetry 2. Seasons—Poetry 3. Poetry—Collections
ISBN 0-15-267100-5   LC 89-20061

A collection of poems about holidays and seasons, organized chronologically from New Year to Christmas

"The verse of such favorite poets as Robert Frost, Aileen Fisher, Langston Hughes, and Carl Sandburg adds depth to the cheerful pages, which are illustrated alternately with color and black-and-white drawings. The artist's sense of humor and attention to detail make the book one that youngsters will enjoy looking at as well as listening to." Booklist

Side by side; poems to read together; collected by Lee Bennett Hopkins; illustrated by Hilary Knight. Simon & Schuster Bks. for Young Readers 1988 80p il lib bdg $14.95; pa $7.95   **808.81**

1. Poetry—Collections
ISBN 0-671-63579-4; 0-671-73622-1 (pa)
     LC 87-33025

A collection of poems especially chosen to be read aloud, by authors ranging from Lewis Carroll and Robert Louis Stevenson to Gwendolyn Brooks and David McCord

"With the rhythmic, sometimes narrative verses, and the joyful antics of the characters prancing across the pages, this collection offers visual as well as aural treats for children and adults to savor together." Booklist

Sing a song of popcorn; every child's book of poems; illustrated by nine Caldecott Medal artists, Marcia Brown [et al.]; selected by Beatrice Schenk de Regniers [et al.] Scholastic 1988 142p il lib bdg $18.95
     808.81

1. Poetry—Collections
ISBN 0-590-40645-0   LC 87-4330

Revised edition of Poems children will sit still for, published 1969

A collection of 128 poems by a variety of well-known authors with illustrations by nine Caldecott medalists

"A pleasant book, still a useful if conservative anthology, this has title, author, and first line indexes, and brief notes on the illustrators." Bull Cent Child Books

Sleep, baby, sleep; lullabies and night poems; selected and illustrated by Michael Hague. Morrow Junior Bks. 1994 unp il $18
     808.81

1. Poetry—Collections 2. Lullabies
ISBN 0-688-10877-6   LC 93-27119

"This collection of 51 bedtime rhymes is divided into lullabies, night poems, and musical arrangements for piano and guitar. There is one selection per page, decorated with star-studded borders in blue, green, and lavender and full-or half-page, full-color paintings of sweet-looking children and nursery animals." SLJ

Sleep rhymes around the world; edited by Jane Yolen; illustrated by 17 international artists. Wordsong 1994 [i.e. 1993] 39p il $16.95   **808.81**

1. Poetry—Collections 2. Lullabies 3. Polyglot materials
ISBN 1-56397-243-3   LC 93-60244

Sleep rhymes around the world—*Continued*

This is a collection of lullabies from seventeen countries. Each lullaby is in its native language with an English translation

"Artists from each of the featured countries illustrate their lullabies, making this the ultimate multicultural bedtime book." Christ Sci Monit

Talking to the sun: an illustrated anthology of poems for young people; selected and introduced by Kenneth Koch and Kate Farrell. Metropolitan Mus. of Art; Holt & Co. 1985 112p il $24.95 **808.81**

1. Poetry—Collections
ISBN 0-8050-0144-1 (Holt & Co.) LC 85-15428

"Poems from a wide variety of times and cultures and reproductions from the Metropolitan Museum of Art are organized by themes that include spring, love, nonsense, animals, and the secrets beneath the ordinary." Booklist

Thanksgiving poems; selected by Myra Cohn Livingston; illustrated by Stephen Gammell. Holiday House 1985 32p il lib bdg $14.95 **808.81**

1. Thanksgiving Day—Poetry 2. Poetry—Collections
ISBN 0-8234-0570-2 LC 85-762

"The two-color illustrations have a soft, melting quality that is given contrast by precision of line on some pages, so that the pictures have a range in technique and mood that matches the poems they illustrate." Bull Cent Child Books

"Shaded pencil drawings tinged with peach and robin's egg blue prove the versatility of the illustrator, who matches the mood of the poetry with stunning Indian portraits, views of the barren November land, and squiggly-line cartoon drawings." Horn Book

Valentine poems; selected by Myra Cohn Livingston; illustrated by Patience Brewster. Holiday House 1987 32p il lib bdg $13.95 **808.81**

1. Valentine's Day—Poetry 2. Poetry—Collections
ISBN 0-8234-0587-7 LC 85-31723

"A short anthology of poems for Valentine's Day that combines first-rate humorous and romantic verses by both contemporary and traditional poets. Both young listeners and independent readers will find the selections appealing. Brewster's humorous red and blue pencil illustrations of animals suit each poem, such as the two rabbits who show Love's strength for Karla Kuskin's 'To You'. . . . A plus for both school and public libraries needing Valentine's Day material." SLJ

Voices on the wind; poems for all seasons; selected by David Booth; illustrated by Michèle Lemieux. Morrow Junior Bks. 1990 41p il $13.95; lib bdg $13.88 **808.81**

1. Seasons—Poetry 2. Nature poetry 3. Poetry—Collections
ISBN 0-688-09554-2; 0-688-09555-0 (lib bdg)
LC 90-5566

This is a "collection of traditional poems celebrating nature and the seasons. Included are many familiar poems by authors such as John Ciardi, Christina Rosetti, and William Blake." Horn Book Guide

"Though the subjects cover the usual round of plants, animals, and activities appropriate to each season, the book has its own bright airiness, due in large part to the beauty of Lemieux's impressionistic watercolors. . . . There is also a refreshing variety in the placement of text and use of white space to offset color. Nice for looking at and sharing aloud." Booklist

When the dark comes dancing; a bedtime poetry book; compiled by Nancy Larrick; illustrated by John Wallner. Philomel Bks. 1983 79p il $17.95 (k-3) **808.81**

1. Poetry—Collections 2. Lullabies
ISBN 0-399-20807-0 LC 81-428

An "anthology of poems and lullabies for young children. . . . Among the contributors are Eleanor Farjeon, Aileen Fisher, Arthur Guiterman, Karla Kuskin, Myra Cohn Livingston, Eve Merriam, Christina Rossetti, and Robert Louis Stevenson." Bull Cent Child Books

"Both old and new poets are represented, folk songs range from as far away as Russia and Africa, and kept throughout is a happy balance of the simplest rhymes with those of more complex imagery. The illustrations, most of them in color, are done in soft pastels, and in their decorative detail and slightly surrealistic flavor they complement the serene and dreamlike quality of the book." Horn Book

Includes bibliography

Why am I grown so cold?; poems of the unknowable; edited by Myra Cohn Livingston. Atheneum Pubs. 1982 269p $14.95 (5 and up) **808.81**

1. Supernatural—Poetry 2. Poetry—Collections
ISBN 0-689-50242-7 LC 82-6646

"A Margaret K. McElderry book"

"Shakespeare, Sandburg, Shel Silverstein, Tolkien, Ted Hughes, Goethe, Felice Holman, Joan Aiken, Pablo Neruda are only a few of the poets represented in the selections that deal with sorcery, devils, fairies, portents, mermaids—the gamut of arcana." Publ Wkly

"An inspired anthology, generous in both quantity and quality, will attract poetry lovers with its rich language and non-poetry lovers with the strong expressions of its eerie theme." Booklist

Winter poems; selected by Barbara Rogasky; illustrated by Trina Schart Hyman. Scholastic 1994 40p il $15.95 **808.81**

1. Winter—Poetry 2. Poetry—Collections
ISBN 0-590-42872-1 LC 91-24419

"Rogasky has selected a wide range of poems—25 in all—dating from 10th-century Japan to the contemporary U.S. The best of the ages is represented, with familiar favorites from Shakespeare, Thomas Hardy, Robert Frost, Emily Dickinson, Carl Sandburg, etc. . . . Hyman's illustrations perfectly capture the spirit of that season, with acrylics in deep, chilling shades. . . . A beautiful presentation of outstanding quality." SLJ

A **Zooful** of animals; selected by William Cole; illustrated by Lynn Munsinger. Houghton Mifflin 1992 88p il $17.95 **808.81**

1. Animals—Poetry 2. Poetry—Collections
ISBN 0-395-52278-1 LC 91-21885

A collection of animal poems by authors including Rachel Field, Shel Silverstein, and John Ciardi

"Not your usual zoo, this happy gathering of poetry and verse is broadly inclusive of its denizens, who live in unfettered joy within handsomely designed pages. . . . Lynn Munsinger's full-color illustrations contribute to making this book outstanding. She has a wonderfully expressive yet delicate line, the ability to be elegant and humorous at the same time." Horn Book

808.82   Drama—Collections

Barchers, Suzanne I.
Scary readers theatre. Teacher Ideas Press
1994 157p pa $20   **808.82**
1. Drama—Collections 2. Drama in education
ISBN 1-56308-292-6   LC 94-31715
A collection of 30 plays for classroom use adapted from
folktales, Greek myths, ghost stories, and modern urban legends
Includes bibliographical references

Bauer, Caroline Feller, 1935-
Presenting reader's theater; plays and poems
to read aloud; drawings by Lynn Gates
Bredeson. Wilson, H.W. 1987 238p il $45
    808.82
1. Drama—Collections 2. Drama in education
ISBN 0-8242-0748-3   LC 87-2105
The author has dramatized poems, folktales and excerpts
from contemporary books to introduce children to reading
This book "provides a wealth of script material for children to read aloud before an audience or for their own pleasure." SLJ

The **Big** book of Christmas plays; 21 modern
and traditional one-act plays for the
celebration of Christmas; edited by Sylvia E.
Kamerman. Plays 1988 357p $18.95
    808.82
1. Christmas—Drama 2. One act plays
ISBN 0-8238-0288-4   LC 88-15691
This collection includes "adaptations of scenes from *Little Women, Les Misérables,* and *A Christmas Carol* . . . [as
well as] more modern offerings. . . . The table of contents,
which seemingly includes something for everyone from lower grades through high school, is arranged by age group. Appended production notes lists characters, playing time,
costumes, props, setting, lighting, and sound effects." Booklist

Play index. Wilson, H.W. 1953-1992 8v
    808.82
1. Drama—Indexes
ISSN 0554-3037
First published 1953, covering the years 1949-1952, and
edited by Dorothy Herbert West and Dorothy Margaret
Peake $20. Additional volumes: 1953-1960 $25 edited by
Estelle A. Fidell and Dorothy Margaret Peake; 1961-1967
$28 edited by Estelle A. Fidell; 1968-1972 $33 edited by Estelle A. Fidell; 1973-1977 $41 edited by Estelle A. Fidell;
1978-1982 $48 edited by Juliette Yaakov; 1983-1987 $58
edited by Juliette Yaakov and John Greenfieldt; 1988-1992
$80 edited by Juliette Yaakov and John Greenfieldt
Play index indexes plays in collections and single plays;
one-act and full-length plays; radio, television, and Broadway plays; plays for amateur production; plays for children,
young adults, and adults. It is divided into four parts. Part
I is an author, title, and subject index; the author or main
entry includes the title of the play, brief synopsis of the
plot, number of acts and scenes, size of cast, number of
sets, and bibliographic information. Part II is a list of collections indexed, and Part III, a cast analysis, lists plays by
the type of cast and number of players required. Part IV is
a directory of publishers and distributors
"This index is an excellent source for locating published
plays." Nichols. Guide to Ref Books for Sch Media Cent.
4th edition

Plays; the drama magazine for young people.
Plays $28 per year   **808.82**
1. Drama—Periodicals 2. College and school drama—
Periodicals
ISSN 0032-1540
Monthly October through May, except January/February
combined. First published 1941
Each issue of this magazine "offers approximately three
plays for junior and senior high school students and three
or more for the middle and lower grades. In addition, there
is a dramatized classic and either a skit, a puppet play, or
a choral reading. Production notes and stage directions accompany each play." Katz. Mag for Libr. 8th edition

808.88   Collections of miscellaneous writings

Bartlett, John, 1820-1905
Familiar quotations. Little, Brown $40
    808.88
1. Quotations
Also available CD-ROM version
First published 1855. (16th edition 1992) Periodically re-
vised. Editors vary
"Comprehensive collection of quotations in chronological
order with author and keyword indexes." N Y Public Libr.
Ref Books for Child Collect. 2d edition

Cole, Joanna
Six sick sheep; 101 tongue twisters;
compiled by Joanna Cole and Stephanie
Calmenson; illustrated by Alan Tiegreen.
Morrow Junior Bks. 1993 64p il $15; lib bdg
$14.93 (3-6)   **808.88**
1. Tongue twisters
ISBN 0-688-11139-4; 0-688-11140-8 (lib bdg)
    LC 92-5715
A collection of all kinds of tongue twisters: some only
two or three words long, some that tell a story, and some
featuring a theme
Includes bibliography

Schwartz, Alvin, 1927-1992
Busy buzzing bumblebees and other tongue
twisters; illustrated by Paul Meisel.
HarperCollins Pubs. 1992 61p il lib bdg
$12.89; pa $3.50 (k-2)   **808.88**
1. Tongue twisters
ISBN 0-06-025269-3 (lib bdg); 0-06-444036-2 (pa)
    LC 91-4799
"An I can read book"
First published 1982 with different illustrations
"Ilustrated in wild, cheerful watercolors and with a mul-
ticultural cast, this . . . collection of tongue twisters is per-
fect for beginning readers." Booklist

Schwartz, Alvin, 1927-1992—*Continued*

A twister of twists, a tangler of tongues; tongue twisters; collected by Alvin Schwartz; illustrated by Glen Rounds. Lippincott 1972 125p il hardcover o.p. paperback available $5.95 (4 and up) **808.88**

1. Tongue twisters
ISBN 0-06-446004-5 (pa)

This is a collection of tongue twisters in both prose and verse, including several in other languages

"The selection of well-known and not-so-well-known tongue twisters should provide endless hours of elocutionary diversion for young and old alike. . . . A helpful series of notes, sources, and bibliographic references give added dimension to a light-hearted, yet incisive, compilation, highlighted by the jovial line drawings." Horn Book

810.8 American literature—Collections

The **Big** book for our planet; written by Aliki [et al.]; illustrated by Aliki [et al.]; edited by Ann Durell, Jean Craighead George, Katherine Paterson; designed by Jane Byers Bierhorst. Dutton Children's Bks. 1993 136p il $17.99 **810.8**

1. American literature—Collections 2. Environmental protection
ISBN 0-525-45119-6 LC 92-33433

Nearly thirty stories, poems, and non-fiction pieces by such notable authors as Natalie Babbitt, Marilyn Sachs, and Jane Yolen illustrated by the likes of Steven Kellogg and Susan Jeffers, demonstrate some of the environmental problems now plaguing our planet

"Consistently lively and readable, this collection delivers its message in imaginative, and therefore effective, ways." SLJ

The **Big** book for peace; edited by Ann Durell and Marilyn Sachs; designed by Jane Byers Bierhorst; written by Lloyd Alexander [et al.]; illustrated by Jon Agee [et al.] Dutton Children's Bks. 1990 120p il music lib bdg $17.50 **810.8**

1. American literature—Collections 2. Peace
ISBN 0-525-44605-2 LC 89-37595

"Contributions by thirty-four well-known authors and illustrators of children's books look at the issues of peace, conflict, war, and resolution from a variety of points of view. The many approaches, the use of humor, and the quality of the selections elevate the collection from the didactic to the inspired." Horn Book Guide

Children of promise; African-American literature and art for young people; edited by Charles Sullivan. Abrams 1991 126p il $24.95 (5 and up) **810.8**

1. African Americans in literature 2. African Americans in art 3. American literature—African American authors—Collections 4. African American artists
ISBN 0-8109-3170-2 LC 91-7566

Poems, prose, folk songs, photographs, sculpture, and paintings explore the African-American experience as seen through art and literature by blacks or about black subjects

"History serves as a backdrop for this carefully chosen anthology. . . . Over eighty colorful photographs and paintings provide additional appeal to this valuable resource. A stunning collection." Horn Book

Diane Goode's American Christmas. Dutton Children's Bks. 1990 80p il lib bdg $14.95 **810.8**

1. Christmas 2. American literature—Collections
ISBN 0-525-44620-6 LC 89-25605

"This generous, festively illustrated collection of stories, poems and songs captures the holiday as celebrated by many different Americans." N Y Times Book Rev

Free to be—you and me; conceived by Marlo Thomas; developed and edited by Carole Hart [et. al]; editor Francine Klagsbrun; art director: Samuel N. Antupit. McGraw-Hill 1974 143p il music o.p.; Bantam Bks. paperback available $10.95 **810.8**

1. American literature—Collections 2. Individuality 3. Social role
ISBN 0-553-34544-3 (pa)

"A project of the Ms. Foundation, Inc." Title page

The theme of this collection of twenty-five songs, stories, poems and a dialogue is that children should develop as individuals and be independent of obsolete sexual and racial role myths. Fifteen of the selections originally were recorded on a 1973 album of the same title

This collection "is a significant step toward filling the need for nonsexist material for children. . . . The total adds up to a qualitatively uneven but still useful endeavor at encouraging children to be themselves." Booklist

From sea to shining sea, a treasury of American folklore and folk songs; illustrated by eleven Caldecott Medal and four Caldecott honor book artists: Molly Bang [et al.]; compiled by Amy L. Cohn. Scholastic 1993 399p il music $29.95 **810.8**

1. American literature—Collections 2. Folklore—United States 3. Folk songs—United States
ISBN 0-590-42868-3 LC 92-30598

A compilation of more than 140 folk songs, tales, poems, non-fiction, and stories telling the history of America and reflecting its multicultural society

This is "a treasure chest that will be dipped into year after year and generation after generation. The attention to detail and love that each illustrator brought to their section is evident as is the research Ms. Cohn did before making her choices. A masterpiece that is also a gorgeous piece of book making." Child Book Rev Serv

Includes glossary and bibliography

Home; a collaboration of thirty distinguished authors and illustrators of children's books to aid the homeless; edited by Michael J. Rosen; written by Franz Brandenberg [et al.]; illustrated by Aliki [et al.] HarperCollins Pubs. 1992 unp il $16; lib bdg $14.89 (k-3) **810.8**

1. American literature—Collections 2. Homeless persons
ISBN 0-06-021788-X; 0-06-021789-8 (lib bdg)
LC 91-29125

"A Charlotte Zolotow book"

"Thirty noted authors and illustrators offer interpretations of home in a collaboration whose proceeds will go to Share Our Strength, an organization that provides food and shelter to the needy. The eclectic mix of poetry, prose and pictures spans a range of distinct styles and emotions. . . .

Home—*Continued*

Many of these author/illustrator duos have worked together before, resulting in particularly solid and polished combinations. . . . Young readers will delight in the variety and may be prompted to ask about the larger social issues that inspired this project." Publ Wkly

Rising voices; writings of young Native Americans; selected by Arlene B. Hirschfelder and Beverly R. Singer. Scribner 1992 115p $13.95 (5 and up)   **810.8**

1. American literature—American Indian authors—Collections 2. Indians of North America 3. Children's writings

ISBN 0-684-19207-1   LC 91-32083

Also available in paperback from Ivy Bks.

A collection of poems and essays in which young Native Americans speak of their identity, their families and communities, rituals, and the harsh realities of their lives

"These 'rising voices' speak eloquently in this important collection. . . . Some pieces are over 100 years old; some are quite current. Some were written by elementary school students, and others by high schoolers. All are poignant and haunting." Voice Youth Advocates

Scared silly!; a book for the brave; [compiled and illustrated by] Marc Brown. Little, Brown 1994 61p il music $18.95 (k-3)   **810.8**

1. American literature—Collections

ISBN 0-316-11360-3   LC 93-13501

An illustrated collection of spooky stories, poems, and riddles including a humorous array of ghosts, monsters, ghouls, and witches

This is "shivery enough to awe a young audience, yet silly enough for them to giggle their apprehensions away. Selections by such well-known authors as Ogden Nash, Jack Prelutsky, and Judith Viorst are included, as well as several original pieces by Brown. . . . Brown scores again with his own brand of warm, engaging watercolor art. . . . Brilliant colors, attention to detail, and the excellent balance of text and art provide a feast for the eye." SLJ

Stone Soup; the magazine by young writers and artists. Children's Art Foundation $24 per year   **810.8**

1. Child authors—Periodicals 2. Child artists—Periodicals

ISSN 0094-579X

Five issues a year. First published 1973

"This is a magazine that encourages children's creativity by giving them a place to publish their stories, poetry, book reviews, and art. . . . Each 48-page issue is filled with stories on a variety of subjects written by children up to the age of 13. Each issue also includes an insert for teachers suggesting activities that relate to the stories in that issue. Although most of the issue is in black and white, a few pictures are reproduced in full color." Katz. Mag for Libr. 8th edition

Thanksgiving: stories and poems; edited by Caroline Feller Bauer; illustrated by Nadine Bernard Westcott. HarperCollins Pubs. 1994 86p il music $14; lib bdg $13.89   **810.8**

1. Thanksgiving Day 2. American literature—Collections

ISBN 0-06-023326-5; 0-06-023327-3 (lib bdg)

LC 93-18631

A collection of stories, poems, and songs about Thanksgiving Day, by such authors as Aileen Fisher, Jack Prelutsky, Eve Merriam, and Yoshiko Uchida

"An amiable collection. . . . Cartoon sketches with gray wash dance across the pages, and recipes for pumpkin pie and cranberry sauce as well as directions for making a turkey garland to decorate the table are included." Horn Book

Includes bibliography

To ride a butterfly; original pictures, stories, poems, & songs for children; by fifty-two distinguished authors and illustrators; edited by Nancy Larrick and Wendy Lamb with a letter from Barbara Bush. Dell 1991 96p il music $17   **810.8**

1. American literature—Collections

ISBN 0-440-50402-3   LC 91-7778

"In celebration of the twenty-fifth anniversary of Reading is Fundamental"

This collection includes works by "Tomie DePaola, Patricia Reilly Giff, Madeleine L'Engle, Patricia McKissack, Cynthia Rylant, Seymour Simon, and Peter Spier." Booklist

This book is "a gem that is sure to be a family favorite for years to come. Appropriately, many of the entries revolve around a love of books or reading. . . . A wonderful book for sharing, for giving, for curling-up alone with." Child Book Rev Serv

Valentine's day: stories and poems; edited by Caroline Feller Bauer; illustrated by Blanche L. Sims. HarperCollins Pubs. 1993 90p il $15; lib bdg $14.89   **810.8**

1. Valentine's Day 2. American literature—Collections

ISBN 0-06-020823-6; 0-06-020824-4 (lib bdg)

LC 91-37641

A collection of stories, poems, and activities by a variety of authors, on the theme of Valentine's Day

"Sims's black-and-white cartoons prove that affection can be humorous without being silly and are a perfect accompaniment for this pleasing anthology." SLJ

Includes bibliography

Yolen, Jane

Here there be dragons; illustrated by David Wilgus. Harcourt Brace & Co. 1993 149p il $16.95 (5 and up)   **810.8**

1. Dragons—Fiction 2. American literature—Collections

ISBN 0-15-209888-7   LC 92-23194

"Yolen has compiled a collection of her poetry and prose about dragons of all sizes, shapes and dispositions. She introduces each piece with a brief description including the circumstances surrounding its writing. . . . The poetry, like the prose, varies in length but will enthrall readers. David Wilgus' pen and ink drawings further enhance the book." Book Rep

Here there be unicorns; illustrated by David Wilgus. Harcourt Brace & Co. 1994 115p il $16.95 (5 and up)   **810.8**

1. Unicorns—Fiction 2. American literature—Collections

ISBN 0-15-209902-6   LC 94-1790

A collection of stories, poems and songs about unicorns

"The poems, which are written in a variety of styles, including some that are quite challenging, are sure to generate interesting discussions about creative expression. In brief notes preceding each selection, Yolen lends insight into the background of the myths and into her own creative process." Booklist

811 American poetry

Adoff, Arnold, 1935-

All the colors of the race: poems; illustrated by John Steptoe. Lothrop, Lee & Shepard Bks. 1982 56p il $15; lib bdg $14.93; pa $4.95 (4-6) **811**

1. Family life—Poetry 2. Race awareness—Poetry
ISBN 0-688-00879-8; 0-688-00880-1 (lib bdg); 0-688-11496-2 (pa) LC 81-11777

This "cycle of poems is written from the viewpoint of a child who has one parent who is black and Protestant, one who is white and Jewish. The poetry is free and flowing, reflecting the facets of the child's feelings. . . . The illustrations, brown and white, are often angular in block print style, speckled and stylized, and they echo the vitality and tenderness of the poems' moods." Bull Cent Child Books

Eats: poems; illustrated by Susan Russo. Lothrop, Lee & Shepard Bks. 1979 unp il $15; lib bdg $14.93; pa $3.95 **811**

1. Food—Poetry
ISBN 0-688-41901-1; 0-688-51901-6 (lib bdg); 0-688-11695-7 (pa) LC 79-11300

All of the "smells, tastes, and obsessive cravings—pizzas, burgers, ice cream, etc.—are evoked in poems and verse-recipes that range in tone from dreamy to passionate. . . . Russo's brown-tone illustrations have sufficient precision to depict each topic but retain a smoky, slight blurriness that carries on the reveries of the verses. Readers of all ages will relate to Adoff's blissful musings and fancies and occasional whimsy." Booklist

In for winter, out for spring; illustrations by Jerry Pinkney. Harcourt Brace Jovanovich 1990 unp il $14.95 (k-3) **811**

1. Seasons—Poetry 2. Family life—Poetry
ISBN 0-15-238637-8 LC 90-33185

This collection of poems, told from the perspective of a young black farm girl, celebrates family life throughout the yearly cycle of seasons

"With his variegated watercolor and pencil illustrations, Pinkney captures the mood or essence of each poem. . . . Because the uninhibited layout of the free verse poetry may be confusing to younger readers, this book would benefit from one-on-one sharing. It certainly invites repeated readings." Bull Cent Child Books

Sports pages; illustrations by Steve Kuzma. Lippincott 1986 79p il lib bdg $14.89; pa $5.95 (4 and up) **811**

1. Sports—Poetry
ISBN 0-397-32103-1 (lib bdg); 0-06-446098-3 (pa) LC 85-45169

Free verse poems about the experiences and feelings of young athletes involved in various sports, illustrated with pencil sketches

"The poems are in the voices of young athletes of both sexes, and they capture hope or despair, excitement or exhaustion, the bonding in a team sport, the isolation of the single participant. Adoff writes with a control of structure that never impedes the movement of the poem. This is one of his best collections." Bull Cent Child Books

Street music; city poems; illustrated by Karen Barbour. HarperCollins Pubs. 1995 unp il $16; lib bdg $15.89 **811**

1. City life—Poetry
ISBN 0-06-021522-4; 0-06-021523-2 (lib bdg) LC 92-28539

"Adoff's poetry celebrates the city the way a child experiences it, primarily through the senses. Garbage trucks clang and crash, cold water gushes from a hydrant, and taxi horns, subway trains, and engines provide the street music of the book's title. . . . Barbour's stylized paintings fill the pages with hot colors and simplified images." Booklist

"An energetic, cosmopolitan, and unapologetic evocation of urban life that skillfully mingles free verse with free association." Horn Book

Agard, John, 1949-

No hickory, no dickory, no dock; Caribbean nursery rhymes; written and remembered by John Agard and Grace Nichols; illustrated by Cynthia Jabar. Candlewick Press 1995 48p il $15.95 (k-3) **811**

1. Caribbean region—Poetry
ISBN 1-56402-156-4 LC 93-24289

A collection of rhymes, both original and traditional, that evoke the rhythms and language of the Caribbean

"The lines have a musical beat, and the scratchboard illustrations capture the island scene with brilliant tropical colors and folk-art exaggeration." Booklist

Angelou, Maya

Life doesn't frighten me; poem by Maya Angelou; paintings by Jean-Michel Basquiat; edited by Sara Jane Boyers. Stewart, Tabori & Chang 1993 unp il $14.95 **811**

ISBN 1-55670-288-4 LC 92-40409

"Angelou's direct, lovely poem is the text of a dramatic large-size picture book with paintings in glowing color. . . . Basquiat's work has the directness of street art, with a bold combination of magic realism and abstract geometric shapes. . . . Also included are long, excellent biographical sketches of Angelou and Basquiat." Booklist

Includes bibliography

Begay, Shonto

Navajo; visions and voices across the Mesa. Scholastic 1995 48p il $15.95 (5 and up) **811**

1. Navajo Indians—Poetry
ISBN 0-590-46153-2 LC 93-31610

The author "presents a very personal view of contemporary Navajo life in this picture-book collection for older readers. Pairing 20 of his paintings with original poetry, Begay moves from the spiritual aspects of Navajo life through personal childhood memories into striking present-day images, concluding with an affirmation of continuing life and rebirth." Booklist

Bodecker, N. M., 1922-1988

Water pennies, and other poems; illustrated by Erik Blegvad. Margaret K. McElderry Bks. 1990 51p il $12.95 **811**

1. Animals—Poetry
ISBN 0-689-50517-5 LC 90-6477

Bodecker, N. M., 1922-1988—Continued

A collection of poems featuring such small creatures as the pollywog, snail, moth, and earthworm

"Many of the poems have the kind of strong, insistent rhythms that appeal instantly to children. . . . Erik Blegvad's dainty line drawings of insects and other small creatures . . . create an added dimension, emphasizing as they do the human point of view." Horn Book

Brooks, Gwendolyn

Bronzeville boys and girls; pictures by Ronni Solbert. Harper & Row 1956 40p il lib bdg $14.89 (2-5)   **811**

1. African Americans—Poetry

ISBN 0-06-020651-9

A collection of thirty-six poems about everyday experiences of children. "While the children are black and the place is Chicago, the place might be anywhere and the children, any children." Natl Counc of Teach of Engl. Adventuring with Books. 2d edition

"Ronni Solbert's sensitive and expressive drawings reflect and extend the mode and beauty of the poetry." Chicago Sunday Trib

Brown, Margaret Wise, 1910-1952

Nibble nibble: poems for children; illustrated by Leonard Weisgard. Harper & Row 1986 c1959 unp il lib bdg $14.89 (k-3)   **811**

1. Nature poetry

ISBN 0-201-09291-3   LC 84-43128

"A Young Scott book"

First published 1959 by W. R. Scott

Twenty-five poems, about insects, fish, animals, birds, and the seasons

"The pleasingly cadenced verses are fresh and childlike, and the illustrations in black, white, and cool green are lovely; together they make a harmonious, evocative whole which young children will enjoy." Booklist

Bruchac, Joseph, 1942-

Thirteen moons on a turtle's back; a Native American year of moons; by Joseph Bruchac and Jonathan London; illustrated by Thomas Locker. Philomel Bks. 1992 unp il $15.95   **811**

1. Indians of North America—Legends 2. Indians of North America—Poetry 3. Seasons—Poetry

ISBN 0-399-22141-7   LC 91-3961

"Native American stories are retold as poems that capture the cycles of the moon. Months slip by as the oil paintings show each moon in the shell of the turtle's back." Child Book Rev Serv

"Locker . . . has created a dramatic oil painting for each short tale. His artwork portrays seasonal changes in the land as well as the specific seasonal activities of humans and animals. The large format with minimal text will appeal to younger children, while the alternative calendar, based on changes in nature, will interest middle readers. An unusual, easy-to-use resource for librarians, teachers, and others wishing to incorporate multicultural activites throughout the year." Booklist

Bryan, Ashley, 1923-

Sing to the sun; poems and pictures by Ashley Bryan. HarperCollins Pubs. 1992 unp il $15; lib bdg $14.89; pa $4.95   **811**

ISBN 0-06-020829-5; 0-06-020833-3 (lib bdg); 0-06-443437-0 (pa)   LC 91-38359

A collection of poems and paintings celebrating the ups and downs of life

"With an energetic beat that's hard to resist, Bryan drums out poetry with a Caribbean sway. These short poems that sing the praises of everyday joys are further charged by the riotous primary colors Bryan splashes around." Booklist

Carlstrom, Nancy White, 1948-

Northern lullaby; illustrated by Leo and Diane Dillon. Philomel Bks. 1992 unp il $15.95 (k-3)   **811**

1. Lullabies

ISBN 0-399-21806-8   LC 90-19719

"A sleepy baby says goodnight to the Alaskan countryside and its inhabitants in a free-verse poem. Each natural element or animal is represented by an anthropomorphized object—Grandpa Mountain, Great Moose Uncle, Auntie Birch. The verse is evocative, filled with subtle imageries of the cold, yet beautiful, country. . . . Each double-page spread effectively humanizes the symbolic text, utilizing the natural colors and patterns of the area." SLJ

Cassedy, Sylvia, 1930-1989

Zoomrimes; poems about things that go; poems by Sylvia Cassedy; pictures by Michele Chessare. HarperCollins Pubs. 1993 50p il $14.95; lib bdg $14.89   **811**

1. Transportation—Poetry

ISBN 0-06-022632-3; 0-06-022633-1 (lib bdg)   LC 90-1463

"Cassedy has built, around an alphabetical framework, a collection of poems that elicit images of movement. Brief and imaginative lyric verses illustrate the vehicular application of subjects as varied as camels, rocking chairs, and feet. The poems remind us of the poet's remarkable ability to create phrases and images that resonate." Horn Book Guide

Child, Lydia Maria Francis, 1802-1880

Over the river and through the wood (k-2)   **811**

1. Thanksgiving Day—Poetry 2. Songs

Some editions are:

HarperCollins Pubs. $14.95; lib bdg $14.89 Illustrated by Nadine Bernard Westcott (ISBN 0-06-021303-5; 0-06-021304-3; LC 92-14979)

Little, Brown lib bdg $15.95 Illustrated by Iris Van Rynbach (ISBN 0-316-13873-8; LC 88-4712)

North-South Bks. $14.95 Illustrated by Christopher Manson (ISBN 1-55858-211-8; LC 93-16614)

Text originally published in volume 2 of the author's Flowers for children, 1844, under title: A boy's Thanksgiving Day

Illustrated versions of a poem about a family's visit to their grandparents for Thanksgiving

Ciardi, John, 1916-1986
The hopeful trout and other limericks; illustrated by Susan Meddaugh. Houghton Mifflin 1989 52p il $13.95 **811**
1. Limericks
ISBN 0-395-43606-0 LC 87-23587
"A posthumous gathering of limericks by the well-known poet offers insight into the traditional pyrotechnics of the form—a saucy blending of wit with rhythmic phrases. Some celebrate disasters; some affront; others introduce characters one hopes never to meet. . . . Susan Meddaugh's black-and-white illustrations complement the irreverent tone, nicely opening up the pages so that the volume will appeal to lovers of joke books, those reluctant to tackle long selections, and even those searching for an offbeat comment to write in an autograph book." Horn Book

The monster den; or, Look what happened at my house—and to it; drawings by Edward Gorey. Wordsong 1991 62p il $13.95 **811**
1. Monsters—Poetry
ISBN 1-878093-35-5 LC 90-85904
A reissue of the title first published 1966 by Lippincott
"A truly delightful collection of humorous verse that celebrates the little monster lurking within every child, with mad-as-a-hatter illustrations by Edward Gorey." SLJ

The reason for the pelican; with new illustrations by Dominic Catalano. Boyds Mills Press 1994 64p il $13.95 **811**
ISBN 1-56397-370-7
A newly illustrated edition of the title first published 1959 by Lippincott
"This slim volume of light nonsense verse, flawlessly executed, makes a worthy shelf companion for Lewis Carroll and W. S. Gilbert." Atlantic

You know who; drawings by Edward Gorey. Wordsong 1991 63p il $13.95 **811**
ISBN 1-878093-34-7 LC 90-85903
A reissue of the title first published 1964 by Lippincott
A humorous collection of poetry about a child who is a sleepy head in the morning and unwilling to go to bed at night
"Mr. Ciardi is painstakingly simple in vocabulary, and admirably unsentimental in attitude." N Y Times Book Rev

You read to me, I'll read to you; drawings by Edward Gorey. Lippincott 1962 64p il hardcover o.p. paperback available $6.95 **811**
1. Humorous poetry
ISBN 0-06-446060-6 (pa)
Thirty-five "imaginative and humorous poems for an adult and a child to read aloud together. Written in a basic first-grade vocabulary, the poems to be read by the child alternate with poems to be read by the adult." Booklist

Cullen, Countee, 1903-1946
The lost zoo; by Christopher Cat and Countee Cullen; illustrated by Brian Pinkney. Silver Burdett Press 1992 95p il $12.95 **811**
1. Mythical animals—Poetry 2. Humorous poetry
ISBN 0-382-24256-4 LC 91-16532
A newly illustrated edition of the title first published 1940 by Harper & Brothers

"Part prose (conversations between Cullen and his loquacious cat) and part poetry, the book describes the animals 'who didn't get into Noah's Ark, even though he sent them all invitations.' There are long nonsense verses about such creatures as the Lapalakes, the Treasuretit, the Squilililigee, and others. . . . [The illustrations] are often more eerie than comic." Bull Cent Child Book

Cumpián, Carlos
Latino rainbow; poems about Latino Americans; illustrated by Richard Leonard. Childrens Press 1994 47p il (Many voices, one song) lib bdg $15.45 (3-6) **811**
1. Hispanic Americans—Poetry
ISBN 0-516-05153-9 LC 94-5069
"This collection of 20 poems in picture-book format introduces aspects of Latino culture in the United States. The chronologically arranged selections range in topic from the colonization of California by the Spanish, to Ellen Ochoa, the first Latina astronaut. . . . The backgrounds, often heavily colored in earth and sepia tones, allude to the subjects' accomplishments." SLJ

Dickinson, Emily, 1830-1886
I'm nobody! who are you? poems of Emily Dickinson for children; illustrated by Rex Schneider; with an introduction by Richard B. Sewall. Stemmer House 1978 84p il $21.95; pa $14.95 (3-6) **811**
ISBN 0-916144-21-6; 0-916144-22-4 (pa)
LC 78-6828
"A Barbara Holdridge book"
This collection of Emily Dickinson's poetry is illustrated with full color drawings depicting life in nineteenth century New England
Includes glossary

Eliot, T. S. (Thomas Stearns), 1888-1965
Growltiger's last stand; with The pekes and the pollicles and The song of the Jellicles; with pictures by Errol Le Cain. Farrar, Straus & Giroux; Harcourt Brace Jovanovich 1987 c1986 unp il $14; pa $4.95 **811**
1. Cats—Poetry
ISBN 0-374-32809-9; 0-374-42811-5 (pa)
An illustrated presentation of three cat poems taken from the author's Old Possum's book of practical cats, first published 1939. This edition first published 1986 in the United Kingdom
This book is "best suited to readers with enough sophistication to appreciate the poet's wide-ranging vocabulary, frequent syntactical inversions and sly humor. Others may not know how to respond to the outward fierceness of the title poem or to the more clearly playful but still bellicose [second poem]. . . . Le Cain's richly textured illustrations are often droll, occasionally rather fearsome and always striking, particularly in his use of symmetry and pattern." Publ Wkly

Mr. Mistoffelees; with, Mungojerrie and Rumpelteazer; with pictures by Errol Le Cain. Harcourt Brace Jovanovich 1991 unp il $13.95 **811**
1. Cats—Poetry
ISBN 0-15-256230-3 LC 90-39856

Eliot, T. S. (Thomas Stearns), 1888-1965—
Continued

An illustrated presentation of two cat poems taken from the author's Old Possum's book of practical cats, first published 1939. This edition first published 1990 in the United Kingdom

"Le Cain portrays Mr. Mistoffelees as a black cat with huge yellow eyes wearing a top hat and a collar of playing cards. In the second poem, Mungojerrie and Rumpelteazer, two conniving cats, wear sly expressions and are dressed like prison convicts." Booklist

This is a "visually rich book that celebrates Eliot's verbal acrobatics and contributes a few capers of its own." Publ Wkly

Esbensen, Barbara Juster

Cold stars and fireflies; poems of the four seasons; illustrated by Susan Bonners. Crowell 1984 70p il lib bdg $14.89 (4 and up)

811

1. Nature poetry 2. Seasons—Poetry

ISBN 0-690-04363-5   LC 83-45051

"Nature and the changing seasons are the subjects of Esbensen's 43 poems, which are arranged according to season and illustrated with evocative, shadowy shapes touched with grays and reds." Booklist

Who shrank my grandmother's house? poems of discovery; pictures by Eric Beddows. HarperCollins Pubs. 1992 47p il $15; lib bdg $14.89

811

ISBN 0-06-021827-4; 0-06-021828-2 (lib bdg)

LC 90-39631

A collection of poems about childhood discoveries concerning everyday objects and things

"The images here are clean, simple, and surprising. The words are arranged on the page for special notice of sound effects and are surrounded by Beddows' brightly lit, full-color images that play on a fifties' tone without getting stuck there. Both the familiar subjects and the bountiful white space open these twenty-three poems to a child's discovery." Bull Cent Child Books

Words with wrinkled knees: animal poems; pictures by John Stadler. Crowell 1986 unp il lib bdg $14.89

811

1. Animals—Poetry

ISBN 0-690-04505-0   LC 85-47886

A collection of poems about words that express the essence of the animals they identify

"The black-and-white drawings are sometimes as inventive as the poems." Bull Cent Child Books

Evans, Lezlie

Rain song; illustrated by Cynthia Jabar. Houghton Mifflin 1995 unp il $14.95 (k-1)

811

1. Rain—Poetry

ISBN 0-395-69865-0   LC 94-17368

"A playful rhyming poem and energetic, lighthearted illustrations show two girls relishing the delights of a rainstorm." Booklist

Farber, Norma

How does it feel to be old? illustrated by Trina Schart Hyman. Dutton 1979 unp il o.p.; Penguin Bks. paperback available $4.99

811

1. Old age—Poetry

ISBN 0-14-054759-2 (pa)   LC 79-11516

"A Unicorn book"

In this poem a grandmother explains to her granddaughter some of the thoughts and feelings, advantages and disadvantages that accompany being old

"The detailed pen-and-ink drawings abound with fascinating clutter—photographs in elaborate frames, twisting candelabras, and ornate china. Poet and artist have achieved a remarkable union of spirit, expressing in verse and evocative illustrations the bittersweet accumulation of a lifetime of memories." Horn Book

When it snowed that night; illustrated by Petra Mathers. HarperCollins Pubs. 1993 unp il $17; lib bdg $16.89

811

1. Jesus Christ—Nativity—Poetry

ISBN 0-06-021707-3; 0-06-021708-1 (lib bdg)

LC 92-27414

"A Laura Geringer book"

A collection of nativity poems featuring animals who travel from afar to be at the manger of baby Jesus and protect him from the snow

"Petra Mathers's deep-toned, elegantly stylized paintings vary from full-page to double-page spreads. . . . A joyful Nativity offering that celebrates one life and many." Horn Book

Fisher, Aileen Lucia, 1906-

Always wondering; some favorite poems of Aileen Fisher; drawings by Joan Sandin. HarperCollins Pubs. 1991 86p il $13.95; lib bdg $13.89 (1-3)

811

ISBN 0-06-022851-2; 0-06-022858-X (lib bdg)

LC 90-23069

"A Charlotte Zolotow book"

The author selects some of the most requested poems from her own work, grouped under such headings as "Think About People," "Suddenly," and "Whoever Planned the World"

"The verses are fresh and simple, half-musing and half-humorous in tone, with satisfying rhythm and rhyme. New readers will find the poetry easy to read and memorize, while young children will enjoy hearing it read aloud." Booklist

Fleischman, Paul

I am phoenix: poems for two voices; illustrated by Ken Nutt. Harper & Row 1985 51p il $14.95; lib bdg $14.89; pa $4.95 (4 and up)

811

1. Birds—Poetry

ISBN 0-06-021881-9; 0-06-021882-7 (lib bdg); 0-06-446092-4 (pa)   LC 85-42615

"A Charlotte Zolotow book"

A collection of poems about birds to be read aloud by two voices

"Devotés of the almost lost art of choral reading should be among the first to appreciate this collection. . . . Printed in script form, the selections . . . have a cadenced pace and dignified flow; their combination of imaginative imagery and realistic detail is echoed by the combination of stylized

Fleischman, Paul—*Continued*
fantasy and representational drawings in the black and white pictures, all soft line and strong nuance." Bull Cent Child Books

Joyful noise: poems for two voices; illustrated by Eric Beddows. Harper & Row 1988 44p il $14.95; lib bdg $14.89; pa $3.95 (4 and up) **811**

1. Insects—Poetry
ISBN 0-06-021852-5; 0-06-021853-3 (lib bdg); 0-06-446093-2 (pa) LC 87-45280
Awarded the Newbery Medal, 1989
"A Charlotte Zolotow book"
"This collection of poems for two voices explores the lives of insects. Designed to be read aloud, the phrases of the poems are spaced vertically on the page in two columns, one for each reader. The voices sometimes alternate, sometimes speak in chorus, and sometimes echo each other." Booklist
"There are fourteen poems in the handsomely designed volume, with stylish endpapers and wonderfully interpretive black-and-white illustrations. Each selection is a gem, polished perfection." Horn Book

Florian, Douglas, 1950-
Beast feast; poems and paintings by Douglas Florian. Harcourt Brace & Co. 1994 48p il $14.95 (k-3) **811**

1. Animals—Poetry
ISBN 0-15-295178-4 LC 93-10720
A collection of humorous poems about such animals as the walrus, anteater, and boa
"Most verses are rhymed and employ standard poetic schemes, but clever wordplay, good rhythm, and liberal humor in word and illustrations make a fine poetic feast." Horn Book Guide

Bing bang boing; poems and drawings by Douglas Florian. Harcourt Brace & Co. 1994 144p il $15.95 (3-5) **811**

1. Nonsense verses
ISBN 0-15-233770-9 LC 94-3894
Also available in paperback from Penguin Bks.
An illustrated collection of more than 150 nonsense verses
"The author's spare, pen-and-ink drawings, like the poems themselves, deftly explore the comic potential in each combination of words. With a few clean lines, he creates an original, funny vision." SLJ

Frost, Robert, 1874-1963
Birches; illustrated by Ed Young. Holt & Co. 1988 unp il $13.95; pa $5.95 **811**

1. Trees—Poetry
ISBN 0-8050-0570-6; 0-8050-1316-4 (pa)
LC 86-4787
An illustrated version of the well-known poem written in 1916, about birch trees and the pleasures of climbing them
"The freedom called for in the sweep and depth of Frost's words should not be hemmed in by rigidly defined illustrations, and Young allows this license, giving the viewer ample opportunity to absorb and be absorbed by the imagery. The text is set two to three lines to a page, with the poem repeated in its entirety at the end." Booklist

Robert Frost; edited by Gary D. Schmidt; illustrated by Henri Sorensen. Sterling 1994 48p il (Poetry for young people) $14.95 (4 and up) **811**

ISBN 0-8069-0633-2 LC 94-11161
"A Magnolia Editions book"
This volume "contains a three-page overview of the poet's life, 29 poems selected and arranged around the seasons of the year, brief and apt commentaries on each, and a useful index of titles and subject matter. The realistic watercolor illustrations capture the delicate beauty of a New England spring and the glory of fall while still suggesting the around-the-corner chill of winter, a disquiet echoing throughout much of Frost's poetry." SLJ

Stopping by woods on a snowy evening; illustrated by Susan Jeffers. Dutton 1978 unp il $13.99 **811**

1. Winter—Poetry
ISBN 0-525-40115-6 LC 78-8134
Illustrations of wintry scenes accompany each line of the well-known poem
"There is such delicate strength to this famous poem that stretching it to book size might easily have become a heavy-handed venture. Fortunately the artist has taken great care to love, honor and faithfully follow the words. Her drawing, which tends at times to prettification, is for the most part softly restrained. You can almost hear the silence of the woods in it." N Y Times Book Rev

Giovanni, Nikki
Ego-tripping and other poems for young people; illustrations by George Ford; foreword by Virginia Hamilton. 2nd ed. Hill Bks. 1993 52p il $14.95; pa $9.95 (5 and up) **811**

1. African Americans—Poetry
ISBN 1-55652-188-X; 1-55652-189-8 (pa)
LC 93-29578
First published 1974
Giovanni has added 10 new poems to her earlier "collection of 23 poems for young people. Ford's illustrations in sepia shades are bold and full of character and dreaming. As Virginia Hamilton says in her foreword, Giovanni's voice is personal and warm, she 'celebrates ordinary folks' and writes of struggle and liberation. She's upbeat and celebratory without minimizing hard times." Booklist

Knoxville, Tennessee; illustrated by Larry Johnson. Scholastic 1994 unp il $14.95 (k-3) **811**

1. African Americans—Poetry 2. Family life—Poetry 3. Summer—Poetry
ISBN 0-590-47074-4 LC 93-8877
Describes the joys of summer spent with family in Knoxville: eating vegetables right from the garden, going to church picnics, and walking in the mountains
"This brief poem, written in free verse and originally included in Giovanni's 1971 *Black Feeling, Black Talk, Black Judgement* (Morrow), speaks to children as directly today as it did when first published. . . . Johnson's full-color, painterly illustrations envelop readers in a wonderful green world suffused with an overwhelming sense of family and community love." Horn Book

Giovanni, Nikki—*Continued*

Spin a soft black song: poems for children; illustrated by George Martins. rev ed. Hill & Wang 1985 57p il $11.95; pa $3.95 (3-6)

811

1. African Americans—Poetry
ISBN 0-8090-8796-0; 0-374-46469-3 (pa)

LC 84-19287

First published 1971

A poetry collection which recounts the feelings of black children about their neighborhoods, American society, and themselves

"A beautifully illustrated book of poems about black children for children of all ages. . . . Simple in theme but a very moving collection nonetheless." Read Ladders for Hum Relat. 5th edition

Graham, Joan Bransfield

Splish splash; illustrated by Steven M. Scott. Ticknor & Fields 1994 unp $13.95 (k-2)

811

1. Water—Poetry
ISBN 0-395-70128-7   LC 94-1237

A collection of poems celebrating water in its various forms, from ice cubes to the ocean

"The variety of text styles, colors and formats is fascinating for young and older readers, and invites aspiring writers to experiment with their own poetry. The graphics are bright, crisp and inviting." Child Book Rev Serv

Greenfield, Eloise, 1929-

Daydreamers; [illustrated by] Tom Feelings. Dial Press (NY) 1981 unp il $13.95; pa $4.95 (3-6)

811

1. Dreams—Poetry 2. African Americans—Poetry
ISBN 0-8037-2137-4; 0-8037-0167-5 (pa)

This is a "poem about the child who daydreams, and who is changed by the introspective quiet of that dreaming." Bull Cent Child Books

"Expressive, soul-searching portraits of Black young people—ranging from early innocent childhood to adolescence on the brink of maturity—are uncannily echoed by the pellucid sensitive words. Done in sepia or in tones of gray, the portrayals display a quiet, pensive vitality." Horn Book

Honey, I love, and other love poems; pictures by Diane and Leo Dillon. Crowell 1978 unp il $13.95; lib bdg $13.89; pa $3.95 (2-4)

811

1. African Americans—Poetry 2. Love poetry
ISBN 0-690-01334-5; 0-690-03845-3 (lib bdg); 0-06-443097-9 (pa)   LC 77-2845

"These 16 poems explore facets of warm, loving relationships with family, friends and schoolmates as experienced by a young Black girl. Central to the theme of the book is the idea that the child loves herself and is very confident in expressing that love." Interracial Books Child Bull

"The Dillons transform this quiet book into magic with soft, grey charcoal renderings of the young girl and her friends, overlaid with child-like brown scratchboard pictures embodying the images in the poems." SLJ

Nathaniel talking; illustrated by Jan Spivey Gilchrist. Black Butterfly Children's Bks. 1989 c1988 unp il $12.95; pa $6.95 (2-4)

811

1. African Americans—Poetry
ISBN 0-86316-200-2; 0-86316-201-0 (pa)

LC 88-51011

Coretta Scott King Award for illustration, 1990

"The rhythm of Greenfield's text is infectious from a very early line: 'It's Nathaniel talking/and Nathaniel's me/I'm talking about/My philosophy/About the things I do/And the people I see/All told in the words/Of Nathaniel B. Free/That's me.' Her sentiments are equally affecting, but in a more sobering way; Nathaniel wonders when he'll ever be old enough not to have to answer a question 'I don't know,' and he remembers his mother, who has died. . . . His experiences are warmly universal, as are Gilchrist's depictions of his joyful and sorrowful moments." Publ Wkly

Night on Neighborhood Street; pictures by Jan Spivey Gilchrist. Dial Bks. for Young Readers 1991 unp il $14.99; lib bdg $13.89 (2-4)

811

1. African Americans—Poetry 2. City life—Poetry 3. Night—Poetry
ISBN 0-8037-0777-0; 0-8037-0778-9 (lib bdg)

LC 89-23480

Also available in paperback from Penguin Bks.

A collection of poems exploring the sounds, sights, and emotions enlivening a black neighborhood during the course of one evening

"Through a series of poems accompanied by sensitive, handsome paintings, executed in gouache with pastel highlighting, readers are brought into a community which is at once unique and universal. Remarkable for unselfconscious use of varied rhyme schemes and verse forms, the text reads aloud beautifully." Horn Book

Under the Sunday tree; paintings by Amos Ferguson; poems by Eloise Greenfield. Harper & Row 1988 38p il lib bdg $14.89; pa $6.95 (2-4)

811

1. Bahamas—Poetry
ISBN 0-06-022257-3 (lib bdg); 0-06-443257-2 (pa)

LC 87-29373

"This collection of poems and paintings present a vivid picture of life in the Bahamas. The poems cover a variety of subjects and occasionally seem to have been written to go with a painting. The folk-art styled paintings are detailed, vibrant and certainly evoke a picture of island life." Child Book Rev Serv

Grimes, Nikki

Meet Danitra Brown; illustrated by Floyd Cooper. Lothrop, Lee & Shepard Bks. 1994 unp il $15; lib bdg $14.93 (2-4)

811

1. African Americans—Poetry 2. Friendship—Poetry
ISBN 0-688-12073-3; 0-688-12074-1 (lib bdg)

LC 92-43707

"A collection of 13 original poems that stand individually and also blend together to tell a story of feelings and friendship between two African-American girls. . . . Cooper's distinguished illustrations in warm dusty tones convey the feeling of closeness. The poignant text and lovely pictures are an excellent collaboration." SLJ

Grimes, Nikki—_Continued_

Something on my mind; [illustrated by] Tom Feelings; words by Nikki Grimes. Dial Bks. 1978 unp il hardcover o.p. paperback available $4.95 **811**

1. African Americans—Poetry
ISBN 0-8037-0273-6 (pa)   LC 77-86266
Also available in hardcover from P. Smith
Coretta Scott King Award for illustrations, 1979
"The black and white drawings of black children by Feelings were used by Grimes as bases for prose poems that interpret the pictures. The drawings are sensitive portraits, some beautifully shaded and soft, others looking like deft, unfinished sketches. The poems vary in depth and treatment, some fragmentary and others imbued with poignant emotion; all are serious, some reflecting the black experience and others—most of the selections—capturing universal longings or reactions of childhood." Bull Cent Child Books

Hale, Sarah Josepha

Mary had a little lamb (k-2)   **811**
1. Nursery rhymes 2. Sheep—Poetry
Some editions are:
Holiday House lib bdg $15.95; pa $5.95 illustrations by Tomie de Paola (ISBN 0-8234-0509-5; 0-8234-0519-2) with musical accompaniment
Orchard Bks. $14.95; lib bdg $14.99 illustrated by Salley Mavor (ISBN 0-531-06875-7; 0-531-08725-5)
Scholastic lib bdg $14.95 photos by Bruce McMillan (ISBN 0-590-43773-9)
First published 1830 by Marsh, Capen & Lyon with title: Mary's lamb
The famous nineteenth-century nursery rhyme about the school-going lamb

Heide, Florence Parry, 1919-

Grim and ghastly goings-on; pictures by Victoria Chess. Lothrop, Lee & Shepard Bks. 1992 unp il $15; lib bdg $14.93   **811**
1. Monsters—Poetry
ISBN 0-688-08319-6; 0-688-08322-6 (lib bdg)
LC 89-8071
A collection of twenty-one humorous poems, about monsters and their ilk
"Unsavory beings of all types inhabit this wickedly funny collection. . . . Poems and art dramatize and wildly exaggerate universal fears—thereby offering some comic relief. . . . Snappy and rhythmic, typically closing with a satisfying twist, Heide's verses find their match in Chess's colorful, elaborately patterned illustrations, which spare no wart nor fang and masterfully convey the spine-tingling sense that something creepy is just a breath away." Publ Wkly

Hoban, Russell

Egg thoughts and other Frances songs; pictures by Lillian Hoban. newly il ed. HarperCollins Pubs. 1994 31p il $15; lib bdg $14.89; pa $4.95 (k-2)   **811**
ISBN 0-06-022331-6; 0-06-022332-4 (lib bdg); 0-06-443378-1 (pa)   LC 92-44004
A newly illustrated edition of the title first publishd 1972
In this collection of poems, Frances the badger focuses "on eggs cooked in various ways, a wellworn favorite doll, string, homework, little sister Gloria, and other joys and tribulations of childhood." Booklist

"Frances' thoughts and observations though not always fluidly expressed, are childlike and unselfconsciously amusing, and the verse is complemented by illustrations that are equally down-to-earth and appealing." SLJ

Hopkins, Lee Bennett, 1938-

Been to yesterdays: poems of a life; illustrations by Charlene Rendeiro. Wordsong 1995 64p il $14.95 (4 and up)   **811**
ISBN 1-56397-467-3   LC 94-73320
Autobiographical poems capture a thirteen-year old boy's feelings, experiences, and aspirations in one tumultuous year of his life

Good rhymes, good times; original poems; pictures by Frané Lessac. HarperCollins Pubs. 1995 unp $14.95; lib bdg $14.89 (k-2)   **811**
ISBN 0-06-023499-7, 0-06-023500-4 (lib bdg)
LC 93-8159
"Hopkins has collected 21 of his own children's poems published over the years. Rooted in the small events of a child's day, from jiggling a loose tooth to cuddling a pet, the poems are very simple, usually no more than one or two words to a line, with some affectionate wordplay and 'good rhymes.' Lessac's brilliantly colored illustrations in folk-art style set the poems in a vital multicultural city neighborhood." Booklist

Hughes, Langston, 1902-1967

The dream keeper and other poems; including seven additional poems; illustrated by Brian Pinkney. Knopf 1994 83p il $12; lib bdg $12.99 (5 and up)   **811**
1. African Americans—Poetry
ISBN 0-679-84421-X; 0-679-94421-4 (lib bdg)
LC 92-10240
First published 1932
"Langston Hughes's poems range from the romantic to the poignant, from the spiritual to the challenging. His lyrical voice asks for recognition of the Negro, offers encouragement, and reminds his African-American brothers of their glorious past. Although the pieces in _The Dream Keeper_ were written over a half-century ago . . . the words have the same strength of meaning and power as if they had been written today." Horn Book

The sweet and sour animal book; illustrations by students of the Harlem School of the Arts; introduction by Ben Vereen; afterword by George P. Cunningham. Oxford Univ. Press 1994 unp il $15.95   **811**
1. Animals—Poetry 2. Child artists
ISBN 0-19-509185-X   LC 94-8779
"The Iona and Peter Opie library of children's literature"
"Twenty-seven previously unpublished, alphabetically arranged verses about animals, written in 1936. . . . Children from The Harlem School of the Arts have created brightly painted, three-dimensional clay or paper creatures to accompany the poems; full-color photographs of these sculptures are placed next to the selections. . . . An inspired artistic collaboration." SLJ

Johnson, James Weldon, 1871-1938

The creation; a poem; pictures by Carla Golembe. Little, Brown 1993 unp il $16.95

811

1. Creation—Poetry 2. Bible stories
ISBN 0-316-46744-8   LC 92-24304

"The biblical story of creation is retold here in resonant, inspiring verse set against a jubilant background of bold colors." Publ Wkly

Joseph, Lynn

Coconut kind of day; island poems; illustrated by Sandra Speidel. Lothrop, Lee & Shepard Bks. 1990 unp il $13.95; lib bdg $13.88

811

1. Trinidad and Tobago—Poetry
ISBN 0-688-09119-9; 0-688-09120-2 (lib bdg)

LC 90-6676

"Joseph's 13 brief poems recall a day in the life of a family in Trinidad. . . . Joseph frequently incorporates island speech patterns into her work. Speidel's illustrations add enormously to the book's appeal. Double-page spreads in soft, muted shades of blue, rose, gold, and green show the poems superimposed on one side. . . . A gentle, nostalgic, loving recollection about growing up in another part of the world." SLJ

Kennedy, X. J.

The beasts of Bethlehem; verse by X. J. Kennedy; drawings by Michael McCurdy. Margaret K. McElderry Bks. 1992 39p il $13.95 (3-6)

811

1. Jesus Christ—Nativity—Poetry 2. Animals—Poetry
ISBN 0-689-50561-2   LC 91-38417

Presents nineteen poems, each in the voice of a creature that was present in the stable at the time of Christ's birth

"These small, quiet verses celebrate the special birth in well-chosen words. Each is accompanied by an equally quietly contained illustration, rendered in scratchboard with colored pencil. Set against black backgrounds, their white lines and dashes of color give them a hint of drama, making each picture an apt partner for the words it accompanies." SLJ

Brats; illustrations by James Watts. Atheneum Pubs. 1986 42p il $12.95; pa $3.95 (3-6)

811

1. Nonsense verses
ISBN 0-689-50392-X; 0-689-71884-5 (pa)

LC 85-20018

"A Margaret K. McElderry book"

"Forty-two brief verses, mostly rhymed quatrains, celebrate or denigrate the actions of mischievous children, many of whom meet fearful fates. These are bright, tight, and inventive, with plenty of playground chanting potential. . . . A few of the selections have a slightly grisly ring (specifically, in the case of Louise, who sneaks up on a snoozing bear), but it's all done in high humor, as are the slapstick black-and-white drawings that illustrate the spacious pages. Neatly crafted poetry that will be highly popular as well." Bull Cent Child Books

Drat these brats! illustrations by James Watts. Margaret K. McElderry Bks. 1993 44p il $12.95 (3-6)

811

1. Nonsense verses
ISBN 0-689-50589-2   LC 92-33686

Forty-four humorous poems which describe the behavior of some annoying children

"This terse and cheeky rogue's gallery in verse abounds with puns and delicious rhymes. Pen-and-ink drawings capture the slightly wicked naughtiness." Publ Wkly

The forgetful wishing well: poems for young people; with illustrations by Monica Incisa. Atheneum Pubs. 1985 88p $12.95 (4 and up)

811

ISBN 0-689-50317-2   LC 84-45977

"A Margaret K. McElderry book"

Seventy poems deal with the challenges of growing up, curious beasts and birds, city life, and other subjects both realistic and fanciful

"Characterized by fresh imagery, related to but not restricted by everyday expressions, these are poems to delight the ear and stimulate the imagination. Strategically placed full-page, pen-and-ink drawings add a restrained decorative note to a handsomely designed small volume." Horn Book

Fresh brats; illustrations by James Watts. Margaret K. McElderry Bks. 1990 44p il $13.95 (3-6)

811

1. Nonsense verses
ISBN 0-689-50499-3   LC 89-38031

This book "contains 44 short comic verses about mischievous children. As in the previous collection, Watts has contributed 16 black-and-white drawings that highlight the actions in the verse." SLJ

"For children who think poetry too sweet and sentimental, Kennedy's acerbic wit is the perfect antidote to their preconceptions." Booklist

Ghastlies, goops & pincushions: nonsense verse; drawings by Ron Barrett. Margaret K. McElderry Bks. 1989 56p il $13.95 (3-6)

811

1. Nonsense verses
ISBN 0-689-50477-2   LC 88-28663

"A diverse collection of short, amusing poems, Kennedy's . . . book takes imagination in many directions. Children will savor his high-flying nonsense and his deliciously malicious wit. . . . Barrett's black-and-white drawings, appearing on nearly every other page, underscore the humor with their lively, exaggerated interpretation of the poetry. A fine choice for children who like their poetry comical, and their comedy droll." Booklist

The kite that braved old Orchard Beach; year-round poems for young people; illustrations by Marian Young. Margaret K. McElderry Bks. 1991 85p il $12.95 (3-6)

811

ISBN 0-689-50507-8   LC 90-20100

A collection of poems, grouped in such categories as "Growing & Dreaming," "Family," "Not So Ordinary Things," and "Birds, Beasts & Fish"

"A fine collection in which there is a variety of mood, tone, theme, rhythm, and purpose, and one that's great fun to read out loud. . . . Young's gentle, realistic black-and-white illustrations introduce each new section of the book." SLJ

Kuskin, Karla

Any me I want to be: poems. Harper & Row 1972 unp il lib bdg $12.89 (k-3)

811

ISBN 0-06-023616-7

Illustrated by the author

These thirty poems "do not describe: instead, the poet has tried—and, with refreshing, edged but gentle humor and not an ounce of condescension, succeeded—'to get inside each subject and briefly be it.' . . . The subjects—and moods and pacing, too—range from a mirror to the moon." Saturday Rev

City noise; illustrated by Renée Flower. HarperCollins Pubs. 1994 unp il $15; lib bdg $14.89 (k-3) **811**

1. City life—Poetry 2. Noise—Poetry

ISBN 0-06-021076-1; 0-06-021077-X (lib bdg)

LC 91-44213

In this poem an old tin can becomes an urban conch shell when, held against a child's ear, it reveals the sounds of a bustling city

"An exuberant explosion of colors and shapes illustrates this rhyming, energetic poem. . . . Purples, reds, golds, and greens dominate the (mainly) single-page, pop-art cartoons." SLJ

Dogs & dragons, trees & dreams: a collection of poems. Harper & Row 1980 85p il lib bdg $12.89; pa $4.95 (2-4) **811**

ISBN 0-06-023544-6; 0-06-446122-X (pa)

A representative collection of Karla Kuskin's poetry with introductory notes on poetry writing and appreciation

"Karla Kuskin's work has imagination and verve, but her diction is not always impeccable; by her own admission, her poems are 'relaxed.' But she exhorts adults to read poetry to children and to encourage them to read and to write." Horn Book

Near the window tree: poems and notes. Harper & Row 1975 63p il lib bdg $14.89 (2-4) **811**

ISBN 0-06-023540-3

"An Ursula Nordstrom book"

Thirty-two poems with notes explaining some of the author's thoughts while writing them

"Not only can one enjoy the poetry, but the drawings and the accompanying notes give a sense of conversing with the author and understanding what goes on before, during, and after a poem. This combination is very useful to a classroom teacher who is interested in stirring children to write." Read Teach

Patchwork island; illustrated by Petra Mathers. HarperCollins Pubs. 1994 unp il $15; lib bdg $14.89 (k-3) **811**

1. Quilts—Poetry

ISBN 0-06-021242-X; 0-06-021284-5 (lib bdg)

LC 92-10344

This story-poem "relates how a mother uses pieces of colored cloth to create a patchwork quilt. When finished, the quilt is used as an island for the baby to play upon or as a cover to keep the infant comfortable. Mathers's use of fresh, clear colors adds to the peaceful aura of the book." Horn Book Guide

Soap soup and other verses. HarperCollins Pubs. 1992 63p il $14.95; lib bdg $14.89; pa $3.50 (k-2) **811**

ISBN 0-06-023571-3; 0-06-023572-1 (lib bdg); 0-06-444174-1 (pa) LC 91-22947

"A Charlotte Zolotow book. An I can read book"

A collection of poems about discovering the world

The author "uses short words and simple reversals that are both surprising and fun to read aloud. . . . The many watercolor illustrations are closely cued to the poems, giving a figurative expression to the verbal imagery that will be helpful to beginning readers. . . . With most rhymes providing some version of a poetic punchline at the end, struggling decoders will quickly learn that reading provides its own rewards." Bull Cent Child Books

Lawrence, Jacob

Harriet and the Promised Land. Simon & Schuster Bks. for Young Readers 1993 unp il $15 **811**

1. Tubman, Harriet, 1815?-1913—Poetry 2. Underground railroad—Poetry

ISBN 0-671-86673-7 LC 92-33740

A newly illustrated edition of the title first published 1968 by Windmill Books

"Simple rhymes tell the story of Harriet Tubman, the slave who led many of her people North to freedom." Adventuring with Books

"The strength of this volume is in the forceful, stylized paintings by the famous black artist, which capture the degradation of slavery." Brooklyn. Art Books for Child

Lee, Dennis, 1939-

The ice cream store; poems by Dennis Lee; pictures by David McPhail. Scholastic 1992 unp il $14.95 (k-3) **811**

ISBN 0-590-45861-2 LC 91-41641

"This collection begins with a celebration of the diversity of children . . . and the entries range from engaging character portraits to descriptions of feelings and whimsical wordplay. McPhail's lively watercolors underscore the joy in each selection." SLJ

Lessac, Frané

Caribbean canvas. Wordsong 1994 unp il $15.95 **811**

1. Poetry—Collections 2. Caribbean region in art

ISBN 1-56397-390-1 LC 93-61864

A reissue of the title first published 1987 in the United Kingdom; first United States edition published 1989 by Lippincott

"This is a collection of Lessac's paintings of island life in Antigua, Barbados, Grenada, St. Kitts, Nevis, Redonda, and the Grenadines. [It also contains] West Indian proverbs and poems from a dozen poets, including Edward Brathwaite, A. L. Hendricks, and Evan Jones." Publisher's note

"The poems and proverbs included seem almost an afterthought to the striking illustrations, which, through brown faces, neon colors, and assorted scenes of buildings, beaches, and people, suggest both the joy and the harsher realities of tropical life." Booklist

Levy, Constance, 1931-

A tree place and other poems; illustrated by Robert Sabuda. Margaret K. McElderry Bks. 1994 40p il $12.95 (3-5) **811**

1. Nature—Poetry
ISBN 0-689-50599-X LC 93-20586

A collection of forty poems about nature and the outdoor world

"Accessible to the most tentative readers, the forty poems in this collection contain delicately nuanced insights into nature, childlike cadences and simplicity of language, and an unaffected tenderness." Horn Book Guide

Lewis, Claudia Louise, 1907-

Up in the mountains, and other poems of long ago; by Claudia Lewis; pictures by Joel Fontaine. HarperCollins Pubs. 1991 55p il $13.95; lib bdg $13.89 (3-5) **811**

1. Family life—Poetry
ISBN 0-06-023810-0; 0-06-023812-7 (lib bdg)
LC 90-4439

"A Charlotte Zolotow book"

A collection of poems depicting the life of a young girl in turn-of-the-century America

"The poems are full of honest feelings and vivid impressions of a sensitive girl who recognized richness, mystery, and joy in her life. Joel Fontaine's soft charcoal drawings reflect both the flavor of the times and the spirit of the poems." Horn Book

Lewis, J. Patrick

Black swan/white crow; illustrated by Chris Manson. Atheneum Bks. for Young Readers 1995 unp $14 **811**

1. Nature—Poetry 2. Haiku
ISBN 0-689-31899-5 LC 94-34984

"With one short verse on each left-hand page and a woodcut print on the right, this attractive volume features 13 poems written in a form of haiku. Noting in his introduction that 'originally, this short poem lived by strict rules' of 17 syllables, three lines, and a word indicating a season, Lewis relaxes the strictures on syllables and looks to all of nature for his subjects." Booklist

Earth verses and water rhymes; illustrated by Robert Sabuda. Atheneum Pubs. 1991 32p il $13.95 (3-5) **811**

1. Nature poetry
ISBN 0-689-31693-3 LC 90-40709

A collection of poems celebrating the natural world

"Enhancing the verses are Sabuda's lovely linoleum-cut prints in softly colorful earth tones." Booklist

The fat-cats at sea; illustrated by Victoria Chess. Knopf 1994 34p il $15 **811**

1. Cats—Poetry 2. Nonsense verses
ISBN 0-679-82639-4 LC 91-31296

"An Apple Soup book"

"Twelve nonsense poems tell of a mission undertaken by a group of seaworthy cats. Commissioned by the Queen of Catmandoo, they set off for distant shores on their ship, *The Frisky Dog*, in search of sticky-buns. . . . Appropriately ludicrous, full-color illustrations of the felines and their misdeeds accompany this nonsensical tale of misadventure." SLJ

A hippopotamusn't and other animal verses; pictures by Victoria Chess. Dial Bks. for Young Readers 1990 unp il $12.95; lib bdg $12.89 **811**

1. Animals—Poetry 2. Humorous poetry
ISBN 0-8037-0518-2; 0-8037-0519-0 (lib bdg)
LC 87-24579

Also available in paperback from Puffin Bks.

This is a collection of light verse that "concentrates on an intriguing selection of birds and beasts. Varied poetic forms include, among others, lively quatrains, couplets, and limericks as well as a charming haiku. . . . The tone is light; the effect genuinely humorous rather than merely funny—a mood complemented by Victoria Chess's colorful, expressive, and at times oh-so-subtly wicked illustrations. Her delicate, agile use of line underscores the quick wit of the poet to perfection." Horn Book

Lindbergh, Reeve

Johnny Appleseed; a poem; paintings by Kathy Jakobsen. Little, Brown 1990 unp il $15.95; pa $5.95 (k-3) **811**

1. Appleseed, Johnny, 1774-1845—Poetry 2. Frontier and pioneer life—Poetry
ISBN 0-316-52618-5; 0-316-52634-7 (pa)
LC 89-35192

"Joy Street books"

Rhymed text and illustrations relate the life of John Chapman, whose distribution of appleseeds and trees across the Midwest made him a legend and left a legacy still enjoyed today

"The folk art paintings add a dimension that enhances the lyrical, moving poem. Together they combine to capture daily pioneer life and the legend." Child Book Rev Serv

View from the air; Charles Lindbergh's earth and sky; photographs by Richard Brown. Viking 1992 31p il $15 **811**

ISBN 0-670-84660-0 LC 92-4062

"A lyrical memory poem by Reeve Lindbergh, dedicated to her father, Charles Lindbergh, accompanies this photographic journey over the New England landscape. His love for the Earth and concern for human impact on it is captured by the spectacular photographs and evocative language. The vision and commitment of this early environmentalist is aptly documented in a careful blending of word and image." Sci Child

Little, Jean, 1932-

Hey world, here I am! illustrations by Sue Truesdell. Harper & Row 1989 88p il lib bdg $13.89; pa $3.95 (4-6) **811**

ISBN 0-06-024006-7 (lib bdg); 0-06-440384-X (pa)
LC 88-10987

Text first published 1986 in Canada

A collection of poems and brief vignettes from the perspective of a girl named Kate Bloomfield, reflecting her views on friendship, school, family life, and the world

"Engaging and often humorous, the vignettes are short enough to capture even the most reluctant reader yet deep enough to make the most sophisticated think. . . . Truesdell's gray line-and-wash illustrations are a fine, funny touch." Booklist

Livingston, Myra Cohn

Birthday poems; illustrated by Margot Tomes. Holiday House 1989 32p il lib bdg $13.95 **811**

1. Birthdays—Poetry
ISBN 0-8234-0783-7 LC 89-2114

"In this collection of poems centered around the festive theme of birthdays, there are games, good things to eat, prizes, and lots of presents. But best of all are Margot Tomes's illustrations of the variety of children who enjoy them. Humorous touches, such as the stuffed monsters who leer out at the reader in 'Pinning the Tail on the Donkey.' make this a special treat." Horn Book

Celebrations; Myra Cohn Livingston, poet; Leonard Everett Fisher, painter. Holiday House 1985 unp il lib bdg $15.95; pa $5.95 **811**

1. Holidays—Poetry
ISBN 0-8234-0550-8 (lib bdg); 0-8234-0654-7 (pa) LC 84-19216

"Sixteen short, mainly rhymed verses celebrate major holidays beginning with New Year's and ending with Christmas. A final page recalls that special event, 'birthday.' The book exhibits a fine variety of moods; all the poems would work with the intended audience. . . . Visually dramatic, the illustrations pack a punch. All but three of the poems appear on double-page spreads with text on one side, the painting encompassing both. In addition, the large page size, lack of margins, brilliant colors and surprising compositions all add a great sense of excitement." SLJ

A circle of seasons; Myra Cohn Livingston, poet; Leonard Everett Fisher, painter. Holiday House 1982 unp il lib bdg $15.95; pa $5.95 **811**

1. Seasons—Poetry
ISBN 0-8234-0452-8 (lib bdg); 0-8234-0696-3 (pa) LC 81-20305

"A cycle of 12 quatrains, each with its own brief refrain, celebrates the four seasons depicted in expressionistic oil paintings." Booklist

"The paintings are stunning, bold and stylized but with delicate details; there is variety in the brushwork and use of color, uniformity in the excellent use of space and shape to achieve effective compositions. Nice to read alone, or aloud, nice to look at." Bull Cent Child Books

Flights of fancy and other poems. Margaret K. McElderry Bks. 1994 40p il $13.95 (5 and up) **811**

ISBN 0-689-50613-9 LC 94-14476

In those forty short poems "Livingston describes sights and insights in simple, direct language, sometimes with an adult's voice and sometimes with a child's, making private observations or addressing a companion. Though the theme of flight recurs, both literally and figuratively, the selections include some post-Christmas thoughts, several 'Highway Haiku,' and tributes to Margot Tomes and Jacques D'Amboise." SLJ

I never told and other poems. Margaret K. McElderry Bks. 1992 42p $11.95 (4-6) **811**

ISBN 0-689-50544-2 LC 91-20475

"Forty-two poems, none more than a page long (and most considerably less) show a range of form (concrete poetry, haiku, cinquains, free verse, etc.) tone, and subject, but Livingston retains her usual sharp focus throughout. . . .

Kids who are bored stiff by discussions of poetic form will unknowingly savor it here, and confirmed poetry fans will revel in the variety at hand." Bull Cent Child Books

Keep on singing; a ballad of Marian Anderson; illustrated by Samuel Byrd. Holiday House 1994 unp il $15.95 (k-3) **811**

1. Anderson, Marian, 1897-1993—Poetry
ISBN 0-8234-1098-6 LC 93-46909

"In this ballad, Myra Cohn Livingston narrates the story of Marian Anderson's life, from her humble beginnings in Philadelphia in the early 1900s to her triumphant career as a world-renowned singer, despite racial barriers." Publisher's note

"The large illustrations, often based on photographs, use details sparingly and employ sweeping backgrounds to lend a feeling of significance to a scene. Adults may want to review Livingston's closing biographical notes before reading the book to children, but the ballad itself still catches the inspiring outlines of Anderson's life and makes her story accessible to a young audience." Booklist

Let freedom ring; a ballad of Martin Luther King, Jr.; illustrated by Samuel Byrd. Holiday House 1992 32p il $15.95 (k-3) **811**

1. King, Martin Luther, 1929-1968—Poetry
ISBN 0-8234-0957-0 LC 91-28245

A poetic treatment of Martin Luther King and his dream

The author's "brief text reads much like a song that features intermittent rhyme, phrases from King's speeches and the repeated refrain: 'From every mountainside, let freedom ring. Your dream is our dream, Martin Luther King.' . . . Complementing this unusual and forceful narrative style are Byrd's . . . strikingly realistic paintings, which depict actual events in King's life." Publ Wkly

Sky songs; Myra Cohn Livingston, poet; Leonard Everett Fisher, painter. Holiday House 1984 31p il lib bdg $14.95 **811**

1. Sky—Poetry
ISBN 0-8234-0502-8 LC 83-12955

"Fourteen poems consisting of three cinquains each address the heavenly bodies—the moon, stars, planets, and shooting stars—and the changing moods of the sky from dawn to sunset, through storms and smog." Horn Book

"The author and artist combine their talents to create a book that is a pleasure to see and to read. Livingston's poems . . . are honed and sensitive, while Fisher's paintings combine, in double-page spreads, vibrant colors, and effective use of space, and wonderful variation of mood in handsomely composed paintings." Bull Cent Child Books

Worlds I know and other poems; drawings by Tim Arnold. Atheneum Pubs. 1985 57p il $13.95 (3-5) **811**

ISBN 0-689-50332-6 LC 85-7344

A Margaret K. McElderry book

A collection of poems reflecting special feelings and events of childhood, including a toboggan ride, a Christmas play, and the love of special objects

The text is "highlighted by Arnold's small, delicate black-and-white drawings. The poems vividly evoke toboggan rides, mosquitos, strange and wonderful relatives, miracles observed and long remembered disappointments." SLJ

Lobel, Arnold

The book of pigericks: pig limericks. Harper & Row 1983 48p il lib bdg $14.89; pa $5.95 (1-3)   **811**

1. Pigs—Poetry 2. Limericks
ISBN 0-06-023983-2 (lib bdg); 0-06-443163-0 (pa)
LC 82-47730

"The heroes and heroines of these rhymes—pictured in soft, subtle colors with affectionate humor and lyric expressiveness—are for the most part middle class, middle aged lady and gentleman pigs in elaborate 19th-century attire. . . . Limerick lovers expect exuberance, inventiveness, literary lunacy—in short, the unexpected. And it is plentiful here." N Y Times Book Rev

Whiskers & rhymes; written and illustrated by Arnold Lobel. Greenwillow Bks. 1985 48p il $13; lib bdg $12.88; pa $4.95 (1-3)   **811**

1. Humorous poetry 2. Nursery rhymes
ISBN 0-688-03835-2; 0-688-03836-0 (lib bdg); 0-688-08291-2 (pa)   LC 83-25424

These poems are "lilting, brief, comic, often nonsensical, occasionally related to a Mother Goose rhyme. . . . They have that fun-to-say/easy-to-memorize quality. . . . There are clever pictures, softly tinted and drawn with panache, on every page, and the layout of illustrations and poems on the pages has been done to make both communications maximally effective." Bull Cent Child Books

Longfellow, Henry Wadsworth, 1807-1882

Hiawatha; pictures by Susan Jeffers. Dial Bks. for Young Readers 1983 unp il $14.95; lib bdg $14.89   **811**

1. Indians of North America—Poetry 2. Indians of North America—Legends
ISBN 0-8037-0013-X; 0-8037-0014-8 (lib bdg)
LC 83-7225

Also available Spanish language edition
Verses excerpted from the poem first published 1855 with title: Song of Hiawatha

"Jeffers has captured the essence of this brief section from the classic poem. . . . The pale tints of the pictures are in complete harmony with nature and with the text and show in detail how Hiawatha might have seen his world. A fine first exposure to the poem for children and a beautiful artistic experience." SLJ

Paul Revere's ride   **811**

1. Revere, Paul, 1735-1818—Poetry 2. Lexington (Mass.), Battle of, 1775—Poetry
Also available Spanish language edition
Some editions are:
Dutton $15.99 Illustrated by Ted Rand (ISBN 0-525-44610-9)
Greenwillow Bks. $14.95; lib bdg $14.88 Illustrated by Nancy Winslow Parker (ISBN 0-688-04014-4; 0-688-04015-2)

The famous narrative poem recreating Paul Revere's midnight ride in 1775 to warn the people of the Boston countryside that the British were coming

"Nancy Winslow Parker's rendering . . . both delights and instructs young and older readers alike. In addition to her simple and charming drawings, she includes an informative note on the setting, a clear map of 1775 Boston, and a section defining difficult words and terms." Child Book Rev Serv

"Rand's illustrations . . . are impressionistic in the use of color and light, yet realistic in historical interpretation. . . . The wide double-page spreads have a panoramic vision and a dramatic impetus that make this the version of choice for reading aloud." Booklist

McCord, David Thompson Watson, 1897-1994

All day long: fifty rhymes of the never was and always is; by David McCord; drawings by Henry B. Kane. Little, Brown 1966 104p il hardcover o.p. paperback available $6.95 (4-6)   **811**

ISBN 0-316-55532-0 (pa)   LC 66-17688
Poems about the haunting delights, surprises and wit of childhood

"The topics are simple but intriguing, the writing has rhythm, humor, and imaginative zest; the black and white illustrations are attractive, many of them also humorous." Bull Cent Child Books

One at a time; his collected poems for the young; with full subject index as well as an index of first lines; [by] David McCord; with illustrations by Henry B. Kane. Little, Brown 1977 494p il $18.95 (4-6)   **811**

ISBN 0-316-55516-9   LC 77-21792
A collection of poems previously published in All day long and Take sky (each entered separately) and in Away and ago (1975); Far and few (1952); and For me to say (1970)

"This one-volume edition, with a short introduction by the poet . . . is likely to be most useful to teachers and school resource persons; children's collections that already hold the five individual titles should find those sufficient for use by young readers." SLJ

Speak up: more rhymes of the never was and always is; by David McCord; illustrated by Marc Simont. Little, Brown 1980 68p il $13.95 (4-6)   **811**

ISBN 0-316-55517-7   LC 80-15260
"The 50 poems, about all sorts of things—butterflies, windshield wipers, long words, joggers, worms—are uneven in quality. Some catch McCord's wit, playfulness and disciplined shaping. Others are merely cute or clever; a few are flat and uninspired. Its pleasant, unintimidating format and the humorous sketches make it attractive." SLJ

Take sky: more rhymes of the never was and always is; by David McCord; drawings by Henry B. Kane. Little, Brown 1962 107p il $12.95 (4-6)   **811**

ISBN 0-316-55509-6   LC 62-12392
A collection of forty-eight humorous poems on various subjects ranging in form from short verses to longer narrative poetry

"Diversity of imagination and humor makes a volume that bears dipping into again and again for quiet enjoyment and for reading aloud. Henry Kane's pencil drawings, make beautiful pages, with great variety in layout." Horn Book

McMillan, Bruce

One sun: a book of terse verse; written & photo-illustrated by Bruce McMillan. Holiday House 1990 unp il lib bdg $15.95; pa $5.95 (k-3)   **811**

1. Beaches—Poetry
ISBN 0-8234-0810-8; 0-8234-0951-1 (pa)
LC 89-24625

Describes a day at the beach in a series of terse verses (verses made up of two monosyllabic words that rhyme) accompanied by photographs

"There is a strong textural element; readers can practical-

McMillan, Bruce—*Continued*

ly feel the sand in their shoes. Teachers may enjoy trying out the rhyming game concepts with their students, while everyone else will simply enjoy the pleasure of a perfect sunny day at the seaside." SLJ

Merriam, Eve, 1916-1992

Bam, bam, bam; illustrated by Dan Yaccarino. Holt & Co. 1995 unp il $14.95 (k-2) **811**

ISBN 0-8050-3527-3 LC 94-20300

A Bill Martin book

In this noisy poem, a wrecking ball demolishes old houses and stores to make way for a skyscraper

"Merriam's rhymes are simple like a sledgehammer blow, with the same rhythmic swing, and Yaccarino's bulky, brightly colored workers make the process look like fun." Booklist

Blackberry ink; pictures by Hans Wilhelm. Morrow 1985 unp il $15; lib bdg $13.93; pa $4.95 (k-2) **811**

1. Humorous poetry 2. Nonsense verses
ISBN 0-688-04150-7; 0-688-04151-5 (lib bdg); 0-688-13080-1 (pa) LC 84-16633

"These 24 simple poems touch everyday objects and occurrences—elusive butterflies, seasonal happenings, favorite foods, bedtime routine, animal antics and more. . . . The smiling teddy on the cover appears throughout the pages in the midst of charming watercolor illustrations featuring delightfully devilish children and whimsical animals. Merriam's poems are great fun to read. . . . Sure to tickle small funnybones everywhere and to provide many moments of pleasure." SLJ

Chortles: new and selected wordplay poems; illustrations by Sheila Hamanaka. Morrow Junior Bks. 1989 53p il $11.95; lib bdg $11.88 (3-6) **811**

ISBN 0-688-08152-5; 0-688-08153-3 (lib bdg)
LC 88-29129

"A selection of forty-seven new and previously published verses by a popular writer that promises to delight pun and poetry lovers, young and old. . . . Humorous pencil drawings appropriately reflect the spirit of the collection." Horn Book

Fresh paint; new poems by Eve Merriam; woodcuts by David Frampton. Macmillan 1986 unp il $13.95 (4 and up) **811**

ISBN 0-02-766860-6 LC 85-23742

Forty-five poems on subjects ranging from the squat mushroom to the new moon

"The variety of rhyming patterns, the freshness of vision, and the deceptive ease with which image and idea are summoned up contribute a liveliness, sophistication, and vitality often missing in poetry for the young. The attractive black-and-white woodcuts nicely complement the quirky and playful quality of the poetry itself." Horn Book

Halloween A B C; illustrations by Lane Smith. Macmillan 1987 unp il $14.95 (k-2) **811**

1. Halloween—Poetry 2. Alphabet
ISBN 0-02-766870-3 LC 86-23772

"These 26 Halloween poems, one for each letter of the alphabet, are, like most of Merriam's work, imaginative, inventive, and playful. Her unusual rhythms, rhythmic

schemes, and twists of word or image are often humorous as well as seasonally spooky. . . . Smith's dark oil paintings on ecru pages match both the mood and the wit of the poems. . . . This is not a book for young children to learn the alphabet, but it is a witty, whimsical, and happily shivery book for Halloween sharing." SLJ

Higgle wiggle; happy rhymes; pictures by Hans Wilhelm. Morrow Junior Bks. 1994 unp il $15; lib bdg $14.93 (k-2) **811**

ISBN 0-688-11948-4; 0-688-11949-2 (lib bdg)
LC 92-29795

This "book of simple poetry is enriched by Merriam's skill in using a variety of rhythmic patterns that invite participation. Wilhelm has captured the spirit of the rhymes in his laughter-filled illustrations—especially the ever-present pink pig." Horn book Guide

A poem for a pickle: funnybone verses; pictures by Sheila Hamanaka. Morrow Junior Bks. 1989 unp il $12.95; lib bdg $12.88 (k-2) **811**

ISBN 0-688-08137-1, 0-688-08138-X (lib bdg)
LC 88-22047

This "collection includes 28 short, witty poems. . . . Using overlapping lines of finely shaded color, Hamanaka creates lively artwork with refreshingly varied composition and points of view. A visually appealing poetry book with lots of classroom potential." Booklist

The singing green; new and selected poems for all seasons; illustrated by Kathleen Collins Howell. Morrow Junior Bks. 1992 102p il $14 (3-6) **811**

ISBN 0-688-11025-8 LC 91-31205

An illustrated collection of poems on a variety of topics

"Celebrating the connection of the sun, the trees, and the child inside us all, this collection is a frolicking wordplay romp in the countryside. . . . Howell's warm, comforting pencil-and-wash drawings invite all to come and join the fun." Booklist

You be good and I'll be night: jump-on-the-bed poems; pictures by Karen Lee Schmidt. Morrow Junior Bks. 1988 unp il $12.95; lib bdg $12.88 (k-2) **811**

ISBN 0-688-06742-5; 0-688-06743-3 (lib bdg)
LC 87-24859

This "collection of twenty-eight poems features mostly jump-rope rhythms and chanting rhymes. . . . Each poem is accompanied with bouncy watercolor scenes, often including comically incongruous animals. . . . A few are too jingly, but on the whole this is nonsense with flair." Bull Cent Child Books

Moore, Clement Clarke, 1779-1863

The night before Christmas (k-3) **811**

1. Santa Claus—Poetry 2. Christmas—Poetry

Also available Spanish language edition

Some editions are:

Clarion Bks. $13.95 Illustrated by Wendy Watson (ISBN 0-395-53624-3)

Holiday House lib bdg $15.95; pa $6.95 Illustrated by Tomie de Paola (ISBN 0-8234-0414-5; 0-8234-0417-X)

Holt & Co. $12.95 Illustrated by Michael Hague (ISBN 0-8050-0900-0)

Houghton Mifflin $14.95 With pictures by Jessie Willcox Smith (ISBN 0-395-06952-1) Has title: 'Twas the night

Moore, Clement Clarke, 1779-1863—*Continued*

before Christmas

Knopf $12 Illustrated by Anita Lobel (ISBN 0-394-86863-3)

Knopf $14 Illustrated by Scott Gustafson (ISBN 0-394-54809-4)

North-South Bks. $16.95 Illustrated by Ted Rand (ISBN 1-55858-465-X)

Philomel Bks. $16.95 (ISBN 0-399-21614-6) An antique reproduction

Random House $15; lib bdg $15.99 Illustrated with paintings by Grandma Moses (ISBN 0-679-81526-0; 0-679-91526-5)

Random House $8.99 Illustrated by Cheryl Harness (ISBN 0-394-82698-1)

Turner Pub. (Atlanta) $19.95 Illustrated by Ruth Sanderson (ISBN 1-57036-040-5)

Text first published 1823 with title: A visit from St. Nicholas

This popular Christmas poem has been a favorite with American children ever since the author wrote it for his children in 1822. It is from this poem that we get the names for the Christmas reindeer

Morrison, Bill, 1935-

Squeeze a sneeze. Houghton Mifflin 1977 32p il lib bdg $14.95; pa $4.95 (k-3)   811

1. Nonsense verses

ISBN 0-395-25151-6 (lib bdg); 0-395-44238-9 (pa)

LC 76-62503

Illustrated by the author

The author "uses nonsense rhyming to teach creative word association as well as word enjoyment. Readers are invited to follow the author's examples of word play such as 'share a pear with a hungry bear' or 'make sure it's dark if you bark at a shark.'" SLJ

"The rhymes are nonsensical, but the illustrations make the word plays work. Young children will delight in hearing, repeating, and seeing this book. It is a book that a child would return to, time and time again." Child Book Rev Serv

Myers, Walter Dean, 1937-

Brown angels; an album of pictures and verse. HarperCollins Pubs. 1993 unp il $16; lib bdg $15.89   811

1. African Americans—Poetry

ISBN 0-06-022917-9; 0-06-022918-7 (lib bdg)

LC 92-36792

A collection of poems, accompanied by antique photographs, about African American children living around the turn of the century

"Myers has created an exquisite album. The 42 superbly sepia prints radiate intensely with the personalities of their subjects. The author's 11 original poems are in various forms and range from humorous to elegiac. The language is simple and reads aloud well." SLJ

Nash, Ogden, 1902-1971

The adventures of Isabel; pictures by James Marshall. Little, Brown 1991 unp il lib bdg $14.95; pa $4.95 (k-3)   811

1. Girls—Poetry

ISBN 0-316-59874-7 (lib bdg); 0-316-59883-6 (pa)

LC 90-13284

"Joy Street books"

The feisty Isabel defeats giants, witches, and other threatening creatures with ease

"The amusing details of the illustrations . . . add to an engaging combination of humor and reassurance." Horn Book

Custard and company: poems; selected and illustrated by Quentin Blake. Little, Brown 1980 128p il hardcover o.p. paperback available $7.95   811

1. Humorous poetry

ISBN 0-316-59855-0 (pa)   LC 79-25742

"The cartoonist-illustrator has assembled this anthology of [84 of] his favorite Nash poems and provided illustrations for each one." SLJ

"The inspired lunacy of Nash's poems is wonderfully echoed by the scratchy, flyaway line drawings." Bull Cent Child Books

The tale of Custard the Dragon; illustrated by Lynn Munsinger. Little, Brown 1995 unp il $14.95 (k-3)   811

1. Dragons—Poetry

ISBN 0-316-59880-1   LC 94-6594

Text first published 1936

In this humorous poem, Custard the cowardly dragon saves the day when a pirate threatens Belinda and her pet animals

"Munsinger does an appealing job of catching the mix of wry humor and affection that has made Ogden's whimsical poem a favorite with audiences young and old for 60 years." Booklist

O'Neill, Mary Le Duc, 1908-1990

Hailstones and halibut bones; adventures in color; newly illustrated by John Wallner. Doubleday 1989 1961 unp il $13.95; pa $6.95 (k-3)   811

1. Color—Poetry

ISBN 0-385-24484-3; 0-385-41078-6 (pa)

LC 88-484

A newly illustrated edition of the title first published 1961

Twelve poems reflect the author's feelings about various colors

"Wallner has created montages of each poem's images and colored them with various hues of the featured color. The results do complement the moods of the poems." SLJ

Oppenheim, Joanne

Have you seen trees? illustrated by Jean and Mou-sien Tseng. Scholastic 1995 unp il $14.95 (k-2)   811

1. Trees—Poetry

ISBN 0-590-46691-7   LC 94-14585

A newly illustrated edition of the title first published 1967

"Oppenheim uses a strong, simple, appealing rhythm in this poem about all kinds of trees. . . . Revolving her theme around the seasons, Oppenheim employs immediacy and repetition to describe such arboreal elements as fruit and berries, wood and bark, and birds and bugs." Booklist

"The Tsengs use small children or animals in each picture to highlight the scale of their subjects. Their watercolors capture the unique light of each season, giving every page a fresh feeling." SLJ

Pomerantz, Charlotte

Halfway to your house; pictures by
Gabrielle Vincent. Greenwillow Bks. 1993 32p
il $14; lib bdg $13.93 (k-3)   **811**

ISBN 0-688-11804-6; 0-688-11805-4 (lib bdg)
                                        LC 92-30083

A collection of short poems about animals, nature, and
home life

"Vincent's delicate watercolor illustrations of dreamy
small kids at play first appeared with a French text published in Europe. Elusive and childlike, the pictures work
well with Pomerantz's poetry, matching mood and feeling
rather than any literal images. The poems are untitled and
informal, expressing quiet, intimate moments with a physical immediacy." Booklist

If I had a paka; poems in eleven languages;
illustrated by Nancy Tafuri. Greenwillow Bks.
1993 unp il $14; lib bdg $13.93; pa $4.95 (k-3)
                                        811

ISBN 0-688-11900-X; 0-688-11901-8 (lib bdg);
0-688-12510-7 (pa)   LC 92-33088

A reissue of the title first published 1982

This "collection of 12 short poems is in English, but each
poem uses a few words from a different language." SLJ

The author "has written some charming poems. . . . The
foreign words are melodious and interesting, and they can
always be understood in the context of the poems. The illustrations by Nancy Tafuri are exquisite combinations of
design, color and feeling." N Y Times Book Rev

The Tamarindo puppy and other poems;
pictures by Byron Barton. Greenwillow Bks.
1993 31p il $14.95; lib bdg $13.93; pa $4.95
(k-3)   **811**

ISBN 0-688-11902-6; 0-688-11903-4 (lib bdg);
0-688-11514-4 (pa)

A reissue of the title first published 1980

"Illustrated with colorful drawings that have an awkward
naivete, this charming collection of poems plays with language, English and Spanish, in a variety of ways; meanings
are made clear by context or repetition in many poems,
while some are in English and use only Spanish names.
This should please and be comprehensible to those small
listeners to whom Spanish is a first language as well as to
those whose first language is English. . . . The poems are
fresh and lilting, appealingly childlike in both subject matter
and approach." Bull Cent Child Books

Prelutsky, Jack

The baby Uggs are hatching; pictures by
James Stevenson. Greenwillow Bks. 1982 32p
il $15; lib bdg $14.93; pa $3.95 (k-3)   **811**

1. Nonsense verses
ISBN 0-688-00922-0; 0-688-00923-9 (lib bdg);
0-688-09239-X (pa)   LC 81-7266

This volume contains humorous poems about imaginary
creatures with names like: Ugg, Quossible, Smasheroo, Flot-
terzott, and Grebbles

"The catchy rhythms, humorous drawings, and deliciously alarming subjects make a splendid book." Horn Book

Beneath a blue umbrella: rhymes; pictures
by Garth Williams. Greenwillow Bks. 1990
64p il lib bdg $15.95 (k-3)   **811**

1. Nonsense verses 2. Nursery rhymes
ISBN 0-688-06429-9   LC 86-19406

A collection of illustrated humorous poems in which a
hungry hippo raids a melon stand, a butterfly tickles a girl's
nose, and children frolic in a Mardi Gras parade

"Prelutsky has an unerring sense of popular appeal; these
verses bounce as rhythmically as children do on a bed or
jumping rope. They also feature plenty of reassurance and
humor, staples for chanting. Garth Williams' homey pen
drawing and luminous colors enliven each full-page illustration with a dramatic simplicity set off by spacious book design." Bull Cent Child Books

Circus; pictures by Arnold Lobel. Macmillan
1974 unp il hardcover o.p. paperback
available $4.95 (k-3)   **811**

1. Circus—Poetry
ISBN 0-689-70806-8 (pa)

Prelutsky "presents the attractions of the big top in
verses and they are made visible in Lobel's witty color pictures. . . . For children who haven't experienced the thrills
of the greatest show on earth, this book tells about the performing seals, the acrobats, sword-swallowers, fire eaters,
human cannonballs and more." Publ Wkly

The dragons are singing tonight; pictures by
Peter Sis. Greenwillow Bks. 1993 39p il $16;
lib bdg $15.93 (2-5)   **811**

1. Dragons—Poetry
ISBN 0-688-09645-X; 0-688-12511-5 (lib bdg)
                                        LC 92-29013

"Dragons are verbally and visually portrayed in this collection with wonder, whimsy, and a touch of wistfulness. .
. . The oil and gouache paintings on a gesso background
have marvelous details and unexpected bursts of humor."
SLJ

The Headless Horseman rides tonight; more
poems to trouble your sleep; illustrated by
Arnold Lobel. Greenwillow Bks. 1980 38p il
$13.95; lib bdg $13.88; pa $4.95 (2-5)
                                        811

1. Monsters—Poetry
ISBN 0-688-80273-7; 0-688-84273-9 (lib bdg);
0-688-11705-8 (pa)   LC 80-10372

"In addition to the perambulating mummy, the author
deals with, among others, a writhing specter on a misty
moor, a zombie, a sorceress, a baleful banshee . . . the
abominable snowman and a headless horseman." Horn
Book

The author's "rhymes are as lethal, lithe, and literate as
ever and Lobel wrings every atmospheric ounce out of
them." SLJ

It's Christmas; pictures by Marylin Hafner.
Greenwillow Bks. 1981 46p il $15; lib bdg
$14.93 (1-3)   **811**

1. Christmas—Poetry
ISBN 0-688-00439-3; 0-688-00440-7 (lib bdg)
                                        LC 81-1100

Also available in paperback from Scholastic

"A Greenwillow read-alone book"

"The poems cover subjects of interest to children—
making a Christmas list, performing in the school assembly,
cutting a Christmas tree . . . [and dealing] with the disappointments that sometimes occur: being sick on Christmas,
getting underwear as a gift and having a new sled but no
snow. Marilyn Hafner's cartoonlike drawings add to the
fun." SLJ

Prelutsky, Jack—*Continued*

It's Halloween; pictures by Marylin Hafner. Greenwillow Bks. 1977 56p il $13.95; lib bdg $13.88 (1-3)   **811**

1. Halloween—Poetry

ISBN 0-688-80102-1; 0-688-84102-3 (lib bdg)

LC 77-2141

"A Greenwillow read-alone book"

"A gathering of thirteen light-hearted verses celebrates for beginning readers the deliciously frightening aspects of Halloween. Although a few seem constrained by the format, the majority demonstrate the inventive use of words and agile rhythms characteristic of the poet's style. . . . The illustrations, most of them in four colors, highlight the contrast between the real and the imagined, thus providing an appropriate visual extension for the simple text." Horn Book

It's snowing! It's snowing! pictures by Jeanne Titherington. Greenwillow Bks. 1984 47p il $12.95 (1-3)   **811**

1. Winter—Poetry 2. Snow—Poetry

ISBN 0-688-01512-3   LC 83-16583

"Soft gray-and-white drawings washed with blue complement seventeen poems that celebrate a child's delight in snow. From 'One Last Little Leaf' to 'The Snowman's Lament' the course of a season is marked by the natural phenomena and human activities of winter. . . . An easy-to-read format and large print suit the facility of the rhyme and accessibility of the imagery. Where more challenging vocabulary is introduced, contextual clues help the beginning reader." Horn Book

It's Thanksgiving; pictures by Marylin Hafner. Greenwillow Bks. 1982 47p il $14; lib bdg $13.93 (1-3)   **811**

1. Thanksgiving Day—Poetry

ISBN 0-688-00441-5; 0-688-00442-3 (lib bdg)

LC 81-1929

Also available in paperback from Scholastic

"A Greenwillow read-alone book"

This "collection of poems about Thanksgiving has rhyme, rhythm, and humor as well as a variety of topics: helping Grandma with the meal, watching Daddy watch a football game, seeing a Thanksgiving Day parade, working on school projects, not being able to eat any of the holiday treats because of braces, and the Pilgrim Thanksgiving. The poems are illustrated by brisk, often comic drawings, line and wash. This isn't great poetry, but it has a bouncy quality that's appealing." Bull Cent Child Books

It's Valentine's Day; pictures by Yossi Abolafia. Greenwillow Bks. 1983 47p il $15; lib bdg $14.93; pa $4.95 (1-3)   **811**

1. Valentine's Day—Poetry

ISBN 0-688-02311-8; 0-688-02312-6 (lib bdg); 0-688-14652-X (pa)   LC 83-1449

"A Greenwillow read-alone book"

"The 14 poems here range from the genuine joy of 'It's Valentine's Day' . . . to the giddy goofiness of 'I love you more than applesauce' or 'Jelly Jill loves Weasel Will'. . . .The rhymes are generally simple but clever and the line drawings in red and blue, with their expressive faces and explanatory vignettes, add tremendously to the enjoyment of the poetry." SLJ

My parents think I'm sleeping: poems; pictures by Yossi Abolafia. Greenwillow Bks. 1985 47p il $16; lib bdg $15.93; pa $4.95 (2-4)   **811**

1. Sleep—Poetry

ISBN 0-688-04018-7; 0-688-04019-5 (lib bdg); 0-688-14028-9 (pa)   LC 84-13640

This is a collection of humorous poems about bedtime

"Sometimes humorous, sometimes thoughtfully quiet, the poems reflect an interesting range of reactions to the night. . . . Illustrations, done for the most part in appropriate shades of gray and blue with occasional glints of yellow light, extend the nuances of the poetry. While some of the selections may seem a bit limper than the poet's usual crisp, fresh fare, the book will probably still find an audience with Prelutsky fans." Horn Book

The new kid on the block: poems; drawings by James Stevenson. Greenwillow Bks. 1984 159p il $17.95; lib bdg $15.88 (3-6)   **811**

1. Humorous poetry

ISBN 0-688-02271-5; 0-688-02272-3 (lib bdg)

LC 83-20621

"Most of the 100-plus poems here are mini-jokes, word-play, and character sketches . . . with liberal doses of monsters and meanies as well as common, garden-variety child mischief." Booklist

"The author's rollicking, silly poems bounce and romp with fun; Stevenson's cartoon-like sketches capture the hilarity with equal skill. A book everyone will enjoy dipping into." Child Book Rev Serv

Nightmares: poems to trouble your sleep; illustrated by Arnold Lobel. Greenwillow Bks. 1976 38p il $14; lib bdg $13.93; pa $4.95 (2-5)   **811**

1. Monsters—Poetry

ISBN 0-688-80053-X; 0-688-84053-1 (lib bdg); 0-688-04589-8 (pa)   LC 76-4820

This "collection of poems is calculated to evoke icy apprehension, and the poems about wizards, bogeymen, ghouls, ogres (well, one poem apiece to each or to others of their ilk) are exaggerated just enough to bring simultaneous grins and shudders. Prelutsky uses words with relish and his rhyme and rhythm are, as usual, deft. Lobel's illustrations are equally adroit, macabre yet elegant." Bull Cent Child Books

The queen of Eene; pictures by Victoria Chess. Greenwillow Bks. 1978 32p il lib bdg $14.88 (k-3)   **811**

1. Nonsense verses

ISBN 0-688-84144-9   LC 77-17311

"Fourteen original poems are presented in . . . picture-book format. Humorous, nonsensical, the verses mostly concern foolish characters like 'The Pancake Collector' who explains, 'I have pancakes in most of my pockets,/and concealed in the linings of suits./There are tiny ones stuffed in my mittens/and larger ones packed in my boots.' . . . Most of the poems are given a double-page spread and all are accompanied by detailed, appropriately droll black-and-white illustrations. It's an attractive package, and most children will enjoy the contents whether they are reading or listening." SLJ

Ride a purple pelican; pictures by Garth Williams. Greenwillow Bks. 1986 64p il $17.95 (k-3)   **811**

1. Nonsense verses 2. Nursery rhymes

ISBN 0-688-04031-4   LC 84-6024

Prelutsky, Jack—*Continued*

A collection of short nonsense verses and nursery rhymes
"Prelutsky has caught the rhythm and spirit of nursery rhymes in 29 short poems about drum-beating bunnies, bullfrogs on parade, Chicago winds, giant sequoias and other wondrous things. Many of these easy-to-remember poems are filled with delicious sounding American and Canadian place names. Garth Williams' full-color, full-page illustrations are good complements to the poems. Highly recommended." Child Book Rev Serv

Rolling Harvey down the hill; illustrated by Victoria Chess. Greenwillow Bks. 1980 30p il $14.95; lib bdg $12.88; pa $4.95 (1-3)

811

1. Friendship—Poetry 2. Humorous poetry
ISBN 0-688-80258-3; 0-688-84258-5 (lib bdg); 0-688-12270-1 (pa)   LC 79-18236
"Fifteen contemporary poems describe the mischievous antics of five apartment-house buddies." Child Book Rev Serv
"Chess' puckish black-and-white scenes cash in on all the text's mischief. The motley cast is suitably disheveled and just bizarre enough in expression. This is fresh, funny, and quite in tune with scampish concerns." Booklist

The sheriff of Rottenshot: poems; pictures by Victoria Chess. Greenwillow Bks. 1982 32p il $12.95; lib bdg $14.93; pa $4.95 (2-5)

811

1. Nonsense verses
ISBN 0-688-00205-6; 0-688-00198-X (lib bdg); 0-688-13635-4 (pa)   LC 81-6420
"Macabre art with a silver lining, the often-gruesome Chess drawings have robust humor of their own, for almost every lumpish human or lurking beast has either enough exaggeration or enough of a twinkle to be funny. Thus the illustrations are admirably suited to the often ghoulish and very funny poems that Prelutsky writes with a strong use of meter and some entertaining wordplay." Bull Cent Child Books

The snopp on the sidewalk, and other poems; pictures by Byron Barton. Greenwillow Bks. 1977 unp il lib bdg $15.93 (k-4)   811

1. Nonsense verses
ISBN 0-688-84084-1   LC 76-46323
Twelve poems about snopps, grobbles, flonsters, and other fantastic creatures
"Employing alliteration, metaphor, repetition, and portmanteau words within the framework of traditional rhymed verse forms, the poet has conjured into reality a menagerie of imaginary beings. . . . Despite the pseudomacabre situations, the tone of the twelve poems is gleefully ghoulish without being gruesome, a mood complemented by the modulating grays and curvilinear patterns of the stylized, cartoonlike illustrations. A delectably bizarre gathering of marvelously outrageous nonsense." Horn Book

Something big has been here; drawings by James Stevenson. Greenwillow Bks. 1990 160p il $17.95 (3-5)   811

1. Humorous poetry
ISBN 0-688-06434-5   LC 89-34773
An illustrated collection of humorous poems on a variety of topics
"Puns and verbal surprises abound. Clever use of alliteration and abundant variety in the sound and texture of words add to the pleasure. . . . Stevenson's small cartoons of snaggle-toothed animals and deadpan children extend and expand the mad humor of the poems, supporting but never overwhelming their good-natured fun. A fine prescription against the blues at any time of year." Horn Book

Tyrannosaurus was a beast; illustrated by Arnold Lobel. Greenwillow Bks. 1988 31p il $13.95; lib bdg $13.88; pa $4.95 (2-5)

811

1. Dinosaurs—Poetry
ISBN 0-688-06442-6; 0-688-06443-4 (lib bdg); 0-688-11569-1 (pa)   LC 87-25131
A collection of humorous poems about dinosaurs
"Fourteen dinosaurs meet their match in this outstanding author/illustrator team. While Prelutsky's short, pithy, often witty verses sum up their essential characters, Lobel's line and watercolor portraits bring the beasts to life, enormous yet endearingly vulnerable." Booklist

Ryder, Joanne

Under your feet; illustrated by Dennis Nolan. Four Winds Press 1990 unp il $14.95 (k-3)   811

1. Nature poetry 2. Seasons—Poetry
ISBN 0-02-777955-6   LC 89-33897
"Following a boy through the seasons, . . . [these poems] tell of the animals beneath his feet: moles race along their tunnels below the ground, fish dart though the lake as he swims, worms huddle together in deep winter burrows, a cricket beneath a stone feels the ground shake as the boy passes." Booklist
"The tone is reverent and hushed, the illustrations splendidly vibrant and accurate. . . . Both language and art offer an intriguing look at the world under children's feet." Publ Wkly

Sandburg, Carl, 1878-1967

Arithmetic; illustrated as an anamorphic adventure by Ted Rand. Harcourt Brace Jovanovich 1993 unp il $15.95 (2-5)   811

1. Arithmetic—Poetry
ISBN 0-15-203865-5   LC 92-5291
Poem first published 1933
A poem about numbers and their characteristics. Features anamorphic, or distorted, drawings which can be restored to normal by viewing from a particular angle or by viewing the image's reflection in the Mylar cone provided with the book
"The drawing is impeccable and the odd perceptual premise gives the book an exuberant zing." Bull Cent Child Books

Carl Sandburg; edited by Frances Schoonmaker Bolin; illustrated by Steve Arcella. Sterling 1995 48p il (Poetry for young people) $14.95 (4 and up)   811

ISBN 0-8069-0818-1   LC 94-30777
"A Magnolia Editions book"
"The 33 poems in *Sandburg* vary in length and theme, but most are the staples of anthologies, e.g., 'Fog,' 'Arithmetic,' and 'We Must Be Polite.' The surrealistic illustrations, which appear to be rendered in pastels, are appealing; the soft edges and warm tones work well with Sandburg's imagery." SLJ

Sandburg, Carl, 1878-1967—*Continued*

Rainbows are made: poems; selected by Lee Bennett Hopkins; wood engravings by Fritz Eichenberg. Harcourt Brace Jovanovich 1982 81p il $17.95; pa $8.95 (5 and up) **811**

ISBN 0-15-265480-1; 0-15-265481-X (pa)

LC 82-47934

This book "offers some 70 short poems by Carl Sandburg and groups them by theme: the seasons, the sea, the imaginative mind, etc. Each theme explores different aspects of poetic creativity as envisioned by Sandburg and illustrated by Fritz Eichenberg's wood engravings. Eichenberg has truly captured the power and vigorousness of Sandburg's verse." SLJ

Schertle, Alice, 1941-

Advice for a frog and other poems; illustrated by Norman Green. Lothrop, Lee & Shepard Bks. 1995 unp il $16; lib bdg $15.93 **811**

1. Animals—Poetry
ISBN 0-688-13486-6; 0-688-13487-4 (lib bdg)

LC 94-33714

"Each of the 14 poems concerns an animal, usually an exotic or endangered one such as the black rhino, cheetah, frilled lizard, or harpy eagle. Schertle delights in playing with language; though not long, the book is extraordinarily varied and filled with linguistic surprise. . . . Green's paintings are double-page spreads with blue, gold, rose, lavender, and green predominating. Imaginative and playful, his pictures capture the essence of each creature." SLJ

How now, brown cow? poems by Alice Schertle; paintings by Amanda Schaffer. Browndeer Press 1994 unp il lib bdg $14.95 **811**

1. Cattle—Poetry
ISBN 0-15-276648-0

LC 93-24052

This "collection of poems about cows abounds with tongue-in-cheek spoofs, verbal acrobatics and lyrical songs that are aptly illustrated by debut artist Schaffer's wry cast of brown and purple cows." Publ Wkly

Scieszka, Jon, 1954-

The book that Jack wrote; illustrated by Daniel Adel. Viking 1994 unp $14.99 (2-4) **811**

1. Nursery rhymes
ISBN 0-670-84330-X

LC 94-10932

"An updated version of 'This Is the House That Jack Built,' this cumulative tale tells of a blind rat who falls into a picture in the book that Jack wrote, thus setting off a chain of events in which the players are done in one by one until nothing is left but the book itself. . . . The dark tones of Adel's full-page oil paintings are a fine match for the irreverent mood of the piece." SLJ

Service, Robert W. (Robert William), 1874-1958

The cremation of Sam McGee; paintings by Ted Harrison; introduction by Pierre Berton. Greenwillow Bks. 1987 c1986 unp il $16 (4 and up) **811**

1. Yukon Territory—Poetry
ISBN 0-688-06903-7

LC 86-14971

Also available in paperback from Hancock House

Text first published 1907. This newly illustrated edition first published 1986 in Canada

"In the tradition of tall tales, the story of Sam McGee is told here in Service's original rollicking verses. Pledged to cremate his friend Sam, the narrator tells how, after carting the frozen body for miles, he stuffs it into a ship's roaring furnace. To his surprise, when he later opens the door he discovers Sam alive . . . and warm for the first time 'since he left Tennessee.'" Publ Wkly

"A fine example of a 20th-Century regional ballad, one that tells of the profound cold of the Yukon and how it affected the lives of two gold miners." SLJ

The shooting of Dan McGrew; paintings by Ted Harrison. Godine 1988 unp il $14.95 (4 and up) **811**

1. Yukon Territory—Poetry
ISBN 0-87923-748-1

LC 88-6124

Text first published 1907

A narrative poem set in the Yukon describing the shootout in a saloon between a trapper and the man who stole his girl

"While the action of the poem is intense and demanding, the painterly illustrations by Harrison are overwhelmingly powerful; they seem to take on a life of their own, drawing readers' attentions away from the text and toward the surrealistic interpretation of events. . . . Harrison creates a pulsating world of hate and destruction; it's a fascinating interpretation of a well-known poem." Publ Wkly

Siebert, Diane

Mojave; paintings by Wendell Minor. Crowell 1988 unp il lib bdg $14.89; pa $4.95 (1-3) **811**

1. Deserts—Poetry
ISBN 0-690-04569-7 (lib bdg); 0-06-443283-1 (pa)

LC 86-24329

"Paintings of the desert and its creatures illustrate a first-person poem in the voice of the Mojave." Bull Cent Child Books

"Regular rhythms and clever rhymes propel us through space and the vagaries of time. Wendell Minor's artistic vision at times parallels that of Georgia O'Keeffe. . . . [This is] a beautifully orchestrated book of illustrated poems." Christ Sci Monit

Sierra; paintings by Wendell Minor. HarperCollins Pubs. 1991 unp il $16; lib bdg $15.89; pa $4.95 (1-3) **811**

1. Sierra Nevada Mountains—Poetry
ISBN 0-06-021639-5; 0-06-021640-9 (lib bdg); 0-06-443441-9 (pa)

LC 90-30522

"In Siebert's rhymed couplets, a mountain speaks of its birth and growth, of the forests and animals it shelters, and of the cycle of life and death it supports." Booklist

"The story of the Sierras is told in lyrical rhymes that are both wonderful to read and full of information. The vivid and beautiful pictures that accompany each page give one the feeling of being in the midst of these delightful mountains." Sci Books Films

Silverstein, Shel

A light in the attic. Harper & Row 1981 167p il $15.95; lib bdg $15.89 **811**

1. Humorous poetry 2. Nonsense verses
ISBN 0-06-025673-7; 0-06-025674-5 (lib bdg)

LC 80-8453

Silverstein, Shel—*Continued*

This collection of more than one hundred poems "will delight lovers of Silverstein's raucous, rollicking verse and his often tender, whimsical, philosophical advice. . . . The poems are tuned in to kids' most hidden feelings, dark wishes and enjoyment of the silly. . . . The witty line drawings are a full half of the treat of this wholly satisfying anthology by the modern successor to Edward Lear and Hilaire Belloc." SLJ

Where the sidewalk ends; the poems & drawings of Shel Silverstein. Harper & Row 1974 166p il $15.95; lib bdg $15.89   **811**

1. Humorous poetry 2. Nonsense verses

ISBN 0-06-025667-2; 0-06-025668-0 (lib bdg)

"There are skillful, sometimes grotesque line drawings with each of the 127 poems, which run in length from a few lines to a couple of pages. The poems are tender, funny, sentimental, philosophical, and ridiculous in turn, and they're for all ages." Saturday Rev

Singer, Marilyn, 1948-

Family reunion; illustrated by R.W. Alley. Macmillan 1994 unp il $14.95 (k-3)   **811**

ISBN 0-02-782883-2   LC 92-40336

"Read in sequence, this collection of 14 free-verse poems tells the story of a great day at a family reunion. Read alone each selection stands on its own. Courageous, silly fun is the theme; and this gathering is full of gregarious, entertaining types. . . . Alley 's watercolor and pen illustrations help to reinforce the free-spirited mood of the day." SLJ

Sky words; illustrated by Deborah Kogan Ray. Macmillan 1994 unp il $14.95 (k-3)   **811**

1. Sky—Poetry

ISBN 0-02-782882-4   LC 92-3765

"Singer finds boundless inspiration in the sky as she creates poems about skywriting and tornadoes, about the world at twilight, about clouds and fog and monarch butterflies filling the air like orange leaves. Subtle internal and end rhyme schemes and rich imagery create a sumptuous flow of words. Reflecting the text, the illustrations vary in tone from abstract expressionism to realism." Horn Book Guide

Turtle in July; illustrated by Jerry Pinkney. Macmillan 1989 unp il $14.95; pa $4.95 (k-3)   **811**

1. Animals—Poetry

ISBN 0-02-782881-6; 0-689-71805-5 (pa)

LC 89-2745

"A bullhead catfish lying in the sediment at the bottom of a pond sets up the underlying rhythm of the changing seasons in this symphony of verses that features an animal for each month of the year. The variety of wildlife and the corresponding changes in meter and tone, combined with Jerry Pinkney's lush, full-page illustrations in full color, create a vivid picture book that is visually as well as auditorily pleasing." Horn Book

Smith, William Jay, 1918-

Birds and beasts; woodcuts by Jacques Hnizdovsky. Godine 1990 unp il $18.95 (4-6)   **811**

1. Animals—Poetry

ISBN 0-87923-865-8

"These 29 short, witty verses about creatures ranging from barnyard ordinaries like sheep and roosters to exotica such as sage grouse and zoo familiars like flamingos have been illustrated with unusually fine, equally witty woodcuts. The book has been elegantly designed and produced by letterpress on rich paper stock, so it is a pleasure to hold as well as to read aloud." N Y Times Book Rev

Laughing time; collected nonsense; pictures by Fernando Krahn. rev ed. Farrar, Straus & Giroux 1990 163p il $14; pa $3.50 (3-5)   **811**

1. Nonsense verses

ISBN 0-374-34366-7; 0-374-44315-7 (pa)

LC 90-55655

A revised and expanded edition of the collection first published 1980 by Delacorte Press/Seymour Lawrence

Contains nonsense poems on a variety of topics

"The poems are bright and breezy, ranging in tone from gentle whimsy to looniness, with an occasional lyrical gleam. . . . Krahn's zesty black-line drawings enhance the verse." Booklist

Soto, Gary

Neighborhood odes; illustrated by David Diaz. Harcourt Brace Jovanovich 1992 68p il $15.95 (4-6)   **811**

1. Hispanic Americans—Poetry

ISBN 0-15-256879-4   LC 91-20710

Also available in paperback from Scholastic

"Twenty-one poems, all odes, celebrate life in a Hispanic neighborhood. Other than the small details of daily life—peoples' names or the foods they eat—these poems could be about any neighborhood. With humor, sensitivity, and insight, Soto explores the lives of children. . . . David Diaz's contemporary black-and-white illustrations, which often resemble cut paper, effortlessly capture the varied moods—happiness, fear, longing, shame, and greed—of this remarkable collection. With a glossary of thirty Spanish words and phrases." Horn Book

Steig, Jeanne

Alpha beta chowder; pictures by William Steig. HarperCollins Pubs. 1992 unp il $15; lib bdg $14.89; pa $5.95   **811**

1. Alphabet—Poetry

ISBN 0-06-205006-0; 0-06-205007-9 (lib bdg); 0-06-205902-5 (pa)   LC 92-52641

"Michael di Capua books"

Each verse in this collection is based on a letter of the alphabet

"Jeanne Steig's verse bubbles merrily along, drolly blending abundant alliterations with downright silliness in a wonderful celebration of language. William Steig's lighthearted illustrations perfectly complement the keen wit while they add depth to the numerous people and animals conjured up in the poetry." Publ Wkly

Stevenson, James, 1929-
Sweet corn. Greenwillow Bks. 1995 63p il
$15   **811**
ISBN 0-688-12647-2   LC 94-4902
"James Stevenson's watercolors give further depth to his
poetry: a pensiveness to the boy using his lemonade stand
as an umbrella. Other poems are a visual experience of typography and colored background. About everyday things
and situations, these poems could be used in classrooms to
encourage students to write their own poetry." Child Book
Rev Serv

Swenson, May, 1919-1989
The complete poems to solve; illustrated by
Christy Hale. Macmillan 1993 115p il $13.95
(5 and up)   **811**
1. Nature poetry
ISBN 0-02-788725-1   LC 92-26183
Includes poems first published in Poems to solve, and
More poems to solve, published 1966 and 1971 respectively
by Scribner
A selection of the author's poetry, largely dealing with
nature, which challenges the reader to guess the subject of
each poem or a meaning not immediately obvious
"The variety in the collection of seventy-two poems . .
. illustrates the scope of Swenson's imaginative powers and
verbal skills." Horn Book Guide

Thayer, Ernest Lawrence, 1863-1940
Casey at the bat   **811**
1. Baseball—Poetry   LC 88-45290
Some editions are:
Atheneum Pubs. $15 Illustrated by Gerald Fitzgerald (ISBN
0-689-31945-2)
Godine pa $10.95 Illustrations by Barry Moser; afterword
by Donald Hall (ISBN 1-56792-072-1)
Putnam lib bdg $14.95 With additional text and illustra-
tions by Patricia Polacco (ISBN 0-399-21585-9)
Smith, P. $17.75 Illustrated by Jim Hull; introduction by
Martin Gardner (ISBN 0-8446-5613-5)
First published 1888
A narrative poem about the celebrated baseball player
who strikes out at the crucial moment of a game

Thomas, Joyce Carol
Brown honey in broomwheat tea; poems by
Joyce Carol Thomas; illustrated by Floyd
Cooper. HarperCollins Pubs. 1993 unp il $15;
lib bdg $14.89; pa $4.95 (k-3)   **811**
1. African Americans—Poetry
ISBN 0-06-021087-7; 0-06-021088-5 (lib bdg);
0-06-443439-7 (pa)   LC 91-46043
"A dozen poems rooted in home, family, and the African
American experience combine with a series of warm and
evocative watercolors in this highly readable and attractive
picture book." Booklist

Viorst, Judith
If I were in charge of the world and other
worries; poems for children and their parents;
illustrated by Lynne Cherry. Atheneum Pubs.
1981 56p il lib bdg $14.95; pa $4.95 (3-6)
      811
ISBN 0-689-30863-9 (lib bdg); 0-689-70770-3 (pa)
     LC 81-2342

"Forty-one lively, funny poems written from a wry, self-
deprecating point of view. Some poems verge on adult
feelings—such as a broken heart or a lyrical appreciation of
spring—but most of them deal with children's worries, to
which the author seems to be specially attuned." Horn
Book

Sad underwear and other complications;
poems; illustrated by Richard Hull. Atheneum
Pubs. 1995 78p $14.95 (3-6)   **811**
1. Humorous poetry
ISBN 0-689-31929-0   LC 94-3357
"From 'The Seventh Swimming Lesson,' in which Sally
finally puts her face in the water, to a practical version of
'Sleeping Beauty,' this is an inspired book of verse guaranteed to tickle the humerus again and again. Yet, poignancy
is present, too. . . . Both humorous and dreamlike pen-and-
ink illustrations are scattered throughout." SLJ

Watson, Clyde, 1947-
Father Fox's pennyrhymes; illustrated by
Wendy Watson. Crowell 1971 56p il
hardcover o.p. paperback available $6.95 (k-3)
      811
1. Nonsense verses 2. Nursery rhymes
ISBN 0-06-443137-1 (pa)
"A collection of short, original nonsense rhymes, illustrated with a bounty of high-spirited pictures. Some of the
verses are impish or boisterous or just plain silly; some are
similar to counting-out rhymes and jump-rope jingles; a few
are as gentle as lullabies. All are highly rhythmic and reminiscent of the traditional rhymes of folklore. The watercolor-and-ink illustrations are somewhat whimsical in their
busyness; tiny pictures printed in sequence—like comic
strips—as well as single, full-page pictures are brimming
with minute detail and activity." Horn Book

Whittier, John Greenleaf, 1807-1892
Barbara Frietchie; illustrated by Nancy
Winslow Parker. Greenwillow Bks. 1992 32p il
maps $14; lib bdg $13.93 (1-3)   **811**
1. Fritchie, Barbara, 1766-1862—Poetry 2. United
States—History—1861-1865, Civil War—Poetry
ISBN 0-688-09829-0; 0-688-09830-4 (lib bdg)
     LC 90-41755
"Set in Frederick, Maryland during the Civil War, Whittier's famous poem features Frietchie, the elderly woman
who defied Confederate orders . . . and flaunted her flag in
front of Stonewall Jackson. . . . Parker's pen-and-marker
artwork offers clean, white pages and clear, uncluttered
compositions that illustrate the poem with a fitting lack of
fuss. . . . Parker provides excellent notes on the setting, the
general, the poet, the war, and the question of whether the
events dramatized in the poem ever took place." Booklist

Wilbur, Richard, 1921-
More opposites; written and illustrated by
Richard Wilbur. Harcourt Brace Jovanovich
1991 34p il $12.95   **811**
1. Humorous poetry
ISBN 0-15-170072-9   LC 91-14411
A collection of humorous poems centering around words
and their opposites
"Each poem is accompanied by a jaunty, mischievous
line drawing. . . . Many of the verses try one's patience with
their arch, self-conscious humor; others have the gimlet wit
and subtle wordplay of Wilbur's finest translations." Publ
Wkly

Wilbur, Richard, 1921-—*Continued*

Opposites; written and illustrated by Richard Wilbur. Harcourt Brace Jovanovich 1991 c1973 39p il $11.95   **811**

1. Humorous poetry

ISBN 0-15-258720-9   LC 90-39844

A reissue of the title first published 1973

A collection of humorous poems about the opposites of various items

"Richard Wilbur's flair for a clever line rarely flags, and his drawings add more humor to these riddling verses. The kooky logic . . . is contagious." Christ Sci Monit

Runaway opposites; illustrated by Henrik Drescher. Harcourt Brace & Co. 1995 unp il $15   **811**

1. Humorous poetry

ISBN 0-15-258722-5   LC 94-13188

A collection of 15 humorous poems culled from the author's Opposites and More opposites

"The artwork, photographed collages including tiny objects, stamps, large assembled objects, and black line as well as full-color water-based drawings, offer layers of meaning and a real interpretative challenge. Together, the text and art create an irresistible synergy for those willing to invest the time to appreciate the sophisticated pairing." SLJ

Willard, Nancy

Pish, posh, said Hieronymus Bosch; illustrations by the Dillons. Harcourt Brace Jovanovich 1991 unp il $18.95 (2-5)   **811**

1. Bosch, Hieronymus, d. 1516—Poetry

ISBN 0-15-262210-1   LC 86-3173

In this poem, the housekeeper for medieval Dutch artist Hieronymus Bosch complains about the weird creatures which inhabit his home

"Once again, the Dillons have tailored their style to perfectly suit—and here, lend waggish twists to—their subject. Rendered in the opulent tones and peculiar, wild spirit of Bosch's works, their parade of fantastical creatures would make the master proud: animate cucumbers, an armorplated, two-headed dragon, a flying fish with wings of pickles. . . . This eccentric work may not be for youngest children, but anyone with unusual vision and an affinity for the quirkiest corners of the imagination will find it a source of endless fascination." Publ Wkly

The sorcerer's apprentice; illustrated by Leo and Diane Dillon. Blue Sky Press (NY) 1993 unp il $15.95 (2-5)   **811**

1. Magicians—Poetry

ISBN 0-590-47329-8   LC 93-19912

Sylvia, the new apprentice to the great magician Tottibo, steals one of his spells to complete an impossible task and accidentally creates chaos

"The dancing, varied rhythms and the alliterative imagery of the poetry make this a read-aloud treasure. The book is a visual prize as well. Preposterous creatures swarm over cream-colored, gilt-bordered pages while small vignettes outside the frames open up each spread and advance the story line." Horn Book

A visit to William Blake's inn; poems for innocent and experienced travelers; illustrated by Alice and Martin Provensen. Harcourt Brace Jovanovich 1981 44p il $14.95; pa $5.95 (2-5)   **811**

1. Nonsense verses

ISBN 0-15-293822-2; 0-15-293823-0 (pa)

LC 80-27403

Awarded the Newbery Medal, 1982 and also a Caldecott Medal honor book for the same year

"This entertaining collection of sixteen nonsense verses describes the lively goings-on among several incongruous travelers who put up at an imaginary inn run by the English poet William Blake. Inspired by Blake's poems and catching their rhythms and something of their oblique way of looking at things, the poems are in various forms and move along with a good beat." Child Book Rev Serv

"The illustrations are full of stylized naïveté—a rather sedate, late-eighteenth-century, middle-class kind of innocence. Done chiefly in glowing tawny colors, the pictures are highly decorative, and the whole book, printed on buff paper speckled to simulate an antique look, presents an elegant appearance." Horn Book

The voyage of the Ludgate Hill; travels with Robert Louis Stevenson; illustrated by Alice and Martin Provensen. Harcourt Brace Jovanovich 1987 unp il $14.95; pa $4.95 (2-5)   **811**

1. Stevenson, Robert Louis, 1850-1894—Poetry

ISBN 0-15-294464-8; 0-15-200119-0 (pa)

LC 86-19502

"Inspired by Stevenson's letters, Nancy Willard has written a poem, part fact part fantasy, about his stormy ocean voyage from London to New York on a cargo-carrying steamer in 1887. Stevenson and his wife, and a few other adventurous passengers, are joined in this journey by a bevy of assorted animals: apes and baboons, monkeys and stallions, not to mention the shipmaster's cat." N Y Times Book Rev

"The Provensens' paintings, brush stroked in buff, brown, and blue, are mannered, with a restrained humor based on a juxtaposition of the mundane with the unreal. A delight to read aloud, this will need some background explanation from adults." Bull Cent Child Books

Worth, Valerie

All the small poems and fourteen more; pictures by Natalie Babbitt. Farrar, Straus & Giroux 1994 194p il $18   **811**

ISBN 0-374-30211-1   LC 94-8810

"As the title implies, all the original collaborations between this poet and artist are collected in this volume, which includes ninety-nine poems and an additional fourteen new ones. The earlier works have been widely praised, for good reason, and the new verses are every bit as worthy as their predecessors." Horn Book

At Christmastime; poems by Valerie Worth; pictures by Antonio Frasconi. HarperCollins Pubs. 1992 unp il $15; lib bdg $14.89   **811**

1. Christmas—Poetry

ISBN 0-06-205019-2; 0-06-205020-6 (lib bdg)

LC 92-52693

"Michael di Capua books"

"In this collection of poems, award-winning poet Worth tackles all the classic images of Christmastime—presents

Worth, Valerie—*Continued*

and Christmas tree, wise men and crèche, stockings and Santa Claus. But her poetry does not end there. She concludes the book with 'New Year's Eve,' 'New Year's Day,' 'Twelfth Night,' and, surprisingly, 'Spring.' The short and lovely poems, enhanced by Frasconi's gorgeous woodcuts in bright inks, are very appealing." Booklist

Still more small poems; pictures by Natalie Babbitt. Farrar, Straus & Giroux 1978 41p il $11   **811**

    ISBN 0-374-37258-6   LC 78-11739

"Sketches, in free verse, of everyday objects, animals, places, sensations, and situations, from sounds a bell makes . . . to a drowsy turtle's speculations . . . to the miraculous ability of a hen, 'all quirk/And freak and whim' to produce so pure and calm an item as an egg." SLJ

"Small is beautiful. The collaborators always prove that economy can result in images rich as Croesus. . . . Ink drawings as understated yet infused with mystery as the lines . . . amplify mood and meaning." Publ Wkly

Yolen, Jane

Animal fare; poems by Jane Yolen; illustrated by Janet Street. Harcourt Brace & Co. 1994 32p il $14.95 (3-5)   **811**

    1. Animals—Poetry 2. Nonsense verses

    ISBN 0-15-203550-8   LC 92-44931

A collection of nonsense poems about the anteloop, the sprinkler spaniel, the rhinocerworse, and other fantastic animals

"In Street's colorful illustrations, the creatures cavort gracefully across the pages in bright pastel watercolors full of movement and mirroring beautifully the lighthearted fun of the poetry." SLJ

The ballad of the pirate queens; illustrated by David Shannon. Harcourt Brace & Co. 1995 unp il $15 (3-5)   **811**

    1. Bonny, Anne, b. 1700—Poetry 2. Read, Mary, 1680-1721—Poetry 3. Pirates—Poetry

    ISBN 0-15-200710-5   LC 94-7874

"A poem about Anne Bonney and Mary Reade, who were real pirates and who sailed on the sloop Vanity and fought the man-of-war Albion. They were tried in Jamaica in 1720 but, some say, were released because they were pregnant. Dramatic seafaring illustrations." N Y Times Book Rev

Best witches: poems for Halloween; illustrated by Elise Primavera. Putnam 1988 45p il $14.95 (3-5)   **811**

    1. Witches—Poetry 2. Halloween—Poetry

    ISBN 0-399-21539-5   LC 88-5866

The author presents her own poetry on witches, ghosts, magic, and other aspects of Halloween

"There's nice control of form, meter, rhyme, and scansion in this collection; there are moments of spine-chill that middle-grades readers will enjoy; there is, as prime appeal, a humor that has verve and sophistication but is never inaccessible. The ebullience of Yolen's poetry is matched by that of Primavera's paintings, which are colorful but pleasantly gruesome, with a great deal of vitality and antic humor." Bull Cent Child Books

Dinosaur dances; illustrated by Bruce Degen. Putnam 1990 39p il $14.95 (3-5)
     811

    1. Dinosaurs—Poetry 2. Humorous poetry

    ISBN 0-399-21629-4   LC 88-11661

Seventeen whimsical poems featuring allosaurus, stegosaurus, tyrannosaurus, and other dancing dinosaurs

"The silly pictures, filled with clever touches and subtle (?) spoof, do more than their share in making the prehistoric party irresistible, especially for dinosaur affecionados." Child Book Rev Serv

How beastly! a menagerie of nonsense poems; pictures by James Marshall. Wordsong 1994 46p il $14.95 (3-5)   **811**

    1. Mythical animals—Poetry 2. Nonsense verses

    ISBN 1-56397-086-4   LC 92-85036

A reissue of the title first published 1980 by Collins

This is a collection of nonsense verses on such imaginary creatures as the alligate, the tuner fish and the canterpillar

"For each of the twenty-two verses, a full-page line drawing washed with gray illuminates and comments on the fanciful fauna." Horn Book

Ring of earth: a child's book of seasons; illustrated by John Wallner. Harcourt Brace Jovanovich 1986 unp il $14.95 (3-6)   **811**

    1. Seasons—Poetry 2. Animals—Poetry

    ISBN 0-15-267140-4   LC 86-4800

The author "has written four short poems about the seasons of the year from the viewpoint of the Weasel in Winter, the Spring-Peeper in the Spring, the Dragonfly in Summer, and the Goose in the Fall." Child Book Rev Serv

"The picture book format is a bit deceptive here, for both the poetry and the art have a more sophisticated appeal. . . . Wallner's mottled paintings are gracefully composed across double-page spreads to pick up Yolen's circle motifs with interlocking rings and overlapping round frames connecting the cyclical flora and fauna reflected in the verses. A rewarding selection for classroom poetry groups or family sharing in a quieter context." Bull Cent Child Books

The three bears holiday rhyme book; written by Jane Yolen; illustrated by Jane Dyer. Harcourt Brace & Co. 1995 32p il $15 (k-2)   **811**

    1. Holidays—Poetry 2. Bears—Poetry

    ISBN 0-15-200932-9   LC 93-17252

"Baby Bear, joined by Mother, Father, or their friend Goldilocks, celebtrates 15 special days throughout the year. Each occasion is featured in a splendid two-page water-color illustration with a short poem honoring the event." SLJ

The three bears rhyme book; illustrated by Jane Dyer. Harcourt Brace Jovanovich 1987 32p il lib bdg $14.95 (k-2)   **811**

    1. Bears—Poetry

    ISBN 0-15-286386-9   LC 86-19514

"The 16 poems offered here assume that Goldilocks and the three bears maintain a close friendship in spite of their initial encounter, which is not mentioned. The verses describe familiar activities such as taking a walk, eating porridge, having a birthday party, and going out in the rain." SLJ

"The universality of the events will certainly appeal to young listeners who'll find the words mirroring their own everyday activities. As for the illustrations, there's just one word for them—delightful. Executed in soft watercolors and colored pencils, the pictures are charming without being cloying, the humor is amusing without being broad." Booklist

Yolen, Jane—*Continued*

Water music; poems for children; photographs by Jason Stemple. Wordsong 1995 unp il $16.95 (3-5)   **811**

1. Water—Poetry

ISBN 1-56397-336-7   LC 94-79163

"Yolen notes that Stemple's stunning full-color photographs were the inspiration for these 17 poems on different aspects of water. Ocean surf, dew drops, soap bubbles, a river, waterfall, icicle, and reflections are among the subjects sensitively wrought in words and pictures. The colors are soft and shimmering, reflecting the mood of quiet contemplation evoked by the verses." SLJ

Zolotow, Charlotte, 1915-

Snippets; a gathering of poems, pictures, and possibilities . . .; illustrations by Melissa Sweet. HarperCollins Pubs. 1993 unp il $16; lib bdg $15.89 (k-3)   **811**

ISBN 0-06-020818-X; 0-06-020819-8 (lib bdg)
      LC 91-37751

"Bits and pieces from over 25 of Zolotow's books are gathered together and set in the fine frame of Sweet's delicate watercolor cartoons. . . . This title will charm those not ready for life's brutal realism and those who find gentle, thoughtful fare reassuring and rewarding." SLJ

811.008 American poetry— Collections

April, bubbles, chocolate; an ABC of poetry; selected by Lee Bennett Hopkins; illustrated by Barrett Root. Simon & Schuster Bks. for Young Readers 1994 40p il $14 (k-3)   **811.008**

1. American poetry—Collections 2. Alphabet

ISBN 0-671-75911-6   LC 92-17100

A collection of poems on things from A to Z, by such authors as Eve Merriam, Carl Sandburg, and Arnold Adoff

"This light, delectable collection of poems . . . has true child appeal. It offers a roster of quality verses. . . . Layout is attractive, with each brief poem whimsically illustrated by either a full-or double-page watercolor painting." SLJ

At the crack of the bat; baseball poems compiled by Lillian Morrison; illustrated by Steve Cieslawski. Hyperion Bks. for Children 1992 64p il $14.95; lib bdg $14.89; pa $5.95 (3-5)   **811.008**

1. Baseball—Poetry 2. American poetry—Collections

ISBN 1-56282-176-8; 1-56282-177-6 (lib bdg); 1-56282-670-0 (pa)   LC 91-28946

An illustrated collection of poems, by a variety of authors, about the game and personalities of baseball

"Line drawings and full-color paintings have a dramatic vitality that should appeal to baseball buffs as much as will this excellent collection of poems by an experienced anthologist. . . . There is variety of style, form, mood, and subject, but a unanimity of theme and high quality." Bull Cent Child Books

Beat the drum; Independence Day has come: poems for the Fourth of July; selected by Lee Bennett Hopkins; illustrations by Tomie de Paola. Wordsong 1993 32p il $9.95 (2-4)   **811.008**

1. Fourth of July—Poetry 2. American poetry—Collections

ISBN 1-878093-60-6   LC 92-85033

A reissue of the title first published 1977 by Harcourt Brace Jovanovich

"Poems from Shel Silverstein, Rachel Field, Lucille Clifton, Lois Lenski, Lee Blair, Carl Sandburg, and others represent the parades, picnics, fireworks, and patriotism of the popular July holiday." Booklist

Birthday rhymes, special times; selected by Bobbye S. Goldstein; pictures by Jose Aruego and Ariane Dewey. Doubleday Bks. for Young Readers 1993 48p il $15 (k-3)   **811.008**

1. Birthdays—Poetry 2. American poetry—Collections

ISBN 0-385-30419-6   LC 90-21488

A collection of poems about birthdays, by such authors as Dr. Seuss, John Ciardi, and Jack Prelutsky

"The poems . . . are relatively short (just right for a young child's short attention span) and range from the semi-serious to the quirkily whimsical to the tickle-your-funny-bone silly. Artists Aruego and Dewey . . . offer amusing, cartoonlike illustrations in bright, eye-catching colors. The drawings are imaginative and witty." Booklist

Blast off!; poems about space; selected by Lee Bennett Hopkins; pictures by Melissa Sweet. HarperCollins Pubs. 1995 48p il $14; lib bdg $13.89 (k-2)   **811.008**

1. American poetry—Collections 2. Outer space—Poetry

ISBN 0-06-024260-4; 0-06-024261-2 (lib bdg)
      LC 93-24536

"An I can read book"

"Hopkins collects twenty poems by a variety of writers on the subject of space: moon, the sun, stars, planets and meteorites. Most, including his own two, are fairly contemporary, except for 'Star light, star bright,' and one by Sara Teasdale from the 1930s. . . . The poems are well chosen and on a topic many children favor, and Sweet's watercolors capture their mix of wonder and joy well." Bull Cent Child Books

A Caribbean dozen; poems from Caribbean poets; edited by John Agard and Grace Nichols; illustrated by Cathie Felstead. Candlewick Press 1994 93p il $19.95 (4-6)   **811.008**

1. Caribbean region—Poetry

ISBN 1-56402-339-7   LC 93-47272

This is a "collection of poems by 13 Caribbean authors. The 54 eloquently written selections share each poet's appreciation of nature and reverence for life. . . . Attractive folk-style collage, watercolor, pastel, gouache, oil, and ink illustrations complement the verses." SLJ

Celebrate America in poetry and art; paintings, sculpture, drawings, photographs, and other works of art from the National Museum of American Art, Smithsonian Institution; edited by Nora Panzer. Hyperion Bks. for Children 1994 96p il $18.95; lib bdg $18.89 (5 and up)

811.008

1. American poetry—Collections 2. American art
3. United States—Poetry
ISBN 1-56282-664-6; 1-56282-665-4 (lib bdg)
          LC 93-32336

"Published in association with the National Museum of American Art, Smithsonian Institution"

A collection of American poetry that celebrates over 200 years of American life and history as illustrated by fine art from the collection of the National Museum of American Art

"There's a terrific cross-section of writers and illustrators—Maya Angelou, Robert Frost, Winslow Homer, Thomas Hart Benton—and there is special pleasure in the pairings. . . . Combined, the art and words are exhilaratingly more than the sum of their parts." Booklist

Christmas in the stable; poems selected and illustrated by Beverly K. Duncan. Harcourt Brace Jovanovich 1990 32p il $14.95 (2-4)

811.008

1. Christmas—Poetry 2. Poetry—Collections
ISBN 0-15-217758-2   LC 88-37953

A collection of poems by Jane Yolen, Elizabeth Coatsworth, Norma Farber, and others, each from the point of view of an animal or about the animals in the stable where the Christ Child lay asleep

"Though suffused with a spirit of peace and wonder, the pieces are refreshingly unsentimental and free of cliche. . . . Each selection and the animal painting that illustrates it are framed together with thin colored borders and centered against a tapestrylike background that is detailed with plants appropriate to the season. The graceful designs were inspired by medieval manuscripts and possess a similar quality of serenity and grace." Booklist

Click, rumble, roar; poems about machines; poems selected by Lee Bennett Hopkins; photographs by Anna Held Audette. Crowell 1987 40p il lib bdg $14.89 (2-5)

811.008

1. Machinery—Poetry 2. American poetry—Collections
ISBN 0-690-04589-1   LC 86-47746

A collection of eighteen poems about machines by Myra Cohn Livingston, Eve Merriam, David McCord, and others

"The eighteen poems in the slim, attractive collection cover the range of the car wash and parking lot, bulldozers, tractors, garbage trucks, escalators, helicopters, and pocket calculators. Some are brief observations; others offer stimulating insights. There is great variety of form and plenty of humor. . . . The often eloquent, full-page photographs accompanying the poems will lure browsers into sampling the poetry." Horn Book

Cool salsa; bilingual poems on growing up Latino in the United States; edited by Lori M. Carlson; introduction by Oscar Hijuelos. Holt & Co. 1994 xx, 123p il $14.95 (5 and up)

811.008

1. American poetry—Hispanic American authors—Collections 2. Bilingual books—English-Spanish
ISBN 0-8050-3135-9   LC 93-45798

"This collection presents poems by 29 Mexican-American, Cuban-American, Puerto Rican, and other Central and South American poets, including Sandra Cisneros, Luis J. Rodriguez, Pat Mora, Gary Soto, Ana Castillo, Oscar Hijuelos, Ed J. Vega, Judith Ortiz-Cofer, and other Latino writers both contemporary and historical. Brief biographical notes on the authors are provided. All the poems deal with experiences of teenagers." Book Rep

Dinosaurs: poems; selected by Lee Bennett Hopkins; illustrated by Murray Tinkleman. Harcourt Brace Jovanovich 1987 46p il $12.95; pa $4.95 (3-5)

811.008

1. Dinosaurs—Poetry 2. American poetry—Collections
ISBN 0-15-223495-0; 0-15-223496-9 (pa)
          LC 86-14818

"In this volume of 18 poems, Hopkins invites us to 'Reflect upon the dinosaur,/A giant that exists no more.' With poems by Myra Cohn Livingston, Lilian Moore, Valerie Worth and others, the collection explores fossils . . . and the museums that house [them]." Publ Wkly

"The collection will offer a spur to the imagination which more scientific material may lack. Minutely crosshatched, black-and-white illustrations effectively recreate the nubbly, grainy skins of the mysterious, ponderous creatures and the swamps and savannas of their remote and shadowy world. Index of authors, titles, and first lines." Horn Book

Extra innings; baseball poems; selected by Lee Bennett Hopkins; illustrated by Scott Medlock. Harcourt Brace Jovanovich 1993 40p il $14.95 (4 and up)

811.008

1. Baseball—Poetry 2. American poetry—Collections
ISBN 0-15-226833-2   LC 92-13013

"A collection of 19 poems about baseball, bolstered by vibrant oil-on-paper illustrations that are sure to attract attention, even from reluctant readers. Poets include May Swenson, Lillian Morrison, Ernest Thayer, and Lee Bennett Hopkins." Booklist

Families; poems celebrating the African American experience; selected by Dorothy S. Strickland and Michael R. Strickland; illustrations by John Ward. Wordsong 1994 31p il $14.95; pa $7.95 (2-4)

811.008

1. African Americans—Poetry 2. American poetry—Collections
ISBN 1-56397-288-3; 1-56397-560-2 (pa)
          LC 93-61162

Family relationships are explored and affirmed in this anthology of poems celebrating the diversity of African-American families

"Offering a variety of poems written by some of the best African-American poets (Langston Hughes, Nikki Giovanni, Gwendolyn Brooks, etc.), this compilation captures the spirit of growing up in an African-American family. Children will enjoy reading and listening to these age-appropriate poems. . . . Colorful, expression-filled illustrations fit the mood." Child Book Rev Serv

For laughing out loud; poems to tickle your funnybone; selected by Jack Prelutsky; illustrated by Marjorie Priceman. Knopf 1991 84p il $14.95; lib bdg $15.99

811.008

1. American poetry—Collections 2. Humorous poetry
ISBN 0-394-82144-0; 0-394-92144-5 (lib bdg)
          LC 90-33010

A collection of humorous poems by writers including Ellen Raskin, Karla Kuskin, Ogden Nash, and Arnold Lobel

For laughing out loud—*Continued*
"These nonsense verses by a wide variety of poets combine the domestic and the gross, deadpan and slapstick, with a lilting rhythm and satisfying rhyme. . . . The design is ebullient, often with several poems appearing on a double-page spread surrounded by wildly energetic wash-and-line illustrations." Booklist

Good books, good times!; selected by Lee Bennett Hopkins; pictures by Harvey Stevenson. Harper & Row 1990 31p il $14; lib bdg $14.89 (1-3) **811.008**
1. Books and reading—Poetry 2. American poetry—Collections
ISBN 0-06-022527-0; 0-06-022528-9 (lib bdg)
LC 89-49108
"A Charlotte Zolotow book"
An anthology of poems about the joys of books and reading. Includes selections by David McCord, Karla Kuskin, Myra Cohn Livingston, and Jack Prelutsky
"The tone of the poems, the majority of which have not yet appeared in anthologies, ranges from exuberant to meditative. The collection will excite any parent, teacher, or librarian looking for brief, accessible poems on the subject of books and reading. Stevenson's lighthearted watercolors perfectly capture the jubilant mood of the book." Horn Book

Hand in hand; an American history through poetry; collected by Lee Bennett Hopkins; illustrated by Peter M. Fiore. Simon & Schuster Bks. for Young Readers 1994 144p il $19.95 (4 and up) **811.008**
1. United States—History—Poetry 2. American poetry—Collections
ISBN 0-671-73315-X
LC 92-24230
"Hopkins divides the country's past into nine arbitrary eras and presents 5-10 selections as representative of each period or theme. He includes patriotic songs, speeches, and individual anthems by a veritable feast of American poets, such as Walt Whitman, Carl Sandburg, Langston Hughes, and Robert Frost. . . . Fiore's bold impressionistic oil paintings, in the form of expansive tableaus and cameo vignettes, provide vivid visuals to go along with the poetic imagery." SLJ

Happy birthday; poems; selected by Lee Bennett Hopkins; illustrated by Hilary Knight. Simon & Schuster Bks. for Young Readers 1991 unp il $11.95; pa $5.95 (k-3) **811.008**
1. Birthdays—Poetry 2. American poetry—Collections
ISBN 0-671-70973-9; 0-671-79851-0 (pa)
LC 90-10086
"Hopkins has assembled a collection of birthday verses from popular children's poets such as Beatrice Schenk de Regniers, Aileen Fisher, Myra Cohn Livingston, and Nancy White Carlstrom. Through watercolor, pen-and-ink, and colored-pencil cartoons, Knight tells the story of a birthday party from preparing the invitations to the writing of thank-you cards." SLJ

I am the darker brother; an anthology of modern poems by Negro Americans; drawings by Benny Andrews; foreword by Charlemae Rollins. Macmillan 1968 128p il hardcover o.p. paperback available $4.95 (5 and up) **811.008**
1. American poetry—African American authors—Collections
ISBN 0-02-041120-0 (pa)
LC 68-12077

Edited by: Arnold Adoff
"A most interesting anthology, with many contributions from such well-known poets as Brooks, Dunbar, Hayden, Hughes, and McKay, and a broad representation of selections from the work of some two dozen other modern authors." Bull Cent Child Books

I thought I'd take my rat to school; poems for September to June; selected by Dorothy M. Kennedy; illustrated by Abby Carter. Little, Brown 1993 63p il $16.95 (3-5) **811.008**
1. Schools—Poetry
ISBN 0-316-48893-3
LC 92-12775
A collection of poems capturing the good and the bad sides of school, by such authors as Russell Hoban, Gary Soto, and Karla Kuskin.
"Carter's gray wash drawings illustrate the poetry with subtlety and wit. An attractive anthology that reflects the day-to-day experiences of school children." Booklist

If you ever meet a whale; poems selected by Myra Cohn Livingston; illustrated by Leonard Everett Fisher. Holiday House 1992 32p il $14.95 (3-5) **811.008**
1. Whales—Poetry 2. American poetry—Collections
ISBN 0-8234-0940-6
LC 91-36265
A collection of poems about whales, by such authors as Jane Yolen, Theodore Roethke, and John Ciardi
"Fisher's majestic full-color paintings depict the underwater world in deep, cool hues shot with warmer or whiter highlights. . . . The spacious design, a necessity for displaying such mammoth creatures, is a fine counterpoint to the pithy poems." Booklist

In the witch's kitchen; poems for Halloween; compiled by John E. Brewton, Lorraine A. Blackburn, George M. Blackburn III; illustrated by Harriett Barton. Crowell 1980 88p il lib bdg $13.89 (3-6) **811.008**
1. Halloween—Poetry 2. American poetry—Collections
ISBN 0-690-04062-8
LC 79-7822
"Familiar Halloween motifs are to be found in the forty-six poems gathered into a gleefully ghoulish medley for younger audiences. Works by such well-known writers for children as John Ciardi, Aileen Fisher, X. J. Kennedy, David McCord, and Jack Prelutsky are included as well as traditional rhymes and chants. . . . The imaginative, slightly cartoonlike illustrations are appropriately executed in black, gray, and white. An inviting and serviceable collection for a varied audience. With indexes of authors, titles, and first lines." Horn Book

It's about time!; poems; selected by Lee Bennett Hopkins; illustrated by Matt Novak. Simon & Schuster Bks. for Young Readers 1993 36p il $14 (k-2) **811.008**
1. Time—Poetry 2. American poetry—Collections
ISBN 0-671-78512-5
LC 92-12128
Sixteen poems by a variety of American poets reflect thoughts about time
"Novak's soft pastel pencil drawings do much to bring unity to the divergent writing styles represented. Well-modulated shifts in tone and mood keep this volume ticking quickly." Publ Wkly

More surprises; selected by Lee Bennett Hopkins; illustrated by Megan Lloyd. Harper & Row 1987 64p il lib bdg $13.89 (k-2)   **811.008**

1. American poetry—Collections

ISBN 0-06-022605-6   LC 86-45335

Companion volume to Surprises

"An I can read book. A Charlotte Zolotow book"

A collection of poems with topics ranging from school to birds to nonsense

"This is the perfect compilation to teach the joys of poetry to very young children. Words and rhyme schemes are simple enough for beginning readers to handle themselves, and the offerings by poets such as Aileen Fisher, William Cole, Karla Kuskin, and Jack Prelutsky are filled with humor and verve." Booklist

My black me; a beginning book of black poetry; edited by Arnold Adoff. [rev. ed.] Dutton Children's Bks. 1994 83p $14.99 (5 and up)   **811.008**

1. American poetry—African American authors—Collections

ISBN 0-525-45216-8

First published 1974

A compilation of poems reflecting thoughts on being black by such authors as Langston Hughes, Lucille Clifton, Nikki Giovanni, and Imamu Amiri Baraka

Never take a pig to lunch and other poems about the fun of eating; selected and illustrated by Nadine Bernard Westcott. Orchard Bks. 1994 64p il $18.95 (k-3)   **811.008**

1. Food—Poetry 2. American poetry—Collections

ISBN 0-531-08634-X   LC 93-11801

"A Melanie Kroupa book"

"A food-oriented collection of limericks, free verse, and other styles of rhyme by such well-known poets and humorists as Ogden Nash, Eve Merriam, Florence Parry Heide, Jack Prelutsky, John Ciardi, David McCord, and others. Poems about popular treats, disgusting eating habits, and outrageous table manners are among the categories included. Westcott's rollicking cartoons, done in ink and acrylics, capture the fun." SLJ

The **Oxford** book of children's verse in America; edited by Donald Hall. Oxford Univ. Press 1985 xxxviii, 319p $29.95; pa $13.95   **811.008**

1. American poetry—Collections

ISBN 0-19-503539-9; 0-19-506761-4 (pa)

LC 84-20755

"Hall's intention, expressed in the introduction, is to create an anthology of American poetry actually written for or adopted by children during a particular historical period. The emphasis is on authenticity rather than personal taste." SLJ

"A fine and carefully winnowed collection of American poetry is gathered in a book that will interest students of children's literature and young people who simply enjoy browsing." Horn Book

Pass it on; African-American poetry for children; selected by Wade Hudson; illustrated by Floyd Cooper. Scholastic 1993 32p il $14.95 (k-3)   **811.008**

1. American poetry—African American authors—Collections

ISBN 0-590-45770-5   LC 92-16034

An illustrated collection of poetry by such Afro-American poets as Langston Hughes, Nikki Giovanni, Eloise Greenfield, and Lucille Clifton

"Cooper's beautifully individualized oil-wash portraits express the energy, the yearning, and the heartfelt emotion of this fine anthology." Booklist

The **Place** my words are looking for; what poets say about and through their work; selected by Paul B. Janeczko. Bradbury Press 1990 150p il $14.95 (4 and up)   **811.008**

1. American poetry—Collections 2. Poetics

ISBN 0-02-747671-5   LC 89-39331

"More than forty contemporary poets are included: Eve Merriam, X. J. Kennedy, Felice Holman, Gary Soto, Mark Vinz, Karla Kuskin, and John Updike, among others. Their contributions vary widely in theme and mood and style, though the preponderance of the pieces are written in modern idiom and unrhymed meter. The accompanying comments frequently are as insightful and eloquent as the poems themselves." Horn Book

Poem stew; poems selected by William Cole; pictures by Karen Ann Weinhaus. Lippincott 1981 84p il o.p.; HarperCollins Pubs. paperback available $4.95 (3-6)   **811.008**

1. Food—Poetry 2. Dining—Poetry 3. American poetry—Collections

ISBN 0-06-440136-7 (pa)   LC 81-47106

"Drawn from anonymous and traditional sources as well as from the works of such poets as Ogden Nash, John Ciardi, Jack Prelutsky, Myra Cohn Livingston, and the selector himself, the poems celebrate the subject of food. But they haven't been chosen for their appeal to gourmet palates; rather they comment on occasions when particular items of food become the impetus for a humorous narrative, lyric, or epigram. . . . With indexes of authors and titles." Horn Book

Poems for Jewish holidays; selected by Myra Cohn Livingston; illustrated by Lloyd Bloom. Holiday House 1986 32p il lib bdg $13.95 (k-3)   **811.008**

1. Jewish holidays—Poetry 2. American poetry—Collections

ISBN 0-8234-0606-7   LC 85-27179

"Sixteen poems celebrate 12 Jewish holidays. The poems vary from the traditional 'Had Gadya' taken from the Passover Haggadah, to the more playful, contemporary 'First Night of Hanukkah' by Ruth Rosten and the more sensitive and moving 'Tisha B'Av,' which commemorates a Jewish day of mourning, by Meyer Hahn. Several of the poems were commissioned for this volume, and therefore do not appear anywhere else. Images effectively convey the moods of different holidays. However, it is Bloom's black-and-white illustrations that make this a truly distinguished book. Each of the ten full-page charcoal paintings captures the different aspects of the Jewish experience while keeping with the spirit of the poem." SLJ

Questions; poems selected by Lee Bennett Hopkins; illustrated by Carolyn Croll. HarperCollins Pubs. 1993 64p il $13; lib bdg $12.89; pa $3.50 (k-2) **811.008**
1. American poetry—Collections
ISBN 0-06-022412-6; 0-06-022413-4 (lib bdg); 0-06-444181-4 (pa) LC 90-21745
"A Charlotte Zolotow book. An I can read book"
A collection of poems that ask questions, by such authors as Aileen Fisher, Lee Bennett Hopkins, Eve Merriam, and Ogden Nash
"Hopkins has gathered a fine collection to introduce new readers to lines that sing. . . . The color illustrations and bright, clear design will draw kids into a book that will make them want to read more." Booklist

Ragged shadows; poems of Halloween night; selected by Lee Bennett Hopkins; illustrated by Giles Laroche. Little, Brown 1993 32p il $15.95 (k-3) **811.008**
1. Halloween—Poetry 2. American poetry—Collections
ISBN 0-316-37276-5 LC 92-1369
A collection of poems about Halloween and its creatures, by such authors as Jane Yolen, Karla Kuskin, and Nancy Willard
"Whether humorous, lyrical, scary, or evocative, in rhyme or free verse, each poem is a gem of its kind, with its effectiveness heightened by the unique artwork; cut-paper figures cast shadows that create interesting three-dimensional effects." Horn Book Guide

Reflections on a gift of watermelon pickle . . . and other modern verse; [compiled by] Stephen Dunning, Edward Lueders, Hugh Smith. Lothrop, Lee & Shepard Bks. 1967 c1966 139p il $16; lib bdg $15.93 (6 and up) **811.008**
1. American poetry—Collections
ISBN 0-688-41231-9; 0-688-51231-3 (lib bdg)
LC 67-29527
First published 1966 by Scott, Foresman in a text edition
"Although some of the [114] selections are by recognized modern writers, many are by minor or unknown poets, and few will be familiar to the reader. Nearly all are fresh in approach and contemporary in expression. . . . Striking photographs complementing or illuminating many of the poems enhance the attractiveness of the volume." Booklist

Singing America; selected with an introduction by Neil Philip; illustrated by Michael McCurdy. Viking 1995 160p il $19.99 (5 and up) **811.008**
1. American poetry—Collections
ISBN 0-670-86150-2
This "collection of poems includes traditional songs and poetry from the eighteenth century through the twentieth century. . . . The voices of poetry represent Native Americans, African Americans, Asian Americans, Hispanic Americans, and European immigrants." Voice Youth Advocates
"McCurdy's bold, beautiful woodcuts, many depicting people at work, extend the energy and individuality of the words." Booklist

Small talk; a book of short poems; selected by Lee Bennett Hopkins; illustrated by Susan Gaber. Harcourt Brace & Co. 1995 48p il $14 (2-4) **811.008**
1. American poetry—Collections
ISBN 0-15-276577-8 LC 94-7601

"Hopkins collects thirty-three poems that together constitute no more than one hundred lines of poetry: these are very short poems, indeed. Twenty-seven authors are represented, ranging from Mother Goose to Carl Sandburg to several of today's poets for children. . . . Gaber illustrates each entry with a watercolor or colored-pencil drawing, each image carefully chosen to extend the poem's meaning." Bull Cent Child Books

Soul looks back in wonder; [illustrated by] Tom Feelings. Dial Bks. 1993 unp il $15.99 (3-6) **811.008**
1. American poetry—African American authors—Collections
ISBN 0-8037-1001-1 LC 93-824
Coretta Scott King award for illustration, 1994
Artwork and poems by such writers as Maya Angelou, Langston Hughes, and Askia Toure portray the creativity, strength, and beauty of their African American heritage
"This thoughtful collection of poetry is unique. . . . Feelings selected sketches done while he was in West Africa, South America, and at home in America. The original drawings were enhanced with colored pencils, colored papers, stencil cut-outs, and other techniques to give a collage effect. Marbled textures bring vibrancy to the work." Horn Book

Star walk; edited by Seymour Simon. Morrow Junior Bks. 1995 unp il $15; lib bdg $14.93 (4 and up) **811.008**
1. Stars—Poetry 2. Outer space—Poetry 3. Poetry—Collections
ISBN 0-688-11887-9; 0-688-11888-7 (lib bdg)
LC 94-16643
A collection of poetry and photographs about stars and space
"This anthology combines "full-and double-page photographs with powerfull poetry. Each photo is briefly captioned to identify the astronomical feature it depicts. Verse by Archibald MacLeish, Sara Teasdale, Stanley Kunitz, May Swenson, and others, along with three anonymous Native American poems (identified by tribal origin), provide a thought-provoking view of the universe." SLJ

Sunflakes; poems for children; selected by Lilian Moore; illustrated by Jan Ormerod. Clarion Bks. 1992 96p il $18.95 (k-2) **811.008**
1. American poetry—Collections
ISBN 0-395-58833-2 LC 90-23760
A collection of poems about universal childhood experiences
"The organization flows organically; the poems seem to group themselves naturally into sections on bugs, rain, food, etc., each titled with a quote and none seeming contrived. Aesthetically and poetically, this will serve as a family or classroom staple." Bull Cent Child Books

Surprises; selected by Lee Bennett Hopkins; illustrated by Megan Lloyd. Harper & Row 1984 64p il lib bdg $14.89; pa $3.50 (k-2) **811.008**
1. American poetry—Collections
ISBN 0-06-022585-8 (lib bdg); 0-06-444105-9 (pa)
LC 83-47712
"An I can read book. A Charlotte Zolotow book"
Hopkins has put together a "collection of poems from the proverbial star-studded cast: X. J. Kennedy, Myra Cohn Livingston, Nikki Giovanni, Russell Hoban, Eve Merriam, Langston Hughes, Christina Rossetti, Carl Sandburg and on and on. These 38 poems, most previously published else-

Surprises—*Continued*

where, employ short words and simple language to tell their
tale or paint their picture and often make good read-alouds
as well as smart choices for beginning readers." SLJ

Through our eyes; poems and pictures about
growing up; poems selected by Lee Bennett
Hopkins; photographs by Jeffrey Dunn.
Little, Brown 1992 32p il $15.95 (2-4)

811.008

1. American poetry—Collections
ISBN 0-316-19654-1   LC 91-13875

Color photographs and poems depict children from diverse backgrounds engaged in contemporary activities and
thoughts

"These 16 poems about growing up are from some old
favorites—Giovanni, Krauss, McCord, Prelutsky—as well
as less frequently anthologized poets. The selections are well
chosen, speaking simply to a range of childhood feelings
and situations. . . . The 'pictures' that get equal billing are
full-color photos whose cropped rectangles share the white
pages with the poems' clean black print." SLJ

Until I saw the sea and other poems; a
collection of seashore poems; [selected and
illustrated by] Alison Shaw. Holt & Co.
1995 32p il $15.95 (k-2)   **811.008**

1. Sea poetry 2. Poetry—Collections
ISBN 0-8050-2755-6   LC 94-28810

"Authors John Masefield, e. e. cummings, and Myra
Cohn Livingston, among others, explore sand castles, fog,
seaweed, shells, and the ineffable lure of the ocean. The 19
poems range in complexity from brief and evocative to
longer and more thoughtful verses. Shaw's expansive photographs dominate the page with their size and glowing colors." Booklist

Weather; poems selected by Lee Bennett
Hopkins; pictures by Melanie Hall.
HarperCollins Pubs. 1994 63p il $14; il bdg
$13.89 (k-2)   **811.008**

1. Weather—Poetry 2. American poetry—Collections
ISBN 0-06-021463-5; 0-06-021462-7 (lib bdg)
     LC 92-14913

"An I can read book"

A collection of poems describing various weather conditions, by such authors as Christina G. Rossetti, Myra Cohn
Livingston, and Aileen Fisher

"Hopkins' excellent choices are easily accessible in large
type with a spacious design and brightly colored illustrations." Booklist

Yours 'til banana splits; 201 autograph
rhymes; compiled by Joanna Cole and
Stephanie Calmenson; illustrated by Alan
Tiegreen. Morrow Junior Bks. 1995 62p il
$15; lib bdg $14.93; pa $6.95 (2-5)

811.008

1. American poetry—Collections 2. Humorous poetry
ISBN 0-688-13185-9; 0-688-13186-7 (lib bdg);
0-688-14019-X (pa)   LC 94-10654

A collection of rhymes suitable for writing in autograph
books

"Kids still like to write in yearbooks and autograph
books. It's a childhood ritual that goes on year after year
and provides lots of good times. All the old favorites are
here, plus some new, or maybe not so new, ideas about secret messages and ingenius ways to leave one's signature.
Amusing black-and-white line drawings add to the appeal."

The selections are great reading, too, for the sounds and
rhythms of language." SLJ

812   American drama

Rockwell, Thomas, 1933-

How to eat fried worms, and other plays;
illustrated by Joel Schick. Delacorte Press
1980 142p il lib bdg $9.89 (4-6)   **812**

ISBN 0-440-03499-X   LC 78-72854

"Though the combination of slapstick humor and ghoulish silliness in these four plays is a winning one, the zaniness often lapses into sheer hysteria. The title play (an
adaptation of Rockwell's popular 1973 novel) is also the
most successful, as the worm eating episodes reach new and
revolting heights. The least successful is 'Myron Mere,' 'a
slight effort in which the villainous Mere captures a queen
and turns her into a butterfly. In 'Aiiieeeeeeeeee' havoc
breaks loose as seven demons attack a town and are finally
overcome by a princess and humble villager. 'The Heiress,
or the Croak of Doom' dramatizes the plight of Helen, being driven insane by two evil paper boys after her inherited
fortune." SLJ

Thane, Adele

Plays from famous stories and fairy tales;
royalty-free dramatizations of favorite
children's stories. Plays 1983 c1967 463p pa
$15 (4-6)   **812**

1. One act plays 2. Folk drama
ISBN 0-8238-0060-1   LC 83-23039

First published 1967

"Twenty-eight royalty-free, one act plays are included in
this collection of adaptations from well-known folktales,
fairy tales, children's classics and old favorites. The dramatizations are simple, often compressing into a scene or two
several incidents from a book; they are adequately written
and some are moderately funny. Because of the appeal of
the sources, a useful collection. Brief notes on costumes,
props, lights, setting, et cetera, are appended." Bull Cent
Child Books

812.008   American drama— Collections

Holiday plays round the year; edited by Sylvia
E. Kamerman. Plays 1983 291p pa $13.95 (4
and up)   **812.008**

1. One act plays 2. Holidays—Drama
ISBN 0-8238-0261-2   LC 83-13218

"The 27 modern holiday plays in this collection have
been taken from various issues of 'Play' magazine; they
cover 12 common holidays. Production notes at the end of
the book list number of characters (2 to more than 23),
playing time, costumes, properties and setting but no age or
grade levels." SLJ

"The contemporary plays do not seem as dated as is
sometimes the case in these anthologies. . . . [These plays]
are royalty free. The staging and costuming are simple, and
ample production notes are provided." Booklist

817.008 American satire and humor—Collections

The **Random** House book of humor for children; selected by Pamela Pollack; illustrated by Paul O. Zelinsky. Random House 1988 310p il $15.95; lib bdg $16.99 (4-6)   **817.008**

ISBN 0-394-88049-8; 0-394-98049-2 (lib bdg)

LC 86-31478

"The list of authors excerpted here reads like a 'Who's Who' of children's literature: Babbitt, Blume, Byars, Cleary, Dahl, Fitzhugh, McCloskey, Singer, Thurber, and Twain, to name just a few. Most of the 34 selections are chapters from longer novels. . . . Although some chapters work better than others out of context, most of the offerings stand quite well on their own, and the stories chosen are fine examples of humorous prose. The best use for the collection might be a sampler from which readers may choose books they want to enjoy in their entirety." Booklist

818 American miscellany

Brown, Margaret Wise, 1910-1952

The fish with the deep sea smile; stories and poems for reading to young children; illustrated by Roberta Rauch. Linnet Bks. 1988 c1938 128p il lib bdg $18 (1-3)   **818**

ISBN 0-208-02193-0   LC 87-26227

A reissue of the title first published 1938 by Dutton

A compilation of the author's stories and poems, illustrated with sketches by her sister

"The author has succeeded in telling stories that young children will find diverting. Some are wildly fantastic, some funny, some a little sad, but all human." Springfield Repub

Sandburg, Carl, 1878-1967

The Sandburg treasury; prose and poetry for young people; introduction by Paula Sandburg; illustrated by Paul Bacon. Harcourt Brace Jovanovich 1970 480p il $25.95 (5 and up)   **818**

ISBN 0-15-270180-X

"Including, ¦Rootabaga stories,' 'Early moon,' 'Wind song,' 'Abe Lincoln grows up,' 'Prairie-town boy.'" Title page

This volume brings together all of Sandburg's books for young people; his whimsical stories, two books of poetry, a version of his biography of Abraham Lincoln, and portions of his autobiography specially edited for children

821 English poetry

Belloc, Hilaire, 1870-1953

Matilda, who told lies, and was burned to death (1-3)   **821**

Some editions are:

Dial Bks. for Young Readers $13 Illustrated by Steven Kellogg (ISBN 0-8037-1101-8)

Knopf $15; lib bdg $15.99 Illustrated by Posy Simmonds (ISBN 0-679-82658-0; 0-679-92658-5)

"Belloc's heroine is one of several figures he conceived in satirizing the moralistic tales used in Edwardian England to instill proper behavior in children. . . . Matilda, an incorrigible fibber, calls the fire brigade out on a false alarm; later, when fire does indeed break out, she is disbelieved and left to burn to death." Publ Wkly

Berry, James

Celebration song; a poem; illustrated by Louise Brierley. Simon & Schuster Bks. for Young Readers 1994 unp il $14 (k-3)   **821**

1. Jesus Christ—Nativity—Poetry 2. Caribbean region—Poetry

ISBN 0-671-86446-3   LC 93-87671

"Jamaican-born writer Berry sets his nativity poem in the West Indies. Baby Jesus is a year old, and his mother sings him a celebratory lullaby about his birth. Brierley's expressive double-spreads watercolors in folk-art style capture the warm brown shades of the people against the sunlit landscape." Booklist

Blake, Quentin, 1932-

All join in. Little, Brown 1991 unp il $14.95 (k-3)   **821**

1. Noise—Poetry

ISBN 0-316-09934-1   LC 90-53308

Also available Spanish language edition

First published 1990 in the United Kingdom

The poems in this volume celebrate the joys of noise and mischief

"The unremittingly boisterous refrains will please younger readers, and the illustrations are . . . as lively as the poems. A cacophonous delight for those with nerves of steel." Horn Book Guide

Blake, William, 1757-1827

The tyger; illustrated by Neil Waldman. Harcourt Brace Jovanovich 1993 unp il $15.95   **821**

1. Tigers—Poetry

ISBN 0-15-292375-6   LC 92-23378

An illustrated version of Blake's well-known poem, viewing the "tyger, tyger, burning bright, in the forests of the night."

"Waldman's acrylic paintings extend [the poem's] sense of wonder. Within each double-page spread of dark swirling forest, he sets one stanza of the poem and one small frame of brilliant color. . . . As animal poem, as creation myth, and as introduction to the music of poetry, this book makes a stirring read-aloud." Booklist

Browning, Robert, 1812-1889

The Pied Piper of Hamelin; with illustrations by Kate Greenaway. Knopf 1993 104p il $12.95   **821**

ISBN 0-679-42812-7   LC 93-11265

A reissue of the edition first published 1880 in the United Kingdom; first United States edition 1882 by Lyman & Curtis

The Pied Piper pipes the village free of rats, and when the villagers refuse to pay him for the service he exacts a terrible revenge

Includes bibliographical references

Carroll, Lewis, 1832-1898

Lewis Carroll's Jabberwocky; illustrated by Jane Breskin Zalben; with annotations by Humpty Dumpty. Warne 1977 unp il $14.95
821

1. Nonsense verses
ISBN 0-7232-6145-8   LC 77-75040

"In Zalben's intricate double-page watercolor illustrations interpreting Lewis Carroll's nonsense poem 'Jabberwocky,' Humpty Dumpty takes readers through a fantasy world in which trees grow candy and cakes, a raccoon-like creature has three tails and an eye patch, and green pigs shed green tears. Zalben uses color well and the nonsense is visualized in a style rich in detail without appearing cluttered. An annotation of the poem, in the form of a discussion between Alice and Humpty Dumpty, appears as a natural extension at the end of this book which could be useful as a handsome starting point for teaching creative poetry or language development." SLJ

Cohen, Barbara, 1932-1992

Canterbury tales; [by] Geoffrey Chaucer; selected, translated, and adapted by Barbara Cohen; illustrated by Trina Schart Hyman. Lothrop, Lee & Shepard Bks. 1988 87p il $17.95 (4 and up)   **821**

ISBN 0-688-06201-6   LC 86-21045
Contents: The nun's priest's tale; The pardoner's tale; The wife of Bath's tale; The franklin's tale

"Cohen's evident love and respect for Chaucer's writing keep her close to the text. Her writing retains the flavor of the times and the spirit of Chaucer's words while her prose retelling, enriched by Hyman's lively full-color paintings, enhances the book's appeal to young people. . . . An excellent introduction to *The Canterbury Tales* for young readers." Booklist

De la Mare, Walter, 1873-1956

Peacock pie; a book of rhymes; with pictures by Louise Brierley. Holt & Co. 1989 111p il $17.95 (4 and up)   **821**

ISBN 0-8050-1124-2   LC 89-1828
De la Mare's collection of poems describing the capers of fairies, princes, beasts, children, witches, farmers, and kings first appeared in the United Kingdom in 1913. This edition contains de la Mare's revised and expanded 1924 text

"The poems are placed cleanly on the page. Brierley's accompanying sketches and watercolors offer a thoughtful counterpoint to the poems." SLJ

Rhymes and verses; collected poems for children; with drawings by Ellinore [sic] Blaisdell. Holt & Co. 1988 c1947 344p $15.95; pa $7.95 (4 and up)   **821**

ISBN 0-8050-0847-0; 0-8050-0848-9 (pa)
     LC 88-45278
A reissue of the title first published 1947
This volume contains selections from the published works of this English poet. The poems are arranged under such headings as: Green grow the rashes, O; All round about the town; All creatures great and small; Fairies—witches—phantoms, etc.

Hughes, Shirley

Rhymes for Annie Rose. Lothrop, Lee & Shepard Bks. 1995 unp il $16 (k-2)   **821**

ISBN 0-688-14220-6   LC 94-37544
Other titles about Annie Rose and Alfie are entered in E section
A collection of more than twenty poems about young Annie Rose and the daily activities of a child

"Annie Rose and her brother, Alfie, play and dream and discover the world. With wonderful domestic detail, Hughes' line-and-watercolor pictures capture the toddler's joy and mischief, fear and affection. The rhymes are a little forced . . . but the words have a physicalness and a beat that children will love." Booklist

Lear, Edward, 1812-1888

The complete nonsense of Edward Lear; edited and introduced by Holbrook Jackson. Dover Publs. 1951 288p il pa $5.95   **821**

1. Nonsense verses
ISBN 0-486-20167-8
Also available in hardcover from Amereon and P. Smith
A reprint of the 1947 Faber edition published in the United Kingdom

"This is a choice contribution to the literature of laughter. Limericks, verses of all kinds, alphabets and botanics are as daft and amusing as the pictures." Adventuring With Books

How pleasant to know Mr. Lear! Edward Lear's selected works; with an introduction and notes by Myra Cohn Livingston. Holiday House 1982 123p il $14.95   **821**

1. Nonsense verses
ISBN 0-8234-0462-5   LC 82-80822

"Each section begins with a note by the compiler, and notes on sources, as well as a combined title/first line index are appended. While the poetry is easily available elsewhere, it is useful to have the combination of poetry by Lear and information about him, each reinforcing the other." Bull Cent Child Books

The Jumblies   **821**

1. Nonsense verses
Some editions are:
Adama Bks. $6.95 Drawings by Edward Gorey (ISBN 0-915361-34-5)
Putnam $14.95 Illustrated by Ted Rand (ISBN 0-399-21632-4)
First published 1900
This collection of nonsense verse features the adventures of the Jumblies who go to sea in a sieve

Of pelicans and pussycats; poems and limericks; pictures by Jill Newton. Dial Bks. for Young Readers 1990 unp il music $12.95   **821**

1. Nonsense verses 2. Limericks
ISBN 0-8037-0728-2   LC 89-37618
A selection of poems and limericks by Edward Lear, including The Quangle Wangle's Hat, The Pelican Chorus, and The Courtship of Yonghy-Bonghy-Bo

"Dappled and delightful, Newton's watercolors remain faithful to the silliness of Lear's original drawings, and the endpapers display her samples of Lear's nonsense botany. . . . This is a fun introduction to Lear's work." Booklist

Lear, Edward, 1812-1888—*Continued*

The owl and the pussycat **821**

1. Nonsense verses LC 84-24897

Some editions are:

Lothrop, Lee & Shepard Bks. $13.95; lib bdg $13.88 Illustrated by Louise Voce (ISBN 0-688-09536-4; 0-688-09537-2)

Putnam $14.95 Illustrated by Jan Brett (ISBN 0-399-21925-0)

First published 1871

After a courtship voyage of a year and a day, Owl and Pussy finally buy a ring from Piggy and are blissfully wed

The pelican chorus and other nonsense; illustrated by Fred Marcellino. HarperCollins Pubs. 1995 unp il $14.95; lib bdg $14.89 **821**

1. Nonsense verses

ISBN 0-06-205062-1; 0-06-205063-X (lib bdg)

LC 94-78570

"Michael di Capua books"

"Three great nonsense rhymes by the inimitable Edward Lear—'The Pelican Chorus,' 'The Owl and the Pussycat,' and 'The New Vestments'—are presented with wildly comic illustrations, uniquely suited to their era and content. . . . Fred Marcellino's bouncy, humorous, and expressive illustrations enlarge and expand the narratives of all three verses. A great treat for lovers of Lear." Horn Book

There was an old man—; a gallery of nonsense rhymes; illustrated by Michèle Lemieux. Morrow Junior Bks. 1994 unp il $15; lib bdg $14.93 **821**

1. Nonsense verses 2. Limericks

ISBN 0-688-10788-5; 0-688-10789-3 (lib bdg)

LC 93-46492

This "collection of 53 of Lear's nonsense limericks invites children to share the poet's look at the foibles of some of the world's silliest people. Lemieux has heightened the humor with her bright, detailed watercolors that echo the sharp noses and strange expressions of Lear's original drawings." SLJ

Milne, A. A. (Alan Alexander), 1882-1956

Now we are six; with decorations by Ernest H. Shepard. Dutton 1961 c1927 104p il $17.50 (k-3) **821**

ISBN 0-525-44960-4

Also available in paperback from Puffin Bks.

First published 1927. "Reprinted September 1961 in this completely new format designed by Warren Chappell." Verso of title page

"The boy or girl who has liked 'When were were very young' and 'Winnie-the-Pooh' will enjoy reading about Alexander Beetle who was mistaken for a match, the knight whose armor didn't squeak, and the old sailor who had so many things which he wanted to do. There are other entertaining poems, also, and many pictures as delightful as the verses." Pittsburgh

When we were very young; with decorations by Ernest H. Shepard. Dutton 1961 c1924 102p il $17.50 (k-3) **821**

ISBN 0-525-44961-2

Also available in paperback from Puffin Bks.

First published 1924. "Reprinted September 1961 in this completely new format designed by Warren Chappell." Verso of title page

Verse "written for Milne's small son Christopher Robin, which for its bubbling nonsense, its whimsy, and the unexpected surprises of its rhymes and rhythms, furnishes immeasurable joy to children." Right Book for the Right Child

"Mr. Milne's gay jingles have found a worthy accompaniment in the charming illustrations of Mr. Shepard." Saturday Rev

The world of Christopher Robin; the complete When we were very young and Now we are six; with decorations and new illustrations in full color, by E. H. Shepard. Dutton 1958 234p il $17.50 (k-3) **821**

ISBN 0-525-44448-3

Also available as part of a boxed set together with: The world of Pooh, entered in the Fiction section, for $29.95 (ISBN 0-525-43348-1)

In this combined edition of the two titles entered separately "the black-and-white illustrations of the original book have been retained and in addition the artist has created end papers and eight full-page illustrations in color." Booklist

Noyes, Alfred, 1880-1958

The highwayman; written by Alfred Noyes; illustrated by Neil Waldman. Harcourt Brace Jovanovich 1990 unp il $14.95 **821**

1. Thieves—Poetry

ISBN 0-15-234340-7 LC 89-30805

An illustrated version of the well-known poem about the highwayman and his true love, the innkeeper's daughter

"Waldman's watercolors, both abstract and realistic, capture the haunting, tragic spirit of the text. His broad palette glows, and his frequent use of shadow and silhouette is magnificent. . . . For older readers, this unusual—and triumphant—treatment provides a striking introduction to an epic work." Publ Wkly

Stevenson, Robert Louis, 1850-1894

Block city; illustrated by Ashley Wolff. Dutton 1988 unp il $12.95 (k-2) **821**

ISBN 0-525-44399-1 LC 87-33397

Also available in paperback from Puffin Bks.

"Wolff's colorful paintings, which resemble block prints, cleverly combine with and enrich Stevenson's poem. Large two-page spreads show a young boy at home reading on a rainy day. As he starts to build with his blocks on the floor he creates an elaborate landscape that comes alive. The hard edges of the cut block contrast with muted colors that fade off into the distance to echo the corresponding relationship in the poem whereby the solid building blocks combine with the child's imagination to create a world of palaces and harbors, sailing ships, and kings." SLJ

A child's garden of verses (k-4) **821**

Some editions are:

Abrams $14.95 Illustrated by Joanna Isles (ISBN 0-8109-3196-6; LC 93-74829)

Knopf (Everyman's library children's classics) $12.95 Illustrated by Charles Robinson (ISBN 0-679-41799-0; LC 92-53175)

Oxford Univ. Press pa $8.95 Illustrated by Brian Wildsmith (ISBN 0-19-276065-3)

Scribner $18.95 (Scribner illustrated classics) Illustrated by Jessie Willcox Smith (ISBN 0-684-20949-7)

First published 1885 in the United Kingdom with title: Penny whistles

Stevenson, Robert Louis, 1850-1894—*Continued*

"Verses known and loved by one generation after another. Among the simpler ones for pre-school children are: Rain; At the Seaside; and Singing." Right Book for the Right Child

My shadow (k-3)   **821**

1. Shades and shadows—Poetry

Some editions are:

Godine $14.95 Illustrations by Glenna Lang (ISBN 0-87923-788-0)

Putnam $14.95 Illustrated by Ted Rand (ISBN 0-399-22216-2)

Illustrated versions of Stevenson's popular poem in which a child tells about her relationship with her shadow

"Lang's flat acrylic paintings eliminate natural shadows and reduce volumes to shapes—as shadows do." SLJ

"Rather than following one child through the activities suggested in this classic poem, Rand skips about the world for a multi-cultural view of children and their shadowplay. The result is an exuberant version that revitalizes the familiar lines. . . . The scenes, which stretch across double-page spreads, are unified by their impressionistic style, subtle colors, and joyful mood." Booklist

Treece, Henry, 1911-1966

The magic wood; a poem by Henry Treece; paintings by Barry Moser. HarperCollins Pubs. 1992 unp il $16; lib bdg $15.89   **821**

1. Supernatural—Poetry 2. Night—Poetry

ISBN 0-06-020802-3; 0-06-020803-1 (lib bdg)

LC 91-29547

"Willa Perlman books"

This poem was originally published in the author's collection The black season (c1945) and in Collected poems (c1946)

A mysterious man befriends an unwitting visitor in a nighttime wood filled with hidden danger

"Treece's poem is haunting enough by itself. . . . With the addition of Moser's paintings, it becomes positively uncanny." Booklist

821.008 English poetry— Collections

Creatures; poems selected by Lee Bennett Hopkins; illustrated by Stella Ormai. Harcourt Brace Jovanovich 1985 32p il lib bdg $14.95 (3-5)   **821.008**

1. Monsters—Poetry 2. English poetry—Collections 3. American poetry—Collections

ISBN 0-15-220875-5   LC 84-15698

"Ghosties, ghoulies and fantastical beings dance through the 18 poems by Rachel Field, Ted Hughes, Karla Kuskin and others, accompanied by Ormai's green and gray pencil drawings that capture the mood of the poems." SLJ

Ghost poems; edited by Daisy Wallace; illustrated by Tomie de Paola. Holiday House 1979 30p il lib bdg $13.95; pa $4.95 (1-4)   **821.008**

1. Ghosts—Poetry 2. English poetry—Collections 3. American poetry—Collections

ISBN 0-8234-0344-0 (lib bdg); 0-8234-0849-3 (pa)

LC 78-11028

"Mostly inducing titters rather than terrors—is this collection by rhymsters with an active sense of the absurd. . . . Among the 17 entertainers are the old Scottish prayers ('Ghosties and Ghoulies'), two American Indian songs and contributions from conjurers of the past and present: Nancy Willard, Lilian Moore. X. J. Kennedy, Jack Prelutsky, et al., as well as anonymous selections from legends." Publ Wkly

"Illustrated with a quick and fearsome flourish by Tomie de Paola. . . . Here are wonderful poems to frighten young children with—but not really." N Y Times Book Rev

A **Great** big ugly man came up and tied his horse to me; a book of nonsense verse; [compiled and] illustrated by Wallace Tripp. Little, Brown 1973 46p il lib bdg $14.95 (k-3)   **821.008**

1. Nonsense verses 2. English poetry—Collections 3. American poetry—Collections

ISBN 0-316-85280-5

This book is "a case of an imaginative illustrator taking a new look at some old words—nursery rhymes, oral chants, verse and occasional doggerel, and coming up with some zany interpretations. Assorted animals and humans frolic through the pages in a lively series of 41 bits of verse spanning several centuries. . . . About half the verses are nursery rhymes; the rest run to oral verse, some limericks and one parody." N Y Times Book Rev

If there were dreams to sell; compiled by Barbara Lalicki; illustrated by Margot Tomes. 2nd ed. Four Winds Press 1994 c1984 unp il $15.95 (k-3)   **821.008**

1. Alphabet 2. English poetry—Collections 3. American poetry—Collections

ISBN 0-02-751251-7   LC 94-10352

A reissue of the title first published 1984 by Lothrop, Lee & Shepard Bks.

In this collection "each letter of the alphabet appears in upper- and lowercase and is represented by a poem, nursery rhyme, phrase, or word. . . . An addendum gives a paragraph's worth of information about each of the textual choices, some of which are by literary lights such as Tennyson, Longfellow, Coleridge, and Pope." Booklist

"Tomes' magical illustrations are glorious, and her scenes of elves, animals and British and Colonial American villages and villagers radiate with energy and activity." SLJ

Knock at a star; a child's introduction to poetry; [compiled by] X. J. Kennedy, Dorothy M. Kennedy; illustrated by Karen Ann Weinhaus. Little, Brown 1982 148p il $15.95; pa $9.95 (3-6)   **821.008**

1. English poetry—Collections 2. American poetry—Collections

ISBN 0-316-48853-4; 0-316-48854-2 (pa)

LC 82-7328

"The anthology is stocked with poems chosen from a myriad of varied poets, ranging from Blake and Herrick to David McCord, Eve Merriam, and Bob Dylan. . . . The commentaries have avoided both pedantry and prettification by stressing the naturalness of the poetic experience." Horn Book

"The abundant illustrations are whimsical and similar to Arnold Lobel's style, and would appeal especially to younger readers. If any book can win young readers to poetry, this one can, for there's not a poem in it that isn't a chuckle, a scare, or an illumination." SLJ

Lifelines; a poetry anthology patterned on the stages of life; selected and introduced by Leonard S. Marcus. Dutton Children's Bks. 1994 116p il $15.99 (4 and up)   **821.008**

1. American poetry—Collections 2. English poetry—Collections

ISBN 0-525-45164-1   LC 93-26413

"A collection of some 80 poems, mostly American, many contemporary, addresses the life cycle from birth to death. Interesting biographical sketches of the poets." N Y Times Book Rev

Miracles: poems by children of the English-speaking world; collected by Richard Lewis. Simon & Schuster 1966 215p il hardcover o.p. paperback available $5.95   **821.008**

1. English poetry—Collections 2. Child authors

ISBN 0-671-42797-0 (pa)

Poems on a variety of subjects by children between the ages if 4 and 13. The authors come from such varied backgrounds as the United States, England, Ireland, New Zealand, Kenya, Uganda, and Australia

"Poems chosen with a keen appreciation of the spontaneity of children's creative expression." Child Books, 1966

Monster poems; edited by Daisy Wallace; illustrated by Kay Chorao. Holiday House 1976 29p il lib bdg $13.95; pa $4.95 (1-4)   **821.008**

1. Monsters—Poetry 2. English poetry—Collections 3. American poetry—Collections

ISBN 0-8234-0268-1 (lib bdg); 0-8234-0848-5 (pa)

"These poems, collected from several sources, feature a Griggle who giggles while eating lunch, a nine-foot Ugstabuggle with hairy, grasping hands, a spangled pandemonium who is missing from the zoo, an Ombley-Gombley who sits upon a train track, and a Slithergadee who crawls out of the sea. Chorao's orange-and-blue creatures swarm over and around the rhymes, which are set off in white blocks, and lurk in corners and margins to add humor and eye-catching novelty for the reader." Booklist

A New treasury of children's poetry; old favorites and new discoveries; selected and introduced by Joanna Cole; illustrated by Judith Gwyn Brown. Doubleday 1984 224p il $18.50   **821.008**

1. English poetry—Collections 2. American poetry—Collections

ISBN 0-385-18539-1   LC 83-20821

This "anthology of more than 200 poems is arranged in nine subject-oriented sections which include animals, holidays, silly rhymes and nature. It is a collection of Cole's personal favorites, and there is an emphasis on 19th- and 20th-Century American poets." SLJ

"Animated line drawings, some soberly representational but most comical and/or grotesque, illustrate a book in which the selections are arranged so that they progress from simple poems for very young children and, with increasing complexity, move on to poems for older readers. . . . There's little unusual here, but it's an anthology of solid worth." Bull Cent Child Books

Of quarks, quasars, and other quirks; quizzical poems for the supersonic age; collected by Sara and John E. Brewton and John Brewton Blackburn; illustrated by Quentin Blake. Crowell 1977 114p il lib bdg $13.89 (5 and up)   **821.008**

1. English poetry—Collections 2. American poetry—Collections

ISBN 0-690-04885-8   LC 76-54747

"An anthology of children's poetry spoofing modern life and scientific progress. Credit card overuse, TV mania, computer craziness, transplants, and atomic bombs are parodied in original and outrageous verse with serious undertones. . . . With such contributors as Eve Merriam, Ogden Nash, and John Updike." SLJ

The Oxford book of children's verse; chosen and edited with notes by Iona and Peter Opie. Oxford Univ. Press 1973 xxxi, 407p il $29.95; pa $14.95   **821.008**

1. English poetry—Collections 2. American poetry—Collections

ISBN 0-19-812140-7; 0-19-282349-3 (pa)

Arranged chronologically, these 332 selections from British and American children's poetry include works by such poets as Chaucer, Charles and Mary Lamb, Kipling, Farjeon, Milne, Eliot and Nash

Poems for the very young; selected by Michael Rosen; illustrated by Bob Graham. Kingfisher (NY) 1993 77p il $15.95 (k-3)   **821.008**

1. Poetry—Collections

ISBN 1-85697-908-3   LC 92-45574

This "is a mix of traditional rhymes, verse by poets, and pieces written by children that ranges over time and cultures, united by a sure sense of the richness of well-chosen words. The obvious care behind each poem's selection is matched by Graham's humorous watercolor cartoons that extend, interpret, and celebrate their subjects." SLJ

The Poetry troupe; an anthology of poems to read aloud; compiled by Isabel Wilner; decorations by Isabel Wilner. Scribner 1977 223p il lib bdg $14.95   **821.008**

1. English poetry—Collections 2. American poetry—Collections

ISBN 0-684-15198-7   LC 77-9439

"During her years as a librarian in an elementary laboratory school on a college campus, the compiler has worked with children in 'poetry troupes' that invite both active participation and passive listening. The groups vary in age, taste, and sophistication; girls and boys help to hunt down the poems to be shared and present them in an assortment of ways to classes of college students as well as of children. The collection represents poetry that has brought great pleasure to readers and to audiences; and while most of the authors are familiar enough, the poems themselves are buoyant and unhackneyed. . . . With indexes of authors, titles, and first lines." Horn Book

Rainbow in the sky; collected and edited by Louis Untermeyer; illustrated by Reginald Birch. Golden anniversary ed. Harcourt Brace Jovanovich 1985 c1935 xxvii, 498p il $19.95 (k-4)   **821.008**

1. English poetry—Collections 2. American poetry—Collections 3. Nursery rhymes

ISBN 0-15-265479-8   LC 84-19306

Rainbow in the sky—*Continued*

A reissue of the title first published 1935

"More than five hundred poems from Mother Goose to modern times are included in this anthology for younger children. Mr. Birch's drawings in black and white are lively and . . . amusing." N Y Public Libr

The **Random** House book of poetry for children; selected and introduced by Jack Prelutsky; illustrated by Arnold Lobel. Random House 1983 248p il $19; lib bdg $17.99   **821.008**

1. American poetry—Collections 2. English poetry—Collections

ISBN 0-394-85010-6; 0-394-95010-0 (lib bdg)

                       LC 83-2990

Opening poems for each section especially written for this anthology by Jack Prelutsky

In this anthology emphasis "is placed on humor and light verse; but serious and thoughtful poems are also included. . . . Approximately two thirds of the selections were written within the past forty years—the splendid contributions of such writers as John Ciardi, Aileen Fisher, Dennis Lee, Myra Cohn Livingston, David McCord, Eve Merriam, and Lilian Moore. [There are] . . . samplings of earlier poets from Shakespeare and Blake to Emily Dickinson and Walter de la Mare." Horn Book

Read-aloud rhymes for the very young; selected by Jack Prelutsky; illustrated by Marc Brown; with an introduction by Jim Trelease. Knopf 1986 98p il $19; lib bdg $17.99 (k-2)   **821.008**

1. English poetry—Collections 2. American poetry—Collections 3. Nursery rhymes

ISBN 0-394-87218-5; 0-394-97218-X (lib bdg)

                       LC 86-7147

"Prelutsky has selected and combined joyous, sensitive poems . . . by such traditional poets as Dorothy Aldis and A. A. Milne, as well as by more contemporary poets such as Karla Kuskin, Dennis Lee, and Prelutsky himself. All are lively, rhythmic poems that young children will enjoy. . . . Brown's bright pastel illustrations effectively use framing, action, and cheerful creatures to echo the light tone of the book. The poems are arranged with others of the same topic and include popular concerns of small children such as animals, bath time, dragons, and play. Teachers and librarians will appreciate poems about seasons, months, holidays, and special events that can be easily incorporated into story hours and classroom life." SLJ

Talking like the rain; a first book of poems; selected by X. J. Kennedy and Dorothy Kennedy; illustrated by Jane Dyer. Little, Brown 1992 96p il $19.95 (k-3)

                            821.008

1. English poetry—Collections 2. American poetry—Collections

ISBN 0-316-48889-5   LC 89-13504

This is an "assortment of classic and contemporary verse for children. From Robert Louis Stevenson to Dennis Lee, with samples of most of the best children's poets ranging among the 123 selections, there's a sense of rolling rhyme that carries the reader from one singing page to another. And there are many pages, each designed to surround the poetry or set it into neat, discreet illustrations that project graphic images from verbal ones. . . . In selection, scope, and visual format, this is likely to be a volume many times revisited." Bull Cent Child Books

Tripp, Wallace, 1940-

Marguerite, go wash your feet. Houghton Mifflin 1985 48p il lib bdg $17.95; pa $8.95 (1-3)   **821.008**

1. Humorous poetry 2. English poetry—Collections 3. American poetry—Collections

ISBN 0-395-35392-0 (lib bdg); 0-395-39894-0 (pa)

                       LC 85-7616

A collection of amusing verses by a variety of poets, including Emily Dickinson, Spike Milligan, Shakespeare, and others less well known

"Tripp's taste in irreverent nonsense is impeccable; his talent for illustrating it is remarkable. . . . There is something here for everyone: young children will enjoy the language rhythms and cartoon drawings, older ones will pick up on the forthright jokes, while adults will enjoy the artistic allusions and sassier poems that require some background for full appreciation." Booklist

Wider than the sky: poems to grow up with; collected and edited by Scott Elledge. Harper & Row 1990 358p lib bdg $19.89 (5 and up)   **821.008**

1. English poetry—Collections 2. American poetry—Collections

ISBN 0-06-021787-1   LC 90-4135

"This substantial, eclectic gathering of diverse forms includes classic and contemporary selections on a variety of subjects, ranging from love to nature, from the sublime to the ridiculous. . . . It is essentially a browsing collection, yet the arrangement is not quite as random as a first glance might indicate. Several poems with similar themes or which benefit from close juxtaposition are sequentially placed." Horn Book

Includes bibliographical references

Witch poems; edited by Daisy Wallace; illustrated by Trina Schart Hyman. Holiday House 1976 30p il lib bdg $13.95; pa $4.95

                            821.008

1. Witches—Poetry 2. English poetry—Collections 3. American poetry—Collections

ISBN 0-8234-0281-9 (lib bdg); 0-8234-0850-7 (pa)

"A collection of 20 short witch poems, most by contemporary authors (X. J. Kennedy, Karla Kuskin, and company) but also including four traditional chants." SLJ

"All the poems are rich in the rhymes, refrains and wordplay of which good incantations are made." N Y Times Book Rev

822.3   William Shakespeare

Lamb, Charles, 1775-1834

Tales from Shakespeare; by Charles & Mary Lamb   **822.3**

1. Shakespeare, William, 1564-1616—Adaptations

Hardcover and paperback editions available from various publishers; Spanish language edition also available

First published 1807

"The *Tales* were the first version of 'Shakespeare' to be published specifically for children. They are written in a clear, vigorous style, not often encumbered by the attempt to make the language resemble that of the original. A lot is left out. . . . But the literary quality of the *Tales* makes them outshine almost every other English children's book of this period, and they proved an immediate and lasting success." Oxford Companion to Child Lit

McCaughrean, Geraldine, 1951-
Stories from Shakespeare; illustrated by Antony Maitland. Margaret K. McElderry Bks. 1995 143p il $19.95   **822.3**

1. Shakespeare, William, 1564-1616—Adaptations

ISBN 0-689-80037-1   LC 94-78244

"McCaughrean provides a cast of characters for each play and a brief statement that sets the work in context. Her rendition of 'Macbeth' is crisp, swiftly paced and properly horripilating—the best of the 10 plays she examines. While the dramas are much condensed, excerpts from the best-known speeches are provided as sidebars on many pages, and at the end of each play a portion of the actual text is attractively set, much as a poem might be." N Y Times Book Rev

Ross, Stewart
Shakespeare and Macbeth; the story behind the play; illustrated by Tony Karpinski and Victor Ambrus; foreword by Kenneth Branagh. Viking 1994 35p il $16.99 (5 and up)   **822.3**

ISBN 0-670-85629-0

The author "tells of the writing and first performance of this turbulent Shakespeare play in 1605 London, including smoothly written information about patronage, historical sources, and habits of theatergoers. He gives the real Macbeth a fair shake too, explaining the differences between Shakespeare's version and known history and suggesting reasons for the playwright's changes. A chronology of Shakespeare, a general note on the play, a list of Shakespeare's works, an index, and a brief bibliography . . . are included." Bull Cent Child Books

828   English miscellany

Carroll, Lewis, 1832-1898
The complete works of Lewis Carroll; with an introduction by Alexander Woollcott; and the illustrations by John Tenniel. Nonesuch Press; distributed by Viking 1990 c1989 1165p il $35   **828**

ISBN 1-871061-14-8   LC 89-60108

Also available Random House edition $15.95 (ISBN 0-394-60485-7)

This edition first published 1939 in the United Kingdom

In addition to Alice's adventures in Wonderland, Through the looking glass, Sylvie and Bruno, Sylvie and Bruno concluded, The hunting of the snark, Phantasmagoria and other poems, and Three sunsets and other poems, this volume collects Carroll's shorter prose, verse, stories, games, puzzles, problems, acrostics and a selection from Symbolic logic

Thomas, Dylan, 1914-1953
A child's Christmas in Wales.   **828**

1. Christmas—Wales

Hardcover and paperback editions available from various publishers

First published 1954

A portrait of Christmas Day in a small Welsh town and of the author's childhood there

For any season of the year "the language is enchanting and the poetry shines with an unearthly radiance." NY Times Book Rev

841   French poetry

Bernos de Gasztold, Carmen
Prayers from the ark; selected poems by Carmen Bernos de Gasztold; translated from the French by Rumer Godden; illustrated by Barry Moser. Viking 1992 unp il $16   **841**

1. Noah's ark—Poetry 2. Animals—Poetry 3. Prayers 4. French poetry

ISBN 0-670-84496-9   LC 92-77

Poems selected from the 1962 Viking edition of the same title which was illustrated by Jean Primrose; the French originals appeared in two books published 1947 and 1955

An illustrated collection of poems, each a prayer by one of the animals in Noah's ark

"These 'prayers' of a selection of animals are poetic reflections on their natures, their functions, and their fates. Each creature is vividly self-characterized, wittily and concisely; at the same time, each unmistakably mirrors human feelings and foibles. . . . Moser contributes a brilliant portrait of every animal, subtly suggesting the very qualities revealed in each one's words. These splendid illustrations exactly suit the wide range of the text." SLJ

Cendrars, Blaise, 1887-1961
Shadow; translated and illustrated by Marcia Brown from the French of Blaise Cendrars. Scribner 1982 unp il $16.95 (1-3)   **841**

ISBN 0-684-17226-7 .   LC 81-9424

Also available in paperback from Aladdin Bks.

Awarded the Caldecott Medal, 1983

Original text first published in France

This is the French poet's "version of a West African folk tale about a spirit that is at once elusive and multiform." N Y Times Book Rev

"Inspired by the exotic atmosphere and the dramatic possibilities of the text, Brown has choreographed a sequence of almost theatrical illustrations, placing human and animal figures—and their shadows—against brilliant, contrasting, always changing settings. Resplendent—yet controlled—in color, texture, and form, the work is an impressive, sophisticated example of the art of the picture book." Horn Book

883   Classical Greek epic poetry and fiction

Hutton, Warwick
The Trojan horse; retold and illustrated by Warwick Hutton. Margaret K. McElderry Bks. 1992 unp il $14.95 (3-5)   **883**

1. Homer—Adaptations 2. Trojan War 3. Classical mythology

ISBN 0-689-50542-6   LC 91-21590

"This picture book humanizes the heroic story without in any way reducing its mystery. . . . Hutton's informal style, with its masterful use of changing perspective, is perfectly suited to his story. The deceptively casual illustrations manage to be both contemporary and historical." Booklist

Picard, Barbara Leonie, 1917-
The Iliad of Homer; retold by Barbara
Leonie Picard; illustrated by Joan
Kiddell-Monroe. Oxford Univ. Press 1960
208p il hardcover o.p. paperback available
$10.95 (6 and up)   **883**
1. Homer—Adaptations 2. Trojan War
ISBN 0-19-274147-0 (pa)
"Rounding out the course of the Trojan War in the ninth
year, as given by Homer, Miss Picard provides a Prologue
explaining how the war with Troy began, and an Epilogue
recounting how the war ended. Finally, she includes a . . .
glossary identifying the long cast of humans and gods taking
part in the conduct of the war." Horn Book

Sutcliff, Rosemary, 1920-1992
Black ships before Troy; the story of the
Iliad; illustrated by Alan Lee. Delacorte Press
1993 128p il $19.95 (5 and up)   **883**
1. Trojan War
ISBN 0-385-31069-2   LC 92-38782
Retells the story of the Trojan War, from the quarrel for
the golden apple, and the flight of Helen with Paris, to the
destruction of Troy
"Sutcliff's strong rhythms and Lee's misty watercolors in
shades of brown, blue, and silvergray make this large-size
volume great for reading aloud." Booklist
Includes bibliography

895.6   Japanese literature

Demi, 1942-
In the eyes of the cat; Japanese poetry for
all seasons; selected and illustrated by Demi;
translated by Tze-si Huang. Holt & Co. 1992
unp il $15.95; pa $5.95   **895.6**
1. Animals—Poetry 2. Japanese poetry—Collections
ISBN 0-8050-1955-3; 0-8050-3383-1 (pa)
     LC 91-27728
"The poems were selected from the works of the Japanese masters and organized according to the seasons. Each
depicts an animal, from the familiar kittens to the less familiar heron and egret. The poems evoke multi-sensory images because of the carefully selected words and the
deceptively simplistic, brilliant illustrations. A book to read,
re-read and treasure." Child Book Rev Serv

Mado, Michio
The animals; selected poems; decorations by
Mitsumasa Anno; translated by the Empress
Michiko of Japan. Margaret K. McElderry
Bks. 1992 47p il $16.95 (4 and up)   **895.6**
1. Animals—Poetry 2. Japanese poetry—Collections
3. Bilingual books—English-Japanese
ISBN 0-689-50574-4   LC 92-10356
"A collection of 20 poems, artfully written and gracefully
staged. Presented in Japanese with the English version on
the facing page, Mado's poems are set against buff-colored
backgrounds that are bordered in white and ornamented
with cut-paper animal friezes. Included are poems about a
variety of animals. . . . An accessible title that will draw a
wide range of readers, this fine combination of content and
design will have a multitude of uses. It is a handsome piece
of bookmaking in which the design beautifully echoes the
elegant restraint of the poetry." Booklist

Red dragonfly on my shoulder; haiku
translated by Sylvia Cassedy and Kunihiro
Suetake; illustrated by Molly Bang.
HarperCollins Pubs. 1992 unp il $15; lib
bdg $14.89   **895.6**
1. Haiku 2. Animals—Poetry
ISBN 0-06-022624-2; 0-06-022625-0 (lib bdg)
     LC 91-18443
"Here are 13 traditional Japanese haiku illustrated by
artwork that is both striking and original. The verse adheres
to the 17-syllable form, the language is concrete, and the
images have vitality. . . . What's new here is Bang's artwork, interpreting the verse not with the usual brushed ink
or watercolor paintings, but with unusual collages combining paper, hardware, and found objects in a series of illustrations as arresting as the poems themselves." Booklist

896   African literatures

Olaleye, Isaac
The distant talking drum; poems from
Nigeria; paintings by Frané Lessac. Wordsong
1995 32p il $14.95 (2-4)   **896**
1. Nigeria—Poetry
ISBN 1-56397-095-3   LC 94-60260
"Each of Olaleye's fifteen poems describes one aspect Nigerian village life, such as farming, washing clothes in the
stream, and dancing in the village square. . . . The blank
verse describes, rather than evokes, the details of village
life. Each poem is accompanied by a full-page illustration
bordered with a colorful geometric pattern, reflecting the
patterns on the bright Nigerian clothing." Horn Book

897   North American native
literatures

Dancing teepees: poems of American Indian
youth; selected by Virginia Driving Hawk
Sneve, with art by Stephen Gammell.
Holiday House 1989 32p il $15.95; pa $5.95
(3-5)   **897**
1. Indians of North America—Poetry
ISBN 0-8234-0724-1; 0-8234-0879-5 (pa)
     LC 88-11075
An illustrated collection of poems from the oral tradition
of Native Americans
This is an "eclectic collection, drawn from a variety of
tribal traditions. Printed on heavy paper, the book is illustrated with a catalogue of marvelously rendered designs and
motifs, ranging from those of the Northwest Coast to the
intricate beadwork patterns of the Great Lakes and the zig-
zag geometric borders of Southwestern pottery." N Y Times
Book Rev

In the trail of the wind; American Indian
poems and ritual orations; edited by John
Bierhorst. Farrar, Straus & Giroux 1971
201p il hardcover o.p. paperback available
$4.95 (5 and up)   **897**
1. Indians—Poetry
ISBN 0-374-43576-6 (pa)
This "collection of poetry, taken from the oral literature
of more than 30 tribes of Indians of North, Central, and
South America and the Eskimos, is arranged topically under
such headings as The beginning, Of rain and birth, The

In the trail of the wind—*Continued*
words of war, and Death. . . . Background information on certain aspects of Indian thought and the problems of translation are discussed in the introduction. Appended are notes on each poem including translator and source; a glossary of tribes, cultures, and languages; and suggestions for further reading." Booklist

"A fascinating book to read, and to reread. . . . Its illustrations, selected from period engravings, makes it a distinguished book to look at as well." Publ Wkly

On the road of stars; Native American night poems and sleep charms; selected by John Bierhorst; pictures by Judy Pedersen. Macmillan 1994 unp il $15.95 (k-3)

897

1. Night—Poetry 2. Sleep—Poetry 3. Indians of North America—Poetry
ISBN 0-02-709735-8   LC 92-20001

A collection of Native American night poems, sleep charms, and other special night songs intended to soothe, heal, bring dreams, or make sleep irresistible

"The shadowy illustrations, mostly in deep blues, browns, and grays, are often full page, and the poems are spaciously arranged, some appearing in handwritten text. The variety in tone and subject will appeal to young listeners, and the book's format and artwork will allow them to find their favorites easily, again and again." Booklist

The **Sacred** path; spells, prayers & power songs of the American Indians; edited by John Bierhorst. Morrow 1983 191p il $15.95; pa $7.95 (5 and up)   **897**

1. Indians—Poetry
ISBN 0-688-01699-5; 0-688-02647-8 (pa)
                                            LC 82-14118

"Containing both traditional and contemporary material, this is a compilation of American Indian poetry that is arranged by stages of the life cycle, beginning with poems and chants of birth and infancy, and progressing through stages and activities of life to prayers and songs for the dying and the dead. . . . The tribal source for each selection is printed below the poem; appended are editorial notes, a bibliography of sources, and a glossary of tribes, cultures and languages." Bull Cent Child Books

Songs are thoughts; poems of the Inuit; edited with an introduction by Neil Philip; illustrated by Maryclare Foa. Orchard Bks. 1995 unp il $15.95 (1-3)   **897**

1. Inuit—Poetry
ISBN 0-531-06893-5   LC 94-27866

"Collected largely by Danish ethnologist Knud Rasmussen during an Arctic expedition, these poems reflect every aspect of Inuit life. Despite their brevity, they project strong visual and emotional images that stay with the listener or reader. Each double-page spread comprises a poem set opposite a full-page oil painting. The strong, colorful paintings, which reflect the mood of the poetry, will intrigue children as much as the poetry itself." Booklist

The **Trees** stand shining; poetry of the North American Indians; selected by Hettie Jones; paintings by Robert Andrew Parker. Dial Bks. 1993 unp il $13.99; lib bdg $13.89 (3-6)

897

1. American poetry—American Indian authors—Collections
ISBN 0-8037-9083-X; 0-8037-9084-8 (lib bdg)
                                            LC 79-142452

A reissue of the title first published 1971

"The poems are grouped by subject, with sources given, most of them reflecting the love and respect for natural things that are part of the great heritage of the Indian cultures of North America; they were originally songs, many of them brief fragments that seem almost chants or lamentations." Bull Cent Child Books

"Fourteen large full-color paintings are provided for this handsome picture book. . . . Some are like rich impressionistic backdrops and illuminate the intense, haikulike word images. . . . Others portray animal or human figures against sweeping brush strokes of color." Horn Book

900 GEOGRAPHY AND HISTORY

905 History—Serial publications

Calliope; world history for young people. Cobblestone Pub. $17.95 per year   **905**

1. History—Periodicals
ISSN 1050-7086

Five issues a year. First published 1981 with title: Classical Calliope

This "is a world history magazine for elementary and junior high-aged children. Each 48-page black-and-white issue focuses on a single theme, such as Judaism, Athens, or epic heroes, and explores the theme through a variety of articles and activities. The magazine uses photos, drawings, diagrams, and charts to enhance its usefulness. Sidebars to the articles provide additional helpful information. Regular features include maps, fun with words, and reviews of books and other materials relating to the issue's theme." Katz. Mag for Libr. 8th edition

909 World history. Civilization

Haskins, James, 1941-
Count your way through the Arab world; by Jim Haskins; illustrations by Dana Gustafson. Carolrhoda Bks. 1987 unp il lib bdg $18.95; pa $5.95 (2-4)   **909**

1. Arab countries
ISBN 0-87614-304-4 (lib bdg); 0-87614-487-3 (pa)
                                            LC 87-6391

Uses Arabic numerals from one to ten to introduce concepts about Arab countries and Arab culture

Knight, Margy Burns
Talking walls; illustrated by Anne Sibley O'Brien. Tilbury House 1992 unp il maps $17.95; pa $8.95 (3-5)   **909**

1. Walls 2. World history
ISBN 0-88448-102-6; 0-88448-154-9 (pa)
                                            LC 91-67867

Also available Spanish language edition
An illustrated description of walls around the world and their significance

"A praiseworthy celebration of similarities and differences among the world's peoples. . . . Young readers will recognize such landmarks as the Great Wall of China, the cave walls of Lascaux, the Wailing Wall and the Vietnam Memorial. More surprising selections feature the work of

Knight, Margy Burns—*Continued*
Australian aborigines, Indian Hindus, Islamic Egyptians, Native Americans and Africans. The narrative is respectful and egalitarian, with the clear intent of valuing no one people over another. O'Brien's . . . well-designed and affecting pastels cover each spread." Publ Wkly

Putnam, James
Pyramid; written by James Putnam; photographed by Geoff Brightling & Peter Hayman. Knopf 1994 63p il (Eyewitness books) $19; lib bdg $18.99 (4 and up)

909

1. Pyramids
ISBN 0-679-86170-X; 0-679-96170-4 (lib bdg)
LC 94-8804
"A Dorling Kindersley book"

This introduction to pyramids of the world features "full-color photographs. The best coverage is given to Egyptian tombs, but pyramids in Nubia, Mexico, and Central America are also described. In addition to sharing information on what is known about the Egyptian pyramids, Putnam also mentions unsolved riddles about them, such as how many workers built them, how the stones were moved, etc." SLJ

The **World** in 1492; by Jean Fritz [et al.]; with illustrations by Stefano Vitale. Holt & Co. 1992 168p il maps $19.95 (5 and up)

909

1. Fifteenth century 2. World history
ISBN 0-8050-1674-0
LC 92-5434

A collection of essays on 15th century life divided by continent. "Jean Fritz writes of Europe; Katherine Paterson, Asia; the McKissacks, Africa; Margaret Mahy, Australia and Oceania; and Jamake Highwater, the Americas. . . . Elegant in format . . . the book is graced with numerous illustrations and reproductions." SLJ

Includes bibliography

909.07 World history — ca. 500-1450/1500

Anno, Mitsumasa, 1926-
Anno's medieval world; adapted from the translation by Ursula Synge. Philomel Bks. 1980 unp il $16.95 (3-6)

909.07

1. Medieval civilization 2. Universe 3. Science and civilization
ISBN 0-399-20742-2
LC 79-28367
Original Japanese edition, 1979

The author describes scientific beliefs concerning the universe in the Middle Ages up to the Age of Reason. Through text and paintings Anno looks at the culture, "fears and superstitions, as well as the growing advances in scientific thought and inquiry." Publisher's note

"The detailed scientific explanation, along with a chronology and notes that are appended, will need adult interpretation. For an older audience than the picture-book format implies, but nonetheless fascinating." Booklist

Hunt, Jonathan
Illuminations; written and illustrated by Jonathan Hunt. Bradbury Press 1989 unp il $16.95 (2-4)

909.07

1. Alphabet 2. Medieval civilization 3. Illumination of books and manuscripts
ISBN 0-02-745770-2
LC 88-38967
Also available in paperback from Aladdin Bks. (NY)

"An oversized, elaborately illustrated, eclectic alphabetic view of the Middle Ages from Alchemist to Zither, with illuminated initials based on a twelfth-century alphabet, this book is for browsing rather than reference, and useful for introducing or complementing history units." Horn Book Guide

Includes bibliography

909.81 World history—19th century, 1800-1899

Industrial revolution; John D. Clare, editor. Harcourt Brace & Co. 1994 64p il maps (Living history) $16.95 (5 and up)

909.81

1. Industrial revolution
ISBN 0-15-200514-5
LC 93-2554
"Gulliver books"

Describes the dramatic technological, industrial, and social changes brought about by the Industrial Revolution in America and Europe

"The combination of dramatic photography and a clear, well-written text makes this period truly come to life." SLJ

Langley, Andrew
The industrial revolution. Viking 1994 48p il (See through history) $15.99 (4 and up)

909.81

1. Industrial revolution
ISBN 0-670-85835-8
LC 94-60549
"An overview of the Industrial Revolution is presented in a series of double-page spreads that show how inventions and technology . . . affected people at every socioeconomic level. The book is illustrated with photographs and attractive color artwork, including four plastic overlays. Time line included." Horn Book Guide

Includes glossary

910 Geography and travel

Bell, Neill, 1946-
The book of where; or, How to be naturally geographic; illustrated by Richard Wilson. Little, Brown 1982 119p il maps hardcover o.p. paperback available $11.95 (4 and up)

910

1. Geography
ISBN 0-316-08831-5 (pa)
LC 81-19315
"A Brown paper school book"

This geography book contains "a series of exercises that are designed to teach children directions, map reading, a . . . spectrum of concepts that concern U.S. and world geography and geology and continental drift." Sci Books Films

"The tone is personable and supportive, and the book's considerable length is tempered by lots of jocular cartoon il-

Bell, Neill, 1946-—*Continued*
lustrations, diagrams, and relevant asides. . . . Ideal for independent study or as a classroom activity source book, this gets some key lessons across in a refreshingly unpedantic fashion." Booklist

Brown, Laurene Krasny
Dinosaurs travel; a guide for families on the go; [by] Laurie Krasny Brown and Marc Brown. Little, Brown 1988 32p il lib bdg $13.95; pa $5.95 (k-3)   **910**

1. Travel
ISBN 0-316-11076-0 (lib bdg); 0-316-11253-4 (pa)
LC 87-36637
Text and illustrations of dinosaur characters discuss the practicalities and pleasures of travel, from packing up and taking off to returning home again
"The advice is practical and straightforward, and the three or four illustrations on each page are delightfully silly. . . . A perfect introduction to armchair traveling, as well as a soaring success as an opener for primary grade units on transportation." SLJ

Heinrichs, Susan
The Pacific Ocean. Childrens Press 1986 45p il lib bdg $18 (2-4)   **910**

1. Pacific Ocean
ISBN 0-516-01295-9   LC 86-9653
"A New true book"
Provides basic information about the Pacific Ocean, including wave formation, currents, tides, marine biology, and the landscape of the ocean floor
Includes glossary

Leedy, Loreen, 1959-
Blast off to Earth! a look at geography. Holiday House 1992 unp il $14.95 (k-3)
910

1. Geography
ISBN 0-8234-0973-2   LC 92-2567
A group of aliens on a field trip visit each of the continents on Earth and learn about some of their unique features
"An unusually appealing geography primer, this useful, lighthearted picture book provides a new perspective on the home planet." Booklist

910.3   Geography—Dictionaries, encyclopedias, gazetteers

Exploring your world; the adventure of geography. rev. National Geographic Soc. 1993 608p il maps $40   **910.3**

1. Geography—Dictionaries
ISBN 0-87044-726-2   LC 93-1849
First published 1989
"A one-volume encyclopedia of geography covering subjects from agriculture through international organization to zone. . . . This book is very attractive, with its glossy pages and many photographs, and provides valuable information on the physical, human, and political geography of the world." Am Ref Books Annu, 1995

Webster's new geographical dictionary. Merriam-Webster il maps $24.95   **910.3**

1. Geography—Dictionaries 2. Gazetteers
First published 1949 with title: Webster's geographical dictionary. Periodically revised
"Concise and easy-to-read gazetteer, listing both ancient and modern place names. Most entries include pronunciation, brief description, population and brief history. Includes numerous charts and lists, some maps and a list of geographical terms from other languages." N Y Public Libr. Ref Books for Child Collect. 2d edition

The **World** Book encyclopedia of people and places. World Bk. 6v il maps set $160
910.3

1. Geography—Dictionaries
First published 1992. Revised annually
This set profiles more than 200 countries. Coverage of each country includes an overview of its history, geography, economy, people, culture and government; a physical/political map; a locator map; and fact box
For a review see: Booklist, Sept. 1, 1992

Worldmark encyclopedia of the nations. Gale Res.; distributed by Wiley 5v il maps set $335   **910.3**

1. Geography—Dictionaries   2. World history—Dictionaries 3. World politics—Dictionaries
First published 1960 by Worldmark Press. (8th edition 1995) Periodically revised
The first volume of this set is devoted to the United Nations, covering its structure, history, organization and agencies. The remaining volumes, divided by geographic area, consist of alphabetically arranged profiles of some 200 countries
For a review see: Booklist, April 1, 1995

910.4   Accounts of travel. Seafaring life. Buried treasure

Ballard, Robert D.
Exploring the Bismarck; by Robert D. Ballard with Rick Archbold. Scholastic 1991 64p il maps (Time quest book) $15.95; pa $6.95 (4 and up)   **910.4**

1. Bismarck (Battleship) 2. Shipwrecks 3. Underwater exploration 4. World War, 1939-1945—Naval operations
ISBN 0-590-44268-6; 0-590-44269-4 (pa)
LC 90-15580
"A Scholastic/Madison Press book"
Recreates the sea battle that sank the German battleship Bismarck in World War II and recounts how the shipwreck was discovered in 1989
"The easy to read text is extremely well illustrated. Important historical photographs are combined with bright, clear, full-color contemporary shots." SLJ
Includes glossary and bibliography

Exploring the Titanic; edited by Patrick Crean; illustrations by Ken Marschall. Scholastic 1988 64p il maps (Time quest book) $15.95; pa $6.95 (4 and up)   **910.4**

1. Titanic (Steamship) 2. Shipwrecks 3. Underwater exploration
ISBN 0-590-41953-6; 0-590-41952-8 (pa)
LC 88-6478

Ballard, Robert D.—*Continued*

"A Scholastic/Madison Press book"

A narrative for young readers based on the author's The discovery of the Titanic

"The technically accurate and lucid explanations are greatly enhanced by Marshall's stunning paintings, as well as by diagrams and current and period photographs." SLJ

Includes glossary and bibliography

The lost wreck of the Isis; by Robert D. Ballard with Rick Archbold. Scholastic 1990 63p il maps (Time quest book) hardcover o.p. paperback available $4.95 (4 and up)

910.4

1. Shipwrecks 2. Underwater exploration 3. Romans
ISBN 0-590-43853-0 (pa)   LC 89-70280

"A Scholastic/Madison Press book"

"The JASON Project's Mediterranean expedition to study the remains of an ancient Roman shipwreck is recounted in an entertaining, skillful blend of scientific exploration, archaeology, and history. Includes flashbacks to the fourth century." Sci Child

Includes glossary and bibliography

Blumberg, Rhoda, 1917-

The remarkable voyages of Captain Cook. Bradbury Press 1991 137p il maps $18.95 (5 and up)   910.4

1. Cook, James, 1728-1779 2. Voyages around the world 3. Explorers
ISBN 0-02-711682-4   LC 91-11219

An account of the historic adventures and achievements of the British explorer and discoverer of Australia, Hawaii, and other Pacific Ocean lands and peoples

"A fascinating, meticulously documented account that reads like an adventure novel. . . . It is profusely illustrated with reproductions of the work of many who accompanied Cook, showing the world as they saw it. It's an amazing gallery that informs, enlightens, and entertains." SLJ

Includes bibliography

Deem, James M.

How to hunt buried treasure; illustrated by True Kelley. Houghton Mifflin 1992 191p il $16.95 (4 and up)   910.4

1. Buried treasure
ISBN 0-395-58799-9   LC 91-21749

Also available in paperback from Avon Bks.

"Deem takes readers on many kinds of treasure hunts, identifying what to look for, where to look, laws governing the return of a find, and scouting techniques. The book is interesting, entertaining, and will make anyone who reads it want to learn more about the art of treasure hunting." SLJ

Includes bibliography

Exquemelin, A. O. (Alexandre Olivier)

Exquemelin and the pirates of the Caribbean; edited with an introduction and additional material by Jane Shuter. Raintree Steck-Vaughn Pubs. 1995 48p il (History eyewitness) $22.80 (5 and up)   910.4

1. Pirates
ISBN 0-8114-8282-0   LC 94-28702

"The text is based on Exquemelin's book, originally published in Dutch and later translated into serveral languages, in which the former slave turned pirate describes his life in the Caribbean between 1666 and 1674." Horn Book Guide

"Shuter supplies background to Exquemelin's writings, which are marked by particular attention to the nuts and bolts of pirating—the money, the raids, and the mayhem." Booklist

Fine, John Christopher

Sunken ships & treasure; written & illustrated with photographs by John Christopher Fine. Atheneum Pubs. 1986 119p il $16.95 (5 and up)   910.4

1. Shipwrecks 2. Buried treasure
ISBN 0-689-31280-6   LC 86-3652

"An International Oceanographic Foundation selection"

The author "describes the investigations of various treasure seekers and ocean explorers and also relates the historical, technical, and environmental information that shipwrecks have provided over the years. Included are comments on ancient Mediterranean wrecks, sunken World War II submarines, as well as the *Titanic* and *Andrea Doria* disasters." Booklist

"The book is short, easily read, and well illustrated with attractive color photographs." SLJ

Includes bibliography

Fritz, Jean

Around the world in a hundred years; from Henry the Navigator to Magellan; illustrated by Anthony Bacon Venti. Putnam 1994 128p il maps $17.95 (4-6)   910.4

1. Explorers
ISBN 0-399-22527-7   LC 92-27042

"Fritz examines the voyages of ten explorers, acknowledging that their contributions, though deserving of recognition, were dearly bought. Opening and closing chapters summarize the fourteenth-century world view and indicate later expansion of geographic understanding. As always, Fritz tempers scholarship with humor in this brief volume—illustrated with drawings in pencil—which reads like an adventure story." Horn Book Guide

Includes bibliography

Gibbons, Gail

Sunken treasure. Crowell 1988 32p il $13.95; lib bdg $14.89; pa $4.95 (k-3)

910.4

1. Nuestra Señora de Atocha (Ship) 2. Buried treasure 3. Shipwrecks
ISBN 0-690-04734-7; 0-690-04736-3 (lib bdg); 0-06-446097-5 (pa)   LC 87-30114

"Gibbons concentrates on the ancient Spanish galleon, the *Atocha*, which sank off the coast of Florida in 1662, describing under labeled headings the sinking, the search, the find, recording, salvage, restoration and preservation, cataloguing, and eventual distribution of the treasure. . . . A handsomely designed book, well organized, and easily accessible to younger readers." Horn Book

Hackwell, W. John

Diving to the past: recovering ancient wrecks. Scribner 1988 54p il $14.95 (4 and up)   910.4

1. Underwater exploration 2. Shipwrecks 3. Archeology
ISBN 0-684-18918-6   LC 87-233529

Hackwell, W. John—*Continued*

"Straightforward, well-honed text, complemented by softly colored pencil sketches, describes how ancient wrecks are excavated by marine archaeologists who, armed with high-tech equipment and scientific expertise, seek clues to our human past." Sci Child

Hidden treasures of the sea. National Geographic Soc. 1988 104p il lib bdg $12.50 (4 and up)   **910.4**

1. Buried treasure 2. Shipwrecks
ISBN 0-87044-663-0   LC 88-5142
"Books for world explorers"

An introduction to nautical archeology, focusing on social, cultural, and political history as exposed by shipwrecks from ancient times to the present

Includes bibliography

Matthews, Rupert

Explorer; written by Rupert Matthews. Knopf 1991 63p il maps (Eyewitness books) $19; lib bdg $16.99 (4 and up)   **910.4**

1. Exploration 2. Explorers
ISBN 0-679-81460-4; 0-679-91460-9 (lib bdg)
                                              LC 91-8428

Also available Spanish language edition

This "is the story of travel and discovery, from the journeys of the Egyptians and Vikings, to the North and South Poles, underwater, and space." Voice Youth Advocates

"The illustrations are accurate and fascinating and include the best examples from each period discussed." Sci Books Films

Platt, Richard, 1953-

Pirate; photographed by Tina Chambers. Knopf 1994 63p il maps (Eyewitness books) $19; lib bdg $20.99 (4 and up)   **910.4**

1. Pirates
ISBN 0-679-87255-8; 0-679-97255-2 (lib bdg)
                                              LC 94-37732

"A Dorling Kindersley book"

"Platt looks at the subject of piracy from the time of ancient Greece to the 19th century. . . . Readers are introduced to privateers, buccaneers, and corsairs, and told how they differ. Illustrations of various types of pirate ships, and the merchant vessels that were most often their targets, are particularly effective." SLJ

Spedden, Daisy Corning Stone, 1872-1950

Polar, the Titanic bear; illustrations by Laurie McGaw; introduction by Leighton H. Coleman. Little, Brown 1994 64p il $16.95 (3-6)   **910.4**

1. Titanic (Steamship)
ISBN 0-316-80625-0   LC 94-75240

"Written in 1913 as a gift to the author's son, this is the story of their true adventures as passengers and survivors of the Titanic. Told through the eyes of Polar, the son's stuffed bear, the book is illustrated with watercolors and actual photographs. An epilogue includes background on the society of the times, facts about the Titanic, and what became of the family." Child Book Rev Serv

"Well designed and thoughtfully researched, the book offers entertainment, history, and a glimpse of a vanished world." SLJ

Sullivan, George

Slave ship; the story of the Henrietta Marie. Cobblehill Bks. 1994 80p il maps $15.99 (5 and up)   **910.4**

1. Henrietta Marie (Ship) 2. Slave trade 3. Shipwrecks 4. Underwater exploration
ISBN 0-525-65174-8   LC 93-47653

"In telling the story of the *Henrietta Marie*, a slave ship that sank 35 miles off the Florida coast in the early 1700s, Sullivan delves into the Atlantic slave trade, conditions aboard slave ships, research into historical records of the *Henrietta Marie*, and the search for the ship itself. Describing methods of underwater archaeology, he discusses the artifacts recovered and some of the inferences that can be drawn from them. . . . Black-and-white photographs, maps, and reproductions of period drawings and engravings illustrate the text. Well-researched and clearly written." Booklist

Includes bibliography

Sunk!; exploring underwater archaeology; prepared by Geography Department. Runestone Press 1994 72p il (Buried worlds) lib bdg $22.95 (5 and up)   **910.4**

1. Underwater exploration 2. Shipwrecks 3. Archeology
ISBN 0-8225-3205-0   LC 93-42008

Revised edition of Elisha Linder and Avner Raben's Introducing underwater archaeology, published 1976 by Lerner

This "provides a general overview of how archaeologists work to bring to light and interpret aspects of ancient trade, commerce, and history. . . . Unique changes that occur underwater, such as the flattening of ships' hulls and encrustation of their bells, are explained in the easy-to-understand text. The illustrations, a combination of photographs, drawings, and diagrams in both black and white and full color, bring the methods and the history to life." SLJ

910.5   Geography—Serial publications

National Geographic World. National Geographic Soc. $14.95 per year (3-6)   **910.5**

1. Geography—Periodicals
ISSN 0361-5499

Monthly. First published 1975

This "publication for children 8 to 13 aims to combine information and entertainment in factual stories and colorful pictures about people and places, science, sports, adventure, and animals. . . . The full-color pictures on glossy-coated paper are in keeping with the well-known parent publication; however, page size is larger here, 8½ by 10½ inches. . . . The subject matter of this splendid and enlightening pictorial magazine is in keeping with the many interests of children." Richardson. Mag for Child. 2d edition

912   Atlases. Maps

Boyle, Bill

My first atlas; illustrated by Dave Hopkins. Dorling Kindersley 1994 45p il maps $14.95 (1-3)   **912**

1. Atlases
ISBN 1-56458-624-3   LC 94-10467

Boyle, Bill—*Continued*

An "illustrated introduction to atlases, maps, and the countries and continents of the world. The easy-to-read text is interactive, as questions are presented that will encourage children to explore and interpret maps. . . . Each double-page topic treatment consists of a locator globe that highlights a region in red; a paragraph-long overview of the area; and a . . . map that shows place names, natural resources, climate, plants, animals, and landmarks." SLJ

For a fuller review see: Booklist, Nov. 11, 1994

Goode's world atlas; editor, Edward B. Espenshade, Jr. Rand McNally il maps $29.95 **912**

1. Atlases

First published 1922 with title: Goode's school atlas. (19th edition 1994) Periodically revised

"Contains thematic maps and tables showing distribution of population, minerals, manufacturing, and other subjects. Also included are metropolitan-area maps, physical-political maps of regions, geographic tables, and ocean-floor maps showing earth movement. Pronouncing index included." N Y Public Libr. Book of How & Where to Look It Up

Lye, Keith

The complete atlas of the world. Raintree Steck-Vaughn Pubs. 1995 160p maps $31.36 **912**

1. Atlases

ISBN 0-8114-5804-0   LC 94-19316

"An Andromeda book"

"The book is divided into two sections: world maps and maps of 23 regions. The volume is rich in thematic maps that feature the various geographical aspects of our planet both as a whole and by specific areas. Each region is explored with basic date and flags for all independent countries. as well as physical, political, habitat, environmental, population, industrial, and agricultural maps. Climate graphs are also included." Libr J

National Geographic atlas of the world. rev 6th ed. National Geographic Soc. 1992 136p il maps $100; pa $65 **912**

1. Atlases

ISBN 0-87044-835-8; 0-87044-834-X (pa)

LC 92-27845

First published 1963

This "atlas begins with a series of thematic and world maps, accompanied by text, that cover such topics as food, minerals, climate, energy, and population. The back of the atlas includes a section that provides brief profiles, including flags, of U.S. states, Canadian provinces, and the nations of the world. Other sections focus on geographic comparisons, climate, and population of selected places around the world. . . . It is the middle portion of this atlas that people recognize and associate with the National Geographic Society. These colorful pages are arranged by continent, followed by sections on the oceans and the heavens." Booklist

National Geographic picture atlas of our fifty states. National Geographic Soc. 1991 264p il maps $29.95; lib bdg $19.95 **912**

1. United States—Maps 2. Atlases

ISBN 0-87044-859-5; 0-87044-860-9 (lib bdg)

LC 91-28084

Includes maps and other pertinent information about the geography, industries, and population of each of the fifty states

National Geographic picture atlas of our world. rev [ed]. National Geographic Soc. 1993 276p il maps $25 **912**

1. Atlases

ISBN 0-87044-960-5   LC 93-4514

Also available CD-ROM version

First published 1979

Maps and text provide information on the geography, industries, and other vital facts of the countries of the world

Rand McNally children's atlas of the United States. Rand McNally il maps $14.95; pa $7.95 (4-6) **912**

1. United States—Maps 2. Atlases

First published 1989. (1994 edition) Frequently revised

Maps and text present information about the topography, population, emblems, and other aspects of the different states in the United States

Rand McNally children's world atlas. Rand McNally il maps $14.95; pa $7.95 (4-6) **912**

1. Atlases

First published 1989. (1995 edition) Frequently revised. Variant title Rand McNally children's atlas of the world

Presents maps showing the world's terrain, climate, major economic activities, and populations

Rand McNally cosmopolitan world atlas. Rand McNally il maps $70 **912**

1. Atlases

First published 1949. (1996 edition) Frequently revised. Title varies

This atlas contains large-scale maps of continents, countries, states and provinces. Features included are thematic maps on two-page spreads, case study maps, photographs and diagrams

Rand McNally picture atlas of the world; illustrated by Brian Delf. Rand McNally il maps $19.95 (4-6) **912**

1. Atlases

First published 1991. (1995 edition) Frequently revised

Maps of the different regions of the world show their geographic, cultural, and economic features. Includes text describing the individual countries

Weiss, Harvey, 1922-

Maps; getting from here to there. Houghton Mifflin 1991 64p il maps $14.95; pa $5.95 (3-5) **912**

1. Maps

ISBN 0-395-56264-3; 0-395-72028-1 (pa)

LC 90-25069

Discusses various aspects of maps including direction, distance, symbols, latitude, and longitude, how maps are made, special purpose maps, and charts

"Weiss provides an excellent introduction to the subject of maps in a clear, concise work. . . . Black-and-tan illustrations, including drawings and a variety of maps, facilitate interest and promote understanding of the material." Booklist

Williams, Brian, 1943-

The Kingfisher reference atlas; an A-Z guide to countries of the world; cartographic consultant, Keith Lye. Kingfisher (NY) 1993 215p il maps $19.95 **912**

1. Atlases

ISBN 1-85697-838-9   LC 92-54829

Includes an illustrated relief map and a brief description of every country in the world along with important facts and figures, flags, population information, and an economic survey for each

"Both the maps and text are clear and easy to understand; countries are arranged in alphabetical order, so one can find them quickly." Recomm Ref Books for Small & Medium-sized Libr & Media Cent, 1994

Wright, David, 1939-

The Facts on File children's atlas; [by] David and Jill Wright. Facts on File il maps $15.95 **912**

1. Atlases

First published 1987. (1993 edition) Frequently revised

This "volume is replete with color photographs, cheerful text, and a *National Geographic* look. The relief maps come with scale, which is well explained in the section on enjoying maps, which also explains the convention for showing topography used in the volume. Besides an index, the atlas includes questions on every other page and a short quiz." Am Ref Books Annu, 1994

920   Biography

Books of biography are arranged as follows: 1. Biographical collections (920) 2. Biographies of individuals alphabetically by name of biographee (92)

Aaseng, Nathan, 1953-

The problem solvers. Lerner Publs. 1989 80p il (Inside business series) lib bdg $9.50 (5 and up) **920**

1. Business people

ISBN 0-8225-0675-0   LC 88-695

"This brief book tells the stories of people who found ways to turn problems into useful products. The names of the companies and products they started are famous now and include Evinrude, Kitchen-Aid, Prudential Insurance, Polaroid, and Astro-Turf. Each story is briefly told in about seven pages with one full page or more of illustrations and pictures of the inventors and the products." Sci Books Films

Includes bibliography

The unsung heroes. Lerner Publs. 1989 80p il (Inside business series) lib bdg $9.50 (5 and up) **920**

1. Business people

ISBN 0-8225-0676-9   LC 88-3022

Introduces little-known individuals responsible for advancing well-known business products, including the originators of Coca-Cola, Hoover vacuum cleaners, and Bingo

Includes bibliography

Altman, Susan R.

Extraordinary black Americans; from colonial to contemporary times; [by] Susan Altman. Childrens Press 1988 208p il lib bdg $31.93; pa $15.95 (5 and up) **920**

1. African Americans—Biography

ISBN 0-516-00581-2; 0-516-40581-0 (pa)

     LC 88-11977

A "collection of 85 short biographies interspersed with explanations of key historical (particularly civil rights) events. The scope is wide ranging: Altman's subjects are men and women recognized for their achievements in exploration, invention, literature, theater, the military, education, politics, science, medicine, music, and sports. . . . A priority choice for black-studies collections." Booklist

Ashabranner, Brent K., 1921-

People who make a difference; [by] Brent Ashabranner; photographs by Paul Conklin. Cobblehill Bks. 1989 135p il $15.95 (5 and up) **920**

1. United States—Biography

ISBN 0-525-65009-1   LC 89-34593

"The fourteen people interviewed here demonstrate a wide variety of concerns, but all share an unwavering commitment to their chosen causes. . . . Mary Joan Willard trains capuchin monkeys to assist quadraplegics; Frank Trejo teaches karate to handicapped children; Beverly Thomas is the principal of an inner-city high school in Detroit that sends its graduates on to Ivy League colleges. Like these heroes, the rest of the subjects—some young people themselves—seem to have been chosen not only as worthy role models, but as people whose accomplishments will have a special meaning for young adults." Bull Cent Child Books

Includes bibliography

Blassingame, Wyatt

The look-it-up book of presidents. Random House il $12; pa $6.99 (5 and up) **920**

1. Presidents—United States

First published 1968 and periodically revised to include new Presidents and administrations

"Each president is (allotted) several pages of readable text that cover his politics and policies and touch upon his personal life. The good-sized print and well-chosen illustrations (black-and-white photographs, lithographs, and cartoons) combine in an easy-to-peruse layout." Booklist

Breen, Karen, 1943-

Index to collective biographies for young readers. 4th ed. Bowker 1988 xxxiii, 494p $50 **920**

1. Biography—Indexes 2. Biography—Bibliography

ISBN 0-8352-2348-5   LC 88-19410

First edition edited by Judith Silverman published 1970 with title: An index to young readers' collective biographies

This "book indexes approximately 9,773 people representing the contents of 1,129 collective biographies. The fourth edition retains most of the titles indexed in the preceding editions and notes out-of-print titles by an 'o.p.' . . . This index and a sizeable collection of the titles included are essential for all libraries serving children." Peterson. Ref Books for Child. 4th edition

Burns, Khephra

Black stars in orbit; NASA's African-American astronauts; [by] Khephra Burns and William Miles. Harcourt Brace & Co. 1995 72p il $18.95; pa $8.95 (4 and up)

920

1. Astronauts 2. African Americans—Biography
ISBN 0-15-200432-7; 0-15-200276-6 (pa)

LC 93-44624

"Gulliver books"

Based on a 1990 television documentary, this book begins "with a chapter on the African American pilots of World War II, the Tuskegee Airmen, and [continues] with the experience of Ed Dwight, a Korean War era pilot who was recommended for the Astronaut Training Program by President Kennedy. . . . The contributions of African American scientists and physicians who worked behind the scenes are documented, as is NASA's campaign, with the advent of the Space Shuttle Program, to recruit minority trainees. The authors use quotations from the television documentary to tell the compelling and at times horrifying story in a full and lively manner." SLJ

Drimmer, Frederick

Born different; amazing stories of very special people. Atheneum Pubs. 1988 182p il $15.95 (6 and up)

920

1. Physically handicapped—Biography
ISBN 0-689-31360-8

LC 87-33354

"A collective biography of seven people (six accounts, since one includes Chang and Eng, Siamese twins) whose anatomical anomalies made them prominent; among them are the midget known as Tom Thumb, Robert Wadlow (the tallest man who ever lived, according to medical records) and the tragic 'elephant man.'" Bull Cent Child Books

"Drimmer relates each well-documented story sympathetically, explains the causes of his subjects' various birth defects and shows that no matter what their deformity most led happy, dignified lives." Booklist

Includes bibliography

Faber, Doris, 1924-

Great lives: American literature; [by] Doris Faber and Harold Faber. Atheneum Bks. for Young Readers 1995 313p il $23 (5 and up)

920

1. Authors, American
ISBN 0-684-19448-1

LC 94-10866

"The lives of thirty American literary figures whose major work was completed by 1960 are covered in this collection. Novelists, poets and playwrights are included. . . . The 1960 parameter for inclusion limits the coverage of many women and minority writers but as a collective biography of major American literary figures, this does a more than adequate job of gathering the type of information needed by middle and junior high students." Voice Youth Advocates

Includes bibliography

Freedman, Russell

Indian chiefs. Holiday House 1987 151p il map lib bdg $18.95; pa $9.95 (6 and up)

920

1. Indians of North America—Biography
ISBN 0-8234-0625-3 (lib bdg); 0-8234-0971-6 (pa)

LC 86-46198

This "book chronicles the lives of six renowned Indian chiefs, each of whom served as a leader during a critical period in his tribe's history. . . . The text relates information about the lives of each chief and aspects of Indian/white relationships that illuminate his actions. . . . The illustrations and photographs and an especially clear map augment the text well and add to the overall appeal of the book." Horn Book

Greenfield, Eloise, 1929-

Childtimes: a three-generation memoir; by Eloise Greenfield and Lessie Jones Little; with material by Pattie Ridley Jones; drawings by Jerry Pinkney and photographs from the authors' family albums. Crowell 1979 175p il lib bdg $13.89; pa $5.95 (4 and up)

920

1. African American women
ISBN 0-690-03875-5 (lib bdg); 0-06-446134-3 (pa)

LC 77-26581

Childhood memoirs of three African American women—grandmother, mother, and daughter—who grew up between the 1880's and the 1950's

"A carefully considered and thoughtful book, moving deliberately, constructed with loving care. The authors respect their child-readers (or listeners) and honor them with candor and honesty, tragedy and tears, providing chuckles and smiles as well." Interracial Books Child Bull

Haskins, James, 1941-

Against all opposition; black explorers in America; [by] Jim Haskins. Walker & Co. 1992 86p il $13.95; lib bdg $14.85 (5 and up)

920

1. African Americans—Biography 2. Explorers 3. America—Exploration
ISBN 0-8027-8137-3; 0-8027-8138-1 (lib bdg)

LC 91-30203

Surveys the lives and adventures of black explorers who helped discover new worlds. James Beckwourth, Matthew Henson and Ronald E. McNair are among those profiled

This is "a readable, informative collective biography. . . . [The author offers] crisp, flowing prose that incorporates telling details and cogent quotations, bringing his subjects to life and giving their toils meaning and relevance." SLJ

Includes bibliography

One more river to cross; the stories of twelve black Americans; by Jim Haskins. Scholastic 1992 204p il $13.95; pa $3.50 (4 and up)

920

1. African Americans—Biography
ISBN 0-590-42896-9; 0-590-42897-7 (pa)

LC 91-8817

This book presents biographical sketches of twelve African Americans who courageously fought against racism to become leaders in their fields, including Marian Anderson, Ralph Bunche, Fannie Lou Hamer, and Malcolm X

"Through clear and dramatic writing, Haskins helps readers to understand the impact of institutional racism. . . . A valuable compilation for reading aloud, for independent recreational reading, and for reports." SLJ

Includes bibliography

Jacobs, William Jay

Great lives: human rights. Scribner 1990 278p il $22.95 (5 and up)   **920**

1. Reformers 2. Civil rights 3. United States—Biography

ISBN 0-684-19036-2   LC 89-37211

This volume presents "biographical portraits of thirty defenders of human rights throughout American history, from Thomas Paine and Anne Hutchinson to Cesar Chavez and Martin Luther King, Jr." Horn Book Guide

"The biographies are well written and paced to keep the reader interested. They convey significant facts with clarity and include curious and exciting anecdotes." Voice Youth Advocates

Includes bibliography

They shaped the game; Ty Cobb, Babe Ruth, Jackie Robinson. Scribner 1994 85p il $15.95 (4 and up)   **920**

1. Cobb, Ty, 1886-1961 2. Ruth, Babe, 1895-1948 3. Robinson, Jackie, 1919-1972 4. Baseball—Biography

ISBN 0-684-19734-0   LC 94-14007

"Jacobs does a commendable job of presenting accurate, interesting information in the 20-plus pages he devotes to each subject. While the majority of the text describes the outstanding athletic careers of the three men, Jacobs pulls no punches when covering the volatile off-field activities of Cobb and Ruth." SLJ

Includes bibliography

Kramer, Sydelle

Baseball's greatest hitters; by S. A. Kramer; illustrated by Jim Campbell. Random House 1995 48p il lib bdg $9.99; pa $3.99 (2-4)   **920**

1. Baseball—Biography

ISBN 0-679-95307-8 (lib bdg); 0-679-85307-3 (pa)   LC 94-16497

"Step into reading. A step 4 book"

"Kramer introduces young readers to five of baseball's greatest hitters—Honus Wagner, Ty Cobb, Babe Ruth, Ted Williams, and Hank Aaron. For each Hall of Famer, the author offers a biographical sketch and a chart of career statistics. . . . A final chapter briefly profiles six other batters. The illustrations, a mix of black-and-white and color photos and drawings, help to clarify the text and, combined with short chapters and large print, make for an attractive and nonthreatening layout." Booklist

Krull, Kathleen, 1952-

Lives of the musicians; good times, bad times (and what the neighbors thought); written by Kathleen Krull; illustrated by Kathryn Hewitt. Harcourt Brace Jovanovich 1993 96p il $18.95 (4 and up)   **920**

1. Composers

ISBN 0-15-248010-2   LC 91-33497

"Twenty (including both Gilbert and Sullivan) composers, from Vivaldi to Gershwin, are here profiled in a series of irreverent, anecdotal vignettes, each stylishly illustrated with an elegant caricature." Bull Cent Child Books

Includes glossary and bibliography

Lives of the writers; comedies, tragedies (and what the neighbors thought); written by Kathleen Krull; illustrated by Kathryn Hewitt. Harcourt Brace & Co. 1994 96p il $18.95 (4 and up)   **920**

1. Authors

ISBN 0-15-248009-9   LC 93-32436

This offers "views of twenty writers . . . from various countries and historical periods. Included are William Shakespeare, Edgar Allan Poe, Mark Twain, Zora Neale Hurston, Isaac Bashevis Singer, and many others." Publisher's note

The "authors profiled are cleverly chosen. . . . Hewitt provides a full-page color portrait, part caricature, part realistic, for each, and Krull's text includes hard facts as well as enough lively anecdotes to make clear that the writers are human." Booklist

Includes glossary and bibliography

Littlefield, Bill

Champions; stories of ten remarkable athletes; paintings by Bernie Fuchs; with a foreword by Frank Deford. Little, Brown 1993 132p il $22.95 (5 and up)   **920**

1. Athletes

ISBN 0-316-52805-6   LC 92-31390

A collection of sports biographies exploring athletes who have made extraordinary achievements, grown beyond their successes, and given something back to their sports. Satchel Paige, Julie Krone, Nate Archibald and Billy Jean King are among the ten athletes profiled

The author's "engrossing prose style makes each entry read like a story. Fuch's paintings are dramatic, depicting the excitement of each sport while offering accurate portraits." SLJ

Includes bibliography

McKissack, Patricia C., 1944-

African-American inventors; by Patricia and Fredrick McKissack. Millbrook Press 1994 96p il (Proud heritage) lib bdg $17.90 (5 and up)   **920**

1. African American inventors 2. Inventions

ISBN 1-56294-468-1   LC 93-42625

"After presenting a brief history of the patent process and the law, the McKissacks provide an overview of African American inventors throughout the 19th and 20th centuries, including those who were free born and those who were slaves. . . . Good-quality black-and-white photographs and reproductions, along with the drawings that accompanied the original patent applications, appear throughout. This title fills a real need; its readable text gives information not often found in books on inventions or on U.S. history." SLJ

Includes bibliography

African-American scientists; by Patricia and Fredrick McKissack. Millbrook Press 1994 96p il (Proud heritage) lib bdg $17.90 (5 and up)   **920**

1. Scientists 2. African Americans—Biography

ISBN 1-56294-372-3   LC 93-11226

McKissack, Patricia C., 1944—*Continued*

Examines the lives and achievements of African-American scientists from colonial days to the present

"Not only do the McKissacks provide documented, fascinating portraits of well-known figures such as Benjamin Banneker and George Washington Carver, but they also consider the remarkable contributions of persons rarely written about, including outstanding women scientists. Black-and-white photographs and artwork illustrate the text." Horn Book Guide

Includes bibliography

Monceaux, Morgan

Jazz: my music, my people; foreword by Wynton Marsalis. Knopf 1994 62p il $18 (4 and up)   **920**

1. Jazz musicians 2. African American musicians
ISBN 0-679-85618-8   LC 93-38177

"Brief biographical sketches not only provide basic facts about the subjects' lives, but also highlights their importance in the field of music and the historical development of this genre. Over 40 instrumentalists and vocalists are discussed, ranging from Buddy Bolden to Nat King Cole, Leadbelly to Charlie Parker, Bessie Smith to Ella Fitzgerald." SLJ

This is "concise, fascinating and stunningly illustrated." N Y Times Book Rev

Includes glossary

Morey, Janet

Famous Asian Americans; [by] Janet Nomura Morey and Wendy Dunn. Cobblehill Bks. 1992 170p il $15.99 (5 and up)   **920**

1. Asian Americans—Biography
ISBN 0-525-65080-6   LC 91-17255

Chronicles the lives and accomplishments of fourteen Asian Americans including Jose Aruego, Michael Chang, An Wang, and Ellison Onizuka

"In an excellent introduction, Harry Kitano . . . gives a brief history of Asian immigration to the U.S. and looks at the discrimination experienced by immigrants and their descendants and the tendency to disregard the unique history, language, and culture of specific Asian American groups." Booklist

Includes bibliography

Famous Mexican Americans; [by] Janet Morey & Wendy Dunn. Cobblehill Bks. 1989 176p il $14.95 (5 and up)   **920**

1. Mexican Americans—Biography
ISBN 0-525-65012-1   LC 89-7218

Also available Spanish language edition

This collection "gives sketches of the lives of fourteen contemporary Mexican Americans; the men and women who are discussed represent such diverse fields as the law, sports, entertainment, business, and public service at the local or federal level." Bull Cent Child Books

"While the intent of the book is to showcase the outstanding contributions of the selected Mexican Americans, the book also provides young readers with role models to be admired and emulated." SLJ

Includes bibliography

Morin, Isobel V., 1928-

Women of the U. S. Congress. Oliver Press 1994 160p il (Profiles) lib bdg $14.95 (5 and up)   **920**

1. United States. Congress—Biography 2. Women in politics
ISBN 1-881508-12-9   LC 93-26068

Describes the lives and political careers of seven women who have served in the Congress: Jeannette Rankin, Margaret Chase Smith, Helen Gahagan Douglas, Shirley Chisholm, Barbara Jordan, Nancy Landon Kassebaum, and Barbara Mikulski, and mentions four more in a chapter titled "The Year of the Woman: 1992"

"All the biographies, which are concise yet interesting, highlight the subject's most significant contributions and contain anecdotes that point out gender-based political inequities without being didactic. Valuable for school projects concerning government, biography, or women's studies, with many high-resolution, full-page black-and-white photos." Booklist

Includes bibliography

Paré, Michael A.

Sports stars. U.X.L 1994 2v il set $38 (6 and up)   **920**

1. Athletes
ISBN 0-8103-9859-1   LC 94-21835

"This two-volume set includes sketches of 80 athletes, most of whom are at the peak of their fame. . . . Each entry includes a section on the childhood of the athlete, an account of obstacles overcome, and a summary of the events giving him or her 'star' status. Every entry closes with a paragraph on the athlete's personal life and a mailing address." Book Rep

For a fuller review see: Booklist, Jan. 15, 1995

Rappaport, Doreen

Living dangerously; American women who risked their lives for adventure. HarperCollins Pubs. 1991 117p il $14.95; lib bdg $14.89 (4 and up)   **920**

1. Women—Biography 2. Adventure and adventurers
ISBN 0-06-025108-5; 0-06-025109-3 (lib bdg)
LC 90-28915

"Annie Edson Taylor, Annie Smith Peck, Bessie Coleman, Delia Akeley, Eugene Clark, and Thecla Mitchell all have one thing in common—they are women who struggled against social conventions and physical challenges to accomplish amazing feats. . . . Each of these women's lives is candidly portrayed, making this an excellent starting point for learning about these little-known figures. Black-and-white photographs clarify and enhance the textual descriptions and add enormously to the overall appeal." SLJ

Includes bibliography

Reef, Catherine

Black fighting men; a proud history. 21st Cent. Bks. (NY) 1994 80p il (African-American soldiers) $14.95 (5 and up)   **920**

1. African American soldiers
ISBN 0-8050-3106-5   LC 93-44279

Reef, Catherine—*Continued*

"Reef chronicles the heroism of individual black soldiers and airmen in the major wars of the U.S., beginning with the American Revolution. Reef's approach is straightforward; the heroic action of each soldier is examined, as well as his life before and—for those who survived—after the conflict." SLJ

Includes bibliographical references

Sandler, Martin W.

Presidents; introduction by James H. Billington. HarperCollins Pubs. 1995 94p il $19.95; lib bdg $20.89 (4 and up)   **920**

1. Presidents—United States
ISBN 0-06-024534-4; 0-06-024535-2 (lib bdg)
LC 93-49403

"A Library of Congress book"

This work presents information about the political and private lives of American presidents. Illustrations include archival photographs, lithographs, paintings, posters and drawings

"Browsers and student researchers will be delighted by the wealth of entertaining information and fascinating photographs." Booklist

Scheller, William

Amazing archaeologists and their finds. Oliver Press 1994 160p il maps lib bdg $14.95 (4 and up)   **920**

1. Archeologists
ISBN 1-881508-17-X   LC 93-46919

The author discusses the lives and careers of Kathleen Kenyon, Hiram Bingham, Austen Henry Layard, Henri Mouhot, Heinrich Schliemann, Sir Arthur Evans, Edward Thompson, and Howard Carter

"Biographical material is appropriately intermingled with history so that readers gain a sense of the eras in which these individuals lived and the settings within which they conducted their explorations. Simple maps help determine locations." SLJ

Includes bibliographical references

Sills, Leslie

Inspirations; stories about women artists: Georgia O'Keeffe, Frida Kahlo, Alice Neel, Faith Ringgold. Whitman, A. 1989 49p il lib bdg $17.95 (5 and up)   **920**

1. Women artists
ISBN 0-8075-3649-0   LC 88-80

A look at the lives and works of "four 20th-century women artists of great talent. There are photographs of the artists as children and adults, and well-chosen examples of their work reproduced in full color." N Y Times Book Rev

Includes bibliography

Visions; stories about women artists: Mary Cassatt, Betye Saar, Leonora Carrington, Mary Frank. Whitman, A. 1993 58p il lib bdg $18.95 (5 and up)   **920**

1. Women artists
ISBN 0-8075-8491-6   LC 92-32909

Presents the lives and works of four pioneering women artists

"Written with clarity, simplicity, and insight. . . . Full-color reproductions of each artist's work are included. The text is further broken up by black-and-white photos of the subjects. Design and layout are carefully planned, resulting in a beautiful book worth sharing with many readers." SLJ

Includes bibliography

Sinnott, Susan

Extraordinary Asian-Pacific Americans. Childrens Press 1993 270p il lib bdg $25.35; pa $15.95 (5 and up)   **920**

1. Asian Americans—Biography
ISBN 0-516-03152-X (lib bdg); 0-516-43152-8 (pa)
LC 93-12678

"More than an extensive collection of minibiographies of Asian Pacific Americans, this title is also a history of Asian Pacific immigration to the U.S., including information on immigration laws and naturalization quotas, essays on Chinese railroad workers, and Japanese detention camps, and more. Biographical sketches, which feature such notables as Seiji Ozawa, Maxine Hong Kingston, and Kristi Yamaguchi, run two or three pages and are accompanied by a photograph. . . . Accessible and interesting for the browser or casual reader, the book also includes notes and a list of further reading that will make it valuable to the report writer." Booklist

Extraordinary Hispanic Americans. Childrens Press 1991 277p il lib bdg $25.35; pa $15.95 (5 and up)   **920**

1. Hispanic Americans—Biography
ISBN 0-516-00582-0 (lib bdg); 0-516-40582-9 (pa)
LC 91-13909

Profiles the lives of Hispanics who helped shape the history of the United States beginning with the age of exploration and leading into the 20th century. Among those profiled are: Hernando de Soto, Father Junípero Serra, Francisco Ramírez, Desi Arnaz, Roberto Clemente and Joan Baez

"The volume is a substantial resource that should be on all library reference shelves." Booklist

Includes bibliography

Sullivan, George

Pitchers: twenty-seven of baseball's greatest. Atheneum Pubs. 1994 74p il $17.95 (4 and up)   **920**

1. Baseball—Biography
ISBN 0-689-31825-1   LC 93-3007

Profiles twenty-seven of the best pitchers in the history of baseball, including Nolan Ryan, Tom Seaver, Whitey Ford, Dizzy Dean, and Cy Young

"A worthwhile addition to the sports or collective biography collection." Book Rep

Torres, John Albert

Home-run hitters; heroes of the four home-run game; by John A. Torres. Macmillan Bks. for Young Readers 1995 120p il $15 (4 and up)   **920**

1. Baseball—Biography
ISBN 0-02-789407-X   LC 94-13554

Torres, John Albert—*Continued*

"Baseball before 1900 is covered in one chapter, while the 20th century is covered chronologically with individual chapters for each of the ten hitters. Included are familiar names—Lou Gehrig, Willie Mays and Mike Schmidt—as well as some of the lesser known—Chuck Klein, Rocky Colavito, Bob Horner." Book Rep

"Torres has put together an interesting collection of profiles. . . . Each player is covered in a breezy, highly readable style." SLJ

Includes bibliography

Vare, Ethlie Ann

Women inventors & their discoveries; [by] Ethlie Ann Vare and Greg Ptacek; foreword by Ruth Handler. Oliver Press 1993 160p il (Profiles) lib bdg $14.95 (5 and up)   **920**

1. Women inventors 2. Inventions

ISBN 1-881508-06-4   LC 92-38268

Surveys the lives and work of such innovative women as Grace Hopper, Fannie Farmer, C. J. Walker, and Stephanie Kwolek

"Interesting facts about 10 obscure American women who invented famous things fill the pages of this very readable book." Booklist

Includes bibliography

Wolf, Sylvia

Focus: five women photographers; Julia Margaret Cameron, Margaret Bourke-White, Flor Garduño, Sandy Skoglund, Lorna Simpson. Whitman, A. 1994 63p il $18.95 (5 and up)   **920**

1. Women photographers

ISBN 0-8075-2531-6   LC 94-1416

A "survey of five accomplished photographers. . . . The black-and-white and color reproductions are excellent; all are described and analyzed in the straightforward, well-paced text. The diversity in background and interests of the photographers makes the book an especially fine resource." Horn Book Guide

Includes bibliography

920.003 Biographical reference works

Authors of books for young people; by Martha E. Ward [et al.] 3rd ed. Scarecrow Press 1990 780p $59.50   **920.003**

1. Authors—Dictionaries 2. Children's literature—Bio-bibliography

ISBN 0-8108-2293-8   LC 90-32569

First published 1964

This work "includes brief biographies of 3,708 authors and illustrators for young adults. Entries give dates and a few sentences about the author and cite several sources. The work's claim to fame is that it lists more authors than any other one-volume source." Nichols. Guide to Ref Books for Sch Media Cent. 4th edition

Children's authors and illustrators: an index to biographical dictionaries. Gale Res. (Gale biographical index series) $156   **920.003**

1. Authors—Dictionaries—Indexes 2. Illustrators—Dictionaries—Indexes

First published 1976. (5th edition 1995) Periodically revised

Provides over 200,000 citations to biographical sketches for some 30,000 authors and illustrators in more than 650 reference sources

Contemporary Spanish-speaking writers and illustrators for children and young adults; a biographical dictionary; edited by Isabel Schon with the collaboration of Lourdes Gavaldón de Barreto; translation from the Spanish by Jason Douglas White. Greenwood Press 1994 248p $49.95   **920.003**

1. Children's literature—Bio-bibliography 2. Authors, Latin American—Dictionaries 3. Authors, Spanish—Dictionaries 4. Illustrators—Dictionaries

ISBN 0-313-29027-X   LC 93-11529

"The title is descriptive of the scope of this unique work. It contains contemporary, not historical, persons; authors who are native Spanish speakers (almost no natives of the United States); and those who write or illustrate for children. . . . More than 200 persons from countries such as Argentina, Bolivia, Chile, Costa Rica, Cuba, Uruguay, Venezuela, Mexico, Peru, and Spain are included." Recomm Ref Books for Small & Medium-sized Libr & Media Cent, 1995

Fifth book of junior authors & illustrators; edited by Sally Holmes Holtze. Wilson, H.W. 1983 357p il $48   **920.003**

1. Authors—Dictionaries 2. Illustrators—Dictionaries 3. Children's literature—Bio-bibliography

ISBN 0-8242-0694-0   LC 83-21828

Offers biographical or autobiographical sketches of 243 noted children's authors and illustrators

Fourth book of junior authors and illustrators; edited by Doris de Montreville and Elizabeth D. Crawford. Wilson, H.W. 1978 370p il $45   **920.003**

1. Authors—Dictionaries 2. Illustrators—Dictionaries 3. Children's literature—Bio-bibliography

ISBN 0-8242-0568-5   LC 78-115

Provides biographical or autobiographical sketches of some 250 authors and illustrators

The **Junior** book of authors; edited by Stanley J. Kunitz and Howard Haycraft. 2nd ed rev. Wilson, H.W. 1951 309p $40   **920.003**

1. Authors—Dictionaries 2. Illustrators—Dictionaries 3. Children's literature—Bio-bibliography

ISBN 0-8242-0028-4

First published 1934. This foundation volume in the series presents biographical and autobiographical sketches of 289 authors and illustrators of books for children and young people

"Each volume in the series focuses on authors and illustrators who have come to prominence since the previous volume. The *Third book* contains the first cumulative index to the series." Guide to Ref Books. 11th edition

"This series belongs on every school and public library shelf as a valuable reference tool." Booklist

Merriam-Webster's biographical dictionary. Merriam-Webster 1995 1170p $27.95

920.003

1. Biography—Dictionaries

Replaces Webster's new biographical dictionary

This work "chronicles the lives of more than 34,000 celebrated, important, and notorious men and women from all parts of the world, all eras, and all fields of endeavor. . . . [Arranged alphabetically, the] entries provide birth and death dates, nationality or ethnic origin, pronunciations, pseudonyms, variant spellings, pertinent information about the individual's career, and more." Publisher's note

More junior authors; edited by Muriel Fuller. Wilson, H.W. 1963 235p il $35

920.003

1. Authors—Dictionaries 2. Illustrators—Dictionaries 3. Children's literature—Bio-bibliography

ISBN 0-8242-0036-5

Offers biographical or autobiographical sketches of 268 noted children's authors and illustrators

The **Oxford** children's book of famous people. Oxford Univ. Press 1994 384p il maps $35

920.003

1. Biography—Dictionaries

ISBN 0-19-910171-X   LC 94-22379

This volume presents "biographies of 1,000 people from all parts of the world and all time periods. . . . The typical 100-word entry begins with a tag that identifies the person ('Saint Thomas Aquinas, Italian religious leader and philosopher'), birth and death dates, and age at death. . . . The subjects are indexed by occupation and by date of birth." Booklist

Rollock, Barbara T., 1924-1992

Black authors & illustrators of children's books; a biographical dictionary. 2nd ed. Garland 1992 234p il (Garland reference library in the humanities) $35   **920.003**

1. Children's literature—Bio-bibliography 2. African American authors—Bio-bibliography 3. Illustrators

ISBN 0-8240-7078-X   LC 91-37402

First published 1988

"This work contains short biographical sketches of some 150 personalities, both living and dead, in the field of children's literature. . . . Noteworthy features of the work . . . are numerous: a simple-to-use dictionary arrangement; a clean, readable format; more than 85 pictures of the authors and illustrators as well as some of their better-known works; and an index of 500 book titles. Appendixes contain a list of children's award and honor books for the authors and illustrators included, with all Coretta Scott King Award recipients given." Am Ref Books Annu, 1993

Saari, Peggy

Explorers & discoverers; from Alexander the Great to Sally Ride; [by] Peggy Saari, Daniel B. Baker. U.X.L 1995 4v 886p il maps set $76

920.003

1. Explorers—Dictionaries   2. Adventure and adventurers—Dictionaries

ISBN 0-8103-9787-8   LC 95-166826

Based on Explorers and discoverers of the world, published 1993 by Gale Res.

Profiles of approximately 170 "geographers, oceanographers,and other assorted travelers are alphabetically arranged by best-known name with an index in each volume covering the whole set. . . . Entries range from three to five pages, usually accompanied by a drawing or photo of the explorer. Effort has been made to include women and non-Westerners. . . . The text is readable and interesting for upper-elementary through middle-school students." Booklist

Seventh book of junior authors & illustrators; edited by Sally Holmes Holtze. Wilson, H.W. 1996 371p il $50   **920.003**

1. Authors—Dictionaries 2. Illustrators—Dictionaries 3. Children's literature—Bio-bibliography

ISBN 0-8242-0873-0   LC 95-47983

Provides biographical or autobiographical sketches of 235 noted children's authors and illustrators

Sixth book of junior authors & illustrators; edited by Sally Holmes Holtze. Wilson, H.W. 1989 345p il $48   **920.003**

1. Authors—Dictionaries 2. Illustrators—Dictionaries 3. Children's literature—Bio-bibliography

ISBN 0-8242-0777-7   LC 89-14815

Lists autobiographical or biographical entries for 236 authors and illustrators of notable children's books

Something about the author; facts and pictures about authors and illustrators of books for young people. Gale Res. il ea $92

920.003

1. Authors—Dictionaries 2. Illustrators—Dictionaries 3. Children's literature—Bio-bibliography

ISSN 0276-816X

First published 1971. Frequency varies

Editors vary

"Each entry includes personal and career information, photographs, bibliography and biographical sources. Starting with V. 15, it includes authors of all periods although focus remains on those currently active." N Y Public Libr. Ref Books for Child Collect. 2d edition

"This attractive and useful series . . . is an essential purchase for elementary and middle school libraries." Nichols. Guide to Ref Books for Sch Media Cent. 4th edition

Something about the author: autobiography series. Gale Res. il ea $92   **920.003**

1. Authors—Dictionaries 2. Illustrators—Dictionaries 3. Children's literature—Bio-bibliography

ISSN 0885-6842

First published 1986

Editors vary

An "ongoing series in which juvenile authors discuss their lives, careers, and published works. Each volume contains essays by 20 established writers or illustrators (e.g., Evaline Ness, Nonny Hogrogian, Betsy Byars, Jean Fritz) who represent all types of literature, preschool to young adult. . . . Some articles focus on biographical information, while others emphasize the writing career. Most, however, address young readers and provide family background, discuss the writing experience, and cite some factors that influenced it. Illustrations include portraits of the authors as children and more recent action pictures and portraits. There are cumulative indexes by authors, important published works, and geographical locations mentioned in the essays." Nichols. Guide to Ref Books for Sch Media Cent. 4th edition

Third book of junior authors; edited by Doris de Montreville and Donna Hill. Wilson, H.W. 1972 320p il $40 **920.003**

1. Authors—Dictionaries 2. Illustrators—Dictionaries 3. Children's literature—Bio-bibliography

ISBN 0-8242-0408-5

Offers biographical and autobiographical sketches of 255 noted children's authors and illustrators

Twentieth-century children's writers. St. James Press $132 **920.003**

1. Authors—Dictionaries 2. Children's literature—Bio-bibliography 3. Children's literature—History and criticism

First published 1978 by St. Martin's Press. (4th edition 1995) Periodically revised

"The entry for each author consists of a biography, a complete list of published works, and a signed critical essay. . . . Coverage is mainly of British and U.S. writers; however, a number of Australian and Canadian authors are included, as are a smattering of Third World authors. For a one-volume quick source for information about children's authors, this is the best source." Am Ref Books Annu, 1996

92 Individual biography

Lives of individuals are arranged alphabetically under the name of the person written about. A number of subject headings have been added to the entries in this section to aid in curriculum work. It is not necessarily recommended that these subjects be used in the library catalog.

Adams, John Quincy, 1767-1848

Kent, Zachary. John Quincy Adams, sixth president of the United States. Childrens Press 1987 98p il (Encyclopedia of presidents) lib bdg $19.20 (4 and up) **92**

1. Presidents—United States

ISBN 0-516-01386-6   LC 86-31022

A biography of the president who continued the family dedication to public service begun by his father, John Adams

"Frequent illustrations include reproductions of historical art, photos, letters, newspapers, and documents, all of which add interest and authenticity to the text. The writing style is easy to read, marked by short declarative sentences." SLJ

Adams, Samuel, 1722-1803

Fritz, Jean. Why don't you get a horse, Sam Adams? illustrated by Trina Schart Hyman. Coward, McCann & Geoghegan 1974 47p il $13.95; pa $7.95 (2-4) **92**

1. United States—History—1775-1783, Revolution

ISBN 0-698-20292-9; 0-698-20545-6 (pa)

A brief biography of Samuel Adams describing his activities in stirring up the revolt against the British and how he was finally persuaded to learn to ride a horse

"A piece of history far more entertaining and readable than most fiction. . . . The author has humanized a figure of the Revolution: Adams emerges a marvelously funny and believable man. The illustrations play upon his foibles; they are, in fact, even more outrageously mocking than the text. A tour de force, for both author and illustrator." Horn Book

Ailey, Alvin

Pinkney, Andrea Davis. Alvin Ailey; illustrated by Brian Pinkney. Hyperion Bks. for Children 1993 unp il $13.95; lib bdg $13.89; pa $4.95 (k-3) **92**

1. African American dancers

ISBN 1-56282-413-9; 1-56282-414-7 (lib bdg); 0-7868-1077-7 (pa)   LC 92-54865

Describes the life, dancing, and choreography of Alvin Ailey, who created his own modern dance company to explore the black experience

"Brian Pinkney's marvelously detailed scratchboard drawings are tinted with pastels to show the sweep and flow of dancers caught in the act of leaping, twirling, and soaring through the air. . . . The book is both informative and inspiring." SLJ

Anderson, Marian, 1897-1993

Ferris, Jeri. What I had was singing: the story of Marian Anderson. Carolrhoda Bks. 1994 96p il (Trailblazers) lib bdg $17.50; pa $6.95 (4 and up) **92**

1. African American singers 2. African American women

ISBN 0-87614-818-6 (lib bdg); 0-87614-634-5 (pa)   LC 93-28502

The author "tracks Anderson's life and career as a singer, from her youth in Philadelphia to her debut at the Metropolitan Opera. Warm and informative, the biography shows how the accomplished contralto, who at first received more recognition in Europe than in her own country because of racism, paved the way for the careers of future African-American singers." Horn Book Guide

Includes bibliography

Appleseed, Johnny, 1774-1845

Aliki. The story of Johnny Appleseed; written and illustrated by Aliki. Prentice-Hall 1963 unp il o.p.; Simon & Schuster Bks. for Young Readers paperback available $5.95 (k-3) **92**

1. Frontier and pioneer life

ISBN 0-671-66746-7 (pa)

Also available Spanish language edition

This is a picture-story of "Johnny Appleseed, the New Englander who wandered through the Middle West in the early days distributing seeds of apple trees for planting, and remaining to share his love for wild creatures, pioneer folk, and nature." Christ Sci Monit

Kellogg, Steven. Johnny Appleseed; a tall tale retold and illustrated by Steven Kellogg. Morrow Junior Bks. 1988 unp il $16; lib bdg $15.93; pa $4.95 (k-3) **92**

1. Frontier and pioneer life

ISBN 0-688-06417-5; 0-688-06418-3 (lib bdg); 0-688-14025-4 (pa)   LC 87-27317

"Oversize pages have given Kellogg a fine opportunity for pictures that are on a large scale, colorful and animated if often busy with details. His version of Chapman's life is more substantial than the subtitle (*A Tall Tale*) would indicate, since the text makes clear the difference between what Chapman really did and what myths grew up about his work, his life, his personality, and his achievements. There's some exaggeration, but on the whole the biography is factual and written with clarity." Bull Cent Child Books

Armstrong, Louis, 1900-1971

Collier, James Lincoln. Louis Armstrong: an American success story. Macmillan 1985 165p il $14.95; pa $5.95 (5 and up)   **92**

1. Jazz musicians 2. African American musicians
ISBN 0-02-722830-4; 0-02-042555-4 (pa)

LC 84-42982

"Evokes Armstrong's life as a poverty-stricken boy from a broken home in New Orleans, a poor, struggling black musician in the South, and one of the outstanding jazz musicians of all time. An intriguing, absorbing portrait that reveals musical genius that could not be denied in an artist who never had a music lesson. Information about recordings is combined with a short annotated bibliography." Soc Educ

Arnold, Benedict, 1741-1801

Wade, Mary Dodson. Benedict Arnold. Watts 1994 63p il lib bdg $13.51 (4 and up)   **92**

1. Generals 2. United States—History—1775-1783, Revolution
ISBN 0-531-20156-2   LC 94-2574

"A First book"

The author "chronicles Arnold's life from his boyhood in Connecticut to his death in London. Special emphasis is placed on his treasonous activities, but the book also includes his heroic deeds that helped the Americans win the Revolution. . . . Attractive, full-color and black-and-white reproductions appear throughout." SLJ

Includes bibliography

Arthur, Chester Alan, 1829-1886

Simon, Charnan. Chester A. Arthur: twenty-first president of the United States. Childrens Press 1989 98p il (Encyclopedia of presidents) lib bdg $14.85 (4 and up)   **92**

1. Presidents—United States
ISBN 0-516-01369-6   LC 89-35386

This book traces the early life, influences, and career of the president "in a straightforward manner with black-and-white photographs or drawings on nearly every page. . . . Includes a chronology of American history." Booklist

Ashe, Arthur

Moutoussamy-Ashe, Jeanne. Daddy and me: a photo story of Arthur Ashe and his daughter, Camera; photographs and words by Jeanne Moutoussamy-Ashe. Knopf 1993 unp il $13; lib bdg $14.99 (k-3)   **92**

1. Fathers and daughters 2. AIDS (Disease) 3. African American athletes
ISBN 0-679-85096-1; 0-679-95096-6 (lib bdg)

LC 93-11513

Text and photographs provide insight into the relationship of tennis great Arthur Ashe and his six-year-old daughter, Camera, showing how young children and their families deal with AIDS

"The matter-of-fact tone of the text is reflected in the clear, expressive black-and-white photos, portraying the loving give and take of father and daughter." Booklist

Quackenbush, Robert M. Arthur Ashe and his match with history; [by] Robert Quackenbush. Simon & Schuster Bks. for Young Readers 1994 35p il $14; pa $4.95 (3-6)   **92**

1. Tennis—Biography 2. African American athletes
ISBN 0-671-86597-8; 0-671-88182-5 (pa)

LC 93-14945

A biography of the African American tennis champion who used his success to work against the racial prejudice he had faced

"Just as Ashe was more than a sports figure, this book is more than a simple sports biography. The last pages show Ashe as author and family man and acknowledge his experiences with heart disease and with AIDS, as both patient and spokesman." Booklist

Includes bibliographical references

Audubon, John James, 1785-1851

Audubon, John James. Capturing nature; the writings and art of John James Audubon; edited by Peter and Connie Roop; with illustrations by Rick Farley. Walker & Co. 1993 39p il $16.95; lib bdg $17.85 (4 and up)   **92**

1. Artists, American 2. Naturalists
ISBN 0-8027-8204-3; 0-8027-8205-1 (lib bdg)

LC 92-15662

Uses the words of Audubon himself, selected from various sources, to present an account of the life and work of this nineteenth-century naturalist

"A beautiful first-person adventure story through nature. Audubon's writing is engaging and easily accepted as authentic. The artwork complements the text, yet each may be enjoyed as separate entities." Sci Child

Includes bibliography

Baker, Sara Josephine, 1873-1945

Ptacek, Greg. Champion for children's health: a story about Dr. S. Josephine Baker; illustrations by Lydia M. Anderson. Carolrhoda Bks. 1994 64p il (Carolrhoda creative minds book) lib bdg $17.50 (3-5)   **92**

1. Women physicians
ISBN 0-87614-806-2   LC 93-10482

A biography of the doctor who, along with other achievements, was among the first to act on the idea that preventative medicine and health care for children is a function of government

"Designed for young readers, well written, and nicely illustrated with black-and-white drawings. . . . It belongs in every elementary and middle school library." Sci Books Films

Includes bibliography

Ballard, Robert D.

Archbold, Rick. Deep-sea explorer: the story of Robert Ballard, discoverer of the Titanic. Scholastic 1994 144p il maps $13.95 (6 and up)   **92**

1. Oceanography—Biography
ISBN 0-590-47232-1   LC 93-1983

Ballard, Robert D.—*Continued*
This is a biography "of the scientist/explorer who discovered the *Titanic*, the *Bismarck*, and shipwrecks from the Battle of Guadalcanal." Booklist
"This is an engaging narrative of a sometimes controversial figure, providing a glimpse of the public frustrations and personal disappointments that pioneers often face." SLJ
Includes glossary and bibliography

Banneker, Benjamin, 1731-1806
Ferris, Jeri. What are you figuring now? a story about Benjamin Banneker; illustrations by Amy Johnson. Carolrhoda Bks. 1988 64p il (Carolrhoda creative minds book) lib bdg $15.95; pa $5.95 (3-5)   **92**

1. Astronomers 2. African Americans—Biography
ISBN 0-87614-331-1 (lib bdg); 0-87614-521-7 (pa)
                LC 88-7267
A biography of the African American farmer and self-taught mathematician, astronomer, and surveyor for the new capital city of the United States in 1791, who also calculated a successful almanac notable for its preciseness
"Ferris' judicious use of dialogue and Johnson's full-page gray washes enhance this smooth, engaging biographical story; the mature style and succinct text make this a good choice for reluctant readers." Booklist

Pinkney, Andrea Davis. Dear Benjamin Banneker; illustrated by Brian Pinkney. Harcourt Brace & Co. 1994 unp il $14.95 (2-4)   **92**

1. Astronomers 2. African Americans—Biography
ISBN 0-15-200417-3   LC 93-31162
"Gulliver books"
"The Pinkneys chronicle Banneker's work on his almanac and, most particularly, his letter to Thomas Jefferson, then secretary of state, protesting the country's—and Jefferson's—involvement in slavery." Bull Cent Child Books
This offers "lucid text and striking illustrations, rendered on scratchboard and colored with oil paint." Publ Wkly

Barrie, J. M. (James Matthew), 1860-1937
Aller, Susan Bivin. J.M. Barrie: the magic behind Peter Pan. Lerner Publs. 1994 128p il lib bdg $21.50 (5 and up)   **92**

1. Authors, Scottish
ISBN 0-8225-4918-2   LC 94-5452
"Aller tells the story of the literary genius who created Peter Pan and Never Land, from his birth and early years in Scotland as the 9th of 10 children through his death at the age of 77 in 1937. The book is written in an interesting manner and will hold readers' attention. . . . The facts are well documented and logically organized. Black-and-white reproductions of photographs, caricatures of Barrie, illustrations from his works, and sketches of his own illustrate the text." SLJ
Includes bibliography

Beethoven, Ludwig van, 1770-1827
Thompson, Wendy. Ludwig van Beethoven. Viking 1991 c1990 48p il music (Composer's world) $17.95 (5 and up)   **92**

1. Composers
ISBN 0-670-83678-8   LC 90-70942

First published 1990 in the United Kingdom
This book describes the life and work of the composer, and the historical time in which he lived
This volume is "well-researched and highly informative. . . . The numerous black-and-white and full-color illustrations, photographs, sketches, maps, and musical excerpts and arrangements, combined with the list of works and picture credits, make [this] irresistible." SLJ
Includes glossary

Bell, Alexander Graham, 1847-1922
Parker, Steve. Alexander Graham Bell and the telephone. Chelsea House 1995 c1994 32p il (Science discoveries) lib bdg $14.95 (4 and up)   **92**

1. Inventors 2. Telephone
ISBN 0-7910-3004-0   LC 94-43925
Also available Spanish language edition
First published 1994 in the United Kingdom
Describes the life and times of the Scottish-born inventor whose interest in communication and sound led him to become the first person to transmit voices from one place to another
Includes glossary

St. George, Judith. Dear Dr. Bell—your friend, Helen Keller. See entry under Keller, Helen, 1880-1968

Bethune, Mary Jane McLeod, 1875-1955
Greenfield, Eloise. Mary McLeod Bethune; illustrated by Jerry Pinkney. Crowell 1977 32p il (Crowell biography) lib bdg $14.89; pa $5.95 (2-5)   **92**

1. African American educators 2. African American women
ISBN 0-690-01129-6 (lib bdg); 0-06-446168-8 (pa)
                LC 76-11522
"Details the life of Mary McLeod Bethune from her childhood in South Carolina to the founding of her school and her active role in the National Youth Administration under Franklin D. Roosevelt." Horn Book
"Written with a simple, natural flow, this biography for younger readers does not have all the fascinating details of the life of the great educator, but it gives salient facts and is nicely balanced in treatment." Bull Cent Child Books

McKissack, Patricia C. Mary McLeod Bethune: a great American educator. Childrens Press 1985 111p il (People of distinction biographies) hardcover o.p. paperback available $5.95 (4 and up)   **92**

1. African American educators 2. African American women
ISBN 0-516-43218-4 (pa)   LC 85-12843
Recounts the life of the black educator, from her childhood in the cotton fields of South Carolina to her success as teacher, crusader, and presidential adviser
This "is a warm story that gives a good view of a slave's life both before and after slaves were freed. Bethune's talents are well described, but her humanness shows through. . . . Photographs and letters . . . are excellent, and time lines are helpful, covering not only the subject's life but also major world events of that time. Indexes are thorough." SLJ

Blériot, Louis, 1872-1936

Provensen, Alice. The glorious flight: across the Channel with Louis Blériot, July 25, 1909; [by] Alice and Martin Provensen. Viking 1983 39p il lib bdg $16.99; pa $5.99 (1-4)   **92**

1. Air pilots 2. Airplanes—Design and construction
ISBN 0-670-34259-9 (lib bdg); 0-14-050729-9 (pa)
                LC 82-7034
Awarded the Caldecott Medal, 1984
This book "recounts the persistence of a Frenchman, Louis Blériot, to build a flying machine to cross the English Channel. For eight years (1901-1909) he tries and tries again to create a kind of contraption light enough to lift him off the ground and yet strong enough to keep from falling apart." SLJ
"A pleasing text recounts Bleriot's adventures with gentle humor and admiration for his earnest, if accident-prone, determination. Best of all, the pictures shine with the illustrator's delight in the wondrous flying machines themselves. Each strut, fin, and wing is lovingly depicted; but the book also tells the story of Bleriot's loyal family; careful readers will observe the five children growing up as they share the ups and downs of Papa's glorious career." Horn Book

Bonheur, Rosa, 1822-1899

Turner, Robyn Montana. Rosa Bonheur. Little, Brown 1991 32p il (Portraits of women artists for children) hardcover o.p. paperback available $6.95 (4-6)   **92**

1. Artists, French 2. Women artists
ISBN 0-316-85653-3 (pa)   LC 90-44135
A biography of the French artist noted for her paintings of animals
"Turner's simple (but not simplistic) style creates a clear and informative narrative. . . . Liberally illustrated with reproductions of Bonheur's painting and sculpture (chiefly in color, and with a few paintings of the artist by others), this is an excellent combination of biography and art history." Bull Cent Child Books

Botticelli, Sandro, 1444 or 5-1510

Venezia, Mike. Botticelli; written and illustrated by Mike Venezia. Childrens Press 1991 32p il (Getting to know the world's greatest artists) lib bdg $18.60; pa $5.95 (k-3)   **92**

1. Artists, Italian
ISBN 0-516-02291-1 (lib bdg); 0-516-42291-X (pa)
              LC 90-21645
Examines the life and work of the Italian painter of the early Renaissance, describing and giving examples of his art

Brady, Mathew B., ca. 1823-1896

Sullivan, George. Mathew Brady: his life and photographs. Cobblehill Bks. 1994 136p il $15.99 (6 and up)   **92**

1. Photographers 2. United States—History—1861-1865, Civil War
ISBN 0-525-65186-1   LC 93-28354

This "biography of the man credited with documenting the American Civil War focuses on Brady's professional life as a photographer." SLJ
"The beauty of the photographs—all taken more than a hundred years ago—eloquently conveys the truth of Brady's insight into the power and dramatic possibilities of the medium. The well-written book is interesting as a history of photography, of the man, and of the nation." Horn Book
Includes bibliographical references

Bridgman, Laura Dewey, 1829-1889

Hunter, Edith Fisher. Child of the silent night; illustrated by Bea Holmes. Houghton Mifflin 1963 124p il $14.95 (3-5)   **92**

1. Blind 2. Deaf
ISBN 0-395-06835-5
"Biographies of persons who have overcome physical handicaps can often reassure and inspire. This is the story of Laura Bridgman, a blind-deaf child whose successful attempts at communication paved the way for Helen Keller." Cincinnati Public Libr

Brown, John, 1800-1859

Everett, Gwen. John Brown; one man against slavery; paintings by Jacob Lawrence. Rizzoli Int. Publs. 1993 32p il $15.95 (4-6)   **92**

1. Abolitionists
ISBN 0-8478-1702-4   LC 92-41973
The views of the abolitionist John Brown and the events leading up to his ill-fated attack on the arsenal at Harpers Ferry are described through the eyes of Brown's daughter, Annie
"Despite the brevity of the narrative, Brown steps out of an historical tableau to become a real human being. . . . The art is stylized, emphasizing strong patterns and bold graphic designs to evoke powerful emotions for a powerful story." Horn Book Guide

Brown, Molly, d. 1934

Blos, Joan W. The heroine of the Titanic: a tale both true and otherwise of the life of Molly Brown; illustrated by Tennessee Dixon. Morrow Junior Bks. 1991 unp il $14.95; lib bdg $14.88 (k-3)   **92**

1. Titanic (Steamship)
ISBN 0-688-07546-0; 0-688-07547-9 (lib bdg)
              LC 90-35369
An anecdotal account of some of the adventurous activities of Molly Brown, with an emphasis on her survival of the sinking of the Titanic
"Illustrated with lavish and vigorous watercolors that sprawl across large double-page spreads, this tall-taleish—and occasionally rhyming—rendition of the Molly Brown saga has the feel and appeal of a folk epic." Bull Cent Child Books

Brueghel, Pieter, the Elder, 1522?-1569

Sterckx, Pierre. Brueghel; a gift for telling stories; illustrations by Claudine Roucha; translation by John Goodman. Chelsea House 1995 56p il (Art for children) lib bdg $14.95 (5 and up)   **92**

1. Artists, Flemish
ISBN 0-7910-2806-2   LC 94-47283

Brueghel, Pieter, the Elder, 1522?-1569—Continued

A book of the life of the Flemish painter best known for his landscapes and peasant scenes

Includes glossary

Venezia, Mike. Pieter Bruegel; written and illustrated by Mike Venezia. Childrens Press 1992 32p il (Getting to know the world's greatest artists) lib bdg $18.60; pa $5.95 (k-3) 92

1. Artists, Flemish

ISBN 0-516-02279-2 (lib bdg); 0-516-42279-0 (pa)

LC 92-4810

Briefly examines the life and work of the sixteenth-century Flemish painter through brief text, full-color reproductions of his paintings, and cartoon drawings

Bulla, Clyde Robert, 1914-

Bulla, Clyde Robert. A grain of wheat: a writer begins. Godine 1985 49p il hardcover o.p. paperback available $7.95 (3-5) 92

1. Authors, American 2. Farm life—Missouri

ISBN 0-87923-717-1 (pa)

LC 84-48750

The author describes "the first ten years of his life on a farm in Missouri. Childhood pranks, accidents, the first day of school (his sister was the teacher) and the death of a pet are some of the memories the author shares, as well as his early decision to be a writer. The book concludes with ten-year-old Clyde winning a dollar in a writing contest." SLJ

"Children familiar with Bulla's books . . . will be pleased, and those coming across this while looking for biographies will be equally intrigued, but the book's greatest use probably will be by librarians seeking ways to introduce the writing of a noteworthy author. A few photographs of Bulla as a child are included." Booklist

Bunting, Eve, 1928-

Bunting, Eve. Once upon a time; photographs by John Pezaris. Owen, R.C. 1995 32p il (Meet the author) $13.95 (1-3) 92

1. Authors, American 2. Women authors

ISBN 1-878450-59-X

LC 94-47220

"Bunting talks about her childhood in Ireland, immigration to the U.S., and her writing career, including how she came to write *The Wall* (1990) and *Smoky Night* (1994) [both entered in class E]. . . . For classes discussing writers and their books, here's the next best thing to meeting Bunting." Booklist

Burns, Anthony, 1834-1862

Hamilton, Virginia. Anthony Burns: the defeat and triumph of a fugitive slave. Knopf 1988 193p lib bdg $12.99; pa $4.99 (5 and up) 92

1. Slavery—United States 2. African Americans—Biography

ISBN 0-394-98185-5 (lib bdg); 0-679-83997-6 (pa)

LC 87-38063

A biography of the slave who escaped to Boston in 1854, was arrested at the instigation of his owner, and whose trial caused a furor between abolitionists and those determined to enforce the Fugitive Slave Act

"This book does exactly what good biography for children ought to do: takes readers directly into the life of the subject and makes them feel what it was like to be that person in those times." Horn Book

Includes bibliography

Butcher, Solomon D.

Conrad, Pam. Prairie visions: the life and times of Solomon Butcher. HarperCollins Pubs. 1991 85p il map lib bdg $16.89; pa $9.95 (5 and up) 92

1. Photographers 2. Nebraska—History 3. Frontier and pioneer life

ISBN 0-06-021375-2; 0-06-446135-1 (pa)

LC 90-38658

A collection of photos and stories about photographer Solomon Butcher and turn-of-the-century Nebraska

"This well-designed, narrated album makes imaginative use of source materials to convey real setting and character, providing a fresh, dramatic view of period and place." Horn Book

Includes bibliography

Byars, Betsy Cromer, 1928-

Byars, Betsy Cromer. The moon and I; [by] Betsy Byars. Messner 1991 96p il $12.95; lib bdg $14.98 (4 and up) 92

1. Authors, American 2. Women authors

ISBN 0-671-74166-7; 0-671-74165-9 (lib bdg)

LC 91-15000

A "personal narrative that gives readers some info about snakes, a fair amount of insight into how writers do what they do, and the unmistakable impression that autobiographies are great entertainment. Byars's genuine, humorous outlook on life shines through on every page." SLJ

Calamity Jane, 1852-1903

Faber, Doris. Calamity Jane; her life and her legend. Houghton Mifflin 1992 62p il $14.95 (5 and up) 92

1. Cowhands 2. West (U.S.)

ISBN 0-395-56396-8

LC 91-40050

Examines the life of the Wild West heroine, born Mary Jane Cannary, who was transformed into a legendary figure in the public mind

"With little reliable fact to go on, Faber's portrait of Cannary remains elusive, but the legend of Calamity Jane comes through strong and clear. . . . The book is spaciously and cleanly designed, with reproductions of old photos and dime novel covers . . . that further the evidence of both life and myth." Bull Cent Child Books

Includes bibliography

Carson, Rachel, 1907-1964

Kudlinski, Kathleen V. Rachel Carson: pioneer of ecology; illustrated by Ted Lewin. Viking Kestrel 1988 55p il (Women of our time) hardcover o.p. paperback available $4.50 (4 and up) 92

1. Women scientists

ISBN 0-14-032242-6 (pa)

LC 87-40671

Carson, Rachel, 1907-1964—*Continued*

A biography of the scientist and writer whose book "Silent spring" warned of the dangers of pesticides and launched a popular movement to control their use

"The tone is appreciative rather than reverential, the balance between Carson's personal and professional lives is nicely maintained, and the writing is clear, direct, and informative." Bull Cent Child Books

Ransom, Candice F. Listening to crickets: a story about Rachel Carson; illustrations by Shelly O. Haas. Carolrhoda Bks. 1993 64p il (Carolrhoda creative minds book) lib bdg $15.95; pa $5.95 (3-5)   **92**

1. Women scientists
ISBN 0-87614-727-9 (lib bdg); 0-87614-615-9 (pa)
LC 92-3470

This book traces "the course of Carson's life, her work, and her influence on ecological awareness." Booklist
This is "well written, and nicely illustrated with black-and-white drawings." Sci Books Films
Includes bibliography

Carter, Jimmy, 1924-

Wade, Linda R. James Carter: thirty-ninth president of the United States. Childrens Press 1989 100p il (Encyclopedia of presidents) lib bdg $14.85 (4 and up)   **92**

1. Presidents—United States
ISBN 0-516-01372-6   LC 89-33754

Describes the life and achievements of the relatively unknown governor from Georgia who became president of the United States in 1977

Carver, George Washington, 1864?-1943

Aliki. A weed is a flower: the life of George Washington Carver; written and illustrated by Aliki. Simon & Schuster Bks. for Young Readers 1988 32p il lib bdg $14; pa $5.95 (k-3)   **92**

1. Scientists 2. African Americans—Biography
ISBN 0-671-66118-3 (lib bdg); 0-671-66490-5 (pa)
LC 87-22864

First published 1965 by Prentice-Hall
Text and pictures present the life of the man, born a slave, who became a scientist and devoted his entire life to helping the South improve its agriculture

Mitchell, Barbara. A pocketful of goobers: a story about George Washington Carver; illustrations by Peter E. Hanson. Carolrhoda Bks. 1986 64p il (Carolrhoda creative minds book) lib bdg $17.50; pa $5.95 (3-5)   **92**

1. Scientists 2. African Americans—Biography
ISBN 0-87614-292-7 (lib bdg); 0-87614-474-1 (pa)
LC 86-2690

Relates the scientific efforts of George Washington Carver, especially his production of more than 300 uses for the peanut

"This book tells his remarkable story accurately, sympathetically, and felicitously." Sci Books Films

Cassatt, Mary, 1844-1926

Turner, Robyn Montana. Mary Cassatt. Little, Brown 1992 32p il (Portraits of women artists for children) $16.95; pa $6.95 (4-6)   **92**

1. Artists, American 2. Women artists
ISBN 0-316-85650-9; 0-316-85640-1 (pa)
LC 91-29557

Celebrates the life and work of the American artist renowned for her luminous paintings of children and mothers

"Through a clear, informative, engaging narration, Cassatt comes vibrantly alive. . . . With a wonderful sense of balance and pacing, the author discusses Cassatt's evolving work and portrays her personal life with immediacy and spirit. . . . The full-color, high-quality reproductions are beautiful; the overall design is handsome." SLJ

Venezia, Mike. Mary Cassatt; written and illustrated by Mike Venezia. Childrens Press 1990 32p il (Getting to know the world's greatest artists) lib bdg $18.60; pa $5.95 (k-3)   **92**

1. Artists, American 2. Women artists
ISBN 0-516-02278-4 (lib bdg); 0-516-42278-2 (pa)
LC 90-2165

Introduces the American Impressionist painter through brief text, full-color reproductions of her work, and cartoon drawings

Catlin, George, 1796-1872

Sufrin, Mark. George Catlin; painter of the Indian West. Atheneum Pubs. 1991 153p il $14.95 (6 and up)   **92**

1. Artists, American
ISBN 0-689-31608-9   LC 90-19813

A biography of the painter, author, and ethnographer who devoted his life to recording Indian life, not only in this country but in South America and Asia

"Sufrin's readable biography is rich in colorful details, lively anecdotes, and intriguing descriptions from Catlin's own journals and letters. The book is liberally illustrated with the artist's paintings." SLJ
Includes bibliography

Chaka, Zulu Chief, 1787?-1828

Stanley, Diane. Shaka, king of the Zulus; [by] Diane Stanley and Peter Vennema; illustrated by Diane Stanley. Morrow Junior Bks. 1988 unp il $16; lib bdg $15.93; pa $4.95 (3-5)   **92**

1. Zulus
ISBN 0-688-07342-5; 0-688-07343-3 (lib bdg); 0-688-13114-X (pa)   LC 87-27376

A biography of the nineteenth-century military genius and Zulu chief

"Diane Stanley and Peter Vennema have culled the massive amount of historical material that exists about this strange and fascinating figure. Their text is lucid; the incidents are tactfully within the scope and decorum of a children's book but representative and true to the facts. . . . The rhythm of the illustrations . . . makes each page not only a realistic representation but also an artistic composition." N Y Times Book Rev
Includes bibliography

Cisneros, Henry

Bredeson, Carmen. Henry Cisneros; building a better America. Enslow Pubs. 1995 128p il (People to know) lib bdg $17.95 (5 and up)
92

1. Mexican Americans 2. Cabinet officers
ISBN 0-89490-546-5   LC 94-41906

This is a biography of the Secretary of the Department of Housing and Urban Development during the Clinton administration and the first Hispanic American mayor of a major U.S. city, San Antonio, Texas

Includes bibliography

Cleopatra, Queen of Egypt, d. 30 B.C.

Stanley, Diane. Cleopatra; [by] Diane Stanley, Peter Vennema; illustrated by Diane Stanley. Morrow Junior Bks. 1994 unp il maps $15; lib bdg $14.93 (3-5)
92

1. Kings, queens, rulers, etc.
ISBN 0-688-10413-4; 0-688-10414-2 (lib bdg)
LC 93-27032

This is a biography of the ancient Egyptian queen

"Lucid writing combines with carefully selected anecdotes, often attributed to the Greek historian Plutarch to create an engaging narrative. . . . Stanley's stunning, full-color gouache artwork is arresting in its large, well-composed images executed in flat Greek style." SLJ

Includes bibliography

Clinton, Bill, 1946-

Kent, Zachary. William Jefferson Clinton; forty-second President of the United States. Childrens Press 1994 98p il (Encyclopedia of presidents) lib bdg $19.20 (4 and up)   92

1. Presidents—United States
ISBN 0-516-01350-5   LC 92-47044

A biography of the Arkansas governor who became the forty-second president of the United States

Columba, Saint, 521-597

Fritz, Jean. The man who loved books; illuminated by Trina Schart Hyman. Putnam 1981 unp il $14.99 (2-4)
92

1. Christian saints
ISBN 0-399-61284-X   LC 80-12614

A biography of the Irish saint who was known for his love of books and his missionary work throughout Scotland

"The telling is direct and spirited, lilting and sensitively balanced. . . . The episodes in [Columba's] adventurous life are humorously reflected in full-page and half-page drawings washed with shades of brown." Horn Book

Columbus, Christopher

Adler, David A. A picture book of Christopher Columbus; illustrated by John and Alexandra Wallner. Holiday House 1991 unp il map lib bdg $15.95; pa $5.95 (1-3)
92

1. Explorers 2. America—Exploration
ISBN 0-8234-0857-4 (lib bdg); 0-8234-0949-X (pa)
LC 90-39211

Also available Spanish language edition

A brief account of the life and accomplishments of Christopher Columbus

"The Wallners' illustrations . . . are framed watercolors that surround the text. They offer a delightful look at Renaissance dress and housing and add immeasurably to the spare text. . . . This title fills the bill for those looking for an attractive picture book presentation of the basic facts." SLJ

Columbus, Christopher. I, Columbus; my journal, 1492-3; edited by Peter and Connie Roop; illustrated by Peter E. Hanson. Walker & Co. 1990 57p il $13.95; lib bdg $14.85 (4-6)
92

1. Explorers 2. America—Exploration
ISBN 0-8027-6977-2; 0-8027-6978-0 (lib bdg)
LC 90-12407

Also available in paperback from Avon Bks.

Follows the voyages of discovery made by Christopher Columbus through excerpts from the journals he kept of his travels

"The Roops provide a readable and fascinating glimpse into Columbus's thoughts. . . . Hanson's excellent pen-and-ink drawings . . . are delicately watercolored in soft blues and golds." SLJ

Fritz, Jean. Where do you think you're going, Christopher Columbus? pictures by Margot Tomes. Putnam 1980 80p il maps $13.95; pa $8.95 (2-4)
92

1. Explorers 2. America—Exploration
ISBN 0-399-20723-6; 0-399-20734-1 (pa)
LC 80-11377

"Reducing a life as well-documented as Columbus's to 80 pages must result in some simplifications of fact or context, but in this case they are not readily apparent. Mrs. Fritz's breezy narrative gives us a highly individual Columbus. . . . Margot Tomes's three-color illustrations are attractive, amusing and informative." N Y Times Book Rev

Sis, Peter. Follow the dream. Knopf 1991 unp il map $15 (k-3)
92

1. Explorers 2. America—Exploration
ISBN 0-679-80628-8   LC 90-45276

Cover title: Follow the dream: the story of Christopher Columbus

In a pictorial retelling, Christopher Columbus overcomes a number of obstacles to fulfill his dream of sailing west to find a new route to the Orient

"The text is smoothly written and informative. Yet it is Sis's illustrations that make Follow the Dream so distinctive; his pictures, executed in oil, ink and watercolor, and gouache, complement and extend the narrative, adding additional facts and capturing young readers' interest by humanizing Columbus and vividly rendering his vision of a new world." Horn Book

Copland, Aaron, 1900-1990

Venezia, Mike. Aaron Copland; written and illustrated by Mike Venezia. Childrens Press 1995 32p il (Getting to know the world's greatest composers) lib bdg $18.60; pa $5.95 (k-3)
92

1. Composers, American
ISBN 0-516-04538-5 (lib bdg); 0-516-44538-3 (pa)
LC 94-36344

Introduces the American composer through brief text, photographs, and cartoon drawings

Cosby, Bill, 1937-

Haskins, James. Bill Cosby: America's most famous father; by Jim Haskins. Walker & Co. 1988 138p il $13.95; lib bdg $14.95 (5 and up) **92**

1. African American entertainers
ISBN 0-8027-6785-0; 0-8027-6786-9 (lib bdg)
LC 87-33951
"Unlike most juvenile biographies of celebrities, this one deals extensively with the problems Bill Cosby faced, both as a youngster growing up in an impoverished family and as a comedian who refused to use race as a source for his material. Prolific writer Jim Haskins has written a biography that gives its readers something to think about as they learn about one of their favorites." Child Book Rev Serv
Includes bibliography

Crazy Horse, Sioux Chief, ca. 1842-1877

St. George, Judith. Crazy Horse. Putnam 1994 180p maps $17.95 (5 and up) **92**

1. Oglala Indians
ISBN 0-399-22667-2
LC 94-12329
"Using transcripts of interviews conducted in the 1930s with people who knew Crazy Horse as well as other primary sources, the author paints a picture of a taciturn but loyal man who felt it was his destiny to defend his people against the encroachment of white settlers. Woven into the narrative is information about the Sioux culture, alliances, and beliefs." SLJ
"Thoroughly researched and filled with passion, the action-packed narrative communicates the author's admiration for her subject." Publ Wkly
Includes bibliography

Crews, Donald

Crews, Donald. Bigmama's. Greenwillow Bks. 1991 unp il $16; lib bdg $15.93 **92**

1. Authors, American 2. African Americans—Biography 3. Country life
ISBN 0-688-09950-5; 0-688-09951-3 (lib bdg)
LC 90-33142
Visiting Bigmama's house in the country, young Donald Crews finds his relatives full of news and the old place and its surroundings just the same as the year before
"This is an evocative celebration of the joy and wonder of childhood; would that every child had such a summer. The last page is a hauntingly lovely remembrance. The illustrations are perfect and make this a truly beautiful book." Child Book Rev Serv

Curie, Marie, 1867-1934

Parker, Steve. Marie Curie and radium. Chelsea House 1995 c1992 32p il (Science discoveries) lib bdg $13.95 (4 and up) **92**

1. Chemists 2. Women scientists
ISBN 0-7910-3011-3
LC 94-20657
Also available Spanish language edition
First published 1992 by HarperCollins Pubs.
Details the life and work of Marie Curie from early childhood to the discovery of radium and her two Nobel Prizes
Includes glossary

Pflaum, Rosalynd. Marie Curie and her daughter Irène. Lerner Publs. 1993 144p il lib bdg $22.95 (5 and up) **92**

1. Joliot-Curie, Irène, 1897-1956 2. Chemists 3. Women scientists
ISBN 0-8225-4915-8
LC 92-2453
Presents the life stories of Marie Curie, discoverer of radium, polonium, and natural radiation, and her daughter Irène Joliot-Curie, discoverer of artificial radiation
Includes bibliographical references

Poynter, Margaret. Marie Curie: discoverer of radium. Enslow Pubs. 1994 128p il maps (Great minds of science) lib bdg $17.95 (4 and up) **92**

1. Chemists 2. Women scientists
ISBN 0-89490-477-9
LC 93-21224
This "biography emphasizes Marie Curie's early life of poverty, desire to study, and contributions to the fields of chemistry, physics, and medicine." Horn Book Guide
"The writing style is straightforward, with a combination of personal detail and scientific explanation. . . . Sure to be in demand for those middle-grade biography and science assignments." Booklist
Includes glossary and bibliography

Dalí, Salvador, 1904-1989

Venezia, Mike. Salvador Dali; written and illustrated by Mike Venezia. Childrens Press 1993 32p il (Getting to know the world's greatest artists) lib bdg $18.60; pa $5.95 (k-3) **92**

1. Artists, Spanish
ISBN 0-516-02296-2 (lib bdg); 0-516-42296-0 (pa)
LC 92-35053
Briefly describes the life and work of the twentieth-century Spanish surrealist painter, and includes examples of his art

Darwin, Charles, 1809-1882

Evans, J. Edward. Charles Darwin; revolutionary biologist. Lerner Publs. 1993 112p il maps lib bdg $22.95 (5 and up) **92**

1. Naturalists 2. Evolution
ISBN 0-8225-4914-X
LC 92-45281
A biography of the English naturalist who, after collecting plants and animals from around the world, came up with the theory of evolution by natural selection
"Important events and facts are well described and his theories explained so as to be easily understood. Black-and-white photographs and drawings of the time enhance the text." Sci Child
Includes bibliography

Parker, Steve. Charles Darwin and evolution. Chelsea House 1995 c1992 32p il (Science discoveries) lib bdg $13.95 (4 and up) **92**

1. Evolution 2. Naturalists
ISBN 0-7910-3007-5
LC 94-20656
Also available Spanish language edition
First published 1992 by HarperCollins Pubs.

Darwin, Charles, 1809-1882—*Continued*

Traces the life of the English naturalist from his early years through his expedition aboard the H.M.S. Beagle and the development of his theory of evolution by natural selection

Includes glossary and bibliographical references

Day, Tom, 1801-ca. 1861

Lyons, Mary E. Master of mahogany: Tom Day, free black cabinetmaker. Scribner 1994 42p il (African-American artists and artisans) $15.95 (4 and up)   92

1. African Americans—Biography 2. Cabinetwork
ISBN 0-684-19675-1   LC 93-37900

"Born in 1801, Day created a profitable business designing and building furniture in North Carolina. Lyons does an excellent job of piecing together the sketchy details of his life. The photographs of Day's graceful furniture and newel posts, now preserved in museum collections and historic homes, contribute to the reader's understanding of his artistry." Horn Book

Includes glossary and bibliography

De Mille, Agnes

Gherman, Beverly. Agnes de Mille: dancing off the earth. Atheneum Pubs. 1990 138p il $13.95 (5 and up)   92

1. Dancers
ISBN 0-689-31441-8   LC 89-6888

Also available in paperback from Collier Bks.

The life and accomplishments of the choreographer, dancer and author best known for the ballets she created on American themes and for the choreography of the musical "Oklahoma"

"In a judicious blend of well-researched text and pithy, candidly revealing quotes from de Mille, the author infuses splendid vitality into her biography of one of America's greatest choreographers." Booklist

Includes bibliography

Debussy, Claude, 1862-1918

Thompson, Wendy. Claude Debussy. Viking 1993 48p il music (Composer's world) $17.99 (5 and up)   92

1. Composers
ISBN 0-670-84482-9   LC 92-85504

This describes Debussy's life, work, and times, illustrated with historical paintings and drawings and musical excerpts

Dickens, Charles, 1812-1870

Stanley, Diane. Charles Dickens; the man who had great expectations; [by] Diane Stanley & Peter Vennema; illustrated by Diane Stanley. Morrow Junior Bks. 1993 unp il $15; lib bdg $14.93 (3-5)   92

1. Authors, English
ISBN 0-688-09110-5; 0-688-09111-3 (lib bdg)
                                    LC 91-41552

"This picture-book biography of the great English novelist is attractive and appealing. Stanley's full-color, full-page gouache paintings are expressive and inviting; the abbreviated text covers all of the major events in Dickens's life." SLJ

Includes bibliography

Douglass, Frederick, 1817?-1895

Kerby, Mona. Frederick Douglass. Watts 1994 63p il lib bdg $13.93 (4 and up)   92

1. Abolitionists 2. African Americans—Biography
ISBN 0-531-20173-2   LC 94-15

"A First book"

Kerby's "biography examines the life of the 19th-century spokesman and abolitionist. She discusses the harsh conditions that constituted Douglass's daily life as a slave, his daring escape to freedom, and his participation in the antislavery movement. . . . The writing is smooth, and the chapters flow nicely. Black-and-white and full-color photographs and reproductions of paintings and documents appear throughout." SLJ

Includes bibliographical references

Miller, Douglas T. Frederick Douglass and the fight for freedom. Facts on File 1988 152p il (Makers of America) lib bdg $16.95; pa $8.95 (6 and up)   92

1. Abolitionists 2. African Americans—Biography
ISBN 0-8160-1617-8 (lib bdg); 0-8160-2996-2 (pa)
                                    LC 87-28806

Traces the life of the black abolitionist, from his early years in slavery to his later success as a persuasive editor, orator, and writer

"This biography is clearly organized and provides a fast-paced narrative which, in addition to being an excellent study of Douglass, presents the issues of south vs. north, slave owners vs. abolitionists, whites vs. blacks. . . . Miller's readable and reliable life of Frederick Douglass is a fine example of biographical writing." SLJ

Includes bibliography

Miller, William. Frederick Douglass; the last day of slavery; illustrated by Cedric Lucas. Lee & Low Bks. 1995 unp il $14.95 (1-3)   92

1. Abolitionists 2. African Americans—Biography
ISBN 1-880000-17-2   LC 94-26542

"This picture-book biography focuses on a crucial episode in the life of the great abolitionist Frederick Douglass: the day he stood up to a vicious overseer and fought back. As the tension builds to that confrontation, Miller tells the story of Douglass' life under slavery." Booklist

"This plain rendering is a powerful introduction to the man and to the tragedy of slavery. Cedric [Lucas's] vigorous figures set against richly colored and textured backgrounds effectively illuminate this thought-provoking biographical tale." Horn Book

Drake, Sir Francis, 1540?-1596

Marrin, Albert. The sea king: Sir Francis Drake and his times. Atheneum Bks. for Young Readers 1995 168p il maps $18 (6 and up)   92

1. Explorers
ISBN 0-689-31887-1   LC 95-60386

Drake, Sir Francis, 1540?-1596—*Continued*

"Sir Francis Drake is seen variously as explorer, naval military genius, and pirate; Marrin paints a picture including all those characteristics and more, tracing Drake's life from his early days on the sea, through his unsuccessful and successful quests for Central American gold and his global circumnavigation, to his unofficial spearheading of the defeat of the Spanish Armada." Bull Cent Child Books

"Marrin does an exemplary job of defining words in context, incorporating quotations, explaining both sides of a conflict, all while retaining the essential drama of Britain's most famous sailor. Marrin's Drake is not just a swashbuckling hero, but a complex character." Voice Youth Advocates

Includes bibliography

Dunbar, Paul Laurence, 1872-1906

McKissack, Patricia C. Paul Laurence Dunbar, a poet to remember. Childrens Press 1984 127p il (People of distinction biographies) hardcover o.p. paperback available $5.95 (4 and up) **92**

1. Poets, American 2. African American authors
ISBN 0-516-43209-5 (pa)   LC 84-7625

A biography of the turn-of-the-century black poet and novelist whose works were among the first to give an honest presentation of black life

The author "makes a good case for the enduring value of Dunbar's dialect poetry, illustrating with excerpts and her own commentary the sensitivity and appreciation which Dunbar expressed for the language and the people who spoke it." SLJ

Dunham, Katherine

Greene, Carol. Katherine Dunham; black dancer. Childrens Press 1992 44p il (Rookie biography) lib bdg $13.28; pa $4.95 (1-3) **92**

1. African American dancers 2. African American women
ISBN 0-516-04252-1 (lib bdg); 0-516-44252-X (pa)
LC 92-8769

Presents the personal experiences and professional achievements of the black dancer, choreographer, and founder of the Dunham Dance Company

This features "a few sentences against plenty of white space, complemented by lots of illustrations using full-color paintings and mostly black-and-white photographs." SLJ

Earhart, Amelia, 1898-1937

Lauber, Patricia. Lost star: the story of Amelia Earhart. Scholastic 1988 106p il maps hardcover o.p. paperback available $3.50 (5 and up) **92**

1. Women air pilots
ISBN 0-590-41159-4 (pa)   LC 88-3043

"Earhart's early life is covered succinctly, including the family problems that resulted from her father's alcoholism. Close to half of the book is concerned with the details of the last flight around the world and the mysterious disappearance, sure to hold the attention of readers. Small but very clear black-and-white photographs are included." SLJ

Includes bibliography

Quackenbush, Robert M. Clear the cow pasture, I'm coming in for a landing!: a story of Amelia Earhart; [by] Robert Quackenbush. Simon & Schuster Bks. for Young Readers 1990 36p il $11.95; pa $3.95 (2-4) **92**

1. Women air pilots
ISBN 0-671-68548-1; 0-671-69218-6 (pa)
LC 89-6164

A biography of the courageous aviatrix who became the first woman to cross the Atlantic by air

"Concisely and amusingly worded, the book includes three separate illustrative styles that complement the volume's admiring yet lighthearted tone. The first consists of single-page scenes picturing Earhart's life; the second is a series of cartoons, set in page corners, that depicts a mother bird introducing the concept of flight to her two babies. The third style is featured on the endpapers, which show a map of Earhart's final, incomplete flight route with added diagrams of aerial maneuvers." Booklist

Earle, Sylvia A., 1935-

Conley, Andrea. Window on the deep: the adventures of underwater explorer Sylvia Earle. Watts 1991 41p il $14.95; lib bdg $15.82 (5 and up) **92**

1. Underwater exploration 2. Submarine diving
ISBN 0-531-15232-4; 0-531-11119-9 (lib bdg)
LC 91-17792

"A New England Aquarium book"

Describes the underwater exploration of Sylvia Earle, a woman who has set many diving records

"It is refreshing to find a book of this quality available to children. The author has managed to portray the rigors of science and exploration, and the enjoyment (the fun!) one gets from them, without being preachy about Earle's gender. This book will hold the interest of any student who has an interest in the sea and its exploration." Sci Books Films

Includes glossary and bibliography

Eastman, George, 1854-1932

Mitchell, Barbara. CLICK!: a story about George Eastman; illustrations by Jan Hosking Smith. Carolrhoda Bks. 1986 56p il (Carolrhoda creative minds book) lib bdg $17.50; pa $5.95 (3-5) **92**

1. Inventors 2. Photography—History
ISBN 0-87614-289-7 (lib bdg); 0-87614-472-5 (pa)
LC 86-2672

Follows the life and career of the man who revolutionized photography by developing a camera simple enough for anyone to use

Edelman, Marian Wright

Siegel, Beatrice. Marian Wright Edelman; the making of a crusader. Simon & Schuster Bks. for Young Readers 1995 159p il $15 (5 and up) **92**

1. African American women 2. Children—Law and legislation
ISBN 0-02-782629-5   LC 94-41245

Edelman, Marian Wright—*Continued*

This is a biography of the "advocate for children and civil rights. . . . Siegel focuses mainly on Edelman's political work and her involvement in the civil rights movement." Voice Youth Advocates

This book "has the advantage of using primary sources, including an interview with the subject herself. . . . An unusually good example of contemporary biography." Booklist

Includes bibliographical references

Edison, Thomas A. (Thomas Alva), 1847-1931

Adler, David A. Thomas Alva Edison; great inventor; illustrated by Lyle Miller. Holiday House 1990 48p il (First biography) lib bdg $14.95 (2-4)   92

1. Inventors
ISBN 0-8234-0820-5   LC 89-77507

A biography of the inventive genius who developed the electric light bulb, the phonograph, and the motion picture

"In sturdy, somewhat grave prose, Adler incorporates telling anecdotes that illustrate Edison's quirky character. . . . A text laced with quotations avoids fictionalizing. Black-and-white pencil drawings, detailed and accurate, appear on each page." SLJ

Nirgiotis, Nicholas. Thomas Edison. Childrens Press 1994 32p il (Cornerstones of freedom) lib bdg $15.93; pa $3.95 (4-6)
                                                                       92

1. Inventors
ISBN 0-516-06676-5 (lib bdg); 0-516-46676-3 (pa)
                                            LC 93-37028

"The author has focused on only a few of those among Edison's inventions of which the general public is aware: the electric light bulb, the phonograph, the motion picture system, and improvements to the telegraph and telephone. The book stresses the importance of learning, even without the benefit of good schooling, and dedication to one's work." Sci Books Films

Parker, Steve. Thomas Edison and electricity. Chelsea House 1995 32p il (Science discoveries) lib bdg $13.95 (4 and up)   92

1. Inventors
ISBN 0-7910-3012-1   LC 94-20658
Also available Spanish language edition
First published 1992 by HarperCollins

Details the life and work of Thomas Edison, who developed such inventions as the stock ticker, the lightbulb, and the phonograph

Includes glossary

Edmonds, S. Emma E. (Sarah Emma Evelyn), 1841-1898

Reit, Seymour. Behind rebel lines: the incredible story of Emma Edmonds, Civil War spy. Harcourt Brace Jovanovich 1988 102p hardcover o.p. paperback available $5 (4 and up)   92

1. United States—History—1861-1865, Civil War
2. Spies
ISBN 0-15-200424-6 (pa)   LC 87-28079
"Gulliver books"

This biography tells of a Canadian-born woman who assumed male dress and served in the Union Army, first in a tent hospital, and then as a spy behind Confederate lines under various disguises

"Working from Emma's memoirs, U.S. Army records, and National Archives files, Reit has woven a suspense-filled account of a brave and loyal feminist." Booklist

Includes bibliography

Stevens, Bryna. Frank Thompson; her Civil War story. Macmillan 1992 144p il lib bdg $13.95 (5 and up)   92

1. United States—History—1861-1865, Civil War
2. Spies
ISBN 0-02-788185-7   LC 91-45382

A biography of the woman who, disguised as a man, moved behind Confederate lines to spy for the Union during the Civil War

"This book contributes information in an area not frequently examined—the role of women in the Union Army." SLJ

Includes bibliographical references

Einstein, Albert, 1879-1955

McPherson, Stephanie Sammartino. Ordinary genius: the story of Albert Einstein. Carolrhoda Bks. 1995 95p il (Trailblazers) lib bdg $13.13 (4 and up)   92

1. Scientists
ISBN 0-87614-788-0   LC 93-1408

Recounts the life of the scientist whose theories of relativity revolutionized the way we look at space and time

"Without trivializing Einstein's genius, McPherson lets readers feel the great scientist's excitement and frustration with his work. Explanations of Einstein's scientific discoveries are clearly presented, as is the social context of Germany between the wars and during the Nazi years. Photographs of Einstein, including one of him at age five, are well chosen to leave some new visual memories of the famous face." Booklist

Includes bibliography

Parker, Steve. Albert Einstein and relativity. Chelsea House 1995 c1994 32p il (Science discoveries) lib bdg $14.95 (4 and up)   92

1. Scientists
ISBN 0-7910-3003-2   LC 94-43924
Also available Spanish language edition
First published 1994 in the United Kingdom

Discusses the life and times of the German-American scientist who revolutionized the study of modern physics

Includes glossary

El Chino

Say, Allen. El Chino. Houghton Mifflin 1990 32p il $14.95 (2-5)   92

1. Bullfights—Biography
ISBN 0-395-52023-1   LC 90-35026

A biography of Bill Wong, a Chinese American who became a famous bullfighter in Spain

"Say's text renders Billy's complex story with simplicity and grace, presenting Billy as an endearing, determined hero; Say's watercolors are luminous, filled with harmonious detail. The first several pages of the book are reproduced in sepia tones, but when Billy attends his first bullfight, the pictures burst into full color." Publ Wkly

Eleanor, of Aquitaine, Queen, consort of Henry II, King of England, 1122?-1204

Brooks, Polly Schoyer. Queen Eleanor: independent spirit of the medieval world; a biography of Eleanor of Aquitaine. Lippincott 1983 183p il map lib bdg $14.89 (6 and up) **92**

1. Great Britain—Kings, queens, rulers, etc. 2. France—Kings, queens, rulers, etc.
ISBN 0-397-31995-9   LC 82-48776

A biography of the twelfth-century queen, first of France, then of England, who was the very lively wife of Henry II and mother of several notable sons, including Richard the Lionhearted

"The biographer has captured the subject's personality in a narrative as elegant and vivacious as Eleanor herself. And while obviously enthusiastic, the author nevertheless presents a balanced portrait: legend is separated from known facts; gossip from evidence." Horn Book

Includes bibliography

Elizabeth I, Queen of England, 1533-1603

Stanley, Diane. Good Queen Bess: the story of Elizabeth I of England; by Diane Stanley and Peter Vennema; illustrated by Diane Stanley. Four Winds Press 1990 unp il $16.95 (3-5) **92**

1. Great Britain—Kings, queens, rulers, etc.
ISBN 0-02-786810-9   LC 88-37501

Follows the life of the strong-willed queen who ruled England in the time of Shakespeare and the defeat of the Spanish Armada

"The handsome illustrations . . . are worthy of their subject. Although the format suggests a picture-book audience, this biography needs to be introduced to older readers who have the background to appreciate and understand this woman who dominated and named an age." SLJ

Includes bibliography

Ellington, Duke, 1899-1974

Collier, James Lincoln. Duke Ellington. Macmillan 1991 144p $13.95; pa $5.95 (5 and up) **92**

1. Jazz musicians 2. African Americans—Biography
ISBN 0-02-722985-8 (lib bdg); 0-02-042675-5 (pa)
     LC 90-26303

The author describes the life and times of the noted jazz musician

"This well-written biography is more panoramic than personal, yet affords a fascinating introduction to the man, his music, and his milieu." Voice Youth Advocates

Includes bibliography

Venezia, Mike. Duke Ellington; written and illustrated by Mike Venezia. Childrens Press 1995 32p il (Getting to know the world's greatest composers) lib bdg $18.60; pa $5.95 (k-3) **92**

1. Jazz musicians 2. African Americans—Biography
ISBN 0-516-04540-7 (lib bdg); 0-516-44540-5 (pa)
     LC 95-2404

Traces the life of the internationally acclaimed musician and composer who helped popularize jazz music

Equiano, Olaudah, b. 1745

Cameron, Ann. The kidnapped prince: the life of Olaudah Equiano; by Olaudah Equiano; adapted by Ann Cameron; with an introduction by Henry Louis Gates, Jr. Knopf 1995 133p il $16 (4 and up) **92**

1. Slavery 2. Blacks—Biography
ISBN 0-679-85619-6   LC 93-29914

Adaptation of The interesting narrative of the life of Olaudah Equiano

This is an "adaptation of an influential slave narrative by an African prince who was kidnapped as a child and later freed from slavery; first published in 1789." N Y Times Book Rev

"The inspired simplicity of Cameron's adaptation quickly allows Equiano's gifted voice to establish a compelling relationship between himself and young readers. Well sculpted with detail." SLJ

Includes glossary and bibliographical references

Eratosthenes, 3rd cent. B.C.

Lasky, Kathryn. The librarian who measured the earth; illustrated by Kevin Hawkes. Little, Brown 1994 48p il $16.95 (2-5) **92**

1. Astronomers
ISBN 0-316-51526-4   LC 92-42656

Describes the life and work of Eratosthenes, the Greek geographer and astronomer who accurately measured the circumference of the Earth

"Illustrating the text with warmth and humor, Hawkes' acrylic paintings capture the period details of the setting and clarify the geometric concepts used in the measurement. The often dramatic compositions vary from page to page, while the sunlit reds, oranges, and yellows glow brightly against the cooler blues and greens. . . . Entertaining as well as instructional." Booklist

Includes bibliography

Flipper, Henry O., 1856-1940

Pfeifer, Kathryn. Henry O. Flipper; [by] Kathryn Browne Pfeifer. 21st Cent. Bks. (NY) 1993 80p il (African-American soldiers) lib bdg $14.95 (5 and up) **92**

1. African American soldiers
ISBN 0-8050-2351-8   LC 93-10631

The author "chronicles the life of the first African American to graduate from West Point. Born a slave, Flipper had loving parents who wanted their son to receive a good education. His years of loneliness mixed with the insults he received at West Point are well detailed, and the circumstances that led to his dishonorable discharge from the army in 1881 are clearly explained. The almost 100-year attempt to have this discharge changed to an honorable one is discussed." SLJ

Includes bibliography

Ford, Henry, 1863-1947

Mitchell, Barbara. We'll race you, Henry: a story about Henry Ford; illustrations by Kathy Haubrich. Carolrhoda Bks. 1986 56p il (Carolrhoda creative minds book) lib bdg $14.95; pa $5.95 (3-5) **92**

1. Automobile industry 2. Inventors
ISBN 0-87614-291-9 (lib bdg); 0-87614-471-7 (pa)
     LC 86-2691

Ford, Henry, 1863-1947—*Continued*

A brief biography of Henry Ford with emphasis on how he came to develop fast, sturdy, and reliable racing cars that eventually gave him the idea for his Model T

"This book stands out from the general run of biographies for children because of the successful integration of a goodly amount of technological information with accurate and interesting biographical information." Appraisal

Foreman, Michael, 1938-

Foreman, Michael. War boy: a country childhood. Arcade Pub. 1990 c1989 92p il $16.95 (5 and up) **92**

1. Authors, English 2. Illustrators 3. World War, 1939-1945—Great Britain—Personal narratives
ISBN 1-55970-049-1   LC 89-48501
First published 1989 in the United Kingdom
"War memories of a childhood spent on the frontline of World War II on the Suffolk coast of England are related . . . by text and illustrations." Child Book Rev Serv
"The stories meander among small, intriguing details. Bomb shelters, local characters and sweetshop treats are remembered and enlivened with beautiful, evocative illustrations. Foreman's sketches and full-color watercolors are sprinkled across the wide format, while reproductions of airplane specifications and other period details keep this from looking like just another picture book." Publ Wkly

Forten, Charlotte L., 1837-1914

Burchard, Peter. Charlotte Forten; a black teacher in the Civil War. Crown 1995 106p il map $16 (5 and up) **92**

1. African American educators 2. African American women
ISBN 0-517-59242-8   LC 94-18305
This is a biography of a "black woman who grew up at the center of the abolitionist movement and worked as a teacher and nurse during the Civil War." Book Rep
"Readers will experience history firsthand as Forten recounts her anxiety over fugitive slave Anthony Burns; her excitement when celebrating Lincoln's Emancipation Proclamation; and her grief over the death of a close friend and heroic leader of the famed 54th Massachusetts Volunteers. A well-documented, effective mix of primary sources and historic information." SLJ
Includes bibliography

Fortune, Amos, 1709 or 10-1801

Yates, Elizabeth. Amos Fortune, free man; illustrations by Nora S. Unwin. Dutton 1950 181p il $15 (4 and up) **92**

1. African Americans—Biography 2. Slavery—United States
ISBN 0-525-25570-2
Also available in paperback from Viking
Awarded the Newbery Medal, 1951
"Born free in Africa, Amos Fortune was sold into slavery in America in 1725. After more than 40 years of servitude Amos was able to purchase his freedom and, in time, that of several others. He died a tanner of enviable reputation, a landowner, and a respected citizen of his community. Based on fact, this is a . . . story of a life dedicated to the fight for freedom and service to others." Booklist

Francis, of Assisi, Saint, 1182-1226

De Paola, Tomie. Francis, the poor man of Assisi; written and illustrated by Tomie de Paola. Holiday House 1982 unp il lib bdg $14.95; pa $6.95 (3-5) **92**

1. Clare, of Assisi, Saint, 1194-1253 2. Christian saints
ISBN 0-8234-0435-8 (lib bdg); 0-8234-0812-4 (pa)
    LC 81-6984
The text "describes how Francis of Assisi changed from a roistering youth, son of a rich merchant, to a beggar for God. There are stories about the miracles that influenced him, of miracles he performed as he inspired others to join his mendicant band. The author also tells about Clare who heard Francis speak and left home to found the order still known as the Little Sisters of the Poor and of the miracles she performed." Publ Wkly
"Tomie de Paola captures the sweetness and gentleness of St. Francis, particularly in the illustrations, whose flattened perspective and muted earth, green and rust tones are obviously inspired by Giotto. . . . The inclusion of the text of Francis' 'Song to the Sun' makes a charming conclusion for the book." N Y Times Book Rev

Hodges, Margaret. Brother Francis and the friendly beasts; pictures by Ted Lewin. Scribner 1991 unp il $14.95 (k-3) **92**

1. Christian saints
ISBN 0-684-19173-3   LC 90-33206
"Hodges tells of the evolution of Saint Francis of Assisi, the son of a merchant who rejected material wealth to preach to the people and animals of Italy." Booklist
"Hodges writes with reverence, drawing the kind man's portrait by skillfully weaving together the many legends surrounding his life and times. Lewin captures in fine detail the old Italian villages and the countryside's verdant, natural beauty." Publ Wkly

Frank, Anne, 1929-1945

Adler, David A. A picture book of Anne Frank; illustrated by Karen Ritz. Holiday House 1993 unp il lib bdg $15.95; pa $6.95 (1-3) **92**

1. Jews—Netherlands 2. Holocaust, 1933-1945
ISBN 0-8234-1003-X (lib bdg); 0-8234-1078-1 (pa)
    LC 92-17283
"Adler introduces Anne Frank and her family to primary grade readers. . . . Ritz's illustrations, some based on actual photographs, allow Anne's lively personality to emerge, and yet never appear undignified. . . . Adler's presentation is both sensitive and appropriate for the age group." Booklist

Frank, Anne. The diary of a young girl; translated from the Dutch by B. M. Mooyaart-Doubleday (6 and up) **92**

1. World War, 1939-1945—Jews 2. Netherlands—History—1940-1945, German occupation 3. Jews—Netherlands
Available in various bindings and editions including Spanish language edition
This is the diary of a "German-Jewish girl who hid from the Nazis with her parents, their friends, and some other fugitives in an Amsterdam warehouse from 1942 to 1944. Her diary, covering the years of hiding, was found by friends and published as *Het achterhus* (1947); it was later published in English as *The Diary of a Young Girl* (1952). . . . Written with humor as well as insight, it shows a growing girl with all the preoccupations of adolescence and first love. The diary ends three days before the Franks and their group were discovered by the Nazis." Reader's Ency. 3d edition

Frank, Anne, 1929-1945—Continued

Frank, Anne. The diary of a young girl: the definitive edition; edited by Otto H. Frank and Mirjam Pressler; translated by Susan Massotty. Doubleday 1995 340p il $25 (6 and up)   **92**

1. World War, 1939-1945—Jews 2. Netherlands—History—1940-1945, German occupation 3. Jews—Netherlands
ISBN 0-385-47378-8   LC 94-41379
Also available G.K. Hall large print edition
"This new translation of Frank's famous diary includes material about her emerging sexuality and her relationship with her mother that was originally excised by Frank's father, the only family member to survive the Holocaust." Libr J

Hurwitz, Johanna. Anne Frank: life in hiding; illustrated by Vera Rosenberry. Jewish Publ. Soc. 1988 62p il map $13.95 (3-5)   **92**

1. Jews—Netherlands 2. Holocaust, 1933-1945
ISBN 0-8276-0311-8   LC 87-35263
Also available in paperback from Morrow
The author "gives a concise explanation of the political and economic background to the Holocaust and provides a map of Europe and a chronology. She ably covers the events of Anne's life before, during, and after the period covered by the 'Diary of Anne Frank,' explaining the significance and importance of the 'Diary' throughout the world." SLJ

Rol, Ruud van der. Anne Frank, beyond the diary; a photographic remembrance; by Ruud van der Rol and Rian Verhoeven; in association with the Anne Frank House; translated by Tony Langham and Plym Peters; with an introduction by Anna Quindlen. Viking 1993 113p il maps $17; pa $7.99 (5 and up)   **92**

1. Jews—Netherlands 2. Holocaust, 1933-1945
ISBN 0-670-84932-4; 0-14-036926-0 (pa)
          LC 92-41528
Original Dutch edition, 1992
Photographs, illustrations, and maps accompany historical essays, diary excerpts, and interviews, providing an insight to Anne Frank and the massive upheaval which tore apart her world
"Readers will become absorbed in the richness of the detail and careful explanation which revisit and expand the familiar, well-loved story." Horn Book

Franklin, Benjamin, 1706-1790

Adler, David A. A picture book of Benjamin Franklin; illustrated by John & Alexandra Wallner. Holiday House 1990 unp il lib bdg $15.95; pa $5.95 (1-3)   **92**

ISBN 0-8234-0792-6 (lib bdg); 0-8234-0882-5 (pa)
          LC 89-20059
Surveys the life of Benjamin Franklin, highlighting his work as an inventor and statesman
"The Wallners' full-color, softly painted illustrations are well executed and add informative details to the text. None of Franklin's life is dealt with in detail. . . . Adler's book will provide an excellent resource for primary readers." SLJ

Aliki. The many lives of Benjamin Franklin; written down and illustrated by Aliki. Simon & Schuster Bks. for Young Readers 1988 unp il $12.95; pa $5.95 (k-3)   **92**

ISBN 0-671-66119-1; 0-671-66491-3 (pa)
          LC 87-22872
First published 1977 by Prentice-Hall
Recounts the story of Benjamin Franklin's life and his many activities and achievements
"Aliki's captioned cartoons—lightly lined and washed—expand or punctuate her easy text. . . . An efficient, lightweight introduction for picturebook readers." Booklist

Fritz, Jean. What's the big idea, Ben Franklin? illustrated by Margot Tomes. Coward, McCann & Geoghegan 1976 46p il $13.95; pa $7.95 (2-4)   **92**

ISBN 0-698-20365-8; 0-698-20543-X (pa)
The text "focuses on Franklin's multifaceted career but also gives personal details and quotes some of his pithy sayings. Enough background information about colonial affairs is given to enable readers to understand the importance of Franklin's contributions to the public good but not so much that it obtrudes on his life story. Although the text is not punctuated by references or footnotes, a page of notes (with numbers for pages referred to) is appended." Bull Cent Child Books

Parker, Steve. Benjamin Franklin and electricity. Chelsea House 1995 32p il (Science discoveries) lib bdg $14.95 (4 and up)   **92**

ISBN 0-7910-3006-7   LC 94-25255
Discusses the life and times of the 18th century statesman, scientist, and inventor
Includes glossary

Fritz, Jean

Fritz, Jean. Homesick: my own story; illustrated with drawings by Margot Tomes and photographs. Putnam 1982 163p il $15.95 (5 and up)   **92**

1. China
ISBN 0-399-20933-6   LC 82-7646
Also available in paperback from Dell
A Newbery Medal honor book, 1983
Companion volume to China homecoming, entered in class 951.05
This is a somewhat fictionalized memoir of the author's childhood in China. "Born in Hankow, where her father was director of the YMCA, Jean loved the city. . . . But she knew she 'belonged on the other side of the world'—in Pennsylvania with her grandmother and her other relations." Horn Book
"The descriptions of places and the times are vivid in a book that brings to the reader, with sharp clarity and candor, the yearnings and fears and ambivalent loyalties of a young girl." Bull Cent Child Books

Galilei, Galileo, 1564-1642

Fisher, Leonard Everett. Galileo. Macmillan 1992 unp il $15.95 (3-5)   **92**

1. Astronomers
ISBN 0-02-735235-8   LC 91-31146
Examines the life and discoveries of the noted mathematician, physicist, and astronomer, whose work changed the course of science

Galilei, Galileo, 1564-1642—*Continued*

"The fact-filled yet graceful narrative places Galileo within the continuum of scientific inquiry even as it reveals considerable information about his valuable discoveries. . . . The characteristic black-and-gray pages throughout—coupled with textured, chiaroscuro acrylic paintings—give the book a distinctive look while emphasizing the story's dramatic elements." Publ Wkly

Gallaudet, T. H. (Thomas Hopkins), 1787-1851

Neimark, Anne E. A deaf child listened: Thomas Gallaudet, pioneer in American education. Morrow 1983 116p $15 (6 and up)
92

1. Deaf—Education
ISBN 0-688-01719-3   LC 82-23942

This biography of the man who established the first school for the deaf in the United States "is both a record of Gallaudet's life and his battles on behalf of deaf children, and a record of the status of treatment and education of the deaf as they changed over the centuries." Bull Cent Child Books

The author presents "a thorough sketch of the man, personally and professionally. She does not end the book with Gallaudet's death, but with the progress deaf education has made . . . including a synopsis of Gallaudet College. A well-researched, readable book." SLJ

Includes bibliography

Gannett, Deborah Sampson, 1760-1827

McGovern, Ann. The secret soldier: the story of Deborah Sampson; illustrated by Ann Grifalconi. Four Winds Press 1987 c1975 62p il $15 (3-5)
92

1. United States—History—1775-1783, Revolution
2. Soldiers—United States 3. Women soldiers
ISBN 0-02-765780-9

Also available in paperback from Scholastic

A reissue of the title first published 1975

A "biography of Deborah Sampson who, disguised as a boy, fought for one and a half years in the Continental army until her true identity was discovered (Deborah then became a wife and mother but still continued to defy convention by traveling and lecturing). History and biography from childhood to young adulthood, paralleling the young nation's fight for freedom with Deborah's own desire for independence and selfhood." SLJ

Gauguin, Paul, 1848-1903

Venezia, Mike. Paul Gauguin; written and illustrated by Mike Venezia. Childrens Press 1992 32p il (Getting to know the world's greatest artists) lib bdg $18.60; pa $5.95 (k-3)
92

1. Artists, French
ISBN 0-516-02295-4 (lib bdg); 0-516-42295-2 (Pa)
LC 91-35054

Briefly describes the life and work of the nineteenth-century French artist known for his paintings of the South Pacific

George III, King of Great Britain, 1738-1820

Fritz, Jean. Can't you make them behave, King George? pictures by Tomie de Paola. Coward, McCann & Geoghegan 1977 45p il $13.95; pa $6.95 (2-4)
92

1. Great Britain—Kings, queens, rulers, etc.
ISBN 0-698-20315-1; 0-698-20542-1 (pa)
LC 75-33722

"As a boy, George is seen to have had struggles in deportment; as King George III, he is mystified that the colonists refuse to be taught. Bits of history, a sense of George's personality, and the loneliness of being king are all conveyed with good humor. The artist's drawings evoke more chuckles." LC. Child Books, 1977

Geronimo, Apache Chief, 1829-1909

Shorto, Russell. Geronimo and the struggle for Apache freedom; written by Russell Shorto; introduction by Alvin M. Josephy, Jr.; illustrated by L.L. Cundiff. Silver Burdett Press 1989 131p il maps (Alvin Josephy's biography series of American Indians) lib bdg $11.98; pa $7.95 (5 and up)
92

1. Apache Indians
ISBN 0-382-09571-5 (lib bdg); 0-382-09760-2 (pa)
LC 88-33687

Recounts the life story of the Apache chief who led one of the last great Indian uprisings

Includes bibliography

Gershwin, George, 1898-1937

Mitchell, Barbara. America, I hear you: a story about George Gershwin; illustrations by Jan Hosking Smith. Carolrhoda Bks. 1987 56p il (Carolrhoda creative minds book) lib bdg $14.95 (3-5)
92

1. Composers, American
ISBN 0-87614-309-5   LC 87-6544

Focuses on the life and musical career of the composer who wrote a number of popular musicals and brought jazz into the realm of acceptable and respectable music

Venezia, Mike. George Gershwin; written and illustrated by Mike Venezia. Childrens Press 1994 32p il (Getting to know the world's greatest composers) lib bdg $13.95; pa $4.95 (k-3)
92

1. Composers, American
ISBN 0-516-04536-9 (lib bdg); 0-516-44536-7 (pa)
LC 94-9478

This is a biography of Gershwin, who expressed a new sound in American music, in such compositions as Rhapsody in blue and the opera Porgy and Bess

"The material is conveyed in an upbeat, if slightly irreverent, manner. . . . Black-and-white and full-color photographs and period art reproductions appear throughout, in addition to numerous colorful cartoons." SLJ

Ginsburg, Ruth Bader

Roberts, Jack L. Ruth Bader Ginsburg; Supreme Court justice. Millbrook Press 1994 48p il (Gateway biography) lib bdg $13.40; pa $6.95 (3-5)   92

1. United States. Supreme Court 2. Women judges
ISBN 1-56294-497-5 (lib bdg); 1-56294-744-3 (pa)
LC 93-39015

Profiles "the women's rights advocate and Supreme Court Justice. Focusing primarily on her law career, Roberts' accurate and tightly written text is enhanced with just enough black-and-white and full-color photographs to keep interest high." SLJ
Includes bibliography

Gish, Lillian, 1893-1993

Gish, Lillian. An actor's life for me; [by] Lillian Gish as told to Selma Lanes; illustrations by Patricia Henderson Lincoln. Viking Kestrel 1987 73p il lib bdg $14.95 (3-5)   92

1. Actors
ISBN 0-670-80416-9   LC 87-8197

"Discipline acquired early is the rock on which Gish built her singular success. But she still enjoyed many good times and adventures while growing up and traveling around the country with fellow performers. Lincoln's illustrations add color. . . . From the outset, the lively telling will engage readers who will discover that Lanes's script of this actor's life is informative and charming." Publ Wkly

Goble, Paul

Goble, Paul. Hau kola: hello friend; photographs by Gerry Perrin. Owen, R.C. 1994 32p il (Meet the author) $13.95 (1-3)   92

1. Authors, American
ISBN 1-878450-44-1   LC 93-48167

"Goble's autobiography provides fascinating insight about this English transplant to Nebraska who has written and illustrated many award-winning books about Native Americans. . . . Clear, color photos on almost every page convey the artistry of one of our most prominent children's book authors and illustrators." Booklist

Goddard, Robert Hutchings, 1882-1945

Streissguth, Thomas. Rocket man: the story of Robert Goddard; [by] Tom Streissguth. Carolrhoda Bks. 1995 88p il (Trailblazers) lib bdg $17.50 (4 and up)   92

1. Scientists
ISBN 0-87614-863-1   LC 94-22836

The author "describes Goddard's pioneering efforts to build rockets capable of leaving Earth's atmosphere that would become the basis of modern astronautical engineering. Explaining potentially difficult scientific principles clearly, he paints a vivid portrait of a brilliant but secretive scientist who refused to share his research and persevered in spite of repeated failures." Booklist
Includes glossary and bibliography

Gogh, Vincent van, 1853-1890

Venezia, Mike. Van Gogh; written and illustrated by Mike Venezia. Childrens Press 1988 32p il (Getting to know the world's greatest artists) lib bdg $18.60; pa $5.95 (k-3)   92

1. Artists, Dutch
ISBN 0-516-02274-1 (lib bdg); 0-516-42274-X (pa)
LC 88-11842

Introduces the nineteenth-century Dutch painter through brief text, full-color reproductions of his art, and cartoon drawings

Goodall, Jane, 1934-

Goodall, Jane. My life with the chimpanzees. Pocket Bks. 1988 123p il map pa $3.95 (3-6)   92

1. Women scientists 2. Chimpanzees
ISBN 0-671-66095-0

"A Byron Preiss book. A Minstrel book"

This autobiography "follows Goodall from her early years in London through her schooling . . . her fortuitous meeting and subsequent work with Louis Leakey, happenings in her personal life, and her . . . studies of chimpanzee behavior." Sci Books Films

"Family snapshots add to the special feeling of being let into Goodall's circle of friends as the famous scientist recounts her adventures with the chimps and illustrates many of her subjects' distinctive personalities. . . . This outstanding autobiography will be a noteworthy choice for school and public libraries." Booklist

Goya, Francisco, 1746-1828

Venezia, Mike. Francisco Goya; written and illustrated by Mike Venezia. Childrens Press 1991 27p il (Getting to know the world's greatest artists) lib bdg $18.60; pa $5.95 (k-3)   92

1. Artists, Spanish
ISBN 0-516-02292-X (lib bdg); 0-516-42292-8 (pa)
LC 90-20887

Introduces the Spanish artist through brief text, full-color reproductions of his works and cartoon drawings

Graham, Martha

Garfunkel, Trudy. Letter to the world: the life and dances of Martha Graham. Little, Brown 1995 92p il $16.95 (4 and up)   92

1. Dancers 2. Choreographers
ISBN 0-316-30413-1   LC 94-16715

Garfunkel "traces Graham's life, from her sheltered childhood in the dreary coal town of Allegheny, Pa., through her unlikely entrance intol professional study at the relatively advanced age of 22 and her subsequent extraordinary career in modern dance. Liberally sprinkled with photos of performances and personal moments." Publ Wkly
Includes bibliography

Grant, Ulysses S. (Ulysses Simpson), 1822-1885

Archer, Jules. A house divided: the lives of Ulysses S. Grant and Robert E. Lee. Scholastic 1995 184p il $14.95 (5 and up)   **92**

1. Lee, Robert E. (Robert Edward), 1807-1870 2. Generals 3. United States—History—1861-1865, Civil War

ISBN 0-590-48325-0   LC 93-38886

"In alternating chapters, Archer looks at Grant and Lee's formative years and early careers. He then highlights their roles in the war, occasionally stopping at particular battles to demonstrate each man's character through his actions. The final two chapters tell of the subjects' postwar lives." SLJ

"This book is a great comparison of two men who lived at the same time in history. Each achieved fame through different routes. Students could use this book as the resource for a comparison and contrast assignment. Further, those with an interest in the Civil War will find the work fascinating." Voice Youth Advocates

Includes bibliography

Griffith Joyner, Florence

Koral, April. Florence Griffith Joyner; track and field star. Watts 1992 64p il lib bdg $18.43 (4 and up)   **92**

1. Women athletes 2. African American athletes 3. Track athletics—Biography

ISBN 0-531-20061-2   LC 91-32827

"A First book"

A biography of the noted sprinter who won three gold medals at the 1988 Olympics

"The presentation is well organized, to the point, and easy to read, allowing even those who aren't particularly sports-oriented to follow without trouble. . . . Koral evokes strong visual images, which gives the text a richness unusual in nonfiction written this simply and indirectly." SLJ

Includes bibliography

Gutenberg, Johann, 1397?-1468

Fisher, Leonard Everett. Gutenberg. Macmillan 1993 unp il $14.95 (3-5)   **92**

1. Printing—History

ISBN 0-02-735238-2   LC 92-26991

"Fisher's biography of Johann Gutenberg, the creator of movable type, is marked by careful research, clear writing, and striking illustrations." Horn Book

Hamilton, Alice

McPherson, Stephanie Sammartino. The workers' detective: a story about Dr. Alice Hamilton; illustrations by Janet Schulz. Carolrhoda Bks. 1992 64p il (Carolrhoda creative minds book) lib bdg $15.95 (3-5)   **92**

1. Women physicians

ISBN 0-87614-699-X   LC 91-23634

A biography of Dr. Alice Hamilton, social worker and doctor, whose work brought attention to the health risks associated with particular jobs

"McPherson has researched her subject thoroughly and does an effective, concise job of combining historical information on the industrial revolution with Hamilton's life and interests. . . . Realistic black-and-white pencil drawings enhance the highly readable text that is stimulating enough for older reluctant readers." SLJ

Includes bibliography

Hancock, John, 1737-1793

Fritz, Jean. Will you sign here, John Hancock? pictures by Trina Schart Hyman. Coward, McCann & Geoghegan 1976 47p il $13.95; pa $7.95 (2-4)   **92**

1. United States—History—1775-1783, Revolution

ISBN 0-698-20308-9; 0-698-20539-1 (pa)

"A straightforward biography of the rich Boston dandy with the gigantic signature. When he signed the Declaration of Independence he quipped, 'There! George the Third can read "that" without his spectacles. Now he can double his reward for my head.'" Saturday Rev

"An affectionate look at a flamboyant, egocentric, but kindly, patriot, the book is a most enjoyable view of history. . . . The delightful illustrations exactly suit the times and the extraordinary character of John Hancock." Horn Book

Handel, George Frideric, 1685-1759

Venezia, Mike. George Handel; written and illustrated by Mike Venezia. Childrens Press 1995 32p il (Getting to know the world's greatest composers) lib bdg $18.60; pa $5.95 (k-3)   **92**

1. Composers

ISBN 0-516-04539-3 (lib bdg); 0-516-44539-1 (pa)   LC 94-36345

Examines the life, career and influence of the German composer Handel through brief text, photographs, and cartoon drawings

Hawking, S. W. (Stephen W.)

Simon, Sheridan. Stephen Hawking; unlocking the universe. Dillon Press 1991 112p il (People in focus) lib bdg $13.95 (5 and up)   **92**

1. Scientists 2. Physically handicapped

ISBN 0-87518-455-3   LC 90-40849

Examines the education, research, and personal life of the renowned British theoretical physicist who has taken the study of cosmology farther than most in his field, despite his need for wheelchair and computer in order to travel and communicate

"The biographical sketch succeeds as a very readable explanation of a complex subject, while illuminating an equally remarkable individual." Sci Books Films

Includes glossary and bibliographical references

Haydn, Joseph, 1732-1809

Thompson, Wendy. Joseph Haydn. Viking 1991 48p il music (Composer's world) $17.95 (5 and up)   **92**

1. Composers

ISBN 0-670-84171-4   LC 91-50212

Haydn, Joseph, 1732-1809—_Continued_
The author discusses the life and work of the composer and the times in which he lived, illustrated with historical paintings and drawings and musical excerpts
Includes glossary

Henry, Infante of Portugal, 1394-1460
Fisher, Leonard Everett. Prince Henry the Navigator. Macmillan 1990 unp il maps $15.95 (3-5)   **92**

1. Explorers
ISBN 0-02-735231-5   LC 89-28068
A biography of that Portuguese prince whose vision and whose school of navigation significantly affected all later explorers who charted the unknown
"Fisher's account of Henry's deeds is clear and informative. . . . The book's strength is in its handsome paintings in black, white, and smoky gray." Booklist

Henry, Patrick, 1736-1799
Fritz, Jean. Where was Patrick Henry on the 29th of May? illustrated by Margot Tomes. Coward, McCann & Geoghegan 1975 47p il $13.95; pa $7.95 (2-4)   **92**

1. United States—History—1600-1775, Colonial period
ISBN 0-698-20307-0; 0-698-20544-8 (pa)
A "portrait of a founding father. Patrick Henry was born on May 29, and the author uses this date to focus on significant periods in his life. Henry's skill at oratory is shown in development as well as his anger at English laws, until they peak in his famous speech." Child Book Rev Serv
"The color pictures are artful evocations of the [18th] century in America and the text presents Patrick Henry as a human being—not a sterilized historic 'figure.'" Publ Wkly

Henson, Matthew Alexander, 1866-1955
Ferris, Jeri. Arctic explorer: the story of Matthew Henson. Carolrhoda Bks. 1989 80p il maps lib bdg $19.95; pa $5.95 (3-6)   **92**

1. Explorers 2. North Pole 3. African Americans—Biography
ISBN 0-87614-370-2 (lib bdg); 0-87614-507-1 (pa)
                                              LC 88-34449
"A high adventure biography of Matthew Henson, the black explorer who accompanied Robert Peary on six expeditions to the North Pole. Henson's great courage, determination, and adaptability were crucial elements in the success of the expeditions. Black-and-white photographs supplement well-written text." Sci Child
Includes bibliography

Hiawatha, 15th cent.
Fradin, Dennis B. Hiawatha: messenger of peace; [by] Dennis Brindell Fradin. Margaret K. McElderry Bks. 1992 40p il map $14.95 (3-5)   **92**

1. Iroquois Indians
ISBN 0-689-50519-1   LC 90-26312

Recounts the life of the fifteenth-century Iroquois Indian who brought five tribes together to form the long-lasting Iroquois Federation
"The book is copiously illustrated with both black-and-white and full-color photographs of Indian artifacts and of paintings and sculpture by Native American artists, all relevant to the text. This attractive volume helps fill the need for good, readable biographies for this age group." SLJ
Includes bibliography

Hopkins, Lee Bennett, 1938-
Hopkins, Lee Bennett. The writing bug; photographs by Diane Rubinger. Owen, R.C. 1993 32p il (Meet the author) $13.95 (1-3)   **92**

1. Authors, American
ISBN 1-878450-38-7   LC 93-11994
"While showing readers his study and his gardens, Hopkins talks about the sights, sounds, memories, and experiences that inspire him to write." Booklist
This book is "ideally suited for younger students seeking to fulfill school assignments." Horn Book Guide

Hopper, Edward, 1882-1967
Venezia, Mike. Edward Hopper; written and illustrated by Mike Venezia. Childrens Press 1989 32p il (Getting to know the world's greatest artists) lib bdg $18.60; pa $5.95 (k-3)   **92**

1. Artists, American
ISBN 0-516-02277-6 (lib bdg); 0-516-42277-4 (pa)
                                              LC 90-2166
Briefly examines the life and work of the American realist painter, describing and giving examples of his art

Horner, John R.
Lessem, Don. Jack Horner: living with dinosaurs; illustrated by Janet Hamlin. Scientific Am. Bks. for Young Readers 1994 47p il (Science superstars) $14.95; pa $4.95 (4 and up)   **92**

1. Scientists 2. Fossils 3. Dinosaurs
ISBN 0-7167-6546-2; 0-7167-6549-7 (pa)
                                              LC 94-17993
This is the biography of the paleontologist who, despite dyslexia and several unsuccessful years in school, has gone on to become one of the world's leading dinosaur experts
The author "writes with zest, showing the determination and excitement that accompanied Horner's explorations. . . . Chapters are short, with many pencil illustrations that add interest and help clarify the science, making the book a good choice for reluctant readers." Bull Cent Child Books
Includes bibliographical references

Houston, Samuel, 1793-1863
Fritz, Jean. Make way for Sam Houston; illustrations by Elise Primavera. Putnam 1986 109p il map $14.95; pa $7.95 (4 and up)   **92**

ISBN 0-399-21303-1; 0-399-21304-X (pa)
                                              LC 85-25601

Houston, Samuel, 1793-1863—*Continued*

This is a biography of the "lawyer, governor of Tennessee, general in the wars against Santa Anna, president of the Republic of Texas, and finally U.S. senator and governor of the state of Texas." Horn Book

"Artfully weaving the threads of fact, Fritz creates a biography that is both interesting and informative. Developing Houston as a human character that readers can identify with as well as admire, and drawing him against the scene of America's own political turmoil, Fritz gives us a book to be read and to be felt." Voice Youth Advocates

Includes bibliography

Howe, James, 1946-

Howe, James. Playing with words; photographs by Michael Craine. Owen, R.C. 1994 32p il (Meet the author) $13.95 (1-3)   92

1. Authors, American
ISBN 1-878450-40-9   LC 93-48166

This is an "easy-to-read, thoughtful autobiography. . . . Sharp color photos on almost every page document Howe's story and provide insight into the behind-the-scenes life of a popular wordsmith." Booklist

Hughes, Langston, 1902-1967

Cooper, Floyd. Coming home: from the life of Langston Hughes. Philomel Bks. 1994 unp il lib bdg $15.95 (2-4)   92

1. Poets, American 2. African American authors
ISBN 0-399-22682-6   LC 93-36332

This "biography highlights pivotal events in Hughes's life, emphasizing his loneliness as a child and his development as a poet. . . . Cooper's hazy illustrations in gold, brown, and sepia tones reveal keen observations of people and neighborhood. The text and art combine to create a fine tribute and introduction to the writer's life." Horn Book

Includes bibliography

Walker, Alice. Langston Hughes, American poet; illustrated by Don Miller. Crowell 1974 33p il (Crowell biography) o.p. (2-5)   92

1. Poets, American 2. African American authors
New edition in preparation

In this biography of the beloved black writer, the author traces Langston Hughes' childhood in Kansas, the discovery of his poems by Vachel Lindsay, his later fame as a writer, and his efforts to bring his work directly to the people

The author "includes a candid assessment of the poet's bitter, biased father that is not usually found in books about Hughes written for children. The illustrations are adequate, the biography as substantial as one for the primary grades reader can be." Bull Cent Child Books

Hurston, Zora Neale, 1891-1960

Miller, William. Zora Hurston and the chinaberry tree; illustrated by Cornelius Van Wright and Ying-hwa Hu. Lee & Low Bks. 1994 unp il $14.95 (k-3)   92

1. African American authors 2. Women authors
ISBN 1-880000-14-8   LC 94-1291

"This biography, which covers a brief period in Zora Neale Hurston's childhood, ends with the young girl grieving over her mother's death but finding inner power and strength from her mother's life." Horn Book

"Conveying the changing expressions on the face of the young Hurston as easily as they show the grandeur of the sky at nightfall, the versatile artists neatly capture the emotions in this lucidly told story." Publ Wkly

Porter, A. P. Jump at de sun: the story of Zora Neale Hurston; foreword by Lucy Ann Hurston. Carolrhoda Bks. 1992 95p il lib bdg $17.50; pa $6.95 (4 and up)   92

1. African American authors 2. Women authors
ISBN 0-87614-667-1 (lib bdg); 0-87614-546-2 (pa)
LC 91-37241

Follows the life of the African American writer known for her novels, plays, articles, and collections of folklore

This is "written in engagingly fresh prose and attractively laid out in a large, clear type. . . . The well-chosen and appropriately placed black-and-white photographs serve not only to extend the text, but also to put faces on the many names that crop up in the story of Hurston's eventful life." SLJ

Includes bibliography

Huynh, Quang Nhuong

Huynh, Quang Nhuong. The land I lost: adventures of a boy in Vietnam; with pictures by Vo-Dinh Mai. Harper & Row 1982 115p il lib bdg $14.89; pa $3.95 (4 and up)   92

1. Vietnam—Social life and customs
ISBN 0-397-32448-0 (lib bdg); 0-06-440183-9 (pa)
LC 80-8437

"Each chapter in this book of reminiscence about the author's boyhood in a hamlet in the Vietnamese highlands, is a separate episode, although the same characters appear in many of the episodes. . . . The writing has an ingenuous quality that adds to the appeal of the strong sense of familial and communal ties that pervades the story." Bull Cent Child Books

Hyman, Trina Schart, 1939-

Hyman, Trina Schart. Self-portrait: Trina Schart Hyman; written and illustrated by Trina Schart Hyman. Harper & Row 1981 unp il lib bdg $15.89 (4 and up)   92

1. Illustrators 2. Women artists
ISBN 0-06-022766-4   LC 80-26662
First published by Addison-Wesley

"Hyman's sense of humor is as evident in her writing as in her drawing as she describes her childhood, her marriage while an art student, the year she and her husband spent in Sweden, where she had her first commission: illustrating a children's book at the behest of editor Astrid Lindgren. . . . Interspersed throughout the personal material are facts about books and other assignments on which Trina Hyman worked. A lively and informative book." Bull Cent Child Books

Ishi

Kroeber, Theodora. Ishi, last of his tribe; drawings by Ruth Robbins. Parnassus Press 1964 209p il maps $14.95 (5 and up)   92

1. Yana Indians
ISBN 0-395-27644-6
Also available in paperback from Bantam Bks.

Ishi—*Continued*

"The true story of a California Yahi Indian [discovered in 1911 by anthropologists] who survives the invasion by the white man, while the rest of his tribe die off." Notable Books, 1964

Written "with a grave simplicity . . . utterly right for the subject. The cultural details are quite unobtrusive: they are simply there, an evidence of the author's knowledge and empathy." Bull Cent Child Books

Includes glossary

Jackson, Bo

Johnson, Rick L. Bo Jackson; baseball/football superstar. Dillon Press 1991 61p il (Taking part) lib bdg $13.95 (4-6)
92

1. Baseball—Biography   2. Football—Biography
3. African American athletes

ISBN 0-87518-489-8   LC 91-17910

A biography of the man who overcame a childhood of poverty to become one of the great stars of professional baseball and football

Includes bibliographical references

Jackson, Jesse L., 1941-

McKissack, Patricia C. Jesse Jackson: a biography. Scholastic 1989 108p il hardcover o.p. paperback available $3.25 (4 and up)
92

1. African Americans—Biography

ISBN 0-590-42395-9 (pa)   LC 89-10133

A biography of the African American minister and civil rights worker who ran for the Democratic presidential nomination in 1984 and 1988

"Occasionally the tone is adulatory. . . . However, the information is factually solid without becoming too detailed, and, in spite of a few stylistic flaws, the text is accessible and easy to read." Bull Cent Child Books

Includes bibliography

Jackson, Stonewall, 1824-1863

Fritz, Jean. Stonewall; with drawings by Stephen Gammell. Putnam 1979 152p il map $15.95 (4 and up)
92

1. Generals 2. United States—History—1861-1865, Civil War

ISBN 0-399-20698-1   LC 79-12506

Also available in paperback from Viking

A biography of the brilliant southern general who gained the nickname Stonewall by his stand at Bull Run during the Civil War

"Fritz's trenchant, compassionate life of General Thomas Jonathan Jackson grips the reader and makes one understand why Stonewall is an honored legend in American history. . . . The tragic irony of his death at age 39 is movingly described." Publ Wkly

Includes bibliography

Jefferson, Thomas, 1743-1826

Adler, David A. A picture book of Thomas Jefferson; illustrated by John & Alexandra Wallner. Holiday House 1990 unp il lib bdg $13.95; pa $5.95 (1-3)
92

1. Presidents—United States

ISBN 0-8234-0791-8 (lib bdg); 0-8234-0881-7 (pa)
LC 89-20076

Traces the life and achievements of the architect, bibliophile, president, and author of the Declaration of Independence

"The book includes an amazing amount of material. An appealing package with simple language and detailed drawings." Horn Book

Giblin, James. Thomas Jefferson; a picture book biography; by James Cross Giblin; illustrated by Michael Dooling. Scholastic 1994 48p il $16.95 (2-4)
92

1. Presidents—United States

ISBN 0-590-44838-2   LC 93-23340

"Giblin records the significant events in Jefferson's long and varied career with enough personal incidents and sidelights to give readers some sense of the man himself, as well as his place in history. . . . Dooling's dramatic oil paintings stretch across each double-page spread. . . . Historically accurate and visually handsome." Booklist

Quackenbush, Robert M. Pass the quill, I'll write a draft: a story of Thomas Jefferson; [by] Robert Quackenbush. Pippin Press 1989 36p il lib bdg $14.95 (2-4)
92

1. Presidents—United States

ISBN 0-945912-07-2   LC 89-8439

Follows the life and accomplishments of the third president, from his birth in 1743 to his retirement to Monticello

"Quackenbush's drawings are witty, expressive, and for the most part appealing. A full-page illustration faces each page of text; small cartoons appear at the bottom of each printed page. . . . These cartoons extend the text with interesting odd facts about Jefferson's many inventions." SLJ

Johnson, William H., 1901-1970

Everett, Gwen. Li'l Sis and Uncle Willie: a story based on the life and paintings of William H. Johnson. Rizzoli Int. Publs. 1991 unp il $14.95 (k-3)
92

1. African American artists

ISBN 0-8478-1462-9   LC 91-14800

Also available in paperback from Hyperion Bks. for Children

Surveys the life of African-American artist William H. Johnson as his young niece might have told it. The artist's paintings provide the illustrations

"The biographical and historical information is blended naturally into the observations of a child whose voice is clear and candid. The pictures themselves are gripping, with heavy lines, sharp angles, and deep colors shaped into direct, pared-down compositions that are spaciously and lavishly reproduced. Johnson's style, although varied according to different periods of his work, has a consistently powerful simplicity that will particularly appeal to children, while his life makes an honestly dramatic story." Bull Cent Child Books

Joliot-Curie, Irène, 1897-1956

Pflaum, Rosalynd. Marie Curie and her daughter Irène. See entry under Curie, Marie, 1867-1934

Jones, Mother, 1830-1930

Colman, Penny. Mother Jones and the march of the mill children. Millbrook Press 1994 47p il lib bdg $15.40 (3-5)   **92**

1. Reformers 2. Labor—United States

ISBN 1-56294-402-9   LC 93-1933

This "biography of the labor organizer who fought for the end of child labor is well illustrated with period photographs and drawings. Focusing on a dramatic protest march Mother Jones organized, the portrait of the strong, determined woman provides a good introduction to the labor movement." Horn Book Guide

Includes bibliography

Kraft, Betsy Harvey. Mother Jones; one woman's fight for labor. Clarion Bks. 1995 116p il $16.95 (4 and up)   **92**

1. Reformers 2. Labor—United States

ISBN 0-395-67163-9   LC 94-19715

"This biography of union organizer Mary Harris Jones, more popularly known as Mother Jones, is as much a history of the American labor movement from the 1870s-1930s as it is the story of one woman's life. Kraft tells about Jones's childhood in Ireland; the tragic death of her husband and children from yellow fever in Memphis; and her defiant commitment to bringing about changes." SLJ

"This scintillating, well-illustrated biography achieves the formidable task of doing justice to its redoubtable subject." Publ Wkly

Includes bibliographical references

Jones, Frederick McKinley, 1893-1961

Swanson, Gloria Borseth. I've got an idea! the story of Frederick McKinley Jones; [by] Gloria M. Swanson, Margaret V. Ott. Runestone Press 1994 95p il lib bdg $17.50; pa $7.95 (3-5)   **92**

1. African American inventors

ISBN 0-8225-3174-7 (lib bdg); 0-8225-9662-8 (pa)
LC 93-7823

A new and revised edition of Man with a million ideas: Fred Jones, genius/inventor, published 1977 by Lerner Publs.

A biography of the black engineer and inventor credited with many inventions, including refrigeration units for trucks and railroad cars, portable X-ray units, and the ticket dispenser

"The succinct biography, illustrated with black-and-white photographs, clearly profiles both the man and his achievements." Horn Book Guide

Includes bibliography

Joplin, Scott, 1868-1917

Mitchell, Barbara. Raggin': a story about Scott Joplin; illustrations by Hetty Mitchell. Carolrhoda Bks. 1987 55p il (Carolrhoda creative minds book) lib bdg $17.50; pa $5.95 (3-5)   **92**

1. Composers, American 2. African American musicians

ISBN 0-87614-310-9 (lib bdg); 0-87614-589-6 (pa)
LC 87-9310

The life story of the black Texan who became a popular composer and sought to elevate ragtime to the level of classical music, only to have his talents fully recognized after his death

Jordan, Michael

Kornbluth, Jesse. Airborne: the triumph and struggle of Michael Jordan. Macmillan Bks. for Young Readers 1995 164p il $15 (5 and up)   **92**

1. Basketball—Biography 2. African American athletes

ISBN 0-02-750922-2   LC 94-12553

In this biography of the basketball player Kornbluth "delves into the controversy, gambling, press problems, marriage, that is part and parcel of Michael Jordan." Voice Youth Advocates

"Written with the cooperation of the subject and his family, Kornbluth's book offers an insider's view of the superstar. . . . Balanced by the athlete's incredible charm, his charity work, and his love of family, the book presents a fascinating portrait of a human being who is a great, but not perfect man." SLJ

Includes bibliographical references

Lipsyte, Robert. Michael Jordan; a life above the rim. HarperCollins Pubs. 1994 106p il (Superstar lineup) lib bdg $14.89; pa $3.95 (5 and up)   **92**

1. Basketball—Biography 2. African American athletes

ISBN 0-06-024235-3 (lib bdg); 0-06-446156-4 (pa)
LC 93-50561

"Rather than focusing solely on the subject's life on and off the court, Lipsyte examines M.J. the multimillion dollar commodity. He puts the Jordan phenomenon into historical perceptive, correlating the man's success with the rise in popularity of the N.B.A. and the changes in the style of the game over the years. In addition, he explores the relationship between athletics and the marketing of products. . . . The text is illustrated with black-and-white photographs of Jordan and other important figures in the history of basketball." SLJ

Includes bibliography

Juana Inés de la Cruz, 1651-1695

Martinez, Elizabeth Coonrod. Sor Juana, a trailblazing thinker. Millbrook Press 1994 32p il (Hispanic heritage) lib bdg $12.90 (3-5)   **92**

1. Authors, Mexican 2. Nuns 3. Women authors

ISBN 1-56294-406-1   LC 93-15095

Juana Inés de la Cruz, 1651-1695—*Continued*

A biography of the seventeenth-century Mexican nun who not only wrote poetry and plays and conducted botanical studies but was world famous for her knowledge of many subjects

The book is "written in a clear, easy-to-read style, and includes interesting tidbits of trivia that will attract readers. The black-and-white and full-color illustrations, both photographs and period reproductions, enhance the overall presentation." SLJ

Includes bibliography

Kahlo, Frida, 1907-1954

Turner, Robyn Montana. Frida Kahlo. Little, Brown 1993 32p il (Portraits of women artists for children) $16.95 (4-6)   **92**

1. Artists, Mexican 2. Women artists
ISBN 0-316-85651-7   LC 91-29556

"Turner introduces Kahlo's life and work in this attractive biography. . . . Black-and-white photos offer glimpses of this Mexican painter and her world, but the full-color reproductions of her paintings will intrigue kids more." Booklist

Kaiulani, Princess of Hawaii, 1875-1899

Stanley, Fay. The last princess: the story of Princess Ka'iulani of Hawai'i; illustrated by Diane Stanley. Four Winds Press 1991 40p il map $16.95; pa $5.95 (3-5)   **92**

1. Princes and princesses 2. Hawaii—History
ISBN 0-02-786785-4; 0-689-71829-2 (pa)
                                                 LC 89-71445

Recounts the story of Hawaii's last heir to the throne, who was denied her right to rule when the monarchy was abolished

"The princess's story sheds new light on long-forgotten history; the vibrant, handsome gouache illustrations establish the lush Hawaiian background and provide historic detail." Horn Book

Includes bibliography

Keats, Ezra Jack, 1916-1983

Engel, Dean. Ezra Jack Keats; a biography with illustrations; [by] Dean Engel and Florence B. Freedman. Silver Moon Press 1995 81p il $17.95 (3-5)   **92**

1. Authors, American 2. Illustrators
ISBN 1-881889-65-3   LC 94-34960

A "profile of a significant creator of twentieth-century children's books, this study of Ezra Jack Keats for young readers is based on reminiscences of conversations with and autobiographical essays by the subject. . . . The illustrations, most from published works, integrate Keats's persona with that of his characters." Horn Book

"This attractive, oversized volume is a must read for Keats's many fans and a marvelous way to introduce (or reintroduce) children to his work." SLJ

Keita, Soundiata, d. 1255

Wisniewski, David. Sundiata; lion king of Mali; story and pictures by David Wisniewski. Clarion Bks. 1992 unp il $16.95 (1-4)   **92**

1. Mali—History
ISBN 0-395-61302-7   LC 91-27931

The story of Sundiata, who overcame physical handicaps, social disgrace, and strong opposition to rule Mali in the thirteenth century

"Passed down through oral tradition, this historical account has the drama and depth of a folktale. The illustrations—elaborate collages inspired by the artifacts and culture of the Malinke—create a series of dramatic images. The intricacy of the paper-cuts and the richness of the colors and patterns give the artwork visual as well as narrative strength." Booklist

Keller, Helen, 1880-1968

Adler, David A. A picture book of Helen Keller; illustrated by John & Alexandra Wallner. Holiday House 1990 unp il lib bdg $15.95; pa $5.95 (1-3)   **92**

1. Blind 2. Deaf
ISBN 0-8234-0818-3 (lib bdg); 0-8234-0950-3 (pa)
                                                 LC 89-77510

A brief biography of the woman who overcame her handicaps of being both blind and deaf

"The Wallners' line and watercolor cartoons match the simple text and are appropriate to the book's tone." SLJ

St. George, Judith. Dear Dr. Bell—your friend, Helen Keller. Putnam 1992 95p il $15.95 (5 and up)   **92**

1. Bell, Alexander Graham, 1847-1922 2. Blind 3. Deaf
ISBN 0-399-22337-1   LC 91-37327

Also available in paperback from Morrow

Follows the parallel lives of Helen Keller and Alexander Graham Bell, who continued to encounter and support each other from that eventful meeting when he recommended she be given a teacher and thus led her to Annie Sullivan

"A lively style and plenty of quotes from each person's writing and letters show the feelings and thoughts behind the friendship. Black-and-white photographs show scenes from both of their lives as well as of their times together." SLJ

Includes bibliography

Kennedy, John F. (John Fitzgerald), 1917-1963

Adler, David A. A picture book of John F. Kennedy; illustrated by Robert Casilla. Holiday House 1991 unp il lib bdg $15.95; pa $5.95 (1-3)   **92**

1. Presidents—United States
ISBN 0-8234-0884-1 (lib bdg); 0-8234-0976-7 (pa)
                                                 LC 90-23589

Depicts the life and career of John F. Kennedy

"Adler presents a brief, clearly written text that provides basic information about his subject in an appealing format. . . . Casilla's watercolors are full-color copies of famous photographs." SLJ

Harrison, Barbara. A twilight struggle: the life of John Fitzgerald Kennedy; [by] Barbara Harrison and Daniel Terris. Lothrop, Lee & Shepard Bks. 1992 159p il $18 (6 and up)

92

1. Presidents—United States
ISBN 0-688-08830-9   LC 91-14926

Kennedy, John F. (John Fitzgerald), 1917-1963—*Continued*

Discusses the childhood, family, and political career of the president who served from 1961 until his assassination in 1963

"The authors, who researched the television documentary 'JFK: In His Own Words,' have achieved a remarkably balanced account of Kennedy's life and Presidency. The tone is conversational, neither condescending nor sensational, the writing crisp." N Y Times Book Rev

Includes bibliography

Kenny, Elizabeth, 1886-1952

Crofford, Emily. Healing warrior: a story about Sister Elizabeth Kenny; illustrations by Steve Michaels. Carolrhoda Bks. 1989 64p il (Carolrhoda creative minds book) lib bdg $17.50 (3-5) 92

1. Nurses
ISBN 0-87614-382-6   LC 89-33474

"This biography traces Sister Kenny's life from childhood, through her nursing career, to her death at age 72 in 1952. Known as the founder of modern physical rehabilitation, the Australian nurse was instrumental in improving treatment of polio patients." Sci Child

This book is "well written and, while a bit of dialogue may have been invented, on the whole, [it] seems to be authoritative and objective. . . . [A] good introduction to [an] admirable medical pioneer that will attract recreational readers and be useful for reports." SLJ

Includes bibliography

Key, Francis Scott, 1779-1843

Whitcraft, Melissa. Francis Scott Key. Watts 1994 63p il lib bdg $19.30 (4 and up) 92

1. Star spangled banner (Song) 2. United States—History—1812-1815, War of 1812
ISBN 0-531-20163-5   LC 94-2571

"A First book"

This is an "introductory biography of the man who authored our national anthem. Whitcraft chronicles Key's life, from his birth on a Maryland plantation until his death, including the events surrounding the writing of 'The Star-Spangled Banner.' This readable volume is well illustrated with full-color reproductions and photographs and is ideal for reports or recreational reading. The full text of Key's poem and a good index are appended." SLJ

Includes bibliographical references

Kherdian, Veron, 1907-

Kherdian, David. The road from home; the story of an Armenian girl. Greenwillow Bks. 1979 238p il map $13.95; lib bdg $13.93; pa $4.95 (6 and up) 92

1. Armenians—Turkey 2. Armenian massacres, 1915-1923
ISBN 0-688-80205-2; 0-688-84205-4 (lib bdg); 0-688-14425-X (pa)   LC 78-72511

A Newbery Medal honor book, 1980

The author presents a "biography of his mother's early life as a young Armenian girl. Veron Dumehjian was part of a prosperous Armenian family in Turkey, but the Armenian minority undergoes a holocaust when the Turkish government persecutes its Christian minorities. In 1915 Veron and her family are deported and, as refugees, live through hardships of disease, starvation, bombing, and fire until, at

sixteen, Veron is able to go to America as a 'mail-order' bride." Babbling Bookworm

King, Coretta Scott, 1927-

Medearis, Angela Shelf. Dare to dream: Coretta Scott King and the civil rights movement ; illustrated by Anna Rich. Lodestar Bks. 1994 60p il (Rainbow biography) $13.99 (3-5) 92

1. King, Martin Luther, 1929-1968 2. African American women 3. African Americans—Civil rights
ISBN 0-525-67426-8   LC 93-33573

This biography "charts the milestones in King's life from her early ambitions to be an opera singer through her marriage, her involvement in the civil rights movement, and her continuation of her husband's work after his death. . . . Illustrated with soft pencil drawings as well as numerous black-and-white photographs." Booklist

Includes bibliography

King, Martin Luther, 1929-1968

Adler, David A. Martin Luther King, Jr.: free at last; illustrated by Robert Casilla. Holiday House 1986 48p il lib bdg $14.95; pa $5.95 (2-4) 92

1. African Americans—Biography 2. African Americans—Civil rights
ISBN 0-8234-0618-0 (lib bdg); 0-8234-0619-9 (pa)
                                       LC 86-4670

"A short, chronological account of the life and major activities of this Civil Rights leader. . . . Preceded by a chronology of the major dates in King's life, the text is divided into four chapters and illustrated very fully with black-and-white paintings. . . . The book is pleasing in appearance, and the didactic thrust of explaining background issues and the value of King's beliefs and actions is well modulated." Horn Book

Adler, David A. A picture book of Martin Luther King, Jr.; illustrated by Robert Casilla. Holiday House 1989 unp il lib bdg $15.95; pa $6.95 (1-3) 92

1. African Americans—Biography 2. African Americans—Civil rights
ISBN 0-8234-0770-5 (lib bdg); 0-8234-0847-7 (pa)
                                       LC 89-1930

Also available Spanish language edition

This "biography takes a look at the life, leadership, and ideals of Dr. Martin Luther King, Jr. Adler examines King's family background, leadership of the Montgomery bus boycott, and the 1963 march on Washington, D.C. By focusing primarily on these events, Adler provides young readers with enough basic information to form a well-rounded picture of King and his ideals. However, the outstanding feature of this book is the vivid watercolor illustrations, which are sure to capture readers' attention. Casilla dramatically reveals the mood and feelings of the era." SLJ

Bray, Rosemary L. Martin Luther King; paintings by Malcah Zeldis. Greenwillow Bks. 1995 47p il $16; lib bdg $15.93 (2-4) 92

1. African Americans—Biography 2. African Americans—Civil rights
ISBN 0-688-13131-X; 0-688-13132-8 (lib bdg)
                                       LC 93-41002

"Vivid full-page paintings in a folk art style give special strength to a straightforward biography of the civil rights leader." N Y Times Book Rev

King, Martin Luther, 1929-1968—*Continued*

Darby, Jean. Martin Luther King, Jr. Lerner Publs. 1990 144p il lib bdg $22.95; pa $6.95 (5 and up)   **92**

1. African Americans—Biography   2. African Americans—Civil rights

ISBN 0-8225-4902-6 (lib bdg); 0-8225-9611-3 (pa)

LC 89-36797

This book "provides an indepth look into King's life and the racial strife and civil rights movement of the sixties. It begins with his childhood and shows the impact that his college and theological education had on his beliefs, actions, and strategies for leadership. This moving account in highly readable prose captures King's spirit, genius, and determination. Frequent and varied black-and-white photos add dramatic appeal." Booklist

Includes glossary and bibliography

Haskins, James. I have a dream: the life and words of Martin Luther King, Jr.; by Jim Haskins. Millbrook Press 1992 111p il lib bdg $19.90; pa $8.95 (5 and up)   **92**

1. African Americans—Biography   2. African Americans—Civil rights

ISBN 1-56294-087-2 (lib bdg); 1-56294-837-7 (pa)

LC 91-42528

Presents the life, words, and principles of the noted civil rights worker through extensive quotations from his speeches and writings

"All quotations are sourced, and Haskins includes a time line of important events in King's life as well as suggestions for further reading. A serviceable, practical biography, this will be a good addition to any size collection." Booklist

Haskins, James. The life and death of Martin Luther King, Jr. Lothrop, Lee & Shepard Bks. 1977 176p il lib bdg $14.93; pa $3.95 (5 and up)   **92**

1. African Americans—Biography   2. African Americans—Civil rights

ISBN 0-688-51802-8 (lib bdg); 0-688-11690-6 (pa)

LC 77-3157

The author "writes about the civil rights leader in a simple, readable manner. Part one describes the development of the civil rights movement; part two describes the assassination, and an inordinate amount of space is given to James Earl Ray and the theory of a conspiracy behind the murder." Horn Book

Marzollo, Jean. Happy birthday, Martin Luther King; illustrated by J. Brian Pinkney. Scholastic 1993 unp il $14.95; lib bdg $19.95 (k-3)   **92**

1. African Americans—Biography   2. African Americans—Civil rights

ISBN 0-590-44065-9; 0-590-72828-8 (lib bdg)

LC 91-42137

Also available Spanish language edition

"This very easy biography of Martin Luther King is distinguished by its succinct explanations of King's achievements. . . . The narrative of King's life is smooth and accessible. Pinkney's scratchboard paintings are fluidly drawn, warm, and dignified." Bull Cent Child Books

McKissack, Patricia C. Martin Luther King, Jr., a man to remember; by Patricia McKissack. Childrens Press 1984 128p il (People of distinction biographies) lib bdg $18.60; pa $5.95 (4 and up)   **92**

1. African Americans—Biography   2. African Americans—Civil rights

ISBN 0-516-03206-2 (lib bdg); 0-516-43206-0 (pa)

LC 83-23933

"McKissack addresses King's relationship with other black leaders, movements, politicians, and the FBI as well as allegations of Communism. King's uncertainties and concerns, particularly with the rise of Black Power, are portrayed in a way that makes his character understandable. Chapters are introduced with poems from various black authors that set the tone for what follows. A time line at the end places King in the perspective of world affairs." SLJ

Patrick, Diane. Martin Luther King, Jr. Watts 1990 64p il lib bdg $13.93 (4 and up)   **92**

1. African Americans—Biography   2. African Americans—Civil rights

ISBN 0-531-10892-9

LC 89-24800

"A First book"

"King's family life, childhood, and schooling are described, along with the major events that established him as a leader. The information provided is general, and terms that readers might not understand are fully explained. . . . Numerous photographs supplement the text, which is arranged in an attractive manner. This book is a good, basic introduction to King." SLJ

Patterson, Lillie. Martin Luther King, Jr., and the freedom movement. Facts on File 1989 178p il (Makers of America) $16.95; pa $8.95 (6 and up)   **92**

1. African Americans—Biography   2. African Americans—Civil rights

ISBN 0-8160-1605-4; 0-8160-2997-0 (pa)

LC 88-26051

"This political biography of King is also a dramatic account of the civil rights movement he led. Beginning with the Montgomery bus boycott in the mid-1950s, through the sit-ins, freedom rides, the march on Washington, the Nobel Prize, Selma, and the Voting Rights Act of 1965, Patterson presents King as a heroic figure." Booklist

Includes bibliography

Klee, Paul, 1879-1940

Venezia, Mike. Paul Klee; written and illustrated by Mike Venezia. Childrens Press 1991 32p il (Getting to know the world's greatest artists) lib bdg $18.60; pa $5.95 (k-3)   **92**

1. Artists, German

ISBN 0-516-02294-6 (lib bdg); 0-516-42294-4 (pa)

LC 91-12554

Discusses, in simple text, the life and work of the abstract painter, focusing on his use of color, shape, and symbolism

Koehn, Ilse, 1929-1991

Koehn, Ilse. Mischling, second degree: my childhood in Nazi Germany; with a foreword by Harrison E. Salisbury. Greenwillow Bks. 1977 240p $15; lib bdg $14.93 (6 and up)   **92**

1. World War, 1939-1945—Jews 2. Germany—History—1933-1945 3. Jews—Germany

ISBN 0-688-80110-2; 0-688-84110-4 (lib bdg)

LC 77-6189

Also available in paperback from Viking

This story "is told in retrospect by an author who did not know why her loving parents separated until after the war, when she learned that it had helped her and her mother avoid the consequences of the fact that her father had one Jewish parent. Liberals and intellectuals, the Koehns coped, as many did, with a government and a philosophy they detested. And Ilse, a young adolescent, was drafted into the Hitler Youth, forced to go through the motions of devotion." Bull Cent Child Books

Kuskin, Karla

Kuskin, Karla. Thoughts, pictures, and words; photographs by Nicholas Kuskin. Owen, R.C. 1995 32p il (Meet the author) $13.95 (1-3)   **92**

1. Authors, American 2. Women authors

ISBN 1-878450-41-7

LC 95-1290

In this book "Kuskin discusses poetry and prose, writing and illustration. Her account is studded with memories, anecdotes, poems, and thoughts of family." Booklist

Lange, Dorothea, 1895-1965

Turner, Robyn Montana. Dorothea Lange. Little, Brown 1994 32p il (Portraits of women artists for children) $15.95 (4-6)   **92**

1. Women photographers

ISBN 0-316-85656-8

LC 93-42573

This is an "introduction to the life and work of this documentary photographer. . . . Turner recounts that this woman, who captured unforgettable images of the human condition during the Great Depression, faced many personal difficulties. . . . Her genius for capturing people in unposed moments is evident in the examples of some of her most famous black-and-white photos that appear throughout the book. The quality of the reproductions is excellent. . . . The text also gives an authentic sense of the 1920s and '30s." SLJ

Lartigue, Jacques-Henri, 1894-1986

Cech, John. Jacques-Henri Lartigue; boy with a camera. Four Winds Press 1994 32p il $15.95 (4 and up)   **92**

1. Photographers

ISBN 0-02-718136-7

LC 94-10210

"Cech provides a glimpse into the life and vision of an artist whose photographs have been termed 'a national treasure in France.' . . . The photographs have been carefully chosen from hundreds taken by Lartigue during his youth. They exhibit the exuberance, adventure, and comic composition that made his work unique." Horn Book

Lear, Edward, 1812-1888

Kamen, Gloria. Edward Lear, king of nonsense; a biography; illustrated by Edward Lear and Gloria Kamen. Atheneum Pubs. 1990 74p il $15 (4-6)   **92**

1. Poets, English 2. Artists, British

ISBN 0-689-31419-1

LC 89-28023

Examines the life and career of the nineteenth-century writer-artist who was renowned for his nonsense verse

"A delightful biography that captures the essence of this man of many talents. . . . Interesting facts about Lear's life are varied by the insertion of his rhymes, nonsense words and sketches. Kamen provides an entertaining and informative glimpse into the humorist's life." Child Book Rev Serv

Includes bibliography

Lee, Robert E. (Robert Edward), 1807-1870

Archer, Jules. A house divided: the lives of Ulysses S. Grant and Robert E. Lee. See entry under Grant, Ulysses S. (Ulysses Simpson), 1822-1885

Weidhorn, Manfred. Robert E. Lee. Atheneum Pubs. 1988 150p il map lib bdg $14.95 (5 and up)   **92**

1. Generals 2. United States—History—1861-1865, Civil War

ISBN 0-689-31340-3

LC 87-14500

"Opening with Lee's decision, in 1861, to resign from the U.S. army rather than accept an offer to command it, Weidhorn flashes back with a brief overview of the Virginian's life. The rest of the book is devoted to Lee's leadership of Confederate forces throughout the Civil War, with two final chapters on his 'reconciliation' and years as a college president." Bull Cent Child Books

"With a quick, fluid pace and sustained tension, Weidhorn describes the battles in a big-picture sense, analyzing Lee's part in the outcome, win or lose, and capturing for the reader Lee's penetrating insight, brilliant maneuvers, and strategy." Booklist

Includes bibliography

Leeuwenhoek, Antoni van, 1632-1723

Kumin, Maxine. The microscope; pictures by Arnold Lobel. Harper & Row 1984 c1968 unp il lib bdg $14.50 (k-3)   **92**

1. Microscopes 2. Scientists

ISBN 0-06-023524-1

LC 82-47728

First published 1968 in the author's collection: The wonderful babies of 1809 and other years

Relates in rhyme the famous Dutch scientist's penchant for viewing things with a microscope, through which he made remarkable observations

This "short, amusing poem . . . deftly sketches Leeuwenhoek's adventures and the wondrous, miniscule world that wriggled to life before his astonished eyes. The somber pen-and-ink drawings, handsomely printed on creamy beige paper, are often humorous parodies of the Dutch painters of Leeuwenhoek's era." Horn Book

Leonardo, da Vinci, 1452-1519

Provensen, Alice. Leonardo da Vinci: the artist, inventor, scientist; in three-dimensional, movable pictures by A. & M. Provensen. Viking 1984 unp il $19.95 (3 and up)   **92**

1. Artists, Italian 2. Inventors 3. Scientists
ISBN 0-670-42384-X   LC 83-26005

This "book contains eight 'pop-up' or movable paintings that dynamically illustrate some of Leonardo da Vinci's great inventions and paintings. The controls on the 'pop-ups' work well and each resulting movement displays some facet of Leonardo's inventiveness. . . . The brief text tells facts and stories about da Vinci." Sci Child

Venezia, Mike. Da Vinci; written and illustrated by Mike Venezia. Childrens Press 1989 32p il (Getting to know the world's greatest artists) lib bdg $18.60; pa $5.95 (k-3)   **92**

1. Artists, Italian
ISBN 0-516-02275-X (lib bdg); 0-516-42275-8 (pa)
LC 88-37715

Venezia introduces the Italian Renaissance artist through brief text, full-color reproductions of works, and cartoon drawings
"This is a useful first look for younger children." SLJ

Lincoln, Abraham, 1809-1865

Adler, David A. A picture book of Abraham Lincoln; illustrated by John & Alexandra Wallner. Holiday House 1989 unp il lib bdg $14.95; pa $5.95 (1-3)   **92**

1. Presidents—United States
ISBN 0-8234-0731-4 (lib bdg); 0-8234-0801-9 (pa)
LC 88-16393

Also available Spanish language edition

Follows the life of the popular president, from his childhood on the frontier to his assassination after the end of the Civil War
"While the author does include details that make the narratives more specific or realistic, he avoids fictionalizing. The Wallners' attractive line-and-watercolor illustrations evoke the past with the narrative quality of American naive painting and a certain gentle charm all their own." Booklist

Freedman, Russell. Lincoln: a photobiography. Clarion Bks. 1987 150p il $16.95; pa $7.95 (4 and up)   **92**

1. Presidents—United States
ISBN 0-89919-380-3; 0-395-51848-2 (pa)
LC 86-33379

Awarded the Newbery Medal, 1988

The author "begins by contrasting the Lincoln of legend to the Lincoln of fact. His childhood, self-education, early business ventures, and entry into politics comprise the first half of the book, with the rest of the text covering his presidency and assassination." SLJ
This is "a balanced work, elegantly designed and enhanced by dozens of period photographs and drawings, some familiar, some refreshingly unfamiliar." Publ Wkly
Includes bibliography

Kunhardt, Edith. Honest Abe; paintings by Malcah Zeldis; words by Edith Kunhardt. Greenwillow Bks. 1993 unp il $15; lib bdg $15.93 (k-3)   **92**

1. Presidents—United States
ISBN 0-688-11189-0; 0-688-11190-4 (lib bdg)
LC 91-47191

This is a "picture book version of Lincoln's life. Zeldis' folk art paintings use bright colors, bold patterns, and repeated shapes to create vibrant scenes that will hold the attention of kids right back to the last row of the classroom. Keeping a good pace, the text hits the high spots and finds time for memorable tidbits. . . . Appended are the Gettysburg Address and a chronology of Lincoln's life." Booklist

Lincoln, in his own words; edited by Milton Meltzer; illustrated by Stephen Alcorn. Harcourt Brace & Co. 1993 226p il $22.95 (6 and up)   **92**

1. United States—History—1861-1865, Civil War 2. Presidents—United States
ISBN 0-15-245437-3   LC 92-17431

Combines background commentary with quotes from Lincoln's letters, speeches, and public papers to provide a personal view of his life, thoughts, and actions
"Meltzer gives Lincoln's words rich historical context by framing them with the facts of his life. Alcorn's powerful black-and-white and color linoleum block prints have impact and majesty." Booklist
Includes bibliographical references

Lindbergh, Charles, 1902-1974

Burleigh, Robert. Flight: the journey of Charles Lindbergh; illustrated by Mike Wimmer; introduction by Jean Fritz. Philomel Bks. 1991 unp il $14.95 (2-4)   **92**

1. Aeronautics—Flights 2. Air pilots
ISBN 0-399-22272-3   LC 90-35401

Describes how Charles Lindbergh achieved the remarkable feat of flying nonstop and solo from New York to Paris in 1927
"Using Charles Lindbergh's autobiography, The Spirit of St. Louis, as the basis for his text, Burleigh vividly creates that first solo flight in words, while Wimmer fashions exhilarating pictures that are, above all else, emotional. . . . This artistic emotion . . . works terrifically with the terseness of the near-poetic text." Booklist

Demarest, Chris L. Lindbergh. Crown 1993 unp il $15; lib bdg $15.99 (k-3)   **92**

1. Air pilots
ISBN 0-517-58718-1; 0-517-58719-X (lib bdg)
LC 92-41845

"The story of how 'The Spirit of St. Louis' came about and how Lindbergh eventually completed the 33-hour trip will entertain, inform and delight readers. Through Demarest's text and brilliant watercolors, some readers may even catch a spark of Lindbergh's creativity." Child Book Rev Serv
Includes bibliography

Ling, Rinpoche

Raimondo, Lois. The little Lama of Tibet. Scholastic 1994 40p il map $15.95 (3-5)   **92**

1. Tibet (China) 2. Buddhism
ISBN 0-590-46167-2   LC 93-13627

Ling, Rinpoche—*Continued*

"In text and color photographs, six-year-old Ling Rinpoche—believed to be the reincarnation of a great teacher—is shown preparing for the day he will assume responsibility for passing on Buddhist teachings to his people." Horn Book Guide

The author "writes a sympathetic account of this unusual life and the religious and cultural beliefs that shape it. However, it's her magnificent full-color photographs that truly capture Rinpoche's world." SLJ

Little, Jean, 1932-

Little, Jean. Little by Little; a writer's education. Viking Kestrel 1988 c1987 233p il $13.95; pa $6.99 (5 and up)   92

1. Authors, Canadian 2. Women authors
ISBN 0-670-81649-3; 0-14-032325-2 (pa)
First published 1987 in Canada

This autobiography covers the life of the Canadian author of children's literature from preschool memories to the publication of her first book

"Jean Little's story is a remarkable one, for it is a celebration of the human spirit. By turns touching and humorous, her autobiographical reminiscence should equal or surpass her fictional works in appeal, for it has the same flow, the same emotional power, the same warm tone as her novels." Horn Book

Louis XIV, King of France, 1638-1715

Aliki. The King's day: Louis XIV of France. Crowell 1989 unp il lib bdg $14.89; pa $4.95 (2-5)   92

1. France—Kings, queens, rulers, etc.
ISBN 0-690-04590-5 (lib bdg); 0-06-443268-8 (pa)
LC 88-38179

This book "introduces Louis XIV, his palaces and his family. It follows him through a typical day from his getting up ritual, to chapel, council, his huge dinner and riding or hunting. After a rest, he entertains and has supper with the royal family before his going to bed ceremony." Child Book Rev Serv

"The book design combines the appeal of a comic format with carefully researched illustration, including elaborate indoor and outdoor scenes of Versailles. A chronology and list of definitions (without pronunciation) for French words are appended. On balance, this is lively and informative biography." Bull Cent Child Books

Love, Nat, 1854-1921

Miller, Robert H. (Robert Henry). The story of Nat Love; by Robert Miller; illustrated by Michael Bryant. Silver Press 1995 unp il $12.95; lib bdg $14.95; pa $4.95 (k-3)   92

1. African Americans—Biography 2. Cowhands—Biography
ISBN 0-382-24398-6; 0-382-24389-7 (lib bdg); 0-382-24393-5 (pa)
LC 93-46287

"This picture-book biography of colorful Old West cowboy Nat Love follows his life from his early days as a slave on a plantation in Tennessee to his death in 1925 after becoming a legendary figure. Young readers will delight in Nat's exciting adventures. . . . Bryant's sprawling watercolor illustrations . . . nicely convey the spacious feeling of the untamed Old West. A great primary storytime selection for black history month." Booklist

Lovelace, Ada King, Countess of, 1815-1852

Wade, Mary Dodson. Ada Byron Lovelace; the lady and the computer. Dillon Press 1994 128p il (People in focus) lib bdg $13.95; pa $7.95 (5 and up)   92

1. Women mathematicians
ISBN 0-87518-598-3 (lib bdg); 0-382-24717-5 (pa)
LC 94-12678

"Wade introduces a talented yet eccentric young woman whose brilliant explanation of Charles Babbage's analytical engine included a computer program and ideas for its use that even the inventor had not imagined. Lovelace, the wife of an English aristocrat and the daughter of poet Lord Byron, declined the traditional roles of housewife and mother, opting instead to pursue the study of mathematics. . . . A good choice for report writers or computer history buffs." Booklist

Includes bibliographical references

Lyon, Mary, 1797-1849

Rosen, Dorothy. A fire in her bones: the story of Mary Lyon; [by] Dorothy Schack Rosen. Carolrhoda Bks. 1995 88p il map (Trailblazers) lib bdg $17.50 (4 and up)   92

1. Mount Holyoke College 2. Women teachers 3. Educators
ISBN 0-87614-840-2   LC 94-1978

Presents "the story of Mary Lyon, a farm girl who loved education and went on to start Mount Holyoke Female Seminary." Booklist

"Rosen presents her subject's story in an easy-to-understand, straightforward manner that emphasizes Lyon's earnest and persevering drive to establish the first college for women in America. . . . The text is augmented with many period black-and-white reproductions." SLJ

Includes bibliography

Madison, James, 1751-1836

Fritz, Jean. The great little Madison. Putnam 1989 159p il $15.95 (5 and up)   92

1. Presidents—United States
ISBN 0-399-21768-1   LC 88-31584

"Small, soft-spoken, and by nature diffident, James Madison found it difficult to speak in the midst of controversy, but his zeal and his convictions in the struggle between Republicans and Federalists gave him confidence, and his successes brought him to the presidency. Fritz has given a vivid picture of the man and an equally vivid picture of the problems—especially the internal dissension—that faced the leaders of the new nation. . . . Notes by the author and a bibliography are appended." Bull Cent Child Books

Magellan, Ferdinand, 1480?-1521

Hargrove, Jim. Ferdinand Magellan. Childrens Press 1990 128p il maps (World's great explorers) lib bdg $26.60 (4-6)   92

1. Explorers 2. Voyages around the world
ISBN 0-516-03051-5   LC 89-15781

Magellan, Ferdinand, 1480?-1521—Continued
The life of the Portuguese navigator and explorer who launched the first voyage around the world in the early 1500's but met his death before his men completed the expedition
"A fascinating history presented in an extremely well-written, accurate book, with a nice complement of factual background and timely sidelights. . . . The full-color illustrations of maps, etchings, woodcuts, and reproductions contain a wealth of information." SLJ
Includes glossary and bibliography

Mahy, Margaret
Mahy, Margaret. My mysterious world; photographs by David Alexander. Owen, R.C. 1995 32p il (Meet the author) $13.95 (1-3)
92
1. Women authors
ISBN 1-878450-58-1 LC 95-1291
"Mahy introduces her New Zealand home 'in the shell of an old volcano' and takes readers along as she writes, plants trees, plays with her dog, answers children's letters, and reads aloud to a school class." Booklist
"Mahy's story is unique because of setting (rural New Zealand), and because of the high quality of the accompanying photographs showing the author at work and play." SLJ

Malcolm X, 1925-1965
Adoff, Arnold. Malcolm X; illustrated by John Wilson. Crowell 1970 41p il (Crowell biography) lib bdg $11.89; pa $5.95 (2-5)
92
1. African Americans—Biography
ISBN 0-690-51414-X (lib bdg); 0-06-446015-0 (pa)
"This short forthright biography vividly outlines the events, both tragic and rewarding, which influenced the life and thought of Malcolm X from childhood to death and clearly evinces his significance as a black leader. The account describes the adverse effects of Malcolm's bitter childhood experiences, the changes which began during his incarceration in the Norfolk Prison Colony, his association with the Black Muslims and his later break with them, and the hostility of both black and white groups toward his Organization of Afro-American Unity." Booklist

Mandela, Nelson
Dell, Pamela. Nelson Mandela; freedom for South Africa. Childrens Press 1994 31p il (Picture story biographies) lib bdg $15.80; pa $3.95 (3-5)
92
1. South Africa—Race relations 2. South Africa—Politics and government
ISBN 0-516-04192-4 (lib bdg); 0-516-44192-2 (pa)
LC 94-3386
This book introduces "the life of Mandela and the struggle against apartheid. The style is clear, the tone is adulatory, the type is large, and the well-chosen photos are nicely reproduced on glossy paper." Booklist

Roberts, Jack L. Nelson Mandela; determined to be free. Millbrook Press 1995 48p il (Gateway biography) lib bdg $13.40 (3-5)
92
1. South Africa—Race relations 2. South Africa—Politics and government
ISBN 1-56294-558-0 LC 94-21519

This biography of the South African president "is a direct, accurate account . . . illustrated with occasional, well-reproduced photographs. The style is straightforward without being simplistic or condescending, so older reluctant readers will also be drawn to the story." Booklist
Includes bibliographical references

Marshall, Thurgood
Haskins, James. Thurgood Marshall; a life for justice. Holt & Co. 1992 163p $14.95; pa $7.95 (6 and up)
92
1. United States. Supreme Court 2. Judges 3. African Americans—Biography
ISBN 0-8050-2095-0; 0-8050-4256-3 (pa)
LC 91-46251
Examines the life and accomplishments of the first black judge to be appointed to the Supreme Court
"Young readers will find the account both readable and inspiring and appreciate the explanations of unfamiliar terms and concepts. The historical, social, and political perspective Haskins incorporates makes the work an illuminating, in-depth portrait of a courageous leader as well as an excellent resource for study of the civil rights movement." Booklist
Includes bibliography

Martin, Rafe, 1946-
Martin, Rafe. A storyteller's story; photographs by Jill Krementz. Owen, R.C. 1992 32p il map (Meet the author) $13.95 (1-3)
92
1. Authors, American
ISBN 0-913461-03-2 LC 92-7794
Children's author Rafe Martin describes his life and writing process and how they are interwoven
"Just the ticket for those librarian-perplexing assignments for autobiographies at the second-grade level. . . . Martin conveys just how long a manuscript can gestate: 'Will's Mammoth [entered in class E] took either three years or thirty seconds to write!'" Bull Cent Child Books

Matzeliger, Jan, 1852-1889
Mitchell, Barbara. Shoes for everyone: a story about Jan Matzeliger; illustrations by Hetty Mitchell. Carolrhoda Bks. 1986 63p il (Carolrhoda creative minds book) lib bdg $17.50; pa $5.95 (3-5)
92
1. Shoe industry 2. African American inventors
ISBN 0-87614-290-0 (lib bdg); 0-87614-473-3 (pa)
LC 86-4157
A biography of the half-Dutch half-black Surinamese man who, despite the hardships and prejudice he found in his new Massachusetts home, invented a shoe-lasting machine that revolutionized the shoe industry in the late nineteenth century
This is "a compelling story of human endeavor. A clear text blessedly allows the extraordinary individual in focus, Jan Matzeliger, . . . to emerge without undue exclamatory adulation." Bull Cent Child Books

Meir, Golda, 1898-1978

Adler, David A. Our Golda: the story of Golda Meir; illustrated by Donna Ruff. Viking 1984 52p il hardcover o.p. paperback available $4.99 (3-5)   **92**

1. Women politicians 2. Israel—Politics and government 3. Zionism

ISBN 0-14-032104-7 (pa)   LC 83-16798

"Adler's biography covers Golda Meir's life, including her Russian birth and American upbringing, through her resignation from the office of Prime Minister of Israel in 1974. Golda's strong-willed personality is Adler's primary focus." SLJ

This is a "compact, thoughtful biography. . . . [The] well-researched narrative exhibits a sensitivity for time and place that is echoed in accompanying soft-pencil drawings." Booklist

Michelangelo Buonarroti, 1475-1564

Richmond, Robin. Introducing Michelangelo. Little, Brown 1992 32p il $14.95 (4 and up)   **92**

1. Artists, Italian

ISBN 0-316-74440-9   LC 91-25602

First published 1991 in the United Kingdom

A biography of the Renaissance artist, illustrated with reproductions of his work

"This volume effortlessly transports the reader back to the Renaissance. . . . The author's discussion of some of Michelangelo's major triumphs—the Great Pietàs, David, and the Sistine Chapel—provides a solid introduction to Michelangelo's art." Booklist

Venezia, Mike. Michelangelo; written and illustrated by Mike Venezia. Childrens Press 1991 32p il (Getting to know the world's greatest artists) lib bdg $18.60; pa $5.95 (k-3)   **92**

1. Artists, Italian

ISBN 0-516-02293-8 (lib bdg); 0-516-42293-6 (pa)
LC 91-555

Introduces the Italian Renaissance artist through brief text, full-color reproductions of his works, and cartoon drawings

Monet, Claude, 1840-1926

Venezia, Mike. Monet; written and illustrated by Mike Venezia. Childrens Press 1993 29p il (Getting to know the world's greatest artists) ilb bdg $18.60; pa $5.95 (k-3)   **92**

1. Artists, French

ISBN 0-516-02276-8 (lib bdg); 0-516-42276-6 (pa)
LC 89-25452

Traces the life of the French Impressionist painter and analyzes some of his paintings

"Venezia offers fine reproductions of full-color paintings judiciously arranged. . . . Half a dozen cartoons with slap-stick humor are interjected in the book in an effort to show readers that art can be 'fun' for them too." SLJ

Moore, Henry, 1898-1986

Gardner, Jane Mylum. Henry Moore; from bones and stones to sketches and sculptures. Four Winds Press 1993 32p il $15.95 (2-4)   **92**

1. Sculptors

ISBN 0-02-735812-7   LC 92-23969

Presents a brief biography of the twentieth-century English sculptor and a discussion of his work

"Combining photographs, drawings and a simple but eloquent text, Gardner's introduction to the sculptor's life and work is itself a small marvel of artistic sensibility." Publ Wkly

Moses, Grandma, 1860-1961

Oneal, Zibby. Grandma Moses: painter of rural America; illustrated by Donna Ruff; paintings by Grandma Moses. Viking Kestrel 1986 58p il (Women of our time) hardcover o.p. paperback available $4.99 (4 and up)   **92**

1. Artists, American 2. Women artists

ISBN 0-14-032220-5 (pa)   LC 86-4071

A biography focusing on the early years of Grandma Moses, who was known for her paintings of rural America

"Though short, this biographical sketch brims with the energy of both the woman and the artist. . . . Oneal does an exemplary job of interpreting the artist's work, giving a semblance of the style and flavor in a brisk, evocative narrative. Recommended not only as a biography of a woman who succeeded in her craft but also as an inspirational source for fledgling artists." Booklist

Mozart, Wolfgang Amadeus, 1756-1791

Thompson, Wendy. Wolfgang Amadeus Mozart. Viking 1991 48p il music (Composer's world) $17.95 (5 and up)   **92**

1. Composers

ISBN 0-670-83679-6   LC 90-70941

First published 1990 in the United Kingdom

This book describes Mozart's life and work and the times in which he lived

The author "has put together an attractive and serious biography for children in the upper grades. Most of the beautiful and informative illustrations are reproductions of historical documents. . . . The text is interspersed with pages of music that look very inviting to play in the context of the unfolding life story." N Y Times Book Rev

Includes glossary

Venezia, Mike. Wolfgang Amadeus Mozart; written and illustrated by Mike Venezia. Childrens Press 1995 32p il (Getting to know the world's greatest composers) lib bdg $18.60; pa $5.95 (k-3)   **92**

1. Composers

ISBN 0-516-04541-5 (lib bdg); 0-516-44541-3 (pa)
LC 95-13366

An illustrated biography of the Austrian child prodigy who wrote more than 800 pieces of music before his untimely death at thirty-five

Mozart, Wolfgang Amadeus, 1756-1791—Continued

Weil, Lisl. Wolferl: the first six years in the life of Wolfgang Amadeus Mozart, 1756-1762. Holiday House 1991 unp il $14.95 (k-3)

92

1. Composers
ISBN 0-8234-0876-0   LC 90-47684

"The early childhood of Mozart is recounted, from his birth to his first command performance for the Empress Maria Theresa of Austria at age six. Lisl Weil's cartoon-like illustrations in ink, crayon, and watercolor provide a charming view of life in eighteenth-century Vienna. A glossary helps explain the more difficult terms and place-names." Adventuring with Books

Muir, John, 1838-1914

Douglas, William O. (William Orville). Muir of the mountains; illustrations by Daniel San Souci. Sierra Club Bks. for Children 1994 105p il $16.95 (4 and up)   92

1. Naturalists 2. Nature conservation
ISBN 0-87156-505-6   LC 93-13680

A newly illustrated and slightly abridged edition of the title first published 1961 by Houghton Mifflin

A biography of John Muir revealing the events and ideas that shaped America's pioneer conservationist and founder of the Sierra Club

Nickens, Bessie, 1906-

Nickens, Bessie. Walking the log; memories of a Southern childhood; paintings and stories by Bessie Nickens. Rizzoli Int. Publs. 1994 30p il $14.95 (2-4)   92

1. Artists, American 2. African American artists 3. Women artists
ISBN 0-8478-1794-6   LC 94-10803

This is an autobiography of "African-American artist Bessie Nickens. Told as a series of reminiscences, accompanied by paintings which combine elements of folk art with impressionistic landscapes, the book has an engaging, personal tone that allows the reader to comprehend what it was like to live in rural America at the turn of the century." Horn Book

Includes glossary

O'Keeffe, Georgia, 1887-1986

Turner, Robyn Montana. Georgia O'Keeffe. Little, Brown 1991 32p il (Portraits of women artists for children) $15.95; pa $6.95 (4-6)

92

1. Artists, American 2. Women artists
ISBN 0-316-85649-5; 0-316-85654-1 (pa)
          LC 90-19352

A biography of a prominent American artist renowned for her images of gigantic flowers, cityscapes, and distinctive desert scenes

This is "a rich, colorful biography. The reproductions chosen to illustrate her life are excellent. . . . Throughout, the succinct, clear prose stresses O'Keeffe's art, her search for ways to express her feelings, her love for nature, and her total subjection of all else to the study and the demands of a creative life." SLJ

Venezia, Mike. Georgia O'Keeffe; written and illustrated by Mike Venezia. Childrens Press 1993 31p il (Getting to know the world's greatest artists) lib bdg $18.60; pa $5.95 (k-3)

92

1. Artists, American 2. Women artists
ISBN 0-516-02297-0 (lib bdg); 0-516-42297-9 (pa)
          LC 93-13004

Briefly examines the life and work of the twentieth-century American artist known for her paintings of flowers and presents examples of her art

O'Neal, Shaquille

Townsend, Brad. Shaquille O'Neal; center of attention. Lerner Publs. 1994 64p il (Achievers) lib bdg $17.50; pa $5.95 (4 and up)   92

1. Basketball—Biography 2. African American athletes
ISBN 0-8225-2879-7 (lib bdg); 0-8225-9655-5 (pa)
          LC 93-35558

"This brief biography of the Orlando Magic's 40-million dollar center, contains five short, easy-to-read chapters. . . A page of statistics reflects his accomplishments. Every double-page spread has at least one black-and-white or full-color photograph. Readers interested in basketball and the stars of the game will find their interests satisfied here." SLJ

Owens, Jesse, 1913-1980

Adler, David A. A picture book of Jesse Owens; [by] David Adler; illustrated by Robert Casilla. Holiday House 1992 unp il lib bdg $15.95; pa $5.95 (1-3)   92

1. African American athletes 2. Track athletics—Biography
ISBN 0-8234-0966-X (lib bdg); 0-8234-1066-8 (pa)
          LC 91-44735

A simple biography of the noted black track star who competed in the 1936 Berlin Olympics

Parker, Charlie, 1920-1955

Raschka, Christopher. Charlie Parker played be bop; [by] Chris Raschka. Orchard Bks. 1992 unp il $14.99; lib bdg $13.99 (k-2)

92

1. Jazz musicians
ISBN 0-531-05999-5; 0-531-08599-6 (lib bdg)
          LC 91-38420

"A Richard Jackson book"

Introduces the famous saxophonist and his style of jazz known as bebop

"Bold, clever illustrations and lyrical verse cause the reader to be caught up in the rhythm of the text." Child Book Rev Serv

Parks, Rosa, 1913-

Adler, David A. A picture book of Rosa Parks; illustrated by Robert Casilla. Holiday House 1993 unp il lib bdg $15.95; pa $5.95 (1-3)   92

1. African American women 2. African Americans—Civil rights
ISBN 0-8234-1041-2 (lib bdg); 0-8234-1177-X (pa)
          LC 92-41826

Parks, Rosa, 1913-—_Continued_

A biography of the Alabama black woman whose refusal to give up her seat on a bus helped establish the civil rights movement

This features "simple narrative text and the dramatic color illustrations." Booklist

Celsi, Teresa Noel. Rosa Parks and the Montgomery bus boycott; by Teresa Celsi. Millbrook Press 1991 28p il (Gateway civil rights) lib bdg $11.90; pa $4.95 (3-5)   **92**

1. African American women 2. African Americans—Civil rights 3. Montgomery (Ala.)—Race relations

ISBN 1-878841-14-9 (lib bdg); 0-878841-34-3 (pa)
                 LC 91-29905

This brief biography of the civil rights leader concentrates on the Montgomery bus boycott and includes information on the Ku Klux Klan, segregated schools, and the Freedom Train

"Illustrated with clear, well-chosen photographs. . . . While excellent for reports [this] should attract some recreational readers as well." SLJ

Includes bibliography

Greenfield, Eloise. Rosa Parks; illustrated by Gil Ashby. HarperCollins Pubs. 1995 41p il lib bdg $13.89; pa $3.95 (2-4)   **92**

1. African American women 2. African Americans—Civil rights

ISBN 0-06-027110-8 (lib bdg); 0-06-442025-6 (pa)
                 LC 95-35497

A newly illustrated edition of the title first published 1973

A biography of the black woman whose acts of civil disobedience led to the 1956 Supreme Court order to desegregate buses in Montgomery, Alabama

Parks, Rosa. Rosa Parks: my story; by Rosa Parks with Jim Haskins. Dial Bks. 1992 192p il $17 (5 and up)   **92**

1. African American women 2. African Americans—Civil rights

ISBN 0-8037-0673-1   LC 89-1124

Rosa Parks describes her early life and experiences with race discrimination, and her participation in the Montgomery bus boycott and the civil rights movement

"A remarkable story, a record of quiet bravery and modesty, a document of social significance, a taut drama told with candor." Bull Cent Child Books

Siegel, Beatrice. The year they walked: Rosa Parks and the Montgomery bus boycott. Four Winds Press 1992 103p il maps $13.95 (4-6)
                       92

1. African American women 2. African Americans—Civil rights 3. Montgomery (Ala.)—Race relations

ISBN 0-02-782631-7   LC 91-14078

"Unlike the more comprehensive _Rosa Parks: My Story_ [entered above] Siegel's considerably shorter book focuses on the immediate repercussions of Parks's refusal in 1955 to give up her bus seat to a white man in Montgomery, Ala. . . . This account effectively documents the overwhelming humiliation experienced by Montgomery's black residents during a year filled with shocking incidents of racism." Publ Wkly

Includes bibliography

Patrick, Saint, 373?-463?

De Paola, Tomie. Patrick: patron saint of Ireland. Holiday House 1992 unp il lib bdg $15.95 (k-3)   **92**

1. Christian saints

ISBN 0-8234-0924-4   LC 91-19417

Relates the life and legends of Patrick, the patron saint of Ireland

"The combination of book design, text, and illustration is suitably reverent but never saccharine; the whole is a well-executed treatment of an appealing subject." Horn Book

Pavlova, Anna, 1881-1931

Levine, Ellen. Anna Pavlova, genius of the dance. Scholastic 1995 132p il $14.95 (5 and up)   **92**

1. Ballet dancers

ISBN 0-590-44304-6   LC 94-7310

This biography of the ballerina covers "Pavlova's early years in Russia, her later settling in England, and then her extensive touring through Europe, the United States, South America, and Asia." Bull Cent Child Books

"Short chapters with lots of dialogue and anecdotes create a lively tension that pulls the reader through the book. Pavlova's sparkling personality is evident at every turn. . . . Ideal for middle grades, Levine's writing style is also interesting enough to capture older reluctant readers." Voice Youth Advocates

Includes glossary and bibliographical references

Peale, Charles Willson, 1741-1827

Tunnell, Michael O. The joke's on George; pictures by Kathy Osborn. Tambourine Bks. 1993 unp il $14; lib bdg $13.93 (k-3)   **92**

1. Washington, George, 1732-1799 2. Artists, American

ISBN 0-688-11758-9; 0-688-11759-7 (lib bdg)
                 LC 92-33312

Briefly surveys the life of the early American portrait painter and describes an incident in which George Washington, visiting his natural history museum, was fooled by a lifelike painting of two of Peale's sons climbing a staircase

"Faintly echoing cubism as well as naive American art, Osborn's paintings have an inviting look that suits the tone of the text. Fresh and funny." Booklist

Peck, Richard

Peck, Richard. Anonymously yours. Messner 1991 122p il (In my own words) o.p.; Morrow paperback available $4.95 (5 and up)   **92**

1. Authors, American

ISBN 0-688-13702-4 (pa)   LC 91-10067

The popular author describes how he grew up in Decatur, Illinois, went into teaching, and eventually became a writer, incorporating his earlier experiences into novels intended to reach and change young readers

"This memoir is . . . engaging and filled with insight into Peck's creative processes." SLJ

Includes bibliography

Peet, Bill

Peet, Bill. Bill Peet: an autobiography. Houghton Mifflin 1989 190p il $17.95; pa $9.95 (4 and up) **92**

1. Walt Disney Productions 2. Authors, American 3. Illustrators

ISBN 0-395-50932-7; 0-395-68982-1 (pa)

LC 88-37067

A Caldecott Medal honor book, 1990

This memoir "describes the life of the well-known children's book author who worked as an illustrator for Walt Disney from the making of 'Dumbo' until 'Mary Poppins.'" N Y Times Book Rev

"Every page of this oversized book is illustrated with Peet's unmistakable black-and-white drawings of himself and the people, places, and events described in the text. Familiar characters from his books and movies appear often." SLJ

Peter I, the Great, Emperor of Russia, 1672-1725

Stanley, Diane. Peter the Great. Four Winds Press 1986 32p il $15.95; pa $4.95 (3-5) **92**

1. Russia—Kings, queens, rulers, etc.

ISBN 0-02-786790-0; 0-689-71548-X (pa)

LC 85-13060

A biography of the tsar who began the transformation of Russia into a modern state in the late seventeenth-early eighteenth centuries

The author's "material is presented with a modicum of oversimplification and a plethora of details that are sure to fascinate children. But what really makes this biography shine are its breathtaking illustrations. The meticulously researched, vivid scenes of Russian life during Peter's reign—courts, countryside, architecture, costumes—are beautifully rendered." Publ Wkly

Picasso, Pablo, 1881-1973

Venezia, Mike. Picasso; written and illustrated by Mike Venezia. Childrens Press 1988 32p il (Getting to know the world's greatest artists) lib bdg $18.60; pa $5.95 (k-3) **92**

1. Artists, French

ISBN 0-516-02271-7 (lib bdg); 0-516-42271-5 (pa)

LC 87-33023

Introduces the French twentieth-century artist through brief text, full-color reproductions of his works, and cartoon drawings

Pinkerton, Allan, 1819-1884

Wormser, Richard. Pinkerton: America's first private eye. Walker & Co. 1990 119p il $19.95; lib bdg $18.85 (5 and up) **92**

1. Detectives

ISBN 0-8027-6964-0; 0-8027-6965-9 (lib bdg)

LC 90-12362

Examines the life of the detective who founded his own agency and introduced a system to help track criminals down and tie them to crimes

"An intriguing subject, lively prose, and in-depth analysis combine to make this a first-rate biography. . . . Wormser never tries to paper over the contradictions or erase Pinkerton's warts. He makes abundant anecdotal use of Pinkerton's detective cases, and the result is fresh and thought provoking, engrossing despite a high ratio of text to illustration." Booklist

Includes bibliography

Pippin, Horace, 1888-1946

Lyons, Mary E. Starting home: the story of Horace Pippin, painter. Scribner 1993 42p il (African-American artists and artisans) $15.95 (4 and up) **92**

1. Artists, American 2. African American artists

ISBN 0-684-19534-8

LC 92-26990

"Horace Pippin was a self-taught painter whose work reflects his personal story. Haunted by his experience as a soldier in World War I, he painted scenes from the trenches years after he returned. . . . The paintings are haunting, and Lyons speaks about them with warm appreciation." Booklist

Pocahontas, d. 1617

Fritz, Jean. The double life of Pocahontas; with illustrations by Ed Young. Putnam 1983 96p il o.p.; Viking paperback available $3.99 (4 and up) **92**

1. Powhatan Indians 2. Jamestown (Va.)—History

ISBN 0-14-032257-4 (pa)

LC 83-9662

"Pocahontas, the daughter of the seventeenth century Indian chief Powhatan, . . . saved the life of Captain John Smith and later married John Rolfe. In tracing the girl's life, the author has explored the history of the Jamestown colony from 1607 to 1622 and has given [an] . . . account of the often unhappy relationship between the colonists and the Indians." Horn Book

Includes bibliography

Polacco, Patricia

Polacco, Patricia. Firetalking; photographs by Lawrence Migdale. Owen, R.C. 1994 32p il (Meet the author) $13.95 (1-3) **92**

1. Women authors 2. Authors, American

ISBN 1-878450-55-7

LC 93-48162

"Polacco explains how childhood evenings of 'firetalking' with her Russian and Irish grandparents formed the basis of many of her stories. The black-and-white and full-color photographs add to the intimacy of the [text]." SLJ

Pollock, Jackson, 1912-1956

Venezia, Mike. Jackson Pollock; written and illustrated by Mike Venezia. Childrens Press 1994 31p il (Getting to know the world's greatest artists) lib bdg $13.95; pa $5.95 (k-3) **92**

1. Artists, American

ISBN 0-516-02298-9 (lib bdg); 0-516-42298-7 (pa)

LC 93-36699

Introduces the American artist through brief text, photographs, full-color reproductions of his paintings, and cartoon drawings

Potter, Beatrix, 1866-1943

Collins, David R. The country artist: a story about Beatrix Potter; illustrations by Karen Ritz. Carolrhoda Bks. 1989 56p il (Carolrhoda creative minds book) lib bdg $17.50; pa $5.95 (3-5) **92**

1. Authors, English 2. Illustrators 3. Women authors 4. Women artists

ISBN 0-87614-344-3 (lib bdg); 0-87614-509-8 (pa)

LC 88-27417

A biography of the English author and illustrator who grew up during the Victorian era and whose detailed drawings of plants and animals found their way into her famous picture books

Taylor, Judy. Beatrix Potter: artist, storyteller and countrywoman. Warne 1987 c1986 224p il $24.95 **92**

1. Authors, English 2. Illustrators 3. Women authors 4. Women artists

ISBN 0-7232-3314-4

LC 86-50799

First published 1986 in the United Kingdom

"In this brief but copiously illustrated biography, Judy Taylor adds much fresh information to what was previously known about her sanguine-spirited and intensely private subject's life. . . . Further insights may be gleaned from the more than 200 illustrations reproduced in this attractive volume, including dozens of family photographs . . . and an abundant sampling of Potter landscapes, botanical studies, picture letters, rough sketches and finished book art." N Y Times Book Rev

Includes bibliography

Powell, Colin L.

Banta, Melissa. Colin Powell. Chelsea House 1995 79p il (Junior world biographies) lib bdg $14.95; pa $4.95 (5 and up) **92**

1. Generals 2. African American soldiers

ISBN 0-7910-1770-2 (lib bdg); 0-7910-2142-4 (pa)

LC 94-8349

This is a biography of the African American "general who became Chairman of the Joint Chiefs of Staff, led the hunt for Noriega in Panama, and engineered the Operation Desert Storm invasion of Kuwait. Well researched, with a bibliography of recent sources, it is of manageable length and has an open format, well-organized chapters, and frequent black-and-white photos." SLJ

Includes glossary

Powers, Harriet, 1837-1911

Lyons, Mary E. Stitching stars: the story quilts of Harriet Powers. Scribner 1993 41p il (African-American artists and artisans) $15.95 (4 and up) **92**

1. Quilts 2. Artists, American 3. Women artists 4. African American artists

ISBN 0-684-19576-3

LC 92-38561

"Harriet Powers was born in slavery and lived in poverty, with few records of her life except her richly imaginative story quilts. In this brief artistic biography, Lyons openly surmises or fictionalizes where the bitter obscurity of slavery and poverty has resulted in an absence of records, but Harriet speaks eloquently through her handiwork depicting Bible stories and natural phenomena. . . . Lyons' lively writing stitches concepts together with smoothness and clarity." Bull Cent Child Books

Includes bibliography

Reiss, Johanna

Reiss, Johanna. The upstairs room. Crowell 1972 196p $15; lib bdg $14.89; pa $3.95 (4 and up) **92**

1. World War, 1939-1945—Jews 2. Netherlands—History—1940-1945, German occupation 3. Jews—Netherlands

ISBN 0-690-85127-8; 0-690-04702-9 (lib bdg); 0-06-440370-X (pa)

Also available Spanish language edition

A Newbery Medal honor book, 1973

"In a vital, moving account the author recalls her experiences as a Jewish child hiding from the Germans occupying her native Holland during World War II. . . . Ten-year-old Annie and her twenty-year-old sister Sini, . . . are taken in by a Dutch farmer, his wife, and mother who hide the girls in an upstairs room of the farm house. Written from the perspective of a child the story affords a child's-eye-view of the war." Booklist

Followed by The journey back (1976)

Rembrandt Harmenszoon van Rijn, 1606-1669

Sturgis, Alexander. Introducing Rembrandt. Little, Brown 1994 32p il maps $15.95 (4-6) **92**

1. Artists, Dutch

ISBN 0-316-82022-9

LC 93-11418

"Full-color reproductions of a representative sampling of Rembrandt's drawings, paintings, and prints enhance an engaging text to create an excellent introduction to the artist's life, work, and importance in the history and development of art. Intriguingly juxtaposed works and probing questions invite active looking and comparison." Horn Book Guide

Venezia, Mike. Rembrandt; written and illustrated by Mike Venezia. Childrens Press 1988 31p il (Getting to know the world's greatest artists) lib bdg $18.60; pa $5.95 (k-3) **92**

1. Artists, Dutch

ISBN 0-516-02272-5 (lib bdg); 0-516-42272-3 (pa)

LC 87-33014

Briefly examines the life and work of the seventeenth-century Dutch painter

Renoir, Auguste, 1841-1919

Skira-Venturi, Rosabianca. A weekend with Renoir. Rizzoli Int. Publs. 1991 61p il $19.95; pa $9.95 (4 and up) **92**

1. Artists, French

ISBN 0-8478-1438-6; 0-8478-1921-3 (pa)

LC 91-12426

The nineteenth century artist talks about his life and work as if entertaining the reader for a weekend

"The author not only succeeds in providing solid information and astute commentary but also seems to capture the individual personality of [the painter]." Horn Book

Includes bibliographical references

Revere, Paul, 1735-1818

Fritz, Jean. And then what happened, Paul Revere? pictures by Margot Tomes. Coward, McCann & Geoghegan 1973 45p il $13.95; pa $6.95 (2-4) **92**

1. United States—History—1775-1783, Revolution

ISBN 0-698-20274-0; 0-698-20541-3 (pa)

This "description of Paul Revere's ride to Lexington is funny, fast-paced, and historically accurate; it is given added interest by the establishment of Revere's character: busy, bustling, versatile, and patriotic, a man who loved people and excitement. The account of his ride is preceded by a description of his life and the political situation in Boston, and it concludes with Revere's adventures after reaching Lexington." Bull Cent Child Books

Richards, Ellen Henrietta Swallow, 1842-1911

Vare, Ethlie Ann. Adventurous spirit: a story about Ellen Swallow Richards; illustrations by Jennifer Hagerman. Carolrhoda Bks. 1992 64p il (Carolrhoda creative minds book) lib bdg $15.95 (3-5) **92**

1. Chemists 2. Women scientists

ISBN 0-87614-733-3 LC 91-39714

A biography of Ellen Swallow Richards, the first woman to study at the Massachusetts Institute of Technology, founder of the American home economics movement, and first professional woman chemist

"An interesting, accurate portrayal of the scientist's life. . . . The full-page, black-and-white pencil drawings are effective and appropriately placed." SLJ

Includes bibliography

Ringgold, Faith

Turner, Robyn Montana. Faith Ringgold. Little, Brown 1993 32p il (Portraits of women artists for children) $16.95 (4-6) **92**

1. Artists, American 2. Women artists 3. African American artists

ISBN 0-316-85652-5 LC 92-42652

Examines the life and work of the artist whose determination to be true to her African-American heritage brought about an influential new art form

"Illustrated on every page, the book features clear black-and-white photographs of the artist and her family and full-color reproductions of Ringgold's paintings and quilts as well as smaller photos of other artists' works that have inspired her." Booklist

Rivera, Diego, 1886-1957

Neimark, Anne E. Diego Rivera, artist of the people. HarperCollins Pubs. 1992 116p il lib bdg $16.89 (6 and up) **92**

1. Artists, Mexican

ISBN 0-06-021784-7 LC 91-25209

Follows the life of the twentieth-century Mexican muralist, from his earliest artistic expressions through his developmental years in Spain, Paris, and Italy to his political activities when he returned to Mexico

"An author's note makes it clear that this is a fictionalized biography with some invented scenes and dialogues. . . . Still, Rivera himself always mingled facts with tall tales, and Neimark's story of Rivera's life in all its fierce contradictions—as revolutionary, womanizer, and artist—is enthralling. . . . The book's design is handsome, with a glowing cover painting, clear type, and many fine reproductions of Rivera's work." Booklist

Includes bibliography

Venezia, Mike. Diego Rivera; written and illustrated by Mike Venezia. Childrens Press 1994 32p il (Getting to know the world's greatest artists) lib bdg $13.95; pa $5.95 (k-3) **92**

1. Artists, Mexican

ISBN 0-516-02299-7 (lib bdg); 0-516-42299-5 (pa)

LC 94-11650

Introduces the Mexican artist through brief text, photographs, full-color reproductions of his paintings, and cartoon drawings

"Venezia's humorous cartoons . . . elaborate on biographical details in a down-to-earth manner. . . . All artworks are meticulously labeled. . . . [This] will enable even preschoolers to begin to relish the worlds's art treasures." Booklist

Winter, Jonah. Diego; [illustrated] by Jeanette Winter; text by Jonah Winter; translated from the English by Amy Prince. Knopf 1991 unp il hardcover o.p. paperback available $5.99 (k-3) **92**

1. Artists, Mexican 2. Bilingual books—English-Spanish

ISBN 0-679-85617-X (pa) LC 90-25923

This book "in both Spanish and English, chronicles the life of Mexican muralist Diego Rivera. . . . Jonah Winter's crisp text and Jeanette Winter's elaborately bordered, dynamic illustrations successfully convey the spirit of the man and his work." Publ Wkly

Robeson, Paul, 1898-1976

Greenfield, Eloise. Paul Robeson; illustrated by George Ford. Crowell 1975 32p il (Crowell biography) lib bdg $15.89 (2-5) **92**

1. African Americans—Biography

ISBN 0-690-00660-8

A biography of the black man who became a famous singer, actor, and spokesman for equal rights for his people

"This format and style are appealing to the beginning reader and useful for the high-interest-low-reading level that many teachers and librarians encounter." Child Book Rev Serv

Robinson, Jackie, 1919-1972

Adler, David A. Jackie Robinson: he was the first; written by David A. Adler; illustrated by Robert Casilla. Holiday House 1989 48p il (First biography) lib bdg $14.95; pa $5.95 (2-4) **92**

1. Baseball—Biography 2. African American athletes

ISBN 0-8234-0734-9 (lib bdg); 0-8234-0799-3 (pa)

LC 88-23294

Robinson, Jackie, 1919-1972—*Continued*

Traces the life of the talented and determined athlete who broke the color barrier in major league baseball in 1947 by joining the Brooklyn Dodgers

This biography is "clearly written, admiring but not adulatory, and succinct without being terse. . . . Adler does a good job in covering the highlights of Robinson's career and maintains a balance between facts about that career and about Robinson's personal life; the information is accurate, the tone subdued, so that any tension and action speak the more volubly for themselves." Bull Cent Child Books

Adler, David A. A picture book of Jackie Robinson; illustrated by Robert Casilla. Holiday House 1994 unp il $15.95 (1-3)
92

1. Baseball—Biography 2. African American athletes

ISBN 0-8234-1122-2   LC 93-27224

"A brief look at the life of baseball great Jackie Robinson. The subject's childhood, sporting accomplishments, and later endeavors are touched upon, as are the bigotry and prejudice he faced as the first African American to play in the major leagues. . . . Casilla's full-and double-page watercolors provide attractive backgrounds for the text. A sound introduction to a significant figure." SLJ

Golenbock, Peter. Teammates; written by Peter Golenbock; designed and illustrated by Paul Bacon. Harcourt Brace Jovanovich 1990 unp il $15.95; pa $4.95 (1-4)   **92**

1. Reese, Pee Wee, 1919- 2. Brooklyn Dodgers (Baseball team) 3. Baseball—Biography 4. African American athletes

ISBN 0-15-200603-6; 0-15-284286-1 (pa)

LC 89-38166

"Gulliver books"

Describes the racial prejudice experienced by Jackie Robinson when he joined the Brooklyn Dodgers and became the first black player in Major League baseball and depicts the acceptance and support he received from his white teammate Pee Wee Reese

"Golenbock's bold and lucid style distills this difficult issue, and brings a dramatic tale vividly to life. Bacon's spare, nostalgic watercolors, in addition to providing fond glimpses of baseball lore, present a haunting portrait of one man's isolation. Historic photographs of the major characters add interest and a touch of stark reality to an unusual story, beautifully rendered." Publ Wkly

Röntgen, Wilhelm Conrad, 1845-1923

Gherman, Beverly. The mysterious rays of Dr. Röntgen; illustrated by Stephen Marchesi. Atheneum Pubs. 1994 24p il lib bdg $14.95 (2-4)   **92**

1. Scientists 2. X rays

ISBN 0-689-31839-1   LC 92-38966

Describes the work of Wilhelm Röntgen, the German physicist who won the first Nobel Prize in Physics in 1901 for his discovery of X rays

This book "combines the excitement of scientific discovery with an accessible explanation of how the rays work. . . . The handsome period color oil illustrations on every page help to personalize the drama." Booklist

Includes bibliography

Roosevelt, Eleanor, 1884-1962

Adler, David A. A picture book of Eleanor Roosevelt; illustrated by Robert Casilla. Holiday House 1991 unp il lib bdg $15.95; pa $5.95 (1-3)   **92**

1. Presidents—United States—Spouses

ISBN 0-8234-0856-6 (lib bdg); 0-8234-1157-5 (pa)

LC 90-39212

A brief account of the life and accomplishments of Eleanor Roosevelt

"A crisply written biography enhanced by realistic watercolors." SLJ

Faber, Doris. Eleanor Roosevelt: first lady of the world; illustrated by Donna Ruff. Viking Kestrel 1985 57p il (Women of our time) hardcover o.p. paperback available $4.99 (4 and up)   **92**

1. Presidents—United States—Spouses

ISBN 0-14-032103-9 (pa)   LC 84-20861

A biography emphasizing the early years of Eleanor Roosevelt, who had enormous political influence and won love and respect as America's first lady

The author "manages to convey the basic events and experience of her subject's life in a clear, interesting and understanding manner." SLJ

Freedman, Russell. Eleanor Roosevelt; a life of discovery. Clarion Bks. 1993 198p il $17.95 (5 and up)   **92**

1. Presidents—United States—Spouses

ISBN 0-89919-862-7   LC 92-25024

A Newbery Medal honor book, 1994

"Readers are made privy to the telling details of a full life through numerous quotes from Roosevelt and her wide inner circle in this frank, well-documented portrait of the 'First Lady of the World.' A superlative biography." SLJ

Includes bibliography

Roosevelt, Franklin D. (Franklin Delano), 1882-1945

Freedman, Russell. Franklin Delano Roosevelt. Clarion Bks. 1990 200p il $16.95; pa $7.95 (5 and up)   **92**

1. Presidents—United States

ISBN 0-89919-379-X; 0-395-62978-0 (pa)

LC 89-34986

Photographs and text trace the life of Franklin Delano Roosevelt

"The carefully researched, highly readable text and extremely effective coordination of black-and-white photographs chronicle Roosevelt's priviledged youth, his early influences, and his maturation. . . . Even students with little or no background in American history will find this an intriguing and inspirational human portrait." SLJ

Includes bibliography

Roosevelt, Theodore, 1858-1919

Fritz, Jean. Bully for you, Teddy Roosevelt! illustrations by Mike Wimmer. Putnam 1991 127p il $15.95 (5 and up)   **92**

1. Presidents—United States

ISBN 0-399-21769-X   LC 90-8142

Roosevelt, Theodore, 1858-1919—*Continued*

Follows the life of the twenty-sixth president, discussing his conservation work, hunting expeditions, family life, and political career

"Jean Fritz gives a rounded picture of her subject and deftly blends the story of a person and a picture of an era." Bull Cent Child Books

Includes bibliography

Whitelaw, Nancy. Theodore Roosevelt takes charge. Whitman, A. 1992 192p il $14.95 (6 and up)   92

1. Presidents—United States
ISBN 0-8075-7849-5   LC 90-29181

Describes the life of the twenty-sixth president of the United States, from his sickly youth through his varied career as rancher, author, and politician

"Liberally illustrated with reproductions of contemporary prints and photographs, this is a lively biography of Roosevelt although the style is serious. The coverage is broad, and the author is candid about Roosevelt's faults or idiosyncrasies but firmly complimentary about his many achievements." Bull Cent Child Books

Includes bibliography

Ross, Betsy, 1752-1836

Wallner, Alexandra. Betsy Ross; written and illustrated by Alexandra Wallner. Holiday House 1994 unp il $15.95 (k-2)   92

1. United States—History—1775-1783, Revolution
2. Flags—United States
ISBN 0-8234-1071-4   LC 93-3559

An introduction to the life of the Philadelphia seamstress credited with sewing the first American flag

"More inviting than most young biographies, this is a good book for taking Ms. Ross from a cameo role to a starring part and using her to explain early American urban life." Bull Cent Child Books

Rylant, Cynthia

Rylant, Cynthia. Best wishes; photographs by Carlo Ontal. Owen, R.C. 1992 32p il map (Meet the author) $13.95 (1-3)   92

1. Authors, American 2. Women authors
ISBN 1-87845-020-4   LC 92-7796

Children's author Cynthia Rylant describes her life and writing process and how they are interwoven

"The color photos . . . have a candid snapshot quality that contributes to the friendly informality of the text." Bull Cent Child Books

Sasaki, Sadako, 1943-1955

Coerr, Eleanor. Sadako; illustrated by Ed Young. Putnam 1993 unp il $17.95 (1-4)
                                        92

1. Leukemia 2. Atomic bomb—Physiological effect
3. Hiroshima (Japan)—Bombardment, 1945
ISBN 0-399-21771-1   LC 92-41483

"This is the same story as the author's *Sadako and the Thousand Paper Cranes*, told through an entirely new text. In this abbreviated version, the beautiful, limpid prose and crisp dialogue further telescope Sadako's fight with leukemia. . . . Young's pastels vividly capture all the moods of the narrative, place, and characters. . . . A masterful collaboration." SLJ

Coerr, Eleanor. Sadako and the thousand paper cranes; paintings by Ronald Himler. Putnam 1977 64p il $14.95 (3-6)   92

1. Leukemia 2. Atomic bomb—Physiological effect
3. Hiroshima (Japan)—Bombardment, 1945
ISBN 0-399-20520-9   LC 76-9872

Also available in paperback from Dell; Spanish language edition also available

"A story about a young girl of Hiroshima who died from leukemia ten years after the dropping of the atom bomb. Her dreams of being an outstanding runner are dimmed when she learns she has the fatal disease. But her spunk and bravery, symbolized in her efforts to have faith in the story of the golden crane, are beautifully portrayed by the author. Sadako was a real person for whom a statue has been erected in the Hiroshima Peace Park. Her legend has been alive to the Japanese for many years and this sensitive book now enables young Americans to share her story." Babbling Bookworm

Schubert, Franz, 1797-1828

Thompson, Wendy. Franz Schubert. Viking 1991 48p il map music (Composer's world) $17.95 (5 and up)   92

1. Composers
ISBN 0-670-84172-2   LC 91-50213

The composer's life, work, and times are described, with musical excerpts, and illustrated with historical paintings and drawings

Includes glossary

Sequoyah, 1770?-1843

Cwiklik, Robert. Sequoyah and the Cherokee alphabet; written by Robert Cwiklik; introduction by Alvin M. Josephy, Jr.; illustrations by T. Lewis. Silver Burdett Press 1989 129p il (Alvin Josephy's biography series of American Indians) lib bdg $12.95; pa $7.95 (5 and up)   92

1. Cherokee Indians
ISBN 0-382-09570-7 (lib bdg); 0-382-09759-9 (pa)
                                        LC 89-30737

A biography of the Cherokee Indian who invented a method for his people to write and read their own language

Includes bibliography

Klausner, Janet. Sequoyah's gift; a portrait of the Cherokee leader; with an afterword by Duane H. King. HarperCollins Pubs. 1993 111p il $15; lib bdg $14.89 (4 and up)   92

1. Cherokee Indians
ISBN 0-06-021235-7; 0-06-021236-5 (lib bdg)
                                        LC 92-24939

"Sequoyah is best remembered for his remarkable feat of creating a Cherokee syllabary that allowed his people to read and write their own language. Klausner's detailed account includes discussion of Sequoyah's role during the Trail of Tears journey, the forced removal in 1838 of the Cherokee nation from Georgia to what became Oklahoma. . . . This is a solid work with many applications for study." Booklist

Includes bibliography

Seuss, Dr.

Weidt, Maryann N. Oh, the places he went;
a story about Dr. Seuss—Theodore Seuss
Geisel; illustrations by Kerry Maguire.
Carolrhoda Bks. 1994 64p il (Carolrhoda
creative minds book) lib bdg $17.50; pa $5.95
(3-5)   92
1. Authors, American 2. Illustrators
ISBN 0-87614-823-2 (lib bdg); 0-87614-627-2 (pa)
                                              LC 93-41370
This is a biography of the popular author and illustrator
of children's picture books
"A lively, straightforward overview of Theodor Geisel's
life and work. . . . Maguire's full-page pencil sketches capture the subject's appearance and personality." SLJ
Includes bibliography

Shakespeare, William, 1564-1616

Stanley, Diane. Bard of Avon: the story of
William Shakespeare; by Diane Stanley and
Peter Vennema; illustrated by Diane Stanley.
Morrow Junior Bks. 1992 unp il $15; lib bdg
$14.93 (3-5)   92
1. Dramatists
ISBN 0-688-09108-3; 0-688-09109-1 (lib bdg)
                                              LC 90-46564
A brief biography of the world's most famous playwright,
using only historically correct information
"A remarkably rounded picture of Shakespeare's life and
the period in which he lived is presented . . . together with
a thoughtful attempt to relate circumstances in his personal
life to the content of his plays. . . . The text is splendidly
supported by the illustrations, which are stylized, yet recognizable, and present a clear view of life in the late sixteenth
century. A discerning, knowledgeable biography, rising far
above the ordinary." Horn Book
Includes bibliography

Singer, Isaac Bashevis, 1904-1991

Kresh, Paul. Isaac Bashevis Singer: the story
of a storyteller; illustrated by Penrod Scofield.
Dutton 1984 149p il (Jewish biography series)
$13.95 (6 and up)   92
1. Authors, American 2. Jews—Biography
ISBN 0-525-67156-0   LC 84-10271
"Lodestar books"
The author "traces Singer's life from the shtetls of Poland, through the ghettos of Warsaw, to his life in the United States where he found literary acceptance and financial
reward. . . . An author who received little notice or recognition until he was in his 40s, he eventually went on to receive the Nobel Prize for literature." Booklist
"Kresh gives full and balanced coverage to personal and
literary aspects of Singer's life . . . writing in a straightforward, capable style. A divided bibliography of Singer's writings is provided." Bull Cent Child Books

Sitting Bull, Dakota Chief, 1831-1890

Bruchac, Joseph. A boy called Slow: the true
story of Sitting Bull; illustrated by Rocco
Baviera. Philomel Bks. 1994 unp il $15.95
(1-3)   92
1. Dakota Indians
ISBN 0-399-22692-3   LC 93-21233

The author "recounts the early years of the young Lakota
boy who grows from an unprepossessing child named
'Slow,' to a youth whose careful and deliberate actions bring
honor to the name, to a young warrior whose courage in de-
feating the Crow earns him his father's vision name Ta-
tan'ka Iyota'ke—Sitting Bull." Bull Cent Child Books
"Baviera's darkly atmospheric, dramatic paintings frequently feature startling bits of bright color, as in the setting
sun or a piece of sky visible through the smoke hole of a
family's tipi. The picture evoke a sense of timelessness and
distance, possessing an almost mythic quality that befits
this glimpse into history." Horn Book

Stanton, Elizabeth Cady, 1815-1902

Fritz, Jean. You want women to vote, Lizzie
Stanton? illustrated by DyAnne DiSalvo-Ryan.
Putnam 1995 88p il $15.95 (2-4)   92
1. Feminism 2. Women—Suffrage
ISBN 0-399-22786-5   LC 94-30018
This is a biography of the 19th century feminist and ad-
vocate of women's suffrage
"With remarkable clarity, sensitivity, and momentum,
Fritz has captured—but never imprisoned [Stanton's] spirit
in an accessible, fascinating portrait." Horn Book
Includes bibliography

Stevenson, James, 1929-

Stevenson, James. Fun, no fun. Greenwillow
Bks. 1994 unp il $14; lib bdg $13.93 (k-2)
                                                        92
1. Authors, American 2. Illustrators
ISBN 0-688-11673-6; 0-688-11674-4 (lib bdg)
                                              LC 93-18187
"An autobiographical picture book revealing the events
of childhood during the 1930's that were fun and not so
fun. Today's children may identify some of the events while
others may raise their curiosity. The thinly washed watercolors combined with muted shades add to the time period
of the story. A perfect choice to encourage children to begin
their own autobiography and share the ups-and-downs of
life." Child Book Rev Serv

Stevenson, James. Higher on the door.
Greenwillow Bks. 1987 unp il $11.75; lib bdg
$11.88 (k-2)   92
1. Authors, American 2. Illustrators
ISBN 0-688-06636-4; 0-688-06637-2 (lib bdg)
                                              LC 86-14925
This is "Stevenson's recollection of growing up in a small
town not too far from New York City." Booklist
"The vigor of the remembrance is in the paintings. The
artist's strokes of color are unaffected and abstract: mere
blots of paint represent children in one context and entire
forests in another. There is humor and the tender irony of
hindsight. . . . Stevenson touches on the color-filled moments of childhood that are at once particular and universal." Publ Wkly

Stevenson, James. July. Greenwillow Bks.
1990 unp il $12.95; lib bdg $12.88 (k-2)
                                                        92
1. Authors, American 2. Illustrators
ISBN 0-688-08822-8; 0-688-08823-6 (lib bdg)
                                              LC 88-37584
The author "looks back to when, as a boy, he and his
brother happily spent the month of July with their grandparents, who lived near the beach." Booklist
"This book of gentle reminiscence combines past yet

Stevenson, James, 1929——*Continued*
timeless joys into one perfect summer memory. . . . This lovingly executed book avoids heavy nostalgia by skillfully evoking universal pleasures of the season. Soft, evocative watercolors capture various moods with minimum detail but maximum emotional impact. With a few splashes and lines of color, Stevenson reveals the pure exuberance of racing bicycles along the boardwalk." SLJ

Stevenson, James. When I was nine. Greenwillow Bks. 1986 unp il $14; lib bdg $13.93 (k-2)   92

1. Authors, American 2. Illustrators
ISBN 0-688-05942-2; 0-688-05943-0 (lib bdg)
                                                  LC 85-9777
"An autobiographical snippet from the prolific children's writer and cartoonist for The New Yorker. The illustrations are graceful watercolor washes—slightly faded, too, like memories. The spare text, about everyday life when he was a boy and then a special vacation trip to New Mexico, is wry and haunting." N Y Times Book Rev

Stowe, Harriet Beecher, 1811-1896

Fritz, Jean. Harriet Beecher Stowe and the Beecher preachers. Putnam 1994 144p il $16.95 (5 and up)   92

1. Beecher family 2. Women authors 3. Authors, American 4. Abolitionists
ISBN 0-399-22666-4   LC 93-6408
This is a biography of the abolitionist author of "Uncle Tom's Cabin," with an emphasis on the influence of her preacher father and her family on her life and work
"Written with vivacity and insight, this readable and engrossing biography is an important contribution to women's history as well as to the history of American letters." Horn Book
Includes bibliography

Tchaikovsky, Peter Ilich, 1840-1893

Thompson, Wendy. Pyotr Ilyich Tchaikovsky. Viking 1993 48p il music (Composer's world) $17.99 (5 and up)   92

1. Composers
ISBN 0-670-84476-4   LC 92-85503
This describes Tchaikovsky's life, work, and times, illustrated with historical paintings and drawings and musical excerpts
"The information is accurate and complete." SLJ
Includes glossary

Venezia, Mike. Peter Tchaikovsky; written and illustrated by Mike Venezia. Childrens Press 1994 32p il (Getting to know the world's greatest composers) lib bdg $18.60; pa $5.95 (k-3)   92

1. Composers
ISBN 0-516-04537-7 (lib bdg); 0-516-04537-7 (pa)
                                                  LC 94-9479
Introduces the nineteenth-century Russian composer of Swan Lake and the 1812 Overture through brief text, photographs, art reproductions, and the author's cartoons

Tecumseh, Shawnee Chief, 1768-1813

Shorto, Russell. Tecumseh and the dream of an American Indian nation; written by Russell Shorto; introduction by Alvin M. Josephy, Jr.; illustrations by Tim Sisco. Silver Burdett Press 1989 123p il maps (Alvin Josephy's biography series of American Indians) lib bdg $12.95; pa $7.95 (5 and up)   92

1. Shawnee Indians
ISBN 0-382-09569-3 (lib bdg); 0-382-09758-0 (pa)
                                                  LC 88-32656
A biography of the Shawnee warrior, orator, and leader who united a confederacy of Indians in an effort to save Indian land from the advance of white soldiers and settlers
Includes bibliography

Thaxter, Celia Laighton, 1835-1894

Krupinski, Loretta. Celia's island journal; written by Celia Thaxter; adapted and illustrated by Loretta Krupinski. Little, Brown 1992 unp $15.95 (k-3)   92

1. Isles of Shoals (Me. and N.H.)
ISBN 0-316-83921-3   LC 91-26707
Adaptation of: Among the Isles of Shoals by Celia Thaxter first published 1873
"When nineteenth-century poet Celia Thaxter was a child, she lived on an island off the coast of New Hampshire, where her father was the lighthouse keeper. There, with her young brother, she explored the rocky surfaces, watched the tidal pools, relished the seasons, and became an astute observer of nature. Thaxter kept her childhood impressions in a journal, describing her days so keenly that other children can share them today. The journal excerpts are bordered by island birds and plants; facing pages interpret the isolation and beauty in the family's life." Adventuring with Books

Thoreau, Henry David, 1817-1862

Reef, Catherine. Henry David Thoreau; a neighbor to nature; illustrated by Larry Raymond. 21st Cent. Bks. (NY) 1992 72p il (Earth keepers) lib bdg $14.95 (4 and up)   92

1. Authors, American 2. Naturalists
ISBN 0-941477-39-8   LC 91-19779
Describes the life of the author who came to value the natural world and whose writings have influenced and inspired others concerning nature
This is "nicely drawn and organized. . . . Highly readable." SLJ
Includes glossary

Thorpe, Jim, 1888-1953

Lipsyte, Robert. Jim Thorpe, 20th-century jock. HarperCollins Pubs. 1993 103p il (Superstar lineup) $14; lib bdg $13.89; pa $3.95 (5 and up)   92

1. Athletes 2. Indians of North America—Biography
ISBN 0-06-022988-8; 0-06-022989-6 (lib bdg); 0-06-446141-6 (pa)   LC 92-44069

Thorpe, Jim, 1888-1953—*Continued*
A biography of the American Indian known as one of the best all-round athletes for his accomplishments as an Olympic medal winner and as an outstanding professional football and baseball player

"Involving and thought provoking, the account has wide applicability across curriculum lines, and it will fill a number of current information needs in the areas of biography, sports, Native Americans, and race relations." Booklist
Includes bibliography

Toulouse-Lautrec, Henri de, 1864-1901
Venezia, Mike. Henri de Toulouse-Lautrec; written and illustrated by Mike Venezia; consultant, Meg Moss. Childrens Press 1995 32p il (Getting to know the world's greatest artists) lib bdg $18.60; pa $5.95 (k-3)   **92**
1. Artists, French
ISBN 0-516-02283-0 (lib bdg); 0-516-42283-9 (pa)
LC 94-36348
This introduction to the life and work of Toulouse-Lautrec includes full-color reproductions of his works

Traylor, Bill, 1856-1947
Lyons, Mary E. Deep blues: Bill Traylor, self-taught artist. Scribner 1994 42p il (African-American artists and artisans) $15.95 (4 and up)   **92**
1. African American artists
ISBN 0-684-19458-9   LC 93-23736
This illustrated "biography explores the life of folk artist Bill Traylor, who in 1856 was born into slavery in Alabama. By the time he died, at the age of ninety-three, he had not only learned to write his name but had created over one thousand pieces of art that reflect his vision of the world." Horn Book
Includes bibliographical references

Truman, Harry S., 1884-1972
Fleming, Thomas J. Harry S Truman, president; [by] Thomas Fleming. Walker & Co. 1993 136p il (Presidential biography series) $14.95; lib bdg $15.85 (5 and up)
          92
1. Presidents—United States
ISBN 0-8027-8267-1; 0-8027-8269-8 (lib bdg)
LC 93-153
A biography of the thirty-third president of the United States
This "is a well-researched, clearly organized biography. Fleming provides a fascinating portrait of Truman's political life as well as insights into his personal life." Voice Youth Advocates
Includes bibliography

Truth, Sojourner, d. 1883
Adler, David A. A picture book of Sojourner Truth; illustrated by Gershom Griffith. Holiday House 1994 unp il $15.95 (1-3)   **92**
1. African American women 2. Abolitionists 3. Feminism
ISBN 0-8234-1072-2   LC 93-7478

An introduction to the life of the woman born into slavery who became a well-known abolitionist and crusader for the rights of African Americans in the United States
The author "portrays his subject in a realistic manner, discussing slavery and other issues in an easy-to-read style. The quotes, while undocumented, are simple enough for the target audience and help to place events in context. Excellent-quality watercolor illustrations capture the action and provide effective representations and details of the time period." SLJ

Ferris, Jeri. Walking the road to freedom: a story about Sojourner Truth; illustrations by Peter E. Hanson. Carolrhoda Bks. 1988 64p il (Carolrhoda creative minds book) lib bdg $15.95; pa $5.95 (3-5)   **92**
1. African American women 2. Feminism 3. Abolitionists
ISBN 0-87614-318-4 (lib bdg); 0-87614-505-5 (pa)
LC 87-18277
"Truth, born into slavery in New York in about 1797, survived several wrenching sales as a child. Securing her freedom, she determined to 'walk up and down the land, telling others about God's goodness.' She sang and spoke out against slavery and in support of women's rights throughout the Midwest, becoming well known and widely respected. . . . Hanson's [illustrations] are more impressionistic, with muted backgrounds." Booklist

Macht, Norman L. (Norman Lee). Sojourner Truth. Chelsea Jrs. 1992 79p il (Junior world biographies) $14.95 (4 and up)   **92**
1. African American women 2. Feminism 3. Abolitionists
ISBN 0-7910-1754-0   LC 91-37268
A biography of the former slave who became an outspoken antislavery and women's rights activist in the United States
Includes bibliographical references

McKissack, Patricia C. Sojourner Truth; a voice for freedom; [by] Patricia and Fredrick McKissack; illustrated by Michael Bryant. Enslow Pubs. 1992 32p il (Great African Americans) lib bdg $12.95 (1-3)   **92**
1. African American women 2. Feminism 3. Abolitionists
ISBN 0-89490-313-6   LC 92-6190
Describes the life of the anti-slavery and women's rights activist, from her beginnings in slavery to her tireless campaign for the rights and welfare of the freedmen
"Short sentences, large, well-spaced text, and a blend of black-and-white photographs and sketches. . . . [This] will give an overview of that great woman's achievements." SLJ
Includes glossary

McKissack, Patricia C. Sojourner Truth: ain't I a woman? [by] Patricia C. McKissack and Fredrick McKissack. Scholastic 1992 186p il $13.95; pa $3.50 (5 and up)   **92**
1. African American women 2. Feminism 3. Abolitionists
ISBN 0-590-44690-8; 0-590-44691-6 (pa)
LC 91-45988

Truth, Sojourner, d. 1883—*Continued*

A biography of the former slave who became well-known as an abolitionist and advocate of women's rights

This "is a great deal more than a biography of a remarkable woman. The forceful narrative also offers a startling portrayal of a pivotal yet appalling era in American history." Publ Wkly

Includes bibliography

Tubman, Harriet, 1815?-1913

Adler, David A. A picture book of Harriet Tubman; illustrated by Samuel Byrd. Holiday House 1992 unp il $15.95; pa $5.95 (1-3)

92

1. African American women 2. Underground railroad
ISBN 0-8234-0926-0; 0-8234-1065-X (pa)
LC 91-19628

Biography of the black woman who escaped from slavery to become famous as a conductor on the Underground Railroad

This book features "brief, easy-to-read text, , , , Byrd's appealing, colorful illustrations convey the quiet dignity of a brave heroine." Booklist

Burns, Bree. Harriet Tubman. Chelsea Jrs. 1992 80p il (Junior world biographies) $13.95 (4 and up)

92

1. African American women 2. Underground railroad
ISBN 0-7910-1751-6
LC 91-28383

A biography of the Afro-American woman best known for her work with the Underground Railroad, describing her childhood as a slave, her escape to the North, her work during the Civil War, and more

Includes bibliographical references

Elish, Dan. Harriet Tubman and the Underground Railroad. Millbrook Press 1993 32p il (Gateway civil rights) lib bdg $13.40; pa $4.95 (3-5)

92

1. African American women 2. Underground railroad
ISBN 1-56294-273-5 (lib bdg); 1-56294-791-5 (pa)
LC 92-9562

A biography of the African American woman who escaped from slavery, led slaves to freedom on the Underground Railroad, aided Northern troops during the Civil War, and worked for women's suffrage

Includes bibliographical references

Ferris, Jeri. Go free or die: a story about Harriet Tubman; illustrations by Karen Ritz. Carolrhoda Bks. 1988 63p il (Carolrhoda creative minds book) $17.50; pa $5.95 (3-5)

92

1. African American women 2. Underground railroad
ISBN 0-87614-317-6; 0-87614-504-7 (pa)
LC 87-18279

This is "the story of Harriet Tubman, born a slave in Maryland in 1820. Fiercely determined to 'go free or die,' Tubman, aided by the Quakers, mastered the intricate maneuvering of the Underground Railroad, and from 1850 to 1861 made 19 trips leading more than 300 slaves to freedom, never losing one. Using a clear direct style, Ferris does not dwell on the brutal injustices . . . but rather on [her] against-all-odds perseverance to fight for equal rights. Ritz' illustrations have a haunting antique-photo quality." Booklist

Turner, Nat, 1800?-1831

Barrett, Tracy. Nat Turner and the slave revolt. Millbrook Press 1993 32p il (Gateway civil rights) lib bdg $13.40; pa $4.95 (3-5)

92

1. African Americans—Biography 2. Slavery—United States
ISBN 1-56294-275-1 (lib bdg); 1-56294-792-3 (pa)
LC 92-12086

This book "recounts Turner's life as slave-turned-revolutionary. . . . Barrett attempts to place the event in its historical context in a concise, noninflammatory text." Booklist

Includes bibliography

Tutankhamen, King of Egypt

Sabuda, Robert. Tutankhamen's gift; written and illustrated by Robert Sabuda. Atheneum Pubs. 1994 unp il $15.95 (k-3)

92

1. Egypt Antiquities
ISBN 0-689-31818-9
LC 93-5401

"His tutor foresees that little Tutankhamen's 'gift for the gods' will someday be revealed. That day comes sooner than expected, when the young boy becomes pharaoh after his brother's death and rebuilds the beautiful temples created by his father and destroyed by his brother. Bold pictures outlined in black against a background of painted, handmade Egyptian papyrus illustrate the book, and an afterword provides historical details." Horn Book Guide

Twain, Mark, 1835-1910

Collins, David R. Mark T-W-A-I-N! a story about Samuel Clemens; illustrations by Vicky Carey. Carolrhoda Bks. 1994 63p il (Carolrhoda creative minds book) lib bdg $17.50; pa $5.95 (3-5)

92

1. Authors, American
ISBN 0-87614-801-1 (lib bdg); 0-87614-640-X (ps)
LC 93-15164

Covers the life of the famed nineteenth-century author from his childhood in Hannibal, Missouri, through his careers as journalist, riverboat pilot, soldier, prospector, and humorist

"Although the intended audience will be too young to have read Clemens' works, this is a lively biography that may well draw readers to them. Illustrated with charcoal drawings and appended with a bibliography and a list of Clemens' writings." Booklist

Uchida, Yoshiko, 1921-1992

Uchida, Yoshiko. The invisible thread. Messner 1991 136p il (In my own words) $12.95 (5 and up)

92

1. Authors, American 2. Japanese Americans—Biography 3. Women authors
ISBN 0-671-74164-0
LC 91-12398

Children's author, Yoshiko Uchida, describes growing up in Berkeley, California, as a Nisei, second generation Japanese American, and her family's internment in a Nevada concentration camp during World War II

The author "writes with mastery of style and an implicit respect for her readers." Bull Cent Child Books

Includes bibliography

Valentine, Saint

Sabuda, Robert. Saint Valentine; retold and illustrated by Robert Sabuda. Atheneum Pubs. 1992 unp il $14.95 (1-3)   92

1. Christian saints
ISBN 0-689-31762-X   LC 91-25012

Recounts an incident in the life of St. Valentine, a physician who lived some 200 years after Christ, in which he treated a small child for blindness

"The fluid, straightforward retelling of the legend is accompanied by evocative, mosaiclike illustrations created from colored cut paper. Varying sizes of illustrations, careful page placement, and effective use of white space create the impression of the large-scale period mosaics. A fine melding of text and art." SLJ

Van Meter, Victoria, 1982-

Van Meter, Victoria. Taking flight; my story; by Vicki Van Meter with Dan Gutman. Viking 1995 134p il maps $14.99 (4 and up)   92

1. Women air pilots
ISBN 0-670-86260-6   LC 94-44067

"This is the story of Vicki Van Meter, a 10-year-old girl who learned to fly airplanes. It reviews her experience in ground school and flight training. Deciding to fly across the United States, starting from Augusta, Maine, she accomplishes the feat in three days, becoming the youngest girl to do so. She recounts modestly her experiences as a celebrity. . . . The book should be of considerable interest to girls of Vicki's age, showing what it is possible for youth to accomplish, albeit with a great deal of parental support." Sci Books Films

Verne, Jules, 1828-1905

Teeters, Peggy. Jules Verne; the man who invented tomorrow. Walker & Co. 1992 120p il $13.95; lib bdg $14.85 (4 and up)   92

1. Authors, French
ISBN 0-8027-8189-6; 0-8027-8191-8 (lib bdg)
                                            LC 92-35457

Examines the life and work of the nineteenth-century French writer whose fantastic novels took his readers to all of the places he had dreamed about as a young boy

"Teeters rightfully pays tribute to her subject's remarkable prescience: technological and scientific wonders that he foretold over a century ago have become or are emerging as today's commonplaces. Black-and-white photographs and sketches complement the text." Adventuring with Books

Includes bibliographical references

Villa, Pancho, 1878-1923

O'Brien, Steven. Pancho Villa. Chelsea House 1994 111p il (Hispanics of achievement) lib bdg $18.95 (5 and up)   92

1. Mexico—History
ISBN 0-7910-1257-3   LC 93-37890

The author "handles the life and lifestyle of Villa, one of Mexico's controversial, legendary heroes, in a candid and unbiased manner. Illustrated with black-and-white photographs, the biography of this revolutionary is an enjoyable, readable, welcome addition." Horn Book Guide

Includes bibliography

Wagner, Honus, 1874-1955

Kavanagh, Jack. Honus Wagner; introduction by Jim Murray. Chelsea House 1994 64p il (Baseball legends) $14.95 (4 and up)   92

1. Baseball—Biography
ISBN 0-7910-1193-3   LC 91-28898

A biography of the Pittsburgh Pirates shortstop who was one of the greatest hitters and fielders in baseball history

This biography includes "enough statistics, baseball history, and black-and-white photographs to satisfy any fan of the game." Horn Book Guide

Includes bibliographical references

Walker, Madame C. J., 1867-1919

McKissack, Patricia C. Madam C.J. Walker; self-made millionaire; [by] Patricia and Fredrick McKissack; series consultant: Russell L. Adams; illustrations by Michael Bryant. Enslow Pubs. 1992 32p il (Great African Americans) $12.95 (1-3)   92

1. African American business people
ISBN 0-89490-311-X   LC 92-6189

Describes the life of the black laundress who founded a cosmetics company and became the first female self-made millionaire in the United States

Wang, Ya-ni, 1975-

Cheng, Chen-sun. A young painter; the life and paintings of Wang Yani—China's extraordinary young artist; by Zheng Zhensun and Alice Low; photographs by Zheng Zhensun; introduction by Jan Stuart. Scholastic 1991 80p il map $17.95 (4 and up)   92

1. Child artists
ISBN 0-590-44906-0   LC 90-29319

"A Byron Preiss/New China Pictures book"

Examines the life and works of the young Chinese girl who started painting animals at the age of three and in her teens became the youngest artist to have a one-person show at the Smithsonian Institution

"Admiring but not hyperbolic, the text gives a rounded picture of the artist as a person and discusses her work in great detail; it is illustrated by color photographs of Yani and myriad reproductions of her paintings." Bull Cent Child Books

Includes glossary

Washington, Booker T., 1856-1915

McKissack, Patricia C. Booker T. Washington; leader and educator; [by] Patricia and Fredrick McKissack; illustrated by Michael Bryant. Enslow Pubs. 1992 32p il (Great African Americans) lib bdg $12.95 (1-3)   92

1. Tuskegee Institute 2. African American educators
ISBN 0-89490-314-4   LC 92-5356

A biography of the former slave who founded Tuskegee University and later became the most powerful African American leader at the turn of the century

Washington, George, 1732-1799

Giblin, James. George Washington; a picture book biography; by James Cross Giblin; illustrated by Michael Dooling. Scholastic 1992 48p il map $14.95 (k-3)
92

1. Presidents—United States
ISBN 0-590-42550-1 LC 91-16614
Examines the family life and career of the first American president, also discussing myths and legends, monuments to Washington, and Mount Vernon
This "simplified yet well-rounded portrait of Washington offers considerable insight into the private man. . . . The appealingly informal text is laced with engaging details. . . . Sharing the credit for the book's success are Dooling's vivid, beautifully textured oil paintings, which add drama to the story of this modest, fair and ultimately devoted man." Publ Wkly

Meltzer, Milton. George Washington and the birth of our nation. Watts 1986 188p il maps lib bdg $15.33 (5 and up) 92

1 Presidents United States
ISBN 0-531-10253-X LC 86-9222
A biography of our first President, from his growing-up years in Virginia to his death at Mount Vernon
This "is a competently written and carefully documented book, well illustrated with reproductions of historic art, manuscript pages, and maps." Bull Cent Child Books
Includes bibliographical references

Osborne, Mary Pope. George Washington; leader of a new nation. Dial Bks. for Young Readers 1991 117p il map lib bdg $13.89 (4-6)
92

1. Presidents—United States
ISBN 0-8037-0949-8 LC 90-42601
A biography of our first President, illustrated with old prints, maps, and photographs
"This very fine biography of Washington gives a clear picture of the man and his achievements. Osborne covers both his personal and public life in straightforward, easy-to-understand chronological order, providing plenty of background information. . . . The real strength of this book, however, is its excellent use of primary sources. . . . High quality black-and-white reproductions of period artwork and a spacious layout help make this an excellent introduction to Washington and the early years of the United States." SLJ
Includes bibliography

Washington, Mary Ball, 1708-1789

Fritz, Jean. George Washington's mother; illustrated by DyAnne DiSalvo-Ryan. Grosset & Dunlap 1992 48p il $7.99; pa $3.50 (1-3)
92

1. Washington, George, 1732-1799
ISBN 0-448-40385-4; 0-448-40384-6 (pa)
LC 91-34247
"All aboard reading"
Describes the life of the mother of our first president and her relationship with her children
"Fritz brings the excitement of history to newly independent readers. . . . Using factual data and funny incidents, the author humorously depicts Mary Ball Washington as a manipulative and stubborn worrywart. The numerous, half- and full-page, pencil-and-watercolor illustrations . . . complement the text and extend the humor." SLJ

Wheatley, Phillis, 1753-1784

Sherrow, Victoria. Phyllis Wheatley. Chelsea Jrs. 1992 80p il $14.95 (4 and up) 92

1. Poets, American 2. African American authors 3. Women poets
ISBN 0-7910-1753-2 LC 91-12767
The life of the woman who, although a slave, gained renown throughout the colonies as the first important black American poet
Includes bibliographical references

White, E. B. (Elwyn Brooks), 1899-1985

Gherman, Beverly. E. B. White; some writer! Atheneum Pubs. 1992 136p il $13.95; pa $4.95 (5 and up) 92

1. Authors, American
ISBN 0-689-31672-0; 0-688-12826-2 (pa)
LC 91-19012
Describes the life of the popular author of poems, essays, short stories for adults, and books for children
"Written with respect for both the subject and the audience, Gherman's biography is meticulously researched and documented, with notes for every one of the numerous quotations and with a generous bibliography that includes primary sources. She has struck an easy balance between discussions of work and of personal life, as well as between descriptions of early and later years." Bull Cent Child Books

White, Ryan

White, Ryan. Ryan White: my own story; by Ryan White and Ann Marie Cunningham. Dial Bks. 1991 277p il $16.95 (5 and up)
92

1. AIDS (Disease)—Personal narratives
ISBN 0-8037-0977-3 LC 90-21038
Also available in paperback from New Am. Lib.
Ryan White describes how he got AIDS, engaged in a legal battle to return to school, and became a celebrity and spokesman for issues concerning the deadly disease
The book contains "surprising snatches of humor and insight that lend dimension to the vulnerable young man whose positive outlook shines through so clearly. Not saccharine, not angry, not bitter, this unusual book, delivered without an ounce of self-pity, seems as honest as it is inspiring. It will touch both adults and teens." Booklist

White, Walter Francis, 1893-1955

Jakoubek, Robert E. Walter White and the power of organized protest. Millbrook Press 1994 32p il (Gateway civil rights) lib bdg $13.40; pa $4.95 (3-5) 92

1. African Americans—Biography 2. African Americans—Civil rights
ISBN 1-56294-378-2 (lib bdg); 1-56294-697-8 (pa)
LC 93-8715
Relates the details of the life and career of the African American reporter and civil rights activist who became secretary of the NAACP
White's "story is told in a straightforward manner. Black-and-white photographs add needed depth and texture." SLJ
Includes bibliography

Whitman, Walt, 1819-1892

Loewen, Nancy. Walt Whitman; text by Nancy Loewen; illustrations by Rob Day. Creative Educ. 1994 45p il (Voices in poetry) $16.95 (5 and up) **92**

1. Poets, American
ISBN 1-56846-096-1   LC 93-15081

"In this combination of poetry, history, and photography, a dozen selections from Whitman's *Leaves of Grass* are juxtaposed with brief biographical vignettes. . . . A carefully crafted volume whose majestic poems, intelligent text, and period illustrations have timeless and ageless appeal." SLJ

Includes bibliographical references

Wiesel, Elie, 1928-

Pariser, Michael. Elie Wiesel; bearing witness. Millbrook Press 1994 48p il (Gateway biography) lib bdg $13.40; pa $6.95 (3-5)
92

1. Authors, French 2. Jews—Biography 3. Holocaust, 1933-1945
ISBN 1-56294-419-3; 1-56294-743-5 (pa)
                LC 93-37126

An account of Wiesel's life as a concentration camp inmate as well as his liberation by Allied forces and his subsequent career as journalist, author, speaker and political activist

Includes bibliographical references

Wilder, Laura Ingalls, 1867-1957

Anderson, William T. Laura Ingalls Wilder; a biography; by William Anderson. HarperCollins Pubs. 1992 240p il $16; lib bdg 15.89; pa $5.95 (4 and up) **92**

1. Authors, American 2. Frontier and pioneer life
3. Women authors
ISBN 0-06-020113-4; 0-06-020114-2 (lib bdg);
0-06-446103-3 (pa)   LC 91-33805

A biography of the writer whose pioneer life on the American prairie became the basis for her "Little House" books

"A readable biography that is easily accessible to middle grade children who are likely to read the Little House books. Particularly interesting are the sections that fill in the gaps in Wilder's stories." Booklist

Wilder, Laura Ingalls. West from home; letters of Laura Ingalls Wilder to Almanzo Wilder, San Francisco, 1915; edited by Roger Lea MacBride; historical setting by Margot Patterson Doss. Harper & Row 1974 124p il $15; lib bdg $14.89; pa $3.95 (6 and up)

92

1. San Francisco (Calif.)—Description 2. Authors, American 3. Women authors
ISBN 0-06-024110-1; 0-06-024111-X (lib bdg);
0-06-440081-6 (pa)   LC 73-14342

This collection is "edited from letters sent to her beloved husband while Laura spent two months in late 1915 visiting their daughter and immersing herself in the sights of bustling San Francisco and the exciting Panama-Pacific Exposition. Wilder readers of all ages will lose themselves in this trip—the adults with nostalgia and wholesome pleasure, the youth with wonder and awe over the sights vividly described in her inimitable combination of homespun literary and journalistic styles." Child Book Rev Serv

Wilson, Edith Bolling Galt, 1872-1961

Giblin, James. Edith Wilson: the woman who ran the United States; by James Cross Giblin; illustrated by Michele Laporte. Viking 1992 52p il (Women of our time) $11; pa $3.99 (4 and up) **92**

1. Wilson, Woodrow, 1856-1924 2. Presidents—United States—Spouses
ISBN 0-670-83005-4; 0-14-034249-4 (pa)
                LC 91-42265

A biography of the First Lady who gave vital support to her husband, President Woodrow Wilson, and to the nation during and after World War I

"For reports or pleasure reading, this simply written, well-organized volume captures this remarkable woman's personality and contributions to society." SLJ

Wood, Grant, 1892-1942

Venezia, Mike. Grant Wood; written and illustrated by Mike Venezia. Childrens Press 1995 32p il (Getting to know the world's greatest artists) lib bdg $18.60; pa $5.95 (k-3)
92

1. Artists, American
ISBN 0-516-02284-9 (lib bdg); 0-516-42284-7 (pa)
                LC 95-7023

Relates the artistic career of the Iowan who painted people, life, and customs of the American Midwest and whose style became known as Regionalism

Wright, Orville, 1871-1948

Freedman, Russell. The Wright brothers: how they invented the airplane; with original photographs by Wilbur and Orville Wright. Holiday House 1991 129p il $18.95; pa $9.95 (5 and up) **92**

1. Wright, Wilbur, 1867-1912 2. Aeronautics—History
ISBN 0-8234-0875-2; 0-8234-1082-X (pa)
                LC 90-48440

A Newbery Medal honor book, 1992

In this "combination of photography and text, Freedman reveals the frustrating, exciting, and ultimately successful journey of these two brothers from their bicycle shop in Dayton, Ohio, to their Kitty Hawk flights and beyond. . . . An essential purchase for younger YAs." Voice Youth Advocates

Includes bibliography

Parker, Steve. The Wright brothers and aviation. Chelsea House 1995 32p il (Science discoveries) $13.95 (4 and up) **92**

1. Wright, Wilbur, 1867-1912 2. Aeronautics—History
ISBN 0-7910-3013-X   LC 94-25254

This illustrated biography looks at the personal achievements of the Wright Brothers and their pioneering work in aeronautics

Wright, Wilbur, 1867-1912

Freedman, Russell. The Wright brothers: how they invented the airplane. See entry under Wright, Orville, 1871-1948

Parker, Steve. The Wright brothers and aviation. See entry under Wright, Orville, 1871-1948

Yeager, Chuck, 1923-

Levinson, Nancy Smiler. Chuck Yeager: the man who broke the sound barrier; a science biography. Walker & Co. 1988 133p il $13.95; lib bdg $14.85 (5 and up)   92

1. Air pilots
ISBN 0-8027-6781-8; 0-8027-6799-0 (lib bdg)
LC 87-25431

"Well-written text describes the boyhood, war experiences, years as a test pilot, and goals and ambitions of the then Air Force captain who first broke the sound barrier." Sci Child

Includes glossary and bibliography

Yep, Laurence

Yep, Laurence. The lost garden. Messner 1991 117p il (In my own words) $12.95; lib bdg $14.98 (5 and up)   92

1. Authors, American 2. Chinese Americans—Biography
ISBN 0-671-74160-8; 0-671-74159-4 (lib bdg)
LC 90-40647

The author describes how he grew up as a Chinese American in San Francisco and how he came to use his writing to celebrate his family and his ethnic heritage

"The writing is warm, wry, and humorous. . . . *The Lost Garden* will be welcomed as a literary autobiography for children and, more, a thoughtful probing into what it means to be an American." SLJ

Yolen, Jane

Yolen, Jane. A letter from Phoenix Farm; photographs by Jason Stemple. Owen, R.C. 1992 32p il map (Meet the author) $13.95 (1-3)   92

1. Authors, American 2. Women authors
ISBN 1-87845-036-0   LC 92-7795

An autobiographical account of the prominent author Jane Yolen and how her daily life and writing process are interwoven

"The color photos . . . have a candid snapshot quality that contributes to the friendly informality of the text." Bull Cent Child Books

Zaharias, Babe Didrikson, 1911-1956

Knudson, R. Rozanne. Babe Didrikson: athlete of the century; by R.R. Knudson; illustrated by Ted Lewin. Viking Kestrel 1985 57p il (Women of our time) hardcover o.p. paperback available $4.99 (4 and up)   92

1. Women athletes
ISBN 0-14-032095-4 (pa)   LC 84-17411

A biography, emphasizing the early years, of Babe Didrikson, who broke records in golf, track and field, and other sports, at a time when there were few opportunities for female athletes

"Knudson comes forth with all sorts of little-known information about one of the greatest athletes of this century. The book's lively, contemporary style will encourage young readers' respect for and admiration of the exuberant Babe. A pleasant addition to any library." Child Book Rev Serv

Zhang, Song Nan

Zhang, Song Nan. A little tiger in the Chinese night; an autobiography in art. Tundra Bks. 1993 48p il $19.95; pa $8.95   92

1. Artists, Chinese
ISBN 0-88776-320-0; 0-88776-356-1 (pa)

"Song Nan Zhang traces his life in China, describing an idyllic childhood after World War II; his youthful idealism during the 'Great Leap Forward,' which entailed years of hard work under harsh conditions; and the even more horrible Cultural Revolution." SLJ

"The writing is so vivid and the story so involving that it is hard to put down. Best of all, colorful, well-composed illustrations appear on nearly every spread, bringing Zhang's experiences more sharply into focus." Booklist

929 Genealogy, names, insignia

Perl, Lila

The great ancestor hunt; the fun of finding out who you are; drawings by Erika Weihs; illustrated with photographs. Clarion Bks. 1989 104p il $15.95; pa $7.95 (5 and up)   929

1. Genealogy
ISBN 0-89919-745-0; 0-395-54790-3 (pa)
LC 88-36211

The author "weaves the how-to of genealogy with a historical perspective on immigration. All the basics are covered: drawing an ancestry chart, conducting interviews with relatives, finding family memorabilia and, for those who wish to continue their quest, writing away for documentation. The format is also a plus. Interesting black-and-white photos alternate with charts, diagrams, and a few (softly executed) drawings by Erika Weihs." Booklist

Includes bibliography

929.4 Personal names

Meltzer, Milton, 1915-

A book about names; drawings by Mischa Richter. Crowell 1984 128p il lib bdg $14.89 (5 and up)   929.4

1. Personal names 2. Nicknames
ISBN 0-690-04381-3   LC 83-45241

"In which custom, tradition, law, myth, history, folklore, foolery, legend, fashion, nonsense, symbol, taboo help explain how we got our names and what they mean." Title page

"A delight for browsing. . . . Meltzer goes all over the world for his information, back and forth through history. He looks at the naming practices of Jews, native Americans, Anglo-Saxons, Chinese, Christians, famous people, the rich and the poor." Booklist

929.9 Flags

Brandt, Sue R., 1916-
State flags; including the Commonwealth of Puerto Rico. Watts 1992 63p il lib bdg $18.43; pa $6.95 (5 and up) **929.9**
1. Flags—United States
ISBN 0-531-20001-9 (lib bdg); 0-531-15630-3 (pa)
LC 92-8948
Describes the history, design, and significance of the fifty state flags
Includes bibliography

Crampton, W. G. (William G.)
Flag; written by William Crampton. Knopf 1989 63p il (Eyewitness books) $19; lib bdg $16.99 (4 and up) **929.9**
1. Flags
ISBN 0-394-82255-2; 0-394-92255-7 (lib bdg)
LC 88-27174
A photographic essay about flags from countries all over the world and such special flags as signal flags for ships and boats, flags for special festivals and sports, political flags and coats of arms. Also includes information about the meaning of shapes and colors on flags

Fisher, Leonard Everett, 1924-
Stars & stripes; our national flag; written and illustrated by Leonard Everett Fisher. Holiday House 1993 unp il $15.95 (1-3)
929.9
1. Flags—United States
ISBN 0-8234-1053-6
LC 93-20176
With the Pledge of Allegiance as accompanying text, presents various American flags and gives brief historical information about each
"In bold graphic style, with appropriately eye-catching red, white, and blue details, Fisher presents a brief, straightforward history of the U.S. flag." Booklist

Haban, Rita D.
How proudly they wave; flags of the fifty states. Lerner Publs. 1989 111p il lib bdg $23.95 (4 and up) **929.9**
1. Flags—United States
ISBN 0-8225-1799-X
LC 89-2302
"Haban presents full-color pictures of the 50 state flags. . . . Two-page descriptions explain who designed the flag, what the design means, and when each flag was officially adopted. . . . A glossary lists flag-related terms, and an accompanying diagram shows the parts of a flag. An enormously useful reference source for both school and public librarians." Booklist

930 History of ancient world

The **Visual** dictionary of ancient civilizations. Dorling Kindersley 1994 64p il map (Eyewitness visual dictionaries) $15.95 (4 and up) **930**
1. Ancient civilization
ISBN 1-56458-701-0
LC 94-8395

Labeled illustrations and text briefly describe ancient artifacts and civilizations of the world. Timelines are included

930.1 Archaeology

Anderson, Joan
From map to museum; uncovering mysteries of the past; photographed by George Ancona; introduction by David Hurst Thomas. Morrow Junior Bks. 1988 63p il maps $12.95; lib bdg $12.88 (5 and up)
930.1
1. Indians of North America—Antiquities 2. Archeology
ISBN 0-688-06914-2; 0-688-06915-0 (lib bdg)
LC 87-31307
"An enjoyable, informative photo essay about the exploration of the site of a Spanish mission off the coast of Georgia enhances the reader's understanding of the relationship between museums and archaeology. Includes an introduction by the archaeologist responsible for the find." Sci Child
Includes glossary

Avi-Yonah, Michael, 1904-1974
Dig this! how archaeologists uncover our past. Runestone Press 1993 96p il (Buried worlds) lib bdg $22.95 (5 and up) **930.1**
1. Archeology 2. Ancient civilization
ISBN 0-8225-3200-X
LC 92-28305
Discusses methods of archaeological excavations, ancient civilizations, the history of archaeology, and pioneers in the field
"The attractive and informative volume features interesting black-and-white and crisp color photographs." Booklist
Includes glossary

Early humans. Knopf 1989 63p il maps (Eyewitness books) $19; lib bdg $20.99 (4 and up) **930.1**
1. Prehistoric man 2. Ancient civilization
ISBN 0-394-82257-9; 0-394-92257-3 (lib bdg)
LC 88-13431
Also available Spanish language edition
Text and photographs present a description of early humans: their origins; their tools and weapons; how they hunted and foraged for food; and the role of family life, money, religion, and magic
"The book is beautifully illustrated, with a paragraph of text at the beginning of each two-page section and an explanatory caption for each artifact pictured. The 25 sections range in topic from the toolmakers to the first artists to bronzeworking." Sci Books Films

Getz, David
Frozen man; illustrated by Peter McCarty. Holt & Co. 1994 68p il maps $14.95 (5 and up) **930.1**
1. Archeology 2. Prehistoric man 3. Mummies
ISBN 0-8050-3261-4
LC 94-9109
"A Redfeather book"

Getz, David—_Continued_

"This is an account of the mummified stone-age corpse who was found in Austria in 1991. . . . Getz's generally well-organized information and smooth exposition makes the effort to understand the Iceman, as this book calls him, into an intriguing detective story. This could well stimulate the interest of kids who didn't think they liked science or archeology. Black-and-white drawings include useful maps and diagrams." Bull Cent Child Books

Includes glossary and bibliography

Hackwell, W. John

Digging to the past: excavations in ancient lands. Scribner 1986 50p il $14.95 (4 and up)
930.1

1. Archeology 2. Ancient civilization
ISBN 0-684-18692-6   LC 86-13115

The author "describes the painstaking process of excavating clues to the past. He sets his story in the Middle East, and outlines the participants, the hardships, the excitement, and the satisfaction. . . . The book includes archeological vocabulary defined in context." Appraisal

"Although this has the horizontal shape of a picture book and is chock-full of handsome full-color and black-and-white illustrations, Hackwell's introduction to archaeology is actually quite sophisticated." Booklist

Lauber, Patricia, 1924-

Tales mummies tell; illustrated with photographs. Crowell 1985 118p il lib bdg $15.89 (5 and up)   **930.1**

1. Mummies 2. Archeology
ISBN 0-690-04389-9   LC 83-46172

"Lauber describes the various ways, intentional or accidental, that animals and human beings have become mummies, and she discusses the various ways (carbon-14 dating, x-rays, analysis of body tissue and stomach contents) that scientists use to establish facts about the individual or the culture or changes over the centuries. Clearly written and well-organized, this is an informative and eminently readable text." Bull Cent Child Books

Includes bibliography

Lessem, Don

The iceman. Crown 1994 32p il maps $14; lib bdg $15.75 (4-6)   **930.1**

1. Archeology 2. Prehistoric man 3. Mummies
ISBN 0-517-59596-6; 0-517-59597-4 (lib bdg)
LC 93-31534

"This is a story of the remarkable discovery of a man who, more than 5,000 years ago, was frozen in an Alpine glacier along with his tools and weapons. Full-page, color photographs accompany a high-interest narrative that will surely captivate even the most reluctant readers." Sci Child

McIntosh, Jane

Archeology; written by Jane McIntosh. Knopf 1994 63p il (Eyewitness books) $19; lib bdg $20.99 (4 and up)   **930.1**

1. Archeology
ISBN 0-679-86572-1; 0-679-96572-6 (lib bdg)
LC 94-9378

"A Dorling Kindersley book"

This volume "touches on aspects of archaeology in many locations around the world. Each double-page spread exam-

ines one or two concepts: preservation and decay, excavation, clues to the past, human remains, fakes and forgeries, etc. . . . Readers are not likely to use this book for research, but will want to make repeated short visits." SLJ

931   China to 420 A.D.

Cotterell, Arthur

Ancient China; written by Arthur Cotterell; photographed by Alan Hills & Geoff Brightling. Knopf 1994 63p il maps (Eyewitness books) $19; lib bdg $20.99 (4 and up)   **931**

1. China—Civilization
ISBN 0-679-86167-X; 0-679-96167-4 (lib bdg)
LC 94-9319

Also available Spanish language edition

"A Dorling Kindersley book"

"This volume touches upon such topics as Chinese history, the first emperor, inventions, health and medicine, waterways, food and drink, clothing, the Silk Road, and arts and crafts. . . . The book will . . . be popular for browsing." SLJ

932   Egypt to 640 A.D.

Bendick, Jeanne, 1919-

Egyptian tombs. Watts 1989 64p il lib bdg $13.93 (4 and up)   **932**

1. Tombs 2. Pyramids 3. Egypt—Antiquities
ISBN 0-531-10462-1   LC 87-27918

"A First book"

The author discusses the design, purpose, and excavation of the pyramids of ancient Egypt, the Egyptians' beliefs about death, how mummies were made, and some legends about the pyramids

"Full-color artwork enlivens the pages, and there are numerous color and black-and-white photos, many bordered in orange. Pronunciations are included in the text (though this does interrupt the flow of the narrative)." Booklist

Includes glossary

Hart, George, 1945-

Exploring the past: ancient Egypt; illustrated by Stephen Biesty. Harcourt Brace Jovanovich 1989 c1988 64p il map $14.95 (4 and up)
932

1. Egypt—History 2. Egypt—Civilization
ISBN 0-15-200449-1   LC 88-30065

"Gulliver books"

First published 1988 in the United Kingdom

Presents an overview of life in ancient Egypt discussing such topics as the Pharaoh, religion, mummification and afterlife, the role of scribes and craftsmen, home and family, and common occupations

"Overall, the book is worth acquiring on the basis of the illustrations alone. The text, though brief, is useful and well written. As an invitation to young readers to explore ancient Egypt further, the book succeeds nicely." Sci Books Films

Reeves, C. N. (Carl Nicholas), 1956-
Into the mummy's tomb; by Nicholas
Reeves with Nan Froman. Scholastic 1992 64p
il (Time quest book) hardcover o.p. paperback
available $6.95 (4 and up)   **932**
1. Tutankhamen, King of Egypt 2. Egypt—Antiquities
ISBN 0-590-45753-5 (pa)   LC 91-46185
"A Scholastic/Madison Press book"
An account of Howard Carter's discovery of the tomb of
King Tutankhamun, descriptions of the artifacts inside and
their importance, the discovery in 1988 of more artifacts,
and theories about the curse associated with the tomb
"Exquisite full-color photos and informative diagrams accompany original black-and-white photos taken by the explorers. . . . Reeves also includes much information about
life in ancient Egypt. This is a thoroughly thrilling book,
and a not-to-be-missed adventure." SLJ
Includes glossary and bibliography

937 Roman Empire

Bisel, Sara
The secrets of Vesuvius; by Sara C. Bisel
with Jane Bisel and Shelley Tanaka; historical
consultant, Paul Denis. Scholastic 1991 64p il
maps (Time quest book) hardcover o.p.
paperback available $6.95 (4 and up)   **937**
1. Herculaneum (Extinct city) 2. Excavations
(Archeology)—Italy
ISBN 0-590-43851-4 (pa)   LC 90-8887
"A Scholastic/Madison Press book"
By "reading" the bones of people killed in the town of
Herculaneum by the eruption of Mount Vesuvius, an an-
thropologist reconstructs their lives
"The stunning illustrations, beginning with a two-page
spread showing the city as it might have looked prior to the
eruption, are intermingled with full-color photographs of
art, artifacts, and the ruins as they look today—all uniform-
ly excellent. A fine choice for collections needing more in
the areas of ancient history and archaeology." SLJ
Includes glossary and bibliography

Corbishley, Mike
Ancient Rome; [by] Michael Corbishley.
Facts on File 1989 96p il maps (Cultural atlas
for young people) $17.95 (5 and up)   **937**
1. Rome—Antiquities 2. Rome—Civilization
ISBN 0-8160-1970-3   LC 88-31687
"An Equinox book"
This topical atlas "begins with a 'Table of Dates,' a chro-
nology of the history, arts, and literature of [Roman] cul-
ture. The remainder of [the] book is made up of double-
page spreads, each covering a different subject." Booklist
Includes glossary and bibliographical references

Goor, Ron, 1940-
Pompeii: exploring a Roman ghost town;
[by] Ron and Nancy Goor. Crowell 1986 118p
il maps lib bdg $14.89 (5 and up)   **937**
1. Pompeii (Extinct city) 2. Excavations (Archeology)—
Italy
ISBN 00690-04516-6   LC 85-47895
"A concise overview of the social, political, cultural, and
religious life in the ancient Roman city of Pompeii that was
destroyed and preserved by the eruption of Mt. Vesuvius in
A.D. 79. Rediscovered in 1748, Pompeii offers a unique
glimpse of everyday life in a Roman city." Soc Educ

Howarth, Sarah
Roman people. Millbrook Press 1995 c1993
47p il (People and places) lib bdg $14.90 (4
and up)   **937**
1. Rome—Social life and customs
ISBN 1-56294-650-1   LC 94-33578
First published 1993 in the United Kingdom
The author "provides generalized information about the
lifestyles of several classes of people, including mothers, the
emperor, hostages, slaves, shopkeepers, Christians, tax collectors, centurions, and surveyors." Booklist
"The clear, concise text and numerous full-color and
black-and-white photos and illustrations make [this book] a
good introduction to this culture." SLJ
Includes glossary and bibliography

Roman places. Millbrook Press 1995 c1993
46p il (People and places) lib bdg $14.90 (4
and up)   **937**
1. Rome
ISBN 1-56294-651-X   LC 94-32663
First published 1993 in the United Kingdom
"Quotations from the works of major Roman writers introduce short chapters on daily life in ancient Rome. . . .
Besides the usual facts about the forum, the villa, and the
city, Howarth discusses the baths, vineyards, shrines, forts,
hospitals, and colonies." Booklist
Includes glossary and bibliography

James, Simon, 1957-
Ancient Rome. Viking 1992 48p il map (See
through history) $15 (4 and up)   **937**
1. Rome—Antiquities 2. Rome—Civilization
ISBN 0-670-84493-4   LC 91-68543
Describing the Roman Empire during the Augustan era,
this book combines "fine illustrations, both photographs
and drawings, with a clearly written text. . . . Clear acetate
pages interspersed throughout [the book] . . . may be lifted
to reveal the inner workings of the structures depicted.
Even more useful is the fact that the captions are fully indexed with the rest of the text." SLJ
Includes glossary

938 Greece to 323 A.D.

Coolidge, Olivia Ensor, 1908-
The golden days of Greece; by Olivia
Coolidge; illustrated by Enrico Arno. Crowell
1968 211p il $14.95 (4-6)   **938**
1. Greece—History 2. Greek civilization
ISBN 0-690-33473-7
"Highlights of Greek history combined with anecdotes
depicting the exploits of gods and men and accounts describing the lives and accomplishments of Greek philoso-
phers, artists, poets, and playwrights provide a lively,
illuminating introduction to ancient Greek civilization."
Booklist
Includes glossary

Odijk, Pamela, 1942-

The Greeks. Silver Burdett Press 1989 47p il map (Ancient world) lib bdg $16.98; pa $7.95 (5 and up) **938**

1. Greece—History 2. Greek civilization
ISBN 0-382-09884-6 (lib bdg); 0-382-24259-9 (pa)
LC 89-33859

Discusses the civilization of ancient Greece, including the hunting, medicine, clothing, religion, laws, legends, and recreation

This book "will prove just the thing at report time. The information . . . is arranged the way young researchers like it. . . . Each topic gets a page or so, and the information is clearly and concisely presented. Especially nice are the color photographs and historical reproductions." Booklist

Includes glossary

Pearson, Anne

Ancient Greece; written by Anne Pearson. Knopf 1992 63p il (Eyewitness books) $19; lib bdg $18.99 (4 and up) **938**

1. Greece—History 2. Greek civilization
ISBN 0-679-81682-8; 0-679-91682-2 (lib bdg)
LC 92-4713

"A Dorling Kindersley book"

Describes the land, history, and civilization of ancient Greece

"One will enjoy this book just for its multitude of visual images. . . . This is a great pictorial presentation of the ancient Greeks and their civilization—their politics, games, dining, clothing, art, and science." Sci Books Films

940.1 Europe—Early history to 1453

Biesty, Stephen

Stephen Biesty's cross-sections: Castle; illustrated by Stephen Biesty; written by Richard Platt. Dorling Kindersley 1994 27p il $16.95 (4 and up) **940.1**

1. Castles 2. Medieval civilization
ISBN 1-56458-467-4
LC 93-30158

This "volume displays pictures of a cutaway medieval castle, revealing how the castle was constructed for protection and showing the way of life shared by those inside its walls." Horn Book Guide

"The duo's trademark humor is evident throughout. . . . Not only is the book guaranteed to attract browsers, but it will also make fun and fruitful work of report research." Booklist

Corbishley, Mike

The Middle Ages. Facts on File 1989 96p il maps (Cultural atlas for young people) $17.95 (5 and up) **940.1**

1. Medieval civilization 2. Middle Ages
ISBN 0-8160-1973-8
LC 88-31692

"An Equinox book"

Maps, charts, illustrations, and text explore the history and culture of the Middle Ages

"Corbishley gives fair and equal coverage to all areas of medieval Europe, including Russia and Scandinavia, which some books omit. The maps are excellent, precise, clear, and easy to read and understand, and the illustrations, particularly those of works of art, are wonderful."

Includes bibliographical references

Gravett, Christopher

Knight; written by Christopher Gravett; photographed by Geoff Dann. Knopf 1993 63p il (Eyewitness books) $19; lib bdg $20.99 (4 and up) **940.1**

1. Knights and knighthood 2. Medieval civilization
ISBN 0-679-83882-1; 0-679-93882-6 (lib bdg)
LC 92-1590

Also available Spanish language edition

"A Dorling Kindersley book"

Discusses the age of knighthood, covering such aspects as arms, armor, training, ceremonies, tournaments, the code of chivalry, and the Crusades

"The strength of the 'Eyewitness' title is, of course, the wonderful full-color photographs." SLJ

Lyttle, Richard B.

Land beyond the river; Europe in the age of migration; with illustrations by the author. Atheneum Pubs. 1986 175p il maps $15.95 (6 and up) **940.1**

1. Europe—History
ISBN 0-689-31199-0
LC 85-28758

"The author aims to show how Europe was affected by Huns, Goths, Vandals, Anglo-Saxons, Vikings, Mongols, and other migrating groups." Voice Youth Advocates

Includes bibliography

Martell, Hazel Mary

Everyday life in Viking times. Watts 1994 32p il (Clues to the past) lib bdg $12.60 (3-5) **940.1**

1. Vikings
ISBN 0-531-14287-6
LC 93-36128

This illustrated look at Viking culture explores places particular emphasis on recreation, food, customs and fashion

940.2 Europe—1453-

Wood, Tim

The Renaissance. Viking 1993 48p il maps (See through history) $14.99 (4 and up) **940.2**

1. Renaissance
ISBN 0-670-85149-3
LC 93-60028

Drawings, photographs, and text describe 15th and 16th century European civilization. Four see-through acetate pages lift to reveal the inner structures of three buildings and Columbus' ship, the Santa Maria

Includes glossary

940.3 World War I, 1914-1918

First World War; John D. Clare, editor. Harcourt Brace & Co. 1995 64p il maps (Living history) $16.95 (5 and up)

940.3

1. World War, 1914-1918

ISBN 0-15-200087-9 LC 94-7875

"Gulliver books"

First published 1994 in the United Kingdom

"Although the emphasis is on military aspects of the war, the social and political forces of the time are not ignored. The author ends with a discussion of the long-reaching consequences that permeated the social and economic fabric of much of the world. Period photographs and full-color dramatizations of scenes reflect conditions endured by military personnel and civilian population." SLJ

Includes bibliographical references

McGowen, Tom

World War I. Watts 1993 64p il maps lib bdg $13.93; pa $5.95 (4 and up) **940.3**

1. World War, 1914-1918

ISBN 0-531-20149-X (lib bdg); 0-531-15660-5 (pa)
LC 92-28329

"A First book"

Provides an overview of the military battles and political changes that occurred during World War I

This features "lots of dramatic photographs; full-page, colorful maps; and a fast-moving narrative, filled with facts, figures, and action." Booklist

Includes bibliography

940.53 World War II, 1939-1945

Abells, Chana Byers

The children we remember; photographs from the Archives of Yad Vashem, the Holocaust Martyrs' and Heroes' Remembrance Authority, Jerusalem, Israel. Greenwillow Bks. 1986 unp il $15; lib bdg $12.93 (3-6) **940.53**

1. Holocaust, 1933-1945

ISBN 0-688-06371-3; 0-688-06372-1 (lib bdg)
LC 85-24876

Text and photographs briefly describe the fate of Jewish children before, during, and after the Holocaust

"This is a book of few words, assuming some background knowledge of World War II and the Holocaust. And in this case, less is more, for the carefully selected photos dominate the unobtrusive statements describing scenes of children helping each other, children dying, children surviving. In acknowledging, along with the book jacket, that this is 'a story that must be told to all of today's children,' one also hopes there is an adult nearby to help share the shock of scenes like the one in which a soldier is shooting a mother and her baby." Bull Cent Child Books

Adler, David A., 1947-

Child of the Warsaw ghetto; illustrated by Karen Ritz. Holiday House 1995 unp il $15.95 (3-5) **940.53**

1. Baum, Froim, 1936- 2. Holocaust, 1933-1945
3. Jews—Poland

ISBN 0-8234-1160-5 LC 94-27779

This "is the story of life in the Warsaw ghetto as seen through the eyes of fourteen-year-old Froim Baum." J Youth Serv Libr

"Adler relates his subject's story in a direct, simple style. . . . It's an impressive tale of courage and survival. The effect of Adler's text is heightened by the large pastel drawings on each gray-toned page." SLJ

Hilde and Eli, children of the Holocaust; illustrated by Karen Ritz. Holiday House 1994 unp il $15.95 (3-5) **940.53**

1. Rosenzweig, Hilde, 1923-1941 2. Lax, Eli, 1932-1944
3. Holocaust, 1933-1945

ISBN 0-8234-1091-9 LC 93-38229

"Through the biographies of two Jewish children, this picture book for older readers will bring home to gradeschoolers what the Holocaust meant to kids like them. Nothing is sensationalized, but the facts are terrifying. . . . The SS murdered Hilde in a freight train filled with poisonous gas. Eli died in the gas chambers in Auschwitz. The text is quiet, the particulars inexorable, drawn from Adler's interviews with the surviving relatives. The illustrations are powerfully realistic." Booklist

Bachrach, Susan D., 1948-

Tell them we remember; the story of the Holocaust. Little, Brown 1994 109p il maps $21.95; pa $12.95 (5 and up) **940.53**

1. United States Holocaust Memorial Museum
2. Holocaust, 1933-1945

ISBN 0-316-69264-6; 0-316-07484-5 (pa)
LC 93-40090

"Intended to extend the experience of the United States Holocaust Memorial Museum beyond its walls, this book reproduces some of its artifacts, photographs, maps, and taped oral and video histories. . . . Bachrach makes the victims of Hitler's cruelty immediate to readers, showing that, like readers, they were individuals with hobbies and desires, friends and families. . . . This is a very personal approach to Holocaust history and a very effective one." SLJ

Includes glossary and bibliography

Greenfeld, Howard

The hidden children. Ticknor & Fields Bks. for Young Readers 1993 118p il $15.95 (4 and up) **940.53**

1. Holocaust, 1933-1945—Personal narratives 2. Jews—Europe

ISBN 0-395-66074-2 LC 93-20326

Describes the experiences of those Jewish children who were forced to go into hiding during the Holocaust and survived to tell about it

"Illustrated with black-and-white photographs, the moving stories and dramatic facts make inspiring, and often troubling, reading. A lovely, important book about heroism and survival." Horn Book Guide

Includes bibliography

Krull, Kathleen, 1952-

V is for victory; America remembers World War II. Apple Soup Bks. 1995 115p il $24; lib bdg $25.99 (4 and up)   **940.53**

    1. World War, 1939-1945
    ISBN 0-679-86198-X; 0-679-96198-4 (lib bdg)
                               LC 94-28309

"Colorful pages replete with archival photos, postcards, posters, letters, and realia present a visual and textual scrapbook of the war years. Krull covers the preliminary events, Pearl Harbor, life at home, military service, the Holocaust, weapons, and lasting changes and effects brought about by the war. . . . All readers will benefit from this visual feast." SLJ

Includes bibliography

Leitner, Isabella

The big lie; a true story; by Isabella Leitner, with Irving A. Leitner; illustrated by Judy Pedersen. Scholastic 1992 79p il lib bdg $13.95; pa $2.95 (3-6)   **940.53**

    1. Holocaust, 1933-1945—Personal narratives 2. Auschwitz (Poland: Concentration camp)
    ISBN 0-590-45569-9 (lib bdg); 0-590-45570-2 (pa)
                               LC 91-40809

Leitner relates "the story of her family's ordeal at the end of World War II. She, her mother, brother, four sisters, and the Jewish citizens of their small Hungarian town are first herded into a ghetto and then transported to Auschwitz, where her mother and youngest sister are immediately gassed. The others survive until three of them escape during a forced march (their oldest sister dies in Bergen-Belsen) and shelter with Russian troops, eventually making their way to the U.S. . . . This is a must for elementary-grades Holocaust units." Bull Cent Child Books

McGowen, Tom

World War II. Watts 1993 64p il maps lib bdg $13.93; pa $5.95 (4 and up)   **940.53**

    1. World War, 1939-1945
    ISBN 0-531-20150-3 (lib bdg); 0-531-15661-3 (pa)
                               LC 92-28328

"A First book"

Provides an overview of the military battles and political changes that occurred during World War II

Includes bibliography

Meltzer, Milton, 1915-

Never to forget: the Jews of the Holocaust. Harper & Row 1976 217p maps lib bdg $15.89; pa $6.95 (6 and up)   **940.53**

    1. Holocaust, 1933-1945
    ISBN 0-06-024175-6 (lib bdg); 0-06-446118-1 (pa)
                               LC 75-25409

"The mass murder of six million Jews by the Nazis during World War II is the subject of this compelling history. Interweaving background information, chilling statistics, individual accounts and newspaper reports, it provides an excellent introduction to its subject." Interracial Books Child Bull

Includes bibliography

Rescue: the story of how Gentiles saved Jews in the Holocaust. Harper & Row 1988 168p maps lib bdg $12.89; pa $6.95 (6 and up)   **940.53**

    1. World War, 1939-1945—Jews 2. Holocaust, 1933-1945
    ISBN 0-06-024210-8 (lib bdg); 0-06-446117-3 (pa)
                               LC 87-47816

A recounting drawn from historic source material of the many individual acts of heroism performed by righteous gentiles who sought to thwart the extermination of the Jews during the Holocaust

"This is an excellent portrayal of a difficult topic. Meltzer manages to both explain without accusing, and to laud without glorifying. . . . The discussion of the complicated relations between countries are clear, but not simplistic. An impressive aspect of this book is its lack of didacticism." Voice Youth Advocates

Includes bibliography

Rosenberg, Maxine B., 1939-

Hiding to survive; stories of Jewish children rescued from the Holocaust. Clarion Bks. 1994 166p il $15.95 (5 and up)   **940.53**

    1. Holocaust, 1933-1945—Personal narratives 2. Jews—Europe
    ISBN 0-395-65014-3   LC 93-28328

First person accounts of fourteen Holocaust survivors who as children were hidden from the Nazis by non-Jews

"Told in the plain, unvarnished language of childhood memories, these harrowing first-person accounts are particularly moving in their straightforward simplicity, and all are accompanied by photos of the survivors as children and as they are today." Voice Youth Advocates

Includes glossary and bibliography

Toll, Nelly S., 1935-

Behind the secret window; a memoir of a hidden childhood during Word War Two. Dial Bks. 1993 161p il $17 (6 and up)   **940.53**

    1. Jews—Poland 2. Holocaust, 1933-1945—Personal narratives
    ISBN 0-8037-1362-2   LC 92-21831

The author recalls her experiences when she and her mother were hidden from the Nazis by a Gentile couple in Lwów, Poland, during World War II

"Toll writes of her experiences in an emotionally controlled, thoughtful manner that only serves to emphasize the horrors she experienced. She relies extensively on a diary she began when she entered hiding at the age of eight, and her story is illustrated with full-color paintings she made during the same period." Booklist

940.54 World War II, 1939-1945 (Military conduct of the war)

Bliven, Bruce, 1916-

The story of D-Day, June 6, 1944; [by] Bruce Bliven, Jr.; with an author's note written especially for this edition. 50th anniversary ed. Random House 1994 140p il $15; pa $4.99   **940.54**

    1. Normandy (France), Attack on, 1944
    ISBN 0-679-84503-8; 0-394-84886-1 (pa)
                               LC 93-24776

Bliven, Bruce, 1916-—*Continued*
First published 1956
An account of the planning and resources of the Allied invasion of Normandy which was the turning point of the Second World War, and of the brave men who implemented it
"A brief, dramatic account . . . recommended for reluctant older readers." Hodges. Books for Elem Sch Libr

Dolan, Edward F., 1924-
America in World War II. Millbrook Press 1991-1993 4v il maps lib bdg ea $15.90 (4-6)
940.54
1. World War, 1939-1945
ISBN 1-878841-05-X (1941); 1-56294-007-4 (1942); 1-56294-113-5 (1943); 1-56294-221-2 (1944)
LC 91-30808
Some volumes also available in paperback
Contents: [v1] 1941; [v2] 1942; [v3] 1943; [v4] 1944
Each volume covers prominent events and personalities of a year from 1941 to 1944
The set "will be valuable for students with a general interest in World War II or those doing research on the topic." Voice Youth Advocates

Maruki, Toshi, 1912-
Hiroshima no pika; words and pictures by Toshi Maruki. Lothrop, Lee & Shepard Bks. 1982 c1980 unp il $16
940.54
1. Hiroshima (Japan)—Bombardment, 1945 2. World War, 1939-1945—Japan
ISBN 0-688-01297-3
LC 82-15365
First published 1980 in Japan
"Impressionistic paintings accompany a realistic account of one child's suffering on the day the atomic bomb was dropped on Hiroshima." Booklist
"The publisher suggests that the book is suitable for twelve-year-olds and up, but twelve-years-olds do not read picture books on their own. I would use this book with grades two and up, and it could also be used with even younger children. . . . Other adults who have read the book to eight-year-olds also report no nightmares, just feelings of deep sorrow. I would not suggest reading the book to large groups of children, however, unless there was a great deal of prior discussion and mood-setting." Interracial Books Child Bull

Morimoto, Junko
My Hiroshima. Viking 1990 unp il $13.95 (2-4)
940.54
1. Hiroshima (Japan)—Bombardment, 1945 2. World War, 1939-1945—Japan—Personal narratives
ISBN 0-670-83181-6
LC 89-51483
First published 1987 in the United Kingdom
"The narrator describes her pre-war childhood before detailing the events of August 6, 1945, when she and her family were lucky enough to survive the blast that destroyed her home. . . . A last page gives facts about the bombing of Hiroshima, and endpapers include historical black-and-white photographs together with an author's note to parents and teachers." Bull Cent Child Books
"This nonfiction title in picture-book format is a frank, powerful story in which both text and illustration work together without sentimentality or sensationalism to show the horror of war." SLJ

Taylor, Theodore, 1921-
Air raid—Pearl Harbor! the story of December 7, 1941; illustrated by W. T. Mars. Crowell 1971 185p il maps o.p.; Harcourt Brace & Co. paperback available $5 (5 and up)
940.54
1. Pearl Harbor (Oahu, Hawaii), Attack on, 1941
ISBN 0-15-201655-4 (pa)
"Well-documented and written with all the suspense of a mystery story, this is a detailed account of the events that led up to the disaster of Pearl Harbor. The story is told both from the American and the Japanese viewpoint, with all of the errors in planning, the gaps in communication, the secrecy of tactics and strategy." Bull Cent Child Books
Includes bibliography

941.6   Ulster. Northern Ireland

Northern Ireland—in pictures; prepared by Geography Department. Lerner Publs. 1991 64p il maps (Visual geography series) lib bdg $19.95 (5 and up)
941.6
1. Northern Ireland
ISBN 0-8225-1898-8
LC 90-24151
Introduces the geography, history, people, economy, and governmental structure of Northern Ireland

942   England and Wales

England—in pictures; prepared by Geography Department. Lerner Publs. 1990 64p il maps (Visual geography series) lib bdg $19.95 (5 and up)
942
1. England
ISBN 0-8225-1874-0
LC 89-78070
Revised edition of the title prepared by James Nach, published 1977 by Sterling
Introduces the topography, history, society, economy, and governmental structure of England
Includes bibliographical references

Goodall, John S., 1908-
The story of a castle. Margaret K. McElderry Bks. 1986 29p il $16 (3-6) **942**
1. Castles—Pictorial works 2. England—Social life and customs—Pictorial works
ISBN 0-689-50405-5
LC 86-70130
"A British castle is the subject of a sequence of paintings aimed at showing the building's history. There is no text; specifics are related in a page of front matter that identifies each of the castle's eras. . . . The paintings are typical of Goodall's style: quick, detailed, and strong in color and composition. The book's design, with half pages advancing the action, will be familiar as well. A wordless lesson that can play to a wider audience, including middle graders studying medieval history or castles." Booklist

The story of a farm. Margaret K. McElderry Bks. 1989 34p il $14.95 (3-6) **942**
1. Farm life—England—Pictorial works 2. England—Social life and customs—Pictorial works
ISBN 0-689-50479-9
LC 88-13398
By following the changes in one house over centuries, the development of farm life in England is depicted

Goodall, John S., 1908-—*Continued*

Goodall's "watercolors capture both particular details and larger impressions, and finely convey a sense of time's inexorable passage. In addition, he makes ingenious use of half-page flaps to portray two faces of a single scene." Publ Wkly

942.03 England—Period of House of Plantagenet, 1154-1399

Sancha, Sheila, 1924-

Walter Dragun's town; crafts and trade in the Middle Ages. Crowell 1989 c1987 64p il lib bdg $15.89 (6 and up)   **942.03**

1. England—Social life and customs 2. Handicraft 3. Medieval civilization

ISBN 0-690-04806-8   LC 88-34066

First published 1987 in the United Kingdom

"This is a superb resource book with engaging text and line art that looks closely, with a great deal of in-depth detail, at life in the English town of Stanford on the river Weland in the year 1274. Events, architecture, cast of characters, are all based on facts found in still-existing Public Records; Ms. Sancha has fashioned these facts into an intimate history covering a few busy days in August. Introduction, epilogue, word origins for place-names and surnames, and glossary add their value to this brief-but-compact oversize volume." Child Book Rev Serv

942.1 London

Fisher, Leonard Everett, 1924-

The Tower of London. Macmillan 1987 unp il $15.95 (4 and up)   **942.1**

1. Tower of London (England) 2. London (England)—History

ISBN 0-02-735370-2   LC 87-1629

"Fisher introduces the history-laden Tower of London and recounts 13 episodes from its bloody history. . . . The tellings are succinct while capturing the essence of the famous structure. Kids will be enticed by the gory goings-on. . . . Fisher provides bold black-and-white artwork throughout in double-page spreads; impressive and dramatic, they add strong flavor to the narrative." Booklist

Munro, Roxie, 1945-

The inside-outside book of London. Dutton 1989 unp il $13.95 (2-4)   **942.1**

1. London (England)—Description

ISBN 0-525-44522-6   LC 89-12023

Also available in paperback from Puffin Bks.

Captioned illustrations depict noted sights in London as seen from the outside and inside. Includes the British Museum, Houses of Parliament, Tower of London, Waterloo Station, St. Paul's Cathedral, and others. Includes a section of text in the back of the book providing information on each sight

"The book displays a high level of craftsmanship and careful research, offering a uniquely personal yet informative view of the city's treasures." SLJ

942.9 Wales

Sutherland, Dorothy B.

Wales. Childrens Press 1987 128p il maps (Enchantment of the world) lib bdg $28.70 (4 and up)   **942.9**

1. Wales

ISBN 0-516-02794-8   LC 86-29954

Explores the geography, history, industry, arts, and everyday life of Wales

943 Central Europe. Germany

Germany—in pictures; prepared by Geography Department. Lerner Publs. 1994 64p il maps (Visual geography series) lib bdg $19.95 (5 and up)   **943**

1. Germany

ISBN 0-8225-1873-2   LC 93-40971

Describes the topography, history, government, society, and economy of Germany

943.7 Czech Republic and Slovakia

Czech Republic—in pictures; prepared by Geography Department. Lerner Publs. 1995 64p il maps (Visual geography series) lib bdg $19.95 (5 and up)   **943.7**

1. Czech Republic

ISBN 0-8225-1879-1   LC 94-37432

An illustrated introduction to the republic which, along with Slovakia, became independent with the 1993 breakup of Czechoslovakia

Slovakia—in pictures; prepared by Geography Department. Lerner Publs. 1995 64p il maps (Visual geography series) lib bdg $19.95 (5 and up)   **943.7**

1. Slovakia

ISBN 0-8225-1912-7   LC 94-45803

Photographs and text introduce the land, history, government, people, industry, and economy of Slovakia

943.9 Hungary

Hungary—in pictures; prepared by Geography Department. Lerner Publs. 1993 64p il maps (Visual geography series) lib bdg $19.95 (5 and up)   **943.9**

1. Hungary

ISBN 0-8225-1883-X   LC 93-3179

Describes the topography, history, society, economy, and governmental structure of Hungary

944   France and Monaco

Munro, Roxie, 1945-
The inside-outside book of Paris. Dutton
1992 unp il $15 (2-4)   **944**
1. Paris (France)—Description
ISBN 0-525-44863-2   LC 91-29318
Captioned illustrations depict noted sights in Paris,
including the Eiffel Tower, the Arch of Triumph, the Metro
subway, and a puppet theater. A section of text provides information on each sight
"Munro uses oversize pages for bright colorful paintings
that pair exterior views with interior close-ups of famous
buildings. . . . The book succeeds in evoking the effervescent atmosphere of Paris and in conveying details, architec-
turally precise and true to the laws of sometimes dizzying
perspective." Bull Cent Child Books

945   Italian Peninsula and adjacent islands. Italy

Travis, David, 1953-
The land and people of Italy. HarperCollins
Pubs. 1992 240p il maps (Portraits of the
nations series) $18; lib bdg 17.89 (5 and up)
     945
1. Italy
ISBN 0-06-022778-8; 0-06-022784-2 (lib bdg)
     LC 91-9771
An introduction to the history, geography, economy, culture, and people of Italy
"Travis's conversational style and strong storytelling are
sure to tempt those involved in quick referencing from the
index to slow down, read, and enjoy. The numerous maps
and generously captioned black-and-white photos do not repeat information from the text but serve as interesting supplement." SLJ
Includes bibliography

946   Iberian Peninsula and adjacent islands. Spain

Shubert, Adrian, 1953-
The land and people of Spain.
HarperCollins Pubs. 1992 244p il maps
(Portraits of the nations series) $18; lib bdg
$17.89 (5 and up)   **946**
1. Spain
ISBN 0-06-020217-3; 0-06-020218-1 (lib bdg)
     LC 91-9971
Introduces the history, geography, people, culture, gov-
ernment, and economy of Spain
Includes bibliography

Spain—in pictures; prepared by Geography
Department. Lerner Publs. 1995 64p il maps
(Visual geography series) lib bdg $19.95 (5
and up)   **946**
1. Spain
ISBN 0-8225-1887-2   LC 94-41990
Revised edition of the title originally published by Ster-
ling

Individual chapters discuss the land, history and government, the people, and the economy of Spain

946.081   Spain—Period of Second Republic, 1931-1939

Katz, William Loren
The Lincoln Brigade; a picture history; by
William Loren Katz and Marc Crawford.
Atheneum Pubs. 1989 84p il map $14.95 (5
and up)   **946.081**
1. Spain—History—1936-1939, Civil War
ISBN 0-689-31406-X   LC 88-27522
Recounts the story of the American contingent which
joined other International Brigades in fighting with the Loyalists during the Spanish Civil War
This book "bills itself as 'a picture history.' The handsome book is that—and many of the photos have never before been published—but it also has a substantial text. It
does not focus on any one hero. Rather, this politically
aware book gives emphasis to the black volunteers who, for
the first time in the history of an American armed force,
served side-by-side with whites." N Y Times Book Rev
Includes bibliography

947   Russia. Eastern Europe

Azerbaijan; prepared by Geography
Department. Lerner Publs. 1993 56p il maps
(Then & now) lib bdg $22.95 (5 and up)
     947
1. Azerbaijan
ISBN 0-8225-2810-X   LC 92-24954
Discusses the topography, location, ethnic makeup, histo-
ry, economic activities, and future of the former Soviet re-
public of Azerbaijan

Belarus; prepared by Geography Department.
Lerner Publs. 1993 56p il maps (Then &
now) lib bdg $22.95 (5 and up)   **947**
1. Belarus
ISBN 0-8225-2811-8   LC 92-33231
Discusses the history, geography, ethnic groups, politics,
economy, and future of the former Soviet republic of Belarus

Chicoine, Stephen
Lithuania; the nation that would be free;
[by] Stephen Chicoine and Brent Ashabranner;
photographs by Stephen Chicoine. Cobblehill
Bks. 1995 64p il maps $16.99 (4 and up)
     947
1. Lithuania
ISBN 0-525-65151-9   LC 94-12782
This book "is part history and part exploration of Lithu-
anian culture. . . . Illustrated with over thirty photographs
taken by co-author Chicoine . . . the book is attractive and
informative, bringing to young readers insight into the lives
of a courageous and steadfast people. The guiding hand of
Brent Ashabranner is evident throughout in the construction of the text." Horn Book
Includes bibliography

Estonia; prepared by Geography Department. Lerner Publs. 1992 56p il maps (Then & now) lib bdg $22.95 (5 and up) **947**

1. Estonia

ISBN 0-8225-2803-7 LC 91-44932

Discusses the history, geography, resources, politics, ethnography, economics, and future of this Baltic country, annexed by the Soviet Union in 1940 and independent once again in 1991

"Large, high-quality, full-color photographs and maps, most of them captioned, greatly enhance the clearly written [text]. Care has been taken to select illustrations that not only provide information about the culture, but also convey the mood of the people." SLJ

Includes glossary

Georgia; prepared by Geography Department. Lerner Publs. 1993 56p il maps (Then & now) lib bdg $22.95 (5 and up) **947**

1. Georgia (Republic)

ISDN 0-8225-2807-X LC 93-19291

Discusses the geography, history, politics, economics, and ecology of the former Soviet republic Georgia

"The presentation of this newly independent nation is accurate, well organized, and beautifully illustrated." SLJ

Includes glossary

Harvey, Miles

The fall of the Soviet Union. Childrens Press 1995 30p il maps (Cornerstones of freedom) lib bdg $12.98 (4-6) **947**

1. Soviet Union—History 2. Former Soviet republics—History

ISBN 0-516-06694-3 LC 94-24371

Beginning with the revolution in 1917, the author traces events through the fall of the former Soviet Union

"An enormous amount of complex history is broken down into a highly readable text enhanced by full-color and black-and-white photographs of Russian life past and present." SLJ

Latvia; prepared by Geography Department. Lerner Publs. 1992 56p il maps (Then & now) lib bdg $21.50 (5 and up) **947**

1. Latvia

ISBN 0-8225-2802-9 LC 92-7260

Discusses the geography, history, ethnography, resources, politics, and future of this Baltic country, annexed by the Soviet Union in 1940 and independent once again in 1991

"The presentation is well done and highly suitable for average readers of the target age group." SLJ

Includes glossary

Lithuania; prepared by Geography Department. Lerner Publs. 1992 56p il maps (Then & now) lib bdg $21.50 (5 and up) **947**

1. Lithuania

ISBN 0-8225-2804-5 LC 92-9698

Discusses Lithuania's geography, ethnic populations, history, political events, economic activities, environmental hazards, relations with neighbors, and future

Includes glossary

Moldova; prepared by Geography Department. Lerner Publs. 1993 56p il maps (Then & now) lib bdg $22.95 (5 and up) **947**

1. Moldova

ISBN 0-8225-2809-6 LC 92-13499

Discusses the history, geography, ethnic mixture, politics, economy, and future of the former Soviet republic of Moldova

Includes glossary

Russia; prepared by Geography Department. Lerner Publs. 1992 64p il maps (Then & now) lib bdg $22.95 (5 and up) **947**

1. Russia (Republic)

ISBN 0-8225-2805-3 LC 92-7833

Discusses the topography, ethnic tensions, history, and current political situation of Russia, the largest republic in the former Soviet Union

Ukraine; prepared by Geography Department. Lerner Publs. 1993 64p il maps (Then & now) lib bdg $21.50 (5 and up) **947**

1. Ukraine

ISBN 0-8225-2808-8 LC 92-10284

Examines the history, geography, ethnic makeup, politics, economy, and future of the former Soviet republic of the Ukraine

947.086 Russia—1991-

Kendall, Russ

Russian girl; life in an old Russian town. Scholastic 1994 40p il $14.95 (3-5) **947.086**

1. Russia (Republic)—Social life and customs

ISBN 0-590-45789-6 LC 93-13198

Text and photographs describe the life of nine-year-old Olga and her family in the small Russian city of Suzdal

"Kendall's observant color photographs and accompanying text makes for a personal, even poignant, introduction to contemporary Russian family life. . . . Condensed background information, recipes, and a brief guide to the Russian alphabet provide interest." Horn Book Guide

Resnick, Abraham

The Commonwealth of Independent States; Russia and the other republics. Childrens Press 1993 144p il maps (Enchantment of the world) $28.70 (4 and up) **947.086**

1. Commonwealth of Independent States 2. Former Soviet republics

ISBN 0-516-02613-5 LC 92-39801

Describes how the Commonwealth of Independent States came about after the collapse of the Soviet Union and introduces the geography, people, and culture of the Commonwealth's republics

"A comprehensive and serviceable volume. . . . [It includes] numerous clear, full-color photographs." SLJ

948 Scandinavia

Margeson, Susan M.
Viking; written by Susan M. Margeso; photographed by Peter Anderson. Knopf 1994 63p il maps (Eyewitness books) $19; lib bdg $18.99 (4 and up) **948**

1. Vikings
ISBN 0-679-86002-9; 0-679-96002-3 (lib bdg)
LC 93-32593
"A Dorling Kindersley book"
This overview of Viking culture ranges from domestic life and social structure "to the more violent aspects of their explorations and expansions into new territories." SLJ
"This book is a very fine supplement to texts dealing with the history of Europe and with the Vikings." Sci Books Films

Pearson, Anne
The Vikings. Viking 1994 c1993 48p il maps (See through history) $15.99 (4 and up)
948

1. Vikings
ISBN 0-670-85834-X
First published 1993 in the United Kingdom
Color artwork, photographs of artifacts, and text describe three centuries of Viking life. Interspersed throughout the book are acetate overlays which lift to reveal the internal structures of a Viking house, a Viking longship, the burial mound of a Viking queen, and a stave church
Includes glossary

The **Vikings**; John D. Clare, editor. Harcourt Brace Jovanovich 1992 64p il (Living history) $16.95 (5 and up) **948**

1. Vikings
ISBN 0-15-200512-9
LC 91-24146
"Gulliver books"
This book uses posed photographs of costumed people in period settings to depict various aspects of Viking culture
"Almost any fact a young person might want to know about the customs and daily life of the Vikings is available in this well-written and visually arresting book." Soc Educ

948.1 Norway

Charbonneau, Claudette, 1936-
The land and people of Norway; by Claudette Charbonneau and Patricia Slade Lander; special photographs by Ola Røe. HarperCollins Pubs. 1993 226p il maps (Portraits of the nations series) $18; lib bdg $17.89 (5 and up) **948.1**

1. Norway
ISBN 0-06-020573-3; 0-06-020583-0 (lib bdg)
LC 91-35029
Photographs and text introduce the history, economy, government, and the social life and customs of Norway
Includes bibliography

Norway—in pictures; prepared by Geography Department. Lerner Publs. 1990 64p il maps (Visual geography series) lib bdg $19.95 (5 and up) **948.1**

1. Norway
ISBN 0-8225-1871-6
LC 89-12118
Revised edition of the title prepared by John B. Burks, published 1980 by Sterling
An introduction to the geography, history, economy, government, culture, and people of Norway

948.9 Denmark and Finland

Denmark—in pictures; prepared by Geography Department. Lerner Publs. 1991 64p il maps (Visual geography series) lib bdg $19.95 (5 and up) **948.9**

1. Denmark
ISBN 0-8225-1880-5
LC 90-41730
Revised edition of the title prepared by Toby A. Reiss, published 1966 by Sterling
Examines the topography, history, society, economy, and governmental structure of Denmark

Hintz, Martin, 1945-
Denmark. Childrens Press 1994 128p il maps (Enchantment of the world) $28.70 (4 and up) **948.9**

1. Denmark
ISBN 0-516-02620-8
LC 93-35487
An illustrated introduction to the history, geography, culture, government, economics and peoples of Denmark

948.97 Finland

Lander, Patricia Slade
The land and people of Finland; by Patricia Slade Lander and Claudette Charbonneau. Lippincott 1990 212p il maps (Portraits of the nations series) $18; lib bdg $17.89 (5 and up) **948.97**

1. Finland
ISBN 0-397-32357-3; 0-397-32358-1 (lib bdg)
LC 88-27144
Introduces the history, geography, people, culture, government, and economy of Finland
Includes bibliography

Lewin, Ted, 1935-
The reindeer people; written and illustrated by Ted Lewin. Macmillan 1994 unp il $14.95 (3-5) **948.97**

1. Sami (European people) 2. Lapland
ISBN 0-02-757390-7
LC 93-19252
Lewin "introduces the Sami people who live north of the Arctic Circle. . . . Six vignettes portray a blue, frozen land teeming with activity. . . . The author's highly descriptive prose is as luxurious as a reindeer coat, and his finely detailed, snapshot-style watercolors will engage readers of any age." Publ Wkly

949.2 Netherlands

Netherlands—in pictures; prepared by Geography Department. Lerner Publs. 1991 64p il (Visual geography series) lib bdg $12.95 (5 and up)   949.2

1. Netherlands
ISBN 0-8225-1893-7   LC 91-10466

Revised edition of Holland in pictures prepared by Lincoln A. Boehm, published 1976 by Sterling

Photographs and text introduce the land, history, government, people, industry, and economy of Holland

949.3 Southern Low Countries. Belgium

Belgium—in pictures; prepared by Geography Department. Lerner Publs. 1991 64p il maps (Visual geography series) $19.95 (5 and up)
                    949.3

1. Belgium
ISBN 0-8225-1889-9   LC 91-15011

Revised edition of Belgium and Luxembourg in pictures prepared by E. W. Egan, published 1966 by Sterling

Describes the topography, history, society, economy, and governmental structure of Belgium

Hargrove, Jim, 1947-
Belgium. Childrens Press 1988 127p il maps (Enchantment of the world) lib bdg $28.70 (4 and up)   949.3

1. Belgium
ISBN 0-516-02701-8   LC 87-36753

An introduction to the geography, history, government, economy, culture, and people of this small country that is often called the "crossroads of Europe"

949.35 Luxembourg

Lepthien, Emilie U. (Emilie Utteg)
Luxembourg. Childrens Press 1989 125p il (Enchantment of the world) lib bdg $28.70 (4 and up)   949.35

1. Luxembourg
ISBN 0-516-02714-X   LC 89-34664

An introduction to the geography, history, government, economy, culture, and people of one of the smallest and oldest independent countries in Europe

949.5 Greece

Greece—in pictures; prepared by Geography Department. Lerner Publs. 1992 64p il maps (Visual geography series) lib bdg $19.95 (5 and up)   949.5

1. Greece
ISBN 0-8225-1882-1   LC 91-23302

Revised edition of the title prepared by Robert V. Masters [i.e. David A. Boehm] published 1980 by Sterling

Describes the topography, history, society, economy, and government of Greece

949.65 Albania

Albania—in pictures; prepared by Geography Department. Lerner Publs. 1995 64p il maps (Visual geography series) lib bdg $18.95 (5 and up)   949.65

1. Albania
ISBN 0-8225-1902-X   LC 94-10616

Individual chapters describe the land, history and government, the people, and the economy of this Balkan nation

949.77 Bulgaria

Bulgaria—in pictures; prepared by Geography Department. Lerner Publs. 1994 64p il maps (Visual geography series) lib bdg $19.95 (5 and up)   949.77

1. Bulgaria
ISBN 0-8225-1890-2   LC 93-23080

Revised edition of the title originally published by Sterling

Describes the topography, history, economy, society, and culture of the country situated on the Balkan Peninsula in southeastern Europe

Resnick, Abraham
Bulgaria. Childrens Press 1995 126p il maps (Enchantment of the world) lib bdg $28.70 (4 and up)   949.77

1. Bulgaria
ISBN 0-516-02631-3   LC 94-37948

This introduction to Bulgaria "discusses the cultural heritage of the people; their folk festivals, cuisine, and arts. By reading about the Balkans, students may begin to understand the war in Bosnia in a larger context." SLJ

949.8 Romania

Romania—in pictures; prepared by Geography Department. Lerner Publs. 1993 64p il maps (Visual geography series) lib bdg $19.95 (5 and up)   949.8

1. Romania
ISBN 0-8225-1894-5   LC 92-32861

Describes the topography, history, society, economy, and governmental structure of Romania

951 China and adjacent areas

Ashabranner, Brent K., 1921-
Land of yesterday, land of tomorrow; discovering Chinese Central Asia; photographs by Paul, David, and Peter Conklin; text by Brent Ashabranner. Cobblehill Bks. 1992 84p il maps $16 (5 and up)   951

1. China
ISBN 0-525-65086-5   LC 91-25145

Ashabranner, Brent K., 1921— *Continued*

Photographs and text explore the Chinese province of Xinjiang, closed to foreigners by the Communist government in 1949 and only reopened in 1984

"A vital and highly informative travel book that cogently combines Xinjiang's historical significance (especially its role in Silk Road politics) with issues of today. . . . The photographs are . . . sharp and well composed; most are in black and white. The dozen or so in full color are so enthralling that one wishes for more. This is an absorbing travelogue with enough substance for reports." SLJ

Includes bibliography

Fisher, Leonard Everett, 1924-

The Great Wall of China. Macmillan 1986 30p il map $14.95 (4 and up)   **951**

1. China—History
ISBN 0-02-735220-X   LC 85-15324

Also available in paperback from Aladdin Bks. (NY)

A brief history of the Great Wall of China, begun about 2,200 years ago to keep out Mongol invaders

"The combination of stunning black-and-white illustrations, calligraphy and the artist's chops (signature seal) in red, plus a spare, narrative text makes this an exciting introduction to one of history's great building projects." N Y Times Book Rev

Haskins, James, 1941-

Count your way through China; by Jim Haskins; illustrations by Dennis Hockerman. Carolrhoda Bks. 1987 unp il lib bdg $17.50; pa $5.95 (2-4)   **951**

1. China
ISBN 0-87614-302-8 (lib bdg); 0-87614-486-5 (pa)
                                       LC 87-5177

Using the numbers from one to ten, this book presents facts about China and Chinese culture. Each double-page spread shows the number, the character for it, the pronunciation, and a full-color illustration

McLenighan, Valjean, 1947-

China, a history to 1949. Childrens Press 1983 127p il maps (Enchantment of the world) lib bdg $28.70 (4 and up)   **951**

1. China—History
ISBN 0-516-02754-9   LC 83-14260

A history of China up to the establishment of the communist state in 1949

951.04   China—Period of Republic, 1912-1949

Fritz, Jean

China's Long March; 6,000 miles of danger; with illustrations by Yang Zhr Cheng. Putnam 1988 124p il maps $16.95 (6 and up)
                                            951.04

1. China—History—1912-1949
ISBN 0-399-21512-3   LC 87-31171

Describes the events of the 6,000 mile march undertaken by Mao Zedong and his Communist followers as they retreated before the forces of Chiang Kai-shek

"Because Fritz is adept at gauging her intended audience, and because most of her material is based on interviews with survivors, the writing has an easy flow and an immediacy that make the ordeal vivid and personal." Bull Cent Child Books

Includes bibliography

951.05   China—Period of People's Republic, 1949-

Fritz, Jean

China homecoming; with photographs by Michael Fritz. Putnam 1985 143p il $16.95 (6 and up)   **951.05**

1. China
ISBN 0-399-21182-9   LC 84-24775

Companion volume to Homesick: my own story, entered in class 92

This account of the author's return to Hankow after four decades "is intended for a slightly older readership than 'Homesick' . . . as it is not only an autobiography, but also a glimpse of Chinese history and a social commentary. It is, however, a book to be read and reread." SLJ

Includes bibliography

951.2   Taiwan, Hong Kong, Macao

Cromie, Alice

Taiwan; with a contribution from Parris H. Chang; consultant for Taiwan, Parris H. Chang; consultant for reading, Robert L. Hillerich. Childrens Press 1994 127p il maps (Enchantment of the world) lib bdg $28.70 (4 and up)   **951.2**

1. Taiwan
ISBN 0-516-02627-5   LC 94-6120

Discusses the geography, history, economics and culture of Taiwan

951.7   Mongolia

Brill, Marlene Targ

Mongolia. Childrens Press 1992 127p il maps (Enchantment of the world) lib bdg $28.70 (4 and up)   **951.7**

1. Mongolia
ISBN 0-516-02605-4   LC 91-34172

Describes the geography, history, culture, industry, and people of Mongolia

Reynolds, Jan, 1956-
Mongolia; vanishing cultures. Harcourt Brace & Co. 1994 unp il (Vanishing cultures series) $16.95; pa $8.95 (2-4)   **951.7**
1. Mongolia 2. Mongols
ISBN 0-15-255312-6; 0-15-255313-4 (pa)
LC 93-1351
Two nomadic Mongolian children listen to stories of the past from their father and yearn for their own horses, creatures essential to their way of life
"Colorful photographs invite the reader to share an active day on the Asian plains with the boys and their extended family. Simply told, the text is direct and informative." Horn Book Guide

951.9 Korea

McMahon, Patricia
Chi-hoon: a Korean girl; with photographs by Michael F. O'Brien. Boyds Mills Press 1993 47p il $16.95 (3-5)   **951.9**
1. Korea—Social life and customs
ISBN 1-56397-026-0   LC 92-81331
"A week in the life of an eight year old Korean girl is presented through diary entries, a wry third-person narration, and full-color photographs. . . . McMahon has produced a vivid portrait of a very real little girl. . . . The photographs are excellent, informative, and sensibly placed." SLJ

Solberg, S. E. (Sammy Edward), 1930-
The land and people of Korea. HarperCollins Pubs. 1991 216p il maps (Portraits of the nations series) lib bdg $18.89 (5 and up)   **951.9**
1. Korea
ISBN 0-06-021649-2   LC 90-5952
An introduction to the history, government, traditions, and way of life of the people of Korea
Includes bibliography

952 Japan

Blumberg, Rhoda, 1917-
Commodore Perry in the land of the Shogun. Lothrop, Lee & Shepard Bks. 1985 144p il map lib bdg $17 (5 and up)   **952**
1. Perry, Matthew Calbraith, 1794-1858 2. United States Naval Expedition to Japan (1852-1854) 3. United States—Foreign relations—Japan 4. Japan—Foreign relations—United States
ISBN 0-688-03723-2   LC 84-21800
A Newbery Medal honor book, 1986
"The diplomatic expeditions of Commodore Matthew C. Perry to secure a treaty to provide for U.S. trade with Japan are described. The black-and-white period illustrations and informative text provide an in-depth and intimate view of nineteenth century Japan, Japanese and U.S. values and attitudes, and treaty negotiations." Soc Educ
Includes bibliography

Haskins, James, 1941-
Count your way through Japan; by Jim Haskins; illustrations by Martin Skoro. Carolrhoda Bks. 1987 unp il lib bdg $18.95; pa $5.95 (2-4)   **952**
1. Japan
ISBN 0-87614-301-X (lib bdg); 0-87614-485-7 (pa)
LC 87-6398
Presents the numbers one to ten in Japanese, using each number to introduce concepts about Japan and its culture

Japan—in pictures; prepared by Geography Department. Lerner Publs. 1989 64p il maps (Visual geography series) lib bdg $18.95 (5 and up)   **952**
1. Japan
ISBN 0-8225-1861-9   LC 88-30461
Revised edition of the title prepared by Robert V. Masters [i.e. David A. Boehm] published 1973 by Sterling
Introduces Japan's geography, history, society, economy, and government structure

952.04 Japan—1945-

Kuklin, Susan
Kodomo; children of Japan. Putnam 1995 48p il $15.95 (3-6)   **952.04**
1. Children—Japan 2. Japan—Social life and customs
ISBN 0-399-22613-3   LC 94-15417
"*Kodomo*, meaning child or children, describes the everyday lives of 6 girls and 1 boy, ranging in age from 8 to 14, in contemporary Japan. The first section, 'A Way of Life,' focuses on daily activities in Hiroshima; the second, 'Traditional Activities,' on sports and the arts in the ancient capital of Kyoto. . . . The full-color photographs are excellent, lively, and sometimes humorous." SLJ

953 Arabian Peninsula and adjacent areas

Fox, Mary Virginia
Bahrain. Childrens Press 1992 126p il maps (Enchantment of the world) lib bdg $28.70 (4 and up)   **953**
1. Bahrain
ISBN 0-516-02608-9   LC 92-8892
Describes the history, geography, culture, government, and industry of the island country in the Persian Gulf
This is "up-to-date, reflecting current problems . . . as well as recent political events. Excellent maps, informative photographs, and 'Mini-Facts at A Glance' augment the broad, well-controlled [text]." SLJ

953.8 Saudi Arabia

Foster, Leila Merrell
Saudi Arabia. Childrens Press 1993 127p il maps (Enchantment of the world) lib bdg $28.70 (4 and up)   **953.8**
1. Saudi Arabia
ISBN 0-516-02611-9   LC 92-8890

Foster, Leila Merrell—*Continued*

Describes the history, geography, culture, industry, and economy of the largest country on the Arabian Peninsula

"A readable, appealing book. . . . Throughout, the well-chosen photographs consistently portray the variety of the terrain, the people, their lifestyles, and work environment." SLJ

954 South Asia. India

Hermes, Jules, 1962-

The children of India. Carolrhoda Bks. 1993 47p il (World's children) lib bdg $19.95; pa $7.95 (3-5) **954**

1. Children—India 2. India

ISBN 0-87614-759-7 (lib bdg); 0-87614-848-8 (pa)

LC 92-35103

This photo-essay "conveys the religious, cultural, and geographic diversity of India. Portraits of over a dozen children from different regions and social levels offer fascinating details about home, dress, food, family, education, and language to portray an ancient culture steeped in religious tradition. The color photographs capture the daily routine and picture India's varied landscape." Horn Book Guide

India—in pictures; prepared by Geography Department. Lerner Publs. 1989 64p il maps (Visual geography series) lib bdg $19.95 (5 and up) **954**

1. India

ISBN 0-8225-1852-X LC 88-9018

Revised edition of the title prepared by Elizabeth Katz, published 1961 by Sterling

Photographs and text introduce the geography, history, government, society, and economy of this diverse nation

Lewin, Ted, 1935-

Sacred river; written and illustrated by Ted Lewin. Clarion Bks. 1995 32p $14.95 (1-4) **954**

1. Ganges River valley (India and Bangladesh)—Description

ISBN 0-395-69846-4 LC 94-18370

"Luminous watercolors and a brief, evocative text create a vista of the Ganges river at Benares, holy goal of millions of Hindu pilgrims." Soc Educ

954.9 Jurisdictions of South Asia other than India

Margolies, Barbara A., 1939-

Kanu of Kathmandu; a journey in Nepal. Four Winds Press 1992 34p il $14.95 (2-4) **954.9**

1. Nepal—Social life and customs

ISBN 0-02-762282-7 LC 92-12482

An eight-year-old boy who lives in the city of Kathmandu takes a tour of several small towns and villages of Nepal, observing many traditional customs and activities

This features "engaging and varied photographs." Soc Educ

954.91 Pakistan

Weston, Mark

The land and people of Pakistan. HarperCollins Pubs. 1992 242p il maps (Portraits of the nations series) $18 (5 and up) **954.91**

1. Pakistan

ISBN 0-06-022789-3 LC 91-2847

An introduction to the history, geography, government, economy, culture, and people of Pakistan

Includes bibliography

Yusufali, Jabeen

Pakistan; an Islamic treasure. Dillon Press 1990 127p il map (Discovering our heritage) lib bdg $14.95 (4 and up) **954.91**

1. Pakistan

ISBN 0-87518-433-2 LC 89-26028

Discusses the history, people, religions, food, cultural heritage, lifestyle, education, sports, industries, major cities, politics, historic sites, festivals, and holidays of Pakistan

"Black-and-white and color photographs of the people, the art, and the landscape of the country strengthen an already informative text; as an added bonus, a few recipes are given. . . . An excellent resource for report writing." Booklist

Includes glossary and bibliography

954.92 Bangladesh

Lauré, Jason, 1940-

Bangladesh. Childrens Press 1992 127p il maps (Enchantment of the world) lib bdg $28.70 (4 and up) **954.92**

1. Bangladesh

ISBN 0-516-02609-7 LC 92-8891

An introduction to the geography, history, economy, culture, and people of Bangladesh, the small, densely populated neighbor of India

This title "presents a wealth of information in an attractive, readable format." SLJ

954.93 Sri Lanka

Sri Lanka—in pictures; prepared by Geography Department. Lerner Publs. 1989 64p il maps (Visual geography series) lib bdg $19.95 (5 and up) **954.93**

1. Sri Lanka

ISBN 0-8225-1853-8 LC 88-15888

Revised edition of Ceylon (Sri Lanka) by E. W. Egan, published 1967 by Sterling

Sri Lanka's topography, history, society, economy, and government are concisely described, augmented by photographs, maps, charts, and captions

954.96 Nepal

Nepal—in pictures; prepared by the Geography Department. Lerner Publs. 1989 64p il maps (Visual geography series) lib bdg $19.95 (5 and up) **954.96**

1. Nepal
ISBN 0-8225-1851-1   LC 88-8347
Revised edition of Nepal, Sikkim and Bhutan (Himalayan kingdoms) in pictures, prepared by Eugene Gordon, published 1972 by Sterling
Discusses the land, history, government, people, and economy of the country whose diverse topography contains the world's highest peak and also lush tropical lowlands

Pitkänen, Matti A.
The children of Nepal; [by] Matti A. Pitkänen, with Reijo Härkönen. Carolrhoda Bks. 1990 48p il map (World's children) lib bdg $19.95 (3-5) **954.96**

1. Nepal 2. Children—Nepal
ISBN 0-87614-395-8   LC 89-23923
Original Finish edition, 1985
An introduction to the history, geography, and people of Nepal with emphasis on the day-to-day life of the children
"This book will make readers fall in love with Nepal. Fifty-nine full-color photographs provide a dazzling introduction to the home of Mt. Everest and the abominable snowman." SLJ

Reynolds, Jan, 1956-
Himalaya; vanishing cultures. Harcourt Brace Jovanovich 1991 unp il map (Vanishing cultures series) $16.95; pa $8.95 (2-4) **954.96**

1. Himalaya Mountains—Social life and customs
ISBN 0-15-234465-9; 0-15-234466-7 (pa)
LC 90-36197
This book describes the customs and day-to-day life of a family living in the Himalaya Mountains
"The text and accompanying beautiful photographs help the reader learn about family life and customs." Child Book Rev Serv

955 Iran

Stein, R. Conrad, 1937-
The Iran hostage crisis. Childrens Press 1994 31p il (Cornerstones of freedom) lib bdg $12.98 (4-6) **955**

1. Iran hostage crisis, 1979-1981
ISBN 0-516-06681-1   LC 94-9492
"Stein begins with the events leading up to the hostile takeover of the American Embassy in Tehran on November 4, 1979. Quotes from former hostages, President Jimmy Carter, and one of the clergymen allowed to meet with the captives gives the compelling narrative an immediacy that transcends the . . . years that have passed since their release." SLJ
Includes bibliographical references

956.1 Turkey

Dalokay, Vedat
Sister Shako and Kolo the goat; memories of my childhood in Turkey; translated by Güner Ener. Lothrop, Lee & Shepard Bks. 1994 96p $14 (5 and up) **956.1**

1. Turkey—Social life and customs 2. Goats
ISBN 0-688-13271-5   LC 93-86329
Original Turkish edition, 1979
This "memoir of the author's childhood in a village in eastern Turkey relates the story of his friendship with an outcast, a woman whose only belongings are her goats. The story of Sister Shako's goat-bound existence, in the hands of the skilled author and translator, soon transcends the details of udders milked and dung dried to become an exquisite portrait of a remarkable soul." Horn Book Guide

956.7 Iraq

Foster, Leila Merrell
Iraq. Childrens Press 1991 128p il maps (Enchantment of the world) lib bdg $28.70 (4 and up) **956.7**

1. Iraq
ISBN 0-516-02723-9   LC 90-2174
Discusses the geography, history, people, and culture of Iraq

956.92 Lebanon

Foster, Leila Merrell
Lebanon. Childrens Press 1992 127p il maps (Enchantment of the world) lib bdg $28.70 (4 and up) **956.92**

1. Lebanon
ISBN 0-516-02612-7   LC 91-32230
Describes the geography, history, culture, industry, and people of Lebanon
"The book's format is attractive with abundant full-color photographs and reproductions. . . . Information is current through early 1992." SLJ

Marston, Elsa
Lebanon; new light in an ancient land. Dillon Press 1994 127p il (Discovering our heritage) lib bdg $14.95 (4 and up) **956.92**

1. Lebanon
ISBN 0-87518-584-3   LC 93-5402
This is an "overview of the geography, history, and culture of Lebanon. The text covers customs, education, and family, and makes distinctions between rural, mountain, and urban life. Marston also covers the impact of Lebanese immigration on the United States. Her love of the country is evident, and her writing is lucid and interesting. . . . The book is illustrated with well-placed and accurately captioned photographs." SLJ
Includes bibliography

956.93 Cyprus

Cyprus—in pictures; prepared by Geography Department. Lerner Publs. 1992 64p il maps (Visual geography series) lib bdg $19.95 (5 and up)   956.93
1. Cyprus
ISBN 0-8225-1910-0   LC 91-43188
Describes the topography, history, society, economy, and governmental structure of Cyprus

Fox, Mary Virginia
Cyprus. Childrens Press 1993 128p il maps (Enchantment of the world) lib bdg $28.70 (4 and up)   956.93
1. Cyprus
ISBN 0-516-02617-8   LC 93-755
Presents the geography, history, and customs of the divided Mediterranean island of Cyprus

956.94 Palestine. Israel

Dolphin, Laurie
Neve shalom/Wahat al-salam: Oasis of peace; photographs by Ben Dolphin. Scholastic 1993 48p il $14.95 (2-4)   956.94
1. Neveh Shalom (School) 2. Jewish-Arab relations 3. Israel—Social life and customs
ISBN 0-590-45799-3   LC 92-15552
Text and photos present the lives of two ten-year-old boys, one Jewish and one Arab, who attend school in a unique community near Jerusalem where Jews and Arabs live together in peace
"With a simple expository narrative and photographs brimming with vitality and candor, the Dolphins create an intimate portrait of two families as well as of the school in which the boys meet." Publ Wkly
Includes glossary

Haskins, James, 1941-
Count your way through Israel; illustrations by Rick Hanson. Carolrhoda Bks. 1990 unp il lib bdg $18.95; pa $5.95 (2-4)   956.94
1. Israel
ISBN 0-87614-415-6 (lib bdg); 0-87614-558-6 (pa)
LC 90-1594
An introduction to the land and people of Israel accompanied by instructions on how to read and pronounce the numbers one through ten in Hebrew

Scharfstein, Sol, 1921-
Understanding Israel. Ktav 1994 144p il maps $19.95; pa $14.95 (5 and up)   956.94
1. Israel
ISBN 0-88125-448-7; 0-88125-428-2 (pa)
LC 94-5791
A "pictorial overview of the modern state from its beginnings in Palestine up to the present. Scharfstein describes the land and peoples of Israel, its history, government, culture, economy, archaeology, and religion. The country's role

in the politics, powerplays, and wars of the Middle East are also summarized. . . . The writing is straightforward with brief declarative sentences and from one to two pages devoted to a topic." SLJ

958 Central Asia

Kazakhstan; prepared by Geography Department. Lerner Publs. 1993 56p il maps (Then & now) lib bdg $21.50 (5 and up)
958
1. Kazakhstan
ISBN 0-8225-2815-0   LC 92-33082
Discusses the topography, location, ethnic mixture, history, and current political climate of the former Soviet republic of Kazakhstan
Includes glossary

Tajikistan; prepared by Geography Department. Lerner Publs. 1993 56p il maps (Then & now) lib bdg $21.50 (5 and up)
958
1. Tajikistan
ISBN 0-8225-2816-9   LC 92-40237
Discusses the geography, history, people, economics, politics, and future of the central Asian country that was the smallest and poorest Soviet republic
Includes glossary

Uzbekistan; prepared by Geography Department. Lerner Publs. 1993 56p il maps (Then & now) lib bdg $21.50 (5 and up)
958
1. Uzbekistan
ISBN 0-8225-2812-6   LC 92-33081
Discusses the topography, location, ethnic mixture, history, and current political situation of the former Soviet republic of Uzbekistan

959.5 Commonwealth of Nations territories. Malaysia

Wright, David K.
Brunei. Childrens Press 1991 127p il maps (Enchantment of the world) lib bdg $28.70 (4 and up)   959.5
1. Brunei
ISBN 0-516-02602-X   LC 91-22511
An introduction to the small and prosperous country of Brunei, which lies on the north coast of the island of Borneo

959.6 Cambodia

Chandler, David P.
The land and people of Cambodia. HarperCollins Pubs. 1991 210p il maps (Portraits of the nations series) $19; lib bdg $18.89 (5 and up)   959.6
1. Cambodia
ISBN 0-06-021129-6; 0-06-021130-X (lib bdg)
LC 90-5907

Chandler, David P.—*Continued*

Introduces the history, geography, people, culture, government, and economy of Cambodia

Includes bibliography

Greenblatt, Miriam

Cambodia. Childrens Press 1995 126p il maps (Enchantment of the world) lib bdg $28.70 (4 and up) **959.6**

1. Cambodia

ISBN 0-516-02632-1 LC 94-37949

"In addition to geography and culture, the religious life of the people is given special attention through clear explanations about Buddhism and Islam. The war in Vietnam and the subsequent events in surrounding countries that have resulted in many immigrants coming to the United States are explained." SLJ

959.7 Vietnam

Vietnam—in pictures; prepared by Geography Dept. Lerner Publs. 1994 64p il maps (Visual geography series) lib bdg $18.95 (5 and up) **959.7**

1. Vietnam

ISBN 0-8225-1909-7 LC 93-21343

This is a "description of Vietnam—its land, history and government, people, and economy—amply illustrated with pictures." Sci Books Films

This is a book "students will find useful for country reports. . . . The text is clear, readable and up to date." Booklist

959.704 Vietnam—1949-

Ashabranner, Brent K., 1921-

Always to remember; the story of the Vietnam Veterans Memorial; [by] Brent Ashabranner; photographs by Jennifer Ashabranner. Dodd, Mead 1988 101p il lib bdg $14.95 (5 and up) **959.704**

1. Vietnam War, 1961-1975 2. Vietnam Veterans Memorial (Washington, D.C.)

ISBN 0-399-22031-3 LC 87-33110

Also available in paperback from Scholastic

"Beginning with a concise (and fair) chapter on the Vietnam War, the author then recounts the hard work of Jan Scruggs, the vet who began the Vietnam Veterans Memorial Fund, and Maya Lin, the 21-year-old architecture student who won the contest to design the monument. While there is plenty in this book to bring tears, Ashabranner is unobtrusive, allowing the veterans, families, and the memorial to speak for themselves. . . . Jennifer Ashabranner's photographs capture the details of flowers and fatigues left along the base of the monument wall but, as the architect intended, viewers will find their attentions primarily caught by the endless rows of names." Bull Cent Child Books

Donnelly, Judy

A wall of names; the story of the Vietnam Veterans Memorial; illustrated with photographs. Random House 1991 48p il lib bdg $9.99; pa $3.99 (2-4) **959.704**

1. Vietnam Veterans Memorial (Washington, D.C.) 2. Vietnam War, 1961-1975

ISBN 0-679-90169-8 (lib bdg); 0-679-80169-3 (pa) LC 90-30275

"Step into reading. A step 4 book"

Surveys the history of the Vietnam War, chronicles the construction of the Vietnam Memorial, and discusses what the Memorial means to many Americans

This book "is a moving, appropriately simple introduction to a major monument. Donnelly's concise text—illustrated with well-chosen file photos—skillfully places the Vietnam War within a continuum of American history." Publ Wkly

Garland, Sherry, 1948-

Vietnam, rebuilding a nation. Dillon Press 1990 127p il map (Discovering our heritage) lib bdg $14.95 (4 and up) **959.704**

1. Vietnam

ISBN 0-87518-422-7 LC 89-29212

The author offers an "overview of Vietnam, describing its landscape, peoples, history, and culture in a text that is aimed at middle graders on the lookout for report material. Color and black-and-white photos support the information. . . . Also included is a chapter on the boat people and the struggles of Vietnamese immigrants making a new life in the U.S." Booklist

Includes glossary and bibliographical references

Schmidt, Jeremy, 1949-

Two lands, one heart; an American boy's journey to his mother's Vietnam; [by] Jeremy Schmidt, Ted Wood; photographs by Ted Wood. Walker & Co. 1995 44p il maps $15.95; lib bdg $16.85 (3-5) **959.704**

1. Sharp, Timothy James 2. Vietnam—Description

ISBN 0-8027-8357-0; 0-8027-8358-9 (lib bdg) LC 94-33648

"After years of hearing stories and seeing pictures of his mother's homeland, young TJ travels to Vietnam to visit the family his mother left behind as a child during the Vietnam War. A narrative rich in detail and striking, full-color photographs capture TJ's adventure and in the process, introduce readers to the Vietnamese culture and landscape." Booklist

959.8 Indonesia

Indonesia—in pictures; prepared by Geography Department. Lerner Publs. 1990 64p il maps (Visual geography series) lib bdg $19.95 (5 and up) **959.8**

1. Indonesia

ISBN 0-8225-1860-0 LC 89-36540

Revised edition of the title prepared by Tom Gerst, published 1974 by Sterling

Text and photographs introduce the topography, history, society, economy, and governmental structure of Indonesia

McNair, Sylvia, 1924-

Indonesia. Childrens Press 1993 126p il maps (Enchantment of the world) lib bdg $28.70 (4 and up)   **959.8**

1. Indonesia
ISBN 0-516-02618-6   LC 93-3401

A survey of the geography, people, history, government, industries, and culture of Indonesia

"It is particularly helpful that definitions of unfamiliar words are seamlessly woven into the text instead of referring readers to a glossary at the back. Abundant and well-chosen black-and-white reproductions and full-color photographs appear throughout." SLJ

960   Africa

Chiasson, John C.

African journey; [by] John Chiasson. Bradbury Press 1987 55p il map $17.95 (4 and up)   **960**

1. Africa—Social life and customs 2. Ethnology—Africa
ISBN 0-02-718530-3   LC 86-8233

"Text describes the culture and habitat of the people in six regions, beginning with the Twareg and WoDaaBe, two herding tribes in desert areas of Niger." Horn Book

"Chiasson creates a stark, compelling picture of this continent. . . . The images themselves are involving and immediate; this is a photoessay deserving of high honors." Publ Wkly

Haskins, James, 1941-

From Afar to Zulu; a dictionary of African cultures; [by] Jim Haskins, and Joann Biondi. Walker & Co. 1995 212p il maps $18.95; lib bdg $19.85 (4 and up)   **960**

1. Africa—Social life and customs—Dictionaries
ISBN 0-8027-8290-6; 0-8027-8291-4 (lib bdg)
    LC 94-11545

This volume describes "more than 30 major and 200 smaller ethnic groups on the African continent. History, social customs, religions, political issues and contemporary events are discussed in each entry." BAYA Book Rev

For a fuller review see: Booklist, March 1, 1995

Includes bibliographical references

Ibazebo, Isimeme

Exploration into Africa. New Discovery Bks. 1994 48p il maps $15.95 (4-6)   **960**

1. Africa—Exploration
ISBN 0-02-718081-6   LC 93-43720

"The history, politics, culture, and religions of . . . Africa are presented in an accessible and focused manner through the use of double-page topic treatments. . . . Beautiful full-color and black-and-white photographs and fine-art reproductions are plentiful." SLJ

Includes glossary

Musgrove, Margaret, 1943-

Ashanti to Zulu: African traditions; pictures by Leo and Diane Dillon. Dial Bks. for Young Readers 1976 unp il $17.99; lib bdg $15.89; pa $4.95 (3-6)   **960**

1. Africa—Social life and customs 2. Ethnology—Africa
ISBN 0-8037-0357-0; 0-8037-0358-9 (lib bdg); 0-8037-0308-2 (pa)

Awarded the Caldecott Medal, 1977

"In brief texts arranged in alphabetical order, each accompanied by a large framed illustration, the author introduces 'the reader to twenty-six African peoples by depicting a custom important to each.' . . . In most of the paintings the artists 'have included a man, a woman, a child, their living quarters, an artifact, and a local animal' and have, in this way, stressed the human and the natural ambience of the various peoples depicted." Horn Book

"The writing is dignified and the material informative, but it is the illustrations that make the book outstanding." Bull Cent Child Books

961   Tunisia and Libya. North Africa

Umm El Madayan; an Islamic city through the ages; [by] Abderrahman Ayoub [et al.]; illustrated by Francesco Corni; translated by Kathleen Leverich. Houghton Mifflin 1994 61p il $16.95 (5 and up)   **961**

1. Cities and towns 2. North Africa
ISBN 0-395-65967-1   LC 93-757

Original Italian edition, 1993

Traces the development of a fictional Islamic city in North Africa through the ages

"Beautifully detailed line drawings fill every page of this informative book." Book Rep

961.1   Tunisia

Fox, Mary Virginia

Tunisia. Childrens Press 1990 123p il maps (Enchantment of the world) lib bdg $28.70 (4 and up)   **961.1**

1. Tunisia
ISBN 0-516-02724-7   LC 90-2199

Discusses the geography, history, people, and culture of Tunisia

964   Northwest African coast and offshore islands. Morocco

Hermes, Jules, 1962-

The children of Morocco. Carolrhoda Bks. 1995 48p il maps (World's children) lib bdg $19.95; pa $7.95 (3-5)   **964**

1. Children—Morocco 2. Morocco
ISBN 0-87614-857-7 (lib bdg); 0-87614-899-2 (pa)
    LC 94-12709

"After an introductory map section, Hermes tells the story of many different Moroccan children—nomadic Berbers, village dwellers, and city children from Casablanca, Rabat,

Hermes, Jules, 1962-—*Continued*
and Tangier. Some of the children are living with families; others are on their own in cities." Booklist
"The author's fine eye for detail makes the book refreshing and stimulating. Layout and design are well balanced." SLJ

965   Algeria

Algeria—in pictures; prepared by Geography Department. Lerner Publs. 1992 64p il maps (Visual geography series) lib bdg $19.95 (5 and up)   **965**

1. Algeria
ISBN 0-8225-1901-1   LC 91-30722

Describes the topography, history, society, economy, and governmental structure of Algeria

966.2   Mali, Burkina Faso, Niger

McKissack, Patricia C., 1944-

The royal kingdoms of Ghana, Mali, and Songhay; life in medieval Africa; [by] Patricia and Fredrick McKissack. Holt & Co. 1993 142p il maps $15.95; pa $7.95 (5 and up)   **966.2**

1. Ghana Empire—History 2. Mali—History 3. Songhai Empire
ISBN 0-8050-1670-8; 0-8050-4259-8 (pa)
                                           LC 93-4838

Examines the civilizations of the Western Sudan which flourished from 700 to 1700 A.D., acquiring such vast wealth that they became centers of trade and culture for a continent
"The McKissacks are careful to distinguish what is known from what is surmised; they draw on the oral tradition, eyewitness accounts, and contemporary scholarship; and chapter source notes discuss various conflicting views of events." Booklist
Includes bibliography

966.23   Mali

O'Toole, Thomas, 1941-

Mali—in pictures; prepared by Thomas O'Toole. Lerner Publs. 1990 64p il maps (Visual geography series) lib bdg $19.95 (5 and up)   **966.23**

1. Mali
ISBN 0-8225-1869-4   LC 89-34527

Text and photographs introduce the topography, history, society, economy, and governmental structure of Mali

966.5   Gambia, Guinea, Guinea-Bissau, Cape Verde

Zimmermann, Robert

The Gambia. Childrens Press 1994 128p il maps (Enchantment of the world) lib bdg $28.70 (4 and up)   **966.5**

1. Gambia
ISBN 0-516-02625-9   LC 94-7008

Text and numerous illustrations present the history, geography, economy and the people of The Gambia
"As with other titles in this series, *The Gambia* offers young researchers the basic information they need for reports." SLJ

967.51   Zaire

Zaire—in pictures; prepared by Geography Department. Lerner Publs. 1992 64p il maps (Visual geography series) lib bdg $19.95 (5 and up)   **967.51**

1. Zaire
ISBN 0-8225-1899-6   LC 91-31006

Describes the topography, history, society, economy, and governmental structure of Zaire

967.8   Tanzania

Margolies, Barbara A., 1939-
Olbalbal; a day in Maasailand. Four Winds Press 1994 32p il maps $15.95 (3-5)   **967.8**

1. Masai (African people)
ISBN 0-02-762284-3   LC 93-19744

"Beginning with the origins of the Maasai and some historical background, Margolies introduces readers to their seminomadic life, family structure, how the Maasai tell time, the important role of women, food, religious beliefs, rites of passage, and the inevitable changes Western education is likely to bring Maasailand. Clear, beautiful photographs accompany the rich narration." Horn Book Guide

968   Southern Africa. Republic of South Africa

Angelou, Maya
My painted house, my friendly chicken, and me; photographs by Margaret Courtney-Clarke. Potter 1994 unp il $16 (k-3)   **968**

1. South Africa—Social life and customs
ISBN 0-517-59667-9   LC 93-45735

"Thandi, an eight-year-old Ndebele girl of South Africa, tells about her family, the fine art of house painting carried out mainly by the women in the village, and the contrast between village and city life. Courtney-Clarke's abundant, brightly colored photographs accompany Angelou's refreshingly warm introduction to the art, culture, and social life of the Ndebele people." Horn Book Guide

968.8 Botswana, Lesotho, Swaziland, Nambia

Brandenburg, Jim
Sand and fog; adventures in Southern Africa; edited by JoAnn Bren Guernsey. Walker & Co. 1994 44p il map $16.95; lib bdg $17.85 (4 and up)   **968.8**

1. Namibia 2. Desert ecology 3. Photography of animals
ISBN 0-8027-8232-9; 0-8027-8233-7 (lib bdg)
LC 93-30425

This is a "collection of images of life—both human and animal—in the desert realms of Namibia." Publ Wkly
The author "combines exquisite color pictures with a first-person narrative to produce a book noteworthy for its craftsmanship, artistry, and perspective." Horn Book Guide

Lauré, Jason, 1940-
Botswana. Childrens Press 1993 128p il maps (Enchantment of the world) $28.70 (4 and up)   **968.8**

1. Botswana
ISBN 0-516-02616-X   LC 93-753
An illustrated introduction to the geography, climate, history, economy, culture, and people of Botswana

968.91 Zimbabwe

Cheney, Patricia
The land and people of Zimbabwe. Lippincott 1990 242p il maps (Portraits of the nations series) lib bdg $15.89 (5 and up)
968.91

1. Zimbabwe
ISBN 0-397-32393-X   LC 89-36244
An introduction to the history, geography, economy, culture, and people of Zimbabwe
"A fairly even account of Zimbabwe's struggle to regain its independence. . . . Detailed but not overburdened with facts, this is a straightforward account that has interesting incidents and information." SLJ
Includes bibliography

968.97 Malawi

Lane, Martha S. B.
Malawi; consultant for Malawi, John Rowe; consultant for reading, Robert L. Hillerich. Childrens Press 1990 126p il maps (Enchantment of the world) lib bdg $28.70 (4 and up)   **968.97**

1. Malawi
ISBN 0-516-02720-4   LC 89-25433
Introduces the geography, history, government, lifestyles, and industries of Malawi

970.004 North American native peoples

Ancona, George, 1929-
Powwow; photographs and text by George Ancona. Harcourt Brace Jovanovich 1993 unp il $16.95; pa $8.95 (3-6)   **970.004**

1. Crow Fair (Crow Agency, Mont.) 2. Indians of North America—Rites and ceremonies
ISBN 0-15-263268-9; 0-15-263269-7 (pa)
LC 92-15912

A photo essay on the pan-Indian celebration called a powwow, this particular one being held on the Crow Reservation in Montana
The book is "illustrated with well-placed, full-color photos that clearly reflect the text. . . . An exquisite kaleidoscope of Native American music, customs, and crafts." SLJ

Andryszewski, Tricia, 1956-
The Seminoles; people of the Southeast. Millbrook Press 1995 64p il map (Native Americans) lib bdg $15.40 (4-6)   **970.004**

1. Seminole Indians
ISBN 1-56294-530-0   LC 94-21819
This book describes the history and culture of the Seminoles of Florida. A traditional recipe, game and story are included
Includes glossary and bibliography

Arnold, Caroline, 1944-
The ancient cliff dwellers of Mesa Verde; photographs by Richard Hewett. Clarion Bks. 1992 64p il $15.95 (4 and up)   **970.004**

1. Pueblo Indians
ISBN 0-395-56241-4   LC 91-8145
Discusses the native Americans known as the Anasazi, who migrated to southwestern Colorado in the first century A.D. and mysteriously disappeared in 1300 A.D. after constructing extensive dwellings in the cliffs of the steep canyon walls
"A thorough and attractive introduction to the Anasazi people with outstanding photographs of the dramatic vistas and ceremonial chambers within this national park." SLJ
Includes glossary

Baylor, Byrd, 1924-
When clay sings; illustrated by Tom Bahti. Scribner 1972 unp il $15 (1-4)   **970.004**

1. Indians of North America—Art 2. Indians of North America—Southwestern States 3. Pottery
ISBN 0-684-18829-5
Also available in paperback from Aladdin Bks. (NY)
A Caldecott Medal honor book, 1973
"A lyrical tribute to an almost forgotten time of the prehistoric Indian of the desert West presents broken bits of pottery from this ancient time. The designs and drawings, done in rich earth tones, are derived from prehistoric pottery found in the American Southwest." Read Ladders for Hum Relat. 6th edition

Bealer, Alex W.

Only the names remain; the Cherokees and the Trail of Tears; illustrated by Kristina Rodanas. Little, Brown 1996 79p il $15.95; pa $4.95 (4-6)   **970.004**

1. Cherokee Indians

ISBN 0-316-08518-9; 0-316-08519-7 (pa)

A reissue with new illustrations of the title first published 1972

The author describes "the rise of the Cherokee Nation, with its written language, constitution, and republican form of government, and its tragic betrayal in the 1830s." Chicago Public Libr

Bonvillain, Nancy

The Navajos; people of the Southwest. Millbrook Press 1995 64p il (Native Americans) lib bdg $15.40 (4-6)   **970.004**

1. Navajo Indians

ISBN 1-56294-495-9   LC 94-21818

An illustrated overview of the history and culture of the largest Native American tribe in contemporary America. A traditional song and recipe are included

Includes bibliographical references

Braine, Susan

Drumbeat—heartbeat; a celebration of the powwow; text and photographs by Susan Braine. Lerner Publs. 1995 48p il (We are still here: Native Americans today) lib bdg $19.95; pa $6.95 (3-6)   **970.004**

1. Indians of North America—Rites and ceremonies

ISBN 0-8225-2656-5 (lib bdg); 0-8225-9711-X (pa)
LC 94-42594

The author explains how powwows "started, when and where they are held, and what one can expect to see there. Detailed descriptions of the various dance styles for both men and women are given, followed by information on the singing and drumming, a special plus. . . . Informative full-color photographs are well placed throughout." SLJ

Includes glossary and bibliography

Brill, Marlene Targ

The Trail of Tears; the Cherokee journey from home. Millbrook Press 1995 64p il maps (Spotlight on American history) lib bdg $15.40 (5 and up)   **970.004**

1. Cherokee Indians

ISBN 1-56294-486-X   LC 94-16988

This is an "account of the history of the Cherokee Nation's conflicts with white colonizers of its tribal lands; the U.S. government's removal of the people from their ancestral homes in 1838; and their forced migration West to Oklahoma. The text is sparingly, but appropriately, illustrated with full-color and black-and-white reproductions and photographs. Solid and useful appendixes are included." SLJ

Includes bibliography

Crum, Robert

Eagle drum; on the powwow trail with a young grass dancer. Four Winds Press 1994 48p il $16.95 (3-6)   **970.004**

1. Kalispel Indians 2. Indians of North America—Rites and ceremonies

ISBN 0-02-725515-8   LC 94-6034

"Nine-year-old Louis Pierre, a member of the Pend Oreile tribe on the Flathead Reservation in Montana, has been dancing since he was four. Combining history with information about tribal dance and Pierre's family, Crum presents the preparation and performance of the powwow dances in colorful photographs and detailed descriptions." Booklist

Duvall, Jill

The Chumash; by Jill D. Duvall. Childrens Press 1994 45p il maps lib bdg $16.60; pa $4.95 (2-4)   **970.004**

1. Chumash Indians

ISBN 0-516-01052-2; 0-516-41052-0 (pa)
LC 93-36672

"A New true book"

Describes the history, customs, religious beliefs, Spanish mission life, and contemporary life of the Chumash of California

Includes glossary

Ehrlich, Amy, 1942-

Wounded Knee: an Indian history of the American West; adapted for young readers by Amy Ehrlich from Dee Brown's Bury my heart at Wounded Knee. Holt & Co. 1974 202p il maps hardcover o.p. paperback available $9.95 (6 and up)   **970.004**

1. Indians of North America—West (U.S.) 2. Indians of North America—Wars 3. West (U.S.)—History

ISBN 0-8050-2700-9 (pa)

This book traces the plight of the Navaho, Apache, Cheyenne and Sioux Indians in their struggles against the white man in the West between 1860 and 1890. It recounts battles and their causes, participants, and consequences during this era

"Some chapters [of the original] have been deleted, others condensed, and in some instances sentence structure and language have been simplified. The editing is good, and this version is interesting, readable, and smooth. " SLJ

Includes bibliographies

Fradin, Dennis B.

The Cheyenne. Childrens Press 1988 45p il lib bdg $16.60; pa $4.95 (2-4)   **970.004**

1. Cheyenne Indians

ISBN 0-516-01211-8 (lib bdg); 0-516-41211-6 (pa)
LC 87-33792

"A New true book"

"Fradin covers in short chapter segments topics such as the early history of the tribe, their beliefs, social and family life, Indian-white relations, and the Cheyenne today. The volume contains color as well as black-and-white photographs." SLJ

Includes glossary

Fradin, Dennis B.—*Continued*

The Pawnee. Childrens Press 1988 45p il map lib bdg $16.60; pa $4.95 (2-4)
        970.004

1. Pawnee Indians
ISBN 0-516-01155-3 (lib bdg); 0-516-41155-1 (pa)
        LC 88-11820
"A New true book"
Discusses Pawnee Indian customs, villages, warfare, religious beliefs, family life, and their place in contemporary American society
Includes glossary

The Shoshoni. Childrens Press 1988 47p il maps lib bdg $16.60; pa $4.95 (2-4)
        970.004

1. Shoshoni Indians
ISBN 0-516-01156-1 (lib bdg); 0-516-41156-X (pa)
        LC 88-11821
"A New true book"
Describes the history, beliefs, customs, homes, and day-to-day life of the Shoshoni Indians. Also discusses how they live today
Includes glossary

Freedman, Russell

Buffalo hunt. Holiday House 1988 52p il lib bdg $18.95; pa $8.95 (4 and up)   **970.004**
1. Indians of North America—Great Plains 2. Bison
ISBN 0-8234-0702-0 (lib bdg); 0-8234-1159-1 (pa)
        LC 87-35303
The author discusses the importance of the buffalo in the lore and day-to-day life of the Indian tribes of the Great Plains. He describes hunting methods, the uses found for each part of the animal, and the near disappearance of the buffalo as white hunters, traders and settlers moved west
"Freedman has hit his stride in terms of selection, style, and illustration: the color reproductions of historical art work form a stunning complement to the carefully researched, graceful presentation of information." Bull Cent Child Books

Griffin-Pierce, Trudy

The encyclopedia of Native America. Viking 1995 192p il $25   **970.004**
1. Indians of North America
ISBN 0-670-85104-3   LC 94-61491
"Each chapter covers a specific geographical area of the United States, such as The Great Plains or the Southwest, and the tribes that resided there. Topics include languages of tribes with a map showing where each language group lived, descriptions of each tribe and its way of life, and European contact with the tribes and the results. Along with historical information about the tribes, Griffin-Pierce has included information on the present-day status of Native Americans." Book Rep

Hoyt-Goldsmith, Diane

Apache rodeo; photographs by Lawrence Migdale. Holiday House 1995 32p il $15.95 (3-5)   **970.004**
1. Apache Indians 2. Rodeos
ISBN 0-8234-1164-8   LC 94-26583

This is an introduction to "the Apache of the Fort Apache Indian Reservation in Whiteriver, Arizona. Using ten-year-old Felecita La Rose as its focus and narrator, the book summarizes Apache history, customs, and daily life, and then goes on to its feature event: the rodeo." Bull Cent Child Books
"The many full-color photographs that appear throughout make it easy for other children to see how Felicita's life is like and unlike their own. An appealing introduction to Apache life today." Booklist
Includes glossary

Arctic hunter; photographs by Lawrence Migdale. Holiday House 1992 30p il $15.95; pa $6.95 (3-5)   **970.004**
1. Inuit
ISBN 0-8234-0972-4; 0-8234-1124-9 (pa)
        LC 92-2563
"Hoyt-Goldsmith follows 10-year-old Reggie Joule and his family as they journey to their spring hunting and fishing camp north of the Arctic Circle. . . . Readers will share in Reggie's excitement as he accompanies the men on a seal hunt and makes his first kill. Hoyt-Goldsmith treats the Iñupiaq culture with great respect. . . . Migdale's photographs illustrate the text beautifully." Booklist
Includes glossary

Cherokee summer; photographs by Lawrence Migdale. Holiday House 1993 32p il $15.95 (3-5)   **970.004**
1. Cherokee Indians
ISBN 0-8234-0995-3   LC 92-54416
"Ten-year-old Bridget, a mixed-blood member of the Cherokee Nation, lives with her family in a small town in Oklahoma. During the summer, Bridget participates in special events of the Cherokee Nation. . . . Double-page spreads focus on tribal history, including information on the Trail of Tears, the development of the Cherokee syllabary, and contemporary Cherokee life. Clear, full-color photographs bring the matter-of-fact text to life." Booklist
Includes glossary

Pueblo storyteller; photographs by Lawrence Migdale. Holiday House 1991 26p il $15.95; pa $6.95 (3-5)   **970.004**
1. Pueblo Indians
ISBN 0-8234-0864-7; 0-8234-1080-3 (pa)
        LC 90-46405
A young Cochiti Indian girl living with her grandparents in the Cochiti Pueblo near Santa Fe, New Mexico, describes her home and family and the day-to-day life and customs of her people
"The bright, crisp, almost shadowless photographs smoothly integrate additional details into the lively text." Publ Wkly
Includes glossary

Totem pole; photographs by Lawrence Migdale. Holiday House 1990 30p il lib bdg $15.95; pa $6.95 (3-5)   **970.004**
1. Indians of North America—Northwest Coast of North America 2. Totems and totemism
ISBN 0-8234-0809-4 (lib bdg); 0-8234-1135-4 (pa)
        LC 89-26720

Hoyt-Goldsmith, Diane— *Continued*

A Tsimshian Indian boy proudly describes how his father carved a totem pole for the Klallam tribe and the subsequent ceremonial celebration

"The writing is simple and direct, the tone of pride is strong, the information is not often found in books for children, and the book is imbued with cultural dignity and a sense of the value of the extended family and community." Bull Cent Child Books

Includes glossary

Jenness, Aylette

In two worlds: a Yup'ik Eskimo family; [by] Aylette Jenness and Alice Rivers; photographs by Aylette Jenness. Houghton Mifflin 1989 84p il $13.95 (4 and up)   **970.004**

1. Inuit
ISBN 0-395-42797-5   LC 88-13887

Text and photographs document the life of a Yup'ik Eskimo family, residents of a small Alaskan town on the coast of the Bering Sea, detailing the changes that have come about in the last fifty years

"More descriptive than analytical, the book includes details of hunting, fishing, trapping and skinning, schooling, family life, and recreation, which includes both women's basketball and traditional dancing. The writing is generally clear although sometimes oddly constructed, and the many black-and-white photographs lack captions but are usually well-placed." Bull Cent Child Books

Includes bibliography

Kalbacken, Joan

The Menominee. Childrens Press 1994 45p il map lib bdg $18; pa $4.95 (2-4)
          970.004

1. Menominee Indians
ISBN 0-516-01054-9; 0-516-41054-7 (pa)
          LC 93-36671

"A New true book"

This brief history of the Menominee Indians of Wisconsin describes their tribal organization, customs and ceremonies, early relations with the French, recent restoration of their lands, reservation life today, and their future

Includes glossary

Keegan, Marcia

Pueblo boy; growing up in two worlds. Cobblehill Bks. 1991 unp il $15.99 (3-5)
          970.004

1. Pueblo Indians
ISBN 0-525-65060-1   LC 90-45187

Text and photographs depict the home, school, and cultural life of a young Indian boy named Timmy growing up on the San Ildefonso Pueblo in New Mexico

"The clear, colorful photographs in this respectful photo essay will attract an enthusiastic audience, and Keegan's text is interesting and readable." Horn Book

Kendall, Russ

Eskimo boy; life in an Inupiaq Eskimo village; written and photographed by Russ Kendall. Scholastic 1991 40p il $14.95 (2-4)
          970.004

1. Inuit
ISBN 0-590-43695-3   LC 90-9157

This "photographic essay introduces Norman Kokeok, a young Inupiaq Eskimo who lives on an Alaskan island where hunting and fishing are for survival. Readers meet Norman's family and neighbors, and follow their daily routines through the changing seasons. . . . Simple text and an afterword offering more detailed information round out a useful and enjoyable book." Adventuring with Books

Includes glossary

King, Sandra

Shannon: an Ojibway dancer; photographs by Catherine Whipple; with a foreword by Michael Dorris. Lerner Publs. 1993 48p il map (We are still here: Native Americans today) lib bdg $19.95; pa $6.95 (3-6)   **970.004**

1. Ojibwa Indians
ISBN 0-8225-2652-2 (lib bdg); 0-8225-9643-1 (pa)
          LC 92-27261

Shannon, a twelve-year-old Ojibwa Indian living in Minneapolis, Minnesota, learns about her tribe's traditional costumes from her grandmother and gets ready to dance at a powwow

"Numerous, colorful photographs show Shannon's daily activities as well as the costumes and dances at the powwow. The photos combine with a contemporary focus and straightforward text to make the book an excellent choice for middle readers." Booklist

Includes glossary and bibliography

Koslow, Philip

The Seminole Indians. Chelsea Jrs. 1994 79p il maps (Junior library of American Indians) $14.95; pa $6.95 (4-6)   **970.004**

1. Seminole Indians
ISBN 0-7910-1672-2; 0-7910-2486-5 (pa)
          LC 93-35441

This is a "general overview of the Seminoles, well illustrated with primarily black-and-white photographs and reproductions. Tribal history is presented chronologically, accompanied by helpful territorial maps and an accurate, complete index. Koslow has a knack for presenting complex ideas in simple, understandable language." SLJ

Krull, Kathleen, 1952-

One nation, many tribes; how kids live in Milwaukee's Indian community; photographs by David Hautzig. Lodestar Bks. 1995 48p il map (World of my own) $15.99 (4 and up)
          970.004

1. Indians of North America—Wisconsin
ISBN 0-525-67440-3   LC 93-39538

This book "introduces an Oneida/Ojibwa girl who is a talented solo hoop dancer and an Ojibwa/Comanche/Mexican boy. They are both students at the Milwaukee Indian Community School, which incorporates Native American cultures into every aspect of its curriculum. . . . Large, full-color photographs, one or more on almost every page, and the use of the subjects' own words bring these children to life." SLJ

Includes bibliography

Landau, Elaine
The Hopi. Watts 1994 63p il lib bdg $13.93; pa $5.95 (4 and up) **970.004**
1. Hopi Indians
ISBN 0-531-20098-1 (lib bdg); 0-531-15684-2 (pa)
LC 93-31964
"A First book"
This describes Hopi Indian families and homes, farming and livestock, ceremonies, crafts, and history
Includes glossary and bibliography

Lepthien, Emilie U. (Emilie Utteg)
The Choctaw. Childrens Press 1987 45p il maps lib bdg $13.27; pa $4.95 (2-4)
970.004
1. Choctaw Indians
ISBN 0-516-01240-1 (lib bdg); 0-516-41240-X (pa)
LC 87-14583
"A New true book"
"The book begins with a brief history of the Choctaw and their legends of how they came to settle in the area that is now Alabama and Mississippi. Descriptions of their daily lives are given, telling what they ate, their respect for nature, and methods of building homes. There is a short chronology of the Choctaw up to present times. . . . Problems and accomplishments of modern life are mentioned, making this a valuable book for native American studies." SLJ
Includes glossary

The Mandans. Childrens Press 1989 45p il lib bdg $13.27; pa $4.95 (2-4) **970.004**
1. Mandan Indians
ISBN 0-516-01180-4 (lib bdg); 0-516-41180-2 (pa)
LC 89-22235
"A New true book"
"Filled with attractive contemporary photographs and informative historical materials such as sketches by George Catlin and N.C. Wyeth, this attractive book contains historical background of the Mandans and their neighbors, the Hidatsa and the Arikara. . . . Well organized, the book offers historical accuracy and readability." SLJ
Includes glossary

Liptak, Karen
North American Indian ceremonies. Watts 1992 63p il lib bdg $13.93; pa $5.95 (4 and up) **970.004**
1. Indians of North America—Rites and ceremonies
ISBN 0-531-20100-7 (lib bdg); 0-531-15639-7 (pa)
LC 91-30263
"A First book"
The author "explains the significance of rituals for American Indians through history and in today's world and shows how modern ceremonies are rooted in tribal history and religious beliefs. The ceremonies presented represent many different tribes and cover a wide range of purposes—puberty rites, healing rituals, and ceremonies used in time of conflict." Booklist
Includes glossary and bibliography

Lucas, Eileen
The Ojibwas: people of the northern forests. Millbrook Press 1994 64p il (Native Americans) lib bdg $16.95 (4-6) **970.004**
1. Ojibwa Indians
ISBN 1-56294-313-8
LC 93-18640

This book describes the historical background, cultural traditions, religious beliefs, and present day way of life of the Ojibwa Indians, also known as the Chippewa
"The narrative is sound and well illustrated with maps, paintings, and photographs." Sci Books Films
Includes glossary and bibliography

McKissack, Patricia C., 1944-
The Apache; by Patricia McKissack. Childrens Press 1984 45p il lib bdg $16.60; pa $5.50 (2-4) **970.004**
1. Apache Indians
ISBN 0-516-01925-2 (lib bdg); 0-516-41925-0 (pa)
LC 84-7803
"A New true book"
Describes the history, customs, religion, government, homes, and day-to-day life of the Apache people of the Southwest

Miller, Jay, 1947-
The Delaware. Childrens Press 1994 45p il map lib bdg $16.60; pa $4.95 (2-4)
970.004
1. Delaware Indians
ISBN 0-516-01053-0 (lib bdg); 0-516-41053-9 (pa)
LC 93-36670
"A New true book"
This introduction to the Delaware Nation describes the history, customs, housing, clan structure, religious ceremonies, treatment by European settlers, and the Delaware today
Includes glossary

Monroe, Jean Guard
First houses; Native American homes and sacred structures; [by] Jean Guard Monroe and Ray A. Williamson; illustrated by Susan Johnston Carlson. Houghton Mifflin 1993 147p il $14.95 (6 and up) **970.004**
1. Indians of North America—Dwellings 2. Indians of North America—Rites and ceremonies 3. Indians of North America—Legends 4. Creation—Fiction
ISBN 0-395-51081-3
LC 92-34900
Presents a variety of North American Indian creation myths and discusses how the "first houses" described in these myths set the pattern used by the tribes for their own homes and ritual structures
"A well-researched and documented book that takes a unique approach to its topic." SLJ
Includes glossary and bibliography

Murdoch, David Hamilton, 1937-
North American Indian; written by David Murdoch; chief consultant, Stanley A. Freed; photographed by Lynton Gardiner. Knopf 1995 62p il (Eyewitness books) $17; lib bdg $18.99 (4 and up) **970.004**
1. Indians of North America
ISBN 0-679-86169-6; 0-679-96169-0 (lib bdg)
LC 94-36193
"A Dorling Kindersley book"
Published in association with the American Museum of Natural History

Murdoch, David Hamilton, 1937— *Continued*

"Brief, scattered information concerning the history and culture of a variety of Native-American peoples is accompanied by sharp color photographs of clothing, tools, weapons, and many other antiquities. Although far from comprehensive, the book is a fine photographic resource on historical and contemporary native artifacts." Horn Book Guide

Osinski, Alice

The Chippewa. Childrens Press 1987 45p il maps lib bdg $16.60; pa $4.95 (2-4)

970.004

1. Ojibwa Indians

ISBN 0-516-01230-4 (lib bdg); 0-516-41230-2 (pa)

LC 86-32687

"A New true book"

Presents a brief history of the Chippewa Indians describing their customs and traditions and how they are maintained in the modern world

Includes glossary

The Navajo. Childrens Press 1987 45p il maps lib bdg $16.60; pa $4.95 (2-4)

970.004

1. Navajo Indians

ISBN 0-516-01236-3 (lib bdg); 0-516-41236-1 (pa)

LC 86-30978

"A New true book"

A brief history of the Navajo Indians describing customs, interactions with white settlers, and changes in traditional ways of life brought on by modern civilization

The author "doesn't back away from the facts; detailing, for example, the 'Long Walk' forced upon the Navajos in 1864-65 as well as discussing the difficulties many native Americans face in today's world." Booklist

Includes glossary

The Nez Perce. Childrens Press 1988 45p il map lib bdg $16.60; pa $4.95 (2-4)

970.004

1. Nez Percé Indians

ISBN 0-516-01154-5 (lib bdg); 0-516-41154-3 (pa)

LC 88-11822

"A New true book"

A brief history of the Nez Percé Indians describing their customs, religious beliefs and their place in contemporary society

Includes glossary

The Sioux. Childrens Press 1984 40p il lib bdg $16.60; pa $4.95 (2-4) **970.004**

1. Dakota Indians

ISBN 0-516-01929-5 (lib bdg); 0-516-41929-3 (pa)

LC 84-7629

"A New true book"

A brief history of the Sioux, or Dakota, Indians of the Great Plains describing their tribal organization, customs, religion, and their encounter with the white settlers

Patterson, Lotsee

Indian terms of the Americas; [by] Lotsee Patterson, Mary Ellen Snodgrass; original illustrations by Dan Timmons. Libraries Unlimited 1994 275p il maps $35

970.004

1. Indians—Dictionaries

ISBN 1-56308-133-4 LC 93-47170

"Each of the approximate 850 entries provides a pronunciation guide for the term, an alternate form or spelling, a definition of Indian vocabulary, people, places, and events, boldface words that refer to other listings in the book, and other related terms for more information. . . . Drawings and photos greatly enhance the meaning of the terms." Book Rep

For a fuller review see: Booklist, Oct. 15, 1994

Peters, Russell M.

Clambake; a Wampanoag tradition; photographs by John Madama; with a foreword by Michael Dorris. Lerner Publs. 1992 48p il (We are still here: Native Americans today) lib bdg $19.95; pa $6.95 (3-6) **970.004**

1. Wampanoag Indians

ISBN 0-8225-2651-4 (lib bdg); 0-8225-9621-0 (pa)

LC 92-8423

"The traditional clambake, or Apponaug, of the Wampanoag Indians of the Northeastern American coast holds important spiritual and cultural meaning for the people of the tribe. This is the story of how young Steven, a Mashpee Wampanoag, celebrates his first Apponaug with friends and relatives on tribal lands of Cape Cod, Massachusetts." Publisher's note

"The full-color photographs illustrate the clearly written text and portray real people who are part of the contemporary world, passing on old traditions to their children." SLJ

Includes glossary and bibliography

Powell, Suzanne I.

The Pueblos; [by] Suzanne Powell. Watts 1993 64p il lib bdg $19.90; pa $5.95 (4 and up) **970.004**

1. Pueblo Indians

ISBN 0-531-20068-X (lib bdg); 0-531-15703-2 (pa)

LC 93-18368

"A First book"

Discusses the traditional and modern way of life of the Pueblos, examining their history, culture, religion, and ability to survive and thrive in difficult conditions

Includes glossary and bibliography

Regguinti, Gordon

The sacred harvest; Ojibway wild rice gathering; photographs by Dale Kakkak; with a foreword by Michael Dorris. Lerner Publs. 1992 48p il maps (We are still here: Native Americans today) lib bdg $19.95; pa $6.95 (3-6) **970.004**

1. Ojibwa Indians 2. Rice

ISBN 0-8225-2650-6 (lib bdg); 0-8225-9620-2 (pa)

LC 92-1167

Regguinti, Gordon—*Continued*

Glen Jackson, Jr., an eleven-year-old Ojibway Indian in northern Minnesota, goes with his father to harvest wild rice, the sacred food of his people

"There is a lot of information here, and readers will gain much from it and the many well-chosen, full-color photographs of the Jackson family." SLJ

Includes glossary and bibliography

Reynolds, Jan, 1956-

Frozen land; vanishing cultures. Harcourt Brace & Co. 1993 unp il maps (Vanishing cultures series) $16.95; pa $8.95 (2-4)

970.004

1. Inuit 2. Canadian Northwest
ISBN 0-15-238787-0; 0-15-238788-9 (pa)

LC 92-30324

Describes the traditional ways of life of an Inuit family living in the Canadian Northwest Territories and some of the changes they have had to face

This offers "appealing full-color photographs and a simple but descriptive text." SLJ

Roessel, Monty

Kinaaldá: a Navajo girl grows up; text and photographs by Monty Roessel; with a foreword by Michael Dorris. Lerner Publs. 1993 48p il map (We are still here: Native Americans today) lib bdg $19.95; pa $6.95 (3-6)

970.004

1. Navajo Indians
ISBN 0-8225-2655-7 (lib bdg); 0-8225-9641-5 (pa)

LC 92-35204

Celinda McKelvey, a Navajo girl, participates in the Kinaalda, the traditional coming-of-age ceremony of her people

"The text is spare but clear, with sufficient detail to inform general readers; the color photographs are crisp and well composed." Horn Book Guide

Includes glossary and bibliography

Sewall, Marcia, 1935-

People of the breaking day; written and illustrated by Marcia Sewall. Atheneum Pubs. 1990 48p il $15.95 (3-6)

970.004

1. Wampanoag Indians
ISBN 0-689-31407-8

LC 89-18194

This is a poetic evocation of the lifestyle and traditional beliefs of the Wampanoag Indians

"Sewall's deftly colored paintings, dominated by earthtones, portray a slice of history with verve and accuracy. . . . The writing, too, is fine and in many places eloquent." Booklist

Includes glossary

Sneve, Virginia Driving Hawk

The Iroquois; illustrated by Ronald Himler. Holiday House 1995 32p il map (First Americans book) $15.95 (3-5)

970.004

1. Iroquois Indians
ISBN 0-8234-1163-X

LC 94-03748

In this illustrated overview of the Six Nations of the Iroquois the author "includes a highly abridged creation story; an account of the traditional government of the people; descriptions of men's, women's, and children's roles; food; spiritual beliefs; the use of wampum; and the people today." SLJ

The Navajos; illustrated by Ronald Himler. Holiday House 1993 32p il (First Americans book) $15.95; pa $6.95 (3-5)

970.004

1. Navajo Indians
ISBN 0-8234-1039-0; 0-8234-1168-0 (pa)

LC 92-40330

Provides an overview of the history, culture, and way of life of the Navajo Indians

"Himler's paintings enliven the matter-of-fact text." Booklist

The Nez Percé; illustrated by Ronald Himler. Holiday House 1994 32p il map (First Americans book) $15.95 (3-5)

970.004

1. Nez Percé Indians
ISBN 0-8234-1090-0

LC 93-38598

This discussion of the Nez Percé Indians "begins with a Chopunnish creation story, followed by descriptions of daily life and an abbreviated history. Himler's paintings beautifully enhance the text." Booklist

The Seminoles; illustrated by Ronald Himler. Holiday House 1994 32p il map (First Americans book) $15.95 (3-5)

970.004

1. Seminole Indians
ISBN 0-8234-1112-5

LC 93-14316

Discusses the history, lifestyle, customs, and current situation of the Seminoles

"The writing is smooth, if necessarily generalized, and Himler's watercolors are especially suited to the swampy backdrops and dramatic action that characterized the Seminoles' struggle to survive." Bull Cent Child Books

The Sioux; illustrated by Ronald Himler. Holiday House 1993 32p il (First Americans book) $15.95; pa $6.95 (3-5)

970.004

1. Dakota Indians
ISBN 0-8234-1017-X; 0-8234-1171-0 (pa)

LC 92-23946

Identifies the different tribes of the Sioux Indians and discusses their beliefs and traditional way of life

"Himler's art work balances the aesthetic with the instructive, the past with the present, in compositions that are steeped in plains . . . hues and are vibrant with action." Bull Cent Child Books

Stein, R. Conrad, 1937-

The Trail of Tears. rev ed. Childrens Press 1993 30p il maps (Cornerstones of freedom) lib bdg $15.27; pa $4.95 (4-6)

970.004

1. Cherokee Indians
ISBN 0-516-06666-8 (lib bdg); 0-516-46666-6 (pa)

LC 92-33422

First published 1985 with title: The story of the Trail of Tears

Describes the federal government's seizure of Cherokee lands in Georgia and the forced migration of the Cherokee Nation to Oklahoma along the route that came to be known as the Trail of Tears

Swentzell, Rina, 1939-

Children of clay; a family of Pueblo potters; photographs by Bill Steen; with a foreword by Michael Dorris. Lerner Publs. 1992 40p il maps (We are still here: Native Americans today) lib bdg $19.95; pa $6.95 (3-6)

970.004

1. Pueblo Indians 2. Pottery
ISBN 0-8225-2654-9 (lib bdg); 0-8225-9627-X (pa)
LC 92-8680

Members of a Tewa Indian family living in Santa Clara Pueblo in New Mexico follow the ages-old traditions of their people as they create various objects of clay

"A beautifully illustrated short work. . . . In addition to the many large, full-color photographs, there are maps of the area and of the 19 pueblos in New Mexico and designs decorating the large-print text. Swentzell does a good job of demonstrating the family's closeness to nature and to other members in the village." SLJ

Includes glossary and bibliography

Thomson, Peggy, 1922-

Katie Henio: Navajo sheepherder; photographs by Paul Conklin. Cobblehill Bks. 1995 51p il $16.99 (4 and up)   **970.004**

1. Henio, Katie 2. Navajo Indians
ISBN 0-525-65160-8
LC 93-40430

This "photo documentary follows Henio as she herds her animals down from sheep camp to the village, shears them, and works with the wool to prepare it for weaving. The text also includes such diverse topics as tribal customs, techniques for dyeing wool, and Henio's special tools. Clear color photographs accompany the text and set the scene in rural New Mexico." Horn Book Guide

Tomchek, Ann Heinrichs

The Hopi. Childrens Press 1987 45p il maps lib bdg $16.60; pa $4.95 (2-4)   **970.004**

1. Hopi Indians
ISBN 0-516-01234-7 (lib bdg); 0-516-41234-5 (pa)
LC 87-8037

"A New true book"

A brief history of the Hopi Indians describing their customs, religious beliefs, interactions with other tribes, and the changes modern civilization has brought to their traditional way of life

Includes glossary

Trimble, Stephen, 1950-

The village of blue stone; words by Stephen Trimble; illustrations by Jennifer Owings Dewey and Deborah Reade. Macmillan 1990 58p il maps $14.95 (4-6)   **970.004**

1. Pueblo Indians 2. Cliff dwellers and cliff dwellings 3. Chaco Culture National Historical Park (N.M.)
ISBN 0-02-789501-7
LC 88-34194

Recreates, in text and illustrations, the day-to-day life throughout a full year in a Chaco Culture Anasazi pueblo, located in what is now New Mexico, in 1100 A.D

"An impressive amount of material is packed into the slim volume. . . . The modest format is pleasant, and, although the fictional-looking narrative will deter some information seekers, the account conveys . . . a respectful view of an intriguing way of life." Horn Book

Includes glossary and bibliography

Wolfson, Evelyn

From Abenaki to Zuni; a dictionary of native American tribes; illustrated by William Sauts Bock. Walker & Co. 1988 215p il maps $18.95; lib bdg $18.85; pa $9.95 (4 and up)

970.004

1. Indians of North America—Dictionaries
ISBN 0-8027-6789-3; 0-8027-6790-7 (lib bdg); 0-8027-7445-8 (pa)
LC 87-27875

An alphabetical identification of sixty-eight of the larger North American Indian tribes, describing their habitats, social life and customs, food, means of travel, and modern descendants

"Although, as the author notes, the book is not exhaustive in terms of tribes covered, Wolfson has provided help for researchers by pulling together data on so many native peoples in such a handy format. Students will be pleased with the concise summaries of information needed for school reports." Booklist

Includes bibliography

From the earth to beyond the sky; Native American medicine; illustrated by Jennifer Hewitson. Houghton Mifflin 1993 96p il $14.95 (5 and up)   **970.004**

1. Indians of North America—Medicine 2. Shamanism 3. Indians of North America—Religion
ISBN 0-395-55009-2
LC 92-46035

An illustrated account of the traditions and customs of Native American medicine men

"Clearly written and spiced with anecdotes, this provides a view of another way of thinking as well as concrete information about medical practices." Booklist

Includes glossary and bibliography

Wood, Ted, 1965-

A boy becomes a man at Wounded Knee; [by] Ted Wood with Wanbli Numpa Afraid of Hawk. Walker & Co. 1992 42p il $15.95; lib bdg $16.85; pa $6.95   **970.004**

1. Dakota Indians 2. Wounded Knee Creek, Battle of, 1890
ISBN 0-8027-8174-8; 0-8027-8175-6 (lib bdg); 0-8027-7446-6 (pa)
LC 92-1218

Describes the events that led to the massacre of Lakota (Sioux) Indians at Wounded Knee in 1890 and the experiences of a young boy as he rides with his people to commemorate this event one hundred years later

"The book's first-rate prose—which nonetheless retains an eight-year-old's voice and sensibilities—emits stylistic elegance, and pride in this youngster's achievement. . . . This singular story offers a gratifying blend of exciting, in-depth reading and learning rarely found in photo essays." Publ Wkly

Worthylake, Mary M.

The Pomo. Childrens Press 1994 45p il map lib bdg $16.60; pa $4.95 (2-4)   **970.004**

1. Pomo Indians
ISBN 0-516-01057-3 (lib bdg); 0-516-41057-1 (pa)
LC 93-36666

"A New true book"

A historical look at the Pomo Indians of northern California, describing their food, shelter, clothing, trade, basketry, games, ceremonies and beliefs. The Pomo of today are also briefly described

Includes glossary

Yue, Charlotte
The Pueblo; [by] Charlotte and David Yue.
Houghton Mifflin 1986 117p il $14.95; pa
$6.95 (4 and up)   **970.004**
1. Pueblo Indians
ISBN 0-395-38350-1; 0-395-54961-2 (pa)
                          LC 85-27087
"A look at the many facets of Pueblo life, not often covered in the many books on Native Americans. Filled with illustrations and diagrams that expand and clarify, it emphasizes the relationship between the people and the land. Superb nonfiction and a boon to report writers." SLJ
Includes bibliography

970.01   North America—Early history to 1599

Brenner, Barbara
If you were there in 1492. Bradbury Press
1991 106p il maps $19.50 (4-6)   **970.01**
1. Columbus, Christopher 2. Fifteenth century 3. America—Exploration
ISBN 0-02-712321-9   LC 90-24099
Readers take a trip back in time to learn about the culture and civilization of 15th century Europe and Spain, and the discovery of America by Columbus
"Fascinating details keep company with a style that may strike some readers as cutesy but that gives a wealth of interesting facts about life in late 15th-century Spain. . . . The numerous black-and-white reproductions of woodcuts, maps, and period paintings are informative as well as decorative." SLJ
Includes bibliography

Lauber, Patricia, 1924-
Who discovered America? mysteries and puzzles of the New World; illustrated by Mike Eagle. new ed. HarperCollins Pubs. 1992 79p il maps $16; lib bdg $15.89 (3-5)   **970.01**
1. America—Antiquities 2. America—Exploration
ISBN 0-06-023728-7; 0-06-023729-5 (lib bdg)
                          LC 90-43604
First published 1970 by Random House
Discusses how information on the settling and exploration of America before Columbus has been compiled from archaeological discoveries
"Ink drawings with watercolor washes brighten the pages of this attractive volume. The text clearly presents both knowledge and surmise, without confusing the two." Booklist
Includes bibliography

Maestro, Betsy, 1944-
The discovery of the Americas; by Betsy and Giulio Maestro. Lothrop, Lee & Shepard Bks. 1990 48p il maps $15; lib bdg $14.93; pa $5.95 (2-4)   **970.01**
1. America—Exploration
ISBN 0-688-06837-5; 0-688-06838-3 (lib bdg); 0-688-11512-8 (pa)   LC 89-32375
Also available Spanish language edition
Discusses both hypothetical and historical voyages of discovery to America by the Phoenicians, Saint Brendan of Ireland, the Vikings, and such later European navigators as

Columbus, Cabot, and Magellan
"The dazzlingly clean and accurate prose and the exhilarating beauty of the pictures combine for an extraordinary achievement in both history and art." SLJ

Exploration and conquest; the Americas after Columbus, 1500-1620; [by] Betsy & Giulio Maestro. Lothrop, Lee & Shepard Bks. 1994 48p il maps $16; lib bdg $15.93 (2-4)
                          970.01
1. America—Exploration
ISBN 0-688-09267-5; 0-688-09268-3 (lib bdg)
                          LC 93-48618
This is a "discussion of the European exploration and conquest of the 'New World.' The author carefully explains that, 'The great gain of one people was the great loss of another' and traces the disastrous effects that the Portuguese, Spanish, English, French, and Dutch had on the native peoples of the Americas, while acknowledging the benefits the Europeans enjoyed." SLJ
"The book's most outstanding feature is its full-color artwork. Large, double-page spreads give scope to dramatic landscapes, while smaller pictures on every page show events, places, and maps pertinent to the text. . . . This book provides a useful overview of the period." Booklist

Marzollo, Jean
In 1492; illustrated by Steve Björkman. Scholastic 1991 unp il hardcover o.p. paperback available $4.95 (k-2)   **970.01**
1. Columbus, Christopher 2. America—Exploration 3. Explorers
ISBN 0-590-49442-2 (pa)   LC 91-100
Rhyming text describes Christopher Columbus's first voyage to the New World
"The tale is surprisingly clear and complete, despite the brief and simple text. . . . Björkman's light-hearted illustrations are top-notch—his oceanscapes are suitably sweeping, his ships imposing, his characters endearing in their naïveté." Publ Wkly

Sattler, Helen Roney
The earliest Americans; illustrated by Jean Day Zallinger. Clarion Bks. 1993 125p il maps $16.95 (5 and up)   **970.01**
1. Indians—Antiquities 2. Prehistoric man 3. America—Antiquities
ISBN 0-395-54996-5   LC 91-9463
Covers the history of early man in America from the earliest known sites to approximately 1492 A.D
"A readable archaeologically based account of pre-Columbian history, profusely illustrated in meticulous detail." SLJ
Includes bibliography

Yue, Charlotte
Christopher Columbus; how he did it; [by] Charlotte and David Yue. Houghton Mifflin 1992 136p il maps $14.95 (5 and up)
                          970.01
1. Columbus, Christopher 2. America—Exploration
ISBN 0-395-52100-9   LC 91-19624
"The authors explain the explorer's reasons for making the journey and the scientific and geographical assumptions upon which he based his plans. In 18 detailed pages, they discuss the construction of his three ships, including the

Yue, Charlotte—*Continued*

size, name, and shape of every sail. The crew is another focus, as are the tools of the trade, armor, the unpleasant living conditions, and the hierarchy of command. Much of this information is not readily available elsewhere. . . .The impressive bibliography as well as the meticulous drawings are evidence of painstaking research. This is a very special book because it answers many questions students often ask." SLJ

971 Canada

Malcolm, Andrew H., 1943-

The land and people of Canada. HarperCollins Pubs. 1991 220p il maps (Portraits of the nations series) $19; lib bdg $17.89 (5 and up) **971**

1. Canada
ISBN 0-06-022494-0; 0-06-022495-9 (lib bdg)
LC 90-47560

Introduces the history, geography, people, culture, government, and economy of Canada

"There are numerous 'fact boxes' and charts, which could provide researchers with quick information and anecdotes. . . . The maps are clear and have good keys." SLJ

Includes bibliography

Manson, Ainslie

A dog came, too; a true story; pictures by Ann Blades. Margaret K. McElderry Bks. 1993 c1992 unp il $13.95 (k-3) **971**

1. Mackenzie, Sir Alexander, 1755?-1820 2. Dogs 3. America—Exploration
ISBN 0-689-50567-1
LC 91-44891

First published 1992 in Canada

Recounts the adventures of Our Dog, the dog who accompanied Scottish explorer Alexander Mackenzie on his journey across Canada to the Pacific Ocean and thus became the first dog to cross the North American continent by land

"This is an intriguing story with an adventurous backdrop. . . . The narration treats the animal with unsentimental respect and generally keeps him authentically doggy. The watercolors are in pale and liquid tones that somehow make the scenes temporally distant despite their modern line." Bull Cent Child Books

971.27 Manitoba

Kurelek, William, 1927-1977

A prairie boy's summer; paintings and story by William Kurelek. Houghton Mifflin 1975 unp il o.p.; Tundra Bks. reprint available $14.95 (3-5) **971.27**

1. Children—Canada 2. Farm life—Canada 3. Summer
ISBN 0-88776-058-9

This book shows "many details of the artist's life when he was a boy growing up on a farm in Western Canada." Horn Book

"It is, of course, the pictures by this distinguished Canadian artist that give the book its distinction; each full-color page glows with life and vigor, and the paintings have both a felicity of small details and a remarkable evocation of the breadth and sweep of the Manitoba prairie." Bull Cent Child Books

A prairie boy's winter; paintings and story by William Kurelek. Houghton Mifflin 1973 unp il $14.95; pa $6.95 (3-5) **971.27**

1. Children—Canada 2. Farm life—Canada 3. Winter
ISBN 0-395-17708-1; 0-395-36609-7 (pa)

The author depicts the rigors and pleasures of boyhood winters on a Manitoba farm in the 1930's including hauling hay, playing hockey, and surviving a blizzard

971.3 Ontario

Greenwood, Barbara

A pioneer sampler; the daily life of a pioneer family in 1840; illustrated by Heather Collins. Ticknor & Fields Bks. for Young Readers 1995 240p il $18.95 (4 and up) **971.3**

1. Frontier and pioneer life
ISBN 0-395-71540-7
LC 94-12829

First published 1994 in Canada with title: A pioneer story

"Using a combination of fiction and fact-filled supplementary commentary, with illustrations inspired by Garth Williams, the author tells the story of the Robertsons, a large, hardworking farm family. Good projects for school or home." N Y Times Book Rev

971.9 Northern territories of Canada

Cooper, Michael L., 1950-

Klondike fever; the famous gold rush of 1898; illustrated with photographs; by Michael Cooper. Clarion Bks. 1989 80p il hardcover o.p. paperback available $6.95 (5 and up) **971.9**

1. Klondike River valley (Yukon)—Gold discoveries
ISBN 0-395-54784-9 (pa)
LC 89-31117

Traces the history of the Klondike gold rush of the late 1890s, describing the men responsible for the initial discovery, the trail to the Klondike gold fields, and the explosive growth and rapid demise of the gold rush town of Dawson

"An oversize book, profusely illustrated with contemporary photographs, with a bibliography and a good index. The provision and arrangement of the material are quite adequate." Bull Cent Child Books

972 Middle America. Mexico

Fisher, Leonard Everett, 1924-

Pyramid of the sun, pyramid of the moon. Macmillan 1988 unp il map $15.95 (4 and up) **972**

1. Aztecs 2. Toltecs 3. Teotihuacán site (San Juan Teotihuacán, Mexico)
ISBN 0-02-735300-1
LC 88-1410

Fisher discusses the history of the pyramids of Teotihuacan, built by the Toltecs and later sacred to the Aztecs. He describes how the Aztecs lived and worshipped, and how they were overcome by the Spaniards

"Shadowy paintings in black, white, and gray—

Fisher, Leonard Everett, 1924——*Continued*
punctuated with brick-red symbols—depict events and ceremonies of monumental grandeur. . . . A dramatic, well-designed introduction." Bull Cent Child Books

Mathews, Sally Schofer
The Sad Night; the story of an Aztec victory and a Spanish loss; written and illustrated by Sally Schofer Mathews. Clarion Bks. 1994 unp il $16.95 (2-4)   **972**
1. Aztecs 2. Mexico—History
ISBN 0-395-63035-5   LC 92-25119
Tells how the Aztecs established an empire in Mexico and what happened when they, led by Montezuma, encountered Cortés and the Spaniards in the early sixteenth century
This is a highly effective melding of graceful, lucid text and stylized art. Designed to resemble Aztec codices . . . the illustrations appear in double-page strips above the bordered text." SLJ

Wood, Tim
The Aztecs. Viking 1992 48p il maps (See through history) $14.99 (4 and up)   **972**
1. Aztecs
ISBN 0-670-84492-6   LC 91-68542
This book describes Aztec civilization
This is "particularly readable and well-designed. Topics are covered adequately and are sensibly arranged, and the better-than-average color illustrations are bolstered by photos of artifacts." Booklist
Includes glossary

972.84   El Salvador

Foley, Erin, 1967-
El Salvador. Marshall Cavendish 1994 128p il maps (Cultures of the world) $21.95 (5 and up)   **972.84**
1. El Salvador
ISBN 1-85435-696-8   LC 94-22567
This book "traces the history of the Spanish Conquest and the influences of Indian languages and liberation theology on the people. The political role of the United States in recent history should prove helpful to anyone trying to understand the country's recent and devastating struggle against abuse and injustice." SLJ
Includes glossary and bibliography

972.85   Nicaragua

Kott, Jennifer, 1971-
Nicaragua. Marshall Cavendish 1994 128p il maps (Cultures of the world) $21.95 (5 and up)   **972.85**
1. Nicaragua
ISBN 1-85435-695-X   LC 94-28809
An illustrated overview of the geography, economy, history, government, politics, and culture of Nicaragua
Includes glossary and bibliography

972.87   Panama

St. George, Judith, 1931-
Panama Canal; gateway to the world; illustrated with photographs. Putnam 1989 159p il maps $16.95 (5 and up)   **972.87**
1. Panama Canal
ISBN 0-399-21637-5   LC 88-11617
Presents a history of the Panama Canal from the time Columbus first anchored off the coast of Panama through the signing of the 1977 United States-Panama treaties
"Brimming with dramatic details and invested with excellent research, St. George recounts the enormous scope and the difficulties of this expansive project, giving weight to each leader's concerns and goals without diminishing its cost to human lives." SLJ

Vazquez, Ana Maria B.
Panama; by Ana María Vazquez. Childrens Press 1991 127p il maps (Enchantment of the world) lib bdg $27.40 (4 and up)   **972.87**
1. Panama
ISBN 0-516-02604-6   LC 91-12667
Discusses the geography, history, economics, and culture of Panama

972.9   West Indies and Bermuda

Jacobs, Francine, 1935-
The Tainos; the people who welcomed Columbus. Putnam 1992 107p il map $15.95 (4 and up)   **972.9**
1. Taino Indians 2. America—Exploration
ISBN 0-399-22116-6   LC 91-3215
"Jacobs describes the history, culture, and annihilation of the Tainos, the people who welcomed Columbus when he first landed in the Americas in 1492." Booklist
This "is a lucid, well-organized account. The author maintains an even hand, almost dispassionately describing the obviously horrendous conduct of the explorers; she allows children, who will find much of the information unfamiliar, to draw their own conclusions about this momentous clash between two cultures." Horn Book
Includes bibliography

972.91   Cuba

Sheehan, Sean
Cuba. Marshall Cavendish 1994 128p il maps (Cultures of the world) $21.95 (5 and up)   **972.91**
1. Cuba
ISBN 1-85435-691-7   LC 94-22574
This introduction to Cuba "covers geography, history, government, economy, population, lifestyle, religion, language, arts, leisure, festivals, and food. . . . The material is well organized in easily readable sections, accurately illustrated with well-placed, full-color photographs on every page." SLJ
Includes glossary and bibliography

972.93 Dominican Republic

Foley, Erin, 1967-
Dominican Republic. Marshall Cavendish 1995 128p il maps (Cultures of the world) $21.95 (5 and up)   972.93

1. Dominican Republic
ISBN 1-85435-694-1   LC 94-29382

This describes the Dominican Republic's "geography, history, government, economy, population, lifestyle, religion, language, arts, leisure, festivals, and food. . . . The material is well organized in easily readable sections, accurately illustrated with well-placed, full-color photographs on every page." SLJ

Includes glossary and bibliography

972.94 Haiti

Cheong-Lum, Roseline Ng, 1962-
Haiti. Marshall Cavendish 1994 128p il maps (Cultures of the world) $21.95 (5 and up)   972.94

1. Haiti
ISBN 1-85435-693-3   LC 94-22572

This survey of Haiti covers "the background of the people, their recent political turmoil, and anticipation of Aristide's return to power. Especially interesting here is the discussion of the various ethnic and language influences, as well as the important role of voodoo." SLJ

Includes glossary and bibliography

Goldish, Meish
Crisis in Haiti. Millbrook Press 1995 c1994 64p il (Headliners) lib bdg $15.90 (5 and up)   972.94

1. Haiti
ISBN 1-56294-553-X   LC 94-36052

This is "an account of politics and government in Haiti from Columbus's landing in 1492 to President Aristide's reinstatement on October 15, 1994. . . . Readable, detailed, and supplemented with charts, graphs, and full-color and black-and-white photographs and reproductions." SLJ

Includes bibliography

973 United States

America the beautiful. Childrens Press 1987-1992 52v il maps lib bdg ea $27.30 (4 and up)   973

Also available as a set for $1419.60

Contents: Alabama, by S. McNair; Alaska, by A. Heinrichs; Arizona, by A. Heinrichs; Arkansas, by A. Heinrichs; California, by R. C. Stein; Colorado, by D. Kent; Connecticut, by D. Kent; Delaware, by D. Kent; Florida, by L. M. Stone; Georgia, by Z. Kent; Hawaii, by S. McNair; Idaho, by Z. Kent; Illinois, by R. C. Stein; Indiana, by R. C. Stein; Iowa, by D. Kent; Kansas, by Z. Kent; Kentucky, by S. McNair; Louisiana, by D. Kent; Maine, by T. Harrington; Maryland, by D. Kent; Massachusetts, by D. Kent; Michigan, by R. C. Stein; Minnesota, by R. C. Stein; Mississippi, by R. Carson; Missouri, by W. R. Sanford; Montana, by A. Heinrichs; Nebraska, by J. Hargrove; Nevada, by D. Lillegard and W. Stoker; New Hampshire, by S. McNair; New

Jersey, by D. Kent; New Mexico, by R. C. Stein; New York, by R. C. Stein; North Carolina, by R. C. Stein; North Dakota, by M. S. Herguth; Ohio, by D. Kent; Oklahoma, by A. Heinrichs; Oregon, by R. C. Stein; Pennsylvania, by D. Kent; Puerto Rico, by D. Kent; Rhode Island, by A. Heinrichs; South Carolina, by D. Kent; South Dakota, by E. U. Lepthien; Tennessee, by S. McNair; Texas, by R. C. Stein; Utah, by B. McCarthy; Vermont, by S. McNair; Virginia, by S. McNair; Washington, by R. C. Stein; Washington, D. C., by D. Kent; West Virginia, by R. C. Stein; Wisconsin, by R. C. Stein; Wyoming, by A. Heinrichs

In this series, "topics covered include geography, history from the pioneer times to today, government and the economy, industry, arts and leisure, and historic sites. Whether utilized for a quick report, appreciative browsing of the outstanding photography, historical research, or armchair-vacation planning, these books are top-notch presentations. Each 30-page reference section is a veritable gold mine—besides the expected statistics, maps, dates, and descriptions there are biographical sketches with accompanying photos." Booklist

Hakim, Joy
A history of US. Oxford Univ. Press 1993-1995 10v il apply to publisher for price (6 and up)   973

1. United States—History   LC 92-50114

Set and individual volumes available in hardcover, library binding and paperback

Contents: bk1 The first Americans; bk2 Making thirteen colonies; bk3 From colonies to country; bk4 The new nation; bk5 Liberty for all?; bk6 War, terrible war; bk7 Reconstruction and reform; bk8 An age of extremes; bk9 War, peace, and all that jazz; bk10 All the people

The volumes in this series present a chronological overview of United States history. "The books are illustrated with period prints and drawings . . . and enhanced by numerous quotations. Hakim's chatty style and personal interjections make for engaging reading." SLJ

Hello USA series. Lerner Publs. 1991-1995 52v il maps lib bdg ea $17.50 (3-6)   973

Contents: Alabama, by D. Brown; Alaska, by J. Johnston; Arizona, by D. Filbin; Arkansas, by D. Di Piazza; California, by K. Pelta; Colorado, by S. Bledsoe; Connecticut, by A. Gelman; Delaware, by D. Brown; Florida, by K. Sirvaitis; Georgia, by R. C. LaDoux; Hawaii, by J. Johnston; Idaho, by K. Pelta; Illinois, by K. P. Anderson; Indiana, by G. Swain; Iowa, by R. C. LaDoux; Kansas, by C. Fredeen; Kentucky, by D. Brown; Louisiana, by R. C. LaDoux; Maine, by L. Engfer; Maryland, by J. Johnston; Massachusetts, by J. F. Warner; Michigan, by K. Sirvaitis; Minnesota, by A. P. Porter; Mississippi, by A. Ready; Missouri, by R. C. LaDoux; Nebraska, by A. P. Porter; Nevada, by K. Sirvaitis; New Hampshire, by D. Brown; New Jersey, by C. Fredeen; New Mexico, by T. S. Early; New York, by A. Gelman; North Carolina, by A. Schulz; North Dakota, by J. M. Verba; Ohio, by D. Brown; Oklahoma, by R. C. LaDoux; Oregon, by G. Bratvold; Pennsylvania, by G. Swain; Puerto Rico, by J. Johnston; Rhode Island, by J. F. Warner; South Carolina, by C. Fredeen; South Dakota, by K. Sirvaitis; Tennessee, by K. Sirvaitis; Texas, by K. Pelta; Utah, by K. Sirvaitis; Vermont, by K. Pelta; Virginia, by K. Sirvaitis; Washington, by E. S. Powell; Washington, D.C., by J. Johnston; West Virginia, by D. Di Piazza; Wisconsin, by G. Bratvold; Wyoming, by C. Frisch

With "full-color illustrations (mainly photographs) on nearly every page, books in the Hello U.S.A. series are both inviting and informative. Geared to the needs of elementary school students writing reports on states, the books follow a standard format, with a chapter each on geography, histo-

Hello USA series—*Continued*

ry, social and economic conditions, and the environment. Features include capsule biographies of famous native sons and daughters, timelines, and fast facts." Booklist

Historical albums series. Millbrook Press 1993-1996 18v il maps lib bdg ea $15.90; pa $6.95 (4 and up)   **973**

Contents: A historical album of Alabama, by C. A. Wills; A historical album of California, by C. A. Wills; A historical album of Colorado, by C. A. Wills; A historical album of Connecticut, by C. A. Wills; A historical album of Florida, by C. A. Wills; A historical album of Illinois, by C. A. Wills; A historical album of Kentucky, by A. Smith and K. S. Smith; A historical album of Massachusetts, by M. Avakian; A historical album of Minnesota by J. D. Carlson; A historical album of Nebraska, by C. A. Wills; A historical album of New Jersey, by F. Topper and C. A. Wills; A historical album of New York, by M. Avakian and C. Smith; A historical album of Ohio, by C. A. Wills; A historical album of Oregon, by C. A. Wills; A historical album of Pennsylvania, by C. A. Wills; A historical album of Texas, by C. A. Wills; A historical album of Virginia, by W. Cocke; A historical album of Washington, by W. Cocke

"These brief series titles are heavily pictorial . . . and offer a clear overview of each state's history from prehistory to the present. Students may find them useful for simple research, or for scanning the pertinent and well-chosen illustrations. The appended pages are great for ready reference." SLJ

Meltzer, Milton, 1915-

Nonfiction for the classroom; Milton Meltzer on writing, history, and social responsibility; edited and with an introduction by E. Wendy Saul. Teachers College Press 1994 201p (Language and literacy series) $38; pa $18.95   **973**

1. Historiography 2. United States—Historiography
ISBN 0-8077-3378-4; 0-8077-3377-6 (pa)

LC 94-25084

This collection contains previously published essays, speeches, articles and interviews that explore ideas about the writing of history and biography

This "is not only an excellent resource for a school's professional collection, but it also represents one more contribution that this writer makes to the lives of both the educator and the young reader." SLJ

Includes bibliography

Weitzman, David L.

My backyard history book; written by David Weitzman; illustrated by James Robertson. Little, Brown 1975 128p il $16.95; pa $10.95 (4 and up)   **973**

1. United States—History—Miscellanea 2. United States—Local history
ISBN 0-316-92901-8; 0-316-92902-6 (pa)

"A Brown paper school book"

Activities and projects, such as making time capsules and rubbings and tracing genealogy, demonstrate that learning about the past begins at home

"Full of fascinating social studies activities to be pursued 'scientifically' by elementary children. The clever, down-to-earth tasks will not only keep children happy and busy for weeks, but will give them a taste of historical research techniques. The illustrations are clear and concise. The humor injected into every page is the kind of slapstick hilarity kids love." Sci Books Films

973.03   United States—History— Encyclopedias and dictionaries

The **Kingfisher** young people's encyclopedia of the United States. Kingfisher (NY) 1994 776p il maps $39.95   **973.03**

1. United States—Dictionaries
ISBN 1-85697-521-5   LC 93-42501

"A comprehensive overview of the United States, this work features 1,200 entries; thousands of color photographs, lists, maps, and graphics; and a variety of subjects—language, plants and animals, religion, economics, sports, Indian tribes, myths and legends, geography, dance, argiculture, and 200 years of history." Recomm Ref Books for Small & Medium-sized Libr & Media Cent, 1995

This offers "brief, well-written entries. . . . The visual aids are spectacular, and these high-quality illustrations and black-and-white and color photos have instructive captions. The maps and diagrams are precise and accurate. Sound cross references are provided, as are subject and general indexes." SLJ

973.05   United States—History— Serial publications

Cobblestone; the history magazine for young people. Cobblestone Pub. $24.95 per year   **973.05**

1. United States—History—Periodicals
ISSN 0199-5197

Nine issues a year. First published 1980

"Each 48-page black-and-white issue focuses on a single theme, such as Irish Americans or Martin Luther King, Jr. The articles, activities, and stories explore the theme from a variety of viewpoints. Photos and drawings enhance the articles. Regular features include games, book reviews, and 'Dear Ebenezer' with readers' contributions. This title would be appropriate to supplement classroom work or for reading for interest." Katz. Mag for Libr. 8th edition

973.2   United States—Colonial period, 1607-1775

Howarth, Sarah

Colonial people. Millbrook Press 1994 47p il (People and places) lib bdg $15.90 (4 and up)   **973.2**

1. United States—Social life and customs—1600-1775, Colonial period
ISBN 1-56294-512-2   LC 94-20608

"Provides brief portraits of the life styles and work of Native Americans, governor, goodwife, apprentice, Puritan, servant, planter, slave, fur trader, constable, smuggler, and patriot. . . . Brief quotations and black-and-white and full-color illustrations and reproductions are interspersed throughout. . . . The material is well organized." SLJ

Includes glossary and bibliography

Colonial places. Millbrook Press 1994 46p il (People and places) lib bdg $15.90 (4 and up)   **973.2**

1. United States—Social life and customs—1600-1775, Colonial period
ISBN 1-56294-513-0   LC 94-25754

Howarth, Sarah—*Continued*

This "describes several sites around which life in early America revolved, including the governor's house, the meetinghouse, the tobacco field, the church, the post office, the harbor, and the fort. . . . Topics [are] presented in short, well-outlined chapters. Large print and numerous photographic reproductions and drawings (some in color) add to the . . . appeal. Chapters also include quotations from period writings." Booklist

Includes glossary and bibliography

Tunis, Edwin, 1897-1973

Colonial living; written and illustrated by Edwin Tunis. Crowell 1976 c1957 155p il o.p. (5 and up)   **973.2**

1. United States—Social life and customs—1600-1775, Colonial period

A reissue of the title first published 1957 by The World Publishing Company

"Common everyday aspects of colonial living from 1564-1770 are highlighted by the detailed descriptions and numerous black and white illustrations of items such as tools, home furnishings, clothing, etc." N Y Public Libr. Ref Books for Child Collect

973.3 United States—Periods of Revolution and Confederation, 1775-1789

The **American** revolutionaries: a history in their own words, 1750-1800; edited by Milton Meltzer. Crowell 1987 210p il lib bdg $14.89; pa $6.95 (6 and up)   **973.3**

1. United States—History—1775-1783, Revolution
2. United States—History—1755-1763, French and Indian War

ISBN 0-690-04643-X (lib bdg); 0-06-446145-9 (pa)
LC 86-47846

"Meltzer has assembled a collage of eyewitness accounts, speech and diary excerpts, letters, and other documents for a chronological account of the half century that included the American Revolution. . . . The voices of women who accompanied the troops and of blacks who fought with the army are both represented." Bull Cent Child Books

Brenner, Barbara

If you were there in 1776. Bradbury Press 1994 136p il $16 (4-6)   **973.3**

1. United States. Declaration of Independence 2. United States—Social life and customs

ISBN 0-02-712322-7   LC 93-24060

Demonstrates how the concepts and principles expressed in the Declaration of Independence were drawn from the experiences of living in America in the late eighteenth century, with emphasis given to how children lived on a New England farm, a Southern plantation, and the frontier

"The author's inclusion of details of how peoples' lives began to change as a result of the Revolution and her accessible style are the selling points here. Both budding historians and report writers will find this title worth their time." SLJ

Includes bibliography

Davis, Burke, 1913-

Black heroes of the American Revolution; foreword by Edward W. Brooke. Harcourt Brace Jovanovich 1976 80p il hardcover o.p. paperback available $4.95 (5 and up)
973.3

1. United States—History—1775-1783, Revolution
2. African American soldiers

ISBN 0-15-208561-0 (pa)   LC 75-42218

"In a very readable style, the author relates the stories of a few of the approximately 5000 Black soldiers who participated in the Revolution, emphasizing their unselfishness fighting a war from which few of them would substantially benefit. In addition, there is an excellent chapter on the exploits of several predominantly Black infantry companies." SLJ

Includes bibliography

Marzollo, Jean

In 1776; illustrated by Steve Björkman. Scholastic 1994 unp il $14.95 (k-2)   **973.3**

1. United States—History—1775-1783, Revolution

ISBN 0-590-46973-8   LC 92-29508

Rhyming text and illustrations describe how the colonists declared their independence from Great Britain in 1776

"This author/illustrator collaboration shows that difficult concepts of history can be made understandable to young children. Björkman's watercolors steal the show here." SLJ

Stein, R. Conrad, 1937-

Valley Forge. Childrens Press 1994 28p il (Cornerstones of freedom) lib bdg $12.98; pa $3.95 (4-6)   **973.3**

1. Washington, George, 1732-1799 2. United States—History—1775-1783, Revolution

ISBN 0-516-06683-8 (lib bdg); 0-516-46683-6 (pa)
LC 94-9490

First published 1985 with title: The story of Valley Forge

The author "describes how, routed at the Battle of Brandywine, Washington's forces retreated to Valley Forge. Quotations personalize their suffering, their resolve, and their loyalty to Washington. The addition of full-color and black-and-white photos, period paintings, and reproductions adds enormously to the book's appeal." SLJ

973.5 United States—1809-1845

Toynton, Evelyn

Growing up in America, 1830-1860. Millbrook Press 1995 96p il lib bdg $16.90 (4 and up)   **973.5**

1. United States—Social life and customs 2. Children—United States—History

ISBN 1-56294-453-3   LC 94-13088

"The first half of this book describes the lives of young people from four distinct sociological groups in the U.S. between 1830-1860: New England farmers, slave families, urban dwellers, and Sioux and pioneer children. The second half covers daily activities: school, work, play, and reading material." SLJ

"Showing contrasts and similarities between then and now, the book is informative, interesting, and filled with period illustrations that beautifully depict activities and dress." Booklist

Includes bibliography

973.7　United States— Administration of Abraham Lincoln, 1861-1865. Civil War

Bolotin, Norm, 1951-

For home and country; a Civil War scrapbook; [by] Norman Bolotin and Angela Herb. Lodestar Bks. 1995 98p il (Young readers' history of the Civil War) $16.99 (5 and up)　　　　　　　　　　　　**973.7**

1. United States—History—1861-1865, Civil War
ISBN 0-525-67495-0　　　　　　　LC 95-7896

"This heavily illustrated volume concentrates on social rather than political history. Organized by chapters chronologically from 'War Fever' to 'Marching Home,' the text discusses broad topics such as the troops' food, sickness, boredom, and letters home. The many reproductions of period photographs, documents, advertisements, and newspaper clippings bring the times into clearer focus." Booklist

Includes glossary and bibliography

Cox, Clinton

Undying glory; the story of the Massachusetts 54th Regiment. Scholastic 1991 167p il hardcover o.p. paperback available $3.25 (6 and up)　　　　　　　　　　**973.7**

1. United States. Army. Massachusetts Infantry Regiment, 54th (1863-1865) 2. United States—History—1861-1865, Civil War 3. African American soldiers
ISBN 0-590-44171-X (pa)　　　　LC 90-22303

"This book discusses the history of the formation of the African-American Fifty-fourth Massachusetts Regiment and its battles from 1863 to 1865. The regiment's unsung heroes found an enemy in both the Confederate army and the Union government, both of which treated them as second-class soldiers." Soc Educ

Includes bibliography

Haskins, James, 1941-

The day Fort Sumter was fired on; a photo history of the Civil War; by Jim Haskins. Scholastic 1995 96p il pa $6.95 (5 and up)　　　　　　　　　　　　**973.7**

1. United States—History—1861-1865, Civil War—Pictorial works
ISBN 0-590-46397-7　　　　　　LC 95-193186

The course of the Civil War from Bull Run to Reconstruction is documented with photographs in this book which considers not just military maneuvers and politics but also the war's effect on women, blacks, and children

"This attractive book opens a valuable window on the period. A chronology and bibliography help make the volume perfect for students." Booklist

Johnson, Neil, 1954-

The Battle of Gettysburg; with photographs from the 125th anniversary reenactment. Four Winds Press 1989 56p il maps $15.95 (5 and up)　　　　　　　　　　　　**973.7**

1. Gettysburg (Pa.), Battle of, 1863
ISBN 0-02-747831-9　　　　　　LC 88-30414

Text recounts the historic Civil War battle at Gettysburg and photographs capture a reenactment of that encounter, performed in 1988 in honor of the 125th anniversary

"Johnson's camera captures an intriguing slice of the action while his text explains how the battle unfolded, skirmish by skirmish, ridge by ridge. . . . Of obvious use to students researching assignments, this handsomely designed photo essay will also appeal to Civil War buffs." Booklist

Includes bibliography

Mettger, Zak

Till victory is won; black soldiers in the Civil War. Lodestar Bks. 1994 118p il (Young readers' history of the Civil War) $16.99 (5 and up)　　　　　　　　　　　　**973.7**

1. African American soldiers 2. United States—History—1861-1865, Civil War
ISBN 0-525-67412-8　　　　　　LC 93-44154

"The two hundred thousand African Americans who fought in the Civil War proved their equality on the battlefield and helped to earn freedom for their families yet also continued to face racism and prejudice. The clear text is highlighted by the soldiers' letters and diary entries and is accompanied by archival illustrations and photographs in black and white." Horn Book Guide

Includes glossary and bibliography

Murphy, Jim, 1947-

The boys' war; Confederate and Union soldiers talk about the Civil War. Clarion Bks. 1990 110p il $15.95; pa $7.95 (5 and up)　　　　　　　　　　　　**973.7**

1. United States—History—1861-1865, Civil War
ISBN 0-89919-893-7; 0-395-66412-8 (pa)
　　　　　　　　　　　　　LC 89-23959

This book includes diary entries, personal letters, and archival photographs to describe the experiences of boys, sixteen years old or younger, who fought in the Civil War

"An excellent selection of more than 45 sepia-toned contemporary photographs augment the text of this informative, moving work." SLJ

Includes bibliography

The long road to Gettysburg. Clarion Bks. 1992 116p il maps $15.95 (5 and up)　　　　　　　　　　　　**973.7**

1. Gettysburg (Pa.), Battle of, 1863
ISBN 0-395-55965-0　　　　　　LC 90-21881

Describes the events of the Battle of Gettysburg in 1863 as seen through the eyes of two actual participants, nineteen-year-old Confederate lieutenant John Dooley and seventeen-year-old Union soldier Thomas Galway. Also discusses Lincoln's famous speech delivered at the dedication of the National Cemetery at Gettysburg

The author "uses all of his fine skills as an information writer—clarity of detail, conciseness, understanding of his age group, and ability to find the drama appealing to readers—to frame a well-crafted account of a single battle in the war." Horn Book

Includes bibliography

Ray, Delia

Behind the Blue and Gray; the soldier's life in the Civil War. Lodestar Bks. 1991 102p il (Young readers' history of the Civil War) $16.99 (5 and up)   **973.7**

1. United States—History—1861-1865, Civil War
ISBN 0-525-67333-4   LC 90-46412

This book traces the events of the Civil War from the first battle to the surrender with emphasis on the experiences of the individual soldier

The author "has chosen many informative, perceptive personal accounts upon which to base her work. The fears, horrors, boredom, and simple, transitory pleasures of these young men are brought into sharp focus by the many first-person writings. . . . Black-and-white historical photographs and reproductions flesh out this highly readable volume." SLJ

Includes glossary and bibliography

Voices from the Civil War; a documentary history of the great American conflict; edited by Milton Meltzer. Crowell 1989 203p il lib bdg $14.89; pa $6.95 (6 and up)   **973.7**

1. United States—History—1861-1865, Civil War—Sources
ISBN 0-690-04802-5 (lib bdg); 0-06-446124-6 (pa)
                 LC 88-34067

Letters, diaries, memoirs, interviews, ballads, newspaper articles, and speeches depict life and events during the four years of the Civil War

"Meltzer has incorporated a good cross-section of material documenting both the Northern and Southern viewpoints. . . . The open format, clean pages, and outstanding black-and-white photographs make this an attractive book that will be a fine resource for reports, as well as informative recreational reading for history buffs." SLJ

Includes bibliography

973.8 United States—Reconstruction period, 1865-1901

Marrin, Albert, 1936-

The Spanish-American War. Atheneum Pubs. 1991 182p il maps $15.95 (6 and up)   **973.8**

1. Spanish-American War, 1898
ISBN 0-689-31663-1   LC 90-935

This book describes the causes and events of the Spanish-American War and how it led to the involvement of the United States in the Philippine Insurrection

"Photos and carefully selected details place battles firmly within the historical context and add the human element that makes history . . . come alive. . . . Readers will find themselves entertained as well as instructed." Booklist

Includes bibliography

Mettger, Zak

Reconstruction; America after the Civil War. Lodestar Bks. 1994 122p il (Young readers' history of the Civil War) $16.99 (5 and up)   **973.8**

1. Reconstruction (1865-1876) 2. United States—Politics and government—1865-1898
ISBN 0-525-67490-X   LC 93-44665

The author explains the "post-Civil War era, a time she defines as 'a period of great hope and crushing disappointment.' She accomplishes her goal with a clearly written, well-explained history. Unflinching in the details about lynchings, the Ku Klux Klan, and corrupt governments, she manages to put a human face on the times." SLJ

Includes glossary and bibliography

974 Northeastern United States

Rylant, Cynthia

Appalachia; the voices of sleeping birds; illustrated by Barry Moser. Harcourt Brace Jovanovich 1991 21p il $15   **974**

1. Appalachian region
ISBN 0-15-201605-8   LC 90-36798

"This is a running narrative description of the dogs, people, houses, seasons, and lifestyles of Appalachia." Bull Cent Child Books

"Taking her subtitle from a passage by James Agee, the author conveys with a marvelous economy of words the essence of the very special part of America where she was raised. A poetic text projects emotion as well as information. . . . Moser's watercolors capture the scene perfectly. . . . The book is a treasure—simply a beautiful combination of text and art." Horn Book

974.1 Maine

Dean, Julia

A year on Monhegan Island. Ticknor & Fields Bks. for Young Readers 1995 46p il $14.95 (4-6)   **974.1**

1. Monhegan Island (Me.)
ISBN 0-395-66476-4   LC 93-24534

The author "chronicles the seasons on Monhegan Island, a small community off the coast of central Maine. Beginning with late fall, she describes how the few permanent inhabitants deal with their isolated life. . . . Crisp, clear photos on nearly every page show many of the island's residents at work and play, as well as the natural beauty of Monhegan's craggy beaches and ancient forests. . . . Useful for geography units and fascinating for would-be visitors." Booklist

Gibbons, Gail

Surrounded by sea; life on a New England fishing island. Little, Brown 1991 unp il $14.95 (k-3)   **974.1**

1. Islands 2. Maine
ISBN 0-316-30961-3   LC 90-31773

By revealing activities of island residents through the four seasons, contemporary everyday life in a New England fishing village is presented

"Gibbons' illustrations both inform . . . and please the eye. Young readers curious about ocean fishing and lobstering, as well as potential island visitors, will find this a fascinating introduction." Booklist

Murphy, Jim, 1947-

Into the deep forest with Henry David Thoreau; illustrated by Kate A. Kiesler. Clarion Bks. 1995 39p il $14.95 (4-6)

        974.1

1. Thoreau, Henry David, 1817-1862 2. Maine—Description

ISBN 0-395-60522-9   LC 94-11791

This "introduction to the naturalist/writer, written as a third-person narrative, has been adapted from Thoreau's own journal entries and an article he wrote about his 1857 trip into the Maine wilderness, during which he climbed Mount Katahdin. Although Thoreau's entries have been condensed, the text is liberally sprinkled with quotes. Traveling with a friend and a Native American guide, he noted his observations of plants and trees, animals and birds." SLJ

974.4   Massachusetts

Anderson, Joan

The first Thanksgiving feast; photographed by George Ancona. Clarion Bks. 1984 unp il $15.95; pa $5.95 (3-5)   **974.4**

1. Massachusetts—History—1600-1775, Colonial period 2. Pilgrims (New England colonists) 3. Thanksgiving Day

ISBN 0-89919-287-4; 0-395-51886-5 (pa)

             LC 84-5804

Recreates the first harvest feast celebrated by the Pilgrims in 1621 using the Pilgrim and Indian actors and the seventeenth-century setting of Plimoth Plantation, a living history museum in Plymouth, Massachusetts

"Narrative and illustrations work together to create a real sense of the people, daily life and culture in 1620s Plymouth. The personalized dialogue and sensitive photographs humanize and enliven a historical legend that has become static and empty from too many textbook tellings." SLJ

Bowen, Gary

Stranded at Plimoth Plantation, 1626; words and woodcuts by Gary Bowen; introduction by David Freeman Hawke. HarperCollins Pubs. 1994 81p il map $19.95; lib bdg $19.89 (3-5)

        974.4

1. Pilgrims (New England colonists) 2. Massachusetts—History—1600-1775, Colonial period

ISBN 0-06-022541-6; 0-06-022542-4 (lib bdg)

             LC 93-31016

The author "gives an account of the year 1626 at the by-then-well-established Pilgrim colony, rendered in the form of a journal kept by an orphaned 13-year-old. Shipwrecked on the way to Jamestown, taken in by the settlers at Plimoth, Christopher Sears observes their customs, planting, harvesting, home tutoring, the eight-hour Sabbath meeting, court day, the use of the stocks, etc." Publ Wkly

"The youthful voice and observations, in language that is a remarkable blend of clarity and period flavor, provide a more intimate and involving picture of the period than more straightforward factual accounts." SLJ

Cherry, Lynne, 1952-

A river ran wild; an environmental history. Harcourt Brace Jovanovich 1992 unp il maps $15 (1-4)   **974.4**

1. Nashua River (Mass. and N.H.) 2. Human influence on nature 3. Water pollution

ISBN 0-15-200542-0   LC 91-12892

"Gulliver books"

An environmental history of the Nashua River, from its discovery by Indians through the polluting years of the Industrial Revolution to the ambitious clean-up that revitalized it

"The main text is a straightforward, readable narrative. The layout is pleasing and informative. . . . Not only are the problems of the river discussed, but an effort is made to understand the points of view of the people who industrialized the area." Horn Book

Fritz, Jean

Who's that stepping on Plymouth Rock? illustrated by J. B. Handelsman. Coward, McCann & Geoghegan 1975 30p il $14.95 (2-4)   **974.4**

1. Plymouth Rock

ISBN 0-698-20325-9

An "account of the Rock which is visited yearly by about one and a half million people. It stands now under a monument on the waterfront of Plymouth, Massachusetts, sacred to the memory of the First Comers (Pilgrims) but it has figured in many adventures since the Pilgrims did—or did not—step upon it in 1620." Publ Wkly

"Both a delightful story and a perceptive commentary on how the mythmaking process works in American history." N Y Times Book Rev

George, Jean Craighead, 1919-

The first Thanksgiving; illustrated by Thomas Locker. Philomel Bks. 1993 unp il $15.95 (3-5)   **974.4**

1. Massachusetts—History—1600-1775, Colonial period 2. Pilgrims (New England colonists) 3. Thanksgiving Day

ISBN 0-399-21991-9   LC 91-46643

Describes how the colonists aboard the Mayflower founded New Plymouth and celebrated their first harvest with a feast of thanksgiving

"Locker crafted stunning oil paintings to complement a well-researched and compellingly told presentation." Child Book Rev Serv

Sewall, Marcia, 1935-

The pilgrims of Plimoth; written and illustrated by Marcia Sewall. Atheneum Pubs. 1986 48p il $15.95 (3-6)   **974.4**

1. Pilgrims (New England colonists) 2. Massachusetts—History—1600-1775, Colonial period

ISBN 0-689-31250-4   LC 86-3362

The author provides a "first-person narrative account of the Mayflower voyage of 1620 and the early years of the Plymouth colony. This is not the personal diary of an individual, but rather a journal of the community." Booklist

"Translating narrative and descriptive details into visual images, the illustrations accompany every page of text, occasionally overspreading double pages for panoramic effects. Combining subtle, modulating color with a spiritual as well as an actual luminosity, the paintings—done in gouache—

Sewall, Marcia, 1935-—*Continued*
are vibrant with the daily pulse of life among an energetic, enterprising people." Horn Book

Waters, Kate

Samuel Eaton's day; a day in the life of a Pilgrim boy; photographs by Russ Kendall. Scholastic 1993 40p il $14.95 (2-4)   **974.4**

1. Pilgrims (New England colonists) 2. Massachusetts—History—1600-1775, Colonial period

ISBN 0-590-46311-X   LC 92-32325

Text and photographs follow a six-year-old Pilgrim boy through a busy day during the spring harvest in 1627

"The photographs, taken at Plimoth Plantation, an outdoor living history museum, entice the reader back into the seventeenth century with their authenticity and detail. A vivid description of the hardships endured as well as the pride felt by these English colonists in their new American community." Horn Book

Includes glossary

Sarah Morton's day; a day in the life of a pilgrim girl; photographs by Russell Kendall. Scholastic 1989 32p il $14.95; pa $4.95 (2-4)   **974.4**

1. Pilgrims (New England colonists) 2. Massachusetts—History—1600-1775, Colonial period

ISBN 0-590-42634-6; 0-590-44871-4 (pa)
                                      LC 88-35581

Text and photographs of Plimouth Plantation follow a pilgrim girl through a typical day as she milks the goats, cooks and serves meals, learns her letters, and adjusts to her new stepfather

This "is a highly accessible account of pilgrim life. Attractive color photographs invigorate the text."

Includes glossary

974.7 New York

Costabel, Eva Deutsch, 1924-

The Jews of New Amsterdam; written and illustrated by Eva Deutsch Costabel. Atheneum Pubs. 1988 32p il $13.95 (2-4)   **974.7**

1. Jews—New York (N.Y.) 2. New York (N.Y.)—History

ISBN 0-689-31351-9   LC 87-27873

Traces the events leading to the arrival of the first group of Jews in the Dutch colony of New Amsterdam in 1654 and describes how they adapted and eventually prospered under Dutch, and later British, rule

"Sprightly hued watercolors alternate with striking black-and-white line drawings as Costabel authentically evokes seventeenth-century New Amsterdam. Alongside her quaint illustrations are brief chapters studded with fascinating historical anecdotes about the Jews' settlements of the colony and the Dutch-influenced life-style they adopted there. This invitingly instructive presentation brightly illuminates one aspect of early American history and the roots of religious tolerance." Booklist

Includes glossary and bibliography

Fisher, Leonard Everett, 1924-

The Statue of Liberty. Holiday House 1985 64p il lib bdg $14.95 (4 and up)   **974.7**

1. Statue of Liberty (New York, N.Y.)

ISBN 0-8234-0586-9   LC 85-42878

Recounts the history of one of the largest monuments in the world, including how it was executed in France, shipped to America, and erected in New York Harbor

Fradin, Dennis B.

The New York Colony. Childrens Press 1988 159p il lib bdg $23.93 (4 and up)   **974.7**

1. New York (State)—History

ISBN 0-516-00389-5   LC 87-35803

"Beginning with the 1300s, when the Algonquian and Iroquois Indians were the dominant tribes, Fradin traces the development of New York state. . . . Fradin's lively word pictures chronicle everyday life as the colony moves from Dutch to English domination, and his account ends in 1790 with the relocation of the nation's capital from New York to Philadelphia. Biographical sketches of historical state figures are interspersed, and the crisply designed book includes a liberal use of portraits and engravings. A colonial America time line is a handy reference; overall, a competent, attractive offering." Booklist

Haskins, James, 1941-

The Statue of Liberty: America's proud lady; [by] Jim Haskins. Lerner Publs. 1986 48p il lib bdg $14.95 (4 and up)   **974.7**

1. Statue of Liberty (New York, N.Y.)

ISBN 0-8225-1706-X   LC 85-18061

"A straightforward account of the people and ideas which inspired Bartholdi's arduous battle to make the Statue of Liberty a reality. The book's many black-and-white photographs and prints are effectively dramatic. The paper is of high quality, and the layout and design are superb. Included is information about vital statistics and a plan of repairs. The index is thorough and makes this an excellent book for beginning researchers." SLJ

Includes glossary

Jakobsen, Kathy, 1952-

My New York. Little, Brown 1993 32p il map $15.95 (k-3)   **974.7**

1. New York (N.Y.)—Description

ISBN 0-316-45653-5   LC 91-33567

Becky, a young New Yorker, takes the reader and a friend from the Midwest on a tour of her favorite places in the city

"Jakobsen's shrewdly chosen sites get terrific treatments in her crowded folk-style art, which makes the city come alive." Booklist

Maestro, Betsy, 1944-

The story of the Statue of Liberty; [by] Betsy & Giulio Maestro. Lothrop, Lee & Shepard Bks. 1986 39p il lib bdg $12.88; pa $5.95 (k-3)   **974.7**

1. Bartholdi, Frédéric Auguste, 1834-1904 2. Statue of Liberty (New York, N.Y.)

ISBN 0-688-05774-8 (lib bdg); 0-688-08746-9 (pa)
                                      LC 85-11324

Maestro, Betsy, 1944-—Continued

"Although Maestro simplifies the story—including only the most important people's names, for example—she still presents an accurate account of what happened. The exceptional drawings are visually delightful—primarily in the blue-green range, although they are in full color—and cover most of every page. Human figures—workers, tourists—are included in many drawings, indicating the statue's tremendous scale. Further, the drawings involve viewers through the use of unusual perspectives and angles and by placing the statue in scenes of city life." SLJ

Includes bibliography

Munro, Roxie, 1945-

The inside-outside book of New York City. Dodd, Mead 1985 unp il o.p.; Puffin Bks. paperback available $4.99 (2-4)   **974.7**

1. New York (N.Y.)—Description

ISBN 0-14-050454-0 (pa)   LC 85-7085

"Paired pictures explore exterior and interior views of various sites in Manhattan (plus the Bronx Zoo)." Bull Cent Child Books

"The book thoughtfully includes a one-page reprise, summarizing salient and interesting facts about each site. Notable for the skill with which design elements emphasize the structural significance and relationship of parts to whole, the book is a stylish yet very human approach to this quintessential metropolis." Horn Book

974.8 Pennsylvania

Fradin, Dennis B.

The Pennsylvania colony. Childrens Press 1988 160p il maps lib bdg $23.93 (4 and up)   **974.8**

1. Pennsylvania—History

ISBN 0-516-00390-9   LC 88-11975

A history of the colony of Pennsylvania, from the time of the earliest European settlers to the aftermath of the battle for independence that resulted in statehood. Includes biographical sketches of some individuals prominent in Pennsylvania history

975.3 District of Columbia (Washington)

Climo, Shirley, 1928-

City! Washington, D.C.; photographs by George Ancona. Macmillan 1991 59p il maps $16.95 (4-6)   **975.3**

1. Washington (D.C.)

ISBN 0-02-719036-6   LC 90-40524

Describes the history and significant sights of Washington, D.C

"Extending the sight-seeing feel are Ancona's color photographs. . . . A friendly, informative introduction." Booklist

Doherty, Craig A.

The Washington Monument; [by] Craig A. Doherty and Katherine M. Doherty. Blackbirch Press 1995 48p il (Building America) lib bdg $14.95 (4-6)   **975.3**

1. Washington Monument (Washington, D.C.)

ISBN 1-56711-110-6   LC 94-24477

This work describes the history, planning, architecture, and construction of The Washington Monument. Illustrated with historical photographs, reproductions and current pictures of the site

Includes bibliographical references

Fisher, Leonard Everett, 1924-

The White House. Holiday House 1989 96p il $15.95 (4 and up)   **975.3**

1. White House (Washington, D.C.)

ISBN 0-8234-0774-8   LC 89-1990

"A fresh, captivating commentary of the conception and evolution of America's most famous residence. Through anecdotal prose and wonderful historical photos, Fisher demystifies the prestigious monument by showing it to be a home—complete with its foibles, quirks, and inconveniences." SLJ

Fradin, Dennis B.

Washington, D.C; by Dennis Brindell Fradin. Childrens Press 1992 64p il map lib bdg $16.50; pa $5.95 (3-5)   **975.3**

1. Washington (D.C.)

ISBN 0-516-03851-6 (lib bdg); 0-516-43851-4 (pa)
          LC 91-32919

"An introduction to our culturally and ethnically diverse capitol, highlighting its history, economy, and historic sites of interest. A timeline, map, glossary, and index make the information easily accessible, while the full-color photographs keep interest high." SLJ

Munro, Roxie, 1945-

The inside-outside book of Washington, D.C. Dutton 1987 unp il $13.95 (2-4)   **975.3**

1. Washington (D.C.)—Description

ISBN 0-525-44298-7   LC 86-24267

Also available in paperback from Puffin Bks.

"Views of familiar—and some less familiar—landmarks in our national capitol are recreated in a series of wonderfully effective, colorful pictures. Using a variety of perspectives and an awe-inspiring multiplicity of detail, the illustrator captures the often ponderous lavishness of Federal buildings with careful attention to architectural motifs and just a touch of humor." Horn Book

975.5 Virginia

Ashabranner, Brent K., 1921-

A grateful nation; the story of Arlington National Cemetery; [by] Brent Ashabranner; photographs by Jennifer Ashabranner. Putnam 1990 117p il $15.95 (5 and up)   **975.5**

1. Arlington National Cemetery (Va.)

ISBN 0-399-22188-3   LC 90-34035

Ashabranner, Brent K., 1921--—*Continued*

Traces the history of our national burial ground and shrine to American heroes

"Ashabranner deftly weaves factual information on the cemetery's history and operations, providing vignettes about the people buried there as well as personal anecdotes from visitors, staff, and members of the military honor guard. . . . His daughter's well-placed, evocative black-and-white photographs enhance his descriptive, personal style, creating a powerful feeling of immediacy." Booklist

Includes bibliography

Fisher, Leonard Everett, 1924-

Monticello. Holiday House 1988 64p il $15.95 (4 and up) **975.5**

1. Jefferson, Thomas, 1743-1826—Homes and haunts

ISBN 0-8234-0688-1   LC 87-25219

"The text opens with summary background on the development of English and American architecture, the specific buildings that influenced Jefferson, and his early planning. Various stages of construction and modification demonstrate Jefferson's ingenuity and wide-ranging intelligence as he adapted classical structures to local landscape. The decay of the property after Jefferson's death and its eventual renovation give as much sense of history as the building's conception. The photographs, reproductions, diagrams, and drawings are a masterly mix of graphic information." Bull Cent Child Books

Richards, Norman, 1932-

Monticello. Childrens Press 1995 30p il (Cornerstones of freedom) lib bdg $12.98 (4-6) **975.5**

1. Jefferson, Thomas, 1743-1826—Homes and haunts

ISBN 0-516-06695-1   LC 94-35654

A revised and newly illustrated edition of The story of Monticello, published 1970

The construction and furnishing of the home of Thomas Jefferson "are described as they relate to the events of Jefferson's life and to the founding of our country. The well-written text is handsomely enhanced by full-color and black-and-white photographs and illustrations of the house, gardens, and Jefferson's inventions. His beliefs and feelings about slavery are briefly discussed." SLJ

975.7 South Carolina

Fradin, Dennis B.

The South Carolina Colony; by Dennis Brindell Fradin; consultant, Stephen Hoffius. Childrens Press 1992 160p il maps lib bdg $23.93 (4 and up) **975.7**

1. South Carolina

ISBN 0-516-00397-6   LC 91-32330

Describes the history and people of South Carolina from its earliest settlements to statehood in 1788

Krull, Kathleen, 1952-

Bridges to change; how kids live on a South Carolina Sea Island; photographs by David Hautzig. Lodestar Bks. 1995 46p il (World of my own) $15.99 (4 and up) **975.7**

1. Saint Helena Island (S.C.)—Social life and customs
2. African Americans—Social life and customs

ISBN 0-525-67441-1   LC 93-42392

This book "profiles two 10-year-old African Americans, Travis and Martha, living on St. Helena, a beautiful coastal Sea Island of South Carolina. Krull strikes a noteworthy balance between the details of the children's everyday lives . . . and a broader set of issues. The latter range from the history of slavery in the region and the related development of the Gullah language, to changes brought about on the once-isolated island by bridge building and real-estate development. . . . The simple, conversational quality of the text is matched by the informal full-color photographs." Booklist

Includes bibliography

975.8 Georgia

Fradin, Dennis B.

The Georgia colony; by Dennis Brindell Fradin. Childrens Press 1990 143p il lib bdg $18.53 (4 and up) **975.8**

1. Georgia

ISBN 0-516-00392-5   LC 89-34954

A historical account of Georgia's early days, from its creation as a colony for debtors in the 1700's until its admission as the fourth state in 1788

"The format features large print, wide margins, and a liberal use of portraits, photos, and engravings. Biographical sketches, set off from the main text, will be a boon to report writers. Because the text reads easily, it will be a good choice for reluctant researchers." Booklist

975.9 Florida

George, Jean Craighead, 1919-

Everglades; paintings by Wendell Minor. HarperCollins Pubs. 1995 unp il $14.95; lib bdg $14.89 (2-4) **975.9**

1. Everglades (Fla.)

ISBN 0-06-021228-4; 0-06-021229-2 (lib bdg)
     LC 92-9517

Also available Spanish language edition

"Though structured as a tale told to five children whom a storyteller has poled into the Everglades, the narrative focuses on the history of that unusual ecosystem. The narrator tells how the Everglades became 'a living kaleidoscope of color and beauty,' filled with plants and animals, and how human involvement has changed the ecology, devastating the area. . . . When the children ask about what happened to the orchids, egrets, and alligators, the storyteller suggests that they can make a happy ending to the story when they grow up." Booklist

"The story and the art create a mystical tale that flows from a serene start to a powerful conclusion." SLJ

977　North Central United States. Lake states

McCall, Edith S.

Biography of a river: the living Mississippi; [by] Edith McCall. Walker & Co. 1990 162p il maps $16.95; lib bdg $17.85 (6 and up)　　**977**

1. Mississippi River
ISBN 0-8027-6914-4; 0-8027-6915-2 (lib bdg)
LC 89-70698

Traces the history of the Mississippi River, presents stories of people whose lives were affected by the river, and describes how humans have changed the Mississippi

The author "writes clearly and comprehensively of people and events. . . . She is very objective in her treatment of native Americans. Black-and-white period illustrations and photos show how people have viewed the river throughout history." SLJ

Includes glossary

977.3　Illinois

Murphy, Jim, 1947-

The great fire. Scholastic 1995 144p il maps $16.95 (5 and up)　　**977.3**

1. Fires—Chicago (Ill.)
ISBN 0-590-47267-4　　LC 94-9963

Newbery honor book, 1996

"Firsthand descriptions by persons who lived through the 1871 Chicago fire are woven into a gripping account of this famous disaster. Murphy also examines the origins of the fire, the errors of judgment that delayed the effective response, the organizational problems of the city's firefighters, and the postfire efforts to rebuild the city. Newspaper lithographs and a few historical photographs convey the magnitude of human suffering and confusion." Horn Book Guide

Includes bibliography

978　Western United States

Bentley, Judith, 1945-

Brides, midwives, and widows. 21st Cent. Bks. (NY) 1995 96p il maps (Settling the West) $16.98 (5 and up)　　**978**

1. Women—West (U.S.) 2. West (U.S.)—Social life and customs 3. Frontier and pioneer life—West (U.S.)
ISBN 0-8050-2994-X　　LC 94-39897

The author "tells the often neglected story of the women who helped settle the West. Making use of diaries and other primary sources, she does an excellent job of introducing these women as well as the ups and downs (often downs) of their lives." Booklist

Includes bibliographical references

Blumberg, Rhoda, 1917-

The incredible journey of Lewis and Clark. Lothrop, Lee & Shepard Bks. 1987 143p il maps $18; pa $9.95 (5 and up)　　**978**

1. Lewis, Meriwether, 1774-1809 2. Clark, William, 1770-1838 3. Lewis and Clark Expedition (1804-1806) 4. West (U.S.)—Exploration
ISBN 0-688-06512-0; 0-688-14421-7 (pa)
LC 87-4235

Describes the expedition led by Lewis and Clark to explore the unknown western regions of America at the beginning of the nineteenth century

"Blumberg's writing is dignified but never dry, and her sense of narrative makes familiar history an exciting story." Bull Cent Child Books

Includes bibliography

Freedman, Russell

Children of the wild West. Clarion Bks. 1983 104p il map $15.95; pa $6.95 (4 and up)　　**978**

1. Children—West (U.S.) 2. Frontier and pioneer life—West (U.S.) 3. West (U.S.)—History
ISBN 0-89919-143-6; 0-395-54785-7 (pa)
LC 83-5133

"A smooth narrative and numerous historical photographs combine for an intriguing backward look at how children fared in pioneer times." Booklist

Cowboys of the wild West. Clarion Bks. 1985 103p il map lib bdg $15.95; pa $7.95 (4 and up)　　**978**

1. Cowhands 2. Frontier and pioneer life—West (U.S.) 3. West (U.S.)—History
ISBN 0-89919-301-3 (lib bdg); 0-395-54800-4 (pa)
LC 85-4200

"Freedman describes the herders' duties on the open range roundups and trail rides, their ranch and line-camp life, the clothes and equipment dictated by their work, and the economic necessities that defined the job in its heyday, from the 1860s to the 1890s." Bull Cent Child Books

"The author does a fine job of presenting us with information without belittling the real place the cowboy has in both history and fiction. Bibliography and index." Horn Book

An Indian winter; paintings and drawings by Karl Bodmer. Holiday House 1992 88p il $21.95; pa $12.95 (6 and up)　　**978**

1. Wied, Maximilian, Prinz von, 1782-1867 2. Indians of North America—Missouri River valley 3. Missouri River valley—Description
ISBN 0-8234-0930-9; 0-8234-1158-3 (pa)
LC 91-24205

Relates the experiences of a German prince, his servant, and a young Swiss artist as they traveled through the Missouri River Valley in 1833 learning about the territory and its inhabitants and recording their impressions in words and pictures

"The pictures are particularly effective in presenting rich details of village life, clothing, ceremonies, and customs. Both the book's specific information about native peoples and its use of primary-source material make it a valuable creation." Horn Book

Includes bibliographical references

Granfield, Linda
Cowboy: an album. Ticknor & Fields 1994
96p il $18.95 (5 and up)   **978**

1. Cowhands 2. West (U.S.)
ISBN 0-395-68430-7   LC 93-11027

An introduction to cowboys, their history, their daily life, famous cowboys and cowgirls, and portrayals of cowboys in modern films

"Offering a broad vision of the subject, yet full of intriguing details, this compendium of cowboy history and lore will satisfy browsers and researchers alike." Booklist

Includes bibliography

Lavender, David Sievert, 1910-
The Santa Fe Trail; [by] David Lavender.
Holiday House 1995 64p il $15.95 (4 and up)
          978

1. Santa Fe Trail
ISBN 0-8234-1153-2   LC 94-16638

This is a "history of the route that, for some sixty years, serviced the commerical and military wagon trade between Missouri and New Mexico. Lavender traces the Trail's expansion from William Becknell's 1821 gamble on over trade with Mexico to the road's demise at the advent of the steam locomotive in 1879." Bull Cent Child Books

"Well-placed, black-and-white reproductions, including historical photographs, complement the text. . . . This is a carefully written and worthwhile purchase." SLJ

Miller, Brandon Marie
Buffalo gals; women of the old West. Lerner Publs. 1995 88p il (People's history series) lib bdg $14.21 (5 and up)   **978**

1. Women—West (U.S.) 2. Frontier and pioneer life—West (U.S.) 3. West (U.S.)—History
ISBN 0-8225-1730-2   LC 94-5063

"Westward migration, housekeeping difficulties, professions, forms of entertainment, and intercultural relations are some of the topics discussed in this . . . overview of women's experiences in getting to and surviving in the West." Bull Cent Child Books

The author "catches both the bone-wearying labor and the excitement that sometimes made living in the West worthwhile. She deftly augments her text with excerpts from journals and memoirs as well as photographs from regional archives, which are especially effective because the images are not familiar ones." Booklist

Includes bibliography

Murdoch, David Hamilton, 1937-
Cowboy; written by David H. Murdoch; photographed by Geoff Brightling. Knopf 1993 63p il (Eyewitness books) $19; lib bdg $18.99 (4 and up)   **978**

1. Cowhands
ISBN 0-679-84014-1; 0-679-94014-6   LC 93-12768

Also available Spanish language edition

"A Dorling Kindersley book"

Text and photographs trace the history and lore of cowboys around the globe

"Each chapter has excellent illustrations, primarily photographs taken from a variety of museums and photo collections from throughout the world. This book gives a good overview of cowboy culture." Sci Books Films

Reef, Catherine
Buffalo soldiers. 21st Cent. Bks. (NY) 1993 80p il (African-American soldiers) $14.95 (5 and up)   **978**

1. African American soldiers 2. West (U.S.)—History
ISBN 0-8050-2372-0   LC 92-34413

Recounts the deeds of the 9th and 10th Cavalry, comprised of African American soldiers who kept peace between Indians and settlers on the western frontier, fought in the Spanish-American War, and pursued the outlaw Pancho Villa through Mexico

This is "written in clear, interest-holding prose and plentifully illustrated with period black-and-white photographs and reproductions." SLJ

Includes bibliography

Rounds, Glen, 1906-
Cowboys. Holiday House 1991 unp il lib bdg $14.95; pa $5.95 (k-2)   **978**

1. Cowhands
ISBN 0-8234-0867-1; 0-8234-1061-7 (pa)
          LC 90-46501

Follows a cowboy from sunup to bedtime as he rounds up cattle, kills a rattlesnake, and plays cards in the bunkhouse after dinner

The author "conveys a surprising amount of information in his deceptively simple narrative, appropriate for even the youngest story-hour audience. His blackline illustrations, shaded in golds, browns, and blues, depict the barren landscape of the Great Plains as well as many details of ranch life." Booklist

Scott, Ann Herbert, 1926-
Cowboy country; pictures by Ted Lewin.
Clarion Bks. 1993 unp il $14.95; pa $5.95 (k-3)   **978**

1. Cowhands 2. West (U.S.)
ISBN 0-395-57561-3; 0-395-76482-3 (pa)
          LC 92-24499

An "old buckaroo" tells how he became a cowboy, what the work was like in the past, and how this life has changed

The author "succinctly captures the laconic speaking rhythms and distinctive jargon of her subject. . . . Lewin's . . . well-lit watercolors suggest the affability of the weathered narrator and the awe of the boy with him." Publ Wkly

Tunis, Edwin, 1897-1973
Frontier living; written and illustrated by Edwin Tunis. Crowell 1976 c1961 165p il maps $26 (5 and up)   **978**

1. Frontier and pioneer life—West (U.S.) 2. West (U.S.)—History
ISBN 0-690-01064-8

A Newbery Medal honor book, 1962

A reprint of the title first published 1961 by World Publishing Company

This volume "portrays the manners and customs of the frontiersman and his family from the beginning of the westward movement through the 19th century in . . . text and more than 200 drawings." Wis Libr Bull

978.9   New Mexico

Petersen, David, 1946-
Carlsbad Caverns National Park. Childrens
Press 1994 45p il lib bdg $13.50; pa $4.95
(2-4)   **978.9**
1. Carlsbad Caverns National Park (N.M.) 2. Caves
ISBN 0-516-01051-4 (lib bdg); 0-516-41051-2 (pa)
                  LC 93-36997
"A New true book"
This briefly describes the history of Carlsbad Caverns
National Park, how its caves were formed, its rock forma-
tions, bats, and other wildlife
"Outstanding color photographs and an engaging narra-
tive well suited to the intended audience make this book
most appealing." Sci Books Films
Includes glossary

979.4   California

Blake, Arthur
The gold rush of 1849; staking a claim in
California; [by] Arthur Blake and Pamela
Dailey. Millbrook Press 1995 63p il maps
(Spotlight on American history) lib bdg $15.40
(5 and up)   **979.4**
1. California—Gold discoveries 2. Overland journeys to
the Pacific 3. Frontier and pioneer life—California
ISBN 1-56294-483-5   LC 94-25773
Describes the discovery of gold in California, the various
routes used to get there, the immigrant groups who migrat-
ed there, and work and social life of miners
"A clear overview of the subject. . . . Illustrations are a
mix of black-and-white and full-color photographs and reproductions." SLJ
Includes bibliography

Blumberg, Rhoda, 1917-
The great American gold rush. Bradbury
Press 1989 135p il $17.95 (5 and up)
                  979.4
1. California—Gold discoveries 2. Overland journeys to
the Pacific 3. Frontier and pioneer life—California
ISBN 0-02-711681-6   LC 89-736
Describes the emigration of people from the East Coast
of the United States and from foreign countries to California to pursue the dream of discovering gold
"Profusely illustrated with cartoons and sketches from
publications of the gold rush years, 1848-1852, this oversize
book is an impressive combination of good bookmaking,
thorough (and documented) research, a lively writing style,
and logical arrangement of material. Source material, cited
in an appended section by chapters, is used within the text;
an extensive relative index is provided, as is a bibliography
that is divided into primary and secondary sources. It is
rare to find so illuminating a new book on an old subject."
Bull Cent Child Books

Climo, Shirley, 1928-
City! San Francisco; photographs by George
Ancona. Macmillan 1990 57p il maps $16.95
(4 and up)   **979.4**
1. San Francisco (Calif.)
ISBN 0-02-719030-7   LC 89-32912

"The author's suggestions for tourist activities in and
around San Francisco are as diversified as they are interesting, and the book offers much more besides. The author
has chosen and arranged her material to produce a superbly
clear picture of the city - its geographical location, history,
ethnic composition, and relationship to other cities that together with San Francisco make up the San Francisco Bay
Area. The design is attractive and enticing. . . . Ancona's
photographs catch San Francisco's lively flavor, its diversity, and its breathtaking views." Horn Book

979.5   Oregon. Pacific Northwest

Bentley, Judith, 1945-
Explorers, trappers, and guides. 21st Cent.
Bks. (NY) 1995 96p il maps (Settling the
West) $16.98 (5 and up)   **979.5**
1. West (U.S.)—Exploration 2. Frontier and pioneer
life—West (U.S.)
ISBN 0-8050-2995-8   LC 94-39895
"Peppered with quotes from well-known (Lewis & Clark,
Kit Carson) as well as rarely encountered figures (Ross Cox,
David Douglas), the book provides an overview of many
westward adventures. . . . Period reproductions and modern
photographs add to the text." SLJ
Includes bibliographical references

Fisher, Leonard Everett, 1924-
The Oregon Trail. Holiday House 1990 64p
il maps $15.95 (4 and up)   **979.5**
1. Overland journeys to the Pacific 2. Oregon Trail
3. West (U.S.)—History
ISBN 0-8234-0833-7   LC 90-55103
Charts the journey of those who followed the Oregon
Trail in the first half of the nineteenth century
"Fisher brings this migration to life with a clear, readable
text that makes generous use of the emigrants' own journal
entries. . . . The illustrations are many and varied, including
maps, photographs, drawings, documents, and paintings."
Booklist

979.8   Alaska

Murphy, Claire Rudolf
A child's Alaska; photographs by Charles
Mason. Alaska Northwest Bks. 1994 47p il
$14.95 (2-5)   **979.8**
1. Alaska
ISBN 0-88240-457-1   LC 93-48164
"Following the seasons from one winter to the next,
Murphy touches on climate, wildlife, and typical activities
of Alaskan children. . . . Mason's intriguing, sharply repro-
duced, full-color photos appear on every page and capture
the essence of the Alaskan experience." Booklist
Includes bibliographical references

981 Brazil

Lewington, Anna
Antonio's rain forest; adapted from an original text by Anna Lewington; photographs by Edward Parker. Carolrhoda Bks. 1993 c1992 48p il maps lib bdg $21.50 (3-5) **981**

1. Rain forests 2. Rubber 3. Brazil
ISBN 0-87614-749-X   LC 91-46972
First published 1992 in the United Kingdom
"The life of a rubber tapper's family living in the north-western Brazilian rain forest is told in the first person from the viewpoint of eight-year-old Antonio José, the son and grandson of rubber tappers. . . . The vivid color photographs illustrate a life lived close to the earth and its resources." Sci Books Films
Includes glossary and bibliography

Reynolds, Jan, 1956-
Amazon basin; vanishing cultures. Harcourt Brace & Co. 1993 unp il (Vanishing cultures series) $16.95; pa $8.95 (2-4) **981**

1. Yanoama Indians 2. Amazon River valley
ISBN 0-15-202831-5; 0-15-202832-3 (pa)
LC 92-21089
"Jan Reynolds's book is a sensitive, first-hand account of the daily life of an Amazonian tribe as seen through the eyes of an Indian child. . . . The simple narrative, which takes the form of extended captions for the photos, is factual and accurate but not overburdened with information difficult for young readers to assimilate. . . . The photographic reproduction and layout are excellent." Sci Books Films

Schwartz, David M., 1951-
Yanomami; people of the Amazon; photographs by Victor Englebert. Lothrop, Lee & Shepard Bks. 1995 48p il (Vanishing peoples) $16; lib bdg $15.93 **981**

1. Yanoama Indians 2. Amazon River valley
ISBN 0-688-11157-2; 0-688-11158-0 (lib bdg)
LC 93-48616
This book "profiles the Yanomami, a tribe indigenous to the Amazon rain forest. . . . Both text and color photos work together to paint an intriguing portrait of village life, and there are scenes of hunting, feasting, and healing." Booklist

Waterlow, Julia
The Amazon; written and photographed by Julia Waterlow. Raintree Steck-Vaughn Pubs. 1994 47p il maps (Rivers of the world) $22.80 (4 and up) **981**

1. Amazon River
ISBN 0-8114-3101-0   LC 92-25446
An overview of the Amazon River, its physical features, plants and wildlife, history, economics, towns and cities, vanishing Indians, and environmental threats
Includes glossary and bibliography

982 Argentina

Brusca, María Cristina
On the pampas. Holt & Co. 1991 unp il $15.95; pa $5.95 (k-3) **982**

1. Argentina—Social life and customs 2. Cowhands 3. Ranch life
ISBN 0-8050-1548-5; 0-8050-2919-2 (pa)
LC 90-40938
Also available Spanish language edition
"Brusca, a city child from Buenos Aires, recounts a summer spent at her grandparents' *estancia* on the Argentine pampas. . . . Brusca's watercolor cartoons, done in a folksy style, are filled with unexpected details of landscape, architecture, clothing, and local flora and fauna, as well as visually pleasing color and form. . . . Her work succeeds on two levels—picture book art and social studies." SLJ

Fox, Geoffrey
The land and people of Argentina. Lippincott 1990 238p il maps (Portraits of the nations series) lib bdg $18.89 (5 and up) **982**

1. Argentina
ISBN 0-397-32381-6   LC 89-37811
Introduces the history, geography, people, culture, government, and economy of Argentina
Includes bibliography

984 Bolivia

Blair, David Nelson
The land and people of Bolivia. Lippincott 1990 208p il maps (Portraits of the nations series) lib bdg $15.89 (5 and up) **984**

1. Bolivia
ISBN 0-397-32383-2   LC 89-39721
An illustrated look at Bolivia's history, geography and place in the modern world
Includes bibliography

Morrison, Marion
Bolivia. Childrens Press 1988 128p il maps (Enchantment of the world) lib bdg $26.60 (4 and up) **984**

1. Bolivia
ISBN 0-516-02705-0   LC 88-10877
Discusses the geography, history, people, culture, politics, daily life, and economy of Bolivia
"The cocaine trade receives open discussion, with a good tie-in to its roots in the impoverished Bolivian economy." SLJ

985 Peru

Kendall, Sarita
The Incas. New Discovery Bks. 1992 64p il maps lib bdg $14.95 (5 and up) **985**

1. Incas
ISBN 0-02-750160-4   LC 91-513

Kendall, Sarita—*Continued*

"A survey of the Incas, with a general description of their way of life before, during, and after their fatal encounter with the Spaniards. Kendall also describes how disease and cultural differences allowed the Spanish conquistadors to defeat these advanced people. In two-page entries, she briefly covers such topics as clothes, medicine and healing, weapons and warfare, crafts, etc." SLJ

Lepthien, Emilie U. (Emilie Utteg)

Peru. Childrens Press 1992 127p il maps (Enchantment of the world) lib bdg $21.53 (4 and up)   **985**

1. Peru
ISBN 0-516-02610-0   LC 92-4813

Describes the history, geography, people, economy, and government of the country which lies along the Pacific coast of South America

"Almost all full-color, the illustrations in this title are spectacular." SLJ

McKissack, Patricia C., 1944-

The Inca; [by] Patricia McKissack. Childrens Press 1985 45p il lib bdg $18; pa $5.50 (2-4)   **985**

1. Incas
ISBN 0-516-01268-1 (lib bdg); 0-516-41268-X (pa)
     LC 85-6712

Also available Spanish language edition

"A New true book"

Traces the rise of the Incan civilization with emphasis on their culture, social structure, government, economy, and the fatal encounter with the Spanish conquistadors which brought about the end of their society

Newman, Shirlee Petkin

The Incas. Watts 1992 61p il lib bdg $19.90; pa $5.95 (4 and up)   **985**

1. Incas
ISBN 0-531-20004-3 (lib bdg); 0-531-15637-0 (pa)
     LC 91-31378

"A First book"

Describes the civilization of the Inca empire that flourished from the thirteenth to the sixteenth century and the present-day lives of the Andean people descended from that empire

Includes bibliographical references

987   Venezuela

Fox, Geoffrey

The land and people of Venezuela. HarperCollins Pubs. 1991 193p il maps (Portraits of the nations series) lib bdg $17.89 (5 and up)   **987**

1. Venezuela
ISBN 0-06-022477-0   LC 90-20431

Introduces the history, geography, people, culture, government, and economy of Venezuela

"Although it is not an in-depth study, it gives a well rounded look at a good friend and important neighbor to the south. . . . An interesting, informative book well worth reading." Voice Youth Advocates

Includes bibliography

988   Guiana

Brill, Marlene Targ

Guyana; consultant for Guyana: George I. Blanksten; consultant for reading: Robert L. Hillerich. Childrens Press 1994 127p il maps (Enchantment of the world) lib bdg $21.53 (4 and up)   **988**

1. Guyana
ISBN 0-516-02626-7   LC 94-7007

Describes the people, land, history, economy, and government of Guyana

989.2   Paraguay

Morrison, Marion

Paraguay. Childrens Press 1993 127p il maps (Enchantment of the world) lib bdg $21.53 (4 and up)   **989.2**

1. Paraguay
ISBN 0-516-02619-4   LC 93-754

Introduces the geography, history, agriculture, industry, and people of the South American country known as "the place with the great river."

This features "abundant and well-chosen black-and-white reproductions and full-color photographs." SLJ

989.5   Uruguay

Morrison, Marion

Uruguay. Childrens Press 1992 128p il maps (Enchantment of the world) lib bdg $26.60 (4 and up)   **989.5**

1. Uruguay
ISBN 0-516-02607-0   LC 91-35144

Presents a history of a small South American country, discussing its people, everyday and cultural life, and problems

993   New Zealand

Fox, Mary Virginia

New Zealand; consultant for New Zealand, S.F. Newman; consultant for reading, Robert L. Hillerich. Childrens Press 1991 127p il maps (Enchantment of the world) lib bdg $21.53 (4 and up)   **993**

1. New Zealand
ISBN 0-516-02728-X   LC 90-20010

Introduces New Zealand, first populated by the Maori, who named the land mass "Land of the Long White Cloud"

New Zealand—in pictures; prepared by Geography Department. Lerner Publs. 1990 64p il maps (Visual geography series) lib bdg $19.95 (5 and up)   **993**

1. New Zealand
ISBN 0-8225-1862-7   LC 89-36541

New Zealand—in pictures—*Continued*
Revised edition of the title prepared by Michael Robson, published 1979 by Sterling
Text and photographs introduce the topography, history, society, economy, and governmental structure of New Zealand

994 Australia

Australia—in pictures; prepared by Geography Department. Lerner Publs. 1990 64p il maps (Visual geography series) lib bdg $19.95 (5 and up) **994**
1. Australia
ISBN 0-8225-1855-4   LC 89-29199
Revised edition of the title prepared by Jo McDonald and Reven Uihlein, published 1979 by Sterling
An introduction to the land, history, government, economy, people, and culture of Australia

Lester, Alison, 1952-
My farm. Houghton Mifflin 1994 unp il $14.95 (1-3) **994**
1. Farm life—Australia
ISBN 0-395-68193-6   LC 93-30894
"Spanning one year of her childhood on an Australian farm overlooking the sea, Lester's narrative begins and ends near Christmas time in the summer. . . . The author's writing and illustrating style is delicate. Her watercolors, neatly lined with ink; the highly stylized figures and faces; and the abundant detailing all contribute to this lovely picture book." SLJ

Reynolds, Jan, 1956-
Down under; vanishing cultures. Harcourt Brace Jovanovich 1992 unp il $16.95; pa $9 (2-4) **994**
1. Australian aborigines
ISBN 0-15-224182-5; 0-15-224183-3 (pa)
    LC 91-9791
Examines the vanishing culture of the Tiwi tribe, aborigines who live on a small island off the coast of Australia
"Reynolds' respect for her subjects is apparent in every photograph, and the simple language of the text is the perfect accompaniment. This photo-essay captures the beauty of an endangered culture and helps us to appreciate it." Booklist

995.3 Papua New Guinea. New Guinea region

Fox, Mary Virginia
Papua New Guinea. Childrens Press 1994 127p il maps (Enchantment of the world) lib bdg $21.53 (4 and up) **995.3**
1. Papua New Guinea
ISBN 0-516-02621-6   LC 93-35493
This volume covers "the Southeast Asian nation's geography, geology, and wildlife; its diverse cultures and ways of life; European settlers and missionaries; the 1930 discovery of a civilization in the highland zone; the independent nation; and Papau New Guinea today. The text is a fine combination of expository, narrative, and descriptive writing

that will motivate students to read further. . . . Full-color and black-and-white photographs show the islands' spectacular scenery, cultural customs, unique flora and fauna, and cities and villages." SLJ

998 Arctic islands and Antarctica

Beattie, Owen
Buried in ice; by Owen Beattie and John Geiger with Shelley Tanaka. Scholastic 1992 64p il maps (Time quest book) $15.95; pa $6.95 (4 and up) **998**
1. Franklin, Sir John, 1786-1847 2. Arctic regions
ISBN 0-590-43848-4; 0-590-43849-2 (pa)
    LC 91-23897
"A Scholastic/Madison Press book"
Probes the tragic and mysterious fate of Sir John Franklin's failed expedition to the Arctic to find the Northwest Passage in 1845
"The narrative is interspersed with an imaginative section that relates the story of the expedition from the point of view of 19-year-old Luke, a member of the crew. While the text is exciting, the book's greatest strength is its superb illustrations: drawings, paintings, and historic and present day photographs are used to enrich each page." SLJ
Includes glossary and bibliography

Billings, Henry
Antarctica. Childrens Press 1994 126p il maps (Enchantment of the world) lib bdg $27.40 (4 and up) **998**
1. Antarctic regions
ISBN 0-516-02624-0   LC 94-9142
Discusses the location, climate, plant and animal life, discovery and exploration, and the cooperation of nations in preserving the fifth-largest continent

Cowcher, Helen
Antarctica. Farrar, Straus & Giroux 1990 unp il $14.95; pa $6.95 (1-3) **998**
1. Antarctic regions 2. Penguins 3. Seals (Animals) 4. Wildlife conservation
ISBN 0-374-30368-1; 0-374-40371-6 (pa)
Also available Spanish language edition
"In story form, Cowcher attempts to describe life for emperor and Adélie penguins and Weddell seals during one Antarctic winter and spring as they nest, give birth, and raise their young. Harsh weather makes survival difficult, but the true enemy may be the men who have a base camp near the Adélies' nesting area; their helicopter frightens the penguins away, allowing the predatory skuas access to their eggs." SLJ
"The superb pictures, with stunning closeups of birds and mammals in colours glowing against the blue and green of ice and water, hold the eye while the mind takes in the crucial conservation message. Grow Point

Ekoomiak, Normee
Arctic memories. Holt & Co. 1990 c1988 unp il $22.25; pa $5.95 (3-5) **998**
1. Inuit 2. Québec (Province) 3. Arctic regions
ISBN 0-8050-1254-0; 0-8050-2347-X (pa)
    LC 89-39194
First published 1988 in Canada

Ekoomiak, Normee—*Continued*

"Ekoomiak, an Inuit who grew up in the James Bay area of Arctic Quebec, depicts scenes from his childhood in a picture book that is essentially a personalized record of a way of life that is now all but extinct. The text is written in both English and Inuktitut, the language of the Inuit people." Horn Book

"These simple commentaries become an unexpectedly resonant voice. . . . Ekoomiak's art is spare and elemental. Clean shapes and stylized figures are the rule, though compositions can become agreeably busy and even complex." Booklist

Hackwell, W. John

Desert of ice; life and work in Antarctica. Scribner 1991 40p il $14.95 (4-6)   **998**

1. Antarctic regions
ISBN 0-684-19085-0   LC 89-35002

Introduces the history and geography of Antarctica and describes life on an Antarctic base and the type of scientific research that is done there

"The writing is clear and competent; the book is a pleasure to read." SLJ

Johnson, Rebecca L.

Science on the ice; an Antarctic journal. Lerner Publs. 1995 128p il lib bdg $22.13 (5 and up)   **998**

1. Antarctic regions
ISBN 0-8225-2852-5   LC 94-41487

A "personal look at scientific investigation and survival in one of the world's harshest ecosystems, Johnson braved the Antarctic cold, wind, and hazardous conditions (including the infamous ozone hole) to accompany biologists, geologists, meterologists, and other scientists while they pursued their work." SLJ

Pringle, Laurence P.

Antarctica; the last unspoiled continent; by Laurence Pringle. Simon & Schuster Bks. for Young Readers 1992 56p il maps $15 (4 and up)   **998**

1. Antarctic regions
ISBN 0-671-73850-X   LC 90-27362

Surveys the plant and animal life, impact on global ecology, history, and politics of the White Continent

"With lavish full-color photographs and a clear, accessible text, this is a must for most libraries." SLJ

Includes glossary

Taylor, Barbara, 1954-

Arctic & Antarctic; written by Barbara Taylor; photographed by Geoff Brightling. Knopf 1995 63p il (Eyewitness books) $17; lib bdg $18.99 (4 and up)   **998**

1. Polar regions
ISBN 0-679-87257-4; 0-679-97257-9 (lib bdg)
          LC 94-37730

"A Dorling Kindersley book"

This overview "features a series of two-page spreads focusing on the history, geology, plant life, wildlife and ecology of the polar regions. Each two-page topic is given a paragraph of explanatory text surrounded by diagrams, maps, charts and photographs with lengthy captions." Appraisal

Fic   Fiction

A number of subject headings have been added to the books in this section to aid in curriculum work. It is not necessarily recommended that these subjects be used in the library catalog.

Ackerman, Karen, 1951-

The night crossing; illustrated by Elizabeth Sayles. Knopf 1994 56p il $14 (3-5)   **Fic**

1. Holocaust, 1933-1945—Fiction 2. Jews—Austria—Fiction
ISBN 0-679-83169-X   LC 94-10805

Also available in paperback from Random House

In 1938, having begun to feel the persecution that all Jews are experiencing in their Austrian city, Clara and her family escape over the mountains into Switzerland

"Ackerman's writing is clear and direct; despite its simplicity, it is never banal. This is an excellent fictional introduction to the Holocaust." SLJ

Adams, Richard, 1920-

Watership Down. Macmillan 1974 c1972 429p $29.95 (6 and up)   **Fic**

1. Rabbits—Fiction 2. Allegories
ISBN 0-02-700030-3

Also available in paperback from Avon Bks.

First published 1972 in the United Kingdom

"Faced with the annihilation of its warren, a small group of male rabbits sets out across the English downs in search of a new home. Internal struggles for power surface in this intricately woven, realistically told adult adventure when the protagonists must coordinate tactics in order to defeat an enemy rabbit fortress. It is clear that the author has done research on rabbit behavior, for this tale is truly authentic." Shapiro. Fic for Youth. 3d edition

Adler, C. S. (Carole S.), 1932-

Youn Hee and me. Harcourt Brace & Co. 1995 183p $11; pa $5 (4-6)   **Fic**

1. Adoption—Fiction 2. Brothers and sisters—Fiction 3. Family life—Fiction 4. Korean Americans—Fiction
ISBN 0-15-200073-9; 0-15-200376-2 (pa)
          LC 94-31060

"Eleven-year-old Caitlin loves her five-year-old brother, Simon, who came from Korea to join her family three years ago. When it turns out Simon has a birth sister Caitlin's age still in a Korean orphanage, Caitlin insists that Youn Hee is part of the family too; when Youn Hee arrives, however, it's clear that making a family is not as simple as Caitlin envisions. . . . Caitlin's narration quietly but effectively addresses questions of racism and the matter of her divorced and distant dad as well as telling the central story in lively and readable style." Bull Cent Child Books

Adler, David A., 1947-

Cam Jansen and the mystery of the stolen diamonds; illustrated by Susanna Natti. Viking 1980 58p il $11.99; pa $3.99 (2-4)   **Fic**

1. Mystery fiction
ISBN 0-670-20039-5; 0-14-034670-8 (pa)
          LC 79-20695

Cam Jansen, a fifth-grader with a photographic memory, and her friend Eric help solve the mystery of the stolen diamonds

This is a "fast-action uncomplicated adventure . . . [with] a touch of humor, a breezy writing style, and some very enjoyable pen-and-ink drawings." Booklist

Other available titles about Cam Jansen are:
Cam Jansen and the chocolate fudge mystery (1993)

Adler, David A., 1947——*Continued*

Cam Jansen and the mystery at the haunted house (1992)
Cam Jansen and the mystery at the monkey house (1985)
Cam Jansen and the mystery of Flight 54 (1989)
Cam Jansen and the mystery of the Babe Ruth baseball (1982)
Cam Jansen and the mystery of the carnival prize (1984)
Cam Jansen and the mystery of the circus clown (1983)
Cam Jansen and the mystery of the dinosaur bones (1981)
Cam Jansen and the mystery of the gold coins (1982)
Cam Jansen and the mystery of the monster movie (1984)
Cam Jansen and the mystery of the stolen corn popper (1986)
Cam Jansen and the mystery of the television dog (1981)
Cam Jansen and the mystery of the UFO (1980)
Cam Jansen and the Triceratops Pops mystery (1995)

Ahlberg, Allan

Ten in a bed; illustrated by André Amstutz. Viking Kestrel 1989 c1983 94p il $12.95; pa $3.99 (3-5)   **Fic**

1 Fairy tales
ISBN 0-670-82042-3; 0-14-032531-X (pa)
First published 1983 in the United Kingdom
"Dinah Price's daytimes may be ordinary but her bedtimes are fantastic. As the sun sets on each of eight consecutive nights, she climbs the stairs and finds in her bed at least one well-known character: the three bears, the Wicked Witch, the cat of 'Hey Diddle, Diddle' fame, Sleeping Beauty, the Big Bad Wolf, Simple Simon, the Frog Prince, or a giant. Each feels right at home beneath Dinah's covers, and it takes all of her inventive powers and patience to chase them out." Booklist

"André Amstutz' illustrations are charming black-and-white line drawings, scattered throughout the text—a benign complement to the wacky stories, and pleasantly moderate in comparison." N Y Times Book Rev

Ahlberg, Janet

It was a dark and stormy night; [by] Janet and Allan Ahlberg. Viking 1993 unp il $13.99 (2-4)   **Fic**

1. Pirates—Fiction
ISBN 0-670-84620-1   LC 94-238786
"Captured by brigands, taken to their mountain cave, and ordered to tell a story, a plucky lad named Antonio entertains his captors with a tale that captivates the childlike chief and his band of dim-witted desperadoes. . . . In its spacious format and humorous tone, this illustrated story offers the satisfaction of an eight-year-old outwitting a band of outlaws more silly than sinister. . . . An appealing read-aloud choice." Booklist

Aiken, Joan, 1924-

Midnight is a place. Viking 1974 287p o.p.; Scholastic paperback available $2.95 (5 and up)   **Fic**

1. Orphans—Fiction 2. Great Britain—Fiction
ISBN 0-590-45496-X (pa)
Fourteen-year-old Lucas leads a lonely, monotonous life in the house of his unpleasant guardian until the unexpected arrival of an unusual little girl presages a series of events that completely change his life

"With her customary vivacity and inventiveness, the author has created another novel steeped in nineteenth-century literary traditions and devices. . . . The melodrama, which manages to avoid even a hint of sentimentality, nev-er flags as it goes from incident to incident and reaches a happy ending." Horn Book

The wolves of Willoughby Chase; illustrated by Pat Marriott. Doubleday 1963 c1962 168p il hardcover o.p. paperback available $3.99 (5 and up)   **Fic**

1. Great Britain—Fiction
ISBN 0-440-49603-9 (pa)
First published 1962 in the United Kingdom
"In this burlesque of a Victorian melodrama, two London children are sent to a country estate while their parents are away. Here they outwit a wicked governess, escape from packs of hungry wolves, and restore the estate to its rightful owner." Hodges. Books for Elem Sch Libr

"Plot, characterization, and background blend perfectly into an amazing whole. . . . Highly recommended." SLJ

Another available title in this series is:
Is underground (1993)

Alcock, Vivien, 1924-

The cuckoo sister. Delacorte Press 1986 c1985 160p $14.95 (6 and up)   **Fic**

1. Sisters—Fiction 2. London (England)—Fiction
ISBN 0-385-29467-0   LC 85-20648
First published 1985 in the United Kingdom
"Eleven year old Kate Seton becomes very upset when an underfed 13-year-old shows up at her parents' home with a letter stating that she is Kate's sister—stolen from a pram outside a store where Mrs. Seton had been shopping. Rosie doesn't believe the story that she is Emma Seton and frantically tries to find her mother who has left with no trace. Kate eventually comes to love Rosie and tries to provide a clue that will enable her to stay. Characterizations are very vivid and although it definitely has a British flavor, students will empathize with Kate and Rosie." Voice Youth Advocates

The monster garden. Delacorte Press 1988 134p hardcover o.p. paperback available $2.95 (4 and up)   **Fic**

1. Monsters—Fiction 2. Fathers and daughters—Fiction 3. Science fiction
ISBN 0-440-40257-3 (pa)
"The story of a young girl who unexpectedly finds herself nurturing a creature of unknown origin. Frankie Stein is the daughter of a scientist whose preoccupation with his work drives a wedge among the family members. When Frankie obtains some unknown genetic 'material,' she finds herself having to cope with a growing 'monster.'" SLJ

"*The Monster Garden* is a deft fantasy; it is also a story of compassionate love and growing self-reliance." Bull Cent Child Books

Singer to the sea god. Delacorte Press 1993 c1992 199p $15; pa $3.99 (6 and up)   **Fic**

1. Adventure fiction
ISBN 0-385-30866-3; 0-440-41003-7 (pa)
       LC 92-9832
First published 1992 in the United Kingdom
When he and his companions flee their island home after the king's court is turned to stone, Phaidon begins to believe in the gods and monsters that his uncle has always scorned

"The setting and text remain true to the epic style, yet the dialogue is sufficiently contemporary to make the book accessible to today's reader. A fine, fast-paced, bold story with enough depth to use as a companion to classic mythology." Horn Book

Alcott, Louisa May, 1832-1888

Little women; or Meg, Jo, Beth and Amy (5 and up) **Fic**

1. Family life—Fiction 2. New England—Fiction

Available from various publishers, including a Holt & Co. edition illustrated by Michael Hague; Spanish language edition also available

First published 1868

The story of the New England home life of the four March sisters. Each 'little woman's' personality differs: Jo's quick temper and restless desire for the freedom of a boy's life; Meg's hatred of poverty and her longing for pretty clothes; Amy's all-engulfing self-interest; and gentle Beth's love of home and family

The tale is "related with sympathy, humour, and sincerity. This lively natural narrative of family experience is as well-loved today as when it first appeared." Toronto Public Libr. Books for Boys & Girls

Other available titles about members of the March family are:

Eight cousins (1875)
Jo's boys (1886)
Little men (1871)
Rose in bloom (1876)

An old-fashioned Thanksgiving (3-5) **Fic**

1. Family life—Fiction 2. Thanksgiving Day—Fiction 3. New England—Fiction

Various editions available

"In this story, which first appeared in 'St. Nicholas' magazine in 1881, Alcott recounts the escapades of a New Hampshire farm family in the 1820s. When the parents are unexpectedly called away on Thanksgiving Day, the children pitch in to make their version of the traditional holiday feast and, with little knowledge and less caution, bumble along toward a culinary catastrophe reminiscent of Meg and Jo's dinner in 'Little Women.'" Booklist

Alexander, Lloyd

The Arkadians. Dutton Children's Bks. 1995 272p $15.99 (5 and up) **Fic**

1. Fantasy fiction

ISBN 0-525-45415-2   LC 94-35025

To escape the wrath of the king and his wicked soothsayers, Lucian joins with Fronto, a poet-turned-jackass, and Joy-in-the-Dance, a young girl with mystical powers, on a series of epic adventures

"On one level, this is a rousing adventure complete with cliffhangers and do-or-die situations. On another, readers familiar with Greek mythology will find clever hints at the myths' purpose and genesis." SLJ

The Beggar Queen. Dutton 1984 221p o.p.; Dell paperback available $4.99 (5 and up) **Fic**

1. Adventure fiction

ISBN 0-440-90548-6 (pa)   LC 83-25502

The concluding volume in the author's Westmark trilogy, begun with Westmark, entered below, and The Kestrel (1982)

"Since the end of the war with Regia, Theo has become a consul to Mickle, now Queen Augusta. However, peace lasts only two years, when Cabbarus invades the country to wrest the kingdom back from Mickle. Theo is forced to take up arms again to help his beloved queen and country." Roman. Sequences

The book of three. Holt & Co. 1964 217p il $16.95 (5 and up) **Fic**

1. Fantasy fiction

ISBN 0-8050-0874-8

Also available in paperback from Dell

"The first of five books about the mythical land of Prydain finds Taran, an assistant pig keeper, fighting with Prince Gwydion against the evil which theatens the kingdom." Hodges. Books for Elem Sch Libr

"Related in a simple, direct style, this fast-paced tale of high adventure has a well-balanced blend of fantasy, realism, and humor. Although the Welsh Mabinogion is the inspiration for the story and some of the characters, the incidents, mood, and characterizations are more reminiscent of Tolkien's trilogy." SLJ

Other available titles about the mythical land of Prydain are:

The black cauldron (1965)
The castle of Llyr (1966)
Taran Wanderer (1967)

Final volume about Prydain: The High King, entered below

The cat who wished to be a man. Dutton 1973 107p o.p.; Dell paperback available $3.50 (4-6) **Fic**

1. Cats—Fiction

ISBN 0-440-40580-7 (pa)   LC 73-77447

When he begins dealing with humanity, Lionel the cat begins to understand why his wizard master was reluctant to change him into a man

This is "a comic and ebullient fantasy; just right for reading aloud." Horn Book

The High King. Holt & Co. 1968 285p il lib bdg $16.95 (5 and up) **Fic**

1. Fantasy fiction

ISBN 0-8050-1114-5

Also available in paperback from Dell

Awarded the Newbery Medal, 1969

Concluding title in the chronicles of Prydain which include: The book of three, The black cauldron, The castle of Llyr, and Taran Wanderer, entered above

In this final volume Taran, the assistant pig-keeper "becomes High King of Prydain, Princess Eilonwy becomes his queen, the predictions of Taran's wizard guardian Dallben are fulfilled, and the forces of black magic led by Arawn, Lord of Annuvin, Land of the Dead, are vanquished forever." SLJ

"The fantasy has the depth and richness of a medieval tapestry, infinitely detailed and imaginative." Saturday Rev

The Illyrian adventure. Dutton 1986 132p o.p.; Dell paperback available $3.50 (5 and up) **Fic**

1. Adventure fiction

ISBN 0-440-94018-4 (pa)   LC 85-30762

"Sixteen-year-old Vesper Holly drags her long-suffering guardian, Brinnie, off to Illyria to vindicate her late father's reputation as a scholar. With humor, beguiling charm, and intelligence she manages to find a treasure, thwart a conspiracy to murder Illyria's King Osman, and guide two rival factions to the peace table." Wilson Libr Bull

"Alexander's archeological mystery has intricate plotting and witty wording." Bull Cent Child Books

Other available adventure titles featuring Vesper Holly are:

The Drackenberg adventure (1988)
The El Dorado adventure (1987)
The Jedera adventure (1989)
The Philadelphia adventure (1990)

Alexander, Lloyd—Continued

The marvelous misadventures of Sebastian; grand extravaganza, including a performance by the entire cast of the Gallimaufry-Theatricus. Dutton 1970 204p o.p.; Dell paperback available $3.50 (4 and up) **Fic**

1. Adventure fiction 2. Musicians—Fiction
ISBN 0-440-40549-1 (pa)   LC 70-116879

"Sebastian, a teenage fiddler, gets involved in court intrigue and muddles his way to eventual success in ousting a cruel usurper from the throne." Natl Counc of Teach of Engl. Adventuring with Books

"The intricacy of plot, the humor and allusiveness of the writing, the exaggerated characterization, and the derring-do of romantic adventures are knit into a lively and elaborate tale that can be enjoyed for its action and appreciated for its subtler significance." Sutherland. The Best in Child Books

The remarkable journey of Prince Jen. Dutton Children's Bks. 1991 273p $15.99 (5 and up) **Fic**

1. Adventure fiction 2. China—Fiction
ISBN 0-525-44826-8   LC 91-13720

Bearing six unusual gifts, young Prince Jen in Tang Dynasty China embarks on a perilous quest and emerges triumphantly into manhood

"Alexander satisfies the taste for excitement, but his vivid characters and the food for thought he offers will nourish long after the last page is turned." SLJ

Westmark. Dutton 1981 184p $15.95 (5 and up) **Fic**

1. Adventure fiction
ISBN 0-525-42335-4

Also available in paperback from Dell

A boy fleeing from criminal charges falls in with a charlatan, his dwarf attendant, and an urchin girl, travels with them about the kingdom of Westmark, and ultimately arrives at the palace where the king is grieving over the loss of his daughter

The author "peoples his tale with a marvelous cast of individuals, and weaves an intricate story of high adventure that climaxes in a superbly conceived conclusion, which, though predictable, is reached through carefully built tension and subtly added comic relief." Booklist

Followed by the Kestrel (1982), and The Beggar Queen, entered above

Andersen, Hans Christian, 1805-1875

Hans Christian Andersen's The fir tree; illustrated by Nancy Ekholm Burkert. Harper & Row 1970 34p il hardcover o.p. paperback available $6.95 (2-5) **Fic**

1. Christmas—Fiction
ISBN 0-06-443109-6 (pa)

This translation of the fairy tale is by H. W. Dulcken

Surrounded by the beauties of the forest, the little fir tree was unhappy and longed for its moment of glory. It came one Christmas Eve but it was neither what the tree expected nor wanted

"The delicacy and meticulousness of the illustrative details of this edition, beautiful in soft colors or in black and white, should please old fans and the felicity of mood should attract new ones." Bull Cent Child Books

The little match girl; illustrated by Rachel Isadora. Putnam 1987 30p il $15.95; pa $5.95 (3-5) **Fic**

ISBN 0-399-21336-8; 0-399-21337-6 (pa)

LC 85-30082

The wares of the poor little match girl illuminate her cold world, bringing some beauty to her brief, tragic life

"Isadora follows Andersen's lead, neither sensationalizing nor apologizing for the tale's potentially sentimental plot. . . . A moving, original picture-book interpretation of the classic tale." Booklist

The nightingale (2-5) **Fic**

1. Nightingales—Fiction 2. Fairy tales

Also available Spanish language edition

Some editions are:

Harcourt Brace Jovanovich pa $3.95 Illustrated by Demi (ISBN 0-15-257428-X)

Harper & Row lib bdg $14.89, pa $7.95 Translated by Eva Le Gallienne; designed and illustrated by Nancy Ekholm Burkert; 0-06-023781-3; 0-06-443070-7)

Picture Bk. Studio $14.95, pa $4.95 Illustrated by Lisbeth Zwerger; translated by Anthea Bell (ISBN 0-907234-51-1; 0-88708-269-6)

This is the "story of the Emperor's nightingale which entertained him with exquisite song. Replaced by a gorgeous jewel-encrusted artificial bird, the nightingale is banished from the empire, only to return later to save the Emperor from sure death." Publ Wkly

The princess and the pea (1-4) **Fic**

1. Fairy tales

Also available Spanish language edition

Some editions are:

Clarion Bks. $14.95 Illustrated by Paul Galdone (ISBN 0-395-28807-X)

North-South Bks. $15.95; pa $6.95 Illustrated by Dorothee Duntze (ISBN 1-55858-034-4; 0-55858-381-5)

Picture Bk. Studio $13.95; pa $4.95 Translated by Anthea Bell; illustrated by Eve Tharlet (ISBN 0-88708-052-9; 0-88708-170-3)

A "well-known prince seeks in vain for a bride but finds no princess who seems real in all the world. When a pretty unknown girl shows up at the royal castle and asks for shelter from a storm . . . [the queen] plans to test the princess for sensitivity. Of course, the stranger becomes the prince's bride when she passed a sleepless night because of the pea under the 20 mattresses and 20 featherbeds towering over her four-poster." Publ Wkly

The Snow Queen (4-6) **Fic**

1. Fairy tales

Some editions are:

Candlewick Press $16.95 Translated by Naomi Lewis; illustrated by Angela Barrett (ISBN 1-56402-215-3)

HarperCollins Pubs. lib bdg $13.89 Translated by Eve Le Gallienne; illustrations by Arieh Zeldich (ISBN 0-06-023695-7)

Lothrop, Lee & Shepard Bks. $14.95, lib bdg $14.88 Illustrated by Sally Holmes; English version by Neil Philip (ISBN 0-688-09047-8; 0-688-09048-6)

"The devil makes a mirror which causes everything good to appear unpleasant and vice versa. The mirror shatters and splinters of its glass fly about the world. Two enter the eyes and heart of Kai, a little boy, who becomes cynical and hard in character, beginning to turn against his former playfellow, the little girl Gerda. Soon he is carried off by the icily beautiful but cruel Snow Queen. Gerda goes in search of him, and has many strange adventures before she finds him and melts the splinters and his frozen heart with her tears." Oxford Companion to Child Lit

Andersen, Hans Christian, 1805-1875—*Continued*

The steadfast tin soldier; newly translated from the Danish by Naomi Lewis; illustrated by P. J. Lynch. Harcourt Brace Jovanovich 1992 unp il $10.95 (1-4)   **Fic**

1. Toys—Fiction 2. Fairy tales
ISBN 0-15-200599-4   LC 91-29953
"Gulliver books"
After being accidentally launched on a perilous voyage, a one-legged toy soldier finds his way back to his true love—a paper dancing girl
"Like closeup camera shots [Lynch's illustrations] are tightly focused on the soldier and show only those bits of the world at large that affect him. These narrow, sometimes startling perspectives give certain illustrations real depth and dimension, creating powerful visual images, while his use of dense, neutral shades underscores the drama of the soldier's journey and provides a sense of hard-edged reality." SLJ

The swineherd; [illustrated by] Lisbeth Zwerger; translated from the Danish by Anthea Bell. North-South Bks. 1995 c1982 unp il $14.95; pa $5.95 (1-4)   **Fic**

1. Fairy tales
ISBN 1-55858-428-5; 1-55858-429-3 (pa)
    LC 94-32153
Also available Spanish language edition
"A Michael Neugebauer book"
A reissue of the 1982 Morrow edition
A prince disguises himself as a swineherd and learns the true character of the princess he desires
The story "is given a comic and earthy tone by Zwerger's expressive line." SLJ

Thumbeline; illustrated by Lisbeth Zwerger; translated by Anthea Bell. Picture Bk. Studio 1985 unp il $14.95 (1-4)   **Fic**

1. Fairy tales
ISBN 0-88708-006-5   LC 85-12062
Also available Spanish language edition
"The delightful adventures of a tiny girl no bigger than a thumb and her many animal friends . . . evocatively interpreted by Austrian illustrator Lisbeth Zwerger." Booklist

The ugly duckling; illustrated by Alan Marks; translated by Anthea Bell. Picture Bk. Studio 1989 unp il $14.95 (1-4)   **Fic**

1. Swans—Fiction
ISBN 0-88708-116-9   LC 89-3975
An ugly duckling spends an unhappy year ostracized by the other animals before he grows into a beautiful swan
"Bell's smoothly translated text fills the left-hand pages of this book, with full-color washes by Marks on the right. His illustrations have an earthy quality, with ruddy colors and bold action." Booklist

Armstrong, Jennifer, 1961-

Steal away. Orchard Bks. 1992 206p $15.95; lib bdg $15.99 (5 and up)   **Fic**

1. Slavery—Fiction 2. African Americans—Fiction 3. Underground railroad—Fiction
ISBN 0-531-05983-9; 0-531-08583-X (lib bdg)
    LC 91-18504
Also available in paperback from Scholastic
"A Richard Jackson book"

In 1855 two thirteen-year-old girls, one white and one black, run away from a southern farm and make the difficult journey north to freedom, living to recount their story forty-one years later to two similar young girls
"Armstrong's novel has pace and suspense, characterization that is solid and consistent, and a crescendo that builds to a logical yet dramatic climax." Bull Cent Child Books

Armstrong, William Howard, 1914-

Sounder; [by] William H. Armstrong; illustrations by James Barkley. Harper & Row 1969 116p il $14; lib bdg $14.89; pa $5 (5 and up)   **Fic**

1. Dogs—Fiction 2. African Americans—Fiction 3. Family life—Fiction
ISBN 0-06-020143-6; 0-06-020144-4 (lib bdg); 0-06-080975-2 (pa)
Also available Cornerstone Bks. large print edition; Spanish language edition also available
Awarded the Newbery Medal, 1970
"Set in the South in the era of sharecropping and segregation, this succinctly told tale poignantly describes the courage of a father who steals a ham in order to feed his undernourished family; the determination of the eldest son, who searches for his father despite the apathy of prison authorities; and the devotion of a coon dog named Sounder." Shapiro. Fic for Youth. 3d edition

Atwater, Richard Tupper, 1892-1948

Mr. Popper's penguins; [by] Richard and Florence Atwater; illustrated by Robert Lawson. Little, Brown 1938 138p il $15.95 (3-5)   **Fic**

1. Penguins—Fiction
ISBN 0-316-05842-4
Also available in paperback from Dell
A Newbery Medal honor book, 1939
When Mr. Popper, a mild little painter and decorator with a taste for books and movies on polar explorations, was presented with a penguin, he named it Captain Cook. From that moment on life was changed for the Popper family
"To the depiction of the penguins in all conceivable moods Robert Lawson [the] artist has brought not only his skill but his individual humor, and his portrayal of the wistful Mr. Popper is memorable." N Y Times Book Rev

Avi, 1937-

The barn. Orchard Bks. 1994 106p $13.95; lib bdg $13.99 (4-6)   **Fic**

1. Fathers and sons—Fiction 2. Farm life—Fiction 3. Frontier and pioneer life—Fiction
ISBN 0-531-06861-7; 0-531-08711-5 (lib bdg)
    LC 94-6920
"A Richard Jackson book"
In an effort to fulfill their dying father's last request, nine-year-old Ben and his brother and sister construct a barn on their land in the Oregon Territory in the 1850s
"While focusing mainly on his characters, Avi presents a vivid picture of the time and place, including fairly involved details about how the barn is constructed. This novel . . . is a thought-provoking and engaging piece of historical fiction." SLJ

Avi, 1937—*Continued*

Blue heron. Bradbury Press 1992 186p $15
(5 and up)   **Fic**

1. Family life—Fiction 2. Herons—Fiction
ISBN 0-02-707751-9   LC 91-4308

Also available in paperback from Avon Bks.

While spending the month of August on the Massachusetts shore with her father, stepmother, and their new baby,
almost thirteen-year-old Maggie finds beauty in and draws
strength from a great blue heron, even as the family around
her unravels

"Maggie emerges as a sensitive heroine whose perceptions are genuine as well as compelling. Reflecting the complexity of people and their emotions, this novel explores
rather than solves the conflicts introduced." Publ Wkly

**Emily Upham's revenge; a Massachusetts
adventure;** illustrated by Paul O. Zelinsky.
Morrow Junior Bks. 1992 c1978 172p il $15;
pa $3.95 (4-6)   **Fic**

1. Thieves—Fiction 2. Massachusetts—Fiction
ISBN 0-688-11898-4; 0-688-11899-2 (pa)
                                           LC 92-390

A reissue of the title first published 1978 by Pantheon
During the summer of 1875, seven-year-old Emily is sent
to live with her wealthy Uncle George in Massachusetts and
becomes involved in a bank robbery with eleven-year-old
Seth Marple

"This fast-paced story . . . succeeds best when taken with
a grain of salt. Though it strains credibility somewhat to be
lieve in seven-year-old Emily's piety and endurance, Seth's
inventive endeavors deserve a decided bravo." Booklist

Encounter at Easton. Morrow Junior Bks.
1994 c1980 138p $14; pa $4.95 (5 and up)
                                                       Fic

1. Runaway children—Fiction 2. Contract labor—
Fiction 3. Pennsylvania—Fiction 4. United States—
History—1600-1775, Colonial period—Fiction
ISBN 0-688-05295-9; 0-688-05296-7 (pa)   LC 94-81
A reissue of the title first published 1980 by Pantheon
Bks.

"Robert and Elizabeth, two indentured servants who fled
their master in *Night Journeys* [entered below], are floundering toward Easton, Pennsylvania, and hoped-for safety.
Elizabeth is gravely ill, however, and Robert is forced to
leave her with Mad Moll, an outcast who wanders the hills.
Thinking he has met a friend, Robert enters the employ of
Nathaniel Hill, a man paid to hunt down the children, and
is caught up in a disastrous climax of events." Booklist

"The tale is told through alternating testimonies of the
major parties involved. . . . In his terse style, Avi manipulates these narratives with skill, sustaining suspense." SLJ

The fighting ground. Lippincott 1984 157p
lib bdg $14.89; pa $4.95 (5 and up)   **Fic**

1. United States—History—1775-1783, Revolution—
Fiction
ISBN 0-397-32074-4 (lib bdg); 0-06-440185-5 (pa)
                                           LC 82-47719

"It's April 1776, and the fighting ground is both the farm
country of Pennsylvania and the heart of a boy which is
'wonderful ripe for war.' Twenty-four hours transform Jonathan from a cocky 13-year-old, eager to take on the British,
into a young man who now knows the horror, the pathos,
the ambiguities of war." Voice Youth Advocates

The author "has written a taut, fast-paced novel that
builds to a shattering climax. His protagonist's painful, inner struggle to understand the intense and conflicting emotions brought on by a war that spares no one is central to
this finely crafted novel." ALAN

The history of helpless Harry; to which is
added a variety of amusing and entertaining
adventures; with pictures by Paul O. Zelinsky.
Morrow Junior Bks. 1995 c1980 179p il $15;
pa $4.95 (4-6)   **Fic**

1. Thieves—Fiction
ISBN 0-688-05302-5; 0-688-05303-3 (pa)
                                           LC 94-26356

A reissue of the title first published 1980 by Pantheon
Bks.

Eleven-year-old Harry's adventures, involving lies, attempted robbery, and the possibility of murder, begin when
his parents go away and he is left in the care of a young
woman

"This has a good deal of nonsense, a good deal of fun
with the orotund language of the period (1845), and a good
deal of action." Bull Cent Child Books

Night journeys. Morrow Junior Bks. 1994
c1979 143p $14; pa $4.95 (5 and up)   **Fic**

1. Society of Friends—Fiction 2. Contract labor—
Fiction 3. Pennsylvania—Fiction 4. United States—
History—1600 1775, Colonial Period—Fiction
5. Orphans—Fiction
ISBN 0-688-05298-3; 0-688-13628-1 (pa)
                                           LC 93-50233

A reissue of the title first published 1979 by Pantheon
Bks.

Set in 1768 on the Pennsylvania-New Jersey border, this
story "concerns 12-year-old Peter York and his guardian,
Everett Shinn, a devout Quaker. . . . News that two runaway indentured servants are in the area prompts Mr.
Shinn . . . to organize a search. Peter assumes that the runaways are swarthy ruffians and   he joins the hunt His
discovery that they are mistreated children sets up a different scenario in which he and then his guardian are emotionally and physically involved." Christ Sci Monit

This is a "fast-paced, suspenseful tale. . . . The tightly
constructed, disaster-laden scenes . . . zestfully carry along
the plot to its satisfying conclusion." Booklist

Followed by Encounter at Easton, entered above

Poppy; illustrated by Brian Floca. Orchard
Bks. 1995 147p il $15.95; lib bdg $15.99 (3-5)
                                                       Fic

1. Animals—Fiction 2. Allegories
ISBN 0-531-09483-9; 0-531-08783-2 (lib bdg)
                                           LC 95-6040

"A Richard Jackson book"
"As ruler of Dimwood Forest, Ocax the hoot owl has
promised to protect the mice occupying an abandoned
farmhouse as long as they ask permission before 'moving
about.' Poppy, a timid dormouse, is a loyal, obedient
subject—until she sees Ocax devour her fiancé and hears
the owl deny her father's request to seek new living quarters. To prove that the intimidating ruler is really a phony,
Poppy embarks on a dangerous and eye-opening quest,
which ends with her one-on-one battle with Ocax. . . . An
engaging blend of romance, suspense and parody." Publ
Wkly

S.O.R. losers. Bradbury Press 1984 90p $14
(5 and up)   **Fic**

1. Soccer—Fiction 2. School stories
ISBN 0-02-793410-1   LC 84-11022

Also available in paperback from Avon Bks.

Each member of the South Orange River eighth-grade
soccer team has qualities of excellence, but not on the soccer field

"Short, pithy chapters highlighting key events maintain
the pace necessary for successful comedy. . . . The style is

Avi, 1937-—*Continued*
vivid, believably articulate, for the narrator and his teammates may be deficient athletically but not intellectually.
Certainly, the team manifesto 'People have a right to be
losers' is as refreshing as it is iconoclastic." Horn Book

Something upstairs; a tale of ghosts.
Orchard Bks. 1988 120p $14.95; lib bdg
$13.99 (5 and up) Fic
1. Ghost stories
ISBN 0-531-05782-8; 0-531-08382-9 (lib bdg)
LC 88-60094
Also available in paperback from Avon Bks.
"A Richard Jackson book"
"When 12-year-old Kenny Huldorf moves with his fami-
ly to Providence, Rhode Island, he finds himself embroiled
in the century-old murder of a teenage slave named Caleb.
Not only is Kenny haunted by the injustice of the murder,
but also by the ghost of Caleb himself, who summons Ken-
ny back in time to the early 19th Century, where the boy
must solve Caleb's murder to return to his own century."
SLJ
"This ghostly tale is exciting and well-written." Child
Book Rev Serv

The true confessions of Charlotte Doyle;
decorations by Ruth E. Murray. Orchard Bks.
1990 215p $15.95; lib bdg $15.99 (6 and up)
Fic
1. Sea stories
ISBN 0-531-05893-X; 0-531-08493-0 (lib bdg)
LC 90-30624
Also available Thorndike Press large print edition and in
paperback from Avon Bks.
A Newbery Medal honor book, 1991
"A Richard Jackson book"
This is a "seafaring adventure, set in 1832. Charlotte
Doyle, 13, returning from school in England to join her
family in Rhode Island, is deposited on a seedy ship with
a ruthless, mad captain and a mutinous crew. Refusing to
heed warnings about Captain Jaggery's brutality, Charlotte
seeks his guidance and approval only to become his victim,
a pariah to the entire crew, and a convicted felon for the
murder of the first mate." SLJ
The author has "fashioned an intriguing, suspenseful,
carefully crafted tale, with nonstop action on the high seas."
Booklist

Babbitt, Natalie
The eyes of the Amaryllis. Farrar, Straus &
Giroux 1977 127p $15; pa $3.95 (5 and up)
Fic
1. Sea stories 2. Grandmothers—Fiction
ISBN 0-374-32241-4; 0-374-42238-9 (pa)
LC 77-11862
"The sea holds countless mysteries and gives up very few
secrets; when she does, it is truly a remarkable event, an
event that eleven-year-old Geneva Reade experiences when
she visits her grandmother who lives in a house by the water's edge. Sent for to tend her Gran through a broken leg,
Jenny is put to work, at once, combing the beach for a sign
from her grandfather, a captain lost at sea with his ship and
crew thirty years ago." Child Book Rev Serv
"The book succeeds as a well-wrought narrative in which
a complex philosophic theme is developed through the balanced, subtle use of symbol and imagery. It is a rare story."
Horn Book

Goody Hall; story and pictures by Natalie
Babbitt. Farrar, Straus & Giroux 1971 176p il
hardcover o.p. paperback available $4.95 (4-6)
Fic
1. Mystery fiction
ISBN 0-374-42767-4 (pa)
In this Gothic mystery "Hercules Feltwright, a would-be
actor, comes to a magnificent house—Goody Hall—to tutor
the young master, Willet Goody. The boy soon announces
his firm conviction that his father is not dead and interred
in the family tomb. In trying to find an answer for Willet,
Hercules' way is marked by chilling events." Wis Libr Bull
"Lightened by humor and colored by suspense, the story
whirls its delightfully just-short-of-burlesqued characters in
a triumphant gavotte of melodrama." Saturday Rev

Kneeknock Rise; story and pictures by
Natalie Babbitt. Farrar, Straus & Giroux 1970
117p il $15; pa $3.95 (4-6) Fic
1. Allegories 2. Superstition—Fiction
ISBN 0-374-34257-1; 0-374-44260-6 (pa)
Also available Spanish language edition
A Newbery Medal honor book, 1971
"Did you ever meet a Megrimum? There is one in
KneeKnock Rise, and on stormy nights the villagers of In-
step tremble in delicious delight as its howls echo over the
Mammoth Mountains. Egan learns a lesson when he climbs
to meet and conquer the Megrimum." Best Sellers
"An enchanting tale imbued with a folk flavor, enlivened
with piquant imagery and satiric wit." Booklist

The search for delicious. Farrar, Straus &
Giroux 1969 167p il $16; pa $3.95 (5 and up)
Fic
ISBN 0-374-36534-2; 0-374-46536-3 (pa)
"An Ariel book"
The Prime Minister is compiling a dictionary and when
no one at court can agree on the meaning of delicious, the
King sends his twelve-year-old messenger to poll the coun-
try
"The theme, foolish arguments can lead to great conflict,
may not be clear to all children who will enjoy this fanta-
sy." Best Sellers

Tuck everlasting. Farrar, Straus & Giroux
1975 139p $15; pa $3.95 (5 and up) Fic
1. Fantasy fiction
ISBN 0-374-37848-7; 0-374-48009-5 (pa)
Also available Spanish language edition
The Tuck family is confronted with an agonizing situation when they discover that a ten-year-old girl and a malicious stranger now share their secret about a spring whose
water prevents one from ever growing any older
"The story is macabre and moral, exciting and excellently written." N Y Times Book Rev

Bagnold, Enid
National Velvet; illustrations by Ted Lewin.
Morrow 1985 c1935 258p il lib bdg $15.95 (5
and up) Fic
1. Horses—Fiction 2. Great Britain—Fiction
ISBN 0-688-05788-8 LC 85-2982
Also available Cornerstone Bks. large print edition and
in paperback from Avon Bks.
First published 1935; first Morrow edition illustrated by
Paul Brown published 1949
An English girl, Velvet Brown, wins a magnificent pie-
bald horse in a lottery and determines to enter and win the

Bagnold, Enid—*Continued*

Grand National Steeplechase even though girls are not allowed to ride in that race

"Numerous vibrant, full-page watercolors and some in shaded, pale washes of gray add new spirit while still keeping the original flavor of the story. An inviting piece." Booklist

Baker, Olaf

Where the buffaloes begin; illustrated by Stephen Gammell. Viking 1985 c1981 unp il $14.95; pa $5.99 (2-4)   Fic

1. Indians of North America—Fiction 2. Bison—Fiction
ISBN 0-670-82760-6; 0-14-050560-1 (pa)
LC 85-5682

A Caldecott Medal honor book, 1982

First published in book form 1981 by Warne

"Originally published in 1915 in 'St. Nicholas Magazine,' the story tells in four short chapters of the adventure of Little Wolf, a ten-year-old Indian boy. He was fascinated by a tribal legend about a lake to the south, a sacred spot where the buffaloes were said to originate. . . . Narrated in cadenced prose rich in imagoo, the story evokes the Plains Indians' feelings of reverence for the buffalo." Horn Book

The illustrations "are an example of the best kind of book art, pictures that extend and complement the story, that are appropriate in mood, and that are distinctive in themselves." Bull Cent Child Books

Barrie, J. M. (James Matthew), 1860-1937

Peter Pan (3-3)   Fic

1. Fairy tales
Some editions are:
Holt & Co. $19.95 Illustrated by Michael Hague (ISBN 0-8050-0276-6)
Potter $7.99 Illustrated by Michael Foreman (ISBN 0-517-66189-6) Has title: Peter Pan & Wendy
Random House lib bdg $8.99; pa $8.95 Illustrated by Diane Goode; edited by Josette Frank (ISBN 0-394-95717-2; 0-394-85717-8)
Scribner $19.95 Illustrations by Trina Schart Hyman (ISBN 0-684-16611-9)

First published 1911 by Scribner with title: Peter and Wendy

This is the story of "how Wendy, John, and Michael flew with Peter Pan, the boy who never grows up, to adventures in the Never-Never Land with pirates, redskins, and the fairy Tinker Bell. [It is] in Barrie's inimitable style, pleasing the child with delightful absurdities and the adult with good-humored satire." Right Book for the Right Child

Bauer, Marion Dane, 1938-

On my honor. Clarion Bks. 1986 90p $14.95 (4 and up)   Fic

1. Accidents—Fiction
ISBN 0-89919-439-7
LC 86-2679

Also available G.K. Hall large print edition and in paperback from Dell; Spanish language edition also available

A Newbery Medal honor book, 1987

When his best friend drowns while they are both swimming in a treacherous river that they had promised never to go near, Joel is devastated and terrified at having to tell both sets of parents the terrible consequences of their disobedience

"Bauer's association of Joel's guilt with the smell of the polluted river on his skin is particularly noteworthy. Its miasma almost rises off the pages. Descriptions are vivid, characterization and dialogue natural, and the style taut but unforced. A powerful, moving book." SLJ

A question of trust. Scholastic 1994 130p $13.95; pa $2.99 (5 and up)   Fic

1. Mothers and sons—Fiction 2. Cats—Fiction
ISBN 0-590-47915-6; 0-390-47923-7 (pa)
LC 93-4611

After his mother leaves the family, Brian copes with his feelings of rejection by secretly taking care of a stray cat and her two newborn kittens

"The coming-of-age novel has powerful scenes, memorable characters, vivid dialogue, and palpable emotions." Horn Book Guide

Rain of fire. Clarion Bks. 1983 153p $14.95 (5 and up)   Fic

1. World War, 1939-1945—Fiction 2. Brothers—Fiction 3. Veterans—Fiction
ISBN 0-89919-190-8
LC 83-2065

"Steve wants to hear about his older brother's World War II experiences, but Matthew is too upset by them to oblige. Steve makes up stories to cover for Matthew, but each story plunges him deeper into trouble. A moral story about the dangers of lying as well as a book that shows the difficulties in adjusting faced by returning veterans." Child Book Rev Serv

"This is a trenchant story of the ways in which children's attitudes toward war, enemies, heroism, and ethical conduct are shaped by events, by the ideas of adults, and by their own needs to be accepted and feel secure . . . it has good pace and momentum within its tight frame." Bull Cent Child Books

Baum, L. Frank (Lyman Frank), 1856-1919

The Wizard of Oz (3-6)   Fic

1. Fantasy fiction
Available from various publishers, including Holt & Co. edition illustrated by Michael Hague; Spanish language edition also available

First published 1900 with title: The wonderful Wizard of Oz

Here are the adventures of Dorothy who, in her dreams, escapes from her bed in Kansas to visit the Emerald City and to meet the wonderful Wizard of Oz, the Scarecrow, the Tin Woodman, and the Cowardly Lion

Other available titles about the land of Oz are:
Dorothy and the Wizard in Oz (1908)
The land of Oz (1904)
Little Wizard stories of Oz (1985)
The magic of Oz (1919)
The marvelous land of Oz (1904)
Ozma of Oz (1907)
The patchwork girl of Oz (1913)
The tin woodsman of Oz (1918)

Bawden, Nina, 1925-

Carrie's war. Lippincott 1973 159p il lib bdg $14.89 (4 and up)   Fic

1. Wales—Fiction
ISBN 0-397-31450-7

"Carrie, recently widowed, takes her children to the small Welsh mining town where she and her younger brother, Nick, had been evacuated during World War II." Libr J

"The pace and the dialogue and the characterization all add up to a whole which could be read with interest and pleasure by any age, and in which the lessons are implied, delicately in the behaviour and relationships of the principal actors, never rammed home." New Statesman

Bawden, Nina, 1925——*Continued*

A handful of thieves. Clarion Bks. 1991 c1967 177p $13.95 (4 and up)   **Fic**

1. Mystery fiction
ISBN 0-395-58634-8   LC 90-21229
A reissue of the title first published 1967 by Lippincott
When a confidence man steals Fred's grandmother's savings, Fred and his four friends set out to find him and steal it back
"Excellent characterization, a thorough-going mystery, fast action, enough suspense to keep 9-12's reading, and convincing dialogue." Christ Sci Monit

Henry; illustrated by Joyce Powzyk. Lothrop, Lee & Shepard Bks. 1988 119p il $15 (5 and up)   **Fic**

1. World War, 1939-1945—Fiction 2. Squirrels—Fiction
ISBN 0-688-07894-X   LC 87-29339
"Henry is a baby squirrel adopted by a family waiting out the London Blitz on a country farm during World War II. With her characteristic subtlety of craft, Bawden develops scenes and dialogue that bring the reader to realize what Henry means to the narrator, her two brothers, and her mother as they all await her father's return from naval duty. . . . This is a story that speaks of family unity in the face of dislocation and separation." Bull Cent Child Books

Humbug. Clarion Bks. 1992 133p $13.95 (4 and up)   **Fic**

1. Truthfulness and falsehood—Fiction
ISBN 0-395-62149-6   LC 91-33900
Also available in paperback from Puffin Bks.
When eight-year-old Cora is sent to stay next door with the seemingly pleasant woman called Aunt Sunday, she is tormented by Aunt Sunday's mean-spirited, deceitful daughter, but finds an ally in Aunt Sunday's elderly mother
"Characters are beautifully and intricately drawn. . . . Bawden deals forthrightly with harsh truths; she acknowledges that children can hate, and she shatters a host of childhood notions about grown-ups, honesty, and fairness. Along with that, she delivers a riveting plot and a totally credible Cora." Booklist

The outside child. Lothrop, Lee & Shepard Bks. 1989 232p $12.95 (5 and up)   **Fic**

1. Brothers and sisters—Fiction
ISBN 0-688-08965-8   LC 88-27349
Also available in paperback from Puffin Bks.
"Suddenly and accidentally, thirteen-year-old Jane Tucker learns that her widowed father—a ship's engineer whom she rarely sees—is remarried and has two younger children. Inevitably, she defies her adoptive aunts to locate her half-sister and brother. What she doesn't expect to find is a dark secret that seems to spark violent hostility from her stepmother." Bull Cent Child Books
"Superb characterizations, the interplay of human relationships, and powerful emotions that lie beneath the surface of everyday life are presented wholly from the girl's ingenuous perspective." Horn Book

The robbers. Lothrop, Lee & Shepard Bks. 1979 155p $12.95 (5 and up)   **Fic**

1. Grandmothers—Fiction 2. Family life—Fiction 3. London (England)—Fiction 4. Friendship—Fiction
ISBN 0-688-41902-X   LC 79-4152
"Solitary and happy, nine-year-old Philip lived with his grandmother in an apartment in a seaside castle; his mother was dead, his father a peripatetic television reporter. When his father married an American, Philip went to London for what he thought was a visit; it proved to be a long stay. Precocious and articulate, Philip made only one friend,

Darcy, a street-wise boy whose family . . . made Philip welcome." Bull Cent Child Books
"Motive, action, setting—everything is simple, clear-cut and selective, and totally adequate for the task of creating a particular corner of London in which believable people speak, act, suffer and learn from their mistakes." Grow Point

The witch's daughter. Clarion Bks. 1991 184p $13.95 (4 and up)   **Fic**

1. Blind—Fiction 2. Scotland—Fiction
ISBN 0-395-58635-6   LC 90-21228
A reissue of the title first published 1966 by Lippincott
This story, set on the Scottish island of Skua, involves "much more than the capture of jewel thieves. Perdita, a lonely orphan, is rejected by the other children because of her unusual power to see into the future. Through the arrival of a blind girl, Janey, and Janey's brother Tim, Perdita comes to realize that her powers are not a sign of witchcraft, but a special talent." Read Ladders for Hum Relat. 6th edition
"A credible suspense story, with a likeable and resourceful cast. A plausible plot, superior dialogue and an appropriate setting." N Y Times Book Rev

Baylor, Byrd, 1924-

I'm in charge of celebrations; pictures by Peter Parnall. Scribner 1986 unp il $14.95; pa $4.95 (3-6)   **Fic**

1. Deserts—Fiction
ISBN 0-684-18579-2; 0-689-80620-5 (pa)
      LC 85-19633
A dweller in the desert celebrates a triple rainbow, a chance encounter with a coyote, and other wonders of the wilderness
Baylor writes in a "conversational, poetic prose that begs to be read aloud. Sky blues, cactus greens, searing sun yellows, desert browns, and bright to burnt oranges are jabbed, streaked, and swirled around Parnall's arresting, expressionistic impressions of Baylor's experiences." Booklist

Beatty, Patricia, 1922-1991

Bonanza girl. Beech Tree Bks. 1993 c1962 210p $16; pa $4.95 (5 and up)   **Fic**

1. Mines and mineral resources—Fiction 2. Idaho—Fiction 3. West (U.S.)—Fiction
ISBN 0-688-12361-9; 0-688-12280-9 (pa)
      LC 92-27682
A reissue of the title first published 1962 by Morrow
Mrs. Scott, a "widow, and her two children, Jemmy and Ann Katherine, head for gold rush territory in Idaho, hoping to find jobs and a new life
This "is believable enough having been based on true events. It has humor, danger, a snow slide, and even romance." Chicago Sunday Tribune

Charley Skedaddle. Morrow 1987 186p $15 (5 and up)   **Fic**

1. United States—History—1861-1865, Civil War—Fiction 2. Farm life—Fiction 3. Virginia—Fiction
ISBN 0-688-06687-9   LC 87-12270
Also available in paperback from Troll Assocs.
"12-year-old Charley Quinn, a cocky boy from the Bowery, runs away and finagles a job as a drummer in the Union army. In his first battle he meets the horrors of war face to face and, without thought to an injured friend, 'skedaddles' into the Virginia mountains." Booklist
"The author notes that she has based Charley's fictional adventures on actual accounts, and her reading and research

Beatty, Patricia, 1922-1991—*Continued*
lend authenticity to her story. . . . Charley's Civil War adventures . . . move at a lively pace and offer an entertaining account of a young city slicker's growing respect for his new surroundings." Horn Book

Eight mules from Monterey. Morrow 1982 192p $15; pa $4.95 (5 and up)   Fic
1. Libraries—Fiction 2. California—Fiction
ISBN 0-688-01047-4; 0-688-12281-7 (pa)
LC 81-22284
"The time is 1916, the place is the Santa Lucia mountains of California, and the story describes the trip that [thirteen-year-old] Fayette and her younger brother take with their widowed mother, who has just graduated from library school, as she travels the mountain trails (by mule) to set up library outposts." Bull Cent Child Books
The author "has created a warm story of perserverance coupled with well-developed believable characters, set in an unusual time period. Her use of slang terms in character conversation is true to the period making this a good book to use in history classes." Voice Youth Advocates

Jayhawker. Morrow Junior Bks. 1991 214p $15; pa $4.95 (5 and up)   Fic
1. United States—History—1861-1865, Civil War—Fiction 2. Underground railroad—Fiction 3. Spies—Fiction
ISBN 0-688-09850-9; 0-688-14422-5 (pa)
LC 91-17890
In the early years of the Civil War, teenage Kansan farm boy Lije Tulley becomes a Jayhawker, an abolitionist raider freeing slaves from the neighboring state of Missouri, and then goes undercover there as a spy
"Peppered with fascinating historical figures, vivid with drama and action, Beatty's story has an accuracy and a realism that are both addictive and illuminating." Booklist

Turn homeward, Hannalee. Morrow 1984 193p $15 (5 and up)   Fic
1. United States—History—1861-1865, Civil War—Fiction   2. Georgia—Fiction   3. Children—Employment—Fiction
ISBN 0-688-03871-9
LC 84-8960
Also available in paperback from Troll Assocs.
This "historical fiction shows how the Civil War affected one segment of the population—the southern mill workers—and is based on fact. . . . The protagonists are Hannalee and Jem, twelve and ten, who are shipped from their Georgia town (and their recently widowed, pregnant mother) to Indiana, where they are offered as workers to anyone who wants them." Bull Cent Child Books
"The story is vintage Beatty, with a forthright, plainspoken heroine who has gumption to spare. As a period piece, it is a vivid, seemingly authentic picture of what times might have been like for a hardworking, white, Southern family." Booklist

Bell, Anthea
The nutcracker; [by] E.T.A. Hoffmann; retold by Anthea Bell; illustrated by Lisbeth Zwerger. Picture Bk. Studio 1987 unp il $14.95; pa $4.95 (2-4)   Fic
1. Fairy tales 2. Christmas—Fiction
ISBN 0-88708-051-0; 0-88708-156-8 (pa)
LC 87-15249
"A Michael Neugebauer book"
First published 1983 by Neugebauer Press with a longer text with title: The nutcracker and the mouse-king

After hearing how her toy nutcracker got his ugly face, a little girl helps break the spell and changes him into a handsome prince
This book "features full pages of text alternating with Lisbeth Zwerger's beautiful full-page, full-color illustrations, including one double-page spread. . . . Anthea Bell's translation for this book is a slightly condensed version of the original story, which, of course, differs substantially from the ballet version." Horn Book

Bellairs, John
The curse of the blue figurine. Dial Bks. for Young Readers 1983 200p o.p.; Bantam Bks. paperback available $3.50 (5 and up)   Fic
1. Mystery fiction
ISBN 0-553-15540-7 (pa)
LC 82-73217
"The terror for young Johnny Dixon begins when cranky eccentric Professor Childermass tells him that St. Michael's Church is haunted by Father Baart, an evil sorcerer who mysteriously disappeared years ago. When Johnny finds a blue Egyptian figurine hidden in the church basement, he takes it home in spite of the warning note from Father Baart threatening harm to anyone who removes it from the church." SLJ
The author "intertwines real concerns with sorcery in a seamless fashion, bringing dimension to his characters and events with expert timing and sharply honed atmosphere." Booklist
Other available titles about Johnny Dixon and Professor Childermass are:
The chessmen of doom (1989)
The eyes of the killer robot (1986)
The mummy, the will and the crypt (1983)
The revenge of the wizard's ghost (1985)
The secret of the underground room (1990)
The spell of the sorcerer's skull (1984)
The trolley to yesterday (1989)

The house with a clock in its walls; pictures by Edward Gorey. Dial Bks. for Young Readers 1973 179p il o.p.; Puffin Bks. paperback available $3.99 (5 and up)   Fic
1. Witchcraft—Fiction
ISBN 0-14-036336-X (pa)
Also available in hardcover from P. Smith
In 1948, Lewis, a ten-year-old orphan, goes to New Zebedee, Michigan with his warlock Uncle Jonathan, who lives in a big mysterious house and practices white magic. Together with their neighbor, Mrs. Zimmerman, a witch, they search to find a clock that is programmed to end the world and has been hidden in the walls of the house by the evil Isaac Izard
"Bellairs's story and Edward Gorey's pictures are satisfyingly frightening." Publ Wkly
Other available titles about Lewis are:
The doom of the haunted opera (1995)
The figure in the shadows (1975)
The ghost in the mirror (1993)
The letter, the witch, and the ring (1976)
The vengeance of the witch-finder (1993)

Berends, Polly Berrien
The case of the elevator duck; illustrated by Diane Allison. Random House 1989 60p il hardcover o.p. paperback available $3.99 (3-5)   Fic
1. Ducks—Fiction 2. Apartment houses—Fiction 3. Mystery fiction
ISBN 0-394-82646-9 (pa)
LC 88-23971

Berends, Polly Berrien—*Continued*

"A Stepping Stone book"

Gilbert finds a lost duck in the elevator of his apartment building, and must do some secret detective work to find its owner, since no pets are allowed in the housing project

A "light mystery for begining readers. The action is humorously illustrated by Washburn's line sketches; and Berends' first-person, short-sentence story is personable, plausible, and useful for librarians needing simple, satisfying material for their easy mystery shelves." Booklist

Betancourt, Jeanne, 1941-

My name is brain Brian. Scholastic 1993 128p $14.95; pa $3.50 (4-6)   **Fic**

1. Dyslexia—Fiction 2. School stories 3. Friendship—Fiction

ISBN 0-590-44921-4; 0-590-44922-2 (pa)

LC 92-16513

On title page the word "brain" appears with an "X" through it

Although he is helped by his new sixth grade teacher after being diagnosed as dyslexic, Brian still has some problems with school and with people he thought were his friends

"Betancourt's depiction of Brian's emotional and psychological growth is believable and involving." Booklist

Bianco, Margery Williams, 1880-1944

The velveteen rabbit; or, How toys become real; by Margery Williams (2-4)   **Fic**

1. Toys—Fiction 2. Rabbits—Fiction 3. Fairy tales

Also available Spanish language edition

Some editions are:

Doubleday $9.95 illustrated by William Nicholson (ISBN 0-385-07725-4)

Holt & Co. $13.95 Illustrated by Michael Hague (ISBN 0-8050-0209-X)

Knopf (An Ariel book) $12.95 Illustrated by Allen Atkinson (ISBN 0-394-53221-X)

First published 1922 by Doran

"The story of a toy rabbit that becomes real through the love of a child and the intervention of a fairy." Bull Cent Child Books

Björk, Christina

Linnea in Monet's garden; text, Christina Björk; drawings, Lena Anderson. R & S Bks. 1987 52p il $13 (3-5)   **Fic**

1. Monet, Claude, 1840-1926—Fiction 2. Paris (France)—Fiction

ISBN 91-29-58314-4   LC 87-45163

Also available Spanish language edition

Original Swedish edition, 1985

"Linnea and her elderly friend Mr. Bloom travel to Paris, visit Monet's home in Giverny, picnic in the artist's garden, and admire the waterlilies and the Japanese bridge which he often painted. In Paris, the two companions stop at a museum to see Impressionist paintings, view the sunlight over the Seine, and chatter about the life and times of the artist. The book ends with a page of information about things to do and see in Paris." SLJ

"In addition to the long but smooth text peppered with dialogue are photographs of Monet's paintings, house, and family as well as colorful drawings of the little girl's excursion. . . . A splendid way to introduce children to impressionism and to the man behind the masterpieces." Booklist

Blos, Joan W., 1928-

A gathering of days: a New England girl's journal, 1830-32; a novel. Scribner 1979 144p $14; pa $3.95 (6 and up)   **Fic**

1. New Hampshire—Fiction

ISBN 0-684-16340-3; 0-689-71419-X (pa)

LC 79-16898

Awarded the Newbery Medal, 1980

The journal of a 14-year-old girl, kept the last year she lived on the family farm, records daily events in her small New Hampshire town, her father's remarriage, and the death of her best friend

"The 'simple' life on the farm is not facilely idealized, the larger issues of the day are felt . . . but it is the small moments between parent and child, friend and friend that are at the fore, and the core, of this lowkey, intense, and reflective book." SLJ

Blume, Judy

Are you there God? it's me, Margaret. Twentieth anniversary ed. Bradbury Press 1990 c1970 149p $15 (5 and up)   **Fic**

1. Adolescence—Fiction 2. Religions—Fiction

ISBN 0-02-710991-7   LC 90-44484

Also available in paperback from Dell; Spanish language edition also available

First published 1970

"A perceptive story about the emotional, physical, and spiritual ups and downs experienced by 12-year-old Margaret, child of a Jewish-Protestant union." Natl Counc of Teach of Engl. Adventuring with Books. 2d edition

"The writing style is lively, the concerns natural, and the problems are treated with both humor and sympathy, but the story is intense in its emphasis on the four girls' absorption in, and discussions of, menstruation and brassieres." Bull Cent Child Books

Freckle juice; illustrated by Sonia O. Lisker. Four Winds Press 1971 40p il lib bdg $13.95 (2-4)   **Fic**

ISBN 0-02-711690-5

Also available in paperback from Dell; Spanish language edition also available

"A gullible second-grader pays 50¢ for a recipe to grow freckles." Best Books for Child

"Spontaneous humor, sure to appeal to the youngest reader." Horn Book

It's not the end of the world. Bradbury Press 1972 169p $14.95 (4-6)   **Fic**

1. Divorce—Fiction 2. Parent and child—Fiction

ISBN 0-02-711050-8

Also available in paperback from Dell

Unwilling to adjust to her parents' impending divorce, twelve-year-old Karen Newman attempts a last ditch effort at arranging a reconciliation. This story tells how her scheme goes awry when an unplanned confrontation between her parents sharply illuminates for Karen the reality of the situation

"A believable first-person story with good characterization, particularly of twelve-year-old Karen, and realistic treatment of the situation." Booklist

Otherwise known as Sheila the Great. Dutton 1972 188p lib bdg $14.99 (4-6)

Fic

1. Fear—Fiction

ISBN 0-525-36455-2

Also available Spanish language edition

Blume, Judy—*Continued*

Ten-year-old Sheila is secretly afraid of dogs, spiders, bees, ghosts and the dark. When she and her family leave New York for their summer home, she has to face up to her problems

"An unusual and merry treatment of the fears of a young girl. . . . This is a truly appealing book in which the author makes her points without a single preachy word." Publ Wkly

Tales of a fourth grade nothing; illustrated by Roy Doty. Dutton 1972 120p il $13.99 (3-6)   **Fic**

1. Brothers—Fiction 2. Family life—Fiction
ISBN 0-525-40720-0

Also available in paperback from Dell

This story describes the trials and tribulations of nine-year-old Peter Hatcher who is saddled with a pesky two-year-old brother named Fudge who is constantly creating trouble, messing things up, and monopolizing their parents' attention. Things come to a climax when Fudge gets at Peter's pet turtle

"The episode structure makes the book a good choice for reading aloud." Saturday Rev

Other available titles about Peter and Fudge are:
Fudge-a-mania (1990)
Superfudge (1980)

Bond, Michael, 1926-

A bear called Paddington; with drawings by Peggy Fortnum. Houghton Mifflin 1960 c1958 128p il $14.95 (2-5)   **Fic**

1. Bears—Fiction 2. Great Britain—Fiction
ISBN 0-395-06636-0

Also available in paperback from Dell; Spanish language edition also available

First published 1958 in the United Kingdom

"Mr. and Mrs. Brown first met Paddington on a railway platform in London. Noticing the sign on his neck reading 'Please look after this bear. Thank you,' they decided to do just that. From there on home was never the same though the Brown children were delighted." Publ Wkly

Other available titles about Paddington Bear are:
More about Paddington
Paddington abroad
Paddington at large
Paddington at work
Paddington helps out
Paddington marches on
Paddington on screen
Paddington on top
Paddington takes the air
Paddington takes the test
Paddington takes to TV

Another book about Paddington Bear with the title: Paddington's storybook, is entered in the Story Collections section; picture books about Paddington are entered in the Easy Books section

The tales of Olga da Polga; illustrated by Hans Helweg. Macmillan 1989 c1971 113p il $13.95 (2-5)   **Fic**

1. Guinea pigs—Fiction
ISBN 0-02-711731-6   LC 88-31444

A reissue of the title first published 1971 in the United Kingdom; first United States edition, 1973

The adventures of Olga da Polga, a vain and talented guinea pig, as she leaves the pet shop to enter the world of the Sawdust People (guinea pigs' name for humans)

"The book will delight . . . [children] who like to imagine

that their pets have their own lives and personalities. The style is easy and the characters flow from the author's pen, but he sketches his animal friends with a much surer stroke than the humans." Jr Bookshelf

Followed by: Olga meets her match (1975 c1973); Olga carries on (1977 c1976); and Olga takes charge (1982)

Bond, Nancy, 1945-

A string in the harp. Atheneum Pubs. 1976 370p il hardcover o.p. paperback available $4.95 (6 and up)   **Fic**

1. Taliesin—Fiction 2. Fantasy fiction 3. Wales—Fiction
ISBN 0-689-80445-8 (pa)   LC 75-28181

"A Margaret K. McElderry book"

"Present-day realism and the fantasy world of sixth-century Taliesin meet in an absorbing novel set in Wales. The story centers around the Morgans—Jen, Peter, Becky, and their father—their adjustment to another country, their mother's death, and especially, Peter's bitter despair, which threatens them all." LC Child Books, 1976

Truth to tell. Margaret K. McElderry Bks. 1994 325p $17.95 (6 and up)   **Fic**

1. Fathers and daughters—Fiction 2. New Zealand—Fiction
ISBN 0-689-50601-5   LC 93-11248

In 1958, having been dragged by her mother from England to a decaying mansion in New Zealand, fourteen-year-old Alice thinks that she has stumbled on a shocking secret involving her long-dead father

"With a sure instinct for recording revealing details and exploring adolescent feelings, Bond aptly conveys what it must be like to be in an alien land, a strange school, and an unfriendly house and adds intrigue with a hidden family secret." Horn Book Guide

Boston, L. M. (Lucy Maria), 1892-1990

The children of Green Knowe; with illustrations by Peter Boston. Harcourt Brace & Co. 1955 157p il hardcover o.p. paperback available $3.95 (4-6)   **Fic**

1. Fantasy fiction 2. Great Britain—Fiction
ISBN 0-15-217151-7 (pa)

Also available in hardcover from P. Smith

First published 1954 in the United Kingdom

"Tolly comes to live with his great-grandmother at Green Knowe, her ancestral mansion in the English countryside. Here the present blends with the past, and the children of another era become his playmates and help him to break the curse put upon the house by a gypsy." Hodges. Books for Elem Sch Libr

"A special book for the imaginative child, in which mood predominates and fantasy and realism are skillfully blended; not the least of the book's charm is the rapport that exists between the lonely little boy and the understanding old woman who lives with her memories." Booklist

Other available titles about Green Knowe are:
An enemy at Green Knowe (1964)
The river at Green Knowe (1959)
A stranger at Green Knowe (1961)
Treasure of Green Knowe (1958)

Boyd, Candy Dawson, 1946-

Charlie Pippin. Macmillan 1987 182p $12.95 (4-6) **Fic**

1. Fathers and daughters—Fiction 2. Vietnam War, 1961-1975—Fiction 3. African Americans—Fiction

ISBN 0-02-726350-9 LC 86-23780

Also available in paperback from Puffin Bks.

"Charlie (Chartreuse) Pippin is eleven, jealous of her older sister Sienna, baffled by her father's stern intransigence. She's black and bright; she's often in trouble at school (and that makes even more trouble at home) because she sets up businesses in school. Charlie wonders why her father is so angry, why he is irked by her school project, which entails a study of the Vietnam War in which he served." Bull Cent Child Books

"Boyd's story probes sensitive issues with remarkable balance. While the story's theme is decidedly antiwar, it presents an affecting portrayal, from a child's standpoint, of the anger, concerns, and painful emotional wounds that many returned veterans still bear. Charlie's family is black, but their relationships and emotional pain reach beyond color, and the story's impact won't quickly fade." Booklist

Briggs, Katharine Mary

Kate Crackernuts; [by] K. M. Briggs. Greenwillow Bks. 1980 c1979 223p $13.50 (6 and up) **Fic**

1. Witchcraft—Fiction 2. Scotland—Fiction 3. Good and evil—Fiction

ISBN 0-688-80240-0 LC 79-9229

First published 1979 in the United Kingdom

"Two Kates, Katherine Lindsay and Kate Maxwell, met when they were quite young and a deep and enduring friendship developed. Later, when Katherine was twelve her father married Kate's mother. Unfortunately for Katherine her stepmother was very jealous of her and not only made her life most unpleasant but used her black arts against her. A high-spirited girl, Kate does her best to shield her stepsister from a witch's wrath. . . . The setting is Scotland in the 17th century during a Scottish/English war." Best Sellers

"History and folklore are melded into a strong, anguished story of evil incarnate pitted against compassion and love. Some difficulties are posed by the complexity of the background events and by the unfamiliar Lowland Scots speech, but with encouragement capable older readers should be able to transcend the obstacles." Horn Book

Brink, Carol Ryrie, 1895-1981

Caddie Woodlawn; illustrated by Trina Schart Hyman. Macmillan 1973 275p il $16; pa $3.95 (4-6) **Fic**

1. Frontier and pioneer life—Fiction 2. Wisconsin—Fiction

ISBN 0-02-713670-1; 0-689-71370-3 (pa)

Also available Cornerstone Bks. large print edition

Awarded the Newbery Medal, 1936

First published 1935

Caddie Woodlawn was eleven in 1864. Because she was frail, she had been allowed to grow up a tomboy. Her capacity for adventure was practically limitless, and there was plenty of adventure on the Wisconsin frontier in those days. The story covers one year of life on the pioneer farm, closing with the news that Mr. Woodlawn had inherited an estate in England, and the unanimous decision of the family to stay in Wisconsin. Based upon the reminiscences of the author's grandmother

The typeface "is eminently clear and readable, and the illustrations in black and white . . . are attractive and expressive." Wis Libr Bull

Brittain, Bill

Devil's donkey; drawings by Andrew Glass. Harper & Row 1981 120p il lib bdg $14.89; pa $3.95 (3-6) **Fic**

1. Witches—Fiction 2. Devil—Fiction 3. New England—Fiction

ISBN 0-06-020683-7 (lib bdg); 0-06-440129-4 (pa) LC 80-7907

Young Dan'l Pitt scoffs at warnings about local witches by his guardian, storekeeper Stewart Meade (Stew Meat), who tells the story. "Having offended Old Magda, the last witch left in the New England town of Coven Tree the boy is put under a spell that turns him into a donkey. . . . The shrewd and courageous efforts of Stew Meat and of a farm girl not only succeed in changing Dan'l back, but culminate in a risky contest in which they win a bet with the devil." SLJ

"Notable for color and grace in the telling and with distinction of format, [this is a] highly original fantasy. . . . The wonder and humor of the story are finely evoked by animated charcoal drawings conveying atmosphere and sense of mystery." Horn Book

Other available titles about Coven Tree are:

Dr. Dredd's wagon of wonders (1987)

Professor Popkin's prodigious polish (1990)

The wish giver (1983)

Shape-changer. HarperCollins Pubs. 1994 108p $14; lib bdg $13.89; pa $4.50 (4 and up) **Fic**

1. Science fiction 2. Extraterrestrial beings—Fiction

ISBN 0-06-024238-8; 0-06-024239-6 (lib bdg); 0-06-440514-1 (pa) LC 93-27268

Two seventh-grade friends help a shape-changing policeman from the planet Rodinam as he tries to recapture an alien master criminal who can also change form

"Funny scenes abound in the fast-paced, enthralling adventure." Horn Book Guide

Brooks, Bruce, 1950-

Everywhere. Harper & Row 1990 70p lib bdg $13.89; pa $3.95 (4 and up) **Fic**

1. Grandfathers—Fiction 2. Death—Fiction

ISBN 0-06-020729-9 (lib bdg); 0-06-440433-1 (pa) LC 90-4073

Afraid that his beloved grandfather will die after suffering a heart attack, a nine-year-old boy agrees to join ten-year-old Dooley in performing a mysterious ritual called soul switching

"Echoes of the great Southern writers with their themes of loneliness and faith can be heard in this masterly novella. . . . Brooks's precise use of language is a tour de force." Horn Book

Brooks, Walter R., 1886-1958

Freddy goes camping; illustrated by Kurt Wiese. Knopf 1986 c1948 258p il lib bdg $9.99; pa $4.95 (3-5) **Fic**

1. Pigs—Fiction 2. Mystery fiction

ISBN 0-394-97602-9 (lib bdg); 0-394-87602-4 (pa) LC 86-139633

A reissue of the title first published 1948

With a new introduction by Michael Cart

A mystery story for boys and girls, in which Freddy the pig goes camping to solve the mystery of a haunted hotel

Brooks, Walter R., 1886-1958—*Continued*

Other available titles about Freddy are:
Freddy and the perilous adventure (1942)
Freddy plays football (1949)
Freddy rides again (1951)
Freddy the cowboy (1950)

Bulla, Clyde Robert, 1914-

Shoeshine girl; illustrated by Leigh Grant. Crowell 1975 84p il lib bdg $14.89 (3-5)   Fic

ISBN 0-690-04830-0
Also available in paperback from HarperCollins
"When ten-and-a-half Sara Ida, a spirited defiant youngster, becomes involved with a friend who steals for kicks, her parents send her to an aunt for the summer. Denied an allowance (for discipline), Sara Ida finds a job as a shoeshine girl and discovers the satisfaction of earning her own pocket money and becomes less self-centered." Child Book Rev Serv
"The willful young heroine is appealing in spite of her bristly disposition; the setting is realistic and the storytelling smooth and economical." Horn Book

The sword in the tree; illustrated by Paul Galdone. Crowell 1956 113p il lib bdg $14.89 (3-5)   Fic

1. Arthur, King—Fiction 2. Knights and knighthood—Fiction
ISBN 0-690-79909-8
A story of England in King Arthur's days. Shan, the son of Lord Weldon, takes on the duties of a knight and seeks redress against his uncle, who had usurped his father's rights. A picture of the Knights of the Round Table and King Arthur develops
"A good story for beginning readers, this is also excellent for the older child who is a slow reader, because of the stimulating combination of exciting adventure, short sentences, and easy vocabulary." N Y Times Book Rev

Bunting, Eve, 1928-

Nasty, stinky sneakers. HarperCollins Pubs. 1994 105p $14; lib bdg $13.89; pa $3.95 (4-6)   Fic

ISBN 0-06-024236-1; 0-06-024237-X (lib bdg); 0-06-440507-9 (pa)   LC 93-34641
Will ten-year-old Colin find his missing stinky sneakers in time to enter The Stinkiest Sneakers in the World contest?
"A fast-paced, funny book that should elicit some delighted groans." Horn Book Guide

Spying on Miss Müller. Clarion Bks. 1995 179p $13.95 (5 and up)   Fic

1. World War, 1939-1945—Fiction 2. School stories 3. Fathers and daughters—Fiction 4. Ireland—Fiction
ISBN 0-395-69172-9   LC 94-15003
At Alveara boarding school in Belfast at the start of World War II, thirteen-year-old Jessie must deal with her suspicions about a teacher whose father was German and with her worries about her own father's drinking problem
"A thoughtful, moving coming-of-age novel, Jessie and her world . . . are portrayed with page-turning immediacy." Horn Book

Burch, Robert, 1925-

Ida Early comes over the mountain. Viking 1980 145p hardcover o.p. paperback available $3.95 (4 and up)   Fic

1. Economic depressions—Fiction 2. Country life—Fiction 3. Georgia—Fiction
ISBN 0-14-034534-5 (pa)   LC 79-20532
Also available in paperback from Avon Bks.
"A strong but rather eccentric non-conforming female character is central to this whimsical novel set in the mountains of rural Georgia during the Depression. Ida Early arrives one day to the motherless Sutton family of four children. Mr. Sutton agrees to hire her as a temporary housekeeper. So the adventure begins." Interracial Books Child Bull
"The book works on two levels—the hilarious account of Ida Early's exotic housekeeping in which real cleverness and skill is as effective and amazing as any fantasy magic, and the gentle, touching story of an ungainly woman's longing for beauty and femininity. That both levels meet, resolve themselves satisfactorily, and leave the characters deeply changed is the true success of this fine book." SLJ
Another available title about Ida Early is:
Christmas with Ida Early (1983)

Queenie Peavy; illustrated by Jerry Lazare. Viking 1966 159p il hardcover o.p. paperback available $3.95 (5 and up)   Fic

1. Parent and child—Fiction 2. Georgia—Fiction
ISBN 0-14-032305-8 (pa)
"Defiant, independent and intelligent, 13-year-old Queenie idolized her father who was in jail and was neglected by her mother who had to work all the time. Growing up in the [Depression] 1930's in Georgia, Queenie eventually understands her father's real character, herself and her relationships to those about her." Wis Libr Bull
"There is no straining here to formulate a story about a problem child. On the surface the account is as dispassionate as a case study, but considerably more convincing, and Queenie is so real that the reader becomes deeply involved in everything that concerns her." Horn Book

Burnett, Frances Hodgson, 1849-1924

A little princess (4-6)   Fic

1. School stories 2. Great Britain—Fiction
Available from various publishers, including a Lippincott edition illustrated by Tasha Tudor
First American edition published 1892 by Scribner in shorter form with title: Sara Crewe
The story of Sara Crewe, a girl who is sent from India to a boarding school in London, left in poverty by her father's death, and rescued by a mysterious benefactor
"The story is inevitably adorned with sentimental curlicues but the reader will hardly notice them since the story itself is such a satisfying one. Tasha Tudor's gentle, appropriate illustrations make this a lovely edition." Publ Wkly

The secret garden (4-6)   Fic

Also available Spanish language edition
Some editions are:
Godine $17.95 Illustrated by Graham Rust (ISBN 0-87923-649-3)
Harper & Row lib bdg $14.89; pa $3.50 Illustrated by Tasha Tudor; 0-397-32162-7; 0-06-440-188-X)
Holt & Co. $19.95 Illustrated by Michael Hague (ISBN 0-8050-0277-4)
Knopf $18.95 Illustrated by Ruth Sanderson (ISBN 0-394-55431-0)
Viking $20.95 Illustrated by Shirley Hughes (ISBN 0-670-82571-9)

Burnett, Frances Hodgson, 1849-1924—Continued

First published 1909 by Stokes

"Neglected by his father because of his mother's death at his birth, Colin lives the life of a spoilt and incurable invalid until, on the arrival of an orphaned cousin, the two children secretly combine to restore his mother's locked garden and Colin to health and his father's affection." Four to Fourteen

Burnford, Sheila, 1918-1984

The incredible journey. Little, Brown 1961 145p o.p.; Amereon reprint available $16.95 (4 and up) **Fic**

1. Cats—Fiction 2. Dogs—Fiction 3. Canada—Fiction
ISBN 0-88410-099-0

Also available in paperback from Bantam Bks.

"A half-blind English bull terrier, a sprightly yellow Labrador retriever, and a feisty Siamese cat have resided for eight months with a friend of their owners, who are away on a trip. Then their temporary caretaker leaves them behind in order to take a short vacation. The lonely trio decides to tackle the harsh 250-mile hike across the Canadian wilderness in search of home, despite the human and wild obstacles the group will encounter." Shapiro. Fic for Youth. 3d edition

Butterworth, Oliver, 1915-1990

The enormous egg; illustrated by Louis Darling. Little, Brown 1956 187p il $16.95; pa $3.95 (4 and up) **Fic**

1. Dinosaurs—Fiction
ISBN 0-316-11904-0; 0-316-11920-2 (pa)

Also available in paperback from Dell

"Up in Freedom, New Hampshire, one of the Twitchell's hens laid a remarkable egg—long, leathery-shelled, and so enormous that she could neither cover it nor turn it. Six weeks later when a live dinosaur hatched from the egg, the hen was dazed and upset, the Twitchells dumbfounded, and the scientific world went crazy. Twelve-year-old Nate who had taken care of the egg and made a pet out of the triceratops tells of the hullabaloo." Booklist

Nate's story, "is not only great fun but, one might say, educational—in a painless way, of course. And if you have any trouble visualizing a Triceratops moving placidly through the twentieth-century world you need only turn to Louis Darling's illustrations to believe." NY Times Book Rev

Byars, Betsy Cromer, 1928-

The 18th emergency; [by] Betsy Byars; illustrated by Robert Grossman. Viking 1973 126p il hardcover o.p. paperback available $3.99 (4-6) **Fic**

1. Fear—Fiction
ISBN 0-14-031451-2 (pa)

Timid Benjie, whose nickname is Mouse, spends two days worrying about Marv a big sixth grader who threatens to beat him up. Mouse "finally confronts Marv and takes two to the stomach, one to the breastbone, and two to the face without landing a punch on his opponent. Standing up like a man (not a Mouse) so impresses his peers that they begin to call him Benjie." Libr J

"For its skillful portrayal of the loneliness of fear as well as a boy's emotional battle with himself—his frantic thoughts, his fantasies of escape, his gradual awakening to the way things are as against the way he wishes they were—

'The 18th Emergency' weighs in . . . as a bantam champion." N Y Times Book Rev

The burning questions of Bingo Brown; [by] Betsy Byars. Viking 1988 166p lib bdg $12.95; pa $3.99 (4 and up) **Fic**

1. School stories
ISBN 0-670-81932-8 (lib bdg); 0-14-032479-8 (pa)
LC 87-21022

Also available G.K. Hall large print edition; Spanish language edition also available

A boy is puzzled by the comic and confusing questions of youth and worried by disturbing insights into adult conflicts

"A fully worked out novel. . . . Readers will recognize the pitfalls, agonies, and joys of elementary school life in this book. . . . The short chapters and comic style are designed to appeal to young readers and to move them right into other books." Christ Sci Monit

Other available titles about Bingo Brown are:
Bingo Brown and the language of love (1989)
Bingo Brown, gypsy lover (1990)
Bingo Brown's guide to romance (1992)

Cracker Jackson; [by] Betsy Byars. Viking Kestrel 1985 147p $12.95; pa $3.99 (5 and up) **Fic**

1. Wife abuse—Fiction 2. Child abuse—Fiction
ISBN 0-670-80546-7; 0-14-031881-X (pa)
LC 84-24684

"Young Jackson discovers that his ex-baby sitter has been beaten by her husband; and, spurred by affection for her, the boy enlists his friend Goat to help drive her to a home for battered women. The pathetic story of Alma, with her adored baby, tidy home, and treasured collection of Barbie dolls, is relieved by flashbacks to the two boys' antics at school and by their hilarious, if potentially lethal, attempt to drive her to safety." Horn Book

"Suspense, danger, near-tragedy, heartbreak and tension-relieving, unwittingly comic efforts at seriously heroic action mark this as the best of middle-grade fiction to highlight the problems of wife-battering and child abuse." SLJ

The Cybil war; [by] Betsy Byars; illustrated by Gail Owens. Viking 1981 126p il $13.99; pa $3.99 (4-6) **Fic**

1. Friendship—Fiction
ISBN 0-670-25248-4; 0-14-034356-3 (pa)
LC 80-26912

"Simon is deeply smitten by Cybil, a fourth-grade classmate, and just as deeply angered by his once-closest friend Tony, a blithely inventive liar who persists in telling fibs to and about Cybil to strengthen his cause: Tony is also smitten by Cybil." Bull Cent Child Books

"In her gently comic style, Byars presents Simon and the other people in her . . . story (even nasty Tony) as subteens who are people dealing with real problems. . . . Owens has illustrated sympathetically, making up a book that readers will take to their hearts." Publ Wkly

The house of wings; [by] Betsy Byars; illustrated by Daniel Schwartz. Viking 1972 142p il lib bdg $14.95; pa $4.99 (4-6) **Fic**

1. Cranes (Birds)—Fiction 2. Grandfathers—Fiction
ISBN 0-670-38025-3 (lib bdg); 0-14-031523-3 (pa)

Also available Spanish language edition

"A young boy reeling from the pain of temporary parental abandonment forges a relationship with an eccentric grandfather whom he despises. In attempting to rescue and mend a wounded crane, they come to respect each other for what they are, and as men." Book World

Byars, Betsy Cromer, 1928——*Continued*

This story "has an unsentimental and potent message about wildlife and draws a telling portrait of a human relationship. Save for the brief appearance of the parents, Sammy and his grandfather are the only characters. The book's spare construction makes it strong." Saturday Rev

The midnight fox; [by] Betsy Byars; illustrated by Ann Grifalconi. Viking 1968 157p il lib bdg $14.99; pa $3.99 (4-6) **Fic**

1. Foxes—Fiction
ISBN 0-670-47473-8 (lib bdg); 0-14-031450-4 (pa)
Also available Spanish language edition

"City-bred Tommy hates the idea of spending the summer on Aunt Millie's farm while his parents bicycle through Europe. Once he is there, however, a black fox shatters his conviction that he and animals share a mutual antipathy; fascinated, he stalks and watches the wild creature for two months—until it steals some of Aunt Millie's poultry and has to be hunted down." Booklist

"What distinguishes the story from many others on the same theme is the simplicity and beauty of the writing and the depth of the characterization." Horn Book

The night swimmers; by Betsy Byars; illustrated by Troy Howell. Delacorte Press 1980 131p il hardcover o.p. paperback available $3.50 (5 and up) **Fic**

1. Single parent family—Fiction 2. Brothers and sisters—Fiction
ISBN 0-440-45857-9 (pa) LC 79-53597
Also available Cornerstone Bks. large print edition

With their mother dead and their father working nights, Retta tries to be mother to her two younger brothers but somehow things just don't seem to be working right

"The plot moves a little slowly but characterization is good." Voice Youth Advocates

The not-just-anybody family; [by] Betsy Byars; illustrated by Jacqueline Rogers. Delacorte Press 1986 149p il hardcover o.p. paperback available $3.99 (5 and up) **Fic**

1. Brothers and sisters—Fiction 2. Family life—Fiction
ISBN 0-440-45951-6 (pa) LC 85-16184
"It's an ordinary day in the Blossom family: Junior, with Maggie and Vernon watching, is poised to fly off the barn in homemade wings; Mom's on the rodeo circuit; and Pap and his dog, Mud, are in town. By evening, Pap's in jail; Junior's in the hospital; Mud is gone; and Maggie helps Vernon break into jail to be with their grandfather." Publisher's note

"The story of the pathetically self-reliant, eccentric, but deeply loving family makes a book that is funny and sad, warm and wonderful." Horn Book
Other available titles about the Blossom family are:
A Blossom promise (1987)
The Blossoms and the Green Phantom (1987)
The Blossoms meet the Vulture Lady (1986)
Wanted: Mud Blossom (1991)

The pinballs; [by] Betsy Byars. Harper & Row 1977 136p $15; lib bdg $14.89; pa $3.95 (5 and up) **Fic**

1. Foster home care—Fiction 2. Friendship—Fiction
ISBN 0-06-020917-8; 0-06-020918-6 (lib bdg); 0-06-440198-7 (pa)
Also available Spanish language edition

"Pinballs go where they're pushed—and life's 'tilts' have thrown together three misfits. Suddenly finding themselves in a warm, loving foster home are Thomas J, eight, who is homeless now that his octogenarian twin guardians are hospitalized; Harvey, 13, whose mother ran off to a commune and whose hard drinking father ran over him in a car; and Carlie, 15, who cannot get along with a succession of step-fathers—or the rest of the world, for that matter." SLJ

"A deceptively simple, eloquent story, its pain and acrimony constantly mitigated by the author's light, offhand style and by Carlie's wryly comic view of life." Horn Book

The summer of the swans; [by] Betsy Byars; illustrated by Ted CoConis. Viking 1970 142p il $15.99; pa $3.99 (5 and up) **Fic**

1. Slow learning children—Fiction 2. Brothers and sisters—Fiction
ISBN 0-670-68190-3, 0-14-031420-2 (pa)
Also available Cornerstone Bks. large print edition; Spanish language edition also available
Awarded the Newbery Medal, 1971

"The thoughts and feelings of a young girl troubled by a sense of inner discontent which she cannot explain are tellingly portrayed in the story of two summer days in the life of fourteen-year-old Sara Godfrey. Sara is jolted out of her self pitying absorption with her own inadequacies by the disappearance of her ten-year-old retarded brother who gets lost while trying to find the swans he had previously seen on a nearby lake. Her agonizing, albeit ultimately successful, search for Charlie and the reactions of others to this traumatic event help Sara gain a new perspective on herself and life." Booklist

Trouble River; [by] Betsy Byars; illustrated by Rocco Negri. Viking 1969 158p il $14.99; pa $3.95 (4-6) **Fic**

1. Frontier and pioneer life—Fiction 2. Rivers—Fiction
ISBN 0-670-73257-5; 0-14-034243-5 (pa)
Dewey Martin and his grandmother must make their way down the Trouble River on a home-made raft to escape the danger of hostile Indians. They find the raft hard to navigate on the river, but they persevere and eventually reach Hunter City and safety

"A philosophy of not giving up amid hardships and a sense of real love and family solidarity predominate." Read Ladders for Hum Relat. 6th edition

Calhoun, Mary, 1926-

Katie John; pictures by Paul Frame. Harper & Row 1960 134p il lib bdg $13.89 (4-6)
Fic

1. Houses—Fiction
ISBN 0-06-020951-8
"When the Tuckers inherited an old house in a Missouri town, they decided to live in it until they could get it ready to sell. Ten-year-old Katie John was gloomy at the prospect—until she made a new friend, helped to solve a mystery, and learned to love the house." Hodges. Books for Elem Sch Libr

A "story with a likable heroine, lively doings, and a credible ending." Booklist
Other available titles about Katie John are:
Depend on Katie John (1961)
Katie John and Heathcliff (1980)

Calvert, Patricia, 1931-

Bigger. Scribner 1994 137p $15 (5 and up)
Fic

1. Frontier and pioneer life—Fiction 2. Fathers and sons—Fiction 3. Dogs—Fiction
ISBN 0-684-19685-9 LC 93-14415

Calvert, Patricia, 1931-—*Continued*

Also available in paperback from Troll Assocs.

When his father disappears near the Mexican border at the end of the Civil War, twelve-year-old Tyler decides to go after him and bring him home, acquiring on the journey a strange dog which he names Bigger

"Calvert's story has many tantalizing elements: Tyler is likable and realistically portrayed, the book raises some provocative issues, and the ending is sad but satisfying. . . . This is an entertaining story even reluctant readers will relish." Booklist

Cameron, Ann, 1943-

The most beautiful place in the world; drawings by Thomas B. Allen. Knopf 1988 57p il $13; lib bdg $12.99; pa $3.50 (2-4) **Fic**

1. Grandmothers—Fiction 2. Guatemala—Fiction

ISBN 0-394-89463-4; 0-394-99463-9 (lib bdg); 0-394-80424-4 (pa) LC 88-532

Growing up with his grandmother in a small Central American town, seven-year-old Juan discovers the value of hard work, the joy of learning, and the location of the most beautiful place in the world

"The easy-to-read text, the handsome pencil drawings, and a setting that will take U.S. children into lives led elsewhere make this a winning choice for reading aloud or alone." Bull Cent Child Books

The stories Julian tells; illustrated by Ann Strugnell. Pantheon Bks. 1981 71p il $8.95; lib bdg $10.97; pa $3.50 (2-4) **Fic**

1. Family life—Fiction 2. African Americans—Fiction

ISBN 0-394-84301-0; 0-394-94301-5 (lib bdg); 0-394-82892-5 (pa) LC 80-18023

"When seven-year-old Julian tells his little brother, Huey, that cats come from catalogues, Huey believes him. But when he flips the pages of the catalogue and doesn't find any cats, he begins to cry and Julian has some fast explaining to do. . . . A loving family is the center for six happy stories about catalog cats, strange teeth, a garden, a birthday fig tree and a new friend." West Coast Rev Books

"Strugnell's delightful drawings depict Julian, his little brother Huey and their parents as black, but they could be members of any family with a stern but loving and understanding father." Publ Wkly

Other available titles about Julian and his family are:
Julian, dream doctor (1990)
Julian, secret agent (1988)
Julian's glorious summer (1987)
More stories Julian tells (1986)

Cameron, Eleanor, 1912-

The court of the stone children. Dutton 1973 191p o.p.; Puffin Bks. paperback available $3.95 (5 and up) **Fic**

1. Museums—Fiction 2. Mystery fiction

ISBN 0-14-034289-3 (pa)

Also available in hardcover from P. Smith

In a San Francisco museum of French art and furniture, Nina encounters the ghost of Dominique, a girl who lived in the nineteenth-century. Spurred on by the appearance of the ghost, Nina sets out to untangle a murder mystery which had remained unsolved since Napoleon's day

"A nice concoction of mystery, fantasy, and realism adroitly blended in a contemporary story. . . . The characters are interesting, the plot threads nicely integrated." Bull Cent Child Books

A room made of windows; illustrated by Trina Schart Hyman. Little, Brown 1971 271p il $15.95 (5 and up) **Fic**

ISBN 0-316-12523-7

Also available in paperback from Puffin Bks.

"An Atlantic Monthly Press book"

"This is the tale of Julia, an aspiring young author, who is highly intelligent but emotionally immature. Although she revels in the satisfactions of good friends and progress in her writing, she is troubled by her mother's desire to remarry, the death of a much-loved elderly friend, and problems of those around her." Wis Libr Bull

"The portrayal and interaction of interesting and diverse characters are given unity and meaning by the genius of a fine storyteller." J Youth Serv Libr

Other available titles about Julia Redfern are:
Julia's magic (1984)
The private worlds of Julia Redfern (1988)

The wonderful flight to the Mushroom Planet; with illustrations by Robert Henneberger. Little, Brown 1954 214p il $15.95; pa $6.95 (4-6) **Fic**

1. Science fiction

ISBN 0-316-12537-7; 0-316-12540-7 (pa)

"An Atlantic Monthly Press book"

Two boys help a neighbor build a space ship in answer to an ad and take off for the dying planet of Basidium. There they help the inhabitants to restore an essential food to their diets and thereby save the life of the planet

"Scientific facts are emphasized in this well-built story. Since they are necessary to the development of the story the reader absorbs them naturally as he soars with the boys on the mission." N Y Times Book Rev

Other available titles about the Mushroom Planet, the boys and Mr. Bass are:
Mr. Bass's planetoid (1958)
Stowaway to the Mushroom Planet (1956)

Carlson, Natalie Savage, 1906-

The family under the bridge; pictures by Garth Williams. Harper & Row 1958 99p il lib bdg $14.89; pa $3.95 (3-5) **Fic**

1. Tramps—Fiction 2. Christmas—Fiction 3. Paris (France)—Fiction

ISBN 0-06-020991-7 (lib bdg); 0-06-440250-9 (pa)

A Newbery Medal honor book, 1959

"Old Armand, a Parisian hobo, enjoyed his solitary, carefree life. . . . Then came a day just before Christmas when Armand, who wanted nothing to do with children because they spelled homes, responsibility, and regular work, found that three homeless children and their working mother had claimed his shelter under the bridge. How the hobo's heart and life become more and more deeply entangled with the little family and their quest for a home is told." Booklist

"Garth Williams' illustrations are perfect for this thoroughly delightful story of humor and sentiment which includes a Christmas Eve party given by the ladies of Notre Dame for the homeless of Paris and an inside view of a gypsy encampment." Libr J

Carrick, Carol

Stay away from Simon! pictures by Donald Carrick. Clarion Bks. 1985 63p il lib bdg $13.95; pa $5.95 (3-5) **Fic**

1. Mentally handicapped—Fiction
ISBN 0-89919-343-9 (lib bdg); 0-89919-849-X (pa)
LC 84-14289

"In a story set on Martha's Vineyard in the 1830's, the children of the Village echo the ignorance of the period and their fear of, and misunderstanding about, those who are retarded. Lucy, eleven, is already afraid of big, shambling Simon and is terrified when she finds he is following her as she stumbles homeward through a snowstorm with her weeping little brother. It is then that Simon saves them, leading the way to the road and carrying Josiah." Bull Cent Child Books

"Because the story is set in a different era and features an intrinsically interesting adventure, its message comes across without being didactic. Involving and moving, the tale also comes alive through Donald Carrick's finely crafted pencil drawings that set the mood as well as the scene." Booklist

What a wimp! drawings by Donald Carrick. Clarion Bks. 1983 89p il hardcover o.p. paperback available $5.95 (3-5) **Fic**

1. School stories 2. Divorce—Fiction
ISBN 0-89919-703-5 (pa)
LC 82-9597

"After their parents were divorced, Barney and his brother Russ moved to the small town where his mother had spent her childhood summers. Barney finds now that coping with a bully in his class, Lenny, makes him unhappy about everything else." Bull Cent Child Books

"Prose and illustrations excel at capturing the classrooom and playground atmosphere of a primary school." SLJ

Carroll, Lewis, 1832-1898

Alice's adventures in Wonderland (4 and up) **Fic**

1. Fantasy fiction
Also available Spanish language edition
Some editions are:
Crown (Children's classics) $12.99 With illustrations in color by Bessie Pease Gutmann and black and white illustrations by John Tenniel (ISBN 0-517-65961-1)
Gramercy Bks. $15.99 Illustrated by Arthur Rackham (ISBN 0-517-12420-3)
Holt & Co. $19.95 Illustrated by Michael Hague (ISBN 0-8050-0212-X)
St. Martin's Press $14.95 Illustrated by John Tenniel (ISBN 0-312-01821-5)

"First told in 1862 to the little Liddell girls. Written out for Alice Liddell, published, and first copy given to her in 1865." Arnold

Variant title: Alice in Wonderland

"A rabbit who took a watch out of his waistcoat pocket seemed well-worth following to Alice so she hurried after him across the field, down the rabbit hole, and into a series of adventures with a group of famous and most unusual characters." Let's Read Together

This fantasy "is one of the most quoted books in the English language. Every child should be introduced to Alice, though its appeal will not be universal." Natl Counc of Teach of Engl. Adventuring with Books

Followed by: Through the looking glass, and what Alice found there

Alice's adventures in Wonderland, and Through the looking glass (4 and up) **Fic**

1. Fantasy fiction
Available from various publishers including a Dell paperback edition illustrated by John Tenniel
A combined edition of the two titles listed separately

Through the looking glass, and what Alice found there. (4 and up) **Fic**

1. Fantasy fiction
Available from various publishers, including a St. Martin's Press edition illustrated by John Tenniel; Spanish language edition also available
First published 1872

In this sequel to Alice's adventures in Wonderland, entered above, Alice climbs through a looking glass into a country where "everything is reversed, just as reflections are reversed in a mirror. Brooks and hedges divide the land into a checkerboard and Alice finds herself a white pawn in the whimsical and fantastic game of chess that constitutes the bulk of the story. . . . The ballad 'Jabberwocky' is found in the tale." Reader's Ency

Cassedy, Sylvia, 1930-1989

Behind the attic wall. Crowell 1983 315p lib bdg $14.89 (5 and up) **Fic**

1. Uncles—Fiction 2. Orphans—Fiction 3. Ghost stories 4. Dolls—Fiction
ISBN 0-690-04337-6
LC 82-43922

Also available in paperback from Avon Bks.

Maggie, a rebellious twelve-year-old orphan "is sent to stay with two elderly great-aunts; like other guardians they are horrified by the behavior of the . . . hostile child. . . . That is the realistic matrix for a fantasy world behind the attic wall, where Maggie finds two dolls who are articulate and who draw her into their world so that she becomes engaged and protective." Bull Cent Child Books

"The gradual merging of the story into fantasy, detail by telling detail, demands patience and attention on the part of the reader, but the wonderfully strange denouement will reward perseverance." Horn Book

Caudill, Rebecca, 1899-1985

A certain small shepherd; with illustrations by William Pène Du Bois. Holt & Co. 1965 48p il lib bdg $14.95 (4 and up) **Fic**

1. Physically handicapped children—Fiction 2. Christmas—Fiction 3. Appalachian Mountains—Fiction
ISBN 0-8050-1323-7

The author tells of "the singleminded enthusiasm of [Jamie], a little mute boy, who is given the part of one of the shepherds in a church celebration. . . . The pageant never takes place as a blizzard immobilizes the poor mountain community where the child lives, but the small shepherd is so deeply committed to his part that he acts it out impulsively [and speaks] when a baby is born to a family of travelers, caught by the storm and obliged to take refuge in the church." Book Week

"Set in the mountains of Appalachia, the tender, moving story, illustrated with poignantly interpretive drawings, expresses anew the age-old Christmas message of love and wonder." Booklist

Caudill, Rebecca, 1899-1985—*Continued*

Did you carry the flag today, Charley?
illustrated by Nancy Grossman. Holt & Co.
1966 94p il lib bdg $15.95; pa $3.95 (2-4)
Fic

1. School stories 2. Appalachian Mountains—Fiction
ISBN 0-8050-1201-X (lib bdg); 0-03-086620-0 (pa)

A "story about a small and lively boy, just turned five,
who has his first encounter with the necessary strictures of
the classroom at a summer school in Appalachia. Charley,
obstreperous youngest in a family of ten, is given a full picture of the joys and the responsibilities he will encounter;
his brothers and sisters tell him that one child 'who has
been specially good that day' has the honor of carrying the
flag at the head of the line to the bus. . . . This is a realistic
and low-keyed story with good dialogue." Bull Cent Child
Books

Childress, Alice, 1920-1994

A hero ain't nothin' but a sandwich.
Coward-McCann 1973 126p $15.95 (6 and up)
Fic

1. Drug abuse—Fiction 2. African Americans—Fiction
3. Harlem (New York, N.Y.)—Fiction
ISBN 0-698-20278-3

Also available in paperback from Avon Bks.

"At the age of thirteen Benjie Johnson is hooked on
'horse.' He believes that he can break the habit whenever
he is ready. When two of Benjie's teachers realize that he
is on drugs, they report him to the principal of the school.
Then begins his seesaw battle to break his addiction. Using
Black English, the author draws a picture of the urban drug
scene." Shapiro. Fic for Youth. 2d edition

Choi, Sook Nyul

Year of impossible goodbyes. Houghton
Mifflin 1991 171p o.p.; Dell paperback
available $3.99 (5 and up)
Fic

1. Korea—Fiction
ISBN 0-440-40759-1 (pa)   LC 91-10502

A young Korean girl survives the oppressive Japanese
and Russian occupation of North Korea during the 1940s,
to later escape to freedom in South Korea

"Tragedies are not masked here, but neither are they
overdramatized. . . . The observations are honest, the details authentic, the characterizations vividly developed."
Bull Cent Child Books

Other available titles about Sookan are:
Echoes of the white giraffe (1993)
Gathering of pearls (1994)

Christopher, John, 1922-

The White Mountains. Macmillan 1967
184p $14.95; pa $3.95 (5 and up)
Fic

1. Science fiction
ISBN 0-02-718360-2; 0-02-042711-5 (pa)

"The world of the future is ruled by huge and powerful
machine-creatures, the Tripods, who control mankind by
implanting metal caps in their skulls when they reach the
age of fourteen. Three boys . . . see that the people about
them are mindless conformists [and] decide to flee to the
White Mountains (Switzerland), where there is a colony of
free men." Saturday Rev

This "remarkable story . . . belongs to the school of sci-
ence-fiction which puts philosophy before technology and is
not afraid of telling an exciting story." Times Lit Suppl

Other available titles about the Tripods are:
The city of gold and lead (1967)
The pool of fire (1968)
When the Tripods came (1988)

Christopher, Matt, 1917-

Fighting tackle; illustrated by Karin
Lidbeck. Little, Brown 1995 147p il $14.95
(4-6)
Fic

1. Football—Fiction 2. Brothers—Fiction 3. Mentally
handicapped—Fiction
ISBN 0-316-14010-4   LC 94-19680

When he becomes stronger but slower, Terry must deal
with being moved from defensive safety to offensive tackle
on his football team and with the fact that his younger
brother, who was born with Down's Syndrome, is becoming
a faster runner

"This is one of Christopher's better sports-theme books.
. . . The conclusion is satisfying." SLJ

The hit-away kid; illustrated by George
Ulrich. Little, Brown 1988 60p il lib bdg
$12.95; pa $3.95 (2-4)
Fic

1. Baseball—Fiction
ISBN 0-316-13995-5 (lib bdg); 0-316-14007-4 (pa)
LC 87-24406

Barry McGee, star batter for the Peach Street Mudders,
enjoys winning so much that he has a tendency to bend the
rules; then the dirty tactics of the pitcher on a rival team
give him a new perspective on sports ethics

"This is predictable in theme if not in plot (Barry's team
loses), but kids will get the reading practice they need on a
subject that's palatable and popular." Bull Cent Child
Books

Tackle without a team; illustrated by
Margaret Sanfilippo. Little, Brown 1989 145p
il $15.95; pa $3.95 (4-6)
Fic

1. Football—Fiction 2. Drugs—Fiction 3. Mystery fic-
tion
ISBN 0-316-14067-8; 0-316-14268-9 (pa)
LC 88-22644

Unjustly dismissed from the football team for drug possession, Scott learns that only by finding out who planted
the marijuana in his duffel bag can he clear himself with his
parents

"Christopher's message—that smoking cigarettes or pot
is a bummer—comes through loud and clear. Lots of action
and enough suspense hold the plot together." Booklist

Clapp, Patricia, 1912-

Constance: a story of early Plymouth; a
story of early Plymouth. Lothrop, Lee &
Shepard Bks. 1968 255p o.p.; Morrow
paperback available $3.95 (5 and up)
Fic

1. Pilgrims (New England colonists)—Fiction
2. Massachusetts—History—1600-1775, Colonial
period—Fiction
ISBN 0-688-10976-4 (pa)

Also available in hardcover from P. Smith

The imaginary "journal kept by Constance Hopkins,
daughter of Stephen Hopkins and ancestress of Patricia
Clapp. Constance began jotting down her impressions and
intimate thoughts at the age of fifteen on the eve of the
'Mayflower's' arrival and continued up to the day of her
wedding five years later." Horn Book

"The characters come alive, the writing style is excellent,
and the historical background is smoothly integrated." Bull
Cent Child Books

Clapp, Patricia, 1912-—_Continued_

Jane-Emily. Lothrop, Lee & Shepard Bks. 1969 160p o.p.; Morrow paperback available $3.95 (5 and up) **Fic**

1. Ghost stories
ISBN 0-688-04592-8 (pa)

"While visiting her grandmother, young Jane finds a crystal ball which reflects the image of Emily, a dead girl. Jane is soon possessed by the ghost of Emily, and the events which follow are chilling." Cincinnati Public Libr

"Well written and with a convincing strong Gothic strain, the story is spellbinding, building up to an exciting climax." Horn Book

Cleary, Beverly

Dear Mr. Henshaw; illustrated by Paul O. Zelinsky. Morrow 1983 133p il $16 (4-6) **Fic**

1. Divorce—Fiction 2. Parent and child—Fiction 3. School stories
ISBN 0-688-02405-X LC 83-5372

Also available in paperback from Avon Bks. and Dell; Spanish language edition also available

Awarded the Newbery Medal, 1984

"Leigh Botts started writing letters to his favorite author, Boyd Henshaw, in the second grade. Now, Leigh is in the sixth grade, in a new school, and his parents are recently divorced. This year he writes many letters to Mr. Henshaw, and also keeps a journal. Through these the reader learns how Leigh adjusts to new situations, and of his triumphs." Child Book Rev Serv

"The story is by no means one of unrelieved gloom, for there are deft touches of humor in the sentient, subtly wrought account of the small triumphs and tragedies in the life of an ordinary boy." Horn Book

Followed by Strider, entered below

Ellen Tebbits; illustrated by Louis Darling. Morrow 1951 160p il $16; lib bdg $15.93 (3-5) **Fic**

1. School stories
ISBN 0-688-21264-6; 0-688-31264-0 (lib bdg)

Also available in paperback from Avon Bks.

"Ellen Tebbits is eight years old, takes ballet lessons, wears bands on her teeth, and has a secret—she wears woolen underwear. But she finds a friend in Austine, a new girl in school, who also wears woolen underwear. They have the usual troubles that beset 'best friends' in grade school plus some that are unusual." Carnegie Libr of Pittsburgh

"Their experiences in the third grade are comical and very appealing to children in the middle grades." Hodges. Books for Elem Sch Libr

Henry Huggins; illustrated by Louis Darling. Morrow 1950 155p $16; lib bdg $15.93 (3-5) **Fic**

ISBN 0-688-21385-5; 0-688-31385-X (lib bdg)

Also available Cornerstone Bks. large print edition and in paperback from Avon Bks.; Spanish language edition also available

"Henry Huggins is a typical small boy who, quite innocently, gets himself into all sorts of predicaments—often with the very apt thought, 'Won't Mom be surprised.' There is not a dull moment but some hilariously funny ones in the telling of Henry's adventures at home and at school." Booklist

Other available titles about Henry Huggins are:
Henry and Beezus (1952)

Henry and Ribsy (1954)
Henry and the clubhouse (1962)
Henry and the paper route (1957)
Ribsy (1964)

Mitch and Amy; illustrated by Bob Marstall. Morrow Junior Bks. 1991 222p il $13.95; lib bdg $13.88 (3-5) **Fic**

1. Twins—Fiction 2. School stories
ISBN 0-688-10806-7; 0-688-10807-5 (lib bdg)
LC 91-25657

Also available in paperback from Avon Bks.

A newly illustrated edition of the title first published 1967

"The twins Mitch and Amy are in the fourth grade. Mitch is plagued by a bully and by reading difficulties, Amy struggles with multiplication tables, and their patient mother mediates their squabbles." SLJ

"The writing style and dialogue, the familial and peer group relationships, the motivations and characterizations all have the ring of truth. Written with ease and vitality, lightened with humor, the story is perhaps most appealing because it is clear that the author respects children." Bull Cent Child Books

The mouse and the motorcycle; illustrated by Louis Darling. Morrow 1965 158p il $16; lib bdg $15.93 (3-5) **Fic**

1. Mice—Fiction
ISBN 0-688-21698-6; 0-688-31698-0 (lib bdg)

Also available Cornerstone Bks. large print edition and in paperback from Avon Bks.

"A fantasy about Ralph, a mouse, who learns to ride a toy motorcycle and goes on wild rides through the corridors of the hotel where he lives. Keith, the boy to whom the motorcycle belongs, becomes fast friends with Ralph and defends him when danger threatens." Hodges. Books for Elem Sch Libr

"The author shows much insight into the thoughts of children. She carries the reader into an imaginative world that contains many realistic emotions." Wis Libr Bull

Other available titles about Ralph are:
Ralph S. Mouse (1982)
Runaway Ralph (1970)

Muggie Maggie; illustrated by Kay Life. Morrow Junior Bks. 1990 70p il $15; lib bdg $14.93 (2-4) **Fic**

1. Handwriting—Fiction 2. School stories
ISBN 0-688-08553-9; 0-688-08554-7 (lib bdg)
LC 89-38959

Also available in paperback from Avon Bks.

Maggie resists learning cursive writing in the third grade, until she discovers that knowing how to read and write cursive promises to open up an entirely new world of knowledge for her

"This deceptively simple story is accessible to primary-grade readers able to read longhand, as some of the text is in script. . . . Everything in this book rings true, and Cleary has created a likable, funny heroine about whom readers will want to know more." SLJ

Otis Spofford; illustrated by Louis Darling. Morrow 1953 191p il $16; lib bdg $14.93 (3-5) **Fic**

1. School stories
ISBN 0-688-21720-6; 0-688-31720-0 (lib bdg)

Also available in paperback from Avon Bks.

"Otis, a mischievous, fun loving boy, is always getting in and out of trouble. His mother, a dancing teacher, is busy and often leaves Otis on his own. This book tells of several

Cleary, Beverly—*Continued*

episodes in Otis's life—from his sneaking vitamins to a white rat to 'disprove' a diet experiment, to getting his final 'come-uppance' when a trick on Ellen Tebbits backfires." Read Ladders for Hum Relat. 6th edition

"This writer has her elementary school down pat, and manages to report her growing boys, teachers, and P.T.A. meetings so that parents chuckle and boys laugh out loud." N Y Her Trib Books

Ramona the pest; illustrated by Louis Darling. Morrow 1968 192p il $16; lib bdg $15.93 (3-5) **Fic**

1. Kindergarten—Fiction 2. School stories

ISBN 0-688-21721-4; 0-688-31721-9 (lib bdg)

Also available Cornerstone Bks. large print edition and in paperback from Avon Bks.; Spanish language edition also available

"Ramona Quimby comes into her own. Beezus keeps telling her to stop acting like a pest, but Ramona is five now, and she is convinced that she is 'not' a pest; she feels very mature, having entered kindergarten, and she immediately becomes enamoured of her teacher. Ramona's insistence on having just the right kind of boots, her matter-of-fact interest in how Mike Mulligan got to a bathroom, her determination to kiss one of the boys in her class, and her refusal to go back to kindergarten because Miss Binney didn't love her any more—all of these incidents or situations are completely believable and are told in a light, humorous, zesty style." Bull Cent Child Books

Other available titles about Ramona are:

Beezus and Ramona (1955)
Ramona and her father (1977)
Ramona and her mother (1979)
Ramona, forever (1984)
Ramona Quimby, age 8 (1981)
Ramona the brave (1975)

Socks; illustrated by Beatrice Darwin. Morrow 1973 156p il $15; lib bdg $14.93 (3-5) **Fic**

1. Cats—Fiction 2. Infants—Fiction

ISBN 0-688-20067-2; 0-688-30067-7 (lib bdg)

Also available in paperback from Avon Bks.

"The Brickers' kitten, Socks, is jealous when they bring a baby home from the hospital. How he copes with this rivalry makes an amusing story true to cat nature." Cleveland Public Libr

"Not being child-centered, this may have a smaller audience than earlier Cleary books, but it is written with the same easy grace, the same felicitous humor and sharply observant eye." Bull Cent Child Books

Strider; illustrated by Paul O. Zelinsky. Morrow Junior Bks. 1991 179p il $16; lib bdg $15.93 (4 and up) **Fic**

1. Dogs—Fiction 2. Divorce—Fiction

ISBN 0-688-09900-9; 0-688-09901-7 (lib bdg)

LC 90-6608

Also available in paperback from Avon Bks.; Spanish language edition also available

Sequel to Dear Mr. Henshaw, entered above

In a series of diary entries, Leigh Botts, now fourteen and beginning high school, tells how he comes to terms with his parents' divorce, acquires joint custody of an abandoned dog, and joins the track team at school

"The development of the narrative is vintage Beverly Cleary, an inimitable blend of comic and poignant moments." Horn Book

Cleaver, Vera

Grover; [by] Vera and Bill Cleaver; illustrated by Frederic Marvin. Lippincott 1970 125p il $13.95 (4-6) **Fic**

1. Death—Fiction

ISBN 0-397-31118-4

Ten-year-old Grover "goes through an agonizing period of adjustment beginning with his mother's sudden departure to the hospital and ending with his eventual acceptance of her death. The strain is increased by adult attempts to 'protect' him from the truth during her illness and by his father's withdrawal into grief after her suicide." Booklist

Although the elements of the story "may sound grim, there's nothing depressing about this book—it seems very real, with its most deeply touching or dramatic moments heightened by superbly comic incidents or dialogue." SLJ

Where the lillies bloom; [by] Vera & Bill Cleaver; illustrated by Jim Spanfeller. Lippincott 1969 174p il lib bdg $14.89 (5 and up) **Fic**

1. Orphans—Fiction 2. Brothers and sisters—Fiction 3. Appalachian Mountains—Fiction

ISBN 0-397-32500-2

Also available Spanish language edition

Mary Call Luther is "fourteen years old and made of granite. When her sharecropper father dies, Mary Call becomes head of the household, responsible for a boy of ten and a retarded, gentle older sister. Mary and her brother secretly bury their father so they can retain their home; [in the Appalachian hills]; tenaciously she fights to keep the family afloat by selling medicinal plants and to keep them together by fending off [Kiser Pease, their landlord], who wants to marry her sister." Saturday Rev

"The setting is fascinating, the characterization good, and the style of the first-person story distinctive." Bull Cent Child Books

Followed by Trial Valley (1977)

Clifford, Eth, 1915-

Help! I'm a prisoner in the library; illustrated by George Hughes. Houghton Mifflin 1979 105p il $14.95 (3-5) **Fic**

1. Libraries—Fiction 2. Blizzards—Fiction

ISBN 0-395-28478-3 LC 79-14447

Also available in paperback from Scholastic

"Caught in a blinding snowstorm with their car out of gas, Mary Rose and Jo-Beth are told to stay put while their father finds fuel for the stalled vehicle. Jo-Beth, however, develops 'an emergency' and Mary Rose takes her to a nearby library to find a restroom. . . . Without warning the girls find themselves locked in when the building closes early. As the storm worsens, the lights and telephone go out and a series of flying objects, creaking noises, and moaning sounds thoroughly frighten the girls. . . . Clifford uses a light touch while evoking a pleasingly scary atmosphere that children will enjoy. Spirited dialogue and swift pace are an additional plus." Booklist

The remembering box; illustrated by Donna Diamond. Houghton Mifflin 1985 70p il $14.95 (3-5) **Fic**

1. Grandmothers—Fiction 2. Jews—Fiction 3. Death—Fiction

ISBN 0-395-38476-1 LC 85-10851

Also available in paperback from Morrow

Nine-year-old Joshua's weekly visits to his beloved grandmother on the Jewish Sabbath give him an understanding of love, family, and tradition which helps him ac-

Clifford, Eth, 1915—*Continued*

cept her death

"This warm and loving relationship between a boy and his grandmother is beautifully depicted. . . . Diamond's silhouettes, used for the stories that Grandma tells Joshua, are dramatic, and her meticulously detailed black-and-white illustrations of Joshua and his grandmother are both expressive and moving." SLJ

Clifton, Lucille, 1936-

The lucky stone; illustrated by Dale Payson. Delacorte Press 1979 64p il $12.50; pa $3.50 (3-5)   Fic

1. African Americans—Fiction 2. Charms
ISBN 0-440-05121-5; 0-440-45110-8 (pa)

LC 78-72862

"Four short stories about four generations of Black women and their dealings with a lucky stone. . . . Clifton uses as a frame device a grandmother telling the history of the stone to her granddaughter; by the end the granddaughter has inherited the stone herself. . . . The story is written in Black dialect." SLJ

"This book contains information on various aspects of Black culture—slavery, religion and extended family—all conveyed in a way that is both positive and accurate." Interracial Books Child Bull

Coatsworth, Elizabeth Jane, 1893-1986

The cat who went to heaven; [by] Elizabeth Coatsworth; illustrated by Lynd Ward. Macmillan 1958 62p il $15; pa $3.95 (4 and up)   Fic

1. Cats—Fiction 2. Japan—Fiction
ISBN 0-02-719710-7; 0-689-71433-5 (pa)

LC 58-10917

Also available Spanish language edition
First published 1930. The 1958 edition is a reprint with new illustrations of the book which won the Newbery Medal award in 1931

"Watched by his little cat, Good Fortune, a Japanese artist paints a picture of the Buddha receiving homage from the animals. By tradition the cat should not be among them, but the artist risks his reputation by adding Good Fortune and is vindicated by a miracle." Hodges. Books for Elem Sch Libr

"Into this lovely and imaginative story the author has put something of the serenity and beauty of the East and of the gentleness of a religion that has a place even for the humblest of living creatures." N Y Times Book Rev

Coerr, Eleanor, 1922-

Mieko and the fifth treasure; calligraphy by Cecil H. Uyehara. Putnam 1993 77p $13.95 (3-5)   Fic

1. Artists—Fiction 2. Nagasaki (Japan)—Bombardment, 1945—Fiction 3. Japan—Fiction
ISBN 0-399-22434-3   LC 92-14660
Also available in paperback from Dell

Staying with her grandparents after the atomic bomb has been dropped on Nagasaki, ten-year-old Mieko feels that the happiness in her heart has departed forever and she will no longer be able to produce a beautiful drawing for the contest at school

"The story conveys a wonderfully delicate sense of Japanese people, customs, and beliefs. Coerr has created an intriguing and beautifully told tale whose strong message about friendship, self-confidence, and hope is inspiring." Booklist

Cohen, Barbara, 1932-1992

The carp in the bathtub; illustrated by Joan Halpern. Lothrop, Lee & Shepard Bks. 1972 48p il lib bdg $14.93 (2-4)   Fic

1. Jews—Fiction 2. Fishes—Fiction
ISBN 0-688-51627-0
Also available in paperback from Kar-Ben Copies

Set in New York City. "Leah and Harry have made friends of Joe, the appealing carp their mother has swimming in the bathtub, awaiting its execution on the Feast of Seder. Joe will make marvelous 'gefilte' fish but the children are determined to save him. They sneak him into the tub of a neighbor, but alas; his change of scene is only a reprieve, not a pardon. A delightfully warm book with pictures equally appealing." Publ Wkly

The long way home; illustrated by Diane de Groat. Lothrop, Lee & Shepard Bks. 1990 170p il lib bdg $12.95 (4-6)   Fic

1. Cancer—Fiction 2. Twins—Fiction 3. Camps—Fiction
ISBN 0-688-09674-3   LC 89-35309

Sally's relationship with an elderly bus driver who recites Shakespeare stories helps her to cope with the problems of her mother's cancer and being separated from her twin sister at summer camp

"Cohen has done a fine job of portraying the confusion of a preadolescent who is trying to deal with her anger and fear within a family who love one another but are afraid to talk about cancer. . . . But rather than focus on death, Cohen has written about a family who will likely survive both a mother's illness and the terrible fear it brings to those close to her." SLJ

Molly's Pilgrim; illustrated by Michael J. Deraney. Lothrop, Lee & Shepard Bks. 1983 unp il $16; lib bdg $15.93 (2-4)   Fic

1. Jews—Fiction 2. School stories 3. Thanksgiving Day—Fiction 4. Immigration and emigration—Fiction
ISBN 0-688-02103-4; 0-688-02104-2 (lib bdg)

LC 83-797

Also available in paperback from Bantam Bks. and Dell; Spanish language edition also available

"It is an unpleasant irony that each generation of Americans demoralizes the incoming immigrant generation and forgets that the Pilgrims were immigrants. Using a Jewish immigrant as the main character, the author develops this irony further, noting that both groups came to this country seeking religious freedom, and that Thanksgiving was a Pilgrim rendering of an Old Testament holiday which Jews call Succos. A sensitive teacher translates this message to the children who torment Molly because of her appearance and lack of familiarity with our Thanksgiving." Child Book Rev Serv

"Pencil drawings, firmly shaded, are strong in characterization and period details. The picture-book format recommends this as a thought-provoking Thanksgiving read-aloud." Booklist

Thank you, Jackie Robinson; drawings by Richard Cuffari. Lothrop, Lee & Shepard Bks. 1974 125p il lib bdg $13.95 (4-6)   Fic

1. Baseball—Fiction 2. Friendship—Fiction 3. African Americans—Fiction
ISBN 0-688-07909-1
Also available in paperback from Scholastic

"When 60-year-old Davey (Black) comes to work at the inn for Sam's mother, Sam (Jewish and fatherless) gains a friend. Davey takes Sam to see the Brooklyn Dodgers (circa 1945), and an avid, statistic-spouting Dodger fan is born. When Davey becomes ill, Sam gets Jackie Robinson and

Cohen, Barbara, 1932-1992—*Continued*
his teammates to autograph a ball for Davey." Child Book
Rev Serv

"Cohen's characters have unusual depth and her story
succeeds as a warm, understanding consideration of friendship and, finally, death." Booklist

Cole, Brock, 1938-

The goats; written and illustrated by Brock
Cole. Farrar, Straus & Giroux 1987 184p il
$15; pa $3.95 (5 and up)   **Fic**

1. Camps—Fiction 2. Friendship—Fiction
ISBN 0-374-32678-9; 0-374-42575-2 (pa)

LC 87-45362

"A boy and the girl have been chosen as 'the goats' at
summer camp. Stripped naked, they are marooned on Goat
Island, as part of an annual prank played on campers who
don't fit in. But the goats have much more spirit than their
fellow campers expect, and they decide to disappear completely." Publ Wkly

"This is an unflinching book, and there is a quality of
raw emotion that may score some discomfort among adults.
Such a first novel restores faith in the cultivation of children's literature." Bull Cent Child Books

Collier, James Lincoln, 1928-

The jazz kid. Holt & Co. 1994 216p $15.95
(5 and up)   **Fic**

1. Jazz   music—Fiction   2. Musicians—Fiction
3. Chicago (Ill.)—Fiction
ISBN 0-8050-2821-8   LC 93-33932
Also available in paperback from Puffin Bks.

Playing the coronet is the first thing that twelve-year-old
Paulie Horvath has taken seriously, but his obsession with
becoming a jazz musician leads him into conflict with his
parents and into the tough underworld of Chicago in the
1920s

"Many references to actual jazz musicians and Chicago
locales add authenticity, and the narrator's voice . . . is intimate and convincing. In an afterword, Collier sorts out the
historic from the fictional elements, and he suggests his
readers seek out early jazz recordings." Bull Cent Child
Books

Jump ship to freedom; [by] James Lincoln
Collier, Christopher Collier. Delacorte Press
1981 198p hardcover o.p. paperback available
$3.99 (6 and up)   **Fic**

1. United   States—History—1783-1809—Fiction
2. Slavery—Fiction 3. African Americans—Fiction
ISBN 0-440-44323-7 (pa)   LC 81-65492
Companion volume to War comes to Willie Freeman
and Who is Carrie, both entered below

In 1787 Dan Arabus, a fourteen-year-old slave, anxious
to buy freedom for himself and his mother, escapes from
his dishonest master and tries to find help in cashing the
soldier's notes received by his father, Jack Arabus, for fighting in the Revolution

"The period seems well researched, and the speech has
an authentic ring without trying to imitate a dialect." SLJ

My brother Sam is dead; by James Lincoln
Collier and Christopher Collier. Four Winds
Press 1985 c1974 216p $15.95 (6 and up)

Fic

1. United States—History—1775-1783, Revolution—
Fiction
ISBN 0-02-722980-7   LC 84-28787

Also available in paperback from Scholastic
A reissue of the title first published 1974

"In 1775 the Meeker family lived in Redding, Connecticut, a Tory community. Sam, the eldest son, allied himself
with the Patriots. The youngest son, Tim, watched a rift in
the family grow because of his brother's decision. Before
the war was over the Meeker family had suffered at the
hands of both the British and the Patriots." Shapiro. Fic for
Youth. 3d edition

War comes to Willy Freeman; [by] James
Lincoln Collier, Christopher Collier. Delacorte
Press 1983 178p hardcover o.p. paperback
available $3.99 (6 and up)   **Fic**

1. United States—History—1775-1783, Revolution—
Fiction 2. African Americans—Fiction 3. Slavery—
Fiction
ISBN 0-440-49504-0 (pa)   LC 82-70317
Also available in hardcover from P. Smith

This deals with events prior to those in Jump ship to
freedom, entered above, and involves members of the same
family. "Willy is thirteen when she begins her story, which
takes place during the last two years of the Revolutionary
War; her father, a free man, has been killed fighting against
the British, her mother has disappeared. Willy makes her
danger-fraught way to Fraunces Tavern in New York, her
uncle, Jack Arabus, having told her that Mr. Fraunces may
be able to help her. She works at the tavern until the war
is over, goes to the Arabus home to find her mother dying,
and participates in the trial (historically accurate save for
the fictional addition of Willy) in which her uncle sues for
his freedom and wins." Bull Cent Child Books

Who is Carrie? [by] James Lincoln Collier,
Christopher Collier. Delacorte Press 1984
158p hardcover o.p. paperback available $3.99
(6 and up)   **Fic**

1. United   States—History—1783-1809—Fiction
2. Slavery—Fiction 3. African Americans—Fiction
ISBN 0-440-49536-9 (pa)   LC 83-23947
Companion volume to Jump ship to freedom, and War
comes to Willy Freeman, both entered above

Carrie "is a kitchen slave in Samuel Fraunces Tavern. .
. . She keeps in touch with her special friend, Dan Arabus,
and he enlists Carrie's help in finding out if the new government will honor the notes with which Dan hopes to purchase his mother's freedom. In so doing, Carrie finds out
the truth about herself." Child Book Rev Serv

"This is historical fiction at its best. The Collier's familiar 'How Much of This Book is True' addendum fills readers in on the essentials concerning fictional and factual
elements of the plot, as well as the research involved in its
composition." SLJ

Collodi, Carlo, 1826-1890

The adventures of Pinocchio (3-6)   **Fic**

1. Puppets and puppet plays—Fiction 2. Fairy tales
Various editions available including Spanish language
edition

An Italian classic for children, written late in the 19th
century. Variant title: Pinocchio

"When Geppetto discovered a piece of wood which
talked, he carved it into a marionette and named him
Pinocchio. Although he is a wooden boy, Pinocchio has a
lively and nimble mind and an ardent curiosity which lead
to unexpected and extraordinary results. A lighthearted and
original fantasy in which children can identify themselves
with Pinocchio and grasp the simple and practical morality
which underlies the story." Toronto Public Libr. Books for
Boys & Girls

Coman, Carolyn

What Jamie saw. Front St. 1995 126p
$13.95 (5 and up) **Fic**

1. Child abuse—Fiction
ISBN 1-886910-02-2 LC 95-23545

A Newbery Medal honor book, 1996

Having fled to a family friend's hillside trailer after his
mother's boyfriend tried to throw his baby sister against a
wall, nine-year-old Jamie finds himself living an existence
full of uncertainty and fear

"Shocking in its simple narration and child's-eye view,
What Jamie Saw is a bittersweet miracle in understated
language and forthright hopefulness." SLJ

Conford, Ellen

A case for Jenny Archer; illustrated by
Diane Palmisciano. Little, Brown 1988 61p il
lib bdg $12.95 (2-4) **Fic**

ISBN 0-316-15266-0 LC 88-14169

"A Springboard book"

After reading three mysteries in a row, Jenny becomes
convinced that the neighbors across the street are up to no
good and decides to investigate

Other available titles about Jenny Archer are:
Can do, Jenny Archer (1991)
Get the picture, Jenny Archer (1994)
Jenny Archer, author (1989)
Jenny Archer to the rescue (1990)
A job for Jenny Archer (1988)
Nibble, nibble, Jenny Archer (1993)
What's cooking, Jenny Archer? (1989)

Dear Lovey Hart: I am desperate. Little,
Brown 1975 170p $14.95 (6 and up) **Fic**

1. College and school journalism—Fiction 2. School stories
ISBN 0-316-15306-0

Also available in paperback from Scholastic

"Carrie is having a great time writing a column of advice
to the lovelorn for her school paper. An added benefit is
that she gets to be around Chip, the paper's handsome editor. But when the letters to 'Lovey Hart' become more serious, Carrie does not know what to do. People are taking her
advice, and trouble is usually the result. What is worse,
though, is that Chip seems to be interested in Carrie's best
friend Claudia. Now Carrie feels she needs some advice!"
Your Read

Followed by: We interrupt this semester for an important
bulletin (1979)

Felicia the critic; illustrated by Arvis
Stewart. Little, Brown 1973 145p il $14.95; pa
$5.95 (4-6) **Fic**

ISBN 0-316-15295-1; 0-316-15358-3 (pa)

"When her negative communications meet with looks of
loathing, Felicia, mostly undaunted and with good inten-
tions, embarks on a career as a constructive critic, hoping
that she will be valued for her talent. . . . Felicia's audacity
continues to be regarded with coldness by her family, her
friends, and many of her victims. Nevertheless, she is so often on target that some people find themselves taking up
her advice in spite of themselves." Booklist

"Fresh, entertaining, and percipient. . . . It all adds up to
a deft, sympathetic portrait of a real child—a loner aware
of the obtuseness and supercritical responses of other people." Horn Book

Me and the terrible two; illustrated by
Charles Carroll. Little, Brown 1974 117p il
hardcover o.p. paperback available $4.95 (3-6)
Fic

1. Friendship—Fiction 2. Twins—Fiction
ISBN 0-316-15366-4 (pa)

"Dorrie, a sixth-grader . . . not only loses her best friend
when the family next door moves to Australia, but must be
plagued by the new incumbents—a pair of zany, prankish,
totally self-sufficient, identical twin boys. Dorrie, predictably, not only manages to survive, but ultimately settles
into a three-way friendship with her tormentors." Horn
Book

"A witty, brisk and altogether effective story." Publ Wkly

Conly, Jane Leslie

Crazy lady! HarperCollins Pubs. 1993 180p
$13.95; lib bdg $13.89; pa $4.50 (5 and up)
Fic

1. Prejudices Fiction 2. Death Fiction
3. Alcoholics—Fiction 4. Mentally handicapped—
Fiction
ISBN 0-06-021357-4; 0-06-021360-4 (lib bdg);
0-06-440571-0 (pa) LC 92-18348

A Newbery Medal honor book, 1994

"A Laura Geringer book"

As he tries to come to terms with his mother's death,
Vernon finds solace in his growing relationship with the
neighborhood outcasts, an alcoholic and her retarded son

The author "is fast and blunt, and the conversations are
lively and true." Bull Cent Child Books

Racso and the rats of NIMH; illustrations
by Leonard Lubin. Harper & Row 1986 278p
il $15; lib bdg $14.89 (4 and up) **Fic**

1. Mice—Fiction 2. Rats—Fiction
ISBN 0-06-021361-2; 0-06-021362-0 (lib bdg)
LC 85-42634

Sequel to Mrs. Frisby and the rats of NIMH by Robert
C. O'Brien, entered below

This book "continues the NIMH saga with a focus on
the second rodent generation: Timothy, Mrs. Frisby's son,
and Racso, son of the rebel rat Jenner. On his way to classes at Thorn Valley, Timothy saves Racso's life but is himself severely injured. Both reach the Utopian colony only to
discover that the valley and surrounding farms are to be
turned into a tourist lake and campgrounds." SLJ

"The book is cleverly and gracefully built upon both the
philosophy of self-sufficiency and the details of the plot of
its predecessor. Given the difficulty of writing good sequels,
Racso and the Rats of NIMH is an outstanding success."
Horn Book

Another available title about the rats of NIMH is:
RT, Margaret, and the rats of NIMH (1990)

Trout summer. Holt & Co. 1995 234p
$15.95 (5 and up) **Fic**

1. Brothers and sisters—Fiction 2. Canoes and
canoeing—Fiction 3. Summer—Fiction
ISBN 0-8050-3933-3 LC 95-16381

"When their father leaves them, Shana, 13, and Cody,
12, move with their mother to Maryland. . . . The kids convince Mama that they should stay in an abandoned cabin
along the Leanna River for the summer. There they meet
Henry, an irascible old man who professes to be a ranger.
Ill and difficult but an excellent canoeist, he teaches Cody
his skills. . . . Shana's fast-paced, first-person narrative is
enhanced by Henry's quirky character and revealing dialogue. . . . Conly succeeds in telling a good story while dem-

Conly, Jane Leslie—*Continued*

onstrating the value of knowing and learning from someone who most people call 'crazy.'" SLJ

Conrad, Pam, 1947-1996

My Daniel. Harper & Row 1989 137p $13.95; lib bdg $13.89; pa $3.95 (5 and up)   **Fic**

1. Brothers and sisters—Fiction 2. Nebraska—Fiction
ISBN 0-06-021313-2; 0-06-021314-0 (lib bdg); 0-06-440309-2 (pa)   LC 88-19850

"When she's 80 years old, Julia Summerwaithe decides to visit her grandchildren, Ellie and Stevie, in New York City, for the first time. She has something important to show them; in the Natural History Museum is the dinosaur she and her brother discovered on their farm in Nebraska when they were young. But even more important to Julia than seeing the dinosaur is sharing her memories of the discovery and excavation with her grandchildren." SLJ

"Rendering scenes from both the past and the present with equal skill, Conrad is at the peak of her storytelling powers." Publ Wkly

Prairie songs; illustrations by Darryl S. Zudeck. Harper & Row 1985 167p il lib bdg $14.89; pa $3.95 (5 and up)   **Fic**

1. Frontier and pioneer life—Fiction 2. Nebraska—Fiction
ISBN 0-06-021337-X (lib bdg); 0-06-440206-1 (pa)   LC 85-42633

"The deterioration of the frail, young wife of a doctor who is unable to adapt to the harshness of prairie life is made more vivid because the reader views it through the eyes of an adolescent girl who lives nearby. Set in Nebraska at the turn of the century, this story is rich with detail about the beauty and hardships of pioneer life in the American West." Soc Educ

Stonewords; a ghost story. Harper & Row 1990 130p $14; lib bdg $14.89 (5 and up)   **Fic**

1. Ghost stories 2. Space and time—Fiction
ISBN 0-06-021315-9; 0-06-021316-7 (lib bdg)   LC 89-36382

Zoe discovers that her house is occupied by the ghost of an eleven-year-old girl, who carries her back to the day of her death in 1870 to try to alter that tragic event

"The supernatural and time-travel elements of the book are viscerally convincing, and the desperate neediness of both girls is fierce and real. The disquieting ending is in the richest gothic tradition, resolving one mystery only to reveal another even more frightening. This is a very scary book." Bull Cent Child Books

Cooper, Susan, 1935-

The boggart. Margaret K. McElderry Bks. 1993 196p $15; pa $3.95 (4-6)   **Fic**

1. Supernatural—Fiction   2. Scotland—Fiction
3. Canada—Fiction
ISBN 0-689-50576-0; 0-689-80173-4 (pa)   LC 92-15527

After visiting the castle in Scotland which her family has inherited and returning home to Canada, twelve-year-old Emily finds that she has accidentally brought back with her a boggart, an invisible and mischievous spirit with a fondness for practical jokes

"Using both electronics and theater as metaphors for magic, Cooper has extended the world of high fantasy into

contemporary children's lives through scenes superimposing the ordinary and the extraordinary." Bull Cent Child Books

Dawn of fear; illustrated by Margery Gill. Harcourt Brace Jovanovich 1970 157p il $14.95 (5 and up)   **Fic**

1. Great Britain—Fiction 2. World War, 1939-1945—Fiction
ISBN 0-15-266201-4

Also available in paperback from Aladdin

During World War II, three English boys' fearless unconcern with the enemy planes that flew daily on their way to bomb London, gradually underwent a change as the night raids grew more severe. This is the story of how, through the destruction—not by bombs—of the secret camp they were building, the boys came face-to-face with grown-up hatred, and then they knew the meaning of fear

"The characterization [is] deft and the dialogue natural [and] the relationship between the boys and a young man who is about to enter the Merchant Navy [is] particularly perceptive." Sutherland. The Best in Child Books

The grey king; illustrated by Michael Heslop. Atheneum Pubs. 1975 208p il $16; pa $3.95 (5 and up)   **Fic**

1. Good and evil—Fiction 2. Fantasy fiction 3. Wales—Fiction
ISBN 0-689-50029-7; 0-689-71089-5 (pa)

Also available Cornerstone Bks. large print edition

Awarded the Newbery Medal, 1976

"A Margaret K. McElderry book"

"In the fourth of Cooper's Arthurian fantasies [series entered below] Will Stanton, last and youngest of the Old Ones, the strange Welsh boy, Bran, and the sheep dogs and ghostly gray foxes of the mountains are drawn into the epic struggles of a world beyond time." SLJ

"So well-crafted that it stands as an entity in itself, the novel . . . is nevertheless strengthened by its relationship to the preceding volumes—as the individual legends within the Arthurian cycles take on deeper significance in the context of the whole. A spellbinding tour de force." Horn Book

Over sea, under stone; illustrated by Margery Gill. Harcourt Brace Jovanovich 1966 c1965 252p il $14.95 (5 and up)   **Fic**

1. Fantasy fiction 2. Good and evil—Fiction 3. Great Britain—Fiction
ISBN 0-15-259034-X

Also available in paperback from Macmillan

First published 1965 in the United Kingdom

In this series about the "conflict between the good of the Servants of Light and the evil of the Powers of Dark, Cooper has created an intricate fantasy. Ancient lore and mythology are believably interwoven into a modern setting. Ostensibly, the three Drew children, on a holiday in Cornwall, find an old map and, aided by their uncle, they begin a search for an ancient treasure linked with King Arthur. With each book, more reliance is placed on folklore and legend. There is much action and excitement included in the carefully wrought stories." Roman. Sequences

Other available titles in the Dark is rising series are:
The dark is rising (1973)
Greenwitch (1974)
Silver on the tree (1977)

Fourth title in series: The grey king, entered above

Seaward. Atheneum Pubs. 1983 167p $16; pa $3.95 (6 and up)   **Fic**

1. Fantasy fiction
ISBN 0-689-50275-3; 0-02-042190-7 (pa)
     LC 83-7055

Cooper, Susan, 1935-—*Continued*

"A Margaret K. McElderry book"

"Fleeing from unhappiness, two young people are cast into a different reality. . . . Cally and West are the two young people. Cally's ancestors may have been seals; West's were probably Shamana. Having nothing better to do, the two set off for the sea, where they expect to find their parents. As they travel, they are hounded by strange creatures. However, they survive and reach the sea where they learn that Life and Death are related by necessity and where they learn to embrace the reality from which they once fled." ALAN

"This metaphysical adventure has appeal for beginning fantasy readers. Cooper's fans however, will find only hints of the rich mythic and folkloric detail they have come to expect of her." SLJ

Corbett, Scott, 1913-

The lemonade trick; illustrated by Paul Galdone. Little, Brown 1960 103p il o.p.; Scholastic paperback available $3.50 (3-5)

Fic

1. Fantasy fiction
ISBN 0-590-32197-8 (pa)

"An Atlantic Monthly Press book"

A brew from his Feats O'Magic chemistry set, given to him by the mysterious Mrs. Graymalkin, changes Kerby into a perfect gentleman; unfortunately, it has the opposite effect on good boys

"An ingenious bit of magic has been mixed by [the author] and dashingly illustrated . . . to please eight-year-old readers . . . and even some a bit older who like a fairly simple story that doesn't take too long to read." N Y Her Trib Books

Cormier, Robert

Tunes for bears to dance to. Delacorte Press 1992 101p $15 (6 and up)

Fic

1. Prejudices—Fiction 2. Jews—Fiction 3. Good and evil—Fiction
ISBN 0-385-30818-3
LC 92-2734

Also available in paperback from Dell

Eleven-year-old Henry escapes his family's problems by watching the woodcarving of Mr. Levine, an elderly Holocaust survivor, but when Henry is manipulated by his employer, Mr. Hairston, into betraying his friend he comes to know true evil

"A powerful book for discussion with readers of all ages. Henry's loss of innocence is a dramatic event, but how he reacts to this event is thought-provoking." Voice Youth Advocates

Coville, Bruce

Jennifer Murdley's toad; a magic shop book; illustrated by Gary A. Lippincott. Harcourt Brace Jovanovich 1992 156p il $16.95 (4-6)

Fic

1. Toads—Fiction 2. Fantasy fiction
ISBN 0-15-200745-8
LC 91-33811

Also available in paperback from Pocket Bks.

"Jane Yolen books"

When an ordinary looking fifth grader purchases a talking toad, she embarks on a series of extraordinary adventures

"This light, fast-paced fantasy has touches of humor (at times low comedy), an implicit moral, and a hint that Jennifer may be in for more adventures." Booklist

Jeremy Thatcher, dragon hatcher; a magic shop book; illustrated by Gary A. Lippincott. Jane Yolen Bks. 1991 148p il $16.95 (4-6)

Fic

1. Dragons—Fiction 2. Fantasy fiction
ISBN 0-15-200748-2
LC 90-5101

Also available in paperback from Pocket Bks.

Small for his age but artistically talented, twelve-year-old Jeremy Thatcher unknowingly buys a dragon's egg

This is "right on target. Not only is the story involving but the reader can really get a feeling for Jeremy as a person. Coville's technique of combining the real world with a fantasy one works well in this story." Voice Youth Advocates

Creech, Sharon

Walk two moons. HarperCollins Pubs. 1994 280p $16; lib bdg $15.89 (6 and up)

Fic

1. Death—Fiction 2. Grandparents—Fiction 3. Family life—Fiction 4. Friendship—Fiction
ISBN 0-06-023334-6; 0-06-023337-0 (lib bdg)
LC 93-31277

Awarded the Newbery Medal, 1995

After her mother leaves home suddenly, thirteen-year-old Sal and her grandparents take a car trip retracing her mother's route. Along the way, Sal recounts the story of her friend Phoebe, whose mother also left

"An engaging story of love and loss, told with humor and suspense. . . . A richly layered novel about real and metaphorical journeys." SLJ

Cresswell, Helen

Ordinary Jack. Macmillan 1977 195p $14.95 (5 and up)

Fic

1. Family life—Fiction
ISBN 0-02-725540-9
LC 77-5146

Eleven-year-old Jack, the only "ordinary" member of the talented and eccentric Bagthorpe family, concocts a scheme to distinguish himself as a modern-day prophet

Another available title about the Bagthorpe family is: Bagthorpes v. the world (1979)

Titles in the series: Absolute zero (1978); Bagthorpes abroad (1984); Bagthorpes haunted (1985); Bagthorpes liberated (1989); Bagthorpes unlimited (1978) o.p.

Crew, Linda

Nekomah Creek; illustrated by Charles Robinson. Delacorte Press 1991 191p il $14; pa $3.50 (4-6)

Fic

1. Family life—Fiction 2. School stories
ISBN 0-385-30442-0; 0-440-40788-5 (pa)
LC 90-49119

Nine-year-old Robby loves his noisy and somewhat unconventional family, but unwanted attention from a counselor and a bully at school make him self-conscious about just how unconventional his family might look to outsiders

"The situations are hilarious, all the while dealing with concerns typical of the targeted audience." SLJ

Another available title about Robby and his family is: Nekomah Creek Christmas (1994)

Curtis, Christopher Paul

The Watsons go to Birmingham—1963; a novel. Delacorte Press 1995 210p $14.95 (4 and up)   **Fic**

1. African Americans—Fiction 2. Family life—Fiction 3. Prejudices—Fiction

ISBN 0-385-32175-9   LC 95-7091

A Newbery Medal honor book, 1996

The ordinary interactions and everyday routines of the Watsons, an African American family living in Flint, Michigan, are drastically changed after they go to visit Grandma in Alabama in the summer of 1963

"Curtis's ability to switch from fun and funky to pinpoint-accurate psychological imagery works unusually well. . . . Ribald humor, sly sibling digs, and a totally believable child's view of the world will make this book an instant hit." SLJ

Cushman, Karen

Catherine, called Birdy. Clarion Bks. 1994 169p $14.95 (6 and up)   **Fic**

1. Middle Ages—Fiction 2. Great Britain—Fiction

ISBN 0-395-68186-3   LC 93-23333

Also available in paperback from HarperCollins

A Newbery Medal honor book, 1995

The fourteen-year-old daughter of an English country knight keeps a journal in which she records the events of her life, particularly her longing for adventures beyond the usual role of women and her efforts to avoid being married off

"In the process of telling the routines of her young life, Birdy lays before readers a feast of details about medieval England. . . . Superb historical fiction." SLJ

The midwife's apprentice. Clarion Bks. 1995 122p $10.95 (6 and up) •   **Fic**

1. Middle Ages—Fiction 2. Midwives—Fiction 3. Great Britain—Fiction

ISBN 0-395-69229-6   LC 94-13792

Awarded the Newbery Medal, 1996

In medieval England, a nameless, homeless girl is taken in by a sharp-tempered midwife, and in spite of obstacles and hardship, eventually gains the three things she most wants: a full belly, a contented heart, and a place in this world

"Earthy humor, the foibles of humans both high and low, and a fascinating mix of superstition and genuinely helpful herbal remedies attached to childbirth make this a truly delightful introduction to a world seldom seen in children's literature." SLJ

Dahl, Roald

The BFG; pictures by Quentin Blake. Farrar, Straus & Giroux 1982 219p il $10.95 (4-6)   **Fic**

1. Giants—Fiction 2. Orphans—Fiction

ISBN 0-374-30469-6   LC 82-15548

Also available in hardcover from Knopf and in paperback from Penguin Bks.; Spanish language edition also available

Kidsnatched from her orphanage by a BFG (Big Friendly Giant), who spends his life blowing happy dreams to children, Sophie concocts with him a plan to save the world from nine other man-gobbling cannybull giants

This "is a book not all adults will like, but most kids will. . . . Highly unusual, often hilarious, and occasionally vulgar, even grisly." Booklist

James and the giant peach; illustrated by Nancy Ekholm Burkert. Knopf 1961 118p il $16; lib bdg $16.99 (4-6)   **Fic**

1. Fantasy fiction

ISBN 0-394-81282-4; 0-394-91282-9 (lib bdg)

Also available Cornerstone Bks. large print edition and in paperback from Puffin Bks.; Spanish language edition also available

After the death of his parents, little James is forced to live with Aunt Sponge and Aunt Spike, two cruel old harpies. A magic potion causes the growing of a giant-sized peach on a puny peach tree. James sneaks inside the peach and finds a new world of insects. With his new family, James heads for many adventures

"A 'juicy' fantasy, 'dripping' with humor and imagination." Commonweal

Matilda; illustrations by Quentin Blake. Viking Kestrel 1988 240p il $15.99; pa $5.99 (4-6)   **Fic**

1. School stories

ISBN 0-670-82439-9; 0-14-034294-X (pa)

LC 88-40312

Also available Cornerstone Bks. large print edition and Everyman's library edition from Knopf; Spanish language edition also available

"Matilda knows how to be extremely and creatively naughty—lining her father's hat with super glue, putting her mother's hair bleach in her father's hair tonic bottle, for example. This streak of imaginative wickedness not only allows her to make a loyal friend, Lavender, but also to wreak revenge on her unloving parents, defeat the fiendish headmistress, Miss Turnbull, and return her victimized teacher, the enchanting Miss Honey, to her rightful place in the world." N Y Times Book Rev

"Dahl has written another fun and funny book with a child's perspective on an adult world. As usual, Blake's comical sketches are the perfect complement to the satirical humor." SLJ

Dalgliesh, Alice, 1893-1979

The bears on Hemlock Mountain; illustrated by Helen Sewell. Scribner 1990 c1952 unp il $13.95; pa $3.95 (1-4)   **Fic**

1. Bears—Fiction

ISBN 0-684-19169-5; 0-689-71604-4 (pa)

LC 89-27651

A Newbery Medal honor book, 1953

A reissue of the title first published 1952

"This is the story of a little boy sent by his mother to borrow an iron from an aunt who lived on the other side of Hemlock Mountain—really only a hill. Jonathan's mother did not believe that there were bears on Hemlock Mountain but Jonathan did. . . . The two-color, somewhat stylized illustrations seem right for the story." Booklist

"Jonathan's adventure is a tall tale passed down in Pennsylvania, which might have happened to a pioneer boy almost anywhere. Full of suspense and humor, it will make good reading aloud." N Y Her Trib Books

The courage of Sarah Noble; illustrations by Leonard Weisgard. Scribner 1986 c1954 52p il $14; pa $4.95 (2-4)   **Fic**

1. Frontier and pioneer life—Fiction 2. Indians of North America—Fiction 3. Connecticut—Fiction

ISBN 0-684-18830-9; 0-689-71540-4 (pa)

LC 54-5922

Also available Spanish language edition

A Newbery Medal honor book, 1955

Dalgliesh, Alice, 1893-1979—*Continued*

"Sarah, though only eight, cooked for her father while he made a new home for the family in the Connecticut wilderness of 1707. When Mr. Noble returned to Massachusetts for the rest of the family, leaving Sarah with a friendly Indian, her courage was sorely tested." Hodges. Books for Elem Sch Libr

"Based on a true incident in Connecticut history—the founding of New Milford—this story is one to be long remembered for its beautiful simplicity and dignity. Leonard Weisgard's pictures add just the right sense of background." N Y Times Book Rev

Danziger, Paula, 1944-

Amber Brown is not a crayon; illustrated by Tony Ross. Putnam 1994 80p il $12.95 (2-4)
Fic

1. Friendship—Fiction 2. Moving—Fiction 3. School stories

ISBN 0-399-22509-9   LC 92-34678

Also available in paperback from Little, Brown; Spanish language edition also available

The year she is in the third grade is a sad time for Amber because her best friend Justin is getting ready to move to a distant state

"Ross's black-and-white sketches throughout add humor and keep the pages turning swiftly. Danzinger reaches out to a younger audience in this funny, touching slice of third-grade life, told in the voice of a feisty, lovable heroine." SLJ

Other available titles about Amber Brown are:
Amber Brown goes fourth (1995)
You can't eat your chicken pox, Amber Brown (1995)

The cat ate my gymsuit. Delacorte Press 1974 147p $14.95; pa $3.99 (5 and up)
Fic

1. School stories 2. Teachers—Fiction

ISBN 0-385-28183-8; 0-440-41612-4 (pa)

Marcy Lewis is bored by school and tyrannized by her father. With the help of an unconventional teacher, she conquers many of her feelings of insecurity and, in turn, rallies the student body in support of the teacher who was fired because of her behavior

"A sad-funny novel. . . . Ms. Danziger has an attractive style; her prose sparkles with wit and originality." Publ Wkly

Everyone else's parents said yes. Delacorte Press 1989 115p $13.95 (4-6)   Fic

1. Family life—Fiction 2. School stories

ISBN 0-385-29805-6   LC 88-37540

Also available in paperback from Dell

Matthew cannot resist the temptation to play practical jokes on his older sister and all the girls in his class at school, so by the time of the big party for his eleventh birthday they have all declared war on him

"Danziger does display a keen sensitivity to the typical concerns and sense of humor of her target audience. Brisk in style and pacing, this lighthearted offering is sure to be popular." Booklist

Other available titles about Matthew are:
Earth to Matthew (1991)
Make like a tree and leave (1990)
Not for a billion gazillion dollars (1992)

There's a bat in bunk five. Delacorte Press 1980 150p hardcover o.p. paperback available $3.99 (5 and up)   Fic

1. Camps—Fiction

ISBN 0-440-40098-8 (pa)   LC 80-15581

"A thinner Marcy than appeared in 'The Cat ate My Gymsuit' [entered above] here eagerly accepts an invitation from Ms. Finney, her favorite teacher, to work as a counselor-in-training at a summer camp. Though wanting to do a good job, particulrly in reaching the abrasive and uncooperative Ginger, Marcy also indulges in a romance with fellow camper Ted and spends time sorting out her own inner conflicts." Booklist

"In some ways this is the usual camping story of pranks, bunkmates, adjustment to separation from parents, etc. This doesn't, however, follow a formula plot; it has depth in the relationships and characterizations; and it's written with vigor and humor." Bull Cent Child Books

De Angeli, Marguerite Lofft, 1889-1987

The door in the wall; by Marguerite de Angeli. Doubleday 1989 c1949 120p il $15.95 (4-6)   Fic

1. Physically handicapped children—Fiction 2. Great Britain—Fiction 3. Middle Ages—Fiction

ISBN 0-385-07283-X

Also available in paperback from Dell; Spanish language edition also available

Awarded the Newbery Medal, 1950

First published 1949

Robin, a crippled boy in fourteenth-century England, proves his courage and earns recognition from the King

"An enthralling and inspiring tale of triumph over handicap. Unusually beautiful illustrations, full of authentic detail, combine with the text to make life in England during the Middle Ages come alive." N Y Times Book Rev

DeClements, Barthe, 1920-

6th grade can really kill you. Viking Kestrel 1985 146p $12.95; pa $3.99 (5 and up)
Fic

1. Learning disabilities—Fiction 2. School stories

ISBN 0-670-80656-0; 0-14-037130-3 (pa)

                                           LC 85-40382

Also available Cornerstone Bks. large print edition

"Helen dreads the first day in sixth grade. Good in math and gifted on the pitcher's mound, she is a nonreader diagnosed as a behavior problem. Against the slice-of-life background of a skating party, pierced ears and overnights at friend Louise's, Helen loses the battle with the printed word." SLJ

This is "a story that amply compensates for its uneven pace by the natural quality of the relationships and the dialogue in the classroom environment and by the insight gained through the first person treatment of a learning disability." Bull Cent Child Books

DeFelice, Cynthia C.

Weasel; [by] Cynthia DeFelice. Macmillan 1990 119p $13.95 (4 and up)   Fic

1. Frontier and pioneer life—Fiction 2. Ohio—Fiction

ISBN 0-02-726457-2   LC 89-37794

Also available in paperback from Avon Bks.

Alone in the Ohio frontier wilderness in the winter of 1839 while his father is recovering from an injury, eleven-year-old Nathan runs afoul of the renegade killer known as Weasel and makes a surprising discovery about the concept

DeFelice, Cynthia C.—*Continued*

of revenge

"Despite its clear point of view, the book is ideal for discussion and debate—a fine choice as a novel to teach in a literature-based curriculum, where children can be stimulated to think about moral choices and about some of the unhappy truths of frontier settlement." Booklist

DeJong, Meindert, 1906-1991

The house of sixty fathers; pictures by Maurice Sendak. Harper & Row 1956 189p il lib bdg $15.75; pa $3.95 (4-6) **Fic**

1. Sino-Japanese Conflict, 1937-1945—Fiction
2. China—Fiction

ISBN 0-06-021481-3 (lib bdg); 0-06-440200-2 (pa)

A Newbery Medal honor book, 1957

This story is set in "China during the early days of the Japanese invasion. Tien Pao, a small Chinese boy, and his family fled inland on a sampan when the Japanese attacked their coastal village, but Tien Pao was separated from his parents during a storm and swept back down the river on the sampan. . . . [The author paints] starkly realistic word pictures that give the reader the full impact of the terror, pain, hunger and finally the joy that Tien Pao knew during his search for his family." Bull Cent Child Books

The wheel on the school; pictures by Maurice Sendak. Harper & Row 1954 298p il $15; lib bdg $14.89; pa $3.95 (4-6) **Fic**

1. Storks—Fiction 2. School stories 3. Netherlands—Fiction

ISBN 0-06-021585-2; 0-06-021586-0 (lib bdg); 0-06-440021-2 (pa)

Also available Spanish language edition

Awarded the Newbery Medal, 1955

"Six Dutch children encouraged by a sensitive schoolmaster search for a wheel to place on the schoolhouse roof as a nesting place for storks. Their efforts and ultimate success lead to better understanding among the children and closer ties to older members of the community." Read Ladders for Hum Relat

"This author goes deeply into the heart of childhood and has written a moving story, filled with suspense and distinguished for the quality of its writing." Child Books Too Good To Miss

Delton, Judy

Angel's mother's wedding; illustrated by Margot Apple. Houghton Mifflin 1987 166p il $14.95 (3-5) **Fic**

1. Weddings—Fiction 2. Family life—Fiction

ISBN 0-395-44470-5 LC 87-16937

"Angel's capacity for worry, added to her friend Edna's knowledge of how a wedding should be properly organized, leads to confusions and misunderstandings that reach almost epic proportions. . . . Humor, affection, and action narrowly skirting disaster mark each chapter in the progress from bridal shower to wedding march. Angel, her family, and friends are all pleasantly ordinary folk with a singular capacity to bring near-chaos into the normally quiet routines and celebrations of their daily life." Horn Book

Other available titles about Angel are:

Angel in charge (1985)

Angel's mother's baby (1989)

Angel's mother's boyfriend (1986)

Back yard Angel (1983)

Dickens, Charles, 1812-1870

A Christmas carol (4 and up) **Fic**

1. Christmas—Fiction 2. Ghost stories 3. Great Britain—Fiction

Also available Spanish language edition

Some editions are:

Holiday House $18.95 Illustrated by Trina Schart Hyman (ISBN 0-8234-0486-2)

Knopf (Everyman's library children's classics) $13.95 Illustrated by Arthur Rackham (ISBN 0-679-43639-1)

Margaret K. McElderry Bks. $19.95 Illustrated by Quentin Blake (ISBN 0-689-80213-7)

Picture Bk. Studio $19.95 Illustrated by Lisbeth Zwerger (ISBN 0-88708-069-3)

Written in 1843

"This Christmas story of nineteenth century England has delighted young and old for generations. In it, a miser, Scrooge, through a series of dreams, finds the true Christmas spirit. . . . The story ends with the much-quoted cry of Tiny Tim, the crippled son of Bob Cratchit, whom Scrooge now aids: 'God bless us, every one!'" Haydn. Thesaurus of Book Dig

"There is perhaps no story in English literature better known and loved, or one that carries a more potent appeal to the Christmas sentiment." Springfield Repub

Dodge, Mary Mapes, 1830-1905

Hans Brinker; or, The silver skates (4 and up) **Fic**

1. Ice skating—Fiction 2. Netherlands—Fiction

Various editions available

First published 1865

A new friend gives Hans and his sister Gretel enough money for one pair of ice skates, so Hans insists that Gretel enter the grand competition for silver skates, while he seeks the great Doctor who consents to try to restore their father's memory

Donahue, John, 1951-

An island far from home. Carolrhoda Bks. 1995 179p lib bdg $19.95 (4 and up) **Fic**

1. United States—History—1861-1865, Civil War—Fiction

ISBN 0-87614-859-3 LC 94-9444

"Adventures in time books"

The twelve-year-old son of a Union army doctor killed during the fighting in Fredericksburg comes to understand the meaning of war and the fine line between friends and enemies when he begins corresponding with a young Confederate prisoner of war

"A page-turner full of emotional turmoil that's wonderful for discussion groups and extremely accessible to reluctant historical fiction readers." SLJ

Dorris, Michael

Morning Girl. Hyperion Bks. for Children 1992 74p $12.95; lib bdg $12.89; pa $3.50 (4-6) **Fic**

1. Taino Indians—Fiction 2. Brothers and sisters—Fiction 3. America—Exploration—Fiction

ISBN 1-56282-284-5; 1-56282-285-3 (lib bdg); 0-56282-661-1 (pa) LC 92-52989

Twelve year old Morning Girl, a Taino Indian who loves the day, and her younger brother Star Boy, who loves the night, take turns describing their life on a Bahamian island in 1492; in Morning Girl's last narrative, she witnesses the arrival of the first Europeans to her world

Dorris, Michael—*Continued*

"The author uses a lyrical, yet easy-to-follow, style to place these compelling characters in historical context. . . . Dorris does a superb job of showing that family dynamics are complicated, regardless of time and place. . . . A touching glimpse into the humanity that connects us all." Horn Book

Du Bois, William Pène, 1916-1993

The twenty-one balloons; written and illustrated by William Pène Du Bois. Viking 1947 179p il $15.99; pa $3.99 (5 and up)
Fic

1. Balloons—Fiction

ISBN 0-670-73441-1; 0-14-032097-0 (pa)

Awarded the Newbery Medal, 1948

"Professor Sherman set off on a flight across the Pacific in a giant balloon, but three weeks later the headlines read 'Professor Sherman in wrong ocean with too many balloons.' This book is concerned with the professor's explanation of this phenomenon. His account of his one stopover on the island of Krakotoa which blew up with barely a minute to spare to allow time for his escape, is the highlight of this hilarious narrative." Ont Libr Rev

Eager, Edward, 1911-1964

Half magic; drawings by N. M. Bodecker. Harcourt Brace & Co. 1954 217p il $15, pa $4.95 (4-6)
Fic

1. Fantasy fiction

ISBN 0-15-233078-X; 0-15-233081-X (pa)

"Three sisters, a brother and widowed mother made up the family. Jane, the eldest, found a magic charm [an ancient coin] which granted half of any wish; after finding that out, and barring accidents, the children wished for twice as much as they wanted. The charm made for a week of adventures." N Y Times Book Rev

"The chief effect of such a book is humor, arising from the ridiculous yet logical situations. . . . [It is] a book whose total contribution is one of fun and relaxation." Saturday Rev

Other available titles in this series are:
Knight's castle (1956)
Magic by the lake (1957)
The time garden (1958)

Seven-day magic; illustrated by N. M. Bodecker. Harcourt Brace & Co. 1962 156p il hardcover o.p. paperback available $5 (4-6)
Fic

1. Fantasy fiction

ISBN 0-15-272916-X (pa)

Also available in hardcover from P. Smith

"A sophisticated fantasy in which five children find a magic book that describes themselves, and realize that they can create their own magic by wishing with the book. In one episode . . . they disrupt a telecast by silencing all the cast except for one member of a male quartet. The children are lively and a bit precocious. . . . [The book has] humor, and some fresh and imaginative situations." Bull Cent Child Books

Eckert, Allan W.

Incident at Hawk's Hill; with illustrations by John Schoenherr. Little, Brown 1971 173p il hardcover o.p. paperback available $5.95 (6 and up)
Fic

1. Badgers—Fiction 2. Wilderness survival—Fiction 3. Saskatchewan—Fiction

ISBN 0-316-20948-1 (pa)

A Newbery Medal honor book, 1972

This account of an actual incident in Saskatchewan at the turn of the century tells of six-year-old Ben Macdonald, more attuned to animals than to people, who gets lost on the prairie and is nurtured by a female badger for two months before being found. Although a strange bond continues between the boy and the badger, the parents' understanding of their son and his communication with them improve as a result of the bizarre experience

"A very deeply moving, well written book." Jr Bookshelf

Ehrlich, Amy, 1942-

The Snow Queen; [by] Hans Christian Andersen; pictures by Susan Jeffers; retold by Amy Ehrlich. Dial Bks. for Young Readers 1982 40p il lib bdg $12.89; pa $4.95 (2-4)
Fic

1. Fairy tales

ISBN 0-8037-8029-X (lib bdg); 0-8037-0692-8 (pa)
LC 82-70199

"A smooth and simplified retelling of Andersen's classic story of the power of love, this is in oversize format that affords the artist an opportunity for stunning paintings, soft and romantic in hues and muted but strong in composition and in the use of imaginative details, often sensuously textured. While the book can be used for reading aloud to younger children, the length of the story and the concept of love's transmuting power indicate the middle grades as prime audience." Bull Cent Child Books

Ellis, Sarah, 1952-

Next-door neighbors. Margaret K. McElderry Bks. 1990 154p $13.95 (4 and up)
Fic

1. Friendship—Fiction 2. Family life—Fiction 3. Canada—Fiction

ISBN 0-689-50495-0
LC 89-37923

Her family's move to a new town in Canada leaves shy twelve-year-old Peggy feeling lonely and uncomfortable, until she befriends the unconventional George and the Chinese servant of her imperious neighbor Mrs. Manning

"The theme of prejudicial scapegoating is confidently woven into an essentially optimistic school-and-family story, with neither characterization nor plot succumbing to didacticism." Bull Cent Child Books

Pick-up sticks. Margaret K. McElderry Bks. 1992 124p $15 (5 and up)
Fic

1. Mothers and daughters—Fiction 2. Moving—Fiction

ISBN 0-689-50550-7
LC 91-26585

Also available in paperback from Puffin Bks.

First published 1991 in Canada

Thirteen-year-old Polly's rebellion against her unmarried, fiercely independent mother comes to a head when they must find a new apartment

Ellis's writing is lean and child-centered; her insights are perceptive and have an unmistakable ring of honesty." Horn Book

Enright, Elizabeth, 1909-1968

Gone-Away Lake; illustrated by Beth and Joe Krush. Harcourt Brace & Co. 1957 192p il hardcover o.p. paperback available $5 (4-6)   **Fic**

ISBN 0-15-231649-3 (pa)

Also available in hardcover from P. Smith

A Newbery Medal honor book, 1958

Tale of an exciting summer when Portia, "beginning to be eleven," and her brother Foster, aged six-and-a-half, went to visit an uncle and aunt in the country. On one of Portia's expeditions with her slightly older cousin Julian they discovered a swamp which had once been a lake, with houses, mostly unoccupied, where the summer people had lived. Life became a happy thing from that moment for the rest of the summer

"Excellent writing, clear in setting of scene and details of nature, and strong in appeal for children." Horn Book

Another available title about Gone-Away Lake is:
Return to Gone-Away Lake (1961)

Erickson, Russell E.

A toad for Tuesday; pictures by Lawrence Di Fiori. Lothrop, Lee & Shepard Bks. 1974 63p il lib bdg $12.93 (2-4)   **Fic**

1. Toads—Fiction 2. Owls—Fiction 3. Mice—Fiction 4. Friendship—Fiction
ISBN 0-688-51569-X

Also available in paperback from Morrow

Warton the toad sets out on skis to visit his aunt during the winter. After rescuing a mouse from danger, he is captured by an owl who threatens to eat him in five days. During this interval, events occur which create friendship between the toad, the owl and a group of mice

The book "stresses friendship, caring for and helping others without motivational self-gain. . . . Real feelings are expressed in this story. Fine illustrations." Child Book Rev Serv

Another available title about Warton and Morton is:
Warton and the contest (1968)

Estes, Eleanor, 1906-1988

Ginger Pye. Harcourt Brace & Co. 1951 250p il $14.95; pa $5 (4-6)   **Fic**

1. Dogs—Fiction
ISBN 0-15-230930-6; 0-15-230933-0 (pa)

Awarded the Newbery Medal, 1952

The Pyes lived in the little New England town of Cranbury. There was Mr. Pye, a famous ornithologist, his pretty young wife, their two children Jerry and Rachel, and Gracie the cat. Later there was the dog Ginger. The story is about the loss of Ginger, and his return to his beloved family, through the cleverness of Uncle Benny, aged three

"Not many writers can give us the mind and heart of a child as Eleanor Estes can. . . . [She] has illustrated [the book] with her own drawings—vivid, amusing sketches that point up and confirm the atmosphere of the story. It is a book to read and reread." Saturday Rev

Another available title about the Pye family is:
Pinky Pye (1958)

The hundred dresses; illustrated by Louis Slobodkin. Harcourt Brace & Co. 1944 80p il $15; pa $5 (4-6)   **Fic**

ISBN 0-15-237374-8; 0-15-642350-2 (pa)

Also available Spanish language edition

A Newbery Medal honor book, 1945

"The 100 dresses are just dream dresses, pictures Wanda Petronski has drawn, but she describes them in self-defense as she appears daily in the same faded blue dress. Not until Wanda, snubbed and unhappy, moves away leaving her pictures at school for an art contest, do her classmates realize their cruelty." Books for Deaf Child

"Written with great simplicity it reveals, in a measure, the pathos of human relationships and the suffering of those who are different. Mr. Slobodkin's water-colors interpret the mood of the story and fulfill the quality of the text." N Y Public Libr

The Moffats; illustrated by Louis Slobodkin. Harcourt Brace & Co. 1941 290p il $14.95 (4-6)   **Fic**

1. Family life—Fiction
ISBN 0-15-255095-X

"The Moffats—Mama and her four children—have a fun-filled and satisfying life in spite of being poor. Their little house on New Dollar Street in Cranbury, Connecticut, is the scene of constant activity and surprises. A captivating family story with highly individual characters. Each chapter is a separate episode, suitable for reading aloud." Hodges. Books for Elem Sch Libr

Other available titles about the Moffats are:
The Moffat Museum (1983)
Rufus M. (1943)

Farjeon, Eleanor, 1881-1965

The glass slipper; Illustrated by Ernest H. Shepard. Viking 1956 c1955 187p il o.p.; HarperCollins Pubs. paperback available $4.95 (3-6)   **Fic**

1. Fairy tales
ISBN 0-06-440561-3 (pa)

Also available in hardcover from Amereon and Buccaneer Bks.

First published 1955 in the United Kingdom

"One of the most famous of fairy tales in the Western world—the Cinderella story—is here retold by a talented storyteller. . . . The result is an expanded version—almost novel length—alive with amusing characters and rich in background detail." N Y Times Book Rev

Farley, Walter, 1915-1989

The Black Stallion; illustrated by Keith Ward. Random House 1941 275p il lib bdg $13.99; pa $4.99 (4 and up)   **Fic**

1. Horses—Fiction
ISBN 0-394-90601-2 (lib bdg); 0-679-81343-8 (pa)

A boy and a wild black stallion, the only survivors from a shipwreck, live for a time on an uninhabited island, and somehow manage to exist until they are rescued. Back in the United States the boy and a retired jockey tame the horse and race him to the entire satisfaction of all concerned

Other available titles about the Black Stallion are:
The Black Stallion and Flame (1960)
The Black Stallion and Satan (1949)
The Black Stallion and the girl (1971)
The Black Stallion challenged! (1964)
The Black Stallion legend (1983)
The Black Stallion mystery (1957)
The Black Stallion returns (1945)
The Black Stallion's Blood Bay colt (c1950)
The Black Stallion's courage (1956)
The Black Stallion's filly (1952)
The Black Stallion's ghost (1969)

Farley, Walter, 1915-1989—*Continued*
Son of the Black Stallion (1947)
The young Black Stallion (1989)

Farmer, Nancy, 1941-
The Ear, the Eye, and the Arm; a novel.
Orchard Bks. 1994 311p $18.95; lib bdg
$18.99 (6 and up)   **Fic**

1. Science fiction 2. Zimbabwe—Fiction
ISBN 0-531-06829-3; 0-531-08679-8 (lib bdg)
                                             LC 93-11814
Also available in paperback from Puffin Bks.
A Newbery Medal honor book, 1995
"A Richard Jackson book"
In 2194 in Zimbabwe, General Matsika's three children
Tendai, Rita, and Kuda, are kidnapped and put to work in
a plastic mine, while three mutant detectives named The
Ear, the Eye and the Arm use their special powers to search
for them
"Throughout the story, it's the thrilling adventure that
will grab readers, who will also like the comic, tender char-
acterizations." Booklist

Feiffer, Jules
The man in the ceiling; entirely written and
illustrated by Jules Feiffer. HarperCollins
Pubs. 1993 185p il $15; lib bdg $14.89; pa
$5.95 (4-6)   **Fic**

1. Artists—Fiction
ISBN 0-06-205035-4; 0-06-205036-2 (lib bdg);
0-06-205907-6 (pa)   LC 92-39953
"Michael Di Capua books"
"With his quest to invent the best-ever superhero, 10-
year-old cartoonist Jimmy Jiggett bids for immortality—or
at least some attention from his type-A father." Publ Wkly
"Feiffer's deft depiction of moments of family dysfunc-
tion are wickedly funny. His rough-drawn, signature cartoon
illustrations are charged with an energy that matches the
briskly paced text." Booklist

Fenner, Carol
Yolonda's genius. Margaret K. McElderry
Bks. 1995 211p $17 (4-6)   **Fic**

1. Brothers and sisters—Fiction 2. Musicians—Fiction
3. African Americans—Fiction
ISBN 0-689-80001-0   LC 94-46962
A Newbery Medal honor book, 1996
After moving from Chicago to Grand River, Michigan,
fifth grader Yolonda, big and strong for her age, determines
to prove that her younger brother is not a slow learner but
a true musical genius
"In this brisk and appealing narrative, readers are intro-
duced to a close-knit, middle-class African-American family.
. . . [This novel] is suffused with humor and spirit." Horn
Book

Field, Rachel, 1894-1942
Hitty: her first hundred years; with
illustrations by Dorothy P. Lathrop.
Macmillan 1929 207p il $14.95 (4 and up)
                                                     Fic

1. Dolls—Fiction
ISBN 0-02-734840-7
Also available in paperback from Dell

Awarded the Newbery Medal, 1930
"Hitty, a doll of real character carved from a block of
mountain ash, writes a story of her eventful life from the
security of an antique-shop window which she shares with
Theobold, a rather over-bearing cat. . . . The illustrations by
Dorothy P. Lathrop are the happiest extension of the text."
Cleveland Public Libr

Fine, Anne
Alias Madame Doubtfire. Little, Brown
1988 199p o.p.; Bantam Bks. paperback
available $3.99 (6 and up)   **Fic**

1. Family life—Fiction 2. Sex role—Fiction
3. Divorce—Fiction
ISBN 0-553-56615-6 (pa)   LC 87-30195
Also available Spanish language edition
"Joy Street books"
Miranda's three children thoroughly enjoy their huge,
overdressed baby sitter/cleaning woman who is actually
their father in disguise, and they dread the day when their
mother discovers Madame Doubtfire is really her ex-
husband
"Miranda, at first seeming a cold career woman, is equally revealed as a mother who works terribly hard at her job
and family. This novel is a special combination of high humor and genuine pain (the first often expressing the second), showing, ironically and perfectly, in this 'broken
home' the bonds of shared history and love that keep a
family together." Bull Cent Child Books

Flour babies. Little, Brown 1994 c1992 178p
$14.95 (6 and up)   **Fic**

1. School stories 2. Parent and child—Fiction
ISBN 0-316-28319-3   LC 93-35698
Also available in paperback from Dell
First published 1992 in the United Kingdom
When his class of underachievers is assigned to spend
three torturous weeks taking care of their own "babies" in
the form of bags of flour, Simon makes amazing discoveries
about himself while coming to terms with his long-absent
father
"There's no mistaking Fine's underlying theme (she's not
a bit subtle), but its couched in such splendid, trenchant
humor—spiffy one-liners, funny, well-devised characters,
and hilarious situations—that the story simply flies along."
Booklist

Fitzgerald, John D., 1907-1988
The Great Brain; illustrated by Mercer
Mayer. Dial Bks. for Young Readers 1967
175p lib bdg $11.89 (4 and up)   **Fic**

1. Utah—Fiction
ISBN 0-8037-3076-4
Also available Cornerstone Bks. large print edition and
in paperback from Dell
"The Great Brain was Tom Dennis ('T.D.') Fitzgerald,
age ten, of Adenville, Utah; the time, 1896. . . . This auto-
biographical yarn is spun by his brother John Dennis
('J.D.'), age seven . . . who can tell stories about himself
and his family with enough tall-tale exaggeration to catch
the imagination." Horn Book
Other available titles about the Great Brain are:
The Great Brain at the academy (1972)
The Great Brain does it again (1975)
The Great Brain is back (1995)
The Great Brain reforms (1973)
Me and my little brain (1971)
More adventures of the Great Brain (1969)
The return of the Great Brain (1974)

Fitzhugh, Louise, 1928-1974

Harriet the spy; written and illustrated by Louise Fitzhugh. Harper & Row 1964 298p il $16; lib bdg $15.89; pa $3.95 (4 and up)   Fic

1. School stories
ISBN 0-06-021910-6; 0-06-021911-4 (lib bdg); 0-06-440331-9 (pa)
Also available Cornerstone Bks. large print edition

"Harriet roams her Manhattan neighborhood spying on everyone who interests her and writing down her opinions in a notebook. When fellow sixth-graders find her notes and read her caustic remarks about them, she is ostracized until she finds a way to make a place for herself in the school." Hodges. Books for Elem Sch Libr

"A very, very funny and a very, very affective story; the characterizations are marvelously shrewd, the pictures of urban life and of the power structure of the sixth grade class are realistic." Bull Cent Child Books

Another available title about Harriet is:
The long secret (1965)

Fleischman, Paul

The borning room. HarperCollins Pubs. 1991 101p $14.95; lib bdg $13.89; pa $3.95 (6 and up)   Fic

1. Frontier and pioneer life—Fiction 2. Ohio—Fiction
ISBN 0-06-023762-7; 0-06-023785-6 (lib bdg); 0-06-447099-7 (pa)   LC 91-4432
"A Charlotte Zolotow book"

Lying at the end of her life in the room where she was born in 1851, Georgina remembers what it was like to grow up on the Ohio frontier

"Fleischman successfully tackles many important themes and once again gifts readers with writing lush with similes, metaphors, and allusions, so subtly woven into the mesh of the narrative that they enrich without distracting. A memorable novel, rich and resonant in familial love and the strength of connection and tradition." SLJ

Bull Run; woodcuts by David Frampton. HarperCollins Pubs. 1993 104p il $14.95; lib bdg $13.89; pa $4.95 (6 and up)   Fic

1. Bull Run, Battle of, 1861—Fiction 2. United States—History—1861-1865, Civil War—Fiction
ISBN 0-06-021446-5; 0-06-021447-3 (lib bdg); 0-06-440588-5 (pa)   LC 92-14745
"A Laura Geringer book"

"In a sequence of sixty one- to two-page narratives, fifteen fictional characters (and one real general) recount their experiences during the Civil War. A few encounter each other, most meet unawares or not at all, but they have in common a battle, Bull Run, that affects—and sometimes ends—their lives." Bull Cent Child Books

"Abandoning the conventions of narrative fiction, Fleischman tells a vivid, many-sided story in this original and moving book. An excellent choice for readers' theater in the classroom or on stage." Booklist

The Half-a-Moon Inn; illustrated by Kathy Jacobi. Harper & Row 1980 88p il lib bdg $14.89; pa $3.95 (4-6)   Fic

1. Kidnapping—Fiction 2. Physically handicapped children—Fiction 3. Hotels and motels—Fiction
ISBN 0-06-021918-1 (lib bdg); 0-06-440364-5 (pa)
     LC 79-2010
"A mute boy, Aaron, leaves the cottage he shares with his mother to search for her when she is days late returning from market. Lost in a blizzard, he seeks shelter at the

Half-A-Moon Inn. Here the evil crone Miss Grackle, who owns the place, forces Aaron to abet her thieving. The boy tries to warn guests against Miss Grackle but none of them can read his hastily written notes. . . . The ending is a terrific twist." Publ Wkly

"Despite the grimness of Aaron's predicament, accentuated by dark scratch drawings of figures in grotesque proportion, the story's tone is hopeful and its style concrete and brisk. Elements of folklore exist in the story's characterization, structure, and narration." SLJ

Saturnalia. Harper & Row 1990 113p $14.95; lib bdg $14.89; pa $3.95 (6 and up)   Fic

1. Narraganset Indians—Fiction 2. Apprentices—Fiction 3. Prejudices—Fiction 4. Boston (Mass.)—Fiction
ISBN 0-06-021912-2; 0-06-021913-0 (lib bdg); 0-06-447089-X (pa)   LC 89-36380
"A Charlotte Zolotow book"

This novel is set in Boston in 1681. Fourteen-year-old William, a Narraganset Indian captured six years earlier in a raid, is apprenticed to Mr. Currie, a printer. "William's accomplishments enrage Mr. Baggot, the tithing-man whose grandsons were killed by Indians. . . . William often wanders the streets after curfew playing an Indian melody on a small bone flute in the hope of finding his lost brother. One night, the melody does bring him to an uncle and young cousin, now servants of a cruel eyeglass maker. When the eyeglass maker is found murdered, . . . [Mr. Baggot] accuses William of the crime." Horn Book

"While William is the main focus of the story, there are several bubbling subplots that illuminate the texture of Puritan colonial life. . . . Especially welcome as a support for history units, this absorbing story exemplifies Fleischman's graceful, finely honed use of the English language." Booklist

Fleischman, Sid, 1920-

By the Great Horn Spoon! illustrated by Eric von Schmidt. Little, Brown 1963 193p il $16.95; pa $5.95 (4-6)   Fic

1. California—Gold discoveries—Fiction
ISBN 0-316-28577-3; 0-316-28612-5 (pa)
Also available Spanish language edition
"An Atlantic Monthly Press book"

"Jack and his aunt's butler, Praiseworthy, stow away on a ship bound for California. Here are their adventures aboard ship and in the Gold Rush of '49." Publ Wkly

Chancy and the grand rascal; illustrated by Eric von Schmidt. Little, Brown 1966 179p il $14.95; pa $4.95 (4-6)   Fic

1. Frontier and pioneer life—Fiction
ISBN 0-316-28575-7; 0-316-26012-6 (pa)
"An Atlantic Monthly Press book"

"A young boy sets out to find his brothers and sisters, separated by the death of their parents in the Civil War, and meets a 'Grand Rascal' who leads him through many adventures in the battle of wits and colorful tall-talking." Bruno. Books for Sch Libr, 1968

"This is one of those rare children's books where language and story are one. It is a world of hyperbole and homely detail, an ebullient, frontier, Bunyanesque world." Christ Sci Monit

The ghost on Saturday night; illustrated by Eric von Schmidt. Little, Brown 1974 57p il $14.95 (3-5)   Fic

1. Thieves—Fiction
ISBN 0-316-28583-8
"An Atlantic Monthly Press book"

Fleischman, Sid, 1920——*Continued*

Opie is working as a guide in order to earn $17.59 for a saddle. He gets the saddle free, however, when he guides a fraudulent ghost-raising bank robber straight into the sheriff's arms

"The short scenario, illustrated with figures as overstated and caricatured as those in the text, is filled with the same kind of hyperbole, piquant phrasing, and bravura that have made the author's other books so delightful and so much fun to read." Horn Book

Jim Ugly; illustrations by Jos. A. Smith. Greenwillow Bks. 1992 130p il $15 (4 and up)   Fic

1. Dogs—Fiction 2. West (U.S.)—Fiction
ISBN 0-688-10886-5   LC 91-14392
Also available in paperback from Dell
The adventures of twelve-year-old Jake and Jim Ugly, his father's part-mongrel, part-wolf dog, as they travel through the Old West trying to find out what really happened to Jake's actor father
"Fleischman wields his magic pen once again in a fast-moving, picaresque adventure with memorable characters, a well-honed descriptive style—perfectly suited to tone, time, and place—and a sure sense of story." Horn Book

McBroom tells the truth; illustrated by Walter Lorraine. Little, Brown 1981 42p il $12.45 (3-5)   Fic

1. Farm life—Fiction 2. Tall tales
ISBN 0-316-28550-1   LC 81-1035
"An Atlantic Monthly Press book"
A reissue with new illustrations of the title first published 1966 by Norton
"A hilarious yarn about a New England farmer who is duped into buying a piece of land 80 acres deep with a pond on top. When a freak drought dries up the pond, however, McBroom discovers the soil underneath is so fertile it will produce four crops of vegetables a day. Beans grow so fast that McBroom has to step lively to keep from getting entangled in the vines and his 11 children have great fun riding pumpkins and using corn stalks as pogo sticks." Booklist
Other available titles about McBroom are:
Here comes McBroom! (1992)
McBroom and the big wind (1967)
McBroom and the great race (1980)
McBroom's almanac (1984)
McBroom's wonderful one-acre farm (1992)

The midnight horse; illustrations by Peter Sis. Greenwillow Bks. 1990 84p il $12.95 (3-6)   Fic

1. Magicians—Fiction 2. Ghost stories 3. Orphans—Fiction
ISBN 0-688-09441-4   LC 89-23441
Also available in paperback from Dell
Touch enlists the help of The Great Chaffalo, a ghostly magician, to thwart his great-uncle's plans to put Touch into the orphan house and swindle The Red Raven Inn away from Miss Sally
"The prose is colorful and earthy. . . . Good and bad are clearly defined, a happy ending is never in doubt, and the reader must accept in good faith the capricious appearances of a deceased but still-practicing magician." Horn Book

The whipping boy; illustrations by Peter Sis. Greenwillow Bks. 1986 90p il $16 (5 and up)   Fic

1. Thieves—Fiction 2. Adventure fiction
ISBN 0-688-06216-4   LC 85-17555

Also available in paperback from Troll; Spanish language edition also available
Awarded the Newbery Medal, 1987
"A round tale of adventure and humor, this follows the fortunes of Prince Roland (better known as Prince Brat) and his whipping boy, Jemmy, who has received all the hard knocks for the prince's mischief. . . . There's not a moment's lag in pace, and the stock characters, from Hold-Your-Nose Billy to Betsy's dancing bear Petunia, have enough inventive twists to project a lively air to it all." Bull Cent Child Books

Fleming, Ian, 1908-1964

Chitty-Chitty-Bang-Bang; the magical car; illustrated by John Burningham. Random House 1964 111p il hardcover o.p. paperback available $3.99 (4-6)   Fic

1. Automobiles—Fiction
ISBN 0-394-81948-9 (pa)
"An ingenious nonsense tale about an English family and their remarkable old car. Gifted with the ability to navigate land, sea, and air, Chitty-Chitty-Bang-Bang rescues the family from floods, traffic jams, and gangsters." Hodges. Books for Elem Sch Libr

Fletcher, Ralph J.

Fig pudding; by Ralph Fletcher. Clarion Bks. 1995 136p $14.95 (4 and up)   Fic

1. Family life—Fiction 2. Death—Fiction
ISBN 0-395-71125-8   LC 94-3654
"Twelve year old Cliff, the oldest of six children . . . recalls the past year in episodes focusing on his brothers and his sister. . . . There were good times, but there were also ones he'd like to forget—among them, the death of one brother." Booklist
"Written with humor, perception, and clarity of language, the book resonates with laughter and sorrow." SLJ

Forbes, Esther, 1891-1967

Johnny Tremain; a novel for old & young; with illustrations by Lynd Ward. Houghton Mifflin 1943 256p il $14.95 (5 and up)   Fic

1. United States—History—1775-1783, Revolution—Fiction 2. Boston (Mass.)—Fiction
ISBN 0-395-06766-9
Also available Cornerstone Bks. large print edition and in paperback from Dell
Awarded the Newbery Medal, 1944
"Johnny, an orphan, works as a favored apprentice to an aging silversmith until he burns his hand severely while working on an important project. During the Revolutionary War he serves as a dispatch rider for the Committee on Public Safety, meeting such men as Paul Revere and John Hancock. An outcast for a time, he finally learns on the battlefield of Lexington that his crippled hand can be put to use." Shapiro. Fic for Youth. 3d edition

Forrester, Sandra

Sound the jubilee. Lodestar Bks. 1995 183p $15.99 (6 and up)   Fic

1. Slavery—Fiction 2. Roanoke Island (N.C.)—Fiction 3. United States—History—1861-1865, Civil War
ISBN 0-525-67486-1   LC 94-32664

Forrester, Sandra—*Continued*

"In 1861, strong-willed Maddie is an eleven-year-old slave. Through her eyes, readers view the life of a family and community that gain economic security in the North Carolina settlement of Roanoke Island after being freed from slavery. Depicting tragic and triumphant episodes during a turbulent time in American history, the novel, which follows the family for four years, is compelling and informative." Horn Book Guide

Fox, Paula

The eagle kite; a novel. Orchard Bks. 1995 127p $15.95; lib bdg $15.99 (6 and up)   **Fic**

1. Homosexuality—Fiction 2. Fathers and sons—Fiction 3. AIDS (Disease)—Fiction 4. Death—Fiction

ISBN 0-531-06892-7; 0-531-08742-5 (lib bdg)

LC 94-26415

"A Richard Jackson book"

Liam's father has AIDS, and his family cannot talk about it until Liam reveals a secret that he has tried to deny ever since he saw his father embracing another man at the beach

"The author's refusal to diminish the tangled emotional issues that underlie her story quietly challenges all preconceptions, and readers cannot help but be deeply affected." Publ Wkly

One-eyed cat; a novel. Bradbury Press 1984 216p $14.95 (5 and up)   **Fic**

1. Firearms—Fiction 2. Cats—Fiction

ISBN 0-02-735540-3   LC 84-10964

Also available in paperback from Dell; Spanish language edition also available

A Newbery Medal honor book, 1985

"Told by his father that he's too young for the air rifle an uncle gives him as a bithday present, Ned sneaks the gun out one night and takes a shot at a shadowy creature. He is subsequently smitten with guilt when he sees a one-eyed feral cat, and the knowledge that he may have been responsible as well as [having disobeyed] his father colors all his days." Bull Cent Child Books

The author's "writing is terse. Her characterization is outstanding, and she creates a strong sense of place and mood. The relationships among the characters are complex and ring true, while often filling readers with a sense of despair. 'One-Eyed Cat' is a deep and demanding psychological novel. Its slow pace may limit its appeal, but those who persevere will be rewarded." SLJ

The slave dancer; a novel; with illustrations by Eros Keith. Bradbury Press 1973 176p il $14.95 (5 and up)   **Fic**

1. Slave trade—Fiction 2. Sea stories

ISBN 0-02-735560-8   LC 73-80642

Also available in paperback from Dell; Spanish language edition also available

Awarded the Newbery Medal, 1974

"Thirteen-year-old Jessie Bollier is kidnapped from New Orleans and taken aboard a slave ship. Cruelly tyrannized by the ship's captain, Jessie is made to play his fife for the slaves during the exercise period into which they are forced in order to keep them fit for sale. When a hurricane destroys the ship, Jessie and Ras, a young slave, survive. They are helped by an old black man who finds them, spirits Ras north to freedom, and assists Jessie to return to his family." Shapiro. Fic for Youth. 3d edition

The stone-faced boy; illustrated by Donald A. Mackay. Bradbury Press 1968 106p il $13.95 (4-6)   **Fic**

1. Brothers and sisters—Fiction 2. Family life—Fiction

ISBN 0-02-735570-5

Also available in paperback from Aladdin; Spanish language edition also available

"The story is a perceptive character study of a lonely, timid middle child in a family of five self-possessed, individualistic children. To save himself from teasing by classmates and siblings, Gus Oliver has learned to mask his feelings so well that he has lost all ability to show emotion. Even the startling and unexpected arrival of an eccentric, outspoken great-aunt appears to leave Gus unmoved but the night his sister inveigles him into going out in the dark and the cold to rescue a stray dog, he gains a new-found confidence in himself." Booklist

The village by the sea. Orchard Bks. 1988 147p $15.95 (5 and up)   **Fic**

1. Aunts—Fiction

ISBN 0-531-05788-7   LC 88-60099

Also available in paperback from Dell

"A Richard Jackson book"

"Emma is sent to stay with her fractious aunt and eccentric uncle, where she experiences the devastating effects of envy and the power of love and forgiveness." SLJ

"Fox's style is compressed without seeming dense, each scene and image allowed space for clean effect. Although the emotional layering is sophisticated, the viewpoint is unfalteringly that of the child. The novel is easy to read and complex to consider, an encounter that moves the reader from Gothic narrative suspense to compassionate illumination of the dark in human nature." Bull Cent Child Books

Fritz, Jean

The cabin faced west; illustrated by Feodor Rojankovsky. Coward-McCann 1958 124p il $13.95 (3-6)   **Fic**

1. Scott, Ann Hamilton—Fiction 2. Frontier and pioneer life—Fiction 3. Pennsylvania—Fiction

ISBN 0-698-20016-0

Also available in paperback from Puffin Bks.

"Ann is unhappy when her family moves from Gettysburg to the Pennsylvania frontier, but she soon finds friends and begins to see that there is much to enjoy about her new home—including a visit from General Washington." Hodges. Books for Elem Sch Libr

Early thunder; illustrated by Lynd Ward. Coward-McCann 1967 255p il o.p.; Puffin Bks. paperback available $4.99 (6 and up)   **Fic**

1. United States—History—1600-1775, Colonial period—Fiction 2. Salem (Mass.)—Fiction

ISBN 0-14-032259-0 (pa)

"The political conflict in Salem, Mass., 1774-75, is realized in the agony of David, the 14-year-old son of a Tory doctor, who struggles to determine where his own allegiance lies." Coughlan. Creating Independence, 1763-1789

"The period details and the historical background are excellent, both in themselves and in the easy way they are incorporated into the story." Bull Cent Child Books

Fritz, Jean—*Continued*

George Washington's breakfast; Paul Galdone drew the pictures. Coward-McCann 1969 unp il hardcover o.p. paperback available $7.95 (2-4)   **Fic**

1. Washington, George, 1732-1799—Fiction
ISBN 0-698-20616-9 (pa)

George W. Allen "was named for George Washington and he had the same birthday. It made him feel almost related. So related he wanted to know everything he could about George Washington. . . . [He especially wanted to] know what George Washington ate for breakfast. He got his grandmother to promise she'd cook George Washington's breakfast if he found out what it was, and he was going to find out—no matter what." About the book

Gage, Wilson, 1922-1992

Mike's toads; illustrated by Glen Rounds. Greenwillow Bks. 1990 85p il $12.95; pa $3.95 (4-6)   **Fic**

1. Toads—Fiction
ISBN 0-688-08834-1; 0-688-10977-2 (pa)
                 LC 88-34907

A newly illustrated edition of the title first published 1970 by World Pub. Co.

A sixth-grade boy volunteers his brother's services once too often without consulting him and ends up having to spend the summer vacation caring for a friend's toads himself

Gannett, Ruth Stiles, 1923

My father's dragon; illustrated by Ruth Chrisman Gannett. Random House 1948 86p il lib bdg $14.95; pa $4.99 (1-4)   **Fic**

1. Dragons—Fiction 2. Fantasy fiction 3. Animals—Fiction
ISBN 0-394-91438-4 (lib bdg); 0-394-89048-5 (pa)

A Newbery Medal honor book, 1949

This is a combination of fantasy, sense, and nonsense. It describes the adventures of a small boy, Elmer Elevator, who befriended an old alley cat and in return heard the story of the captive baby dragon on Wild Island. Right away Elmer decided to free the dragon. The tale of Elmer's voyage to Tangerina and his arrival on Wild Island, his encounters with various wild animals, and his subsequent rescue of the dragon follows

Other available titles in this series are:
The dragons of Blueland (1951)
Elmer and the dragon (1950)

Gantos, Jack

Heads or tails; stories from the sixth grade. Farrar Straus Giroux 1994 151p il $16; pa $3.95 (5 and up)   **Fic**

1. Diaries—Fiction 2. Family life—Fiction 3. School stories
ISBN 0-374-32909-5; 0-374-42923-5 (pa)
                 LC 93-43117

"Jack is trying to survive his sixth-grade year, and he narrates, through a series of short-stories-cum-chapters, his difficulties in dodging the obstacles life throws in his path. . . . The writing is zingy and specific, with snappily authentic dialogue and a vivid sense of juvenile experience. . . . Jack and his family have a recognizably thorny relationship. This is a distinctive and lively sequence of everyday-life stories." Bull Cent Child Books

Gardam, Jane

The hollow land; illustrated by Janet Rawlins. Greenwillow Bks. 1982 c1981 152p il $10.25 (5 and up)   **Fic**

1. Farm life—Fiction 2. Friendship—Fiction 3. Great Britain—Fiction
ISBN 0-688-00873-9   LC 81-6620

First published 1981 in the United Kingdom

The episodes in this story about two families "focus on the relationship between the Teesdales, a local farming family, and the Batemans, a London family who rents a house from the Teesdales and continues to return for part of every year. The enduring friendship between Bell Teesdale, a boy of eight at the beginning of the first narrative, and Harry Bateman, two or three years younger, rounds out the story." Horn Book

"With humor and mystery and realistic detail Gardam lovingly evokes the Cumbrian fells area in northern England." SLJ

Gardiner, John Reynolds, 1944

Stone Fox, illustrated by Marcia Sewall. Crowell 1980 81p il $14.95; lib bdg $14.89; pa $3.95 (2-5)   **Fic**

1. Sled dog racing—Fiction 2. Dogs—Fiction
ISBN 0-690-03983-2; 0-690-03984-0 (lib bdg); 0-06-440132-4 (pa)   LC 79-7895

"When his usually spry grandfather won't get out of bed Willy searches for a remedy. Back taxes are the problem and the only way to get the money is to win the dogsled race. Stone Fox, a towering Indian who has never lost a race, is primary competition. Both want the prize money for the government—Willy for taxes and Stone Fox to buy his native land back." SLJ

This story "is rooted in a Rocky Mountain legend, a locale faithfully represented in Sewall's wonderful drawings. . . . In Gardiner's bardic chronicle, the tension is teeth rattling, with the tale flying to a conclusion that is almost unbearably moving, one readers won't soon forget." Publ Wkly

Gates, Doris, 1901-1987

Blue willow; illustrated by Paul Lantz. Viking 1940 172p il $14.99; pa $3.99 (4 and up)   **Fic**

1. Migrant labor—Fiction 2. California—Fiction
ISBN 0-670-17557-9; 0-14-030924-1 (pa)

Also available Spanish language edition

"Having to move from one migrant camp to another intensifies Janey Larkin's desire for a permanent home, friends, and school. The only beautiful possession the family has is a blue willow plate handed down from generation to generation. It is a reminder of happier days in Texas and represents dreams and promises for a better future. Reading about this itinerant family's ways of life, often filled with despair and yet always hopeful, leaves little room for the reader's indifference." Read Ladders for Hum Relat. 6th edition

Gauch, Patricia Lee

This time, Tempe Wick? [illustrated by] Margot Tomes. Putnam 1992 43p il $13.95 (3-5)   **Fic**

1. United States—History—1775-1783, Revolution—Fiction
ISBN 0-399-21880-7   LC 91-30894

Gauch, Patricia Lee—*Continued*

A reissue of the title first published 1974 by Coward, McCann & Geoghegan

Based on a Revolutionary War legend about a real girl, this story tells how Tempe Wick helped feed and clothe the thousands of American soldiers who spent the winters of 1780 and 1781 in Jockey Hollow, New Jersey. When the soldiers mutinied, Tempe had to use her wits and courage to prevent two of them from stealing her horse

"The book presents a realistic and humane view of the war and of the people who fought it. . . . The writing is the perfect vehicle for the illustrations—in the artist's inimitable style—which capture the down-to-earth, unpretentious, and humorous quality of the storytelling." Horn Book

Thunder at Gettysburg; drawings by Stephen Gammell. Putnam 1990 c1975 46p il map $14.95 (3-5)   Fic

1. Gettysburg (Pa.), Battle of, 1863—Fiction

ISBN 0-399-22201-4   LC 89-70047

Also available in paperback from Bantam Bks. and Dell

A reissue of the title first published 1975 by Coward, McCann & Geoghegan

Fourteen-year-old Tillie becomes involved in the tragic battle of July 1-3, 1863

"Gauch has drawn on the experiences of a real person, in this case Tillie Pierce Alleman, whose 1889 book 'At Gettysburg' provided the basis of the story. Gammell's thorough pencilled scenes are full of atmosphere and acute emotion, their escalating drama effectively congruent with that of the story." Booklist

Gee, Maurice

The champion. Simon & Schuster Bks. for Young Readers 1993 c1989 212p $14 (6 and up)   Fic

1. World War, 1939-1945—Fiction 2. New Zealand—Fiction

ISBN 0-671-86561-7   LC 92-37670

First published 1989 in New Zealand

In 1943 twelve-year-old Rex sees his quiet New Zealand village dramatically changed by the arrival of a black American soldier on leave from the war

"Gee fills his book with memorable characters. . . . The ending is neither predictable nor contrived; it leaves the reader hoping to meet some of these people again." Booklist

George, Jean Craighead, 1919-

Julie; illustrated by Wendell Minor. HarperCollins Pubs. 1994 226p il $15; lib bdg $14.89; pa $4.50 (6 and up)   Fic

1. Inuit—Fiction 2. Arctic regions—Fiction 3. Wolves—Fiction

ISBN 0-06-023528-4; 0-06-023529-2 (lib bdg); 0-06-440573-7 (pa)   LC 93-27738

This sequel to Julie of the wolves "details Julie's adjustment to family and modernization after returning home. Her father's musk oxen enterprise depicts the problems inherent to environment-versus-economics issues as Julie struggles to save her wolf friends." Sci Child

Julie of the wolves; pictures by John Schoenherr. Harper & Row 1972 170p il $15; lib bdg $14.89; pa $4.50 (6 and up)   Fic

1. Inuit—Fiction 2. Wolves—Fiction 3. Arctic regions—Fiction 4. Wilderness survival—Fiction

ISBN 0-06-021943-2; 0-06-021944-0 (lib bdg); 0-06-440058-1 (pa)

Also available Spanish language edition

Awarded the Newbery Medal, 1973

"Lost in the Alaskan wilderness thirteen-year old Miyax [Julie in English] an Eskimo girl, is gradually accepted by a pack of Arctic wolves that she comes to love." Booklist

"The superb narration includes authentic descriptions and details of the Eskimo way-of-life and of Eskimo rituals. . . . The whole book has a rare, intense reality which the artist enhances beautifully with animated drawings." Horn Book

My side of the mountain; written and illustrated by Jean Craighead George. Dutton 1988 177p il $15; pa $4.95 (5 and up)   Fic

1. Outdoor life—Fiction 2. Catskill Mountains (N.Y.)—Fiction

ISBN 0-525-44392-4; 0-525-44395-9 (pa)

LC 87-27556

Also available in paperback from Puffin Bks.; Spanish language edition also available

A reissue of the title first published 1959

"Sam Gribley feels closed in by the city and his large family so he runs away to the Catskills and the land that had belonged to his grandfather. He tells the story of his year in the wilderness—the loneliness, the struggle to survive, and the need for companionship." Read Ladders for Hum Relat. 6th edition

"The book is all the more convincing for the excellence of style, the subtlety of humor, aptness of phrases, and touches of poetry." Horn Book

Followed by On the far side of the mountain

On the far side of the mountain; written and illustrated by Jean Craighead George. Dutton Children's Bks. 1990 170p il $15 (5 and up)   Fic

1. Outdoor life—Fiction 2. Catskill Mountains (N.Y.)—Fiction

ISBN 0-525-44563-3   LC 89-25988

Also available in paperback from Puffin Bks.

Sam's peaceful existence in his wilderness home is disrupted when his sister runs away and his pet falcon is confiscated by a conservation officer

"A tense, believable plot; likable characters; and a strong, positive message about the joys and beauty of the mountains . . . combine to make this story a jewel." Booklist

Giff, Patricia Reilly

Love, from the fifth-grade celebrity; illustrated by Leslie Morrill. Delacorte Press 1986 117p il hardcover o.p. paperback available $3.50 (4-6)   Fic

1. Friendship—Fiction 2. School stories

ISBN 0-440-44948-0 (pa)   LC 85-46075

Casey enjoyed Tracy's company during summer vacation but becomes increasingly jealous of her irrepressible new friend when she joins Casey's fifth-grade class

"This pleasant book appealingly presents the ups and downs of friendship—how it can founder on jealousy and misunderstanding. A subplot underscores conflicting feelings

Giff, Patricia Reilly—*Continued*
children may have when a new baby joins the family." Publ Wkly

Gilson, Jamie, 1933-
4B goes wild; illustrated by Linda Strauss Edwards. Lothrop, Lee & Shepard Bks. 1983 160p il lib bdg $15 (4-6)   Fic
1. Camping—Fiction 2. School stories
ISBN 0-688-02236-7   LC 83-948
Also available in paperback from Pocket Bks.
"Hobie Hanson, a sensitive fourth grader, tells of the time two fourth grade classes went on a three day camping trip. Along with learning about the country, they learned how to work together, and developed new relationships with each other and the adults with them." Child Book Rev Serv
"There are sustaining threads, but the plot is episodic; the writing style is breezy and comic, occasionally a bit cute; the characters are drawn with variable depth and some exaggeration; the dialogue is natural, one of the strong points of Gilson's writing." Bull Cent Child Books
Other available titles about Hobie Hanson are:
Double dog dare (1988)
Hobie Hanson, greatest hero of the mall (1989)
Hobie Hanson, you're weird (1987)
Soccer circus (1993)
Sticks and stones and skeleton bones (1991)
Thirteen ways to sink a sub (1982)

Do bananas chew gum? Lothrop, Lee & Shepard Bks. 1980 158p $15; lib bdg $14.93 (4-6)   Fic
1. Reading—Fiction 2. Learning disabilities—Fiction
ISBN 0-688-41960-7; 0-688-51960-1 (lib bdg)
          LC 80-11414
Also available in paperback from Pocket Bks.
Able to read and write at only a second grade level, sixth-grader Sam Mott considers himself dumb until he is prompted to cooperate with those who think something can be done about his problem
"This is a wonderfully written story, with real situations and a main character for whom the reader feels anguish at his fear of his learning disability being discovered, but also exultation when he correctly reads a long and difficult word. . . . This is a story that leaves you feeling good." Voice Youth Advocates

Hello, my name is Scrambled Eggs; illustrated by John Wallner. Lothrop, Lee & Shepard Bks. 1985 159p il $15 (4 and up)   Fic
1. Vietnamese—United States—Fiction
ISBN 0-688-04095-0   LC 84-10075
Also available in paperback from Pocket Bks.
"A humorous account of what happens when a Vietnamese family, sponsored by the church, moves into Harvey's home temporarily. To make himself feel more important, Harvey decides to make educating and Americanizing the 12-year-old boy his project. By the end of the book, Tuan is not the only one who has received an education. . . . Child characters are believable and intuitive because they understand the sense of isolation that Tuan's father and grandmother feel about being in a strange culture with a different language, customs and food. Adult characters are well-meaning and kindly but not as strongly portrayed as the children." SLJ
Another available title about Harvey is:
Harvey, the beer can king (1978)

Itchy Richard; illustrated by Diane de Groat. Clarion Bks. 1991 52p il $13.95 (2-4)   Fic
1. Lice—Fiction 2. School stories
ISBN 0-395-59282-8   LC 91-6567
Also available in paperback from Pocket Bks.
"Most of the children in Richard's second-grade class have heard of head lice, and some of them have contracted them. Richard is mortified to discover that he may have the itchy creatures in his own hair (he doesn't)." SLJ
"Loaded with kid-appealing humor and personalities straight out of a grade-school classroom . . . Gilson's sensitive story takes a fairly common elementary school problem and makes it seem, if no less 'yucky,' at least less scary." Booklist
Another available title about Richard and his classmates is:
It goes eeeeeeeeeeeee! (1994)

Gipson, Frederick Benjamin, 1903-1973
Old Yeller; [by] Fred Gipson; drawings by Carl Burger. Harper & Row 1956 158p il $22; pa $5.50 (6 and up)   Fic
1. Dogs—Fiction 2. Texas—Fiction 3. Frontier and pioneer life—Fiction
ISBN 0-06-011545-9; 0-06-080002-X (pa)
          LC 56-8780
A Newbery Medal honor book, 1957
"Travis at fourteen was the man of the family during the hard summer of 1860 when his father drove his herd of cattle from Texas to the Kansas market. It was the summer when an old yellow dog attached himself to the family and won Travis' reluctant friendship. Before the summer was over, Old Yeller proved more than a match for thieving raccoons, fighting bulls, grizzly bears, and mad wolves. This is a skilful tale of a boy's love for a dog as well as a description of a pioneer boyhood and it can't miss with any dog lover." Horn Book

Goble, Paul
Beyond the ridge; story and illustrations by Paul Goble. Bradbury Press 1989 unp il $14.95 (2-4)   Fic
1. Indians of North America—Fiction
ISBN 0-02-736581-6   LC 87-33113
Also available in paperback from Aladdin
At her death an elderly Plains Indian woman experiences the afterlife believed in by her people, while the surviving family members prepare her body according to their custom
"Goble's illustrations—in a double spread of gray rocks, smoothly surfaced in a skyscape of flying vultures—make a dignified context for a moving, direct discussion of death. Goble has managed to make personal what might have been anthropological." Bull Cent Child Books

Godden, Rumer, 1907-
Candy Floss; illustrated by Nonny Hogrogian. Philomel Bks. 1991 54p il music $16.95 (2-4)   Fic
1. Dolls—Fiction 2. Fairs—Fiction
ISBN 0-399-21807-6   LC 90-19469
A newly illustrated edition of the title first published 1960 by Viking
A doll named Candy Floss is very happy serving as Jack's lucky charm at his stall at the fair, until a spoiled rich girl steals her

Godden, Rumer, 1907- —*Continued*

"Hogrogian's new illustrations, executed in chalk, show serenity in the garden scenes, and the moments at the carnival have a colorful vitality. A fine collaboration between an author who writes enchantingly and an artist who can paint enchantment." Booklist

The doll's house; illustrated by Tasha Tudor. Viking 1962 c1947 136p il hardcover o.p. paperback available $4.50 (2-4)   **Fic**

1. Dollhouses—Fiction 2. Dolls—Fiction

ISBN 0-14-030942-X (pa)

Also available in hardcover from P. Smith

First published 1947 in the United Kingdom; first United States edition illustrated by Dana Saintsbury published 1948

Adventures of a brave little hundred-year-old Dutch farthing doll, her family, their Victorian dollhouse home and the two little English girls to whom they all belonged. Tottie's great adventure was when she went to the exhibition, Dolls through the ages, and was singled out for notice by the Queen who opened the exhibition

"Each doll has a firmly drawn, recognizably true character; the children think and behave convincingly. . . . The story is enthralling, and complete in every detail." Spectator

The story of Holly and Ivy; pictures by Barbara Cooney. Viking Kestrel 1985 31p il lib bdg $15.99; pa $5.99 (2-4)   **Fic**

1. Orphans—Fiction 2. Christmas—Fiction 3. Dolls—Fiction

ISBN 0-670-80622-6 (lib bdg); 0-14-050723-X (pa)
                LC 84-25799

A newly illustrated edition of the title first published 1959

Orphaned Ivy finds her Christmas wish fulfilled with the help of a lonely couple and a doll named Holly

"One of the author's most winsome doll stories has been revitalized by an abundance of luminous new paintings, precisely detailed and full of authentic atmosphere, sensitivity, and beauty." Horn Book

Grahame, Kenneth, 1859-1932

The reluctant dragon (3-5)   **Fic**

1. Dragons—Fiction 2. Fairy tales

Some editions are:

Holiday House $12.95; pa $4.95 Illustrated by Ernest H. Shepard (ISBN 0-8234-0093-X; 0-8234-0755-1)

Holt & Co. $16.95; pa $6.95 Illustrated by Michael Hague (ISBN 0-8050-1112-9; 0-8050-0802-0)

This chapter from Dream days was first published 1938 by Holiday House

This "is the droll tale of a peace-loving dragon who is forced to fight St. George. The dragon's friend, called simply the Boy, arranges a meeting between St. George and the dragon, and a mock fight is planned. St. George is the hero of the day, the dragon is highly entertained at a banquet, and the Boy is pleased to have saved both the dragon and St. George." Huck. Child Lit in the Elem Sch. 3d edition

The wind in the willows (4-6)   **Fic**

1. Animals—Fiction

Also available Spanish language edition

Some editions are:

Holt & Co. $19.95 Illustrated by Michael Hague (ISBN 0-8050-0213-8)

Knopf (Everyman's library children's classics) $13.95 Illustrated by Arthur Rackham (ISBN 0-679-41802-4)

Scribner $25 Illustrated by Ernest H. Shepard (ISBN 0-684-19345-0)

St. Martin's Press $18.95 Illustrated by Patrick Benson (ISBN 0-312-13624-2)

Viking $15.75; pa $2.95 Pictures by John Burningham (ISBN 0-670-77120-1; 0-14-031544-6)

First published 1908 by Scribner

In this fantasy "the characters are Mole, Water Rat, Mr. Toad, and other small animals, who live and talk like humans but have charming individual animal characters. The book is a tender portrait of the English countryside." Reader's Ency

Gray, Luli

Falcon's egg. Houghton Mifflin 1995 133p $13.95 (3-5)   **Fic**

1. Dragons—Fiction 2. New York (N.Y.)—Fiction

ISBN 0-395-71128-2   LC 94-16731

"Falcon is an 11-year-old girl in New York City and the egg is red, hot, and discovered in Central Park. Falcon enlists the help of an older friend and neighbor to hide it until it hatches, fearing that her mother won't let her keep it. Soon elderly Aunt Emily; her ornithologist friend, Fernando Maldonado; and Falcon's younger brother join the cozy group that gathers to ponder the egg. When Egg hatches, she is a dragon. . . . Each of the characters is rich in wit, wisdom, and human foibles. . . . The real world blends well with the fantasy elements as tidbits of lore and locale are woven seamlessly." SLJ

Greene, Bette, 1934-

Philip Hall likes me, I reckon maybe; pictures by Charles Lilly. Dial Bks. for Young Readers 1974 135p il o.p.; Dell paperback available $3.99 (4-6)   **Fic**

1. Friendship—Fiction 2. African Americans—Fiction 3. Arkansas—Fiction

ISBN 0-440-45755-6 (pa)

A Newbery Medal honor book, 1975

Eleven-year-old Beth, an African American girl from Arkansas, thinks that Philip Hall likes her, but their on-again, off-again relationship sometimes makes her wonder

"The action is sustained; the narration, in first person Black dialect, is good or bad, depending on your linguistic stance; the illustrations are excellent black-and-white pencil sketches." Read Teach

Followed by Get on out of here, Philip Hall (1981)

Summer of my German soldier. Dial Bks. for Young Readers 1973 230p $14.99 (6 and up)   **Fic**

1. World War, 1939-1945—Fiction 2. German prisoners of war—Fiction 3. Arkansas—Fiction

ISBN 0-8037-8321-3

Also available Cornerstone Bks. large print edition and in paperback from Dell

"Patty knows the pain of loneliness, rejection, and beatings in a family where she is the ugly duckling, unable to gain her parents' love. This is in contrast to the affection shown to her beautiful and submissive sister. Anton Reiker is a German prisoner-of-war in a camp outside of Jenkinsville, Arkansas, and when he escapes, Patty helps him. Because her family is Jewish, she pays dearly for this intervention." Shapiro. Fic for Youth. 3d edition

Followed by Morning is a long time coming (1978)

Greene, Constance C.

Beat the turtle drum; illustrated by Donna Diamond. Viking 1976 119p il hardcover o.p. paperback available $3.99 (5 and up)   Fic

1. Sisters—Fiction 2. Death—Fiction

ISBN 0-14-036850-7 (pa)

Also available Cornerstone Bks. large print edition

"Joss saves money for her 11th birthday so that she can rent a horse for a week. She and her older sister, who narrates the story, have the happiest week of their lives until Joss falls from the apple tree and breaks her neck. Joss's death stuns the family." SLJ

"Written with an eloquent and moving simplicity." N Y Times Book Rev

A girl called Al; illustrated by Byron Barton. Viking 1969 127p il hardcover o.p. paperback available $4.50 (5 and up)   Fic

1. Friendship—Fiction

ISBN 0-14-034786-0 (pa)

Also available Cornerstone Bks. large print edition

"Written in an amusing first-person style, this is the story of a friendship between two seventh grade girls. Al (short for Alexandra) and the unnamed narrator of the story learn much from Mr. Richards, the elderly assistant superintendent of their apartment house, as he helps build their self-confidence and reveals his own ability to accept life's problems as well as its joys." Read Ladders for Hum Relat. 6th edition

Other available titles about Al are:
Al(exandra) the Great (1982)
Al's blind date (1989)

Isabelle the itch; illustrated by Emily A. McCully. Viking 1973 126p il hardcover o.p. paperback available $4.50 (4-6)   Fic

ISBN 0-14-036028-X (pa)

Isabelle, a hyperactive fifth grader, spends a great deal of time getting nowhere, until she realizes that she must channel her energy in order to reach her goals, which include taking over her brother's paper route and winning the fifty-yard dash at school

"This has lively characters described in good style and is written with abundant humor." Bull Cent Child Books

Nora; maybe a ghost story. Browndeer Press 1993 202p $10.95; pa $3.95 (6 and up)   Fic

1. Sisters—Fiction 2. Mothers and daughters—Fiction 3. Fathers and daughters—Fiction 4. Remarriage—Fiction

ISBN 0-15-277696-6; 0-15-276895-5 (pa)

LC 92-44929

While Nora, thirteen, and her younger sister Patsy deal with their father's plans to remarry and their competition over a new boy at school, Nora alone senses the presence of her mother who died three years before

"From the first page, masterly comic timing and sharp, witty observations . . . firmly establish that the reader has entered Greene territory. . . . Believable characters and snappy dialogue keep the pace brisk." Publ Wkly

Greenfield, Eloise, 1929-

Sister; drawings by Moneta Barnett. Crowell 1974 83p il $15; pa $3.95 (4 and up)   Fic

1. Sisters—Fiction 2. Single parent family—Fiction 3. African Americans—Fiction

ISBN 0-690-00497-4; 0-06-440199-5 (pa)

A 13-year-old black girl whose father is dead watches her 16-year-old sister drifting away from her and her mother and fears she may fall into the same self-destructive behavior herself. While waiting for her sister's return home, she leafs through her diary, reliving both happy and unhappy experiences while gradually recognizing her own individuality

"The book is strong . . . strong in perception, in its sensitivity, in its realism." Bull Cent Child Books

Greenwald, Sheila

Give us a great big smile, Rosy Cole. Little, Brown 1981 76p il $14.95 (3-5)   Fic

1. Violinists, violoncellists, etc.—Fiction 2. Photographers—Fiction

ISBN 0-316-32672-0

Also available in paperback from Pocket Bks.

"An Atlantic Monthly Press book"

"Rosy's uncle, an author-photographer, has made Rosy's sisters, with their dancing and equestrian talents, the subject of two famous books. Now, to her dismay, it's 10-year-old Rosy's turn to gild Uncle Ralph's bank account, and he begins making regular visits to her violin class with his camera." Booklist

"The author never loses touch with her heroine, a refreshingly ordinary child whose basic good sense saves her from the foibles of adults. Lively, scratchy ink drawings extending the text's considerable humor, aptly picture Rosy's true feelings as she is led down the path to stardom." Horn Book

Other available titles about Rosy Cole are:
Here's Hermione: a Rosy Cole production (1991)
Rosy Cole discovers America! (1992)
Rosy Cole: she walks in beauty (1994)

Grifalconi, Ann

Not home; a novel. Little, Brown 1995 136p $15.95 (4 and up)   Fic

1. Foster home care—Fiction 2. Brothers—Fiction 3. African Americans—Fiction

ISBN 0-316-32905-3   LC 94-16708

"An African-American boy named Tom narrates this contemporary novel in which he and his brother are sent to a church-run home when their widowed mother is hospitalized. After befriending a self-sufficient but lonely older boy much admired by the home's residents, Tom learns the meaning of both family and home." Horn Book Guide

"Those drawn into Tommy's story will be moved by its emotionally charged, bitter-sweet conclusion." Publ Wkly

Griffin, Peni R.

Switching well. Margaret K. McElderry Bks. 1993 218p $16 (5 and up)   Fic

1. Space and time—Fiction 2. Texas—Fiction

ISBN 0-689-50581-7   LC 92-38442

Also available in paperback from Puffin Bks.

Two twelve-year-old girls in San Antonio, Texas, Ada in 1891 and Amber in 1991, switch places through a magic well and try desperately to return to their own times

"A fine blend of time travel and friendship, laced with insight into social history and attitudes." SLJ

Haas, Jessie

Beware the mare; pictures by Martha Haas. Greenwillow Bks. 1993 64p il $13 (3-5) **Fic**

1. Horses—Fiction 2. Grandfathers—Fiction
ISBN 0-688-11762-7   LC 92-14505

Gramps gets a good bargain on an apparently perfect bay mare for Lily, but because the horse is named Beware he suspects that there may be something wrong with her

"The book will capture young horse lovers with its believable characters and realistic dialogue." SLJ

Hahn, Mary Downing, 1937-

Daphne's book. Clarion Bks. 1983 177p $14.95 (5 and up) **Fic**

1. School stories 2. Friendship—Fiction 3. Authorship—Fiction 4. Family life—Fiction
ISBN 0-89919-183-5   LC 83-7348

Also available in paperback from Avon Bks.

As author Jessica and artist Daphne collaborate on a picture book for a seventh-grade English class contest, Jessica becomes aware of conditions in Daphne's home life that seem to threaten her health and safety

"The story is compelling in its portrayal of peer group cruelty and the disturbing dilemma Daphne faces. Jessica's own conflict about how long to shield Daphne will provoke its share of thought too. Characterizations are strong and the situations pressing, so that although the development has a weak spot or two, the story's capacity to move a reader is strong." Booklist

The dead man in Indian Creek. Clarion Bks. 1990 130p $14.95 (5 and up) **Fic**

1. Mystery fiction
ISBN 0-395-52397-4   LC 89-22162

Also available in paperback from Avon Bks.

When Matt and Parker learn the body they found in Indian Creek is a drug-related death, they fear Parker's mother may be involved

"Though readers will respond viscerally to the action, what sets the book apart are Hahn's insightful character sketches, especially her portrayal of Matt, whose first-person musings will both entertain and give pause." Booklist

December stillness. Clarion Bks. 1988 181p $14.95 (6 and up) **Fic**

1. Veterans—Fiction 2. Homeless persons—Fiction 3. Vietnam Veterans Memorial (Washington, D.C.)—Fiction
ISBN 0-89919-758-2   LC 88-2572

Also available in paperback from Avon Bks.

Thirteen-year-old Kelly tries to befriend Mr. Weems, a disturbed, homeless Vietnam War veteran who spends his days in her suburban library, though the man makes it clear he wants to be left alone

"The author's skillful use of dialogue in defining her characters rescues what could have been a maudlin ending to a fine story, and her depiction of teenagers and their concerns is, as always, right on the mark." Horn Book

The doll in the garden; a ghost story. Clarion Bks. 1989 128p $14.95 (4-6) **Fic**

1. Space and time—Fiction 2. Ghost stories
ISBN 0-89919-848-1   LC 88-20365

Also available in paperback from Avon Bks.

After Ashley and Kristi find an antique doll buried in old Miss Cooper's garden, they discover that they can enter a ghostly turn-of-the-century world by going through a hole in the hedge

"Hahn's elegant use of language, as well as her ability to probe complex emotions at a child's level, elevates this above-the-ordinary ghost tale into a story with universal themes." Booklist

Stepping on the cracks. Clarion Bks. 1991 216p $14.95 (5 and up) **Fic**

1. World War, 1939-1945—Fiction
ISBN 0-395-58507-4   LC 91-7706

Also available in paperback from Avon Bks.

In 1944, while her brother is overseas fighting in World War II, eleven-year-old Margaret gets a new view of the school bully Gordy when she finds him hiding his own brother, an army deserter, and decides to help him

"Well-drawn characters and a satisfying plot. . . . There is plenty of action and page-turning suspense to please those who want a quick read, but there is much to ponder and reflect on as well." SLJ

Time for Andrew; a ghost story. Clarion Bks. 1994 165p $14.95 (5 and up) **Fic**

1. Ghost stories 2. Space and time—Fiction
ISBN 0-395-66556-6   LC 93-2877

Also available in paperback from Avon Bks.

When he goes to spend the summer with his great-aunt in the family's old house, eleven-year-old Drew is drawn eighty years into the past to trade places with his great-great-uncle who is dying of diptheria

"There's plenty to enjoy in this delightful time-slip fantasy: a fascinating premise, a dastardly cousin, some good suspense, and a roundup of characters to care about." Booklist

Wait till Helen comes; a ghost story. Clarion Bks. 1986 184p $14.95 (4-6) **Fic**

1. Ghost stories 2. Stepchildren—Fiction
ISBN 0-89919-453-2   LC 86-2648

Also available in paperback from Avon Bks.

Molly and Michael dislike their spooky new stepsister Heather but realize that they must try to save her when she seems ready to follow a ghost child to her doom

"Intertwined with the ghost story is the question of Molly's moral imperative to save a child she truly dislikes. Though the emotional turnaround may be a bit quick for some, this still scores as a first-rate thriller." Booklist

Hall, Lynn, 1937-

Dagmar Schultz and the angel Edna. Scribner 1989 86p hardcover o.p. paperback available $3.95 (6 and up) **Fic**

1. Adolescence—Fiction
ISBN 0-689-71615-X (pa)   LC 88-36862

"Dagmar Schultz, the girl from New Berlin, Iowa, who has had more than her share of supernatural adventures, meets her guardian angel. . . . Fast-talking Dagmar is turning 13 and ready for a boyfriend, but her plans are stymied when long-dead Aunt Edna suddenly materializes." Booklist

"The book is written, as are the others about Dagmar, in a chatty, friendly style—a cross between recounting adventures to a best friend and musing aloud. Dagmar's hilarious and frustrating ventures into the new world of being a teenager at long last and finding her very first boyfriend are sure to be a hit with preteens." SLJ

Other available titles about Dagmar Schultz are:
Dagmar Schultz and the powers of darkness (1989)
The secret life of Dagmar Schultz (1988)

Hamilton, Virginia, 1936-

The bells of Christmas; illustrations by Lambert Davis. Harcourt Brace Jovanovich 1989 59p $17.95 (4-6) **Fic**

1. Christmas—Fiction 2. Family life—Fiction 3. African Americans—Fiction 4. Ohio—Fiction
ISBN 0-15-206450-8 LC 89-7468

"On Christmas Day, 1890, in Ohio, the Bell family comes along the National Road to spend the holiday with Jason and his family. The gentle story is stuffed like a proper plum pudding with specific details of rural life almost a century ago." N Y Times Book Rev

Cousins. Philomel Bks. 1990 125p $14.95 (5 and up) **Fic**

1. Death—Fiction 2. Cousins—Fiction 3. Grandmothers—Fiction 4. African Americans—Fiction
ISBN 0-399-22164-6 LC 90-31451

Also available in paperback from Scholastic; Spanish language edition also available

"Cammy feels things strongly, whether it's the immeasurable love she has for her Gram Tut, or the jealousy and anger she feels for her perfect, sometimes patronizing cousin Patty Ann. But while those intense emotions make her a strong-willed, feisty girl, they also cause her a great deal of pain when Patty Ann drowns saving another cousin. Only through the wisdom and love of Gram and the return of her estranged father is Cammy able to work her way through the guilt and grief." SLJ

"The book deals essentially with emotions and sensations, and the writing reverberates with honesty and truth. Virginia Hamilton encases the story in family tradition, which offsets the instabilities of contemporary life, and she beautifully counterposes superstition and rationality, separation and reconciliation, love and death." Horn Book

Drylongso; written by Virginia Hamilton; illustrated by Jerry Pinkney. Harcourt Brace Jovanovich 1992 54p il $18.95 (3-5) **Fic**

1. Droughts—Fiction 2. Farm life—Fiction 3. African Americans—Fiction
ISBN 0-015224241-4 LC 91-25575

As a great wall of dust moves across their drought-stricken farm, a family's distress is relieved by a young man called Drylongso, who literally blows into their lives with the storm

"In an understated story of drought and hard times and longing for rain, a great writer and a great artist have pared down their rich, exuberant styles to something quieter but no less intense. . . . The characters are vital and lovingly individualized, set against a landscape washed in thick drifts of pale red dust. Pinkney's paintings in watercolor, pastel, and pencil have a flowing softness, like snow." Booklist

The house of Dies Drear; illustrated by Eros Keith. Macmillan 1968 246p il $15.95; pa $3.95 (5 and up) **Fic**

1. African Americans—Fiction 2. Mystery fiction 3. Ohio—Fiction
ISBN 0-02-742500-2; 0-02-043520-7 (pa)

"A hundred years ago, Dies Drear and two slaves he was hiding in his house, an Underground Railroad station in Ohio, had been murdered. The house, huge and isolated, was fascinating, Thomas thought, but he wasn't sure he was glad Papa had bought it—funny things kept happening, frightening things." Bull Cent Child Books

"The answer to the mystery comes in a startling dramatic dénouement that is pure theater. This is gifted writing; the characterization is unforgettable, the plot imbued with mounting tension." Saturday Rev

Followed by The mystery of Drear House

M. C. Higgins the great. Macmillan 1974 278p $17; pa $3.95 (6 and up) **Fic**

1. African Americans—Fiction 2. Family life—Fiction 3. Appalachian Mountains—Fiction
ISBN 0-02-742480-4; 0-02-043490-1 (pa)

Awarded the Newbery Medal, 1975

M.C. Higgins, a 13-year-old black boy "dreams of saving his family's house from an Ohio strip mining slag heap and finds that the answer to his dreams lies in coming to terms with his family heritage and his own identity." Publisher's note

"This is a deeply involving story possessing a folklorish quality. Superstition and magic are deeply rooted in its telling. Characterizations are highly original. The unusual setting and uniqueness of story line make this outstanding juvenile literature." Child Book Rev Serv

The mystery of Drear House; the conclusion of the Dies Drear chronicle. Greenwillow Bks. 1987 217p $15.95 (5 and up) **Fic**

1. African Americans—Fiction 2. Buried treasure—Fiction 3. Mystery fiction
ISBN 0-688-04026-8 LC 86-9829

Also available in paperback from Macmillan

"Professor Small, Thomas' father is engaged in cataloging a treasure house of antiques which have been hidden in one of the caverns on the property, which is a maze of tunnels and caves. He must protect these treasures from discovery by a neighboring family who are searching for them in order to sell them." Voice Youth Advocates

"Ingredients such as secret rooms and passages, moving walls, and awesome treasure will play well to a popular audience; yet substantive portrayals of characters and relationships provide the depth one associates with Hamilton. This solid tale displays a sensitivity toward feelings, emotions, and conflicting values—all in the context of a fantastic mystery laid to rest." Booklist

Plain City. Blue Sky Press (NY) 1993 194p $13.95; pa $3.99 (5 and up) **Fic**

1. Fathers and daughters—Fiction 2. African Americans—Fiction
ISBN 0-590-47364-6; 0-590-47365-4 (pa)
LC 93-19910

Also available Spanish language edition

Twelve-year-old Buhlaire, a "mixed" child who feels out of place in her community, struggles to unearth her past and her family history as she gradually discovers more and more about her long-missing father

"Richly textured with a cast of unforgettable characters, this extraordinary novel offers a rare glimpse of unconditional love, family loyalty and compassion." Publ Wkly

The planet of Junior Brown. Macmillan 1971 210p $14.95; pa $3.95 (6 and up) **Fic**

1. Friendship—Fiction 2. African Americans—Fiction
ISBN 0-02-742510-X; 0-02-043540-1 (pa)

"This is the story of a crucial week in the lives of two black, eighth-grade dropouts who have been spending their time with the school janitor. Each boy is presented as a distinct individual. Jr. is a three-hundred pound musical prodigy as neurotic as his overprotective mother. Buddy has learned to live by his wits in a world of homeless children. Buddy becomes Jr. Brown's protector and says to the other boys, 'We are together because we have to learn to live for each other.'" Read Ladders for Hum Relat. 6th edition

Hamilton, Virginia, 1936——*Continued*

Willie Bea and the time the Martians landed. Greenwillow Bks. 1983 208p $15 (5 and up)   Fic

1. Family life—Fiction 2. African Americans—Fiction 3. Halloween—Fiction
ISBN 0-688-02390-8   LC 83-1659

Also available in paperback from Aladdin Bks.

"Set in Ohio in 1938, this is the story of Willie Bea and her family, who have gathered for a festive Sunday dinner. Willie Bea and her cousins are anticipating Halloween trick or treating, but the evening takes an unexpected turn as Orson Welles' radio broadcast 'War of the Worlds' terrifies Willie Bea's family. A wonderful portrayal of a warm, extended black family." Soc Educ

Zeely; illustrated by Symeon Shimin. Macmillan 1967 122p il $13.95; pa $3.95 (4 and up)   Fic

1. African Americans—Fiction
ISBN 0-02-742470-7; 0-689-71695-8 (pa)

"Imaginative eleven-year-old Geeder is stirred when she sees Zeely Tayber, who is dignified, stately, and six-and-a-half feet tall. Geeder thinks Zeely looks like the magazine picture of the Watusi queen. Through meeting Zeely personally and getting to know her, Geeder finally returns to reality." Read Ladders for Hum Relat. 5th edition

Hansen, Joyce

The captive. Scholastic 1994 195p $13.95; pa $3.50 (5 and up)   Fic

1. Slavery—Fiction
ISBN 0-590-41625-1; 0-590-41624-3 (pa)

"Modeled after an actual slave narrative, this moving first-person tale follows twelve-year-old Kofi from his kidnapping in West Africa to his cruel enslavement in Massachusetts and his subsequent freedom and career as a sailor. The well-crafted and compelling survival story juxtaposes two cultures and gives a unique account of slavery from the sufferer's perspective." Horn Book Guide

The gift-giver. Clarion Bks. 1980 118p o.p.; Ticknor & Fields paperback available $6.95 (4-6)   Fic

1. School stories 2. African Americans—Fiction 3. New York (N.Y.)—Fiction
ISBN 0-89919-852-X (pa)   LC 80-12969

"Ten-year-old Doris lives in the ghetto, but has a loving family and teachers and parents who set forth important values in her life. In fact, Doris believes her life is too protected and restricted until Amir moves into the neighborhood. Amir shows her that she does not have to be exactly like everyone else and helps Doris and others in their class to develop their own special talents. The author gives a non-stereotypical view of life in a ghetto." Read Ladders for Hum Relat. 6th edition

Followed by: Yellow Bird and me (1985)

Which way freedom? Walker & Co. 1986 120p $14.95 (5 and up)   Fic

1. African Americans—Fiction 2. United States—History—1861-1865, Civil War—Fiction
ISBN 0-8027-6623-4   LC 85-29547

Also available in paperback from Avon Bks.

"Walker's American history series for young readers"

The author "describes the way in which one young black man, Obi, struggles over a period of three years (1861-1864) politically and ideologically toward the goal of being a free man. . . . [He] eventually joins a Union regiment and is one of the few to escape from the bloody battle at Fort Pillow, Tennessee." Bull Cent Child Books

"There is sufficient action to sustain readers' interest, but it is in the book's characterization that the chief strength lies. . . . A sensitive, thought-provoking historical novel." SLJ

Followed by Out from this place (1988)

Härtling, Peter, 1933-

Crutches; translated from the German by Elizabeth D. Crawford. Lothrop, Lee & Shepard Bks. 1988 163p $12.95 (5 and up)   Fic

1. Friendship—Fiction 2. Austria—Fiction
ISBN 0-688-07991-1   LC 88-80400

Original German edition, 1986

A young boy, searching vainly for his mother in post-war Vienna, is befriended by a man on crutches, a former German officer, and together they find hope for the future

"Because of its pacing, the book, while re-creating a specific time in history, has the intensity of an adventure story; it is equally remarkable for its development of theme without sacrificing believability or sense of story. When Thomas is finally reunited with his mother, for example, the moment is tinged with sadness, as it means that he will be parted from Crutches. The bittersweet ending is poignant but not manipulative." Horn Book

Old John; translated from the German by Elizabeth D. Crawford. Lothrop, Lee & Shepard Bks. 1990 120p lib bdg $11.95 (4 and up)   Fic

1. Grandfathers—Fiction 2. Old age—Fiction 3. Death—Fiction
ISBN 0-688-08734-3   LC 89-12976

Original German edition, 1981

"When Jacob's family invite their 75-year-old maternal grandfather, Old John, to come and live with them, he's hale and hearty, asserting himself in ways the family finds eccentric, but tolerable. Old John makes a place for himself within his family and about the town, even enjoying a romance. Then one fateful day, he has a stroke, and though he returns home from the hospital, he never regains his former strength." Booklist

"Härtling deftly sketches simple chapters, each unfolding into the next, with an economy of vocabulary and a storyteller's sense of timing. Even in translation the story crackles with energy and poignancy. A book to be savored, read aloud, and used to entice older but less skillful readers." SLJ

Harvey, Brett

Cassie's journey; going West in the 1860s; illustrated by Deborah Kogan Ray. Holiday House 1988 unp il lib bdg $13.95; pa $5.95 (2-4)   Fic

1. Overland journeys to the Pacific—Fiction 2. Frontier and pioneer life—Fiction 3. West (U.S.)—Fiction
ISBN 0-8234-0684-9 (lib bdg); 0-8234-1172-9 (pa)
         LC 87-23599

A young girl relates the hardships and dangers of traveling with her family in a covered wagon from Illinois to California during the 1860's

"Harvey has based this story of westward migration on the diaries of pioneer women . . . a fascinating piece of historical fiction. . . . Ray's soft charcoal drawings carry a solemnity that gives the account a serious edge while evoking the loneliness and breadth of the landscape." Booklist

Harvey, Brett—*Continued*

My prairie Christmas; illustrations by Deborah Kogan Ray. Holiday House 1990 unp il $15.95; pa $5.95 (2-4)   **Fic**

1. Christmas—Fiction 2. Frontier and pioneer life—Fiction 3. West (U.S.)—Fiction
ISBN 0-8234-0827-2; 0-8234-1064-1 (pa)
                                    LC 90-55104
On the first Christmas after Eleanor's family moves to a house on the prairie, everyone becomes worried when Papa goes out to cut down a Christmas tree and does not come back
"Ray's soft-edged illustrations capture the prairie vistas and the warm family interactions well. The narrative is flowing and comfortable." Booklist

My prairie year; based on the diary of Elenore Plaisted; written by Brett Harvey; illustrated by Deborah Kogan Ray. Holiday House 1986 unp il $13.95; pa $5.95 (2-4)   **Fic**

1. Frontier and pioneer life—Fiction 2. West (U.S.)—Fiction
ISBN 0-8234-0604-0; 0-8234-1028-5 (pa)
                                    LC 85-27177
Nine-year old Elenore describes her experiences living with her family in the Dakota Territory in the late nineteenth century
"Brett Harvey has shaped her grandmother's diary into a brief, flowing text. . . . Balanced and warm, with quiet intensity, the book offers new dimensions each time it is read." Horn Book
Followed by My prairie Christmas, entered above

Haseley, Dennis, 1950-

Shadows; pictures by Leslie Bowman. Farrar, Straus & Giroux 1991 72p il $12.95; pa $3.95 (3-5)   **Fic**

1. Grandfathers—Fiction 2. Country life—Fiction
ISBN 0-374-36761-2; 0-374-46611-4 (pa)
                                    LC 90-56149
Jamie's lonely life with his aunt changes when Grandpa comes to visit and teaches him to make shadow pictures
"The narrative is selectively but vividly detailed, the dialogue natural, and the shadow motif projected on both literal and symbolic levels." Bull Cent Child Books

Hautzig, Esther Rudomin, 1930-

A gift for Mama; [by] Esther Hautzig; illustrated by Donna Diamond. Viking 1981 56p il hardcover o.p. paperback available $3.95 (3-6)   **Fic**

1. Gifts—Fiction 2. Jews—Poland—Fiction 3. Poland—Fiction
ISBN 0-14-032384-8 (pa)   LC 80-24973
Also available in hardcover from P. Smith
"Sara, an only child, determines to buy her mother a gift for Mother's Day rather than make one as she has in the past. . . . She manages to earn the nine zlotys for the satin slippers with blue leather trim by mending and repairing the clothes of her aunt's friends at the university." Child Book Rev Serv
"The book is set in Poland [in the 1930s] the author's homeland, and the reader learns much about Jewish customs and Polish lifestyle. The illustrations are beautiful, high-quality monoprints, which are pictures painted on

glass and then transferred to paper by using an etching press." Interracial Books Child Bull

Riches; [by] Esther Hautzig; illustrated by Donna Diamond. HarperCollins Pubs. 1992 43p il lib bdg $13.89; pa $3.95 (4 and up)   **Fic**

1. Jews—Fiction
ISBN 0-06-022260-3 (lib bdg); 0-06-440550-8 (pa)
                                    LC 89-26904
"A Charlotte Zolotow book"
After following the advice of the wisest rabbi in the area, a rich storekeeper discovers that giving of himself is better than merely giving money
"With the ring of a traditional Jewish folktale, this beautiful book features cream-colored pages and meticulous black-ink-wash artwork that extends the appeal of the story well beyond middle grade readers. . . . A story to be shared across generations." Booklist

Heide, Florence Parry, 1919-

The shrinking of Treehorn; drawings by Edward Gorey. Holiday House 1971 unp il lib bdg $13.95; pa $4.95 (2-5)   **Fic**

ISBN 0-8234-0189-8 (lib bdg); 0-8234-0975-9 (pa)
Treehorn spends an unhappy day and night shrinking. Yet when he tells his mother, father, teacher and principal of his problem they're all too busy to do anything about it. To Treehorn's great relief he finally discovers a magical game that restores him to his natural size, but then he starts turning green!
This "is an imaginative little whimsy, whose sly humor and macabre touches are perfectly matched in Edward Gorey's illustrations." Book World
Another available title about Treehorn is:
Treehorn's wish (1984)

Henkes, Kevin, 1960-

Protecting Marie. Greenwillow Bks. 1995 195p $15 (5 and up)   **Fic**

1. Fathers and daughters—Fiction 2. Dogs—Fiction
ISBN 0-688-13958-2   LC 94-16387
Relates twelve-year-old Fanny's love-hate relationship with her father, a temperamental artist, who has given Fanny a new dog
"The characters ring heartbreakingly true in this quiet, wise story; they are complex and difficult—like all of us—and worthy of our attention." Horn Book

Words of stone. Greenwillow Bks. 1992 152p $15 (5 and up)   **Fic**

1. Friendship—Fiction
ISBN 0-688-11356-7   LC 91-28543
Also available in paperback Puffin Bks.; Spanish language edition also available
Busy trying to deal with his many fears and his troubled feelings for his dead mother, ten-year-old Blaze has his life changed when he meets the boisterous and irresistible Joselle
"A story rich in characterization, dramatic subplots, and some very creepy moments." SLJ

Henry, Marguerite, 1902-

Brighty of the Grand Canyon; illustrated by Wesley Dennis. Macmillan 1991 222p il $15; pa $3.95 (4 and up)   Fic

1. Donkeys—Fiction 2. Grand Canyon (Ariz.)—Fiction
ISBN 0-02-743664-0; 0-689-71485-8 (pa)

LC 90-28636

First published 1953 by Rand McNally

Drawn from a real-life incident, this is the story of "Brighty, the shaggy little burro who roamed the canyons of the Colorado River [and] had a will of his own. He liked the old prospector and Uncle Jim and he helped solve a mystery, but chiefly he was the freedom loving burro." Chicago Public Libr

"Only those who are unfamiliar with the West would say it is too packed with drama to be true. And the author's understanding warmth for all of God's creatures still shines through her superb ability as a story teller making this a vivid tale." Christ Sci Monit

Justin Morgan had a horse. Macmillan 1991 169p il $12.95; pa $3.95 (4 and up)   Fic

1. Horses—Fiction 2. Vermont—Fiction
ISBN 0-02-689322-3; 0-689-71534-X (pa)

LC 91-13973

A Newbery Medal honor book, 1946

An expanded version of the book first published 1945 by Wilcox & Follett; this is a reissue of the 1957 edition published by Rand McNally

Story of the brave little Vermont work horse from which came the famous American breed of Morgan horses. Justin Morgan first owned the horse, but it was the boy Joel Goss who loved 'Little Bub', later called 'Justin Morgan', followed him through his career, rescued him from a cruel master, and finally had the pleasure of having him ridden by James Monroe when he was President of the United States

A horse story "in a book that is rich in human values—the sort of book that makes you proud and sometimes brings a lump to your throat." Book Week

King of the wind; illustrated by Wesley Dennis. Macmillan 1991 172p il $14; pa $3.95 (4 and up)   Fic

1. Horses—Fiction
ISBN 0-02-743629-2; 0-689-71486-6 (pa)

LC 91-13474

Awarded the Newbery Medal, 1949

A reissue of the title first published 1948 by Rand McNally

"A beautiful, sympathetic story of the famous [ancestor of a line of great thoroughbred horses] . . . and the little mute Arabian stable boy who accompanies him on his journey across the seas to France and England [in the eighteenth century]. The lad's fierce devotion to his horse and his great faith and loyalty are skillfully woven into an enthralling tale which children will long remember. The moving quality of the writing is reflected in the handsome illustrations." Wis Libr Bull

Misty of Chincoteague; illustrated by Wesley Dennis. Macmillan 1991 173p il $14; pa $3.95 (4 and up)   Fic

1. Horses—Fiction 2. Chincoteague Island (Va.)—Fiction 3. Assateague Island National Seashore (Md. and Va.)—Fiction
ISBN 0-02-743622-5; 0-689-71492-0 (pa)

LC 90-27237

Also available Spanish language edition
A Newbery Medal honor book, 1948
First published 1947 by Rand McNally

"The islands of Chincoteague and Assateague, just off the coast of Virginia, are the setting. . . . Two children have their hearts set on owning a wild pony and her colt, descendants, so legend says, of the Moorish ponies who were survivors of a Spanish galleon wrecked there long ago." Booklist

"The beauty and pride of the wild horses is the highpoint in the story, and skillful drawings of them reveal their grace and swiftness." Ont Libr Rev

Other available titles about the ponies of Chincoteague Island are:
Sea star, orphan of Chincoteague (1949)
Stormy, Misty's foal (1963)

White stallion of Lipizza; illustrated by Wesley Dennis. Macmillan 1994 112p il $14.95; pa $9.95 (4 and up)   Fic

1. Horses—Fiction
ISBN 0-02-743628-4; 0-689-71824-1 (pa)

LC 93-86024

A reissue of the title first published 1964 by Rand McNally

"The son of a baker, enamored with the famous Lipizzaners in his native Vienna, has his dream come true when he is given the chance to train at the renowned riding school. The old-fashioned story is well researched and will appeal to fans of the beloved author-illustrator team." Horn Book

Henry, O., 1862-1910

The gift of the Magi (5 and up)   Fic

1. Christmas—Fiction
Also available Spanish language edition
Some editions are:
Picture Bk. Studio $16.95; pa $5.95 Illustrated by Lisbeth Zwerger; script by Michael Neugebauer (ISBN 0-907234-17-8; 0-88708-276-9)
Simon & Schuster Bks. for Young Readers $14 Illustrated by Kevin King (ISBN 0-671-64706-7)
"The tale of a poor young couple who sacrifice their dearest possessions to buy each other Christmas gifts." Bull Cent Child Books

Hermes, Patricia, 1936-

You shouldn't have to say good-bye. Harcourt Brace Jovanovich 1982 117p o.p.; Scholastic paperback available $3.25 (5 and up)   Fic

1. Mothers—Fiction 2. Parent and child—Fiction 3. Death—Fiction
ISBN 0-590-44174-9 (pa)   LC 82-47933

"Sarah's always healthy mother is struck with sudden and fatal cancer. The book depicts Sarah and her family trying to understand and cope with this situation, and ends with the mother's death after a five month illness." Child Book Rev Serv

"Characters are credible and their behaviors realistic." SLJ

Hesse, Karen

Letters from Rifka. Holt & Co. 1992 148p $14.95 (5 and up)   Fic

1. Immigration and emigration—Fiction 2. Jews—Fiction 3. Letters—Fiction
ISBN 0-8050-1964-2   LC 91-48007

Also available in paperback from Puffin Bks.

Hesse, Karen—*Continued*

In letters to her cousin, Rifka, a young Jewish girl, chronicles her family's flight from Russia in 1919 and her own experiences when she must be left in Belgium for a while when the others emigrate to America

"Based on the true story of the author's great-aunt, the moving account of a brave young girl's story brings to life the day-to-day trials and horrors experienced by many immigrants as well as the resourcefulness and strength they found within themselves." Horn Book

Sable; illustrated by Marcia Sewall. Holt & Co. 1994 81p il $14.95 (2-4)   Fic

1. Dogs—Fiction
ISBN 0-8050-2416-6   LC 93-33646
"A Redfeather book"

Tate Marshall is delighted when a stray dog turns up in the yard one day, but Sable, named for her dark, silky fur, causes trouble with the neighbors and has to go

"The early chapter book relates a dog tale sweet and scary enough for any budding pet lover." Horn Book Guide

Hickman, Janet

Jericho; a novel. Greenwillow Bks. 1994 135p $14 (5 and up)   Fic

1. Grandmothers—Fiction 2. Family life—Fiction 3. Old age—Fiction
ISBN 0-688-13398-3   LC 93-37309

An account of twelve-year-old Angela's visit to help take care of her great-grandmother alternates with the story of the old woman's life

"The author's unsentimental narrative reveals a sharp eye for detail, a profound understanding of the aging pro cess and a deep love for humanity." Publ Wkly

Hodges, Margaret

Gulliver in Lilliput; retold by Margaret Hodges from Gulliver's travels by Jonathan Swift; illustrated by Kimberly Bulcken Root. Holiday House 1995 unp il $15.95 (3-6)   Fic

1. Fantasy fiction
ISBN 0-8234-1147-8   LC 94-15037

On a voyage in the South Seas, an Englishman finds himself shipwrecked in Lilliput, a land of people only six inches high

"Hodges's adaptation of Part I of *Gulliver's Travels* is a masterful retelling of the 18th-century classic. While condensing the story considerably, she has retained not only the important details of the involved plot, but also the flavor of Swift's rich, descriptive language. . . . Root's stunning pen-and-watercolor illustrations do much to bring the fanciful tale to life." SLJ

Hoffmann, E. T. A. (Ernst Theodor Amadeus), 1776-1822

Nutcracker; pictures by Maurice Sendak; translated by Ralph Manheim. Crown 1984 102p il $16 (4 and up)   Fic

1. Fairy tales 2. Christmas—Fiction
ISBN 0-517-58659-2   LC 83-25266

This "book stems from Sendak's costume and set designs for the Pacific Northwest Ballet's 1981 production. That production, and this volume, differ from the traditional ballet as they are based on Hoffmann's original 1816 long short story, rather than a French version of Hoffmann's tale." SLJ

"The smooth, elegant, new translation re-creates the flavor of the period and does justice to the story. . . . The occasional quirkiness of the pictures . . . eerily reflect the mysterious story. Altogether a magnificent, splendid combination of talents." Horn Book

Holling, Holling C., 1900-1973

Paddle-to-the-sea; written and illustrated by Holling Clancy Holling. Houghton Mifflin 1941 unp il lib bdg $17.95; pa $7.95 (4-6)   Fic

1. Great Lakes region—Fiction
ISBN 0-395-15082-5 (lib bdg); 0-395-29203-4 (pa)
A Caldecott Medal honor book, 1942

A toy canoe with a seated Indian figure is launched in Lake Nipigon by the Indian boy who carved it and in four years travels thru all the Great Lakes and the St. Lawrence River to the Atlantic. An interesting picture of the shore life of the lakes and the river with striking full page pictures in bright colors and marginal pencil drawings

"The canoe's journey is used to show the flow of currents and of traffic, and each occurrence is made to seem plausible. . . . There are also diagrams of a sawmill, a freighter, the canal locks at the Soo, and Niagara Falls." Libr J

Holm, Anne, 1922-

North to freedom; translated from the Danish by L. W. Kingsland. Harcourt Brace 1965 190p hardcover o.p. paperback available $4.95 (6 and up)   Fic

1. Refugees—Fiction
ISBN 0-15-257553-7 (pa)
Also available in hardcover from P. Smith
First published 1963 in Denmark; first United States edition published 1965

"Twelve-year-old David, whose only memory is of life in a prison camp, escapes and makes his way across Europe alone. Before he is reunited with his mother, his prisonbred fear of people has gradually faded, and he has learned that goodness as well as evil exists in the world." Hodges. Books for Elem Sch Libr

Holman, Felice

Slake's limbo. Scribner 1974 117p $14.95; pa $3.95 (6 and up)   Fic

1. Runaway children—Fiction 2. Subways—Fiction 3. New York (N.Y.)—Fiction
ISBN 0-684-13926-X; 0-689-71066-6 (pa)

Aremis Slake, at the age of thirteen, takes to the New York City subways as a refuge from an abusive home life and oppressive school system

"The economically told chronicle of Slake's adventures is more than a survival saga: it is also an eloquent study of poverty, of fear, and finally of hope." Horn Book

Honeycutt, Natalie

The all new Jonah Twist. Bradbury Press 1986 110p $13.95 (3-5)   Fic

1. School stories 2. Friendship—Fiction
ISBN 0-02-744840-1   LC 85-28048
Also available in paperback from Avon Bks.

Jonah's efforts to survive the third grade are complicated by the new boy in class, who has the potential for either be-

Honeycutt, Natalie—*Continued*

coming a friend or beating him up

"Although things fall predictably into place at the end, the novel is satisfying in its depiction of third-grade culture in general and Jonah in particular. Other characters are drawn in a more cursory fashion, but in Jonah, Honeycutt creates a sympathetic figure who grows with the help of circumstances, friends, and his own will to change. With only 110 pages and a dash of humor, this novel will be a welcome addition to many collections." Booklist

Another available title about Jonah Twist is: The best-laid plans of Jonah Twist (1988)

Invisible Lissa. Bradbury Press 1985 168p $14.95 (3-5)   **Fic**

1. School stories 2. Clubs—Fiction

ISBN 0-02-744360-4   LC 84-20466

Also available in paperback from Avon Bks.

"Not only is Lissa the victim of Debra's snubbing campaign, but also the only girl in fifth grade excluded from the secret 'FUNCHY' club. Even friends Katie and Joel seem to have succumbed to Debra's phony charms. Hurt and isolated, Lissa throws herself into a school project that leads to a decisive confrontation and brings her back to social visibility." Publisher's note

"There are many middle-grades stories about classroom power struggles; this is not unusual in structure but it is better written than most, is nicely balanced by other facets of Lissa's life, and has a cheerful, lively tone." Bull Cent Child Books

Hooks, William H.

The ballad of Belle Dorcas; illustrated by Brian Pinkney. Knopf 1990 unp il lib bdg $14.99 (3-5)   **Fic**

1. African Americans—Fiction 2. Slavery—Fiction 3. Magic—Fiction

ISBN 0-394-94645-6   LC 89-2715

Also available in paperback from D. McKay

"Belle Dorcas, a free issue, marries Joshua, a slave. When his master decides to sell him, Belle Dorcas seeks the help of Granny Lizzard, a conjure woman. A tree by day, Joshua is transformed back into a man each night so he can be reunited with his love. Both are happy until the master cuts down the Joshua tree and uses the lumber to build a smokehouse." Child Book Rev Serv

"Hooks's graceful prose captures all the drama and poignancy of this tale of star-crossed lovers, and Pinkney's brooding illustrations, reminiscent of woodcuts, provide the perfect accompaniment." Publ Wkly

Circle of fire. Atheneum Pubs. 1982 147p $13.95 (5 and up)   **Fic**

1. Ku Klux Klan—Fiction 2. North Carolina—Fiction 3. Prejudices—Fiction

ISBN 0-689-50241-9   LC 82-3982

"A Margaret K. McElderry book"

"Harrison Hawkins is an eleven-year-old white boy growing up in 1936 rural coastal North Carolina. His best friends are Kitty Fisher, an eleven-year-old black boy, and Kitty's sister, Scrap. A band of gypsies camps in his father's hollow. Harrison overhears a local bigot planning a Ku Klux Klan attack on the tinkers, the gypsies' name for themselves, on Christmas. Harrison begins to suspect his father is involved in the Klan plot. He wrestles with his conscience over whether or not to warn the gypsies." Voice Youth Advocates

The story "is crisp with dialogue and beautifully shaded with a variety of vivid characters. Its mystery aspects propel the story's momentum, while the ethical decisions inherent in the plot give readers a sense of history and of moral obligation." Booklist

The girl who could fly; illustrated by Kees de Kiefte. Macmillan Bks. for Young Readers 1995 53p il $14 (2-4)   **Fic**

1. Extraterrestrial beings—Fiction 2. Friendship—Fiction

ISBN 0-02-744433-3   LC 94-4582

"Tom can read minds, make living maps of the continents, stop a baseball in midair, and fly. Adam Lee's new neighbor is out of this world—literally. Worse than being an alien, however, Tom (short for Tomasina) is a girl and doesn't know that going-on-ten-year-old boys don't have girls for 'best friends.' . . . This is light and breezy science fiction fun." Booklist

Hoover, H. M., 1935-

Away is a strange place to be. Dutton 1989 167p $14.95 (4-6)   **Fic**

1. Science fiction

ISBN 0-525-44505-6   LC 89-34455

When she is kidnapped from the Earth in 2349 to serve as slave labor on an artificial world under construction, twelve-year-old Abby must cooperate with her fellow prisoner Bryan, a spoiled rich boy, in order to plan an escape

"Hoover's crisp writing creates a gripping story with believable settings." Publ Wkly

The winds of Mars. Dutton Children's Bks. 1995 181p $14.99 (5 and up)   **Fic**

1. Science fiction

ISBN 0-525-45359-8   LC 94-32095

When rebel forces strike against her father, the all-powerful president of Mars, teenage Annalyn finds her comfortable existence turned upside-down and her life threatened from unexpected sources

"Hoover sets up a convincing society and several memorable characters in a story that moves swiftly to its conclusion." Booklist

Houston, James A., 1921-

Frozen fire; a tale of courage; by James Houston; drawings by the author. Atheneum Pubs. 1977 149p il $14; pa $4.95 (6 and up) **Fic**

1. Wilderness survival—Fiction 2. Arctic regions—Fiction 3. Inuit—Fiction

ISBN 0-689-50083-1; 0-689-71612-5 (pa)

LC 77-6366

"A Margaret K. McElderry book"

"Based on the true and dramatic ordeal of an Eskimo boy in the 1960's, this adventure story is set . . . in the far north. Kayak, a classmate of Matthew Morgan's in their Baffin Island school, suggests to his new friend Mattoosie (Matthew) that they take a snowmobile and go to the rescue of Mattoosie's father when the latter, a prospector, disappears. The spare can of gasoline leaks, and the two boys face a homeward trek through seventy-five miles of whirling snow and bitter cold." Bull Cent Child Books

"Convincing dialogue, good pace, and lean style mark this as first-class adventure with a partial basis in fact." SLJ

Followed by Black diamonds (1982)

Howard, Ellen

Edith herself; illustrated by Ronald Himler. Atheneum Pubs. 1987 131p il $13.95; pa $3.95 (4-6)   **Fic**

1. Epilepsy—Fiction 2. Farm life—Fiction 3. Orphans—Fiction

ISBN 0-689-31314-4; 0-689-71795-4 (pa)

LC 86-10826

"A Jean Karl book"

Orphaned by her mother's death, Edith goes to live with her older sister and dour brother-in-law in their stern Christian farming household, where the strain of adjusting seems to aggravate Edith's epileptic seizures

"The black-and-white drawings which head each chapter lend an old-fashioned, homespun touch to the quiet appeal of a young girl's triumph over her handicap and her ability to find joy and pleasure in her new surroundings." Horn Book

Howe, Deborah, 1946-1978

Bunnicula; a rabbit-tale of mystery; by Deborah and James Howe; illustrated by Alan Daniel. Atheneum Pubs. 1979 98p il $14 (4-6)   **Fic**

1. Animals—Fiction 2. Mystery fiction

ISBN 0-689-30700-4

LC 78-11472

Also available in paperback from Avon Bks.; Spanish language edition also available

"When the Monroes add a new pet to their household and vegetables are drained of their juices and turn white overnight, all the clues point to the little bunny they found in the theater the night they went to see a Dracula movie. The Monroes do not suspect Bunnicula, but their bookish cat, Chester, does. He sits up late reading Edgar Allan Poe and 'The Mark of the Vampire.' and he enlists the help of Harold, the dog, in getting to the bottom of the mystery." Child Book Rev Serv

"The plot is less important in the story than the style: blithe, sophisticated, and distinguished for the wit and humor of the dialogue. If readers like shaggy dog stories at all, they'd have to search hard for a funnier one." Bull Cent Child Books

Other available titles about Harold and Chester are entered below under James Howe; titles in picture book format are entered in Easy Section

Howe, James, 1946-

The celery stalks at midnight; illustrated by Leslie Morrill. Atheneum Pubs. 1983 111p il $14 (4-6)   **Fic**

1. Animals—Fiction 2. Mystery fiction

ISBN 0-689-30987-2

LC 83-2665

Also available in paperback from Avon Bks.

"Convinced that Bunnicula, the Monroe family's pet rabbit, is a kind of vegetarian vampire, Chester becomes alarmed when the object of his suspicions mysteriously disappears. His overworked imagination begins to envision the possible consequences of Bunnicula's appetite for vegetable juices. . . . With his two canine companions—Harold, the narrator, and Howie, a naïve dachshund—Chester sets forth to locate Bunnicula and to save the victims." Horn Book

"The amusing and skillful black-and-white sketches capture the animals' antics and expressions of alternating doubt, skepticism, disgust and worry in this clever tale abounding with puns, wild chases and slapstick humor." SLJ

Other available titles about Harold and Chester are:
Howliday Inn (1982)
Nighty-nightmare (1987)
Return to Howliday Inn (1992)

Dew drop dead; a Sebastian Barth mystery. Atheneum Pubs. 1990 156p $14 (4-6)   **Fic**

1. Mystery fiction 2. Homeless persons—Fiction

ISBN 0-689-31425-6

LC 89-34697

Also available in paperback from Avon Bks.

"A Jean Karl book"

"Sebastian Barth and his friends Corrie and David discover what appears to be a dead body in the long-abandoned Dew Drop Inn. But when they return with the police, the body has vanished. Police theory—that the 'body' was a homeless man passed-out drunk—is refuted when the kids find the body again in the woods, undeniably dead and possibly murdered." SLJ

"The story is well crafted and has substance beyond escapist fare as a result of Howe's inclusion of secondary storylines involving the homeless and Sebastian's own worries about his father's pending job loss." Booklist

Other available titles about Sebastian Barth are:
Eat your poison, dear (1986)
Stage fright (1986)
What Eric knew (1985)

Hughes, Ted, 1930-

The iron giant; a story in five nights; illustrations by Dirk Zimmer. Harper & Row 1988 58p il lib bdg $12.89; pa $4.95 (4-6)   **Fic**

1. Science fiction

ISBN 0-06-022639-0 (lib bdg); 0-06-440214-2 (pa)

LC 87-45089

A newly illustrated edition of the title first published 1968; published in the United Kingdom with title: The iron man

This is the story of an Iron Giant "who appears from nowhere and stalks the earth, devouring tractors and barbed wire for his supper. . . . But in the end he has to save the world from a creature from Outer Space." N Y Times Book Rev

"A clever, inventive fantasy." Booklist

Hunt, Irene, 1907-

Across five Aprils. Silver Burdett Press 1993 c1964 212p $10.95; lib bdg $12.95; pa $5.45 (5 and up)   **Fic**

1. United States—History—1861-1865, Civil War—Fiction 2. Farm life—Fiction 3. Illinois—Fiction

ISBN 0-382-24367-6; 0-382-24358-7 (lib bdg); 0-8136-7202-3 (pa)   LC 92-46736

Also available in paperback from Berkley Bks.

A reissue of the title first published 1964 by Follett

Young Jethro Creighton grows from a boy to a man when he is left to take care of the family farm in Illinois during the difficult years of the Civil War

"Authentic background, a feeling for the people of that time, and a story that never loses the reader's interest." Wilson Libr Bull

Up a road slowly; cover painting by Don Bolognese. Modern Curriculum Press c1966 192p $10.95 (5 and up)   **Fic**

ISBN 0-382-24366-8

Also available in paperback from Berkley Bks.

Hunt, Irene, 1907-—*Continued*

Awarded the Newbery Medal, 1967

First published 1996 by Follett

"Julie Trelling describes her life from the time her mother dies until her high school graduation: ten years. Aunt Cordelia's ramrod soul seems hard to live with, but Julie finds, to her surprise, when her father remarries and wants his daughter at home again, that she has become used to Aunt Cordelia and loves her dearly. The problems of jealousy, first love, parental relations, and snobbishness are handled with ease and honesty; the more serious problems of alcoholism and of emotional disturbance in adult characters are handled with dignity. A moving and beautifully written book." Sutherland. The Best in Child Books

Hunter, Mollie, 1922-

The mermaid summer. Harper & Row 1988 118p lib bdg $14.89; pa $3.95 (4 and up) Fic

1. Mermaids and mermen—Fiction 2. Grandfathers—Fiction

ISBN 0-06-022628-5 (lib bdg); 0-06-440344-0 (pa)

LC 87-45984

"A Charlotte Zolotow book"

With the help of her brother, Jon, nine-year-old Anna daringly seeks to discover the secret means to undo a mermaid's curse upon their grandfather

"Hunter's atmospherically rich story, set about a century ago, unfolds against a tapestry of local color. The delicately intertwining plot skeins reveal both tightly controlled suspense and an intriguing puzzle. Characters are well realized and fit the time and setting as well as the folkloric mold that Hunter once again uses to thoroughly enchant her readers." Booklist

A sound of chariots. Harper & Row 1972 242p lib bdg $12.89; pa $3.95 (5 and up) Fic

1. Death—Fiction 2. Authorship—Fiction 3. Scotland—Fiction

ISBN 0-06-022669-2 (lib bdg); 0-06-440235-5 (pa)

Also available in hardcover from P. Smith

A story set in post World War I Scotland. Bridie McShane's happy early childhood is interrupted by the death of her beloved father whose favorite child she was. Her sorrow colors her life as she matures, leading her to morbid reflections on time and death which she finally learns to deal with through her desire to write poetry

"The rich flavor of time and place, the details of poverty, hard work, and religious and political fervor add strength to the story." Horn Book

A stranger came ashore; a story of suspense. Harper & Row 1975 163p lib bdg $14.89; pa $3.95 (6 and up) Fic

1. Mythical animals—Fiction 2. Shetland (Scotland)—Fiction

ISBN 0-06-022652-8 (lib bdg); 0-06-440082-4 (pa)

The author "mingles the reality of the lives of fishermen-crofters and the legends of the Selkies, the seal-folk of the Shetland Islands. A young man, Finn Learson, appears during a fierce storm. Is he the lone survivor of a shipwreck or is he—as young Rob suspects—a seal-man who plans to take Rob's sister to his ocean home? The folklore of the Selkies and the customs of the islands are woven throughout the tale, which culminates in a suspense-filled struggle between the forces of good and evil." Bull Cent Child Books

The wicked one; a story of suspense. Harper & Row 1977 136p lib bdg $17.50; pa $3.95 (4 and up) Fic

1. Fairy tales 2. Scotland—Fiction

ISBN 0-06-022648-X (lib bdg); 0-06-440117-0 (pa)

"The Grollican, an otherworld creature, delights in tormenting fiery-tempered Colin Grant. Even a trip from Scotland to America doesn't rid the crofter of this persistent, almost likeable, pest." LC. Child Books, 1977

"The book exudes a fine Highland flavor and is an excellent example of the author's ability to interplay strong, solid characters with creatures from the Otherworld in tales of excitement and humor." Horn Book

Hurwitz, Johanna

The adventures of Ali Baba Bernstein; illustrated by Gail Owens. Morrow 1985 82p il $15; lib bdg $14.93 (2-4) Fic

1. Personal names—Fiction

ISBN 0-688-04161-2; 0-688-04345-3 (lib bdg)

LC 84-27387

Also available in paperback from Avon Bks.

"Tired of his ordinary name, David Bernstein, age eight, decides he wants to be called Ali Baba, and he has a series of . . . adventures, culminating in a birthday party to which he invites every David Bernstein in the Manhattan telephone directory. That's when he realizes how different people with the same name can be, and he decides that some day he might go back to calling himself David." Bull Cent Child Books

"Hurwitz' characters, as always, are believable, the situations realistic and the plot well developed." SLJ

Other available titles about Ali Baba Bernstein are:

Ali Baba Bernstein, lost and found (1992)

Hooray for Ali Baba Bernstein (1989)

Baseball fever; illustrated by Ray Cruz. Morrow 1981 128p il $15; lib bdg $14.93; pa $3.95 (3-5) Fic

1. Baseball—Fiction 2. Fathers and sons—Fiction

ISBN 0-688-00710-4; 0-688-00711-2 (lib bdg); 0-688-10495-9 (pa)

LC 81-5633

"Ten-year-old Ezra suffers from 'Baseball Fever' and a father who has no interest in the sport. Mr. Feldman is constantly nagging Ezra to show an interest in chess. A weekend trip that takes the pair to Cooperstown and the Hall of Fame sets the stage for father-and-son rapprochement." SLJ

"A brisk, breezy story about a believable family is told with warmth and humor." Bull Cent Child Books

Busybody Nora; illustrated by Lillian Hoban. Morrow Junior Bks. 1990 63p il $15; lib bdg $12.88 (2-4) Fic

1. Apartment houses—Fiction 2. New York (N.Y.)—Fiction

ISBN 0-688-09092-3; 0-688-09093-1 (lib bdg)

LC 89-13649

Also available in paperback from Puffin Bks.

A newly illustrated edition of the title first published 1976

"To five-year-old Nora and her little brother Teddy, their large apartment building in New York City is an exciting place to be. After learning there are as many as 200 people living 'in the same house,' Nora resolves to learn all their names and bring everyone together like one big happy family. Readers view big and little episodes in Nora and Teddy's lives through a nearly unblemished window on childhood." Booklist

Hurwitz, Johanna—*Continued*

Other available titles about Nora are:
New neighbors for Nora (1979)
Nora and Mrs. Mind-Your-Own-Business (1977)

Class clown; illustrated by Sheila Hamanaka. Morrow 1987 98p il $15 (2-4)

Fic

1. School stories
ISBN 0-688-06723-9   LC 86-23624
Also available in paperback from Scholastic
Lucas Cott "is the problem child in class; although extremely bright, he acts out involuntarily at the most inopportune moments. Even when he is trying his best to do assignments properly, things go wrong." Horn Book
"There are some very funny moments here, as well as some gentle and touching ones. . . . Realistic dialogue, short sentences in large print, and commonplace situations that sparkle with humor combine to make this a fine choice for children just beginning chapter books." SLJ
Other available titles in this series are:
Class president (1990)
School spirit (1994)
School's out (1990)
Teacher's pet (1988)

The hot & cold summer; illustrated by Gail Owens. Morrow 1984 160p il lib bdg $15 (3-5)

Fic

1. Friendship—Fiction
ISBN 0-688-02746-6   LC 83-19336
Also available in paperback from Scholastic
"Ten year olds Rory and Dere are best friends—a unit that does not need outsiders. So when their neighbor tells them that her neice is coming for the summer and that she expects they'll be great chums, Rory decides that the best attack is to ignore the girl from the start. But Bolivia . . . is not to be shunted aside. With the help of her talking parrot, she knows how to get attention and, once gotten, how to keep it. . . . This episodic novel is cheerful and perceptive—right on target for both boys and girls." Booklist
Other available titles about Rory, Derek, and Bolivia are:
The cold & hot winter (1988)
The up & down spring (1993)

Much ado about Aldo; pictures by John Wallner. Morrow 1978 95p il lib bdg $13.93 (3-5)

Fic

1. Vegetarianism—Fiction
ISBN 0-688-32160-7   LC 78-5434
Also available in paperback from Puffin Bks.
"Aldo ponders on the meanings of everything in his orbit, especially relationships. He enters enthusiastically into a class project, a terrarium with crickets. When the teacher adds chameleons to the tank, however, Aldo realizes the purpose of the project: to teach how living things feed on each other. In shock and horror, Aldo becomes a vegetarian and gets into a fix when he stealthily rescues the crickets." Publ Wkly
"Aldo is an earnest and likeable character in a convincing family story with a pleasant urban setting. The author has a remarkable ability to project the amusements and worries of childhood, conveying them in a deceptively simple style." Horn Book
Other available titles about Aldo are:
Aldo Applesauce (1979)
Aldo Ice Cream (1981)
Aldo Peanut Butter (1990)

Rip-roaring Russell; illustrated by Lillian Hoban. Morrow 1983 80p il $15; lib bdg $14.93 (2-4)

Fic

1. Family life—Fiction 2. School stories 3. Nursery schools—Fiction
ISBN 0-688-02347-9; 0-688-02348-7 (lib bdg)
                                      LC 83-1019
Also available in paperback from Puffin Bks.
Russell the four-year-old neighbor of Busybody Nora, entered above "faces the challenges of growing up in his own inimitable way. . . . Being a big brother disturbs him because baby Elisa takes altogether too much of his mother's time, but by the book's end, he decides that it isn't so bad." SLJ
"The action is low-keyed. . . . This is both realistic and sunny, with good adult-child relationships, the appeal of everyday life experiences, and a light, humorous treatment." Bull Cent Child Books
Other available titles about Russell and Elisa are:
E is for Elisa (1991)
Elisa in the middle (1995)
Make room for Elisa (1993)
Russell and Elisa (1989)
Russell rides again (1985)
Russell sprouts (1987)

Irving, Washington, 1783-1859

Rip Van Winkle (5 and up)   **Fic**

1. New York (State)—Fiction
Some editions are:
Dial Bks. $19 Illustrated by Arthur Rackham (ISBN 0-8037-1264-2)
Morrow (Books of Wonder) $20 Illustrated by N. C. Wyeth (ISBN 0-688-07459-6)
Originally appeared 1819 in Irving's The sketch book of Geoffrey Crayon, Gent.
Rip Van Wrinkle "is based on a folk tale. Henpecked Rip and his dog Wolf wander into the Catskill mountains before the Revolutionary War. There they meet a dwarf, whom Rip helps to carry a keg. They join a group of dwarfs playing ninepins. When Rip drinks from the keg, he falls asleep and wakes 20 years later, an old man. Returning to his town, he discovers his termagant wife dead, his daughter married, and the portrait of King George replaced by one of George Washington. Irving uses the folk tale to present the contrast between the new and old societies." Reader's Ency. 3d edition

Irwin, Hadley

Jim-Dandy. Margaret K. McElderry Bks. 1994 135p $15 (5 and up)   **Fic**

1. Custer, George Armstrong, 1839-1876—Fiction 2. Frontier and pioneer life—Fiction 3. Kansas—Fiction 4. Horses—Fiction
ISBN 0-689-50594-9   LC 93-22611
Also available in paperback from Troll
Living after the Civil War on a Kansas homestead with his stern stepfather, thirteen-year-old Caleb raises a beloved colt and becomes involved in General Custer's raids on the Cheyenne
"A thought-provoking read that's sure to promote discussion." SLJ

The original Freddie Ackerman. Margaret K. McElderry Bks. 1992 183p $15; pa $3.99 (5 and up)   **Fic**

1. Aunts—Fiction 2. Islands—Fiction 3. Maine—Fiction
ISBN 0-689-50562-0; 0-689-80389-3 (pa)
                                      LC 91-43145

Irwin, Hadley—*Continued*

Twelve-year-old Trevor Frederick Ackerman refuses to spend another summer with his extended family of divorced parents, step-parents, and step-brothers and step-sisters, so he is sent up to Maine to stay with two eccentric great aunts and there gets involved in a series of adventures

"This is a beautiful coming-of-age story with wonderful characterizations. Trevor's loneliness and low self-esteem are palpable as he escapes painful realities through a series of fantasies of himself as a war hero. . . . A fine book with a winning combination of humor and poignancy." SLJ

Jacques, Brian

Redwall; illustrated by Gary Chalk. Philomel Bks. 1986 351p il $17.95 (6 and up)
Fic

1. Mice—Fiction 2. Animals—Fiction 3. Fantasy fiction
ISBN 0-399-21424-0   LC 86-25467

Also available in paperback from Avon Bks.

"Only the lost sword of Martin the Warrior can save Redwall Abbey from the evil rat Cluny and his greedy horde. The young mouse Matthias (formerly Redwall's most awkward novice) vows to recover the legendary weapon." Publ Wkly

"Thoroughly engrossing, this novel captivates despite its length. . . . The theme will linger long after the story is finished." Booklist

Other available titles about Redwall Abbey are:
The Bellmaker (1995)
Mariel of Redwall (1992)
Martin the Warrior (1994)
Mattimeo (1990)
Mossflower (1988)
Salamandastron (1993)

James, Mary, 1927-

Shoebag. Scholastic 1990 135p $13.95; pa $3.25 (5 and up)   Fic

1. Cockroaches—Fiction 2. Fantasy fiction
ISBN 0-590-43029-7; 0-590-43030-0 (pa)
                                    LC 89-10828

Shoebag, a happy young cockroach who finds himself suddenly changed into a little boy, changes the lives of those around him before returning to his former life as an insect

"Fans of the improbable will find this cockroach fantasy holds appeal, while the combination of humor and possible discussion topics offers opportunities for interchange." Booklist

Jansson, Tove, 1914-

Moominsummer madness; translated by Thomas Warburton. Farrar, Straus & Giroux 1991 c1955 159p il $13.95; pa $4.50 (4-6)
Fic

1. Fantasy fiction
ISBN 0-374-35039-6; 0-374-45310-1 (pa)
                                    LC 90-56150

Original Swedish edition 1954; this translation first published 1955 in the United Kingdom; first United States edition 1961 by Henry Z. Walck

A flood hits Moomin Valley and triggers a series of adventures for the Moomins

"Newcomers to the long-established Moominvalley series might first glance at the simple, playfully illustrated appendix—'Moomin Gallery'—to acquaint themselves with the host of Moomin-species that adorn the plot. Once initi-ated, it's difficult not to be drawn in by the inventive adventures of Moomintroll and his family." Publ Wkly

Other available titles about the Moomintrolls are:
Comet in Moominland (1990)
Finn Family Moomintroll (1990)
Moominland midwinter(1992)
Moominpapa at sea (1993)
Moominpapa's memoirs (1994)
Tales from Moominvalley (1995)

Johnson, Annabel, 1921-

The grizzly; pictures by Gilbert Riswold. Harper & Row 1964 160p il hardcover o.p. paperback available $3.95 (5 and up)   Fic

1. Bears—Fiction 2. Camping—Fiction 3. Parent and child—Fiction
ISBN 0-06-440036-0 (pa)

"Eleven-year-old David, living with his divorced mother, is doubtful about going on a camping trip with his father. When a grizzly injures the father and disables the truck, David surprises both himself and his father by his resourcefulness." Hodges. Books for Elem Sch Libr

"Through a fine balance of descriptive detail and dialogue between the characters, the authors offer much insight into human relationships, especially those between father and son." Adventuring with Books. 2d edition

Johnston, Julie

Hero of lesser causes. Little, Brown 1993 c1992 194p $15.95 (5 and up)   Fic

1. Poliomyelitis—Fiction 2. Physically handicapped—Fiction 3. Brothers and sisters—Fiction
ISBN 0-316-46988-2   LC 92-37268

Also available in paperback from Penguin Bks.

"Joy Street books"

First published 1992 in Canada

In 1946 twelve-year-old Keely is devastated when her older brother Patrick is paralyzed by polio, and she starts a campaign to reawaken his waning interest in life

"Johnston's particular gift is the authenticity of her characters and relationships. . . . This is a touching and funny story of sibling maturation." Bull Cent Child Books

Jones, Diana Wynne

Castle in the air. Greenwillow Bks. 1991 199p $15 (6 and up)   Fic

1. Fantasy fiction
ISBN 0-688-09686-7   LC 90-30266

In this "follow-up to *Howl's Moving Castle* [entered below] . . . the protagonist is a young carpet merchant called Abdullah, who spends much of his time creating a richly developed daydream in which he is the long-lost son of a great prince, kidnapped as a child by a villainous bandit. . . . Feisty Sophie and the Wizard Howl (from *Howl's Moving Castle*) do not become apparent till late in the story, but their fortunes do link up with those of Abdullah and his love. Jones maintains both suspense and wit throughout, demonstrating once again that frequently nothing is what it seems to be." Booklist

Dogsbody. Greenwillow Bks. 1988 c1975 242p $11.95 (6 and up)   Fic

1. Dogs—Fiction 2. Fantasy fiction
ISBN 0-688-08191-6

Also available in paperback from Random House

A reissue of the title first published 1975 in the United Kingdom; 1977 in the United States

Jones, Diana Wynne—*Continued*

"Sirius, the Dog Star, falsely accused in the heavens of losing the Zoi, is sentenced to earth as a pup in order to search for this sacred object, which has fallen as a meteorite. Rescued from drowning by Kathleen, an Irish waif abused by her uncle's family, Sirius develops a close bond of affection with the girl. However, it is the search for the Zoi that compels Sirius, a quest that seems futile until help comes from Sol, Earth, and Moon. [The author] . . . intricately weaves contemporary family tensions with the evil powers' struggle to gain control of the Zoi and incidentally portrays a touching child-dog relationship. Her ability to tell the story through a dog's eyes in a believable way is to her credit." Booklist

Howl's moving castle. Greenwillow Bks. 1986 212p $13 (6 and up)   Fic

1. Fantasy fiction
ISBN 0-688-06233-4   LC 85-21981

"When the wicked Witch of the Waste turns Sophie Hatter into an ugly crone, the girl seeks refuge in Wizard Howl's moving castle. To her surprise and dismay, she finds herself embroiled in a contest between the witch and the wizard, in the tangled love affairs of the wizard, and in a perplexing mystery." Child Book Rev Serv

"Satisfyingly, Sophie meets a fate far exceeding her dreary expectations. This novel is an exciting, multi-faceted puzzle, peopled with vibrant, captivating characters. A generous sprinkling of humor adds potency to this skillful author's spell." Voice Youth Advocates

Jukes, Mavis

Blackberries in the dark; pictures by Thomas B. Allen. Knopf 1985 unp il $15 (2-4)
Fic

1. Grandmothers—Fiction 2. Death—Fiction
ISBN 0-394-87599-0   LC 85-4259

Also available in paperback from Random House

Nine-year-old Austin visits his grandmother the summer after his grandfather dies and together they try to come to terms with their loss

"This spare story vividly captures the emotions of painful times and shows how they ease with sharing and remembering. . . . Poignant and perceptive, this has impressive resonance for so brief a story, and readers won't easily shed its warm afterglow. Heavily shaped pencil drawings are scattered throughout." Booklist

Like Jake and me; pictures by Lloyd Bloom. Knopf 1984 unp il hardcover o.p. paperback available $7.99 (2-4)   Fic

1. Stepfathers—Fiction 2. Spiders—Fiction
ISBN 0-394-89263-1 (pa)   LC 83-8380

A Newbery Medal honor book, 1985

In this book "timid Alex strives to be like his rugged cowboy stepfather, and the two find a common bond when Alex demonstrates his bravery by 'rescuing' Jake from a wolf spider that is crawling on his clothes." SLJ

"The humorous short story is illustrated picture-book fashion with a series of misty, soft-edged paintings that pose slightly caricatured figures largely on the pages. The story might be an excellent springboard for discussion of relationships and emotions; at the very least it's a satisfying vignette of the tender spots left when families take new shapes." Booklist

Juster, Norton, 1929-

The phantom tollbooth; illustrated by Jules Feiffer. Random House 1961 255p il $18; pa $3.95 (5 and up)   Fic

1. Fantasy fiction
ISBN 0-394-81500-9; 0-394-82037-1 (pa)

Also available G.K. Hall large print edition

"Milo, a boy who receives a surprise package which, when put together, is a toll-booth, goes off in a toy automobile on a tour of an imaginary country." Bull Cent Child Books

"It's all very clever. The author plays most ingeniously on words and phrases . . . and on concepts of averages and infinity and such . . . while the pictures are even more diverting than the text, for they add interesting details." N Y Her Trib Books

Keith, Harold, 1903-

Rifles for Watie. Crowell 1957 332p $15.75; pa $3.95 (6 and up)   Fic

1. Watie, Stand, 1806-1871 Fiction 2. United States—History—1861-1865, Civil War—Fiction
ISBN 0-690-70181-0; 0-06-447030-X (pa)

Awarded the Newbery Medal, 1958

"Young Jeff Bussey longs for the life of a Union soldier during the Civil War, but before long he realizes the cruelty and savagery of some men in the army situation. The war loses its glamor as he sees his very young friends die. When he is made a scout, his duties take him into the ranks of Stand Watie, leader of the rebel troops of the Cherokee Indian Nation, as a spy." Stensland. Lit By & About the Am Indian

Kerley, Barbara

Songs of Papa's island; illustrated by Katherine Tillotson. Houghton Mifflin 1995 59p il $14.95 (3-5)   Fic

1. Mothers and daughters—Fiction 2. Guam—Fiction
ISBN 0-395-71548-2   LC 94-24581

A mother tells her daughter a series of stories about life on Guam before the daughter was born and when she was a baby

"Told in a leisurely pace in simple, gently cadenced language, these personal reminiscences display a lively sense of humor and a deep appreciation and respect for nature. . . . Wide margins, heavy cream paper, and handsome black-and-white woodblock prints—one per chapter—make the book a joy to hold." SLJ

Kerr, Judith

When Hitler stole Pink Rabbit; illustrated by the author. Coward-McCann 1972 c1971 191p il o.p.; Dell paperback available $3.99 (4 and up)   Fic

1. Jewish refugees—Fiction
ISBN 0-440-49017-0 (pa)

Also available Spanish language edition

First published 1971 in the United Kingdom

"Anna, aged nine, finds that her family suddenly has to leave Berlin for Switzerland because the Nazis have won an election. In packing, she has to choose between two stuffed animals—an old beloved pink rabbit and a new dog. She chooses the dog, assuming that their exile will be temporary. Only gradually as her family moves from Switzerland to France to England in search of a meager living does she realize that she will never return to Germany and that she

Kerr, Judith—*Continued*

will never see the rabbit again." Economist

"This tale of a refugee family is based on the author's childhood experience and, although anti-Semitism in Germany and financial depression everywhere are a somber backdrop, the book is warm and cozy, filled with the small, homely details of events that are important in a child's life." Saturday Rev

Followed by The other way around (1975)

Kimmel, Margaret Mary

Magic in the mist; illustrated by Trina Schart Hyman. Atheneum Pubs. 1975 unp il $13.95 (1-4)   **Fic**

1. Dragons—Fiction 2. Magic—Fiction 3. Wales—Fiction

ISBN 0-689-50026-2

"A Margaret K. McElderry book"

"Practicing to be a wizard, a boy named Thomas lived alone in a damp, cold Welsh cottage with his pet toad. One day a great mist came and Thomas found a tiny dragon in the grass; the dragon breathed on the fire and the logs burned brightly as they never had. The next day the dragon was gone, but the fire has burned cheerfully ever since." Bull Cent Child Books

"Hyman's pen-and-ink drawings effectively convey the chill starkness of marshlands and bogs." SLJ

King-Smith, Dick, 1922-

Ace, the very important pig; illustrations by Lynette Hemmant. Crown 1990 134p il $13; lib bdg $13.99 (3-5)   **Fic**

1. Pigs—Fiction

ISBN 0-517-57832-8; 0-517-57833-6 (lib bdg)

LC 90-1447

Also available in paperback from Knopf

Farmer Tubbs' amazing pig, Ace of Clubs, eventually winds up on television for his cleverness

"The author exploits his joyful sense of the absurd to the hilt, combining a gentle ribbing of country folk and their animal counterparts with a genuine affection." Horn Book

Babe: the gallant pig; written by Dick King-Smith, illustrated by Mary Rayner. Crown 1985 c1983 118p il $13 (3-5)   **Fic**

1. Pigs—Fiction

ISBN 0-517-55556-5   LC 84-11429

Also available in paperback from Dell

First published 1983 in the United Kingdom with title: The sheep-pig

A piglet destined for eventual butchering arrives at the farmyard, is adopted by an old sheep dog, and discovers a special secret to success

"Mary Rayner's engaging black-and-white drawings capture the essence of Babe and the skittishness of sheep and enhance this splendid book—which should once and for all establish the intelligence and nobility of pigs." Horn Book

The cuckoo child; illustrated by Leslie W. Bowman. Hyperion Bks. for Children 1993 127p il $13.95; pa $3.50 (3-5)   **Fic**

1. Ostriches—Fiction 2. Geese—Fiction 3. Farm life—Fiction

ISBN 1-56282-350-7; 0-7868-1001-7 (pa)

LC 92-72029

"Eight-year-old Jack steals a huge ostrich egg that is about to be fed to a snake in Wildlife Park. Jack sets the

egg under the farmyard goose; it hatches, and Jack raises Oliver, the ostrich chick, until he's two years old. . . . King-Smith has a lot of fun with the way humans and animals resemble each other. He characterizes the farmyard with comedy and warmth, and Bowman's illustrations capture the cackles and chaos." Booklist

The fox busters; illustrated by Jon Miller. Delacorte Press 1988 c1978 117p il o.p.; Dell paperback available $2.95 (3-5)   **Fic**

1. Chickens—Fiction 2. Foxes—Fiction

ISBN 0-440-40288-3 (pa)   LC 87-37409

First published 1978 in the United Kingdom

"The fox busters are three extraordinary pullets, whose heritage, upbringing and intelligence combine to make them attempt a daring plan. Their enemies, four smart poultry-loving foxes, have hatched a murderous plan of their own. While the odds seem to favor the carnivores, the chickens have discovered an ingenious way to harden their unlaid eggs and to use them as weapons. Suspenseful, engrossing, and so carefully structured as to render it entirely believable, the story is an ideal read-aloud." Publ Wkly

Martin's mice; illustrations by Jez Alborough. Crown 1989 c1988 122p il $13 (3-5)   **Fic**

1. Cats—Fiction 2. Mice—Fiction

ISBN 0-517-57113-7   LC 88-20359

Also available in paperback from Dell

First published 1988 in the United Kingdom

"Martin, a kitten, is branded 'wimp' by his siblings and 'stupid' by other farm animals for his friendly interest in mice. When he captures the pregnant mouse Drusilla, he makes her and her eventual brood his pets. He loves caring for them and can't understand their desire for freedom. Only when he becomes the pet of a big city apartment dweller does he realize why his pets deserted him." SLJ

"Dick King-Smith is at his anthropomorphic jolliest and the perspective of the farmyard allows him to explore a number of issues, such as the relationship between humans and animals. . . . Martin is also the kind of child/kitten who constantly asks questions. As a result, this book will teach you the differences between omnivores, herbivores and carnivores; the relative intelligence of sheep, cows and pigs; and how to keep a pet mouse." Times Lit Suppl

Pigs might fly; a novel; drawings by Mary Rayner. Viking 1982 158p il hardcover o.p.; paperback available $4.99 (3-5)   **Fic**

1. Pigs—Fiction 2. Farm life—Fiction 3. Physically handicapped—Fiction 4. Great Britain—Fiction

ISBN 0-14-034537-X (pa)   LC 81-11525

Also available in paperback from Scholastic

First published 1980 in the United Kingdom with title: Daggie Dogfoot

"Daggie Dogfoot (his front trotters are formed like paws) is the nickname bestowed on the runt of a litter born on a pig farm in England. Daggie overhears, out of its ironic context, the comment that 'pigs might fly' and this becomes his goal. His attempts to fly lead to his learning how to swim, with the help of a Muscovy duck and a happy-go-lucky otter. After a fierce rainstorm bursts the dam upstream, flooding most of the farm and carrying the food-storage shed downstream, it is Daggie who must swim to get help." SLJ

"Written with wit and controlled ebullience, this has excellent characterization, pithy dialogue, good pace, and admirable line drawings." Bull Cent Child Books

King-Smith, Dick, 1922-—_Continued_
Sophie's Tom; illustrated by David Parkins. Candlewick Press 1991 110p il $13.95 (3-5)
Fic

1. Cats—Fiction 2. Great Britain—Fiction
ISBN 1-56402-107-6   LC 91-58756

Sophie "finds a stray cat and tries to talk her parents into letting her keep it. Set against the backdrop of this story are Sophie's first experiences with school. . . . A good readaloud for Sophie's contemporaries, this is a funny chronicle of a rugged and interesting little girl." Bull Cent Child Books

Other available titles about Sophie are:
Sophie hits six (1993)
Sophie in the saddle (1994)
Sophie is seven (1995)

Three terrible trins; illustrated by Mark Teague. Crown 1994 105p il $15; lib bdg $15.99 (3-5)
Fic

1. Mice—Fiction 2. Cats—Fiction
ISBN 0-517-59828-0; 0-517-59829-9 (lib bdg)
LC 93-44157

Three mice brothers, ignoring the class system separating the four clans of rodents in their farmhouse, befriend a lower class mouse and form a team to fight cats

"King-Smith excels in creating vivid characters and a fast-paced plot. . . . All in all, a delightful romp, illustrated with humorous black-and-white drawings, that will appeal to readers who enjoy fantastic animal stories." SLJ

Kinsey-Warnock, Natalie
The Canada geese quilt; illustrated by Leslie W. Bowman. Dutton 1989 60p il $13 (3-5)
Fic

1. Quilts—Fiction 2. Grandmothers—Fiction 3. Family life—Fiction 4. Vermont—Fiction
ISBN 0-525-65004-0   LC 88-32661

Also available in paperback from Dell

Worried that the coming of a new baby and her grandmother's serious illness will change the warm familiar life on her family's Vermont farm, ten-year-old Ariel combines her artistic talent with her grandmother's knowledge to make a very special quilt

"Written in simple language, this intergenerational love story succeeds in touching the heart through its rare combination of sensitivity and grit. Bowman's softly shaded pencil drawings subtly suggest the 1940s Vermont setting, characters, and mood." Booklist

Kipling, Rudyard, 1865-1936
The beginning of the armadilloes   Fic

1. Armadillos—Fiction
Some editions are:
Harcourt Brace Jovanovich $14.95; pa $5 Illustrated by Lorinda Bryan Cauley (ISBN 0-15-206380-3; 0-15-206381-1)
North-South Bks. $15.95; lib bdg $15.88 Illustrated by John A. Rowe (ISBN 1-55858-482-X; 1-55858-483-8)

Story originally published 1902 as part of Kipling's Just so stories

A tortoise and a hedgehog combine their natural assets and transform themselves into armadillos to escape the hungry attention of a young jaguar

The elephant's child   Fic

1. Elephants—Fiction
Also available Spanish language edition

Some editions are:
Harcourt Brace Jovanovich $14; pa $5 Illustrated by Lorinda Bryan Cauley (ISBN 0-15-225385-8; 0-15-225386-6)
North-South Bks. $14.95; lib bdg $14.88 Illustrated by John A. Rowe (ISBN 1-55858-369-6; 1-55858-370-X)

Originally published 1902 as part of Kipling's Just so stories

"This well-known whimsical fantasy that explains how the insatiably curious elephant child got his trunk is a fine example of one of Kipling's greatest classics." Adventuring with Books

How the camel got his hump; written by Rudyard Kipling ; illustrated by Tim Raglin. Rabbit Ears Bks. 1989 unp il $14.95   Fic

1. Camels—Fiction
ISBN 0-88708-096-0   LC 88-33366

Originally published 1902 as part of Kipling's Just so stories

When the world was new, the camel, a creature of 'scruciating idleness, said "Humph!" too often and received for all time a hump[h] from the Djinn of All Deserts

Klause, Annette Curtis
Alien secrets. Delacorte Press 1993 227p $15.95; pa $4.50 (5 and up)   Fic

1. Science fiction 2. Mystery fiction
ISBN 0-385-30928-7; 0-440-41061-4 (pa)
LC 92-31326

On her journey to the distant planet where her parents are working, twelve-year-old Puck befriends a troubled alien and becomes involved in a dangerous mystery involving a precious artifact

"This fast-paced adventure novel features a smart heroine, an appealing alien, plenty of intrigue, and a noble mission that readers won't be able to resist." SLJ

Kline, Suzy, 1943-
Herbie Jones; illustrated by Richard Williams. Putnam 1985 95p il $13.95 (3-5)
Fic

1. School stories
ISBN 0-399-21183-7   LC 84-24915

Also available in paperback from Puffin Bks.

Herbie's experiences in the third grade include finding bones in the boy's bathroom, wandering away from his class on their field trip, and being promoted to a higher reading group

This is "filled with light humor in its accounts of classroom incidents." Bull Cent Child Books

Other available titles about Herbie Jones are:
Herbie Jones and Hamburger Head (1989)
Herbie Jones and the birthday showdown (1993)
Herbie Jones the the class gift (1987)
Herbie Jones and the dark attic (1992)
Herbie Jones and the monster ball (1988)
What's the matter with Herbie Jones? (1986)

Horrible Harry in room 2B; pictures by Frank Remkiewicz. Viking Kestrel 1988 56p il lib bdg $12.99; pa $2.99 (2-4)   Fic

1. School stories
ISBN 0-670-82176-4 (lib bdg); 0-14-032825-4 (pa)
LC 88-14204

Harry "is the devilish second grader who plays pranks and gets into mischief but can still end up a good friend. In a series of brief scenes, children meet Harry as he shows a garter snake to Song Lee and later ends up being a snake

Kline, Suzy, 1943——*Continued*

himself for Halloween. His trick to make scary people out of pencil stubs backfires when no one is scared, and his budding romance with Song Lee goes nowhere on the trip to the aquarium. . . . This story should prove to be popular with those just starting chapter books." SLJ

Other available titles about Horrible Harry and Song Lee are:

Horrible Harry and the ant invasion (1989)
Horrible Harry and the Christmas surprise (1991)
Horrible Harry and the green slime (1989)
Horrible Harry and the kickball wedding (1992)
Horrible Harry's secret (1990)
Song Lee and Leech Man (1995)
Song Lee and the hamster hunt (1994)
Song Lee in room 2B (1993)

Mary Marony, mummy girl; illustrations by Blanche Sims. Putnam 1994 78p il $13.95 (2-4)   **Fic**

1. Halloween—Fiction 2. School stories 3. Speech disorders—Fiction
ISBN 0-399-22609-5   LC 93-14348

Second-grader Mary Marony wants to be something scary for Halloween so she can get back at Marvin, who makes fun of Mary's stuttering

"Kline's characters deal with real problems in upbeat, yet believable ways. . . . A fine addition to the burgeoning easy-chapter-book genre as well as a popular offering for Halloween." Booklist

Other available titles about Mary Marony are:
Mary Marony and the chocolate surprise (1995)
Mary Marony and the snake (1992)
Mary Marony hides out (1993)

Orp and the FBI. Putnam 1995 94p il $14.95 (4-6)   **Fic**

1. Mystery fiction
ISBN 0-399-22664-8   LC 94-24552

"When Orp and his friend Derrick start a detective agency, Famous Bathtub investigators (FBI), Orp's little sister, Chloe, starts a rival one, Chloe's investigation Agency (CIA). So when the children notice strange lights and sounds coming from the next-door neighbor's house, both the FBI . . . and CIA turn out to investigate." Booklist

"The plot develops smoothly and believably with many amusing turns along the way, and the level of suspense is well maintained." SLJ

Other available titles about Orp are:
Orp (1989)
Orp and the chop suey burgers (1990)
Orp goes to the hoop (1991)
Who's Orp's girlfriend? (1993)

Koertge, Ronald

Tiger, tiger, burning bright; a novel. Orchard Bks. 1994 179p $15.95; lib bdg $16.99 (6 and up)   **Fic**

1. Grandfathers—Fiction   2. Old   age—Fiction 3. California—Fiction
ISBN 0-531-06840-4; 0-531-08690-9 (lib bdg)
                                                 LC 93-37758

Also available in paperback from Avon Bks.
"A Melanie Kroupa book"

Worried that his mother will send his beloved grandfather to a nursing home "for his own good," Jesse and some of his eighth-grade classmates accompany Pappy into the mountains near their small California town to look for the tiger tracks he claims to have seen

"Koertge has created a quirky, often hilarious, cast of characters in a small central California town. . . . The dialogue, whether between Jesse and his family members or between Jesse and his cronies, sounds exactly right." Book Rep

Konigsburg, E. L.

About the B'nai Bagels; written and illustrated by E. L. Konigsburg. Atheneum Pubs. 1969 172p il $14.95 (4-6)   **Fic**

1. Jews—Fiction 2. Baseball—Fiction
ISBN 0-689-20631-3

Also available in paperback from Dell

A "story of a Jewish Little League team. Twelve-year-old Mark Stezer has problems: his mother is manager of the team; his brother is coach. This makes some sticky situations and 'overlaps' in his life. And he has worries about losing his best friend. Mark matures, having to make some difficult decisions on his own." Read Ladders for Hum Relat. 5th edition

"Penetrating characterizations emerge by implication; and the author's unfailing humor and her deep understanding of human nature are as noticeable as ever." Horn Book

From the mixed-up files of Mrs. Basil E. Frankweiler; written and illustrated by E. L. Konigsburg. Atheneum Pubs. 1967 162p il $15; pa $3.95 (4-6)   **Fic**

1. Metropolitan Museum of Art (New York, N.Y.)—Fiction
ISBN 0-689-20586-4; 0-689-71181-6 (pa)

Also available in paperback from Dell
Awarded the Newbery Medal, 1968

"Claudia, feeling misunderstood at home, takes her younger brother and runs away to New York where she sets up housekeeping in the Metropolitan Museum of Art, making ingenius arrangements for sleeping, bathing, and laundering. She and James also look for clues to the authenticity of an alleged Michelangelo statue, the true story of which is locked in the files of Mrs. Frankweiler, its former owner. Claudia's progress toward maturity is also a unique introduction to the Metropolitan Museum." Moorachian. What is a City?

Jennifer, Hecate, Macbeth, William McKinley, and me, Elizabeth; written and illustrated by E. L. Konigsburg. Atheneum Pubs. 1967 117p il $15 (4-6)   **Fic**

1. Friendship—Fiction 2. Witchcraft—Fiction 3. African Americans—Fiction
ISBN 0-689-30007-7

Also available in paperback from Dell
A Newbery Medal honor book, 1968

"Two fifth grade girls, one of whom is the first black child in a middle-income suburb, play at being apprentice witches in this amusing and perceptive story." NY Public Libr. Black Exper in Child Books

Journey to an 800 number. Atheneum Pubs. 1982 138p $15 (5 and up)   **Fic**

1. Fathers—Fiction 2. Parent and child—Fiction 3. Social classes—Fiction
ISBN 0-689-30901-5   LC 81-10829

Also available in paperback from Dell

Bo learns about kindness, love, loyalty, appearances, and pretense from the unusual characters he meets when he is sent to live with his father after his mother decides to remarry

"With a fine display of irony yet without aiming over the heads of young readers, the author has written a splendid

Konigsburg, E. L.—*Continued*

satire on modern American life and has peopled it with some of her most original and eccentric characters." Horn Book

A proud taste for scarlet and miniver; written and illustrated by E. L. Konigsburg. Atheneum Pubs. 1973 201p il $14.95 (5 and up) **Fic**

1. Eleanor, of Aquitaine, Queen, consort of Henry II, King of England, 1122?-1204—Fiction

ISBN 0-689-30111-1

Also available in paperback from Dell

This is an historical novel about the 12th century queen, Eleanor of Aquitaine, wife of kings of France and England and mother of King Richard the Lion Heart and King John. Impatiently awaiting the arrival of her second husband, King Henry II, in heaven, she recalls her life with the aid of some contemporaries

The author "has succeeded in making history amusing as well as interesting. . . . The characterization is superb. . . . The black-and-white drawings are skillfully as well as appropriately modeled upon medieval manuscript illuminations and add their share of joy to the book." Horn Book

Up from Jericho Tel. Atheneum Pubs. 1986 178p $15.95 (5 and up) **Fic**

1. Actors—Fiction 2. Mystery fiction

ISBN 0-689-31194-X   LC 85-20061

"Jeanmarie and Malcolm are both unpopular, both bossy, both latchkey children, both live in a trailer park, and both want to be famous. Jeanmarie knows that she will be a famous actress and that Malcolm will one day be a famous scientist. These two friends embark on a series of adventures encouraged by the spirit of the long dead actress, Tallulah. Yes, presumably 'the' Tallulah! Tallulah, as a ghost, has the ability to make them invisible, and in that state the kids are sent to find the missing Regina Stone." Voice Youth Advocates

"Konigsburg always provides fresh ideas, tart wit and humor, and memorable characters. As for style, she is a natural and gifted storyteller. . . . This is a lively, clever, and very funny book." Bull Cent Child Books

Krasnopolsky, Fara Lynn

I remember; illustrated by Gennady Schikarioff and Tatyana Mamonova. Clarion Bks. 1995 165p il $15.95 (4 and up) **Fic**

1. Family life—Fiction 2. Jews—Russia—Fiction 3. Russia—Fiction

ISBN 0-395-67401-8   LC 94-21542

First published 1992 in the United Kingdom

This is a fictionalized account of the author's own childhood in the small Russian town of Pochep. Set "against a backdrop of the prejudice and political upheaval preceding World War I, a series of vignettes chronicle the difficult daily life and struggle toward adulthood of a young Jewish girl named Hannah." Horn Book Guide

"A full-page ink drawing appears at the beginning of each chapter, adding visual interest and helping to define the historical setting." Booklist

Krensky, Stephen, 1953-

The printer's apprentice; illustrated by Madeline Sorel. Delacorte Press 1995 103p il $13.95 (4-6) **Fic**

1. Zenger, John Peter, 1697-1746—Fiction 2. New York (N.Y.)—Fiction 3. United States—History—1600-1775, Colonial period—Fiction

ISBN 0-385-32095-7   LC 94-36721

In 1735 in New York City, a young printer's apprentice learns about the importance of freedom of speech when the printer Peter Zenger is arrested and tried for writing articles criticizing the government

The author "creates a lively adventure story, making skillful use of the boy's struggle of conscience to introduce the principle of freedom of the press. . . . Madeline Sorel's humorous full-page pen drawings add a vigorous sense of the time and place. An afterword further explains the historical events." Horn Book

Krumgold, Joseph, 1908-1980

Onion John; illustrated by Symeon Shimin. Crowell 1959 248p il lib bdg $14.89; pa $3.95 (5 and up) **Fic**

1. Friendship—Fiction

ISBN 0-690-04698-7 (lib bdg); 0-06-440144-8 (pa)

Awarded the Newbery Medal, 1960

The story "of Andy Rusch, twelve, and European-born Onion John, the town's odd-jobs man and vegetable peddler who lives in a stone hut and frequents the dump. Andy . . . tells of their . . . friendship and of how he and his father, as well as Onion John, are affected when the Rotary Club, at his father's instigation, attempts to transform Onion John's way of life." Booklist

"The writing has dignity and strength. There is conflict, drama, and excellent character portrayal." SLJ

Langton, Jane

The fledgling. Harper & Row 1980 182p il lib bdg $20.75; pa $3.95 (5 and up) **Fic**

1. Geese—Fiction 2. Fantasy fiction

ISBN 0-06-023679-5 (lib bdg); 0-06-440121-9 (pa)
LC 79-2008

A Newbery Medal honor book, 1981

"An Ursula Nordstrom book"

"Quiet, introspective Georgie . . . yearns to fly. An encounter with a large, old Canadian goose, which stops at Walden Pond on its migratory journey south, brings her that chance. . . . Then neighboring Mr. Preek, who tries to save Georgie from what he thinks is an attacking predator, and Miss Prawn, who sees the girl's feat as a saintly sign, interfere." Booklist

The writing is alternately solemn and funny, elevated and colloquial. It is mythic, almost sacred, in passages involving Georgie and the goose; it is satiric, almost irreverent, when it relates to Mr. Preek and Miss Prawn." Horn Book

The fragile flag. Harper & Row 1984 275p il hardcover o.p. paperback available $4.95 (5 and up) **Fic**

1. Protests, demonstrations, etc.—Fiction 2. Arms control—Fiction

ISBN 0-06-440311-4 (pa)   LC 83-49471

A nine-year-old girl leads a march of children from Massachusetts to Washington, in protest against the President's new missile which is capable of destroying the Earth

"There may be differences of opinion about the political-military implications of the story; there can be little dis-

Langton, Jane—*Continued*

agreement about its effectiveness as a piece of dramatic and polished writing. The book has good pace, momentum, strong characters, and a sturdy story line." Bull Cent Child Books

Lasky, Kathryn

The night journey; with drawings by Trina Schart Hyman. Warne 1981 149p il o.p.; Penguin Bks. paperback available $4.99 (4 and up)   Fic

1. Jews—Fiction 2. Russia—Fiction
ISBN 0-14-032048-2 (pa)   LC 81-2225

This novel "describes the escape of a Jewish family from the persecutions and pogroms of Tsarist Russia. . . . It is told as a story-within-a-story, as thirteen-year-old Rachel learns, bit by bit, what her great-grandmother went through as a child." Bull Cent Child Books

"The novel shifts back and forth from the dangerous journey out of Russia to Rachel's own casual, secure life at home and school. These transitions are handled with a smoothness that doesn't break the intrinsic tension of the story, and the contrast between the two lives demonstrates with poignant clarity the real meaning of freedom. The portrayal of warm, supportive families in both stories becomes a link between past and present." SLJ

Lawlor, Laurie

Gold in the hills. Walker & Co. 1995 146p $15.95 (4-6)   Fic

1. Frontier and pioneer life—Fiction 2. Brothers and sisters—Fiction 3. Gold mines and mining—Fiction 4. Colorado—Fiction
ISBN 0-8027-8371-6   LC 94-35267

When they are left with relatives while their father goes prospecting for gold in the Colorado mountains, ten-year-old Hattie and her older brother depend on their friendship with a recluse who lives nearby to make their lives bearable

The book offers "some excellent characterization. . . . A nicely developed story with some primary and secondary matters that can be discussed or thought about long after the book is finished." SLJ

Lawson, Robert, 1892-1957

Ben and me; a new and astonishing life of Benjamin Franklin, as written by his good mouse Amos; lately discovered, edited and illustrated by Robert Lawson. Little, Brown 1939 113p il $15.95; pa $5.95 (5 and up)   Fic

1. Franklin, Benjamin, 1706-1790—Fiction 2. Mice—Fiction
ISBN 0-316-51732-1; 0-316-51730-5 (pa)

"How Amos, a poor church mouse, oldest son of a large family, went forth into the world to make his living, and established himself in Benjamin Franklin's old fur cap, 'a rough frontier-cabin type of residence,' and made himself indispensable to Ben with his advice and information, and incidentally let himself in for some very strange experiences is related here in a merry compound of fact and fancy." Bookmark

"The sophisticated and clever story is illustrated by even more sophisticated and clever line drawings." Roundabout of Books

Mr. Revere and I; set down and embellished with numerous drawings by Robert Lawson. Little, Brown 1953 152p il $16.95; pa $5.95 (5 and up)   Fic

1. Revere, Paul, 1735-1818—Fiction 2. Horses—Fiction 3. United States—History—1775-1783, Revolution—Fiction
ISBN 0-316-51739-9; 0-316-51729-1 (pa)

"Being an account of certain episodes in the career of Paul Revere, Esq., as recently revealed by his horse, Scheherazade, late pride of His Royal Majesty's 14th Regiment of Foot." Subtitle

"A delightful tale which is perfect for reading aloud to the whole family. The make-up is excellent, illustrations are wonderful, and the reader will get a very interesting picture of the American Revolution." Libr J

Rabbit Hill. Viking 1944 127p il lib bdg $15.99; pa $3.99 (3-6)   Fic

1. Rabbits—Fiction 2. Animals—Fiction
ISBN 0-670-58675-7 (lib bdg); 0-14-031010-X (pa)
Awarded the Newbery Medal, 1945

"Story of the great rejoicing among the wild creatures when the news goes round that new people are coming to live in the big house. For people in the big house will mean a garden and a garden means food. Their hopes are rewarded. The new people are 'planting folks' and the garden is big enough to provide for all." Wis Libr Bull

"Robert Lawson, because he loves the Connecticut country and the little animals of field and wood and looks at them with the eye of an artist, a poet and a child, has created for the boy and girl, indeed for the sensitive reader of any age, a whole, fresh, lively, amusing world." N Y Times Book Rev

Followed by The tough winter, entered below

The tough winter. Viking 1954 128p il o.p.; Smith, P. reprint available $16.75 (3-6)

Fic

1. Rabbits—Fiction 2. Animals—Fiction
ISBN 0-8446-6565-7

"When the 'folks' go south for the winter and the caretaker arrives with a 'mean and ornery' dog, the small animals experience a tough winter that is made bearable by the spirit of friendliness among them." Adventuring with Books. 2d edition

Le Guin, Ursula K., 1929-

Catwings; illustrations by S. D. Schindler. Orchard Bks. 1988 39p il $13.95 (2-4)

Fic

1. Cats—Fiction
ISBN 0-531-05759-3   LC 87-33104
Also available in paperback from Scholastic
"A Richard Jackson book"

"When four kittens with wings are born in a rough city neighborhood, their mother nurtures and protects them as they grow and learn to fly. At her urging they soon escape the dangerous streets and alleys, flying to a forest where they find more enemies but, finally, new friends." Booklist

"Le Guin's adroit writing style, the well-observed feline detail, the thematic concern for natural victims of human environment, and the gentle humor make this a prime choice for reading aloud, although one would not want children to miss the fine-line hatch drawings that further project the satisfying sense of reality." Bull Cent Child Books

Other available titles about Catwings are:
Catwings return (1989)
Wonderful Alexander and the Catwings (1994)

Le Guin, Ursula K., 1929-—*Continued*

A wizard of Earthsea. Atheneum Pubs. 1991
197p $16.95 (6 and up)   **Fic**
1. Fantasy fiction
ISBN 0-689-31720-4   LC 90-23884
Also available in paperback from Bantam Bks.
"A Parnassus Press book"
A reissue of the title first published 1968 by Parnassus
Press
"An imaginary archipelago is the setting for . . . [this]
fantasy. . . . In a willful misuse of his limited powers, the
novice wizard unleashes a shadowy, malevolent creature
that endangers his life and the world of Earthsea." Booklist
A "powerful fantasy-allegory. Though set as prose, the
rhythms of the langauge are truly and consistently poetical."
Read Ladders for Hum Relat. 5th edition
Other available titles about Earthsea are:
The farthest shore (1984)
Tehanu (1990)
The tombs of Atuan (1988)

L'Engle, Madeleine, 1918-

Meet the Austins. Vanguard Press 1960
191p o.p.; Dell paperback available $3.99 (5
and up)   **Fic**
1. Family life—Fiction 2. Orphans—Fiction
ISBN 0-440-95777-X (pa)
A "story of the family of a country doctor, told by the
twelve-year-old daughter, during a year in which a spoiled
young orphan, Maggy, comes to live with them. . . . [This
is an] account of the family's adjustment to Maggy and hers
to them." Horn Book
Other available titles about the Austins are:
The moon by night (1963)
The ring of endless light (1980)
Troubling a star (1994)

A wrinkle in time. Farrar, Straus & Giroux
1962 211p $17 (5 and up)   **Fic**
1. Fantasy fiction
ISBN 0-374-38613-7
Also available Cornerstone Bks. large print edition and
in paperback from Dell; Spanish language edition also available
Awarded the Newbery Medal, 1963
"A brother and sister, together with a friend, go in search
of their scientist father who was lost while engaged in secret
work for the government on the tesseract problem. A tesseract is a wrinkle in time. The father is a prisoner on a for-
bidding planet, and after awesome and terrifying
experiences, he is rescued, and the little group returns safely
to Earth and home." Child Books Too Good To Miss
"It makes unusual demands on the imagination and consequently gives great rewards." Horn Book
Other available titles in this series are:
Many waters (1986)
A swiftly tilting planet (1978)
A wind in the door (1973)

Levitin, Sonia, 1934-

Journey to America; illustrated by Charles
Robinson. Atheneum Pubs. 1993 c1970 150p
il $13.95; pa $3.95 (4 and up)   **Fic**
1. World War, 1939-1945—Fiction 2. Jewish refugees—
Fiction 3. Family life—Fiction
ISBN 0-689-31829-4; 0-689-71130-1 (pa)
                                  LC 93-163980

A reissue of the title first published 1970
"In a strong immigration story, Lisa Platt, the middle
daughter, tells how her family is forced to leave Nazi Germany and make a new life in the United States. First their
father leaves, then the others escape to Switzerland, where
they endure harsh conditions. After months of separation,
the family is reunited in New York." Rochman. Against
borders
Followed by Silver days (1989)

The return. Atheneum Pubs. 1987 213p map
$14.95 (6 and up)   **Fic**
1. Jews—Ethiopia—Fiction 2. Antisemitism—Fiction
ISBN 0-689-31309-8   LC 86-25891
Also available in paperback from Fawcett Bks.
"In a docunovel of a Jewish Ethiopian family's flight to
Israel, Levitin focuses on an orphan, Desta, whose older
brother, Joas, persuades her to leave the village where hunger and political recriminations constantly threaten their
lives." Bull Cent Child Books
"A vivid and compelling book. . . . Levitin's tour de
force is sensitively written; her command of the language is
impressive and she uses Ethiopian terms effectively, inter-
spersing them in ways readers will understand." Booklist

Levoy, Myron

Alan and Naomi. Harper & Row 1977 192p
hardcover o.p. paperback available $3.95 (6
and up)   **Fic**
1. Friendship—Fiction 2. Jews—Fiction 3. Mentally
ill—Fiction 4. World War, 1939-1945—Fiction
ISBN 0-06-440209-6 (pa)
"After reluctantly agreeing to befriend Naomi, a disturbed war refugee who has crumbled under the memory of
seeing her father beaten to death by Nazis, Alan breaks
through her defenses and begins truly to like her—only to
lose her when a violent incident shatters her fragile sanity."
Booklist
"This warming story with its ethnic humor, its compassionate families, and its heart-wrenching ending is one of
the more honest approaches to the repercussions of
W.W.II." SLJ

Lewis, C. S. (Clive Staples), 1898-1963

The lion, the witch, and the wardrobe;
illustrated by Pauline Baynes. HarperCollins
Pubs. 1994 189p il $15; lib bdg $14.89; pa
$5.95 (4 and up)   **Fic**
1. Fantasy fiction
ISBN 0-06-023481-4; 0-06-023482-2 (lib bdg);
0-06-440499-4 (pa)   LC 93-8889
Also available Spanish language edition
A reissue of the title first published 1950 by Macmillan
Four English schoolchildren find their way through the
back of a wardrobe into the magic land of Narnia and assist
Aslan, the golden lion, to triumph over the White Witch,
who has cursed the land with eternal winter
This begins "the 'Narnia' stories, outstanding modern
fairy tales with an underlying theme of good overcoming
evil." Child Books Too Good to Miss
Other available titles about Narnia are:
The horse and his boy (1954)
The last battle (1956)
The magician's nephew (1956)
Prince Caspian (1951)
The silver chair (1953)
The voyage of the Dawn Treader (1952)

Lindgren, Astrid, 1907-

Pippi Longstocking; translated from the Swedish by Florence Lamborn; illustrated by Louis S. Glanzman. Viking 1950 158p il lib bdg $13.99; pa $3.95 (3-6)   **Fic**

1. Sweden—Fiction
ISBN 0-670-55745-5 (lib bdg); 0-14-032772-4 (pa)
Also available Spanish language edition
Original Swedish edition, 1945
"There were no more dull days for Tommy and Annika after they made the acquaintance of Pippi Longstocking. Pippi was nine years old, her strength—and her imagination—was prodigious, and except for her monkey and horse, she lived alone unrestrained by adults." Booklist
Other available titles about Pippi Longstocking are:
Pippi goes on board (1957)
Pippi in the South Seas (1959)

Ronia, the robber's daughter; translated by Patricia Crampton. Viking 1983 c1981 176p il hardcover o.p. paperback available $4.99 (4-6)   **Fic**

1. Thieves—Fiction 2. Middle Ages—Fiction
ISBN 0-14-031720-1 (pa)   LC 82-60081
Also available in hardcover from P. Smith
Original Swedish edition, 1981
"Ronia, the robber's daughter, meets Birk, son of her father's rival, and the result is a benefit to all in both camps. Thanks to a shrewd older friend, the young people bring about the union of their parents' forces and, even better, learn to make a living legally." Publ Wkly
"The book is full of high adventure, hairsbreadth escapes, droll earthy humor, and passionate emotional energy; and cast over the whole narrative is a primitive, ecstatic response to the changing seasons and the wonders of nature." Horn Book

Lisle, Janet Taylor, 1947-

Afternoon of the elves. Orchard Bks. 1989 122p $14.95; lib bdg $14.99 (4-6)   **Fic**

1. Friendship—Fiction 2. Mentally ill—Fiction
ISBN 0-531-05837-9; 0-531-08437-X (lib bdg)
                    LC 88-35099
Also available in paperback from Scholastic
A Newbery Medal honor book, 1990
"Nine-year-old Hillary has a happy home, all the material possessions she wants, and plenty of friends at school. Eleven-year-old Sara-Kate is an outcast, thin, poorly dressed, with failing grades, a decrepit house, and a weedy yard adjoining Hillary's neat garden. But Sara-Kate has an elf village, and with it she hooks Hillary into a friendship that thrives on elf stories but suffers from Sara-Kate's stormy moods and prickly pride. It is for Hillary to discover that Sara-Kate alone is caring for a mother who is mentally ill, penniless, and unable to provide the most basic physical or emotional necessities." Bull Cent Child Books
"'Afternoon of the elves' is a distinctive portrayal of the way children figure out ways to inhabit the world when there aren't any adults around." N Y Times Book Rev

Forest. Orchard Bks. 1993 150p $15.95; lib bdg $15.99 (5 and up)   **Fic**

1. Squirrels—Fiction 2. Fantasy fiction
ISBN 0-531-06803-X; 0-531-08653-4 (lib bdg)
                    LC 93-9630
Also available in paperback from Scholastic
"A Richard Jackson book"
Twelve-year-old Amber's invasion of an organized forest community of squirrels starts a war between humans and beasts, despite the protests of an unconventional and imaginative squirrel named Woodbine
"Lisle has created a world of innocence marked with heartache, truth infused with absurdity, and wisdom relinquished to recklessness—all in the guise of animal fantasy." Bull Cent Child Books

Little, Jean, 1932-

Different dragons; illustrated by Laura Fernandez. Viking Kestrel 1987 c1986 123p il hardcover o.p. paperback available $3.95 (3-5)   **Fic**

1. Fear—Fiction 2. Dogs—Fiction
ISBN 0-14-031998-0 (pa)   LC 86-50710
First published 1986 in the United Kingdom
"On his first stay away from home without his family, timid Ben faces many challenges: Aunt Rose, whom his brother said was mean; sleeping alone; the bossy girl next door; a thunderstorm; but most of all—a big dog." SLJ
"Simply told, this features a true-to-life situation with very realistic characters. The story is compact, taking place over just one weekend; the rapid movement of events and the handling of a common problem—childhood fears—ensure a ready audience." Booklist

From Anna; pictures by Joan Sandin. Harper & Row 1972 201p il $14.89; pa $3.95 (4-6)   **Fic**

1. Vision disorders—Fiction 2. Family life—Fiction 3. Germans—Canada—Fiction
ISBN 0-06-023912-3; 0-06-440044-1 (pa)
"Often ridiculed by her older brothers and sisters and chided by her mother for her awkwardness and lack of ability nine-year-old Anna is prickly and uncommunicative, but when her family moves to Canada in 1933 to get away from the growing oppression in their native Germany a doctor discovers that Anna has an acute vision problem. Fitted with glasses and sent to a special school for visually handicapped children Anna is slowly drawn out of her shell by an understanding teacher and new friends. . . . This is an engaging story of Anna's adjustment to life and her family's to a new homeland." Booklist
Followed by Listen for the singing (1977)

Look through my window; pictures by Joan Sandin. Harper & Row 1970 258p il lib bdg $14.89 (4-6)   **Fic**

1. Family life—Fiction 2. Friendship—Fiction
ISBN 0-06-023924-7
Emily's very predictable life as an only child suddenly changes when her family moves into an eighteen-room house and her cousins come to stay with them. She discovers that life in a big family can be rewarding if sometimes exasperating and after meeting Kate she discovers both the hurts and the joys of true friendship
"The small but absorbing crises of family life are described with vitality, and the book is garlanded with Emily's and Kate's rapt discussions of books and their candid exploration of what it means to be Jewish (as Kate is)." Saturday Rev
Followed by Kate (1971)

Mine for keeps. Viking 1995 c1962 213p $13.99 (4-6)   **Fic**

1. Cerebral palsy—Fiction 2. Physically handicapped children—Fiction
ISBN 0-670-85967-2   LC 95-152141
A reissue without illustrations of the title first published 1962 by Little, Brown

Little, Jean, 1932—*Continued*

"Sally Copeland adjusts to living at a special school for children with physical handicaps. When she learns she is going home to live, she is filled with fear and apprehension for she knows being the only cerebral palsied child in a family and a school would cause many difficulties." Read Ladders for Hum Relat. 6th edition

Lively, Penelope, 1933-

The ghost of Thomas Kempe; illustrated by Antony Maitland. Dutton 1973 186p il $14.95 (4-6)   Fic

1. Ghost stories 2. Great Britain—Fiction
ISBN 0-525-30495-9
Also available in paperback from Puffin Bks.

"Workmen getting an English cottage ready for its new tenants break an old bottle and let loose the spirit of Thomas Kempe, a sorcerer whose mortal remains have been buried since 1639. Thus begin the persecutions and perils of young James Harrison, a prankish boy who moves into the house and is blamed for the high jinks of the ghost. Aware that he can't convince his pragmatic parents that the house is haunted and that he is not to blame for the tricks played when the vicar comes to call, as well as other disasters, Jim seeks out an exorcist." Publ Wkly

"Although the British vocabulary and spelling may seem strange at times to middle graders, they are sure to enjoy this exciting and involving tale of the supernatural." SLJ

Lobel, Arnold

Fables; written and illustrated by Arnold Lobel. Harper & Row 1980 40p il $15; lib bdg $14.89; pa $5.95 (3-5)   Fic

1. Animals—Fiction
ISBN 0-06-023973-5; 0-06-023974-3 (lib bdg); 0-06-443046-4 (pa)   LC 79-2004
Also available Spanish language edition
Awarded the Caldecott Medal, 1981

"Short, original fables, complete with moral, poke subtle fun at human foibles through the antics of 20 memorable animal characters. . . . Despite the large picture-book format, the best audience will be older readers who can understand the innuendos and underlying messages. Children of all ages, however, will appreciate and be intrigued by the artist's fine, full-color illustrations. Tones are deftly blended to luminescent shadings, and the pictorial simplicity of ideas, droll expressions, and caricature of behavior work in many instances as complete and humorous stories in themselves." Booklist

London, Jack, 1876-1916

The call of the wild (5 and up)   Fic

1. Dogs—Fiction 2. Alaska—Fiction
Hardcover and paperback editions available from various publishers. Illustators include Barry Moser and Philippe Munch

First published 1903 by Macmillan

"The dog hero, Buck, is stolen from his comfortable home and pressed into service as a sledge dog in the Klondike. At first he is abused by both men and dogs, but he learns to fight ruthlessly and finally finds in John Thornton a master whom he can respect and love. When Thornton is murdered, he breaks away to the wilds and becomes the leader of a pack of wolves." Reader's Ency

White Fang (5 and up)   Fic

1. Dogs—Fiction 2. Alaska—Fiction
Various editions available

First published 1906

White Fang "is about a dog, a cross-breed, sold to Beauty Smith. This owner tortures the dog to increase his ferocity and value as a fighter. A new owner Weedom Scott, brings the dog to California, and, by kind treatment, domesticates him. White Fang later sacrifices his life to save Scott." Haydn. Thesaurus of Book Dig

Lord, Bette Bao

In the Year of the Boar and Jackie Robinson; illustrations by Marc Simont. Harper & Row 1984 169p il $14.89; pa $3.95 (4-6)   Fic

1. Chinese Americans—Fiction 2. School stories
ISBN 0-06-024003-2; 0-06-440175-8 (pa)
LC 83-48440

"In a story based in part on the author's experience as an immigrant, Shirley Temple Wong . . . arrives in Brooklyn and spends her first year in public school." Bull Cent Child Books

"Warm-hearted, fresh, and dappled with humor, the episodic book, which successfully encompasses both Chinese dragons and the Brooklyn Dodgers, stands out in the bevy of contemporary problem novels. And the unusual flavor of the text infiltrates the striking illustrations picturing the pert, pigtailed heroine making her way in 'Mei Guo'—her new 'Beautiful Country.'" Horn Book

Lovelace, Maud Hart, 1892-1980

Betsy-Tacy; illustrated by Lois Lenski. HarperCollins Pubs. 1994 c1940 112p il $9.95; lib bdg $14.89; pa $3.95 (2-4)   Fic

1. Friendship—Fiction 2. Minnesota—Fiction
ISBN 0-06-024415-1; 0-690-13805-9 (lib bdg); 0-06-440096-4 (pa)
A reissue of the title first published 1940 by Crowell

Betsy and Tacy (short for Anastacia) were two little five-year-olds, such inseparable friends that they were regarded almost as one person. This is the story of their friendship in a little Minnesota town in the early 1900's

The author "has written a story of real literary merit as well as one with good story interest." Libr J

Other available titles about Betsy through adolescence and young womanhood with reading levels to grade 5 and up are:

Betsy and Joe (1948)
Betsy and Tacy go downtown (1943)
Betsy and Tacy go over the big hill (1942)
Betsy and the great world (1952)
Betsy in spite of herself (1946)
Betsy-Tacy and Tib (1941)
Betsy was a junior (1947)
Betsy's wedding (1955)
Heaven to Betsy (1945)

Lowry, Lois

Anastasia Krupnik. Houghton Mifflin 1979 113p $14.95 (4-6)   Fic

1. Family life—Fiction
ISBN 0-395-28629-8
Also available in paperback from Dell; Spanish language edition also available

This book describes the tenth year in the life of fourth-grader Anastasia. As she "experiences rejection of a long labored-over poem, fights acceptance of the coming arrival of a baby sibling, deliberates about becoming Catholic (in order to change her name), has a crush on Washburn Cummings who constantly dribbles an imaginary basketball, and

Lowry, Lois—*Continued*

learns to understand her senile grandmother's inward eye, she grows and matures." Booklist

"Anastasia's father and mother—an English professor and an artist—are among the most humorous, sensible, and understanding parents to be found in . . . children's fiction, and Anastasia herself is an amusing and engaging heroine." Horn Book

Other available titles about Anastasia Krupnik and her family are:

All about Sam (1988)
Anastasia, absolutely (1995)
Anastasia again! (1981)
Anastasia, ask your analyst (1984)
Anastasia at this address (1991)
Anastasia at your service (1982)
Anastasia has the answers (1986)
Anastasia on her own (1985)
Anastasia's chosen career (1987)
Attaboy Sam! (1992)

Autumn Street. Houghton Mifflin 1980 188p $14.95 (4 and up)   **Fic**

1. World War, 1939-1945—Fiction 2. Friendship—Fiction

ISBN 0-395-27812-0   LC 80-376

Also available in paperback from Dell

"Elizabeth, the teller of the story, feels danger around her when her father goes to fight in World War II. She, her older sister, and her pregnant mother go to live with her grandparents on Autumn Street. Tatie, the black cook-housekeeper, and her street-wise grandson Charley love Elizabeth and reassure her during this difficult time." Child Book Rev Serv

"Characters, dialogue, believable plot combine in this well written story to capture the mind and heart of all who read this memorable and touching book." Voice Youth Advocates

The giver. Houghton Mifflin 1993 180p $14.95 (6 and up)   **Fic**

1. Science fiction

ISBN 0-395-64566-2   LC 92-15034

Also available Thorndike Press large print edition and in paperback from Dell; Spanish language edition also available

Awarded the Newbery Medal, 1994

Given his lifetime assignment at the Ceremony of Twelve, Jonas becomes the receiver of memories shared by only one other in his community and discovers the terrible truth about the society in which he lives

"A riveting, chilling story that inspires a new appreciation for diversity, love, and even pain. Truly memorable." SLJ

Number the stars. Houghton Mifflin 1989 137p $14.95 (4 and up)   **Fic**

1. World War, 1939-1945—Fiction 2. World War, 1939-1945—Jews 3. Friendship—Fiction 4. Denmark—Fiction

ISBN 0-395-51060-0   LC 88-37134

Also available in paperback from Dell; Spanish language edition also available

Awarded the Newbery Medal, 1990

"Best friends Annemarie Johansen and Ellen Rosen must suddenly pretend to be sisters one night when Ellen's parents go into hiding to escape a Nazi roundup in wartime Copenhagen. With the help of a young resistance fighter, the Johansens smuggle the Rosens aboard Annemarie's uncle's fishing boat bound for freedom in Sweden. But it is Annemarie who actually saves all their lives by transporting a handkerchief coated with blood and cocaine to deaden the

search dogs' sense of smell." Bull Cent Child Books

"The appended author's note details the historical incidents upon which Lowry bases her plot. . . . The whole work is seamless, compelling, and memorable." Horn Book

The one hundredth thing about Caroline. Houghton Mifflin 1983 150p $15.95 (5 and up)   **Fic**

1. Single parent family—Fiction 2. Brothers and sisters—Fiction

ISBN 0-395-34829-3   LC 83-12629

Also available in paperback from Dell

"Caroline, fascinated by dinosaurs, spends much of her free time prowling New York's Museum of Natural History; her best friend, Stacy, practices being an investigative reporter. The combination proves disastrous when Caroline's mother becomes interested in Frederick Fiske, the mysterious man in the fifth-floor apartment who looks, Caroline is convinced, like the evil 'Tyrannosaurus rex' and who seemingly wants to eliminate Caroline and her brother, J.P." Booklist

"Lowry's style is bright, fast-paced and funny, with skillfully-drawn, believable characters." SLJ

Followed by Switcharound, entered below

Rabble Starkey. Houghton Mifflin 1987 192p $13.95 (5 and up)   **Fic**

1. Friendship—Fiction 2. Mothers and daughters—Fiction

ISBN 0-395-43607-9   LC 86-27542

Also available G.K. Hall large print edition and in paperback from Dell

"Parable Starkey and her mother, Sweet Hosanna, move into the Bigelows' house to take charge of the children after Mrs. Bigelow's hospitalization for mental illness. . . . [This is] a smooth first-person narrative that quietly takes on class as well as individual differences. In the end, Lowry has managed to portray a large, diverse cast by carefully and consistently focusing the point of view as one of a maturing observer." Bull Cent Child Books

A summer to die; illustrated by Jenni Oliver. Houghton Mifflin 1977 154p il $14.95 (5 and up)   **Fic**

1. Sisters—Fiction 2. Death—Fiction

ISBN 0-395-25338-1   LC 77-83

Also available in paperback from Bantam Bks.

"Meg, 13, envies her older sister's popularity and prettiness and finds it difficult to cope with Molly's degenerating illness and eventual death." Booklist

"As told by Meg, the chronicle of this experience is a sensitive exploration of the complex emotions underlying the adolescent's first confrontation with human mortality; the author suggests nuances of contemporary conversation and situations without sacrificing the finesse with which she limns her characters." Horn Book

Switcharound. Houghton Mifflin 1985 118p il $14.95 (5 and up)   **Fic**

1. Brothers and sisters—Fiction 2. Family life—Fiction

ISBN 0-395-39536-4   LC 85-14576

Also available in paperback from Dell

Sequel to The one hundredth thing about Caroline, entered above

Forced to spend a summer with their father and his "new" family, Caroline, age eleven, and J.P., age thirteen, are given unpleasant responsibilities for which they are determined to get revenge

"There is a bit too convenient an all-ends-tied final chapter, but the strong characterization, the humorous style and yeasty dialogue, and the change and development (including

Lowry, Lois—*Continued*

some shaking of stereotypical sex roles) in the two main characters give the story both substance and appeal." Bull Cent Child Books

Your move, J.P.! Houghton Mifflin 1990 122p $13.95 (5 and up) **Fic**

1. School stories
ISBN 0-395-53639-1   LC 89-24707

Caroline's older brother, twelve-year-old J.P. Tate who appeared in The one hundredth thing about Caroline and Switcharound (both entered above), has a "crush on Angela Galsworthy, newly arrived at his private school from London, England. . . . Anxious to sustain Angela's interest, J.P. tells her that he is suffering from triple framosis, a rare but fatal disease. Angela believes him and J.P. is stuck with his lie." Bull Cent Child Books

"The author makes the most of the humor in J.P.'s antics but maintains a rueful sympathy throughout for his plight and for his eventual admission of truth." Horn Book

Lunn, Janet Louise Swoboda, 1928-

The root cellar; [by] Janet Lunn. Scribner 1983 c1981 229p $14.95 (5 and up) **Fic**

1. Space and time—Fiction 2. Orphans—Fiction 3. Farm life—Fiction 4. United States—History—1861-1865, Civil War—Fiction
ISBN 0-684-17855-9   LC 83-3246

Also available in paperback from Puffin Bks.
First published 1981 in Canada

"Rose, a twelve-year-old orphan, is unhappy in her new home. When she goes down into the root cellar she finds herself back in Civil War days. She makes friends with the former tenants of the old house and becomes involved in their war-torn lives. She finally decides she belongs in modern times and returns with a better spirit." Child Book Rev Serv

"It's hard not to feel for Rose as she learns, for the first time in her life, how to be part of a family and have companions her own age. The descriptions of the physical surroundings and conditions in the post-Civil War time period are particularly vivid, and the pieces fit together well in this fast-paced, readable novel." SLJ

Lyon, George Ella, 1949-

Borrowed children. Orchard Bks. 1988 154p $15.95; lib bdg $15.99 (5 and up) **Fic**

1. Economic depressions—Fiction 2. Family life—Fiction 3. Kentucky—Fiction
ISBN 0-531-05751-8; 0-531-08351-9 (lib bdg)
                                       LC 87-22700

Also available in paperback from Bantam Bks.
"A Richard Jackson book"

"Twelve-year-old Amanda, the oldest girl in a large, poor Kentucky family during the Depression, has to quit school to take care of the house and new baby after her mother's difficult delivery. As a reward, she's sent to her grandparents' comfortable home in Memphis for a [rest]. Observing her alcoholic aunt's unhappy marriage makes her realize how rich her mountain background is." Bull Cent Child Books

"There is a tender and unusual quality to both Amanda's story and the novel itself. The author has imbued her narrator with lyricism, which somehow doesn't feel out of place. Instead, it helps create a sense of the past: slightly formal and suggestively nostalgic." N Y Times Book Rev

Lyons, Mary E.

Letters from a slave girl; the story of Harriet Jacobs. Scribner 1992 146p il $15; pa $4.95 (6 and up) **Fic**

1. Jacobs, Harriet A. (Harriet Ann), 1813-1896 or 7—Fiction 2. Slavery—Fiction 3. African Americans—Fiction 4. Letters—Fiction
ISBN 0-684-19446-5; 0-689-80015-0 (pa)
                                       LC 91-45778

A fictionalized version of the life of Harriet Jacobs, told in the form of letters that she might have written during her slavery in North Carolina and as she prepared for escape to the North in 1842

This "is historical fiction at its best. . . . Mary Lyons has remained faithful to Jacobs's actual autobiography throughout her readable, compelling novel. . . . Her observations of the horrors of slavery are concise and lucid. The letters are written in dialect, based on Jacobs's own writing and on other slave narrations of the period." Horn Book

MacDonald, Betty, d. 1958

Mrs. Piggle-Wiggle; illustrated by Hilary Knight. Lippincott 1957 c1947 118p il $14.95; pa $3.95 (2-4) **Fic**

ISBN 0-397-31712-3; 0-06-440148-0 (pa)
First published 1947

Chapters follow "the amazing versatility of Mrs. Piggle-Wiggle who loves children good or bad, who never scolds but who has positive cures for 'Answer-Backers,' 'Never-Want-To-Go-To-Bedders,' and other children with special problems." Books for Deaf Child

The author "mixes a little psychology with a lot of common sense, and seasons with nonsense, to produce the most palatable type of lecture on good behavior. Hilary Knight's illustrations catch the mood of the whole delightful business." Chicago Sunday Trib

Other available titles about Mrs. Piggle-Wiggle are:
Hello, Mrs. Piggle-Wiggle (1957)
Mrs. Piggle-Wiggle's farm (1954)
Mrs. Piggle-Wiggle's magic (1949)

MacDonald, George, 1824-1905

At the back of the North Wind (4-6) **Fic**

1. Fairy tales
Some editions are:
Godine $18.95 Illustrated by Lauren A. Mills (ISBN 0-87923-703-1)
Morrow lib bdg $17.95 Illustrated by Jessie Willcox Smith (ISBN 0-688-07808-7)
First published 1871

"There is a rare quality in Macdonald's lovely fairy tales which relates spiritual ideals with the everyday things of life. This one tells of Diamond, the little son of a coachman, and his friendship with the North Wind who appears to him in various guises." Toronto Public Libr. Books for Boys & Girls

The light princess; with pictures by Maurice Sendak. 2nd ed. Farrar, Straus & Giroux 1977 c1969 110p il $15; pa $4.95 (3-6) **Fic**

1. Fairy tales
ISBN 0-374-34455-8; 0-374-44458-7 (pa)
"An Ariel book"

This fairy story originally appeared 1864 in the author's novel Adela Cathcart and was reprinted in his 1867 story collection Dealings with the fairies. First published with these illustrations in 1969

MacDonald, George, 1824-1905—*Continued*

"The problems of the princess who had been deprived, as an infant, of her gravity and whose life hung in the balance when she grew up are amusing as ever and the sweet capitulation to love that brings her (literally) to her feet, just as touching. All of the best of Macdonald is reflected in the Sendak illustrations: the humor and wit, the sweetness and tenderness, and the sophistication—and they are beautiful." Sutherland. The Best in Child Books

The princess and the goblin (3-6)   **Fic**

1. Fairy tales

Some editions are:

Knopf (Everyman's library children's classics) $12.95 Illustrated by Arthur Hughes (ISBN 0-679-42810-0)

Morrow (Books of Wonder) $20 Illustrated by Jessie Willcox Smith (ISBN 0-688-06604-6)

First published 1872

"Living in a great house on the side of a mountain in a country where hideous spiteful goblins inhabit the dark caverns below the mines, little Princess Irene and Curdie the miner's son have many strange adventures. . . . To adults Macdonald's stories have an allegorical significance, to each succeeding generation of children they are wonderful fairytale adventures." Four to Fourteen

Followed by The princess and Curdie

MacLachlan, Patricia

Arthur, for the very first time; illustrated by Lloyd Bloom. Harper & Row 1980 117p il lib bdg $14.89; pa $3.95 (4-6)   **Fic**

ISBN 0-06-024047-4 (lib bdg); 0-06-440288-6 (pa)
LC 79-2007

A "recounting of ten-year-old Arthur's activities and introspections during a summer spent with a great-uncle and a great-aunt. The offbeat relatives cultivate equally offbeat friends, climb trees, and speak French to their pet chicken. Arthur also enjoys the companionship of a veterinarian's granddaughter." Horn Book

"Good-hearted good humor. . . . The colorfulness of the characters is unrelenting; each is more exaggeratedly unique and zany than the other." SLJ

Baby. Delacorte Press 1993 132p $14.95 (5 and up)   **Fic**

1. Infants—Fiction 2. Death—Fiction 3. Islands—Fiction

ISBN 0-385-31133-8   LC 93-22117

Also available in paperback from Dell

Taking care of a baby left with them at the end of the tourist season helps a family come to terms with the death of their own infant son

"Short, spare, powerful, this is a story which touches deep emotions and lingers in the heart." Horn Book

The facts and fictions of Minna Pratt. Harper & Row 1988 136p $12.95; lib bdg $12.89; pa $3.95 (4 and up)   **Fic**

1. Musicians—Fiction

ISBN 0-06-024114-4; 0-06-024117-9 (lib bdg); 0-06-440265-7 (pa)   LC 85-45388

"A Charlotte Zolotow book"

"Minna Pratt plays the cello and wishes she would get her vibrato. She wishes someone would answer her questions about herself and life and love. . . . Then she meets Lucas Ellerby. His life seems so perfect and he has a vibrato. As their friendship develops Minna finds that life is not always as it seems and even when you think you know someone or something there may be a hidden side that will surprise you." Voice Youth Advocates

"Ms. MacLachlan's skillful handling of her subject, and above all her vivid characterization . . . place her story in the ranks of outstanding middle-grade fiction." N Y Times Book Rev

Journey. Delacorte Press 1991 83p $13.95; pa $3.99 (4 and up)   **Fic**

1. Family life—Fiction

ISBN 0-385-30427-7; 0-440-40809-1 (pa)
LC 90-21052

When their mother goes off, leaving her two children with their grandparents, they feel as if their past has been erased until Grandfather finds a way to restore it to them

"This is a spellbinding tale, lean only in its length. The author's clipped dialogue and meticulously pared-down descriptions convey a deceptive simplicity—there are deep, intricate rumblings beneath the surface calm of MacLachlan's words." Publ Wkly

Sarah, plain and tall. Harper & Row 1985 58p $12.95; lib bdg $12.89; pa $3.95 (3-5)   **Fic**

1. Stepmothers—Fiction 2. Frontier and pioneer life—Fiction

ISBN 0-06-024101-2; 0-06-024102-0 (lib bdg); 0-06-440205-3 (pa)   LC 83-49481

Also available Cornerstone Bks. large print edition; Spanish language edition also available

Awarded the Newbery Medal, 1986

"A Charlotte Zolotow book"

When their father invites a mail-order bride to come live with them in their prairie home, Caleb and Anna are captivated by their new mother and hope that she will stay

"It is the simplest of love stories expressed in the simplest of prose. Embedded in these unadorned declarative sentences about ordinary people, actions, animals, facts, objects and colors are evocations of the deepest feelings of loss and fear, love and hope." N Y Times Book Rev

Seven kisses in a row; pictures by Maria Pia Marrella. Harper & Row 1983 56p il lib bdg $13.89; pa $3.95 (2-4)   **Fic**

1. Aunts—Fiction 2. Uncles—Fiction 3. Family life—Fiction

ISBN 0-06-024084-9 (lib bdg); 0-06-440231-2 (pa)
LC 82-47718

"A Charlotte Zolotow book"

"How different life is for Emma and Zachary when Aunt Evelyn and Uncle Elliott babysit for them while their parents attend an 'eyeball meeting'! No seven kisses before breakfast or divided grapefruit with cherry. Nevertheless both learn from the others—Emma learns to eat broccoli and her aunt and uncle learn about babies and what they do." Child Book Rev Serv

"The brief understated story makes few demands on the reader, but it is full of humor and the warmth of family caring and mutual affection. Informal, offhand pen-and-ink drawings reflect the tone of both story and style." Horn Book

Skylark. HarperCollins Pubs. 1994 86p $12.95; lib bdg $12.89 (3-5)   **Fic**

1. Stepmothers—Fiction 2. Droughts—Fiction 3. Frontier and pioneer life—Fiction

ISBN 0-06-023328-1; 0-06-023333-8 (lib bdg)
LC 93-33211

Sequel to Sarah, plain and tall, entered above

Also available Spanish language edition

"Sarah and the two children travel to Maine to visit her aunts—leaving Jacob behind. Only letters connect them—until, just before school starts, Jacob reappears, and the old

MacLachlan, Patricia—*Continued*

bonds are strengthened with the promise of a new baby in the spring. . . . The book is suffused with joy and, ultimately, hope." Horn Book Guide

Unclaimed treasures. Harper & Row 1984 118p $14; lib bdg $14.89; pa $3.95 (5 and up) **Fic**

ISBN 0-06-024093-8; 0-06-024094-6 (lib bdg); 0-06-440189-8 (pa)　　　　　　LC 83-47714

"A Charlotte Zolotow book"

This story "describes the summer when Willa, aged eleven, longs to find her true love. This search she knows has nothing to do with her parents' comfortable relationship but a lot to do . . . with her infatuation with her friend Horace's father—a painter for whom she poses—and with Ted and Wanda, the self-absorbed characters in a mindless romance written by one of her father's students." Horn Book

The author "has crafted an extraordinary story from ordinary daily events and filled it with unique neighborhood characters. . . . MacLachlan's penetration into the dreams of youth merges with her keen sense of humor and fluid writing style." SLJ

Magorian, Michelle, 1947-

Good night, Mr. Tom. Harper & Row 1981 318p lib bdg $15.89; pa $3.95 (6 and up) **Fic**

1. Child abuse—Fiction 2. Adoption—Fiction 3. Great Britain—Fiction
ISBN 0-06-024079-2 (lib bdg); 0-06-440174-X (pa)　　　　　　LC 80-8444

"When children are evacuated from London during World War II, Tom Oakley, a taciturn near-recluse who has never recovered from the deaths of his wife and child, takes in and forms a mutually healing relationship with eight-year-old Willie, a sickly, quiet boy who bears the marks of brutal beatings." Booklist

"The ending is tense, dramatic, believable, and satisfying. . . . Magorian uses dialogue and dialect well, giving local color as well as using them to establish character." Bull Cent Child Books

Maguire, Gregory

Seven spiders spinning; illustrated by Dirk Zimmer. Clarion Bks. 1994 132p il $13.95 (4-6) **Fic**

1. Spiders—Fiction 2. School stories
ISBN 0-395-68965-1　　　　　　LC 93-30478

Also available in paperback from HarperCollins

Seven prehistoric spiders that had been trapped in ice for thousands of years bring excitement to rural Vermont and briefly unite two rival clubs at a local elementary school

"There is quite a bit of tongue-in-cheek humor here. . . . Characters are almost caricatures. . . . Yet, somehow it all comes together to create a funny, shivery story." SLJ

Mahy, Margaret

Aliens in the family. Scholastic 1986 174p hardcover o.p. paperback available $3.25 (6 and up) **Fic**

1. Science fiction 2. Stepfamily—Fiction
ISBN 0-590-44898-6 (pa)　　　　　　LC 86-3908

"In a science fantasy set in New Zealand, Jacqueline (Jake) Raven comes to visit her father and the family he's acquired with a second marriage. His wife, Philippa, is fine,

and her son Lewis isn't bad, but her daughter Dora is the ultra-feminine type Jake despises. What finally draws them together is the protective circle they feel they must draw around Bond, an extraterrestrial visitor whose identity must be hidden from their parents and whose time-travel project is threatened by the evil forces who pursue him." Bull Cent Child Books

"Using Bond and Jake as aliens in their own situations, Mahy has written a story of families learning to accept and believe in each other in spite of, and even because of, their differences." Voice Youth Advocates

Dangerous spaces. Viking 1991 154p $12.95; pa $3.99 (5 and up) **Fic**

1. Fantasy fiction 2. Ghost stories
ISBN 0-670-83734-2; 0-14-036362-9 (pa)　　　　　　LC 90-50565

"Sturdy, earth-bound Flora resents her glamourous cousin. Newly orphaned Anthea has come to live with Flora's family in the house that is haunted by the girls' grandfather, Lionel. Unsure of her place in this chaotic adoptive family, Anthea retreats to Viridian, a strange dream landscape that was created and is inhabited by ghostly Lionel's long-dead younger brother." Publ Wkly

"This is a moving story, told with great psychological insight and imagination." N Y Times Book Rev

The Good Fortunes Gang; illustrated by Marian Young. Delacorte Press 1993 100p il $13.95 (3-5) **Fic**

1. Moving—Fiction 2. Cousins—Fiction 3. New Zealand—Fiction
ISBN 0-385-31015-3　　　　　　LC 92-38784

Also available in paperback from Dell

After living like a gypsy in Australia all of his life, ten-year-old Pete Fortune tries to adjust to living in a permanent place—his father's New Zealand hometown where Pete must pass a test to belong to his cousins' exclusive gang

"Mahy's usual subtlety and understanding raises this simple plot several notches above its apparent level in this first book in a projected four-volume series about the Fortune family." Horn Book

The great piratical rumbustification & The librarian and the robbers; illustrated by Quentin Blake. Godine 1986 c1978 63p il $13.50 (3-6) **Fic**

ISBN 0-87923-629-9　　　　　　LC 85-45966

Also available in paperback from Morrow

First published 1978 in the United Kingdom

A "pair of humorous pieces, one a novella, the other a short story. In *The Great Piratical Rumbustification*, the boys of the Terrapin family find themselves with a pirate babysitter who wants to use their house for a long-delayed pirate party. In *The Librarian and the Robbers*, Serena Laburnum, the beautiful librarian, is kidnapped and held for ransom by a gang of ill-read robbers." SLJ

"These are splendid read-alouds, but listeners should not miss Quentin Blake's exuberantly ridiculous, black-and-white cartoons, which tumble across the pages with much the same verve as Mahy's text—a matchless combo of childlike irreverence." Bull Cent Child Books

The haunting. Atheneum Pubs. 1983 c1982 135p $15 (5 and up) **Fic**

1. Family life—Fiction 2. Extrasensory perception—Fiction
ISBN 0-689-50243-5　　　　　　LC 82-3983

"A Margaret K. McElderry book"

"Barney, eight, is terrified by the repetition of images and messages that proclaim 'Barney is dead,' but . . . he

Mahy, Margaret—*Continued*

discovers that he had had a great-uncle who had been a 'magician,' not only having ESP but able to evoke illusions. This was Cole, who had a beloved brother, another Barney. Presumed dead for many years, Cole suddenly appears and there is an interfamilial confrontation." Bull Cent Child Books

The principal characters "are beautifully drawn. . . . Their growth and development as individuals and as members of a family unit are as important to the story as its supernatural chills, thrills and puzzlements, a fact that lends this genre book unusual richness." SLJ

Underrunners. Viking 1992 169p $14; pa $3.99 (5 and up)   Fic

1. Mystery fiction 2. New Zealand—Fiction
ISBN 0-670-84179-X; 0-14-036869-8 (pa)

LC 91-27864

"Amid a network of underrunners—tunnels that create crumbling holes in the New Zealand Peninsula where Tris lives with his father—Tris finds a refuge to indulge in fantasies and forget events that fractured his family. Then Tris meets Winola, the perfect partner for his games. But someone is watching them, a man as dangerous as the underrunners." Publisher's note

"The story's pattern is intricate yet clearly defined, dazzling in its complexity, and satisfying in the brilliance of its resolution. . . . Unique and unforgettable—cerebral but never pretentious, exquisitely crafted but never self-conscious." Horn Book

Marino, Jan

The Mona Lisa of Salem Street; a novel. Little, Brown 1995 155p $14.95 (5 and up)
Fic

1. Brothers and sisters—Fiction 2. Orphans—Fiction 3. Grandfathers—Fiction 4. Boston (Mass.)—Fiction
ISBN 0-316-54614-3   LC 94-34666

Nettie and John Peter have been passed from one relative to another ever since their parents died, so when they go to live in Boston with their grandfather, Nettie doubts he really wants them

This is "a natural and affecting narrative. . . . Marino is skilled at revealing her characters economically and with great sympathy. In this . . . novel, she has also rooted them firmly within their setting, realistically evoking the Italian flavor of Boston's North End." Horn Book

Matas, Carol, 1949-

Lisa's war. Scribner 1989 c1987 111p $13.95 (5 and up)   Fic

1. World War, 1939-1945—Fiction 2. Jews—Fiction 3. Denmark—Fiction
ISBN 0-684-19010-9   LC 88-29525

Also available in paperback from Scholastic

During the Nazi occupation of Denmark, Lisa and other teenage Jews become involved in an underground resistance movement and eventually must flee for their lives

"'Lisa's War' poses such sophisticated concerns with an honorable simplicity rare even in adult fiction. And at the same time it builds a great deal of excitement, as the German menace spreads and intensifies, growing from a sinister fear to lethal reality." N Y Times Book Rev

Mathis, Sharon Bell, 1937-

Sidewalk story; illustrated by Leo Carty. Viking 1971 71p il hardcover o.p. paperback available $3.99 (3-5)   Fic

1. Friendship—Fiction 2. African Americans—Fiction
ISBN 0-14-032165-9 (pa)   LC 86-4075

"An affecting easy-to-read story of a persistent little black girl to whom friendship means caring and helping a friend in trouble. Upset because her best friend Tanya and her family are being evicted and their belongings piled on the sidewalk and frustrated by her own mother's unwillingness to become involved, Lilly Etta phones first the police and then the newspaper for help and in the night creeps out to cover the things with sheets and blankets—and herself—to protect them from the wind and rain. Enhanced by several sensitive double-spread paintings in black and white." Booklist

Mayerson, Evelyn Wilde, 1934-

The cat who escaped from steerage; a bubbemeiser. Scribner 1990 66p $14 (3-5)
Fic

1. Immigration and emigration—Fiction 2. Cats—Fiction
ISBN 0-684-19209-8   LC 90-32890

Living in the steerage section of a steamship bound for America, Chanah, a nine-year-old Polish girl, tries to keep her newly found cat a secret

"Written with drama, emotion, and a touch of humor, this is a first-rate piece of historical fiction." Booklist

Mayne, William, 1928-

Hob and the goblins; illustrated by Norman Messenger. Dorling Kindersley 1994 c1993 140p il $12.95 (4 and up)   Fic

1. Fairies—Fiction 2. Fantasy fiction
ISBN 1-56458-713-4   LC 94-7029

First published 1993 in the United Kingdom

Hob, the friendly spirit who lives under the stairs and protects the house, must do battle with a variety of evil beings trying to take control of his family's home

"Mayne's writing style is deceptively simple, presenting a complex, fanciful world in a matter-of-fact manner. His quiet humor enhances the book's appeal, as do the cleverly illustrated initials at the start of each chapter." SLJ

McCaffrey, Anne

Dragonsong. Atheneum Pubs. 1976 202p o.p.; Bantam Bks. paperback available $5.99 (6 and up)   Fic

1. Fantasy fiction
ISBN 0-553-25852-4 (pa)   LC 75-30530

"Forbidden by her stern father to make the music she loves, Menolly runs away from Half-Circle Sea Hold on the Planet Pern, takes shelter with fire lizards, and finds a new life opening up for her." LC. Child Books, 1976

"The author explores the ideas of alienation, rebellion, love of beauty, the role of women and the role of the individual in society with some sensitivity in a generally well-structured plot with sound characterizations." SLJ

Others available titles in the Harper Hall series are:
Dragondrums (1979)
Dragonsinger (1977)

McCloskey, Robert, 1914-

Homer Price. Viking 1943 149p il $14.99; pa $3.99 (4-6) **Fic**

ISBN 0-670-37729-5; 0-14-030927-6 (pa)

Six "stories about the exploits of young Homer Price, who divides his time between school and doing odd jobs at his father's filling station and in his mother's tourist lunchroom two miles outside of Centerburg." Bookmark

"Text and pictures are pure Americana, hilarious and convincing in their portrayal of midwestern small-town life." Child Books Too Good to Miss

Another available title about Homer Price is: Centerburg tales (1951)

McDonnell, Christine, 1949-

Toad food & measle soup; pictures by Diane de Groat. Dial Bks. 1982 109p il o.p.; Puffin Bks. paperback available $3.99 (2-4) **Fic**

1. Family life—Fiction
ISBN 0-14-031724-4 (pa) LC 82-70204

Also available in hardcover from P. Smith

"Leo, introduced as a supporting player in 'Don't Be Mad, Ivy' [1981] is the star of these five . . . episodes. In one, Leo's imagination gets him in trouble; in another, he is dissatisfied with his longed-for pet chameleon. But the funniest chapter is the first, in which Leo's mom becomes a vegetarian cook and introduces the family to what Leo thinks is toad food and measle soup ('tofu and miso soup')." Booklist

"The author presents a very human boy, beset by the insecurities of youth, but helped by loving parents and she does so with clever, gentle humor. McDonnell is particularly good at describing Leo's thoughts and feelings, and the text is illustrated with 11 realistic pencil drawings." SLJ

Followed by Lucky charms & birthday wishes (1984)

McEwan, Ian

The daydreamer; illustrated by Anthony Browne. HarperCollins Pubs. 1994 192p il $14; lib bdg $13.89 (4-6) **Fic**

1. Family life—Fiction
ISBN 0-06-024426-7; 0-06-024427-5 (lib bdg)
LC 93-44476

"Peter Fortune, 10, is a dreamer, and not everyone understands that. . . . Each of the seven stories following the introduction is a separate adventure, probably occurring mostly in Peter's imagination but including an unusual twist to link it to a real situation. . . . Peter's adventures include trading bodies with his cat, taming a bully, catching a burglar, and even waking up in the dreaded world of grown-ups. . . . Brown's illustrations, one per chapter, capture the eeriness of the selections. A delightful blend of serious whimsy and hilarious gravity." SLJ

McKay, Hilary

Dog Friday. Margaret K. McElderry Bks. 1995 135p $15 (4-6) **Fic**

1. Dogs—Fiction 2. Great Britain—Fiction
ISBN 0-689-80383-4 LC 95-4446

First published 1994 in the United Kingdom

Ten-year-old Robin Brogan is determined to keep the dog he finds abandoned on the beach from being impounded by the police

"The sharply realized characters, fast-paced story, and witty dialogue make this English novel both distinctive and refreshing." Booklist

The exiles. Margaret K. McElderry Bks. 1992 217p $14.95 (5 and up) **Fic**

1. Sisters—Fiction 2. Grandmothers—Fiction
ISBN 0-689-50555-8 LC 91-38220

The four Conroy sisters spend a wild summer at the seaside with Big Grandma, who tries to break them of their reading habit by substituting fresh air and hard work for books and gets unexpected results

This is an "extremely and continuously funny book." Bull Cent Child Books

Another available title about The exiles is: The exiles at home (1994)

McKenzie, Ellen Kindt

Under the bridge. Holt & Co. 1994 140p $14.95 (4-6) **Fic**

1. Brothers and sisters—Fiction 2. Parent and child—Fiction
ISBN 0 8050 3398 X LC 94-3415

Also available in paperback from HarperCollins

When Ritchie's younger sister Rosie gets very sick after their mother suddenly goes away, Rosie begins to receive letters from a lonely troll, and these letters help Ritchie cope with his mother's absence, his father's seeming indifference, and the fifth-grade class bully

"McKenzie weaves her threads together elegantly, giving the troll's story a certain poignancy and giving Ritchie dignity without losing his childlike outlook. . . . Rich material for class discussion as well as individual contemplation." Bull Cent Child Books

McKinley, Robin

Beauty: a retelling of the story of Beauty & the beast. Harper & Row 1978 247p $16; lib bdg $15.89; pa $4.95 (5 and up) **Fic**

1. Fairy tales
ISBN 0-06-024149-7; 0-06-024150-0 (lib bdg); 0-06-440477-3 (pa) LC 77-25636

"McKinley's version of this folktale is embellished with rich descriptions and settings and detailed characterizations. The author has not modernized the story but varied the traditional version to attract modern readers. The values of love, honor, and beauty are placed in a magical setting that will please the reader of fantasy." Shapiro. Fic for Youth. 3d edition

The hero and the crown. Greenwillow Bks. 1985 246p lib bdg $16 (6 and up) **Fic**

1. Fantasy fiction
ISBN 0-688-02593-5 LC 84-4074

Also available Cornerstone Bks. large print edition and in paperback from Ace Bks.

Awarded the Newbery Medal, 1985

"A prequel rather than sequel to 'The Blue Sword' [1982] McKinley's second novel set in the . . . mythical kingdom of Damar centers on Aerin, daughter of a Damarian king and his second wife, a witchwoman from the feared, demon-ridden North. The narrative follows Aerin as she seeks her birthright, becoming first a dragon killer and eventually the savior of the kingdom." Booklist

The author "has in this suspenseful prequel . . . created an utterly engrossing fantasy, replete with a fairly mature romantic subplot as well as adventure." N Y Times Book Rev

Mead, Alice

Crossing the Starlight Bridge. Bradbury Press 1994 122p il $14.95; pa $3.95 (3-5)

Fic

1. Penobscot Indians—Fiction 2. Fathers and daughters—Fiction
ISBN 0-02-765950-X; 0-689-80105-X (pa)

LC 93-40978

Nine-year-old Rayanne's life turns upside down when her father leaves and she has to move off the Penobscot reservation and go to live with her grandmother

"Mead deftly establishes a child's point of view with simple and unpretentious language. . . . This is a gentle and understanding story of a young girl's adjustment to change." Bull Cent Child Books

Menotti, Gian Carlo, 1911-

Amahl and the night visitors; illustrated by Michèle Lemieux. Morrow 1986 64p il $19.95; lib bdg $14.88 (2-4)   Fic

1. Jesus Christ—Nativity—Fiction 2. Magi
ISBN 0-688-05426-9; 0-688-05427-7 (lib bdg)

LC 84-27196

Also available Spanish language edition

Relates how a crippled young shepherd comes to accompany the three Kings on their way to pay hommage to the newborn Jesus

"Some of the pictures, which are dominated by reddish brown, have rich tension and composition, as in the one of Amahl's mother contemplating theft, or in the portrait of Melchior describing the Christ child. . . . There is a great deal to look at, and the story, popular since the opera's 1951 debut, has sentimental appeal, humor, and some commanding moments." Bull Cent Child Books

Merrill, Jean, 1923-

The pushcart war; with illustrations by Ronni Solbert. HarperCollins Pubs. 1992 c1964 222p il $14.89 (5 and up)   Fic

1. Trucks—Fiction 2. New York (N.Y.)—Fiction
ISBN 0-06-020822-8

Also available in paperback from Dell

A reissue of the title first published 1964 by W.R. Scott

In the near future, "arrogant, mammoth trucks threaten to crowd people, small cars, pushcarts, and peddlers off the streets of New York. When a truck contemptuously runs down a pushcart, the peddlers rebel and wage a guerrilla war against the trucks, using a primitive, but effective, secret weapon. Funny, dramatic, tongue-in-cheek satire on the sheer bigness which is overwhelming urban life but which is here, for once, defeated by the little people who 'are' the city." Moorachian. What is a City?

The toothpaste millionaire; prepared by the Bank Street College of Education. Houghton Mifflin 1974 c1972 90p il $14.95; pa $4.95 (4-6)   Fic

1. Business—Fiction
ISBN 0-395-18511-4; 0-395-66954-5 (pa)
First copyright 1972
Illustrated by Jan Palmer

The author recounts the adventures of twelve-year-old Rufus Mayflower who starts manufacturing and selling toothpaste when he is in the sixth grade. By the time he is an eighth grader, he is a millionaire and ready to retire

This story "is laden rather heavily with arithmetic and business details, but rises above it. . . . The illustrations are engaging, the style is light, the project interesting (with more than a few swipes taken at advertising and business practices in our society) and Rufus a believable genius." Bull Cent Child Books

Miles, Betty, 1928-

The trouble with thirteen. Knopf 1979 108p lib bdg $12.99 (5 and up)   Fic

1. Friendship—Fiction
ISBN 0-394-93930-1   LC 78-31678

"Annie, who tells the story, and her best friend Rachel are twelve and in no hurry to grow up too fast. . . . When Rachel's parents decide to get a divorce, Rachel and her mother move to the city. While Annie's adjustment to her friend's departure, to the fact that they are each going to have other close friends, and to the death of a beloved pet gives the story some continuity, this is primarily an account of changes that are peculiar to adolescent girlhood." Bull Cent Child Books

"Annie and Rachel are distinct, fully drawn characters, not meant to stand for Everygirl nor needlessly quirky. They are authentic, the plot is balanced and believable, the pace is sure, and the book is a winner." SLJ

Miles, Miska, 1899-1986

Annie and the Old One; illustrated by Peter Parnall. Little, Brown 1971 44p il hardcover o.p. paperback available $7.95 (1-4)   Fic

1. Navajo Indians—Fiction 2. Death—Fiction
ISBN 0-316-57120-2 (pa)
Also available Spanish language edition
A Newbery Medal honor book, 1972
"An Atlantic Monthy Press book"

"Annie, a young Navajo girl, struggles with the realization that her grandmother, the Old One, must die. Slowly and painfully, she accepts the fact that she cannot change the cyclic rhythms of the earth to which the Old One has been so sensitively attuned." Wis Libr Bull

This is "a poignant, understated, rather brave story of a very real child, set against a background of Navajo traditions and contemporary Indian life. Fine expressive drawings match the simplicity of the story." Horn Book

Mills, Claudia, 1954-

Dynamite Dinah. Macmillan 1990 120p $13.95; pa $3.95 (3-5)   Fic

1. Friendship—Fiction 2. School stories 3. Infants—Fiction
ISBN 0-02-767101-1; 0-689-71591-9 (pa)

LC 89-13300

Mischievous Dinah struggles to remain the center of attention when her baby brother comes home from the hospital and her best friend gets a lead role in the class play

"The writing is both savvy and sparkling, making Dinah a distinctive and memorable individual with broad appeal." Bull Cent Child Books

Other available titles about Dinah are:
Dinah for President (1992)
Dinah forever (1995)
Dinah in love (1993)

Milne, A. A. (Alan Alexander), 1882-1956

The house at Pooh Corner; with decorations by Ernest H. Shepard. Dutton 1961 c1928 180p il $9.95 (1-4)   **Fic**

1. Bears—Fiction 2. Animals—Fiction 3. Toys—Fiction

ISBN 0-525-32302-3

Also available in paperback from Puffin Bks.; Spanish language edition also available

First published 1928

"Pooh and Piglet built a house for Eeyore at Pooh Corner. They called it that because it was shorter and sounded better than did Poohanpiglet Corner. Christopher Robin, Rabbit, and other old acquaintances of 'Winnie-the-Pooh' appear, and a new friend, Tigger, is introduced." Carnegie Libr of Pittsburgh

"It is hard to tell what Pooh Bear and his friends would have been without the able assistance of Ernest H. Shepard to see them and picture them so cleverly. . . . They are, and should be, classics." N Y Times Book Rev

The Pooh story book; with decorations and illustrations in full color by E. H. Shepard. Dutton 1965 77p il $13.99 (1-4)   **Fic**

1. Bears—Fiction 2. Animals—Fiction 3. Toys—Fiction

ISBN 0-525-37546-5

Excerpts from: The house at Pooh Corner and Winnie-the-Pooh

Contents: In which a house is built at Pooh Corner for Eeyore; In which Piglet is entirely surrounded by water; In which Pooh invents a new game and Eeyore joins in

Winnie-the-Pooh; illustrated by Ernest H. Shepard, colored by Hilda Scott. Dutton 1974 c1926 161p il $10.99 (1-4)   **Fic**

1. Bears—Fiction 2. Animals—Fiction 3. Toys—Fiction

ISBN 0-525-44443-2

Also available in paperback from Puffin Bks.; Spanish language edition also available

First published 1926

"The kindly, lovable Pooh is one of an imaginative cast of animal characters which includes Eeyore, the wistfully gloomy donkey, Tigger, Piglet, Kanga, and Roo, all living in a fantasy world presided over by Milne's young son, Christopher Robin. Many of the animals are drawn from figures in Milne's life, though each emerges as a universally recognizable type." Reader's Ency

The world of Pooh; the complete Winnie-the-Pooh and The House at Pooh Corner; with decorations and new illustrations in full color by E. H. Shepard. Dutton 1957 314p il $19.99 (1-4)   **Fic**

1. Bears—Fiction 2. Animals—Fiction 3. Toys—Fiction

ISBN 0-525-44447-5

Also available as part of a boxed set together with: The world of Christopher Robin, entered separately in class 821, for $29.95 (ISBN 0-525-43348-1)

This combined edition of the two titles entered separately above contains the original black and white "illustrations and eight delightful new full-page pictures printed in lovely soft colors." Publ Wkly

Moeri, Louise

Save Queen of Sheba. Dutton 1981 116p o.p.; Avon Bks. paperback available $3.50 (4 and up)   **Fic**

1. Survival after airplane accidents, shipwrecks, etc.—Fiction 2. Brothers and sisters—Fiction 3. West (U.S.)—Fiction

ISBN 0-380-71154-0 (pa)   LC 80-23019

Also available in paperback from Puffin Bks.

"A marauding band of Sioux have botched the job of scalping twelve-year-old King David. He awakes with a massive head wound to find that he is alone amidst the wreckage of the wagon train and the bodies of the other travelers. Searching desperately, he finds his six-year-old sister, Queen of Sheba, unharmed but mightily unhappy. Collecting scant food supplies, a rifle, and a plow horse who has returned, the two children set off across the prairie to seek the remnants of a wagon train that might be a few days ahead." Child Book Rev Serv

"Vivid scenes are held taut by a continuity of background. . . . Memorable for reading aloud, with discussion, or alone." Booklist

Mohr, Nicholasa, 1935-

Going home. Dial Bks. for Young Readers 1986 192p lib bdg $13.89 (4-6)   **Fic**

1. Puerto Ricans—New York (N.Y.)—Fiction 2. Puerto Rico—Fiction

ISBN 0-8037-0338-4   LC 85-20621

Also available in paperback from Bantam Bks.

Feeling like an outsider when she visits her relatives in Puerto Rico for the first time, eleven-year-old Felita tries to come to terms with the heritage she always took for granted

"This is a convincing story that captures the universality of preteen relationships." Rochman. Against borders

Another available title about Felita is:
Felita (1979)

Montgomery, L. M. (Lucy Maud), 1874-1942

Anne of Green Gables (5 and up)   **Fic**

Also available Spanish language edition

Some editions are:

Grosset & Dunlap (Illustrated junior lib) $13.95 Illustrated by Jody Lee (ISBN 0-448-06030-2)

Holt & Co. (Henry Holt little classics) $15.95 Illustrated by Inga Moore (ISBN 0-8050-3126-X)

Knopf (Everyman's library children's classics) $13.95 Illustrated by Sybil Tawse (ISBN 0-679-44475-0)

First published 1908 by Page

"Daily doings and dreams from her 10th to 17th year of a lively, imaginative child, adopted by an elderly brother and sister on a Prince Edward island farm." N Y State Libr

Other available titles about Anne are:
Anne of Avonlea (1909)
Anne of Ingleside (1939)
Anne of the island (1915)
Anne of Windy Poplars (1936)
Anne's house of dreams (1917)

Morey, Walt, 1907-1992

Gentle Ben; illustrated by John Schoenherr. Dutton 1965 191p il o.p.; Avon Bks. paperback available $2.95 (5 and up)   **Fic**

1. Bears—Fiction 2. Alaska—Fiction

ISBN 0-380-00743-6 (pa)

Also available in paperback from Puffin Bks.

Morey, Walt, 1907-1992—*Continued*

Set in Alaska before statehood, this is the story of 13-year-old Mark Anderson who befriends a huge brown bear which has been chained in a shed since it was a cub. Finally Mark's father buys the bear, but Orca City's inhabitants eventually insist that the animal, named Ben, be shipped to an uninhabited island. However, the friendship of Mark and Ben endures

The author "has written a vivid chronicle of Alaska, its people and places, challenges and beauties. Told with simplicity and dignity which befits its characters, human and animal, [it] is a memorable reading experience." SLJ

Morpurgo, Michael

Arthur, high king of Britain; illustrated by Michael Foreman. Harcourt Brace & Co. 1995 137p il $19.95 (4 and up)   **Fic**

1. Arthur, King—Fiction 2. Arthurian romances
ISBN 0-15-200080-1   LC 93-33620

First published 1994 in the United Kingdom

A twelve-year-old boy comes across Arthur Pendragon, who has just awakened from his long sleep beneath the earth, and hears from him some of the exciting stories of his past

"The sweep of this version encompasses a rich array of beloved stories . . . as well as some of their noteworthy yet lesser-known kin. . . . Although he offers no source notes, Morpurgo has clearly done wide research. . . . He follows in a time-honored tradition of adaptation and abridgement, but he never neglects the integrity and authenticity of the stories he tells. . . . [Foreman's] soft watercolor scenes are pricked with a cool freshness; blues, greens, golds, and purples shimmer together into variances of seasonal changes, windswept hilltops, and shadowed castles." Bull Cent Child Books

Waiting for Anya. Viking 1991 c1990 172p $13.99 (5 and up)   **Fic**

1. World War, 1939-1945—Fiction 2. Jews—France—Fiction 3. France—History—1940-1945, German occupation—Fiction
ISBN 0-670-83735-0   LC 90-50560

First published 1990 in the United Kingdom

"A World War II adventure story set in Vichy, France, this centers on a young shepherd, Jo, who becomes involved in smuggling Jewish children across the border from his mountain village to Spain. Morpurgo has injected the basic conventions of heroism and villainy with some complexities of character. . . . Independent readers will appreciate the simple, clear style and fast-paced plot of the book, which will also hold up well in group read-alouds, commanding attention to ethics as well as action." Bull Cent Child Books

Moser, Barry

The tinderbox; [by] Hans Christian Andersen; adapted, illustrated, and designed by Barry Moser. Little, Brown 1990 29p il $14.95   **Fic**

1. Fairy tales 2. Tennessee—Fiction
ISBN 0-316-03938-1   LC 90-30279

"Moser retells Andersen's classic fairy tale as it might have happened in the Tennessee mountains just after the Civil War. A young soldier on his way home meets an old codger (rather than the traditional witch). The mountain man lowers the soldier down a rock cliff to a cave where he finds three magical dogs atop their treasure chests and, of course, the tinderbox. Preserving the main elements of the story, Moser uses dialogue along with the illustrations to create the Southern setting." Booklist

"Moser's superb watercolors are chiefly portraits of the principals. . . . Their vivid individuality convincingly links the real, the historic, and the fantastic, giving a new, distinctly American life to the tale." SLJ

Myers, Walter Dean, 1937-

Fast Sam, Cool Clyde, and Stuff. Viking 1975 190p $17.25; pa $3.99 (6 and up)
                    Fic

1. Friendship—Fiction 2. African Americans—Fiction 3. Harlem (New York, N.Y.)—Fiction
ISBN 0-670-30874-9; 0-14-032613-8 (pa)

"In an affectionate, colloquial narrative, Stuff, now 18, recalls the time when he was 13, hanging out on 116th Street, and enjoying being part of a circle of dependable friends, the best of whom were Fast Sam and Cool Clyde." Booklist

"A funny, fast-paced story of teenagers in the ghetto. The characters are memorable." Read Teach

Me, Mop, and the Moondance Kid; illustrated by Rodney Pate. Delacorte Press 1988 154p il hardcover o.p. paperback available $3.99 (4-6)   **Fic**

1. Baseball—Fiction   2. Adoption—Fiction 3. Friendship—Fiction
ISBN 0-440-40396-0 (pa)   LC 88-6503

"Eleven-year-old T. J. and his younger brother Billy, a.k.a. the Moondance Kid, have been living with their adoptive parents for about six months, and are settling in well. They are worried that their friend Mop, a girl who has not yet been adopted, may be transferred to an orphanage some distance away. Mop decides to join T. J.'s little league team in order to get close to the coach and his wife, whom she suspects are interested in adopting her." SLJ

"Myers's keen sense of humor, quick, natural dialogue and irresistible protagonists make this novel a winner." Publ Wkly

Another available title about T. J., Moondance, and Mop is:

Mop, Moondance, and the Nagasaki Knights (1992)

Naidoo, Beverley

Chain of fire; illustrations by Eric Velasquez. Lippincott 1990 c1989 245p il lib bdg $14.89; pa $3.95 (5 and up)   **Fic**

1. South Africa—Race relations—Fiction
ISBN 0-397-32427-8 (lib bdg); 0-06-440468-4 (pa)
                    LC 89-27551

First published 1989 in the United Kingdom

"The political awakening of fifteen-year-old Naledi, who first appeared in *Journey to Jóburg* [entered below], is recounted with passion and eloquence as the author describes the resettling of Black villagers to their new and barren 'homeland'—the result of South Africa's policy of apartheid." Horn Book Guide

Journey to Jo'burg; a South African story; illustrations by Eric Velasquez. Lippincott 1986 80p il $14.95; lib bdg $13.89; pa $3.95 (5 and up)   **Fic**

1. South Africa—Race relations—Fiction
ISBN 0-397-32168-6; 0-397-32169-4 (lib bdg); 0-06-440237-1 (pa)   LC 85-45508

"This touching novel graphically depicts the plight of Africans living in the horror of South Africa. Thirteen-year-old Maledi and her 9-year-old brother leave their small vil-

Naidoo, Beverley—*Continued*

lage, take the perilous journey to the city, and encounter, firsthand, the painful struggle for justice, freedom, and dignity in the 'City of Gold.' A provocative story with a message readers will long remember." Soc Educ

Followed by Chain of fire, entered above

Namioka, Lensey

Yang the third and her impossible family; illustrated by Kees de Kiefte. Little, Brown 1995 143p il $15.95 (4-6) Fic

1. Chinese Americans—Fiction 2. Family life—Fiction 3. Friendship—Fiction 4. Cats—Fiction

ISBN 0-316-59726-0 LC 94-30110

This features Third Sister, also known as Mary, introduced in Yang the youngest and his terrible ear, entered below. "Determined to fit in with her American friends, she tries hard to establish a friendship with popular Holly, even adopting a kitten from her although Mary's parents don't allow pets in the house. Mary's attempts . . . to hide the kitten from the rest of the family make for an amusing story." Horn Book

Yang the youngest and his terrible ear; illustrated by Kees de Kiefte. Little, Brown 1992 134p il $15.95 (4-6) Fic

1. Chinese—United States—Fiction 2. Family life—Fiction

ISBN 0-316-59701-5 LC 91-30345

Also available in paperback from Dell

"Joy Street books"

Recently arrived in Seattle from China, musically untalented Yingtao is faced with giving a violin performance to attract new students for his father when he would rather be working on friendships and playing baseball

"Namioka explores issues of diversity, self-realization, friendship, and duty with sensitivity and a great deal of humor." Horn Book

Napoli, Donna Jo, 1948-

The prince of the pond; otherwise known as De Fawg Pin; illustrated by Judy Schachner. Dutton Children's Bks. 1992 151p il $13.99 (4-6) Fic

1. Frogs—Fiction

ISBN 0-525-44976-0 LC 91-40340

Also available in paperback from Puffin Bks.

This story based on the frog prince motif is "told from the point of view of Jade, a female frog. . . . Pin (as the Prince calls himself, hampered in his speech by a long, fat tongue attached at the front of his mouth) is handsome, but strangely ignorant of everything . . . so Jade must teach him the ropes. . . . Eventually, when the opportunity of kissing a princess represents itself, Pin leaps at it and disappears from Jade's life forever." Booklist

"Point of view is all here, and Napoli uses it to involve the reader in a touching story. . . . The consistency and mini-drama of a frog's-eye view (one at a time), coupled with a poignant ending that doesn't shy away from loss, makes this an animal fantasy that fairy tale readers will relish. . . . Schachner's numerous ink-and-wash drawings go far in supporting the characterization." Bull Cent Child Books

When the water closes over my head; illustrated by Nancy Poydar. Dutton Children's Bks. 1994 132p il $13.99 (3-5) Fic

1. Fear—Fiction 2. Swimming—Fiction 3. Family life—Fiction

ISBN 0-525-45083-1 LC 93-14486

Also available in paperback from Puffin Bks.

"Afraid of the water because he can't swim, fourth-grader Mikey dreads the start of summer vacation and swimming lessons. With encouragement and understanding from his family, Mikey over-comes his fear and gains confidence in his water-safety skills. Likable characters and lively dialogue, as well as Napoli's sensitive treatment of Mikey's problem, make for a touching, amusing story." Horn Book Guide

Naylor, Phyllis Reynolds, 1933-

The agony of Alice. Atheneum Pubs. 1985 131p $15 (5 and up) Fic

1. Teachers—Fiction 2. School stories

ISBN 0-689-31143-5 LC 85-7957

Also available in paperback from Dell

Eleven-year-old, motherless Alice decides she needs a gorgeous role model who does everything right; and when placed in homely Mrs. Plotkins's class she is greatly disappointed until she discovers it's what people are inside that counts

"The lively style exhibits a deft touch at capturing the essence of an endearing heroine growing up without a mother." SLJ

Other available titles about Alice are:
Alice in April (1993)
Alice in rapture, sort of (1989)
Alice in-between (1994)
Alice the brave (1995)
All but Alice (1992)
Reluctantly Alice (1991)

The fear place. Atheneum Pubs. 1994 118p $14.95 (5 and up) Fic

1. Brothers—Fiction 2. Pumas—Fiction 3. Camping—Fiction

ISBN 0-689-31866-9 LC 93-38891

When he and his older brother Gordon are left camping alone in the Rocky Mountains, twelve-year-old Doug faces his fear of heights and his feelings about Gordon--with the help of a cougar

This is "a solid action story, tense and involving. . . . A satisfying wilderness adventure." Publ Wkly

The grand escape; illustrated by Alan Daniel. Atheneum Pubs. 1993 148p il $14 (4-6) Fic

1. Cats—Fiction 2. Adventure fiction

ISBN 0-689-31722-0 LC 91-40816

Also available in paperback from Dell

After years of being strictly house cats, Marco and Polo escape into the wonderful, but dangerous outside world and are sent on three challenging adventures by a group of cats known as the Club of Mysteries

"While Naylor's feline explorers are amusing and lovable, their behavior is always catlike, and their interpretation of human foibles is often hilarious." Booklist

Naylor, Phyllis Reynolds, 1933——*Continued*

Maudie in the middle; [by] Phyllis Reynolds Naylor and Lura Schield Reynolds; illustrated by Judith Gwyn Brown. Atheneum Pubs. 1988 161p il $16 (3-5)   **Fic**

1. Family life—Fiction 2. Iowa—Fiction
ISBN 0-689-31395-0   LC 87-3470
Also available in paperback from Dell
"A Jean Karl book"
"Maudie, who is eight when the story begins, is the middle child of seven, either too young or too old for everything, she feels. And, since she is a lively child and often in trouble, she despairs of ever being appreciated, or being special in any way. This turn-of-the-century family story is based on the childhood of Lura Reynolds, Phyllis Naylor's mother, and it's adequately told and structured but expectably episodic in the way most reminiscences are." Bull Cent Child Books

Shiloh. Atheneum Pubs. 1991 144p $13.95 (4-6)   **Fic**

1. Dogs—Fiction 2. West Virginia—Fiction
ISBN 0-689-31614-3   LC 90-603
Also available Cornerstone Bks. large print edition and in paperback from Dell
Awarded the Newbery Medal, 1992
When he finds a lost beagle in the hills behind his West Virginia home, Marty tries to hide it from his family and the dog's real owner, a mean-spirited man known to shoot deer out of season and to mistreat his dogs
"A credible plot and characters, a well-drawn setting, and nicely paced narration combine in a story that leaves the reader feeling good." Horn Book

The witch's eye; illustrated by Joe Burleson. Delacorte Press 1990 179p il hardcover o.p. paperback available $3.50 (5 and up)   **Fic**

1. Witchcraft—Fiction
ISBN 0-440-40514-9 (pa)   LC 89-77237
Though suspected witch-neighbor Mrs. Tuggle has died, her glass eye resurfaces, bringing new dangers and terrors to Lynn's family and her friend Mouse
"The quality of writing and characterization makes this a truly scary story. . . . The personaity changes of characters who come under the influence of the witch or her eye sustain a convincingly threatening atmosphere." SLJ
Other available titles about Lynn, Mouse, and Mrs. Tuggle are:
The witch herself (1978)
The witch returns (1992)
Witch water (1977)
Witch weed (1991)
Witch's sister (1975)

Nelson, Theresa, 1948-

The 25¢ miracle. Bradbury Press 1986 214p $14.95; pa $3.95 (5 and up)   **Fic**

1. Fathers and daughters—Fiction
ISBN 0-02-724370-2; 0-689-71326-6 (pa)
                 LC 85-17061
"Complex characterizations illuminate the anguish of a widowed father and his plucky motherless daughter, unable to discuss their true feelings. It's a story filled with childhood angst, heartache, and joy." SLJ

And one for all. Orchard Bks. 1989 182p $15.95 (5 and up)   **Fic**

1. Vietnam War, 1961-1975—Fiction 2. Brothers and sisters—Fiction
ISBN 0-531-05804-2   LC 88-22490
Also available in paperback from Dell
"A Richard Jackson book"
Geraldine, the twelve-year-old narrator of this Vietnam War novel, tells the story of her older brother Wing who enlists in the Marines, and his best friend Sam, an antiwar activist. When Wing is killed at Khe Sanh, "Geraldine blames Sam and hops a bus to Washington, D.C., where she confronts him among peace protestors at the foot of the Washington Monument. Finally, her grief and fury give way to understanding that Sam was always on Wing's side in trying to end the war." SLJ
"Plot, dialogue, and setting are effortlessly authentic and never overwhelmed by the theme. . . . Smoothly written and easily read, this also manages to challenge assumptions in a thought-provoking probe of the past." Bull Cent Child Books

Devil storm. Orchard Bks. 1987 212p il $15.95; lib bdg $15.99 (5 and up)   **Fic**

1. Hurricanes—Fiction 2. Tramps—Fiction 3. Texas—Fiction
ISBN 0-531-05711-9; 0-531-08311-X (lib bdg)
                 LC 87-5493
"A Richard Jackson book"
"Is the old tramp really the son of pirate Jean LaFitte, and why does he wander through Bolivar and Galveston and up and down the Gulf Coast? Buried treasure? Against their father's explicit instructions, 13-year-old Walter and his younger sister Alice befriend old Tom, giving him food in exchange for marvelous stories, and they find their kindness repaid when Bolivar is hit by a hurricane that threatens to kill the family." Bull Cent Child Books
"The writing is powerful, reflecting the force of the great storm; the scenes in Galveston and the father's helpless anguish are deeply impressive. The setting is clearly drawn, and the author has a light but accurate hand with the local dialect and culture." Horn Book

Earthshine; a novel. Orchard Bks. 1994 182p $15.95; lib bdg $15.99 (5 and up)   **Fic**

1. AIDS (Disease)—Fiction 2. Fathers and daughters—Fiction 3. Homosexuality—Fiction
ISBN 0-531-06867-6; 0-531-08717-4 (lib bdg)
                 LC 94-8793
"A Richard Jackson book"
"Slim—real name Margery—is twelve, living with her actor father and her father's lover, Larry; her father is dying of AIDS, and Slim participates in a church youth group for kids close to people with the disease." Bull Cent Child Books
"Major and minor charcters are real people and never case studies. And the author's use of language expresses both the action and underlying feelings while remaining true to the voice of the narrator. . . . This special book should find a wide audience." SLJ

Nesbit, E. (Edith), 1858-1924

The enchanted castle; illustrated by Paul O. Zelinsky; afterword by Peter Glassman. Morrow Junior Bks. 1992 292p il lib bdg $20 (4-6)   **Fic**

1. Fantasy fiction 2. Great Britain—Fiction
ISBN 0-688-05435-8   LC 91-46267

Nesbit, E. (Edith), 1858-1924—*Continued*

First published 1907 in the United Kingdom; first United States edition 1908 by Harper & Brothers

Four English children find a wonderful world of magic through an enchanted wishing ring

"With fine, cross-hatched lines tinted in luminous colors, Zelinsky's artwork is as lively as the story and very much of the period." Booklist

The railway children (4-6)   Fic

1. Family life—Fiction 2. Brothers and sisters—Fiction 3. Railroads—Fiction 4. Country life—Fiction 5. Great Britain—Fiction

Some editions are:

Holt & Co. (Henry Holt little classics) $14.95 Illustrated by Shirley Hughes (ISBN 0-8050-3129-4)

Knopf (Everyman's library children's classics) $12.95 Illustrated by C. E. Brock (ISBN 0-679-42534-9)

First published 1906 by Macmillan

When their father is sent away to prison, Roberta, Peter, and Phyllis move with their mother from London to the country where they keep busy preventing accidents on the nearby railway, making many new friends, and generally learning a good deal about themselves

Neuberger, Anne E., 1953-

The girl-son. Carolrhoda Bks. 1995 131p il lib bdg $19.95 (4 and up)   Fic

1. Pahk, Induk—Fiction 2. Sex role—Fiction 3. Korea—Fiction

ISBN 0-87614-846-1   LC 94-6725

"Adventures in time books"

Based on the life of Induk Pahk, a Korean educator, whose widowed mother disguised her as a boy at the age of eight in order for her to attend school, a choice forbidden to girls in the early twentieth century in that country

"This is a riveting, true story." Soc Educ

Neufeld, John, 1938-

Almost a hero. Atheneum Bks. for Young Readers 1995 147p $15; pa $3.95 (5 and up)   Fic

1. Child abuse—Fiction 2. Homeless persons—Fiction 3. Death—Fiction

ISBN 0-689-31971-1; 0-689-80740-6 (pa)

LC 94-12785

"Ben Derby is a 12-year-old whose teacher has assigned to him a week of charitable work during spring break. Ben works at a day care center for homeless children, one of whom Ben thinks he sees being abused in the grocery story. When 'the system' is too cautious in its response, Ben and his friends plan a bold rescue of the child." Booklist

"Ben ponders some difficult questions in ways that young readers, who may face similar moral challenges themselves, will relate to." Bull Cent Child Books

Neville, Emily Cheney, 1919-

It's like this, Cat; [by] Emily Neville; pictures by Emil Weiss. Harper & Row 1963 180p il $15; lib bdg $14.89; pa $3.95 (5 and up)   Fic

1. Cats—Fiction 2. New York (N.Y.)—Fiction

ISBN 0-06-024390-2; 0-06-024391-0 (lib bdg); 0-06-440073-5 (pa)

Awarded the Newbery Medal, 1964

This is the "story of a fourteen-year-old growing up in the neighborhood of Gramercy Park in New York City. He tells of life in the city and his relationships with his parents, neighbors, and friends. It is his pet, a stray tom cat whom he adopts, that brings him two new friends, one a troubled boy and the other his first girl." Wis Libr Bull

"A story told with a great amount of insight into human relationships. . . . This all provides a wonderfully real picture of a city boy's outlets and of one likable adolescent's inner feelings. An exceedingly fresh, honest, and well-rounded piece of writing." Horn Book

Newman, Robert, 1909-1988

The case of the Baker Street Irregular; a Sherlock Holmes story. Atheneum Pubs. 1978 216p hardcover o.p. paperback available $4.95 (5 and up)   Fic

1. Mystery fiction 2. London (England)—Fiction

ISBN 0-689-70766-5 (pa)   LC 77-15463

Also available in hardcover from P. Smith

Brought to London under mysterious circumstances by his tutor, young Andrew Tillett seeks the help of Sherlock Holmes when his tutor is kidnapped and he himself is threatened with the same fate

"The author is as urbane and fluent as the legendary Mr. Holmes; he seems thoroughly comfortable with the characters, the atmosphere, and the turn-of-the century London setting; and the story moves along with unflagging energy." Horn Book

Other available titles involving Andrew Tillett, his friend Sara Wiggins and Scotland Yard's Inspector Peter Wyatt are:

The case of the vanishing corpse (1980)

The case of the watching boy (1987)

Nichol, Barbara

Beethoven lives upstairs; illustrated by Scott Cameron. Orchard Bks. 1994 c1993 unp il $15.95 (3-5)   Fic

1. Beethoven, Ludwig van, 1770-1827—Fiction 2. Uncles—Fiction 3. Letters—Fiction

ISBN 0-531-06828-5   LC 93-5774

Also available Spanish language edition

First published 1993 in Canada

The letters that ten-year-old Christoph and his uncle exchange show how Christoph's feelings for Mr. Beethoven, the eccentric boarder that shares his house, change from anger and embarrassment to compassion and admiration

"The oil pictures are rich and dark, with glowing, candlelit interiors; they define the period while giving a strong sense of character. But it's the story that holds you, as tension builds until the triumphant first performance of the Ninth." Booklist

Nixon, Joan Lowery, 1927-

A family apart. Bantam Bks. 1987 162p hardcover o.p. paperback available $4.50 (5 and up)   Fic

1. Foster home care—Fiction 2. Brothers and sisters—Fiction 3. United States—History—1783-1865—Fiction

ISBN 0-553-27478-3 (pa)   LC 87-12563

The first volume in the "Orphan train" series "this is based on a real program, the Children's Aid Society's placement of orphans who travelled from New York City to the West to be adopted by residents there. In this story, set in 1860, widowed Mrs. Kelley realizes she cannot support her six children and gives them up for adoption. The protago-

Nixon, Joan Lowery, 1927-—*Continued*

nist is the oldest girl, Frances, who disguises herself as a boy so that she can be paired with her baby brother for adoption, and they are indeed taken together by a very nice family." Bull Cent Child Books

"The plot is rational and well paced; the characters are real and believable; the time setting important to U.S. history, and the values all that anyone could ask for." Voice Youth Advocates

Other titles available in the Orphan train series are:
Caught in the act (1988)
In the face of danger (1988)
Keeping secrets (1995)
A place to belong (1989)

Nordstrom, Ursula, 1910-1988

The secret language; pictures by Mary Chalmers. Harper & Row 1960 167p il lib bdg $12.89; pa $3.95 (3-5)   Fic

1. School stories
ISBN 0-06-024576-X (lib bdg); 0-06-440022-0 (pa)

A "story about two eight-year-old girls at boarding school. None of the experiences that Vicky and Martha have are unusual; none dramatic; yet all of the details of their year make absorbing reading. Vicky is homesick and Martha is a rebel; as they adjust to each other and as they adapt themselves to the pattern of school life, both girls find satisfactions and both grow up a little. The writing style has a gentle humor, a warm understanding, and an easy narrative flow that seems effortless." Bull Cent Child Books

Norton, Andre, 1912-

Fur magic; illustrated by Alicia Austin. Grant, D.M. 1992 173p il $30 (4-6)   Fic

1. Fantasy fiction
ISBN 1-880418-20-7

A newly illustrated edition of the title first published 1968 by World Pub. Co.

A city-bred boy "is sent to spend the summer on a ranch in Idaho with an Indian foster uncle. Cory's enthusiasm fades quickly when he finds that he is afraid. . . . When he stumbles upon an old cave and touches an ancient medicine bag, a chain of adventures begins. Transformed into an [animal], he is transported into the past. . . . As Yellow Shell, [the beaver,] Cory endures great hardship . . . before he regains his boy-shape." Horn Book

Norton, Mary, 1903-1992

Bed-knob and broomstick; illustrated by Erik Blegvad. Harcourt Brace 1957 189p il hardcover o.p. paperback available $3.95 (3-5)   Fic

1. Fantasy fiction 2. Witchcraft—Fiction
ISBN 0-15-206231-9 (pa)

Also available G.K. Hall large print edition

A combined edition of: The magic bed-knob, first published 1943 by Putnam and Bonfires and broomsticks, first published 1947 in the United Kingdom

The story is about "two brothers and a sister who receive from their neighbor Miss Price, because they have uncovered her secret efforts to become a witch, a magic bed-knob which can grant their wishes to be anywhere in the present or, with a different twist, in the past." Horn Book

"While there is one unpleasant note in text and illustration of Negroid cannibals, the story has the same quiet humor and calm acceptance of the fantastic as does 'The Borrowers' [entered below]." Bull Cent Child Books

The Borrowers; illustrated by Beth and Joe Krush. Harcourt Brace 1953 180p il $13.95; pa $4.95 (3-6)   Fic

1. Fairy tales
ISBN 0-15-209987-5; 0-15-209990-5 (pa)

Also available with illustrations by Michael Hague $22.95 (ISBN 0-15-209991-3)

First published 1952 in the United Kingdom

A "fascinating fantasy about a tiny family that lived beneath the kitchen floor of an old English country house and 'borrowed' from the larger human residents to fill their modest needs. Their sudden discovery by a small boy visitor almost proves to be their undoing. The imaginative details about the activities of the miniature people have tremendous appeal for children." Child Books Too Good to Miss

Other available titles about the Borrowers are:
The Borrowers afield (1955)
The Borrowers afloat (1959)
The Borrowers aloft (1961)
The Borrowers avenged (1982)

O'Brien, Robert C., 1918-1973

Mrs. Frisby and the rats of NIMH; illustrated by Zena Bernstein. Atheneum Pubs. 1971 223p il lib bdg $16; pa $3.95 (4 and up)   Fic

1. Mice—Fiction 2. Rats—Fiction
ISBN 0-689-20651-8 (lib bdg); 0-689-71068-2 (pa)

Also available Spanish language edition

Awarded the Newbery Medal, 1972

"Mrs. Frisby, a widowed mouse, is directed by an owl to consult with the rats that live under the rosebush about her problem of moving her sick son from the family's endangered home. Upon entering that rats' quarters, Mrs. Frisby discovers to her astonishment that the rats are not ordinary rodents, but highly intelligent creatures that escaped from an NIMH laboratory after being taught to read." Booklist

"The story is fresh and ingenious, the style witty, and the plot both hilarious and convincing." Saturday Rev

Followed by Racso and the rats of NIMH by Jane Leslie Conly, entered above

O'Dell, Scott, 1898-1989

The black pearl; illustrated by Milton Johnson. Houghton Mifflin 1967 140p il $14.95 (6 and up)   Fic

1. Pearlfisheries—Fiction 2. Baja California (Mexico: Peninsula)—Fiction
ISBN 0-395-06961-0

Also available in paperback from Dell; Spanish language edition also available

A Newbery Medal honor book, 1968

"The people of Baja California feared a demon creature, a giant ray—El Manta Diablo. He was believed to live in a cave at the end of a lagoon. . . . Yet Ramón Salazar, goaded by the taunts of the greatest pearl diver of his father's fleet, dared to enter the cave to dive for a pearl even more wonderful than the one El Sevillano had boasted of. And he found it—the Paragon of Pearls, the Pearl of Heaven. Then came the encounter with the Manta." Horn Book

"The stark simplicity of the story and the deeper significance it holds in the triumph of good over evil add importance to the book, but even without that the book would be enjoyable as a rousing adventure tale with supernatural overtones and beautifully maintained tempo and suspense." Bull Cent Child Books

O'Dell, Scott, 1898-1989—*Continued*

The captive. Houghton Mifflin 1979 210p
$14.95 (6 and up) **Fic**

1. Mayas—Fiction 2. Mexico—Fiction
ISBN 0-395-27811-2   LC 79-15809

This story set in the 16th century, "centers on the adventures of a young Jesuit seminarian who goes to the New World as part of a Spanish expedition. Full of Christian idealism, Julián Escobar believes his role is to convert the savages. Instead, he succumbs to the temptation to pose as the reincarnated Mayan deity [Kukulcán]." Child Book Rev Serv

"Characterizations are all finely drawn, and Julián's transformation from insecure, humane seminarian to pretend god is remarkable in its honest development." SLJ

Another available title in The City of the Seven Serpents series is:
The feathered serpent (1981)

Island of the Blue Dolphins; illustrated by
Ted Lewin. Houghton Mifflin 1990 181p il
$18.95 (5 and up) **Fic**

1. Indians of North America—Fiction 2. Wilderness survival—Fiction 3. San Nicolas Island (Calif.)—Fiction
ISBN 0-395-53680-4   LC 90-35331

Also available in paperback from Dell; Spanish language edition also available

Awarded the Newbery Medal, 1961

A reissue with new illustrations of the title first published 1960

"Unintentionally left behind by members of her California Native American tribe who fled a tragedy-ridden island, young Karana must construct a life for herself. Without bitterness or self-pity, she is able to extract joy and challenge from her eighteen years of solitude." Shapiro. Fic for Youth. 2d edition

Followed by Zia, entered below

The King's fifth; decorations and maps by
Samuel Bryant. Houghton Mifflin 1966 264p
$15.95 (5 and up) **Fic**

1. Estevan, d. 1539—Fiction 2. Mexico—Fiction
ISBN 0-395-06963-7

Also available Spanish language edition

A Newbery Medal honor book, 1967

"Fifteen-year-old Esteban sailed with Admiral Alarcon as a cartographer; carrying supplies for Coronado, the expedition went astray and a small group was put ashore to find Coronado's camp. Thus begins a harrowing story of the exciting and dangerous journey in search of the fabled gold of Cibola." Sutherland. The Best in Child Books

Sarah Bishop. Houghton Mifflin 1980 184p
$14.95 (6 and up) **Fic**

1. United States—History—1775-1783, Revolution—Fiction 2. American loyalists—Fiction 3. New York (State)—Fiction
ISBN 0-395-29185-2   LC 79-28394

Also available in paperback from Scholastic

"Surrounded by war, prejudice, and fear, fifteen-year-old Sarah Bishop quietly determines to live her own kind of life in the wilderness that was Westchester County, New York, during the Revolution. Orphaned Sarah plucks up her courage when she is wrongfully dealt with by both the American and British forces, and she creates a home for herself and her animal friends in the forest near Long Pond." Child Book Rev Serv

"Despite a series of highly dramatic incidents, the story line is basically sharp and clear; O'Dell's messages about the bitterness and folly of war, the dangers of superstition, and the courage of the human spirit are smoothly woven into the story, as are the telling details of period and place." Bull Cent Child Books

Sing down the moon. Houghton Mifflin
1970 137p $14.95 (5 and up) **Fic**

1. Navajo Indians—Fiction
ISBN 0-395-10919-1

Also available Cornerstone Bks. large print edition and in paperback from Dell; Spanish language edition also available

A Newbery Medal honor book, 1971

This story is told "through the eyes of a young Navaho girl as she sees the rich harvest in the Canyon de Chelly in 1864 destroyed by Spanish slavers and the subsequent destruction by white soldiers which forces the Navahos on a march to Fort Sumner." Publ Wkly

"There is a poetic sonority of style, a sense of identification, and a note of indomitable courage and stoicism that is touching and impressive." Saturday Rev

Streams to the river, river to the sea; a
novel of Sacagawea. Houghton Mifflin 1986
191p $14.95 (5 and up) **Fic**

1. Sacagawea, b. 1786—Fiction 2. Lewis and Clark Expedition (1804-1806)—Fiction 3. Indians of North America—Fiction
ISBN 0-395-40430-4   LC 86-936

Also available G.K. Hall large print edition and in paperback from Fawcett Bks.

This novel "tells the story of the Lewis and Clark expedition through the eyes of the young Shoshone woman who served as interpreter and, often, guide." Soc Educ

"An informative and involving choice for American history students and pioneer-adventure readers." Bull Cent Child Books

Zia. Houghton Mifflin 1976 179p $14.95 (5
and up) **Fic**

1. Indians of North America—Fiction 2. Christian missions—Fiction
ISBN 0-395-24393-9   LC 75-44156

Also available in paperback from Dell; Spanish language edition also available

In this sequel to Island of the Blue Dolphins, the author invents a niece for Karana "in the character of Zia, a young Indian who lives at the Santa Barbara Mission and who dreams of sailing to the island to rescue her aunt. After one thwarted attempt to get there, and imprisonment for helping some fellow Indians flee the Mission, Zia finds her dream realized." N Y Times Book Rev

"Zia is an excellent story in its own right, written in a clear, quiet, and reflective style which is in harmony with the plot and characterization." SLJ

Orgel, Doris

The devil in Vienna. Dial Bks. for Young
Readers 1978 246p o.p.; Puffin Bks. paperback
available $4.99 (6 and up) **Fic**

1. Austria—Fiction 2. Jews—Austria—Fiction 3. Holocaust, 1933-1945—Fiction 4. Friendship—Fiction
ISBN 0-14-032500-X (pa)   LC 78-51319

Also available in hardcover from P. Smith

"Although fictional, the events in this story about the Nazi occupation of Austria are based on the author's experiences as a child in Vienna. Inge is Jewish, her best friend Lieselotte is the daughter of a Nazi officer so devoted to Hitler that he had moved his family to Germany, returning only after the anschluss. Although the girls have been forbidden to meet by both sets of parents, Inge knows her

Orgel, Doris—*Continued*

friend is loyal; when her parents are having difficulty in leaving the country, Inge turns to Lieselotte's uncle, a Catholic priest, for help. The story ends with the refugees' safe arrival in Yugoslavia." Bull Cent Child Books

"The book arouses in its readers anguish, fury, admiration, scorn—it couldn't be a more effective story or a more powerful illustration of the reason 'never to forget.'" Publ Wkly

Orlev, Uri, 1931-

The island on Bird Street; translated by Hillel Halkin. Houghton Mifflin 1984 162p $14.95 (5 and up)   **Fic**

1. Holocaust, 1933-1945—Fiction 2. Jews—Poland—Fiction 3. World War, 1939-1945—Fiction 4. Poland—Fiction

ISBN 0-395-33887-5   LC 83-26524

Original Hebrew edition, copyright 1981

This is the "story of an 11-year-old boy's life during the Holocaust. Alex, entirely on his own in an empty Polish ghetto, is sustained by his father's admonition to wait for him. Over rooftops, through attics and basements he traverses the deserted sector in his struggle for life." SLJ

"The author has written a book that offers on one level a first-rate survival story and on another a haunting glimpse of the war's effects on individual people. . . . Although the tone of the book reflects the boy's cheerful, logical disposition, the loneliness and utter desperation of his situation come through with a piercing clarity." Horn Book

Lydia, Queen of Palestine; translated from the Hebrew by Hillel Halkin. Houghton Mifflin 1993 170p $13.95 (5 and up)   **Fic**

1. Jews—Romania—Fiction 2. World War, 1939-1945—Fiction 3. Divorce—Fiction 4. Romania—Fiction 5. Israel—Fiction

ISBN 0-395-65660-5   LC 93-12488

Also available in paperback from Puffin Bks.

Original Hebrew edition, 1991

A young Rumanian Jewish girl describes her childhood in pre-World War II Romania, her struggles to understand her parents divorce amid the chaos of the war, and her life on a kibbutz in Palestine. Based on the life of the Israeli poet Arianna Haran

"Young readers will especially enjoy Lydia's flip, often irreverent humor. . . . Orlev gives us an offbeat perspective here, showing family strife as dominating a child's view of the catastrophic events surrounding her." Bull Cent Child Books

The man from the other side; translated from the Hebrew by Hillel Halkin. Houghton Mifflin 1991 186p $13.95 (6 and up)   **Fic**

1. World War, 1939-1945—Fiction 2. Holocaust, 1933-1945—Fiction

ISBN 0-395-53808-4   LC 90-47898

Also available in paperback from Puffin Bks.

Living on the outskirts of the Warsaw Ghetto during World War II, fourteen-year-old Marek and his grandparents shelter a Jewish man in the days before the Jewish uprising

"Strong emotions and swift actions bombard the reader in this fact based book. The well-done translation projects the book's intensity." Child Book Rev Serv

Park, Barbara, 1947-

Beanpole. Knopf 1983 147p hardcover o.p. paperback available $3.50 (5 and up)   **Fic**

ISBN 0-394-84746-6 (pa)   LC 83-111

Also available in paperback from Avon Bks.

"Lillian begins her . . . story just as she turns thirteen; five feet six, she's called 'Beanpole' by her classmates in seventh grade. She has a three-part birthday wish; to get a bra, to dance with a boy, to become a member of the Pom Squad." Bull Cent Child Books

"Told in a first-person rambling style, 'Beanpole' features common sense outlined in humor with a three-dimensional supporting cast of relatives and friends." SLJ

Mick Harte was here. Apple Soup Bks. 1995 89p $15; lib bdg $16.99 (4-6)   **Fic**

1. Brothers and sisters—Fiction 2. Death—Fiction

ISBN 0-679-87088-1; 0-679-97088-6 (lib bdg)
                                        LC 94-27272

Thirteen-year-old Phoebe recalls her younger brother Mick and his death in a bicycle accident

"The author is adept at portraying the stages of grief and the effects of this sudden tragedy on the family. The book's tone of sadness is mitigated by humor, reassurance, and hope." SLJ

My mother got married (and other disasters). Knopf 1989 138p lib bdg $13.99; pa $4.50 (4-6)   **Fic**

1. Stepfamily—Fiction

ISBN 0-394-92149-6 (lib bdg); 0-394-85059-9 (pa)
                                        LC 88-27257

Twelve-year-old Charles experiences many difficulties in adjusting to a new stepfather, stepsister, and stepbrother

"Stories about divorce are nothing new, but Parks does a superb job of giving this one a fresh feel. Charlie's first-person dialogue is humorous but also realistically bitter. . . . A story of surprising depth." Booklist

Skinnybones. Knopf 1982 112p lib bdg $10.99; pa $3.99 (4-6)   **Fic**

1. School stories 2. Baseball—Fiction

ISBN 0-394-94988-9 (lib bdg); 0-394-94988-9 (pa)
                                        LC 81-20791

The novel's hero "Alex Frankovitch (short, thin 'Skinnybone'), is a realist who knows that winning the Most Improved Player awards for six years only means that each year he has started out 'stink-o' and gone to 'smelly.' His particular nemesis this year is T.J. Stoner; T.J.'s brother plays for the Chicago Cubs, and T.J.'s so good he could be suiting up with them momentarily himself. At least that's the way it seems to Alex, who always manages to be on T.J.'s wrong side and in the middle of a disaster because of it. Alex finally comes into his own when he wins the Kitty Fritters TV Contest and thus gets his own taste of what being a celebrity is like." Booklist

Another available title about Skinnybones is:
Almost starring Skinnybones (1988)

Park, Ruth

Playing Beatie Bow. Atheneum Pubs. 1982 c1980 196p $16 (5 and up)   **Fic**

1. Family life—Fiction 2. Space and time—Fiction 3. Australia—Fiction

ISBN 0-689-30889-2   LC 81-8097

Also available in paperback from Puffin Bks.

"An Argo book"

First published 1980 in Australia

Park, Ruth—*Continued*

"'Beatie Bow' is the name of a game that Abigail sees younger children playing, and she notices one waif-like girl who watches but never joins the play. Abigail's fourteen, resenting the fact that her mother is more than willing to take back the husband who'd deserted her for another woman, resenting even more her parents' decision to move from Sydney to Norway. . . . [In this] time-slip story, the waif proves to be the Beatie Bow for whom the game was named—but she doesn't know why her name is known. Only when Abigail goes back to Beatie's time, a century ago, does a pattern emerge that answers both their questions." Bull Cent Child Books

Patent, Dorothy Hinshaw

Return of the wolf; illustrated by Jared Taylor Williams. Clarion Bks. 1995 67p il $15.95 (5 and up)   **Fic**

1. Wolves—Fiction
ISBN 0-395-72100-8   LC 94-26798

"Sedra, a she-wolf banished from her pack, finds new territory and a mate, and begins a new pack with her first litter the following spring." SLJ

"Based on the author's first-hand observations, this dramatic story is realistic and fast-paced. Many intriguing details of animal communication, wolf pups' birth and training, and a pack's hunting and survival techniques enliven this unforgettable story." Sci Child

Paterson, Katherine

Bridge to Terabithia; illustrated by Donna Diamond. Crowell 1977 128p il $14.95; lib bdg $14.89; pa $3.95 (4 and up)   **Fic**

1. Friendship—Fiction 2. Death—Fiction 3. Virginia—Fiction
ISBN 0-690-01359-0; 0-690-04635-9 (lib bdg); 0-06-440184-7 (pa)   LC 77-2221

Also available Cornerstone Bks. large print edition; Spanish language edition also available

Awarded the Newbery Medal, 1978

The life of Jess, a ten-year-old boy in rural Virginia expands when he becomes friends with a newcomer who subsequently meets an untimely death trying to reach their hideaway, Terabithia, during a storm

"Jess and his family are magnificently characterized; the book abounds in descriptive vignettes, humorous sidelights on the clash of cultures, and realistic depictions of rural school life." Horn Book

Come sing, Jimmy Jo. Lodestar Bks. 1985 193p $14.99 (5 and up)   **Fic**

1. Country music—Fiction 2. Family life—Fiction
ISBN 0-525-67167-6   LC 84-21123

Also available in paperback from Avon Bks. and Puffin Bks.

When his family becomes a successful country music group and makes him a featured singer, eleven-year-old James has to deal with big changes in all aspects of his life, even his name

"What Katherine Paterson does so well is catch the cadence of the locale without sounding fake. There isn't a false note in her diction. She has created a West Virginian world that is entirely believable: homely, honest, goodhearted. . . . This book is James's personal inward journey, and it is deeply felt." Christ Sci Monit

Flip-flop girl. Lodestar Bks. 1994 120p $14.99 (4-6)   **Fic**

1. Brothers and sisters—Fiction 2. Death—Fiction 3. Friendship—Fiction
ISBN 0-525-67480-2   LC 93-31591

Also available in paperback from Puffin Bks.

Uprooted following the death of their father, nine-year-old Vinnie and her five-year-old brother, Mason, cope in different ways—one in silence—but both with the help of Lupe, the flip-flop girl

"Vinnie and her family are drawn with exquisite candor in scenes that combine love, anger, and sudden comedy." Booklist

The great Gilly Hopkins. Crowell 1978 148p $14.95; lib bdg $13.89; pa $3.95 (5 and up)   **Fic**

1. Foster home care—Fiction
ISBN 0-690-03837-2; 0-690-03838-0 (lib bdg); 0-06-440201-0 (pa)   LC 77-27075

Also available Spanish language edition

"Cool, scheming, and deliberately obstreperous, 11-year-old Gilly is ready to be her usual obnoxious self when she arrives at her new foster home. . . . But Gilly's old tricks don't work against the all-encompassing love of the huge, half-illiterate Mrs. Trotter. . . . Determined not to care she writes a letter full of wild exaggerations to her real mother that brings, in return, a surprising visit from an unknown grandmother." Booklist

"A well-structured story [this] has vitality of writing style, natural dialogue, deep insight in characterization, and a keen sense of the fluid dynamics in human relationships." Bull Cent Child Books

Lyddie. Lodestar Bks. 1991 182p $15 (5 and up)   **Fic**

1. United States—History—1815-1861—Fiction 2. Massachusetts—Fiction 3. Factories—Fiction
ISBN 0-525-67338-5   LC 90-42944

Also available Thorndike Press large print edition and in paperback from Puffin Bks.

Impoverished Vermont farm girl Lyddie Worthen is determined to gain her independence by becoming a factory worker in Lowell, Massachusetts, in the 1840s

"Not only does the book contain a riveting plot, engaging characters, and a splendid setting, but the language—graceful, evocative, and rhythmic—incorporates the rural speech patterns of Lyddie's folk, the simple Quaker expressions of the farm neighbors, and the lilt of fellow mill girl Bridget's Irish brogue. . . . A superb story of grit, determination, and personal growth." Horn Book

The master puppeteer; illustrated by Haru Wells. Crowell 1976 c1975 179p il $15; lib bdg $14.89; pa $3.95 (6 and up)   **Fic**

1. Puppets and puppet plays—Fiction 2. Japan—Fiction
ISBN 0-690-00913-5; 0-690-04905-6 (lib bdg); 0-06-440281-9 (pa)

Also available in paperback from Avon Bks.

"In 18th-century Osaka, Japan, Jiro, son of a starving puppetmaker, runs away from home to apprentice himself to Yoshida, the ill-tempered master of the Hanaza puppet theater. As Jiro works to learn the art of the puppeteer and travels among the savage, hunger-crazed bands of night rovers in search of his parents, he becomes aware of a mysterious connection between Saboro, a Robin Hood-like figure, and the Hanaza theater itself." SLJ

"The make-believe world of the Japanese puppet theatre merges excitingly with the hungry, desperate realities of 18th century Osaka in this better-than-average junior novel." Bull Cent Child Books

Paterson, Katherine—*Continued*

Of nightingales that weep; illustrated by Haru Wells. Crowell 1974 170p il $14; pa $3.95 (6 and up)   **Fic**

1. Japan—Fiction

ISBN 0-690-00485-0; 0-06-440282-7 (pa)

"Takiko, daughter of a famous samurai killed in the wars, is taken into the court of the boy emperor Antoku as a musician and personal servant. Takiko's conflicting loyalties to the Heike-supported court, a dashing Genji warrior, and her physically grotesque but goodhearted peasant stepfather form the impetus for her internal development while the war rages around her." Booklist

Park's quest. Lodestar Bks. 1988 148p $13.99 (5 and up)   **Fic**

1. Farm life—Fiction 2. Vietnamese Americans—Fiction

ISBN 0-525-67258-3   LC 87-32422

Also available in paperback from Puffin Bks.; Spanish language edition also available

Eleven-year-old Park makes some startling discoveries when he travels to his grandfather's farm in Virginia to learn about his father who died in the Vietnam War and meets a Vietnamese-American girl named Thanh

The author "confronts the complexity, the ambiguity, of the war and the emotions of those it involved with an honesty that young readers are sure to recognize and appreciate." N Y Times Book Rev

Paton Walsh, Jill, 1937-

Fireweed. Farrar, Straus & Giroux 1970 c1969 133p hardcover o.p. paperback available $3.50 (5 and up)   **Fic**

1. World War, 1939-1945—Fiction 2. London (England)—Fiction

ISBN 0-374-42316-4 (pa)

First published 1969 in the United Kingdom

During World War II, "Bill and Julie had found each other by chance, each of them lurking around London after having started off with a group of children being evacuated. Julie had money, Bill could cope, and together the two made a clandestine home in the rubble of a building. Only when Julie was caught by a raid did Bill, staring in anguish at the fresh ruins, realize how important she had become to him." Saturday Rev

"The development of a relationship . . . is one of the two main achievements of this book. . . . The second achievement is the setting, the picture given without squeamishness or apparent over-emphasis of London in the blitz—the humour, the fear, the misery, the sometimes uncanny normality." Times Lit Suppl

Unleaving. Farrar, Straus & Giroux 1976 145p hardcover o.p. paperback available $3.50 (6 and up)   **Fic**

1. Cornwall (England)—Fiction

ISBN 0-374-48068-0 (pa)

Sequel to Goldengrove (1972)

"Young Madge rents most of her house for the summer to two college professors, their families, and students for an intellectual retreat. She becomes friendly with the group, especially Patrick and his young mongoloid sister, and enters into their discussions of life, death, and God. Woven in are episodes of Gran, now years later, again at summertime, sharing the same house with her family and examining the same topics as the young Madge did." Child Book Rev Serv

"Drawing upon the changing surface of the ocean by the beach house, Walsh creates intense descriptive passages which provide a shimmering background for the constantly shifting perspectives of the plot. The result is a tantalizing

evocative book, skillfully interweaving themes of love, death, and the continuity of the soul." SLJ

Patron, Susan

Maybe yes, maybe no, maybe maybe; pictures by Dorothy Donahue. Orchard Bks. 1993 87p il $14.95; lib bdg $14.99 (3-5)   **Fic**

1. Moving—Fiction 2. Sisters—Fiction 3. Mothers and daughters—Fiction

ISBN 0-531-05482-9; 0-531-08632-1 (lib bdg)

LC 92-34067

Also available in paperback from Dell

"A Richard Jackson book"

When her hardworking mother decides to move, eight-year-old PK uses her imagination and storytelling to help her older and younger sisters adjust

"The author's distinctive voice and characters drive this engaging novel, with its easy vocabulary, large type, and scattered, full-page wash paintings." Horn Book Guide

Paulsen, Gary

The cookcamp. Orchard Bks. 1991 115p $14.95; lib bdg $14.99 (5 and up)   **Fic**

1. Grandmothers—Fiction 2. World War, 1939-1945—Fiction

ISBN 0-531-05927-8; 0-531-08527-9 (lib bdg)

LC 90-7734

Also available in paperback from Dell

"A Richard Jackson book"

During World War II, a little boy is sent to live with his grandma, a cook in a camp for workers building a road through the wilderness

"Paulsen's simply told story strikes extraordinary emotional chords. . . . Those hungry for adventure stories, as well as more introspective readers, will be spellbound by this stirring novel." Publ Wkly

Dogsong. Bradbury Press 1985 177p $15 (6 and up)   **Fic**

1. Inuit—Fiction 2. Arctic regions—Fiction

ISBN 0-02-770180-8   LC 84-20443

Also available in paperback from Puffin Bks.

A Newbery Medal honor book, 1986

A fourteen-year-old Eskimo boy who feels assailed by the modernity of his life takes a 1400-mile journey by dog sled across ice, tundra, and mountains seeking his own "song" of himself

The author's "mystical tone and blunt prose style are well suited to the spare landscape of his story, and his depictions of Russell's icebound existence add both authenticity and color to a slick rendition of the vision-quest plot, which incorporates human tragedy as well as promise." Booklist

The haymeadow; illustrated by Ruth Wright Paulsen. Delacorte Press 1992 195p il $15; pa $4.50 (6 and up)   **Fic**

1. Ranch life—Fiction 2. Sheep—Fiction 3. Wyoming—Fiction

ISBN 0-385-30621-0; 0-440-40923-3 (pa)

LC 91-36666

Fourteen-year-old John comes of age and gains self-reliance during the summer he spends up in the Wyoming mountains tending his father's herd of sheep

"The protagonist is clearly imagined; the style is both consciously simple and dramatic. . . . There's even a touch of humor." Bull Cent Child Books

Paulsen, Gary—*Continued*

Mr. Tucket. Delacorte Press 1994 166p
$15.95; pa $4.50 (5 and up)   **Fic**

1. Frontier and pioneer life—Fiction 2. West (U.S.)—
Fiction
ISBN 0-385-31169-9; 0-440-41133-5 (pa)

LC 93-31180

In 1848, while on a wagon train headed for Oregon, fourteen-year-old Francis Tucket is kidnapped by Pawnee Indians and then falls in with a one-armed trapper who teaches
him how to live in the wild

"Superb characterizations, splendidly evoked setting and
thrill-a-minute plot make this book a joy to gallop
through." Publ Wkly

Another available title about Francis Tucket is:
Call me Francis Tucket (1995)

The winter room. Orchard Bks. 1989 103p
$11.95; lib bdg $14.99 (5 and up)   **Fic**

1. Farm life—Fiction 2. Minnesota—Fiction
ISBN 0-531-05839-5; 0-531-08439-6 (lib bdg)

LC 89-42541

Also available in paperback from Dell
A Newbery Medal honor book, 1990
"A Richard Jackson book"

A young boy growing up on a northern Minnesota farm
describes the scenes around him and recounts his old Norwegian uncle's tales of an almost mythological logging past

"While this seems at first to be a collection of anecdotes
organized around the progression of the farm calendar,
Paulsen subtly builds a conflict that becomes apparent in
the last brief chapters, forceful and well-prepared. . . . Lyrical and only occasionally sentimental, the prose is clean,
clear, and deceptively simple." Bull Cent Child Books

Pearce, Philippa, 1920-

Tom's midnight garden; illustrated by Susan
Einzig. Lippincott 1959 c1958 229p il lib bdg
$13.89; pa $4.95 (4 and up)   **Fic**

1. Fantasy fiction 2. Space and time—Fiction
ISBN 0-397-30477-3 (lib bdg); 0-06-440445-5 (pa)

First published 1958 in the United Kingdom

"Daytime life for Tom at his aunt's home in England is
dull, but each night he participates through fantasy in the
lives of the former inhabitants of the interesting old house
in which he is spending an enforced vacation. The book is
British in setting and atmosphere. The element of mystery
is well sustained, and the reader is left to make his own interpretation of the reality of the story." Adventuring with
Books

Peck, Richard

The ghost belonged to me; a novel. Viking
1975 183p o.p.; Dell paperback available $3.99
(5 and up)   **Fic**

1. Ghost stories
ISBN 0-440-42861-0 (pa)

"Although he tries to avoid her, thirteen-year-old Alexander Armsworth relates how his classmate and neighbor,
Blossom Culp, involves him in a ghost mystery. Later,
Blossom relates her own stories with a most convincing air.
Humor and excitement play a big role in the stories, which
are set in 1913. The characters are unusual and unforgettable. Peck writes with a flair for the dramatic." Roman. Sequences

Other available titles about Blossom Culp are:
Blossom Culp and the sleep of death (1986)
The dreadful future of Blossom Culp (1983)
Ghosts I have been (1977)

Peck, Robert Newton, 1928-

A day no pigs would die. Knopf 1973 c1972
150p $20; pa $4.99 (6 and up)   **Fic**

1. Shakers—Fiction 2. Farm life—Fiction 3. Vermont—
Fiction

ISBN 0-394-48235-2; 0-679-85306-5 (pa)

"Rob lives a rigorous life on a Shaker farm in Vermont
in the 1920s. Since farm life is earthy, this book is filled
with Yankee humor and explicit descriptions of animals
mating. A painful incident that involves the slaughter of
Rob's beloved pet pig is instrumental in urging him toward
adulthood. The death of his father completes the process of
his accepting responsibility." Shapiro. Fic for Youth. 3d edition

Soup; illustrated by Charles C. Gehm.
Knopf 1974 96p il lib bdg $12.99 (5 and up)
Fic

1. Friendship—Fiction 2. Vermont—Fiction

ISBN 0-394-92700-1

Also available in paperback from Dell

"Soup was Robert Peck's best friend during his boyhood,
and this is an episodic account of some of the ploys and
scrapes the two shared when they were in elementary
school." Bull Cent Child Books

"Rural Vermont during the 1920's is the setting for this
nostalgic account. . . . In a laconic and wryly humorous
style, the author relates the activities of the mischievous
twosome. . . . The black-and-white pencil drawings, artistically executed in the manner of Norman Rockwell, reflect
the understated story." SLJ

Other available titles about the author and his friend Soup
are:
Soup 1776 (1995)
Soup & me (1975)
Soup ahoy (1994)
Soup for president (1978)
Soup in love (1992)
Soup in the saddle (1983)
Soup on ice (1985)
Soup on wheels (1981)
Soup's hoop (1990)
Soup's uncle (1988)

Perl, Lila

Fat Glenda turns fourteen. Clarion Bks.
1991 168p $13.95 (5 and up)   **Fic**

1. Reducing—Fiction 2. Fashion models—Fiction

ISBN 0-395-53341-4   LC 90-40438

Fourteen-year-old Glenda, extremely unhappy after re-
gaining the pounds she worked so hard to lose, meets the
very overweight Giselle and discovers the world of plus-size
modeling, but she will have to stay fat to keep working as
such a model

"The snappy dialogue and realistic situations are entertaining and humorous. A hint of romance and an upbeat
ending add to the appeal of the book." Voice Youth Advocates

Other available titles about Fat Glenda are:
Fat Glenda's summer romance (1986)
Hey, remember Fat Glenda? (1981)

Petry, Ann Lane

Tituba of Salem Village; [by] Ann Petry. Crowell 1964 254p lib bdg $14.89; pa $3.95 (6 and up)   **Fic**

1. Tituba—Fiction   2. Salem   (Mass.)—Fiction
3. Witchcraft—Fiction 4. African Americans—Fiction
ISBN 0-690-04766-5 (lib bdg); 0-06-440403-X (pa)

"From the beauty of the island of Barbados, Tituba is uprooted to the dreary, gray cold of Boston. As the slave in the household of the minister, Samuel Parris, Tituba cooks, nurses, and attends to his sickly wife, daughter, and niece. When the minister moves to a new post in Salem Village, Tituba becomes the central figure in a witchcraft trial." Shapiro. Fic for Youth. 3d edition

Pevsner, Stella

And you give me a pain, Elaine. Clarion Bks. 1978 182p o.p.; Pocket Bks. paperback available $2.99 (4 and up)   **Fic**

1. Brothers and sisters—Fiction 2. Family life—Fiction
ISBN 0-671-68838-3 (pa)   LC 78-5857

First published by Seabury Press

"Thirteen-year-old Andrea, who tells the story, is the youngest of three; her adored brother Joe is away at college and her sister Elaine, sixteen, is the bane of Andrea's life, a sulky and rebellious adolescent who can't get along with Andrea or with their parents. Depressed by her own plodding personality and resentful of the attention Elaine gets when she defies her parents, Andrea is jolted into despair when Joe is killed in a motorcycle accident. This . . . is convincing as a first-person record, it is perceptive in establishing the fluctuations in personal relationships, [and] it has excellent dialogue." Bull Cent Child Books

Pinkney, Andrea Davis

Hold fast to dreams. Morrow Junior Bks. 1995 106p $15 (5 and up)   **Fic**

1. Moving—Fiction 2. Prejudices—Fiction 3. African Americans—Fiction
ISBN 0-688-12832-7   LC 94-32909

"When 12-year-old Deirdre's father gets a new job in New York City, the family relocates from Baltimore to suburban Connecticut. There are few blacks in Wexford and the white kids whisper and stare. . . . Deirdre, however, pursues her interest in photography and makes a friend." SLJ

"Pinkney is candid about the pain and loss as well as the achievement, and the docunovel is enlivened by characters drawn with warmth and wit." Booklist

Pinkwater, Daniel Manus, 1941-

Fat men from space; written and illustrated by Daniel Manus Pinkwater. Dodd, Mead 1977 57p il o.p.; Dell paperback available $3.25 (3-6)   **Fic**

1. Food—Fiction 2. Science fiction
ISBN 0-440-44542-6 (pa)   LC 77-6091

"Young William goes to the dentist and comes out with a filling that receives radio programs. Exploring the infinite possibilities of a tooth radio, he attaches a wire to a chain-link fence, touches it to his molar, and tunes in on an invading 'spaceburger' from the planet Spiegel. Before he can warn anyone of earth's peril, he is captured and 'floated' up to the spaceburger where he meets the invaders—fat men with glasses, wearing plaid sport jackets. Their raid is successful—Earth is stripped of all its junk food." SLJ

"Message books aren't usually this much fun, but Pinkwater makes his a polished romp." Bull Cent Child Books

Another available title in this series is:
Attila the pun (1981)

The Hoboken chicken emergency; by D. Manus Pinkwater. Prentice-Hall 1977 83p il hardcover o.p. paperback available $4.95 (3-6)   **Fic**

1. Chickens—Fiction

ISBN 0-671-66447-6 (pa)   LC 76-41910

Arthur goes to pick up the turkey for Thanksgiving dinner but comes back with a 260-pound chicken

"A contemporary tall tale that will stretch middle graders' imagination, sense of humor, and enthusiasm for reading. For absurdity with perfect timing, not many can match the author." Booklist

Lizard music; written and illustrated by D. Manus Pinkwater. Dodd, Mead 1976 157p il o.p.; Bantam Bks. paperback available $3.99 (4 and up)   **Fic**

1. Science fiction

ISBN 0-553-15605-5 (pa)

"Left alone when his parents go on a vaction, Victor discovers, through late-night TV, a community of intelligent lizards and the Chicken Man. The succeeding adventures take Victor through some strange but thought-provoking escapades. Children associate with the ending—a return to normal but dull life when the rest of the family returns. A good read-aloud book." Read Teach

Pinkwater, Jill

Tails of the Bronx; a tale of the Bronx. Macmillan 1991 208p $14.95; pa $3.95 (4-6)   **Fic**

1. Homeless persons—Fiction 2. Bronx (New York, N.Y.)—Fiction

ISBN 0-02-774652-6; 0-689-71671-0 (pa)

LC 90-48914

In their search for a group of missing cats, a group of children in the Bronx encounters the problems of homelessness firsthand

"By turns outrageously funny and heartbreaking, Pinkwater's . . . riveting book is solid, thought-provoking entertainment." Publ Wkly

Polikoff, Barbara Garland

Life's a funny proposition, Horatio. Holt & Co. 1992 103p $13.95 (5 and up)   **Fic**

1. Death—Fiction 2. Grandfathers—Fiction
ISBN 0-8050-1972-3   LC 91-46724

Also available in paperback from Puffin Bks.

As Horatio tries to adjust to the death of his father from lung cancer, O.P., Horatio's grandfather, mourns the loss of his dog Mollie

"While capable of great tenderness, the understated writing style is both bracing and poignantly funny." Bull Cent Child Books

Pope, Elizabeth Marie, 1917-
The Perilous Gard; illustrated by Richard
Cuffari. Houghton Mifflin 1974 280p il o.p.;
Puffin Bks. paperback available $4.99 (6 and
up)   **Fic**
1. Great Britain—Fiction 2. Druids and Druidism—
Fiction 3. Fantasy fiction
ISBN 0-14-034912-X (pa)
A Newbery Medal Honor book, 1975
In 1558 while imprisoned in a remote castle, a young girl
becomes involved in a series of events that leads to an un-
derground labyrinth peopled by the last practitioners of
Druidic magic.
"The description of the Fairy Folk's life and customs is
fascinating and the plot is mystical and exciting enough for
all fantasy lovers." SLJ

Raskin, Ellen, 1928-1984
Figgs & phantoms. Dutton 1989 c1974 152p
il lib bdg $15.95 (5 and up)   **Fic**
1. Family life—Fiction
ISBN 0-525-29680-8   LC 88-29910
Also available in paperback from Puffin Bks.
A Newbery Medal honor book, 1974
A reissue of the title first published 1974
"This concerns Mona Lisa Newton, fat and frustrated
member of the Figg Newton family in the town of Pineapple. Of the Figg Newton family, which includes ex-variety
show stars Truman the Human Pretzel and uncles Romulus
and Remus, Mona loves only Uncle Florence Italy Figg—a
book dealer who dreams of dying and going to Capri, the
Figg fantasy heaven. When Florence dies, Mona embarks
on a clue-solving search for Capri, takes a wild mind trip,
and returns a wiser and happier person." Booklist

The mysterious disappearance of Leon (I
mean Noel). Dutton 1989 149p il o.p.; Puffin
Bks. paperback available $4.99 (4 and up)   **Fic**
1. New York (N.Y.)—Fiction 2. Mystery fiction
ISBN 0-14-032945-5 (pa)   LC 88-30658
A reissue of the title first published 1971
"Wed at the age of five to a seven-year-old husband (it
solved a business difficulty for their two families), the very
young Mrs. Leon Carillon immediately loses her spouse,
who is sent off to boarding school. This is the hilarious account of her search for Leon, aided by adopted twins, when
she is older. With clever clues to stimulate the reader's participation, the story is a bouquet of wordplay garnished
with jokes, sly pokes at our society, daft characters, and
soupcon of slapstick. Fresh and funny, it's the kind of book
that passes from child to child." Saturday Rev

The Westing game. Dutton 1978 185p lib
bdg $15.99 (5 and up)   **Fic**
1. Mystery fiction
ISBN 0-525-42320-6   LC 77-18866
Also available in paperback from Avon Bks. and Puffin
Bks.
Awarded the Newbery Medal, 1979
"This mystery puzzle . . . centers on the challenge set
forth in the will of eccentric multimillionaire Samuel Westing. Sixteen heirs of diverse backgrounds and ages are assembled in the old 'Westing house,' paired off, and given
clues to a puzzle they must solve—apparently in order to
inherit." SLJ
"The rules of the game make eight pairs of the players;
each oddly matched couple is given a ten thousand dollar
check and a set of clues. The result is a fascinating medley

of word games, disguises, multiple aliases and subterfuges—
in a demanding but rewarding book." Horn Book

Rawlings, Marjorie Kinnan, 1896-1953
The yearling; with pictures by N. C. Wyeth.
Scribner 1985 c1938 400p il $25; pa $5.95 (6
and up)   **Fic**
1. Deer—Fiction 2. Florida—Fiction
ISBN 0-684-18461-3; 0-02-044931-3 (pa)
     LC 85-40301
Also available G.K. Hall large print edition
First published 1938; this is a reissue of the 1939 edition
"Young Jody Baxter lives a lonely life in the scrub forest
of Florida until his parents unwillingly consent to his adopting an orphan fawn. The two become inseparable until the
fawn destroys the meager crops. Then Jody realizes that this
situation offers no compromise. In the sacrifice of what he
loves best, he leaves his own yearling days behind." Read
Ladders for Hum Relat. 5th edition

Rawls, Wilson, 1913-
Where the red fern grows; the story of two
dogs and a boy. Doubleday 1992 c1961 212p
$16.95; pa $4.50   **Fic**
1. Dogs—Fiction 2. Ozark Mountains—Fiction
ISBN 0-553-08900-5; 0-553-27429-5 (pa)
First published 1961
"Looking back more than 50 years to his boyhood in the
Ozarks, the narrator recalls how he achieved his heart's desire in the ownership of two redbone hounds, how he
taught them all the tricks of hunting, and how they won the
championship coon hunt before Old Dan was killed by a
mountain lion and Little Ann died of grief. Although some
readers may find this novel hackneyed and entirely too sentimental, others will enjoy the fine coon-hunting episodes
and appreciate the author's feelings for nature." Booklist

Reaver, Chap, 1935-1993
Bill. Delacorte Press 1994 216p $15.95; pa
$3.99 (5 and up)   **Fic**
1. Dogs—Fiction 2. Fathers and daughters—Fiction
3. Prohibition—Fiction
ISBN 0-385-31175-3; 0-440-41153-X (pa)
     LC 93-35491
With the help of her faithful dog Bill and the officer responsible for putting her father in jail, thirteen-year-old Jessica faces changes in her life when she realizes that her
father will not stop drinking and making moonshine
"The story contains everything a reader could want—
spunky, intriguing characters; a smart, loyal dog; hidden
treasure; a raft trip; and a happy ending. Never lapsing into
melodrama, the gripping novel depicts a girl and her dog
who never give up and never let go of each other." Horn
Book Guide

Reeder, Carolyn, 1937-
Shades of gray. Macmillan 1989 152p $15 (4
and up)   **Fic**
1. Orphans—Fiction 2. Uncles—Fiction 3. United
States—History—1861-1865, Civil War—Fiction
ISBN 0-02-775810-9   LC 89-31976
Also available in paperback from Avon Bks.
At the end of the Civil War, twelve-year-old Will, having
lost all his immediate family, reluctantly leaves his city
home to live in the Virginia countryside with his aunt and

Reeder, Carolyn, 1937-—*Continued*
the uncle he considers a "traitor" because he refused to take part in the war

"Minor plot threads (Will's adjustment to rural life, his relationships with the local boys and his affection for his cousin Meg) provide changes of tone and tempo in a novel that has, despite an uneven pace, both momentum and nuance." Bull Cent Child Books

Reid Banks, Lynne, 1929-
The Indian in the cupboard. Doubleday 1980 181p il $15.95 (5 and up)   **Fic**
1. Indians of North America—Fiction 2. Fantasy fiction
ISBN 0-385-17051-3   LC 79-6533
Also available Cornerstone Bks. large print edition and in paperback from Avon Bks.
Illustrated by Brock Cole
A nine-year-old boy receives a plastic Indian, a cupboard, and a little key for his birthday and finds himself involved in adventure when the Indian comes to life in the cupboard and befriends him
Other available titles in this series are:
The mystery of the cupboard (1993)
The return of the Indian (1986)
The secret of the Indian (1989)

Riskind, Mary, 1944-
Apple is my sign. Houghton Mifflin 1981 146p hardcover o.p. paperback available $4.95 (5 and up)   **Fic**
1. Deaf—Fiction
ISBN 0-395-65747-4 (pa)
"The story is set in Pennsylvania at the time of the first horseless carriages . . . in a school for the deaf. Ten-year-old Harry is at first homesick, but he soon makes friends, becomes excited about learning to draw and learning to talk. Aware that his father is ashamed of his own deafness (both parents are deaf) and that his mother is not, Harry learns to accept his situation as his mother has: a handicap rather than a stigma." Bull Cent Child Books
"In a lengthy note the author explains that she had deaf parents and learned sign language before she learned to speak. She also explores some characteristics of sign language, which has been translated into print via sentence syntax and spelling. A warm, unpretentious story that rises above bibliotherapeutic intent to become simple, effective storytelling." Booklist

Roberts, Willo Davis
The girl with the silver eyes. Atheneum Pubs. 1980 181p $16 (4-6)   **Fic**
1. Psychokinesis—Fiction
ISBN 0-689-30786-1   LC 80-12391
Also available in paperback from Scholastic
"Silver eyes are not all that set ten-year-old Katie apart from her peers—she's able to move things by thinking about them and talk to animals. Living with her mother for the first time since she was three, Katie tries to adjust to the other adults in the building, to her mom's male friend, and to her own strange situation." SLJ
"Much of the book's first half relies on diverting readers with examples of Katie's powers . . . while the second section builds more suspensefully around her efforts to track down the source of her problem, other children who might share it, and someone who will help her deal with it. . . . Roberts' smooth writing will lure them right to the end." Booklist

Scared stiff. Atheneum Pubs. 1991 188p $14.95 (5 and up)   **Fic**
1. Mystery fiction 2. Amusement parks—Fiction 3. Brothers—Fiction
ISBN 0-689-31692-5   LC 90-37732
"A Jean Karl book"
When their mother disappears, two brothers go to stay with a great uncle in a mobile home park next to an abandoned amusement park and begin a search which puts themselves in danger
"The brisk pace, fluid style, and excitement of the novel are sure to entertain readers, while the sensitive handling of such issues as separation and alcoholism, and the not-perfect ending make the book a cut above the general fare." SLJ

The view from the cherry tree. Atheneum Pubs. 1975 181p $15.95; pa $3.95 (5 and up)   **Fic**
1. Mystery fiction
ISBN 0-689-30483-8; 0-689-71131-X (pa)
"Thoroughly disgruntled by the furor which accompanies his sister's wedding, eleven-year-old Rob Mallory retires to his favorite perch in the cherry tree. There, he is a horrified witness to the murder of an unpleasant neighborhood recluse. Because of the wedding preparations and the arrival of hordes of relatives, no adult will believe Rob's story. Soon, he finds that someone knows—and is trying to kill him, too." Child Book Rev Serv
"Although written in a direct and unpretentious style, this is essentially a sophisticated story, solidly constructed, imbued with suspense, evenly paced, and effective in conveying the atmosphere of a household coping with the last-minute problems and pressures of a family wedding." Bull Cent Child Books

Robertson, Keith, 1914-1991
Henry Reed, Inc.; illustrated by Robert McCloskey. Viking 1958 239p il hardcover o.p. paperback available $4.99 (4-6)   **Fic**
ISBN 0-14-034144-7 (pa)
"Henry Reed, on vacation from the American School in Naples, keeps a record of his research into the American free-enterprise system, to be used as a school report on his return. With a neighbor, Midge Glass, he starts a business in pure and applied research, which results in some very free and widely enterprising experiences, all recorded deadpan in his journal. Very funny and original escapades." Hodges. Books for Elem Sch Libr
Other available titles about Henry Reed are:
Henry Reed's babysitting service (1966)
Henry Reed's journey (1963)

Robinet, Harriette Gillem, 1931-
If you please, President Lincoln. Atheneum Bks. for Young Readers 1995 149p $15 (5 and up)   **Fic**
1. African Americans—Fiction 2. Slavery—Fiction 3. Haiti—Fiction
ISBN 0-689-31969-X   LC 95-2126
"A Jean Karl book"
"In December 1863 Moses, a 14-year-old slave, runs away from his Maryland master rather than be sold South. He befriends Goshen, a blind free black, and the two are enticed onto a ship with promises of work. The voyage, however, takes them—and 400 others—to an uninhabited island off Haiti, as part of an ill-conceived colonization scheme." SLJ

Robinet, Harriette Gillem, 1931-—*Continued*
"A historical novel with an exciting plot, convincing characters, and a most original setting. . . . In the appended Author's Note, Robinet details her research into the history of the actual Isle à Vache expedition." Booklist

Robinson, Barbara
The best Christmas pageant ever; pictures by Judith Gwyn Brown. Harper & Row 1972 80p il $14.95; lib bdg $14.89; pa $3.95 (4-6)
        Fic
1. Christmas—Fiction 2. Pageants—Fiction
ISBN 0-06-025043-7; 0-06-025044-5 (lib bdg); 0-06-440275-4 (pa)
In this story the six Herdmans, "absolutely the worst kids in the history of the world," discover the meaning of Christmas when they bully their way into the leading roles of the local church nativity play
"Although there is a touch of sentiment at the end . . . the story otherwise romps through the festive preparations with comic relish, and if the Herdmans are so gauche as to seem exaggerated, they are still enjoyable, as are the not-so-subtle pokes at pageant-planning in general." Bull Cent Child Books
Another available title about the Herdmans is:
The best school year ever (1994)

Rockwell, Thomas, 1933-
How to eat fried worms; pictures by Emily McCully. Watts 1973 115p il lib bdg $14.77 (3-6)
        Fic
1. Worms—Fiction
ISBN 0-531-02631-0
Also available in paperback from Dell
"The stakes are high when Alan bets $50 that his friend Billy can't eat 15 worms (one per day). . . . Billy's mother, instead of upchucking, comes to her son's aid by devising gourmet recipes like Alsatian Smothered Worm. Alan wants to win as desperately as Billy, who is itching to buy a used minibike, and few holds are barred in the contest." SLJ
"A hilarious story that will revolt and delight bumptious, unreachable, intermediate-grade boys and any other less particular mortals that read or listen to it. . . . The characters and their families and activities are natural to a T, and this juxtaposed against the uncommon plot, makes for some colorful, original writing in a much-needed comic vein." Booklist

Rodda, Emily, 1948-
Finders keepers; illustrated by Noela Young. Greenwillow Bks. 1991 c1990 184p il $12.95; pa $3.95 (4-6)
        Fic
1. Fantasy fiction 2. Computer games—Fiction
ISBN 0-688-10516-5; 0-688-11846-1 (pa)
        LC 90-47850
First published 1990 in Australia
While playing a computer game, Patrick is transported to a parallel world and invited to participate in a game show in which he must find three lost items to win several fabulous prizes
"Rodda serves up at least one riotous situation per chapter and keeps her adventure moving at lightning speed—making for an uncommonly satisfying read. Young's line drawings deftly keep pace with the story's changing moods." Publ Wkly

Rodgers, Mary, 1931-
Freaky Friday. Harper & Row 1972 145p $14.95; lib bdg $13.89; pa $3.95 (4 and up)
        Fic
1. Mothers and daughters—Fiction
ISBN 0-06-025048-8; 0-06-025049-6 (lib bdg); 0-06-440046-8 (pa)
Also available Cornerstone Bks. large print edition; Spanish language edition also available
"'When I woke up this morning, I found I'd turned into my mother.' So begins the most bizarre day in the life of 13-year-old Annabel Andrews, who discovers one Friday morning she has taken on her mother's physical characteristics while retaining her own personality. Readers will giggle in anticipation as Annabel plunges madly from one disaster to another trying to cope with various adult situations." Publ Wkly
"A fresh, imaginative, and entertaining story." Bull Cent Child Books
Other available titles about Annabel Andrews and her family are:
A billion for Boris (1974)
Summer switch (1982)

Rodowsky, Colby F., 1932-
The gathering room; [by] Colby Rodowsky. Farrar, Straus & Giroux 1981 185p $11.95 (5 and up)
        Fic
1. Family life—Fiction 2. Cemeteries—Fiction 3. Aunts—Fiction
ISBN 0-374-32520-0
After Aunt Ernestus comes to visit, a family living in seclusion as caretakers for a cemetery find the time has come to rejoin the mainstream of society
"Lacking in fast-moving action and flawed with a slow start, the story relies on an electric atmosphere and on the carefully developed anticipation of change to gain its considerable hold on the reader's interest." Horn Book

Hannah in between; [by] Colby Rodowsky. Farrar, Straus & Giroux 1994 151p $15 (5 and up)
        Fic
1. Alcoholism—Fiction 2. Mothers and daughters—Fiction
ISBN 0-374-32837-4
        LC 93-35478
Also available in paperback from Dell
As she starts seventh grade, twelve-year-old Hannah can no longer ignore her mother's increasingly erratic behavior caused by drinking
"This heartrending novel offers a frank, sensitive depiction of alcoholism and its effects." Publ Wkly

Rosen, Michael J., 1954-
Elijah's angel; a story for Chanukah and Christmas; illustrated by Aminah Brenda Lynn Robinson. Harcourt Brace Jovanovich 1992 unp il $13.95
        Fic
1. Pierce, Elijah, 1892-1984—Fiction 2. Artists—Fiction 3. Jews—Fiction 4. Christmas—Fiction 5. Hanukkah—Fiction
ISBN 0-15-225394-7
        LC 91-37552
At Christmas-Hanukkah time, Elijah Pierce, a black Christian woodcarver gives a carved angel to Michael, a young Jewish friend, who struggles with accepting the Christmas gift until he realizes that friendship means the same thing in any religion
"Perhaps because it's based on reality, Michael and Elijah's relationship rings sweetly true. The naive-style paint-

Rosen, Michael J., 1954-—*Continued*

ings, done in house paint on scrap rags, boldly simulate
woodcuts, and though the artwork is not pretty, it, too, has
the feel of reality." Booklist

A school for Pompey Walker; illustrated by
Aminah Brenda Lynn Robinson. Harcourt
Brace & Co. 1995 unp il $16   **Fic**

1. Slavery—Fiction 2. African Americans—Fiction
ISBN 0-15-200114-X   LC 94-6240

This "story is based on the life of Gussie West, a slave
who sold himself into slavery again and again, escaped each
time with the help of his white friend, and used the money
to build a school for freed black children. . . . Drawing on
slave memoirs, Rosen imagines Pompey Walker telling his
story, an elderly man remembering and talking to the children in his school." Booklist
"The narrator's voice is startlingly clear and natural. . .
. Using dyes and bold, sinuous lines to suggest the rich,
transparent coloring and stylized figures of stained glass,
Robinson's full- and half-page illustrations convey strong
feelings through facial expressions and gnarled, slightly
oversized hands." SLJ

Ross, Ramon Royal, 1930-

Harper & Moon. Atheneum Pubs. 1993
181p $14.95 (6 and up)   **Fic**

1. Friendship—Fiction 2. Orphans—Fiction 3. Child
abuse—Fiction
ISBN 0-689-31803-0   LC 92-17216

Also available in paperback from Avon Bks.
"A Jean Karl book"
Although twelve-year-old Harper has always liked Moon,
an abused, orphaned older boy, their friendship is tested by
a discovery Harper makes when Moon joins the Army in
1943
"The book . . . has lots of action and suspense. While the
story is written simply enough for the older middle grades,
it deals with heavy issues: child abuse, animal abuse, suspected murder, and a suicide attempt." Booklist

Roth-Hano, Renée, 1931-

Touch wood; a girlhood in occupied France.
Four Winds Press 1988 297p $16.95 (6 and
up)   **Fic**

1. Holocaust, 1933-1945—Fiction 2. France—History—
1940-1945, German occupation—Fiction 3. Jews—
France—Fiction
ISBN 0-02-777340-X   LC 87-34326

Also available in paperback from Puffin Bks.
This "novel in diary format tells the experiences of a
pre-adolescent Jewish girl in occupied France. Renée Roth's
family has fled from Alsace to find safety in Paris, but the
Nazi restrictions and round-ups force her parents to send
their three daughters to a convent in Normandy, where
they're lonely but cared for in relative comfort until caught
in the bombing that fronts the Allied invasion." Bull Cent
Child Books
"An immediate and moving memoir, the book adds still
another dimension to understanding the impact of the
1940s not only on world events but on the lives of individuals." Horn Book

Ruckman, Ivy, 1931-

Night of the twisters. Crowell 1984 153p
$14; lib bdg $14.89; pa $3.95 (3-6)   **Fic**

1. Tornadoes—Fiction 2. Nebraska—Fiction
ISBN 0-690-04408-9; 0-690-04409-7 (lib bdg);
0-06-440176-6 (pa)   LC 83-46168

"Twelve-year-old Dan describes the events leading up to
the hour that his town was struck seven times by tornadoes.
Alone at home, [in Grand Island, Nebraska] Dan, his baby
brother, and his best friend Arthur ride out the storm hud-
dled in the shower stall in Dan's basement and then begin
the search for their parents." Sci Child
"Ruckman does a good job of creating and maintaining
suspense, produces dialogue that sounds appropriate for a
stress situation, and gives her characters some depth and
differentiation." Bull Cent Child Books

Rylant, Cynthia

A blue-eyed daisy. Bradbury Press 1985 99p
$13.95 (5 and up)   **Fic**

1. Family life—Fiction 2. West Virginia—Fiction
ISBN 0-02-777960-2   LC 84-21554

Also available in paperback from Dell
This story "describes a year in a child's life. . . . Ellie is
eleven, youngest of five girls. She wishes her father didn't
drink but understands his frustration. . . . It is a bond between them when they acquire a hunting dog. . . . She also
acquires a best friend during the year, gets her first kiss
(and is surprised to see that she enjoys it) and adjusts to the
fact that some of the events in her life will be sad ones."
Bull Cent Child Books
"Episodic in nature, the story captures, as if in a frozen
frame, the brief moments between childhood and adolescence." Horn Book

A fine white dust. Bradbury Press 1986
106p $14.95; pa $3.95 (5 and up)   **Fic**

1. Religion—Fiction 2. Friendship—Fiction 3. Family
life—Fiction
ISBN 0-02-777240-3; 0-689-80462-8 (pa)
                                           LC 86-1003

Also available in paperback from Dell
A Newbery Medal honor book, 1987
The visit of the traveling Preacher Man to his small
North Carolina town gives new impetus to thirteen-year-old
Peter's struggle to reconcile his own deeply felt religious belief with the beliefs and non-beliefs of his family and
friends
"Blending humor and intense emotion with a poetic use
of language, Cynthia Rylant has created a taut, finely drawn
portrait of a boy's growth from seeking for belief, through
seduction and betrayal, to a spiritual acceptance and a readiness 'for something whole.'" Horn Book

Missing May. Orchard Bks. 1992 89p
$14.95; lib bdg $13.99 (5 and up)   **Fic**

1. Death—Fiction 2. West Virginia—Fiction
ISBN 0-531-05996-0; 0-531-08596-1 (lib bdg)
                                           LC 91-23303

Also available in paperback from Dell
Awarded the Newbery Medal, 1993
"A Richard Jackson book"
After the death of the beloved aunt who has raised her,
twelve-year-old Summer and her uncle Ob leave their West
Virginia trailer in search of the strength to go on living
"There is much to ponder here, from the meaning of life
and death to the power of love. That it all succeeds is a
tribute to a fine writer who brings to the task a natural
grace of language, an earthly sense of humor, and a well-
grounded sense of the spiritual." SLJ

Rylant, Cynthia—*Continued*
The Van Gogh Cafe. Harcourt Brace & Co.
1995 53p $14 (4-6)   **Fic**

1. Restaurants—Fiction 2. Magic—Fiction
ISBN 0-15-200843-8   LC 94-43348

This consists of "seven vignettes of life at the Van Gogh
Café. Situated off I-70 in Flowers, Kansas, the café (formerly an old movie theater) is run by Marc and his 10-year-old
daughter, Clara, who appreciate the magic that comes from
the café's very walls." Booklist
The author "breaks new ground in producing this whimsical tale, dextrously weaving extraordinary events into the
fabric of ordinary life. . . . The strength of her imagination
and the depth of her sensitivity will impress even the reluctant reader." Publ Wkly

Sachar, Louis, 1954-
Marvin Redpost, kidnapped at birth?
illustrated by Neal Hughes. Random House
1992 68p il lib bdg $9.99; pa $3.99 (2-4)
Fic

ISBN 0-679-91946-5 (lib bdg); 0-679-81946-0 (pa)
LC 91-51105

"A First Stepping Stone book"
Red-haired Marvin is convinced that the reason he looks
different from the rest of his family is that he is really the
lost prince of Shampoon
"Written almost completely in dialogue, the story is fast
paced, easy to read, and full of humor." SLJ
Other available titles about Marvin Redpost are:
Marvin Redpost, alone in his teacher's house (1994)
Marvin Redpost, is he a girl? (1993)
Marvin Redpost, why pick on me? (1993)

Wayside School gets a little stranger;
illustrated by Joel Schick. Morrow Junior Bks.
1995 168p il $15 (3-6)   **Fic**

1. School stories
ISBN 0-688-13694-X   LC 94-25448

This is "about the zany goings-on in [an] unorthodox 30-
story-tall school. . . . The narrative revolves around the
wacky substitute teachers who take Mrs. Jewls's place when
she is on maternity leave." Publ Wkly
"Sachar's offering contains hilarity, malevolence, romance, relentless punning, goofiness, inspiration, revenge,
and poignancy." SLJ
Other available titles about Wayside School are:
Sideways stories from Wayside School (1978)
Wayside School is falling down (1989)

Sachs, Marilyn, 1927-
The bears' house. Dutton 1987 c1971 67p
o.p.; Avon Bks. paperback available $2.99
(4-6)   **Fic**

1. Family life—Fiction 2. Dollhouses—Fiction
ISBN 0-380-70582-6 (pa)   LC 86-29267

First published 1971 by Doubleday in an illustrated edition
"Life is grim for nine-year-old Fran Ellen. Father has
deserted the family, mother has retreated into apathy and
tears, and the five children shift for themselves. Fran Ellen's only joy is Baby Flora. Rejected at home and taunted
at school, Fran Ellen adopts as her own the classroom doll
house, compensating for her unhappiness with . . . fantasies
in which its tenants, the three bears, adore her." Saturday
Rev
"Superb characterizations and uncommonly skilled writing draw the reader completely into the realities and fantasies of Fran Ellen's world." Libr J

Another available title about Fran Ellen is:
Fran Ellen's house (1987)

What my sister remembered. Dutton
Children's Bks. 1992 122p $15 (5 and up)
Fic

1. Sisters—Fiction 2. Adoption—Fiction
ISBN 0-525-44953-1   LC 91-32263

Also available in paperback from Puffin Bks.
While visiting her younger sister Mollie, Beth confronts
painful memories of the sudden death of her parents and
the subsequent adoption of the sisters by different families
"Nuances of love and angst are revealed with a rare
combination of perception, compassion, and dramatic conviction. . . . Taut and powerful." Bull Cent Child Books

Saint-Exupéry, Antoine de, 1900-1944
The little prince; written and drawn by
Antoine de Saint-Exupéry; translated from the
French by Katherine Woods. Harcourt Brace
& Co. 1943 91p il $15; pa $7 (4 and up)
Fic

ISBN 0-15-246503-0; 0-15-646511-6 (pa)
Also available G.K. Hall large print edition; Spanish language edition also available
First published by Reynal & Hitchcock
"This many-dimensional fable of an airplane pilot who
has crashed in the desert is for readers of all ages. The pilot
comes upon the little prince soon after the crash. The
prince tells of his adventures on different planets and on
Earth as he attempts to learn about the universe in order to
live peacefully on his own small planet. A spiritual quality
enhances the seemingly simple observations of the little
prince." Shapiro. Fic for Youth. 3d edition

Salten, Felix, 1869-1945
Bambi; a life in the woods il (4-6)   **Fic**

1. Deer—Fiction
Original German edition, 1923; first United States edition published 1928 by Simon & Schuster
Various editions available
"Bambi is a young deer, growing up in a forest, at first
a curious child playing about his mother in glade and
meadow, conversing with grasshoppers, squirrels and his
own little cousins, Faline and Gobo." N Y Libr
"Felix Stalten's story of deer life in the woods that fringe
the Danube is neither sentimental nor used to point a moral. It derives its dramatic value, legitimately, from the animals' fear and terror of their historic enemy—man. . . . In
his absorption with details that author has brought his
whole forest to life, yet these details are selected with a
poet's intuition for delicacy of effect." N Y Her Trib Books

Sargent, Sarah, 1937-
Weird Henry Berg. Crown 1980 113p o.p.;
Knopf paperback available $3.50 (4-6)
Fic

1. Dragons—Fiction 2. Fantasy fiction
ISBN 0-679-80703-9 (pa)   LC 80-13651

"Henry Berg doesn't know that the 'lizard' he has is a
baby dragon; all he knows is that the odd, endearing pet has
hatched from an ancient egg that had belonged to his great-
grandfather. Elderly Millie Levenson doesn't know Henry,
but she gets in touch with him because she has had a visit
from a dragon, a sophisticated creature sent over from
Wales to find the baby that had been left behind a century

Sargent, Sarah, 1937-—*Continued*

ago. Henry wants to keep his pet; Millie, knowing that the dragon is in danger, wants to get him back to Wales." Bull Cent Child Books

"The conjunction of fantasy with reality is made believable by the author's narrative skill and by her ability to suggest character through economical description. A fascinating and original tale." Horn Book

Sawyer, Ruth, 1880-1970

Roller skates; written by Ruth Sawyer and illustrated by Valenti Angelo. Viking 1995 c1936 186p il $14.99; pa $4.99 (4-6)   **Fic**

1. New York (N.Y.)—Fiction
ISBN 0-670-60310-4; 0-14-030358-8 (pa)

               LC 85-43418

Awarded the Newbery Medal, 1937

A reissue of the title first published 1936

"For one never-to-be forgotten year Lucinda Wyman (ten years old) was free to explore New York on roller skates. She made friends with Patrick Gilligan and his hansom cab, with Policeman M'Gonegal, with the fruit vendor, Vittore Coppicco and his son Tony, and with many others. All Lucinda's adventures are true and happened to the author herself as is borne out by the occasional pages of Lucinda's diary which are a part of the story." Horn Book

Schnur, Steven

The shadow children; illustrated by Herbert Tauss. Morrow Junior Bks. 1994 86p il $14; lib bdg $13.93 (5 and up)   **Fic**

1. Holocaust, 1933-1945—Fiction 2. Ghost stories 3. France—Fiction
ISBN 0-688-13281-2; 0-688-13831-4 (lib bdg)

               LC 94-5098

While spending the summer on his grandfather's farm in the French countryside, eleven-year-old Etienne discovers a secret dating back to World War II and encounters the ghosts of Jewish children who suffered a dreadful fate under the Nazis

"The prose is spare and beautiful, and the expressive charcoal illustrations move from the warm affection of the present to the shadowy horror that won't go away." Booklist

Schur, Maxine, 1948-

The circlemaker; by Maxine Rose Schur. Dial Bks. for Young Readers 1994 179p $14.99 (5 and up)   **Fic**

1. Jews—Russia—Fiction 2. Russia—Fiction
ISBN 0-8037-1354-1   LC 93-17983

Also available in paperback from Viking

In mid-nineteenth century Russia, Mendel Cholinsky, a twelve-year-old Jewish boy tries to escape to America to avoid being taken into the Czar's army for twenty-five years of military service

"The action and suspense will draw readers to a book that could also be used by teachers and librarians for units on Russia, Judaism, multiculturalism, and prejudice." Book Rep

Scieszka, Jon, 1954-

Knights of the kitchen table; illustrated by Lane Smith. Viking 1991 55p il $11.99; pa $2.99 (3-5)   **Fic**

1. Fantasy fiction
ISBN 0-670-83622-2; 0-14-034603-1 (pa)

               LC 90-51009

At head of title: The Time Warp Trio

"Transported to the Middle Ages, three friends save themselves from a dragon and a giant through quick thinking. The tongue-in-cheek narrative makes for laugh-out-loud enjoyment, and the easy-to-read sentences and zany dialogue perfectly suit the breathless pace." SLJ

Other available titles about The Time Warp Trio are: 2095 (1995)
The good, the bad, and the goofy (1992)
The not-so-jolly Roger (1991)
Your mother was a Neanderthal (1993)

Sebestyen, Ouida, 1924-

Out of nowhere; a novel. Orchard Bks. 1994 183p $15.95; lib bdg $15.99 (5 and up)   **Fic**

1. Dogs—Fiction 2. Foster home care—Fiction
ISBN 0-531-06839-0; 0-531-08689-5 (lib bdg)

               LC 93-37759

Also available in paperback from Puffin Bks.

"A Melanie Kroupa book"

When he no longer fits into his vagabond mother's life, thirteen-year-old Harley adopts an abandoned dog and falls in with an outspoken old woman, a cantakerous junk collector, and an energetic and loving teenage girl

"This poignant story is beautifully written, and readers will delight in it." SLJ

Words by heart. Little, Brown 1979 162p $15.95 (5 and up)   **Fic**

1. African Americans—Fiction 2. Race relations—Fiction 3. Family life—Fiction
ISBN 0-316-77931-8   LC 78-27847

Also available in paperback from Bantam Bks.

"An Atlantic Monthly Press book"

"It is 1910, and Lena's family is the only black family in her small Southwestern town. When Lena wins a scripture reciting contest that a white boy is supposed to win, her family is threatened. Lena's father tries to make her understand that by hating the people who did this, the problems that cause their behavior are not solved. Only more hatred and violence cause Lena and the village to understand the words of her father." ALAN

Followed by On fire (1985)

Seidler, Tor, 1952-

The steadfast tin soldier; [by] Hans Christian Andersen; illustrated by Fred Marcellino; retold by Tor Seidler. HarperCollins Pubs. 1992 28p il $15; lib bdg $14.89 (1-4)   **Fic**

1. Toys—Fiction 2. Fairy tales
ISBN 0-06-205000-1; 0-06-205001-X (lib bdg)

               LC 92-52690

Also available Spanish language edition

"Michael di Capua books"

This is a retelling of Andersen's fairy tale in which the one-legged tin soldier falls in love with a paper ballerina

The text is "lively and readable. . . . Marcellino . . . creates an exceptionally handsome version of the tale. Set

Seidler, Tor, 1952-—*Continued*
in the nineteenth century, presumably in Denmark, the book includes impressive outdoor scenes under a pewter gray winter sky and domestic indoor scenes golden with the diffuse light of candles. Softly delineated forms and figures appear in a series of formally composed scenes sometimes reminiscent of dramatic tableaux. Designed with a sense of quiet elegance." Booklist

The Wainscott weasel; illustrated by Fred Marcellino. HarperCollins Pubs. 1993 193p il $20; lib bdg $19.89; pa $9.95 (4-6)   **Fic**

1. Weasels—Fiction 2. Animals—Fiction
ISBN 0-06-205032-X; 0-06-205033-8 (lib bdg); 0-06-205911-4 (pa)   LC 92-54526

"The weasels' summer begins with the visiting Wendy being charmed by both Zeke and Bagley, Jr. . . . But Bagley pines for Bridget, a beautiful fish who lives in the nearby brook. . . . When Bridget's life is in danger, Bagley learns he can be a hero." Child Book Rev Serv

"Seidler's pacing is superb; he builds a solid structure within each chapter. A dry wit inspires his characterizations. . . . Marcellino enhances and even extends the beguiling ambiance with his exceptionally expressive art." Publ Wkly

Selden, George, 1929-1989
The cricket in Times Square; illustrated by Garth Williams. Farrar, Straus & Giroux 1960 151p il $15 (3-6)   **Fic**

1. Cats—Fiction 2. Crickets—Fiction 3. Mice—Fiction 4. New York (N.Y.)—Fiction
ISBN 0-374-31650-3

Also available Cornerstone Bks. large print edition and in paperback from Dell; Spanish language edition also available

A Newbery Medal honor book, 1961
"An Ariel book"

"A touch of magic comes to Times Square subway station with Chester, a cricket from rural Connecticut. He is introduced to the distinctive character of city life by three friends: Mario Bellini, whose parents operate a newsstand; Tucker, a glib Broadway mouse; and Harry, a sagacious cat. Chester saves the Bellinis' business by giving concerts from the newsstand, bringing to rushing commuters moments of beauty and repose. This modern fantasy shows that, in New York, anything can happen." Moorachian. What is a City?

Other available titles about Chester and his friends are:
Chester Cricket's new home (1983)
Chester Cricket's pigeon ride (1981)
Harry Cat's pet puppy (1974)
Harry Kitten and Tucker Mouse (1986)
The old meadow (1987)
Tucker's countryside (1969)

The genie of Sutton Place. Farrar, Straus & Giroux 1973 175p hardcover o.p. paperback available $4.95 (4 and up)   **Fic**

ISBN 0-374-42530-2 (pa)

Also available in hardcover from P. Smith

Adapted from the television play written by the author and Kenneth Heuer

"Tim turns to his dead father's diaries for some occult wisdom to help him keep Sam, a beloved mongrel his aunt has banished from their apartment. What he finds is a spell that summons the genie Abdullah from a thousand years' captivity in a woven carpet." Booklist

"The speedy action and clever dialogue in this witty book are sure to entice readers." SLJ

Selznick, Brian
The Houdini box. Knopf 1991 unp il lib bdg $13.99; pa $2.99 (2-4)   **Fic**

1. Houdini, Harry, 1874-1926—Fiction 2. Magicians—Fiction
ISBN 0-679-91429-3 (lib bdg); 0-679-85448-7 (pa)   LC 90-5387

A chance encounter with Harry Houdini leaves Victor in possession of a mysterious box—one that might hold the secrets to the greatest magic tricks ever performed

"The abundant pen-and-ink drawings capture the era perfectly. A book written with humor, excitement and most of all, magic." Child Book Rev Serv

Seredy, Kate, 1899-1975
The Good Master; written and illustrated by Kate Seredy. Viking 1935 210p il hardcover o.p. paperback available $4.99 (4-6)   **Fic**

1. Farm life—Fiction 2. Hungary—Fiction
ISBN 0-14-030133-X (pa)

A Newbery Medal honor book, 1936

Into this story of Jancsi, a ten-year-old Hungarian farm boy and his little hoyden of a cousin Kate from Budapest, is woven a description of Hungarian farm life, fairs, festivals, and folk tales. Under the tutelage of Jancsi's kind father, called by the neighbors The Good Master, Kate calms down and becomes a more docile young person

"The steady warm understanding of the wise father, the Good Master, is a shining quality throughout." Horn Book

Followed by: The singing tree (1939)

The white stag; written and illustrated by Kate Seredy. Viking 1937 94p il $14.99; pa $4.99 (4-6)   **Fic**

1. Hungary—Fiction
ISBN 0-670-76375-6; 0-14-031258-7 (pa)

Awarded the Newbery Medal, 1938

"Striking illustrations interpret this hero tale of the legendary founding of Hungary, when a white stag and a red eagle led the people to their promised land." Hodges. Books for Elem Sch Libr

Serraillier, Ian, 1912-
The silver sword; illustrated by C. Walter Hodges. Phillips 1959 c1956 187p il $26.95 (5 and up)   **Fic**

1. World War, 1939-1945—Fiction 2. Polish refugees—Fiction
ISBN 0-87599-104-1

First published 1956 in the United Kingdom; first United States edition published 1959 by Criterion Books

"As a result of World War II, the Balicki family of Warsaw are separated from one another. Living in bombed-out cellars or the countryside the children are helped by Edek until his arrest for smuggling and from then on by Jan, a sullen orphan. The privations of each member of the family, especially the children, are graphically described as each works toward their rendezvous, Switzerland, and freedom. A suspense-filled, exciting story." Read Ladders for Hum Relat. 5th edition

Service, Pamela F.
Stinker from space. Scribner 1988 83p $13.95 (4-6)   **Fic**

1. Science fiction
ISBN 0-684-18910-0   LC 87-25266

Service, Pamela F.—_Continued_

Also available in paperback from Fawcett Bks.

An agent of the Sylon Confederacy, fleeing from enemy ships, crash lands on Earth, transfers his mind to the body of a skunk, and enlists the aid of two children in getting back to his home planet

"A first-class, funny science fantasy that will hook middle-grade readers right from the first scene. . . . The situation is gratifyingly absurd, the development satisfyingly natural." Bull Cent Child Books

Storm at the edge of time. Walker & Co. 1994 179p $16.95 (5 and up)   **Fic**

1. Scotland—Fiction 2. Fantasy fiction

ISBN 0-8027-8306-6   LC 93-50816

"In the Orkney Islands, a sorcerer waits through the millennia for three young descendants to answer his call and fend off a destructive force reclaiming three stolen staffs of power. Aided by Urkar's magic. Arni, a Viking; Jamie, a girl from the present; and Tyaak, of the 26th century, pool their talents to outwit evil opponents in their own times." Publisher's note

"The story is fast paced and intriguing." Voice Youth Advocates

Sewell, Anna, 1820-1878

Black Beauty (4-6)   **Fic**

1. Horses—Fiction 2. Great Britain—Fiction

Also available Spanish language edition

Some editions are:

Farrar, Straus & Giroux $19.95 Pictures by Charles Keeping (ISBN 0-374-30776-8)

Grosset & Dunlap (Illustrated junior library) $14.95 Illustrated by Fritz Eichenberg (ISBN 0-448-40942-9)

Holt & Co. (Henry Holt little classics) $14.95 Illustrated by Victor Ambrus (ISBN 0-8050-2772-6)

Knopf (Everyman's library children's classics) $13.95 Illustrated by Lucy Kemp-Welch (ISBN 0-679-42811-9)

First published 1877 in the United Kingdom; first United States edition, 1891

This is "the most celebrated 'Animal Story' of the 19th cent., an account of a horse's experiences at the hands of many owners, ranging from the worthy Squire Gordon to a cruel cab-owner." Oxford Companion to Child Lit

Shalant, Phyllis

Beware of kissing Lizard Lips. Dutton Children's Bks. 1995 183p $13.99 (4-6)   **Fic**

1. School stories 2. Martial arts—Fiction 3. Korean Americans—Fiction

ISBN 0-525-45199-4   LC 94-44389

"Zach wants to stop being Mouseboy, the smallest in the sixth grade, and at the mercy of Lizard Lips, the tallest girl. He finds some hope, physically and spiritually, from learning tae kwon do and becomes interested in a girl in his class." SLJ

"This is a laugh-out-loud story about growing up male, written without a trace of condescension." Booklist

Sharmat, Marjorie Weinman, 1928-

Getting something on Maggie Marmelstein; pictures by Ben Shecter. Harper & Row 1971 101p il lib bdg $15.75 (3-5)   **Fic**

1. School stories

ISBN 0-06-025552-8

"This story of boy/girl rivalry involves the trouble that develops when Thad calls Maggie Marmelstein a mouse. She retaliates by threatening to tell that she has seen him helping her mother cook. His desperate search for something on Maggie leads to his discovery that she writes mushy fan letters to movie stars." SLJ

"Simple black-and-white illustrations provide a natural extension of the text which combines genuine character and plot development with amusing dialog." Publ Wkly

Another available title about Maggie Marmelstein is:
Maggie Marmelstein for president (1975)

Sharp, Margery, 1905-1991

The rescuers; with illustrations by Garth Williams. Little, Brown 1959 149p il hardcover o.p. paperback available $4.95 (3-6)   **Fic**

1. Mice—Fiction

ISBN 0-316-78355-2 (pa)

Also available in hardcover from P. Smith

This is "a story featuring animals. The Prisoners' Aid Society of mice [one of whose members is Miss Bianca, the pampered pet of an ambassador's son] want to free a Norwegian poet held captive in the Black Castle in a barbarous country." Publ Wkly

Shreve, Susan Richards

The flunking of Joshua T. Bates; [by] Susan Shreve; illustrated by Diane de Groat. Knopf 1984 82p il lib bdg $13.99; pa $4.50 (3-5)   **Fic**

1. School stories 2. Teachers 3. Family life—Fiction

ISBN 0-394-96380-6 (lib bdg); 0-679-84187-3 (pa)
     LC 83-19636

"Sometimes children, especially boys, are held back in school even if they are smart. To his dismay, Joshua T. Bates was supposed to repeat the whole third grade, but he was lucky enough to have a very sympathetic teacher." N Y Times Book Rev

"In addition to the warm depiction of a teacher-pupil relationship, the story has other relationships, astutely drawn: Joshua's parents, the former classmate who teases Joshua, the best friend who stoutly defends him. The dialogue is particularly good, often contributing to characterization, just as often crisply humorous." Bull Cent Child Books

Another available title about Joshua is:
Joshua T. Bates takes charge (1993)

Shyer, Marlene Fanta

Welcome home, Jellybean. Scribner 1978 152p hardcover o.p. paperback available $3.95 (5 and up)   **Fic**

1. Mentally handicapped children—Fiction 2. Brothers and sisters—Fiction

ISBN 0-689-71213-8 (pa)   LC 77-17970

"'When my sister turned thirteen the school where she lived got her toilet-trained and my mother decided she ought to come home to live, once and for all.' So begins Neil Oxley's story of how it was to have his profoundly retarded sister re-enter the family circle." Booklist

Shyer, Marlene Fanta—*Continued*

"Painful, honest, and convincing, this is quietly written and very effective in evoking sympathy and understanding for retarded children and for their families." Bull Cent Child Books

Singer, Isaac Bashevis, 1904-1991

The fools of Chelm and their history; pictures by Uri Shulevitz; translated by the author and Elizabeth Shub. Farrar, Straus & Giroux 1973 57p il $14 (4 and up)   Fic

1, Jews—Fiction

ISBN 0-374-32444-1

The "town of Chelm is just like every place else, only worse, as numerous shortages, foolish citizens, and inept leaders combine to make life thoroughly miserable. . . . Singer mocks the 'advantages'—such as war, crime, and revolution—that civilization brings to Chelm, as the leadership changes but never improves." Booklist

"An amusing story, well-told. The pen-and-ink illustrations embellish the text, adding droll touches of their own." Horn Book

Skurzynski, Gloria

Good-bye, Billy Radish. Bradbury Press 1992 138p il $14.95 (5 and up)   Fic

1. World War, 1914-1918—United States—Fiction 2. Friendship—Fiction 3. Ukrainian Americans—Fiction 4. Pennsylvania—Fiction

ISBN 0-02-782921-9   LC 92-7577

In 1917, as the United States enters World War I, ten-year-old Hank sees change all around him in his western Pennsylvania steel mill town and feels his older Ukrainian friend Billy drifting apart from him

"In this story permeated with the realities of life in World War I Pittsburgh, characters, time, and place spring vividly to life from the very first pages. And scene after scene—from the boys' first meeting to Hank's final feverish farewell—will remain etched in readers' memory through the unfolding of this richly textured, lovingly crafted historical novel." SLJ

Sleator, William

The duplicate. Dutton 1988 154p $13.99 (6 and up)   Fic

1. Science fiction

ISBN 0-525-44390-8   LC 87-30562

Also available in paperback from Bantam Bks.

Sixteen-year-old David, finding a strange machine that creates replicas of living organisms, duplicates himself and suffers the horrible consequences when the duplicate turns against him

"There are some points in the story when the roles of the clones (referred to as Duplicates A and B) become congested to the detriment of the book's pace, but fantasy fans will doubtless find the concept fresh enough and eerie enough to compensate for this, and Sleator is, as always, economical in casting and structuring his story." Bull Cent Child Books

Interstellar pig. Dutton 1984 197p $12.95 (5 and up)   Fic

1. Science fiction

ISBN 0-525-44098-4   LC 84-4132

Also available in paperback from Puffin Bks.

"Solitary and bored, Barney is quickly attracted by the exotic appearance and protean personalities of Zena, Manny, and Joe, who have rented the summer house next door.

The interest of the sophisticated adults in sixteen-year-old Barney at first flatters, then intrigues, and finally terrifies him as he becomes absorbed in their compulsion to possess 'The Piggy.' When he realizes that the talisman has power, the game expands in significance." Horn Book

The author "draws the reader in with intimations of danger and horror, but the climactic battle is more slapstick than horrific, and the victor's prize could scarcely be more ironic. Problematic as straight science fiction but great fun as a spoof on human-alien contact." Booklist

Into the dream; illustrated by Ruth Sanderson. Dutton 1979 137p il $13.95 (5 and up)   Fic

1. Extrasensory perception—Fiction 2. Psychokinesis—Fiction 3. Unidentified flying objects—Fiction

ISBN 0-525-32583-2   LC 78-11825

Also available in paperback from Knopf

When two youngsters realize they are having the same frightening dream, they begin searching for an explanation for this mysterious coincidence

"Tightly woven suspense and an ingenious, totally involving plot line . . . make this a thriller of top-notch quality." Booklist

Strange attractors. Dutton 1990 169p $13.95 (5 and up)   Fic

1. Space and time—Fiction 2. Science fiction

ISBN 0-525-44530-7   LC 89-33840

Also available in paperback from Puffin Bks.

"The strange attractors are people from a parallel universe: a brilliant scientist, Sylvan, and his beautiful daughter, Eve, whose reckless manipulation of time travel has plunged their timeline into chaos. Their search for a stable timeline brings them to our world, where they must destroy their doppelgängers, the 'real' Sylvan and Eve, or drag this world into chaos, too. Max, a teenage science student, is forced to become their unwilling ally or be destroyed himself." SLJ

"Sleator's talent for fascinating scientific manipulation is fully in evidence and exceptionally well conceived here. . . . Along with the clever science, Sleator turns in some good suspense." Booklist

Slepian, Jan, 1921-

The Alfred summer. Macmillan 1980 119p $15 (5 and up)   Fic

1. Friendship—Fiction 2. Handicapped children—Fiction 3. Brooklyn (New York, N.Y.)—Fiction

ISBN 0-02-782920-0   LC 79-24097

The story is "set in Brooklyn in 1937. . . . Lester, who suffers from cerebral palsy; Alfred, who is crippled and mentally retarded; Myron, clumsy and ineffectual—along with Claire, their athletic tomboy friend, find friendship and spend a happy summer building a boat." Horn Book

"The narrator's intelligent voice, with its youthful, touching irony, is the perfect voice. . . . Most remarkable is that the author is not handing out leaflets and guilt. She is not talking about US and Them. . . . She is saying that we are all a little bent somewhere, a little palsied. . . . A point worth making, a book worth reading." N Y Times Book Rev

Followed by Lester's turn (1981)

The Broccoli tapes. Philomel Bks. 1989 157p $14.95 (5 and up)   Fic

1. Cats—Fiction 2. Death—Fiction 3. Brothers and sisters—Fiction 4. Hawaii—Fiction

ISBN 0-399-21712-6   LC 88-25490

Also available in paperback from Scholastic

Slepian, Jan, 1921--—*Continued*

"Both 12-year-old Sara and her 13-year-old brother, Sam, have trouble adjusting to Hawaii during the five months that their family is living there. . . . When Sara and Sam rescue a wild cat (who is later named Broccoli), they meet Eddie Nutt. At first Eddie is as suspicious and untrusting as Broccoli until the bonds of friendship gradually develop. The story unfolds through Sara's cassette tapes sent to her teacher and classmates back home." SLJ

"Slepian is a fine writer, and the elements of her story are smoothly meshed, the action and characterization mutually affective. The message that love is worth the chance of pain is given by the people in her story, not didactically imposed by the author." Bull Cent Child Books

Risk 'n' roses. Philomel Bks. 1990 175p $14.95 (5 and up)   Fic

1. Friendship—Fiction   2. Mentally handicapped children—Fiction 3. Sisters—Fiction
ISBN 0-399-22219-7   LC 90-31460

Also available in paperback from Scholastic

In this "novel set after World War II, Skip, eleven, is as enthralled as the other neighborhood children with Jean, who is tough, daring, and domineering. Sharp-tongued Jean is a manipulator, and one of the people she manipulates is Angela, the beautiful and retarded older sister of Skip." Bull Cent Child Books

"Readers will see something of themselves in Skip, and, perhaps in Jean, and should come away from this story with much food for thought. An excellent choice for the middle grades." SLJ

Slote, Alfred

Finding Buck McHenry. HarperCollins Pubs. 1991 250p lib bdg $13.89; pa $3.95 (4-6)
Fic

1. Baseball—Fiction 2. African Americans—Fiction
ISBN 0-06-021653-0 (lib bdg); 0-06-440469-2 (pa)
LC 90-39190

Eleven-year-old Jason, believing the school custodian Mack Henry to be Buck McHenry, a famous pitcher from the old Negro League, tries to enlist him as a coach for his Little League team by revealing his identity to the world

"Slote skillfully blends comedy, suspense and baseball in a highly entertaining tale." Publ Wkly

Hang tough, Paul Mather. Lippincott 1973 156p lib bdg $14.89; pa $3.95 (4-6)   Fic

1. Leukemia—Fiction 2. Baseball—Fiction
ISBN 0-397-32509-6 (lib bdg); 0-06-440153-7 (pa)

"Paul Mather, a Little League star pitcher before he contracted leukemia, is unable to resist the temptation to demonstrate his skill when his family moves to Michigan and he ends up in the hospital." Booklist

"The story of Paul's candor and courage is convincing, sad but never morbid, in a book that has depth and integrity." Bull Cent Child Books

The trading games. Lippincott 1990 200p lib bdg $14.89; pa $4.50 (4-6)   Fic

1. Baseball cards—Fiction 2. Fathers and sons—Fiction 3. Grandfathers—Fiction
ISBN 0-397-32398-0 (lib bdg); 0-06-440438-2 (pa)
LC 89-12851

"Andy Harris' baseball-card collection, inherited from his recently deceased father, contains some valuable items, including a 1952 Mickey Mantle card worth $2500. He's willing, however, to trade Mantle for a 25-cent card that pictures his grandfather, Jim 'Ace 459' Harris, whom Andy idolizes. . . . It's not until Grampa coaches Andy that he

learns why the relationship between his father and grandfather was strained." SLJ

"Slote does a masterful job grounding the moral dilemmas of growing up within the rigorously measured world of the baseball diamond. Friendship, father-son intimacy, and the rough edges of adult life are all examined and filtered through the eyes of a boy who instinctively understands more than he knows." Booklist

Smith, Doris Buchanan

Best girl. Viking 1993 144p $13.99; pa $3.99 (4-6)   Fic

1. Mothers and daughters—Fiction
ISBN 0-670-83752-0; 0-14-034686-4 (pa)
LC 92-25931

As she struggles to cope with a difficult mother and finding her place in the world, young Nealy Compton finds solace in the relative solitude and safety beneath her neighbor's porch

The author "weaves another intricate web of emotions in this intimate story of loss and survival." Publ Wkly

The pennywhistle tree. Putnam 1991 144p $14.95 (4-6)   Fic

1. Friendship—Fiction
ISBN 0-399-21840-8   LC 90-23119

A rift develops in the closeness shared by eleven-year-old Jonathon and his best friends when Sanders, a new boy, moves onto the street and insists on pushing himself into Jonathon's life

"Smith meticulously reveals the changing levels of behavior and attitude in each character with a fine intertwining of action and reaction, misconception and perception. Thoughtful readers will find truths in this story worth pondering alone or discussing in a group." SLJ

Return to Bitter Creek; a novel. Viking Kestrel 1986 174p hardcover o.p. paperback available $3.95 (5 and up)   Fic

1. Family life—Fiction 2. Appalachian Mountains—Fiction
ISBN 0-14-032223-X (pa)   LC 85-40838

"After living in Colorado for most of her life, twelve-year-old Lacey returns with her mother, Campbell, and her mother's friend, David, to the North Carolina mountain village where she was born. Life is difficult there, for Lacey's grandmother has never forgiven her daughter for being an unwed mother and for taking her granddaughter away from her." Child Book Rev Serv

"Neither harsh in the portrayal of Grandmom's stubborn conventionality nor critical of Campbell's waywardness, the author shows that love survives in unlikely surroundings and that acknowledging its existence can be almost as difficult as grieving for its absence." Horn Book

A taste of blackberries; illustrated by Charles Robinson. Crowell 1973 58p il lib bdg $13.89; pa $3.95 (4-6)   Fic

1. Death—Fiction 2. Friendship—Fiction
ISBN 0-690-80512-8 (lib bdg); 0-06-440238-4 (pa)

A "portrayal of the death of a close friend. While gathering Japanese beetles to help a neighbor, Jamie is stung by a bee and falls screaming and writhing to the ground. His best friend (never named) disgustedly stalks off, only to find later that Jamie is dead of the bee sting. The boy feels guilty because he thought Jamie was clowning and didn't try to help. The boy is very withdrawn the week of the funeral, but comes to grips with the tragedy and learns to manage his grief." SLJ

"A difficult and sensitive subject, treated with taste and

Smith, Doris Buchanan—*Continued*

honesty, is woven into a moving story about a believable little boy. The black-and-white illustrations are honest, affective, and sensitive." Horn Book

Smith, Janice Lee, 1949-

The kid next door and other headaches; stories about Adam Joshua; drawings by Dick Gackenbach. Harper & Row 1984 143p il lib bdg $13.89; pa $3.95 (2-4)   Fic

1. Friendship—Fiction

ISBN 0-06-025793-8 (lib bdg); 0-06-440182-0 (pa)
                                                LC 83-47689

"Adam Joshua and Nelson, who are best friends as well as next-door neighbors, play and battle as best friends do. Their finest hour is coping with a visit from Nelson's truly horrid cousin Cynthia." N Y Times Book Rev

"This book has all the ingredients necessary for the often reluctant transition from easy readers to chapter books: large print and an ample supply of dialogue, humor and wonderfully funny black-and-white illustrations." SLJ

Other available titles about Adam Joshua are:

The baby blues (1994)
It's not easy being George (1989)
The monster in the third dresser drawer and other stories about Adam Joshua (1981)
Nelson in love (1992)
Serious science (1993)
The show-and-tell war and other stories about Adam Joshua (1988)
There's a ghost in the coatroom (1991)
The turkeys' side of it (1990)

Smith, Robert Kimmel, 1930-

Bobby Baseball; illustrated by Alan Tiegreen. Delacorte Press 1989 165p il $13.95; pa $3.99 (4-6)   Fic

1. Fathers and sons—Fiction 2. Baseball—Fiction

ISBN 0-385-29807-2; 0-440-40417-7 (pa)
                                                LC 89-1175

Ten-year-old Bobby is passionate about baseball and convinced that he is a great player. The only problem is to get a chance to prove his skill, especially to his father

"Baseball fans who share Bobby's fantasies will admire his determination and empathize with his stinging realization. Smith's crisp dialogue vivifies the book's appealing characters, and Tiegreen's illustrations lend an antic touch to Bobby's predicaments. This is an upbeat, refreshing celebration of the spirit of our national pastime." Publ Wkly

Chocolate fever; illustrated by Gioia Fiammenghi. Putnam 1989 c1972 93p il o.p.; Dell paperback available $3.99 (4-6)   Fic

ISBN 0-440-41369-6 (pa)   LC 88-23508

A reissue of the title first published 1972 by Coward-McCann

"You've heard of too much of a good thing? You've never heard of it the way it happens to Henry Green. Henry's a chocolate maven, first class. No, that's too mild. Henry's absolutely freaky over chocolate, loco over cocoa. He can't get enough, until—aaarrrfh! Brown spots, brown bumps all over Henry. It's (gulp) 'Chocolate Fever.'" N Y Times Book Rev

"It's all quite preposterous and lots of laughs, and so are the cartoon illustrations." Publ Wkly

The war with Grandpa; illustrated by Richard Lauter. Delacorte Press 1984 141p il hardcover o.p. paperback available $3.99 (4-6)
                                                Fic

1. Grandfathers—Fiction 2. Family life—Fiction

ISBN 0-440-49276-9 (pa)   LC 83-14366

"Pete's Grandpa comes to live with the family and bumps Pete out of the room he's had 'forever.' Egged on by his buddies, Pete starts a war of notes and practical jokes. To his surprise, Grandpa enjoys the skirmishes and the two carry on a quiet campaign for a while. In the final episode, Pete realizes just how wrong he has been and Grandpa comes up with a happy solution. This should be a winner with the middle grade set." Child Book Rev Serv

Snyder, Zilpha Keatley

Below the root; illustrated by Alton Raible. Atheneum Pubs. 1975 231p il o.p.; Dell paperback available $3.50 (5 and up)   Fic

1. Fantasy fiction

ISBN 0-440-21266-9 (pa)

Chosen to become one of a group of civil and religious leaders ruling the land of Green-Sky, thirteen-year-old Raamo's experiences make him question their teachings and lead him to uncover age-old deceptions

"There are long passages of description and explanation establishing Green Sky as a believable world, and though at times the allegory is a little heavy-handed, this is still an interesting suspenseful fantasy." SLJ

Other available titles about the land of Green-Sky are:
And all between (1976)
Until the celebration (1977)

Cat running. Delacorte Press 1994 168p $15.95; pa $3.99 (4 and up)   Fic

1. Economic depressions—Fiction 2. Running—Fiction

ISBN 0-385-31056-0; 0-440-41152-1 (pa)
                                                LC 94-447

"Sixth grader Cat Kinsey is sure she is the fastest runner in Brownwood School until Zane Perkins arrives barefoot and clothed in ragged overalls. He's an 'Okie,' and to most Californians during the Great Depression, that automatically translates to 'lazy, dirty, and shiftless.' When Cat's father forbids her to wear slacks because he feels they are unseemly, she ignores Zane's challenge and refuses to race during the school's annual Play Day. . . . This story is both appealing and informative. The characters are well drawn and beautifully motivated." SLJ

The Egypt game; drawings by Alton Raible. Atheneum Pubs. 1967 215p il $16 (5 and up)
                                                Fic

ISBN 0-689-30006-9

Also available in paperback from Dell

A Newbery Medal honor book, 1968

"Six children of different ethnic backgrounds secretly play a game invented by a white girl and a [black] girl who are fascinated by their own imaginations and by ancient Egypt. The Egypt game helps solve one girl's personal problems and it leads to the capture of a mentally ill murderer who attacks one of the girls." Wis Libr Bull

This book "is strong in characterization, the dialogue is superb, the plot is original, and the sequences in which the children are engaged in sustained imaginative play are fascinating, and often very funny." Saturday Rev

Snyder, Zilpha Keatley—*Continued*

The headless cupid; illustrated by Alton Raible. Atheneum Pubs. 1971 203p il $15.95 (5 and up)   **Fic**

1. Occultism—Fiction
ISBN 0-689-20687-9

Also available in paperback from Dell

A Newbery Medal honor book, 1972

"Story of an unhappy adolescent's preoccupation with the occult, her relationships with her step-siblings, and her eventual acceptance of the tangible world. Set in present-day California." Publisher's note

"The author portrays children with acute understanding, evident both in her delineation of Amanda and David and of the distinctively different younger children. Good style, good characterization, good dialogue, good story." Sutherland. The Best in Child Books

Other available titles about the Stanley family are:
Blair's nightmare (1984)
The famous Stanley kidnapping case (1979)

Libby on Wednesdays. Delacorte Press 1990 196p hardcover o.p. paperback available $3.99 (5 and up)   **Fic**

1. Authorship—Fiction 2. Friendship—Fiction 3. School stories
ISBN 0-440-40498-3 (pa)   LC 89-34959

"Libby, age eleven, very bright and the only child in an unconventional but strong household, has heretofore been home-educated. She is enrolled in public school for 'socialization' but soon finds that her peers tease her and mock her enormous wealth of knowledge. Only when she is selected for a writer's group does she forge ties to some equally gifted students." Child Book Rev Serv

"Vivid descriptions and clear portraits of the characters give an honest, forthright picture of these classmate-turned-friends who come to accept their difficulties and to care about each other. It's an absorbing story, filled with real young people and genuine concerns." SLJ

Song of the gargoyle. Delacorte Press 1991 232p hardcover o.p. paperback available $3.99 (5 and up)   **Fic**

1. Adventure fiction 2. Fools and jesters—Fiction
ISBN 0-440-40898-9 (pa)   LC 90-3772

When mysterious men in black abduct his father, the court jester of Austerneve, thirteen-year-old Tymmon flees into the forest, where he acquires a strange animal companion and plots to rescue his father

"This tale, a mixture of magic and hard-won truths, is deeply layered and affecting." Booklist

The velvet room; drawings by Alton Raible. Atheneum Pubs. 1965 216p il o.p.; Dell paperback available $3.50 (5 and up)   **Fic**

1. Migrant labor—Fiction 2. Economic depressions—Fiction 3. California—Fiction
ISBN 0-440-40042-2 (pa)

Also available in hardcover from P. Smith

"Beset by the problems of growing up [in California during the Depression] in a migrant worker's family, Robin finds refuge from the real world in a deserted mansion with a book-lined room and a mysterious past." Adventuring with Books

The witches of Worm; illustrated by Alton Raible. Atheneum Pubs. 1972 183p il $14.95 (5 and up)   **Fic**

1. Witchcraft—Fiction 2. Cats—Fiction
ISBN 0-689-30066-2

Also available in paperback from Dell

A Newbery Medal honor book, 1973

Jessica, the neglected child of a divorcee, "finds a deserted, new-born kitten which she calls 'Worm' since it is virtually hairless and blind. When this Worm turns—daily becoming more dominant over its mistress—Jessica is convinced she is in the grip of a hellish force that makes her play harmful tricks on her mother and on her few friends." Publ Wkly

"This is a haunting story of the power of mind and ritual, as well as of misunderstanding, anger, loneliness and friendship. It is written with humor, pace, a sure feeling for conversation and a warm understanding of human nature." Commonweal

Sobol, Donald J., 1924-

Encyclopedia Brown, boy detective; illustrated by Leonard Shortall. Dutton Children's Bks. 1963 88p il $13.99 (3-5)   **Fic**

1. Mystery fiction
ISBN 0-525-67200-1

Also available in paperback from Bantam Bks.

First published by Thomas Nelson

"Leroy Brown earns his nickname by applying his encyclopedic learning to community mysteries. The reader is asked to anticipate solutions before checking them in the back of the book." Natl Counc of Teach of Engl. Adventuring with Books. 2d edition

"The answers are logical; some are tricky, but there are no trick questions, and readers who like puzzles should enjoy the . . . challenge. The episodes are lightly humorous, brief, and simply written." Bull Cent Child Books

Other available titles about Encyclopedia Brown are:
Encyclopedia Brown and the case of the dead eagles (1975)
Encyclopedia Brown and the case of the disgusting sneakers (1990)
Encyclopedia Brown and the case of the midnight visitor (1977)
Encyclopedia Brown and the case of the mysterious hand-prints (1985)
Encyclopedia Brown and the case of the secret pitch (1965)
Encyclopedia Brown and the case of the treasure hunt (1988)
Encyclopedia Brown and the case of the two spies (1994)
Encyclopedia Brown carries on (1980)
Encyclopedia Brown finds the clues (1966)
Encyclopedia Brown gets his man (1967)
Encyclopedia Brown keeps the peace (1969)
Encyclopedia Brown lends a hand (1974)
Encyclopedia Brown saves the day (1970)
Encyclopedia Brown sets the pace (1982)
Encyclopedia Brown shows the way (1972)
Encyclopedia Brown solves them all (1968)
Encyclopedia Brown takes the cake! (1983)
Encyclopedia Brown takes the case (1973)
Encyclopedia Brown tracks them down (1971)

Soto, Gary

Crazy weekend. Scholastic 1994 144p $13.95; pa $3.50 (4 and up)   **Fic**

1. Thieves—Fiction 2. Friendship—Fiction 3. Hispanic Americans—Fiction 4. California—Fiction
ISBN 0-590-47814-1; 0-590-47076-0 (pa)
     LC 93-13967

Soto, Gary—*Continued*

After their photograph of a robbery is published in the newspaper, Hector and Mando find themselves pursued by two goofy thieves

"The lighthearted and fast-paced style and the use of slang expressions and Spanish words provide an amusing read." Horn Book Guide

Another available title about Hector and Mando is: Summer on wheels (1995)

The pool party; illustrated by Robert Casilla. Delacorte Press 1993 104p il $13.95; pa $3.50 (3-5) **Fic**

1. Mexican Americans—Fiction 2. Family life—Fiction 3. California—Fiction
ISBN 0-385-30890-6; 0-440-41010-X (pa)
LC 92-34407

While helping his father and grandfather work as gardeners in Fresno, California, ten-year-old Rudy sees some differences between his Mexican-American family and the wealthy families that live nearby

"A few elements make this story special: the poetic perfection Soto exhibits both in description and in authentic dialogue and the immersion of readers into the bosom of a loving, hard-working Mexican-American family." SLJ

Another available title about Rudy is: Boys at work (1995)

Taking sides. Harcourt Brace Jovanovich 1991 138p $15.95; pa $8 (5 and up) **Fic**

1. Hispanic Americans—Fiction 2. Basketball—Fiction
ISBN 0-15-284076-1; 0-15-284077-X (pa)
LC 91-11082

Fourteen year old Lincoln Mendoza, an aspiring basketball player, must come to terms with his divided loyalties when he moves from the Hispanic inner city to a white suburban neighborhood

This is a "light but appealing story. . . . Because of its subject matter and its clear, straightforward prose, it will be especially good for reluctant readers." SLJ

Includes glossary

Speare, Elizabeth George, 1908-1994

The bronze bow. Houghton Mifflin 1961 255p $14.95; pa $7.95 (6 and up) **Fic**

1. Jesus Christ—Fiction 2. Christianity—Fiction 3. Palestine—Fiction
ISBN 0-395-07113-5; 0-395-13719-5 (pa)
Awarded the Newbery Medal, 1962

"A book about the days of the early Christians. A vividly written story of a young Jewish rebel who was won over to the gentle teachings of Jesus. Daniel had sworn vengence against the Romans who had killed his parents, and he had become one of a band of outlaws. Forced to return to the village to care for his sister, Daniel found ways—dangerous ways—to work against the Roman soldiers. Each time he saw the Rabbi Jesus, the youth was drawn to his cause; at last he resolved his own conflict by giving up his hatred and, as a follower of the Master, accepting his enemies. The story has drama and pace, fine characterization, and colorful background detail; the theme of conflict and conversion is handled with restraint and perception." Bull Cent Child Books

The sign of the beaver. Houghton Mifflin 1983 135p $14.95 (5 and up) **Fic**

1. Frontier and pioneer life—Fiction 2. Indians of North America—Fiction 3. Friendship—Fiction
ISBN 0-395-33890-5
LC 83-118

Also available Cornerstone Bks. large print edition and in paperback from Dell; Spanish language edition also available

A Newbery Medal honor book, 1984

Left alone to guard the family's wilderness home in eighteenth-century Maine, Matt is hard-pressed to survive until local Indians teach him their skills

Matt "begins to understand the Indians' ingenuity and respect for nature and the devastating impact of the encroachment of the white man. In a quiet but not unsuspenseful story . . . the author articulates historical facts along with the adventures and the thoughts, emotions, and developing insights of a young adolescent." Horn Book

The witch of Blackbird Pond. Houghton Mifflin 1958 249p $14.95 (6 and up) **Fic**

1. Connecticut—History—1600-1775, Colonial period—Fiction 2. Witchcraft—Fiction 3. Puritans—Fiction
ISBN 0-395-07114-3
LC 58-11063

Also available Cornerstone Bks. large print edition and in paperback from Dell; Spanish language edition also available

Awarded the Newbery Medal, 1959

"Headstrong and undisciplined, Barbados-bred Kit Tyler is an embarrassment to her Puritan relatives, and her sincere attempts to aid a reputed witch soon bring her to trial as a suspect." Child Books Too Good to Miss

Sperry, Armstrong, 1897-1976

Call it courage; illustrations by the author. Macmillan 1940 95p il $15; pa $3.95 (5 and up) **Fic**

1. Polynesia—Fiction
ISBN 0-02-786030-2; 0-689-71391-6 (pa)

Also available Cornerstone Bks. large print edition; Spanish language edition also available

Awarded the Newbery Medal, 1941

"Because he fears the ocean, a Polynesian boy is scorned by his people and must redeem himself by an act of courage. His lone journey to a sacred island and the dangers he faces there earn him the name Mafatu, 'Stout Heart.' Dramatic illustrations add atmosphere and mystery." Hodges. Books for Elem Sch Libr

Spinelli, Jerry, 1941-

Maniac Magee; a novel. Little, Brown 1990 184p $14.95 (5 and up) **Fic**

1. Orphans—Fiction 2. Homeless persons—Fiction 3. Race relations—Fiction
ISBN 0-316-80722-2
LC 89-27144

Also available Thorndike Press large print edition and in paperback from HarperCollins

Awarded the Newbery Medal, 1991

"Orphaned at three, Jeffery Lionel Magee, after eight unhappy years with relatives, one day takes off running. A year later, he ends up 200 miles away in Two Mills, a highly segregated community. Part tall tale and part contemporary realistic fiction, this unusual novel magically weaves timely issues of homelessness, racial prejudice, and illiteracy into an energetic story that bursts with creativity enthusiasm, and hope for the future. In short, it's a celebration of life." Booklist

Spinelli, Jerry, 1941-—*Continued*

There's a girl in my hammerlock. Simon &
Schuster Bks. for Young Readers 1991 199p
$14; pa $3.95 (5 and up) **Fic**

1. Wrestling—Fiction 2. Sex role—Fiction 3. School stories
ISBN 0-671-74684-7; 0-671-86695-8 (pa)

LC 91-8765

Thirteen-year-old Maisie joins her school's formerly all-
male wrestling team and tries to last through the season, despite opposition from other students, her best friend, and
her own teammates

The author "tackles a meaty subject—traditional gender
roles—with his usual humor and finesse. The result, written
in a breezy, first-person style, is a rattling good sports story
that is clever, witty and tightly written." Publ Wkly

Spyri, Johanna, 1827-1901
Heidi (4 and up) **Fic**

1. Alps—Fiction 2. Switzerland—Fiction
Also available Spanish language edition
Some editions are:
Grosset & Dunlap (Illustrated junior library) $13.95 Illus-
trated by William Sharp (ISBN 0-448-40563-6)
Holt & Co. (Henry Holt little classics) $14.95 Illustrated by
Ted Rand (ISBN 0-8050-3565-6)
Morrow Junior Bks. (Books of Wonder) $22 Illustrated by
Jessie W. Smith (ISBN 0-688-14519-1)
First published 1880

"The story of Heidi is the story of the greatness of her
affection for her pet goats, for Peter and her grandfather,
and for her mountain home. Permeating the whole tale is
the play of sunshine and shadow on the slopes of the jagged
peaks of the great, glittering, snow-capped mountains of
Heidi's [Swiss] Alpine home. A book which finds a responsive chord in every young heart." Toronto Public Libr

Stanek, Muriel

I speak English for my mom; illustrations
by Judith Friedman. Whitman, A. 1989 unp il
lib bdg $12.95 (2-4) **Fic**

1. Mexican Americans—Fiction 2. Mothers and
daughters—Fiction
ISBN 0-8075-3659-8

LC 88-20546

Lupe, a young Mexican American, must translate for her
mother who speaks only Spanish until Mrs. Gomez decides
to learn English in order to get a better job

"Stanek provides a nicely rounded look at a situation
common to immigrant families." Booklist

Steig, William, 1907-
Abel's island. Farrar, Straus & Giroux 1976
117p il $15; pa $4.95 (3-5) **Fic**

1. Mice—Fiction 2. Survival after airplane accidents,
shipwrecks, etc.—Fiction
ISBN 0-374-30010-0; 0-374-40016-4 (pa)
Also available Spanish language edition

"Abel is a mouse who lives in cultured comfort on an inherited income and dotes on his bride Amanda. Ever gen-
tlemanly, Abel leaves the safety of a cave (they've taken
shelter while on a picnic) to rescue Amanda's gauzy scarf.
He is swept off by wind and rain, catapulted into a torrent
of water, and lands on an island. This is really sort of a
Robinson Crusoe Tale, as the heretofore pampered and in-
dolent Abel learns to cope with solitude, find food and shelter, avoid a predatory owl, and eventually find his way
back—a year later—to his loving wife and luxurious home."

Bull Cent Child Books

"The line drawings washed with gray faithfully and delightfully record not only the rigors of Abel's experiences
but the refinement of his domestic existence." Horn Book

Dominic; story and pictures by William
Steig. Farrar, Straus & Giroux 1972 145p il
hardcover o.p. paperback available $3.95 (3-5)
Fic

1. Dogs—Fiction
ISBN 0-374-41826-8 (pa)
Also available Spanish language edition

Dominic, a gregarious dog, sets out on the high road one
day, going no place in particular, but moving along to find
whatever he can. And that turns out to be plenty, including
an invalid pig who leaves Dominic his fortune; a variety of
friends and adventures; and even—in the end—his life's
companion

"A singular blend of naïveté and sophistication, comic
commentary and philosophizing, the narrative handles situation clichés with humor and flair—perhaps because of the
author's felicitous turn of phrase, his verbal cartooning, and
his integration of text and illustrations. A chivalrous and
optimistic tribute to gallantry and romance." Horn Book

The real thief; story and pictures by William
Steig. Farrar, Straus & Giroux 1973 58p il
$12.95; pa $3.95 (3-5) **Fic**

1. Animals—Fiction 2. Thieves—Fiction
ISBN 0-374-36217-3; 0-374-46208-9 (pa)
Also available Spanish language edition

"Proud of his job as guard to the Royal Treasury, loyal
to his king (Basil the bear) Gawain the goose is baffled by
the repeated theft of gold and jewels from the massive
building to which only Gawain and Basil have keys. He is
heartsick when the king dismisses him publicly and calls
him a disgrace to the kingdom. Sentenced to prison, the
goose flies off to isolation. The true thief, a mouse, is peni-
tent and decides that he will go on stealing so that the king
will know Gawain is innocent." Bull Cent Child Books

"Steig's gray line-and-wash drawings provide a charming
accompaniment to a wholly winning story." SLJ

Stevenson, Robert Louis, 1850-1894
Treasure Island (6 and up) **Fic**

1. Buried treasure—Fiction 2. Pirates
Also available Spanish language edition
Some editions are:
Grosset & Dunlap (Illustrated junior library) $13.95 Illus-
trated by Norman Price (ISBN 0-448-06025-6)
Holt & Co. (Henry Holt little classics) $15.95; pa $4.95 Il-
lustrated by Colin McNaughton (ISBN 0-8050-2773-4; 0-
8114-6844-5)
Knopf (Everyman's library children's classics) $12.95 Illus-
trated by Mervyn Peake (ISBN 0-679-41800-8)
Scribner $25 Illustrated by N. C. Wyeth (ISBN 0-684-
17160-0)
Viking $20 Illustrated by Robert Ingpen (ISBN 0-670-
84685-6)
First published 1882

Young Jim Hawkins discovers a treasure map in the
chest of an old sailor who dies under mysterious circum-
stances at his mother's inn. He shows it to Dr. Livesey and
Squire Trelawney who agree to outfit a ship and sail to
Treasure Island. Among the crew are the pirate Long John
Silver and his followers who are in pursuit of the treasure

"A masterpiece among romances. . . . Pew, Black Dog,
and Long John Silver are a villainous trio, strongly individualized, shedding an atmosphere of malignancy and terror.
The scenery of isle and ocean contrasts vividly with the
savagery of the action." Baker. Guide to the Best Fic

Stockton, Frank, 1834-1902

The Bee-man of Orn; pictures by Maurice Sendak. Harper & Row 1986 c1964 44p il $13.95; lib bdg $13.89; pa $4.95 (4-6)   **Fic**

1. Fairy tales
ISBN 0-06-025818-7; 0-06-025819-5 (lib bdg); 0-06-433125-8 (pa)   LC 85-45813

A reissue of the title first published 1964 by Holt, Rinehart & Winston; the story originally appeared in the author's The Bee-man of Orn, and other fanciful tales, published 1887 by Scribner

"Completely content, living a simple and busy life with his omnipresent bees, the Bee-Man becomes perturbed when a Junior Sorcerer informs him that he has undoubtedly been transformed from some other sort of being. What kind of being that is, he is not qualified to say—so the Bee-Man sets out to find his previous incarnation." Bull Cent Child Books

The story "has been illustrated to perfection. . . . A delightful and imaginative piece of bookmaking." Publ Wkly

The Griffin and the Minor Canon; by Frank R. Stockton; with illustrations by Maurice Sendak. Harper & Row 1986 c1963 55p il $14.95; lib bdg $13.89; pa $4.95 (4-6)   **Fic**

1. Mythical animals
ISBN 0-06-025816-0; 0-06-025817-9 (lib bdg); 0-06-443126-6 (pa)   LC 85-45827

A reissue of the title first published 1963 by Holt; the story originally appeared in the author's Fanciful tales, published 1894 by Scribner

"The last of the griffins visits a medieval cathedral town and through his ferocity, and his friendship for the gentle minor canon, reforms both young and old alike." Common weal

"The fine flow of language . . . will please those who read aloud to children as well as the children themselves; and on their own the fairy tale ages will be drawn naturally to this fully illustrated book. Sendak's carefully detailed gothic sketches and his prefacing words reveal his work to have been a labor of love." Horn Book

Stolz, Mary, 1920-

Bartholomew Fair; decorations by Pamela Johnson. Greenwillow Bks. 1990 152p $15; pa $3.95 (5 and up)   **Fic**

1. Elizabeth I, Queen of England, 1533-1603—Fiction 2. Fairs—Fiction 3. Great Britain—History—1485-1603, Tudors—Fiction
ISBN 0-688-09522-4; 0-688-11501-2 (pa)
                                                    LC 89-27230

On an August day in 1598 six people, including Queen Elizabeth, a wealthy cloth merchant, a scullery maid, two schoolboys, and an overworked apprentice, attend London's Bartholomew's Fair and come away with unforgettable experiences

"Stolz's characterizations ring clear as the bells of London, her style is strongly knit with humor, and the plot wends enticingly to a close not entirely foreseen. Picaresque and picturesque, this will enrich many a historical unit with human dimensions." Bull Cent Child Books

A dog on Barkham Street; pictures by Leonard Shortall. Harper & Row 1960 184p il lib bdg $14.89; pa $3.95 (4-6)   **Fic**

1. Dogs—Fiction
ISBN 0-06-025841-1 (lib bdg); 0-06-440160-X (pa)

"Fifth-grader Edward Frost has two seemingly insurmountable problems—to rid himself of the constant tormenting by the bully who lives next door and to convince his parents that he is responsible enough to have a dog. It is the coming of his irresponsible vagabond uncle with a beautiful young collie that precipitates the solution of Edward's problems." Booklist

"Simple, everyday events and very familiar people make up this story, but there is nothing ordinary about the way those ingredients are assembled. . . . This author has a remarkable ability to get inside her characters, whether they are young boys, adolescent girls, parents or hobos, and the result in this book is a reading experience as sharp as reality." Horn Book

Other available titles about Edward Frost and Martin Hastings are:
The bully of Barkham Street (1963)
The explorer of Barkham Street (1985)

Go fish; illustrated by Pat Cummings. HarperCollins Pubs. 1991 69p il lib bdg $12.89; pa $3.95 (2-4)   **Fic**

1. Grandfathers—Fiction 2. Fishing—Fiction 3. African Americans—Fiction
ISBN 0-06-025822-5 (lib bdg); 0-06-440466-8 (pa)
                                                    LC 90-4860

Companion volume to Storm in the night, entered in E section

After spending the day fishing in the Gulf of Mexico with Grandfather, eight-year-old Thomas has a quiet evening on the porch hearing more about his African heritage

"The text is easy to read, laced with gentle humor, and designed with rounded, black-and-white pictures in a popart style. . . . A book that's all the more effective for its low-key, companionable tone." Bull Cent Child Books

Another available title about Thomas and his grandfather is:
Stealing home (1992)

Streatfeild, Noel, 1895-1986

Ballet shoes; illustrated by Diane Goode. Random House 1991 281p il hardcover o.p. paperback available $4.99 (5 and up)   **Fic**

1. Ballet—Fiction 2. Theater—Fiction 3. London (England)—Fiction
ISBN 0-679-84759-6 (pa)   LC 89-24390

A newly illustrated edition of the title first published 1936 in the United Kingdom; first United States edition 1937

Relates the fortunes of three adopted sisters who take dancing and stage training at the Children's Academy of Dancing in London, Pauline to become an actress, Posy a ballerina, and Petrova an aviatrix

"By pointing out some of the things which make up stage magic [the author] has done a real service to the theater for its young audience." N Y Her Trib Books

Theatre shoes, or other people's shoes; illustrated by Richard Floethe. Random House 1945 282p il o.p.; Bullseye Bks. paperback available $4.99 (5 and up)   **Fic**

1. Theater—Fiction 2. Family life—Fiction 3. Great Britain—Fiction
ISBN 0-679-85434-7 (pa)

"Sorrel, Mark, and Holly Forbes are sent to their maternal grandmother's when their father's plane is shot down during World War II. They are thrust into the middle of a theatrical family, none of whom they know, but the children's own talents manage to come to light. Solid family fare." Booklist

Sutcliff, Rosemary, 1920-1992

Flame-colored taffeta. Farrar, Straus & Giroux 1986 129p $11.95; pa $3.50 (5 and up) **Fic**

1. Smuggling—Fiction 2. Great Britain—History—0-1066—Fiction

ISBN 0-374-32344-5; 0-374-42341-5 (pa)

LC 86-18351

This is a "tale of a girl who rescues a mysterious, wounded man. Twelve-year-old Damaris, who lives on a seaside Sussex farm, discovers a young man who has been shot in the leg. She and 13-year-old Peter hide the man, who calls himself Tom Wildgoose, in their secret meeting place—a half-ruined cottage in the forest." Publ Wkly

"The suspenseful story involves its characters less in historical events than in personal interplay. . . . Rosemary Sutcliff is still a superbly evocative storyteller, conveying a vibrant sense of seasons and of place." Horn Book

Talbert, Marc, 1953-

A sunburned prayer. Simon & Schuster Bks. for Young Readers 1995 108p $14 (5 and up) **Fic**

1. Grandmothers—Fiction 2. Mexican Americans—Fiction 3. Dogs—Fiction

ISBN 0-689-80125-4 LC 94-38682

As he makes a seventeen-mile pilgrimage to the Santuario de Chimayó that he hopes will save his beloved grandmother from cancer, eleven-year-old Eloy is joined by a friendly dog that helps him keep going

"Talbert's earthy, metaphorical prose (spiced with Spanish words defined in a short glossary at the end of the book) adds color and depth to this poignant story." SLJ

Tate, Eleanora E., 1948-

Thank you, Dr. Martin Luther King, Jr.! Watts 1990 237p o.p.; Bantam Bks. paperback available $3.99 (4 and up) **Fic**

1. African Americans—Fiction

ISBN 0-553-15886-4 (pa) LC 89-70665

"Fourth grader Mary Elouise Avery struggles with a low self-image in this consciousness-raising story of black pride. When Gumbo Grove Elementary School prepares for its annual Presidents' Month play, Mary Elouise is selected as narrator for the new black history segment. . . . By story's end, her part in the play has given Mary Elouise a better understanding of her heritage." SLJ

"Tate tackles a sensitive issue, taking pains to keep characters multidimensional and human. . . . Clear-eyed and accessible." Booklist

Another available title about Gumbo Grove is:
The secret of Gumbo Grove (1967)

Taylor, Mildred D.

The friendship; pictures by Max Ginsburg. Dial Bks. for Young Readers 1987 53p il $13.95; lib bdg $13.89 (4 and up) **Fic**

1. African Americans—Fiction 2. Race relations—Fiction 3. Mississippi—Fiction

ISBN 0-8037-0417-8; 0-8037-0418-6 (lib bdg)

LC 86-29309

Also available in paperback from Bantam Bks., bound with The gold Cadillac

Coretta Scott King Award for text, 1988

This "story about race relations in rural Mississippi during the Depression focuses on an incident between an old

Black man, Mr. Tom Bee, and a white storekeeper, Mr. John Wallace. Indebted to Tom for saving his life as a young man, John had promised they would always be friends. But now, years later, John insists that Tom call him 'Mister' and shoots the old man for defiantly—and publicly—calling him by his first name. Narrator Cassie Logan and her brothers . . . are verbally abused by Wallace's villainous sons before witnessing the encounter." Bull Cent Child Books

The gold Cadillac; pictures by Michael Hays. Dial Bks. for Young Readers 1987 43p il $14.99; lib bdg $12.89 (4 and up) **Fic**

1. African Americans—Fiction 2. Prejudices—Fiction 3. Race relations—Fiction

ISBN 0-8037-0342-2; 0-8037-0343-0 (lib bdg)

LC 86-11526

Also available in paperback from Bantam Bks., bound with The friendship

"The shiny gold Cadillac that Daddy brings home one summer evening marks a stepping stone in the lives of Wilma and 'lois, two black sisters growing up in Ohio during the fifties. At first neighbors and relatives shower them with attention. But when the family begins the long journey to the South to show off the car to their Mississippi relatives, the girls, for the first time, encounter the undisguised ugliness of racial prejudice." Horn Book

"Full-page sepia paintings effectively portray the characters, setting, and mood of the story events as Hays ably demonstrates his understanding of the social and emotional environments which existed for blacks during this period." SLJ

Let the circle be unbroken. Dial Bks. for Young Readers 1981 394p $16.99 (4 and up) **Fic**

1. African Americans—Fiction 2. Mississippi—Fiction 3. Economic depressions—Fiction

ISBN 0-8037-4748-9 LC 81-65854

Also available in paperback from Penguin Bks.

This novel featuring the Logans covers "a series of tangential events so that it is a family record, a picture of the depression years in rural Mississippi, and an indictment of black-white relations in the Deep South. A young friend is convicted of a murder of which he is innocent, a pretty cousin is insulted by some white boys and her father taunted because he married a white woman, an elderly neighbor tries to vote, the government pays farmers to plow their crops under, etc." Bull Cent Child Books

The author "provides her readers with a literal sense of witnessing important American history. . . . Moreover, [she] never neglects the details of her volatile 9-year-old heroine's interior life. The daydreams, the jealousy, the incredible ardor of that age come alive." N Y Times Book Rev

Mississippi bridge; by Mildred Taylor; pictures by Max Ginsburg. Dial Bks. for Young Readers 1990 62p il $15.99; lib bdg $13.89 (4 and up) **Fic**

1. Race relations—Fiction 2. African Americans—Fiction 3. Prejudices—Fiction 4. Mississippi—Fiction

ISBN 0-8037-0426-7; 0-8037-0427-5 (lib bdg)

LC 89-27898

Also available in paperback from Bantam Bks.

In this story featuring the children of Mississippi's Logan family, "Jeremy Simms, a 10-year-old white neighbor, describes a harrowing incident after the Logans and other blacks are ordered off the weekly bus in a foggy rainstorm." N Y Times Book Rev

"Taylor has shaped this episode into a haunting meditation that will leave readers vividly informed about segregation practices and the unequal rights that prevailed in that

Taylor, Mildred D.—*Continued*

era. The conclusion comes abruptly—it's almost as if Taylor ran out of things to say—but the incident and its context constitute a telling piece of social history." Booklist

The road to Memphis; by Mildred Taylor. Dial Bks. 1989 290p $15 (4 and up)   **Fic**

1. Race relations—Fiction 2. African Americans—Fiction 3. Mississippi—Fiction

ISBN 0-8037-0340-6   LC 88-33654

Also available in paperback from Puffin Bks.

Coretta Scott King award for text, 1989

Sadistically teased by two white boys in 1940's rural Mississippi, Cassie's friend, Moe, severely injures one of the boys with a tire iron and enlists Cassie's help in trying to flee the state

"Reading the previous books of the series is not necessary in order to understand and enjoy this volume. Taylor's continued smooth, easy language provides readability for all ages, with a focus on universal human pride, worthy values, and individual responsibility. This action-packed drama is highly recommended." Voice Youth Advocates

Roll of thunder, hear my cry; frontispiece by Jerry Pinkney. Dial Bks. for Young Readers 1976 276p $15.99 (4 and up)   **Fic**

1. African Americans—Fiction 2. Economic depressions—Fiction 3. Mississippi—Fiction

ISBN 0-8037-7473-7

Also available Cornerstone Bks. large print edition and in paperback from Puffin Bks.; Spanish language edition also available

Awarded the Newbery Medal, 1977

"The time is 1933. The place is Spokane, Mississippi where the Logans, the only black family who own their own land, wage a courageous struggle to remain independent, displeasing a white plantation owner bent on taking their land. But this suspenseful tale is also about the story's young narrator, Cassie, and her three brothers who decide to wage their own personal battles to maintain the self-dignity and pride with which they were raised. . . . Ms. Taylor's richly textured novel shows a strong, proud black family . . . resisting rather than succumbing to oppression." Child Book Rev Serv

Song of the trees; pictures by Jerry Pinkney. Dial Bks. for Young Readers 1975 48p il $14.99; lib bdg $11.89 (4 and up)   **Fic**

1. African Americans—Fiction 2. Economic depressions—Fiction 3. Mississippi—Fiction

ISBN 0-8037-5452-3; 0-8037-5453-1 (lib bdg)

Also available in paperback from Bantam Bks.

Eight-year-old Cassie Logan tells how her family "leaving Mississippi during the Depression was cheated into selling for practically nothing valuable and beautiful giant old pines and hickories, beeches and walnuts in the forest surrounding their house." Adventuring with Books

The well; David's story. Dial Bks. for Young Readers 1995 92p $14.99; lib bdg $14.89 (4 and up)   **Fic**

1. African Americans—Fiction 2. Race relations—Fiction 3. Mississippi—Fiction

ISBN 0-8037-1802-0; 0-8037-1803-9 (lib bdg)

LC 94-25360

"David Logan (Cassie's father) tells this story from his childhood. . . . There's a drought, and the Logans possess the only well in the area that has not gone dry. Black and white alike come for water freely given by the family, but the Simms boys can't seem to stand the necessary charity, and their resentment explodes when David's big brother

Hammer beats Charlie Simms after Charlie hits David." Bull Cent Child Books

This story "delivers an emotional wallop in a concentrated span of time and action. . . . This story reverberates in the heart long after the final paragraph is read." Horn Book

Taylor, Sydney, 1904-1978

All-of-a-kind family; illustrated by Helen John. Follett 1951 192p il o.p.; Taylor Productions reprint available $14.95 (4-6)   **Fic**

1. Jews—Fiction 2. New York (N.Y.)—Fiction

ISBN 0-929093-00-3 (pa)

Also available in paperback from Dell and in hardcover from P. Smith

"Five little Jewish girls grow up in New York's lower east side in a happy home atmosphere before the first World War." Carnegie Libr of Pittsburgh

"A genuine and delightful picture of a Jewish family . . . with an understanding mother and father, rich in kindness and fun though poor in money. The important part the public library played in the lives of these children is happily evident; and the Jewish holiday celebrations are particularly well described." Horn Book

Other available titles about this family are:

All-of-a-kind family downtown (1957)
All-of-a-kind family uptown (1957)
Ella of all-of-a-kind family (1978)
More all-of-a-kind family (1954)

Taylor, Theodore, 1921-

The cay. Doubleday 1969 137p $15.95 (5 and up)   **Fic**

1. Race relations—Fiction 2. Caribbean region—Fiction 3. Survival after airplane accidents, shipwrecks, etc.—Fiction 4. Blind—Fiction

ISBN 0-385-07906-0

Also available in paperback from Avon Bks.

"When the freighter which was to take Phillip and his mother from wartime Curacao to the United States is torpedoed, Phillip finds himself afloat on a small raft with a hugh, old, very black West Indian man. Phillip becomes blind from injuries and resents his dependence upon old Timothy. Through exciting adventures on a very small cay (coral island), Phillip learns to overcome his prejudice toward Timothy and to see him as a man and a friend. Following the aftermath of a fierce tropical storm, Timothy dies. Phillip survives to live a more complete life because of his friend and because he has grown with the changes that occurred in his life." Read Ladders for Hum Relat. 5th edition

"Starkly dramatic, believable and compelling." Saturday Rev

Followed by Timothy of the cay

Timothy of the cay. Harcourt Brace & Co. 1993 161p $13.95 (5 and up)   **Fic**

1. Race relations—Fiction 2. Caribbean region—Fiction 3. Survival after airplane accidents, shipwrecks, etc.—Fiction 4. Blind—Fiction

ISBN 0-15-288358-4   LC 93-7898

Also available in paperback from Avon Bks.

Having survived being blinded and shipwrecked on a tiny Caribbean island with the old black man Timothy, twelve-year-old white Phillip is rescued and hopes to regain his sight with an operation. Alternate chapters follow the life of Timothy from his days as a young cabin boy

"Somewhat more thoughtful than its well-loved antecedent, this boldly drawn novel is no less commanding." Publ Wkly

Taylor, Theodore, 1921-—*Continued*

The trouble with Tuck. Doubleday 1981
110p $13.95 (5 and up)   **Fic**
1. Dogs—Fiction 2. Blind—Fiction
ISBN 0-385-17774-7   LC 81-43139
Also available in paperback from Avon Bks.

Helen trains her blind dog Tuck to follow and trust a
seeing-eye companion dog

This is "a touching dog story, written with good flow,
pace, and structure." Bull Cent Child Books

Another available title about Helen and Tuck is:
Tuck triumphant (1991)

Temple, Frances, 1945-1995

Grab hands and run. Orchard Bks. 1993
165p $15.95; lib bdg $15.99 (6 and up)
                                      Fic
1. El   Salvador—Fiction   2. Refugees—Fiction
3. Canada—Fiction
ISBN 0-531-05480-2; 0-531-08630-5 (lib bdg)
                                      LC 92-34063
Also available in paperback from HarperCollins
"A Richard Jackson book"

After his father disappears, twelve-year-old Felipe, his
mother, and his younger sister set out on a difficult and
dangerous journey, trying to make their way from their
home in El Salvador to Canada

"The taut and absorbing escape is made all the more real
by the fully fleshed out characters and heart-stopping situations." SLJ

The Ramsay scallop; a novel. Orchard Bks.
1994 310p $17.95; lib bdg $17.99 (6 and up)
                                      Fic
1. Middle Ages—Fiction 2. Pilgrims and pilgrimages—
Fiction
ISBN 0-531-06836-6; 0-531-08686-0 (lib bdg)
                                      LC 93-29697
Also available in paperback from HarperCollins
"A Richard Jackson book"

At the turn of the fourteenth century in England, fourteen-year-old Elenor finds her betrothal to an ambitious
lord's son launching her on a memorable pilgrimage to far-
off Spain

"With a nod to *The Canterbury Tales*, the book highlights the stories that their fellow pilgrims share with Elenor
and Thomas; the stories are sad, romantic, and instructive,
and all help shape the journey into the special thing it becomes for the duo. . . . The leisurely pace of the pilgrimage
allows the author to introduce a large cast of characters and
to decorate her story with historical details that enlighten
and intrigue." Booklist

Tonight, by sea; a novel. Orchard Bks. 1995
152p $15.95; lib bdg $15.99 (6 and up)
                                      Fic
1. Haiti—Fiction 2. Refugees—Fiction
ISBN 0-531-06899-4; 0-531-08749-2 (lib bdg)
                                      LC 94-32167
"A Richard Jackson book"

As governmental brutality and poverty become unbearable, Paulie joins with others in her small Haitian village to
help her uncle secretly build a boat they will use to try to
escape to the United States

"In an elegant prose style [the author] captures the lyrical
cadence of Creole speech and paints an affecting portrait of
a proud, resourceful people trying to survive in the face of
lawlessness and tyranny." SLJ

Thesman, Jean

When the road ends. Houghton Mifflin 1992
184p $14.95 (5 and up)   **Fic**
1. Foster home care—Fiction 2. Handicapped—Fiction
ISBN 0-395-59507-X   LC 91-14950
Also available in paperback from Avon Bks.

Sent to spend the summer in the country, three foster
children and an older woman recovering from a serious accident are abandoned by their slovenly caretaker and must
try to survive on their own

This "is enlivened by humor, strong characterization,
and a hopeful ending." SLJ

Thomas, Jane Resh, 1936-

The comeback dog; drawings by Troy
Howell. Clarion Bks. 1981 62p il $13.95 (3-5)
                                      Fic
1. Dogs—Fiction 2. Farm life—Fiction
ISBN 0-395-29432-0   LC 80-12886
Also available in paperback from Bantam Bks.

"Grieving over the loss of his dog, Daniel claims he
doesn't want another dog, but when he finds one that is
near death, he takes her home and gives her loving care.
The dog, Lady, gets well but seems fearful and hostile; irritated, Daniel lets her off the leash to run away. When she
comes back, some weeks later, her face bristling with porcupine quills, he's again irritated but quickly decides to help
Lady and is then gratified when she shows trust and affection." Bull Cent Child Books

"The matter-of-fact, life-must-go-on attitude of Daniel's
concerned parents is particularly well communicated. . . .
Numerous soft pencil drawings greatly enhance the exceptionally gentle, poignant story." Horn Book

Thurber, James, 1894-1961

Many   moons;   illustrated   by   Louis
Slobodkin. Harcourt Brace 1943 unp il $15; pa
$6 (1-4)   **Fic**
1. Fairy tales
ISBN 0-15-251873-8; 0-15-251877-9 (pa)
Also available with illustrations by Marc Simont for
$14.95 (ISBN 0-15-251872-X)

Awarded the Caldecott Medal, 1944

This is "the story of a little princess who fell ill of a surfeit of raspberry tarts and would get well only if she could
have the moon. The solving of this baffling court problem,
how to get the moon, results in an original and entertaining
picture-storybook." Booklist

"Louis Slobodkin's pictures float on the pages in four
colors: black and white cannot represent them. They are the
substance of dreams . . . the long thoughts little children,
and some adults wise as they, have about life." N Y Her
Trib Books

Titus, Eve

Basil of Baker Street; illustrated by Paul
Galdone. McGraw-Hill 1958 96p il lib bdg
$8.95 (3-5)   **Fic**
1. Doyle, Sir Arthur Conan, 1859-1930—Parodies,
travesties, etc. 2. Mice—Fiction 3. Mystery fiction
ISBN 0-07-064907-3 (lib bdg)
Also available in paperback from Pocket Bks.
"Whittlesey House publications"

"Basil of Baker Street is the Sherlock Holmes of the
mouse world, having studied scientific sleuthing at the feet
of the famous English detective. Here in an entertaining, de-

Titus, Eve—*Continued*

lightfully illustrated story Basil's assistant, Dr. Dawson, tells how the great Basil solves a baffling kidnapping case, restores the children to their parents, and brings the dangerous kidnappers to justice. Acquaintance with Sherlock Holmes and Dr. Watson is not essential to the enjoyment of this small-scale detective story." Booklist

Other available titles about Basil are:
Basil and the pygmy cats (1971)
Basil in Mexico (1976)
Basil in the Wild West (1982)

Tolan, Stephanie S., 1942-

Save Halloween! Morrow Junior Bks. 1993 168p $14 (5 and up) **Fic**

1. Halloween—Fiction 2. Christian life—Fiction 3. School stories
ISBN 0-688-12168-3   LC 93-10635

Eleven-year-old Johnna, who is deeply involved in the sixth grade Halloween pageant although her family views it as a celebration of an un-Christian holiday, decides that she must follow her own beliefs

"Thoughtful, pithy, and entertaining, this will intrigue readers from cover to cover." Booklist

Tolkien, J. R. R. (John Ronald Reuel), 1892-1973

The hobbit; or, There and back again; illustrated by the author. Houghton Mifflin 1938 310p il $14.95; pa $11.95 (4 and up) **Fic**

1. Fantasy fiction
ISBN 0-395-07122-4; 0-395-28265-9 (pa)

Also available from Houghton Mifflin in an edition with illustrations by Michael Hague for $24.95 (ISBN 0-395-36290-3); paperback $16.95 (ISBN 0-395-52021-5); Spanish language edition also available

First published 1937 in the United Kingdom

"This fantasy features the adventures of hobbit Bilbo Baggins, who joins a band of dwarfs led by Gandalf the Wizard. Together they seek to recover the stolen treasure that is hidden in Lonely Mountain and guarded by Smaug the Dragon." Shapiro. Fic for Youth. 2d edition

Followed by The lord of the rings, a trilogy intended for older readers

Tomlinson, Theresa

The Forestwife. Orchard Bks. 1995 170p $15.95; lib bdg $16.99 (6 and up) **Fic**

1. Maid Marian (Legendary character)—Fiction 2. Robin Hood (Legendary character)—Fiction 3. Great Britain—Fiction
ISBN 0-531-09450-2; 0-531-08750-6 (lib bdg)
LC 94-33007

In England during the reign of King Richard I, fifteen-year-old Marian escapes from an arranged marriage to live with a community of forest folk that includes a daring young outlaw named Robert

"This exciting book is based on Medieval folk tales of the Green Lady and Green Man and Robin Hood. . . . The book is full of strong, memorable characters, action, and vivid descriptions with an underlying love story." Voice of Youth Advocates

Travers, P. L. (Pamela L.), 1899-1996

Mary Poppins; illustrated by Mary Shepard. rev ed. Harcourt Brace Jovanovich 1981 206p il o.p.; Dell paperback available $4.50 (4-6) **Fic**

1. Fantasy fiction
ISBN 0-440-04046-1 (pa)   LC 81-7273

Also available in hardcover from Bucaneer Bks.

First published 1934

"The chapter 'Bad Tuesday,' in which Mary and the Banks children travel to the four corners of the earth and meet the inhabitants, has been criticized for portraying minorities in an unfavorable light. In 1971 when the paperback edition came out, Travers altered the language of the Africans but has felt it necessary to revise the chapter completely in order to eliminate the negative stereotypical elements. The revised edition accomplishes this by having the entourage meet up with a polar bear, macaw, panda, and dolphin instead of Eskimos, Africans, Chinese, and American Indians. The change is fortuitous, and should put the matter to rest." Booklist

Other available titles about Mary Poppins are:
Mary Poppins comes back (1935)
Mary Poppins from A to Z (1962)
Mary Poppins in Cherry Tree Lane (1982)
Mary Poppins opens the door (1943)

Treviño, Elizabeth Borton de, 1904-

I, Juan de Pareja. Farrar, Straus & Giroux 1993 c1965 180p $16; pa $3.95 (6 and up) **Fic**

1. Juan, de Pareja—Fiction 2. Velázquez, Diego, 1599-1660—Fiction
ISBN 0-374-33531-1; 0-374-43525-1 (pa)

Also available Spanish language edition

Awarded the Newbery Medal, 1966

First published 1965

The black slave boy, Juan de Pareja, "began a new life when he was taken into the household of the Spanish painter, Velázquez. As he worked beside the great artist learning how to grind and mix colors and prepare canvases, there grew between them a warm friendship based on mutual respect and love of art. Created from meager but authentic facts, the story, told by Juan, depicts the life and character of Velázquez and the loyalty of the talented seventeenth-century slave who eventually won his freedom and the right to be an artist." Booklist

Trevor, William, 1928-

Juliet's story. Simon & Schuster 1994 105p $15 (5 and up) **Fic**

1. Travel—Fiction 2. Ireland—Fiction
ISBN 0-671-87442-X   LC 93-21790

"Juliet, an Irish girl from County Tipperary, loves Paddy Old's tales. . . . When Paddy dies, Juliet feels lost, but her grief slowly dissipates when her Grandmamma takes her on a fanciful trip from Dublin to the south of France. Along the way she tells Juliet her own unique stories." Publ Wkly

"The tales that are woven into the narrative—from fairy tale to realistic comedy—are rich with character. In the end Juliet finds her own adventure and makes it happen, and she does it with spirit and style." Booklist

Tunis, John R., 1889-1975
The kid from Tomkinsville. Harcourt Brace
Jovanovich 1987 278p (Baseball diamonds, 1)
$14.95; pa $3.95 (5 and up)   **Fic**
1. Baseball—Fiction
ISBN 0-15-242568-3; 0-15-242567-5 (pa)
                                    LC 86-27104
Also available from P. Smith
A reissue of the title first published 1943
As the newest addition to the Brooklyn Dodgers, young
Roy Tucker's pitching helps pull the team out of a slump;
but, a freak accident ends his career as a pitcher, he
must try to find another place for himself on the team
Other available titles about Roy Tucker and the Brooklyn
Dodgers are:
Keystone kids (1943)
The kid comes back (1946)
Rookie of the year (1944)
World Series (1941)

Turner, Ann Warren, 1945-
Grasshopper summer. Macmillan 1989 166p
$14.95 (4-6)   **Fic**
1. Frontier and pioneer life—Fiction 2. South Dakota—
Fiction
ISBN 0-02-789511-4   LC 88-13847
Also available in paperback from Dell
In 1874 eleven-year-old Sam and his family move from
Kentucky to the southern Dakota Territory, where harsh
conditions and a plague of hungry grasshoppers threaten
their chances for survival
"Carefully selected details, skillfully woven into the story
line, evoke a sense of place and time by documenting the
building of a sod house, the distances between neighbors,
the grandeur of the Dakota landscape, the modest pleasures
of a celebration, and the destructive force of a locust
plague. This latter event is a particularly fine example of exposition as an integral part of plot, for it builds to the
dénouement even as it provides further insight into character. Both a family story and an account of pioneer living,
the book is accessible as well as informative." Horn Book

Nettie's trip South; [by] Ann Turner;
illustrated by Ronald Himler. Macmillan 1987
unp il $14; pa $4.95 (3-5)   **Fic**
1. Slavery—Fiction
ISBN 0-02-789240-9; 0-689-80117-3 (pa)
                                    LC 86-18135
"In 1859 Nettie is allowed to accompany her brother,
who has been assigned his first newspaper story, and an
older sister on the trip from Albany, New York, to Richmond. The text appears in the form of a letter Nettie writes
to a friend, and while more smoothly written and articulate
than one might expect from the young girl depicted in the
illustrations, the story recounts her poignantly felt reactions
to the viewing of slave quarters and an auction of black
men and women." Horn Book
"Himler's charcoal drawings fashion scenes rich with
character and emotion. In this case, black and white is as
powerful as color. A vivid piece of history for early elementary students or older picture-book audiences." Booklist

One brave summer; [by] Ann Turner.
HarperCollins Pubs. 1995 163p $13.95; lib bdg
$13.89 (3-5)   **Fic**
1. Friendship—Fiction
ISBN 0-06-023732-5; 0-06-023875-5 (lib bdg)
                                    LC 94-18702

"Timid, quiet Katy anticipates that her mother's decision
to rent a mountain cabin will mean a long, dull summer.
But she changes her mind when she meets Lena May. . . .
With Lena May, Katy finds more than her share of adventure. . . . When the girls discuss the mysteries of kissing,
birth, and death, Lena May is the authority; but, one night,
when they see Lena May's Gram sleepwalking down the
road, it is Katy who steps forward to comfort her friend
and get her settled in bed before walking home alone in the
dark." Horn Book
"Using language rich in metaphor and punctuated by
vivid descriptions of nature's beauty, the author spins a
lively, amusing, and tightly woven story." SLJ

Rosemary's witch; [by] Ann Turner.
HarperCollins Pubs. 1991 164p $14.95; lib bdg
$14.89; pa $3.95 (5 and up)   **Fic**
1. Witchcraft—Fiction
ISBN 0-06-026127-7; 0-06-026128-5 (lib bdg);
0-06-440494-3 (pa)   LC 90-39779
"A Charlotte Zolotow book"
After moving into an old house in a small New England
town, 9-year-old Rosemary discovers that the nearby woods
conceal a 150-year-old witch, who once lived in the house
and is using her magic to take it back
"A chanteuse of a storyteller, Turner uses poetic prose to
caress the plot while keeping the tension turned high. . . .
Character development is superb." SLJ

Twain, Mark, 1835-1910
The adventures of Huckleberry Finn (5 and
up)   **Fic**
1. Mississippi River—Fiction 2. Missouri—Fiction
Also available Spanish language edition
Some editions are:
Morrow Junior Bks. (Books of Wonder) $20 Illustrated by
Steven Kellogg (ISBN 0-688-10656-0)
University of Calif. Press $38 Illustrated by Barry Moser
(ISBN 0-520-05338-9)
First published in 1885
"Huck, escaping from his blackguardly father, who had
imprisoned him in a lonely cabin, meets Jim, a runaway
slave, on Jackson's Island in the Mississippi River. Together they float on a raft down the mighty stream. . . . Two
confidence men join them and they drift into many extraordinary adventures, in the course of which Tom Sawyer reappears. Tom's Aunt Sally wants to adopt Huck, who
decides he had better disappear again, lest he be 'sivilized'.
. . . The struggle in Huck's soul between his 'respectable'
Southern prejudices and his growing appreciation of Jim's
value and dignity as a human being is an ironic and powerful indictment of the moral blindness of a slaveholding society." Herzberg. Reader's Ency of Am Lit

The adventures of Tom Sawyer (5 and up)
                                    Fic
1. Mississippi River—Fiction 2. Missouri—Fiction
Also available Spanish language edition
Some editions are:
Grosset & Dunlap (Illustrated junior library) $13.95 Illus-
trated by Donald McKay (ISBN 0-448-40560-1)
Morrow Junior Bks. (Books of wonder) $21.95 Illustrated
by Barry Moser (ISBN 0-688-07510-X)
First published 1876
The plot "is episodic, dealing in part with Tom's pranks
in school, Sunday school, and the respectable world of his
Aunt Polly, and in part with his adventures with Huck
Finn, the outcaste son of the local ne'er-do-well. . . . Tom
and Huck witness a murder and, in terror of the murderer,
Injun Joe, secretly flee to Jackson's island. They are

Twain, Mark, 1835-1910—*Continued*
searched for, are finally mourned for dead, and return to town in time to attend their own funeral. Tom and his sweetheart, Becky Thatcher get lost in a cave in which Injun Joe is hiding. . . . The story closely follows incidents involving Twain and his friends that occured in Hannibal, Mo." Herzberg. Reader's Ency of Am Lit

Followed by Tom Sawyer abroad (1894) and Tom Sawyer, detective (1896)

Uchida, Yoshiko, 1921-1992
A jar of dreams. Atheneum Pubs. 1981 131p $14.95; pa $3.95 (5 and up)   Fic

1. Japanese Americans—Fiction 2. Family life—Fiction 3. Prejudices—Fiction 4. California—Fiction
ISBN 0-689-50210-9; 0-689-71672-9 (pa)
LC 81-3480

"A Margaret K. McElderry book"
"A story of the Depression Era is told by eleven-year-old Rinko, the only girl in a Japanese-American family living in Oakland and suffering under the double burden of financial pressure and the prejudice that had increased with the tension of economic competition. Into the household comes a visitor who is a catalyst for change." Bull Cent Child Books

"Rinko in her guilelessness is genuine and refreshing, and her worries and concerns seem wholly natural, honest, and convincing." Horn Book

Other available titles about Rinko Tsujimura and her family are:
The best bad thing (1983)
The happiest ending (1985)

Journey home; illustrated by Charles Robinson. Atheneum Pubs. 1978 131p il $15; pa $3.95 (5 and up)   Fic

1. Japanese Americans—Fiction 2. Prejudices—Fiction 3. Family life—Fiction
ISBN 0-689-50126-9; 0-689-70755-X (pa)
LC 78-8792

"A Margaret K. McElderry book"
The "story of a Japanese-American family's struggle to return to a normal life after their relocation camp experience in Utah [described in Journey to Topaz]. . . . Seen through the eyes of twelve-year-old Yuki, the plight of her parents, who want to return to California, the disillusionment of her brother, who returns from the war with shattered dreams, and the despair of her friends, who want to rebuild their lives in spite of the hostility outside the camp, take on a special poignancy." Child Book Rev Serv

Journey to Topaz; a story of the Japanese-American evacuation; illustrated by Donald Carrick. Scribner 1971 149p il o.p.; Creative Art Publs. paperback available $8.95 (5 and up)   Fic

1. Japanese Americans—Evacuation and relocation, 1942-1945—Fiction
ISBN 0-916870-85-5 (pa)
This is the story of eleven-year-old Yuki, her eighteen-year-old brother and her mother, who were uprooted, evacuated and interned in Topaz, the War Relocation Center in Utah during World War II

"This tragic herding of innocent people is described with dignity and a sorrowful sense of injustice that never becomes bitter." Saturday Rev

Followed by Journey home

Van Leeuwen, Jean
Bound for Oregon; pictures by James Watling. Dial Bks. for Young Readers 1994 167p il map $14.99; lib bdg $14.89 (4-6)   Fic

1. Todd, Mary Ellen, 1843-1924—Fiction 2. Overland journeys to the Pacific—Fiction 3. Oregon Trail—Fiction
ISBN 0-8037-1526-9; 0-8037-1527-7 (lib bdg)
LC 93-26709

A fictionalized account of the journey made by nine-year-old Mary Ellen Todd and her family from their home in Arkansas westward over the Oregon Trail in 1852

"The appealing narrator, the forthright telling, and the concrete details of life along the Oregon Trail will draw readers into the story." Booklist

The great Christmas kidnapping caper; pictures by Steven Kellogg. Dial Bks. for Young Readers 1975 133p il $12.95 (3-5)   Fic

1. Mice—Fiction 2. Christmas—Fiction 3. New York (N.Y.)—Fiction
ISBN 0-8037-5415-9
"Narrated by one mouse named Marvin the Magnificent, it tells of the disappearance of Mr. Dunderhoff, Macy's Santa Claus for 18 years. It happens just after Marvin and his two friends . . . have moved into a dollhouse in the toy department and made friends with the kindly gentleman." N Y Times Book Rev

"Steven Kellogg makes the most of his endearing subjects in pictures which are as zestful and surprising as the author's make-believe." Publ Wkly

Other available titles about Marvin the Magnificent are:
The great rescue operation (1982)
The great summer camp catastrophe (1992)

Verne, Jules, 1828-1905
Twenty thousand leagues under the sea (5 and up)   Fic

1. Submarines—Fiction 2. Sea stories 3. Science fiction
Various editions available including Spanish language edition
Original French edition, 1869
This romance is "remarkable for its prognostication of the invention of submarines. The central characters of the tale, in the process of exploring marine disturbances, are captured by the megalomaniacal Captain Nemo. An undersea tour in a strange craft and their ensuing escape conclude the work." Reader's Ency

Vining, Elizabeth Gray, 1902-
Adam of the road; illustrated by Robert Lawson. Viking 1942 317p il $16.99; pa $4.99 (5 and up)   Fic

1. Minstrels—Fiction 2. Middle Ages—Fiction 3. Great Britain—Fiction
ISBN 0-670-10435-3; 0-14-032464-X (pa)
Awarded the Newbery Medal, 1943
Tale of a minstrel and his son Adam, who wandered through southeastern England in the thirteenth century. Adam's adventures in search of his lost dog and his beloved father led him from St. Alban's Abbey to London, and thence to Winchester, back to London, and then to Oxford where the three were at last reunited

Voigt, Cynthia

Come a stranger. Atheneum Pubs. 1986
190p $15.95; pa $3.95 (6 and up)   Fic

1. African Americans—Fiction 2. Race relations—
Fiction

ISBN 0-689-31289-X; 0-689-80444-X (pa)

LC 86-3610

Also available in paperback from Fawcett Bks.

"Mina Smiths, the assertive, intelligent young black girl
whom readers caught a glimpse of in 'Dicey's Song' [entered
below] is the central figure in this thoughtful coming-of-age
novel. Mina is young, only 11 at the story's beginning, and
thoroughly involved in ballet. She attends a special ballet
camp on a scholarship but is bounced out the following
year; in the midst of puberty she has become ungainly—but
she wonders if the real reason is that she is black. The
shock of rejection and the resulting preoccupation with her
identity as a young black woman shadow Mina as her life
proceeds on a new course centered on family and friends;
there is also her quiet, intense but hopeless love for Tamer
Shipp, the summer replacement minister who understands
her heart in a way no one else can." Booklist

Dicey's song. Atheneum Pubs. 1982 196p
$14.95 (6 and up)   Fic

1. Grandmothers—Fiction 2. Brothers and sisters—
Fiction

ISBN 0-689-30944-9   LC 82-3882

Also available Cornerstone Bks. large print edition and
in paperback from Fawcett Bks.

Awarded the Newbery Medal, 1983

Sequel to Homecoming, entered below

Dicey "had brought her siblings to the grandmother
they'd never seen when their mother (now in a mental institution) had been unable to cope. This is the story of the
children's adjustment to Gram (and hers to them) and to a
new school and a new life—but with some of the old problems. Dicey, in particular, has a hard time since she must
abandon her role of surrogate mother and share the responsibility with Gram." Bull Cent Child Books

"The vividness of Dicey is striking; Voigt has plumbed
and probed her character inside out to fashion a memorable
protagonist. Unlike most sequels, this outdoes its predecessor by being more fully realized and consequently more resonant." Booklist

Homecoming. Atheneum Pubs. 1981 312p
$15.95 (6 and up)   Fic

1. Brothers and sisters—Fiction 2. Abandoned
children—Fiction

ISBN 0-689-30833-7   LC 80-36723

Also available in paperback from Fawcett Bks.; Spanish
language edition also available

"When their momma abandons them in a shopping center, Dicey Tillerman and her three younger brothers and sisters set out on foot for where momma was ostensibly taking
them—to Great-Aunt Cilla's in Bridgeport, Connecticut.
They arrive to find only Cousin Eunice; Priscilla has died.
Eunice, mindlessly religious and insensitive to their needs,
agrees to look after them. But Dicey knows she has to take
another chance and another journey, this time to Crisfield,
Maryland, where she hopes their unknown grandmother
might provide a better home." Booklist

"The characterizations of the children are original and
intriguing, and there are a number of interesting minor
characters encountered in their travels." SLJ

Followed by Dicey's song

Vos, Ida, 1931-

Anna is still here; translated by Terese
Edelstein and Inez Smidt. Houghton Mifflin
1993 139p $13.95 (4 and up)   Fic

1. Holocaust, 1933-1945—Fiction 2. Jews—
Netherlands—Fiction 3. Netherlands—Fiction

ISBN 0-395-65368-1   LC 92-1618

Also available in paperback from Puffin Bks.

Original Dutch edition, 1986

In this sequel to Hide and seek, Anna now thirteen "has
been reunited with her parents, who are loving but still unable to speak of their own time in hiding or of the loss of
family and friends. . . . The story mainly concerns the rebuilding of her relationship with her parents and a tenuous
friendship with Mrs. Neumann, a woman who is searching
for her little daughter, lost in the tides of war. . . . A striking, and ultimately hopeful, account of how the human spirit survives and recovers." Horn Book

Hide and seek; translated by Terese
Edelstein and Inez Smidt. Houghton Mifflin
1991 132p $13.95 (4 and up)   Fic

1. Holocaust, 1933-1945—Fiction 2. Jews—
Netherlands—Fiction 3. Netherlands—Fiction

ISBN 0-395-56470-0   LC 90-4980

Also available in paperback from Puffin Bks.

Original Dutch edition, 1981

Anna, a young Jewish girl living in Holland, tells of her
experiences during the Nazi occupation, her years in hiding,
and the after shock when the war finally ends

"Drawing on her own experiences during WW II, Vos
fills the narrative with understated but painfully realistic
moments. . . . Vos's novel deserves special attention for its
sensitive and deeply affecting consideration of life after liberation." Publ Wkly

Followed by Anna is still here

Wagner, Jane

J. T.; With pictures by Gordon Parks, Jr.
Van Nostrand Reinhold 1969 63p il o.p.; Dell
paperback available $3.99 (3-6)   Fic

1. Cats—Fiction 2. African Americans—Fiction
3. Harlem (New York, N.Y.)—Fiction

ISBN 0-440-44275-3 (pa)

"J. T., a constant worry to his anxious mother since his
father has left, is running from neighborhood toughs [who
are] after the radio he has stolen, when he finds a badly
wounded one-eyed alley cat. Secretly and ingeniously J. T.
builds a shelter for the cat in an abandoned stove and feeds
and nurses it until it is killed by a car. His brief association
with the cat and the resultant understanding of the adults
in his life are sharply felt." Booklist

Wallace, Barbara Brooks, 1922-

The twin in the tavern. Atheneum Pubs.
1993 179p $15 (4-6)   Fic

1. Orphans—Fiction 2. Twins—Fiction 3. Mystery
fiction

ISBN 0-689-31846-4   LC 92-36429

"A Jean Karl book"

Taddy, a young orphan, afraid of being sent to the work-
house, finds himself at the mercy of the unsavory owner of
a tavern in Alexandria, Virginia, while he tries to solve the
mystery surrounding his past and a missing twin

"With a fine hand for Gothic embroidery and a nifty
surprise conclusion that ties up all the loose ends, Wallace
has delivered [a] . . . very satisfying read." SLJ

Wallace, Bill, 1947-

Beauty. Holiday House 1988 177p $14.95 (4-6)   **Fic**

1. Horses—Fiction 2. Farm life—Fiction

ISBN 0-8234-0715-2   LC 88-6422

Also available in paperback from Pocket Bks.

Unhappy about his parents splitting up and moving with his mother to Grandpa's farm, eleven-year-old Luke finds comfort in riding and caring for a horse named Beauty

"Wallace's horse story is strong on sentiment, and its tear-jerker finale packs a wallop. . . . The story will stir up genuine emotion." Booklist

A dog called Kitty. Holiday House 1980 153p $14.95 (4-6)   **Fic**

1. Dogs—Fiction 2. Farm life—Fiction

ISBN 0-8234-0376-9   LC 80-16293

Also available in paperback from Archway and Minstrel Bks.

Afraid of dogs since he was attacked by a mad one as a baby, Ricky resists taking in a homeless pup that shows up at the farm

"Some minor plot elements are contrived enough to strain credibility, but Ricky is real, as are his family and friends, and there is no lack of action. Recommended also for older reluctant readers for its fast pace, popular appeal, and second-to-third-grade reading level." Booklist

Walter, Mildred Pitts, 1922-

Justin and the best biscuits in the world; with illustrations by Catherine Stock. Lothrop, Lee & Shepard Bks. 1986 122p il $14.95 (3-6)   **Fic**

1. Sex role—Fiction 2. Grandfathers—Fiction 3. Family life—Fiction 4. African Americans—Fiction

ISBN 0-688-06645-3   LC 86-7148

Also available in paperback from Knopf

Coretta Scott King Award for text, 1987

"Justin can't seem to do anything right at home. His sisters berate his dishwashing and his mother despairs of his ever properly tidying his room. As for Justin, he angrily rejects the tasks as 'women's work.' Enter now Justin's widowed grandfather, who sizes up the situation, invites Justin for a visit to his ranch, and through daily routines quietly shows Justin that 'it doesn't matter who does the work, man or woman, when it needs to be done." Booklist

"The strong, well-developed characters and humorous situations in this warm family story will appeal to intermediate readers; the large print will draw slow or reluctant readers." SLJ

Mariah keeps cool. Bradbury Press 1990 139p il $14 (3-6)   **Fic**

1. Family life—Fiction 2. Sisters—Fiction 3. African Americans—Fiction

ISBN 0-02-792295-2   LC 89-23981

Twelve-year-old Mariah envisions a great summer competing as a diver and planning a surprise party for her sister Lynn but half-sister Denise proves a cloud in Mariah's sunny summer

"The story plays out comfortably. . . . The strong portrayal of a warm, close-knit family is a real virtue, and Mariah's character will have broad appeal." Booklist

Another available title about Mariah is:
Mariah loves rock (1988)

Ward, Lynd Kendall, 1905-1985

The silver pony; a story in pictures; by Lynd Ward. Houghton Mifflin 1973 174p il $17.95; pa $6.95 (2-4)   **Fic**

1. Horses—Fiction 2. Stories without words

ISBN 0-395-14753-0; 0-395-64377-5 (pa)

"Eighty pictures in shades of gray, black, and white tell the story of a lonely farm boy whose dreams of his adventures on a winged horse become confused with reality. One night the boy leans out his window fantasizing that the horse is carrying him to the moon; but the dream turns into a nightmare as rockets and missiles fill the air around them, then explode, killing the horse and sending the boy hurtling through space—really out the window to his own yard below. The boy recovers physically and, with the help of his parents, doctor, and a real colt, emotionally. This is a complex story subtly conveyed without words—a unique experience for readers and nonreaders alike." Booklist

Watkins, Yoko Kawashima

My brother, my sister, and I. Bradbury Press 1994 275p $17; pa $3.95 (6 and up)   **Fic**

1. World War, 1939-1945—Fiction 2. Japan—Fiction

ISBN 0-02-792526-9; 0-689-80656-6 (pa)

LC 93-23535

"The author continues her autobiographical account begun in So Far from the Bamboo Grove with the story of how the two sisters, Ko and Yoko, now reunited with their brother Hideyo, try to survive in postwar Japan." Horn Book

"Watkins's first-person narrative is beautifully direct and emotionally honest." Publ Wkly

So far from the bamboo grove. Lothrop, Lee & Shepard Bks. 1986 183p map $15 (6 and up)   **Fic**

1. World War, 1939-1945—Fiction 2. Korea—Fiction 3. Japan—Fiction

ISBN 0-688-06110-9   LC 85-15939

Also available in paperback from Penguin Bks.

A fictionalized autobiography in which eight-year-old Yoko escapes from Korea to Japan with her mother and sister at the end of World War II

"An admirably told and absorbing novel." Horn Book

Followed by My brother, my sister and I

Waugh, Sylvia

The Mennyms. Greenwillow Bks. 1994 c1993 212p $14 (5 and up)   **Fic**

1. Dolls—Fiction 2. Family life—Fiction 3. Great Britain—Fiction

ISBN 0-688-13070-4   LC 93-15901

Also available in paperback from Avon Bks.

First published 1993 in the United Kingdom

The Mennyms, a family of life-size rag dolls living in a house in England and pretending to be human, see their peaceful existence threatened when the house's owner announces he is coming from Australia for a visit

"The suspenseful, seamless fantasy is rich in detail and imagination." Horn Book Guide

Another title about the Mennyms is:
Mennyms in the wilderness (1995)

Wells, Rosemary, 1943-

Through the hidden door; with drawings by the author. Dial Bks. for Young Readers 1987 264p il o.p.; Scholastic paperback available $3.50 (5 and up) **Fic**

1. Fantasy fiction 2. Friendship—Fiction

ISBN 0-590-44013-6 (pa) LC 86-24273

"When five brutish boys feel that Barney has betrayed them, he becomes a pariah in the small world of a boarding school for younger boys and eventually more than ready to receive the offer of friendship from another outcast, Snowy Cobb. Snowy offers more than friendship; he shares a prized and extraordinary discovery, a secret cave which houses the remains of a miniature civilization." Horn Book

"Like the meshed cogs of two wheels, the small but important element of fantasy and the larger one of reality together spin smoothly to create a story that has pace and suspense, strong relationships, and a sturdy structure." Bull Cent Child Books

Westall, Robert, 1929-1993

Ghost abbey. Scholastic 1989 c1988 169p $12.95; pa $3.25 (5 and up) **Fic**

1. Ghost stories 2. Great Britain—Fiction

ISBN 0-590-41692-8; 0-590-41693-6 (pa)

LC 88-23945

First published 1988 in the United Kingdom

"When Dad accepts a job repairing a run-down old manor house, Maggi is delighted. She hopes the absorbing work will help him recover from Mum's death and that the move out of the city will keep her mischievous twin brothers out of trouble. None of them know that the old house has its own plans for effecting its restoration and preservation." Horn Book

"Here's a haunted house story that, from the spooky cover to the happy but unsettling ending, delivers the goods." Bull Cent Child Books

The machine gunners. Greenwillow Bks. 1976 c1975 186p lib bdg $13.88 (6 and up) **Fic**

1. World War, 1939-1945—Fiction 2. Great Britain—Fiction

ISBN 0-688-84055-8

First published 1975 in the United Kingdom

"Garmouth, England, is under constant bombing attack by the Germans in World War II. Charles McGill finds a machine gun in a downed German plane and, with that weapon as protection, he and his friends construct a fortress in preparation for an enemy attack. They capture a German soldier who becomes their friend. Instead of the expected Nazis, other gangs and their families become the enemy. An attack mistakenly thought to be by Nazis leaves their only ally, the German soldier, dead." Shapiro. Fic for Youth. 2d edition

Followed by Fathom five (1980)

Whelan, Gloria

Goodbye, Vietnam. Knopf 1992 135p $13; lib bdg $13.99 (4 and up) **Fic**

1. Refugees—Fiction 2. Vietnamese—Fiction

ISBN 0-679-82263-1; 0-679-92263-6 (lib bdg)

LC 91-3660

Also available in paperback from Bullseye Bks.

Thirteen-year-old Mai and her family embark on a dangerous sea voyage from Vietnam to Hong Kong to escape the unpredictable and often brutal Vietnamese government

"While the book has the suspense and appeal of any good escape story, Whelan is neither melodramatic nor sentimental, and the sometimes horrific details of the scary voyage are plain but understated." Bull Cent Child Books

White, E. B. (Elwyn Brooks), 1899-1985

Charlotte's web; pictures by Garth Williams. Harper & Row 1952 184p il $13.95; lib bdg $13.89; pa $3.95 (3-6) **Fic**

1. Pigs—Fiction 2. Spiders—Fiction

ISBN 0-06-026385-7; 0-06-026386-5 (lib bdg); 0-06-440055-7 (pa)

Also available Spanish language edition

A Newbery Medal honor book, 1953

The story of a little girl who could talk to animals, but especially the story of the pig, Wilbur, and his friendship with Charlotte, the spider, who could not only talk but write as well

"Illustrated with amusing sketches . . . [this] story is a fable for adults as well as children and can be recommended to older children and parents as an amusing story and a gentle essay on friendship." Libr J

Stuart Little; pictures by Garth Williams. Harper & Row 1945 131p il $13.95; lib bdg $13.89; pa $4.50 (3-6) **Fic**

1. Mice—Fiction

ISBN 0-06-026395-4; 0-06-026396-2 (lib bdg); 0-06-440056-5 (pa)

Also available Spanish language edition

This is "the story of a 'Tom Thumb'-like child born to a New York couple who is to all intents and purposes a mouse. . . . The first part of the book explores, with deadpan humour, the advantages and disadvantages of having a mouse in one's family circle. Then Stuart sets out on a quest in search of his inamorata, a bird named Margalo, and the story ends in mid-air. The book is outstandingly funny and sometimes touching." Oxford Companion to Child Lit

The trumpet of the swan; pictures by Edward Frascino. Harper & Row 1970 210p il $13.95; lib bdg $13.89; pa $3.95 (3-6) **Fic**

1. Swans—Fiction

ISBN 0-06-026397-0; 0-06-026398-9 (lib bdg); 0-06-440048-4 (pa)

Also available Spanish language edition

"The focus of this book is Louis, a trumpeter swan who was born mute. Unable to court a lovely swan, Serena, Louis is saved from a lonely fate by his father, who steals a trumpet so that his son may communicate better. Because he is talented and resourceful, Louis is able to earn enough money as a professional musician to pay for the instrument, and most importantly, to win Serena." Wis Libr Bull

The author "deftly blends true birdlore with fanciful adventures in a witty, captivating fantasy." Booklist

White, T. H. (Terence Hanbury), 1906-1964

The sword in the stone; with illustrations by Dennis Nolan. Putnam 1993 256p il $19.95

Fic

1. Arthur, King—Fiction 2. Merlin (Legendary character)

ISBN 0-399-22502-1 LC 92-24808

Also available in paperback from Dell

A newly illustrated edition of the title first published 1938 in the United Kingdom; first United States edition 1939 by G.P Putnam's Sons

White, T. H. (Terence Hanbury), 1906-1964—
Continued

"In White's classic story about the boyhood of King Arthur, Wart—unaware of his true identity—is tutored by Merlyn, who occasionally transform the young boy into various animals as part of his schooling. Contemporary children will still enjoy the text, which is both fantastical and down-to-earth." Horn Book Guide

Wibberley, Leonard, 1915-1983

John Treegate's musket. Farrar, Straus & Giroux 1959 188p hardcover o.p. paperback available $3.95 (6 and up)   **Fic**

1. United States—History—1775-1783, Revolution—Fiction 2. Boston (Mass.)—Fiction

ISBN 0-374-43788-2 (pa)

Also available in hardcover from P. Smith

The first of a series of books about the Treegate family set during the Revolutionary War. Other titles: Peter Treegate's war (1960), Sea captain from Salem (1961) and Treegate's raiders (1962)

In 1769, just after his pro-Royalist father has sailed for England on business, 11-year-old Peter Treegate of Boston unwittingly becomes involved in a dock murder. Fleeing arrest, he takes refuge on an American cargo ship which is subsequently wrecked off the South Carolina coast. Peter is rescued by a Scotsman who, in 1775, helps him rejoin his father, now an embattled American patriot, ready to fight at Bunker Hill

An "unusually clear presentation of the political and military mind of the period." Bookmark

Wiggin, Kate Douglas Smith, 1856-1923

The Bird's Christmas Carol; by Kate Douglas Wiggin; illustrated by Jessie Gillespie. Memorial ed. Houghton Mifflin 1941 84p il $14.95 (3-5)   **Fic**

1. Christmas—Fiction

ISBN 0-395-07205-0

Also available from Buccaneer Bks.

First published 1888

"The story of Carol Bird, an invalid girl so named because she was born at Christmas." Oxford Companion to Child Lit

Rebecca of Sunnybrook Farm; with illustrations by Helen Mason Grose; afterword by Peter Glassman. Morrow 1994 291p il $17 (4 and up)   **Fic**

1. Aunts—Fiction 2. New England—Fiction

ISBN 0-688-13481-5   LC 94-9899

Also available various hardcover reprint and paperback editions

A reissue of the title first published 1903 by Houghton, Mifflin

Talkative, ten-year-old Rebecca goes to live with her spinster aunts, one harsh and demanding, the other soft and sentimental, with whom she spends seven difficult but rewarding years growing up

"Six full-color illustrations and numerous pen-and-ink drawings attractively depict the familiar characters and old-time setting of the classic novel. Wiggin's story . . . continues to hold appeal." Horn Book Guide

Wilde, Oscar, 1854-1900

The selfish giant (2-5)   **Fic**

1. Fairy tales 2. Giants—Fiction

Also available Spanish language edition

Some editions are:

Picture Bk. Studio $15.95 Illustrated by Lisbeth Zwerger (ISBN 0-907234-30-5)

Putnam & Grosset Group $15.95 Illustrated by Saelig Gallagher (ISBN 0-399-22448-3)

This is the "story of a giant whose garden is wrapped in winter until he shares it with the children who live nearby." Booklist

Wilder, Laura Ingalls, 1867-1957

Little house in the big woods; illustrated by Garth Williams. newly illustrated, uniform ed. Harper & Row 1953 237p il $15.95; lib bdg $15.89; pa $3.50 (4-6)   **Fic**

1. Frontier and pioneer life—Fiction 2. Wisconsin—Fiction

ISBN 0-06-026430-6, 0-06-026431-4 (lib bdg); 0-06-107005-X (pa)

First published 1932

This book "tells the story of the author's earliest days 'in the Big Woods of Wisconsin, in a little grey house made of logs.' The style of narrative is simple, almost naive, but the pioneer life is described unsqueamishly, with attention to such details as the butchering of the family hog. As in later books, the author refers to herself in the third person as 'Laura.' The record of daily life far from any town is punctuated with stories told in the evenings by Pa, who is also a great singer of folk-songs," Oxford Companion to Child Lit

Other available titles in the Little House series are:
By the shores of Silver Lake (1939)
Farmer boy (1933)
The first four years (1971)
Little house on the prairie (1935)
Little town on the prairie (1941)
The long winter (1940)
On the banks of Plum Creek (1937)
These happy golden years (1943)

Williams, Vera B.

Scooter. Greenwillow Bks. 1993 147p il $15; lib bdg $14.93 (3-5)   **Fic**

1. Moving—Fiction 2. Divorce—Fiction 3. Friendship—Fiction 4. Mothers and daughters—Fiction

ISBN 0-688-09376-0; 0-688-09377-9 (lib bdg)

           LC 90-38489

After her parent's divorce "Elana Rose Rosen and her mother relocate to an apartment in a big city housing project where 'Lanny' spends the summer making friends and practicing her favorite scooter tricks." Publ Wkly

"The voice is totally authentic, and Williams peppers the pages with ink drawings that have an equally authentic childlike zest." Bull Cent Child Books

Wilson, Nancy Hope, 1947-

The reason for Janey. Macmillan 1994 160p $14.95 (5 and up)   **Fic**

1. Mentally handicapped—Fiction 2. Divorce—Fiction 3. Family life—Fiction

ISBN 0-02-793127-7   LC 93-22930

Also available in paperback from Avon Bks.

Wilson, Nancy Hope, 1947-—*Continued*

Philly's life changes greatly when, after her parents' divorce, her mother takes in Janey, a retarded adult, to live with them

"Written in the first person, the story smoothly draws the diverse, complex characters and shows the bitter feelings that divorce can cause. . . . A dramatic plot without melodramatic treatment." SLJ

Winthrop, Elizabeth

The castle in the attic; frontispiece and chapter title decorations by Trina Schart Hyman. Holiday House 1985 179p il $15.95 (4-6)   **Fic**

1. Fantasy fiction
ISBN 0-8234-0579-6   LC 85-5607
Also available in paperback from Dell

"William is ten, both of his parents work, and he has always been taken care of by Mrs. Phillips; when she tells him she is going home to England, he is distraught, even though her farewell gift is a large replica of a castle, a toy that has been in her family for generations. There's one little figurine, Sir Simon, and a tale that he will some day come to life. For William, he does, and the boy becomes completely involved with Sir Simon and then with a Mrs. Phillips that William has caused to shrink, by a magic token, to Sir Simon's size. The only way that he can show repentance and rescue her is to shrink himself." Bull Cent Child Books

"Well-crafted, easy to follow, this excursion into knightly times and affairs is further enhanced by the cover art, chapter decorations, and, most important of all, a thoughtful floor plan of the castle." Horn Book

Another available title about William and Sir Simon is: The battle for the castle (1993)

Wiseman, David, 1916-

Jeremy Visick. Houghton Mifflin 1981 170p hardcover o.p. paperback available $5.95 (5 and up)   **Fic**

1. Space and time—Fiction 2. Supernatural—Fiction 3. Miners—Fiction 4. Great Britain—Fiction
ISBN 0-395-56153-1 (pa)   LC 80-28116
"Sent by his teacher to explore some local gravestones, Matthew is inexorably drawn to the message on the 1852 Visick family marker, with its tragic tag line, 'And to Jeremy Visick, . . . aged 12 years, whose body still lies in Wheal Maid.' Numerous nocturnal ramblings find Matthew firmly entrenched in the long-dead family's affairs and their work in the Wheal Maid mine. One night, Matthew compulsively follows young Jeremy into the mine, where he learns how the boy died and, though barely escaping death himself, finally brings peace to the boys restless ghost." Booklist

"This story blends the mystery and awe of the supernatural with the real terror and peril of descending the shaft of an 1850 Cornish copper mine." SLJ

Wisler, G. Clifton, 1950-

Mr. Lincoln's drummer. Lodestar Bks. 1995 131p $14.99 (4 and up)   **Fic**

1. Johnston, William J., b. 1850—Fiction 2. United States—History—1861-1865, Civil War—Fiction
ISBN 0-525-67463-2   LC 94-20328
Recounts the courageous exploits of Willie Johnston, an eleven-year-old Civil War drummer, who became the youngest recipient of the Congressional Medal of Honor

"Lively dialogue, vivid battle scenes, unsentimentalized heroism, and a fair amount of wry humor make this an especially good choice for history-shy readers." Bull Cent Child Books

Red Cap. Lodestar Bks. 1991 160p $15 (4 and up)   **Fic**

1. Powell, Ransom J., 1849-1899—Fiction 2. Andersonville Prison—Fiction 3. United States—History—1861-1865, Civil War—Fiction
ISBN 0-525-67337-7   LC 90-21944
Also available in paperback from Puffin Bks.

A young Yankee drummer boy displays great courage when he's captured and sent to Andersonville Prison

The author "presents a well-researched view of the war. He effectively interweaves the known facts of Powell's life with first-person accounts of other soldiers and prisoners to create an exciting story." SLJ

Wojciechowska, Maia, 1927-

Shadow of a bull; drawings by Alvin Smith. Atheneum Pubs. 1964 165p il $15; pa $3.95 (6 and up)   **Fic**

1. Bullfights—Fiction 2. Spain—Fiction
ISBN 0-689-30042-5; 0-689-71132-8 (pa)
Awarded the Newbery Medal, 1965

"Manolo was the son of the great bullfighter Juan Olivar. Ever since his father's death the town of Arcangel [Spain] has waited for [the time] when Manolo would be twelve and face his first bull. From the time he was nine and felt in his heart that he was a coward, Manolo worked and prayed that he might at least face this moment with honor, knowing it could well bring his death." Publ Wkly

"In spare, economical prose [the author] makes one feel, see, smell the heat, endure the hot Andalusian sun and shows one the sand and glare of the bullring. Above all, she lifts the veil and gives glimpses of the terrible loneliness in the soul of a boy. . . . Superbly illustrated." N Y Times Book Rev

Wolff, Virginia Euwer

The Mozart season. Holt & Co. 1991 249p $22.25 (6 and up)   **Fic**

1. Violinists, violoncellists, etc.—Fiction
ISBN 0-8050-1571-X   LC 90-23635
Also available in paperback from Scholastic

Allegra spends her twelfth summer practicing a Mozart concerto for a violin competition and finding many significant connections in her world

"With a clear, fresh voice that never falters, Wolff gives readers a delightful heroine, a fully realized setting, and a slowly building tension that reaches a stunning climax." SLJ

Woodruff, Elvira

Dear Levi; letters from the Overland Trail; illustrated by Beth Peck. Knopf 1994 119p il $14; lib bdg $14.99 (4-6)   **Fic**

1. Overland journeys to the Pacific—Fiction 2. Frontier and pioneer life—Fiction 3. Letters—Fiction
ISBN 0-679-84641-7; 0-679-94641-1 (lib bdg)
     LC 93-5315
Twelve-year-old Austin Ives writes letters to his younger brother describing his three-thousand-mile journey from their home in Pennsylvania to Oregon in 1851

"Atmospheric black-and-white pencil sketches illustrate a few of the story's major events, and a clearly drawn map traces the wagon's route on the Overland Trail. The well-paced story is a page turner." Horn Book Guide

Woodson, Jacqueline

I hadn't meant to tell you this. Delacorte Press 1994 115p $15.95 (6 and up)   **Fic**

1. African Americans—Fiction 2. Friendship—Fiction 3. Incest—Fiction 4. Child sexual abuse—Fiction
ISBN 0-385-32031-0   LC 93-8733
Also available in paperback from Dell

Marie, the only black girl in the eighth grade willing to befriend her white classmate Lena, discovers that Lena's father is doing horrible things to her in private

"Woodson's characters are deftly drawn, whole individuals; her spare prose and crystal images create a haunting, poetic novel." Horn Book Guide

Wrede, Patricia C., 1953-

Dealing with dragons. Harcourt Brace Jovanovich 1990 212p (Enchanted Forest Chronicles) $15.95 (6 and up)   **Fic**

1. Fairy tales 2. Dragons—Fiction
ISBN 0-15-222900-0   LC 89-24599
Also available in paperback from Scholastic
"Jane Yolen books"

Bored with traditional palace life, a princess goes off to live with a group of dragons and soon becomes involved with fighting against some disreputable wizards who want to steal away the dragons' kingdom

"A decidedly diverting novel with plenty of action and many slightly skewed fairy-tale conventions that add to the laugh-out-loud reading pleasure and give the story a wide appeal. The good news is that this is book one in the Enchanted Forest Chronicles." Booklist

Other available titles in the Enchanted Forest Chronicles are:
Calling on dragons (1993)
Searching for dragons (1991)
Talking to dragons (1993)

Wright, Betty Ren

The dollhouse murders. Holiday House 1983 149p $14.95 (4 and up)   **Fic**

1. Mystery fiction
ISBN 0-8234-0497-8   LC 83-6147
Also available in paperback from Scholastic

A dollhouse filled with a ghostly light in the middle of the night and dolls that have moved from where she last left them lead Amy and her retarded sister to unravel the mystery surrounding grisly murders that took place years ago

"More than just a mystery, this offers keen insight into the relationship between handicapped and nonhandicapped siblings and glimpses into the darker adult emotions of guilt and anger. A successful, full-bodied work." Booklist

The ghost comes calling. Scholastic 1994 83p $13.95 (4 and up)   **Fic**

1. Ghost stories
ISBN 0-590-47353-0   LC 93-13969

While vacationing at a spooky cabin on Perch Lake, nine-year-old Chad tries to clear the name of Tim Tapper, the cabin's ghostly inhabitant, who was blamed for a truck accident in the 1930s

"With a taut sense of timing and shivery suspense, Wright revitalizes the story of the mean ghost who cannot rest." Booklist

A ghost in the house. Scholastic 1991 164p hardcover o.p. paperback available $2.95 (4 and up)   **Fic**

1. Ghost stories
ISBN 0-590-43603-1 (pa)   LC 90-23089
Also available Spanish language edition

Strange things happen when twelve-year-old Sarah is alone in the house with Great Aunt Margaret, who appears to be the victim of a ghost seeking revenge for a death in the past

"Wright is an expert at haunted-house effects. . . . The haunting . . . convincingly escalates, climaxing with a scary materialization and confrontation. . . . Genre fans will be pleased to discover more than they bargained for." Bull Cent Child Books

The ghosts of Mercy Manor. Scholastic 1993 172p $13.95; pa $3.50 (4 and up)   **Fic**

1. Ghost stories 2. Orphans—Fiction 3. Mystery fiction
ISBN 0-590-43601-5; 0-590-43602-3 (pa)
LC 92-21557

Twelve-year-old Gwen, an orphan who comes to live with the Mercy family, discovers that the house is haunted by the ghost of a sad-looking young girl and is determined to solve the mystery behind her appearances

"Superbly written and suspenseful throughout." Voice Youth Advocates

Nothing but trouble; drawings by Jacqueline Rogers. Holiday House 1995 119p il $14.95 (4 and up)   **Fic**

1. Aunts—Fiction 2. Dogs—Fiction 3. Mystery fiction
ISBN 0-8234-1175-3   LC 94-34285

"When Vannie Kirkland is dropped off with an aged aunt she's never met while her parents search for work in California, things don't look great. For one, aunt Bert thinks Vannie's diminutive dog, Muffy, is a noisy, destructive little bundle. But Aunt Bert's less prickly side is revealed when mysterious prowlers start vandalizing her farm." Booklist

"The plot is cleanly structured and should hold readers' interest. . . . Overall, a satisfying story for a wide range of mystery fans." SLJ

Out of the dark. Scholastic 1995 149p $13.95 (4 and up)   **Fic**

1. Ghost stories 2. Grandmothers—Fiction
ISBN 0-590-43598-1   LC 93-48025

"Jessie and her parents have recently moved to her grandmother's rural home, but her enjoyment of the house is marred by nightmares that are chillingly real. Her parents' frustrations with unemployment have put a strain on the whole family, and she doesn't feel able to share her terror as the threatening ghost of her dreams begins to appear while she is awake. . . . Relationships built on well-defined characters add realism to this supernatural tale. Effective and well crafted." SLJ

Wrightson, Patricia, 1921-

The Nargun and the stars. Margaret K. McElderry Bks. 1986 c1970 184p o.p.; Penguin Bks. paperback available $3.95 (5 and up)   **Fic**

1. Fantasy fiction 2. Australia—Fiction
ISBN 0-14-030780-X (pa)   LC 86-10600

A reissue of the title first published 1973 in the United Kingdom; first United States edition published 1974 by Atheneum Pubs.

Wrightson, Patricia, 1921— *Continued*

This is a fantasy set in Northern Australia. An ancient stone monster called the Nargun "threatens to crush the home of orphaned Simon's middle-aged cousins, Charlie and Edie. To rid themselves of the Nargun they seek help from other supernatural beings." Libr J

"The characters, seemingly plain and uncomplicated people, subtly come to life as complex human beings; and the essentially simple plot is worked into the rich fabric of a story that begins serenely, arches up to a great crescendo of suspense, and then falls away at the end to 'a whisper in the dark.'" Horn Book

Wyss, Johann David, 1743-1818

The Swiss family Robinson (5 and up)
                                                    Fic

1. Survival after airplane accidents, shipwrecks, etc.—Fiction

Some editions are:

Grosset & Dunlap (Illustrated junior library) $15.95 Illustrated by Lynd Kendall Ward (ISBN 0-448-06022-1)

Knopf (Everyman's library children's classics) $13.95 Illustrated by Louis Rhead (ISBN 0-679-43640-5)

Originally published 1813 in Switzerland

"A Swiss family—a pastor, his wife, and four boys—are shipwrecked on an uninhabited island. They gradually establish an attractive way of life for themselves, and their many adventures are used by their father to form the basis of lessons in natural history and the physical sciences." Oxford Companion to Child Lit

Yarbrough, Camille, 1938-

The shimmershine queens. Putnam 1988 142p $14.95 (4-6)   **Fic**

1. African Americans—Fiction 2. School stories 3. Prejudices—Fiction

ISBN 0-399-21465-8   LC 88-11539

Also available in paperback from Knopf

"Angie and her friend Michelle are in fifth grade, where Angie is taunted because her skin is so dark. It's an elderly visiting relative . . . who makes Angie feel her own worth and who explains 'shimmershine' as the glow you get when you feel good about yourself." Bull Cent Child Books

"This story carries a clear message about the dire need for students to respect themselves, each other, and education. The dialogue (rendered in black English) rings true, and the characterizations have depth." Booklist

Yep, Laurence

Child of the owl. Harper & Row 1977 217p lib bdg $13.89; pa $3.95 (5 and up)   **Fic**

1. Chinese Americans—Fiction 2. Grandmothers—Fiction 3. San Francisco (Calif.)—Fiction

ISBN 0-06-026743-7 (lib bdg); 0-06-440336-X (pa)
                                        LC 76-24314

"Casey, a 12-year-old Chinese American girl, is more American than Chinese. When her father, a compulsive gambler, is hospitalized after a severe beating, Casey moves in with her grandmother in San Francisco's Chinatown. Although she is a street-smart child, Casey finds that she is an outsider in this community. Her grandmother teaches her something of her heritage and what it means to be 'a child of the owl.'" Shapiro. Fic for Youth. 3d edition

Dragon's gate. HarperCollins Pubs. 1993 273p $15; lib bdg $14.89; pa $3.95 (6 and up)
                                        Fic

1. Chinese—United States—Fiction 2. Railroads—Fiction

ISBN 0-06-022971-3; 0-06-022972-1 (lib bdg); 0-06-440489-7 (pa)   LC 92-43649

Sequel to The serpent's children (1984) and Mountain light (1985)

A Newbery Medal honor book, 1994

When he accidentally kills a Manchu, a fifteen-year-old Chinese boy is sent to America to join his father, an uncle, and other Chinese working to build a tunnel for the transcontinental railroad through the Sierra Nevada mountains in 1867

"Yep has succeeded in realizing the primary characters and the irrepressibly dramatic story. . . . The carefully researched details will move students to thought and discussion." Bull Cent Child Books

Dragonwings. Harper & Row 1975 248p lib bdg $14.89; pa $4.95 (5 and up)   **Fic**

1. Chinese Americans—Fiction 2. San Francisco (Calif.)—Fiction 3. Fathers and sons—Fiction

ISBN 0-06-026738-0 (lib bdg); 0-06-440085-9 (pa)

Also available Cornerstone Bks. large print edition

"In 1903 Moon Shadow, eight years old, leaves China for the 'Land of the Golden Mountains,' San Francisco, to be with his father, Windrider, a father he has never seen. There, beset by the trials experienced by most foreigners in America, Moonrider shares his father's dream—to fly. This dream enables Windrider to endure the mockery of the other Chinese, the poverty he suffers in this hostile place—the land of the white demons—and his loneliness for his wife and his own country." Shapiro. Fic for Youth. 3d edition

Later, gator. Hyperion Bks. for Children 1995 122p $13.95; lib bdg $13.89 (4-6)
                                        Fic

1. Chinese Americans—Fiction 2. Brothers—Fiction 3. Alligators—Fiction

ISBN 0-7868-0059-3; 0-7868-2083-7 (lib bdg)
                                        LC 94-11254

"Teddy resents his goody-goody brother, Bobby. Urged to get Bobby a suitable pet for his eighth birthday, Teddy buys an alligator instead. Bobby unexpectedly adores Oscar—sharp teeth, voracious appetite, and all. The challenge of feeding Oscar unites the boys, but also gets Teddy in trouble . . . again." Publisher's note

"The characterizations of the family and portrayal of the culture of San Francisco's Chinatown are plausible and likable. Yep acknowledges the peril and cruelty of exotic pet ownership in a brief afterword." Horn Book

The star fisher. Morrow Junior Bks. 1991 150p $15 (6 and up)   **Fic**

1. Chinese Americans—Fiction 2. Moving—Fiction 3. Prejudices—Fiction

ISBN 0-688-09365-5   LC 90-23785

Also available in paperback from Puffin Bks.

Fifteen-year-old Joan Lee and her family find the adjustment hard when they move from Ohio to West Virginia in the 1920s

"Based on experiences from Laurence Yep's own family history, the story offers unique insight into the plight of ethnic minorities. It is disturbing but never depressing, poignant but not melancholy. . . . The book is a pleasure to read, entertaining its audience even as it educates their hearts." Horn Book

Yep, Laurence—*Continued*

Sweetwater; pictures by Julia Noonan. Harper & Row 1973 201p il hardcover o.p. paperback available $3.50 (6 and up)   **Fic**

1. Science fiction

ISBN 0-06-440135-9 (pa)

"Young Tyree is torn between pursuing an interest in music encouraged by Amadeus, an Argan (the oldest race on the planet Harmony), and obeying his father, elected captain of the Silkies, descendants of the starship crews from Earth, who are fighting for a life in harmony with the dominant sea. A distinctive narrative that unexpectedly and winningly combines a richly imagined world and its ecology, a boy's rite of passage, and wide-ranging allusions to music and the Old Testament." Anatomy of Wonder. 3d edition

Thief of hearts. HarperCollins Pubs. 1995 197p $14.95; lib bdg $14.89 (5 and up)   **Fic**

1. Chinese Americans—Fiction 2. Friendship—Fiction 3. San Francisco (Calif.)—Fiction

ISBN 0-06-023341-X; 0-06-023342-8 (lib bdg)

LC 94-18703

"Stacy is not pleased that she's been elected by her parents to show a new girl from China around school, particularly when it turns out that Hong Ch'un is snotty and difficult, even calling Stacy *t'ung chung,* 'mixed seed.' Stacy's mother (whose story was told in *Child of the Owl*) . . . is of Chinese descent, and her father Caucasian, and when Hong Ch'un is accused by the other kids of stealing, Stacy feels torn between parental instruction, ethnic loyalty, and peer acceptance." Bull Cent Child Books

"Told with candor and controlled emotion, this first person narrative presents a difficult topic in a manner accessible to a wide audience." Horn Book

Yolen, Jane

The devil's arithmetic. Viking Kestrel 1988 170p $15.99; pa $3.99 (4 and up)   **Fic**

1. Jews—Fiction 2. Holocaust, 1933-1945—Fiction

ISBN 0-670-81027-4; 0-14-034535-3 (pa)

LC 88-14235

"During a Passover Seder, 12-year-old Hannah finds herself transported from America in 1988 to Poland in 1942, where she assumes the life of young Chaya. Within days the Nazis take Chaya and her neighbors off to a concentration camp, mere components in the death factory. As days pass, Hannah's own memory of her past, and the prisoners' future, fades until she is Chaya completely." Publ Wkly

"Through Hannah, with her memories of the present and the past, Yolen does a fine job of illustrating the importance of remembering. She adds much to children's understanding of the effects of the Holocaust." SLJ

The dragon's boy. Harper & Row 1990 120p $14.95; lib bdg $14.89 (5 and up)   **Fic**

1. Arthur, King—Fiction 2. Merlin (Legendary character)—Fiction

ISBN 0-06-026789-5; 0-06-026790-9 (lib bdg)

LC 89-24642

"This is a retelling of the education and coming of age of 13-year-old Artos (Arthur). Old Linn (Merlin) is to be his teacher, but, doubting he can command the boy's attention, he constructs a fire-breathing dragon as a façade." SLJ

"Scattered throughout the book are broad hints of Artos's identity, but even children unfamiliar with the legendary King Arthur should find the crisply told story accessible and entertaining." Horn Book

S C   Story Collections

Books in this class include collections of short stories by one author and collections by more than one author. Folk tales are entered in class 398.2. Collections of general literature, American literature, English literature, etc.—which may include but are not limited to short stories—are entered in classes 808.8, 810.8, 820.8, etc.

Aiken, Joan, 1924-

A foot in the grave; [by] Joan Aiken and Jan Pieńkowski. Viking 1991 c1989 128p il $15.95; pa $3.99 (6 and up)   **S C**

1. Ghost stories 2. Short stories

ISBN 0-670-84169-2; 0-14-036111-1 (pa)

First published 1989 in the United Kingdom

"At Pienkowski's request, Aiken has written a series of ghost stories—sometimes spooky-funny and sometimes disturbingly eerie—to accompany the artist's stark, surrealistic paintings. In 'A Foot in the Grave,' developers are prevented from turning a graveyard into a cricket pitch (field) by Aunt Millie and her mangy dog, who rise from the grave to do battle. 'Amberland' is a fantasy island seen by two brothers in their dreams. When Dolph dies because of a lie Randy told, Dolph haunts Randy's dreams, seeming to occupy a cave on the island. . . . This book, with its black dust jacket showing a creature in torment, makes an enticing addition to the spooky-story shelf." Booklist

Give yourself a fright: thirteen tales of the supernatural. Delacorte Press 1989 180p hardcover o.p. paperback available $3.99 (6 and up)   **S C**

1. Horror fiction 2. Short stories

ISBN 0-440-41014-2 (pa)

LC 88-20366

"A magic duck, ghosts, the devil, a confused muse, and human evil haunt these 13 unusual stories that hover between fantasy and reality; humor and psychological terror. The styles vary, giving an interesting texture to the collection." SLJ

Andersen, Hans Christian, 1805-1875

Hans Christian Andersen fairy tales; selected & illustrated by Lisbeth Zwerger; translated by Anthea Bell. Picture Bk. Studio 1992 65p il $19.95 (4-6)   **S C**

1. Fairy tales 2. Short stories

ISBN 0-88708-182-7

LC 91-13132

Also available Spanish language edition

"A Michael Neugebauer book".

Original German edition published 1991 in Austria

"This collection of eight stories includes relatively unknown stories, such as 'The Rose Tree Regiment,' along with such familiar favorites as 'The Princess & the Pea.' Bell's finesse in writng is well matched by Zwerger's delicate, understated approach in the illustrations, which are introspective rather than dramatic." Booklist

Twelve tales; selected, translated, and illustrated by Erik Blegvad. Margaret K. McElderry Bks. 1994 92p il $18.95 (4-6)   **S C**

1. Fairy tales 2. Short stories

ISBN 0-689-50584-1

LC 93-6927

"The twelve chosen tales are mostly the familiar ones, such as 'The Swineherd,' 'The Emperor's New Clothes,' and

Andersen, Hans Christian, 1805-1875—_Continued_

'The Tinderbox,' but several lesser-known tales are included—'The Pixie at the Grocer's,' 'The Sweethearts,' 'Twelve by Coach.'" Horn Book

Blegvad's "translation is smooth and inviting, and the accompanying watercolor and pen-and-ink illustrations add to the high quality of the overall design. But it is Blegvad's selection of tales that makes this a strong addition to even the most complete Andersen collection." Booklist

Babbitt, Natalie

The Devil's other storybook; stories and pictures by Natalie Babbitt. Farrar, Straus & Giroux 1987 81p il $13; pa $3.50 (4-6)

S C

1. Devil—Fiction 2. Short stories
ISBN 0-374-31767-4; 0-374-41704-0 (pa)

LC 86-32760

Also available Spanish language edition

"Michael di Capua books"

Featuring the same creature as in The Devil's storybook, entered below, this companion volume contains 10 additional tales

The Devil's storybook; stories and pictures by Natalie Babbitt. Farrar, Straus & Giroux 1974 101p il $13; pa $3.95 (4-6)   S C

1. Devil—Fiction 2. Short stories
ISBN 0-374-31770-4; 0-374-41708-3 (pa)

Also available Spanish language edition

Ten "stories about the machinations of the Devil to increase the population of his realm. He is not always successful and, despite his clever ruses, meets frustration as often as his intended victims do." Horn Book

"Twists of plot within traditional themes and a briskly witty style distinguish this book, illustrated amusingly with black-and-white line drawings." Booklist

Berry, James

The future-telling lady and other stories. Perlman Bks. 1993 c1991 139p $14; lib bdg $13.89; pa $3.95 (5 and up)   S C

1. Jamaica—Fiction 2. Short stories
ISBN 0-06-021434-1; 0-06-021435-X (lib bdg); 0-06-440471-4 (pa)

LC 92-13759

First published 1991 in the United Kingdom in a slightly different form with title: The future-telling lady

This is a collection of six stories set in contemporary Jamaica

"This collection offers a wealth of detail about life in the West Indies, and Berry's language sings with grace, beauty, and respect." Horn Book Guide

Bond, Michael, 1926-

Paddington's storybook; illustrated in color and black and white by Peggy Fortnum. Houghton Mifflin 1984 c1983 159p il $19.95 (2-5)   S C

1. Bears—Fiction 2. Great Britain—Fiction 3. Short stories
ISBN 0-395-36667-4

LC 84-12900

For other titles about Paddington see Fiction Section

First published 1983 in the United Kingdom

"A selection of some of the very best stories about a very fine bear published over the past 25 years. Watercolor has been added to the original line drawings." N Y Times Book Rev

Brooke, William J.

Teller of tales. HarperCollins Pubs. 1994 170p $15; lib bdg $14.89; pa $5.95 (4 and up)

S C

1. Fairy tales 2. Short stories
ISBN 0-06-023399-0; 0-06-023400-8 (lib bdg); 0-06-440511-7 (pa)

LC 93-43421

"The background story is that of an old man who is learning to tell old stories through the new medium of type; he is encouraged, taunted, and eventually loved as a father by a tough and streetwise young girl whom he takes into his home. Using these two characters sometimes as tale-telling mouthpieces and sometimes as folkloric _dramatis personae_, Brooke tells versions of 'The Emperor's New Clothes,' 'Goldilocks,' 'Little Red Riding Hood,' and 'Rumpelstiltskin.'" Bull Cent Child Books

A telling of the tales: five stories; drawings by Richard Egielski. Harper & Row 1990 132p il lib bdg $13.89; pa $5.95 (4 and up)

S C

1. Short stories
ISBN 0-06-020689-6 (lib bdg); 0-06-440467-6 (pa)

LC 89-36588

A retelling of five classic folk/fairy tales, including Cinderella, Sleeping Beauty, Paul Bunyan, John Henry, and Jack and the Beanstalk, from a contemporary perspective

"Brooke has succeeded in making these old familiar tales his own, softening their make-believe, playing with their meanings, but leaving their magic utterly intact. . . . A perceptive and engaging collection that's ideal for reading aloud." SLJ

Conrad, Pam, 1947-1996

Our house; the stories of Levittown; illustrations by Brian Selznick. Scholastic 1995 65p il $14.95 (4-6)   S C

1. Short stories 2. Levittown (N.Y.)—Fiction
ISBN 0-590-46523-6

LC 94-42126

Six stories, one from each decade from the 1940s to the 1990s, about children growing up in Levittown, New York

"Vivid descriptions and poignant observations leave indelible impressions. . . . Conrad's fresh, imaginative approach to the concept of 'home' makes this an ideal starting point for discussion, creative writing, and other class activities." Booklist

Coville, Bruce

Oddly enough; stories by Bruce Coville; illustrations by Michael Hussar. Harcourt Brace & Co. 1994 122p $15.95 (6 and up)

S C

1. Horror fiction 2. Short stories
ISBN 0-15-200093-3

LC 94-16286

"Jane Yolen books"

A collection of nine short stories featuring an angel, unicorn, vampire, werewolf, and other unusual creatures

"The stories are well written. . . . The plots . . . are always clear and characterizations deftly drawn. . . . A worthwhile purchase, particularly for classroom discussions." SLJ

Fleischman, Paul

Coming-and-going men; four tales; illustrations by Randy Gaul. Harper & Row 1985 147p il lib bdg $12.89 (6 and up)

S C

1. New England—Fiction 2. Short stories
ISBN 0-06-021884-3   LC 84-48336

"A Charlotte Zolotow book"

"Four loosely connected stories present the adventures of itinerant artisans and tradesmiths as they travel through the small town of New Canaan, Vermont, in the year 1800. Each tale involves a young person as a major character, and Fleischman creates a pleasing motif by setting each adventure in a different season." SLJ

Graven images; 3 stories; illustrations by Andrew Glass. Harper & Row 1982 85p il lib bdg $13.89 (6 and up)   S C

1. Supernatural—Fiction 2. Short stories
ISBN 0-06-021907-6   LC 81-48649

A Newbery Medal honor book, 1983

"A Charlotte Zolotow book"

Three stories about people whose lives are influenced by sculptured figures. In Saint Crispin's follower, "Nicholas, an apprentice cobbler, believes the statue of St. Crispin in his village square is guiding him to a successful courtship with a comely lass. . . . The other two tales are grim examples of retribution. A wooden figurehead, 'The Binnacle Boy,' unmasks a killer in an old whaling port, and a statue commissioned by a ghost proves that a father has murdered his son in 'The Man of Influence.'" Publ Wkly

Geras, Adèle

Golden windows and other stories of Jerusalem. Perlman Bks. 1993 148p $14.95; lib bdg $13.89 (4 and up)   S C

1. Jews—Fiction 2. Jerusalem—Fiction 3. Short stories
ISBN 0-06-022941-1; 0-06-022942-X (lib bdg)
LC 92-39885

Five short stories which describe what it was like to grow up in Jerusalem in the first half of the twentieth century

"Well-written, laced with subtleties of history, and rich in personal emotion, this lovely collection of stories lends reality and humanity to a not too distant time and place." Booklist

Godden, Rumer, 1907-

Four dolls; illustrated by Pauline Baynes. Greenwillow Bks. 1984 c1983 137p il $15 (3-5)

S C

1. Dolls—Fiction 2. Short stories
ISBN 0-688-02801-2   LC 83-14157

This collection was first published 1983 in the United Kingdom; the stories were originally published separately Impunity Jane (1955); The fairy doll (1956); The story of Holly and Ivy (1959); Candy Floss (1960)

These "are timeless tales featuring plucky little dolls and their resourceful owners. The new black-and-white and color artwork is not terribly exciting but serves pleasantly." Booklist

Hamilton, Virginia, 1936-

The all Jahdu storybook; illustrations by Barry Moser. Harcourt Brace Jovanovich 1991 108p il $19.95 (4-6)   S C

1. Magic—Fiction 2. Short stories
ISBN 0-15-239498-2   LC 90-47847

A collection of stories about Jahdu, the magical Afro-American trickster who can change his shape. Eleven of the stories appeared previously in the author's The Time-ago tales of Jahdu (1969), Time-ago lost: more tales of Jahdu (1973), and Jahdu (1973) and have been revised

"Hamilton manages to combine elements of myth, fairy tale, and modern life with no more sense of incongruity than a child at play. This beautifully designed book features watercolor paintings that suggest the power and mystery of the story." Booklist

Jennings, Paul, 1943-

Unreal! eight surprising stories. Viking 1991 c1985 107p $14; pa $3.95 (4 and up)

S C

1. Short stories
ISBN 0-670-84175-7; 0-14-037577-5 (pa)
LC 91-50286

First published 1985 in Australia

This is an "assortment of short stories—some scary, some funny, some just plain gross—each told by a young male protagonist." Booklist

"Jennings has found the perfect formula for the scary and supernatural sprinkled with just the right touch of hilarity." SLJ

Kennedy, Richard, 1932-

Richard Kennedy: collected stories; illustrations by Marcia Sewall. Harper & Row 1987 270p il o.p. (3-5)   S C

1. Short stories   LC 86-45495

A collection of two poems and 14 stories, previously published separately in picture book format

Kennedy "introduces each story with a brief paragraph answering the inevitable question, 'Where do you get your ideas?' As individual as its source, each story is remarkably different from the others which surround it. . . . What the stories do have in common—aside from the richness of their language—is vivid and loving characterization, levels of meaning which speak to a multi-generational audience, the timeless, enduring appeal of stories which have been told around long generations of campfires, and an astonishing gift of imagination." SLJ

Kipling, Rudyard, 1865-1936

The jungle books (4 and up)   S C

1. Animals—Fiction 2. India—Fiction 3. Short stories

Hardcover and paperback editions available from various publishers; Spanish language edition also available

A collection of fifteen animal stories first published 1894 and 1895 in two volumes by Macmillan with titles: The jungle book and The second jungle book. The jungle books also available from Grosset & Dunlap illustrated by Fritz Eichenberg and from Knopf illustrated by Kurt Wiese

The central figure in the stories is the human Mowgli, brought up in the jungle in India by Mother Wolf

Just so stories (3-6)   S C

1. Animals—Fiction 2. India—Fiction 3. Short stories
Also available Spanish language edition

Kipling, Rudyard, 1865-1936—*Continued*

Some editions are:

Holt & Co. $17.95 Illustrated by Safaya Salter (ISBN 0-8050-0439-4)

Knopf (Everyman's library children's classics) $12.95 Illustrated by the author (ISBN 0-679-41797-4)

Viking Kestrel $15 Illustrated by Michael Foreman; 0-670-80242-5)

The book consists of twelve animal fables

"While Kipling's original and humorous elucidation of how the elephant got his trunk and the leopard his spots are barely believable, he has nevertheless drawn animal characteristics and habits 'just so.' First published in 1902." Toronto Public Libr. Books for Boys & Girls

Several of the Just so stories are entered separately in the Fiction Section

Konigsburg, E. L.

Altogether, one at a time; illustrated by Gail E. Haley [et al.] Atheneum Pubs. 1971 79p il $13.95; pa $3.95 (4-6)   S C

1. Short stories
ISBN 0-689-20638-0; 0-689-71290-1 (pa)

"Compelled to invite a child he doesn't want to his birthday party in 'Inviting Jason,' Stanley likes the boy even less afterwards, but for a different reason. A 10-year-old boy learns something about old age in 'The Night of the Leonids' when he realizes his grandmother has lost her chance to see a shower of stars that occurs only once every 33¼ years. The spirit of a long dead camp counselor helps an obese girl make up her mind that she will never have to attend Camp Fat again. In 'Momma at the Pearly Gates,' Momma tells the story of how, as a girl, she was called a 'dirty nigger' by a white classmate." Libr J

Throwing shadows. Atheneum Pubs. 1979 151p hardcover o.p. paperback available $3.95 (5 and up)   S C

1. Short stories
ISBN 0-02-044140-1 (pa)   LC 79-10422
Also available in hardcover from P. Smith

"This is a collection of five original short stories. Each of the stories is told in the first person and concerns a preadolescent boy as he learns a little about his identity. The boys come from a variety of geographical backgrounds, races, and cultures. . . . As each boy discovers a new facet of his personality or accepts an old one, he throws a shadow that is uniquely his own." Child Book Rev Serv

"The stories each occupy about 30 pages but have the spacious quality of a novel; characters and events have a chance to develop naturally rather than seeming pushed along." SLJ

Levoy, Myron

The witch of Fourth Street, and other stories; pictures by Gabriel Lisowski. Harper & Row 1972 110p il hardcover o.p. paperback available $3.95 (4-6)   S C

1. New York (N.Y.)—Fiction 2. Short stories
ISBN 0-06-440059-X (pa)
Also available in hardcover from P. Smith

"The eight stories [set on the Lower East Side of New York in the 1920's] tell about a group of neighbors, young and old. . . . Tales and characters are highly original, sometimes humorous, sometimes poignant, and often profound. . . . The soft drawings are exactly right." Horn Book

MacLachlan, Patricia

Tomorrow's wizard; illustrations by Kathy Jacobi. Harper & Row 1982 80p il lib bdg $13.89 (3-6)   S C

1. Witchcraft—Fiction 2. Short stories
ISBN 0-06-024074-1   LC 81-47733
"A Charlotte Zolotow book"

This collection of six stories "follows the adventures of three . . . characters: Tomorrow's Wizard, his young apprentice Murdoch and a philosophical horse saved from an ill-tempered owner. The Wizard and Murdoch are charged with fulfilling the most important wishes and curses uttered by the humans who inhabit the nearby villages of this unnamed land. Watched over by the High Wizard, the three companions go about making surprising matches between very different individuals." SLJ

This "is a quietly stunning book, filled with poetry and parables. Kathy Jacobi's illustrations perfectly complement Patricia MacLachlan's lyrical storytelling. A book that should stand permanently on every child's shelf." Christ Sci Monit

Mahy, Margaret

The girl with the green ear; stories about magic in nature; illustrations by Shirley Hughes. Knopf 1992 97p il $15; lib bdg $15.99; pa $3.25 (3-5)   S C

1. Nature—Fiction 2. Magic—Fiction 3. Short stories
ISBN 0-679-82231-3; 0-679-92231-8 (lib bdg); 0-679-84000-1 (pa)   LC 91-14992

A collection of nine stories in which characters encounter talking plants, a pine-tree man, a merry-go-round with flying horses, mystical midnight birds, and a cake-eating tree

"The collection provides funny dialogue, luscious descriptions (matched by Hughes' ink sketches), a generous ecological lesson, and fair evidence of Mahy's abundant imagination." Bull Cent Child Books

Tick tock tales; stories to read around the clock; illustrated by Wendy Smith. Margaret K. McElderry Bks. 1994 c1993 92p il $16.95 (k-3)   S C

1. Short stories
ISBN 0-689-50604-X
First published 1993 in the United Kingdom

"Kings, wizards, pirates, orphans, and an assortment of animals grace this fanciful collection, which is great for bedtime reading. Mahy's skill as a storyteller and Smith's well-placed color illustrations will carry readers through to the last page." Horn Book Guide

Marshall, James, 1942-1992

Rats on the range and other stories. Dial Bks. for Young Readers 1993 80p $12.99; lib bdg $12.89 (2-4)   S C

1. Animals—Fiction 2. Short stories
ISBN 0-8037-1384-3; 0-8037-1385-1 (lib bdg)
          LC 92-28918

In eight animal stories the reader meets a rat family that vacations at a dude ranch, a pig who takes lessons in table manners, a mouse who keeps house for a tomcat, and a buzzard who leaves his money to the Society for Stray Cats—or does he?

"In this collection, which brilliantly demonstrates Marshall's gift for humor, there are eight gems." Horn Book Guide

Marshall, James, 1942-1992—*Continued*

Rats on the roof, and other stories. Dial Bks. for Young Readers 1991 79p il $13; lib bdg $12.89 (2-4) **S C**

1. Animals—Fiction 2. Short stories
ISBN 0-8037-0834-3; 0-8037-0835-1 (lib bdg)
LC 90-44084

An illustrated collection of seven stories about various animals, including a frog with magnificent legs, a hungry brontosaurus, and a mouse who gets married

"Marshall's fertile imagination gets lots of exercise here as does his sardonic wit, and he's included plenty of expressive illustrations, all done in his signature style." Booklist

McKissack, Patricia C., 1944-

The dark-thirty; Southern tales of the supernatural; illustrated by Brian Pinkney. Knopf 1992 122p il $16; lib bdg $15.99 (4 and up) **S C**

1. Ghost stories 2. African Americans—Fiction 3. Short stories
ISBN 0-679-81863-4; 0-679-91863-9 (lib bdg)
LC 92-3021

A Newbery Medal honor book, 1993; Coretta Scott King Award for text, 1993

A collection of ghost stories with African American themes, designed to be told during the Dark Thirty—the half hour before sunset—when ghosts seem all too believable

"Strong characterizations are superbly drawn in a few words. The atmosphere of each selection is skillfully developed and sustained to the very end. Pinkney's stark scratchboard illustrations evoke an eerie mood, which heightens the suspense of each tale. This is a stellar collection for both public and school libraries looking for absorbing books to hook young readers. Storytellers also will find it a goldmine." SLJ

The **Oxford** treasury of children's stories; [compiled by] Michael Harrison and Christopher Stuart-Clark. Oxford Univ. Press 1994 159p il $20 (3-5) **S C**

ISBN 0-19-278133-2

This anthology includes twenty-six stories by such authors as Julius Lester, James Berry, Joan Aiken, and Margaret Mahy

"The selections are suitable for reading aloud and are mostly fantastic, with a generous sprinkling of dragons, giants, and other magical beings, and the tone is predominantly humorous. Six different illustrators contribute full-page and smaller watercolors." SLJ

Paterson, Katherine

Angels & other strangers: family Christmas stories. Crowell 1979 118p $14; lib bdg $13.89; pa $3.95 (5 and up) **S C**

1. Christmas—Fiction 2. Short stories
ISBN 0-690-03992-1; 0-690-04911-0 (lib bdg); 0-06-440283-5 (pa)
LC 79-63797

"The author weaves stories about miracles of the Christmas season—miracles that take place on a truly human level. Each story is based on the Christian message of the birth of Christ and the significance that message takes on for the characters. She writes of the poor, the desolate, and the lonely as well as of the arrogant, the complacent, and the proud." Horn Book

Porte-Thomas, Barbara Ann

A turkey drive and other tales; by Barbara Ann Porte; pictures by Yossi Abolafia. Greenwillow Bks. 1993 63p il $14 (2-4) **S C**

1. Short stories
ISBN 0-688-11336-2
LC 91-48032

A sister and brother who enjoy storytelling like their father, and art like their mother, join in making up stories about different pictures around their house

These stories "include exotic adventures, slightly fractured fables, and tall hometown tales, all of which have a loopy luster that kids will relish as a readaloud or readalone. Abolafia's cheerfully matter-of-fact line-and-wash drawings give the idiosyncratic narrative a connection to the real world." Bull Cent Child Books

Rylant, Cynthia

Children of Christmas; stories for the season; drawings by S. D. Schindler. Orchard Bks. 1987 38p il $13.95; pa $5.95 (4 and up) **S C**

1. Christmas—Fiction 2. Short stories
ISBN 0-531-05706-2; 0-531-07042-5 (pa)
LC 87-1690

These Christmas stories are "about lost things: a stray cat, a stray bachelor, a grandfather who has lost the connection to the youngest generation, a misunderstood boy who receives a cowboy set instead of a doctor kit and who tries to hold onto a lost dream." Read Teach

"Rylant's Christmas is a sad and lonely one, but her ability to summon the joys of the season through her writing is extraordinary. Schindler's illustrations, appropriately, are both reserved and inciting." Publ Wkly

Every living thing; stories; decorations by S. D. Schindler. Bradbury Press 1985 81p $14; pa $3.95 (5 and up) **S C**

1. Animals—Fiction 2. Short stories
ISBN 0-02-777200-4; 0-689-71263-4 (pa)
LC 85-7701

"This book tells twelve stories about lonely people whose lives have been changed for the better by an association with an animal. Many of the stories are heartwarming and meant to be read aloud. Through a parrot, a twelve-year-old boy learns how much his father loves him; a retired schoolteacher and an old collie renew their life by becoming friends with young children. While some of the stories are overly sentimental, the majority realistically show the importance of animals in our lives." Okla State Dept of Educ

Sandburg, Carl, 1878-1967

More rootabagas; stories by Carl Sandburg; pictures by Paul O. Zelinsky; collected and with a foreword by George Hendrick. Knopf 1993 94p il $18; lib bdg $18.99 **S C**

1. Fairy tales 2. Short stories
ISBN 0-679-80070-0; 0-679-90070-5 (lib bdg)
LC 92-14930

A selection of Sandburg's fanciful, humorous short stories peopled with such characters as the Potato Face Blind Man, Susan Slackentwist, and Dippy the Wisp

"These 10 previously unpublished stories are chock-full of the wisdom and whimsy of Sandburg's classic *Rootabaga Stories,* and have the added attraction of Zelinsky's fine colored-pencil interpretations of the fanciful characters and scenes." SLJ

Sandburg, Carl, 1878-1967—*Continued*

Rootabaga stories; illustrated by Michael Hague. Harcourt Brace Jovanovich 1988-1989 2v il ea $19.95; pa $4.95   **S C**

1. Fairy tales 2. Short stories
ISBN 0-15-269061-1 (v1); 0-15-269065-4 (v1 pa); 0-15-269062-X (v2); 0-15-269063-8 (v2 pa)
LC 88-935

Singer, Isaac Bashevis, 1904-1991

Naftali the storyteller and his horse, Sus, and other stories; pictures by Margot Zemach. Farrar, Straus & Giroux 1976 129p il hardcover o.p. paperback available $3.50 (4 and up)   **S C**

1. Jews—Poland—Fiction 2. Poland—Fiction 3. Short stories
ISBN 0-374-45487-6 (pa)   LC 76-26917

Three of the stories "continue the adventures of the fools of Chelm, characters whose zaniness has tickled readers of all ages in earlier collections by the author [including The fools of Chelm and their history, entered in the Fiction Section]. The title story, however, is a moving account of Naftali who lived long ago in Poland, of his inordinate love of stories." Publ Wkly

The power of light; eight stories for Hanukkah; with illustrations by Irene Lieblich. Farrar, Straus & Giroux 1980 86p il hardcover o.p. paperback available $7.95 (4 and up)   **S C**

1. Hanukkah—Fiction 2. Jews—Fiction 3. Short stories
ISBN 0-374-45984-3 (pa)   LC 80-20263
Also available in paperback from Avon Bks.

"The stories, bound together by recurring Hanukkah motifs—the lamp, the dreidel, and the pancakes, tell chiefly of events affecting the lives of Eastern European Jews. Ranging from such somber happenings as the drafting of small Jewish boys to serve in the Russian army during the nineteenth century through the bombing and burning of the Warsaw ghetto, the harrowing events are seen in the context of the celebration of Hanukkah." Horn Book

"The stories vary from realism to incorporation of the miraculous . . . but are united in their strong piety as they are in the polished craftsmanship and warmth with which they are written." Bull Cent Child Books

Stories for children. Farrar, Straus & Giroux 1984 337p $22.95; pa $13 (4 and up)   **S C**

1. Jews—Fiction 2. Short stories
ISBN 0-374-37266-7; 0-374-46489-8 (pa)
LC 84-13612

This collection of thirty-six stories includes "parables, beast fables, allegories and reminiscences. Some stories are silly and charming, while others are wildly fantastic, dealing with savagery and miracles in mythical, medieval Poland. Frequently they are about scary situations, but all tend to end happily, with an edifying idea. Most appealing is the Nobel Prize winner's sheer story-telling power. In this respect, he has no equal among contemporaries." N Y Times Book Rev

Soto, Gary

Baseball in April, and other stories. Harcourt Brace Jovanovich 1990 111p $14.95; pa $4.95 (5 and up)   **S C**

1. Mexican Americans—Fiction 2. California—Fiction 3. Short stories
ISBN 0-15-205720-X; 0-15-205721-8 (pa)
LC 89-36460
Also available Spanish language edition

A collection of eleven short stories focusing on the everyday adventures of Hispanic young people growing up in Fresno, California

Each story "gets at the heart of some aspect of growing up. The insecurities, the embarrassments, the triumphs, the inequities of it all are chronicled with wit and charm. Soto's characters ring true and his knowledge of, and affection for, their shared Mexican-American heritage is obvious and infectious." Voice Youth Advocates

Where angels glide at dawn; new stories from Latin America; edited by Lori M. Carlson and Cynthia Ventura; introduction by Isabel Allende; illustrations by José Ortega. Lippincott 1990 114p il hardcover o.p. paperback available $3.95 (5 and up)   **S C**

1. Latin America—Fiction 2. Short stories
ISBN 0-06-440464-1 (pa)   LC 90-6697

"Tinged with the surreal quality of dreams and fairy tales, this collection of translated stories amplifies the richness of Latin American culture. Reflecting a history of social upheaval and political changes, the selections reveal the quiet wisdom and deep emotions of a strong, enduring people. . . . Bolstered by a glossary of terms and brief explanations of each entry's setting, these 10 tales are as accessible as they are intriguing." Publ Wkly

Wilde, Oscar, 1854-1900

The fairy tales of Oscar Wilde; illustrated by Isabelle Brent; edited with an introduction by Neil Philip. Viking 1994 141p il $19.99 (3-6)   **S C**

1. Fairy tales 2. Short stories
ISBN 0-670-85585-5
Also available an Everyman's library reissue of the 1888 edition with illustrations by Charles Robinson

"The stories were originally published as 'The Happy Prince and other Tales' (1888) and 'A House of Pomegranates' (1891)." Verso of title page

Wilder, Laura Ingalls, 1867-1957

A Little house Christmas; holiday stories from the Little house books; illustrated by Garth Williams. HarperCollins Pubs. 1994 89p il music $18.95; lib bdg $18.89; pa $8.95   **S C**

1. Christmas—Fiction 2. Frontier and pioneer life—Fiction 3. Family life—Fiction 4. Short stories
ISBN 0-06-024269-8; 0-06-024270-1 (lib bdg); 0-06-440615-6 (pa)   LC 93-24537

A collection of stories describing the experiences of a pioneer girl and her family as they celebrate various Christmases, selected from Little house in the big woods, Little house on the prairie, and On the banks of Plum Creek, entered in Fiction section

Wynne-Jones, Tim

The book of changes; stories. Orchard Bks. 1995 c1994 143p $14.95; lib bdg $14.99 (4 and up)   S C

1. Short stories

ISBN 0-531-09489-8; 0-531-08789-1 (lib bdg)
LC 95-6034

Also available in paperback from Penguin Bks.

"A Melanie Kroupa book"

First published 1994 in Canada

The stories "focus on what seem to be ordinary events: a frantic search for inspiration for a class project, a chance to appear a hero to a younger child, the tyranny of a class bully. Yet with his prowess for crafting each tale so that it neatly comes full circle, Wynne-Jones makes the quotidian well worth reading about. . . . The characters' on-target thoughts and banter attest to the author's familiarity with—and compassion for—today's kids." Publ Wkly

Some of the kinder planets: stories. Orchard Bks. 1995 c1993 130p $14.95; lib bdg $14.99 (4 and up)   S C

1. Short stories

ISBN 0-531-09451-0; 0-531-08751-4 (lib bdg)
LC 94-33009

First published 1993 in Canada

"This collection of nine short stories offers offbeat vignettes of contemporary life as well as tales of ghosts, aliens, and historical figures. Clear writing combines with clever concepts and varied subject matter to make the book accessible and enjoyable to a wide audience." SLJ

Yee, Paul

Tales from Gold Mountain; stories of the Chinese in the New World; paintings by Simon Ng. Macmillan 1989 64p il $15.95 (4 and up)   S C

1. Chinese—North America—Fiction 2. Short stories

ISBN 0-02-793621-X   LC 89-12643

"The eight stories in this collection are . . . rooted in the real experiences of the Chinese who came to North America seeking the prosperity of Gold Mountain. Though Mr. Yee has drawn on tales he heard growing up in Vancouver's Chinatown and on research into the lives of the Chinese who settled in Canada, the stories contain many parallels with the experiences of the Chinese in the United States." Horn Book

These "brief, pithy tales strikingly reflect traditional Chinese beliefs and customs in new world circumstances. . . . Romance, family loyalty, and justice are important themes, and an element of surprise is never far away. Ng's cool, brooding full-page paintings have an intense presence that enhances the stories' exotic flavor." Booklist

E   Easy Books

This section consists chiefly of fiction books that would interest children from pre-school through third grade. Easy books that have a definite nonfiction subject content are usually classified with other nonfiction books. Easy books listed here include:
1. Picture books, whether fiction or nonfiction, that the young child can use independently
2. Fiction books with very little or scattered text, with large print and with vocabulary suitable for children with reading levels of grades 1-3
3. Picture storybooks with a larger amount of text to be used primarily by or with children in pre-school through grade 3

Ackerman, Karen, 1951-

By the dawn's early light; illustrated by Catherine Stock. Atheneum Pubs. 1994 unp il $14.95   E

1. Mothers—Fiction   2. Factories—Fiction
3. Grandmothers—Fiction

ISBN 0-689-31788-3   LC 92-35633

Also available Spanish language edition

Rachel and Josh stay with their grandmother while their mother works at night in a factory

"Told from the eight or nine-year-old daughter's perspective, the text is honest without being maudlin or bitter. . . . Warm, often impressionistic watercolor illustrations accurately convey the misty, wee-small hour setting as well as the glow of family relationships. Characters are predominantly African-American females." SLJ

Song and dance man; illustrated by Stephen Gammell. Knopf 1988 unp il $15; lib bdg $15.99; pa $5.99   E

1. Entertainers—Fiction 2. Grandfathers—Fiction

ISBN 0-394-89330-1; 0-394-99330-6 (lib bdg); 0-679-81995-9 (pa)   LC 87-3200

Awarded the Caldecott Medal, 1989

"Grandpa takes three grandchildren up to the attic, where he arranges lights and gives a performance that enchants his audience. They tell him they wish they could have seen him dance in 'the good old days' but he says he wouldn't trade a million good old days for the time he spends with the narrators." Bull Cent Child Books

The illustrator "captures all the story's inherent joie de vivre with color pencil renderings that fairly leap off the pages." Booklist

Adams, Adrienne

The Easter egg artists. Scribner 1976 unp il $13.95; pa $4.95   E

1. Rabbits—Fiction   2. Easter—Fiction   3. Egg decoration—Fiction

ISBN 0-684-14652-5; 0-684-71481-5 (pa)

"The Abbotts, rabbits who design Easter Eggs, are worried that son Orson will not follow the family trade. On a winter vacation Orson and the family paint a car, a house, an airplane, a bridge, and Orson becomes a committed Easter Egg Artist. Children rated this charming story with its lovely illustrations one of the most beautiful picture books of the year." Read Teach

Adoff, Arnold, 1935-

Black is brown is tan; pictures by Emily Arnold McCully. Harper & Row 1973 31p il $15; lib bdg $14.89; pa $3.25　　E

1. Stories in rhyme 2. Family life—Fiction 3. Race relations—Fiction
ISBN 0-06-020083-9; 0-06-020084-7 (lib bdg); 0-06-443269-6 (pa)

This story in rhyme describes "a warm, racially-mixed family who reads, cuts wood, plays, and eats together." Booklist

"Arnold Adoff's spare free verse combines familiar images in a startling original way . . . and Emily McCully's beautiful watercolors are radiant with feeling and life." SLJ

Agee, Jon

The incredible painting of Felix Clousseau. Farrar, Straus & Giroux 1988 unp il $15; pa $4.95　　E

ISBN 0-374-33633-4; 0-374-43582-0 (pa)
LC 87-046072

"When the Royal Palace holds a competition, Clousseau . . . is ridiculed for his simple painting of a duck—until it goes 'QUACK!' and walks out of the frame. . . . Suddenly Paris is agog, all of the man's paintings are coming alive." Booklist

"A well-defined drawing style is enhanced by dark, rich colors, thickly and boldly applied. Agee provides much food for the spirit with his spare storytelling and distinctive artwork." Publ Wkly

Ahlberg, Janet

The baby's catalogue; [by] Janet and Allan Ahlberg. Little, Brown 1982 unp il $15.95; pa $5.95　　E

1. Infants—Fiction 2. Vocabulary
ISBN 0-316-02037-0; 0-316-02038-9 (pa)
LC 82-9928

"An Atlantic Monthly press book"

"Titles and labels are the only print on the pages of a book that begins with a page headed 'Babies' and goes through the objects and activities and people that most babies see on a typical day. There are Moms, Dads, brothers and sisters, toys, high chairs, diapers, meals, books, baths, bedtimes, etc. The softly colored paintings are cheerful and amusing, the format is clean and uncluttered, and the whole should provide hours of pointing, identification, and naming." Bull Cent Child Books

Each peach pear plum; an 'I spy' story; [by] Janet and Allan Ahlberg. Viking 1979 c1978 unp il $12.95; pa $3.99　　E

1. Stories in rhyme
ISBN 0-670-28705-9; 0-14-050639-X (pa)
LC 78-16726

First published 1978 in the United Kingdom

This book "invites children to play 'I spy' and point out nursery rhyme and story characters such as Jack and Jill, the Three Bears, Cinderella, etc. who are semi-hidden within . . . [the] illustrations." SLJ

The characters hide "in a pleasant, rural, watercolor world that's decorative but never precious or self-regarding. This is a lovely small book, well-conceived and very well drawn, gentle, humorous, unsentimental." N Y Times Book Rev

Funnybones; [by] Janet and Allan Ahlberg. Greenwillow Bks. 1981 c1980 unp il $15; lib bdg $14.93; pa $3.95　　E

1. Skeleton—Fiction
ISBN 0-688-80238-9; 0-688-84238-0 (lib bdg); 0-688-09927-0 (pa)

Three skeletons—a grown-up, a child, and a dog—live in a dark cellar. They wake one night and decide "to go out and frighten someone, and though no one is in the park, the adult and child skeletons have a good time on the swings." SLJ

"What happens in the story is of less importance than the basic situation and the way in which the story's told, in a book in comic strip format. . . . The Ahlbergs have fun with words and with the concept of skeletons at play, and their communicable zest precludes any note of the macabre." Bull Cent Child Books

Other available titles about the three skeletons, written by Allan Ahlberg, are:
The black cat (1990)
Dinosaur dreams (1991)
The ghost train (1992)
Mystery tour (1991)
The pet shop (1990)
Skeleton crew (1992)

Peek-a-boo! by Janet & Allan Ahlberg. Viking 1981 unp il $11.95; pa $4.99　　E

1. Infants—Fiction 2. Family life—Fiction 3. Stories in rhyme
ISBN 0-670-54598-8; 0-670-82383-9 (pa)

Published in the United Kingdom with title: Peepo!

Brief rhyming clues invite the reader to look through holes in the pages for a baby's view of the world from breakfast to bedtime

"Perfectly tuned for a first-book experience. . . . The full-color paintings reveal a reassuringly disorganized but loving family in pastel-framed scenes that feature tiny familiar objects as part of the border." Booklist

Alexander, Lloyd

The fortune-tellers; illustrated by Trina Schart Hyman. Dutton Children's Bks. 1992 unp il $15.99　　E

1. Fortune telling—Fiction 2. Cameroon—Fiction
ISBN 0-525-44849-7
LC 91-30684

A carpenter goes to a fortune teller and finds the predictions about his future coming true in an unusual way

"Alexander's rags-to-riches story combines universal elements of the trickster character and the cumulative disaster tale. Hyman's pictures set it all in a vibrant community in Cameroon, West Africa. . . . The energetic, brilliantly colored paintings are packed with people and objects that swirl around the main characters. . . . With its ups and downs, this is a funny, playful story that evokes the irony of the human condition." Booklist

Alexander, Martha G.

How my library grew, by Dinah; story and pictures by Martha Alexander. Wilson, H.W. 1983 unp il $18　　E

1. Libraries—Fiction
ISBN 0-8242-0679-7
LC 82-20204

"Told through the eyes of a young girl talking to her stuffed friend, Teddy, this softly colored, child-like story describes a library being built across the street. Through the seasons, Dinah and Teddy watch a hole being dug and the building going up; they wonder about its use and delight in

Alexander, Martha G.—*Continued*
designing a surprise for opening day. . . . Small vignettes, often grouped two or three to a page, enticingly depict the library's construction and open-for-business scenes, making the library a very inviting and stimulating place to be." Booklist

Nobody asked me if I wanted a baby sister; story and pictures by Martha Alexander. Dial Bks. for Young Readers 1971 unp il hardcover o.p. paperback available $3.95   E
1. Brothers and sisters—Fiction 2. Infants—Fiction
ISBN 0-8037-6410-3 (pa)
"Jealous of the fuss made over his baby sister, Oliver bundles Bonnie into his wagon and, wheeling her around the neighborhood, tries to give her away. He changes his mind, however, and decides to keep her when the baby, unhappy at being held by strangers, cries until he takes her." Booklist
"Not a brand-new theme, but pictures and text together make a charming variation, the precise little drawings affectionate and humorous, the writing ingenious and direct." Bull Cent Child Books

When the new baby comes, I'm moving out; story and pictures by Martha Alexander. Dial Bks. for Young Readers 1979 unp il hardcover o.p. paperback available $3.99   E
1. Brothers and sisters—Fiction 2. Infants—Fiction
ISBN 0-1405-4723-1 (pa)   LC 79-4275
"Although this is a companion to 'Nobody asked me if I wanted a baby sister,' the action precedes the first book in that the object of Oliver's sibling jealousy hasn't been born yet. Mom is due any day and Oliver is feeling hostile. So hostile in fact, that he fantasizes stuffing his pregnant mother into a garbage can and taking it to the dump." SLJ
"The clean, small-scale pictures echo the warmth and humor of the story." Bull Cent Child Books

You're a genius, Blackboard Bear; [by] Martha Alexander. Candlewick Press 1995 unp il $12.95   E
1. Space flight to the moon—Fiction 2. Bears—Fiction
ISBN 1-56402-238-2   LC 94-11060
Blackboard Bear helps a small boy build a spaceship for a trip to the moon, but when the boy packs so many supplies that there is no room for him, the bear goes alone
"Spare text and soft, pastel watercolor illustrations add just the right touch to this tale of fantasy and friendship. A story that will delight young listeners." SLJ
Other available titles about Blackboard Bear are:
Blackboard Bear (1969)
I sure am glad to see you, Blackboard Bear (1976)

Aliki
Overnight at Mary Bloom's. Greenwillow Bks. 1987 unp il $15; lib bdg $14.93   E
1. Friendship—Fiction 2. Night—Fiction
ISBN 0-688-06764-6; 0-688-06765-4 (lib bdg)
LC 86-7719
"'Come spend the night,' says Mary Bloom to her young friend, and the excited child packs her bags as quickly as she can." Booklist
"A visit with Mary Bloom is a kid's idea of adventure, creative play and independence. Aliki's . . . technique of full color with ink outline conveys the fun and excitement of every kid's sleepover dream." Publ Wkly
Another available title about Mary Bloom is:
At Mary Bloom's (1976)

The two of them; written and illustrated by Aliki. Greenwillow Bks. 1979 unp il $16.95; lib bdg $15.93; pa $4.95   E
1. Grandfathers—Fiction 2. Death—Fiction
ISBN 0-688-80225-7; 0-688-84225-9 (lib bdg); 0-688-07337-9 (pa)   LC 79-10161
Describes the relationship of a grandfather and his granddaughter from her birth to his death
"The eloquent illustrations in muted full color and the smaller soft-pencil drawings show the life the two shared as well as the tenderness and pure pleasure implicit in their relationship. . . . The book transcends the labored introductions to geriatrics which have proliferated in contemporary children's literature and describes with sensitivity and truth the changing seasons of human life." Horn Book

Use your head, dear. Greenwillow Bks. 1983 unp il $15; lib bdg $13.93   E
1. Alligators—Fiction
ISBN 0-688-01811-4; 0-688-01812-2 (lib bdg)
LC 82-11911
Charles, a young alligator, means well, but gets things mixed up until his father gives him an invisible thinking cap for his birthday
"Both text and illustrations are notable for the care with which they develop the thoroughly childlike story. The words are fresh and funny, precise complements for expressive line drawings highlighted by the authoritative green shapes of the alligator characters and by the quarter-inch borders defining each double-page spread." Horn Book

We are best friends. Greenwillow Bks. 1982 unp il $16; lib bdg $15.93; pa $3.95   E
1. Friendship—Fiction
ISBN 0-688-00822-4; 0-688-00823-2 (lib bdg); 0-688-07037-X (pa)   LC 81-6549
When Robert's best friend Peter moves away, both are unhappy, but they learn that they can make new friends and still remain best friends
"Brightly lit pictures in cheerful primary colors portray with just a stroke of the pen the misery of losing a friend who must move away and the tentative beginnings of a new companionship. . . . Details of school and home abound in the lively pictures." Horn Book

Welcome, little baby. Greenwillow Bks. 1987 unp il $15; lib bdg $13.93   E
1. Infants—Fiction 2. Mothers—Fiction
ISBN 0-688-06810-3; 0-688-06811-1 (lib bdg)
LC 86-7648
A mother welcomes her newborn infant, and tells what life will be like as the child grows older
"Tender pictures in pastel colors are appropriate for a minimal text, not substantial but effective in its message of love." Bull Cent Child Books

Allard, Harry, 1928-
Bumps in the night; pictures by James Marshall. Doubleday 1979 32p il o.p.; Bantam Bks. paperback available $3.25   E
1. Ghost stories 2. Animals—Fiction
ISBN 0-553-15711-6 (pa)   LC 78-22301
"Dudley the Stork hears noises in his house at night and encounters a ghost. In order to find out what the ghost wants, Dudley and his friends have Madam Kreepy hold a seance. The story is humorous and spooky. The illustrations show us an unusual assortment of characters and add to the story line." Children's Bk Rev Serv

Allard, Harry, 1928— *Continued*

Miss Nelson is missing! [by] Harry Allard, James Marshall. Houghton Mifflin 1977 32p il $14.95; pa $4.95   E

1. School stories 2. Teachers—Fiction
ISBN 0-395-25296-2; 0-395-40146-1 (pa)
                   LC 76-55918

Illustrated by James Marshall

"The kids in room 207 were so fresh and naughty that they lost their sweet-natured teacher, the blonde Miss Nelson, and got in her place the sour-souled Miss Swamp." N Y Times Book Rev

"Humor and suspense fill the pages of [this book]." Christ Sci Monit

Other available titles about Miss Nelson are:
Miss Nelson has a field day (1985)
Miss Nelson is back (1982)

Andrews, Jan, 1942-

Very last first time; illustrated by Ian Wallace. Atheneum Pubs. 1986 unp il lib bdg $16   E

1. Inuit—Fiction
ISBN 0-689-50388-1   LC 85-71606
"A Margaret K. McElderry book"

"In her Inuit village in northern Canada, Eva Padlyat prepares to 'walk on the bottom of the sea' alone for the first time. For years, after the tide goes out, she and her mother have gone under the ice to collect mussels, but doing it by herself is a rite of passage that becomes a mini-adventure. . . . The paintings, dominated by deep purple glinting here and there with gold or green, are impressionistic in texture and give an eerie sense of the shadowy shapes, crevasses, and sense of isolation surrounding the child." Bull Cent Child Books

Anno, Mitsumasa, 1926-

Anno's alphabet; an adventure in imagination. Crowell 1975 c1974 unp il $16; lib bdg $15.89; pa $7.95   E

1. Alphabet
ISBN 0-690-00540-7; 0-690-00541-5 (lib bdg); 0-06-443190-8 (pa)

"In this unusual alphabet book, large letters, painted to look like carved wood, have a three-dimensional, optically challenging appearance. Borders, embellished with plants and hidden creatures, surround the pictured letters and objects." LC. Child Books, 1975

Anno's counting book. Crowell 1977 c1975 unp il $16; lib bdg $15.89; pa $5.95   E

1. Counting 2. Seasons—Fiction 3. Stories without words
ISBN 0-690-01287-X; 0-690-01288-8 (lib bdg); 0-06-443123-1 (pa)   LC 76-28977
Original Japanese edition, 1975

"A distinctive, beautifully conceived counting book in which twelve full-color doublespreads show the same village and surrounding countryside during different hours (by the church clock) and months. Both the seasons and community changes are studied, as such components of the scene as flowers, trees, animals, people, and buildings increase from one to twelve." LC. Child Books, 1977

Anno's counting house. Philomel Bks. 1982 unp il $16.95   E

1. Counting 2. Moving—Fiction 3. Stories without words
ISBN 0-399-20896-8   LC 82-617

One by one, ten children move from their old house into their new house with all their possessions. Die-cut windows reveal the interiors of the houses and the book can also be read from back to front

"The paintings are precisely and beautifully detailed, and the book has a game element that should appeal to children although the initial interest may depend on guidance. A note to adults is appended, discussing the fostering of mathematical concepts in the early years." Bull Cent Child Books

Anno's journey. Philomel Bks. 1981 c1977 unp il $15.95   E

1. Europe—Pictorial works 2. Stories without words
ISBN 0-399-20762-7

Original Japanese edition, 1977; first United States edition published 1978 by Collins

"In a panorama which unrolls wordlessly, a traveler rides horseback over a landscape that seems distinctly European, shown in meticulously detailed illustrations of everyday life, artifacts, and architecture." Horn Book

"Most children will need the help of informed adults to decipher the puzzles. But even beginners should enjoy turning the pages of an exceptional book and responding to the beauties depicted." Publ Wkly

Anno's U.S.A. Philomel Bks. 1983 unp il $16.95; pa $7.95   E

1. United States—Pictorial works 2. Stories without words
ISBN 0-399-20974-3; 0-399-21595-6 (pa)
                   LC 83-13107

In wordless panoramas a lone traveler approaches the New World from the West in the present day and journeys the width of the country backward through time, departing the east coast as the Santa Maria appears over the horizon

"Anno deliberately mixes costumes, vehicles, and other representations of various periods in the handsome double-page spreads that are beautifully composed; his use of color and perspective are admirable; his command of architectural drawing is impressive. What may appeal most to readers, however, are the small visual jokes that enliven the pages." Bull Cent Child Books

Appelt, Kathi, 1954-

Bayou lullaby; pictures by Neil Waldman. Morrow Junior Bks. 1995 unp il $16; lib bdg $15.93   E

1. Lullabies 2. Stories in rhyme
ISBN 0-688-12856-4; 0-688-12857-2 (lib bdg)
                   LC 94-16639

This is "a rhythmic, soothing lullaby for a little girl who lives in a house by the banks of the bayou. . . . The verse is evocative and lovely, but the true merit of the book lies in Waldman's double-page acrylic paintings. Each scene is a self-contained work of art and a visual feast. He has set the swamp's luminous flora and fauna against a velvety black background, and richly fluorescent shades of greens, purples, blues, and teals decorate the pages." SLJ

Armstrong, Jennifer, 1961-

Chin Yu Min and the ginger cat; illustrated by Mary Grandpré. Crown 1993 unp il $15; lib bdg $15.99; pa $5.99 **E**

1. China—Fiction 2. Cats—Fiction
ISBN 0-517-58656-8; 0-517-58657-6 (lib bdg); 0-517-88549-2 (pa) LC 92-8658

Through her friendship with a ginger cat, a haughty Chinese widow learns to be humble and to provide for herself
"The rich, graceful text is complemented by Grandpré's stylish, cinematic illustrations. The use of dramatic lighting and unusual perspective lends an animated look to the characters, who act in a vibrant landscape saturated with brilliant colors." Booklist

Arnosky, Jim

Deer at the brook. Lothrop, Lee & Shepard Bks. 1986 unp il $16; lib bdg $15.93; pa $4.95 **E**

1. Deer
ISBN 0-688-04099-3; 0-688-04100-0 (lib bdg); 0-688-10488-6 (pa) LC 84-12239

The "illustrations are everything here, amplifying the sparest of texts with dramatic scenes of deer coming to a woodland brook to drink, eat, play, and nap. The full-color pictures are soft and compelling, focusing on a doe and her two fawns, which are masterfully drawn and imbued with nearly as much presence as real-life creatures would have. Other wildlife are artistically integrated into the drawings." Booklist

Every autumn comes the bear. Putnam 1993 unp il $15.95 **E**

1. Bears
ISBN 0-399-22508-0 LC 92-30515

Every autumn a bear shows up behind the farm, and goes through a series of routines before finding a den among the hilltop boulders where he sleeps all winter long
"The lean, powerful text uses an intimate, conversational tone. . . . Each of the full-page watercolors is vibrant, translucent and strikingly composed." Publ Wkly

Raccoons and ripe corn. Lothrop, Lee & Shepard Bks. 1987 unp il $16; lib bdg $12.88; pa $4.95 **E**

1. Raccoons
ISBN 0-688-05455-2; 0-688-05456-0 (lib bdg); 0-688-10489-4 (pa) LC 87-4243

"A mother raccoon and two older kits come in autumn dusk to a farmer's field, enjoy a star-lit romp and feed, then skulk off at dawn. A trail of fall leaves across the title pages leads to 11 double-spreads of open pencil sketches and color washes of woods and farm." SLJ
"Arnosky's pictures have a way of making nature larger than life. His raccoons are a strong focus of attention, and the hushed nighttime mood is almost palpable. The nature lesson implicit in the depicted episode is not romantic; these raccoons are greedy and somewhat destructive." Booklist

Aruego, Jose

Look what I can do. Scribner 1971 unp il o.p. paperback available $3.95 **E**

1. Water buffalo—Fiction
ISBN 0-689-71205-7 (pa)

"The story of two carabaos who get carried away trying to outdo each other and almost come to a sad end." Booklist
"There are just fifteen words in this story . . . whose valuable message should be intelligible to the young nonreader. . . . Sprightly, cartoon-like drawings are the focal point." Book World

We hide, you seek; by Jose Aruego and Ariane Dewey. Greenwillow Bks. 1979 unp il $14.95; lib bdg $15.93; pa $4.95 **E**

1. Camouflage (Biology)—Fiction
ISBN 0-688-80201-X; 0-688-84201-1 (lib bdg); 0-688-07815-X (pa) LC 78-13638

"An oafishly good-natured rhino, invited into a junglewide game of hide and seek, bumbles from one scene to the next, accidentally exposing would-be hiders (leopards, crocodiles, lions) at every stop; then turning the tables on his playmates, cleverly hides himself. Readers are served up a wealth of information in 27 words (plus end-papers that give a page-by-page identification of the species pictured) and droll scenes drenched in the vibrant tones of an East African palette." SLJ

Asch, Frank

Sand cake; a Frank Asch bear story. Parents Mag. Press 1979 c1978 unp il $5.95; lib bdg $5.95 **E**

1. Bears—Fiction 2. Beaches—Fiction 3. Fathers and sons—Fiction
ISBN 0-8193-0985-0; 0-8193-0986-9 (lib bdg) LC 78-11183

Also available in paperback from Grosset & Dunlap
Papa Bear uses his culinary skills and a little imagination to concoct a sand cake
Other available titles about Baby Bear and his family are:
Bread and honey (1982)
Goodbye house (1985)
Just like Daddy (1981)
Milk and cookies (1982)
Other available titles about a similar looking character called Bear are:
Bear shadow (1985)
Bear's bargain (1985)
Happy birthday, Moon (1982)
Mooncake (1983)
Moongame (1984)
Popcorn (1979)
Skyfire (1984)

Auch, Mary Jane

Peeping Beauty; written and illustrated by Mary Jane Auch. Holiday House 1993 unp il $15.95; pa $6.95 **E**

1. Chickens—Fiction 2. Foxes—Fiction 3. Ballet—Fiction
ISBN 0-8234-1001-3; 0-8234-1170-2 (pa) LC 92-16374

Poulette the dancing hen falls into the clutches of a hungry fox, who exploits her desire to become a great ballerina
"The language is lively, and filled with witty phrases and ballet references. Using bright colors and just enough detail, Auch sets her cast of characters against a simple backdrop." SLJ

Aylesworth, Jim, 1943-

Country crossing; illustrated by Ted Rand. Atheneum Pubs. 1991 unp il $13.95; pa $4.95

E

1. Railroads—Fiction 2. Night—Fiction

ISBN 0-689-31580-5; 0-689-71895-0 (pa)

LC 89-78184

Recreates the sights and sounds at a country crossing one summer night, as an old car patiently awaits the passing of a long and noisy freight train

"Times past are evoked in a combination of onomatopoeic text and richly hued illustrations. . . . The effect of text and pictures is powerful—as close as one can come to total sensory involvement through the pages of a book." Horn Book

My son John; woodcuts by David Frampton. Holt & Co. 1994 unp il $15.95

E

1. Nursery rhymes

ISBN 0-8050-1725-9   LC 92-27192

"In the tradition of 'Diddle Diddle Dumpling, My Son John.' Aylesworth offers 14 new verses." Booklist

"This book is a feast for the eyes and ears. Aylesworth amplifies the simple nursery classic with a rainbow of rich, descriptive verses on additional names, evoking all of the five senses in the process. The rhymes are enhanced by an exceptional layout using brilliant woodcuts done with brightly colored oils." SLJ

Old black fly; illustrations by by Stephen Gammell. Holt & Co. 1992 unp il $19.95; pa $5.95

E

1. Flies—Fiction 2. Alphabet 3. Stories in rhyme

ISBN 0-8050-1401-2; 0-8050-3924-4 (pa)

LC 91-26825

Rhyming text and illustrations follow a mischievous old black fly through the alphabet as he has a very busy bad day landing where he should not be

"Ayleworth's snappy couplets constitute a waggish presentation of a basic concept. . . . Gammell's paintings are exuberant splashes of mayhem—rainbows of splattered hues from which truly memorable characters emerge. His appropriately bug-eyed (and cross-eyed) fly and gap-toothed humans sporting crazy hairdos provide a level of dementia that children will relish." Publ Wkly

One crow; a counting rhyme; illustrated by Ruth Young. Lippincott 1988 unp il o.p.; HarperCollins Pubs. paperback available $5.95

E

1. Counting 2. Animals—Fiction 3. Stories in rhyme

ISBN 0-06-443242-4 (pa)   LC 85-45856

"Simple four-line counting rhymes from one to ten (zero's there, too, but without a verse) take readers on a morning-to-night barnyard tour twice, once for a sunny summer day and once for a cold, snowy winter day. The first two lines of each quatrain focus on the animals representing the given number, while the second two comment on some aspect of nature in the setting. . . . The clear colors, clean line, and open composition of the illustrations convey a cheerful mood that's in keeping with the text." SLJ

Azarian, Mary

A farmer's alphabet. Godine 1981 61p il $16.95; pa $12.95

E

1. Alphabet 2. Farm life—Fiction

ISBN 0-87923-394-X; 0-87923-397-4 (pa)

LC 80-84938

"Large, bold woodcuts make up an album of farming scenes obviously from New England—for example, 'M' is for maple sugar. A few scenes look cold and stern—showing winter and icicles—but there are children jumping in hay and flying a kite as well as . . . 'N' for neighbor and 'G' for a garden bursting with vegetables." Horn Book

Babbitt, Natalie

Nellie: a cat on her own; story and pictures by Natalie Babbitt. Farrar, Straus & Giroux 1989 unp il $14; pa $4.95

E

1. Cats—Fiction

ISBN 0-374-35506-1; 0-374-45496-5 (pa)

LC 89-61248

"Michael Di Capua books"

"Nellie is a marionette who can only dance when the old woman pulls her strings. Big Tom is a real cat who dashes in and out at all times leaving Nellie to wonder where he goes. When the old woman dies, Tom leads Nellie into the world to meet his friends. She becomes inspired to learn to dance in the moonshine by herself." Child Book Rev Serv

"This tale of independence achieved, certainly the epitome of catlike behavior, is enhanced by delicate watercolors of the dubious Nellie and competent Big Tom. A small tale, charmingly rendered." Horn Book

Babcock, Chris, 1963-

No moon, no milk! illustrated by Mark Teague. Crown 1993 unp il hardcover o.p. paperback available $5.99

E

1. Cattle—Fiction 2. Moon—Fiction

ISBN 0-517-88540-9 (pa)   LC 92-40697

Martha the cow refuses to give milk until she can visit the moon like her great-great-grandmother before her, the Cow Who Jumped Over the Moon

"Teague's ebullient artwork captures a very determined cow in a variety of decidedly uncowlike settings, and he illustrates all the settings with humor and panache." Booklist

Baker, Jeannie

Home in the sky; story and pictures by Jeannie Baker. Greenwillow Bks. 1984 unp il $13; lib bdg $11.96

E

1. Pigeons—Fiction 2. New York (N.Y.)—Fiction

ISBN 0-688-03841-7; 0-688-03842-5 (lib bdg)

LC 83-25379

Also available in paperback from Scholastic

"The story of a day in the life of a New York City pigeon recounts his trauma as he faces the perils of the weather and the subway system before being united with the gentle Black man who feeds him. . . . The illustrations are utterly fascinating. Made of such items as grasses, leaves, pigeon feathers, fabric, and human hair and then painted, these collage constructions give an incredible feeling of three dimensions to the two-dimensional surface of the page." Horn Book

Baker, Jeannie—*Continued*

Where the forest meets the sea; story and pictures by Jeannie Baker. Greenwillow Bks. 1988 c1987 unp il $16; lib bdg $15.93   E

1. Australia—Fiction 2. Rain forests—Fiction
ISBN 0-688-06363-2; 0-688-06364-0 (lib bdg)
LC 87-7551

Also available in paperback from Scholastic
First published 1987 in the United Kingdom

On a camping trip in an Australian rain forest with his father, a young boy thinks about the history of the plant and animal life around him and wonders about their future

The illustrations "are relief collages 'constructed from a multitude of materials, including modeling clay, papers, textured materials, preserved natural materials, and paints.' Integrated by the artist's vision, the collages create three-dimensional effects on two-dimensional pages drawing the reader into each scene as willing observer and explorer." Horn Book

Window. Greenwillow Bks. 1991 unp il $16; lib bdg $13.93   E

1. Stories without words 2. Human ecology—Fiction 3. Australia—Fiction
ISBN 0-688-08917-8; 0-688-08918-6 (lib bdg)
LC 90-3922

Also available in paperback from Puffin Bks.

"The story in this wordless book is told through the outdoor scene viewed over time from one child's bedroom window. Initially, a mother holding her infant son gazes out at the lush Australian bush; as the boy gets older, civilization swallows up the wilderness." Horn Book Guide

"Filled with marvelous detail, the textured collages make an affecting statement about the erosion of the planet Earth." SLJ

Baker, Keith, 1953-

The magic fan; written and illustrated by Keith Baker. Harcourt Brace Jovanovich 1989 unp il $14.95; pa $5   E

1. Japan—Fiction
ISBN 0-15-250750-7; 0-15-200983-3 (pa)
LC 88-18727

Despite the laughter of his fellow villagers, Yoshi uses his building skills to make a boat to catch the moon, a kite to reach the clouds, and a bridge that mimics the rainbow

"The artwork, acrylics on illustration board, is framed within the outline of an open fan. The text appears outside this frame, and fan-shaped die-cuts allow the reader to turn the inner page and see a second picture on each double-page spread. . . . An entertaining tale as well as an elegant addition to the picture-book shelf." Booklist

Balian, Lorna

Humbug witch. Abingdon Press 1965 unp il o.p.; Humbug Bks. reprint available $12.95   E

1. Witches—Fiction
ISBN 1-881772-24-1

This book is about "a little witch and her unsuccessful attempts at witchcraft. One evening she wearily takes off piece after piece of comical attire—the last of which proves to be a mask, revealing a hilarious little girl underneath! Too good to miss." Adventuring with Books. 2d edition

Bang, Molly, 1943-

The Grey Lady and the Strawberry Snatcher. Four Winds Press 1980 unp il $14.95   E

1. Strawberries—Fiction 2. Stories without words
ISBN 0-02-708140-0
LC 79-21243

A Caldecott Medal honor book, 1981

The strawberry snatcher tries to wrest the strawberries from the grey lady but as he follows her through shops and woods he discovers some delicious blackberries instead

"Bang's illustrations are unparalleled in effects, full-color paintings and collages in which the surrealistic and the representational combine to tell a story without words." Publ Wkly

The paper crane. Greenwillow Bks. 1985 unp il $16; lib bdg $15.93; pa $4.95   E

ISBN 0-688-04108-6; 0-688-04109-4 (lib bdg); 0-688-07333-6 (pa)
LC 84-13346

"Bang gives a modern setting and details to the consoling story of a good man, deprived by unlucky fate of his livelihood, whose act of kindness and generosity is repaid by the restoration of his fortunes, through the bringing to life of a magical animal—the paper crane." SLJ

"Every detail of the restaurant interior, from the strawberries on the cake to the floral centerpieces, is a delight to the eye and imagination. . . . The book successfully blends Asian folklore themes with contemporary Western characterization." Horn Book

Ten, nine, eight. Greenwillow Bks. 1983 unp il $16; lib bdg $15.93; pa $4.95   E

1. Lullabies 2. Counting
ISBN 0-688-00906-9; 0-688-00907-7 (lib bdg); 0-688-10480-0 (pa)
LC 81-20106

A Caldecott Medal honor book, 1984

"In countdown style, the text of this counting book begins with '10 small toes all washed and warm,' and ends with '1 big girl all ready for bed.' The captions rhyme . . . and the pictures—warm, bright paintings—show a black father and child snuggling in a chair, the child yawning, and the child hugging her toy bear after some loving good night kisses." Bull Cent Child Books

Bányai, István, 1949-

Zoom. Viking 1995 unp il $13.99   E

1. Stories without words
ISBN 0-670-85804-8
LC 94-33181

A wordless picture book presents a series of scenes, each one from farther away, showing, for example, a girl playing with toys which is actually a picture on a magazine cover, which is part of a sign on a bus, and so on

"If the concept is not wholly new, the execution is superior. Readers are in for a perpetually surprising—and even philosophical—adventure." Publ Wkly

Barber, Antonia, 1932-

Gemma and the baby chick; written by Antonia Barber; illustrated by Karin Littlewood. Scholastic 1993 c1992 unp il $14.95   E

1. Eggs—Fiction 2. Chickens—Fiction 3. Farm life—Fiction
ISBN 0-590-45479-X
LC 91-36550

First published 1992 in the United Kingdom with title: Gemma and the broody hen

Barber, Antonia, 1932-—*Continued*

Gemma, who collects eggs from the hen house, discovers a hen sitting on her eggs and helps save a chick that is slow to hatch

"Barber's direct yet warm text demonstrates a keen awareness of a child's perspective. . . . Littlewood's soft, soothing watercolors are in close accord." Publ Wkly

The Mousehole cat; illustrated by Nicola Bayley. Macmillan 1990 unp il $14.95   E

1. Cats—Fiction 2. Sea stories

ISBN 0-02-708331-4   LC 90-31533

Also available Spanish language edition

"In the village of Mowzel lives a proud, determined cat named Mowzer. Her 'pet' is an old fisherman who provides her with succulent fresh fish. When the Storm Cat blocks the village, Tom and Mowzer venture forth anyhow. Mowzer's eloquent purring tames the ferocious giant and enables Tom to pull in a boat-load of fish." Child Book Rev Serv

"This delicate, charming tale and the exquisite illustrations of stormy seas, gleaming fish, and delightful cats and townspeople make an extremely handsome book, splendid for reading aloud." Horn Book

Barber, Barbara E., 1943-

Saturday at The New You; illustrated by Anna Rich. Lee & Low Bks. 1994 unp il $14.95   E

1. African Americans—Fiction 2. Mothers and daughters—Fiction 3. Beauty shops—Fiction

ISBN 1-880000-06-7   LC 93-5165

Shauna, a young African American girl, wishes she could do more to help Momma with the customers at her beauty salon. Then one day she gets her chance

"Rich's paintings are just right, matching the warm story with warm, soft colors, and the depiction of the African-American cast has an expansive spirit." Bull Cent Child Books

Barracca, Debra

The adventures of Taxi Dog; by Debra and Sal Barracca; pictures by Mark Buehner. Dial Bks. for Young Readers 1990 30p il $14.99; lib bdg $12.89   E

1. Dogs—Fiction 2. Stories in rhyme

ISBN 0-8037-0671-5; 0-8037-0672-3 (lib bdg)

LC 89-1056

"In snappy, rhymed lines, Maxi recalls his days as a stray and his adoption by taxi-driving Jim. Applying oil paint over acrylics, Buehner creates color with lush character. The hues' intense depth, coupled with the artist's finesse with perspective, will draw readers into the action." Booklist

Other available titles about Maxi, the Taxi Dog are:

Maxi, the hero (1991)
Maxi, the star (1993)
A Taxi Dog Christmas (1994)

Barrett, Judi, 1941-

Benjamin's 365 birthdays; written by Judi Barrett and drawn by Ron Barrett. Atheneum Pubs. 1974 unp il $13.95; pa $4.95   E

1. Birthdays—Fiction

ISBN 0-689-31791-3; 0-689-71635-4 (pa)

"Benjamin loves birthdays so much that the thought of waiting a whole year after his ninth till his next one makes

him weep and then inspires him to rewrap his presents, one each day, and go on to wrap everything in his house." Booklist

Benjamin's "solution to prolonging pleasure will amuse preschoolers familiar with post-party blues. . . . The theme is familiar, but its execution both in text and humorously detailed illustrations is fresh and spontaneous." Horn Book

Barton, Byron

Bones, bones, dinosaur bones. Crowell 1990 unp il $15; lib bdg $14.89   E

1. Dinosaurs

ISBN 0-690-04825-4; 0-690-04827-0 (lib bdg)

LC 89-71306

"From the field search for dinosaur bones to reconstructed skeletons for museum display, paleontology as process is revealed in simple text, bold print, and flat illustrations with heavy, black outlines. Includes labeled illustrations of eight dinosaurs." Sci Child

Dinosaurs, dinosaurs. Crowell 1989 unp il $10.95; lib bdg $14.89; pa $4.95   E

1. Dinosaurs

ISBN 0-694-00269-0; 0-690-04768-1 (lib bdg); 0-06-443298-X (pa)   LC 88-22938

Also available HarperCollins Big book edition $21.95 (ISBN 0-06-020410-9)

This book examines the many different kinds of dinosaurs, big and small, those with spikes and those with long, sharp teeth

"Barton conveys the primordial sense of excitement that draws children to these beasts. Despite the illustrations' simplicity, Barton's dinosaurs' expressions are not mammalian smiles; they have a saurian quality all their own. The endpapers identify the creatures by scientific name and pronunciation. Barton wisely keeps his text simple, describing dinosaurs only by size and physical features." SLJ

The wee little woman. HarperCollins Pubs. 1995 unp il $13.95; lib bdg $13.89   E

1. Cats—Fiction 2. Milk—Fiction

ISBN 0-06-023387-7; 0-06-023388-5 (lib bdg)

LC 94-18683

When a wee little woman milks her wee little cow and leaves the bowl of milk on her wee little table, the situation proves too tempting for a mischievous wee little cat

"This reassuring story is told in simple words with lots of repetition. The large paper cuts are done in primary colors against vivid green and yellow backgrounds in designs that are simple yet humorous and expressive. A satisfying and attractive choice for the very young." Booklist

Bartone, Elisa

Peppe the lamplighter; illustrations by Ted Lewin. Lothrop, Lee & Shepard Bks. 1993 unp il $14; lib bdg $13.93   E

1. Italian Americans—Fiction 2. Fathers and sons—Fiction 3. Brothers and sisters—Fiction 4. New York (N.Y.)—Fiction

ISBN 0-688-10268-9; 0-688-10269-7 (lib bdg)

LC 92-1397

A Caldecott Medal honor book, 1994

Peppe's father is upset when he learns that Peppe has taken a job lighting the gas street lamps in his New York City neighborhood

"Peppe's quiet quest for familial respect and pleasure in his work is touching and rhythmically written. The early-American city scenes are dark but have a nice period luminescence in the myriad street and table lamps, and the

Bartone, Elisa—*Continued*

earth-toned watercolors lend the bustling streets and interiors of Little Italy an air both somber and lively." Bull Cent Child Books

Bates, Artie Ann

Ragsale; written by Artie Ann Bates; illustrated by Jeff Chapman-Crane. Houghton Mifflin 1995 unp il $14.95   E

1. Shopping—Fiction 2. Appalachian Mountains—Fiction
ISBN 0-395-70030-2   LC 94-17366

Jessann and her family spend Saturday going to the ragsales of their Appalachian town

"Author and artist give a strong, unsentimental sense of individual people in an Appalachian community. The full-page framed pictures have the precise realism and character of Edward Hopper's small-town scenes, but there's no melancholy here." Booklist

Bauer, Marion Dane, 1938-

When I go camping with Grandma; pictures by Allen Garns. BridgeWater Bks. 1994 unp il lib bdg $14.95   E

1. Camping—Fiction 2. Grandmothers—Fiction
ISBN 0-8167-3448-8   LC 93-33809

A child enjoys a camping trip with Grandma that includes hiking, canoeing, fishing, and cooking out

"An idyllic mood piece combines Bauer's simple descriptive text and Garns' lush pastel landscapes and portraits." Booklist

Bayer, Jane, d. 1985

A my name is Alice; pictures by Steven Kellogg. Dial Bks. for Young Readers 1984 unp il $15.99; lib bdg $14.89; pa $4.95   E

1. Stories in rhyme 2. Alphabet
ISBN 0-8037-0123-3; 0-8037-0124-1 (lib bdg); 0-8037-0130-6 (pa)   LC 84-7059

"Each page contains (in the border above the illustration) the name of an animal ('A my name is Alice') and its spouse ('and my husband's name is Alex.'), their locale ('We come from Alaska') and occupation ('and we sell ants.'). Two sentences appear beneath the illustrations on each page identifying the kind of animals in the verse ('Alice is an 'Ape.' Alex is an 'Anteater.')." SLJ

"It is a superlative blend of visual and textual nonsense because the visual surprises keep the repetitive pattern in the text from becoming tedious. The verbal parts gradually expand in their ludicrousness, in their cataloging of zany characters and occupations." Wilson Libr Bull

Baylor, Byrd, 1924-

Desert voices. Scribner 1981 unp il $14.95; pa $3.95   E

1. Desert animals
ISBN 0-684-16712-3; 0-689-71691-5 (pa)

Ten desert creatures "each speak a poetic (free form) piece about their lives, homes and place in the desert world. The essential nature of each animal, whether patient or playful, alert or ominous, is conveyed with simplicity and energy in the well-phrased text and is further illuminated in Parnall's drawings, which are at once bold and delicate." SLJ

Hawk, I'm your brother; illustrated by Peter Parnall. Scribner 1976 unp il lib bdg $14.95   E

1. Hawks—Fiction
ISBN 0-684-14571-5

Also available in paperback from Aladdin Bks.; Spanish language edition also available

A Caldecott Medal honor book, 1977

"Driven by the desire to fly, Rudy Soto steals a baby hawk from its nest in the hope that having a hawk as his 'brother' will somehow enable him to take flight. Seeing the hawk's frustration in confinement, the boy finally releases it." Interracial Books Child Bull

"In the poetic simplicity of the writing, Baylor echoes the quietness of the desert and she captures the essence of the desert people's affinity for natural things. Both are reflected in Parnall's spacious illustrations, as clean and poetic as is the writing." Bull Cent Child Books

Belton, Sandra, 1939-

May'naise sandwiches & sunshine tea; story by Sandra Belton; illustrations by Gail Gordon Carter. Four Winds Press 1994 unp il $14.95
E

1. Grandmothers—Fiction 2. African Americans—Fiction
ISBN 0-02-709035-3   LC 93-46781

Big Mama reminisces with her grandchild about a childhood experience that helped inspire her to be the first member of her family to attend college

"Belton and Carter's combination of poignant words and delicate, warm, pastel-hued watercolors creates a story with universal appeal that imparts the beauty and importance of intergenerational sharing." SLJ

Bemelmans, Ludwig, 1898-1962

Madeline; story and pictures by Ludwig Bemelmans. Viking 1985 c1939 unp il $15; pa $4.99   E

1. Paris (France)—Fiction 2. Stories in rhyme
ISBN 0-670-44580-0; 0-14-050198-3 (pa)

Also available Spanish language edition

A Caldecott Medal honor book, 1940

A reissue of the title first published 1939 by Simon & Schuster

"Madeline is a nonconformist in a regimented world—a Paris convent school. This rhymed story tells how she made an adventure out of having appendicitis." Hodges. Books for Elem Sch Libr

Other available titles about Madeline are:
Madeline and the bad hat (1957)
Madeline and the gypsies (1959)
Madeline in London (1961)
Madeline's Christmas (1985)

Another available title about Madeline is: Madeline's rescue, entered below

Madeline's rescue; story and pictures by Ludwig Bemelmans. Viking 1985 c1953 unp il $14.99; pa $4.99   E

1. Dogs—Fiction 2. Paris (France)—Fiction 3. Stories in rhyme
ISBN 0-670-44716-1; 0-14-050207-6 (pa)

Awarded the Caldecott Medal, 1954

First published 1953

A picture-story book with rhymed text about little Madeline in Paris. This time she falls into the Seine and is res-

Bemelmans, Ludwig, 1898-1962—*Continued*
cued by 'a dog that kept its head.' The dog, named
Genevieve, was promptly adopted by Madeline's boarding
school mistress and her twelve pupils. When Genevieve was
turned out by snobbish trustees the little girls were incon-
solable, until Genevieve solved their problem

Benchley, Nathaniel, 1915-1981
A ghost named Fred; pictures by Ben
Shecter. Harper & Row 1968 unp il lib bdg
$14.89; pa $3.50   E
1. Ghost stories
ISBN 0-06-020474-5 (lib bdg); 0-06-444022-2 (pa)
"An I can read mystery"
"George, an imaginative child used to playing alone,
went into an empty house to get out of the rain; there he
met an absent-minded ghost named Fred, who knew there
was a treasure but had forgotten where. Only when Fred
opened an umbrella for George's homeward journey did the
treasure materialize." Bull Cent Child Books
"More humorous than scary . . . this is a pleasing and
acceptable ghost story for beginning readers." Booklist

Small Wolf; story by Nathaniel Benchley;
pictures by Joan Sandin. HarperCollins Pubs.
1994 64p il $14.95; lib bdg $14.89; pa $3.50
                                              E
1. Indians of North America—Fiction 2. United
States—History—1600-1775, Colonial period—Fiction
ISBN 0-06-020491-5; 0-06-020492-3 (lib bdg);
0-06-444180-6 (pa)   LC 93-26717
"An I can read book"
A newly illustrated edition of the title first published
1972
A young Native American boy sets out to hunt on Manhattan Island and discovers some strange people with white
faces and very different ideas about land
"Simply written but not stilted, the book has dramatic
and humanitarian interest as well as historical use, and the
illustrations have the same dramatic simplicity." Bull Cent
Child Books

Berenstain, Stan, 1923-
Bears on wheels; by Stan and Jan
Berenstain. Random House 1969 unp il $7.99;
lib bdg $9.99   E
1. Bears—Fiction 2. Counting
ISBN 0-394-80967-X; 0-394-90967-4 (lib bdg)
Titles about the bears are available in various series on
different reading levels. For complete listing see publisher's
catalog
"A Bright & early book"
The authors' illustrations are used with numbers in this
counting book which tells the story of a small bear who
goes out for a ride on one small wheel. As the bear rides
on, traffic and unwanted passengers accumulate

Berenzy, Alix, 1957-
A Frog Prince; written and illustrated by
Alix Berenzy. Holt & Co. 1989 unp il $14.95;
pa $5.95   E
1. Fairy tales 2. Frogs—Fiction
ISBN 0-8050-0426-2; 0-8050-1848-4 (pa)
                                      LC 88-29628
"Based on the original story: Der Froschkönig." Verso of
title page

"Beginning like Grimm's fairy tale 'The Frog Prince,'
this story takes an unusual twist, leading to new adventures
and a surprise ending. Told from the frog's point of view."
Booklist
"Berenzy's palette of deep rich color, alternately gilded
with light and cloaked in darkness, displays a magnificent
utilization of light and shadow. A wonderful book—wry,
touching, funny, and completely satisfying." SLJ

Berger, Barbara, 1945-
Grandfather Twilight. Philomel Bks. 1984
unp il $15.95; pa $5.95   E
1. Night—Fiction
ISBN 0-399-20996-4; 0-399-21596-4 (pa)
                                      LC 83-19490
"The coming of night is fancifully explained via the
glowing figure of Grandfather Twilight, a benign, mysterious figure who walks shimmering through the woods to the
seaside to release an incandescent pearl that becomes the
moon. The slight story gets a lift from the attractive illustrations, which are full-color paintings with soft textures,
and deep, rich color." Booklist

Beskow, Elsa, 1874-1953
Pelle's new suit; picture book by Elsa
Beskow; translated by Marion Letcher
Woodburn. Harper & Row 1929 unp il o.p.;
Gryphon House reprint available $14.95
                                              E
1. Sweden—Fiction
ISBN 0-86315-092-6
"Charming pictures tell the story of how Pelle earned his
new suit. He is shown raking hay, bringing in wood, feeding
pigs, going on errands and at the same time, each process
in the making of the suit is followed, beginning with the
shearing of the lamb. The coloring of the pictures (which
show both Swedish peasant house interiors and out-of-door
scenes) is quite lovely." N Y Public Libr

Binch, Caroline
Gregory Cool; story and pictures by
Caroline Birch. Dial Bks. for Young Readers
1994 unp il $14.99   E
1. Cousins—Fiction 2. Islands—Fiction 3. Trinidad and
Tobago—Fiction
ISBN 0-8037-1577-3   LC 93-11845
When he goes to visit his grandparents and his cousin,
Lennox, on the island of Tobago, Gregory misses home at
first, but as he gets to know both the island ways and his
relatives, Gregory begins to enjoy himself
"Binch's story is thoughtful, and the multicultural message is handled with finesse, but it is the refreshingly clear
and beautiful illustrations that make this book a delight.
From the gorgeous turquoise-and-white waterfilled endpapers to the poignantly alive faces of Gregory and his family,
these pictures fairly burst off the page." SLJ

Birdseye, Tom
Airmail to the moon; illustrated by Stephen
Gammell. Holiday House 1988 unp il lib bdg
$14.95; pa $5.95   E
1. Teeth—Fiction
ISBN 0-8234-0683-0 (lib bdg); 0-8234-0754-3 (pa)
                                      LC 87-21199

Birdseye, Tom—*Continued*

"Ora Mae, better known as Oreo because she's such a sweet cookie, has been worrying at a loose tooth like mad until, finally, one night it plops into her plate of spaghetti. Hurrying to bed to dream of all the wonderful things she'll buy with the tooth fairy's money, she's outraged in the morning to find that her tooth has been stolen. From one member of her family to the next, Oreo investigates the dastardly deed, vowing that when she catches the villain she'll 'open up a can of gotcha and send 'em airmail to the moon!'" Horn Book

"Gammell's colorful pencil drawings carry out the down-home rickety flavor from the title page outhouse to the pig waller. If the country flavor is spread a bit thick, the underlying story does work." SLJ

Blake, Quentin, 1932-

Cockatoos. Little, Brown 1992 unp il $14.95

E

1. Birds—Fiction 2. Counting
ISBN 0-316-09951-1   LC 91-46555

To avoid Professor Dupont's monotonous daily greeting, his ten pet cockatoos hide in his house

"Kids will love spotting the colorful plumage behind every corner and cushion—easily visible to everyone but the hapless professor. . . . Blake's characteristically effusive drawings enhance the silliness of this thoroughly engaging ditty." Publ Wkly

Blegvad, Lenore

Anna Banana and me; illustrated by Erik Blegvad. Atheneum Pubs. 1985 unp il lib bdg $13.95; pa $3.95

E

1. Fear—Fiction
ISBN 0-689-50274-5 (lib bdg); 0-689-71114-X (pa)
                                               LC 84-457

"A Margaret K. McElderry book"

"Anna Banana is fearless; she thrives on adventure and eagerly explores new situations. When this free spirit meets a cautious, timid male playmate in a city park, he is drawn into her exciting yet scary world. . . . Erik Blegvad's pen-and-ink and watercolor illustrations complement the simple, poetic text." SLJ

Blood, Charles L., 1929-

The goat in the rug; as told to Charles L. Blood & Martin Link by Geraldine; illustrated by Nancy Winslow Parker. Four Winds Press 1980 1976 unp il $14.95

E

1. Goats—Fiction 2. Navajo Indians—Fiction 3. Rugs—Fiction
ISBN 0-02-710920-8   LC 80-17315

Also available in paperback from Aladdin Bks.

A reissue of the 1976 edition published by Parents Magazine Press

"A goat's-eye view of how a Navajo rug is made, from the shearing of our supposed narrator ('Geraldine') to the dyeing and weaving. By the time the rug is finished, Geraldine has grown enough wool to start another one." Saturday Rev

"Parker's vivid primary colored illustrations are as enjoyable and humorous as the instructive text." SLJ

Blos, Joan W., 1928-

The grandpa days; illustrated by Emily Arnold McCully. Simon & Schuster Bks. for Young Readers 1989 unp il $8.95; pa $3.95

E

1. Grandfathers—Fiction
ISBN 0-671-64640-0; 0-671-88244-9 (pa)
                                               LC 88-19801

Philip comes up with just the right project to build with Grandpa during their week together, but first he has to learn the difference between wishes and good planning

"Besides celebrating the link between old and young, the story also explores the creative process in a fashion young children can easily understand. McCully's pen-and-wash drawings capture the good feelings between Philip and his Grandpa in warm scenes of the two planning, working, and puttering about. Unassuming and sweet." Booklist

Old Henry; illustrated by Stephen Gammell. Morrow 1987 unp il $16; lib bdg $15.93; pa $4.95

E

1. Stories in rhyme
ISBN 0-688-06399-3; 0-688-06400-0 (lib bdg); 0-688-09935-1 (pa)   LC 86-21745

A "poem-portrait of an old man who offends the neighbors with his raggedy house and renegade ways. When Old Henry moves in, people expect him 'to fix things up a bit. He did not think of it.' Instead, he spreads his paraphernalia over the uncut grass, rejects offers of help shoveling snow, and finally moves out. Amazingly, he and the community come to miss each other." Bull Cent Child Books

"This very lightly told story about social tolerance and the merits of diversity is deftly illustrated in soft, colored-pencil drawings that capture the characters perfectly." N Y Times Book Rev

Blume, Judy

The one in the middle is the green kangaroo; illustrated by Irene Trivas. rev American ed. Bradbury Press 1991 unp il $14.95

E

1. Family life—Fiction 2. Brothers and sisters—Fiction
ISBN 0-02-711055-9   LC 91-154236

Also available in paperback from Dell

Original edition illustrated by Lois Axeman published 1969 by Reilly & Lee; this is a newly illustrated reissue of the 1981 edition

Freddy hates being the middle one in the family until he gets a part in the school play

"Trivas' bouncy, good-natured illustrations seem destined to charm even the most critical viewers. . . . This edition seems better designed for reading aloud to children." Booklist

The Pain and the Great One; illustrations by Irene Trivas. Bradbury Press 1984 unp il lib bdg $14.95

E

1. Brothers and sisters—Fiction
ISBN 0-02-711100-8   LC 84-11009

Also available in paperback from Dell

A six-year-old (The Pain) and his eight-year-old sister (The Great One) see each other as troublemakers and the best-loved in the family

"Young readers, depending on their position within the family, will readily identify with either character and may learn empathy for the other. Used in a group, this will provide much healthy discussion. . . . Trivas' vibrant colors add depth and humor to a valuable book on sibling relationships." SLJ

Bodkin, Odds

The Banshee train; illustrated by Ted Rose. Clarion Bks. 1995 unp il $14.95   E

1. Ghost stories 2. Railroads—Fiction

ISBN 0-395-69426-4   LC 93-39635

"A spectral train saves a locomotive from hurtling over a flooded Rocky Mountain trestle. Based on folklore that Irish immigrant railroad workers brought to America in the nineteenth century, the riveting tale features the eerie warning of a Gaelic banshee. Purple-hued, luminescent watercolors capture the tension in this retelling by a master storyteller." Horn Book Guide

Bond, Felicia, 1954-

Poinsettia & her family. Crowell 1981 32p il lib bdg $14.89; pa $4.95   E

1. Family life—Fiction 2. Pigs—Fiction

ISBN 0-690-04145-4 (lib bdg); 0-06-443076-6 (pa)

"Irritated when all her favorite retreats . . . have been pre-empted by one or another of her six brothers and sisters, Poinsettia Pig makes herself thoroughly disagreeable and is sent to bed early 'for general misbehavior.' But when, on the following day, father pig announces that they will look for a new and larger home, she deliberately remains behind, convinced that the size of the family, not the size of the house, is responsible for their discomfort." Horn Book

"What makes this . . . story unexpectedly entertaining is Bond's slightly potty pen-and-wash drawings and her success at portraying Poinsettia as a connoisseur of privacy." Booklist

Another available title about Poinsettia is:
Poinsettia and the firefighters (1984)

Bond, Michael, 1926-

Paddington's colors; illustrated by John Lobban; devised by Carol Watson. Viking 1991 unp il $11.99; pa $4.99   E

1. Color—Fiction

ISBN 0-670-84102-1; 0-14-055764-4 (pa)

LC 93-129083

First published 1990 in the United Kingdom

"Paddington does his spring cleaning. Putting a RED blanket in the washer on one large double-page spread, he adds a WHITE sheet on the next. The third shows the sheet, now PINK, hanging on the line. A GRAY cloud threatens rain, but Paddington pulls out his trusty BLACK umbrella, and so on. On the last pages, the genial bear invites readers to name the colors of his paw prints, tells 'what happens when you mix the colors'. . . and talks about the number, names, and order of colors in the rainbow. The first pages would be fun for very young children, while giving older kids a running start for the more challenging questions at the end." Booklist

Some other available titles about Paddington in picture book format are:
Paddington's 1 2 3 (1991)
Paddington's ABC (1991)
Paddington's opposites (1991)

Other available titles about Paddington for older readers are entered in the Fiction Section

Bonners, Susan, 1947-

The wooden doll. Lothrop, Lee & Shepard Bks. 1991 unp il $13.95; lib bdg $13.88   E

1. Dolls—Fiction 2. Grandparents—Fiction

ISBN 0-688-08280-7; 0-688-08282-3 (lib bdg)

LC 90-33647

"Stephanie feels excited but strange staying with her grandparents by herself and hopes that her uncommunicative grandfather will understand when she secretly plays with his treasured Polish doll. Well-delineated emotions and believable characters come to life in a pensive intergenerational story, with evocative, full-color paintings." Horn Book Guide

Bonsall, Crosby Newell, 1921-1995

The case of the hungry stranger; by Crosby Bonsall. HarperCollins Pubs. 1992 64p $13; lib bdg $12.89; pa $3.75   E

1. Mystery fiction

ISBN 0-06-020570-9; 0-06-020571-7 (lib bdg); 0-06-444026-5 (pa)   LC 91-13345

Also available Spanish language edition

"An I can read book"

A reissue of the title first published 1963. This edition has full color illustrations

Wizard and his friends are clueless when they are sent on the trail of a blueberry pie thief, until Wizard hits on a plan that is sure to nab the sweet-toothed pilferer

This offers "suspense and humor." Horn Book

Other available titles in this series are:
The case of the cat's meow (1965)
The case of the double cross (1980)
The case of the dumb bells (1966)
The case of the scaredy cats (1971)

The day I had to play with my sister. Harper & Row 1972 32p il lib bdg $14.89; pa $3.50   E

1. Brothers and sisters—Fiction

ISBN 0-06-020576-8 (lib bdg); 0-06-444117-2 (pa)

"An Early I can read book"

A young boy finds trying to teach his little sister to play hide-and-seek very frustrating

"The extremely simple text, written from the boy's point of view, is one with which children can readily identify. Pastel illustrations on every page add touches of humor to the text, which is divided into chapters. The realistic atmosphere makes Bonsall's book an excellent addition to the very early reading shelves." SLJ

Who's a pest? Harper & Row 1962 64p il lib bdg $14.89; pa $3.50   E

ISBN 0-06-020621-7 (lib bdg); 0-06-444099-0 (pa)

"An I can read book"

"In this truly funny . . . book a small boy named Homer proves that he is not a pest as his four sisters, a rabbit, chipmunk, and lizard claim. The drawings are as laughable as the text and the tongue-twisting dialog begs to be read aloud." Booklist

Another available title about Homer is:
Piggle (1973)

Who's afraid of the dark? by Crosby Bonsall. Harper & Row 1980 32p il lib bdg $14.89; pa $3.50   E

1. Night—Fiction 2. Fear—Fiction

ISBN 0-06-020599-7 (lib bdg); 0-06-444071-0 (pa)

LC 79-2700

Bonsall, Crosby Newell, 1921-1995—*Continued*

"An Early I can read book"

"A little boy describes to a friend the nighttime fears of his dog Stella. Stella shivers in the dark, he claims; she sees shapes and hears scary sounds. The doubting but sympathetic friend offers a suggestion—hug Stella in the night and comfort her until her fears go away. . . . The illustrations in shades of light blue and brown are filled with as much life and warmth as ever." Horn Book

Borden, Louise, 1949-

Caps, hats, socks, and mittens; a book about the four seasons; illustrated by Lillian Hoban. Scholastic 1989 unp il hardcover o.p. paperback available $3.95   E

1. Seasons—Fiction
ISBN 0-590-44872-2 (pa)   LC 87-28776

"Borden takes children around the calendar and introduces them to the uniqueness of each season. . . . The simple prose is illustrated by Hoban's distinctive drawings, featuring groups of round-cheeked children. . . . Cheery colors add to the book's ebullient feel." Booklist

Bottner, Barbara, 1943-

Bootsie Barker bites; illustrated by Peggy Rathmann. Putnam 1992 unp il $15.95   E
ISBN 0-399-22125-5   LC 91-12182

"When Bootsie comes to play, she casts herself as a dinosaur, and the intimidated narrator as a turtle or salamander to be eaten. The girl dreams that her enemy will go away on her own, but faced with a possible sleepover, she uses her wits to make Bootsie-the-dinosaur a thing of the past." Publisher's note

"Bottner's tone is a model of simplicity and matter-of-factness, sometimes droll but never coy. Rathmann's neon-bright, full-color artwork extends the emotional tenor and the humor of the text." Booklist

Boulton, Jane

Only Opal; the diary of a young girl; by Opal Whiteley; selected [and adapted] by Jane Boulton; illustrations by Barbara Cooney. Philomel Bks. 1994 unp il $14.95   E

1. Whiteley, Opal Stanley 2. Frontier and pioneer life 3. Oregon
ISBN 0-399-21990-0   LC 91-38581

"Opal Whiteley's diary was first published in 1920 by the Atlantic Monthly Press and is available in a longer form, *Opal: The Journal of an Understanding Heart,* published by Tioga Publishing Company, adapted by Jane Boulton"

"Orphaned at five, Opal was taken in by an Oregon family who gave her shelter but little else. Transcribed into a lyrical text with luminous watercolors, the account captures the life of a turn-of-the-century child who, despite the odds, remains true to herself and the memories of her 'Angel Mother and Angel Father.'" Horn Book Guide

Bowen, Betsy

Antler, bear, canoe; a northwoods alphabet year. Little, Brown 1991 unp il lib bdg $15.95; pa $4.95   E

1. Alphabet 2. Nature 3. Seasons
ISBN 0-316-10376-4 (lib bdg); 0-316-10315-2 (pa)
LC 90-33754

"Joy Street books"

Introduces the letters of the alphabet in woodcut illustrations and brief text depicting the changing seasons in the northern woods

"From its memorable, unusually fine woodcuts, to the telling glimpse it offers of a life that is close to the rhythms of nature, this debut is no garden variety ABC book." Publ Wkly

Bradby, Marie

More than anything else; story by Marie Bradby; pictures by Chris K. Soentpiet. Orchard Bks. 1995 unp il $14.95; lib bdg $15.99   E

1. Washington, Booker T., 1856-1915—Fiction 2. African Americans—Fiction 3. Books and reading—Fiction
ISBN 0-531-09464-2; 0-531-08764-6 (lib bdg)
LC 94-48804

"A Richard Jackson book"

Nine-year-old Booker works with his father and brother at the saltworks but dreams of the day when he'll be able to read

"An evocative text combines with well-crafted, dramatic watercolors to provide a stirring, fictionalized account of the early life of Booker T. Washington." Horn Book

Brandenberg, Franz, 1932-

Aunt Nina and her nephews and nieces; illustrated by Aliki. Greenwillow Bks. 1983 unp il $15; lib bdg $15.93   E

1. Aunts—Fiction 2. Parties—Fiction 3. Birthdays—Fiction 4. Cats—Fiction
ISBN 0-688-01869-6; 0-688-01870-X (lib bdg)
LC 82-12004

"Fun-loving Aunt Nina, who lives alone, invites her six nephews and nieces to a birthday celebration for her cat, Fluffy. When the honored guest fails to appear, the children search the house for her, from cellar to attic. . . . After lunch, they prepare for naps and discover the missing Fluffy in Aunt Nina's bed with six newborns that look just like her." Child Book Rev Serv

"Aliki's chipper, brightly colored watercolor paintings of children making the most of Aunt Nina's cozy home underscore the story's warmth." Booklist

Other available titles about Aunt Nina are:
Aunt Nina, goodnight (1989)
Aunt Nina's visit (1984)

Leo and Emily; illustrated by Aliki. Greenwillow Bks. 1981 55p il $15   E

1. Friendship—Fiction
ISBN 0-688-80292-3

"A Greenwillow read-alone book"

"Emily often wakes her pal Leo before dawn, encouraging him to dress in the dark and join her to swap treasures (a rabbit for Grandmother's wig) or just to talk. Dressing in the dark results in inside-out clothes, untied spaghetties (shoestrings) and the omission of socks. Emily's grandmother is so understanding about her wig being borrowed, she buys Emily her own rabbit and Leo and Emily put on a magic show." SLJ

"In three chapters, this book for beginning independent readers incorporates humor, friendship values, enterprise, and some excellent familial relationships. . . . Aliki's people are small, brisk, and amusing." Bull Cent Child Books

Other available titles about Leo and Emily are:
Leo and Emily and the dragon (1984)
Leo and Emily's big ideas (1982)
Leo and Emily's zoo (1988)

Brandenberg, Franz, 1932-—*Continued*

Nice new neighbors; illustrated by Aliki.
Greenwillow Bks. 1977 56p il lib bdg $13.88;
pa $4.95   E

1. Friendship—Fiction 2. Mice—Fiction
ISBN 0-688-84105-8 (lib bdg); 0-688-10997-7 (pa)
LC 77-1651
Also available in paperback from Scholastic
"A Greenwillow read-alone book"
"A newly moved-in family of fieldmouse children makes
vain attempts to join other youngsters in game playing. After being rebuffed by juvenile representatives of each nearby
household, the resourceful mouse children decide to create
their own play." Booklist
"Aliki uses pale pinks and greens in combination with
black and white for her lively, scrawly drawings of small
animals; her illustrations have some touches (balloon captions, framed sequence drawing for a play) that will be familiar to cartoon-conscious beginning independent readers."
Bull Cent Child Books

Brenner, Barbara

Wagon wheels; pictures by Don Bolognese.
Harper & Row 1978 64p il $14.95; lib bdg
$14.89; pa $3.75   E

1. Frontier and pioneer life—Fiction 2. African
Americans—Fiction
ISBN 0-06-020668-3; 0-06-020669-1 (lib bdg);
0-06-444052-4 (pa)
"An I can read history book"
A "frontier story for beginning independent readers describes the experiences of a black family which comes from
Kentucky to Kansas in the 1870's. The story is told by one
of the three boys; the writing is simple and direct, yet it has
a narrative flow and gives a vivid picture of both the hardships of pioneer life and of the love and courage of the family. The book is based on fact." Bull Cent Child Books

Brett, Jan, 1949-

Annie and the wild animals; written and
illustrated by Jan Brett. Houghton Mifflin
1985 unp il lib bdg $14.95; pa $4.95   E

1. Animals—Fiction 2. Cats—Fiction
ISBN 0-395-37800-1 (lib bdg); 0-395-51006-6 (pa)
LC 84-19818
When Annie's cat disappears, she attempts friendship
with a variety of unsuitable woodland animals, but with the
emergence of Spring, everything comes right
"Miss Brett uses colorful borders filled with detail to
provide miniature previews of the narrative action and a
story around a story, so that the reader instantly becomes
an insider. The small glimpses of the world outside Annie's
cottage move the tale forward and embellish the pages with
grace and skill." N Y Times Book Rev

Berlioz the bear; written and illustrated by
Jan Brett. Putnam 1991 unp il $14.95; pa
$5.95   E

1. Bears—Fiction 2. Animals—Fiction 3. Musicians—
Fiction
ISBN 0-399-22248-0; 0-399-22846-2 (pa)
LC 90-37634
Berlioz the bear and his fellow musicians are due to play
for the town ball when the mule pulling their bandwagon
refuses to move. A strange buzzing in Berlioz's double bass
turns into a surprise that saves the day
"In tone, Brett's cumulative story has elements of tradi-
tional folklore, and her spare text begs to be read aloud.
Her pen-and-ink, watercolor, and colored-pencil illustrations
are richly, often humorously, detailed." SLJ

Trouble with trolls. Putnam 1992 unp il
$15.95   E

1. Fairy tales
ISBN 0-399-22336-3   LC 91-41061
While climbing Mt. Baldy, Treva outwits some trolls
who want to steal her dog
"Bursting with energy and fine detail, the double-page
spreads, which escape their cross-stitch borders, depict a
beautiful mountain landscape, dotted with trees and rocks
that make excellent hiding places for the pesky trolls. Cutaway scenes beneath the spreads tell a concurrent story, picturing the trolls readying their home for Tuffi while an
uninvited guest works its way down the chimney, then inside. Playful and funny, with a valiant female protagonist,
this is a first-rate read." Booklist

The wild Christmas reindeer; written and
illustrated by Jan Brett. Putnam 1990 unp il
$15.95   E

1. Reindeer—Fiction 2. Christmas—Fiction
ISBN 0-399-22192-1   LC 89-36095
"The story's heroine is Teeka, who is asked by Santa to
get the reindeer ready to fly. . . . Only when she realizes
that hugging works better than bossing, do the reindeer
unite into the working team that Santa needs to bring
Christmas to the world. . . . Brett provides ornamental pictures, heavily detailed and decoratively bordered. . . . Beautifully conceived and finely wrought." Booklist

Briggs, Raymond, 1934-

Father Christmas. Coward-McCann 1973
unp il o.p.; Penguin Bks. paperback available
$4.50   E

1. Santa Claus—Fiction 2. Christmas—Fiction
ISBN 0-14-050125-8 (pa)
Illustrated by the author in cartoon format, this book
"portrays Christmas Eve as Santa sees it. Dreaming of trop-
ic weather, he grumbles his way through the preparations
for a long, cold night of work: feeding the animals, loading
the sleigh, packing a snack. He grumbles at chimneys,
catches cold, wearily distributes gifts, and rides home to a
steaming bath and a solitary Christmas dinner." Bull Cent
Child Books
"Each small picture is precisely detailed, convincingly
well-drawn, and alive with action; the longer and larger
frames—including some full-page spreads—offer a lot of visual contrast in size, color, and contents." Booklist

The snowman. Random House 1978 unp il
$16; pa $4.95   E

1. Stories without words 2. Dreams—Fiction 3. Snow—
Fiction
ISBN 0-394-83973-0; 0-394-88466-3 (pa)
LC 78-55904
Also available Spanish language edition
A "wordless picture book about a small boy who expertly fashions a snowman and then dreams that his splendid
creation comes alive. Affably greeting the child, the snowman enters the house and is introduced to the delights and
dangers of gadgetry. . . . Finally, no longer earthbound, the
two friends go soaring over city and countryside, magical in
their snowy beauty." Horn Book
"The pastel-toned pencil-and-crayon pictures in their
neat rectangular frames will hold the attention of primary
'readers.'" SLJ

Bright, Robert, 1902-1988

My red umbrella. Morrow 1985 c1959 unp il $12   E

1. Umbrellas and parasols—Fiction

ISBN 0-688-05249-5

A reissue of the title first published 1959

"A good read-aloud story for very young listeners, about a little girl whose red umbrella grew to accommodate all the creatures who sought shelter under it. Cheerful colored pictures by the author." Hodges. Books for Elem Sch Libr

Brinckloe, Julie

Fireflies! story and pictures by Julie Brinckloe. Macmillan 1985 unp il $13.95; pa $3.95   E

1. Fireflies—Fiction

ISBN 0 02-713310-9; 0-689-71055-0 (pa)

LC 84-20158

A young boy is proud of having caught a jar full of fireflies, which seems to him like owning a piece of moonlight, but as the light begins to dim he realizes he must set the insects free or they will die

"The tale is embellished with lovely, wistful pencil drawings of the boy and his friends leaping about in the twilight and of his expressive face showing his mingled joy and sadness. A simple, basic story, very gracefully presented." Horn Book

Brown, Jeff, 1926-

Flat Stanley; pictures by Tomi Ungerer. Harper & Row 1964 unp il lib bdg $14.89; pa $4.95   E

ISBN 0-06-020681-0 (lib bdg); 0-06-440293-2 (pa)

"When an enormous bulletin board fell on him as he lay in bed Stanley Lambchop emerged as flat as a pancake. Once he got used to his half-inch thickness Stanley came to enjoy it and so did his parents— he could be lowered through sidewalk gratings, mailed to California, rolled up like wallpaper and tied with a string for carrying, and disguised as a framed picture to help catch art thieves in the museum. Comical colored pictures accentuate the humor of this rib-tickling story." Booklist

Brown, Laurene Krasny

Rex and Lilly family time; stories by Laurie Krasny Brown; pictures by Marc Brown. Little, Brown 1995 32p il lib bdg $12.95

E

1. Dinosaurs—Fiction 2. Brothers and sisters—Fiction

ISBN 0-316-11385-9   LC 93-24162

"A Dino easy reader"

This book includes three adventures of a dinosaur brother and sister, Rex and Lilly "making a birthday surprise for mom, getting a housekeeping robot that goes wild, choosing the best pet. . . . [The text is] straightforward, often using repetitive sentence structure and phrases, and [lays] the groundwork for the humorous (and sometimes silly) watercolor-and-ink illustrations." SLJ

Another available title about Rex and Lilly is:
Rex and Lilly playtime (1995)

Brown, Marc Tolon

Arthur's nose; by Marc Brown. Little, Brown 1976 32p il $14.95; pa $4.95   E

1. Nose—Fiction 2. Aardvark—Fiction

ISBN 0-316-11193-7; 0-316-11070-1 (pa)

"An Atlantic Monthly Press book"

"Arthur the aardvark is unhappy with his long nose. When he finally decides to visit a rhinologist to have it changed, he discovers that he can't come up with a different kind of nose that suits him. No alterations are done, for Arthur comes to realize that 'I'm just not me without my nose.' The overworked lesson is pleasantly conveyed with surprisingly little text and large and colorful illustrations so that independent readers may be tempted to pick this up." SLJ

Other available titles about Arthur are:
Arthur babysits (1992)
Arthur goes to camp (1982)
Arthur meets the president (1991)
Arthur's April Fool (1983)
Arthur's baby (1987)
Arthur's birthday (1989)
Arthur's chicken pox (1994)
Arthur's Christmas (1985)
Arthur's eyes (1979)
Arthur's family vacation (1993)
Arthur's first sleepover (1994)
Arthur's Halloween (1982)
Arthur's new puppy (1993)
Arthur's pet business (1990)
Arthur's teacher trouble (1986)
Arthur's Thanksgiving (1983)
Arthur's tooth (1985)
Arthur's TV trouble (1995)
Arthur's valentine (1980)

D.W. all wet; [by] Marc Brown. Little, Brown 1988 unp il $10.95; pa $4.95   E

1. Beaches—Fiction 2. Brothers and sisters—Fiction 3. Aardvark—Fiction

ISBN 0-316-11077-9; 0-316-11268-2 (pa)

LC 87-15752

"Joy Street books"

"Arthur the Aardvark's little sister D.W. stars in the second book (the first was D.W. flips [1987]) of her own series that features the likable, cheeky young heroine. This time D.W. . . . announces, 'I don't like the beach, and I don't like to get wet.' She asks to leave the minute she arrives, she won't play and she's afraid of getting sunburned. It's Arthur who helps change D.W.'s mind about the beach by unexpectedly tossing her into very shallow water." Publ Wkly

"A simple, even predictable vignette, but entertaining nonetheless because of Brown's warm pictures." Booklist

Other available titles about D.W. are:
D.W. rides again (1993)
D.W. the picky eater (1995)
D.W. thinks big (1993)

Brown, Margaret Wise, 1910-1952

Baby animals; illustrated by Susan Jeffers. Random House 1989 unp il $16   E

1. Animals—Fiction

ISBN 0-394-82040-1   LC 88-18481

Text originally published 1941 in longer version

Relates the morning, noon, and evening activities of several young animals and a little girl

"Paintings and text are interspersed on each page, creating a lovely whole. Illustrations range from full-page and double-page spreads to several smaller ones on a page surrounded by crisp white space. Young children will delight

Brown, Margaret Wise, 1910-1952—*Continued*

in the lilting, often repetitive, question-and-answer format of the text." SLJ

Big red barn; pictures by Felicia Bond. Newly illustrated ed. Harper & Row 1989 unp il $14.95; lib bdg $14.89   E

1. Animals—Fiction 2. Farm life—Fiction 3. Stories in rhyme
ISBN 0-06-020748-5; 0-06-020749-3 (lib bdg)
LC 85-45814

Also available Spanish language edition
A newly illustrated edition of the title first published 1956

Rhymed text and illustrations introduce the many different animals that live in the big red barn

"The large illustrations are somewhat stylized, but still have a strong sense of detail and reality. The bright colors will attract young readers. The short text on each page is superimposed on the picture, but always in a way that is easy to read. Children will enjoy studying each of the pages as the day progresses from early morning to night." SLJ

A child's good night book; pictures by Jean Charlot. HarperCollins Pubs. 1992 unp il $10; lib bdg $9.89   E

1. Night—Fiction
ISBN 0-06-021028-1; 0-06-020752-3 (lib bdg)
LC 91-45340

A Caldecott Medal honor book, 1944
A reissue of the title first published 1943 by W. R. Scott

As an invitation to sleepiness the author writes of birds and animals, sailboats, automobiles and little children as they settle down for the night
The brief text is accompanied by full-page softly colored lithographs

Four fur feet; illustrated by Woodleigh Marx Hubbard. Hyperion Bks. for Children 1994 unp il $12.95; lib bdg $[2.89   E

1. Animals—Fiction
ISBN 0-7868-0002-X; 0-7868-2000-4 (lib bdg)
LC 93-31523

A newly illustrated edition of the title first published 1961 by W. R. Scott
Poetic text and illustrations describe an animal's journey around the world on his four fur feet

This is "a simple, repetitive tale with the sort of serious whimsy Brown wrote so well. . . . Hubbard's new artwork depicts the creature itself—and a magnificent beast it is, too—with bright squiggles of red adorning its yellow coat and luxurious curly black whiskers." SLJ

Goodnight moon; pictures by Clement Hurd. Harper & Row 1947 unp il $13.95; lib bdg $13.89; pa $4.95   E

1. Rabbits—Fiction 2. Night—Fiction 3. Stories in rhyme
ISBN 0-06-020705-1; 0-06-020706-X (lib bdg); 0-06-443017-0 (pa)

Also available Spanish language edition
"The coming of night is shown in pictures which change from bright to dark as a small rabbit says good night to the familiar things in his nest." Hodges. Books for Elem Sch Libr
"A clever goodnight book in which pages are progressively darker as the leaves are turned. There are many objects to identify and children enjoy picking out familiar words." Books for Deaf Child

The indoor noisy book; pictures by Leonard Weisgard. HarperCollins Pubs. 1994 unp il lib bdg $15.89   E

1. Sound—Fiction 2. Dogs—Fiction
ISBN 0-06-020821-X   LC 92-46879

A reissue of the title first published 1942 by W. R. Scott
A little dog who has a cold stays indoors all day and listens to the sounds of housecleaning, meals being eaten, and the wind and rain beating on the window pane
This "bright, boldly designed [book features] strikingly modern, angular, posterlike illustrations." Horn Book Guide

Little Fur family; illustrated by Garth Williams. HarperCollins Pubs. 1991 unp il $14; lib bdg $14.89   E

ISBN 0-06-020745-0; 0-06-020746-9 (lib bdg)

First published 1946; this is a reissue of the 1951 edition
"This story of a little fur child's day in the woods ends when his parents sing him to sleep with a lovely bedtime song." Publisher's note
This "book will still charm readers. . . . Williams's softly lit illustrations are enchanting." Horn Book

The noisy book; pictures by Leonard Weisgard. HarperCollins Pubs. 1993 unp il hardcover o.p. paperback available $4.95   E

1. Sound—Fiction 2. Dogs—Fiction
ISBN 0-06-443001-4 (pa)   LC 92-8322

A reissue of the title first published 1939 by W. R. Scott
Muffin the dog is blindfolded for a day and tries to identify things by the sounds they make

Red light, green light; illustrated by Leonard Weisgard. Scholastic 1992 unp il $14.95; pa $4.95   E

ISBN 0-590-44558-8; 0-590-44559-6 (pa)
LC 91-14589

A newly illustrated edition of the title first published 1944 by Doubleday
All day and night the traffic signal blinks its messages of stop and go
"This picture book still appeals to young children. While the composition of the pictures remains the same and the setting is still the 1940s, the new illustrations are just a little bigger, brighter, and more distinct than in the earlier edition." Booklist

The runaway bunny; pictures by Clement Hurd. Harper & Row 1972 c1942 unp il $13.95; lib bdg $13.89; pa $3.95   E

1. Rabbits—Fiction
ISBN 0-06-020765-5; 0-06-020766-3 (lib bdg); 0-06-443018-9 (pa)

Also available Spanish language edition
A reissue, with some illustrations redrawn, of the title first published 1942
"Within a framework of mutual love, a bunny tells his mother how he will run away and she answers his challenge by indicating how she will catch him." SLJ
"The text has the simplicity of a folk tale and the illustrations are black and white or double page drawings in startling colour." Ont Libr Rev

Brown, Margaret Wise, 1910-1952—*Continued*

Wheel on the chimney; illustrated by Tibor Gergely. Lippincott 1985 c1954 unp il $14; lib bdg $13.89   E

1. Storks—Fiction
ISBN 0-397-30288-6; 0-397-30296-7 (lib bdg)
LC 84-48379

A Caldecott Medal honor book, 1955

A reissue of the title first published 1954

"First there was one stork, then there were two. They built their nest on a wheel on the chimney of a little Hungarian house, thus promising good luck to the family. This annual ritual inspired Gergely's tracing of the stork's migration from their summer European habitat to their winter sojourn in Africa." Second Educ Board

"The simple text tells of the ways of storks and of the hazards of their long flight south, while the illustrations in strong contrasting colours show much of the beauty and interest of the seas and continents the great birds cross in their journey." Ont Libr Rev

Brown, Ruth

The big sneeze. Lothrop, Lee & Shepard Bks. 1985 unp il $16; lib bdg $15.93   E

1. Farm life—Fiction
ISBN 0-688-04665-7; 0-688-04666-5 (lib bdg)
LC 84-23385

A farmer sneezes a fly off his nose and causes havoc in the barnyard

"The deep, rich colour and naturalistic style of the illustrations lead the eye agreeably along the line of cumulative disaster in an energetic and diverting picture-book." Grow Point

A dark, dark tale; story and pictures by Ruth Brown. Dial Bks. for Young Readers 1981 unp il $14.99; lib bdg $12.89; pa $3.95   E

1. Cats—Fiction
ISBN 0-8037-1672-9; 0-8037-1673-7 (lib bdg); 0-8037-0093-8 (pa)

In a "style used by storytellers of ghostly tales, Brown begins 'Once upon a time there was a dark, dark moor' and goes on to describe the 'dark, dark wood' on the moor, the 'dark, dark house' in the wood and the stygian rooms in the huge place. A nimble black cat accompanies explorers of the mansion and leaps with them in gleeful terror when the final 'dark, dark thing' is discovered." Publ Wkly

"The book's mysterious power is engendered by the illustrations of weed-choked gardens and abandoned, echoing halls, of mullioned windows and blowing curtains." Time

One stormy night. Dutton Children's Bks. 1993 c1992 unp il $13.99   E

1. Ghost stories
ISBN 0-525-45091-2
LC 92-27004

First published 1992 in the United Kingdom

"One stormy night . . . a mysterious white dog roams the grounds of an old English estate. But, with the coming of morning's first light, the ghost dog finally settles, rejoining its master and mistress long at rest in their tomb. . . . The text is poetically spare. . . . Brown's scratched and smudgy watercolor illustrations create a darkly romantic landscape within which she has wrought a gentle, gothic ghost story that is spooky yet not frightening." Booklist

The picnic. Dutton Children's Bks. 1993 unp il $14   E

1. Animals—Fiction
ISBN 0-525-45012-2
LC 92-5718

"A picnic in a meadow as seen by the resident creatures who run for cover—rabbits, moles and mice." NY Times Book Rev

"Brown makes use of unusual perspectives in her energetic, earth-toned watercolors. The economically told story has a gentle message just right for sharing with young animal lovers." Horn Book Guide

Browne, Anthony

Gorilla. Knopf 1985 c1983 unp il lib bdg $13.99; pa $6.99   E

1. Gorillas—Fiction 2. Fathers and daughters—Fiction
ISBN 0-394-97525-1 (lib bdg); 0-394-82225-0 (pa)
LC 85-13

Also available Spanish language edition

First published 1983 in the United Kingdom

Neglected by her busy father, a lonely young girl receives a toy gorilla for her birthday and together they take a miraculous trip to the zoo

"Despite the fantasy, Browne has created a picture book that explores real emotions with a beautifully realized child protagonist. Using his artistic skills, he's fashioned the visual metaphors that help us transcend superficial meanings and feel the power of the more archetypical emotions that bind children to parents and people to the other animals." Horn Book

Piggybook. Knopf 1986 unp il hardcover o.p. paperback available $6.99   E

1. Mothers—Fiction 2. Family life—Fiction
ISBN 0-679-80837-X (pa)
LC 86-3008

Also available Spanish language edition

When Mrs. Piggott unexpectedly leaves one day, her demanding family begins to realize just how much she did for them

"As in most of Browne's art, there is more than a touch of irony and visual humor here, bringing off the didactic with a light touch and turning the lesson into satire." Bull Cent Child Books

Willy the wimp. Knopf 1985 c1984 unp il hardcover o.p. paperback available $7.99   E

1. Chimpanzees—Fiction 2. Bodybuilding—Fiction
ISBN 0-394-82610-8 (pa)
LC 84-14320

Also available Spanish language edition

First published 1984 in the United Kingdom

A young chimpanzee named Billy, tired of being bullied by the suburban gorilla gang, decides to build up his muscles so he won't be a wimp anymore

The book offers "delicious tongue-in-cheek humor and skillfully executed color artwork that has a crisp, polished look." Booklist

Other available titles about Willy are:
Willy and Hugh (1991)
Willy the champ (1986)
Willy the wizard (1995)

Zoo. Knopf 1992 unp il $15   E

1. Zoos—Fiction
ISBN 0-679-83946-1
LC 92-11708

Also available Spanish language edition

"A young narrator relates the incidents surrounding a day spent at the zoo with his brother and his parents. . . . The artwork is superb. . . . Nothing is ever quite as it ap-

Browne, Anthony—*Continued*

pears. The naturalistic representations of the zoo inhabitants are juxtaposed with animate features and expressions of the visitors." SLJ

Browne, Philippa-Alys

African animals ABC. Sierra Club Bks. for Children 1995 unp il $15.95   E

1. Animals—Africa 2. Alphabet

ISBN 0-87156-372-X   LC 95-4032

"This animal alphabet book is dominated by full-page paintings that are vibrantly, almost fluorescently, colored. With thick black lines and textures that resemble woodcuts, the compositions are underscored by patterns incorporating African motifs and characterizations that are whimsical. . . . The simple rhyming text has an appealing jauntiness. . . . The substantive information is relegated to an afterword, where size, classification, social group, diet, habitat, and gestation are noted." Booklist

Brunhoff, Jean de, 1899-1937

The story of Babar, the little elephant; translated from the French by Merle S. Haas. Random House 1937 c1933 47p il $13; lib bdg $11.99   E

1. Elephants—Fiction

ISBN 0-394-80575-5; 0-394-90575-X (lib bdg)

Also available facsmile reprint of the original oversized United States edition $19 (ISBN 0-394-86823-4); Spanish language edition also available

Original French edition, 1931; this is a reduced format version of the 1933 United States edition

"Babar runs away from the jungle and goes to live with an old lady in Paris, where he adapts quickly to French amenities. Later he returns to the jungle and becomes king. Much of the charm of the story is contributed by the author's gay pictures." Hodges. Books for Elem Sch Libr

Other available titles about Babar by Jean de Brunhoff are:
Babar and Father Christmas (1940)
Babar and his children (1938)
Babar the king (1935)
Travels of Babar (1934)

Other available titles about Babar by Laurent de Brunhoff are:
Babar and the ghost (1981)
Babar learns to cook (1978)
Babar loses his crown (1967)
Babar saves the day (1976)
Babar's ABC (1983)
Babar's anniversary album (1981)
Babar's birthday surprise (1970)
Babar's book of color (1984)
Babar's busy year (1989)
Barbar's family album (1991)
Babar's French lessons (1963)
Babar's little circus star (1988)
Babar's little girl (1987)
Babar's mystery (1978)
Babar's picnic (1991)
Meet Babar and his family (1973)

Brutschy, Jennifer

The winter fox; illustrated by Allen Garns. Knopf 1993 unp il $15; lib bdg $15.99   E

1. Rabbits—Fiction 2. Foxes—Fiction 3. Winter—Fiction

ISBN 0-679-81524-4; 0-679-91524-9 (lib bdg)

LC 92-33467

During a very cold winter, Rosemary's pet rabbit is taken by a hungry fox

This is "written in spare and sparkling prose. . . . Rosemary's tears, shed both for her rabbit and for its hungry predator, are utterly believable. Equally affecting in Allen Garns's richly textured illustrations is Rosemary's quiet, straightforward Papa." N Y Times Book Rev

Buckley, Helen E. (Helen Elizabeth)

Grandfather and I; [illustrated by] Jan Ormerod. Lothrop, Lee & Shepard Bks. 1994 unp il $13; lib bdg $12.93   E

1. Grandfathers—Fiction

ISBN 0-688-12533-6; 0-688-12534-4 (lib bdg)

LC 93-22936

A newly illustrated edition of the title first published 1959

A child considers how Grandfather is the perfect person to spend time with because he is never in a hurry

"Ormerod's full-color paintings teem with the warmth of a loving intergenerational family and fairly burst from the pages." SLJ

Grandmother and I; [illustrated by] Jan Ormerod. Lothrop, Lee & Shepard Bks. 1994 unp il $13; lib bdg $12.93   E

1. Grandmothers—Fiction

ISBN 0-688-12531-X; 0-688-12532-8 (lib bdg)

LC 93-22937

A newly illustrated edition of the title first published 1961

A child considers how Grandmother's lap is just right for those times when lightning is coming in the window or the cat is missing

"The watercolor art, done mostly in earth tones, varies from soft to sassy, but most of all, it is honest. Any child who has shared the unconditional love of a grandparent will see that love reflected here." Booklist

Bulla, Clyde Robert, 1914-

The chalk box kid; illustrated by Thomas B. Allen. Random House 1987 unp il $6.99; pa $3.99   E

ISBN 0-394-99102-8; 0-394-89102-3 (pa)

LC 87-4683

"Gregory's family moves to a smaller house in a poorer part of town; the father has lost his factory job. There is no yard at the new house in which to play, but Gregory explores a nearly burnt-out building that formerly was a chalk factory. Gregory finds plenty of chalk in the debris as he cleans up, and the artist in him soars." Publ Wkly

"As usual, Bulla manages a poignant depth within the confines of simple style and narrative. Understated and easy to read, this nevertheless tackles problems that are not easy to solve without exercising the imagination." Bull Cent Child Books

Daniel's duck; pictures by Joan Sandin. Harper & Row 1979 60p il lib bdg $15.75; pa $3.50   E

1. Wood carving—Fiction

ISBN 0-06-020909-7 (lib bdg); 0-06-444031-1 (pa)

LC 77-25647

"An I can read book"

"Daniel, who lived in 'a cabin on a mountain in Tennessee,' wanted 'to make something for the spring fair,' as the rest of the family were doing. Using the block of wood and the knife his father gave him, the boy carved a duck with

Bulla, Clyde Robert, 1914-—*Continued*
its head looking backward. At the fair, people laughed when they saw the carving, and Daniel thought his work was being ridiculed: but he was more than consoled by a famous local wood-carver, who not only praised Daniel's duck but offered to buy it. The easy-to-read story and the simple format are excellently served by the subdued three-color illustrations, which round out the account of a traditional Appalachian family." Horn Book

Bunting, Eve, 1928-
The day before Christmas; paintings by Beth Peck. Clarion Bks. 1992 unp il $14.95　　E
　1. Christmas—Fiction　　2. Ballet—Fiction
　3. Grandfathers—Fiction
　ISBN 0-89919-866-X　　　　LC 91-35099
Four years after the death of her mother, seven-year-old Allie goes with her grandfather to a performance of "The Nutcracker" on Christmas Eve, hears about the special day he had with her mother going to her first "Nutcracker," and shares his loving memory of her
"A gentle, simple story. . . . The California scenery, the presentation of the ballet, and Allie's delight are beautifully portrayed in sometimes strong, sometimes romantic, paintings." Horn Book

Flower garden; written by Eve Bunting; illustrated by Kathryn Hewitt. Harcourt Brace & Co. 1994 unp il $14　　E
　1. Flowers—Fiction 2. Birthdays—Fiction 3. Stories in rhyme
　ISBN 0-15-228776-0　　　　LC 92-25766
"The young narrator has, with the help of her father, assembled a 'garden in a shopping cart' to take home and plant in a window box high above the city as a birthday gift for her mother." Horn Book Guide
"The simple rhymed verse, which skips along in pace with the child's anticipation, is smoothly integrated with the vibrant, lifelike paintings." Booklist

Fly away home; illustrated by Ronald Himler. Clarion Bks. 1991 32p il $13.95; pa $5.95　　E
　1. Homeless persons—Fiction 2. Airports—Fiction
　3. Fathers and sons—Fiction
　ISBN 0-395-55962-6; 0-395-66415-2 (pa)
　　　　　　　　　　　　　　LC 90-42353
A homeless boy who lives in an airport with his father, moving from terminal to terminal and trying not to be noticed, is given hope when he sees a trapped bird find its freedom
"Himler's quiet paintings echo the economy and the touching quality of the story, which is all the more effective in depicting the plight of the homeless because it is so low-keyed." Bull Cent Child Books

Ghost's hour, spook's hour; illustrated by Donald Carrick. Clarion Bks. 1987 unp il lib bdg $14.95; pa $7.95　　E
　1. Night—Fiction 2. Fear—Fiction
　ISBN 0-89919-484-2 (lib bdg); 0-395-56244-9 (pa)
　　　　　　　　　　　　　　LC 86-31674
"A little boy, frightened by a howling wind and by a bedside lamp that doesn't turn on, creeps down to his parents' room only to find their bed empty and to hear more strange slitherings and thumpings on their window." Horn Book
"Bunting masterfully paces her story, with each fear of the child climaxing in his discovery of the basis for the sound. . . . The text is extended by Carrick's paintings,

most of which brood with the darkness and . . . change completely when the boy, with his parents, is no longer afraid: warm, comforting gold tones then enrobe the family. A book that provides the perfect blend of chills and comfort." SLJ

How many days to America? a Thanksgiving story; illustrated by Beth Peck. Clarion Bks. 1988 unp il lib bdg $15.95; pa $5.95　　E
　1. Refugees—Fiction 2. Thanksgiving Day—Fiction
　ISBN 0-89919-521-0 (lib bdg); 0-395-54777-6 (pa)
　　　　　　　　　　　　　　LC 88-2590
Refugees from an unnamed Caribbean island embark on a dangerous boat trip to America where they have a special reason to celebrate Thanksgiving
"Bunting's simple tale focuses on the hardships of the journey and on the American ideals of freedom and safety. She wisely leaves aside the issues of politics in the homeland or in this country. Her prose is poetically spare. . . . Peck's richly colored crayon drawings yield added enjoyment. . . . A poignant story and a thought-provoking discussion starter." SLJ

In the haunted house; illustrated by Susan Meddaugh. Clarion Bks. 1990 unp il $14.95; pa $5.95　　E
　1. Halloween—Fiction
　ISBN 0-395-51589-0; 0-395-69942-8 (pa)
　　　　　　　　　　　　　　LC 89-77663
"Skeletons pop out of closets and a bandaged mummy winks at two people—identified only by their red and blue high-top sneakers—as they explore a haunted house. Accompanying the pictures of green-faced witches and swirling ghosts is a rhyming text that relates what the two are seeing and their mutual assurances that they are really not frightened at all. Nice details in the pictures add to the ghoulish fun." Horn Book

The man who could call down owls; illustrated by Charles Mikolaycak. Macmillan 1984 unp il $14.95; pa $4.95　　E
　1. Owls—Fiction
　ISBN 0-02-715380-0; 0-689-71837-3 (pa)
　　　　　　　　　　　　　　LC 83-17568
"Every evening an old man carrying a willow wand, wearing a flowing white cape and a large hat, walks into the woods and calls the owls to him. And every evening a boy watches him, marveling at his mastery of the mysterious birds. An evil stranger, covetous but not respectful of the power the man wields, kills the owl-man and attempts to use his secrets, but it is the boy who inherits the cape at the end of the tale." Horn Book
"A haunting story, lyrically narrated, is realized in powerful pencil drawings that effortlessly draw viewers into their spell." Booklist

The Mother's Day mice; illustrated by Jan Brett. Clarion Bks. 1986 unp il lib bdg $14.95; pa $5.95　　E
　1. Gifts—Fiction 2. Mice—Fiction
　ISBN 0-89919-387-0 (lib bdg); 0-89919-702-7 (pa)
　　　　　　　　　　　　　　LC 85-13991
"Three little mice go out on a spring morning in search of Mother's Day presents. After suitable adventures they return with a dandelion, a strawberry and a song." N Y Times Book Rev
"The story is a sweet one, saved from being too sugary by Brett's wonderful full-color illustrations." Booklist

Bunting, Eve, 1928-—*Continued*

Night of the gargoyles; illustrated by David Wiesner. Clarion Bks. 1994 unp il $14.95

E

1. Monsters—Fiction 2. Museums—Fiction

ISBN 0-395-66553-1   LC 93-8160

In the middle of the night, the gargoyles that adorn a museum building come to life and frighten the night watchman

"This is an unusually sophisticated work, playful but dark-edged. Its language is both economical and rich, its mood a complex blend of the eerie, the sensuous . . . the innocent . . . and the melancholic. . . . Wiesner captures all these moods and more in marvelously textured charcoal-powder illustrations that powerfully infuse the stone-solid watersprouts with life." Publ Wkly

Night tree; illustrated by Ted Rand. Harcourt Brace Jovanovich 1991 unp il $15; pa $5

E

1. Trees—Fiction 2. Christmas—Fiction

ISBN 0-15-257425-5; 0-15-200121-2 (pa)

LC 90-36178

A family makes its annual pilgrimage to decorate an evergreen tree with food for the forest animals at Christmastime

"Bunting's quiet text and Rand's watercolors have just the right nighttime mood, capturing the mystery of the woods where there are 'secrets all around us.'" Bull Cent Child Books

A perfect Father's Day; illustrated by Susan Meddaugh. Clarion Bks. 1991 unp il $13.95; pa $5.95

E

1. Father's Day—Fiction 2. Fathers and daughters—Fiction

ISBN 0-395-52590-X; 0-395-66416-0 (pa)

LC 90-42355

When four-year-old Susie treats her father to a series of special activities for Father's Day, they just happen to be all of her own favorite things

"Bunting's simple, witty text sketches a warm father-daughter relationship and affectionately glances at the four-year-old mind at work. Meddaugh's bright watercolor and pencil illustrations add to the humor." Booklist

Red fox running; paintings by Wendell Minor. Clarion Bks. 1993 unp il $15.95

E

1. Foxes—Fiction 2. Stories in rhyme 3. Winter—Fiction

ISBN 0-395-58919-3   LC 92-27

Rhyming text follows the experiences of a red fox as it searches across a wintery landscape for food

"As naturalistic and delicate as the text, Minor's full-color artwork captures with precision the sights of the rural landscape. . . . From the typography to the picture borders to the shadowy figure of a fox that appears on each page of text, the design elements here show thoughtful attention to detail." Booklist

Scary, scary Halloween; pictures by Jan Brett. Clarion Bks. 1986 unp il $14.95; pa $5.95

E

1. Halloween—Fiction 2. Cats—Fiction 3. Stories in rhyme

ISBN 0-89919-414-1; 0-89919-799-X (pa)

LC 86-2642

A band of trick-or-treaters and a mother cat and her kittens spend a very scary Halloween

"Tailored for nursery and pre-school holiday read-aloud sessions, this is a slightly spooky picturebook with bright graphics on a black background showing costumed creepies prancing through the night, all watched by four pairs of green eyes hiding under a porch. . . . The faces on the creatures, the pumpkins, and even the trees will inspire shivers of delight in any darkened room." Bull Cent Child Books

Smoky night; written by Eve Bunting; illustrated by David Diaz. Harcourt Brace & Co. 1994 unp il $15

E

1. Riots—Fiction 2. Los Angeles (Calif.)—Fiction 3. African Americans—Fiction 4. Korean Americans—Fiction

ISBN 0-15-269954-6   LC 93-14885

Awarded the Caldecott Medal, 1995

When the Los Angeles riots break out in the streets of their neighborhood, Daniel and his mother, African Americans, make friends with Mrs. Kim, a Korean grocer from across the street

"Diaz's bold artwork is a perfect match for the intensity of the story. Thick black lines border vibrant acrylic paintings. . . . Diaz places these dynamic paintings on collages of real objects that, for the most part, reinforce the narrative action. . . . Both author and illustrator insist on a headlong confrontation with the issue of rapport between different races, and the result is a memorable, thought-provoking book." Horn Book

Someday a tree; illustrated by Ronald Himler. Clarion Bks. 1993 unp il $14.95; pa $5.95

E

1. Trees—Fiction 2. Pollution—Fiction

ISBN 0-395-61309-4; 0-395-76478-5 (pa)

LC 92-24074

Alice, her parents, and their neighbors try to save an old oak tree that has been poisoned by pollution

"Himler's soft, realistic watercolors spread over double pages and complement the sensitive, poetic mood of the story." SLJ

Sunshine Home; illustrated by Diane de Groat. Clarion Bks. 1994 32p il $14.95   E

1. Grandmothers—Fiction 2. Nursing homes—Fiction 3. Old age—Fiction

ISBN 0-395-63309-5   LC 93-570

When he and his parents visit his grandmother in the nursing home where she is recovering from a broken hip, everyone pretends to be happy until Tim helps them express their true feelings

"A rare and perceptive book on an increasingly important topic. . . . Bunting tells of one family's transition with dignity, honesty, sensitivity, and just enough humor to make it bearable. . . . de Groat's realistic watercolor illustrations are appropriately heavy on institutional green and poignantly support the text." SLJ

A turkey for Thanksgiving; illustrated by Diane de Groat. Clarion Bks. 1991 31p il lib bdg $13.95

E

1. Thanksgiving Day—Fiction 2. Turkeys—Fiction 3. Moose—Fiction

ISBN 0-89919-793-0   LC 90-21871

Mr. and Mrs. Moose invite a turkey to their Thanksgiving feast

"Young readers will be as thrilled as Turkey to hear that Mrs. Moose wants him *at* her table, not *on* it. Together, Bunting's good-natured tale and de Groat's autumn-hued, richly detailed watercolors convey the animals' warm friendship and the humor resulting from the misunderstanding." Publ Wkly

Bunting, Eve, 1928-—_Continued_

The Wall; illustrated by Ronald Himler. Clarion Bks. 1990 unp il $14.95; pa $5.95

E

1. Fathers and sons—Fiction 2. Vietnam Veterans Memorial (Washington, D.C.)—Fiction
ISBN 0-395-51588-2; 0-395-62977-2 (pa)

LC 89-17429

"A father and his young son come to the Vietnam Veterans Memorial to find the name of the grandfather the boy never knew. This moving account is beautifully told from a young child's point of view; the watercolors capture the impressive mass of the wall of names as well as the poignant reactions of the people who visit there." Horn Book Guide

The Wednesday surprise; illustrated by Donald Carrick. Clarion Bks. 1989 unp il lib bdg $14.95; pa $5.95

E

1. Grandmothers—Fiction 2. Reading—Fiction
ISBN 0-89919-721-3 (lib bdg); 0-395-54776-8 (pa)

LC 88-12117

This "first-person account tells of the special gift that seven-year-old Anna and her grandmother have planned for her dad's birthday; secretly, the two read books together until finally, the grandmother has learned to read." SLJ

"Bunting's writing is simple and warm and direct, showing rather than telling the book's audience that reading is both a skill and a joy. Carrick's pictures echo the warmth, especially in the faces of the family, painted in realistically detailed watercolors with a careful attention to familial resemblance. A gentle charmer." Bull Cent Child Books

Burningham, John, 1936-

Aldo. Crown 1992 c1991 unp il $15; lib bdg $15.99

E

1. Imaginary playmates—Fiction
ISBN 0-517-58701-7; 0-517-58699-1 (lib bdg)

LC 91-19589

First published 1991 in the United Kingdom

A small girl reflects on the comfort she gets from her imaginary rabbit friend Aldo

"A poignant outsider story. . . . The contrast between the spare, pale drawings of her real world and the richly colored, impressionistic double-page spreads of her imaginary play speaks of the intensity beneath her unobtrusive appearance. . . . Every child will recognize the loneliness." Booklist

The baby. Candlewick Press 1994 unp il $6.95; pa $3.99

E

1. Brothers and sisters—Fiction 2. Infants—Fiction
ISBN 1-56402-334-6; 1-56402-689-2 (pa)

LC 93-24277

A reissue of the title first published 1974 in the United Kingdom; first United States edition 1975 by Crowell

"A big brother finds that sometimes he likes the baby—and sometimes he doesn't!." Publisher's note

The blanket. Candlewick Press 1994 unp il $6.95

E

1. Blankets—Fiction 2. Bedtime—Fiction
ISBN 1-56402-337-0

LC 93-24288

A reissue of the title first published 1975 in the United Kingdom; first United States edition 1976 by Crowell

Unable to find the blanket he always takes to bed with him, a child enlists the aid of his family to help him look for it

"Burningham's realizations are completely uncluttered, befitting the smallest listeners' perceptions of their own small world. . . . With charmingly naive crayon illustrations." Booklist

Come away from the water, Shirley. Crowell 1977 unp il lib bdg $14.89

E

1. Pirates—Fiction 2. Beaches—Fiction
ISBN 0-690-01361-2

LC 77-483

"A little girl uses her imagination to rise above all-too-familiar parental warnings at the beach." LC. Child Books, 1977

Another available title about Shirley is:
Time to get out of the bath, Shirley (1978)

The dog. Candlewick Press 1994 unp il $6.95; pa $2.99

E

1. Dogs—Fiction
ISBN 1-56402-326-5; 1-56402-435-0 (pa)

LC 93-10341

A reissue of the title first published 1975 in the United Kingdom; first United States edition 1976 by Crowell

A small boy enjoys looking after a dog that is staying at his home awhile

This book offers "small size . . . clean design, and Burningham's vigorous illustrations." Horn Book

The friend. Candlewick Press 1994 unp il $6.95

E

1. Friendship—Fiction
ISBN 1-56402-327-3

LC 93-10331

A reissue of the title first published 1975 in the United Kingdom; first United States edition 1976 by Crowell

"The young narrator knows that Arthur is his best friend, even when they fight and Arthur goes home." Horn Book

Granpa. Crown 1985 c1984 unp il $14; pa $5.99

E

1. Grandfathers—Fiction
ISBN 0-517-55643-X; 0-517-58797-1 (pa)

LC 84-17464

First published 1984 in the United Kingdom

"The special relationship between a little girl and her grandfather is lovingly portrayed in a series of double-page vignettes. . . . Text is minimal; it is the illustrations in pastel crayon and pen-and-ink that bring to life the activities of the two and their love for each other. The book is an exaltation of a glorious relationship with the life/continuum viewed as the natural progression of things." SLJ

John Burningham's ABC. Crown 1993 unp il $13; lib bdg $13.99

E

1. Alphabet
ISBN 0-517-59503-6; 0-517-59504-4 (lib bdg)

LC 92-42765

A reissue of the title first published 1964 in the United Kingdom; first United States edition 1967 by Bobbs-Merrill

Upper and lower case letters and labeled pictures depict dogs, flowers, umbrellas, a wasp, and other animals and objects from A to Z

"Lively, vigorous, glowing, John Burningham's alphabet book demands attention. . . . In addition to the brilliance of color and boldness of form, there are also touches of the unexpected." Horn Book

Mr. Gumpy's outing. Holt & Co. 1971 c1970 unp il $14.95; pa $5.95

E

1. Animals—Fiction
ISBN 0-8050-0708-3; 0-8050-1315-6 (pa)

First published 1970 in the United Kingdom

Burningham, John, 1936—*Continued*

"Mr. Gumpy is about to go off for a boat ride and is asked by two children, a rabbit, a cat, a dog, and other animals if they may come. To each Mr. Gumpy says yes, if— if the children don't squabble, if the rabbit won't hop, if the cat won't chase the rabbit or the dog tease the cat, and so on. Of course each does exactly what Mr. Gumpy forbade, the boat tips over, and they all slog home for tea in friendly fashion." Sutherland. The Best in Child Books

Another available title about Mr. Gumpy is:
Mr. Gumpy's motor car (1976)

Burton, Virginia Lee, 1909-1968

Katy and the big snow; story and pictures by Virginia Lee Burton. Houghton Mifflin 1943 32p il $14.95; pa $4.95   E

1. Tractors—Fiction 2. Snow—Fiction
ISBN 0-395-18155-0; 0-395-18562-9 (pa)

"Katy was a beautiful red crawler tractor. In summer she wore a bulldozer to push dirt with. In winter she wore a snowplow. She was big and strong and the harder the job the better she liked it. When the Big Snow covered the city of Geoppolis like a thick blanket, Katy cleared the city from North to South and East to West." Ont Libr Rev

The little house; story and pictures by Virginia Lee Burton. Houghton Mifflin 1942 40p il $14.95; pa $4.95   E

1. Houses—Fiction 2. Cities and towns—Fiction
ISBN 0-395-18156-9; 0-395-25938-X (pa)

Also available Spanish language edition

Awarded the Caldecott Medal, 1943

"The little house was very happy as she sat on the quiet hillside watching the changing seasons. As the years passed, however, tall buildings grew up around her, and the noise of city traffic disturbed her. She became sad and lonely until one day someone who understood her need for twinkling stars overhead and dancing apple blossoms moved her back to just the right little hill." Child Books Too Good to Miss

Mike Mulligan and his steam shovel; story and pictures by Virginia Lee Burton. Houghton Mifflin 1939 unp il $14.95; lib bdg $11.95; pa $4.95   E

1. Steam-shovels—Fiction
ISBN 0-395-16961-5; 0-395-06681-6 (lib bdg); 0-395-25939-8 (pa)

"Mike Mulligan remains faithful to his steam shovel, Mary Anne, against the threat of the new gas and Diesel-engine contraptions and digs his way to a surprising and happy ending." New Yorker

"One of the most convincing personifications of a machine ever written. Lively pictures, dramatic action, and a satisfying conclusion." Adventuring with Books. 2d edition

Butler, Dorothy, 1925-

My brown bear Barney; illustrated by Elizabeth Fuller. Greenwillow Bks. 1989 unp il $16; lib bdg $13.93   E

1. Teddy bears—Fiction
ISBN 0-688-08567-9; 0-688-08568-7 (lib bdg)
LC 88-21199

First published 1988 in New Zealand

"As a wide-eyed, straight-haired little girl enumerates all the places she takes her brown bear, Barney, her faithful teddy is spied amid the weeds in the wheelbarrow, sunning at the beach, and—of course—tucked into bed. . . . But

when the youngster itemizes the things she'll carry to school, the omnipresent Barney is conspicuously absent." Booklist

"Every item on the little girl's checklists is first pictured clearly for easy identification and then imaginatively placed in its proper narrative context in an inviting, bright full-page illustration with just enough detail to fascinate but not overwhelm." Horn Book

Another available title about Barney is:
My brown bear Barney in trouble (1993)

Byars, Betsy Cromer, 1928-

Go and hush the baby; by Betsy Byars; illustrated by Emily A. McCully. Viking 1971 unp il hardcover o.p. paperback available $4.99   E

1. Brothers and sisters—Fiction 2. Infants—Fiction
ISBN 0-14-050396-X (pa)

"Just as he is about to leave the house, bat in hand, Will is asked by his mother to pacify the baby. He performs and the baby smiles, but as soon as Will leaves the crying resumes. Play a game, mother suggests. Finally Will launches on a story that quiets the baby and so intrigues the storyteller that he is surprised when he loses his audience to a nursing bottle. 'Well, I have to play this game of baseball anyway,' he announces as he goes off." Bull Cent Child Books

"A charming little picture book, told with simplicity and illustrated with appealing two-color drawings." Booklist

The Golly sisters go West; by Betsy Byars; pictures by Sue Truesdell. Harper & Row 1986 c1985 64p il lib bdg $14.89; pa $3.50   E

1. Entertainers—Fiction 2. Frontier and pioneer life—Fiction 3. West (U.S.)—Fiction
ISBN 0-06-020884-8 (lib bdg); 0-06-444132-6 (pa)
LC 84-48474

"An I can read book"

May-May and Rose, the singing, dancing Golly sisters, travel west by covered wagon, entertaining people along the way

"In the first story, they learn the hard way how to make a horse move forward; in the second, they give their first road show to an audience of two dogs; in the third, they get lost; in the fourth, try to incorporate the horse into their act; in the fifth, make up after one of their constant arguments; in the sixth, talk themselves out of a nighttime scare. The dialogue and antics are convincingly like those of rivalrous young siblings anywhere on the block. The story lines are cleverer than much easy-to-read fare, and the old-West setting adds flair. The accompanying watercolors, too, add a generous dollop of humor." Bull Cent Child Books

Other available titles about the Golly sisters are:
The Golly sisters ride again (1994)
Hooray for the Golly sisters! (1990)

Caines, Jeannette Franklin, 1938-

Abby; pictures by Steven Kellogg. Harper & Row 1973 32p il lib bdg $13.89; pa $4.95   E

1. Adoption—Fiction 2. Brothers and sisters—Fiction 3. African Americans—Fiction
ISBN 0-06-020922-4 (lib bdg); 0-06-443049-9 (pa)

Abby, an adopted pre-schooler, "loves to look at her baby book, even more, to listen to stories told by her mother and by her brother, Kevin, about the day she became part of the family. . . . A crisis arises when Kevin announces he can't be bothered with her because she's a girl. But the clouds roll by when big brother says he was only

Caines, Jeannette Franklin, 1938——*Continued*
fooling and that he loves her. In fact, he will even take her to school with him and feature Abby at show-and-tell time." Publ Wkly

This "story of a warm and loving black family living in a city apartment could be used to introduce the subject of adoption. . . . Shaded drawings showing the family at home perfectly complement the story." SLJ

I need a lunch box; by Jeannette Caines; pictures by Pat Cummings. Harper & Row 1988 unp il $15; lib bdg $14.89; pa $4.95
E
1. African Americans—Fiction
ISBN 0-06-020984-4; 0-06-020985-2 (lib bdg); 0-06-443341-2 (pa)
LC 85-45829
"A little boy's big sister has just gotten a lunch box, and he wants one too. Mama says no, because unlike his sister, he isn't about to start school. Still, the boy covets one, thinking about what he could keep in it—his crayons, marbles, bug collection, or toy animals—and dreaming of a different model for each day of the week. . . . Cummings' pictures are exuberant paintings that don't stint on strident displays of strong color." Booklist

Just us women; by Jeannette Caines; illustrated by Pat Cummings. Harper & Row 1982 32p il $14.95; pa $4.95
E
1. Aunts—Fiction 2. Travelers—Fiction 3. African Americans—Fiction
ISBN 0-06-020942-9; 0-06-443056-1 (pa)
LC 81-48655
This is the "story of a Black little girl planning a long car trip with her favorite aunt. Enjoying being together, 'no boys and no men, just us women,' they pack carefully and buy two road maps (because last year Aunt Martha forgot their lunch and the map on the kitchen table)." SLJ

"The pleasure of that trip and the warm relationship it represents shine through in realistic, sometimes photograph-like pictures." Booklist

Calhoun, Mary, 1926-
Cross-country cat; illustrated by Erick Ingraham. Morrow 1979 unp il $12.95; lib bdg $15.93; pa $4.95
E
1. Cats—Fiction
ISBN 0-688-22186-6; 0-688-32186-0 (lib bdg); 0-698-06519-8 (pa)
LC 78-31718
When he becomes lost in the mountains, Henry, a cat with the unusual ability of walking on two legs finds his way home on cross-country skis

"Only the careful blending of skills by a talented author and illustrator could turn such a farfetched plot into a warm, rich, and rewarding story. The realistic illustrations seem to be enveloped in a glowing light and invite the reader to step right into the story." Child Book Rev Serv

Other available titles about Henry are:
Henry the sailor cat (1994)
High-wire Henry (1991)
Hot-air Henry (1981)

Calmenson, Stephanie
The principal's new clothes; illustrated by Denise Brunkus. Scholastic 1989 unp il $12.95; pa $3.95
E
1. School stories
ISBN 0-590-41822-X; 0-590-44778-5 (pa)
LC 88-30314

In this version of the Andersen tale the vain principal of P.S. 88 is persuaded by two tailors that they will make him an amazing, one-of-a-kind, suit that will be visible only to intelligent people who are good at their jobs

"Sly expressions spice these cartooned watercolors that will have children giggling through to the very end." Booklist

Cannon, Janell, 1957-
Stellaluna. Harcourt Brace Jovanovich 1993 unp il $15
E
1. Bats—Fiction 2. Birds—Fiction
ISBN 0-15-280217-7
LC 92-16439
Also available Spanish language edition
After she falls headfirst into a bird's nest, a baby bat is raised like a bird until she is reunited with her mother

"Cannon's delightful story is full of gentle humor. . . . [She] provides good information about bats in the story, amplifying it in two pages of notes at the end of the book. Her full-page colored-pencil-and-acrylic paintings fairly glow." Booklist

Carle, Eric
Do you want to be my friend? Crowell 1971 unp il $15; lib bdg $14.89; pa $5.95
E
1. Mice—Fiction 2. Stories without words
ISBN 0-690-24276-X; 0-690-01137-7 (lib bdg); 0-06-443127-4 (pa)
"The only text is the title question at the start and a shy 'Yes!' at the close. The pictures do the rest, as the hopeful mouse overtakes one large creature after another. With each encounter, the mouse sees (on the right-hand page) an interesting tail. Turn the page, and there is a huge lion, or a malevolent fox, or a peacock, and then, at last another wee mouse." Saturday Rev

"Good material for discussion and guessing games. . . . The pictures tell an amusing story and they are good to look at as well." Times Lit Suppl

The grouchy ladybug. Crowell 1977 unp il $15; lib bdg $14.89; pa $5.95
E
1. Ladybugs—Fiction
ISBN 0-690-01391-4; 0-690-01392-2 (lib bdg); 0-06-443116-9 (pa)
LC 77-3170
Also available Spanish language edition
"Hour by hour, a hungry, irritable ladybug challenges everyone she meets to a fight. As the creatures encountered by the ladybug become larger, so do the pages and the accompanying print. The climax is reached on the tail of a Blue Whale. The story is resolved with the ladybug returning to her starting point, contrite and pleasant at last." Child Book Rev Serv

"The finger paint and collage illustrations—as bold as the feisty hero—are satisfyingly placed on pages sized to suit the successsive animals that appear (one is cut in the fan shape of the whale's tail). Tiny clocks show the time of each enjoyable encounter, with the sun rising and setting as the action proceeds." SLJ

A house for Hermit Crab. Picture Bk. Studio 1988 c1987 unp il $15.95; pa $4.95
E
1. Crabs—Fiction
ISBN 0-88708-056-1; 0-88708-168-1 (pa)
LC 87-29261
"Hermit Crab, having outgrown his old shell, sets out to find a new one. He's a bit frightened at first, but over the course of the next year acquires not only a shell, but also an array of sea creatures to decorate, clean, and protect his

Carle, Eric—*Continued*

new home. The story ends with him once again outgrowing his shell." SLJ

"The bright illustrations in Carle's familiar style, which seems particularly suited to undersea scenes, and the cumulative story are splendid, and one of the book's greatest strengths is the encouraging, hopeful view that the outside world is full of exciting possibilities." Horn Book

The mixed-up chameleon; by Eric Carle. Crowell 1984 unp il $15; lib bdg $14.89; pa $5.95 E

1. Chameleons—Fiction
ISBN 0-690-04396-1; 0-690-04397-X (lib bdg); 0-06-443162-2 (pa) LC 83-45950

A revised and newly illustrated edition of the title first published 1975

"A chameleon goes to a zoo where it wishes it could become like the different animals it sees. It does, but then isn't happy until it wishes it could be itself again." Child Book Rev Serv

The author "has replaced the heavy-lined, childlike, scrawled colors with crisp, appealing collages and has streamlined the text. The cutaway pages have been retained, and none of the humor has been lost. The simpler text results in a smoother flow, and children will enjoy the resulting repetition." Booklist

The very busy spider. Philomel Bks. 1984 unp il $19.95; pa $6.95 E

1. Spiders—Fiction
ISBN 0-399-21166-7; 0-399-21592-1 (pa)
LC 84-5907

"Blown by the wind across the book's first pages and onto a fence post near a farm yard, a spider begins to spin a web. Her task allows her no time to answer barnyard animals, each of whom invites her to join in a favorite activity. Finally, her web completed, she snags the pesty fly that's been annoying all of the animals and, exhausted, falls asleep." SLJ

This book "has a disarming ingenuousness and a repetitive structure that will capture the response of pre-school audiences. Of special note is the book's use of raised lines for the spider, its web, and an unsuspecting fly. Both sighted and blind children will be able to follow the action with ease." Booklist

The very hungry caterpillar. Philomel Bks. 1981 c1970 unp il $16.95; lib bdg $17.95; pa $4.95 E

1. Caterpillars—Fiction
ISBN 0-399-20853-4; 0-399-22753-9 (lib bdg); 0-399-21301-5 (pa)

Also available Spanish language edition

First published 1970 by World Publishing Company

"This caterpillar is so hungry he eats right through the pictures on the pages of the book—and after leaving many holes emerges as a beautiful butterfly on the last page." Best Books for Child, 1972

The very lonely firefly. Philomel Bks. 1995 unp il $19.95 E

1. Fireflies—Fiction
ISBN 0-399-22774-1 LC 94-27827

A lonely firefly goes out into the night searching for other fireflies

"The illustrations are painted cut-paper collages, designed to draw the eye to the page. This is a compelling accomplishment." SLJ

The very quiet cricket. Philomel Bks. 1990 unp il $19.95 E

1. Crickets—Fiction
ISBN 0-399-21885-8 LC 89-78317

A very quiet cricket who wants to rub his wings together and make a sound as do so many other animals finally achieves his wish

"The text is skillfully shaped; the illustrations convey energy and immediacy; and, in a surprise ending, a microchip inserted in the last page replicates the cricket's chirp." Horn Book Guide

Carlson, Nancy L., 1953-

I like me! [by] Nancy Carlson. Viking Kestrel 1988 unp il $18.99; lib bdg $14.99; pa $3.99 E

1. Pigs—Fiction
ISBN 0-14-054846-1; 0-670-82062-8 (lib bdg); 0-14-050819-8 (pa) LC 87-32616

By admiring her finer points and showing that she can take care of herself and have fun even when there's no one else around, a charming pig proves the best friend you can have is yourself

This book is "visually interesting, with sturdy animals drawn in a deliberately artless style. Simple shapes, strong lines, and clear colors, with lots of pattern mixing, show what is not described in the minimal text. The text is hand-lettered." SLJ

Carlson, Natalie Savage, 1906-

Spooky night; illustrated by Andrew Glass. Lothrop, Lee & Shepard Bks. 1982 unp il $16; lib bdg $13.88 E

1. Cats—Fiction 2. Witches—Fiction 3. Halloween—Fiction
ISBN 0-688-00934-4; 0-688-00935-2 (lib bdg)
LC 82-54

A witch's black cat who wishes to become a family pet must perform one last bit of magic before he can be free

"Just the right ingredients—a cat, a witch, and a spooky night—are brewed into a gentle Halloween story. . . . The shadowy crosshatched illustrations show to advantage the dark night with shooting stars, the mean witch, and Spooky's emerald green eyes." Horn Book

Carlstrom, Nancy White, 1948-

Jesse Bear, what will you wear? illustrations by Bruce Degen. Macmillan 1986 unp il $15 E

1. Bears—Fiction 2. Stories in rhyme
ISBN 0-02-717350-X LC 85-10610

Also available in paperback from Aladdin Bks.

"The happy, singsong verse of the title follows Jesse Bear through the changes of clothes and activities of his day, even to bath and bed." N Y Times Book Rev

"The big, cheerful watercolor paintings show the baby bear in loving relation to his family and world. Without crossing the line into sentimentality, this offers a happy, humorous soundfest that will associate reading aloud with a sense of play." Bull Cent Child Books

Other available titles about Jesse Bear are:
Better not get wet, Jesse Bear (1988)
Happy birthday, Jesse Bear (1994)
How do you say it today, Jesse Bear? (1992)
It's about time, Jesse Bear, and other rhymes (1990)

Carrick, Carol

Big old bones; a dinosaur tale; illustrated by Donald Carrick. Clarion Bks. 1989 unp il $14.95; pa $6.95 E

1. Fossils—Fiction
ISBN 0-89919-734-5; 0-395-61582-8 (pa)

LC 88-16967

"In this tale the learned professor Potts and his family are traveling out West when he finds a fascinating site with quantities of very large, very old bones. He takes them home and tries different ways of assembling them, but the resulting skeletons are too absurd to be believed. . . . The book is a gentle spoof of early paleontologists who were a little unsure of exactly what they had found. It will be a treat for almost every child over the age of three, who will have an enjoyable feeling of superiority as the professor bungles about, making ridiculous mistakes." Horn Book

The foundling; pictures by Donald Carrick. Seabury Press 1977 unp il lib. bdg $14.95; pa $4.95 E

1. Dogs—Fiction
ISBN 0-8164-3199-X; 0-89919-466-4 (pa)

LC 77-1587

"A Clarion book"
Memories of his dog, killed in an accident, cause Christopher to resist his parents' efforts to adopt a puppy
"Christopher's emotions will speak directly to readers. With Donald Carrick's snug, appealing, detailed pencil and watercolor illustrations." Booklist
Other available titles about Christopher are:
The accident (1976)
Ben and the porcupine (1981)
Dark and full of secrets (1984)
Left behind (1988)
Sleep out (1973)
The washout (1978)

In the moonlight, waiting; illustrated by Donald Carrick. Clarion Bks. 1990 unp il lib bdg $13.95 E

1. Sheep—Fiction 2. Farm life—Fiction
ISBN 0-89919-867-8 LC 89-17430

In the spring during lambing time, a family wakes in the middle of the night to welcome Clover the sheep's new baby
"The story—full of a sense of life and the renewal of spring—captures the shivery excitement of waking during the night for a special event. The watercolor sketches made by Donald Carrick before his death have a fresh, spontaneous, and unformed quality that heightens the emotional intensity of newness and birth." Horn Book

Patrick's dinosaurs; pictures by Donald Carrick. Clarion Bks. 1983 unp il lib bdg $14.95; pa $5.95 E

1. Dinosaurs—Fiction 2. Brothers—Fiction
ISBN 0-89919-189-4 (lib bdg); 0-89919-402-8 (pa)

LC 83-2049

"During a zoo visit, Patrick's older brother Hank compares the size, habits, and ferocity of dinosaurs to the animals in the zoo, blithely unaware that Patrick is becoming increasingly afraid. . . . Only at home over peanut-butter-and-jelly sandwiches, when Hank assures him that 'dinosaurs have been gone for sixty million years,' can Patrick relax." Booklist
"The Carricks do a particularly good job of creating an impressive array of creatures both in text and illustrations—realistic pencil drawings washed in muted greens, browns and oranges." SLJ
Another available title about Patrick is entered below

What happened to Patrick's dinosaurs? pictures by Donald Carrick. Clarion Bks. 1986 unp il lib bdg $15.95; pa $5.95 E

1. Dinosaurs—Fiction 2. Brothers—Fiction
ISBN 0-89919-406-0 (lib bdg); 0-89919-797-3 (pa)

LC 85-13989

"While he and his brother Hank rake leaves, Patrick unfolds the true life and times of dinosaurs. They were friends with people once, you see, picnicking and fishing, building houses, operating car wind-up (not fill-up) service stations and presenting carnival shows to bored humans. Patrick recounts the sad fact that people did not want to learn from the dinosaurs, as they were only interested in recess and lunch, so the dinosaurs left on a spaceship, keeping a celestial check on the people they miss so dearly." SLJ
"A kindly, funny book, wonderfully evocative of the imagination of children, with a theme that will appear perfectly probable to young readers." Horn Book

Carrick, Donald

Harald and the great stag. Clarion Bks. 1988 unp il lib bdg $15.95 E

1. Deer—Fiction 2. Hunting—Fiction 3. Middle Ages—Fiction
ISBN 0-89919-514-8 LC 87-17875

Sequel to Harald and the giant knight (1982)
When Harald, who lives in medieval England, hears that the Baron and his royal guests are planning to hunt the legendary Great Stag, he devises a clever scheme to protect the animal
"The clear antihunting statement reaches across the ages. Carrick's rendering of the characters and details of the period add depth to the simple tale. In full color the illustrations capture the lush forest from misty morning through sunset." Horn Book

Carson, Jo, 1946-

You hold me and I'll hold you; story by Jo Carson; pictures by Annie Cannon. Orchard Bks. 1992 unp il $14.95; lib bdg $14.99 E

1. Death—Fiction 2. Fathers and daughters—Fiction
ISBN 0-531-05895-6; 0-531-08495-7 (lib bdg)

LC 91-16370

"A Richard Jackson book"
When a great-aunt dies, a young girl finds comfort in being held by her father and in holding, too
The author "has created an engaging and straightforward heroine to dramatize the impact of death on a child—this girl thinks, reacts and talks in a remarkably believable fashion, making her narration all the more touching. . . . Lightly tinted watercolors with collaged-in materials provide an unthreatening setting, and Cannon . . . paints a family of reassuringly lovable people. . . . A moving and sensitive exploration of a difficult topic." Publ Wkly

Caseley, Judith, 1951-

Dear Annie. Greenwillow Bks. 1991 unp il $15; lib bdg $14.93; pa $4.95 E

1. Grandfathers—Fiction 2. Letters—Fiction
ISBN 0-688-10010-4; 0-688-10011-2 (lib bdg); 0-688-13575-7 (pa) LC 90-39793

Presents a series of postcards and letters Annie sends to or receives from her loving grandfather from the time she is born
"The line-and-watercolor illustrations of the letters and the cozy details of Grandpa's and Annie's lives are bright

Caseley, Judith, 1951-—*Continued*

vignettes set within lots of white space, giving the book an open and friendly tone. The affection between a grandparent and child is rarely captured with such easygoing warmth." Bull Cent Child Books

Mama, coming and going. Greenwillow Bks. 1994 unp il $14; lib bdg $13.93   E

1. Infants—Fiction 2. Mothers and daughters—Fiction 3. Brothers and sisters—Fiction

ISBN 0-688-11441-5; 0-688-11442-3 (lib bdg)

LC 92-29402

Big sister Jenna recalls the funny things that Mama forgot to do after baby Mickey was born

"The cheerful watercolor-and-pencil drawings are filled with bright yellows, blues, and reds. . . . A lighthearted glance at a loving family during a topsy-turvy time." SLJ

Mr. Green Peas. Greenwillow Bks. 1995 unp il $15; lib bdg $14.93   E

1. Iguanas—Fiction 2. Pets—Fiction 3. Nursery schools—Fiction

ISBN 0-688-12859-9; 0-688-12860-2 (lib bdg)

LC 93-24183

Norman is sad because he's the only one in his nursery school class who doesn't have a pet, until he gets a pet iguana

"Everything about this book is charming: the tantalizing subject, the large text in bold print, the decorative borders, and the colorful illustrations, which brim with interesting details to hold children's attention." Booklist

Sophie and Sammy's library sleepover. Greenwillow Bks. 1993 unp il $15; lib bdg $14.93   E

1. Books and reading—Fiction 2. Brothers and sisters—Fiction 3. Libraries—Fiction

ISBN 0-688-10615-3; 0-688-10616-1 (lib bdg)

LC 91-48160

"When Sophie goes with her mother to a library sleepover, her little brother Sammy (who demolishes books) stays at home. . . . The next night, she sets up a similar sleepover for Sammy on her bed." SLJ

"Caseley does an admirable job capturing the energetic fun of the library; throughout she uses bright, inviting patterns and colors and features sturdy, appealing looking children." Horn Book

Castañeda, Omar S., 1954-

Abuela's weave; illustrated by Enrique O. Sanchez. Lee & Low Bks. 1993 unp il $14.95; pa $5.95   E

1. Grandmothers—Fiction 2. Guatemala—Fiction 3. Weaving—Fiction

ISBN 1-880000-00-8; 0-880000-20-2 (pa)

LC 92-71927

Also available Spanish language edition

A young Guatemalan girl and her grandmother grow closer as they weave some special creations and then make a trip to the market in hopes of selling them

"Castañeda affectingly portrays the loving rapport between a child and her grandmother, as well as the beauty of his homeland's cultural traditions. Sanchez's bright, richly grained acrylic-on-canvas paintings bring dimension to the characters and authenticity to the setting." Publ Wkly

Cauley, Lorinda Bryan, 1951-

Clap your hands. Putnam 1992 unp il $15.95   E

1. Animals—Fiction 2. Stories in rhyme

ISBN 0-399-22118-2   LC 91-12863

Rhyming text instructs the listener to find something yellow, roar like a lion, give a kiss, tell a secret, spin in a circle, and perform other playful activities along with the human and animal characters pictured

"In a series of lively double-page spreads, the illustrations feature glowing colors and make good use of Cauley's gift for characterization. . . . Some parts of the book would be fun as action rhymes for preschool story time. . . . Parent-child sharing would also be fun, though not at bedtime: this book's bugle call is not taps, but reveille." Booklist

Cech, John

My grandmother's journey; illustrated by Sharon McGinley-Nally. Bradbury Press 1991 unp il $14.95   E

1. Grandmothers—Fiction 2. Russian Americans—Fiction 3. Immigration and emigration—Fiction

ISBN 0-02-718135-9   LC 90-35731

A grandmother tells the story of her eventful life in early twentieth-century Russia and her arrival in the United States after World War II

"Based on the life of Cech's mother-in-law, the book is illustrated with bright, colorful pictures that have folk-art borders and complement the text beautifully. A well-told tale of love and survival and the continuing goodness of people." Child Book Rev Serv

Chapman, Cheryl, 1948-

Snow on snow on snow; paintings by Synthia Saint James. Dial Bks. for Young Readers 1994 unp il $14.99; lib bdg $14.89   E

1. Snow—Fiction 2. Dogs—Fiction

ISBN 0-8037-1456-4; 0-8037-1457-2 (lib bdg)

LC 93-6278

The author uses repetitive word play to tell the story of an African American boy who loses and then recovers his dog while sledding in the snow

"The concrete, physical words have a spare poetry. Saint James' very bright paintings, with flat, clear shapes, look like cutouts and emphasize the beauty of layers and connections." Booklist

Charlip, Remy

Thirteen. Four Winds Press 1975 unp il $14.95   E

1. Stories without words

ISBN 0-02-718120-0

Also available in paperback from Macmillan

First published by Parents Magazine Press

"Each double-page spread contains thirteen different illustrations that are part of thirteen graphic sequences. Some of these are narrative, but most of them are concerned with changing and evolving visual forms. . . . All of these images, beautifully executed in pastels, have been carefully arranged on the pages. The book may have to be introduced to children because it is not immediately obvious." Horn Book

Cherry, Lynne, 1952-
The great kapok tree; a tale of the Amazon rainforest. Harcourt Brace Jovanovich 1990 unp il $14.95   E

1. Rain forests—Fiction 2. Conservation of natural resources—Fiction
ISBN 0-15-200520-X   LC 89-2208
Also available Spanish language edition
"Gulliver books"

The many different animals that live in a great kapok tree in the Brazilian rainforest try to convince a man with an ax of the importance of not cutting down their home

"A carefully researched picture book about the Brazilian rain forest is strikingly illustrated and presented in a large format. Cherry captures the Amazonian proportions of the plants and animals that live there by using vibrant colors, intricate details, and dramatic perspectives. . . . The writing is simple and clear, yet makes a serious point about humans' destructive ways." Booklist

Choi, Sook Nyul
Halmoni and the picnic; illustrated by Karen Milone. Houghton Mifflin 1993 31p il $14.95   E

1. Korean Americans—Fiction 2. Grandmothers—Fiction
ISBN 0-395-61626-3   LC 91-34121
A Korean American girl's third grade class helps her newly arrived grandmother feel more comfortable with her life in the United States

"Choi's text, sentimental but never saccharine, captures a jumble of emotions. . . . With a light hand Choi delivers a happy ending. Dugan's serviceable pencil and watercolor illustrations are warm in spirit and accurate in their detail." Publ Wkly

Christelow, Eileen, 1943-
Five little monkeys jumping on the bed; retold and illustrated by Eileen Christelow. Clarion Bks. 1989 unp il $14.95   E

1. Monkeys—Fiction 2. Counting
ISBN 0-89919-769-8   LC 88-22839
Also available in paperback from Houghton Mifflin

A counting book in which one by one the five little monkeys jump on the bed only to fall off and bump their heads

"Squiggling, swirling lines of color capture the sense of unbridled motion as the monkeys bounce and, one by one, topple from the bed. After all five bandaged youngsters finally fall asleep, a relaxed mama gratefully retires to her room . . . to bounce on 'her' bed. An amusingly presented counting exercise." Booklist

Other available titles about the five little monkeys are:
Don't wake up Mama! (1992)
Five little monkeys sitting in a tree (1991)

Christiansen, Candace
The ice horse; paintings by Thomas Locker. Dial Bks. for Young Readers 1993 unp il $15.99; lib bdg $15.89   E

1. Horses—Fiction
ISBN 0-8037-1400-9; 0-8037-1401-7 (lib bdg)
                                     LC 92-28964
While harvesting ice on the Hudson River with his uncle one winter, a boy uses quick thinking to save his uncle's horse

"Readers gain a nearly tactile appreciation of this van-ished industry, thanks to the solid details . . . included in the text. . . . The simple and unvarying page design focuses attention on the lush paintings of the artist's beloved Hudson Valley." Publ Wkly

Clifton, Lucille, 1936-
Everett Anderson's 1-2-3; illustrations by Ann Grifalconi. Holt & Co. 1992 unp il $14.95   E

1. Remarriage—Fiction 2. African Americans—Fiction 3. Stories in rhyme
ISBN 0-8050-2310-0   LC 92-8031
A reissue of the title first published 1977 by Holt, Rinehart & Winston

As a small boy's mother considers remarriage, he considers the numbers one, two, and three--sometimes they're lonely, sometimes crowded, but sometimes just right

"The illustrations, strongly drawn with bold, broken lines, are large in scale, almost all pictures of the three characters with only minimal background details. The text is tender, artful in the simplicity and brevity with which it gets to the gist of the matter." Bull Cent Child Books

Other available titles about Everett Anderson are:
Everett Anderson's Christmas coming (c1971)
Everett Anderson's friend (c1976)
Everett Anderson's goodbye (c1983)
Everett Anderson's nine month long (c1978)
Everett Anderson's year (c1974)
Some of the days of Everett Anderson (c1970)

Climo, Shirley, 1928-
The cobweb Christmas; illustrated by Joe Lasker. Crowell 1982 unp il lib bdg $14.89; pa $4.50   E

1. Christmas—Fiction 2. Spiders—Fiction
ISBN 0-690-04216-7 (lib bdg); 0-06-443110-X (pa)
                                     LC 81-43879
"Every year Tante shooed the animals and spiders from her cottage so that she could prepare for Christmas. But every year . . . she would ask the animals back to her cottage, for she had heard that on Christmas Eve they might speak. . . . This year, as always, the old woman . . . fell asleep. She never heard 'the rusty, squeaky voices' of the neglected spiders, hoping to be let in. But Christkindel . . . opened the door for the spiders, who covered the tree with sticky webs; then . . . Christkindel transformed the webs into strands of gold and silver." Horn Book

"Lasker's watercolor paintings fill each page they occupy with glowing color. The scenes he sets are contained but full, with sparely composed rustic interiors and appropriate touches of glory when Christkindel works his magic. A good-looking, involving story for the Christmas shelf." Booklist

Coerr, Eleanor, 1922-
The big balloon race; pictures by Carolyn Croll. Harper & Row 1981 62p il $14; lib bdg $12.89; pa $3.75   E

1. Balloons—Fiction 2. Parent and child—Fiction
ISBN 0-06-021352-3; 0-06-021353-1 (lib bdg); 0-06-444053-2 (pa)   LC 80-8368
"An I can read book"

The author "recounts the winning of a hydrogen balloon race by Carlotta Myers, a famous aeronaut, and her stowaway daughter Ariel. Balloon facts are slipped naturally and painlessly into the story, which moves cogently along. The novel subject matter, straightforward mother-daughter relationship, and clear composition of the orange, blue and gray

Coerr, Eleanor, 1922-—*Continued*
illustrations . . . make for a high-flying new look at a piece
of the past." SLJ

Chang's paper pony; pictures by Deborah
Kogan Ray. Harper & Row 1988 64p il lib
bdg $13.89; pa $3.75   E

1. Chinese Americans—Fiction 2. Horses—Fiction
3. Gold mines and mining—Fiction
ISBN 0-06-021329-9 (lib bdg); 0-06-444163-6 (pa)
                                    LC 87-45679
"An I can read book"
This story is "set at the time of California's Gold Rush.
Chang and his grandfather work in the kitchen of a mining
camp. As a result of hard work and honesty, not to mention
fair play by one of the miners, Chang gets the pony of his
dreams. But the story does not prettify the ugly way many
immigrant Chinese were treated." N Y Times Book Rev
"Ray's forceful drawings support the text well and firmly
establish the dusty mining-town environment. She is particularly adept at showing the vulnerability of children, as well
as the ways in which large and small joys affect them."
Publ Wkly

The Josefina story quilt; pictures by Bruce
Degen. Harper & Row 1986 64p il $14.95; lib
bdg $14.89; pa $3.75   E

1. Quilts—Fiction 2. Overland journeys to the Pacific—
Fiction
ISBN 0-06-021348-5; 0-06-021349-3 (lib bdg);
0-06-444129-6 (pa)   LC 85-45260
Also available Spanish language edition
"An I can read book"
While traveling west with her family in 1850, a young
girl makes a patchwork quilt chronicling the experiences of
the journey and reserves a special patch for her pet hen
Josefina
"The story makes the history go down easily, and an author's note at the end fills in facts about the western trip
and the place of quilts as pioneer diaries. The charcoal and
blue/yellow wash illustrations are clear and natural . . . a
good introduction to historical fiction that children can read
for themselves." SLJ

Cohen, Miriam, 1926-
See you in second grade! story by Miriam
Cohen; pictures by Lillian Hoban.
Greenwillow Bks. 1989 unp il $15; lib bdg
$14.93   E

1. School stories
ISBN 0-688-07138-4; 0-688-07139-2 (lib bdg)
                                    LC 87-14869
Also available in paperback from Dell
At an end-of-the-year beach picnic, Anna Maria, Jim,
and the other children realize they will miss First Grade
and their teacher, but decide they are ready for Second
Grade after all
"There's a dash of poignant nostalgia, but no sentimen-
tality, as they remember events of the year and say goodbye
to their beloved teacher and to each other." Bull Cent Child
Books
Other available titles about Jim and his classmates are:
"Bee my valentine!" (1978)
Best friends (1971)
Don't eat too much turkey! (1987)
First grade takes a test (1980)
It's George! (1988)
Jim meets The Thing (1981)
Jim's dog Muffins (1984)
Liar, liar, pants on fire! (1985)

Lost in the museum (1979)
The new teacher (1972)
No good in art (1980)
The real skin rubber monster mask (1990)
See you tomorrow, Charles (1983)
So what? (1982)
Starring first grade (1985)
When will I read? (1977)
Will I have a friend? (1967)

Cole, Brock, 1938-
No more baths; written and illustrated by
Brock Cole. Doubleday 1980 unp il o.p.;
Farrar, Straus & Giroux paperback available
$3.95   E

1. Baths—Fiction 2. Animals—Fiction
ISBN 0-374-45514-7 (pa)   LC 78-22790
"When Jessie McWhistle's unreasonable family tries to
make her have a bath 'in the middle of the day,' the out-
rage is too much, and she decides to leave home. She tries
being a chicken 'frazzling' in the sand but it makes her feel
gritty. Next she tries copying her cat, licking her paws and
smoothing her hair; that doesn't work either. So she attempts to follow the example of the happy pig in her deep,
oozy wallow, with predictably uncomfortable results. At
last, Jessie gives up the unequal struggle, marches home,
and surrenders to the hot bath, the shampoo, the towel."
SLJ
"The author-artist tells a fresh, funny story with a clear
text, well-paced for reading aloud. The watercolor illustrations add detail and humor and help create a lively sense
of farm life." Horn Book

Conrad, Pam, 1947-1996
The Tub People; illustrations by Richard
Egielski. Harper & Row 1989 unp il $15; lib
bdg $14.89; pa $4.95   E

1. Toys—Fiction
ISBN 0-06-021340-X; 0-06-021341-8 (lib bdg);
0-06-443306-4 (pa)   LC 88-32804
"The Tub People are a family of seven wooden toys that
are always perched on the edge of the bathtub. One evening
during one of their favorite games, the Tub Child is sucked
down the drain. Fortune arrives in the form of a plumber
who rescues the tired Tub Child. The whole family is given
a new, safer (and dry) home where some things are very different." Child Book Rev Serv
"In its combination of the dramatic and the subtle, this
is a masterful picture book. The narrative takes for its patterns the rituals of play, heightening the reality and inject-
ing it with drama by excluding humans from the action.
The art, too, juggles the effects of order and chaos, the neat
shapes offset by strong color contrasts and lively patterns."
Bull Cent Child Books
Another title about the Tub People is:
The Tub Grandfather (1993)

Cooney, Barbara, 1917-
Chanticleer and the fox; adapted and
illustrated by Barbara Cooney. Crowell 1958
unp il $14.95; lib bdg $14.89; pa $3.95   E

1. Fables 2. Foxes—Fiction 3. Roosters—Fiction
ISBN 0-690-18561-8; 0-690-18562-6 (lib bdg);
0-690-04318-X (pa)
Awarded the Caldecott Medal, 1959
"Adaptation of the 'Nun's Priest's Tale' from the Canter-
bury Tales." Verso of title page

Cooney, Barbara, 1917——*Continued*

"Chanticleer, the rooster, learns the pitfalls of vanity, while the fox who captures, then loses him, learns the value of self-control." Books for Deaf Child

This adaptation "retains the spirit of the original in its telling and in the beautiful, strongly colored illustrations softened by detailed lines. . . . [It] will be excellent for reading aloud to children." Libr J

Hattie and the wild waves. Viking 1990 unp il $14.95; pa $4.99   E

1. Beaches—Fiction 2. Artists—Fiction
ISBN 0-670-83056-9; 0-14-054193-4 (pa)
LC 90-32577

"A little girl recounts the story of her family's life in Brooklyn at the beginning of the century. Her prosperous father builds houses so they can afford to vacation on Coney Island and Long Island, where her imagination blooms. She wishes with the waves and decides to pursue her love of drawing and become an artist when she grows up." SLJ

"The exquisite paintings, done in acrylics and pastels, reflect the solid comfort and cultivation of turn-of-the-century affluent life in Brooklyn." Horn Book

Island boy; story and pictures by Barbara Cooney. Viking Kestrel 1988 unp il lib bdg $15; pa $5.99   E

1. Islands—Fiction 2. Growth—Fiction 3. Family life—Fiction
ISBN 0-670-81749-X (lib bdg); 0-14-050756-6 (pa)
LC 88-175

"Lyrical in its telling and flawless in its visualization, Cooney's book shows the interdependence of three generations of life off the New England coast. This island is a treasure." SLJ

Miss Rumphius; story and pictures by Barbara Cooney. Viking 1982 unp il hardcover o.p. paperback available $4.99   E

ISBN 0-14-050539-3 (pa)   LC 82-2837

Also available Spanish language edition

As a child Great-aunt Alice Rumphius resolved that when she grew up she would go to faraway places, live by the sea in her old age, and do something to make the world more beautiful—and she does all those things, the last being the most difficult of all

"The idea of offering beauty as one's heritage is appealing, the story is nicely told, and the illustrations are quite lovely, especially the closing scenes of a hill covered with flowers being gathered by children." Bull Cent Child Books

Cooper, Susan, 1935-

Matthew's dragon; illustrated by Jos. A. Smith. Margaret K. McElderry Bks. 1991 unp il $14.95; pa $4.95   E

1. Dragons—Fiction
ISBN 0-689-50512-4; 0-689-71794-6 (pa)
LC 90-31532

The dragon in Matthew's picture book comes to life and takes him for an amazing nocturnal ride

"Filled with imaginative creatures, incandescent colors and thrilling motion, Smith's paintings of the dragon-crowded sky are truly breathtaking. This is an inspired pairing of author and illustrator." Publ Wkly

Cowcher, Helen

Tigress. Farrar, Straus & Giroux 1991 unp il $14.95; pa $5.95   E

1. Tigers—Fiction 2. Wildlife refuges—Fiction
ISBN 0-374-37567-4; 0-374-47781-7 (pa)
LC 91-12513

Also available Spanish language edition

Herdsmen work with a wildlife sanctuary ranger to keep their animals safe from a marauding tigress

"Stunning illustrations of magnificent beasts and a substantive story line reinforce the importance of maintaining nature's delicate balance." SLJ

Cowen-Fletcher, Jane

It takes a village; written and illustrated by Jane Cowen-Fletcher. Scholastic 1994 unp il $15.95   E

1. Brothers and sisters—Fiction 2. Benin—Fiction
ISBN 0-590-46573-2   LC 92-32324

On market day in a small village in Benin, Yemi tries to watch her little brother Kokou and finds that the entire village is watching out for him too

"The bright watercolors depict the people's multicolored garb and show various aspects of village life, especially the workings of an open-air market. . . . A lovely, gentle, visually appealing book that conveys a sense of what it means to belong to a community." SLJ

Crampton, Patricia

Peter and the wolf; [by] Sergei Prokofiev; illustrated by Josef Palecek; retold by Patricia Crampton. Picture Bk. Studio 1987 unp il $13.95; pa $4.95   E

1. Wolves—Fiction 2. Fairy tales
ISBN 0-88708-049-9; 0-88708-226-2 (pa)
LC 87-13915

"A Michael Neugebauer book"

Retells the orchestral fairy tale of the boy who, ignoring his grandfather's warnings proceeds to capture a wolf

"Palacek uses warm, bright colors; flat backgrounds; and exaggerated expressionistic forms." SLJ

Crews, Donald

Carousel. Greenwillow Bks. 1982 unp il lib bdg $15.93   E

ISBN 0-688-00909-3   LC 82-3062

"Crews uses both color photography of words and paintings in Art Deco style of the carousel; a brief text describes the ride, from the horses waiting, silent and still, to the end of a whirling ride. The speeded, blurred pictures of the carousel in motion and of the words (boom, too) that signify the calliope sounds are very effective. Despite the lack of story line, this should appeal to children because of the brilliant color, the impression of speed, and the carousel itself." Bull Cent Child Books

Freight train. Greenwillow Bks. 1978 unp il $16; lib bdg $15.93; pa $3.95   E

1. Railroads 2. Color
ISBN 0-688-80165-X; 0-688-84165-1 (lib bdg); 0-688-11701-5 (pa)   LC 78-2303
A Caldecott Medal honor book, 1979

"Crews, with a minimum of descriptive words, has drawn a stylized freight train passing by, slowly at first, then in a blur of black and bright color." Babbling Bookworm

Crews, Donald—*Continued*

"The young child can learn to identify the engine, the caboose and the different cars. . . . A delightful introduction to railroad transportation and to the colors in the spectrum." America

Harbor. Greenwillow Bks. 1982 unp il $11.75; lib bdg $14.93; pa $3.95 **E**

1. Harbors 2. Ships
ISBN 0-688-00861-5; 0-688-00862-3 (lib bdg); 0-688-07332-8 (pa) LC 81-6607

"Liners, tankers, barges, and freighters move in and out. Ferryboats shuttle from shore to shore. Busiest of all are the tugboats as they push and tow the big ships to their docks. The New York harbor is full of action." Publisher's note

This book "is an exciting, educational and beautiful show-and-tell. . . . The full-page, full-color paintings will delight children. . . . Crew's outstanding feat here . . . is demonstrating the widely different sizes of the boats in pictures matching and contrasting them with trucks and other land vehicles." Publ Wkly

Parade. Greenwillow Bks. 1983 unp il $16; lib bdg $15.93; pa $3.95 **E**

1. Parades
ISBN 0-688-01995-1; 0-688-01996-X (lib bdg); 0-688-06520-1 (pa) LC 82-20927

"Full-color illustrations and a brief text combine to present the various elements of a city parade. Beginning with an early morning empty street and then readying street vendors, excitement mounts as crowds swell to greet a parade of bright images; flags, floats, a marching band, baton twirlers, antique cars and bicycles and a new fire engine. The parade ends and crowds thin; a street cleaning machine sweeps up the remains." SLJ

The author/illustrator's "refined poster-art approach to evoking an event works again here. . . . A polished assembly of crisp shapes, effective compositions, and pure, bright color." Booklist

Sail away. Greenwillow Bks. 1995 unp il $15; lib bdg $14.93 **E**

1. Sailing—Fiction
ISBN 0-688-11053-3; 0-688-11054-1 (lib bdg) LC 94-6004

"A family rows a small dinghy out to a sailboat to spend the day on the water, only to have the bright sky turn dark as high winds churn up an angry sea. Calm finally returns, and the sail ends with light from the setting sun and a lighthouse leading the boat to a safe mooring." Booklist

"To read any Crews book is to be immersed in sights and sounds vividly rendered and perfectly phrased, and this book proves no exception. The paintings move and swell; the words are haiku-like in their efficiency and implication." Horn Book

School bus. Greenwillow Bks. 1984 unp il $15; lib bdg $14.93; pa $4.95 **E**

1. School stories 2. Buses—Fiction
ISBN 0-688-02807-1; 0-688-02808-X (lib bdg); 0-688-12267-1 (pa) LC 83-18681

"The book takes readers through the morning hours, when the buses roll to collect children from their parents and deposit them at different schools, to the end of the day, when they return to gather their riders together again and bring them back to the corners where mothers and fathers are awaiting the homeward-bound scholars." Publ Wkly

"The author-artist cleverly avoids monotony in his subject matter by using different size buses and a pleasing variety of background, perspectives, and the directions in which they travel. Even the potentially tiresome yellow of the buses provides both a unifying element and a contrast for the cheerful colors of the children's clothing and for the bustle of city streets." Horn Book

Shortcut. Greenwillow Bks. 1992 unp il $14; lib bdg $14.93 **E**

1. Railroads—Fiction 2. African Americans—Fiction
ISBN 0-688-06436-1; 0-688-06437-X (lib bdg) LC 91-36312

Children taking a shortcut by walking along a railroad track find excitement and danger when a train approaches

"The story . . . is a perfect foil for the artist's masterful renderings of trains. . . . Scenes portraying the frightened children are equally effective in this out of the ordinary drama set forth with uncommon artistry." Publ Wkly

Ten black dots. rev ed. Greenwillow Bks. 1986 unp il $16; lib bdg $15.93; pa $4.95 **E**

1. Counting 2. Stories in rhyme
ISBN 0-688-06067-6; 0-688-06068-4 (lib bdg); 0-688-13574-9 (pa) LC 85-14871

A revision of the title first published 1968

"In this basic counting book . . . large black dots appear as an integral part of each illustrated subject. For example, 'Five dots can make buttons on a coat . . . or the port-holes of a boat.' This simple concept succeeds admirably through the bold, flat colors and briskly delineated graphics of Crews' illustrations." Booklist

Truck. Greenwillow Bks. 1980 unp il $16; lib bdg $15.93; pa $3.95 **E**

1. Trucks
ISBN 0-688-80244-3; 0-688-84244-5 (lib bdg); 0-688-10481-9 (pa) LC 79-19031

A Caldecott Medal honor book, 1981

A bright red tractor-trailer truck "sporting a chalk-white 'Trucking' label affixed to its side . . . pushes its way across the United States to deliver its prized cargo of tricycles." Christ Sci Monit

"Although there is no text, the story is far from wordless; trucks, buses, and vans are emblazoned with letters and emblems, the streets are lined with familiar traffic signs, and a truck stop is festooned with advertisements in neon lights. The artist depicts no people; the silent red truck is the main character of an imaginative, almost pop-art view of mobile America." Horn Book

We read: A to Z. Greenwillow Bks. 1984 c1967 26p il $16; lib bdg $15.93 **E**

1. Alphabet
ISBN 0-688-03843-3; 0-688-03844-1 (lib bdg) LC 83-25453

A reissue of the title first published 1967 by Harper & Row

"Instead of the conventional approach to the alphabet, the author has combined the letters and the illustrations with definite concepts that a child can see and use. The format is good, the print excellent, and the use of colors unusual and very appealing to a child's imagination." Bruno. Books for Sch Libr, 1968

Crowe, Robert L.

Clyde monster; illustrated by Kay Chorao. Dutton 1976 unp il hardcover o.p. paperback available $3.95 **E**

1. Monsters—Fiction 2. Night—Fiction 3. Fear—Fiction
ISBN 0-525-44289-8 (pa)

Also available in paperback from Puffin Bks.

Crowe, Robert L.—*Continued*

"In an amusing reversal of roles, a young monster is afraid of the dark because he believes that a person may be lurking under the bed or in a corner." LC. Child Books, 1976

"The now familiar table-turning theme for children afraid of monsters takes on effective, rational proportions in a very amusing tale. . . . Chorao's softly grotesque portraits add character without chill." Booklist

Cummings, Pat, 1950-

C.L.O.U.D.S. Lothrop, Lee & Shepard Bks. 1986 unp il $12.95; lib bdg $18   E

1. Fantasy fiction 2. New York (N.Y.)—Fiction
ISBN 0-688-04682-7; 0-688-04683-5 (lib bdg)
LC 85-9719

Chuku the angel is given the job of painting the skies of New York City, an assignment he approaches with reluctance, but grows to love

"The strong colors and futuristic tone of the art, with its (sometimes cluttered) designer-style comment on the subject of graphic design, turn this into a spoof on several levels. Young listeners will miss the jabs at corporate bureaucracy but probably enjoy the story level, which, like the art, is fairly sophisticated in itself." Bull Cent Child Books

Carousel. Bradbury Press 1994 unp il $14.95
E

1. Birthdays—Fiction 2. Fathers and daughters—Fiction
ISBN 0-02-725512-3   LC 93-8708

"The exquisite toy carousel Alex's father gives her fails to soften her disappointment and anger when he misses her birthday party. However, the carousel animals come to life that night and take Alex on a fun-filled jaunt, and, in the morning, Alex quickly forgives her apologetic father. The richly colored artwork features an African-American family." Horn Book Guide

Clean your room, Harvey Moon! Bradbury Press 1991 unp il $14.95; pa $4.95   E

1. African Americans—Fiction 2. Stories in rhyme
ISBN 0-02-725511-5; 0-689-71798-9 (pa)
LC 89-23863

Harvey tackles a big job: cleaning his room

"Cummings's art is a boisterous clutter of color, providing just the right mood for her bouncy, rhyming text." Publ Wkly

Daly, Niki, 1946-

My dad; story and pictures by Niki Daly. Margaret K. McElderry Bks. 1995 unp il $16
E

1. Alcoholism—Fiction 2. Fathers—Fiction
ISBN 0-689-50620-1   LC 94-14455

"Though the brother and sister featured here dearly love their father, they are embarrassed and increasingly anxious about his drinking. . . . A Friday-night school concert becomes the turning point; Dad shows up drunk and humiliates his children. . . . The tale ends on a hopeful note, however, with Dad persuaded to join Alcoholics Anonymous. Daly's gentle touch extends to both words and pictures: her sensitive, graceful prose is coupled with soft-focus watercolors that underscore the poignancy of her characters' struggles." Publ Wkly

Not so fast, Songololo; written & illustrated by Niki Daly. Atheneum Pubs. 1986 c1985 unp il $13.95   E

1. Blacks—Fiction 2. Grandmothers—Fiction 3. South Africa—Fiction
ISBN 0-689-50367-9   LC 85-71034

Also available in paperback from Puffin Bks.

"A Margaret K. McElderry book"

First published 1985 in the United Kingdom

"The setting is South Africa and the names of the people are like poetry: Uzuti, Mongi, Mr. Motiki. Malusi is now old enough to accompany his grandmother, Gogo, into the city to shop. She is an old woman—ample, proud, not quite in step with modern technology, and she no longer moves quickly. Malusi (Songololo to his grandmother) helps her with her shopping." Publ Wkly

"The watercolor illustrations are splendidly evocative of the affection between the generations and of the South African city scene, which, surprisingly, is hardly distinguishable from an American city. The beautiful, gentle book about the ordinary occurrences of daily life has an extraordinary effect." Horn Book

Papa Lucky's shadow, story and pictures by Niki Daly. Margaret K. McElderry Bks. 1992 unp il $14.95   E

1. Dancing—Fiction 2. Grandfathers—Fiction
ISBN 0-689-50541-8   LC 91-24283

With his granddaughter's help, Papa Lucky takes his love of dancing onto the street and makes some extra money

"Daly presents a loving relationship between grandparent and child that will touch any kid who's experienced that special kind of unconditional love. Adding spice to a story that might otherwise have been too sweet is the exuberant artwork. The lift of dancing comes across clearly in colorful paintings that have their own rhythm and bounce. This is a book that's hard to resist." Booklist

Daugherty, James Henry, 1889-1974

Andy and the lion; by James Daugherty. Viking 1938 unp il $14.99; pa $4.99   E

1. Lions—Fiction
ISBN 0-670-12433-8; 0-14-050277-7 (pa)

A Caldecott Medal honor book, 1939

A modern picture story of Androcles and the lion in which Andy, who read a book about lions, was almost immediately plunged into action. The next day he met a circus lion with a thorn in his paw. Andy removed the thorn and earned the lion's undying gratitude

"This is a tall tale for little children. It is typically American in its setting and its fun. The large full page illustrations are in yellow, black and white and the brief, hand-lettered text on the opposite page is clear and readable." Libr J

Day, Alexandra

Carl goes shopping. Farrar, Straus & Giroux 1990 unp il $12.95   E

1. Dogs—Fiction 2. Department stores—Fiction 3. Stories without words
ISBN 0-374-31110-2   LC 88-46216

Carl the dog "is told to mind the baby at a department store while the mother does an errand. Carl and baby go browsing instead, in wordless vignettes that take them all over the store, in and out of mischief." N Y Times Book Rev

"Painted with rich texture and subdued colors, the illustrations tell the largely wordless story with ample action

Day, Alexandra—*Continued*

and humor to sustain children's and adults' repeated enjoyment." Booklist

Other available titles about Carl are:
Carl goes to daycare (1993)
Carl makes a scrapbook (1994)
Carl's afternoon in the park (1991)
Carl's birthday (1995)
Carl's Christmas (1990)
Carl's masquerade (1992)
Good dog, Carl (1985)

Frank and Ernest. Scholastic 1988 unp il
$14.95; pa $3.95   E

1. Elephants—Fiction   2. Bears—Fiction
3. Restaurants—Fiction
ISBN 0-590-41557-3; 0-590-41556-5 (pa)

LC 88-1966

"Frank, a bear, and Ernest, an elephant, specialize in taking care of small businesses while the owner is away. When Mrs. Miller hires them to run her diner for three days, they assure her that they will take good care of it. Then Frank decides they must learn diner lingo before they begin." Publ Wkly

"A four-page glossary of restaurant language may encourage children to invent their own picturesque nomenclature. Carrying the text are the watercolor illustrations, rich in diner detail and humor. A novelty offering with nostalgia appeal." Booklist

Other available titles about Frank and Ernest are:
Frank and Ernest on the road (1994)
Frank and Ernest play ball (1990)

De Paola, Tomie, 1934-

The art lesson; written and illustrated by
Tomie dePaola. Putnam 1989 unp il $15.95;
pa $5.95   E

ISBN 0-399-21688-X; 0-399-22761-X (pa)

LC 88-27617

Also available Spanish language edition

Having learned to be creative in drawing pictures at home, young Tommy is dismayed when he goes to school and finds the art lesson there much more regimented

"How Tommy learns to express his own individuality and listen to his own creative impulses and imagination makes for engrossing reading. DePaola's characteristic bright illustrations complement and enliven his tale of growing up." Horn Book

Bill and Pete; story and pictures by Tomie
de Paola. Putnam 1978 unp il $14.95; pa
$5.95   E

1. Crocodiles—Fiction 2. Birds—Fiction
ISBN 0-399-20646-9; 0-399-20650-7 (pa)

"Near the Nile River, long ago, William Everett Crocodile chooses Pete the plover for his toothbrush, and they become friends as well. When the reptile scholar despairs of writing all the letters in his name, Pete has an idea and William passes the test by penning 'Bill.' Then, the Bad Guy (a human trapper) captures Bill and plans to make a suitcase of him. The solution to that problem is heady fun." Publ Wkly

"De Paola has again created an imaginative, humorous tale which he illustrates in happy pinks, greens, yellows, and blues." SLJ

Another available title about Bill and Pete is:
Bill and Pete go down the Nile (1987)

An early American Christmas; written and
illustrated by Tomie dePaola. Holiday House
1987 unp il lib bdg $14.95; pa $6.95   E

1. Christmas—Fiction 2. German Americans
ISBN 0-8234-0617-2 (lib bdg); 0-8234-0979-1 (pa)

LC 86-3102

"A German family moves from the old country to a small New England town in the 1800's. The town doesn't celebrate Christmas, but the family forges ahead with bayberry candles, evergreen decorations, a Christmas tree in the parlor, and carols on the night air. Gradually, all the households become 'Christmas families'." Child Book Rev Serv

"This provides a fascinating look at Christmas as it once was: a holiday whose customs were entwined with the season's natural bounty. . . . This is a warm and beautifully realized tribute to the spirit and traditions of the season." Publ Wkly

Helga's dowry; a troll love story; story and
pictures by Tomie de Paola. Harcourt Brace
Jovanovich 1977 unp il $15.95; pa $5   E

1. Fairy tales
ISBN 0-15-233701-6; 0-15-640010-3 (pa)

LC 76-54953

"Helga . . . is 'the loveliest Troll in three parishes' but she is also the poorest. Handsome Lars loves her—but not enough to resist the lure of Plain Inge's enormous dowry. Upon hearing the news of their engagement . . . she clomps off to earn, through the use of her wits . . . an estate fit for a queen—which she promptly becomes, after a hilarious confrontation with her rival." SLJ

"Humor bubbles through text and pictures with squatty, buck-toothed, detailed trolls amd bemused bystanders cavorting across richly colored paintings trimmed with hearts-and-flowers." Booklist

The knight and the dragon; story and
pictures by Tomie de Paola. Putnam 1980 unp
il $15.95; pa $5.95   E

1. Knights and knighthood—Fiction 2. Dragons—Fiction
ISBN 0-399-20707-4; 0-399-22401-7 (pa)

LC 79-18131

"A boy knight feels he really ought to fight a dragon and, in a cave far away, a dragon begins to feel he ought to defend his species' honor by a duel with a knight. . . . When the foes finally meet, the encounter becomes something else." Publ Wkly

"Very few words and typical de Paola illustrations make this lighthearted jest. . . . There's a chuckle on every page, especially for librarians, as the castle librarian saves both warriors from disgrace with the right books from her horse-drawn bookmobile!" Child Book Rev Serv

Nana Upstairs & Nana Downstairs; story
and pictures by Tomie de Paola. Putnam 1973
unp il $13.95   E

1. Grandmothers—Fiction 2. Death—Fiction
ISBN 0-399-21417-8   LC 72-77965
Also available in paperback from Puffin Bks.

"Small Tommy calls his ninety-four-year-old grandmother 'Nana Upstairs' because she is bedridden; downstairs her daughter is busily keeping house, she's 'Nana Downstairs.' When great-grandmother dies, Tommy learns about death and, years later, he is better prepared when Nana Downstairs dies in her old age." Bull Cent Child Books

"In a quietly touching story, the author-illustrator depicts loving family relationships so that even the very young reader can understand the concepts." Publ Wkly

De Paola, Tomie, 1934-—*Continued*

Now one foot, now the other; story and pictures by Tomie de Paola. Putnam 1981 unp il $13.95; pa $6.95   E

1. Grandfathers—Fiction
ISBN 0-399-20774-0; 0-399-20775-9 (pa)
                        LC 80-22239
Also available Spanish language edition
"Bobby's much loved grandfather has had a stroke. After a long hospitalization, the man returns home unable to speak, walk or care for himself. . . . Their roles reversed, the youngster helps his grandfather learn to walk again 'now one foot, now the other.'" SLJ
"De Paola sensitively provides an understanding portrayal about grandparents' illness. . . . Soft blues and tans, textured with pencil shadings, provide a tranquil backdrop for the emotion-filled faces that expressively suggest the changing relationship of the old man and the boy." Booklist

Strega Nona; an old tale; retold and illustrated by Tomie de Paola. Simon & Schuster 1988 c1975 unp il $15; pa $6.95   E

1. Witches—Fiction 2. Italy—Fiction
ISBN 0-671-66283-X; 0-671-66606-1 (pa)
                        LC 88-11438
Also available Spanish language edition
A Caldecott Medal honor book, 1976
A reissue of the title first published 1975 by Prentice-Hall
In this Italian folk-tale set in Calabria, "Strega Nona, 'Grandma Witch,' leaves Big Anthony alone with her magic pasta pot. He decides to give the townspeople a treat. . . . Big Anthony doesn't know how to make the pot stop. The town is practically buried in spaghetti before Strega Nona returns to save the day." SLJ
"Tomie de Paola has used simple colors, simple line, and medieval costume and architecture in his spaciously composed humorous pictures." Bull Cent Child Books
Other available titles about Strega Nona and Big Anthony are:
Big Anthony and the magic ring (1979)
Strega Nona meets her match (1993)
Strega Nona's magic lessons (1982)

Tom; written and illustrated by Tomie dePaola. Putnam 1993 unp il $15.95   E

1. Grandfathers—Fiction
ISBN 0-399-22417-3
                        LC 92-1022
"In a story based on his own childhood, Tomie dePaola tells about little Tommy's regular Sunday visits with his grandfather, Tom. . . . With gentle humor and his usual mastery of line and composition, dePaola conveys the strong bond of affection between Tom and little Tommy." Horn Book Guide

De Regniers, Beatrice Schenk

A little house of your own; illustrated by Irene Haas. Harcourt Brace Jovanovich 1987 unp il $12.95   E

ISBN 0-15-245787-9   LC 86-27013
A reissue of the title first published 1954
"This book describes and explains the need to be alone at times. Everyone must have a 'house of his own,' boys and girls, mothers and fathers." Read Ladders for Hum Relat. 5th edition
"This is a delightful book by an author who obviously understands children well and has observed them very carefully. . . . The illustrations are perfectly matched to the text." Publ Wkly

May I bring a friend? illustrated by Beni Montresor. Atheneum Pubs. 1964 unp il $15; pa $4.95   E

1. Animals—Fiction
ISBN 0-689-20615-1; 0-689-71353-3 (pa)
Awarded the Caldecott Medal, 1965
"Each time the little boy in this picture book is invited to take tea or dine with the King and Queen, he brings along a somewhat difficult animal friend. Their Highnesses always cope and are wonderfully rewarded in the end." Publ Wkly
"Rich color and profuse embellishment adorn an opulent setting. Absurdities and contrasts are so imaginatively combined in a hilarious comedy of manners that the merriment can be enjoyed on several levels." Horn Book

Deedy, Carmen Agra

The library dragon; illustrated by Michael P. White. Peachtree Pubs. 1994 unp il $16.95   E

1. Librarians—Fiction 2. Dragons—Fiction 3. Books and reading—Fiction 4. School stories
ISBN 1-56145-091-X   LC 94-14754
Miss Lotta Scales is a dragon who believes her job is to protect the school's library books from the children, but when she finally realizes that books are meant to be read, the dragon turns into Miss Lotty, librarian and storyteller
Deedy "is an accomplished storyteller, and kids will likely enjoy her frequent puns and wordplay. White heads off imminent cutesiness with droll, stylized illustrations, filled with vibrant color and lots of comical details." Publ Wkly

Degen, Bruce, 1945-

Jamberry; story and pictures by Bruce Degen. Harper & Row 1983 unp il $14.95; lib bdg $14.89; pa $3.95   E

1. Stories in rhyme 2. Berries—Fiction
ISBN 0-06-021416-3; 0-06-021417-1 (lib bdg); 0-06-443068-5 (pa)   LC 82-47708
"Boy meets bear, and together they go berry-picking by canoe, through fields and by pony and 'Boys-in-Berries' train, all the way to Berryland." Child Book Rev Serv
"Berries and jam are roundly celebrated in a lilting rhyme that, coupled with the jaunty colored pictures, makes it . . . a good pick for sharing one on one, or fun to read aloud as a poetry introduction." Booklist

Demi, 1942-

Demi's Find-the-animal A.B.C.; an alphabet-game book. Grosset & Dunlap 1985 unp il hardcover o.p. paperback available $5.95   E

1. Alphabet 2. Animals—Fiction
ISBN 0-448-19165-2 (pa)   LC 85-70285
The author/illustrator uses animals from A to Z to introduce the letters of the alphabet. Readers are also asked to spot additional animals hidden in the illustrations
"Not just a showcase for the artist's talent, this engaging puzzle book will sharpen the basic prereading skill of discrimination. . . . Alternating with well-designed black-and-white spreads are those in color, their bright but harmonious hues adding gaiety to the already animated scenes." Booklist

Denslow, Sharon Phillips, 1947-
Bus riders; pictures by Nancy Carpenter. Four Winds Press 1993 unp il $14.95   E
1. Buses—Fiction
ISBN 0-02-728682-7   LC 92-14109
When their regular bus driver gets sick, Warren, Louise, and the other bus riders must endure a string of substitute drivers
"Carpenter uses oil paint and colored pencil to create a homey cast of characters and richly hued, robust views of life in the 'squash-colored bus.'" Horn Book Guide

DiSalvo-Ryan, DyAnne, 1954-
Uncle Willie and the soup kitchen. Morrow Junior Bks. 1991 unp il $16; lib bdg $15.93   E
1. Uncles—Fiction 2. Poverty—Fiction
ISBN 0-688-09165-2; 0-688-09166-0 (lib bdg)
LC 90-6375
A boy spends the day with Uncle Willie in the soup kitchen where he works preparing and serving food for the hungry
"The color-pencil and wash illustrations observe . . . [a] balance between attracting the viewer with softly blended colors and avoiding the sentimentality of glamorizing an essentially sad situation. Without sacrifice of story, the total effect leaves young listeners with new considerations of society and social service, a theme too often neglected in picture books." Bull Cent Child Books

Dorros, Arthur
Abuela; illustrated by Elisa Kleven. Dutton Children's Bks. 1991 unp il $14.99   E
1. Hispanic Americans—Fiction 2. Grandmothers—Fiction
ISBN 0-525-44750-4   LC 90-21459
Also available Spanish language edition
While riding on a bus with her Hispanic grandmother, a little girl named Rosalba imagines that they are carried up into the sky and fly over the sights of New York City
"Each illustration is a masterpiece of color, line, and form that will mesmerize youngsters. . . . The smooth text, interspersed with Spanish words and phrases, provides ample context clues, so the glossary, while helpful, is not absolutely necessary." Booklist

Radio Man. Don Radio; a story in English and Spanish; Spanish translation by Sandra Marulanda Dorros. HarperCollins Pubs. 1993 unp il $16; lib bdg $15.89   E
1. Migrant labor—Fiction 2. Mexican Americans—Fiction 3. Bilingual books—English-Spanish
ISBN 0-06-021547-X; 0-06-021548-8 (lib bdg)
LC 92-28369
As he travels with his family of migrant farmworkers, Diego relies on his radio to provide him with companionship and help connect him to all the different places in which he lives
"Spot art separates English and Spanish on text pages that alternate with affecting, primitive-like acrylic paintings." Publ Wkly

Tonight is Carnaval; illustrated with arpilleras sewn by the Club de Madres Virgen del Carmen of Lima, Peru. Dutton Children's Bks. 1991 unp il $14.99   E
1. Festivals—Fiction 2. Peru—Fiction
ISBN 0-525-44641-9   LC 90-32391

Also available in paperback from Puffin Bks.; Spanish language edition also available
A family in South America eagerly prepares for the excitement of Carnaval
"Dorros' text is appealing and informative, emphasizing the strong communal life of the village. However, the real star of this book is its illustration. The action is shown in *arpilleras*, the distinctive South American wall hangings made from cut-and-sewn pieces of cloth. The Club de Madres Virgen del Carmen of Lima, Peru, has created about a dozen of these cheerful fabric pictures in bright primary colors. . . . Appended are a short glossary of foreign-language terms and an illustrated explanation of how *arpilleras* are made." Booklist

Dragonwagon, Crescent
Half a moon and one whole star; illustrations by Jerry Pinkney. Macmillan 1986 unp il $14.95; pa $3.95   E
1. Night—Fiction 2. Sleep—Fiction 3. Stories in rhyme
ISBN 0-02-733120-2; 0-689-71415-7 (pa)
LC 85-13818
The summer night is full of wonderful sounds and scents as Susan falls asleep
"The poem has some lilting phrases and some sharp images; occasionally the rhyme or meter falters, but the concept of night activity and the sleeping household should appeal to the read-aloud audience." Bull Cent Child Books

Drescher, Henrik, 1955-
Simon's book. Lothrop, Lee & Shepard Bks. 1983 unp il $16; lib bdg $14.88; pa $3.95   E
1. Drawing—Fiction 2. Monsters—Fiction
ISBN 0-688-02085-2; 0-688-02086-0 (lib bdg); 0-688-10484-3 (pa)   LC 82-24931
"A frightening yet humorous-looking monster . . . chases young Simon through the pages of his drawing pad. Despite the aid of snake-like pens and an antennae-equipped ink bottle, Simon eventually becomes trapped at the bottom of the page. Surprisingly, a big sloppy kiss reveals the beast's friendly feelings, so boy, beast, pens and ink can relax and peacefully retire. A finished book—'Simon's Book'—is left upon the table for the real Simon to discover when he wakes in the morning." SLJ
"Using the story-within-a-story format, the author-artist embarks on an exhilarating exploration, in a childlike yet sophisticated manner, of the elusive border separating dream and reality. . . . Original, fresh, and engaging, the book is deliciously thrilling but never terrifying." Horn Book

Drucker, Malka, 1945-
Grandma's latkes; written by Malka Drucker; illustrated by Eve Chwast. Harcourt Brace Jovanovich 1992 unp il $13.95   E
1. Hanukkah—Fiction 2. Jews—Fiction
ISBN 0-15-200468-8   LC 91-30086
"Gulliver books"
Grandma explains the meaning of Hanukkah while showing Molly how to cook latkes for the holiday. Recipe included
"The dark lines of the woodcut illustrations, painted with pale watercolors, have a warm, old-fashioned quality that enhances the idea of passing a people's history from one generation to the next." Horn Book

Dubanevich, Arlene, 1950-

Pigs in hiding. Four Winds Press 1983 unp il $13.95 **E**

1. Pigs—Fiction
ISBN 0-02-732140-1 LC 83-1409
Also available in paperback from Scholastic

"One pig initiates a game of hide-and-seek. He's 'it' while the other 99 porkers go and hide among the house's swine artifacts. He can't find his friends anywhere until he gets an idea. Laying out a spread of tasty goodies he lures his fellows from their nooks and crannies while he hides under a nearby umbrella. When they have assembled, he gleefully shouts he has found them all." Booklist

"The imagination displayed in the sharply detailed, bravely colored pictures and the whirling happenings can't fail to make readers laugh out loud." Publ Wkly

Another available title about the pigs is:
Pigs at Christmas (1986)

Dugan, Barbara

Leaving home with a pickle jar; pictures by Karen Lee Baker. Greenwillow Bks. 1993 unp il $14; lib bdg $13.93 **E**

1. Moving—Fiction 2. Grasshoppers—Fiction
ISBN 0-688-10836-9; 0-688-10837-7 (lib bdg)
LC 91-48256

Ernest P. doesn't want to move to Minnesota, but he hopes that taking his grasshopper along will help on the long trip

"The text is illustrated with soft, watercolor paintings framed with white space, allowing the reader to view the story as if through windows, particularly when the characters are traveling on their long car trip. A realistic, sensitive tale." Horn Book

Loop the loop; pictures by James Stevenson. Greenwillow Bks. 1992 unp il $14; lib bdg $14.93 **E**

1. Old age—Fiction 2. Friendship—Fiction
ISBN 0-688-09647-6; 0-688-09648-4 (lib bdg)
LC 90-21727

Also available in paperback from Puffin Bks.
Annie and old Mrs. Simpson form a friendship that lasts even after the woman enters a nursing home

"Dugan develops her story line with a sure and light touch, which is echoed in Stevenson's simple, congenial cartoon sketches, roughly shaded in light watercolors. The dénouement is both poignant and upbeat." Horn Book

Duke, Kate

The guinea pig ABC. Dutton 1983 unp il o.p.; Puffin Bks. paperback available $5.99 **E**

1. Alphabet 2. Guinea pigs
ISBN 0-14-054756-8 (pa) LC 83-1410
Each letter of the alphabet is illustrated by a word which applies to pictured guinea pigs

Another available title about the guinea pigs is:
Guinea pigs far and near (1984)

Dunrea, Olivier, 1953-

The painter who loved chickens. Farrar, Straus & Giroux 1995 unp il $15 **E**

1. Artists—Fiction 2. Chickens—Fiction
ISBN 0-374-35729-3 LC 94-27562

An artist, who loves to paint chickens, finally finds someone that appreciates his pictures

Dunrea's "unassuming text straightforwardly conveys his emotion-filled, clearly delineated story. His sunny gouache paintings, liberally splashed with oranges, yellows and reds, are a chicken-lover's delight." Publ Wkly

Durán, Cheli

Hildilid's night; by Cheli Durán Ryan; illustrated by Arnold Lobel. Macmillan 1986 c1971 unp il $13.95; pa $4.95 **E**

1. Night—Fiction
ISBN 0-02-777260-8; 0-689-80538-1 (pa)
LC 86-5294

A Caldecott Medal honor book, 1972
A reissue of the title first published 1971

"Hating the night, [an old woman named] Hildilid tries to sweep it away with a broom, spanks it, digs a grave for it, tries to stuff it into a sack, and so on. Exhausted by her vain endeavors, she falls asleep just as the sun comes up and the detested darkness is gone." Bull Cent Child Books

"The black-and-white line drawings, into which yellow is occasionally but strategically inserted, perfectly illustrate the rhythmically narrative lines." Horn Book

Duvoisin, Roger, 1904-1980

Petunia; written and illustrated by Roger Duvoisin. Knopf 1950 unp il lib bdg $13.99 **E**

1. Geese—Fiction
ISBN 0 394 90865 1

A picture story book about Petunia, the silly goose, who found a book and carried it around because she thought it would make her wise. After a catastrophe brought on by Petunia's silliness she suddenly discovered that it's what is inside the book that counts

"Not since 'The Little Red Hen' has there been written such an engaging story of a poultry heroine. . . . Delightfully illustrated by the author in black-and-white and color wash." Libr J

Other available titles about Petunia are:
Petunia, beware! (1958)
Petunia takes a trip (1953)

Eastman, P. D. (Philip D.), 1909-1986

Are you my mother? written and illustrated by P. D. Eastman. Beginner Bks. 1960 63p il $7.99; lib bdg $9.99 **E**

1. Birds—Fiction 2. Bilingual books—English-Spanish
ISBN 0-394-80018-4; 0-394-90018-9 (lib bdg)
Also available Spanish-English edition

"A small bird falls from his nest and searches for his mother. He asks a kitten, a hen, a dog, a cow, a boat, [and] a plane . . . 'Are you my mother?' Repetition of words and phrases and funny pictures are just right for beginning readers." Chicago. Public Libr

Edwards, Michelle

A baker's portrait. Lothrop, Lee & Shepard Bks. 1991 unp il $13.95; lib bdg $13.88 **E**

1. Artists—Fiction 2. Jews—Fiction
ISBN 0-688-09712-X; 0-688-09713-8 (lib bdg)
LC 90-41926

Edwards, Michelle—*Continued*

Michelin paints portraits that do not flatter her sitters but she learns an enduring lesson when she must paint her kindly aunt and uncle

"Edwards is an artist who can also write. Her story radiates warmth and, at the same time, deals with the age-old problem of how to be honest yet kind. Her sturdy art, with dark colors and definite shapes, has humor, too, as it takes a close look at the ironies of the human condition. A picture book with something to say." Booklist

Edwards, Richard, 1949-

Ten tall oaktrees; pictures by Caroline Crossland. Tambourine Bks. 1993 unp il $15; lib bdg $14.93   E

1. Trees—Fiction 2. Counting 3. Stories in rhyme
ISBN 0-688-04620-7; 0-688-04621-5 (lib bdg)

LC 92-41771

Over a period of time, a stand of ten oak trees is cut down one by one, until there are none

"The theme of tree conservation is presented in a subtle and poetic manner." Sci Child

Egielski, Richard

Buz. HarperCollins Pubs. 1995 unp il $14.95; lib bdg $14.89   E

1. Insects—Fiction
ISBN 0-06-023566-7; 0-06-023567-5 (lib bdg)

LC 94-36033

"A Laura Geringer book"

When a little boy swallows a bug along with his cereal, pandemonium breaks out as the bug searches for an escape, the boy searches for an antidote, and Keystone Cops-like pills search for the bug

"The text is minimal, although amusing, but the real treat is the bright, gaudy, almost plastic-looking illustrations." Horn Book

Ehlert, Lois, 1934-

Circus. HarperCollins Pubs. 1992 unp il $15; lib bdg $14.89   E

1. Circus—Fiction 2. Animals—Fiction
ISBN 0-06-020252-1; 0-06-020253-X (lib bdg)

LC 91-12067

Leaping lizards, marching snakes, a bear on the high wire, and others perform in a somewhat unusual circus

"The book approximates a light show in visual intensity, with neon-bright illustrations set against black or bold backgrounds. The figures . . . are a hodgepodge of geometric shapes. . . . The use of complementary colors and interlocking shapes also gives the illustrations energy. . . . The sprightly rhythm of Ms. Ehlert's text complements her Day-Glo palette. Echoing a ringmaster's speech, she's afraid of neither alliteration . . . nor hyperbole." N Y Times Book Rev

Color farm. Lippincott 1990 unp il $14; lib bdg $12.89   E

1. Color 2. Size and shape
ISBN 0-397-32440-5; 0-397-32441-3 (lib bdg)

LC 89-13561

"A delightful die-cut exploration of how shapes and colors can be layered and overlapped to create the faces of farm animals. Includes geometric pictures of a rooster, a chicken, a goose, a duck, a cat, a dog, a sheep, a pig, and a cow." Sci Child

Color zoo. Lippincott 1989 unp il $15; lib bdg $14.89   E

1. Color 2. Size and shape
ISBN 0-397-32259-3; 0-397-32260-7 (lib bdg)

LC 87-17065

A Caldecott Medal honor book, 1990

This "book features a series of cutouts stacked so that with each page turn, a layer is removed to reveal yet another picture. Each configuration is an animal: a tiger's face (a circle shape) and two ears disappear with a page turn to leave viewers with a square within which is a mouse. . . . There are three such series, and each ends with a small round-up of the shapes used so far. . . . On the reverse of the turned page is the shape cutout previously removed with the shape's printed name." SLJ

"Not only an effective method for teaching basic concepts, the book is also a means for sharpening visual perception, which encourages children to see these shapes in other contexts." Horn Book

Eating the alphabet; fruits and vegetables from A to Z. Harcourt Brace Jovanovich 1989 unp il $14.95; pa $4.95   E

1. Alphabet 2. Fruit 3. Vegetables
ISBN 0-15-224435-2; 0-15-224436-0 (pa)

LC 88-10906

An alphabetical tour of the world of fruits and vegetables, from apricot and artichoke to yam and zucchini

"The objects depicted, shown against a white ground, are easily identifiable for the most part, and represent the more common sounds of the letter shown. . . . Both upper- and lower-case letters are printed in large, black type. A nice added touch is the glossary which includes the pronunciation and interesting facts about the origin of each fruit and vegetable, how it grows, and its uses. An exuberant, eye-catching alphabet book." SLJ

Feathers for lunch. Harcourt Brace Jovanovich 1990 unp il $13.95; pa $5   E

1. Cats—Fiction 2. Birds—Fiction 3. Stories in rhyme
ISBN 0-15-230550-5; 0-15-200986-8 (pa)

LC 89-29459

Also available Spanish language edition

This "book is both a story and a beginning nature guide. A pet cat wants to vary his diet with wild birds, but each attempt gains him only feathers. Twelve different bird species are . . . illustrated. . . . On each page, the bird's typical call is printed and plants pictured are named." SLJ

"Ehlert has attempted many things in these pages—for instance, the birds are all drawn life-size—and has succeeded in all of them; her lavish use of bold color against generous amounts of white space is graphically appealing, and the large type, nearly one-half-inch tall, invites attempts by those just beginning to read. An engaging, entertaining, and recognizably realistic story." Horn Book

Growing vegetable soup; written and illustrated by Lois Ehlert. Harcourt Brace Jovanovich 1987 unp il $13.95; pa $4.95   E

1. Vegetable gardening—Fiction
ISBN 0-15-232575-1; 0-15-232580-8 (pa)

LC 86-22812

Also available Spanish language edition

"Brightly-colored large illustrations and a boldly-worded text show how to plant and grow vegetables for Dad's soup. Shocking pinks, reds and greens give the illustrations an almost three-dimensional quality and will be good for large audiences of preschoolers." Child Book Rev Serv

Ehlert, Lois, 1934- —*Continued*

Mole's hill; a woodland tale. Harcourt Brace & Co. 1994 unp il $14.95   **E**

1. Moles (Animals)—Fiction
ISBN 0-15-255116-6   LC 93-31151

When Fox tells Mole she must move out of her tunnel to make way for a new path, Mole finds an ingenious way to save her home

"Ehlert's language is compact and telling. . . . The art . . . is dark-hued, appropriately nocturnal without losing spirit or contrast, and the beads stippled across the cutout cloth shapes lend interesting texture to the planes of color. . . . The story (which Ehlert says she based on a fragment of a Seneca tale, with source completely cited in the book) has charm and vigor." Bull Cent Child Books

Nuts to you! Harcourt Brace Jovanovich 1993 unp il $14.95   **E**

1. Squirrels—Fiction 2. Stories in rhyme
ISBN 0-15-257647-9   LC 92-19441

"A frisky squirrel digs up bulbs and steals birdseed from a nearby feeder; in his boldest act, he enters the young narrator's apartment through a tear in the window screen. The quick thinking child entices the mischievous squirrel back outside with some peanuts. . . . The story, told in brisk rhyme, is a fast-paced romp, and the large, dramatically styled collages will dazzle even the largest audiences. . . . The four concluding pages offer basic information about squirrels." Horn Book

Planting a rainbow; written and illustrated by Lois Ehlert. Harcourt Brace Jovanovich 1988 unp il lib bdg $14.95; pa $4.95   **E**

1. Gardening—Fiction 2. Flowers—Fiction
ISBN 0-15-262609-3 (lib bdg); 0-15-262610-7 (pa)
    LC 87-8528

A mother and daughter plant a rainbow of flowers in the family garden

"The stylized forms of the plants are clearly and beautifully designed, and the primary, blazing colors of the blossoms dazzle in their resplendence. The minimal text, in very large print, is exactly right to set off the glorious illustrations, making a splendid beginning book of colors and flowers cleverly arranged for young readers." Horn Book

Ehrlich, Amy, 1942-

Leo, Zack, and Emmie together again; pictures by Steven Kellogg. Dial Bks. for Young Readers 1987 56p il $9.95; pa $3.95
    E

1. Friendship—Fiction
ISBN 0-8037-0381-3; 0-8037-0837-8 (pa)
    LC 86-16810

"An Easy-to-read book"

In this title "three second graders are involved . . . in four loosely connected episodes that take place in the winter: they play in the snow, meet Santa Claus, suffer through chicken pox . . . and make Valentine cards. . . . Ehrlich's writing is direct and uncluttered. There is just enough conflict in the plot to create interest. Kellogg's full-color illustrations consistently add humor to the text and make this book hard to put down." SLJ

Maggie and Silky and Joe; pictures by Robert J. Blake. Viking 1994 unp il $14.99
    E

1. Dogs—Fiction 2. Death—Fiction 3. Farm life—Fiction
ISBN 0-670-83387-8   LC 94-9149

Joe, a young boy who grows up under the protection and companionship of his family's cow dog, Maggie, and later with a stray puppy called Silky, must learn how to cope with loss when Maggie dies during a thunderstorm

This "tender story of the death of a beloved pet respects the bitterness of grief by avoiding sentimentality and letting honest facts speak for themselves. . . . Blake's . . . glorious and realistic paintings echo both the joy and sorrow in the story." Publ Wkly

Parents in the pigpen, pigs in the tub; pictures by Steven Kellogg. Dial Bks. for Young Readers 1993 unp il $14.99; lib bdg $14.89   **E**

1. Animals—Fiction 2. Farm life—Fiction
ISBN 0-8037-0933-1; 0-8037-0928-5 (lib bdg)
    LC 91-15601

Tired of their usual routine, the farm animals insist on moving into the house, so the family decides to move into barn, but eventually everyone tires of this new arrangement

"Ehrlich's text begs to be read aloud in an exaggerated country twang, while Kellogg's watercolor illustrations are rambling and full of humorous details." SLJ

The wild swans; [by] Hans Christian Andersen; pictures by Susan Jeffers; retold by Amy Ehrlich. Dial Bks. for Young Readers 1981 40p il $16.95   **E**

1. Fairy tales
ISBN 0-8037-9381-2   LC 81-65843

"An extra-large but truly magnificent version of this old favorite. The illustrations superbly convey the tale of a young princess trying to free her eleven brothers from a spell. With this lively adaptation youngsters will be thrilled anew by this story." Child Book Rev Serv

Eichenberg, Fritz, 1901-1990

Ape in a cape; an alphabet of odd animals. Harcourt Brace & Co. 1952 unp il $15.95; pa $4.95   **E**

1. Animals 2. Alphabet
ISBN 0-15-203722-5; 0-15-607830-9 (pa)

A Caldecott Medal honor book, 1953

"Each letter of the alphabet from A for ape to Z for zoo is represented by a full-page picture of an animal with a brief nonsense rhyme caption explaining it. For example: mouse in a blouse, pig in a wig, toad on the road, whale in a gale." Publ Wkly

"The skill of a craftsman distinguishes this picture book illustrated with bold and lively drawings printed in three colors." N Y Public Libr

Emberley, Ed

Go away, big green monster! Little, Brown 1992 unp il $12.95   **E**

1. Monsters—Fiction 2. Fear—Fiction 3. Bedtime—Fiction
ISBN 0-316-23653-5   LC 92-6231

"In the first half of this fear-dispelling book, graphically distinctive die-cut pages reveal, bit by bit, a monster with 'sharp white teeth' and 'scraggly purple hair.' The process is then reversed as the text commands each scary feature to 'go away,' until there is nothing at all left of the monster but a black page instructing 'Don't Come Back! Until I say so.' Entertaining and empowering for young children." Horn Book Guide

Emberley, Michael, 1960-
Ruby. Little, Brown 1990 unp il $14.95; lib
bdg $14.95; pa $4.95   E

1. Mice—Fiction 2. Cats—Fiction
ISBN 0-316-88859-1; 0-316-23643-8 (lib bdg);
0-316-23660-8 (pa)   LC 89-12108

"Ruby [a mouse] is given some pies to deliver to her sick
grandmother and to a neighbor, Mrs. Mastiff. She is warned
not to talk to strangers and especially never to trust a cat.
Of course, Ruby forgets this sound advice and gets smart-
alecky with a slimy reptile who steals her goodie bag. She
is rescued by a well-dressed, smooth-talking cat whose drool
drips down his whiskers at the sight of Ruby. When Ruby
tells the cat exactly where her grandma lives, readers will be
aghast, yet Ruby has a plan. All ends well—except for the
cat." SLJ

"Emberley brings this urbanized Red Riding Hood vividly to life, with multicolored, intensely detailed paintings
capturing the clutter and constant motion of city life."
Booklist

Welcome back sun. Little, Brown 1993 unp
il lib bdg $14.95   E

1. Sun—Fiction 2. Spring—Fiction 3. Norway—Fiction
ISBN 0-316-23647-0   LC 92-9786

"The sunless Norwegian winter has seemed endless, and
a little girl longs to see the sun. . . . This little girl, her family, and the other villagers climb Mount Gausta for a first
glimpse of springtime on the other side." Bull Cent Child
Books

"With its secure tone and satisfying ending, this evocative and beautifully illustrated story is an ideal choice to
share with any child experiencing a difficult, dark time."
Booklist

Ericsson, Jennifer A.
No milk! pictures by Ora Eitan.
Tambourine Bks. 1993 unp il $15; lib bdg
$14.93   E

1. Cattle—Fiction
ISBN 0-688-11306-0; 0-688-11307-9 (lib bdg)
       LC 92-21806

"A city boy tries to coax milk out of a cow by scratching
her ear, kissing her nose, feeding her, and even doing magic
tricks. Nothing works, and his frustration increases until he
throws a tantrum. Animals and boy are drawn with childlike, simplified shapes, displaying a high level of observation and a strong sense of motion and humor." Horn Book
Guide

Ernst, Lisa Campbell, 1957-
Sam Johnson and the blue ribbon quilt.
Lothrop, Lee & Shepard Bks. 1983 32p il lib
bdg $13.93; pa $3.95   E

1. Quilts—Fiction
ISBN 0-688-01517-4 (lib bdg); 0-688-11505-5 (pa)
       LC 82-9980

While mending the awning over the pig pen, Sam discovers that he enjoys sewing the various patches together but
meets with scorn and ridicule when he asks his wife if he
could join her quilting club

The illustrations "bring an old-timey, bucolic scene to
life and show steps in an equal-rights issue." Publ Wkly

When Bluebell sang. Bradbury Press 1989
unp il $15   E

1. Cattle—Fiction
ISBN 0-02-733561-5   LC 88-22262

Also available in paperback from Aladdin Bks.

Bluebell the cow's talent for singing brings her stardom
but she soon longs to be back at the farm—if she can get
away from her greedy manager

"An amusing, lighthearted tale ideal for early grades' story hours, and also an enjoyable read-alone for third and
fourth graders. The pastel-hued, cartoon-like illustrations
are humorous without being silly. The text, which appears
opposite the illustrations, is decorated with drawings of
Bluebell's mementos—photos, tickets and posters—which
add to the fun." SLJ

Zinnia and Dot. Viking 1992 unp il $14.99;
pa $4.99   E

1. Chickens—Fiction
ISBN 0-670-83091-7; 0-14-054199-3 (pa)
       LC 91-36178

Zinnia and Dot, self-satisfied hens who bicker constantly
about who lays better eggs, put aside their differences to
protect a prime specimen from a marauding weasel

"Ernst has an easy storytelling style and a flair for grouchy dialogue that clucks to be read aloud, and her line-and-
wash paintings, lighted with gentle yellow tones, warm the
comedy." Bull Cent Child Books

Ets, Marie Hall, 1893-1984
Gilberto and the Wind. Viking 1963 32p il
$14.99; pa $4.99   E

1. Winds—Fiction
ISBN 0-670-34025-1; 0-14-050276-9 (pa)
Also available Spanish language edition

"I am Gilberto and this is the story of me and the
Wind." Title page

"A little Mexican boy thinks aloud about all the things
his playmate the wind does with him, for him, and against
him. The wind calls him to play, floats his balloon, refuses
to fly his kite, blows his soap bubble into the air, races with
him, and rests with him under a tree." SLJ

"In brown, black, and white against soft gray pages, this
author-artist has caught in a very appealing book . . . the
emotions and attitudes of childhood." Horn Book

Just me; written and illustrated by Marie
Hall Ets. Viking 1965 32p il $15.99; pa $4.99
       E

ISBN 0-670-41109-4; 0-14-050325-0 (pa)
A Caldecott Medal honor book, 1966

"A little boy plays a game commonly enjoyed by small
children for its imaginative as well as muscular demands.
He goes from one animal to another, mimicking its ambula-
tion, moving 'just like' it. When there is a chance to take
a boat ride with Dad, the game ends abruptly, and another
kind of imitation begins—emulation of father." Horn Book

"Strong, simply designed illustrations and brief, rhythmic
text." LC. Child Books, 1965

Play with me; story and pictures by Marie
Hall Ets. Viking 1955 31p il $13.95; pa $4.99
       E

1. Animals—Fiction
ISBN 0-670-55977-6; 0-14-050178-9 (pa)
A Caldecott Medal honor book, 1956

On a sunny morning in the meadow an excited little girl
tries to catch the meadow creatures and play with them.
But, one by one, they all run away. Finally, when she learns
to sit quietly and wait, there is a happy ending

The "pictures done in muted tones of brown, gray and
yellow . . . accurately reflect the little girl's rapidly changing
moods of eagerness, bafflement, disappointment and final
happiness." N Y Times Book Rev

Evans, Katie

Hunky Dory found it; pictures by Janet Morgan Stoeke. Dutton Children's Bks. 1994 unp il $13.99   E

1. Dogs—Fiction 2. Stories in rhyme
ISBN 0-525-45192-7   LC 93-15826

A playful dog named Hunky Dory carries off all sorts of things, including a sock, a ball, a book, and a toy boat

"Simple, bright Tempera illustrations capture the action, giving readers easy clues for deciphering the text. This fine combination of a sprightly narrative and uncluttered, child-like illustrations is certain to attract the youngest of readers, while preschoolers will enjoy it as a read-aloud." SLJ

Everitt, Betsy

Mean soup. Harcourt Brace Jovanovich 1992 unp il $15; pa $5   E
ISBN 0-15-253146-7; 0-15-200227-8 (pa)
     LC 91-15244

Horace feels really mean at the end of a bad day, until he helps his mother make Mean Soup

"The text features short sentences and easy but effective vocabulary, so the story bubbles with a building excitement. Everitt's . . . stylized paintings and bold palette—hot pinks, purples and black predominate—convey all of the feisty emotion of a frustrated youngster." Publ Wkly

Farber, Norma

As I was crossing Boston Common; illustrated by Arnold Lobel. Dutton 1991 unp il $14.95   E

1. Alphabet
ISBN 0-525-25960-0

A reissue of the title first published 1975

"An alphabetical parade of meticulously drawn exotic creatures is accompanied by quizzical verses which are simple in diction and refrainlike in progress. The twenty-six rather uncommon creatures are again cast in a green-and-yellow tint, and their existence is supported by a glossary at the end of the book." Horn Book

Feelings, Muriel, 1938-

Jambo means hello; Swahili alphabet book; pictures by Tom Feelings. Dial Bks. for Young Readers 1981 unp il $15.99; lib bdg $13.89; pa $4.99   E

1. Alphabet 2. Swahili language 3. East Africa
ISBN 0-8037-4346-7; 0-8037-4350-5 (lib bdg); 0-8037-4428-5 (pa)

Also available in paperback from Puffin Bks.

A Caldecott Medal honor book, 1975

This book "gives a word for each letter of the alphabet (the Swahili alphabet has 24 letters) save for 'q' and 'x', and a sentence or two provides additional information. A double-page spread of soft black and white drawings illustrates each word. . . . The text gives a considerable amount of information about traditional East African life as well as some acquaintance with the language that is used by approximately 45 million people." Bull Cent Child Books

"Integrated totally in feeling and mood, the book has been engendered by an intense personal vision of Africa—one that is warm, all-enveloping, quietly strong and filled with love." Horn Book

Moja means one; Swahili counting book; pictures by Tom Feelings. Dial Bks. for Young Readers 1971 unp il o.p.; Puffin Bks. paperback available $4.99   E

1. Counting 2. Swahili language 3. East Africa
ISBN 0-14-054662-6 (pa)

A Caldecott Medal honor book, 1972

The book "uses double-page spreads for each number, one to ten, with beautiful illustrations that depict aspects of East African culture as well as numbers of objects in relation to the various numbers." Publ Wkly

"A short introduction explaining the importance of Swahili and providing a map of the areas in which it is spoken expands the book's use beyond the preschool level of the text into the first three school grades." SLJ

Fisher, Leonard Everett, 1924-

The ABC exhibit. Macmillan 1991 unp il $15.95   E

1. Alphabet
ISBN 0-02-735251-X   LC 90-6639

Introduces the letters of the alphabet in paintings of subjects from Acrobat to Zinnia

"The intensity of color and precision of detail invite readers to linger, to identify, and to observe. The alphabet is merely the framework; the lesson is in the appreciation of art." SLJ

Flack, Marjorie, 1897-1958

Ask Mr. Bear. Macmillan 1958 c1932 unp il $13; pa $4.95   E

1. Animals—Fiction 2. Birthdays—Fiction
ISBN 0-02-735390-7; 0-02-043090-6 (pa)

First published 1932

Danny did not know what to give his mother for a birthday present, so he set out to ask various animals—the hen, the duck, the goose, the lamb, the cow and others, but he met with very little success until he met Mr. Bear

This "will have a strong appeal to very young children because of its repetition, its use of the most familiar animals, its gay pictures and the cumulative effect of the story." N Y Times Book Rev

Fleischman, Paul

Time train; illustrations by Claire Ewart. HarperCollins Pubs. 1991 unp il $15; lib bdg $14.89; pa $4.95   E

1. Dinosaurs—Fiction 2. Fantasy fiction
ISBN 0-06-021709-X; 0-06-021710-3 (lib bdg); 0-06-443351-X (pa)   LC 90-27357

"A Charlotte Zolotow book"

A class takes a field trip back through time to observe living dinosaurs in their natural habitat

"The deadpan humor and gloriously animated watercolors provide unlimited entertainment." SLJ

Fleischman, Sid, 1920-

The scarebird; pictures by Peter Sis. Greenwillow Bks. 1988 unp il $15; lib bdg $14.93; pa $4.95   E

1. Friendship—Fiction 2. Farm life—Fiction
ISBN 0-688-07317-4; 0-688-07318-2 (lib bdg); 0-688-13105-0 (pa)   LC 87-4099

Fleischman, Sid, 1920-—*Continued*

A lonely old farmer realizes the value of human friendship when a young man comes to help him and his scarecrow with their farm

"The oil paintings by Peter Sis are wonderfully evocative. They capture the quiet dignity of the sturdy old farmer and of the farm set in a vast expanse of field and sky. Together, words and pictures create a memorable portrait of a loving human being." Horn Book

Fleming, Denise, 1950-

Barnyard banter. Holt & Co. 1994 unp il $15.95   E

1. Animals—Fiction 2. Stories in rhyme

ISBN 0-8050-1957-X   LC 93-11032

All the farm animals are where they should be, clucking and mucking, mewing and cooing, except for the missing goose

"Strong rhythm and rhyme, plus fun onomatopoetic animal sounds, demand reading aloud. But even more delightful than the engaging text are Fleming's spectacular illustrations. . . . They create realistically textured, bold, bright settings for the whimsical critters to romp through." SLJ

Count! Holt & Co. 1992 unp il $14.95; pa $5.95   E

1. Counting 2. Animals

ISBN 0-8050-1595-7; 0-8050-4252-0 (pa)

               LC 91-25686

The antics of lively and colorful animals present the numbers one to ten, twenty, thirty, forty, and fifty

"A fresh, upbeat concept book. Lizards, giraffes, toucans, butterflies are available for counting—if only they'll hold still long enough! Fuchsias and oranges, teals and purples, roll over the pages blending into each other in Fleming's beautiful couched paper with hand cut-stencil illustrations. Her explosions of color and motion are captivating and energizing." SLJ

In the small, small pond. Holt & Co. 1993 unp il $15.95   E

1. Pond ecology—Fiction 2. Stories in rhyme

ISBN 0-8050-2264-3   LC 92-25770

A Caldecott Medal honor book, 1994

Illustrations and rhyming text describe the activities of animals living in and near a small pond as spring progresses to autumn

"The brilliant, primitive illustrations were made by pouring colored cotton pulp through hand-cut stencils. Against the eye-catching colors, the four-word rhymes in bold black print dance, each double-page spread picturing and describing a different creature. Text, pictures, layout, and design are all beautifully done." SLJ

In the tall, tall grass. Holt & Co. 1991 unp il $15.95; pa $5.95   E

1. Animals—Fiction 2. Stories in rhyme

ISBN 0-8050-1635-X; 0-8050-3941-4 (pa)

               LC 90-26444

Rhymed text (crunch, munch, caterpillars lunch) presents a toddler's view of creatures found in the grass from lunchtime till nightfall, such as bees, ants, and moles

"Boldly colored in grassy greens, sunny yellows, and evening blues, the impressionistic illustrations make this a real treat for eyes as well as ears." Booklist

Lunch. Holt & Co. 1993 unp il $14.95   E

1. Mice—Fiction 2. Color

ISBN 0-8050-1636-8   LC 92-178

"A very hungry mouse nibbles and crunches his way through the various components of a vegetarian repast, while the text introduces readers to the individual foods and their respective colors." Publ Wkly

"Fleming continues to work in the medium of handmade paper built from layers of colored pulp that has been forced through a stencil. A huge typeface and the judicious use of large blocks of bold, solid color give this book a fresh look. Delectable fun, and, with its simple yet engaging plot, sure to be requested over and over by the youngest readers." Horn Book

Flora, James, 1914-

The Fabulous Firework Family; story and pictures by James Flora. Margaret K. McElderry Bks. 1994 unp il $14.95   E

1. Fireworks—Fiction 2. Mexico—Fiction

ISBN 0-689-50596-5   LC 93-11472

"A completely different version (both text and art) of *The Fabulous Firework Family* by James Flora was published by Harcourt Brace & World in 1955." Verso of title page

"Engaged to make fireworks for the celebration of the village saint's day, the Fabulous Firework Family works to create the best display ever and then enjoys the village festival, highlighted by their own handiwork." Booklist

"Flora's bright blues, pinks, and yellows capture the festive atmosphere, and the busy, detailed drawings are fun to pore over. An entertaining story that gives children a glimpse of another culture." SLJ

Florian, Douglas, 1950-

At the zoo. Greenwillow Bks. 1992 unp il $14; lib bdg $13.93   E

1. Zoos 2. Animals

ISBN 0-688-09628-X; 0-688-09629-8 (lib bdg)

               LC 89-77727

Labeled drawings portray animals at the zoo

"Though the allure of the book is its simplicity, adults will notice how much Florian accomplishes with plain, pleasing art and a minimum of text. A fun visit for the youngest." Booklist

City street. Greenwillow Bks. 1990 32p il $15; lib bdg $14.93   E

1. City life—Fiction

ISBN 0-688-09543-7; 0-688-09544-5 (lib bdg)

               LC 89-28694

Pictures and minimal text present life on a city street, where skateboards roll, pigeons fly, and traffic moves

"The sights and sounds, the bustling activity and rare quiet moments are depicted with precision and élan. . . . Whether at work or play, Florian's thickly defined figures capture just the right city attitudes. In a style that seems both childlike and sophisticated, his vibrant palette washes each scene with a rainbow of color." Publ Wkly

Nature walk. Greenwillow Bks. 1989 32p il $12.95; lib bdg $12.88   E

1. Nature

ISBN 0-688-08266-1; 0-688-08269-6 (lib bdg)

               LC 88-39430

Florian, Douglas, 1950-—*Continued*

"A walk through the forest in simple, rhyming text and black pen and crayon drawings. Trail-side discoveries identified on the last page encourage rereading and observation." Sci Child

Turtle day. Crowell 1989 unp il lib bdg $14.89   **E**

1. Turtles—Fiction
ISBN 0-690-04745-2   LC 88-30321
"A turtle's typical day is recounted in simple, predictable text and childlike, full-color drawings. Format invites readers to anticipate what the turtle will do next." Sci Child

A year in the country. Greenwillow Bks. 1989 unp il $12.95; lib bdg $12.88   **E**

1. Farm life 2. Seasons
ISBN 0-688-08186-X; 0-688-08187-8 (lib bdg)
     LC 88-16026
"Utilizing a single landscape, Florian visually chronicles the monthly changes that occur on a farm and its surrounding countryside. The name of each month appears in boldface type in the upper left-hand corner of each double-page watercolor-and-ink spread." SLJ
"The simple drawn pictures, bask in a golden glow year round. Florian once again demonstrates that less can be more." Booklist

Flournoy, Valerie, 1952-

The patchwork quilt; pictures by Jerry Pinkney. Dial Bks. for Young Readers 1985 unp il $14.99; lib bdg $14.89   **E**

1. Quilts—Fiction 2. Family life—Fiction 3. African Americans—Fiction
ISBN 0-8037-0097-0; 0-8037-0098-9 (lib bdg)
     LC 84-1711
Coretta Scott King Award for illustrations, 1986
Using scraps cut from the family's old clothing, Tanya helps her grandmother and mother make a beautiful quilt that tells the story of her Afro-American family's life
"Plentiful full-page and double-page paintings in pencil, graphite and watercolor are vivid yet delicately detailed, bespeaking the warm physical bonds among members of this family. Giving a sense of dramatization to the text, which is longer than most picture books, the illustrations provide just the right style and mood for the story and are well placed within the text." SLJ

Folsom, Michael

Easy as pie; a guessing game of sayings; by Marcia and Michael Folsom; pictures by Jack Kent. Clarion Bks. 1985 unp il lib bdg $14.95; pa $5.95   **E**

1. Alphabet
ISBN 0-89919-303-X (lib bdg); 0-89919-351-X (pa)
     LC 84-14978
Introduces the letters of the alphabet with such familiar sayings as A "Straight as an arrow", B "Snug as a bug in a rug"
"The collection is . . . infused with freshness and vitality by artful Kent's color cartoons. . . . In the authors' note, a discussion of comparisons ends with examples that encourage young people to make up new 'old sayings' instead of using inherited ones." Publ Wkly

Ford, Miela

Little elephant; story by Miela Ford; photographs by Tana Hoban. Greenwillow Bks. 1994 unp il $14; lib bdg $13.93   **E**

1. Elephants—Fiction 2. Zoos—Fiction
ISBN 0-688-13140-9; 0-688-13141-7 (lib bdg)
     LC 93-25208
"Told from the point of view of an infant elephant, this simple story documents the zoo baby's adventures of going into and getting out of the pool in its cage with mother close by. The large-print text of one short sentence or phrase per page, underneath spectacular color photos, makes this a perfect choice for reading one-on-one or with a small group." Booklist

Fox, Mem, 1946-

Hattie and the fox; illustrated by Patricia Mullins. Bradbury Press 1987 c1986 unp il $14.95   **E**

1. Chickens—Fiction 2. Foxes—Fiction
ISBN 0-02-735470-9   LC 86-18849
Also available in paperback from Aladdin Bks.
First published 1986 in Australia
"Hattie is a fine, portly, and observant hen, and she knows there is something wrong when she spies a sharp foxy nose in the bushes. Her alarmist and ever escalating announcements, however, bring nothing but bored and languid replies." Horn Book
"Bright, whimsical tissue collage and crayon illustrations add zest to this simple cumulative tale, and reveal more action than is expressed by the text alone." SLJ

Koala Lou; illustrated by Pamela Lofts. Harcourt Brace Jovanovich 1989 c1988 unp il $13.95; pa $5   **E**

1. Koalas—Fiction
ISBN 0-15-200502-1; 0-15-200076-3 (pa)
     LC 88-26810
"Gulliver books"
First published 1988 in Australia
This story is "set in the Australian bush. Koala Lou feels bereft when her mother becomes preoccupied with a growing brood of younger koala children. In her desire to recapture her mother's attention and affection, the enterprising Koala Lou decides to become a contestant in the Bush Olympics." Horn Book
"A reassuring story for the child who feels neglected when siblings arrive." Child Book Rev Serv

Night noises; written by Mem Fox; illustrated by Terry Denton. Harcourt Brace Jovanovich 1989 unp il $13.95; pa $4.95   **E**

1. Night—Fiction 2. Sleep—Fiction
ISBN 0-15-200543-9; 0-15-257421-2 (pa)
     LC 89-2162
"Gulliver books"
Old Lily Laceby dozes by the fire with her faithful dog Butch Aggie at her feet as strange night noises herald a surprising awakening
"With an almost joltingly bright palette . . . Denton has divided up many of the double-page spreads into three scenes: the main one depicting Lily Laceby and Butch Aggie in various stages of alertness, another showing the chronology of Lily's life, and the third cleverly revealing clues to the mysterious activity outdoors. The text, in Mem Fox's Houdini-like hands, reads beautifully—the language, pacing, tension, and sparks of excitement absolutely at one with the artwork." Horn Book

Fox, Mem, 1946-—*Continued*

Shoes from Grandpa; illustrated by Patricia Mullins. Orchard Bks. 1990 unp il $14.95; pa $5.95   E

1. Clothing and dress—Fiction 2. Stories in rhyme

ISBN 0-531-05848-4; 0-531-07031-X (pa)

LC 89-35401

First published 1989 in Australia

In a cumulative rhyme, family members describe the clothes they intend to give Jessie to go with her shoes from Grandpa

"The illustrations, torn-paper collages, are as lively as the text, giving concrete reality to the catalogue of garments. The choice of medium was inspired, for it allows the artist to extend the text, adding subtly to the characterization of each participant through his or her selections." Horn Book

Sophie; illustrated by Aminah Brenda Lynn Robinson. Harcourt Brace & Co. 1994 c1989 unp il $13.95   E

1. Grandfathers—Fiction 2. African Americans—Fiction

ISBN 0-15-277160-3   LC 94-1976

First published 1989 in Australia

"In this cyclical tale, Grandpa welcomes infant Sophie into the world; much later, Sophie is saddened when 'there was no Grandpa.' The birth of Sophie's own child completes the circle." Publ Wkly

"The artwork is rich, expressionist, heavily lined oil. . . . The oversized hands depicted in many drawings exemplify the handholding theme, and the sunny hues of earth and garden convey with warmth a loving and extended African-American family." Bull Cent Child Books

Tough Boris; illustrated by Kathryn Brown. Harcourt Brace & Co. 1994 unp il $15   E

1. Pirates—Fiction 2. Parrots—Fiction

ISBN 0-15-289612-0   LC 92-8015

Boris von der Borch is a tough pirate but he weeps when his parrot dies

"The text is deceptively simple, but the observant child will quickly fill in the details, aptly provided in the illustrations. The reassuring message, although understated, is clear and effective." Horn Book Guide

Freeman, Don, 1908-1978

Corduroy; story and pictures by Don Freeman. Viking 1968 32p il lib bdg $13.99; pa $4.99   E

1. Teddy bears—Fiction

ISBN 0-670-24133-4 (lib bdg); 0-14-050173-8 (pa)

Also available Spanish language edition

"One day Corduroy, a toy bear who lives in a big department store, discovers he has lost a button. That night he goes to look for it and in his search he sees many strange and wonderful things. He does not find his button, but the following morning he finds what he has always wanted—a friend, Lisa." Read Ladders for Hum Relat. 6th edition

"The art and story are direct and just right for the very young who like bears and escalators." Book World

Another available title about Corduroy is:
A pocket for Corduroy (1978)

Dandelion; story and pictures by Don Freeman. Viking 1964 48p il lib bdg $14.99; pa $4.99   E

1. Lions—Fiction

ISBN 0-670-25532-7 (lib bdg); 0-14-050218-1 (pa)

"Dandelion, properly invited by note to Jennifer Giraffe's tea-and-taffy party, pays no heed to the words, 'Come as you are.' At his regular haircut appointment he allows Lou Kangaroo and helper to do him up properly, according to the new fashions for lions. But pride goeth before a fall—and it is not surprising that Jennifer's tall door is closed on the unrecognizable stranger; nor that after being restored by a heavy rainfall to something nearer his usual state, he makes the party, after all. Mr. Freeman cleverly depicts an assortment of personalities in his many animal characters. The party scenes and the barber shop are wonderfully amusing." Horn Book

Friedman, Ina R.

How my parents learned to eat; illustrated by Allen Say. Houghton Mifflin 1984 30p il $14.95; pa $4.95   E

1. Dining—Fiction 2. Japan—Fiction

ISBN 0-395-35379-3; 0-395-44235-4 (pa)

LC 83-18553

An American sailor courts a Japanese girl and each tries, in secret, to learn the other's way of eating

"The illustrations have precise use of line and soft colors, and the composition is economical. A warm and gentle story of an interracial family." Bull Cent Child Books

Froehlich, Margaret Walden, 1930-

That Kookoory! written by Margaret Walden Froehlich; illustrated by Marla Frazee. Browndeer Press 1995 unp il $15   E

1. Roosters—Fiction 2. Fairs—Fiction

ISBN 0-15-277650-8   LC 93-41833

In his excitement about Edgerton Fair, Kookoory wakes his friends and inadvertently attracts the attention of a hungry weasel

"Both artwork and text are outstanding. Frazee's pen-and-colored-ink illustrations portray night scenes and the dawn spectrum with equal effectiveness, and the animals appear small but distinctive against expansive backgrounds of fields and buildings. Froehlich's text has a folksy feel . . . and it's pleasingly specific." Booklist

Gackenbach, Dick, 1927-

What's Claude doing? Clarion Bks. 1984 unp il hardcover o.p. paperback available $4.95   E

1. Dogs—Fiction

ISBN 0-89919-464-8 (pa)   LC 83-14983

"Claude, a 'do-good' hound, can't be persuaded by his friends to come outside and join their fun. Suspense builds as the animals (and children) wonder just what Claude is doing." SLJ

"Large three-color pictures featuring a perky cast of animal characters and a pared-down text make this cozy, mildly suspenseful winter story a prime read-aloud choice for the toddler set." Booklist

Other available titles about Claude are:
Claude has a picnic (1993)
Claude the dog (1974)

Gág, Wanda, 1893-1946

The A B C bunny; hand lettered by Howard Gág. Coward-McCann 1933 unp il $15.95; pa $6.95   E

1. Rabbits—Fiction 2. Alphabet 3. Stories in rhyme
ISBN 0-698-20000-4; 0-698-20465-4 (pa)
A Newbery Medal honor book, 1934
An alphabet book which tells in verse and pictures the story of a little rabbit's adventures. The verse has been set to music by the author's sister
"The book has the freshness of invention, and the drawings, the beauty, humor and originality characteristic of this artist's work. The illustrations are original lithographs." N Y Times Book Rev

Millions of cats. Coward-McCann 1928 unp il $10.95; pa $4.95   E

1. Cats—Fiction
ISBN 0-698-20091-8; 0-698-20637-1 (pa)
A Newbery Medal honor book, 1929
"An unusual story-picture book about a very old man and a very old woman who wanted one little cat and who found themselves with 'millions and billions and trillions of cats.'" St Louis Public Libr
It is "a perennial favorite among children and takes a place of its own, both for the originality and strength of its pictures and the living folktale quality of its text." N Y Her Trib Books

Gage, Wilson, 1922-1992

Cully Cully and the bear; pictures by James Stevenson. Greenwillow Bks. 1983 unp il lib bdg $14.93; pa $3.95   E

1. Hunting—Fiction 2. Bears—Fiction
ISBN 0-688-01769-X (lib bdg); 0-688-07043-4 (pa)
LC 82-11715
"Cully Cully, a hunter armed with bow and arrows, decided he needed a bearskin to lie on. Nicking a bear's nose with an arrow, the hunter became fearful and tried to run away. Man and beast began to chase each other around the trunk of a huge tree, each never completely certain as to who was chasing whom. Ultimately, the bear walked away, and Cully Cully was happy to lie on the rough ground." Horn Book
"Stevenson's robust pictures are a great asset, and the book is a guaranteed story-hour success." Child Book Rev Serv

Mrs. Gaddy and the ghost; by Wilson Gage; pictures by Marylin Hafner. Greenwillow Bks. 1979 55p il $14.95   E

1. Ghost stories
ISBN 0-688-80179-X   LC 78-16366
Also available in paperback from Scholastic
"A Greenwillow read-alone book"
"Plump Mrs. Gaddy is very happy living on her farm. . . . But she . . . has an unwanted boarder—a hungry ghost who keeps her awake with its nocturnal feasting. Mrs. Gaddy tries many ploys to rid her house of 'the ghosty thing.' . . . The simple text is spiced with such colorful expressions as 'bless my big toe!' and 'tarnation.' The illustrations in warm tones of pink and sepia ink are full of witty and imaginative detail." Horn Book
Another available title about Mrs. Gaddy is:
The crow and Mrs. Gaddy (1984)

Gantos, Jack

Rotten Ralph; written by Jack B. Gantos; illustrated by Nicole Rubel. Houghton Mifflin 1976 unp il lib bdg $14.95; pa $5.95   E

1. Cats—Fiction
ISBN 0-395-24276-2 (lib bdg); 0-395-29202-6 (pa)
"The protagonist of this story is a mean and nasty cat, Ralph. As his young owner, Sarah, and her family say, he is very difficult to love. Finally on a trip to the circus his behavior becomes unforgivable and they leave him. There he is treated as miserably as he has treated everyone else and he comes home a week later a wiser, more benevolent cat—well, almost." Child Book Rev Serv
The "bright watercolor scenes . . . capturing Ralph's demonic meanness and his family's chagrin are a perfect complement to the text." SLJ
Other available titles about Ralph the cat are:
Happy birthday Rotten Ralph (1990)
Not so Rotten Ralph (1994)
Rotten Ralph's rotten Christmas (1984)
Rotten Ralph's show and tell (1989)
Rotten Ralph's trick or treat! (1986)
Worse than rotten, Ralph (1978)

Garland, Michael, 1952-

Dinner at Magritte's. Dutton Children's Bks. 1995 unp il $14.99   E

1. Magritte, René, 1898-1967—Fiction 2. Dalí, Salvador, 1904-1989—Fiction 3. Artists—Fiction 4. France—Fiction
ISBN 0-525-45336-9   LC 94-28257
"Pierre's family spends the summer in the country, where their neighbors are René and Georgette Magritte. The artist and his wife befriend the boy and introduce him to their surreal way of looking at things, and also to their friend Salvador Dali. Witty illustrations make this a sophisticated entertainment." N Y Times Book Rev

Garland, Sherry, 1948-

The summer sands; illustrated by Robert J. Lee. Harcourt Brace & Co. 1995 unp il $15   E

1. Seashore ecology—Fiction
ISBN 0-15-282492-8   LC 94-6978
"A Gulliver green book"
"All summer, a girl and her little brother play on the dunes and beach behind ther grandfather's house, but one day, a violent storm washes the sand hills away. When the children and their parents return to Grandpa's after New Year's Day, they take their Christmas tree to the beach and line it up with others to catch the sand and form new dunes." Booklist
"Detailed watercolors portray the natural beauty of the seashore as well as the ravages of coastal storms, and convey the sensitivity of the story. Excellent for showing the delicate ecological balance of our planet, as well as a good read." SLJ

Garten, Jan

The alphabet tale; illustrated by Muriel Batherman. new ed. Greenwillow Bks. 1994 unp il $15; lib bdg $14.93   E

1. Animals 2. Alphabet
ISBN 0-688-12702-9; 0-688-12703-7 (lib bdg)
LC 93-4879
First published 1964 by Random House

Garten, Jan—*Continued*

"Accompanied by simple, bright illustrations, this rhyming tale of tails will appeal to young children who delight in solving puzzles. Readers have the opportunity to identify the owners of the tails presented for each letter of the alphabet." Horn Book Guide

Gauch, Patricia Lee

Christina Katerina and the time she quit the family; illustrated by Elise Primavera. Putnam 1987 unp il $14.95   E

1. Family life—Fiction
ISBN 0-399-21408-9   LC 86-18658

"It all begins on a 'perfectly good' Saturday morning when Christina Katerina, who has been unjustly accused of just about everything, changes her name to Agnes and quits on the spot. 'You go your way. We'll go ours,' announces Mildred (a k a Mother)." N Y Times Book Rev

"Primavera's spiffy watercolors pulse with reality, and although the scenarios are at times inevitably exaggerated, no one should mind the dramatic license when the situation, in words and pictures, comes right from the heart." Booklist

Other available titles about Christina Katerina are:
Christina Katerina & the box (1971)
Christina Katerina and the great bear train (1990)

Dance, Tanya; [illustrations by] Satomi Ichikawa; story by Patricia Lee Gauch. Philomel Bks. 1989 unp il $15.95   E

1. Ballet—Fiction
ISBN 0-399-21521-2   LC 88-9935

Tanya loves ballet dancing, repeating the moves she sees her older sister using when practicing for class or a recital, and soon Tanya is big enough to go to ballet class herself

"Gauch's sweet story gains strength from Ichikawa's soft watercolor paintings, which celebrate Tanya's enthusiasm with a sharp sense of how small children move. . . . A gentle, knowing book." Booklist

Other available titles about Tanya are:
Bravo Tanya (1992)
Tanya and Emily in a dance for two (1994)

Geisert, Arthur

After the flood. Houghton Mifflin 1994 32p il $16.95   E

1. Noah's ark—Fiction
ISBN 0-395-66611-2   LC 93-758

After surviving the Flood, Noah and his family settle in a sheltered valley with the animals they have saved and begin the glorious experience of repopulating the Earth

"The minimalist statements are extended in marvelously intricate, sensitively rendered, full-color etchings." Horn Book Guide

Oink. Houghton Mifflin 1991 unp il $13.95; pa $4.95   E

1. Pigs—Fiction 2. Stories without words
ISBN 0-395-55329-6; 0-395-74516-0 (pa)
                                           LC 90-46123

"The only word in this book is OINK! Mother pig takes her piglets exploring but always makes certain they return with her. But one day, as she sleeps, they romp away and find themselves stranded in a tree. When mother finds them, her one OINK brings them down and they are marched back, safe but subdued." Child Book Rev Serv

"Children of all ages will love this porcine family, so appealingly etched in pale pink and black and white. The droll illustrations exude an understated hilarity." Publ Wkly

Another available title about mother pig and her piglets is:
Oink, oink (1993)

Pigs from 1 to 10. Houghton Mifflin 1992 32p il $14.95   E

1. Counting 2. Pigs—Fiction
ISBN 0-395-58519-8   LC 92-5097

Ten pigs go on an adventurous quest. The reader is asked to find all ten of them, and the numerals from zero to nine, in each picture

"Geisert's inventiveness knows no bounds, and his illustrations both inspire the imagination and convey a homey charm. The final page, a triumphant aggregation of pigs and numbers, is especially endearing." Publ Wkly

Pigs from A to Z. Houghton Mifflin 1986 unp il $16.95   E

1. Alphabet 2. Pigs—Fiction
ISBN 0-395-38509-1   LC 86-18542

Seven piglets cavort through a landscape of hidden letters as they build a tree house

"At the back of the book is a key that shows where the artist has secreted all the letters in each illustration; some are plain, some are subtle and every picture has, in addition to its principal letter, one or two from the alphabetical surroundings. . . . So 'Pigs From A to Z' succeeds as narrative, alphabet book, counting book (are all seven piglets in each etching?), puzzle book and as art." N Y Times Book Rev

George, Lindsay Barrett

In the woods: who's been here? Greenwillow Bks. 1995 unp il $15; lib bdg $14.93   E

1. Forest animals
ISBN 0-688-12318-X; 0-688-12319-8 (lib bdg)
                                           LC 93-16244

A boy and girl in the autumn woods find an empty nest, a cocoon, gnawed bark, and other signs of unseen animals and their activities

"Children will be drawn to George's vivid gouache paintings, especially those depicting the animals in their natural surroundings. . . . For most childen this will be an excellent introduction to classroom nature units and the perfect prelude to a walk in the woods." Booklist

George, William T.

Box Turtle at Long Pond; pictures by Lindsay Barrett George. Greenwillow Bks. 1989 unp il $16; lib bdg $15.93   E

1. Turtles—Fiction
ISBN 0-688-08184-3; 0-688-08185-1 (lib bdg)
                                           LC 88-18787

On a busy day at Long Pond, Box Turtle searches for food, basks in the sun, and escapes a raccoon

"A beautifully illustrated book that introduces a pond environment. . . . The reader learns of other plants, animals, and insects that inhabit the pond." Sci Child

Other available titles about Long Pond are:
Beaver at Long Pond (1988)
Christmas at Long Pond (1992)
Fishing at Long Pond (1991)

Geringer, Laura

A three hat day; pictures by Arnold Lobel. Harper & Row 1985 30p il lib bdg $14.89; pa $4.95   E

1. Hats—Fiction
ISBN 0-06-021989-0 (lib bdg); 0-06-443157-6 (pa)
LC 85-42640

This "is about R.R. Pottle the Third, an inveterate collector of hats. Wearing one at a time usually suits him, but on days when he is depressed, he wears three all at once. It is on such a day that he meets Ida, the shop clerk, and not long after, R.R. Pottle the Fourth is born—an inveterate collector of shoes." Wilson Libr Bull

"Lobel's energetic line drawings with warm, full-color washes contribute their own dignity and humor to the characters . . . With its light touch, good pacing, and satisfying symmetry, this is a pleasing choice to read aloud." Booklist

Gerrard, Roy, 1935-

Mik's mammoth. Farrar, Straus & Giroux 1990 unp il $15; pa $4.95   E

1. Cave dwellers—Fiction 2. Mammoths—Fiction 3. Stories in rhyme
ISBN 0-374-31891-3; 0-374-44843-4 (pa)
LC 90-55189

"Mik the caveman is a timid sort who befriends a woolly mammoth. He and the beast save the tribe from 'hordes of hairy men,' and Mik becomes their leader." SLJ

"Gerrard's . . . paintings, subtly shaded watercolors on a white ground, create a sturdy, pleasing, understated vision of the tale. Handsomely illustrated in full color, the book is sophisticated in design and disarmingly childlike in content. Touches of droll humor in both artwork and verse will endear it to readers young and old." Booklist

Gershator, David

Bread is for eating; [by] David and Phillis Gershator; illustrated by Emma Shaw-Smith. Holt & Co. 1995 unp il music $14.95   E

1. Bread—Fiction 2. Songs 3. Hispanic Americans—Fiction
ISBN 0-8050-3173-1   LC 94-28811
Also available Spanish language edition

A mother "explains, poetically, how wheat is planted, grown, harvested, milled, and baked to loaves of life-giving bread. A little song, El pan es para comer (music included) accompanies each step in the process. Spanish and English are blended seamlessly with the graceful narrative. Shaw-Smith's heroic-style pictures, filled with rich, glowing reds and yellows, are crammed with disparate details." SLJ

Gerstein, Mordicai, 1935-

Arnold of the Ducks; by Mordicai Gerstein. Harper & Row 1983 unp il lib bdg $12.89
E

1. Ducks—Fiction
ISBN 0-06-022003-1   LC 82-47735

"Snatched as an infant by a pelican, Arnold is dropped from the bird's beak into a nest of ducklings, and adopted by Mrs. Leda Duck as one of her own. An odd duckling, but she loves him. With mud and marsh slime, the others paste feathers over Arnold so that he won't look so odd, and that's how Arnold is able to fly. . . . Nicely told, with a wistful ending that rounds out the concept of the fantasy." Bull Cent Child Books

The mountains of Tibet. Harper & Row 1987 unp il $14; pa $5.95   E

1. Reincarnation—Fiction 2. Tibet (China)—Fiction
ISBN 0-06-022144-5; 0-06-443211-4 (pa)
LC 85-45684

The author "has created a tale of reincarnation inspired by his reading of the Tibetan Book of the Dead. A little boy is born in a valley high in the mountains of Tibet. . . . Looking at the stars, he dreams of visiting other worlds and seeing other countries and peoples. . . . After his death a voice offers him a chance to live another life; he chooses from the galaxies, star systems, planets, and life forms." Horn Book

"As the illustrator of his own spare text, Mr. Gerstein . . . makes tasteful allusions to Tibetan art, creating a colorful, well-balanced picture book in the classic mold. Every element complements the story or, indeed, adds to it." N Y Times Book Rev

Roll over! by Mordicai Gerstein. Crown 1984 unp il $12   E

1. Nursery rhymes 2. Counting
ISBN 0-517-55209-4   LC 83-18884

The author "injects fresh jollity into the old counting chant. A yawning tyke in pajamas approaches his huge bed where 10 'guests' are already snuggled and the 'little one said,' 'ROLL OVER!'" Publ Wkly

"The book's design features a folded-over flap on the right-hand side; youngsters will have the surprise of peeking beneath to see who the latest ejected creature is. Full-color pen-and-wash drawings create a cozy-looking, very broad bed with a star-and-moon-covered quilt." Booklist

Gibbons, Gail

The seasons of Arnold's apple tree. Harcourt Brace Jovanovich 1984 unp il $15; pa $4.95
E

1. Seasons—Fiction 2. Trees—Fiction
ISBN 0-15-271246-1; 0-15-271245-3 (pa)
LC 84-4484

Arnold enjoys his apple tree through the changing year: its springtime blossoms, the swing and tree-house it supports, its summer shade, its autumn harvest; in the winter, the tree's branches hold strings of popcorn and berries for the birds

"Two major concepts emerge here, the first being the passage of the seasons, the second the valuable resource Arnold has in his apple tree. . . . Gibbons' crisp pictures ensure that the multifaceted lesson is explicit, bright and cheery." Booklist

Giff, Patricia Reilly

Watch out, Ronald Morgan! illustrated by Susanna Natti. Viking Kestrel 1985 24p il hardcover o.p. paperback available $5.99
E

1. Eyeglasses—Fiction 2. School stories
ISBN 0-14-050638-1 (pa)   LC 84-19623

Ronald has many humorous mishaps until he gets a pair of eyeglasses. Includes a note for adults about children's eye problems

"Told in a forthright manner but with appreciation for children's candor, the book's dialogue rings true with catchy humor. . . . Natti's illustrations show the characters to be bright, colorful informal figures who move with the text." SLJ

Giff, Patricia Reilly—*Continued*
Other available titles about Ronald Morgan are:
Happy birthday, Ronald Morgan! (1986)
Ronald Morgan goes to bat (1988)
Ronald Morgan goes to camp (1995)
Today was a terrible day (1980)

Giganti, Paul, Jr.
Each orange had 8 slices; a counting book; by Paul Giganti, Jr.; pictures by Donald Crews. Greenwillow Bks. 1992 unp il $15; lib bdg $14.93 E
1. Counting 2. Mathematics
ISBN 0-688-10428-2; 0-688-10429-0 (lib bdg)
LC 90-24167
This volume presents a series of statements about the illustrations: "'On my way to Grandma's I saw 2 fat cows. Each cow had 2 calves. Each calf had 4 skinny legs,' and the questions follow: 'How many fat cows . . . calves . . . legs were there in all?'" SLJ
"This bright, well-designed book challenges young children to think analytically about what's on its pages. . . . Since the objects are organized into sets and subsets, this could be used to introduce the concept of multiplication as well as counting and addition." Booklist

How many snails? a counting book; by Paul Giganti, Jr.; pictures by Donald Crews. Greenwillow Bks. 1988 unp il $16; lib bdg $15.93; pa $4.95 E
1. Counting
ISBN 0-688-06369-1; 0-688-06370-5 (lib bdg); 0-688-13639-7 (pa)
LC 87-26281
"Instead of inviting children to count static objects, Mr. Giganti poses a series of simple, direct questions designed to encourage youngsters to determine the often subtle differences between those objects. Donald Crews . . . concentrates here on decorating each page with objects that supply the necessary links to the text. Some of the pages—depicting a collection of motley dogs at the park or beautiful toy boats and trucks, cars and airplanes at a toy store—are a joy to look at." N Y Times Book Rev

Ginsburg, Mirra
Asleep, asleep; inspired by a verse of A. Vvedensky; illustrated by Nancy Tafuri. Greenwillow Bks. 1992 unp il $14; lib bdg $13.93 E
1. Sleep—Fiction
ISBN 0-688-09153-9; 0-688-09154-7 (lib bdg)
LC 91-14383
Everything everywhere is asleep except for the wind and one wakeful child
"The brief, rhythmic text is simple and repetitive, with just enough variation to avoid monotony. The watercolor pictures, bordered with simple bands of quiet color, illuminate the words beautifully." SLJ

The chick and the duckling; translated [and adapted] from the Russian of V. Suteyev; pictures by Jose & Ariane Aruego. Macmillan 1972 unp il $14.95; pa $4.95 E
1. Ducks—Fiction 2. Chickens—Fiction
ISBN 0-02-735940-9; 0-689-71226-X (pa)
"The adventures of a duckling who is a leader and a chick who follows suit. When the chick decides that an aquatic life is not for him, this brief selection for reading aloud comes to a humorous conclusion." Wis Libr Bull
"The sunny simplicity of the illustrations is just right for a slight but engaging text, and they add a note of humor that is a nice foil for the bland directness of the story." Bull Cent Child Books

Good morning, chick; by Mirra Ginsburg, adapted from a story by Korney Chukovsky; pictures by Byron Barton. Greenwillow Bks. 1980 unp il $14; lib bdg $13.93; pa $3.95 E
1. Chickens—Fiction
ISBN 0-688-80284-2; 0-688-84284-4 (lib bdg); 0-688-08741-8 (pa)
LC 80-11352
"In this simple preschool tale . . . a chick hatches out of an egg ('like this'), learns to eat worms ('like this'), is scared by a cat ('like this'), falls in a pond ('like this'), and is coddled back to fluffiness by Mom ('like this')." SLJ
"Based upon a tale by the great Russian poet and storyteller, the totally childlike picture book for the very young employs an engaging device: The text, illustrated with a bright vignette, appears on each of the left-hand pages; then, after pausing briefly and leading the eye to the right, a sentence runs to completion on the opposite page with two words contained in a large storytelling picture done in bold, brilliant color." Horn Book

Goble, Paul
Death of the iron horse; story and illustrations by Paul Goble. Bradbury Press 1987 unp il $14.95 E
1. Cheyenne Indians—Fiction 2. Railroads—Fiction
ISBN 0-02-737830-6
LC 85-28011
Also available in paperback from Aladdin Bks.
The author "has taken several accounts of the 1867 Cheyenne attack of a Union Pacific freight train . . . and combined them into a story from the Indians' viewpoint. As the Cheyenne Prophet Sweet Medicine had foretold, strange hairy people were invading the land, killing women and children and driving off the horses. Descriptions of the iron horse inspired curiosity and fear in the young braves who decided to go out and protect their village from this new menace. Keeping fairly close to actual Indian accounts, Goble presents the braves' bold attack on the train, glossing over the deaths of the train crew." SLJ

Dream wolf; story and illustrations by Paul Goble. Bradbury Press 1990 unp il $14.95 E
1. Indians of North America—Fiction 2. Wolves—Fiction
ISBN 0-02-736585-9
LC 89-687
Revised edition of: The friendly wolf, published 1974
When two Plains Indian children become lost, they are cared for and guided safely home by a friendly wolf
"*Dream Wolf* is filled with glowing imagery—the illustrations showing nightfall, the children's search for shelter and the wolf's first, dreamlike appearance are particularly riveting. Once again, Goble has captured the lives and legends of this tribe in a magnificent picture book." Publ Wkly

The girl who loved wild horses; story and illustrations by Paul Goble. Bradbury Press 1978 unp il $14.95 E
1. Indians of North America—Fiction 2. Horses—Fiction
ISBN 0-02-736570-0
LC 77-20500
Also available in paperback from Aladdin Bks.
Awarded the Caldecott Medal, 1979

Goble, Paul—*Continued*

"After becoming lost in a storm, a young Indian girl joins and lives with a herd of wild horses until finally, she becomes one herself." SLJ

"Elaborate double-page spreads burst with life, revealing details of flowers and insects, animals and birds. . . . The story is told in simple language, and the author has included verses of a Navaho and Sioux song about horses. Both storytelling and art express the harmony with and the love of nature which characterize Native American culture." Horn Book

Goldin, Barbara Diamond

Cakes and miracles; a Purim tale; illustrated by Erika Weihs. Viking 1991 unp il lib bdg $15; pa $4.99   E

1. Purim—Fiction 2. Blind—Fiction 3. Jews—Fiction
ISBN 0-670-83047-X (lib bdg); 0-14-054871-8 (pa)
           LC 90-42048

Young, blind Hershel finds that he has special gifts he can use to help his mother during the Jewish holiday of Purim

"This original tale, set in Eastern Europe in the late 19th century, satisfies on many levels. The fluid writing has grace and beauty. . . . Appended is the story of Purim and a recipe for *hamantashen*, those delectable three cornered pastries. Weihs's perfectly composed, folk-type illustrations are rich, yet subtle." SLJ

Just enough is plenty: a Hanukkah tale; paintings by Seymour Chwast. Viking Penguin 1988 unp il lib bdg $12.95; pa $4.99   E

1. Hanukkah—Fiction 2. Jews—Fiction
ISBN 0-670-81852-6 (lib bdg); 0-14-050787-6 (pa)
           LC 88-3953

"Malka's family is too poor to have a proper Hanukkah celebration, but when a mysterious stranger knocks on their door, he is welcomed in anyway. He rewards their generosity by weaving enough stories and magic to last a lifetime. The stranger's sudden disappearance leaves everyone wondering if they had not been blessed by a visit from the prophet Elijah." Child Book Rev Serv

"Goldin's tale and Chwast's vibrant, primitive paintings are masterfully combined." Publ Wkly

The magician's visit; a Passover tale; adapted from a story by I.L. Peretz; retold by Barbara Diamond Goldin; illustrated by Robert Andrew Parker. Viking 1993 unp il $14.99; pa $4.99   E

1. Passover—Fiction 2. Jews—Fiction
ISBN 0-670-84840-9; 0-14-054455-0 (pa)
           LC 92-22903

A poor Jewish couple is rewarded for its faith and charity by a mysterious magician

"Goldin has simplified Peretz' tale without losing—or trying to explain—the sense of mystical wonder. Parker picks up on the tone with his expressionistic, thickly textured paintings, in which mottled colors are subtly juggled against dark backgrounds." Bull Cent Child Books

The world's birthday; a Rosh Hashanah story; pictures by Jeanette Winter. Harcourt Brace Jovanovich 1990 unp il $13.95; pa $5   E

1. Rosh ha-Shanah—Fiction 2. Jews—Fiction
ISBN 0-15-299648-6; 0-15-200045-3 (pa)
           LC 89-29208

"To celebrate Rosh Hashanah, the Jewish holiday commemorating the birth of the world, young Daniel wants to host a birthday party and invite the world as guest of honor." Booklist

"This is a delightful holiday story about a young child making his own personal connection to belief and ritual. Each full-page watercolor illustration is juxtaposed to a full page of text; the gentle colors and earnest, wide-eyed expressions add greatly to the strength of the text." SLJ

Gollub, Matthew, 1960-

The twenty-five Mixtec cats; pictures by Leovigildo Martinez. Tambourine Bks. 1993 unp il $15; lib bdg $14.93   E

1. Cats—Fiction 2. Mexico—Fiction
ISBN 0-688-11639-6; 0-688-11640-X (lib bdg)
           LC 92-13585

The inhabitants of a mountain village in Oaxaca, Mexico are suspicious of the twenty-five cats who come to live with their healer, until the cats are able to help lift a curse placed on the butcher

"The story is told in an easy colloquial English that has the cadenced feel of Spanish. The illustrations are remarkable. Done in predominantly desert hues of yellow, ocher, blue, and pink, in a primitive, folk style, the bordered watercolors bring the text to life." SLJ

Goode, Diane

Where's our mama? Dutton Children's Bks. 1991 unp il $13.95   E

1. Mothers—Fiction 2. Paris (France)—Fiction
ISBN 0-525-44770-9   LC 91-2158

Also available in paperback from Puffin Bks.

A kindly gendarme conducts two young children around Paris in search of their lost mother

"The original Gare d'Orsay Train Station in Paris circa 1920 is the setting for this winning tribute to the enduring belief that one's own mother is the best in the world. . . . Goode has crafted a book that is both elegant and childlike. The full-color art authentically evokes a glamourous, multiethnic Parisian milieu; marbleized endpapers and a classic border contribute to the handsome design." SLJ

Gould, Deborah

Aaron's shirt; illustrated by Cheryl Harness. Bradbury Press 1989 unp il $13.95   E

1. Clothing and dress—Fiction
ISBN 0-02-736351-1   LC 88-10414

"Aaron really likes the red-and-white striped shirt he's chosen at a department store. He gives it up only through necessity (laundering or seasonal storage) and wears it until it's uncomfortably tight. Eventually he admits defeat, passing the shirt on to his stuffed bear." Bull Cent Child Books

"Vivid watercolors believably portray Aaron's growth over three years. Dealing with change and parting with favorite things are familiar themes, and children will recognize Aaron's dilemma and solution as just right." SLJ

Gove, Doris

One rainy night; illustrated by Walter Lyon Krudop. Atheneum Pubs. 1994 unp il $14.95   E

1. Nature conservation—Fiction 2. Mothers and sons—Fiction
ISBN 0-689-31800-6   LC 93-13900

Gove, Doris—*Continued*

A boy and his mother go out on a rainy night to collect animals for a nature center that releases its specimens to the wild after two weeks

"This is fine nature writing, with handsome impressionistic paintings that extend both the physical immediacy and the careful observation of the story." Booklist

Gramatky, Hardie, 1907-1979

Little Toot; pictures and story by Hardie Gramatky. Putnam c1939 unp il $14.95; pa $8.95   E

1. Tugboats—Fiction

ISBN 0-399-22419-X; 0-399-22418-X (pa)

Story and pictures describe the early career of a saucy little tug-boat too pleased with himself to do any real work until one day when he found himself out on the ocean in a storm. Then Little Toot earned the right to be called a hero

"Mr. Gramatky tells his story with humor and enjoyment, giving, too, a genuine sense of the water front in both pictures and story." Horn Book

Gray, Libba Moore

My mama had a dancing heart; illustrated by Raúl Colón. Orchard Bks. 1995 unp il $15.95; lib bdg $15.99   E

1. Dancing—Fiction 2. Mothers and daughters—Fiction 3. Seasons—Fiction

ISBN 0-531-09470-7; 0-531-08770-0 (lib bdg)

LC 94-48802

"A Melanie Kroupa book"

"In spring, summer, fall and winter, a mother leads her young daughter in dancing a celebratory ballet, a hymn to the season. When the girl is older, she is a ballerina and remembers that her mother gave her a dancing heart. . . . Colón's etched watercolors in earth and muted jewel tones give the book an old-fashioned ambiance. . . . Gray's writing lends itself to reading aloud, but independent readers will also enjoy it." SLJ

Small Green Snake; pictures by Holly Meade. Orchard Bks. 1994 unp il $14.95; lib bdg $14.99   E

1. Snakes—Fiction

ISBN 0-531-06844-7; 0-531-08694-1 (lib bdg)

LC 93-49396

Despite his mother's warning not to wander, Small Green Snake wiggles away to investigate the new sound from across the garden wall

"This is a romping, rhyming delight of a story that must be read aloud so that the many S's and the great words and catchy phrases can be fully enjoyed. The fresh and funny tornpaper collages are a perfect complement to the spirited text." SLJ

Greenberg, Melanie Hope

Aunt Lilly's laundromat. Dutton Children's Bks. 1994 unp il $13.99   E

1. Haitian Americans—Fiction 2. Laundry—Fiction

ISBN 0-525-45211-7   LC 93-42597

Aunt Lilly thinks about her island home, Haiti, while she works in her laundromat in Brooklyn

"Busy illustrations in bold, luminous colors capture Lilly's joie de vivre. . . . Greenberg's work has a childlike zest and, at the same time, is imbued with a strong sense of order and design." Publ Wkly

Greenfield, Eloise, 1929-

Africa dream; illustrated by Carole Byard. Crowell 1977 unp il lib bdg $14.89; pa $4.95   E

1. Africa—Fiction

ISBN 0-690-04776-2 (lib bdg); 0-06-443277-7 (pa)

LC 77-5080

Coretta Scott King Award, 1978

"As ethereal as the title implies, this sparsely worded prose-poem relates the benign dream experience of a young child who transports her mind to 'Long-ago Africa.'" Booklist

Grandmama's joy; illustrated by Carole Byard. Philomel Bks. c1980 unp il $14.95   E

1. African Americans—Fiction 2. Grandmothers—Fiction

ISBN 0-399-21064-4   LC 79-11403

First published 1980 by Collins

This is the story of the relationship between Grandmama and Rhondy. Rhondy has lived with Grandmama since she "was a baby and her parents died in a car accident. Rhondy's attempts to cheer the sad woman fail, and Rhondy learns why; they must move to a cheaper home. But the girl is persistent and cheers her by reminding her of the love they share." SLJ

"This extremely gifted and sensitive writer consistently . . . illuminates key aspects of the Black experience in a way that underlines both its uniqueness and universality. . . . Carole Byard's beautiful expressive drawings match the tone of the story." Interracial Books Child Bull

Grandpa's face; illustrated by Floyd Cooper. Philomel Bks. 1988 unp il lib bdg $15.95; pa $5.95   E

1. Grandfathers—Fiction 2. Actors—Fiction

ISBN 0-399-21525-5 (lib bdg); 0-399-22106-9 (pa)

LC 87-16729

Also available Spanish language edition

"Tamika fears that her grandfather, an actor, is incapable of loving her when she sees him practicing a cruel expression. The young girl's turmoil and its resolution are keenly felt through evocative text and striking pictures." SLJ

Me and Neesie; illustrated by Moneta Barnett. Crowell 1975 unp il lib bdg $16.75; pa $4.95   E

1. African Americans—Fiction 2. Imaginary playmates—Fiction

ISBN 0-690-00715-9 (lib bdg); 0-06-443057-X (pa)

"An enjoyable story of a little girl and her imaginary, mischievous friend. Janell's mother wishes she would abandon her modern day 'Binker,' but it's not until Janell goes to school where she meets many new friends that Neesie disappears from her life." SLJ

"This story about a Black family has a very warm texture. Janell's mother and father are portrayed as being sensitive and sympathetic regarding their daughter's growing pains. Moneta Barnett's illustrations are lively and expressive." Interracial Books Child Bull

Greenfield, Eloise, 1929-—*Continued*
She come bringing me that little baby girl;
illustrated by John Steptoe. Lippincott 1974
unp il $16; lib bdg $15.89; pa $5.95   E
1. Brothers and sisters—Fiction 2. Infants—Fiction
3. African Americans—Fiction
ISBN 0-397-31586-4; 0-397-32478-2 (lib bdg);
0-06-443296-3 (pa)
"For Kevin, who had wanted a baby brother, the arrival
of his pink-shawled baby sister proved a bitter disappointment. Not only was she the wrong sex, she also cried too
much, had too many wrinkles to look new, and most provoking of all she occupied everyone's attention. How he
changed his opinion about his sister is developed in a sensitive first-person text, complemented and extended by the
poignant, darkly brilliant, three-color illustrations. A familiar situation handled with rare charm, culminating in a visual and verbal paean to familial love." Horn Book

Gretz, Susanna
Teddy bears 1 to 10. Four Winds Press
1986 c1969 unp il $13.95   E
1. Counting ? Teddy bears—Fiction
ISBN 0-02-738140-4   LC 86-4795
A reissue of the title first published 1969 by Follett
As teddy bears are washed, dried, take the bus, and have
tea they introduce the numbers one to ten
Other available titles about the teddy bears are:
Teddy bears ABC (1986)
Teddy bears at the seaside (1989)
Teddy bears cure a cold (1984)
Teddy bears' moving day (1981)
Teddy bears stay indoors (1987)
Teddy bears take the train (1987)

Grifalconi, Ann
Darkness and the butterfly. Little, Brown
1987 unp il lib bdg $16.95   E
1. Fear—Fiction 2. Night—Fiction 3. Africa—Fiction
ISBN 0-316-32863-4   LC 86-27561
Small Osa is fearless during the day, climbing trees or
exploring the African valley where she lives, but at night
she becomes afraid of the things that might be hiding in the
dark
Another available title about Osa is:
Osa's pride (1990)

Griffith, Helen V.
Alex and the cat; pictures by Joseph Low.
Greenwillow Bks. 1982 63p il $13.95; lib bdg
$13.88   E
1. Dogs—Fiction 2. Cats—Fiction
ISBN 0-688-00420-2; 0-688-00421-0 (lib bdg)
LC 81-11608
"A Greenwillow read-alone book"
This is a book "about Alex, a puppy still wet behind the
ears, and his wise housemate, the cat. Three chapters in the
book reveal the cat as Alex's mentor and champion. In the
first, the puppy decides to be a cat. . . . In the second episode, the dog discovers that running away from home isn't
all it's cracked up to be, and in the third . . . the cat saves
Alex from a furious hen." Publ Wkly
"The stories are appropriate in length, vocabulary difficulty, and concept for the beginning reader, the illustrations
are amusing, almost aqueous wash and line. . . . What
makes the book a joy to read aloud or alone is the terse humor of the talks between Alex and his blasé companion."
Bull Cent Child Books

Followed by: Alex remembers (1983) and More Alex and
the cat (1983)

Grandaddy's place; pictures by James
Stevenson. Greenwillow Bks. 1987 unp il $15;
lib bdg $13.88; pa $4.95   E
1. Farm life—Fiction 2. Grandfathers—Fiction
ISBN 0-688-06253-9; 0-688-06254-7 (lib bdg);
0-688-10491-6 (pa)   LC 86-19573
"Janetta accompanies her mother to the country to meet
her grandfather for the first time. . . . This vacation in the
country seems doomed until her grandfather tells of some
absolutely incredible incidents that happened to him on this
very farm. . . . Imaginative, tall-tale humor abounds
throughout the smooth, well-paced text. . . . Watercolor illustrations, executed in warm pastels, lend visual clarity, exuding warmth and satisfaction." SLJ
Other available titles about Janetta and her grandfather
are:
Georgia music (1986)
Grandaddy and Janetta (1993)
Grandaddy's stars (1995)

Guarino, Deborah, 1954-
Is your mama a llama? illustrated by Steven
Kellogg. Scholastic 1989 unp il $14.95; pa
$4.95   E
1. Llamas—Fiction 2. Animals—Fiction 3. Stories in
rhyme
ISBN 0-590-41387-2; 0-590-44725-4 (pa)
LC 87-32315
Also available Spanish language edition
A young llama asks his friends if their mamas are llamas
and finds out, in rhyme, that their mothers are other types
of animals
"The lines are clean as well as exuberant, the colors well-
blended as well as bright, and the compositions uncluttered
as well as appealing. An ingenious page design invites choral participation, and the ending will encourage a cozy hia-
tus for bed/nap time." Bull Cent Child Books

Guback, Georgia
Luka's quilt. Greenwillow Bks. 1994 unp il
$14; lib bdg $13.93   E
1. Quilts—Fiction 2. Grandmothers—Fiction
3. Hawaii—Fiction
ISBN 0-688-12154-3; 0-688-12155-1 (lib bdg)
LC 93-12241
When Luka's grandmother makes a traditional Hawaiian
quilt for her, she and Luka disagree over the colors it
should include
"Eye-catching collages of brightly painted papers, the illustrations express the characters' emotions and show a delight in the Hawaiian landscape and traditions. . . . An
involving story that's all the more satisfying because the
ending offers no mere emotional patch up but a real solution." Booklist

Guiberson, Brenda Z.
Lobster boat; illustrated by Megan Lloyd.
Holt & Co. 1993 unp il $14.95   E
1. Lobsters—Fiction 2. Sea stories
ISBN 0-8050-1756-9   LC 92-4055
Tommy spends the day on a lobster boat helping Uncle
Russ tend the traps, set bait, pull up the traps, and sell their
catch
"Guiberson's writing style is pleasant and easy to read,

Guiberson, Brenda Z.—*Continued*

with evocative descriptions of the sights and sounds of the sea. She manages to combine realistic details and factual information about lobsters and lobstering with an appealingly told fictional account of a young boy's exciting adventures. An appended note gives additional information." Booklist

Haas, Jessie

No foal yet; pictures by Jos. A. Smith. Greenwillow Bks. 1995 unp il $16; lib bdg $15.93   E

1. Horses—Fiction
ISBN 0-688-12925-0; 0-688-12926-9 (lib bdg)
LC 94-6265

"Nora, who lives on a farm with her grandparents, is waiting for the mare Bonnie to give birth. The story conveys both the excitement and the emotional exhaustion of that wait. . . . The pictures are touched with gentle, golden light, like the light of a springtime twilight." Booklist

Hader, Berta, 1891-1976

The big snow. Macmillan 1948 unp il $14.95; pa $4.95   E

1. Animals 2. Winter
ISBN 0-02-737910-8; 0-02-043300-X (pa)
Awarded the Caldecott Medal, 1949

This book shows "the birds and animals which come for the food put out by an old couple after a big snow." Hodges. Books for Elem Sch Libr

Hall, Donald, 1928-

I am the dog, I am the cat; pictures by Barry Moser. Dial Bks. for Young Readers 1994 unp il $15.99; lib bdg $15.89   E

1. Dogs—Fiction 2. Cats—Fiction
ISBN 0-8037-1504-8; 0-8037-1505-6 (lib bdg)
LC 93-28060

"Two of the most common pets, Dog and Cat, philosophize alternately about life in their human household. Naturally, differences abound. . . . Poet Hall carefully chooses his words, while Moser's deft paintbrush captures the two animals with precision. . . . Although the main characters are the focal point of the paintings, Moser's well-designed backgrounds, both indoors and out, in muted tones are the perfect complement to this rhythmical, whimsical duet." Booklist

Lucy's Christmas; written by Donald Hall; illustrated by Michael McCurdy. Browndeer Press; Harcourt Brace Jovanovich 1994 unp il $14.95   E

1. Christmas—Fiction 2. Gifts—Fiction
ISBN 0-15-276870-X
LC 92-46292

"A charming look back at an early-twentieth-century Christmas, when gifts were handmade. The story follows Lucy and her family through the snowy days of paper chain and calendar construction, jars of homemade applesauce, and the popcorn and ribbon candy gifts to be distributed at the church. The colored scratchboard illustrations imbue the scenes with warmth and lively family activity." Horn Book Guide

Ox-cart man; pictures by Barbara Cooney. Viking 1979 unp il $15; pa $4.99   E

1. New England—Fiction
ISBN 0-670-53328-9; 0-14-050441-9 (pa)
LC 79-14466

Awarded the Caldecott Medal, 1980

"It is fall and a farmer loads a cart with the year's produce, journeys to market, sells, buys, and returns to his family to begin the year's work anew. The journey, and the ensuing year, unfold at a stately pace against the rich 19th-century New England backdrop alive with the subtly changing colors and activities of the succeeding seasons." SLJ

"The stunning combination of text and illustrations, suggesting early American paintings on wood, depict the countryside through which [the farmer] travels, the jostle of the marketplace, and the homely warmth of family life." Horn Book

Hall, Zoe, 1957-

It's pumpkin time! illustrated by Shari Halpern. Blue Sky Press (NY) 1994 unp il $13.95   E

1. Pumpkin—Fiction   2. Halloween—Fiction
3. Gardening—Fiction
ISBN 0-590-47833-8
LC 93-35909

A sister and brother plant and tend their own pumpkin patch so they will have jack-o-lanterns for Halloween

"Painted paper collages accompany a simple, but effective, story." Child Book Rev Serv

Halpern, Shari

My river. Macmillan 1992 unp il $15
E

1. Freshwater animals 2. River ecology
ISBN 0-02-741980-0
LC 91-33582

Frogs, fish, a turtle, and other creatures who live in or around a river state their need for the river, making a plea for protecting this natural resource

"Bold collage cutouts and simple, large text make this a dramatically inviting book to share with preschoolers and beginning readers." Sci Child

Hamanaka, Sheila

All the colors of the earth. Morrow Junior Bks. 1994 unp il $15; lib bdg $14.93   E

ISBN 0-688-11131-9; 0-688-11132-7 (lib bdg)
LC 93-27118

Reveals in verse that despite outward differences children everywhere are essentially the same and all are lovable

"A poetic picture book and an exemplary work of art. . . . Hamanaka's oil paintings are all double-page spreads filled with the colors of earth, sky, and water, and the texture of the artist's canvas shines through. The text is arranged in undulant waves across each painting." SLJ

Hartman, Gail

As the crow flies; a first book of maps; illustrated by Harvey Stevenson. Bradbury Press 1991 32p il maps $13.95   E

1. Animals—Fiction 2. Maps—Fiction
ISBN 0-02-743005-7
LC 90-33982

Also available in paperback from Aladdin Bks.

"Simple words and pictures describe the travels of an eagle, a rabbit, a crow, a police horse, a seagull, and the moon. A pictorial map for each animal is given; all maps are joined in 'The Big Map' at the end." SLJ

"Stevenson's bright pen-and-ink with watercolor illustrations contain many interesting details, yet never seem overcluttered. . . . This is an attractive picture book that should find a niche in story hours and classrooms." Booklist

Hartman, Gail—*Continued*

As the roadrunner runs; a first book of maps; illustrated by Cathy Bobak. Bradbury Press 1994 unp il maps $14.95   E

1. Deserts—Fiction 2. Animals—Fiction 3. Maps—Fiction
ISBN 0-02-743092-8   LC 94-13

Simple maps show how different animals, including a lizard, a jackrabbit, a roadrunner, mules, and deer, travel through an area of the Southwest

"Attractive full-color illustrations appear on every page, allowing young readers to grasp the connection between snapshots of individual sites and their corresponding graphic representations. . . . An excellent addition to primary map units, this will also find a niche in story hours." Booklist

Hautzig, Deborah, 1956-

The nutcracker ballet; retold by Deborah Hautzig; illustrated by Carolyn Ewing. Random House 1992 48p il lib bdg $9.99; pa $3.99   E

1. Fairy tales
ISBN 0-679-92385-3 (lib bdg); 0-679-82385-9 (pa)
                LC 92-3320

"Step into reading"
A little girl helps break the spell on her toy nutcracker and changes him into a handsome prince

"Hautzig retells the story of *The Nutcracker*, concentrating on the narrative content of the first act. . . . The simple vocabulary makes this edition accessible to beginning readers; bright watercolor artwork adds an immediate appeal." Booklist

Havill, Juanita

Jamaica's find; illustrations by Anne Sibley O'Brien. Houghton Mifflin 1986 32p il $14.95; pa $4.95   E

1. African Americans—Fiction 2. Toys—Fiction
ISBN 0-395-39376-0; 0-395-45357-7 (pa)
                LC 85-14542

Also available Spanish language edition
"When Jamaica discovers a raggedy stuffed dog at the park, she decides to take it home. Her family's reaction is lukewarm at best . . . and she broods over her mother's suggestion that she return it to the park desk. Reluctantly, she does. Just after that, Jamaica encounters a little girl named Kristin, who has come to search for her missing toy dog." Booklist

"This is a pleasant picture book with warm, expressive pictures and an appealing story line that encourages values clarification." Interracial Books Child Bull

Other available titles about Jamaica are:
Jamaica and Brianna (1993)
Jamaica tag-along (1989)
Jamaica's blue marker (1995)

Hayes, Sarah

Happy Christmas, Gemma; illustrated by Jan Ormerod. Lothrop, Lee & Shepard Bks. 1986 unp il $15; pa $4.95   E

1. Christmas—Fiction 2. Blacks—Fiction
ISBN 0-688-06508-2; 0-688-11702-3 (pa)
                LC 85-23674

A "story of a black family preparing for and celebrating Christmas. It is told from the perspective of the older brother as he contrasts his proper and helpful behavior with that of his mischievous toddler sister, Gemma." SLJ

"Ormerod's clean, brightly-colored illustrations effectively placed against a white background capture the warmth of the black family and of their shared holiday experience along with the pleasure they take in their smallest member." Horn Book

Another available title about Gemma is:
Eat up, Gemma (1988)

Hazelaar, Cor

Dogs everywhere. Knopf 1995 unp il $13; lib bdg $13.99   E

1. Dogs—Fiction
ISBN 0-679-85439-8; 0-679-95439-2 (lib bdg)
                LC 93-32597

"Pulling their masters by the leash, the city's canines descend brownstone steps and hurry to the park. There they frolic with their friends, fetch sticks, and hunt fields for imaginary prey." Booklist

"The pizazz comes from Hazelaar's quaint and fanciful illustrations, which convey the energy and spunk of a spectrum of canines. . . . [The artist uses] an intriguing, soft palette that is at once subtle and luminescent." Publ Wkly

Hazen, Barbara Shook, 1930-

The gorilla did it; illustrated by Ray Cruz. Atheneum Pubs. 1974 unp il $13.95; pa $3.95   E

1. Gorillas—Fiction
ISBN 0-689-30138-3; 0-689-71214-6 (pa)
Also available Spanish language edition
"An imaginary ape interrupts the boy's nap, and together they make a wreck of his room, to his mother's annoyance. She can hardly believe him when he lays the blame on a gorilla she can't see." Saturday Rev

"The absolute pitch of familiarity in the dialog and line drawings, which contrast the huge, innocent-but-destructive gorilla in blue with everything unimagined in black and white, makes a picture book humorously tuned into a child's fantasy friend without making fun of it." Booklist

Turkey in the straw; pictures by Brad Sneed. Dial Bks. for Young Readers 1993 unp il $13.99; lib bdg $13.89   E

1. Farm life—Fiction 2. Square dancing—Fiction
ISBN 0-8037-1298-7; 0-8037-1299-5 (lib bdg)
                LC 92-27516

When things are looking bad, a farmer who would rather fiddle than do his chores invites his neighbors to a hoedown where he plays such a lively tune that his shy daughter's pet turkey starts dancing, with happy results

The author's "lively text, imbued with the rhythm of dance-call phrases, is as friendly and carefree as a do-si-do. Sneed's watercolors, with their tilted perspectives and sharp planes, visually echo the carefree, syncopated tune." Publ Wkly

Heath, Amy

Sofie's role; story by Amy Heath; pictures by Sheila Hamanaka. Four Winds Press 1992 unp il $14.95   E

1. Bakers and bakeries—Fiction 2. Family life—Fiction 3. Christmas—Fiction
ISBN 0-02-743505-9   LC 91-33488

On the day before Christmas, Sofie makes her big debut serving customers in her family's busy Broadway Bakery

Heath, Amy—*Continued*

"The story is vividly told, and the special names of the German pastries are a mouth-watering litany. . . . Hamanaka . . . paints an interracial family and multiethnic cast in glowing oils. The double-spread pictures vary dramatically in perspective. . . . For readers who want to join in, two simple recipes frame the story." Booklist

Heide, Florence Parry, 1919-

The day of Ahmed's secret; [by] Florence Parry Heide & Judith Heide Gilliland; illustrated by Ted Lewin. Lothrop, Lee & Shepard Bks. 1990 unp il $16; lib bdg $15.93
        E

1. Cairo (Egypt)—Fiction
ISBN 0-688-08894-5; 0-688-08895-3 (lib bdg)
        LC 90-52694

Also available in paperback from Morrow

"Ahmed has monumental news to share with his family, but first he must complete the age-old duties of a butagaz boy, delivering cooking gas to customers all over Cairo. The juxtaposition of old and new is a repeated theme in Heide and Gilliland's thoughtful story of a young boy living in the bustling metropolis surrounded by thousand-year-old walls and buildings. . . . Enhanced by Lewin's distinguished photorealistic watercolors, the sights, sounds, and smells of the exotic setting come to life. . . . At home at last, surrounded by his loving family, Ahmed demostrates his newly acquired facility, proudly writing his name in Arabic." SLJ

Sami and the time of the troubles; [by] Florence Parry Heide & Judith Heide Gilliland; illustrated by Ted Lewin. Clarion Bks. 1992 unp il $15.95
        E

1. Family life—Fiction 2. Lebanon—Fiction
ISBN 0-395-55964-2   LC 91-14343

A ten-year-old Lebanese boy in Beirut goes to school, helps his mother with chores, plays with his friends, and lives with his family in a basement shelter when bombings occur and fighting begins on his street

"Three marvelously talented collaborators offer a powerful, poignant book. Heide and Gilliland's lyrically written, haunting story makes clear that war threatens not only physical existence but affects the human spirit as well. Lewin's watercolor illustrations capture contemporary Beirut with stunning clarity and drama." SLJ

Heilbroner, Joan, 1922-

This is the house where Jack lives; illustrated by Aliki. Harper & Row 1962 62p il $14.89
        E

1. Nonsense verses
ISBN 0-06-022286-7

"An I can read book"

"A city apartment building is the setting for this modern version of the old cumulative nonsense rhyme about Jack and his house." Cincinnati Public Libr

"The illustrations are gay and humorous, echoing in the drawings the cumulative parts of the rhyme." Bull Cent Child Books

Heine, Helme

Friends; written and illustrated by Helme Heine. Atheneum Pubs. 1982 unp il lib bdg $14.95; pa $4.95
        E

1. Friendship—Fiction 2. Animals—Fiction
ISBN 0-689-50256-7 (lib bdg); 0-689-71083-6 (pa)
        LC 82-45313

"A Margaret K. McElderry book"

This is an "account of the friendship between three animals, a mouse, a cock and a pig. . . . They do everything together like true friends should, but at bedtime, having all tried in turn the mousehole, the pigsty and the perch, they decide that they are after all quite different, and each sets off to his own bed to dream happy dreams of one another." Times Lit Suppl

"Heine's visual imagination makes the images extraordinary. . . . Watercolors take full advantage of the white page. The double-page scene at dusk with silhouetted cottage and tree is a fine restful transition from the frenetic daytime fun to the final funny efforts to bed down." SLJ

Another available title about the friends is:
Friends go adventuring (1995)

The most wonderful egg in the world; written and illustrated by Helme Heine. Atheneum Pubs. 1983 unp il $14.95; pa $4.95
        E

1. Chickens—Fiction
ISBN 0-689-50280-X; 0-689-71117-4 (pa)
        LC 82-49350

"A Margaret K. McElderry book"

"Three proud hens—Dotty, with the most beautiful feathers; Stalky, with the most beautiful legs; and Plumy, with the most beautiful crest—quarrel about which one of them is the most beautiful." Horn Book

"The message here—'What you can do is more important than what you look like'—is conveyed simply but effectively, with the theme of uniqueness and individuality nicely underplayed. The watercolor illustrations, mostly in pale tones with much open white space, are full of fun. . . . Children will be rewarded with new, humorous details on each rereading." SLJ

Hendershot, Judith, 1940-

In coal country; illustrated by Thomas B. Allen. Knopf 1987 unp il $16; pa $5.99
        E

1. Coal mines and mining—Fiction
ISBN 0-394-88190-7; 0-679-83479-6 (pa)
        LC 86-15311

A child growing up in a coal mining community finds both excitement and hard work, in a life deeply affected by the local industry

"The power of the book . . . lies in the deep, dark counterpoint that underlies the light melody of the childhood reminiscence. Using charcoal and pastels on earth-tone paper, Thomas Allen creates the illusion that coal dust permeates every illustration. The text is set in a box of grayed color centered on a stark white page. . . . Though the text is spare, the dark, eloquent pictures speak volumes." Horn Book

Hendrick, Mary Jean

If anything ever goes wrong at the zoo; illustrated by Jane Dyer. Harcourt Brace Jovanovich 1993 unp il $14; pa $5   E

1. Zoos—Fiction
ISBN 0-15-238007-8; 0-15-201009-2 (pa)
LC 91-25566

After Leslie tells the zookeepers to send the animals to her house should anything go wrong at the zoo, a series of zoo emergencies results in some unusual houseguests for the girl and her family

"A crisp and conversational text makes this a good choice for reading aloud, and children will be quick to anticipate the animals' arrival. Dyer's spirited watercolors skillfully capture the understated humor and add sparkle to a winning tale." SLJ

Henkes, Kevin, 1960-

Chester's way. Greenwillow Bks. 1988 unp il $16; lib bdg $15.93   E

1. Mice—Fiction
ISBN 0-688-07607-6; 0-688-07608-4 (lib bdg)
LC 87-14882

Also available in paperback from Puffin Bks.

The mice Chester and Wilson share the exact way of doing things, until Lilly moves into the neighborhood and shows them that new ways can be just as good

"Henkes' charming cartoons are drawn with pen-and-ink, washed over with cheerful watercolors. They give witty expressions to his characters." SLJ

Chrysanthemum. Greenwillow Bks. 1991 unp il $16; lib bdg $15.93   E

1. Personal names—Fiction 2. School stories 3. Mice—Fiction
ISBN 0-688-09699-9; 0-688-09700-6 (lib bdg)
LC 90-39803

Also available Spanish language edition

Chrysanthemum, a mouse, loves her name, until she starts going to school and the other children make fun of it

"The text, precise and evocative, uses contrast and repetition to achieve rhythm and balance; the illustrations are forthright yet delicately colored, remarkable for the agility of the fine line which creates setting and characters." Horn Book

Jessica. Greenwillow Bks. 1989 unp il $15; lib bdg $11.93   E

1. Imaginary playmates—Fiction
ISBN 0-688-07829-X; 0-688-07830-3 (lib bdg)
LC 87-38087

"A shy preschooler insists that her friend Jessica is not imaginary—and, in the end, she's absolutely correct. Henkes' depiction of play-alone and play-together time brims with buoyant camaraderie in this upbeat story of friendship fulfilled." SLJ

Julius, the baby of the world. Greenwillow Bks. 1990 unp il $16; lib bdg $15.93   E

1. Mice—Fiction
ISBN 0-688-08943-7; 0-688-08944-5 (lib bdg)
LC 88-34904

Also available Spanish language edition

Lilly, the girl mouse who debuted in Chester's way, entered above, "may still be the queen of the world, but her new brother 'Julius is the baby of the world.' Suffering from a severe case of sibling-itis, she warns pregnant strangers: 'You will live to regret that bump under your dress.' While her understanding parents shower her with 'compliments

and praise and niceties of all shapes and sizes,' nothing works until snooty Cousin Garland comes for a visit." Booklist

"Magically, Henkes conveys a world of expressions and a wide range of complex emotions with a mere line or two upon the engaging mousey faces of Lilly and her family. A reassuring, funny book for all young children who suffer from new-sibling syndrome." SLJ

Owen. Greenwillow Bks. 1993 unp il $15   E

1. Blankets—Fiction
ISBN 0-688-11449-0
LC 92-30084

A Caldecott Medal honor book, 1994

Owen's parents try to get him to give up his favorite blanket before he starts school, but when their efforts fail, they come up with a solution that makes everyone happy

This is "imbued with Henkes's characteristically understated humor, spry text and brightly hued watercolor-and-ink pictures." Publ Wkly

Sheila Rae, the brave. Greenwillow Bks. 1987 unp il $16; lib bdg $14.93   E

1. Mice—Fiction
ISBN 0-688-07155-4; 0-688-07156-2 (lib bdg)
LC 86-25761

Also available in paperback from Puffin Bks.

"A mouse both boastful and fearless, Sheila Rae decides to go home from school by taking a new route. She walks backwards with her eyes closed, growls at dogs and cats, climbs trees, turns new corners and crosses different streets—and ends up in the middle of unfamiliar territory." Publ Wkly

"Bouncy watercolors in spring-like colors with some pen-and-ink detailing highlight Sheila Rae's bravado in an engaging and amusing way, and Henkes provides Sheila Rae, Louise, and their school friends with highly expressive faces." SLJ

Hennessy, B. G. (Barbara G.)

The missing tarts; pictures by Tracey Campbell Pearson. Viking Kestrel 1989 unp il $12.95; pa $3.95   E

1. Stories in rhyme
ISBN 0-670-82039-3; 0-14-050815-5 (pa)
LC 88-28809

When the Queen of Hearts discovers that her strawberry tarts have been stolen, she enlists the help of many popular nursery rhyme characters in order to find them

"Bright colors pick out the scampering figures which are sketched in with humor and bubbling vitality and seem to leap from one page to the next. Youngsters will enjoy spotting Bo Peep and Little Jack Horner in the illustrations and confirming their identities in the rhymed text." Horn Book

Herold, Maggie Rugg

A very important day; illustrated by Catherine Stock. Morrow Junior Bks. 1995 unp il $16; lib bdg $15.93   E

1. Naturalization—Fiction 2. Immigration and emigration—Fiction 3. New York (N.Y.)—Fiction
ISBN 0-688-13065-8; 0-688-13066-6 (lib bdg)
LC 94-16647

Two-hundred nineteen people from thirty-two different countries make their way to downtown New York in a snowstorm to be sworn in as citizens of the United States

"After the first quiet, gray-tone painting, which pictures a solitary face staring out at a city dawn dotted with snowflakes, this book bursts forth in a riot of color and activity.

Herold, Maggie Rugg—*Continued*
. . . A glossary supplies guidance for pronouncing names, and a clear, nicely detailed overview of the process of naturalization rounds things out. Pictures and story combine to make the joy of the day contagious." Booklist

Herriot, James
Moses the kitten; illustrated by Peter Barrett. St. Martin's Press 1984 unp il $13; pa $6.95   **E**
1. Cats—Fiction 2. Farm life—Fiction
ISBN 0-312-54905-9; 0-312-06419-5 (pa)
                    LC 84-50930
"Found by Herriot among the frozen rushes, the kitten was quickly adopted by a farm family, warmed back to liveliness in an [open] oven, and named Moses. What the veterinarian-author found, on his next visit, was that Moses had inserted himself into a litter of piglets and been accepted as one of the family, both at feeding times and at sleep-in-a-heap naptime." Bull Cent Child Books
"Patience, kindness and caring are the dominant themes here, and the storyline and characterizations never deviate from this. The text is complemented throughout with appropriate, well-placed soft pastel watercolors [depicting] in detail the northern English countryside." SLJ

Hesse, Karen
Lester's dog; illustrated by Nancy Carpenter. Crown 1993 unp il $15; lib bdg $13.99   **E**
1. Dogs—Fiction 2. Friendship—Fiction 3. Cats—Fiction
ISBN 0-517-58357-7; 0-517-58358-5 (lib bdg)
                    LC 92-27674
This is a "story about a boy who, with the help of a deaf friend, conquers his fear of a neighbor's dog that bit him years earlier. In the process, he saves a kitten and befriends an elderly, recently widowed man. Carpenter's pictures give vivid life to Hesse's gripping story, set in a 1940s neighborhood. The prose reverberates with powerful words." SLJ

Hest, Amy
The crack-of-dawn walkers; pictures by Amy Schwartz. Macmillan 1984 unp il $13.95
                         E
1. Grandfathers—Fiction 2. Walking—Fiction
ISBN 0-02-743710-8   LC 83-19597
Also available in paperback from Puffin Bks.
"Before anyone else in the neighborhood is up, Sadie and her grandfather begin their biweekly walk to the bakery for onion rolls, to Fabio for cocoa, and to pick up the paper. Next week this treat will be her younger brother's, but now Sadie has her grandfather all to herself." Child Book Rev Serv
"Soft pencil drawings project the tranquil mood of a picture book that communicates the love and companionship of a small girl and her grandfather. . . . The unpretentious, somewhat stylized drawings are well-suited to depicting the details of Sadie's neighborhood." Horn Book

The midnight eaters; illustrated by Karen Gundersheimer. Four Winds Press 1989 unp il $13.95   **E**
1. Grandmothers—Fiction 2. Old age—Fiction
ISBN 0-02-743630-6   LC 88-24381
Also available in paperback from Aladdin Bks.
Despite the doctor's warning that she is too frail, Samantha's grandmother zestfully joins her in a midnight raid

on the kitchen, where they make fabulous ice cream sundaes and look at old photographs
"The neatly contained illustrations rely on selective detailing of interior scenes that consistently highlight the two diminutive characters. The art is quietly toned, befitting secrets." Bull Cent Child Books

Nana's birthday party; pictures by Amy Schwartz. Morrow Junior Bks. 1993 unp il $15; lib bdg $14.93   **E**
1. Grandmothers—Fiction 2. Birthdays—Fiction 3. Cousins—Fiction
ISBN 0-688-07497-9; 0-688-07498-7 (lib bdg)
                    LC 92-10260
Maggie who writes stories, and her cousin Brette, who paints pictures, combine their talents to create the grandest present ever for their grandmother Nana's birthday.
"Schwartz's fluid yet exuberant watercolors perfectly capture the cousins—as friends and as competitors—in all their differences and make a beautiful show of Nana's cozy apartment, busy with color and pattern. . . . A warm, wise story about cousins that captures continuity and affection across generations." Booklist

The purple coat; pictures by Amy Schwartz. Four Winds Press 1986 unp il $14.95   **E**
1. Coats—Fiction 2. Grandfathers—Fiction
ISBN 0-02-743640-3   LC 85-29186
Also available in paperback from Aladdin Bks.
"Gabrielle has always gotten a navy coat in the fall, but, this year, to Mama's dismay, she yearns for a purple one. Grandpa, their favorite tailor, discovers a solution to please all." Child Book Rev Serv
"The artwork is full color, and the deep shades and vibrant colors (especially that purple) are arresting. The numerous details and patternings catch the eye and make for pictures that can be looked at over and over; each time the story's satisfying conclusion rings sweetly true." Booklist

Heyward, DuBose, 1885-1940
The country bunny and the little gold shoes; as told to Jenifer; pictures by Marjorie Flack. Houghton Mifflin 1939 unp il lib bdg $14.95; pa $4.95   **E**
1. Rabbits—Fiction 2. Easter—Fiction
ISBN 0-395-15990-3 (lib bdg); 0-395-18557-2 (pa)
This is an Easter story for young readers which grew out of a story the author has told and retold to his young daughter. It is of the little country rabbit who wanted to become one of the five Easter bunnies, and how she managed to realize her ambition
"It is really imaginative and well written. . . . The colored pictures are just right too." New Yorker

Hill, Elizabeth Starr
Evan's corner; story by Elizabeth Starr Hill; pictures by Sandra Speidel. Viking 1991 unp il $13.99; pa $4.99   **E**
1. Family life—Fiction 2. African Americans—Fiction
ISBN 0-670-82830-0; 0-14-054406-2 (pa)
                    LC 89-24839
A revised and newly illustrated edition of the title first published 1967 by Holt, Rinehart and Winston
Needing a place to call his own, Evan is thrilled when his mother points out that their crowded apartment has eight corners, one for each family member
"The new illustrations are bright and suit the text." Horn Book

Hines, Anna Grossnickle, 1946-

Daddy makes the best spaghetti. Clarion Bks. 1986 unp il lib bdg $13.95; pa $5.95

E

1. Fathers and sons—Fiction
ISBN 0-89919-388-9 (lib bdg); 0-89919-794-9 (pa)
LC 85-13993

"Corey and his father enjoy a close relationship that is aptly demonstrated in picture and story. He teases Corey and they spend time together doing things such as shopping for groceries and making a pot of spaghetti or being silly at bath time and getting ready for bed. Hines' simple but warm pencil drawings play out the scenes by capitalizing on the incidents described in the text; the strong sense of family (Mother is here too) is evident." Booklist

Gramma's walk. Greenwillow Bks. 1993 unp il $14; lib bdg $13.93

E

1. Grandmothers—Fiction   2. Seashore—Fiction
3. Physically handicapped—Fiction
ISBN 0-688-11480-6; 0-688-11481-4 (lib bdg)
LC 92-30085

Donnie and Gramma, who is in a wheelchair, take an imagined walk to the seashore and smell the salty breeze, walk barefoot on the warm sand, observe animals, and build a sand castle

"Softlined, muted watercolors and colored pencils create pristine, full-page seascapes. No big deal is made of Gramma's condition, nor is the reason for it given; what comes through is total acceptance and intergenerational love." SLJ

It's just me, Emily. Clarion Bks. 1987 unp il hardcover o.p. paperback available $4.95

E

1. Mothers and daughters—Fiction 2. Stories in rhyme
ISBN 0-89919-853-8 (pa)   LC 86-34352

"In this simple rhyming story, young Emily is either squirming under Mother's blanket, splashing around in the tub, or thumping under the table. At each juncture Mother comes up with a fanciful reason for all the noises." Booklist

"The text is full of rhymes and rhythms that will delight children. Hines has added to her story with fine line illustrations filled in with creamy pastel colors on white backgrounds that exhibit the familiar items and environment of a normal preschool child's world." SLJ

What Joe saw. Greenwillow Bks. 1994 unp il $15; lib bdg $14.93

E

1. Nature—Fiction 2. School stories
ISBN 0-688-13123-9; 0-688-13124-7 (lib bdg)
LC 93-26583

Joe is the last one in his class to line up for a walk to the park, and he lags behind all the others, but he sees a lot more than they do

"The realistic watercolor and colored-pencil depictions of the ethnically diverse class alternate with attractive, naturalistic scenes. The text is well placed and well written for a satisfying read-aloud with wide appeal." SLJ

Hoban, Lillian

Arthur's Christmas cookies; words and pictures by Lillian Hoban. Harper & Row 1972 63p il lib bdg $14.89; pa $3.50

E

1. Chimpanzees—Fiction   2. Christmas—Fiction
3. Baking—Fiction
ISBN 0-06-022368-5 (lib bdg); 0-06-444055-9 (pa)
"An I can read book"

When Arthur decides to make Christmas cookies for his parents, a "disastrous mistake in the ingredients makes the cookies inedible but the story ends happily when Arthur turns them into holiday decorations." Publ Wkly

The characters are chimpanzees but "are endearingly like human children. . . . The Christmas setting is appealing, the plot has problem, conflict, and solution yet is not too complex for the beginning independent reader, and the simplicity and humor make the book an appropriate one for reading aloud to preschool children also." Bull Cent Child Books

Other available titles about Arthur are:
Arthur's camp-out (1993)
Arthur's funny money (1981)
Arthur's great big valentine (1989)
Arthur's Halloween costume (1984)
Arthur's Honey Bear (1974)
Arthur's loose tooth (1985)
Arthur's pen pal (1976)
Arthur's prize reader (1978)

Silly Tilly's Thanksgiving dinner; story and pictures by Lillian Hoban. Harper & Row 1990 63p il $14; lib bdg $14.89

E

1. Thanksgiving Day—Fiction 2. Moles (Animals)—Fiction 3. Animals—Fiction
ISBN 0-06-022422-3; 0-06-022423-1 (lib bdg)
LC 89-29287

"An I can read book"

Forgetful Silly Tilly Mole nearly succeeds in ruining her Thanksgiving dinner, but her animal friends come to the rescue with tasty treats

"Watercolors in vibrant autumn hues accentuate this comedy of errors with quirky characterizations and fine brushwork." Booklist

Another available title about Silly Tilly is:
Silly Tilly and the Easter Bunny (1987)

Hoban, Russell

Bedtime for Frances; pictures by Garth Williams. HarperCollins Pubs. 1995 c1960 31p il $14; lib bdg $13.89; pa $4.95

E

1. Badgers—Fiction 2. Bedtime—Fiction
ISBN 0-06-022350-2; 0-06-022351-0 (lib bdg); 0-06-443005-7 (pa)   LC 94-43809

Also available Spanish language edition

A reissue of the title first published 1960

"A little badger with a lively imagination comes up with one scheme after another to put off going to sleep but father badger proves himself as smart as his daughter." Bookmark

"The soft humorous pictures of these lovable animals in human predicaments are delightful." Horn Book

Other available titles about Frances are:
A baby sister for Frances (1964)
A bargain for Frances (1970)
Best friends for Frances (1969)
A birthday for Frances (1968)
Bread and jam for Frances (1964)

Another book about Frances, Egg thoughts and other Frances songs, is entered in class 811

Dinner at Alberta's; pictures by James Marshall. Crowell 1975 unp il lib bdg $14.89

E

1. Crocodiles—Fiction 2. Etiquette—Fiction
ISBN 0-690-23993-9 (lib bdg)

Arthur Crocodile cannot seem to learn table manners until his sister brings her new girlfriend to visit

Arthur's "concentrated practice sessions for dining out according to accepted standards are hilariously documented in an absurd combination of tongue-in-cheek text and droll, brown-toned drawings." Horn Book

Hoban, Russell—*Continued*

Another available title about Arthur is:
Arthur's new power (1978)

Hoban, Tana

26 letters and 99 cents. Greenwillow Bks.
1987 unp il $16; lib bdg $15.93; pa $4.95
                                                    E

1. Alphabet 2. Counting 3. Coins
ISBN 0-688-06361-6; 0-688-06362-4 (lib bdg);
0-688-14389-X (pa)   LC 86-11993

This concept book "is really two books in one. *26 Letters*
is a delightful ABC handbook. Each page shows two letters
(in both upper- and lowercase) paired with objects from airplane to zipper. Turning the book around reveals the even
more creative *99 Cents*. Here Hoban clearly shows youngsters how to count by pairing photos of numbers with pennies, nickels, dimes and quarters in a variety of
combinations. The book counts ones from 1¢ to 30¢, by
fives from 30¢ to 50¢, by tens from 50¢ to 90¢, culminating
in 99¢. . . . An extremely inventive approach that will be
hailed by parents, teachers and librarians." Publ Wkly

A, B, see! Greenwillow Bks. 1982 unp il lib
bdg $14.93   E

1. Alphabet
ISBN 0-688-00833-X   LC 81-6890

A collection of black and white silhouette photographs of
objects beginning with a particular letter of the alphabet

"Artistically arranged to provide rhythm and balance, the
pictures are also exercises in object recognition and visual
discrimination—intriguing puzzles to be solved rather than
just lessons to be learned. Some objects are instantly recognizable; others demand somewhat sophisticated understanding; and still others require some mental agility to identify.
. . . An exciting, original, and carefully conceived book."
Horn Book

All about where. Greenwillow Bks. 1991
unp il $13.95; lib bdg $13.88   E

1. Vocabulary
ISBN 0-688-09697-2; 0-688-09698-0 (lib bdg)
                                       LC 90-30849

Photographs illustrate location words such as above, between, in, under, and behind

The book's "interesting and practical design allows young
children to pore over the pictures and consider the several
possibilities for describing relative spatial relationships
among the objects, people, and animals they see. . . . Composed with an unerring eye for the aesthetic, the photographs will spark discussion and encourage long
contemplation." Horn Book

Black on white. Greenwillow Bks. 1993 unp
il $4.95   E
ISBN 0-688-11918-2   LC 92-18897

Black illustrations against a white background depict
such objects as an elephant, butterfly, and leaf

This board book features "the stunning, sophisticated
photography of Tana Hoban. . . . Simply the best for babies." Horn Book Guide

A children's zoo. Greenwillow Bks. 1985
unp il $16; lib bdg $15.93; pa $4.95   E

1. Animals
ISBN 0-688-05202-9; 0-688-05204-5 (lib bdg);
0-688-07044-2 (pa)   LC 84-25318

This is a photographic "portfolio of zoo denizens. . . .
Each species is matted with a narrow white line, framed in
black, and placed opposite a black page against which . . .
white sans serif letters list three of that species' characteristics as well as its name." Horn Book

"For the most part, the photographs are standard zoo
fare, but a few are truly different and amusing." SLJ
Includes glossary

Circles, triangles and squares. Macmillan
1974 unp il $14   E

1. Size and shape
ISBN 0-02-744830-4   LC 72-93305

"There is no division of the material into sections and
no text here, simply a series of photographs in which the
three most familiar geometric forms occur. Often more than
one shape appears on the photograph." Bull Cent Child
Books

"An imaginative exercise for the development of visual
awareness." Horn Book

Colors everywhere. Greenwillow Bks. 1995
unp il $16; lib bdg $15.93   E

1. Color
ISBN 0-688-12762-2; 0-688-12763-0 (lib bdg)
                                       LC 93-24847

"On each page of this wordless picture book is a color
photograph accompanied by a bar graph that displays the
spectrum of colors found in the photo." Booklist

"Very young children will enjoy naming the pictured objects, while older readers will be drawn into exploring the
colors' varying tones. A book children will come back to
over and over." Horn Book

Dots,   spots,   speckles,   and   stripes.
Greenwillow Bks. 1987 unp il $14; lib bdg
$15.93   E
ISBN 0-688-06862-6; 0-688-06863-4 (lib bdg)
                                       LC 86-22919

Photographs show dots, spots, speckles, and stripes as
found on clothing, flowers, faces, animals, and other places

"Not only are the photos in this title technically superb,
but the composition and the subjects are imaginative yet
clearly identifiable. . . . Going beyond a concept book on
patterns, *Dots, Spots, Speckles, and Stripes* becomes a
thought-provoking photo essay that can be appreciated by
older children." Horn Book

Exactly the opposite. Greenwillow Bks. 1990
unp il $15; lib bdg $14.93   E

1. English language—Synonyms and antonyms
ISBN 0-688-08861-9; 0-688-08862-7 (lib bdg)
                                       LC 89-27227

"Using a variety of people, animals, and objects found in
outdoor settings of both the city and the country, [the au-
thor] introduces and expands on the concept of opposites in
this wordless photographic book. The photographs are clear,
bright, and enticing. Pairs of opposites are presented on facing pages." SLJ

Is it larger? Is it smaller? Greenwillow Bks.
1985 unp il $14.95; lib bdg $15.93   E

1. Size and shape
ISBN 0-688-04027-6; 0-688-04028-4 (lib bdg)
                                       LC 84-13719

"In each full-color photograph of the wordless picture
book Hoban juxtaposes similar objects of differing size. In
the simplest pictures only one kind of object is shown, such
as three bright plastic sand cups in graduated sizes or three
maple leaves. More complex compositions group several related items: measuring cups, bowls, and utensils; fish, shells,

Hoban, Tana—*Continued*
and pebbles in an aquarium. Still others contrast dissimilar objects that have common features. . . . In the photographs, Hoban demonstrates once again her mastery of the elements of composition, such as color, texture, and balance." Horn Book

Is it red? Is it yellow? Is it blue? An adventure in color. Greenwillow Bks. 1978 unp il $16; lib bdg $16.88; pa $4.95   E

1. Color 2. Size and shape
ISBN 0-688-80171-4; 0-688-84171-6 (lib bdg); 0-688-07034-5 (pa)   LC 78-2549
Illustrations and brief text introduce colors and the concepts of shape and size
"The wordless book is simply designed and opens the eye to the marvelous world of color; each stark-white page contains one photograph which nearly fills it. In the bottom margin the predominant colors in the photograph are indicated by a row of corresponding circles." Horn Book

Is it rough? Is it smooth? Is it shiny? Greenwillow Bks. 1984 unp il $16; lib bdg $15.93   E

ISBN 0-688-03823-9; 0-688-03824-7 (lib bdg)   LC 83-25460
Color photographs without text introduce objects of many different textures, such as pretzels, foil, hay, mud, kitten, and bubbles
"Extraordinarily crisp, clean color photographs allow Hoban to call attention to textures." Booklist

Look again! Macmillan 1971 unp il $15   E

ISBN 0-02-744050-8
"This captivating book of photographs invites the reader to look once through a two-inch cut-out square at a pattern or portion of something larger. On the next page, the complete picture of the object is revealed. On the verso of the second page is another view of the object. And so, as each set is displayed, one is impelled to look again and again and again." Wis Libr Bull

Look! look! look! Greenwillow Bks. 1988 unp il $16; lib bdg $15.93   E

ISBN 0-688-07239-9; 0-688-07240-2 (lib bdg)   LC 87-25655
Photographs of familiar objects are first viewed through a cut-out hole, then in their entirety
"The author employs an element of trickery that will intrigue older children: for instance, showing a bit of a Ferris wheel that children in a story hour first guessed as the Statue of Liberty. Hoban's photographs are crystal clear, beautifully composed, and a treat to view." Horn Book

Look up, look down. Greenwillow Bks. 1992 unp il $14; lib bdg $13.93   E

1. Perception
ISBN 0-688-10577-7; 0-688-10578-5 (lib bdg)   LC 91-12613
Photographs present objects and scenes from different perspectives, some viewed from below and some from above
"Another first-rate concept book by Hoban. . . . In a few cases, it'll take readers some time to figure out what they're looking at, even though they'll be certain of the perspective. The two large, vivid photos on each double-page spread are related in content (for example, a martin house and the imprint of birds' feet on sand) or in composition (the radiating spiral of a snail's shell and the pattern of an open umbrella). This connection between pictures gives observers even

more food for thought. For this reason, the book will challenge primary graders as well as preschoolers." SLJ

Of colors and things. Greenwillow Bks. 1989 unp il $16; lib bdg $15.93   E

1. Color
ISBN 0-688-07534-7; 0-688-07535-5 (lib bdg)   LC 88-11101
Photographs of toys, food, and other common objects are grouped on each page according to color
"Hoban hits on a simple device to heighten a child's awareness, but what lifts this above the average concept book is the quality of its design and illustration." Booklist

Over, under & through, and other spatial concepts. Macmillan 1973 unp il $15; pa $3.95   E

1. Vocabulary
ISBN 0-02-744820-7, 0-689-71111-5 (pa)
In brief text and photographs, the author depicts several spatial concepts—over, under, through, on, in, around, across, between, beside, below, against, and behind
"Children who are confused by these concepts may need help understanding that many of the pictures illustrate more than one concept. However, both the photographs and the format, with the words printed large on broad yellow bands at the beginning of each section, are uncluttered and appealing." Booklist

Push pull, empty full; a book of opposites. Macmillan 1972 unp il $13.95   E

1. English language—Synonyms and antonyms
ISBN 0-02-744810-X
Brief text and black and white photographs illustrate fifteen pairs of opposites—push pull, empty full, wet dry, in out, up down, thick thin, whole broken, front back, big little, first last, many few, heavy light, together apart, left right, and day night
"Most of the meanings are immediately apparent from the pictures although some children may have difficulty with thick (elephants) and thin (flamingos)." Booklist

Round & round & round. Greenwillow Bks. 1983 unp il $14.95; lib bdg $14.93   E

1. Size and shape
ISBN 0-688-01813-0; 0-688-01814-9 (lib bdg)   LC 82-11984
Color photos without text feature objects that are round
"This is a good choice for encouragement of a child's powers of observation as well as to emphasize a concept of shape, and the pictures of a scoop of ice cream, a raccoon peering out of a hole in a tree, bright balloons, irridescent soap bubbles, and a seal balancing a ball should appeal to young children." Bull Cent Child Books

Shadows and reflections. Greenwillow Bks. 1990 unp il $12.95; lib bdg $12.88   E

1. Shades and shadows
ISBN 0-688-07089-2; 0-688-07090-6 (lib bdg)   LC 89-30461
Photographs without text feature shadows and reflections of various objects, animals, and people
"This imaginative, wordless book of color photographs is a visual treat, offering witty and subtle sets of images for enriching the eyes of children and adults." SLJ

Hoban, Tana—*Continued*

Shapes, shapes, shapes. Greenwillow Bks. 1986 unp il $16; lib bdg $22.25; pa $4.95
E

1. Size and shape
ISBN 0-688-05832-9; 0-688-05833-7 (lib bdg); 0-688-14740-2 (pa)   LC 85-17569

Photographs of familiar objects such as chair, barrettes, and manhole cover present a study of rounded and angular shapes

"Tana Hoban has created an excellent concept book that will encourage children to look for specific shapes in everyday urban scenes. There are triangles, circles, trapezoids, and so on, in photographs of such varied subjects as buildings, laundries and street vendor's wares. The photographs not only serve to teach shapes and colors but are works of art themselves. . . . This book not only succeeds in helping children learn shapes, but helps to instill in them observational instincts that are such an important, integral part of many disciplines, especially science." Appraisal

Spirals, curves, fanshapes & lines. Greenwillow Bks. 1992 unp il $14; lib bdg $13.93
E

ISBN 0-688-11228-5; 0-688-11229-3 (lib bdg)
LC 91-30159

Introduces the concepts of spirals, curves, fanshapes, and lines through photographs of bananas, a broom, birds, and other objects and things

"With her usual practiced eye, Hoban searches out the geometric form and grace in the everyday objects that surround us. Her photographs are saturated with color. . . . White borders frame each high-quality reproduction." Booklist

Take another look. Greenwillow Bks. 1981 40p il $15.93
E

ISBN 0-688-84298-4   LC 80-21342

By viewing nine subjects both in full-page photos and through die-cut pages, the reader learns that things maybe perceived in different ways

"The objects are as familiar as a daisy, a cat, an umbrella, et cetera, with only one perhaps less familiar object, a lizard. A nice concept book, this has a guessing game appeal." Bull Cent Child Books

Where is it? Macmillan 1974 unp il $15
E

1. Rabbits—Fiction 2. Easter—Fiction 3. Stories in rhyme
ISBN 0-02-744070-2

In this story in rhyme, illustrated with photographs, a rabbit searches for its own Easter basket full of garden vegetables

"The type is large and the scanning lines short while some end words rhyme—all factors considered helpful to the decoding practice of the youngest readers as well as older reluctants." SLJ

White on black. Greenwillow Bks. 1993 unp il $4.95
E

ISBN 0-688-11919-0   LC 92-20092

In this board book, white illustrations against a black background depict such objects as a horse, baby bottle, and sailboat

"Hoban's compositions are so supple and her layouts so well balanced that she casts a kind of spell." Publ Wkly

Hoestlandt, Jo

Star of fear, star of hope; illustrations by Johanna Kang; translated from the French by Mark Polizzotti. Walker & Co. 1995 unp il $15.95
E

1. Holocaust, 1933-1945—Fiction 2. Jews—Fiction 3. Paris (France)—Fiction
ISBN 0-8027-8373-2   LC 94-32378

Nine-year-old Helen is confused by the disappearance of her Jewish friend during the German occupation of Paris

"The pastel pictures in sepia tones are understated, with an old-fashioned, almost childlike simplicity. . . . Without being maudlin or sensational, the story brings the genocide home." Booklist

Hoff, Syd, 1912-

Danny and the dinosaur; story and pictures by Syd Hoff. Harper & Row 1958 64p il $14.95; lib bdg $14.89; pa $3.50
E

1. Dinosaurs—Fiction
ISBN 0-06-022465-7; 0-06-022466-5 (lib bdg); 0-06-444002-8 (pa)

Also available Spanish language edition
"An I can read book"

The story is "about an amiable dinosaur who leaves his home in the museum to stroll about town and play with Danny, a small boy who loves dinosaurs." Bull Cent Child Books

"The bold, humorous, colored pictures convey the imaginative story. . . . Because of the simple vocabulary and sentence structure, first-graders can actually read this story." Libr J

Another available title about Danny and the dinosaur is:
Happy birthday, Danny and the dinosaur! (1995)

Hoffman, Mary, 1945-

Amazing Grace; pictures by Caroline Binch. Dial Bks. for Young Readers 1991 unp il $14.99
E

1. African Americans—Fiction 2. Theater—Fiction
ISBN 0-8037-1040-2   LC 90-25108

Also available Spanish language edition

Although her classmates say that she cannot play Peter Pan in the school play because she is black and a girl, Grace discovers that she can do anything she sets her mind to do

"Gorgeous watercolor illustrations portraying a determined, talented child and her warm family enhance an excellent text and positive message of self-affirmation. Grace is an amazing girl and this is an amazing book." SLJ

Another available title about Grace is:
Boundless Grace (1995)

Hogrogian, Nonny

The cat who loved to sing. Knopf 1988 unp il music lib bdg $13.99
E

1. Cats—Fiction
ISBN 0-394-99004-8   LC 86-27358

"Hogrogian presents this cumulative tale of a carefree cat who trades with those he meets: a thorn for bread, then for a hen, and so on until he winds up with a mandolin, which he keeps 'for he is a cat who loves to sing'." SLJ

"The words and music of the cat's song conclude the book, which is designed with woodsy endpapers that extend the verdant scenery of the cat's capers. The fused effects of the backgrounds contrast nicely with the pencilled lines tex-

Hogrogian, Nonny—*Continued*

turing the cat's fur for a gentle effect to which young listeners will respond by quickly picking up the chant." Bull Cent Child Books

Hoguet, Susan Ramsay

I unpacked my grandmother's trunk; a picture book game. Dutton 1983 unp il $13.95
E

1. Alphabet 2. Games
ISBN 0-525-44069-0   LC 83-1701

"This familiar word game is usually played without a book, but Hoguet's rendition is so charmingly illustrated that even veteran players will welcome it. Just a few of the articles that tumble out of the trunk include: a curious bear, a melting igloo, an adept acrobat, and a mimicking kangaroo. Executed in precise pastel drawings, the objects illustrate each letter of the alphabet, provide lots to look at, and cumulatively tell a story of sorts. The clever use of half pages exposes the trunk's contents imaginatively, adding to the fun. Also included are directions for playing the memory game without the book." Booklist

Holabird, Katharine

Angelina ballerina; illustrations by Helen Craig; text by Katharine Holabird. Potter 1983 unp il $16
E

1. Mice—Fiction 2. Ballet—Fiction
ISBN 0-517-55083-0   LC 83-8233

Also available miniature edition $4.99 (ISBN 0-517-57668-6)

"Though Angelina is a little mouse, she could be any child who has dreamed of taking lessons in a special subject. When she starts ballet class, instead of dreaming and trying, she can concentrate on chores and school. Later, her talent and hard work enable her to become a famous ballerina. Touches of humor, attention to detail, a feel for dance and truly anthropomorphic mice make the illustrations a major part of the book." Child Book Rev Serv

Other available titles about Angelina are:
Angelina and Alice (1987)
Angelina and the princess (1984)
Angelina at the fair (1985)
Angelina ice skates (1993)
Angelina on stage (1986)
Angelina's baby sister (1991)
Angelina's birthday surprise (1989)
Angelina's Christmas (1985)

Hopkinson, Deborah

Sweet Clara and the freedom quilt; paintings by James Ransome. Knopf 1993 unp il $16; lib bdg $16.99; pa $6.99
E

1. Slavery—Fiction 2. Quilts—Fiction
ISBN 0-679-82311-5; 0-679-92311-X (lib bdg); 0-679-87472-0 (pa)   LC 91-11601

Clara, a young slave stitches a quilt with a map pattern which guides her to freedom in the North

"The smooth, optimistic, first-person vernacular of the story is ably accompanied by Ransome's brightly colored, full-page paintings." Horn Book Guide

Hort, Lenny

How many stars in the sky? paintings by James E. Ransome. Tambourine Bks. 1991 unp il $16; lib bdg $15.93
E

1. Stars—Fiction 2. Fathers and sons—Fiction
ISBN 0-688-10103-8; 0-688-10104-6 (lib bdg)
LC 90-36044

One night when Mama is away, Daddy and child seek a good place to count the stars in the night sky

"Ransome uses thick, visible strokes in his dense oil paintings that completely fill each large-format page. In general they present a nice variety of scenes to match the flow of the text, and the closeness between the black father and son is warmly portrayed. A fresh look at an age-old concept." SLJ

Houston, Gloria

My great-aunt Arizona; illustrated by Susan Condie Lamb. HarperCollins Pubs. 1992 unp il $15; lib bdg $14.89
E

1. Teachers 2. Appalachian region
ISBN 0-06-022606-4; 0-06-022607-2 (lib bdg)
LC 90-44112

The author tells the life story of "her great aunt Arizona who never traveled farther than the next town where she trained as a teacher before returning to her small Appalachian community's one-room schoolhouse. Though not well-traveled, Arizona encouraged her students to dream of faraway places and was always there to give them hugs and kisses." Child Book Rev Serv

"The pleasant, conversational rhythm of the prose, the unobtrusive use of repetition, and the ability to sum up the unique quality of a life in a few telling phrases give the writing its substance. . . . Sunny and lively, the watercolor paintings have a naive quality that suits the story well." Booklist

The year of the perfect Christmas tree; an Appalachian story; pictures by Barbara Cooney. Dial Bks. for Young Readers 1988 unp il $15.99; lib bdg $14.89
E

1. Christmas—Fiction 2. Appalachian Mountains—Fiction
ISBN 0-8037-0299-X; 0-8037-0300-7 (lib bdg)
LC 87-24551

"It's 1918 in the mountains of North Carolina, and the custom in the village is for one family to select and donate the Christmas tree each year. In the spring Ruthie and her father select a perfect balsam high on a rocky crag. Then Father goes to war. Still, on Christmas Eve the tree is in the church and Ruthie plays the angel. The winning illustrations perfectly match the tone of this affecting story, which comes from the author's family." N Y Times Book Rev

Howard, Elizabeth Fitzgerald, 1927-

Aunt Flossie's hats (and crab cakes later); paintings by James Ransome. Clarion Bks. 1991 31p il $15.95; pa $5.95
E

1. Hats—Fiction 2. Aunts—Fiction 3. African Americans—Fiction
ISBN 0-395-54682-6; 0-395-72077-X (pa)
LC 90-33332

Sara and Susan share tea, cookies, crab cakes, and stories about hats when they visit their favorite relative, Aunt Flossie

"This is an affecting portrait of a black American family and of the ways in which shared memories can be a thread, invisible yet strong, that ties generations together. Howard's

Howard, Elizabeth Fitzgerald, 1927——_Continued_

quiet, sure telling is well matched by Ransome's art—elegant, expressive oil paintings that convey warmth, joy, tenderness and love." Publ Wkly

Chita's Christmas tree; illustrated by Floyd Cooper. Bradbury Press 1989 unp il $14.95
E

1. Christmas—Fiction 2. Family life—Fiction 3. African Americans—Fiction

ISBN 0-02-744621-2   LC 88-26250

Also available in paperback from Aladdin Bks.

"A turn-of-the-century story begins on the Saturday before Christmas, when Chita and her father go out of the city (Baltimore) to choose a tree. Papa marks it with Chita's name and assures her that Santa Claus will get it to their house. The story continues, quietly, with preparations for the holiday, a dinner for the black family and relatives on Christmas Eve, and Chita's happy discovery the next morning that the big, decorated tree does indeed have her name carved on it." Bull Cent Child Books

"The paintings that surround the almost-poetic text are softly unfocused and glow with a golden color that suffuses the scenes. Yet despite the dreamy feeling of the art, carefully delineated characters play their parts perfectly in the family scenes." Booklist

Another available title about Chita is:
Papa tells Chita a story (1995)

The train to Lulu's; illustrated by Robert Casilla. Bradbury Press 1988 unp il $14.95
E

1. Railroads—Fiction 2. Sisters—Fiction 3. African Americans—Fiction

ISBN 0-02-744620-4   LC 86-33429

Also available in paperback from Macmillan

This story "describes two young sisters' nine-hour train ride from Boston to Baltimore. Although the girls are travelling alone, the Travelers' Aid ladies and conductors assure them safe passage, and it's only boredom that mars the trip. Beppy does her best to entertain Babs, but both are relieved when they finally arrive to be claimed by grandmotherly Lulu for the summer." Bull Cent Child Books

"Even though this story takes place in the late 1930s, its themes of self-reliance and readiness are timeless. . . . Casilla deftly captures the warmth existing in this extended black family and also the appealing aspects of railroad travel." SLJ

Howe, James, 1946-

The day the teacher went bananas; illustrated by Lillian Hoban. Dutton 1984 unp il $13.99; pa $3.95
E

1. Teachers—Fiction 2. School stories 3. Gorillas—Fiction

ISBN 0-525-44107-7; 0-525-44321-5 (pa)

LC 84-1536

"A mix-up places a gorilla and a new teacher in the wrong places, and the class of children find that the gorilla is a fine teacher. They learn to count on their toes and swing on trees before the error is matter-of-factly righted, and the following day the class goes to the zoo to have lunch with their favorite teacher." SLJ

"Hoban's artistic perceptions of children are, as usual, right on target, and in a book where integration of text and picture is crucial, the two mesh with colorful vigor and aplomb." Booklist

Pinky and Rex; illustrated by Melissa Sweet. Atheneum Pubs. 1990 38p il $12.95   E

1. Museums—Fiction 2. Friendship—Fiction 3. Toys—Fiction

ISBN 0-689-31454-X   LC 89-30786

Also available in paperback from Avon Bks.

"Pinky, a boy named for his favorite color, and Rex, a girl whose name reflects her interest in dinosaurs, live next door to each other; they each have twenty-seven stuffed animals and are best friends. . . . They go to the museum and discover that even best friends can vie with each other for the last remaining pink dinosaur in the museum store." Horn Book

"Sweet's gently washed, jovial illustrations reflect the unpretentious sincerity of Rex and Pinky's relationship, while Howe's readable text blending natural dialogue with narrative, is divided into individual chapters." Booklist

Other available titles about Pinky and Rex are:
Pinky and Rex and the double-dad weekend (1995)
Pinky and Rex and the mean old witch (1991)
Pinky and Rex and the new baby (1993)
Pinky and Rex and the spelling bee (1991)
Pinky and Rex get married (1990)
Pinky and Rex go to camp (1992)

Scared silly: a Halloween treat; illustrated by Leslie Morrill. Morrow Junior Bks. 1989 unp il $16; lib bdg $15.93   E

1. Halloween—Fiction 2. Animals—Fiction

ISBN 0-688-07666-1; 0-688-07667-X (lib bdg)

LC 88-7837

Also available in paperback from Avon Bks.

At head of title: Harold & Chester in

The Monroes leave their cat, Chester, and two dogs, Harold and Howe, alone on Halloween night, unaware that their pets are about to be visited by a strange figure who might be a wicked witch

"Howe's pacing is perfect, and the ending is unexpected. But it is Morrill's artwork that really enhances the drama. Exciting watercolors capture the individuality of the animals and the creepiness of the setting as shadows gradually fall." Booklist

Other picture books about Harold and Chester are:
Creepy-crawly birthday (1991)
The fright before Christmas (1988)
Hot fudge (1990)
Rabbit-Cadabra! (1993)

Other available titles about Harold and Chester are entered in Fiction Section under Deborah Howe and James Howe

There's a dragon in my sleeping bag; illustrated by David S. Rose. Atheneum Pubs. 1994 unp il $14.95   E

1. Brothers—Fiction 2. Imaginary playmates—Fiction

ISBN 0-689-31873-1   LC 93-26572

Also available Spanish language edition

Alex is intimidated by his older brother Simon's imaginary dragon, until he is able to create his own friend—a camel named Calvin

"The story is humorous and heartwarming without being overly cute, and Rose's acrylic illustrations are colorful and imaginative." Booklist

Another available title about Simon is:
There's a monster under my bed (1986)

Hughes, Shirley

Alfie gets in first. Lothrop, Lee & Shepard Bks. 1982 c1981 unp il $16; lib bdg $14.93; pa $4.95
E

1. Locks and keys—Fiction
ISBN 0-688-00848-8; 0-688-00849-6 (lib bdg); 0-688-07036-1 (pa)   LC 81-8427

Another title about Annie Rose and Alfie is entered in class 821

"Alfie, racing ahead of his mother and his baby sister as they return from grocery shopping, reaches the front door first; after Mom has unlocked the door and gone down the steps to get the baby, Alfie dashes into the hall shouting 'I've won!' Unfortunately, he slams the door. Unfortunately, Mom's key is inside with Alfie. Crisis! Just as the milkman brings a ladder for the window cleaner to use in getting to an upstairs window, the door opens: a beaming Alfie has thought of a way to solve the problem." Bull Cent Child Books

"Inventive use of the double spreads establishes the simultaneous display of indoor and outdoor actions. The setting is English and the prose understated, and the illustrations, in full color, manage to be pleasing in a slightly scruffy way." SLJ

Other available titles about Alfie and his family are:
Alfie gives a hand (1983)
Alfie's feet (1982)
An evening at Alfie's (1985)
The big Alfie and Annie Rose storybook (1989)
The big Alfie out of doors storybook (1992)

Angel Mae: a tale of Trotter Street. Lothrop, Lee & Shepard Bks. 1989 unp il $12.95; lib bdg $12.88; pa $4.95
E

1. Infants—Fiction 2. Christmas—Fiction
ISBN 0-688-08538-5; 0-688-08539-3 (lib bdg); 0-688-11847-X (pa)   LC 89-45288

"Christmas is coming, and so is a new baby for the Morgan family of Trotter Street. Mum, Dad, Grandma, Frankie, and little sister Mae are getting ready for both events, preparing a room, a crib, toys, and more for the baby at home, and rehearsing a Christmas play at school." SLJ

"Set in an English working-class, multiethnic neighborhood, this warm, humorous, well-told story also has holiday appeal. Hughes' pictures are, as always, delightful; realistically rendered in ink and watercolors, they are placed on the page in a pleasantly varied manner, and both art and text are appropriately childlike." Booklist

Other available titles in the Trotter Street series are:
The big concrete lorry (1990)
The snow lady (1990)
Wheels (1991)

Bouncing. Candlewick Press 1993 unp il $12.95
E

1. Brothers and sisters—Fiction
ISBN 1-56402-128-9   LC 92-53001

A "little girl teaches her baby brother everything there is to know about bouncing." Horn Book Guide

"Soft pencil and paint illustrations succinctly capture familiar situations . . . and Hughes is especially adept at portraying the undercurrents of emotion in the simplest of actions." Publ Wkly

Other available titles in this series are:
Chatting (1994)
Giving (1993)
Hiding (1994)

Dogger. Lothrop, Lee & Shepard Bks. 1988 c1977 unp il $15; lib bdg $14.93; pa $4.95
E

1. Toys—Fiction
ISBN 0-688-07980-6; 0-688-07981-4 (lib bdg); 0-688-11704-X (pa)   LC 87-33787

First published 1977 in the United Kingdom. First United States edition published 1978 by Prentice-Hall with title: David and Dog

A youngster is upset by the loss of his favorite stuffed dog

"Hughes' story . . . is warmly satisfying, due in part to the way the illustrations capture the comfortable disarray that seems to rule wherever children are present. . . . Hughes has a way of zeroing in on the foibles of childhood with remarkable accuracy; this doesn't miss its mark." Booklist

Moving Molly. Lothrop, Lee & Shepard Bks. 1988 c1978 unp il $11.95; lib bdg 11.88
E

1. Moving—Fiction
ISBN 0-688-07982-2; 0-688-07984-9 (lib bdg)   LC 87-34250

First published 1978 in the United Kingdom; first United States edition published 1979 by Prentice-Hall

Molly is lonely after her family's move from the city to the country but she adjusts with the help of her two new next-door-neighbors

"The illustrations showing comfortable family life are very English in appearance but universal in appeal and add immeasurably to the warm, simple story." Horn Book

The nursery collection. Lothrop, Lee & Shepard Bks. 1994 unp il $16
E

1. Stories in rhyme
ISBN 0-688-13583-5   LC 93-47395

Five previously published titles "*Bathwater's Hot* and *Noisy* and *When We Went to the Park* (1985) and *Colors* and *All Shapes and Sizes* (1986)—have been collected into one big, handsome volume that will give preschoolers hours of fun. . . . The simple rhyming text makes you savor the words, and each cheerful line-and-watercolor illustration tells a story to talk about." Booklist

Out and about. Lothrop, Lee & Shepard Bks. 1988 unp il $16; lib bdg $14.88
E

1. Seasons—Fiction 2. Stories in rhyme
ISBN 0-688-07690-4; 0-688-07691-2 (lib bdg)   LC 87-17000

Rhyming text depicts the pleasures of the outdoors in all kinds of weather, through the four seasons

"The children who romp through these non-stop family scenes are rosy, cared-for, active, and enthusiastically messy. Hughes' drawing is always good, but the composition and coloration here mark some of her most cohesive book design and art work." Bull Cent Child Books

Stories by firelight. Lothrop, Lee & Shepard Bks. 1993 unp il $16
E

1. Winter—Fiction 2. Short stories
ISBN 0-688-04568-5   LC 92-38207

In a series of brief winter episodes, a child learns about a mythical sea creature, a boy and his grandfather build a bonfire, and Mrs. Toomly Stones pays a scary visit

"No one captures the real innocence and emotions of childhood with less sentimentality than Hughes. Designed with an appealing jacket and full-color illustrations on every page, this book will be in demand for reading aloud or reading alone." Booklist

Hughes, Shirley—*Continued*

Two shoes, new shoes. Lothrop, Lee & Shepard Bks. 1986 unp il $4.95   **E**

1. Clothing and dress—Fiction 2. Stories in rhyme

ISBN 0-688-04207-4   LC 86-2733

"The rhyme informs as the pictures celebrate the pleasures of dressing up: 'Slippers, warm by the fire, lace-ups in the street./Gloves are for hands and socks are for feet.' These are nice for sharing one on one; their down-to-earth ambience is most appealing." Booklist

Hurd, Edith Thacher, 1910-

I dance in my red pajamas; pictures by Emily Arnold McCully. Harper & Row 1982 unp il lib bdg $14.89   **E**

1. Grandparents—Fiction

ISBN 0-06-022700-1   LC 81-47721

Jenny visits with her grandparents and enjoys a beautiful noisy day

"McCully's drawings are buoyant and as lively as the day described. Her pen drawings give form and vibrance, while the colored washes provide the gentleness of a child's view of grandparents." SLJ

Johnny Lion's book; pictures by Clement Hurd. Harper & Row 1965 63p il lib bdg $13.89   **E**

1. Lions—Fiction

ISBN 0-06-022706-0

"An I can read book"

"A small lion, told to stay home and read his new book while his parents are out hunting, reads about another small lion. Less dutiful than the reader, the lion cub in the book wanders off and is later put to bed early. Johnny Lion pretends to his parents that he has strayed, but quickly informs them that he has really stayed home and read his book." Bull Cent Child Books

The "book-within-a-book technique is admirably handled, though it may be a bit sophisticated for the youngest readers without some guidance. More experienced readers . . . will enjoy the gay pictures and understand the central idea that adventures in a book are almost as exciting and interesting as real ones." N Y Times Book Rev

Other available titles about Johnny Lion are:

Johnny Lion's bad day (1970)

Johnny Lion's rubber boots (1972)

Last one home is a green pig; pictures by Clement Hurd. Harper & Row 1959 63p il lib bdg $11.89   **E**

1. Ducks—Fiction 2. Monkeys—Fiction

ISBN 0-06-022716-8

"An I can read book"

"A duck and a monkey use many ingenious means of transportation when they race each other home." Hodges. Books for Elem Sch Libr

Hurd, Thacher

Little Mouse's big valentine. Harper & Row 1990 unp il $13.95; $12.89; pa $3.95   **E**

1. Mice—Fiction 2. Valentine's Day—Fiction

ISBN 0-06-026192-7; 0-06-026193-5 (lib bdg); 0-06-443281-5 (pa)   LC 89-34515

After several unsuccessful attempts to give his special valentine to someone, Little Mouse finally finds just the right recipient

"The plot of boy mouse meets girl mouse may be simple, but it is offset by delightful characterizations. The book's small size gives it added appeal for its intended audience." Publ Wkly

Another available title about Little Mouse is:

Little Mouse's birthday cake (1992)

Mama don't allow; starring Miles and the Swamp Band. Harper & Row 1984 unp il $16; lib bdg $15.89; pa $4.95   **E**

1. Bands (Music)—Fiction 2. Alligators—Fiction

ISBN 0-06-022689-7; 0-06-022690-0 (lib bdg); 0-06-443078-2 (pa)   LC 83-47703

Miles and the Swamp Band have the time of their lives playing at the Alligator Ball, until they discover the menu includes Swamp Band soup

"The multi-colored full-spread watercolor illustrations are stunningly bright and full of movement, far outpacing the story line in energy and imagination." SLJ

Mystery on the docks. Harper & Row 1983 unp il lib bdg $14.89; pa $4.95   **E**

1. Mystery fiction 2. Rats—Fiction

ISBN 0-06-022702-8 (lib bdg); 0-06-443058-8 (pa)   LC 82-48261

Ralph, a short order cook, rescues a kidnapped opera singer from Big Al and his gang of nasty rats

Hurd "creates real excitement (albeit tongue-in-cheek) with his colorful pictures and fast-paced plot. There's a mysterious aura to the docks, and the stereotyped good and bad guys are hilarious. The unabashed fun and excitement make it perfect for reading aloud." Child Book Rev Serv

Hurwitz, Johanna

New shoes for Silvia; illustrated by Jerry Pinkney. Morrow Junior Bks. 1993 unp il $15; lib bdg $14.93   **E**

1. Shoes—Fiction 2. Latin America—Fiction

ISBN 0-688-05286-X; 0-688-05287-8 (lib bdg)   LC 92-40868

Silvia receives a pair of beautiful red shoes from her Tia Rosita and finds different uses for them until she grows enough for them to fit

"This simple story, told in spare prose, speaks universally to the imagination and emotions. Pinkney's spirited watercolors animate the narrative and are large enough for group sharing." SLJ

Hutchins, Pat, 1942-

1 hunter. Greenwillow Bks. 1982 unp il $16; lib bdg $15.93; pa $4.95   **E**

1. Counting 2. Animals—Fiction

ISBN 0-688-00614-0; 0-688-00615-9 (lib bdg); 0-688-06522-8 (pa)   LC 81-6352

This is "a 1 to 10 and back again counting book. . . . Here, a Mr. Magoo-type hunter blunders through the jungle entirely missing the camouflaged elephants (2), giraffes (3), ostriches (4), etc." SLJ

"Humorous illustrations done in a flat, clear style make an outstanding counting book." Horn Book

Changes, changes. Macmillan 1971 unp il $14.95; pa $4.95   **E**

1. Toys—Fiction 2. Dolls—Fiction 3. Stories without words

ISBN 0-02-745870-9; 0-689-71137-9 (pa)

This wordless book shows how two wooden dolls rearrange a child's building blocks to form various objects

"Another book for the very young child who delights in

Hutchins, Pat, 1942-—*Continued*

'reading' by himself, the lack of text amply compensated for by the bright, bold pictures and the imaginative use of blocks and two stiff little dolls." Bull Cent Child Books

Clocks and more clocks. Macmillan 1994 c1970 unp il $13.95; pa $4.95   E

1. Clocks and watches—Fiction
ISBN 0-02-745921-7; 0-689-71769-5 (pa)
A reissue of the title first published 1970

"After buying four clocks, Mr. Higgins is still not sure which one is right because there is always a few minutes difference between them." Booklist
"A minimum of well-chosen words and bright colored pictures tell the droll tale." Horn Book

Don't forget the bacon! Greenwillow Bks. 1976 unp il $16; lib bdg $15.93; pa $4.95   E

ISBN 0-688-06787-5; 0-688-06788-3 (lib bdg); 0-688-08743-4 (pa)

"Surely anyone could remember four items on a grocery list! A play on words, however, leads the shopper into interesting predicaments. Children gleefully follow the strange replacements that result. A great book for developing visual literacy and word play." Read Teach

The doorbell rang. Greenwillow Bks. 1986 unp il $16; lib bdg $22.25; pa $3.95   E

ISBN 0-688-05251-7; 0-688-05252-5 (lib bdg); 0-688-09234-9 (pa)   LC 85-12615
Also available Spanish language edition

"Victoria and Sam are delighted when Ma bakes a tray of a dozen cookies, even though Ma insists that her cookies aren't as good as Grandma's. They count them and find that each can have six. But the doorbell rings, friends arrive and the cookies must be re-divided. This happens again and again, and the number of cookies on each plate decreases as the visitors' pile of gear in the corner of the kitchen grows larger." SLJ
"Bright, joyous, dynamic, this wonderfully humorous piece of realism for the young is presented simply but with style and imagination." Horn Book

Good-night, Owl! Macmillan 1972 unp il $14.95; pa $3.95   E

1. Owls—Fiction
ISBN 0-02-745900-4; 0-689-71371-1 (pa)
Owl takes revenge on the birds and the animals who have not let him sleep during the day
"The ending is perky, the pictures funny, and the simplicity and repetition of pattern in the text are encouraging for the pre-reader." Bull Cent Child Books

Happy birthday, Sam. Greenwillow Bks. 1978 unp il lib bdg $14.93; pa $3.95   E

1. Birthdays—Fiction
ISBN 0-688-84160-0 (lib bdg); 0-688-10482-7 (pa)
LC 78-1295
Sam "wakes to find that being a year older hasn't changed the fact that he can't reach a light switch, or the clothes in his closet, or the tap above the sink where he'd like to play with the boat he's received as a present from his parents. Then Grandpa's present arrives; it's a small sturdy chair, and it enables Sam to reach everything." Bull Cent Child Books
"Sunny yellow and bright green predominate in this cheerfully stylized, full-color picture book." Booklist

Rosie's walk. Macmillan 1968 unp il $14.95; pa $4.95   E

1. Chickens—Fiction 2. Foxes—Fiction
ISBN 0-02-745850-4; 0-02-043750-1 (pa)
"Rosie the hen goes for a walk around the farm and gets home in time for dinner, completely unaware that a fox has been hot on her heels every step of the way. The viewer knows, however, and is not only held in suspense but tickled by the ways in which the fox is foiled at every turn by the unwitting hen. A perfect choice for the youngest." Booklist

Titch. Macmillan 1971 unp il $14.95; pa $4.95   E

1. Brothers and sisters—Fiction
ISBN 0-02-745880-6; 0-689-71688-5 (pa)
"How does it feel to be the youngest child in the family? To have an older brother and sister who lead a more exciting life? . . . [The author] has, with a minimum of well-chosen words and bright, engaging illustrations, triumphantly related the story of a small boy who surpasses his brother and sister with one simple action." Publ Wkly
Other available titles about Titch are:
Tidy Titch (1991)
You'll soon grow into them, Titch (1983)

What game shall we play? Greenwillow Bks. 1990 unp il $12.95; lib bdg $12.88; pa $4.95   E

1. Animals—Fiction
ISBN 0-688-09196-2; 0-688-09197-0 (lib bdg); 0-688-13573-0 (pa)   LC 89-34621
"Frog and Duck want to play but can't think of a game, so they search for Fox to ask for help, and so it goes until the animals seek Owl's advice. In their childlike naivete, they don't realize that Owl has been watching them the whole time, and when he suggests a game of 'Hide and Seek,' they enthusiastically agree." SLJ
"Stylized decorative details are incorporated into the animal characters of Hutchins' ink and watercolor pictures. . . . The story line is simple, and young children will enjoy the accumulation of animals, the fact that they have been seeking hidden friends all along, and the fact that they all can easily be seen by Owl from his high perch and by readers from theirs." Bull Cent Child Books
Another available title about these animal friends is:
The surprise party (1969)

Where's the baby? Greenwillow Bks. 1988 unp il $12.95; lib bdg $12.84   E

1. Monsters—Fiction   2. Infants—Fiction
3. Cleanliness—Fiction
ISBN 0-688-05933-3; 0-688-05934-1 (lib bdg)
LC 86-33566
When Grandma, Ma, and Hazel Monster want to find Baby Monster, they follow the messy trail he has left
"Delightful. . . . Each brightly decked illustration is cluttered with everyday objects for the young reader to identify and the text is a loping doggerel entirely in keeping with the rough-and-ready storyline." Times Lit Suppl
Other available titles about the Monster family are:
Silly Billy (1882)
Three-star Billy (1994)
The very worst monster (1985)

The wind blew. Macmillan 1974 unp il $14.95; pa $4.95   E

1. Winds—Fiction 2. Stories in rhyme
ISBN 0-02-745910-1; 0-689-71744-X (pa)
"Full-color paintings illustrate a rhymed cumulative text depicting the frantic efforts of unwary pedestrians to recov-

Hutchins, Pat, 1942-—*Continued*
er possessions snatched away by a mischievous and unpredictable wind. . . . Although the brief text is a pleasant,
rhythmic accompaniment to the pictures, the story can be
'read' from the doublespread illustrations. A humorous and
imaginative treatment of a familiar situation." Horn Book

Isaacs, Anne
Swamp Angel; illustrated by Paul O.
Zelinsky. Dutton Children's Bks. 1994 unp il
$15.99   E
  1. Tall tales 2. Frontier and pioneer life—Fiction
  3. Tennessee—Fiction
  ISBN 0-525-45271-0   LC 93-43956
  A Caldecott Medal honor book, 1995
  Along with other amazing feats, Angelica Longrider, also
known as Swamp Angel, wrestles a huge bear, known as
Thundering Tarnation, to save the winter supplies of the
settlers in Tennessee
  "Isaacs tells her original story with the glorious exaggeration and uproarious farce of the traditional tall tale and
with its typical laconic idiom—you just can't help reading
it aloud. . . . Zelinsky's detailed oil paintings in folk-art
style are exquisite, framed in cherry, maple, and birch wood
grains. They are also hilarious, making brilliant use of perspective to extend the mischief and the droll understate-
ment." Booklist

Isadora, Rachel
At the crossroads. Greenwillow Bks. 1991
unp il $16; lib bdg $15.93; pa $4.95   E
  1. Fathers—Fiction 2. South Africa—Fiction
  ISBN 0-688-05270-3; 0-688-05271-1 (lib bdg);
  0-688-13103-4 (pa)   LC 90-30751
  South African children gather to welcome home their fathers who have been away for ten months working in the
mines
  "The characters' anticipation, patience, and joy speak
loudest here, both in text and in brilliantly lit watercolor
paintings." Bull Cent Child Books

Ben's trumpet. Greenwillow Bks. 1979 unp
il $16; pa $4.95   E
  1. Musicians—Fiction 2. African Americans—Fiction
  ISBN 0-688-80194-3; 0-688-10988-8 (pa)
                                          LC 78-12885
  A Caldecott Medal honor book, 1980
  This is the story of Ben, a boy whose dream is to be a
jazz trumpeter but who is too poor to own an instrument
until a real musician, remembering his own dreams, puts
one into the boy's hands
  "The art is astonishingly varied in its brilliant
recreation—in the margins, in the urban backgrounds—of
the commercial art of the 20's and 30's." N Y Times Book
Rev

City seen from A to Z. Greenwillow Bks.
1983 unp il lib bdg $15.93; pa $3.95   E
  1. City life 2. Alphabet
  ISBN 0-688-01803-3 (lib bdg); 0-688-12032-6 (pa)
                                          LC 82-11966
  Twenty-six black-and-white drawings of scenes of city life
suggest words beginning with each letter of the alphabet
  "The activities or objects or concepts in this urban alphabet book . . . reflect the multiethnic composition of a
city, and they seldom include words that are not easily
comprehensible. The first letter of each word (sometimes
two words, like 'Roller skate') is in brown, the rest of the
word in black, adequately distinguished from, but blending

with the soft, soft illustrations that are highly textured, often stippled, dramatic in composition." Bull Cent Child
Books

Lili at ballet. Putnam 1993 unp il $15.95
                                             E
  1. Ballet—Fiction
  ISBN 0-399-22423-8   LC 92-8429
  Lili dreams of becoming a ballerina and goes to her ballet lessons four afternoons a week
  "Isadora uses pastel shades of purple, pink, green, and
blue with bold splashes of black. This is a prettily illustrated book that captures the magic and hard work involved in
ballet." SLJ
  Another available title about Lili is:
Lili on stage (1995)

Max; story & pictures by Rachel Isadora.
Macmillan 1976 unp il $13.95; pa $3.95
                                             E
  1. Baseball—Fiction 2. Ballet—Fiction
  ISBN 0-02-747450-X; 0-02-043800-1 (pa)
                                          LC 76-9088
  Max "is the star of his baseball team. On a Saturday
morning, he has time to spare before his game and accepts
(with some hidden disdain) the invitation of his sister, Lisa,
to watch her ballet class in action. Max is surprised to find
himself interested and happy to join the students at teacher's suggestion. . . . The experience pays off at the ball park
where Max hits a home run. Now he warms up for the
game each week at Lisa's dancing class. The pictures are an
ebullient combination of grace and comedy, with the leggy
students dipping and soaring, in contrast to Max in his uniform." Publ Wkly

Over the green hills. Greenwillow Bks. 1992
unp il $14; lib bdg $13.93   E
  1. South Africa—Fiction
  ISBN 0-688-10509-2; 0-688-10510-6 (lib bdg)
                                          LC 91-12761
  Zolani, who lives in a rural black homeland in South Africa, goes with his mother to visit his Grandma Zindzi
  "The kindness of the South African people is at the heart
of this affecting story, told as much through Isadora's vibrantly hued, arresting watercolors—spotlighting the local
landscape, wildlife and customs—as her eloquent writing."
Publ Wkly

Swan Lake; adapted and illustrated by
Rachel Isadora. Putnam 1989 unp il $14.95
                                             E
  1. Ballet—Stories, plots, etc. 2. Fairy tales
  ISBN 0-399-21730-4   LC 88-29843
  A prince's love for a swan queen overcomes an evil sorcerer's spell in this fairy tale adaptation of the classic ballet
  "The illustrations and the text (which is clear and
straightforward) effectively re-create the ballet, with all its
mystery and romanticism." N Y Times Book Rev

Ivimey, John W. (John William), 1868-1961
The complete story of the three blind mice;
illustrated by Paul Galdone. Clarion Bks. 1987
unp il lib bdg $13.95; pa $5.95   E
  1. Mice—Fiction 2. Stories in rhyme
  ISBN 0-89919-481-8 (lib bdg); 0-395-51585-8 (pa)
                                          LC 87-689
  First published 1909 in the United Kingdom with title:
Complete version of ye three blind mice

Ivimey, John W. (John William), 1868-1961—
Continued

"Galdone found this story—Ivimey's tale of the three blind mice—in a collection of antique British children's stories and knew he wanted to reillustrate it. . . . The sprightly text is written in the same rhyme as the song (which is given with the music on the dust jacket), making this a perfect read-aloud for story hours. Galdone's familiar, jaunty artwork is done in rich colors and catches all the humorous nuances of a tale that will appeal greatly to young children."
Booklist

Iwamatsu, Atushi Jun, 1908-1994
Crow Boy; [by] Taro Yashima. Viking 1955 37p il lib bdg $15.99; pa $4.99   E
1. School stories 2. Japan—Fiction
ISBN 0-670-24931-9 (lib bdg); 0-14-050172-X (pa)
Also available Spanish language edition
A Caldecott Medal honor book, 1956
"A young boy from the mountain area of Japan goes to school in a nearby village, where he is taunted by his classmates and feels rejected and isolated. Finally an understanding teacher helps the boy gain acceptance. The other students recognize how wrong they have been and nickname him 'Crow Boy' because he can imitate the crow's calls with such perfection." Adventuring with Books. 2d edition
"A moving story interpreted by the author's distinctive illustrations, valuable for human relations and for its picture of Japanese school life." Hodges. Books for Elem Sch Libr

Umbrella; [by] Taro Yashima. Viking 1958 30p il lib bdg $15.99; pa $4.99   E
1. Umbrellas and parasols—Fiction
ISBN 0-670-73858-1 (lib bdg); 0-14-050240-8 (pa)
A Caldecott Medal honor book, 1959
"Momo, given an umbrella and a pair of red boots on her third birthday, is overjoyed when at last it rains and she can wear her new rain togs." Hodges. Books for Elem Sch Libr
In this simple tale, young children "will be carried along by their identification with the actions of this very real little girl. . . . The beauty of the book makes this worthwhile." Horn Book
Another available title about Momo is:
Momo's kitten (1961)

Jackson, Ellen B., 1943-
Brown cow, green grass, yellow mellow sun; illustrated by Victoria Raymond. Hyperion Bks. for Children 1995 unp il $14.95; lib bdg $14.89   E
1. Color—Fiction 2. Farm life—Fiction
ISBN 0-7868-0010-0; 0-7868-2006-3 (lib bdg)
LC 93-37091
"This picture book relates how the sun helps the grass grow, the cow eats the grass, the boy milks the cow, and the granny churns the milk to make . . . butter! Jackson is a gifted writer who can make the simplest language rhythmic and interesting. The intriguing illustrations, created with a modeling compound that is baked and then painted, are fabulous: everything is curved and rounded and full of movement and texture. . . . The book ends with two recipes, one for 'big brown pancakes,' and another for 'yellow mellow butter.'" SLJ

Cinder Edna; by Ellen Jackson; illustrated by Kevin O'Malley. Lothrop, Lee & Shepard Bks. 1994 unp il $15; lib bdg $14.93   E
1. Fairy tales
ISBN 0-688-12322-8; 0-688-12323-6 (lib bdg)
LC 92-44160
Cinderella and Cinder Edna, who live with cruel stepmothers and stepsisters, have different approaches to life; and, although each ends up with the prince of her dreams, one is a great deal happier than the other
"O'Malley's full-page, full-color illustrations are exuberant and funny. Ella is suitably bubble-headed and self-absorbed while Edna is plain, practical, and bound to enjoy life." SLJ

Jaffe, Nina
In the month of Kislev; a story for Hanukkah; illustrated by Louise August. Viking 1992 30p il $15; pa $4.99   E
1. Hanukkah—Fiction 2. Jews—Fiction
ISBN 0-670-82863-7; 0-14-055654-0 (pa)
LC 91-45804
A rich, arrogant merchant takes the family of a poor peddler to court and learns a lesson about the meaning of Hanukkah
"A story rich in folkloric tradition, crisply told and firmly placed in an old-world setting. . . . The illustrations, prepared as woodcuts painted in oils on paper with warm browns, soft blues, and lots of black shading, have the rich look of rubbed wood." SLJ

James, Betsy
Mary Ann. Dutton Children's Bks. 1994 unp il $13.99   E
1. Praying mantis—Fiction 2. Friendship—Fiction
ISBN 0-525-45077-7   LC 93-13364
"Amy is miserable when her best friend moves away and wishes she could have 'hundreds of Mary Anns'—so that if one moved away, she would still have more. Then Amy finds a praying mantis, whom she names Mary Ann, and, when her new friend's eggs hatch, she gets her wish: 'hundreds and hundreds of Mary Anns!'" Horn Book Guide
"A shining example of a science lesson couched within an evocative story. . . . The pleasantly warm tones of the watercolor-and-ink illustrations portray the full gamut of emotions from true sadness to unabated joy. . . . The book concludes with a valuable author's note that presents fascinating facts and hints for raising these intriguing creatures." SLJ

Johnson, Angela
Do like Kyla; paintings by James E. Ransome. Orchard Bks. 1990 unp il $14.95; lib bdg $14.99; pa $5.95   E
1. Sisters—Fiction 2. African Americans—Fiction
ISBN 0-531-05852-2; 0-531-08452-3 (lib bdg); 0-531-07040-9 (pa)   LC 89-16229
"A Richard Jackson book"
A little girl imitates her big sister Kyla all day, until in the evening Kyla imitates her
"Ransome's solid oil paintings feature two lively black girls firmly placed in a loving home, with both father and mother, and a neighborhood that pulses with realism." Booklist

Johnson, Angela—*Continued*

Julius; story by Angela Johnson; pictures by Dav Pilkey. Orchard Bks. 1993 unp il $14.95; lib bdg $14.99

                E

1. Pigs—Fiction
ISBN 0-531-05465-9; 0-531-08615-1 (lib bdg)
                LC 92-24175

"A Richard Jackson book"
"Young Maya receives a gift from her grandfather, which he believes will help her learn about fun and sharing—a playful pig named Julius. The multimedia collages contain many artistic references. . . . They feature large areas of bright color or pattern, juxtaposed to create a visually dazzling, childlike vision of the world. An exuberant, joyful collaboration." Horn Book Guide

Tell me a story, Mama; pictures by David Soman. Orchard Bks. 1989 unp il $14.95; lib bdg $14.99; pa $5.95
                E

1. Mothers and daughters—Fiction 2. African Americans—Fiction
ISBN 0-531-05794-1; 0-531-08394-2 (lib bdg); 0-531-07032-8 (pa)
                LC 88-17917

A young girl and her mother remember together all the girl's favorite stories about her mother's childhood
"Soman's vivid, lively watercolors capture the essence of the mood and message as they deftly portray the quotidian portraits of two generations of a black family. Both language and art are full of subtle wit and rich emotion, resulting in a beautifully realized evocation of treasured childhood and family moments." SLJ

When I am old with you; story by Angela Johnson; pictures by David Soman. Orchard Bks. 1990 unp il $14.95; lib bdg $14.99; pa $5.95
                E

1. Grandfathers—Fiction 2. Old age—Fiction
ISBN 0-531-05884-0; 0-531-08484-1 (lib bdg); 0-531-07035-2 (pa)
                LC 89-70928

"A Richard Jackson book"
A young black boy imagines being old with Grandaddy and joining him in such activities as playing cards all day, visiting the ocean, and eating bacon on the porch
"A warm, affectionate portrait of a special relationship with impressive watercolors that are full of life." Horn Book Guide

Johnson, Crockett, 1906-1975

Harold and the purple crayon. Harper & Row 1955 unp il lib bdg $12.89; pa $3.95
                E

ISBN 0-06-022936-5 (lib bdg); 0-06-443022-7 (pa)

Also available Spanish language edition
"As Harold goes for a moonlight walk, he uses his purple crayon to draw a path and the things he sees along the way, then draws himself back home." Hodges. Books for Elem Sch Libr
Other available titles about Harold are:
Harold's ABC (1963)
Harold's circus (1959)
Harold's fairy tale (1986)
Harold's trip to the sky (1957)
A picture for Harold's room (1960)

Johnson, Paul Brett

The cow who wouldn't come down; story and pictures by Paul Brett Johnson. Orchard Bks. 1993 unp il $14.95; lib bdg $14.99
                E

1. Cattle—Fiction
ISBN 0-531-05481-0; 0-531-08631-3 (lib bdg)
                LC 92-27592

"A Richard Jackson book"
Miss Rosemary tries everything to coax her flying cow Gertrude down from the sky
"A rib-tickling read-aloud about a cow who defies gravity and logic, complemented by comical, light-dappled illustrations." SLJ

Johnson, Stephen, 1964-

Alphabet city; [by] Stephen T. Johnson. Viking 1995 unp il $14.99
                E

1. Alphabet
ISBN 0-670-85631-2
                LC 95-12335

A Caldecott Medal honor book, 1995
"Beginning with the *A* formed by a construction site's sawhorse and ending with the *Z* found in the angle of a fire escape, Johnson draws viewers' eyes to tiny details within everyday objects to find letters." SLJ
"Only after careful scrutiny will viewers realize that these arresting images aren't photographs but compositions of pastels, watercolors, gouache and charcoal. A visual tour de force, Johnson's ingenious alphabet book transcends the genre by demanding close inspection of not just letters, but the world." Publ Wkly

Johnston, Tony

Alice Nizzy Nazzy, the Witch of Santa Fe; illustrated by Tomie dePaola. Putnam 1995 unp il $15.95
                E

1. Witches—Fiction 2. New Mexico—Fiction
ISBN 0-399-22788-1
                LC 93-44375

Johnson and dePaola "transport Baba Yaga, one of Russia's great folklore figures, to the American Southwest. Incarnated here as Alice Nizzy Nazzy, the child-eating witch lives in an adobe hut perched on 'skinny roadrunner feet' and surrounded by a fence of prickly pear cactus. When Manuela wanders by in search of her lost sheep, she ends up in Alice's soup caldron." Publ Wkly
"Johnston's writing snaps with life. . . . dePaola has filled the book with the bright colors of the Southwest, using brick red borders and lots of teal, purple, and orange. Alice is a satisfying blend of spookiness and silliness." Bull Cent Child Books

The cowboy and the black-eyed pea; illustrated by Warren Ludwig. Putnam 1992 unp il $15.95
                E

1. Fairy tales 2. Cowhands—Fiction 3. West (U.S.)—Fiction
ISBN 0-399-22330-4
                LC 91-21606

In this adaptation of "The Princess and the Pea," the wealthy daughter of a Texas rancher devises a plan to find a real cowboy among her many suitors
"Rich with the language and details of the Wild West. Ludwig's colorful illustrations heighten the story's exaggerated humor (especially in facial expressions) and contrast nicely with the deadpan text. A great choice for a read-aloud." Booklist

Johnston, Tony—*Continued*

Grandpa's song; pictures by Brad Sneed. Dial Bks. for Young Readers 1991 unp il $13.99; lib bdg $12.89   E

1. Grandfathers—Fiction 2. Old age—Fiction
ISBN 0-8037-0801-7; 0-8037-0802-5 (lib bdg)
LC 90-43836
Also available in paperback from Puffin Bks.

When a young girl's beloved, exuberant grandfather becomes forgetful, she helps him by singing their favorite song

"Sneed's offbeat, distinctive watercolors emphasize Grandpa's 'kettledrum' size and zest for life. . . . Johnston's story is poignant without being sentimental, and joyously celebrates the love between grandparents and grandchildren." Publ Wkly

The quilt story; pictures by Tomie dePaola. Putnam 1985 unp il $15.95; pa $5.95   E

1. Quilts—Fiction 2. Mothers and daughters—Fiction
ISBN 0-399-21009-1; 0-399-21008-3 (pa)
LC 84-18212
A pioneer mother lovingly stitches a beautiful quilt which warms and comforts her daughter Abigail; many years later another mother mends and patches it for her little girl

"DePaola's full-color tempera illustrations add much to the story—the folk-art style matches the text perfectly and will grab the attention of young 'book browsers.'" SLJ

The soup bone; illustrated by Margot Tomes. Harcourt Brace Jovanovich 1990 unp il $12.95; pa $4.95   E

1. Skeleton—Fiction 2. Halloween—Fiction
ISBN 0-15-277255-3; 0-15-277256-1 (pa)
LC 89-19900
Looking for a soup bone on Halloween, a little old lady finds a hungry skeleton instead

"The folkloric quality of the text, with its repetitive alliterative phrases, is ably complemented by Margot Tomes's superb illustrations. The two principals come alive against richly textured backgrounds in the interplay of light and shadow which creates dimension and defines space." Horn Book

The vanishing pumpkin; pictures by Tomie dePaola. Putnam 1983 unp il hardcover o.p. paperback available $6.95   E

1. Halloween—Fiction 2. Witches—Fiction
ISBN 0-399-22436-X
LC 83-3122
"A 700-year-old woman and an 800-year-old man feel in the mood for some pumpkin pie on Halloween night, but they can't find their pumpkin. Fearing it's been 'snitched,' the two set off to find it." Booklist

"A not-very-scary—but very funny—Halloween story which the youngest trick-or-treaters will enjoy. . . . The illustrations are large and colorful, done in unusual but pleasing shades of green, orange and blue and clearly outlined in black ink." SLJ

Yonder; pictures by Lloyd Bloom. Dial Bks. for Young Readers 1988 unp il $12.95; lib bdg $12.89; pa $4.95   E

1. Seasons—Fiction 2. Country life—Fiction 3. Family life—Fiction
ISBN 0-8037-0277-9; 0-8037-0278-7 (lib bdg); 0-8037-0987-0 (pa)
LC 86-11549
"A young farmer brings a new wife home. The couple plant a tree and say a prayer, then set about being fruitful and multiplying. To commemorate each birth, a new 'tree of life' is planted, and over the years an entire orchard takes root in the fertile soil. The old farmer, by now a grandpa many times over, dies, and it turns out that family deaths are commemorated the same way as births—twin ceremonies based on the author's own family tradition." N Y Times Book Rev

"Lloyd Bloom's lush palette of verdant green and earth tones wakens all the senses. . . . Together, art and text convey an archetypical image of rural American life in an earlier, simpler time." Horn Book

Jonas, Ann

The 13th clue. Greenwillow Bks. 1992 unp il $14; lib bdg $14.93   E

1. Puzzles 2. Birthdays—Fiction 3. Parties—Fiction
ISBN 0-688-09742-1; 0-688-09743-X (lib bdg)
LC 91-34586
Also available in paperback from Dell

A young girl follows thirteen clues to a surprise birthday party

"Puzzles the girl and the reader must decipher include a rebus, words formed by clothes hanging on a clothesline, letters that spell out different words upside down and right side up, and words with their letters scrambled. . . . The full-color artwork, with its delightful changes of perspective, shows a sure sense of design. While the book looks 'young,' it will appeal most to those early and middle elementary school children who are fascinated by wordplay." Booklist

Aardvarks, disembark! Greenwillow Bks. 1990 unp il $16; lib bdg $14.88   E

1. Noah's ark 2. Rare animals 3. Alphabet
ISBN 0-688-07206-2; 0-688-07207-0 (lib bdg)
LC 89-27225
Also available in paperback from Puffin Bks.

After the flood, Noah calls out of the ark a variety of little-known animals, many of which are now endangered

"The book concludes with a list of the 132 species pictured, and one line of information about each. Those now extinct or endangered are indicated. Realistic, accurate watercolors; an impressive, special book." Horn Book Guide

Color dance. Greenwillow Bks. 1989 unp il $16; lib bdg $15.93   E

1. Color
ISBN 0-688-05990-2; 0-688-05991-0 (lib bdg)
LC 88-5446
Three dancers show how colors combine to create different colors

"The clean, spare design of the white background and horizontal spreads makes the contrasting hues all the more striking. An effective picture book for children ready to move beyond mere color labeling." Booklist

Holes and peeks. Greenwillow Bks. 1984 unp il $16; lib bdg $15.93   E

1. Size and shape—Fiction
ISBN 0-688-02537-4; 0-688-02538-2 (lib bdg)
LC 83-14128
"A sparkling, white-tiled bathroom decorated with touches of warm color provides the setting for a preschooler's view of scary holes and welcome peeks in this reassuring story of fears, pleasures and objects common to very young children." SLJ

"The crisp lines of black-and-white tile floor and the horizontally tiled white walls form a patterned expanse against which are set people and objects colored in smooth pastels and bright primary colors." Horn Book

Jonas, Ann—*Continued*

Now we can go. Greenwillow Bks. 1986 unp il $12.95; lib bdg $18   **E**

1. Toys—Fiction
ISBN 0-688-04802-1; 0-688-04803-X (lib bdg)
LC 85-12614

"The small narrator can't leave the house until he has transferred all his treasures—ball, skates, teddy, book, truck, doll—from their special box to his travel bag." N Y Times Book Rev

"A fine black line, used in conjunction with colored dyes, defines each object with precision and clarity. The colors are bright without being garish; the perspective such that the relative position of each toy in the box or bag is easily discernible. This approach adds still another dimension—predicting which object will be selected next." Horn Book

The quilt. Greenwillow Bks. 1984 unp il $16; lib bdg $15.93   **E**

1. Quilts—Fiction
ISBN 0-688-03825-5; 0-688-03826-3 (lib bdg)
LC 83-25385
Also available in paperback from Puffin Bks.

"A little girl is given a new patchwork quilt, and at bedtime she amuses herself by identifying the materials used in its making. Later, she has a colorful dream in which she almost loses her stuffed dog, Sally (a piece of Sally is in the quilt, too)." Child Book Rev Serv

"The intricate illustrations in Jonas's book can be described only in superlatives. Backed by a length of golden-yellow calico imprinted with small red flowers, a quilt fashioned from squares in a variety of colors is the prize shown to readers by a dear little girl." Publ Wkly

Reflections. Greenwillow Bks. 1987 unp il $16; lib bdg $14.93   **E**

1. Seashore—Fiction
ISBN 0-688-06140-0; 0-688-06141-9 (lib bdg)
LC 86-33545

"Imaginative book about a day at the seashore. At what is the end in most books, this book is reversed and read from back to front with re-interpreted artwork and new captions. Clever idea executed with skill, flare, and appealing, full-color illustrations. Excellent for encouraging observation and making predictions." Sci Child

Round trip. Greenwillow Bks. 1983 unp il $16; lib bdg $15.93; pa $3.95   **E**

1. Cities and towns—Fiction
ISBN 0-688-01772-X; 0-688-01781-9 (lib bdg);
0-688-09986-6 (pa) LC 82-12026

Black and white illustrations and text record the sights on a day trip to the city and back home again to the country. The trip to the city is read from front to back and the return trip, from back to front, upside down

"Although one or two pictures too easily suggest their upside-down images and the device is occasionally strained, the author-artist displays a fine sense of graphic design and balance, and pictorial beauty is never sacrificed for mere cleverness." Horn Book

Splash! Greenwillow Bks. 1995 unp il $15; lib bdg $14.93   **E**

1. Counting 2. Animals—Fiction
ISBN 0-688-11051-7; 0-688-11052-5 (lib bdg)
LC 94-4110

A little girl's turtle, fish, frogs, dog, and cat jump in and out of a backyard pond, constantly changing the answer to the question "How many are in my pond?"

"A clever concept book with physical humor and exciting acrylic paintings that capture the heat and drama of a sunny summer day." Booklist

The trek. Greenwillow Bks. 1985 unp il $14.95; lib bdg $14.88; pa $3.95   **E**

ISBN 0-688-04799-8; 0-688-04800-5 (lib bdg);
0-688-08742-6 (pa) LC 84-25962

The author-illustrator presents the story of a young girl's daydream on her way to school. Familiar objects are transformed by her imagination as the walk turns into a jungle journey where exotic animals lie in wait

"It's up to the reader to find and identify all the animals [the girl] sees lurking on a lawn, along a fence, in a grove of trees, or popping out of a fruit stand. The last two pages picture and identify all the creatures camouflaged in the illustrations, and many a viewer will be forced to flip back for further investigation of a hiding place." Bull Cent Child Books

Two bear cubs. Greenwillow Bks. 1982 unp il lib bdg $14.93   **E**

1. Bears—Fiction
ISBN 0-688-01408-9 LC 82-2860

"Two bear cubs, bent on exploration, stray from their mother in pursuit of adventure (a skunk) and wind up lost. They try their luck getting honey from a bee tree and fish from a stream, and the text repeats, 'Where is their mother?' Mother, meanwhile, appears in the background of each illustration, keeping a watchful eye on the proceedings and revealing herself in the end for a joyful reunion." SLJ

"The illustrations in Jonas's story demonstrate her unerring sense of how to use boldly contrasting colors and uncluttered shapes for maximum effect." Publ Wkly

When you were a baby. Greenwillow Bks. 1982 unp il $15; lib bdg $14.93; Puffin Bks. pa $3.95   **E**

1. Infants
ISBN 0-688-00863-1; 0-688-00864-X (lib bdg);
0-14-050574-1 (pa) LC 81-12800

This book shows, "at the beginning, a baby's plump, brown feet waving in the air above its crib . . . and, at the end, two sturdy legs in socks and shoes planted firmly, independently on the floor. In between, there's a list of all the things you couldn't do when you were a baby . . . 'But now you can't the text ends." Bull Cent Child Books

"What a nice simple book, with large primary pictures, to remind a child what it was like to be a baby." Child Book Rev Serv

Jones, Rebecca C., 1947-

Matthew and Tilly; illustrated by Beth Peck. Dutton Children's Bks. 1991 unp il $13.95   **E**

1. Friendship—Fiction
ISBN 0-525-44684-2 LC 90-3730

Also available in paperback from Puffin Bks.; Spanish language edition also available

"Living in a multicultural city neighborhood, Matthew (who's white) and Tilly (who's black) are best friends, riding bikes, playing games, and selling lemonade together. After an argument, each tries to play alone but finds it unsatisfying, so they make up and play together again." Booklist

"This is not an unfamiliar tale, but it is told here with simple eloquence and poignancy. Text and illustrations are beautifully balanced." Publ Wkly

Joosse, Barbara M., 1949-

Mama, do you love me? illustrated by Barbara Lavallee. Chronicle Bks. 1991 unp il $13.95   E

1. Mothers and daughters—Fiction 2. Inuit—Fiction
ISBN 0-87701-759-X   LC 90-1863

"A young girl asks how much her mother loves her, even when she is naughty, and receives warm, reassuring answers. The twist on this familiar theme is that the two are Inuits, and the text and pictures draw on their unique culture. . . . Two pages of back matter define and explain the functions of various terms in Inuit life past and present. Charming, vibrant watercolor illustrations expand the simple rhythmic text, adding to the characters' personalities and to the cultural information." SLJ

Nobody's cat; pictures by Marcia Sewall. HarperCollins Pubs. 1992 unp il lib bdg $14.89   E

1. Cats—Fiction
ISBN 0-06-020835-X   LC 91-37619

A starving cat who has been living in the wild seeks food and shelter for her kittens and herself by going to the home of a learning disabled boy

"Sewall's strong, plain paintings add a feeling of solidity and rightness to the story. Realistic and heartwarming." Horn Book

Joseph, Lynn

An island Christmas; illustrated by Catherine Stock. Clarion Bks. 1992 30p il $14.95   E

1. Christmas—Fiction 2. Trinidad and Tobago—Fiction
ISBN 0-395-58761-1   LC 91-16178

Rosie's preparations for Christmas on the island of Trinidad include picking red petals for the sorrel drink, mixing up the black currant cake, and singing along with the parang band

"Stock's fluent watercolors stream radiant island sunlight onto Joseph's lilting evocation of Christmas traditions in Trinidad and Tobago." Bull Cent Child Books

Jasmine's parlour day; [illustrated by] Ann Grifalconi. Lothrop, Lee & Shepard Bks. 1994 unp il $15; lib bdg $14.93   E

1. Trinidad and Tobago—Fiction
ISBN 0-688-11487-3; 0-688-11488-1 (lib bdg)

"On 'Parlour Day,' Jasmine and her mother bring their goods to the beach to sell. Jasmine and her friends run through the market at Maracas Bay, Trinidad, but she hurries back to her parlour—a food stand—just in time to help her mother. The simple story has an especially rich and satisfying setting, and, together, the text and the glowing illustrations make an exuberant package." Horn Book Guide

Joyce, William

Bently & egg; story and pictures by William Joyce. HarperCollins Pubs. 1992 unp il $15; lib bdg $14.89   E

1. Frogs—Fiction 2. Ducks—Fiction 3. Eggs—Fiction
ISBN 0-06-020385-4; 0-06-020386-2 (lib bdg)
LC 91-55499

"A Laura Geringer book"

"Bently Hopperton, a singing frog, baby-sits a duck egg for his friend Kack Kack. The egg is kidnapped, and in the process of rescuing it, Bently and the egg have a series of adventures." Child Book Rev Serv

"The illustrations, painted in the palest of springtime palettes, feature animals that are large on the page and comically expressive but rendered with a softness that is not typical of Joyce's previous work. The playful language, full-bodied and musical, is a pleasure to read aloud and will fall deliciously on the ears of eager young listeners." Horn Book

A day with Wilbur Robinson. Harper & Row 1990 unp il $14.95; lib bdg $14.89; pa $5.95   E

ISBN 0-06-022967-5; 0-06-022968-3 (lib bdg); 0-06-443339-0 (pa)   LC 90-4066

"A young narrator, going to see his best friend Wilbur, remarks, 'His house is the greatest place to visit.' Readers soon see why. Wilbur's large household includes an aunt whose train set is life-sized, an uncle who shares his 'deep thoughts' . . . and a grandfather who trains a dancing frog band. There's not much in the way of formal plot here—save a slight mystery involving Grandfather's missing false teeth—but Joyce's wonderfully strange paintings abound with hilarious, surprising details and leave the impression that a lot has happened." Publ Wkly

Dinosaur Bob and his adventures with the family Lazardo. new ed. HarperCollins Pubs. 1995 unp il music $15; lib bdg $14.89   E

1. Dinosaurs—Fiction
ISBN 0-06-021074-5; 0-06-021075-3 (lib bdg)
LC 94-19100

"A Laura Geringer book"

A revised and enlarged edition of the title first published 1988

"The Lazardo family goes on safari to Africa where they find a dinosaur. They name him Bob and take him back to Pimlico Hills. . . . Bob soon becomes famous because he can play the trumpet, dance, and most importantly play baseball." Child Book Rev Serv [review of 1988 edition]

George shrinks; story and pictures by William Joyce. Harper & Row 1985 unp il $15; lib bdg $14.89; pa $4.95   E

1. Size and shape—Fiction 2. Fantasy fiction
ISBN 0-06-023070-3; 0-06-023071-1 (lib bdg); 0-06-443129-0 (pa)   LC 83-47697

"A young boy named George awakes from his nap to discover he has become as small as a mouse. . . . Resting against the alarm clock is a piece of poster-size paper on which parental instructions are written telling George all that he should do after getting up. . . . Most of the book's text consists of this note's contents." N Y Times Book Rev

"The colorful illustrations, executed with painstaking attention to detail, create a surreal landscape from an ordinary breakfast-cereal world, as familiar objects become monumental structures through which the diminutive George moves with panache." Horn Book

Santa calls. HarperCollins Pubs. 1993 unp il $18; lib bdg $17.89   E

1. Brothers and sisters—Fiction 2. Santa Claus—Fiction 3. Christmas—Fiction
ISBN 0-06-021133-4; 0-06-021134-2 (lib bdg)
LC 92-52691

"A Laura Geringer book"

Art Aimesworth receives a mysterious summons from Santa Claus in 1908 Texas and he shares a Christmas adventure with his sister that brings them closer together

"Seasoned with contemporary expressions and illustrated with figures resembling carved wooden toys, this animated melodrama could be a year-round success." SLJ

Jukes, Mavis

I'll see you in my dreams; illustrated by Stacey Schuett. Knopf 1993 unp il $15; lib bdg $15.99 E

1. Airplanes—Fiction 2. Uncles—Fiction 3. Death—Fiction

ISBN 0-679-82690-4; 0-679-92690-9 (lib bdg)

LC 91-47605

A girl preparing to visit her seriously ill uncle in the hospital imagines being a skywriter and flying over his bed with a message of love

"Jukes looks at a sensitive subject in a fresh, innovative way, matching the experience to her audience's level of understanding. . . . Schuett has mirrored the author's simply written, touching piece with bright acrylic paintings in tones of sunset and daybreak—farewell and rebirth—orange and purple, turquoise and teal." SLJ

Kalan, Robert

Blue sea; illustrated by Donald Crews. Greenwillow Bks. 1979 unp il $14.95; lib bdg $14.93; pa $3.95 E

1. Size and shape—Fiction 2. Fishes—Fiction

ISBN 0-688-80184-6; 0-688-84184-8 (lib bdg); 0-688-11509-8 (pa) LC 78-18396

Several fishes of varying size introduce space relationships and size differences

"On a deep-blue background, the words 'blue sea' appear in a paler shade and then the first of Crews's eye-filling paintings, 'little fish,' in bright yellow. While Kalan keeps his text to an irreducible minimum, the pictures increase in color and complexity." Publ Wkly

Jump, frog, jump! pictures by Byron Barton. Greenwillow Bks. 1995 c1981 unp il $15; pa $4.95 E

1. Frogs—Fiction 2. Stories in rhyme

ISBN 0-688-13954-X; 0-688-09241-1 (pa)

Also available Spanish language edition

First published 1981

"For the frog, life in the swampy pond was hazardous in the extreme. Everyone, it seemed was out to get him—first a fish; then a snake, a turtle, a net, and finally some boys. The resourceful frog, however, had one big advantage—he was a champion jumper." Horn Book

"The excitement generated by the tale is matched by the humor in Barton's pictures. They resemble naive art but demonstrate superior skill in vibrant juxtaposition of colors and in the masterful composition that intensifies the story's momentum." SLJ

Rain; illustrated by Donald Crews. Greenwillow Bks. 1978 unp il lib. bdg $14.93; pa $3.95 E

1. Rain

ISBN 0-688-84139-2 (lib bdg); 0-688-10479-7 (pa)

LC 77-25312

Brief text and illustrations describe a rainstorm, beginning with a blue sky, yellow sun and white clouds being replaced by gray sky and rain and ending with a bright rainbow-spanned scene

Kasza, Keiko

The pigs' picnic. Putnam 1988 unp il hardcover o.p. paperback available $5.95

E

1. Pigs—Fiction 2. Animals—Fiction

ISBN 0-399-21883-1 (pa) LC 87-22691

Mr. Pig, on his way to call on Miss Pig, allows his animal friends to persuade him to don various handsome portions of their own bodies, with an alarming result

"Working in watercolor, Kasza's spacious design and well-proportioned characters make this simple tale about being oneself ideal for a young storyhour. The character's facial expressions add to the humor." Booklist

The wolf's chicken stew. Putnam 1987 unp il $15.95; pa $5.95 E

1. Wolves—Fiction 2. Chickens—Fiction

ISBN 0-399-21400-3; 0-399-22000-9 (pa)

LC 86-12303

Also available Spanish language edition

"An old plot takes a new turn after the wolf, determined to fatten a chicken for his stew, bakes goodies for her every day only to find them consumed by a horde of baby chicks who shame 'Uncle Wolf' with their adoring gratitude." Bull Cent Child Books

"Kasza combines quivery line and shaded color to turn Wolf and Chicken into scuptural forms. Landscape images are treated similarly, and produce an open, expansive feeling when placed asymmetrically, making the flimflamming refrains sound just right for such a charismatic rascal." Wilson Libr Bull

Keats, Ezra Jack, 1916-1983

Apt. 3. Macmillan 1971 unp il hardcover o.p. paperback available $4.95 E

1. City life—Fiction 2. Brothers—Fiction 3. Blind—Fiction

ISBN 0-689-71059-3 (pa)

Set in a dingy tenement house, this book describes "the encounter of two young and lonely boys with a blind musician whose beautiful music helps them learn that communication is possible through ways other than words." Wolfe. About 100 Books

"The subtle colors of Keats's paintings and his restrained use of detail to establish atmosphere make Apt. 3 a pleasure to look at, but it is less of a story than a situation picture book." Saturday Rev

Jennie's hat. Harper & Row 1985 unp il lib bdg $14.89; pa $5.95 E

1. Hats—Fiction

ISBN 0-06-023114-9 (lib bdg); 0-06-443072-3 (pa)

"Jennie is counting on a new hat from her aunt—and dreaming of its beauty. A very plain hat comes, and after unsuccessful attempts to make herself a hat, Jennie goes to church in the drab one. In the interval she has fed her friends the birds, and they save the day by flying down and trimmming the hat for her." Saturday Rev

This fantasy "has a sense of freshness, of spring, about it. Attractive, colorful pictures make most telling use of collage." Christ Sci Monit

Louie. Greenwillow Bks. 1983 c1975 unp il lib bdg $14.93 E

1. Puppets and puppet plays—Fiction

ISBN 0-688-02383-5

First published 1975

A shy, withdrawn boy loses his heart to a puppet

"This story is illustrated with the same glowing colors . . . and with some of the postercollage that is the artist's trademark. The aura is touching without being maudlin, the writing simple and informal. . . . The elements of kindness to others, imaginative play, and a fervent wish granted should have a strong appeal to the picture book audience." Sutherland. The Best in Child Books

Keats, Ezra Jack, 1916-1983—*Continued*
Other available titles about Louie are:
Louie's search (1980)
Regards to the man in the moon (1981)
The trip (1978)

The snowy day. Viking 1962 31p il lib bdg
$14.99; pa $4.99 E
1. Snow—Fiction
ISBN 0-670-65400-0 (lib bdg); 0-14-050182-7 (pa)
Also available Spanish language edition
Awarded the Caldecott Medal, 1963
A small "boy's ecstatic enjoyment of snow in the city is
shown in vibrant pictures. Peter listens to the snow crunch
under his feet, makes the first tracks in a clean patch of
snow, makes angels and a snowman. At night in his warm
bed he thinks over his adventures, and in the morning wak-
ens to the promise of another lovely snowy day." Moorachi-
an. What is a City?
Other available titles about Peter and his friends are:
Goggles (1969)
Hi, cat! (1970)
A letter to Amy (1968)
Pet show! (1972)
Peter's chair (1967)
Whistle for Willie (1964)

Keister, Douglas
Fernando's gift; El regalo de Fernando.
Sierra Club Bks. for Children 1995 32p il
$16.95 E
1. Rain forests—Fiction 2. Costa Rica—Fiction
3. Bilingual books—English-Spanish
ISBN 0-87156-414-9 LC 94-38041
One day young Fernando, who lives in the rain forest of
Costa Rica with his family, goes with his friend Carmina to
look for her favorite climbing tree only to find it cut down
"Large, crystal-clear full-color photographs and an engag-
ing first-person bilingual narrative bring this simple story to
life." SLJ

Keller, Holly
Geraldine's blanket. Greenwillow Bks. 1984
unp il $15; lib bdg $14.93; pa $3.95 E
1. Blankets—Fiction
ISBN 0-688-02539-0; 0-688-02540-4 (lib bdg);
0-688-07810-9 (pa) LC 83-14062
"Geraldine's pink blanket was a baby present from Aunt
Bessie. It's worn now and patched, and when Aunt Bessie
sends her a doll, Geraldine preserves and transfers her af-
fections simultaneously by using the scraps for a doll dress."
N Y Times Book Rev
"Simply but wonderfully expressive line drawings washed
with pastel colors capture the gentleness and humor of the
story." SLJ
Other available titles about Geraldine are:
Geraldine's baby brother (1994)
Geraldine's big snow (1988)

Grandfather's dream. Greenwillow Bks.
1994 unp il $14; lib bdg $13.93 E
1. Cranes (Birds)—Fiction 2. Grandfathers—Fiction
3. Vietnam—Fiction
ISBN 0-688-12339-2; 0-688-12340-6 (lib bdg)
LC 93-18186
After the end of the war in Vietnam, a young boy's
grandfather dreams of restoring the wetlands of the Mekong
delta, hoping that the large cranes that once lived there will

return
"Keller uses simple, direct storytelling and vivid watercolor and ink illustrations to present a complex theme in a
story of hope and rebirth." Horn Book Guide

Harry and Tuck. Greenwillow Bks. 1993
unp il $14; lib bdg $13.93 E
1. Twins—Fiction 2. School stories
ISBN 0-688-11462-8; 0-688-11463-6 (lib bdg)
LC 91-45674
Harrison and Tucker always act and think alike as they
are growing up, but when they go to kindergarten and end
up in different classrooms they start to develop differences
"The cheery, bold colors and flat, stylistic characters on
uncluttered pages suit the story, whose uplifting statement
about individuality will be sure to strike home with children, be they twins or not." Horn Book Guide

Horace. Greenwillow Bks. 1991 unp il $15;
lib bdg $14.93; pa $4.95 E
1. Adoption Fiction
ISBN 0-688-09831-2; 0-688-09832-0 (lib bdg);
0-688-11844-5 (pa) LC 90-30750
"Horace is adopted. He is also spotted, and he is loved
and cared for by his new mother and father—who are
striped. But . . . Horace feels the need to search out his
roots. And although he does find a brood that resembles
him physically, it is not a family that truly loves him. . . .
Keller . . . deals with a sensitive subject in a way that is
perceptive but not sentimental. . . . The bright, boldly colored illustrations feature a lively animal cast and numerous
amusing details." Publ Wkly

Island baby. Greenwillow Bks. 1992 unp il
$15; lib bdg $13.93; pa $4.95 E
1. Birds—Fiction 2. Caribbean region—Fiction
ISBN 0-688-10579-3; 0-688-10580-7 (lib bdg);
0-688-13617-6 (pa) LC 91-32491
Pops, a man who runs a bird hospital on a Caribbean island, and his young helper Simon nurse an injured baby flamingo back to health
"Child-pleasing paintings in vibrant tropical hues illustrate an affectionate and reassuring story. . . . Surrounded
by decorative borders containing handsomely plumed birds,
each full page of text faces a full-page illustration in watercolor and black pen that shows expressive characters amid
the lovely island landscape." Booklist

Kelley, True, 1946-
I've got chicken pox; written and illustrated
by True Kelley. Dutton Children's Bks. 1994
unp il $13.99 E
1. Chickenpox—Fiction 2. Sick—Fiction
ISBN 0-525-45185-4 LC 93-11685
When Jess gets chicken pox it seems glamorous at first,
but soon she gets tired of being stuck at home
"The text very realistically portrays the various emotional stages of chicken pox. . . . The illustrations are rendered
in bright, engaging watercolors—many have charming details. . . . Each of the illustrations has a border that reflects
the stage of Jess's progressing chicken pox. Another welcome feature is the inclusion of a 'pox fact' at the bottom
of each page, many of which answer the most commonly
asked questions of patients or parents regarding chicken
pox." Sci Books Films

Kellogg, Steven, 1941-

Aster Aardvark's alphabet adventures. Morrow 1987 unp il $15; lib bdg $14.93; pa $3.95   E

1. Alphabet 2. Animals—Fiction
ISBN 0-688-07256-9; 0-688-07257-7 (lib bdg); 0-688-11571-3 (pa)   LC 87-5715

Alliterative text and pictures present adventures of animals from A to Z

"Glowing with bright, harmonious hues, the lively, if sometimes crowded, watercolor scenes display plots, subplots, and myriad details. . . . Children will delight in this zany celebration of the sound and sense of words and will savor the sight of so many silly situations so clearly out of hand." Booklist

Best friends; story and pictures by Steven Kellogg. Dial Bks. for Young Readers 1986 unp il $14.99; lib bdg $13.89; pa $4.99   E

1. Friendship—Fiction
ISBN 0-8037-0099-7; 0-8037-0101-2 (lib bdg); 0-8037-0829-7 (pa)   LC 85-15971

Kathy feels lonely and betrayed when her best friend Louise goes away for the summer and has a wonderful time

"The watercolor and ink illustrations are appealingly bright and magical. Kathy and Louise's daydreams are vividly and flamboyantly portrayed, with 'reality' just as attractively pictured." SLJ

Can I keep him? story and pictures by Steven Kellogg. Dial Bks. for Young Readers 1971 unp il $13.99; lib bdg $12.89   E

1. Pets—Fiction
ISBN 0-8037-0988-9; 0-8037-0989-7 (lib bdg)

"Lonely Arnold wants a playmate but his mother objects to every one he suggests—grandma is allergic to cat fur, bears have a disagreeable odor, pythons shed their skins which clog the vacuum cleaner, and so on." Booklist

"Finely detailed pictures of Arnold's real and imagined pets and an amusing cummulative storyline." Libr J

Much bigger than Martin; story and pictures by Steven Kellogg. Dial Bks. for Young Readers 1976 unp il $14.99; lib bdg $11.89; pa $3.95   E

1. Brothers—Fiction
ISBN 0-8037-5809-X; 0-8037-5810-3 (lib bdg); 0-8037-5811-1 (pa)

"Henry doesn't like being Martin's little brother when he's victim in games, gets the smallest piece of cake, or finds the basketball loop too high for his shots. . . . The imagination scenes, where Henry perceives himself as a giant towering over Martin, are where Kellogg's touches of subtle humor and whimiscal detail are most effective. The black line drawings are washed in hues of gold, green, and blue." Booklist

The mysterious tadpole. Dial Bks. for Young Readers 1977 unp il $15.99; pa $4.95   E

1. Pets—Fiction
ISBN 0-8037-6245-3; 0-8037-6244-5 (pa)
                                            LC 77-71517

"Lively details in the author's full-color illustrations portray the fantastic growth and lovable behavior of a tadpole sent Louis from Loch Ness, Scotland, for his birthday." LC. Child Books, 1977

The mystery of the missing red mitten; story and pictures by Steven Kellogg. Dial Bks. for Young Readers 1974 unp il hardcover o.p. paperback available $3.50   E

ISBN 0-8037-5749-2 (pa)   LC 73-15439

"Annie loses a red mitten and sets out to search for it with her dog, Oscar. She fantasizes about the mitten's possible fate . . . and imagines planting her remaining mitten and reaping a multitude from the resultant mitten tree. Annie's search ends when what appears to be the heart of a snowman is revealed to be the missing mitten." SLJ

"Kellogg's imagination extends from a clever story to captivating black-and-white drawings with accents of red. His use of a bubble to show the little girl's thoughts is perfect." Babbling Bookworm

Pinkerton, behave! story and pictures by Steven Kellogg. Dial Bks. for Young Readers 1979 unp il $15.99; lib bdg $13.89; pa $3.95
                                                       E

1. Dogs—Fiction
ISBN 0-8037-6573-8; 0-8037-6575-4 (lib bdg); 0-8037-7250-5 (pa)   LC 78-31794

"Pinkerton is a large dog modeled after the author-artist's harlequin Great Dane. He appears to be untrainable, both at home and at obedience school. Actually, he responds consistently to commands, but when he is told to fetch, he tears the newspaper to shreds; and when he is told to get the burglar, he licks the face of the dummy he is expected to destroy. One day, when a real burglar appears, Pinkerton's small owner remembers the dog's idiosyncracies, commands him to fetch, and all ends well." SLJ

"Kellogg wittily captures expressions and movements of animal and human, wisely allowing the focal humor to emanate through the faces and action and forgoing the background detail usually found in his work." Booklist

Other available titles about Pinkerton are:
Prehistoric Pinkerton (1987)
A Rose for Pinkerton (1981)
Tallyho, Pinkerton! (1982)

Ralph's secret weapon; story and pictures by Steven Kellogg. Dial Bks. for Young Readers 1983 unp il $13.95; pa $3.95   E

1. Sea monsters—Fiction
ISBN 0-8037-7086-3; 0-8037-0307-4 (pa)
                                            LC 82-22115

"Ralph visits his zany Aunt Georgina who insists that the 4th grader learn to play the bassoon during his stay with her. He wins a snake-charming contest with his new-found musical skill, then aids the Navy in teaching a lesson to a bothersome sea serpent." Child Book Rev Serv

The author/illustrator "includes an extravaganza of detail to pore over. Line work, expanded with lively color, leads the eye, and humor electrically explodes from every picture. . . . To top it off, Kellogg fashions a most clever conclusion." Booklist

Kesey, Ken

Little Tricker, the squirrel, meets Big Double, the bear; illustrated by Barry Moser. Viking 1990 26p il $14.95; pa $4.99   E

1. Squirrels—Fiction 2. Bears—Fiction
ISBN 0-670-81136-X; 0-14-050623-3 (pa)
                                            LC 90-32362

Little Tricker the squirrel watches as Big Double the bear terrorizes the forest animals one by one, but then Little Tricker gets revenge

"It all works superbly, due in equal measure to Kesey's

Kesey, Ken—*Continued*

graceful handling of the folk idiom . . . and to Moser's evocative watercolors, which appear in rich, deep colors on the book's right-hand pages and capture both the story's humor and its sense of peril." Booklist

Kesselman, Wendy Ann

Emma; illustrated by Barbara Cooney. Doubleday 1980 unp il o.p.; Dell paperback available $5.95   E

1. Painting—Fiction 2. Old age—Fiction
ISBN 0-440-40847-4 (pa)   LC 77-15161

This book is "about a lonely grandmother named Emma, who, after her 72d birthday, began to paint pictures, starting with images of the village where she had lived as a girl. The illustrations capture Emma's personal and artistic style with charm." N Y Times Book Rev

Kessler, Leonard P., 1920-

Here comes the strikeout. newly il ed HarperCollins Pubs. 1992 64p il $14.95; lib bdg $14.89; pa $3.75   E

1. Baseball—Fiction
ISBN 0-06-023155-6; 0-06-023156-4 (lib bdg); 0-06-444011-7 (pa)   LC 91-14717

Also available Spanish language edition

"An I can read book"

A revised and newly illustrated edition of the title first published 1965

This "concerns a boy who can't hit a baseball until he follows the advice of a friend 'Lucky helmets won't do it. Lucky bats won't do it. Only hard work will do it.' . . . A winner." Booklist

Kick, pass, and run; by Leonard Kessler. Harper & Row 1966 64p il lib bdg $14.89; pa $3.50   E

1. Football—Fiction
ISBN 0-06-023160-2 (lib bdg); 0-06-444012-5 (pa)

"A Sports I can read book"

"Football rules and terms are tackled in easy-to-read, easy-to-remember terms and reinforced by the illustrated glossary that follows the comic story of animal teams imitating the Giants and the Jets." Best Books for Child, 1968

"May [also] appeal to the older reluctant reader." Hodges. Books for Elem Sch Libr

Last one in is a rotten egg; by Leonard Kessler. Harper & Row 1969 64p il lib bdg $14.89; pa $3.50   E

1. Swimming—Fiction
ISBN 0-06-023158-0 (lib bdg); 0-06-444118-0 (pa)

Also available Spanish language edition

"A Sports I can read book"

Because Freddy can't swim, he must stay in the shallow water while his friends have fun diving and racing. Support from his mother and from his friends Bobby and Willy, and lessons from Tom the lifeguard enable Freddy to overcome his fear of the water

Old Turtle's soccer team; [by] Leonard Kessler. Greenwillow Bks. 1988 47p il $14; lib bdg $13.93   E

1. Soccer—Fiction 2. Animals—Fiction
ISBN 0-688-07157-0; 0-688-07158-9 (lib bdg)   LC 87-14870

"A Greenwillow read-alone book"

Under Old Turtle's guidance, the animals learn how to play soccer and the meaning of good sportsmanship

"Brief sentences, controlled vocabulary, and illustrations reflecting the play-by-play action make this a surefire choice." Booklist

Another available title about Old Turtle is:
Old Turtle's baseball stories (1982)

Ketteman, Helen, 1945-

The year of no more corn; pictures by Robert Andrew Parker. Orchard Bks. 1993 unp il $14.95; lib bdg $14.99   E

1. Corn—Fiction 2. Grandfathers—Fiction 3. Tall tales
ISBN 0-531-05950-2; 0-531-08550-3 (lib bdg)   LC 90-29092

Beanie's grandfather tells him about the failure of the corn crop in 1928 and how he was able to make corn trees grow from whittled corn kernels

"The storytelling is as smooth and straightfacedly funny as the pen and wash art." Bull Cent Child Books

Khalsa, Dayal Kaur

Cowboy dreams. Potter 1990 unp il $16; lib bdg $18.99; pa $5.99   E

1. Cowhands—Fiction
ISBN 0-517-57490-X; 0-517-57491-8 (lib bdg); 0-517-88744-4 (pa)   LC 89-22782

"A young city girl dreams of being a cowgirl and riding horses in the Wild West. Unable to do so, the basement banister, pieces of clothesline and an old blanket become her horse and its trappings." Child Book Rev Serv

"Humorous touches are many. . . . 'Cowboy Dreams' showcases the author-illustrator's special gift for discerning and communicating what is important to children, and since this book is as much about the power of dreams and imagination as it is about the West, it will fascinate young people from coast to coast." Horn Book

How pizza came to Queens. Potter 1989 unp il $15; pa $5.99   E

1. New York (N.Y.)—Fiction
ISBN 0-517-57126-9; 0-517-88538-7 (pa)

LC 88-22452

May, of My family vacation (1988) is visiting her good friends the Penny sisters. An Italian visitor to their Queens home bemoans the unavailability of pizza until the thoughtful girls enable her to make some

"It is a straightforward little story, with bright, bold, naïve paintings. Any young pizza lover will relish it." N Y Times Book Rev

I want a dog; story and pictures by Dayal Kaur Khalsa. Potter 1987 unp il $15; pa $5.99   E

1. Dogs—Fiction
ISBN 0-517-56532-3; 0-517-88199-3 (pa)

LC 86-30329

"This is the story of a little girl [named May] who desperately wants a dog. Her parents are not too thrilled about the idea, and as a result she pretends that her roller skate is a dog instead. . . . If the plot seems minimal and somewhat static . . . the illustrations are anything but. They are beautiful, inspired, detailed, naïvely drawn and painted and extremely colorful." NY Times Book Rev

Kimmel, Eric A.

The Chanukkah guest; illustrated by Giora Carmi. Holiday House 1990 unp il $15.95; pa $5.95   E

1. Hanukkah—Fiction 2. Bears—Fiction
ISBN 0-8234-0788-8; 0-8234-0978-3 (pa)
    LC 89-20073

On the first night of Chanukkah, Old Bear wanders into Bubba Brayna's house and receives a delicious helping of potato latkes when she mistakes him for the rabbi
"In this comical story, Kimmel captures the kindness of an old woman and the innocence of a hungry bear in an unusual visit. Carmi's airy pastel illustrations shade the tale with a golden glow appropriate for the Festival of Lights." Publ Wkly

Four dollars and fifty cents; illustrated by Glen Rounds. Holiday House 1990 unp il lib bdg $14.95; pa $5.95   E

1. Cowhands—Fiction 2. West (U.S.)—Fiction
ISBN 0-8234-0817-5 (lib bdg); 0-8234-1024-2 (pa)
    LC 89-77515

Story first published in Cricket, The Magazine for Children

To avoid paying the Widow Macrae the four dollars and fifty cents he owes her, deadbeat cowboy Shorty Long plays dead and almost gets buried alive
"Rounds's outrageous, bold, line-and-crayon drawings perfectly suit the tale's Western flavor. A fast-paced, funny story." Horn Book

Hershel and the Hanukkah goblins; written by Eric A. Kimmel; illustrated by Trina Schart Hyman. Holiday House 1989 unp il $15.95; pa $6.95   E

1. Hanukkah—Fiction 2. Fairies—Fiction 3. Jews—Fiction
ISBN 0-8234-0769-1; 0-8234-1131-1 (pa)
    LC 89-1954

A Caldecott Medal honor book, 1990
"The setting is an Eastern European village, and the plot is a little like Halloween Hanukkah—it seems that goblins are occupying the synagogue on the hill. Along comes plucky Hershel of Ostropol, and he cleverly outwits the demons." N Y Times Book Rev
This "will fit companionably with haunted castle variants. Hyman is at her best with windswept landscapes, dark interiors, close portraiture, and imaginatively wicked creatures. Both art and history are charged with energy." Bull Cent Child Books

I took my frog to the library; pictures by Blanche Sims. Viking Penguin 1990 unp il $14; pa $4.99   E

1. Pets—Fiction 2. Libraries—Fiction
ISBN 0-670-82418-6; 0-14-050916-X (pa)
    LC 89-37866

"Havoc reigns when Bridgett's animal friends accompany her to the library." SLJ
"Sims plays with the inherent humor of Kimmel's brief story, painting young patrons' horror at a python shedding her skin all over the picture books or their uneasy amusement as a giraffe reads over their shoulders. Finally young Bridgett agrees to the librarian's suggestion that she come alone to the library, leaving her animal friends content at home with the elephant reading to them. A hilariously enjoyable introduction to library manners for young patrons." Booklist

Kinsey-Warnock, Natalie

The bear that heard crying; [by] Natalie Kinsey-Warnock, and Helen Kinsey; illustrated by Ted Rand. Cobblehill Bks. 1993 unp il $14.99   E

1. Survival after airplane accidents, shipwrecks, etc.—Fiction 2. Frontier and pioneer life—Fiction 3. Bears—Fiction
ISBN 0-525-65103-9   LC 91-33114

A fictionalized retelling of the true story of three-year-old Sarah Whitcher, who, in 1783, became lost in the woods of New Hampshire and was protected by a bear until her rescue four days later
"Competent writing makes a viable picture book out of the incident, while Rand's appealing watercolor illustrations bring out the drama and emotion of the story." Booklist

Kitchen, Bert

Animal alphabet. Dial Bks. for Young Readers 1984 unp il o.p. paperback available $4.95   E

1. Alphabet 2. Animals
ISBN 0-8037-0431-3 (pa)   LC 83-23929

The reader is invited to guess the identity of twenty-six unusual animals illustrating the letter of the alphabet
"Color and line are masterfully manipulated to produce a three-dimensional effect so that each animal seems to have been arrested in motion. Skillful rendering of textures provides effective contrast with the stark, glossy paper, adds visual excitement, and imbues each species with vitality, while the oversized format, allowing for generous expanses of white, is particularly suited to the elegance of the concept." Horn Book

Animal numbers. Dial Bks. 1987 unp il $12.95; pa $4.95   E

1. Counting 2. Animals
ISBN 0-8037-0459-3; 0-8037-0910-2 (pa)
    LC 87-5365

A counting book in which animals both exotic and familiar are shown with the specified number of infants
"Arranged against starkly white pages, the illustrations combine a scientific authenticity of detail with strong visual appeal. . . . A concluding page of facts about the animals gives brief information for those who would know more, but the appeal of the book lies in its pictorial representations and, as such, is a handsome addition to the number-book genre." Horn Book

Gorilla/Chinchilla and other animal rhymes. Dial Bks. 1990 unp il lib bdg $13.89   E

1. Animals 2. Stories in rhyme
ISBN 0-8037-0771-1   LC 89-16851

Rhymed text and illustrations describe a variety of animals whose names rhyme but are of very different habits and appearance
Kitchen has "produced a book overflowing with stunning, attention-demanding visuals. His realistic renderings of animals are executed with exacting attention to detail." SLJ

Kleven, Elisa

The paper princess. Dutton Children's Bks. 1994 unp il $14.99   E

1. Drawing—Fiction
ISBN 0-525-45231-1   LC 93-32612

Kleven, Elisa—*Continued*

A little girl makes a picture of a princess that comes to life and is carried off by the wind

"The jubilant, communicative collage art captivates the reader, as the winning text beguiles. A delightful reading experience." Horn Book Guide

Koontz, Robin Michal

Chicago and the cat: the camping trip; written and illustrated by Robin Michal Koontz. Cobblehill Bks. 1994 unp il $12.99
E

1. Rabbits—Fiction 2. Cats—Fiction 3. Camping—Fiction

ISBN 0-525-65137-3   LC 92-46685

"A Little chapter book"

Chicago the rabbit and her friend the cat go on a camping trip that includes hiking, river rafting, and some surprises

"Beginning readers will enjoy the enthusiastic rabbit and the reluctant feline's funny camping adventures. The cuddly characters, depicted in watercolors with pen detail, are placed effectively on the pages; the visual effect is very appealing." SLJ

Other available titles about Chicago the rabbit and his friend the cat are:

Chicago and the cat (1993)

Chicago and the cat: the Halloween party (1994)

Krasilovsky, Phyllis, 1926-

The cow who fell in the canal; illustrated by Peter Spier. Doubleday 1957 unp il o.p.; Dell paperback available $4.99
E

1. Cattle—Fiction 2. Netherlands—Fiction

ISBN 0-440-40825-3   LC 56-8236

Picture story about Hendrika, a fat cow living in Holland. Hendrika loved her master and was usually content to eat a great deal and produce rich creamy milk—though she sometimes got bored. But after she fell into the canal and floated down to the distant city on a raft she was never bored again, because she had so much to think about

The artist's "watercolor illustrations are remarkable for details lovingly recalled, panoramic scenes of town and country, and colors as fresh and clean as a newly scrubbed Dutch floor." Cincinnati Public Libr

The man who was too lazy to fix things; pictures by John Emil Cymerman. Tambourine Bks. 1992 unp il $15; lib bdg $14.93
E

1. Repairing—Fiction

ISBN 0-688-10394-4; 0-688-10395-2 (lib bdg)

LC 91-435

"A man and his cat move into a new house, but as time passes things begin to fall apart. He ignores the problems or makes do until his relatives arrive, fix everything and even make him a birthday cake." N Y Times Book Rev

"The full-page pen and ink and watercolor illustrations frame the text and portray the action. Cheery colors and expressive facial features accentuate the story's broad humor." SLJ

Kraus, Robert, 1925-

Whose mouse are you? pictures by José Aruego. Macmillan 1970 unp il $15; pa $4.95
E

1. Mice—Fiction 2. Stories in rhyme

ISBN 0-02-751190-1; 0-689-71142-5 (pa)

A lonely little mouse has to be resourceful in order to bring his family back together

"This is an absolute charmer of a picture book, original, tender, and childlike. The rhyming text is so brief, so catchy, and so right that a child will remember the words after one or two readings, and the large, uncluttered illustrations are gay and appealing." Booklist

Other available titles about the mouse and his family are:

Come out and play, little mouse (1987)

Where are you going, little mouse? (1986)

Krauss, Ruth, 1911-1993

The carrot seed; pictures by Crockett Johnson. Harper & Row 1945 unp il $13.95; lib bdg $13.89; pa $3.95
E

ISBN 0-06-023350-8; 0-06-023351-6 (lib bdg); 0-06-443210-6 (pa)

Also available Spanish language edition

Simple text and picture show how the faith of a small boy, who planted a carrot seed, was rewarded

"Crockett Johnson's pictures are perfect and the brief text is just right." Book Week

The growing story; pictures by Phyllis Rowand. Harper & Row 1947 unp il $11.95
E

1. Growth—Fiction

ISBN 0-06-023380-X

"Watching the animals and plants growing through the seasons, a little boy worries considerably about his own seeming lack of growth—until he puts on last year's clothes and sees actual proof that he too has grown. The subject, the simply written text, and the detailed, stylized pictures should prove satisfying fare for little children." Booklist

A very special house; pictures by Maurice Sendak. Harper & Row 1953 unp il $15.89; pa $4.95
E

ISBN 0-06-023456-3; 0-06-443228-9 (pa)

A Caldecott Medal honor book, 1954

"The very special house is a house which exists in the imagination of a small boy—a house where the chairs are for climbing, the walls for writing on, and the beds for jumping on; a house where a lion, a giant, or a dead mouse is welcome, and where nobody ever says stop. Told in a chanting rhythm that demands participation by the reader; the imaginary characters, objects, and doings are pictured in line drawings almost as a child would scribble them while the real little boy stands out boldly in bright blue overalls." Booklist

Krensky, Stephen, 1953-

Lionel at large; pictures by Susanna Natti. Dial Bks. for Young Readers 1986 56p il hardcover o.p. paperback available $4.95
E

1. Family life—Fiction

ISBN 0-8037-0556-5 (pa)   LC 85-15930

"Dial easy-to-read"

Krensky, Stephen, 1953— *Continued*

"Five simply written stories for the beginning independent reader are illustrated by full-color drawings, line-and-wash, that have a cheerful vitality and humor. Each story is a modest anecdote about Lionel: a visit to the doctor, a confrontation with the necessity of eating vegetables, a nervous hunt for an older sister's pet snake . . . in other words, experiences similar to those most children have. There's a quiet humor in the writing, so that readers can enjoy the joke while they are empathizing with Lionel's problems and with his success in overcoming or tolerating them." Bull Cent Child Books

Other available titles about Lionel are:

Lionel and Louise (1992)
Lionel in the fall (1987)
Lionel in the spring (1990)
Lionel in the winter (1994)

Kroll, Steven

The biggest pumpkin ever; illustrated by Jeni Bassett. Holiday House 1984 unp il $15.95   E

1. Pumpkin—Fiction 2. Halloween—Fiction 3. Mice—Fiction
ISBN 0-8234-0505-2   LC 83-18492

Also available in paperback from Scholastic

"A village mouse and a field mouse fall in love with the same pumpkin. Clayton feeds and waters it by day, while Desmond tends it at night. What a surprise when the two finally bump into each other! Whose pumpkin is it—Clayton's for the pumpkin contest, or Desmond's for a jack-o'-lantern?" Publisher's note

"The cheerful, bright watercolor illustrations are as captivating as the text. Children will delight in reading or hearing this story at any time of the year." Child Book Rev Serv

Mary McLean and the St. Patrick's Day parade; illustrated by Michael Dooling. Scholastic 1991 unp il $13.95; pa $3.95   E

1. Saint Patrick's Day—Fiction 2. Irish Americans—Fiction
ISBN 0-590-43701-1; 0-590-43702-X (pa)
                                               LC 90-37409

In order to march with Mr. Finnegan in the St. Patrick's Day Parade, Mary must find a perfect shamrock in Manhattan in the middle of winter. Set in the 1850s

"Filling each right-hand page, the expressive, full-color paintings will draw children right into the story. . . . The story would be good as a St. Patrick's Day read-aloud for primary grade children." Booklist

One tough turkey; a Thanksgiving story; illustrated by John Wallner. Holiday House 1982 unp il lib bdg $14.95   E

1. Turkeys—Fiction 2. Thanksgiving Day—Fiction
ISBN 0-8234-0457-9   LC 82-2925

"Sent by the Governor of the Pilgrim colony to hunt turkeys for the first Thanksgiving dinner, the bumbling troop of hunters is outwitted easily by the tough turkey of the title, Solomon. He, his wife Regina, and their children Alfred and Lavinia taunt and trick the hunters, putting up signs (among other ploys) that say 'NO TURKEYS! TURKEYS FLOWN SOUTH FOR THE WINTER!' or 'PILGRIMS GO HOME!' Eventually the weary hunters trudge back and decide to have squash instead of turkey, and that's why, the book ends, 'Everyone just thinks they ate turkey.'" Bull Cent Child Books

"The attractive and lively illustrations complement the story, creating a charming aberration from the usual Thanksgiving tale." Child Book Rev Serv

Santa's crash-bang Christmas; illustrated by Tomie de Paola. Holiday House 1977 unp il $14.95; pa $5.95   E

1. Santa Claus—Fiction 2. Christmas—Fiction
ISBN 0-8234-0302-5; 0-8234-0621-0 (pa)
                                               LC 77-3025

"As if Santa Claus wasn't having a hard enough time on Christmas Eve with falling out of the sleigh, on top of the fireplace ashes, into the Christmas tree, and against the hanging chandelier, he finds a misplaced polar bear in his pack and Gerald, a stowaway elf, in his sleigh. . . . De Paola extracts full measure from this amusing tale with a clumsy Santa, wide-eyed elf, and lovable polar bear. The three characters are done in red, brown, and white against gray wash until the present-strewn Christmas morning scene splashes forth in full color." Booklist

Kroll, Virginia L.

Masai and I; by Virginia Kroll; illustrations by Nancy Carpenter. Four Winds Press 1992 unp il $15   E

1. Masai (African people)—Fiction 2. African Americans—Fiction
ISBN 0-02-751165-0   LC 91-24561

Linda, a little girl who lives in the city, learns about East Africa and the Masai in school, and imagines what her life might be like if she were Masai

"The book's creative design—a Western scene on one page of each spread faces a typical Masai scene on the other—seamlessly blends corroborative colors and details." Publ Wkly

Sweet Magnolia; by Virginia Kroll; illustrated by Laura Jacques. Charlesbridge Pub. 1995 unp il $14.95; lib bdg $15.88; pa $6.95   E

1. Marshes—Fiction 2. Louisiana—Fiction
ISBN 0-88106-415-7; 0-88106-416-5 (lib bdg); 0-88106-414-9 (pa)   LC 93-11966

"Denise visits her grandmother, a wildlife rehabilitator, in the Louisiana bayou. A lush, vibrant environment is the scene for this exceptional story of generational love, cultural diversity, and ecological stewardship." Sci Child

Krudop, Walter, 1966-

Something is growing; [by] Walter Lyon Krudop. Atheneum Bks. for Young Readers 1995 ump il $15   E

1. Plants—Fiction 2. Gardening—Fiction
ISBN 0-689-31940-1   LC 94-12794

Also available Spanish language edition

This story "follows the growth of a seed Peter plants in a dirt patch in the city. The plant, Gigantus floriticus, grows everywhere, its root system infiltrating the train track, its trunk holding up traffic until finally Peter is commended for his good work." Child Book Rev Serv

"Larger-than-life acrylic paintings burst with greens, browns, and blues. Humorous details in the art will appeal to both children and adults, and perhaps lead to some reflection on city v. rain forest." SLJ

Krupinski, Loretta, 1940-

Bluewater journal; the voyage of the Sea Tiger. HarperCollins Pubs. 1995 unp il $14.95; lib bdg $14.89   E

1. Sea stories 2. Diaries—Fiction

ISBN 0-06-023436-9; 0-06-023437-7 (lib bdg)

LC 94-13241

Twelve-year-old Benjamin Slocum keeps his own journal as he travels with his family from Boston to Honolulu in the clipper ship Sea Tiger

"An engrossing, fact-filled capsule of seafaring life in 1860. . . . Authentic details . . . make the story rich and memorable. The experiences Benjamin relates are based on thorough research. . . . Rendered mostly in gouache and colored pencil, the illustrations are clear yet slightly stylized, projecting a warmly idiosyncratic vision of a vanished world." Publ Wkly

Kuskin, Karla

City dog; written and illustrated by Karla Kuskin. Clarion Bks. 1994 30p il $14.95

    E

1. Dogs—Fiction 2. Stories in rhyme

ISBN 0-395-66138-2   LC 93-8252

A rhyming tale of a city dog's first outing in the country

"Kuskin's soft-edged, sun-dappled watercolors make a spacious setting for the verses, which appear in one piece for a cohesive reading at the book's end. Words and pictures that at first glance appear naive accrue a rhythmic warmth that deepens with each runthrough." Bull Cent Child Books

The Dallas Titans get ready for bed; illustrations by Marc Simont. Harper & Row 1986 36p il hardcover o.p. paperback available $4.95   E

1. Football—Fiction

ISBN 0-06-443180-0 (pa)   LC 83-49470

"A Charlotte Zolotow book"

Follows a fictitious football team off the field, into the locker room, and to their homes, describing the normal routine after a game and examining the uniforms and pieces of equipment as they are removed

As the "players undress, Kuskin and Simont reveal an enormous amount of information about the game and gear, providing at the same time a sophisticated counting book. . . . Kuskin's text throughout is a poetic, energetic romp, and Simon's robust pictures . . . and the glorious upheaval of the locker room are a perfect match." Bull Cent Child Books

The Philharmonic gets dressed; by Karla Kuskin; illustrations by Marc Simont. Harper & Row 1982 unp il $14; lib bdg $14.89; pa $4.95   E

1. Clothing and dress 2. Orchestra

ISBN 0-06-023622-1; 0-06-023623-X (lib bdg); 0-06-443124-X (pa)   LC 81-48658

"A Charlotte Zolotow book"

"The 105 members of the orchestra (92 men and 13 women) are shown showering, dressing, traveling and setting themselves up on stage for an evening's concert." SLJ

"The vigor and humor of Simont's illustrations add vitality to a direct, simple text." Bull Cent Child Books

Lamorisse, Albert, 1922-1970

The red balloon. Doubleday 1957 c1956 unp il $16.95; pa $10.95   E

1. Balloons—Fiction 2. Paris (France)—Fiction

ISBN 0-385-00343-9; 0-385-14297-8 (pa)

Original French edition, 1956

"The chief feature of this book is the stunning photographs, many in color, which were taken during the filming of the French movie of the same name. A little French schoolboy Pascal catches a red balloon which turns out to be magic. The streets of Paris form a backdrop for a charming story and superb photographs." Libr J

Lankford, Mary D., 1932-

Is it dark? is it light? illustrated by Stacey Schuett. Knopf 1991 unp il $13; lib bdg $13.99   E

1. Moon—Fiction 2. English language—Synonyms and antonyms

ISBN 0-679-81579-1; 0-679-91579-6 (lib bdg)

LC 90-21492

While describing the moon's appearance, two children introduce pairs of opposites. The book lists the word for "moon" in 16 languages

"Beautiful, luminous illustrations, done with bold acrylics, creatively portray the pairs of opposites along with the recurring, dazzling, velvet blue sky and twinkling silver stars, perfectly complementing the simply stated text." SLJ

Lasky, Kathryn

A baby for Max, text by Kathryn Lasky; in the words of Maxwell B. Knight; photographs by Christopher G. Knight. Scribner 1984 48p il hardcover o.p. paperback available $4.95

    E

1. Infants 2. Brothers and sisters

ISBN 0-689-71118-2 (pa)   LC 84-5307

Text and photographs record a five-year-old as he awaits the birth of the family's new baby and enjoys her afterward

"Illustrated with photographs of excellent quality by the author's husband, this is a modest photodocumentary about the advent of the couple's second child, as told by five-year-old Max. The text is easy enough for beginning independent readers but so simplified in tone and concept that it seems more appropriate for the preschool child." Bull Cent Child Books

My island grandma; illustrated by Amy Schwartz. Morrow Junior Bks. 1993 unp il $15; lib bdg $14.93   E

1. Islands—Fiction 2. Grandmothers—Fiction

ISBN 0-688-07946-6; 0-688-07948-2 (lib bdg)

LC 91-31000

A revised and newly illustrated edition of the title first published 1979 by Warne

Abbey spends every summer with her parents and her grandmother on an island, where the leisurely activities include swimming in the ocean, picking blueberries, and finding the constellations

This is a "delightful intergenerational story . . . with fresh, new, brightly colored paintings." Booklist

Pond year; illustrated by Mike Bostock. Candlewick Press 1995 unp il $13.95   E

1. Ponds—Fiction 2. Friendship—Fiction

ISBN 1-56402-187-4   LC 94-14834

Lasky, Kathryn—*Continued*

Two young girls enjoy playing and exploring in the near-by pond where they discover tadpoles, insects, wildflowers in the summer, and a place to ice skate in the winter

"Laced with informative facts and brimming with Bos-tock's . . . at once exuberant and delicate watercolors, this book is both a comical salute to friendship and a field guide." Publ Wkly

Sea swan; illustrated by Catherine Stock. Macmillan 1988 unp il $14.95   **E**

1. Old age—Fiction 2. Grandmothers—Fiction
3. Swimming—Fiction
ISBN 0-02-751700-4   LC 88-1444

"Elzibah Swan lives quietly on Boston's Beacon Hill with her cat Zanzibar, her housekeeper, and her chauffeur. When her two grandchildren come for a visit she takes them to the beach and marvels at the way they swim. After they leave, she misses them, but the time on her hands prompts an amazing decision: Elzibah herself decides to learn how to swim." Booklist

"This is a quiet, pleasant story, but like Elzibah's life, filled with small surprises. . . . Her special relationship with her grandchildren through letters will strike a responsive chord in many. The book is illustrated with wonderful, warm, mostly full-page pencil plus watercolor paintings." SLJ

She's wearing a dead bird on her head! illustrated by David Catrow. Hyperion Bks. for Children 1995 unp il $14.95; lib bdg $14.89   **E**

1. Hemenway, Harriet, d. 1960—Fiction 2. Hall, Minna—Fiction 3. Birds—Protection—Fiction
ISBN 0-7868-0065-8; 0-7868-2052-7 (lib bdg)
       LC 94-18204

"Lasky tells the story of two strong-willed women who started the Audubon Society in Massachusetts around the turn of the century. When wearing dead birds as hat decora-tions became a raging fashion, Harriet Hemenway and her cousin Minna Hall were outraged. They contacted other la-dies of fashion to start a club, named it after John James Audubon and began the Bird Hat Campaign. . . . Most, but not all, of the incidents are based on actual events." SLJ

"Reflecting humorous touches in the text, the colorful ink-and-watercolor artwork pokes fun at the extremes of fashion and the haughty pretensions of society. Based on exaggeration and caricature, the broad humor is carried off in a good-natured way." Booklist

Leaf, Margaret

The eyes of the dragon; illustrated by Ed Young. Lothrop, Lee & Shepard Bks. 1987 unp il $18; lib bdg $16.93   **E**

1. Dragons—Fiction 2. Artists—Fiction 3. China—Fiction
ISBN 0-688-06155-9; 0-688-06156-7 (lib bdg)
       LC 85-11670

"This is the story of a Chinese magistrate who commis-sions a painter to decorate the new village wall with a drag-on. The painter agrees, with the stipulation that the painting be accepted unconditionally. The finished art is breathtak-ing, but, in spite of warnings, the magistrate insists the art-ist add eyes to the dragon, whereupon the dragon shakes loose from the wall and flies away in a storm." Bull Cent Child Books

"Powerfully told and touched with humor, the tale works on several levels. . . . The pictures are astonishing. Done in pastels, they are all double-page spreads vibrant with life and color." SLJ

Leaf, Munro, 1905-1976

The story of Ferdinand; illustrated by Robert Lawson. Viking 1936 unp il $13.99; pa $9.95   **E**

1. Bulls—Fiction 2. Bullfights—Fiction 3. Spain—Fiction
ISBN 0-670-67424-9; 0-14-095075-3 (pa)

Also available Spanish language edition

"Ferdinand was a peace-loving little bull who preferred smelling flowers to making a reputation for himself in the bull ring. His story is told irresistbly in pictures and few words." Wis Libr Bull

"The drawings picture not only Ferdinand but Spanish scenes and characters as well." N Y Public Libr

Lee, Jeanne M.

Silent Lotus. Farrar, Straus & Giroux 1991 unp il $14.95; pa $4.95   **E**

1. Dancing—Fiction 2. Deaf—Fiction 3. Cambodia—Fiction
ISBN 0-374-36911-9; 0-374-46646-7 (pa)
       LC 90-55141

Although she cannot speak or hear, Lotus, a young Cam-bodian girl, trains as a Khmer court dancer and becomes el-oquent in dancing out the legends of the gods

"Lee tells her story with simple, undecorated prose, care-fully balancing all the story elements. Her flat, stylized paintings are reminiscent of Far-Eastern art and do much to capture the ambiance of the ancient setting." Horn Book

Leighton, Maxinne Rhea

An Ellis Island Christmas; illustrated by Dennis Nolan. Viking 1992 31p il $15; pa $4.99   **E**

1. Immigration and emigration—Fiction 2. Polish Americans—Fiction 3. Christmas—Fiction
ISBN 0-670-83182-4; 0-14-055344-4 (pa)
       LC 91-47731

Having left Poland and braved ocean storms to join her father in America, Krysia arrives at Ellis Island on Christ-mas Eve

"Nolan's soft-textured watercolors express Krysia's bewil-derment and hope. . . . Leighton's language is quiet, and the incidents are general enough for children and those who read to them to fill in the details of their own family jour-neys." Booklist

Lessac, Frané

Caribbean alphabet. Tambourine Bks. 1994 c1989 unp il $15; lib bdg $14.93   **E**

1. Alphabet 2. Caribbean region
ISBN 0-688-12952-8; 0-688-12953-6 (lib bdg)
       LC 93-15833

First published 1989 in the United Kingdom

Presents an alphabet of images from the Caribbean, such as hibiscus, mangoes, and reggae

"Exuberant gouache paintings in tropical colors and na-ive style celebrate Caribbean culture. . . . On each page, kids will identify things they know and also find something new and exciting." Booklist

Lester, Helen
Three cheers for Tacky; illustrated by Lynn Munsinger. Houghton Mifflin 1994 32p il $13.95 E
1. Penguins—Fiction 2. Contests—Fiction 3. Cheerleading—Fiction
ISBN 0-395-66841-7 LC 93-14342
"Practicing with his classmates for a cheerleading contest, Tacky the penguin falls over his own feet, can't remember the right words, and looks simply slovenly. He finally gets it right, but, on the big day, he reverts to his usual form." Horn Book Guide
This "is a smooth, fun read. Munsinger's full-color illustrations are charming and subtle." SLJ
Another available title about Tacky is:
Tacky the penguin (1988)

Levine, Arthur A., 1962-
Pearl Moscowitz's last stand; pictures by Robert Roth. Tambourine Bks. 1993 unp il $14; lib bdg $13.93 E
1. Trees—Fiction 2. City life—Fiction
ISBN 0-688-10753-2; 0-688-10754-0 (lib bdg)
LC 91-10652
Pearl Moscowitz takes a stand when the city government tries to chop down the last ginko tree on her street
"Levine . . . details the dynamics of Pearl's urban streets as it is settled by Jewish immigrants and, later, by African Americans, Latinos and Asians. . . . Roth exaggerates the characters' proportions. . . . His animated watercolors portray the goings-on with as much humor and goodwill as does Levine's affectionate text." Publ Wkly

Levine, Ellen
I hate English! illustrated by Steve Björkman. Scholastic 1989 unp il hardcover o.p. paperback available $3.95 E
1. Chinese—United States—Fiction 2. Immigration and emigration—Fiction
ISBN 0-590-42304-5 (pa) LC 88-38265
When her family moves to New York from Hong Kong, Mei Mei finds it difficult to adjust to school and learn the alien sounds of English
"This story of cultural adjustment rings true, and Mei Mei's dilemma is strongly affecting. Her disgruntlement with English, the fun of an outing to Jones Beach, to cite two contrasting examples, are brought vividly to life by Björkman's cartoon-style illustrations (watercolor with pen-and-ink outline)." Publ Wkly

Levinson, Nancy Smiler, 1938-
Snowshoe Thompson; pictures by Joan Sandin. HarperCollins Pubs. 1992 64p il map $14; lib bdg $13.89; pa $3.75 E
1. Thompson, Snowshoe—Fiction 2. Postal service—Fiction 3. Frontier and pioneer life—Fiction 4. Skiing—Fiction
ISBN 0-06-023801-1; 0-06-023802-X (lib bdg); 0-06-444206-3 (pa) LC 90-37401
"An I can read book"
One winter John Thompson skis across the Sierra Nevada Mountains and creates a path upon which mail and people may travel, thus earning his nickname "Snowshoe Thompson"
"Based on a real Gold Rush hero, Levinson's story is a satisfying blend of heartache . . . and action. . . . Sandin's

paintings amplify the contrasts between the warm browns of cozy, wood-stove interiors and the gray-white sweep of snow and mountains." Bull Cent Child Books

Levinson, Riki
I go with my family to Grandma's; illustrated by Diane Goode. Dutton 1986 unp il hardcover o.p. paperback available $3.95 E
1. Grandmothers—Fiction 2. Family life—Fiction 3. Transportation—Fiction 4. New York (N.Y.)—Fiction
ISBN 0-525-44557-9 (pa) LC 86-4490
Also available in paperback from Puffin Bks.
As five cousins and their families arrive by various means of transportation, Grandma's home in Brooklyn gets livelier and livelier
"With an exceptional elegance of design, each of the five family groups is shown at home, en route, and then being welcomed by the relatives who have already arrived at Grandma's. The warm, pastel-colored drawings are jam-packed with the most humorous details as each family is hugged, admired, fed, and retrieved from under tables and out of tree branches. . . . The details in the illustrations will be a source of endless fascination to the child reading the book and to the adult lucky enough to share it." Horn Book

Our home is the sea; paintings by Dennis Luzak. Dutton 1988 unp il $13.95 E
1. Hong Kong—Fiction
ISBN 0-525-44406-8 LC 87-36419
Also available in paperback from Puffin Bks.
A Chinese boy hurries home from school to his family's houseboat in Hong Kong harbor. It is the end of the school year, and he is anxious to join his father and grandfather in their family profession, fishing
The book shows "the universality of children's interests and concerns. Here the never-named child moves with curiosity and perceptual acuteness through the city scene to the warmth and security of home and family." Bull Cent Child Books

Watch the stars come out; illustrated by Diane Goode. Dutton 1985 unp il $15 E
1. Immigration and emigration—Fiction
ISBN 0-525-44205-7 LC 84-28672
Also available in paperback from Puffin Bks.; Spanish language edition also available
Grandma tells about her mama's journey to America by boat, years ago
"Because the story doesn't actually pinpoint the nationality or religion of its characters, it could be read as a portrait of any number of immigrant groups that streamed into this country between the 1880's and 1920's. . . . Diane Goode's beautiful, dreamlike paintings with their charmingly expressive figures manage to capture—even for the very young—the depth and emotion of the immigrant experience." N Y Times Book Rev

Levy, Elizabeth, 1942-
Something queer is going on (a mystery); illustrated by Mordicai Gerstein. Delacorte Press 1973 unp il hardcover o.p. paperback available $3.50 E
1. Mystery fiction
ISBN 0-440-47974-6 (pa)
Also available in hardcover from P. Smith
"Jill arrives home to find her dog Fletcher missing; armed with sets of identifying pictures of Fletcher from all

Levy, Elizabeth, 1942-—*Continued*

angles, she and friend Gwen conduct a house-to-house search. The finger of guilt points to television commercial producer Fiedler Fernbach, who denies knowing Fletcher before he has even seen the dog's picture. The next day the girls, accompanied by Jill's mother, follow Fernbach to his television studio where they find Fletcher on camera for a dog food commercial. For the youngest fans a patly plausible story with zany illustrations." Booklist

Other available titles in this mystery series are:
Something queer at the ball park (1975)
Something queer at the birthday party (1990)
Something queer at the haunted school (1982)
Something queer at the lemonade stand (1982)
Something queer at the library (1977)
Something queer at the scary movie (1995)
Something queer in outer space (1993)
Something queer in the cafeteria (1994)
Something queer on vacation (1980)

Lewin, Betsy, 1937-

Booby hatch. Clarion Bks. 1995 32p il $14.95   **E**

1. Birds—Fiction 2. Galapagos Islands—Fiction
ISBN 0-395-68703-9   LC 94-19309

Pépe, a young blue-footed booby, is born on a tiny island and grows until he is old enough to mate and help create a new little booby

"Although the tone is more leisurely than dramatic, the narrative is totally satisfying. . . . Lewin's watercolor landscapes are spare and evocative." SLJ

Lewin, Hugh, 1939-

Jafta; story by Hugh Lewin; pictures by Lisa Kopper. Carolrhoda Bks. 1983 c1981 unp il lib bdg $15.95; pa $4.95   **E**

1. Animals—Fiction 2. South Africa—Fiction
ISBN 0-87614-207-2 (lib bdg); 0-87614-494-6 (pa)
     LC 82-12847

First published 1981 in the United Kingdom

"A small boy in South Africa, Jafta, says 'When I'm happy I purr like a lion cub, or skip like a spider, or laugh like a hyena. And sometimes I want to jump like an impala, and dance like a zebra . . .' and so on. . . . The illustrations have no background clutter, showing only the attractive brown child and the appealing animals." Bull Cent Child Books

Other available titles about Jafta are:
Jafta and the wedding (1983)
Jafta—the homecoming (1994)
Jafta—the journey (1984)
Jafta—the town (1984)
Jafta's father (1983)
Jafta's mother (1983)

Lewin, Ted, 1935-

Amazon boy; written and illustrated by Ted Lewin. Macmillan 1993 unp il $14.95   **E**

1. Environmental protection—Fiction 2. Brazil—Fiction 3. Amazon River Valley—Fiction
ISBN 0-02-757383-4   LC 92-15798

As a Brazilian boy makes his first trip up the Amazon to the port city of Belém, he learns something about the river's many treasures

"Lewin's paintings are spread across double pages in energetic scenes set against softly rendered, verdant backgrounds. An attractive and thought-provoking portrait of a way of life." Horn Book Guide

Lewis, J. Patrick

The moonbow of Mr. B. Bones; illustrated by Dirk Zimmer. Knopf 1992 unp il $16; lib bdg $16.99   **E**

1. Peddlers and peddling—Fiction
ISBN 0-394-85365-2; 0-394-95365-7 (lib bdg)
     LC 88-37107

A new boy in a small mountain village tries to discredit the old peddler who sells magic jars of sundrops, moonbows, and the like; but though he drives the old man away, something remarkable does happen in the sky

"Lewis tells the story with a lilting, colloquial rhythm. . . . Zimmer's illustrations, in pen and color with detailed cross-hatching, depict the characters in boisterous, comic-book style." Booklist

Lewison, Wendy Cheyette

Going to sleep on the farm; pictures by Juan Wijngaard. Dial Bks. for Young Readers 1992 unp il $14.99; lib bdg $13.89   **E**

1. Animals—Fiction 2. Sleep—Fiction 3. Stories in rhyme
ISBN 0-8037-1096-8; 0-8037-1097-6 (lib bdg)
     LC 91-3737

"A small boy in pajamas, playing with toy farm animals, asks his dad how animals sleep. One by one, the father explains how the cow, the duck, the horse, the pig, and the hen sleep, and, finally, how his (now dozing) son snuggles down in his nice warm bed. The simple text, with its repetition and rhyme, works well, but the real strength of the book is the large color paintings, which capture a farm from various perspectives as an animal comes into focus. . . . The artist's sense of detail and viewpoint result in a cozy book that begs to be shared at bedtime." Booklist

Lexau, Joan M.

Come here, cat; by Joan L. Nødset; pictures by Steven Kellogg. HarperCollins Pubs. 1993 c1973 unp il $10; lib bdg $9.89   **E**

1. Cats—Fiction
ISBN 0-06-024557-3; 0-06-024558-1 (lib bdg)
     LC 92-39005

A reissue of the title first published 1973

"By trial and error, a young girl and a cat discover how to treat each other—no tail-pulling, no biting—and a friendship is born. Nodset's gentle text is well matched with Kellogg's pictures of the persistent and affectionate pair." Horn Book Guide

Go away, dog; by Joan L. Nødset; pictures by Crosby Bonsall. HarperCollins Pubs. 1993 c1963 unp il $10; lib bdg $9.89   **E**

1. Dogs—Fiction
ISBN 0-06-024555-7; 0-06-024556-5 (lib bdg)

A reissue of the title first published 1963

"A boy who dislikes dogs undergoes a change of heart when a four-legged present from his uncle charms him with its waggish ways. . . . The small-sized book's simple text and expressive art remain appealing." Horn Book Guide

The rooftop mystery; pictures by Syd Hoff. Harper & Row 1968 64p il lib bdg $13.89   **E**

1. African Americans—Fiction 2. Mystery fiction
ISBN 0-06-023865-8

"An I can read mystery"

Lexau, Joan M.—*Continued*

"Sam and Albert are helping Sam's family move to another home within walking distance; unfortunately Sam finds any distance too long in which he can be seen in public carrying his sister's large, conspicuous doll." Sutherland. The Best in Child Books

"The cartoon illustrations show the children to be both blacks and whites." N Y Public Libr. Black Exper in Child Books

Who took the farmer's [hat]? [by] Joan L. Nodset; pictures by Fritz Siebel. Harper & Row 1963 unp il lib bdg $14.89; pa $5.95

E

1. Animals—Fiction
ISBN 0-06-024566-2 (lib bdg); 0-06-443174-6 (pa)

"Away flew the farmer's hat. In his search for it he found that his hat could be many things to many animals including, most permanently, a bird's nest." Publ Wkly

Lillie, Patricia

Everything has a place; pictures by Nancy Tafuri. Greenwillow Bks. 1993 unp il $14; lib bdg $13.93

E

ISBN 0-688-10082-1; 0-688-10083-X (lib bdg)

LC 90-23497

Text and pictures assign a cow to a barn, a dish to a cupboard, a family to a house, and other things to their place

"This is one of those rare gems to use with the toddler just beginning to bring order to a bewildering world. The text is simplicity itself. . . . The parallel constructions have a rhythmic, soothing effect extended by Tafuri's glowing, stylized illustrations." Horn Book Guide

Lindbergh, Reeve

Benjamin's barn; paintings by Susan Jeffers. Dial Bks. for Young Readers 1990 unp il $13.95

E

1. Barns—Fiction 2. Farm life—Fiction 3. Stories in rhyme
ISBN 0-8037-0613-8

LC 88-23690

Also available in paperback from Puffin Bks.

"One rainy spring day, a small boy named Benjamin sets off for his big red barn, where he spends hours with the flesh-and-blood animals of the farm and the exotic creatures of his imagination. . . . The rhyming text has a comforting circular flow, well-suited to Benjamin's flight of fancy and subsequent return to reality. Jeffers' lifelike illustrations enhance the theme, lending as much reality to the leathery texture of a pterodactyl's wing as to the downy softness of goose feathers." SLJ

The day the goose got loose; pictures by Steven Kellogg. Dial Bks. for Young Readers 1990 unp il $14.99; lib bdg $12.89

E

1. Animals—Fiction 2. Stories in rhyme
ISBN 0-8037-0408-9; 0-8037-0409-7 (lib bdg)

LC 87-28959

Also available in paperback from Puffin Bks.

The day the goose gets loose, havoc reigns at the farm as all the animals react

"The line-and-watercolor pictures are active and humorous; they are as out of control as the story, spilling into the margins of each page. The young narrator of the rhyme has the last word, setting herself loose with the goose in a wild and wonderful dream; at the end they both come home to roost in a cozy bed, sleepy and smiling." Horn Book

Linden, Anne Marie

One smiling grandma; a Caribbean counting book; illustrated by Lynne Russell. Dial Bks. for Young Readers 1992 unp il o.p.; Puffin Bks. paperback available $4.99

E

1. Counting 2. Stories in rhyme 3. Caribbean region
ISBN 0-14-055341-X (pa)

LC 91-30826

Introduces the numbers one to ten as a young girl describes various sights on her Caribbean island

"The bright, borderless paintings present lush views of the tropical landscape; images seem to spill off the book's vibrant pages. Colors and shapes offer a rich texture filled with the warmth and light of the setting. The spare text sways with a lilting cadence and imaginative use of language." Publ Wkly

Lindgren, Astrid, 1907-

The Tomten; adapted by Astrid Lindgren from a poem by Viktor Rydberg; illustrated by Harald Wiberg. Coward-McCann 1961 unp il $15.95; pa $5.95

E

1. Winter—Fiction 2. Fairy tales
ISBN 0-698-20147-7; 0-689-20680-0 (pa)

"Snowy farm pictures and warm scenes inside barn, sheds, and house show the Tomten, a little Swedish troll, going quietly about to the animals on cold winter nights comforting them with the promise that spring will come. The text was adapted from a nineteenth-century poem by Viktor Rydberg, and the pictures are by an outstanding Swedish painter of animals and nature. An unusual and beautiful picture book." Horn Book

Another available title about the Tomten is:
The Tomten and the fox (1966)

Lindgren, Barbro, 1937-

Sam's car; illustrated by Eva Eriksson. Morrow 1982 unp il $6.95

E

1. Toys—Fiction
ISBN 0-688-01263-9

LC 82-3437

Also available Spanish language edition

When Sam and Lisa fight over Sam's red car, Sam's mother resolves the conflict by providing another car

"There is but one simple sentence per page, and the facing illustrations portray precisely what the words convey. The language and situations are totally childlike; the pictures are endearing. These are sure to be welcomed by the youngest listeners." Child Book Rev Serv

Other available titles about Sam are:
Sam's ball (1983)
Sam's bath (1983)
Sam's cookie (1982)
Sam's potty (1986)
Sam's teddy bear (1982)
Sam's wagon (1986)

The wild baby; pictures by Eva Eriksson; adapted from the Swedish by Jack Prelutsky. Greenwillow Bks. 1981 unp il lib bdg $15.93

E

1. Mothers and sons—Fiction 2. Stories in rhyme
ISBN 0-688-00601-9

LC 81-2151

"The story of baby Ben: always where he shouldn't be, never where he should. He sleeps in the clock and the chandelier, swims in the sink and wanders off at every opportunity. Things tend to get broken around Ben, but Mama loves him dearly." SLJ

"The Swedish text has been adapted into rhythmic

Lindgren, Barbro, 1937—_Continued_

rhymed nonsense verse accompanying a series of lightly caricatured water-color illustrations detailed in pen and ink. The effect is broadly humorous to complement the mood of the situations and reflect the nature of the young protagonist." Horn Book

Another available title about Baby Ben and his mother is: The wild baby gets a puppy (1988)

Lionni, Leo, 1910-

Alexander and the wind-up mouse. Pantheon Bks. 1970 c1969 unp il $15; lib bdg $15.99 **E**

1. Mice—Fiction

ISBN 0-394-80914-9; 0-394-90914-3 (lib bdg)

A Caldecott Medal honor book, 1970

"Alexander wants to be a wind-up mouse like Willie, who is the little girl's favorite toy. A magic lizard can change him, but then he learns that Willie's key is broken and decides to turn Willie into a real mouse like himself." Adventuring With Books. 2d edition

The author's "collage illustrations are dazzling in their color and bold design and contribute to a beautiful and appealing picture book." Booklist

The biggest house in the world. Pantheon Bks. 1968 unp il lib bdg $14.99; pa $4.99 **E**

1. Snails—Fiction

ISBN 0-394-90944-5 (lib bdg); 0-394-82740-6 (pa)

"In this picture book a small snail has a very large wish. He wants the largest house in the world. But by telling the youngster a story, his wise father helps him to see the impracticality of being encased in a magnificent monstrosity too big to move." Book Week

A color of his own. Knopf 1993 c1975 unp il $8.99; lib bdg $9.99 **E**

1. Chameleons—Fiction 2. Color—Fiction

ISBN 0-679-84197-0; 0-679-94197-5 (lib bdg)

A reissue of the title first published 1975 by Pantheon

"When a young chameleon grows tired of constantly changing color, he decides to sit on a leaf and stay green forever. But even the leaf changes color in the fall. After he meets another chameleon and makes a friend, he learns to accept himself. Lionni's simple print illustrations work well with the short text to achieve a satisfying whole." Horn Book Guide

An extraordinary egg. Knopf 1994 unp il $16; lib bdg $16.99 **E**

1. Frogs—Fiction 2. Alligators—Fiction 3. Friendship—Fiction

ISBN 0-679-85840-7; 0-679-95840-1 (lib bdg)

LC 93-28565

Jessica the frog befriends an alligator that hatches from an egg she brought home, thinking it is a chicken

"Lionni's understated text perfectly complements his signature illustrations, which are a skillful combination of collage, crayon, and watercolors." SLJ

Fish is fish. Pantheon Bks. 1970 unp il lib bdg $13.99; pa $5.99 **E**

1. Frogs—Fiction 2. Fishes—Fiction

ISBN 0-394-90440-0 (lib bdg); 0-394-82799-6 (pa)

The frog tells the fish all about the world above the sea. The fish, however, can only visualize it in terms of fishpeople, fish-birds and fish-cows

"The story is slight but pleasantly and simply told, the illustrations are page-filling, deft, colorful, and amusing." Bull Cent Child Books

Frederick. Pantheon Bks. 1967 unp il $17; lib bdg $16.99; pa $4.99 **E**

1. Mice—Fiction

ISBN 0-394-81040-6; 0-394-91040-0 (lib bdg); 0-394-82614-0 (pa)

Also available Spanish language edition

A Caldecott Medal honor book, 1968

"While other mice are gathering food for the winter, Frederick seems to daydream the summer away. When dreary winter comes, it is Frederick the poet-mouse who warms his friends and cheers them with his words." Wis Libr Bull

"This captivating book . . . sings a hymn of praise to poets in a gentle story that is illustrated with gaiety and charm." Saturday Rev

Inch by inch. Astor-Honor 1960 unp il $10.95 **E**

1. Worms—Fiction 2. Birds—Fiction

ISBN 0-8392-3010-9

Also available in paperback from Mulberry Bks.; French language and Spanish language editions also available

A Caldecott Medal honor book, 1961

This is a "small tale about an inchworm who liked to measure the robin's tail, the flamingo's neck, the whole of a hummingbird but not a nightingale's song." Christ Sci Monit

"This is a book to look at again and again. The semiabstract forms are sharply defined, clean and strong, the colors subtle and glowing, and the grassy world of the inchworm is a special place of enchantment." N Y Times Book Rev

It's mine! Knopf 1986 c1985 unp il $15; lib bdg $15.99 **E**

1. Frogs—Fiction

ISBN 0-394-87000-X; 0-394-97000-4 (lib bdg)

LC 85-190

Original German edition, 1985

"Three childlike frogs spend their days bickering and baiting each other: It's mine, claims one about the water. Another purports ownership of the earth—or a worm—or a butterfly—or whatever. It isn't until disaster almost strikes and they are saved by a toad that Milton, Rupert and Lydia realize that private ownership isn't that important. . . . Collages of marbled-textured paper, all in cool, crisp, springlike colors against a stark white background, are a perfect match for this story of selfishness on the pond." SLJ

Little blue and little yellow; a story for Pippo and Ann and other children. Astor-Honor 1959 unp il $10.95 **E**

1. Color—Fiction

ISBN 0-8392-3018-4

Also available in paperback from Mulberry Bks.

The author uses "splashes of color and abstract forms to tell the story of little blue and his friend little yellow who hugged and hugged each other until they were green—and unrecognizable to their parents." Booklist

"So well are the dots handled on the pages that little blue and little yellow and their parents seem to have real personalities. It should inspire interesting color play and is a very original picture book by an artist." N Y Her Trib Books

Lionni, Leo, 1910-—*Continued*

Matthew's dream. Knopf 1991 unp il hardcover o.p. paperback available $4.99

E

1. Mice—Fiction 2. Artists—Fiction
ISBN 0-679-87318-X (pa)   LC 90-34242
Also available Spanish language edition
A visit to an art museum inspires a young mouse named Matthew to become a painter
"Lionni brings his own joyful shapes and colors into play here. . . . The text is direct yet abundantly meaningful—poetic without becoming sappy." Publ Wkly

Swimmy. Pantheon Bks. c1963 unp il $16; lib bdg $15.99; pa $5.99

E

1. Fishes—Fiction
ISBN 0-394-81713-3; 0-394-91713-8 (lib bdg); 0-394-82620-5 (pa)
Also available Spanish language edition
A Caldecott Medal honor book, 1964
"Swimmy, an insignificant fish, escapes when a whole school of small fish are swallowed by a larger one. As he swims away from danger he meets many wonderful, colorful creatures and later saves another school of fish from the jaws of the enemy." Ont Libr Rev
"To illustrate his clever, but very brief story, Leo Lionni has made a book of astonishingly beautiful pictures, full of undulating, watery nuances of shape, pattern, and color." Horn Book

Lobel, Anita, 1934-

Alison's zinnia. Greenwillow Bks. 1990 unp il $16; lib bdg $15.93

E

1. Flowers—Fiction 2. Alphabet
ISBN 0-688-08865-1; 0-688-08866-X (lib bdg)
LC 89-23700
"More than two dozen little girls, a full alphabet of them, pick flowers for their friends: 'Alison acquired an Amaryllis for Beryl' and 'Nancy noticed a Narcissus for Olga' and so on till 'Zena zeroed in on a Zinnia for Alison.' Underneath each large handsome floral illustration is a smaller picture of the named child and her flower. Charming." N Y Times Book Rev

Away from home. Greenwillow Bks. 1994 unp il $16; lib bdg $15.93

E

1. Travel—Fiction 2. Alphabet
ISBN 0-688-10354-5; 0-688-10355-3 (lib bdg)
LC 93-36521
Proceeds through the alphabet using boys' names and the names of exotic places in alliterative fashion
"Lobel's watercolor and gouache art is lavish, comic, and joyful; and the handsome book design, with a group of kids looking up at the stage and applauding the show, makes clear that each page is a changing stage set." Booklist

Lobel, Arnold

Frog and Toad are friends. Harper & Row 1970 64p il $14.95; lib bdg $14.89; pa $3.75

E

1. Frogs—Fiction 2. Toads—Fiction
ISBN 0-06-023957-3; 0-06-023958-1 (lib bdg); 0-06-444020-6 (pa)
Also available Spanish language edition
A Caldecott Medal honor book, 1971
"An I can read book"

Here are five stories . . . which recount the adventures of two best friends—Toad and Frog. The stories are: Spring; The story; A lost button; A swim; The letter
The stories are told "with humor and perception. Illustrations in soft green and brown enhance the smooth flowing and sensitive story." SLJ
Other available titles about Frog and Toad are:
Days with Frog and Toad (1979)
Frog and Toad all year (1976)
Frog and Toad together (1972)

Grasshopper on the road. Harper & Row 1978 62p il lib bdg $14.89; pa $3.50

E

1. Locusts—Fiction 2. Animals—Fiction
ISBN 0-06-023962-X (lib bdg); 0-06-444094-X (pa)
LC 77-25653
"An I can read book"
"Grasshopper's journey is divided into six chapters. In each chapter he meets a different animal or animals attending to a spectrum of tasks. The chapters weave a tale of habit—doing without questioning. Grasshopper gives his need-for-change reaction to each one, but only a worm in his apple home is open to change." Child Book Rev Serv
"The contemporary version of the fable of the ant and the grasshopper is told in a repetitive I-Can-Read text and extended in three-color illustrations which delicately capture the grasshopper's microcosmic world view." Horn Book

Ming Lo moves the mountain; written and illustrated by Arnold Lobel. Greenwillow Bks. 1982 unp il lib bdg $15.93; pa $4.95

E

1. Mountains—Fiction 2. Houses—Fiction
ISBN 0-688-00611-6 (lib bdg); 0-688-10995-0 (pa)
LC 81-13327
"Ming Lo and his wife love their house, but not the mountain that overshadows it. So, at his wife's bidding, Ming Lo undertakes to move the mountain by following the advice of a wise man." Child Book Rev Serv
"An original tale utilizing folkloric motifs, the book is Chinese-like rather than Chinese, for the artist has created an imagined landscape. The setting, shown in flowing lines and tones of delicate watercolors, provides a source of inspiration drawn from an ancient artistic tradition; particularly effective in conveying a sense of distance are the panoramic double-page spreads." Horn Book

Mouse soup. Harper & Row 1977 63p il $14.95; lib bdg $13.89; pa $3.50

E

1. Mice—Fiction
ISBN 0-06-023967-0; 0-06-023968-9 (lib bdg); 0-06-444041-9 (pa)   LC 76-41517
Also available Spanish language edition
"An I can read book"
"In an effort to save himself from a weasel's stew pot, a little mouse tells the weasel four separate stories." West Coast Rev Books
"An artistic triumph with enough suspense, humor and wisdom to hold any reader who has a trace of curiosity and compassion. . . . The little one triumphs over the big one, and every child will rejoice. The exquisite wash drawings in mousey shades of grays, blues, greens and golds, have enough humor and pathos to exact repeated scrutiny. Like the stories, they improve with each reading." N Y Times Book Rev

Mouse tales. Harper & Row 1972 61p il $14.95; lib bdg $14.89; pa $3.50

E

1. Mice—Fiction
ISBN 0-06-023941-7; 0-06-023942-5 (lib bdg); 0-06-444013-3 (pa)
Also available Spanish language edition

Lobel, Arnold—*Continued*

"An I can read book"

Papa Mouse tells seven bedtime stories, one for each of his sons

Contents: The wishing well; Clouds; Very tall mouse and very short mouse; The mouse and the winds; The journey; The odd mouse; The bath

"The illustrations have soft colors and precise, lively little drawings of the imaginative and humorous events in the stories. The themes are familiar to children: cloud shapes, wishing, a tall and a short friend who observe—and greet—natural phenomena on a walk, taking a bath, et cetera." Bull Cent Child Books

On Market Street; pictures by Anita Lobel; words by Arnold Lobel. Greenwillow Bks. 1981 c1980 unp il $16; lib bdg $15.93; pa $4.95　　　　　　　　E

1. Shopping—Fiction 2. Alphabet 3. Stories in rhyme

ISBN 0-688-80309-1; 0-688-84309-3 (lib bdg); 0-688-08745-0 (pa)　　　　　　　LC 80-21418

A Caldecott Medal honor book, 1982

In this "alphabet book, a boy trots down Market Street buying presents for a friend, each one starting with a letter of the alphabet. Every letter is illustrated by a figure . . . composed of, for instance, apples or wigs or quilts or Xmas trees." Horn Book

"The artist has adapted the style of old French trade engravings, infusing it with a wonderful sense of color and detail. . . . Arnold Lobel's words ring of old rhymes, but it is these intricate, lovely drawings that take the day, and truly make it brighter." N Y Times Book Rev

On the day Peter Stuyvesant sailed into town. Harper & Row 1971 unp il hardcover o.p. paperback available $5.95　　　　　　E

1. Stuyvesant, Peter, 1592-1672—Fiction 2. New York (N.Y.)—History—Fiction 3. Stories in rhyme

ISBN 0-06-443144-4 (pa)

This is the "story of Peter Stuyvesant who, arriving in New Amsterdam in 1647, found the whole dirty place a total disgrace, and angrily set the Dutchmen to work transforming the village into a pleasant place in which to live." Booklist

"The illustrations, many framed like Dutch tiles, are done in yellow and blue and have a rhythm and humor that complement the verse exactly. The double-page spread at the end of the book—showing the future of Peter's tidy city—provides an unexpected shock of recognition." Horn Book

Owl at home. Harper & Row 1982 64p il lib bdg $14.89; pa $3.50　　　　　　E

1. Owls—Fiction

ISBN 0-06-023949-2 (lib bdg); 0-06-444034-6 (pa)

Also available Spanish language edition

"An I can read book"

Five stories describe the adventures of a lovably foolish owl

"A child reader or listener in a kind of one-upmanship over wide-eyed tufted Owl will bristle with anxiety to have him perceive what causes two bewildering bumps under the blanket at the foot of his bed. The best scope for Lobel's inventiveness in drawing is, however, the opening episode where 'poor old' Winter makes a pushy entry into Owl's home. Muted browns and greys are countered by an animation that fully reveals Owl's distresses and contentments." Wash Post Child Book World

The rose in my garden; pictures by Anita Lobel. Greenwillow Bks. 1984 unp il $16; lib bdg $15.93; pa $4.95　　　　　　E

1. Flowers—Fiction 2. Stories in rhyme

ISBN 0-688-02586-2; 0-688-02587-0 (lib bdg); 0-688-12265-5 (pa)　　　　　　LC 83-14097

"A cumulative poem tells of a lovely garden, starting with 'this is the rose in my garden,' continuing through the lilies, bluebells, daisies, and other flowers, and culminating with a cat chasing a field mouse. A bee on the rose awakens and stings the cat, thus allowing the mouse to escape, and the text ends with the opening lines." Horn Book

"Lovely to look at, and enjoyable for reading aloud." Bull Cent Child Books

Small pig; story and pictures by Arnold Lobel. Harper & Row 1969 63p il lib bdg $14.89; pa $3.75　　　　　　E

1. Pigs—Fiction

ISBN 0-06-023932-8 (lib bdg); 0-06-444120-2 (pa)

"An I can read book"

This "is the story of a pig who, finding the clean farm unbearable, runs away to look for mud—and ends up stuck in cement. His facial expressions alone are worth the price of the book; the illustrations, in blue, green, and gold, are a perfect complement to the story. Humor, adventure, and short, simple sentences provide a real treat for beginning readers." SLJ

A treeful of pigs; pictures by Anita Lobel. Greenwillow Bks. 1979 unp il $16; lib bdg $15.93　　　　　　E

1. Pigs—Fiction 2. Farm life—Fiction

ISBN 0-688-80177-3; 0-688-84177-5 (lib bdg)
　　　　　　LC 78-1810

Also available in paperback from Scholastic

A "story about a farmer's wife who tries everything to pry her lazy husband out of bed. He says he'll come to help her when the pigs grow on trees, fall from the sky, or 'bloom in the garden like flowers.' His wife knows how to work magic, and she makes each one of them happen with the help of a cooperative brood of piglets." Child Book Rev Serv

"The framed, full-color illustrations, characterized by intricately detailed designs in costumes and setting, are as elaborate as the diction is simple. The total effect, however, is one of unity, for the two are combined into a true picture book in which words and illustrations are interdependent." Horn Book

Uncle Elephant. Harper & Row 1981 62p il $14; lib bdg $14.89; pa $3.75　　　　　　E

1. Elephants—Fiction 2. Uncles—Fiction

ISBN 0-06-023979-4; 0-06-023980-8 (lib bdg); 0-06-444104-0 (pa)　　　　　　LC 80-8944

"An I can read book"

Uncle Elephant takes care of his nephew whose parents are lost at sea. This book describes the way they lived together until the parents are rescued and little elephant rejoins them

"Nine gentle stories for the beginning independent reader; the soft grey, peach, and green tones of the deft pictures are an appropriate echo of the mood." Bull Cent Child Books

Locker, Thomas, 1937-
The land of Gray Wolf. Dial Bks. 1991 unp
il $16.99; lib bdg $15.89　　　　　E
1. Indians of North America—Fiction 2. Human
influence on nature—Fiction 3. Conservation of natural
resources—Fiction
ISBN 0-8037-0936-6; 0-8037-0937-4 (lib bdg)
　　　　　　　　　　　　　　　LC 90-3915
Also available in paperback from NAL/Dutton
Running Deer and his fellow tribesmen take special care
of their land until they lose it to invading white settlers,
who wear it out and leave it to recover on its own
"Magnificent illustrations enhance this poignant story of
Native Americans and the tragic experience they had at the
hands of early settlers." Sci Child

The mare on the hill. Dial Bks. for Young
Readers 1985 unp il $15.89　　　　　E
1. Horses—Fiction
ISBN 0-8037-0208-6　　　　　　LC 85-1684
Also available in paperback from Puffin Bks.
Grandfather brings home a fearful mare to breed, hoping
that his grandsons can teach her to trust people again
"Locker tells a solid story, in a minimum of well-chosen
words. . . . Each event is printed on the reader's mind by
Locker's ineffable paintings of the matchless terrain of the
Hudson River Valley. The artist's rich colors emphasize
changes wrought by the four seasons in the country, largely
undisturbed by 'progress,' where people live in harmony
with nature." Publ Wkly

Sailing with the wind. Dial Bks. for Young
Readers 1986 unp il lib bdg $14.89　　　　E
1. Sailing—Fiction 2. Uncles—Fiction
ISBN 0-8037-0312-0　　　　　　LC 85-23381
Also available in paperback from Puffin Bks.
"A young girl's uncle, a sailor who has been around the
world, comes to visit. He arrives by sailboat, having come
up the river from the port, where his ship has docked. Ever
since his niece was small, Uncle Jack has promised her a
sailboat trip to the ocean, and now that promise is about to
be fulfilled. Their day begins at dawn; they share a picnic
lunch, weather a storm, and then sail back home beneath a
red-and-yellow sky." Booklist
"Besides painting exquisite Constable-esque country
scenes, Mr. Locker carefully chooses a particular rhythm of
Nature to illustrate the passage of time and to provide his
palette with the full spectrum of color, light and shadow.
What makes his books so spectacularly successful is the harmonious marriage of textual theme and Nature's theme."
Child Book Rev Serv

Where the river begins. Dial Bks. for Young
Readers 1984 unp il $16.95; lib bdg $14.89
　　　　　　　　　　　　　　　E
1. Grandfathers—Fiction　　2. Camping—Fiction
3. Rivers—Fiction
ISBN 0-8037-0089-X; 0-8037-0090-3 (lib bdg)
　　　　　　　　　　　　　　　LC 84-1709
Also available in paperback from Puffin Bks.
"Two young boys journey with their grandfather to find
the beginning of the river that flows by their house. In full-
page landscape paintings and simple prose, Thomas Locker
follows the journey." Sci Child
"Admittedly, the simple narrative text is overshadowed
by the magnificence of its illustrations. But their limpid
beauty and exquisite detail are—to paraphrase Emerson—
their own excuse for being. Reminiscent of the work of
great landscape painters like Turner, Constable, and the
American George Inness, the paintings follow not only the
course of the river but the nearly three-day journey of the
old man and the boys." Horn Book

Loh, Morag Jeanette, 1935-
Tucking Mommy in; by Morag Loh;
illustrated by Donna Rawlins. Orchard Bks.
1988 c1987 unp il $14.95; lib bdg $12.99; pa
$5.95　　　　　　　　　　　　　　E
1. Sisters—Fiction 2. Mothers and daughters—Fiction
3. Sleep—Fiction
ISBN 0-531-05740-2; 0-531-08340-3 (lib bdg);
0-531-07025-5 (pa)　　　　　　LC 87-16740
First published 1987 in Australia
Two sisters tuck their mother into bed one evening when
she is especially tired
"The amusing turnabout on standard bedtime routines is
a sweet reflection of the spontaneous love and generosity
children sometimes show. Rawlins' pictures depict a raven-
haired family at ease with each other's company. Her scenes
show an eye for the dishevelment that follows children's
footsteps, and the warm, sunny colors that dominate add to
the story's good vibrations." Booklist

Lomas Garza, Carmen
Family pictures; paintings by Carmen
Lomas Garza; stories by Carneb Lomas Garza;
as told to Harriet Rohmer; version in Spanish,
Rosalma Zubizarreta. Children's Bk. Press
1990 30p il lib bdg $14.95; pa $6.95　　　E
1. Hispanic Americans—Fiction 2. Bilingual books—
English-Spanish
ISBN 0-89239-050-6 (lib. bdg.); 0-89239-108-1 (pa)
　　　　　　　　　　　　　　　LC 89-27845
Text in English and Spanish
The author describes her experiences growing up in a
Hispanic community in Texas
"An inspired celebration of American cultural diversity.
. . . The English text is simple and reads smoothly, but it
is Zubizarreta's Spanish rendition that has real verve and
style. From the exquisite cut-paper images on the text
pages, to the brilliant paintings, to the strong family bonds
expressed in the text, Family Pictures/Cuadros de familia is
a visual feast, and an aural delight." SLJ

London, Jonathan, 1947-
Froggy learns to swim; illustrated by Frank
Remkiewicz. Viking 1995 unp il $12.99
　　　　　　　　　　　　　　　E
1. Swimming—Fiction 2. Frogs—Fiction
ISBN 0-670-85551-0　　　　　　LC 94-43077
Froggy is afraid of the water until his mother, along with
his flippers, snorkle, and mask, help him learn to swim
"Vivid watercolor cartoons add the humor, showing the
comical facial expressions and hilarious beachwear. Froggy's
childlike dialogue and the sound words—'zook! zik!'; 'flop
flop . . . splash!'—make this story a wonderful read-aloud."
SLJ
Other available titles about Froggy are:
Froggy gets dressed (1992)
Let's go, Froggy! (1994)

Lord, John Vernon, 1939-
The giant jam sandwich; story and pictures
by John Vernon Lord, with verses by Janet
Burroway. Houghton Mifflin 1973 c1972 32p
il lib bdg $16.95; pa $4.95　　　　　　E
1. Wasps—Fiction 2. Stories in rhyme
ISBN 0-395-16033-2 (lib bdg); 0-395-44237-0 (pa)
First published 1972 in the United Kingdom

Lord, John Vernon, 1939-—*Continued*

This is a story in rhymed verse "about the citizens of Itching Down, who, attacked by four million wasps, make a giant jam sandwich to attract and trap the insects. With dump truck, spades, and hoes the people spread butter and strawberry jam across an enormous slice of bread; then, when the wasps settle, they drop the other slice from five helicopters and a flying tractor." Booklist

"Highly amusing in the details of John Vernon Lord's illustrations. . . . The figures are deliciously grotesque, their expressions wickedly accurate and the colours cheerfully vivid." Jr Bookshelf

Low, Joseph, 1911-

Mice twice; story & pictures by Joseph Low. Atheneum Pubs. 1980 unp il hardcover o.p. paperback available $4.95   E

1. Animals—Fiction
ISBN 0-689-71060-7 (pa)   LC 79-23274

A Caldecott Medal honor book, 1981

"A Margaret K. McElderry book"

"Mouse asks to bring a friend when Cat invites her to dinner, and while Cat licks his whiskers at the thought of more than one mouse, Mouse has in mind her friend Dog. And so begins a round of very hospitable and polite dinners with a slightly more outrageous friend brought along every night." SLJ

"Wit triumphant is the motif of an original tale which combines an elegantly crafted text with colorful illustrations." Horn Book

Lowery, Linda

Twist with a burger, jitter with a bug; illustrated by Pat Dypold. Houghton Mifflin 1994 unp il $14.95   E

1. Dancing 2. Stories in rhyme
ISBN 0-395-67022-5   LC 93-38236

"Bold, brash cut-paper collages in bright neon colors illustrate an exuberant rhyme about music and dance—all kinds of dance, from polka and mambo to jitterbug, waltz, and ballet. The pages bounce with play and movement." Booklist

Luenn, Nancy, 1954-

Nessa's fish; illustrated by Neil Waldman. Atheneum Pubs. 1990 unp il $14.95   E

1. Inuit—Fiction 2. Grandmothers—Fiction
ISBN 0-689-31477-9   LC 89-15048

Also available Spanish language edition

"Nessa, an Inuit girl, and her grandmother go on an ice-fishing expedition. When Grandmother falls ill, Nessa uses her wits, her courage, and the remembered advice of her father and her grandfather to defend their catch from a fox, a pack of wolves, and a bear. Luminous watercolor paintings set the action within a remarkable variety of land- and snowscapes seen in the same place at different times of the day and night. . . . Well designed, the book invites readers to linger over its many striking visual images." Booklist

Another available title about Nessa is:
Nessa's story (1994)

Lyon, George Ella, 1949-

A B Cedar; an alphabet of trees; designed and illustrated by Tom Parker. Orchard Bks. 1989 unp il lib bdg $14.99   E

1. Alphabet 2. Trees
ISBN 0-395-08395-0   LC 88-22797

"A Richard Jackson book"

"Here is a grove of trees alphabetically arranged—aspen, butternut, cedar to xolisma, yew and zebrawood. The trees are in silhouette and in proportion to cavorting human beings on the bottom of each page. The leaves and seeds are in larger, fixed scale across the pages." N Y Times Book Rev

"Easily the basis for a nature lesson, this will intrigue children usually considered too old for alphabet books. The art is cleanly executed." Booklist

Cecil's story; paintings by Peter Catalanotto. Orchard Bks. 1991 unp il $15.95; lib bdg $15.99; pa $5.95   E

1. United States—History—1861-1865, Civil War—Fiction
ISBN 0-531-05912-X; 0-531-08512-0 (lib bdg); 0-531-07063-8 (pa)   LC 90-7775

"A Richard Jackson book"

A boy thinks about the possible scenarios that exist for him at home if his father goes off to fight in the Civil War

"The trauma of separation is sensitively explored . . . in this evocative picture book. . . . Each page has a simple line or two of text, complemented dramatically by double-page watercolor paintings of extraordinary quality." SLJ

Come a tide; story by George Ella Lyon; pictures by Stephen Gammell. Orchard Bks. 1990 unp il $15.95; lib bdg $15.99; pa $5.95   E

1. Floods—Fiction 2. Country life—Fiction
ISBN 0-531-05854-9; 0-531-08454-X (lib bdg); 0-531-07036-0 (pa)   LC 89-35650

"A Richard Jackson book"

"'It'll come a tide,' says Grandma after a four-day deluge. She's right: as the streams and creeks rush down the hill to the river, the water rises, sending residents of the hollows packing. The narrator's family hightails it up the hill to Grandma's house." Booklist

"Capturing the diction and homely imagery of a down-to-earth rural community, the first-person text richly evokes the sturdy qualities of folks who, beset by spring floods, respond to nature's challenges with common sense and wry humor. . . . In combination with Stephen Gammell's energetic illustrations, remarkable for their expressive lines and elegant use of watercolor, it becomes an exemplary picture story book, regional in setting but universal in appeal." Horn Book

Dreamplace; paintings by Peter Catalanotto. Orchard Bks. 1993 unp il $15.95; lib bdg $15.99   E

1. Pueblo Indians—Fiction
ISBN 0-531-05466-7; 0-531-08616-X (lib bdg)   LC 92-25102

"A Richard Jackson book"

Present-day visitors describe what they see when they visit the pueblos where the Anasazi lived long ago

"Simple and direct, Lyon's poetic text sketches the main ideas, while the illustrations define and defy places, people, and times. . . . Rich with atmosphere, delicate with sensitivity, and dreamlike in its evocation of dual realities, this would be an imaginative choice to read before a class trip to any historic site." Booklist

Lyon, George Ella, 1949—*Continued*

Mama is a miner; story by George Ella Lyon; paintings by Peter Catalanotto. Orchard Bks. 1994 unp il $15.95; lib bdg $15.99

E

1. Mothers and daughters—Fiction 2. Miners—Fiction
ISBN 0-531-06853-6; 0-531-08703-4 (lib bdg)

LC 93-49398

"A Richard Jackson book"

"Mama is a coal miner in Appalachia. From the warmth of the family kitchen, a child thinks about her mother's job, and words and pictures set the worlds of home and work side by side. . . . Children will hear the poetry that leaps from the particulars of the workplace, both in the child's simple narrative and in the miners' rhymes. . . . Catalanotto's double-page-spread watercolors focus on the loving bond between the child and her mother, when they're together in the light-filled house, and when they're thinking of each other above and below ground." Booklist

Who came down that road? story by George Ella Lyon; paintings by Peter Catalanotto. Orchard Bks. 1992 unp il $15.95; lib bdg $15.99; pa $5.95

E

1. Roads—Fiction
ISBN 0-531-05987-1; 0-531-08587-2 (lib bdg); 0-531-07073-5 (pa)

LC 91-20742

"A Richard Jackson book"

Mother and child ponder the past in discussing who might have traveled down an old, old road, looking backwards from pioneer settlers all the way to prehistoric animals

"The spare and elegant text creates a poetic yet childlike mood. . . . Catalanotto's double-page watercolor paintings, which make extensive use of light and shadow for dramatic effect, are dreamy, romanticized representations of each scenario." SLJ

Macaulay, David, 1946-

Black and white. Houghton Mifflin 1990 unp il $14.95

E

ISBN 0-395-52151-3

LC 89-28888

Awarded the Caldecott Medal, 1990

Four brief "stories" about parents, trains, and cows, or is it really all one story? The author recommends careful inspection of words and pictures to both minimize and enhance confusion

"The magic of *Black and White* comes not from each story, . . . but from the mysterious interactions between them that creates a fifth story. . . . Eventually, the stories begin to merge into a surrealistic tale spanning several levels of reality. . . . *Black and White* challenges the reader to use text and pictures in unexpected ways." Publ Wkly

Shortcut. Houghton Mifflin 1995 unp il $15.95

E

ISBN 0-395-52436-9

LC 95-2542

"This picture book concerns six humans whose paths cross and recross in the eight chapters of brief text and distinctive artwork. Albert and his horse, June, take their wagon of melons to market, sell them, and go home. . . . Patty's pet pig, Pearl, wanders onto an abandoned railroad line. . . . Professor Tweet is studying birds when suddenly his hot air balloon breaks free and heads toward a nearby cathedral spire. . . . Seemingly inconsequential details in one story become the moving forces in another." Booklist

"Because *Shortcut* is not linear in its progression but rather an exploration of simultaneity and concepts of time and space, it is a picture book for sophisticated readers who

enjoy puzzles and unraveling clues. . . . David Macaulay deserves applause for challenging his readers as well as entertaining them through boldly conceived illustrations with a cast of wonderfully caricatured characters." Horn Book

Why the chicken crossed the road. Houghton Mifflin 1987 31p il lib bdg $13.95; pa $6.95

E

ISBN 0-395-44241-9 (lib bdg); 0-395-58411-6 (pa)

LC 87-2908

"A ridiculous chicken sets off a circular story involving a herd of cows, a bridge, a train, a robber, the fire department and some hydrangeas. Chaos. The illustrations are suitably wild—painted with brilliant color and almost palpable energy." N Y Times Book Rev

Macdonald, Suse, 1940-

Alphabatics. Bradbury Press 1986 unp il $16.95; pa $6.95

E

1. Alphabet
ISBN 0-02-761520-0; 0-689-71625-7 (pa)

LC 85-31429

A Caldecott Medal honor book, 1987

MacDonald "maneuvers each letter to create a visual image as well as an object that begins with that letter." Child Book Rev Serv

The "*A* tilts, flops over, and literally becomes an ark as it turns itself around. An *N* turns over, glides up a tree trunk, and becomes a nest for three young birds. Crisp, fresh, and totally effective, it's a unique way of looking at the alphabet. This is a book for creative thinking and sheer enjoyment of MacDonald's precise graphics, rather than for object identification among the very young." SLJ

Sea shapes. Harcourt Brace & Co. 1994 unp il $13.95

E

1. Size and shape 2. Marine animals
ISBN 0-15-200027-5

LC 93-27957

"Gulliver books"

"Each double-page spread is devoted to a different shape. On each left-hand page, a sequence of simple pictures shows a basic shape evolving into the shape of a marine animal. The opposite page pictures the animal in the sea. The brightly colored paper collages make it easy to follow along as the sea animal develops. The shapes chosen go beyond the ordinary to include, for example, a fan shape, a diamond, a crescent, and a hexagon. MacDonald uses the three final pages to present some information about each animal." Booklist

MacLachlan, Patricia

All the places to love; paintings by Mike Wimmer. HarperCollins Pubs. 1994 unp il $15; lib bdg $14.89

E

1. Farm life—Fiction 2. Family life—Fiction
ISBN 0-06-021098-2; 0-06-021099-0 (lib bdg)

LC 92-794

A young boy describes the favorite places that he shares with his family on his grandparents' farm and in the nearby countryside

Wimmer's "paintings beautifully convey the splendor of nature, as well as the deep affection binding three generations. This inspired pairing of words and art is a timeless, uplifting portrait of rural family life." Publ Wkly

MacLachlan, Patricia—*Continued*

Mama One, Mama Two; pictures by Ruth Lercher Bornstein. Harper & Row 1982 unp il $13; lib bdg $14.89   E

1. Foster home care—Fiction 2. Mothers and daughters—Fiction 3. Mental illness—Fiction
ISBN 0-06-024081-4; 0-06-024082-2 (lib bdg)
               LC 81-47795

"When Maudie is awakened by the baby's crying, her foster mother tells her the story of how she came to live in this temporary home. Together they describe the girl's mother's increasingly withdrawn behavior that led to the institutionalization of the girl's 'Mama One' and her subsequent placement with Katherine, whom she calls 'Mama Two.' They discuss Maudie's feelings and her hopes for her mother's quick recovery. This articulation of her fears calms the troubled child." SLJ

"Softly-crayoned pastel pictures, simply and tenderly composed and nicely fitting the mood of the story, show the love that is the mortar of the text." Bull Cent Child Books

Three Names; pictures by Alexander Pertzoff. Harper & Row 1991 31p il lib bdg $14.89; pa $4.95   E

1. Grandfathers—Fiction 2. Dogs—Fiction 3. Frontier and pioneer life—Fiction
ISBN 0-06-024036-9 (lib bdg); 0-06-443360-9 (pa)
               LC 90-4444

"A Charlotte Zolotow book"

Great-grandfather reminisces about going to school on the prairie with his dog Three Names

"A rhythmic text, remarkable for subtle, exact imagery and complemented by luminous, impressionistic watercolors." Horn Book

Maestro, Betsy, 1944-

Delivery van; words for town and country; [by] Betsy and Giulio Maestro. Clarion Bks. 1990 unp il $14.95   E

1. Vocabulary 2. Country life
ISBN 0-395-51119-4   LC 89-23992

The reader is introduced to typical town and country words such as "roadside stand," "village," "dairy farm," and "marina" as a delivery van and its woman driver travel through a busy workday

"Maestro's watercolor illustrations are colorful and detailed, with white space skillfully used to give the book a fresh, uncluttered look. . . . A visually appealing and useful introduction to town and country." SLJ

Ferryboat; by Betsy and Giulio Maestro. Crowell 1986 unp il map lib bdg $14.89
      E

1. Boats and boating—Fiction
ISBN 0-690-04520-4   LC 85-47887

A family crosses the Connecticut River on a ferryboat and observes how the ferry operates

Illustrated with "sunny watercolor paintings in realistically detailed double-page spreads. . . . Children who are familiar with the procedure should enjoy this recreation of their experience, and others may be intrigued. . . . An appended note gives historical information about the ferry on which the book is based, the Chester-Hadlyme Ferry, which began operating in 1769." Bull Cent Child Books

Snow day; illustrated by Giulio Maestro. Scholastic 1989 unp il hardcover o.p. paperback available $4.95   E

1. Snow—Fiction
ISBN 0-590-46083-8 (pa)   LC 88-19480

Text and illustrations describe what happens after a major snowstorm, from plowing driveways and rescuing stranded motorists to clearing train tracks, airports, and harbors

"The charcoal-and-wash drawings, which nicely carry forth the mood, are realistic in style, in contrast to the bright, slick colors and cartoonlike drawings seen in much of Maestro's other work. An unpretentious wintertime choice." Booklist

Taxi; a book of city words; by Betsy & Giulio Maestro. Clarion Bks. 1989 unp il lib bdg $14.95; pa $5.95   E

1. Vocabulary 2. City life
ISBN 0-89919-528-8 (lib bdg); 0-395-54811-X (pa)
               LC 88-22867

"A taxi moves through a city in the course of an ordinary day. The text describes what happens in the action-oriented pictures. The best illustrations strive to capture a quality of urban motion and lively urban streets." N Y Times Book Rev

Mahy, Margaret

17 kings and 42 elephants; pictures by Patricia MacCarthy. Dial Bks. for Young Readers 1987 26p il $15.99; pa $4.95   E

1. Animals—Fiction 2. Stories in rhyme
ISBN 0-8037-0458-5; 0-8037-0781-9 (pa)
               LC 87-5311

A newly illustrated edition of the title first published 1972 in the United Kingdom

Seventeen kings and forty-two elephants romp with a variety of jungle animals during their mysterious journey through a wild, wet night

"This book takes you on a jungle journey you will never forget. . . . The text is lyrical, humorous, and full of nonsense and fantasy. Children and adults will be charmed by the melodic use of language and the beautiful batik illustrations." Child Book Rev Serv

The boy who was followed home; pictures by Steven Kellogg. Dial Bks. for Young Readers 1986 c1975 unp il $14.99; pa $4.95
      E

1. Hippopotamus—Fiction 2. Witches—Fiction
ISBN 0-8037-0286-8; 0-8037-0903-4 (pa)
First published 1975 by Franklin Watts

In this "story, Robert, for some unexplained reason, is adopted by a growing number of hippopotami. His parents are most patient with the situation until the number of hippos reaches twenty-seven. Robert's father calls in the services of a local witch to rid the boy of his rapidly growing horde of friends." Child Book Rev Serv

"Swathes of lemon yellow and pinkish lavender are balanced with lots of clean white space and fine line work. The artist's sense of the absurd has made connections with an author's experience in what appeals to children." Booklist

The dragon of an ordinary family; pictures by Helen Oxenbury. Dial Bks. for Young Readers 1992 unp il $14   E

1. Dragons—Fiction
ISBN 0-8037-1062-3   LC 91-2513

Mahy, Margaret—*Continued*

A reissue of the title first published 1969 by Watts

When Mr. Belsaki chooses a dragon as a pet for his son, what was a very ordinary family begins some extraordinary adventures

"This is vintage Mahy, with her witty juxtaposition of wild magic and domestic order. Oxenbury's exuberant, swirling illustrations, dense with color and cross-hatching, reveal the incipient chaos bursting the bonds of a 'very ordinary' family home on a very ordinary street." Booklist

The great white man-eating shark; a cautionary tale; pictures by Jonathan Allen. Dial Bks. for Young Readers 1990 unp il $13.99   E

1. Sharks—Fiction

ISBN 0-8037-0749-5   LC 89-1514

Also available in paperback from Puffin Bks.

Greedy to have the cove where he swims all to himself, Norvin, who looks a bit like a shark, pretends to be one, scaring off the other swimmers and leaving him in happy aquatic solitude—until he is discovered by an amorous female shark

"Mahy's amusing tongue-in-cheek tale meets its match in Allen's droll drawings. Norvin's wonderfully shifty eyes and the vivid expressions on the faces of his victims are certain to tickle funnybones." Publ Wkly

Keeping house; illustrated by Wendy Smith. Margaret K. McElderry Bks. 1991 unp il $13.95   E

ISBN 0-689-50515-9   LC 90-37591

Ashamed to let the housekeeper, Robin Puckertucker, see how untidy her house has become, Lizzie Firkin cleans it herself

"Mahy's eccentric story-telling style and Smith's ramblingly explicit drawings are a perfect match." Publ Wkly

Making friends; illustrated by Wendy Smith. Margaret K. McElderry Bks. 1990 unp il $13.95   E

1. Dogs—Fiction 2. Friendship—Fiction

ISBN 0-689-50498-5   LC 89-13246

Small Mrs. de Vere's large dog Titania and large Mr. Derry's small dog Oberon serve as the instruments that bring their masters together in an unexpected but quite successful friendship

"The illustrations are a perfect match for the humor and affection for the nice old couple that suffuse the text." Horn Book

The pumpkin man and the crafty creeper; illustrated by Helen Craig. Lothrop, Lee & Shepard Bks. 1990 unp il $14.95; lib bdg $14.88   E

1. Plants—Fiction

ISBN 0-688-10347-2; 0-688-10348-0 (lib bdg)

LC 90-40401

A bossy and demanding plant insists on going home with Mr. Parkin, who usually only tends quiet pumpkins, and from that moment his peaceful existence is changed

"A humorous and intriguing story that is both gentle and satisfying. . . . Craig's watercolors are restrained but expressive." SLJ

The rattlebang picnic; pictures by Steven Kellogg. Dial Bks. for Young Readers 1994 unp il $14.99; lib bdg $14.89   E

1. Family life—Fiction 2. Automobiles—Fiction

ISBN 0-8037-1318-5; 0-8037-1319-3 (lib bdg)

LC 93-36294

The McTavishes, their seven children, and Granny McTavish take their old rattlebang of a car on a picnic up Mt. Fogg and have an exciting adventure

"An original tall tale with an outrageously bizarre plot. . . . . Only Mahy could concoct a story about an overcooked pizza saving a family from rivers of hot lava. Her writing is vivid, funny, and full of details that will be dear to a child's heart. And Kellogg's watercolors are a perfect match, adding to the air of deadpan chaos." SLJ

Manushkin, Fran

Latkes and applesauce; a Hanukkah story; illustrated by Robin Spowart. Scholastic 1990 unp il $12.95; pa $4.95   E

1. Hanukkah—Fiction 2. Jews—Fiction

ISBN 0-590-42261-8; 0-590-42265-0 (pa)

LC 88-38916

When a blizzard leaves a family housebound one Hanukkah, they share what little food they have with a stray kitten and dog

"To their surprise and delight, the dog digs in the snow and unearths some potatoes, and the kitten has to be rescued from a tree that still has apples on its branches. . . . The two new pets are named Latke and Applesauce. The dark, slightly impressionistic illustrations in warm tones capture the feeling of a time past and of a family that has an abundance of affection. The story of the holiday, a recipe for latkes, instructions for the dreidel game, and the names of a few other books about the holiday are appended." Horn Book

The matzah that Papa brought home; illustrated by Ned Bittinger. Scholastic 1995 unp il $14.95   E

1. Jews—Fiction 2. Passover—Fiction 3. Stories in rhyme

ISBN 0-590-47146-5   LC 94-9952

A cumulative rhyme in the style of "The House That Jack Built" describes the traditions connected to a family's celebration of the Passover seder

"While the text is well done and great fun, the illustrations, rendered in oils, are stellar. Each masterful painting has a subtext. The family members are constantly moving or gesturing. . . . Three pages at the end tell the story of Passover. A unique, lively offering." SLJ

Peeping and sleeping; illustrated by Jennifer Plecas. Clarion Bks. 1994 31p il $14.95   E

1. Frogs—Fiction 2. Night—Fiction 3. Fathers and sons—Fiction

ISBN 0-395-64339-2   LC 93-26297

Barry and his father take an evening walk, exploring the strange peeping sounds they hear and finding a surprise down at the pond

"Gently effervescent sound effects of the peepers peeping and plopping and hopping punctuate the mild story, and the pastel and colored-pencil illustrations have lots of nighttime mystery made safe by Daddy's comfortable presence and the lemony glow of the flashlight's beam." Bull Cent Child Books

Maris, Ron

Is anyone home? Greenwillow Bks. 1985 unp il lib bdg $16   **E**

ISBN 0-688-05899-X   LC 85-5436

"Every other page is a half-page door to open. The first half-page is a garden gate to be opened (turned) by the reader. The next door opens to the hen house. The doors lead the reader to the last door which is the door to grandma's house where she is waiting for you to come in and visit. The art work is well done and very colorful. A good book to read aloud, one which lends itself to creative writing as well." Okla State Dept of Educ

Marshall, Edward, 1942-1992

Fox and his friends; pictures by James Marshall. Dial Bks. for Young Readers 1982 56p il hardcover o.p. paperback available $4.95   **E**

1. Foxes—Fiction
ISBN 0-8037-2668-6 (pa)   LC 81-68769

Also available in paperback from Puffin Bks.; Spanish language edition also available

"Dial easy-to-read"

"Fox has one objective—having fun with his motley group of friends. Unfortunately, his desires regularly conflict with his mother's insistence that he care for his younger sister Louise or with his responsibilities when assigned to traffic patrol." Horn Book

"The sibling exchanges and situations are comically true to life, as is Fox's duty/pleasure conflict. The red, green and black illustrations, showing a defiant Louise, a beleaguered Fox, a wonderful assortment of creature friends and a hilariously feeble group of old hounds pick the story up and add character embellishment and humor." SLJ

Other available titles about Fox are:
Fox all week (1984)
Fox at school (1983)
Fox in love (1982)
Fox on wheels (1983)
Other available titles about Fox written by the author using the name James Marshall are:
Fox be nimble (1990)
Fox on stage (1993)
Fox on the job (1988)
Fox outfoxed (1992)

Space case; pictures by James Marshall. Dial Bks. for Young Readers 1980 unp il $14.99; lib bdg $12.89   **E**

1. Science fiction 2. Halloween—Fiction
ISBN 0-8037-8005-2; 0-8037-8007-9 (lib bdg)   LC 80-13369

Also available in paperback from Puffin Bks.

"The 'thing'—a neon yellow robot-like creature from space—arrives on Halloween for a look around and is promptly mistaken for a costumed trick-or-treater. It spends the night with a friendly child . . . visits at school (the teacher takes it for a science project) and leaves promising to return for the next fun holiday, Christmas." SLJ

"The open ending of the brief story is as satisfying as it is original, for the small space traveler is thoroughly childlike in its insouciance, curiosity, and concern for self-gratification. The text is an economical, tongue-in-cheek accompaniment to the various levels of humor depicted in the illustrations." Horn Book

Another available title in this series written by the author using the name James Marshall is:
Merry Christmas, space case (1986)

Three by the sea; pictures by James Marshall. Dial Bks. for Young Readers 1981 48p il lib bdg $12.89   **E**

ISBN 0-8037-8687-5

Also available in paperback from Puffin Bks.

"Dial easy-to-read"

"When Lolly, on a beach picnic with friends Sam and Spider, reads a story ('The rat saw the cat and the dog.') aloud, it is rated dull. So Sam uses the same rat and cat characters to tell one of his own, and Spider tops Sam's managing to scare the other two with his tale of a monster that passes by the rat and cat to find some tasty kids." SLJ

"The mild lunacy of the illustrations (an almost vertical hill, a neatly striped cat) with their ungainly, comical figures is nicely matched with the bland directness of the writing. This is good-humored and amusing." Bull Cent Child Books

Another available title about Spider, Sam, and Lolly is:
Four on the shore (1985)
Another available title about Spider, Sam, and Lolly written by the author using the name James Marshall is:
Three up a tree (1986)

Marshall, James, 1942-1992

The cut-ups. Viking Kestrel 1984 unp il lib bdg $14.99; pa $4.99   **E**

ISBN 0-670-25195-X (lib bdg); 0-14-050637-3 (pa)   LC 84-40256

Practical jokers Spud and Joe get away with every trick in the book until the day they meet a little girl named Mary Frances Hooley

"This book may not show the subtle wit of Marshall at his best . . . but it is good-humored fun that will certainly entice readers and listeners." SLJ

Other available titles about Spud and Joe are:
The cut-ups at Camp Custer (1989)
The cut-ups carry on (1990)
The cut-ups crack up (1992)
The cut-ups cut loose (1987)

George and Martha; written and illustrated by James Marshall. Houghton Mifflin 1972 46p il lib bdg $14.95; pa $4.95   **E**

1. Hippopotamus—Fiction 2. Friendship—Fiction
ISBN 0-395-16619-5 (lib bdg); 0-395-19972-7 (pa)

In these five short episodes which include a misunderstanding about split pea soup, invasion of privacy and a crisis over a missing tooth, two not very delicate hippopotamuses reveal various aspects of friendship

"The pale pictures of these creatures and their adventures—in yellows, pinks, greens, and grays—capture the directness and humor of the stories." Horn Book

Other available titles about George and Martha are:
George and Martha back in town (1984)
George and Martha encore (1973)
George and Martha, one fine day (1978)
George and Martha rise and shine (1976)
George and Martha round and round (1988)
George and Martha, tons of fun (1980)

Wings; a tale of two chickens. Viking Kestrel 1986 unp il $14.99; pa $4.99   **E**

1. Chickens—Fiction 2. Foxes—Fiction
ISBN 0-670-80961-6; 0-14-050579-2 (pa)   LC 85-40953

Harriet the chicken rescues her foolish, uneducated friend from the clutches of a wily fox

"Marshall's pictures are even roomier and more expressive than usual in a story perfectly suited for the young audience who has just discovered the difference between

Marshall, James, 1942-1992—*Continued*
chickens and foxes and who will therefore delight in these
sly reversals." Bull Cent Child Books

Yummers! Houghton Mifflin 1973 30p il lib
bdg $14.95; pa $5.95　　　　　　　　　　　E
1. Pigs—Fiction 2. Turtles—Fiction 3. Reducing—
Fiction
ISBN 0-395-14757-3 (lib bdg); 0-395-39590-9 (pa)
Worried about her weight, Emily Pig "jumps rope; her
friend Eugene [Turtle] suggests a walk as better exercise, but
the walk is interrupted by a series of snacks. Emily, who
has said 'Yummers,' to everything, finally has a tummy
ache. She thinks it must have been due to all the walking,
and agrees with Eugene when he suggests that she stay in
bed and eat plenty of good food." Bull Cent Child Books
"Corpulent, amiable Emily moves with monumental
charm in the humorous, bright pastel pictures." Horn Book
Other available titles about Emily Pig and Eugene Turtle
are;
Taking care of Carruthers (1981)
What's the matter with Carruthers? (1972)
Yummers too: the second course (1986)

Martin, Ann M., 1955-
Rachel Parker, kindergarten show-off; by
Ann Martin; illustrated by Nancy Poydar.
Holiday House 1992 unp il $15.95; pa $6.95
　　　　　　　　　　　　　　　　　　　E
1. Friendship—Fiction 2. School stories
ISBN 0-8234-0935-X; 0-8234-1067-6 (pa)
　　　　　　　　　　　　　LC 91-25793
Five-year-old Olivia's new neighbor Rachel is in her kin-
dergarten class, and they must overcome feelings of jealousy
and competitiveness to be friends
"Olivia's first-person narrative, chatty and comic, im-
parts a breath of fresh air to a common situation. (Commendably, no point is made of the fact that Olivia is
African American while her eventual pal is white.) Filled
with entertaining touches, Poydar's true-to-life illustrations
scattered throughout the text adroitly capture the girls'
changeable emotions." Publ Wkly

Martin, Bill, 1916-
Barn dance! by Bill Martin, Jr. and John
Archambault; illustrated by Ted Rand. Holt &
Co. 1986 unp il $15.95; pa $4.95　　　　　E
1. Stories in rhyme 2. Dancing—Fiction 3. Country
life—Fiction
ISBN 0-8050-0089-5; 0-8050-0799-7 (pa)
　　　　　　　　　　　　　LC 86-14225
Unable to sleep on the night of a full moon, a young boy
follows the sound of music across the fields and finds an
unusual barn dance in progress
"The bouncy rhyme will be a pleasure for listeners and
tellers as they pick up the twang and the barn-dance beat.
Rand's raucous two-page watercolor spreads are as spirited
as the story poem." Booklist

Brown bear, brown bear what do you see?
pictures by Eric Carle. Holt & Co. 1992 unp
il $15.95　　　　　　　　　　　　　　　E
1. Color—Fiction 2. Animals—Fiction 3. Stories in
rhyme
ISBN 0-8050-1744-5　　　　　　LC 91-29115
A newly illustrated edition of the title first published
1967 by Holt, Rinehart & Winston

A chant in which a variety of animals, each one a different color, answers the question, "What do you see?"
"Carle's large, brilliantly colored animals set against a
white background make the book perfect for sharing with a
group of preschoolers, while Martin's repetitious text is eminently chantable—a boon for beginning readers." Horn
Book

Chicka chicka boom boom; by Bill Martin,
Jr. and John Archambault; illustrated by Lois
Ehlert. Simon & Schuster Bks. for Young
Readers 1989 unp il $14　　　　　　　　E
1. Alphabet 2. Stories in rhyme
ISBN 0-671-67949-X　　　　　　LC 89-4315
An alphabet rhyme/chant that relates what happens
when the whole alphabet tries to climb a coconut tree
"Ehlert's illustrations—bold, colorful shapes—are contained by broad polka-dotted borders, like a proscenium
arch through which the action explodes. Tongue-tingling, visually stimulating, with an insistent repetitive chorus of
'chicka chicka boom boom,' the book demands to be read
again and again and again." Horn Book

The ghost-eye tree; by Bill Martin, Jr. and
John Archambault; illustrated by Ted Rand.
Holt & Co. 1985 unp il $13.95; pa $5.95
　　　　　　　　　　　　　　　　　　　E
1. Ghost stories 2. Fear—Fiction 3. Brothers and
sisters—Fiction
ISBN 0-8050-0208-1; 0-8050-0947-7 (pa)
　　　　　　　　　　　　　LC 85-8422
"On a dark and ghostly night a brother and sister are
sent to fetch a pail of milk from the other end of town.
They must pass the fearful ghost-eye tree, old and horribly
twisted, looking like a monster, with a gap in the branches
where the moon shines through like an eye. . . . The story
is rhythmically told, sometimes rhyming, always moving
ahead, sharp with the affectionate teasing of the brother and
sister. The realistic watercolor illustrations are superb—
strong, striking, very dark, with highlights of moonlight and
lantern light that cast a spooky, scary spell. A splendidly
theatrical book for storytelling and reading aloud." Horn
Book

Knots on a counting rope; by Bill Martin,
Jr. and John Archambault; illustrated by Ted
Rand. Holt & Co. 1987 unp il $14.95　　　E
1. Indians of North America—Fiction 2. Grandfathers—
Fiction 3. Blind—Fiction
ISBN 0-8050-0571-4　　　　　　LC 87-14858
A different version of the title illustrated by Joe Smith
was published in 1966
"Boy-Strength-of-Blue-Horses begs his grandfather to tell
him again the story of the night he was born. In a question-
and-answer litany, the boy and his grandfather share the
telling of the events on that special night." SLJ
"The powerful spare poetic text is done full justice by
Rand's fine full-color illustrations, which capture both the
drama and brilliance of vast southwestern space and the intimacy of starlit camp-fire scenes. While classified as an Indian story the love, hope, and courage expressed are
universal, meriting a wide audience." Booklist

The maestro plays; by Bill Martin, Jr.;
pictures by Vladimir Radunsky. Holt & Co.
1994 unp il $15.95　　　　　　　　　　　E
1. Musicians—Fiction
ISBN 0-8050-1746-1　　　　　　LC 94-1916
"At center stage is a clown-like creature, 'The Maestro,'
who plays a progression of instruments. And how does he
play? In an intriguing variety of ways, including some that

E

Martin, Bill, 1916- —*Continued*

are easy enough to understand ('flowingly, glowingly, knowingly, showingly, goingly') and some that will require youngsters to use their imaginations ('nippingly, drippingly, zippingly, clippingly, pippingly'." Publ Wkly

"Radunsky's wonderfully bizarre illustrations, created from hand-colored cut paper, are a visual delight. . . . An infectious rhythm builds, at times lapsing into nonsense, but resulting in an almost perfect coupling of text and illustration." SLJ

Old devil wind; illustrated by Barry Root. Harcourt Brace & Co. 1993 unp il $13.95

E

1. Ghost stories
ISBN 0-15-257768-8   LC 92-37908

A newly illustrated edition of the title first published 1970 by Holt, Rinehart & Winston

On a dark and stormy night one object after another joins in making eerie noises in the old house

"Emphasis on lengthened inflection in the climactic lines detailing the wind's power to eliminate the noisy assemblage from 'BROOOM' to 'WIIIIIITCH' makes this a wonderful excursion into vocalization, well suited to interactive story hours. In a fine book for reading aloud, Barry Root's illustrations, featuring a dark palette, limited content, and surreal distortion, are deliciously ghoulish without being too scary." Horn Book

Polar bear, polar bear, what do you hear? by Bill Martin, Jr.; pictures by Eric Carle. Holt & Co. 1991 unp il $15.95   **E**

1. Animals—Fiction 2. Stories in rhyme
ISBN 0-8050-1759-3   LC 91-13322

Zoo animals from polar bear to walrus make their distinctive sounds for each other, while children imitate the sounds for the zookeeper

"Carle's characteristically inventive, jewel-toned artwork forms a seamless succession of images that fairly leap off the pages." Publ Wkly

Martin, C. L. G.

Three brave women; illustrated by Peter Elwell. Macmillan 1991 unp il $13.95   **E**

1. Mothers and daughters—Fiction 2. Grandmothers—Fiction 3. Spiders—Fiction
ISBN 0-02-762445-5   LC 89-77770

Also available Spanish language edition

Mama and Grammy's humorous childhood anecdotes help Caitlin come to terms with her fear of spiders

"This has touches of humor in both text and illustrations, and Elwell uses understated hues effectively in appealing ink-and-watercolor artwork. A warm family story showing that sisterhood can be intergenerational." Booklist

Martin, Rafe, 1946-

Will's mammoth; illustrated by Stephen Gammell. Putnam 1989 unp il $15.95; pa $4.95   **E**

1. Mammoths—Fiction
ISBN 0-399-21627-8; 0-399-22603-6 (pa)
          LC 88-11651

"Will loves mammoths—huge, hairy, woolly mammoths. His parents explain that there are no mammoths left in the world, but Will knows better. Off he goes into an iridescent, snowbound world of his own creation, where he quickly finds all manner of woolly prehistoric beasts." SLJ

"Gammell's depiction of a child's rich imagination is il-

lustrated in vivid colors. The fantasy spreads use winter whites and blues as background for subtly individualized animals who move energetically across the pages." Booklist

Marzollo, Jean

Close your eyes; pictures by Susan Jeffers. Dial Bks. 1978 unp il lib bdg $12.89; pa $4.95
          E

1. Lullabies
ISBN 0-8037-1610-9 (lib bdg); 0-8037-1617-6 (pa)
          LC 76-42935

A lullaby interspersed with illustrations of a father's efforts to put his reluctant child to bed

"The text is interpreted in magnificent full-color pastel-toned illustrations, remarkable for their clarity, meticulous detail, and delicate line. . . . The book is a charming production in the old-fashioned tradition of a warm and reassuring bedtime story." Horn Book

Pretend you're a cat; pictures by Jerry Pinkney. Dial Bks. for Young Readers 1990 unp il $14.99; lib bdg $12.89   **E**

1. Animals—Fiction 2. Stories in rhyme
ISBN 0-8037-0773-8; 0-8037-0774-6 (lib bdg)
          LC 89-34546

"Each double spread consists of a large painting of an animal, a smaller painting—boxed—of children imitating the animal, and of a series of questions [in verse]. Sample 'Can you climb? Can you leap? Can you stretch? Can you sleep? Can you hiss? Can you scat? Can you purr like a cat? What else can you do like a cat?'" Bull Cent Child Books

"The rhymed verses are vivid and straightforward, and Pinkney's inventive watercolor and pencil drawings are as engaging as the characters and animals he portrays." Publ Wkly

Mathers, Petra

Sophie and Lou. HarperCollins Pubs. 1991 unp il $15; lib bdg $14.89   **E**

1. Mice—Fiction
ISBN 0-06-024071-7; 0-06-024072-5 (lib bdg)
          LC 90-37562

"When a dance studio opens across the street, painfully shy Sophie [a mouse] learns to dance alone in her own apartment. Lou watches her from afar until one day he asks her to dance." Child Book Rev Serv

"A naïve, almost childlike style of art illustrates this tale. . . . The text is uncomplicated and charming." SLJ

Maxner, Joyce

Nicholas Cricket; illustrated by William Joyce. Harper & Row 1989 unp il $14; lib bdg $13.89; pa $4.95   **E**

1. Crickets—Fiction 2. Bands (Music)—Fiction 3. Animals—Fiction 4. Stories in rhyme
ISBN 0-06-024216-7; 0-06-024222-1 (lib bdg); 0-06-443275-0 (pa)   LC 88-33076

Nicholas Cricket and the other members of the Bug-a-Wug Cricket Band lead all the forest creatures in a musical celebration of the night

"Joyce's imaginative pictures, . . . depart from the expected by casting much of the action in a decidedly uptown mode. Top-hatted gents squire ladies in gowns in and out of clubs that ooze sophistication—no mean feat, considering these are insects and animals. The palette is dark, the creatures sleek and distinctive—Nicholas and company sport four suit-coated limbs, the better to fiddle and strum. A splendid toe-tapping night for all." Booklist

Mayer, Mercer, 1943-

A boy, a dog, and a frog. Dial Bks. for Young Readers 1967 unp il lib bdg $9.89; pa $3.50   **E**

1. Frogs—Fiction 2. Stories without words
ISBN 0-8037-0767-3 (lib bdg); 0-8037-0769-X (pa)

"Without the need for a single word, humorous, very engaging pictures tell the story of a little boy who sets forth with his dog and a net on a summer day to catch an enterprising and personable frog. Even very young preschoolers will 'read' the tiny book with the greatest satisfaction and pleasure." Horn Book

Other available titles in this series are:
A boy, a dog, a frog, and a friend (1971)
Frog goes to dinner (1974)
Frog on his own (1973)
Frog, where are you? (1969)
One frog too many (1975)

There's a nightmare in my closet. Dial Bks. for Young Readers 1968 unp il $14.99; lib bdg $13.89; pa $4.95   **E**

1. Fear—Fiction
ISBN 0-8037-8682-4; 0-8037-8683-2 (lib bdg); 0-8037-8574-7 (pa)

Also available Spanish language edition

A young boy confronts the frightening creature lurking in his closet

"Childhood fear of the dark and the resulting exercise in imaginative exaggeration are given that special Mercer Mayer treatment in this dryly humorous fantasy. Young children will easily empathize with the boy and can be comforted by his experience." SLJ

Another available title about this boy is:
There's an alligator under my bed (1987)

McBratney, Sam

Guess how much I love you; illustrated by Anita Jeram. Candlewick Press 1995 unp il $14.95   **E**

1. Rabbits—Fiction 2. Fathers and sons—Fiction
ISBN 1-56402-473-3   LC 94-1599

Also available Spanish language edition

During a bedtime game, every time Little Nutbrown Hare demonstrates how much he loves his father, Big Nutbrown Hare gently shows him that the love is returned even more

"Neither sugary nor too cartoonlike, the watercolors, in soft shades of brown and greens with delicate ink-line details, warmly capture the loving relationship between parent and child as well as the comedy that stems from little hare's awe of his wonderful dad." Booklist

McCloskey, Robert, 1914-

Blueberries for Sal. Viking 1948 54p il $14.95; pa $4.99   **E**

1. Bears—Fiction 2. Maine—Fiction
ISBN 0-670-17591-9; 0-14-050169-X (pa)

A Caldecott Medal honor book, 1949

"The author-artist tells what happens on a summer day in Maine when a little girl and a bear cub, wandering away from their blueberry-picking mothers, each mistakes the other's mother for its own. The Maine hillside and meadows are real and lovely, the quiet humor is entirely childlike, and there is just exactly the right amount of suspense for small children." Wis Libr Bull

Another available title about Sal is: One morning in Maine, entered below

Lentil. Viking 1940 unp il $14.95; pa $4.99   **E**

1. Harmonicas—Fiction 2. Ohio—Fiction
ISBN 0-670-42357-2; 0-14-050287-4 (pa)

Picture-story book about a small boy who could not sing, but who could work wonders on a simple harmonica, especially on the day when the great Colonel Carter returned to his home town

"Big, vigorous, amusing pictures in black-and-white, with an Ohio small-town background." New Yorker

Make way for ducklings. Viking 1941 unp $14.99; pa $4.99   **E**

1. Ducks—Fiction 2. Boston (Mass.)—Fiction
ISBN 0-670-45149-5; 0-14-050171-1 (pa)

Also available Spanish language edition

Awarded the Caldecott Medal, 1942

"A family of baby ducks was born on the Charles River near Boston. When they were old enough to follow, Mother Duck, with some help from a friendly policeman, trailed them through Boston traffic to the pond in the Public Garden." Bookmark

"There are some very beautiful drawings in this book." Horn Book

One morning in Maine. Viking 1952 64p il $14.99; pa $4.99   **E**

1. Maine—Fiction
ISBN 0-670-52627-4; 0-14-050174-6 (pa)

A Caldecott Medal honor book, 1953

The events of this "story—Sal's discovery of her first loose tooth, the loss of the tooth while digging clams, the consequent wish on a gull's feather, and the wish come true—occur in the course of one morning in Maine. The lovely Maine seacoast scenes and the doings of Sal with her family and friends are drawn with enticing detail in beautiful, big double-spread lithographs printed in dark blue." Booklist

Time of wonder. Viking 1957 63p il $16.99; pa $5.99   **E**

1. Maine—Fiction
ISBN 0-670-71512-3; 0-14-050201-7 (pa)

Awarded the Caldecott Medal, 1958

"A summer on an island in Maine is described through the simple everyday experiences of children, but also reveals the author's deep awareness of an attachment to all the shifting moods of season and weather, and the salty, downright character of the New England people." Top News

McCully, Emily Arnold

The amazing Felix. Putnam 1993 unp il $14.95   **E**

1. Magic—Fiction 2. Musicians—Fiction
ISBN 0-399-22428-9   LC 92-10929

Felix has been practicing a magic trick instead of the piano and is worried about disappointing his musician father, but then he gets to be a hero in the castle where his father is performing

"McCully handles watercolors with facility and panache, using impressionistic dapples of color to delineate forms. The 1920s settings on board ship and in an English castle lend themselves to a variety of intriguing illustrations, but even more impressive are her subtle characterizations of adults and children. McCully's original story, with its involving pictures and sense of childhood concerns, is an especially fine choice for reading aloud." Booklist

McCully, Emily Arnold—*Continued*

The grandma mix-up; story and pictures by Emily Arnold McCully. Harper & Row 1988 63p il lib bdg $14.89; pa $3.50 **E**

1. Grandmothers—Fiction
ISBN 0-06-024202-7 (lib bdg); 0-06-444150-4 (pa)
LC 87-29378

"An I can read book"

Young Pip doesn't know what to do when two very different grandmothers come to baby sit, each with her own way of doing things

"McCully's two-color, line-and-wash drawings emphasize the personality differences by consciously flouting stereotypes: Pip's laid-back Grandma Sal has white hair and glasses, while his strict Grandma Nan dresses like a teenager. Choice of words and sentence length will make the sly humor easy for beginning readers to grasp." Booklist

Other available titles about Pip and his grandmothers are:
Grandmas at bat (1993)
Grandmas at the lake (1990)

Mirette on the high wire. Putnam 1992 unp il $15.95 **E**

1. Tightrope walking—Fiction 2. Paris (France)—Fiction
ISBN 0-399-22130-1 LC 91-36324

Awarded the Caldecott Medal, 1993

Mirette learns tightrope walking from Monsieur Bellini, a guest in her mother's boarding house, not knowing that he is a celebrated tightrope artist who has withdrawn from performing because of fear

"With a rich palette of deep colors, the artist immerses the reader in 19th-century Paris. Colorful theatrical personalities . . . fill the glowing interiors with robust life. And the exterior scenes . . . are filled with the magic of a Paris night when anything can happen. . . . An exuberant and uplifting picture book." N Y Times Book Rev

McDermott, Gerald

Papagayo; the mischief maker; written and illustrated by Gerald McDermott. Harcourt Brace Jovanovich 1992 unp il $16.95; pa $6.95 **E**

1. Parrots—Fiction
ISBN 0-15-259465-5; 0-15-259464-7 (pa)
LC 91-40364

A reissue of the title first published 1980 by Windmill Bks.

Papagayo, the noisy parrot, helps the night animals save the moon from being eaten up by the moon dog

"McDermott's original story assumes folktale proportions. . . . Art for the story is striking; deep tropical colors seem intensified by glossy page surfaces, and they nearly vibrate against the intermittent deep-blue backdrop of a night sky." Booklist

Tim O'Toole and the wee folk; an Irish tale; told and illustrated by Gerald McDermott. Viking 1990 unp il $13.95; pa $4.99 **E**

1. Fairy tales 2. Ireland—Fiction
ISBN 0-670-80393-6; 0-14-050675-6 (pa)
LC 89-8913

A very poor Irishman is provided with magical things by the "wee folk", but he must then keep his good fortune out of the hands of the greedy McGoons

"McDermott's characteristic illustrations are a perfect accompaniment to the cheery good humor of the story; flocks of tiny leprechauns resembling fields of shamrocks cavort over the bright green hillsides. The comical folk art and the economical use of language, as well as its slight hint of brogue, will make this book a pleasurable choice for story hour." Horn Book

McDonald, Megan, 1959-

The great pumpkin switch; story by Megan McDonald; pictures by Ted Lewin. Orchard Bks. 1992 unp il $15.95; lib bdg $14.99; pa $5.95 **E**

1. Pumpkin—Fiction 2. Brothers and sisters—Fiction
ISBN 0-531-05450-0; 0-531-08600-3 (lib bdg); 0-531-07065-4 (pa) LC 91-39660

"A Richard Jackson book"

An old man tells his grandchildren how he and a friend accidentally smashed the pumpkin his sister was growing and had to find a replacement

"The extraordinary watercolors depict the period with bold, sure strokes and add nuances and depth to the story; the portraits, especially that of a broadly smiling, youthful Grandpa, are unabashedly joyful. A book that cuts across generations with its sensitivity and gentle wit." Booklist

Insects are my life; story by Megan McDonold; pictures by Paul Brett Johnson. Orchard Bks. 1995 unp il $14.95; lib bdg $14.99 **E**

1. Insects—Fiction
ISBN 0-531-06874-9; 0-531-08724-7 (lib bdg)
LC 94-21960

"A Richard Jackson book"

No one at home or school understands Amanda Frankenstein's devotion to insects until she meets Maggie

"Factual tidbits slipped surreptitiously into the appealing text add information to this spirited tale. . . . Full-page and vignette illustrations rendered in soft-hued watercolors, colored pencils, and pastels complement and add humor to the story." SLJ

The potato man; story by Megan McDonald; pictures by Ted Lewin. Orchard Bks. 1991 unp il $14.95; lib bdg $14.99; pa $5.95 **E**

1. Peddlers and peddling—Fiction
ISBN 0-531-05914-6; 0-531-08514-7 (lib bdg); 0-531-07053-0 (pa) LC 90-7758

"A Richard Jackson book"

Grandpa tells stories of the fruit and vegetable peddler in his childhood neighborhood, a man he learns to appreciate after a rocky start

"McDonald and Lewin have created a lovely, evocative period piece. The artist's horse-drawn wagons, rugged faces and turn-of-the-century kitchen are perfectly matched by the gentle homespun writing style." Publ Wkly

McGuire, Richard

Night becomes day. Viking 1994 unp il $13.99 **E**

1. Time—Fiction 2. Day—Fiction
ISBN 0-670-85547-2 LC 94-9923

McGuire "takes readers from country to city, summer to spring, dawn to dark. 'Night becomes day/And day becomes bright/Bright becomes sun/And sun becomes shine,' begins the volume." Publ Wkly

"What seems deceptively simple often demands a second or third thought in the creative picture book. . . . Illustrating all this movement of life are post-modern pictures that use geometric design work and pure colors—red, brown, yellow, green, and blue—to catch your eye. But as striking

McGuire, Richard—*Continued*

as the art work is, it's really the words that will spark the imagination." Booklist

McKissack, Patricia C., 1944-

Flossie & the fox; pictures by Rachel Isadora. Dial Bks. for Young Readers 1986 unp il $14; lib bdg $13.89 E

1. Foxes—Fiction 2. African Americans—Fiction

ISBN 0-8037-0250-7; 0-8037-0251-5 (lib bdg)

LC 86-2024

A wily fox notorious for stealing eggs meets his match when he encounters a bold little girl in the woods who insists upon proof that he is a fox before she will be frightened

"The watercolor and ink illustrations, with realistic figures set on impressionistic backgrounds, enliven this humorous and well-structured story which is told in the black language of the rural south. The language is true, and the illustrations are marvelously complementary in their interpretation of the events. This spirited little girl will capture readers from the beginning, and they'll adore her by the end of this delightful story." SLJ

A million fish—more or less; illustrated by Dena Schutzer. Knopf 1992 unp il $14; lib bdg $14.99; pa $5.99 E

1. Tall tales 2. Fishing—Fiction 3. Louisiana—Fiction 4. African Americans—Fiction

ISBN 0 679 80692 X; 0 679 90692 4 (lib bdg), 0-679-88086-0 (pa) LC 91-17323

"While Hugh Thomas is fishing, Papa-Daddy and Elder Abbajon row out of the fog swapping bayou tales. He doesn't believe their stories, but when he catches a million fish and has all but three taken by a giant gator, raccoon pirates, and a cat, he has his own whopping good story about the Bayou Clapateaux." Publisher's note

"The play between fantasy and reality is neatly handled, with action following exaggeration in an ambiguous way that leaves the ending open as to who's telling the truth and who believes what. The African-American characters and swamp setting swirl across the pages in thick, rounded strokes of brazen-hued paint, well-matched with the story's brassy flash." Bull Cent Child Books

Mirandy and Brother Wind; illustrated by Jerry Pinkney. Knopf 1988 unp il $16; lib bdg $16.99 E

1. Dancing—Fiction 2. Winds—Fiction 3. African Americans—Fiction

ISBN 0-394-88765-4; 0-394-98765-9 (lib bdg)

LC 87-349

A Caldecott Medal honor book, 1989; Coretta Scott King award for illustrations, 1989

"Mirandy is sure that she'll win the cake walk if she can catch Brother Wind for her partner, but he eludes all the tricks her friends advise. When she finally does catch him with her own quick wits, she ends up wishing instead for her boyfriend Ezel to overcome his clumsiness. Sure enough, the two children finish first in high style." Bull Cent Child Books

"Although this is not a history book, the past lives within these pages. Ms. McKissack and Mr. Pinkney's ebullient collaboration captures the texture of rural life and culture 40 years after the end of slavery. . . . Each page of 'Mirandy and Brother Wind' sparkles with life." N Y Times Book Rev

McLeod, Emilie, 1926-1982

The bear's bicycle; by Emilie Warren McLeod; illustrated by David McPhail. Little, Brown 1975 31p il lib bdg $14.95; pa $5.95 E

1. Bears—Fiction 2. Cycling—Fiction

ISBN 0-316-56203-3 (lib bdg); 0-316-56206-8 (pa)

"An Atlantic Monthly Press book"

"Bicycle safety is demonstrated through colorful pictures leavened by a parallel set of humorous pictures of a teddy-bear-turned-real who takes the hazardous consequences of ignoring the safety rules." Read Teach

McLerran, Alice, 1933-

Roxaboxen; illustrated by Barbara Cooney. Lothrop, Lee & Shepard Bks. 1991 unp il $16; lib bdg $14.88 E

ISBN 0-688-07592-4; 0-688-07593-2 (lib bdg)

LC 89-8057

Also available in paperback from Puffin Bks.

A hill covered with rocks and wooden boxes in the desert becomes an imaginary town named Roxaboxen for Marian, her sisters, and their friends

"A celebration of the transforming magic of the imagination, the story was inspired by McLerran's mother's reminiscences of her childhood in Yuma, Arizona. . . . The story, told as though from the memory of a Roxaboxenite, brings their play to life through concrete details and a spare, understated style. Equally vivid, Cooney's full-color artwork evokes the striking variety of colors and moods found in the desert landscape." Booklist

McMillan, Bruce

Counting wildflowers. Lothrop, Lee & Shepard Bks. 1986 unp il $16; lib bdg $22.25; pa $4.95 E

1. Counting 2. Wild flowers

ISBN 0-688-02859-4; 0-688-02860-8 (lib bdg); 0-688-14027-0 (pa) LC 85-16607

A counting book with photographs of wildflowers illustrating the numbers one through twenty

"Dazzling photographs of twenty-three wildflowers are the major feature of this deftly constructed, multipurpose concept book. On the simplest level this is a counting book. . . . The book is also a simple identification guide, with the popular name of each variety appearing just above the photograph; all the flowers are listed again at the end along with the scientific name, months of blooming, and type of terrain where found." Horn Book

Growing colors. Lothrop, Lee & Shepard Bks. 1988 32p il $16; lib bdg $15.93; pa $4.95 E

1. Color 2. Vegetables 3. Fruit

ISBN 0-688-07844-3; 0-688-07845-1 (lib bdg); 0-688-13112-3 (pa) LC 88-2767

"A colors book using fruits and vegetables of every hue. Each double-page spread has a small photograph of the whole plant and a large close-up of the fruit or vegetable. The colors are announced in bold type tinted in the appropriate shade. . . . At the end of the book, there is a picture glossary of all the colors and plants used." Publ Wkly

"A luscious-looking book that will help children identify colors. . . . This is notably a treat for kids and an example of photography as an art form in picture books." Bull Cent Child Books

McMillan, Bruce—*Continued*

Mouse views; what the class pet saw; written and photo-illustrated by Bruce McMillan. Holiday House 1993 32p il $15.95; pa $5.95   E

1. Mice—Fiction
ISBN 0-8234-1008-0; 0-8234-1132-X (pa)

LC 92-25921

Photographic puzzles follow an escaped pet mouse through a school while depicting such common school items as scissors, paper, books, and chalk. Readers are challenged to identify the objects as seen from the mouse's point of view

"Children will see this brightly illustrated puzzle book, with its combination of story and game, as pure fun. Teachers will appreciate the chance to hone their students' observational skills and also to introduce mapping through the map at the book's conclusion." Booklist

One, two, one pair! written and photo-illustrated by Bruce McMillan. Scholastic 1991 unp il $12.95   E

1. Counting
ISBN 0-590-43767-4   LC 90-37410

"Color photographs show the two parts of a pair on one side of each two-page spread, with the words 'one' and 'two' under them, and on the other side the two together as 'one pair.' As the pictures progress, children will realize that the illustrations are showing preparations for going ice skating. However, only at the end will they realize that the child pictured is actually two children—a pair of twins. While text is limited to the words of the title, the book will give young readers much to talk about and describe in these pictures." SLJ

Step by step. Lothrop, Lee & Shepard Bks. 1987 unp il $13.95; lib bdg $11.88   E

1. Infants—Fiction 2. Growth—Fiction
ISBN 0-688-07233-X; 0-688-07234-8 (lib bdg)

LC 87-4195

"A tiny infant sleeps, rolls over, stands up, walks and then, at 14 months, runs, in this photographic portrait of a child's first moves." Publ Wkly

"Families with one and two year olds will enjoy looking at these familiar moments, unposed and natural. This book works not so much of itself, but because of the response it will call from children looking at it and the opportunity for discussion that may follow." SLJ

McPhail, David M.

The bear's toothache; written and illustrated by David McPhail. Little, Brown 1972 31p il $14.95; pa $5.95   E

1. Bears—Fiction 2. Teeth—Fiction
ISBN 0-316-56312-9; 0-316-56325-0 (pa)

"An Atlantic Monthly Press book"

"In this delightful fantasy, a small boy receives a nocturnal visit from a bear with a sore tooth. Pulling on the tooth doesn't work, eating fails to loosen it, and hitting it with a pillow breaks a lamp and wakes up father. The boy's cowboy rope is securely fastened to tooth and bedpost and, as the bear jumps out the window, the tooth finally pops out. The grateful bear then gives it to the boy to put under his pillow. The simple text is accompanied by full-page pastel pictures which are filled with action and detail and are superbly suited to this imaginative bedtime tale." SLJ

Farm boy's year; by David McPhail. Atheneum Pubs. 1992 unp il $13.95   E

1. Farm life—Fiction 2. New England—Fiction
ISBN 0-689-31679-8   LC 91-4982

"A year in the life of a late-nineteenth-century New England farm boy is lovingly chronicled in softly nostalgic paintings and a brief text styled as journal entries. . . . The author skillfully blends a great deal of material about the time and atmosphere. The book conveys information through both word and image as we learn about rural life and the chores on a farm, from apple-picking to toolmaking in the home forge." Horn Book

Fix-it; by David McPhail. Dutton 1984 unp il $13.99; pa $3.95   E

1. Bears—Fiction
ISBN 0-525-44093-3; 0-525-44323-1 (pa)

LC 83-16459

"Distraught when the television set won't work, little Emma, a bear, gets her parents out of bed one morning with the demand that they fix the set. They try and fail. Emma weeps. They call a repairman, who also fails to find out what's wrong. Emma's parents do what they can to distract and amuse her; by the time her father fixes the television set (it had been unplugged) Emma is busy 'reading' to her doll." Bull Cent Child Books

"McPhail's black line and watercolor wash illustrations tell half the story and provide most of the humor." SLJ

Other available titles about Emma are:
Emma's pet (1985)
Emma's vacation (1987)

Pig Pig grows up; by David McPhail. Dutton 1980 unp il hardcover o.p. paperback available $3.95   E

1. Pigs—Fiction
ISBN 0-525-44195-6 (pa)

"A Unicorn book"

Only when faced with a dire emergency does Pig Pig finally react like a grown-up and admit he is not a baby any more

"Large drawings in subdued full color are uncluttered and go straight to the point; full of humor and action, they virtually tell the story by themselves." Horn Book

Other availables titles about Pig Pig are:
Pig Pig and the magic photo album (1986)
Pig Pig gets a job (1990)
Pig Pig goes to camp (1983)
Pig Pig rides (1982)

Pigs aplenty, pigs galore! [by] David McPhail. Dutton Children's Bks. 1993 unp il $13.99; pa $4.99   E

1. Pigs—Fiction 2. Stories in rhyme
ISBN 0-525-45079-3; 0-14-055313-4 (pa)

LC 92-27986

"As pigs of every size, shape, and dress (including Elvis) arrive at his house in every possible vehicle, a riotous party begins and lasts through the night as the perplexed narrator looks on." SLJ

"The rhyme is bouncy enough, but it's the pictures that will have parents and kids howling. Using deep watercolors set against a black background, McPhail presents a magnificent group of porkers, whose capacity for costumes and capers is truly wondrous." Booklist

Meddaugh, Susan

Martha speaks. Houghton Mifflin 1992 unp il $14.95; pa $4.95   E

1. Dogs—Fiction
ISBN 0-395-63313-3; 0-395-72024-9 (pa)

LC 91-48455

Problems arise when Martha, the family dog, learns to speak after eating alphabet soup

"Good-natured and amusing, with cheerful illustrations of the delightfully stocky Martha and her amazed family." Horn Book

Another available title about Martha is:
Martha calling (1994)

Merrill, Jean, 1923-

The Girl Who Loved Caterpillars; a twelfth century tale from Japan; adapted by Jean Merrill; illustrated by Floyd Cooper. Philomel Bks. 1992 unp il $15.95   E

1. Fairy tales 2. Japan—Fiction
ISBN 0-399-21871-8

LC 91-29054

In this retelling of an anonymous twelfth-century Japanese story, the young woman Izumi resists social and family pressures as she befriends caterpillars and other socially unacceptable creatures

"This story of an independent girl has a surprisingly contemporary tone. . . . Merrill's adaptation is cleanly yet elegantly styled, as are Cooper's pastel double spreads, which elaborate on the many vivid images in the story." Bull Cent Child Books

Micklethwait, Lucy

I spy; an alphabet in art; devised & selected by Lucy Micklethwait. Greenwillow Bks. 1992 unp il $19   E

1. Art appreciation 2. Alphabet
ISBN 0-688-11679-5

LC 91-42212

Presents objects for the letters of the alphabet through paintings by such artists as Magritte, Picasso, Botticelli, and Vermeer

"The author's stated intention of introducing young children to fine art, her choice of paintings, the handsome book design, and the quality of paper and reproduction take this beyond the usual alphabet book." Booklist

Miller, Margaret, 1945-

Guess who? Greenwillow Bks. 1994 unp il $15; lib bdg $14.93   E

1. Occupations
ISBN 0-688-12783-5; 0-688-12784-3 (lib bdg)

LC 93-26704

A child is asked who delivers the mail, gives haircuts, flies an airplane, and performs other important tasks. Each question has several different answers from which to choose

"Gender and ethnic representation are deftly handled. The author's sharp, clear full-color photographs are well composed, and her use of cropped photos and white space alternating with bled photos is an effective tool for involving youngsters." SLJ

My five senses. Simon & Schuster 1994 unp il $15   E

1. Senses and sensation
ISBN 0-671-79168-0

LC 93-1956

"Five attractive preschoolers of different races narrate this simple photographic survey of sensory activities. In a succession of four-page sequences, each child engages in a variety of experiences that demonstrates each of the senses. The clear, uncluttered design is effective and inviting in this beautifully conceived and executed book." Horn Book Guide

Who uses this? Greenwillow Bks. 1990 unp il $12.95; lib bdg $12.88   E

1. Tools 2. Occupations
ISBN 0-688-08278-5; 0-688-08279-3 (lib bdg)

LC 89-30456

"Brilliant color photographs introducing common objects such as a hammer, a football, and a rolling pin are accompanied by the question, 'Who uses this?' The object is then pictured being used by an adult and by a child. This concept book—quietly nonsexist—is ideal for reading aloud to the youngest listeners." Horn Book Guide

Whose shoe? Greenwillow Bks. 1991 unp il $13.95; lib bdg $13.88   E

1. Shoes
ISBN 0-688-10008-2; 0-688-10009-0 (lib bdg)

LC 90-38491

Illustrates a variety of footwear and matches each wearer with the appropriate shoe

"Miller has consciously avoided stereotypes, picturing a male ballet dancer and children from many racial groups. She understands children's fascination with make-believe and dress-up, and this newest book should spark much imaginative play." Horn Book

Mills, Claudia, 1954-

A visit to Amy-Claire; illustrated by Sheila Hamanaka. Macmillan 1992 unp il $14.95   E

1. Sisters—Fiction 2. Cousins—Fiction
ISBN 0-02-766991-2

LC 91-280

"Rachel is looking forward to a visit at her older cousin's house, but she's in for a rude surprise when it appears that this time around Amy-Claire has eyes only for Rachel's two-year-old sister Jessie." Publ Wkly

"Both the joy of family relations and the problematic moods of childhood are strikingly conveyed in this fine book's contemporary oil paintings. . . . The paintings use off-center perspective and unusual cropping to direct readers' attention. The faces of the adults and children in these two Asian-American families are animated and sensitive in expression. Mills's first picture book handles childhood rivalry with a subtle, deft, and sympathetic touch that Hamanaka lovingly mirrors." SLJ

Minarik, Else Holmelund

Little Bear; pictures by Maurice Sendak. Harper & Row 1957 63p il $14.95; lib bdg $14.89; pa $3.50   E

1. Bears—Fiction
ISBN 0-06-024240-X; 0-06-024241-8 (lib bdg); 0-06-444004-4 (pa)
Also available Spanish language edition

"An I can read book"

Four episodes "about Little Bear . . . as he persuades his mother to make him a winter outfit—only to discover his fur coat is all he needs; makes himself some birthday soup—and then is surprised with a birthday cake; takes an imaginary trip to the moon, and finally goes happily off to sleep as his mother tells him a story about 'Little Bear.'" Bull Cent Child Books

The pictures "depict all the warmth of feeling and the

Minarik, Else Holmelund—*Continued*
special companionship that exists between a small child and
his mother." Publ Wkly

Other available titles about Little Bear are:
Father Bear comes home (1959)
A kiss for Little Bear (1968)
Little Bear's friend (1960)
Little Bear's visit (1961)

No fighting, no biting! pictures by Maurice
Sendak. Harper & Row 1958 62p il $13; lib
bdg $14.89; pa $3.50   E

1. Alligators—Fiction
ISBN 0-06-024290-6; 0-06-024291-4 (lib bdg);
0-06-444015-X (pa)
"An I can read book"
"A young lady who is unable to read in peace because of
two children squabbling beside her tells them a story about
two little alligators whose fighting and biting almost lead to
disastrous consequences with a big hungry alligator. Children are sure to accept and enjoy the lesson in this little adventure tale and be amused by the expressive old-fashioned
drawings." Booklist

Mitchell, Margaree King, 1953-
Uncle Jed's barbershop; illustrated by James
Ransome. Simon & Schuster Bks. for Young
Readers 1993 unp il $15   E

1. Uncles—Fiction 2. Barbers and barbershops—Fiction
3. African Americans—Fiction
ISBN 0-671-76969-3   LC 91-44148
Despite serious obstacles and setbacks Sarah Jean's Uncle Jed, the only black barber in the county, pursues his
dream of saving enough money to open his own barbershop
"The author's convivial depictions of family life are enhanced by Ransome's . . . spirited oil paintings, which set
the affectionate intergenerational cast against brightly patterned walls and crisp, leaf-strewn landscapes." Publ Wkly

Mitchell, Rita Phillips
Hue Boy; pictures by Caroline Binch. Dial
Bks. for Young Readers 1993 unp il $13.99
                                                        E

1. Caribbean region—Fiction 2. Growth—Fiction
ISBN 0-8037-1448-3   LC 92-18560
Everyone in little Hue Boy's island village has suggestions on how to help him grow, but he learns to stand tall
in a way all his own
"Mitchell's sympathetic story and fluid, lilting prose are
a fitting springboard for Binch . . . whose supremely expressive watercolors make the most of the tale's Caribbean setting." Publ Wkly

Mochizuki, Ken, 1954-
Baseball saved us; written by Ken
Mochizuki; illustrated by Dom Lee. Lee &
Low Bks. 1993 unp il $14.95; pa $5.95   E

1. Japanese Americans—Evacuation and relocation,
1942-1945—Fiction 2. World War, 1939-1945—Fiction
3. Baseball—Fiction 4. Prejudices—Fiction
ISBN 1-880000-01-6; 0-880000-19-9 (pa)
                                           LC 92-73215
Also available Spanish language edition
A Japanese American boy learns to play baseball when
he and his family are forced to live in an internment camp
during World War II, and his ability to play helps him after
the war is over
"Fences and watchtowers are in the background of many
of Lee's moving illustrations, some of which were inspired
by Ansel Adams' 1943 photographs of Manzanar. . . . The
baseball action will grab kids—and so will the personal experience of bigotry." Booklist

Heroes; written by Ken Mochizuki;
illustrated by Dom Lee. Lee & Low Bks. 1995
unp il $14.95   E

1. Japanese Americans—Fiction 2. Prejudices—Fiction
ISBN 1-880000-16-4   LC 94-26541
"In the 1960's Donnie Okada took a lot of razzing from
the other boys in the neighborhood; they insisted that he
had to be the enemy in their war games because he looked
like the enemy, and they did not believe his father and uncle had served in the American military. Dad and Uncle
Yosh give those boys a dignified and effective lesson." N Y
Times Book Rev
"The book is a powerful exploration of the cruelty children can inflict upon one another and of the confusion and
pain borne by the target of such unthinking racism." Horn
Book

Modell, Frank
One zillion valentines. Greenwillow Bks.
1981 unp il $14; lib bdg $13.93; pa $3.95
                                                        E

1. Valentine's Day—Fiction
ISBN 0-688-00565-9; 0-688-00569-1 (lib bdg);
0-688-07329-8 (pa)   LC 81-2215
"Milton and Marvin decide that valentines are for everybody and proceed to distribute the simple hearts they have
drawn up to everyone in the neighborhood. The leftovers
they sell for a nickel and with the money they've made, buy
a giant box of candy to share." Booklist
"The plot is impeccably logical, and its execution—both
in text and drawings—completely childlike. From the opening gambit to a thoroughly satisfying conclusion, the story
moves briskly; the author-illustrator captures the essence of
youthful optimism in the situation and a comic spirit in the
exuberant, cartoonlike illustrations." Horn Book

Monjo, F. N., 1924-1978
The drinking gourd; a story of the
Underground Railroad; pictures by Fred
Brenner. Newly illustrated ed. HarperCollins
Pubs. 1993 62p il $14.95; lib bdg $14.89; pa
$3.50   E

1. Underground railroad—Fiction
ISBN 0-06-024329-5; 0-06-024330-9 (lib bdg);
0-06-444042-7 (pa)   LC 92-10823
"An I can read book"
First published 1970
Set in New England in the decade before the Civil War.
For mischievous behavior in church, Tommy is sent home
to his room, but wanders instead into the barn. There he
discovers that his father is helping runaway slaves escape to
Canada
"The simplicity of dialogue and exposition, the level of
concepts, and the length of the story [makes] it most suit-
able for the primary grades reader. The illustrations are
deftly representational, the whole a fine addition to the
needed body of historical books for the very young." Bull
Cent Child Books

Morozumi, Atsuko

One gorilla; a counting book. Farrar, Straus & Giroux 1990 unp il $15; pa $4.95   E

1. Gorillas—Fiction 2. Counting
ISBN 0-374-35644-0; 0-374-45646-1 (pa)

Published in the United Kingdom with title: And one gorilla

The author begins this counting book "with the words: 'Here is a list of things I love. One gorilla.' He goes on to accumulate a number of other things he loves: 'Two butterflies among the flowers and one gorilla. Three budgerigars in my house and one gorilla.'" Quill Quire

"The illustrations, delicately drawn but vividly colored, have a misty quality to them that adds to the air of fantasy. . . . The pictures delightfully capture the personality of each animal. Searching out the creatures in each two-page spread is enjoyable and moderately challenging." SLJ

Moss, Lloyd

Zin! zin! zin! a violin; illustrated by Marjorie Priceman. Simon & Schuster Bks. for Young Readers 1995 unp il $15   E

1. Musical instruments 2. Counting 3. Stories in rhyme
ISBN 0-671-88239-2   LC 93-37902

A Caldecott Medal honor book, 1996

"Rhyming couplets present 10 instruments and their characteristics. . . . In the process of adding instruments, the book teaches the names of musical groups up to a chamber group of 10 as well as the categories into which the instruments fall: strings, reeds, and brasses. Amazingly, Moss conveys this encyclopedic information while keeping the poem streamlined and peppy. Priceman's sprightly, sunny hued gouache paintings should take a bow, too." Booklist

Most, Bernard, 1937-

Whatever happened to the dinosaurs? written and illustrated by Bernard Most. Harcourt Brace Jovanovich 1984 unp il lib bdg $13.95; pa $4.95   E

1. Dinosaurs—Fiction
ISBN 0-15-295295-0 (lib bdg); 0-15-295296-9 (pa)
LC 84-3779

The author "offers various fantastic explanations to answer his title question. 'Did the dinosaurs go to another planet? . . . did a magician make them disappear? . . . Are the dinosaurs in the hospital?'" SLJ

"A hilarious book, sure to be popular for individual reading or with groups." Child Book Rev Serv

Mullins, Patricia

V for vanishing; an alphabet of endangered animals. HarperCollins Pubs. 1994 c1993 unp il $15; lib bdg $14.89   E

1. Endangered species 2. Extinct animals 3. Alphabet
ISBN 0-06-023556-X; 0-06-023557-8 (lib bdg)
LC 93-8181

First published 1993 in Australia

An ABC book featuring illustrations of endangered and extinct animals from around the world

"Careful scholarship, intelligent presentation, and gorgeous artwork combine to make this a fascinating book for a wide audience." Horn Book

Includes bibliographical references

Murphy, Jill, 1949-

Peace at last. Dial Bks. for Young Readers 1980 unp il hardcover o.p. paperback available $3.95   E

1. Night—Fiction 2. Bears—Fiction
ISBN 0-8037-6964-4 (pa)   LC 80-15659

Mr. Bear spends the night searching for enough peace and quiet to go to sleep

"The story appears on the verso pages with line drawings; facing pages are in full color; the pictures have warmth and humor and the story is told in brisk, forthright style with an appealing refrain that will probably elicit listener-participation, 'Oh, NO! I can't stand THIS.'" Bull Cent Child Books

A quiet night in. Candlewick Press 1994 c1993 unp il $12.95; pa $4.99   E

1. Elephants—Fiction 2. Bedtime—Fiction
ISBN 1-56402-248-X; 1-56402-673-6 (pa)
LC 93-875

First published 1993 in the United Kingdom

Mr. and Mrs. Large's attempt to put the children to bed early and have a quiet night on their own has an unexpected ending

"The illustrations are first rate; especially priceless are the expressions on the elephants' faces. The text is full of humor and instantly recognizable as true to life." SLJ

What next, Baby Bear! Dial Bks. for Young Readers 1984 unp il hardcover o.p. paperback available $3.95   E

1. Bears—Fiction 2. Space flight to the moon—Fiction
ISBN 0-685-37306-1 (pa)   LC 83-7316

"Baby Bear methodically goes about finding a rocket, space helmet, boots, companionship, and food for his journey to the moon. He returns in time for his bath and bedtime on Earth." Bull Cent Child Books

"The story is simple, yet teases young listeners with the question, was the trip purely imaginary? Baby Bear is, after all, very sooty in the end. But most appealing is the artwork; cleverly wrought black-and-white drawings alternate with charming full-page pictures in jewellike colors." Booklist

Mwenye Hadithi

Crafty Chameleon; illustrated by Adrienne Kennaway. Little, Brown 1987 unp il lib bdg $15.95; pa $4.95   E

1. Chameleons—Fiction
ISBN 0-316-33723-4 (lib bdg); 0-316-33771-4 (pa)
LC 87-3867

A chameleon bedeviled by a leopard and a crocodile uses his wits to get them to leave him alone

"The drawings of the animals in the jungle setting are dramatically bold and exciting, and the words add their own rhythmic accent. . . . There are humorous details of jungle life, such as the ants marching in columns along branches. Finding Chameleon as he sits against a background of gray stones, leans from a bush, or hides among green leaves will be a special challenge for young readers." Horn Book

Hot Hippo; illustrated by Adrienne Kennaway. Little, Brown 1986 unp il $14.95; pa $4.95   E

1. Hippopotamus—Fiction
ISBN 0-316-33722-6; 0-316-33718-8 (pa)   LC 86-65

"Using the narrative structure of the *pourquoi* tale, Mwenye Hadithi has composed an economical yet marvel-

Mwenye Hadithi—*Continued*

ously evocative and rhythmic text to describe the circumstances which determined the habitat of the hippopotamus. . . . The illustrations are more than a striking accompaniment to the text; they share equally in the development of plot, setting, and characters. Warm colors, skillfully merging one into another, create a hot, arid atmosphere so that Hippo's longing is thoroughly understandable." Horn Book

Myers, Walter Dean, 1937-

The story of the three kingdoms; illustrated by Ashley Bryan. HarperCollins Pubs. 1995 unp il $14.95; lib bdg $14.89   E

1. Animals—Fiction

ISBN 0-06-024286-8; 0-06-024287-6 (lib bdg)

LC 94-2685

"An original fable tells of the day when the elephant ruled the forest, the shark ruled the sea and the hawk ruled the sky. Then people discovered that they could think, solve problems and tell stories. With wisdom, they learned, there is no need to rule the earth." N Y Times Book Rev

"The hot colors, sweeping lines and stylized figures that characterize Bryan's art form a bold backdrop for the author's equally dramatic original fable." Publ Wkly

Myrick, Mildred

The Secret Three; drawings by Arnold Lobel. Harper & Row 1963 64p il $14.89   E

1. Clubs—Fiction 2. Ciphers—Fiction 3. Seashore—Fiction

ISBN 0-06-024356-2

"An I can read book"

"Three boys, two on the mainland and one on an island lighthouse, exchange messages in a bottle carried by the tide. They organize a club with a secret code, handshake, and name. On a trip to the island the boys explore the lighthouse and camp out overnight." SLJ

"The cryptography is elementary enough for the age of the readers, and should delight girls as well as boys. The illustrations are charming." Bull Cent Child Books

Narahashi, Keiko

I have a friend. Margaret K. McElderry Bks. 1987 unp il $19.50   E

1. Shades and shadows—Fiction

ISBN 0-689-50432-2   LC 86-27628

A small boy tells about his friend who lives with him, who follows him, who sometimes is very tall, but who disappears when the sun goes down—his shadow

"A deceptively simple picture book is full of graphic echoes that capture the eye as effectively as the text will catch children's fancy." Bull Cent Child Books

Neitzel, Shirley

The bag I'm taking to Grandma's; pictures by Nancy Winslow Parker. Greenwillow Bks. 1995 unp il $15; lib bdg $14.93   E

1. Stories in rhyme

ISBN 0-688-12960-9; 0-688-12961-7 (lib bdg)

LC 94-4115

This story is presented in "simple cumulative verse and rebuses. A young boy is packing for a trip to visit his grandmother. He fills a shopping bag with his mitt, cars, space ship, wooden animals, his favorite stuffed rabbit, his pillow,

a book, a flashlight. But then along comes mom with ideas of her own." SLJ

"Nancy Winslow Parker's spare, softly-colored sketches are comic and expressive, supplying the humor in deft conjunction with the text. . . . The rhyming rebus invites shared reading with individual children and groups." Horn Book

The dress I'll wear to the party; pictures by Nancy Winslow Parker. Greenwillow Bks. 1992 unp il $14; lib bdg $13.93; pa $4.95   E

1. Clothing and dress—Fiction 2. Stories in rhyme

ISBN 0-688-09959-9; 0-688-09960-2 (lib bdg); 0-688-14261-3 (pa)   LC 91-30906

In cumulative verses and rebuses a girl describes how she is dressing up in her mother's party things

"The perky, crisp cartoons executed in ink, watercolor, and colored-pencil, are exactly right for capturing the sprightly objects and events. The rollicking rhythm, vivid language, and appealing art make a handsome package." SLJ

The jacket I wear in the snow; pictures by Nancy Winslow Parker. Greenwillow Bks. 1989 unp il $16; lib bdg $13.93   E

1. Clothing and dress—Fiction 2. Snow—Fiction 3. Stories in rhyme

ISBN 0-688-08028-6; 0-688-08030-8 (lib bdg)

LC 88-18767

A young girl names all the clothes that she must wear to play in the snow

"Written in cheerful, cumulative verse that recalls the well-known favorite nursery rhyme 'The House That Jack Built,' the text, with its easy-going rhythm, will be simple for children to recite from memory. . . . The artist's drawings are executed in her familiar style using watercolor, pencil, and pen; they combine with the large typeface and a generous amount of white space to create a tremendously appealing book." Horn Book

Ness, Evaline, 1911-1986

Sam, Bangs & Moonshine; written and illustrated by Evaline Ness. Holt & Co. 1966 unp il $14.95; pa $5.95   E

ISBN 0-8050-0314-2; 0-8050-0315-0 (pa)

Also available Spanish language edition

Awarded the Caldecott Medal, 1967

Young Samantha, or Sam, "the fisherman's daughter, finally learns to draw the line between reality and the 'moonshine' [her fantasies] in which her mother is a mermaid, she owns a baby kangaroo, and can talk to her cat." Publisher's note

"In this unusually creative story the fantasy in which many, many children indulge is presented in a realistic and sympathetic context. The illustrations in ink and pale color wash (mustard, grayish-aqua) have a touching realism, too. This is an outstanding book." SLJ

Neumeier, Marty

Action alphabet; by Marty Neumeier and Byron Glaser. Greenwillow Bks. 1985 unp il $15; lib bdg $14.93   E

1. Alphabet

ISBN 0-688-05703-9; 0-688-05704-7 (lib bdg)

LC 84-25322

The letters of the alphabet appear as parts of pictures representing sample words, such as a drip formed by a D

Neumeier, Marty—*Continued*

coming out of a faucet and a vampire with two V's for fangs

"This clever concept book, created by an award-winning pair of graphic designers, is bold, brash and as promised by the title, 'full' of action. . . . A mere description doesn't do the smashing graphics justice. To call this alphabet vivid is to understate the case. No matter how many ABC's you have already, you 'need' this one." SLJ

Newberry, Clare Turlay, 1903-1970

April's kittens. HarperCollins Pubs. 1993 c1940 32p il $17; lib bdg $16.89   E

1. Cats—Fiction

ISBN 0-06-024400-3; 0-06-024401-1 (Lib bdg)

A Caldecott Medal honor book, 1941

A reissue of the title first published 1940

"Though old-fashioned, the story of a small girl's yearning to keep both a mother cat and one of her kittens still speaks to pet owners young and old. Newberry's simple, charcoal drawings of the felines are as elegant and endearing as ever." Horn Book

Marshmallow; story and pictures by Clare Turlay Newberry. Harper & Row 1990 c1942 unp il $17   E

1. Rabbits—Fiction 2. Cats—Fiction

ISBN 0-06-024460-7   LC 89-20052

A Caldecott Medal honor book, 1943

A reissue of the title first published 1942

"A little white bunny, looking as soft as a marshmallow, comes to live in the house with a pampered bachelor cat who at first does not know whether or not to accept so strange a thing. But before long the big black cat and the little white bunny are such friends that, cuddled up together, asleep, and playing, they give the artist an excuse for some of her best work." Bookmark

"It is a delightful combination of beauty, understanding of children and animals, and droll humor." N Y Times Book Rev

Newman, Lesléa

Too far away to touch; illustrated by Catherine Stock. Clarion Bks. 1995 32p il $14.95   E

1. AIDS (Disease)—Fiction 2. Uncles—Fiction 3. Death—Fiction

ISBN 0-395-68968-6   LC 93-30327

"Zoe and her uncle Leonard always go someplace special and today they're off to the planetarium. While there, Zoe learns that Uncle Leonard has AIDS. He reassures Zoe that when he dies, he will be like the stars—too far to touch but close enough to see." Child Book Rev Serv

Stock's "soft-focus watercolors provide a delicate foil for this exceptionally thoughtful story. . . . Despite the sombre theme, the story ends on an uplifting note, and it's hard to imagine a more appropriate book for young readers that deals so gently and insightfully with such an important topic." Publ Wkly

Nixon, Joan Lowery, 1927-

Beats me, Claude; story by Joan Lowery Nixon; pictures by Tracey Campbell Pearson. Viking Kestrel 1986 unp il lib bdg $11.95; pa $4.99   E

1. Frontier and pioneer life—Fiction

ISBN 0-670-80781-8 (lib bdg); 0-14-050847-3 (pa)

LC 86-5465

"In this sequel to *If You Say So, Claude* (1980), Shirley and Claude continue to enjoy their new found peace in the cabin in the great state of Texas. When Shirley, who has never been a very good cook, tries her hand at baking an apple pie, the result is a surprise for her and for readers." SLJ

"Nixon's story has a down-home verve, and Pearson's illustrations of the farfetched antics are as full of spice as a real apple pie." Publ Wkly

Other available titles about Claude and Shirley are:

Fat chance, Claude (1987)

That's the spirit, Claude (1993)

Noble, Trinka Hakes

The day Jimmy's boa ate the wash; pictures by Steven Kellogg. Dial Bks. for Young Readers 1980 unp il $14.99; lib bdg $13.89; pa $4.95   E

1. Farm life—Fiction 2. Snakes—Fiction 3. School stories

ISBN 0-8037-1723-7; 0-8037-1724-5 (lib bdg); 0-8037-0094-6 (pa)   LC 80-15098

Also available in paperback from Puffin Bks.

"One small girl, reporting to her mother after a class visit to a farm, nonchalantly describes the frenzied day; she works backward from effects to causes, beginning with the statement that the day was kind of dull and boring until the cow started crying. Why? A haystack fell on her. How? The farmer hit it with his tractor. Why? He was busy yelling at the pigs to get off the school bus . . . and she goes on to unfold the tale of how Jimmy's boa escaped, set the hens in a flurry, precipitated an egg-throwing match, and so on." Bull Cent Child Books

"The illustrations, which depict disgruntled chickens, expressive pigs, and smiling cats as well as other individualized animal and human characters, show the artist's flair for humorous detail." Horn Book

Other available titles about Jimmy's boa are:

Jimmy's boa and the big splash birthday bash (1989)

Jimmy's boa bounces back (1984)

Meanwhile back at the ranch; pictures by Tony Ross. Dial Bks. for Young Readers 1987 unp il $14; lib bdg $13.89   E

1. Ranch life—Fiction

ISBN 0-8037-0353-8; 0-8037-0354-6 (lib bdg)

LC 86-11651

"Rancher Hicks leads a life so uneventful that he takes a trip to town just to see what is happening. Wife Elna stays home. While the rancher is amusing himself with the high life in Sleepy Gulch—getting his whiskers trimmed, having lunch at Millie Mildew's, and watching a turtle cross Main Street—Elna is home winning contests, inheriting fortunes, starring in movies, and entertaining the President." SLJ

"Noble's tongue-in-cheek story fits rollickingly into the tall-tale genre while Ross' exuberant full-color pictures wring every bit of humor from the already funny tale." Booklist

Nolen, Jerdine

Harvey Potter's balloon farm; [illustrated by] Mark Buehner. Lothrop, Lee & Shepard Bks. 1994 unp il $15; lib bdg $14.93 E

1. Tall tales 2. Balloons—Fiction 3. Farm life—Fiction
ISBN 0-688-07887-7; 0-688-07888-5 (lib bdg)
        LC 91-38129
"Harvey Potter's unusual crop is balloons—which grow just like corn on long, sturdy stalks. Harvey Potter himself is not at all unusual, and his friend, a young African-American girl, is determined to uncover the secret of his curious harvest. The story is lively, but of even greater attraction are the vivid, air-brushed illustrations of balloons with expressive faces in every size, color, and shape." Horn Book Guide

Numeroff, Laura Joffe

If you give a moose a muffin; illustrated by Felicia Bond. HarperCollins Pubs. 1991 unp il $14.95; lib bdg $14.89 E

1. Moose—Fiction
ISBN 0-06-024405-4; 0-06-024406-2 (lib bdg)
        LC 91-2207
Also available Spanish language edition
"A Laura Geringer book"
Chaos can ensue if you give a moose a muffin and start him on a cycle of urgent requests
"The text provides just the right springboard for Bond's distinct, pen-and-ink and watercolor drawings. The moose is a riot. He is at once dainty and exuberant with a heart-warming, ever-smiling face." SLJ

If you give a mouse a cookie; by Laura Numeroff; illustrated by Felicia Bond. Harper & Row 1985 unp il $13.95; lib bdg $13.89
            E

1. Mice—Fiction
ISBN 0-06-024586-7; 0-06-024587-5 (lib bdg)
        LC 84-48343
Also available Spanish language edition
Relating the cycle of requests a mouse is likely to make after you give him a cookie takes the reader through a young child's day
"Children love to indulge in supposition or to ask 'what will happen if. . .?' and here there is a long, satisfying chain of linked and enjoyably nonsensical causes and effects. . . . The illustrations, neatly drawn, spaciously composed, and humorously detailed, extend the story just the way picture book illustrations should." Bull Cent Child Books

Nunes, Susan, 1937-

The last dragon; by Susan Miho Nunes; illustrated by Chris K. Soentpiet. Clarion Bks. 1995 unp il $14.95 E

1. Chinese Americans—Fiction
ISBN 0-395-67020-9   LC 93-30631
While spending the summer in Chinatown with his great-aunt, a young boy finds an old ten-man dragon in a shop and gets a number of people to help him repair it
"Nunes' text builds to a satisfying conclusion. . . . The expansive watercolor illustrations are warm, colorful, and full of details unique to Chinatown. An endnote provides information on Chinese dragon lore."

Oakes, Bill

Puzzlers; [by] Bill Oakes, Suse MacDonald. Dial Bks. for Young Readers 1989 unp il lib bdg $13.89 E

1. Counting
ISBN 0-8037-0690-1   LC 88-33392
"A colorful menagerie comprising number collages introduces concepts including widest, backward, upside down and sequence. A left-hand page uses three squares to demonstrate the concept of overlap; on the right side, a cow's face is made up of overlapping numbers. A key at the end of the book informs the reader of other things to look for in that cow, such as a pattern and numbers shown back-to-back. MacDonald and Oakes use beautiful marbelized papers in bright hues to create the festive images." Publ Wkly

Oakley, Graham

The church mouse. Atheneum Pubs. 1972 unp il $13.95 E

1. Mice—Fiction 2. Cats—Fiction
ISBN 0-689-30058-1
"Arthur, the church mouse at first view seems to live an idyllic existence. . . . He has an easy relationship with the parson—and even with Sampson, the church cat. . . . And he is lonely. One day, while reading 'Exodus' . . . he is inspired to invite all the town mice to come live with him in the church." N Y Times Book Rev
"Full-color paintings with an abundance of activity and detail contribute much to the telling of the story. . . . Very British allusions give the fulsome text a certain sophistication; but the action and the clever illustrations are wholly childlike in their fun." Horn Book
 Other available titles about the church mice and Sampson, the church cat are:
The church mice and the moon (1974)
The church mice and the ring (1992)
The church mice in action (1983)
The church mice spread their wings (1976)

Oberman, Sheldon

The always prayer shawl; illustrated by Ted Lewin. Boyds Mills Press 1994 unp il $14.95
            E

1. Jews—Fiction 2. Immigration and emigration—Fiction
ISBN 1-878093-22-3
This story "tells of the Jewish boy Adam, growing up in a shtetl, whose life drastically changes when famine and chaos in old Russia force his parents to immigrate to America. At parting, Adam's beloved grandfather gives the boy a gift, a prayer shawl ('my always prayer shawl'), which was presented to the grandfather by *his* grandfather, for whom Adam was named. . . . As good as any of Lewin's best work, the watercolors are abundantly detailed and wonderfully expressive. . . . The pictures enrich the tranquil telling, which harks back to the biblical Adam, as it movingly depicts how memory and tradition add texture and richness to our lives—even as other things around us change." Booklist

O'Connor, Jane, 1947-

Super Cluck; by Jane O'Connor and Robert O'Connor; pictures by Megan Lloyd. HarperCollins Pubs. 1991 64p il $11.95; lib bdg $14.89; pa $3.50 E

1. Chickens—Fiction
ISBN 0-06-024594-8; 0-06-024595-6 (lib bdg); 0-06-444162-8 (pa)   LC 90-32832

O'Connor, Jane, 1947-— *Continued*
"An I can read book"

Chuck Cluck, an alien chick living on Earth, earns the name Super Cluck when he uses his super strength to save baby chicks from a rat

"Bursting with energy, Lloyd's bright, detailed illustrations lend humor and verve to this I Can Read book." Publ Wkly

Olaleye, Isaac
Bitter bananas; illustrated by Ed Young. Boyds Mills Press 1994 unp il $14.95 E
1. Baboons—Fiction 2. Rain forests—Fiction 3. Africa—Fiction
ISBN 1-56397-039-2 LC 93-73306
Also available in paperback from Puffin Bks.

"Baboons are stealing the sweet palm sap that the young African boy Yusuf sells at market, and it takes patience, ingenuity, and several trials before Yusuf outwits his forest rivals with a lure of tempting sap and bananas—laced with wormwood." Bull Cent Child Books

"Olaleye's eminently readable text naturally calls for audience participation. Young renders the story beautifully in cut-paper collages of vibrant pink and lush green." Booklist

Onyefulu, Ifeoma, 1959-
Emeka's gift; an African counting story. Cobblehill Bks. 1995 unp il $14.99 E
1. Counting 2. Nigeria
ISBN 0-525-65205-1 LC 94-30700

This "counting book cum photoessay weaves into its narrative details of life among the Igala people of southern Nigeria. 'One boy'—Emeka— walks to the neighboring village to visit his grandmother, wondering about a suitable gift for her. He passes various possibilities along the way . . . and imagines how Granny might react to each one. . . . Onyefulu . . . sprinkles informative sidebars alongside her tale of Emeka's journey. . . . Lucid, attractively composed photographs of Igala people and their artifacts add to the book's multicultural import." Publ Wkly

Oppenheim, Shulamith Levey
The lily cupboard; illustrated by Ronald Himler. HarperCollins Pubs. 1992 unp il lib bdg $14.89; pa $4.95 E
1. World War, 1939-1945—Fiction 2. Netherlands—Fiction 3. Jews—Fiction
ISBN 0-06-024670-7 (lib bdg); 0-06-443393-5 (pa)
LC 90-38592

"A Charlotte Zolotow book"

Miriam, a young Jewish girl, is forced to leave her parents and hide with strangers in the country during the German occupation of Holland

"The golden glow of the illustrations light both the painful scenes of the family parting and the wholesome scenes of the kindly, solid farm family and their home. This gentle story for young children is a welcome addition to the tales of heroism during World War II." Horn Book

Ormerod, Jan
101 things to do with a baby. Lothrop, Lee & Shepard Bks. 1984 unp il lib bdg $13.88; pa $4.95 E
1. Infants 2. Brothers and sisters
ISBN 0-688-03802-6 (lib bdg); 0-688-12770-3 (pa)
LC 84-4401

A six-year-old girl tells 101 things she can do with her baby brother

"Jan Ormerod's illustrations are magnificent—evoking both the tenderness and the tumult with which each day in a two-sibling household is filled. They are also painfully realistic." N Y Times Book Rev

Moonlight. Lothrop, Lee & Shepard Bks. 1982 unp il $15; lib bdg $14.93; Penguin Bks. pa $3.50 E
1. Stories without words
ISBN 0-688-00846-1; 0-688-00847-X (lib bdg); 0-14-050372-2 (pa) LC 81-8290

"This wordless book about bedtime is a companion to the author's 'Sunshine' [entered below]. In a similar format, with lovely, detailed watercolor paintings that are warm and human, Ormerod describes one bedtime in the life of the same family. Here we see dinner, the making of two boats from fruit leftovers, a bath, a bedtime story and a few not-able-to-sleep ups-and-downs." SLJ

Sunshine. Lothrop, Lee & Shepard Bks. 1981 unp il hardcover o.p. paperback available $3.95 E
1. Stories without words
ISBN 0-688-09353-1 (pa) LC 80-84971
Also available in paperback from Puffin Bks.

"Without benefit of words, this book follows the four or five year old as she rubs her eyes awake . . . and tiptoes into her sleeping parents' bedroom. The book ends with a picture of mother and daughter hand in hand on the way to work and school. The action in between describes all the activities of a first leisurely, then rushed preparation for the day's events." SLJ

"The illustrations are simply composed, with large but quiet areas of color and with realistic details; they are distinctive in the use of light and shadow . . . as the sunlight creeps across the shadowed bedrooms." Bull Cent Child Books

Osofsky, Audrey
Dreamcatcher; illustrated by Ed Young. Orchard Bks. 1992 unp il $15.95; lib bdg $15.99 E
1. Indians of North America—Fiction 2. Infants—Fiction 3. Family life—Fiction
ISBN 0-531-05988-X; 0-531-08588-0 (lib bdg)
LC 91-20029

"All day, an Ojibwa baby watches from a cradle as little boys play and Mother, big sister, Grandmother, and Father work nearby. At night, baby sleeps peacefully, for sister has made a dreamcatcher, a small willow hoop woven with a taut net of nettle fibers that catches bad dreams and holds them until the sun destroys their power, while letting good dreams slip through." Booklist

"Young's pastels are vibrantly colored but as tender as the text. . . . The artist's treatment emphasizes the universally human as well as the culturally particular in this empathic glimpse of Ojibway life." SLJ

Owens, Mary Beth
A caribou alphabet; written & illustrated by Mary Beth Owens. Dog Ear Press 1988 unp il $16.95 E
1. Caribou 2. Alphabet
ISBN 0-937966-25-8 LC 88-70631
Also available in paperback from Farrar, Straus & Giroux

Owens, Mary Beth—*Continued*

An alphabet book depicting the characteristics and ways of caribou

"A wonderful blending of the impressionist's palette with the graphic designer's authority, the illustrations transcend the utilitarian to become aesthetic statements. The artist has an uncanny ability to execute each so that without distortion the caribou are an essential part of the particular letter." Horn Book

Oxenbury, Helen, 1938-

Beach day. Dial Bks. for Young Readers 1982 unp il $3.95 **E**

1. Beaches—Fiction
ISBN 0-8037-0992-7   LC 81-69273
"Very first books"

Sand play at the beach is featured in this wordless board book

"Youngsters will enjoy the familiar details Oxenbury depicts so humorously without a word. Her clean lines, warm colors, and simple scenes lend themselves to parent-child picture reading." Booklist

The birthday party. Dial Bks. for Young Readers 1983 unp il o.p.; Puffin Bks. paperback available $3.99 **E**

1. Birthdays—Fiction 2. Parties—Fiction
ISBN 0-14-054947-1 (pa)   LC 82-19792
Also available Spanish language edition
"Out-and-about books"

"A child chooses a present but hates to give it away, is miffed at the casual way the gift is received, has a splendidly messy time, and walks home triumphantly, enjoying the souvenir balloon all the more because it's clear that the birthday child didn't want to give it up." Bull Cent Child Books

"The pictures are humorous and lively, with the left-hand page featuring the central item to be found in the right-hand scene." Publ Wkly

The car trip. Dial Bks. for Young Readers 1983 unp il $3.95 **E**

1. Automobiles—Fiction
ISBN 0-8037-0009-1   LC 83-5255
Also available in paperback from Puffin Bks.; Spanish language edition also available
"Out-and-about books"

"The hapless family in [this story] experiences every mishap imaginable. . . . The contrast between the child's sense of adventure and adult's desire for no surprises couldn't be greater. The bright, exuberant drawings catch each moment at the most emotional peak of each incident. A happy romp sure to prompt discussions about whether delight and disaster are relative terms." SLJ

First day of school. Dial Bks. for Young Readers 1983 unp il o.p.; Puffin Bks. paperback available $3.99 **E**

1. Nursery schools—Fiction
ISBN 0-14-054977-3 (pa)   LC 83-7452
Also available Spanish language edition
"Out-and-about books"

"On the first day of nursery school, a wailing child is pried away from her mother, makes a friend, and has a fine time. The cleanly drawn, unclutered pictures are small, bright, deft, and hilarious." Bull Cent Child Books

Helen Oxenbury's ABC of things. Macmillan 1993 c1971 unp il $3.95 **E**

1. Alphabet
ISBN 0-689-71761-X   LC 94-141790

A reissue of the title first published 1971 in the United Kingdom; first United States edition published 1972 by Franklin Watts

"Large letters and the words that begin them appear on pages bedizened by illustrations in full color of supreme silliness: 'O o' for an ostrich with an otter clinging to its long neck and both looking befuddled by their situation; 'W w' showing the wedding of a weasel and a wolf and the wasp that worries the couple. The originality and fun make this ABC a standout among the numerous offerings in the genre." Publ Wkly

It's my birthday. Candlewick Press 1994 c1993 unp il $9.95; pa $3.99 **E**

1. Cake—Fiction 2. Birthdays—Fiction 3. Animals—Fiction
ISBN 1-56402-412-1; 0-56402-602-7 (pa)
          LC 93-39667

First published 1993 in the Netherlands

The birthday child's animal friends bring ingredients and help make a birthday cake

"Oxenbury tells a cumulative story for the very young child with clear watercolors and a simple, cheerful text. The telling has a satisfying rhythm and repetition." Booklist

Our dog. Dial Bks. for Young Readers 1984 unp il o.p.; Puffin Bks. paperback available $3.99 **E**

1. Dogs—Fiction
ISBN 0-14-050392-7 (pa)   LC 84-5829
Also available Spanish language edition
"Out-and-about books"

A small boy and his mother try to cope with a dog that loves to go for walks, jump into dirty water, and roll in mud

Pippo gets lost. Aladdin Bks. (NY) 1989 unp il $5.95 **E**

1. Toys—Fiction
ISBN 0-689-71336-3   LC 89-340

Tom is very worried when he searches the house and can't find his stuffed monkey Pippo

Other available titles about Tom and Pippo are:
Tom and Pippo and the bicycle (1994)
Tom and Pippo and the dog (1989)
Tom and Pippo and the washing machine (1988)
Tom and Pippo go for a walk (1988)
Tom and Pippo go shopping (1989)
Tom and Pippo in the garden (1989)
Tom and Pippo in the snow (1989)
Tom and Pippo make a friend (1989)
Tom and Pippo make a mess (1988)
Tom and Pippo on the beach (1993)
Tom and Pippo read a story (1988)
Tom and Pippo see the moon (1989)
Tom and Pippo's day (1989)

Playing. Wanderer Bks. 1981 unp il $3.95 **E**

ISBN 0-671-42109-3   LC 80-52217
"Baby board books"

Illustrations of objects that infants play with appear alone on one page facing another page showing the baby using them. Included are blocks, a wagon, a pot, a box, a book (held upside down by the fledgling reader), a teddy bear, and a ball

Oxenbury, Helen, 1938-—*Continued*

Shopping trip. 2d ed. Dial Bks. for Young Readers 1991 c1982 unp il $3.95   **E**

1. Shopping—Fiction 2. Stories without words

ISBN 0-8037-0997-8   LC 81-69274

"Dial very first books"

First published 1982

The baby in this book "manages to achieve a good bit of independent investigation and some damage, all of which leaves Mama limp by the end of a shopping trip. A foray into a clothes rack, a broken packet of what looks like sugar, a raid on Mama's purse in a fitting booth followed by a sociable pulling back of its curtain, revealing Mama just emerging from the garment she's been trying on. . . . This has no words and needs none; it is drawn with simplicity, humor, and flair." Bull Cent Child Books

Palatini, Margie

Piggie pie! illustrated by Howard Fine. Clarion Bks. 1995 unp il $13.95   **E**

1. Witchcraft—Fiction 2. Pigs—Fiction 3. Wolves—Fiction

ISBN 0-395-71691-8   LC 94-19726

"Gritch the Witch sets out for Old MacDonald's Farm to get herself a meal of plump piggies. Alerted, however, . . . the swine hastily don sheep, cow, and other barnyard disguises and fool her. . . . The still-hungry Gritch is persuaded to give up by a Big Bad Wolf . . . and the two go off for lunch, each picturing the other made into a sandwich. . . . The exuberant illustrations are colorful and action-filled. Greedy (but not too bright) witch and wolf both get what they deserve in this thoroughly enjoyable romp." SLJ

Parish, Peggy, 1927-1988

Amelia Bedelia; pictures by Fritz Siebel. HarperCollins Pubs. 1992 63p il $14.95; lib bdg $14.89; pa $3.50   **E**

ISBN 0-06-020186-X; 0-06-020187-8 (lib bdg); 0-06-444155-5 (pa)   LC 91-10163

Also available Spanish language edition

"An I can read book"

A newly illustrated edition of the title first published 1963

"Amelia Bedelia is a maid whose talent for interpreting instructions literally results in comical situations, such as dressing the chicken in fine clothes." Hodges. Books for Elem Sch Libr

Other available titles about Amelia Bedelia are:
Amelia Bedelia and the baby (1981)
Amelia Bedelia and the surprise shower (1966)
Amelia Bedelia goes camping (1985)
Amelia Bedelia helps out (1979)
Amelia Bedelia's family album (1988)
Come back, Amelia Bedelia (1971)
Good driving, Amelia Bedelia (1995)
Good work, Amelia Bedelia (1976)
Merry Christmas, Amelia Bedelia (1986)
Play ball, Amelia Bedelia (1972)
Teach us, Amelia Bedelia (1977)
Thank you, Amelia Bedelia (1964)

Park, Barbara, 1947-

Junie B. Jones and her big fat mouth; illustrated by Denise Brunkus. Random House 1993 69p il lib bdg $9.99; pa $3.99   **E**

1. Kindergarten—Fiction 2. School stories

ISBN 0-679-94407-9 (lib bdg); 0-679-84407-4 (pa)   LC 92-50957

"A First stepping stone book"

When her kindergarten class has Job Day, Junie B. goes through much confusion and excitement before deciding on the "bestest" job of all

"Brunkus' energetic drawings pick up the slapstick action and the spunky comic hero." Booklist

Other available titles about Junie B. Jones are:
Junie B. Jones and a little monkey business (1993)
Junie B. Jones and the stupid smelly bus (1992)
Junie B. Jones and the yucky blucky fruitcake (1995)
Junie B. Jones and some sneaky peeky spying (1994)

Parker, Nancy Winslow

Working frog. Greenwillow Bks. 1992 39p il $14; lib bdg $13.93   **E**

1. Frogs—Fiction 2. Zoos—Fiction

ISBN 0-688-09918-1; 0-688-09919-X (lib bdg)   LC 90-24173

Winston the bullfrog describes his life at the Reptile House at the Bronx Zoo

"Throughout the book, pleasant, colorful pictures illustrate Winston's words and give intriguing backstage glimpses of his keepers and their jobs. A great way to prepare for a class trip to the zoo." Booklist

Parkin, Rex

The red carpet; story and pictures by Rex Parkin. Macmillan 1988 c1948 unp il hardcover o.p. paperback available $4.95   **E**

1. Carpets—Fiction 2. Stories in rhyme

ISBN 0-689-71678-8 (pa)   LC 88-5192

A reissue of the title first published 1948

A tale in rhyme and colorful pictures about a runaway carpet. When it was rolled out of the hotel to receive a visiting duke, it rolled on and on, down the street, along the highway and over the country roads, bringing excitement wherever it went

Paul, Ann Whitford

Eight hands round; a patchwork alphabet; illustrated by Jeanette Winter. HarperCollins Pubs. 1991 unp il $15; lib bdg $14.89; pa $4.95   **E**

1. Quilts 2. Alphabet 3. Frontier and pioneer life

ISBN 0-06-024689-8; 0-06-024704-5 (lib bdg); 0-06-443464-8 (pa)   LC 88-745

Introduces the letters of the alphabet with names of early American patchwork quilt patterns and explains the origins of the designs by describing the activity or occupation they derive from

"The slightly stylized pictures have a crayonlike texture, and throughout, colors are soft and fresh. Attractive and informative, this could easily perk up a unit on pioneer life." Booklist

Payne, Emmy, 1919-

Katy No-Pocket; pictures by H. A. Rey. Houghton Mifflin 1944 unp il lib bdg $14.95; pa $5.95 **E**

1. Kangaroos—Fiction 2. Animals—Fiction
ISBN 0-395-17104-0 (lib bdg); 0-395-13717-9 (pa)

Katy Kangaroo was most unfortunately unprovided with a pocket in which to carry her son Freddy. She asked other animals with no pockets how they carried their children but none of their answers seemed satisfactory. Finally a wise old owl advised her to try to find a pocket in the City, and so off she went and in the City she found just what she and Freddy needed

Peet, Bill

Big bad Bruce. Houghton Mifflin 1977 38p il 14.95; pa $5.95 **E**

1. Bears—Fiction 2. Witches—Fiction
ISBN 0-395-25150-8; 0-395-32922-1 (pa)

LC 76-62502

Bruce, a bear bully, never picks on anyone his own size until he is diminished in more ways than one by a small but very independent witch

"The language of the text is almost musical, with lots of words used for the sheer pleasure or appropriateness of their sounds. The illustrations are colorful and amusing." Child Book Rev Serv

Cowardly Clyde. Houghton Mifflin 1979 38p il $14.95; pa $5.95 **E**

1. Horses—Fiction 2. Courage—Fiction
ISBN 0-395-27802-3; 0-395-36171-0 (pa)

LC 78-24343

"Brave Sir Galavant and his cowardly steed Clyde take up the challenge to rid the farmers of the terrible 'giant owl-eyed ox-footed ogre.' Clyde, who quivers at a scarecrow, is terrified, but finds that by acting brave, you become brave." Read Teach

"The writing is brisk and casual; the illustrations are colorful and vigorous." Bull Cent Child Books

Eli; illustrated by the author. Houghton Mifflin 1978 38p il $14.95; pa $5.95 **E**

1. Lions—Fiction 2. Vultures—Fiction 3. Friendship—Fiction
ISBN 0-395-26454-5; 0-395-36611-9 (pa)

LC 77-17500

"The story of pathetic Eli, a 'king of the jungle' who's too old to fight. Feeding on leftovers one day, Eli is disgusted by hovering vultures, but 'noblesse oblige' compels him to rescue one bird, Vera, from a jackal who snatches her. Eli routs the jackal and earns the unwelcome friendship of the birds. . . . Comes the day when the hunters are closing in on him; Vera and the flock persuade Eli to play dead. . . . The hunters see no glory in hauling off a dead body, apparently the feast of vultures, and the old cat is saved." Publ Wkly

This offers "the author-artist's flair for exaggerated expressions, plentiful action, and bold use of color." Booklist

Huge Harold; written and illustrated by Bill Peet. Houghton Mifflin 1961 unp il lib bdg $14.95; pa $5.95 **E**

1. Rabbits—Fiction 2. Stories in rhyme
ISBN 0-395-18449-5 (lib bdg); 0-395-32923-X (pa)

"Harold the rabbit grows and grows—to dimensions which deprive him of normal hiding places but help him, after a bizarre chase, to an astonishing and wonderful achievement." Horn Book

This story, "told in rhyming couplets and colored drawings, is action filled and laughable." Booklist

The whingdingdilly; written and illustrated by Bill Peet. Houghton Mifflin 1970 60p il $14.95; pa $5.95 **E**

1. Dogs—Fiction 2. Witches—Fiction
ISBN 0-395-24729-2; 0-395-31381-3 (pa)

"Scamps, the dog, wants to be a horse, but a well-meaning witch turns him into a Whingdingdilly with the hump of a camel, zebra's tail, giraffe's neck, elephant's front legs and ears, rhinoceros' nose, and reindeer's horns." Adventuring With Books. 2d edition

Penn, Malka

The miracle of the potato latkes; a Hanukkah story; illustrated by Giora Carmi. Holiday House 1994 unp il $15.95; pa $6.95 **E**

1. Hanukkah—Fiction 2. Jews—Russia—Fiction
ISBN 0-8234-1118-4; 0-8234-1204-0 (pa)

LC 93-29921

"Every Hanukkah Tante Golda makes potato latkes for all her friends. One year, when all but one potato are gone, she makes latkes for a starving beggar. Trusting in God to provide, she finds one potato on the first day, two on the second and so on. Each day she invites an additional friend to share her meal. The crayon illustrations suit the Russian location and somewhat folktale quality of the story. A recipe for latkes is provided." Child Book Rev Serv

Petersham, Maud, 1890-1971

The circus baby; a picture book by Maud and Miska Petersham. Macmillan 1950 unp il $13.95; pa $3.95 **E**

1. Elephants—Fiction 2. Clowns—Fiction 3. Circus—Fiction
ISBN 0-02-771670-8; 0-689-71295-2 (pa)

A picture book all about the circus elephant and her baby, and the circus clown family. When the mother elephant tried to train her child to eat at table, like the clown baby, the results were disastrous

The authors "have combined talents again to make a delightful picture book. The four-color circus scenes are bright and simple. Mother and Baby are wonderfully expressive but still quite real elephants, rather than the stuffed-toy variety so familiar in the nursery books." NY Times Book Rev

Peterson, Jeanne Whitehouse

My mama sings; illustrated by Sandra Speidel. HarperCollins Pubs. 1994 unp il $15; lib bdg $14.89 **E**

1. Mothers and sons—Fiction 2. Singing—Fiction 3. African Americans—Fiction
ISBN 0-06-023854-2; 0-06-023859-3 (lib bdg)

LC 91-72

"To a little boy, it seems that his mama has an inexhaustible supply of songs. Some she learned from her mother; some are original; and others come from gospel and blues. When Mama loses her job, she stops singing, and the little boy realizes that he must now sing a happy song for her." Horn Book Guide

The book portrays a "warm, upbeat African American family. . . . The characters move sonorously through Speidel's lush pastel spreads, which beautifully complement the story." Publ Wkly

Pfeffer, Wendy, 1929-

Marta's magnets; illustrated by Gail Piazza. Silver Press 1995 unp il $13.95; lib bdg $15.95; pa $5.95   E

1. Magnets—Fiction 2. Collectors and collecting—Fiction 3. Friendship—Fiction
ISBN 0-382-24931-3; 0-382-24930-5 (lib bdg); 0-382-24932-1 (pa)   LC 94-37223

Includes one magnet in pocket

"Marta's collection of magnets, which her sister calls junk, provides the vehicles for Marta's acceptance into her new multicultural neighborhood." Sci Child

Pilkey, Dav, 1966-

When cats dream; story and paintings by Dav Pilkey. Orchard Bks. 1992 unp il $15.95; lib bdg $15.99   E

1. Cats—Fiction 2. Dreams—Fiction
ISBN 0-531-05997-9; 0-531-08597-X (lib bdg)
LC 91-31355

"A Richard Jackson book"

When cats dream, they can do anything they want, from combing their hair with the moon to swinging from vines in the jungle

"Pilkey's fantastical vision is one of tropical colors and unfettered movement, a whirling world of abandon and energy, a Chagallian landscape of inverted reality. Language soars between the mystical, the poetic and the down-to-earth as the felines slip in and out of slumber, but Pilkey's sharp wit is ever-present. A celebration of the imagination and the extraordinary." Publ Wkly

Pinczes, Elinor J.

One hundred hungry ants; illustrated by Bonnie MacKain. Houghton Mifflin 1993 unp il $14.95   E

1. Ants—Fiction 2. Mathematics—Fiction 3. Stories in rhyme
ISBN 0-395-63116-5   LC 91-45415

One hundred hungry ants head towards a picnic to get yummies for their tummies, but stop to change their line formation, illustrating the various ways one hundred may be divided

"Kids will enjoy the bouncy rhyme and the comical portrayal of the ants, while teachers will appreciate the entertaining demonstration of a math concept. The illustrations, which look like linocuts tinted with flat colors, have a distinctive style and a definite sense of humor." Booklist

Pinkney, Gloria Jean

Back home; pictures by Jerry Pinkney. Dial Bks. for Young Readers 1992 unp il $15.99; lib bdg $14.89   E

1. Farm life—Fiction 2. North Carolina—Fiction 3. African Americans—Fiction
ISBN 0-8037-1168-9; 0-8037-1169-7 (lib bdg)
LC 91-22610

Eight-year-old Ernestine returns to visit relatives on the North Carolina farm where she was born

"Gloria Pinkney's text has a relaxed pace that is perfectly suited to the summer setting. Her characterizations are particularly well drawn, and her dialogue thoroughly convincing. In some of Jerry Pinkney's finest work, sunlight filters through his pencil and watercolor illustrations, imbuing them with a feathery soft glow." Publ Wkly

The Sunday outing; pictures by Jerry Pinkney. Dial Bks. for Young Readers 1994 unp il $14.99; lib bdg $14.89   E

1. Railroads—Fiction 2. African Americans—Fiction
ISBN 0-8037-1198-0; 0-8037-1199-9 (lib bdg)
LC 93-25383

"When Ernestine confides to her great-aunt how much she wishes her parents could afford to send her by train to visit her North Carolina relatives, Aunt Odessa advises her to find a way to make up the fare by saving her parents some money. . . . Gloria Jean Pinkney's quiet story and Jerry Pinkney's illustrations provides a loving portrait of an African-American family working to make a dream come true." Horn Book Guide

Pinkwater, Daniel Manus, 1941-

Aunt Lulu; by Daniel Pinkwater. Macmillan 1988 unp il $13.95, pa $3.95   E

1. Aunts—Fiction 2. Librarians—Fiction 3. Dogs—Fiction
ISBN 0-02-774661-5; 0-689-71413-0 (pa)
LC 88-1736

Tired of working as a librarian in Alaska, Aunt Lulu takes her sled and her fourteen Huskies and moves to Parsippany, New Jersey

"Skeletal but energetic drawings are accomplished with colored felt-tip pens. The seemingly tossed-off lines are filled in with flat color that gives a mottling effect. The story's language is simple and its exposition rhythmic in a way that is tailor-made for young children." Booklist

Guys from space; [by] Daniel Pinkwater. Macmillan 1989 unp il $15; pa $3.95   E

1. Science fiction
ISBN 0-02-774672-0; 0-689-71590-0 (pa)
LC 88-13485

A boy accompanies some guys from space on a visit to another planet, where they discover such incredibly amazing things as talking rocks and root beer with ice cream

"Daniel Pinkwater has once again put his offbeat imagination to work to create a silly story that will have readers smiling, chuckling and laughing. . . . The full-colored, vivid pictures convey the absurd antics in this out-of-this-world story." Child Book Rev Serv

I was a second grade werewolf; by Daniel Pinkwater. Dutton 1983 unp il hardcover o.p. paperback available $3.95   E

1. Werewolves—Fiction
ISBN 0-525-44194-8 (pa)   LC 82-17715

"Lawrence Talbot changes into a werewolf one morning but nobody at home or in school notices, even though Lawrence snarls, bites, growls and eats his milk carton and a Twinkie with the cellophane on it and a pencil." Publ Wkly

"Pinkwater has stepped right into a little boy's imagination and has illustrated the episode in his own inimitable style. The good-size pictures are brightly colored and funny enough to make kids laugh out loud. And in keeping with the title, a strong second-grade reader should be able to handle this one alone." Booklist

Piper, Watty

The little engine that could; retold by Watty Piper; illustrated by George & Doris Hauman. 60th anniversary edition. Platt & Munk Pubs. 1990 c1930 unp il $14.95; pa $5.95   E

1. Railroads—Fiction
ISBN 0-448-40041-3; 0-448-40520-2 (pa)
LC 89-81287
Also available Spanish language edition
First published 1930
"When a train carrying good things to children breaks down, the little blue engine proves his courage and determination. The rhythmic, repetitive text encourages children to help tell the story." Hodges. Books for Elem Sch Libr

Platt, Kin, 1911-

Big Max; illustrated by Robert Lopshire. HarperCollins Pubs. 1992 64p il $13; lib bdg $12.89; pa $3.50   E

1. Mystery fiction 2. Elephants—Fiction
ISBN 0-06-024750-9; 0-06-024751-7 (lib bdg); 0-06-444006-0 (pa)   LC 91-14742
"An I can read book"
A newly illustrated edition of the title first published 1965
Big Max, the world's greatest detective, helps a king find his missing elephant
"Clever side play and a logical resolution of the major plot event keep readers interested in the story. Lopshire's newly colorized, cartoonlike drawings add to the humor." Horn Book Guide

Polacco, Patricia

Babushka's doll. Simon & Schuster Bks. for Young Readers 1990 unp il $15; pa $5.95   E

1. Dolls—Fiction
ISBN 0-671-68343-8; 0-689-80255-2 (pa)
LC 89-6122
"When Natasha wants something, she wants it now—not after her grandmother, Babushka, has finished her chores. Babushka gets tired of this attitude, and finally goes off to the market, leaving Natasha to play with a special doll that she keeps on a high shelf. The doll comes to life and subjects Natasha to the same sort of insistent whining that Natasha used on Babushka." SLJ
"Polacco's distinctive artwork interprets the story with style and verve. Using pencil, marker, and paint, she creates a series of varied compositions, highlighting muted shades with an occasional flare of bright colors and strong patterns. . . . A good, original story, illustrated with panache." Booklist

The bee tree. Philomel Bks. 1993 unp il $15.95   E

1. Books and reading—Fiction 2. Bees—Fiction
ISBN 0-399-21965-X   LC 92-8660
To teach his daughter the value of books, a father leads a growing crowd in search of the tree where the bees keep all their honey
"With a lively plot and a beautifully depicted backdrop of a rural Michigan community early in the twentieth century, this book delivers its lovely sentiment with originality and verve." Booklist

Chicken Sunday. Philomel Bks. 1992 unp il $15.95   E

1. Easter—Fiction 2. Friendship—Fiction
ISBN 0-399-22133-6   LC 91-16030
Also available Spanish language edition
To thank old Eula for her wonderful Sunday chicken dinners, her two grandsons and their friend, a girl who has "adopted" her since her own "babushka" died, sell decorated eggs and buy her a beautiful Easter hat
"Without being heavy-handed, Polacco's text conveys a tremendous pride of heritage as it brims with rich images from her characters' African American and Russian Jewish cultures. Her vibrant pencil-and-wash illustrations glow—actual family photographs have been worked into several spreads." Publ Wkly

Just plain Fancy. Bantam Bks. 1990 unp il $15.95   E

1. Amish—Fiction 2. Peacocks—Fiction
ISBN 0-553-05884-3   LC 89-27856
Also available in paperback from Dell
"In Naomi's Amish community, plainness is a way of life; still, Naomi would like just once to have something fancy. So when a peacock is mysteriously hatched among her chickens, Naomi's feelings are mixed. Delighted with Fancy's plumage, she also worries that her colorful bird will be shunned." Booklist
"The author-illustrator offers a lively story in a nontraditional setting that is depicted faithfully in both text and illustration." Horn Book

The keeping quilt. Simon & Schuster Bks. for Young Readers 1988 unp il lib bdg $15   E

1. Quilts—Fiction 2. Jews—Fiction
ISBN 0-671-64963-9   LC 88-4507
A homemade quilt ties together the lives of four generations of an immigrant Jewish family, remaining a symbol of their enduring love and faith
"Jewish customs and the way they've shifted through the years are portrayed unobtrusively in the story, which is illustrated in sepia pencil, except for the quilt, which sparks every page with its strong colors." Booklist

Mrs. Katz and Tush. Bantam Bks. 1992 unp $15   E

1. Friendship—Fiction 2. Jews—Fiction 3. African Americans—Fiction
ISBN 0-553-08122-5   LC 91-18710
Also available in paperback from Dell
"A Bantam little rooster book"
A long-lasting friendship develops between Larnel, a young African-American, and Mrs. Katz, a lonely, Jewish widow, when Larnel presents Mrs. Katz with a scrawny kitten without a tail
"Polacco has used loving details in both words and art work to craft a moving and heartfelt story of a friendship that reaches across racial and generational differences." Horn Book

My rotten redheaded older brother. Simon & Schuster Bks. for Young Readers 1994 unp il $15   E

1. Brothers and sisters—Fiction
ISBN 0-671-72751-6   LC 93-13980
"Featuring an obnoxious, freckle-faced, bespectacled boy and a comforting, tale-telling grandmother, this autobiographical story is as satisfying as a warm slice of apple pie. Patricia can't quite understand how anyone could possibly like her older brother Richard. Whether picking blackber-

Polacco, Patricia—*Continued*

ries or eating raw rhubarb, he always manages to outdo her, rubbing it in with one of his 'extra-rotten, weasel-eyed, greeny-toothed grins.' When their Bubbie teaches Patricia to wish on a falling star, she knows just what to ask for." SLJ

Pink and Say. Philomel Bks. 1994 unp il
$15.95   E
1. Friendship—Fiction 2. United States—History—1861-1865, Civil War—Fiction
ISBN 0-399-22671-0   LC 93-36340
Say Curtis describes his meeting with Pinkus Aylee, a black soldier, during the Civil War, and their capture by Southern troops
"Polacco pulls out all the stops in this heart-wrenching tale of Civil War valor which has been passed through several generations of the author's family. . . . Say's narration rings true, incorporating rough-edged grammar and idiomatic vocabulary. Polacco's signature line-and-watercolor paintings epitomize heroism, tenderness, and terror. . . . Unglamorized details of the conventions and atrocities of the Civil War target readers well beyond customary picture book age." Horn Book

Rechenka's eggs; written and illustrated by Patricia Polacco. Philomel Bks. 1988 unp il lib bdg $15.95   E
1. Geese—Fiction 2. Easter—Fiction 3. Eggs—Fiction 4. Russia—Fiction
ISBN 0-399-21501-8   LC 87-16588
An injured goose rescued by Babushka, having broken the painted eggs intended for the Easter Festival in Moscva, lays thirteen marvelously colored eggs to replace them, then leaves behind one final miracle in egg form before returning to her own kind
"Polacco achieves optimal dramatic contrast by using bold shapes against uncluttered white space and by contrasting rich colors and design details with faces in black and white." Bull Cent Child Books

Thunder cake. Philomel Bks. 1990 unp il
$15.95   E
1. Thunderstorms—Fiction 2. Fear—Fiction 3. Grandmothers—Fiction
ISBN 0-399-22231-6   LC 89-33405
"Polacco illustrates a first-person narrative about a little girl's experience on her grandmother's farm in Michigan. A Russian immigrant, Baboushka placates her granddaughter's fears by baking a 'Thunder Cake' that requires the two of them to gather ingredients to the count of the approaching booms." Bull Cent Child Books
"Polacco succeeds with both words and art. . . . The carefully drawn faces, done in pencil, contrast with the rest of the colorful folk art." Booklist

Tikvah means hope; written and illustrated by Patricia Polacco. Doubleday Bks. for Young Readers 1994 unp il $15.95   E
1. Jews—Fiction 2. Fires—Fiction 3. Sukkoth—Fiction 4. Cats—Fiction
ISBN 0-385-32059-0   LC 93-32311
"Justine's neighbor, elderly Mr. Roth, is preparing for the Jewish harvest holiday Sukkoth. Justine and her friend Duane help Mr. Roth build his Sukkah in the yard. . . . They see the orange glow and realize that the hills of Oakland, where they live, are on fire. They stay in a school gym while the fire burns for two days, and when they return to their neighborhood, they find it completely devastated. Miraculously, the Sukkah has survived untouched, as has Mr. Roth's cat, Tikvah, whose name in Hebrew means 'hope.'" Bull Cent Child Books
"Polacco's vibrantly colored illustrations pulse with ener-

gy and emotion. . . . Good Sukkoth stories are rare; rooted in an actual event as well as in ages-old tradition, this one is a priceless gem." Booklist

Politi, Leo, 1908-1996

Song of the swallows. Scribner 1987 c1949 unp il music $14.95; pa $4.95   E
1. Swallows—Fiction 2. California—Fiction 3. Missions—Fiction
ISBN 0-684-18831-7; 0-689-71140-9 (pa)
Awarded the Caldecott Medal, 1950
A reissue of title first published 1949
"The swallows always appeared at the old Mission of Capistrano on St. Joseph's Day and Juan who lived nearby wondered how they could tell that from all others. This tender poetic story of the coming of springtime is touched by the kindliness of the good Fathers of the Mission as a little boy knew it. Lovely pictures in soft colors bring out the charm of the southern California landscape and the melody of the swallow song adds to the feeling of Spring." Horn Book

Polushkin, Maria

Who said meow? illustrated by Ellen Weiss. Bradbury Press 1988 unp il $13.95   E
1. Dogs—Fiction 2. Animals—Fiction
ISBN 0-02-774770-0   LC 87-28073
Adaptation of a Russian story by V. Suteev
"A puppy is awakened from his nap by a teasing kitten, and in pursuit he encounters a mouse, a dog, a bee and other creatures. He finds the kitten back in the house, and sure enough, it does say meow." N Y Times Book Rev
"The pictures, while simple, colorful, and pleasant, lack polish. Still, little ones should like the hide-and-seek aspect of the book, and the occasional glimpses of kitty hiding in the corners will keep them turning the pages." Booklist

Pomerantz, Charlotte

The chalk doll; pictures by Frané Lessac. Lippincott 1989 30p il lib bdg $14.89; pa $4.75   E
1. Dolls—Fiction 2. Mothers and daughters—Fiction 3. Jamaica—Fiction
ISBN 0-397-32319-0 (lib bdg); 0-06-443333-1 (pa)
LC 88-872
"Rose has a cold and must stay in bed. Before she settles in for a nap, she coaxes her mother to tell stories of her Jamaican childhood. The scene shifts from Rose's colorful room filled with toys to a simple little house in the village where her mother grew up. The stories are touching for the contrast between the poverty and yearning of these childhood memories and the obvious comfort of their present lives." Horn Book
"The stylized illustrations by the West Indian artists Frané Lessac are primitive in bright, oscillating colors, evoking poverty in a tropical paradise as well as mother-daughter affection in a well-appointed home." N Y Times Book Rev

The outside dog; story by Charlotte Pomerantz; pictures by Jennifer Plecas. HarperCollins Pubs. 1993 62p il $14.95; lib bdg $14.89; pa $3.75   E
1. Dogs—Fiction 2. Grandfathers—Fiction 3. Puerto Rico—Fiction
ISBN 0-06-024782-7; 0-06-024783-5 (lib bdg); 0-06-444187-3 (pa)   LC 91-6351

Pomerantz, Charlotte—*Continued*

"An I can read book"

Marisol, who lives in Puerto Rico, wants a dog very much but her grandfather will not let her have one, until a skinny mutt wins him over

"Unlike most easy readers, not everything is spelled out in the story, and kids will have to make connections, the very thing that will increase their reading ability. Some Spanish words and phrases (defined at the beginning of the book) also deepen the story. But most importantly, this is lively, fun, and filled with pen-and-watercolor art that captures the affection that binds this new family." Booklist

The piggy in the puddle; pictures by James Marshall. Macmillan 1974 unp il $14.95; pa $4.95   **E**

1. Pigs—Fiction 2. Stories in rhyme

ISBN 0-02-774900-2; 0-689-71293-6 (pa)

The "rhythmic tale of a small pig that scorns soap and refuses to leave her puddle. Her pleasure is infectious and finally mother, father, and brother join her in 'the very merry middle' of the 'muddy little puddle.'" Booklist

"The soft pastel drawings add just the right touch to the humorous bedtime story which demands to be read aloud." Child Book Rev Serv

Where's the bear? pictures by Byron Barton; words by Charlotte Pomerantz. Greenwillow Bks. 1984 unp il $15; lib bdg $14.93; pa $3.95   **E**

1. Bears—Fiction 2. Stories in rhyme

ISBN 0-688-01752-5; 0-688-01753-3 (lib bdg); 0-688-10999-3 (pa)   LC 83-1697

"A woman runs back into her village and alerts the people to something lurking in the woods. 'Where's the bear?' they ask, and follow her armed with hoes, hammers, and brooms. Back in the forest, they ask again 'Where?' 'There's the bear, there's the bear.' At least that's what the villagers think, but it's only rabbits, racoons, and birds making the noise. Then the bear really does appear, and it's a mad scramble to get back to the safety of home." Booklist

"This is ideal for the youngest children: brilliantly colored pictures, clear expressions, simple activities, and repetitive words that can be chanted. Preschool and kindergarten teachers could easily turn this into a game or skit. Children just learning to read can enjoy this on their own." Child Book Rev Serv

Porte-Thomas, Barbara Ann

Chickens! chickens! story by Barbara Ann Porte; paintings by Greg Henry. Orchard Bks. 1995 unp il $14.95; lib bdg $14.99   **E**

1. Artists—Fiction 2. Chickens—Fiction

ISBN 0-531-06877-3; 0-531-08727-1 (lib bdg)

LC 94-19552

"A Richard Jackson book"

A man who loves to draw chickens fortunately meets and marries a woman who not only appreciates his art, but also find a way to put it to good use

"With rhythmic prose and occasional internal rhymes meted out by a practical storyteller, this buoyant story will snag listeners with its infectious silliness. . . . A contemporary fairy tale with down-home twists of humor that are extended in Henry's paintings, stylized in a naïve mode with flat perspectives and brilliant color contrasts. . . . The characters are African American, the theme is follow your dream, and the book is a lot of fun." Bull Cent Child Books

Harry in trouble; [by] Barbara Ann Porte; pictures by Yossi Abolafia. Greenwillow Bks. 1989 47p il $15; lib bdg $14.93   **E**

ISBN 0-688-07633-5; 0-688-07722-6 (lib bdg)

LC 87-21253

Harry is upset about losing his library card three times in a row, but feels better when he learns that his father and his friend Dorcas sometimes lose things

"Porte's story has an easy-to-read format which nicely fits the present tense childlike first-person narration. Abolafia's expressive cartoon style illustrations ably convey characters' emotions." SLJ

Other available titles about Harry are:

Harry gets an uncle (1991)

Harry's birthday (1994)

Harry's dog (1984)

Harry's mom (1985)

When grandma almost fell off the mountain & other stories; by Barbara Ann Porte; pictures by Maxie Chambliss. Orchard Bks. 1993 unp il $14.95; lib bdg $14.99   **E**

1. Vacations—Fiction 2. Grandmothers—Fiction 3. Family life—Fiction

ISBN 0-531-05965-0; 0-531-08565-1 (lib bdg)

LC 91-41174

"A Richard Jackson book"

Grandma tells surprising and unusual stories about a vacation she took with her family when she was a little girl

"Chambliss' simple, bright watercolor and color-pencil illustrations on every page express the exuberance and farce of the stories and the warmth of the telling, the rich sense of character and place." Booklist

Potter, Beatrix, 1866-1943

The pie and the patty-pan. Warne il o.p.; Dover Publs. paperback available $1.95   **E**

1. Cats—Fiction 2. Dogs—Fiction

ISBN 0-486-23383-9 (pa)

First published 1905 with title: A tale of the pie and the patty-pan

"Ribby, a pussy cat, invites a little dog named Duchess to tea." Toronto Public Libr. Books for Boys & Girls

The story of Miss Moppet. Warne il $5.95; pa $2.25   **E**

1. Cats—Fiction 2. Mice—Fiction

ISBN 0-7232-3480-9; 0-7232-3505-8 (pa)

First published 1906

Miss Moppet is a kitten who uses her wiles to capture a curious mouse. But her trickery amounts to naught when she herself is outwitted

Other available titles about Moppet's brother Tom and sister Mittens are:

The complete adventures of Tom Kitten and his friends (1984)

The roly-poly pudding (1908)

The tale of Tom Kitten (1935)

The tailor of Gloucester. Warne il $5.95; pa $2.25   **E**

1. Tailoring—Fiction 2. Mice—Fiction 3. Christmas—Fiction

ISBN 0-7232-3462-0; 0-7232-3487-6 (pa)

Also available Spanish language edition

First published in 1903

Potter, Beatrix, 1866-1943—*Continued*
"The cat Simpkin looked after his master when he was ill, but it was the nimble-fingered mice who used snippets of cherry-coloured twist and so finished the embroidered waist coat for the worried tailor. A Christmas-time story set in old Gloucester." Four to Fourteen
"A read-aloud classic in polished style, perfectly complemented by the author's exquisite watercolor illustrations." Hodges. Books for Elem Sch Libr

The tale of Jemima Puddle-duck   E
1. Ducks—Fiction
Also available Spanish language edition
Some editions are:
Simon & Schuster $3.95 (ISBN 0-671-63236-1)
Warne $13; pa $4.95 (ISBN 0-7232-3468-X; 0-7232-3425-6)
First published 1908 by Warne
"Jemima Puddle-duck's obstinate determination to hatch her own eggs, makes a story of suspense and sly humor." Toronto Public Libr. Books for Boys & Girls

The tale of Mr. Jeremy Fisher   E
1. Frogs—Fiction
Also available Spanish language edition
Some editions are:
Simon & Schuster $14.95 (ISBN 0-88708-094-4)
Warne $5.95; pa $2.25 (ISBN 0-7232-3466-3; 0-7232-3491-4)
First published 1906 by Warne
A frog fishing from his lilly pad boat doesn't catch any fish, but one catches him

The tale of Mrs. Tiggy-Winkle. Warne il $5.95; pa $2.25   E
1. Hedgehogs—Fiction
ISBN 0-7232-3465-5; 0-7232-3490-6 (pa)
Also available Spanish language edition
First published 1905
Lucie visits the laundry of Mrs. Tiggy-Winkle, a hedgehog, and finds her lost handerchiefs

The tale of Mrs. Tittlemouse. Warne il $5.95; pa $2.25   E
1. Mice—Fiction
ISBN 0-7232-3470-1; 0-7232-3495-7 (pa)
Also available Spanish language edition
First published 1910
The story of a little mouse's funny house, the visitors she has there, and how she finally rids herself of the untidy, messy ones

The tale of Peter Rabbit. Warne il $5.95; pa $2.25   E
1. Rabbits—Fiction
ISBN 0-7232-3460-4; 0-7232-3485-X (pa)
Also available French language and Spanish language editions
First published 1903
All about the famous rabbit family consisting of Flopsy, Mopsy, Cotton-tail and especially Peter Rabbit who disobeys Mother Rabbit's admonishment not to go into Mr. McGregor's garden
"Distinctive writing and a strong appeal to a small child's sense of justice and his sympathies make this an outstanding story. The water color illustrations add charm to the narrative by their simplicity of detail and delicacy of color." Child Books Too Good to Miss

Other available titles about Peter Rabbit and his family are:
The tale of Benjamin Bunny (1904)
The tale of Mr. Tod (1912)
The tale of the flopsy bunnies (1909)

The tale of Pigling Bland. Warne il $5.95; pa $2.25   E
1. Pigs—Fiction
ISBN 0-7232-3474-4; 0-7232-3499-X (pa)
First published 1913
"Pigling's story ends happily with a perfectly lovely little black Berkshire pig called Pigwig." Toronto Public Libr. Books for Boys & Girls

The tale of Squirrel Nutkin. Warne il $5.95; pa $2.25   E
1. Squirrels—Fiction
ISBN 0-7232-3461-2; 0-7232-6226-8 (pa)
Also available Spanish language edition
First published 1903
Each day the squirrels gather nuts, Nutkin propounds a riddle to Mr. Brown, the owl, until impertinent Nutkin, over-estimating Mr. Brown's patience, gets his due

The tale of Timmy Tiptoes. Warne il $5.95; pa $2.25   E
1. Squirrels—Fiction
ISBN 0-7232-3471-X; 0-7232-3496-5 (pa)
First published 1911
An innocent squirrel accused of stealing nuts is forced down a hole in a tree, where he meets a friendly chipmunk

The tale of two bad mice. Warne il $5.95; pa $2.25   E
1. Mice—Fiction
ISBN 0-7232-3464-7; 0-7232-3489-2 (pa)
Also available Spanish language edition
First published 1904
"Two mischievous little mice pilfer a doll's house to equip their own. They are caught and finally make amends for what they have done. Perfectly charming illustrations and a most enticing tale." Adventuring With Books. 2d edition

Preston, Edna Mitchell
Squawk to the moon, Little Goose; illustrated by Barbara Cooney. Viking 1974 unp il o.p.; Puffin Bks. paperback available $3.95   E
1. Geese—Fiction 2. Moon—Fiction
ISBN 0-14-050546-6 (pa)
"Tucked in for the night, Little Goose steals out for a night ramble; she sees the moon covered by a cloud and wakes the farmer with her squawking; it happens again when she sees the moon reflected in the pond and decides it has fallen. When she's caught by a fox, Little Goose squawks, but the disgruntled farmer won't get up a third time. However, Little Goose uses her wits and outfoxes the fox." Bull Cent Child Books
"Ms. Cooney has infused her watercolor illustrations with so much personality, drollery and beauty that fortunate owners of this book will find themselves gazing at the pictures again and again, finding new aspects at which to marvel each time." Publ Wkly

Priceman, Marjorie

How to make an apple pie and see the world. Knopf 1994 unp il $16; lib bdg $16.99

    E

1. Baking—Fiction 2. Voyages and travels—Fiction
ISBN 0-679-83705-1; 0-679-93705-6 (lib bdg)

    LC 93-12341

Since the market is closed, the reader is led around the world to gather the ingredients for making an apple pie

"The perfect blend of whimsical illustrations and tongue-in-cheek humor makes this an irresistable offering. The recipe is included." Child Book Rev Serv

Prokofiev, Sergey, 1891-1953

Peter and the wolf; translated by Maria Carlson; illustrated by Charles Mikolaycak. Viking 1982 unp il hardcover o.p. paperback available $3.95

    E

1. Wolves—Fiction 2. Fairy tales
ISBN 0-14-050633-0 (pa)

    LC 81-70402

This book retells the orchestral fairy tale of the boy who, ignoring his grandfather's warnings, proceeds to capture a wolf

"Prokofiev's classic, designed to teach children the instruments of an orchestra, has been published in picture book form before, but never better illustrated. The translation is smooth. . . . The paintings are rich in color, dramatic in details of costume or architecture, strong in composition, with distinctive individuality in the faces of people and of the wolf." Bull Cent Child Books

Provensen, Alice, 1918-

Shaker Lane; by Alice and Martin Provensen. Viking Kestrel 1987 unp il lib bdg $14.95

    E

ISBN 0-670-81568-3

    LC 87-6283

"As the Herkimer sisters, rural inhabitants, grew old, they sold off parts of their land to those with modest incomes and a laid-back lifestyle. Then land developers arrived, created a reservoir, and forced the poor to move out to be replaced by middle-class families." SLJ

"It's always autumn in the Provensens' paintings of this quiet rural drama, with the browns and russets of land and sky providing a comfortable background for the rickety houses and piled-up yards of Shaker Lane's inhabitants. There's plenty of wry humor here, and the whole has a tone of inevitability rather than tragedy." Bull Cent Child Books

The year at Maple Hill Farm; [by] Alice and Martin Provensen. Atheneum Pubs. 1978 unp il hardcover o.p. paperback available $4.95

    E

1. Seasons—Fiction 2. Farm life—Fiction 3. Animals—Fiction
ISBN 0-689-71270-7 (pa)

    LC 77-18518

"A Jonathan Cape book"

Describes the seasonal changes on a farm and surrounding countryside throughout the year

"Each of the twelve double-page spreads has a running line of general comment across the tops of the pages . . . and captions for the other pictures, of which there may be one or several. The text is direct, mildly humorous, and informative; the illustrations are perky and amusing, with soft, bright colors and the appeal of animals, animals, animals." Bull Cent Child Books

Another available title about Maple Hill Farm is:
An owl and three pussycats (1981)

Purdy, Carol

Mrs. Merriwether's musical cat; illustrated by Petra Mathers. Putnam 1994 unp il $15.95

    E

1. Pianists—Fiction 2. Cats—Fiction
ISBN 0-399-22543-9

    LC 92-43934

Mrs. Merriwether takes in a stray cat that proves to have an amazing effect on her piano students

"Accompanied by appealing illustrations that feature bold colors and strong lines, Purdy's engaging tale will strike a chord with cat fanciers and music students alike." Booklist

Raschka, Christopher

Yo! Yes? by Chris Raschka. Orchard Bks. 1993 unp il $14.95; lib bdg $14.99

    E

1. Friendship—Fiction 2. Race relations—Fiction 3. African Americans—Fiction
ISBN 0-531-05469-1; 0-531-08619-4 (lib bdg)

    LC 92-25644

A Caldecott Medal honor book, 1994

"A Richard Jackson book"

Two lonely characters, one black and one white, meet on the street and become friends

"The design and drawing are bold, spare and expressive; the language has the strength and rhythm of a playground chant." Bull Cent Child Books

Raskin, Ellen, 1928-1984

Nothing ever happens on my block. Atheneum Pubs. 1966 unp il hardcover o.p. paperback available $4.95

    E

ISBN 0-689-71335-5 (pa)

"Chester Filbert, the personification of the 'grass is greener,' sits on the curb longing to see fierce lions, monsters, or other fantastic sights. Meanwhile he misses all the fantastic events, including robberies and fires transpiring around him. Much of the fun is in combing the illustrations for all the things Chester is missing." Minnesota. Dept of Educ. Libr Div

"In all fairness to Chester all those thefts and parachute jumps never happened on my block either. This in no way detracts from the inventive excellence of the book, which is a delight." N Y Times Book Rev

Spectacles. Atheneum Pubs. 1968 unp il hardcover o.p. paperback available $4.95

    E

1. Eyeglasses—Fiction
ISBN 0-689-71271-5 (pa)

Even though nearsighted "Iris swears that there's a fire-breathing dragon at the door, a giant pygmy nuthatch on the lawn, a chestnut mare in the parlor, her readers will see, by flipping the page each time, that it's only Great-aunt Fanny, her friend Chester, and the baby sitter respectively. Iris detests specs but gets them, anyway." SLJ

"Laughable picture book, conceived and illustrated with imagination and humor. May be useful with children resisting needed glasses." Booklist

Rathmann, Peggy

Good night, Gorilla. Putnam 1994 unp il $13.95

    E

1. Zoos—Fiction
ISBN 0-399-22445-9

    LC 92-29020

Rathmann, Peggy—*Continued*

An unobservant zookeeper is followed home by all the animals he thinks he has left behind in the zoo

"In a book economical in text and simple in illustration, the many amusing, small details, as well as the tranquil tone of the story, make this an outstanding picture book." Horn Book Guide

Officer Buckle and Gloria. Putnam 1995 unp il $15.95   **E**

1. School stories 2. Dogs—Fiction 3. Safety education—Fiction

ISBN 0-399-22616-8   LC 93-43887

Awarded the Caldecott Medal, 1996

"When rotund, good-natured officer Buckle visits school assemblies to read off his sensible safety tips, the children listen, bored and polite, dozing off one by one. But when the new police dog, Gloria, stands behind him, secretly miming the dire consequences of acting imprudently, the children suddenly become attentive, laughing uproariously and applauding loudly. . . . The deadpan humor of the text and slapstick wit of the illustrations make a terrific combination. Large, expressive line drawings illustrate the characters with finesse, and the Kool-Aid-bright washes add energy and pizzazz." Booklist

Rattigan, Jama Kim

Dumpling soup; illustrated by Lillian Hsu-Flanders. Little, Brown 1993 unp il $15.95   **E**

1. Family life—Fiction 2. New Year—Fiction 3. Hawaii—Fiction

ISBN 0-316-73445-4   LC 91-42949

"Marisa, a seven-year-old Asian-American girl who lives in Hawaii, explains the traditions that exist in her family to celebrate the New Year. Her family . . . consists of people who are Japanese, Chinese, Korean, Hawaiian, and *haole* (Hawaiian for white person). . . . A glossary of English, Hawaiian, Japanese, and Korean words provides pronunciations and definitions for many of the possibly unfamiliar terms that weave in and out of the text. A thoroughly enjoyable celebration of family warmth and diverse traditions, illustrated with cheery watercolors." Horn Book

Rayner, Mary, 1933-

Mr. and Mrs. Pig's evening out. Atheneum Pubs. 1976 unp il $14.95   **E**

1. Pigs—Fiction

ISBN 0-689-30530-3   LC 76-4476

"Even though Mrs. Pig assures them she has hired a very nice lady from the babysitting agency, her 10 piglets moan and groan in protest. She goes to the door and ushers in a cloaked, sinister figure, the babysitter who answers to the name of Mrs. Wolf. Tension mounts as Mrs. Wolf turns on the oven and makes for the piglets' bedroom, where she grabs one brother and heads back to the preheated oven. The piglets rally round to rescue their brother for an exciting and victorious ending." N Y Times Book Rev

"If humour and terror (resolved) are the ingredients of treasured nursery-stories, Mary Rayner's [book] will be loved till its sturdy binding falls off. . . . [The] book has style, wit, excitement, high drama, and pathos." Times Lit Suppl

Other available titles about Mr. and Mrs. Pig and their piglets are:

Garth Pig and the ice cream lady (1977)
Garth Pig steals the show (1993)
Mrs. Pig gets cross and other stories (1987)
Mrs. Pig's bulk buy (1981)

Reiser, Lynn

The surprise family. Greenwillow Bks. 1994 unp il $14; lib bdg $13.93   **E**

1. Chickens—Fiction 2. Ducks—Fiction

ISBN 0-688-11671-X; 0-688-11672-8 (lib bdg)

     LC 93-16249

A baby chicken accepts a young boy as her mother and later becomes a surrogate mother for some ducklings that she has hatched

"Complemented by amusing watercolor and ink illustrations, the story promotes unconditional love within families without sounding didactic." Horn Book Guide

Rey, H. A. (Hans Augusto), 1898-1977

Curious George. Houghton Mifflin 1941 unp il $13.95; pa $4.95   **E**

1. Monkeys—Fiction

ISBN 0-395-15993-8; 0-395-15023-X (pa)

Also available Spanish language edition

Also available book form adaptations from the Curious George film series, edited by Margaret Rey and Alan J. Shalleck

Curious George goes to the hospital was written by Margaret Rey and H. A. Rey in collaboration with the Children's Hospital Medical Center; and Curious George flies a kite was written by Margaret Rey with pictures by H. A. Rey

Colored picture book, with simple text, describing the adventures of a curious small monkey, and the difficulties he had in getting used to city life, before he went to live in the zoo

"The bright lithographs in red, yellow, and blue, are gay and lighthearted, following the story closely with the same speed and animated humour." Ont Libr Rev

Other available titles about Curious George are:

Curious George flies a kite (1958)
Curious George gets a medal (1957)
Curious George goes to the hospital (1966)
Curious George learns the alphabet (1963)
Curious George rides a bike (1952)
Curious George takes a job (1947)

Rice, Eve, 1951-

Benny bakes a cake; story and pictures by Eve Rice. Greenwillow Bks. 1993 c1981 unp il $14; lib bdg $[3.93; pa $4.95   **E**

1. Birthdays—Fiction 2. Cake—Fiction

ISBN 0-688-11579-9; 0-688-11580-2 (lib bdg); 0-688-07814-1 (pa)

A reissue of the title first published 1981

"It is Benny's birthday, and Mama lets him help bake the cake. But when Benny's cake is done, Ralph, the dog, helps himself to the biggest piece. Luckily Papa saves the day." SLJ

"A reassuring domestic story spiced with Ralph's mischief; a perennial favorite just right for its preschool audience." Horn Book

City night; pictures by Peter Sis. Greenwillow Bks. 1987 unp il $11.75; lib bdg $11.88   **E**

1. City life—Fiction 2. Night—Fiction 3. Stories in rhyme

ISBN 0-688-06856-1; 0-688-06857-X (lib bdg)

     LC 86-12021

The rhyming text follows a family as they set out for a nighttime jaunt through city streets

"Urban life after dark shines and glows in this book,

Rice, Eve, 1951-—*Continued*

with a texture and depth to the rough-hewn illustrations that will charm city-dwellers and country kids alike." Publ Wkly

Goodnight, goodnight. Greenwillow Bks. 1980 unp il $15; lib bdg $14.93; pa $3.95
E

1. Night—Fiction
ISBN 0-688-80254-0; 0-688-84254-2 (lib bdg); 0-688-11707-4 (pa)   LC 79-17253
Everyone in town, including the cats, prepare for sleep
"Rice uses black and white, tempered by grainy textures for shadow and depth, brightened and warmed by spots of primary yellow wherever light shines from room or sky. Once again, the author-artist succeeds uniquely in conveying a happy, self-contained world satisfying to the souls of young children." Booklist

Peter's pockets; pictures by Nancy Winslow Parker. Greenwillow Bks. 1989 unp il $15; lib bdg $14.93
E

ISBN 0-688-07241-0; 0-688-07242-9 (lib bdg)
LC 87-15640
Peter's new pants don't have any pockets, so Uncle Nick lets Peter use his until Peter's mother solves the problem in a clever and colorful way
"Parker's sturdy, rounded shapes and colored-pencil shading conserve the simplicity of Rice's story, which characteristically—and successfully—portrays the world from a young child's viewpoint." Bull Cent Child Books

Sam who never forgets. Greenwillow Bks. 1977 unp il lib bdg $13.93; pa $3.95
E

1. Zoos—Fiction 2. Animals—Fiction
ISBN 0-688-84088-4 (lib bdg); 0-688-07335-2 (pa)
LC 76-30370
Sam is "a zoo keeper who 'never, never forgets' to feed the animals promptly at three o'clock. The beasts have their doubts when it looks like Sam has neglected to feed poor Elephant who is both hungry and crestfallen. Happily, Sam returns with a whole wagon of hay." SLJ
"A simple, unpretentious story with child appeal that lies in the naive, straightforward telling and elemental emotional interactions of the characters. . . . Rice has forsaken her pen drawings for bright, unlined colored shapes. The figures are pleasantly stylized, the scenes evenly composed." Booklist

Ringgold, Faith

Aunt Harriet's Underground Railroad in the sky. Crown 1992 unp il $16; lib bdg $17.99; pa $5.99
E

1. Tubman, Harriet, 1815?-1913—Fiction 2. Slavery—Fiction 3. Underground railroad—Fiction
ISBN 0-517-58767-X; 0-517-58768-8 (lib bdg); 0-517-88543-3 (pa)   LC 92-20072
With Harriet Tubman as her guide, Cassie [featured in Tar Beach] retraces the steps escaping slaves took on the Underground Railroad in order to reunite with her younger brother
"Ringgold's dynamic paintings combine historical fact with strongly realized emotions. . . . Two pages of historical notes on Tubman and the Underground Railroad, including a map and bibliography, round out the volume." Booklist

Tar Beach. Crown 1991 unp il $18; lib bdg $16.99; pa $5.99
E

1. African Americans—Fiction 2. Dreams—Fiction 3. Harlem (New York, N.Y.)—Fiction
ISBN 0-517-58030-6; 0-517-58031-4 (lib bdg); 0-517-58984-2 (pa)   LC 90-40410
A Caldecott Medal honor book, 1992; Coretta Scott King Award for illustration, 1992
Eight-year-old Cassie dreams of flying above her Harlem home, claiming all she sees for herself and her family. Based on the author's quilt painting of the same name
"Part autobiographical, part fictional, this allegorical tale sparkles with symbolic and historical references central to African-American culture. The spectacular artwork, a combination of primitive naive figures in a flattened perspective against a boldly patterned cityscape, resonates with color and texture." Horn Book

Robins, Joan

Addie meets Max; pictures by Sue Truesdell. Harper & Row 1985 31p il lib bdg $14.89
E

1. Friendship—Fiction
ISBN 0-06-025064-X   LC 84-48329
"An Early I can read book"
Addie discovers that the new boy next door, Max, and his dog are not so terrible when she helps him bury his newly lost tooth
"A realistic, mildly funny story is pleasant for reading aloud as well as for the beginning independent reader. The illustrations, line and wash, have vigor and humor." Bull Cent Child Books
Other available titles about Addie and Max are:
Addie runs away (1989)
Addie's bad day (1993)

Rockwell, Anne F., 1934-

At the beach; [by] Anne & Harlow Rockwell. Macmillan 1987 unp il $13.95; pa $3.95
E

1. Beaches
ISBN 0-02-777940-8; 0-689-71494-7 (pa)
LC 86-2943
"A young preschooler accompanies her mother to the beach and in a first-person narrative describes familiar beach activities such as putting on sunscreen and chasing sandpipers." SLJ
"Harlow Rockwell is at his best with the deceptively naive arrangements of pleasing shapes and strong primary colors, but the more crowded beach scenes afford a welcome contrast in their busy, if controlled, activity." Horn Book

First comes spring; [by] Anne Rockwell. Crowell 1985 unp il hardcover o.p. paperback available $4.95
E

1. Seasons—Fiction 2. Bears—Fiction
ISBN 0-06-107412-8 (pa)   LC 84-45331
Bear Child notices that the clothes he wears, the things everyone does at work and play, and other parts of his world all change with the seasons
"The pen-and-ink drawings, glowing with Rockwell's soft yet brilliant watercolors, create a world that young children will want to explore again and again." Booklist

Rockwell, Anne F., 1934-—*Continued*

The first snowfall; [by] Anne & Harlow Rockwell. Macmillan 1987 unp il $13.95; pa $3.95   E

1. Snow—Fiction
ISBN 0-02-777770-7; 0-689-71614-1 (pa)
LC 86-23712

A child enjoys the special sights and activities of a snow-covered world with her father

"Children will vicariously enjoy the fragrance and warmth of the steaming hot cocoa the young girl drinks upon her return home. Only the illustration of her mother in an incorrect and awkward skiing position mars this otherwise inviting and useful introduction to the joys of the season." Horn Book

Happy birthday to me; [by] Anne & Harlow Rockwell. Macmillan 1981 unp il $10.95
E

1. Birthdays—Fiction
ISBN 0-02-777680-8
LC 81-3738
"My world"

This book utilizes "the authors' characteristic soft lines, rounded shapes and spectrum of primary colors washed to make the world lively but not startlingly bright. The text appears to be hand lettered, but is distinct and sized correctly for the pages. . . . [It] shows mother, father and son making preparations for the boy's party, children enjoying the festivities and the final thank-yous and goodbyes. The book expresses a very positive experience, with the many aspects of a party." SLJ

How my garden grew; [by] Anne & Harlow Rockwell. Macmillan 1982 unp il $10.95
E

1. Gardening—Fiction
ISBN 0-02-777660-3
LC 81-17145
"My world"

This book "presents a small child showing the reader where his lettuce and marigolds and pumpkins and sunflowers have come from." Christ Sci Monit

The book is "alive with realism and color. . . . The simple vocabulary and format clearly relate the process of planting, growing and harvesting a garden. Preschoolers can easily understand the theories of ecology and nature as bugs eat the insects and natural fish fertilizer is used to make a garden grow." SLJ

Our garage sale; by Anne Rockwell; pictures by Harlow Rockwell. Greenwillow Bks. 1984 unp il $10.25; lib bdg $10.88   E

1. Garage sales—Fiction
ISBN 0-688-80278-8; 0-688-84278-X (lib bdg)
LC 80-16704

"This gives a clear account of what a garage sale is and why people have them. . . . The speaker is the younger child in a family that clears unwanted objects from attic, cellar, and garage to hold a sale in their driveway." Bull Cent Child Books

"Rockwell's plain lines and open compositions make everything look fresh and inviting. This should have its share of takers, especially among children whose streets and alleys have boasted such events." Booklist

Pots and pans; by Anne Rockwell; illustrated by Lizzy Rockwell. Macmillan 1993 unp il $13.95   E

1. Household equipment and supplies
ISBN 0-02-777631-X
LC 91-4976

Introduces the shiny, colorful utensils in a kitchen cupboard, including the tea kettle, omelette pan, and cake mold

"The glowing watercolors are dynamically balanced, and the layout is well varied. . . . The simple text mentions a few shapes, sizes, and construction materials but mainly names the items. Preschoolers who know the joys of pulling out kitchen things will appreciate this book." SLJ

Sick in bed; [by] Anne & Harlow Rockwell. Macmillan 1982 unp il $10.95   E

1. Sick—Fiction 2. Medical care—Fiction
ISBN 0-02-777730-8
LC 81-15637
"My world"

This book documents a "small boy's bout with illness from initial crankiness to joyful recovery. Painful elements—sore throat, fever, medication—are not minimized, but the sympathetic attention and special privileges accorded to homebound young patients offer cozy reassurance." Horn Book

"The Rockwells show through description and colorful pen-and-wash art the details of thermometers, throat-culture tubes and a medical examination. The illustrations create opportunities for discussion." SLJ

Rohmann, Eric

Time flies. Crown 1994 unp il $15; lib bdg $15.99   E

1. Stories without words   2. Birds—Fiction
3. Dinosaurs—Fiction
ISBN 0-517-59598-2; 0-517-59599-0 (lib bdg)
LC 93-28200

A Caldecott Medal honor book, 1995

A wordless tale in which a bird flying around the dinosaur exhibit in a natural history museum has an unsettling experience when the dinosaur seems to come alive and view the bird as a potential meal

"The handsome, atmospheric paintings heighten the drama as they tell their simple, somewhat mysterious, and quite short story." Booklist

Rosen, Michael, 1946-

We're going on a bear hunt; retold by Michael Rosen; illustrated by Helen Oxenbury. Margaret K. McElderry Bks. 1989 unp il $15.95; pa $5.95   E

1. Bears—Fiction 2. Hunting—Fiction
ISBN 0-689-50476-4; 0-689-71653-2 (pa)
LC 88-13338

Also available Spanish language edition

"Glorious puddles of watercolor alternate with impish charcoal sketches in this refreshing interpretation of an old hand rhyme in which a man, four children, and a dog stalk the furry beast through mud and muck, high and low. A book with a genuine atmosphere of togetherness and boundless enthusiasm for the hunt." SLJ

Rosenberg, Liz

Monster mama; story by Liz Rosenberg; illustrations by Stephen Gammell. Philomel Bks. 1993 unp il $15.95   E

1. Mothers and sons—Fiction 2. Monsters—Fiction
ISBN 0-399-21989-7
LC 91-46825

"Patrick loves his strange and powerful mother, and when the local bullies insult her, his anger transforms him, and he chases them with glowing eyes and 'truly monstrous' laughter. Gammell's splattered paintings in brilliant watercolors and frenetic lines express all the mad energy and transformation of the story." Booklist

Ross, Pat

Meet M and M; pictures by Marylin Hafner. Pantheon Bks. 1980 41p il o.p.; Puffin Bks. paperback available $3.99   E

1. Friendship—Fiction
ISBN 0-14-032651-0 (pa)   LC 79-190
"An I am reading book"

"Because they look so much alike, Mandy and Mimi like to pretend they're twins; they share everything, including bubble baths and toys. . . . Total amity. Then, 'one crabby day,' they have a squabble, it takes several miserable days more before they make up, and there is a happy reunion as they meet on the stairs halfway between their apartments." Bull Cent Child Books

"Beginning readers will have no difficulty with the humorously told, very real incidents, and the way in which the impasse is breached and friendship restored is particularly childlike. The many black-and-white pencil drawings capture the girls' facial expressions especially well." Horn Book

Other available titles about M and M (Mandy and Mimi) are:

M and M and the bad news babies (1983)
M and M and the Halloween monster (1991)
M and M and the haunted house game (1980)
M and M and the Santa secrets (1980)
M and M and the super child afternoon (1987)

Rounds, Glen, 1906-

Washday on Noah's ark; a story of Noah's ark. Holiday House 1985 unp il $14.95; pa $5.95   E

1. Noah's ark—Fiction 2. Tall tales
ISBN 0-8234-0555-9; 0-8234-0880-9 (pa)
LC 84-22380

When the forty-first day on the ark dawns bright and clear, Mrs. Noah decides to do the wash, and having no rope long enough, devises an ingenious clothesline

"This goes far afield from the original; Noah gets his information on the impending storm from weather reports, not God. And, as in many tall tales, animals are not given the best of treatment . . . but the simple shapes and softly textured colors make a nice combination. The art radiates a sense of movement and fun that young children will find appealing." Booklist

Russo, Marisabina

A visit to Oma. Greenwillow Bks. 1991 unp il $13.95; lib bdg $13.88   E

1. Grandmothers—Fiction
ISBN 0-688-09623-9; 0-688-09624-7 (lib bdg)
LC 89-77716

"Every week Celeste visits her great grandmother Oma who doesn't speak English. As she chatters to Celeste in her native tongue, the young girl patiently listens as she creates a story about the old lady. This day, she pictures her as a young woman forced to marry a man she hates. She flees on her wedding night and is ostracized by her village. With the triumph of love and understanding between the two, both Oma and Celeste are satisfied." Child Book Rev Serv

"The illustrations are easily recognizable as Russo's; large areas of deep, warm, flat color are suffused with Old-World charm. . . . Russo's story will engage young readers with its warmth, love, and mysterious sense of personal history." Horn Book

Waiting for Hannah. Greenwillow Bks. 1989 unp il $12.95; lib bdg $14.93   E

1. Infants—Fiction 2. Mothers and daughters—Fiction
ISBN 0-688-08015-4; 0-688-08016-2 (lib bdg)
LC 87-37201

Hannah's mother recounts events during the summer when she was expecting her daughter. A universal story and a beautiful vignette of daily life in a family." Horn Book Guide

Ryder, Joanne

My father's hands; illustrated by Mark Graham. Morrow Junior Bks. 1994 unp il $15; lib bdg $14.93   E

1. Fathers and daughters—Fiction 2. Gardening—Fiction
ISBN 0-688-09189-X; 0-688-09190-3 (lib bdg)
LC 93-27116

"A little girl and her father share the wonders of nature as they examine several small creatures in the garden—a pink worm, a golden beetle, a sliding snail, and a praying mantis. Graham's lovely double-page, impressionistic oil paintings clearly focus on the man and his daughter, with closeups of faces and hands in nearly every illustration. The garden in the background, lush with flowers and vegetable plants, provides a picturesque setting for this simple, straightforward description of a special parent/child outing." SLJ

Rylant, Cynthia

All I see; story by Cynthia Rylant; pictures by Peter Catalanotto. Orchard Bks. 1988 unp il $16.95; lib bdg $15.99; pa $5.95   E

1. Artists—Fiction 2. Painting—Fiction
ISBN 0-531-05777-1; 0-531-08377-2 (lib bdg);
0-531-07048-4 (pa)   LC 88-42547
"A Richard Jackson book"

"The story of a shy boy, Charlie, who, while summering by a lake, becomes fascinated with the work of a painter named Gregory. Secretly watching Gregory paint and hum Beethoven's Fifth symphony to his white cat, Charlie eventually communicates by canvas, leaving first a picture and then messages before coming out into the open for lessons, a gift of paints, and friendship." Bull Cent Child Books

"Soft-focus, soft-color illustrations—double-page watercolors—are full of sun and shadow, leaves and water, and gentle peace punctuated by bursts of energy, as when Gregory's cat springs while geese take flight. The pictures carry a sense of the mystery of art. This is romantic, but not sentimental." Libr J

An angel for Solomon Singer; story by Cynthia Rylant; paintings by Peter Catalanotto. Orchard Bks. 1992 unp il $15.95; lib bdg $14.99   E

1. Restaurants—Fiction 2. New York (N.Y.)—Fiction
ISBN 0-531-05978-2; 0-531-08578-3 (lib bdg)
LC 91-15957

A lonely New York City resident finds companionship and good cheer at the Westway Cafe where dreams come true

"Rylant has sketched a spare portrait, in her flawless, graceful prose, of a man weighted down by hopelessness. . . . Catalanotto's signature watercolors have never been more affecting. He captures the smudgy nighttime murkiness of urban streets illuminated by artificial lights that float upward to become stars and bleed downward onto wet pavements to become a vision of midwestern wheat fields." SLJ

Rylant, Cynthia—*Continued*

Henry and Mudge; the first book of their adventures; story by Cynthia Rylant; pictures by Suçie Stevenson. Bradbury Press 1987 39p il $13; pa $3.95   E

1. Dogs—Fiction

ISBN 0-02-778001-5; 0-689-71399-1 (pa)

LC 86-13615

This book tells "about a boy named Henry and his dog, Mudge. . . . Henry yearns for a dog and convinces his parents to get one. Mudge is small at first, but soon grows 'out of seven collars in a row' to become enormous, and Henry's best friend. Then comes a day when Mudge is lost, and boy and dog realize what they mean to each other." N Y Times Book Rev

"The stories are lighthearted and affectionate. Backed by line-and-wash cartoon drawings, they celebrate the familiar in a down-to-earth way that will please young readers." Booklist

Other available titles about Henry and Mudge are:

Henry and Mudge and the bedtime thumps (1991)
Henry and Mudge and the best day of all (1995)
Henry and Mudge and the careful cousin (1994)
Henry and Mudge and the forever sea (1989)
Henry and Mudge and the happy cat (1990)
Henry and Mudge and the long weekend (1992)
Henry and Mudge and the wild wind (1993)
Henry and Mudge get the cold shivers (1989)
Henry and Mudge in puddle trouble (1987)
Henry and Mudge in the green time (1987)
Henry and Mudge in the sparkle days (1988)
Henry and Mudge take the big test (1991)
Henry and Mudge under the yellow moon (1987)

Mr. Griggs' work; illustrated by Julie Downing. Orchard Bks. 1989 unp il $14.95; lib bdg $15.99; pa $5.95   E

1. Postal service—Fiction

ISBN 0-531-05769-0; 0-531-08369-1 (lib bdg); 0-531-07037-9 (pa)

LC 88-1484

Mr. Griggs so loves his work at the post office that he thinks of it all the time and everything reminds him of it

"Line drawings and the controlled brightness of restrained crayon work are the media for pictures that have clean composition and that are nicely synchronized with the text. . . . Nice to have a story about someone who enjoys a job that is not glamorous." Bull Cent Child Books

Mr. Putter and Tabby pour the tea; illustrated by Arthur Howard. Harcourt Brace & Co. 1994 unp il $10.95; pa $4.95   E

1. Cats—Fiction 2. Old age—Fiction

ISBN 0-15-256255-9; 0-15-200901-9 (pa)

LC 93-21470

"Mr. Putter, a lonely old man, finds a friend in Tabby, an elderly cat he gets from the pound." Booklist

"Rylant's charming story of two elderly characters is complemented and enhanced by Howard's delightful illustrations, done in pencil, watercolor, and gouache." SLJ

Other available titles about Mr. Putter and Tabby are:
Mr. Putter and Tabby bake the cake (1994)
Mr. Putter and Tabby pick the pears (1995)
Mr. Putter and Tabby walk the dog (1994)

Night in the country; pictures by Mary Szilagyi. Bradbury Press 1986 unp il lib bdg $14.95; pa $4.95   E

1. Night—Fiction 2. Country life—Fiction

ISBN 0-02-777210-1 (lib bdg); 0-689-71473-4 (pa)

LC 85-70963

Text and illustrations describe the sights and sounds of nighttime in the country

"Rich with nuances, the images and sounds evoked by the text have brought forth deeply shadowed drawings by the artist; likewise, the text will conjure up vivid imaginings in the minds of young children. The journey through nighttime fittingly concludes that night animals 'will spend a day in the country listening to you.' Each page invites children to look, listen and explore." SLJ

The relatives came; story by Cynthia Rylant; illustrated by Stephen Gammell. Bradbury Press 1985 unp il lib bdg $14.95; pa $4.95   E

1. Family life—Fiction

ISBN 0-02-777220-9 (lib bdg); 0-689-71738-5 (pa)

LC 85-10929

A Caldecott Medal honor book, 1986

"The relatives have come—in an old station wagon that smells 'like a real car'—bringing with them hugs and laughs, quiet talk, and, at night when all are asleep hither and yon, 'all that new breathing.'" Booklist

"If there's anything more charming than the tone of voice in this story, it's the drawings that go with it. Stephen Gammell . . . fills the pages with bright, crayony pictures teeming with details that children should enjoy poring over for hours." N Y Times Book Rev

This year's garden; pictures by Mary Szilagyi. Bradbury Press 1984 unp il $13.95; pa $4.95   E

1. Gardens—Fiction 2. Seasons—Fiction

ISBN 0-02-777970-X; 0-689-71122-0 (pa)

LC 84-10974

This book tells "about a family's planning of its summer vegetable garden, the seeding and harvesting, and the enjoyment of the preserved crop through the summer and fall—and then the planning again, as the bare brown garden patch waits, like the family, for next year's garden." Bull Cent Child Books

"Rylant's words are set against Szilagyi's richly colored pictures. Deep hues from a multicolored palette make the visual landscape as fertile as the story. Even city-bred readers will come away with a sense of what it's all about." Booklist

When I was young in the mountains; illustrated by Diane Goode. Dutton 1982 unp il $14.99; pa $3.95   E

ISBN 0-525-42525-X; 0-525-44198-0 (pa)

LC 81-5359

A Caldecott Medal honor book, 1983

"Based on the author's memories of an Appalachian childhood, this is a nostalgic piece. . . . There is no story line, but a series of memories, each beginning, 'When I was young in the mountains . . .' as the author reminisces about the busy, peaceful life of an extended family and their community." Bull Cent Child Books

"The people in the story are poor in material things, but rich in family pleasures. The title becomes a pleasing refrain that is used to herald a change in topic. Illustrations and text are placed on a bed of white space, without borders, which makes them look uncrowded and imparts a great feeling of freedom." SLJ

Sadler, Marilyn

Alistair's elephant; illustrated by Roger Bollen. Prentice-Hall 1983 unp il $14; pa $5.95   E

1. Elephants—Fiction
ISBN 0-671-66680-0; 0-13-022773-0 (pa)

LC 82-23091

"Alistair Grittle is an extremely intelligent, highly organized little boy who, we are told, has 'no time for nonsense.' Into his carefully structured existence comes an elephant, who follows Alistair home from the zoo one Saturday and proceeds to make the following week a bewildering series of frustrations for Alistair. The elephant follows him everywhere, even to school, and is not only nosy but midly destructive. At the end of the week, having taught the elephant a few manners, Alistair returns him to the zoo and gratefully heads for home . . . only to be followed by a giraffe." SLJ

"The story has the sort of humor children find appealing, and the full-color illustrations are bright and clean." Booklist

Other available titles about Alistair are:
Alistair and the alien invasion (1994)
Alistair in outer space (1984)
Alistair underwater (1990)
Alistair's time machine (1986)

Samuels, Barbara

Duncan & Dolores. Bradbury Press 1986 unp il $13.95; pa $3.95   E

1. Cats—Fiction
ISBN 0-02-778210-7; 0-689-71294-4 (pa)

LC 85-17119

This is "the story of a small girl's adjustment to a newly-acquired cat. And vice versa. Duncan avoids her noisy roughness; she feels rebuffed and is jealous because the cat clearly prefers her older sister. However, Dolores gets the point, and the longed-for rapport ensues." Bull Cent Child Books

"The cheerful, childlike illustrations are remarkably expressive, clearly showing the rapidly alternating feelings of Duncan and the pleasant, sisterly relationship of sensible Faye and bouncy Dolores. The whole book is a charming illustration of the old aphorism that in getting to know cats, less is more." Horn Book

Sanders, Scott R. (Scott Russell), 1945-

Aurora means dawn; illustrated by Jill Kastner. Bradbury Press 1989 unp il $13.95

E

1. Frontier and pioneer life—Fiction 2. Ohio—Fiction
ISBN 0-02-778270-0   LC 88-24127

"Mr. and Mrs. Sheldon, traveling from Connecticut by covered wagon, arrive in Aurora, Ohio in 1800; they have been told that Aurora is a village with homes, a mill, and a store. What they find, using the land-company's map, is a surveyor's post. Trapped by debris from a storm, the family is able to reach their site when settlers from a nearby village help clear the road." Bull Cent Child Books

"The use of detail is engaging, yet it never slows the pace. Sentences are placed so that the action corresponds to that depicted in the luminous, vital, and well-composed watercolor paintings." Horn Book

Warm as wool; by Scott Russell Sanders; illustrated by Helen Cogancherry. Bradbury Press 1992 unp il $14.95   E

1. Frontier and pioneer life—Fiction 2. Ohio—Fiction
ISBN 0-02-778139-9   LC 91-34987

When Betsy Ward's family moves to Ohio from Connecticut in 1803, she brings along a sockful of coins to buy sheep so that she can gather wool, spin cloth, and make clothes to keep her children warm

"Cogancherry's watercolors, done in earth tones that reflect natural colors and lighting, convey a sure sense of pioneer life. This is a warm book about the struggle to stay warm, and a strong heroine is captured in both story and pictures." Booklist

Sandin, Joan, 1942-

The long way westward. Harper & Row 1989 63p il lib bdg $19.50; pa $3.50   E

1. Immigration and emigration—Fiction 2. Swedish Americans—Fiction
ISBN 0-06-025207-3 (lib bdg); 0-06-444198-9 (pa)

LC 89-2024

Also available prior volume The long way to a new land (1981)

"An I can read book"

Relates the experiences of two young brothers and their family, immigrants from Sweden, from their arrival in New York through the journey to their new home in Minnesota

"The text does a nice job of evoking the mix of excitement and apprehension that gripped newcomers to the U.S. Details of the long train ride from New York pace the book and inform readers unobtrusively as the nicely detailed pen-and-wash drawings bring the story to life. A fine bit of historical fiction for beginning readers." Booklist

Say, Allen, 1937-

The bicycle man. Parnassus Press 1982 unp il lib bdg $14.95; pa $5.95   E

1. Cycling—Fiction 2. Japan—Fiction
ISBN 0-395-32254-5 (lib bdg); 0-395-50652-2 (pa)

LC 82-2980

The amazing tricks two American soldiers do on a borrowed bicycle are a fitting finale for the school sports day festivities in a small village in occupied Japan

"The kindly, openhearted story is beautifully pictured in a profusion of delicate pen-and-ink drawings washed in gentle colors. Meticulously hatched and cross-hatched, they reflect the guileless joy and exuberance of adults and children alike in a book that celebrates human friendship." Horn Book

Grandfather's journey; written and illustrated by Allen Say. Houghton Mifflin 1993 32p il $16.95   E

1. Japanese Americans—Fiction 2. Grandfathers—Fiction 3. Voyages and travels—Fiction 4. Japan—Fiction
ISBN 0-395-57035-2   LC 93-18836

Awarded the Caldecott Medal, 1994

A Japanese American man recounts his grandfather's journey to America which he later also undertakes, and the feelings of being torn by a love for two different countries

"The brief text is simple and unaffected, but the emotions expressed are deeply complex. The paintings are astonishingly still, like the captured moments found in a family photo album. Each translucent watercolor is suffused with light. . . . Flawless in his execution, Say has chronicled three generations of a family whose hearts have been divided between two nations." SLJ

The lost lake. Houghton Mifflin 1989 32p il $14.95; pa $4.95   E

1. Fathers and sons—Fiction 2. Camping—Fiction
ISBN 0-395-50933-5; 0-395-63036-3 (pa)

LC 89-11026

Say, Allen, 1937-—*Continued*

"Luke is disappointed in his relationship with his taciturn, work-absorbed father, with whom he is spending the summer. Early one morning his father awakens him with exciting news of a camping trip: they are going to find the Lost Lake, a very special and secret place Luke's father used to visit with his own father. But their arduous hike brings them to a lake that has since been discovered by many people; they agree to blaze a new trail and find their own private place." Horn Book

"Using colors as crisp and clean as the outdoors, Say effectively alternates between scenes where father and son are the focus and those where the landscape predominates. Both in story and art, a substantial piece." Booklist

Tree of cranes; written and illustrated by Allen Say. Houghton Mifflin 1991 32p il $17.95   E

1. Christmas—Fiction 2. Mothers and sons—Fiction 3. Japan—Fiction
ISBN 0-395-52024-X   LC 91-14107

A Japanese boy learns of Christmas when his mother decorates a pine tree with paper cranes

"The quiet, graciously told picture book is a perfect blend of text and art. Fine-lined and handsome, Say's watercolors not only capture fascinating details of the boy's far away home . . . but also depict, with simple grace, the rich and complex bond between mother and child that underlies the story." Booklist

Scheer, Julian

Rain makes applesauce; by Julian Scheer & Marvin Bileck. Holiday House 1964 unp il $15.95   E

ISBN 0-8234-0091-3

A Caldecott Medal honor book, 1965

"A book of original nonsense, illustrated with intricate drawings. Small children live the refrains, 'Rain makes applesauce' and 'You're just talking silly talk,' and enjoy the fantastic details in the pictures." Hodges. Books for Elem Sch Libr

Schertle, Alice, 1941-

Down the road; illustrated by E.B. Lewis. Browndeer Press 1995 unp il $16   E

1. Eggs—Fiction 2. Country life—Fiction 3. Parent and child—Fiction
ISBN 0-15-276622-7   LC 94-9901

Hetty "makes her first solo jaunt to Mr. Birdie's store for fresh eggs, determined to prove how responsible she is. On the way home, temptation beckons in the guise of an apple tree; Hetty breaks the eggs while picking fruit, then hides among the branches in shame. Papa and Mama take her failure better than she expects and, instead of scolding, join her in the tree and share apple pie for breakfast." Bull Cent Child Books

"The story is remarkable for its evocative imagery, and the loving interchange between the characters set a charming tone. The words are perfectly complemented by Lewis' dazzling, impressionistic watercolors." Booklist

Witch Hazel; illustrated by Margot Tomes. HarperCollins Pubs. 1991 unp il $15; lib bdg $14.89; pa $4.95   E

ISBN 0-06-025140-9; 0-06-025141-7 (lib bdg); 0-06-443368-4 (pa)   LC 90-39630

A young boy uses a witch hazel branch to make a scarecrow and has a mysterious encounter on the night of the harvest moon

"An alliterative telling and homespun autumnal-toned watercolors contribute to this magical tale about the mysteries of nature." SLJ

Schnur, Steven

The tie man's miracle; a Chanukah tale; illustrated by Stephen T. Johnson. Morrow Junior Bks. 1995 unp il $16; lib bdg $15.93   E

1. Hanukkah—Fiction 2. Jews—Fiction
ISBN 0-688-13463-7; 0-688-13464-5 (lib bdg)
LC 94-39854

On the last night of Chanukah, after hearing how an old man lost his family in the Holocaust, a young boy makes a wish that is carried to God as the menorah candles burn down

"This touching tale links remembrance of the Holocaust with the Jewish celebration of Hanukkah in a sensitive and accessible way. The watercolor illustrations are especially moving." Horn Book

Schotter, Roni

Captain Snap and the children of Vinegar Lane; illustrations by Marcia Sewall. Orchard Bks. 1989 unp il $15.95; lib bdg $15.99; pa $5.95   E

1. Friendship—Fiction
ISBN 0-531-05797-6; 0-531-08397-7 (lib bdg); 0-531-07038-7 (pa)   LC 88-22489

The children of Vinegar Lane discover that bad-tempered old Captain Snap has a wonderful secret

"The twitchy, wiggly children of Vinegar Lane scamper through Sewall's woodcutesque paintings in this crackling good story of pint-sized neighbors who melt the Captain's hard heart with a couple of good deeds and a whole lot of high spirits." SLJ

Passover magic; written by Roni Schotter; illustrated by Marylin Hafner. Little, Brown 1995 unp il $14.95   E

1. Passover—Fiction 2. Jews—Fiction
ISBN 0-316-77468-5   LC 93-20053

A young girl and her relatives celebrate Passover with the traditional seder, a dinner with special foods and special meaning

"Vibrant watercolors evoke the warmth and affection of a family's celebration of this special holiday. Tradition, laced with humor and fun, characterizes the observance and reminds relatives of a shared heritage." Soc Educ

Schroeder, Alan, 1961-

Carolina shout! pictures by Bernie Fuchs. Dial Bks. for Young Readers 1995 unp il $14.99; lib bdg $14.89   E

1. African Americans—Fiction 2. South Carolina—Fiction
ISBN 0-8037-1676-1; 0-8037-1678-8 (lib bdg)
LC 94-17125

This describes a "facet of pre-World War II African American life. All day long, Delia hears the music of Charleston, South Carolina. She finds it in the sounds of raindrops, the croaking of bullfrogs, and the squeaking of the rusty iron gate. Most musical of all are the shouts—the short, rhythmic songs of street vendors and work crews." Booklist

Schroeder, Alan, 1961-—*Continued*

"Fuchs's distinctive, sun-drenched paintings are filled with period details and characters so lively that the reader can almost hear them sing. A joyful collection of rhythmic music, luminous paintings and image-rich language." Publ Wkly

Ragtime Tumpie; paintings by Bernie Fuchs. Little, Brown 1989 unp il lib bdg $15.95; pa $4.95   **E**

1. Baker, Josephine, 1906-1975—Fiction 2. African Americans—Fiction 3. Dancing—Fiction
ISBN 0-316-77497-9 (lib bdg); 0-316-77504-5 (pa)
LC 87-37221

"Joy Street books"

A fictionalized account of "the childhood of Josephine Baker, the St. Louis girl who became the toast of Paris and, for many, epitomized the Jazz Age." Bull Cent Child Books

"This book evokes the magic of ragtime St. Louis, its down-and-out places and its joys. Both the prose and paintings are bursts of color." N Y Times Book Rev

Schwartz, Amy, 1954-

Annabelle Swift, kindergartner; story and pictures by Amy Schwartz. Orchard Bks. 1988 unp il $14.95; pa $5.95   **E**

1. School stories 2. Sisters—Fiction
ISBN 0-531-05737-2; 0-531-07027-1 (pa)
LC 87-15403

"Annabelle is starting school and her older sister Lucy prepares Annabelle for kindergarten, but some of her training backfires. In spite of some embarrassment in the classroom, Annabelle makes a hit with her fellow classmates." Child Book Rev Serv

"In illustrations that carefully evoke the naive and awkward drawings of children, Schwartz captures the essence of childhood complete with pedal-pushers, pinafores, and 6¢ milk. Line and wash illustrations in crayon-bright colors reveal a classroom that is cheerful, warm, and inviting. The children pictured are universal yet individual, while the adults are solid and supportive." SLJ

Bea and Mr. Jones; story and pictures by Amy Schwartz. Bradbury Press 1982 unp il $13.95; pa $3.95   **E**

1. Fathers—Fiction 2. School stories 3. Business—Fiction
ISBN 0-02-781430-0; 0-689-71796-2 (pa)
LC 81-18031

"Bea is tired of kindergarten, and Mr. Jones is fed up with being chained to a desk all day. So the two decide to change places, a pleasure for both." Booklist

"A nice treatment of role reversal, this junior tall tale is told with simplicity and humor, and is illustrated with soft pencil drawings that have pudgy people, nice textural quality, and some funny details, such as Mr. Jones, lying on the floor and using blocks to spell out 'antidisestablishmentarianism.'" Bull Cent Child Books

Oma and Bobo; story and pictures by Amy Schwartz. Bradbury Press 1987 unp il $14.95
      E

1. Dogs—Fiction 2. Grandmothers—Fiction
ISBN 0-02-781500-5   LC 86-10665

"When Alice is told she can have a dog for her birthday, she hurries down to the pound and picks out an old black-and-white mutt she names Bobo. Oma, Alice's grandmother, is not keen on the idea of a dog." Booklist

"This is a fresh portrait of an unlikely friendship that al-

lows room for both humor and dignity. Schwartz's eccentric illustrations have a 50's mood colored by an 80's sensibility, and are filled with witty details and patterns . . . exactly suiting the dry tone of the text." Bull Cent Child Books

A teeny, tiny baby. Orchard Bks. 1994 unp il $15.95; lib bdg $15.99   **E**

1. Infants—Fiction 2. City life—Fiction
ISBN 0-531-06818-8; 0-531-08668-2 (lib bdg)
LC 93-4876

"A Richard Jackson book"

"'I'm a teeny tiny baby and I know how to get anything I want.' So begins an infant's hilarious narration of his many needs and pleasures. . . . Everyone who has had a baby in the family will respond to the gentle humor in Schwartz's gouache paintings." SLJ

Schwartz, David M., 1951-

How much is a million? pictures by Steven Kellogg. Lothrop, Lee & Shepard Bks. 1985 unp il $17; lib bdg $15.93; pa $4.95   **E**

1. Million (The number) 2. Billion (The number) 3. Trillion (The number)
ISBN 0-688-04049-7; 0-688-04050-0 (lib bdg); 0-688-09933-5 (pa)   LC 84-5736

"Marvelosissimo the Mathematical Magician leads the reader through Steven Kellogg's scenes of fantasy to express the concepts of a million, a billion and a trillion. The text is all printed in capital letters to point out the expanding scenes portrayed in the fabulous illustrations. The idea is to make possible to children the awesome concept of large numbers. It is a delightful fantasy as a picture book, but it is even more compelling as a first reader." Okla State Dept of Educ

If you made a million; pictures by Steven Kellogg. Lothrop, Lee & Shepard Bks. 1989 unp il $16; lib bdg $16.93; pa $4.95   **E**

1. Personal finance
ISBN 0-688-07017-5; 0-688-07018-3 (lib bdg); 0-688-13634-6 (pa)   LC 88-12819

The author examines "how one earns money, how checks are used instead of cash, why banks pay interest on money deposited, [and] why interest is charged on loans." Booklist

"The concepts of banks and banking . . . are all explained with absurd and humorous examples involving Ferris wheels, ogres, and rhinoceroses. . . . The best advice of all is 'Enjoying your work is more important than money.' Steven Kellogg's splendidly funny illustrations contain a troupe of two cats, one dog, numerous kids, a unicorn, and the wonderful magician Marvelosissimo." Horn Book

Schwartz, Henry

Albert goes Hollywood; story by Henry Schwartz; pictures by Amy Schwartz. Orchard Bks. 1992 unp il $15.95; lib bdg $14.99
      E

1. Dinosaurs—Fiction 2. Motion pictures—Fiction
ISBN 0-531-05980-4; 0-531-08580-5 (lib bdg)
LC 91-18495

"A Richard Jackson book"

Liz gets to keep her pet dinosaur Albert when she finds him a job in the movies

"Amy Schwartz's fresh and funny illustrations are a perfect complement for her father's wry and understated text." SLJ

Another available title about Liz and Albert is:
How I captured a dinosaur (1989)

Scieszka, Jon, 1954-

The Frog Prince continued; story by Jon Scieszka; paintings by Steve Johnson. Viking 1991 unp il $14.95; pa $4.99   E

1. Fairy tales 2. Frogs—Fiction
ISBN 0-670-83421-1; 0-14-054285-X (pa)

LC 90-26537

After the frog turns into a prince, he and the Princess do not live happily ever after and the Prince decides to look for a witch to help him turn back into a frog

"The dialogue is witty; the plot, as logical as it is offbeat. Steve Johnson's paintings, executed in a rich and somber palette, are like stage settings; his depiction of the various characters is inspired." Horn Book

Math curse; illustrated by Lane Smith. Viking 1995 unp il $16.99   E

1. Mathematics—Fiction
ISBN 0-670-86194-4   LC 95-12341

When the teacher tells her class that they can think of almost everything as a math problem, one student acquires a math anxiety which becomes a real curse

"Bold in design and often bizarre in expression, Smith's paintings clearly express the child's feelings of bemusement, frustration, and panic as well as her eventual joy when she overcomes the math curse. . . . A child-centered, witty picture book." Booklist

The Stinky Cheese Man and other fairly stupid tales; [by Jon Scieszka & Lane Smith] Viking 1992 unp il $16.99   E

ISBN 0-670-84487-X   LC 91-48194

A Caldecott Medal honor book, 1993

"Cinderumpelstiltskin and The Really Ugly Duckling are among the tales that Jack the narrator tries to present. But the Dedication is upside down; the Table of Contents is late; and Little Red Running Shorts and the wolf quit." Publisher's note

"The picture-book set will probably recognize the stories enough to know that what's going on isn't what's 'supposed' to happen. But *The Stinky Cheese Man* isn't a book for little ones. It will take older children (that's teens along with 10s) to follow the disordered story lines and appreciate the narrative's dry wit, wordplay, and wacky, sophomoric jokes. . . . Smith's New Wave art is an intricate part of the whole, extending as well as reinforcing the narrative; the pictures are every bit as comically insolent and deliberately clever as the words." Booklist

Scott, Ann Herbert, 1926-

Hi; illustrated by Glo Coalson. Philomel Bks. 1994 unp il $15.95   E

1. Postal service—Fiction
ISBN 0-399-21964-1   LC 91-42978

"Margarita calls an exuberant 'Hi' to each person in line at the post office, but no one responds. With each failed attempt, the toddler's greeting becomes softer and more hesitant, but when her whispered 'Hi' elicits a big smile and a warm greeting from the 'post-office lady,' Margarita cheerfully calls, 'Bye!' all the way out the door. A perfect meld of a childhood incident with tender and expressive watercolors." Horn Book Guide

On Mother's lap; illustrated by Glo Coalson. Clarion Bks. 1992 32p il $14.95; pa $5.95   E

1. Inuit—Fiction 2. Parent and child—Fiction
ISBN 0-395-58920-7; 0-395-62976-4 (pa)

LC 91-17765

A newly illustrated edition of the title first published 1972 by McGraw-Hill

"Sitting on his mother's lap, a young Eskimo boy gathers his belongings until he, some toys, his puppy, and a blanket are all crowded together in the rocking chair. When his baby sister cries, the boy claims there is no room for her, but Mother proves him wrong, and the threesome settle comfortably in the chair. Soft illustrations depict a cozy scene and a loving family." Horn Book

Segal, Lore Groszmann

Tell me a Mitzi; [by] Lore Segal; pictures by Harriet Pincus. Farrar, Straus & Giroux 1970 unp il $17; pa $5.95   E

1. Family life—Fiction
ISBN 0-374-37392-2; 0-374-47502-4 (pa)

The author injects an element of fantasy into these three stories of family life, the first of which deals with Mitzi's safari to grandma's and grandpa's house, the second with a confrontation with the common cold, and the third with her brother Jacob's encounter with a Presidential motorcade

"The illustrations, while they do not boast attractive children, are full of vitality and humor, the busy urban neighborhood and homely people having a rueful charm." Sutherland. The Best in Child Books

Tell me a Trudy; [by] Lore Segal; pictures by Rosemary Wells. Farrar, Straus & Giroux 1977 unp il $15; pa $4.95   E

1. Family life—Fiction
ISBN 0-374-37395-7; 0-374-47504-0 (pa)

LC 77-24123

"Following the same format as 'Tell Me a Mitzi,' [entered above] a little girl named Martha cajoles her mother and her father into telling stories. Each tale features Trudy, her younger brother Jacob, and her parents and gently satirizes a common family situation. In the first story Trudy's grandma lures stubborn children to bed; in the second, parents are found squabbling over toys; the third story deals with Trudy's fear of robbers in the bathroom. . . . Flamboyant color and caricatured figures heighten the humor of a straight-faced text." Horn Book

Sendak, Maurice

Alligators all around; an alphabet. Harper & Row 1962 unp il lib bdg $13.89; pa $3.95   E

1. Alphabet
ISBN 0-06-025530-7 (lib bdg); 0-06-443254-8 (pa)

Originally published in smaller format as volume one of the "Nutshell library"

An alphabet book of alligators doing dishes, juggling jelly beans, throwing tantrums and wearing wigs, all from A to Z

Chicken soup with rice; a book of months. Harper & Row 1962 30p il lib bdg $13.89; pa $3.95   E

1. Seasons—Fiction
ISBN 0-06-025535-8 (lib bdg); 0-06-443253-X (pa)

Originally published in smaller format as volume two of the "Nutshell library"

Pictures and verse illustrate the delight of eating chicken soup with rice in every season of the year

Sendak, Maurice—*Continued*

Higglety pigglety pop! or, There must be more to life; story and pictures by Maurice Sendak. Harper & Row 1967 69p il $15; lib bdg $14.89; pa $5.95   E

1. Dogs—Fiction
ISBN 0-06-025487-4; 0-06-025488-2 (lib bdg); 0-06-443021-9 (pa)

In this modern fairy tale "Jennie, the Sealyham terrier, leaves home because 'there must be more to life than having everything.' When she applies for a job as the leading lady of the World Mother Goose Theater, she discovers that what she lacks is experience. What follows are her adventures and her gaining of experience; finally Jennie becomes the leading lady of the play." Wis Libr Bull

"The story has elements of tenderness and humor; it also has . . . typically macabre Sendak touches. . . . The illustrations are beautiful, amusing, and distinctive." Sutherland. The Best in Child Books

In the night kitchen. 25th anniversary ed. HarperCollins Pubs. 1996 c1970 unp il $15.95; lib bdg $15.89; pa $5.95   E

1. Fantasy fiction
ISBN 0-06-026668-6; 0-06-026669-4 (lib bdg); 0-06-443436-2 (pa)

Also available Spanish language edition
A Caldecott Medal honor book, 1971
First published 1970

"A small boy falls through the dark, out of his clothes, and into the bright, night kitchen where he is stirred into the cake batter and almost baked, jumps into the bread dough, kneads and shapes it into an airplane, and flies up over the top of the Milky Way to get milk for the bakers." Booklist

"A perfect midnight fantasy. The feelings, smells, sights, and comforting emotions which young children experience are here in lovely dream colors." Brooklyn. Art Books for Child

One was Johnny; a counting book. Harper & Row 1962 unp il lib bdg $13.89; pa $3.95   E

1. Counting
ISBN 0-06-025540-4 (lib bdg); 0-06-443251-3 (pa)

Originally published in smaller format as volume three of the "Nutshell library"

Counting from one to ten and back again to one, Johnny, who starts off alone, acquires too many numbered visitors for his own comfort, until they disappear one by one

Outside over there. Harper & Row 1981 unp il $20; lib bdg $19.89; pa $8.95   E

1. Fairy tales 2. Sisters—Fiction
ISBN 0-06-025523-4; 0-06-025524-2 (lib bdg); 0-06-443185-1 (pa)   LC 79-2682

A Caldecott Medal honor book, 1982
"An Ursula Nordstrom book"

With Papa off to sea and Mama despondent, Ida must go outside over there to rescue her baby sister from goblins who steal her to be a goblin's bride

"A gentle yet powerful story in the romantic tradition. . . . Soft in tones, rich in the use of light and color . . . the pictures are particularly distinctive for the tenderness with which the children's faces are drawn, the classic handling of texture, the imaginative juxtaposition of infant faces and the baroque landscape details that might have come from Renaissance paintings." Bull Cent Child Books

Pierre; a cautionary tale in five chapters and a prologue. Harper & Row 1962 48p il lib bdg $13.89; pa $3.95   E

ISBN 0-06-025965-5 (lib bdg); 0-06-443252-1 (pa)

Originally published in smaller format as volume four of the "Nutshell library"

A story in verse about a little boy called Pierre who insisted upon saying 'I don't care' until he said it once too often and learned a well needed lesson

The sign on Rosie's door; story and pictures by Maurice Sendak. Harper & Row 1960 46p il $14; lib bdg $14.89   E

ISBN 0-06-025505-6; 0-06-025506-4 (lib bdg)

The sign on imaginative Rosie's door read, 'If you want to know a secret, knock three times.' The secret was that Rosie was now Alinda. With her friends Kathy, Sol, Pudgy, Dolly, and Lenny, and with the help of the Music Man, Alinda has a Fourth of July celebration. Then Alinda the lady singer leaves as Rosie becomes someone else

Where the wild things are; story and pictures by Maurice Sendak. Harper & Row 1963 unp il $15; lib bdg $14.89; pa $4.95   E

1. Fantasy fiction
ISBN 0-06-025492-0; 0-06-025493-9 (lib bdg); 0-06-443178-9 (pa)

Also available Spanish language edition
Awarded the Caldecott Medal, 1964

"A tale of very few words about Max, sent to his room for cavorting around in his wolf suit, who dreamed of going where the wild things are, to rule them and share their rumpus. Then a longing to be 'where someone loved him best of all' swept over him." Book Week

"This vibrant picture book in luminous, understated full color has proved utterly engrossing to children with whom it has been shared. . . . A sincere, preceptive contribution which bears repeated examination." Horn Book

Serfozo, Mary

Rain talk; illustrated by Keiko Narahashi. Margaret K. McElderry Bks. 1990 unp il $15; pa $4.95   E

1. Rain—Fiction
ISBN 0-689-50496-9; 0-689-71699-9 (pa)
    LC 89-12178

A child enjoys a glorious day in the rain, listening to the varied sounds it makes as it comes down

"The text fine tunes readers' ears to the different sounds of rain on umbrellas, ponds, roofs, and highways. Such vivid sensory images have immediate appeal for even the youngest read-aloud audience. Equally appealing are the watercolor illustrations. . . . Bright yellow and green dominate the pages, providing the perfect backdrop for the brown-limbed girl in her red galoshes and flowered dress." SLJ

Who said red? illustrated by Keiko Narahashi. Margaret K. McElderry Bks. 1988 unp il $13.95; pa $4.95   E

1. Color
ISBN 0-689-50455-1; 0-689-71592-7 (pa)
    LC 88-9345

This "picture book about colors also has a storyline as an extra treat for its preschool audience. The jaunty, rhyming text is a conversation between two playmates, a little boy searching for his lost red kite and his older sister." Booklist

Serfozo, Mary—*Continued*

This book has "very little text, and the door is wide open to the imagination. For the smallest child, familiar objects can be labeled and identified. Keiko Narahashi's watercolors are misty and delicate, but so accurate when looked at closely that children can identify not only types of leaves but a woodpecker, a monarch butterfly and a tiger lily. In several cases, finding the creatures becomes a hide-and-seek game that playfully builds a child's powers of observation." N Y Times Book Rev

Seuss, Dr.

The 500 hats of Bartholomew Cubbins. Random House 1990 c1938 unp il $14; lib bdg $15.99   E

1. Hats—Fiction

ISBN 0-394-84484-X; 0-394-94484-4 (lib bdg)

LC 88-38412

"A Vanguard Press book"

A reissue of the title first published 1938 by Vanguard Press

"A read-aloud story telling what happened to Bartholomew Cubbins when he couldn't take his hat off before the King." Hodges. Books for Elem Sch Libr

"It is a lovely bit of tomfoolery which keeps up the suspense and surprise until the last page, and of the same ingenious and humorous imagination are the author's black and white illustrations in which a red cap and then an infinite number of red caps titillate the eye." N Y Times Book Rev

Another available title about Bartholomew Cubbins is Bartholomew and the oobleck, entered below

And to think that I saw it on Mulberry Street. Random House 1989 c1937 unp il $14; lib bdg $11.99   E

1. Nonsense verses 2. Stories in rhyme

ISBN 0-394-84494-7; 0-394-94494-1 (lib bdg)

LC 88-38411

"A Vanguard Press book"

A reissue of the title first published 1937 by Vanguard Press

This book tells in rhyme accompanied by pictures how little Marco saw a horse and wagon on Mulberry Street. Then "how that horse became a zebra, then a reindeer, then an elephant, and how the cart turned into a band wagon with a retinue of police to guide it through the traffic on Mulberry Street, only the book can properly explain." Christ Sci Monit

"A fresh, inspiring picture-story book in bright colors. . . . As convincing to a child as to the psychologist in quest of a book with an appeal to the child's imaginations." Horn Book

Another available title about Marco is McElligot's pool, entered below

Bartholomew and the oobleck; written and illustrated by Dr. Seuss. Random House 1949 unp il $14; lib bdg $15.99   E

ISBN 0-394-80075-3; 0-394-90075-8 (lib bdg)

A Caldecott Medal honor book, 1950

"King Derwin, dissatisfied with only rain, sunshine, fog and snow, orders the royal magicians to produce oobleck. The greenish, sticky stuff was alost disastrous and it is Bartholomew Cubbins who rescues the kingdom." Wis Libr Bull

The cat in the hat. Random House 1957 61p il $7.99; lib bdg $9.99   E

1. Cats—Fiction 2. Nonsense verses 3. Stories in rhyme 4. Bilingual books—English-Spanish

ISBN 0-394-80001-X; 0-394-90001-4 (lib bdg)

Also available in a bilingual Spanish-English edition

A nonsense story in verse illustrated by the author about an unusual cat and his tricks which he displayed for the children one rainy day

Another available title about The cat in the hat is: The cat in the hat comes back! (1958)

Green eggs and ham. Beginner Bks. 1960 62p il $7.99; lib bdg $9.99; pa $7.95   E

1. Food—Fiction 2. Nonsense verses 3. Stories in rhyme

ISBN 0-394-80016-8; 0-394-90016-2 (lib bdg); 0-394-89220-8 (pa)

Also available Spanish language edition

This book is about "Sam-I-Am who wins a determined campaign to make another Seuss character eat a plate of green eggs and ham." Libr J

"The happy theme of refusal-to-eat changing to relish will be doubly enjoyable to the child who finds many common edibles as nauseating as the title repast. The pacing throughout is magnificent, and the opening five pages, on which the focal character introduces himself with a placard: 'I am Sam,' are unsurpassed in the controlled-vocabulary literature." Saturday Rev

Horton hatches the egg. Random House 1940 unp il $14; lib bdg $14.99   E

1. Elephants—Fiction 2. Nonsense verses 3. Stories in rhyme

ISBN 0-394-80077-X; 0-394-90077-4 (lib bdg)

"Horton, the elephant, is faithful one hundred percent as he carries out his promise to watch a bird's egg while she takes a rest. Hilarious illustrations and a surprise ending." Adventuring with Books. 2d edition

Horton hears a Who! Random House 1954 unp il $14; lib bdg $15.99   E

1. Elephants—Fiction 2. Nonsense verses 3. Stories in rhyme

ISBN 0-394-80078-8; 0-394-90078-2 (lib bdg)

"Although considered the biggest blame fool in the Jungle of Nool, the faithful and kindhearted elephant of 'Horton hatches the egg' [entered above] believing that a person's a person no matter how small, stanchly defends the Whos, too-small-to-be-seen inhabitants of Whoville, a town which exists on a dust speck." Booklist

"The verses are full of the usual lively, informal language and amazing rhymes that have delighted such a world-wide audience in the good 'doctor's' other books." N Y Her Trib Books

How the Grinch stole Christmas. Random House 1957 unp il $14; lib bdg $11.99   E

1. Christmas—Fiction 2. Nonsense verses 3. Stories in rhyme

ISBN 0-394-80079-6; 0-394-90079-0 (lib bdg)

"The Grinch lived on a mountain where it was able to ignore the people of the valley except at Christmas time when it had to endure the sound of their singing. One year it decided to steal all the presents so there would be no Christmas, but much to its amazement discovered that people did not need presents to enjoy Christmas. It there-upon reformed, returned the presents and joined in the festivities." Bull Cent Child Books

"The verse is as lively and the pages are as bright and colorful as anyone could wish." Saturday Rev

Seuss, Dr.—*Continued*

If I ran the circus. Random House 1956 unp
il $14; lib bdg $14.99   E

1. Circus—Fiction 2. Nonsense verses 3. Stories in
rhyme
ISBN 0-394-80080-X; 0-394-90080-4 (lib bdg)

The author-illustrator "presents the fabulous Circus Mc-
Gurkus with its highly imaginative young owner, Morris
McGurk and its intrepid performer, Sneelock, behind whose
store the circus is to be housed. There are the expected
number of strange creatures with nonsensical names, but
the real humor lies in the situations, and especially those
involving Mr. Sneelock. There is fun for the entire family
here." Bull Cent Child Books

If I ran the zoo. Random House 1950 unp
il $14; lib bdg $15.99   E

1. Zoos—Fiction 2. Nonsense verses 3. Stories in rhyme
ISBN 0-394-80081-8; 0-394-90081-2 (lib bdg)

A Caldecott Medal honor book, 1951

"Assembled here are the rare and wonderful creatures
which young Gerald McGrew collects from far and unusual
places for the 'gol-darndest zoo on the face of the earth.'"
Booklist

"As you turn the pages, the imaginings get wilder and
funnier, the rhymes more hilarious. There will be no age
limits for this book, because families will be forced to share
rereading and quotation, for a long long time." N Y Her
Trib Books

McElligot's pool; written and illustrated by
Dr. Seuss. Random House 1947 unp il $14; lib
bdg $13.99   E

1. Fishing—Fiction 2. Nonsense verses 3. Stories in
rhyme
ISBN 0-394-80083-4; 0-394-90083-9 (lib bdg)

A Caldecott Medal honor book, 1948

"In spite of warnings that there are no fish in McElligot's
Pool, a boy continues to fish and to imagine the rare and
wonderful denizens of the deep which he just 'might'
catch." Hodges. Books for Elem Sch Libr

"Fine color surrounding a host of strange creatures enlivens this amazing fish story for all ages." Horn Book

Oh, the places you'll go! Random House
1990 unp il $16; lib bdg $16.99   E

1. Stories in rhyme
ISBN 0-679-80527-3; 0-679-90527-8 (lib bdg)
      LC 89-36892

Also available Spanish language edition

Advice in rhyme for proceeding in life; weathering fear,
loneliness, and confusion; and being in charge of your actions

"The combination of the lively text and wacky, offbeat
pictures will delight both children and their parents." Child
Book Rev Serv

Seymour, Tres

Hunting the white cow; story by Tres
Seymour; pictures by Wendy Anderson
Halperin. Orchard Bks. 1993 unp il $15.95; lib
bdg $15.99   E

1. Cattle—Fiction 2. Farm life—Fiction
ISBN 0-531-05496-9; 0-531-08646-1 (lib bdg)
      LC 92-43757

"A Richard Jackson book"

A child watches as more and more people join in the attempts to catch the family cow that has gotten loose, each

remarking on how special the cow is

"Wendy Halperin's soft colored-pencil drawings of fields
and woods that drift far back into the distant hills add to
the mythic aura. A unique and imaginative book." Horn
Book

Shannon, George, 1952-

Dance away! illustrated by Jose Aruego and
Ariane Dewey. Greenwillow Bks. 1982 unp il
$15; lib bdg $13.93; pa $3.95   E

1. Rabbits—Fiction 2. Foxes—Fiction 3. Dancing—
Fiction
ISBN 0-688-00838-0; 0-688-00839-9 (lib bdg);
0-688-10483-5 (pa)   LC 81-6391

"One day Rabbit discovers his friends in the paws of a
hungry fox but through his dance is able to outwit the rascal and save them all." Booklist

"The synthesis of well-defined, identifiable characters
with the text is irresistible. The brevity of the plot, the per-
ceivable conflict, and the humor of the illustrations suggest
a special appeal to preschoolers." Horn Book

Sharmat, Marjorie Weinman, 1928-

The 329th friend; illustrations by Cyndy
Szekeres. 2nd ed. Four Winds Press 1992
c1979 unp il $14.95   E

1. Friendship—Fiction   2. Raccoons—Fiction
3. Animals—Fiction
ISBN 0-02-782259-1

A reissue of the title first published 1979

Bored with his own company, Emery Raccoon invites
328 guests to lunch but finds that none of them have time
to listen to him

"Szekeres' expressive detail is magnified with humorous
touches executed in watercolors that reflect the gala festivities." Booklist

Gila monsters meet you at the airport;
pictures by Byron Barton. Macmillan 1980
unp il $14.95; pa $4.95   E

1. Moving—Fiction 2. West (U.S.)—Fiction
ISBN 0-02-782450-0; 0-689-71383-5 (pa)
      LC 80-12264

A New York City boy's preconceived ideas of life in the
West make him very apprehensive about the family's move
there

"The exaggeration is amusing, the style yeasty, with a
nice final touch; the illustrations are comic and awkward,
but add little that's not inherent in the story." Bull Cent
Child Books

Nate the Great; illustrated by Marc Simont.
Coward, McCann & Geoghegan 1972 60p il
$14.95   E

1. Mystery fiction
ISBN 0-698-20627-4

Also available in paperback from Dell

"A Break-of-day book"

Nate the Great, a junior detective who has found missing
balloons, books, slippers, chickens and even a goldfish, is
now in search of a painting of a dog by Annie, the girl
down the street

"The illustrations capture the exaggerated, tongue-in-
cheek humor of the story." Booklist

Other available titles about Nate the Great are:
Nate the Great and the boring beach bag (1987)
Nate the Great and the fishy prize (1985)
Nate the Great and the Halloween hunt (1989)

Sharmat, Marjorie Weinman, 1928-—*Continued*

Nate the Great and the lost list (1975)
Nate the Great and the missing key (1981)
Nate the Great and the mushy valentine (1994)
Nate the Great and the musical note (1990)
Nate the Great and the phony clue (1977)
Nate the Great and the pillowcase (1993)
Nate the Great and the snowy trail (1982)
Nate the Great and the sticky case (1978)
Nate the Great and the stolen base (1992)
Nate the Great and the tardy tortoise (1995)
Nate the Great goes down in the dumps (1989)
Nate the Great goes undercover (1974)
Nate the Great stalks stupidweed (1986)

Sharmat, Mitchell, 1927-

Gregory, the terrible eater; illustrated by Jose Aruego and Ariane Dewey. Four Winds Press 1985 c1980 unp il $15   E
1. Goats—Fiction 2. Diet—Fiction
ISBN 0-02-782250-8   LC 85-29290
Also available in paperback from Scholastic
A reissue of the title first published 1980
"Gregory is not your average goat. In fact, he's the original goat gourmet, abandoning bottle caps in favor of bananas and trading last year's boots for bread and butter." SLJ
"Aruego and Dewey's illustrations are highly amusing, thanks to their goats' dot-eyed facial expressions. . . . There is energy in the pictures; they are beguiling and help to carry the humor." Booklist

Shaw, Charles, 1892-1974

It looked like spilt milk. Harper & Row 1947 unp il $13.95; lib bdg $13.85; pa $4.95
    E

ISBN 0-06-025566-8; 0-06-025565-X (lib bdg); 0-06-443159-2 (pa)
White silhouettes on a blue background with simple captions: "sometimes it looked like a tree," "Sometimes it looked like a bird," etc. lead to a surprise ending "sometimes it looked like split milk, but what it was was—"
"What one thing could look like all of these? On the last page you are told, and I could no more tell you now than I could spoil an adult mystery by a review that gives away its solution." N Y Her Trib Books

Shaw, Nancy

Sheep in a jeep; illustrated by Margot Apple. Houghton Mifflin 1986 32p il lib bdg $13.95; pa $3.95   E
1. Sheep—Fiction 2. Stories in rhyme
ISBN 0-395-41105-X (lib bdg); 0-395-47030-7 (pa)
     LC 86-3101
"When five sheep pile into one little jeep, there is trouble . . . [as] the poor woolly travelers push, shove, and attempt to drive their way from one calamity to another." Horn Book
"Shaw demonstrates a promising capacity for creating nonsense rhymes. . . . Veteran illustrator Apple's whimsical portraits of the sheep bring the story to life. Pleasing and lighthearted, this has much appeal for young readers." Publ Wkly

Other available titles about the sheep are:
Sheep in a shop (1991)
Sheep on a ship (1989)
Sheep out to eat (1992)
Sheep take a hike (1994)

Shelby, Anne

Homeplace; illustrations by Wendy Anderson Halperin. Orchard Bks. 1995 unp il $15.95; lib bdg $15.99   E
1. Farm life—Fiction 2. Family life—Fiction
ISBN 0-531-06882-X; 0-531-08732-8 (lib bdg)
     LC 94-24856
"A Richard Jackson book"
"A grandmother is able to trace her family back to 1810 when her homestead was built by her great-great-great-grandpa. She shares this legacy with her granddaughter as she describes the way each generation lived." Child Book Rev Serv
"The text is brief, but poetic—a fitting accompaniment to the rhythm of life presented in the earth-toned watercolors." SLJ

Sheldon, Dyan

The whales' song; paintings by Gary Blythe. Dial Bks. for Young Readers 1991 c1990 unp il $15.99   E
1. Whales—Fiction
ISBN 0-8037-0972-2   LC 90-46722
Also available Spanish language edition
First published 1990 in the United Kingdom
Enthralled by her grandmother's story of seeing and hearing whales singing in the sea long ago, Lilly hopes to see them herself and to hear their mysterious songs
"Infused with the cadences of real speech, Sheldon's poetic text manages to overlay a homespun practicality with an ethereal, fairy-tale magic. . . . Blythe's paintings are extraordinary . . . Rendered in unusual perspectives, these vibrant panoramas of the sea and of the whales leaping from the moonlit water possess a rare luminosity and beauty that should not be missed." Publ Wkly

Showers, Paul, 1910-

The listening walk; illustrated by Aliki. new ed. HarperCollins Pubs. 1991 unp il $14.95; lib bdg $14.89; pa $4.95   E
1. Fathers and daughters—Fiction
ISBN 0-06-021637-9; 0-06-021638-7 (lib bdg); 0-06-443322-6 (pa)   LC 90-30526
Also available Spanish language edition
A revised and newly illustrated edition of the title first published 1961 by Crowell
A little girl and her father take a quiet walk and identify the sounds around them
Aliki's "artwork features active scenes, all created with an array of spring colors. A fine resource for preschool and primary grades studying the senses and worth reading just for fun." Booklist

Shub, Elizabeth

The white stallion; illustrated by Rachel Isadora. Greenwillow Bks. 1982 56p il $15.95; lib bdg $15.93   E
1. Horses—Fiction 2. West (U.S.)—Fiction
ISBN 0-688-01210-8; 0-688-01211-6 (lib bdg)
     LC 81-20308

Shub, Elizabeth—*Continued*

Also available in paperback from Bantam Bks.

"A Greenwillow read-alone book"

Retold from James Frank Dobie's Tales of the mustang

Carried away from her wagon train in Texas in 1845 by the old mare she is riding, a little girl is befriended by a white stallion

"The quietly compelling story, framed by the grandmother's opening and closing lines to her granddaughter, is riveting without ever sensationalizing or anthropomorphizing. Elizabeth Shub's straightforward, lean text is part of the book's quality and appeal, but even more credit goes to the superb ink drawings." SLJ

Shulevitz, Uri, 1935-

Dawn; words and pictures by Uri Shulevitz. Farrar, Straus & Giroux 1974 unp il $16; pa $5.95   E

ISBN 0-374-31707-0; 0-374-41689-3 (pa)

"Drawn from a Chinese poem, the spare text tells of an old man and his grandson asleep by the shore of a mountain lake. With the approach of daylight, the watercolor illustrations, which start out small, dark, and blurred, slowly become more focused and detailed: the moon casts a soft glow; a breeze riffles the water; mists rise. As the old man and the boy push out on to the lake in their boat, a hint of color suffuses the scene; and finally . . . the sun rises over the mountain and they are bathed in full color." SLJ

"The purity of the hues, well-produced on ample spreads, the subtle graphic development from scene to scene, and the sharply focused simplicity of the few words make this a true art experience." Horn Book

Hanukah money; by Sholem Aleichem; translated and adapted by Uri Shulevitz and Elizabeth Shub; illustrated by Uri Shulevitz. Greenwillow Bks. 1978 30p il o.p.; Mulberry Bks. paperback available $3.95   E

1. Jews—Fiction 2. Hanukkah—Fiction

ISBN 0-688-10993-4 (pa)

"A vignette of pre-World War I Eastern European Jewish life, in which the home ritual of lighting Hanukah candles and the traditional practice of frying potato pancakes becomes intertwined with the holiday custom of giving money to children as a gift for a joyous season." Horn Book

"Some passages seem to echo chanted prayer rhythms. . . . Such an atmospheric piece will evoke nostalgia in adults reading aloud and will further acculturate children involved in their own traditional celebrations." Booklist

One Monday morning. Scribner 1967 unp il lib bdg $14.95; pa $4.95   E

ISBN 0-684-13195-1 (lib bdg); 0-689-71062-3 (pa)

"'One Monday morning, the king, the queen, and the little prince came to visit me. But I wasn't home. . . .' So goes the daydream of a small child in a drab tenement. As the week progresses, the royal entourage, in the panoply of playing card figures, increases. Their pageantry blots out the grey background while commonplace activities play counterpoint to the fantasy theme." Moorachian. What is a City?

"Humor, dignity, imagination, and a remarkable interplay between text and illustration make . . . [this] a beautiful book that is easy and fun to read. . . . Children will be able to identify, understand, and enjoy both worlds of [the book's] imaginative child." Wis Libr Bull

Rain, rain, rivers; words and pictures by Uri Shulevitz. Farrar, Straus & Giroux 1969 unp il $16; pa $3.95   E

1. Rain

ISBN 0-374-36171-1; 0-374-46195-3 (pa)

A child indoors watches the rain on the window and in the streets and tells how it falls on the fields, hills, and seas

"There is no story line but interest is captured and held by the beauty of the striking illustrations and the strong, pervasive mood they evoke." Booklist

Siebert, Diane

Plane song; paintings by Vincent Nasta. HarperCollins Pubs. 1993 unp il lib bdg $14.89; pa $5.95   E

1. Airplanes—Fiction 2. Stories in rhyme

ISBN 0-06-021467-8 (lib bdg); 0-06-443367-6 (pa)

LC 92-17359

Rhymed text and illustrations describe different kinds of planes and their unique abilities

"Using words that rise and fall in the rhythm of flight, the poet conjures up images of different aircraft. Nasta's stunning illustrations realize these images beautifully in oil paintings of planes soaring through the clouds, highlighted against the changing colors of the sky." SLJ

Train song; paintings by Mike Wimmer. Crowell 1990 unp il $15; lib bdg $14.89; pa $5.95   E

1. Railroads—Fiction 2. Stories in rhyme

ISBN 0-690-04726-6; 0-690-04728-2 (lib bdg); 0-06-443340-4 (pa)   LC 88-389

Rhymed text and illustrations describe the journey of a transcontinental train

"Wimmer's luminous, nostalgic paintings will enable readers to grasp the beauty and power of the trains and the landscape across which they travel." Publ Wkly

Truck song; pictures by Byron Barton. Crowell 1984 unp il lib bdg $14.89; pa $4.95   E

1. Trucks—Fiction 2. Stories in rhyme

ISBN 0-690-04411-9 (lib bdg); 0-06-443134-7 (pa)

LC 83-46173

"Vivid illustrations and a rhythmic text describe the transcontinental journey of a truck driver. Readers/listeners get a sense of overland travel and the diverse American landscape it provides." Soc Educ

Silverman, Erica

Don't fidget a feather; illustrated by S.D. Schindler. Macmillan 1994 unp il $14.95   E

1. Contests—Fiction 2. Ducks—Fiction 3. Geese—Fiction 4. Friendship—Fiction

ISBN 0-02-782685-6   LC 93-8707

"After they compete at swimming and flying, a duck and a gander hold a freeze-in-place contest. Bees, rabbits, and crows pester them and a fox drags them off to his cave; still neither moves. But when Gander's life is in danger, Duck shows that she's the 'true and forever champion of champions.'" Publisher's note

"Schindler's delicate pastel illustrations lend a soft quality to the humor and warmth of Silverman's tale of friendship." Booklist

Sis, Peter

Beach ball. Greenwillow Bks. 1990 unp il $14; lib bdg $12.93   **E**

1. Beaches—Fiction
ISBN 0-688-09181-4; 0-688-09182-2 (lib bdg)

LC 89-2076

"A happy child follows her beach ball down the beach, passing sections of seashore filled with, for example, shapes or colors or objects starting with each letter of the alphabet." Horn Book Guide

The author's "inimitably cheerful illustrations fuse a riot of unsullied color with deft details and endless invention." Publ Wkly

Komodo! Greenwillow Bks. 1993 unp il $16; lib bdg $14.93   **E**

1. Komodo dragon—Fiction 2. Indonesia—Fiction
ISBN 0-688-11583-7; 0-688-11584-5 (lib bdg)

LC 92-25811

A young boy who loves dragons goes with his parents to the Indonesian island of Komodo in hopes of seeing a real dragon. Includes factual information about the Komodo dragon

"The story, assisted by the art in its moodily surreal tone, is simply written but implies worlds." Bull Cent Child Books

An ocean world. Greenwillow Bks. 1992 unp il $15; lib bdg $13.93   **E**

1. Whales—Fiction
ISBN 0-688-09067-2; 0-688-09068-0 (lib bdg)

LC 89-11692

A whale sails new seas and, after several unsuccessful attempts, makes a friend

"In this practically wordless picture book, a whale that has been raised in captivity is returned to the open ocean. . . . Sis illustrates this gentle, quixotic tale with shimmering watercolors in all the hues of the sea and sky. . . . A rich invitation to experiment with seeing and imagining the world in new and unexpected ways." Publ Wkly

Slepian, Jan, 1921-

Lost moose; illustrated by Ted Lewin. Philomel Bks. 1995 unp il $15.95   **E**

1. Moose—Fiction
ISBN 0-399-22749-0   LC 94-6738

A moose calf separated from his mother encounters a boy who follows him on a long walk through the woods, until they are both reclaimed by their respective mothers

"Lewin's distinguished watercolors capture the mood of the two young creatures' adventure in the sun-splashed forest. The text, light letters on dark background and dark on light, floats directly on the pictures; this unity of words and art emphasizes the quiet intensity of the experience." SLJ

Slobodkina, Esphyr, 1908-

Caps for sale; a tale of a peddler, some monkeys & their monkey business; told and illustrated by Esphyr Slobodkina. Addison-Wesley 1947 unp il $13.95; lib bdg $13.89; pa $3.95   **E**

1. Monkeys—Fiction 2. Peddlers and peddling—Fiction
ISBN 0-201-09147-X; 0-06-025778-4 (lib bdg); 0-06-443143-6 (pa)

Also available Spanish language edition

A picture book story which "provides hilarious confusion. A cap peddler takes a nap under a tree. When he wakes up, his caps have disappeared. He looks up in the tree and sees countless monkeys, each wearing a cap and grinning." Parent's Guide To Child Read

Small, David, 1945-

George Washington's cows. Farrar Straus Giroux 1994 unp il $15   **E**

1. Washington, George, 1732-1799—Fiction 2. Animals—Fiction 3. Stories in rhyme
ISBN 0-374-32535-9   LC 93-39989

Humorous rhymes about George Washington's farm where the cows wear dresses, the pigs wear wigs, and the sheep are scholars

"Small's watercolors immeasurably extend his zany poem and make maximum use of the double-page spreads. Cleverly designed and well-executed scenes are filled with silly details that children will love." Booklist

Imogene's antlers; written and illustrated by David Small. Crown 1985 unp il $15; pa $4.99   **E**

ISBN 0-517-55564-6; 0-517-56242-1 (pa)

LC 84-12085

One Thursday Imogene wakes up with a pair of antlers growing out of her head and causes a sensation wherever she goes

The author "maximizes the inherent humor of the absurd situation by allowing the imaginative possibilities of Imogene's predicament to run rampant. The brief text is supported by Small's expansive watercolors. They brim with humorous details." SLJ

Smith, Lane

Glasses: who needs 'em? Viking 1991 unp il $14; pa $4.99   **E**

1. Eyeglasses—Fiction
ISBN 0-670-84160-9; 0-14-054484-4 (pa)

LC 91-9827

Also available Spanish language edition

"When a young patient states, 'I'm worried about looking like a dork,' the optometrist lists others who wear spectacles—'monster-movie' stuntpeople, famous inventors, entire planets. Just when he decides the doctor is crazy, the boy looks through the glasses and sees what he's been missing (almost everyone and everything in the world wearing glasses)." SLJ

The author's "outlandish, surreal illustrations combine with a loopy layout and fanciful type design to provide an abundance of laughter." Publ Wkly

Smucker, Anna Egan

No star nights; paintings by Steve Johnson. Knopf 1989 unp il hardcover o.p. paperback available $4.99   **E**

1. Steel industry—Fiction
ISBN 0-679-86724-4 (pa)   LC 88-2782

A young girl growing up in a steel mill town in the 1950s describes her childhood and how it was affected by the local industry

"The book is handsomely designed, from gray endpapers to full-page paintings alternating a dusky glow with scenes hazed by air pollution." Bull Cent Child Books

Sorensen, Henri, 1950-
New Hope. Lothrop, Lee & Shepard Bks.
1995 unp il $15; lib bdg $14.93   E
1. Danish Americans—Fiction 2. Frontier and pioneer
life—Fiction
ISBN 0-688-13925-6; 0-688-13926-4 (lib bdg)
       LC 94-78939
"Jimmy loves to hear his grandpa tell the story of how
their ancestors came from Denmark and started their journey across America. The town of New Hope began when
the Jensen's axle broke before they crossed the river. Soon
others decided to build a store, hotel and a newspaper office in the now booming town." Child Book Rev Serv
"The realistic portraits of the pioneer family are set
against light-filled views of the wide plains and then scenes
of the crowded streets. Many kids will want to go from here
to their own family stories of coming to America." Booklist

Soto, Gary
Chato's kitchen; illustrated by Susan
Guevara. Putnam 1995 unp il $15.95   E
1. Cats—Fiction 2. Mice—Fiction
ISBN 0-399-22658-3   LC 93-43503
To get the "ratoncitos," little mice, who have moved
into the barrio to come to his house, Chato the cat prepares
all kinds of good food: fajitas, frijoles, salsa, enchiladas, and
more
"Soto adeptly captures the flavor of life in *el barrio* in
this amusing tale. The animal characters have distinct personalities, and their language, sprinkled with Spanish
phrases and expressions, credibly brings them to life. Best
of all, though, are Guevara's striking illustrations that enrich the text with delightful, witty details. Each page exudes
'East L.A. culture,' creating vivid scenes in which bold colors and shapes combine to increase the humor and tension
in the narrative." SLJ

Too many tamales; illustrated by Ed
Martinez. Putnam 1992 unp il $15.95   E
1. Christmas—Fiction 2. Mexican Americans—Fiction
ISBN 0-399-22146-8   LC 91-19229
Also available Spanish language edition
Maria tries on her mother's wedding ring while helping
make tamales for a Christmas family get together, but panic
ensues when hours later, she realizes the ring is missing
This is "a very funny story, full of delicious surprise. The
handsome, realistic oil paintings, in rich shades of brown,
red, and purple, are filled with light, evoking the togetherness of an extended family." Booklist

Spier, Peter, 1927-
Bored—nothing to do! Doubleday 1978 unp
il hardcover o.p. paperback available $5.95
       E
1. Airplanes—Fiction
ISBN 0-385-24104-6 (pa)   LC 77-20726
"A mother orders her young sons to 'do' something: 'I
was never bored at your age!' So they do. Guided by a
handbook, the boys misappropriate the wheels from a baby
carriage, bed sheets, wire from a fence and every essential
requirement to construct an airplane—including the engine
from the family car." Publ Wkly
"The text is almost superfluous, but the colorful, detailed
drawings offer great scope for discussion, poring over, and
enjoying a fantasy to which young children will relate."
Child Book Rev Serv

Fast-slow, high-low; a book of opposites.
Doubleday 1972 unp il hardcover o.p.
paperback available $5.95   E
1. English language—Synonyms and antonyms
ISBN 0-385-24093-7 (pa)
"Pages filled with delightful drawings, in pairs, that illustrate objects or concepts like fast or slow, young or old,
over or under, heavy or light, dark or light, and so on."
Bull Cent Child Books

Peter Spier's circus! Doubleday 1992 unp il
$16; pa $5.99   E
1. Circus—Fiction
ISBN 0-385-41969-4; 0-440-40935-7 (pa)
      LC 90-23282
A traveling circus arrives, sets up its village of tents, performs for the crowd, and then moves on again
"Peter Spier fills every bit of the volume with busy
scenes. . . . The reader is shown a multitude of trucks,
house trailers, railroad cars, cages, animals, people, and paraphernalia. . . . Peter Spier's characteristic sketches, lightly
tinted in watercolor, are an energetic tour de force. . . . The
book is masterful in capturing the amazing complexity of
the circus world." Horn Book

Spinelli, Eileen, 1942-
Thanksgiving at the Tappletons'; illustrated
by Maryann Cocca-Leffler. newly il ed.
HarperCollins Pubs. 1992 c1982 unp il $15;
lib bdg $14.89; pa $4.95   E
1. Thanksgiving Day—Fiction
ISBN 0-06-020871-6; 0-06-020872-4 (lib bdg);
0-06-443204-1 (pa)   LC 91-33250
A newly illustrated edition of the title first published
1982 by Addison-Wesley
"'Thanksgiving at the Tappletons' was always a big day.
But one year, when each member of the family is unable to
contribute his usual part of the meal—the turkey falls in a
pond; the salad makings are fed to pet rabbits—they make
do with liverwurst and cheese sandwiches and are thankful
for being together. The light, humorous illustrations are a
match for the droll text." Horn Book Guide

Stanley, Diane, 1943-
The gentleman and the kitchen maid;
pictures by Dennis Nolan. Dial Bks. for
Young Readers 1994 unp il $14.99; lib bdg
$14.89   E
1. Painting—Fiction 2. Museums—Fiction
ISBN 0-8037-1320-7; 0-8037-1321-5 (lib bdg)
      LC 93-157
Also available Spanish language edition
When two paintings hanging across from each other in a
museum fall in love, a resourceful art student finds a way
to unite the lovers
"Nolan uses a light touch to create paintings that resemble the work of several masters, and Stanley's text is breezy
and fresh." Horn Book Guide

Steig, William, 1907-
The amazing bone. Farrar, Straus & Giroux
1976 unp il $17; pa $4.95   E
1. Pigs—Fiction 2. Bones—Fiction
ISBN 0-374-30248-0; 0-374-40358-9 (pa)
Also available Spanish language edition

Steig, William, 1907——*Continued*

A Caldecott Medal honor book, 1977

On her way home from school, Pearl finds an unusual bone that has unexpected powers

"Steig's marvelously straightfaced telling comes with a panoply of ultra-spring landscapes for pink-dressed Pearl to tiptoe through. And there's no holding back the chortles at the wonderfully expressive faces the artist delights in. This is a tight mesh of witty storytelling and art bound to please any audience." Booklist

Brave Irene. Farrar, Straus & Giroux 1986 unp il $17; pa $4.95　E

ISBN 0-374-30947-7; 0-374-40927-7 (pa)

LC 86-80957

Also available Spanish language edition

"Hardworking Mrs. Bobbin has just finished a beautiful ballgown for the duchess, but she has a headache and can't deliver it. Brave and devoted daughter Irene takes charge, tucking her mother snugly into bed and determinedly marching out into a raging snowstorm with the dress. Howling 'GO HO-WO-WOME' at poor Irene, the fierce wind rips the box open and the gown sails out, 'waltzing through the powdered air with tissue-paper attendants.'" Publ Wkly

"With sure writing and well composed, riveting art, Steig keeps readers with Irene every step of the long way. The pictures, which take up about two-thirds of each page, are done in winter blues, purples, and grays that gradually get darker as Irene trudges on. An overlay of swirling white snow adds appropriate atmosphere." Booklist

Caleb & Kate. Farrar, Straus & Giroux 1977 unp il $11.95; pa $4.95　E

1. Dogs—Fiction 2. Witches—Fiction

ISBN 0-374-31016-5; 0-374-41038-0 (pa)

LC 77-4947

"Though Caleb the carpenter loves Kate the weaver very much, he leaves her one day because of a quarrel. In the deep woods where he is resting Yedida the witch turns him into a dog. The tale of his faithfulness and love for his wife, even though he is a dog, is . . . told. Their love is shared to the end, when a remarkable turn of events enables him to return to his former self." Child Book Rev Serv

"The well-cadenced storytelling has a certain old-fashioned elegance of language, and the humor is emphasized by an atmosphere of mock-pathos. William Steig is a superb artist with the literary ingenuity to produce durable, energetic stories." Horn Book

Doctor De Soto. Farrar, Straus & Giroux 1982 unp il $16　E

1. Dentists—Fiction 2. Mice—Fiction 3. Animals—Fiction

ISBN 0-374-31803-4　　　　LC 82-15701

Also available Spanish language edition

A Newbery Medal honor book, 1983

"Dr. De Soto is a mouse dentist who, with his assistant Mrs. De Soto, treats all creatures large and small but none that are injurious to mice. When Fox begs for help, the couple face a dilemma. He is in pain and professional ethics demand that they pull his aching tooth and replace it with a sound one." Publ Wkly

This "book goes beyond the usual tale of wit versus might; the story achieves comic heights partly through the delightful irony of the situation. . . . Watercolor paintings, with the artist's firm line and luscious color, depict with aplomb the eminently dentistlike mouse as he goes about his business." Horn Book

Another available title about Doctor De Soto is:
Doctor De Soto goes to Africa (1992)

Farmer Palmer's wagon ride; story and pictures by William Steig. Farrar, Straus & Giroux 1974 unp il hardcover o.p. paperback available $4.95　E

1. Pigs—Fiction 2. Donkeys—Fiction

ISBN 0-374-42268-0 (pa)

"Farmer Palmer (a pig) and his hired hand (a donkey) have a catastrophe-ridden return from market." LC. Child Books, 1974

"The text . . . boasts some captivating and original onomatopoeia, lending itself to reading aloud. Full-color illustrations add action, expression, and countryside colors appropriate to the story." Booklist

Solomon the rusty nail. Farrar, Straus & Giroux 1985 unp il $16; pa $5.95　E

1. Rabbits—Fiction

ISBN 0-374-37131-8; 0-374-46903-2 (pa)

LC 85-81024

"If he scratches his nose and wiggles his toes at the same time, young Solomon rabbit turns into a rusty nail. He uses his trick lightly, but one day taunts a smart cat who catches and eventually nails him to the side of a clapboard house." N Y Times Book Rev

"The illustrations are inimitably Steig, although a trifle quieter in color than his work usually is." Horn Book

Sylvester and the magic pebble. Simon & Schuster 1969 unp il $14; pa $5.95　E

1. Donkeys—Fiction

ISBN 0-671-66154-X; 0-671-66269-4 (pa)

LC 80-12314

Also available Spanish language edition

Awarded the Caldecott Medal, 1970

"Sylvester the young donkey was a pebble collector; one day he found a flaming red stone, shiny and round—and quite unaccountably able to grant wishes. Overjoyed, Sylvester was planning to share his magic with his family when 'a mean, hungry lion' appeared. Startled and panicky, Sylvester wished himself transformed into a rock. In vain his grieving parents searched for their beloved child; all worried animals took up the hunt. Then, after months of sorrow and mourning, poor Sylvester was fortuitously but logically restored. A remarkable atmosphere of childlike innocence pervades the book; beautiful pictures in full, natural color show daily and seasonal changes in the lush countryside and greatly extend the kindly humor and the warm, unselfconscious tenderness." Horn Book

Zeke Pippin. HarperCollins Pubs. 1994 unp il $15; lib bdg $20.75　E

1. Pigs—Fiction 2. Harmonicas—Fiction

ISBN 0-06-205076-1; 0-06-205077-X (lib bdg)

LC 94-76111

"Michael di Capua books"

"The harmonica that Zeke Pippin, a young pig, finds in the street has magical powers. Of course he doesn't understand that it is the special music that causes his family to fall asleep when he plays, so he crossly runs away from home. He ends up both a local hero and a fine musician." N Y Times Book Rev

"Colorful and cartoonlike, Steig's watercolor and pen-and-ink illustrations add to the humorous story." Booklist

Stein, Sara Bonnett

Oh, baby! [by] Sara Stein; photographs by Holly Ann Shelowitz. Walker & Co. 1993 unp il $14.95; lib bdg $15.85; pa $5.95   **E**

1. Infants

ISBN 0-8027-8261-2; 0-8027-8262-0 (lib bdg); 0-8027-7464-4 (pa)   LC 93-12677

Text and photographs of different infants describe many things babies can do

"Full-color photographs, bordered by crayon lines, lay on the pages as if in a photo album. The clearly written text describes all of the babies' accomplishments as they develop and grow. . . . African Americans, Asians, and Caucasians are all represented." SLJ

Steptoe, John, 1950-1989

Baby says. Lothrop, Lee & Shepard Bks. 1988 unp il $15; lib bdg $13.93; pa $3.95   **E**

1. Brothers—Fiction 2. Infants—Fiction

ISBN 0-688-07423-5; 0-688-07424-3 (lib bdg); 0-688-11858-0 (pa)   LC 87-17296

"Little brother keeps throwing his Teddy bear until he finally topples the block city Big Brother is building. All ends well when understanding Big Brother realizes that Little Brother only wants to help. After hugs and kisses, the project is started over again—together." Child Book Rev Serv

"With simplicity of style and soft, pastel colored pencil drawings the author-artist depicts the tender, caring relationship of an older brother for his baby brother." Horn Book

Birthday. Holt & Co. 1991 c1972 unp il $14.95   **E**

1. Birthdays—Fiction 2. African Americans—Fiction 3. Africa—Fiction

ISBN 0-8050-1849-2   LC 91-18436

A reissue of the title first published 1972 by Holt, Rinehart & Winston

"Eight-year-old Javaka celebrates his birthday in the imaginary utopian farming community to which he and his parents have moved to escape the racism of the 'Old America.' Effectively told in the black vernacular, the book is illustrated with vibrant, glowing paintings that capture the intimacy and warmth of Javaka's community." Horn Book

Stevie. Harper & Row 1969 unp il lib bdg $14.89; pa $5.95   **E**

1. African Americans—Fiction

ISBN 0-06-025764-4 (lib bdg); 0-06-443122-3 (pa)

Also available Spanish language edition

A small black boy, Robert "tells the story of the intruder, Stevie, who comes to stay at his house because both parents are working. Stevie is a pest. He tags along after Robert, he messes up toys, he wants everything he sees. Worst of all, 'my momma never said nothin' to him.' But Robert is an only child, and after Stevie goes, the house is still. He remembers the games they played, the way Stevie looked up to him." Saturday Rev

"Warm and touching, the first-person story is effectively told in idiomatic language and is illustrated with expressive lifelike paintings in dark and brilliant colors." Booklist

Stevenson, Harvey

Grandpa's house. Hyperion Bks. for Children 1994 unp il $14.95; lib bdg $14.89   **E**

1. Grandfathers—Fiction

ISBN 1-56282-588-7; 1-56282-589-5 (lib bdg)   LC 93-6318

"Before he visits his grandfather, Woody cannot remember exactly what he is like, but, once he and his parents get there, Woody is delighted by Grandpa's playful teasing. Stevenson creates a wonderful and warm relationship between them, and readers will laugh at Grandpa's silliness. Lively pen-and-ink and watercolor illustrations add to the cheerful mood." Horn Book Guide

Stevenson, James, 1929-

"Could be worse!". Greenwillow Bks. 1977 unp il $15; lib bdg $14.95   **E**

1. Grandfathers—Fiction 2. Dreams—Fiction

ISBN 0-688-80075-0; 0-688-84075-2 (lib bdg)   LC 76-28534

MaryAnn and Louie "comment on the fact that their grandfather . . . goes through the same routine every morning. . . . But one day Grandpa fools them and tells a long, involved story of a dream-fantasy in which he went from one peril to another." Bull Cent Child Books

"Stevenson's sketchy watercolors, arranged in panels, trace Grandpa's adventures. . . . A read-aloud picture story guaranteed to tickle young funny bones." Booklist

Other available titles about Grandpa, Mary Ann, and Louie are:

Brrr! (1991)
Grandpa's great city tour (1983)
Grandpa's too-good garden (1989)
The great big especially beautiful Easter egg (1983)
No friends (1986)
That dreadful day (1985)
That terrible Halloween night (1980)
That's exactly the way it wasn't (1991)
There's nothing to do! (1986)
We hate rain! (1988)
What's under my bed? (1983)
Will you please feed our cat? (1987)
Worse than Willy! (1984)

Don't you know there's a war on? Greenwillow Bks. 1992 unp il $14; lib bdg $13.93   **E**

1. World War, 1939-1945—United States 2. Authors, American 3. Illustrators

ISBN 0-688-11383-4; 0-688-11384-2 (lib bdg)   LC 91-31461

The author recalls his efforts to win the Second World War, including planting a victory garden, collecting tin foil, and looking for spies

The author's "combination of casual, poetic text and small, blurry watercolor sketches, several to a page, creates an exquisite memoir that also communicates what it's like to remember." Booklist

Emma. Greenwillow Bks. 1985 unp il $11.75; lib bdg $11.88; pa $3.95   **E**

1. Witches—Fiction

ISBN 0-688-04020-9; 0-688-04021-7 (lib bdg); 0-688-07336-0 (pa)   LC 84-4141

"Stevenson tells the story of two green-faced broom-flying witches, Lavinia and Dolores, who are looking for something terrible to do, and a pint-sized amiable witch named Emma, who wants to fly." SLJ

"The exaggerated humor, obvious characterization,

Stevenson, James, 1929-—*Continued*
straightforward plotline, and 'right over might' theme are well suited to the comic-book format, balloon-encased dialogue, agile line, and no-nonsense colors. . . . This book should enthrall a restless audience." Horn Book

Other available titles about Emma, Lavinia, and Dolores are:
Emma at the beach(1990)
Fried feathers for Thanksgiving (1986)
Happy Valentine's Day, Emma! (1987)
Un-Happy New Year, Emma! (1989)
Yuck! (1984)

Monty. Greenwillow Bks. 1992 unp il $15; pa $4.95   E

1. Alligators—Fiction 2. Animals—Fiction
ISBN 0-688-11241-2; 0-688-11288-9 (pa)

LC 91-20657

Also available Spanish language edition
A reissue of the title first published 1979

"Tom, Doris, and Arthur (a rabbit, a duck, and a frog) always call for their alligator friend Monty when it's time to cross the river to get to school. One day Monty decides he's had enough of being taken for granted, enough of listening to his three friends order him about with 'Don't wobble so much,' 'Let's see some more speed,' and 'More to the right!' He announces he's taking a vacation. The efforts the three students make to find another way to cross the river are hilarious." Bull Cent Child Books

Another available title about Monty is:
No need for Monty (1987)

The Mud Flat Olympics. Greenwillow Bks. 1994 56p il $15; lib bdg $14.93   E

1. Animals—Fiction 2. Games—Fiction
ISBN 0-688-12923-4; 0-688-12924-2 (lib bdg)

LC 93-28118

At the Mud Flat Olympics if the animals don't win the Deepest Hole Contest, the All-Snail High Hurdles, or the River-Cross Freestyle, they can still come to the picnic after the games and have ice cream for dessert

"This is a great example of the author-artist's mischievous verbal wit. It also shows off Stevenson's remarkable ability to turn splashes of watercolor and a few freewheeling ink lines into expressive cartoon characters." Booklist

The night after Christmas. Greenwillow Bks. 1981 unp il $16; lib bdg $15.93; pa $4.95   E

1. Teddy bears—Fiction 2. Dolls—Fiction 3. Dogs—Fiction
ISBN 0-688-00547-0; 0-688-00548-9 (lib bdg); 0-688-04590-1 (pa)

"Replaced by new toys, an old teddy bear and a worn-out doll are thrown away the day after Christmas. They try to make a new life for themselves, but it is a stray dog who befriends them and finds a way for them to become beloved toys again." Child Book Rev Serv

"The author's style is casual but smooth, his structure tight, and his illustrations, especially the snow-swirled outdoor scenes, evocative." Bull Cent Child Books

The Sea View Hotel. Greenwillow Bks. 1994 unp il $15; lib bdg $14.93   E

1. Mice—Fiction 2. Vacations—Fiction 3. Animals—Fiction
ISBN 0-688-13469-6; 0-688-13470-X (lib bdg)

A newly illustrated edition of the title first published 1978

As the only child at the Sea View Hotel, Hubert the mouse is having a miserable two-week vacation until he en-counters the hotel handyman

"A story with simplicity, harmony, and ease in the telling. . . . The characters, whose bodies in their turn-of-the-century clothing seem human, have heads of birds, turtles, dogs, or whatever suits their personality or Stevenson's whimsy." SLJ

Other available titles about Hubert (Hubie) and his family are:
All aboard! (1995)
The stowaway (1990)

A village full of valentines. Greenwillow Bks. 1995 39p il $15; lib bdg $14.93   E

1. Valentine's Day—Fiction 2. Animals—Fiction
ISBN 0-688-13602-8; 0-688-13603-6 (lib bdg)

LC 94-624

"A series of simple vignettes all center around Valentine's Day. Clifford, the turtle, doesn't believe in sending a valentine until he gets one. As a result, he's been waiting for fifty-six years. On the other hand, Mona, Tina, and Mary Lou are all so anxious to make valentines, they quarrel about how to divide the work fairly. . . . Though the first six chapters seem to tell unrelated stories about making, giving, and receiving valentines, the last chapter ties all the stories together when everyone in the village gathers at Sidney's barn for a party." Horn Book

"Stevenson has done a masterful job of creating stories easy enough for new readers to read alone, each with a twist or joke based on a character's personality." Bull Cent Child Books

The worst person in the world. Greenwillow Bks. 1978 unp il lib bdg $13.93; pa $4.95   E

1. Friendship—Fiction
ISBN 0-688-84127-9 (lib bdg); 0-688-14394-6 (pa)

LC 77-22141

"A grumpy old man known as the worst person in the world lives alone in a neglected old house until a friendly creature named Ugly follows him home, tidies up, and invites the neighborhood children to a party." Publisher's note

"A blithe if predictable story illustrated by cartoon-style drawings. . . . The style is jaunty and the pictures amusing." Bull Cent Child Books

Other available titles about the worst person are:
Worse than the worst (1994)
The worst goes South (1995)
The worst person's Christmas (1991)

Stewart, Sarah

The library; pictures by David Small. Farrar, Straus & Giroux 1995 unp il $15   E

1. Books and reading—Fiction 2. Stories in rhyme
ISBN 0-374-34388-8   LC 94-30320

Elizabeth Brown loves to read more than anything else, but when her collection of books grows and grows, she must make a change in her life

"Framed watercolors give the book an old-fashioned, scrapbooklike appearance. . . . Small black-ink line drawings decorate the verses below and often add an additional touch of humor. This is a funny, heartwarming story about a quirky woman with a not-so-peculiar obsession." SLJ

Stock, Catherine

Armien's fishing trip. Morrow Junior Bks. 1990 unp il $13.95; lib bdg $13.88   E

1. Fishing—Fiction 2. South Africa—Fiction

ISBN 0-688-08395-1; 0-688-08396-X (lib bdg)

LC 89-3266

While visiting his aunt and uncle in the little South African village of Kalk Bay, Armien stows away in his uncle's fishing boat and becomes an unexpected hero

"This is universal adventure specifically set. The town and Armien's friends are an ethnic and cultural mix, a fishing community united by their bond with the sea. Double-page spreads of all the neighbors at the dock are likewise multi-colorful, a strong and sunny contrast to the stormy, blue-washed pages of Armien's heroic rescue of fisherman Sam." Bull Cent Child Books

Stoeke, Janet Morgan

A hat for Minerva Louise. Dutton Children's Bks. 1994 unp il $12.99   E

1. Chickens—Fiction 2. Hats—Fiction

ISBN 0-525-45328-8   LC 94-2139

Minerva Louise, a snow-loving chicken, mistakes a pair of mittens for two hats to keep both ends warm

This "is a rare find: a picture book exactly on target for preschoolers that sacrifices none of the essential elements of plot, character, and humor. . . . The pictures, in large rectangles of bright primary colors, are easy for preschoolers to 'read' and contain most of the book's considerable humor." Horn Book

Another available title about Minerva Louise is:
Minerva Louise (1988)

Stolz, Mary, 1920-

Emmett's pig; pictures by Garth Williams. Harper & Row 1959 61p il lib bdg $14.89

    E

1. Pigs—Fiction

ISBN 0-06-025856-X

"An I can read book"

"Although Emmett lives in a city apartment and is surrounded by toy pigs, pictures and books about pigs, his great desire for a real live pig is finally granted as a birthday present—a pig to be his own, but to be boarded on a farm outside the city." Wis Libr Bull

This book is "far above the average in both interest and illustration." Bookmark

Storm in the night; illustrated by Pat Cummings. Harper & Row 1988 unp il lib bdg $14.89; pa $4.95   E

1. Thunderstorms—Fiction 2. Grandfathers—Fiction 3. Fear—Fiction

ISBN 0-06-025913-2 (lib bdg); 0-06-443256-4 (pa)

LC 85-45838

After a power failure during a thunderstorm, Thomas, his grandfather and Ringo the cat go out on the porch. Grandfather tells Thomas a story of his own childhood fear of storms and how concern for his equally frightened pet helped him to overcome it

"Presenting a glorified portrayal of a white cat, a beautiful black child, and a gentle old man, the dark, shadowy paintings are made luminous by 'the carrot-colored flames in the wood stove' or by lightning slashing across the navy-blue sky; every illustration is imbued with the boy's sensory awareness during a night of wonder and discovery." Horn Book

Stutson, Caroline

By the light of the Halloween moon; [by] Caroline Stutson, Kevin Hawkes. Lothrop, Lee & Shepard Bks. 1993 unp il $16; lib bdg $15.93   E

1. Halloween—Fiction

ISBN 0-688-12045-8; 0-688-12046-6 (lib bdg)

LC 92-10258

Also available in paperback from Puffin Bks.

"A lively cumulative Halloween poem sets forth a series of scary Halloween creatures trying to catch a mysterious toe. . . . Not only is the text rhythmically bouncy and appealing, but the illustrations are of the least fearful and most amusing of ghastly creatures, very effectively set against a black and gloomy background. A sure Halloween hit." Horn Book

Sutcliff, Rosemary, 1920-1992

The minstrel and the dragon pup; written by Rosemary Sutcliff; illustrated by Emma Chichester Clark. Candlewick Press 1993 42p il $16.95; pa $6.99   E

1. Dragons—Fiction 2. Minstrels—Fiction

ISBN 1-564-02098-3; 1-56402-603-5 (pa)

LC 92-53012

When a minstrel's adopted dragon pup is stolen by a wicked showman, the minstrel's songs suffer accordingly

"Sutcliff has written a beautifully crafted, magical, mesmerizing tale with an original twist. . . . Each page of the book is highly stylized and original, with marbleized borders, decorative panels, and richly colored illustrations reminiscent of Renaissance art." Booklist

Swift, Hildegarde Hoyt, d. 1977

The little red lighthouse and the great gray bridge; by Hildegarde H. Swift and Lynd Ward. Harcourt Brace Jovanovich 1942 unp il $16; pa $5   E

1. George Washington Bridge (N.Y. and N.J.)—Fiction 2. Lighthouses—Fiction

ISBN 0-15-247040-9; 0-15-652840-1 (pa)

"After the great beacon atop the . . . George Washington Bridge was installed, the little red lighthouse feared he would no longer be useful, but when an emergency arose, the little lighthouse proved that he was still important." Hodges. Books for Elem Sch Libr

"The story is written with imagination and a gift for bringing alive this little lighthouse and its troubles. . . . [Lynd Ward's] illustrations have some distinction and one in particular, the fog creeping over the river clutching at the river boats, has atmosphere, rhythm and good colour." Ont Libr Rev

Tafuri, Nancy

Do not disturb. Greenwillow Bks. 1987 unp il $12.95; lib bdg $11.88   E

1. Camping—Fiction 2. Animals—Fiction 3. Stories without words

ISBN 0-688-06541-4; 0-688-06542-2 (lib bdg)

LC 86-357

"A few succinct words—'It was the first day of summer'—help to establish the fact that a family of one dog, two parents, and three children are setting up camp near a woodland lake. Now the narrative becomes purely pictorial, with definitive line drawing, enticing color, and interesting perspectives." Horn Book

Tafuri, Nancy—*Continued*

Early morning in the barn. Greenwillow Bks. 1983 unp il $16; lib bdg $15.93; pa $3.95; Puffin Bks. pa $3.95   E

1. Animals—Fiction 2. Stories without words
ISBN 0-688-02328-2; 0-688-02329-0 (lib bdg); 0-688-11710-4 (pa); 0-14-050511-3 (pa)

LC 83-1436

"With sunup on the farm comes a cock crowing, a mother hen and chicks running outside, and an array of other familiar barnyard animals all greeting the morning with their respective vocalizations." Booklist

"This boldly colorful, wordless picture book (the only text is some animal sounds) is a perfect beginning book for the nursery set. The colors have the impact of poster paint but with some of the subtle gradations of watercolors. The young reader can watch the travels of new chicks past quacking ducks, baaing lambs, and slurping pigs as they go to their mother. A charmer." Child Book Rev Serv

Follow me! Greenwillow Bks. 1990 unp il $16; lib bdg $13.88   E

1. Seals (Animals)—Fiction 2. Crabs—Fiction 3. Stories without words
ISBN 0-688-08773-6; 0-688-08774-4 (lib bdg)

LC 89-23259

"A baby sea lion exhibits the curiosity of a youngster as the baby explores a crab's world. Children will have no trouble following the wordless story told in Tafuri's usual direct, appealing style. Mama sea lion's careful observation of the journey is the ultimate reassurance." Horn Book Guide

Have you seen my duckling? Greenwillow Bks. 1984 unp il $15.95; lib bdg $13.88; pa $3.95   E

1. Ducks—Fiction
ISBN 0-688-02797-0; 0-688-02798-9 (lib bdg); 0-688-10994-2 (pa)   LC 83-17196

A Caldecott Medal honor book, 1985

"In a picture book virtually wordless except for the repeated question of the title, seven ducklings obediently cluster in their nest, while the eighth—more daring and more curious—scrambles after an errant butterfly." Horn Book

"Tafuri's artwork . . . features clean lines, generous figures, and clear, cool colors. She also adds nice detail—feathers, for instance, that you can almost feel under your hands." Booklist

Rabbit's morning. Greenwillow Bks. 1985 unp il lib bdg $22.25   E

1. Rabbits—Fiction 2. Stories without words
ISBN 0-688-04064-0   LC 84-10229

"In a nearly wordless picture book, a young rabbit explores the meadow, sighting neighboring beavers, deer, mice, pheasants and other animals in the course of its journey. Tafuri's watercolors contain the essence of a summer dawn's translucence, incorporating minimal text into borderless double-page spreads filled with animals and their babies that are certain to appeal to preschoolers and beginning readers." SLJ

Spots, feathers, and curly tails. Greenwillow Bks. 1988 unp il $16; lib bdg $16   E

1. Domestic animals
ISBN 0-688-07536-3; 0-688-07537-1 (lib bdg)

LC 87-15638

Questions and answers highlight some outstanding characteristics of farm animals, such as a chicken's feathers and a horse's mane

"In the watercolor illustrations with black pen outline,

Nancy Tafuri manages in the simplest style to give energy and personality to the animals through the angle of a head or the set of a snout. The story will provide a successful experience for both child and adult reader and is an ideal book for the beginning reader to entertain a younger sibling in a game they'll both enjoy." Horn Book

This is the farmer. Greenwillow Bks. 1994 unp il $15; lib bdg $14.93   E

1. Farm life—Fiction
ISBN 0-688-09468-6; 0-688-09469-4 (lib bdg)

LC 92-30082

A farmer's kiss causes an amusing chain of events on the farm

"The well-defined, watercolor-and-ink double-spread illustrations are . . . of the highest quality. The brief story is rhythmic, predictable, and printed in extra-large type." SLJ

Teague, Mark, 1963-

The field beyond the outfield. Scholastic 1992 unp il $14.95; pa $4.95   E

1. Fear—Fiction 2. Baseball—Fiction
ISBN 0-590-45173-1; 0-590-45174-X (pa)

LC 91-18055

"Ludlow Grebe sees monsters everywhere. His worried parents . . . urge him to try Little League. But playing outfield encourages flights of fancy, and before Ludlow knows what's happened, he's up to bat for a team of strange green flying critters. . . . Flat, bright colors coupled with expert use of depth give the paintings a uniform solidity that makes even Ludlow's imaginings seem real, and children will stare at the game's unusual spectators and delight in the fact that they seem to be staring right back." Booklist

Pigsty. Scholastic 1994 unp il $13.95   E

1. Pigs—Fiction 2. Cleanliness—Fiction
ISBN 0-590-45915-5   LC 93-21179

When Wendell doesn't clean up his room, a whole herd of pigs comes to live with him

"Much of the tale's fun resides in Teague's quirky acrylic art. . . . Whether Wendell and his friends are jumping on the bed or playing Monopoly on the rug, their antics are rendered in the bold palette of a gleefully inventive imagination. Highly recommended for neat-freaks and messmakers alike." Publ Wkly

Testa, Fulvio, 1947-

If you take a paintbrush; a book of colors. Dial Bks. for Young Readers 1983 unp il hardcover o.p. paperback available $4.95
                    E

1. Color
ISBN 0-8037-0282-5 (pa)   LC 82-45512

"The book begins with endpapers that have tubes of paint, rulers, compasses, and other art supplies scattered in delightful disarray. Following this are short but clear statements about a color—'yellow is the color of the sun.' This faces a bordered picture that features the sun beating down on the sands of the desert as two children atop a camel ride by. 'Brown is the color of chocolate' is illustrated by two young bakers watching as a third oozes frosting down the side of a cake." Booklist

"Simple, yet imaginative, the book deals with the concept of color in an attractive, appealing manner." Child Book Rev Serv

Testa, Fulvio, 1947- —*Continued*

If you take a pencil. Dial Bks. for Young Readers 1982 unp il hardcover o.p. paperback available $4.95   E

1. Drawing—Fiction 2. Counting
ISBN 0-8037-0165-9 (pa)   LC 82-1505

This story describes "the busy day of two friends who take a pencil and draw two cats. Three, four and more numbers follow, represented by bright scenes in a garden (six orange trees), until the playmates land on a desert island with 12 treasure chests, empty except for one with 'a small treasure—a pencil.'" Publ Wkly

"In the guise of a counting book, this is actually an exceedingly handsome and amusing gallery of pictures by Fulvio Testa. . . . Funny, mysterious, playful, hiding numerous puzzles within the pictures, anticipating later pictures in earlier ones, the book serves as much to elicit stories out of its perusers as to tell stories to them." SLJ

Thayer, Jane, 1904-

The popcorn dragon; written by Jane Thayer; illustrated by Lisa McCue. Morrow Junior Bks. 1989 unp il $16; lib bdg $15.93   E

1. Dragons—Fiction
ISBN 0-688-08340-4; 0-688-08876-7 (lib bdg)
    LC 88-39855

A newly illustrated edition of the title first published 1953

Though his hot breath is the envy of all the other animals, a young dragon learns that showing off does not make friends

"McCue's new full-color illustrations capture the whimsical mood of the fable. The animals, although too coy, have appealing humanlike expressions which convey their envy and contempt." SLJ

The puppy who wanted a boy; illustrated by Lisa McCue. Morrow 1986 unp il $14; lib bdg $13.93; pa $4.95   E

1. Dogs—Fiction 2. Christmas—Fiction
ISBN 0-688-05944-9; 0-688-05945-7 (lib bdg); 0-688-08293-9 (pa)   LC 85-15465

A newly illustrated edition of the title first published 1958

"More than anything in the world, Petey, a puppy, wanted a boy for Christmas. Nothing else his mother suggested would do, and none of the other dogs would give him their boys. Dejected, Petey passes the Home for Boys where a lonely newcomer sits on the steps. Petey has found not one boy, but 50 boys full of love." SLJ

"It is the same, somewhat sentimental but certainly appealing tale that Thayer fashioned in 1958, when this was originally published; however, McCue's affectionately drawn, warmly colored illustrations go a long way toward perking up the story." Booklist

Thomas, Jane Resh, 1936-

Saying good-bye to Grandma; illustrated by Marcia Sewall. Clarion Bks. 1988 48p il lib bdg $15.95; pa $6.95   E

1. Death—Fiction 2. Grandmothers—Fiction
ISBN 0-89919-645-4; 0-395-54779-2 (pa)
    LC 87-20826

"An anecdotal account of seven-year-old Suzie's trip to her grandparent's house to attend her grandmother's funeral. Activities with her cousins, her feelings about her grandmother, and relating to her grieving grandfather are all

conveyed." Child Book Rev Serv

"Marcia Sewall's colorful, loose, almost faceless illustrations are just sketchy enough to contribute to the book's universality; a child could picture himself or herself in any of these scenes." N Y Times Book Rev

Thomassie, Tynia

Feliciana Feydra LeRoux; a Cajun tall tale; illustrated by Cat Bowman Smith. Little, Brown 1995 unp il lib bdg $14.95   E

1. Alligators—Fiction 2. Cajuns—Fiction 3. Louisiana—Fiction
ISBN 0-316-84125-0   LC 93-30347

"Feliciana's grandpa won't let her go alligator hunting in the Louisiana Cajun bayou. When she sneaks out, Feliciana causes fun and excitement, and even becomes a heroine." Soc Educ

This "combines breezy watercolors and a swinging text that's perfect for reading aloud. A note on Cajun culture, a glossary, and a pronunciation guide are included." Booklist

Thurber, James, 1894-1961

The great Quillow; illustrated by Steven Kellogg. Harcourt Brace Jovanovich 1994 56p il $17.95   E

1. Fairy tales
ISBN 0-15-232544-1   LC 91-20586

"An HBJ contemporary classic"

A newly illustrated edition of the title first published 1944

Quillow, a tiny toymaker, defeats a ferocious giant named Hunder and saves his town from destruction

"The lively full-color illustrations are pure Kellogg: energetic line, sunlit color, broad humor, subtle detail, and exuberant spirit. . . . The artwork captures the bustle and the bickering of the story as well as the terror and the wonder." Booklist

Titherington, Jeanne, 1951-

Pumpkin, pumpkin. Greenwillow Bks. 1986 23p il $15; lib bdg $14.93; pa $3.95   E

ISBN 0-688-05695-4; 0-688-05696-2 (lib bdg); 0-688-09930-0 (pa)   LC 84-25334

"Softly colored pencil illustrations in a realistic style effectively communicate Jamie's pride as a very young gardener. He plants a seed, then grows and harvests a pumpkin from which he saves seeds for next year. The large, detailed drawings capture Jamie's anticipation and pleasure just right. The garden creatures appearing on every page and grandpa, whom we catch sight of now and then, are a delightful supporting cast. Nonreaders can easily follow the story in pictures alone. Very large, clear print on facing pages makes the simple narrative inviting for beginning readers, too." SLJ

Tompert, Ann, 1918-

Grandfather Tang's story; illustrated by Robert Andrew Parker. Crown 1990 unp il $16; lib bdg $16.99   E

1. Foxes—Fiction
ISBN 0-517-57487-X; 0-517-57272-9 (lib bdg)
    LC 89-22205

"An old Chinese man sits beneath a tree with his granddaughter, telling her the tale of two foxes who change themselves into ever-fiercer animals as they compete for

Tompert, Ann, 1918-—*Continued*

dominance. As he speaks, he rearranges two tangram puzzles to form the shapes of the animals. . . . Directions for making tangrams, described as ancient Chinese puzzles, appear on the book's last page." Booklist

"Parker's watercolor washes complement the text, adding energy and tension, as well as evoking oriental brushwork technique. However, the text is strong enough to stand on its own, and will be valued by storytellers and listeners alike." SLJ

Torres, Leyla

Subway sparrow. Farrar, Straus & Giroux 1993 unp il $20   E

1. Subways—Fiction 2. Birds—Fiction 3. New York (N.Y.)—Fiction
ISBN 0-374-37285-3   LC 92-55104
Also available Spanish language edition

Although the passengers of a New York City subway train speak different languages, they work together to rescue a frightened bird

"Colorful watercolor paintings illustrate this multicultural story. . . . The brief text, which includes phrases in Spanish and Polish, advances the plot while allowing the double-spread illustrations to convey the action. . . . The expressive pictures and the caring tone transcend any particular place or time." SLJ

Tresselt, Alvin R., 1916-

Hide and seek fog; by Alvin Tresselt; illustrated by Roger Duvoisin. Lothrop, Lee & Shepard Bks. 1965 unp il lib bdg $15.93; pa $3.95   E

1. Fog
ISBN 0-688-51169-4 (lib bdg); 0-688-07813-3 (pa)
A Caldecott Medal honor book, 1966

"This is not a plotted story but rather a mood picture book . . . describing a fog which rolls in from the sea to veil an Atlantic seacoast village for three days. The beautiful paintings, most of them double-spreads, and the brief, poetic text sensitively and effectively evoke the atmosphere of the 'worst fog in twenty years' and depict the reactions of children and grown-ups to it." Booklist

Rain drop splash; by Alvin Tresselt; pictures by Leonard Weisgard. Lothrop, Lee & Shepard Bks. 1946 unp il lib bdg $15.88; pa $3.95   E

1. Rain
ISBN 0-688-51165-1 (lib bdg); 0-688-09352-3 (pa)
A Caldecott Medal honor book, 1947

"The brief, poetic text follows the falling raindrops as they form first a puddle and then a pond, spilling over into a brook, tumbling into a lake, overflowing into a river until, just before the sun comes out, the river flows into the sea." Bookmark

"Striking pictures in tones of yellow and brown . . . describe a rainstorm in terms a small child can understand." Booklist

Sun up; [by] Alvin Tresselt; illustrated by Henri Sorensen. Lothrop, Lee & Shepard Bks. 1991 unp il $14.95; lib bdg $14.88   E

1. Farm life—Fiction 2. Summer—Fiction
ISBN 0-688-08656-X; 0-688-08657-8 (lib bdg)
LC 90-35144
A revised and newly illustrated edition of the title first published 1949

Follows the activities of a farmer and his son from sunrise to sunset on a hot summer day

"Sorensen provides strong, sunlit paintings that sensitively interpret the mood and sense of Tresselt's rhythmic text." Booklist

Wake up, city! [by] Alvin Tresselt; pictures by Carolyn Ewing. Lothrop, Lee & Shepard Bks. 1990 unp il $12.95; lib bdg $13.88   E

1. City life—Fiction
ISBN 0-688-08652-7; 0-688-08653-5 (lib bdg)
LC 89-45901
A revised and newly illustrated edition of the title first published 1957

"Tresselt's description of some of the things that happen when the day starts in a large city are just as applicable now as then; Ewing's paintings add some touches that will please feminists (a policewoman, a woman bus driver—at least, a bus driver who could be a woman) and some that relect the architectural variety, the bustle of various activities, and the multiracial composition of the urban scene." Bull Cent Child Books

Wake up, farm! [by] Alvin Tresselt; pictures by Carolyn Ewing. Lothrop, Lee & Shepard Bks. 1990 unp il $14.95; lib bdg $14.88   E

1. Farm life—Fiction
ISBN 0-688-08654-3; 0-688-08655-1 (lib bdg)
LC 90-33646
A revised and newly illustrated edition of the title first published 1955

Relates the morning activities and sounds of a variety of farm animals

"Tresselt's updated, lyrical text is longer and more sophisticated. . . . [The book includes] lush, realistic paintings in colors that are rich and muted." Booklist

White snow, bright snow; by Alvin Tresselt; illustrated by Roger Duvoisin. Lothrop, Lee & Shepard Bks. 1988 c1947 unp il $16; lib bdg $15.93; pa $4.95   E

1. Snow—Fiction
ISBN 0-688-41161-4; 0-688-51161-9 (lib bdg); 0-688-08294-7 (pa)   LC 88-10018
Awarded the Caldecott Medal, 1948
A reissue of the title first published 1947

When it begins to look, feel, and smell like snow, everyone prepares for a winter blizzard

Trivizas, Eugene, 1946-

The three little wolves and the big bad pig; illustrated by Helen Oxenbury. Margaret K. McElderry Bks. 1993 unp il $16   E

1. Pigs—Fiction 2. Wolves—Fiction
ISBN 0-689-50569-8   LC 92-24829
Also available Spanish language edition

"In this reverse of 'The Three Little Pigs' the wolves build with cement, barbed wire and reinforced chains. In response, the 'big bad pig' uses a sledgehammer, pneumatic drill and dynamite." Child Book Rev Serv

"Trivizas laces the text with funny, clever touches. . . . Oxenbury's watercolors capture the story's broad humor and add a wealth of supplementary details, with exquisite renderings of the wolves' comic temerity and the pig's bellicose stances." Publ Wkly

Turkle, Brinton Cassaday, 1915-

Deep in the forest; by Brinton Turkle. Dutton 1976 unp il $13.99; pa $3.95　　E

1. Bears—Fiction 2. Stories without words
ISBN 0-525-28617-9; 0-525-44322-3 (pa)

"An inquisitive bear cub wanders away from his mother and discovers an attractive, well-kept log cabin in the forest. Like Goldilocks in the fairy tale, he samples food, chairs, and beds, and the havoc he raises is discovered by the little girl and her parents upon their return from a walk. Except for the names on the porridge bowls, the book is wordless. The gray, yellow, and white illustrations not only give a rustic early American charm to the interior scenes but graphically portray the emotions of the bears and of the human beings." Horn Book

Do not open; by Brinton Turkle. Dutton 1981 unp il $14.99; pa $3.95　　E

1. Seashore—Fiction 2. Cats—Fiction 3. Magic—Fiction
ISBN 0-525-28785-X; 0-525-44224-3 (pa)

"Elderly Miss Moody and her cat, Captain Kidde, find a bottle on the seashore. Miss Moody ignores the label warning 'DO NOT OPEN' and liberates a horror. But the spunky woman tells the thing only mice scare her so it becomes a mouse that Kidde takes care of 'tout de suite.'" Publ Wkly

"The strong, simple composition that is typical of Turkle is especially well suited to the still isolation of deserted beaches, and the combination of rich color used with restraint and the framed squares of clear print adds to the visual appeal of the pages. The story is a nice blend of realism and fantasy." Bull Cent Child Books

Obadiah the Bold; story and pictures by Brinton Turkle. Viking 1965 unp il hardcover o.p. paperback available $4.99　　E

1. Society of Friends—Fiction 2. Nantucket (Mass.)—Fiction
ISBN 0-14-050233-5 (pa)

"This story, with its setting in Nantucket about one hundred years ago, shows young Obadiah in the midst of a happy Quaker family. Brothers will tease, however, and when Obadiah wants to 'play pirate' (in hopes of someday being one), he is not spared a little fright. An understanding father helps his son think about following in the footsteps of another kind of seafarer, his grandfather, Captain Obadiah Starbuck." Read Ladders for Hum Relat. 6th edition

Other available titles about Obadiah are:
The adventures of Obadiah (1972)
Rachel and Obadiah (1978)
Thy friend, Obadiah (1969)

Turner, Ann Warren, 1945-

Katie's trunk; by Ann Turner; illustrations by Ron Himler. Macmillan 1992 unp il $15　　E

1. United States—History—1775-1783, Revolution—Fiction
ISBN 0-02-789512-2　　LC 91-20409

Katie, whose family is not sympathetic to the rebel soldiers during the American Revolution, hides under the clothes in her mother's wedding trunk when they invade her home

"Based on a true incident, this bit of historical fiction . . . is unusual because the perspective is from a Tory family's point of view. . . . The story begins reflectively as Katie remembers her growing tension and fear; the narrative then speeds through the gripping action of the attack and ends succinctly with Katie's new-found understanding of the gray areas of life. The illustrations are lovely period paintings that complement, but never overpower, the story." Horn Book

Through moon and stars and night skies; by Ann Turner; pictures by James Graham Hale. Harper & Row 1989 unp il $13.95; lib bdg $12.89; pa $4.95　　E

1. Adoption—Fiction 2. Parent and child—Fiction
ISBN 0-06-026189-7; 0-06-026190-0 (lib bdg); 0-06-443308-0 (pa)　　LC 87-35044

"A Charlotte Zolotow book"

A boy who came from Southeast Asia to be adopted by a couple in this country remembers how unfamiliar and frightening some of the things were in his new home, before he accepted the love to be found there

"This touching, memorable tale is illustrated in warm watercolor-and-ink pictures that gently contrast the narrator's Asian home with his new life in America. It will serve as a meaningful introduction to adoption as well as a starting point for a discussion on cultural transitions." SLJ

Uchida, Yoshiko, 1921-1992

The bracelet; story by Yoshiko Uchida; illustrated by Joanna Yardley. Philomel Bks. 1993 unp il $15.95　　E

1. Japanese Americans—Evacuation and relocation, 1942-1945—Fiction 2. World War, 1939-1945—Fiction 3. Friendship—Fiction
ISBN 0-399-22503-X　　LC 92-26196

Emi, a Japanese American in the second grade, is sent with her family to an internment camp during World War II, but the loss of the bracelet her best friend has given her proves that she does not need a physical reminder of that friendship

"The book (previously published as a short story) is a gentle, honest introduction to the treatment of the Japanese-Americans during the war, and Yardley's delicate pencil-and-watercolor paintings are cleanly drawn and richly colored, with scant pencil lines softly framing the sad scenes. A brief afterword gives a context for the story." Bull Cent Child Books

Udry, Janice May

A tree is nice; pictures by Marc Simont. Harper & Row 1956 unp il $14.95; lib bdg $14.89; pa $4.95　　E

1. Trees—Fiction
ISBN 0-06-026155-2; 0-06-026156-0 (lib bdg); 0-06-443147-9 (pa)

Also available Spanish language edition

Awarded the Caldecott Medal, 1957

"In childlike terms and in enticing pictures, colored and black and white, author and artist set forth reasons why trees are nice to have around—trees fill up the sky, they make everything beautiful, cats get away from dogs in them, leaves come down and can be played in, and trees are nice to climb in, to hang a swing in, or to plant. A picture book sure to please young children." Booklist

What Mary Jo shared; pictures: Eleanor Mill. Whitman, A. 1966 unp il lib bdg $14.95　　E

1. African Americans—Fiction 2. School stories
ISBN 0-8075-8842-3

Also available in paperback from Scholastic

"Whenever Mary Jo selected something to 'show and tell', her classmates had already chosen it. Finally she brought a very special person to share with the class—her

Udry, Janice May—*Continued*

father." N Y Public Libr. Black Exper in Child Books

"The writing is smooth and natural, and the illustrations, done in soft colors and black and white, are charming." We Build Together

Ungerer, Tomi, 1931-

Crictor. Harper & Row 1958 32p il $14; lib bdg $13.89; pa $4.95   E

1. Snakes—Fiction

ISBN 0-06-026180-3; 0-06-026181-1 (lib bdg); 0-06-443044-8 (pa)

"An entertaining bit of nonsense about the boa constrictor that was sent to Madame Bodot, who lived and taught school in a little French town. She called the snake Crictor and he became a great pet, learned, debonair and brave. The boys used him for a slide and the girls for a jump-rope. When Crictor captured a burglar by coiling around him until the police came, he was awarded impressive tokens of esteem and affection of the townspeople. Engaging line drawings echo the restrained and elegant absurdities of the text." Bull Cent Child Books

The three robbers. Atheneum Pubs. 1987 c1962 unp il lib bdg $14.95; pa $4.95   E

1. Thieves—Fiction

ISBN 0-689-31391-8 (lib bdg); 0-689-71511-0 (pa)
LC 87-11549

Also available Spanish language edition

A reissue of the title first published 1962

Three robbers who roam the countryside are subdued by the charm of a little girl named Tiffany

"With vigorous, sweeping design and stained glass colors on black and midnight blue Tomi Ungerer presents three of the most charming fierce robbers." Christ Sci Monit

Van Allsburg, Chris

Bad day at Riverbend. Houghton Mifflin 1995 unp il $17.95   E

ISBN 0-395-67347-X   LC 95-4154

When Sheriff Hardy investigates the source of a brilliant light and shiny slime afflicting Riverbend, he finds that the village is becoming part of a child's coloring book streaked with greasy crayons

"Van Allsburg cuts loose with this inventive spoof that will keep readers guessing right up to the end. . . . Van Allsburg clearly had fun with his one, and readers likely will too." Publ Wkly

Ben's dream; story and pictures by Chris Van Allsburg. Houghton Mifflin 1982 31p il lib bdg $15.95   E

1. Dreams—Fiction

ISBN 0-395-32084-4   LC 81-20029

"When rain spoils Ben's ball game with Margaret, he returns to an empty house, falls asleep in his father's chair, and embarks on a dream. In a marvelous series of double-page black-and-white pictures meticulously textured with hatching, one shares Ben's voyage past such sights as the Statue of Liberty, the Sphinx, and the Mount Rushmore presidents, all with flood waters lapping about their respective chins and waists. Dramatic angles, closeups from above and below, and careful architectural details which recall the work of David Macaulay dazzle the eye and the imagination as Ben's little house floats upon the waters on its splendid excursion. . . . A visual tour de force." Horn Book

The garden of Abdul Gasazi; written and illustrated by Chris Van Allsburg. Houghton Mifflin 1979 unp il lib bdg $17.95   E

1. Magic—Fiction 2. Dogs—Fiction

ISBN 0-395-27804-X

A Caldecott Medal honor book, 1980

"When Fritz, the naughty dog, ran into the garden of Abdul Gasazi, a retired magician, Alan was terrified, for he knew that dogs were not allowed beyond the vine-covered wall. Fritz eluded Alan, who ultimately requested the return of the dog. His request was granted, but Fritz, who had been turned into a duck, compounded his original naughtiness by flying away with Alan's cap." Horn Book

The full page "lithographlike drawings are astonishing—eerie, monumental, surreal and witty all at once—and the effect of the whole is original and unforgettable." Books of the Times

Jumanji; written and illustrated by Chris Van Allsburg. Houghton Mifflin 1981 unp il $17.95   E

1. Games—Fiction

ISBN 0-395-30448-2   LC 80-29632

Also available in paperback from Scholastic; Spanish language edition also available

Awarded the Caldecott Medal, 1982

"Two children, alone at home while their parents are gone for the afternoon, play a game they have found lying under a tree. Judy reads the rules for the game, 'Jumanji,' and realizes that it must be played to the end; not until they begin play do she and Peter know why that's true. With each roll of the dice, there's a new hazard: a menacing lion, a troop of destructive monkeys, a torrential monsoon, a herd of rhinos, etc." Bull Cent Child Books

"Through the masterly use of light and shadow, the interplay of design elements, and audacious changes in perspective and composition, the artist conveys an impression of color without losing the dramatic contrast of black and white." Horn Book

Just a dream. Houghton Mifflin 1990 unp il $17.95   E

1. Environmental protection—Fiction 2. Pollution—Fiction 3. Dreams—Fiction

ISBN 0-395-53308-2   LC 90-41343

"Walter, an environmental ignoramus of a 10-year-old, is careless or scornful of such elementary actions as recycling or tree planting. One nightmarish evening, however, he visits a future where his daydreams of technological paradise are demolished. Instead, there is merely a horrifically exacerbated continuation of today's eco-problems: landfills, expressways, smog, lifeless oceans, and vanished wilderness. Walter awakens reformed, and is rewarded with another dream: the future redeemed." SLJ

"Once again Van Allsburg demonstrates his unique artistic magic in combining foresight, wisdom and striking artwork to deliver an ecological message concerning conservation and renewal. . . . The full-color, striking paintings evoke the intense revelations of Walter's dreams." Child Book Rev Serv

The mysteries of Harris Burdick. Houghton Mifflin 1984 unp il lib bdg $17.95   E

ISBN 0-395-35393-9   LC 84-9006

Presents a series of loosely related drawings each accompanied by a title and a caption which the reader may use to make up his or her own story

Rendered in the author's "signature velvet black and white . . . the pictures are nothing short of spectacular. . . . While some may find this just an excuse for handsome artwork, others will see its great potential for stretching a

Van Allsburg, Chris—*Continued*

child's imagination. Although the book could be used in countless ways, primarily it will make storytellers of children. They will need little prompting once they set their eyes on Van Allsburg's provocative scenes. An inventive, useful concoction." Booklist

The Polar Express; written and illustrated by Chris Van Allsburg. Houghton Mifflin 1985 unp il $17.95   E

1. North Pole—Fiction   2. Santa Claus—Fiction 3. Christmas—Fiction
ISBN 0-395-38949-6   LC 85-10907
Also available Spanish language edition
Awarded the Caldecott Medal, 1986

A magical train ride on Christmas Eve takes a boy to the North Pole to receive a special gift from Santa Claus
This offers "stunning paintings in which Van Allsburg uses dark, rich colors and misty shapes in contrast with touches of bright white-gold light to create scenes, interior and exterior, that have a quality of mystery that imbues the strong composition to achieve a soft, evocative mood." Bull Cent Child Books

The stranger. Houghton Mifflin 1986 unp il lib bdg $17.95   E

ISBN 0-395-42331-7   LC 86-15235
"A mysterious figure, accidentally struck down by a farmer's truck, stays with the farmer's family until he recovers his memory, participating in the life of the farm. The man—it seems—is Jack Frost, or the spirit of winter; the weather cannot continue its change without him, and when he recalls his function, he takes his leave of his human friends with tears in his eyes." N Y Times Book Rev
"The full-color illustrations, framed in white, evoke an old-fashioned New England landscape at the end of summer; some are remarkably peaceful in tone, others slightly spooky by virtue of brooding colors, unexpected perspectives, or the stranger's peculiar expressions." Bull Cent Child Books

The sweetest fig. Houghton Mifflin 1993 unp il $17.95   E

1. Dreams—Fiction 2. Magic—Fiction 3. Dogs—Fiction
ISBN 0-395-67346-1   LC 93-12692
Also available Spanish language edition

After being given two magical figs that make his dreams come true, Monsieur Bibot sees his plans for future wealth upset by his long-suffering dog
"The full-color, expressive illustrations are filled with nuance, detail and mystery. Once again, Van Allsburg weaves a spell with ultimate skill and creativity." Child Book Rev Serv

The widow's broom. Houghton Mifflin 1992 unp il $17.95   E

1. Magic—Fiction 2. Witchcraft—Fiction
ISBN 0-395-64051-2   LC 92-7110
Also available Spanish language edition

A witch's worn-out broom serves a widow well, until her neighbors decide the thing is wicked and dangerous
"In addition to being a neatly understated piece of storytelling, this fuels Van Allsburg's best kind of illustration—darkly rounded, speckle-textured art with eerie effects. . . . The doubling of the unexpectedly beautiful young witch and the sensible heroine delivers a healthy dose of female power, which kids can subconsciously digest while enjoying the slightly scary images tempered with a text given to straight-faced humor." Bull Cent Child Books

The wreck of the Zephyr; written and illustrated by Chris Van Allsburg. Houghton Mifflin 1983 unp il lib bdg $17.95   E

ISBN 0-395-33075-0   LC 82-23371
"The story-within-a-story is a fantasy told by an old man, a tale of a boy who sees flying boats and is determined that he, too, will learn to make his boat, the Zephyr, fly. He succeeds, but the boat is wrecked, and he suffers a broken leg. The tale over, the old man limps away." Bull Cent Child Books
This "displays recognizable hallmarks of the artist's work: beauty of composition, striking contrasts of light and shadow, and especially the fascinating ambiguity of illusion and reality." Horn Book

The wretched stone. Houghton Mifflin 1991 unp il $17.95   E

1. Sea stories
ISBN 0-395-53307-4   LC 91-11525

A strange glowing stone picked up on a sea voyage captivates a ship's crew and has a terrible transforming effect on them
"Although Van Allsburg clearly has a message to convey, he has added to the book an enjoyable and necessary dollop of humor. The story has a quiet, understated, yet suspenseful tone; most of the plot's considerable drama is conveyed in the impressive illustrations." Horn Book

The Z was zapped; a play in twenty-six acts; performed by the Caslon Players; written and directed by Chris Van Allsburg. Houghton Mifflin 1987 unp il $17.95   E

1. Alphabet
ISBN 0-395-44612-0   LC 87-14988

At head of title: The Alphabet Theatre proudly presents
This book presents a "series of beautifully executed full-page black-and-white illustrations showing letters undergoing varieties of existential *Angst* on a tasteful little stage, each with an explanatory line of copy printed on its backside." N Y Times Book Rev
"Children can try to guess what action has occured, thereby increasing their vocabulary and the fun, or they can turn the page and read the text, or better yet—do both. This clever romp resembles old vaudeville theater, with one curious act following the next." SLJ

Van Laan, Nancy

Possum come a-knockin'; illustrated by George Booth. Knopf 1990 unp il lib bdg $14.99   E

1. Opossums—Fiction 2. Stories in rhyme
ISBN 0-394-92206-9 (lib bdg)   LC 88-12751

The narrator "sees a possum a-knockin' at the door. While Granny is a-rockin' and a-knittin', and Ma's a-cookin' and Pa's a-fixin', . . . [the boy] unsuccessfully tries to tell them about the possum." Booklist
The author has produced a wonderfully rhythmic and funny trickster tale told in a controlled dialect that is consistent throughout. Booth's critters—possum, cat, and dog—are priceless. Friend possum is the wiliest and slyest varmint one could imagine. The humans are pretty funny, too, while the stage set is appropriately countrified. The story is a raucous romp." Horn Book

Van Leeuwen, Jean

Going West; pictures by Thomas B. Allen. Dial Bks. for Young Readers 1991 unp il $15; lib bdg $14.89 **E**

1. Frontier and pioneer life—Fiction 2. Family life—Fiction

ISBN 0-8037-1027-5; 0-8037-1028-3 (lib bdg)

LC 90-20694

Follows a family's emigration by prairie schooner from the East, across the plains to Kansas

"Into a gentle text brimming with family warmth and love, Van Leeuwen . . . packs a wealth of emotional moments. . . . Allen's . . . scumbled, subdued pastel drawings, on sepia stock, masterfully conjure up the expanse of land and feelings." Publ Wkly

Tales of Oliver Pig; pictures by Arnold Lobel. Dial Bks. for Young Readers 1979 64p il lib bdg $9.89; pa $4.95 **E**

1. Pigs—Fiction 2. Family life—Fiction

ISBN 0-8037-8736-7 (lib bdg); 0-8037-8737-5 (pa)

LC 79-4276

Also available Spanish language edition

"Dial easy-to-read"

"Oliver encounters many true-to-life situations and decides how to cope with them: what to do on a rainy day, how to make a bad day into a good one, what to do when Grandma comes, how to dress for the snow, and most confusing, what to do when Mother cries." Child Book Rev Serv

The book is "filled with the warmth of the commonplace, the jostling joys and sorrows of siblings and the love of a pig family. . . . Arnold Lobel's illustrations, often in miniature, carry on the tender, yet never sentimental tone." SLJ

Other available titles about the Pig family are:

Amanda Pig and her big brother Oliver (1982)
Amanda Pig on her own (1991)
More tales of Amanda Pig (1985)
More tales of Oliver Pig (1981)
Oliver, Amanda, and Grandmother Pig (1987)
Oliver and Amanda and the big snow (1995)
Oliver and Amanda's Christmas (1989)
Oliver and Amanda's Halloween (1992)
Oliver Pig at school (1990)
Tales of Amanda Pig (1983)

Varley, Susan

Badger's parting gifts. Lothrop, Lee & Shepard Bks. 1984 unp il $15; lib bdg $14.93; pa $4.95 **E**

1. Death—Fiction 2. Badgers—Fiction 3. Animals—Fiction

ISBN 0-688-02699-0; 0-688-02703-2 (lib bdg); 0-688-11518-7 (pa) LC 83-17500

Also available Spanish language edition

"Badger is an old animal who has been an inspiration to the other animals throughout his life. Knowing he will soon travel the 'Long Tunnel,' his great desire is to leave something for the others to remember. His legacy is revealed through the accomplishments of the others, all having learned their skills from him." Child Book Rev Serv

"The animal world Varley creates is a gentle place, her pen-and-ink drawings delicately etched, alive with grace and movement and washed with watercolors that register the moods and temperatures and textures of her pastoral setting in this tale of death and friendship." SLJ

Vaughan, Marcia, 1951-

Whistling Dixie; illustrated by Barry Moser. HarperCollins Pubs. 1995 31p il $15; lib bdg $14.89 **E**

1. Animals—Fiction 2. Marshes—Fiction 3. Supernatural—Fiction

ISBN 0-06-021030-3; 0-06-021029-X (lib bdg)

LC 91-45831

Dixie Lee brings home an alligator, a snake, and an owl as pets to protect her family from such spooky creatures as the churn-turners, the bogeyman, and the mist-sisters

"Spiced with Cajun dialect and sayings that conjure up vivid images and a wonderful look at Southern life, this read-aloud combines realism and fantasy in a humorous way that will delight youngsters. The pictures are bright and colorful." Child Book Rev Serv

Vincent, Gabrielle

Ernest and Celestine. Greenwillow Bks. 1982 unp il hardcover o.p. paperback available $3.95 **E**

1. Bears—Fiction 2. Mice—Fiction 3. Toys—Fiction

ISBN 0-688-06525-2 (pa) LC 81-6392

"Ernest, is a portly bear who lives with Celestine, a mouse child, in a humble but cozy house. . . . Celestine loses her beloved duck-doll named Gideon in the snow. Ernest finds it beyond repair and tries unsuccessfully to console Celestine with new stuffed animals. Finally with Celestine's help, he designs a new Gideon just in time for Christmas." Booklist

"The illustrations are watercolors full of whimsy and warmth, which, with the text, convey a great sense of mutual appreciation and pleasure shared. Because the text is entirely written in uncluttered dialogue, eyes are pulled to the detailed illustrations. The books are translated from the French, and their origin is apparent in the character's environment and dress." SLJ

Other available titles about Ernest and Celestine are:

Ernest and Celestine at the circus (1989)
Ernest and Celestine's patchwork quilt (1985)
Ernest and Celestine's picnic (1982)
Feel better, Ernest! (1988)
Merry Christmas, Ernest and Celestine (1984)
Smile, Ernest and Celestine (1982)
Where are you, Ernest and Celestine? (1986)

Viorst, Judith

Alexander and the terrible, horrible, no good, very bad day; illustrated by Ray Cruz. Atheneum Pubs. 1972 unp il $14; pa $3.95

E

ISBN 0-689-30072-7; 0-689-71173-5 (pa)

Also available Spanish language edition

The author "describes the plight of a boy for whom everything goes wrong from the moment he steps out of bed and discovers he has gum stuck in his hair to his return to bed that night when he has to wear his hated railroad-train pajamas and the cat decides to sleep with one of his brothers instead of with him. His mother consoles him by remarking that some days are like that." Booklist

"Small listeners can enjoy the litany of disaster, and perhaps be stimulated to discuss the possibility that one contributes by expectation. The illustrations capture the grumpy dolor of the story, ruefully funny." Sutherland. The Best In Child Books

Other available titles about Alexander are:

Alexander, who is not (do you hear me?) going (I mean it) to move (1995)
Alexander, who used to be rich last Sunday (1978)

Viorst, Judith—*Continued*

Earrings! illustrated by Nola Langner Malone. Atheneum Pubs. 1990 unp il $15; pa $4.95   E

ISBN 0-689-31615-1; 0-689-71669-9 (pa)

LC 89-17846

"The curly-haired protagonist pleads, cajoles and bargains to get pierced ears; she points out that she is the only girl in 'her class, the world or the solar system' without them. She promises to walk the dog, clean her room, read a book a week for a year and be nice to her little brother if she is only granted her wish." Publ Wkly

"Viorst homes in on minor childhood crises with the perfect blend of humor and insight, and Malone's expressive and comic figures are miniature character studies in themselves." Horn Book

My mama says there aren't any zombies, ghosts, vampires, creatures, demons, monsters, fiends, goblins, or things. Atheneum Pubs. 1973 unp il $15; pa $3.95   E

1. Monsters—Fiction 2. Mothers—Fiction
ISBN 0-689-30102-2; 0-689-71204-9 (pa)

This book deals humorously with the childhood sense of being threatened by "imaginary monsters and a mother's reassurances that they don't exist. While wanting to believe his mother, Nick is also aware that she often makes mistakes . . . like the time she made Nick wear his boots on a sunny day." SLJ

Rosie and Michael; illustrated by Lorna Tomei. Atheneum Pubs. 1974 unp il $13.95; pa $3.95   E

1. Friendship—Fiction
ISBN 0-689-30439-0; 0-689-71272-3 (pa)

"Rosie and Michael catalog the humorous, sometimes elaborate particulars of their eventful friendship: she likes him even when he's dopey and he likes her even when she's grouchy. . . . In the same vein further testimonials reflecting magnanimity and loyal support dispatch any chagrin that either buddy might harbor. Though repetition begins to weigh heavily, the serio-comic message is buoyed by Tomei's detailed, grotesquely interpretive pen-and-ink caricatures that lend a 'Mad' magazine touch to the whole panoply." Booklist

The tenth good thing about Barney; illustrated by Erik Blegvad. Atheneum Pubs. 1971 25p il $13.95; pa $3.95   E

1. Death—Fiction 2. Cats—Fiction
ISBN 0-689-20688-7; 0-689-71203-0 (pa)

"A little boy saddened by the death of his cat thinks of nine good things about Barney to say at his funeral. Later his father helps him discover a tenth good thing: Barney is in the ground helping grow flowers and trees and grass and 'that's a pretty nice job for a cat.'" Booklist

"The author succinctly and honestly handles both the emotions stemming from the loss of a beloved pet and the questions about the finality of death which naturally arise in such a situation. . . . An unusually good book that handles a difficult subject straightforwardly and with no trace of the macabre." Horn Book

Waber, Bernard

Ira sleeps over. Houghton Mifflin 1972 48p il lib bdg $14.95; pa $4.95   E

ISBN 0-395-13893-0 (lib bdg); 0-395-20503-4 (pa)

Also available Spanish language edition

"A small boy's joy in being asked to spend the night with a friend who lives next door is unrestrained until his sister raises the question of whether or not he should take his teddy bear. Torn between fear of being considered babyish and fear of what it may be like to sleep without his bear, Ira has a hard time deciding what to do. His dilemma is resolved happily, however, when he discovers that his friend Reggie also has a nighttime bear companion. An appealing picture book which depicts common childhood qualms with empathy and humor in brief text and colorful illustrations." Booklist

Another available title about Ira is:
Ira says goodbye (1988)

Lyle, Lyle, crocodile. Houghton Mifflin 1965 48p il $14.95   E

1. Crocodiles—Fiction 2. New York (N.Y.)—Fiction
ISBN 0-395-16995-X

Lyle the crocodile who lives in New York City "wants desperately to win the friendship of the cat Loretta two doors away but every time Loretta catches a glimpse of him she flings herself into a nervous fit." Booklist

"The illustrations are cartoon-like, lively, and colorful. . . . The situation is nicely exploited with a bland daffiness." Bull Cent Child Books

Other available titles about Lyle are:
Funny, funny Lyle (1987)
The house on East 88th Street (1962)
Lovable Lyle (1969)
Lyle and the birthday party (1966)
Lyle at the office (1994)
Lyle finds his mother (1974)

Waddell, Martin

Can't you sleep, Little Bear? illustrated by Barbara Firth. 2nd U.S. ed. Candlewick Press 1992 unp il $14.95; pa $4.99   E

1. Bears—Fiction 2. Bedtime—Fiction
ISBN 1-56402-007-X; 1-56402-262-5 (pa)

LC 91-71858

Also available Spanish language edition

First published 1988 in the United Kingdom

When bedtime comes Little Bear is afraid of the dark, until Big Bear brings him lights and love

"Firth's brightly lit watercolor and soft pencil illustrations, framed in the dark blue of the night, capture the cozy, physical affection of the story, the playfulness of Little Bear, . . . the shadowy mystery of the moonlit landscape, and the huge comforting presence of a parent who is always there when you call." Booklist

Another available title about Little Bear is:
Let's go home, Little Bear (1993)

Farmer duck; illustrated by Helen Oxenbury. Candlewick Press 1992 c1991 unp il $15.95   E

1. Ducks—Fiction 2. Farm life—Fiction
ISBN 1-56402-009-6   LC 91-71855

First published 1991 in the United Kingdom

When a kind and hardworking duck nearly collapses from overwork, while taking care of a farm because the owner is too lazy to do so, the rest of the animals get together and chase the farmer out of town

"Hilarious art masterfully captures the expressions of the put-upon duck, the supportive cast, and the slovenly ergophobic who reads the newspaper and chomps on bonbons in bed. . . . With its lilting, large-print text and satisfying resolution, it's is as perfect for beginning readers as it is for story hours." SLJ

Waddell, Martin—_Continued_

Owl babies; illustrated by Patrick Benson. Candlewick Press 1992 unp il $14.95 **E**

1. Owls—Fiction
ISBN 1-56402-101-7 LC 91-58750
Also available Spanish language edition
Three owl babies whose mother has gone out in the night try to stay calm while she is gone
"The illustrations, executed in black ink and watercolor, capture in every feather and expression the little owls' worry and watchfulness as well as their complete joy when Owl Mother returns." Horn Book

Walsh, Ellen Stoll, 1942-

Mouse count. Harcourt Brace Jovanovich 1991 unp il lib bdg $12; pa $5 **E**

1. Mice—Fiction 2. Snakes—Fiction 3. Counting
ISBN 0-15-256023-8 (lib bdg); 0-15-200223-5 (pa)
LC 90-35915
Ten mice outsmart a hungry snake
"Children will delight in this counting game that is couched in an exciting, original story. . . . The torn paper collage and tempra illustrations are lively and depict the story's unerring drama through an uncluttered form and line." SLJ
Another available title about the mice is:
Mouse paint (1989)

Walter, Mildred Pitts, 1922-

Brother to the wind; pictures by Diane and Leo Dillon. Lothrop, Lee & Shepard Bks. 1985 unp il lib bdg $15.93 **E**

1. Flight—Fiction 2. Africa—Fiction
ISBN 0-688-03812-3 LC 83-26800
With the help of Good Snake, Emeke, a young African boy gets his dearest wish
"Elements of folk legend—such as the wise woman, the oracular snake and its magic talismans, talking animals—contribute a timeless power to Emeke's lessons of faith and self-reliance. The illustrations emphasize the coalition of dream and necessity, which fuels Emeke's ingenuity. Vibrantly colored scenes of Emeke's daily life in the village are superimposed against personifications of the surreal forces which inspire his imagination." Horn Book

My mama needs me; pictures by Pat Cummings. Lothrop, Lee & Shepard Bks. 1983 unp il $16; lib bdg $15.93 **E**

1. Infants—Fiction 2. Parent and child—Fiction 3. African Americans—Fiction
ISBN 0-688-01670-7; 0-688-01671-5 (lib bdg)
LC 82-12654
Coretta Scott King Award for illustration, 1984
"A warm portrayal of a young black child's reaction to the arrival of his baby sister. Jason is invited out to play with friends, go over to a neighbor's for cookies, and feed the ducks in the pond. And while he reluctantly participates in some of these activities, Jason's overriding concern is to be home in case his mama needs him." Booklist
"The decorative illustrations show a warm family situation, and at the end one sees a cheerful view of Jason in a multi-racial neighborhood. An encouraging book, especially for the child who is a trifle uncertain about the arrival of a new sibling." Horn Book

Ward, Lynd Kendall, 1905-1985

The biggest bear; by Lynd Ward. Houghton Mifflin 1988 84p il lib bdg $14.95; pa $5.95 **E**

1. Bears—Fiction
ISBN 0-395-14806-5 (lib bdg); 0-395-15024-8 (pa)
LC 88-176366
Awarded the Caldecott Medal, 1953
A reissue of the title first published 1952
"Johnny Orchard never did acquire the bearskin for which he boldly went hunting. Instead, he brought home a cuddly bear cub, which grew in size and appetite to mammoth proportions and worried his family and neighbors half to death." Child Books Too Good to Miss

Watson, Clyde, 1947-

Applebet: an ABC; pictures by Wendy Watson. Farrar, Straus & Giroux 1982 unp il hardcover o.p. paperback available $3.95 **E**

1. Alphabet 2. Stories in rhyme
ISBN 0-374-40427-5 (pa) LC 81-19399
"Alphabetical sequence becomes the organizing principle for an . . . original picture book recounting the adventures of a farmer and her daughter Bet as they journey one sunny day to the distant town where the marvels of a harvest exposition—from potables to puppets, magicians to malefactors—dazzle their senses." Horn Book
"The sing-song rhyme pattern is chant-worthy, but it's the pictures that make this a standout. The small-scale drawings are ablaze with autumnal colors. The use of light and shadow makes readers aware of the warm Indian summer sunshine casting its glow on the whole affair." Booklist

Valentine foxes; pictures by Wendy Watson. Orchard Bks. 1989 unp il $14.95; lib bdg $14.99; pa $5.95 **E**

1. Foxes—Fiction 2. Valentine's Day—Fiction
ISBN 0-531-05800-X; 0-531-08400-0 (lib bdg); 0-531-07033-6 (pa) LC 88-22392
Four little foxes prepare a cake and a Valentine surprise for their parents
"Rosy, pleasant illustrations accompany the story, as does a recipe for pound cake." Publ Wkly

Watson, Wendy

Thanksgiving at our house. Clarion Bks. 1991 unp il $14.95; pa $5.95 **E**

1. Thanksgiving Day—Fiction 2. Family life—Fiction
ISBN 0-395-53626-X; 0-395-69944-4 (pa)
LC 90-26138
The family busily prepares for Thanksgiving and has a grand feast with visiting relatives. Includes Thanksgiving poems
"The homey details are told in an easy-to-read narrative and pictured in Watson's usual crisp, lively ink-and-watercolor quasi-comic-strip illustrations in warm, muted tones. The rounded, robust, active figures of the children and adults of all ages express the happiness and comfort of a close, loving family." SLJ

Weiss, Nicki, 1954-

Maude and Sally. Greenwillow Bks. 1983 unp il $13.95; lib bdg $13.88 **E**

1. Friendship—Fiction
ISBN 0-688-01635-9; 0-688-01638-3 (lib bdg)
LC 82-12003

Weiss, Nicki, 1954-—*Continued*

When her best friend Sally goes to summer camp, Maude finds she can become best friends with Emmylou also

"Bright, cheerful pictures of varying shapes and sizes are contained within a line border, and the straightforward text is creatively placed throughout. Filled with details but not cluttered, the pale-colored illustrations often include conversational asides which add extra interest to a book designed with taste and originality." Horn Book

Where does the brown bear go? Greenwillow Bks. 1989 unp il $15; lib bdg $14.93 **E**

1. Animals—Fiction 2. Night—Fiction
ISBN 0-688-07862-1; 0-688-07863-X (lib bdg)
LC 87-36980

Also available in paperback from Puffin Bks.

When the lights go down on the city street and the sun sinks far behind the seas, the animals of the world are on their way home for the night

"The rich, dark colors of a velvet night sky, polka dotted with stars, form the background for this enchanting lullaby. . . . Repetition and alliteration are skillfully employed in the verses; the rhythm and rhymes are so perfect that it takes only a reading or two before the poem is committed to memory. . . . Altogether, an exquisite book to end a young one's day." Horn Book

Wells, Rosemary, 1943-
Fritz and the Mess Fairy. Dial Bks. for Young Readers 1991 unp il $14; lib bdg $13.89 **E**

1. Fairies—Fiction 2. Skunks—Fiction
ISBN 0-8037-0981-1; 0-8037-0983-8 (lib bdg)
LC 90-26671

Also available in paperback from Puffin Bks.

Fritz, a skunk and a master at creating terrible messes, meets his match when his science project goes wrong and the Mess Fairy emerges

"An unexpected twist caps this spirited tale, illustrated with Wells's distinctive watercolors that brim with droll details. As ever, her childlike sensibilities and zany sense of humor are perfectly on target." Publ Wkly

Hazel's amazing mother. Dial Bks. for Young Readers 1985 unp il $14.99; lib bdg $13.89; pa $3.95 **E**

1. Mothers—Fiction
ISBN 0-8037-0209-4; 0-8037-0210-8 (lib bdg); 0-8037-0703-7 (pa)
LC 85-1447

When Hazel and her beloved doll Eleanor are set upon by bullies, Hazel's mother comes to the rescue in a surprising way

"The power of maternal love may be exaggerated here, but the lap audience will understand that mothers are their defenders and will do extraordinary things for their young. As is true of other books by Wells, the characters are small animals in appearance; in behavior they are people. . . . Breezy and funny, but also touching, this should appeal to children's sense of justice as well as their faith in parental omnipotence." Bull Cent Child Books

Max's first word. Dial Bks. for Young Readers 1979 unp il $4.50 **E**

1. Vocabulary—Fiction 2. Brothers and sisters—Fiction 3. Rabbits—Fiction
ISBN 0-8037-6066-3
LC 79-59745

"Very first books"

The book depicts "the trials of put-upon Ruby and her infant brother, Max. . . . Ruby puts a cup on Max's highchair tray and orders him to say 'cup.' Slamming the cup firmly down, Max shouts 'Bang!' And 'Bang!' is what he responds to all Ruby's teaching as she points out things in the kitchen. . . . When she hands Max an apple, she says 'yumyum,' whereupon the tricky baby hollers 'Delicious!'" Publ Wkly

Other available titles about Max and Ruby are:
Max and Ruby's first Greek myth: Pandora's box (1993)
Max and Ruby's Midas: another Greek myth (1995)
Max's bath (1985)
Max's bedtime (1985)
Max's birthday (1985)
Max's breakfast (1985)
Max's chocolate chicken (1989)
Max's Christmas (1986)
Max's dragon shirt (1991)
Max's new suit (1979)
Max's ride (1979)
Max's toys (1979)

Morris's disappearing bag; a Christmas story. Dial Bks. for Young Readers 1975 unp il $11.99 **E**

1. Rabbits—Fiction 2. Christmas—Fiction
ISBN 0-8037-5441-8

Also available in paperback from Puffin Bks.

"Christmas day can be full of disappointments, especially if you only get a teddy bear, and your older brother and sisters get nifty gifts like a hockey stick, a beauty kit, and a chemistry set. . . . Morris is so frustrated with his gift that he invents a disappearing bag, one that becomes an instant hit with his brother and sisters. With new bargaining power due to his bag, Morris finally gets his chance to share the older children's gifts." Babbling Bookworm

"Christmas, magic, and getting the family temporarily to disappear add up to three irresistible themes, and Wells treats them imaginatively. The author-artist does, along with careful color and line work, some wonderful things with Morris' ears and eyes, expressing exactly the sentiments of a putout preschool rabbit." Booklist

Moss pillows; a voyage to The Bunny Planet. Dial Bks. for Young Readers 1992 unp il lib bdg $12.89 **E**

1. Rabbits—Fiction
ISBN 0-8037-1177-8
LC 91-41600

Also available in miniature boxed set edition with two other titles in the series for $13 (ISBN 0-8037-1174-3)

Robert's visit to relatives is disastrous, but a visit to the Bunny Planet cheers him up as he experiences the day that should have been

"As always, Wells shows her empathy for children's feelings of helplessness and their dreams of escape. . . . The bad day is described in a weary impersonal voice. . . . In contrast, the idyllic planet visit is recounted in an upbeat first-person narrative in rhyme. . . . Not many books could make both the shame and the happiness so entertaining. Wells evokes the embarrassment and pain with touching comedy and without a trace of condescension." Booklist

Other available titles about The Bunny Planet are:
First tomato (1992)
The island light (1992)

Night sounds, morning colors; pictures by David McPhail. Dial Bks. for Young Readers 1994 unp il $14.99; lib bdg $14.89 **E**

1. Senses and sensation—Fiction
ISBN 0-8037-1301-0; 0-8037-1302-9 (lib bdg)
LC 93-31815

Wells, Rosemary, 1943-—*Continued*

"In several short 'chapters,' a young boy describes moments in which he experiences the sensations of smell, color, sound, taste, and touch. . . . The incidents are related in spare, blank verse without much plotting, and are illustrated in sometimes surrealistic, always impressionistic full-page opaque acrylic paintings. . . . While there's not much story here, the feelings are deeply felt, true to life, comforting, and invigorating." SLJ

Noisy Nora; story and pictures by Rosemary Wells. Dial Bks. for Young Readers 1973 unp il $11.99; lib bdg $10.89; pa $3.99   E

1. Mice—Fiction 2. Stories in rhyme
ISBN 0-8037-6638-6; 0-8037-6639-4 (lib bdg); 0-8037-6193-7 (pa)
Also available Spanish language edition
Little Nora, tired of being ignored, tries to gain her family's attention by being noisy. When this doesn't work Nora disappears but returns when she is sure she has been missed
"A small book with rhymed verses and anthropomorphic mice has been illustrated with buoyant pastel drawings that add humorous details to the story. . . . The universal emotion of a child's feeling slighted because of its siblings has been given life in a simple book." Horn Book

Shy Charles; written and illustrated by Rosemary Wells. Dial Bks. for Young Readers 1988 unp il $13.99; lib bdg $11.89   E

1. Mice—Fiction 2. Stories in rhyme
ISBN 0-8037-0563-8; 0-8037-0564-6 (lib bdg)
LC 87-27247
Also available in paperback from Puffin Bks.
"Charles, a young mouse, is perfectly happy playing by himself, and social contacts are an endless ordeal. He can't or won't say 'thank you' in public places, can't or won't cope with dancing lessons or football. But when the baby sitter falls down the stairs, Charles is able to comfort her and call for help, before resuming his shy silence." N Y Times Book Rev
"Wells' illustrations . . . show the plump, large-eared cast to be full of charm and cleverness. Facial expressions, posture, and background details substantially extend the humor of the story. The simple rhythm of the rhyming text is subtle and playful." SLJ

Timothy goes to school; story and pictures by Rosemary Wells. Dial Bks. for Young Readers 1981 unp il $14.99; lib bdg $11.89   E

1. School stories 2. Raccoons—Fiction
ISBN 0-8037-8948-3; 0-8037-8949-1 (lib bdg)
LC 80-20785
Also available in paperback from Puffin Bks.; Spanish language edition also available
"Timothy, a little raccoon, runs eagerly to school on his first day, only to suffer weeks of pure torture. Best-dressed, over-achieving Claude puts Timothy down at every turn and nothing the poor victim's loving mother can do or say is any comfort. Timothy prays in vain that Claude will disgrace himself somehow and is about to quit school at the time of a class entertainment. Claude suavely plays the saxophone; Grace toe dances. Timothy hears Violet, sitting beside him, say she can't stand it any more, with that smarmy Grace. Thus a morale-boosting friendship is born between the snubbed ones." Publ Wkly
"It is amazing that the illustrator can show so much emotion—Timothy's misery, his mother's anxiety, and Claude's scorn—in their beady little eyes. In a small gem of a book the outcome inspires the reader with a sense of jubilation." Horn Book

Westcott, Nadine Bernard, 1949-

The lady with the alligator purse; adapted and illustrated by Nadine Bernard Westcott. Little, Brown 1988 unp il $15.95; pa $4.95   E

1. Nonsense verses
ISBN 0-316-93135-7; 0-316-93136-5 (pa)
LC 87-21368
"Joy Street books"
"Westcott adapts a jump rope rhyme about the misadventures of Tiny Tim to create a zany book of nonsense that demands reading aloud. After the mischievous baby drinks his bathwater, eats the soap, and tries to stuff the bathtub down his throat, his mother calls the doctor, the nurse, and the lady with the alligator purse. When medical cures fail, the lady produces pizza. The colorful illustrations filled with frenzied activities sustain the silliness and the absurdity of the story." SLJ

Wiesner, David

Free fall. Lothrop, Lee & Shepard Bks. 1988 unp il $16; lib bdg $15.93; pa $4.95   E

1. Dreams—Fiction 2. Stories without words
ISBN 0-688-05583-4; 0-688-05584-2 (lib bdg); 0-688-10990-X (pa)
LC 87-22834
A Caldecott Medal honor book, 1989
A young boy dreams of daring adventures in the company of imaginary creatures inspired by the things surrounding his bed
"Technical virtuosity is the trademark of the double-page watercolor spreads. Especially notable is the solidity of forms and architectural details." SLJ

Hurricane. Clarion Bks. 1990 unp il $15.95; pa $5.95   E

1. Hurricanes—Fiction 2. Brothers—Fiction
ISBN 0-395-54382-7; 0-395-62974-8 (pa)
LC 90-30070
"A family weathers a hurricane; the next day, in the post-hurricane yard, the two boys in the family play on a great fallen elm, imagining it to be a jungle, a pirate ship, and a space ship. A handsome book, affording opportunities for sharing fears and dreams of adventure." Horn Book Guide

June 29, 1999. Clarion Bks. 1992 unp il $15.95; pa $5.95   E

1. Vegetables—Fiction
ISBN 0-395-59762-5; 0-395-72767-7 (pa)
LC 91-34854
"Either Holly Evans's science project that sent vegetable seedlings into the ionosphere is enormously successful—or else something unearthly is going on." SLJ
"Here an understated, fairly straightforward text is a perfect foil for the outrageous scenes of vegetables run amok. Realistic watercolors reveal red peppers that need to be roped down, beans with bemused Arizona sheep clambering over them, and gargantuan peas floating down the Mississippi like logs to the sawmill. Fans of Wiesner's offbeat sense of humor will be delighted." Horn Book

Tuesday. Clarion Bks. 1991 unp il $15.95   E

1. Frogs—Fiction
ISBN 0-395-55113-7
LC 90-39358
Awarded the Caldecott Medal, 1992
Frogs rise on their lily pads, float through the air, and explore the nearby houses while their inhabitants sleep
"Wiesner offers a fantasy watercolor journey accom-

Wiesner, David—*Continued*

plished with soft-edged realism. Studded with bits of humor, the narrative artwork tells a simple, pleasant story with a consistency and authenticity that makes the fantasy convincing." Booklist

Wild, Margaret, 1948-

Our granny; story by Margaret Wild; pictures by Julie Vivas. Ticknor & Fields 1994 c1993 unp il $14.95   **E**

1. Grandmothers—Fiction

ISBN 0-395-67023-3   LC 93-11950

First published 1993 in Australia

"Two young children present a catalog of all the varying sizes, shapes, and types of grandmothers, interspersed with loving comments about their own granny, who has 'a wobbly bottom' and wears a funny bathing suit. . . . Vivas's lively illustrations capture the grandmothers in their most comic moments." Horn Book Guide

The very best of friends; written by Margaret Wild; illustrated by Julie Vivas. Harcourt Brace Jovanovich 1990 unp il lib bdg $13.95; pa $4.95   **E**

1. Cats—Fiction 2. Farm life—Fiction 3. Death—Fiction

ISBN 0-15-200625-7 (lib bdg); 0-15-200077-1 (pa)

   LC 89-36464

"Gulliver books"

Since Jessie has never cared for her farmer husband's cat William, her difficult adjustment period after her husband's death makes William doubt if he is still welcome on the farm

"Young listeners will be held by the loss and recovery of a vulnerable pet. . . . Vivas' spare watercolor spreads are strong on expressive postures and unexpected perspectives." Bull Cent Child Books

Wilde, Oscar, 1854-1900

The Happy Prince; from the fairy tale by Oscar Wilde; [abridged and illustrated by] Jane Ray. Dutton Children's Bks. 1995 c1994 unp il $15.99   **E**

1. Fairy tales

ISBN 0-525-45367-9   LC 94-25888

First published 1994 in the United Kingdom

A beautiful, golden, jewel-studded statue and a little swallow give all they have to help the poor

"Using most of the author's words and all of his intent [Ray has] . . . omitted the more flowery and verbose prose and subplots. The result is a tightened tale that expresses compassion in a simple, heartfelt story. . . . Ray has put enormous detail into her paintings, and each one is burnished with a kind of verdigris gold." SLJ

Wildsmith, Brian, 1930-

Brian Wildsmith's birds. Watts 1967 unp il o.p.; Oxford Univ. Press paperback available $7.50   **E**

1. Birds

ISBN 0-19-272117-8 (pa)

"Mr. Wildsmith has tied a series of pictures of birds . . . to their group names: a watch of nightingales, a nye of pheasants, a congregation of plover, et cetera. There is no other text." Saturday Rev

"Birds—how well the subject lends itself to this artist's exquisite use of color!. . . The child will have fun with the terms while absorbing truly beautiful illustrations." Horn Book

Brian Wildsmith's circus. Watts 1970 unp il o.p.; Oxford Univ. Press paperback available $7.50   **E**

1. Circus

ISBN 0-19-272102-X (pa)

First published 1970 in the United kingdom. Paperback edition has title: The circus

"Enclosed between a notice that the circus is coming to town and an announcement of its move to the next place is a series of pictures with no text. In double-page spreads Brian Wildsmith has painted vibrant, beautiful illustrations of animals and acrobats, clowns and jugglers, birds on a seesaw, and the full panoply of a circus parade. The pictures have action and humor and . . . are remarkable for the quality of the colors." Saturday Rev

Brian Wildsmith's wild animals. Watts 1967 unp il o.p.; Oxford Univ. Press paperback available $7.50   **E**

1. Mammals

ISBN 0-19-272103-8 (pa)

First published 1967 in the United Kingdom. Paperback edition has title: Wild animals

"A pride of lions, a lepe of leopards, a skulk of foxes, and a cete of badgers are among the cleverly captured groups of wild beasts that stalk the vivid, glowing pages of this fascinating picture book. A splendid, eyecatching . . . volume." Booklist

A Christmas story. Knopf 1989 unp il o.p.

   E

1. Jesus Christ—Nativity—Fiction 2. Donkeys—Fiction

   LC 89-7959

Only available edition is miniature edition (ISBN 0-679-84726-X) $6.99

A young donkey reunites with her mother in a Bethlehem stable and witnesses a miracle

"Spectacular illustrations show the Nativity as backdrop for a story of a small donkey whose mother carries Mary to Bethlehem. A neighbor, Rebecca, offers to care for the donkey, but he pines so for his mother that she promises to take him to her. At each stop on the road, Rebecca asks if anyone has seen a donkey and two people, and is improbably but miraculously steered in the directions of the stable. . . . For children who already know the Christmas story, this is a chance to see it from another point of view." SLJ

Fishes. Oxford Univ. Press 1985 c1968 unp $16.75; pa $7.50   **E**

1. Fishes

ISBN 0-19-279639-9; 0-19-272151-8 (pa)

First United States edition published 1968 by Franklin Watts with title: Brian Wildsmith's fishes

The author "presents groups of fishes. A cluster of porcupine fish, a hover of trout, a spread of sticklebacks, and flocks, schools, and streams of other fish swim across the pages in a riot of color." Booklist

Willard, Nancy

The high rise glorious skittle skat roarious sky pie angel food cake; illustrated by Richard Jesse Watson. Harcourt Brace Jovanovich 1990 unp il $15.95; pa $5   E

1. Cake—Fiction 2. Birthdays—Fiction 3. Mothers and daughters—Fiction
ISBN 0-15-234332-6; 0-15-201019-X (pa)
LC 89-15230

"A young girl, wishing to make her mother a birthday surprise, searches for her great-grandmother's secret recipe for the cake of the title. The recipe is found in an old diary, the secret ingredient turns up under the grand piano, and at midnight the cake is baked. Following directions, the girl spells LOVE backwards in the sugar, and three angels appear in the kitchen to add a spectacular icing and a golden thimble to the birthday morning surprise." SLJ

"Setting off the tale are Watson's paintings that range from precisely drafted pictures of objects and people (and some very original angels) to drifts of eclectic images that float freely across the page. A fresh, amusing piece that's also handsomely designed." Booklist

Simple pictures are best; story by Nancy Willard; pictures by Tomie de Paola. Harcourt Brace Jovanovich 1977 unp il hardcover o.p. paperback available $4.95   E

1. Photography—Fiction
ISBN 0-15-682625-9 (pa)
LC 76-4923

A shoemaker and his wife being photographed for their wedding anniversary keep adding items to the picture despite the photographer's admonition that "Simple pictures are best"

"De Paola's colorful, deadpan illustrations perfectly complement Willard's funny tale in the folk tradition. . . . The smooth flowing cumulative story, simple and direct but rich in pithy descriptions and similes, is certain to be a story time hit." SLJ

Williams, Barbara

Albert's toothache; illustrated by Kay Chorao. Dutton 1974 unp il hardcover o.p. paperback available $3.95   E

1. Turtles—Fiction
ISBN 0-525-45037-8 (pa)

This is the "story of a small turtle, toothless as are all of his kind, who takes to his bed with an announced toothache. His mother worries; his father thunders incredulous impatience; his siblings cast scorn. So it goes until grandmother investigates and discovers 'where' he has a toothache." Libr J

"The humor of the concise dialogue and of the stylized repetitions of the narrative is carefully reflected in the sepia-line and half-tone drawings that reveal the anthropomorphically domestic life of the turtles." Horn Book

Williams, Jay, 1914-1978

Everyone knows what a dragon looks like; illustrated by Mercer Mayer. Four Winds Press 1976 unp il $14.95; pa $5.95   E

1. Dragons—Fiction 2. China—Fiction
ISBN 0-02-793090-4; 0-02-045600-X (pa)

Because of the road sweeper's belief in him, a dragon saves the city of Wu from the Wild Horsemen of the north

"The theme of this story is that appearances can be deceiving. Mercer Mayer provides a series of emotionally expressive illustrations scaled down to a child's eye level. The humanized characters realistically portray fear, anger or joy.

. . . Careful attention has been paid to the background detail, perspective and layout, drawing the eye into each superb illustration and creating a three-dimensional effect." N Y Times Book Rev

Williams, Karen Lynn

Galimoto; illustrated by Catherine Stock. Lothrop, Lee & Shepard Bks. 1990 unp il $16; lib bdg $15.93; pa $4.95   E

1. Toys—Fiction 2. Malawi—Fiction
ISBN 0-688-08789-2; 0-688-08790-6 (lib bdg); 0-688-10991-8 (pa)
LC 89-2258

"In Malawi, Africa, according to the author's note, *galimoto* are intricate and popular push toys crafted by children. Williams tells the story of seven-year-old Kondi's quest to find ample scrap material to fashion his own toy pickup truck. Visits to his uncle's shop, the miller, and the trash heap yield enough wire to allow him to create a plaything which he proudly uses to lead his friends in their evening game. Kondi's perseverance and the pleasure he takes in his accomplishment are just two of the delights of this appealing story. Stock's graceful watercolors portray life in a bustling village and include enough detail . . . to give readers the flavor of a day in this southern African nation." Horn Book

When Africa was home; pictures by Floyd Cooper. Orchard Bks. 1991 unp il $15.95; lib bdg $15.99; pa $5.95   E

1. Africa—Fiction
ISBN 0-531-05925-1; 0-531-08525-2 (lib bdg); 0-531-07043-3 (pa)
LC 90-7684

"A Richard Jackson book"

After returning to the United States, Peter's whole family misses the warmth and friendliness of their life in Africa; so Peter's father looks for another job there

"The joyful text and Cooper's boldly drawn, glowing oil-wash pictures evoke the intensely physical experience of the small child, his delight in the place and culture, what it feels like to belong there." Booklist

Williams, Linda

The little old lady who was not afraid of anything; illustrated by Megan Lloyd. Crowell 1986 unp il $15; lib bdg $14.89; pa $4.95

E

ISBN 0-690-04584-0; 0-690-04586-7 (lib bdg); 0-06-443183-5 (pa)
LC 85-48250

Also available Spanish language edition

A little old lady who is not afraid of anything must deal with a pumpkin head, a tall black hat, and other spooky objects that follow her through the dark woods trying to scare her

"A delightful picture book, perfect for both independent reading pleasure and for telling aloud." SLJ

Williams, Sherley Anne, 1944-

Working cotton; written by Sherley Anne Williams; illustrated by Carole Byard. Harcourt Brace Jovanovich 1992 unp il $14.95

E

1. Migrant labor—Fiction 2. Cotton—Fiction 3. African Americans—Fiction
ISBN 0-15-299624-9
LC 91-21586

A Caldecott Medal honor book, 1993

Williams, Sherley Anne, 1944-—*Continued*

A young black girl relates the daily events of her family's migrant life in the cotton fields of central California

"Byard's acrylic paintings contribute weight and emotion to Williams's spare text. The fields and family members fill each full-page spread, drawing the reader very close to the action of the story. The mural-like paintings glow with blue and brown tones, recreating the textures and hues of the cotton fields. Williams's text, based on her poems, has a lyrical, rhythmic quality." Horn Book

Williams, Vera B.

A chair for my mother. Greenwillow Bks. 1982 unp il $16; lib bdg $15.93; pa $4.95   E

1. Family life—Fiction 2. Saving and thrift—Fiction 3. Chairs—Fiction

ISBN 0-688-00914-X; 0-688-00915-8 (lib bdg); 0-688-04074-8 (pa)   LC 81-7010

Also available Spanish language edition

A Caldecott Medal honor book, 1983

A child, her waitress mother, and her grandmother save dimes to buy a comfortable armchair after all their furniture is lost in a fire

"The cheerful paintings take up the full left-hand page and face, in most cases, a small chunk of the text set against a modulated wash of a complementing color; a border containing a pertinent motif surrounds the two pages, further unifying the design. The result is a superbly conceived picture book expressing the joyful spirit of a loving family." Horn Book

Other available titles about Rosa and her family are:
Music, music for everyone (1984)
Something special for me (1983)

Cherries and cherry pits. Greenwillow Bks. 1986 unp il $13.95; lib bdg $13.88   E

1. African Americans—Fiction 2. Drawing—Fiction

ISBN 0-688-05145-6; 0-688-05146-4 (lib bdg)   LC 85-17156

"Bidemmi, a young black child, draws splendid pictures. 'As she draws, she tells the story of what she is drawing,' always starting with the word 'this.' . . . Finally, Bidemmi tells her story, revealing her wish for her neighborhood and her world. Each story involves cherries—buying, sharing, and enjoying them." SLJ

"Williams' portraits of Bidemmi drawing are done in watercolor; the drawings Bidemmi makes are done with bright markers, some being simple sketches, others filling the page with color, looking like naive, but glorious icons. The interior stories are well integrated with each other, and the whole adds up to a study of child as artist that is fresh, vibrant, and exciting." Bull Cent Child Books

"More more more" said the baby; 3 love stories. Greenwillow Bks. 1990 unp il $16; lib bdg $15.93   E

1. Infants—Fiction 2. Parent and child—Fiction

ISBN 0-688-09173-3; 0-688-09174-1 (lib bdg)   LC 89-2023

A Caldecott Medal honor book, 1991

Three babies are caught up in the air and given loving attention by a father, grandmother, and mother

"The pages reverberate with bright colors and vigorous forms, and the rhythmic language begs to be read aloud." Horn Book Guide

Stringbean's trip to the shining sea; greetings from Vera B. Williams, story and pictures; and Jennifer Williams, more pictures. Greenwillow Bks. 1987 unp il $15; lib bdg $13.93   E

1. West (U.S.)—Fiction

ISBN 0-688-07161-9; 0-688-07162-7 (lib bdg)   LC 86-29502

Also available in paperback from Scholastic

"Stringbean and big brother Fred (joined en route by Potato, Stringbean's dog) take a car trip from their home in Kansas to the Pacific Ocean, and their pilgrimage is recorded herein in the form of a mock photo and postcard album." Bull Cent Child Books

"The use of mixed media—watercolors, Magic Markers, and colored pencils—is as aesthetically pleasing as it is skillful. Nothing has been forgotten; nothing more needs to be added. Not for the usual picture-book set, this travelogue storybook will appeal to slightly older audiences." Horn Book

Three days on a river in a red canoe. Greenwillow Bks. 1984 unp il $16; lib bdg $11.88; pa $3.95   E

1. Canoes and canoeing—Fiction 2. Camping—Fiction

ISBN 0-688-80307-5; 0-688-84307-7 (lib bdg); 0-688-04072-1 (pa)   LC 80-23893

In this book, a "canoe trip for two children and two adults is recorded with all its interesting detail in a spontaneous first-person account and engaging full-color drawings on carefully designed pages. Driving to a river site, making camp, paddling the craft, negotiating a waterfall, swimming, fishing, dealing with a sudden storm, and even rescuing one overboard child are all described as important incidents in a summertime adventure." Horn Book

Willis, Jeanne

Earthlets, as explained by Professor Xargle; illustrated by Tony Ross. Dutton 1989 unp il $14.99   E

1. Extraterrestrial beings—Fiction 2. Infants—Fiction

ISBN 0-525-44465-3   LC 88-23692

Also available in paperback from Puffin Bks.

Professor Xargle's class of extraterrestrials learns about the physical characteristics and behavior of the human baby

"This funny view of babies is fraught with Professor Xargle's well-meaning, zany misinterpretations. Willis's clever and original text will particularly delight older siblings who may also find that babies are a separate species. Ross's inspired paintings bristle with out-of-this-world color and imagination." Publ Wkly

Other available titles about Professor Xargle are:
Earth hounds, as explained by Professor Xargle (1990)
Earth mobiles, as explained by Professor Xargle (1992)
Earth tigerlets, as explained by Professor Xargle (1991)
Earth weather, as explained by Professor Xargle (1993)
Relativity, as explained by Professor Xargle (1994)

Wilner, Isabel

B is for Bethlehem; a Christmas alphabet; illustrated by Elisa Kleven. Dutton Children's Bks. 1990 unp il $14.99   E

1. Jesus Christ—Nativity—Poetry 2. Alphabet

ISBN 0-525-44622-2   LC 89-49481

Also available in paperback from Puffin Bks.

Rhyming verses introduce the letters of the alphabet and the events surrounding the birth of Jesus

Wilner, Isabel—*Continued*

This book includes "unique and appealing pictures. Kleven offers mixed-media collage using watercolor, cut paper, and drawings, giving her artwork a radiant, folkloric look. . . . Wilner first wrote the piece for second graders to perform. Though it certainly could be used in this manner, the book seems a natural in its present, lovely form." Booklist

Winter, Jeanette

Follow the drinking gourd; story and pictures by Jeanette Winter. Knopf 1988 unp il music lib bdg $17.99; pa $6.99   E

1. Slavery—Fiction 2. Underground railroad—Fiction 3. African Americans—Fiction

ISBN 0-394-99694-1 (lib bdg); 0-679-81997-5 (pa)
LC 88-9661

By following directions in a song, taught them by an old sailor, runaway slaves journey north along the Underground Railroad to freedom in Canada

"Complementing the few lines of text per page are dark-hued illustrations horizontally framed with a fine black line and plenty of white space. . . . The art carries the weight of introducing children to a riveting piece of U.S. history, and the music included at the end of the book will fix it in their minds." Bull Cent Child Books

Winthrop, Elizabeth

Shoes; illustrated by William Joyce. Harper & Row 1986 19p il $14; lib bdg $14.89; pa $4.95   E

1. Shoes—Fiction 2. Stories in rhyme

ISBN 0-06-026591-4; 0-06-026592-2 (lib bdg); 0-06-443171-1 (pa)
LC 85-45841

"A jaunty rhyme about shoes of all kinds—'shoes for fishing, shoes for wishing, shoes for muddy squishing.' The roly-poly figures are drawn from a child's perspective." N Y Times Book Rev

"This lilting rhyme about shoes and feet easily pleases. . . . Backing the verses are full-color drawings of children busily involved with one kind of shoe or another. Joyce's pictures are animated, energetic, and warmly colored." Booklist

Wise, William, 1923-

Ten sly piranhas; a counting story in reverse (a tale of wickedness—and worse!); pictures by Victoria Chess. Dial Bks. for Young Readers 1993 unp il $13.99; lib bdg $13.89   E

1. Fishes—Fiction 2. Counting 3. Stories in rhyme

ISBN 0-8037-1200-6; 0-8037-1201-4 (lib bdg)
LC 91-33704

A school of ten sly piranhas gradually dwindles as they waylay and eat each other, and the last is eaten by a crocodile

"The combination of a jaunty, rhymed text and gleefully fiendish illustrations demonstrates with delicious derring-do that the wicked frequently receive their just deserts." Horn Book

Wiseman, Bernard

Morris and Boris at the circus; by B. Wiseman. Harper & Row 1988 64p il $14.95; lib bdg $14.89; pa $3.50   E

1. Moose—Fiction 2. Bears—Fiction 3. Circus—Fiction

ISBN 0-06-026477-2; 0-06-026478-0 (lib bdg); 0-06-444143-1 (pa)
LC 87-45682

"An I can read book"

"Morris the Moose and his friend Boris the Bear . . . take a trip to the circus. Morris has never gone before, so he doesn't quite have the big picture. He thinks the clown's nose is red because he has a cold, and when they join the performers in the ring, Morris rides 'bearback' on Boris, instead of on a horse." Booklist

"The cartoon illustrations with bold colors provide ample context clues for beginning readers. This delightful combination of text and illustrations will entice children to read and re-read this book." SLJ

Other available titles about Morris and Boris are:
Halloween with Morris and Boris (1975)
Morris goes to school (1970)
Morris the moose (1989)

Wisniewski, David

Elfwyn's saga; story and pictures by David Wisniewski. Lothrop, Lee & Shepard Bks. 1990 unp il $13.95; lib bdg $13.88   E

1. Fairy tales 2. Vikings—Fiction

ISBN 0-688-09589-5; 0-688-09590-9 (lib bdg)
LC 89-35308

"Elfwyn is born blind, but she grows up to destroy that original curse as well as a subsequent one threatening her clan. Loosely based on the legends and history of Iceland, the story is full of elements and motifs—magic, the battle between good and evil—which entrance young people. Cut-paper illustrations dazzle the eye and bring power and drama to an exciting folkloric tale." Horn Book Guide

Rain player; story and pictures by David Wisniewski. Clarion Bks. 1991 unp il $16.95; pa $5.95   E

1. Mayas—Fiction 2. Games—Fiction

ISBN 0-395-55112-9; 0-395-72083-4 (pa)
LC 90-44101

To bring rain to his thirsty village, Pik challenges the rain god to a game of pok-a-tok

"This original tale combines research on Mayan history and legend with a suspenseful sports story. . . . Intricate and dramatic cut-paper illustrations powerfully re-create the foliage, landscape, architecture, and clothing of the Mayan classical period. . . . An author's note provides fascinating background information on Mayan civilization and gives in-depth explanations of some of the words and phrases used in the text." Horn Book

The warrior and the wise man; story and pictures by David Wisniewski. Lothrop, Lee & Shepard Bks. 1989 unp il $16; lib bdg $15.93   E

1. Fairy tales 2. Japan—Fiction

ISBN 0-688-07889-3; 0-688-07890-7 (lib bdg)
LC 88-21678

This original fairy tale "describes the quests of the twin sons of the emperor of Japan for five magical elements of the world: earth, water, fire, wind, and cloud. The brother who returns first will inherit the throne." Booklist

"The striking cut-paper illustrations, executed and reproduced with virtuosity, make use of black silhouettes against emotionally charged colors that modulate and change from

Wisniewski, David—*Continued*
page to page and create a dynamic, almost cinematographic effect. In a detailed end note Wisniewski explicates the visual references to be seen in the costumes, decorations, and artifacts and thus establishes the historical, religious, and artistic authenticity of his work." Horn Book

The wave of the Sea-Wolf; story and pictures by David Wisniewski. Clarion Bks. 1994 unp il $16.95   E

1. Tlingit Indians—Fiction
ISBN 0-395-66478-0   LC 93-18265
Kchokeen, a Tlingit princess, is rescued from drowning by a guardian spirit that later enables Kchokeen to summon a great wave and save her people from hostile strangers
"Vivid storytelling is complemented by textured cut-paper illustrations that paint the forest landscape in lacy layers. . . . Wisniewski's ability to convey both high drama and simple emotion lends a sense of authenticity to this original tale." Publ Wkly

Wojciechowski, Susan
The Christmas miracle of Jonathan Toomey; illustrated by P.J. Lynch. Candlewick Press 1995 unp il $15.95   E

1. Wood carving—Fiction   2. Christmas—Fiction
3. Friendship—Fiction
ISBN 1-56402-320-6   LC 94-48917
The widow McDowell and her seven-year-old son Thomas ask the gruff Jonathan Toomey, the best wood-carver in the valley, to carve the figures for a Christmas creche
"The story verges on the sentimental, but it's told with feeling and lyricism. . . . Lynch's sweeping illustrations, in shades of wood grain, are both realistic and gloriously romantic, focusing on faces and hands at work before the fire and in the lamplight." Booklist

Wolff, Ashley, 1956-
Come with me. Dutton 1990 unp il lib bdg $12.95   E

1. Dogs—Fiction
ISBN 0-525-44555-2   LC 89-34482
A little boy tells a newborn puppy all the things they'll do in the meadow and by the sea when the puppy is old enough to come to live with him
"Double-page watercolors in a wide but misted palette, with soft contours and no harsh lines, perfectly suit the quietly joyful mood of innocent love. . . . Words and pictures present the California coastal setting and the boy's rehearsal of this important childhood relationship with a romantic affection that stops short of cloying. A book that's well-suited for both read-aloud and one-on-one sharing." SLJ

Only the cat saw. Dodd, Mead 1985 unp il $13.95   E

1. Night—Fiction 2. Cats—Fiction 3. Family life—Fiction
ISBN 0-399-21698-7   LC 85-7031
As Amy and her family get ready to settle down for the night, the cat gets ready to explore and sees many things
"This not only portrays a warm family but also gives a sense of the nocturnal cycle picking up after most children consider everything to have wound down. The oil paintings are rich in texture with surprising blends of color, dramatic shapes, and satisfying compositions." Bull Cent Child Books

Stella & Roy. Dutton Children's Bks. 1993 unp il $12.99   E

1. Cycling—Fiction
ISBN 0-525-45081-5   LC 92-27005
Also available in paperback from Puffin Bks.
"In true 'Hare and Tortoise' fashion, older, overconfident Stella takes her time pedalling round a lake, stopping to check out the flora and fauna, while toddler Roy repeatedly rolls 'right on by.' The luminously tinted linoleum prints perfectly capture the thrill of the race." SLJ

A year of beasts. Dutton 1986 unp il $11.95   E

1. Animals 2. Seasons
ISBN 0-525-44240-5   LC 85-27419
"Again focusing on the family from the author's earlier *A Year of Birds* [entered below] the linoleum block prints with clear black lines and bright but translucent washes record the changing seasons of a New England landscape and its nonhuman as well as human inhabitants." SLJ
"Warm but never cute, handsome without becoming pretentious, commanding attention without overwhelming the subject, this is a child's calendar, a celebration of family, and an evocation of nature's wonders—all scaled to the preschooler's perception. A satisfying and handsome production." Horn Book

A year of birds. Dodd, Mead 1984 unp il o.p.; Penguin Bks. paperback available $3.95   E

1. Birds 2. Seasons
ISBN 0-14-050854-6 (pa)   LC 83-27470
"Handsome, vividly colored linoleum block prints are the artistic centerpieces of this month-by-month catalog of birds that 'visit Ellie's house' in the course of a year. The succinct text simply states names of birds and the month they are likely to be seen ('Grosbeaks, purple finches, and black-capped chickadees in January . . .'), while charming two-page spreads evoke seasonal characteristics of each month. . . . The pictures of Ellie and her parents have a cozy warmth and tell a wordless story besides, showing Ellie's mother's advancing pregnancy until, in July, a new baby appears. . . . A quietly appealing, well-conceived introduction to the months of the year and changing seasons." Booklist

Wolff, Patricia Rae
The toll-bridge troll; illustrated by Kimberly Bulcken Root. Harcourt Brace & Co.; Browndeer Press 1995 unp il $14   E

1. Fairy tales
ISBN 0-15-277665-6   LC 93-32298
A troll tries to prevent Trigg from crossing the bridge on the way to school only to be outwitted by the boy's riddles
"While the humor of the text lies partly in the slyly matter-of-fact tone, the illustrations ground the whimsy in a wealth of detail—like the troll's knobby, skinned knees and his petulant expression." Horn Book

Wood, Audrey
Elbert's bad word; illustrated by Audrey and Don Wood. Harcourt Brace Jovanovich 1988 unp il $13.95   E

1. Parties—Fiction
ISBN 0-15-225320-3   LC 86-7557
"A bad word, spoken by a small boy at a fashionable garden party, creates havoc, and the child, Elbert, gets his mouth scrubbed out with soap. The bad word, in the shape

Wood, Audrey—*Continued*
of a long-tailed furry monster, will not go away until a wiz-ard-gardener cooks up some really delicious, super-long words that everyone at the party applauds. This single-idea cautionary tale has lively, absurdist pictures of tiara-crowned, formally dressed adults recoiling in horror or ca-vorting with glee when Elbert, the only child at the party, speaks a word." SLJ

Heckedy Peg; illustrated by Don Wood. Harcourt Brace Jovanovich 1987 unp il lib bdg $15; pa $6   E

1. Fairy tales 2. Witches—Fiction
ISBN 0-15-233678-8 (lib bdg); 0-15-233679-6 (pa)
LC 86-33639

"The poor mother of seven children, each named for a day of the week, goes off to market promising to return with individual gifts that each child has requested and ad-monishing them to lock the door to strangers and not to touch the fire. The gullible children are tricked into dis-obeying their mother by the witch, Heckedy Peg, who turns them all into various kinds of food. The mother can rescue her children only by guessing which child is the fish, the roast rib, the bread. . . . This story, deep and rich with folk wisdom, is stunningly illustrated with Don Wood's lumi-nous paintings. . . . With variety of color and line he en-hances every nuance of the text, from the individuality of the children and the stalwart mother to the unrelenting evil of the witch. A tour de force in every way." SLJ

King Bidgood's in the bathtub; written by Audrey Wood; illustrated by Don Wood. Harcourt Brace Jovanovich 1985 unp il lib bdg $15   E

1. Kings, queens, rulers, etc.—Fiction 2. Baths—Fiction
ISBN 0-15-242730-9   LC 85-5472
A Caldecott Medal honor book, 1986
Despite pleas from his court, a fun-loving king refuses to get out of his bathtub to rule his kingdom
"The few simple words of text per large, well-designed page invite story-telling—but keep the group very small, so the children can be close enough to pore over the brilliant, robust illustrations." SLJ

The napping house; illustrated by Don Wood. Harcourt Brace Jovanovich 1984 unp il lib bdg $15   E

1. Sleep—Fiction
ISBN 0-15-256708-9   LC 83-13035
Also available Spanish language edition
"In this sleepytime cumulative tale, all are pleasantly napping until a pesky flea starts the clamor that wakes up the whole family—mouse, cat, dog, child, and granny." Child Book Rev Serv
"The cool blues and greens are superseded by warm col-ors and bursts of action as each sleeper wakes, ending in an eruption of color and energy as naptime ends. A deft matching of text and pictures adds to the appeal of cumula-tion, and to the silliness of the mound of sleepers—just the right kind of humor for the lap audience." Bull Cent Child Books

Wood, Don, 1945-
Piggies; written by Don and Audrey Wood; illustrated by Don Wood. Harcourt Brace Jovanovich 1991 unp il $13.95; pa $5.95

E

1. Bedtime—Fiction 2. Pigs—Fiction
ISBN 0-15-256341-5; 0-15-200217-0 (pa)
LC 89-24598

Ten little piggies dance on a young child's fingers and toes before finally going to sleep
"A happy text and luxuriant, witty pictures make this a book to pore over again and again." Booklist

Wyeth, Sharon Dennis
Always my Dad; illustrated by Raúl Colón. Knopf 1995 unp il $15; lib bdg $15.99   E

1. Fathers and daughters—Fiction 2. African Americans—Fiction
ISBN 0-679-83447-8; 0-679-93447-2 (lib bdg)
LC 93-43755

"An Apple soup book"
This is "about a young African-American girl's longing for her father, almost always away looking for work. Once, while staying at her grandparents' farm for the summer, the girl and her two younger brothers do get to see their father for awhile, and she learns that although he has to leave yet again, he always thinks of her and will come back 'soon.'" Bull Cent Child Books
This is a "poignant, lyrical story. . . . The etched water-color, charcoal, colored-pencil, and lithograph-pencil art has a dreamy, statuesque quality that reflects the feeling of pre-cious and subsequent '. . . leftover summer days.'" SLJ

Yarbrough, Camille, 1938-
Cornrows; illustrated by Carole Byard. Coward, McCann & Geoghegan 1979 unp il hardcover o.p. paperback available $6.95

E

1. African Americans—Fiction 2. Hair—Fiction
ISBN 0-698-20709-2 (pa)   LC 78-74011
Coretta Scott King Award for illustration, 1980
This story illustrates how the hair style of cornrows, a symbol in Africa since ancient times, can today in this country symbolize the courage of Afro-Americans
"Dialect is used but not overused. Byard's black-and-white drawings . . . are attractive and welcome." SLJ

Yep, Laurence
The boy who swallowed snakes; illustrated by Jean and Mou-Sien Tseng. Scholastic 1994 unp il $14.95   E

1. China—Fiction 2. Snakes—Fiction
ISBN 0-590-46168-0   LC 93-21822
"Little Chou discovers a poisonous ku snake in a basket of silver coins, and to make sure no one is injured by it, he swallows it. . . . Finally, the deadly snake winds up where it needs to be to fulfill its destiny—in the house of the greedy wealthy man who abandoned it in the first place. The story is rich in elements that will appeal to children. Its comedy is reflected not only in the text, but also in the ac-companying watercolors." Booklist

The Butterfly Boy; pictures by Jeanne M. Lee. Farrar, Straus & Giroux 1993 unp il $16

E

1. Butterflies—Fiction 2. China—Fiction
ISBN 0-374-31003-3
"'There once was a boy who dreamed he was a butterfly, and, as a butterfly, he always dreamed he was a boy.' The rhythmic text has a poetic simplicity in this delicate trans-formation story, which draws on the writings of an ancient Chinese philosopher. . . . The different ways of seeing are expressed in different kinds of brightly colored illustrations, from the formal style of Chinese woodcuts to the sensuous, surreal images of dreams." Booklist

Yolen, Jane

Commander Toad in space; pictures by Bruce Degen. Coward, McCann & Geoghegan 1980 63p il hardcover o.p. paperback available $6.95   E

1. Toads—Fiction

ISBN 0-698-20522-7 (pa)

A "beginning-to-read book with brave space explorers, a ship named the 'Star Warts,' and a monster who calls himself Deep Wader. . . . The adventure of Commander Toad and his colleagues is a clever spoof and really funny reading. . . . Degen picks up on [the spoof] by drawing mock-serious amphibious characters and a horrible, yet somehow foolish, Wader. This hits the nail on the countdown button for primary as well as some older problem readers." Booklist

Other available titles about Commander Toad are:
Commander Toad and the big black hole (1983)
Commander Toad and the dis-asteroid (1985)
Commander Toad and the intergalactic spy (1986)
Commander Toad and the Planet of the Grapes (1982)
Commander Toad and the space pirates (1987)

The girl who loved the wind; pictures by Ed Young. Crowell 1972 unp il hardcover o.p. paperback available $5.95   E

1. Winds—Fiction

ISBN 0-06-443088-X (pa)   LC 71-171012

"The bittersweet tale of a wealthy merchant's daughter, Danina, protected from the world so carefully that her exquisite palace becomes a prison, and she finally flies away with the wind. The striking illustrations, combining watercolor and collage, are stylized and oriental. The story unfolds at a measured pace, with a subtly implied message that life must be a mixture of happiness and sadness." Booklist

Greyling; illustrated by David Ray. Philomel Bks. 1991 unp il $14.95   E

1. Seals (Animals)—Fiction 2. Scotland—Fiction

ISBN 0-399-22262-6   LC 90-35395

A newly illustrated edition of the title first published 1968 by World Publishing Company

A selchie, a seal transformed into human form, lives on land in Scotland with a lonely fisherman and his wife, until the day a great storm threatens the fisherman's life

This story "shows Yolen's ability to give her work the power and language of legend. . . . Ray has created a romantic, fairy-tale landscape and characters of swirling lines and large expanses of color." SLJ

Letting Swift River go; illustrated by Barbara Cooney. Little, Brown 1992 unp il $15.95; pa $4.95   E

1. Country life—Fiction 2. Massachusetts—Fiction

ISBN 0-316-96899-4; 0-316-96860-9 (pa)

LC 90-47909

Relates Sally Jane's experience of changing times in rural America, as she lives through the drowning of the Swift River towns in western Massachusetts to form the Quabbin Reservoir

"Yolen's descriptions of life in rural western Massachusetts are redolent with the sights and sounds of a childhood spent outdoors. . . . The watercolor, pencil, and pastel paintings by Barbara Cooney lovingly proclaim the pleasures of each season and capture the joys of a rural way of life many children can no longer experience firsthand." Horn Book

Owl moon; illustrated by John Schoenherr. Philomel Bks. 1987 unp il lib bdg $15.95   E

1. Owls—Fiction 2. Fathers and daughters—Fiction

ISBN 0-399-21457-7   LC 87-2300

Awarded the Caldecott Medal, 1988

"The poetic narrative is told from the point of view of a child who 'has been waiting to go owling with Pa for a long, long time.' The father and child venture forth on a cold winter night not to capture, but to commune with, the great horned owl." SLJ

This book "conveys the scary majesty of winter woods at night in language that seldom overreaches either character or subject. . . . Jane Yolen and John Schoenherr, who are both prolific, have done excellent work in the past, but this book has a magic that is extremely rare in books for any age." N Y Times Book Rev

Piggins and the royal wedding; illustrated by Jane Dyer. Harcourt Brace Jovanovich 1989 c1988 unp il $13.95; pa $4.95   E

1. Mystery fiction 2. Pigs—Fiction

ISBN 0-15-261687-X; 0-15-200078-X (pa)

LC 88-5399

"Piggins, the imperturbable butler, is summoned to solve the mystery of a missing wedding ring. The royal family, the well-dressed Reynard family, and their cozy Edwardian period home are all amusingly depicted in the busy and colorful illustrations." Horn Book

Other available titles about Piggins are:
Piggins (1987)
Picnic with Piggins (1988)

The seeing stick; pictures by Remy Charlip and Demetra Maraslis. Crowell 1977 unp il lib bdg $14.89   E

1. Blind—Fiction 2. China—Fiction

ISBN 0-690-00596-2   LC 75-6949

"Yolen tells a sensitive and graceful story of a small, blind [Chinese] princess whose rich, powerful father, the Emperor, cannot give her the most precious gift of all—her sight. A tattered, old wood carver brings her the wide world, however, by telling stories of wonders he has seen on his travels and carving them into the golden wood of a stick. As he invites her to feel not only the cane but objects surrounding her, she begins to see with 'eyes on the tips of her fingers.'" SLJ

"The illustrators worked in concert to create pencil drawings and misty pastel-crayon scenes that look like watercolors." Publ Wkly

Sleeping ugly; by Jane Yolen; pictures by Diane Stanley. Coward, McCann & Geoghegan 1981 64p il hardcover o.p. paperback available $7.95   E

1. Fairy tales

ISBN 0-698-20617-7 (pa)

"A Break-of-day book"

When beautiful Princess Miserella, Plain Jane, and a fairy fall under a sleeping spell, a prince undoes the spell in a surprising way

"Diane Stanley's expressive illustrations, jumping from once upon a time to right now, add an intriguing perspective to the tale's witty text and humorous play with fairy tale conventions." SLJ

Yorinks, Arthur, 1953-

Company's coming; illustrated by David Small. Crown 1988 unp il hardcover o.p. paperback available $4.99　　　E

1. Extraterrestrial beings—Fiction
ISBN 0-517-58858-7 (pa)　　　LC 87-13579

"Shirley has invited her relatives to dinner and Moe is tinkering in the backyard when a flying saucer lands. The hilarious dialogue in this storybook 'is as well timed as the best comedy act,' and pen-and-ink illustrations capture the mayhem perfectly." N Y Times Book Rev

Hey, Al; story by Arthur Yorinks; pictures by Richard Egielski. Farrar, Straus & Giroux 1986 unp il $16; pa $4.95　　　E

1. Fantasy fiction
ISBN 0-374-33060-3; 0-374-42985-5 (pa)
　　　LC 86-80955
Awarded the Caldecott Medal, 1987

"Al, a janitor, and his faithful dog, Eddie, live in a single room on the West Side. . . . Their tiny home is crowded and cramped; their life is an endless struggle. Al and Eddie are totally miserable until a large and mysterious bird offers them a change of fortune." Publisher's note

"Egielski's solid naturalism provides just the visual foil needed to establish the surreal character of this fantasy. The muted earth tones of the one-room flat contrast symbolically with the bright hues of the birds' plumage and the foliage of the floating paradise. The anatomical appropriateness of Al and Eddie plays neatly against the flamboyant depiction of the plants. Text and pictures work together to challenge readers' concept of reality." SLJ

It happened in Pinsk; story by Arthur Yorinks; pictures by Richard Egielski. Farrar, Straus & Giroux 1983 unp il $14; pa $3.95
　　　E

1. Head—Fiction
ISBN 0-374-33651-2; 0-374-43649-5 (pa)
　　　LC 83-1727

"Shoe salesman Irv Irving and his wife have all of life's comforts—nice clothes, good food, a telephone—but Irv, jealous of nearly everyone else, simply is not satisfied. When he awakes one morning and finds he is missing his head, his pragmatic wife outfits him with a new one, made of old socks and a pillowcase; Irv then has the chance to find out what it is like to be someone else." SLJ

"The artist's distinctive almost caricatured treatment of human figures is perfectly suited to the offbeat nature of the tale. With enthusiasm and wit the lavish illustrations match the rhythm and humor of the text." Horn Book

Young, Ruth

Golden Bear; illustrations by Rachel Isadora. Viking 1992 unp il $15.99; pa $4.99
　　　E

1. Bears—Fiction 2. Stories in rhyme
ISBN 0-670-82577-8; 0-14-050959-3 (pa)
　　　LC 89-24843

"Golden Bear and his friend (an unnamed African-American child) do many things together—rocking in the rocking chair, ice-skating and playing the violin." Child Book Rev Serv

"While the rhyming text is agreeable, Isadora's winsome artwork steals the show. Her chalk drawings fill the pages with simple shapes and deep-toned colors. . . . A good bedtime book and, for those who can read the music on the endpapers, a bedtime song as well." Booklist

Who says moo? illustrated by Lisa Campbell Ernst. Viking 1994 unp il $13.99
　　　E

1. Animals
ISBN 0-670-85162-0　　　LC 94-11878

Simple questions in rhyme invite young children to identify animals by sound, color, or other description

"It is Ernst's lively art that places this above the usual riddle books. Using large, rounded shapes and a layout that has the air of action (monkeys swinging and horses galloping across spreads), Ernst provides delightful pictures that will work especially well for groups. A key at the end identifies all the creatures. Fun for little ones." Booklist

Zelinsky, Paul O.

The maid and the mouse and the odd-shaped house; a story in rhyme; adapted and illustrated by Paul O. Zelinsky. Dutton Children's Bks. 1993 unp il $14.99　　　E

1. Houses—Fiction 2. Mice—Fiction 3. Stories in rhyme
ISBN 0-525-45095-5　　　LC 89-3512

Also available in paperback from Puffin Bks.

A reissue of the title first published 1981 by Dodd, Mead

"In this rhyming tell-and-draw story, cleverly disguised eyes, ears, whiskers, legs, and a tail result from improvements that the maid and the mouse make in their odd-shaped house." SLJ

"Superb design and masterful pacing." Horn Book Guide

Zemach, Harve

The judge; an untrue tale; with pictures by Margot Zemach. Farrar, Straus & Giroux 1969 unp il $17; pa $5.95　　　E

1. Judges—Fiction 2. Stories in rhyme
ISBN 0-374-33960-0; 0-374-43962-1 (pa)

A Caldecott Medal honor book, 1970

"Enthroned on his bench, a curmudgeon of a judge hears a prisoner plead that he didn't know that what he did was against the law, but that he had seen a horrible beast. 'This man has told an untrue tale. Throw him in jail!' Each additional prisoner adds to the story; each infuriates the judge." Sutherland. The Best in Child Books

Mommy, buy me a china doll; pictures by Margot Zemach. Farrar, Straus & Giroux 1975 c1966 unp il hardcover o.p. paperback available $4.95　　　E

1. Folk songs—United States
ISBN 0-374-45286-5 (pa)

A reprint of the title first published 1966 by Follett

A "picture book version of the cumulative folk song that has the appeals of repetition, of a chain of mildly nonsensical actions, and of a warmly satisfying ending. Eliza Lou's request for a china doll leads to proposals that it be bought with Daddy's feather bed, so Daddy would have to sleep in the horsey's bed, and the horsey would have to sleep in Sister's bed, and so on, and so on. Each page of print is faced by a full-page illustration in color, humorous in mood." Bull Cent Child Books

Zemach, Harve—*Continued*

The princess and Froggie; stories by Harve and Kaethe Zemach; pictures by Margot Zemach. Farrar, Straus & Giroux 1975 unp il hardcover o.p. paperback available $4.95 E

1. Frogs—Fiction 2. Friendship—Fiction

ISBN 0-374-46011-6 (pa)

"Three disarming vignettes starring 'the princess' and her friend Froggie, who is adept at easing crisis situations. . . . Coupled with Margot Zemach's unconventional graphic interpretation, the stories become droll farce. The frumpy princess in a shapeless Sunday dress with a be-draggled ribbon in her hair is a merry departure from the usual type; and Mama doesn't recall any royal matrons on the scene lately. Blithe tongue-in-cheek comedy for the very young." Booklist

Ziefert, Harriet

A new coat for Anna; pictures by Anita Lobel. Knopf 1986 unp il lib bdg $12.99; pa $5.99 E

1. Coats—Fiction

ISBN 0-394-97426-3 (lib bdg); 0-394-89861-3 (pa)
LC 86-2722

Set in a war-torn town in post-World War II Eastern Europe. Even though there is no money, Anna's mother finds a way to make Anna a badly needed winter coat

"Ziefert's writing is clear and succinct, but it is in Lobel's brightly colored paintings that the story truly unfolds. . . . The expressiveness of the faces in Lobel's paintings brings life to the story. Ziefert's tale, based on a true story, carries a simple lesson that will be understood and cherished by all ages." SLJ

Zion, Gene

Harry the dirty dog; pictures by Margaret Bloy Graham. Harper & Row 1956 unp il $15; lib bdg $14.89; pa $4.95 E

1. Dogs—Fiction

ISBN 0-06-026865-4; 0-06-026866-2 (lib bdg); 0-06-443009-X (pa)

Also available Spanish language edition

"A runaway dog becomes so dirty his family almost doesn't recognize him. Harry's flight from scrubbing brush and bath water takes him on a tour of the city. Road repairs, railroad yards, construction sites, and coal deliveries contribute to his grimy appearance and show aspects of city life that contrast with the tidy suburb that is 'home.'" Moorachian. What is a City?

"Harry's fun and troubles are told simply, and the drawings are full of action and humor. The combination will have great appeal for the very young." Horn Book

Other available titles about Harry are:
Harry and the lady next door (1960)
Harry by the sea (1965)
No roses for Harry! (1958)

Zolotow, Charlotte, 1915-
The hating book; pictures by Ben Shecter. Harper & Row 1969 32p il $14.95; lib bdg $14.89; pa $3.95 E

1. Friendship—Fiction

ISBN 0-06-026923-5; 0-06-026924-3 (lib bdg); 0-06-443197-5 (pa)

"A little girl tells of several instances of being rebuffed by her friend, ending with the comment, 'I hated my friend.' Finally, at the urging of her mother, she goes to see the friend and asks her why she's been so 'rotten.' The answer is that 'Sue said Jane said you said I looked like a freak.' The actual remark had been that she looked 'neat.' The point of the book is clear as the two friends make plans to play together the following day." Read Ladders for Hum Relat. 6th edition

I know a lady; pictures by James Stevenson. Greenwillow Bks. 1984 unp il $14.95; lib bdg $14.88; pa $4.95; Penguin Bks. pa $3.95 E

1. Old age—Fiction

ISBN 0-688-03837-9; 0-688-03838-7 (lib bdg); 0-688-11519-5 (pa); 0-14-050550-4 (pa)
LC 83-25361

Sally describes a loving and lovable old lady in her neighborhood who grows flowers, waves to children when they pass her house, and bakes cookies for them at Christmas

"With virtuoso skill the artist uses scratchy lines to catch just the right tilt of a dog's tail and the bulge of a cookie-filled cheek. The amiable old lady is brought to life, complete with her slight stoop, sensible shoes, and shapeless but still spry body. Her house is a perfectly conceived setting as the illustrator lovingly pictures her stove and comfortable rocking chairs. A feeling of warmth and affection suffuses the pictures." Horn Book

Mr. Rabbit and the lovely present; pictures by Maurice Sendak. Harper & Row 1962 unp il hardcover o.p. paperback available $4.95 E

1. Birthdays—Fiction 2. Color—Fiction 3. Rabbits—Fiction

ISBN 0-06-443020-0 (pa)

Also available Spanish language edition

A Caldecott Medal honor book, 1963

"A serious little girl and a tall, other-worldly white rabbit converse about a present for her mother. 'But what?' said the little girl. 'Yes, what?' said Mr. Rabbit.' It requires a day of searching—for red, yellow, green, and blue, all things the mother likes, to make a basket of fruit for the present." Horn Book

"The quiet story, told in dialogue, is illustrated in richly colored pictures which exactly fit the fanciful mood." Hodges. Books for Elem Sch Libr

My grandson Lew; pictures by William Pène Du Bois. Harper & Row 1974 30p il lib bdg $14.89; pa $4.95 E

1. Death—Fiction 2. Grandfathers—Fiction

ISBN 0-06-026962-6 (lib bdg); 0-06-443066-9 (pa)

"An Ursula Nordstrom book"

"Warm, rich, and beautiful, a comforting consideration of death. Lew, now six, awakes and remembers back to when he was two and his grandfather came to him in the night when he called. . . . Lew recounts the images he has retained and then his mother tells of her remembrances, concluding, 'We will remember him together and neither of us will be so lonely as we would be if we had to remember

Zolotow, Charlotte, 1915-—*Continued*

him alone.' Pène du Bois' finely washed illustrations exude a serenity and understanding perfectly in tune with the story." Booklist

The quarreling book; pictures by Arnold Lobel. Harper & Row 1963 unp il lib bdg $13.89; pa $3.95   E

ISBN 0-06-026976-6 (lib bdg); 0-06-443034-0 (pa)

"Father forgets to kiss Mother goodbye when starting to work one morning, so Mother is unhappy and becomes cross with Jonathan James who takes out his feelings on his sister, and the chain continues until reversed by the dog who thinks being shoved off the bed is just a game and lots of fun. The sequence, then starts in happy reverse until at five, with the rain ending, Mr. James comes home and kisses Mrs. James." SLJ

It is "a worthwhile book which clearly demonstrates the far-reaching effects one's actions have on others. Even the youngest child will grasp its lesson easily. The illustrations are whimsical, detailed and expressive." NY Times Book Rev

The seashore book; paintings by Wendell Minor. HarperCollins Pubs. 1992 unp il $15; lib bdg $14.89; pa $5.95   E

1. Seashore—Fiction 2. Mothers and sons—Fiction
ISBN 0-06-020213-0; 0-06-020214-9 (lib bdg); 0-06-443364-1 (pa)   LC 91-22783

A mother's words help a little boy imagine the sights and sounds of the seashore, even though he's never seen the ocean

"Minor's crisply detailed watercolors evoke place with imaginative accuracy and visual grace, and Zolotow's . . . spare, poetic text provides a lyrical and nostalgic paean to the wonders of seaside life." Publ Wkly

Sleepy book; illustrations by Ilse Plume. newly il ed. Harper & Row 1988 unp il lib bdg $13.89; pa $5.95   E

1. Sleep 2. Animals
ISBN 0-06-026968-5 (lib bdg); 0-06-443239-4 (pa)
LC 87-45861

A newly illustrated edition of the title first published 1958 by Lothrop

Describes how each animal sleeps in its own special place, in its own special way

"Plume's full-page drawings on the right are windows into a great green room of childhood from which human sleepy-heads can look outward onto an enchanting world of nature. Her top and bottom borders on the left pages frame the spare, poetic narrative." SLJ

Something is going to happen; pictures by Catherine Stock. Harper & Row 1988 unp il hardcover o.p. paperback available $4.95
E

1. Snow—Fiction 2. Family life—Fiction
ISBN 0-06-443274-2 (pa)   LC 87-26661

"One by one, as the members of a family awaken on a cold November Monday, they are all stirred by the feeling that 'something is going to happen.' When they open the front door together, they discover, to their surprise and delight, the first snow of winter. . . . Rhythm and repetition empower short, simple sentences, skillfully paced to build anticipation. The rounded shapes and muted hues of Stock's watercolor paintings enhance the story's sense of homey security, and contrast successfully with the snowy white double-page spread which serves as its climax." SLJ

A tiger called Thomas; pictures by Catherine Stock. Lothrop, Lee & Shepard Bks. 1988 c1963 unp il lib bdg $12.88   E

1. Halloween—Fiction
ISBN 0-688-06697-6   LC 86-20878

A newly illustrated edition of the title first published 1963

"Shy Thomas thinks that no one in his new neighborhood will like him, so he just sits on his new porch and watches, instead of trying to make friends—until Halloween night. Dressed in his tiger outfit, Thomas makes his first foray into the new neighborhood . . . and returns—surprised—with a whole passel of new friends." SLJ

"The story has a simple but satisfying plot, light writing style, and a gentle message." Bull Cent Child Books

When the wind stops; illustrated by Stefano Vitale. rev and newly illustrated ed. HarperCollins Pubs. 1995 unp il $14.95; lib bdg $14.89   E

1. Nature—Fiction
ISBN 0-06-026971-5; 0-06-026972-3 (lib bdg)
LC 94-14477

A revised and newly illustrated edition of the title first published 1962 by Abelard-Schuman

A mother explains to her son that in nature an end is also a beginning as day gives way to night, winter ends and spring begins, and, after it stops falling, rain makes clouds for other storms

"The full-color scenes, painted on wood, gloriously depict heaven and earth and give concrete meaning to abstract concepts. Not only wonderful for lap sharing, this beautiful book will also be a rich supplement for a science unit on the elements or the seasons." Booklist

William's doll; pictures by William Pène Du Bois. Harper & Row 1972 30p il $14.95; lib bdg $14.89; pa $4.95   E

1. Dolls—Fiction 2. Sex role—Fiction
ISBN 0-06-027047-0; 0-06-027048-9 (lib bdg); 0-06-443067-7 (pa)

When little William asks for a doll, the other boys scorn him and his father tries to interest him in conventional boys' playthings such as a basketball and a train. His sympathetic grandmother buys him the doll, explaining his need to have it to love and care for so that he can practice being a father

"Very, very special. The strong, yet delicate pictures . . . convey a gentleness of spirit and longing most effectively, as William pantomimes his craving." N Y Times Book Rev

AUTHOR, TITLE, SUBJECT AND ANALYTICAL INDEX

This index to the books in the Classified Catalog includes author, title, subject, and analytical entries; added entries for publishers' series, illustrators, joint authors, and editors of works entered under title; and name and subject cross-references, all arranged in one alphabet.

The number in bold face type at the end of each entry refers to the Dewey Decimal Classification or to the Fiction, Story Collection, or Easy Books section where the main entry for the book will be found. Works classed in 92 will be found under the name of the person written about. The parenthetical notation following the title of a work indicates the grade level at which the item is likely to be of interest.

For further directions for use of this index and for examples of entries, see How to Use Children's Catalog.

1 hunter. Hutchins, P.   E
3-2-1 Contact   505
The 3-D paper book. Tofts, H.   745.54
4B goes wild. Gilson, J.   Fic
4th of July See Fourth of July
6th grade can really kill you. DeClements, B.
                                                   Fic
12 ways to get to 11. Merriam, E.   510
The 13th clue. Jonas, A.   E
A 16th century mosque. Macdonald, F.
                                                   297
17 kings and 42 elephants. Mahy, M.   E
18th century clothing. Kalman, B.   391
The 18th emergency. Byars, B. C.   Fic
19th century clothing. Kalman, B.   391
25 birds every child should know, Crinkle-
    root's. Arnosky, J.   598
25 fish every child should know, Crinkleroot's.
    Arnosky, J.   597
25 great moments. Ward, G. C.   796.357
The 25¢ miracle. Nelson, T.   Fic
26 letters and 99 cents. Hoban, T.   E
50 simple things kids can do to recycle (4 and
    up)   363.7
50 simple things kids can do to save the earth
    (4 and up)   363.7
75 years of Children's Book Week posters
                                              808.06
101 science tricks. Richards, R.   507.8
101 things to do with a baby. Ormerod, J.
                                                   E
201 awesome, magical, bizarre & incredible
    experiments, Janice VanCleave's. Van-
    Cleave, J. P.   507.8
The 329th friend. Sharmat, M. W.   E
The 500 hats of Bartholomew Cubbins. Seuss,
    Dr.   E
1,000 miles in 12 days. Hautzig, D.   796.6
The 11:59. McKissack, P. C.
    In McKissack, P. C. The dark-thirty p35-
    42   S C
1400-1499 (15th century) See Fifteenth century
1492 blues. Priore, F. V.
    In Holiday plays round the year p229-38
                                              812.008

2095. Scieszka, J. See note under Scieszka, J.
    Knights of the kitchen table   Fic

A

The A B C bunny. Gág, W.   E
A.B.C.'s See Alphabet
A B Cedar. Lyon, G. E.   E
A, B, see!. Hoban, T.   E
A-hunting we will go. See Langstaff, J. M. Oh,
    a-hunting we will go   782.42
A.I.D.S. (Disease) See AIDS (Disease)
A my name is Alice. Bayer, J.   E
A. Nonny Mouse writes again! (1-3)
                                              808.81
A to Zen. Wells, R.   495.6
A to zoo. Lima, C. W.   011.6
A was an archer and shot at a frog
    In A Nursery companion p10-15
                                              820.8
AAAS See American Association for the Ad-
    vancement of Science
AACR See Anglo-American cataloguing rules
Aamodt, Alice
    (jt. auth) Johnson, S. A. Wolf pack
                                              599.74
Aardema, Verna
    Anansi finds a fool (k-3)   398.2
    Bimwili & the Zimwi (k-3)   398.2
    Borreguita and the coyote (k-3)   398.2
    Bringing the rain to Kapiti Plain (k-3)
                                              398.2
    Misoso (3-5)   398.2
    Contents: Leelee Goro; Anansi and the phantom food;
    The Boogey Man's wife; Half-a-Ball-of-Kenki; The hen and
    the dove; The Sloogey Dog and the stolen aroma; The cock
    and the jackal; No, Boconono!; Toad's trick; Goso the
    teacher; Hapendeki and Binti the Bibi; Kindai and the ape
    Oh, Kojo! How could you! (k-3)   398.2
    Rabbit makes a monkey of lion (k-3)
                                              398.2
    Traveling to Tondo (k-3)   398.2
    What's so funny, Ketu? (k-3)   398.2
    Who's in Rabbit's house? (k-3)   398.2
    Why mosquitoes buzz in people's ears (k-3)
                                              398.2

Adler, David A., 1947——Continued

Cam Jansen and the mystery of the circus clown. See note under Adler, D. A. Cam Jansen and the mystery of the stolen diamonds **Fic**

Cam Jansen and the mystery of the dinosaur bones. See note under Adler, D. A. Cam Jansen and the mystery of the stolen diamonds **Fic**

Cam Jansen and the mystery of the gold coins. See note under Adler, D. A. Cam Jansen and the mystery of the stolen diamonds **Fic**

Cam Jansen and the mystery of the monster movie. See note under Adler, D. A. Cam Jansen and the mystery of the stolen diamonds **Fic**

Cam Jansen and the mystery of the stolen corn popper. See note under Adler, D. A. Cam Jansen and the mystery of the stolen diamonds **Fic**

Cam Jansen and the mystery of the stolen diamonds (2-4) **Fic**

Cam Jansen and the mystery of the television dog. See note under Adler, D. A. Cam Jansen and the mystery of the stolen diamonds **Fic**

Cam Jansen and the mystery of the UFO. See note under Adler, D. A. Cam Jansen and the mystery of the stolen diamonds **Fic**

Cam Jansen and the Triceratops Pops mystery. See note under Adler, D. A. Cam Jansen and the mystery of the stolen diamonds **Fic**

The carsick zebra and other animal riddles (1-3) **793.73**

Child of the Warsaw ghetto (3-5) **940.53**

Hilde and Eli, children of the Holocaust (3-5) **940.53**

Jackie Robinson: he was the first (2-4) **92**

Martin Luther King, Jr.: free at last (2-4) **92**

Our Golda: the story of Golda Meir (3-5) **92**

A picture book of Abraham Lincoln (1-3) **92**

A picture book of Anne Frank (1-3) **92**

A picture book of Benjamin Franklin (1-3) **92**

A picture book of Christopher Columbus (1-3) **92**

A picture book of Eleanor Roosevelt (1-3) **92**

A picture book of Harriet Tubman (1-3) **92**

A picture book of Helen Keller (1-3) **92**

A picture book of Jackie Robinson (1-3) **92**

A picture book of Jesse Owens (1-3) **92**

A picture book of John F. Kennedy (1-3) **92**

A picture book of Martin Luther King, Jr. (1-3) **92**

A picture book of Rosa Parks (1-3) **92**

A picture book of Sojourner Truth (1-3) **92**

A picture book of Thomas Jefferson (1-3) **92**

Roman numerals (2-4) **513**

A teacher on roller skates and other school riddles (1-3) **793.73**

Thomas Alva Edison (2-4) **92**

The twisted witch, and other spooky riddles (1-3) **793.73**

(jt. auth). Cam Jansen and the mystery of the stolen diamonds **Fic**

Adoff, Arnold, 1935-

All the colors of the race: poems (4-6) **811**

Black is brown is tan **E**

Eats: poems **811**

In for winter, out for spring (k-3) **811**

Malcolm X (2-5) **92**

Sports pages (4 and up) **811**

Street music **811**

(ed) I am the darker brother. See I am the darker brother **811.008**

(ed) My black me. See My black me **811.008**

Adolescence

Bourgeois, P. Changes in you and me: a book about puberty, mostly for boys (4 and up) **612.6**

Bourgeois, P. Changes in you and me: a book about puberty, mostly for girls (4 and up) **612.6**

Madaras, L. The what's happening to my body? book for boys: a growing up guide for parents and sons (4 and up) **613.9**

Madaras, L. The what's happening to my body? book for girls: a growing up guide for parents and daughters (4 and up) **613.9**

Fiction

Blume, J. Are you there God? it's me, Margaret (5 and up) **Fic**

Hall, L. Dagmar Schultz and the angel Edna (6 and up) **Fic**

Adopted by the eagles. Goble, P. **398.2**

Adoption

Banish, R. A forever family (k-3) **362.7**

Krementz, J. How it feels to be adopted (4 and up) **362.7**

Rogers, F. Adoption (k-2) **362.7**

Fiction

Adler, C. S. Youn Hee and me (4-6) **Fic**

Caines, J. F. Abby **E**

Keller, H. Horace **E**

Magorian, M. Good night, Mr. Tom (6 and up) **Fic**

Myers, W. D. Me, Mop, and the Moondance Kid (4-6) **Fic**

Sachs, M. What my sister remembered (5 and up) **Fic**

Turner, A. W. Through moon and stars and night skies **E**

Adoption, Interracial See Interracial adoption

Adventure and adventurers
  Rappaport, D. Living dangerously (4 and up) **920**
Dictionaries
Saari, P. Explorers & discoverers
  920.003
Fiction
  See Adventure fiction
Adventure fiction
  See also Science fiction; Sea stories
  Alcock, V. Singer to the sea god (6 and up) **Fic**
  Alexander, L. The Beggar Queen (5 and up) **Fic**
  Alexander, L. The Illyrian adventure (5 and up) **Fic**
  Alexander, L. The marvelous misadventures of Sebastian (4 and up) **Fic**
  Alexander, L. The remarkable journey of Prince Jen (5 and up) **Fic**
  Alexander, L. Westmark (5 and up) **Fic**
  Fleischman, S. The whipping boy (5 and up) **Fic**
  Naylor, P. R. The grand escape (4-6) **Fic**
  Snyder, Z. K. Song of the gargoyle (5 and up) **Fic**
Adventure in space. Scott, E. **522**
An **Adventure** in the Amazon (3-6) **508**
The **adventure** of the German student. San Souci, R.
  In San Souci, R Short & shivery p96-102 **398.2**
Adventures in time books [series]
  Donahue, J. An island far from home **Fic**
  Neuberger, A. E. The girl-son **Fic**
The **adventures** of a fisher lad. Quayle, E.
  In Quayle, E. The shining princess, and other Japanese legends p57-68 **398.2**
The **adventures** of Ali Baba Bernstein. Hurwitz, J. **Fic**
The **Adventures** of Haroun-al-Raschid, Caliph of Bagdad
  In The Arabian nights entertainments p316-19 **398.2**
The **adventures** of High John the Conqueror. Sanfield, S. **398.2**
The **adventures** of Huckleberry Finn. Twain, M. **Fic**
The **adventures** of Isabel. Nash, O. **811**
The **Adventures** of Jack and Jill and Old Dame Gill
  In A Nursery companion p38-39 **820.8**
The **adventures** of Little Mouse. Mahy, M.
  In Mahy, M. Tick tock tales p24-30 **S C**
The **adventures** of Obadiah. Turkle, B. C. See note under Turkle, B. C. Obadiah the Bold **E**

The **adventures** of Pinocchio. Collodi, C. **Fic**
The **Adventures** of Prince Camaralzaman and the Princess Badoura
  In The Arabian nights entertainments p216-66 **398.2**
The **adventures** of Taxi Dog. Barracca, D. **E**
The **adventures** of Tom Sawyer. Twain, M. **Fic**
The **adventures** of Tom Sawyer [excerpt]. Twain, M.
  In The Random House book of humor for children p293-300 **817.008**
Adventuring with books **011.6**
Adventurous spirit: a story about Ellen Swallow Richards. Vare, E. A. **92**
Advertising
  See/See also pages in the following book(s):
  Schmitt, L. Smart spending p1-13 (5 and up) **640.73**
Advice for a frog and other poems. Schertle, A. **811**
Advocate. See The New Advocate **028.505**
AECT *See* Association for Educational Communications and Technology
Aeken, Hieronymus van *See* Bosch, Hieronymus, d. 1516
Aeneas (Legendary character)
  See/See also pages in the following book(s):
  Hamilton, E. Mythology p319-42 (6 and up) **292**
Aeronautics
  See also Airplanes; Airships; Flight; Rocketry
  The Visual dictionary of flight (4 and up) **629.133**
Flights
Burleigh, R. Flight: the journey of Charles Lindbergh (2-4) **92**
Taylor, R. L. The first unrefueled flight around the world (4 and up) **629.13**
History
Berliner, D. Before the Wright brothers (5 and up) **629.13**
Boyne, W. J. The Smithsonian book of flight for young people (4 and up) **629.13**
Freedman, R. The Wright brothers: how they invented the airplane (5 and up) **92**
Gibbons, G. Flying (k-3) **629.13**
Nahum, A. Flying machine (4 and up) **629.133**
Parker, S. The Wright brothers and aviation (4 and up) **92**
Aeronautics, High speed *See* High speed aeronautics
Aesop
  Aesop's fables [illus. by Heidi Holder] **398.2**
  Aesop's fables [illus. by Lisbeth Zwerger] **398.2**

Aesop—*Continued*

Brett, J. Town mouse, country mouse
    398.2

Clark, M. The best of Aesop's fables
    398.2

Craig, H. The town mouse and the country mouse
    398.2

Galdone, P. Three Aesop fox fables
    398.2

McClintock, B. Animal fables from Aesop
    398.2

Paxton, T. Aesop's fables   **398.2**

Paxton, T. Androcles and the lion and other Aesop's fables
    398.2

Paxton, T. Belling the cat and other Aesop's fables
    398.2

Paxton, T. Birds of a feather and other Aesop's fables
    398.2

Stevens, J. The town mouse and the country mouse
    398.2

Aesop's fables. Paxton, T.   **398.2**

Aesop's fables [illus. by Heidi Holder]. Aesop
    398.2

Aesop's fables [illus. by Lisbeth Zwerger]. Aesop
    398.2

Aesthetics

    See also Art appreciation

Afanas´ev, A. N. (Aleksandr Nikolaevich), 1826-1871

Russian fairy tales (4 and up)   **398.2**
Contents: The wondrous wonder, the marvelous marvel; The fox physician; The death of the cock; Misery; The castle of the fly; The turnip; Riddles; The enchanted ring; The just reward; Salt; The golden slipper; Emelya the simpleton; The three kingdoms; The pike with the long teeth; The bad wife; The miser; The nobleman and the peasant; Ivanushka the Little Fool; The crane and the heron; Aliosha Popovich; The fox confessor; The bear; The spider; Baba Yaga and the brave youth; Prince Ivan and Princess Martha; The cat, the cock, and the fox; Baldak Borisievich; Know Not; The magic shirt; The three pennies; The princess who wanted to solve riddles; A soldier's riddle; The dead body; The frog princess; The speedy messenger; Vasilisa, the priest's daughter; The wise maiden and the seven robbers; The mayoress; Ivan the Simpleton; Father Nicholas and the thief; Burenshka, the little red cow; The jester; The precious hide; The cross is pledged as security; The daydreamer; The taming of the shrew; Quarrelsome Demyan; The magic box; Bukhtan Bukhtanovich; The fox and the woodcock; The fox and the crane; The two rivers; Nodey, the priest's grandson; The poor wretch; The fiddler in hell; The old woman who ran away; The singing tree and the talking bird; The ram who lost half his skin; The fox, as midwife; The fox, the hare, and the cock; Baba Yaga; The ram, the cat, and the twelve wolves; The fox and the woodpecker; The snotty goat; Right and wrong; The potter; The self-playing gusla; Marco the Rich and Vasily the Luckless; Ivanko the bear's son; The secret ball; The indiscreet wife; The cheater cheated; The Maiden Tsar; Ivan the Cow's Son; The wolf and the goat; The wise little girl; Danilo the Luckless; Ivan the peasant's son and thumb-sized man; Death of a miser; The footless champion and the handless champion; Old favors are soon forgotten; The sheep, the fox, and the wolf; The brave laborer; Daughter and stepdaughter; The stubborn wife; Snow White and the fox; Foma Berennikov; The peasant, the bear, and the fox; Good advice; Horns; The armless maiden; Frolka Stay-at-Home; The milk of wild beasts; How a husband weaned his wife from fairy tales; The cock and the hen; The fox and the lobster; Nikita the Tanner; The wolf; The goat shedding on one side; The bold knight, the apples of youth, and the water of life; Two out of the sack; The man who did not know fear; The merchant's daughter and the maidservant; The priest's laborer; The peasant and the corpse; The arrant fool; Lutoniushka; Barter; The grumbling old woman; The white duck; If you

don't like it don't listen; The magic swan geese; Prince Danila Govorila; The wicked sisters; The princess who never smiled; Baba Yaga; Jack Frost; Husband and wife; Little Sister Fox and the wolf; The three kingdoms, copper, silver, and golden; The cock and the hand mill; Tereschichka; King Bear; Magic; The one-eyed evil; Sister Alionushka, brother Ivanushka; The seven Semyons; The merchant's daughter and the slanderer; The robbers; The lazy maiden; The miraculous pipe; The Sea King and Vasilisa the Wise; The fox as mourner; Vasilisa the Beautiful; The bun; The foolish wolf; The bear, the dog, and the cat; The bear and the cock; Dawn, Evening, and Midnight; Two Ivans, soldier's sons; Prince Ivan and Byely Polyanin; The crystal mountain; Koshchey the Deathless; The Firebird and Princess Vasilisa; Beasts in a pit; The dog and the woodpecker; Two kinds of luck; Go I know not whither—fetch I know not what; The wise wife; The goldfish; The golden-bristled pig, the golden-feathered duck, and the golden-maned mare; The duck with golden eggs; Elena the Wise; Treasure-trove; Maria Morevna; The soldier and the king; The sorceress; Ilya Muromets and the dragon; The devil who was a potter; Clever answers; Dividing the goose; The feather of Finist, the Bright Falcon; The Sun, the Moon, and the Raven; The bladder, the straw, and the shoe; The thief; The vampire; The beggar's plan; Woman's way; The foolish German; The enchanted princess; The raven and the lobster; Prince Ivan, the firebird, and the gray wolf; Shemiaka the judge

Afanas´ev, Aleksandr Nikolaevich *See* Afanas´ev, A. N. (Aleksandr Nikolaevich), 1826-1871

Africa

Exploration
Ibazebo, I. Exploration into Africa (4-6)
    960

Fiction
Greenfield, E. Africa dream   **E**

Grifalconi, A. Darkness and the butterfly
    E

Olaleye, I. Bitter bananas   **E**

Steptoe, J. Birthday   **E**

Walter, M. P. Brother to the wind   **E**

Williams, K. L. When Africa was home
    E

Folklore
See Folklore—Africa

History
See/See also pages in the following book(s):
The World in 1492 p67-95 (5 and up)
    909

Natural history
See Natural history—Africa

Social life and customs
Chiasson, J. C. African journey (4 and up)
    960

Musgrove, M. Ashanti to Zulu: African traditions (3-6)   **960**

Social life and customs—Dictionaries
Haskins, J. From Afar to Zulu (4 and up)
    960

Africa, East *See* East Africa

Africa, North *See* North Africa

Africa, South *See* South Africa

Africa dream. Greenfield, E.   **E**

Africa in literature

Bibliography
Khorana, M. Africa in literature for children and young adults   **016.9**

Africa in literature for children and young adults. Khorana, M.   **016.9**

African Americans—Fiction—*Continued*

Hamilton, V. The house of Dies Drear (5 and up)   Fic

Hamilton, V. M. C. Higgins the great (6 and up)   Fic

Hamilton, V. The mystery of Drear House (5 and up)   Fic

Hamilton, V. Plain City (5 and up)   Fic

Hamilton, V. The planet of Junior Brown (6 and up)   Fic

Hamilton, V. Willie Bea and the time the Martians landed (5 and up)   Fic

Hamilton, V. Zeely (4 and up)   Fic

Hansen, J. The gift-giver (4-6)   Fic

Hansen, J. Which way freedom? (5 and up)   Fic

Havill, J. Jamaica's find   E

Hill, E. S. Evan's corner   E

Hoffman, M. Amazing Grace   E

Hooks, W. H. The ballad of Belle Dorcas (3-5)   Fic

Howard, E. F. Aunt Flossie's hats (and crab cakes later)   E

Howard, E. F. Chita's Christmas tree   E

Howard, E. F. The train to Lulu's   E

Isadora, R. Ben's trumpet   E

Johnson, A. Do like Kyla   E

Johnson, A. Tell me a story, Mama   E

Konigsburg, E. L. Jennifer, Hecate, Macbeth, William McKinley, and me, Elizabeth (4-6)   Fic

Kroll, V. L. Masai and I   E

Lexau, J. M. The rooftop mystery   E

Lyons, M. E. Letters from a slave girl (6 and up)   Fic

Mathis, S. B. Sidewalk story (3-5)   Fic

McKissack, P. C. The dark-thirty (4 and up)   S C

McKissack, P. C. Flossie & the fox   E

McKissack, P. C. A million fish—more or less   E

McKissack, P. C. Mirandy and Brother Wind   E

Mitchell, M. K. Uncle Jed's barbershop   E

Myers, W. D. Fast Sam, Cool Clyde, and Stuff (6 and up)   Fic

Peterson, J. W. My mama sings   E

Petry, A. L. Tituba of Salem Village (6 and up)   Fic

Pinkney, A. D. Hold fast to dreams (5 and up)   Fic

Pinkney, G. J. Back home   E

Pinkney, G. J. The Sunday outing   E

Polacco, P. Mrs. Katz and Tush   E

Raschka, C. Yo! Yes?   E

Ringgold, F. Tar Beach   E

Robinet, H. G. If you please, President Lincoln (5 and up)   Fic

Rosen, M. J. A school for Pompey Walker   Fic

San Souci, R. Sukey and the mermaid (1-4)   398.2

Schroeder, A. Carolina shout!   E

Schroeder, A. Ragtime Tumpie   E

Sebestyen, O. Words by heart (5 and up)   Fic

Slote, A. Finding Buck McHenry (4-6)   Fic

Steptoe, J. Birthday   E

Steptoe, J. Stevie   E

Stolz, M. Go fish (2-4)   Fic

Tate, E. E. Thank you, Dr. Martin Luther King, Jr.! (4 and up)   Fic

Taylor, M. D. The friendship (4 and up)   Fic

Taylor, M. D. The gold Cadillac (4 and up)   Fic

Taylor, M. D. Let the circle be unbroken (4 and up)   Fic

Taylor, M. D. Mississippi bridge (4 and up)   Fic

Taylor, M. D. The road to Memphis (4 and up)   Fic

Taylor, M. D. Roll of thunder, hear my cry (4 and up)   Fic

Taylor, M. D. Song of the trees (4 and up)   Fic

Taylor, M. D. The well (4 and up)   Fic

Udry, J. M. What Mary Jo shared   E

Voigt, C. Come a stranger (6 and up)   Fic

Wagner, J. J. T. (3-6)   Fic

Walter, M. P. Justin and the best biscuits in the world (3-6)   Fic

Walter, M. P. Mariah keeps cool (3-6)   Fic

Walter, M. P. My mama needs me   E

Williams, S. A. Working cotton   E

Williams, V. B. Cherries and cherry pits   E

Winter, J. Follow the drinking gourd   E

Woodson, J. I hadn't meant to tell you this (6 and up)   Fic

Wyeth, S. D. Always my Dad   E

Yarbrough, C. Cornrows   E

Yarbrough, C. The shimmershine queens (4-6)   Fic

Folklore

Bang, M. Wiley and the Hairy Man (1-4)   398.2

Faulkner, W. J. Brer Tiger and the big wind (k-3)   398.2

Hamilton, V. The people could fly: American black folktales (4 and up)   398.2

Haskins, J. The headless haunt and other African-American ghost stories (4 and up)   398.2

Lester, J. Further tales of Uncle Remus (4-6)   398.2

Lester, J. John Henry (k-3)   398.2

Lester, J. The knee-high man, and other tales (k-3)   398.2

Lester, J. The last tales of Uncle Remus (4-6)   398.2

Lester, J. More tales of Uncle Remus (4-6)   398.2

Lester, J. The tales of Uncle Remus (4-6)   398.2

Aher, Jackie
(il) Madaras, L. The what's happening to my body? book for boys: a growing up guide for parents and sons **613.9**
(il) Madaras, L. The what's happening to my body? book for girls: a growing up guide for parents and daughters **613.9**

Ahlberg, Allan
The black cat. See note under Ahlberg, J. Funnybones **E**
Dinosaur dreams. See note under Ahlberg, J. Funnybones **E**
The ghost train. See note under Ahlberg, J. Funnybones **E**
Mystery tour. See note under Ahlberg, J. Funnybones **E**
The pet shop. See note under Ahlberg, J. Funnybones **E**
Skeleton crew. See note under Ahlberg, J. Funnybones **E**
Ten in a bed (3-5) **Fic**
(jt. auth) Ahlberg, J. The baby's catalogue **E**
(jt. auth) Ahlberg, J. Each peach pear plum **E**
(jt. auth) Ahlberg, J. Funnybones **E**
(jt. auth) Ahlberg, J. It was a dark and stormy night **Fic**
(jt. auth) Ahlberg, J. Peek-a-boo! **E**

Ahlberg, Janet
The baby's catalogue **E**
Each peach pear plum **E**
Funnybones **E**
It was a dark and stormy night (2-4) **Fic**
Peek-a-boo! **E**

Aïda. Price, L. **792.5**

AIDS (Disease)
Greenberg, L. AIDS (4 and up) **616.97**
Hausherr, R. Children and the AIDS virus (1-3) **616.97**
Moutoussamy-Ashe, J. Daddy and me: a photo story of Arthur Ashe and his daughter, Camera (k-3) **92**
See/See also pages in the following book(s):
Ashabranner, B. K. People who make a difference p41-46 (5 and up) **920**
Facklam, H. Viruses p41-47 (5 and up) **576**
Fry, V. L. Part of me died, too p133-58 (5 and up) **155.9**
Fiction
Fox, P. The eagle kite (6 and up) **Fic**
Nelson, T. Earthshine (5 and up) **Fic**
Newman, L. Too far away to touch **E**
Personal narratives
White, R. Ryan White: my own story (5 and up) **92**

Aiiieeeeeeeeeee!. Rockwell, T.
In Rockwell, T. How to eat fried worms, and other plays p79-107 **812**

Aiken, Joan, 1924-
A foot in the grave (6 and up) **S C**
Contents: Cold harbour; Movable eyes; Beezlebub's baby; A foot in the grave; Light work; An ill wind; Bindweed; Amberland

Give yourself a fright: thirteen tales of the supernatural (6 and up) **S C**
Contents: Wing Quack Flap; The old poet; Do not alight here; The lame king; The jealous apprentice; A rhyme for silver; The ill-natured muse; The Erl King's daughter; The end of silence; The King of Nowhere; Aunt Susan; Find me; Give yourself a fright

Is underground. See note under Aiken, J. The wolves of Willoughby Chase **Fic**
Midnight is a place (5 and up) **Fic**
Think of a word
In The Oxford treasury of children's stories p82-90 **S C**
The wolves of Willoughby Chase (5 and up) **Fic**

Ailey, Alvin
About
Pinkney, A. D. Alvin Ailey (k-3) **92**

Air
Branley, F. M. Air is all around you (k-1) **551.5**
Devonshire, H. Air (3-5) **533**
Robbins, K. Air (4-6) **551.5**
Experiments
Ardley, N. The science book of air (3-5) **507.8**
White, L. B. Air (2-4) **507.8**

Air is all around you. Branley, F. M. **551.5**

Air pilots
See also African American pilots; Women air pilots
Burleigh, R. Flight: the journey of Charles Lindbergh (2-4) **92**
Demarest, C. L. Lindbergh (k-3) **92**
Levinson, N. S. Chuck Yeager: the man who broke the sound barrier (5 and up) **92**
Provensen, A. The glorious flight: across the Channel with Louis Blériot, July 25, 1909 (1-4) **92**

Air pollution
See/See also pages in the following book(s):
Langone, J. Our endangered earth p28-36 (6 and up) **363.7**

Air raid—Pearl Harbor!. Taylor, T. **940.54**

Airborne: the triumph and struggle of Michael Jordan. Kornbluth, J. **92**

Airmail to the moon. Birdseye, T. **E**

Airplanes
Barton, B. Airplanes (k-1) **387.7**
Barton, B. Airport (k-1) **387.7**
Johnstone, M. Planes (4 and up) **629.133**
Magee, D. Let's fly from A to Z (k-2) **629.133**
Maynard, C. Airplane (k-3) **629.136**
Parker, S. What's inside airplanes? **629.133**
Rockwell, A. F. Planes (k-1) **629.133**
The Visual dictionary of flight (4 and up) **629.133**

Alcott, Louisa May, 1832-1888—*Continued*
An old-fashioned Thanksgiving (3-5)   **Fic**
Rose in bloom. See note under Alcott, L. M.
Little women   **Fic**
See/See also pages in the following book(s):
Faber, D. Great lives: American literature
p91-99 (5 and up)   **920**
Krull, K. Lives of the writers p52-55 (4 and
up)   **920**
Aldiborontiphoskyphorniostikos. Stennet, R.
In A Nursery companion p108-12
820.8
Aldo. Burningham, J.   **E**
Aldo Applesauce. Hurwitz, J. See note under
Hurwitz, J. Much ado about Aldo
Fic
Aldo Ice Cream. Hurwitz, J. See note under
Hurwitz, J. Much ado about Aldo
Fic
Aldo Peanut Butter. Hurwitz, J. See note un-
der Hurwitz, J. Much ado about Aldo
Fic
Alef-bet. Edwards, M.   **492.4**
Aleichem, Sholem *See* Sholem Aleichem,
1859-1916
Alex and the cat. Griffith, H. V.   **E**
Alexander, the Great, 356-323 B.C.
See/See also pages in the following book(s):
Coolidge, O. E. The golden days of Greece
p178-95 (4-6)   **938**
Alexander, David, 1956-
(il) Mahy, M. My mysterious world   **92**
Alexander, Ellen
Llama and the great flood (1-3)   **398.2**
(il) Hawes, J. Fireflies in the night
595.7
Alexander, Lloyd
The Arkadians (5 and up)   **Fic**
The Beggar Queen (5 and up)   **Fic**
The Big book for peace. See The Big book
for peace   **810.8**
The black cauldron. See note under Alexan-
der, L. The book of three   **Fic**
The book of three (5 and up)   **Fic**
The castle of Llyr. See note under Alexan-
der, L. The book of three   **Fic**
The Cat-king's daughter
In Valentine's Day: stories and poems
p51-70   **810.8**
The cat who wished to be a man (4-6)
Fic
The Drackenberg adventure. See note under
Alexander, L. The Illyrian adventure
Fic
The El Dorado adventure. See note under
Alexander, L. The Illyrian adventure
Fic
The fortune-tellers   **E**
The High King (5 and up)   **Fic**
The Illyrian adventure (5 and up)   **Fic**
The Jedera adventure. See note under Alex-
ander, L. The Illyrian adventure   **Fic**
The marvelous misadventures of Sebastian
(4 and up)   **Fic**

The Philadelphia adventure. See note under
Alexander, L. The Illyrian adventure
Fic
The remarkable journey of Prince Jen (5
and up)   **Fic**
Taran Wanderer. See note under Alexander,
L. The book of three   **Fic**
The two brothers
In The Big book for peace p6-16
810.8
Westmark (5 and up)   **Fic**
See/See also pages in the following book(s):
Newbery and Caldecott Medal books, 1966-
1975 p48-55   **028.5**
Alexander, Martha G.
Blackboard Bear. See note under Alexander,
M. G. You're a genius, Blackboard Bear
E
How my library grew, by Dinah   **E**
I sure am glad to see you, Blackboard Bear.
See note under Alexander, M. G. You're
a genius, Blackboard Bear   **E**
Nobody asked me if I wanted a baby sister
E
When the new baby comes, I'm moving out
E
You're a genius, Blackboard Bear   **E**
Alexander, Sally Hobart
Mom can't see me (3-5)   **362.4**
Mom's best friend (3-5)   **362.4**
Alexander and the terrible, horrible, no good,
very bad day. Viorst, J.   **E**
Alexander and the wind-up mouse. Lionni, L.
E
Alexander Graham Bell and the telephone.
Parker, S.   **92**
Alexander, who is not (do you hear me?) going
(I mean it) to move. Viorst, J. See note
under Viorst, J. Alexander and the terri-
ble, horrible, no good, very bad day
E
Alexander, who used to be rich last Sunday.
Viorst, J. See note under Viorst, J. Alex-
ander and the terrible, horrible, no good,
very bad day   **E**
Al(exandra) the Great. Greene, C. C. See note
under Greene, C. C. A girl called Al
Fic
Alexeieff, Alexander, 1901-1982
(il) Afanas'ev, A. N. Russian fairy tales
398.2
Alfie gets in first. Hughes, S.   **E**
Alfie gives a hand. Hughes, S. See note under
Hughes, S. Alfie gets in first   **E**
Alfie's feet. Hughes, S. See note under Hughes,
S. Alfie gets in first   **E**
The **Alfred** summer. Slepian, J.   **Fic**
Alger, Leclaire *See* Leodhas, Sorche Nic,
1898-1968
Algeria
Algeria—in pictures (5 and up)   **965**
Algeria—in pictures (5 and up)   **965**

Algonquian Indians
See also Delaware Indians

Ali, Muhammad, 1942-
See/See also pages in the following book(s):
Littlefield, B. Champions p81-92 (5 and up)
920

Ali Baba and the forty thieves. Philip, N.
In Philip, N. The Arabian nights p131-42
398.2

Ali Baba Bernstein, lost and found. Hurwitz, J. See note under Hurwitz, J. The adventures of Ali Baba Bernstein **Fic**

Alias Madame Doubtfire. Fine, A. **Fic**

Alice in April. Naylor, P. R. See note under Naylor, P. R. The agony of Alice **Fic**

Alice in-between. Naylor, P. R. See note under Naylor, P. R. The agony of Alice **Fic**

Alice in rapture, sort of. Naylor, P. R. See note under Naylor, P. R. The agony of Alice **Fic**

Alice in Wonderland. See Carroll, L. Alice's adventures in Wonderland **Fic**

Alice Nizzy Nazzy, the Witch of Santa Fe. Johnston, T. **E**

Alice the brave. Naylor, P. R. See note under Naylor, P. R. The agony of Alice **Fic**

Alice's adventures in Wonderland. Carroll, L. **Fic**
also in Carroll, L. The complete works of Lewis Carroll p9 120 **828**

Alice's adventures in Wonderland, and Through the looking glass. Carroll, L. **Fic**

Alien secrets. Klause, A. C. **Fic**

Aliens from outer space *See* Extraterrestrial beings

Aliens in the family. Mahy, M. **Fic**

Aliki
At Mary Bloom's. See note under Aliki. Overnight at Mary Bloom's **E**
Communication (k-3) **302.2**
Corn is maize (k-3) **633.1**
Digging up dinosaurs (k-3) **567.9**
Dinosaur bones (k-3) **567.9**
Dinosaurs are different (k-3) **567.9**
Feelings (k-3) **152.4**
Fossils tell of long ago (k-3) **560**
The gods and goddesses of Olympus (2-5) **292**
How a book is made (2-5) **686**
I'm growing! (k-1) **612.6**
The King's day: Louis XIV of France (2-5) **92**
Manners (k-3) **395**
The many lives of Benjamin Franklin (k-3) **92**
A medieval feast (2-5) **394.1**
Milk from cow to carton (k-3) **637**
My feet (k-1) **612**
My five senses (k-1) **612.8**
My hands (k-1) **612**
My visit to the aquarium (k-3) **639.3**
Overnight at Mary Bloom's **E**

The story of Johnny Appleseed (k-3) **92**
The two of them **E**
Use your head, dear **E**
We are best friends **E**
A weed is a flower: the life of George Washington Carver (k-3) **92**
Welcome, little baby **E**
Wild and woolly mammoths (k-3) **569**
(il) Brandenberg, F. Aunt Nina and her nephews and nieces **E**
(il) Brandenberg, F. Leo and Emily **E**
(il) Brandenberg, F. Nice new neighbors **E**
(il) Cole, J. Evolution **575**
(il) Heilbroner, J. This is the house where Jack lives **E**
(il) Home. See Home **810.8**
(il) Showers, P. The listening walk **E**

Aliosha Popovich. Afanas'ev, A. N.
In Afanas'ev, A. N. Russian fairy tales p67-71 **398.2**

Alison's zinnia. Lobel, A. **E**

Alistair and the alien invasion. Sadler, M. See note under Sadler, M. Alistair's elephant **E**

Alistair in outer space. Sadler, M. See note under Sadler, M. Alistair's elephant **E**

Alistair underwater. Sadler, M. See note under Sadler, M. Alistair's elephant **E**

Alistair's elephant. Sadler, M. **E**

Alistair's time machine. Sadler, M. See note under Sadler, M. Alistair's elephant **E**

All aboard!. Stevenson, J. See note under Stevenson, J. The Sea View Hotel **E**

All aboard overnight. Maestro, B. **428**

All about allergies. Terkel, S. N. **616.97**

All about alligators. Arnosky, J. **597.9**

All about asthma. Ostrow, W. **616.2**

All about basketball. Sullivan, G. **796.323**

All about football. Sullivan, G. **796.332**

All about owls. Arnosky, J. **598**

All about Sam. Lowry, L. See note under Lowry, L. Anastasia Krupnik **Fic**

All about where. Hoban, T. **E**

All-American Girls Professional Baseball League
Galt, M. F. Up to the plate (5 and up) **796.357**

All but Alice. Naylor, P. R. See note under Naylor. P. R. The agony of Alice **Fic**

All day long: fifty rhymes of the never was and always is. McCord, D. T. W. **811**

All God's critters got a place in the choir. Staines, B. **782.42**

All Hallows' Eve *See* Halloween

All I see. Rylant, C. **E**

The all Jahdu storybook. Hamilton, V. **S C**

All join in. Blake, Q. **821**

The **all** new Jonah Twist. Honeycutt, N.
    Fic

All night, all day   **782.25**

All-of-a-kind family. Taylor, S.   Fic

All-of-a-kind family downtown. Taylor, S. See note under Taylor, S. All-of-a-kind family
    Fic

All-of-a-kind family uptown. Taylor, S. See note under Taylor, S. All-of-a-kind family
    Fic

All of our noses are here. Schwartz, A.
    In Schwartz, A. All of our noses are here, and other noodle tales p22-37
    398.2

All of our noses are here, and other noodle tales. Schwartz, A.   **398.2**

All of you was singing. Lewis, R.   **398.2**

All pigs are beautiful. King-Smith, D.
    636.4

All shapes and sizes. Hughes, S.
    In Hughes, S. The nursery collection
    E

All Souls' Day
    Ancona, G. Pablo remembers (k-3)
    394.2
    Hoyt-Goldsmith, D. Day of the Dead (3-5)
    394.2
    Lasky, K. Days of the Dead (4-6)   **394.2**

All the colors of the earth. Hamanaka, S.
    E

All the colors of the race: poems. Adoff, A.
    811

All the king's animals. Kessler, C.   **639.9**

All the places to love. MacLachlan, P.   E

All the small poems and fourteen more. Worth, V.   **811**

All the stars in the sky. Rylant, C.
    In Rylant, C. Children of Christmas p32-38   S C

All times, all peoples: a world history of slavery. Meltzer, M.   **326**

Allard, Harry, 1928-
    Bumps in the night   E
    It's so nice to have a wolf around the house
    In The Laugh book p111-18   **808.8**
    Miss Nelson has a field day. See note under Allard, H. Miss Nelson is missing!   E
    Miss Nelson is back. See note under Allard, H. Miss Nelson is missing!   E
    Miss Nelson is missing!   E

Allegories
    See also Fables
    Adams, R. Watership Down (6 and up)
    Fic
    Avi. Poppy (3-5)   Fic
    Babbitt, N. Kneeknock Rise (4-6)   Fic

Allen, Gary
    (il) George, J. C. One day in the tropical rain forest   **574.5**
    (il) George, J. C. One day in the woods
    574.5

Allen, Jonathan, 1957-
    (il) Mahy, M. The great white man-eating shark   E

Allen, Thomas B., 1928-
    On Granddaddy's farm (1-3)   **630.1**
    (il) Bulla, C. R. The chalk box kid   E
    (il) Cameron, A. The most beautiful place in the world   Fic
    (il) Hendershot, J. In coal country   E
    (il) Jukes, M. Blackberries in the dark
    Fic
    (il) Van Leeuwen, J. Going West   E

Aller, Susan Bivin
    J.M. Barrie: the magic behind Peter Pan (5 and up)   **92**

Allergy
    See also Hay fever
    Seixas, J. S. Allergies (1-3)   **616.97**
    Terkel, S. N. All about allergies (2-4)
    616.97

Allerleirauh. Grimm, J.
    In The Green fairy book p276-81
    398.2
    In Grimm, J. The complete Grimm's fairy tales p326-31   **398.2**

Alley, R. W. (Robert W.)
    (il) Singer, M. Family reunion   **811**

Alley, Robert W. *See* Alley, R. W. (Robert W.)

Alligators
    Arnosky, J. All about alligators (1-3)
    597.9
    George, J. C. The moon of the alligators (3-6)   **597.9**
    Guiberson, B. Z. Spoonbill swamp (k-3)
    591.5
    Lauber, P. Alligators: a success story (3-5)
    597.9
    Patent, D. H. The American alligator (4 and up)   **597.9**
    Staub, F. J. Alligators (2-4)   **597.9**
    Stone, L. M. Alligators and crocodiles (2-4)
    597.9

    Fiction
    Aliki. Use your head, dear   E
    Hurd, T. Mama don't allow   E
    Lionni, L. An extraordinary egg   E
    Minarik, E. H. No fighting, no biting!
    E
    Stevenson, J. Monty   E
    Thomassie, T. Feliciana Feydra LeRoux
    E
    Yep, L. Later, gator (4-6)   Fic

Alligators all around. Sendak, M.   E

Alligators and crocodiles. Stone, L. M.
    597.9

Allison, Diane Worfolk
    (il) Berends, P. B. The case of the elevator duck   Fic

Allison, Linda, 1948-
    Eenie meenie miney math!   **510**
    Gee, Wiz! (4 and up)   **507.8**

Anancy and Dog and Puss and friendship. Berry, J.
In Berry, J. Spiderman Anancy p87-93
398.2

Anancy and friend. Berry, J.
In Berry, J. Spiderman Anancy p36-38
398.2

Anancy and looking for a wife. Berry, J.
In Berry, J. Spiderman Anancy p1-5
398.2

Anancy and storm and the Reverend Man-Cow. Berry, J.
In Berry, J. Spiderman Anancy p78-86
398.2

Anancy and the Hide-Away-Garden. Berry, J.
In Berry, J. Spiderman Anancy p39-44
398.2

Anancy and the making of the Bro title. Berry, J.
In Berry, J. Spiderman Anancy p11-21
398.2

Anancy, Dog and Old Higue Dry-Skull. Berry, J.
In Berry, J. Spiderman Anancy p22-26
398.2

Anancy, Lion and Tiger's last day. Berry, J.
In Berry, J. Spiderman Anancy p116-19
398.2

Anancy, Old Witch and King-Daughter. Berry, J.
In Berry, J. Spiderman Anancy p6-10
398.2

Anancy runs into Tiger's trouble. Berry, J.
In Berry, J. Spiderman Anancy p69-71
398.2

Anancy, Tiger and the Shine-Dancer-Shine. Berry, J.
In Berry, J. Spiderman Anancy p107-15
398.2

Ananse the Spider in search of a fool. Bryan, A.
In Bryan, A. The ox of the wonderful horns and other African folktales p3-10 **398.2**

Anansi (Legendary character)
Aardema, V. Anansi finds a fool (k-3)
398.2
Aardema, V. Oh, Kojo! How could you! (k-3) **398.2**
Berry, J. Spiderman Anancy (5 and up)
398.2
Haley, G. E. A story, a story (k-3)
398.2
Kimmel, E. A. Anansi and the talking melon (k-3) **398.2**
Kimmel, E. A. Anansi goes fishing (k-3)
398.2
McDermott, G. Anansi the spider (k-3)
398.2
Rohmer, H. Brother Anansi and the cattle ranch **398.2**
Temple, F. Tiger soup (k-3) **398.2**

Anansi and Candlefly. Sherlock, Sir P. M.
In Sherlock, Sir P. M. West Indian folktales p97-104 **398.2**

Anansi and his visitor, Turtle. Kaula, E. M.
In The Laugh book p201-03 **808.8**

Anansi and Nothing go hunting for wives. Courlander, H.
In Courlander, H. The cow-tail switch, and other West African stories p95-102 **398.2**

Anansi and Snake the postman. Sherlock, Sir P. M.
In Sherlock, Sir P. M. West Indian folktales p71-76 **398.2**

Anansi and the phantom food. Aardema, V.
In Aardema, V. Misoso p9-13 **398.2**

Anansi and the talking melon. Kimmel, E. A.
398.2

Anansi finds a fool. Aardema, V. **398.2**

Anansi goes fishing. Kimmel, E. A. **398.2**

Anansi hunts with Tiger. Sherlock, Sir P. M.
In Sherlock, Sir P. M. West Indian Folktales p118-24 **398.2**

Anansi rides tiger. Kherdian, D.
In Kherdian, D. Feathers and tails p31-32
398.2

Anansi the spider. McDermott, G. **398.2**

Anansi's fishing expedition. Courlander, H.
In Courlander, H. The cow-tail switch, and other West African stories p47-58
398.2

Anansi's hat-shaking dance. Courlander, H.
In The Scott, Foresman anthology of children's literature p313-14 **808.8**

Anansi's old riding-horse. Sherlock, Sir P. M.
In Sherlock, Sir P. M. West Indian folktales p105-11 **398.2**

Anasazi culture *See* Pueblo Indians

Anastasia, absolutely. Lowry, L. See note under Lowry, L. Anastasia Krupnik **Fic**

Anastasia again!. Lowry, L. See note under Lowry, L. Anastasia Krupnik **Fic**

Anastasia, ask your analyst. Lowry, L. See note under Lowry, L. Anastasia Krupnik
Fic

Anastasia at this address. Lowry, L. See note under Lowry, L. Anastasia Krupnik
Fic

Anastasia at your service. Lowry, L. See note under Lowry, L. Anastasia Krupnik
Fic

Anastasia has the answers. Lowry, L. See note under Lowry, L. Anastasia Krupnik
Fic

Anastasia Krupnik. Lowry, L. **Fic**

Anastasia on her own. Lowry, L. See note under Lowry, L. Anastasia Krupnik **Fic**

Anastasia's chosen career. Lowry, L. See note under Lowry, L. Anastasia Krupnik
Fic

Anatomy
See also Physiology
Llamas Ruiz, A. Animals on the inside (4 and up) **591.4**

Anatomy, Human *See* Human anatomy

The **ancestors** are all around us. Belting, N. M.
In Belting, N. M. Moon was tired of walking on air p42-43 **398.2**

Ancient astronomy. See Asimov, I. Astronomy in ancient times **520**

Ancient China. Cotterell, A. **931**

Ancient civilization
Avi-Yonah, M. Dig this! (5 and up) **930.1**
Early humans (4 and up) **930.1**
Hackwell, W. J. Digging to the past: excavations in ancient lands (4 and up) **930.1**
The Visual dictionary of ancient civilizations (4 and up) **930**

The **ancient** cliff dwellers of Mesa Verde. Arnold, C. **970.004**

Ancient Egypt. See Hart, G. Exploring the past: ancient Egypt **932**

The **ancient** fortress. Spariosu, M.
In Spariosu, M. Ghosts, vampires, and werewolves p59-64 **398.2**

Ancient Greece. Pearson, A. **938**

An **ancient** heritage. Ashabranner, B. K. **305.8**

Ancient ones. Bash, B. **585**

Ancient Rome. Corbishley, M. **937**

Ancient Rome. James, S. **937**

Ancient world [series]
Odijk, P. The Greeks **938**

The **ancient** world of the Bible. Day, M. **221.9**

Ancona, George, 1929-
The American family farm (5 and up) **630.1**
The aquarium book (3-5) **639.3**
Bananas (3-5) **641.3**
Cutters, carvers & the cathedral (3-5) **693**
The golden lion tamarin comes home (3-5) **639.9**
Handtalk zoo (k-3) **419**
Man and mustang (3-6) **636.1**
My camera (3-6) **771**
Pablo remembers (k-3) **394.2**
The piñatamaker: El piñatero (k-3) **745.594**
Powwow (3-6) **970.004**
Riverkeeper (3-6) **333.91**
Sheep dog (4 and up) **636.7**
Turtle watch (2-4) **597.9**
(il) Alexander, S. H. Mom can't see me **362.4**
(il) Alexander, S. H. Mom's best friend **362.4**
(il) Anderson, J. Earth keepers **363.7**

(il) Anderson, J. The first Thanksgiving feast **974.4**
(il) Anderson, J. From map to museum **930.1**
(il) Anderson, J. Twins on toes **792.8**
(jt. auth) Charlip, R. Handtalk **419**
(il) Charlip, R. Handtalk birthday **419**
(il) Climo, S. City! San Francisco **979.4**
(il) Climo, S. City! Washington, D.C. **975.3**
(jt. auth) Mary Beth. Handtalk school **419**
(il) Rosenberg, M. B. Being a twin, having a twin **155.4**
(il) Rosenberg, M. B. Being adopted **362.7**
(il) Rosenberg, M. B. Brothers and sisters **306.8**
(il) Rosenberg, M. B. Finding a way **362.4**
(il) Rosenberg, M. B. Making a new home in America **325.73**
(il) Rosenberg, M. B. My friend Leslie **362.4**

Ancona, Mary Beth *See* Mary Beth

And all between. Snyder, Z. K. See note under Snyder, Z. K. Below the root **Fic**

And one for all. Nelson, T. **Fic**

And one gorilla. See Morozumi, A. One gorilla **E**

And the green grass grew all around. Schwartz, A. **398.2**

And then there was one. Facklam, M. **591.5**

And then what happened, Paul Revere?. Fritz, J. **92**

And to think that I saw it on Mulberry Street. Seuss, Dr. **E**

And you give me a pain, Elaine. Pevsner, S. **Fic**

Andersen, Hans Christian, 1805-1875
Blockhead Hans
In The Yellow fairy book p313-18 **398.2**

The emperor's new clothes
In Tomie dePaola's favorite nursery tales p87-95 **398.2**
In The Yellow fairy book p21-25 **398.2**

The fir tree
In Take joy! The Tasha Tudor Christmas book p14-22 **394.2**
Hans Christian Andersen fairy tales (4-6) **S C**
Contents: The sandman; The Emperor's new clothes; The princess & the pea; The tinderbox; The rose tree regiment; The naughty boy; The jumpers; The little match girl
Hans Christian Andersen's The fir tree (2-5) **Fic**

How to tell a true princess
In The Yellow fairy book p254-55 **398.2**

The little match girl (3-5) **Fic**

Andreas and the magic bells. Levoy, M.
  In Levoy, M. The witch of Fourth Street, and other stories **S C**

Andreasen, Dan
  (il) Kroll, S. By the dawn's early light **782.42**

Andrews, Benny, 1930-
  (il) I am the darker brother. See I am the darker brother **811.008**

Andrews, Charles J.
  Hughes, R. P. Fell's United States coin book **737.4**

Andrews, Jan, 1942-
  Very last first time **E**

Androcles and the lion and other Aesop's fables. Paxton, T. **398.2**

Andryszewski, Tricia, 1956-
  The Seminoles (4-6) **970.004**

Andy and the lion. Daugherty, J. H. **E**

Anecdotes
  See also Wit and humor

Anecdotes and adventures of fifteen gentlemen. Sharpe, R. S.
  In A Nursery companion p70-74 **820.8**

Angel Falls. Jordan, M. **508**

An **angel** for Solomon Singer. Rylant, C. **E**

Angel in charge. Delton, J. See note under Delton, J. Angel's mother's wedding **Fic**

Angel Mae: a tale of Trotter Street. Hughes, S. **E**

Angelina and Alice. Holabird, K. See note under Holabird, K. Angelina ballerina **E**

Angelina and the princess. Holabird, K. See note under Holabird, K. Angelina ballerina **E**

Angelina at the fair. Holabird, K. See note under Holabird, K. Angelina ballerina **E**

Angelina ballerina. Holabird, K. **E**

Angelina ice skates. Holabird, K. See note under Holabird, K. Angelina ballerina **E**

Angelina on stage. Holabird, K. See note under Holabird, K. Angelina ballerina **E**

Angelina's baby sister. Holabird, K. See note under Holabird, K. Angelina ballerina **E**

Angelina's birthday surprise. Holabird, K. See note under Holabird, K. Angelina ballerina **E**

Angelina's Christmas. Holabird, K. See note under Holabird, K. Angelina ballerina **E**

Angelo, Valenti, 1897-
  (il) Sawyer, R. Roller skates **Fic**

Angelou, Maya
  Life doesn't frighten me **811**
  My painted house, my friendly chicken, and me (k-3) **968**

Angels & other strangers: family Christmas stories. Paterson, K. **S C**

Angels and other strangers. Paterson, K.
  In Paterson, K. Angels & other strangers: family Christmas stories p1-16 **S C**

Angel's mother's baby. Delton, J. See note under Delton, J. Angel's mother's wedding **Fic**

Angel's mother's boyfriend. Delton, J. See note under Delton, J. Angel's mother's wedding **Fic**

Angel's mother's wedding. Delton, J. **Fic**

Angels, prophets, rabbis & kings from the stories of the Jewish people. Patterson, J. **296.1**

The **angel's** wings. Schwartz, H.
  In Schwartz, H. The diamond tree p107-13 **398.2**

Anglo-American cataloguing rules
  Gorman, M. The concise AACR2, 1988 revision **025.3**

Anglo-American cataloguing rules, 2nd edition, 1988 revision. See Gorman, M. The concise AACR2, 1988 revision **025.3**

Anglo-Argentine War, 1982 *See* Falkland Islands War, 1982

Anglo-Saxons
  See/See also pages in the following book(s):
  Lyttle, R. B. Land beyond the river p62-76 (6 and up) **940.1**

Angus and the cat. Flack, M.
  In The Read-aloud treasury p156-78 **808.8**

Animal abuse *See* Animal welfare

Animal alphabet. Kitchen, B. **E**

Animal architecture. Dewey, J. **591.5**

Animal babies
  Heller, R. Chickens aren't the only ones (k-1) **591.1**
  Hirschi, R. A time for babies (k-2) **591.5**
  Hirschland, R. B. How animals care for their babies (k-3) **591.5**
  Johnston, G. Slippery babies (3-5) **597.6**
  McMillan, B. The baby zoo **590.74**
  Patent, D. H. Baby horses (3-6) **636.1**
  Smith, R. Inside the zoo nursery (4 and up) **590.74**
  Sobol, R. Seal journey (3-5) **599.74**

Animal behavior
  See also Animal defenses
  Arnosky, J. Secrets of a wildlife watcher (4 and up) **591.5**
  Brooks, B. Predator! (5 and up) **591.5**
  Cutchins, J. Parenting papas (3-5) **591.5**
  Emory, J. Nightprowlers (3-6) **591.5**
  Evans, L. G. An elephant never forgets its snorkel (3-5) **591.5**
  Facklam, M. Partners for life (3-6) **591.5**
  Hirschi, R. A time for playing (k-2) **591.5**
  Kitchen, B. Somewhere today (k-3) **591.5**

Any me I want to be: poems. Kuskin, K.
811

The **Apache**. McKissack, P. C.   970.004

Apache Indians
Hoyt-Goldsmith, D. Apache rodeo (3-5)
970.004
McKissack, P. C. The Apache (2-4)
970.004
Shorto, R. Geronimo and the struggle for Apache freedom (5 and up)   92
See/See also pages in the following book(s):
Ehrlich, A. Wounded Knee: an Indian history of the American West (6 and up)
970.004
Hofsinde, R. Indian costumes p13-20 (3-6)
391

Apache rodeo. Hoyt-Goldsmith, D.
970.004

Apartment houses
Fiction
Berends, P. B. The case of the elevator duck (3-5)   Fic
Hurwitz, J. Busybody Nora (2-4)   Fic

Ape in a cape. Eichenberg, F.   E

Apes
See also Chimpanzees; Gorillas; Orangutan
Grace, E. S. Apes (4-6)   599.88
Lemmon, T. Apes (2-4)   599.88
Selsam, M. E. A first look at monkeys and apes (1-3)   599.8

Apfel, Necia H., 1930-
Nebulae (4 and up)   523.1
Orion, the Hunter (4 and up)   523.8
Voyager to the planets (4 and up)   523.4

Aphrodite (Greek deity)
Hodges, M. The arrow and the lamp (2-4)
292

Apiculture *See* Bees

Appalachia. Rylant, C.   974

Appalachian Mountain region *See* Appalachian region

Appalachian Mountains
Fiction
Bates, A. A. Ragsale   E
Caudill, R. A certain small shepherd (4 and up)   Fic
Caudill, R. Did you carry the flag today, Charley? (2-4)   Fic
Cleaver, V. Where the lillies bloom (5 and up)   Fic
Hamilton, V. M. C. Higgins the great (6 and up)   Fic
Houston, G. The year of the perfect Christmas tree   E
Smith, D. B. Return to Bitter Creek (5 and up)   Fic
Folklore
See Folklore—Appalachian Mountains

Appalachian region
Houston, G. My great-aunt Arizona   E
Rylant, C. Appalachia   974

Appaloosa horses. Patent, D. H.   636.1

Appelbaum, Diana Karter
Giants in the land (2-4)   634.9

Appelt, Kathi, 1954-
Bayou lullaby   E

Appetite disorders *See* Eating disorders

Apple, Margot
(il) Delton, J. Angel's mother's wedding
Fic
(il) Shaw, N. Sheep in a jeep   E

Apple
Johnson, S. A. Apple trees (4 and up)
634
Maestro, B. How do apples grow? (k-3)
634
Micucci, C. The life and times of the apple (2-4)   634
Schnieper, C. An apple tree through the year (3-6)   634

Apple is my sign. Riskind, M.   Fic

The **apple** of contentment. Thane, A.
In Thane, A. Plays from famous stories and fairy tales p153-68   812

An **apple** tree through the year. Schnieper, C.
634

Apple trees. Johnson, S. A.   634

Applebet: an ABC. Watson, C.   E

Appleseed, Johnny, 1774-1845
About
Aliki. The story of Johnny Appleseed (k-3)
92
Kellogg, S. Johnny Appleseed (k-3)   92
Poetry
Lindbergh, R. Johnny Appleseed (k-3)
811

Applied arts *See* Decorative arts

The **appointment**. Schwartz, A.
In Schwartz, A. Scary stories 3 p7
398.2

Appraisal   016.5

Apprentices
Fiction
Fleischman, P. Saturnalia (6 and up)
Fic

April, bubbles, chocolate (k-3)   811.008

April's kittens. Newberry, C. T.   E

Apt. 3. Keats, E. J.   E

Apuleius
Hodges, M. The arrow and the lamp
292

Aquaculture
Koch, F. K. Mariculture (5 and up)   639

The **aquarium** book. Ancona, G.   639.3

Aquariums
See also Marine aquariums
Evans, M. Fish (2-5)   639.3
Johnston, G. Windows on wildlife (3-6)
590.74

Aquatic animals *See* Marine animals

Aquatic birds *See* Water birds

Aquatic plants *See* Marine plants

Arab Americans
Ashabranner, B. K. An ancient heritage (5 and up) **305.8**

Arab countries
Haskins, J. Count your way through the Arab world (2-4) **909**

Arab-Jewish relations *See* Jewish-Arab relations

Arabian nights
Aladdin and other tales from the Arabian nights **398.2**
The **Arabian** nights. Philip, N. **398.2**
The **Arabian** nights entertainments (5 and up) **398.2**

Arabs
See/See also pages in the following book(s):
Lyttle, R. B. Land beyond the river p71-91 (6 and up) **940.1**
Folklore
Aladdin and other tales from the Arabian nights **398.2**
The Arabian nights entertainments (5 and up) **398.2**
Philip, N. The Arabian nights (4 and up) **398.2**

Arachne (Greek mythology)
See/See also pages in the following book(s):
Climo, S. Someone saw a spider p5-12 (4 and up) **398.2**

Arachne's gift. Climo, S.
In Climo, S. Someone saw a spider p5-12 **398.2**

Arachnida *See* Spiders

Arai, Kazuyoshi
(il) Brown, T. Konnichiwa! **305.8**

Arapaho Indians
See/See also pages in the following book(s):
Ehrlich, A. Wounded Knee: an Indian history of the American West (6 and up) **970.004**

Arawak Indians *See* Taino Indians

Arbuthnot, May Hill, 1884-1969
(jt. auth) Sutherland, Z. Children and books **028.5**

The **Arbuthnot** lectures, 1970-1979/1980-1989 **028.5**

Arcella, Steve
(il) Sandburg, C. Carl Sandburg **811**

Archaeology *See* Archeology

Archambault, John
(jt. auth) Martin, B. Barn dance! **E**
(jt. auth) Martin, B. Chicka chicka boom boom **E**
(jt. auth) Martin, B. The ghost-eye tree **E**
(jt. auth) Martin, B. Knots on a counting rope **E**

Archbold, Rick, 1950-
Deep-sea explorer: the story of Robert Ballard, discoverer of the Titanic (6 and up) **92**
(jt. auth) Ballard, R. D. Exploring the Bismarck **910.4**

(jt. auth) Ballard, R. D. The lost wreck of the Isis **910.4**

Archeological specimens *See* Antiquities

Archeologists
Scheller, W. Amazing archaeologists and their finds (4 and up) **920**

Archeology
See also Antiquities; Excavations (Archeology); Prehistoric man; Rock drawings, paintings, and engravings; names of extinct cities; and names of groups of people and of cities (except extinct cities), countries, regions, etc., with the subdivision Antiquities
Anderson, J. From map to museum (5 and up) **930.1**
Avi-Yonah, M. Dig this! (5 and up) **930.1**
Getz, D. Frozen man (5 and up) **930.1**
Hackwell, W. J. Digging to the past: excavations in ancient lands (4 and up) **930.1**
Hackwell, W. J. Diving to the past: recovering ancient wrecks (4 and up) **910.4**
Lauber, P. Tales mummies tell (5 and up) **930.1**
Lessem, D. The iceman (4-6) **930.1**
McIntosh, J. Archeology (4 and up) **930.1**
Sunk! (5 and up) **910.4**

Archer, Jules
A house divided: the lives of Ulysses S. Grant and Robert E. Lee (5 and up) **92**

Archibald, Nate, 1948-
See/See also pages in the following book(s):
Littlefield, B. Champions p53-66 (5 and up) **920**

Architectural engineering *See* Building

Architecture
Biesty, S. Stephen Biesty's incredible cross-sections (4 and up) **600**
Brown, D. J. The Random House book of how things were built (4 and up) **720**
Isaacson, P. M. Round buildings, square buildings, & buildings that wiggle like a fish (4 and up) **720**
The Visual dictionary of buildings (4 and up) **720**
Details
See also Woodwork

Architecture, Domestic *See* Domestic architecture

Architecture, Gothic *See* Gothic architecture

Architecture, Roman *See* Roman architecture

Arctic & Antarctic. Taylor, B. **998**

Arctic explorer: the story of Matthew Henson. Ferris, J. **92**

Arctic hunter. Hoyt-Goldsmith, D. **970.004**

Arctic memories. Ekoomiak, N. **998**

Arctic regions
See also North Pole

Arnosky, Jim—*Continued*
Secrets of a wildlife watcher (4 and up)
591.5
Watching foxes (k-2) **599.74**

Arnott, Kathleen
Unanana and the elephant
In Womenfolk and fairy tales p127-34
398.2

Aronson, Billy
They came from DNA (5 and up)
575.1

Around the world in 80 dishes. Linde, P. van
der **641.5**

Around the world in a hundred years. Fritz, J.
910.4

Arquette, Mary F.
(il) Medicine Story. The Children of the
Morning Light: Wampanoag tales
398.2

The **arrant** fool. Afanas´ev, A. N.
In Afanas´ev, A. N. Russian fairy tales
p334-36 **398.2**

The **arrow** and the lamp. Hodges, M. **292**

Arrow to the sun. McDermott, G. **398.2**

Arrowhead Finger. Bruchac, J.
In Bruchac, J. The girl who married the
Moon p13-20 **398.2**

Arroz con leche (k-3) **782.42**

Art
See also Decoration and ornament
Davidson, R. Take a look (5 and up)
701
Isaacson, P. M. A short walk around the
pyramids & through the world of art (5
and up) **700**
See/See also pages in the following book(s):
Bauer, C. F. Celebrations p1-24 **808.8**
Museums
See Art museums

Art, American *See* American art

Art, Indian *See* Indians of North America—
Art

Art, Jewish *See* Jewish art and symbolism

Art, Medieval *See* Medieval art

Art, Renaissance *See* Renaissance art

The **art** and industry of sandcastles. Adkins, J.
728.8

Art and science
Devonshire, H. Air (3-5) **533**
Devonshire, H. Color (3-5) **535.6**
Devonshire, H. Light (3-5) **535**
Devonshire, H. Water (3-5) **553.7**

Art appreciation
Beckett, W. A child's book of prayer in art
(3-6) **242**
Brown, L. K. Visiting the art museum (k-3)
708
Greenberg, J. The painter's eye (6 and up)
759.13
Greenberg, J. The sculptor's eye (6 and up)
730.9

Micklethwait, L. A child's book of art (k-3)
701
Micklethwait, L. I spy **E**
Roalf, P. Looking at paintings (5 and up)
750
Tucker, J. S. Come look with me: discovering photographs with children (4 and up)
779

Art for children [series]
Raboff, E. Albrecht Dürer **759.3**
Sterckx, P. Brueghel **92**

Art industries and trade *See* Decorative arts

The **art** lesson. De Paola, T. **E**

Art museums
See also names of individual art museums
Brown, L. K. Visiting the art museum (k-3)
708

The **art** of Maurice Sendak. Lanes, S. G.
741.6

The **art** of the story-teller. Shedlock, M. L.
372.6

Arthropoda
Facklam, H. Insects (5 and up) **595.7**

Arthur, King
About
Green, R. L. King Arthur and his Knights
of the Round Table (5 and up) **398.2**
Hodges, M. Of swords and sorcerers (4-6)
398.2
Sutcliff, R. The light beyond the forest (4
and up) **398.2**
Sutcliff, R. The road to Camlann (4 and up)
398.2
Sutcliff, R. The sword and the circle (4 and
up) **398.2**
See/See also pages in the following book(s):
Shedlock, M. L. The art of the story-teller
p173-78 **372.6**
Fiction
Bulla, C. R. The sword in the tree (3-5)
Fic
Morpurgo, M. Arthur, high king of Britain
(4 and up) **Fic**
White, T. H. The sword in the stone
Fic
Yolen, J. The dragon's boy (5 and up)
Fic

Arthur, Alex
Shell (4 and up) **594**

Arthur, Chester Alan, 1829-1886
About
Simon, C. Chester A. Arthur: twenty-first
president of the United States (4 and up)
92

Arthur, Kay, 1933-
Mother goes modern
In Holiday plays round the year p267-84
812.008

Arthur Ashe and his match with history.
Quackenbush, R. M. **92**

Arthur babysits. Brown, M. T. See note under
Brown, M. T. Arthur's nose **E**

Arthur, for the very first time. MacLachlan, P.
Fic

Arthur goes to camp. Brown, M. T. See note under Brown, M. T. Arthur's nose   E

Arthur, high king of Britain. Morpurgo, M.
Fic

Arthur in the cave. Thomas, W. J.
In Shedlock, M. L. The art of the story-teller p173-78   **372.6**

Arthur meets the president. Brown, M. T. See note under Brown, M. T. Arthur's nose   E

Arthurian romances
See also Grail
Green, R. L. King Arthur and his Knights of the Round Table (5 and up)   **398.2**
Hastings, S. Sir Gawain and the Green Knight (3 and up)   **398.2**
Hastings, S. Sir Gawain and the loathly lady (3 and up)   **398.2**
Hodges, M. The kitchen knight (3 and up)   **398.2**
Hodges, M. Of swords and sorcerers (4-6)   **398.2**
Morpurgo, M. Arthur, high king of Britain (4 and up)   Fic
Sutcliff, R. The light beyond the forest (4 and up)   **398.2**
Sutcliff, R. The road to Camlann (4 and up)   **398.2**
Sutcliff, R. The sword and the circle (4 and up)   **398.2**

Arthur's April Fool. Brown, M. T. See note under Brown, M. T. Arthur's nose   E

Arthur's April Fool. Brown, M. T.
In The Family read-aloud holiday treasury p30-37   **808.8**

Arthur's baby. Brown, M. T. See note under Brown, M. T. Arthur's nose   E

Arthur's birthday. Brown, M. T. See note under Brown, M. T. Arthur's nose   E

Arthur's camp-out. Hoban, L. See note under Hoban, L. Arthur's Christmas cookies   E

Arthur's chicken pox. Brown, M. T. See note under Brown, M. T. Arthur's nose   E

Arthur's Christmas. Brown, M. T. See note under Brown, M. T. Arthur's nose   E

Arthur's Christmas cookies. Hoban, L.   E

Arthur's eyes. Brown, M. T. See note under Brown, M. T. Arthur's nose   E

Arthur's family vacation. Brown, M. T. See note under Brown, M. T. Arthur's nose   E

Arthur's first sleepover. Brown, M. T. See note under Brown, M. T. Arthur's nose   E

Arthur's funny money. Hoban, L. See note under Hoban, L. Arthur's Christmas cookies   E

Arthur's great big valentine. Hoban, L. See note under Hoban, L. Arthur's Christmas cookies   E

Arthur's Halloween. Brown, M. T. See note under Brown, M. T. Arthur's nose   E

Arthur's Halloween costume. Hoban, L. See note under Hoban, L. Arthur's Christmas cookies   E

Arthur's Honey Bear. Hoban, L. See note under Hoban, L. Arthur's Christmas cookies   E

Arthur's loose tooth. Hoban, L. See note under Hoban, L. Arthur's Christmas cookies   E

Arthur's new power. Hoban, R. See note under Hoban, R. Dinner at Alberta's   E

Arthur's new puppy. Brown, M. T. See note under Brown, M. T. Arthur's nose   E

Arthur's nose. Brown, M. T.   E

Arthur's pen pal. Hoban, L. See note under Hoban, L. Arthur's Christmas cookies   E

Arthur's pet business. Brown, M. T. See note under Brown, M. T. Arthur's nose   E

Arthur's prize reader. Hoban, L. See note under Hoban, L. Arthur's Christmas cookies   E

Arthur's teacher trouble. Brown, M. T. See note under Brown, M. T. Arthur's nose   E

Arthur's Thanksgiving. Brown, M. T. See note under Brown, M. T. Arthur's nose   E

Arthur's tooth. Brown, M. T. See note under Brown, M. T. Arthur's nose   E

Arthur's TV trouble. Brown, M. T. See note under Brown, M. T. Arthur's nose   E

Arthur's valentine. Brown, M. T. See note under Brown, M. T. Arthur's nose   E

Artistic photography
Tucker, J. S. Come look with me: discovering photographs with children (4 and up)   **779**

Artists
See also African American artists; Child artists; Illustrators; Sculptors; Women artists

Fiction
Coerr, E. Mieko and the fifth treasure (3-5)   Fic
Cooney, B. Hattie and the wild waves   E
Dunrea, O. The painter who loved chickens   E
Edwards, M. A baker's portrait   E
Feiffer, J. The man in the ceiling (4-6)   Fic
Garland, M. Dinner at Magritte's   E
Leaf, M. The eyes of the dragon   E
Lionni, L. Matthew's dream   E
Porte-Thomas, B. A. Chickens! chickens!   E
Rosen, M. J. Elijah's angel   Fic
Rylant, C. All I see   E

Artists, American
Audubon, J. J. Capturing nature (4 and up)   **92**

Automobile racing
Sullivan, G. Racing Indy cars (5 and up)
796.7

Automobile service stations *See* Service stations

Automobiles
Cole, J. Cars and how they go (k-3)
629.222
Johnstone, M. Cars (4 and up)   629.222
Rockwell, A. F. Cars (k-1)   629.222
Sutton, R. Car (4 and up)   629.222
The Visual dictionary of cars (4 and up)
629.222
Fiction
Fleming, I. Chitty-Chitty-Bang-Bang (4-6)
Fic
Mahy, M. The rattlebang picnic   E
Oxenbury, H. The car trip   E
Maintenance and repair
Florian, D. An auto mechanic (k-1)
629.28

Autumn
Hirschi, R. Fall (k-2)   508
Maestro, B. Why do leaves change color?
(k-3)   582.16
Markle, S. Exploring autumn (4 and up)
508
Simon, S. Autumn across America (3-5)
508
Autumn across America. Simon, S.   508
Autumn Street. Lowry, L.   Fic
AV market place   371.3025
Avakian, Monique
A historical album of Massachusetts
In Historical albums series   973
A historical album of New York
In Historical albums series   973
Avery, Gillian, 1926-
(ed) Children and their books. See Children
and their books   028.5
Avi, 1937-
The barn (4-6)   Fic
Blue heron (5 and up)   Fic
Emily Upham's revenge (4-6)   Fic
Encounter at Easton (5 and up)   Fic
The fighting ground (5 and up)   Fic
The history of helpless Harry (4-6)   Fic
Night journeys (5 and up)   Fic
Poppy (3-5)   Fic
S.O.R. losers (5 and up)   Fic
Something upstairs (5 and up)   Fic
The true confessions of Charlotte Doyle (6
and up)   Fic
Avi-Yonah, Michael, 1904-1974
Dig this! (5 and up)   930.1
Aviation *See* Aeronautics
Aviators *See* Air pilots
Awards, Literary *See* Literary prizes
Away from home. Lobel, A.   E
Away is a strange place to be. Hoover, H. M.
Fic
Awful aardvark. Mwalimu   398.2

Awkward aardvark. See Mwalimu. Awful aardvark   398.2
Axelrod, Alan, 1952-
Songs of the Wild West. See Songs of the
Wild West   782.42
Aylesworth, Jim, 1943-
The completed hickory dickory dock (k-2)
398.8
Country crossing   E
My son John   E
Old black fly   E
One crow   E
Aymara Indians
See/See also pages in the following book(s):
Newman, S. P. The Incas (4 and up)
985
Ayoub, Abderrahman
Umm El Madayan. See Umm El Madayan
961
Azarian, Mary
A farmer's alphabet   E
Azerbaijan
Azerbaijan (5 and up)   947
Azerbaijan (5 and up)   947
Aztecs
See also Toltecs
Fisher, L. E. Pyramid of the sun, pyramid
of the moon (4 and up)   972
Mathews, S. S. The Sad Night (2-4)
972
Wood, T. The Aztecs (4 and up)   972
Legends
Bierhorst, J. Doctor Coyote (1-4)   398.2
Lewis, R. All of you was singing   398.2

B

B is for Bethlehem. Wilner, I.   E
Baba Yaga. Afanas'ev, A. N.
In Afanas'ev, A. N. Russian fairy tales
p194-95   398.2
Baba Yaga [another story]. Afanas'ev, A. N.
In Afanas'ev, A. N. Russian fairy tales
p363-65   398.2
Baba Yaga. Lent, B.   398.2
Baba Yaga and the brave youth. Afanas'ev, A.
N.
In Afanas'ev, A. N. Russian fairy tales
p76-79   398.2
Baba Yaga and Vasilisa the brave. Mayer, M.
398.2
Baba Yaga Bony-Legs. Mayo, M.
In Mayo, M. Magical tales from many
lands p105-15   398.2
Baba Yaga, the terrible. Hamilton, V.
In Hamilton, V. The dark way p14-22
398.2
Babar and Father Christmas. Brunhoff, J. de
See note under Brunhoff, J. de. The story
of Babar, the little elephant   E

Babar and his children. Brunhoff, J. de See note under Brunhoff, J. de. The story of Babar, the little elephant **E**

Babar and the ghost. Brunhoff, L. de See note under Brunhoff, J. de. The story of Babar, the little elephant **E**

Babar learns to cook. Brunhoff, L. de See note under Brunhoff, J. de. The story of Babar, the little elephant **E**

Babar loses his crown. Brunhoff, L. de See note under Brunhoff, J. de. The story of Babar, the little elephant **E**

Babar saves the day. Brunhoff, L. de See note under Brunhoff, J. de. The story of Babar, the little elephant **E**

Babar the king. Brunhoff, J. de See note under Brunhoff, J. de. The story of Babar, the little elephant **E**

Babar's ABC. Brunhoff, L. de See note under Brunhoff, J. de. The story of Babar, the little elephant **E**

Babar's anniversary album. Brunhoff, L. de See note under Brunhoff, J. de. The story of Babar, the little elephant **E**

Babar's birthday surprise. Brunhoff, L. de See note under Brunhoff, J. de. The story of Babar, the little elephant **E**

Babar's book of color. Brunhoff, L. de See note under Brunhoff, J. de. The story of Babar, the little elephant **E**

Babar's busy year. Brunhoff, L. de See note under Brunhoff, J. de. The story of Babar, the little elephant **E**

Babar's family album. Brunhoff, L. de See note under Brunhoff, J. de. The story of Babar, the little elephant **F**

Babar's French lessons. Brunhoff, L. de See note under Brunhoff, J. de. The story of Babar, the little elephant **E**

Babar's little circus star. Brunhoff, L. de See note under Brunhoff, J. de. The story of Babar, the little elephant **E**

Babar's little girl. Brunhoff, L. de See note under Brunhoff, J. de. The story of Babar, the little elephant **E**

Babar's mystery. Brunhoff, L. de See note under Brunhoff, J. de. The story of Babar, the little elephant **E**

Babar's picnic. Brunhoff, L. de See note under Brunhoff, J. de. The story of Babar, the little elephant **E**

Babbitt, Natalie
The bus for Deadhorse
In The Big book for peace p52-56
810.8

The Devil's other storybook (4-6)
S C
Contents: The fortunes of Madame Organza; Justice; The soldier; Boating; How Akbar went to Bethlehem; The signpost; Lessons; The fall and rise of Bathbone; Simple sentences; The ear

The Devil's storybook (4-6) **S C**

Contents: Wishes; The very pretty lady; The harps of Heaven; The imp in the basket; Nuts; A palindrome; Ashes; Perfection; The rose and the minor demon; The power of speech

The eyes of the Amaryllis (5 and up)
Fic

Goody Hall (4-6) **Fic**

The harps of Heaven
In The Random House book of humor for children p134-43 **817.008**

Kneeknock Rise (4-6) **Fic**

The last days of the Giddywit
In The Big book for our planet p12-19
810.8

Nellie: a cat on her own **E**
The search for delicious (5 and up) **Fic**
Tuck everlasting (5 and up) **Fic**
(il) Worth, V. All the small poems and fourteen more **811**
(il) Worth, V. Still more small poems
811

Babcock, Chris, 1963-
No moon, no milk! **E**

Babe Didrikson: athlete of the century. Knudson, R. R. **92**

Babe: the gallant pig. King-Smith, D. **Fic**

Babies *See* Infants

Baboons
Fiction
Olaleye, I. Bitter bananas **E**

Baboushka
In The Family read-aloud Christmas treasury p32-33 **808.8**

Baboushka and the three kings. Robbins, R.
398.2

Babushka. Mikolaycak, C. **398.2**

Babushka's doll. Polacco, P. **E**

The **baby.** Burningham, J. **E**

Baby. MacLachlan, P. **Fic**

Baby animals. Brown, M. W. **E**

Baby Beluga. Raffi **782.42**

The **baby** blues. Smith, J. L. See note under Smith, J. L. The kid next door and other headaches **Fic**

Baby dinosaurs. Sattler, H. R. **567.9**

A **baby** for Max. Lasky, K. **E**

Baby horses. Patent, D. H. **636.1**

Baby rattlesnake. Moroney, L. **398.2**

Baby says. Steptoe, J. **E**

A **baby** sister for Frances. Hoban, R. See note under Hoban, R. Bedtime for Frances
E

The **baby** Uggs are hatching. Prelutsky, J.
811

Baby whales drink milk. Esbensen, B. J.
599.5

The **baby** zoo. McMillan, B. **590.74**

The **Baby's** bedtime book **808.81**

The **baby's** catalogue. Ahlberg, J. **E**

The **Baby's** good morning book **808.81**

The **Baby's** lap book (k-1) **398.8**

Bacchus *See* Dionysus (Greek deity)

Bach, Johann Sebastian, 1685-1750
See/See also pages in the following book(s):
Krull, K. Lives of the musicians p14-17 (4 and up)   920

Bachrach, Susan D., 1948-
Tell them we remember (5 and up)
                               940.53

Back home. Pinkney, G. J.   E

Back in the beforetime. Curry, J. L.   398.2

Back yard Angel. Delton, J. See note under Delton, J. Angel's mother's wedding
                               Fic

Backyard. Silver, D. M.   574.5

Backyard birds. Pine, J.   598

Backyard birds of winter. Lerner, C.   598

Backyard hunter: the praying mantis. Lavies, B.   595.7

Backyard sunflower. King, E.   635.9

Bacon, Joan Chase See Bowden, Joan Chase, 1925-

Bacon, Josephine, 1942-
Cooking the Israeli way
In Easy menu ethnic cookbooks
                               641.5

Bacon, Paul, 1923-
(il) Golenbock, P. Teammates [biography of Jackie Robinson]   92
(il) Sandburg, C. The Sandburg treasury
                               818

Bacteria
Balkwill, F. R. Cell wars (3-6)   616.9
Berger, M. Germs make me sick! (k-3)
                               616.9
Facklam, H. Bacteria (5 and up)   589.9

The **Bad** compadre
In The Monkey's haircut, and other stories told by the Maya p94-106
                               398.2

Bad day at Riverbend. Van Allsburg, C.
                               E

The **bad** news. Schwartz, A.
In From sea to shining sea p311
                               810.8

A **bad** road for cats. Rylant, C.
In Rylant, C. Every living thing p56-65
                               S C

The **bad** wife. Afanas'ev, A. N.
In Afanas'ev, A. N. Russian fairy tales p56-57   398.2

The **badger** and the magic fan. Johnston, T.
                               398.2

Badgers
                    Fiction
Eckert, A. W. Incident at Hawk's Hill (6 and up)   Fic
Hoban, R. Bedtime for Frances   E
Varley, S. Badger's parting gifts   E

Badger's parting gifts. Varley, S.

Baer, Edith, 1924-
This is the way we go to school (k-2)
                               629.04

The **bag** I'm taking to Grandma's. Neitzel, S.
                               E

Bagnold, Enid
National Velvet (5 and up)   Fic

Bags are big!. Renfro, N.   745.54

Bagthorpes v. the world. Cresswell, H. See note under Cresswell, H. Ordinary Jack
                               Fic

Bahamas
                    Poetry
Greenfield, E. Under the Sunday tree (2-4)
                               811

Bahrain
Fox, M. V. Bahrain (4 and up)   953

Bahti, Tom, 1926-1972
(il) Baylor, B. When clay sings   970.004

Bailey, Carolyn Sherwin, 1875-1961
See/See also pages in the following book(s):
Newbery Medal books, 1922-1955 p290-99
                               028.5

Bailey, Donna
Judo (1-4)   796.8

Bailey, Jill
Birds (3-5)   598

Bailey, Philip H.
What shall we do when we all go out? See What shall we do when we all go out?
                               782.42

Baillie, Marilyn
(ed) Magic fun. See Magic fun   793.8

Baines, John D. (John David), 1943-
Acid rain (5 and up)   363.7

Baird, Anne
Space Camp (4 and up)   629.45

Baja California (Mexico: Peninsula)
                    Fiction
O'Dell, S. The black pearl (6 and up)
                               Fic

Baker, Augusta, 1911-
Storytelling: art and technique   372.6

Baker, Charles
The Christmas doubters
In The Big book of Christmas plays p265-74   808.82

Baker, Daniel B.
(jt. auth) Saari, P. Explorers & discoverers
                               920.003

Baker, Jeannie
Home in the sky   E
The story of rosy dock (k-3)   508
Where the forest meets the sea   E
Window   E

Baker, Josephine, 1906-1975
                    Fiction
Schroeder, A. Ragtime Tumpie   E

Baker, Karen, 1965-
(il) Dugan, B. Leaving home with a pickle jar   E

Baker, Keith, 1953-
Big fat hen (k-1)   398.8
The magic fan   E

Baker, Olaf
  Where the buffaloes begin (2-4)   **Fic**

Baker, Pamela J., 1947-
  My first book of sign (k-3)   **419**

Baker, Sara Josephine, 1873-1945
About
  Ptacek, G. Champion for children's health: a story about Dr. S. Josephine Baker (3-5)   **92**

See/See also pages in the following book(s):
  Vare, E. A. Women inventors & their discoveries p67-81 (5 and up)   **920**

Bakers and bakeries
Fiction
  Heath, A. Sofie's role   **E**

The **baker's** daughter. Crossley-Holland, K.
  In Crossley-Holland, K. British folk tales p331-33   **398.2**

A **Baker's** dozen
  In Diane Goode's American Christmas p43-45   **810.8**

The **baker's** dozen. Forest, H.   **398.2**

A **baker's** portrait. Edwards, M.   **E**

Baking
  See also Bread; Cake
Fiction
  Hoban, L. Arthur's Christmas cookies   **E**

  Priceman, M. How to make an apple pie and see the world   **E**

Balance
  Zubrowski, B. Mobiles (4 and up)   **531**

Balboa, Vasco Núñez de, 1475-1519
See/See also pages in the following book(s):
  Fritz, J. Around the world in a hundred years p83-93 (4-6)   **910.4**

Bald eagle
  Craighead, C. The eagle and the river (3-5)   **591.5**

  Johnson, S. A. Raptor rescue! (4 and up)   **639.9**

  Patent, D. H. Where the bald eagles gather (4 and up)   **598**

Baldak Borisievich. Afanas'ev, A. N.
  In Afanas'ev, A. N. Russian fairy tales p90-96   **398.2**

Baldwin, Edward *See* Godwin, William, 1756-1836

Balestrino, Philip
  The skeleton inside you (k-3)   **611**

Balian, Lorna
  Humbug witch   **E**

Balkwill, Frances R.
  Cell wars (3-6)   **616.9**
  Cells are us (3-6)   **611**
  DNA is here to stay (3-6)   **574.87**

Ball, Mary *See* Washington, Mary Ball, 1708-1789

The **ballad** of Belle Dorcas. Hooks, W. H.   **Fic**

The **ballad** of the pirate queens. Yolen, J.   **811**

Ballard, Robert D.
  Exploring the Bismarck (4 and up)   **910.4**
  Exploring the Titanic (4 and up)   **910.4**
  The lost wreck of the Isis (4 and up)   **910.4**
About
  Archbold, R. Deep-sea explorer: the story of Robert Ballard, discoverer of the Titanic (6 and up)   **92**

Ballerinas and bears. Rylant, C.
  In Rylant, C. Children of Christmas p20-25   **S C**

Ballet
  Anderson, J. Twins on toes (4 and up)   **792.8**
  Bussell, D. The young dancer (4 and up)   **792.8**
  Isadora, R. My ballet class (1-3)   **792.8**
  Kuklin, S. Going to my ballet class (k-3)   **792.8**
  Morris, A. On their toes (3-5)   **792.8**
  Switzer, E. E. The nutcracker (4 and up)   **792.8**
Fiction
  Auch, M. J. Peeping Beauty   **E**
  Bunting, E. The day before Christmas   **E**
  Gauch, P. L. Dance, Tanya   **E**
  Holabird, K. Angelina ballerina   **E**
  Isadora, R. Lili at ballet   **E**
  Isadora, R. Max   **E**
  Streatfeild, N. Ballet shoes (5 and up)   **Fic**
Stories, plots, etc.
  Isadora, R. Swan Lake   **E**
  McCaughrean, G. The Random House book of stories from the ballet (4 and up)   **792.8**
  Verdy, V. Of swans, sugarplums, and satin slippers (4-6)   **792.8**

Ballet dancers
  Levine, E. Anna Pavlova, genius of the dance (5 and up)   **92**

Ballet shoes. Streatfeild, N.   **Fic**

Balloons
  Johnson, N. Fire & silk: flying in a hot air balloon (1-4)   **797.5**
Fiction
  Coerr, E. The big balloon race   **E**
  Du Bois, W. P. The twenty-one balloons (5 and up)   **Fic**
  Lamorisse, A. The red balloon   **E**
  Nolen, J. Harvey Potter's balloon farm   **E**

Balloons, Dirigible *See* Airships

Bam, bam, bam. Merriam, E.   **811**

La **Bamba.** Soto, G.
  In Soto, G. Baseball in April, and other stories p81-89   **S C**

Bambi. Salten, F.   **Fic**

The **bamboo** beads. Joseph, L.
  In Joseph, L. A wave in her pocket p37-44   **398.2**

Bamboo hats and a rice cake. Tompert, A.
398.2

Banana
Ancona, G. Bananas (3-5)   641.3

Banana-day trip. Berry, J.
In Berry, J. The future-telling lady and
other stories p34-84   S C

Bancroft, Bronwyn
(il) Oodgeroo. Dreamtime   398.2

Bands (Music)
Hayes, A. Meet the Marching Smithereens
(k-3)   784.19
Fiction
Hurd, T. Mama don't allow   E
Maxner, J. Nicholas Cricket   E

Bang, Molly, 1943-
The Grey Lady and the Strawberry Snatcher
    E
The paper crane   E
Ten, nine, eight   E
Wiley and the Hairy Man (1-4)   398.2
(il) From sea to shining sea. See From sea
to shining sea   810.8
(il) Red dragonfly on my shoulder. See Red
dragonfly on my shoulder   895.6

Bang and rattle. Hewitt, S.
In Hewitt, S. Get set—go! [Music &
sound series]   784.19

Bangladesh
Lauré, J. Bangladesh (4 and up)   954.92

Bangs, Edward, 1756-1818
Steven Kellogg's Yankee Doodle (k-3)
    782.42

Banish, Roslyn, 1942-
A forever family (k-3)   362.7

Bank Street College of Education
Merrill, J. The toothpaste millionaire
    Fic

Bank Street museum book [series]
Oppenheim, J. Oceanarium   591.92

Banks, Lynne Reid *See* Reid Banks, Lynne,
1929-

Bannan, Jan Gumprecht
Sand dunes (3-6)   551.3

Banneker, Benjamin, 1731-1806
About
Ferris, J. What are you figuring now? a story
about Benjamin Banneker (3-5)   92
Pinkney, A. D. Dear Benjamin Banneker
(2-4)   92
See/See also pages in the following book(s):
McKissack, P. C. African-American scien-
tists p15-30 (5 and up)   920

Banning, Herman, d. 1933
See/See also pages in the following book(s):
Hart, P. S. Flying free p28-39 (4 and up)
    629.13

The **Banshee**. Hamilton, V.
In Hamilton, V. The dark way p1-4
    398.2

The **Banshee** train. Bodkin, O.   E

Banta, Melissa
Colin Powell (5 and up)   92

Bányai, István, 1949-
Zoom   E

The **banza**. Wolkstein, D.   398.2

Baobab
Bash, B. Tree of life: the world of the African baobab (3-5)   583

Bar mitzvah
Kimmel, E. A. Bar mitzvah (5 and up)
    296.4

Barbara Frietchie. Whittier, J. G.   811

Barbary States *See* North Africa

Barber, Antonia, 1932-
Gemma and the baby chick   E
The Mousehole cat   E

Barber, Barbara E., 1943-
Saturday at The New You   E

Barber, Daniel Wynn
Tiger in the snow
In The Oxford book of scary tales p36-43
    808.8

Barberis, Juan Carlos
(il) Cole, J. The human body: how we
evolved   573.2

Barbers and barbershops
Fiction
Mitchell, M. K. Uncle Jed's barbershop
    E

Barbie. Soto, G.
In Soto, G. Baseball in April, and other
stories p33-42   S C

Barbour, Karen
(il) Adoff, A. Street music   811

Barchers, Suzanne I.
Scary readers theatre   808.82

Bard of Avon: the story of William Shakespeare. Stanley, D.   92

Bare, Colleen Stanley
Guinea pigs don't read books (k-2)
    636.088

A **bargain** for Frances. Hoban, R. See note under Hoban, R. Bedtime for Frances   E

Baring, Maurice, 1874-1945
The blue rose
In Shedlock, M. L. The art of the story-
teller p204-12   372.6

Barkin, Carol, 1944-
Happy Thanksgiving! (4-6)   394.2
Happy Valentine's Day! (4-6)   394.2
Jobs for kids (5 and up)   650.1
The scary Halloween costume book (3-6)
    391
(jt. auth) James, E. How to be school smart
    371.3
(jt. auth) James, E. Sincerely yours   808

Barkley, James
(il) Armstrong, W. H. Sounder   Fic

Barlowe, Dorothea *See* Barlowe, Dot, 1926-

Barlowe, Dot, 1926-
(il) Zim, H. S. Seashores   574.92
(il) Zim, H. S. Trees   582.16

Barlowe, Sy
(il) Zim, H. S. Seashores   574.92

Barton, Byron—*Continued*
(il) Adler, D. A. Roman numerals **513**
(il) Ginsburg, M. Good morning, chick
E
(il) Greene, C. C. A girl called Al **Fic**
(il) Kalan, R. Jump, frog, jump! **E**
(il) Pomerantz, C. The Tamarindo puppy
and other poems **811**
(il) Pomerantz, C. Where's the bear? **E**
(il) Prelutsky, J. The snopp on the sidewalk,
and other poems **811**
(il) Sharmat, M. W. Gila monsters meet you
at the airport **E**
(il) Siebert, D. Truck song **E**
(il) Simon, S. The paper airplane book
745.592

Barton, Clara, 1821-1912
See/See also pages in the following book(s):
Jacobs, W. J. Great lives: human rights
p138-46 (5 and up) **920**

Barton, Harriett
(il) Branley, F. M. Rain & hail **551.57**
(il) Hoffman, C. Sewing by hand **646.2**
(il) In the witch's kitchen. See In the witch's
kitchen **811.008**

Bartone, Elisa
Peppe the lamplighter **E**

Baseball
Brashler, W. The story of Negro league
baseball (5 and up) **796.357**
Cooper, M. L. Playing America's game (5
and up) **796.357**
Egan, T. The Macmillan book of baseball
stories (4 and up) **796.357**
Galt, M. F. Up to the plate (5 and up)
796.357
Gardner, R. The forgotten players (5 and
up) **796.357**
Healy, D. The illustrated rules of baseball
(3-4) **796.357**
Hughes, D. Baseball tips (3-5) **796.357**
Kreutzer, P. Little League's official how-to-
play baseball book (4 and up)
796.357
McKissack, P. C. Black diamond (6 and up)
796.357
Ritter, L. S. Leagues apart (2-4)
796.357
Ward, G. C. 25 great moments (4 and up)
796.357
Ward, G. C. Shadow ball (4 and up)
796.357
Ward, G. C. Who invented the game? (4
and up) **796.357**
See/See also pages in the following book(s):
Bauer, C. F. Celebrations p25-42 **808.8**
Biography
Adler, D. A. Jackie Robinson: he was the
first (2-4) **92**
Adler, D. A. A picture book of Jackie Rob-
inson (1-3) **92**
Golenbock, P. Teammates [biography of
Jackie Robinson] (1-4) **92**
Jacobs, W. J. They shaped the game (4 and
up) **920**

Johnson, R. L. Bo Jackson (4-6) **92**
Kavanagh, J. Honus Wagner (4 and up)
92
Kramer, S. Baseball's greatest hitters (2-4)
920
Sullivan, G. Pitchers: twenty-seven of base-
ball's greatest (4 and up) **920**
Torres, J. A. Home-run hitters (4 and up)
920
Fiction
Christopher, M. The hit-away kid (2-4)
Fic
Cohen, B. Thank you, Jackie Robinson (4-6)
Fic
Hurwitz, J. Baseball fever (3-5) **Fic**
Isadora, R. Max **E**
Kessler, L. P. Here comes the strikeout
E
Konigsburg, E. L. About the B'nai Bagels
(4-6) **Fic**
Mochizuki, K. Baseball saved us **E**
Myers, W. D. Me, Mop, and the Moon-
dance Kid (4-6) **Fic**
Park, B. Skinnybones (4-6) **Fic**
Slote, A. Finding Buck McHenry (4-6)
Fic
Slote, A. Hang tough, Paul Mather (4-6)
Fic
Smith, R. K. Bobby Baseball (4-6) **Fic**
Teague, M. The field beyond the outfield
E
Tunis, J. R. The kid from Tomkinsville (5
and up) **Fic**
Poetry
At the crack of the bat (3-5) **811.008**
Extra innings (4 and up) **811.008**
Thayer, E. L. Casey at the bat **811**

Baseball cards
Fiction
Slote, A. The trading games (4-6) **Fic**
Baseball diamonds [series]
Tunis, J. R. The kid from Tomkinsville
Fic
Baseball fever. Hurwitz, J. **Fic**
Baseball in April. Soto, G.
In Soto, G. Baseball in April, and other
stories p13-22 **S C**
Baseball in April, and other stories. Soto, G.
S C
Baseball legends [series]
Kavanagh, J. Honus Wagner **92**
Baseball saved us. Mochizuki, K. **E**
Baseball, the American epic [series]
Ward, G. C. 25 great moments **796.357**
Ward, G. C. Shadow ball **796.357**
Ward, G. C. Who invented the game?
796.357
Baseball tips. Hughes, D. **796.357**
Baseball's greatest hitters. Kramer, S. **920**
Bash, Barbara
Ancient ones (3-5) **585**
Desert giant (3-5) **583**
Shadows of night (1-3) **599.4**

Bash, Barbara—*Continued*
Tree of life: the world of the African baobab
(3-5) **583**
Urban roosts: where birds nest in the city
(1-4) **598**
Basic rights *See* Civil rights
Basil and the pygmy cats. Titus, E. See note
under Titus, E. Basil of Baker Street
Fic
Basil in Mexico. Titus, E. See note under Ti-
tus, E. Basil of Baker Street **Fic**
Basil in the Wild West. Titus, E. See note un-
der Titus, E. Basil of Baker Street
Fic
Basil of Baker Street. Titus, E. **Fic**
Basketball
Anderson, D. The story of basketball (5 and
up) **796.323**
Sullivan, G. All about basketball (4 and up)
796.323
Biography
Kornbluth, J. Airborne: the triumph and
struggle of Michael Jordan (5 and up)
92
Lipsyte, R. Michael Jordan (5 and up)
92
Townsend, B. Shaquille O'Neal (4 and up)
92
Fiction
Soto, G. Taking sides (5 and up) **Fic**
Baskin, Barbara Holland, 1929-
More notes from a different drummer
016.8
Notes from a different drummer **016.8**
Baskin, Leonard, 1922-
(il) Segal, L. G. The book of Adam to Mo-
ses **222**
Basquiat, Jean-Michel, 1960-1988
(il) Angelou, M. Life doesn't frighten me
811
Bassett, Jeni
(il) Kroll, S. The biggest pumpkin ever
E
Bates, Artie Ann
Ragsale **E**
Batherman, Muriel
(il) Garten, J. The alphabet tale **E**
Bathrooms
History
Colman, P. Toilets, bathtubs, sinks, and
sewers (5 and up) **643**
Baths
Fiction
Cole, B. No more baths **E**
Wood, A. King Bidgood's in the bathtub
E
Bathwater's hot. Hughes, S.
In Hughes, S. The nursery collection
E
Batman. Pringle, L. P. **599.4**
Bats
Bash, B. Shadows of night (1-3) **599.4**
Maestro, B. Bats (k-3) **599.4**

Pringle, L. P. Batman (4 and up) **599.4**
Selsam, M. E. A first look at bats (1-3)
599.4
Stuart, D. Bats (3-6) **599.4**
Fiction
Cannon, J. Stellaluna **E**
Bats, bugs, and biodiversity. Goodman, S.
574.5
Batten, John D. (John Dickson), 1860-1932
(il) Jacobs, J. English fairy tales **398.2**
Battered children *See* Child abuse
Battering of wives *See* Wife abuse
The **battle** for the castle. Winthrop, E. See
note under Winthrop, E. The castle in the
attic **Fic**
The **Battle** of Gettysburg. Johnson, N.
973.7
Battling dragons **028.5**
Bauer, Caroline Feller, 1935-
Caroline Feller Bauer's new handbook for
storytellers **372.6**
Celebrations **808.8**
Marika the snowmaiden
In Snowy day: stories and poems p45-49
808.8
The poetry break **372.6**
Presenting reader's theater **808.82**
Read for the fun of it **027.62**
Supermarket Thanksgiving
In Thanksgiving: stories and poems p57-
68 **810.8**
This way to books **028.5**
(ed) Halloween: stories and poems. See Hal-
loween: stories and poems **808.8**
(ed) Rainy day: stories and poems. See
Rainy day: stories and poems **808.8**
(ed) Snowy day: stories and poems. See
Snowy day: stories and poems **808.8**
(ed) Thanksgiving: stories and poems. See
Thanksgiving: stories and poems
810.8
(ed) Valentine's day: stories and poems. See
Valentine's day: stories and poems
810.8
(ed) Windy day: stories and poems. See
Windy day: stories and poems **808.8**
Bauer, Marion Dane, 1938-
On my honor (4 and up) **Fic**
A question of trust (5 and up) **Fic**
Rain of fire (5 and up) **Fic**
What's your story? (5 and up) **808.3**
When I go camping with Grandma **E**
Baum, Froim, 1936-
About
Adler, D. A. Child of the Warsaw ghetto
(3-5) **940.53**
Baum, L. Frank (Lyman Frank), 1856-1919
Dorothy and the Wizard in Oz. See note un-
der Baum, L. F. The Wizard of Oz
Fic
The land of Oz. See note under Baum, L. F.
The Wizard of Oz **Fic**
Little Wizard stories of Oz. See note under
Baum, L. F. The Wizard of Oz **Fic**

Baum, L. Frank (Lyman Frank), 1856-1919—
Continued
  The magic of Oz. See note under Baum, L.
    F. The Wizard of Oz   **Fic**
  The marvelous land of Oz. See note under
    Baum, L. F. The Wizard of Oz   **Fic**
  Ozma of Oz. See note under Baum, L. F.
    The Wizard of Oz   **Fic**
  The patchwork girl of Oz. See note under
    Baum, L. F. The Wizard of Oz   **Fic**
  The tin woodsman of Oz. See note under
    Baum, L. F. The Wizard of Oz   **Fic**
  The Wizard of Oz (3-6)   **Fic**

Baum, Lyman Frank *See* Baum, L. Frank (Lyman Frank), 1856-1919

Baumann, Karen
  (il) Ring out, wild bells. See Ring out, wild
    bells   **808.81**

Baumfree, Isabella *See* Truth, Sojourner, d. 1883

Baumli, Othmar, 1936-
  (il) Schnieper, C. An apple tree through the
    year   **634**

Baviera, Rocco
  (il) Bruchac, J. A boy called Slow: the true
    story of Sitting Bull   **92**

Bawden, Nina, 1925-
  Carrie's war (4 and up)   **Fic**
  A handful of thieves (4 and up)   **Fic**
  Henry (5 and up)   **Fic**
  Humbug (4 and up)   **Fic**
  The outside child (5 and up)   **Fic**
  The robbers (5 and up)   **Fic**
  The witch's daughter (4 and up)   **Fic**

Bayer, Jane, d. 1985
  A my name is Alice   **E**

Bayley, Nicola, 1949-
  (il) Barber, A. The Mousehole cat   **E**

Baylor, Byrd, 1924-
  The desert is theirs (1-4)   **574.5**
  Desert voices   **E**
  Hawk, I'm your brother   **E**
  I'm in charge of celebrations (3-6)   **Fic**
  Moon song (1-4)   **398.2**
  The way to start a day (1-4)   **291.4**
  When clay sings (1-4)   **970.004**

Baynes, Pauline, 1922-
  (il) Godden, R. Four dolls   **S C**
  (il) Lewis, C. S. The lion, the witch, and the
    wardrobe   **Fic**

Bayou lullaby. Appelt, K.   **E**

Be a friend to trees. Lauber, P.   **582.16**

Be a kid physicist. Wellnitz, W. R.   **530**

Be seated: a book about chairs. Giblin, J.
                    749

Be the judge/Be the jury [series]
  Rappaport, D. Tinker vs. Des Moines
                  342

Bea and Mr. Jones. Schwartz, A.   **E**

Beach ball. Sis, P.   **E**

Beach ball—left, right. McMillan, B.
                  152.3

Beach day. Oxenbury, H.   **E**

A **beach** for the birds. McMillan, B.   **598**

Beaches
  Rockwell, A. F. At the beach   **E**
             Fiction
  Asch, F. Sand cake   **E**
  Brown, M. T. D.W. all wet   **E**
  Burningham, J. Come away from the water,
    Shirley   **E**
  Cooney, B. Hattie and the wild waves
                  E
  Oxenbury, H. Beach day   **E**
  Sis, P. Beach ball   **E**
             Poetry
  McMillan, B. One sun: a book of terse verse
    (k-3)   **811**

Beacons of light: lighthouses. Gibbons, G.
                  387.1

Bealer, Alex W.
  Only the names remain (4-6)   **970.004**

The **beam.** Grimm, J.
  In Grimm, J. The complete Grimm's
    fairy tales p645   **398.2**

Beano *See* Bingo

Beanpole. Park, B.   **Fic**

The **bear.** Afanas'ev, A. N.
  In Afanas'ev, A. N. Russian fairy tales
    p74-75   **398.2**

The **bear** and the children. Schwartz, H.
  In Schwartz, H. The diamond tree p93-96
                  398.2

The **bear** and the cock. Afanas'ev, A. N.
  In Afanas'ev, A. N. Russian fairy tales
    p455-56   **398.2**

The **bear** boy. Bruchac, J.
  In Bruchac, J. Flying with the eagle, rac-
    ing with the great bear p78-82
                  398.2

A **bear** called Paddington. Bond, M.   **Fic**

The **bear-child.** MacDonald, M. R.
  In MacDonald, M. R. Look back and see
    p107-14   **372.6**

Bear dines with Rabbit. Ross, G.
  In Ross, G. How Rabbit tricked Otter and
    other Cherokee trickster stories p58-
    61   **398.2**

Bear shadow. Asch, F. See note under Asch,
  F. Sand cake   **E**

The **bear** that heard crying. Kinsey-Warnock,
  N.   **E**

The **bear,** the dog, and the cat. Afanas'ev, A.
  N.
  In Afanas'ev, A. N. Russian fairy tales
    p453-55   **398.2**

The **Bear** Woman. Bruchac, J.
  In Bruchac, J. The girl who married the
    Moon p75-83   **398.2**

Bearden, Romare, 1914-1988
See/See also pages in the following book(s):
  Haskins, J. One more river to cross (4 and
  up)   **920**

Beardsley, Aubrey, 1872-1898
(il) Green, R. L. King Arthur and his Knights of the Round Table   **398.2**

Bearhead. Kimmel, E. A.   **398.2**

Bearman: exploring the world of black bears. Pringle, L. P.   **599.74**

Bears

  See also Grizzly bear; Polar bear

Arnosky, J. Every autumn comes the bear   E

Clark, M. G. The threatened Florida black bear (4 and up)   **599.74**

George, J. C. The moon of the bears (3-6)   **599.74**

Greenaway, T. Amazing bears (2-4)   **599.74**

Patent, D. H. Looking at bears (3-5)   **599.74**

Pringle, L. P. Bearman: exploring the world of black bears (4 and up)   **599.74**

Schwartz, A. Fat man in a fur coat, and other bear stories (4 and up)   **599.74**

Stirling, I. Bears (4-6)   **599.74**

Fiction

Alexander, M. G. You're a genius, Blackboard Bear   E

Asch, F. Sand cake   E

Barton, B. The three bears (k-1)   **398.2**

Berenstain, S. Bears on wheels   E

Bond, M. A bear called Paddington (2-5)   Fic

Bond, M. Paddington's storybook (2-5)   S C

Brett, J. Berlioz the bear   E

Carlstrom, N. W. Jesse Bear, what will you wear?   E

Dalgliesh, A. The bears on Hemlock Mountain (1-4)   Fic

Day, A. Frank and Ernest   E

Gage, W. Cully Cully and the bear   E

Galdone, P. The three bears (k-2)   **398.2**

Johnson, A. The grizzly (5 and up)   Fic

Jonas, A. Two bear cubs   E

Kesey, K. Little Tricker, the squirrel, meets Big Double, the bear   E

Kimmel, E. A. The Chanukkah guest   E

Kinsey-Warnock, N. The bear that heard crying   E

Marshall, J. Goldilocks and the three bears (k-2)   **398.2**

McCloskey, R. Blueberries for Sal   E

McLeod, E. The bear's bicycle   E

McPhail, D. M. The bear's toothache   E

McPhail, D. M. Fix-it   E

Milne, A. A. The house at Pooh Corner (1-4)   Fic

Milne, A. A. The Pooh story book (1-4)   Fic

Milne, A. A. Winnie-the-Pooh (1-4)   Fic

Milne, A. A. The world of Pooh (1-4)   Fic

Minarik, E. H. Little Bear   E

Morey, W. Gentle Ben (5 and up)   Fic

Murphy, J. Peace at last   E

Murphy, J. What next, Baby Bear!   E

Peet, B. Big bad Bruce   E

Pomerantz, C. Where's the bear?   E

Rockwell, A. F. First comes spring   E

Rosen, M. We're going on a bear hunt   E

Stevens, J. Tops and bottoms (k-3)   **398.2**

Turkle, B. C. Deep in the forest   E

Vincent, G. Ernest and Celestine   E

Waddell, M. Can't you sleep, Little Bear?   E

Ward, L. K. The biggest bear   E

Wiseman, B. Morris and Boris at the circus   E

Young, R. Golden Bear   E

Poetry

Yolen, J. The three bears holiday rhyme book (k-2)   **811**

Yolen, J. The three bears rhyme book (k-2)   **811**

Bear's bargain. Asch, F. See note under Asch, F. Sand cake   E

The **bear's bicycle.** McLeod, E.   E

The **bears' house.** Sachs, M.   Fic

The **bears on Hemlock Mountain.** Dalgliesh, A.   Fic

Bears on wheels. Berenstain, S.   E

The **bear's speech.** Cortázar, J.
  In Where angels glide at dawn p3-5   S C

The **bear's toothache.** McPhail, D. M.   E

Bearskin. Grimm, J.
  In Grimm, J. The complete Grimm's fairy tales p467-72   **398.2**

Bearskin. Pyle, H.
  In Pyle, H. The wonder clock p1-14   **398.2**

Beast feast. Florian, D.   **811**

Beastly neighbors. Rights, M.   **508**

Beasts in a pit. Afanas'ev, A. N.
  In Afanas'ev, A. N. Russian fairy tales p498   **398.2**

The **beasts of Bethlehem.** Kennedy, X. J.   **811**

Beat the drum (2-4)   **811.008**

Beat the story-drum, pum-pum. Bryan, A.   **398.2**

Beat the turtle drum. Greene, C. C.   Fic

Beats me, Claude. Nixon, J. L.   E

Beattie, Owen
Buried in ice (4 and up)   **998**

Beatty, Patricia, 1922-1991
Bonanza girl (5 and up)   Fic
Charley Skedaddle (5 and up)   Fic
Eight mules from Monterey (5 and up)   Fic
Jayhawker (5 and up)   Fic
Turn homeward, Hannalee (5 and up)   Fic

Beatty (Clyde)-Cole Bros. Circus *See* Clyde Beatty-Cole Bros. Circus

Beezus and Ramona. Cleary, B. See note under Cleary, B. Ramona the pest **Fic**

Beezus and Ramona [excerpt]. Cleary, B.
In The Random House book of humor for children p100-19 **817.008**

Befana (Legendary character)
De Paola, T. The legend of Old Befana (k-3) **398.2**

Before the sun dies. Gallant, R. A. **575**

Before the Wright brothers. Berliner, D. **629.13**

Begay, Shonto
Ma'ii and cousin Horned Toad (k-3) **398.2**
Navajo (5 and up) **811**
(il) Cohen, C. L. The mud pony **398.2**

The **Beggar** Queen. Alexander, L. **Fic**

The **beggar's** plan. Afanas'ev, A. N.
In Afanas'ev, A. N. Russian fairy tales p599 **398.2**

A **beginning**. Sanfield, S.
In Sanfield, S. The feather merchants & other tales of the fools of Chelm p2-7 **398.2**

Beginning golf. Jensen, J. **796.352**

The **beginning** of the armadilloes. Kipling, R. **Fic**
also in Kipling, R. Just so stories **S C**

Beginning soccer. Jensen, J. **796.334**

Beginning sports [series]
Jensen, J. Beginning golf **796.352**
Jensen, J. Beginning soccer **796.334**
Jensen, J. Beginning tennis **796.342**
Jensen, J. Beginning volleyball **796.325**

Beginning tennis. Jensen, J. **796.342**

Beginning volleyball. Jensen, J. **796.325**

Beginning with books. DeSalvo, N. **027.62**

Behavior *See* Human behavior

Behind rebel lines: the incredible story of Emma Edmonds, Civil War spy. Reit, S. **92**

Behind the attic wall. Cassedy, S. **Fic**

Behind the Blue and Gray. Ray, D. **973.7**

Behind the headlines. Fleming, T. J. **071**

Behind the secret window. Toll, N. S. **940.53**

Being a twin, having a twin. Rosenberg, M. B. **155.4**

Being adopted. Rosenberg, M. B. **362.7**

Being born. Kitzinger, S. **612.6**

Beisner, Monika
Catch that cat! **793.73**

Belaney, Archibald Stansfeld *See* Grey Owl, 1888-1938

Belarus
Belarus (5 and up) **947**

Belarus (5 and up) **947**

Belgium
Belgium—in pictures (5 and up) **949.3**

Hargrove, J. Belgium (4 and up) **949.3**

Belgium and Luxembourg in pictures. See Belgium—in pictures **949.3**

Belgium—in pictures (5 and up) **949.3**

Bell, Alexander Graham, 1847-1922
About
Parker, S. Alexander Graham Bell and the telephone (4 and up) **92**
St. George, J. Dear Dr. Bell—your friend, Helen Keller (5 and up) **92**

Bell, Anthea
The nutcracker (2-4) **Fic**

Bell, Cool Papa
See/See also pages in the following book(s):
Brashler, W. The story of Negro league baseball (5 and up) **796.357**

Bell, Currer *See* Brontë, Charlotte, 1816-1855

Bell, Ellis *See* Brontë, Emily, 1818-1848

Bell, Neill, 1946-
The book of where (4 and up) **910**

Bellairs, John
The chessmen of doom. See note under Bellairs, J. The curse of the blue figurine **Fic**
The curse of the blue figurine (5 and up) **Fic**
The doom of the haunted opera. See note under Bellairs, J. The house with a clock in its walls **Fic**
The eyes of the killer robot. See note under Bellairs, J. The curse of the blue figurine **Fic**
The figure in the shadows. See note under Bellairs, J. The house with a clock in its walls **Fic**
The ghost in the mirror. See note under Bellairs, J. The house with a clock in its walls **Fic**
The house with a clock in its walls (5 and up) **Fic**
The letter, the witch, and the ring. See note under Bellairs, J. The house with a clock in its walls **Fic**
The mummy, the will and the crypt. See note under Bellairs, J. The curse of the blue figurine **Fic**
The revenge of the wizard's ghost. See note under Bellairs, J. The curse of the blue figurine **Fic**
The secret of the underground room. See note under Bellairs, J. The curse of the blue figurine **Fic**
The spell of the sorcerer's skull. See note under Bellairs, J. The curse of the blue figurine **Fic**
The trolley to yesterday. See note under Bellairs, J. The curse of the blue figurine **Fic**
The vengeance of the witch-finder. See note under Bellairs, J. The house with a clock in its walls **Fic**

Bellamy, David, 1933-
The rock pool (1-4) **574.92**

Bellan-Gillen, Patricia
(il) Baker, P. J. My first book of sign
419

Belling the cat and other Aesop's fables. Paxton, T. **398.2**

The **Bellmaker**. Jacques, B. See note under Jacques, B. Redwall **Fic**

Belloc, Hilaire, 1870-1953
Matilda, who told lies, and was burned to death (1-3) **821**

The **bells** of Christmas. Hamilton, V. **Fic**

Bellville, Cheryl Walsh, 1944-
(il) Berman, R. American bison **599.73**
(il) Burns, D. L. Cranberries: fruit of the bogs **634**

Belly laughs. Keller, C. **793.73**

Below the root. Snyder, Z. K. **Fic**

Belpré, Pura
The Three Magi
In The Family read-aloud Christmas treasury p82-89 **808.8**

Belting, Natalia Maree, 1915-
Moon was tired of walking on air (4 and up) **398.2**
Contents: Moon was tired of walking on air; The traveling sky baskets; What happened when fox opened the bottle tree; Daughter of rain; Why rainbow is bent; Why sun has a headdress and moon has none; When Orekeke wrestled Tornado; Ghost and souls; Fox and the parakeet women; Worlds above, worlds below; How Averiri made the night and the seasons; What happened when armadillo dug a hole in the sky; The ancestors are all around us; How the birds got new beaks and men got teeth

Belton, Sandra, 1939-
May'naise sandwiches & sunshine tea **E**

Beltrami, Giacomo Constantino, 1779-1855
See/See also pages in the following book(s):
McCall, E. S. Biography of a river: the living Mississippi p67-75 (6 and up)
977

Bemelmans, Ludwig, 1898-1962
Madeline **E**
Madeline and the bad hat. See note under Bemelmans, L. Madeline **E**
Madeline and the gypsies. See note under Bemelmans, L. Madeline **E**
Madeline in London. See note under Bemelmans, L. Madeline **E**
Madeline's Christmas. See note under Bemelmans, L. Madeline **E**
Madeline's rescue **E**
See/See also pages in the following book(s):
Caldecott Medal books, 1938-1957 p255-65
028.5

Ben & Jerry's Homemade Inc.
Jaspersohn, W. Ice cream (3-5) **637**

Ben and me. Lawson, R. **Fic**

Ben and the porcupine. Carrick, C. See note under Carrick, C. The foundling **E**

Bencastro, Mario
A clown's story
In Where angels glide at dawn p57-65
S C

Benchley, Nathaniel, 1915-1981
A ghost named Fred **E**

Small Wolf **E**

Bendemolena
In Diane Goode's book of silly stories & songs p21-27 **398.2**

Bender, Lionel
Invention (4 and up) **609**

Bendick, Jeanne, 1919-
Egyptian tombs (4 and up) **932**
Exploring an ocean tide pool (3-5)
574.92
Tombs of the ancient Americas (4 and up)
393

Beneath a blue umbrella: rhymes. Prelutsky, J.
811

Benedek, Dezsö
(jt. auth) Spariosu, M. Ghosts, vampires, and werewolves **398.2**

Beneficial insects
See also Insect pests

Benin
Fiction
Cowen-Fletcher, J. It takes a village **E**

Benizara and Kakezara. MacDonald, M. R.
In MacDonald, M. R. Celebrate the world p10-19 **372.6**

Benjamin, Carol Lea
Cartooning for kids (4-6) **741.5**

Benjamin and the caliph. Jaffe, N.
In Jaffe, N. While standing on one foot p33-37 **296.1**

Benjamin Franklin and electricity. Parker, S.
92

Benjamin's 365 birthdays. Barrett, J. **E**

Benjamin's barn. Lindbergh, R. **E**

Benne, Mae, 1924-
Principles of children's services in public libraries **027.62**

Bennett, Jill, 1947-
(comp) A Cup of starshine. See A Cup of starshine **808.81**

Bennett, Linda, 1942-
(il) Jobb, J. The night sky book **523**

Bennett Cerf's book of riddles. Cerf, B.
793.73

Benny bakes a cake. Rice, E. **E**

Benoit, Joan *See* Samuelson, Joan

Ben's dream. Van Allsburg, C. **E**

Ben's trumpet. Isadora, R. **E**

Benson, Islay
Long live Christmas
In The Big book of Christmas plays p213-27 **808.82**

Benson, Patrick
(il) Grahame, K. The wind in the willows
Fic
(il) Waddell, M. Owl babies **E**

Bent, Jennifer
(il) Dee, R. Tower to heaven **398.2**

Bentley, Judith, 1945-
Brides, midwives, and widows (5 and up)
978

Berry, James—*Continued*
Spiderman Anancy (5 and up)　　**398.2**
Contents: Anancy and looking for a wife; Anancy, Old Witch and King-Daughter; Anancy and the making of the Bro title; Anancy, Dog and Old Higue Dry-Skull; Monkey, Tiger and the Magic Trials; Tiger and Anancy meet for war; Anancy and friend; Anancy and the Hide-Away Garden; Tiger and the Stump-a-Foot Celebration Dance; Mrs Anancy, chicken soup and Anancy; Ratbat and Tacooma's tree; Bro Tiger goes dead; Anancy runs into Tiger's trouble; Mrs Dog first-child and Monkey-Mother; Anancy and storm and the Reverend Man-Cow; Anancy and Dog and Puss and friendship; Anancy and bad news to Cow-Mother; Mrs Puss, Dog and thieves; Anancy, Tiger and the Shine-Dancer-Shine; Anancy, Lion and Tiger's last day

(comp) Classic poems to read aloud. See Classic poems to read aloud　　**808.81**

Beshore, George W.
Science in ancient China (4 and up)
　　509

Beskow, Elsa, 1874-1953
Pelle's new suit　　**E**

Besmehn, Bobby
Juggling step-by-step (4 and up)　　**793.8**

Bess. Schwartz, A.
In Schwartz, A. Scary stories 3 p27-29
　　398.2

Bess Call. San Souci, R.
In San Souci, R. Cut from the same cloth p13-18　　**398.2**

The **best** bad thing. Uchida, Y. See note under Uchida, Y. A jar of dreams　　**Fic**

Best books *See* Books and reading—Best books

Best books for children, 1992-1995, Science books & films'　　**016.5**

Best books for children: preschool through grade 6　　**011.6**

The **best** boy in the world. Schwartz, A.
In Schwartz, A. All of our noses are here, and other noodle tales p38-57
　　398.2

The **best** Christmas pageant ever. Robinson, B.　　**Fic**

The **best** Christmas pageant ever [excerpt]. Robinson, B.
In The Random House book of humor for children p144-53　　**817.008**

Best encyclopedias, Kister's. Kister, K. F.
　　016

Best friends. Cohen, M. See note under Cohen, M. See you in second grade!　　**E**

Best friends. Kellogg, S.　　**E**

Best friends for Frances. Hoban, R. See note under Hoban, R. Bedtime for Frances
　　E

Best girl. Smith, D. B.　　**Fic**

The **best**: high/low books for reluctant readers. Pilla, M. L.　　**011.6**

Best holiday books [series]
Macmillan, D. Chinese New Year　　**394.2**
Macmillan, D. Ramadan and Id al-Fitr
　　297

The **Best** in children's books　　**028.1**

The **best-laid** plans of Jonah Twist. Honeycutt, N. See note under Honeycutt, N. The all new Jonah Twist　　**Fic**

The **best** of Aesop's fables. Clark, M.
　　398.2

The **best** of Bookfinder. Dreyer, S. S.
　　011.6

The **best** school year ever. Robinson, B. See note under Robinson, B. The best Christmas pageant ever　　**Fic**

Best that life has to give. Pyle, H.
In Pyle, H. The wonder clock p305-18
　　398.2

The **best** way to carry water. Bernier-Grand, C. T.
In Bernier-Grand, C. T. Juan Bobo p6-12
　　398.2

Best wishes. Rylant, C.　　**92**

Best witches: poems for Halloween. Yolen, J.
　　811

Bet you can! science possibilities to fool you. Cobb, V.　　**793.8**

Bet you can't! science impossibilities to fool you. Cobb, V.　　**793.8**

Betancourt, Jeanne, 1941-
My name is brain Brian (4-6)　　**Fic**

Bethune, Mary Jane McLeod, 1875-1955
About
Greenfield, E. Mary McLeod Bethune (2-5)
　　92

McKissack, P. C. Mary McLeod Bethune: a great American educator (4 and up)
　　92

Betsy and Joe. Lovelace, M. H. See note under Lovelace, M. H. Betsy-Tacy　　**Fic**

Betsy and Tacy go downtown. Lovelace, M. H. See note under Lovelace, M. H. Betsy-Tacy　　**Fic**

Betsy and Tacy go over the big hill. Lovelace, M. H. See note under Lovelace, M. H. Betsy-Tacy　　**Fic**

Betsy and the great world. Lovelace, M. H. See note under Lovelace, M. H. Betsy-Tacy　　**Fic**

Betsy in spite of herself. Lovelace, M. H. See note under Lovelace, M. H. Betsy-Tacy
　　Fic

Betsy-Tacy. Lovelace, M. H.　　**Fic**

Betsy-Tacy and Tib. Lovelace, M. H. See note under Lovelace, M. H. Betsy-Tacy
　　Fic

Betsy was a junior. Lovelace, M. H. See note under Lovelace, M. H. Betsy-Tacy
　　Fic

Betsy's wedding. Lovelace, M. H. See note under Lovelace, M. H. Betsy-Tacy　　**Fic**

Better Homes and Gardens step-by-step kids' cook book (4 and up)　　**641.5**

Better not get wet, Jesse Bear. Carlstrom, N. W. See note under Carlstrom, N. W. Jesse Bear, what will you wear?　　**E**

Better wait till Martin comes. Hamilton, V.
In Hamilton, V. The people could fly: American black folktales p133-37
398.2

Betz, Adrienne
(comp) Diane Goode's book of silly stories & songs. See Diane Goode's book of silly stories & songs **398.2**

Beware of kissing Lizard Lips. Shalant, P.
Fic

Beware the mare. Haas, J. **Fic**

Beyond picture books. Barstow, B. **011.6**

Beyond the cross-stitch mountains. 1948. Geras, A.
In Geras, A. Golden windows and other stories of Jerusalem p61-106
S C

Beyond the ridge. Goble, P. **Fic**

The **BFG**. Dahl, R. **Fic**

Bial, Raymond
Amish home (3-5) **289.7**
Shaker home (3-5) **289**
The Underground Railroad (4 and up) **326**

Bianco, Margery Williams, 1880-1944
The velveteen rabbit (2-4) **Fic**

Bible
The Holy Bible [King James Bible. Oxford Univ. Press] **220.5**
The Holy Bible: new revised standard version **220.5**
History of Biblical events
Day, M. The ancient world of the Bible (4 and up) **221.9**
Natural history
Bible. Selections. Animals of the Bible (1-4) **220.8**
Paterson, J. B. Consider the lilies (5 and up) **220.8**

Bible. N.T. Selections
The Christmas story (k-3) **232.9**
The Christmas story: told through paintings (4 and up) **232.9**
The first Christmas (4 and up) **232.9**

Bible. O.T. Genesis
The story of the creation (k-3) **222**

Bible. O.T. Psalms
Eisler, C. T. David's songs (4 and up) **223**

Bible. Selections
Animals of the Bible (1-4) **220.8**
Tomie dePaola's book of Bible stories **220.9**

Bible stories
Bible. O.T. Genesis. The story of the creation (k-3) **222**
Bible. Selections. Tomie dePaola's book of Bible stories **220.9**
Brent, I. Noah's ark (k-3) **222**
Brown, M. W. Christmas in the barn (k-2) **232.9**
Chaikin, M. Children's Bible stories from Genesis to Daniel (4 and up) **221.9**

Chaikin, M. Exodus (2-4) **222**
Chaikin, M. Joshua in the Promised Land (4 and up) **222**
Cohen, B. David (5 and up) **222**
De Paola, T. The miracles of Jesus (k-3) **232.9**
Fisher, L. E. David and Goliath (k-3) **222**
Fisher, L. E. Moses (k-3) **222**
Fisher, L. E. The seven days of creation (k-3) **222**
Fisher, L. E. The Wailing Wall (4 and up) **221.9**
Geisert, A. The ark (k-3) **222**
Gellman, M. Does God have a big toe? (4-6) **221.9**
Hutton, W. Adam and Eve (k-3) **222**
Hutton, W. Moses in the bulrushes (k-3) **222**
Johnson, J. W. The creation **811**
Patterson, G. Jonah and the whale (1-3) **224**
Patterson, J. Angels, prophets, rabbis & kings from the stories of the Jewish people (4-6) **296.1**
Segal, L. G. The book of Adam to Moses (4-6) **222**
Spier, P. Noah's ark (k-2) **222**
Stoddard, S. A child's first Bible (k-2) **220.9**
Stoddard, S. The Doubleday illustrated children's Bible (4-6) **220.9**
Waddell, M. Stories from the Bible **221.9**
Wildsmith, B. The Easter story (k-3) **232.9**
Winthrop, E. A child is born: the Christmas story (k-3) **232.9**
Winthrop, E. He is risen: the Easter story (k-3) **232.9**

Bibliographic instruction
Assessment and the school library media center **027.8**

Bibliographies and indexes in world literature [series]
Khorana, M. Africa in literature for children and young adults **016.9**

Bibliography
See also Books
Best books
See Books and reading—Best books

The **bicycle** man. Say, A. **E**

Bicycle racing
Hautzig, D. 1,000 miles in 12 days (4-6) **796.6**

Bicycles
See also Cycling
Rockwell, A. F. Bikes (k-1) **629.227**
Stine, M. Wheels! the kids' bike book (4 and up) **796.6**

Bicycles and bicycling *See* Cycling

Bierhorst, John
Doctor Coyote (1-4) **398.2**

Bierhorst, John—*Continued*
Why there is death: a native American story
In The Big book for our planet p68-72
810.8
The woman who fell from the sky (k-3)
398.2
(ed) In the trail of the wind. See In the trail
of the wind **897**
(ed) The Monkey's haircut, and other stories
told by the Maya. See The Monkey's haircut, and other stories told by the Maya
398.2
(ed) The Naked bear. See The Naked bear
398.2
(comp) On the road of stars. See On the
road of stars **897**
(ed) The Sacred path. See The Sacred path
897

Biesty, Stephen
Stephen Biesty's cross-sections: Castle (4
and up) **940.1**
Stephen Biesty's cross-sections: Man-of-war
(4 and up) **359.1**
Stephen Biesty's incredible cross-sections (4
and up) **600**
(il) Hart, G. Exploring the past: ancient
Egypt **932**

The **big** Alfie and Annie Rose storybook.
Hughes, S. See note under Hughes, S. Al-
fie gets in first **E**
The **big** Alfie out of doors storybook. Hughes,
S. See note under Hughes S. Alfie gets in
first **E**
Big Anthony and the magic ring. De Paola, T.
See note under De Paola, T. Strega Nona
E
Big Apple Circus
Machotka, H. The magic ring (3-6)
791.3
Big bad Bruce. Peet, B. **E**
The **big** balloon race. Coerr, E. **E**
Big bang theory *See* Universe
The **big** beast book. Booth, J. **567.9**
The **big** black umbrella. Leach, M.
In The Oxford book of scary tales p86-87
808.8
The **Big** book for our planet **810.8**
The **Big** book for peace **810.8**
The **Big** book of Christmas plays **808.82**
The **big** bug book. Facklam, M. **595.7**
Big cats. Simon, S. **599.74**
The **big** concrete lorry. Hughes, S. See note
under Hughes, S. Angel Mae: a tale of
Trotter Street **E**
Big Dipper *See* Ursa Major
The **Big** Dipper. Branley, F. M. **523.8**
Big fat hen. Baker, K. **398.8**
Big feet of the Empress Tu Chin. Carpenter,
F.
In Carpenter, F. Tales of a Chinese grand-
mother p81-88 **398.2**
Big foot *See* Sasquatch

Big game hunting *See* Hunting
Big green drawing book, Ed Emberley's. Em-
berley, E. **741.2**
Big Jack and Little Jack
In The Jack tales p67-75 **398.2**
The **big** lie. Leitner, I. **940.53**
Big Max. Platt, K. **E**
Big men, big country. Walker, P. R.
398.2
Big Mose and the Lady Washington. Walker,
P. R.
In Walker, P. R. Big men, big country
p29-35 **398.2**
Big old bones. Carrick, C. **E**
Big red barn. Brown, M. W. **E**
Big red drawing book, Ed Emberley's. Ember-
ley, E. **741.2**
Big rigs. Marston, H. I. **629.224**
Big Sixteen
In Raw Head, bloody bones p65-67
398.2
The **big** sneeze. Brown, R. **E**
The **big** snow. Hader, B. **E**
The **big** storm. Hiscock, B. **551.55**
Big-top circus. Johnson, N. **791.3**
The **big** tree. Hiscock, B. **582.16**
The **Big** worm
In Raw Head, bloody bones p51-53
398.2
Bigfoot *See* Sasquatch
Bigfoot and other legendary creatures. Walker,
P. R. **001.9**
Bigger. Calvert, P. **Fic**
The **biggest** bear. Ward, L. K. **E**
The **biggest** house in the world. Lionni, L.
E
The **biggest** pumpkin ever. Kroll, S. **E**
Biggest, strongest, fastest. Jenkins, S. **591**
Biggin, Gary
(il) Butterfield, M. Bulldozers **629.225**
(il) Butterfield, M. Space **629.47**
Bigmama's. Crews, D. **92**
Bikes. Rockwell, A. F. **629.227**
Bileck, Marvin, 1920-
(jt. auth) Scheer, J. Rain makes applesauce
E
Bilingual books
English-French
The Cat in the Hat beginner book dictio-
nary in French (k-3) **443**
English-Japanese
Mado, M. The animals (4 and up)
895.6
English-Korean
Han, S. C. The rabbit's escape (k-3)
398.2
English-Spanish
Ancona, G. The piñatamaker: El piñatero
(k-3) **745.594**
Arroz con leche (k-3) **782.42**

Bird. Tolan, S. S.
In The Big book for our planet p73-81
810.8

The **bird** atlas. Taylor, B.   **598**

The **Bird** bride
In The Monkey's haircut, and other stories told by the Maya p25-31
398.2

The **Bird** Child. Mahy, M.
In Mahy, M. Tick tock tales p17-23
S C

A **bird** in the hand. Jaffe, N.
In Jaffe, N. While standing on one foot p87-90   **296.1**

The **bird** of fortune. Walker, B. K.
In Walker, B. K. A treasury of Turkish folktales for children p108-13
398.2

The **bird** that made milk. Lester, J.
In Lester, J. How many spots does a leopard have? and other tales p5-11
398.2

Bird watching
Pine, J. Backyard birds (3-5)   **598**

The **bird** who spoke three times. Sawyer, R.
In Sawyer, R. The way of the storyteller p297-304   **372.6**

Bird Woman *See* Sacagawea, b. 1786

Birds
    See also Birds of prey; Cage birds; Canaries; Condors; Water birds
Arnold, C. Ostriches and other flightless birds (3-5)   **598**
Arnosky, J. Crinkleroot's 25 birds every child should know (k-3)   **598**
Arnosky, J. Crinkleroot's guide to knowing the birds (k-3)   **598**
Bailey, J. Birds (3-5)   **598**
Burnie, D. Bird (4 and up)   **598**
Burton, M. Birds (5 and up)   **598**
Cole, J. A bird's body   **598**
George, J. C. One day in the woods (4-6)
574.5
Legg, G. Amazing tropical birds (2-4)
598
Lerner, C. Backyard birds of winter (3-6)
598
Markle, S. Outside and inside birds (2-4)
598
Parsons, A. Amazing birds (2-4)   **598**
Patent, D. H. Feathers (4 and up)   **598**
Pine, J. Backyard birds (3-5)   **598**
Rockwell, A. F. Our yard is full of birds (k-2)   **598**
Taylor, B. The bird atlas (5 and up)
598
Wildsmith, B. Brian Wildsmith's birds
E
Witmer, L. M. The search for the origin of birds (4 and up)   **568**
Wolff, A. A year of birds   **E**
Zim, H. S. Birds (4 and up)   **598**

See/See also pages in the following book(s):
Chrystie, F. N. Pets p129-42 (4 and up)
636.088

Eggs and nests
Bash, B. Urban roosts: where birds nest in the city (1-4)   **598**
Demuth, P. Cradles in the trees (1-3)
598
Jenkins, P. B. A nest full of eggs (k-1)
598
Selsam, M. E. A first look at bird nests (1-3)
598

Fiction
Blake, Q. Cockatoos   **E**
Cannon, J. Stellaluna   **E**
De Paola, T. Bill and Pete   **E**
Eastman, P. D. Are you my mother?   **E**
Ehlert, L. Feathers for lunch   **E**
Keller, H. Island baby   **E**
Lewin, B. Booby hatch   **E**
Lionni, L. Inch by inch   **E**
Rohmann, E. Time flies   **E**
Torres, L. Subway sparrow   **E**

Migration
Peters, L. W. This way home (k-3)   **598**

Poetry
Fleischman, P. I am phoenix: poems for two voices (4 and up)   **811**
See/See also pages in the following book(s):
Piping down the valleys wild p127-38
808.81
Rainbow in the sky p217-29 (k-4)
821.008

Protection
Arnold, C. Saving the peregrine falcon (3-5)
598
Friedman, J. Operation Siberian crane (5 and up)   **639.9**
Patent, D. H. The whooping crane (4 and up)   **639.9**
Silverstein, A. The spotted owl (4 and up)
598

Protection—Fiction
Lasky, K. She's wearing a dead bird on her head!   **E**

North America
Peterson, R. T. A field guide to the birds
598
Robbins, C. S. Birds of North America (4 and up)   **598**

West (U.S.)
Peterson, R. T. A field guide to western birds   **598**

Birds and beasts. Smith, W. J.   **811**

A **bird's** body. Cole, J.   **598**

Birds, Brian Wildsmith's. Wildsmith, B.
E

The **Bird's** Christmas Carol. Wiggin, K. D. S.
Fic

Birds of a feather and other Aesop's fables. Paxton, T.   **398.2**

Birds of North America. Robbins, C. S.
598

Birds of prey
    See also names of birds of prey

Björk, Christina
  Linnea in Monet's garden (3-5)   **Fic**
  Linnea's almanac (2-5)   **508**
  Linnea's windowsill garden (3-6)   **635**
Björkman, Steve
  (il) Baer, E. This is the way we go to school
        629.04
  (il) Levine, E. I hate English!   **E**
  (il) Marzollo, J. In 1492   **970.01**
  (il) Marzollo, J. In 1776   **973.3**
Black Americans *See* African Americans
The **Black** Americans: a history in their own
  words, 1619-1983 (6 and up)   **305.8**
Black and white. Macaulay, D.   **E**
Black art (Magic) *See* Witchcraft
Black authors
    See also African American authors
Black authors & illustrators of children's
  books. Rollock, B. T.   **920.003**
Black Beauty. Sewell, A.   **Fic**
The **Black** Bull of Norroway
  In The Blue fairy book p380-84
        398.2
Black Bull of Norroway. Jacobs, J.
  In Jacobs, J. English fairy tales p242-48
        398.2
The **Black** Bull of Norway. Crossley-Holland,
  K.
  In Crossley-Holland, K. British folk tales
  p59-70   **398.2**
The **black** cat. Ahlberg, A. See note under Ahl-
  berg, J. Funnybones   **E**
The **black** cauldron. Alexander, L. See note
  under Alexander, L. The book of three
        Fic
Black diamond. McKissack, P. C.   **796.357**
The **black** dog. Schwartz, A.
  In Schwartz, A. Scary stories 3 p17-19
        398.2
Black eagles. Haskins, J.   **629.13**
The **Black** experience in children's books
        016.3058
Black fighting men. Reef, C.   **920**
Black heroes of the American Revolution. Da-
  vis, B.   **973.3**
Black holes (Astronomy)
  Branley, F. M. Journey into a black hole
  (k-3)   **523.8**
Black is brown is tan. Adoff, A.   **E**
Black literature (American) *See* American
  literature—African American authors
Black magic (Witchcraft) *See* Magic
Black music
    See also African American music
Black musicians
    See also African American musicians
Black on white. Hoban, T.   **E**
The **black** pearl. O'Dell, S.   **Fic**
Black poetry (American) *See* American
  poetry—African American authors

Black ships before Troy. Sutcliff, R.   **883**
The **Black** Stallion. Farley, W.   **Fic**
The **Black** Stallion and Flame. Farley, W. See
  note under Farley, W. The Black Stallion
        Fic
The **Black** Stallion and Satan. Farley, W. See
  note under Farley, W. The Black Stallion
        Fic
The **Black** Stallion and the girl. Farley, W. See
  note under Farley, W. The Black Stallion
        Fic
The **Black** Stallion challenged!. Farley, W. See
  note under Farley, W. The Black Stallion
        Fic
The **Black** Stallion legend. Farley, W. See note
  under Farley, W. The Black Stallion
        Fic
The **Black** Stallion mystery. Farley, W. See
  note under Farley, W. The Black Stallion
        Fic
The **Black** Stallion returns. Farley, W. See
  note under Farley, W. The Black Stallion
        Fic
The **Black** Stallion's Blood Bay colt. Farley,
  W. See note under Farley, W. The Black
  Stallion   **Fic**
The **Black** Stallion's courage. Farley, W. See
  note under Farley, W. The Black Stallion
        Fic
The **Black** Stallion's filly. Farley, W. See note
  under Farley, W. The Black Stallion
        Fic
The **Black** Stallion's ghost. Farley, W. See
  note under Farley, W. The Black Stallion
        Fic
Black stars in orbit. Burns, K.   **920**
Black swan/white crow. Lewis, J. P.   **811**
The **Black** Thief and Knight of the Glen
  In The Red fairy book p54-66   **398.2**
Blackberries in the dark. Jukes, M.   **Fic**
Blackberry ink. Merriam, E.   **811**
Blackboard Bear. Alexander, M. G. See note
  under Alexander, M. G. You're a genius,
  Blackboard Bear   **E**
Blackburn, G. Meredith
  (comp) In the witch's kitchen. See In the
  witch's kitchen   **811.008**
  (comp) Index to poetry for children and
  young people. See Index to poetry for
  children and young people   **808.81**
Blackburn, John Brewton
  (comp) Of quarks, quasars, and other quirks.
  See Of quarks, quasars, and other quirks
        821.008
Blackburn, Lorraine A.
  (comp) In the witch's kitchen. See In the
  witch's kitchen   **811.008**
  (comp) Index to poetry for children and
  young people. See Index to poetry for
  children and young people   **808.81**
Blackfoot Indians *See* Siksika Indians

Blacklock, Craig
(il) Nicholson, D. Wild boars   **599.73**
Blacks
Bibliography
The Black experience in children's books
    016.3058
Biography
See also African Americans—Biography
Cameron, A. The kidnapped prince: the life
of Olaudah Equiano (4 and up)   **92**
Fiction
Daly, N. Not so fast, Songololo   **E**
Hayes, S. Happy Christmas, Gemma   **E**
United States
See African Americans
Blacks in art
See also African Americans in art
Blacks in literature
See also African Americans in literature
The **bladder**, the straw, and the shoe. Afanas-
'ev, A. N.
In Afanas'ev, A. N. Russian fairy tales
p590   **398.2**
Blades, Ann, 1947-
(il) Manson, A. A dog came, too   **971**
Blair, David Nelson
The land and people of Bolivia (5 and up)
    984
Blair's nightmare. Snyder, Z. K. See note un-
der Snyder, Z. K. The headless cupid
    Fic
Blaisdell, Elinore
(il) De la Mare, W. Rhymes and verses
    821
Blake, Arthur
The gold rush of 1849 (5 and up)   **979.4**
Blake, Quentin, 1932-
All join in (k-3)   **821**
Cockatoos   **E**
(il) Dahl, R. The BFG   **Fic**
(il) Dahl, R. Matilda   **Fic**
(il) Dickens, C. A Christmas carol   **Fic**
(il) Mahy, M. The great piratical rumbustifi-
cation & The librarian and the robbers
    Fic
(il) Nash, O. Custard and company: poems
    811
(il) Of quarks, quasars, and other quirks. See
Of quarks, quasars, and other quirks
    821.008
(il) Yeoman, J. The singing tortoise and oth-
er animal folktales   **398.2**
Blake, Robert J.
(il) Ehrlich, A. Maggie and Silky and Joe
    E
Blake, William, 1757-1827
The tyger   **821**
The **blanket**. Burningham, J.   **E**
Blankets
Fiction
Burningham, J. The blanket   **E**
Henkes, K. Owen   **E**

Keller, H. Geraldine's blanket   **E**
Blassingame, Wyatt
The look-it-up book of presidents (5 and up)
    920
Blast off! (k-2)   **811.008**
Blast off to Earth!. Leedy, L.   **910**
A **blaze** of glory. Coville, B.
In Coville, B. Oddly enough p105-18
    S C
Bledsoe, Sara
Colorado
In Hello USA series   **973**
Blegvad, Erik
(jt. auth) Andersen, H. C. Twelve tales
    S C
(il) Blegvad, L. Anna Banana and me   **E**
(il) Bodecker, N. M. Water pennies, and
other poems   **811**
(il) Langton, J. The fragile flag   **Fic**
(il) Norton, M. Bed knob and broomstick
    Fic
(il) Viorst, J. The tenth good thing about
Barney   **E**
See/See also pages in the following book(s):
Sendak, M. Caldecott & Co.: notes on books
and pictures p129-30   **028.5**
Blegvad, Lenore
Anna Banana and me   **E**
Blériot, Louis, 1872-1936
About
Provensen, A. The glorious flight: across the
Channel with Louis Blériot, July 25, 1909
(1-4)   **92**
Blessed are you. Edwards, M.   **296.4**
Blia Xiong
Spagnoli, C. Nine-in-one, Grr! Grr!
    398.2
Blimps *See* Airships
Blimps. Munro, R.   **629.133**
Blind
Adler, D. A. A picture book of Helen Keller
(1-3)   **92**
Alexander, S. H. Mom can't see me (3-5)
    362.4
Alexander, S. H. Mom's best friend (3-5)
    362.4
Arnold, C. A guide dog puppy grows up
(3-5)   **362.4**
Hunter, E. F. Child of the silent night [biog-
raphy of Laura Dewey Bridgman] (3-5)
    92
St. George, J. Dear Dr. Bell—your friend,
Helen Keller (5 and up)   **92**
Books and reading—Bibliography
For younger readers: braille and talking
books   **011.6**
Fiction
Bawden, N. The witch's daughter (4 and up)
    Fic
Goldin, B. D. Cakes and miracles   **E**
Keats, E. J. Apt. 3   **E**
Martin, B. Knots on a counting rope   **E**
Taylor, T. The cay (5 and up)   **Fic**

Blind—Fiction—*Continued*

Taylor, T. Timothy of the cay (5 and up)
    Fic

Taylor, T. The trouble with Tuck (5 and up)
    Fic

Yolen, J. The seeing stick   **E**

Blind, Dogs for the *See* Guide dogs

The **blinded** giant. Jacobs, J.
    In Jacobs, J. English fairy tales p303-04
    398.2

Bliven, Bruce, 1916-
The story of D-Day, June 6, 1944
    940.54

Blizzards
    Fiction
Clifford, E. Help! I'm a prisoner in the library (3-5)   **Fic**

Block city. Stevenson, R. L.   **821**

Blockhead Hans. Andersen, H. C.
    In The Yellow fairy book p313-18
    398.2

Blood, Charles L., 1929-
The goat in the rug   **E**

Blood
Cole, J. Cuts, breaks, bruises, and burns (2-4)   **612**
Showers, P. A drop of blood (k-3)
    612.1

    Circulation
Parker, S. The heart and blood (4 and up)
    612.1
Silverstein, A. The circulatory system (5 and up)   **612.1**

    Diseases
    See also Leukemia

Bloody bones
    In Raw Head, bloody bones p43-46
    398.2

Bloom, Lloyd
(il) Johnston, T. Yonder   **E**
(il) Jukes, M. Like Jake and me   **Fic**
(il) MacLachlan, P. Arthur, for the very first time   **Fic**
(il) Poems for Jewish holidays. See Poems for Jewish holidays   **811.008**

Bloomers!. Blumberg, R.   **305.4**

Blos, Joan W., 1928-
A gathering of days: a New England girl's journal, 1830-32 (6 and up)   **Fic**
The grandpa days   **E**
The heroine of the Titanic: a tale both true and otherwise of the life of Molly Brown (k-3)   **92**
Old Henry   **E**
See/See also pages in the following book(s):
Newbery and Caldecott Medal books, 1976-1985 p65-73   **028.5**

Blossom Culp and the sleep of death. Peck, R. See note under Peck, R. The ghost belonged to me   **Fic**

A **Blossom** promise. Byars, B. C. See note under Byars, B. C. The not-just-anybody family   **Fic**

The **Blossoms** and the Green Phantom. Byars, B. C. See note under Byars, B. C. The not-just-anybody family   **Fic**

The **Blossoms** meet the Vulture Lady. Byars, B. C. See note under Byars, B. C. The not-just-anybody family   **Fic**

Blue Beard. Perrault, C.
    In The Blue fairy book p290-95
    398.2
    In The Classic fairy tales p106-09
    398.2

The **Blue** Bird. Aulnoy, Madame d'
    In The Green fairy book p1-26   **398.2**

Blue Coyote. Mayo, G.
    In Mayo, G. That tricky Coyote! p16-20
    398.2

A **blue-eyed** daisy. Rylant, C.   **Fic**

The **Blue** fairy book (4-6)   **398.2**

Blue heron. Avi   **Fic**

The **blue** jackal. Kherdian, D.
    In Kherdian, D. Feathers and tails p80-87
    398.2

The **blue** light. Grimm, J.
    In Grimm, J. The complete Grimm's fairy tales p530-34   **398.2**

The **Blue** Mountains
    In The Yellow fairy book p256-64
    398.2

Blue potatoes, orange tomatoes. Creasy, R.
    635

The **blue** rose. Baring, M.
    In Shedlock, M. L. The art of the storyteller p204-12   **372.6**

Blue sea. Kalan, R.   **E**

Blue silver. Sandburg, C.
    In Sandburg, C. Rootabaga stories pt 2 p175-79   **S C**
    In Sandburg, C. The Sandburg treasury p159-60   **818**

Blue Sun
    In The Monkey's haircut, and other stories told by the Maya p107-12
    398.2

Blue willow. Gates, D.   **Fic**

Bluebeard. Perrault, C.
    In Perrault, C. The complete fairy tales of Charles Perrault p35-44   **398.2**

Blueberries for Sal. McCloskey, R.   **E**

Blues music
    See also Jazz music

Bluewater journal. Krupinski, L.   **E**

Bluford, Guion S., 1942-
See/See also pages in the following book(s):
Haskins, J. Against all opposition p62-71 (5 and up)   **920**
Haskins, J. Black eagles p146-63 (5 and up)
    629.13

Blum, Raymond
Math tricks, puzzles & games (4 and up)
    793.7

Blumberg, Rhoda, 1917-
Bloomers! (k-3)   **305.4**

Blumberg, Rhoda, 1917——_Continued_
Commodore Perry in the land of the Shogun (5 and up) **952**
The great American gold rush (5 and up) **979.4**
The incredible journey of Lewis and Clark (5 and up) **978**
The remarkable voyages of Captain Cook (5 and up) **910.4**

Blume, Judy
Are you there God? it's me, Margaret (5 and up) **Fic**
Freckle juice (2-4) **Fic**
Fudge-a-mania. See note under Blume, J. Tales of a fourth grade nothing **Fic**
It's not the end of the world (4-6) **Fic**
The one in the middle is the green kangaroo **E**
Otherwise known as Sheila the Great (4-6) **Fic**
The Pain and the Great One **E**
Superfudge. See note under Blume, J. Tales of a fourth grade nothing **Fic**
Tales of a fourth grade nothing (3-6) **Fic**
Tales of a fourth grade nothing [excerpt]
_In_ The Random House book of humor for children p3-14 **817.008**

Blythe, Gary, 1959-
(il) Sheldon, D. The whales' song **E**
Boar out there. Rylant, C.
_In_ Rylant, C. Every living thing p15-18 **S C**

Boars
Nicholson, D. Wild boars (3-6) **599.73**
The **boasting** contest. Yep, L.
_In_ Yep, L. The rainbow people p106-15 **398.2**

Boat. Kentley, E. **387.2**
Boat book. Gibbons, G. **387.2**
Boatbuilding
See also Shipbuilding
Boating. Babbitt, N.
_In_ Babbitt, N. The Devil's other storybook p25-32 **S C**
Boats, Submarine _See_ Submarines; Submersibles
Boats. Barton, B. **387.2**
Boats. Rockwell, A. F. **387.2**
Boats and boating
See also Sailing; Ships
Barton, B. Boats (k-1) **387.2**
Gibbons, G. Boat book (k-3) **387.2**
Kentley, E. Boat (4 and up) **387.2**
Rockwell, A. F. Boats (k-1) **387.2**
The Visual dictionary of ships and sailing (4 and up) **387.2**
Fiction
Maestro, B. Ferryboat **E**
Bob and Ray
Prodigy Street
_In_ The Random House book of humor for children p176-80 **817.008**

Bobak, Cathy
(il) Hartman, G. As the roadrunner runs **E**
(il) Poetry from A to Z. See Poetry from A to Z **808.1**
Bobby Baseball. Smith, R. K. **Fic**
Bock, William Sauts, 1939-
(il) Wolfson, E. From Abenaki to Zuni **970.004**
Bodart, Joni Richards
Booktalk! 2-5. See Booktalk! 2-5 **028**
(ed) Booktalking the award winners. See Booktalking the award winners **028.5**
Bodart-Talbot, Joni
See Bodart, Joni Richards
Bodecker, N. M., 1922-1988
Water pennies, and other poems **811**
(il) Eager, E. Half magic **Fic**
(il) Eager, E. Seven-day magic **Fic**
Bodkin, Odds
The Banshee train **E**
Bodmer, Karl, 1809-1893
(il) Freedman, R. An Indian winter **978**
Body, Human _See_ Human anatomy; Physiology
The **body** atlas. Parker, S. **611**
Body books [series]
Sandeman, A. Bones **612.7**
Sandeman, A. Breathing **612.2**
Body in action [series]
Parker, S. Catching a cold **616.2**
Parker, S. Eating a meal **612.3**
Parker, S. Running a race **796.42**
Parker, S. Singing a song **612.7**
Body talk [series]
Bryan, J. Sound and vision **612.8**
Bodybuilding
Fiction
Browne, A. Willy the wimp **E**
Boehm, David A. (David Alfred), 1914-
Greece—in pictures. See Greece—in pictures **949.5**
Japan—in pictures. See Japan—in pictures **952**
The **boggart.** Cooper, S. **Fic**
Bogs _See_ Marshes; Wetlands
Bohlman, Herman
About
Fraser, M. A. Sanctuary (3-5) **639.9**
Boiko, Claire
We interrupt this program—
_In_ The Big book of Christmas plays p200-12 **808.82**
The **bold** knight, the apples of youth, and the water of life. Afanas'ev, A. N.
_In_ Afanas'ev, A. N. Russian fairy tales p314-20 **398.2**
Bolick, Nancy O'Keefe
Shaker inventions (5 and up) **289**
Bolivia
Blair, D. N. The land and people of Bolivia (5 and up) **984**

Bolivia—*Continued*
Morrison, M. Bolivia (4 and up) **984**

Bollen, Marilyn Sadler *See* Sadler, Marilyn

Bollen, Roger
(il) Sadler, M. Alistair's elephant **E**

Bolognese, Don
The way to draw and color monsters (4 and up) **743**
(il) Brenner, B. Wagon wheels **E**

Bolotin, Norm, 1951-
For home and country (5 and up)
973.7

Bolton, A. C.
The friendly ghost
In The Oxford book of scary tales p137-43 **808.8**

Bomans, Godfried, 1913-1971
The thrush girl
In The Oxford treasury of children's stories p23-27 **S C**

Bonanza girl. Beatty, P. **Fic**

Bond, Felicia, 1954-
Poinsettia & her family **E**
Poinsettia and the firefighters. See note under Bond, F. Poinsettia & her family
E
(il) Branley, F. M. The sky is full of stars
523.8
(il) Brown, M. W. Big red barn **E**
(il) Kramer, S. How to think like a scientist
507
(il) Numeroff, L. J. If you give a moose a muffin **E**
(il) Numeroff, L. J. If you give a mouse a cookie **E**

Bond, Michael, 1926-
A bear called Paddington (2-5) **Fic**
More about Paddington. See note under Bond, M. A bear called Paddington
Fic
Paddington abroad. See note under Bond, M. A bear called Paddington **Fic**
Paddington at large. See note under Bond, M. A bear called Paddington **Fic**
Paddington at work. See note under Bond, M. A bear called Paddington **Fic**
Paddington helps out. See note under Bond, M. A bear called Paddington **Fic**
Paddington marches on. See note under Bond, M. A bear called Paddington
Fic
Paddington on screen. See note under Bond, M. A bear called Paddington **Fic**
Paddington on top. See note under Bond, M. A bear called Paddington **Fic**
Paddington takes the air. See note under Bond, M. A bear called Paddington
Fic
Paddington takes the test. See note under Bond, M. A bear called Paddington
Fic
Paddington takes to TV. See note under Bond, M. A bear called Paddington
Fic

Paddington's 1 2 3. See note under Bond, M. Paddington's colors **E**
Paddington's A B C. See note under Bond, M. Paddington's colors **E**
Paddington's colors **E**
Paddington's opposites. See note under Bond, M. Paddington's colors **E**
Paddington's storybook (2-5) **S C**
Contents: A spot of decorating; Paddington cleans up; Paddington dines out; A visit to the bank; A day by the sea; Something nasty in the kitchen; Paddington and the "finishing touch"; Paddington steps out; Paddington and the "cold snap"; Paddington and the Christmas pantomime
The tales of Olga da Polga (2-5) **Fic**

Bond, Nancy, 1945-
A string in the harp (6 and up) **Fic**
Truth to tell (6 and up) **Fic**

Bond, Ruskin
Eyes of the cat
In The Oxford book of scary tales p76-78
808.8

Bonds of affection. DuBois, G.
In Holiday plays round the year p151-60
812.008

Boneless. San Souci, R.
In San Souci, R. Short & shivery p127-32
398.2

Bones
Balestrino, P. The skeleton inside you (k-3)
611
Parker, S. Skeleton (4 and up) **596**
Sandeman, A. Bones (k-3) **612.7**
Silverstein, A. The skeletal system (5 and up) **612.7**
The Visual dictionary of the skeleton (4 and up) **591.4**
Fiction
Steig, W. The amazing bone **E**

Bones, bones, dinosaur bones. Barton, B.
E

Bonfires and broomsticks. Norton, M.
In Norton, M. Bed-knob and broomstick p97-189 **Fic**

Bong Way Wong *See* El Chino

Bonheur, Rosa, 1822-1899
About
Turner, R. M. Rosa Bonheur (4-6) **92**

Bonne, Rose
I know an old lady who swallowed a fly. See I know an old lady who swallowed a fly
782.42

Bonners, Susan, 1947-
Hunter in the snow: the lynx (2-4)
599.74
The wooden doll **E**
(il) Esbensen, B. J. Cold stars and fireflies
811

Bonnet, Robert L.
Space and astronomy: 49 science fair projects (6 and up) **520**

Bonny, Anne, b. 1700
Poetry
Yolen, J. The ballad of the pirate queens (3-5) **811**

Bonsall, Crosby Newell, 1921-1995
The case of the cat's meow. See note under Bonsall, C. N. The case of the hungry stranger   **E**
The case of the double cross. See note under Bonsall, C. N. The case of the hungry stranger   **E**
The case of the dumb bells. See note under Bonsall, C. N. The case of the hungry stranger   **E**
The case of the hungry stranger   **E**
The case of the scaredy cats. See note under Bonsall, C. N. The case of the hungry stranger   **E**
The day I had to play with my sister   **E**
Piggle. See note under Bonsall, C. N. Who's a pest?   **E**
Who's a pest?   **E**
Who's afraid of the dark?   **E**

Bonson, Richard
(il) Van Rose, S. The earth atlas   **550**

Bonvillain, Nancy
The Navajos (4-6)   **970.004**

Bony-Legs. Cole, J.   **398.2**

Boo!. Crossley-Holland, K.
In Crossley-Holland, K. British folk tales p338   **398.2**

Boo! Coyote. Mayo, G.
In Mayo, G. That tricky Coyote! p1-4   **398.2**

Boo Mama. McKissack, P. C.
In McKissack, P. C. The dark thirty p78-94   **S C**

Boobies, iguanas & other critters. Litteral, L. L.   **508**

Booby hatch. Lewin, B.   **E**

The Boogey Man's wife. Aardema, V.
In Aardema, V. Misoso p15-23   **398.2**

A book about names. Meltzer, M.   **929.4**

Book awards *See* Literary prizes
The **book** finder. See Dreyer, S. S. The bookfinder   **011.6**

Book illustration *See* Illustration of books

Book industries
See also Publishers and publishing
Aliki. How a book is made (2-5)   **686**

Book Links   **028.505**

Book of a thousand and one nights *See* Arabian nights

The **book** of Adam to Moses. Segal, L. G.   **222**

Book of Bible stories, Tomie dePaola's. Bible. Selections   **220.9**

The **book** of changes. Wynne-Jones, T.   **S C**
also in Wynne-Jones, T. The book of changes p47-66   **S C**

Book of children's verse in America, The Oxford   **811.008**

Book of children's verse, The Oxford   **821.008**

Book of Christmas carols, Tomie dePaola's   **782.28**

The **book** of eagles. Sattler, H. R.   **598**

Book of flight for young people, The Smithsonian. Boyne, W. J.   **629.13**

Book of Greek gods and heroes, The Macmillan. Low, A.   **292**

Book of humor for children, The Random House   **817.008**

Book of Kells
Lattimore, D. N. The sailor who captured the sea (2-5)   **745.6**

The **Book** of knowledge. See The New book of knowledge   **031**

The **book** of North American owls. Sattler, H. R.   **598**

The **book** of pigericks: pig limericks. Lobel, A.   **811**

Book of poetry for children, The Random House   **821.008**

Book of popular science, The New   **503**

Book of scary stories and songs, Diane Goode's   **398.2**

Book of silly stories & songs, Diane Goode's   **398.2**

The **book** of think. Burns, M.   **153.4**

The **book** of three. Alexander, L.   **Fic**

The **book** of where. Bell, N.   **910**

A **book** of your own. Stevens, C.   **808**

Book report (Periodical)
Marantz, S. S. Multicultural picture books   **016**

The **book** that Jack wrote. Scieszka, J.   **811**

Book trade *See* Book industries

Bookbird   **028.505**

The **bookfinder.** Dreyer, S. S.   **011.6**

Booklist   **028.1**

Books
See also Printing
Aliki. How a book is made (2-5)   **686**
Brookfield, K. Book (4 and up)   **070.5**
Conservation and restoration
Greenfield, J. Books: their care and repair   **025.7**
Reviews
Appraisal   **016.5**
The Best in children's books   **028.1**
Bookbird   **028.505**
Booklist   **028.1**
Bulletin of the Center for Children's Books   **028.1**
Children's literature review   **028.5**
Emergency Librarian   **027.6205**
Five Owls   **028.505**
Gillespie, J. T. Juniorplots   **028.5**
Gillespie, J. T. More juniorplots   **028.5**
Gillespie, J. T. Juniorplots 3   **028.5**
Gillespie, J. T. Juniorplots 4   **028.5**
Gillespie, J. T. Middleplots 4   **028.5**
The Horn Book Guide to Children's and Young Adult Books   **028.505**
The Horn Book Magazine   **028.505**
Journal of Youth Services in Libraries   **027.6205**

The **bookworm**. Chaloner, G.
In Holiday plays round the year p212-19
812.008
Boondoggle. See Gryski, C. Lanyard
746.42
Booth, D. W. *See* Booth, David, 1938-
Booth, David, 1938-
(comp) Voices on the wind. See Voices on the wind **808.81**
Booth, David W. (David Wallace) *See* Booth, David, 1938-
Booth, George, 1926-
(il) Van Laan, N. Possum come a-knockin'
E
Booth, Jerry
The big beast book (4 and up) **567.9**
Boots *See* Shoes
Boots & the glass mountain. Martin, C.
398.2
Boots and his brothers. Kimmel, E. A.
398.2
The **boots** of buffalo-leather. Grimm, J.
In Grimm, J. The complete Grimm's fairy tales p808-11 **398.2**
Bootsie Barker bites. Bottner, B. **E**
Borden, Louise, 1949-
Caps, hats, socks, and mittens **E**
Bored—nothing to do!. Spier, P. **E**
Borglum, Gutzon, 1867-1941
About
Doherty, C. A. Mount Rushmore (4-6)
730.9
Born a monkey, live a monkey. Sherlock, Sir P. M.
In Sherlock, Sir P. M. West Indian folktales p135-43 **398.2**
Born different. Drimmer, F. **920**
The **borning** room. Fleischman, P. **Fic**
Bornstein, Ruth Lercher, 1927-
(il) MacLachlan, P. Mama One, Mama Two **E**
Borreguita and the coyote. Aardema, V.
398.2
Borrowed children. Lyon, G. E. **Fic**
The **Borrowers**. Norton, M. **Fic**
The **Borrowers** afield. Norton, M. See note under Norton, M. The Borrowers **Fic**
The **Borrowers** afloat. Norton, M. See note under Norton, M. The Borrowers **Fic**
The **Borrowers** aloft. Norton, M. See note under Norton, M. The Borrowers **Fic**
The **Borrowers** avenged. Norton, M. See note under Norton, M. The Borrowers **Fic**
Borski, Lucia Merecka
The jolly tailor
In Rainy day: stories and poems p23-33
808.8
Borton, Elizabeth *See* Treviño, Elizabeth Borton de, 1904-
Bortz, Alfred B.
Catastrophe! (5 and up) **620**

Bosch, Hieronymus, d. 1516
Poetry
Willard, N. Pish, posh, said Hieronymus Bosch (2-5) **811**
Boschung, Herbert T., Jr.
The Audubon Society field guide to North American fishes, whales, and dolphins. See The Audubon Society field guide to North American fishes, whales, and dolphins **597**
Bostock, Mike
(il) Lasky, K. Pond year **E**
(il) Wallace, K. Think of an eel **597**
Boston, L. M. (Lucy Maria), 1892-1990
The children of Green Knowe (4-6) **Fic**
An enemy at Green Knowe. See note under Boston, L. M. The children of Green Knowe **Fic**
The river at Green Knowe. See note under Boston, L. M. The children of Green Knowe **Fic**
A stranger at Green Knowe. See note under Boston, L. M. The children of Green Knowe **Fic**
Treasure of Green Knowe. See note under Boston, L. M. The children of Green Knowe **Fic**
Boston, Lucy Maria *See* Boston, L. M. (Lucy Maria), 1892-1990
Boston, Peter, 1918-
(il) Boston, L. M. The children of Green Knowe **Fic**
Boston (Mass.)
Fiction
Fleischman, P. Saturnalia (6 and up) **Fic**
Forbes, E. Johnny Tremain (5 and up) **Fic**
Marino, J. The Mona Lisa of Salem Street (5 and up) **Fic**
McCloskey, R. Make way for ducklings **E**
Wibberley, L. John Treegate's musket (6 and up) **Fic**
Boston Children's Museum activity book [series]
Zubrowski, B. Clocks **681.1**
Zubrowski, B. Making waves **532**
Zubrowski, B. Mirrors **535**
Zubrowski, B. Mobiles **531**
Zubrowski, B. Shadow play **778.7**
Zubrowski, B. Wheels at work **621.8**
Boston Massacre, 1770
See/See also pages in the following book(s):
Davis, B. Black heroes of the American Revolution p33-40 (5 and up) **973.3**
Boston Post Road. See Gibbons, G. From path to highway: the story of the Boston Post Road **388.1**
Botany
See also Plants
Lerner, C. Plant families (4 and up)
582
Botany, Medical *See* Medical botany

Boyle, Bill
My first atlas (1-3)   **912**

Boyne, Walter J., 1929-
The Smithsonian book of flight for young
people (4 and up)   **629.13**

Boys
Employment
See Children—Employment

Boys at work. Soto, G. See note under Soto,
G. The pool party   **Fic**

A **boy's** Thanksgiving Day. See Child, L. M.
F. Over the river and through the wood
811

The **boys'** war. Murphy, J.   **973.7**

The **bracelet**. Uchida, Y.   **E**

Bradby, Marie
More than anything else   **E**

Brady, April A.
Kwanzaa karamu (4-6)   **641.5**

Brady, Irene, 1943-
(il) McClung, R. M. Lili: a giant panda of
Sichuan   **599.74**
(il) Pringle, L. P. Living treasure   **333.95**

Brady, Mathew B., ca. 1823-1896
About
Sullivan, G. Mathew Brady: his life and
photographs (6 and up)   **92**

Brahms, Johannes, 1833-1897
See/See also pages in the following book(s):
Krull, K. Lives of the musicians p48-53 (4
and up)   **920**

Braille books *See* Blind—Books and reading

Brain
Bruun, R. D. The brain—what it is, what it
does (1-3)   **612.8**
Funston, S. It's all in your brain (4 and up)
612.8
Parker, S. The brain and nervous system (4
and up)   **612.8**
Stafford, P. Your two brains (5 and up)
612.8

The **brain** and nervous system. Parker, S.
612.8

The **brain—what** it is, what it does. Bruun, R.
D.   **612.8**

Braine, Susan
Drumbeat—heartbeat (3-6)   **970.004**

Brainstorm!. Tucker, T.   **609**

Bramwell, Martyn
Glaciers and ice caps (4-6)   **551.3**
Mammals: the small plant-eaters (4 and up)
599
Mountains (4 and up)   **551.4**
The oceans (4-6)   **551.46**
Rivers and lakes (4-6)   **551.48**
Volcanoes and earthquakes (4-6)   **551.2**
Weather (4-6)   **551.5**

Brandenberg, Aliki *See* Aliki

Brandenberg, Franz, 1932-
Aunt Nina and her nephews and nieces
E

Aunt Nina, goodnight. See note under Bran-
denberg, F. Aunt Nina and her nephews,
and nieces   **E**
Aunt Nina's visit. See note under Branden-
berg, F. Aunt Nina and her nephews, and
nieces   **E**
Home. See Home   **810.8**
Leo and Emily   **E**
Leo and Emily and the dragon. See note un-
der Brandenberg, F. Leo and Emily   **E**
Leo and Emily's big ideas. See note under
Brandenberg, F. Leo and Emily   **E**
Leo and Emily's zoo. See note under Bran-
denberg, F. Leo and Emily   **E**
Nice new neighbors   **E**

Brandenburg, Jim
An American safari (4 and up)   **574.5**
Sand and fog (4 and up)   **968.8**
To the top of the world (4 and up)
599.74

Brandon *See* Brendan, Saint, the Voyager, ca.
483-577

Brandt, Sue R., 1916-
State flags (5 and up)   **929.9**

Branley, Franklyn Mansfield, 1915-
Air is all around you (k-1)   **551.5**
The Big Dipper (k-1)   **523.8**
Earthquakes (k-3)   **551.2**
Eclipse: darkness in daytime (k-3)   **523.7**
Flash, crash, rumble, and roll (k-3)
551.5
Gravity is a mystery (k-3)   **531**
Is there life in outer space? (k-3)
574.999
It's raining cats and dogs (3-6)   **551.5**
Journey into a black hole (k-3)   **523.8**
Keeping time (4-6)   **529**
The moon seems to change (k-3)   **523.3**
Neptune (3-6)   **523.4**
Rain & hail (k-3)   **551.57**
Shooting stars (k-1)   **523.6**
The sky is full of stars (k-3)   **523.8**
Snow is falling (k-1)   **551.57**
Star guide (3-6)   **523.8**
The sun (k-3)   **523.7**
Sun dogs and shooting stars (5 and up)
523
Sunshine makes the seasons (k-3)   **525**
Uranus (3-6)   **523.4**
Venus (3-6)   **523.4**
Volcanoes (k-3)   **551.2**
What makes day and night (k-3)   **525**
What the moon is like (k-3)   **523.3**

Braren, Loretta Trezzo
(il) Hauser, J. F. Kids' crazy concoctions
745.5
(il) Press, J. The little hands art book
745.5

Brashler, William
The story of Negro league baseball (5 and
up)   **796.357**

Brats. Kennedy, X. J.   **811**

Bratvold, Gretchen, 1959-
Oregon
In Hello USA series   **973**

Brittain, Bill—*Continued*
Dr. Dredd's wagon of wonders. See note under Brittain, B. Devil's donkey   **Fic**
Professor Popkin's prodigious polish. See note under Brittain, B. Devil's donkey   **Fic**
Shape-changer (4 and up)   **Fic**
The wish giver. See note under Brittain, B. Devil's donkey   **Fic**
Bro Tiger goes dead. Berry, J.
In Berry, J. Spiderman Anancy p66-68   **398.2**
In The Oxford treasury of children's stories p45-46   **S C**
Broadcasting
See also Television broadcasting
The **brocaded** slipper. Vuong, L. D.
In Vuong, L. D. The brocaded slipper, and other Vietnamese tales   **398.2**
The **brocaded** slipper and other Vietnamese tales. Vuong, L. D.   **398.2**
The **Broccoli** tapes. Slepian, J.   **Fic**
Brock, C. E. (Charles Edmond), 1870-1938
(il) Nesbit, E. The railway children   **Fic**
Brock, Charles Edmond *See* Brock, C. E. (Charles Edmond), 1870-1938
Brock, Juliet Clutton- *See* Clutton-Brock, Juliet
Brodie, Carolyn S., 1958-
(ed) Many faces, many voices. See Many faces, many voices   **028.5**
Broeck, Fabricio Vanden, 1954-
(il) Dupré, J. The mouse bride   **398.2**
Broekel, Ray, 1923-
Hocus pocus: magic you can do (3-5)   **793.8**
Snakes (2-4)   **597.9**
(jt. auth) White, L. B. Math-a-magic: number tricks for magicians   **793.8**
(jt. auth) White, L. B. Shazam! simple science magic   **793.8**
Broken chain. Soto, G.
In Soto, G. Baseball in April, and other stories p1-12   **S C**
Broken windows. Paterson, K.
In Paterson, K. Angels & other strangers: family Christmas stories p105-18   **S C**
Brolga. Rosen, M.
In Rosen, M. How the animals got their colors p24-26   **398.2**
Brontë, Charlotte, 1816-1855
See/See also pages in the following book(s):
Krull, K. Lives of the writers p42-47 (4 and up)   **920**
Brontë, Emily, 1818-1848
See/See also pages in the following book(s):
Krull, K. Lives of the writers p42-47 (4 and up)   **920**
Bronwen and the crows. Leonard, A.
In The Oxford book of scary tales p98-105   **808.8**

Bronx (New York, N.Y.)
Fiction
Pinkwater, J. Tails of the Bronx (4-6)   **Fic**
The **bronze** bow. Speare, E. G.   **Fic**
The **Bronze** ring
In The Blue fairy book p1-11   **398.2**
Bronzeville boys and girls. Brooks, G.   **811**
Brooke, Leonard Leslie, 1862-1940
The golden goose book (k-3)   **398.2**
Contents: The golden goose; The three bears; The three little pigs; Tom Thumb
(il) Ring o' roses. See Ring o' roses   **398.8**
See/See also pages in the following book(s):
A Horn Book sampler on children's books and reading p60-69, 224-27   **028.5**
Brooke, William J.
Teller of tales (4 and up)   **S C**
Contents: The Emperor's clothes are news; Rumpelstiltskin by any other name; Gold in locks; Little Well Read Riding Hood; Teller's tale; Tale of tellers
A telling of the tales: five stories (4 and up)   **S C**
Contents: The waking of the prince; The growin' of Paul Bunyan; The fitting of the slipper; The working of John Henry; The telling of a tale
Brookfield, Karen
Book (4 and up)   **070.5**
Brooklyn (New York, N.Y.)
Fiction
Slepian, J. The Alfred summer (5 and up)   **Fic**
Brooklyn Dodgers (Baseball team)
Golenbock, P. Teammates [biography of Jackie Robinson] (1-4)   **92**
Brooks, Bruce, 1950-
Everywhere (4 and up)   **Fic**
Nature by design (5 and up)   **591.5**
Predator! (5 and up)   **591.5**
Brooks, Gwendolyn
Bronzeville boys and girls (2-5)   **811**
Brooks, Polly Schoyer
Queen Eleanor: independent spirit of the medieval world (6 and up)   **92**
Brooks, Walter R., 1886-1958
Freddy and the perilous adventure. See note under Brooks, W. R. Freddy goes camping   **Fic**
Freddy goes camping (3-5)   **Fic**
Freddy plays football. See note under Brooks, W. R. Freddy goes camping   **Fic**
Freddy rides again. See note under Brooks, W. R. Freddy goes camping   **Fic**
Freddy the cowboy. See note under Brooks, W. R. Freddy goes camping   **Fic**
See/See also pages in the following book(s):
Cart, M. What's so funny? p27-67   **028.5**
The **broomstick** beauty. Miller, H. L.
In Holiday plays round the year p129-40   **812.008**
Brother Anansi and the cattle ranch. Rohmer, H.   **398.2**

Brother and sister. Grimm, J.
  In Grimm, J. The complete Grimm's
    fairy tales p67-73   **398.2**
  In The Red fairy book p82-88   **398.2**
Brother and sister. San Souci, R.
  In San Souci, R. Short & shivery p117-22
    398.2
Brother eagle, sister sky. Jeffers, S.   **304.2**
Brother Francis and the friendly beasts.
  Hodges, M.   **92**
Brother Lustig. Grimm, J.
  In Grimm, J. The complete Grimm's
    fairy tales p367-77   **398.2**
Brother to the wind. Walter, M. P.   **E**
Brotherhood of Sleeping Car Porters
  McKissack, P. C. A long hard journey (5
    and up)   **331.8**
Brothers
        Fiction
  Bauer, M. D. Rain of fire (5 and up)
    Fic
  Blume, J. Tales of a fourth grade nothing
    (3-6)   **Fic**
  Carrick, C. Patrick's dinosaurs   **E**
  Carrick, C. What happened to Patrick's di-
    nosaurs?   **E**
  Christopher, M. Fighting tackle (4-6)
    Fic
  Freedman, F. B. Brothers: a Hebrew legend
    (k-3)   **398.2**
  Grifalconi, A. Not home (4 and up)   **Fic**
  Howe, J. There's a dragon in my sleeping
    bag   **E**
  Keats, E. J. Apt. 3   **E**
  Kellogg, S. Much bigger than Martin   **E**
  Naylor, P. R. The fear place (5 and up)
    Fic
  Roberts, W. D. Scared stiff (5 and up)
    Fic
  Steptoe, J. Baby says   **E**
  Wiesner, D. Hurricane   **E**
  Yep, L. Later, gator (4-6)   **Fic**
Brothers: a Hebrew legend. Freedman, F. B.
    398.2
Brothers and bone. Hamilton, V.
  In Hamilton, V. The dark way p132-36
    398.2
Brothers and sisters
    See also Twins
  Lasky, K. A baby for Max   **E**
  Ormerod, J. 101 things to do with a baby
    E
  Rosenberg, M. B. Brothers and sisters (k-2)
    306.8
  Rosenberg, M. B. Finding a way (2-4)
    362.4
        Fiction
  Adler, C. S. Youn Hee and me (4-6)
    Fic
  Alexander, M. G. Nobody asked me if I
    wanted a baby sister   **E**
  Alexander, M. G. When the new baby
    comes, I'm moving out   **E**
  Bartone, E. Peppe the lamplighter   **E**

Bawden, N. The outside child (5 and up)
    Fic
Blume, J. The one in the middle is the
  green kangaroo   **E**
Blume, J. The Pain and the Great One
    E
Bonsall, C. N. The day I had to play with
  my sister   **E**
Brown, L. K. Rex and Lilly family time
    E
Brown, M. T. D.W. all wet   **E**
Burningham, J. The baby   **E**
Byars, B. C. Go and hush the baby   **E**
Byars, B. C. The night swimmers (5 and up)
    Fic
Byars, B. C. The not-just-anybody family (5
  and up)   **Fic**
Byars, B. C. The summer of the swans (5
  and up)   **Fic**
Caines, J. F. Abby   **E**
Caseley, J. Mama, coming and going   **E**
Caseley, J. Sophie and Sammy's library
  sleepover   **E**
Cleaver, V. Where the lillies bloom (5 and
  up)   **Fic**
Conly, J. L. Trout summer (5 and up)
    Fic
Conrad, P. My Daniel (5 and up)   **Fic**
Cowen-Fletcher, J. It takes a village   **E**
Dorris, M. Morning Girl (4-6)   **Fic**
Fenner, C. Yolonda's genius (4-6)   **Fic**
Fox, P. The stone-faced boy (4-6)   **Fic**
Greenfield, E. She come bringing me that
  little baby girl   **E**
Hughes, S. Bouncing   **E**
Hutchins, P. Titch   **E**
Johnston, J. Hero of lesser causes (5 and up)
    Fic
Joyce, W. Santa calls   **E**
Lawlor, L. Gold in the hills (4-6)   **Fic**
Lowry, L. The one hundredth thing about
  Caroline (5 and up)   **Fic**
Lowry, L. Switcharound (5 and up)   **Fic**
Marino, J. The Mona Lisa of Salem Street
  (5 and up)   **Fic**
Martin, B. The ghost-eye tree   **E**
McDonald, M. The great pumpkin switch
    E
McKenzie, E. K. Under the bridge (4-6)
    Fic
Moeri, L. Save Queen of Sheba (4 and up)
    Fic
Nelson, T. And one for all (5 and up)
    Fic
Nesbit, E. The railway children (4-6)
    Fic
Nixon, J. L. A family apart (5 and up)
    Fic
Park, B. Mick Harte was here (4-6)   **Fic**
Paterson, K. Flip-flop girl (4-6)   **Fic**
Pevsner, S. And you give me a pain, Elaine
  (4 and up)   **Fic**
Polacco, P. My rotten redheaded older
  brother   **E**
Shyer, M. F. Welcome home, Jellybean (5
  and up)   **Fic**

Brown, Marc Tolon—*Continued*
(il) Bowden, J. C. Why the tides ebb and flow **398.2**
(jt. auth) Brown, L. K. Dinosaurs alive and well!: a guide to good health **613**
(jt. auth) Brown, L. K. Dinosaurs divorce **306.89**
(jt. auth) Brown, L. K. Dinosaurs to the rescue! **363.7**
(jt. auth) Brown, L. K. Dinosaurs travel **910**
(il) Brown, L. K. Rex and Lilly family time **E**
(il) Brown, L. K. Toddler time **649**
(jt. auth) Brown, L. K. Visiting the art museum **708**
(jt. auth) Krensky, S. Dinosaurs, beware! **613.6**
(jt. auth). Your first garden book **635**
(il) The Family read-aloud Christmas treasury. See The Family read-aloud Christmas treasury **808.8**
(il) The Family read-aloud holiday treasury. See The Family read-aloud holiday treasury **808.8**
(il) Read-aloud rhymes for the very young. See Read-aloud rhymes for the very young **821.008**
(comp) Scared silly! See Scared silly! **810.8**
(il) Wolkstein, D. The banza **398.2**

Brown, Marcia, 1918-
Once a mouse (k-3) **398.2**
Stone soup (k-3) **398.2**
(il) Cendrars, B. Shadow **841**
(il) Perrault, C. Cinderella **398.2**
(il) Sing a song of popcorn. See Sing a song of popcorn **808.81**
(il) Verdy, V. Of swans, sugarplums, and satin slippers **792.8**
See/See also pages in the following book(s):
Caldecott Medal books, 1938-1957 p267-83 **028.5**
Newbery and Caldecott Medal books, 1976-1985 p239-53 **028.5**

Brown, Margaret Wise, 1910-1952
Baby animals **E**
Big red barn **E**
A child's good night book **E**
Christmas in the barn (k-2) **232.9**
The fish with the deep sea smile (1-3) **818**
Stories included are: The shy little horse; The good little bad little pig; The steam roller: a fantasy; The garden; Sneakers, that rapscallion cat; Sneakers comes to town; The sky follows Sneakers to town; Sneakers and the Easter flowers; The Easter surprise; Sneakers and the Easter bunnies; The country happens to Sneakers again; The dead bird; The fierce yellow pumpkin; Christmas Eve; How the little city boy changed places with the little country boy for a year; The rat that said boo to the cat; The children's clock; The little girl's medicine; The polite little polar bear; The wonderful kitten; The wild black crows—a circular song; The little black cat who went to Mattituck; The pale blue flower; The wonderful day
Four fur feet **E**
Goodnight moon **E**
The indoor noisy book **E**
Little Fur family **E**

Nibble nibble: poems for children (k-3) **811**
The noisy book **E**
Red light, green light **E**
The runaway bunny **E**
Wheel on the chimney **E**
See/See also pages in the following book(s):
Sendak, M. Caldecott & Co.: notes on books and pictures p125-27 **028.5**

Brown, Mary Barrett
Wings along the waterway (4-6) **598**
(il) Esbensen, B. J. Playful slider **599.74**
(il) Esbensen, B. J. Tiger with wings **598**

Brown, Molly, d. 1934
About
Blos, J. W. The heroine of the Titanic: a tale both true and otherwise of the life of Molly Brown (k-3) **92**

Brown, Richard, 1945-
(il) Lindbergh, R. View from the air **811**

Brown, Risa W.
(jt. auth) Totten, H. L. Culturally diverse library collections for children **011.6**

Brown, Ruth
The big sneeze **E**
A dark, dark tale **E**
One stormy night **E**
The picnic **E**

Brown, Tricia
Chinese New Year (1-4) **394.2**
Konnichiwa! (1-4) **305.8**

Brown angels. Myers, W. D. **811**

Brown bear, brown bear what do you see?. Martin, B. **E**

Brown cow, green grass, yellow mellow sun. Jackson, E. B. **E**

Brown honey in broomwheat tea. Thomas, J. C. **811**

Brown paper preschool book [series]
Allison, L. Eenie meenie miney math! **510**

Brown paper school book [series]
Allison, L. Gee, Wiz! **507.8**
Bell, N. The book of where **910**
Booth, J. The big beast book **567.9**
Burns, M. The book of think **153.4**
Burns, M. I am not a short adult! **305.23**
Burns, M. The I hate mathematics! book **513**
Burns, M. Math for smarty pants **513**
Burns, M. This book is about time **529**
Jobb, J. The night sky book **523**
Rights, M. Beastly neighbors **508**
Walther, T. Make mine music! **784.19**
Weitzman, D. L. My backyard history book **973**
Wilkinson, E. Making cents **332.024**

Browne, Anthony
Gorilla **E**
Piggybook **E**

Browne, Anthony—*Continued*

Willy and Hugh. See note under Browne, A. Willy the wimp   **E**

Willy the champ. See note under Browne, A. Willy the wimp   **E**

Willy the wimp   **E**

Willy the wizard. See note under Browne, A. Willy the wimp   **E**

Zoo   **E**

(il) McEwan, I. The daydreamer   **Fic**

Browne, George

The wonderful tar baby

In The Oxford treasury of children's stories p47-49   **S C**

Browne, Philippa-Alys

African animals ABC   **E**

Browning, Robert, 1812-1889

The Pied Piper of Hamelin   **821**

The Pied Piper of Hamelin; dramatization. See Thane, A. The Pied Piper of Hamelin

The Browns take the day off. Schwartz, A.

In Schwartz, A. There is a carrot in my ear, and other noodle tales p9-14   **398.2**

Brrr!. Stevenson, J. See note under Stevenson, J. "Could be worse"   **E**

Bruchac, Joseph, 1942-

A boy called Slow: the true story of Sitting Bull (1-3)   **92**

The boy who lived with the bears and other Iroquois stories (3-5)   **398.2**
Contents: Rabbit and Fox; The boy who lived with the bears; How the birds got their feathers; Turtle makes war on man; Chipmunk and Bear; Rabbit's snow dance

The first strawberries (k-3)   **398.2**

Flying with the eagle, racing the great bear (5 and up)   **398.2**
Contents: The dream fast; White Weasel; Racing the great bear; Granny Squannit and the Bad Young Man; How the game animals were set free; The wild boy; The underwater lodge; The wisdom of the willow tree; The Owl-Man Giant and the Monster Elk; How the hero twins found their father; The bear boy; The ghost society; The light-haired boy; Star Boy; Salmon Boy; Tommy's whale

The girl who married the Moon (5 and up)   **398.2**
Contents: Arrowhead Finger; The abandoned girl; The girl and the Chenoo; The girl who escaped; Stonecoat; The girl who helped Thunder; The girl who married an Osage; The girls who almost married an owl; The poor Turkey Girl; The girl who gave birth to Water-Jar Boy; The Bear Woman; The Beauty Way—the ceremony of White-Painted Woman; How Pelican Girl was saved; Where the girl rescued her brother; Chipmunk Girl and Owl Woman; The girl who married the Moon

Gluskabe and the four wishes (k-3)   **398.2**

The great ball game (k-3)   **398.2**

Thirteen moons on a turtle's back   **811**

Turtle makes war on Man

In From sea to shining sea p252-55   **810.8**

(jt. auth) Caduto, M. J. Keepers of the night   **398.2**

Bruegel, Pieter *See* Brueghel, Pieter, the Elder, 1522?-1569

Brueghel, Pieter, the Elder, 1522?-1569

About

Mühlberger, R. What makes a Bruegel a Bruegel? (5 and up)   **759**

Sterckx, P. Brueghel (5 and up)   **92**

Venezia, M. Pieter Bruegel (k-3)   **92**

Bruemmer, Fred

(il) Pandell, K. Land of dark, land of light   **508**

Bruh Alligator and Bruh Deer. Hamilton, V.

In Hamilton, V. The people could fly: American black folktales p26-30   **398.2**

Bruh Alligator meets Trouble. Hamilton, V.

In Hamilton, V. The people could fly: American black folktales p35-42   **398.2**

Bruh Lizard and Bruh Rabbit. Hamilton, V.

In Hamilton, V. The people could fly: American black folktales p31-34   **398.2**

Brunei

Wright, D. K. Brunei (4 and up)   **959.5**

Brunhoff, Jean de, 1899-1937

Babar and Father Christmas. See note under Brunhoff, J. de. The story of Babar, the little elephant   **E**

Babar and his children. See note under Brunhoff, J. de. The story of Babar, the little elephant   **E**

Babar the king. See note under Brunhoff, J. de. The story of Babar, the little elephant   **E**

The story of Babar, the little elephant   **E**

Travels of Babar. See note under Brunhoff, J. de. The story of Babar, the little elephant   **E**

See/See also pages in the following book(s):

Sendak, M. Caldecott & Co.: notes on books and pictures p95-105   **028.5**

Brunhoff, Laurent de, 1925-

Babar and the ghost. See note under Brunhoff, J. de. The story of Babar, the little elephant   **E**

Babar learns to cook. See note under Brunhoff, J. de. The story of Babar, the little elephant   **E**

Babar loses his crown. See note under Brunhoff, J. de. The story of Babar, the little elephant   **E**

Babar saves the day. See note under Brunhoff, J. de. The story of Babar, the little elephant   **E**

Babar's ABC. See note under Brunhoff, J. de. The story of Babar, the little elephant   **E**

Babar's anniversary album. See note under Brunhoff, J. de. The story of Babar, the little elephant   **E**

Babar's birthday surprise. See note under Brunhoff, J. de. The story of Babar, the little elephant   **E**

Brunhoff, Laurent de, 1925-—_Continued_
Babar's book of color. See note under Brunhoff, J. de. The story of Babar, the little elephant   E
Babar's busy year. See note under Brunhoff, J. de. The story of Babar, the little elephant   E
Babar's family album. See note under Brunhoff, J. de. The story of Babar, the little elephant   E
Babar's French lessons. See note under Brunhoff, J. de. The story of Babar, the little elephant   E
Babar's little circus star. See note under Brunhoff, J. de. The story of Babar, the little elephant   E
Babar's little girl. See note under Brunhoff, J. de. The story of Babar, the little elephant   E
Babar's mystery. See note under Brunhoff, J. de. The story of Babar, the little elephant   E
Babar's picnic. See note under Brunhoff, J. de. The story of Babar, the little elephant   E
Meet Babar and his family. See note under Brunhoff, J. de. The story of Babar, the little elephant   E

Brunkus, Denise
(il) Calmenson, S. The principal's new clothes   E
(il) Park, B. Junie B. Jones and her big fat mouth   E

Brusca, María Cristina
On the pampas (k-3)   982
When jaguars ate the moon and other stories about animals and plants of the Americas (2-4)   398.2
(il) Medearis, A. S. The zebra-riding cowboy
                                              782.42

Brutschy, Jennifer
The winter fox   E

Bruun, Bertel
(jt. auth) Bruun, R. D. The brain—what it is, what it does   612.8
(jt. auth) Robbins, C. S. Birds of North America   598

Bruun, Peter
(il) Bruun, R. D. The brain—what it is, what it does   612.8

Bruun, Ruth Dowling
The brain—what it is, what it does (1-3)
                                              612.8

Bryan, Ashley, 1923-
Beat the story-drum, pum-pum (1-4)
                                              398.2
Contents: Hen and Frog; Why Bush Cow and Elephant are bad friends; The husband who counted the spoonfuls; Why Frog and Snake never play together; How animals got their tails
The cat's purr (k-2)   398.2
also in From sea to shining sea p260-63
                                              810.8
The ox of the wonderful horns and other African folktales (4-6)   398.2

Contents: Ananse the Spider in search of a fool; Frog and his two wives; Elephant and Frog go courting; Tortoise, Hare, and the sweet potatoes; The ox of the wonderful horns
Sing to the sun   811
The story of Lightning & Thunder (3-5)
                                              398.2
Tortoise, Hare, and the sweet potatoes
_In_ Bauer, C. F. Celebrations p231-34
                                              808.8
(comp) All night, all day. See All night, all day   782.25
(il) Christmas gif'. See Christmas gif'
                                              394.2
(il) Climbing Jacob's ladder. See Climbing Jacob's ladder   782.25
(il) Myers, W. D. The story of the three kingdoms   E
(il) What a morning! See What a morning!
                                              782.25

Bryan, Jenny
Sound and vision (4-6)   612.8

Bryan, William Jennings, 1860-1925
See/See also pages in the following book(s):
Jacobs, W. J. Great lives: human rights p182-88 (5 and up)   920

Bryant, Michael
(il) McKissack, P. C. Booker T. Washington
                                              92
(il) McKissack, P. C. Sojourner Truth
                                              92
(il) Medearis, A. S. Our people   305.8
(il) Miller, R. H. The story of Nat Love
                                              92

Bubble trouble & other poems and stories. Mahy, M.   808.8

Buchanan, Yvonne
(il) Branley, F. M. Uranus   523.4

Bucher, Katherine Toth, 1947-
Computers & technology in school library media centers   027.8

Buchstab, Michael See Avi-Yonah, Michael, 1904-1974

Buck, Pearl S. (Pearl Sydenstricker), 1892-1973
See/See also pages in the following book(s):
Faber, D. Great lives: American literature p173-82 (5 and up)   920

Buckley, Helen E. (Helen Elizabeth)
Grandfather and I   E
Grandmother and I   E

Buddhism
Raimondo, L. The little Lama of Tibet [biography of Ling Rinpoche] (3-5)   92

Budgets, Personal See Personal finance

Buehner, Caralyn
It's a spoon, not a shovel (k-3)   395

Buehner, Mark
(il) Barracca, D. The adventures of Taxi Dog   E
(il) Buehner, C. It's a spoon, not a shovel
                                              395
(il) Nolen, J. Harvey Potter's balloon farm
                                              E

Buffalo, American *See* Bison

Buffalo. Lepthien, E. U.	**599.73**
Buffalo. Patent, D. H.	**599.73**
Buffalo dance. Van Laan, N.	**398.2**
Buffalo gals. Miller, B. M.	**978**
Buffalo hunt. Freedman, R.	**970.004**
Buffalo soldiers. Reef, C.	**978**
Buffalo woman. Goble, P.	**398.2**
Bugs. Parker, N. W.	**595.7**

Buholzer, Theres
Life of the snail (3-6) **594**

Build it with boxes. Irvine, J. **745.54**

Building
    See also Carpentry; House construction
Barton, B. Building a house (k-1) **690**
Barton, B. Machines at work (k-1) **690**
Gibbons, G. How a house is built (k-3)
690
Gibbons, G. Up goes the skyscraper! (k-3)
690
Macaulay, D. Unbuilding (4 and up)
690
Macaulay, D. Underground (4 and up)
624.1
Walker, L. Housebuilding for children
690

Building. Wilkinson, P. **690**
Building a house. Barton, B. **690**

Building America [series]
Doherty, C. A. The Golden Gate Bridge
624
Doherty, C. A. Hoover Dam **627**
Doherty, C. A. Mount Rushmore **730.9**
Doherty, C. A. The Sears Tower **725**
Doherty, C. A. The Washington Monument
975.3

Building materials
Wilkinson, P. Building (4 and up) **690**

Buildings
    See also Apartment houses; Houses;
Skyscrapers

Bukhtan Bukhtanovich. Afanas'ev, A. N.
In Afanas'ev, A. N. Russian fairy tales
p168-70 **398.2**

Bulfinch, Thomas, 1796-1867
Bulfinch's mythology (6 and up) **291**
Bulfinch's mythology. Bulfinch, T. **291**

Bulgaria
Bulgaria—in pictures (5 and up) **949.77**
Resnick, A. Bulgaria (4 and up) **949.77**
Bulgaria—in pictures (5 and up) **949.77**

Bull Run, Battle of, 1861
        Fiction
Fleischman, P. Bull Run (6 and up) **Fic**

Bulla, Clyde Robert, 1914-
The chalk box kid **E**
Daniel's duck **E**
A grain of wheat: a writer begins (3-5)
92
Shoeshine girl (3-5) **Fic**
The sword in the tree (3-5) **Fic**

What makes a shadow? (k-1) **535**
Bulldozers. Butterfield, M. **629.225**

Bulletin boards
Skaggs, G. Off the wall! **027.8**

Bulletin of the Center for Children's Books
028.1

Bullfights
        Biography
Say, A. El Chino (2-5) **92**
        Fiction
Leaf, M. The story of Ferdinand **E**
Wojciechowska, M. Shadow of a bull (6 and
up) **Fic**

Bullock, Kathleen, 1946-
She'll be comin' round the mountain (k-3)
782.42

Bulls
        Fiction
Leaf, M. The story of Ferdinand **E**
Bully for you, Teddy Roosevelt!. Fritz, J.
92
The bully of Barkham Street. Stolz, M. See
note under Stolz, M. A dog on Barkham
Street **Fic**
Bumps in the night. Allard, H. **E**

The bun. Afanas'ev, A. N.
In Afanas'ev, A. N. Russian fairy tales
p447-49 **398.2**

Bunche, Ralph J. (Ralph Johnson), 1904-1971
See/See also pages in the following book(s):
Haskins, J. One more river to cross (4 and
up) **920**

Bunker, Chang, 1811-1874
See/See also pages in the following book(s):
Drimmer, F. Born different p92-121 (6 and
up) **920**

Bunker, Eng, 1811-1874
See/See also pages in the following book(s):
Drimmer, F. Born different p92-121 (6 and
up) **920**

Bunnicula. Howe, D. **Fic**

Bunnies and bonnets. McGowan, J.
In Holiday plays round the year p255-66
812.008

Bunting, Anne Eve *See* Bunting, Eve, 1928-

Bunting, Edward
(ed) The Visual dictionary of prehistoric life.
See The Visual dictionary of prehistoric
life **560**

Bunting, Eve, 1928-
The day before Christmas **E**
Flower garden **E**
Fly away home **E**
Ghost's hour, spook's hour **E**
How many days to America? **E**
In the haunted house **E**
The man who could call down owls **E**
The Mother's Day mice **E**
Nasty, stinky sneakers (4-6) **Fic**
Night of the gargoyles **E**
Night tree **E**
Once upon a time (1-3) **92**
A perfect Father's Day **E**

Bunting, Eve, 1928—*Continued*
Red fox running   E
Scary, scary Halloween   E
Smoky night   E
Someday a tree   E
Spying on Miss Müller (5 and up)   Fic
Sunshine Home   E
A turkey for Thanksgiving   E
The Wall   E
The Wednesday surprise   E

Bunting, Jane
The children's visual dictionary (k-3)
    423

Bunyan, Paul (Legendary character)
Kellogg, S. Paul Bunyan (k-3)   398.2
Rounds, G. Ol' Paul, the mighty logger (3-6)
    398.2

Buonarroti, Michel Angelo *See* Michelangelo
Buonarroti, 1475-1564

Burch, Robert, 1925-
Christmas with Ida Early. See note under
Burch, R. Ida Early comes over the
mountain   Fic
Ida Early comes over the mountain (4 and
up)   Fic
Queenie Peavy (5 and up)   Fic

Burchard, Peter
Charlotte Forten (5 and up)   92

Burenushka, the little red cow. Afanas'ev, A.
N.
In Afanas'ev, A. N. Russian fairy tales
p146-50   398.2

Burger, Carl, 1888-1967
(il) Gipson, F. B. Old Yeller   Fic

Burgie, Irving
Caribbean carnival (k-3)   782.42

Burglon, Nora, 1896-
The Christmas coin
In Take joy! The Tasha Tudor Christmas
book p23-29   394.2

Buried in ice. Beattie, O.   998

The buried moon. Jacobs, J.
In Jacobs, J. English fairy tales p321-27
    398.2

Buried treasure
Deem, J. M. How to hunt buried treasure (4
and up)   910.4
Fine, J. C. Sunken ships & treasure (5 and
up)   910.4
Gibbons, G. Sunken treasure (k-3)
    910.4
Hidden treasures of the sea (4 and up)
    910.4
Fiction
Hamilton, V. The mystery of Drear House
(5 and up)   Fic
Stevenson, R. L. Treasure Island (6 and up)
    Fic

The buried treasure. Yep, L.
In Yep, L. The tree of dreams   398.2

Buried worlds [series]
Avi-Yonah, M. Dig this!   930.1
Sunk!   910.4

Burke, Susan Slattery
(il) Peterson, S. K. Plugged in   793.73

Burkert, Nancy Ekholm
(il) Andersen, H. C. Hans Christian Andersen's The fir tree   Fic
(il) Andersen, H. C. The nightingale   Fic
(il) Dahl, R. James and the giant peach
    Fic

Burks, John B., 1942-
Norway—in pictures. See Norway—in pictures   948.1

Burleigh, Robert, 1936-
Flight: the journey of Charles Lindbergh
(2-4)   92

Burleson, Joe
(il) Naylor, P. R. The witch's eye   Fic

Burnett, Frances Hodgson, 1849-1924
A little princess (4-6)   Fic
A little princess; dramatization. See Thane,
A. The little princess
The secret garden (4-6)   Fic
See/See also pages in the following book(s):
Krull, K. Lives of the writers p62-65 (4 and
up)   920

Burnford, Sheila, 1918-1984
The incredible journey (4 and up)   Fic

Burnie, David
Bird (4 and up)   598
Flowers (3-5)   582.13
How nature works (4 and up)   508
Light (4 and up)   535
Machines and how they work (5 and up)
    621.8
Plant (4 and up)   581
Seashore (3-5)   574.92
Tree (4 and up)   582.16
(jt. auth) Bailey, J. Birds   598

The **burning** questions of Bingo Brown. Byars,
B. C.   Fic

Burningham, John, 1936-
Aldo   E
The baby   E
The blanket   E
Come away from the water, Shirley   E
The dog   E
The friend   E
Granpa   E
John Burningham's ABC   E
Mr. Gumpy's motor car. See note under
Burningham, J. Mr. Gumpy's outing
    E
Mr. Gumpy's outing   E
Time to get out of the bath, Shirley. See
note under Burningham, J. Come away
from the water, Shirley   E
(il) Fleming, I. Chitty-Chitty-Bang-Bang
    Fic
(il) Grahame, K. The wind in the willows
    Fic

Burns, Anthony, 1834-1862
About
Hamilton, V. Anthony Burns: the defeat and
triumph of a fugitive slave (5 and up)
    92

Burns, Bree
Harriet Tubman (4 and up)   92

Burns, Diane L.
Cranberries: fruit of the bogs (3-5)   634

Burns, Ken
(jt. auth) Ward, G. C. 25 great moments
    796.357
(jt. auth) Ward, G. C. Shadow ball
    796.357
(jt. auth) Ward, G. C. Who invented the
game?   **796.357**

Burns, Khephra
Black stars in orbit (4 and up)   920

Burns, Marilyn
The book of think (4 and up)   **153.4**
The Hanukkah book (4 and up)   **296.4**
I am not a short adult! (4 and up)
    305.23
The I hate mathematics! book (4 and up)
    513
Math for smarty pants (4 and up)   **513**
This book is about time (4 and up)
    529

Burros *See* Donkeys

Burroway, Janet, 1936-
(jt. auth) Lord, J. V. The giant jam sandwich   E

Burton, Jane, 1933-
Chick (k-2)   **636.5**
Coral reef (3-6)   **574.92**
(il) Burton, R. Egg   **591.3**

Burton, Maurice, 1898-
Birds (5 and up)   **598**
(ed) Marshall Cavendish international wildlife encyclopedia. See Marshall Cavendish
international wildlife encyclopedia
    591

Burton, Robert, 1941-
Egg (3-5)   **591.3**
(ed) Marshall Cavendish international wildlife encyclopedia. See Marshall Cavendish
international wildlife encyclopedia
    591

Burton, Virginia Lee, 1909-1968
Katy and the big snow   E
The little house   E
Mike Mulligan and his steam shovel   E
See/See also pages in the following book(s):
Caldecott Medal books, 1938-1957 p88-97
    028.5
The Illustrator's notebook p45-49   **741.6**

Burying grounds *See* Cemeteries

The **bus** for Deadhorse. Babbitt, N.
In The Big book for peace p52-56
    810.8

Bus riders. Denslow, S. P.   E

The **bus** stop. Schwartz, A.
In Schwartz, A. Scary stories 3 p8-9
    398.2

Busenberg, Bonnie
Vanilla, chocolate, & strawberry (5 and up)
    664

Buses
Crews, D. School bus   E
    Fiction
Denslow, S. P. Bus riders   E

Bush lion. Scott, R.
In The Oxford book of scary tales p74-75
    808.8

Bushe, Claire
(il) Patterson, J. Angels, prophets, rabbis &
kings from the stories of the Jewish people   **296.1**

Bushy bride. Moe, J. E.
In The Red fairy book p322-28   **398.2**

Business
    Fiction
Merrill, J. The toothpaste millionaire (4-6)
    Fic
Schwartz, A. Bea and Mr. Jones   E

Business people
Aaseng, N. The problem solvers (5 and up)
    920
Aaseng, N. The unsung heroes (5 and up)
    920

Business people, African American *See* African
American business people

Bussell, Darcey
The young dancer (4 and up)   **792.8**

Busy buzzing bumblebees and other tongue
twisters. Schwartz, A.   **808.88**

The **Busy** farmer's wife
In Juba this and Juba that   **372.6**

Busybody Nora. Hurwitz, J.   Fic

Butcher, Solomon D.
    About
Conrad, P. Prairie visions: the life and times
of Solomon Butcher (5 and up)   92

Butcher, Susan
    About
Dolan, E. M. Susan Butcher and the Idita-
rod Trail (5 and up)   **798**
See/See also pages in the following book(s):
Littlefield, B. Champions p67-80 (5 and up)
    920

Butler, Dorothy, 1925-
Cushla and her books   **362.4**
My brown bear Barney   E
My brown bear Barney in trouble. See note
under Butler, D. My brown bear Barney
    E

Butler, John, 1952-
(il) Lemmon, T. Apes   **599.88**

Butterfield, Moira
Bulldozers (4 and up)   **629.225**
Fun with paint (4 and up)   **745.7**
Ships (4 and up)   **623.8**
Space (4 and up)   **629.47**
(jt. auth) Orr, R. Nature cross-sections
    574.5

Butterflies
    See also Caterpillars
Feltwell, J. Butterflies and moths (3-5)
    595.7

Byrd, Samuel
  (il) Adler, D. A. A picture book of Harriet
    Tubman   **92**
  (il) Livingston, M. C. Keep on singing
    811
  (il) Livingston, M. C. Let freedom ring
    811

C

C D C?. Steig, W.   **793.73**
C.L.O.U.D.S.. Cummings, P.   **E**
The **cabbage** donkey. Grimm, J.
  In The Yellow fairy book p42-49
    398.2
The **cabin** faced west. Fritz, J.   **Fic**
Cabinet officers
  Bredeson, C. Henry Cisneros (5 and up)
    92
  Parker, N. W. The president's cabinet and
    how it grew (3-5)   **353.04**
Cabinetwork
  Lyons, M. E. Master of mahogany: Tom
    Day, free black cabinetmaker (4 and up)
    92
Cabot, John, 1450-1498
  See/See also pages in the following book(s):
  Fritz, J. Around the world in a hundred
    years p63-67 (4-6)   **910.4**
Cabral, Pedro Alvares, 1460?-1526?
  See/See also pages in the following book(s):
  Fritz, J. Around the world in a hundred
    years p59-61 (4-6)   **910.4**
A **cache** of jewels and other collective nouns.
  Heller, R.   **428**
Cactus
  Bash, B. Desert giant (3-5)   **583**
  Guiberson, B. Z. Cactus hotel (k-3)   **583**
  Lerner, C. Cactus (4 and up)   **583**
Cactus desert. Silver, D. M.   **574.5**
Cactus hotel. Guiberson, B. Z.   **583**
Caddie Woodlawn. Brink, C. R.   **Fic**
Caddie's Independence Day. Brink, C. R.
  In The Family read-aloud holiday trea-
    sury p76-85   **808.8**
Caduto, Michael J.
  Keepers of the night   **398.2**
  Includes the following stories: How the bat came to be;
  Moth, the fire dancer; Oot-Kwah-Tah, the seven star danc-
  ers; Chipmunk and the Owl Sisters; The great Lacrosse
  game; How Grizzly Bear climbed the mountain
Caffeine
  Perry, R. L. Focus on nicotine and caffeine
    (3-6)   **616.86**
Cage birds
  See also Canaries
  See/See also pages in the following book(s):
  Chrystie, F. N. Pets p63-88 (4 and up)
    636.088
Cain, David, 1951-
  (il) Cobb, V. Science experiments you can
    eat   **507.8**

  (il) Fleischman, P. Copier creations   **760**
Caines, Jeannette Franklin, 1938-
  Abby   **E**
  I need a lunch box   **E**
  Just us women   **E**
Cairo (Egypt)
  Fiction
  Heide, F. P. The day of Ahmed's secret
    E
Cajuns
  Fiction
  Thomassie, T. Feliciana Feydra LeRoux
    E
Cake
  Fiction
  Forest, H. The woman who flummoxed the
    fairies (k-3)   **398.2**
  Oxenbury, H. It's my birthday   **E**
  Rice, E. Benny bakes a cake   **E**
  Willard, N. The high rise glorious skittle
    skat roarious sky pie angel food cake
    E
Cakes and miracles. Goldin, B. D.   **E**
Calamity Jane, 1852-1903
  About
  Faber, D. Calamity Jane (5 and up)   **92**
Caldecott, Randolph, 1846-1886
  See/See also pages in the following book(s):
  Caldecott Medal books, 1938-1957 p1-5
    028.5
  The Illustrator's notebook p30-40   **741.6**
  Illustrators of children's books p66-75 (v1)
    741.6
  Sendak, M. Caldecott & Co.: notes on books
    and pictures p21-25   **028.5**
Caldecott & Co.: notes on books and pictures.
  Sendak, M.   **028.5**
Caldecott Medal
  Caldecott Medal books, 1938-1957
    028.5
  The Newbery and Caldecott awards
    028.5
  Newbery and Caldecott Medal books, 1966-
    1975   **028.5**
  Newbery and Caldecott Medal books, 1976-
    1985   **028.5**
Caldecott Medal books, 1938-1957   **028.5**
Caldecott Medal titles
  Bemelmans, L. See Bemelmans, L. Made-
    line's rescue (1954)   **E**
  Brown, M. See Brown, M. Once a mouse
    (1962)   **398.2**
  Brown, M. See Cendrars, B. Shadow (1983)
    841
  Brown, M. See Perrault, C. Cinderella
    (1955)   **398.2**
  Burton, V. L. See Burton, V. L. The little
    house (1943)   **E**
  Cooney, B. See Cooney, B. Chanticleer and
    the fox (1959)   **E**
  Cooney, B. See Hall, D. Ox-cart man (1980)
    E
  Diaz, D. See Bunting, E. Smoky night
    (1995)   **E**

California—*Continued*

Fiction

Beatty, P. Eight mules from Monterey (5 and up)   **Fic**

Gates, D. Blue willow (4 and up)   **Fic**

Koertge, R. Tiger, tiger, burning bright (6 and up)   **Fic**

Politi, L. Song of the swallows   **E**

Snyder, Z. K. The velvet room (5 and up)   **Fic**

Soto, G. Baseball in April, and other stories (5 and up)   **S C**

Soto, G. Crazy weekend (4 and up)   **Fic**

Soto, G. The pool party (3-5)   **Fic**

Uchida, Y. A jar of dreams (5 and up)   **Fic**

Gold discoveries

Blake, A. The gold rush of 1849 (5 and up)   **979.4**

Blumberg, R. The great American gold rush (5 and up)   **979.4**

Gold discoveries—Fiction

Fleischman, S. By the Great Horn Spoon! (4-6)   **Fic**

California condors *See* Condors

The **caliph** and the cobbler. Kimmel, E. A.

    In Kimmel, E. A. The spotted pony: a collection of Hanukkah stories p50-55   **398.2**

Calisthenics *See* Gymnastics

Call it courage. Sperry, A.   **Fic**

Call me Francis Tucket. Paulsen, G. See note under Paulsen, G. Mr. Tucket   **Fic**

The **call** of the wild. London, J.   **Fic**

Callanan, Cecelia C.

    Cupid and Company

    In Holiday plays round the year p189-91   **812.008**

Callen, Larry

    Fifteen minutes

    In The Random House book of humor for children p283-92   **817.008**

Calling on dragons. Wrede, P. C. See note under Wrede, P. C. Dealing with dragons   **Fic**

Calliope   **905**

Calmenson, Stephanie

    Dinner guests

    In The Read-aloud treasury p100-11   **808.8**

    The lion and the mouse

    In The Read-aloud treasury p188-89   **808.8**

    The principal's new clothes   **E**

    Rosie (k-3)   **636.7**

    What am I? (k-2)   **793.73**

    (jt. auth) Cole, J. Crazy eights and other card games   **795.4**

    (jt. auth) Cole, J. Pin the tail on the donkey and other party games   **793**

    (jt. auth) Cole, J. Six sick sheep   **808.88**

    (jt. auth) Cole, J. Why did the chicken cross the road? and other riddles, old and new   **793.73**

    (comp) The Eentsy, weentsy spider. See The Eentsy, weentsy spider   **796.1**

    (comp) The Laugh book. See The Laugh book   **808.8**

    (comp) Miss Mary Mack and other children's street rhymes. See Miss Mary Mack and other children's street rhymes   **796.1**

    (comp) Pat-a-cake and other play rhymes. See Pat-a-cake and other play rhymes   **398.8**

    (comp) The Read-aloud treasury. See The Read-aloud treasury   **808.8**

    (comp) Yours 'til banana splits. See Yours 'til banana splits   **811.008**

Calvert, Patricia, 1931-

    Bigger (5 and up)   **Fic**

Calvin Copley and the widow. Haskins, J.

    In Haskins, J. The headless haunt and other African American ghost stories p52-53   **398.2**

Cam Jansen and the chocolate fudge mystery. Adler, D. A. See note under Adler, D. A. Cam Jansen and the mystery of the stolen diamonds   **Fic**

Cam Jansen and the mystery at the haunted house. Adler, D. A. See note under Adler, D. A. Cam Jansen and the mystery of the stolen diamonds   **Fic**

Cam Jansen and the mystery at the monkey house. Adler, D. A. See note under Adler, D. A. Cam Jansen and the mystery of the stolen diamonds   **Fic**

Cam Jansen and the mystery of Flight 54. Adler, D. A. See note under Adler, D. A. Cam Jansen and the mystery of the stolen diamonds   **Fic**

Cam Jansen and the mystery of the Babe Ruth baseball. Adler, D. A. See note under Adler, D. A. Cam Jansen and the mystery of the stolen diamonds   **Fic**

Cam Jansen and the mystery of the carnival prize. Adler, D. A. See note under Adler, D. A. Cam Jansen and the mystery of the stolen diamonds   **Fic**

Cam Jansen and the mystery of the circus clown. Adler, D. A. See note under Adler, D. A. Cam Jansen and the mystery of the stolen diamonds   **Fic**

Cam Jansen and the mystery of the dinosaur bones. Adler, D. A. See note under Adler, D. A. Cam Jansen and the mystery of the stolen diamonds   **Fic**

Cam Jansen and the mystery of the gold coins. Adler, D. A. See note under Adler, D. A. Cam Jansen and the mystery of the stolen diamonds   **Fic**

Cam Jansen and the mystery of the monster movie. Adler, D. A. See note under Adler, D. A. Cam Jansen and the mystery of the stolen diamonds   **Fic**

Cam Jansen and the mystery of the stolen corn popper. Adler, D. A. See note under Adler, D. A. Cam Jansen and the mystery of the stolen diamonds **Fic**

Cam Jansen and the mystery of the stolen diamonds. Adler, D. A. **Fic**

Cam Jansen and the mystery of the television dog. Adler, D. A. See note under Adler, D. A. Cam Jansen and the mystery of the stolen diamonds **Fic**

Cam Jansen and the mystery of the UFO. Adler, D. A. See note under Adler, D. A. Cam Jansen and the mystery of the stolen diamonds **Fic**

Cam Jansen and the Triceratops Pops mystery. Adler, D. A. See note under Adler, D. A. Cam Jansen and the mystery of the stolen diamonds **Fic**

Cambodia
Chandler, D. P. The land and people of Cambodia (5 and up) **959.6**
Greenblatt, M. Cambodia (4 and up)
959.6

Fiction
Lee, J. M. Silent Lotus **E**

Folklore
See Folklore—Cambodia

Cambodian Americans
Graff, N. P. Where the river runs (4-6)
305.8

Camels
Arnold, C. Camel (3-5) **599.73**
See/See also pages in the following book(s):
Facklam, M. Who harnessed the horse? p93-102 (3-6) **636**

Fiction
Kipling, R. How the camel got his hump
Fic

Cameras
Ancona, G. My camera (3-6) **771**

Cameron, Ann, 1943-
A day when frogs wear shoes
In The Family read-aloud holiday treasury p62-69 **808.8**
Julian, dream doctor. See note under Cameron, A. The stories Julian tells **Fic**
Julian, secret agent. See note under Cameron, A. The stories Julian tells **Fic**
Julian's glorious summer. See note under Cameron, A. The stories Julian tells
Fic
The kidnapped prince: the life of Olaudah Equiano (4 and up) **92**
More stories Julian tells. See note under Cameron, A. The stories Julian tells
Fic
The most beautiful place in the world (2-4)
Fic
The stories Julian tells (2-4) **Fic**
The stories Julian tells [excerpt]
In The Random House book of humor for children p44-50 **817.008**

Cameron, Eleanor, 1912-
The court of the stone children (5 and up)
Fic
Julia's magic. See note under Cameron, E. A room made of windows **Fic**
Mr. Bass's planetoid. See note under Cameron, E. The wonderful flight to the Mushroom Planet **Fic**
The private worlds of Julia Redfern. See note under Cameron, E. A room made of windows **Fic**
A room made of windows (5 and up)
Fic
The seed and the vision **028.5**
Stowaway to the Mushroom Planet. See note under Cameron, E. The wonderful flight to the Mushroom Planet **Fic**
The wonderful flight to the Mushroom Planet (4-6) **Fic**

Cameron, Julia Margaret Pattle, 1815-1879
See/See also pages in the following book(s):
Wolf, S. Focus: five women photographers p6-15 (5 and up) **920**

Cameron, Scott
(il) Nichol, B. Beethoven lives upstairs
Fic

Cameroon
Fiction
Alexander, L. The fortune-tellers **E**

Camouflage (Biology)
Arnosky, J. I see animals hiding (k-2)
591.5
Martin, J. Hiding out **591.5**
Powzyk, J. A. Animal camouflage (3-6)
591.5

Fiction
Aruego, J. We hide, you seek **E**

Camp Fat. Konigsburg, E. L.
In Konigsburg, E. L. Altogether, one at a time p29-59 **S C**

Campbell, Jim, 1942-
(il) Kramer, S. Baseball's greatest hitters
920

Camping
Carlson, L. M. Kids camp! (3-6) **796.54**
Fiction
Bauer, M. D. When I go camping with Grandma **E**
Gilson, J. 4B goes wild (4-6) **Fic**
Johnson, A. The grizzly (5 and up) **Fic**
Koontz, R. M. Chicago and the cat: the camping trip **E**
Locker, T. Where the river begins **E**
Naylor, P. R. The fear place (5 and up)
Fic
Say, A. The lost lake **E**
Tafuri, N. Do not disturb **E**
Williams, V. B. Three days on a river in a red canoe **E**
The **camping** trip. Koontz, R. M. **E**

Camps
Fiction
Cohen, B. The long way home (4-6) **Fic**
Cole, B. The goats (5 and up) **Fic**

Camps—Fiction—*Continued*
Danziger, P. There's a bat in bunk five (5 and up) **Fic**
Can do, Jenny Archer. Conford, E. See note under Conford, E. A case for Jenny Archer **Fic**
Can I keep him?. Kellogg, S. **E**
Canada
Malcolm, A. H. The land and people of Canada (5 and up) **971**
Children
See Children—Canada
Fiction
Burnford, S. The incredible journey (4 and up) **Fic**
Cooper, S. The boggart (4-6) **Fic**
Ellis, S. Next-door neighbors (4 and up) **Fic**
Temple, F. Grab hands and run (6 and up) **Fic**
Social life and customs
Kurelek, W. A northern nativity (4 and up) **232.9**
The **Canada** geese quilt. Kinsey-Warnock, N. **Fic**
Canada goose *See* Geese
Canadian authors *See* Authors, Canadian
Canadian Northwest
Reynolds, J. Frozen land (2-4) **970.004**
Canaries
See/See also pages in the following book(s):
Chrystie, F. N. Pets p63-71 (4 and up) **636.088**
Cancer
See also Leukemia
Landau, E. Cancer (6 and up) **616.99**
Terkel, S. N. Understanding cancer (3-5) **616.99**
Fiction
Cohen, B. The long way home (4-6) **Fic**
Candles
See/See also pages in the following book(s):
Burns, M. The Hanukkah book p27-39 (4 and up) **296.4**
Candy Floss. Godden, R. **Fic**
also in Godden, R. Four dolls p108-37 **S C**
Cannibal Island
In The Naked bear p44-51 **398.2**
Cannon, Annie
(il) Carson, J. You hold me and I'll hold you **E**
(il) Emory, J. Nightprowlers **591.5**
(il) McNulty, F. With love from Koko **599.88**
Cannon, Janell, 1957-
Stellaluna **E**
A **canoe** trip. Kalman, B. **797.1**
Canoes and canoeing
Kalman, B. A canoe trip (2-4) **797.1**
Fiction
Conly, J. L. Trout summer (5 and up) **Fic**

Williams, V. B. Three days on a river in a red canoe **E**
Can't you make them behave, King George? [biography of George III, King of Great Britain]. Fritz, J. **92**
Can't you sleep, Little Bear?. Waddell, M. **E**
Canterbury tales. Cohen, B. **821**
Cap o' Rushes. Jacobs, J.
In Jacobs, J. English fairy tales p57-62 **398.2**
In Womenfolk and fairy tales p77-82 **398.2**
Caponigro, John Paul, 1962-
(il) Cohen, D. Ghost in the house **133.1**
Cappelloni, Nancy
Ethnic cooking the microwave way
In Easy menu ethnic cookbooks **641.5**
Caps for sale. Slobodkina, E. **E**
Caps, hats, socks, and mittens. Borden, L. **E**
Captain Snap and the children of Vinegar Lane. Schotter, R. **E**
The **captive.** Hansen, J. **Fic**
The **captive.** O'Dell, S. **Fic**
Capturing nature. Audubon, J. J. **92**
Car. Sutton, R. **629.222**
The **car** trip. Oxenbury, H. **E**
Caras, Steven
(il) Switzer, E. E. The nutcracker **792.8**
The **caravan.** Sawyer, R.
In Take joy! The Tasha Tudor Christmas book p43-46 **394.2**
Carbohydrates
Silverstein, A. Carbohydrates (3-6) **612.3**
Carbon 14 dating *See* Radiocarbon dating
Carbon dioxide greenhouse effect *See* Greenhouse effect
Card games
Cole, J. Crazy eights and other card games (3-5) **795.4**
Cardboard boxes full of America. 1954. Geras, A.
In Geras, A. Golden windows and other stories of Jerusalem p128-48 **S C**
Cardiovascular system
See also Blood—Circulation; Heart
Care, Medical *See* Medical care
Careers *See* Occupations
Carey, Vicky
(il) Collins, D. R. Mark T-W-A-I-N! **92**
Caribbean alphabet. Lessac, F. **E**
Caribbean canvas. Lessac, F. **811**
Caribbean carnival. Burgie, I. **782.42**
A **Caribbean** dozen (4-6) **811.008**
Caribbean region
Lessac, F. Caribbean alphabet **E**

Cataloging nonbook materials with AACR2 and MARC. McCroskey, M. J. **025.3**

Catalogs *See* Audiovisual materials—Catalogs; Motion pictures—Catalogs; School libraries—Catalogs; Videotapes—Catalogs

Catalogs, Classified *See* Classified catalogs

Catalogs, Library *See* Library catalogs

Catalogs, Subject *See* Subject catalogs

Catastrophe!. Bortz, A. B. **620**

Catastrophes (Geology)
Vogt, G. The search for the killer asteroid (4-6) **523.4**

Catch that cat!. Beisner, M. **793.73**

Catch the wind!. Gibbons, G. **796.1**

The **catchee.** Konigsburg, E. L.
In Konigsburg, E. L. Throwing shadows **S C**

Catching a cold. Parker, S. **616.2**

Caterpillars

Fiction
Carle, E. The very hungry caterpillar **E**

Cathedral of St. John the Divine (New York, N.Y.)
Ancona, G. Cutters, carvers & the cathedral (3-5) **693**

Cathedral: the story of its construction. Macaulay, D. **726**

Cathedrals
Ancona, G. Cutters, carvers & the cathedral (3-5) **693**
Macaulay, D. Cathedral: the story of its construction (4 and up) **726**

Cather, Willa, 1873-1947
See/See also pages in the following book(s):
Faber, D. Great lives: American literature p183-92 (5 and up) **920**

Catherine, called Birdy. Cushman, K. **Fic**

Catlett, Elizabeth
(il) Johnson, J. W. Lift every voice and sing **782.42**

Catlin, George, 1796-1872
About
Sufrin, M. George Catlin (6 and up) **92**

Catrow, David
(il) Lasky, K. She's wearing a dead bird on her head! **E**

Cats
Arnold, C. Cats: in from the wild (3-5) **599.74**
Clutton-Brock, J. Cat (4 and up) **599.74**
Cole, J. A cat's body **636.8**
Cole, J. My new kitten (k-2) **636.8**
De Paola, T. The kids' cat book (2-4) **636.8**
Hausherr, R. My first kitten (1-3) **636.8**
Jessel, C. The kitten book (k-3) **636.8**
Kuklin, S. Taking my cat to the vet (k-3) **636.8**
Parsons, A. Amazing cats (2-4) **599.74**
Patterson, F. Koko's kitten (1-4) **599.88**
Petersen-Fleming, J. Kitten care and critters, too! (k-3) **636.8**

Ryden, H. Your cat's wild cousins (4-6) **599.74**
See/See also pages in the following book(s):
Chrystie, F. N. Pets p25-39 (4 and up) **636.088**
Facklam, M. Who harnessed the horse? p17-28 (3-6) **636**

Fiction
Alexander, L. The cat who wished to be a man (4-6) **Fic**
Armstrong, J. Chin Yu Min and the ginger cat **E**
Babbitt, N. Nellie: a cat on her own **E**
Barber, A. The Mousehole cat **E**
Barton, B. The wee little woman **E**
Bauer, M. D. A question of trust (5 and up) **Fic**
Brandenberg, F. Aunt Nina and her nephews and nieces **E**
Brett, J. Annie and the wild animals **E**
Brown, R. A dark, dark tale **E**
Bryan, A. The cat's purr (k-2) **398.2**
Bunting, E. Scary, scary Halloween **E**
Burnford, S. The incredible journey (4 and up) **Fic**
Calhoun, M. Cross-country cat **E**
Carlson, N. S. Spooky night **E**
Cleary, B. Socks (3-5) **Fic**
Coatsworth, E. J. The cat who went to heaven (4 and up) **Fic**
Ehlert, L. Feathers for lunch **E**
Emberley, M. Ruby **E**
Fox, P. One-eyed cat (5 and up) **Fic**
Gág, W. Millions of cats **E**
Galdone, P. King of the Cats (k-2) **398.2**
Gantos, J. Rotten Ralph **E**
Gollub, M. The twenty-five Mixtec cats **E**
Griffith, H. V. Alex and the cat **E**
Hall, D. I am the dog, I am the cat **E**
Herriot, J. Moses the kitten **E**
Hesse, K. Lester's dog **E**
Hogrogian, N. The cat who loved to sing **E**
Joosse, B. M. Nobody's cat **E**
King-Smith, D. Martin's mice (3-5) **Fic**
King-Smith, D. Sophie's Tom (3-5) **Fic**
King-Smith, D. Three terrible trins (3-5) **Fic**
Koontz, R. M. Chicago and the cat: the camping trip **E**
Le Guin, U. K. Catwings (2-4) **Fic**
Levine, A. A. The boy who drew cats (k-3) **398.2**
Lexau, J. M. Come here, cat **E**
Mayerson, E. W. The cat who escaped from steerage (3-5) **Fic**
Namioka, L. Yang the third and her impossible family (4-6) **Fic**
Naylor, P. R. The grand escape (4-6) **Fic**
Neville, E. C. It's like this, Cat (5 and up) **Fic**
Newberry, C. T. April's kittens **E**
Newberry, C. T. Marshmallow **E**

Cats—Fiction—*Continued*
Oakley, G. The church mouse   E
Pilkey, D. When cats dream   E
Polacco, P. Tikvah means hope   E
Potter, B. The pie and the patty-pan   E
Potter, B. The story of Miss Moppet   E
Purdy, C. Mrs. Merriwether's musical cat   E
Rylant, C. Mr. Putter and Tabby pour the tea   E
Samuels, B. Duncan & Dolores   E
Selden, G. The cricket in Times Square (3-6)   Fic
Seuss, Dr. The cat in the hat   E
Slepian, J. The Broccoli tapes (5 and up)   Fic
Snyder, Z. K. The witches of Worm (5 and up)   Fic
Soto, G. Chato's kitchen   E
Turkle, B. C. Do not open   E
Viorst, J. The tenth good thing about Barney   E
Wagner, J. J. T. (3-6)   Fic
Wild, M. The very best of friends   E
Wolff, A. Only the cat saw   E
Poetry
Beisner, M. Catch that cat!   **793.73**
Cat poems   **808.81**
Cats are cats   **808.81**
Eliot, T. S. Growltiger's last stand   **811**
Eliot, T. S. Mr. Mistoffelees; with, Mungojerrie and Rumpelteazer   **811**
Galdone, P. Three little kittens (k-1)   **398.8**
Lewis, J. P. The fat-cats at sea   **811**

Cats, Wild *See* Wild cats

Cats. Roalf, P.
In Roalf, P. Looking at paintings   **750**

Cats are cats   **808.81**

Cat's baptism
In The Magic orange tree, and other Haitian folktales p123-26   **398.2**

A **cat's** body. Cole, J.   **636.8**

Cat's cradle *See* String figures

Cat's cradle, owl's eyes. Gryski, C.   **793.9**

The **cat's** elbow, and other secret languages. Schwartz, A.   **652**

Cats in art
Frame, P. Drawing cats and kittens (4 and up)   **743**

The **cat's** purr. Bryan, A.   **398.2**
also in From sea to shining sea p260-63   **810.8**

Catskill Mountains (N.Y.)
Fiction
George, J. C. My side of the mountain (5 and up)   Fic
George, J. C. On the far side of the mountain (5 and up)   Fic

Catskin. Jacobs, J.
In Jacobs, J. English fairy tales p403-08   **398.2**

Catskin. Reeves, J.
In Reeves, J. English fables and fairy stories p81-96   **398.2**

Catskinella. Hamilton, V.
In Hamilton, V. Her stories p23-27   **398.2**

Catskins
In Grandfather tales p106-14   **398.2**

Cattle
See also Bulls
Aliki. Milk from cow to carton (k-3)   **637**
Gibbons, G. The milk makers (k-3)   **637**
See/See also pages in the following book(s):
Facklam, M. Who harnessed the horse? p58-71 (3-6)   **636**
Fiction
Babcock, C. No moon, no milk!   E
Cooper, S. The silver cow: a Welsh tale (1-4)   **398.2**
Ericsson, J. A. No milk!   E
Ernst, L. C. When Bluebell sang   E
Johnson, P. B. The cow who wouldn't come down   E
Krasilovsky, P. The cow who fell in the canal   E
Seymour, T. Hunting the white cow   E
Van Laan, N. The tiny, tiny boy and the big, big cow (k-3)   **398.2**
Poetry
Schertle, A. How now, brown cow?   **811**

Catwings. Le Guin, U. K.   Fic

Catwings return. Le Guin, U. K. See note under Le Guin, U. K. Catwings   Fic

Caudill, Rebecca, 1899-1985
A certain small shepherd (4 and up)   Fic
Did you carry the flag today, Charley? (2-4)   Fic

Caught in the act. Nixon, J. L. See note under Nixon, J. L. A family apart   Fic

The **Cauld** Lad of Hilton. Jacobs, J.
In Jacobs, J. English fairy tales p200-02   **398.2**

Cauley, Lorinda Bryan, 1951-
Clap your hands   E
(il) Kipling, R. The beginning of the armadilloes   Fic
(il) Kipling, R. The elephant's child   Fic

Cavan, Seamus
The Irish-American experience (4 and up)   **305.8**

The **cave.** Jaramillo Levi, E.
In Where angels glide at dawn p43-48   S C

Cave. Silver, D. M.   **574.5**

Cave drawings
See also Rock drawings, paintings, and engravings

Cave dwellers
Fiction
Gerrard, R. Mik's mammoth   E

The **chapter** of kings. Collins, J.
In A Nursery companion p80-89
820.8

Charbonneau, Claudette, 1936-
The land and people of Norway (5 and up)
948.1
(jt. auth) Lander, P. S. The land and people
of Finland **948.97**

The **Charcoal** cruncher
In The Monkey's haircut, and other stories told by the Maya p113-17
398.2

Chardiet, Bernice
(jt. auth) Brenner, B. Where's that insect?
595.7

Charger. Crossley-Holland, K.
In Crossley-Holland, K. British folk tales
p307-08 **398.2**

Charlemagne, Emperor, 742-814
See/See also pages in the following book(s):
Bulfinch, T. Bulfinch's mythology (6 and
up) **291**

Charles Darwin and evolution. Parker, S.
92

Charles the Great *See* Charlemagne, Emperor,
742-814

Charley Skedaddle. Beatty, P. **Fic**

Charlie Parker played be bop. Raschka, C.
92

Charlie Pippin. Boyd, C. D. **Fic**

Charlip, Remy
Handtalk (k-3) **419**
Handtalk birthday (k-3) **419**
Thirteen **E**
(il) Yolen, J. The seeing stick **E**

Charlot, Jean, 1898-1979
(il) Brown, M. W. A child's good night book
E

See/See also pages in the following book(s):
Sendak, M. Caldecott & Co.: notes on books
and pictures p125-27 **028.5**

Charlotte's web. White, E. B. **Fic**

Charms
Clifton, L. The lucky stone (3-5) **Fic**

Chartier, Normand, 1945-
(il) Peters, L. W. This way home **598**

Chase, Richard, 1904-1988
The split dog
In From sea to shining sea p230-31
810.8
(ed) Grandfather tales. See Grandfather tales
398.2
(ed) The Jack tales. See The Jack tales
398.2

Chase's annual events. See Chase's calendar of
events **394.2**

Chase's calendar of events **394.2**

Chastain, Madye Lee
(il) Courlander, H. The cow-tail switch, and
other West African stories **398.2**

Chato's kitchen. Soto, G. **E**

Chatting. Hughes, S. See note under Hughes,
S. Bouncing **E**

Chaucer, Geoffrey, d. 1400
Canterbury tales; adaptation. See Cohen, B.
Canterbury tales **821**
Nun's priest's tale; adaptation. See Cooney,
B. Chanticleer and the fox **E**

Chavez, Cesar, 1927-1993
See/See also pages in the following book(s):
Jacobs, W. J. Great lives: human rights
p238-44 (5 and up) **920**
Morey, J. Famous Mexican Americans p1-
13 (5 and up) **920**

Cheaper by the dozen [excerpt]. Gilbreth, F.
B.
In The Random House book of humor
for children p242-47 **817.008**

The **cheater** cheated. Afanas'ev, A. N.
In Afanas'ev, A. N. Russian fairy tales
p228-29 **398.2**

Check it out! the book about libraries. Gibbons, G. **027**

Cheepii keeps himself safe. Medicine Story
In Medicine Story. The Children of the
Morning Light p62-66 **398.2**

Cheerleading
Fiction
Lester, H. Three cheers for Tacky **E**

Cheese
Peterson, C. Extra cheese, please! (k-3)
637

Cheetahs
Arnold, C. Cheetah (3-5) **599.74**

Chelm and their history, The fools of. Singer,
I. B. **Fic**

Chemical pollution *See* Pollution

Chemistry
Cobb, V. Gobs of goo (2-4) **547**
Newmark, A. Chemistry (4 and up) **540**
Experiments
Gardner, R. Kitchen chemistry: science ex-
periments to do at home (4 and up)
540.7
Kramer, A. How to make a chemical volca-
no and other mysterious experiments (4-6)
540.7

Chemists
Parker, S. Marie Curie and radium (4 and
up) **92**
Pflaum, R. Marie Curie and her daughter
Irène (5 and up) **92**
Poynter, M. Marie Curie: discoverer of radi-
um (4 and up) **92**
Vare, E. A. Adventurous spirit: a story
about Ellen Swallow Richards (3-5)
92

Chen, Ju-hong
(il) Birdseye, T. A song of stars **398.2**
(il) Wang, R. C. The fourth question
398.2
(il) Yacowitz, C. The jade stone **398.2**

Chen, Tony
(il) Stoddard, S. A child's first Bible
220.9

Cheney, Patricia
The land and people of Zimbabwe (5 and up) **968.91**

Cheng, Chen-sun
A young painter [biography of Wang Yani] (4 and up) **92**

Cheng's fighting cricket. Carpenter, F.
In Carpenter, F. Tales of a Chinese grandmother p217-25 **398.2**

Cheong-Lum, Roseline Ng, 1962-
Haiti (5 and up) **972.94**

Chernobyl Nuclear Accident, Chernobyl, Ukraine, 1986
See/See also pages in the following book(s):
Pringle, L. P. Nuclear energy: troubled past, uncertain future p62-76 (5 and up) **621.48**

Chernoff, Goldie Taub
Easy costumes you don't have to sew (3-5) **391**

Cherokee Indians
Bealer, A. W. Only the names remain (4-6) **970.004**
Brill, M. T. The Trail of Tears (5 and up) **970.004**
Cwiklik, R. Sequoyah and the Cherokee alphabet (5 and up) **92**
Hoyt-Goldsmith, D. Cherokee summer (3-5) **970.004**
Klausner, J. Sequoyah's gift (4 and up) **92**
Stein, R. C. The Trail of Tears (4-6) **970.004**

Legends
Bruchac, J. The first strawberries (k-3) **398.2**
Ross, G. How Rabbit tricked Otter and other Cherokee trickster stories (4-6) **398.2**
Ross, G. How Turtle's back was cracked (k-3) **398.2**

Cherokee summer. Hoyt-Goldsmith, D. **970.004**

Cherries and cherry pits. Williams, V. B. **E**

Cherry, Lynne, 1952-
From island to island
In The Big book for our planet p98-106 **810.8**
The great kapok tree **E**
A river ran wild (1-4) **974.4**
(il) Ryder, J. Where butterflies grow **595.7**
(il) Viorst, J. If I were in charge of the world and other worries **811**

Chess, Victoria, 1939-
(il) Adler, D. A. The twisted witch, and other spooky riddles **793.73**
(il) Heide, F. P. Grim and ghastly goings-on **811**
(il) Lewis, J. P. The fat-cats at sea **811**
(il) Lewis, J. P. A hippopotamusn't and other animal verses **811**
(il) Prelutsky, J. The queen of Eene **811**

(il) Prelutsky, J. Rolling Harvey down the hill **811**
(il) Prelutsky, J. The sheriff of Rottenshot: poems **811**
(il) Schwartz, A. Ghosts! **398.2**
(il) Wise, W. Ten sly piranhas **E**

Chessare, Michele
(il) Cassedy, S. Zoomrimes **811**
(il) Rainy day: stories and poems. See Rainy day: stories and poems **808.8**

The **chessmen** of doom. Bellairs, J. See note under Bellairs, J. The curse of the blue figurine **Fic**

Chester. Heide, F. P.
In Thanksgiving: stories and poems p49-50 **810.8**

Chester Cricket's new home. Selden, G. See note under Selden, G. The cricket in Times Square **Fic**

Chester Cricket's pigeon ride. Selden, G. See note under Selden, G. The cricket in Times Square **Fic**

Chester's way. Henkes, K. **E**

Chestnut pudding
In The Naked bear p3-10 **398.2**

Chesworth, Michael
(il) Weiss, J. H. Breathe easy **616.2**

Chewning, Randy
(il) Showers, P. Where does the garbage go? **363.7**
(il) Simon, S. Space words **500.5**

Cheyenne Indians
Fradin, D. B. The Cheyenne (2-4) **970.004**
See/See also pages in the following book(s):
Ehrlich, A. Wounded Knee: an Indian history of the American West (6 and up) **970.004**

Fiction
Goble, P. Death of the iron horse **E**

Legends
Goble, P. Her seven brothers (2-4) **398.2**

Chi-hoon. McMahon, P. **951.9**

The **Ch'i-lin** purse. Fang, L. **398.2**
In Fang, L. The Ch'i-lin purse p3-15 **398.2**

Chiasson, John C.
African journey (4 and up) **960**

Chibcha Indians
Legends
Van Laan, N. The legend of El Dorado (k-3) **398.2**

Chicago (Ill.)
Fiction
Collier, J. L. The jazz kid (5 and up) **Fic**

Chicago and the cat. Koontz, R. M. See note under Koontz, R. M. Chicago and the cat: the camping trip **E**

Chicago and the cat: the camping trip. Koontz, R. M. **E**

Chicago and the cat: the Halloween party. Koontz, R. M. See note under Koontz, R. M. Chicago and the cat: the camping trip E

Chicago Strike, 1894
Altman, L. J. The Pullman strike of 1894 (5 and up) 331.8

Chicanos *See* Mexican Americans

Chichester-Clark, Emma, 1955-
(il) Gilbert, W. S. "I have a song to sing, O!" 782.42
(il) McCaughrean, G. Greek myths 292
(il) Sutcliff, R. The minstrel and the dragon pup E

Chick. Burton, J. 636.5

The **chick** and the duckling. Ginsburg, M. E

A **chick** hatches. Cole, J. 636.5

Chicka chicka boom boom. Martin, B. E

Chickadee 505

Chickasaw Indians
Legends
Moroney, L. Baby rattlesnake (k-2) 398.2

The **chicken-coop** monster. McKissack, P. C. *In* McKissack, P. C. The dark-thirty p111-122 S C

Chicken Licken
In The Tall book of nursery tales p55-61 398.2

Chicken Licken. Asbjørnsen, P. C.
In Tomie dePaola's favorite nursery tales p105-11 398.2

Chicken Little. Kellogg, S. 398.2

Chicken soup with rice. Sendak, M. E

Chicken Sunday. Polacco, P. E

Chickenpox
Fiction
Kelley, T. I've got chicken pox E

Chickens
See also Roosters
Burton, J. Chick (k-2) 636.5
Cole, J. A chick hatches (k-3) 636.5
Hariton, A. Egg story (k-3) 636.5
Johnson, S. A. Inside an egg (4 and up) 598
Selsam, M. E. Egg to chick (k-3) 636.5
See/See also pages in the following book(s):
Facklam, M. Who harnessed the horse? p82-92 (3-6) 636
Fiction
Auch, M. J. Peeping Beauty E
Baker, K. Big fat hen (k-1) 398.8
Barber, A. Gemma and the baby chick E
Barton, B. The little red hen (k-2) 398.2
Dunrea, O. The painter who loved chickens E
Ernst, L. C. Zinnia and Dot E
Fox, M. Hattie and the fox E
Galdone, P. The little red hen (k-2) 398.2

Ginsburg, M. The chick and the duckling E
Ginsburg, M. Good morning, chick E
Heine, H. The most wonderful egg in the world E
Hutchins, P. Rosie's walk E
Kasza, K. The wolf's chicken stew E
King-Smith, D. The fox busters (3-5) Fic
Marshall, J. Wings E
O'Connor, J. Super Cluck E
Pinkwater, D. M. The Hoboken chicken emergency (3-6) Fic
Porte-Thomas, D. A. Chickens! chickens! E
Reiser, L. The surprise family E
Stoeke, J. M. A hat for Minerva Louise E
Zemach, M. The little red hen (k-2) 398.2

Chickens aren't the only ones. Heller, R. 591.1

Chickens! chickens!. Porte-Thomas, B. A. E

Chicoine, Stephen
Lithuania (4 and up) 947

Chief Joseph *See* Joseph, Nez Percé Chief, 1840-1904

Child, Lydia Maria Francis, 1802-1880
Over the river and through the wood (k-2) 811

Child abuse
See also Child sexual abuse
Fiction
Byars, B. C. Cracker Jackson (5 and up) Fic
Coman, C. What Jamie saw (5 and up) Fic
Magorian, M. Good night, Mr. Tom (6 and up) Fic
Neufeld, J. Almost a hero (5 and up) Fic
Ross, R. R. Harper & Moon (6 and up) Fic

Child and parent *See* Parent and child

Child artists
Cheng, C.-S. A young painter [biography of Wang Yani] (4 and up) 92
Hughes, L. The sweet and sour animal book 811
—I never saw another butterfly— 741.9
Periodicals
Stone Soup 810.8

Child authors
—I never saw another butterfly— 741.9
Miracles: poems by children of the English-speaking world 821.008
Periodicals
Stone Soup 810.8

Child care
See also Child rearing

A **child** is born: the Christmas story. Winthrop, E. 232.9

Child labor *See* Children—Employment

Child molesting *See* Child sexual abuse

The **child** of calamity. Yep, L.
In Yep, L. The rainbow people p46-52
398.2

Child of the owl. Yep, L.   Fic

Child of the silent night [biography of Laura Dewey Bridgman]. Hunter, E. F.   92

Child of the Warsaw ghetto. Adler, D. A.
940.53

Child psychology
See also Child rearing

Child rearing
Brown, L. K. Toddler time   649

Child sexual abuse
Terkel, S. N. Feeling safe, feeling strong (4 and up)   362.7

Fiction
Woodson, J. I hadn't meant to tell you this (6 and up)   Fic

Childbirth
Cole, J. How you were born (k-2)   612.6
Frasier, D. On the day you were born (k-3)
508
Ganeri, A. Birth and growth (k-2)   612.6
Kitzinger, S. Being born (3-5)   612.6

Childcraft dictionary. See The World Book student dictionary   423

Childe Rowland. Jacobs, J.
In Jacobs, J. English fairy tales p120-26
398.2

Childe Rowland and Burd Ellen. Hamilton, V.
In Hamilton, V. The dark way p65-72
398.2

Childhood Education   372.05

Children
See also Abandoned children; Girls; Handicapped children; Infants; Runaway children
Burns, M. I am not a short adult! (4 and up)
305.23

Abuse
See Child abuse

Adoption
See Adoption

Books and reading
75 years of Children's Book Week posters
808.06
Bauer, C. F. Read for the fun of it
027.62
Benne, M. Principles of children's services in public libraries   027.62
Fasick, A. M. Managing children's services in the public library   027.62
Greene, E. Books, babies, and libraries
027.62
Hey! listen to this   028.5
McElmeel, S. L. Great new nonfiction reads
028.5
Rollock, B. T. Public library services for children   027.62

Employment
See also Moneymaking projects for children
Barkin, C. Jobs for kids (5 and up)
650.1
Freedman, R. Kids at work (5 and up)
331.3
See/See also pages in the following book(s):
Colman, P. Mother Jones and the march of the mill children (3-5)   92

Employment—Fiction
Beatty, P. Turn homeward, Hannalee (5 and up)   Fic

Law and legislation
Siegel, B. Marian Wright Edelman (5 and up)   92

Management
See Child rearing

Pictorial works
Kindersley, B. Children just like me (3-6)
305.23

Training
See Child rearing

Canada
Kurelek, W. A prairie boy's summer (3-5)
971.27
Kurelek, W. A prairie boy's winter (3-5)
971.27

India
Hermes, J. The children of India (3-5)
954

Japan
Kuklin, S. Kodomo (3-6)   952.04

Morocco
Hermes, J. The children of Morocco (3-5)
964

Nepal
Pitkänen, M. A. The children of Nepal (3-5)
954.96

United States—History
Toynton, E. Growing up in America, 1830-1860 (4 and up)   973.5

West (U.S.)
Freedman, R. Children of the wild West (4 and up)   978

Children, Retarded *See* Mentally handicapped children; Slow learning children

Children. Roalf, P.
In Roalf, P. Looking at paintings   750

Children and adults
See also Conflict of generations

Children and books. Sutherland, Z.   028.5

Children and the AIDS virus. Hausherr, R.
616.97

The **children** and the Zimwi. See Aardema, V. Bimwili & the Zimwi   398.2

Children and their books   028.5

Children just like me. Kindersley, B.
305.23

Children of alcoholics
Rosenberg, M. B. Not my family: sharing the truth about alcoholism (4 and up)
362.29

China—Fiction—*Continued*
Leaf, M. The eyes of the dragon   E
Williams, J. Everyone knows what a dragon looks like   E
Yep, L. The boy who swallowed snakes   E
Yep, L. The Butterfly Boy   E
Yolen, J. The seeing stick   E

Folklore
See Folklore—China
History
Fisher, L. E. The Great Wall of China (4 and up)   951
McLenighan, V. China, a history to 1949 (4 and up)   951
History—1912-1949
Fritz, J. China's Long March (6 and up)   951.04

Science
See Science—China

China (Republic of China, 1949-) *See* Taiwan

China, a history to 1949. McLenighan, V.   951

China homecoming. Fritz, J.   951.05

China's Long March. Fritz, J.   951.04

Chinatown (New York, N.Y.)
Social life and customs
Krull, K. City within a city (4 and up)   305.8

Chincoteague Island (Va.)
Fiction
Henry, M. Misty of Chincoteague (4 and up)   Fic

Chinese
North America—Fiction
Yee, P. Tales from Gold Mountain (4 and up)   S C
United States—Fiction
Levine, E. I hate English!   E
Namioka, L. Yang the youngest and his terrible ear (4-6)   Fic
Yep, L. Dragon's gate (6 and up)   Fic

The **Chinese-American** experience. Wu, Dana Y.-H.   305.8

The **Chinese** American family album. Hoobler, D.   305.8

Chinese Americans
See also Chinese—United States
Hoobler, D. The Chinese American family album (5 and up)   305.8
Krull, K. City within a city (4 and up)   305.8
Kuklin, S. How my family lives in America (k-3)   305.8
Sinnott, S. Chinese railroad workers (4 and up)   331.7
Wu, Dana Y.-H. The Chinese-American experience (4 and up)   305.8
Biography
Yep, L. The lost garden (5 and up)   92
Fiction
Coerr, E. Chang's paper pony   E

Lord, B. B. In the Year of the Boar and Jackie Robinson (4-6)   Fic
Namioka, L. Yang the third and her impossible family (4-6)   Fic
Nunes, S. The last dragon   E
Yep, L. Child of the owl (5 and up)   Fic
Yep, L. Dragonwings (5 and up)   Fic
Yep, L. Later, gator (4-6)   Fic
Yep, L. The star fisher (6 and up)   Fic
Yep, L. Thief of hearts (5 and up)   Fic
Social life and customs
Brown, T. Chinese New Year (1-4)   394.2
Macmillan, D. Chinese New Year (2-4)   394.2
Waters, K. Lion dancer: Ernie Wan's Chinese New Year (k-3)   394.2

Chinese artists *See* Artists, Chinese

Chinese civilization *See* China—Civilization

A **Chinese** fairy tale. Housman, L.
In Bauer, C. F. Celebrations p4-11   808.8

Chinese language
Lee, H. V. At the beach (k-3)   495.1

The **Chinese** mirror. Ginsburg, M.   398.2

Chinese New Year
Brown, T. Chinese New Year (1-4)   394.2
Macmillan, D. Chinese New Year (2-4)   394.2
Waters, K. Lion dancer: Ernie Wan's Chinese New Year (k-3)   394.2

Chinese railroad workers. Sinnott, S.   331.7

The **Chinese** Red Riding Hood. Chang, I. C.
In Womenfolk and fairy tales p14-19   398.2

Chinese science *See* Science—China

Chinook Indians
Legends
Martin, R. The boy who lived with the seals (1-4)   398.2
Taylor, H. P. Coyote places the stars (k-3)   398.2

Chipmunk and Bear. Bruchac, J.
In Bruchac, J. The boy who lived with the bears and other Iroquois stories p53-56   398.2

Chipmunk and the Owl Sisters. Caduto, M. J.
In Caduto, M. J. Keepers of the night p93-96   398.2

Chipmunk Girl and Owl Woman. Bruchac, J.
In Bruchac, J. The girl who married the Moon p108-15   398.2

The **Chippewa**. Osinski, A.   970.004

Chippewa Indians *See* Ojibwa Indians

Chirping insects. Johnson, S. A.   595.7

Chisholm, Shirley, 1924-
See/See also pages in the following book(s):
Haskins, J. One more river to cross (4 and up)   920

Christina Katerina and the time she quit the family. Gauch, P. L.   E

Christmas

    See also Jesus Christ—Nativity

Barth, E. Holly, reindeer, and colored lights (3-6)   **394.2**

Christmas gif' (3-6)   **394.2**

Diane Goode's American Christmas   **810.8**

The Family read-aloud Christmas treasury   **808.8**

Giblin, J. The truth about Santa Claus (4 and up)   **394.2**

McKissack, P. C. Christmas in the big house, Christmas in the quarters (4-6)   **394.2**

Presilla, M. E. Feliz Nochebuena, Feliz Navidad (k-3)   **394.2**

Take joy! The Tasha Tudor Christmas book   **394.2**

Yolen, J. Hark! a Christmas sampler   **808.8**

See/See also pages in the following book(s):
Bauer, C. F. Celebrations p257-78   **808.8**

Drama

The Big book of Christmas plays   **808.82**

Fiction

Andersen, H. C. Hans Christian Andersen's The fir tree (2-5)   **Fic**

Bell, A. The nutcracker (2-4)   **Fic**

Brett, J. The wild Christmas reindeer   E

Briggs, R. Father Christmas   E

Bunting, E. The day before Christmas   E

Bunting, E. Night tree   E

Carlson, N. S. The family under the bridge (3-5)   **Fic**

Caudill, R. A certain small shepherd (4 and up)   **Fic**

Climo, S. The cobweb Christmas   E

De Paola, T. The clown of God (k-3)   **398.2**

De Paola, T. An early American Christmas   E

De Paola, T. The legend of Old Befana (k-3)   **398.2**

De Paola, T. The legend of the poinsettia (k-3)   **398.2**

Dickens, C. A Christmas carol (4 and up)   **Fic**

Godden, R. The story of Holly and Ivy (2-4)   **Fic**

Greene, E. The legend of the Christmas rose (2-4)   **398.2**

Hall, D. Lucy's Christmas   E

Hamilton, V. The bells of Christmas (4-6)   **Fic**

Harvey, B. My prairie Christmas (2-4)   **Fic**

Hayes, S. Happy Christmas, Gemma   E

Heath, A. Sofie's role   E

Henry, O. The gift of the Magi (5 and up)   **Fic**

Hoban, L. Arthur's Christmas cookies   E

Hoffmann, E. T. A. Nutcracker (4 and up)   **Fic**

Houston, G. The year of the perfect Christmas tree   E

Howard, E. F. Chita's Christmas tree   E

Hughes, S. Angel Mae: a tale of Trotter Street   E

Joseph, L. An island Christmas   E

Joyce, W. Santa calls   E

Kroll, S. Santa's crash-bang Christmas   E

Leighton, M. R. An Ellis Island Christmas   E

Paterson, K. Angels & other strangers: family Christmas stories (5 and up)   **S C**

Potter, B. The tailor of Gloucester   E

Robbins, R. Baboushka and the three kings (1-4)   **398.2**

Robinson, B. The best Christmas pageant ever (4-6)   **Fic**

Rosen, M. J. Elijah's angel   **Fic**

Rylant, C. Children of Christmas (4 and up)   **S C**

Sawyer, R. The remarkable Christmas of the cobbler's sons (k-3)   **398.2**

Say, A. Tree of cranes   E

Seuss, Dr. How the Grinch stole Christmas   E

Soto, G. Too many tamales   E

Thayer, J. The puppy who wanted a boy   E

Van Allsburg, C. The Polar Express   E

Van Leeuwen, J. The great Christmas kidnapping caper (3-5)   **Fic**

Wells, R. Morris's disappearing bag   E

Wiggin, K. D. S. The Bird's Christmas Carol (3-5)   **Fic**

Wilder, L. I. A Little house Christmas   **S C**

Wojciechowski, S. The Christmas miracle of Jonathan Toomey   E

See/See also pages in the following book(s):
Take joy! The Tasha Tudor Christmas book p14-55   **394.2**

Poetry

Christmas in the stable (2-4)   **811.008**

Christmas poems   **808.81**

Moore, C. C. The night before Christmas (k-3)   **811**

The Oxford book of Christmas poems (4 and up)   **808.81**

Prelutsky, J. It's Christmas (1-3)   **811**

Worth, V. At Christmastime   **811**

See/See also pages in the following book(s):
Take joy! The Tasha Tudor Christmas book p56-64   **394.2**

Wales

Thomas, D. A child's Christmas in Wales   **828**

Christmas. Wilder, L. I.
In Wilder, L. I. A Little house Christmas p3-21   **S C**

The **Christmas** apple. Sawyer, R.
In Bauer, C. F. Celebrations p259-64   **808.8**

Clare, John D., 1952-
(ed) Industrial revolution. See Industrial
revolution **909.81**
(ed) The Vikings. See The Vikings **948**

Clark, Ann Nolan, 1896-1995
See/See also pages in the following book(s):
Newbery Medal books, 1922-1955 p390-404
028.5

Clark, Christopher Stuart- *See* Stuart-Clark,
Christopher

Clark, Emma Chichester- *See* Chichester-
Clark, Emma, 1955-

Clark, Eugenie
See/See also pages in the following book(s):
Rappaport, D. Living dangerously p71-86 (4
and up) **920**

Clark, Margaret
The best of Aesop's fables (k-3) **398.2**
Contents: The hare and the tortoise; The fox and the
crow; The cat and the mice; The fox and the stork; The boy
who cried wolf; The grasshopper and the ants; The farmer's
daughter; The fox and the grapes; The dog and the bone;
The fox and the goat; The bear and the friends; The fat
hens and the thin hens; The lion and the mouse; The wolf
and his shadow; The crab and his mother; The north wind
and the sun; The town mouse and the country mouse; The
monkey and the camel; The lion and the bull; The wolf and
the heron; The hen and the fox; The lion and the hare; The
ass and the wolf; Zeus and the jackdaw; The dog in the
manger; The miller, his son, and their donkey; The wolf
and the shepherd

Clark, Margaret Goff
The endangered Florida panther (4 and up)
599.74
The threatened Florida black bear (4 and
up) **599.74**
The vanishing manatee (4 and up)
599.5

Clark, William, 1770-1838
About
Blumberg, R. The incredible journey of
Lewis and Clark (5 and up) **978**

The **Clark** Beans man. Wynne-Jones, T.
In Wynne-Jones, T. The book of changes
p1-23 **S C**

Clarke, Barry
Amazing frogs & toads (2-4) **597.8**
Amphibian (4 and up) **597.6**

Clarke, Gus
(il) Old MacDonald had a farm. See Old
MacDonald had a farm **782.42**

Clarke, Margaret Courtney- *See* Courtney-
Clarke, Margaret, 1949-

Class clown. Hurwitz, J. **Fic**

Class president. Hurwitz, J. See note under
Hurwitz, J. Class clown **Fic**

The **Classic** fairy tales **398.2**

Classic poems to read aloud (4 and up)
808.81

Classical antiquities
See also Rome—Antiquities
Classical Calliope. See Calliope **905**
Classical music *See* Music

Classical mythology
See also Aphrodite (Greek deity); Dio-
nysus (Greek deity); Eros (Greek deity);
Persephone (Greek deity); Psyche (Greek
deity)
Aliki. The gods and goddesses of Olympus
(2-5) **292**
Asimov, I. Words from the myths (6 and
up) **292**
Colum, P. The Golden Fleece and the he-
roes who lived before Achilles (5 and up)
292
Fisher, L. E. Cyclops (3-5) **292**
Fisher, L. E. The Olympians (3-5) **292**
Hamilton, E. Mythology (6 and up) **292**
Hodges, M. The arrow and the lamp (2-4)
292
Hutton, W. Perseus (3-5) **292**
Hutton, W. The Trojan horse (3-5) **883**
Low, A. The Macmillan book of Greek gods
and heroes (3-6) **292**
McCaughrean, G. Greek myths (4-6)
292
Osborne, M. P. Favorite Greek myths (3-6)
292
Rockwell, A. F. The robber baby (3-5)
292
Dictionaries
Daly, K. N. Greek and Roman mythology A
to Z (5 and up) **292**

Classification
Books
Subject headings for children **025.4**

Classification, Dewey Decimal *See* Dewey
Decimal Classification

Classified catalogs
The Elementary school library collection
011.6
Middle and junior high school library catalog **011.6**

Claude has a picnic. Gackenbach, D. See note
under Gackenbach, D. What's Claude doing? **E**

Claude the dog. Gackenbach, D. See note under Gackenbach, D. What's Claude doing?
E

Clay, Cassius *See* Ali, Muhammad, 1942-

Clean as a whistle. Coville, B.
In Coville, B. Oddly enough p43-59
S C

Clean your room, Harvey Moon!. Cummings,
P. **E**

Cleanliness
See also Hygiene; Sanitation
Fiction
Hutchins, P. Where's the baby? **E**
Teague, M. Pigsty **E**

Clear the cow pasture, I'm coming in for a
landing!: a story of Amelia Earhart.
Quackenbush, R. M. **92**

The **clearing**. Wynne-Jones, T.
In Wynne-Jones, T. Some of the kinder
planets: stories p83-100 **S C**

Clifton, Lucille, 1936——*Continued*
Everett Anderson's friend. See note under
Clifton, L. Everett Anderson's 1-2-3
        E
Everett Anderson's goodbye. See note under
Clifton, L. Everett Anderson's 1-2-3
        E
Everett Anderson's nine month long. See
note under Clifton, L. Everett Anderson's
1-2-3   E
Everett Anderson's year. See note under
Clifton, L. Everett Anderson's 1-2-3
        E
The lucky stone (3-5)   Fic
Some of the days of Everett Anderson. See
note under Clifton, L. Everett Anderson's
1-2-3   E
Three wishes [short story]
  In Free to be—you and me p114-18
        810.8

Climate
  See also Greenhouse effect; Meteorology; Weather

The **climb**. McKissack, P. C.
  In To ride a butterfly p71-73   810.8

Climbing Jacob's ladder   782.25

Climo, Shirley, 1928-
Atalanta's race (3-5)   292
City! San Francisco (4 and up)   979.4
City! Washington, D.C. (4-6)   975.3
The cobweb Christmas   E
Cobweb Christmas [excerpt]
  In The Family read-aloud Christmas treasury p122-31   808.8
The Egyptian Cinderella (k-3)   398.2
The Korean Cinderella (k-3)   398.2
Someone saw a spider (4 and up)   398.2
  Contents: Arachne's gift; The cloud spinner; The spider
brothers make the rainbow; How spider got his waistline;
The prophet and the spider; The spider and the king; Father spider comes to dinner; The spellbound spider; Sally-Maud, Zachary Dee, and the dream spinner
Stolen thunder (3-5)   293

Clinton, Bill, 1946-
About
Kent, Z. William Jefferson Clinton (4 and
up)   92

Clinton, William Jefferson *See* Clinton, Bill,
1946-

Clocks. Zubrowski, B.   681.1

Clocks and more clocks. Hutchins, P.   E

Clocks and watches
Branley, F. M. Keeping time (4-6)   529
Zubrowski, B. Clocks (4 and up)   681.1
Fiction
Hutchins, P. Clocks and more clocks   E

Close up: a focus on nature [series]
Hunt, J. P. Insects   595.7

Close your eyes. Marzollo, J.   E

Cloth *See* Fabrics

Clothing and dress
  See also Coats; Costume
Kuskin, K. The Philharmonic gets dressed
        E

Perl, L. From top hats to baseball caps,
from bustles to blue jeans (4 and up)
        391
Rowland-Warne, L. Costume (4 and up)
        391
Fiction
Fox, M. Shoes from Grandpa   E
Gould, D. Aaron's shirt   E
Hughes, S. Two shoes, new shoes   E
Neitzel, S. The dress I'll wear to the party
        E
Neitzel, S. The jacket I wear in the snow
        E

The **cloud** book. De Paola, T.   551.57

The **cloud** spinner. Climo, S.
  In Climo, S. Someone saw a spider p17-
24   398.2

Clouds
De Paola, T. The cloud book (k-3)
        551.57
McMillan, B. The weather sky (4 and up)
        551.57

CLOUDS. See Cummings, P. C.L.O.U.D.S.
        E

Cloudy with a chance of meatballs. Barrett, J.
  In Rainy day: stories and poems p3-11
        808.8

The **clover** and the bee. Dowden, A. O. T.
        582

The **clown** of God. De Paola, T.   398.2

Clowns
Fiction
Petersham, M. The circus baby   E

A **clown's** story. Bencastro, M.
  In Where angels glide at dawn p57-65
        S C

**Club de Madres Virgen del Carmen of Lima,
Peru**
Dorros, A. Tonight is Carnaval   E

Clubs
Fiction
Honeycutt, N. Invisible Lissa (3-5)   Fic
Myrick, M. The Secret Three   E

Clues to the past [series]
Martell, H. M. Everyday life in Viking times
        940.1

Clutton-Brock, Juliet
Cat (4 and up)   599.74
Horse (4 and up)   636.1

Clyde Beatty-Cole Bros. Circus
Johnson, N. Big-top circus (1-4)   791.3

Clyde monster. Crowe, R. L.   E

Coal mines and mining
Fiction
Hendershot, J. In coal country   E

Coalson, Glo
(il) Scott, A. H. Hi   E
(il) Scott, A. H. On Mother's lap   E

Coat o' clay. Jacobs, J.
  In Jacobs, J. English fairy tales p294-99
        398.2

Cohen, Barbara, 1932-1992—*Continued*
God's bread
  In To ride a butterfly p68-70   **810.8**
The long way home (4-6)   **Fic**
Molly's Pilgrim (2-4)   **Fic**
Thank you, Jackie Robinson (4-6)   **Fic**
Yussel's prayer (3-5)   **398.2**

Cohen, Caron Lee
The mud pony (k-3)   **398.2**
Sally Ann Thunder Ann Whirlwind Crockett
  meets Mike Fink, Snappin' Turkle
  In From sea to shining sea p118-20
       810.8

Cohen, Daniel, 1936-
Ghost in the house (4 and up)   **133.1**
Ghosts of the deep (4 and up)   **133.1**
The ghosts of war (4 and up)   **133.1**
Great ghosts (4 and up)   **133.1**
Where to find dinosaurs today (5 and up)
       567.9
(jt. auth) Cohen, S. What kind of dog is
  that?   **636.7**

Cohen, Miriam, 1926-
"Bee my valentine!". See note under Cohen,
  M. See you in second grade!   **E**
Best friends. See note under Cohen, M. See
  you in second grade!   **E**
Don't eat too much turkey! See note under
  Cohen, M. See you in second grade!
       E
First grade takes a test. See note under Co-
  hen, M. See you in second grade!   **E**
It's George! See note under Cohen, M. See
  you in second grade!   **E**
Jim meets The Thing. See note under Co-
  hen, M. See you in second grade!   **E**
Jim's dog Muffins. See note under Cohen,
  M. See you in second grade!   **E**
Liar, liar, pants on fire! See note under Co-
  hen, M. See you in second grade!   **E**
Lost in the museum. See note under Cohen,
  M. See you in second grade!   **E**
The new teacher. See note under Cohen, M.
  See you in second grade!   **E**
No good in art. See note under Cohen, M.
  See you in second grade!   **E**
The real skin rubber monster mask. See
  note under Cohen, M. See you in second
  grade!   **E**
See you in second grade!   **E**
See you tomorrow, Charles. See note under
  Cohen, M. See you in second grade!
       E
So what? See note under Cohen, M. See you
  in second grade!   **E**
Starring first grade. See note under Cohen,
  M. See you in second grade!   **E**
When will I read? See note under Cohen,
  M. See you in second grade!   **E**
Will I have a friend? See note under Cohen,
  M. See you in second grade!   **E**

Cohen, Susan, 1938-
What kind of dog is that? (4 and up)
       636.7

(jt. auth) Cohen, D. Where to find dinosaurs
  today   **567.9**

Cohn, Amy
Casey Jones, railroad man
  In From sea to shining sea p170-71
       810.8
Jack and the two-bullet hunt
  In From sea to shining sea p90-91
       810.8
Strong as Annie Christmas
  In From sea to shining sea p277-79
       810.8
With a way, hey, Mister Stormalong
  In From sea to shining sea p104-06
       810.8
(comp) From sea to shining sea. See From
  sea to shining sea   **810.8**

Cohn, Ronald H.
(il) Patterson, F. Koko's kitten   **599.88**
(il) Patterson, F. Koko's story   **599.88**

Coiley, John
Train (4 and up)   **625.1**

Coins
Hoban, T. 26 letters and 99 cents   **E**
Hughes, R. P. Fell's United States coin book
       737.4

Colavito, Rocky, 1933-
See/See also pages in the following book(s):
Torres, J. A. Home-run hitters p61-70 (4
  and up)   **920**

Colborn, Candy, 1942-
What do children read next?   **016.8**

Cold
Ardley, N. The science book of hot & cold
  (3-5)   **536**

Cold (Disease)
Parker, S. Catching a cold (3-5)   **616.2**
The **cold** & hot winter. Hurwitz, J. See note
  under Hurwitz, J. The hot & cold summer
       Fic

Cold harbour. Aiken, J.
  In Aiken, J. A foot in the grave p7-26
       S C

Cold stars and fireflies. Esbensen, B. J.
       811

Coldrey, Jennifer
Shells (3-5)   **594**

Cole, Ann
I saw a purple cow, and 100 other recipes
  for learning   **372.1**

Cole, Brock, 1938-
The goats (5 and up)   **Fic**
No more baths   **E**
(il) Reid Banks, L. The Indian in the cupboard   **Fic**

Cole, Davis *See* Elting, Mary, 1909-

Cole, Joanna
A bird's body   **598**
Bony-Legs (k-3)   **398.2**
Cars and how they go (k-3)   **629.222**
A cat's body   **636.8**
A chick hatches (k-3)   **636.5**

Conflict of generations
LeShan, E. J. Grandparents: a special kind of love (4 and up) **306.8**
LeShan, E. J. When grownups drive you crazy (4 and up) **306.8**

Conford, Ellen
Can do, Jenny Archer. See note under Conford, E. A case for Jenny Archer **Fic**
A case for Jenny Archer (2-4) **Fic**
Dear Lovey Hart: I am desperate (6 and up) **Fic**
Felicia the critic (4-6) **Fic**
Get the picture, Jenny Archer. See note under Conford, E. A case for Jenny Archer **Fic**
Jenny Archer, author. See note under Conford, E. A case for Jenny Archer **Fic**
Jenny Archer to the rescue. See note under Conford, E. A case for Jenny Archer **Fic**
A job for Jenny Archer. See note under Conford, E. A case for Jenny Archer **Fic**
Me and the terrible two (3-6) **Fic**
Nibble, nibble, Jenny Archer. See note under Conford, E. A case for Jenny Archer **Fic**
What's cooking, Jenny Archer? See note under Conford, E. A case for Jenny Archer **Fic**

Congress (U.S.) See United States. Congress

The **conjure** brother. McKissack, P. C.
In McKissack, P. C. The dark-thirty p66-71 **S C**

The **Conjure** wives
In Diane Goode's book of scary stories & songs p42-47 **398.2**

The **conjure** wives. MacDonald, M. R.
In MacDonald, M. R. When the lights go out p79-85 **372.6**

Conjuring See Magic tricks

Conklin, David
(il) Ashabranner, B. K. Land of yesterday, land of tomorrow **951**

Conklin, Paul
(il) Ashabranner, B. K. An ancient heritage **305.8**
(il) Ashabranner, B. K. Land of yesterday, land of tomorrow **951**
(il) Ashabranner, B. K. People who make a difference **920**
(il) Thomson, P. Katie Henio: Navajo sheepherder **970.004**
(il) Thomson, P. Keepers and creatures at the National Zoo **590.74**

Conklin, Peter
(il) Ashabranner, B. K. Land of yesterday, land of tomorrow **951**

Conley, Andrea
Window on the deep: the adventures of underwater explorer Sylvia Earle (5 and up) **92**
(jt. auth) Mallory, K. Rescue of the stranded whales **639.9**

Conly, Jane Leslie
Crazy lady! (5 and up) **Fic**
Racso and the rats of NIMH (4 and up) **Fic**
RT, Margaret, and the rats of NIMH. See note under Conly, J. L. Rasco and the rats of NIMH **Fic**
Trout summer (5 and up) **Fic**

Conly, Robert L. *See* O'Brien, Robert C., 1918-1973

Connecticut
Gelman, A. Connecticut
In Hello USA series **973**
Kent, D. Connecticut
In America the beautiful **973**
Wills, C. A. A historical album of Connecticut
In Historical albums series **973**
Fiction
Dalgliesh, A. The courage of Sarah Noble (2-4) **Fic**
History 1600-1775, Colonial period—Fiction
Speare, E. G. The witch of Blackbird Pond (6 and up) **Fic**

The **Connecticut** peddler. Leach, M.
In From sea to shining sea p218 **810.8**

Conner, Kenyon
About
Schmidt, D. I am a Jesse White tumbler (3-6) **796.47**

Conover, Chris, 1950-
Mother Goose and the sly fox (k-2) **398.2**

Conrad, Pam, 1947-1996
The Earth game
In The Big book for our planet p55-59 **810.8**
My Daniel (5 and up) **Fic**
Our house (4-6) **S C**
Contents: Boy fossil; Night photograph; Dead flies; The longest summer on record; Writer's notebook; The second bad thing
Prairie songs (5 and up) **Fic**
Prairie visions: the life and times of Solomon Butcher (5 and up) **92**
Stonewords (5 and up) **Fic**
The Tub grandfather. See note under Conrad, P. The Tub People **E**
The Tub People **E**

Conservation of energy See Energy conservation

Conservation of forests See Forests and forestry

Conservation of natural resources
See also Nature conservation; Wildlife conservation
Fiction
Cherry, L. The great kapok tree **E**
Locker, T. The land of Gray Wolf **E**

Conservation of plants See Plant conservation

Conserving our world
Baines, J. D. Acid rain **363.7**
Consider the lilies. Paterson, J. B. **220.8**

Constance: a story of early Plymouth. Clapp, P. **Fic**

Constellations

See also Astrology

The **constellations,** how they came to be. Gallant, R. A. **523.8**

Constitutional history

See also United States—Constitutional history

Constitutional rights *See* Civil rights

Construction *See* Building

Construction, House *See* House construction

Consumer education

Schmitt, L. Smart spending (5 and up) **640.73**

Periodicals

Zillions **640.73**

Contagious diseases *See* Communicable diseases

Container gardening

See also House plants

Containers, Box *See* Boxes

Contemporary Spanish-speaking writers and illustrators for children and young adults **920.003**

The **contest.** Hogrogian, N. **398.2**

Contests

Fiction

Lester, H. Three cheers for Tacky **E**

Silverman, E. Don't fidget a feather **E**

Continental drift

Sattler, H. R. Our patchwork planet (5 and up) **551.1**

Contract labor

Fiction

Avi. Encounter at Easton (5 and up) **Fic**

Avi. Night journeys (5 and up) **Fic**

Conundrums *See* Riddles

"A **convention** of delegates". Hauptly, D. J. **342**

Cook, Elizabeth

The ordinary and the fabulous **028.5**

Cook, James, 1728-1779

About

Blumberg, R. The remarkable voyages of Captain Cook (5 and up) **910.4**

Cook, Sybilla Avery, 1930-

Books, battles, and bees **027.8**

The **cookcamp.** Paulsen, G. **Fic**

Cookies

Jaspersohn, W. Cookies (3-5) **664**

Cooking

See also Baking; Food; types of cooking, e.g. Microwave cooking; cooking of particular countries, e.g. French cooking, etc.

American Heart Association kids' cookbook (3-6) **641.5**

Better Homes and Gardens step-by-step kids' cook book (4 and up) **641.5**

Brady, A. A. Kwanzaa karamu (4-6) **641.5**

Cobb, V. More science experiments you can eat (5 and up) **507.8**

Cobb, V. Science experiments you can eat (5 and up) **507.8**

D'Amico, J. The science chef (5 and up) **641.3**

Easy menu ethnic cookbooks (5 and up) **641.5**

Hautzig, E. R. Holiday treats (3-6) **641.5**

Linde, P. van der. Around the world in 80 dishes (3-6) **641.5**

McMillan, B. Eating fractions (k-2) **513**

Penner, L. R. A Native American feast (4 and up) **394.1**

Perl, L. Hunter's stew and hangtown fry: what pioneer America ate and why (4 and up) **641.5**

Perl, L. Slumps, grunts, and snickerdoodles: what Colonial America ate and why (4 and up) **641.5**

Presilla, M. E. Feliz Nochebuena, Feliz Navidad (k-3) **394.2**

Scobey, J. The Fannie Farmer junior cook book (6 and up) **641.5**

Walker, B. M. The Little House cookbook (5 and up) **641.5**

Wilkes, A. The children's step by step cookbook (4-6) **641.5**

See/See also pages in the following book(s):

Barkin, C. Happy Valentine's Day! (4-6) **394.2**

Penner, L. R. Eating the plates p89-105 (4 and up) **394.1**

Cool salsa (5 and up) **811.008**

Coolidge, Olivia Ensor, 1908-

The golden days of Greece (4-6) **938**

The **Coomacka-Tree.** Sherlock, Sir P. M.

In Sherlock, Sir P. M. West Indian folktales p7-12 **398.2**

Coombs, Karen Mueller, 1947-

Flush! (3-6) **628.3**

Cooney, Barbara, 1917-

Chanticleer and the fox **E**

Hattie and the wild waves **E**

Island boy **E**

Miss Rumphius **E**

(il) Boulton, J. Only Opal **E**

(il) Brown, M. W. Christmas in the barn **232.9**

(il) Godden, R. The story of Holly and Ivy **Fic**

(il) Hall, D. Ox-cart man **E**

(il) Houston, G. The year of the perfect Christmas tree **E**

(il) Kesselman, W. A. Emma **E**

(il) McLerran, A. Roxaboxen **E**

(il) Preston, E. M. Squawk to the moon, Little Goose **E**

(il) Sawyer, R. The remarkable Christmas of the cobbler's sons **398.2**

Cooney, Barbara, 1917— *Continued*
(il) Seeger, R. C. American folk songs for children in home, school and nursery school   **782.42**
(il) Seeger, R. C. Animal folk songs for children   **782.42**
(il) Tortillitas para mamá and other nursery rhymes. See Tortillitas para mamá and other nursery rhymes   **398.8**
(il) Yolen, J. Letting Swift River go   **E**
See/See also pages in the following book(s):
Newbery and Caldecott Medal books, 1976-1985 p211-19   **028.5**

Cooper, Chris
Matter (4 and up)   **530**

Cooper, Floyd
Coming home: from the life of Langston Hughes (2-4)   **92**
(il) Greenfield, E. Grandpa's face   **E**
(il) Grimes, N. Meet Danitra Brown   **811**
(il) Hausman, G. Coyote walks on two legs   **398.2**
(il) Howard, E. F. Chita's Christmas tree   **E**
(il) Merrill, J. The Girl Who Loved Caterpillars   **E**
(il) Pass it on. See Pass it on   **811.008**
(il) Thomas, J. C. Brown honey in broomwheat tea   **811**
(il) Williams, K. L. When Africa was home   **E**

Cooper, James Fenimore, 1789-1851
See/See also pages in the following book(s):
Faber, D. Great lives: American literature p3-10 (5 and up)   **920**

Cooper, Lee Pelham
Fun with German (4 and up)   **438**

Cooper, Martha
(il) Gordon, G. My two worlds   **305.8**
(il) Waters, K. Lion dancer: Ernie Wan's Chinese New Year   **394.2**

Cooper, Michael L., 1950-
Klondike fever (5 and up)   **971.9**
Playing America's game (5 and up)   **796.357**

Cooper, Susan, 1935-
The boggart (4-6)   **Fic**
The dark is rising. See note under Cooper, S. Over sea, under stone   **Fic**
Dawn of fear (5 and up)   **Fic**
Greenwitch. See note under Cooper, S. Over sea, under stone   **Fic**
The grey king (5 and up)   **Fic**
Matthew's dragon   **E**
Over sea, under stone (5 and up)   **Fic**
Seaward (6 and up)   **Fic**
The selkie girl (1-4)   **398.2**
The silver cow: a Welsh tale (1-4)   **398.2**
Silver on the tree. See note under Cooper, S. Over sea, under stone   **Fic**
Tam Lin (1-4)   **398.2**

See/See also pages in the following book(s):
Newbery and Caldecott Medal books, 1976-1985 p6-17   **028.5**

Copier creations. Fleischman, P.   **760**

Copland, Aaron, 1900-1990
About
Venezia, M. Aaron Copland (k-3)   **92**

Coppélia (Ballet)
See/See also pages in the following book(s):
McCaughrean, G. The Random House book of stories from the ballet p18-28 (4 and up)   **792.8**

Copway, George, ca. 1818-ca. 1863
Esbensen, B. J. Ladder to the sky   **398.2**

Copy art
Fleischman, P. Copier creations (4 and up)   **760**

Coral reef. Burton, J.   **574.92**

Coral reefs. Johnson, S. A.   **574.92**

Coral reefs and islands
Arnold, C. A walk on the Great Barrier Reef (3-5)   **574.92**
Burton, J. Coral reef (3-6)   **574.92**
Johnson, R. L. The Great Barrier Reef (5 and up)   **574.92**
Johnson, S. A. Coral reefs (4 and up)   **574.92**
Lampton, C. Coral reefs in danger (4 and up)   **574.92**
Sargent, W. Night reef (5 and up)   **574.92**

Coral reefs in danger. Lampton, C.   **574.92**

Corbella, Luciano
(il) Ganeri, A. The oceans atlas   **551.46**

Corbett, Scott, 1913-
The lemonade trick (3-5)   **Fic**

Corbishley, Mike
Ancient Rome (5 and up)   **937**
The Middle Ages (5 and up)   **940.1**

Cordier, Mary Hurlbut, 1930-
(jt. auth) Pérez-Stable, M. A. Understanding American history through children's literature: instructional units and activities for grades k-8   **372.8**

Corduroy. Freeman, D.   **E**
also in The Read-aloud treasury p190-206   **808.8**

The Coretta Scott King Awards book   **028.5**

Cormier, Robert
Tunes for bears to dance to (6 and up)   **Fic**

Corn
Aliki. Corn is maize (k-3)   **633.1**
See/See also pages in the following book(s):
Barth, E. Turkeys, Pilgrims, and Indian corn p79-83 (3-6)   **394.2**
Fiction
Ketteman, H. The year of no more corn   **E**

Counting—*Continued*

Crews, D. Ten black dots	E
Edwards, R. Ten tall oaktrees	E
Feelings, M. Moja means one	E
Fleming, D. Count!	E
Geisert, A. Pigs from 1 to 10	E
Gerstein, M. Roll over!	E
Giganti, P., Jr. Each orange had 8 slices	E
Giganti, P., Jr. How many snails?	E
Gretz, S. Teddy bears 1 to 10	E
Hoban, T. 26 letters and 99 cents	E
Hutchins, P. 1 hunter	E
Jonas, A. Splash!	E
Kitchen, B. Animal numbers	E
Langstaff, J. M. Over in the meadow (k-2)	782.42
Linden, A. M. One smiling grandma	E
McMillan, B. Counting wildflowers	E
McMillan, B. One, two, one pair!	E
Merriam, E. 12 ways to get to 11 (k-3)	510
Morozumi, A. One gorilla	E
Moss, L. Zin! zin! zin! a violin	E
Oakes, B. Puzzlers	E
Onyefulu, I. Emeka's gift	E
Rayner, M. One by one (k-3)	782.42
Rayner, M. Ten pink piglets (k-3)	782.42
Sendak, M. One was Johnny	E
Testa, F. If you take a pencil	E
Walsh, E. S. Mouse count	E
Wise, W. Ten sly piranhas	E

Counting books *See* Counting

Counting house, Anno's. Anno, M.   E

Counting wildflowers. McMillan, B.   E

Country and western music *See* Country music

The **country** artist: a story about Beatrix Potter. Collins, D. R.   92

The **country** bunny and the little gold shoes. Heyward, D.   E

Country crossing. Aylesworth, J.   E

The **country** happens to Sneakers again. Brown, M. W.
   In Brown, M. W. The fish with the deep sea smile p60-61   818

Country life

Crews, D. Bigmama's	92
Maestro, B. Delivery van	E

Fiction

Burch, R. Ida Early comes over the mountain (4 and up)	Fic
Haseley, D. Shadows (3-5)	Fic
Johnston, T. Yonder	E
Lyon, G. E. Come a tide	E
Martin, B. Barn dance!	E
Nesbit, E. The railway children (4-6)	Fic
Rylant, C. Night in the country	E
Schertle, A. Down the road	E
Yolen, J. Letting Swift River go	E

Country music

See also Cowhands—Songs

Fiction

Paterson, K. Come sing, Jimmy Jo (5 and up)   **Fic**

Country pay. Fleischman, P.
   In Fleischman, P. Coming-and-going men p123-47   **S C**

Coupe, Robert
   (jt. auth) Coupe, S. M. Sharks   597

Coupe, Sheena M.
   Sharks (5 and up)   597

Courage

Fiction

Peet, B. Cowardly Clyde   E

The **courage** of Kazan. Walker, B. K.
   In Walker, B. K. A treasury of Turkish folktales for children p67-74
   398.2

The **courage** of Sarah Noble. Dalgliesh, A.   **Fic**

Courlander, Harold, 1908-1996
   Anansi's hat-shaking dance
      In The Scott, Foresman anthology of children's literature p313-14   808.8
   The cow-tail switch, and other West African stories (4-6)   398.2
   Contents: The cow-tail switch; Kaddo's wall; Talk; The one you don't see coming; Kassa, the strong one; Anansi's fishing expedition; Younde goes to town; The singing tortoise; Time; The messenger to Maftam; Guinea Fowl and Rabbit get justice; Anansi and Nothing go hunting for wives; How Soko brought debt to Ashanti; Hungry Spider and the Turtle; Throw Mountains; Ansige Karamba, the glutton; Don't shake hands with everybody
   Coyote helps decorate the night
      In From sea to shining sea p16-17   810.8
   The fire on the mountain
      In The Scott, Foresman anthology of children's literature p303-04   808.8
   Sharing the crops
      In From sea to shining sea p219-21   810.8
   Uncle Bouqui and Godfather Malice
      In The Scott, Foresman anthology of children's literature p394-96   808.8

The **court** jester's last wish. Jaffe, N.
   In Jaffe, N. While standing on one foot p23-25   296.1

The **court** of the stone children. Cameron, E.   **Fic**

Courtney
   (il) Elting, M. Volcanoes and earthquakes   551.2

Courtney-Clarke, Margaret, 1949-
   (il) Angelou, M. My painted house, my friendly chicken, and me   968

Courts and courtiers
   See also Fools and jesters
   Aliki. A medieval feast (2-5)   394.1

Cousin Greylegs, the great red fox and Grandfather Mole. Pyle, H.
   In Pyle, H. The wonder clock p77-88   398.2

Cousins, Lucy
(il) The Little dog laughed. See The Little dog laughed   **398.8**

Cousins

Fiction
Binch, C. Gregory Cool   **E**
Hamilton, V. Cousins (5 and up)   **Fic**
Hest, A. Nana's birthday party   **E**
Mahy, M. The Good Fortunes Gang (3-5)
                                                                    Fic
Mills, C. A visit to Amy-Claire   **E**

Cousteau Society
An Adventure in the Amazon. See An Adventure in the Amazon   **508**
Turtles. See Turtles   **597.9**

Coverlets See Quilts

Coville, Bruce
Dapplegrim
In Herds of thunder, manes of gold p149-56   **808.8**
Jennifer Murdley's toad (4-6)   **Fic**
Jeremy Thatcher, dragon hatcher (4-6)
                                                                    Fic
Oddly enough (6 and up)   **S C**
Contents: The box; Duffy's jacket; Homeward bound; With his head tucked underneath his arm; Clean as a whistle; The language of blood; Old glory; The passing of the pack; A blaze of glory
The taming of Bucephalus
In Herds of thunder, manes of gold p65-70   **808.8**
(ed) Herds of thunder, manes of gold. See Herds of thunder, manes of gold
                                                                    808.8

Coville, Katherine
(il) Barkin, C. The scary Halloween costume book   **391**
(il) San Souci, R. More short & shivery
                                                                    398.2
(il) San Souci, R. Short & shivery   **398.2**

Cow dung custard. Jennings, P.
In Jennings, P. Unreal! p51-67   **S C**

The **cow-tail** switch. Courlander, H.
In Courlander, H. The cow-tail switch, and other West African stories p5-12
                                                                    398.2

The **cow-tail** switch, and other West African stories. Courlander, H.   **398.2**

The **cow** that ate the piper. Crossley-Holland, K.
In Crossley-Holland, K. British folk tales p283-86   **398.2**

The **cow** who fell in the canal. Krasilovsky, P.
                                                                    E

The **cow** who wouldn't come down. Johnson, P. B.   **E**

Cowardly Clyde. Peet, B.   **E**

Cowboy. Murdoch, D. H.   **978**

Cowboy: an album. Granfield, L.   **978**

The **cowboy** and the black-eyed pea. Johnston, T.   **E**

Cowboy country. Scott, A. H.   **978**

Cowboy dreams. Khalsa, D. K.   **E**

Cowboys. Rounds, G.   **978**

Cowboys of the wild West. Freedman, R.
                                                                    978

Cowcher, Helen
Antarctica (1-3)   **998**
Tigress   **E**
Whistling thorn (k-3)   **583**

Cowen-Fletcher, Jane
It takes a village   **E**

Cowhands
Brusca, M. C. On the pampas (k-3)   **982**
Christian, M. B. Hats are for watering horses (3-5)   **391**
Faber, D. Calamity Jane (5 and up)   **92**
Freedman, R. Cowboys of the wild West (4 and up)   **978**
Granfield, L. Cowboy: an album (5 and up)
                                                                    978
Murdoch, D. H. Cowboy (4 and up)
                                                                    978
Rounds, G. Cowboys (k-2)   **978**
Scott, A. H. Cowboy country (k-3)   **978**
Biography
Miller, R. H. The story of Nat Love (k-3)
                                                                    92

Fiction
Johnston, T. The cowboy and the black-eyed pea   **E**
Khalsa, D. K. Cowboy dreams   **E**
Kimmel, E. A. Four dollars and fifty cents
                                                                    E

Songs
Medearis, A. S. The zebra-riding cowboy (k-3)   **782.42**
Songs of the Wild West   **782.42**

Cowles, Kathleen See Krull, Kathleen, 1952-

Cows See Cattle

Cows in the parlor. McFarland, C.   **636.2**

Cox, Clinton
Undying glory (6 and up)   **973.7**

Cox, Daniel J., 1960-
(il) Hirschi, R. Loon lake   **591.5**

Coxe, Molly, 1959-
(il) Branley, F. M. The Big Dipper
                                                                    523.8

Coyote (Legendary character)
Aardema, V. Borreguita and the coyote (k-3)
                                                                    398.2
Baylor, B. Moon song (1-4)   **398.2**
Begay, S. Ma'ii and cousin Horned Toad (k-3)
                                                                    398.2
Bierhorst, J. Doctor Coyote (1-4)   **398.2**
Curry, J. L. Back in the beforetime (4-6)
                                                                    398.2
Hausman, G. Coyote walks on two legs (2-4)
                                                                    398.2
Johnston, T. The tale of Rabbit and Coyote (k-3)
                                                                    398.2
Mayo, G. That tricky Coyote! (k-3)
                                                                    398.2
McDermott, G. Coyote: a trickster tale from the American Southwest (k-3)   **398.2**
Stevens, J. Coyote steals the blanket (k-3)
                                                                    398.2

Coyote (Legendary character)—*Continued*
Taylor, H. P. Coyote and the laughing butterflies (k-3) **398.2**
Taylor, H. P. Coyote places the stars (k-3) **398.2**

Coyote. Rosen, M.
In Rosen, M. How the animals got their colors p6-9 **398.2**

Coyote and Badger. Curry, J. L.
In Curry, J. L. Back in the beforetime p78-88 **398.2**

Coyote and the acorns. Kherdian, D.
In Kherdian, D. Feathers and tails p41-42 **398.2**

The Coyote and the bear
In The Diane Goode book of American folk tales and songs p25-31 **398.2**

Coyote and the blackbirds. Van Laan, N.
In Van Laan, N. In a circle long ago p68-75 **398.2**

Coyote and the laughing butterflies. Taylor, H. P. **398.2**

The coyote and the ravens. Yeoman, J.
In Yeoman, J. The singing tortoise and other animal folktales p19-25 **398.2**

Coyote and the salmon. Curry, J. L.
In Curry, J. L. Back in the beforetime p42-47 **398.2**

Coyote helps decorate the night. Courlander, H.
In From sea to shining sea p16-17 **810.8**

Coyote places the stars. Taylor, H. P. **398.2**

Coyote rides a star. Curry, J. L.
In Curry, J. L. Back in the beforetime p48-51 **398.2**

Coyote rides the Sun. Curry, J. L.
In Curry, J. L. Back to the beforetime p100-106 **398.2**

Coyote steals the blanket. Stevens, J. **398.2**

Coyote walks on two legs. Hausman, G. **398.2**

Coyotes
Winner, C. Coyotes (3-6) **599.74**

Coyote's crying song. MacDonald, M. R.
In MacDonald, M. R. Twenty tellable tales p10-19 **372.6**

Coyote's rain song. MacDonald, M. R.
In MacDonald, M. R. Twenty tellable tales p20-23 **372.6**

Coyote's squirrel hunt. Curry, J. L.
In Curry, J. L. Back in the beforetime p74-77 **398.2**

The Crab and the monkey
In The Rainbow fairy book p269-72 **398.2**

The crab that played with the sea. Kipling, R.
In Kipling, R. Just so stories **S C**

Crabapples [series]
Kalman, B. A canoe trip **797.1**

Crabs
Johnson, S. A. Hermit crabs (4 and up) **595.3**
Kite, L. P. Down in the sea, The crab (2-4) **595.3**
McDonald, M. Is this a house for Hermit Crab? (k-2) **595.3**
Fiction
Carle, E. A house for Hermit Crab **E**
Tafuri, N. Follow me! **E**

Crack (Drug)
Shulman, J. Focus on cocaine and crack (3-6) **362.29**

Crack cocaine *See* Crack (Drug)

The crack-of-dawn walkers. Hest, A. **E**

Cracker Jackson. Byars, B. C. **Fic**

The cradle didn't rock. Lester, J.
In Lester, J. The tales of Uncle Remus p106-09 **398.2**

Cradles in the trees. Demuth, P. **598**

Craft, Kinuko, 1940-
(il) Mayer, M. Baba Yaga and Vasilisa the brave **398.2**

Crafts (Arts) *See* Handicraft

Crafts for Kwanzaa. Ross, K. **745.5**

Crafts for Valentine's Day. Ross, K. **745.5**

Crafty Chameleon. Mwenye Hadithi **E**

Craig, Helen
I see the moon, and the moon sees me... . (k-2) **398.8**
The town mouse and the country mouse (k-3) **398.2**
(il) Holabird, K. Angelina ballerina **E**
(il) Mahy, M. The pumpkin man and the crafty creeper **E**

Craighead, Charles
The eagle and the river (3-5) **591.5**

Craine, Michael
(il) Howe, J. Playing with words **92**

Crampton, Patricia
Peter and the wolf **E**

Crampton, W. G. (William G.)
Flag (4 and up) **929.9**

Crampton, William G. *See* Crampton, W. G. (William G.)

Cranberries
Burns, D. L. Cranberries: fruit of the bogs (3-5) **634**
Jaspersohn, W. Cranberries (3-5) **634**

Crane, Jeff Chapman- *See* Chapman-Crane, Jeff

Crane. Rosen, M.
In Rosen, M. How the animals got their colors p36-38 **398.2**

The crane and the heron. Afanas'ev, A. N.
In Afanas'ev, A. N. Russian fairy tales p66 **398.2**

The crane wife. Yagawa, S. **398.2**

The **crow** and Mrs. Gaddy. Gage, W. See note
under Gage, W. Mrs. Gaddy and the
ghost **E**

The **crow** and the snake. Walker, B. K.
In Walker, B. K. A treasury of Turkish
folktales for children p17-19
398.2

Crow Boy. Iwamatsu, A. J. **E**

Crow chief. Goble, P. **398.2**

Crow Fair (Crow Agency, Mont.)
Ancona, G. Powwow (3-6) **970.004**

Crow Indians
See/See also pages in the following book(s):
Hofsinde, R. Indian costumes p33-39 (3-6)
391

Crowe, Robert L.
Clyde monster **E**

Crowell biography [series]
Adoff, A. Malcolm X **92**
Greenfield, E. Mary McLeod Bethune
92
Greenfield, E. Paul Robeson **92**
Walker, A. Langston Hughes, American poet
92

Cruelty to animals *See* Animal welfare

Crum, Robert
Eagle drum (3-6) **970.004**

The **crumbs** on the table. Grimm, J.
In Grimm, J. The complete Grimm's
fairy tales p768-69 **398.2**

Crusades
See/See also pages in the following book(s):
Brooks, P. S. Queen Eleanor: independent
spirit of the medieval world p31-50 (6 and
up) **92**

Crutches. Härtling, P. **Fic**

Crutchfield, Jimmie, 1910-1993
See/See also pages in the following book(s):
Brashler, W. The story of Negro league
baseball (5 and up) **796.357**

Cruz, Alejandro
The woman who outshone the sun (k-3)
398.2

Cruz, Juana Inés de la *See* Juana Inés de la
Cruz, 1651-1695

Cruz, Ray
(il) Hazen, B. S. The gorilla did it **E**
(il) Hurwitz, J. Baseball fever **Fic**
(il) Viorst, J. Alexander and the terrible,
horrible, no good, very bad day **E**

Cryptography
Huckle, H. The secret code book (4 and up)
652
Janeczko, P. B. Loads of codes and secret
ciphers (5 and up) **652**
Mango, K. N. Codes, ciphers, and other secrets (4 and up) **652**
Schwartz, A. The cat's elbow, and other secret languages (4 and up) **652**

Crystal & gem. Symes, R. F. **548**

The **crystal** ball. Grimm, J.
In Grimm, J. The complete Grimm's
fairy tales p798-801 **398.2**

The **crystal** coffin. Grimm, J.
In The Green fairy book p290-95
398.2

The **crystal** mountain. Afanas'ev, A. N.
In Afanas'ev, A. N. Russian fairy tales
p482-84 **398.2**

Crystallography
Maki, C. Snowflakes, sugar, and salt (1-3)
548
Stangl, J. Crystals and crystal gardens you
can grow (4 and up) **548**
Symes, R. F. Crystal & gem (4 and up)
548

Crystals and crystal gardens you can grow.
Stangl, J. **548**

CT (Computerized tomography) *See* Tomography

Cuba
Sheehan, S. Cuba (5 and up) **972.91**

Cuban Americans
Mendez, A. Cubans in America
In The In America series **305.8**

Cubans in America. Mendez, A.
In The In America series **305.8**

The **cuckoo** child. King-Smith, D. **Fic**

The **cuckoo** sister. Alcock, V. **Fic**

Cuffari, Richard, 1925-1978
(il) Cohen, B. Thank you, Jackie Robinson
Fic
(il) Perl, L. Hunter's stew and hangtown fry:
what pioneer America ate and why
641.5
(il) Perl, L. Slumps, grunts, and snickerdoodles: what Colonial America ate and
why **641.5**
(il) Pope, E. M. The Perilous Gard **Fic**

Cullen, Countee, 1903-1946
The lost zoo **811**

Cully Cully and the bear. Gage, W. **E**

Cultivated plants *See* House plants

Cultural anthropology *See* Ethnology

Cultural atlas for young people [series]
Corbishley, M. Ancient Rome **937**
Corbishley, M. The Middle Ages **940.1**

Cultural pluralism *See* Multiculturalism

Culturally diverse library collections for children. Totten, H. L. **011.6**

Cultures of the world [series]
Cheong-Lum, R. N. Haiti **972.94**
Foley, E. Dominican Republic **972.93**
Foley, E. El Salvador **972.84**
Kott, J. Nicaragua **972.85**
Sheehan, S. Cuba **972.91**

Cultures outside the United States in fiction.
Anderson, V. **016.8**

Cummings, Pat, 1950-
C.L.O.U.D.S. **E**
Carousel **E**
Clean your room, Harvey Moon! **E**
(il) Caines, J. F. I need a lunch box **E**
(il) Caines, J. F. Just us women **E**
(il) Stolz, M. Go fish **Fic**

De Paola, Tomie, 1934- —*Continued*
The miracles of Jesus (k-3) **232.9**
Nana Upstairs & Nana Downstairs **E**
Now one foot, now the other **E**
Patrick: patron saint of Ireland (k-3) **92**
The popcorn book (k-3) **641.3**
The quicksand book (k-3) **552**
Strega Nona **E**
Strega Nona meets her match. See note under De Paola, T. Strega Nona **E**
Strega Nona's magic lessons. See note under De Paola, T. Strega Nona **E**
Tom **E**
Tomie dePaola's book of Christmas carols. See Tomie dePaola's book of Christmas carols **782.28**
Tomie dePaola's Favorite nursery tales. See Tomie dePaola's Favorite nursery tales **398.2**
Tony's bread: an Italian folktale (k-3) **398.2**
(il) Adler, D. A. The carsick zebra and other animal riddles **793.73**
(il) Beat the drum. See Beat the drum **811.008**
(il) The Comic adventures of Old Mother Hubbard and her dog. See The Comic adventures of Old Mother Hubbard and her dog **398.8**
(il) Easter buds are springing. See Easter buds are springing **808.81**
(il) Fritz, J. Can't you make them behave, King George? [biography of George III, King of Great Britain] **92**
(il) Fritz, J. Shhh! we're writing the Constitution **342**
(il) Ghost poems. See Ghost poems **821.008**
(il) Good morning to you, Valentine. See Good morning to you, Valentine **808.81**
(il) Hale, S. J. Mary had a little lamb **811**
(il) Johnston, T. Alice Nizzy Nazzy, the Witch of Santa Fe **E**
(il) Johnston, T. The badger and the magic fan **398.2**
(il) Johnston, T. The quilt story **E**
(il) Johnston, T. The tale of Rabbit and Coyote **398.2**
(il) Johnston, T. The vanishing pumpkin **E**
(il) Kroll, S. Santa's crash-bang Christmas **E**
(il) Moore, C. C. The night before Christmas **811**
(il) Tomie dePaola's Mother Goose. See Tomie dePaola's Mother Goose **398.8**
(il) Willard, N. Simple pictures are best **E**
(il) Yolen, J. Hark! a Christmas sampler **808.8**

De Regniers, Beatrice Schenk
A little house of your own **E**
Little Sister and the Month Brothers (k-3) **398.2**

May I bring a friend? **E**
(comp) Sing a song of popcorn. See Sing a song of popcorn **808.81**
De Rosas, Juan Manuel José Domingo Ortiz See Rosas, Juan Manuel José Domingo Ortiz de, 1793-1877
De Sable, Jean Baptiste Pointe See Pointe de Sable, Jean Baptiste, 1745?-1818
De Saint-Exupéry, Antoine See Saint-Exupéry, Antoine de, 1900-1944
De Sauza, James
Rohmer, H. Brother Anansi and the cattle ranch **398.2**
De Soto, Hernando See Soto, Hernando de, ca. 1500-1542
De Treviño, Elizabeth Borton See Treviño, Elizabeth Borton de, 1904-
De Villeneuve, Madame See Villeneuve, Madame de
The **deacon's** ghost. San Souci, R.
In San Souci, R. Short & shivery p88-91 **398.2**
Dead Aaron
In Raw Head, bloody bones p23-27 **398.2**
Dead Aaron. Haskins, J.
In Haskins, J. The headless haunt and other African American ghost stories p99-104 **398.2**
The **dead** bird. Brown, M. W.
In Brown, M. W. The fish with the deep sea smile p62-63 **818**
The **dead** body. Afanas'ev, A. N.
In Afanas'ev, A. N. Russian fairy tales p118-19 **398.2**
Dead flies. Conrad, P.
In Conrad, P. Our house p22-28 **S C**
The **dead** hand. Schwartz, A.
In Schwartz, A. Scary stories 3 p35-38 **398.2**
The **dead** man in Indian Creek. Hahn, M. D. **Fic**
The **dead** mother. San Souci, R.
In San Souci, R. More short & shivery p143-47 **398.2**
The **dead** tree. See Tresselt, A. R. The gift of the tree **574.5**
The **Dead** wife
In The Yellow fairy book p149-51 **398.2**
Deaf
Adler, D. A. A picture book of Helen Keller (1-3) **92**
Bergman, T. Finding a common language (1-3) **362.4**
Hunter, E. F. Child of the silent night [biography of Laura Dewey Bridgman] (3-5) **92**
Levine, E. S. Lisa and her soundless world (1-3) **617.8**
Peterson, J. W. I have a sister—my sister is deaf (k-3) **362.4**

Deaf—*Continued*

St. George, J. Dear Dr. Bell—your friend, Helen Keller (5 and up)   **92**

Education

Neimark, A. E. A deaf child listened: Thomas Gallaudet, pioneer in American education (6 and up)   **92**

Walker, L. A. Hand, heart, & mind (5 and up)   **371.9**

Fiction

Lee, J. M. Silent Lotus   **E**

Riskind, M. Apple is my sign (5 and up)   **Fic**

Means of communication

See also Sign language

A **deaf** child listened: Thomas Gallaudet, pioneer in American education. Neimark, A. E.   **92**

Deafness

Levine, E. S. Lisa and her soundless world (1-3)   **617.8**

Dealing with dragons. Wrede, P. C.   **Fic**

Dean, Julia

A year on Monhegan Island (4-6)   **974.1**

Dear Annie. Caseley, J.   **E**

Dear Benjamin Banneker. Pinkney, A. D.   **92**

Dear Dr. Bell—your friend, Helen Keller. St. George, J.   **92**

Dear Jane. Lavelle, S.

In The Oxford book of scary tales p8-13   **808.8**

Dear Levi. Woodruff, E.   **Fic**

Dear Lovey Hart: I am desperate. Conford, E.   **Fic**

Dear Mr. Henshaw. Cleary, B.   **Fic**

Death

Bernstein, J. E. Loss and how to cope with it (5 and up)   **155.9**

Fry, V. L. Part of me died, too (5 and up)   **155.9**

Hyde, M. O. Meeting death (4 and up)   **155.9**

The Kids' book about death and dying (5 and up)   **155.9**

Krementz, J. How it feels when a parent dies (4 and up)   **155.9**

LeShan, E. J. Learning to say good-by (4 and up)   **155.9**

Stein, S. B. About dying (k-3)   **155.9**

Fiction

Aliki. The two of them   **E**

Brooks, B. Everywhere (4 and up)   **Fic**

Carson, J. You hold me and I'll hold you   **E**

Cleaver, V. Grover (4-6)   **Fic**

Clifford, E. The remembering box (3-5)   **Fic**

Conly, J. L. Crazy lady! (5 and up)   **Fic**

Creech, S. Walk two moons (6 and up)   **Fic**

De Paola, T. Nana Upstairs & Nana Downstairs   **E**

Ehrlich, A. Maggie and Silky and Joe   **E**

Fletcher, R. J. Fig pudding (4 and up)   **Fic**

Fox, P. The eagle kite (6 and up)   **Fic**

Greene, C. C. Beat the turtle drum (5 and up)   **Fic**

Hamilton, V. Cousins (5 and up)   **Fic**

Härtling, P. Old John (4 and up)   **Fic**

Hermes, P. You shouldn't have to say good-bye (5 and up)   **Fic**

Hunter, M. A sound of chariots (5 and up)   **Fic**

Jukes, M. Blackberries in the dark (2-4)   **Fic**

Jukes, M. I'll see you in my dreams   **E**

Lowry, L. A summer to die (5 and up)   **Fic**

MacLachlan, P. Baby (5 and up)   **Fic**

Miles, M. Annie and the Old One (1-4)   **Fic**

Neufeld, J. Almost a hero (5 and up)   **Fic**

Newman, L. Too far away to touch   **E**

Park, B. Mick Harte was here (4-6)   **Fic**

Paterson, K. Bridge to Terabithia (4 and up)   **Fic**

Paterson, K. Flip-flop girl (4-6)   **Fic**

Polikoff, B. G. Life's a funny proposition, Horatio (5 and up)   **Fic**

Rylant, C. Missing May (5 and up)   **Fic**

Slepian, J. The Broccoli tapes (5 and up)   **Fic**

Smith, D. B. A taste of blackberries (4-6)   **Fic**

Thomas, J. R. Saying good-bye to Grandma   **E**

Varley, S. Badger's parting gifts   **E**

Viorst, J. The tenth good thing about Barney   **E**

Wild, M. The very best of friends   **E**

Zolotow, C. My grandson Lew   **E**

Death of a miser. Afanas'ev, A. N.

In Afanas'ev, A. N. Russian fairy tales p268   **398.2**

The **death** of Brer Fox. Lester, J.

In Lester, J. The tales of Uncle Remus p57-60   **398.2**

The **death** of Brer Wolf. Lester, J.

In Lester, J. The tales of Uncle Remus p40-42   **398.2**

The **death** of Koschei the Deathless. Ralston, W.

In The Red fairy book p42-53   **398.2**

The **death** of the cock. Afanas'ev, A. N.

In Afanas'ev, A. N. Russian fairy tales p17-19   **398.2**

Death of the iron horse. Goble, P.   **E**

also in From sea to shining sea p160-63   **810.8**

The **death** of the little hen. Grimm, J.

In Grimm, J. The complete Grimm's fairy tales p365-67   **398.2**

The **Death** of the Sun-Hero

In The Yellow fairy book p213-15   **398.2**

Dinner, Sherry H.
Nothing to be ashamed of: growing up with mental illness in your family (5 and up)
362.2

Dinner at Alberta's. Hoban, R. **E**

Dinner at Magritte's. Garland, M. **E**

Dinner guests. Calmenson, S.
In The Read-aloud treasury p100-11
808.8

Dino easy reader [series]
Brown, L. K. Rex and Lilly family time
E

Dinosaur. Norman, D. **567.9**

Dinosaur Bob and his adventures with the family Lazardo. Joyce, W. **E**

Dinosaur bones. Aliki **567.9**

Dinosaur dances. Yolen, J. **811**

Dinosaur dig. Lasky, K. **567.9**

Dinosaur discoveries. West, R. **745.54**

Dinosaur dreams. Ahlberg, A. See note under Ahlberg, J. Funnybones **E**

Dinosaur encore. Mullins, P. **567.9**

The **dinosaur** is the biggest animal that ever lived, and other wrong ideas you thought were true. Simon, S. **500**

Dinosaur mountain. Arnold, C. **567.9**

Dinosaur National Monument (Colo. and Utah)
Arnold, C. Dinosaur mountain (4 and up)
567.9

The **dinosaur** question and answer book. Funston, S. **567.9**

Dinosaur tree. Henderson, D. **560**

Dinosaurs
Aliki. Digging up dinosaurs (k-3) **567.9**
Aliki. Dinosaur bones (k-3) **567.9**
Aliki. Dinosaurs are different (k-3)
567.9
Arnold, C. Dinosaur mountain (4 and up)
567.9
Arnold, C. Dinosaurs all around (4 and up)
567.9
Arnold, C. Dinosaurs down under and other fossils from Australia (4 and up)
567.9
Barton, B. Bones, bones, dinosaur bones
E
Barton, B. Dinosaurs, dinosaurs **E**
Benton, M. J. How do we know dinosaurs existed? (4 and up) **567.9**
Booth, J. The big beast book (4 and up)
567.9
Cole, J. The magic school bus: in the time of the dinosaurs (2-4) **567.9**
Dixon, D. Dougal Dixon's dinosaurs (4 and up) **567.9**
Dodson, P. An alphabet of dinosaurs (k-3)
567.9
Funston, S. The dinosaur question and answer book (4-6) **567.9**
Gillette, J. L. The search for Seismosaurus (4-6) **567.9**
Henderson, D. Dinosaur tree (2-4) **560**

Horner, J. R. Digging up Tyrannosaurus rex (3-5) **567.9**
Lasky, K. Dinosaur dig (3-6) **567.9**
Lauber, P. Dinosaurs walked here, and other stories fossils tell (3-5) **560**
Lauber, P. Living with dinosaurs (3-6)
567.9
Lauber, P. The news about dinosaurs (3-6)
567.9
Lessem, D. Jack Horner: living with dinosaurs (4 and up) **92**
Lindsay, W. Barosaurus (4 and up)
567.9
Lindsay, W. Corythosaurus (4 and up)
567.9
Lindsay, W. Triceratops (4 and up)
567.9
Lindsay, W. Tyrannosaurus (4 and up)
567.9
Most, B. How big were the dinosaurs (k-2)
567.9
Most, B. The littlest dinosaurs (k-2)
567.9
Most, B. Where to look for a dinosaur (k-2)
567.9
Mullins, P. Dinosaur encore (k-3) **567.9**
Norman, D. Dinosaur (4 and up) **567.9**
Pringle, L. P. Dinosaurs! (k-3) **567.9**
Sattler, H. R. Baby dinosaurs (1-4)
567.9
Sattler, H. R. Dinosaurs of North America (5 and up) **567.9**
Sattler, H. R. Stegosaurs (3-6) **567.9**
Sattler, H. R. Tyrannosaurus rex and its kin: the Mesozoic monsters (3-6) **567.9**
Simon, S. The largest dinosaurs (1-3)
567.9
Simon, S. New questions and answers about dinosaurs (3-6) **567.9**
The Visual dictionary of dinosaurs (4 and up) **567.9**
The Visual dictionary of prehistoric life (4 and up) **560**
West, R. Dinosaur discoveries (3-5)
745.54
Whitfield, P. J. Macmillan children's guide to dinosaurs and other prehistoric animals (3-6) **567.9**

Collections
Cohen, D. Where to find dinosaurs today (5 and up) **567.9**

Dictionaries
Sattler, H. R. The new illustrated dinosaur dictionary (5 and up) **567.9**

Fiction
Brown, L. K. Rex and Lilly family time
E
Butterworth, O. The enormous egg (4 and up) **Fic**
Carrick, C. Patrick's dinosaurs **E**
Carrick, C. What happened to Patrick's dinosaurs? **E**
Fleischman, P. Time train **E**
Hoff, S. Danny and the dinosaur **E**
Joyce, W. Dinosaur Bob and his adventures with the family Lazardo **E**

Dixon, Ann, 1954-
How Raven brought light to people (k-3)
398.2

Dixon, Dougal, 1947-
Dougal Dixon's dinosaurs (4 and up)
567.9

Dixon, Tennessee
(il) Blos, J. W. The heroine of the Titanic:
a tale both true and otherwise of the life
of Molly Brown **92**

DNA
Aronson, B. They came from DNA (5 and
up) **575.1**
Balkwill, F. R. DNA is here to stay (3-6)
574.87

DNA is here to stay. Balkwill, F. R.
574.87

Do bananas chew gum?. Gilson, J. **Fic**

Do fishes get thirsty? (5 and up) **597**

Do like Kyla. Johnson, A. **E**

Do not alight here. Aiken, J.
In Aiken, J. Give yourself a fright: thir-
teen tales of the supernatural p31-43
S C

Do not disturb. Facklam, M. **591.5**

Do not disturb. Tafuri, N. **E**

Do not open. Turkle, B. C. **E**

Do not sneeze, do not scratch . . . do not eat!.
Bernier-Grand, C. T.
In Bernier-Grand, C. T. Juan Bobo p26-
41 **398.2**

Do you know the difference?. Bischhoff-
Miersch, A. **596**

Do you want to be my friend?. Carle, E.
E

Dobie, J. Frank (James Frank), 1888-1964
The mezcla man
In From sea to shining sea p30-32
810.8

Dobie, James Frank *See* Dobie, J. Frank
(James Frank), 1888-1964

Doc Rabbit, Bruh Fox, and Tar Baby. Hamilton, V.
In Hamilton, V. The people could fly:
American Black folktales p13-19
398.2

Dockray, Tracy
(il) Tomb, H. Microaliens **574**

Doctor Coyote. Bierhorst, J. **398.2**

Doctor De Soto. Steig, W. **E**

Doctor De Soto goes to Africa. Steig, W. See
note under Steig, W. Doctor De Soto
E

Doctor Knowall. Grimm, J.
In Grimm, J. The complete Grimm's
fairy tales p456-58 **398.2**

Doctors *See* Physicians

Dodge, Mary Mapes, 1830-1905
Hans Brinker; or, The silver skates (4 and
up) **Fic**

Dodgers (Baseball team) *See* Brooklyn
Dodgers (Baseball team)

Dodgson, Charles Lutwidge *See* Carroll, Lewis,
1832-1898

Dodson, Bert
(il) Evslin, B. Jason and the Argonauts
292
(il) Smith, E. S. A guide dog goes to school
362.4

Dodson, Peter
An alphabet of dinosaurs (k-3) **567.9**

Does God have a big toe?. Gellman, M.
221.9

The **dog**. Burningham, J. **E**

The **dog** and the sparrow. Grimm, J.
In Grimm, J. The complete Grimm's
fairy tales p280-82 **398.2**

The **dog** and the woodpecker. Afanas'ev, A. N.
In Afanas'ev, A. N. Russian fairy tales
p499-500 **398.2**

A **dog** called Kitty. Wallace, B. **Fic**

A **dog** came, too. Manson, A. **971**

Dog Friday. McKay, H. **Fic**

A **dog** on Barkham Street. Stolz, M. **Fic**

Dog poems **808.81**

Dog racing
See also Iditarod Trail Sled Dog Race,
Alaska; Sled dog racing

Dog steals and Rooster crows. Fang, L.
In Fang, L. The Ch'i-lin purse p16-26
398.2

Dogger. Hughes, S. **E**

Dogs
See also Sheep dogs
American Kennel Club. The complete dog
book **636.7**
Calmenson, S. Rosie (k-3) **636.7**
Cohen, S. What kind of dog is that? (4 and
up) **636.7**
Cole, J. A dog's body **636.7**
Cole, J. My puppy is born (k-3) **636.7**
Hausherr, R. My first puppy (1-3)
636.7
Kuklin, S. Taking my dog to the vet (k-3)
636.7
Manson, A. A dog came, too (k-3) **971**
Patent, D. H. Dogs: the wolf within (3-6)
599.74
Patent, D. H. Hugger to the rescue (2-4)
636.7
Petersen-Fleming, J. Puppy care and critters,
too! (k-3) **636.7**
Pinkwater, J. Superpuppy: how to choose,
raise, and train the best possible dog for
you (5 and up) **636.7**
Ryden, H. Your dog's wild cousins (4-6)
599.74
Silverstein, A. Dogs: all about them (5 and
up) **636.7**
See/See also pages in the following book(s):
Chrystie, F. N. Pets p1-24 (4 and up)
636.088

Dogs—*Continued*

Facklam, M. Who harnessed the horse? p1-16 (3-6)   **636**

Fiction

Armstrong, W. H. Sounder (5 and up)   **Fic**

Barracca, D. The adventures of Taxi Dog   **E**

Bemelmans, L. Madeline's rescue   **E**

Brown, M. W. The indoor noisy book   **E**

Brown, M. W. The noisy book   **E**

Burnford, S. The incredible journey (4 and up)   **Fic**

Burningham, J. The dog   **E**

Calvert, P. Bigger (5 and up)   **Fic**

Carrick, C. The foundling   **E**

Chapman, C. Snow on snow on snow   **E**

Cleary, B. Strider (4 and up)   **Fic**

Day, A. Carl goes shopping   **E**

Ehrlich, A. Maggie and Silky and Joe   **E**

Estes, E. Ginger Pye (4-6)   **Fic**

Evans, K. Hunky Dory found it   **E**

Fleischman, S. Jim Ugly (4 and up)   **Fic**

Gackenbach, D. What's Claude doing?   **E**

Gardiner, J. R. Stone Fox (2-5)   **Fic**

Gipson, F. B. Old Yeller (6 and up)   **Fic**

Griffith, H. V. Alex and the cat   **E**

Hall, D. I am the dog, I am the cat   **E**

Hazelaar, C. Dogs everywhere   **E**

Henkes, K. Protecting Marie (5 and up)   **Fic**

Hesse, K. Lester's dog   **E**

Hesse, K. Sable (2-4)   **Fic**

Jones, D. W. Dogsbody (6 and up)   **Fic**

Kellogg, S. Pinkerton, behave!   **E**

Khalsa, D. K. I want a dog   **E**

Kuskin, K. City dog   **E**

Lexau, J. M. Go away, dog   **E**

Little, J. Different dragons (3-5)   **Fic**

London, J. The call of the wild (5 and up)   **Fic**

London, J. White Fang (5 and up)   **Fic**

MacLachlan, P. Three Names   **E**

Mahy, M. Making friends   **E**

McKay, H. Dog Friday (4-6)   **Fic**

Meddaugh, S. Martha speaks   **E**

Naylor, P. R. Shiloh (4-6)   **Fic**

Oxenbury, H. Our dog   **E**

Peet, B. The whingdingdilly   **E**

Pinkwater, D. M. Aunt Lulu   **E**

Polushkin, M. Who said meow?   **E**

Pomerantz, C. The outside dog   **E**

Potter, B. The pie and the patty-pan   **E**

Rathmann, P. Officer Buckle and Gloria   **E**

Rawls, W. Where the red fern grows   **Fic**

Reaver, C. Bill (5 and up)   **Fic**

Rylant, C. Henry and Mudge   **E**

Schwartz, A. Oma and Bobo   **E**

Sebestyen, O. Out of nowhere (5 and up)   **Fic**

Sendak, M. Higglety pigglety pop!   **E**

Steig, W. Caleb & Kate   **E**

Steig, W. Dominic (3-5)   **Fic**

Stevenson, J. The night after Christmas   **E**

Stolz, M. A dog on Barkham Street (4-6)   **Fic**

Talbert, M. A sunburned prayer (5 and up)   **Fic**

Taylor, T. The trouble with Tuck (5 and up)   **Fic**

Thayer, J. The puppy who wanted a boy   **E**

Thomas, J. R. The comeback dog (3-5)   **Fic**

Van Allsburg, C. The garden of Abdul Gasazi   **E**

Van Allsburg, C. The sweetest fig   **E**

Wallace, B. A dog called Kitty (4-6)   **Fic**

Wolff, A. Come with me   **E**

Wright, B. R. Nothing but trouble (4 and up)   **Fic**

Zion, G. Harry the dirty dog   **E**

Poetry

Dog poems   **808.81**

Training

Jones, R. F. Jake (3-5)   **636.7**

Smith, E. S. A service dog goes to school (3-5)   **636.7**

See/See also pages in the following book(s):

Pinkwater, J. Superpuppy: how to choose, raise, and train the best possible dog for you p144-87 (5 and up)   **636.7**

Dogs, Wild *See* Wild dogs

Dogs. Roalf, P.

In Roalf, P. Looking at paintings   **750**

Dogs & dragons, trees & dreams: a collection of poems. Kuskin, K.   **811**

A dog's body. Cole, J.   **636.7**

Dog's choice. Curry, J. L.

In Curry, J. L. Back in the beforetime p128-31   **398.2**

Dogs everywhere. Hazelaar, C.   **E**

Dogs for the blind *See* Guide dogs

The dog's nose is cold. Sherlock, Sir P. M.

In Sherlock, Sir P. M. West Indian folktales p34-38   **398.2**

Dogsbody. Jones, D. W.   **Fic**

Dogsong. Paulsen, G.   **Fic**

Doherty, Craig A.

The Golden Gate Bridge (4-6)   **624**

Hoover Dam (4-6)   **627**

Mount Rushmore (4-6)   **730.9**

The Sears Tower (4-6)   **725**

The Washington Monument (4-6)   **975.3**

Doherty, Katherine M.

(jt. auth) Doherty, C. A. The Golden Gate Bridge   **624**

(jt. auth) Doherty, C. A. Hoover Dam   **627**

(jt. auth) Doherty, C. A. Mount Rushmore   **730.9**

(jt. auth) Doherty, C. A. The Sears Tower   **725**

Doherty, Katherine M.—*Continued*
(jt. auth) Doherty, C. A. The Washington
Monument **975.3**

Doherty, Paul
(il) Moore, P. Comets and shooting stars
523.6
(il) Moore, P. The planets **523.4**
(il) Moore, P. The stars **523.8**
(il) Moore, P. The sun and moon **523.7**

Dolan, Edward F., 1924-
America in World War II (4-6) **940.54**

Dolan, Ellen M.
Susan Butcher and the Iditarod Trail (5 and
up) **798**

The **doll** in the garden. Hahn, M. D. **Fic**

The **dollar** watch and the five jack rabbits.
Sandburg, C.
In Sandburg, C. Rootabaga stories pt 1
p117-24 **S C**
In Sandburg, C. The Sandburg treasury
p57-61 **818**

The **dollhouse** murders. Wright, B. R. **Fic**

Dollhouses
Fiction
Godden, R. The doll's house (2-4) **Fic**
Sachs, M. The bears' house (4-6) **Fic**

Dolls
Kuklin, S. From head to toe (k-3)
745.592
See/See also pages in the following book(s):
Pellowski, A. The story vine p77-91
372.6

Fiction
Bonners, S. The wooden doll **E**
Cassedy, S. Behind the attic wall (5 and up)
Fic
Field, R. Hitty: her first hundred years (4
and up) **Fic**
Godden, R. Candy Floss (2-4) **Fic**
Godden, R. The doll's house (2-4) **Fic**
Godden, R. Four dolls (3-5) **S C**
Godden, R. The story of Holly and Ivy (2-4)
Fic
Hutchins, P. Changes, changes **E**
Polacco, P. Babushka's doll **E**
Pomerantz, C. The chalk doll **E**
Stevenson, J. The night after Christmas
E
Waugh, S. The Mennyms (5 and up)
Fic
Zolotow, C. William's doll **E**

The **doll's** house. Godden, R. **Fic**

Dolphin, Ben
(il) Dolphin, L. Neve shalom/Wahat al-
salam: Oasis of peace **956.94**

Dolphin, Laurie
Neve shalom/Wahat al-salam: Oasis of
peace (2-4) **956.94**

Dolphin adventure. Grover, W. **599.5**

Dolphins
The Audubon Society field guide to North
American fishes, whales, and dolphins (5
and up) **597**

Grover, W. Dolphin adventure (3-5)
599.5
Patent, D. H. Dolphins and porpoises (5
and up) **599.5**
Patent, D. H. Looking at dolphins and porpoises (3-5) **599.5**
Schomp, V. The bottlenose dolphin (3-5)
599.5

Dolphins and porpoises. Patent, D. H.
599.5

Domestic animals
See also Pets; Working animals
Facklam, M. Who harnessed the horse? (3-6)
636
Ryden, H. Out of the wild (4 and up)
636
Tafuri, N. Spots, feathers, and curly tails
E
See/See also pages in the following book(s):
Chrystie, F. N. Pets p165-93 (4 and up)
636.088

Domestic architecture
See also House construction
Dorros, A. This is my house (k-3) **728**
Ventura, P. Houses (4 and up) **728**

Domestic economic assistance
See also Community development

Domestic finance *See* Personal finance

Domestic relations
See also Family

Domingo siete. MacDonald, M. R.
In MacDonald, M. R. Look back and see
p37-44 **372.6**

Dominic. Steig, W. **Fic**

Dominican Americans
Gordon, G. My two worlds (k-3) **305.8**

Dominican Republic
Foley, E. Dominican Republic (5 and up)
972.93

Donahue, Dorothy
(il) Patron, S. Maybe yes, maybe no, maybe
maybe **Fic**

Donahue, John, 1951-
An island far from home (4 and up)
Fic

Donavin, Denise P.
(ed) American Library Association best of
the best for children. See American Library Association best of the best for children **011.6**

The **donkey.** Grimm, J.
In Grimm, J. The complete Grimm's
fairy tales p632-35 **398.2**

Donkey cabbages. Grimm, J.
In Grimm, J. The complete Grimm's
fairy tales p551-58 **398.2**

The **donkey,** the table, and the stick. Reeves,
J.
In Reeves, J. English fables and fairy sto-
ries p195-210 **398.2**

Donkeys
See/See also pages in the following book(s):
Henry, M. Album of horses p98-101 (4 and up) **636.1**

Fiction
Henry, M. Brighty of the Grand Canyon (4 and up) **Fic**
Steig, W. Farmer Palmer's wagon ride **E**
Steig, W. Sylvester and the magic pebble **E**
Wildsmith, B. A Christmas story **E**

Donkeyskin. Perrault, C.
In Perrault, C. The complete fairy tales of Charles Perrault p108-17 **398.2**

Donnelly, Judy
A wall of names (2-4) **959.704**

Donnelly, Marlene Hill
(il) Rood, R. N. Wetlands **574.5**
(il) Selsam, M. E. How to be a nature detective **591.5**

Don't cut the lawn!. Mahy, M.
In Mahy, M. The girl with the green ear p95-100 **S C**

Don't eat too much turkey!. Cohen, M. See note under Cohen, M. See you in second grade! **E**

Don't fidget a feather. Silverman, E. **E**

Don't forget the bacon!. Hutchins, P. **E**

Don't shake hands with everybody. Courlander, H.
In Courlander, H. The cow-tail switch, and other West African stories p129-32 **398.2**

Don't sing before breakfast, don't sleep in the moonlight. Perl, L. **398**

Don't turn away [series]
Bergman, T. Finding a common language **362.4**
Bergman, T. Going places **362.4**
Bergman, T. Meeting the challenge **362.4**
Bergman, T. Moments that disappear **362.4**
Bergman, T. On our own terms **362.4**
Bergman, T. One day at a time **616.99**

Don't wake up Mama!. Christelow, E. See note under Christelow, E. Five little monkeys jumping on the bed **E**

Don't you know there's a war on?. Stevenson, J.

Dooling, Michael
(il) Giblin, J. George Washington **92**
(il) Giblin, J. Thomas Jefferson **92**
(il) Kroll, S. Mary McLean and the St. Patrick's Day parade **E**

Doolittle, Michael J.
(il) Goodman, S. Bats, bugs, and biodiversity **574.5**

The **doom** of the haunted opera. Bellairs, J. See note under Bellairs, J. The house with a clock in its walls **Fic**

The **door** in the wall. De Angeli, M. L. **Fic**

The **doorbell** rang. Hutchins, P. **E**

Dorfman, Ariel
The rebellion of the magical rabbits
In Where angels glide at dawn p7-25 **S C**

The **Dorling** Kindersley children's illustrated dictionary. McIllwain, J. **423**

The **Dorling** Kindersley science encyclopedia (5 and up) **503**

Dorothy and the Wizard in Oz. Baum, L. F. See note under Baum, L. F. The Wizard of Oz **Fic**

Dorris, Michael
Morning Girl (4-6) **Fic**

Dorros, Arthur
Abuela **E**
Animal tracks (k-3) **591.5**
Ant cities (k-3) **595.7**
Elephant families (k-3) **599.6**
Feel the wind (k-3) **551.5**
Follow the water from brook to ocean (k-3) **551.48**
Radio Man. Don Radio **E**
Rain forest secrets (k-3) **574.5**
This is my house (k-3) **728**
Tonight is Carnaval **E**
(il) Branley, F. M. What makes day and night **525**
(il) Wyler, R. Magic secrets **793.8**

Dots, spots, speckles, and stripes. Hoban, T. **E**

Doty, Roy, 1922-
(il) Blume, J. Tales of a fourth grade nothing **Fic**
(il) James, E. How to be school smart **371.3**
(il) Zubrowski, B. Clocks **681.1**
(il) Zubrowski, B. Making waves **532**
(il) Zubrowski, B. Mirrors **535**
(il) Zubrowski, B. Mobiles **531**
(il) Zubrowski, B. Wheels at work **621.8**

Double dog dare. Gilson, J. See note under Gilson, J. 4B goes wild **Fic**

The **double** life of Pocahontas. Fritz, J. **92**

The **Doubleday** children's dictionary. Grisewood, J. **423**

The **Doubleday** illustrated children's Bible. Stoddard, S. **220.9**

Doucette, Concetta C.
A lamb on the table
In The Family read-aloud holiday treasury p46-51 **808.8**

Dougal Dixon's dinosaurs. Dixon, D. **567.9**

Douglas, Helen Gahagan, 1900-1980
See/See also pages in the following book(s):
Morin, I. V. Women of the U. S. Congress p49-65 (5 and up) **920**

Douglas, William O. (William Orville), 1898-1980
Muir of the mountains (4 and up) **92**

The **dragons** of Blueland. Gannett, R. S. See note under Gannett, R. S. My father's dragon **Fic**

Dragonsinger. McCaffrey, A. See note under McCaffrey, A. Dragonsong **Fic**

Dragonsong. McCaffrey, A. **Fic**

Dragonwagon, Crescent
Half a moon and one whole star **E**

Dragonwings. Yep, L. **Fic**

Drake, Sir Francis, 1540?-1596
About
Marrin, A. The sea king: Sir Francis Drake and his times (6 and up) **92**

Drake, Jane
The kids' summer handbook (4 and up) **790.1**

Drakestail. Marelle, C.
In The Red fairy book p202-07 **398.2**

Drama
See also College and school drama; Folk drama; One act plays
Collections
Barchers, S. I. Scary readers theatre **808.82**
Bauer, C. F. Presenting reader's theater **808.82**
Indexes
Play index **808.82**
Periodicals
Plays **808.82**

Drama in education
Barchers, S. I. Scary readers theatre **808.82**
Bauer, C. F. Presenting reader's theater **808.82**

Dramatists
Stanley, D. Bard of Avon: the story of William Shakespeare (3-5) **92**

Drat these brats!. Kennedy, X. J. **811**

The **draug**. San Souci, R.
In San Souci, R. More short & shivery p22-26 **398.2**

[**Draw** 50 series]. Ames, L. J. **743**

Drawing
Ames, L. J. [Draw 50 series] (4 and up) **743**
Arnosky, J. Drawing from nature (4 and up) **743**
Arnosky, J. Drawing life in motion (4 and up) **743**
Benjamin, C. L. Cartooning for kids (4-6) **741.5**
Bolognese, D. The way to draw and color monsters (4 and up) **743**
Emberley, E. Ed Emberley's big green drawing book (2-5) **741.2**
Emberley, E. Ed Emberley's big red drawing book (2-5) **741.2**
Emberley, E. Ed Emberley's drawing book: make a world (2-5) **741.2**
Emberley, E. Ed Emberley's drawing book of faces (2-5) **743**

Emberley, E. Ed Emberley's great thumbprint drawing book (2-5) **743**
Emberley, E. Ed Emberley's picture pie: a circle drawing book (2-5) **741.2**
Frame, P. Drawing cats and kittens (4 and up) **743**
Jenkins, P. Animation **741.5**
Fiction
Drescher, H. Simon's book **E**
Kleven, E. The paper princess **E**
Testa, F. If you take a pencil **E**
Williams, V. B. Cherries and cherry pits **E**

Drawing. Thomson, R.
In Thomson, R. Get set—go! [Arts & crafts series] **745.5**
Drawing book: make a world, Ed Emberley's. Emberley, E. **741.2**
Drawing book of faces, Ed Emberley's. Emberley, E. **743**
Drawing cats and kittens, Frame, P **743**
Drawing from nature. Arnosky, J. **743**
Drawing life in motion. Arnosky, J. **743**

The **dreadful** future of Blossom Culp. Peck, R. See note under Peck, R. The ghost belonged to me **Fic**

The **dream**. Schwartz, A.
In Schwartz, A. Scary stories 3 p53-54 **398.2**

The **dream** fast. Bruchac, J.
In Bruchac, J. Flying with the eagle, racing with the great bear p3-5 **398.2**

Dream flier. Yep, L.
In Yep, L. The rainbow people p154-60 **398.2**

Dream girl. Yep, L.
In Yep, L. The tree of dreams **398.2**

The **dream** keeper and other poems. Hughes, L. **811**

The **dream** tree. Yep, L.
In Yep, L. The tree of dreams **398.2**

Dream wolf. Goble, P. **E**

Dreamcatcher. Osofsky, A. **E**

Dreaming and dreams. Stafford, P. **154.6**

Dreamplace. Lyon, G. E. **E**

Dreams
See also Sleep
Silverstein, A. The mystery of sleep (4-6) **154.6**
Stafford, P. Dreaming and dreams (5 and up) **154.6**
See/See also pages in the following book(s):
Stafford, P. Your two brains p49-57 (5 and up) **612.8**
Fiction
Briggs, R. The snowman **E**
Pilkey, D. When cats dream **E**
Ringgold, F. Tar Beach **E**
Stevenson, J. "Could be worse!" **E**
Van Allsburg, C. Ben's dream **E**
Van Allsburg, C. Just a dream **E**
Van Allsburg, C. The sweetest fig **E**

Dreams—Fiction—*Continued*
Wiesner, D. Free fall   **E**
Yep, L. The tree of dreams (4 and up)
    398.2

Poetry
Greenfield, E. Daydreamers (3-6)   **811**

Dreams of fire. 1950. Geras, A.
In Geras, A. Golden windows and other
stories of Jerusalem p107-27
    S C

Dreamtime. Oodgeroo   **398.2**

Dreiser, Theodore, 1871-1945
See/See also pages in the following book(s):
Faber, D. Great lives: American literature
p111-20 (5 and up)   **920**

Drescher, Henrik, 1955-
Simon's book   **E**
(il) Poems of A. Nonny Mouse. See Poems
of A. Nonny Mouse   **808.81**
(il) Wilbur, R. Runaway opposites   **811**

Dress *See* Clothing and dress

The **dress** I'll wear to the party. Neitzel, S.
    E

Drew, Charles Richard, 1904-1950
See/See also pages in the following book(s):
Haskins, J. One more river to cross (4 and
up)   **920**

Dreyer, Sharon Spredemann
The best of Bookfinder   **011.6**
The bookfinder   **011.6**

Drimmer, Frederick
Born different (6 and up)   **920**

The **drinking** gourd. Monjo, F. N.   **E**

Drinking problem *See* Alcoholism

A **drop** of blood. Showers, P.   **612.1**

Drop Star. San Souci, R.
In San Souci, R. Cut from the same cloth
p21-26   **398.2**

Droughts
Lampton, C. Drought (4-6)   **551.57**
Fiction
Aardema, V. Bringing the rain to Kapiti
Plain (k-3)   **398.2**
Hamilton, V. Drylongso (3-5)   **Fic**
MacLachlan, P. Skylark (3-5)   **Fic**

Drucker, Malka, 1945-
Grandma's latkes   **E**

Drug abuse
See also Alcoholism
Friedman, D. P. Focus on drugs and the
brain (3-6)   **616.86**
Seixas, J. S. Drugs—what they are, what
they do (1-3)   **616.86**
Shulman, J. Focus on cocaine and crack
(3-6)   **362.29**
Fiction
Childress, A. A hero ain't nothin' but a
sandwich (6 and up)   **Fic**

Drug-alert book [series]
Friedman, D. P. Focus on drugs and the
brain   **616.86**
O'Neill, C. Focus on alcohol   **362.29**

Perry, R. L. Focus on nicotine and caffeine
    616.86
Shulman, J. Focus on cocaine and crack
    362.29
Zeller, P. K. Focus on marijuana
    362.29

Drug plants *See* Medical botany

Drugs
See also Psychotropic drugs
Friedman, D. P. Focus on drugs and the
brain (3-6)   **616.86**
Seixas, J. S. Drugs—what they are, what
they do (1-3)   **616.86**
Fiction
Christopher, M. Tackle without a team (4-6)
    Fic

Drugs, Psychotropic *See* Psychotropic drugs

Druids and Druidism
Fiction
Pope, E. M. The Perilous Gard (6 and up)
    Fic

Drumbeat—heartbeat. Braine, S.   **970.004**

The **drummer.** Grimm, J.
In Grimm, J. The complete Grimm's
fairy tales p781-91   **398.2**

Drummer Hoff. Emberley, B.   **398.8**

Drummond, Karen Eich
(jt. auth) D'Amico, J. The science chef
    641.3

Dry-Bone and Anansi. Sherlock, Sir P. M.
In Sherlock, Sir P. M. West Indian folktales p77-85   **398.2**

Dry goods *See* Fabrics

Dryden, John Fairfield, 1839-1911
See/See also pages in the following book(s):
Aaseng, N. The problem solvers p19-24 (5
and up)   **920**

Drying out. Rylant, C.
In Rylant, C. Every living thing p34-41
    S C

Drylongso. Hamilton, V.   **Fic**

Du Bois, William Pène, 1916-1993
The twenty-one balloons (5 and up)   **Fic**
(il) Caudill, R. A certain small shepherd
    Fic
(il) Zolotow, C. My grandson Lew   **E**
(il) Zolotow, C. William's doll   **E**
See/See also pages in the following book(s):
Newbery Medal books, 1922-1955 p302-17
    028.5

Dubanevich, Arlene, 1950-
Pigs at Christmas. See note under Du-
banevich, A. Pigs in hiding   **E**
Pigs in hiding   **E**

DuBois, Graham
Bonds of affection
In Holiday plays round the year p151-60
    812.008
The end of the road
In Holiday plays round the year p179-88
    812.008

Durant, William Crapo, 1861-1947
See/See also pages in the following book(s):
Aaseng, N. The unsung heroes p29-37 (5 and up) **920**

The **duration** of life. Grimm, J.
In Grimm, J. The complete Grimm's fairy tales p716-18 **398.2**

Durell, Ann, 1930-
(ed) The Big book for our planet. See The Big book for our planet **810.8**
(ed) The Big book for peace. See The Big book for peace **810.8**
(comp) The Diane Goode book of American folk tales and songs. See The Diane Goode book of American folk tales and songs **398.2**

Durenceau, Andre
(il) Mitchell, R. T. Butterflies and moths **595.7**

Dürer, Albrecht, 1471-1528
About
Raboff, E. Albrecht Dürer (5 and up) **759.3**

Dutch artists *See* Artists, Dutch

Duvall, Jill
The Chumash (2-4) **970.004**

Duvoisin, Roger, 1904-1980
The Christmas whale
In The Family read-aloud Christmas treasury p72-79 **808.8**
Petunia **E**
Petunia, beware! See note under Duvoisin, R. Petunia **E**
Petunia takes a trip. See note under Duvoisin, R. Petunia **E**
(il) Tresselt, A. R. Hide and seek fog **E**
(il) Tresselt, A. R. White snow, bright snow **E**
See/See also pages in the following book(s):
Caldecott Medal books, 1938-1957 p166-83 **028.5**

Dyer, Jane
(il) Hendrick, M. J. If anything ever goes wrong at the zoo **E**
(il) Talking like the rain. See Talking like the rain **821.008**
(il) Yolen, J. Piggins and the royal wedding **E**
(il) Yolen, J. The three bears holiday rhyme book **811**
(il) Yolen, J. The three bears rhyme book **811**

Dynamite Dinah. Mills, C. **Fic**

Dypold, Pat
(il) Lowery, L. Twist with a burger, jitter with a bug **E**

Dyslexia
Fiction
Betancourt, J. My name is brain Brian (4-6) **Fic**

E

E I E I O: the story of Old MacDonald, who had a farm. See Old MacDonald had a farm **782.42**

E is for Elisa. Hurwitz, J. See note under Hurwitz, J. Rip-roaring Russell **Fic**

E.S.P. *See* Extrasensory perception

Each orange had 8 slices. Giganti, P., Jr. **E**

Each peach pear plum. Ahlberg, J. **E**

Eads, James Buchanan, 1820-1887
See/See also pages in the following book(s):
McCall, E. S. Biography of a river: the living Mississippi p101-05, 117-21 (6 and up) **977**

Eager, Edward, 1911-1964
Half magic (4-6) **Fic**
Half magic [excerpt]
In The Random House book of humor for children p154-72 **817.008**
Knight's castle. See note under Eager, E. Half magic **Fic**
Magic by the lake. See note under Eager, E. Half magic **Fic**
Seven-day magic (4-6) **Fic**
The time garden. See note under Eager, E. Half magic **Fic**

Eagle, Ellen, 1953-
(il) Branley, F. M. Star guide **523.8**

Eagle, Michael
(il) Lauber, P. Voyagers from space **523.5**
(il) Lauber, P. Who discovered America? **970.01**

The **eagle** and the river. Craighead, C. **591.5**

Eagle drum. Crum, R. **970.004**

The **eagle** kite. Fox, P. **Fic**

Eagles
See also Bald eagle
Bernhard, E. Eagles (k-3) **598**
Lang, A. Eagles (4-6) **598**
Patent, D. H. Eagles of America (4 and up) **598**
Sattler, H. R. The book of eagles (4 and up) **598**

Eagles, hawks, and other birds of prey. DeWitt, L. **598**

Eagles of America. Patent, D. H. **598**

Ear
Parker, S. The ear and hearing (4 and up) **612.8**
Showers, P. Ears are for hearing (k-3) **612.8**

The **ear**. Babbitt, N.
In Babbitt, N. The Devil's other storybook p73-81 **S C**

The **ear** and hearing. Parker, S. **612.8**

The **ear** of corn. Grimm, J.
In Grimm, J. The complete Grimm's fairy tales p791-92 **398.2**

The **Ear,** the Eye, and the Arm. Farmer, N.
           Fic

Earhart, Amelia, 1898-1937
         About
  Lauber, P. Lost star: the story of Amelia
    Earhart (5 and up)   **92**
  Quackenbush, R. M. Clear the cow pasture,
    I'm coming in for a landing!: a story of
    Amelia Earhart (2-4)   **92**

Earl Mar's daughter. Jacobs, J.
  In Jacobs, J. English fairy tales p159-63
             398.2

Earle, Sylvia A., 1935-
         About
  Conley, A. Window on the deep: the adven-
    tures of underwater explorer Sylvia Earle
    (5 and up)   **92**

The **earliest** Americans. Sattler, H. R.
            970.01

Early, Margaret, 1951-
  William Tell   **398.2**

Early, Theresa S., 1957-
  New Mexico
  In Hello USA series   **973**

An **early** American Christmas. De Paola, T.
              E

Early bird nature books [series]
  Powell, E. S. Rats   **599.32**
  Staub, F. J. Alligators   **597.9**
  Staub, F. J. Mountain goats **599.73**
  Staub, F. J. Sea turtles   **597.9**

Early humans (4 and up)   **930.1**

Early I can read book [series]
  Bonsall, C. N. The day I had to play with
    my sister   **E**
  Bonsall, C. N. Who's afraid of the dark?
              E
  Robins, J. Addie meets Max   **E**

Early moon. Sandburg, C.
  In Sandburg, C. The Sandburg treasury
    p161-207   **818**

Early morning in the barn. Tafuri, N. **E**

Early thunder. Fritz, J.   **Fic**

Earrings!. Viorst, J.   **E**

Ears are for hearing. Showers, P. **612.8**

Earth
  Branley, F. M. What makes day and night
    (k-3)   **525**
  Fradin, D. B. Earth (2-4)   **525**
  Frasier, D. On the day you were born (k-3)
              508
  Lauber, P. How we learned the earth is
    round (k-3)   **525**
  Lauber, P. Seeing Earth from space (4 and
    up)   **525**
  Ride, S. K. The third planet (4 and up)
              525
  Simon, S. Earth, our planet in space (1-4)
              525
       Internal structure
  Cole, J. The magic school bus inside the
    Earth (2-4)   **551.1**

McNulty, F. How to dig a hole to the other
  side of the world (2-4)   **551.1**
         Poetry
The Earth is painted green (4-6) **808.81**
Earth alive!. Markle, S.   **550**
The **earth** atlas. Van Rose, S.   **550**
Earth Day
  Ross, K. Every day is Earth Day (1-3)
             745.58
The **Earth** game. Conrad, P.
  In The Big book for our planet p55-59
             810.8
Earth hounds, as explained by Professor Xar-
  gle. Willis, J. See note under Willis, J.
  Earthlets, as explained by Professor Xar-
  gle   **E**
The **Earth** is painted green (4-6) **808.81**
Earth keepers. Anderson, J.   **363.7**
  Reef, C. Henry David Thoreau **92**
Earth mobiles, as explained by Professor Xar-
  gle. Willis, J. See note under Willis, J.
  Earthlets, as explained by Professor Xar-
  gle   **E**
The **earth** on Turtle's back. Van Laan, N.
  In Van Laan, N. In a circle long ago p96-
    97   **398.2**
Earth, our planet in space. Simon, S. **525**
Earth science for every kid, Janice Van-
  Cleave's. VanCleave, J. P.   **550**
Earth science library [series]
  Bramwell, M. Glaciers and ice caps
             551.3
  Bramwell, M. Mountains   **551.4**
  Bramwell, M. The oceans   **551.46**
  Bramwell, M. Rivers and lakes **551.48**
  Bramwell, M. Volcanoes and earthquakes
             551.2
  Bramwell, M. Weather   **551.5**
Earth sciences
  See also Geology
  Lauber, P. Seeing Earth from space (4 and
    up)   **525**
  Robbins, K. Earth (4-6)   **550**
  Van Rose, S. Earth (4 and up) **550**
  The Visual dictionary of the earth (4 and
    up)   **550**
       Experiments
  VanCleave, J. P. Janice VanCleave's earth
    science for every kid (3-5) **550**
Earth tigerlets, as explained by Professor Xar-
  gle. Willis, J. See note under Willis, J.
  Earthlets, as explained by Professor Xar-
  gle   **E**
Earth to Matthew. Danziger, P. See note un-
  der Danziger, P. Everyone else's parents
  said yes   **Fic**
Earth verses and water rhymes. Lewis, J. P.
              811
Earth weather, as explained by Professor Xar-
  gle. Willis, J. See note under Willis, J.
  Earthlets, as explained by Professor Xar-
  gle   **E**
Earth words. Simon, S.   **363.7**

Echoes of the white giraffe. Choi, S. N. See note under Choi, S. N. Year of impossible goodbyes **Fic**

Eckart, Chuck
(il) Jaspersohn, W. How the forest grew **574.5**

Eckert, Allan W.
Incident at Hawk's Hill (6 and up) **Fic**

Eclipse: darkness in daytime. Branley, F. M. **523.7**

Eclipses, Lunar *See* Lunar eclipses

Eclipses, Solar *See* Solar eclipses

Ecology

> *See also* Biogeography; Environmental protection; Food chains (Ecology); Habitat (Ecology); types of ecology, e.g. Marine ecology

Facklam, M. Partners for life (3-6) **591.5**

Godkin, C. Wolf island (k-3) **574.5**

Kuhn, D. More than just a flower garden (2-4) **635.9**

Kuhn, D. More than just a vegetable garden (2-4) **635**

Lavies, B. Mangrove wilderness (4-6) **574.5**

Lavies, B. Tree trunk traffic (k-2) **591.5**

Luenn, N. Squish! (k-2) **574.5**

Norsgaard, E. J. Nature's great balancing act (4-6) **574.5**

Orr, R. Nature cross-sections (4 and up) **574.5**

Pollock, S. Ecology (4 and up) **574.5**

Quinlan, S. E. The case of the mummified pigs and other mysteries in nature (4 and up) **508**

Silver, D. M. Backyard (3-5) **574.5**

Dictionaries

Simon, S. Earth words (3-5) **363.7**

Ecology, Human *See* Human ecology

Economic botany

> *See also* Plant conservation

Economic depressions

Stanley, J. Children of the Dust Bowl (5 and up) **371.9**

Fiction

Burch, R. Ida Early comes over the mountain (4 and up) **Fic**

Lyon, G. E. Borrowed children (5 and up) **Fic**

Snyder, Z. K. Cat running (4 and up) **Fic**

Snyder, Z. K. The velvet room (5 and up) **Fic**

Taylor, M. D. Let the circle be unbroken (4 and up) **Fic**

Taylor, M. D. Roll of thunder, hear my cry (4 and up) **Fic**

Taylor, M. D. Song of the trees (4 and up) **Fic**

Economic entomology *See* Insect pests

Economic zoology

> *See also* Insect pests; Working animals

Ed Emberley's big green drawing book. Emberley, E. **741.2**

Ed Emberley's big red drawing book. Emberley, E. **741.2**

Ed Emberley's drawing book: make a world. Emberley, E. **741.2**

Ed Emberley's drawing book of faces. Emberley, E. **743**

Ed Emberley's great thumbprint drawing book. Emberley, E. **743**

Ed Emberley's picture pie: a circle drawing book. Emberley, E. **741.2**

Edelman, Marian Wright
About
Siegel, B. Marian Wright Edelman (5 and up) **92**

Eden, Maxwell
Kiteworks: explorations in kite building & flying (5 and up) **796.1**

Edens, Cooper, 1945-
(comp) The Glorious Mother Goose. See The Glorious Mother Goose **398.8**

Edible plants
Sekido, I. Fruits, roots, and fungi (1-3) **581.6**

The **edible** pyramid. Leedy, L. **613.2**

Edison, Thomas A. (Thomas Alva), 1847-1931
About
Adler, D. A. Thomas Alva Edison (?-4) **92**

Nirgiotis, N. Thomas Edison (4-6) **92**

Parker, S. Thomas Edison and electricity (4 and up) **92**

Edith herself. Howard, E. **Fic**

Edmonds, S. Emma E. (Sarah Emma Evelyn), 1841-1898
About
Reit, S. Behind rebel lines: the incredible story of Emma Edmonds, Civil War spy (4 and up) **92**

Stevens, B. Frank Thompson (5 and up) **92**

Edmonds, Sarah Emma Evelyn *See* Edmonds, S. Emma E. (Sarah Emma Evelyn), 1841-1898

Edmonds, Walter Dumaux, 1903-
See/See also pages in the following book(s):
Newbery Medal books, 1922-1955 p210-24 **028.5**

Education
> *See also* Elementary education; Schools
Social aspects
Stanley, J. Children of the Dust Bowl (5 and up) **371.9**

United States—History
Loeper, J. J. Going to school in 1776 (4 and up) **370.9**

Loeper, J. J. Going to school in 1876 (4 and up) **370.9**

See/See also pages in the following book(s):
Freedman, R. Children of the wild West p59-69 (4 and up) **978**

Education, Elementary *See* Elementary education

Education, Preschool *See* Preschool education

Education, Segregation in *See* Segregation in education

Education on the Internet. Ellsworth, J. H.
371.3

Educational media centers *See* Instructional materials centers

Educators

See also African American educators

Rosen, D. A fire in her bones: the story of Mary Lyon (4 and up) 92

Educators guide to free films, filmstrips and slides 016.3713

Edward Lear, king of nonsense. Kamen, G.
92

Edwards, Dorothy, 1914-1982

My naughty little sister makes a bottle-tree
In The Oxford treasury of children's stories p35-38 S C

Edwards, Linda

(il) Gilson, J. 4B goes wild Fic

Edwards, Michelle

Alef-bet (k-3) 492.4
A baker's portrait E
Blessed are you (k-3) 296.4

Edwards, Richard, 1949-

Ten tall oaktrees E

Eels

Wallace, K. Think of an eel (k-3) 597

The **eel's** disguise. Yep, L.
In Yep, L. The rainbow people p38-44
398.2

Eenie meenie miney math!. Allison, L.
510

The **Eentsy,** weentsy spider 796.1

Egan, E. W. (Edward Welstead), 1922-

Belgium—in pictures. See Belgium—in pictures 949.3
Sri Lanka—in pictures. See Sri Lanka—in pictures 954.93

Egan, Edward Welstead *See* Egan, E. W. (Edward Welstead), 1922-

Egan, Terry, 1957-

The Macmillan book of baseball stories (4 and up) 796.357

Egg. Burton, R. 591.3

Egg decoration

Fiction

Adams, A. The Easter egg artists E

Egg story. Hariton, A. 636.5

Egg thoughts and other Frances songs. Hoban, R. 811

Egg to chick. Selsam, M. E. 636.5

Eggs

Burton, R. Egg (3-5) 591.3
Cole, J. A chick hatches (k-3) 636.5
Hariton, A. Egg story (k-3) 636.5
Johnson, S. A. Inside an egg (4 and up)
598

Selsam, M. E. Egg to chick (k-3) **636.5**
See/See also pages in the following book(s):
Markle, S. Exploring spring p43-51 (4 and up) **508**

Fiction

Barber, A. Gemma and the baby chick
E
Joyce, W. Bently & egg E
Polacco, P. Rechenka's eggs E
Schertle, A. Down the road E

Egielski, Richard

Buz E
(il) Brooke, W. J. A telling of the tales: five stories S C
(il) Conrad, P. The Tub People E
(il) Yorinks, A. Hey, Al E
(il) Yorinks, A. It happened in Pinsk E
See/See also pages in the following book(s):
Sendak, M. Caldecott & Co.: notes on books and pictures p139-41 **028.5**

Ego-tripping and other poems for young people. Giovanni, N. **811**

Egoff, Sheila A.

Worlds within **028.5**
(ed) Only connect: readings on children's literature. See Only connect: readings on children's literature **028.5**

Egypt

Antiquities

Bendick, J. Egyptian tombs (4 and up)
932
Perl, L. Mummies, tombs, and treasure (4 and up) **393**
Reeves, C. N. Into the mummy's tomb (4 and up) **932**
Sabuda, R. Tutankhamen's gift (k-3) **92**

Civilization

Hart, G. Exploring the past: ancient Egypt (4 and up) **932**
Macaulay, D. Pyramid (4 and up) **726**

Folklore

See Folklore—Egypt

History

Hart, G. Exploring the past: ancient Egypt (4 and up) **932**

The **Egypt** game. Snyder, Z. K. Fic

The **Egyptian** Cinderella. Climo, S. **398.2**

Egyptian language

Giblin, J. The riddle of the Rosetta Stone (5 and up) **493**
Katan, N. J. Hieroglyphs, the writing of ancient Egypt (4 and up) **493**

Egyptian tombs. Bendick, J. **932**

Ehlert, Lois, 1934-

Circus E
Color farm E
Color zoo E
Eating the alphabet E
Feathers for lunch E
Growing vegetable soup E
Mole's hill E
Moon rope. Un lazo a la luna (k-3)
398.2
Nuts to you! E

The **Elementary** school library collection
011.6

Elements [series]
Robbins, K. Air **551.5**
Robbins, K. Earth **550**

Elena and the black geese. Pooley, S.
In Pooley, S. It's raining, it's pouring p45-49 **808.8**

Elena the Wise. Afanas'ev, A. N.
In Afanas'ev, A. N. Russian fairy tales p545-49 **398.2**

Elephant and Frog go courting. Bryan, A.
In Bryan, A. The ox of the wonderful horns and other African folktales p15-21 **398.2**

Elephant families. Dorros, A. **599.6**

Elephant Man *See* Merrick, Joseph Carey, 1862 or 3-1890

An **elephant** never forgets its snorkel. Evans, L. G. **591.5**

Elephant seals. Johnson, S. A. **599.74**

Elephants
Arnold, C. Elephant (3-5) **599.6**
Dorros, A. Elephant families (k-3) **599.6**
Grace, E. S. Elephants (4-6) **599.6**
Macmillan, D. Elephants (3-6) **599.6**
McClung, R. M. America's first elephant (k-3) **599.6**
Patent, D. H. African elephants (3-5) **599.6**
Payne, K. Elephants calling (3-5) **599.6**
Fiction
Brunhoff, J. de. The story of Babar, the little elephant **E**
Day, A. Frank and Ernest **E**
Ford, M. Little elephant **E**
Kipling, R. The elephant's child **Fic**
Lobel, A. Uncle Elephant **E**
Murphy, J. A quiet night in **E**
Petersham, M. The circus baby **E**
Platt, K. Big Max **E**
Sadler, M. Alistair's elephant **E**
Seuss, Dr. Horton hatches the egg **E**
Seuss, Dr. Horton hears a Who! **E**
Young, E. Seven blind mice (k-3) **398.2**
History
See/See also pages in the following book(s):
Facklam, M. Who harnessed the horse? p125-33 (3-6) **636**

Elephants calling. Payne, K. **599.6**

The **elephant's** child. Kipling, R. **Fic**
also in Kipling, R. Just so stories **S C**
also in The Random House book of humor for children p83-92 **817.008**

Elephants swim. Riley, L. C. **591.5**

The **Elf** maiden
In The Rainbow fairy book p242-49 **398.2**

Elfwyn's saga. Wisniewski, D. **E**

Eli. Peet, B. **E**

Elijah the slave. Singer, I. B.
In Singer, I. B. Stories for children p206-09 **S C**

Elijah's angel. Rosen, M. J. **Fic**

Elimination (Physiology) *See* Excretion

Eliot, T. S. (Thomas Stearns), 1888-1965
Growltiger's last stand **811**
Mr. Mistoffelees; with, Mungojerrie and Rumpelteazer **811**

Eliot, Thomas Stearns *See* Eliot, T. S. (Thomas Stearns), 1888-1965

Elisa in the middle. Hurwitz, J. See note under Hurwitz, J. Rip-roaring Russell **Fic**

Elish, Dan, 1960-
Harriet Tubman and the Underground Railroad (3-5) **92**

Elizabeth I, Queen of England, 1533-1603
About
Stanley, D. Good Queen Bess: the story of Elizabeth I of England (3-5) **92**
Fiction
Stolz, M. Bartholomew Fair (5 and up) **Fic**

Elk
Arnold, C. Tule elk (3-5) **599.73**
Patent, D. H. Deer and elk (4 and up) **599.73**

The **elk** and the wren. MacDonald, M. R.
In MacDonald, M. R. Look back and see p103-06 **372.6**

Elkington, John
Going green. See Going green **363.7**

Ella of all of a kind family. Taylor, S. See note under Taylor, S. All-of-a-kind family **Fic**

Elledge, Scott
(ed) Wider than the sky: poems to grow up with. See Wider than the sky: poems to grow up with **821.008**

Ellen Tebbits. Cleary, B. **Fic**

Ellie's valentine. Rylant, C.
In Valentine's Day: stories and poems p21-36 **810.8**

Ellington, Duke, 1899-1974
About
Collier, J. L. Duke Ellington (5 and up) **92**
Venezia, M. Duke Ellington (k-3) **92**

Elliot, Marion
My party book (3-5) **745.594**

Elliot's house. Lowry, L.
In The Big book for our planet p116-21 **810.8**

Elliott, Bob
See also Bob and Ray

Ellis, Jan Davey
(il) Cobb, M. The quilt-block history of pioneer days **746.46**

Ellis, Sarah, 1952-
Next-door neighbors (4 and up) **Fic**
Pick-up sticks (5 and up) **Fic**

Emotions
Aliki. Feelings (k-3)　　　**152.4**
See/See also pages in the following book(s):
Funston, S. It's all in your brain p23-32 (4
and up)　　　**612.8**
Emperors *See* Kings, queens, rulers, etc.
The **Emperor's** clothes are news. Brooke, W. J.
In Brooke, W. J. Teller of tales p1-45
　　　S C
The **Emperor's** new clothes. Andersen, H. C.
In Andersen, H. C. Hans Christian Ander-
sen fairy tales p29-34　　　**S C**
In Andersen, H. C. Twelve tales p63-69
　　　S C
In Tomie dePaola's favorite nursery tales
p87-95　　　**398.2**
In The Yellow fairy book p21-25
　　　398.2
The **Emperor's** nightingale. Thane, A.
In Thane, A. Plays from famous stories
and fairy tales p3-19　　　**812**
Empire State Building (New York, N.Y.)
Macaulay, D. Unbuilding (4 and up)
　　　690
Employees
Training
See also Apprentices
Employment of children *See* Children—
Employment
Employment of women *See* Women—
Employment
The **empty** pot. Demi　　　**398.2**
Emrich, Marion Vallet
Johnny Appleseed! Johnny Appleseed!
In From sea to shining sea p274-76
　　　810.8
The **enchanted** canary. Deulin, C.
In The Red fairy book p257-73　　　**398.2**
The **enchanted** cap. Osborne, M. P.
In Osborne, M. P. Mermaid tales from
around the world p19-23　　　**398.2**
The **enchanted** castle. Nesbit, E.　　　**Fic**
Enchanted Forest Chronicles [series]
Wrede, P. C. Dealing with dragons　　　**Fic**
The **Enchanted** horse
In The Arabian nights entertainments
p358-89　　　**398.2**
The **Enchanted** pig
In The Red fairy book p104-15　　　**398.2**
The **enchanted** princess. Afanas'ev, A. N.
In Afanas'ev, A. N. Russian fairy tales
p600-11　　　**398.2**
The **enchanted** ring. Afanas'ev, A. N.
In Afanas'ev, A. N. Russian fairy tales
p31-37　　　**398.2**
The **enchanted** ring. Fénelon, F. de S. de L. M.
In The Green fairy book p137-44
　　　398.2
The **Enchanted** snake
In The Green fairy book p186-93
　　　398.2

The **enchanted** tapestry. San Souci, R.
　　　398.2
The **enchanted** watch. Deulin, C.
In The Green fairy book p43-47
　　　398.2
Enchantment of the world [series]
Billings, H. Antarctica　　　**998**
Brill, M. T. Guyana　　　**988**
Brill, M. T. Mongolia　　　**951.7**
Cromie, A. Taiwan　　　**951.2**
Foster, L. M. Iraq　　　**956.7**
Foster, L. M. Lebanon　　　**956.92**
Foster, L. M. Saudi Arabia　　　**953.8**
Fox, M. V. Bahrain　　　**953**
Fox, M. V. Cyprus　　　**956.93**
Fox, M. V. New Zealand　　　**993**
Fox, M. V. Papua New Guinea　　　**995.3**
Fox, M. V. Tunisia　　　**961.1**
Greenblatt, M. Cambodia　　　**959.6**
Hargrove, J. Belgium　　　**949.3**
Hintz, M. Denmark　　　**948.9**
Lane, M. S. B. Malawi　　　**968.97**
Lauré, J. Bangladesh　　　**954.92**
Lauré, J. Botswana　　　**968.8**
Lepthien, E. U. Luxembourg　　　**949.35**
Lepthien, E. U. Peru　　　**985**
McLenighan, V. China, a history to 1949
　　　951
McNair, S. Indonesia　　　**959.8**
Morrison, M. Bolivia　　　**984**
Morrison, M. Paraguay　　　**989.2**
Morrison, M. Uruguay　　　**989.5**
Resnick, A. Bulgaria　　　**949.77**
Resnick, A. The Commonwealth of Inde-
pendent States　　　**947.086**
Sutherland, D. B. Wales　　　**942.9**
Vazquez, A. M. B. Panama　　　**972.87**
Wright, D. K. Brunei　　　**959.5**
Zimmermann, R. The Gambia　　　**966.5**
Encounter at Easton. Avi　　　**Fic**
Encyclopedia Brown and the case of the dead
eagles. Sobol, D. J. See note under Sobol,
D. J. Encyclopedia Brown, boy detective
　　　Fic
Encyclopedia Brown and the case of the dis-
gusting sneakers. Sobol, D. J. See note un-
der Sobol, D. J. Encyclopedia Brown, boy
detective　　　**Fic**
Encyclopedia Brown and the case of the mid-
night visitor. Sobol, D. J. See note under
Sobol, D. J. Encyclopedia Brown, boy detective　　　**Fic**
Encyclopedia Brown and the case of the mysterious handprints. Sobol, D. J. See note
under Sobol, D. J. Encyclopedia Brown,
boy detective　　　**Fic**
Encyclopedia Brown and the case of the secret
pitch. Sobol, D. J. See note under Sobol,
D. J. Encyclopedia Brown, boy detective
　　　Fic
Encyclopedia Brown and the case of the treasure hunt. Sobol, D. J. See note under Sobol, D. J. Encyclopedia Brown, boy
detective　　　**Fic**

Every day is Earth Day. Ross, K.   **745.58**

Every day is Thanksgiving. DuBois, G.
  In Holiday plays round the year p47-58
  812.008

Every living thing. Rylant, C.   **S C**

Everyday life in Viking times. Martell, H. M.
  940.1

Everyone else's parents said yes. Danziger, P.
  Fic

Everyone knows what a dragon looks like.
  Williams, J.   **E**

Everything has a place. Lillie, P.   **E**

Everywhere. Brooks, B.   **Fic**

Eve's various children. Grimm, J.
  In Grimm, J. The complete Grimm's
  fairy tales p734-36   **398.2**

Evil *See* Good and evil

Evinrude, Ole, 1877-1934
  See/See also pages in the following book(s):
  Aaseng, N. The problem solvers p39-45 (5
  and up)   **920**

Evolution
  Cole, J. Evolution (k-3)   **575**
  Cole, J. The human body: how we evolved
  (4 and up)   **573.2**
  Evans, J. E. Charles Darwin (5 and up)
  92
  Gallant, R. A. Before the sun dies (6 and
  up)   **575**
  Gamblin, L. Evolution (4 and up)   **575**
  Lindsay, W. Prehistoric life (4 and up)
  560
  Parker, S. Charles Darwin and evolution (4
  and up)   **92**
  Sandak, C. R. Living fossils (4 and up)
  575
  See/See also pages in the following book(s):
  Litteral, L. L. Boobies, iguanas & other crit-
  ters p20-25 (5 and up)   **508**

Evslin, Bernard, 1922-1993
  Hercules (5 and up)   **292**
  Jason and the Argonauts (5 and up)
  292

Ewart, Claire
  (il) De Paola, T. The legend of the Persian
  carpet   **398.2**
  (il) Fleischman, P. Time train   **E**

Ewing, C. S.
  (il) Hautzig, D. The nutcracker ballet   **E**
  (il) Tresselt, A. R. Wake up, city!   **E**
  (il) Tresselt, A. R. Wake up, farm!   **E**

Ewing, Juliana Horatia, 1841-1885
  Murdoch's rath
  In Bauer, C. F. Celebrations p183-88
  808.8

Ex-service men *See* Veterans

Exactly the opposite. Hoban, T.   **E**

Excavations (Archeology)
  Italy
  Bisel, S. The secrets of Vesuvius (4 and up)
  937
  Goor, R. Pompeii: exploring a Roman ghost
  town (5 and up)   **937**

Exceptional children
  See also Handicapped children

Excretion
  Silverstein, A. The excretory system (5 and
  up)   **612.4**

The **excretory** system. Silverstein, A.
  612.4

Exercise
  See also Bodybuilding; Physical fitness
  Reef, C. Stay fit (4 and up)   **613.7**

Exercises, Reducing *See* Reducing

Exhibitions
  See also Fairs

Exiles *See* Refugees

The **exiles**. McKay, H.   **Fic**

The **exiles** at home. McKay, H. See note under McKay, H. The exiles   **Fic**

Exit. Miles, P.
  In The Oxford book of scary tales p152-
  [56]   **808.8**

Exodus. Chaikin, M.   **222**

Expanding universe *See* Universe

Experiments
  White, L. B. Air (2-4)   **507.8**
  White, L. B. Energy (2-4)   **507.8**
  White, L. B. Gravity (2-4)   **507.8**

Exploration
  See also Africa—Exploration
  Matthews, R. Explorer (4 and up)   **910.4**

Exploration and conquest. Maestro, B.
  970.01

Exploration into Africa. Ibazebo, I.   **960**

The **explorer** of Barkham Street. Stolz, M. See
  note under Stolz, M. A dog on Barkham
  Street   **Fic**

Explorers
  Adler, D. A. A picture book of Christopher
  Columbus (1-3)   **92**
  Blumberg, R. The remarkable voyages of
  Captain Cook (5 and up)   **910.4**
  Columbus, C. I, Columbus (4-6)   **92**
  Ferris, J. Arctic explorer: the story of Mat-
  thew Henson (3-6)   **92**
  Fisher, L. E. Prince Henry the Navigator
  (3-5)   **92**
  Fritz, J. Around the world in a hundred
  years (4-6)   **910.4**
  Fritz, J. Where do you think you're going,
  Christopher Columbus? (2-4)   **92**
  Hargrove, J. Ferdinand Magellan (4-6)
  92
  Haskins, J. Against all opposition (5 and up)
  920
  Marrin, A. The sea king: Sir Francis Drake
  and his times (6 and up)   **92**
  Marzollo, J. In 1492 (k-2)   **970.01**
  Matthews, R. Explorer (4 and up)   **910.4**
  Sis, P. Follow the dream [biography of
  Christopher Columbus] (k-3)   **92**
  Dictionaries
  Saari, P. Explorers & discoverers
  920.003

Explorers & discoverers. Saari, P.   **920.003**

Explorers, trappers, and guides. Bentley, J.   **979.5**

Exploring an ocean tide pool. Bendick, J.   **574.92**

Exploring autumn. Markle, S.   **508**

Exploring Earth's biomes [series]
Sayre, A. P. Desert   **574.5**
Sayre, A. P. Grassland   **574.5**
Sayre, A. P. Taiga   **574.5**
Sayre, A. P. Temperate deciduous forest   **574.5**
Sayre, A. P. Tropical rain forest   **574.5**
Sayre, A. P. Tundra   **574.5**

Exploring spring. Markle, S.   **508**

Exploring summer. Markle, S.   **508**

Exploring the Bismarck. Ballard, R. D.   **910.4**

Exploring the Great Lakes States through literature
In Exploring the United States through literature series   **016.973**

Exploring the Mountain States through literature
In Exploring the United States through literature series   **016.973**

Exploring the Northeast States through literature
In Exploring the United States through literature series   **016.973**

Exploring the Pacific States through literature
In Exploring the United States through literature series   **016.973**

Exploring the past: ancient Egypt. Hart, G.   **932**

Exploring the Plains States through literature
In Exploring the United States through literature series   **016.973**

Exploring the Southeast States through literature
In Exploring the United States through literature series   **016.973**

Exploring the Southwest States through literature
In Exploring the United States through literature series   **016.973**

Exploring the Titanic. Ballard, R. D.   **910.4**

Exploring the United States through literature series   **016.973**

Exploring winter. Markle, S.   **508**

Exploring your world   **910.3**

Exquemelin, A. O. (Alexandre Olivier)
Exquemelin and the pirates of the Caribbean (5 and up)   **910.4**

Exquemelin, Alexandre Olivier *See* Exquemelin, A. O. (Alexandre Olivier)

Exquemelin and the pirates of the Caribbean. Exquemelin, A. O.   **910.4**

Extinct animals
See also Prehistoric animals; Rare animals

Facklam, M. And then there was one (3-6)   **591.5**

Mullins, P. V for vanishing   **E**

Extinct plants *See* Fossil plants

The **extinguished** lights. Singer, I. B.
In Singer, I. B. The power of light p13-20   **S C**
In Singer, I. B. Stories for children p15-21   **S C**

Extra cheese, please!. Peterson, C.   **637**

Extra! Extra!. Granfield, L.   **071**

Extra innings (4 and up)   **811.008**

Extraordinary Asian-Pacific Americans. Sinnott, S.   **920**

Extraordinary black Americans. Altman, S. R.   **920**

An **extraordinary** egg. Lionni, L.   **E**

Extraordinary Hispanic Americans. Sinnott, S.   **920**

Extrasensory perception
Fiction
Mahy, M. The haunting (5 and up)   **Fic**
Sleator, W. Into the dream (5 and up)   **Fic**

Extraterrestrial beings
Fiction
Brittain, B. Shape-changer (4 and up)   **Fic**
Hooks, W. H. The girl who could fly (2-4)   **Fic**
Willis, J. Earthlets, as explained by Professor Xargle   **E**
Yorinks, A. Company's coming   **E**

Exupéry, Antoine de Saint- *See* Saint-Exupéry, Antoine de, 1900-1944

Exxon Valdez (Ship)
Carr, T. Spill!: the story of the Exxon Valdez (4 and up)   **363.7**

Eye
Parker, S. The eye and seeing (4 and up)   **612.8**
Showers, P. Look at your eyes (k-1)   **612.8**

The **eye** and seeing. Parker, S.   **612.8**

Eyeglasses
Fiction
Giff, P. R. Watch out, Ronald Morgan!   **E**
Raskin, E. Spectacles   **E**
Smith, L. Glasses: who needs 'em?   **E**

Eyeopeners II. Kobrin, B.   **028.5**

Eyes of jade. Yep, L.
In Yep, L. Tongues of jade p176-85   **398.2**

Eyes of marriage. Terada, A. M.
In Terada, A. M. Under the starfruit tree p64-68   **398.2**

The **eyes** of the Amaryllis. Babbitt, N.   **Fic**

Eyes of the cat. Bond, R.
In The Oxford book of scary tales p76-78   **808.8**

F

Faber, Doris, 1924-
Calamity Jane (5 and up)   92
Eleanor Roosevelt: first lady of the world (4 and up)   92
Great lives: American literature (5 and up)   920

Faber, Harold
(jt. auth) Faber, D. Great lives: American literature   920

Fables
Aesop. Aesop's fables [illus. by Heidi Holder]   398.2
Aesop. Aesop's fables [illus. by Lisbeth Zwerger]   398.2
Bierhorst, J. Doctor Coyote (1-4)   398.2
Brett, J. Town mouse, country mouse (k-3)   398.2
Brown, M. Once a mouse (k-3)   398.2
Clark, M. The best of Aesop's fables (k-3)   398.2
Cooney, B. Chanticleer and the fox   E
Craig, H. The town mouse and the country mouse (k-3)   398.2
Galdone, P. The monkey and the crocodile (k-2)   398.2
Galdone, P. Three Aesop fox fables (k-3)   398.2
Ginsburg, M. Merry-go-round (k-2)   398.2
Heins, E. L. The cat and the cook and other fables of Krylov (1-4)   398.2
Kherdian, D. Feathers and tails (2-5)   398.2
McClintock, B. Animal fables from Aesop (1-4)   398.2
Paxton, T. Aesop's fables (3-5)   398.2
Paxton, T. Androcles and the lion and other Aesop's fables (3-5)   398.2
Paxton, T. Belling the cat and other Aesop's fables (3-5)   398.2
Paxton, T. Birds of a feather and other Aesop's fables (3-5)   398.2
Stevens, J. The town mouse and the country mouse (k-2)   398.2
Tomie dePaola's Favorite nursery tales (k-3)   398.2
Wildsmith, B. The hare and the tortoise (k-2)   398.2
Wildsmith, B. The miller, the boy and the donkey (k-2)   398.2
Young, E. Seven blind mice (k-3)   398.2

Fables. Lobel, A.   Fic

Fabrics
Keeler, P. A. Unraveling fibers (3-5)   677

The Fabulous Firework Family. Flora, J.   E

Face
Haldane, S. Painting faces (4-6)   745.5
Intrater, R. G. Two eyes, a nose, and a mouth (k-2)   573

Face in art
Emberley, E. Ed Emberley's drawing book of faces (2-5)   743

Face to face with science [series]
Horner, J. R. Digging up Tyrannosaurus rex   567.9
Payne, K. Elephants calling   599.6
Ride, S. K. Voyager   523.4

Faces   306.05

Facklam, Howard
Bacteria (5 and up)   589.9
Insects (5 and up)   595.7
Parasites (5 and up)   574.5
Viruses (5 and up)   576

Facklam, Margery, 1927-
And then there was one (3-6)   591.5
Bees dance and whales sing (3-6)   591.5
The big bug book (3-6)   595.7
Do not disturb (3-6)   591.5
Partners for life (3-6)   591.5
What does the crow know? (3-6)   591.5
Who harnessed the horse? (3-6)   636
(jt. auth) Chrystie, F. N. Pets   636.088
(jt. auth) Facklam, H. Bacteria   589.9
(jt. auth) Facklam, H. Insects   595.7
(jt. auth) Facklam, H. Parasites   574.5
(jt. auth) Facklam, H. Viruses   576

Facklam, Paul
(il) Facklam, M. The big bug book   595.7

Factorials
Anno, M. Anno's mysterious multiplying jar (2-5)   512

Factories
          Fiction
Ackerman, K. By the dawn's early light   E
Paterson, K. Lyddie (5 and up)   Fic

Facts, Miscellaneous *See* Curiosities and wonders

The facts and fictions of Minna Pratt. MacLachlan, P.   Fic

The Facts on File children's atlas. Wright, D.   912

Faidley, Warren
(il) Kramer, S. Lightning   551.5

Fair Gruagach. Crossley-Holland, K.
In Crossley-Holland, K. British folk tales p228-43   398.2

Fair Katrinelje and Pif-paf-Poltrie. Grimm, J.
In Grimm, J. The complete Grimm's fairy tales p593-94   398.2

Fair shares. Philip, N.
In Philip, N. The Arabian nights p22-23   398.2

Fair-weather Pig. Marshall, J.
In Marshall, J. Rats on the range and other stories p51-56   S C

Fairclough, Chris
(il) Wright, L. Masks   745.59

Fairer-than-a-fairy
In The Yellow fairy book p126-33   398.2

Fairies

Dictionaries

Briggs, K. M. An encyclopedia of fairies
398.03

Fiction

Kimmel, E. A. Hershel and the Hanukkah
goblins **E**

Mayne, W. Hob and the goblins (4 and up)
Fic

Wells, R. Fritz and the Mess Fairy **E**

The **fairies**. Perrault, C.
In Perrault, C. The complete fairy tales of
Charles Perrault p54-59 **398.2**

Fairs

Fiction

Froehlich, M. W. That Kookoory! **E**

Godden, R. Candy Floss (2-4) **Fic**

Stolz, M. Bartholomew Fair (5 and up)
Fic

The **fairy**. Perrault, C.
In The Classic fairy tales p100-02
398.2

The **fairy** doll. Godden, R.
In Godden, R. Four dolls p32-65
S C

Fairy dusters and blazing stars. Samson, S. M.
582.13

Fairy gifts. Caylus, A. C. P. de T., comte de
In The Green fairy book p64-67
398.2

The **fairy** grotto. Vuong, L. D.
In Vuong, L. D. The brocaded slipper,
and other Vietnamese tales **398.2**

Fairy ointment. Crossley-Holland, K.
In Crossley-Holland, K. British folk tales
p287-92 **398.2**

Fairy ointment. Jacobs, J.
In Jacobs, J. English fairy tales p208-10
398.2

Fairy tale. Mujica, B. L.
In Where angels glide at dawn p77-97
S C

Fairy tales

See also Fantasy fiction

Afanas'ev, A. N. Russian fairy tales (4 and
up) **398.2**

Ahlberg, A. Ten in a bed (3-5) **Fic**

Aladdin and other tales from the Arabian
nights **398.2**

Andersen, H. C. Hans Christian Andersen
fairy tales (4-6) **S C**

Andersen, H. C. The nightingale (2-5)
Fic

Andersen, H. C. The princess and the pea
(1-4) **Fic**

Andersen, H. C. The Snow Queen (4-6)
Fic

Andersen, H. C. The steadfast tin soldier
(1-4) **Fic**

Andersen, H. C. The swineherd (1-4)
Fic

Andersen, H. C. Thumbeline (1-4) **Fic**

Andersen, H. C. Twelve tales (4-6)
S C

Anno, M. Anno's twice told tales (3-5)
398.2

The Arabian nights entertainments (5 and
up) **398.2**

Asbjornsen, P. C. East o' the sun and west
o' the moon (3-6) **398.2**

Asbjornsen, P. C. East of the sun and west
of the moon: old tales from the North
(3-6) **398.2**

Barrie, J. M. Peter Pan (3-5) **Fic**

Bell, A. The nutcracker (2-4) **Fic**

Berenzy, A. A Frog Prince **E**

Bianco, M. W. The velveteen rabbit (2-4)
Fic

The Blue fairy book (4-6) **398.2**

Brett, J. Beauty and the beast (1-3)
398.2

Brett, J. Trouble with trolls **E**

Brooke, W. J. Teller of tales (4 and up)
S C

Carpenter, F. Tales of a Chinese grandmother (4 and up) **398.2**

The Classic fairy tales **398.2**

Climo, S. The Egyptian Cinderella (k-3)
398.2

Climo, S. The Korean Cinderella (k-3)
398.2

Cole, J. Bony-Legs (k-3) **398.2**

Collodi, C. The adventures of Pinocchio
(3-6) **Fic**

Cooper, S. Tam Lin (1-4) **398.2**

Crampton, P. Peter and the wolf **E**

De Paola, T. Helga's dowry **E**

De Regniers, B. S. Little Sister and the
Month Brothers (k-3) **398.2**

DeFelice, C. C. Three perfect peaches (k-3)
398.2

Ehrlich, A. The Snow Queen (2-4) **Fic**

Ehrlich, A. The wild swans **E**

Farjeon, E. The glass slipper (3-6) **Fic**

Fonteyn, Dame M. Swan lake (3-5)
792.8

Galdone, P. The elves and the shoemaker
(k-2) **398.2**

Galdone, P. The gingerbread boy (k-2)
398.2

Galdone, P. King of the Cats (k-2)
398.2

Galdone, P. Puss in boots (k-2) **398.2**

Grahame, K. The reluctant dragon (3-5)
Fic

The Green fairy book (4-6) **398.2**

Grimm, J. About wise men and simpletons
(3-6) **398.2**

Grimm, J. The complete Grimm's fairy
tales (4 and up) **398.2**

Grimm, J. The fisherman and his wife (k-3)
398.2

Grimm, J. Hansel and Gretel [Dial Press]
(k-3) **398.2**

Grimm, J. Hansel and Gretel [Picture Book
Studio] (k-3) **398.2**

Grimm, J. The seven ravens (k-3)
398.2

Grimm, J. Snow White & Rose Red (1-4)
398.2

Family life—Fiction—*Continued*

Levitin, S. Journey to America (4 and up)
Fic

Little, J. From Anna (4-6)   Fic

Little, J. Look through my window (4-6)
Fic

Lowry, L. Anastasia Krupnik (4-6)   Fic

Lowry, L. Switcharound (5 and up)   Fic

Lyon, G. E. Borrowed children (5 and up)
Fic

MacLachlan, P. All the places to love
E

MacLachlan, P. Journey (4 and up)   Fic

MacLachlan, P. Seven kisses in a row (2-4)
Fic

Mahy, M. The haunting (5 and up)   Fic

Mahy, M. The rattlebang picnic   E

McDonnell, C. Toad food & measle soup
(2-4)   Fic

McEwan, I. The daydreamer (4-6)   Fic

Namioka, L. Yang the third and her impossible family (4-6)   Fic

Namioka, L. Yang the youngest and his terrible ear (4-6)   Fic

Napoli, D. J. When the water closes over my head (3-5)   Fic

Naylor, P. R. Maudie in the middle (3-5)
Fic

Nesbit, E. The railway children (4-6)
Fic

Osofsky, A. Dreamcatcher   E

Park, R. Playing Beatie Bow (5 and up)
Fic

Paterson, K. Come sing, Jimmy Jo (5 and up)   Fic

Pevsner, S. And you give me a pain, Elaine (4 and up)   Fic

Porte-Thomas, B. A. When grandma almost fell off the mountain & other stories
E

Raskin, E. Figgs & phantoms (5 and up)
Fic

Rattigan, J. K. Dumpling soup   E

Rodowsky, C. F. The gathering room (5 and up)   Fic

Rylant, C. A blue-eyed daisy (5 and up)
Fic

Rylant, C. A fine white dust (5 and up)
Fic

Rylant, C. The relatives came   E

Sachs, M. The bears' house (4-6)   Fic

Sebestyen, O. Words by heart (5 and up)
Fic

Segal, L. G. Tell me a Mitzi   E

Segal, L. G. Tell me a Trudy   E

Shelby, A. Homeplace   E

Shreve, S. R. The flunking of Joshua T. Bates (3-5)   Fic

Smith, D. B. Return to Bitter Creek (5 and up)   Fic

Smith, R. K. The war with Grandpa (4-6)
Fic

Soto, G. The pool party (3-5)   Fic

Streatfeild, N. Theatre shoes, or other people's shoes (5 and up)   Fic

Uchida, Y. A jar of dreams (5 and up)
Fic

Uchida, Y. Journey home (5 and up)
Fic

Van Leeuwen, J. Going West   E

Van Leeuwen, J. Tales of Oliver Pig   E

Walter, M. P. Justin and the best biscuits in the world (3-6)   Fic

Walter, M. P. Mariah keeps cool (3-6)
Fic

Watson, W. Thanksgiving at our house
E

Waugh, S. The Mennyms (5 and up)
Fic

Wilder, L. I. A Little house Christmas
S C

Williams, V. B. A chair for my mother
E

Wilson, N. H. The reason for Janey (5 and up)   Fic

Wolff, A. Only the cat saw   E

Zolotow, C. Something is going to happen
E

Poetry

Adoff, A. All the colors of the race: poems (4-6)   811

Adoff, A. In for winter, out for spring (k-3)
811

Giovanni, N. Knoxville, Tennessee (k-3)
811

Lewis, C. L. Up in the mountains, and other poems of long ago (3-5)   811

Family pictures. Lomas Garza, C.   E

The **Family** read-aloud Christmas treasury
808.8

The **Family** read-aloud holiday treasury
808.8

Family reunion. Singer, M.   811

The **family** storytelling handbook. Pellowski, A.   372.6

The **family** under the bridge. Carlson, N. S.
Fic

Family violence
See also Child abuse; Wife abuse

Famous Amos Chocolate Chip Cookie Corp.
Jaspersohn, W. Cookies (3-5)   664

Famous Asian Americans. Morey, J.   920

Famous first facts: a record of first happenings, discoveries, and inventions in American history. Kane, J. N.   031.02

Famous Mexican Americans. Morey, J.
920

A **famous** painting. Porte-Thomas, B. A.
In Porte-Thomas, B. A turkey drive and other tales p49-56   S C

The **famous** Stanley kidnapping case. Snyder, Z. K. See note under Snyder, Z. K. The headless cupid   Fic

Fancy dress *See* Costume

Fang, Linda
The Ch'i-lin purse (5 and up)   **398.2**
Contents: The Ch'i-lin purse; Dog steals and Rooster crows; Two Miss Peonys; The Ho Shi jade; The prime minister and the General; The clever magistrate; Mr. Yeh's New Year; The miracle doctor; The royal bridegroom

The **Fannie** Farmer junior cook book. Scobey, J.   **641.5**

Fantastic fiction *See* Fantasy fiction

Fantasy fiction
See also Fairy tales; Science fiction
Alexander, L. The Arkadians (5 and up)
        Fic
Alexander, L. The book of three (5 and up)
        Fic
Alexander, L. The High King (5 and up)
        Fic
Babbitt, N. Tuck everlasting (5 and up)
        Fic
Baum, L. F. The Wizard of Oz (3-6)
        Fic
Bond, N. A string in the harp (6 and up)
        Fic
Boston, L. M. The children of Green Knowe (4-6)   **Fic**
Carroll, L. Alice's adventures in Wonderland (4 and up)   **Fic**
Carroll, L. Alice's adventures in Wonderland, and Through the looking glass (4 and up)   **Fic**
Carroll, L. Through the looking glass, and what Alice found there (4 and up)
        Fic
Cooper, S. The grey king (5 and up)
        Fic
Cooper, S. Over sea, under stone (5 and up)
        Fic
Cooper, S. Seaward (6 and up)   **Fic**
Corbett, S. The lemonade trick (3-5)
        Fic
Coville, B. Jennifer Murdley's toad (4-6)
        Fic
Coville, B. Jeremy Thatcher, dragon hatcher (4-6)   **Fic**
Cummings, P. C.L.O.U.D.S.   **E**
Dahl, R. James and the giant peach (4-6)
        Fic
Eager, E. Half magic (4-6)   **Fic**
Eager, E. Seven-day magic (4-6)   **Fic**
Fleischman, P. Time train   **E**
Gannett, R. S. My father's dragon (1-4)
        Fic
Hodges, M. Gulliver in Lilliput (3-6)
        Fic
Jacques, B. Redwall (6 and up)   **Fic**
James, M. Shoebag (5 and up)   **Fic**
Jansson, T. Moominsummer madness (4-6)
        Fic
Jones, D. W. Castle in the air (6 and up)
        Fic
Jones, D. W. Dogsbody (6 and up)   **Fic**
Jones, D. W. Howl's moving castle (6 and up)   **Fic**
Joyce, W. George shrinks   **E**
Juster, N. The phantom tollbooth (5 and up)   **Fic**

Langton, J. The fledgling (5 and up)
        Fic
Le Guin, U. K. A wizard of Earthsea (6 and up)   **Fic**
L'Engle, M. A wrinkle in time (5 and up)
        Fic
Lewis, C. S. The lion, the witch, and the wardrobe (4 and up)   **Fic**
Lisle, J. T. Forest (5 and up)   **Fic**
Mahy, M. Dangerous spaces (5 and up)
        Fic
Mayne, W. Hob and the goblins (4 and up)
        Fic
McCaffrey, A. Dragonsong (6 and up)
        Fic
McKinley, R. The hero and the crown (6 and up)   **Fic**
Nesbit, E. The enchanted castle (4-6)
        Fic
Norton, A. Fur magic (4-6)   **Fic**
Norton, M. Bed-knob and broomstick (3-5)
        Fic
Pearce, P. Tom's midnight garden (4 and up)   **Fic**
Pope, E. M. The Perilous Gard (6 and up)
        Fic
Reid Banks, L. The Indian in the cupboard (5 and up)   **Fic**
Rodda, E. Finders keepers (4-6)   **Fic**
Sargent, S. Weird Henry Berg (4-6)   **Fic**
Scieszka, J. Knights of the kitchen table (3-5)   **Fic**
Sendak, M. In the night kitchen   **E**
Sendak, M. Where the wild things are
        E
Service, P. F. Storm at the edge of time (5 and up)   **Fic**
Snyder, Z. K. Below the root (5 and up)
        Fic
Tolkien, J. R. R. The hobbit (4 and up)
        Fic
Travers, P. L. Mary Poppins (4-6)   **Fic**
Wells, R. Through the hidden door (5 and up)   **Fic**
Winthrop, E. The castle in the attic (4-6)
        Fic
Wrightson, P. The Nargun and the stars (5 and up)   **Fic**
Yorinks, A. Hey, Al   **E**
Bibliography
Lynn, R. N. Fantasy literature for children and young adults   **016.8**
History and criticism
Egoff, S. A. Worlds within   **028.5**
See/See also pages in the following book(s):
Crosscurrents of criticism p169-96   **028.5**
Only connect: readings on children's literature p164-91, 288-300   **028.5**
Fantasy for children. See Lynn, R. N. Fantasy literature for children and young adults
        016.8

Fantasy literature for children and young adults. Lynn, R. N.   **016.8**

Farber, Norma
As I was crossing Boston Common   **E**
How does it feel to be old?   **811**

Farmer, Fannie Merritt, 1857-1915
Scobey, J. The Fannie Farmer junior cook
book **641.5**
See/See also pages in the following book(s):
Vare, E. A. Women inventors & their dis-
coveries p39-49 (5 and up) **920**

Farmer, Nancy, 1941-
The Ear, the Eye, and the Arm (6 and up)
Fic

The **farmer** and the boggart. Crossley-Holland,
K.
In Crossley-Holland, K. British folk tales
p224-27 **398.2**

The **farmer** and the snake. Lester, J.
In Lester, J. The knee-high man, and other tales p24-26 **398.2**

Farmer boy. Wilder, L. I. See note under Wilder, L. I. Little house in the big woods
Fic

Farmer duck. Waddell, M. **E**

Farmer Palmer's wagon ride. Steig, W. **E**

Farmer Weatherbeard. Asbjornsen, P. C.
In The Red fairy book p294-302
398.2

A **farmer's** alphabet. Azarian, M. **E**

Farming *See* Agriculture

Farming. Gibbons, G. **630.1**

Farms
Epstein, S. You call that a farm? (4-6)
636
Jordan, S. Christmas tree farm (k-3)
635.9

Farrell, Kate
(comp) Talking to the sun: an illustrated anthology of poems for young people. See
Talking to the sun: an illustrated anthology of poems for young people **808.81**

The **farthest** shore. Le Guin, U. K. See note
under Le Guin, U. K. A wizard of Earthsea **Fic**

Fashion
See also Clothing and dress; Costume

Fashion models
Fiction
Perl, L. Fat Glenda turns fourteen (5 and
up) **Fic**

Fasick, Adele M., 1930-
Managing children's services in the public library **027.62**

Fast & funny paper toys you can make.
Churchill, E. R. **745.592**

Fast Sam, Cool Clyde, and Stuff. Myers, W.
D. **Fic**

Fast-slow, high-low. Spier, P. **E**

Faster and faster. Schwartz, A.
In Schwartz, A. Scary stories 3 p10-11
398.2

The **fastest** horse in the world. Porte-Thomas,
B. A.
In Porte-Thomas, B. A turkey drive and
other tales p44-48 **S C**

Fasts and feasts
Judaism
See Jewish holidays

The **fat-cats** at sea. Lewis, J. P. **811**

Fat chance, Claude (1987). Nixon, J. L. See
note under Nixon, J. L. Beats me, Claude
E

Fat Glenda turns fourteen. Perl, L. **Fic**

Fat Glenda's summer romance. Perl, L. See
note under Perl, L. Fat Glenda turns fourteen **Fic**

Fat man in a fur coat, and other bear stories.
Schwartz, A. **599.74**

Fat men from space. Pinkwater, D. M.
Fic

The **fatal** flower. Yep, L.
In Yep, L. Tongues of jade p138-49
398.2

Father Bear comes home. Minarik, E. H. See
note under Minarik, E. H. Little Bear
E

Father Christmas. Briggs, R. **E**

Father Fox's feast of songs. Watson, C.
782.42

Father Fox's pennyrhymes. Watson, C.
811

Father Grumbler
In The Rainbow fairy book p181-91
398.2

Father Nicholas and the thief. Afanas'ev, A.
N.
In Afanas'ev, A. N. Russian fairy tales
p145-46 **398.2**

Father spider comes to dinner. Climo, S.
In Climo, S. Someone saw a spider p77-
86 **398.2**

Fathers
Fiction
Daly, N. My dad **E**
Isadora, R. At the crossroads **E**
Konigsburg, E. L. Journey to an 800 num-
ber (5 and up) **Fic**
Schwartz, A. Bea and Mr. Jones **E**

Fathers, Single parent *See* Single parent family

Fathers and daughters
Moutoussamy-Ashe, J. Daddy and me: a
photo story of Arthur Ashe and his
daughter, Camera (k-3) **92**
Fiction
Alcock, V. The monster garden (4 and up)
Fic
Bond, N. Truth to tell (6 and up) **Fic**
Boyd, C. D. Charlie Pippin (4-6) **Fic**
Browne, A. Gorilla **E**
Bunting, E. A perfect Father's Day **E**
Bunting, E. Spying on Miss Müller (5 and
up) **Fic**
Carson, J. You hold me and I'll hold you
E
Cummings, P. Carousel **E**
Greene, C. C. Nora (6 and up) **Fic**
Hamilton, V. Plain City (5 and up) **Fic**

Fathers and daughters—Fiction—*Continued*
Henkes, K. Protecting Marie (5 and up)
             Fic
Mead, A. Crossing the Starlight Bridge (3-5)
             Fic
Nelson, T. The 25¢ miracle (5 and up)
             Fic
Nelson, T. Earthshine (5 and up)   Fic
Reaver, C. Bill (5 and up)   Fic
Ryder, J. My father's hands   E
Showers, P. The listening walk   E
Wyeth, S. D. Always my Dad   E
Yolen, J. Owl moon   E

Fathers and sons
      Fiction
Asch, F. Sand cake   E
Avi. The barn (4-6)   Fic
Bartone, E. Peppe the lamplighter   E
Bunting, E. Fly away home   E
Bunting, E. The Wall   E
Calvert, P. Bigger (5 and up)   Fic
Fox, P. The eagle kite (6 and up)   Fic
Hines, A. G. Daddy makes the best spaghetti   E
Hort, L. How many stars in the sky?   E
Hurwitz, J. Baseball fever (3-5)   Fic
Manushkin, F. Peeping and sleeping   E
McBratney, S. Guess how much I love you
             E
Say, A. The lost lake   E
Slote, A. The trading games (4-6)   Fic
Smith, R. K. Bobby Baseball (4-6)   Fic
Yep, L. Dragonwings (5 and up)   Fic

Father's Day
      Fiction
Bunting, E. A perfect Father's Day   E

Fats. Silverstein, A.   612.3

Faulkner, William, 1897-1962
See/See also pages in the following book(s):
Faber, D. Great lives: American literature
  p193-202 (5 and up)   920

Faulkner, William J.
Brer Tiger and the big wind (k-3)   398.2
How the slaves helped each other
  In From sea to shining sea p130-31
            810.8

Favorite Greek myths. Osborne, M. P.
            292

Favorite nursery tales, Tomie dePaola's
            398.2

Favorite science experiments, Robert Gardner's. Gardner, R.   507.8

Fayerweather Street School. Unit
The Kids' book about death and dying. See
  The Kids' book about death and dying
            155.9

Fear
      Fiction
Blegvad, L. Anna Banana and me   E
Blume, J. Otherwise known as Sheila the
  Great (4-6)   Fic
Bonsall, C. N. Who's afraid of the dark?
            E
Bunting, E. Ghost's hour, spook's hour
            E

Byars, B. C. The 18th emergency (4-6)
            Fic
Crowe, R. L. Clyde monster   E
Emberley, E. Go away, big green monster!
            E
Grifalconi, A. Darkness and the butterfly
            E
Little, J. Different dragons (3-5)   Fic
Martin, B. The ghost-eye tree   E
Mayer, M. There's a nightmare in my closet
            E
Napoli, D. J. When the water closes over
  my head (3-5)   Fic
Polacco, P. Thunder cake   E
Stolz, M. Storm in the night   E
Teague, M. The field beyond the outfield
            E

Fear and fly. Crossley-Holland, K.
  In Crossley-Holland, K. British folk tales
  p175-77   398.2

The **fear** place. Naylor, P. R.   Fic

The **fearsome** inn. Singer, I. B.
  In Singer, I. B. Stories for children p290-
  307   S C

Feast of Lights *See* Hanukkah

Feast of Tabernacles *See* Sukkoth

The **feather** merchants. Sanfield, S.
  In Sanfield, S. The feather merchants &
  other tales of the fools of Chelm p76-
  83   398.2

The **feather** merchants & other tales of the
  fools of Chelm. Sanfield, S.   398.2

The **feather** of Finist, the Bright Falcon. Afanas'ev, A. N.
  In Afanas'ev, A. N. Russian fairy tales
  p580-88   398.2

Feather Woman and the morning star. Mayo,
  M.
  In Mayo, M. Magical tales from many
  lands p18-24   398.2

The **feathered** serpent. O'Dell, S. See note under O'Dell, S. The captive   Fic

Feathers. Patent, D. H.   598

Feathers and tails. Kherdian, D.   398.2

Feathers for lunch. Ehlert, L.   E

Febold Feboldson. Osborne, M. P.
  In Osborne, M. P. American tall tales
  p63-71   398.2

Febold Feboldson, first citizen of Nebraska.
  Schmidt, S.
  In From sea to shining sea p178-79
            810.8

Feder, Jane
  Table, chair, bear (k-2)   413

Feeding yourself. Cobb, V.   394.1

Feel better, Ernest!. Vincent, G. See note under Vincent, G. Ernest and Celestine
            E

Feel the wind. Dorros, A.   551.5

Feeling safe, feeling strong. Terkel, S. N.
            362.7

Finding Buck McHenry. Slote, A.   Fic

Fine, Anne
  Alias Madame Doubtfire (6 and up)   Fic
  Flour babies (6 and up)   Fic

Fine, Howard
  (il) Palatini, M. Piggie pie!   E

Fine, John Christopher
  Sunken ships & treasure (5 and up)
        910.4

The **fine** field of flax. Crossley-Holland, K.
  In Crossley-Holland, K. British folk tales
    p218-23   **398.2**

A **fine** white dust. Rylant, C.   Fic

Finger, Charles Joseph, 1869-1941
See/See also pages in the following book(s):
  Newbery Medal books, 1922-1955 p37-38
        028.5

The **finger** Lock. MacDonald, M. R.
  In MacDonald, M. R. Celebrate the world
    p128-34   **372.6**

Finger play
  Brown, M. T. Finger rhymes   **796.1**
  Brown, M. T. Hand rhymes   **796.1**
  Brown, M. T. Play rhymes   **796.1**
  Clap your hands   **796.1**
  Defty, J. Creative fingerplays & action
    rhymes   **796.1**
  The Eentsy, weentsy spider   **796.1**
  Grayson, M. F. Let's do fingerplays
        796.1
  The Lap-time song and play book
        782.42
  Pat-a-cake and other play rhymes   **398.8**
  Trot, trot to Boston: play rhymes for baby
        398.8
See/See also pages in the following book(s):
  Pellowski, A. The story vine p92-98
        372.6

Fink, Mike, 1770-1823?
        Fiction
  Kellogg, S. Mike Fink (k-3)   **398.2**

Finland
  Lander, P. S. The land and people of Fin-
    land (5 and up)   **948.97**

Finley, William L. (William Lovell), 1876-1953
        About
  Fraser, M. A. Sanctuary (3-5)   **639.9**

Finn Family Moomintroll. Jansson, T. See
  note under Jansson, T. Moominsummer
  madness   Fic

Fiore, Peter M.
  (il) Hand in hand. See Hand in hand
        811.008

Fir, Douglas *See* Douglas fir

The **fir** tree. Andersen, H. C.
  In Andersen, H. C. Twelve tales p74-85
        S C
  In Take joy! The Tasha Tudor Christmas
    book p14-22   **394.2**
The **fir** tree, Hans Christian Anderson's. An-
  dersen, H. C.   Fic

Fire & silk: flying in a hot air balloon. Johnson, N.   **797.5**

Fire engines
  Bingham, C. Fire truck (k-3)   **628.9**
  Rockwell, A. F. Fire engines (k-1)   **628.9**

Fire fighters
  Kuklin, S. Fighting fires (k-3)   **628.9**
  Maass, R. Fire fighters (k-3)   **628.9**

Fire fighting
  Gibbons, G. Fire! Fire! (k-3)   **363.3**

Fire! Fire!. Gibbons, G.   **363.3**

A **fire** in her bones: the story of Mary Lyon.
  Rosen, D.   **92**

Fire in the forest. Pringle, L. P.   **574.5**

Fire! in Yellowstone. Ekey, R.   **574.5**

The **fire** on the mountain. Courlander, H.
  In The Scott, Foresman anthology of chil-
    dren's literature p303-04   **808.8**

Fire on the mountain. Kurtz, J.   **398.2**

Fire truck. Bingham, C.   **628.9**

Firearms
        Fiction
  Fox, P. One-eyed cat (5 and up)   Fic

Firebird (Ballet)
See/See also pages in the following book(s):
  McCaughrean, G. The Random House book
    of stories from the ballet p85-94 (4 and
    up)   **792.8**

The **Firebird**. Demi   **398.2**

The **firebird**. Hastings, S.   **398.2**

Firebird. Isadora, R.   **398.2**

The **Firebird** and Princess Vasilisa. Afanas'ev,
  A. N.
  In Afanas'ev, A. N. Russian fairy tales
    p494-97   **398.2**

Fireflies
  Hawes, J. Fireflies in the night (k-1)
        595.7
  Johnson, S. A. Fireflies (4 and up)
        595.7
        Fiction
  Brinckloe, J. Fireflies!   E
  Carle, E. The very lonely firefly   E

Fireflies!. Brinckloe, J.   E

Fireflies. Johnson, S. A.   **595.7**

Fireflies in the night. Hawes, J.   **595.7**

Fires
        Fiction
  Polacco, P. Tikvah means hope   E
        Chicago (Ill.)
  Murphy, J. The great fire (5 and up)
        977.3

Firetalking. Polacco, P.   **92**

Fireweed. Paton Walsh, J.   Fic

Fireworks
        Fiction
  Flora, J. The Fabulous Firework Family
        E

Fireworks, picnics, and flags. Giblin, J.
        394.2

Firstman. Medicine Story
  In Medicine Story. The Children of the Morning Light p25-29   **398.2**

Firth, Barbara
  (il) Waddell, M. Can't you sleep, Little Bear?   **E**

Fischer-Nagel, Andreas, 1951-
  (jt. auth) Fischer-Nagel, H. An ant colony   **595.7**
  (jt. auth) Fischer-Nagel, H. The housefly   **595.7**
  (jt. auth) Fischer-Nagel, H. Life of the butterfly   **595.7**
  (jt. auth) Fischer-Nagel, H. Life of the honeybee   **595.7**
  (jt. auth) Fischer-Nagel, H. Life of the ladybug   **595.7**
  (jt. auth) Fischer-Nagel, H. A look through the mouse hole   **599.32**

Fischer-Nagel, Heiderose, 1956-
  An ant colony (3-6)   **595.7**
  The housefly (3-6)   **595.7**
  Life of the butterfly (3-6)   **595.7**
  Life of the honeybee (3-6)   **595.7**
  Life of the ladybug (3-6)   **595.7**
  A look through the mouse hole (3-6)   **599.32**

Fish, Helen Dean
  (ed) Bible. Selections. Animals of the Bible   **220.8**

The **fish** and the ring. Jacobs, J.
  In Jacobs, J. English fairy tales p189-92   **398.2**

The **fish** and the ring. Reeves, J.
  In Reeves, J. English fables and fairy stories p35-48   **398.2**

Fish and Wildlife Service (U.S.) *See* U.S. Fish and Wildlife Service

The **fish** angel. Levoy, M.
  In Levoy, M. The witch of Fourth Street, and other stories   **S C**

The **fish** cart. Manning-Sanders, R.
  In The Oxford treasury of children's stories p19-22   **S C**

Fish culture
  See also Aquariums

Fish heads. Yep, L.
  In Yep, L. Tongues of jade p60-69   **398.2**

The **fish** husband. Osborne, M. P.
  In Osborne, M. P. Mermaid tales from around the world p33-36   **398.2**

Fish in a flash!. Arnosky, J.   **799.1**

Fish is fish. Lionni, L.   **E**

The **fish** with the deep sea smile. Brown, M. W.   **818**

Fisher, Aileen Lucia, 1906-
  Always wondering (1-3)   **811**
  Sing the songs of Thanksgiving
  In Holiday plays round the year p101-11   **812.008**

A tree to trim
  In The Big book of Christmas plays p59-79   **808.82**

Fisher, Dorothy Canfield, 1879-1958
  Thanksgiving Day
  In Bauer, C. F. Celebrations p243-48   **808.8**
  In Thanksgiving: stories and poems p11-22   **810.8**
  Understood Betsy [excerpt]
  In The Random House book of humor for children p31-35   **817.008**

Fisher, James
  See/See also pages in the following book(s):
  Children and their books p79-94   **028.5**

Fisher, Leonard Everett, 1924-
  The ABC exhibit   **E**
  Alphabet art: thirteen ABCs from around the world (4 and up)   **745.6**
  Calendar art (4 and up)   **529**
  Cyclops (3-5)   **292**
  David and Goliath (k-3)   **222**
  Ellis Island (4 and up)   **325.73**
  Galileo (3-5)   **92**
  The Great Wall of China (4 and up)   **951**
  Gutenberg (3-5)   **92**
  Jason and the golden fleece (3-5)   **292**
  Monticello (4 and up)   **975.5**
  Moses (k-3)   **222**
  Number art: thirteen 1 2 3s from around the world (4 and up)   **513**
  The Olympians (3-5)   **292**
  The Oregon Trail (4 and up)   **979.5**
  Prince Henry the Navigator (3-5)   **92**
  Pyramid of the sun, pyramid of the moon (4 and up)   **972**
  The seven days of creation (k-3)   **222**
  Stars & stripes (1-3)   **929.9**
  The Statue of Liberty (4 and up)   **974.7**
  Symbol art (4 and up)   **302.2**
  Theseus and the Minotaur (3-5)   **292**
  The Tower of London (4 and up)   **942.1**
  Tracks across America (5 and up)   **385.09**
  The Wailing Wall (4 and up)   **221.9**
  The White House (4 and up)   **975.3**
  (il) If you ever meet a whale. See If you ever meet a whale   **811.008**
  (il) Kimmel, E. A. The three princes   **398.2**
  (il) Livingston, M. C. Celebrations   **811**
  (il) Livingston, M. C. A circle of seasons   **811**
  (il) Livingston, M. C. Sky songs   **811**
  (il) Meltzer, M. All times, all peoples: a world history of slavery   **326**

A **fisher**. Florian, D.   **639.2**

The **Fisherman** and his soul. Wilde, O.
  In Wilde, O. The fairy tales of Oscar Wilde p94-123   **S C**

The **fisherman** and his wife. Grimm, J.   **398.2**
  also in Anno, M. Anno's twice told tales   **398.2**

Flags—*Continued*

United States

Brandt, S. R. State flags (5 and up)
929.9

Fisher, L. E. Stars & stripes (1-3)   929.9

Haban, R. D. How proudly they wave (4 and up)   929.9

Wallner, A. Betsy Ross (k-2)   92

The **flail** from heaven. Grimm, J.
In Grimm, J. The complete Grimm's fairy tales p514-15   398.2

Flame-colored taffeta. Sutcliff, R.   Fic

Flamingos

Arnold, C. Flamingo (3-5)   598

Flanders, Bruce L.

(ed) Automation for school libraries. See Automation for school libraries   027.8

Flanders, Lillian Hsu- *See* Hsu-Flanders, Lillian

Flapdoodle: pure nonsense from American folklore. Schwartz, A.   398

Flash, crash, rumble, and roll. Branley, F. M.
551.5

Flat Stanley. Brown, J.   E

Flavoring essences

Busenberg, B. Vanilla, chocolate, & strawberry (5 and up)   664

The **fledgling.** Langton, J.   Fic

Fleischman, Albert Sidney *See* Fleischman, Sid, 1920-

Fleischman, Paul

The borning room (6 and up)   Fic
Bull Run (6 and up)   Fic
Coming-and-going men (6 and up)
S C
Contents: The shade cutter; Enemies of the eye; Slaves of sham; Country pay
Copier creations (4 and up)   760
Graven images (6 and up)   S C
Contents: The binnacle boy; Saint Crispin's follower; The man of influence
The Half-a-Moon Inn (4-6)   Fic
I am phoenix: poems for two voices (4 and up)   811
Joyful noise: poems for two voices (4 and up)   811
Saturnalia (6 and up)   Fic
Time train   E
Townsend's warbler (4 and up)   508

Fleischman, Sid, 1920-

By the Great Horn Spoon! (4-6)   Fic
Chancy and the grand rascal (4-6)   Fic
The ghost on Saturday night (3-5)   Fic
Here comes McBroom! See note under Fleischman, S. McBroom tells the truth
Fic
Jim Ugly (4 and up)   Fic
McBroom and the big wind. See note under Fleischman, S. McBroom tells the truth
Fic
McBroom and the big wind
In The Oxford treasury of children's stories p105-13   S C

McBroom and the great race. See note under Fleischman, S. McBroom tells the truth   Fic
McBroom tells the truth (3-5)   Fic
McBroom's almanac. See note under Fleischman, S. McBroom tells the truth
Fic
McBroom's almanac [excerpt]
In The Random House book of humor for children p173-75   817.008
McBroom's wonderful one-acre farm. See note under Fleischman, S. McBroom tells the truth   Fic
The midnight horse (3-6)   Fic
The scarebird   E
The whipping boy (5 and up)   Fic
See/See also pages in the following book(s):
Cart, M. What's so funny? p136-53
028.5

Fleisher, Paul

The master violinmaker (3-5)   787.2

Fleming, Bill

(jt. auth) Petersen-Fleming, J. Kitten care and critters, too!   636.8
(jt. auth) Petersen-Fleming, J. Puppy care and critters, too!   636.7

Fleming, Denise, 1950-

Barnyard banter   E
Count!   E
In the small, small pond   E
In the tall, tall grass   E
Lunch   E

Fleming, Ian, 1908-1964

Chitty-Chitty-Bang-Bang (4-6)   Fic

Fleming, Judy Petersen- *See* Petersen-Fleming, Judy

Fleming, Ronald Lee

(jt. auth) Von Tscharner, R. New Providence   307.7

Fleming, Thomas J., 1927-

Behind the headlines (5 and up)   071
Harry S Truman, president (5 and up)
92

Flemish artists *See* Artists, Flemish

Fletcher, Jane Cowen- *See* Cowen-Fletcher, Jane

Fletcher, Ralph J.

Fig pudding (4 and up)   Fic

Fletcher, Sarah *See* Greene, Carol

Flies

Fischer-Nagel, H. The housefly (3-6)
595.7

Fiction

Aylesworth, J. Old black fly   E

Flies in the water, fish in the air. Arnosky, J.
799.1

Flight

Experiments

Ardley, N. The science book of air (3-5)
507.8

Fiction

Walter, M. P. Brother to the wind   E

Folklore—*Continued*

Nigeria

Bryan, A. Beat the story-drum, pum-pum (1-4)   **398.2**

Daly, N. Why the Sun & Moon live in the sky (k-3)   **398.2**

Gerson, M.-J. Why the sky is far away (k-3)   **398.2**

Norway

Asbjornsen, P. C. East o' the sun and west o' the moon (3-6)   **398.2**

Asbjornsen, P. C. East of the sun and west of the moon: old tales from the North (3-6)   **398.2**

Galdone, P. The three Billy Goats Gruff (k-2)   **398.2**

Kimmel, E. A. Boots and his brothers (k-3)   **398.2**

Martin, C. Boots & the glass mountain (2-4)   **398.2**

Rounds, G. Three billy goats Gruff (k-3)   **398.2**

Pakistan

Shepard, A. The gifts of Wali Dad (2-4)   **398.2**

Persia

See Folklore—Iran

Peru

Alexander, E. Llama and the great flood (1-3)   **398.2**

Ehlert, L. Moon rope. Un lazo a la luna (k-3)   **398.2**

Poland

Sanfield, S. The feather merchants & other tales of the fools of Chelm (4-6)   **398.2**

Puerto Rico

Bernier-Grand, C. T. Juan Bobo (k-2)   **398.2**

Crespo, G. How the sea began (2-4)   **398.2**

Romania

Spariosu, M. Ghosts, vampires, and were-wolves (5 and up)   **398.2**

Russia

See also Folklore—Ukraine

Afanas'ev, A. N. Russian fairy tales (4 and up)   **398.2**

Cole, J. Bony-Legs (k-3)   **398.2**

Demi. The Firebird (k-3)   **398.2**

Hastings, S. The firebird (1-4)   **398.2**

Isadora, R. Firebird (1-4)   **398.2**

Kimmel, E. A. Bearhead (k-3)   **398.2**

Kimmel, E. A. I-know-not-what, I-know-not-where (4-6)   **398.2**

Lent, B. Baba Yaga (k-3)   **398.2**

Lewis, J. P. The frog princess (1-4)   **398.2**

Mayer, M. Baba Yaga and Vasilisa the brave (3-5)   **398.2**

Mikolaycak, C. Babushka (k-3)   **398.2**

Morgan, P. The turnip (k-2)   **398.2**

Ransome, A. The Fool of the World and the flying ship (k-3)   **398.2**

Reyher, R. H. My mother is the most beautiful woman in the world (1-4)   **398.2**

Robbins, R. Baboushka and the three kings (1-4)   **398.2**

Werner, V. L. Petrouchka (4-6)   **398.2**

Winthrop, E. Vasilissa the beautiful (2-5)   **398.2**

Wolkstein, D. Oom Razoom (2-5)   **398.2**

Scotland

Cooper, S. Tam Lin (1-4)   **398.2**

Forest, H. The woman who flummoxed the fairies (k-3)   **398.2**

Hunter, M. Gilly Martin the Fox (k-3)   **398.2**

Van Laan, N. The tiny, tiny boy and the big, big cow (k-3)   **398.2**

Yolen, J. Tam Lin (3-6)   **398.2**

Senegal

Guy, R. Mother Crocodile (k-3)   **398.2**

Southern States

Bang, M. Wiley and the Hairy Man (1-4)   **398.2**

Grandfather tales (4 and up)   **398.2**

Harper, W. The Gunniwolf (k-1)   **398.2**

The Jack tales (4-6)   **398.2**

San Souci, R. The talking eggs (k-3)   **398.2**

Spain

Hancock, S. Esteban and the ghost (k-3)   **398.2**

Sudan

Aardema, V. What's so funny, Ketu? (k-3)   **398.2**

Sweden

Greene, E. The legend of the Christmas rose (2-4)   **398.2**

Trinidad and Tobago

Joseph, L. The mermaid's twin sister: more stories from Trinidad (4 and up)   **398.2**

Joseph, L. A wave in her pocket (4 and up)   **398.2**

Turkey

Walker, B. K. A treasury of Turkish folktales for children (4 and up)   **398.2**

Ukraine

Brett, J. The mitten (k-2)   **398.2**

Tresselt, A. R. The mitten (k-2)   **398.2**

United States

DeFelice, C. C. The dancing skeleton (k-3)   **398.2**

The Diane Goode book of American folk tales and songs (2-5)   **398.2**

Faulkner, W. J. Brer Tiger and the big wind (k-3)   **398.2**

Forest, H. The baker's dozen (k-3)   **398.2**

From sea to shining sea   **810.8**

Galdone, J. The tailypo (k-3)   **398.2**

Haley, G. E. Mountain Jack tales (4 and up)   **398.2**

Hooks, W. H. The three little pigs and the fox (k-3)   **398.2**

Lester, J. John Henry (k-3)   **398.2**

Osborne, M. P. American tall tales (3-6)   **398.2**

The **fortune-tellers**. Alexander, L. **E**

Fortune telling
> **Fiction**
Alexander, L. The fortune-tellers **E**

The **fortunes** of Madame Organza. Babbitt, N.
In Babbitt, N. The Devil's other story-book p3-9 **S C**

The **Forty** thieves
In The Blue fairy book p242-50 **398.2**

The **forty** thieves. Lang, A.
In Womenfolk and fairy tales p51-64 **398.2**

Fossil mammals
Arnold, C. Trapped in tar (3-5) **560**

Fossil plants
Henderson, D. Dinosaur tree (2-4) **560**

Fossil reptiles
> *See also* Dinosaurs
Lasky, K. Dinosaur dig (3-6) **567.9**
Lindsay, W. Barosaurus (4 and up) **567.9**
Lindsay, W. Corythosaurus (4 and up) **567.9**
Lindsay, W. Triceratops (4 and up) **567.9**
Lindsay, W. Tyrannosaurus (4 and up) **567.9**

Fossils
> *See also* Fossil mammals; Fossil reptiles; Prehistoric animals
Aliki. Dinosaur bones (k-3) **567.9**
Aliki. Fossils tell of long ago (k-3) **560**
Arnold, C. Dinosaurs down under and other fossils from Australia (4 and up) **567.9**
Cole, J. Evolution (k-3) **575**
Gibbons, G. Prehistoric animals (k-3) **560**
Gillette, J. L. The search for Seismosaurus (4-6) **567.9**
Horner, J. R. Digging up Tyrannosaurus rex (3-5) **567.9**
Lauber, P. Dinosaurs walked here, and other stories fossils tell (3-5) **560**
Lessem, D. Jack Horner: living with dinosaurs (4 and up) **92**
Lindsay, W. Prehistoric life (4 and up) **560**
Rand McNally picture atlas of prehistoric life (4 and up) **560**
Taylor, P. D. Fossil (4 and up) **560**
Thompson, S. E. Death trap (4 and up) **560**
The Visual dictionary of prehistoric life (4 and up) **560**
> *See/See also pages in the following book(s):*
Gallant, R. A. Before the sun dies p61-71 (6 and up) **575**
> **Fiction**
Carrick, C. Big old bones **E**

Fossils tell of long ago. Aliki **560**

Foster, Joanna
Cartons, cans, and orange peels (4-6) **363.7**

Foster, Leila Merrell
Iraq (4 and up) **956.7**
Lebanon (4 and up) **956.92**
Saudi Arabia (4 and up) **953.8**

Foster, Stephen Collins, 1826-1864
> *See/See also pages in the following book(s):*
Krull, K. Lives of the musicians p44-47 (4 and up) **920**

Foster home care
Banish, R. A forever family (k-3) **362.7**
> **Fiction**
Byars, B. C. The pinballs (5 and up) **Fic**
Grifalconi, A. Not home (4 and up) **Fic**
MacLachlan, P. Mama One, Mama Two **E**
Nixon, J. L. A family apart (5 and up) **Fic**
Paterson, K. The great Gilly Hopkins (5 and up) **Fic**
Sebestyen, O. Out of nowhere (5 and up) **Fic**
Thesman, J. When the road ends (5 and up) **Fic**

The **foundling**. Carrick, C. **E**

Four clever brothers. Grimm, J.
In Anno, M. Anno's twice told tales **398.2**

Four dollars and fifty cents. Kimmel, E. A. **E**

Four dolls. Godden, R. **S C**

The **four** friends. Kherdian, D.
In Kherdian, D. Feathers and tails p11-22 **398.2**

Four fur feet. Brown, M. W. **E**

Four hairs from the beard of the Devil
In The Magic orange tree, and other Haitian folktales p43-48 **398.2**

Four on the shore. Marshall, E. See note under Marshall, E. Three by the sea **E**

The **four** questions. Schwartz, L. S. **296.4**

The **four** skillful brothers. Grimm, J.
In Grimm, J. The complete Grimm's fairy tales p580-84 **398.2**

Fourth book of junior authors and illustrators **920.003**

The **fourth** day. Wilder, L. I.
In Wilder, L. I. A Little house Christmas p71-82 **S C**

Fourth of July
Giblin, J. Fireworks, picnics, and flags (3-6) **394.2**
> **Poetry**
Beat the drum (2-4) **811.008**

The **fourth** question. Wang, R. C. **398.2**

Fowler, Jim
(il) Grover, W. Dolphin adventure **599.5**

Frasconi, Antonio, 1919-
(il) If the owl calls again. See If the owl calls
again **808.81**
(il) Worth, V. At Christmastime **811**

Fraser, Betty, 1928-
(il) Simon, S. Pets in a jar **639**

Fraser, Claud Lovat, 1890-1921
See/See also pages in the following book(s):
Sendak, M. Caldecott & Co.: notes on books
and pictures p93-94 **028.5**

Fraser, Mary Ann
Sanctuary (3-5) **639.9**

Frasier, Debra, 1953-
On the day you were born (k-3) **508**

Frau Trude. Grimm, J.
In Grimm, J. The complete Grimm's
fairy tales p208-09 **398.2**

Fraud
Graham, I. Fakes and forgeries (5 and up)
001.9

Frazee, Marla
(il) Froehlich, M. W. That Kookoory! **E**

Freaky Friday. Rodgers, M. **Fic**

Freaky Friday [excerpt]. Rodgers, M.
In The Random House book of humor
for children p262-67 **817.008**

Freckle juice. Blume, J. **Fic**

Freddy and the perilous adventure. Brooks, W.
R. See note under Brooks, W. R. Freddy
goes camping **Fic**

Freddy goes camping. Brooks, W. R. **Fic**

Freddy plays football. Brooks, W. R. See note
under Brooks, W. R. Freddy goes camp-
ing **Fic**

Freddy rides again. Brooks, W. R. See note
under Brooks, W. R. Freddy goes camping **Fic**

Freddy the cowboy. Brooks, W. R. See note
under Brooks, W. R. Freddy goes camping **Fic**

Fredeen, Charles, 1956-
Kansas
In Hello USA series **973**
New Jersey
In Hello USA series **973**
South Carolina
In Hello USA series **973**

Frederick. Lionni, L. **E**

Frederick and Catherine. Grimm, J.
In Grimm, J. The complete Grimm's
fairy tales p283-89 **398.2**

Frederick Douglass and the fight for freedom.
Miller, D. T. **92**

Free fall. Wiesner, D. **E**

Free material
Educators guide to free films, filmstrips and
slides **016.3713**

The free spirits, Bouki and Malice. Hamilton,
V.
In Hamilton, V. The dark way p102-07
398.2

Free to be—you and me **810.8**

Freedman, Florence B. (Florence Bernstein)
Brothers: a Hebrew legend (k-3) **398.2**
(jt. auth) Engel, D. Ezra Jack Keats **92**

Freedman, Russell
Buffalo hunt (4 and up) **970.004**
Children of the wild West (4 and up)
978
Cowboys of the wild West (4 and up)
978
Eleanor Roosevelt (5 and up) **92**
Franklin Delano Roosevelt (5 and up)
92
Immigrant kids (4 and up) **325.73**
Indian chiefs (6 and up) **920**
An Indian winter (6 and up) **978**
Kids at work (5 and up) **331.3**
Killer snakes (2-5) **597.9**
Lincoln: a photobiography (4 and up)
92
Sharks (3-5) **597**
The Wright brothers: how they invented the
airplane (5 and up) **92**

Freedom. Sanfield, S.
In Sanfield, S. The adventures of High
John the Conqueror **398.2**

Freedom of information
See also Censorship
Weiss, A. E. Who's to know? (5 and up)
323.44

Freedom of speech
Rappaport, D. Tinker vs. Des Moines (5
and up) **342**

Freedom of the press
Weiss, A. E. Who's to know? (5 and up)
323.44

Freedom Rides. Haskins, J. **323.1**

Freedom's children. Levine, E. **323.1**

Freeman, Don, 1908-1978
Corduroy **E**
also in The Read-aloud treasury p190-206
808.8
Dandelion **E**
A pocket for Corduroy. See note under Freeman, D. Corduroy **E**

Freeman, Judy
Books kids will sit still for **011.6**
More books kids will sit still for **011.6**

Freight train. Crews, D. **E**

Frekko, Janet
(jt. auth) Katz, P. Great science fair projects
507.8

French Americans
Kunz, V. B. The French in America
In The In America series **305.8**

French and Indian War *See* United States—
History—1755-1763, French and Indian
War

French artists *See* Artists, French

French authors *See* Authors, French

French Cameroons *See* Cameroon

French-English bilingual books *See* Bilingual
books—English-French

Frogs—Fiction—*Continued*
Zemach, H. The princess and Froggie   E
A **frog's** body. Cole, J.   **597.8**
Frogs, toads, lizards, and salamanders. Parker, N. W.   **597.6**
Frolka Stay-at-Home. Afanas'ev, A. N.
   In Afanas'ev, A. N. Russian fairy tales p299-302   **398.2**
From Abenaki to Zuni. Wolfson, E.   **970.004**
From Afar to Zulu. Haskins, J.   **960**
From Anna. Little, J.   **Fic**
From flower to fruit. Dowden, A. O. T.   **582**
From hand to mouth. Giblin, J.   **394.1**
From head to toe. Kuklin, S.   **745.592**
From island to island. Cherry, L.
   In The Big book for our planet p98-106   **810.8**
From map to museum. Anderson, J.   **930.1**
From page to screen   **016.79143**
From path to highway: the story of the Boston Post Road. Gibbons, G.   **388.1**
From pictures to words. Stevens, J.   **741.6**
From sea to shining sea   **810.8**
From seed to plant. Gibbons, G.   **581**
From tadpole to frog. Pfeffer, W.   **597.8**
From the earth to beyond the sky. Wolfson, E.   **970.004**
From the mixed-up files of Mrs. Basil E. Frankweiler. Konigsburg, E. L.   **Fic**
From top hats to baseball caps, from bustles to blue jeans. Perl, L.   **391**
Froman, Nan
   (jt. auth) Reeves, C. N. Into the mummy's tomb   **932**
Frontier and pioneer life
   Aliki. The story of Johnny Appleseed (k-3)   **92**
   Anderson, W. T. Laura Ingalls Wilder (4 and up)   **92**
   Boulton, J. Only Opal   **E**
   Cobb, M. The quilt-block history of pioneer days (2-5)   **746.46**
   Conrad, P. Prairie visions: the life and times of Solomon Butcher (5 and up)   **92**
   Greenwood, B. A pioneer sampler (4 and up)   **971.3**
   Kalman, B. 19th century clothing (3-6)   **391**
   Kellogg, S. Johnny Appleseed (k-3)   **92**
   Paul, A. W. Eight hands round   **E**
   Rounds, G. Sod houses on the Great Plains (k-3)   **693**
   Walker, B. M. The Little House cookbook (5 and up)   **641.5**
Fiction
   Avi. The barn (4-6)   **Fic**
   Brenner, B. Wagon wheels   **E**
   Brink, C. R. Caddie Woodlawn (4-6)   **Fic**

Byars, B. C. The Golly sisters go West   **E**
Byars, B. C. Trouble River (4-6)   **Fic**
Calvert, P. Bigger (5 and up)   **Fic**
Conrad, P. Prairie songs (5 and up)   **Fic**
Dalgliesh, A. The courage of Sarah Noble (2-4)   **Fic**
DeFelice, C. C. Weasel (4 and up)   **Fic**
Fleischman, P. The borning room (6 and up)   **Fic**
Fleischman, S. Chancy and the grand rascal (4-6)   **Fic**
Fritz, J. The cabin faced west (3-6)   **Fic**
Gipson, F. B. Old Yeller (6 and up)   **Fic**
Harvey, B. Cassie's journey (2-4)   **Fic**
Harvey, B. My prairie Christmas (2-4)   **Fic**
Harvey, B. My prairie year (2-4)   **Fic**
Irwin, H. Jim-Dandy (5 and up)   **Fic**
Isaacs, A. Swamp Angel   **E**
Kinsey-Warnock, N. The bear that heard crying   **E**
Lawlor, L. Gold in the hills (4-6)   **Fic**
Levinson, N. S. Snowshoe Thompson   **E**
MacLachlan, P. Sarah, plain and tall (3-5)   **Fic**
MacLachlan, P. Skylark (3-5)   **Fic**
MacLachlan, P. Three Names   **E**
Nixon, J. L. Beats me, Claude   **E**
Paulsen, G. Mr. Tucket (5 and up)   **Fic**
Sanders, S. R. Aurora means dawn   **E**
Sanders, S. R. Warm as wool   **E**
Sorensen, H. New Hope   **E**
Speare, E. G. The sign of the beaver (5 and up)   **Fic**
Turner, A. W. Grasshopper summer (4-6)   **Fic**
Van Leeuwen, J. Going West   **E**
Wilder, L. I. A Little house Christmas   **S C**
Wilder, L. I. Little house in the big woods (4-6)   **Fic**
Woodruff, E. Dear Levi (4-6)   **Fic**
Poetry
Lindbergh, R. Johnny Appleseed (k-3)   **811**
California
Blake, A. The gold rush of 1849 (5 and up)   **979.4**
Blumberg, R. The great American gold rush (5 and up)   **979.4**
West (U.S.)
Bentley, J. Brides, midwives, and widows (5 and up)   **978**
Bentley, J. Explorers, trappers, and guides (5 and up)   **979.5**
Freedman, R. Children of the wild West (4 and up)   **978**
Freedman, R. Cowboys of the wild West (4 and up)   **978**
Miller, B. M. Buffalo gals (5 and up)   **978**
Tunis, E. Frontier living (5 and up)   **978**
Frontier living. Tunis, E.   **978**

Gambling Hansel. Grimm, J.
In Grimm, J. The complete Grimm's
fairy tales p378-80 **398.2**

Game protection
See also Birds—Protection

Games
See also Card games; Computer games;
Indoor games; Singing games; Sports; Video games; Word games; names of individual games
Anna Banana: 101 jump-rope rhymes (2-4)
398.8
Cole, J. Pin the tail on the donkey and other party games (k-2) **793**
Hoguet, S. R. I unpacked my grandmother's trunk **E**
Kaye, P. Games for reading **372.4**
Miss Mary Mack and other children's street rhymes **796.1**
Opie, I. A. Children's games in street and playground **796.1**
Sportworks (4 and up) **796**
Stamp your feet **796.1**

Fiction
Stevenson, J. The Mud Flat Olympics
E
Van Allsburg, C. Jumanji **E**
Wisniewski, D. Rain player **E**

Games for reading. Kaye, P. **372.4**

Games, puzzles, and toys
In Hands-on science [series] **507**

Gammell, Stephen, 1943-
(il) Ackerman, K. Song and dance man
E
(il) Aylesworth, J. Old black fly **E**
(il) Baker, O. Where the buffaloes begin
Fic
(il) Birdseye, T. Airmail to the moon **E**
(il) Blos, J. W. Old Henry **E**
(il) Dancing teepees: poems of American Indian youth. See Dancing teepees: poems of American Indian youth **897**
(il) Fritz, J. Stonewall [biography of Stonewall Jackson] **92**
(il) Gauch, P. L. Thunder at Gettysburg
Fic
(il) Halloween poems. See Halloween poems
808.81
(il) Lyon, G. E. Come a tide **E**
(il) Martin, R. Will's mammoth **E**
(il) Rosenberg, L. Monster mama **E**
(il) Rylant, C. The relatives came **E**
(il) Schwartz, A. More scary stories to tell in the dark **398.2**
(il) Schwartz, A. Scary stories 3 **398.2**
(il) Schwartz, A. Scary stories to tell in the dark **398.2**
(il) Thanksgiving poems. See Thanksgiving poems **808.81**

The **gamut** and time-table in verse. Finch, C.
In A Nursery companion p90-93
820.8

Ganeri, Anita, 1961-
Birth and growth (k-2) **612.6**

Breathing (k-2) **612.2**
Eating (k-2) **612.3**
Moving (k-2) **612.7**
The oceans atlas (5 and up) **551.46**

Ganges River valley (India and Bangladesh)
Description
Lewin, T. Sacred river (1-4) **954**

Gannett, Deborah Sampson, 1760-1827
About
McGovern, A. The secret soldier: the story of Deborah Sampson (3-5) **92**

Gannett, Ruth Chrisman, 1896-1979
(il) Gannett, R. S. My father's dragon
Fic
(il) Reyher, R. H. My mother is the most beautiful woman in the world **398.2**

Gannett, Ruth Stiles, 1923-
The dragons of Blueland. See note under Gannett, R. S. My father's dragon
Fic
Elmer and the dragon. See note under Gannett, R. S. My father's dragon **Fic**
My father's dragon (1-4) **Fic**

Gans, Roma, 1894-
Rock collecting (k-3) **552**

Gantos, Jack
Happy birthday Rotten Ralph. See note under Gantos, J. Rotten Ralph **E**
Heads or tails (5 and up) **Fic**
Not so Rotten Ralph. See note under Gantos, J. Rotten Ralph **E**
Rotten Ralph **E**
Rotten Ralph's rotten Christmas. See note under Gantos, J. Rotten Ralph **E**
Rotten Ralph's show and tell. See note under Gantos, J. Rotten Ralph **E**
Rotten Ralph's trick or treat! See note under Gantos, J. Rotten Ralph **E**
Worse than rotten, Ralph. See note under Gantos, J. Rotten Ralph **E**

The **Gaping,** wide-mouthed waddling frog
In A Nursery companion p54-57
820.8

Garage sales
Fiction
Rockwell, A. F. Our garage sale **E**

Garbage *See* Refuse and refuse disposal

Garbage!. Hadingham, E. **363.7**

Gardam, Jane
The hollow land (5 and up) **Fic**

The **garden.** Brown, M. W.
In Brown, M. W. The fish with the deep sea smile p33-38 **818**

Garden crafts for kids. Rhoades, D. **635**

Garden ecology
Godkin, C. What about ladybugs? (k-3)
595.7

The **garden** of Abdul Gasazi. Van Allsburg, C.
E

Garden pests *See* Insect pests

Gherman, Beverly
Agnes de Mille: dancing off the earth (5 and up)   **92**
E. B. White (5 and up)   **92**
The mysterious rays of Dr. Röntgen (2-4)   **92**

Ghost abbey. Westall, R.   **Fic**

The **Ghost** and the watermelon
In Raw Head, bloody bones p34-36   **398.2**

The **ghost** belonged to me. Peck, R.   **Fic**

The **ghost** comes calling. Wright, B. R.   **Fic**

Ghost dance
See/See also pages in the following book(s):
Ehrlich, A. Wounded Knee: an Indian history of the American West (6 and up)   **970.004**

The **ghost-eye** tree. Martin, B.   **E**

Ghost in the house. Cohen, D.   **133.1**

A **ghost** in the house. Wright, B. R.   **Fic**

The **ghost** in the mirror. Bellairs, J. See note under Bellairs, J. The house with a clock in its walls   **Fic**

The **ghost** log cabin. Haskins, J.
In Haskins, J. The headless haunt and other African American ghost stories p20-22   **398.2**

A **ghost** named Fred. Benchley, N.   **E**

The **ghost** of a man the Yankees killed. Haskins, J.
In Haskins, J. The headless haunt and other African American ghost stories p94-96   **398.2**

The **ghost** of Eddy Longo. Wynne-Jones, T.
In Wynne-Jones, T. The book of changes p83-108   **S C**

The **ghost** of Jean Lafitte. Schmidt, S.
In From sea to shining sea p320-21   **810.8**

The **ghost** of Misery Hill. San Souci, R.
In San Souci, R. Short & shivery p139-43   **398.2**

The **ghost** of the Yankee soldier. Haskins, J.
In Haskins, J. The headless haunt and other African American ghost stories p91-93   **398.2**

The **ghost** of Thomas Kempe. Lively, P.   **Fic**

The **ghost** on Saturday night. Fleischman, S.   **Fic**

Ghost poems (1-4)   **821.008**

The **ghost** society. Bruchac, J.
In Bruchac, J. Flying with the eagle, racing with the great bear p83-90   **398.2**

Ghost stories
Aiken, J. A foot in the grave (6 and up)   **S C**
Allard, H. Bumps in the night   **E**
Avi. Something upstairs (5 and up)   **Fic**
Benchley, N. A ghost named Fred   **E**

Bodkin, O. The Banshee train   **E**
Brown, R. One stormy night   **E**
Cassedy, S. Behind the attic wall (5 and up)   **Fic**
Clapp, P. Jane-Emily (5 and up)   **Fic**
Conrad, P. Stonewords (5 and up)   **Fic**
Diane Goode's book of scary stories & songs (2-5)   **398.2**
Dickens, C. A Christmas carol (4 and up)   **Fic**
Fleischman, S. The midnight horse (3-6)   **Fic**
Gage, W. Mrs. Gaddy and the ghost   **E**
Galdone, P. The teeny-tiny woman (k-2)   **398.2**
Hahn, M. D. The doll in the garden (4-6)   **Fic**
Hahn, M. D. Time for Andrew (5 and up)   **Fic**
Hahn, M. D. Wait till Helen comes (4-6)   **Fic**
Hancock, S. Esteban and the ghost (k-3)   **398.2**
Haskins, J. The headless haunt and other African-American ghost stories (4 and up)   **398.2**
Lively, P. The ghost of Thomas Kempe (4-6)   **Fic**
Mahy, M. Dangerous spaces (5 and up)   **Fic**
Martin, B. The ghost-eye tree   **E**
Martin, B. Old devil wind   **E**
McKissack, P. C. The dark-thirty (4 and up)   **S C**
Peck, R. The ghost belonged to me (5 and up)   **Fic**
San Souci, R. More short & shivery (4 and up)   **398.2**
Schnur, S. The shadow children (5 and up)   **Fic**
Schwartz, A. Ghosts! (k-2)   **398.2**
Schwartz, A. In a dark, dark room, and other scary stories (k-2)   **398.2**
Schwartz, A. More scary stories to tell in the dark (4 and up)   **398.2**
Schwartz, A. Scary stories 3 (4 and up)   **398.2**
Schwartz, A. Scary stories to tell in the dark (4 and up)   **398.2**
Westall, R. Ghost abbey (5 and up)   **Fic**
Wright, B. R. The ghost comes calling (4 and up)   **Fic**
Wright, B. R. A ghost in the house (4 and up)   **Fic**
Wright, B. R. The ghosts of Mercy Manor (4 and up)   **Fic**
Wright, B. R. Out of the dark (4 and up)   **Fic**
Yep, L. The man who tricked a ghost (k-3)   **398.2**

The **ghost** train. Ahlberg, A. See note under Ahlberg, J. Funnybones   **E**

The **ghostly** little girl. San Souci, R.
In San Souci, R. Short & shivery p48-52   **398.2**

The **ghostly** rhyme. Yep, L.
 In Yep, L. Tongues of jade p186-91
          398.2

Ghosts
 Cohen, D. Ghost in the house (4 and up)
          133.1
 Cohen, D. Ghosts of the deep (4 and up)
          133.1
 Cohen, D. The ghosts of war (4 and up)
          133.1
 Cohen, D. Great ghosts (4 and up)
          133.1

     Poetry
 Ghost poems (1-4)   821.008

Ghosts!. Schwartz, A.   398.2

Ghosts and souls. Belting, N. M.
 In Belting, N. M. Moon was tired of
  walking on air p29   398.2

The **ghost's** bride. Yep, L.
 In Yep, L. The rainbow people p54-59
          398.2

The **ghost's** cap. San Souci, R.
 In San Souci, R. Short & shivery p22-27
          398.2

Ghost's hour, spook's hour. Bunting, E. E

Ghosts I have been. Peck, R. See note under
 Peck, R. The ghost belonged to me
          Fic

Ghosts I have been [excerpt]. Peck, R.
 In The Random House book of humor
  for children p36-43 817.008

The **ghosts** of Cedar Creek. Haskins, J.
 In Haskins, J. The headless haunt and
  other African American ghost stories
  p88-90   398.2

The **ghosts** of Mercy Manor. Wright, B. R.
          Fic

Ghosts of the deep. Cohen, D. 133.1

The **ghosts** of war. Cohen, D. 133.1

Ghosts, vampires, and werewolves. Spariosu,
 M.   398.2

The **giant** and the tailor. Grimm, J.
 In Grimm, J. The complete Grimm's
  fairy tales p745-47 398.2

The **giant** jam sandwich. Lord, J. V. E

The **giant** Og and the ark. Schwartz, H.
 In Schwartz, H. The diamond tree p13-20
          398.2

Giant panda
 Arnold, C. Panda (3-5)   599.74
 Greenaway, T. Amazing bears (2-4)
          599.74
 McClung, R. M. Lili: a giant panda of Sich-
  uan (3-6)   599.74
 Schlein, M. Project panda watch (4 and up)
          599.74

The **giant** who threw tantrums. Harrison, D.
 L.
 In The Oxford treasury of children's sto-
  ries p28-32   S C

Giants
 See also Cyclopes (Greek mythology)

     Fiction
 Dahl, R. The BFG (4-6)   Fic
 Kellogg, S. Jack and the beanstalk (k-3)
          398.2
 Wilde, O. The selfish giant (2-5) Fic

The **Giants** and the herd-boy
 In The Yellow fairy book p75-77
          398.2

Giants in the land. Appelbaum, D. K.
          634.9

Gib Morgan brings in the well. Walker, P. R.
 In Walker, P. R. Big men, big country
  p62-68   398.2

Gibbons, Gail
 Beacons of light: lighthouses (k-3) 387.1
 Boat book (k-3)   387.2
 Catch the wind! (k-3)   796.1
 Check it out! the book about libraries (k-3)
          027
 Easter (k-3)   394.2
 Emergency! (k-3)   363.3
 Farming (k-3)   630.1
 Fill it up! (k-3)   629.28
 Fire! Fire! (k-3)   363.3
 Flying (k-3)   629.13
 Frogs (k-3)   597.8
 From path to highway: the story of the Bos-
  ton Post Road (k-3) 388.1
 From seed to plant (k-3)   581
 The great St. Lawrence Seaway (k-3)
          386
 Halloween (k-3)   394.2
 Happy birthday! (k-3)   394.2
 How a house is built (k-3) 690
 Lights! Camera! Action! (k-3) 791.43
 The milk makers (k-3)   637
 Monarch butterfly (k-3) 595.7
 Nature's green umbrella (k-3) 574.5
 New road! (k-3)   625.7
 The planets (k-3)   523.4
 Playgrounds (k-3)   796
 Prehistoric animals (k-3) 560
 Puff—flash—bang! (k-3) 302.2
 The puffins are back! (k-3) 598
 The reasons for seasons (k-3) 525
 Recycle! (k-3)   363.7
 Sea turtles (k-3)   597.9
 The seasons of Arnold's apple tree E
 Sharks (k-3)   597
 St. Patrick's Day (k-3)   394.2
 Sun up, sun down (k-3) 523.7
 Sunken treasure (k-3)   910.4
 Surrounded by sea (k-3) 974.1
 Thanksgiving Day (k-3) 394.2
 Tool book (k-3)   621.9
 Trains (k-3)   625.1
 Tunnels (k-3)   624.1
 Up goes the skyscraper! (k-3) 690
 Valentine's Day (k-3)   394.2
 Weather forecasting (k-3) 551.6
 Weather words and what they mean (k-3)
          551.6
 Whales (k-3)   599.5
 Wolves (k-3)   599.74
 Zoo (k-3)   590.74

Gilson, Jamie, 1933-—_Continued_
Hobie Hanson, greatest hero of the mall.
See note under Gilson, J. 4B goes wild
Fic
Hobie Hanson, you're weird. See note under
Gilson, J. 4B goes wild **Fic**
It goes eeeeeeeeeeeee! See note under Gil-
son, J. Itchy Richard **Fic**
Itchy Richard (2-4) **Fic**
Soccer circus. See note under Gilson, J. 4B
goes wild **Fic**
Sticks and stones and skeleton bones. See
note under Gilson, J. 4B goes wild
Fic
Thirteen ways to sink a sub. See note under
Gilson, J. 4B goes wild **Fic**
Ginger for the heart. Yee, P.
_In_ Yee, P. Tales from Gold Mountain
p33-38 **S C**
Ginger Pye. Estes, E. **Fic**
Gingerbread boy
_In_ The Tall book of nursery tales p16-22
398.2
The **gingerbread** boy. Galdone, P. **398.2**
The **Gingerbread** man
_In_ The Read-aloud treasury p135-43
808.8
The **gingerbread** man. Kimmel, E. A.
398.2
Gingerbread man. Pooley, S.
_In_ Pooley, S. It's raining, it's pouring p10-
13 **808.8**
The **gingi.** McKissack, P. C.
_In_ McKissack, P. C. The dark-thirty p95-
110 **S C**
Ginsburg, Max
(il) Taylor, M. D. The friendship **Fic**
(il) Taylor, M. D. Mississippi bridge
Fic
Ginsburg, Mirra
Asleep, asleep **E**
The chick and the duckling **E**
The Chinese mirror (k-3) **398.2**
Good morning, chick **E**
Merry-go-round (k-2) **398.2**
Contents: The strongest one of all; What kind of bird is
that?; Where does the sun go at night?; The fox and the
hare
Ginsburg, Ruth Bader
About
Roberts, J. L. Ruth Bader Ginsburg (3-5)
92
Giovanni, Nikki
Ego-tripping and other poems for young
people (5 and up) **811**
Knoxville, Tennessee (k-3) **811**
Spin a soft black song: poems for children
(3-6) **811**
Giovanopoulos, Paul
(il) LeShan, E. J. Learning to say good-by
155.9
Gipsies _See_ Gypsies
Gipson, Frederick Benjamin, 1903-1973
Old Yeller (6 and up) **Fic**

Giraffes
Arnold, C. Giraffe (3-5) **599.73**
Sattler, H. R. Giraffes (5 and up)
599.73
See/See also pages in the following book(s):
Thomson, P. Auks, rocks and the odd dino-
saur p27-31 (5 and up) **508**
The **girl** and the Chenoo. Bruchac, J.
_In_ Bruchac, J. The girl who married the
Moon p29-36 **398.2**
The **girl** and the plat-eye. Haskins, J.
_In_ Haskins, J. The headless haunt and
other African American ghost stories
p70-72 **398.2**
A **girl** called Al. Greene, C. C. **Fic**
A **girl** named Silver Pitchers tells a story
about Egypt, Jesse James and Spanish on-
ions. Sandburg, C.
_In_ Sandburg, C. More rootabagas p9-18
S C
Girl Scouts
World Association of Girl Guides and Girl
Scouts. Trefoil round the world
369.463
The **girl-son.** Neuberger, A. E. **Fic**
The **girl** who could fly. Hooks, W. H. **Fic**
The **Girl** who could think
_In_ Windy day: stories and poems p2-9
808.8
The **girl** who escaped. Bruchac, J.
_In_ Bruchac, J. The girl who married the
Moon p37-43 **398.2**
The **girl** who gave birth to Water-Jar Boy.
Bruchac, J.
_In_ Bruchac, J. The girl who married the
Moon p69-74 **398.2**
The **girl** who helped Thunder. Bruchac, J.
_In_ Bruchac, J. The girl who married the
Moon p51-54 **398.2**
The **Girl** Who Loved Caterpillars. Merrill, J.
E
The **girl** who loved the wind. Yolen, J. **E**
The **girl** who loved wild horses. Goble, P.
E
The **girl** who married an Osage. Bruchac, J.
_In_ Bruchac, J. The girl who married the
Moon p55-57 **398.2**
The **girl** who married the Moon. Bruchac, J.
398.2
The **girl** who married the Moon [story].
Bruchac, J.
_In_ Bruchac, J. The girl who married the
Moon p116-22 **398.2**
The **girl** who was swallowed by the earth.
Hamilton, V.
_In_ Hamilton, V. The dark way p108-12
398.2
The **girl** with the green ear. Mahy, M.
S C
The **girl** with the green ear [story]. Mahy, M.
_In_ Mahy, M. The girl with the green ear
p11-28 **S C**

The **girl** with the silver eyes. Roberts, W. D.
        Fic
The **girl** without hands. Grimm, J.
  In Grimm, J. The complete Grimm's
    fairy tales p160-66   **398.2**
Girls
        Employment
  See Children—Employment
        Poetry
  Nash, O. The adventures of Isabel (k-3)
        811
Girls' clubs
  See also Girl Scouts
The **girls** who almost married an owl.
  Bruchac, J.
  In Bruchac, J. The girl who married the
    Moon p58-61   **398.2**
GIs *See* Soldiers—United States
Giselle (Ballet)
  See/See also pages in the following book(s):
  McCaughrean, G. The Random House book
    of stories from the ballet p29-35 (4 and
    up)   **792.8**
Gish, Lillian, 1893-1993
  An actor's life for me (3-5)   **92**
Githens, Elizabeth M.
  (il) Cooper, L. P. Fun with German
        438
Give us a great big smile, Rosy Cole. Green-
  wald, S.   **Fic**
Give yourself a fright. Aiken, J.
  In Aiken, J. Give yourself a fright: thir-
    teen tales of the supernatural p160-80
        S C
Give yourself a fright: thirteen tales of the su-
  pernatural. Aiken, J.   **S C**
Giveaways *See* Free material
The **giver.** Lowry, L.   **Fic**
Giving. Hughes, S. See note under Hughes, S.
  Bouncing   **E**
The **Gizzard**
  In The Magic orange tree, and other Hai-
    tian folktales p99-112   **398.2**
Glacier National Park (Mont.)
  Patent, D. H. Where the bald eagles gather
    (4 and up)   **598**
Glaciers
  Bramwell, M. Glaciers and ice caps (4-6)
        551.3
  Simon, S. Icebergs and glaciers (3-5)
        551.3
  Walker, S. M. Glaciers (3-6)   **551.3**
Glaciers and ice caps. Bramwell, M.
        551.3
Glanzman, Louis S., 1922-
  (il) Lindgren, A. Pippi Longstocking   **Fic**
Glaser, Byron
  (jt. auth) Neumeier, M. Action alphabet
        E
Glass, Andrew
  (il) Brittain, B. Devil's donkey   **Fic**
  (il) Carlson, N. S. Spooky night   **E**

  (il) Fleischman, P. Graven images
        S C
  (il) San Souci, R. Larger than life   **398.2**
The **glass** coffin. Grimm, J.
  In Grimm, J. The complete Grimm's
    fairy tales p672-78   **398.2**
The **Glass** mountain
  In The Yellow fairy book p114-18
        398.2
The **glass** slipper. Farjeon, E.   **Fic**
Glasses: who needs 'em?. Smith, L.   **E**
Glazer, Tom
  Tom Glazer's Treasury of songs for children
    (3-5)   **782.42**
Gleeson, Brian
  Ride 'em, round 'em, rope 'em: the story of
    Pecos Bill
  In From sea to shining sea p286-88
        810.8
Global warming *See* Greenhouse effect
Global warming. Pringle, L. P.   **363.7**
Glockner-Ferrari, Deborah A.
  (il) Patent, D. H. Humpback whales
        599.5
Glooskap gets two surprises. Norman, H.
  In Norman, H. How Glooskap outwits
    the Ice Giants, and other tales of the
    Maritime Indians p29-37   **398.2**
Gloria. Wynne-Jones, T.
  In Wynne-Jones, T. The book of changes
    p134-43   **S C**
The **glorious** flight: across the Channel with
  Louis Blériot, July 25, 1909. Provensen,
  A.   **92**
The **Glorious** Mother Goose (k-2)   **398.8**
Glossaries *See* Encyclopedias and dictionaries
Glosskap and Wasis. Garner, A.
  In From sea to shining sea p210-11
        810.8
Glubok, Shirley, 1933-
  Olympic games in ancient Greece (5 and up)
        796.48
Gluskabe and the four wishes. Bruchac, J.
        398.2
GM *See* General Motors Corp.
The **gnome.** Grimm, J.
  In Grimm, J. The complete Grimm's
    fairy tales p420-24   **398.2**
Gnus
  Lindblad, L. The Serengeti migration (3-6)
        599.73
Go and hush the baby. Byars, B. C.   **E**
Go away, big green monster!. Emberley, E.
        E
Go away, dog. Lexau, J. M.   **E**
Go fish. Stolz, M.   **Fic**
Go for it! series
  Gutman, B. Field hockey   **796.35**
  Gutman, B. Wrestling   **796.8**
Go free or die: a story about Harriet Tubman.
  Ferris, J.   **92**

Golden guide [series]—*Continued*
Reid, G. K. Pond life   **574.92**
Zim, H. S. Birds   **598**
Zim, H. S. Fishes   **597**
Zim, H. S. Flowers   **582.13**
Zim, H. S. Insects   **595.7**
Zim, H. S. Mammals   **599**
Zim, H. S. Rocks and minerals   **549**
Zim, H. S. Seashores   **574.92**
Zim, H. S. Trees   **582.16**

The **golden** key. Grimm, J.
In Grimm, J. The complete Grimm's
fairy tales p812   **398.2**

The **golden** lads. Grimm, J.
In The Green fairy book p311-18
    398.2

The **golden** lion tamarin comes home. Ancona, G.   **639.9**

Golden Lion Tamarin Conservation Program
Ancona, G. The golden lion tamarin comes
home (3-5)   **639.9**

The **golden** mermaid Grimm, J.
In The Green fairy book p328-38
    398.2

The **golden** slipper. Afanas'ev, A. N.
In Afanas'ev, A. N. Russian fairy tales
p44-46   **398.2**

The **golden** snuff-box. Reeves, J.
In Reeves, J. English fables and fairy stories p157-76   **398.2**

Golden windows. 1910. Geras, A.
In Geras, A. Golden windows and other
stories of Jerusalem p1-31   **S C**

Golden windows and other stories of Jerusalem. Geras, A.   **S C**

The **goldfish**. Afanas'ev, A. N.
In Afanas'ev, A. N. Russian fairy tales
p528-32   **398.2**

Goldilocks and the three bears
In The Read-aloud treasury p214-24
    808.8

Goldilocks and the three bears. Crossley-
Holland, K.
In Crossley-Holland, K. British folk tales
p135-39   **398.2**

Goldilocks and the three bears. Marshall, J.
    398.2

Goldin, Barbara Diamond
Cakes and miracles   **E**
Just enough is plenty: a Hanukkah tale
    E
The magician's visit   **E**
The Passover journey (4 and up)   **296.4**
The world's birthday   **E**

Goldish, Meish
Crisis in Haiti (5 and up)   **972.94**

Goldman, Emma, 1869-1940
See/See also pages in the following book(s):
Jacobs, W. J. Great lives: human rights
p191-98 (5 and up)   **920**

Goldner, Kathryn Allen
(jt. auth) Vogel, C. G. The great Yellowstone fire   **574.5**

Goldsmith, Diane Hoyt- *See* Hoyt-Goldsmith,
Diane

Goldstein, Bobbye S.
(il) Birthday rhymes, special times. See
Birthday rhymes, special times
    811.008

The **golem**. San Souci, R.
In San Souci, R. Short & shivery p149-54
    398.2

Golembe, Carla
(il) Gerson, M.-J. Why the sky is far away
    398.2
(il) Johnson, J. W. The creation   **811**

Golenbock, Peter, 1946-
Teammates [biography of Jackie Robinson]
(1-4)   **92**

Golf
Jensen, J. Beginning golf (3-5)   **796.352**
Krause, P. Fundamental golf (5 and up)
    796.352

Goliath (Biblical figure)
About
Fisher, L. E. David and Goliath (k-3)
    222

Gollub, Matthew, 1960-
The twenty-five Mixtec cats   **E**

The **Golly** sisters go West. Byars, B. C.   **E**

The **Golly** sisters ride again. Byars, B. C. See
note under Byars, B. C. The Golly sisters
go West   **E**

Gompers, Samuel, 1850-1924
See/See also pages in the following book(s):
Jacobs, W. J. Great lives: human rights
p165-72 (5 and up)   **920**

Gone-Away Lake. Enright, E.   **Fic**

Gonna sing my head off!   **782.42**

González, Lucía M.
El gallo de bodas: the rooster on the way to
the wedding
In From sea to shining sea p364-65
    810.8
Juan Bobo and the buñuelos
In From sea to shining sea p240-41
    810.8

Good advice. Afanas'ev, A. N.
In Afanas'ev, A. N. Russian fairy tales
p289-91   **398.2**

Good and evil
Fiction
Briggs, K. M. Kate Crackernuts (6 and up)
    Fic
Cooper, S. The grey king (5 and up)
    Fic
Cooper, S. Over sea, under stone (5 and up)
    Fic
Cormier, R. Tunes for bears to dance to (6
and up)   **Fic**

The **good** bargain. Grimm, J.
In Grimm, J. The complete Grimm's
fairy tales p51-55   **398.2**

The **graveyard** jumbies. Joseph, L.
 In Joseph, L. A wave in her pocket p13-
 19 **398.2**

Graveyards *See* Cemeteries

Gravitation
 Branley, F. M. Gravity is a mystery (k-3)
 531
 Skurzynski, G. Zero gravity (2-4) **531**
 Experiments
 Ardley, N. The science book of gravity (3-5)
 531
 White, L. B. Gravity (2-4) **507.8**

Gravity is a mystery. Branley, F. M. **531**

Gray, Elizabeth Janet *See* Vining, Elizabeth
 Gray, 1902-

Gray, Libba Moore
 My mama had a dancing heart **E**
 Small Green Snake **E**

Gray, Luli
 Falcon's egg (3-5) **Fic**

Gray wolf, red wolf. Patent, D. H. **599.74**

Grayson, Marion F., 1906-1976
 Let's do fingerplays **796.1**

Great African Americans [series]
 McKissack, P. C. Booker T. Washington
 92
 McKissack, P. C. Madam C.J. Walker
 92
 McKissack, P. C. Sojourner Truth **92**

The **great** American gold rush. Blumberg, R.
 979.4

The **great** ancestor hunt. Perl, L. **929**

Great-aunts *See* Aunts

The **great** ball game. Bruchac, J. **398.2**

Great Barrier Reef (Australia)
 Arnold, C. A walk on the Great Barrier Reef
 (3-5) **574.92**
 Johnson, R. L. The Great Barrier Reef (5
 and up) **574.92**
 McGovern, A. Down under, down under
 (3-6) **574.92**

The **great** big especially beautiful Easter egg.
 Stevenson, J. See note under Stevenson, J.
 "Could be worse!" **E**

A **Great** big ugly man came up and tied his
 horse to me (k-3) **821.008**

The **Great Brain**. Fitzgerald, J. D. **Fic**

The **Great Brain** at the academy. Fitzgerald, J.
 D. See note under Fitzgerald, J. D. The
 Great Brain **Fic**

The **Great Brain** does it again. Fitzgerald, J.
 D. See note under Fitzgerald, J. D. The
 Great Brain **Fic**

The **Great Brain** is back. Fitzgerald, J. D. See
 note under Fitzgerald, J. D. The Great
 Brain **Fic**

The **Great Brain** reforms. Fitzgerald, J. D. See
 note under Fitzgerald, J. D. The Great
 Brain **Fic**

Great Britain
 See also England

Fiction
 Aiken, J. Midnight is a place (5 and up)
 Fic
 Aiken, J. The wolves of Willoughby Chase
 (5 and up) **Fic**
 Bagnold, E. National Velvet (5 and up)
 Fic
 Bond, M. A bear called Paddington (2-5)
 Fic
 Bond, M. Paddington's storybook (2-5)
 S C
 Boston, L. M. The children of Green Knowe
 (4-6) **Fic**
 Burnett, F. H. A little princess (4-6) **Fic**
 Cooper, S. Dawn of fear (5 and up) **Fic**
 Cooper, S. Over sea, under stone (5 and up)
 Fic
 Cushman, K. Catherine, called Birdy (6 and
 up) **Fic**
 Cushman, K. The midwife's apprentice (6
 and up) **Fic**
 De Angeli, M. L. The door in the wall (4-6)
 Fic
 Dickens, C. A Christmas carol (4 and up)
 Fic
 Gardam, J. The hollow land (5 and up)
 Fic
 King-Smith, D. Pigs might fly (3-5) **Fic**
 King-Smith, D. Sophie's Tom (3-5) **Fic**
 Lively, P. The ghost of Thomas Kempe
 (4-6) **Fic**
 Magorian, M. Good night, Mr. Tom (6 and
 up) **Fic**
 McKay, H. Dog Friday (4-6) **Fic**
 Nesbit, E. The enchanted castle (4-6)
 Fic
 Nesbit, E. The railway children (4-6)
 Fic
 Pope, E. M. The Perilous Gard (6 and up)
 Fic
 Sewell, A. Black Beauty (4-6) **Fic**
 Streatfeild, N. Theatre shoes, or other peo-
 ple's shoes (5 and up) **Fic**
 Tomlinson, T. The Forestwife (6 and up)
 Fic
 Vining, E. G. Adam of the road (5 and up)
 Fic
 Waugh, S. The Mennyms (5 and up)
 Fic
 Westall, R. Ghost abbey (5 and up) **Fic**
 Westall, R. The machine gunners (6 and up)
 Fic
 Wiseman, D. Jeremy Visick (5 and up)
 Fic

Folklore
 See Folklore—Great Britain
 History—0-1066—Fiction
 Sutcliff, R. Flame-colored taffeta (5 and up)
 Fic

 History—1485-1603, Tudors—Fiction
 Stolz, M. Bartholomew Fair (5 and up)
 Fic

 History—1800-1899 (19th century)
 See also Industrial revolution

Gryski, Camilla, 1948——*Continued*
Many stars & more string games (4-6)
793.9
Super string games (4-6) **793.9**

Guam

Fiction

Kerley, B. Songs of Papa's island (3-5)
Fic

The **guardians**. Yep, L.
In Yep, L. Tongues of jade p16-25
398.2

Guardians of the gate. Carpenter, F.
In Carpenter, F. Tales of a Chinese grandmother p47-55 **398.2**

Guarino, Deborah, 1954-
Is your mama a llama? **E**

Guatemala

Fiction

Cameron, A. The most beautiful place in the world (2-4) **Fic**
Castañeda, O. S. Abuela's weave **E**

Guback, Georgia
Luka's quilt **E**

Guess, George *See* Sequoyah, 1770?-1843

Guess again: more weird & wacky inventions. Murphy, J. **609**

Guess how much I love you. McBratney, S.
E

Guess who?. Miller, M. **E**

Guests. Paterson, K.
In Paterson, K. Angels & other strangers: family Christmas stories p17-25 **S C**

Guevara, Susan
(il) Soto, G. Chato's kitchen **E**

Guiberson, Brenda Z.
Cactus hotel (k-3) **583**
Lobster boat **E**
Salmon story (3-5) **597**
Spoonbill swamp (k-3) **591.5**
Spotted owl (3-5) **598**

A **guide** dog goes to school. Smith, E. S.
362.4

A **guide** dog puppy grows up. Arnold, C.
362.4

Guide dogs
Alexander, S. H. Mom's best friend (3-5)
362.4
Arnold, C. A guide dog puppy grows up (3-5) **362.4**
Smith, E. S. A guide dog goes to school (3-5) **362.4**
See/See also pages in the following book(s):
Silverstein, A. Dogs: all about them p188-96 (5 and up) **636.7**

Guide to reference books for school media centers. Nichols, M. I. **011.6**

Guinea fowl

Fiction

Knutson, B. How the guinea fowl got her spots (k-3) **398.2**

Guinea Fowl and Rabbit get justice. Courlander, H.
In Courlander, H. The cow-tail switch, and other West African stories p87-94
398.2

The **guinea** pig ABC. Duke, K. **E**

Guinea pigs
Bare, C. S. Guinea pigs don't read books (k-2) **636.088**
Duke, K. The guinea pig ABC **E**
Hansen, E. Guinea pigs (3-6) **636.088**
King-Smith, D. I love guinea pigs (k-3)
636.088

Fiction

Bond, M. The tales of Olga da Polga (2-5)
Fic

Guinea pigs don't read books. Bare, C. S.
636.088

Guinea pigs far and near. Duke, K. See note under Duke, K. The guinea pig ABC
E

The **Guinness** book of answers **032.02**

Guinness book of records **032.02**

The **Guinness** book of sports records **796**

Guinness book of world records. See Guinness book of records **032.02**

Guinness sports record book. See The Guinness book of sports records **796**

Gulliver in Lilliput. Hodges, M. **Fic**

Gundersheimer, Karen, 1939-
(il) Calmenson, S. What am I? **793.73**
(il) Hest, A. The midnight eaters **E**

The **Gunniwolf**. Harper, W. **398.2**

The **gunny** wolf. MacDonald, M. R.
In MacDonald, M. R. Twenty tellable tales p68-74 **372.6**

Gustafson, Dana
(il) Haskins, J. Count your way through the Arab world **909**

Gustafson, John
Stars, clusters, and galaxies (4 and up)
523.8

Gustafson, Scott, 1956-
(il) Moore, C. C. The night before Christmas
811

Gutenberg, Johann, 1397?-1468

About

Fisher, L. E. Gutenberg (3-5) **92**

Guthrie, Marjorie Mazia, d. 1983
(jt. auth) Guthrie, W. Woody's 20 grow big songs **782.42**

Guthrie, Woody, 1912-1967
Woody's 20 grow big songs **782.42**
See/See also pages in the following book(s):
Krull, K. Lives of the musicians p90-93 (4 and up) **920**

Gutierrez, Alan
(il) Oppenheim, J. Oceanarium **591.92**

Gutman, Bill
Field hockey (4-6) **796.35**
Wrestling (4-6) **796.8**

Hahn, Mary Downing, 1937-
Daphne's book (5 and up)   **Fic**
The dead man in Indian Creek (5 and up)
     Fic
December stillness (6 and up)   **Fic**
The doll in the garden (4-6)   **Fic**
Stepping on the cracks (5 and up)   **Fic**
Time for Andrew (5 and up)   **Fic**
Wait till Helen comes (4-6)   **Fic**

Haiku
Lewis, J. P. Black swan/white crow   **811**
Red dragonfly on my shoulder   **895.6**

Hail
Branley, F. M. Rain & hail (k-3)   **551.57**

Hailstones and halibut bones. O'Neill, M. L.
D.   **811**

Haing S. Ngor *See* Ngor, Haing S.

Hair
Patent, D. H. Why mammals have fur (4
and up)   **599**
     Fiction
Yarbrough, C. Cornrows   **E**

Hairston, Martha
(il) Burns, M. The I hate mathematics! book
     513

The **Hairy** toe, a story
In Halloween: stories and poems p20-21
     808.8

Haiti
Cheong-Lum, R. N. Haiti (5 and up)
     972.94
Goldish, M. Crisis in Haiti (5 and up)
     972.94
     Fiction
Robinet, H. G. If you please, President Lin-
coln (5 and up)   **Fic**
Temple, F. Tonight, by sea (6 and up)
     Fic
     Folklore
See Folklore—Haiti

Haitian Americans
     Fiction
Greenberg, M. H. Aunt Lilly's laundromat
     E

Hakim, Joy
A history of US (6 and up)   **973**
Titles in series are: The first Americans; Making thirteen
colonies; From colonies to country; The new nation; Liberty
for all?; War, terrible war; Reconstruction and reform; An
age of extremes; War, peace, and all that jazz; All the people

Haldane, Suzanne
Helping hands (4 and up)   **362.4**
Painting faces (4-6)   **745.5**

Hale, Christy
(il) Swenson, M. The complete poems to
solve   **811**

Hale, James Graham
(il) Turner, A. W. Through moon and stars
and night skies   **E**
(il) Zoehfeld, K. W. How mountains are
made   **551.4**

Hale, Lucretia Peabody, 1820-1900
The Peterkins' Christmas tree
In Diane Goode's American Christmas
p11-15   **810.8**

Hale, Sarah Josepha
Mary had a little lamb (k-2)   **811**

Haley, Gail E.
Mountain Jack tales (4 and up)   **398.2**
Contents: Poppyseed's invitation; Jack and the Northwest
Wind; The lion and the unicorn; The longest story; Jack
and Catherine; Jack and Uncle Thimblewit; Jack and the
flying ship; Jack of Hearts and King Marock; Muncimeg
and the giant; Jack and Old Raggedy Bones
A story, a story (k-3)   **398.2**
(il) Konigsburg, E. L. Altogether, one at a
time   **S C**
See/See also pages in the following book(s):
Newbery and Caldecott Medal books, 1966-
1975 p223-29, 232-35   **028.5**

Half-a-Ball-of-Kenki. Aardema, V.
In Aardema, V. Misoso p25-31   **398.2**

Half a moon and one whole star. Dragonwagon, C.   **E**

The **Half-a-Moon** Inn. Fleischman, P.   **Fic**

The **Half-chick**
In The Green fairy book p27-31
     398.2

Half-chick. See Barnes, H. The proud cock

The **half-clad** ghost. Haskins, J.
In Haskins, J. The headless haunt and
other African American ghost stories
p73-74   **398.2**

Half magic. Eager, E.   **Fic**

Half magic [excerpt]. Eager, E.
In The Random House book of humor
for children p154-72   **817.008**

Halfway home. Rylant, C.
In Rylant, C. Children of Christmas p6-12
     S C

Halfway to your house. Pomerantz, C.
     811

Hall, Donald, 1928-
I am the dog, I am the cat   **E**
Lucy's Christmas   **E**
Ox-cart man   **E**
(ed) The Oxford book of children's verse in
America. See The Oxford book of chil-
dren's verse in America   **811.008**

Hall, Katy, 1947-
Snakey riddles (k-2)   **793.73**

Hall, Lynn, 1937-
Dagmar Schultz and the angel Edna (6 and
up)   **Fic**
Dagmar Schultz and the powers of darkness.
See note under Hall, L. Dagmar Schultz
and the angel Edna   **Fic**
The secret of life of Dagmar Schultz. See
note under Hall, L. Dagmar Schultz and
the angel Edna   **Fic**

Hall, Melanie W.
(il) Weather. See Weather   **811.008**

Hamilton, Virginia, 1936-
The all Jahdu storybook (4-6) **S C**
Contents: How Jahdu found his power; How Jahdu took care of trouble; How Jahdu outwits Young Owl; How Jahdu changed Grass and fixed Old Ocean; How Jahdu became a boy; Jahdu in a little bit of trouble; How Jahdu lost his voice; How Jahdu uncovered CIGAM; Jahdu in the far woods; Jahdu meets the big chicken; Jahdu runs through the dark; How Jahdu found what he wished he hadn't; Jahdu lights the way; Jahdu becomes another boy; Jahdu sees the true light

Anthony Burns: the defeat and triumph of a fugitive slave (5 and up) **92**
The bells of Christmas (4-6) **Fic**
Cousins (5 and up) **Fic**
The dark way (4 and up) **398.2**
Contents: The Banshee; Rolling Rio, the gray man, and Death; Baba Yaga, the terrible; The One-Inch Boy; Manabozo; The horned women; The Flying Dutchman; Medusa; The wicked stepmother; The tiny thing; The pretender; Childe Rowland and Burd Ellen; Everlasting life; Tanuki magic teakettle; Fenris, the wolf; Joseph Golem; The very large son; The free spirits, Bouki and Malice; The girl who was swallowed by the earth; The witch's boar; The argument; The magician's fellow; Brothers and bone; Yama, the God of Death; The witch's skinny

Drylongso (3-5) **Fic**
Her stories (4 and up) **398.2**
Includes the following stories: Little Girl and Buh Rabby; Lena and Big One Tiger; Marie and Redfish; Miz Hattie gets some company; Catskinella; Good Blanche, bad Rose, and the talking eggs; Mary Belle and the mermaid; Mom Bett and the little ones a-glowing; Who you!; Macie and boo hag; Lonna and Cat Woman; Malindy and little devil; Woman and Man started even; Luella and the tame parrot; The mer-woman out of the sea; Annie Christmas

The house of Dies Drear (5 and up) **Fic**
In the beginning; creation stories from around the world (5 and up) **291**
M. C. Higgins the great (6 and up) **Fic**
Many thousand gone (5 and up) **326**
The mystery of Drear House (5 and up) **Fic**
The peculiar such thing
In From sea to shining sea p338-39 **810.8**
The people could fly [story]
In From sea to shining sea p144-47 **810.8**
The people could fly: American black folktales (4 and up) **398.2**
Contents: He Lion, Bruh Bear and Bruh Rabbit; Doc Rabbit, Bruh Fox, and Tar Baby; Tappin, the land turtle; Bruh Alligator and Bruh Deer; Bruh Lizard and Bruh Rabbit; Bruh Alligator meets Trouble; Wolf and birds and the Fish-Horse; The beautiful girl of the moon tower; A wolf and Little Daughter; Manuel had a riddle; Papa John's tall tale; The two Johns; Wiley, his mama, and the Hairy Man; John and the Devil's daughter; The peculiar such thing; Little Eight John; Jack and the Devil; Better wait till Martin comes; Carrying the running-aways; How Nehemiah got free; The talking cooter; The riddle tale of freedom; The most useful slave; The people could fly

Plain City (5 and up) **Fic**
The planet of Junior Brown (6 and up) **Fic**
Willie Bea and the time the Martians landed (5 and up) **Fic**
Zeely (4 and up) **Fic**
See/See also pages in the following book(s):
Newbery and Caldecott Medal books, 1966-1975 p129-40 **028.5**

Hamley, Dennis, 1935-
Supermarket
In The Oxford book of scary tales p106-11 **808.8**
Hamlin, Janet
(il) Lessem, D. Jack Horner: living with dinosaurs **92**
Hamsters
Silverstein, A. Hamsters: all about them (5 and up) **636.088**
Han, Suzanne Crowder, 1953-
The rabbit's escape (k-3) **398.2**
Hancock, John, 1737-1793
About
Fritz, J. Will you sign here, John Hancock? (2-4) **92**
Hancock, Sibyl
Esteban and the ghost (k-3) **398.2**
Hand
Aliki. My hands (k-1) **612**
Hand, heart, & mind. Walker, L. A. **371.9**
Hand in hand (4 and up) **811.008**
Hand rhymes. Brown, M. T. **796.1**
Handbook for storytellers. See Bauer, C. F. Caroline Feller Bauer's new handbook for storytellers **372.6**
Handedness See Left- and right-handedness
Handel, George Frideric, 1685-1759
About
Venezia, M. George Handel (k-3) **92**
Handelsman, J. B.
(il) Fritz, J. Who's that stepping on Plymouth Rock? **974.4**
Handforth, Thomas, 1897-1948
See/See also pages in the following book(s):
Caldecott Medal books, 1938-1957 p23-43 **028.5**
A **handful** of thieves. Bawden, N. **Fic**
Handicapped
See also Mentally handicapped; Physically handicapped
Bibliography
Friedberg, J. B. Portraying persons with disabilities: an annotated bibliography of nonfiction for children and teenagers **016**
Fiction
Thesman, J. When the road ends (5 and up) **Fic**
Fiction—Bibliography
Baskin, B. H. More notes from a different drummer **016.8**
Baskin, B. H. Notes from a different drummer **016.8**
Robertson, D. Portraying persons with disabilities: an annotated bibliography of fiction for children and teenagers **016.8**
Handicapped and animals See Animals and the handicapped
Handicapped children
See also Mentally handicapped children; Physically handicapped children

The **Hedley** Kow. Jacobs, J.
In Jacobs, J. English fairy tales p271-74
398.2

Heide, Dirk van der *See* Young, Stanley, 1906-1975

Heide, Florence Parry, 1919-
Chester
In Thanksgiving: stories and poems p49-50 **810.8**
The day of Ahmed's secret **E**
Grim and ghastly goings-on **811**
Sami and the time of the troubles **E**
The shrinking of Treehorn (2-5) **Fic**
also in The Oxford treasury of children's stories p135-43 **S C**
Treehorn's wish. See note under Heide, F. P. The shrinking of Treehorn **Fic**

Heidi. Spyri, J. **Fic**

Heidi. Thane, A.
In Thane, A. Plays from famous stories and fairy tales p315-34 **812**

The **Heifer** hide
In The Jack tales p161-71 **398.2**

Heilbroner, Joan, 1922-
This is the house where Jack lives **E**

Heine, Helme
Friends **E**
Friends go adventuring. See note under Heine, H. Friends **E**
The most wonderful egg in the world **E**

Heinrichs, Ann
Alaska
In America the beautiful **973**
Arizona
In America the beautiful **973**
Arkansas
In America the beautiful **973**
Montana
In America the beautiful **973**
Oklahoma
In America the beautiful **973**
Rhode Island
In America the beautiful **973**
Wyoming
In America the beautiful **973**

Heinrichs, Susan
The Pacific Ocean (2-4) **910**

Heins, Ethel L., 1918-
The cat and the cook and other fables of Krylov (1-4) **398.2**

Heins, Paul, 1909-1996
(ed) Crosscurrents of criticism. See Crosscurrents of criticism **028.5**

The **heiress,** or the croak of doom. Rockwell, T.
In Rockwell, T. How to eat fried worms, and other plays p109-42 **812**

Hekeke. San Souci, R.
In San Souci, R. Cut from the same cloth p103-09 **398.2**

Helbig, Alethea
This land is our land **016.8**

Helen Oxenbury's ABC of things. Oxenbury, H. **E**

Helga's dowry. De Paola, T. **E**

Hellard, Susan
(il) Asher, S. Where do you get your ideas? **808**

Heller, Ruth
A cache of jewels and other collective nouns (2-4) **428**
Chickens aren't the only ones (k-1) **591.1**
Color color color color (1-4) **752**
Kites sail high: a book about verbs (k-2) **428**
Many luscious lollipops: a book about adjectives (k-2) **428**
Merry-go-round (k-2) **428**
Up, up and away (k-2) **428**
(il) Climo, S. The Egyptian Cinderella **398.2**
(il) Climo, S. The Korean Cinderella **398.2**
(il) Creasy, R. Blue potatoes, orange tomatoes **635**
(il) Renberg, D. H. King Solomon and the bee **398.2**

Hello friend. Goble, P. **92**

Hello, Kate!. Schwartz, A.
In Schwartz, A. Scary stories 3 p15-16 **398.2**

Hello, Mrs Piggle Wiggle. MacDonald, B. See note under MacDonald, B. Mrs. Piggle-Wiggle **Fic**

Hello, my name is Scrambled Eggs. Gilson, J. **Fic**

Hello USA series (3-6) **973**

Help! I'm a prisoner in the library. Clifford, E. **Fic**

The **helpful** badger. Yep, L.
In Yep, L. The tree of dreams **398.2**

Helping hands. Haldane, S. **362.4**

Helweg, Hans H., 1917-
(il) Bond, M. The tales of Olga da Polga **Fic**

Hemenway, Harriet, d. 1960
Fiction
Lasky, K. She's wearing a dead bird on her head! **E**

Hemingway, Ernest, 1899-1961
See/See also pages in the following book(s):
Faber, D. Great lives: American literature p221-30 (5 and up) **920**

Hemmant, Lynette, 1938-
(il) King-Smith, D. Ace, the very important pig **Fic**

Hen and Frog. Bryan, A.
In Bryan, A. Beat the story-drum, pum-pum p3-13 **398.2**

The **hen** and the dove. Aardema, V.
In Aardema, V. Misoso p33-35 **398.2**

Hendershot, Judith, 1940-
In coal country **E**

Henderson, Douglas
Dinosaur tree (2-4)   **560**
(il) Lauber, P. Living with dinosaurs
    567.9

Henderson, Kathy
The Great Lakes (2-4)   **551.4**

Hendrick, Mary Jean
If anything ever goes wrong at the zoo
    E

Hendry, Linda
(il) Foodworks. See Foodworks   **641.3**
(il) Gryski, C. Lanyard   **746.42**
(il) Irvine, J. Build it with boxes   **745.54**
(il) Irvine, J. How to make super pop-ups
    736

Heng O, the moon lady. Carpenter, F.
In Carpenter, F. Tales of a Chinese grandmother p206-16   **398.2**

Henio, Katie
About
Thomson, P. Katie Henio: Navajo sheep-
herder (4 and up)   **970.004**

Henkes, Kevin, 1960-
Chester's way   **E**
Chrysanthemum   **E**
Jessica   **E**
Julius, the baby of the world   **E**
Owen   **E**
Protecting Marie (5 and up)   **Fic**
Sheila Rae, the brave   **E**
Words of stone (5 and up)   **Fic**

Henneberger, Robert, 1921-
(il) Cameron, E. The wonderful flight to the
Mushroom Planet   **Fic**

Hennessy, B. G. (Barbara G.)
The missing tarts   **E**
Road builders (k-2)   **625.7**

Hennessy, Barbara G. *See* Hennessy, B. G.
(Barbara G.)

Henny Penny. Galdone, P.   **398.2**

Henny-penny. Jacobs, J.
In Jacobs, J. English fairy tales p116-19
    398.2

Henrietta Marie (Ship)
Sullivan, G. Slave ship (5 and up)
    910.4

Henriquez, Elsa
(il) The Magic orange tree, and other Haitian folktales. See The Magic orange tree,
and other Haitian folktales   **398.2**

Henry, Infante of Portugal, 1394-1460
About
Fisher, L. E. Prince Henry the Navigator
(3-5)   **92**
See/See also pages in the following book(s):
Fritz, J. Around the world in a hundred
years p19-29 (4-6)   **910.4**

Henry, the Navigator *See* Henry, Infante of
Portugal, 1394-1460

Henry, Gregory A.
(il) Porte-Thomas, B. A. Chickens! chickens!
    E

Henry, Marguerite, 1902-
Album of horses (4 and up)   **636.1**
Brighty of the Grand Canyon (4 and up)
    Fic
Justin Morgan had a horse (4 and up)
    Fic
King of the wind (4 and up)   **Fic**
Misty of Chincoteague (4 and up)   **Fic**
Sea Star, orphan of Chincoteague. See note
under Henry, M. Misty of Chincoteague
    Fic
Stormy, Misty's foal. See note under Henry,
M. Misty of Chincoteague   **Fic**
White stallion of Lipizza (4 and up)   **Fic**
See/See also pages in the following book(s):
Newbery Medal books, 1922-1955 p320-24,
327-34   **028.5**

Henry, O., 1862-1910
The gift of the Magi (5 and up)   **Fic**
also in Take joy! The Tasha Tudor Christmas book p47-51   **394.2**
See/See also pages in the following book(s):
Faber, D. Great lives: American literature
p121-29 (5 and up)   **920**

Henry, Patrick, 1736-1799
About
Fritz, J. Where was Patrick Henry on the
29th of May? (2-4)   **92**

Henry. Bawden, N.   **Fic**

Henry and Beezus. Cleary, B. See note under
Cleary, B. Henry Huggins   **Fic**

Henry and Mudge. Rylant, C.   **E**

Henry and Mudge and the bedtime thumps.
Rylant, C. See note under Rylant, C. Henry and Mudge   **E**

Henry and Mudge and the best day of all. Rylant, C. See note under Rylant, C. Henry
and Mudge   **E**

Henry and Mudge and the careful cousin. Rylant, C. See note under Rylant, C. Henry
and Mudge   **E**

Henry and Mudge and the forever sea. Rylant,
C. See note under Rylant, C. Henry and
Mudge   **E**

Henry and Mudge and the happy cat. Rylant,
C. See note under Rylant, C. Henry and
Mudge   **E**

Henry and Mudge and the long weekend. Rylant, C. See note under Rylant, C. Henry
and Mudge   **E**

Henry and Mudge and the wild wind. Rylant,
C. See note under Rylant, C. Henry and
Mudge   **E**

Henry and Mudge get the cold shivers. Rylant,
C. See note under Rylant, C. Henry and
Mudge   **E**

Henry and Mudge in puddle trouble. Rylant,
C. See note under Rylant, C. Henry and
Mudge   **E**

Henry and Mudge in the green time. Rylant,
C. See note under Rylant, C. Henry and
Mudge   **E**

Henry and Mudge in the sparkle days. Rylant, C. See note under Rylant, C. Henry and Mudge **E**

Henry and Mudge take the big test. Rylant, C. See note under Rylant, C. Henry and Mudge **E**

Henry and Mudge under the yellow moon. Rylant, C. See note under Rylant, C. Henry and Mudge **E**

Henry and Ribsy. Cleary, B. See note under Cleary, B. Henry Huggins **Fic**

Henry and the clubhouse. Cleary, B. See note under Cleary, B. Henry Huggins **Fic**

Henry and the paper route. Cleary, B. See note under Cleary, B. Henry Huggins **Fic**

Henry Huggins. Cleary, B. **Fic**

Henry Reed, Inc. Robertson, K. **Fic**

Henry Reed's babysitting service. Robertson, K. See note under Robertson, K. Henry Reed, Inc. **Fic**

Henry Reed's journey. Robertson, K. See note under Robertson, K. Henry Reed, Inc. **Fic**

Henry Street Settlement (New York, N.Y.) Wolf, B. Homeless (2-4) **362.5**

Henry the sailor cat. Calhoun, M. See note under Calhoun, M. Cross-country cat **E**

Henson, Matthew Alexander, 1866-1955
About
Ferris, J. Arctic explorer; the story of Matthew Henson (3-6) **92**
See/See also pages in the following book(s):
Haskins, J. Against all opposition p46-61 (5 and up) **920**
Haskins, J. One more river to cross (4 and up) **920**

Heo, Yumi
(il) Han, S. C. The rabbit's escape **398.2**

Hepler, Susan Ingrid
(jt. auth) Huck, C. S. Children's literature in the elementary school **028.5**

Her. Crossley-Holland, K.
In Crossley-Holland, K. British folk tales p58 **398.2**

Her husband's ghost. Haskins, J.
In Haskins, J. The headless haunt and other African American ghost stories p50 **398.2**

Her Majesty's servants. Kipling, R.
In Kipling, R. The jungle books **S C**

Her seven brothers. Goble, P. **398.2**

Her stories. Hamilton, V. **398.2**

Heracles (Legendary character) *See* Hercules (Legendary character)

Herb, Angela
(jt. auth) Bolotin, N. For home and country **973.7**

Herb, Sara Willoughby- *See* Willoughby-Herb, Sara

Herb, Steven
Using children's books in preschool settings **372.4**

Herbal medicine *See* Medical botany

Herbie Jones. Kline, S. **Fic**

Herbie Jones and Hamburger Head. Kline, S. See note under Kline, S. Herbie Jones **Fic**

Herbie Jones and the birthday showdown. Kline, S. See note under Kline, S. Herbie Jones **Fic**

Herbie Jones and the class gift. Kline, S. See note under Kline, S. Herbie Jones **Fic**

Herbie Jones and the dark attic. Kline, S. See note under Kline, S. Herbie Jones **Fic**

Herbie Jones and the monster ball. Kline, S. See note under Kline, S. Herbie Jones **Fic**

Herbivores
Bramwell, M. Mammals: the small plant-eaters (4 and up) **599**
Stidworthy, J. Mammals: the large plant-eaters (4 and up) **599**

Herculaneum (Extinct city)
Bisel, S. The secrets of Vesuvius (4 and up) **937**

Hercules (Legendary character)
Evslin, B. Hercules (5 and up) **292**
See/See also pages in the following book(s):
Colum, P. The Golden Fleece and the heroes who lived before Achilles p244-94 (5 and up) **292**
Hamilton, E. Mythology p224-43 (6 and up) **292**

Herds of thunder, manes of gold (4 and up) **808.8**

Here come the monster trucks. Sullivan, G. **629.223**

Here comes McBroom!. Fleischman, S. See note under Fleischman, S. McBroom tells the truth **Fic**

Here comes the strikeout. Kessler, L. P. **E**

Here is the southwestern desert. Dunphy, M. **574.5**

Here is the tropical rainforest. Dunphy, M. **574.5**

Here there be dragons. Yolen, J. **810.8**

Here there be unicorns. Yolen, J. **810.8**

Hereafterthis. Jacobs, J.
In Jacobs, J. English fairy tales p230-33 **398.2**

Heredity
See/See also pages in the following book(s):
Gallant, R. A. Before the sun dies p72-81 (6 and up) **575**

Here's Hermione: a Rosy Cole production. Greenwald, S. See note under Greenwald, S. Give us a great big smile, Rosy Cole **Fic**

Herguth, Margaret S.
North Dakota
In America the beautiful 973

Hermes, Jules, 1962-
The children of India (3-5) 954
The children of Morocco (3-5) 964

Hermes, Patricia, 1936-
You shouldn't have to say good-bye (5 and up) Fic

Hermit crabs *See* Crabs

Hermit crabs. Johnson, S. A. 595.3

Hermod and Hadvor
In The Yellow fairy book p301-07 398.2

A **hero** ain't nothin' but a sandwich. Childress, A. Fic

The **hero** and the crown. McKinley, R. Fic

The **Hero** Makóma
In The Rainbow fairy book p137-45 398.2

The **hero** of Bremen. Hodges, M. 398.2

Hero of lesser causes. Johnston, J. Fic

Heroes. Mochizuki, K. E

The **heroine** of the Titanic: a tale both true and otherwise of the life of Molly Brown. Blos, J. W. 92

Heroism *See* Courage

Herold, Maggie Rugg
A very important day E

The **heron** and the hummingbird. Kherdian, D.
In Kherdian, D. Feathers and tails p77-78 398.2

Heron woos crane. Kherdian, D.
In Kherdian, D. Feathers and tails p27-29 398.2

Herons
Fiction
Avi. Blue heron (5 and up) Fic

Herr Korbes. Grimm, J.
In Grimm, J. The complete Grimm's fairy tales p205-06 398.2

Herridge, Steve
(il) Bowler, M. Trains 625.1

Herriot, James
Moses the kitten E

Hershel and the Hanukkah goblins. Kimmel, E. A. E

Hershel and the nobleman. Jaffe, N.
In Jaffe, N. While standing on one foot p56-61 296.1

Hershele and Hanukkah. Singer, I. B.
In Singer, I. B. The power of light p63-72 S C
In Singer, I. B. Stories for children p184-93 S C

Herzog, George, 1901-1984
(jt. auth) Courlander, H. The cow-tail switch, and other West African stories 398.2

Heslop, Michael
(il) Cooper, S. The grey king Fic

Hesse, Karen
Lester's dog E
Letters from Rifka (5 and up) Fic
Sable (2-4) Fic

Hest, Amy
The crack-of-dawn walkers E
The midnight eaters E
Nana's birthday party E
The purple coat E

Hewett, Joan
Tiger, tiger, growing up (1-4) 599.74
Tunnels, tracks, and trains (4-6) 625.4

Hewett, Richard
(il) Arnold, C. The ancient cliff dwellers of Mesa Verde 970.004
(il) Arnold, C. Camel 599.73
(il) Arnold, C. Cats: in from the wild 599.74
(il) Arnold, C. Cheetah 599.74
(il) Arnold, C. Dinosaur mountain 567.9
(il) Arnold, C. Dinosaurs all around 567.9
(il) Arnold, C. Dinosaurs down under and other fossils from Australia 567.9
(il) Arnold, C. Elephant 599.6
(il) Arnold, C. Flamingo 598
(il) Arnold, C. Giraffe 599.73
(il) Arnold, C. A guide dog puppy grows up 362.4
(il) Arnold, C. Hippo 599.73
(il) Arnold, C. House sparrows everywhere 598
(il) Arnold, C. Kangaroo 599.2
(il) Arnold, C. Killer whale 599.5
(il) Arnold, C. Koala 599.2
(il) Arnold, C. Llama 599.73
(il) Arnold, C. Monkey 599.8
(il) Arnold, C. Orangutan 599.88
(il) Arnold, C. Ostriches and other flightless birds 598
(il) Arnold, C. Panda 599.74
(il) Arnold, C. Penguin 598
(il) Arnold, C. Pets without homes 636.088
(il) Arnold, C. Rhino 599.72
(il) Arnold, C. Saving the peregrine falcon 598
(il) Arnold, C. Sea lion 599.74
(il) Arnold, C. Snake 597.9
(il) Arnold, C. Trapped in tar 560
(il) Arnold, C. Tule elk 599.73
(il) Arnold, C. Zebra 599.72
(il) Hewett, J. Tiger, tiger, growing up 599.74
(il) Hewett, J. Tunnels, tracks, and trains 625.4
(il) Meyers, S. Insect zoo 595.7
(il) Scott, E. Look alive 791.43

Hewitson, Jennifer
(il) Wolfson, E. From the earth to beyond the sky 970.004

Hewitt, Kathryn
(il) Bunting, E. Flower garden   E
(il) Krull, K. Lives of the musicians
    920
(il) Krull, K. Lives of the writers   920

Hewitt, Sally
Bang and rattle
  In Hewitt, S. Get set—go! [Music &
  sound series]   784.19
Get set—go! [Music & sound series] (k-3)
    784.19
Pluck and scrape
  In Hewitt, S. Get set—go! [Music &
  sound series]   784.19
Puff and blow
  In Hewitt, S. Get set—go! [Music &
  sound series]   784.19
Squeak and roar
  In Hewitt, S. Get set—go! [Music &
  sound series]   784.19

Hey, Al Yorinks, A.   E
Hey, hay!. Terban, M.   793.73
Hey! I'm reading!. Miles, B.   372.4
Hey! listen to this   028.5
Hey, remember Fat Glenda?. Perl, L. See note
  under Perl, L. Fat Glenda turns fourteen
    Fic
Hey world, here I am!. Little, J.   811
Heyer, Carol, 1950-
(il) Pringle, L. P. Dinosaurs!   567.9
Heyer, Marilee, 1942-
The weaving of a dream (3-5)   398.2
Heyman, Ken, 1930-
(il) Morris, A. Bread, bread, bread
    641.8
(il) Morris, A. Hats, hats, hats   391
(il) Morris, A. Houses and homes   728
(il) Morris, A. On their toes   792.8
Heyward, DuBose, 1885-1940
The country bunny and the little gold shoes
    E
Hi. Scott, A. H.   E
Hi, cat!. Keats, E. J. See note under Keats, E.
  J. The snowy day   E
Hiawatha, 15th cent.
         About
Fradin, D. B. Hiawatha: messenger of peace
  (3-5)   92
Hiawatha. Longfellow, H. W.   811
Hibernation
Facklam, M. Do not disturb (3-6)   591.5
Hic! Hic! Hic!. MacDonald, M. R.
  In MacDonald, M. R. Twenty tellable
  tales p142-53   372.6
Hickman, Janet
Jericho (5 and up)   Fic
(jt. auth) Huck, C. S. Children's literature in
  the elementary school   028.5
Hickock, Martha Jane Canary See Calamity
  Jane, 1852-1903
The **hidden** children. Greenfeld, H.   940.53

The **hidden** life of the pond. Schwartz, D. M.
    574.92
Hidden treasures of the sea (4 and up)
    910.4
Hidden worlds. Simon, S.   500
Hide & seek science [series]
Brenner, B. Where's that insect?   595.7
Hide and seek. Vos, I.   Fic
Hide and seek fog. Tresselt, A. R.   E
Hiding. Hughes, S. See note under Hughes, S.
  Bouncing   E
Hiding out. Martin, J.   591.5
Hiding to survive. Rosenberg, M. B.
    940.53
Hieroglyphics
Giblin, J. The riddle of the Rosetta Stone (5
  and up)   493
Katan, N. J. Hieroglyphs, the writing of an-
  cient Egypt (4 and up)   493
Hieroglyphs, the writing of ancient Egypt. Ka-
  tan, N. J.   493
Higgens, Paul
(il) Bowler, M. Trains   625.1
Higgle wiggle. Merriam, E.   811
Higglety pigglety pop!. Sendak, M.   E
High interest-low vocabulary books
         Bibliography
Pilla, M. L. The best: high/low books for re-
  luctant readers   011.6
High John the Conquerer. Sanfield, S.
  In From sea to shining sea p134-35
    810.8
High John the Conqueror, The adventures of.
  Sanfield, S.   398.2
The **High** King. Alexander, L.   Fic
The **high** rise glorious skittle skat roarious sky
  pie angel food cake. Willard, N.   E
High school libraries
  See also Young adults' library services
High speed aeronautics
Aaseng, N. Breaking the sound barrier (6
  and up)   629.132
Taylor, R. L. The first supersonic flight (4
  and up)   629.132
High tech *See* Technology
High-wire Henry. Calhoun, M. See note under
  Calhoun, M. Cross-country cat   E
Higher on the door. Stevenson, J.   92
Highlights for Children   051
The **highwayman.** Noyes, A.   821
Highways *See* Roads
Hiiaka. San Souci, R.
  In San Souci, R. Cut from the same cloth
  p121-28   398.2
Hiking
  See also Walking
Hilde and Eli, children of the Holocaust. Ad-
  ler, D. A.   940.53
Hildilid's night. Durán, C.   E

"Hold him, Tabb!". San Souci, R.
In San Souci, R. More short & shivery
p1-4 **398.2**

Holder, Heidi
(il) Aesop. Aesop's fables [illus. by Heidi
Holder] **398.2**

"Hold'im down, Brer Fox". Lester, J.
In Lester, J. The tales of Uncle Remus
p6-8 **398.2**

Holes and peeks. Jonas, A. **E**

Holiday cooking around the world
In Easy menu ethnic cookbooks
641.5

Holiday crafts for kids [series]
Ross, K. Crafts for Kwanzaa **745.5**
Ross, K. Crafts for Valentine's Day
745.5
Ross, K. Every day is Earth Day
745.58

Holiday plays round the year (4 and up)
812.008

Holiday treats. Hautzig, E. R. **641.5**

Holidays
See also Christmas; Father's Day;
Fourth of July; Kwanzaa; Saint Patrick's
Day; Thanksgiving Day; Valentine's Day
The American book of days **394.2**
Bauer, C. F. Celebrations **808.8**
Chase's calendar of events **394.2**
The Family read-aloud holiday treasury
808.8
The Folklore of world holidays **394.2**
Gregory, R. W. Anniversaries and holidays
394.2
Perl, L. Piñatas and paper flowers (4 and
up) **394.2**
Drama
Holiday plays round the year (4 and up)
812.008
Poetry
Livingston, M. C. Celebrations **811**
Ring out, wild bells **808.81**
Yolen, J. The three bears holiday rhyme
book (k-2) **811**

Holidays, Jewish *See* Jewish holidays

Holland, Isabelle
See/See also pages in the following book(s):
Crosscurrents of criticism p137-43 **028.5**

Holland, Kevin Crossley- *See* Crossley-
Holland, Kevin

Holland *See* Netherlands

Holland in pictures. See Netherlands—in pictures
tures **949.2**

Holling, Holling C., 1900-1973
Paddle-to-the-sea (4-6) **Fic**

The **hollow** land. Gardam, J. **Fic**

Holly, reindeer, and colored lights. Barth, E.
394.2

Holm, Anne, 1922-
North to freedom (6 and up) **Fic**

Holm, Sharon Lane, 1955-
(il) Lang, S. S. Nature in your backyard
508

(il) Ross, K. Crafts for Kwanzaa **745.5**
(il) Ross, K. Crafts for Valentine's Day
745.5
(il) Ross, K. Every day is Earth Day
745.58

Holman, Felice
Slake's limbo (6 and up) **Fic**

Holmes, Anita, 1937-
Flowers for you (4 and up) **635.9**

Holmes, Bea
(il) Hunter, E. F. Child of the silent night
[biography of Laura Dewey Bridgman]
92

Holmes, Sally
(il) Andersen, H. C. The Snow Queen
Fic
(il) Perrault, C. The complete fairy tales of
Charles Perrault **398.2**

Holocaust, 1933-1945
See also World War, 1939-1945—Jews
Abells, C. B. The children we remember
(3-6) **940.53**
Adler, D. A. Child of the Warsaw ghetto
(3-5) **940.53**
Adler, D. A. Hilde and Eli, children of the
Holocaust (3-5) **940.53**
Adler, D. A. A picture book of Anne Frank
(1-3) **92**
Bachrach, S. D. Tell them we remember (5
and up) **940.53**
Hurwitz, J. Anne Frank: life in hiding (3-5)
92
Meltzer, M. Never to forget: the Jews of the
Holocaust (6 and up) **940.53**
Meltzer, M. Rescue: the story of how Gen-
tiles saved Jews in the Holocaust (6 and
up) **940.53**
Pariser, M. Elie Wiesel (3-5) **92**
Rol, R. van der. Anne Frank, beyond the di-
ary (5 and up) **92**
Toll, N. S. Behind the secret window (6 and
up) **940.53**
Fiction
Ackerman, K. The night crossing (3-5)
Fic
Hoestlandt, J. Star of fear, star of hope
E
Orgel, D. The devil in Vienna (6 and up)
Fic
Orlev, U. The island on Bird Street (5 and
up) **Fic**
Orlev, U. The man from the other side (6
and up) **Fic**
Roth-Hano, R. Touch wood (6 and up)
Fic
Schnur, S. The shadow children (5 and up)
Fic
Vos, I. Anna is still here (4 and up)
Fic
Vos, I. Hide and seek (4 and up) **Fic**
Yolen, J. The devil's arithmetic (4 and up)
Fic
Personal narratives
Greenfeld, H. The hidden children (4 and
up) **940.53**

Holocaust, 1933-1945—Personal narratives—
Continued
Leitner, I. The big lie (3-6)   **940.53**
Rosenberg, M. B. Hiding to survive (5 and up)   **940.53**

Holocaust Museum (U.S.) *See* United States Holocaust Memorial Museum

Holtze, Sally Holmes
(ed) Fifth book of junior authors & illustrators. See Fifth book of junior authors & illustrators   **920.003**
(ed) Seventh book of junior authors & illustrators. See Seventh book of junior authors & illustrators   **920.003**
(ed) Sixth book of junior authors & illustrators. See Sixth book of junior authors & illustrators   **920.003**

Holub, Joan
(il) American Heart Association kids' cookbook. See American Heart Association kids' cookbook   **641.5**

The **Holy Bible** [King James Bible. Oxford Univ. Press]. Bible   **220.5**

The **Holy** Bible: new revised standard version. Bible   **220.5**

Holy Grail *See* Grail

The **holy night.** Lagerlöf, S.
In Take joy! The Tasha Tudor Christmas book p52-54   **394.2**

Hom, Nancy
(il) Spagnoli, C. Nine-In-one, Grr! Grr!   **398.2**

Home (k-3)   **810.8**

Home in the sky. Baker, J.   **E**

Home life *See* Family life

Home-run hitters. Torres, J. A.   **920**

Homecoming. Voigt, C.   **Fic**

The **homecoming.** Yep, L.
In Yep, L. The rainbow people p144-51   **398.2**

Homeless. Wolf, B.   **362.5**

Homeless or hopeless?. Nichelason, M. G.   **362.5**

Homeless persons
See also Refugees; Runaway children; Tramps
Berck, J. No place to be (5 and up)   **362.7**
Home (k-3)   **810.8**
Nichelason, M. G. Homeless or hopeless? (5 and up)   **362.5**
Wolf, B. Homeless (2-4)   **362.5**
See/See also pages in the following book(s):
Ashabranner, B. K. People who make a difference p101-06 (5 and up)   **920**
Fiction
Bunting, E. Fly away home   **E**
Hahn, M. D. December stillness (6 and up)   **Fic**
Howe, J. Dew drop dead (4-6)   **Fic**
Neufeld, J. Almost a hero (5 and up)   **Fic**

Pinkwater, J. Tails of the Bronx (4-6)   **Fic**
Spinelli, J. Maniac Magee (5 and up)   **Fic**

Homeplace. Shelby, A.   **E**

Homer
Adaptations
Hutton, W. The Trojan horse (3-5)   **883**
Picard, B. L. The Iliad of Homer (6 and up)   **883**

Homer Price. McCloskey, R.   **Fic**

Homer Price [excerpt]. McCloskey, R.
In The Random House book of humor for children p181-94   **817.008**

Homesick: my own story. Fritz, J.   **92**

Homeward bound. Coville, B.
In Coville, B. Oddly enough p19-31   **S C**

Homicide
See/See also pages in the following book(s):
Fry, V. L. Part of me died, too p185-206 (5 and up)   **155.9**

Hominids: a look back at our ancestors. Sattler, H. R.   **573.3**

Homosexuality
Fiction
Fox, P. The eagle kite (6 and up)   **Fic**
Nelson, T. Earthshine (5 and up)   **Fic**

Honest Abe [biography of Abraham Lincoln]. Kunhardt, E.   **92**

Honesty
See also Truthfulness and falsehood

Honey
Johnson, S. A. A beekeeper's year (4 and up)   **638**
Micucci, C. The life and times of the honeybee (2-4)   **595.7**

Honey, I love, and other love poems. Greenfield, E.   **811**

Honeybee. Watts, B.   **595.7**

Honeycutt, Natalie
The all new Jonah Twist (3-5)   **Fic**
The best-laid plans of Jonah Twist. See note under Honeycutt, N. The all new Jonah Twist   **Fic**
Invisible Lissa (3-5)   **Fic**

Hong, Lily Toy, 1958-
How the ox star fell from heaven (k-3)   **398.2**
Two of everything (k-3)   **398.2**

Hong Kong
Fiction
Levinson, R. Our home is the sea   **E**

Hoobler, Dorothy
The African American family album (5 and up)   **305.8**
The Chinese American family album (5 and up)   **305.8**
The Irish American family album (5 and up)   **305.8**
The Italian American family album (5 and up)   **305.8**

Horace. Keller, H. **E**

The **Horn** Book Guide to Children's and
Young Adult Books **028.505**

Horn book magazine
Crosscurrents of criticism **028.5**
Horn Book reflections on children's books
and reading **028.5**
A Horn Book sampler on children's books
and reading **028.5**

The **Horn** Book Magazine **028.505**

Horn Book reflections on children's books and
reading **028.5**

A **Horn** Book sampler on children's books and
reading **028.5**

Horne, Daniel
(il) San Souci, R. Young Merlin **398.2**

The **horned** women. Hamilton, V.
In Hamilton, V. The dark way p32-37
398.2

Horner, Bob
See/See also pages in the following book(s):
Torres, J. A. Home-run hitters p93-104 (4
and up) **920**

Horner, Jack *See* Horner, John R.

Horner, John R.
Digging up Tyrannosaurus rex (3-5)
567.9
About
Lessem, D. Jack Horner: living with dino-
saurs (4 and up) **92**

Horns Afanas'ev, A. N.
In Afanas'ev, A. N. Russian fairy tales
p292-94 **398.2**

Horrible Harry and the ant invasion. Kline, S.
See note under Kline, S. Horrible Harry
in room 2B **Fic**

Horrible Harry and the Christmas surprise.
Kline, S. See note under Kline, S. Horrible Harry in room 2B **Fic**

Horrible Harry and the green slime. Kline, S.
See note under Kline, S. Horrible Harry
in room 2B **Fic**

Horrible Harry and the kickball wedding.
Kline, S. See note under Kline, S. Horrible Harry in room 2B **Fic**

Horrible Harry in room 2B. Kline, S. **Fic**

Horrible Harry's secret. Kline, S. See note under Kline, S. Horrible Harry in room 2B
Fic

Horror fiction
Aiken, J. Give yourself a fright: thirteen
tales of the supernatural (6 and up)
S C
Coville, B. Oddly enough (6 and up)
S C
MacDonald, M. R. When the lights go out
372.6
Schwartz, A. In a dark, dark room, and oth-
er scary stories (k-2) **398.2**
Schwartz, A. More scary stories to tell in the
dark (4 and up) **398.2**
Schwartz, A. Scary stories 3 (4 and up)
398.2

Schwartz, A. Scary stories to tell in the dark
(4 and up) **398.2**

The **horse** and his boy. Lewis, C. S. See note
under Lewis, C. S. The lion, the witch,
and the wardrobe **Fic**

Horse and toad
In The Magic orange tree, and other Haitian folktales p143-50 **398.2**

Horseback riding *See* Horsemanship

Horsemanship
See also Rodeos
Green, L. The young rider (4 and up)
798.2
Rodenas, P. The Random House book of
horses and horsemanship (4 and up)
636.1

Horses
See also Ponies
Ancona, G. Man and mustang (3-6)
636.1
Clutton-Brock, J. Horse (4 and up)
636.1
Cole, J. A horse's body **636.1**
Henry, M. Album of horses (4 and up)
636.1
Isenbart, H.-H. Birth of a foal (3-6)
636.1
Jurmain, S. Once upon a horse (6 and up)
636.1
LaBonte, G. The miniature horse (3-5)
636.1
McFarland, C. Hoofbeats (3-5) **636.1**
Patent, D. H. Appaloosa horses (4 and up)
636.1
Patent, D. H. Baby horses (3-6) **636.1**
Patent, D. H. Horses (3-6) **636.1**
Patent, D. H. Horses of America (4 and up)
636.1
Patent, D. H. Where the wild horses roam
(4 and up) **639.9**
Rodenas, P. The Random House book of
horses and horsemanship (4 and up)
636.1
The Visual dictionary of the horse (4 and
up) **636.1**
See/See also pages in the following book(s):
Chrystie, F. N. Pets p194-215 (4 and up)
636.088
Facklam, M. Who harnessed the horse? p29-
44 (3-6) **636**
Fiction
Bagnold, E. National Velvet (5 and up)
Fic
Christiansen, C. The ice horse **E**
Coerr, E. Chang's paper pony **E**
Cohen, C. L. The mud pony (k-3)
398.2
Farley, W. The Black Stallion (4 and up)
Fic
Goble, P. The gift of the sacred dog (2-4)
398.2
Goble, P. The girl who loved wild horses
E
Haas, J. Beware the mare (3-5) **Fic**
Haas, J. No foal yet **E**

How the rhinoceros got his skin. Kipling, R.
In Kipling, R. Just so stories   S C
In The Oxford treasury of children's stories p127-29   S C

How the sea began. Crespo, G.   **398.2**

How the slaves helped each other. Faulkner, W. J.
In From sea to shining sea p130-31   **810.8**

How the three wild Babylonian Baboons went away in the rain eating bread and butter. Sandburg, C.
In Sandburg, C. Rootabaga stories pt 2 p43-47   S C
In Sandburg, C. The Sandburg treasury p106-07   **818**

How the tiger got its stripes. Terada, A. M.
In Terada, A. M. Under the starfruit tree p7-9   **398.2**

How the turtle got his shell. Yeoman, J.
In Yeoman, J. The singing tortoise and other animal folktales p51-57   **398.2**

How the whale got his throat. Kipling, R.
In Kipling, R. Just so stories   S C

How they are good to the green hat-eating horses. Sandburg, C.
In Sandburg, C. More rootabagas p65-70   S C

How they bring back the Village of Cream Puffs when the wind blows it away. Sandburg, C.
In Sandburg, C. Rootabaga stories pt 1 p13-19   S C
In Sandburg, C. The Sandburg treasury p17-19   **818**

How they broke away to go to the Rootabaga Country. Sandburg, C.
In Sandburg, C. Rootabaga stories pt 1 p3-12   S C
In Sandburg, C. The Sandburg treasury p10-16   **818**

How things work, The Random House book of. Parker, S.   **600**

How three went out into the wide world. Pyle, H.
In Pyle, H. The wonder clock p39-48   **398.2**

How to be a nature detective. Selsam, M. E.   **591.5**

How to be an ocean scientist in your own home. Simon, S.   **551.46**

How to be naturally geographic. *See* Bell, N. The book of where   **910**

How to be school smart. James, E.   **371.3**

How to break a bad habit. MacDonald, M. R.
In MacDonald, M. R. Twenty tellable tales p75-78   **372.6**

How to cook a gooseberry fool. Vaughan, M.
In Easy menu ethnic cookbooks   **641.5**

How to dig a hole to the other side of the world. McNulty, F.   **551.1**

How-to-do-it manuals for libraries [series]
Feinberg, S. Running a parent/child workshop   **027.62**
Nespeca, S. M. Library programming for families with young children   **027.62**

How-to-do-it manuals for school and public librarians [series]
Herb, S. Using children's books in preschool settings   **372.4**

How-to-draw book [series]
Frame, P. Drawing cats and kittens   **743**

How to eat fried worms. Rockwell, T.   **Fic**

How to eat fried worms [excerpt]. Rockwell, T.
In The Random House book of humor for children p301-05   **817.008**

How to eat fried worms; dramatization. Rockwell, T.
In Rockwell, T. How to eat fried worms, and other plays p21-78   **812**

How to eat fried worms, and other plays. Rockwell, T.   **812**

How to hang up the telephone. Ephron, D.
In The Random House book of humor for children p268-69   **817.008**

How to hunt buried treasure. Deem, J. M.   **910.4**

How to make a chemical volcano and other mysterious experiments. Kramer, A.   **540.7**

How to make an apple pie and see the world. Priceman, M.   **E**

How to make super pop-ups. Irvine, J.   **736**

How to really fool yourself. Cobb, V.   **152.1**

How to tell a true princess. Andersen, H. C.
In The Yellow fairy book p254-55   **398.2**

How to tell corn fairies if you see 'em. Sandburg, C.
In Sandburg, C. Rootabaga stories pt 1 p169-76   S C
In Sandburg, C. The Sandburg treasury p81-86   **818**

How to think like a scientist. Kramer, S.   **507**

How Turtle's back was cracked. Ross, G.   **398.2**

How two sweetheart dippies sat in the moonlight on a lumberyard fence and heard about the sooners and the boomers. Sandburg, C.
In Sandburg, C. Rootabaga stories pt 2 p111-20   S C
In Sandburg, C. The Sandburg treasury p134-39   **818**

How two went into partnership. Pyle, H.
In Pyle, H. The wonder clock p279-90   **398.2**

How we learned the earth is round. Lauber, P.   **525**

I

I was dreaming to come to America (4 and up) **325.73**

I went to the library
In Juba this and Juba that **372.6**

I win!. Mayo, G.
In Mayo, G. That tricky Coyote! p21-27 **398.2**

Ibargüengoitia, Jorge, 1928-1983
Paletón and the musical elephant
In Where angels glide at dawn p51-55 **S C**

Ibazebo, Isimeme
Exploration into Africa (4-6) **960**

IBBY *See* International Board on Books for Young People

Iblis. Oppenheim, S. L. **297**

Ibn Ezra and the archbishop. Kimmel, E. A.
In Kimmel, E. A. The spotted pony: a collection of Hanukkah stories p12-17 **398.2**

Ice cream, ices, etc.
Jaspersohn, W. Ice cream (3-5) **637**

The ice cream store. Lee, D. **811**

The ice horse. Christiansen, C. **E**

Ice skating
Fiction
Dodge, M. M. Hans Brinker; or, The silver skates (4 and up) **Fic**

Icebergs
Simon, S. Icebergs and glaciers (3-5) **551.3**

Icebergs and glaciers. Simon, S. **551.3**

The iceman. Lessem, D. **930.1**

Ichikawa, Satomi, 1949-
(il) Gauch, P. L. Dance, Tanya **E**
(il) Laird, E. Rosy's garden: a child's keepsake of flowers **635.9**

Ida Early comes over the mountain. Burch, R. **Fic**

Idaho
Kent, Z. Idaho
In America the beautiful **973**
Pelta, K. Idaho
In Hello USA series **973**
Fiction
Beatty, P. Bonanza girl (5 and up) **Fic**

Identity *See* Individuality

Idioms *See* English language—Idioms

Iditarod Trail Sled Dog Race, Alaska
Dolan, E. M. Susan Butcher and the Iditarod Trail (5 and up) **798**

If anything ever goes wrong at the zoo. Hendrick, M. J. **E**

If I had a paka. Pomerantz, C. **811**

If I ran the circus. Seuss, Dr. **E**

If I ran the zoo. Seuss, Dr. **E**

If I were in charge of the world and other worries. Viorst, J. **811**

If the owl calls again (6 and up) **808.81**

If there were dreams to sell (k-3) **821.008**

If you don't like it don't listen. Afanas'ev, A. N.
In Afanas'ev, A. N. Russian fairy tales p345-48 **398.2**

If you ever meet a whale (3-5) **811.008**

If you give a moose a muffin. Numeroff, L. J. **E**

If you give a mouse a cookie. Numeroff, L. J. **E**

If you made a million. Schwartz, D. M. **E**

If you please, President Lincoln. Robinet, H. G. **Fic**

If you take a paintbrush. Testa, F. **E**

If you take a pencil. Testa, F. **E**

If you were there in 1492. Brenner, B. **970.01**

If you were there in 1776. Brenner, B. **973.3**

. . . if your name was changed at Ellis Island. Levine, E. **325.73**

If you're happy and you know it. Weiss, N. **782.42**

Igloos
Yue, C. The igloo (3-6) **728**

Iguanas
Fiction
Caseley, J. Mr. Green Peas **E**

Iktome and the ducks. Lame Deer, A. F.
In From sea to shining sea p208-09 **810.8**

Iktomi and the berries. Goble, P. See note under Goble, P. Iktomi and the boulder **E**

Iktomi and the boulder. Goble, P. **398.2**

Iktomi and the buffalo skull. Goble, P. See note under Goble, P. Iktomi and the boulder **E**

Iktomi and the buzzard. Goble, P. See note under Goble, P. Iktomi and the boulder **E**

Iktomi and the ducks. Goble, P. See note under Goble, P. Iktomi and the boulder **E**

The Iliad of Homer. Picard, B. L. **883**

The ill-natured muse. Aiken, J.
In Aiken, J. Give yourself a fright: thirteen tales of the supernatural p89-108 **S C**

I'll see you in my dreams. Jukes, M. **E**

An ill wind. Aiken, J.
In Aiken, J. A foot in the grave p71-96 **S C**

Illinois
Anderson, K. P. Illinois
In Hello USA series **973**
Stein, R. C. Illinois
In America the beautiful **973**
Wills, C. A. A historical album of Illinois
In Historical albums series **973**

The **incautious** fox and the foolish wolf. Kherdian, D.
In Kherdian, D. Feathers and tails p62-63 **398.2**

Incest
See/See also pages in the following book(s):
Terkel, S. N. Feeling safe, feeling strong p32-43 (4 and up) **362.7**
Fiction
Woodson, J. I hadn't meant to tell you this (6 and up) **Fic**

The **inch** boy. Morimoto, J. **398.2**

Inch by inch. Lionni, L. **E**

Inch by inch. Mallett, D. **782.42**

Incident at Hawk's Hill. Eckert, A. W. **Fic**

Incisa, Monica
(il) Kennedy, X. J. The forgetful wishing well: poems for young people **811**
Incredible cross-sections, Stephen Biesty's. Biesty, S. **600**

The **incredible** journey. Burnford, S. **Fic**

The **incredible** journey of Lewis and Clark. Blumberg, R. **978**

The **incredible** painting of Felix Clousseau. Agee, J. **E**

Indentured servants *See* Contract labor

Independence Day (United States) *See* Fourth of July

Index to children's poetry **808.81**

Index to children's songs. Peterson, C. S. **782.42**

Index to collective biographies for young readers. Breen, K. **920**

Index to fairy tales **398.2**

Index to poetry for children and young people **808.81**

An **index** to young readers' collective biographies. See Breen, K. Index to collective biographies for young readers **920**

India
Hermes, J. The children of India (3-5) **954**
India—in pictures (5 and up) **954**
Children
See Children—India
Fiction
Kipling, R. The jungle books (4 and up) **S C**
Kipling, R. Just so stories (3-6) **S C**
Folklore
See Folklore—India
India—in pictures (5 and up) **954**
Indian chiefs. Freedman, R. **920**
Indian costumes. Hofsinde, R. **391**
The **Indian** in the cupboard. Reid Banks, L. **Fic**

Indian literature (American) *See* American literature—American Indian authors

Indian sign language. Hofsinde, R. **419**

Indian terms of the Americas. Patterson, L. **970.004**
An **Indian** winter. Freedman, R. **978**
Indiana
Stein, R. C. Indiana
In America the beautiful **973**
Swain, G. Indiana
In Hello USA series **973**
Indians
Bendick, J. Tombs of the ancient Americas (4 and up) **393**
Antiquities
Sattler, H. R. The earliest Americans (5 and up) **970.01**
Dictionaries
Patterson, L. Indian terms of the Americas **970.004**
Legends
Brusca, M. C. When jaguars ate the moon and other stories about animals and plants of the Americas (2-4) **398.2**
Poetry
In the trail of the wind (5 and up) **897**
The Sacred path (5 and up) **897**
Indians of Central America
See also Mayas; Mosquito Indians
Indians of Mexico
See also Aztecs; Mayas; Papago Indians; Toltecs; Zapotec Indians
Indians of North America
See also names of Indian peoples and linguistic families
Griffin-Pierce, T. The encyclopedia of Native America **970.004**
Jones, J. C. The American Indians in America
In The In America series **305.8**
Murdoch, D. H. North American Indian (4 and up) **970.004**
Rising voices (5 and up) **810.8**
See/See also pages in the following book(s):
Barth, E. Turkeys, Pilgrims, and Indian corn p60-69 (3-6) **394.2**
Freedman, R. Children of the wild West p38-57 (4 and up) **978**
McCall, E. S. Biography of a river: the living Mississippi (6 and up) **977**
Antiquities
Anderson, J. From map to museum (5 and up) **930.1**
La Pierre, Y. Native American rock art (4 and up) **709.01**
Art
Baylor, B. When clay sings (1-4) **970.004**
Biography
Freedman, R. Indian chiefs (6 and up) **920**
Lipsyte, R. Jim Thorpe, 20th-century jock (5 and up) **92**
Claims
Jeffers, S. Brother eagle, sister sky **304.2**
Costume
Hofsinde, R. Indian costumes (3-6) **391**

Indians of North America—*Continued*
Dictionaries
Wolfson, E. From Abenaki to Zuni (4 and up)   **970.004**

Dwellings
Monroe, J. G. First houses (6 and up)
                                    970.004

Fiction
Baker, O. Where the buffaloes begin (2-4)
                                    Fic
Benchley, N. Small Wolf   **E**
Dalgliesh, A. The courage of Sarah Noble (2-4)   **Fic**
Goble, P. Beyond the ridge (2-4)   **Fic**
Goble, P. Dream wolf   **E**
Goble, P. The girl who loved wild horses
                                       E
Locker, T. The land of Gray Wolf   **E**
Martin, B. Knots on a counting rope   **E**
O'Dell, S. Island of the Blue Dolphins (5 and up)   **Fic**
O'Dell, S. Streams to the river, river to the sea (5 and up)   **Fic**
O'Dell, S. Zia (5 and up)   **Fic**
Osofsky, A. Dreamcatcher   **E**
Reid Banks, L. The Indian in the cupboard (5 and up)   **Fic**
Speare, E. G. The sign of the beaver (5 and up)   **Fic**

Fiction—Bibliography
Anderson, V. Native Americans in fiction
                                    016.8

Folklore
See also Indians of North America—Legends

Languages
See also Indians of North America—Sign language

Legends
Bruchac, J. Flying with the eagle, racing the great bear (5 and up)   **398.2**
Bruchac, J. The girl who married the Moon (5 and up)   **398.2**
Bruchac, J. Thirteen moons on a turtle's back   **811**
Caduto, M. J. Keepers of the night
                                    398.2
Curry, J. L. Back in the beforetime (4-6)
                                    398.2
De Paola, T. The legend of the Indian paintbrush (k-3)   **398.2**
Goble, P. Buffalo woman (2-4)   **398.2**
Goble, P. Crow chief (2-4)   **398.2**
Goble, P. The gift of the sacred dog (2-4)
                                    398.2
Goble, P. The great race of the birds and animals (2-4)   **398.2**
Goble, P. Love flute (2-4)   **398.2**
Longfellow, H. W. Hiawatha   **811**
Mayo, G. That tricky Coyote! (k-3)
                                    398.2
McDermott, G. Coyote: a trickster tale from the American Southwest (k-3)   **398.2**
McDermott, G. Raven (k-3)   **398.2**

Monroe, J. G. First houses (6 and up)
                                    970.004
The Naked bear (4 and up)   **398.2**
Norman, H. How Glooskap outwits the Ice Giants, and other tales of the Maritime Indians (3-6)   **398.2**
Roth, S. L. The story of light (k-3)
                                    398.2
Steptoe, J. The story of Jumping Mouse (1-3)   **398.2**
Van Laan, N. In a circle long ago (3-5)
                                    398.2
Young, E. Moon mother (2-4)   **398.2**

Medicine
Wolfson, E. From the earth to beyond the sky (5 and up)   **970.004**

Mythology
See Indians of North America—Legends

Poetry
Bruchac, J. Thirteen moons on a turtle's back   **811**
Dancing teepees: poems of American Indian youth (3-5)   **897**
Longfellow, H. W. Hiawatha   **811**
On the road of stars (k-3)   **897**

Religion
Wolfson, E. From the earth to beyond the sky (5 and up)   **970.004**

Rites and ceremonies
Ancona, G. Powwow (3-6)   **970.004**
Braine, S. Drumbeat—heartbeat (3-6)
                                    970.004
Crum, R. Eagle drum (3-6)   **970.004**
Liptak, K. North American Indian ceremonies (4 and up)   **970.004**
Monroe, J. G. First houses (6 and up)
                                    970.004

Sign language
Hofsinde, R. Indian sign language (3-6)
                                    419

Social life and customs
Penner, L. R. A Native American feast (4 and up)   **394.1**

Wars
See also United States—History—1755-1763, French and Indian War; Wounded Knee Creek, Battle of, 1890
Ehrlich, A. Wounded Knee: an Indian history of the American West (6 and up)
                                    970.004

Great Plains
Freedman, R. Buffalo hunt (4 and up)
                                    970.004

Missouri River valley
Freedman, R. An Indian winter (6 and up)
                                    978

Northwest Coast of North America
Hoyt-Goldsmith, D. Totem pole (3-5)
                                    970.004

Southwestern States
Baylor, B. When clay sings (1-4)
                                    970.004

The **Inn** of the Stolen Moon. Sanfield, S.
  In Sanfield, S. The feather merchants &
  other tales of the fools of Chelm p60-
  69   **398.2**

Inns *See* Hotels and motels

Innuit *See* Inuit

Inouye, Daniel K.
  See/See also pages in the following book(s):
  Morey, J. Famous Asian Americans p58-68
  (5 and up)   **920**

Insane *See* Mentally ill

Insect metamorphosis. Goor, R.   **595.7**

Insect pests
  Godkin, C. What about ladybugs? (k-3)
                                        595.7

Insect zoo. Meyers, S.   **595.7**

Insectivorous plants *See* Carnivorous plants

Insects
  See also Ants; Butterflies; Dragonflies;
      Grasshoppers; Moths; Wasps
  Brenner, B. Where's that insect? (k-3)
                                        595.7
  Facklam, H. Insects (5 and up)   **595.7**
  Facklam, M. The big bug book (3-6)
                                        595.7
  Goor, R. Insect metamorphosis (2-6)
                                        595.7
  Hunt, J. P. Insects (5 and up)   **595.7**
  Johnson, S. A. Chirping insects (4 and up)
                                        595.7
  Johnson, S. A. Water insects (4 and up)
                                        595.7
  Meyers, S. Insect zoo (4-6)   **595.7**
  Mound, L. A. Amazing insects (2-4)
                                        595.7
  Mound, L. A. Insect (4 and up)   **595.7**
  Parker, N. W. Bugs (1-3)   **595.7**
  Parker, S. Insects (3-5)   **595.7**
  Souza, D. M. Insects around the house (4-6)
                                        595.7
  Souza, D. M. Insects in the garden (4-6)
                                        595.7
  Zim, H. S. Insects (4 and up)   **595.7**
  See/See also pages in the following book(s):
  Norsgaard, E. J. Nature's great balancing act
  p21-41 (4-6)   **574.5**
              Fiction
  Egielski, R. Buz   **E**
  McDonald, M. Insects are my life   **E**
              Poetry
  Fleischman, P. Joyful noise: poems for two
  voices (4 and up)   **811**
  Flit, flutter, fly! (1-4)   **808.81**

Insects, Injurious and beneficial *See* Insect
  pests

Insects are my life. McDonald, M.   **E**

Insects around the house. Souza, D. M.
                                        595.7

An **insect's** body. Cole, J.   **595.7**

Insects in the garden. Souza, D. M. **595.7**

Inside an egg. Johnson, S. A.   **598**

Inside business series
  Aaseng, N. The problem solvers   **920**

Aaseng, N. The unsung heroes   **920**

The **inside-outside** book of London. Munro,
  R.   **942.1**

The **inside-outside** book of New York City.
  Munro, R.   **974.7**

The **inside-outside** book of Paris. Munro, R.
                                        944

The **inside-outside** book of Washington, D.C.
  Munro, R.   **975.3**

Inside story [series]
  Macdonald, F. A 16th century mosque
                                        297
  Macdonald, F. A Roman fort   **355.7**

Inside the bright red gate. Carpenter, F.
  In Carpenter, F. Tales of a Chinese grandmother p1-13   **398.2**

Inside the zoo nursery. Smith, R.   **590.74**

Inspirations. Sills, L.   **920**

Instant paper airplanes. Churchill, E. R.
                                      745.592

Instructional materials centers
  See also School libraries
  American Association of School Librarians.
  Information power   **027.8**
  Assessment and the school library media
  center   **027.8**
  Berger, P. CD-ROM for schools   **025.2**
  Bucher, K. T. Computers & technology in
  school library media centers   **027.8**
  Craver, K. W. School library media centers
  in the 21st century   **027.8**
              Periodicals
  School Library Media Annual   **027.805**
  School Library Media Quarterly
                                    027.805

Instructor   **372.05**

Integration in education *See* School integration

Intellectual freedom
  See also Freedom of information
  Intellectual freedom manual   **323.44**
              Periodicals
  Newsletter on Intellectual Freedom
                                      323.44

Intellectual freedom manual   **323.44**

Intelligence of animals *See* Animal intelligence

**International Board on Books for Young Peo-
ple**
  Bookbird. See Bookbird   **028.505**

International Crane Foundation
  See/See also pages in the following book(s):
  Friedman, J. Operation Siberian crane (5
  and up)   **639.9**

International politics *See* World politics

International relations
  See also World politics

International Wildlife   **591.05**

The **international** wildlife encyclopedia. See
  Marshall Cavendish international wildlife
  encyclopedia   **591**

Internet (Computer network)
  Ellsworth, J. H. Education on the Internet
                                        371.3

Italy
  Travis, D. The land and people of Italy (5 and up) **945**
    Fiction
  De Paola, T. Strega Nona **E**
    Folklore
  See Folklore—Italy
Itchy Richard. Gilson, J. **Fic**
It's a spoon, not a shovel. Buehner, C. **395**
It's about time! (k-2) **811.008**
It's about time, Jesse Bear, and other rhymes. Carlstrom, N. W. See note under Carlstrom, N. W. Jesse Bear, what will you wear? **E**
It's all in your brain. Funston, S. **612.8**
It's an armadillo. Lavies, B. **599.3**
It's Christmas. Prelutsky, J. **811**
It's George!. Cohen, M. See note under Cohen, M. See you in second grade! **E**
It's Halloween. Prelutsky, J. **811**
It's "Him!". Schwartz, A.
  In Schwartz, A. Scary stories 3 p84-85 **398.2**
It's just me, Emily. Hines, A. G. **E**
It's like this, Cat. Neville, E. C. **Fic**
It's mine!. Lionni, L. **E**
It's my birthday. Oxenbury, H. **E**
It's not easy being George. Smith, J. L. See note under Smith, J. L. The kid next door and other headaches **Fic**
It's not the end of the world. Blume, J. **Fic**
It's our world, too!. Hoose, P. M. **302**
It's perfectly normal. Harris, R. H. **613.9**
It's pumpkin time!. Hall, Z. **E**
It's raining cats and dogs. Branley, F. M. **551.5**
It's raining, it's pouring. Pooley, S. **808.8**
It's snowing! It's snowing!. Prelutsky, J. **811**
It's so nice to have a wolf around the house. Allard, H.
  In The Laugh book p111-18 **808.8**
It's Thanksgiving. Prelutsky, J. **811**
It's Valentine's Day. Prelutsky, J. **811**
Ituri Forest (Zaire)
  Jenike, D. A walk through a rain forest (4-6) **574.5**
Ivan the Cow's Son. Afanas'ev, A. N.
  In Afanas'ev, A. N. Russian fairy tales p234-49 **398.2**
Ivan the peasant's son and the thumb-sized man. Afanas'ev, A. N.
  In Afanas'ev, A. N. Russian fairy tales p262-68 **398.2**
Ivan the Simpleton. Afanas'ev, A. N.
  In Afanas'ev, A. N. Russian fairy tales p142-45 **398.2**

Ivanko the bear's son. Afanas'ev, A. N.
  In Afanas'ev, A. N. Russian fairy tales p221-23 **398.2**
Ivanushka the Little Fool. Afanas'ev, A. N.
  In Afanas'ev, A. N. Russian fairy tales p62-65 **398.2**
I've got an idea! the story of Frederick McKinley Jones. Swanson, G. B. **92**
I've got chicken pox. Kelley, T. **E**
Ives, Charles Edward, 1874-1954
  See/See also pages in the following book(s):
  Krull, K. Lives of the musicians p70-73 (4 and up) **920**
Ivimey, John W. (John William), 1868-1961
  The complete story of the three blind mice **E**

Iwamatsu, Atushi Jun, 1908-1994
  Crow Boy **E**
  Momo's kitten. See note under Iwamatsu, A. J. Umbrella **E**
  Umbrella **E**

J

J. T. Wagner, J. **Fic**
Jabar, Cynthia
  (il) Agard, J. No hickory, no dickory, no dock **811**
  (il) Evans, L. Rain song **811**
Jabberwocky, Lewis Carroll's. Carroll, L. **821**
Jack and Catherine. Haley, G. E.
  In Haley, G. E. Mountain Jack tales p37-46 **398.2**
Jack and his golden snuff-box. Jacobs, J.
  In Jacobs, J. English fairy tales p85-96 **398.2**
Jack and King Marock
  In The Jack tales p135-50 **398.2**
Jack and Old Raggedy Bones. Haley, G. E.
  In Haley, G. E. Mountain Jack tales p99-116 **398.2**
Jack and the bean tree
  In The Jack tales p31-39 **398.2**
Jack and the beanstalk
  In The Rainbow fairy book p192-206 **398.2**
  In The Red fairy book p133-45 **398.2**
Jack and the beanstalk. Crossley-Holland, K.
  In Crossley-Holland, K. British folk tales p118-31 **398.2**
Jack and the beanstalk. Jacobs, J.
  In Jacobs, J. English fairy tales p65-72 **398.2**
Jack and the beanstalk. Kellogg, S. **398.2**
Jack and the beanstalk. Reeves, J.
  In Reeves, J. English fables and fairy stories p127-46 **398.2**
Jack and the beanstalk. Rockwell, A. F.
  In Rockwell, A. F. Puss in boots, and other stories p1-11 **398.2**

Jahdu in a little bit of trouble. Hamilton, V.
In Hamilton, V. The all Jahdu storybook
p40-46   **S C**

Jahdu in the far woods. Hamilton, V.
In Hamilton, V. The all Jahdu storybook
p60-65   **S C**

Jahdu lights the way. Hamilton, V.
In Hamilton, V. The all Jahdu storybook
p87-90   **S C**

Jahdu meets the big chicken. Hamilton, V.
In Hamilton, V. The all Jahdu storybook
p66-73   **S C**

Jahdu outwits Young Owl. Hamilton, V.
In Hamilton, V. The all Jahdu storybook
p25-29   **S C**

Jahdu runs through the dark. Hamilton, V.
In Hamilton, V. The all Jahdu storybook
p76-81   **S C**

Jahdu sees the true light. Hamilton, V.
In Hamilton, V. The all Jahdu storybook
p97-104   **S C**

Jake. Jones, R. F.   **636.7**

Jakobsen, Kathy, 1952-
My New York (k-3)   **974.7**
(il) Lindbergh, R. Johnny Appleseed
     811

Jakoubek, Robert E.
Walter White and the power of organized
protest (3-5)   **92**

Jamaica
Fiction
Berry, J. The future-telling lady and other
stories (5 and up)   **S C**
Pomerantz, C. The chalk doll   **E**
Folklore
See Folklore—Jamaica

Jamaica and Brianna. Havill, J. See note under Havill, J. Jamaica's find   **E**

Jamaica tag-along. Havill, J. See note under Havill, J. Jamaica's find   **E**

Jamaica's blue marker. Havill, J. See note under Havill, J. Jamaica's find   **E**

Jamaica's find. Havill, J.   **E**

Jamberry. Degen, B.   **E**

Jambo means hello. Feelings, M.   **E**

James, Betsy
Mary Ann   **E**

James, Diane
(jt. auth) Tofts, H. The 3-D paper book
     745.54
(jt. auth) Tofts, H. The paint book
     745.5
(jt. auth) Tofts, H. The print book   **760**

James, Elizabeth
How to be school smart (5 and up)
     371.3
Sincerely yours (4 and up)   **808**
(jt. auth) Barkin, C. Happy Thanksgiving!
     394.2
(jt. auth) Barkin, C. Happy Valentine's Day!
     394.2
(jt. auth) Barkin, C. Jobs for kids   **650.1**

(jt. auth) Barkin, C. The scary Halloween
costume book   **391**

James, Henry, 1843-1916
See/See also pages in the following book(s):
Children and their books p317-36   **028.5**
Faber, D. Great lives: American literature
p130-40 (5 and up)   **920**

James, Mary, 1927-
Shoebag (5 and up)   **Fic**

James, Simon, 1957-
Ancient Rome (4 and up)   **937**

James, Will, 1892-1942
See/See also pages in the following book(s):
Newbery Medal books, 1922-1955 p47-48
     028.5

James and the giant peach. Dahl, R.   **Fic**

James Marshall's Mother Goose (k-3)
     398.8

Jamestown (Va.)
History
Fritz, J. The double life of Pocahontas (4
and up)   **92**

Jamie O'Rourke and the big potato. De Paola,
T.   **398.2**

Jane, Calamity *See* Calamity Jane, 1852-1903

Jane-Emily. Clapp, P.   **Fic**

Jane gets a donkey. Schwartz, A.
In Schwartz, A. All of our noses are here,
and other noodle tales p8-17
     398.2

Jane grows a carrot. Schwartz, A.
In Schwartz, A. There is a carrot in my
ear, and other noodle tales p40-43
     398.2

Jane Yolen's Mother Goose songbook
     782.42

Janeczko, Paul B., 1945-
Loads of codes and secret ciphers (5 and up)
     652
(comp) The Place my words are looking for.
See The Place my words are looking for
     811.008
(comp) Poetry from A to Z. See Poetry from
A to Z   **808.1**

Janice VanCleave's 201 awesome, magical, bizarre & incredible experiments. VanCleave, J. P.   **507.8**

Janice VanCleave's earth science for every
kid. VanCleave, J. P.   **550**

Janice VanCleave's electricity. VanCleave, J.
P.   **537**

Janice VanCleave's geometry for every kid.
VanCleave, J. P.   **516**

Janice VanCleave's the human body for every
kid. VanCleave, J. P.   **612**

Janovitz, Marilyn
(il) McClung, R. M. America's first elephant
     599.6

Jansson, Tove, 1914-
Comet in Moominland. See note under Jansson, T. Moominsummer madness
     Fic

Jerusalem

Fiction

Geras, A. Golden windows and other stories of Jerusalem (4 and up)   **S C**

Jesse Bear, what will you wear?. Carlstrom, N. W.   **E**

Jesse White Tumbling Team

Schmidt, D. I am a Jesse White tumbler (3-6)   **796.47**

Jessel, Camilla, 1937-

The kitten book (k-3)   **636.8**

Jessica. Henkes, K.   **E**

The jester. Afanas'ev, A. N.

In Afanas'ev, A. N. Russian fairy tales p151-55   **398.2**

Jesters *See* Fools and jesters

Jesus Christ

About

De Paola, T. The miracles of Jesus (k-3)   **232.9**

Wildsmith, B. The Easter story (k-3)   **232.9**

Winthrop, E. He is risen: the Easter story (k-3)   **232.9**

Birth

See Jesus Christ—Nativity

Fiction

Speare, E. G. The bronze bow (6 and up)   **Fic**

Nativity

Bible. N.T. Selections. The Christmas story (k-3)   **232.9**

Bible. N.T. Selections. The Christmas story: told through paintings (4 and up)   **232.9**

Bible. N.T. Selections. The first Christmas (4 and up)   **232.9**

Brown, M. W. Christmas in the barn (k-2)   **232.9**

Kurelek, W. A northern nativity (4 and up)   **232.9**

Winthrop, E. A child is born: the Christmas story (k-3)   **232.9**

Nativity—Fiction

Menotti, G. C. Amahl and the night visitors (2-4)   **Fic**

Wildsmith, B. A Christmas story   **E**

Nativity—Poetry

Berry, J. Celebration song (k-3)   **821**

Farber, N. When it snowed that night   **811**

Kennedy, X. J. The beasts of Bethlehem (3-6)   **811**

Wilner, I. B is for Bethlehem   **E**

The Jew among thorns. Grimm, J.

In Grimm, J. The complete Grimm's fairy tales p503-08   **398.2**

Jewelry

Gryski, C. Friendship bracelets (4 and up)   **746.42**

Jewels *See* Precious stones

The Jewish American family album. Hoobler, D.   **305.8**

The Jewish Americans: a history in their own words, 1650-1950 (6 and up)   **305.8**

Jewish-Arab relations

Dolphin, L. Neve shalom/Wahat al-salam: Oasis of peace (2-4)   **956.94**

Jewish art and symbolism

Chaikin, M. Menorahs, mezuzas, and other Jewish symbols (5 and up)   **296.4**

Jewish biography series

Kresh, P. Isaac Bashevis Singer: the story of a storyteller   **92**

Jewish cooking

See/See also pages in the following book(s):

Burns, M. The Hanukkah book p57-69 (4 and up)   **296.4**

Jewish holidays

See also Hanukkah; Passover; Purim; Rosh ha-Shanah; Sukkoth; Yom Kippur

Jaffe, N. The uninvited guest and other Jewish holiday tales (4-6)   **296.4**

Poetry

Poems for Jewish holidays (k-3)   **811.008**

Jewish holocaust (1933-1945) *See* Holocaust, 1933-1945

Jewish legends

Jaffe, N. The uninvited guest and other Jewish holiday tales (4-6)   **296.4**

Jaffe, N. While standing on one foot (4 and up)   **296.1**

Patterson, J. Angels, prophets, rabbis & kings from the stories of the Jewish people (4-6)   **296.1**

Jewish New Year *See* Rosh ha-Shanah

Jewish refugees

Fiction

Kerr, J. When Hitler stole Pink Rabbit (4 and up)   **Fic**

Levitin, S. Journey to America (4 and up)   **Fic**

Jewish wit and humor

See/See also pages in the following book(s):

Bauer, C. F. Celebrations p119-34   **808.8**

Jews

Biography

Kresh, P. Isaac Bashevis Singer: the story of a storyteller (6 and up)   **92**

Pariser, M. Elie Wiesel (3-5)   **92**

Festivals

See Jewish holidays

Fiction

Clifford, E. The remembering box (3-5)   **Fic**

Cohen, B. The carp in the bathtub (2-4)   **Fic**

Cohen, B. Molly's Pilgrim (2-4)   **Fic**

Cormier, R. Tunes for bears to dance to (6 and up)   **Fic**

Drucker, M. Grandma's latkes   **E**

Edwards, M. A baker's portrait   **E**

Geras, A. Golden windows and other stories of Jerusalem (4 and up)   **S C**

Goldin, B. D. Cakes and miracles   **E**

Jews—Fiction—*Continued*

Goldin, B. D. Just enough is plenty: a Hanukkah tale   E

Goldin, B. D. The magician's visit   E

Goldin, B. D. The world's birthday   E

Hautzig, E. R. Riches (4 and up)   Fic

Hesse, K. Letters from Rifka (5 and up)   Fic

Hoestlandt, J. Star of fear, star of hope   E

Jaffe, N. In the month of Kislev   E

Kimmel, E. A. Hershel and the Hanukkah goblins   E

Konigsburg, E. L. About the B'nai Bagels (4-6)   Fic

Lasky, K. The night journey (4 and up)   Fic

Levoy, M. Alan and Naomi (6 and up)   Fic

Manushkin, F. Latkes and applesauce   E

Manushkin, F. The matzah that Papa brought home   E

Matas, C. Lisa's war (5 and up)   Fic

Oberman, S. The always prayer shawl   E

Oppenheim, S. L. The lily cupboard   E

Polacco, P. The keeping quilt   E

Polacco, P. Mrs. Katz and Tush   E

Polacco, P. Tikvah means hope   E

Rosen, M. J. Elijah's angel   Fic

Schnur, S. The tie man's miracle   E

Schotter, R. Passover magic   E

Shulevitz, U. Hanukah money   E

Singer, I. B. The fools of Chelm and their history (4 and up)   Fic

Singer, I. B. The power of light (4 and up)   S C

Singer, I. B. Stories for children (4 and up)   S C

Taylor, S. All-of-a-kind family (4-6)   Fic

Yolen, J. The devil's arithmetic (4 and up)   Fic

Folklore

Cohen, B. Yussel's prayer (3-5)   398.2

Freedman, F. B. Brothers: a Hebrew legend (k-3)   398.2

Kimmel, E. A. The spotted pony: a collection of Hanukkah stories (3-6)   398.2

Renberg, D. H. King Solomon and the bee (k-3)   398.2

Rothenberg, J. Yettele's feathers (k-3)   398.2

Sanfield, S. Bit by bit (k-3)   398.2

Sanfield, S. The feather merchants & other tales of the fools of Chelm (4-6)   398.2

Sanfield, S. Strudel, strudel, strudel (k-3)   398.2

Schwartz, H. The diamond tree (3-5)   398.2

Singer, I. B. Mazel and Shlimazel (2-5)   398.2

Singer, I. B. When Shlemiel went to Warsaw & other stories (4 and up)   398.2

Singer, I. B. Zlateh the goat, and other stories (4 and up)   398.2

History

Fisher, L. E. The Wailing Wall (4 and up)   221.9

Legends

See Jewish legends

Persecutions

See also Holocaust, 1933-1945

Rites and ceremonies

See Judaism—Customs and practices

Austria—Fiction

Ackerman, K. The night crossing (3-5)   Fic

Orgel, D. The devil in Vienna (6 and up)   Fic

Ethiopia—Fiction

Levitin, S. The return (6 and up)   Fic

Europe

Greenfeld, H. The hidden children (4 and up)   940.53

Rosenberg, M. B. Hiding to survive (5 and up)   940.53

France—Fiction

Morpurgo, M. Waiting for Anya (5 and up)   Fic

Roth-Hano, R. Touch wood (6 and up)   Fic

Germany

Koehn, I. Mischling, second degree: my childhood in Nazi Germany (6 and up)   92

Netherlands

Adler, D. A. A picture book of Anne Frank (1-3)   92

Frank, A. The diary of a young girl (6 and up)   92

Frank, A. The diary of a young girl: the definitive edition (6 and up)   92

Hurwitz, J. Anne Frank: life in hiding (3-5)   92

Reiss, J. The upstairs room (4 and up)   92

Rol, R. van der. Anne Frank, beyond the diary (5 and up)   92

Netherlands—Fiction

Vos, I. Anna is still here (4 and up)   Fic

Vos, I. Hide and seek (4 and up)   Fic

New York (N.Y.)

Costabel, E. D. The Jews of New Amsterdam (2-4)   974.7

Poland

Adler, D. A. Child of the Warsaw ghetto (3-5)   940.53

Toll, N. S. Behind the secret window (6 and up)   940.53

Poland—Fiction

Hautzig, E. R. A gift for Mama (3-6)   Fic

Orlev, U. The island on Bird Street (5 and up)   Fic

Singer, I. B. Naftali the storyteller and his horse, Sus, and other stories (4 and up)   S C

Jews—*Continued*
Romania—Fiction
Orlev, U. Lydia, Queen of Palestine (5 and up)   **Fic**
Russia—Fiction
Krasnopolsky, F. L. I remember (4 and up)   **Fic**
Penn, M. The miracle of the potato latkes   **E**
Schur, M. The circlemaker (5 and up)   **Fic**
United States
Butwin, F. The Jews in America
In The In America series   **305.8**
Hoobler, D. The Jewish American family album (5 and up)   **305.8**
United States—History—Sources
The Jewish Americans: a history in their own words, 1650-1950 (6 and up)   **305.8**

Jews and Gentiles
See also Antisemitism
The Jews in America. Butwin, F.
In The In America series   **305.8**
Jews in literature
See/See also pages in the following book(s):
Crosscurrents of criticism p150-58   **028.5**
The Jews of New Amsterdam. Costabel, E. D.   **974.7**
The **jigsaw** puzzle, a story. Stamper, J. B.
In Halloween: stories and poems p25-35   **808.8**
Jim-Dandy. Irwin, H.   **Fic**
Jim meets The Thing. Cohen, M. See note under Cohen, M. See you in second grade!   **E**
Jim Thorpe, 20th-century jock. Lipsyte, R.   **92**
Jim Ugly. Fleischman, S.   **Fic**
Jimmy's boa and the big splash birthday bash. Noble, T. H. See note under Noble, T. H. The day Jimmy's boa ate the wash   **E**
Jimmy's boa bounces back. Noble, T. H. See note under Noble, T. H. The day Jimmy's boa ate the wash   **E**
Jim's dog Muffins. Cohen, M. See note under Cohen, M. See you in second grade!   **E**
A **job** for Jenny Archer. Conford, E. See note under Conford, E. A case for Jenny Archer   **Fic**
Jobb, Jamie
The night sky book (4 and up)   **523**
Jobs *See* Occupations
Jobs for kids. Barkin, C.   **650.1**
JoeSam
(il) Rohmer, H. The invisible hunters   **398.2**
Johanson, Donald C.
See/See also pages in the following book(s):
Lasky, K. Traces of life p12-20 (5 and up)   **573.2**

John, Helen
(il) Taylor, S. All-of-a-kind family   **Fic**
John and the Devil's daughter. Hamilton, V.
In Hamilton, V. The people could fly: American black folktales p107-15   **398.2**
John Burningham's ABC. Burningham, J.   **E**
John Darling and the skeeter chariot. Walker, P. R.
In Walker, P. R. Big men, big country p37-41   **398.2**
John Henry (Legendary character)
Keats, E. J. John Henry (k-3)   **398.2**
Lester, J. John Henry (k-3)   **398.2**
John Henry. Osborne, M. P.
In Osborne, M. P. American tall tales p87-95   **398.2**
John Henry. Winter, B.
In Holiday plays round the year p239-46   **812.008**
John Henry races the steam drill. Walker, P. R.
In Walker, P. R. Big men, big country p55-61   **398.2**
John Henry: the steel-driving man. San Souci, R.
In San Souci, R. Larger than life p1-12   **398.2**
John in court. Sanfield, S.
In Sanfield, S. The adventures of High John the Conqueror   **398.2**
John Treegate's musket. Wibberley, L.   **Fic**
John wins a bet. Sanfield, S.
In Sanfield, S. The adventures of High John the Conqueror   **398.2**
Johnny and the three goats
In Tomie dePaola's favorite nursery tales p70-74   **398.2**
Johnny Appleseed. Osborne, M. P.
In Osborne, M. P. American tall tales p25-35   **398.2**
Johnny Appleseed! Johnny Appleseed!. Emrich, M. V.
In From sea to shining sea p274-76   **810.8**
Johnny-cake. Jacobs, J.
In Jacobs, J. English fairy tales p155-58   **398.2**
In Tomie dePaola's favorite nursery tales p11-15   **398.2**
Johnny Gloke. Jacobs, J.
In Jacobs, J. English fairy tales p291-93   **398.2**
Johnny Gloke. Reeves, J.
In Reeves, J. English fables and fairy stories p23-34   **398.2**
Johnny Lion's bad day. Hurd, E. T. See note under Hurd, E. T. Johnny Lion's book   **E**
Johnny Lion's book. Hurd, E. T.   **E**

The **juniper** tree. Grimm, J.
In Grimm, J. The complete Grimm's
fairy tales p220-29 **398.2**

Junk food—what it is, what it does. Seixas, J.
S. **641.3**

Jupiter (Planet)
Simon, S. Jupiter (3-6) **523.4**
Vogt, G. Jupiter (2-4) **523.4**
See/See also pages in the following book(s):
Harris, A. The great Voyager adventure p21-
32 (5 and up) **523.4**
Kelch, J. W. Small worlds: exploring the 60
moons of our solar system p51-65 (6 and
up) **523.9**

Jurmain, Suzanne
Once upon a horse (6 and up) **636.1**

Just a dream. Van Allsburg, C. **E**

Just delicious. Schwartz, A.
In Schwartz, A. Scary stories 3 p12-14
398.2

Just enough is plenty: a Hanukkah tale.
Goldin, B. D. **E**

Just like Daddy. Asch, F. See note under
Asch, F. Sand cake **E**

Just me. Ets, M. H. **E**

Just one ghost. Terada, A. M.
In Terada, A. M. Under the starfruit tree
p128-29 **398.2**

Just plain Fancy. Polacco, P. **E**

The **just** reward. Afanas'ev, A. N.
In Afanas'ev, A. N. Russian fairy tales
p39-40 **398.2**

Just say hiç!. Walker, B. K.
In Walker, B. K. A treasury of Turkish
folktales for children p76-79
398.2

Just so stories. Kipling, R. **S C**

Just us women. Caines, J. F. **E**

Juster, Norton, 1929-
As: a surfeit of similes (3-5) **427**
The phantom tollbooth (5 and up) **Fic**
The phantom tollbooth [excerpt]
In The Random House book of humor
for children p130-33 **817.008**

Justice. Babbitt, N.
In Babbitt, N. The Devil's other storybook p11-17 **S C**

Justice. McKissack, P. C.
In McKissack, P. C. The dark-thirty p22-
34 **S C**

Justin and the best biscuits in the world. Walter, M. P. **Fic**

Justin Morgan had a horse. Henry, M.
Fic

The **Juvenile** numerator
In A Nursery companion p36-37
820.8

K

Kaa's hunting. Kipling, R.
In Kipling, R. The jungle books
S C

The **kabil's** donkey. Kimmel, E. A.
In Kimmel, E. A. The spotted pony: a
collection of Hanukkah stories p19-23
398.2

Kaddo's wall. Courlander, H.
In Courlander, H. The cow-tail switch,
and other West African stories p13-24
398.2

Kahl, Jonathan D.
Storm warning (4-6) **551.55**
Thunderbolt (4-6) **551.5**
Weatherwise (4-6) **551.6**
Wet weather (4-6) **551.57**

Kahlo, Frida, 1907-1954
About
Turner, R. M. Frida Kahlo (4-6) **92**
See/See also pages in the following book(s):
Sills, L. Inspirations p18-27 (5 and up)
920

Kahukura and the fairies. Te Kanawa, K.
In Te Kanawa, K. Land of the long white
cloud p45-50 **398.2**

Kaiulani, Princess of Hawaii, 1875-1899
About
Stanley, F. The last princess: the story of
Princess Ka'iulani of Hawai'i (3-5) **92**

Kakkak, Dale
(il) Regguinti, G. The sacred harvest
970.004

Kalan, Robert
Blue sea **E**
Jump, frog, jump! **E**
Rain **E**

Kalbacken, Joan
The Menominee (2-4) **970.004**

Kaleidoscope **011.6**

Kalish, Lionel
(il) Cobb, V. Magic—naturally! **793.8**

Kalispel Indians
Crum, R. Eagle drum (3-6) **970.004**

Kalman, Bobbie, 1947-
18th century clothing (3-6) **391**
19th century clothing (3-6) **391**
A canoe trip (2-4) **797.1**

Kamen, Gloria
Edward Lear, king of nonsense (4-6) **92**
(il) Levine, E. S. Lisa and her soundless
world **617.8**

Kamerman, Sylvia E.
(ed) The Big book of Christmas plays. See
The Big book of Christmas plays
808.82
(ed) Holiday plays round the year. See Holiday plays round the year **812.008**

Kampuchea *See* Cambodia

Kane, Henry Bugbee
(il) McCord, D. T. W. All day long: fifty rhymes of the never was and always is
811
(il) McCord, D. T. W. One at a time
811
(il) McCord, D. T. W. Take sky: more rhymes of the never was and always is
811

Kane, Joseph Nathan, 1899-
Famous first facts: a record of first happenings, discoveries, and inventions in American history
031.02

Kanellos, Nicolás
(ed) Hispanic American almanac. See Hispanic American almanac [junior version]
305.8

Kang, Johanna
(il) Hoestlandt, J. Star of fear, star of hope
E

Kangaroos
Arnold, C. Kangaroo (3-5)
599.2
Darling, K. Kangaroos on location (3-5)
599.2
Fiction
Payne, E. Katy No-Pocket
E

Kangaroos on location. Darling, K.
599.2

Kanji-jo, the nestlings. MacDonald, M. R.
In MacDonald, M. R. Look back and see p24-36
372.6

Kansas
Fredeen, C. Kansas
In Hello USA series
973
Kent, Z. Kansas
In America the beautiful
973
Fiction
Irwin, H. Jim-Dandy (5 and up)
Fic

Kanu above and Kanu below. MacDonald, M. R.
In MacDonald, M. R. The storyteller's start-up book p167-75
372.6

Kanu of Kathmandu. Margolies, B. A.
954.9

Kaplan, Mark, 1953-
(il) Simon, S. Earth words
363.7

Karaçor and the giants. Walker, B. K.
In Walker, B. K. A treasury of Turkish folktales for children p52-61
398.2

Karas, G. Brian
(il) I know an old lady who swallowed a fly. See I know an old lady who swallowed a fly
782.42

Karate
Brimner, L. D. Karate (4 and up)
796.8
Goedecke, C. J. The wind warrior (4 and up)
796.8
Queen, J. A. Karate for kids (4 and up)
796.8

Karate for kids. Queen, J. A.
796.8

The **Karate** Kid. Soto, G.
In Soto, G. Baseball in April, and other stories p69-80
S C

Kari Woodengown. Asbjornsen, P. C.
In The Red fairy book p189-201
398.2

Karlin, Barbara
Cinderella (k-2)
398.2

Karlin, Bernie, 1927-
(il) Merriam, E. 12 ways to get to 11
510

Karmi, Giyora *See* Carmi, Giora

Karpinski, Tony
(il) Ross, S. Shakespeare and Macbeth
822.3

Kassa, the strong one. Courlander, H.
In Courlander, H. The cow-tail switch, and other West African stories p41-46
398.2

Kassebaum, Nancy Landon
See/See also pages in the following book(s):
Morin, I. V. Women of the U. S. Congress p99-113 (5 and up)
920

Kastner, Jill
(il) Sanders, S. R. Aurora means dawn
E

Kasza, Keiko
The pigs' picnic
E
The wolf's chicken stew
E

Katan, Norma Jean
Hieroglyphs, the writing of ancient Egypt (4 and up)
493

Katanya. Schwartz, H.
In Schwartz, H. The diamond tree p35-43
398.2

Katchi Katchi Blue Jay. MacDonald, M. R.
In MacDonald, M. R. Look back and see p81-89
372.6

Kate Crackernuts. Briggs, K. M.
Fic

Kate Crackernuts. Jacobs, J.
In Jacobs, J. English fairy tales p196-99
398.2
In Womenfolk and fairy tales p65-70
398.2

Kate Crackernuts. Mayo, M.
In Mayo, M. Magical tales from many lands p44-53
398.2

Kate Crackernuts. Rockwell, A. F.
In Rockwell, A. F. Puss in boots, and other stories p19-26
398.2

Katie Henio: Navajo sheepherder. Thomson, P.
970.004

Katie John. Calhoun, M.
Fic

Katie John and Heathcliff. Calhoun, M. See note under Calhoun, M. Katie John
Fic

Katie's trunk. Turner, A. W.
E

Katy and the big snow. Burton, V. L.
E

Katy No-Pocket. Payne, E.
E

Katz, Bill *See* Katz, William A., 1924-

Katz, David, 1928-
(jt. auth) Allison, L. Gee, Wiz!
507.8

Katz, Elizabeth, 1933-
India—in pictures. See India—in pictures
954

Kesey, Ken
Little Tricker, the squirrel, meets Big Double, the bear   E

Kessell, Walter Gaffney- *See* Gaffney-Kessell, Walter

Kesselman, Wendy Ann
Emma   E

Kessler, Cristina
All the king's animals (4-6)   639.9

Kessler, Leonard P., 1920-
Here comes the strikeout   E
Kick, pass, and run   E
Last one in is a rotten egg   E
Old Turtle's 90 knock-knocks, jokes, and riddles (1-3)   793.73
Old Turtle's baseball stories. See note under Kessler, L. P. Old Turtle's soccer team   E
Old Turtle's riddle and joke-book (1-3)   793.73
Old Turtle's soccer team   E

Kettelkamp, Larry, 1933-
Living in space (5 and up)   629.4
Magic made easy (4 and up)   793.8

Ketteman, Helen, 1945-
The year of no more corn   E

Key, Francis Scott, 1779-1843
The Star-Spangled Banner   782.42
About
Kroll, S. By the dawn's early light (3-5)   782.42
Whitcraft, M. Francis Scott Key (4 and up)   92

Keys *See* Locks and keys
The keys of destiny. Philip, N.
In Philip, N. The Arabian nights p145-55   398.2
The keys to my kingdom. Dabcovich, L.   398.8

Keystone kids. Tunis, J. R. See note under Tunis, J. R. The kid from Tomkinsville   Fic

Khalsa, Dayal Kaur
Cowboy dreams   E
How pizza came to Queens   E
I want a dog   E

Kherdian, David, 1931-
Feathers and tails (2-5)   398.2
Includes the following stories: The four friends; Heron woos crane; Anansi rides tiger; Pig and bear; The monkey and the crocodile; Coyote and the acorns; The wolf and the seven little kids; The incautious fox and the foolish wolf; The heron and the hummingbird; Monkey; The blue jackal; The stolen moon
The road from home [biography of Veron Kherdian] (6 and up)   92
Terence Toad and the visitor
In To ride a butterfly p35-36   810.8

Kherdian, Nonny Hogrogian *See* Hogrogian, Nonny

Kherdian, Veron, 1907-
About
Kherdian, D. The road from home (6 and up)   92

Khorana, Meena
Africa in literature for children and young adults   016.9

Kick, pass, and run. Kessler, L. P.   E

The **kid** comes back. Tunis, J. R. See note under Tunis, J. R. The kid from Tomkinsville   Fic

The **kid** from Tomkinsville. Tunis, J. R.   Fic

The **kid** next door and other headaches. Smith, J. L.   Fic

Kiddell-Monroe, Joan, 1908-1972
(il) Picard, B. L. The Iliad of Homer   883
(il) Reeves, J. English fables and fairy stories   398.2
(il) Sherlock, Sir P. M. West Indian folktales   398.2

The **kidnapped** prince: the life of Olaudah Equiano. Cameron, A.   92

Kidnapping
Fiction
Fleischman, P. The Half-a-Moon Inn (4-6)   Fic

Kids at work. Freedman, R.   331.3

The **Kids'** book about death and dying (5 and up)   155.9

Kids camp! Carlson, L. M.   796.54

The **kids'** cat book. De Paola, T.   636.8

Kids' cookbook, American Heart Association   641.5

The **kids** cottage book. See Drake, J. The kids' summer handbook   790.1

Kids' crazy concoctions. Hauser, J. F.   745.5

The **kid's** guide to social action. Lewis, B. A.   361.2

A **kid's** guide to the brain. See Funston, S. It's all in your brain   612.8

The **kids'** nature almanac. Smith, A.   508

The **kids'** summer handbook. Drake, J.   790.1

Kiefte, Kees de
(il) Hooks, W. H. The girl who could fly   Fic
(il) Namioka, L. Yang the third and her impossible family   Fic
(il) Namioka, L. Yang the youngest and his terrible ear   Fic

Kiesler, Kate
(il) Murphy, J. Into the deep forest with Henry David Thoreau   974.1

Kiitos! Kiitos!. Hands, R.
In The Oxford book of scary tales p144-49   808.8

Kilcup, Rick
Randy the red-horned rainmoose
In The Big book of Christmas plays p228-39   808.82

Killer bees. Lavies, B.   595.7
Killer snakes. Freedman, R.   597.9
Killer whale. Arnold, C.   599.5

Kline, Suzy, 1943-—*Continued*

Herbie Jones and the class gift. See note under Kline, S. Herbie Jones   **Fic**

Herbie Jones and the dark attic. See note under Kline, S. Herbie Jones   **Fic**

Herbie Jones and the monster ball. See note under Kline, S. Herbie Jones   **Fic**

Horrible Harry and the ant invasion. See note under Kline, S. Horrible Harry in room 2B   **Fic**

Horrible Harry and the Christmas surprise. See note under Kline, S. Horrible Harry in room 2B   **Fic**

Horrible Harry and the green slime. See note under Kline, S. Horrible Harry in room 2B   **Fic**

Horrible Harry and the kickball wedding. See note under Kline, S. Horrible Harry in room 2B   **Fic**

Horrible Harry in room 2B (2-4)   **Fic**

Horrible Harry's secret. See note under Kline, S. Horrible Harry in room 2B   **Fic**

Mary Marony and the chocolate surprise. See note under Kline, S. Mary Marony, mummy girl   **Fic**

Mary Marony and the snake. See note under Kline, S. Mary Marony, mummy girl   **Fic**

Mary Marony hides out. See note under Kline, S. Mary Marony, mummy girl   **Fic**

Mary Marony, mummy girl (2-4)   **Fic**

Orp. See note under Kline, S. Orp and the FBI   **Fic**

Orp and the chop suey burgers. See note under Kline, S. Orp and the FBI   **Fic**

Orp and the FBI (4-6)   **Fic**

Orp goes to the hoop. See note under Kline, S. Orp and the FBI   **Fic**

Song Lee and the hamster hunt. See note under Kline, S. Horrible Harry in room 2B   **Fic**

Song Lee and the Leech Man. See note under Kline, S. Horrible Harry in room 2B   **Fic**

Song Lee in room 2B. See note under Kline, S. Horrible Harry in room 2B   **Fic**

What's the matter with Herbie Jones? See note under Kline, S. Herbie Jones   **Fic**

Who's Orp's girlfriend. See note under Kline, S. Orp and the FBI   **Fic**

Klondike fever. Cooper, M. L.   **971.9**

Klondike River valley (Yukon)
Gold discoveries
Cooper, M. L. Klondike fever (5 and up)   **971.9**

Klotzbeacher, Donovan
(il) Kettelkamp, L. Magic made easy   **793.8**

The **knapsack,** the hat, and the horn. Grimm, J.
In Grimm, J. The complete Grimm's fairy tales p258-64   **398.2**

The **Knee-high** man
In The Diane Goode book of American folk tales and songs p19-21   **398.2**

The **knee-high** man. Lester, J.
In Lester, J. The knee-high man, and other tales p27-29   **398.2**
In The Oxford treasury of children's stories p33-34   **S C**

The **knee-high** man, and other tales. Lester, J.   **398.2**

Kneeknock Rise. Babbitt, N.   **Fic**

Knight, Christopher G.
(il) Lasky, K. A baby for Max   **E**
(il) Lasky, K. Days of the Dead   **394.2**
(il) Lasky, K. Dinosaur dig   **567.9**
(il) Lasky, K. Monarchs   **595.7**
(il) Lasky, K. Sugaring time   **633.6**
(il) Lasky, K. Surtscy   **508**
(il) Lasky, K. Think like an eagle   **778.9**

Knight, Hilary
(il) Happy birthday. See Happy birthday   **811.008**
(il) MacDonald, B. Mrs. Piggle-Wiggle   **Fic**
(il) Side by side. See Side by side   **808.81**

Knight, Kathryn Lasky
See Lasky, Kathryn

Knight, Margy Burns
Talking walls (3-5)   **909**
Welcoming babies (k-2)   **392**

Knight, Maxwell B.
(jt. auth) Lasky, K. A baby for Max   **E**

The **knight** and the dragon. De Paola, T.   **E**

Knights and knighthood
Gravett, C. Knight (4 and up)   **940.1**
Lasker, J. A tournament of knights (1-3)   **394**
Yue, C. Armor (4 and up)   **355.8**
Fiction
Bulla, C. R. The sword in the tree (3-5)   **Fic**
De Paola, T. The knight and the dragon   **E**
Hodges, M. Saint George and the dragon (2-5)   **398.2**

Knight's castle. Eager, E. See note under Eager, E. Half magic   **Fic**

Knights of the kitchen table. Scieszka, J.   **Fic**

Knights of the Round Table *See* Arthurian romances

Knock at a star (3-6)   **821.008**

Knock . . . knock . . . knock. San Souci, R.
In San Souci, R. More short & shivery p148-52   **398.2**

Knoist and his three sons. Grimm, J.
In Grimm, J. The complete Grimm's fairy tales p622   **398.2**

Knots on a counting rope. Martin, B.   **E**

Know about smoking. Hyde, M. O.   **616.86**

Lang, Andrew, 1844-1912
The forty thieves
In Womenfolk and fairy tales p51-64
398.2

The Terrible Head
In The Blue fairy book p182-92
398.2

(ed) The Arabian nights entertainments. See
The Arabian nights entertainments
398.2

(ed) The Blue fairy book. See The Blue fairy
book **398.2**

(ed) The Green fairy book. See The Green
fairy book **398.2**

(ed) The Rainbow fairy book. See The Rainbow fairy book **398.2**

(ed) The Red fairy book. See The Red fairy
book **398.2**

(ed) The Yellow fairy book. See The Yellow
fairy book **398.2**

Lang, Aubrey
Eagles (4-6) **598**
(il) Stirling, I. Bears **599.74**

Lang, Glenna
(il) Stevenson, R. L. My shadow **821**

Lang, Susan S.
Nature in your backyard (2-4) **508**

Lange, Dorothea, 1895-1965
About
Turner, R. M. Dorothea Lange (4-6) **92**

Langford, Alton
(il) Milton, J. Whales **599.5**

Langley, Andrew
The industrial revolution (4 and up)
909.81

Langley, Jonathan
(il) Root, B. My first dictionary **423**

Langone, John, 1929-
Our endangered earth (6 and up) **363.7**

Langstaff, John M., 1920-
Frog went a-courtin' (k-3) **782.42**
Oh, a-hunting we will go (k-2) **782.42**
Over in the meadow (k-2) **782.42**
(ed) Climbing Jacob's ladder. See Climbing
Jacob's ladder **782.25**
(ed) Gilbert, W. S. "I have a song to sing,
O!" **782.42**
(ed) What a morning! See What a morning!
782.25

Langston Hughes, American poet. Walker, A.
92

Langton, Jane
The fledgling (5 and up) **Fic**
The fragile flag (5 and up) **Fic**

Language and languages
See also Sign language

Language and literacy series
Meltzer, M. Nonfiction for the classroom
973

Language arts
See also Creative writing

Language Arts **372.605**

The **language** of blood. Coville, B.
In Coville, B. Oddly enough p61-78
S C

Languages
Vocabulary
See Vocabulary

Lankford, Mary D., 1932-
Hopscotch around the world (3-5) **796.2**
Is it dark? is it light? **E**

Lanting, Frans
(il) Johnson, S. A. Elephant seals
599.74

The **Lantuch**. Singer, I. B.
In Singer, I. B. Naftali the storyteller and
his horse, Sus, and other stories p39-46 **S C**
In Singer, I. B. Stories for children p231-36 **S C**

Lantz, Paul, 1908-
(il) Gates, D. Blue willow **Fic**

Lanyard. Gryski, C. **746.42**

Laos
Folklore
See Folklore—Laos

The **Lap-time** song and play book **782.42**

Lapland
Lewin, T. The reindeer people (3-5)
948.97

Laplanders *See* Sami (European people)

Laporte, Michele
(il) Giblin, J. Edith Wilson: the woman who
ran the United States **92**

Large print books
Armstrong, W. H. Sounder **Fic**
Avi. The true confessions of Charlotte
Doyle **Fic**
Bagnold, E. National Velvet **Fic**
Bauer, M. D. On my honor **Fic**
Bible. The Holy Bible: new revised standard
version **220.5**
Brink, C. R. Caddie Woodlawn **Fic**
Byars, B. C. The burning questions of Bingo
Brown **Fic**
Byars, B. C. The night swimmers **Fic**
Byars, B. C. The summer of the swans
Fic
Cleary, B. Henry Huggins **Fic**
Cleary, B. The mouse and the motorcycle
Fic
Cleary, B. Ramona the pest **Fic**
Cooper, S. The grey king **Fic**
Dahl, R. James and the giant peach **Fic**
Dahl, R. Matilda **Fic**
DeClements, B. 6th grade can really kill you
Fic
Fitzgerald, J. D. The Great Brain **Fic**
Fitzhugh, L. Harriet the spy **Fic**
Forbes, E. Johnny Tremain **Fic**
Frank, A. The diary of a young girl: the definitive edition **92**
Greene, B. Summer of my German soldier
Fic
Greene, C. C. Beat the turtle drum **Fic**

Contents: Brer Fox and Mr. Man; King Lion and Mr. Man; Brer Fox and Brer Turtle; Brer Fox gets tricked by the frogs; Brer Bear gets tricked by Brer Frog; Brer Bear, Brer Turtle, and the rope-pulling contest; Brer Buzzard takes care of Brer Buzzard; Brer Fox wants to make music; The Pimmerly Plum; Brer Turtle takes flying lessons; Brer Buzzard and Brer Hawk; Brer Buzzard bites the dust—again; The Wise Bird and the Foolish Bird; The most-beautiful-bird in-the-world contest; Brer Fox and Uncle Mud Turtle; The creature with no claws; Brer Polecat finds a winter home; Brer Bear and Brer Rabbit take care of Brer Fox and Brer Wolf; Brer Fox gets away for once; Taily-po; Brer Rabbit, Brer Fox, and the chickens; Brer Fox tries to get revenge; Brer Wolf and the pigs; Mr. Benjamin Ram and his wonderful fiddle; Mr. Benjamin Ram triumphs again; How the Bear nursed the Alligators; Brer Turtle and Brer Mink; Brer Billy Goat tricks Brer Wolf; Brer Fox takes Miz Cricket to dinner; Miz Cricket makes the creatures run; The story of the Doodang; Brer Deer and King Sun's daughter; Teenchy-Tiny Duck's magical satchel

Contents: Why the Sun and the Moon live in the sky; The bird that made milk; The monster who swallowed everything; Tug-of-war; Why dogs chase cats; The town where snoring was not allowed; The town where sleeping was not allowed; The woman and the tree children; Why monkeys live in trees; What is the most important part of the body?; How many spots does a leopard have?; The wonderful healing leaves

Lester, Julius—_Continued_

John Henry (k-3) **398.2**

The Knee-High Man

_In_ The Oxford treasury of children's stories p33-34 **S C**

The knee-high man, and other tales (k-3) **398.2**

Contents: What is trouble?; Why dogs hate cats; Mr. Rabbit and Mr. Bear; Why the waves have whitecaps; The farmer and the snake; The knee-high man

The last tales of Uncle Remus (4-6) **398.2**

Contents: Why the cricket has elbows on his legs; Why the earth is mostly water; The origin of the ocean; Brer Rabbit and Miss Nancy; The old king and the new king; Brer Bear comes to the community; The snake; A ghost story; Brer Bear exposes Brer Rabbit; Brer Rabbit teaches Brer Bear to comb his hair; Why Brer Possum has no hair on his tail; Why Brer Possum loves peace; The baby who loved pumpkins; Impty-Umpty and the blacksmith; The angry woman; Brer Rabbit throws a party; Why Brer Fox's legs are black; How the witch was caught; The man who almost married a witch; Why dogs are tame; How Tinktum Tidy recruited an army for the king; Why guinea fowls are speckled; Why the Guineas stay awake; Brer Fox and the white grapes; Why the hawk likes to eat chickens; The little boy and his dogs; The man and the wild cattle; "Cutta cord-la"; Why Brer Bull growls and grumbles; Brer Rabbit, King Polecat, and the gingercakes; The fool; How Brer Lion lost his hair; The man and the boots; Why the goat has a short tail; Brer Buzzard and Brer Crow; The blacksmith and the Devil; Why chickens scratch in the dirt; Brer Rabbit and Aunt Nancy; The adventures of Simon and Susanna

The man who knew too much (2-4) **398.2**

More tales of Uncle Remus (4-6) **398.2**

Contents: Brer Rabbit gets Brer Fox's dinner; Brer Rabbit and Brer Fox kill a cow; Brer Fox and the grapes; Brer Rabbit falls in love; The Ol' African helps out; The courting contest; Brer Rabbit, Brer Coon, and the frogs; Brer Rabbit's laughing place; Brer Rabbit gets the house to himself; Miz Partridge tricks Brer Rabbit; The famine; Brer Rabbit, Brer Bear, and the honey; Brer Snake catches Brer Wolf; Brer Rabbit gets the meat; Brer Rabbit scares everybody; Grinny Granny Wolf; The fire test; Brer Rabbit catches Wattle Weasel; Brer Rabbit and Mr. Man's chickens; The barbecue; Brer Alligator learns about trouble; Brer Fox gets tricked again; Brer Rabbit and Brer Bullfrog; Brer Rabbit meets up with Cousin Wildcat; Brer Rabbit gets a little comeuppance; Brer Rabbit advises Brer Lion; Brer Rabbit's money mint; Brer Rabbit makes a deal with Mr. Man; Brer Rabbit doctors Brer Fox's burns; Brer Fox sets a fire; Brer Rabbit builds a tower; Brer Rabbit saves Brer Wolf—maybe; Mammy-Bammy Big-Money takes care of Brer Wolf; Brer Rabbit and the gizzard eater; Why dogs are always sniffing; Being fashionable ain't always healthy; The race

The tales of Uncle Remus (4-6) **398.2**

Contents: How the animals came to Earth; How Brer Fox and Brer Dog became enemies; "Hold'im down, Brer Fox"; Brer Rabbit comes to dinner; Brer Rabbit and the Tar Baby; Brer Rabbit gets even; Brer Rabbit and Sister Cow; Brer Turtle, Brer Rabbit, and Brer Fox; Brer Wolf tries to catch Brer Rabbit; Brer Rabbit finally gets beaten; Mr. Jack Sparrow meets his end; Brer Rabbit gets caught one more time; The death of Brer Wolf; Brer Fox and Brer Rabbit go hunting; Brer Rabbit tricks Brer Fox again; Brer Rabbit eats the butter; Brer Rabbit saves his meat; Brer Rabbit's children; The death of Brer Fox; Brer Rabbit and Brer Lion; Brer Rabbit takes care of Brer Tiger; Brer Lion meets the creature; The talking house; Brer Rabbit gets beaten again; Brer Rabbit tricks Brer Bear; The end of Brer Bear; Brer Fox gets tricked again; Brer Rabbit and the little girl; Brer Rabbit goes back to Mr. Man's garden; Brer Possum hears the singing; Brer Rabbit's riddle; The Moon in the pond; Why Brer Bear has no tail; Wiley Wolf and Riley Rabbit; Brer Rabbit gets the money; The cradle didn't rock; Brer Rabbit to the rescue; The noise in the woods; Brer Rabbit gets the meat again; Brer Wolf gets in more trouble; Brer

Rabbit tells on Brer Wolf; Brer Rabbit and the mosquitoes; How Brer Rabbit became a scary monster; Brer Fox, Brer Rabbit, and King Deer's daughter; Brer Rabbit breaks up the party; Brer Rabbit outwits Mr. Man; Brer Wolf, Brer Fox, and the little Rabbits; Brer Rabbit's luck

To be a slave (6 and up) **326**

Lester's dog. Hesse, K. **E**

Let freedom ring. Livingston, M. C. **811**

Let George do it. Pendleton, E.

_In_ Holiday plays round the year p169-78 **812.008**

Let the circle be unbroken. Taylor, M. D. **Fic**

Let's do fingerplays. Grayson, M. F. **796.1**

Let's fly from A to Z. Magee, D. **629.133**

Let's get a pet. Ziefert, H. **636.088**

Let's go Froggy. London, J. See note under London, J. Froggy learns to swim **E**

Let's go home, Little Bear. Waddell, M. See note under Waddell, M. Can't you sleep, Little Bear? **E**

Let's go/Vamos. Emberley, R. **463**

Let's-read-and-find-out science books [series]

Aliki. Corn is maize **633.1**

Aliki. Digging up dinosaurs **567.9**

Aliki. Dinosaur bones **567.9**

Aliki. Dinosaurs are different **567.9**

Aliki. Fossils tell of long ago **560**

Aliki. I'm growing! **612.6**

Aliki. Milk from cow to carton **637**

Aliki. My feet **612**

Aliki. My five senses **612.8**

Aliki. My hands **612**

Balestrino, P. The skeleton inside you **611**

Berger, M. Germs make me sick! **616.9**

Berger, M. Look out for turtles! **597.9**

Berger, M. Oil spill! **363.7**

Berger, M. Switch on, switch off **537**

Berger, M. Why I cough, sneeze, shiver, hiccup, & yawn **612.8**

Branley, F. M. Air is all around you **551.5**

Branley, F. M. The Big Dipper **523.8**

Branley, F. M. Earthquakes **551.2**

Branley, F. M. Eclipse: darkness in daytime **523.7**

Branley, F. M. Flash, crash, rumble, and roll **551.5**

Branley, F. M. Gravity is a mystery **531**

Branley, F. M. Is there life in outer space? **574.999**

Branley, F. M. Journey into a black hole **523.8**

Branley, F. M. The moon seems to change **523.3**

Branley, F. M. Rain & hail **551.57**

Branley, F. M. Shooting stars **523.6**

Branley, F. M. The sky is full of stars **523.8**

Branley, F. M. Snow is falling **551.57**

Branley, F. M. The sun **523.7**

Levine, Arthur A., 1962-
The boy who drew cats (k-3)   **398.2**
Pearl Moscowitz's last stand   **E**

Levine, Edna Simon, 1910-1992
Lisa and her soundless world (1-3)
    617.8

Levine, Ellen
Anna Pavlova, genius of the dance (5 and up)   **92**
Freedom's children (6 and up)   **323.1**
I hate English!   **E**
. . . if your name was changed at Ellis Island (3-5)   **325.73**

Levine, Joe
(il) Hirst, R. My place in space   **520**

Levine, Mike
(jt. auth) Egan, T. The Macmillan book of baseball stories   **796.357**

Levinson, Nancy Smiler, 1938-
Chuck Yeager: the man who broke the sound barrier (5 and up)   **92**
Snowshoe Thompson   **E**

Levinson, Riki
I go with my family to Grandma's   **E**
Our home is the sea   **E**
Watch the stars come out   **E**

Levitin, Sonia, 1934-
Journey to America (4 and up)   **Fic**
The return (6 and up)   **Fic**

Levittown (N.Y.)
    Fiction
Conrad, P. Our house (4-6)   **S C**

Levoy, Myron
Alan and Naomi (6 and up)   **Fic**
The witch of Fourth Street, and other stories (4-6)   **S C**
Contents: The witch of Fourth Street; Vincent-the-Good and the electric train; Andreas and the magic bells; Mrs. Dunn's lovely, lovely farm; Keplik, the match man; The fish angel; Aaron's gift; The Hanukkah Santa Claus

Levy, Constance, 1931-
A tree place and other poems (3-5)   **811**

Levy, Elizabeth, 1942-
Something queer at the ball park. See note under Levy, E. Something queer is going on (a mystery)   **E**
Something queer at the birthday party. See note under Levy, E. Something queer is going on (a mystery)   **E**
Something queer at the haunted school. See note under Levy, E. Something queer is going on (a mystery)   **E**
Something queer at the lemonade stand. See note under Levy, E. Something queer is going on (a mystery)   **E**
Something queer at the library. See note under Levy, E. Something queer is going on (a mystery)   **E**
Something queer at the scary movie. See note under Levy, E. Something queer is going on (a mystery)   **E**
Something queer in outer space. See note under Levy, E. Something queer is going on (a mystery)   **E**

Something queer in the cafeteria. See note under Levy, E. Something queer is going on (a mystery)   **E**
Something queer is going on (a mystery)
    E
Something queer on vacation. See note under Levy, E. Something queer is going on (a mystery)   **E**

Lewin, Betsy, 1937-
Booby hatch   **E**
Walk a green path (2-5)   **581**

Lewin, Hugh, 1939-
Jafta   **E**
Jafta and the wedding. See note under Lewin, H. Jafta   **E**
Jafta—the homecoming. See note under Lewin, H. Jafta   **E**
Jafta—the journey. See note under Lewin, H. Jafta   **E**
Jafta—the town. See note under Lewin, H. Jafta   **E**
Jafta's father. See note under Lewin, H. Jafta   **E**
Jafta's mother. See note under Lewin, H. Jafta   **E**

Lewin, Ted, 1935-
Amazon boy   **E**
The reindeer people (3-5)   **948.97**
Sacred river (1-4)   **954**
Tiger trek (2-4)   **599.74**
(il) Bagnold, E. National Velvet   **Fic**
(il) Bartone, E. Peppe the lamplighter   **E**
(il) Heide, F. P. The day of Ahmed's secret
    E
(il) Heide, F. P. Sami and the time of the troubles   **E**
(il) Herds of thunder, manes of gold. See Herds of thunder, manes of gold
    808.8
(il) Hodges, M. Brother Francis and the friendly beasts   **92**
(il) Knudson, R. R. Babe Didrikson: athlete of the century   **92**
(il) Kudlinski, K. V. Rachel Carson: pioneer of ecology   **92**
(il) McDonald, M. The great pumpkin switch   **E**
(il) McDonald, M. The potato man   **E**
(il) Oberman, S. The always prayer shawl
    E
(il) O'Dell, S. Island of the Blue Dolphins
    Fic
(il) Scott, A. H. Cowboy country   **978**
(il) Slepian, J. Lost moose   **E**

Lewington, Anna
Antonio's rain forest (3-5)   **981**

Lewis, Amy
(ed) Encyclopedias, atlases & dictionaries. See Encyclopedias, atlases & dictionaries
    011

Lewis, Barbara A., 1943-
The kid's guide to social action (4 and up)
    361.2

Literature
See also African Americans in literature; Children's literature; Jews in literature; Young adults' literature; names of national literatures, e.g. *English literature*
Collections
Bauer, C. F. Celebrations   **808.8**
The Family read-aloud Christmas treasury   **808.8**
The Family read-aloud holiday treasury   **808.8**
Halloween: stories and poems (2-4)   **808.8**
Herds of thunder, manes of gold (4 and up)   **808.8**
Hey! listen to this   **028.5**
Juba this and Juba that   **372.6**
The Laugh book (4-6)   **808.8**
Mahy, M. Bubble trouble & other poems and stories (3-5)   **808.8**
The Oxford book of scary tales (5 and up)   **808.8**
Pooley, S. It's raining, it's pouring   **808.8**
Rainy day: stories and poems (2-4)   **808.8**
The Read-aloud treasury   **808.8**
Sawyer, R. The way of the storyteller   **372.6**
Shedlock, M. L. The art of the story-teller   **372.6**
Snowy day: stories and poems (2-4)   **808.8**
Windy day: stories and poems (2-4)   **808.8**
Yolen, J. Hark! a Christmas sampler   **808.8**
Dictionaries
Brewer's dictionary of phrase and fable   **803**

History and criticism
See also Authors
Stories, plots, etc.
Gillespie, J. T. Juniorplots   **028.5**
Gillespie, J. T. More juniorplots   **028.5**
Gillespie, J. T. Juniorplots 3   **028.5**
Gillespie, J. T. Juniorplots 4   **028.5**
Rochman, H. Tales of love and terror   **028**
Thomas, R. L. Primaryplots   **028**
Thomas, R. L. Primaryplots 2   **028**
Study and teaching
Hall, S. Using picture storybooks to teach literary devices   **016.8**

Lithography
See/See also pages in the following book(s):
The Illustrator's notebook p109-14   **741.6**

Lithuania
Chicoine, S. Lithuania (4 and up)   **947**
Lithuania (5 and up)   **947**
Lithuania (5 and up)   **947**

Litteral, Linda Lambert, 1949-
Boobies, iguanas & other critters (5 and up)   **508**

Little, Jean, 1932-
Different dragons (3-5)   **Fic**
From Anna (4-6)   **Fic**
Hey world, here I am! (4-6)   **811**
Little by Little (5 and up)   **92**
Look through my window (4-6)   **Fic**
Mine for keeps (4-6)   **Fic**

Little, Lessie Jones, 1906-1986
(jt. auth) Greenfield, E. Childtimes: a three-generation memoir   **920**

Little, Malcolm *See* Malcolm X, 1925-1965

Little Bald-Headed
In Raw Head, bloody bones p73-77   **398.2**

Little Bear. Minarik, E. H.   **E**

Little Bear goes to the moon. Minarik, E. H.
In The Read-aloud treasury p70-83   **808.8**

Little Bear's friend. Minarik, E. H. See note under Minarik, E. H. Little Bear   **E**

Little Bear's visit. Minarik, E. H. See note under Minarik, E. H. Little Bear   **E**

The **little** black cat who went to Mattituck. Brown, M. W.
In Brown, M. W. The fish with the deep sea smile p115-20   **818**

Little blue and little yellow. Lionni, L.   **E**

The **Little** blue dishes
In The Family read-aloud Christmas treasury p52-53   **808.8**

Little Briar-Rose. Grimm, J.
In Grimm, J. The complete Grimm's fairy tales p237-41   **398.2**

The **little** bull-calf. Jacobs, J.
In Jacobs, J. English fairy tales p388-92   **398.2**

Little Buttercup. MacDonald, M. R.
In MacDonald, M. R. When the lights go out p7-20   **372.6**

Little by Little. Little, J.   **92**

Little Cosette and Father Christmas. Thane, A.
In The Big book of Christmas plays p313-31   **808.82**

Little crab and his magic eyes. MacDonald, M. R.
In MacDonald, M. R. Twenty tellable tales p24-34   **372.6**

Little Cricket's marriage. MacDonald, M. R.
In MacDonald, M. R. Look back and see p55-67   **372.6**

The **Little** dog laughed (k-2)   **398.8**

Little Eight John. Hamilton, V.
In Hamilton, V. The people could fly: American black folktales p121-25   **398.2**

Little elephant. Ford, M.   **E**

The **little emperor.** Yep, L.
In Yep, L. Tongues of jade p40-47   **398.2**

The **little engine that could.** Piper, W.   **E**

Loch Ness monster
Landau, E. The Loch Ness monster (3-5)
001.9

Locker, Thomas, 1937-
The land of Gray Wolf   E
The mare on the hill   E
Sailing with the wind   E
Sky tree (1-3)   582.16
Where the river begins   E
(il) Bruchac, J. Thirteen moons on a turtle's back   811
(il) Christiansen, C. The ice horse   E
(il) George, J. C. The first Thanksgiving
974.4

Locks and keys
Fiction
Hughes, S. Alfie gets in first   E
Locusts
See/See also pages in the following book(s):
Johnson, S. A. Chirping insects (4 and up)
595.7
Fiction
Lobel, A. Grasshopper on the road   E
Locusts, Seventeen-year *See* Cicadas
Lodge boy and thrown away
In The Naked bear p79-86   398.2
Loehle, Richard
(il) Tucker, T. Brainstorm!   609
Loeper, John J.
Going to school in 1776 (4 and up)
370.9
Going to school in 1876 (4 and up)
370.9
Loewen, Nancy, 1964-
Walt Whitman (5 and up)   92
Loft the enchanter. San Souci, R.
In San Souci, R. More short & shivery p115-20   398.2
Lofting, Hugh, 1886-1947
See/See also pages in the following book(s):
Horn Book reflections on children's books and reading p218-24   028.5
Newbery Medal books, 1922-1955 p21-27
028.5
Lofts, Pamela
(il) Fox, M. Koala Lou   E
Logging *See* Lumber and lumbering
Logic
Nozaki, A. Anno's hat tricks (1-4)   153.4
Loh, Morag Jeanette, 1935-
Tucking Mommy in   E
Lomas Garza, Carmen
Family pictures   E
Lon Po Po. Young, E.   398.2
London, Jack, 1876-1916
The call of the wild (5 and up)   Fic
White Fang (5 and up)   Fic
See/See also pages in the following book(s):
Faber, D. Great lives: American literature p141-50 (5 and up)   920
Krull, K. Lives of the writers p70-73 (4 and up)   920

London, Jonathan, 1947-
Froggy gets dressed. See note under London, J. Froggy learns to swim   E
Froggy learns to swim   E
Let's go Froggy. See note under London, J. Froggy learns to swim   E
(jt. auth) Bruchac, J. Thirteen moons on a turtle's back   811
London (England)
Description
Munro, R. The inside-outside book of London (2-4)   942.1
Fiction
Alcock, V. The cuckoo sister (6 and up)
Fic
Bawden, N. The robbers (5 and up)   Fic
Newman, R. The case of the Baker Street Irregular (5 and up)   Fic
Paton Walsh, J. Fireweed (5 and up)
Fic
Streatfeild, N. Ballet shoes (5 and up)
Fic
History
Fisher, L. E. The Tower of London (4 and up)   942.1
London (England). Tower *See* Tower of London (England)
London Bridge is falling down! (k-2)
782.42
Long, Kim
The astronaut training book for kids (5 and up)   629.45
A **long** hard journey. McKissack, P. C.
331.8
Long live Christmas. Benson, I.
In The Big book of Christmas plays p213-27   808.82
The **long** road to Gettysburg. Murphy, J.
973.7
The **long** secret. Fitzhugh, L. See note under Fitzhugh, L. Harriet the spy   Fic
Long-term care facilities
See also Nursing homes
The **long** way home. Cohen, B.   Fic
The **long** way westward. Sandin, J.   E
The **long** winter. Van Laan, N.
In Van Laan, N. In a circle long ago p24-33   398.2
The **long** winter. Wilder, L. I. See note under Wilder, L. I. Little house in the big woods
Fic
The **longest** story. Haley, G. E.
In Haley, G. E. Mountain Jack tales p34-36   398.2
The **longest** summer on record. Conrad, P.
In Conrad, P. Our house p29-39
S C
Longevity
See also Old age
Longfellow, Henry Wadsworth, 1807-1882
Hiawatha   811
Paul Revere's ride   811

Louis XIV, King of France, 1638-1715
About
Aliki. The King's day: Louis XIV of France
(2-5)   **92**

Louisiana
Kent, D. Louisiana
In America the beautiful   **973**
LaDoux, R. Louisiana
In Hello USA series   **973**
Fiction
Kroll, V. L. Sweet Magnolia   **E**
McKissack, P. C. A million fish—more or
less   **E**
Thomassie, T. Feliciana Feydra LeRoux
                                              E

The **loup-garou**. San Souci, R.
In San Souci, R. Short & shivery p144-48
                                              398.2

Louse *See* Lice

The **louse** and the flea. Grimm, J.
In Grimm, J. The complete Grimm's
fairy tales p158-60   **398.2**

Lovable Lyle. Waber, B. See note under Waber, B. Lyle, Lyle, crocodile   **E**

Love, Ann, 1947-
(jt. auth) Drake, J. The kids' summer handbook   **790.1**

Love, Nat, 1854-1921
About
Miller, R. H. The story of Nat Love (k-3)
                                              92

Love flute. Goble, P.   **398.2**
Love, from the fifth-grade celebrity. Giff, P. R.
                                              Fic

Love poetry
Greenfield, E. Honey, I love, and other love
poems (2-4)   **811**

Lovelace, Ada King, Countess of, 1815-1852
About
Wade, M. D. Ada Byron Lovelace (5 and
up)   **92**

Lovelace, Maud Hart, 1892-1980
Betsy and Joe. See note under Lovelace, M.
H. Betsy-Tacy   **Fic**
Betsy and Tacy go downtown. See note un-
der Lovelace, M. H. Betsy-Tacy   **Fic**
Betsy and Tacy go over the big hill. See
note under Lovelace, M. H. Betsy-Tacy
                                              Fic
Betsy and the great world. See note under
Lovelace, M. H. Betsy-Tacy   **Fic**
Betsy in spite of herself. See note under
Lovelace, M. H. Betsy-Tacy   **Fic**
Betsy-Tacy (2-4)   **Fic**
Betsy-Tacy and Tib. See note under Love-
lace, M. H. Betsy-Tacy   **Fic**
Betsy was a junior. See note under Lovelace,
M. H. Betsy-Tacy   **Fic**
Betsy's wedding. See note under Lovelace,
M. H. Betsy-Tacy   **Fic**
Heaven to Betsy. See note under Lovelace,
M. H. Betsy-Tacy   **Fic**

The **lovers** of Dismal Swamp. San Souci, R.
In San Souci, R. Short & shivery p123-26
                                              398.2

Low, Alice, 1926-
The Macmillan book of Greek gods and heroes (3-6)   **292**
(jt. auth) Cheng, C.-S. A young painter [bi-
ography of Wang Yani]   **92**
(comp) The Family read-aloud Christmas
treasury. See The Family read-aloud
Christmas treasury   **808.8**
(comp) The Family read-aloud holiday treasury. See The Family read-aloud holiday
treasury   **808.8**

Low, Joseph, 1911-
Mice twice   **E**
(il) Griffith, H. V. Alex and the cat   **E**

Low, Madeline Slovenz- *See* Slovenz-Low,
Madeline

Low vocabulary-high interest books *See* High
interest-low vocabulary books

Lowe, Edwin S., 1910-1986
See/See also pages in the following book(s):
Aaseng, N. The unsung heroes p45-51 (5
and up)   **920**

Lowery, Linda
Twist with a burger, jitter with a bug   **E**

Lowry, Lois
All about Sam. See note under Lowry, L.
Anastasia Krupnik   **Fic**
Anastasia, absolutely. See note under Lowry,
L. Anastasia Krupnik   **Fic**
Anastasia again! See note under Lowry, L.
Anastasia Krupnik   **Fic**
Anastasia, ask your analyst. See note under
Lowry, L. Anastasia Krupnik   **Fic**
Anastasia at this address. See note under
Lowry, L. Anastasia Krupnik   **Fic**
Anastasia at your service. See note under
Lowry, L. Anastasia Krupnik   **Fic**
Anastasia has the answers. See note under
Lowry, L. Anastasia Krupnik   **Fic**
Anastasia Krupnik (4-6)   **Fic**
Anastasia on her own. See note under Low-
ry, L. Anastasia Krupnik   **Fic**
Anastasia's chosen career. See note under
Lowry, L. Anastasia Krupnik   **Fic**
Attaboy, Sam! See note under Lowry, L. An-
astasia Krupnik   **Fic**
Autumn Street (4 and up)   **Fic**
Elliot's house
In The Big book for our planet p116-21
                                              810.8
The giver (6 and up)   **Fic**
Number the stars (4 and up)   **Fic**
The one hundredth thing about Caroline (5
and up)   **Fic**
Rabble Starkey (5 and up)   **Fic**
A summer to die (5 and up)   **Fic**
Switcharound (5 and up)   **Fic**
The tree house
In The Big book for peace p30-38
                                              810.8
Your move, J.P.! (5 and up)   **Fic**

Loya, Olga
Tía Miseria
In From sea to shining sea p202-05
810.8

Loyalists, American *See* American Loyalists

Lubin, Leonard B., 1943-
(il) Conly, J. L. Racso and the rats of NIMH **Fic**

Lucas, Cedric
(il) Miller, W. Frederick Douglass **92**

Lucas, Eileen
The Ojibwas: people of the northern forests (4-6) **970.004**

Lucht, Irmgard, 1937-
The red poppy (k-3) **583**

Lucientes, Francisco José de Goya y *See* Goya, Francisco, 1746-1828

Lucky lips. Jennings, P.
In Jennings, P. Unreal! p39-50 **S C**

Lucky mouse. Ring, E. **599.32**

The lucky stone. Clifton, L. **Fic**

Lucy's Christmas. Hall, D. **E**

Ludwig, Warren
(il) Johnston, T. The cowboy and the black-eyed pea **E**

Lueders, Edward
(comp) Reflections on a gift of watermelon pickle . . . and other modern verse. See Reflections on a gift of watermelon pickle . . . and other modern verse **811.008**

Luella and the tame parrot. Hamilton, V.
In Hamilton, V. Her stories p75-77
398.2

Luenn, Nancy, 1954-
Nessa's fish **E**
Nessa's story. See note under Luenn, N.
Nessa's fish **E**
Squish! (k-2) **574.5**

Luka's quilt. Guback, G. **E**

Lullabies
Appelt, K. Bayou lullaby **E**
The Baby's bedtime book **808.81**
Bang, M. Ten, nine, eight **E**
Carlstrom, N. W. Northern lullaby (k-3)
811
Lullabies and night songs (k-3) **782.42**
The Lullaby songbook (1-3) **782.42**
Marzollo, J. Close your eyes **E**
Paxton, T. The animals' lullaby (k-2)
782.42
Sleep, baby, sleep **808.81**
Sleep rhymes around the world **808.81**
When the dark comes dancing (k-3)
808.81
See/See also pages in the following book(s):
Rainbow in the sky p421-33 (k-4)
821.008

Lullabies and night songs (k-3) **782.42**

The Lullaby songbook (1-3) **782.42**

Lum, Roseline Ng Cheong- *See* Cheong-Lum, Roseline Ng, 1962-

Lumber and lumbering
Appelbaum, D. K. Giants in the land (2-4)
634.9
Kurelek, W. Lumberjack (3-5) **634.9**
See/See also pages in the following book(s):
Guiberson, B. Z. Spotted owl p12-23 (3-5)
598
Silverstein, A. The spotted owl (4 and up)
598

The lumber-room. Saki
In The Random House book of humor for children p74-82 **817.008**

Lumberjack. Kurelek, W. **634.9**

Lumps, bumps, and rashes. Nourse, A. E.
616

Lunar eclipses
See/See also pages in the following book(s):
Gallant, R. A. Rainbows, mirages and sundogs p65-72 (4 and up) **551.5**

Lunar expeditions *See* Space flight to the moon

Lunch. Fleming, D. **E**

Lunn, Janet Louise Swoboda, 1928-
The root cellar (5 and up) **Fic**

Lupiloff-Brazz, Marlene
(jt. auth) Terkel, S. N. Understanding cancer
616.99

Lutoniushka. Afanas'ev, A. N.
In Afanas'ev, A. N. Russian fairy tales p336-37 **398.2**

Luxembourg
Lepthien, E. U. Luxembourg (4 and up)
949.35

Luzak, Dennis
(il) Levinson, R. Our home is the sea
E

Lyall, Dennis
(il) Hughes, D. Baseball tips **796.357**

Lyddie. Paterson, K. **Fic**

Lydia, Queen of Palestine. Orlev, U. **Fic**

Lye, Keith
The complete atlas of the world **912**

Lying *See* Truthfulness and falsehood

Lyle and the birthday party. Waber, B. See note under Waber, B. Lyle, Lyle, crocodile **E**

Lyle at the office. Waber, B. See note under Waber, B. Lyle, Lyle, crocodile **E**

Lyle finds his mother. Waber, B. See note under Waber, B. Lyle, Lyle, crocodile **E**

Lyle, Lyle, crocodile. Waber, B. **E**

Lyme disease
Landau, E. Lyme disease (4 and up)
616.9
Silverstein, A. Lyme disease, the great imitator (6 and up) **616.9**

Lynch, Patrick James
(il) Andersen, H. C. The steadfast tin soldier
Fic
(il) Asbjornsen, P. C. East o' the sun and west o' the moon [Picture book]
398.2

Mahy, Margaret—*Continued*
The seven Chinese brothers (1-3) **398.2**
Tick tock tales (k-3) **S C**
Contents: Poodlum hoodlum; The Bird Child; The adventures of Little Mouse; The boy who made things up; Sailor Jack and the twenty orphans; Tom Tib goes shopping; Cat and Mouse; The king's toys; The strange egg; The boy who bounced; The kings of the broom cupcoard; The Tick Tock party
Underrunners (5 and up) **Fic**
The **maid** and the mouse and the odd-shaped house. Zelinsky, P. O. **E**
Maid in the mirror. Carpenter, F.
In Carpenter, F. Tales of a Chinese grandmother p226-34 **398.2**
Maid Maleen. Grimm, J.
In Grimm, J. The complete Grimm's fairy tales p801-07 **398.2**
Maid Marian (Legendary character)
Fiction
Tomlinson, T. The Forestwife (6 and up) **Fic**
The **Maid** of Brakel. Grimm, J.
In Grimm, J. The complete Grimm's fairy tales p623 **398.2**
The **Maiden** Tsar. Afanas'ev, A. N.
In Afanas'ev, A. N. Russian fairy tales p229-34 **398.2**
Ma'ii and cousin Horned Toad. Begay, S. **398.2**
Maine
Engfer, L. Maine
In Hello USA series **973**
Gibbons, G. Surrounded by sea (k-3) **974.1**
Harrington, T. Maine
In America the beautiful **973**
Description
Murphy, J. Into the deep forest with Henry David Thoreau (4-6) **974.1**
Fiction
Irwin, H. The original Freddie Ackerman (5 and up) **Fic**
McCloskey, R. Blueberries for Sal **E**
McCloskey, R. One morning in Maine **E**
McCloskey, R. Time of wonder **E**
Maitland, Antony, 1935-
(il) Lively, P. The ghost of Thomas Kempe **Fic**
(il) McCaughrean, G. Stories from Shakespeare **822.3**
Majeski, Bill
Whatever happened to good old Ebenezer Scrooge?
In The Big book of Christmas plays p151-68 **808.82**
Mak, Kam
(il) George, J. C. The moon of the monarch butterflies **595.7**
Make a world. See Emberley, E. Ed Emberley's drawing book: make a world **741.2**
Make-believe playmates *See* Imaginary playmates

Make it with boxes. See Irvine, J. Build it with boxes **745.54**
Make like a tree and leave. Danziger, P. See note under Danziger, P. Everyone else's parents said yes **Fic**
Make mine music!. Walther, T. **784.19**
Make noise, make merry. Chaikin, M. **296.4**
Make room for Elisa. Hurwitz, J. See note under Hurwitz, J. Rip-roaring Russell **Fic**
Make way for ducklings. McCloskey, R. **E**
Make way for Sam Houston. Fritz, J. **92**
Make your own animated movies and videotapes. Andersen, Y. **778.5**
Makers of America [series]
Miller, D. T. Frederick Douglass and the fight for freedom **92**
Patterson, L. Martin Luther King, Jr., and the freedom movement **92**
Makeup (Cosmetics) *See* Cosmetics
Maki, Chū, 1929-
Snowflakes, sugar, and salt (1-3) **548**
Making a new home in America. Rosenberg, M. B. **325.73**
Making cents. Wilkinson, E. **332.024**
Making friends. Mahy, M. **E**
Making friends. Rogers, F. **155.4**
Making music. Oates, E. H. **784.19**
Making musical things. Wiseman, A. S. **784.19**
The **making** of First Man. Curry, J. L.
In Curry, J. L. Back in the beforetime p107-15 **398.2**
Making waves. Zubrowski, B. **532**
Malawi
Lane, M. S. B. Malawi (4 and up) **968.97**
Fiction
Williams, K. L. Galimoto **E**
Malcolm, Andrew H., 1943-
The land and people of Canada (5 and up) **971**
Malcolm X, 1925-1965
About
Adoff, A. Malcolm X (2-5) **92**
See/See also pages in the following book(s):
Haskins, J. One more river to cross (4 and up) **920**
Male role *See* Sex role
Mali
O'Toole, T. Mali—in pictures (5 and up) **966.23**
History
McKissack, P. C. The royal kingdoms of Ghana, Mali, and Songhay (5 and up) **966.2**
Wisniewski, D. Sundiata (1-4) **92**
Malindy and little devil. Hamilton, V.
In Hamilton, V. Her stories p61-65 **398.2**

Mallett, David
Inch by inch (k-2)   782.42
Mallory, Kenneth
Rescue of the stranded whales (5 and up)
     639.9
Water hole (5 and up)   574.5
(jt. auth) Kraus, S. D. The search for the
right whale   599.5
Malone, Nola Langner
(il) Viorst, J. Earrings!   E
Mama, coming and going. Caseley, J.   E
Mama, do you love me?. Joosse, B. M.   E
Mama don't allow. Hurd, T.   E
Mama is a miner. Lyon, G. E.   E
Mama One, Mama Two. MacLachlan, P.
     E
Mammals
     See also Fossil mammals; groups of
     mammals; and names of mammals
Arnosky, J. Crinkleroot's 25 mammals every
child should know (k-3)   599
Esbensen, B. J. Baby whales drink milk (k-1)
     599.5
Kerrod, R. Mammals: primates, insect eat-
ers, and baleen whales (4 and up)
     599
Maynard, T. Saving endangered mammals
(4-6)   639.9
O'Toole, C. Mammals: the hunters (4 and
up)   599
Parker, S. Mammal (4 and up)   599
Parsons, A. Amazing mammals (2-4)
     599
Patent, D. H. Why mammals have fur (4
and up)   599
The Sierra Club book of great mammals (4
and up)   599
Snedden, R. What is a mammal? (3-6)
     599
Wildsmith, B. Brian Wildsmith's wild ani-
mals   E
Yamashita, K. Paws, wings, and hooves
(1-3)   599
Zim, H. S. Mammals (4 and up)   599
Mammals: primates, insect eaters, and baleen
whales. Kerrod, R.   599
Mammals: the large plant-eaters. Stidworthy,
J.   599
Mammals: the small plant-eaters. Bramwell,
M.   599
Mammoths
Aliki. Wild and woolly mammoths (k-3)
     569
         Fiction
Gerrard, R. Mik's mammoth   E
Martin, R. Will's mammoth   E
Mamonova, Tatyana, 1943-
(il) Krasnopolsky, F. L. I remember   Fic
Man
       Influence on nature
     See Human influence on nature
         Origin
     See Human origins

Man, Prehistoric *See* Prehistoric man
Man and mustang. Ancona, G.   636.1
The **man** from the other side. Orlev, U.
     Fic
The **man** in the ceiling. Feiffer, J.   Fic
Man in the red suit. Moessinger, W.
     In Holiday plays round the year p37-46
     812.008
The **man** of influence. Fleischman, P.
     In Fleischman, P. Graven images p61-85
     S C
Man-of-war, Stephen Biesty's cross-sections.
Biesty, S.   359.1
The **man** who could call down owls. Bunting,
E.   E
The **man** who did not know fear. Afanas'ev,
A. N.
     In Afanas'ev, A. N. Russian fairy tales
     p325-27   398.2
The **man** who didn't wash his dishes. Kra-
silovsky, P.
     In The Read-aloud treasury p179-87
     808.8
The **man** who knew too much. Lester, J.
     398.2
The **man** who loved books [biography of Saint
Columba]. Fritz, J.   92
The **man** who tricked a ghost. Yep, L.
     398.2
The **Man** who was afraid of nothing
     In Diane Goode's book of scary stories &
     songs p26-31   398.2
The **man** who was too lazy to fix things. Kra-
silovsky, P.   E
Man with a million ideas: Fred Jones, ge-
nius/inventor. See Swanson, G. B. I've got
an idea! the story of Frederick McKinley
Jones   92
Manabozo. Hamilton, V.
     In Hamilton, V. The dark way p27-31
     398.2
Managing children's services in the public li-
brary. Fasick, A. M.   027.62
Manatee on location. Darling, K.   599.5
Manatees
Clark, M. G. The vanishing manatee (4 and
up)   599.5
Darling, K. Manatee on location (3-5)
     599.5
Sibbald, J. H. The manatee (3-5)   599.5
Mancrow, bird of darkness. Sherlock, Sir P.
M.
     In Sherlock, Sir P. M. West Indian folk-
tales p65-70   398.2
Mandan Indians
Lepthien, E. U. The Mandans (2-4)
     970.004
Mandarin and the butterflies. Carpenter, F.
     In Carpenter, F. Tales of a Chinese grand-
mother p198-205   398.2

Marcus, Leonard S., 1950-
75 years of Children's Book Week posters. See 75 years of Children's Book Week posters **808.06**
(ed) Lifelines. See Lifelines **821.008**
The **mare** on the hill. Locker, T. **E**
Marelle, Charles
Drakestail
In The Red fairy book p202-07 **398.2**
The ratcatcher
In The Red fairy book p208-14 **398.2**
The true history of Little Golden-hood
In The Red fairy book p215-19 **398.2**
Mare's eggs. Crossley-Holland, K.
In Crossley-Holland, K. British folk tales p153-54 **398.2**
Margeson, Susan M.
Viking (4 and up) **948**
Margolies, Barbara A., 1939-
Kanu of Kathmandu (2-4) **954.9**
Olbalbal (3-5) **967.8**
Marguerite, go wash your feet. Tripp, W. **821.008**
Maria Morevna. Afanas'ev, A. N.
In Afanas'ev, A. N. Russian fairy tales p553-62 **398.2**
Mariah keeps cool. Walter, M. P. **Fic**
Mariah loves rock. Walter, M. P. See note under Walter, M. P. Mariah keeps cool **Fic**
Marian, Maid (Legendary character) *See* Maid Marian (Legendary character)
Mariculture. Koch, F. K. **639**
Marie and Redfish. Hamilton, V.
In Hamilton, V. Her stories p11-14 **398.2**
Marie Curie and her daughter Irène. Pflaum, R. **92**
Marie Curie and radium. Parker, S. **92**
Mariel of Redwall. Jacques, B. See note under Jacques, B. Redwall **Fic**
Marijuana
Zeller, P. K. Focus on marijuana (3-6) **362.29**
Marika the snowmaiden. Bauer, C. F.
In Snowy day: stories and poems p45-49 **808.8**
Marine animals
See also Freshwater animals
Aliki. My visit to the aquarium (k-3) **639.3**
Arnold, C. A walk on the Great Barrier Reef (3-5) **574.92**
Burnie, D. Seashore (3-5) **574.92**
Cole, J. The magic school bus on the ocean floor (2-4) **591.92**
Johnson, S. A. Coral reefs (4 and up) **574.92**
Macdonald, S. Sea shapes **E**
Oppenheim, J. Oceanarium (3-5) **591.92**
Parker, S. Seashore (4 and up) **574.92**
Stolz, M. Night of ghosts and hermits (3-5) **574.92**

Marine aquariums
Aliki. My visit to the aquarium (k-3) **639.3**
Ancona, G. The aquarium book (3-5) **639.3**
Oppenheim, J. Oceanarium (3-5) **591.92**
Marine biology
Bramwell, M. The oceans (4-6) **551.46**
Johnson, R. L. The Great Barrier Reef (5 and up) **574.92**
Kricher, J. C. Peterson first guide to seashores (6 and up) **574.92**
McGovern, A. Down under, down under (3-6) **574.92**
Swanson, D. Safari beneath the sea (4 and up) **574.92**
Waters, J. F. Deep-sea vents (4 and up) **551.46**
Zim, H. S. Seashores (4 and up) **574.92**
Marine Corps (U.S.) *See* United States. Marine Corps
Marine ecology
Bellamy, D. The rock pool (1-4) **574.92**
Bendick, J. Exploring an ocean tide pool (3-5) **574.92**
Lampton, C. Coral reefs in danger (4 and up) **574.92**
Silverstein, A. Life in a tidal pool (4-6) **574.92**
Marine mammals
See also Dolphins; Porpoises; Seals (Animals); Whales
Marine plants
Burnie, D. Seashore (3-5) **574.92**
Parker, S. Seashore (4 and up) **574.92**
Marine pollution
See also Oil spills
Mariner project *See* Project Mariner
Marines (U.S.) *See* United States. Marine Corps
Marino, Jan
The Mona Lisa of Salem Street (5 and up) **Fic**
Marino, Jane
Mother Goose time **027.62**
Maris, Ron
Is anyone home? **E**
Mark, Jan
No-good Claus
In The Oxford book of scary tales p123-29 **808.8**
William's version
In The Oxford treasury of children's stories p144-50 **S C**
Markle, Sandra, 1946-
Earth alive! (4-6) **550**
Exploring autumn (4 and up) **508**
Exploring spring (4 and up) **508**
Exploring summer (4 and up) **508**
Exploring winter (4 and up) **508**
Math mini-mysteries (4 and up) **510**
Outside and inside birds (2-4) **598**
Outside and inside snakes (2-4) **597.9**

Martinique

Folklore

See Folklore—Martinique

Martins, George
(il) Giovanni, N. Spin a soft black song: poems for children   **811**

Martin's mice. King-Smith, D.   **Fic**

Maruki, Toshi, 1912-
Hiroshima no pika   **940.54**

The **marvellous** musician. Grimm, J.
In The Red fairy book p354-56   **398.2**

The **marvelous** land of Oz. Baum, L. F. See note under Baum, L. F. The Wizard of Oz   **Fic**

The **marvelous** misadventures of Sebastian. Alexander, L.   **Fic**

Marvin, Frederic
(il) Cleaver, V. Grover   **Fic**

Marvin Redpost, alone in his teacher's house. Sachar, L. See note under Sachar, L. Marvin Redpost, kidnapped at birth?   **Fic**

Marvin Redpost, is he a girl?. Sachar, L. See note under Sachar, L. Marvin Redpost, kidnapped at birth?   **Fic**

Marvin Redpost, kidnapped at birth?. Sachar, L.   **Fic**

Marvin Redpost, why pick on me?. Sachar, L. See note under Sachar, L. Marvin Redpost, kidnapped at birth?   **Fic**

Mary Ann. James, B.   **E**

Mary Belle and the mermaid. Hamilton, V.
In Hamilton, V. Her stories p33-37   **398.2**

Mary Beth
Handtalk school (k-3)   **419**
(jt. auth) Ancona, G. Handtalk zoo   **419**
(jt. auth) Charlip, R. Handtalk   **419**
(jt. auth) Charlip, R. Handtalk birthday   **419**

Mary had a little lamb. Hale, S. J.   **811**

Mary Marony and the chocolate surprise. Kline, S. See note under Kline, S. Mary Marony, mummy girl   **Fic**

Mary Marony and the snake. Kline, S. See note under Kline, S. Mary Marony, mummy girl   **Fic**

Mary Marony hides out. Kline, S. See note under Kline, S. Mary Marony, mummy girl   **Fic**

Mary Marony, mummy girl. Kline, S.   **Fic**

Mary McLean and the St. Patrick's Day parade. Kroll, S.   **E**

Mary Poppins. Travers, P. L.   **Fic**

Mary Poppins comes back. Travers, P. L. See note under Travers, P. L. Mary Poppins   **Fic**

Mary Poppins from A to Z. Travers, P. L. See note under Travers, P. L. Mary Poppins   **Fic**

Mary Poppins in Cherry Tree Lane. Travers, P. L. See note under Travers, P. L. Mary Poppins   **Fic**

Mary Poppins opens the door. Travers, P. L. See note under Travers, P. L. Mary Poppins   **Fic**

Maryland
Johnston, J. Maryland
In Hello USA series   **973**
Kent, D. Maryland
In America the beautiful   **973**

Marzollo, Jean
Close your eyes   **E**
Getting your period (5 and up)   **612.6**
Happy birthday, Martin Luther King (k-3)   **92**
In 1492 (k-2)   **970.01**
In 1776 (k-2)   **973.3**
Pretend you're a cat   **E**
(jt. auth) Wick, W. I spy   **793.73**
(jt. auth) Wick, W. I spy Christmas   **793.73**
(jt. auth) Wick, W. I spy fantasy   **793.73**
(jt. auth) Wick, W. I spy fun house   **793.73**
(jt. auth) Wick, W. I spy mystery   **793.73**
(jt. auth) Wick, W. I spy school days   **793.73**

Masai (African people)
Margolies, B. A. Olbalbal (3-5)   **967.8**
Fiction
Kroll, V. L. Masai and I   **E**
Folklore
Aardema, V. Who's in Rabbit's house? (k-3)   **398.2**
Mollel, T. M. The orphan boy (k-3)   **398.2**

Masai and I. Kroll, V. L.   **E**

Masks (Facial)
Wright, L. Masks (4 and up)   **745.59**

Mason, Charles, 1958-
(il) Murphy, C. R. A child's Alaska   **979.8**

Mass communication *See* Communication; Telecommunication

Massachusetts
Avakian, M. A historical album of Massachusetts
In Historical albums series   **973**
Kent, D. Massachusetts
In America the beautiful   **973**
Warner, J. F. Massachusetts
In Hello USA series   **973**
Fiction
Avi. Emily Upham's revenge (4-6)   **Fic**
Paterson, K. Lyddie (5 and up)   **Fic**
Yolen, J. Letting Swift River go   **E**
History—1600-1775, Colonial period
See also Plymouth Rock
Anderson, J. The first Thanksgiving feast (3-5)   **974.4**
Bowen, G. Stranded at Plimoth Plantation, 1626 (3-5)   **974.4**

Mayer, Marianna, 1945-
Baba Yaga and Vasilisa the brave (3-5)
398.2
Beauty and the beast (1-4) **398.2**

Mayer, Mercer, 1943-
A boy, a dog, and a friend. See note under
Mayer, M. A boy, a dog, and a frog
E
A boy, a dog, and a frog **E**
Frog goes to dinner. See note under Mayer,
M. A boy, a dog, and a frog **E**
Frog on his own. See note under Mayer, M.
A boy, a dog, and a frog **E**
Frog, where are you? See note under Mayer,
M. A boy, a dog, and a frog **E**
One frog too many. See note under Mayer,
M. A boy, a dog, and a frog **E**
There's a nightmare in my closet **E**
There's an alligator under my bed. See note
under Mayer, M. There's a nightmare in
my closet **E**
(il) Fitzgerald, J. D. The Great Brain
Fic
(il) Mayer, M. Beauty and the beast
398.2
(il) Williams, J. Everyone knows what a
dragon looks like **E**

Mayerson, Evelyn Wilde, 1934-
The cat who escaped from steerage (3-5)
Fic

Mayhew, James
(il) Classic poems to read aloud. See Classic
poems to read aloud **808.81**

May'naise sandwiches & sunshine tea. Belton,
S. **E**

Maynard, Christopher
Airplane (k-3) **629.136**

Maynard, Thane
Primates (4-6) **599.8**
Saving endangered mammals (4-6)
639.9

Mayne, William, 1928-
Hob and the goblins (4 and up) **Fic**
See/See also pages in the following book(s):
Children and their books p381-98 **028.5**

Mayo, Gretchen
Meet tricky Coyote! See note under Mayo,
G. That tricky Coyote! **398.2**
That tricky Coyote! (k-3) **398.2**
Contents: Boo! Coyote; The sky is falling!; Where is my
song?; Blue Coyote; I win!

Mayo, Margaret, 1935-
Magical tales from many lands (3-6)
398.2
Contents: The Lemon Princess; Feather Woman and the
morning star; The Kingdom Under the Sea; Unanana and
the enormous one-tusked elephant; Kate Crackernuts; The
king who wanted to touch the moon; Three golden apples;
The magic fruit; Seven clever brothers; The prince and the
flying carpet; The Halloween witches; Koala; Baba Yaga
Bony-Legs; The yellow thunder dragon

The **mayoress**. Afanas'ev, A. N.
In Afanas'ev, A. N. Russian fairy tales
p141 **398.2**

Mays, Willie, 1931-
See/See also pages in the following book(s):
Torres, J. A. Home-run hitters p71-80 (4
and up) **920**

Mazel and Shlimazel. Singer, I. B. **398.2**
also in Singer, I. B. Stories for children
p22-40 **S C**

McBratney, Sam
Guess how much I love you **E**

McBroom and the big wind. Fleischman, S.
See note under Fleischman, S. McBroom
tells the truth **Fic**

McBroom and the big wind. Fleischman, S.
In The Oxford treasury of children's stories p105-13 **S C**

McBroom and the great race. Fleischman, S.
See note under Fleischman, S. McBroom
tells the truth **Fic**

McBroom tells the truth. Fleischman, S.
Fic

McBroom's almanac. Fleischman, S. See note
under Fleischman, S. McBroom tells the
truth **Fic**

McBroom's almanac [excerpt]. Fleischman, S.
In The Random House book of humor
for children p173-75 **817.008**

McBroom's wonderful one-acre farm. Fleischman, S. See note under Fleischman, S.
McBroom tells the truth **Fic**

McCaffrey, Anne
Dragondrums. See note under McCaffrey, A.
Dragonsong **Fic**
Dragonsinger. See note under McCaffrey, A.
Dragonsong **Fic**
Dragonsong (6 and up) **Fic**

McCall, Edith S.
Biography of a river: the living Mississippi
(6 and up) **977**

McCall, Francis X., Jr.
(jt. auth) Keeler, P. A. Unraveling fibers
677

McCarthy, Betty
Utah
In America the beautiful **973**

McCarthy, Colin, 1951-
Reptile (4 and up) **597.9**

McCarty, Peter
(il) Getz, D. Frozen man **930.1**

McCaughrean, Geraldine, 1951-
The fisherman and the bottle
In The Oxford treasury of children's sto-
ries p114-20 **S C**
The Great Swallowing Monster
In The Oxford book of scary tales p64-69
808.8
Greek myths (4-6) **292**
The Random House book of stories from
the ballet (4 and up) **792.8**
Stories from Shakespeare **822.3**

McCay, Winsor, 1871-1934
See/See also pages in the following book(s):
Sendak, M. Caldecott & Co.: notes on books
and pictures p77-85 **028.5**

Meggendorfer, Lothar
See/See also pages in the following book(s):
Sendak, M. Caldecott & Co.: notes on books and pictures p51-60 **028.5**

Meier, Max
(il) Schnieper, C. Amazing spiders **595.4**
(il) Schnieper, C. Chameleons **597.9**
(il) Schnieper, C. Lizards **597.9**

Meigs, Cornelia Lynde, 1884-1972
See/See also pages in the following book(s):
Newbery Medal books, 1922-1955 p117-24 **028.5**

Meir, Golda, 1898-1978
About
Adler, D. A. Our Golda: the story of Golda Meir (3-5) **92**

Meisel, Paul
(il) Cole, J. Your insides **612**
(il) Schwartz, A. Busy buzzing bumblebees and other tongue twisters **808.88**

Melcher, Frederic Gershom, 1879-1963
See/See also pages in the following book(s):
Newbery Medal books, 1922-1955 p1-5 **028.5**

Meltzer, Milton, 1915-
All times, all peoples: a world history of slavery (4 and up) **326**
The amazing potato (4 and up) **635**
A book about names (5 and up) **929.4**
George Washington and the birth of our nation (5 and up) **92**
Gold (4 and up) **553.4**
Never to forget: the Jews of the Holocaust (6 and up) **940.53**
Nonfiction for the classroom **973**
Rescue: the story of how Gentiles saved Jews in the Holocaust (6 and up) **940.53**
(ed) The American revolutionaries: a history in their own words, 1750-1800. See The American revolutionaries: a history in their own words, 1750-1800 **973.3**
(ed) The Black Americans: a history in their own words, 1619-1983. See The Black Americans: a history in their own words, 1619-1983 **305.8**
(ed) The Jewish Americans: a history in their own words, 1650-1950. See The Jewish Americans: a history in their own words, 1650-1950 **305.8**
(ed) Lincoln, in his own words. See Lincoln, in his own words **92**
(ed) Voices from the Civil War. See Voices from the Civil War **973.7**

Melville, Herman, 1819-1891
See/See also pages in the following book(s):
Faber, D. Great lives: American literature p49-58 (5 and up) **920**

Memoirs of the little man and the little maid. See The Little man & the little maid

Memory
See/See also pages in the following book(s):
Funston, S. It's all in your brain p33-44 (4 and up) **612.8**

Menana of the waterfall. Osborne, M. P.
In Osborne, M. P. Mermaid tales from around the world p7-11 **398.2**

Menaseh's dream. Singer, I. B.
In Singer, I. B. Stories for children p313-21 **S C**
In Singer, I. B. When Shlemiel went to Warshaw & other stories p83-96 **398.2**

Menashe and Rachel. Singer, I. B.
In Singer, I. B. The power of light p31-39 **S C**
In Singer, I. B. Stories for children p122-29 **S C**

Mendez, Adriana
Cubans in America
In The In America series **305.8**

Mendez, Raymond A.
(il) Cole, J. An insect's body **595.7**

Mennonites
See also Amish

The **Mennyms.** Waugh, S. **Fic**

Mennyms in the wilderness. Waugh, S. See note under Waugh, S. The Mennyms **Fic**

Menominee Indians
Kalbacken, J. The Menominee (2-4) **970.004**

Menorahs, mezuzas, and other Jewish symbols. Chaikin, M. **296.4**

Menotti, Gian Carlo, 1911-
Amahl and the night visitors (2-4) **Fic**

Menstruation
Marzollo, J. Getting your period (5 and up) **612.6**

Mental illness
Dinner, S. H. Nothing to be ashamed of: growing up with mental illness in your family (5 and up) **362.2**
Fiction
MacLachlan, P. Mama One, Mama Two **E**

Mentally handicapped
Fiction
Carrick, C. Stay away from Simon! (3-5) **Fic**
Christopher, M. Fighting tackle (4-6) **Fic**
Conly, J. L. Crazy lady! (5 and up) **Fic**
Wilson, N. H. The reason for Janey (5 and up) **Fic**

Mentally handicapped children
See also Slow learning children
Fiction
Shyer, M. F. Welcome home, Jellybean (5 and up) **Fic**
Slepian, J. Risk 'n' roses (5 and up) **Fic**

Mentally ill
Fiction
Levoy, M. Alan and Naomi (6 and up) **Fic**
Lisle, J. T. Afternoon of the elves (4-6) **Fic**

The **mer-woman** out of the sea. Hamilton, V.
In Hamilton, V. Her stories p78-83
398.2

The **merchant's** daughter and the maidservant.
Afanas'ev, A. N.
In Afanas'ev, A. N. Russian fairy tales
p327-31 **398.2**

The **merchant's** daughter and the slanderer.
Afanas'ev, A. N.
In Afanas'ev, A. N. Russian fairy tales
p415-18 **398.2**

Mercury (Planet)
Simon, S. Mercury (3-6) **523.4**
Vogt, G. Mercury (2-4) **523.4**

Merit students encyclopedia **031**

Merkin, Richard, 1938-
(il) Ritter, L. S. Leagues apart **796.357**

Merlin (Legendary character)
San Souci, R. Young Merlin (2-5) **398.2**
White, T. H. The sword in the stone
Fic

Fiction
Yolen, J. The dragon's boy (5 and up)
Fic

The **Mermaid**
In Diane Goode's book of scary stories &
songs p32-35 **398.2**
In Raw Head, bloody bones p31-33
398.2

The **mermaid** in the millpond. Osborne, M. P.
In Osborne, M. P. Mermaid tales from
around the world p63-69 **398.2**

The **mermaid** summer. Hunter, M. **Fic**

Mermaid tales from around the world. Osborne, M. P. **398.2**

Mermaids and mermen
Osborne, M. P. Mermaid tales from around
the world (4-6) **398.2**
San Souci, R. Sukey and the mermaid (1-4)
398.2

Fiction
Hunter, M. The mermaid summer (4 and
up) **Fic**

The **mermaid's** revenge. Osborne, M. P.
In Osborne, M. P. Mermaid tales from
around the world p45-48 **398.2**

The **mermaid's** twin sister. Joseph, L.
In Joseph, L. The mermaid's twin sister:
more stories from Trinidad p10-17
398.2

The **mermaid's** twin sister: more stories from
Trinidad. Joseph, L. **398.2**

Merriam, Eve, 1916-1992
12 ways to get to 11 (k-3) **510**
Bam, bam, bam (k-2) **811**
Blackberry ink (k-2) **811**
Chortles: new and selected wordplay poems
(3-6) **811**
Fresh paint (4 and up) **811**
Halloween A B C (k-2) **811**
Higgle wiggle (k-2) **811**
A poem for a pickle: funnybone verses (k-2)
811

The singing green (3-6) **811**
You be good and I'll be night: jump-on-the-
bed poems (k-2) **811**

Merriam-Webster's biographical dictionary
920.003

Merriam-Webster's elementary dictionary
(4-6) **423**

Merriam-Webster's intermediate dictionary (5
and up) **423**

Merrick, Joseph Carey, 1862 or 3-1890
See/See also pages in the following book(s):
Drimmer, F. Born different p122-49 (6 and
up) **920**

Merrill, Jean, 1923-
The Girl Who Loved Caterpillars **E**
The pushcart war (5 and up) **Fic**
The toothpaste millionaire (4-6) **Fic**

The **merry** adventures of Robin Hood of great
renown in Nottinghamshire. Pyle, H.
398.2

A **merry** Christmas. Hackett, W.
In The Big book of Christmas plays p332-
48 **808.82**

A **merry** Christmas. Wilder, L. I.
In Wilder, L. I. A Little house Christmas
p49-55 **S C**

Merry Christmas, Amelia Bedelia. Parish, P.
See note under Parish, P. Amelia Bedelia
E

Merry Christmas, Ernest and Celestine. Vincent, G. See note under Vincent, G. Ernest and Celestine **E**

Merry Christmas, space case. Marshall, J. See
note under Marshall, E. Space case **E**

Merry-go-round. Ginsburg, M. **398.2**

Merry-go-round. Heller, R. **428**

The **merry-go-round.** Mahy, M.
In Mahy, M. The girl with the green ear
p58-70 **S C**

Mesopotamia *See* Iraq

Messages in the mailbox. Leedy, L. **808**

Messenger, Norman
(il) Mayne, W. Hob and the goblins **Fic**

The **messenger** to Maftam. Courlander, H.
In Courlander, H. The cow-tail switch,
and other West African stories p79-86
398.2

Messiness *See* Cleanliness

Meteorology
See also Droughts; Weather; Weather
forecasting
Branley, F. M. Sun dogs and shooting stars
(5 and up) **523**
Gallant, R. A. Rainbows, mirages and sundogs (4 and up) **551.5**
Simon, S. Weather (3-6) **551.5**

Meteors
Branley, F. M. Shooting stars (k-1)
523.6
Lauber, P. Voyagers from space (4 and up)
523.5

The **miller,** the boy and the donkey. Wildsmith, B. **398.2**

Millinery

See also Hats

Million (The number)

Schwartz, D. M. How much is a million?
E

A **million** fish—more or less. McKissack, P. C.
E

Millions of cats. Gág, W. **E**

Mills, Alan

I know an old lady who swallowed a fly. See
I know an old lady who swallowed a fly
782.42

Mills, Claudia, 1954-

Dinah for president. See note under Mills,
C. Dynamite Dinah **Fic**

Dinah forever. See note under Mills, C. Dynamite Dinah **Fic**

Dinah in love. See note under Mills, C. Dynamite Dinah **Fic**

Dynamite Dinah (3-5) **Fic**

A visit to Amy-Claire **E**

Mills, Lauren A.

(il) MacDonald, G. At the back of the North
Wind **Fic**

Mills, Yaroslava Surmach *See* Yaroslava,
1925-

Mills

Macaulay, D. Mill (4 and up) **690**

Mills and millwork *See* Mills

Milne, A. A. (Alan Alexander), 1882-1956

The house at Pooh Corner (1-4) **Fic**

also in Milne, A. A. The world of Pooh
p153-314 **Fic**

Now we are six (k-3) **821**

also in Milne, A. A. The world of Christopher Robin p119-234 **821**

The Pooh story book (1-4) **Fic**

When we were very young (k-3) **821**

also in Milne, A. A. The world of Christopher Robin p1-118 **821**

Winnie-the-Pooh (1-4) **Fic**

also in Milne, A. A. The world of Pooh
p7-149 **Fic**

The world of Christopher Robin (k-3)
821

The world of Pooh (1-4) **Fic**

Milne, Alan Alexander *See* Milne, A. A. (Alan
Alexander), 1882-1956

Milner, Angela

(jt. auth) Norman, D. Dinosaur **567.9**

Milone, Karen *See* Dugan, Karen M.

Milton, Joyce

Whales (1-3) **599.5**

Mime

Straub, C. Mime: basics for beginners (6 and
up) **792.3**

Minard, Rosemary, 1939-

(ed) Womenfolk and fairy tales. See Womenfolk and fairy tales **398.2**

Minarik, Else Holmelund

Father Bear comes home. See note under
Minarik, E. H. Little Bear **E**

A kiss for Little Bear. See note under Minarik, E. H. Little Bear **E**

Little Bear **E**

Little Bear goes to the moon

In The Read-aloud treasury p70-83
808.8

Little Bear's friend. See note under Minarik,
E. H. Little Bear **E**

Little Bear's visit. See note under Minarik,
E. H. Little Bear **E**

No fighting, no biting! **E**

Mine for keeps. Little, J. **Fic**

Mineralogy

See also Mines and mineral resources

Podendorf, I. Rocks and minerals (2-4)
549

Symes, R. F. Rocks & minerals (4 and up)
549

Zim, H. S. Rocks and minerals (4 and up)
549

Miners

Fiction

Lyon, G. E. Mama is a miner **E**

Wiseman, D. Jeremy Visick (5 and up)
Fic

Minerva Louise. Stoeke, J. M. See note under
Stoeke, J. M. A hat for Minerva Louise
E

Mines and mineral resources

See also Coal mines and mining

Fiction

Beatty, P. Bonanza girl (5 and up) **Fic**

Ming Lo moves the mountain. Lobel, A.
E

The **miniature** horse. LaBonte, G. **636.1**

Minnesota

Carlson, J. D. A historical album of Minnesota

In Historical albums series **973**

Porter, A. P. Minnesota

In Hello USA series **973**

Stein, R. C. Minnesota

In America the beautiful **973**

Fiction

Lovelace, M. H. Betsy-Tacy (2-4) **Fic**

Paulsen, G. The winter room (5 and up)
Fic

Minnikin. Moe, J. E.

In The Red fairy book p307-21 **398.2**

Minor, Wendell

(il) Bunting, E. Red fox running **E**

(il) George, J. C. Everglades **975.9**

(il) George, J. C. Julie **Fic**

(il) George, J. C. The moon of the owls
598

(il) Siebert, D. Mojave **811**

(il) Siebert, D. Sierra **811**

(il) Zolotow, C. The seashore book **E**

Minorities

The In America series (5 and up) **305.8**

Minorities—*Continued*
Bibliography
Helbig, A. This land is our land   **016.8**
Kaleidoscope   **011.6**
Many faces, many voices   **028.5**
Miller-Lachmann, L. Our family, our friends, our world   **011.6**
Rochman, H. Against borders   **011.6**
Totten, H. L. Culturally diverse library collections for children   **011.6**
Venture into cultures   **011.6**

Minotaur (Greek mythology)
Fisher, L. E. Theseus and the Minotaur (3-5)   **292**
Hutton, W. Theseus and the Minotaur (3-5)   **292**

The **minstrel** and the dragon pup. Sutcliff, R.   **E**

Minstrels
Fiction
Sutcliff, R. The minstrel and the dragon pup   **E**
Vining, E. G. Adam of the road (5 and up)   **Fic**

Mintz, Barbara
(jt. auth) Katan, N. J. Hieroglyphs, the writing of ancient Egypt   **493**

The **miracle** doctor. Fang, L.
In Fang, L. The Ch'i-lin purse p85-100   **398.2**

The **miracle** of Purun Bhagat. Kipling, R.
In Kipling, R. The jungle books   **S C**

The **miracle** of the potato latkes. Penn, M.   **E**

Miracles
Fiction
De Paola, T. The clown of God (k-3)   **398.2**

The **miracles** of Jesus. De Paola, T.   **232.9**

Miracles on the sea. Jaffe, N.
In Jaffe, N. The uninvited guest and other Jewish holiday tales p18-22   **296.4**

Miracles: poems by children of the English-speaking world   **821.008**

The **miraculous** banyan tree. Vuong, L. D.
In Vuong, L. D. Sky legends of Vietnam p38-53   **398.2**

The **miraculous** pipe. Afanas'ev, A. N.
In Afanas'ev, A. N. Russian fairy tales p425-27   **398.2**

Mirages
See/See also pages in the following book(s):
Gallant, R. A. Rainbows, mirages and sundogs p14-22 (4 and up)   **551.5**

Mirandy and Brother Wind. McKissack, P. C.   **E**

Mirette on the high wire. McCully, E. A.   **E**

Mirocha, Paul
(il) Berger, M. Oil spill!   **363.7**

A **mirror**, a carpet, and a lemon. Walker, B. K.
In Walker, B. K. A treasury of Turkish folktales for children p132-34   **398.2**

Mirror magic. Simon, S.   **535**

Mirrors
Simon, S. Mirror magic (k-3)   **535**
Zubrowski, B. Mirrors (4 and up)   **535**

Miscellaneous facts *See* Curiosities and wonders

Mischling, second degree: my childhood in Nazi Germany. Koehn, I.   **92**

The **miser**. Afanas'ev, A. N.
In Afanas'ev, A. N. Russian fairy tales p58-59   **398.2**

The **Miser's** jar
In The Monkey's haircut, and other stories told by the Maya p32-36   **398.2**

Misery. Afanas'ev, A. N.
In Afanas'ev, A. N. Russian fairy tales p20-24   **398.2**

Miskito Indians *See* Mosquito Indians

Misoso. Aardema, V.   **398.2**

Miss Jones. Marshall, J.
In Marshall, J. Rats on the roof, and other stories p63-79   **S C**

Miss Lin, the sea goddess. Carpenter, F.
In Carpenter, F. Tales of a Chinese grandmother p235-41   **398.2**

Miss Lonelyheart. McGowan, J.
In Holiday plays round the year p198-211   **812.008**

Miss Mary Mack and other children's street rhymes   **796.1**

Miss Mouse. Marshall, J.
In Marshall, J. Rats on the range and other stories p7-23   **S C**

Miss Nelson has a field day. Allard, H. See note under Allard, H. Miss Nelson is missing!   **E**

Miss Nelson is back. Allard, H. See note under Allard, H. Miss Nelson is missing!   **E**

Miss Nelson is missing!. Allard, H.   **E**

Miss Rumphius. Cooney, B.   **E**

Missing children
See also Runaway children

Missing May. Rylant, C.   **Fic**

The **missing** tarts. Hennessy, B. G.   **E**

Missions
Fiction
Politi, L. Song of the swallows   **E**

Missions, Christian *See* Christian missions

Mississippi
Carson, R. Mississippi
In America the beautiful   **973**
Ready, A. Mississippi
In Hello USA series   **973**

Money

See also Paper money

Cribb, J. Money (4 and up)   **332.4**

Maestro, B. The story of money (3-5)   **332.4**

Money, money, money. Parker, N. W.   **769.5**

Moneymaking projects for children

Barkin, C. Jobs for kids (5 and up)   **650.1**

Wilkinson, E. Making cents (4 and up)   **332.024**

Monfried, Lucia

(comp) Diane Goode's book of scary stories & songs. See Diane Goode's book of scary stories & songs   **398.2**

(comp) Diane Goode's book of silly stories & songs. See Diane Goode's book of silly stories & songs   **398.2**

Mongolia

Brill, M. T. Mongolia (4 and up)   **951.7**

Reynolds, J. Mongolia (2-4)   **951.7**

Mongolians *See* Mongols

Mongols

Reynolds, J. Mongolia (2-4)   **951.7**

See/See also pages in the following book(s):

Lyttle, R. B. Land beyond the river p135-46 (6 and up)   **940.1**

Monhegan Island (Me.)

Dean, J. A year on Monhegan Island (4-6)   **974.1**

Monjo, F. N., 1924-1978

The drinking gourd   **E**

Monkey. Kherdian, D.

In Kherdian, D. Feathers and tails p65-73   **398.2**

Monkey and Crab. Watkins, Y. K.

In Watkins, Y. K. Tales from the bamboo grove p37-44   **398.2**

The **monkey** and the crocodile. Galdone, P.   **398.2**

The **monkey** and the crocodile. Kherdian, D.

In Kherdian, D. Feathers and tails p45-48   **398.2**

Monkey, Tiger and the Magic Trials. Berry, J.

In Berry, J. Spiderman Anancy p27-33   **398.2**

The **Monkey** who asked for Misery

In The Magic orange tree, and other Haitian folktales p113-16   **398.2**

Monkeys

See also Baboons

Arnold, C. Monkey (3-5)   **599.8**

Haldane, S. Helping hands (4 and up)   **362.4**

Selsam, M. E. A first look at monkeys and apes (1-3)   **599.8**

Steedman, S. Amazing monkeys (2-4)   **599.8**

Fiction

Christelow, E. Five little monkeys jumping on the bed   **E**

Hurd, E. T. Last one home is a green pig   **E**

Rey, H. A. Curious George   **E**

Slobodkina, E. Caps for sale   **E**

The **Monkey's** haircut

In The Monkey's haircut, and other stories told by the Maya p138-43   **398.2**

The **Monkey's** haircut, and other stories told by the Maya (5 and up)   **398.2**

Monroe, Jean Guard

First houses (6 and up)   **970.004**

Monroe, Joan Kiddell- *See* Kiddell-Monroe, Joan, 1908-1972

Monsanto Company

See/See also pages in the following book(s):

Aaseng, N. The problem solvers p69-75 (5 and up)   **920**

Monson, Dianne L.

(jt. auth) Sutherland, Z. Children and books   **028.5**

The **monster** den. Ciardi, J.   **811**

The **monster** garden. Alcock, V.   **Fic**

The **monster** in the third dresser drawer and other stories about Adam Joshua. Smith, J. L. See note under Smith, J. L. The kid next door and other headaches   **Fic**

Monster mama. Rosenberg, L.   **E**

Monster poems (1-4)   **821.008**

The **monster** who swallowed everything. Lester, J.

In Lester, J. How many spots does a leopard have? and other tales p13-15   **398.2**

Monsters

Walker, P. R. Bigfoot and other legendary creatures (4-6)   **001.9**

Fiction

Alcock, V. The monster garden (4 and up)   **Fic**

Bunting, E. Night of the gargoyles   **E**

Crowe, R. L. Clyde monster   **E**

Drescher, H. Simon's book   **E**

Emberley, E. Go away, big green monster!   **E**

Hutchins, P. Where's the baby?   **E**

Rosenberg, L. Monster mama   **E**

Viorst, J. My mama says there aren't any zombies, ghosts, vampires, creatures, demons, monsters, fiends, goblins, or things   **E**

Poetry

Ciardi, J. The monster den   **811**

Creatures (3-5)   **821.008**

Heide, F. P. Grim and ghastly goings-on   **811**

Monster poems (1-4)   **821.008**

Prelutsky, J. The Headless Horseman rides tonight (2-5)   **811**

Prelutsky, J. Nightmares: poems to trouble your sleep (2-5)   **811**

Monsters in art

Bolognese, D. The way to draw and color monsters (4 and up)   **743**

Montana
Heinrichs, A. Montana
In America the beautiful   **973**
LaDoux, R. Montana
In Hello USA series   **973**

Monteith, Ann
(il) Cole, J. A dog's body   **636.7**

Monteith, Jim
(il) Cole, J. A dog's body   **636.7**

Montez, Michele
(il) 50 simple things kids can do to recycle. See 50 simple things kids can do to recycle   **363.7**
(il) 50 simple things kids can do to save the earth. See 50 simple things kids can do to save the earth   **363.7**

Montgomery, L. M. (Lucy Maud), 1874-1942
Anne of Avonlea. See note under Montgomery, L. M. Anne of Green Gables   **Fic**
Anne of Green Gables (5 and up)   **Fic**
Anne of Ingleside. See note under Montgomery, L. M. Anne of Green Gables   **Fic**
Anne of the island. See note under Montgomery, L. M. Anne of Green Gables   **Fic**
Anne of Windy Poplars. See note under Montgomery, L. M. Anne of Green Gables   **Fic**
Anne's house of dreams. See note under Montgomery, L. M. Anne of Green Gables   **Fic**

Montgomery, Lucy Maud *See* Montgomery, L. M. (Lucy Maud), 1874-1942

Montgomery (Ala.)
Race relations
Celsi, T. N. Rosa Parks and the Montgomery bus boycott (3-5)   **92**
Siegel, B. The year they walked: Rosa Parks and the Montgomery bus boycott (4-6)   **92**

See/See also pages in the following book(s):
Levine, E. Freedom's children p17-31 (6 and up)   **323.1**

The **Month-Brothers**. Marshak, S.   **398.2**

Monticello. Fisher, L. E.   **975.5**

Monticello. Richards, N.   **975.5**

Montresor, Beni, 1926-
(il) De Regniers, B. S. May I bring a friend?   **E**

Monty. Stevenson, J.   **E**

Moominland midwinter. Jansson, T. See note under Jansson, T. Moominsummer madness   **Fic**

Moominpapa at sea. Jansson, T. See note under Jansson, T. Moominsummer madness   **Fic**

Moominpapa's memoirs. Jansson, T. See note under Jansson, T. Moominsummer madness   **Fic**

Moominsummer madness. Jansson, T.   **Fic**

Moon
Branley, F. M. The moon seems to change (k-3)   **523.3**
Branley, F. M. What the moon is like (k-3)   **523.3**
Moore, P. The sun and moon (k-3)   **523.7**
Simon, S. The moon (1-4)   **523.3**
See/See also pages in the following book(s):
Kelch, J. W. Small worlds: exploring the 60 moons of our solar system p24-37 (6 and up)   **523.9**

Eclipses
See Lunar eclipses
Fiction
Babcock, C. No moon, no milk!   **E**
Baylor, B. Moon song (1-4)   **398.2**
Daly, N. Why the Sun & Moon live in the sky (k-3)   **398.2**
Ehlert, L. Moon rope. Un lazo a la luna (k-3)   **398.2**
Lankford, M. D. Is it dark? is it light?   **E**
Preston, E. M. Squawk to the moon, Little Goose   **E**
Young, E. Moon mother (2-4)   **398.2**

Moon, Voyages to *See* Space flight to the moon

The **moon**. Grimm, J.
In Grimm, J. The complete Grimm's fairy tales p713-15   **398.2**

The **moon** and I. Byars, B. C.   **92**

The **moon** by night. L'Engle, M. See note under L'Engle, M. Meet the Austins   **Fic**

The **moon** fairy. Vuong, L. D.
In Vuong, L. D. Sky legends of Vietnam p13-37   **398.2**

The **Moon** in the pond. Lester, J.
In Lester, J. The tales of Uncle Remus p96-99   **398.2**

Moon mother. Young, E.   **398.2**

The **moon** of the alligators. George, J. C.   **597.9**

The **moon** of the bears. George, J. C.   **599.74**

The **moon** of the chickarees. George, J. C.   **599.32**

The **moon** of the fox pups. George, J. C.   **599.74**

The **moon** of the gray wolves. George, J. C.   **599.74**

The **moon** of the monarch butterflies. George, J. C.   **595.7**

The **moon** of the mountain lions. George, J. C.   **599.74**

The **moon** of the owls. George, J. C.   **598**

The **moon** of the salamanders. George, J. C.   **597.6**

The **moon** of the winter bird. George, J. C.   **598**

Moon rope. Un lazo a la luna. Ehlert, L.   **398.2**

Mosques
Macdonald, F. A 16th century mosque (5 and up) **297**

The **mosquito** and the water buffalo. Walker, B. K.
In Walker, B. K. A treasury of Turkish folktales for children p14 **398.2**

Mosquito Indians
Legends
Rohmer, H. The invisible hunters (2-4) **398.2**
Rohmer, H. Mother Scorpion country (2-4) **398.2**

Mosquitoes
Patent, D. H. Mosquitoes (4 and up) **595.7**
Fiction
Aardema, V. Why mosquitoes buzz in people's ears (k-3) **398.2**

Moss, Joyce, 1951-
(ed) From page to screen. See From page to screen **016.79143**

Moss, Lloyd
Zin! zin! zin! a violin **E**

Moss gown. Hooks, W. H. **398.2**

Moss pillows. Wells, R. **E**

Mossflower. Jacques, B. See note under Jacques, B. Redwall **Fic**

Mossycoat. Crossley-Holland, K.
In Crossley-Holland, K. British folk tales p86-99 **398.2**

Most, Bernard, 1937-
How big were the dinosaurs (k-2) **567.9**
The littlest dinosaurs (k-2) **567.9**
Whatever happened to the dinosaurs? **E**
Where to look for a dinosaur (k-2) **567.9**

The **most** beautiful place in the world. Cameron, A. **Fic**

The **most** precious thing. Jaffe, N.
In Jaffe, N. While standing on one foot p26-32 **296.1**

The **most** useful slave. Hamilton, V.
In Hamilton, V. The people could fly: American black folktales p160-65 **398.2**

The **most** wonderful egg in the world. Heine, H. **E**

Motels *See* Hotels and motels

The **moth** and the star. Thurber, J.
In The Random House book of humor for children p93-94 **817.008**

Moth, the fire dancer. Caduto, M. J.
In Caduto, M. J. Keepers of the night p43-45 **398.2**

Mother and daughter. Soto, G.
In Soto, G. Baseball in April, and other stories p60-68 **S C**

Mother Crocodile. Guy, R. **398.2**

Mother goes modern. Arthur, K.
In Holiday plays round the year p267-84 **812.008**

Mother Goose
The Comic adventures of Old Mother Hubbard and her dog **398.8**
Craig, H. I see the moon, and the moon sees me. . . . **398.8**
The Glorious Mother Goose **398.8**
Granfa' Grig had a pig, and other rhymes without reason from Mother Goose **398.8**
James Marshall's Mother Goose **398.8**
The Random House book of Mother Goose **398.8**
The Real Mother Goose **398.8**
Ring o' roses **398.8**
Tomie dePaola's Mother Goose **398.8**
Wendy Watson's Mother Goose **398.8**
See/See also pages in the following book(s):
Sendak, M. Caldecott & Co.: notes on books and pictures p11-20 **028.5**

Mother Goose [illus. by Tasha Tudor] (k-2) **398.8**

Mother Goose [illus. by Brian Wildsmith] (k-2) **398.8**

Mother Goose and the sly fox. Conover, C. **398.2**

Mother Goose magic. Chorao, K. **398.8**

Mother Goose songbook, Jane Yolen's **782.42**

Mother Goose time. Marino, J. **027.62**

Mother Hildegarde. Pyle, H.
In Pyle, H. The wonder clock p189-202 **398.2**

Mother Holle. Grimm, J.
In Grimm, J. The complete Grimm's fairy tales p133-36 **398.2**
In The Red fairy book p303-06 **398.2**

Mother Jones *See* Jones, Mother, 1830-1930

Mother Jones and the march of the mill children. Colman, P. **92**

The **Mother** of Ghosts
In The Naked bear p37-43 **398.2**

Mother of the waters
In The Magic orange tree, and other Haitian folktales p151-56 **398.2**

Mother Scorpion country. Rohmer, H. **398.2**

Mother Swan's daughters
In The Naked bear p72-78 **398.2**

Mothers
Fiction
Ackerman, K. By the dawn's early light **E**
Aliki. Welcome, little baby **E**
Browne, A. Piggybook **E**
Goode, D. Where's our mama? **E**
Hermes, P. You shouldn't have to say goodbye (5 and up) **Fic**
Viorst, J. My mama says there aren't any zombies, ghosts, vampires, creatures, demons, monsters, fiends, goblins, or things **E**
Wells, R. Hazel's amazing mother **E**

Mothers, Single parent *See* Single parent family

Mothers and daughters
Alexander, S. H. Mom can't see me (3-5) **362.4**
Alexander, S. H. Mom's best friend (3-5) **362.4**

Fiction
Barber, B. E. Saturday at The New You **E**
Caseley, J. Mama, coming and going **E**
Ellis, S. Pick-up sticks (5 and up) **Fic**
Gray, L. M. My mama had a dancing heart **E**
Greene, C. C. Nora (6 and up) **Fic**
Hines, A. G. It's just me, Emily **E**
Johnson, A. Tell me a story, Mama **E**
Johnston, T. The quilt story **E**
Joosse, B. M. Mama, do you love me? **E**
Kerley, B. Songs of Papa's island (3-5) **Fic**
Loh, M. J. Tucking Mommy in **E**
Lowry, L. Rabble Starkey (5 and up) **Fic**
Lyon, G. E. Mama is a miner **E**
MacLachlan, P. Mama One, Mama Two **E**
Martin, C. L. G. Three brave women **E**
Patron, S. Maybe yes, maybe no, maybe maybe (3-5) **Fic**
Pomerantz, C. The chalk doll **E**
Rodgers, M. Freaky Friday (4 and up) **Fic**
Rodowsky, C. F. Hannah in between (5 and up) **Fic**
Russo, M. Waiting for Hannah **E**
Smith, D. B. Best girl (4-6) **Fic**
Stanek, M. I speak English for my mom (2-4) **Fic**
Willard, N. The high rise glorious skittle skat roarious sky pie angel food cake **E**
Williams, V. B. Scooter (3-5) **Fic**

Mothers and sons
Fiction
Bauer, M. D. A question of trust (5 and up) **Fic**
Gove, D. One rainy night **E**
Lindgren, B. The wild baby **E**
Peterson, J. W. My mama sings **E**
Rosenberg, L. Monster mama **E**
Say, A. Tree of cranes **E**
Zolotow, C. The seashore book **E**
The **Mother's** Day mice. Bunting, E. **E**

Moths
See also Caterpillars
Feltwell, J. Butterflies and moths (3-5) **595.7**
Mitchell, R. T. Butterflies and moths (4 and up) **595.7**
Still, J. Amazing butterflies & moths (2-4) **595.7**
Whalley, P. E. S. Butterfly & moth (4 and up) **595.7**

See/See also pages in the following book(s):
Zim, H. S. Insects (4 and up) **595.7**

Motion
Cobb, V. Why doesn't the earth fall up? (3-5) **531**
Lafferty, P. Force & motion (4 and up) **531**
Experiments
Ardley, N. The science book of motion (3-5) **531**

Motion picture actors *See* Actors

Motion picture direction *See* Motion pictures—Production and direction

Motion picture production *See* Motion pictures—Production and direction

Motion pictures
Catalogs
From page to screen **016.79143**
Fiction
Schwartz, H. Albert goes Hollywood **E**
Production and direction
Gibbons, G. Lights! Camera! Action! (k-3) **791.43**
Scott, E. Look alive (4 and up) **791.43**

Motivation (Psychology)
See also Wishes

Mouhot, Henri, 1826-1861
See/See also pages in the following book(s):
Scheller, W. Amazing archaeologists and their finds (4 and up) **920**

Mound, L. A. (Laurence Alfred), 1934-
Amazing insects (2-4) **595.7**
Insect (4 and up) **595.7**

Mound, Laurence Alfred *See* Mound, L. A. (Laurence Alfred), 1934-

Mounseer Nongtongpaw. Shelley, M. W.
In A Nursery companion p118-22 **820.8**

Mount Holyoke College
Rosen, D. A fire in her bones: the story of Mary Lyon (4 and up) **92**

Mount Rushmore National Memorial (S.D.)
Doherty, C. A. Mount Rushmore (4-6) **730.9**

Mount Saint Helens (Wash.)
Lauber, P. Volcano: the eruption and healing of Mount St. Helens (4 and up) **551.2**

Mountain ecology
George, J. C. One day in the alpine tundra (4-6) **574.5**

Mountain goats. Staub, F. J. **599.73**
Mountain Jack tales. Haley, G. E. **398.2**
Mountain lions *See* Pumas
Mountain-making. Curry, J. L.
In Curry, J. L. Back in the beforetime p22-25 **398.2**

Mountains
See also Appalachian Mountains; Catskill Mountains (N.Y.); Himalaya Mountains; Ozark Mountains; Sierra Nevada Mountains

Music appreciation
See also Music—History and criticism

Music education *See* Music—Study and teaching

Music, music for everyone. Williams, V. B. See note under Williams, V. B. A chair for my mother   E

Musical instruments
Ardley, N. Music (4 and up)   **784.19**
Hayes, A. Meet the Marching Smithereens (k-3)   **784.19**
Hayes, A. Meet the orchestra (k-3)   **784.19**
Hewitt, S. Get set—go! [Music & sound series] (k-3)   **784.19**
Moss, L. Zin! zin! zin! a violin   E
Oates, E. H. Making music (3-5)   **784.19**
Walther, T. Make mine music! (4 and up)   **784.19**
Wiseman, A. S. Making musical things (3-6)   **784.19**

Musicals
See also Operetta

The musician. Terada, A. M.
In Terada, A. M. Under the starfruit tree p132-34   **398.2**

Musicians
See also Composers
Fiction
Alexander, L. The marvelous misadventures of Sebastian (4 and up)   Fic
Brett, J. Berlioz the bear   E
Collier, J. L. The jazz kid (5 and up)   Fic
Fenner, C. Yolonda's genius (4-6)   Fic
Isadora, R. Ben's trumpet   E
MacLachlan, P. The facts and fictions of Minna Pratt (4 and up)   Fic
Martin, B. The maestro plays   E
McCully, E. A. The amazing Felix   E

Musicians, African American *See* African American musicians

Musicians. Roalf, P.
In Roalf, P. Looking at paintings   **750**

Muskrats
Arnosky, J. Come out, muskrats (k-2)   **599.32**

Muslimism *See* Islam

Mutel, Cornelia Fleischer, 1947-
Tropical rain forests (4 and up)   **574.5**

Mutsmag
In Grandfather tales p40-51   **398.2**

Mwalimu
Awful aardvark (k-2)   **398.2**

Mwenye Hadithi
Crafty Chameleon   E
Hot Hippo   E

My backyard history book. Weitzman, D. L.   **973**

My ballet class. Isadora, R.   **792.8**

My big toe
In Diane Goode's book of scary stories & songs p12-13   **398.2**

My black me (5 and up)   **811.008**

My brother, my sister, and I. Watkins, Y. K.   Fic

My brother Sam is dead. Collier, J. L.   Fic

My brown bear Barney. Butler, D.   E

My brown bear Barney in trouble. Butler, D. See note under Butler, D. My brown bear Barney   E

My camera. Ancona, G.   **771**

My dad. Daly, N.   E

My Daniel. Conrad, P.   Fic

My day/Mi día. Emberley, R.   **463**

My dentist. Rockwell, H.   **617.6**

My doctor. Rockwell, H.   **610.69**

My farm. Lester, A.   **994**

My father's dragon. Gannett, R. S.   Fic

My father's hands. Ryder, J.   E

My feet. Aliki   **612**

My first activity book. Wilkes, A.   **745.5**

My first atlas. Boyle, B.   **912**

My first book of nature. Kuhn, D.   **574.3**

My first book of sign. Baker, P. J.   **419**

My first dictionary. Root, B.   **423**

My first garden book. Wilkes, A.   **635**

My first kitten. Hausherr, R.   **636.8**

My first Kwanzaa book. Chocolate, D. M. N.   **394.2**

My first magic book. Leyton, L.   **793.8**

My first nature book. Wilkes, A.   **508**

My first photography book. King, D.   **771**

My first picture dictionary. See Words for new readers   **423**

My first puppy. Hausherr, R.   **636.7**

My five senses. Aliki   **612.8**

My five senses. Miller, M.   E

My friend Flicka. O'Hara, M.
In Herds of thunder, manes of gold p111-35   **808.8**

My friend Leslie. Rosenberg, M. B.   **362.4**

My grandmother's journey. Cech, J.   E

My grandson Lew. Zolotow, C.   E

My great-aunt Arizona [biography of Arizona Houston Hughes]. Houston, G.   E

My great-grandfather's grave-digging. Price, S.
In The Oxford book of scary tales p94-95   **808.8**

My hands. Aliki   **612**

My Hiroshima. Morimoto, J.   **940.54**

My hometown library. Jaspersohn, W.   **027.4**

My house/Mi casa: a book in two languages. Emberley, R.   **463**

My household. Grimm, J.
 In Grimm, J. The complete Grimm's fairy tales p624   **398.2**

My island grandma. Lasky, K.   **E**

My life with the chimpanzees. Goodall, J.   **92**

My Lord Bag-o'-Rice. Quayle, E.
 In Quayle, E. The shining princess, and other Japanese legends p33-43   **398.2**

My mama had a dancing heart. Gray, L. M.   **E**

My mama needs me. Walter, M. P.   **E**

My mama says there aren't any zombies, ghosts, vampires, creatures, demons, monsters, fiends, goblins, or things. Viorst, J.   **E**

My mama sings. Peterson, J. W.   **E**

My mother got married (and other disasters). Park, B.   **Fic**

My mother is the most beautiful woman in the world. Reyher, R. H.   **398.2**

My mysterious world. Mahy, M.   **92**

My name is brain Brian. Betancourt, J.   **Fic**

My naughty little sister makes a bottle-tree. Edwards, D.
 In The Oxford treasury of children's stories p35-38   **S C**

My new kitten. Cole, J.   **636.8**

My New York. Jakobsen, K.   **974.7**

My own self. Jacobs, J.
 In Jacobs, J. English fairy tales p238-41   **398.2**

My painted house, my friendly chicken, and me. Angelou, M.   **968**

My parents think I'm sleeping: poems. Prelutsky, J.   **811**

My party book. Elliot, M.   **745.594**

My place in space. Hirst, R.   **520**

My prairie Christmas. Harvey, B.   **Fic**

My prairie year. Harvey, B.   **Fic**

My puppy is born. Cole, J.   **636.7**

My red umbrella. Bright, R.   **E**

My river. Halpern, S.   **E**

My rotten redheaded older brother. Polacco, P.   **E**

My shadow. Stevenson, R. L.   **821**

My side of the mountain. George, J. C.   **Fic**

My son John. Aylesworth, J.   **E**

My song is beautiful (k-3)   **808.81**

My two worlds. Gordon, G.   **305.8**

My visit to the aquarium. Aliki   **639.3**

My world [series]
 Rockwell, A. F. Happy birthday to me   **E**
 Rockwell, A. F. How my garden grew   **E**
 Rockwell, A. F. Sick in bed   **E**

Myers, Lou, 1915-
 See/See also pages in the following book(s):
 Sendak, M. Caldecott & Co.: notes on books and pictures p131-32   **028.5**

Myers, Walter Dean, 1937-
 Brown angels   **811**
 Fast Sam, Cool Clyde, and Stuff (6 and up)   **Fic**
 Me, Mop, and the Moondance Kid (4-6)   **Fic**
 Mop, Moondance, and the Nagasaki Knights. See note under Myers, W. D. Me, Mop, and the Moondance Kid   **Fic**
 Now is your time! (6 and up)   **305.8**
 The story of the three kingdoms   **E**

Myrick, Mildred
 The Secret Three   **E**

Myron Mere. Rockwell, T.
 In Rockwell, T. How to eat fried worms, and other plays p1-20   **812**

The mysteries of Harris Burdick. Van Allsburg, C.   **E**

Mysteries of science [series]
 Landau, E. The Loch Ness monster   **001.9**
 Landau, E. Sasquatch   **001.9**
 Landau, E. Yeti   **001.9**

The mysterious disappearance of Leon (I mean Noel). Raskin, E.   **Fic**

Mysterious multiplying jar, Anno's. Anno, M.   **512**

The mysterious rays of Dr. Röntgen. Gherman, B.   **92**

The mysterious tadpole. Kellogg, S.   **E**

Mystery and detective stories *See* Mystery fiction

Mystery and magic
 In Hands-on science [series]   **507**

Mystery fiction
 Adler, D. A. Cam Jansen and the mystery of the stolen diamonds (2-4)   **Fic**
 Babbitt, N. Goody Hall (4-6)   **Fic**
 Bawden, N. A handful of thieves (4 and up)   **Fic**
 Bellairs, J. The curse of the blue figurine (5 and up)   **Fic**
 Berends, P. B. The case of the elevator duck (3-5)   **Fic**
 Bonsall, C. N. The case of the hungry stranger   **E**
 Brooks, W. R. Freddy goes camping (3-5)   **Fic**
 Cameron, E. The court of the stone children (5 and up)   **Fic**
 Christopher, M. Tackle without a team (4-6)   **Fic**
 Hahn, M. D. The dead man in Indian Creek (5 and up)   **Fic**
 Hamilton, V. The house of Dies Drear (5 and up)   **Fic**
 Hamilton, V. The mystery of Drear House (5 and up)   **Fic**
 Howe, D. Bunnicula (4-6)   **Fic**

Mystery fiction—*Continued*

Howe, J. The celery stalks at midnight (4-6) **Fic**

Howe, J. Dew drop dead (4-6) **Fic**

Hurd, T. Mystery on the docks **E**

Klause, A. C. Alien secrets (5 and up) **Fic**

Kline, S. Orp and the FBI (4-6) **Fic**

Konigsburg, E. L. Up from Jericho Tel (5 and up) **Fic**

Levy, E. Something queer is going on (a mystery) **E**

Lexau, J. M. The rooftop mystery **E**

Mahy, M. Underrunners (5 and up) **Fic**

Newman, R. The case of the Baker Street Irregular (5 and up) **Fic**

Platt, K. Big Max **E**

Raskin, E. The mysterious disappearance of Leon (I mean Noel) (4 and up) **Fic**

Raskin, E. The Westing game (5 and up) **Fic**

Roberts, W. D. Scared stiff (5 and up) **Fic**

Roberts, W. D. The view from the cherry tree (5 and up) **Fic**

Sharmat, M. W. Nate the Great **E**

Sobol, D. J. Encyclopedia Brown, boy detective (3-5) **Fic**

Titus, E. Basil of Baker Street (3-5) **Fic**

Wallace, B. B. The twin in the tavern (4-6) **Fic**

Wright, B. R. The dollhouse murders (4 and up) **Fic**

Wright, B. R. The ghosts of Mercy Manor (4 and up) **Fic**

Wright, B. R. Nothing but trouble (4 and up) **Fic**

Yolen, J. Piggins and the royal wedding **E**

The **mystery** of Drear House. Hamilton, V. **Fic**

The **mystery** of Melusine. Osborne, M. P.
In Osborne, M. P. Mermaid tales from around the world p1-5 **398.2**

The **mystery** of sleep. Silverstein, A. **154.6**

The **mystery** of the cupboard. Reid Banks, L. See note under Reid Banks, L. The Indian in the cupboard **Fic**

The **mystery** of the missing red mitten. Kellogg, S. **E**

Mystery on the docks. Hurd, T. **E**

Mystery tour. Ahlberg, A. See note under Ahlberg, J. Funnybones **E**

Mythical animals

See also Dragons; Mermaids and mermen

Stockton, F. The Griffin and the Minor Canon (4-6) **Fic**

Fiction

Hunter, M. A stranger came ashore (6 and up) **Fic**

Poetry

Carle, E. Eric Carle's dragons dragons and other creatures that never were **808.81**

Cullen, C. The lost zoo **811**

Yolen, J. How beastly! (3-5) **811**

Mythology

See also Gods and goddesses; Mythical animals; mythology of particular national or ethnic groups or of particular geographic areas, e.g. Celtic mythology

Bulfinch, T. Bulfinch's mythology (6 and up) **291**

Gallant, R. A. The constellations, how they came to be (5 and up) **523.8**

Hamilton, V. In the beginning; creation stories from around the world (5 and up) **291**

See/See also pages in the following book(s):

Cook, E. The ordinary and the fabulous **028.5**

Indexes

Index to fairy tales **398.2**

Mythology, Norse *See* Norse mythology

Mythology. Hamilton, E. **292**

N

NAACP *See* National Association for the Advancement of Colored People

Nabookin
In Diane Goode's book of silly stories & songs p55-57 **398.2**

Nabwire, Constance R.
Cooking the African way
In Easy menu ethnic cookbooks **641.5**

Nach, James
England—in pictures. See England—in pictures **942**

Naden, Corinne J.
(ed) Best books for children: preschool through grade 6. See Best books for children: preschool through grade 6 **011.6**

(jt. auth) Gillespie, J. T. Juniorplots 3 **028.5**

(jt. auth) Gillespie, J. T. Juniorplots 4 **028.5**

(jt. auth) Gillespie, J. T. Middleplots 4 **028.5**

Naftali the storyteller and his horse, Sus. Singer, I. B.
In Singer, I. B. Naftali the storyteller and his horse, Sus, and other stories p3-23 **S C**

In Singer, I. B. Stories for children p167-83 **S C**

Naftali the storyteller and his horse, Sus, and other stories. Singer, I. B. **S C**

Nagasaki (Japan)
Bombardment, 1945—Fiction
Coerr, E. Mieko and the fifth treasure (3-5) **Fic**

Nagel, Andreas Fischer- *See* Fischer-Nagel, Andreas, 1951-

Nagel, Heiderose Fischer- *See* Fischer-Nagel, Heiderose, 1956-

Nahum, Andrew
Flying machine (4 and up)   **629.133**

Naidoo, Beverley
Chain of fire (5 and up)   **Fic**
Journey to Jo'burg (5 and up)   **Fic**

The nail. Grimm, J.
In Grimm, J. The complete Grimm's fairy tales p748-49   **398.2**

Nail Soup. MacDonald, M. R.
In MacDonald, M. R. Celebrate the world p115-23   **372.6**

Nail soup. Rockwell, A. F.
In Rockwell, A. F. Puss in boots, and other stories p12-18   **398.2**

The Naked bear (4 and up)   **398.2**

Nally, Sharon McGinley- *See* McGinley-Nally, Sharon

The Name
In The Magic orange tree, and other Haitian folktales p117-22   **398.2**

The name of the tree. Lottridge, C. B.
    398.2

Names, Personal *See* Personal names

Namibia
Brandenburg, J. Sand and fog (4 and up)
    968.8

Naming colors. Dewey, A.   **535.6**

Namioka, Lensey
Yang the third and her impossible family (4-6)   **Fic**
Yang the youngest and his terrible ear (4-6)   **Fic**

Nana Upstairs & Nana Downstairs. De Paola, T.   **E**

Nana's birthday party. Hest, A.   **E**

Nantucket (Mass.)
     Fiction
Turkle, B. C. Obadiah the Bold   **E**

Napoli, Donna Jo, 1948-
The prince of the pond (4-6)   **Fic**
When the water closes over my head (3-5)   **Fic**

The napping house. Wood, A.   **E**

Narahashi, Keiko
I have a friend   **E**
(il) Serfozo, M. Rain talk   **E**
(il) Serfozo, M. Who said red?   **E**
(il) Uchida, Y. The magic purse   **398.2**

Narcotics
See also Cocaine; Marijuana

The Nargun and the stars. Wrightson, P.
    Fic

Narraganset Indians
     Fiction
Fleischman, P. Saturnalia (6 and up)
    Fic

NASA *See* United States. National Aeronautics and Space Administration

Nash, Ogden, 1902-1971
The adventures of Isabel (k-3)   **811**
Custard and company: poems   **811**
The tale of Custard the Dragon (k-3)
    811

Nashua River (Mass. and N.H.)
Cherry, L. A river ran wild (1-4)   **974.4**

Nasreddin Hoca and the third shot. Walker, B. K.
In Walker, B. K. A treasury of Turkish folktales for children p43-44
    398.2

Nasreddin Hoca, seller of wisdom. Walker, B. K.
In Walker, B. K. A treasury of Turkish folktales for children p37-42
    398.2

Nasta, Vincent
(il) George, J. C. The moon of the winter bird   **598**
(il) Siebert, D. Plane song   **E**

Nastasia of the sea. Osborne, M. P.
In Osborne, M. P. Mermaid tales from around the world p25-30   **398.2**

Nasty, stinky sneakers. Bunting, E.   **Fic**

Nat Turner and the slave revolt. Barrett, T.
    92

Natchev, Alexi
(il) San Souci, R. The Hobyahs   **398.2**

Nate the Great. Sharmat, M. W.   **E**

Nate the Great and the boring beach bag. Sharmat, M. W. See note under Sharmat, M. W. Nate the Great   **E**

Nate the Great and the fishy prize. Sharmat, M. W. See note under Sharmat, M. W. Nate the Great   **E**

Nate the Great and the Halloween hunt. Sharmat, M. W. See note under Sharmat, M. W. Nate the Great   **E**

Nate the Great and the lost list. Sharmat, M. W. See note under Sharmat, M. W. Nate the Great   **E**

Nate the Great and the missing key. Sharmat, M. W. See note under Sharmat, M. W. Nate the Great   **E**

Nate the Great and the mushy valentine. Sharmat, M. W. See note under Sharmat, M. W. Nate the Great   **E**

Nate the Great and the musical note. Sharmat, M. W. See note under Sharmat, M. W. Nate the Great   **E**

Nate the Great and the phony clue. Sharmat, M. W. See note under Sharmat, M. W. Nate the Great   **E**

Nate the Great and the pillowcase. Sharmat, M. W. See note under Sharmat, M. W. Nate the Great   **E**

Nate the Great and the snowy trail. Sharmat, M. W. See note under Sharmat, M. W. Nate the Great   **E**

Nature conservation—*Continued*

Douglas, W. O. Muir of the mountains (4 and up)   92

Mutel, C. F. Tropical rain forests (4 and up)
574.5

Fiction
Gove, D. One rainy night   E

Nature craft

Drake, J. The kids' summer handbook (4 and up)   790.1

Rhoades, D. Garden crafts for kids (4-6)
635

Nature cross-sections. Orr, R.   574.5

Nature got there first. Gates, P.   508

Nature in action [series]

Kramer, S. Caves   551.4
Kramer, S. Lightning   551.5
Kramer, S. Tornado   551.55
Souza, D. M. Northern lights   538
Souza, D. M. Powerful waves   551.47

Nature in your backyard. Lang, S. S.   508

Nature photography

See also Photography of animals

Nature poetry

Brown, M. W. Nibble nibble: poems for children (k-3)   811

Esbensen, B. J. Cold stars and fireflies (4 and up)   811

Lewis, J. P. Earth verses and water rhymes (3-5)   811

Ryder, J. Under your feet (k-3)   811

Swenson, M. The complete poems to solve (5 and up)   811

Voices on the wind   808.81

See/See also pages in the following book(s):

Piping down the valleys wild p161-74
808.81

Nature spy. Rotner, S.   508

Nature study

Arnosky, J. Crinkleroot's guide to walking in wild places (k-3)   796.5

Arnosky, J. Secrets of a wildlife watcher (4 and up)   591.5

Björk, C. Linnea's almanac (2-5)   508

Burnie, D. How nature works (4 and up)
508

Caduto, M. J. Keepers of the night
398.2

Lang, S. S. Nature in your backyard (2-4)
508

Potter, J. Nature in a nutshell for kids (2-4)
508

Rights, M. Beastly neighbors (4 and up)
508

Selsam, M. E. How to be a nature detective (k-1)   591.5

Silver, D. M. Backyard (3-5)   574.5

Smith, A. The kids' nature almanac
508

Wilkes, A. My first nature book (1-4)
508

Nature walk. Florian, D.   E

Nature's great balancing act. Norsgaard, E. J.
574.5

Nature's green umbrella. Gibbons, G.
574.5

The **naughty** boy. Andersen, H. C.

In Andersen, H. C. Hans Christian Andersen fairy tales p53-56   S C

Navaho Indians *See* Navajo Indians

Navajo. Begay, S.   811

Navajo Indians

Bonvillain, N. The Navajos (4-6)
970.004

Osinski, A. The Navajo (2-4)   970.004

Roessel, M. Kinaaldá: a Navajo girl grows up (3-6)   970.004

Sneve, V. D. H. The Navajos (3-5)
970.004

Thomson, P. Katie Henio: Navajo sheepherder (4 and up)   970.004

See/See also pages in the following book(s):

Ehrlich, A. Wounded Knee: an Indian history of the American West (6 and up)
970.004

Fiction

Blood, C. L. The goat in the rug   E

Miles, M. Annie and the Old One (1-4)
Fic

O'Dell, S. Sing down the moon (5 and up)
Fic

Legends

Begay, S. Ma'ii and cousin Horned Toad (k-3)   398.2

Hausman, G. Coyote walks on two legs (2-4)
398.2

Poetry

Begay, S. Navajo (5 and up)   811

Naval architecture

See also Shipbuilding

Las **Navidades** (k-3)   782.42

Naylor, Phyllis Reynolds, 1933-

The agony of Alice (5 and up)   Fic

Alice in April. See note under Naylor, P. R. The agony of Alice   Fic

Alice in-between. See note under Naylor. P. R. The agony of Alice   Fic

Alice in rapture, sort of. See note under Naylor, P. R. The agony of Alice   Fic

Alice the brave. See note under Naylor, P. R. The agony of Alice   Fic

All but Alice. See note under Naylor. P. R. The agony of Alice   Fic

The fear place (5 and up)   Fic

The grand escape (4-6)   Fic

Maudie in the middle (3-5)   Fic

Reluctantly Alice. See note under Naylor, P. R. The agony of Alice   Fic

Shiloh (4-6)   Fic

The witch herself. See note under Naylor, P. R. The witch's eye   Fic

The witch returns. See note under Naylor, P. R. The witch's eye   Fic

Witch water. See note under Naylor, P. R. The witch's eye   Fic

Witch weed. See note under Naylor, P. R. The witch's eye   Fic

The witch's eye (5 and up)   Fic

The New Grolier student encyclopedia
031

New Hampshire
  Brown, D. New Hampshire
    In Hello USA series   973
  McNair, S. New Hampshire
    In America the beautiful   973
      Fiction
  Blos, J. W. A gathering of days: a New England girl's journal, 1830-32 (6 and up)
        Fic

New handbook for storytellers, Caroline Feller Bauer's. Bauer, C. F.   372.6

New Hope. Sorensen, H.   E

The **new** illustrated dinosaur dictionary. Sattler, H. R.   567.9

New Jersey
  Fredeen, C. New Jersey
    In Hello USA series   973
  Kent, D. New Jersey
    In America the beautiful   973
  Topper, F. A historical album of New Jersey
    In Historical albums series   973

The **new** kid on the block: poems. Prelutsky, J.   811

The **new** king. Rappaport, D.   398.2

New Mexico
  Early, T. S. New Mexico
    In Hello USA series   973
  Stein, R. C. New Mexico
    In America the beautiful   973
      Fiction
  Johnston, T. Alice Nizzy Nazzy, the Witch of Santa Fe   E

New neighbors for Nora. Hurwitz, J. See note under Hurwitz, J. Busybody Nora   Fic

New Orleans (La.)
See/See also pages in the following book(s):
  McCall, E. S. Biography of a river: the living Mississippi (6 and up)   977
      Race relations
  Coles, R. The story of Ruby Bridges (1-3)
        370.19

New patches for old. Walker, B. K.
    In Walker, B. K. A treasury of Turkish folktales for children p135-38
        398.2

New Providence. Von Tscharner, R.   307.7

New questions and answers about dinosaurs. Simon, S.   567.9

New road!. Gibbons, G.   625.7

New shoes for Silvia. Hurwitz, J.   E

The **new** teacher. Cohen, M. See note under Cohen, M. See you in second grade!
        E

A **New** treasury of children's poetry
        821.008

New true book [series]
  Broekel, R. Snakes   597.9
  Duvall, J. The Chumash   970.004
  Erlbach, A. Hurricanes   551.55
  Erlbach, A. Tornadoes   551.55
  Fradin, D. B. The Cheyenne   970.004

  Fradin, D. B. Earth   525
  Fradin, D. B. The Pawnee   970.004
  Fradin, D. B. The Shoshoni   970.004
  Heinrichs, S. The Pacific Ocean   910
  Henderson, K. The Great Lakes   551.4
  Kalbacken, J. The Menominee   970.004
  Lepthien, E. U. Buffalo   599.73
  Lepthien, E. U. The Choctaw   970.004
  Lepthien, E. U. The Mandans   970.004
  Lepthien, E. U. Opossums   599.2
  Lepthien, E. U. Rabbits and hares
        599.32
  Lepthien, E. U. Reindeer   599.73
  McKissack, P. C. The Apache   970.004
  McKissack, P. C. The Inca   985
  Miller, J. The Delaware   970.004
  Osinski, A. The Chippewa   970.004
  Osinski, A. The Navajo   970.004
  Osinski, A. The Nez Perce   970.004
  Osinski, A. The Sioux   970.004
  Petersen, D. Carlsbad Caverns National Park   978.9
  Podendorf, I. Rocks and minerals   549
  Stone, L. M. Alligators and crocodiles
        597.9
  Tomchek, A. H. The Hopi   970.004
  Worthylake, M. M. The Pomo   970.004
New World dictionary of computer terms, Webster's   004

New Year
      Fiction
  Rattigan, J. K. Dumpling soup   E
      Poetry
  New Year's poems   808.81

New Year, Chinese *See* Chinese New Year

New Year's hats for the statues. Uchida, Y.
    In Snowy day: stories and poems p3-11
        808.8

New Year's poems   808.81

New York (N.Y.)
      Description
  Huff, B. A. Greening the city streets (4-6)
        635
  Jakobsen, K. My New York (k-3)   974.7
  Munro, R. The inside-outside book of New York City (2-4)   974.7
      Fiction
  Baker, J. Home in the sky   E
  Bartone, E. Peppe the lamplighter   E
  Cummings, P. C.L.O.U.D.S.   E
  Gray, L. Falcon's egg (3-5)   Fic
  Hansen, J. The gift-giver (4-6)   Fic
  Herold, M. R. A very important day   E
  Holman, F. Slake's limbo (6 and up)
        Fic
  Hurwitz, J. Busybody Nora (2-4)   Fic
  Khalsa, D. K. How pizza came to Queens
        E
  Krensky, S. The printer's apprentice (4-6)
        Fic
  Levinson, R. I go with my family to Grandma's
        E

Nichols, Grace—*Continued*
(ed) A Caribbean dozen. See A Caribbean dozen **811.008**

Nichols, Margaret Irby
Guide to reference books for school media centers **011.6**

Nicholson, Darrel
Wild boars (3-6) **599.73**

Nicholson, Sir William, 1872-1949
(il) Bianco, M. W. The velveteen rabbit **Fic**

Nickens, Bessie, 1906-
Walking the log (2-4) **92**

Nicknames
Meltzer, M. A book about names (5 and up) **929.4**

Nielsen, Kay Rasmus, 1886-1957
(il) Asbjornsen, P. C. East of the sun and west of the moon: old tales from the North **398.2**

Nielsen, Nancy J.
Carnivorous plants (4 and up) **583**

Nieves, Ernesto Ramos See Ramos Nieves, Ernesto

Nigeria
Onyefulu, I. Emeka's gift **E**
Folklore
See Folklore—Nigeria
Poetry
Olaleye, I. The distant talking drum (2-4) **896**

Night
See also Bedtime; Day
Branley, F. M. What makes day and night (k-3) **525**
Emory, J. Nightprowlers (3-6) **591.5**
Fiction
Aliki. Overnight at Mary Bloom's **E**
Aylesworth, J. Country crossing **E**
Berger, B. Grandfather Twilight **E**
Bonsall, C. N. Who's afraid of the dark? **E**
Brown, M. W. A child's good night book **E**
Brown, M. W. Goodnight moon **E**
Bunting, E. Ghost's hour, spook's hour **E**
Caduto, M. J. Keepers of the night **398.2**
Crowe, R. L. Clyde monster **E**
Dragonwagon, C. Half a moon and one whole star **E**
Durán, C. Hildilid's night **E**
Fox, M. Night noises **E**
Grifalconi, A. Darkness and the butterfly **E**
Manushkin, F. Peeping and sleeping **E**
Murphy, J. Peace at last **E**
Rice, E. City night **E**
Rice, E. Goodnight, goodnight **E**
Rylant, C. Night in the country **E**
Weiss, N. Where does the brown bear go? **E**
Wolff, A. Only the cat saw **E**

Poetry
Greenfield, E. Night on Neighborhood Street (2-4) **811**
The Night of the whippoorwill **808.81**
On the road of stars (k-3) **897**
Treece, H. The magic wood **821**

The **night** after Christmas. Stevenson, J. **E**

A **night** and day in the desert. Dewey, J. **574.5**

A **night** at Pickey's. Haskins, J.
In Haskins, J. The headless haunt and other African American ghost stories p39-46 **398.2**

Night becomes day. McGuire, R. **E**

The **night** before Christmas. Moore, C. C. **811**

The **night** crossing. Ackerman, K. **Fic**

The **Night** doctor
In Raw Head, bloody bones p47-50 **398.2**

Night in the country. Rylant, C. **E**

The **night** it rained. Schwartz, A.
In Schwartz, A. In a dark, dark room, and other scary stories p42-49 **398.2**

The **night** journey. Lasky, K. **Fic**

Night journeys. Avi **Fic**

Night noises. Fox, M. **E**

Night of ghosts and hermits. Stolz, M. **574.92**

Night of the gargoyles. Bunting, E. **E**

The **Night** of the Leonids. Konigsburg, E. L.
In Konigsburg, E. L. Altogether, one at a time p13-28 **S C**

The **night** of the pomegranate. Wynne-Jones, T.
In Wynne-Jones, T. Some of the kinder planets: stories p1-7 **S C**

Night of the twisters. Ruckman, I. **Fic**

The **Night** of the whippoorwill **808.81**

Night on Neighborhood Street. Greenfield, E. **811**

Night photograph. Conrad, P.
In Conrad, P. Our house p12-21 **S C**

Night reef. Sargent, W. **574.92**

Night sky. Stott, C. **520**

The **night** sky book. Jobb, J. **523**

Night sounds, morning colors. Wells, R. **E**

The **night** swimmers. Byars, B. C. **Fic**

Night tree. Bunting, E. **E**

The **nightingale**. Andersen, H. C. **Fic**
also in The Rainbow fairy book p161-72 **398.2**
also in Shedlock, M. L. The art of the story-teller p243-58 **372.6**
also in The Yellow fairy book p291-300 **398.2**

The **Nightingale** and the rose. Wilde, O.
 In Wilde, O. The fairy tales of Oscar Wilde p24-31 **S C**

Nightingales
Fiction
Andersen, H. C. The nightingale (2-5) **Fic**

Nightmares: poems to trouble your sleep. Prelutsky, J. **811**

Nightprowlers. Emory, J. **591.5**

Nights of the pufflings. McMillan, B. **598**

Nighty-nightmare. Howe, J. See note under Howe, J. The celery stalks at midnight **Fic**

Nikita the Tanner. Afanas'ev, A. N.
 In Afanas'ev, A. N. Russian fairy tales p310-11 **398.2**

Nilsson, Lennart, 1922-
 (il) Kitzinger, S. Being born **612.6**

Nine-in-one, Grr! Grr!. Spagnoli, C. **398.2**

Nineteenth century clothing. See Kalman, B. 19th century clothing **391**

Ningun. MacDonald, M. R.
 In MacDonald, M. R. The storyteller's start-up book p185-92 **372.6**

Nirgiotis, Nicholas
 Erie Canal (4 and up) **386**
 Thomas Edison (4-6) **92**

Nix nought nothing. Jacobs, J.
 In Jacobs, J. English fairy tales p41-46 **398.2**

The **nixie** of the mill-pond. Grimm, J.
 In Grimm, J. The complete Grimm's fairy tales p736-42 **398.2**

Nixon, Joan Lowery, 1927-
 Beats me, Claude **E**
 Caught in the act. See note under Nixon, J. L. A family apart **Fic**
 A family apart (5 and up) **Fic**
 Fat chance, Claude (1987). See note under Nixon, J. L. Beats me, Claude **E**
 In the face of danger. See note under Nixon, J. L. A family apart **Fic**
 Keeping secrets. See note under Nixon, J. L. A family apart **Fic**
 A place to belong. See note under Nixon, J. L. A family apart **Fic**
 That's the spirit, Claude. See note under Nixon, J. L. Beats me, Claude **E**

The **Nixy**
 In The Rainbow fairy book p146-52 **398.2**
 In The Yellow fairy book p108-13 **398.2**

NLS/BPH *See* Library of Congress. National Library Service for the Blind and Physically Handicapped

No beasts! no children! [excerpt]. Keller, B.
 In The Random House book of humor for children p270-75 **817.008**

No, Bocono no!. Aardema, V.
 In Aardema, V. Misoso p51-57 **398.2**

No fighting, no biting!. Minarik, E. H. **E**

No foal yet. Haas, J. **E**

No friends. Stevenson, J. See note under Stevenson, J. "Could be worse!" **E**

No frogs at all. Van Laan, N.
 In Van Laan, N. In a circle long ago p44-47 **398.2**

No-good Claus. Mark, J.
 In The Oxford book of scary tales p123-29 **808.8**

No good in art. Cohen, M. See note under Cohen, M. See you in second grade! **E**

The **no-guitar** blues. Soto, G.
 In Soto, G. Baseball in April, and other stories p43-51 **S C**

No hickory, no dickory, no dock. Agard, J. **811**

No milk!. Ericsson, J. A. **E**

No moon, no milk!. Babcock, C. **E**

No more baths. Cole, B. **E**

No need for Monty. Stevenson, J. See note under Stevenson, J. Monty **E**

No place to be. Berck, J. **362.7**

No roses for Harry!. Zion, G. See note under Zion, G. Harry the dirty dog **E**

No star nights. Smucker, A. E. **E**

No, thanks. Schwartz, A.
 In Schwartz, A. Scary stories 3 p65 **398.2**

Noah's ark
 Brent, I. Noah's ark (k-3) **222**
 Geisert, A. The ark (k-3) **222**
 Jonas, A. Aardvarks, disembark! **E**
 Spier, P. Noah's ark (k-2) **222**
Fiction
 Geisert, A. After the flood **E**
 Rounds, G. Washday on Noah's ark **E**
Poetry
 Bernos de Gasztold, C. Prayers from the ark **841**

Nobel Prize winners [series]
 Aaseng, N. The inventors: Nobel prizes in chemistry, physics, and medicine **609**

Nobel Prizes
 Aaseng, N. The inventors: Nobel prizes in chemistry, physics, and medicine (5 and up) **609**

Noble, Trinka Hakes
 The day Jimmy's boa ate the wash **E**
 Jimmy's boa and the big splash birthday bash. See note under Noble, T. H. The day Jimmy's boa ate the wash **E**
 Jimmy's boa bounces back. See note under Noble, T. H. The day Jimmy's boa ate the wash **E**
 Meanwhile back at the ranch **E**

The **nobleman** and the peasant. Afanas'ev, A. N.
 In Afanas'ev, A. N. Russian fairy tales p59-61 **398.2**

Nobody asked me if I wanted a baby sister. Alexander, M. G. **E**

Nobody believes in witches. Watkins, M. S.
In Holiday plays round the year p141-50
812.008

Nobody's cat. Joosse, B. M. **E**

Nodey, the priest's grandson. Afanas'ev, A. N.
In Afanas'ev, A. N. Russian fairy tales
p173-77 **398.2**

Nodset, Joan L. *See* Lexau, Joan M.

Nogales, Luis
See/See also pages in the following book(s):
Morey, J. Famous Mexican Americans p75-
87 (5 and up) **920**

Noise
Poetry
Blake, Q. All join in (k-3) **821**
Kuskin, K. City noise (k-3) **811**

The **noise** in the woods. Lester, J.
In Lester, J. The tales of Uncle Remus
p113-15 **398.2**

Noisy. Hughes, S.
In Hughes, S. The nursery collection
E

The **noisy** book. Brown, M. W. **E**

Noisy Nora. Wells, R. **E**

Nolan, Dennis, 1945-
(il) Leighton, M. R. An Ellis Island Christmas **E**
(il) Ryder, J. Under your feet **811**
(il) Stanley, D. The gentleman and the kitch-
en maid **E**
(il) White, T. H. The sword in the stone
Fic

Nolan, Jeannette Covert
Happy Christmas to all
In The Big book of Christmas plays p137-
50 **808.82**

Nolan, Paul T., 1919-
Sherlock Holmes' Christmas goose
In The Big book of Christmas plays p298-
312 **808.82**

Nolen, Jerdine
Harvey Potter's balloon farm **E**

Nomura, Janet *See* Morey, Janet

Non-proliferation of nuclear weapons *See* Arms
control

Nonbook materials *See* Audiovisual materials

Nonfiction for the classroom. Meltzer, M.
973

Nonsense verses
See also Limericks; Tongue twisters
Carroll, L. Lewis Carroll's Jabberwocky
821
Florian, D. Bing bang boing (3-5) **811**
A Great big ugly man came up and tied his
horse to me (k-3) **821.008**
Heilbroner, J. This is the house where Jack
lives **E**
Kennedy, X. J. Brats (3-6) **811**
Kennedy, X. J. Drat these brats! (3-6)
811
Kennedy, X. J. Fresh brats (3-6) **811**
Kennedy, X. J. Ghastlies, goops & pincush-
ions: nonsense verse (3-6) **811**

Lear, E. The complete nonsense of Edward
Lear **821**
Lear, E. How pleasant to know Mr. Lear!
821
Lear, E. The Jumblies **821**
Lear, E. Of pelicans and pussycats **821**
Lear, E. The owl and the pussycat **821**
Lear, E. The pelican chorus and other non-
sense **821**
Lear, E. There was an old man— **821**
Lewis, J. P. The fat-cats at sea **811**
Merriam, E. Blackberry ink (k-2) **811**
Morrison, B. Squeeze a sneeze (k-3)
811
Prelutsky, J. The baby Uggs are hatching
(k-3) **811**
Prelutsky, J. Beneath a blue umbrella:
rhymes (k-3) **811**
Prelutsky, J. The queen of Eene (k-3)
811
Prelutsky, J. Ride a purple pelican (k-3)
811
Prelutsky, J. The sheriff of Rottenshot: po-
ems (2-5) **811**
Prelutsky, J. The snopp on the sidewalk,
and other poems (k-4) **811**
Seuss, Dr. And to think that I saw it on
Mulberry Street **E**
Seuss, Dr. The cat in the hat **E**
Seuss, Dr. Green eggs and ham **E**
Seuss, Dr. Horton hatches the egg **E**
Seuss, Dr. Horton hears a Who! **E**
Seuss, Dr. How the Grinch stole Christmas
E
Seuss, Dr. If I ran the circus **E**
Seuss, Dr. If I ran the zoo **E**
Seuss, Dr. McElligot's pool **E**
Silverstein, S. A light in the attic **811**
Silverstein, S. Where the sidewalk ends
811
Smith, W. J. Laughing time (3-5) **811**
Watson, C. Father Fox's pennyrhymes (k-3)
811
Westcott, N. B. The lady with the alligator
purse **E**
Willard, N. A visit to William Blake's inn
(2-5) **811**
Yolen, J. Animal fare (3-5) **811**
Yolen, J. How beastly! (3-5) **811**
See/See also pages in the following book(s):
Piping down the valleys wild p21-36
808.81
Rainbow in the sky p351-82 (k-4)
821.008

Noodles *See* Pasta products

Noonan, Julia
(il) Yep, L. Sweetwater **Fic**

Noonan, William, 1923-
(il) Walker, P. R. Bigfoot and other legendary creatures **001.9**

Noonuccal, Oodgeroo *See* Oodgeroo, 1920-
1993

Nora. Greene, C. C. **Fic**

Nora and Mrs. Mind-Your-Own-Business.
Hurwitz, J. See note under Hurwitz, J.
Busybody Nora   Fic
Nordstrom, Ursula, 1910-1988
The secret language (3-5)   Fic
The **Norka**
In The Red fairy book p116-22   398.2
Norman, David
Dinosaur (4 and up)   567.9
Norman, Howard
How Glooskap outwits the Ice Giants, and
other tales of the Maritime Indians (3-6)
     398.2
Contents: How Glooskap made human beings; How
Glooskap outwits the Ice Giants; Why the sea winds are the
strength they are today; Glooskap gets two surprises; How
magic friend fox helped Glooskap against the panther-witch;
How Glooskap sang through the rapids and found a new
home
Normandy (France), Attack on, 1944
Bliven, B. The story of D-Day, June 6, 1944
     940.54
Norodom Sihanouk, King of Cambodia, 1922-
See/See also pages in the following book(s):
Chandler, D. P. The land and people of
Cambodia p110-31 (5 and up)   959.6
Norse mythology
Climo, S. Stolen thunder (3-5)   293
Colum, P. The children of Odin (5 and up)
     293
Hamilton, E. Mythology (6 and up)   292
Norsemen *See* Vikings
Norsgaard, Campbell
(il) Norsgaard, E. J. Nature's great balancing
act   574.5
Norsgaard, E. Jaediker (Ernestine Jaediker)
Nature's great balancing act (4-6)   574.5
Norsgaard, Ernestine Jaediker *See* Norsgaard,
E. Jaediker (Ernestine Jaediker)
North, Sterling, 1906-1974
Rascal (5 and up)   599.74
North Africa
Umm El Madayan (5 and up)   961
North America
     Natural history
See Natural history—North America
North American Indian. Murdoch, D. H.
     970.004
North American Indian ceremonies. Liptak, K.
     970.004
North American Indians *See* Indians of North
America
North Carolina
Schulz, A. North Carolina
In Hello USA series   973
Stein, R. C. North Carolina
In America the beautiful   973
     Fiction
Hooks, W. H. Circle of fire (5 and up)
     Fic
Pinkney, G. J. Back home   E
North Dakota
Herguth, M. S. North Dakota
In America the beautiful   973

Verba, J. M. North Dakota
In Hello USA series   973
North Pole
See also Arctic regions
Ferris, J. Arctic explorer: the story of Mat-
thew Henson (3-6)   92
     Fiction
Van Allsburg, C. The Polar Express   E
The **North** Pole computer caper. Priore, F. V.
In The Big book of Christmas plays p189-
99   808.82
North to freedom. Holm, A.   Fic
Northern Ireland
Northern Ireland—in pictures (5 and up)
     941.6
Northern Ireland—in pictures (5 and up)
     941.6
Northern lights *See* Auroras
Northern lights. Souza, D. M.   538
Northern lullaby. Carlstrom, N. W.   811
A **northern** nativity. Kurelek, W.   232.9
Northmen *See* Vikings
Northwest, Canadian *See* Canadian Northwest
Northwest Coast of North America
Swanson, D. Safari beneath the sea (4 and
up)   574.92
Norton, Alice Mary *See* Norton, Andre, 1912-
Norton, Andre, 1912-
Fur magic (4-6)   Fic
Norton, Mary, 1903-1992
Bed-knob and broomstick (3-5)   Fic
Bonfires and broomsticks
In Norton, M. Bed-knob and broomstick
p97-189   Fic
The Borrowers (3-6)   Fic
The Borrowers afield. See note under Nor-
ton, M. The Borrowers   Fic
The Borrowers afloat. See note under Nor-
ton, M. The Borrowers   Fic
The Borrowers aloft. See note under Norton,
M. The Borrowers   Fic
The Borrowers avenged. See note under
Norton, M. The Borrowers   Fic
The magic bed-knob
In Norton, M. Bed-knob and broomstick
p11-94   Fic
Paul's tale
In The Oxford treasury of children's sto-
ries p151-59   S C
Norway
Charbonneau, C. The land and people of
Norway (5 and up)   948.1
Norway—in pictures (5 and up)   948.1
     Fiction
Emberley, M. Welcome back sun   E
     Folklore
See Folklore—Norway
Norway—in pictures (5 and up)   948.1
Norwegian Americans
Hillbrand, P. V. Norwegians in America
In The In America series   305.8

Old Fire Dragaman
In The Jack tales p106-13   **398.2**

Old ghosts at home. Murray, J.
In Holiday plays round the year p112-28   **812.008**

Old glory. Coville, B.
In Coville, B. Oddly enough p79-85   **S C**

Old Henry. Blos, J. W.   **E**

Old Hildebrand. Grimm, J.
In Grimm, J. The complete Grimm's fairy tales p440-44   **398.2**

The **old** jar. Yep, L.
In Yep, L. The rainbow people p96-105   **398.2**

Old John. Härtling, P.   **Fic**

Old MacDonald had a farm   **782.42**

The **old** man and his grandson. Grimm, J.
In Grimm, J. The complete Grimm's fairy tales p363-64   **398.2**

The **old** man made young again. Grimm, J.
In Grimm, J. The complete Grimm's fairy tales p640-42   **398.2**

The **old** man who made dead trees bloom. Quayle, E.
In Quayle, E. The shining princess, and other Japanese legends p69-76   **398.2**

The **old** meadow. Selden, G. See note under Selden, G. The cricket in Times Square   **Fic**

Old Mother Hubbard and her dog, The comic adventures of   **398.8**

Old Mother Hubbard and her wonderful dog (k-2)   **398.8**

Old Old One's birthday. Carpenter, F.
In Carpenter, F. Tales of a Chinese grandmother p252-61   **398.2**

Old One-Eye
In Grandfather tales p205-07   **398.2**

Old one-eye. MacDonald, M. R.
In MacDonald, M. R. Twenty tellable tales p43-51   **372.6**

The **old** poet. Aiken, J.
In Aiken, J. Give yourself a fright: thirteen tales of the supernatural p19-30   **S C**

Old Rinkrank. Grimm, J.
In Grimm, J. The complete Grimm's fairy tales p796-98   **398.2**

Old Roaney
In Grandfather tales p195-204   **398.2**

Old Sally Cato. San Souci, R.
In San Souci, R. Cut from the same cloth p67-73   **398.2**

Old sow and the three shoats
In Grandfather tales p81-87   **398.2**

Old Stormalong finds a man-sized ship. Walker, P. R.
In Walker, P. R. Big men, big country p22-28   **398.2**

Old Stormalong: the deep-water sailor. San Souci, R.
In San Souci, R. Larger than life p13-22   **398.2**

Old Sultan. Grimm, J.
In Grimm, J. The complete Grimm's fairy tales p230-32   **398.2**

Old Turtle's 90 knock-knocks, jokes, and riddles. Kessler, L. P.   **793.73**

Old Turtle's baseball stories. Kessler, L. P. See note under Kessler, L. P. Old Turtle's soccer team   **E**

Old Turtle's riddle and joke book. Kessler, L. P.   **793.73**

Old Turtle's soccer team. Kessler, L. P.   **E**

The **old** witch. Jacobs, J.
In Jacobs, J. English fairy tales p312-17   **398.2**

The **old** woman and her dumpling. Hearn, L.
In Womenfolk and fairy tales p44-50   **398.2**

The **old** woman and her pig. Jacobs, J.
In Jacobs, J. English fairy tales p31-33   **398.2**

The **old** woman in a pumpkin shell. MacDonald, M. R.
In MacDonald, M. R. Celebrate the world p61-66   **372.6**

The **old** woman in the wood. Grimm, J.
In Grimm, J. The complete Grimm's fairy tales p558-60   **398.2**

The **old** woman who ran away. Afanas'ev, A. N.
In Afanas'ev, A. N. Russian fairy tales p182-83   **398.2**

Old Yeller. Gipson, F. B.   **Fic**

The **oldest** of them all. Crossley-Holland, K.
In Crossley-Holland, K. British folk tales p178-81   **398.2**

Ole & Trufa. Singer, I. B.
In Singer, I. B. Stories for children p249-53   **S C**

O'Leary, Danny
(il) Aronson, B. They came from DNA   **575.1**

Olfson, Lewy
Christmas coast to coast
In The Big book of Christmas plays p80-98   **808.82**

Olimpia, Cucol, and the door. Fox, P.
In Fox, P. Amzat and his brothers: three Italian tales p45-67   **398.2**

Oliver, Jenni
(il) Lowry, L. A summer to die   **Fic**

Oliver, Amanda, and Grandmother Pig. Van Leeuwen, J. See note under Van Leeuwen, J. Tales of Oliver Pig   **E**

Oliver and Amanda and the big snow. Van Leeuwen, J. See note under Van Leeuwen, J. Tales of Oliver Pig   **E**

One nation, many tribes. Krull, K.
970.004

One Ox, Two Ox, Three Ox, and the Dragon King. Yolen, J.
In Yolen, J. Here there be dragons p118-47　**810.8**

One parent family *See* Single parent family

One rainy night. Gove, D.　E

One small square [series]
Silver, D. M. African savanna　574.5
Silver, D. M. Arctic tundra　574.5
Silver, D. M. Backyard　574.5
Silver, D. M. Cactus desert　574.5
Silver, D. M. Cave　574.5
Silver, D. M. Pond　574.5
Silver, D. M. Seashore　574.5
Silver, D. M. Woods　574.5

One smiling grandma. Linden, A. M.　E

One stormy night. Brown, R.　E

One sun: a book of terse verse. McMillan, B.
811

One thousand miles in 12 days. See Hautzig, D. 1,000 miles in 12 days　796.6

One tough turkey. Kroll, S.　E

One, two, one pair!. McMillan, B.　E

One was Johnny. Sendak, M.　E

The One who would not listen to his own dream
In The Magic orange tree, and other Haitian folktales p71-74　**398.2**

The one you don't see coming. Courlander, H.
In Courlander, H. The cow-tail switch, and other West African stories p31-40
398.2

One zillion valentines. Modell, F.　E

Oneal, Elizabeth *See* Oneal, Zibby, 1934-

O'Neal, Shaquille
About
Townsend, B. Shaquille O'Neal (4 and up)
92

Oneal, Zibby, 1934-
Grandma Moses: painter of rural America (4 and up)　92

O'Neill, Catherine, 1950-
Focus on alcohol (3-6)　362.29
You won't believe your eyes! (4 and up)
152.14

O'Neill, Eugene, 1888-1953
See/See also pages in the following book(s):
Faber, D. Great lives: American literature p250-58 (5 and up)　920

O'Neill, Laurie, 1949-
Little Rock (5 and up)　370.19

O'Neill, Mary Le Duc, 1908-1990
Hailstones and halibut bones (k-3)　811

Onion John. Krumgold, J.　Fic

Onizuka, Ellison S., 1946-1986
See/See also pages in the following book(s):
Morey, J. Famous Asian Americans p115-27 (5 and up)　920

Only a fair day's huntin'
In Grandfather tales p180-85　398.2

Only connect: readings on children's literature
028.5

Only Opal. Boulton, J.　E

Only the cat saw. Wolff, A.　E

Only the names remain. Bealer, A. W.
970.004

Ontal, Carlo
(il) Rylant, C. Best wishes　92

Ontario Science Centre
Foodworks. See Foodworks　641.3

Onyefulu, Ifeoma, 1959-
Emeka's gift　E

Oodgeroo, 1920-1993
Dreamtime (4 and up)　398.2
Includes the following stories: The beginning of life; Biami and Bunyip; Mirrabooka; The midden; Burr-Nong; Wonga and Nudu; Curlew; Oodgeroo; Tuggan-Tuggan; Talwalpin and Kowinka; Pomera; Tia-Gam; Boonah; Mai

Ooh-la-la. Marshall, J.
In Marshall, J. Rats on the roof, and other stories p55-61　S C

Uom Razoom. Wolkstein, D.　398.2

Oot-Kwah-Tah, the seven star dancers. Caduto, M. J.
In Caduto, M. J. Keepers of the night p63-65　398.2

Opal: the journey of an understanding heart. See Boulton, J. Only Opal　E

Opera
Stories, plots, etc.
Price, L. Aïda (4 and up)　792.5
Rosenberg, J. Sing me a story (4-6)
792.5

Operation Siberian crane. Friedman, J.
639.9

Operations research
See also Simulation methods

Operetta
Gilbert, W. S. "I have a song to sing, O!" (4 and up)　782.42

Ophir, Uri
Songs of Chanukah. See Songs of Chanukah
782.42

Opie, Iona Archibald
Children's games in street and playground
796.1
The lore and language of schoolchildren
398
(ed) The Classic fairy tales. See The Classic fairy tales　398.2
(ed) I saw Esau. See I saw Esau　398.8
(ed) A Nursery companion. See A Nursery companion　398.8
(ed) The Oxford book of children's verse. See The Oxford book of children's verse
821.008
(ed) The Oxford dictionary of nursery rhymes. See The Oxford dictionary of nursery rhymes　398.8
(comp) The Oxford Nursery rhyme book. See The Oxford Nursery rhyme book
398.8
About
Children and their books　028.5

Ormerod, Jan—*Continued*
(il) Sunflakes. See Sunflakes   **811.008**

Ornament *See* Decoration and ornament

Orp. Kline, S. See note under Kline, S. Orp and the FBI   **Fic**

Orp and the chop suey burgers. Kline, S. See note under Kline, S. Orp and the FBI   **Fic**

Orp and the FBI. Kline, S.   **Fic**

Orp goes to the hoop. Kline, S. See note under Kline, S. Orp and the FBI   **Fic**

Orphan. McNulty, F.   **599.32**

The **orphan** boy. Mollel, T. M.   **398.2**

Orphans
Fiction
Aiken, J. Midnight is a place (5 and up)   **Fic**
Avi. Night journeys (5 and up)   **Fic**
Cassedy, S. Behind the attic wall (5 and up)   **Fic**
Cleaver, V. Where the lillies bloom (5 and up)   **Fic**
Dahl, R. The BFG (4-6)   **Fic**
Fleischman, S. The midnight horse (3-6)   **Fic**
Godden, R. The story of Holly and Ivy (2-4)   **Fic**
Howard, E. Edith herself (4-6)   **Fic**
L'Engle, M. Meet the Austins (5 and up)   **Fic**
Lunn, J. I. S. The root cellar (5 and up)   **Fic**
Marino, J. The Mona Lisa of Salem Street (5 and up)   **Fic**
Reeder, C. Shades of gray (4 and up)   **Fic**
Ross, R. R. Harper & Moon (6 and up)   **Fic**
Spinelli, J. Maniac Magee (5 and up)   **Fic**
Wallace, B. B. The twin in the tavern (4-6)   **Fic**
Wright, B. R. The ghosts of Mercy Manor (4 and up)   **Fic**

Orr, Richard
Nature cross-sections (4 and up)   **574.5**
(il) Taylor, B. The bird atlas   **598**

Ortega, Jose
(il) Where angels glide at dawn. See Where angels glide at dawn   **S C**

Ortega, Kay
See/See also pages in the following book(s):
Morey, J. Famous Mexican Americans p98-105 (5 and up)   **920**

Ortiz, Fran
(il) Brown, T. Chinese New Year   **394.2**

Osa's pride. Grifalconi, A. See note under Grifalconi, A. Darkness and the butterfly   **E**

Osborn, Kathy
(il) Tunnell, M. O. The joke's on George [biography of Charles Willson Peale]   **92**

Osborne, Mary Pope, 1949-
American tall tales (3-6)   **398.2**
Contents: Davy Crockett; Sally Ann Thunder Ann Whirlwind; Johnny Appleseed; Stormalong; Mose; Febold Feboldson; Pecos Bill; John Henry; Paul Bunyan
Favorite Greek myths (3-6)   **292**
George Washington (4-6)   **92**
Mermaid tales from around the world (4-6)   **398.2**
Contents: The mystery of Melusine; Menana of the waterfall; The sea nymph and the Cyclops; The enchanted cap; Nastasia of the sea; The fish husband; The serpent and the Sea Queen; The mermaid's revenge; The princess of the Tung Lake; The sea princess of Persia; The mermaid in the millpond; The little mermaid
Paul Bunyan, the mightiest logger of them all
In From sea to shining sea p280-83   **810.8**

O'Shaughnessy, Tam
(jt. auth) Ride, S. K. The third planet   **525**
(jt. auth) Ride, S. K. Voyager   **523.4**

Osinski, Alice
The Chippewa (2-4)   **970.004**
The Navajo (2-4)   **970.004**
The Nez Perce (2-4)   **970.004**
The Sioux (2-4)   **970.004**

Osofsky, Audrey
Dreamcatcher   **E**

Ospreys
Patent, D. H. Ospreys (4 and up)   **598**

Osseo-Asare, Fran
A good soup attracts chairs (4 and up)   **641.5**

Ostriches
Arnold, C. Ostriches and other flightless birds (3-5)   **598**
Fiction
King-Smith, D. The cuckoo child (3-5)   **Fic**

Ostriches and other flightless birds. Arnold, C.   **598**

Ostrow, Vivian
(jt. auth) Ostrow, W. All about asthma   **616.2**

Ostrow, William
All about asthma (3-5)   **616.2**

Otani, June
(il) Bulla, C. R. What makes a shadow?   **535**

Otero, Ben
(il) Haskins, J. The headless haunt and other African-American ghost stories   **398.2**

The **other** side. Krull, K.   **305.8**

Otherwise known as Sheila the Great. Blume, J.   **Fic**

Otis Spofford. Cleary, B.   **Fic**

O'Toole, Christopher
Mammals: the hunters (4 and up)   **599**

O'Toole, Thomas, 1941-
Mali—in pictures (5 and up)   **966.23**

Oxenbury, Helen, 1938-—*Continued*
Tom and Pippo read a story. See note under Oxenbury, H. Pippo gets lost   **E**
Tom and Pippo see the moon. See note under Oxenbury, H. Pippo gets lost   **E**
Tom and Pippo's day. See note under Oxenbury, H. Pippo gets lost   **E**
(il) Mahy, M. The dragon of an ordinary family   **E**
(il) Rosen, M. We're going on a bear hunt   **E**
(il) Trivizas, E. The three little wolves and the big bad pig   **E**
(il) Waddell, M. Farmer duck   **E**

The **Oxford** book of children's verse   **821.008**

The **Oxford** book of children's verse in America   **811.008**

The **Oxford** book of Christmas poems (4 and up)   **808.81**

The **Oxford** book of scary tales (5 and up)   **808.8**

The **Oxford** children's book of famous people   **920.003**

Oxford children's encyclopedia   **032**

The **Oxford** companion to children's literature. Carpenter, H.   **028.5**

The **Oxford** dictionary of nursery rhymes   **398.8**

The **Oxford** first companion to music. McLeish, K.   **780**

Oxford Illustrators Ltd.
Simon, S. Science dictionary   **503**
Oxford junior encyclopedia. See Oxford children's encyclopedia   **032**

Oxford myths and legends [series]
Reeves, J. English fables and fairy stories   **398.2**
Sherlock, Sir P. M. West Indian folk-tales   **398.2**

The **Oxford** Nursery rhyme book   **398.8**

Oxford Scientific Films
Snedden, R. What is a mammal?   **599**
Snedden, R. What is a reptile?   **597.9**
Snedden, R. What is an amphibian?   **597.6**

The **Oxford** treasury of children's stories (3-5)   **S C**

Oxlade, Chris
Bridges and tunnels (4-6)   **624**
Houses and homes (4-6)   **690**
Science magic with light (4-6)   **793.8**
Science magic with sound (4-6)   **793.8**

Oyzar the Scholar. Sanfield, S.
In Sanfield, S. The feather merchants & other tales of the fools of Chelm p18-29   **398.2**

Ozark Mountains
Fiction
Rawls, W. Where the red fern grows   **Fic**

Ozma of Oz. Baum, L. F. See note under Baum, L. F. The Wizard of Oz   **Fic**

Ozone layer
Johnson, R. L. Investigating the ozone hole (5 and up)   **363.7**
Pringle, L. P. Vanishing ozone (4 and up)   **363.7**

P

Pablo remembers. Ancona, G.   **394.2**
Pacific Ocean
Heinrichs, S. The Pacific Ocean (2-4)   **910**

The **pack** of ragamuffins. Grimm, J.
In Grimm, J. The complete Grimm's fairy tales p65-66   **398.2**
Packaging
See also Boxes

Paddington abroad. Bond, M. See note under Bond, M. A bear called Paddington   **Fic**

Paddington and the Christmas pantomime. Bond, M.
In Bond, M. Paddington's storybook p146-[60]   **S C**

Paddington and the "cold snap". Bond, M.
In Bond, M. Paddington's storybook p131-45   **S C**

Paddington and the "finishing touch". Bond, M.
In Bond, M. Paddington's storybook p97-111   **S C**

Paddington at large. Bond, M. See note under Bond, M. A bear called Paddington   **Fic**

Paddington at work. Bond, M. See note under Bond, M. A bear called Paddington   **Fic**

Paddington cleans up. Bond, M.
In Bond, M. Paddington's storybook p21-36   **S C**

Paddington dines out. Bond, M.
In Bond, M. Paddington's storybook p37-51   **S C**

Paddington helps out. Bond, M. See note under Bond, M. A bear called Paddington   **Fic**

Paddington marches on. Bond, M. See note under Bond, M. A bear called Paddington   **Fic**

Paddington on screen. Bond, M. See note under Bond, M. A bear called Paddington   **Fic**

Paddington on top. Bond, M. See note under Bond, M. A bear called Paddington   **Fic**

Paddington steps out. Bond, M.
In Bond, M. Paddington's storybook p112-30   **S C**

Paddington takes the air. Bond, M. See note under Bond, M. A bear called Paddington   **Fic**

Parker, Quanah, Comanche Chief, 1854?-1911
See/See also pages in the following book(s):
Freedman, R. Indian chiefs p52-71 (6 and up)   **920**

Parker, Robert Andrew, 1927-
(il) Bierhorst, J. The woman who fell from the sky   **398.2**
(il) DeFelice, C. C. The dancing skeleton   **398.2**
(il) Freedman, F. B. Brothers: a Hebrew legend   **398.2**
(il) Goldin, B. D. The magician's visit   **E**
(il) Ketteman, H. The year of no more corn   **E**
(il) Kuskin, K. A great miracle happened there   **296.4**
(il) The Monkey's haircut, and other stories told by the Maya. See The Monkey's haircut, and other stories told by the Maya   **398.2**
(il) Tompert, A. Grandfather Tang's story   **E**
(il) The Trees stand shining. See The Trees stand shining   **897**
(il) Wolkstein, D. The magic wings   **398.2**

Parker, Ron
(il) George, J. C. The moon of the bears   **599.74**
(il) George, J. C. The moon of the mountain lions   **599.74**

Parker, Steve
Albert Einstein and relativity (4 and up)   **92**
Alexander Graham Bell and the telephone (4 and up)   **92**
Benjamin Franklin and electricity (4 and up)   **92**
The body atlas (5 and up)   **611**
The brain and nervous system (4 and up)   **612.8**
Catching a cold (3-5)   **616.2**
Charles Darwin and evolution (4 and up)   **92**
The ear and hearing (4 and up)   **612.8**
Eating a meal (3-5)   **612.3**
Electricity (4 and up)   **537**
The eye and seeing (4 and up)   **612.8**
Eyewitness natural world (4 and up)   **591**
Fish (4 and up)   **597**
Food and digestion (4 and up)   **612.3**
The heart and blood (4 and up)   **612.1**
Human body (3-5)   **612**
Insects (3-5)   **595.7**
Mammal (4 and up)   **599**
Marie Curie and radium (4 and up)   **92**
Medicine (4 and up)   **610**
Pond & river (4 and up)   **574.92**
The Random House book of how things work (4 and up)   **600**
Running a race (3-5)   **796.42**
Seashore (4 and up)   **574.92**
Singing a song (3-5)   **612.7**
Skeleton (4 and up)   **596**

The skeleton and movement (4 and up)   **612.7**
Thomas Edison and electricity (4 and up)   **92**
Touch, taste and smell (4 and up)   **612.8**
What's inside airplanes?   **629.133**
The Wright brothers and aviation (4 and up)   **92**
(jt. auth) Bramwell, M. Mammals: the small plant-eaters   **599**

Parker, Tom, 1950-
(il) Lyon, G. E. A B Cedar   **E**

Parkin, Rex
The red carpet   **E**

Parkins, David
(il) King-Smith, D. Sophie's Tom   **Fic**

Parks, Gordon
(il) Wagner, J. J. T.   **Fic**

Parks, Rosa, 1913-
Rosa Parks: my story (5 and up)   **92**
About
Adler, D. A. A picture book of Rosa Parks (1-3)   **92**
Celsi, T. N. Rosa Parks and the Montgomery bus boycott (3-5)   **92**
Greenfield, E. Rosa Parks (2-4)   **92**
Siegel, B. The year they walked: Rosa Parks and the Montgomery bus boycott (4-6)   **92**

Parks, Van Dyke
Jump! the adventures of Brer Rabbit (1-4)   **398.2**
Contents: The comeuppance of Brer Wolf; Brer Fox goes hunting but Brer Rabbit bags the game; Brer Rabbit finds his match; Brer Rabbit grossly deceives Brer Fox; The moon in the millpond
Jump again! more adventures of Brer Rabbit (1-4)   **398.2**
Contents: Brer Rabbit, he's a good fisherman; The wonderful Tar-Baby story; How Brer Weasel was caught; Brer Rabbit and the mosquitoes; Brer Rabbit's courtship
Jump on over! the adventures of Brer Rabbit and his family (1-4)   **398.2**
Contents: How Brer Rabbit frightened his neighbors; Brer Rabbit and Brer Bear; Why Brer Wolf didn't eat the little rabs; Another story about the little rabs; Brer Fox gets outfoxed

Parks
See also National parks and reserves

Park's quest. Paterson, K.   **Fic**

Parley Garfield and the frogs. MacDonald, M. R.
In MacDonald, M. R. Twenty tellable tales p52-56   **372.6**

Parliamentary practice
Robert, H. M. The Scott, Foresman Robert's Rules of order newly revised   **060.4**
Sturgis, A. Standard code of parliamentary procedure   **060.4**

Parmenter, Wayne
(il) Levine, E. . . . if your name was changed at Ellis Island   **325.73**

Parnall, Peter
(il) Baylor, B. The desert is theirs   **574.5**

Paulsen, Ruth Wright
  (il) Paulsen, G. The haymeadow **Fic**
  (il) Paulsen, G. The tortilla factory
  641.8

Pauses **028.5**

Pavlova, Anna, 1881-1931
  About
  Levine, E. Anna Pavlova, genius of the dance (5 and up) **92**

Pawnee Indians
  Fradin, D. B. The Pawnee (2-4)
  970.004
  Legends
  Cohen, C. L. The mud pony (k-3)
  398.2

Paws, wings, and hooves. Yamashita, K.
  599

Paxton, Tom, 1937-
  Aesop's fables (3-5) **398.2**
  Androcles and the lion and other Aesop's fables (3-5) **398.2**
  The animals' lullaby (k-2) **782.42**
  Belling the cat and other Aesop's fables (3-5)
  398.2
  Birds of a feather and other Aesop's fables (3-5) **398.2**

Paying with shadows. Yep, L.
  In Yep, L. The tree of dreams **398.2**

Payne, Emmy, 1919-
  Katy No-Pocket **E**

Payne, Katharine
  Elephants calling (3-5) **599.6**

Payson, Dale
  (il) Clifton, L. The lucky stone **Fic**

Peace
  The Big book for peace **810.8**

Peace at last. Murphy, J. **E**

Peace on earth. Le Tord, B. **242**

Peacock. Rosen, M.
  In Rosen, M. How the animals got their colors p32-35 **398.2**

Peacock pie. De la Mare, W. **821**

Peacocks
  Fiction
  Polacco, P. Just plain Fancy **E**

Peake, Mervyn Laurence, 1911-1968
  (il) Stevenson, R. L. Treasure Island
  Fic

Peale, Charles Willson, 1741-1827
  About
  Tunnell, M. O. The joke's on George (k-3)
  92

Pearce, Philippa, 1920-
  Mrs. Cockle's cat
  In The Oxford treasury of children's stories p91-104 **S C**
  Tom's midnight garden (4 and up) **Fic**

Pearl Harbor (Oahu, Hawaii), Attack on, 1941
  Taylor, T. Air raid—Pearl Harbor! (5 and up)
  940.54

Pearl Moscowitz's last stand. Levine, A. A.
  E

Pearlfisheries
  Fiction
  O'Dell, S. The black pearl (6 and up)
  Fic

Pearson, Anne
  Ancient Greece (4 and up) **938**
  The Vikings (4 and up) **948**

Pearson, Tracey Campbell
  (il) Hennessy, B. G. The missing tarts
  E
  (il) Nixon, J. L. Beats me, Claude **E**
  (il) We wish you a merry Christmas. See We wish you a merry Christmas **782.28**

The peasant and the corpse. Afanas'ev, A. N.
  In Afanas'ev, A. N. Russian fairy tales p333-34 **398.2**

The peasant and the Devil. Grimm, J.
  In Grimm, J. The complete Grimm's fairy tales p767-68 **398.2**

The peasant in heaven. Grimm, J.
  In Grimm, J. The complete Grimm's fairy tales p695-96 **398.2**

The peasant, the bear, and the fox. Afanas'ev, A. N.
  In Afanas'ev, A. N. Russian fairy tales p288-89 **398.2**

The peasant's wise daughter. Grimm, J.
  In Grimm, J. The complete Grimm's fairy tales p437-40 **398.2**

Peck, Annie Smith, 1850-1935
  See/See also pages in the following book(s):
  Rappaport, D. Living dangerously p17-38 (4 and up) **920**

Peck, Beth
  (il) Bunting, E. The day before Christmas
  E
  (il) Bunting, E. How many days to America?
  E
  (il) Jones, R. C. Matthew and Tilly **E**
  (il) Woodruff, E. Dear Levi **Fic**

Peck, Richard
  Anonymously yours (5 and up) **92**
  Blossom Culp and the sleep of death. See note under Peck, R. The ghost belonged to me **Fic**
  The dreadful future of Blossom Culp. See note under Peck, R. The ghost belonged to me **Fic**
  The ghost belonged to me (5 and up)
  Fic
  Ghosts I have been. See note under Peck, R. The ghost belonged to me **Fic**
  Ghosts I have been [excerpt]
  In The Random House book of humor for children p36-43 **817.008**

Peck, Robert Newton, 1928-
  A day no pigs would die (6 and up)
  Fic
  Soup (5 and up) **Fic**
  Soup [excerpt]
  In The Random House book of humor for children p235-41 **817.008**
  Soup & me. See note under Peck, R. N. Soup **Fic**

Peck, Robert Newton, 1928-—*Continued*

Soup 1776. See note under Peck, R. N. Soup   Fic

Soup ahoy. See note under Peck, R. N. Soup   Fic

Soup for president. See note under Peck, R. N. Soup   Fic

Soup in love. See note under Peck, R. N. Soup   Fic

Soup in the saddle. See note under Peck, R. N. Soup   Fic

Soup on ice. See note under Peck, R. N. Soup   Fic

Soup on wheels. See note under Peck, R. N. Soup   Fic

Soup's hoop. See note under Peck, R. N. Soup   Fic

Soup's uncle. See note under Peck, R. N. Soup   Fic

Pecos Bill (Legendary character)

Kellogg, S. Pecos Bill (k-3)   398.2

Pecos Bill. Osborne, M. P.

In Osborne, M. P. American tall tales p73-85   398.2

Pecos Bill finds a ranch but loses a wife. Walker, P. R.

In Walker, P. R. Big men, big country p69-76   398.2

The **peculiar** such thing. Hamilton, V.

In From sea to shining sea p338-39   810.8

In Hamilton, V. The people could fly: American black folktales p116-20   398.2

The **peddler** of Ballaghadereen. Sawyer, R.

In Sawyer, R. The way of the storyteller p239-47   372.6

Peddlers and peddling

Fiction

Lewis, J. P. The moonbow of Mr. B. Bones   E

McDonald, M. The potato man   E

Slobodkina, E. Caps for sale   E

Pedersen, Judy

(il) Leitner, I. The big lie   940.53

(il) On the road of stars. See On the road of stars   897

The **pedlar** of Swaffham. Crossley-Holland, K.

In Crossley-Holland, K. British folk tales p251-64   398.2

The **pedlar** of Swaffham. Jacobs, J.

In Jacobs, J. English fairy tales p309-11   398.2

The **pedlar's** dream. Reeves, J.

In Reeves, J. English fables and fairy stories p71-80   398.2

Peek-a-boo!. Ahlberg, J.   E

Peeping and sleeping. Manushkin, F.   E

Peeping Beauty. Auch, M. J.   E

Peepo!. See Ahlberg, J. Peek-a-boo!   E

Peet, Bill

Big bad Bruce   E

Bill Peet: an autobiography (4 and up)   92

Cowardly Clyde   E

Eli   E

Huge Harold   E

The whingdingdilly   E

Pei, I. M., 1917-

See/See also pages in the following book(s):

Morey, J. Famous Asian Americans p128-38 (5 and up)   920

Peigan Indians *See* Piegan Indians

Pelé, 1940-

See/See also pages in the following book(s):

Littlefield, B. Champions p25-38 (5 and up)   920

Pelham, David

(il) Miller, J. The human body   612

The **pelican** chorus and other nonsense. Lear, E.   821

Pelicans

Patent, D. H. Pelicans (4 and up)   598

Pelle's new suit. Beskow, E.   E

Pellowski, Anne

The family storytelling handbook   372.6

The story vine   372.6

The storytelling handbook   372.6

The world of storytelling   372.6

Pelta, Kathy

California

In Hello USA series   973

Idaho

In Hello USA series   973

Texas

In Hello USA series   973

Vermont

In Hello USA series   973

Pemberton, John Styth

See/See also pages in the following book(s):

Aaseng, N. The unsung heroes p10-18 (5 and up)   920

Pend d'Oreille Indians *See* Kalispel Indians

Pendleton, Edrie

Let George do it

In Holiday plays round the year p169-78   812.008

Pène du Bois, William *See* Du Bois, William Pène, 1916-1993

Penguins

Arnold, C. Penguin (3-5)   598

Cowcher, H. Antarctica (1-3)   998

McMillan, B. Penguins at home (2-4)   598

McMillan, B. Puffins climb, penguins rhyme (k-2)   598

Paladino, C. Pomona: the birth of a penguin (2-4)   598

Patent, D. H. Looking at penguins (3-5)   598

Fiction

Atwater, R. T. Mr. Popper's penguins (3-5)   Fic

Lester, H. Three cheers for Tacky   E

Penguins at home. McMillan, B.   598

Pinkney, Jerry, 1939-
(il) Aardema, V. Rabbit makes a monkey of lion **398.2**
(il) Adoff, A. In for winter, out for spring **811**
(il) Dragonwagon, C. Half a moon and one whole star **E**
(il) Eisler, C. T. David's songs **223**
(il) Flournoy, V. The patchwork quilt **E**
(il) Greenfield, E. Childtimes: a three-generation memoir **920**
(il) Greenfield, E. Mary McLeod Bethune **92**
(il) Hamilton, V. Drylongso **Fic**
(il) Hurwitz, J. New shoes for Silvia **E**
(il) Lester, J. Further tales of Uncle Remus **398.2**
(il) Lester, J. John Henry **398.2**
(il) Lester, J. The last tales of Uncle Remus **398.2**
(il) Lester, J. More tales of Uncle Remus **398.2**
(il) Lester, J. The tales of Uncle Remus **398.2**
(il) Marzollo, J. Pretend you're a cat **E**
(il) McKissack, P. C. Mirandy and Brother Wind **E**
(il) Pinkney, G. J. Back home **E**
(il) Pinkney, G. J. The Sunday outing **E**
(il) San Souci, R. The talking eggs **398.2**
(il) Singer, M. Turtle in July **811**
(il) Taylor, M. D. Song of the trees **Fic**

Pinkwater, Daniel Manus, 1941-
Attila the pun. See note under Pinkwater, D. M. Fat men from space **Fic**
Aunt Lulu **E**
Fat men from space (3-6) **Fic**
Guys from space **E**
The Hoboken chicken emergency (3-6) **Fic**
I was a second grade werewolf **E**
Lizard music (4 and up) **Fic**
(jt. auth) Pinkwater, J. Superpuppy: how to choose, raise, and train the best possible dog for you **636.7**

Pinkwater, Jill
Superpuppy: how to choose, raise, and train the best possible dog for you (5 and up) **636.7**
Tails of the Bronx (4-6) **Fic**

Pinkwater, Manus *See* Pinkwater, Daniel Manus, 1941-

Pinky and Rex. Howe, J. **E**

Pinky and Rex and the double-dad weekend. Howe, J. See note under Howe, J. Pinky and Rex **E**

Pinky and Rex and the mean old witch. Howe, J. See note under Howe, J. Pinky and Rex **E**

Pinky and Rex and the new baby. Howe, J. See note under Howe, J. Pinky and Rex **E**

Pinky and Rex and the spelling bee. Howe, J. See note under Howe, J. Pinky and Rex **E**

Pinky and Rex get married. Howe, J. See note under Howe, J. Pinky and Rex **E**

Pinky and Rex go to camp. Howe, J. See note under Howe, J. Pinky and Rex **E**

Pinky Pye. Estes, E. See note under Estes, E. Ginger Pye **Fic**

Pinocchio. See Collodi, C. The adventures of Pinocchio **Fic**

Pinocchio goes to school. Thane, A.
In Thane, A. Plays from famous stories and fairy tales p352-65 **812**

Pinto, Ralph
(il) Lester, J. The knee-high man, and other tales **398.2**

Pioneer life *See* Frontier and pioneer life

A pioneer sampler. Greenwood, B. **971.3**

A pioneer story *See* Greenwood, B. A pioneer sampler **971.3**

Pioneering ocean depths. Markle, S. **551.46**

Piper, Watty
The little engine that could **E**

The piper and the pooka. Crossley-Holland, K.
In Crossley-Holland, K. British folk tales p17-23 **398.2**

Piping down the valleys wild **808.81**

Pippi goes on board. Lindgren, A. See note under Lindgren, A. Pippi Longstocking **Fic**

Pippi in the South Seas. Lindgren, A. See note under Lindgren, A. Pippi Longstocking **Fic**

Pippi Longstocking. Lindgren, A. **Fic**

Pippin, Horace, 1888-1946
About
Lyons, M. E. Starting home: the story of Horace Pippin, painter (4 and up) **92**

Pippo gets lost. Oxenbury, H. **E**

The pirate. San Souci, R.
In San Souci, R. More short & shivery p97-102 **398.2**

The pirate. Schwartz, A.
In Schwartz, A. In a dark, dark room, and other scary stories p50-59 **398.2**

Pirates
Exquemelin, A. O. Exquemelin and the pirates of the Caribbean (5 and up) **910.4**
Platt, R. Pirate (4 and up) **910.4**
Stevenson, R. L. Treasure Island (6 and up) **Fic**
Fiction
Ahlberg, J. It was a dark and stormy night (2-4) **Fic**
Burningham, J. Come away from the water, Shirley **E**
Fox, M. Tough Boris **E**
Poetry
Yolen, J. The ballad of the pirate queens (3-5) **811**

Prayers—*Continued*
Prayers, praises, and thanksgivings (3-6)
    242

Fiction
Cohen, B. Yussel's prayer (3-5)   **398.2**
Prayers from the ark. Bernos de Gasztold, C.
    841
Prayers, praises, and thanksgivings (3-6)
    242

Praying mantis
Lavies, B. Backyard hunter: the praying
   mantis (2-4)   **595.7**
Fiction
James, B. Mary Ann   **E**
The **precious** hide. Afanas'ev, A. N.
   In Afanas'ev, A. N. Russian fairy tales
   p156-58   **398.2**
Precious stones
Symes, R. F. Crystal & gem (4 and up)
    548
Precipitation (Meteorology) *See* Rain; Snow
Predator!. Brooks, B.   **591.5**
Pregnancy
Cole, J. How you were born (k-2)   **612.6**
Kitzinger, S. Being born (3-5)   **612.6**
Prehistoric animals
   See also Dinosaurs; Extinct animals
Gibbons, G. Prehistoric animals (k-3)
    560
Rand McNally picture atlas of prehistoric
   life (4 and up)   **560**
Whitfield, P. J. Macmillan children's guide
   to dinosaurs and other prehistoric animals
   (3-6)   **567.9**
Witmer, L. M. The search for the origin of
   birds (4 and up)   **568**
Prehistoric art
   See also Rock drawings, paintings, and
   engravings
Prehistoric life. Lindsay, W.   **560**
Witmer, L. M. The search for the origin of
   birds   **568**
Prehistoric man
   See also Cave dwellers
Cole, J. The human body: how we evolved
   (4 and up)   **573.2**
Early humans (4 and up)   **930.1**
Getz, D. Frozen man (5 and up)   **930.1**
Lasky, K. Traces of life (5 and up)
    573.2
Lessem, D. The iceman (4-6)   **930.1**
Sattler, H. R. The earliest Americans (5 and
   up)   **970.01**
Sattler, H. R. Hominids: a look back at our
   ancestors (5 and up)   **573.3**
The Visual dictionary of prehistoric life (4
   and up)   **560**
Prehistoric Pinkerton. Kellogg, S. See note un-
   der Kellogg, S. Pinkerton, behave!   **E**
Prejudices
   See also Antisemitism
Fiction
Conly, J. L. Crazy lady! (5 and up)   **Fic**

Cormier, R. Tunes for bears to dance to (6
   and up)   **Fic**
Curtis, C. P. The Watsons go to
   Birmingham—1963 (4 and up)   **Fic**
Fleischman, P. Saturnalia (6 and up)
    Fic
Hooks, W. H. Circle of fire (5 and up)
    Fic
Mochizuki, K. Baseball saved us   **E**
Mochizuki, K. Heroes   **E**
Pinkney, A. D. Hold fast to dreams (5 and
   up)   **Fic**
Taylor, M. D. The gold Cadillac (4 and up)
    Fic
Taylor, M. D. Mississippi bridge (4 and up)
    Fic
Uchida, Y. A jar of dreams (5 and up)
    Fic
Uchida, Y. Journey home (5 and up)
    Fic
Yarbrough, C. The shimmershine queens
   (4-6)   **Fic**
Yep, L. The star fisher (6 and up)   **Fic**
Prelutsky, Jack
The baby Uggs are hatching (k-3)   **811**
Beneath a blue umbrella: rhymes (k-3)
    811
Circus (k-3)   **811**
The dragons are singing tonight (2-5)
    811
The Headless Horseman rides tonight (2-5)
    811
It's Christmas (1-3)   **811**
It's Halloween (1-3)   **811**
It's snowing! It's snowing! (1-3)   **811**
It's Thanksgiving (1-3)   **811**
It's Valentine's Day (1-3)   **811**
My parents think I'm sleeping: poems (2-4)
    811
The new kid on the block: poems (3-6)
    811
Nightmares: poems to trouble your sleep
   (2-5)   **811**
The queen of Eene (k-3)   **811**
Ride a purple pelican (k-3)   **811**
Rolling Harvey down the hill (1-3)   **811**
The sheriff of Rottenshot: poems (2-5)
    811
The snopp on the sidewalk, and other po-
   ems (k-4)   **811**
Something big has been here (3-5)   **811**
Tyrannosaurus was a beast (2-5)   **811**
(comp) A. Nonny Mouse writes again! See
   A. Nonny Mouse writes again! **808.81**
(comp) For laughing out loud. See For
   laughing out loud   **811.008**
Lindgren, B. The wild baby   **E**
(comp) Poems of A. Nonny Mouse. See Poems of A. Nonny Mouse   **808.81**
(ed) The Random House book of poetry for
   children. See The Random House book of
   poetry for children   **821.008**
(comp) Read-aloud rhymes for the very
   young. See Read-aloud rhymes for the
   very young   **821.008**

Q

Quechua Indians
See/See also pages in the following book(s):
Newman, S. P. The Incas (4 and up)
985

Queen, J. Allen
Karate for kids (4 and up)   **796.8**

The **queen** bee. Grimm, J.
In Grimm, J. About wise men and simpletons p55-57   **398.2**
In Grimm, J. The complete Grimm's fairy tales p317-19   **398.2**

Queen Eleanor: independent spirit of the medieval world. Brooks, P. S.   **92**

The **queen** of Eene. Prelutsky, J.   **811**

Queenie Peavy. Burch, R.   **Fic**

Queens *See* Kings, queens, rulers, etc.

A **question** of trust. Bauer, M. D.   **Fic**

Questions (k-2)   **811.008**

Questions and answers
Buehner, C. It's a spoon, not a shovel (k-3)   **395**

Quicksand
De Paola, T. The quicksand book (k-3)   **552**

The **quicksand** book. De Paola, T.   **552**

A **quiet** night in. Murphy, J.   **E**

The **quilt**. Jonas, A.   **E**

The **quilt-block** history of pioneer days. Cobb, M.   **746.46**

The **Quilt** of men's eyes
In The Naked bear p101-09   **398.2**

The **quilt** story. Johnston, T.   **E**

Quilts
Cobb, M. The quilt-block history of pioneer days (2-5)   **746.46**
Lyons, M. E. Stitching stars: the story quilts of Harriet Powers (4 and up)   **92**
Paul, A. W. Eight hands round   **E**
Fiction
Coerr, E. The Josefina story quilt   **E**
Ernst, L. C. Sam Johnson and the blue ribbon quilt   **E**
Flournoy, V. The patchwork quilt   **E**
Guback, G. Luka's quilt   **E**
Hopkinson, D. Sweet Clara and the freedom quilt   **E**
Johnston, T. The quilt story   **E**
Jonas, A. The quilt   **E**
Kinsey-Warnock, N. The Canada geese quilt (3-5)   **Fic**
Polacco, P. The keeping quilt   **E**
Poetry
Kuskin, K. Patchwork island (k-3)   **811**

Quinlan, Susan E.
The case of the mummified pigs and other mysteries in nature (4 and up)   **508**

Quiquern. Kipling, R.
In Kipling, R. The jungle books   **S C**

Quotations
See also subjects, classes of persons, and ethnic groups with the subdivision Quotations
Bartlett, J. Familiar quotations   **808.88**

R

Ra, Carol F., 1939-
(comp) Trot, trot to Boston: play rhymes for baby. See Trot, trot to Boston: play rhymes for baby   **398.8**

The **rabbi**. Sanfield, S.
In Sanfield, S. The feather merchants & other tales of the fools of Chelm p12-17   **398.2**

Rabbi Leib & the witch Cunegunde. Singer, I. B.
In Singer, I. B. Stories for children p89-97   **S C**
In Singer, I. B. When Shlemiel went to Warsaw & other stories p29-42   **398.2**

Rabbit (Legendary character)
Johnston, T. The tale of Rabbit and Coyote (k-3)   **398.2**
Ross, G. How Rabbit tricked Otter and other Cherokee trickster stories (4-6)   **398.2**

Rabbit and Coyote
In The Monkey's haircut, and other stories told by the Maya p72-76   **398.2**

Rabbit and Fox. Bruchac, J.
In Bruchac, J. The boy who lived with the bears and other Iroquois stories p15-21   **398.2**

Rabbit and Puma
In The Monkey's haircut, and other stories told by the Maja p77-80   **398.2**

The **rabbit** and the elephants. Yeoman, J.
In Yeoman, J. The singing tortoise and other animal folktales p89-93   **398.2**

Rabbit and the tar wolf. Ross, G.
In Ross, G. How Rabbit tricked Otter and other Cherokee trickster stories p48-53   **398.2**

The **rabbit** and the well. MacDonald, M. R.
In MacDonald, M. R. Twenty tellable tales p126-41   **372.6**

Rabbit and the willow. Van Laan, N.
In Van Laan, N. In a circle long ago p98-103   **398.2**

The **rabbit** and the wolf. Walker, B. K.
In Walker, B. K. A treasury of Turkish folktales for children p15   **398.2**

Rabbit-Cadabra!. Howe, J. See note under Howe, J. Scared silly: a Halloween treat   **E**

Rabbit dances with the people. Ross, G.
In Ross, G. How Rabbit tricked Otter and other Cherokee trickster stories p71-75   **398.2**

Rabbit escapes from the wolves. Ross, G.
In Ross, G. How Rabbit tricked Otter and other Cherokee trickster stories p24-28   **398.2**

Rabbit gets married
In The Monkey's haircut, and other stories told by the Maya p81-83   **398.2**

Rabbit goes duck hunting. Ross, G.
In Ross, G. How Rabbit tricked Otter and other Cherokee trickster stories p43-47   **398.2**

Rabbit helps Wildcat hunt turkeys. Ross, G.
In Ross, G. How Rabbit tricked Otter and other Cherokee trickster stories p38-41   **398.2**

Rabbit Hill. Lawson, R.   **Fic**

Rabbit makes a monkey of lion. Aardema, V.   **398.2**

Rabbit races with Turtle. Ross, G.
In Ross, G. How Rabbit tricked Otter and other Cherokee trickster stories p54-56   **398.2**

Rabbit sends Wolf to the sunset. Ross, G.
In Ross, G. How Rabbit tricked Otter and other Cherokee trickster stories p67-69   **398.2**

Rabbit steals from Fox. Ross, G.
In Ross, G. How Rabbit tricked Otter and other Cherokee trickster stories p62-66   **398.2**

Rabbits
Lepthien, E. U. Rabbits and hares (2-4)   **599.32**

Fiction
Adams, A. The Easter egg artists   **E**
Adams, R. Watership Down (6 and up)   **Fic**
Bianco, M. W. The velveteen rabbit (2-4)   **Fic**
Brown, M. W. Goodnight moon   **E**
Brown, M. W. The runaway bunny   **E**
Brutschy, J. The winter fox   **E**
Gág, W. The A B C bunny   **E**
Heyward, D. The country bunny and the little gold shoes   **E**
Hoban, T. Where is it?   **E**
Knutson, B. Sungura and Leopard (k-3)   **398.2**
Koontz, R. M. Chicago and the cat: the camping trip   **E**
Lawson, R. Rabbit Hill (3-6)   **Fic**
Lawson, R. The tough winter (3-6)   **Fic**
McBratney, S. Guess how much I love you   **E**
McDermott, G. Zomo the Rabbit (k-3)   **398.2**
Newberry, C. T. Marshmallow   **E**
Peet, B. Huge Harold   **E**
Potter, B. The tale of Peter Rabbit   **E**

Shannon, G. Dance away!   **E**
Steig, W. Solomon the rusty nail   **E**
Stevens, J. Tops and bottoms (k-3)   **398.2**
Tafuri, N. Rabbit's morning   **E**
Wells, R. Max's first word   **E**
Wells, R. Morris's disappearing bag   **E**
Wells, R. Moss pillows   **E**
Wildsmith, B. The hare and the tortoise (k-2)   **398.2**
Zolotow, C. Mr. Rabbit and the lovely present   **E**

Rabbits and hares. Lepthien, E. U.   **599.32**

The **rabbit's** escape. Hall, J. C.   **398.2**

Rabbit's morning. Tafuri, N.   **E**

Rabbit's snow dance. Bruchac, J.
In Bruchac, J. The boy who lived with the bears and other Iroquois stories p57-63   **398.2**

Rabble Starkey. Lowry, L.   **Fic**

Rabies
Landau, E. Rabies (4 and up)   **616.9**
See/See also pages in the following book(s):
Facklam, H. Viruses p26-29 (5 and up)   **576**

Rabin, Mindy
(il) West, R. Dinosaur discoveries   **745.54**

Rabinowitz, Sholem Yakov *See* Sholem Aleichem, 1859-1916

Raboff, Ernest
Albrecht Dürer (5 and up)   **759.3**

Raccoons
Arnosky, J. Raccoons and ripe corn   **E**
North, S. Rascal (5 and up)   **599.74**
Fiction
Sharmat, M. W. The 329th friend   **E**
Wells, R. Timothy goes to school   **E**

Raccoons and ripe corn. Arnosky, J.   **E**

Race awareness
Poetry
Adoff, A. All the colors of the race: poems (4-6)   **811**

Race relations
See also Multiculturalism; names of countries, cities, etc., with the subdivision Race relations
Fiction
Adoff, A. Black is brown is tan   **E**
Raschka, C. Yo! Yes?   **E**
Sebestyen, O. Words by heart (5 and up)   **Fic**
Spinelli, J. Maniac Magee (5 and up)   **Fic**
Taylor, M. D. The friendship (4 and up)   **Fic**
Taylor, M. D. The gold Cadillac (4 and up)   **Fic**
Taylor, M. D. Mississippi bridge (4 and up)   **Fic**
Taylor, M. D. The road to Memphis (4 and up)   **Fic**
Taylor, M. D. The well (4 and up)   **Fic**
Taylor, T. The cay (5 and up)   **Fic**

Rawlings, Marjorie Kinnan, 1896-1953
The yearling (6 and up)   Fic

Rawlins, Donna
(il) Loh, M. J. Tucking Mommy in   E

Rawlins, Janet
(il) Gardam, J. The hollow land   Fic

Rawls, James
The Pilgrim painting
In Holiday plays round the year p91-100
812.008

Rawls, Wilson, 1913-
Where the red fern grows   Fic

Ray, David, 1940-
(il) The Night of the whippoorwill. See The
Night of the whippoorwill   808.81
(il) Yolen, J. Greyling   E

Ray, Deborah Kogan, 1940-
(il) Coerr, E. Chang's paper pony   E
(il) Harvey, B. Cassie's journey   Fic
(il) Harvey, B. My prairie Christmas
Fic
(il) Harvey, B. My prairie year   Fic
(il) Peterson, J. W. I have a sister—my sister is deaf   362.4
(il) Singer, M. Sky words   811

Ray, Delia
Behind the Blue and Gray (5 and up)
973.7

Ray, James Earl, 1928-
See/See also pages in the following book(s):
Haskins, J. The life and death of Martin Lu-
ther King, Jr (5 and up)   92

Ray, Jane
(il) Bible. O.T. Genesis. The story of the
creation   222
(il) Mayo, M. Magical tales from many
lands   398.2
(il) Wilde, O. The Happy Prince [abridged
version]   E

Rayevsky, Robert
(il) Kimmel, E. A. Three sacks of truth
398.2
(il) Paxton, T. Aesop's fables   398.2
(il) Paxton, T. Androcles and the lion and
other Aesop's fables   398.2
(il) Paxton, T. Belling the cat and other Aesop's fables   398.2
(il) Paxton, T. Birds of a feather and other
Aesop's fables   398.2

Raymond, Larry
(il) Reef, C. Henry David Thoreau   92

Raymond, Victoria
(il) Jackson, E. B. Brown cow, green grass,
yellow mellow sun   E

Rayner, Mary, 1933-
Garth Pig and the ice cream lady. See note
under Rayner, M. Mr. and Mrs. Pig's eve-
ning out   E
Garth Pig steals the show. See note under
Rayner, M. Mr. and Mrs. Pig's evening
out   E
Mr. and Mrs. Pig's evening out   E

Mrs. Pig gets cross and other stories. See
note under Rayner, M. Mr. and Mrs. Pig's
evening out   E
Mrs. Pig's bulk buy. See note under Rayner,
M. Mr. and Mrs. Pig's evening out   E
One by one (k-3)   782.42
Ten pink piglets (k-3)   782.42
(il) King-Smith, D. Babe: the gallant pig
Fic
(il) King-Smith, D. Pigs might fly   Fic

Read, Mary, 1680-1721
Poetry
Yolen, J. The ballad of the pirate queens
(3-5)   811

The **read-aloud** handbook. Trelease, J.
028.5

Read-aloud rhymes for the very young (k-2)
821.008

The **Read-aloud** treasury   808.8

Read and wonder [series]
King-Smith, D. All pigs are beautiful
636.4
King-Smith, D. I love guinea pigs
636.088
Wallace, K. Think of an eel   597

Read for the fun of it. Bauer, C. F.
027.62

Reade, Deborah, 1949-
(il) Trimble, S. The village of blue stone
970.004

Reading
Goforth, F. S. Using folk literature in the
classroom   372.6
Herb, S. Using children's books in preschool
settings   372.4
Kaye, P. Games for reading   372.4
Miles, B. Hey! I'm reading! (k-2)   372.4
Fiction
Bunting, E. The Wednesday surprise   E
Gilson, J. Do bananas chew gum? (4-6)
Fic
Periodicals
The Reading Teacher   372.405

Reading interests of children *See* Children—
Books and reading

Reading Is Fundamental, Inc.
To ride a butterfly. See To ride a butterfly
810.8

The **Reading** Teacher   372.405

Ready, Anna
Mississippi
In Hello USA series   973

Ready-to-read [series]
Bang, M. Wiley and the Hairy Man
398.2

The **Real** Mother Goose (k-2)   398.8

The **real** skin rubber monster mask. Cohen,
M. See note under Cohen, M. See you in
second grade!   E

The **real** thief. Steig, W.   Fic

The **reason** for Janey. Wilson, N. H. Fic

The **reason** for the pelican. Ciardi, J. 811

Reeves, James, 1909-1978
  English fables and fairy stories (4-6)
  398.2
  Contents: Jack Hannaford; Tattercoats; Johnny Gloke; The fish and the ring; The two princesses; The story of Tom Thumb; The pedlar's dream; Catskin; The tulip bed; Simpleton Peter; The well of the three heads; Jack and the beanstalk; Tom Tit Tot; The golden snuffbox; The stars in the sky; Molly Whipple; The donkey, the table, and the stick; The Well of the World's End; Dick Whittington and his cat

Reeves, Nicholas *See* Reeves, C. N. (Carl Nicholas), 1956-

Reference books
  Bibliography
  Nichols, M. I. Guide to reference books for school media centers **011.6**
  Peterson, C. S. Reference books for children **011.6**

Reference Books Bulletin. See Booklist
  028.1

Reference books for children. Peterson, C. S.
  011.6

Reference books for elementary and junior high school libraries. See Peterson, C. S. Reference books for children **011.6**

Reference books for young readers. See Encyclopedias, atlases & dictionaries **011**

Reflections. Jonas, A. **E**

Reflections on a gift of watermelon pickle . . . and other modern verse (6 and up)
  811.008

Reflexes
  Berger, M. Why I cough, sneeze, shiver, hiccup, & yawn (k-3) **612.8**

Reformers
  Colman, P. Mother Jones and the march of the mill children (3-5) **92**
  Jacobs, W. J. Great lives: human rights (5 and up) **920**
  Kraft, B. H. Mother Jones (4 and up)
  92

Refugees
  Fiction
  Bunting, E. How many days to America?
  E
  Holm, A. North to freedom (6 and up)
  Fic
  Temple, F. Grab hands and run (6 and up)
  Fic
  Temple, F. Tonight, by sea (6 and up)
  Fic
  Whelan, G. Goodbye, Vietnam (4 and up)
  Fic

Refugees, Jewish *See* Jewish refugees

Refugees, Polish *See* Polish refugees

Refuges, Wildlife *See* Wildlife refuges

Refuse and refuse disposal
  See also Recycling; Sewage disposal
  Foster, J. Cartons, cans, and orange peels (4-6) **363.7**
  Hadingham, E. Garbage! (4 and up)
  363.7
  Showers, P. Where does the garbage go? (k-3) **363.7**

See/See also pages in the following book(s):
  Langone, J. Our endangered earth p56-90 (6 and up) **363.7**

Regards to the man in the moon. Keats, E. J. See note under Keats, E. J. Louie **E**

Regguinti, Gordon
  The sacred harvest (3-6) **970.004**

Reid, George K.
  Pond life (4 and up) **574.92**

Reid Banks, Lynne, 1929-
  The Indian in the cupboard (5 and up)
  Fic
  The mystery of the cupboard. See note under Reid Banks, L. The Indian in the cupboard **Fic**
  The return of the Indian. See note under Reid Banks, L. The Indian in the cupboard **Fic**
  The secret of the Indian. See note under Reid Banks, L. The Indian in the cupboard **Fic**

Reincarnation
  Fiction
  Gerstein, M. The mountains of Tibet **E**

Reindeer
  Lepthien, E. U. Reindeer (2-4) **599.73**
  Fiction
  Brett, J. The wild Christmas reindeer **E**

The **reindeer** people. Lewin, T. **948.97**

Reingold, Michael
  (il) Tiger, S. Diabetes **616.4**

Reingold-Reiss, Debra
  (il) Petersen-Fleming, J. Kitten care and critters, too! **636.8**
  (il) Petersen-Fleming, J. Puppy care and critters, too! **636.7**

Reisberg, Veg
  (il) Moroney, L. Baby rattlesnake **398.2**
  (il) Rohmer, H. Uncle Nacho's hat
  398.2

Reiser, Lynn
  The surprise family **E**

Reiss, Debra Reingold- *See* Reingold-Reiss, Debra

Reiss, Johanna
  The upstairs room (4 and up) **92**

Reiss, Toby A.
  Denmark—in pictures. See Denmark—in pictures **948.9**

Reit, Seymour
  Behind rebel lines: the incredible story of Emma Edmonds, Civil War spy (4 and up) **92**

The **relatives** came. Rylant, C. **E**

Relativity, as explained by Professor Xargle. Willis, J. See note under Willis, J. Earthlets, as explained by Professor Xargle
  E

Releasing pigeons. Porte-Thomas, B. A.
  In Porte-Thomas, B. A turkey drive and other tales p23-27 **S C**

The **rescue**. Yep, L.
In Yep, L. The tree of dreams   **398.2**

Rescue of the stranded whales. Mallory, K.
639.9

Rescue: the story of how Gentiles saved Jews in the Holocaust. Meltzer, M.   **940.53**

Rescue vehicles. Somerville, L.   **629.04**

Rescue work
Patent, D. H. Hugger to the rescue (2-4)
636.7

The **rescuers**. Sharp, M.   **Fic**

Residential construction *See* House construction

Resnick, Abraham
Bulgaria (4 and up)   **949.77**
The Commonwealth of Independent States (4 and up)   **947.086**

Respiration
Ganeri, A. Breathing (k-2)   **612.2**
Sandeman, A. Breathing (k-3)   **612.2**
Silverstein, A. The respiratory system (5 and up)   **612.2**

The **respiratory** system. Silverstein, A.
612.2

Ressner, Phil
Dudley Pippin and the principal [short story]
In Free to be—you and me p88-89
810.8

Restaurants
Fiction
Day, A. Frank and Ernest   **E**
Rylant, C. An angel for Solomon Singer
E
Rylant, C. The Van Gogh Cafe (4-6)
Fic

Retarded children *See* Mentally handicapped children; Slow learning children

Retired. Rylant, C.
In Rylant, C. Every living thing p8-14
S C

Rettich, Margret
The Christmas roast
In Bauer, C. F. Celebrations p265-67
808.8
Television in the snow
In Bauer, C. F. Celebrations p218-20
808.8

The **return**. Levitin, S.   **Fic**

The **return** of the Great Brain. Fitzgerald, J. D. See note under Fitzgerald, J. D. The Great Brain   **Fic**

The **return** of the Indian. Reid Banks, L. See note under Reid Banks, L. The Indian in the cupboard   **Fic**

Return of the wolf. Patent, D. H.   **Fic**

Return to Bitter Creek. Smith, D. B.   **Fic**

Return to Gone-Away Lake. Enright, E. See note under Enright E. Gone-Away Lake
Fic

Return to Howliday Inn. Howe, J. See note under Howe, J. The celery stalks at midnight   **Fic**

Reusable space vehicles *See* Space shuttles

The **revenge** of the Iron Chink. Yee, P.
In Yee, P. Tales from Gold Mountain p57-62   **S C**

The **revenge** of the wizard's ghost. Bellairs, J. See note under Bellairs, J. The curse of the blue figurine   **Fic**

Revere, Paul, 1735-1818
About
Fritz, J. And then what happened, Paul Revere? (2-4)   **92**
Fiction
Lawson, R. Mr. Revere and I (5 and up)
Fic
Poetry
Longfellow, H. W. Paul Revere's ride
811

Revolution, Industrial *See* Industrial revolution

Rex and Lilly family time. Brown, L. K.
E

Rex and Lilly playtime. Brown, L. K. See note under Brown, L. K. Rex and Lilly family time   **E**

Rey, H. A. (Hans Augusto), 1898-1977
Curious George   **E**
Curious George gets a medal. See note under Rey, H. A. Curious George   **E**
Curious George goes to the hospital. See note under Rey, H. A. Curious George
E
Curious George learns the alphabet. See note under Rey, H. A. Curious George
E
Curious George rides a bike. See note under Rey, H. A. Curious George   **E**
Curious George takes a job. See note under Rey, H. A. Curious George   **E**
Find the constellations   **523.8**
(il) Payne, E. Katy No-Pocket   **E**

Rey, Hans Augusto *See* Rey, H. A. (Hans Augusto), 1898-1977

Rey, Margaret
Curious George flies a kite. See note under Rey, H. A. Curious George   **E**
Curious George goes to the hospital. See note under Rey, H. A. Curious George
E

Reyher, Rebecca Hourwich, 1897-1987
My mother is the most beautiful woman in the world (1-4)   **398.2**

Reynolds, Jan, 1956-
Amazon basin (2-4)   **981**
Down under (2-4)   **994**
Frozen land (2-4)   **970.004**
Himalaya (2-4)   **954.96**
Mongolia (2-4)   **951.7**

Reynolds, Lura Schield
(jt. auth) Naylor, P. R. Maudie in the middle   **Fic**

Rockwell, Anne F., 1934-
At the beach E
Bikes (k-1) 629.227
Boats (k-1) 387.2
Cars (k-1) 629.222
The cat who went to the castle
 In To ride a butterfly p20-23 810.8
The emergency room (k-2) 362.1
Fire engines (k-1) 628.9
First comes spring E
The first snowfall E
Happy birthday to me E
How my garden grew E
Machines (k-1) 621.8
Our garage sale E
Our yard is full of birds (k-2) 598
Planes (k-1) 629.133
Pots and pans E
Puss in boots, and other stories (2-4)
 398.2

Contents: Jack and the beanstalk; Nail soup; Kate Crackernuts; The miller, his son, and the donkey; The golden goose; The boy who cried wolf; The fisherman and his wife; Briar Rose; Mr. Vinegar; The frog prince; The cat on the Dovrefell; Puss in boots

The robber baby (3-5) 292
Sick in bed E
Things that go (k-1) 629.04
Things to play with (k-1) 793
The toolbox (k-1) 621.9
Trains (k-1) 625.1
Trucks (k-1) 629.224
(il) Showers, P. What happens to a hamburger 612.3

Rockwell, Harlow, 1910-1988
My dentist (k-1) 617.6
My doctor (k-1) 610.69
(jt. auth) Rockwell, A. F. At the beach
 E
(jt. auth) Rockwell, A. F. The emergency room 362.1
(jt. auth) Rockwell, A. F. The first snowfall
 E
(jt. auth) Rockwell, A. F. Happy birthday to me E
(jt. auth) Rockwell, A. F. How my garden grew E
(jt. auth) Rockwell, A. F. Machines
 621.8
(il) Rockwell, A. F. Our garage sale E
(jt. auth) Rockwell, A. F. Sick in bed E
(jt. auth) Rockwell, A. F. The toolbox
 621.9

Rockwell, Lizzy
(il) Jenkins, P. B. A nest full of eggs
 598
(il) Rockwell, A. F. Our yard is full of birds
 598
(il) Rockwell, A. F. Pots and pans E

Rockwell, Thomas, 1933-
How to eat fried worms (3-6) Fic
How to eat fried worms [excerpt]
 In The Random House book of humor
  for children p301-05 817.008
How to eat fried worms, and other plays
 (4-6) 812

Contents: Myron Mere; How to eat fried worms; Ai-iieeeeeeeeee!; The heiress, or the croak of doom

Rodanas, Kristina
(il) Bealer, A. W. Only the names remain
 970.004

Rodda, Emily, 1948-
Finders keepers (4-6) Fic

Rodell, Don
(il) George, J. C. The moon of the chickarees 599.32

Rodenas, Paula
The Random House book of horses and horsemanship (4 and up) 636.1

Rodeos
Hoyt-Goldsmith, D. Apache rodeo (3-5)
 970.004

Rodgers, Mary, 1931-
A billion for Boris. See note under Rodgers, M. Freaky Friday Fic
Freaky Friday (4 and up) Fic
Freaky Friday [excerpt]
 In The Random House book of humor
  for children p262-67 817.008
Ladies first [short story]
 In Free to be—you and me p39-45
 810.8
Summer switch. See note under Rodgers, M. Freaky Friday Fic

Rodgers, Mary M. (Mary Madeline), 1954-
(jt. auth) Mutel, C. F. Tropical rain forests
 574.5

Rodman, Maia *See* Wojciechowska, Maia, 1927-

Rodowsky, Colby F., 1932-
The gathering room (5 and up) Fic
Hannah in between (5 and up) Fic

Roentgen, Wilhelm Conrad *See* Röntgen, Wilhelm Conrad, 1845-1923

Roessel, Monty
Kinaaldá: a Navajo girl grows up (3-6)
 970.004

Rofes, Eric E., 1954-
(ed) The Kids' book about death and dying. See The Kids' book about death and dying 155.9

Rogasky, Barbara
Rapunzel (1-3) 398.2
The water of life (1-3) 398.2
(comp) Winter poems. See Winter poems
 808.81

Rogers, Fred
Adoption (k-2) 362.7
Going to the dentist (k-2) 617.6
Going to the hospital (k-2) 362.1
Making friends (k-1) 155.4
Moving (k-1) 155.4

Rogers, Jacqueline
(il) Byars, B. C. The not-just-anybody family
 Fic
(il) San Souci, R. More short & shivery
 398.2
(il) Wright, B. R. Nothing but trouble
 Fic

Rosen, Michael, 1946-
How the animals got their colors (3-5)

        398.2

Contents: Coyote; Flying fish; Frog; Tiger; Brolga; Leopard; Peacock; Crane; How the animals got their colors

We're going on a bear hunt   **E**
(comp) Poems for the very young. See Poems for the very young   **821.008**

Rosen, Michael J., 1954-
Elijah's angel   **Fic**
A school for Pompey Walker   **Fic**
(ed) Home. See Home   **810.8**

Rosenberg, Jane, 1949-
Sing me a story (4-6)   **792.5**

Rosenberg, Liz
Monster mama   **E**

Rosenberg, Maxine B., 1939-
Being a twin, having a twin (2-4)   **155.4**
Being adopted (2-4)   **362.7**
Brothers and sisters (k-2)   **306.8**
Finding a way (2-4)   **362.4**
Hiding to survive (5 and up)   **940.53**
Living with a single parent (4 and up)

        306.8

Making a new home in America (4-6)

        325.73

My friend Leslie (1-3)   **362.4**
Not my family: sharing the truth about alcoholism (4 and up)   **362.29**
Talking about stepfamilies (4 and up)

        306.8

Rosenberry, Vera
(il) Hurwitz, J. Anne Frank: life in hiding

        92

Rosenblum, Richard, 1928-
(il) Branley, F. M. Earthquakes   **551.2**

Rosenzweig, Hilde, 1923-1941
        About
Adler, D. A. Hilde and Eli, children of the Holocaust (3-5)   **940.53**

Roser, Nancy
(ed) Adventuring with books. See Adventuring with books   **011.6**

Roses red, violets blue. Johnson, S. A.

        582.13

Rosetta stone
Giblin, J. The riddle of the Rosetta Stone (5 and up)   **493**

Rosh ha-Shanah
Kimmel, E. A. Days of Awe (3-6)   **296.4**
        Fiction
Goldin, B. D. The world's birthday   **E**

Rosie. Calmenson, S.   **636.7**

Rosie and Michael. Viorst, J.   **E**

Rosie the riveter. Colman, P.   **331.4**

Rosie's walk. Hutchins, P.   **E**

Ross, Betsy, 1752-1836
        About
Wallner, A. Betsy Ross (k-2)   **92**

Ross, Gayle
How Rabbit tricked Otter and other Cherokee trickster stories (4-6)   **398.2**

Contents: Flint visits Rabbit; How Rabbit tricked Otter; Why Possum's tail is bare; Rabbit escapes from the wolves; How Deer won his antlers; Why Deer's teeth are blunt; Rabbit helps Wildcat hunt turkeys; Rabbit goes duck hunting; Rabbit and the tar wolf; Rabbit races with Turtle; Bear dines with Rabbit; Rabbit steals from Fox; Rabbit sends Wolf to the sunset; Rabbit dances with the people; What became of Rabbit

How Turtle's back was cracked (k-3)

        398.2

(jt. auth) Bruchac, J. The girl who married the Moon   **398.2**

Ross, Kathy, 1948-
Crafts for Kwanzaa (1-3)   **745.5**
Crafts for Valentine's Day (1-3)   **745.5**
Every day is Earth Day (1-3)   **745.58**

Ross, Pat
M and M and the bad news babies. See note under Ross, P. Meet M and M   **E**
M and M and the Halloween monster. See note under Ross, P. Meet M and M

        E

M and M and the haunted house game. See note under Ross, P. Meet M and M

        E

M and M and the Santa secrets. See note under Ross, P. Meet M and M   **E**
M and M and the super child afternoon. See note under Ross, P. Meet M and M

        E

Meet M and M   **E**

Ross, Ramon Royal, 1930-
Harper & Moon (6 and up)   **Fic**

Ross, Stewart
Shakespeare and Macbeth (5 and up)

        822.3

Ross, Tony, 1938-
(il) Danziger, P. Amber Brown is not a crayon   **Fic**
(il) Going green. See Going green   **363.7**
(il) Noble, T. H. Meanwhile back at the ranch   **E**
(il) Willis, J. Earthlets, as explained by Professor Xargle   **E**

Rosy Cole discovers America!. Greenwald, S. See note under Greenwald, S. Give us a great big smile, Rosy Cole   **Fic**

Rosy Cole: she walks in beauty. Greenwald, S. See note under Greenwald, S. Give us a great big smile, Rosy Cole   **Fic**

Rosy dock, The story of. Baker, J.   **508**

Rosy's garden: a child's keepsake of flowers. Laird, E.   **635.9**

Rosy's romance. Greenwald, S. See note under Greenwald, S. Give us a great big smile, Rosy Cole   **Fic**

Roth, Robert
(il) Levine, A. A. Pearl Moscowitz's last stand   **E**

Roth, Susan L.
The story of light (k-3)   **398.2**
(il) Bruchac, J. The great ball game

        398.2

Roth-Hano, Renée, 1931-
Touch wood (6 and up)   **Fic**

Ruff, Donna
(il) Adler, D. A. Our Golda: the story of Golda Meir   **92**
(il) Faber, D. Eleanor Roosevelt: first lady of the world   **92**
(il) Oneal, Z. Grandma Moses: painter of rural America   **92**

Ruffins, Reynold, 1930-
(il) Aardema, V. Misoso   **398.2**
(jt. auth) Sarnoff, J. Words: a book about the origins of everyday words and phrases   **422**

Rufus M. Estes, E. See note under Estes, E. The Moffats   **Fic**

Rugs
See also Carpets
Fiction
Blood, C. L. The goat in the rug   **E**

Ruins *See* Excavations (Archeology)

Ruiz, Andrés Llamas *See* Llamas Ruiz, Andrés

Rulers *See* Kings, queens, rulers, etc.

Rules of order *See* Parliamentary practice

Rumania *See* Romania

Rumpelstiltskin. Grimm, J.
In The Classic fairy tales p197-98   **398.2**
In Grimm, J. About wise men and simpletons p77-79   **398.2**
In Grimm, J. The complete Grimm's fairy tales p264-68   **398.2**
In Tomie dePaola's favorite nursery tales p46-52   **398.2**

Rumpelstiltskin. Thane, A.
In Thane, A. Plays from famous stories and fairy tales p58-76   **812**

Rumpelstiltskin. Zelinsky, P. O.   **398.2**

Rumpelstiltskin by any other name. Brooke, W. J.
In Brooke, W. J. Teller of tales p47-72   **S C**

Rumpelstiltzkin. Grimm, J.
In The Blue fairy book p96-99   **398.2**
In The Rainbow fairy book p63-67   **398.2**

The **runaway** bunny. Brown, M. W.   **E**

Runaway children
Fiction
Avi. Encounter at Easton (5 and up)   **Fic**
Holman, F. Slake's limbo (6 and up)   **Fic**

Runaway opposites. Wilbur, R.   **811**

Runaway Ralph. Cleary, B. See note under Cleary, B. The mouse and the motorcycle   **Fic**

Running
Parker, S. Running a race (3-5)   **796.42**
Fiction
Snyder, Z. K. Cat running (4 and up)   **Fic**

Running a parent/child workshop. Feinberg, S.   **027.62**

Running a race. Parker, S.   **796.42**

Rural life *See* Country life; Farm life

Rush, Barbara
(jt. auth) Schwartz, H. The diamond tree   **398.2**

Rushen Coatie. Jacobs, J.
In Jacobs, J. English fairy tales p367-71   **398.2**

Russell, John
A saga
In Shedlock, M. L. The art of the storyteller p165-67   **372.6**

Russell, Lynne
(il) Linden, A. M. One smiling grandma   **E**

Russell and Elisa. Hurwitz, J. See note under Hurwitz, J. Rip-roaring Russell   **Fic**

Russell rides again. Hurwitz, J. See note under Hurwitz, J. Rip-roaring Russell   **Fic**

Russell sprouts. Hurwitz, J. See note under Hurwitz, J. Rip-roaring Russell   **Fic**

Russia
See also Russia (Republic); Soviet Union
Fiction
Krasnopolsky, F. L. I remember (4 and up)   **Fic**
Lasky, K. The night journey (4 and up)   **Fic**
Polacco, P. Rechenka's eggs   **E**
Schur, M. The circlemaker (5 and up)   **Fic**
Folklore
See Folklore—Russia
Kings, queens, rulers, etc.
Stanley, D. Peter the Great (3-5)   **92**

Russia (Republic)
See also Commonwealth of Independent States; Russia; Soviet Union
Russia (5 and up)   **947**
Social life and customs
Kendall, R. Russian girl (3-5)   **947.086**
Russia (5 and up)   **947**

Russian Americans
Fiction
Cech, J. My grandmother's journey   **E**

Russian Empire *See* Russia

Russian fairy tales. Afanas'ev, A. N.   **398.2**

Russian girl. Kendall, R.   **947.086**

Russo, Marisabina
A visit to Oma   **E**
Waiting for Hannah   **E**

Russo, Susan, 1947-
(il) Adoff, A. Eats: poems   **811**

Rust, Graham
(il) Burnett, F. H. The secret garden   **Fic**

Rustin, Bayard, 1910-1987
See/See also pages in the following book(s):
Jacobs, W. J. Great lives: human rights p229-37 (5 and up)   **920**

Rutan, Dick
About
Taylor, R. L. The first unrefueled flight around the world (4 and up)   **629.13**

Ruth, Babe, 1895-1948
About
Jacobs, W. J. They shaped the game (4 and up)   **920**
See/See also pages in the following book(s):
Kramer, S. Baseball's greatest hitters p22-29 (2-4)   **920**

Ruth, George Herman *See* Ruth, Babe, 1895-1948

Ruth Law thrills a nation. Brown, D.
629.13

Ryan, Bryan
(ed) Hispanic American almanac. See Hispanic American almanac [junior version]
305.8

Ryan, Cheli Durán *See* Durán, Cheli

Ryan, DyAnne DiSalvo- *See* DiSalvo-Ryan, DyAnne, 1954-

Rydberg, Abraham Viktor *See* Rydberg, Viktor, 1828-1895

Rydberg, Viktor, 1828-1895
Lindgren, A. The Tomten   **E**

Ryden, Hope
The beaver (3-5)   **599.32**
Out of the wild (4 and up)   **636**
Your cat's wild cousins (4-6)   **599.74**
Your dog's wild cousins (4-6)   **599.74**

Ryder, Joanne
Lizard in the sun (k-2)   **597.9**
My father's hands   **E**
Under your feet (k-3)   **811**
Where butterflies grow (k-2)   **595.7**
White bear, ice bear (k-2)   **599.74**

Rylant, Cynthia
All I see   **E**
An angel for Solomon Singer   **E**
Appalachia   **974**
Best wishes (1-3)   **92**
A blue-eyed daisy (5 and up)   **Fic**
Children of Christmas (4 and up)
S C
Contents: The Christmas tree man; Halfway home; For being good; Ballerinas and bears; Silver packages; All the stars in the sky
Ellie's valentine
In Valentine's Day: stories and poems p21-36   **810.8**
Every living thing (5 and up)   **S C**
Contents: Slower than the rest; Retired; Boar out there; Papa's parrot; A pet; Spaghetti; Drying out; Stray; Planting things; A bad road for cats; Safe; Shells
A fine white dust (5 and up)   **Fic**
Henry and Mudge   **E**
Henry and Mudge and the bedtime thumps. See note under Rylant, C. Henry and Mudge   **E**
Henry and Mudge and the best day of all. See note under Rylant, C. Henry and Mudge   **E**

Henry and Mudge and the careful cousin. See note under Rylant, C. Henry and Mudge   **E**
Henry and Mudge and the forever sea. See note under Rylant, C. Henry and Mudge   **E**
Henry and Mudge and the happy cat. See note under Rylant, C. Henry and Mudge   **E**
Henry and Mudge and the long weekend. See note under Rylant, C. Henry and Mudge   **E**
Henry and Mudge and the wild wind. See note under Rylant, C. Henry and Mudge   **E**
Henry and Mudge get the cold shivers. See note under Rylant, C. Henry and Mudge   **E**
Henry and Mudge in puddle trouble. See note under Rylant, C. Henry and Mudge   **E**
Henry and Mudge in the green time. See note under Rylant, C. Henry and Mudge   **E**
Henry and Mudge in the sparkle days. See note under Rylant, C. Henry and Mudge   **E**
Henry and Mudge take the big test. See note under Rylant, C. Henry and Mudge   **E**
Henry and Mudge under the yellow moon. See note under Rylant, C. Henry and Mudge   **E**
Missing May (5 and up)   **Fic**
Mr. Griggs' work   **E**
Mr. Putter and Tabby bake the cake. See note under Rylant, C. Mr. Putter and Tabby pour the tea   **E**
Mr. Putter and Tabby pick the pears. See note under Rylant, C. Mr. Putter and Tabby pour the tea   **E**
Mr. Putter and Tabby pour the tea   **E**
Mr. Putter and Tabby walk the dog. See note under Rylant, C. Mr. Putter and Tabby pour the tea   **E**
Night in the country   **E**
The relatives came   **E**
This year's garden   **E**
The Van Gogh Cafe (4-6)   **Fic**
When I was young in the mountains   **E**

S

S.O.R. losers. Avi   **Fic**
S.S.T.'s *See* Supersonic transport planes
Saar, Betye, 1926-
See/See also pages in the following book(s):
Sills, L. Visions p32-45 (5 and up)   **920**
Saari, Peggy
Explorers & discoverers   **920.003**
Saavedra, Dane
(jt. auth) Madaras, L. The what's happening to my body? book for boys: a growing up guide for parents and sons   **613.9**

Sam's car. Lindgren, B.   E

Sam's cookie. Lindgren, B. See note under
Lindgren, B. Sam's car   E

Sam's girl friend. Schwartz, A.
In Schwartz, A. All of our noses are here,
and other noodle tales p58-63
398.2

Sam's new pet. Schwartz, A.
In Schwartz, A. Scary stories 3 p55-56
398.2

Sam's potty. Lindgren, B. See note under
Lindgren, B. Sam's car   E

Sam's rooster. Porte-Thomas, B. A.
In Porte-Thomas, B. A turkey drive and
other tales p17-22   S C

Sam's story. Porte-Thomas, B. A.
In Porte-Thomas, B. A turkey drive and
other tales p37-43   S C

Sam's teddy bear. Lindgren, B. See note under
Lindgren, B. Sam's car   E

Sam's wagon. Lindgren, B. See note under
Lindgren, B. Sam's car   E

Samson, Suzanne M.
Fairy dusters and blazing stars   582.13

Samuel Eaton's day. Waters, K.   974.4

Samuel Todd's book of great inventions.
Konigsburg, E. L.   608

Samuels, Barbara
Duncan & Dolores   E

Samuel's ghost. Crossley-Holland, K.
In Crossley-Holland, K. British folk tales
p73-76   398.2

Samuelson, Joan
See/See also pages in the following book(s):
Littlefield, B. Champions p39-52 (5 and up)
920

The **samurai's** daughter. San Souci, R.
398.2

San Diego (Calif.)
Social life and customs
Krull, K. The other side (4 and up)
305.8

San Francisco (Calif.)
Climo, S. City! San Francisco (4 and up)
979.4
Description
Wilder, L. I. West from home (6 and up)
92
Fiction
Yep, L. Child of the owl (5 and up)
Fic
Yep, L. Dragonwings (5 and up)   Fic
Yep, L. Thief of hearts (5 and up)   Fic
Social life and customs
Brown, T. Konnichiwa! (1-4)   305.8

San Francisco Insect Zoo
Meyers, S. Insect zoo (4-6)   595.7

San Nicolas Island (Calif.)
Fiction
O'Dell, S. Island of the Blue Dolphins (5
and up)   Fic

San Souci, Daniel
(il) Douglas, W. O. Muir of the mountains
92
(il) San Souci, R. Sootface   398.2
(il) Shepard, A. The gifts of Wali Dad
398.2

San Souci, Robert, 1946-
Cut from the same cloth (4-6)   398.2
Contents: The Star Maiden; Bess Call; Drop Star; Molly
Cottontail; Annie Christmas; Susanna and Simon; Sal Fink;
Sweet Betsey from Pike; Old Sally Cato; Pale-Face Light-
ning; Pohaha; Sister Fox and Brother Coyote; Hekeke;
Otoonah; Hiiaka
The enchanted tapestry (k-3)   398.2
The faithful friend (2-4)   398.2
The Hobyahs (k-3)   398.2
Larger than life (4-6)   398.2
Contents: John Henry: the steel-driving man; Old Stor-
malong: the deep-water sailor; Slue-foot Sue and Pecos Bill;
Strap Buckner: the Texas fighter; Paul Bunyan and Babe the
Blue Ox
More short & shivery (4 and up)   398.2
Contents: "Hold him, Tabb!"; The witches' eyes; The
duppy; Two snakes; The draug; The vampire cat; Windigo
Island; The haunted inn; The rolling head; The Croglin
Grange vampire; The Yara; "Me, myself"; Island of fear;
Three who sought death; Sister Death and the healer; The
mouse tower; The devil and Tom Walker; The greedy
daughter; The pirate; The golden arm; The serpent woman;
Loft the enchanter; The accursed house; Escape up the tree;
The headrest; The thing in the woods; King of the Cats;
The dead mother; Knock . . . knock . . . knock . . .; Twice
surprised
The samurai's daughter (1-4)   398.2
Short & shivery (4 and up)   398.2
Contents: The robber bridegroom; Jack Frost; The waterfall of ghosts; The ghost's cap; The witch cat; The green
mist; The Cegua; The ghostly little girl; The midnight mass
of the Dead; Tailypo; Lady Eleanore's mantle; The soldier
and the vampire; The skeleton's dance; Scared to death;
Swallowed alive; The deacon's ghost; Nuckelavee; The ad-
venture of the German student; Billy Mosby's night ride;
The hunter in the haunted forest; Brother and sister; The
lovers of Dismal Swamp; Boneless; The death waltz; The
ghost of Misery Hill; The loup-garou; The golem; Lavender;
The goblin spider; The Halloween pony
The snow wife (2-4)   398.2
Sootface (1-4)   398.2
Sukey and the mermaid (1-4)   398.2
The talking eggs (k-3)   398.2
The white cat (2-4)   398.2
Young Merlin (2-5)   398.2

Sancha, Sheila, 1924-
Walter Dragun's town (6 and up)
942.03

Sanchez, Enrique O., 1942-
(il) Castañeda, O. S. Abuela's weave   E

Sanctuaries, Wildlife *See* Wildlife refuges

Sanctuary. Fraser, M. A.   639.9

Sanctuary movement
See also Refugees

Sand
See also Quicksand

Sand and fog. Brandenburg, J.   968.8

Sand cake. Asch, F.   E

Sand Creek, Battle of, 1864
See/See also pages in the following book(s):
Ehrlich, A. Wounded Knee: an Indian history of the American West (6 and up)
970.004

Schnur, Steven
  The shadow children (5 and up)   Fic
  The tie man's miracle   E

Schoenherr, John, 1935-
  (il) Eckert, A. W. Incident at Hawk's Hill
       Fic
  (il) George, J. C. Julie of the wolves
       Fic
  (il) Morey, W. Gentle Ben   Fic
  (il) North, S. Rascal   599.74
  (il) Yolen, J. Owl moon   E

The **scholar** Be. Terada, A. M.
  In Terada, A. M. Under the starfruit tree
    p42-49   398.2

Schomp, Virginia
  The bottlenose dolphin (3-5)   599.5

Schon, Isabel
  Books in Spanish for children and young
    adults: an annotated guide [series I-VI]
       011.6
  (ed) Contemporary Spanish-speaking writers
    and illustrators for children and young
    adults. See Contemporary Spanish-
    speaking writers and illustrators for chil-
    dren and young adults   920.003

School bus. Crews, D.   E

School drama *See* College and school drama

A **school** for Pompey Walker. Rosen, M. J.
       Fic

School integration
  Coles, R. The story of Ruby Bridges (1-3)
       370.19
  O'Neill, L. Little Rock (5 and up)
       370.19

School journalism *See* College and school journalism

School libraries
  See also Children's libraries
  American Association of School Librarians.
    Information power   027.8
  Berger, P. CD-ROM for schools   025.2
  Bucher, K. T. Computers & technology in
    school library media centers   027.8
  Craver, K. W. School library media centers
    in the 21st century   027.8
  Skaggs, G. Off the wall!   027.8
  Van Orden, P. J. The collection program in
    schools   027.8
      Activity projects
  Cook, S. A. Books, battles, and bees
       027.8
      Automation
  Automation for school libraries   027.8
      Catalogs
  The Elementary school library collection
       011.6
  Middle and junior high school library cata-
    log   011.6
      Periodicals
  Emergency Librarian   027.6205
  Library Talk   027.805
  School Library Journal   027.805
  School Library Media Annual   027.805

School Library Media Quarterly
       027.805
School Library Journal   027.805
School Library Media Annual   027.805
School library media centers in the 21st centu-
  ry. Craver, K. W.   027.8
School Library Media Quarterly   027.805
School media centers *See* Instructional materi-
  als centers
School science projects *See* Science projects
School spirit. Hurwitz, J. See note under Hur-
  witz, J. Class clown   Fic
School stories
  Allard, H. Miss Nelson is missing!   E
  Avi. S.O.R. losers (5 and up)   Fic
  Betancourt, J. My name is brain Brian (4-6)
       Fic
  Bunting, E. Spying on Miss Müller (5 and
    up)   Fic
  Burnett, F. H. A little princess (4-6)   Fic
  Byars, B. C. The burning questions of Bingo
    Brown (4 and up)   Fic
  Calmenson, S. The principal's new clothes
       E
  Carrick, C. What a wimp! (3-5)   Fic
  Caudill, R. Did you carry the flag today,
    Charley? (2-4)   Fic
  Cleary, B. Dear Mr. Henshaw (4-6)   Fic
  Cleary, B. Ellen Tebbits (3-5)   Fic
  Cleary, B. Mitch and Amy (3-5)   Fic
  Cleary, B. Muggie Maggie (2-4)   Fic
  Cleary, B. Otis Spofford (3-5)   Fic
  Cleary, B. Ramona the pest (3-5)   Fic
  Cohen, B. Molly's Pilgrim (2-4)   Fic
  Cohen, M. See you in second grade!   E
  Conford, E. Dear Lovey Hart: I am desper-
    ate (6 and up)   Fic
  Crew, L. Nekomah Creek (4-6)   Fic
  Crews, D. School bus   E
  Dahl, R. Matilda (4-6)   Fic
  Danziger, P. Amber Brown is not a crayon
    (2-4)   Fic
  Danziger, P. The cat ate my gymsuit (5 and
    up)   Fic
  Danziger, P. Everyone else's parents said yes
    (4-6)   Fic
  DeClements, B. 6th grade can really kill you
    (5 and up)   Fic
  Deedy, C. A. The library dragon   E
  DeJong, M. The wheel on the school (4-6)
       Fic
  Fine, A. Flour babies (6 and up)   Fic
  Fitzhugh, L. Harriet the spy (4 and up)
       Fic
  Gantos, J. Heads or tails (5 and up)
       Fic
  Giff, P. R. Love, from the fifth-grade celeb-
    rity (4-6)   Fic
  Giff, P. R. Watch out, Ronald Morgan!
       E
  Gilson, J. 4B goes wild (4-6)   Fic
  Gilson, J. Itchy Richard (2-4)   Fic
  Hahn, M. D. Daphne's book (5 and up)
       Fic
  Hansen, J. The gift-giver (4-6)   Fic

School stories—*Continued*

Henkes, K. Chrysanthemum   E

Hines, A. G. What Joe saw   E

Honeycutt, N. The all new Jonah Twist (3-5)   Fic

Honeycutt, N. Invisible Lissa (3-5)   Fic

Howe, J. The day the teacher went bananas   E

Hurwitz, J. Class clown (2-4)   Fic

Hurwitz, J. Rip-roaring Russell (2-4)   Fic

Iwamatsu, A. J. Crow Boy   E

Keller, H. Harry and Tuck   E

Kline, S. Herbie Jones (3-5)   Fic

Kline, S. Horrible Harry in room 2B (2-4)   Fic

Kline, S. Mary Marony, mummy girl (2-4)   Fic

Lord, B. B. In the Year of the Boar and Jackie Robinson (4-6)   Fic

Lowry, L. Your move, J.P.! (5 and up)   Fic

Maguire, G. Seven spiders spinning (4-6)   Fic

Martin, A. M. Rachel Parker, kindergarten show-off   E

Mills, C. Dynamite Dinah (3-5)   Fic

Naylor, P. R. The agony of Alice (5 and up)   Fic

Noble, T. H. The day Jimmy's boa ate the wash   E

Nordstrom, U. The secret language (3-5)   Fic

Park, B. Junie B. Jones and her big fat mouth   E

Park, B. Skinnybones (4-6)   Fic

Rathmann, P. Officer Buckle and Gloria   E

Sachar, L. Wayside School gets a little stranger (3-6)   Fic

Schwartz, A. Annabelle Swift, kindergartner   E

Schwartz, A. Bea and Mr. Jones   E

Shalant, P. Beware of kissing Lizard Lips (4-6)   Fic

Sharmat, M. W. Getting something on Maggie Marmelstein (3-5)   Fic

Shreve, S. R. The flunking of Joshua T. Bates (3-5)   Fic

Snyder, Z. K. Libby on Wednesdays (5 and up)   Fic

Spinelli, J. There's a girl in my hammerlock (5 and up)   Fic

Tolan, S. S. Save Halloween! (5 and up)   Fic

Udry, J. M. What Mary Jo shared   E

Wells, R. Timothy goes to school   E

Yarbrough, C. The shimmershine queens (4-6)   Fic

Schools

> *See also* Education; Nursery schools

Fiction

> *See* School stories

Law and legislation

See/See also pages in the following book(s):

Burns, M. I am not a short adult! p41-52 (4 and up)   305.23

Poetry

I thought I'd take my rat to school (3-5)   **811.008**

United States—History

Loeper, J. J. Going to school in 1776 (4 and up)   370.9

Loeper, J. J. Going to school in 1876 (4 and up)   370.9

See/See also pages in the following book(s):

Freedman, R. Children of the wild West p59-69 (4 and up)   978

School's out. Hurwitz, J. See note under Hurwitz, J. Class clown   Fic

Schotter, Roni

Captain Snap and the children of Vinegar Lane   E

Passover magic   E

Schouweiler, Tom, 1965-

Germans in America

In The In America series   305.8

Schroeder, Alan, 1961-

Carolina shout!   E

Ragtime Tumpie   E

Schubert, Franz, 1797-1828

About

Thompson, W. Franz Schubert (5 and up)   92

Schuett, Stacey

(il) Jukes, M. I'll see you in my dreams   E

(il) Lankford, M. D. Is it dark? is it light?   E

Schulz, Andrea

North Carolina

In Hello USA series   973

Schulz, Janet

(il) McPherson, S. S. The workers' detective: a story about Dr. Alice Hamilton   92

Schumann, Clara, 1819-1896

See/See also pages in the following book(s):

Krull, K. Lives of the musicians p40-43 (4 and up)   920

Schur, Maxine, 1948-

The circlemaker (5 and up)   Fic

Schutzer, Dena

(il) McKissack, P. C. A million fish—more or less   E

Schwartz, Alvin, 1927-1992

All of our noses are here, and other noodle tales (k-2)   398.2

Contents: Jane gets a donkey; Grandpa misses the boat; All of our noses are here; The best boy in the world; Sam's girl friend

And the green grass grew all around   398.2

The bad news

In From sea to shining sea p311   810.8

Busy buzzing bumblebees and other tongue twisters (k-2)   808.88

Schwartz, Alvin, 1927-1992—*Continued*
The cat's elbow, and other secret languages (4 and up) 652
Cross your fingers, spit in your hat: superstitions and other beliefs (4 and up) 398
Fat man in a fur coat, and other bear stories (4 and up) **599.74**
Flapdoodle: pure nonsense from American folklore (4 and up) 398
Ghosts! (k-2) **398.2**
Contents: The haunted house; Susie; A little green bottle; The umbrella; Three little ghosts; The teeny-tiny woman; Ghost, get lost
I saw you in the bathtub, and other folk rhymes (k-2) **398.2**
In a dark, dark room, and other scary stories (k-2) **398.2**
Contents: The teeth; In the graveyard; The green ribbon; In a dark, dark room; The night it rained; The pirate
More scary stories to tell in the dark (4 and up) **398.2**
Scary stories 3 (4 and up) **398.2**
Contents: The appointment; The bus stop; Faster and faster; Just delicious; Hello, Kate!; The black dog; Footsteps; Like cats' eyes; Bess; Harold; The dead hand; Such things happen; The wolf girl; The dream; Sam's new pet; Maybe you will remember; The red spot; No, thanks; The trouble; Strangers; The hog; Is something wrong?; It's "Him!"; T-H-U-P-P-P-P-P-P-P!; You may be the next . . .
Scary stories to tell in the dark (4 and up) **398.2**
There is a carrot in my ear, and other noodle tales (k-2) **398.2**
Contents: The Browns take the day off; Sam and Jane go camping; Mr. Brown washes his underwear; Jane grows a carrot; Grandpa buys a pumpkin egg; It is time to go to sleep
Tomfoolery: trickery and foolery with words (4 and up) 398
A twister of twists, a tangler of tongues (4 and up) **808.88**
Unriddling: all sorts of riddles to puzzle your guessery (4 and up) **398.6**
The wendigo
In Schwartz, A. Scary stories to tell in the dark p49-53 **398.2**
Witcracks: jokes and jests from American folklore (4 and up) 398

Schwartz, Amy, 1954-
Annabelle Swift, kindergartner E
Bea and Mr. Jones E
Oma and Bobo E
A teeny, tiny baby E
(il) Hest, A. The crack-of-dawn walkers E
(il) Hest, A. Nana's birthday party E
(il) Hest, A. The purple coat E
(il) Lasky, K. My island grandma E
(il) Schwartz, H. Albert goes Hollywood E

Schwartz, Carol, 1954-
(il) Brenner, B. Where's that insect? **595.7**

Schwartz, Daniel Bennett, 1929-
(il) Byars, B. C. The house of wings Fic

Schwartz, David M., 1951-
The hidden life of the pond (3-5) **574.92**

How much is a million? E
If you made a million E
Yanomami **981**

Schwartz, Henry
Albert goes Hollywood E
How I captured a dinosaur. See note under Schwartz, H. Albert goes Hollywood E

Schwartz, Howard, 1945-
The diamond tree (3-5) **398.2**
Contents: The giant Og and the ark; The magic pitcher; Chusham and the wind; Katanya; The magic sandals of Abu Kassim; The water witch; The enormous frog; A tale of two chickens; A palace of bird beaks; The diamond tree; Moving a mountain; The bear and the children; The goblin; The prince who thought he was a rooster; The angel's wings

Schwartz, Lynne Sharon
The four questions (k-3) **296.4**

Schweninger, Ann
(il) The Read-aloud treasury. See The Read-aloud treasury **808.8**

Science
Graham, I. Fakes and forgeries (5 and up) **001.9**
Markle, S. Science to the rescue (4 and up) **507.8**
Simon, S. The dinosaur is the biggest animal that ever lived, and other wrong ideas you thought were true (3-6) **500**

Bibliography
Kennedy, D. M. Science & technology in fact and fiction a guide to children's books **016.5**
Outstanding science trade books for children **016.5**
Science books & films' Best books for children, 1992-1995 **016.5**

Bibliography—Periodicals
Appraisal **016.5**
Science Books & Films **016.5**

Dictionaries
The Dorling Kindersley science encyclopedia (5 and up) **503**
The New book of popular science **503**
Simon, S. Science dictionary (4 and up) **503**

Exhibitions
Katz, P. Great science fair projects (3-6) **507.8**

Experiments
See also particular branches of science with the subdivision Experiments, e.g. Chemistry—Experiments; etc.
Allison, L. Gee, Wiz! (4 and up) **507.8**
Amato, C. Super science fair projects (4 and up) **507.8**
Ardley, N. The science book of hot & cold (3-5) **536**
Ardley, N. The science book of the senses (3-5) **612.8**
Burnie, D. How nature works (4 and up) **508**
Cobb, V. Gobs of goo (2-4) **547**
Cobb, V. More science experiments you can eat (5 and up) **507.8**

Serraillier, Ian, 1912-
The silver sword (5 and up)   Fic

Service, Pamela F.
Stinker from space (4-6)   Fic
Storm at the edge of time (5 and up)
    Fic

Service, Robert W. (Robert William), 1874-1958
The cremation of Sam McGee (4 and up)
    811
The shooting of Dan McGrew (4 and up)
    811

A service dog goes to school. Smith, E. S.
    636.7

Service stations
Gibbons, G. Fill it up! (k-3)   629.28

Serving special needs series
Friedberg, J. B. Portraying persons with disabilities: an annotated bibliography of nonfiction for children and teenagers
    016
Robertson, D. Portraying persons with disabilities: an annotated bibliography of fiction for children and teenagers   016.8
Rudman, M. K. Books to help children cope with separation and loss   016.3627

Serving special populations series
Baskin, B. H. More notes from a different drummer   016.8

Servitude *See* Slavery

Settling the West [series]
Bentley, J. Brides, midwives, and widows
    978
Bentley, J. Explorers, trappers, and guides
    979.5

Seuss, Dr.
The 500 hats of Bartholomew Cubbins
    E
And to think that I saw it on Mulberry Street   E
Bartholomew and the oobleck   E
The cat in the hat   E
The Cat in the Hat beginner book dictionary. See The Cat in the Hat beginner book dictionary   423
The Cat in the Hat beginner book dictionary in French. See The Cat in the Hat beginner book dictionary in French
    443
The Cat in the Hat beginner book dictionary in Spanish. See The Cat in the Hat beginner book dictionary in Spanish
    463
The cat in the hat comes back! See note under Seuss, Dr. The cat in the hat   E
Green eggs and ham   E
Horton hatches the egg   E
Horton hears a Who!   E
How the Grinch stole Christmas   E
If I ran the circus   E
If I ran the zoo   E
McElligot's pool   E
Oh, the places you'll go!   E

About
Weidt, M. N. Oh, the places he went (3-5)
    92

Seven blind mice. Young, E.   398.2

Seven candles for Kwanzaa. Pinkney, A. D.
    394.2

The seven Chinese brothers. Mahy, M.
    398.2

Seven clever brothers. Mayo, M.
In Mayo, M. Magical tales from many lands p76-84   398.2

Seven-day magic. Eager, E.   Fic

The seven days of creation. Fisher, L. E.
    222

The seven foals. Moe, J. E.
In The Red fairy book p346-53   398.2

The Seven-headed serpent
In The Yellow fairy book p60-63
    398.2

Seven kisses in a row. MacLachlan, P.
    Fic

The seven ravens. Grimm, J.   398.2
also in Grimm, J. The complete Grimm's fairy tales p137-39   398.2

The seven Semyons. Afanas'ev, A. N.
In Afanas'ev, A. N. Russian fairy tales p410-14   398.2

Seven spiders spinning. Maguire, G.   Fic

The seven Swabians. Grimm, J.
In Grimm, J. The complete Grimm's fairy tales p538-42   398.2

The Seven voyages of Sindbad the sailor
In The Arabian nights entertainments p122-86   398.2

The seven weavers. Vuong, L. D.
In Vuong, L. D. Sky legends of Vietnam p71-93   398.2

Seventeen kings and forty-two elephants. Mahy, M.   E

Seventh book of junior authors & illustrators
    920.003

Seventh grade. Soto, G.
In Soto, G. Baseball in April, and other stories p52-59   S C

Seventy-five years of Children's Book Week posters. See 75 years of Children's Book Week posters   808.06

Sewage disposal
Coombs, K. M. Flush! (3-6)   628.3

Sewall, Marcia, 1935-
People of the breaking day (3-6)
    970.004
The pilgrims of Plimoth (3-6)   974.4
(il) Gardiner, J. R. Stone Fox   Fic
(il) Hesse, K. Sable   Fic
(il) Joosse, B. M. Nobody's cat   E
(il) Kennedy, R. Richard Kennedy: collected stories   S C
(il) Schotter, R. Captain Snap and the children of Vinegar Lane   E
(il) Thomas, J. R. Saying good-bye to Grandma   E

Shaw, Alison, 1953-
(comp) Until I saw the sea and other poems.
See Until I saw the sea and other poems
811.008

Shaw, Annette
(il) Terkel, S. N. Understanding cancer
616.99

Shaw, Charles, 1892-1974
It looked like spilt milk   E

Shaw, Nancy
Sheep in a jeep   E
Sheep in a shop. See note under Shaw, N.
Sheep in a jeep   E
Sheep on a ship. See note under Shaw, N.
Sheep in a jeep   E
Sheep out to eat. See note under Shaw, N.
Sheep in a jeep   E
Sheep take a hike. See note under Shaw, N.
Sheep in a jeep   E

Shaw-Smith, Emma
(il) Gershator, D. Bread is for eating   E

Shawn and Uncle John. Steptoe, J.
In To ride a butterfly p53-55   810.8

Shawnee Indians
Shorto, R. Tecumseh and the dream of an
American Indian nation (5 and up)
92

Shay, Frank
The Salem ghost ship
In From sea to shining sea p113-14
810.8

She come bringing me that little baby girl.
Greenfield, E.   E

Shecter, Ben
(il) Benchley, N. A ghost named Fred
E
(il) Sharmat, M. W. Getting something on
Maggie Marmelstein   Fic
(il) Zolotow, C. The hating book   E

Shedlock, Marie L., 1854-1935
The art of the story-teller   372.6
Filial piety
In Shedlock, M. L. The art of the story-
teller p229-32   372.6
The folly of panic
In Shedlock, M. L. The art of the story-
teller p222-24   372.6
Hafiz, the stone-cutter
In Shedlock, M. L. The art of the story-
teller p179-82   372.6
Snegourka
In Shedlock, M. L. The art of the story-
teller p195-97   372.6
The true spirit of a festival day
In Shedlock, M. L. The art of the story-
teller p225-28   372.6

Sheehan, Sean
Cuba (5 and up)   972.91

Sheep
Paladino, C. Spring fleece (3-6)   636.3
Fiction
Aardema, V. Borreguita and the coyote (k-3)
398.2
Carrick, C. In the moonlight, waiting   E

Paulsen, G. The haymeadow (6 and up)
Fic
Shaw, N. Sheep in a jeep   E
Poetry
Hale, S. J. Mary had a little lamb (k-2)
811

Sheep dogs
Ancona, G. Sheep dog (4 and up)   636.7

Sheep in a jeep. Shaw, N.   E

Sheep in a shop. Shaw, N. See note under
Shaw, N. Sheep in a jeep   E

Sheep on a ship. Shaw, N. See note under
Shaw, N. Sheep in a jeep   E

Sheep out to eat. Shaw, N. See note under
Shaw, N. Sheep in a jeep   E

Sheep take a hike. Shaw, N. See note under
Shaw, N. Sheep in a jeep   E

The **sheep,** the fox, and the wolf. Afanas'ev, A.
N.
In Afanas'ev, A. N. Russian fairy tales
p275-76   398.2

A **sheepish** tale. Marshall, J.
In Marshall, J. Rats on the roof, and other stories p19-27   S C

Sheila Rae, the brave. Henkes, K.   E

Shelby, Anne
Homeplace   E

Sheldon, Dyan
The whales' song   E

She'll be comin' round the mountain. Bullock,
K.   782.42

The **shell** woman & the king. Yep, L.
398.2

Shelley, Mary Wollstonecraft, 1797-1851
Mounseer Nongtongpaw
In A Nursery companion p118-22
820.8

Shellfish
See also Crabs; Lobsters; Mollusks

Shells
Abbott, R. T. Seashells of the world (5 and
up)   594
Arthur, A. Shell (4 and up)   594
Coldrey, J. Shells (3-5)   594
Florian, D. Discovering seashells (1-3)
594
Selsam, M. E. A first look at seashells (1-3)
594
Zoehfeld, K. W. What lives in a shell? (k-1)
591.4

Shells. Rylant, C.
In Rylant, C. Every living thing p73-81
S C

Shelowitz, Holly Ann
(il) Stein, S. B. Oh, baby!   E

Shemiaka the judge. Afanas'ev, A. N.
In Afanas'ev, A. N. Russian fairy tales
p625-27   398.2

Shepard, Aaron
The gifts of Wali Dad (2-4)   398.2

Simple Seng and the parrot. Carpenter, F.
In Carpenter, F. Tales of a Chinese grandmother p242-51   **398.2**

Simple sentences. Babbitt, N.
In Babbitt, N. The Devil's other storybook p63-71   **S C**

Simpleton and his little black hen. Pyle, H.
In Pyle, H. The wonder clock p217-28   **398.2**

Simpleton Peter. Reeves, J.
In Reeves, J. English fables and fairy stories p103-14   **398.2**

Simpson, Carol Mann, 1949-
Internet for library media specialists   **004**

Simpson, Lorna, 1960-
See/See also pages in the following book(s):
Wolf, S. Focus: five women photographers p50-59 (5 and up)   **920**

Sims, Blanche
(il) Kimmel, E. A. I took my frog to the library   **E**
(il) Kline, S. Mary Marony, mummy girl   **Fic**
(il) Ostrow, W. All about asthma   **616.2**
(il) Valentine's day: stories and poems. See Valentine's day: stories and poems   **810.8**

Sims, Rudine *See* Bishop, Rudine Sims, 1937-

Simulation methods
Skurzynski, G. Almost the real thing (5 and up)   **620**

Sinbad the sailor, The voyages of See note under Aladdin and other tales from the Arabian nights p187-246   **398.2**

Sincerely yours. James, E.   **808**

Sinclair, Jeff, 1958-
(il) Blum, R. Math tricks, puzzles & games   **793.7**

Sing a song of popcorn   **808.81**

Sing down the moon. O'Dell, S.   **Fic**

Sing me a story. Rosenberg, J.   **792.5**

The **sing-song** of Old Man Kangaroo. Kipling, R.
In Kipling, R. Just so stories   **S C**

Sing the songs of Thanksgiving. Fisher, A. L.
In Holiday plays round the year p101-11   **812.008**

Sing to the sun. Bryan, A.   **811**

Singer, Arthur, 1917-1990
(il) Robbins, C. S. Birds of North America   **598**

Singer, Beverly R.
(comp) Rising voices. See Rising voices   **810.8**

Singer, Isaac Bashevis, 1904-1991
The first Shlemiel
In The Laugh book p132-40   **808.8**
The fools of Chelm and the stupid carp
In The Random House book of humor for children p205-11   **817.008**

The fools of Chelm and their history (4 and up)   **Fic**
Mazel and Shlimazel (2-5)   **398.2**
Naftali the storyteller and his horse, Sus, and other stories (4 and up)   **S C**
Contents: Naftali the storyteller and his horse, Sus; Dalfunka, where the rich live forever; The Lantuch; A Hanukkah Eve in Warsaw; The fools of Chelm and the stupid carp; Lemel and Tzipa; The cat who thought she was a dog and the dog who thought he was a cat; Growing up
The power of light (4 and up)   **S C**
Contents: A Hanukkah evening in my parents' house; The extinguished lights; The parakeet named Dreidel; Menashe and Rachel; The squire; The power of light; Hershele and Hanukkah; Hanukkah in the poorhouse
Shrewd Todie and Lyzer the miser
In Bauer, C. F. Celebrations p121-25   **808.8**
The snow in Chelm
In Snowy day: stories and poems p25-29   **808.8**
Stories for children (4 and up)   **S C**
Contents: The elders of Chelm & Genendel's key; A tale of three wishes; The extinguished lights; Mazel & Shlimazel; Why Noah chose the dove; Zlateh the goat; A Hanukkah Eve in Warsaw; The fools of Chelm & the stupid carp; The wicked city; Rabbi Leib & the witch Cunegunde; The parakeet named Dreidel; Lemel & Tzipa; The day I got lost; Menashe & Rachel; Shlemiel the businessman; Joseph & Koza; A Hanukkah evening in my parents' house; Tsirtsur & Peziza; Naftali the storyteller & his horse, Sus; Hershele & Hanukkah; When Shlemiel went to Warsaw; Elijah the slave; The power of light; Growing up; The Lantuch; Utzel & his daughter, Poverty; The squire; Ole & Trufa; Dalfunka, where the rich live forever; Topiel & Tekla; Hanukkah in the poorhouse; Shrewd Todie & Lyzer the miser; The fearsome inn; The cat who thought she was a dog & the dog who thought he was a cat; Menasch's dream; Tashlik
When Shlemiel went to Warsaw & other stories (4 and up)   **398.2**
Contents: Shrewd Todie & Lyzer the miser; Tsirtsur & Peziza; Rabbi Leib & the witch Cunegunde; The elders of Chelm & Genendel's key; Shlemiel, the businessman; Utzel & his daughter Poverty; Menaseh's dream; When Shlemiel went to Warsaw
Zlateh the goat, and other stories (4 and up)   **398.2**
Contents: Fool's paradise; Grandmother's tale; The snow in Chelm; The mixed-up feet and the silly bridegroom; The first shlemiel; The Devil's trick; Zlateh the goat
About
Kresh, P. Isaac Bashevis Singer: the story of a storyteller (6 and up)   **92**
See/See also pages in the following book(s):
Krull, K. Lives of the writers p90-93 (4 and up)   **920**

Singer, Marilyn, 1948-
Family reunion (k-3)   **811**
Sky words (k-3)   **811**
Turtle in July (k-3)   **811**

Singer to the sea god. Alcock, V.   **Fic**

Singers
See also African American singers

Singing
Parker, S. Singing a song (3-5)   **612.7**
Fiction
Peterson, J. W. My mama sings   **E**

Singing a song. Parker, S.   **612.7**

Singing America (5 and up)   **811.008**

Singing bee!   **782.42**

The **Singing** bone
  In The Magic orange tree, and other Haitian folktales p91-97   **398.2**
The **singing** bone. Grimm, J.
  In Grimm, J. The complete Grimm's fairy tales p148-50   **398.2**
Singing games
  The Lap-time song and play book
        782.42
  Seeger, R. C. American folk songs for children in home, school and nursery school
        782.42
The **singing** green. Merriam, E.   **811**
The **singing** snake. Czernecki, S.   **398.2**
The **singing**, soaring lark. Grimm, J.
  In Grimm, J. The complete Grimm's fairy tales p399-404   **398.2**
The **singing** tortoise. Courlander, H.
  In Courlander, H. The cow-tail switch, and other West African stories p65-72
        398.2
The **singing** tortoise. Yeoman, J.
  In Yeoman, J. The singing tortoise and other animal folktales p27-33
        398.2
The **singing** tortoise and other animal folktales. Yeoman, J.   **398.2**
The **singing** tree and the talking bird. Afanas'ev, A. N.
  In Afanas'ev, A. N. Russian fairy tales p184-88   **398.2**
The **singing** turtle. MacDonald, M. R.
  In MacDonald, M. R. Look back and see p137-46   **372.6**
Single parent family
  Rosenberg, M. B. Living with a single parent (4 and up)   **306.8**
    Fiction
  Byars, B. C. The night swimmers (5 and up)
        Fic
  Greenfield, E. Sister (4 and up)   **Fic**
  Lowry, L. The one hundredth thing about Caroline (5 and up)   **Fic**
Sinnott, Susan
  Chinese railroad workers (4 and up)
        331.7
  Extraordinary Asian-Pacific Americans (5 and up)   **920**
  Extraordinary Hispanic Americans (5 and up)   **920**
Sino-Japanese Conflict, 1937-1945
    Fiction
  DeJong, M. The house of sixty fathers (4-6)
        Fic
Siouan Indians
  See also Dakota Indians; Mandan Indians; Oglala Indians
The **Sioux.** Osinski, A.   **970.004**
The **Sioux.** Sneve, V. D. H.   **970.004**
Sioux Indians *See* Dakota Indians
Sir Gammer Vans. Jacobs, J.
  In Jacobs, J. English fairy tales p261-63
        398.2

Sir Gawain and the Green Knight. Hastings, S.   **398.2**
Sir Gawain and the loathly lady. Hastings, S.   **398.2**
Sirvaitis, Karen, 1961-
  Florida
    In Hello USA series   **973**
  Michigan
    In Hello USA series   **973**
  Nevada
    In Hello USA series   **973**
  South Dakota
    In Hello USA series   **973**
  Tennessee
    In Hello USA series   **973**
  Utah
    In Hello USA series   **973**
  Virginia
    In Hello USA series   **973**
Sis, Peter
  Beach ball   **E**
  Follow the dream [biography of Christopher Columbus] (k-3)   **92**
  Komodo!   **E**
  An ocean world   **E**
  (il) Fleischman, S. The midnight horse
        Fic
  (il) Fleischman, S. The scarebird   **E**
  (il) Fleischman, S. The whipping boy
        Fic
  (il) Halloween: stories and poems. See Halloween: stories and poems   **808.8**
  (il) Prelutsky, J. The dragons are singing tonight   **811**
  (il) Rice, E. City night   **E**
  (il) Shannon, G. More stories to solve
        398.2
  (il) Shannon, G. Still more stories to solve
        398.2
  (il) Shannon, G. Stories to solve   **398.2**
Sisco, Tim
  (il) Shorto, R. Tecumseh and the dream of an American Indian nation   **92**
Sister. Greenfield, E.   **Fic**
Sister Alionushka, brother Ivanushka. Afanas'ev, A. N.
  In Afanas'ev, A. N. Russian fairy tales p406-10   **398.2**
Sister Death and the healer. San Souci, R.
  In San Souci, R. More short & shivery p78-82   **398.2**
Sister Fox and Brother Coyote. San Souci, R.
  In San Souci, R. Cut from the same cloth p93-99   **398.2**
Sister Shako and Kolo the goat. Dalokay, V.
        956.1
Sisters
  Peterson, J. W. I have a sister—my sister is deaf (k-3)   **362.4**
    Fiction
  Alcock, V. The cuckoo sister (6 and up)
        Fic
  Greene, C. C. Beat the turtle drum (5 and up)   **Fic**

Soccer circus. Gilson, J. See note under Gilson, J. 4B goes wild   **Fic**

Social action
Hoose, P. M. It's our world, too! (5 and up)   **302**
Lewis, B. A. The kid's guide to social action (4 and up)   **361.2**

Social anthropology *See* Ethnology

Social behavior *See* Human behavior

Social classes
            Fiction
Konigsburg, E. L. Journey to an 800 number (5 and up)   **Fic**

Social customs *See* Manners and customs

Social life and customs *See* Manners and customs

Social role
Free to be—you and me   **810.8**

Social sciences
            Bibliography
Notable children's trade books in the field of social studies   **016.3**

Societies
    See also Clubs

Society of Friends
            Fiction
Avi. Night journeys (5 and up)   **Fic**
Turkle, B. C. Obadiah the Bold   **E**

Socks. Cleary, B.   **Fic**

Socrates
See/See also pages in the following book(s):
Coolidge, O. E. The golden days of Greece p113-27 (4-6)   **938**

Sod houses on the Great Plains. Rounds, G.   **693**

Sody saleratus
In Juba this and Juba that   **372.6**

Sody Sallyratus. Compton, J.   **398.2**

Sody Sallyraytus
In Grandfather tales p75-80   **398.2**

Sody sallyrytus. MacDonald, M. R.
In MacDonald, M. R. Twenty tellable tales p79-89   **372.6**

Soekarno, 1901-1970
See/See also pages in the following book(s):
Indonesia—in pictures p30-34 (5 and up)   **959.8**

Soentpiet, Chris K.
(il) Bradby, M. More than anything else   **E**
(il) Nunes, S. The last dragon   **E**

Sofie's role. Heath, A.   **E**

Soil ecology
Lavies, B. Compost critters (4 and up)   **591.5**

Sojourner Truth *See* Truth, Sojourner, d. 1883

Solar eclipses
Branley, F. M. Eclipse: darkness in daytime (k-3)   **523.7**
See/See also pages in the following book(s):
Gallant, R. A. Rainbows, mirages and sundogs p72-81 (4 and up)   **551.5**

Solar radiation
    See also Greenhouse effect

Solar system
    See also Satellites
Leedy, L. Postcards from Pluto (k-3)   **523.2**
Simon, S. Our solar system (3-6)   **523.2**

Solberg, S. E. (Sammy Edward), 1930-
The land and people of Korea (5 and up)   **951.9**

Solberg, Sammy Edward *See* Solberg, S. E. (Sammy Edward), 1930-

Solbert, Ronni
(il) Brooks, G. Bronzeville boys and girls   **811**
(il) Merrill, J. The pushcart war   **Fic**

The **soldier**. Babbitt, N.
In Babbitt, N. The Devil's other storybook p19-23   **S C**

The **soldier** and the king. Afanas'ev, A. N.
In Afanas'ev, A. N. Russian fairy tales p563-67   **398.2**

The **soldier** and the vampire. San Souci, R.
In San Souci, R. Short & shivery p68-72   **398.2**

Soldier Jack
In The Jack tales p172-79   **398.2**

Soldiers
    See also Women soldiers; names of countries with the subdivision *Army—Military life*
            United States
McGovern, A. The secret soldier: the story of Deborah Sampson [Gannett] (3-5)   **92**

A **soldier's** riddle. Afanas'ev, A. N.
In Afanas'ev, A. N. Russian fairy tales p117-18   **398.2**

The **sole**. Grimm, J.
In Grimm, J. The complete Grimm's fairy tales p709   **398.2**

Solga, Kim
(il) Rights, M. Beastly neighbors   **508**

Solomon, King of Israel
            Fiction
Renberg, D. H. King Solomon and the bee (k-3)   **398.2**

Solomon the rusty nail. Steig, W.   **E**

Soman, David
(il) Johnson, A. Tell me a story, Mama   **E**
(il) Johnson, A. When I am old with you   **E**

Some body!. Rowan, P.   **611**

Some of the days of Everett Anderson. Clifton, L. See note under Clifton, L. Everett Anderson's 1-2-3   **E**

Some of the kinder planets [story]. Wynne-Jones, T.
In Wynne-Jones, T. Some of the kinder planets: stories p101-17   **S C**

Soup ahoy. Peck, R. N. See note under Peck,
R. N. Soup **Fic**

The **soup** bone. Johnston, T. **E**

Soup for president. Peck, R. N. See note under
Peck, R. N. Soup **Fic**

Soup in love. Peck, R. N. See note under
Peck, R. N. Soup **Fic**

Soup in the saddle. Peck, R. N. See note under Peck, R. N. Soup **Fic**

Soup on ice. Peck, R. N. See note under Peck,
R. N. Soup **Fic**

Soup on wheels. Peck, R. N. See note under
Peck, R. N. Soup **Fic**

Soup's hoop. Peck, R. N. See note under Peck,
R. N. Soup **Fic**

Soup's uncle. Peck, R. N. See note under
Peck, R. N. Soup **Fic**

South (U.S.) *See* Southern States

South Africa
Fiction
Daly, N. Not so fast, Songololo **E**
Isadora, R. At the crossroads **E**
Isadora, R. Over the green hills **E**
Lewin, H. Jafta **E**
Stock, C. Armien's fishing trip **E**
Politics and government
Dell, P. Nelson Mandela (3-5) **92**
Roberts, J. L. Nelson Mandela (3-5) **92**
Race relations
Dell, P. Nelson Mandela (3-5) **92**
Roberts, J. L. Nelson Mandela (3-5) **92**
Race relations—Fiction
Naidoo, B. Chain of fire (5 and up) **Fic**
Naidoo, B. Journey to Jo'burg (5 and up)
Fic
Social life and customs
Angelou, M. My painted house, my friendly
chicken, and me (k-3) **968**

South America
Natural history
See Natural history—South America

South American Indians *See* Indians of South
America

South branch. Yep, L.
In Yep, L. The tree of dreams **398.2**

South Carolina
Fradin, D. B. The South Carolina Colony (4
and up) **975.7**
Fredeen, C. South Carolina
In Hello USA series **973**
Kent, D. South Carolina
In America the beautiful **973**
Fiction
Schroeder, A. Carolina shout! **E**

The **South** Carolina Colony. Fradin, D. B.
975.7

South Dakota
Lepthien, E. U. South Dakota
In America the beautiful **973**
Sirvaitis, K. South Dakota
In Hello USA series **973**

Fiction
Turner, A. W. Grasshopper summer (4-6)
Fic

South Pacific Region *See* Oceania

South Pole
See also Antarctic regions

South Sea Islands *See* Oceania

South Seas *See* Oceania

Southern Rhodesia *See* Zimbabwe

Southern States
Folklore
See Folklore—Southern States
Race relations
Haskins, J. Freedom Rides (5 and up)
323.1

Southey, Robert, 1774-1843
The story of the three bears
In The Classic fairy tales p201-05
398.2
In The Green fairy book p234-37
398.2

The **southpaw** [short story]. Viorst, J.
In Free to be—you and me p71-75
810.8

Southwest Pacific Region *See* Oceania

Souza, D. M. (Dorothy M.)
Frogs, frogs everywhere (4-6) **597.8**
Insects around the house (4-6) **595.7**
Insects in the garden (4-6) **595.7**
Northern lights (4-6) **538**
Powerful waves (4-6) **551.47**
Shy salamanders (4-6) **597.6**

Souza, Dorothy M. *See* Souza, D. M. (Dorothy
M.)

Sovereigns *See* Kings, queens, rulers, etc.

Soviet Union
See also Commonwealth of Independent States; Former Soviet republics; Russia; Russia (Republic)
History
Harvey, M. The fall of the Soviet Union
(4-6) **947**

Space, Outer *See* Outer space

Space. Butterfield, M. **629.47**

Space and astronomy: 49 science fair projects.
Bonnet, R. L. **520**

Space and time
Fiction
Conrad, P. Stonewords (5 and up) **Fic**
Griffin, P. R. Switching well (5 and up)
Fic
Hahn, M. D. The doll in the garden (4-6)
Fic
Hahn, M. D. Time for Andrew (5 and up)
Fic
Lunn, J. L. S. The root cellar (5 and up)
Fic
Park, R. Playing Beatie Bow (5 and up)
Fic
Pearce, P. Tom's midnight garden (4 and
up) **Fic**

Space and time—Fiction—*Continued*
Sleator, W. Strange attractors (5 and up)
Fic
Wiseman, D. Jeremy Visick (5 and up)
Fic
Space biology
Kettelkamp, L. Living in space (5 and up)
629.4
Space Camp. Baird, A.   629.45
Space case. Marshall, E.   E
Space debris
Asimov, I. Pollution in space (3-5)
363.7
Space flight
Mullane, R. M. Liftoff! (4 and up)
629.45
Ride, S. K. To space & back (4 and up)
629.45
Space flight to the moon
Fiction
Alexander, M. G. You're a genius, Blackboard Bear   E
Murphy, J. What next, Baby Bear!   E
Space garbage. See Asimov, I. Pollution in space   363.7
Space pollution *See* Space debris
Space probes
See also Project Mariner
Space shuttles
Kettelkamp, L. Living in space (5 and up)
629.4
Ride, S. K. To space & back (4 and up)
629.45
Space stations
Kettelkamp, L. Living in space (5 and up)
629.4
Space Telescope *See* Hubble Space Telescope
Space vehicles
See also Space shuttles
Graham, I. Spacecraft (4 and up)   629.4
Space words. Simon, S.   500.5
Spacecraft *See* Space vehicles
Spacecraft. Graham, I.   629.4
Spaghetti *See* Pasta products
Spaghetti. Rylant, C.
In Rylant, C. Every living thing p31-33
S C
Spagnoli, Cathy, 1950-
Nine-in-one, Grr! Grr! (k-2)   398.2
Spain
Shubert, A. The land and people of Spain (5 and up)   946
Spain—in pictures (5 and up)   946
Fiction
Leaf, M. The story of Ferdinand   E
Wojciechowska, M. Shadow of a bull (6 and up)   Fic
Folklore
See Folklore—Spain
History—1898, War of 1898
See Spanish-American War, 1898

History—1936-1939, Civil War
Katz, W. L. The Lincoln Brigade (5 and up)
946.081
Spain—in pictures (5 and up)   946
Spanfeller, Jim (James J.), 1930-
(il) Cleaver, V. Where the lillies bloom
Fic
Spangler, James Murray
See/See also pages in the following book(s):
Aaseng, N. The unsung heroes p39-44 (5 and up)   920
Spangler, Stella S.
(jt. auth) Kennedy, D. M. Science & technology in fact and fiction: a guide to children's books   016.5
Spanish America *See* Latin America
Spanish-American War, 1898
Marrin, A. The Spanish-American War (6 and up)   973.8
Spanish artists *See* Artists, Spanish
Spanish authors *See* Authors, Spanish
Spanish-English bilingual books *See* Bilingual books—English-Spanish
Spanish language
Emberley, R. Let's go/Vamos (k-3)   463
Emberley, R. My day/Mi día (k-3)   463
Emberley, R. My house/Mi casa: a book in two languages (k-3)   463
Emberley, R. Taking a walk/Caminando: a book in two languages (k-3)   463
Dictionaries
The Cat in the Hat beginner book dictionary in Spanish (k-3)   463
Spanish language editions
Spanish language editions of the following titles are available from original publishers or distributors of Spanish language material
Ackerman, K. By the dawn's early light
E
Adler, D. A. A picture book of Abraham Lincoln   92
Adler, D. A. A picture book of Christopher Columbus   92
Adler, D. A. A picture book of Martin Luther King, Jr.   92
Aesop. Aesop's fables (illus. by Lisbeth Zwerger)   398.2
Alcott, L. M. Little women   Fic
Aliki. Communication   302.2
Aliki. Dinosaurs are different   567.9
Aliki. Fossils tell of long ago   560
Aliki. How a book is made   686
Aliki. Manners   395
Aliki. A medieval feast   394.1
Aliki. Milk from cow to carton   637
Aliki. My five senses   612.8
Aliki. The story of Johnny Appleseed
92
Ancona, G. Pablo remembers   394.2
Andersen, H. C. Hans Christian Andersen fairy tales   S C
Andersen, H. C. The nightingale   Fic
Andersen, H. C. The princess and the pea
Fic

Spanish literature
  Bibliography
Schon, I. Books in Spanish for children and young adults: an annotated guide [series I-VI] **011.6**

Spariosu, Mihai
Ghosts, vampires, and werewolves (5 and up) **398.2**
<small>Contents: The white cross; The forest; The bitang; The jealous vampire; Special delivery; The three partners; The gypsy fiddlers; The female snake; The six-fingered hand; The red rose; The ancient fortress; The dark stranger; The red emperor's son; The wheel of fire; The wicked queen; The stone statue</small>

The **sparrow** and his four children. Grimm, J.
 In Grimm, J. The complete Grimm's fairy tales p657-60 **398.2**

Sparrows
Arnold, C. House sparrows everywhere (3-5)
  598

George, J. C. The moon of the winter bird (3-6) **598**

Sparrow's luck!. MacDonald, M. R.
 In MacDonald, M. R. Celebrate the world p162-71 **372.6**

Spastic paralysis *See* Cerebral palsy

Speak up: more rhymes of the never was and always is. McCord, D. T. W. **811**

The **speaking** bird, the singing tree, and the golden water. Philip, N.
 In Philip, N. The Arabian nights p99-112
  398.2

Staub, Frank J.—*Continued*
Mountain goats (2-4)   **599.73**
Sea turtles (2-4)   **597.9**
Yellowstone's cycle of fire (3-6)   **574.5**

Stay away from Simon!. Carrick, C.   **Fic**

Stay fit. Reef, C.   **613.7**

The **steadfast** tin soldier. Andersen, H. C.
    Fic
also in Andersen, H. C. Twelve tales p13-
19   **S C**
also in The Rainbow fairy book p18-24
    398.2
also in The Yellow fairy book p308-12
    398.2

The **steadfast** tin soldier. Seidler, T.   **Fic**

Steal away. Armstrong, J.   **Fic**

Stealing home. Stolz, M. See note under Stolz,
M. Go fish   **Fic**

Steam
Jacobs, L. Letting off steam (3-6)
    621.44

The **steam** roller: a fantasy. Brown, M. W.
In Brown, M. W. The fish with the deep
sea smile p25-31   **818**

Steam-shovels
Fiction
Burton, V. L. Mike Mulligan and his steam
shovel   **E**

Steamboats
See/See also pages in the following book(s):
McCall, E. S. Biography of a river: the liv-
ing Mississippi (6 and up)   **977**

Stearns, Virginia
(il) Rohmer, H. Mother Scorpion country
    398.2

Stebbins, Robert C. (Robert Cyril), 1915-
A field guide to western reptiles and amphibians   **597.6**
(jt. auth) Conant, R. Peterson first guide to
reptiles and amphibians   **597.6**

Steedman, Scott
Amazing monkeys (2-4)   **599.8**

Steel industry
Fiction
Smucker, A. E. No star nights   **E**

Steel trade *See* Steel industry

Steele, Philip
Castles (4 and up)   **728.8**

Steen, Bill
(il) Swentzell, R. Children of clay
    970.004

Stegosaurs. Sattler, H. R.   **567.9**

Steig, Jeanne
Alpha beta chowder   **811**

Steig, William, 1907-
Abel's island (3-5)   **Fic**
The amazing bone   **E**
Brave Irene   **E**
C D C? (3-6)   **793.73**
Caleb & Kate   **E**
Doctor De Soto   **E**

Doctor De Soto goes to Africa. See note un-
der Steig, W. Doctor De Soto   **E**
Dominic (3-5)   **Fic**
Farmer Palmer's wagon ride   **E**
The real thief (3-5)   **Fic**
Solomon the rusty nail   **E**
Sylvester and the magic pebble   **E**
also in The Read-aloud treasury p112-34
    808.8
Zeke Pippin   **E**
(il) Steig, J. Alpha beta chowder   **811**
See/See also pages in the following book(s):
Newbery and Caldecott Medal books, 1966-
1975 p218-22   **028.5**

Stein, Gertrude, 1874-1946
See/See also pages in the following book(s):
A Horn Book sampler on children's books
and reading p128-32   **028.5**

Stein, R. Conrad, 1937-
California
In America the beautiful   **973**
Illinois
In America the beautiful   **973**
Indiana
In America the beautiful   **973**
The Iran hostage crisis (4-6)   **955**
Michigan
In America the beautiful   **973**
Minnesota
In America the beautiful   **973**
New Mexico
In America the beautiful   **973**
New York
In America the beautiful   **973**
North Carolina
In America the beautiful   **973**
Oregon
In America the beautiful   **973**
The powers of Congress (4-6)   **328.73**
The powers of the Supreme Court (4-6)
    347
Texas
In America the beautiful   **973**
The Trail of Tears (4-6)   **970.004**
Valley Forge (4-6)   **973.3**
Washington
In America the beautiful   **973**
West Virginia
In America the beautiful   **973**
Wisconsin
In America the beautiful   **973**

Stein, Sara Bonnett
About dying (k-3)   **155.9**
Oh, baby!   **E**
On divorce (k-3)   **306.89**

Steinbeck, John, 1902-1968
See/See also pages in the following book(s):
Faber, D. Great lives: American literature
p259-67 (5 and up)   **920**

Stella & Roy. Wolff, A.   **E**

Stellaluna. Cannon, J.   **E**

Stemple, Adam
The Lullaby songbook. See The Lullaby
songbook   **782.42**

Stemple, Jane H. Yolen *See* Yolen, Jane

The **story** of Negro league baseball. Brashler, W. **796.357**

The **story** of Peter Potato Blossom wishes and how she went down into Rootabaga Country and came back with five sky blue whispering cats. Sandburg, C.
In Sandburg, C. More rootabagas p19-26 **S C**

The **story** of Pretty Goldilocks. Aulnoy, Madame d'
In The Blue fairy book p193-205 **398.2**

The **Story** of Prince Ahmed and the Fairy Paribanou
In The Blue fairy book p342-73 **398.2**

The **story** of Rags Habakuk, the two blue rats, and the circus man who came with spot cash money. Sandburg, C.
In Sandburg, C. Rootabaga stories pt 1 p72-78 **S C**
In Sandburg, C. The Sandburg treasury p39-42 **818**

The **story** of rosy dock. Baker, J. **508**

The **story** of Ruby Bridges. Coles, R. **370.19**

The **story** of Schlauraffen Land. Grimm, J.
In Grimm, J. The complete Grimm's fairy tales p660-61 **398.2**

The **Story** of Sidi-Nouman
In The Arabian nights entertainments p331-45 **398.2**

The **Story** of Sigurd
In The Red fairy book p357-67 **398.2**

The **Story** of the barber's fifth brother
In The Arabian nights entertainments p196-208 **398.2**

The **Story** of the barber's sixth brother
In The Arabian nights entertainments p209-15 **398.2**

Story of the blind Baba-Abdalla
In The Arabian nights entertainments p320-30 **398.2**

The **story** of the creation. Bible. O.T. Genesis **222**

The **story** of the enchanted horse See note under Aladdin and other tales from the Arabian nights p285-314 **398.2**

The **Story** of the envious man and of him who was envied
In The Arabian nights entertainments p86-101 **398.2**

The **Story** of the first calender, son of a king
In The Arabian nights entertainments p68-74 **398.2**

The **Story** of the first old man and of the hind
In The Arabian nights entertainments p13-18 **398.2**

The **Story** of the fisherman
In The Arabian nights entertainments p23-28 **398.2**

The **story** of the fisherman and his wife. Grimm, J.
In The Green fairy book p343-52 **398.2**

The **story** of the fisherman and the genie See note under Aladdin and other tales from the Arabian nights p315-46 **398.2**

The **Story** of the husband and the parrot
In The Arabian nights entertainments p32-33 **398.2**

The **Story** of the merchant and the genius
In The Arabian nights entertainments p6-12 **398.2**

The **story** of the powers of Congress. See Stein, R. C. The powers of Congress **328.73**

The **story** of the powers of the Supreme Court. See Stein, R. C. The powers of the Supreme Court **347**

The **Story** of the second calender, son of a king
In The Arabian nights entertainments p75-85 **398.2**

The **Story** of the second old man and of the two black dogs
In The Arabian nights entertainments p19-22 **398.2**

The **story** of the Statue of Liberty. Maestro, B. **974.7**

Story of the sweat lodge. Medicine Story
In Medicine Story. The Children of the Morning Light p30-34 **398.2**

The **Story** of the third calender, son of a king
In The Arabian nights entertainments p102-21 **398.2**

The **story** of the three bears. Jacobs, J.
In Jacobs, J. English fairy tales p97-101 **398.2**

The **story** of the three bears. Southey, R.
In The Classic fairy tales p201-05 **398.2**
In The Green fairy book p234-37 **398.2**

The **Story** of the three calenders, sons of kings, and of five ladies of Bagdad
In The Arabian nights entertainments p54-67 **398.2**

The **story** of the three kingdoms. Myers, W. D. **E**

The **story** of the three little pigs. Jacobs, J.
In Jacobs, J. English fairy tales p73-76 **398.2**

The **story** of the Trail of Tears. See Stein, R. C. The Trail of Tears **970.004**

The **story** of the treasure seekers [excerpt]. Nesbit, E.
In The Random House book of humor for children p195-204 **817.008**

The **Story** of the vizier who was punished
In The Arabian nights entertainments p34-47 **398.2**

The **story** of the women's movement. Ash, M. **305.4**

Straub, Cindie
Mime: basics for beginners (6 and up)
792.3

Straub, Matthew
(jt. auth) Straub, C. Mime: basics for beginners **792.3**

Straus, Nathan, 1848-1931
See/See also pages in the following book(s):
Giblin, J. Milk: the fight for purity p44-58 (5 and up) **637**

Strauss, Lindy *See* Edwards, Linda

Stravinsky, Igor, 1882-1971
See/See also pages in the following book(s):
Krull, K. Lives of the musicians p74-77 (4 and up) **920**

The **Straw** ox
In Tomie dePaola's favorite nursery tales p75-82 **398.2**

The **Straw, the coal, and the bean**
In The Tall book of nursery tales p90-91 **398.2**

The **straw, the coal, and the bean**. Grimm, J.
In Grimm, J. The complete Grimm's fairy tales p102-03 **398.2**

Strawberries
See/See also pages in the following book(s):
Busenberg, B. Vanilla, chocolate, & strawberry p73-105 (5 and up) **664**
Fiction
Dang, M. The Grey Lady and the Strawberry Snatcher **E**
Bruchac, J. The first strawberries (k-3) **398.2**

The **strawberries** of the little men. MacDonald, M. R.
In MacDonald, M. R. Look back and see p95-102 **372.6**

Stray. Rylant, C.
In Rylant, C. Every living thing p42-47 **S C**

Stream animals
Craighead, C. The eagle and the river (3-5) **591.5**

Streams to the river, river to the sea. O'Dell, S. **Fic**

Streatfeild, Mary Noel *See* Streatfeild, Noel, 1895-1986

Streatfeild, Noel, 1895-1986
Ballet shoes (5 and up) **Fic**
Theatre shoes, or other people's shoes (5 and up) **Fic**

Street, Janet
(il) Yolen, J. Animal fare **811**

Street music. Adoff, A. **811**

The **street** musicians. Grimm, J.
In The Rainbow fairy book p280-85 **398.2**

Street people *See* Homeless persons

Strega Nona. De Paola, T. **E**

Strega Nona meets her match. De Paola, T. See note under De Paola, T. Strega Nona **E**

Strega Nona's magic lessons. De Paola, T. See note under De Paola, T. Strega Nona **E**

Streissguth, Thomas
Rocket man: the story of Robert Goddard (4 and up) **92**

Stren, Patti, 1949-
Hug me
In Valentine's Day: stories and poems p9-12 **810.8**

The **strength** of the hills. Graff, N. P. **630.1**

Strickland, Dorothy S.
(comp) Families. See Families **811.008**

Strickland, Michael R., 1965-
(comp) Families. See Families **811.008**

Strictly Puritan. Miller, H. L.
In Holiday plays round the year p83-90 **812.008**

Strider. Cleary, B. **Fic**

String beans. Hurwitz, J.
In Bauer, C. F. Celebrations p65-67 **808.8**

String figures
Gryski, C. Cat's cradle, owl's eyes (4-6) **793.9**
Gryski, C. Many stars & more string games (4-6) **793.9**
Gryski, C. Super string games (4-6) **793.9**
See/See also pages in the following book(s):
Pellowski, A. The story vine p3-46 **372.6**

A **string** in the harp. Bond, N. **Fic**

Stringbean's trip to the shining sea. Williams, V. B. **E**

Stringed instruments
Hewitt, S. Pluck and scrape
In Hewitt, S. Get set—go! [Music & sound series] **784.19**

Strong as Annie Christmas. Cohn, A.
In From sea to shining sea p277-79 **810.8**

Strong but quirky: the birth of Davy Crockett. Shapiro, I.
In From sea to shining sea p85-87 **810.8**

Strong Hans. Grimm, J.
In Grimm, J. The complete Grimm's fairy tales p688-95 **398.2**

The **strongest** one of all. Ginsburg, M.
In Ginsburg, M. Merry-go-round p4-11 **398.2**

Structural engineering
Wilkinson, P. Building (4 and up) **690**

Strudel, strudel, strudel. Sanfield, S. **398.2**

Strugnell, Ann
(il) Cameron, A. The stories Julian tells **Fic**

Stuart, Dee
The astonishing armadillo (3-6) **599.3**
Bats (3-6) **599.4**

Sullivan, Charles, 1933-
(ed) Children of promise. See Children of promise **810.8**

Sullivan, George
All about basketball (4 and up) **796.323**
All about football (4 and up) **796.332**
The day we walked on the moon (4 and up) **629.45**
Here come the monster trucks (3-6) **629.223**
How an airport really works (4 and up) **387.7**
In-line skating (4 and up) **796.2**
Mathew Brady, his life and photographs (6 and up) **92**
Pitchers: twenty-seven of baseball's greatest (4 and up) **920**
Racing Indy cars (5 and up) **796.7**
Slave ship (5 and up) **910.4**

Summer
Hirschi, R. Summer (k-2) **508**
Kurelek, W. A prairie boy's summer (3-5) **971.27**
Markle, S. Exploring summer (4 and up) **508**

Fiction
Conly, J. L. Trout summer (5 and up) **Fic**
Tresselt, A. R. Sun up **E**
Poetry
Giovanni, N. Knoxville, Tennessee (k-3) **811**

Summer camps See Camps
Summer ice. McMillan, B. **508**
Summer of fire. Lauber, P. **574.5**
Summer of my German soldier. Greene, B. **Fic**
The **summer** of the swans. Byars, B. C. **Fic**
Summer on wheels. Soto, G. See note under Soto, G. Crazy weekend **Fic**
The **summer** sands. Garland, S. **E**
Summer switch. Rodgers, M. See note under Rodgers, M. Freaky Friday **Fic**
A **summer** to die. Lowry, L. **Fic**

Sun
Asimov, I. How did we find out about sunshine? (5 and up) **523.7**
Branley, F. M. The sun (k-3) **523.7**
Daily, R. The sun (4 and up) **523.7**
Gibbons, G. Sun up, sun down (k-3) **523.7**
Moore, P. The sun and moon (k-3) **523.7**
Simon, S. The sun (3-6) **523.7**
Eclipses
See Solar eclipses
Fiction
Daly, N. Why the Sun & Moon live in the sky (k-3) **398.2**
Emberley, M. Welcome back sun **E**

Sun (in religion, folklore, etc.) See Sun worship

The **sun** and moon. Moore, P. **523.7**
Sun dogs and shooting stars. Branley, F. M. **523**
The **Sun**, the Moon, and the Raven. Afanas'ev, A. N.
In Afanas'ev, A. N. Russian fairy tales p588-89 **398.2**
The **sun**, the wind and the rain. Peters, L. W. **551.4**
Sun up. Tresselt, A. R. **E**
Sun up, sun down. Gibbons, G. **523.7**
Sun worship
Baylor, B. The way to start a day (1-4) **291.4**

A **sunburned** prayer. Talbert, M. **Fic**
The **Sunday** outing. Pinkney, G. J. **E**
Sundew stranglers. Wexler, J. **583**
Sundials
Anno, M. Anno's sundial (4 and up) **529**
Sundiata See Keita, Soundiata, d. 1255
Sundiata. Wisniewski, D. **92**
Sunflakes (k-2) **811.008**
Sunflowers
King, E. Backyard sunflower (k-3) **635.9**
Sungura and Leopard. Knutson, B. **398.2**
Sunk! (5 and up) **910.4**
Sunken ships & treasure. Fine, J. C. **910.4**
Sunken treasure. Gibbons, G. **910.4**
Sunrise. Stanton, M.
In Herds of thunder, manes of gold p138-48 **808.8**
Sunshine. Ormerod, J. **E**
Sunshine Home. Bunting, E. **E**
Sunshine makes the seasons. Branley, F. M. **525**
Super Cluck. O'Connor, J. **E**
Super science fair projects. Amato, C. **507.8**
Super string games. Gryski, C. **793.9**
Super, super, superwords. McMillan, B. **422**
Superdupers! really funny real words. Terban, M. **427**
Superfudge. Blume, J. See note under Blume, J. Tales of a fourth grade nothing **Fic**
The **superior** pet. Yep, L.
In Yep, L. The rainbow people p80-85 **398.2**
Superman (Comic strip)
See/See also pages in the following book(s):
Aaseng, N. The unsung heroes p53-59 (5 and up) **920**
Supermarket. Hamley, D.
In The Oxford book of scary tales p106-11 **808.8**
Supermarket Thanksgiving. Bauer, C. F.
In Thanksgiving: stories and poems p57-68 **810.8**

Switzerland
    Fiction
Spyri, J. Heidi (4 and up)   Fic
    Legends
    See Legends—Switzerland
The **sword** and the circle. Sutcliff, R.
         398.2
The **sword** in the stone. White, T. H.   Fic
The **sword** in the stone [excerpt]. White, T. H.
    In The Random House book of humor
        for children p212-34   817.008
The **sword** in the tree. Bulla, C. R.   Fic
La sylphide (Ballet)
    See/See also pages in the following book(s):
McCaughrean, G. The Random House book
    of stories from the ballet p48-56 (4 and
    up)   792.8
Sylvain and Jocosa. Caylus, A. C. P. de T.,
    comte de
    In The Green fairy book p56-63
         398.2
Sylvester and the magic pebble. Steig, W.
         E
    also in The Read-aloud treasury p112-34
         808.8
Sylvie and Bruno. Carroll, L.
    In Carroll, L. The complete works of
        Lewis Carroll p251-456   828
Sylvie and Bruno concluded. Carroll, L.
    In Carroll, L. The complete works of
        Lewis Carroll p457-674   828
Symbol art. Fisher, L. E.   302.2
Symbols *See* Signs and symbols
Symbols, a silent language. Adkins, J.
         302.2
Symes, R. F.
    Crystal & gem (4 and up)   548
    Rocks & minerals (4 and up)   549
System simulation *See* Simulation methods
Szekeres, Cyndy, 1933-
    (il) Sharmat, M. W. The 329th friend   E
Szilagyi, Mary
    (il) Rylant, C. Night in the country   E
    (il) Rylant, C. This year's garden   E

T

T-H-U-P-P-P-P-P-P-P!. Schwartz, A.
    In Schwartz, A. Scary stories 3 p86-88
         398.2
Taback, Simms, 1932-
    (il) Hall, K. Snakey riddles   793.73
    (il) Hennessy, B. G. Road builders
         625.7
    (il) McGovern, A. Too much noise
         398.2
Tabernacles, Feast of *See* Sukkoth
Table, chair, bear. Feder, J.   413
Table etiquette
    Giblin, J. From hand to mouth (4 and up)
         394.1

Tableware
    Cobb, V. Feeding yourself (1-3)   394.1
    Giblin, J. From hand to mouth (4 and up)
         394.1
Tackle without a team. Christopher, M.
         Fic
Tacky the penguin. Lester, H. See note under
    Lester, H. Three cheers for Tacky   E
Tadpoles *See* Frogs
Tafuri, Nancy
    Do not disturb   E
    Early morning in the barn   E
    Follow me!   E
    Have you seen my duckling?   E
    Rabbit's morning   E
    Spots, feathers, and curly tails   E
    This is the farmer   E
    (il) Ginsburg, M. Asleep, asleep   E
    (il) Lillie, P. Everything has a place   E
    (il) Pomerantz, C. If I had a paka   811
Taggart, Tricia
    (il) LeShan, E. J. Grandparents: a special
        kind of love   306.8
Taiga. Sayre, A. P.   574.5
The **tailor** in heaven. Grimm, J.
    In Grimm, J. The complete Grimm's
        fairy tales p175-77   398.2
The **tailor** of Gloucester. Potter, B.   E
Tailoring
    Fiction
    Potter, B. The tailor of Gloucester   E
Tails of the Bronx. Pinkwater, J.   Fic
The **tailypo.** Galdone, J.   398.2
Tailypo. San Souci, R.
    In San Souci, R. Short & shivery p58-61
         398.2
Taino Indians
    Jacobs, F. The Tainos (4 and up)   972.9
    Fiction
    Dorris, M. Morning Girl (4-6)   Fic
    Legends
    Crespo, G. How the sea began (2-4)
         398.2
'Tain't so
    In Diane Goode's book of scary stories &
        songs p22-25   398.2
Taiwan
    Cromie, A. Taiwan (4 and up)   951.2
Tajikistan
    Tajikistan (5 and up)   958
    Tajikistan (5 and up)   958
Take a look. Davidson, R.   701
Take a look at snakes. Maestro, B.   597.9
Take another look. Hoban, T.   E
Take joy! The Tasha Tudor Christmas book
         394.2
Take sky: more rhymes of the never was and
    always is. McCord, D. T. W.   811
Taking a walk/Caminando: a book in two lan-
    guages. Emberley, R.   463
Taking care of Carruthers. Marshall, J. See
    note under Marshall, J. Yummers!   E

Tightrope walking
    Fiction
McCully, E. A. Mirette on the high wire
                                  E

Tigress. Cowcher, H.   **E**
Tikki Tikki Tembo. Mosel, A.   **398.2**
Tikvah means hope. Polacco, P.   **E**
Till victory is won. Mettger, Z.   **973.7**
Tillotson, Katherine
  (il) Kerley, B. Songs of Papa's island
                                  Fic
Tim O'Toole and the wee folk. McDermott,
  G.   **E**
Time
    See also Day; Night
  Anno, M. Anno's sundial (4 and up)
                               529
  Branley, F. M. Keeping time (4-6)   **529**
  Burns, M This book is about time (4 and
  up)   **529**
    Fiction
  McGuire, R. Night becomes day   **E**
    Poetry
  It's about time! (k-2)   **811.008**
Time. Courlander, H.
  In Courlander, H. The cow-tail switch,
    and other West African stories p73-78
                              398.2
Time and space *See* Space and time
Time detectives [series]
  Berrill, M. Mummies, masks, & mourners
                               393
Time flies. Rohmann, E.   **E**
Time for Andrew. Hahn, M. D.   **Fic**
A time for babies. Hirschi, R.   **591.5**
A time for playing. Hirschi, R.   **591.5**
A time for singing. Hirschi, R.   **591.5**
The time garden. Eager, E. See note under Ea-
  ger, E. Half magic   **Fic**
Time of wonder. McCloskey, R.   **E**
Time quest book [series]
  Ballard, R. D. Exploring the Bismarck
                             910.4
  Ballard, R. D. Exploring the Titanic
                             910.4
  Ballard, R. D. The lost wreck of the Isis
                             910.4
  Beattie, O. Buried in ice   **998**
  Bisel, S. The secrets of Vesuvius   **937**
  Reeves, C. N. Into the mummy's tomb
                             932
  Tanaka, S. The disaster of the Hindenburg
                         629.133
Time to get out of the bath, Shirley. Burn-
  ingham, J. See note under Burningham, J.
  Come away from the water, Shirley
                              E
Time train. Fleischman, P.   **E**
Timmons, Dan
  (il) Patterson, L. Indian terms of the Ameri-
  cas   **970.004**

Timmy. Prince, A.
  In The Oxford book of scary tales p79-83
                             808.8
Timothy goes to school. Wells, R.   **E**
Timothy of the cay. Taylor, T.   **Fic**
The tin woodsman of Oz. Baum, L. F. See
  note under Baum, L. F. The Wizard of Oz
                              Fic
The tinder box. Andersen, H. C.
  In Andersen, H. C. Hans Christian Ander-
    sen fairy tales p39-48   **S C**
  In Andersen, H. C. Twelve tales p30-39
                              S C
  In The Classic fairy tales p207-15
                              398.2
  In The Oxford treasury of children's sto-
    ries p55-63   **S C**
  In The Rainbow fairy book p231-41
                              398.2
  In The Yellow fairy book p265-73
                              398.2
The tinderbox. Moser, B.   **Fic**
Ting, S. C. C. (Samuel Chao-chung), 1936-
  See/See also pages in the following book(s):
  Morey, J. Famous Asian Americans p139-49
  (5 and up)   **920**
Ting, Samuel Chao-chung *See* Ting, S. C. C.
  (Samuel Chao-chung), 1936-
Ting Lan and the lamb. Carpenter, F
  In Carpenter, F. Tales of a Chinese grand-
  mother p66-71   **398.2**
Tinkelman, Murray, 1933-
  (il) Dinosaurs: poems. See Dinosaurs: poems
                           811.008
Tinker, John Frederick
    About
  Rappaport, D. Tinker vs. Des Moines (5
  and up)   **342**
The tinker and the ghost. MacDonald, M. R.
  In MacDonald, M. R. When the lights go
  out p69-78   **372.6**
Tinker vs. Des Moines. Rappaport, D.
                             342
Tiny Mouse goes traveling. MacDonald, M. R.
  In MacDonald, M. R. Look back and see
  p130-36   **372.6**
The tiny thing. Hamilton, V.
  In Hamilton, V. The dark way p54-59
                            398.2
The tiny, tiny boy and the big, big cow. Van
  Laan, N.   **398.2**
Tisquantum *See* Squanto, d. 1622
Titanic (Steamship)
  Ballard, R. D. Exploring the Titanic (4 and
  up)   **910.4**
  Blos, J. W. The heroine of the Titanic: a
  tale both true and otherwise of the life of
  Molly Brown (k-3)   **92**
  Spedden, D. C. S. Polar, the Titanic bear
  (3-6)   **910.4**

Tom. De Paola, T.   E

Tom and Pippo and the bicycle. Oxenbury, H. See note under Oxenbury, H. Pippo gets lost   E

Tom and Pippo and the dog. Oxenbury, H. See note under Oxenbury, H. Pippo gets lost   E

Tom and Pippo and the washing machine. Oxenbury, H. See note under Oxenbury, H. Pippo gets lost   E

Tom and Pippo go for a walk. Oxenbury, H. See note under Oxenbury, H. Pippo gets lost   E

Tom and Pippo go shopping. Oxenbury, H. See note under Oxenbury, H. Pippo gets lost   E

Tom and Pippo in the garden. Oxenbury, H. See note under Oxenbury, H. Pippo gets lost   E

Tom and Pippo in the snow. Oxenbury, H. See note under Oxenbury, H. Pippo gets lost   E

Tom and Pippo make a friend. Oxenbury, H. See note under Oxenbury, H. Pippo gets lost   E

Tom and Pippo make a mess. Oxenbury, H. See note under Oxenbury, H. Pippo gets lost   E

Tom and Pippo on the beach. Oxenbury, H. See note under Oxenbury, H. Pippo gets lost   E

Tom and Pippo read a story. Oxenbury, H. See note under Oxenbury, H. Pippo gets lost   E

Tom and Pippo see the moon. Oxenbury, H. See note under Oxenbury, H. Pippo gets lost   E

Tom and Pippo's day. Oxenbury, H. See note under Oxenbury, H. Pippo gets lost   E

Tom Glazer's Treasury of folk songs. See Glazer, T. Tom Glazer's Treasury of songs for children   782.42

Tom Glazer's Treasury of songs for children. Glazer, T.   782.42

Tom Hickathrift. Jacobs, J.
In Jacobs, J. English fairy tales p264-70   398.2

Tom Sawyer, pirate. Thane, A.
In Thane, A. Plays from famous stories and fairy tales p77-89   812

Tom Thumb. Brooke, L. L.
In Brooke, L. L. The golden goose book   398.2

Tom Thumb. Watson, R. J.   398.2

Tom Tib goes shopping. Mahy, M.
In Mahy, M. Tick tock tales p49-55   S C

Tom Tit Tot. Crossley-Holland, K.
In Crossley-Holland, K. British folk tales p47-54   398.2

Tom Tit Tot. Jacobs, J.
In Jacobs, J. English fairy tales p13-20   398.2

Tom Tit Tot. Reeves, J.
In Reeves, J. English fables and fairy stories p147-56   398.2

Tomatoes
Watts, B. Tomato (k-3)   635

Tomb, Howard, 1959-
Microaliens (5 and up)   574

Tombs
See also Cemeteries
Bendick, J. Egyptian tombs (4 and up)   932
Bendick, J. Tombs of the ancient Americas (4 and up)   393

The **tombs** of Atuan. Le Guin, U. K. See note under Le Guin, U. K. A wizard of Earthsea   Fic

Tombs of the ancient Americas. Bendick, J.   393

Tomchek, Ann Heinrichs
The Hopi (2-4)   970.004

Tomei, Lorna
(il) Viorst, J. Rosie and Michael   E

Tomes, Margot, 1917-1991
(il) De Regniers, B. S. Little Sister and the Month Brothers   398.2
(il) Fritz, J. And then what happened, Paul Revere?   92
(il) Fritz, J. Homesick: my own story   92
(il) Fritz, J. What's the big idea, Ben Franklin?   92
(il) Fritz, J. Where do you think you're going, Christopher Columbus?   92
(il) Fritz, J. Where was Patrick Henry on the 29th of May?   92
(il) Gauch, P. L. This time, Tempe Wick?   Fic
(il) Giblin, J. Chimney sweeps: yesterday and today   697
(il) If there were dreams to sell. See If there were dreams to sell   821.008
(il) Johnston, T. The soup bone   E
(il) The Lap-time song and play book. See The Lap-time song and play book   782.42
(il) Livingston, M. C. Birthday poems   811
(il) New Year's poems. See New Year's poems   808.81
(il) Schertle, A. Witch Hazel   E
(il) Snowy day: stories and poems. See Snowy day: stories and poems   808.8

Tomfoolery: trickery and foolery with words. Schwartz, A.   398

Tomie dePaola's book of Bible stories. Bible. Selections   220.9

Tomie dePaola's book of Christmas carols   782.28

Tomie dePaola's Favorite nursery tales (k-3)   398.2

Tomie dePaola's Mother Goose (k-2)
398.8

Tomlinson, Theresa
The Forestwife (6 and up)   Fic

Tommelise. Andersen, H. C.
In The Classic fairy tales p221-29
398.2

Tommy's whale. Bruchac, J.
In Bruchac, J. Flying with the eagle, racing with the great bear p118-24
398.2

Tomography
See/See also pages in the following book(s):
Aaseng, N. The inventors: Nobel prizes in chemistry, physics, and medicine p69-74 (5 and up)   609

Tomorrow's wizard. MacLachlan, P.
S C

Tompert, Ann, 1918-
Bamboo hats and a rice cake (k-3)
398.2
Grandfather Tang's story   E

Tom's midnight garden. Pearce, P.   Fic

The **Tomten**. Lindgren, A.   E

The **Tomten** and the fox. Lindgren, A. See note under Lindgren, A. The Tomten
E

Tong, Gary, 1942-
(il) Bortz, A. B. Catastrophe!   620

The **tongue-cut** sparrow. Ishii, M.   398.2

The **tongue-cut** sparrow. Quayle, E.
In Quayle, E. The shining princess, and other Japanese legends p44-56
398.2

The **tongue-twister**. Wiseman, B.
In The Laugh book p239-41   808.8

Tongue twisters
Cole, J. Six sick sheep (3-6)   808.88
Schwartz, A. Busy buzzing bumblebees and other tongue twisters (k-2)   808.88
Schwartz, A. A twister of twists, a tangler of tongues (4 and up)   808.88

Tongues of jade. Yep, L.   398.2

Tonight, by sea. Temple, F.   Fic

Tonight is Carnaval. Dorros, A.   E

Tony's bread: an Italian folktale. De Paola, T.
398.2

Too far away to touch. Newman, L.   E

Too many tamales. Soto, G.   E

Too much noise. McGovern, A.   398.2

Tool book. Gibbons, G.   621.9

The **toolbox**. Rockwell, A. F.   621.9

Toolchest. Adkins, J.   684

Tools
Gibbons, G. Tool book (k-3)   621.9
Miller, M. Who uses this?   E
Rockwell, A. F. The toolbox (k-1)   621.9

Toomai of the elephants. Kipling, R.
In Kipling, R. The jungle books
S C

The **toothpaste** millionaire. Merrill, J.   Fic

Top of the News. See Journal of Youth Services in Libraries   027.6205

Topiel & Tekla. Singer, I. B.
In Singer, I. B. Stories for children p260-70   S C

Topper, Frank
A historical album of New Jersey
In Historical albums series   973

Tops and bottoms. Sanfield, S.
In Sanfield, S. The adventures of High John the Conqueror   398.2

Tops and bottoms. Stevens, J.   398.2

Tories, American *See* American Loyalists

Tornadoes
Erlbach, A. Tornadoes (2-4)   551.55
George, J. C. One day in the prairie (4-6)
574.5
Kahl, J. D. Storm warning (4-6)   551.55
Kramer, S. Tornado (4-6)   551.55
    Fiction
Ruckman, I. Night of the twisters (3-6)
Fic

Torrence, Jackie, 1944-
Brer Possum's dilemma
In From sea to shining sea p249-51
810.8

Torres, John Albert
Home-run hitters (4 and up)   920

Torres, Leyla
Subway sparrow   E

The **tortilla** factory. Paulsen, G.   641.8

Tortillas
Paulsen, G. The tortilla factory (k-3)
641.8

Tortillitas para mamá and other nursery rhymes (k-2)   398.8

Tortoise and the hare
In The Tall book of nursery tales p105-07
398.2

Tortoise, Hare, and the sweet potatoes. Bryan, A.
In Bauer, C. F. Celebrations p231-34
808.8
In Bryan, A. The ox of the wonderful horns and other African folktales p22-28   398.2

Tortoises *See* Turtles

The **Tory's** conversion
In From sea to shining sea p64-65
810.8

Totanguak. MacDonald, M. R.
In MacDonald, M. R. When the lights go out p118-28   372.6

Totem pole. Hoyt-Goldsmith, D.   970.004

Totems and totemism
Hoyt-Goldsmith, D. Totem pole (3-5)
970.004

Totten, Herman L., 1938-
Culturally diverse library collections for children   011.6

Trees—*Continued*
Ehlert, L. Red leaf, yellow leaf (k-3)
582.16
Gackenbach, D. Mighty tree (k-2)
582.16
Hiscock, B. The big tree (k-3) 582.16
Lauber, P. Be a friend to trees (k-3)
582.16
Lavies, B. Tree trunk traffic (k-2) 591.5
Locker, T. Sky tree (1-3) 582.16
Lyon, G. E. A B Cedar E
Markle, S. Outside and inside trees (2-4)
582.16
Pine, J. Trees (3-5) 582.16
Romanova, N. Once there was a tree (2-4)
582.16
Fiction
Bunting, E. Night tree E
Bunting, E. Someday a tree E
Edwards, R. Ten tall oaktrees E
Gibbons, G. The seasons of Arnold's apple
tree E
Levine, A. A. Pearl Moscowitz's last stand
E
Udry, J. M. A tree is nice E
Poetry
Frost, R. Birches 811
Oppenheim, J. Have you seen trees? (k-2)
811
United States
Zim, H. S. Trees (4 and up) 582.16
The **trees**. Mahy, M.
In Mahy, M. The girl with the green ear
p49-57 S C
The **Trees** stand shining (3-6) 897
Trefoil round the world. World Association of
Girl Guides and Girl Scouts 369.463
The **trek**. Jonas, A. E
Trelease, Jim
The read-aloud handbook 028.5
(ed) Hey! listen to this. See Hey! listen to
this 028.5
The **tremendous** tree book. Brenner, B.
582.16
Tresselt, Alvin R., 1916-
The gift of the tree (k-3) 574.5
Hide and seek fog E
The mitten (k-2) 398.2
Rain drop splash E
Sun up E
Wake up, city! E
Wake up, farm! E
White snow, bright snow E
Treviño, Elizabeth Borton de, 1904-
I, Juan de Pareja (6 and up) Fic
See/See also pages in the following book(s):
Newbery and Caldecott Medal books, 1966-
1975 p5-19 028.5
Trevor, William, 1928-
Juliet's story (5 and up) Fic
Trial in the dragon's palace. Terada, A. M.
In Terada, A. M. Under the starfruit tree
p88-94 398.2
Triceratops. Lindsay, W. 567.9

Tricks
See also Juggling; Magic tricks
Thomson, D. Visual magic (5 and up)
793.8
Tricks of the trade for kids (5 and up)
790.1
Triggs, Barbara
Wombats (4-6) 599.2
Trillion (The number)
Schwartz, D. M. How much is a million?
E
Trimble, Stephen, 1950-
The village of blue stone (4-6) 970.004
Trinidad and Tobago
Fiction
Binch, C. Gregory Cool E
Joseph, L. An island Christmas E
Joseph, L. Jasmine's parlour day E
Folklore
See Folklore—Trinidad and Tobago
Poetry
Joseph, L. Coconut kind of day 811
The **trip**. Keats, E. J. See note under Keats, E.
J. Louie E
Tripp, Wallace, 1940-
Marguerite, go wash your feet (1-3)
821.008
(il) Granfa' Grig had a pig, and other
rhymes without reason from Mother
Goose. See Granfa' Grig had a pig, and
other rhymes without reason from Mother
Goose 398.8
(comp) A Great big ugly man came up and
tied his horse to me. See A Great big ugly
man came up and tied his horse to me
821.008
Trivas, Irene
(il) Blume, J. The one in the middle is the
green kangaroo E
(il) Blume, J. The Pain and the Great One
E
(il) DeFelice, C. C. Three perfect peaches
398.2
Trivia *See* Curiosities and wonders
Trivizas, Eugene, 1946-
The three little wolves and the big bad pig
E
The **Trojan** horse. Hutton, W. 883
Trojan War
Hutton, W. The Trojan horse (3-5) 883
Picard, B. L. The Iliad of Homer (6 and up)
883
Sutcliff, R. Black ships before Troy (5 and
up) 883
See/See also pages in the following book(s):
Asimov, I. Words from the myths p177-201
(6 and up) 292
Hamilton, E. Mythology p197-342 (6 and
up) 292
The **trolley** to yesterday. Bellairs, J. See note
under Bellairs, J. The curse of the blue
figurine Fic
Tropical rain forest. Sayre, A. P. 574.5

Tropical rain forests *See* Rain forests

Tropical rain forests. Mutel, C. F.   **574.5**

Trot, trot to Boston: play rhymes for baby   **398.8**

The **trouble.** Schwartz, A.
> *In* Schwartz, A. Scary stories 3 p69-76   **398.2**

Trouble River. Byars, B. C.   **Fic**

Trouble snake. Yep, L.
> *In* Yep, L. The rainbow people p118-23   **398.2**

The **trouble** with thirteen. Miles, B.   **Fic**

Trouble with trolls. Brett, J.   **E**

The **trouble** with Tuck. Taylor, T.   **Fic**

Troubling a star. L'Engle, M. See note under L'Engle, M. Meet the Austins   **Fic**

Trousers Mehmet and the sultan's daughter. Walker, B. K.
> *In* Walker, B. K. A treasury of Turkish folktales for children p91-96   **398.2**

Trout summer. Conly, J. L.   **Fic**

Truck. Crews, D.   **E**

Truck song. Siebert, D.   **E**

Trucks
> Barton, B. Trucks (k-1)   **629.224**
> Crews, D. Truck   **E**
> Hennessy, B. G. Road builders (k-2)   **625.7**
> Llewellyn, C. Truck (k-3)   **629.224**
> Marston, H. I. Big rigs (1-3)   **629.224**
> Rockwell, A. F. Trucks (k-1)   **629.224**
> Salter, A. Trucks (4 and up)   **629.224**
> Sullivan, G. Here come the monster trucks (3-6)   **629.223**
>> **Fiction**
> Merrill, J. The pushcart war (5 and up)   **Fic**
> Siebert, D. Truck song   **E**

The **true** book of rocks and minerals. See Podendorf, I. Rocks and minerals   **549**

The **true** bride. Grimm, J.
> *In* Grimm, J. The complete Grimm's fairy tales p752-60   **398.2**

The **true** confessions of Charlotte Doyle. Avi   **Fic**

The **true** history of Little Golden-hood. Marelle, C.
> *In* The Red fairy book p215-19   **398.2**

True knowledge. Philip, N.
> *In* Philip, N. The Arabian nights p113-15   **398.2**

The **true** spirit of a festival day. Shedlock, M. L.
> *In* Shedlock, M. L. The art of the storyteller p225-28   **372.6**

Truesdell, Sue
> (il) Byars, B. C. The Golly sisters go West   **E**
> (il) Little, J. Hey world, here I am!   **811**
> (il) Robins, J. Addie meets Max   **E**

(il) Schwartz, A. And the green grass grew all around   **398.2**

(il) Schwartz, A. Unriddling: all sorts of riddles to puzzle your guessery   **398.6**

Truman, Harry S., 1884-1972
> **About**
> Fleming, T. J. Harry S Truman, president (5 and up)   **92**

The **trumpet** of the swan. White, E. B.   **Fic**

Truong Ba and the butcher's skin. Terada, A. M.
> *In* Terada, A. M. Under the starfruit tree p75-77   **398.2**

Trusty John. Grimm, J.
> *In* The Blue fairy book p296-303   **398.2**

Truth, Sojourner, d. 1883
> **About**
> Adler, D. A. A picture book of Sojourner Truth (1-3)   **92**
> Ferris, J. Walking the road to freedom: a story about Sojourner Truth (3-5)   **92**
> Macht, N. L. Sojourner Truth (4 and up)   **92**
> McKissack, P. C. Sojourner Truth (1-3)   **92**
> McKissack, P. C. Sojourner Truth: ain't I a woman? (5 and up)   **92**
> *See/See also pages in the following book(s):*
> Jacobs, W. J. Great lives: human rights p107-16 (5 and up)   **920**

The **truth** about Santa Claus. Giblin, J.   **394.2**

The **truth** about unicorns. Giblin, J.   **398**

Truth to tell. Bond, N.   **Fic**

Truthfulness and falsehood
> **Fiction**
> Bawden, N. Humbug (4 and up)   **Fic**

Tseng, Jean
> (il) Garland, S. Why ducks sleep on one leg   **398.2**
> (il) Ho, M. The two brothers   **398.2**
> (il) Mahy, M. The seven Chinese brothers   **398.2**
> (il) Oppenheim, J. Have you seen trees?   **811**
> (il) Stamm, C. Three strong women   **398.2**
> (il) Watkins, Y. K. Tales from the bamboo grove   **398.2**
> (il) Yep, L. The boy who swallowed snakes   **E**

Tseng, Mou-sien
> (il) Garland, S. Why ducks sleep on one leg   **398.2**
> (il) Ho, M. The two brothers   **398.2**
> (il) Mahy, M. The seven Chinese brothers   **398.2**
> (il) Oppenheim, J. Have you seen trees?   **811**
> (il) Stamm, C. Three strong women   **398.2**

The **very** large son. Hamilton, V.
In Hamilton, V. The dark way p97-101
398.2

Very last first time. Andrews, J.   **E**

The **very** lonely firefly. Carle, E.   **E**

The **very** pretty lady. Babbitt, N.
In Babbitt, N. The Devil's storybook p13-20   **S C**

The **very** quiet cricket. Carle, E.   **E**

A **very** special house. Krauss, R.   **E**

Very Tall Mouse and Very Short Mouse. Lobel, A.
In The Read-aloud treasury p207-13
808.8

The **very** worst monster. Hutchins, P. See note under Hutchins, P. Where's the baby?
E

A **very** young musician. Krementz, J.   **788**

Vespucci, Amerigo, 1451-1512
See/See also pages in the following book(s):
Fritz, J. Around the world in a hundred years p69-75 (4-6)   **910.4**

Veterans
      Fiction
Bauer, M. D. Rain of fire (5 and up)
Fic
Hahn, M. D. December stillness (6 and up)
Fic

Veterinary medicine
Kuklin, S. Taking my cat to the vet (k-3)
636.8
Kuklin, S. Taking my dog to the vet (k-3)
636.7
See/See also pages in the following book(s):
Chrystie, F. N. Pets p216-61 (4 and up)
636.088

Vidal, Beatriz
(il) Van Laan, N. Buffalo dance   **398.2**
(il) Van Laan, N. The legend of El Dorado
398.2

Vidaure, Morris
(jt. auth) Rohmer, H. The invisible hunters
398.2

Video Christmas. Dias, E. J.
In The Big book of Christmas plays p26-40   **808.82**

Video games
Skurzynski, G. Know the score (4-6)
794.8

Videotapes
      Catalogs
From page to screen   **016.79143**

Vietnam
Garland, S. Vietnam, rebuilding a nation (4 and up)   **959.704**
Vietnam—in pictures (5 and up)   **959.7**
      Description
Schmidt, J. Two lands, one heart (3-5)
959.704
      Fiction
Keller, H. Grandfather's dream   **E**
      Folklore
See Folklore—Vietnam

      Social life and customs
Huynh, Q. N. The land I lost: adventures of a boy in Vietnam (4 and up)   **92**
Vietnam—in pictures (5 and up)   **959.7**

Vietnam, rebuilding a nation. Garland, S.
959.704

Vietnam Veterans Memorial (Washington, D.C.)
Ashabranner, B. K. Always to remember (5 and up)   **959.704**
Donnelly, J. A wall of names (2-4)
959.704
      Fiction
Bunting, E. The Wall   **E**
Hahn, M. D. December stillness (6 and up)
Fic

Vietnam War, 1961-1975
Ashabranner, B. K. Always to remember (5 and up)   **959.704**
Donnelly, J. A wall of names (2-4)
959.704
      Fiction
Boyd, C. D. Charlie Pippin (4-6)   **Fic**
Nelson, T. And one for all (5 and up)
Fic
      Protests, demonstrations, etc.
Rappaport, D. Tinker vs. Des Moines (5 and up)   **342**

Vietnamese
      Fiction
Whelan, G. Goodbye, Vietnam (4 and up)
Fic
      United States—Fiction
Gilson, J. Hello, my name is Scrambled Eggs (4 and up)   **Fic**

Vietnamese Americans
Hoyt-Goldsmith, D. Hoang Anh (3-5)
305.8
      Fiction
Paterson, K. Park's quest (5 and up)
Fic

View from the air. Lindbergh, R.   **811**

The **view** from the cherry tree. Roberts, W. D.
Fic

Viguers, Ruth Hill
(comp) Illustrators of children's books. See Illustrators of children's books   **741.6**

Vikings
Margeson, S. M. Viking (4 and up)   **948**
Martell, H. M. Everyday life in Viking times (3-5)   **940.1**
Pearson, A. The Vikings (4 and up)
948
The Vikings (5 and up)   **948**
See/See also pages in the following book(s):
Lyttle, R. B. Land beyond the river p106-24 (6 and up)   **940.1**
      Fiction
Wisniewski, D. Elfwyn's saga   **E**

The **Vikings** (5 and up)   **948**

Villa, Pancho, 1878-1923
      About
O'Brien, S. Pancho Villa (5 and up)   **92**

The **village** by the sea. Fox, P.   **Fic**

A **village** full of valentines. Stevenson, J.
E

The **village** of blue stone. Trimble, S.
970.004

A **village** of fools. Crossley-Holland, K.
In Crossley-Holland, K. British folk tales
p36-37 **398.2**

The **village** of round and square houses. Grifalconi, A.
398.2

Villages
Provensen, A. Town & country (k-2)
307.7

Villanueva Collado, Alfredo
The day we went to see snow
In Where angels glide at dawn p27-33
S C

Villeneuve, Madame de
Beauty and the beast
In The Blue fairy book p100-19
398.2

Villios, Lynne W.
Cooking the Greek way
In Easy menu ethnic cookbooks
641.5

Vincent, Gabrielle
Ernest and Celestine **E**
Ernest and Celestine at the circus. See note under Vincent, G. Ernest and Celestine
E
Ernest and Celestine's patchwork quilt. See note under Vincent, G. Ernest and Celestine
E
Ernest and Celestine's picnic. See note under Vincent, G. Ernest and Celestine **E**
Feel better, Ernest! See note under Vincent, G. Ernest and Celestine **E**
Merry Christmas, Ernest and Celestine. See note under Vincent, G. Ernest and Celestine
E
Smile, Ernest and Celestine. See note under Vincent, G. Ernest and Celestine **E**
Where are you, Ernest and Celestine? See note under Vincent, G. Ernest and Celestine
E
(il) Pomerantz, C. Halfway to your house
811

Vincent-the-Good and the electric train. Levoy, M.
In Levoy, M. The witch of Fourth Street, and other stories **S C**

Vinci, Leonardo da *See* Leonardo, da Vinci, 1452-1519

Vining, Elizabeth Gray, 1902-
Adam of the road (5 and up) **Fic**
See/See also pages in the following book(s):
Newbery Medal books, 1922-1955 p227-41
028.5

Violinists, violoncellists, etc.
Fiction
Greenwald, S. Give us a great big smile, Rosy Cole (3-5) **Fic**
Wolff, V. E. The Mozart season (6 and up)
Fic

Violins
Fleisher, P. The master violinmaker (3-5)
787.2

Viorst, Judith
Alexander and the terrible, horrible, no good, very bad day **E**
Alexander, who is not (do you hear me?) going (I mean it) to move. See note under Viorst, J. Alexander and the terrible, horrible, no good, very bad day **E**
Alexander, who used to be rich last Sunday. See note under Viorst, J. Alexander and the terrible, horrible, no good, very bad day **E**
Earrings! **E**
If I were in charge of the world and other worries (3-6) **811**
My mama says there aren't any zombies, ghosts, vampires, creatures, demons, monsters, fiends, goblins, or things **E**
Rosie and Michael **E**
Sad underwear and other complications (3-6) **811**
The southpaw [short story]
In Free to be—you and me p71-75
810.8
The tenth good thing about Barney **E**

Virginia
Cocke, W. A historical album of Virginia
In Historical albums series **973**
McNair, S. Virginia
In America the beautiful **973**
Sirvaitis, K. Virginia
In Hello USA series **973**
Fiction
Beatty, P. Charley Skedaddle (5 and up)
Fic
Paterson, K. Bridge to Terabithia (4 and up)
Fic

Virtue goes to town. Yep, L.
In Yep, L. The rainbow people p136-42
398.2

Viruses
See also Chickenpox
Balkwill, F. R. Cell wars (3-6) **616.9**
Berger, M. Germs make me sick! (k-3)
616.9
Facklam, H. Viruses (5 and up) **576**
Vision
Bryan, J. Sound and vision (4-6) **612.8**
Lauber, P. What do you see? (4 and up)
535
Parker, S. The eye and seeing (4 and up)
612.8
Wright, L. Seeing (k-2) **612.8**
Vision disorders
Fiction
Little, J. From Anna (4-6) **Fic**
Visions. Sills, L. **920**
A **visit** from St. Nicholas. Moore, C. C.
In Diane Goode's American Christmas p74-78 **810.8**
See also Moore, C. C. The night before Christmas **811**

Vuong, Lynette Dyer, 1938——*Continued*
Sky legends of Vietnam (4-6)   **398.2**
Contents: Why the rooster crows at sunrise; How the moon became ivory; The moon fairy; The miraculous banyan tree; The Weaver Fairy and the Buffalo Boy; The seven weavers

W

Waber, Bernard
Funny, funny Lyle. See note under Waber, B. Lyle, Lyle, crocodile   **E**
The house on East 88th Street. See note under Waber, B. Lyle, Lyle, crocodile   **E**
Ira says goodbye. See note under Waber, B. Ira sleeps over   **E**
Ira sleeps over   **E**
Lovable Lyle. See note under Waber, B. Lyle, Lyle, crocodile   **E**
Lyle and the birthday party. See note under Waber, B. Lyle, Lyle, crocodile   **E**
Lyle at the office. See note under Waber, B. Lyle, Lyle, crocodile   **E**
Lyle finds his mother. See note under Waber, B. Lyle, Lyle, crocodile   **E**
Lyle, Lyle, crocodile   **E**

Waddell, Martin
Can't you sleep, Little Bear?   **E**
Farmer duck   **E**
Let's go home, Little Bear. See note under Waddell, M. Can't you sleep, Little Bear?   **E**
Owl babies   **E**
Stories from the Bible   **221.9**

Wade, Linda R.
James Carter: thirty-ninth president of the United States (4 and up)   **92**

Wade, Mary Dodson
Ada Byron Lovelace (5 and up)   **92**
Benedict Arnold (4 and up)   **92**

Wadlow, Robert Pershing, 1918-1940
See/See also pages in the following book(s):
Drimmer, F. Born different p48-71 (6 and up)   **920**

Wagner, Honus, 1874-1955
About
Kavanagh, J. Honus Wagner (4 and up)   **92**

See/See also pages in the following book(s):
Kramer, S. Baseball's greatest hitters p8-13 (2-4)   **920**

Wagner, Jane
J. T. (3-6)   **Fic**

Wagon wheels. Brenner, B.   **E**
Wagons *See* Carriages and carts
Wahat al-salam. Dolphin, L.   **956.94**
Wailing Wall (Jerusalem) *See* Western Wall (Jerusalem)
The **Wailing** Wall. Fisher, L. E.   **221.9**
The **Wainscott** weasel. Seidler, T.   **Fic**
Wait till Emmett comes. Haskins, J.
    In Haskins, J. The headless haunt and other African American ghost stories p3-6   **398.2**

Wait till Helen comes. Hahn, M. D.   **Fic**
Wait till Martin comes
    In The Diane Goode book of American folk tales and songs p35-37   **398.2**
Waiting for Anya. Morpurgo, M.   **Fic**
Waiting for Hannah. Russo, M.   **E**
Wake up, city!. Tresselt, A. R.   **E**
Wake up, farm!. Tresselt, A. R.   **E**
The **waking** of Men. Curry, J. L.
    In Curry, J. L. Back in the beforetime p116   **398.2**
The **waking** of the prince. Brooke, W. J.
    In Brooke, W. J. A telling of the tales: five stories p3-33   **S C**

Waldee, Lynne Marie
Cooking the French way
    In Easy menu ethnic cookbooks   **641.5**

Waldman, Bryna
(il) Aardema, V. Anansi finds a fool   **398.2**

Waldman, Neil, 1947-
(il) Appelt, K. Bayou lullaby   **E**
(il) Blake, W. The tyger   **821**
(il) Goldin, B. D. The Passover journey   **296.4**
(il) Luenn, N. Nessa's fish   **E**
(il) Noyes, A. The highwayman   **821**

Wales
Sutherland, D. B. Wales (4 and up)   **942.9**

Fiction
Bawden, N. Carrie's war (4 and up)   **Fic**
Bond, N. A string in the harp (6 and up)   **Fic**
Cooper, S. The grey king (5 and up)   **Fic**
Kimmel, M. M. Magic in the mist (1-4)   **Fic**

Folklore
See Folklore—Wales

Walk a green path. Lewin, B.   **581**
A **walk** on the Great Barrier Reef. Arnold, C.   **574.92**
A **walk** through a rain forest. Jenike, D.   **574.5**
Walk two moons. Creech, S.   **Fic**

Walker, Alice, 1944-
Langston Hughes, American poet (2-5)   **92**

Walker, Barbara K.
A treasury of Turkish folktales for children (4 and up)   **398.2**
Contents: The mouse and the elephant; Who's there? And what do you want?; Hasan, the heroic mouse-child; The magpie and the milk; The mosquito and the water buffalo; The rabbit and the wolf; The lion's den; The crow and the snake; Lazy Keloğlan and the sultan's daughter; The three brothers and the hand of fate; Keloğlan and the twelve dancing princesses; I know what I'll do; Nasreddin Hoca, seller of wisdom; Nasreddin Hoca and the third shot; The Hoca as Tamerlane's tax collector; The Hoca and the candle; Teeny-Tiny and the witch-woman; Karaçor and the giants; The wonderful pumpkin; The courage of Kazan; Just say hiç!; How Deli kept his part of the bargain; Two fools

The **white** dove. Grimm, J.
In Grimm, J. About wise men and simpletons p52-53   **398.2**

The **White** duck
In The Yellow fairy book p155-60   **398.2**

The **white** duck. Afanas'ev, A. N.
In Afanas'ev, A. N. Russian fairy tales p342-45   **398.2**

White Fang. London, J.   **Fic**

The **white** hare and the crocodiles. Quayle, E.
In Quayle, E. The shining princess, and other Japanese legends p24-32   **398.2**

The **White** Horse Girl and the Blue Wind Boy. Sandburg, C.
In Herds of thunder, manes of gold p29-34   **808.8**
In Sandburg, C. Rootabaga stories pt 1 p131-37   **S C**
In Sandburg, C. The Sandburg treasury p63-65   **818**

White horses. Crompton, A. E.
In Herds of thunder, manes of gold p55-64   **808.8**

White House (Washington, D.C.)
Fisher, L. E. The White House (4 and up)   **975.3**

The **White** Mountains. Christopher, J.   **Fic**

White on black. Hoban, T.   **E**

The **white** seal. Kipling, R.
In Kipling, R. The jungle books   **S C**

White snake. Carpenter, F.
In Carpenter, F. Tales of a Chinese grandmother p159-65   **398.2**

The **white** snake. Grimm, J.
In The Green fairy book p319-23   **398.2**
In Grimm, J. The complete Grimm's fairy tales p98-101   **398.2**

White snow, bright snow. Tresselt, A. R.   **E**

The **white** stag. Seredy, K.   **Fic**

The **white** stallion. Shub, E.   **E**

White stallion of Lipizza. Henry, M.   **Fic**

White Weasel. Bruchac, J.
In Bruchac, J. Flying with the eagle, racing with the great bear p6-14   **398.2**

Whitebear Whittington
In Grandfather tales p52-64   **398.2**

Whitelaw, Nancy
Theodore Roosevelt takes charge (6 and up)   **92**

Whiteley, Opal Stanley
About
Boulton, J. Only Opal   **E**

Whiten, Mark
See/See also pages in the following book(s):
Torres, J. A. Home-run hitters p105-10 (4 and up)   **920**

Whitfield, Philip J.
Macmillan children's guide to dinosaurs and other prehistoric animals (3-6)   **567.9**

Whitman, Walt, 1819-1892
About
Loewen, N. Walt Whitman (5 and up)   **92**
See/See also pages in the following book(s):
Faber, D. Great lives: American literature p161-69 (5 and up)   **920**

Whitney, Elinor, 1889-
(ed) Caldecott Medal books, 1938-1957. See Caldecott Medal books, 1938-1957   **028.5**
(ed) Horn Book reflections on children's books and reading. See Horn Book reflections on children's books and reading   **028.5**
(ed) Newbery Medal books, 1922-1955. See Newbery Medal books, 1922-1955   **028.5**

Whittier, John Greenleaf, 1807-1892
Barbara Frietchie (1-3)   **811**

Whittington and his cat. Jacobs, J.
In Jacobs, J. English fairy tales p167-76   **398.2**

Whittling *See* Wood carving

Who came down that road?. Lyon, G. E.   **E**

Who discovered America?. Lauber, P.   **970.01**

Who eats what?. Lauber, P.   **574.5**

Who harnessed the horse?. Facklam, M.   **636**

Who invented the game?. Ward, G. C.   **796.357**

Who is Carrie?. Collier, J. L.   **Fic**

Who killed Cock Robin
In A Nursery companion p32-35   **820.8**

Who lives in the skull?. MacDonald, M. R.
In MacDonald, M. R. When the lights go out p143-47   **372.6**

Who said meow?. Polushkin, M.   **E**

Who said red?. Serfozo, M.   **E**

Who says moo?. Young, R.   **E**

Who shrank my grandmother's house?. Esbensen, B. J.   **811**

Who took the farmer's [hat]?. Lexau, J. M.   **E**

Who uses this?. Miller, M.   **E**

Who you!. Hamilton, V.
In Hamilton, V. Her stories p45-50   **398.2**

The **whooping** crane. Patent, D. H.   **639.9**

Whooping cranes *See* Cranes (Birds)

Who's a pest?. Bonsall, C. N.   **E**

Who's afraid of the dark?. Bonsall, C. N.   **E**

Who's in Rabbit's house?. Aardema, V.   **398.2**

Wild flowers—*Continued*

Samson, S. M. Fairy dusters and blazing stars **582.13**

Zim, H. S. Flowers (4 and up) **582.13**

Conservation

See Plant conservation

Wild rice *See* Rice

The **wild** swans. Ehrlich, A. **E**

Wild turkey, tame turkey. Patent, D. H. **598**

Wild words!. Asher, S. **808**

Wilde, Oscar, 1854-1900

The fairy tales of Oscar Wilde (3-6) **S C**

Contents: The happy prince; The Nightingale and the rose; The selfish Giant; The devoted friend; The remarkable rocket; The young king; The birthday of the Infanta; The Fisherman and his soul; The Star-Child

The Happy Prince [abridged version] **E**

The selfish giant (2-5) **Fic**

also in The Oxford treasury of children's stories p121-26 **S C**

Wildebeests *See* Gnus

Wilder, Alec, 1907-1980

Lullabies and night songs. See Lullabies and night songs **782.42**

Wilder, Laura Ingalls, 1867-1957

By the shores of Silver Lake. See note under Wilder, L. I. Little house in the big woods **Fic**

Farmer boy. See note under Wilder, L. I. Little house in the big woods **Fic**

The first four years. See note under Wilder, L. I. Little house in the big woods **Fic**

A Little house Christmas **S C**

Contents: Christmas; Mr. Edwards meets Santa Claus; The Christmas horses; A merry Christmas; Surprise; The fourth day; Christmas Eve

Little house in the big woods (4-6) **Fic**

Little house on the prairie. See note under Wilder, L. I. Little house in the big woods **Fic**

Little town on the prairie. See note under Wilder, L. I. Little house in the big woods **Fic**

The long winter. See note under Wilder, L. I. Little house in the big woods **Fic**

Mr. Edwards meets Santa Claus

In The Family read-aloud holiday treasury p136-45 **808.8**

On the banks of Plum Creek. See note under Wilder, L. I. Little house in the big woods **Fic**

These happy golden years. See note under Wilder, L. I. Little house in the big woods **Fic**

West from home (6 and up) **92**

(ed) The Laura Ingalls Wilder songbook. See The Laura Ingalls Wilder songbook **782.42**

About

Anderson, W. T. Laura Ingalls Wilder (4 and up) **92**

Walker, B. M. The Little House cookbook (5 and up) **641.5**

Wilderness areas

Arnosky, J. Crinkleroot's guide to walking in wild places (k-3) **796.5**

Wilderness survival

Fiction

Eckert, A. W. Incident at Hawk's Hill (6 and up) **Fic**

George, J. C. Julie of the wolves (6 and up) **Fic**

Houston, J. A. Frozen fire (6 and up) **Fic**

O'Dell, S. Island of the Blue Dolphins (5 and up) **Fic**

Wildlife Center (Española, N.M.)

Dewey, J. Wildlife rescue (4-6) **639.9**

Wildlife conservation

See also Birds—Protection

Ancona, G. The golden lion tamarin comes home (3-5) **639.9**

Ancona, G. Turtle watch (2-4) **597.9**

Arnold, C. On the brink of extinction (4 and up) **598**

Arnold, C. Sea lion (3-5) **599.74**

Clark, M. G. The endangered Florida panther (4 and up) **599.74**

Cone, M. Come back, salmon (3-6) **639.3**

Cowcher, H. Antarctica (1-3) **998**

DaVolls, A. Tano & Binti (k-3) **599.88**

Dewey, J. Wildlife rescue (4-6) **639.9**

Facklam, M. And then there was one (3-6) **591.5**

Few, R. Macmillan children's guide to endangered animals (4 and up) **591.5**

Fraser, M. A. Sanctuary (3-5) **639.9**

Friedman, J. Operation Siberian crane (5 and up) **639.9**

The Grolier student encyclopedia of endangered species (4 and up) **591.5**

Kessler, C. All the king's animals (4-6) **639.9**

Kraus, S. D. The search for the right whale (5 and up) **599.5**

Lasky, K. Monarchs (4 and up) **595.7**

Mallory, K. Rescue of the stranded whales (5 and up) **639.9**

Maynard, T. Saving endangered mammals (4-6) **639.9**

McMillan, B. A beach for the birds (2-4) **598**

Patent, D. H. Ospreys (4 and up) **598**

Patent, D. H. Where the wild horses roam (4 and up) **639.9**

Patent, D. H. The whooping crane (4 and up) **639.9**

Pringle, L. P. Living treasure (4 and up) **333.95**

Schlein, M. Project panda watch (4 and up) **599.74**

Smith, R. Sea otter rescue (5 and up) **639.9**

See/See also pages in the following book(s):

Johnson, S. A. Raptor rescue! (4 and up) **639.9**

Langone, J. Our endangered earth p126-50 (6 and up) **363.7**

Wit and humor—*Continued*

Schwartz, A. There is a carrot in my ear, and other noodle tales (k-2) **398.2**

History and criticism

See/See also pages in the following book(s):

Crosscurrents of criticism p197-216

028.5

The **Witch**

In The Yellow fairy book p216-21

398.2

The **Witch** and her servants

In The Yellow fairy book p161-77

398.2

The **witch** cat. San Souci, R.

In San Souci, R. Short & shivery p28-34

398.2

Witch Hazel. Schertle, A.   **E**

The **witch** herself. Naylor, P. R. See note under Naylor, P. R. The witch's eye   **Fic**

Witch hunt. Krensky, S.   **133.4**

The **Witch** in the stone boat

In The Yellow fairy book p274-78

398.2

The **witch** of Blackbird Pond. Speare, E. G.   **Fic**

The **witch** of Fourth Street. Levoy, M.

In Levoy, M. The witch of Fourth Street, and other stories   **S C**

The **witch** of Fourth Street, and other stories. Levoy, M.   **S C**

Witch poems   **821.008**

The **witch** returns. Naylor, P. R. See note under Naylor, P. R. The witch's eye   **Fic**

Witch water. Naylor, P. R. See note under Naylor, P. R. The witch's eye   **Fic**

Witch weed. Naylor, P. R. See note under Naylor, P. R. The witch's eye   **Fic**

Witchcraft

See also Magic

Jackson, S. The witchcraft of Salem Village (4 and up)   **133.4**

Krensky, S. Witch hunt (2-4)   **133.4**

Fiction

Bellairs, J. The house with a clock in its walls (5 and up)   **Fic**

Briggs, K. M. Kate Crackernuts (6 and up)   **Fic**

Konigsburg, E. L. Jennifer, Hecate, Macbeth, William McKinley, and me, Elizabeth (4-6)   **Fic**

MacLachlan, P. Tomorrow's wizard (3-6)   **S C**

Naylor, P. R. The witch's eye (5 and up)   **Fic**

Norton, M. Bed-knob and broomstick (3-5)   **Fic**

Palatini, M. Piggie pie!   **E**

Petry, A. L. Tituba of Salem Village (6 and up)   **Fic**

Snyder, Z. K. The witches of Worm (5 and up)   **Fic**

Speare, E. G. The witch of Blackbird Pond (6 and up)   **Fic**

Turner, A. W. Rosemary's witch (5 and up)   **Fic**

Van Allsburg, C. The widow's broom   **E**

The **witchcraft** of Salem Village. Jackson, S.   **133.4**

Witches

Fiction

Balian, L. Humbug witch   **E**

Brittain, B. Devil's donkey (3-6)   **Fic**

Carlson, N. S. Spooky night   **E**

De Paola, T. Strega Nona   **E**

Johnston, T. Alice Nizzy Nazzy, the Witch of Santa Fe   **E**

Johnston, T. The vanishing pumpkin   **E**

Mahy, M. The boy who was followed home   **E**

Peet, B. Big bad Bruce   **E**

Peet, B. The whingdingdilly   **E**

Steig, W. Caleb & Kate   **E**

Stevenson, J. Emma   **E**

Wood, A. Heckedy Peg   **E**

Poetry

Witch poems   **821.008**

Yolen, J. Best witches: poems for Halloween (3-5)   **811**

The **witches** [excerpt]. Dahl, R.

In The Random House book of humor for children p120-29   **817.008**

The **witches'** eyes. San Souci, R.

In San Souci, R. More short & shivery p5-10   **398.2**

The **witches** of Worm. Snyder, Z. K.   **Fic**

Witches, pumpkins, and grinning ghosts. Barth, E.   **394.2**

The **witch's** boar. Hamilton, V.

In Hamilton, V. The dark way p113-18   **398.2**

The **witch's** daughter. Bawden, N.   **Fic**

The **witch's** eye. Naylor, P. R.   **Fic**

Witch's sister. Naylor, P. R. See note under Naylor, P. R. The witch's eye   **Fic**

The **witch's** skinny. Hamilton, V.

In Hamilton, V. The dark way p143-48   **398.2**

Witcomb, Gerald

(il) Salter, A. Trucks   **629.224**

Witcracks: jokes and jests from American folklore. Schwartz, A.   **398**

With a way, hey, Mister Stormalong. Cohn, A.

In From sea to shining sea p104-06   **810.8**

With Bert & Ray. Konigsburg, E. L.

In Konigsburg, E. L. Throwing shadows   **S C**

With his head tucked underneath his arm. Coville, B.

In Coville, B. Oddly enough p33-41   **S C**

With love from Koko. McNulty, F.   **599.88**

With my eyes closed. Arenas, R.

In Where angels glide at dawn p35-41   **S C**

Wolves—*Continued*

George, J. C. The moon of the gray wolves (3-6) **599.74**

Gibbons, G. Wolves (k-3) **599.74**

Johnson, S. A. Wolf pack (4 and up) **599.74**

Lawrence, R. D. Wolves (4-6) **599.74**

Patent, D. H. Dogs: the wolf within (3-6) **599.74**

Patent, D. H. Gray wolf, red wolf (4 and up) **599.74**

Silverstein, A. The red wolf (4 and up) **599.74**

Simon, S. Wolves (3-6) **599.74**

Fiction

Crampton, P. Peter and the wolf **E**

George, J. C. Julie (6 and up) **Fic**

George, J. C. Julie of the wolves (6 and up) **Fic**

Goble, P. Dream wolf **E**

Grimm, J. Little Red Cap (k-3) **398.2**

Hyman, T. S. Little Red Riding Hood (k-2) **398.2**

Kasza, K. The wolf's chicken stew **E**

Marshall, J. Red Riding Hood (k-2) **398.2**

Marshall, J. The three little pigs (k-2) **398.2**

Palatini, M. Piggie pie! **E**

Patent, D. H. Return of the wolf (5 and up) **Fic**

Prokofiev, S. Peter and the wolf **E**

Rounds, G. Three little pigs and the big bad wolf (k-3) **398.2**

Trivizas, E. The three little wolves and the big bad pig **E**

Young, E. Lon Po Po (1-3) **398.2**

Zemach, M. The three little pigs (k-2) **398.2**

The **wolves** of Willoughby Chase. Aiken, J. **Fic**

Woman and Man started even. Hamilton, V.
In Hamilton, V. Her stories p69-74 **398.2**

The **woman** and the changeling elf. Grimm, J.
In Grimm, J. About wise men and simpletons p34 **398.2**

The **woman** and the tree children. Lester, J.
In Lester, J. How many spots does a leopard have? and other tales p37-39 **398.2**

The **woman** in the snow. McKissack, P. C.
In McKissack, P. C. The dark-thirty p55-65 **S C**

The **woman** who fell from the sky. Bierhorst, J. **398.2**

The **woman** who flummoxed the fairies. Forest, H. **398.2**

The **woman** who flummoxed the fairies. Leodhas, S. N.
In Womenfolk and fairy tales p135-45 **398.2**

The **woman** who outshone the sun. Cruz, A. **398.2**

The **woman** with the golden arm. Twain, M.
In From sea to shining sea p342-43 **810.8**

Woman's way. Afanas'ev, A. N.
In Afanas'ev, A. N. Russian fairy tales p599 **398.2**

Wombats

Triggs, B. Wombats (4-6) **599.2**

Women

> *See also* women of particular racial or ethnic groups, e.g. *African American women;* and women in various occupations and professions

Biography

Rappaport, D. Living dangerously (4 and up) **920**

Civil rights

See Women's rights

Employment

Colman, P. Rosie the riveter (5 and up) **331.4**

Folklore

San Souci, R. Cut from the same cloth (4-6) **398.2**

Political activity

See also Women politicians

Suffrage

Fritz, J. You want women to vote, Lizzie Stanton? (2-4) **92**

West (U.S.)

Bentley, J. Brides, midwives, and widows (5 and up) **978**

Miller, B. M. Buffalo gals (5 and up) **978**

Women air pilots

Brown, D. Ruth Law thrills a nation (k-3) **629.13**

Lauber, P. Lost star: the story of Amelia Earhart (5 and up) **92**

Quackenbush, R. M. Clear the cow pasture, I'm coming in for a landing!: a story of Amelia Earhart (2-4) **92**

Van Meter, V. Taking flight (4 and up) **92**

Women artists

Collins, D. R. The country artist: a story about Beatrix Potter (3-5) **92**

Hyman, T. S. Self-portrait: Trina Schart Hyman (4 and up) **92**

Lyons, M. E. Stitching stars: the story quilts of Harriet Powers (4 and up) **92**

Nickens, B. Walking the log (2-4) **92**

Oneal, Z. Grandma Moses: painter of rural America (4 and up) **92**

Sills, L. Inspirations (5 and up) **920**

Sills, L. Visions (5 and up) **920**

Taylor, J. Beatrix Potter: artist, storyteller and countrywoman **92**

Turner, R. M. Faith Ringgold (4-6) **92**

Turner, R. M. Frida Kahlo (4-6) **92**

Turner, R. M. Georgia O'Keeffe (4-6) **92**

Turner, R. M. Mary Cassatt (4-6) **92**

Turner, R. M. Rosa Bonheur (4-6) **92**

The **wonderful** day. Brown, M. W.
In Brown, M. W. The fish with the deep
sea smile p126-27   **818**

The **wonderful** flight to the Mushroom Planet.
Cameron, E.   **Fic**

The **wonderful** healing leaves. Lester, J.
In Lester, J. How many spots does a leopard have? and other tales p59-68
   398.2

The **wonderful** kitten. Brown, M. W.
In Brown, M. W. The fish with the deep
sea smile p106-10   **818**

Wonderful pear tree. Carpenter, F.
In Carpenter, F. Tales of a Chinese grandmother p142-49   **398.2**

The **wonderful** pumpkin. Walker, B. K.
In Walker, B. K. A treasury of Turkish
folktales for children p62-66
   398.2

Wonderful pussy willows. Wexler, J.   **583**

The **wonderful** shamir. Kimmel, E. A.
In Kimmel, E. A. The spotted pony: a
collection of Hanukkah stories p34-41
   398.2

The **wonderful** sheep. Aulnoy, Madame d'
In The Blue fairy book p214-30
   398.2

The **wonderful** tar baby. Browne, G.
In The Oxford treasury of children's stories p47-49   **S C**

The **wonderful** Wizard of Oz. See Baum, L. F.
The Wizard of Oz   **Fic**

Wonders *See* Curiosities and wonders

The **wondrous** wonder, the marvelous marvel.
Afanas'ev, A. N.
In Afanas'ev, A. N. Russian fairy tales
p13-15   **398.2**

Wong, Jennifer Jordan- *See* Jordan-Wong,
Jennifer

Wood, Audrey
Elbert's bad word   **E**
Heckedy Peg   **E**
King Bidgood's in the bathtub   **E**
The napping house   **E**
(jt. auth) Wood, D. Piggies   **E**

Wood, Don, 1945-
Piggies   **E**
(il) Wood, A. Elbert's bad word   **E**
(il) Wood, A. Heckedy Peg   **E**
(il) Wood, A. King Bidgood's in the bathtub
   E
(il) Wood, A. The napping house   **E**

Wood, Gerald, 1938-
(il) Macdonald, F. A Roman fort   **355.7**

Wood, Gerry *See* Wood, Gerald, 1938-

Wood, Grant, 1892-1942
About
Venezia, M. Grant Wood (k-3)   **92**

Wood, Robert Muir
Rand McNally picture atlas of prehistoric
life. See Rand McNally picture atlas of
prehistoric life   **560**

Wood, Robert W., 1933-
What? (4 and up)   **507.8**
When? (4 and up)   **507.8**
Where? (4 and up)   **507.8**

Wood, Ted, 1965-
A boy becomes a man at Wounded Knee
   970.004

Wood, Tim
The Aztecs (4 and up)   **972**
The Renaissance (4 and up)   **940.2**

Wood
Miller, C. Woodlore (3-5)   **674**

Wood carving
Fiction
Bulla, C. R. Daniel's duck   **E**
Wojciechowski, S. The Christmas miracle of
Jonathan Toomey   **E**

Woodchucks *See* Marmots

Woodcuts
See/See also pages in the following book(s):
The Illustrator's notebook p92-94   **741.6**

The **wooden** bowl. Quayle, E.
In Quayle, E. The shining princess, and
other Japanese legends p97-102
   398.2

The **wooden** bowl. Vittorini, D.
In Bauer, C. F. Celebrations p68-70
   808.8

The **wooden** doll. Bonners, S.   **E**

The **Wooden** Indian and the Shaghorn Buffalo.
Sandburg, C.
In Sandburg, C. Rootabaga stories pt 1
p125-27   **S C**
In Sandburg, C. The Sandburg treasury
p61-62   **818**

Woodlore. Miller, C.   **674**

Woodrow Kennington works practically a miracle. Paterson, K.
In Paterson, K. Angels & other strangers:
family Christmas stories p90-104
   S C

Woodruff, Elvira
Dear Levi (4-6)   **Fic**

Woods, Granville, 1856-1910
See/See also pages in the following book(s):
McKissack, P. C. African-American inven-
tors p71-75 (5 and up)   **920**

Woods *See* Forests and forestry

Woods. Silver, D. M.   **574.5**

Woodson, Jacqueline
I hadn't meant to tell you this (6 and up)
   Fic

Woodward, Martin
(il) Bowler, M. Trains   **625.1**

Woodwork
See also Carpentry
Adkins, J. Toolchest (5 and up)   **684**
Miller, C. Woodlore (3-5)   **674**

Woody's 20 grow big songs. Guthrie, W.
   782.42

Yeager, Chuck, 1923-
About
Levinson, N. S. Chuck Yeager: the man who broke the sound barrier (5 and up)
92

Taylor, R. L. The first supersonic flight (4 and up) **629.132**
See/See also pages in the following book(s):
Aaseng, N. Breaking the sound barrier p77-97 (6 and up) **629.132**

Yeager, Jeana
About
Taylor, R. L. The first unrefueled flight around the world (4 and up) **629.13**

The **year** at Maple Hill Farm. Provensen, A. **E**

A **year** in the country. Florian, D. **E**

A **year** of beasts. Wolff, A. **E**

A **year** of birds. Wolff, A. **E**

Year of impossible goodbyes. Choi, S. N. **Fic**

The **year** of no more corn. Ketteman, H. **E**

The **year** of the perfect Christmas tree. Houston, G. **E**

A **year** on Monhegan Island. Dean, J. **974.1**

The **year** they walked: Rosa Parks and the Montgomery bus boycott. Siegel, B. **92**

The **yearling**. Rawlings, M. K. **Fic**

Yee, Paul
Tales from Gold Mountain (4 and up) **S C**

Contents: Spirits of the railway; Sons and daughters; The friends of Kwan Ming; Ginger for the heart; Gambler's eyes; Forbidden fruit; Rider Chan and the night river; The revenge of the Iron Chink

Yeh-Shen. Louie, A.-L. **398.2**

The **yellow** dwarf. Aulnoy, Madame d'
In The Blue fairy book p30-50 **398.2**
In The Classic fairy tales p68-80 **398.2**

The **Yellow** fairy book (4-6) **398.2**

Yellow Lily. Crossley-Holland, K.
In Crossley-Holland, K. British folk tales p313-30 **398.2**

The **Yellow** ribbon
In Juba this and Juba that **372.6**

The **yellow** thunder dragon. Mayo, M.
In Mayo, M. Magical tales from many lands p116-26 **398.2**

Yellowstone fires. Patent, D. H. **574.5**

Yellowstone National Park
Ekey, R. Fire! in Yellowstone (2-4) **574.5**
Lauber, P. Summer of fire (4 and up) **574.5**
Patent, D. H. Yellowstone fires (2-4) **574.5**
Pringle, L. P. Fire in the forest (4-6) **574.5**

Staub, F. J. Yellowstone's cycle of fire (3-6) **574.5**
Vogel, C. G. The great Yellowstone fire (3-6) **574.5**

Yellowstone's cycle of fire. Staub, F. J. **574.5**

Yeoman, Cushla, 1971-
About
Butler, D. Cushla and her books **362.4**

Yeoman, John
The singing tortoise and other animal folktales (4-6) **398.2**
Contents: The crocodile and the jackal; The young leopard and the ram; The coyote and the ravens; The singing tortoise; The impudent little bird; The turkey girl; How the turtle got his shell; The Ranee and the cobra; The cat and the mice; Animal language; The rabbit and the elephants

Yep, Laurence
The boy who swallowed snakes **E**
The Butterfly Boy **E**
Child of the owl (5 and up) **Fic**
Dragon's gate (6 and up) **Fic**
Dragonwings (5 and up) **Fic**
Later, gator (4-6) **Fic**
The lost garden (5 and up) **92**
The man who tricked a ghost (k-3) **398.2**
The rainbow people (4 and up) **398.2**
Contents: Bedtime snacks; Natural enemies; The professor of smells; The eel's disguise; The child of calamity; The ghost's bride; The butterfly man; We are all one; The superior pet; Snake-spoke; The old jar; The boasting contest; Trouble snake; Breaker's bridge; Virtue goes to town; The homecoming; Dream flier; Slippers; The changeling; The rainbow people
The shell woman & the king (2-4) **398.2**
The star fisher (6 and up) **Fic**
Sweetwater (6 and up) **Fic**
Thief of hearts (5 and up) **Fic**
Tongues of jade (4 and up) **398.2**
Contents: The green magic; The guardians; The cure; The little emperor; Royal robes; Fish heads; The phantom heart; The snake's revenge; The foolish wish; Waters of gold; The tiger cat; The rat in the wall; The fatal flower; The teacher's underwear; The magical horse; Eyes of jade; The ghostly rhyme
The tree of dreams (4 and up) **398.2**
Contents: The helpful badger; Dream girl; Fighting cricket; South branch; The rescue; Paying with shadows; The dream tree; The loom of night; The buried treasure; The fool's dream

Yeti
Landau, E. Yeti (3-5) **001.9**

Yettele's feathers. Rothenberg, J. **398.2**

Yo! Yes?. Raschka, C. **E**

Yolen, Jane
Animal fare (3-5) **811**
The ballad of the pirate queens (3-5) **811**
Best witches: poems for Halloween (3-5) **811**
Commander Toad and the big black hole. See note under Yolen, T. Commander Toad in space **E**
Commander Toad and the dis-asteroid. See note under Yolen, T. Commander Toad in space **E**

Yolen, Jane—*Continued*
Commander Toad and the intergalactic spy. See note under Yolen, T. Commander Toad in space   E
Commander Toad and the Planet of the Grapes. See note under Yolen, T. Commander Toad in space   E
Commander Toad and the space pirates. See note under Yolen, T. Commander Toad in space   E
Commander Toad in space   E
The devil's arithmetic (4 and up)   Fic
Dinosaur dances (3-5)   811
The dragon's boy (3 and up)   Fic
The girl who loved the wind   E
Greyling   E
Hark! a Christmas sampler   808.8
Here there be dragons (5 and up)   810.8
Includes the following stories: Great-Grandfather Dragon's tale; The dragon woke and stretched; "Story," the old man said; Cockfight; Dragonfield; The king's dragon; The dragon's boy; One Ox, Two Ox, Three Ox, and the Dragon King
Here there be unicorns (5 and up)   810.8
How beastly! (3-5)   811
A letter from Phoenix Farm (1-3)   92
Letting Swift River go   E
Owl moon   E
Picnic with Piggins. See note under Yolen, J. Piggins and the royal wedding   E
Piggins. See note under Yolen, J. Piggins and the royal wedding   E
Piggins and the royal wedding   E
Ring of earth: a child's book of seasons (3-6)   811
The seeing stick   E
The sleeping beauty (k-2)   398.2
Sleeping ugly   E
Tam Lin (3-6)   398.2
The three bears holiday rhyme book (k-2)   811
The three bears rhyme book (k-2)   811
Touch magic   028.5
Water music (3-5)   811
(ed) Jane Yolen's Mother Goose songbook. See Jane Yolen's Mother Goose songbook   782.42
(ed) The Lap-time song and play book. See The Lap-time song and play book   782.42
(ed) The Lullaby songbook. See The Lullaby songbook   782.42
(ed) Sleep rhymes around the world. See Sleep rhymes around the world   808.81
Yolonda's genius. Fenner, C.   Fic
Yom Kippur
Kimmel, E. A. Days of Awe (3-6)   296.4
Fiction
Cohen, B. Yussel's prayer (3-5)   398.2
Yonder. Johnston, T.   E
Yonjwa seeks a bride. MacDonald, M. R.
In MacDonald, M. R. The storyteller's start-up book p195-99   372.6

Yorinks, Arthur, 1953-
Company's coming   E
Hey, Al   E
It happened in Pinsk   E
See/See also pages in the following book(s):
Sendak, M. Caldecott & Co.: notes on books and pictures p139-41   028.5
York
See/See also pages in the following book(s):
Haskins, J. Against all opposition p23-40 (5 and up)   920
Yoshi
(il) Wells, R. A to Zen   495.6
Yoshida, Toshi, 1911-
Young lions (1-3)   599.74
Yossel and Sossel. Sanfield, S.
In Sanfield, S. The feather merchants & other tales of the fools of Chelm p44-49   398.2
You be good and I'll be night: jump-on-the-bed poems. Merriam, E.   811
"You better not do it". Sanfield, S.
In Sanfield, S. The adventures of High John the Conqueror   398.2
You call that a farm?. Epstein, S.   636
You can't eat your chicken pox, Amber Brown. Danziger, P. See note under Danziger, P. Amber Brown is not a crayon   Fic
You hold me and I'll hold you. Carson, J.   E
You know who. Ciardi, J.   811
You may be the next ... Schwartz, A.
In Schwartz, A. Scary stories 3 p89   398.2
You must be joking! [series]
Peterson, S. K. Plugged in   793.73
You read to me, I'll read to you. Ciardi, J.   811
You shouldn't have to say good-bye. Hermes, P.   Fic
You want women to vote, Lizzie Stanton?. Fritz, J.   92
You won't believe your eyes!. O'Neill, C.   152.14
You'll soon grow into them, Titch. Hutchins, P. See note under Hutchins, P. Titch   E
Youn Hee and me. Adler, C. S.   Fic
Younde goes to town. Courlander, H.
In Courlander, H. The cow-tail switch, and other West African stories p59-64   398.2
Young, Ed
Little Plum (k-3)   398.2
Lon Po Po (1-3)   398.2
Moon mother (2-4)   398.2
Red thread (2-4)   398.2
Seven blind mice (k-3)   398.2
(il) Cats are cats. See Cats are cats   808.81

PART 3

SELECT LIST OF RECOMMENDED CD-ROM REFERENCE WORKS

SELECT LIST OF RECOMMENDED CD-ROM REFERENCE WORKS

Cartopedia. DK Multimedia, Inc., 95 Madison Avenue, New York, NY 10016 1995 sd., col $49.95

System requirements for Windows: 386DX or higher; 4MB RAM; Windows 3.1 or higher; SVGA; 8- or 16-bit sound card
System requirements for Macintosh: LC II; 4MB RAM; System 7; SVGA; 8-bit sound card

This multimedia package combines an atlas (physical and political), a gazetteer, and an almanac with the resources of an encyclopedia. Over 7,000 pop-up windows present overviews of every country, as well as specific information on such aspects as population, natural resources, and climate

Compton's interactive encyclopedia. SoftKey International Inc., 1 Athenaeum St., Cambridge, MA 02142 1996 sd., col. $37

System requirements for Windows: 486SX or higher; 4MB RAM (8MB recommended); Windows 3.1 or higher; SVGA; Sound Blaster compatible sound card; speakers or headphones; mouse
Includes Small blue planet CD-ROM

Contains over 33,000 articles, 8,000 pictures, 100 full-motion videos, 3-D animations and presentations, interactive atlas and timelines, online dictionary and thesaurus. Includes the editing room, a feature that turns articles, pictures, videos and sounds into a personal multimedia presentation

Encarta encyclopedia. Microsoft Corp., One Microsoft Way, Redmond, WA 98052 1996 sd., col. $54.95

System requirements for Windows: 486SX or higher; 8MB RAM; 9MB free hard drive space for Windows 95 or 11MB for Windows 3.1; DOS 3.1 or higher; Windows 3.1 or higher, or Windows 95 or Windows NT Workstation 3.51 or higher; SVGA; mouse; speakers or headphones
System requirements for Macintosh: LC II or higher; 8MB RAM; 7MB free hard drive space (11MB recommended); System 7.0 or higher; SVGA

Includes over 26,000 articles, 100 videos, 900 maps, 8,000 photos, 40 country fact boxes, a timeline, and nearly 10 hours of sound. Offers easy ways to browse with nearly 300,000 links between related articles. When it is integrated with a word processor it offers creative opportunites to incorporate text, images and sound in reports and other documents

Eyewitness encyclopedia of nature. DK Multimedia, Inc., 95 Madison Avenue, New York, NY 10016 1995 sd., col. $39.95

System requirements for Windows: 386DX or higher; 4MB RAM; Windows 3.1 or higher; SVGA; 8- or 16-bit sound card
System requirements for Macintosh: LC II; 4MB RAM; System 7; SVGA; 8-bit sound card

Covers the behavior of animals in their natural habitat, the calls of birds of prey, environmental systems of the natural world, microscopic life, and the effects of climate. Introduces over 250 plants and animals through video sequences and sound clips

Eyewitness encyclopedia of science. DK Multimedia, Inc., 95 Madison Avenue, New York, NY 10016 1995 sd., col. $39.95

System requirements for Windows: 386DX or higher; 4MB RAM; Windows 3.1 or higher; SVGA; 8- or 16-bit sound card
System requirements for Macintosh: LC II; 4MB RAM; System 7; SVGA; 8-bit sound card

Contains more than 1,700 entries organized into five major categories: Chemistry, Mathematics, Physics, Life Sciences, and Who's Who of Science. Includes full-color photographs, full-motion video sequences, sound clips, and animations

First connections: The Golden Book encyclopedia. Hartley Courseware, 9920 Pacific Heights Blvd. #500, San Diego, CA 92121 1996 sd., col. $79.95

System requirements for Windows: 486; 4MB RAM; 4MB free hard drive space; Windows 3.1 or higher; SVGA; sound card (optional)
System requirements for Macintosh: Color Mac; 4MB RAM; 4MB free hard drive space; System 6.0.7 or higher; SVGA

Students can listen to or read articles, watch short movies, and listen to animal sounds and music selections. On-line audio instructions explain what is on the screen and a built-in notebook allows students to take notes, transfer text from an article, print or save

Grolier multimedia encyclopedia. Version 8.1. Grolier Interactive Inc., 90 Sherman Turnpike, Danbury CT 06816 1996 sd., col. $59.95

System requirements for Windows: 486DX or higher; 8MB RAM for Windows 95 or 4MB for Windows 3.1; 8MB free hard drive space for Windows 95 or 10MB for Windows 3.1; DOS 5.0 or higher; Windows 3.1 or higher or Windows 95; SVGA; sound card; mouse; speakers or headphones; printer (optional)
System requirements for Macintosh: LC III or higher; 5MB RAM; 6MB free hard disk space; System 7.1 or higher; SVGA; printer (optional)
Online access available for both Windows and Macintosh

Contains the full text of the Academic American Encyclopedia. It has over 34,000 new or revised articles, color maps, thousands of pictures, graphs, interactive animation, 3-D models, sounds, videos, a Knowledge Tree, a timeline of world history, "links" by cross-referencing, tables, fact boxes, outlines, bibliographies

Mammals: a multimedia encyclopedia. National Geographic Soc., 1145 17th St. N.W., Washington, D.C. 20036 1993 c1990 sd., col. $69.95

System requirements for DOS: IBM compatible PC; 640K RAM; DOS 3.3 or higher; color monitor; mouse; speakers or headphones
System requirements for Macintosh: Color Mac; 4MB RAM; System 6.0.8 or higher; mouse; speakers or headphones

Mammals: a multimedia encyclopedia—*Continued*

More than 200 animals come to life through 700 full-screen photos, 150 range maps, 150 fact screens, 150 vital statistics screens, 155 authentic vocalizations, 45 full-motion video clips, and many essays. Hypertext leads to cross-references, pronunciations and definitions

Microsoft bookshelf. Microsoft Corp., One Microsoft Way, Redmond, WA 98052 1995 sd., col. $54.95

System requirements for Windows: 486SX or higher; 4MB RAM (8MB recommended); 4MB freehard drive space; Windows 3.1 or higher; SVGA; sound card; mouse; speakers or headphones

System requirements for Macintosh: LC II or higher; 4MB RAM; 4MB free hard disk space; System 7 or higher

A multimedia reference library that provides access to updated versions of The American Heritage Dictionary, The Columbia Dictionary of Quotations, The National Five-Digit Zip Code and Post Office Directory, The Hammond World Atlas, The Original Roget's Thesaurus, The Concise Columbia Encyclopedia, The Peoples' Chronology, and The World Almanac and Book of Facts

Microsoft Encarta *See* Encarta encyclopedia

Multimedia animals encyclopedia. RomTech Inc., 3534 Empleo St., Suite A, San Luis Obispo, CA 93401 1994 sd., col. $59.95

System requirements for Windows: 386SX or higher; 2MB RAM; Windows 3.1 or Windows 95; SVGA; sound card

System requirements for Macintosh: Color Mac; 4MB RAM; 512K VRAM; System 7

Includes illustrations, sounds, correct pronunciations, and cross-referenced facts of 2,000 birds, fish, mammals, reptiles, and amphibians

My first incredible, amazing dictionary 1994 (WIN); 1995 (MAC) sd., col. $29.95

System requirements for Windows: 386DX or higher; 4MB RAM, Windows 3.1 or higher; SVGA; 8- or 16-bit sound card

System requirements for Macintosh: LC II; 4MB RAM; System 7; SVGA; 8-bit sound card

Introduces more than 1,000 words and meanings spoken with text, pictures, sounds and animation

The Presidents: a picture history of our nation. National Geographic Soc., 1145 17th St. N.W., Washington, D.C. 20036 1991 sd., col. $69.95

System requirements for DOS: IBM compatible PC; 640K RAM; DOS 3.3 or higher; color monitor; sound card; mouse; speakers or headphones

This interactive encyclopedia features full-screen captioned photos, video clips of historic moments, text and audio of famous speeches, a multimedia timeline, election maps, and a political party index

The San Diego Zoo presents—The animals!. Version 2.0. Mindscape, 88 Rowland Way, Novato, CA 94945 1994 sd., col. $14.99

System requirements for Windows: 386 (486 recommended); 4MB RAM (8MB recommended); 13MB free hard drive space; DOS 5.0 or higher; Windows 3.1 or higher; SVGA; sound card

System requirements for Macintosh: Power Mac, LC II or higher or Mac II, Performa, or Quadra series; 2.5MB RAM (3MB recommended); 10MB free hard drive space; System 7

Covers hundreds of exotic birds, mammals and reptiles. Includes 120 full-motion videos, photographs, and excellent sound

Simple machines. Science for Kids, Inc., 9950 Concord Church Road, Lewisville, N.C. 27023 1994 sd., col. $129; $199 (teacher's edition with manual)

System requirements for Windows: 386SX or higher; 4MB RAM; DOS 5.0; Windows 3.1 or higher; SVGA; sound card; mouse

System requirements for Macintosh: LC II or higher; 2.5MB RAM; System 6.0.7 or higher; color monitor

Also available English/Spanish edition (MAC only)

This introduction to the physical sciences examines six simple machines: inclined plane, wedge, screw, lever, pulley, and wheel. The program visits six foreign countries to learn how different civilizations progressed through the use of these machines

Small blue planet *See* under Compton's interactive encyclopedia

The ultimate human body. Version 2.0. DK Multimedia, Inc., 95 Madison Avenue, New York, NY 10016 1996 sd., col. $39.95

System requirements for Windows: 386DX or higher; 4MB RAM; Windows 3.1 or higher; SVGA; 8- or 16-bit sound card

System requirements for Macintosh: LC II; 4MB RAM; System 7; SVGA; 8-bit sound card

Three search paths: "The Body Machine," "The Body Organs," and "The Body Systems" make it easy to discover what every part of the human body looks like, where it is situated, what it is called and how it works. Includes microphotography, 3-D images, illustrations, animations, sound and text

DIRECTORY OF PUBLISHERS AND DISTRIBUTORS

21st Cent. Bks. (NY): 21st Cent. Bks., 115 W. 18th St., New York, N.Y. 10011 Tel 212-886-9200 Fax 212-633-0748; refer orders to Henry Holt Distr. Center, 4375 W. 1980 S., Salt Lake City, Utah 84104 Tel 801-972-2221; 800-488-5233 Fax 801-977-9712

Abingdon Press, 201 8th Ave S., P.O. Box 801, Nashville, Tenn. 37202-0801 Tel 615-749-6000; 800-251-3320 (orders) Fax 615-749-6512; 749-6577 (orders)

Abrams: Harry N. Abrams Inc., 100 5th Ave., New York, N.Y. 10011 Tel 212-206-7715; 800-345-1359 Fax 212-645-8437

Adama Bks., P.O. Box 1202, Bellmore, N.Y. 11710-0485 Tel 516-679-1380 Fax 516-679-1448

Addison-Wesley Pub. Co., Jacob Way, Reading, Mass. 01867 Tel 617-944-3700; 800-447-2226 (orders only)

Aladdin Bks. (NY): Aladdin Bks., 1230 Ave. of the Americas, New York, N.Y. 10020 Tel 212-698-7000; 800-257-5755; refer orders to Simon & Schuster Children's Ordering Dept., 200 Old Tappan Rd., Old Tappan, N.J. 07675 Tel 800-223-2336 (orders) Fax 800-445-6991

Alaska Northwest Bks., 2208 N.W. Market St., Suite 300, Seattle, Wash. 98107 Tel 206-784-5071; refer orders to Graphic Arts Center Pub. Co., P.O. Box 10306, Portland, Or. 97210 Tel 503-226-2402; 800-452-3032 Fax 503-223-1410

Amereon Ltd., P.O. Box 1200, Mattituck, N.Y. 11952-9500 Tel 516-298-5100 Fax 516-298-5631

American Assn. for the Advancement of Science, 1333 H St. N.W., 11th Floor, Washington, D.C. 20005 Tel 202-326-6400

American Guidance Service Inc., 4201 Woodland Rd., Circle Pines, Minn. 55014-1796 Tel 612-786-4343; 800-328-2560 Fax 612-786-5603

American Kestrel Press, 500 N. Steamboat Blvd., Steamboat Springs, Colo. 80477-4723 Tel 303-879-1941 Fax 303-879-2086

American Lib. Assn., 50 E. Huron St., Chicago, Ill. 60611 Tel 312-280-2424; 800-545-2433

Andrews & McMeel Inc., 4900 Main St., Kansas City, Mo. 64112 Tel 816-932-6700; 800-826-4216 Fax 816-932-6706

Apple Soup Bks., 201 E. 50th St., New York, N.Y. 10022 Tel 212-751-2600; 800-726-0600

Arcade Pub., 141 5th Ave., New York, N.Y. 10010 Tel 212-475-2633; 800-343-9204 Fax 212-353-8148; refer orders to Little, Brown & Co., 200 West St., Waltham, Mass. 02254 Tel 617-890-0250; 800-343-9204 Fax 617-890-0875

Artists & Writers Guild, 850 3rd Ave., 7th Floor, New York, N.Y. 10022 Tel 212-753-8500; refer orders to 5945 Erie St., Racine, Wis. 53402 Tel 800-225-9514

Association for Childhood Educ. Int., 11501 Georgia Ave., No. 315, Wheaton, Md. 20902-1924 Tel 301-942-2443; 800-423-3563

Association for Educ. Communications & Technology, 1126 16th St. N.W., Washington, D.C. 20036 Tel 202-466-4780

Astor-Honor Inc. Pubs., 48 E. 43rd St., New York, N.Y. 10017

Atheneum Bks. for Young Readers, 1230 Ave. of the Americas, New York, N.Y. 10020 Tel 212-698-7000; 800-223-2348 Fax 800-445-6991; refer orders to Simon & Schuster, 200 Old Tappan Rd., Old Tappan, N.J. 07675 Tel 800-223-2336 (orders) Fax 800-445-6991

Atheneum Pubs., 1230 Ave. of the Americas, New York, N.Y. 10020 Tel 212-698-7000; 800-223-2348 Fax 800-445-6991; refer orders to Simon & Schuster, 200 Old Tappan Rd., Old Tappan, N.J. 07675 Tel 800-223-2336 (orders) Fax 800-445-6991

Atlantic Monthly Press See Grove/Atlantic

August House Inc., P.O. Box 3223, Little Rock, Ark. 72203-3223 Tel 501-372-5450; 800-284-8784 Fax 501-372-5579

Avon Bks., 1350 Ave. of the Americas, 2nd Floor, New York, N.Y. 10019 Tel 212-261-6800; 800-238-0658 Fax 212-261-6895; refer orders to P.O. Box 767, Dresden, Tenn. 38225 Tel 800-223-0690

AVSTAR Pub. Corp., 34C Burlinghoff Lane, P.O. Box 537, Lebanon, N.J. 08833 Tel 908-236-6210

Bantam Bks. Inc., 1540 Broadway, New York, N.Y. 10036 Tel 212-354-6500; 800-323-9872; 800-223-6834 (outside NY) Fax 212-492-9698

Barron's Educ. Ser. Inc., 250 Wireless Blvd., Hauppauge, N.Y. 11788 Tel 516-434-3311; 800-257-5729; 800-645-3476 (outside NY) Fax 516-434-3723

Bedrick Bks.: Peter Bedrick Bks. Inc., 2112 Broadway, Room 318, New York, N.Y. 10023 Tel 212-496-0751 Fax 212-496-1158

Beech Tree Bks., 1350 Ave. of the Americas, New York, N.Y. 10019 Tel 212-261-6500; 800-843-9389 Fax 212-779-0965

Beginner Bks., 201 E. 50th St., New York, N.Y. 10022 Tel 212-751-2600; 800-726-0600 Fax 212-872-8026; refer orders to Random House, 400 Hahn Rd., Westminster, Md. 21157 Tel 410-848-1900; 800-733-3000 Fax 800-659-2436

Bell Bks. (Honesdale): Bell Bks., 815 Church St., Honesdale, Pa. 18431 Tel 717-253-1164; 800-949-7777 Fax 717-253-0179

Black Butterfly Children's Bks., 625 Broadway, Suite 903, New York, N.Y. 10012 Tel 212-982-3158; refer orders to Consortium Bk. Sales & Distr., 287 E. 6th St., Suite 365, St. Paul, Minn. 55101 Tel 612-221-9035; 800-283-3572

Blackbirch Press Inc., 260 Amity Rd., Woodbridge, Conn. 06525 Tel 203-387-7525; 800-831-9183 Fax 203-389-1596

Blue Sky Press (NY): Blue Sky Press, 555 Broadway, New York, N.Y. 10012-3999 Tel 212-343-6100; refer orders to P.O. Box 120, Bergenfield, N.J. 07621 Tel 800-325-6149 (orders only)

Books of Wonder, 132 7th Ave., New York, N.Y. 10011 Tel 212-989-3475; 800-207-6968 Fax 212-989-1203

Bowker: R. R. Bowker Co., 121 Chanlon Rd., New Providence, N.J. 07974 Tel 908-464-6800; 800-521-8110 Fax 908-464-3553; refer orders to Reed Ref. Pub., P.O. Box 31, New Providence, N.J. 07974

Boyds Mills Press, 815 Church St., Honesdale, Pa. 18431 Tel 717-253-1164; 800-949-7777 Fax 717-253-0179

Bradbury Press Inc., 1230 Ave. of the Americas, New York, N.Y. 10020 Tel 212-698-7200; 800-223-2348; refer orders to Simon & Schuster Children's Order Dept., 200 Old Tappan Rd., Old Tappan, N.J. 07675 Tel 800-223-2336 Fax 800-445-6991

BridgeWater Bks., 100 Corporate Dr., Mahwah, N.J. 07430 Tel 201-529-4000; 800-526-5289 Fax 201-529-9347; refer orders to Penguin USA, 375 Hudson St., New York, N.Y. 10014-3657 Tel 212-366-2000; 800-331-4624; 800-253-6476 (orders)

Brodart Co., 500 Arch St., Williamsport, Pa. 17705 Tel 717-326-2461; 800-233-8467

Browndeer Press, P.O. Box 80160, Portland, Or. 97280-1160 Tel 503-452-1795 Fax 503-452-1940

Bullseye Bks., 201 E. 50th St., New York, N.Y. 10022 Tel 212-751-2600; 800-726-0600; refer orders to 400 Hahn Rd., Westminster, Md. 21157 Tel 301-848-2436; 800-733-3000 Fax 800-659-2436

Cahners Pub. Co., 249 W. 17th St., New York, N.Y. 10011 Tel 212-645-0067 Fax 212-463-6560

Cambridge Univ. Press, Edinburgh Bldg., Shaftesbury Rd., Cambridge CB2 2RU, Eng. Tel (01223) 312 393 Fax (01223) 315 052

Branch offices

U.S.: Cambridge Univ. Press, 40 W. 20th St., New York, N.Y. 10011-4211 Tel 212-924-3900; refer orders to 110 Midland Ave., Port Chester, N.Y. 10573-4930 Tel 914-937-9600; 800-872-7423 (orders only) Fax 914-937-4712

Camelot Pub. Co., P.O. Box 1357, Ormond Beach, Fla. 32175-1357 Tel 904-672-5672

Candlewick Press, 2067 Massachusetts Ave., Cambridge, Mass. 02140 Tel 617-661-3330 Fax 617-661-0565; refer orders to Penguin USA, P.O. Box 120, Bergenfield, N.J. 07621-0120 Tel 800-526-0275 Fax 201-385-6521; 800-227-9604

Caroline House (Honesdale): Caroline House, 815 Church St., Honesdale, Pa. 18431 Tel 717-253-1164; 800-949-7777 Fax 717-253-0179

Carolrhoda Bks. Inc., 241 1st Ave. N., Minneapolis, Minn. 55401 Tel 612-332-3344; 800-328-4929 Fax 612-332-7615

Cartwheel Bks., 555 Broadway, New York, N.Y. 10012-3999 Tel 212-343-6100; refer orders to P.O. Box 120, Bergenfield, N.J. 07621 Tel 800-325-6149 (orders only)

Carus Corp., 315 5th St., Peru, Ill. 61354

Charlesbridge Pub., 85 Main St., Watertown, Mass. 02172-4411 Tel 617-926-0329; 800-225-3214

Checkerboard Press, 30 Vesey St., New York, N.Y. 10007 Tel 212-571-6300

Chelsea House Pubs., P.O. Box 914, 1974 Sproul Rd., Suite 400, Broomall, Pa. 19008-0914 Tel 610-353-5166; 800-362-9786 Fax 610-359-1439

Chelsea Jrs., P.O. Box 914, 1974 Sproul Rd., Suite 400, Broomall, Pa. 19008-0914 Tel 610-353-5166; 800-362-9786 Fax 610-359-1439

Chicago Review Press, 814 N. Franklin St., Chicago, Ill. 60610 Tel 312-337-0747; 800-888-4741 (orders only) Fax 312-337-5985

Children's Art Foundation, P.O. Box 83, Santa Cruz, Calif. 95063 Tel 408-426-5557; 800-447-4569

Children's Bk. Council Inc., 568 Broadway, Suite 404, New York, N.Y. 10012 Tel 212-966-1990 Fax 212 966 2073

Children's Bk. Press, 6400 Hollis St., Emeryville, Calif. 94608 Tel 510-655-3395; refer orders to Bookpeople, 7900 Edgewater Dr., Oakland, Calif. 94621 Tel 510-632-4700; 800-999-4650

Childrens Press, Sherman Turnpike, Danbury, Conn. 06801 Tel 203-797-3500

Children's Science Bk. Review Com., 605 Commonwealth Ave., Boston, Mass. 02215

Children's Television Workshop, 1 Lincoln Plaza, New York, N.Y. 10023 Tel 212-595-3456 Fax 212-875-6101

Chronicle Bks., 275 5th St., San Francisco, Calif. 94103 Tel 415-777-7240; 800-445-7577; 800-722-6657 (outside Calif.) Fax 415-777 8887; 800-858-7787 (orders)

Clarion Bks., 215 Park Ave. S., New York, N.Y. 10003 Tel 212-420-5800; refer orders to Houghton Mifflin Co., Wayside Rd., Burlington, Mass. 01803 Tel 617-272-1500; 800-225-3362

Cobblehill Bks., 375 Hudson St., New York, N.Y. 10014-2666 Tel 212-366-2000 Fax 212-366-2020; refer orders to Penguin USA, P.O. Box 999, Dept. 17109, Bergenfield, N.J. 07621 Tel 800-253-6476

Cobblestone Pub. Inc., 7 School St., Peterborough, N.H. 03458 Tel 603-924-7209; 800-821-0115 Fax 603-924-7380

Columbia Univ. Press, 562 W. 113th St., New York, N.Y. 10025 Tel 212-666-1000 Fax 212-316-3100; refer orders to 136 S. Broadway, Irvington, N.Y. 10533 Tel 914-591-9111; 800-944-8648 Fax 914-591-9201; 800-944-1844

Consumers Union of U.S. Inc., 101 Truman Ave., Yonkers, N.Y. 10703 Tel 914-378-2000; 800-272-0722 (orders) Fax 914-378-2901

Contemporary Bks. Inc., 2 Prudential Plaza, Suite 1200, Chicago, Ill. 60601 Tel 312-540-4500; 800-621-1918 Fax 312-540-4687

Copper Beech Bks., 2 Old New Milford Rd., Brookfield, Conn. 06804 Tel 203-740-2220; 800-462-4703 Fax 203-740-8412

Coward-McCann Inc., 200 Madison Ave., New York, N.Y. 10016 Tel 212-951-8400; 800-631-8571; refer orders to 390 Murray Hill Parkway, East Rutherford, N.J. 07073

Coward, McCann & Geoghegan See Coward-McCann

Crabtree Pub. Co., 350 5th Ave., Suite 3308, New York, N.Y. 10118 Tel 212-496-5040; 800-387-7650 Fax 800-355-7166

Creative Art Publs., 301 Riverland Rd., Fort Lauderdale, Fla. 33312 Tel 305-583-9207

Creative Educ. Inc., 123 S. Broad St., P.O. Box 227, Mankato, Minn. 56001 Tel 507-388-6273; 800-445-6209 Fax 507-388-2746

Crowell See HarperCollins Pubs.

Crown Pubs. Inc., 201 E. 50th St., New York, N.Y. 10022 Tel 212-751-2600 Fax 212-572-6192; refer orders to 400 Hahn Rd., Westminster, Md. 21157 Tel 410-848-1900; 800-733-3000 Fax 800-659-2436

Crown Trade Paperbacks, 201 E. 50th St., New York, N.Y. 10022 Tel 212-751-2600 Fax 212-572-6192; refer orders to Random House Inc., 400 Hahn Rd., Westminster, Md. 21157 Tel 410-848-1900; 800-733-3000 Fax 800-659-2436

Delacorte Press, 1540 Broadway, New York, N.Y. 10036 Tel 212-354-6500; 800-221-4676 Fax 212-765-3869

Dell Pub. Co. Inc., 1540 Broadway, New York, N.Y. 10036 Tel 212-354-6500; 800-323-9872; 800-223-6834 (outside NY) Fax 212-492-9698

Dial Bks., 375 Hudson St., New York, N.Y. 10014 Tel 212-366-2000 Fax 212-366-2020; refer orders to Penguin USA, P.O. Box 120, Bergenfield, N.J. 07261 Tel 201-387-0600; 800-526-0275

Dial Bks. for Young Readers, 375 Hudson St., New York, N.Y. 10014 Tel 212-366-2000 Fax 212-366-2020; refer orders to Penguin USA, P.O. Box 120, Bergenfield, N.J. 07261 Tel 201-387-0600; 800-526-0275

Dial Press (NY): The Dial Press, 1540 Broadway, New York, N.Y. 10036 Tel 212-354-6500; 800-323-9872; 800-223-6834 (outside NY) Fax 212-492-9698

Dillon Press, 299 Jefferson Rd., P.O. Box 480, Parsippany, N.J. 07054-0480 Tel 201-739-8000

DK Pub. Inc., 95 Madison Ave., New York, N.Y. 10016 Tel 212-213-4800 Fax 212-213-5240 refer orders to Houghton Mifflin Co., Wayside Rd., Burlington, Mass. 01803 Tel 617-272-1500; 800-225-3362

Dodd, Mead
Out of business; Children's list acquired by Putnam & Grosset Group

Dog Ear Press (The), 132 Water St., Gardiner, Me. 04345 Tel 207-582-1899; refer orders to Consortium Bk. Sales & Distr., 1045 Westgate Dr., Suite 90, St. Paul, Minn. 55114-1065 Tel 612-221-9035; 800-283-3572 Fax 612-221-0124

Dorling Kindersley (US) See DK Pub. Inc.

Doubleday, 1540 Broadway, 18th Floor, New York, N.Y. 10036 Tel 212-354-6500; 800-223-6834 (outside NY); 800-223-5780 (orders) Fax 212-302-7985; 800-258-4233 (orders)

Doubleday Bks. for Young Readers, 1540 Broadway, New York, N.Y. 10036 Tel 212-354-6500; 800-323-9872; 800-223-6834 (outside NY) Fax 212-492-9698

Dover Publs. Inc., 180 Varick St., 9th Floor, New York, N.Y. 10014 Tel 212-255-3755 Fax 212-626-9670; refer orders to 31 E. 2nd St., Mineola, N.Y. 11501 Tel 516-294-7000; 800-223-3130 Fax 516-742-5049

Dutton, 375 Hudson St., New York, N.Y. 10014-3657 Tel 212-366-2000 Fax 212-366-2020; refer orders to Penguin USA, P.O. Box 999, Dept. 17109, Bergenfield, N.J. 07621 Tel 800-253-6476

Dutton Children's Bks., 375 Hudson St., New York, N.Y. 10014 Tel 212-366-2000 Fax 212-366-2020; refer orders to Penguin USA, P.O. Box 120, Bergenfield, N.J. 07261 Tel 201-387-0600; 800-526-0275

Earthworks Press, 1400 Shattuck Ave., Suite 25, Berkeley, Calif. 94709 Tel 510-652-8533 Fax 510-652-8114; refer orders to Publishers Group West, P.O. Box 8843, Emeryville, Calif. 94662 Tel 800-788-3123

Educators Progress Service Inc., 214 Center St., Randolph, Wis. 53956 Tel 414-326-3126

Eight Bit Bks., 462 Danbury Rd., Wilton, Conn. 06897-2125 Tel 203-761-1466; 800-248-8466 Fax 203-761-1444

Encyclopaedia Britannica Inc., 310 S. Michigan Ave., Chicago, Ill. 60604 Tel 312-347-7000; 800-554-9862 Fax 312-294-2191

Enslow Pubs., Box 699, 44 Fadem Rd., Springfield, N.J. 07081-0699 Tel 201-379-8890; 800-398-2504 Fax 201-379-7940

Facts on File Inc., 11 Penn Plaza, New York, N.Y. 10001 Tel 212-967-8800; 800-322-8755 (except Alaska & Hawaii) Fax 212-683-3633; 800-678-3633 (except Alaska & Hawaii)

Farrar, Straus & Giroux Inc., 19 Union Sq. W., New York, N.Y. 10003 Tel 212-741-6900; 800-631-8571 Fax 212-633-9385

Firefly Bks. (Willowdale): Firefly Bks. Ltd., 250 Sparks Ave., Willowdale, Ont., Can. M2H 2S4 Tel 416-499-8412; 800-387-5085; 800-387-6192 (orders only) Fax 416-499-8313; 800-565-6034
Branch offices
U.S.: Firefly Bks. (NY)

Forest House Pub. Co. Inc., 1284 W. Fork Dr., Lake Forest, Ill. 60045 Tel 708-295-8287; 800-394-7323

Forest Press (Albany): Forest Press, 85 Watervliet Ave., Albany, N.Y. 12206 Tel 518-489-8549

Four Winds Press, 1230 Ave. of the Americas, New York, N.Y. 10020 Tel 212-698-7000; 800-257-5755; refer orders to Simon & Schuster Children's Ordering Dept., 200 Old Tappan Rd., Old Tappan, N.J. 07675 Tel 800-223-2336 (orders) Fax 800-445-6991

Free Spirit Pub. Inc., 400 1st Ave. N., Suite 616, Minneapolis, Minn. 55401 Tel 612-338-2068; 800-735-7323 Fax 612-337-5050

Front St., P.O. Box 280, Arden, N.C. 28704 Tel 704-681-0811 Fax 704-681-0508

Fulcrum Pub., 350 Indiana St., Suite 350, Golden, Colo. 80401 Tel 303-277-1623; 800-992-2908 Fax 303-279-7111

Gale Res. Co., 835 Penobscot Bldg., 645 Griswold St., Detroit, Mich. 48226-4094 Tel 313-961-2242 Fax 313-961-6083; refer orders to P.O. Box 33477, Detroit, Mich. 48232-5477 Tel 800-877-4253 Fax 800-414-5043

Gallaudet Univ. Press, 800 Florida Ave. N.E., Washington, D.C. 20002-3625 Tel 202-651-5051; 800-451-1073 Fax 202-651-5489

Gareth Stevens Children's Bks., 1555 N. River Center Dr., River Center Bldg., Suite 201, Milwaukee, Wis. 53212 Tel 414-225-0333; 800-341-3569 Fax 414-225-0377

Garland Pub. Inc., 717 5th Ave., Suite 2500, New York, N.Y. 10022 Tel 212-751-7447 Fax 212-308-9399; refer orders to 1000A Sherman Ave., Hamden, Conn. 06514 Tel 203-281-4487; 800-627-6273 (orders only) Fax 203-230-1186

Godine: David R. Godine Pub., 9 Lewis St., Lincoln, Mass. 01773 Tel 617-259-0700; 800-344-4771 Fax 617-259-9198

Golden Bks., 850 3rd Ave., 7th Floor, New York, N.Y. 10022 Tel 212-753-8500; refer orders to Western Pub. Co. Inc., 1220 Mound Ave., Racine, Wis. 53404 Tel 414-633-2431

Gramercy Bks., 40 Engelhard Ave., Avenel, N.J. 07001 Tel 908-827-2700; 800-223-6804; refer orders to Random House Inc., 400 Hahn Rd., Westminster, Md. 21157 Tel 410-848-1900; 800-733-3000 Fax 800-659-2436

Grant, D.M.: Donald M. Grant Pub. Inc., 19 Surrey Lane, Hampton Falls, N.H. 03844 Tel 603-778-7191; refer orders to Baker & Taylor Bks., 50 Kirby Ave., Somerville, N.J. 08876-0734 Tel 908-722-8000; 800-352-4833; 800-775-2300 (outside N.J.)

Groen, K.: Kendall Green Publs., 800 Florida Ave. N.E., Washington, D.C. 20002 Tel 202-651-5488; 800-451-1073 Fax 202-651-5489

Greenwillow Bks., 1350 Ave. of the Americas, New York, N.Y. 10019 Tel 212-261-6500; 800-237-0657 Fax 212-261-6549; refer orders to William Morrow & Co. Inc., 39 Plymouth St., P.O. Box 1219, Fairfield, N.J. 07007 Tel 800-843-9389

Greenwood Press, 88 Post Rd. W., P.O. Box 5007, Westport, Conn. 06881 Tel 203-226-3571; 800-225-5800 Fax 203-222-1502

Grolier Inc., Sherman Turnpike, Danbury, Conn. 06816 Tel 203-797-3500; 800-356-5590

Grosset & Dunlap Pubs., 200 Madison Ave., New York, N.Y. 10016 Tel 212-951-8400; 800-631-8571 Fax 212-532-3693

Grove/Atlantic, 841 Broadway, New York, N.Y. 10003-4793 Tel 212-614-7850; 800-638-6460 Fax 212-614-7886; refer orders to Publishers Group West, P.O. Box 8843, Emeryville, Calif. 94662 Tel 800-788-3123

Gryphon House, P.O. Box 207, Beltsville, Md. 20704-0207 Tel 301-595-9500; 800-638-0928 Fax 301-595-0051

Harcourt Brace & Co., 1250 6th Ave., San Diego, Calif. 92101 Tel 619-231-6616; 800-543-1918 Fax 800-235-0256

Harcourt Brace College Pubs., 301 Commerce St., Suite 3700, Fort Worth, Tex. 76102; refer orders to 6277 Sea Harbor Dr., Orlando, Fla. 32887 Tel 800-782-4479

Harcourt Brace Jovanovich *See* Harcourt Brace & Co.

Harper & Row See HarperCollins Pubs.

HarperCollins Pubs., 10 E. 53rd St., New York, N.Y. 10022-5299 Tel 212-207-7000; 800-242-7737 Fax 212-207-7145; refer orders to 1000 Keystone Ind. Park, Scranton, Pa. 18512 Tel 717-343-4761; 800-982-4377 Fax 800-822-4090

Heinemann (Portsmouth): Heinemann, 361 Hanover St., Portsmouth, N.H. 03801-3912 Tel 603-431-7894; 800-541-2086 Fax 603-431-7840

Hendrick-Long Pub. Co., 4811 W. Lovers Lane, Dallas, Tex. 75209 Tel 214-358-1677; 800-544-3770 Fax 214-352-4768

Highsmith Press, P.O. Box 800, Highway 106 E., Fort Atkinson, Wis. 53538 Tel 414-563-9571; 800-558-2110 Fax 414-563-7395

Hill & Wang Inc., 19 Union Sq. W., New York, N.Y. 10003 Tel 212-741-6900 Fax 212-741-6973; refer orders to P.O. Box 506, East Rutherford, N.J. 07073 Tel 800-788-6262 Fax 201-933-2316

Hill Bks.: Lawrence Hill Bks., 611 Broadway, Suite 530, New York, N.Y. 10012 Tel 212-260-0576 Fax 212-260-0853; refer orders to Independent Pubs. Group, 814 N. Franklin St., Chicago, Ill. 60610 Tel 312-337-0747; 800-888-4741 Fax 800-337-5985

Holiday House Inc., 425 Madison Ave., New York, N.Y. 10017 Tel 212-688-0085 Fax 212-421-6134; 688-0395 (orders only)

Holt & Co.: Henry Holt & Co., 115 W. 18th St., New York, N.Y. 10011 Tel 212-886-9200 Fax 212-633-0748; refer orders to 4375 W. 1980 S., Salt Lake City, Utah 84104 Tel 800-488-5233 Fax 801-977-9712

Horn Bk. Inc., 14 Beacon St., Boston, Mass. 02108 Tel 617-227-1555; 800-325-1170

Houghton Mifflin Co., 222 Berkeley St., Boston, Mass. 02116 Tel 617-351-5000; refer orders to Wayside Rd., Burlington, Mass. 01803 Tel 617-272-1500; 800-225-3362

Howell Bk. House Inc., 15 Columbus Circle, New York, N.Y. 10023 Tel 212-654-1000 Fax 212-373-8484

Human Sciences Press Inc., 233 Spring St., New York, N.Y. 10013-1578 Tel 212-620-8000; 800-221-9369 Fax 212-807-1047

Humbug Bks., 202 W. Main St., Watertown, Wis. 53094 Tel 414-261-7707; 800-648-6284 Fax 414-261-6026

Hyperion Bks. for Children, 114 5th Ave., New York, N.Y. 10011 Tel 212-633-4400 Fax 212-633-4833; refer orders to Little, Brown & Co. Inc., 200 West St., Waltham, Mass. 02254 Tel 617-890-0250; 800-343-9204 Fax 617-890-0875

Ideals Children's Bks., 1501 County Hospital Rd., Nashville, Tenn. 37218 Tel 615-254-2480; 800-336-6438

International Reading Assn., 800 Barksdale Rd., P.O. Box 8139, Newark, Del. 19714-8139 Tel 302-731-1600; 800-336-7323 (orders) Fax 302-731-1057

Jane Yolen Bks., 525 B St., Suite 1900, San Diego, Calif. 92101 Tel 800-346-8648

Jewish Publ. Soc., 1930 Chestnut St., Philadelphia, Pa. 19103-4599 Tel 215-564-5925; 800-234-3151 Fax 215-564-6640; refer orders to JPS, O'Neil Highway, Dunmore, Pa. 18512 Tel 800-355-1165 Fax 717-348-9297

Kingfisher (NY): Kingfisher, 95 Madison Ave., Suite 1205, New York, N.Y. 10016 Tel 212-686-1060; 800-497-1657 Fax 212-686-1082

Knopf: Alfred A. Knopf Inc., 201 E. 50th St., New York, N.Y. 10022 Tel 212-751-2600; 800-726-0600; refer orders to Random House Inc., 400 Hahn Rd., Westminster, Md. 21157 Tel 410-848-1900; 800-733-3000 Fax 800-659-2436

Ktav Pub. House Inc., 900 Jefferson St., Box 6249, Hoboken, N.J. 07030 Tel 201-963-9524 Fax 201-963-0102

Lee & Low Bks. Inc., 95 Madison Ave., New York, N.Y. 10016 Tel 212-779-4400 Fax 212-683-1894

Lerner Publs. Co., 241 1st Ave. N., Minneapolis, Minn. 55401 Tel 612-332-3344; 800-328-4929 Fax 612-332-7615

Libraries Unlimited Inc., P.O. Box 6633, Englewood, Colo. 80155-6633 Tel 303-770-1200; 800-237-6124 Fax 303-220-8843

Library of Congress, Washington, D.C. 20540 Tel 202-707-6095 Fax 202-707-9898; refer orders to U.S. Govt. Ptg. Office, Washington, D.C. 20402 Tel 202-783-3238

Library of Congress. Natl. Lib. Service for the Blind & Physically Handicapped, 1291 Taylor St. N.W., Washington, D.C. 20542 Tel 202-707-5100

Library Professional Publs., 2 Linsley St., North Haven, Conn. 06473-2517 Tel 203-239-2702 Fax 203-239-2568

Lifetime Bks. (Hollywood): Lifetime Bks. Inc., 2131 Hollywood Blvd., Suite 204, Hollywood, Fla. 33020 Tel 305-925-5242; 800-771-3355 Fax 800-931-7411; refer orders to National Bk. Network, 4720 Boston Way, Lanham, Md. 20706 Tel 301-459-3366; 800-462-6420 Fax 301-459-2118

Linnet Bks., 2 Linsley St., North Haven, Conn. 06473-2517 Tel 203-239-2702 Fax 203-239-2568

Linworth Pub. Inc., 480 E. Wilson Bridge Rd., Suite L, Worthington, Ohio 43085-2372 Tel 614-436-7107 Fax 614-436-9490

Lion Bks., 210 Nelson Rd., Suite B, Scarsdale, N.Y. 10583 Tel 914-725-2280

Lippincott See HarperCollins Pubs.

Little, Brown & Co. Inc., 34 Beacon St., Boston, Mass. 02108 Tel 617-227-0730 Fax 617-227-0790; refer orders to 200 West St., Waltham, Mass. 02254 Tel 617-890-0250; 800-343-9204 Fax 617-890-0875

Little Simon, 1230 Ave. of the Americas, New York, N.Y. 10020 Tel 212-698-7000; 800-257-5755; refer orders to Simon & Schuster Children's Ordering Dept., 200 Old Tappan Rd., Old Tappan, N.J. 07675 Tel 800-223-2336 (orders) Fax 800-445-6991

Lodestar Bks., 375 Hudson St., New York, N.Y. 10014 Tel 212-366-2000 Fax 212-366-2020; refer orders to Penguin USA, P.O. Box 120, Bergenfield, N.J. 07261 Tel 201-387-0600; 800-526-0275

Lothrop, Lee & Shepard Bks., 1350 Ave. of the Americas, New York, N.Y. 10019 Tel 212-261-6500; 800-843-9389 Fax 212-261-6549

Lowell House Juvenile, 2029 Century Park E., Suite 3290, Los Angeles, Calif. 90067 Tel 310-552-7555

Luce, R.B.: Robert B. Luce Inc., 540 Bornum Ave., Bridgeport, Conn. 06608

Lyons & Burford, 31 W. 21st St., New York, N.Y. 10010 Tel 212-620-9580 Fax 212-929-1836

Macmillan, 1633 Broadway, New York, N.Y. 10019 Tel 212-654-3000; refer orders to 201 W. 103rd St., Indianapolis, Ind. 46290 Tel 800-858-7674 Fax 317-871-6728; 800-835-3202

Macmillan Bks. for Young Readers, 1230 Ave. of the Americas, New York, N.Y. 10020 Tel 212-698-7000 Fax 212-698-4350; refer orders to Simon & Schuster, 200 Old Tappan Rd., Old Tappan, N.J. 07675 Tel 800-223-2336 Fax 800-445-6991

Macmillan Educ. Co., 1230 Ave. of the Americas, New York, N.Y. 10020 Tel 212-698-7000 Fax Tappan, N.J. 07675 Tel 800-223-2336 Fax 800-445-6991

Magination Press, 19 Union Sq. W., New York, N.Y. 10003 Tel 212-924-3344; 800-825-3089 (orders) Fax 212-242-6339

Margaret K. McElderry Bks., 1230 Ave. of the Americas, New York, N.Y. 10020 Tel 212-698-7000; 800-257-5755; refer orders to Simon & Schuster Children's Ordering Dept., 200 Old Tappan Rd., Old Tappan, N.J. 07675 Tel 800-223-2336 (orders)

Marshall Cavendish Bks. Ltd., 119 Wardour St., London W1V 3TD, Eng. Tel (0171) 734 6710 Fax (0171) 439 1423

Branch offices

U.S.: Marshall Cavendish Corp., 99 White Plains Rd., Tarrytown, N.Y. 10591-9001 Tel 914-332-8888; 800-821-9881 Fax 914-332-1888

McFarland & Co. Inc. Pubs., P.O. Box 611, Jefferson, N.C. 28640-0611 Tel 910-246-4460; 800-253-2187 (orders only) Fax 910-246-5018

McGraw-Hill Int. Bk. Co., 1221 Ave. of the Americas, New York, N.Y. 10020 Tel 212-512-2000; 800-722-4726; refer orders to McGraw-Hill/Tab Direct Marketing Orders, 860 Taylor Station Rd., Blacklick, Ohio 43004 Tel 800-822-8158 Fax 614-759-3641

Meredith Corp., 1716 Locust St., Des Moines, Iowa 50309-3023 Tel 515-284-3000; 800-678-8091 Fax 515-284-2700

Merriam-Webster Inc., 47 Federal St., P.O. Box 281, Springfield, Mass. 01102 Tel 413-734-3134; 800-828-1880 Fax 413-731-5979

Messner: Julian Messner, 299 Jefferson Rd., P.O. Box 480, Parsippany, N.J. 0754-0480 Tel 201-739-8000

Metropolitan Mus. of Art, 1000 5th Ave., New York, N.Y. 10028 Tel 212-879-5500 Fax 212-535-4830

Millbrook Press Inc. (The), 2 Old New Milford Rd., Brookfield, Conn. 06804-0335 Tel 203-740-2220; 800-462-4703 Fax 203-740-2526; 740-2223 (orders)

Modern Curriculum Press Inc., 13900 Prospect Rd., Cleveland, Ohio 44136 Tel 216-238-2222; 800-321-3106 Fax 216-238-0460

Morrow: William Morrow & Co. Inc., 1350 Ave. of the Americas, New York, N.Y. 10019 Tel 212-261-6500; 800-843-9389 Fax 212-779-0965; refer orders to Wilmor Warehouse, P.O. Box 1219, 39 Plymouth St., Fairfield, N.J. 07007 Tel 201-227-7200

Morrow Junior Bks., 1350 Ave. of the Americas, New York, N.Y. 10019 Tel 212-261-6500; 800-237-0657 Fax 212-261-6689; refer orders to Wilmor Warehouse, P.O. Box 1219, 39 Plymouth St., Fairfield, N.J. 07007 Tel 201-227-7200

Mulberry Bks., 1350 Ave. of the Americas, New York, N.Y. 10019 Tel 212-261-6500; 800-843-9389 Fax 212-779-0965; refer orders to Wilmor Warehouse, P.O. Box 1219, 39 Plymouth St., Fairfield, N.J. 07007 Tel 201-227-7200

Nancy Renfro Studios, P.O. Box 164226, Austin, Tex. 78716 Tel 512-327-9588

National Council of Teachers of English, 1111 W. Kenyon Rd., Urbana, Ill. 61801-1096 Tel 217-328-3870; 800-369-6283 Fax 217-328-9645

National Council of Teachers of Mathematics, 1906 Association Dr., Reston, Va. 22091 Tel 703-620-9840; 800-235-7566 (orders only) Fax 703-476-2970

National Geographic Soc., 1145 17th St. N.W., Washington, D.C. 20036 Tel 202-857-7000; 800-368-2728; refer orders to P.O. Box 1640, Washington, D.C. 20013-9861 Tel 301-921-1200; 800-638-4077

National Science Teachers Assn., 3140 N. Washington Blvd., Arlington, Va. 22201 Tel 703-243-7100 Fax 703-243-7177; refer orders to 1742 Connecticut Ave. N.W., Washington, D.C. 20009 Tel 202-328-5800; 800-722-6782

National Wildlife Federation, 8925 Leesburg Pike, Vienna, Va. 22184 Tel 703-790-4000; 800-432-6564 (orders) Fax 703-442-7332

Neal-Schuman Pubs. Inc., 100 Varick St., New York, N.Y. 10013 Tel 212-925-8650 Fax 212-219-8916; 800-584-2414

Nelson, T.: Thomas Nelson Pubs., P.O. Box 14100, Nashville, Tenn. 37214 Tel 615-889-9000; 800-251-4000 Fax 615-883-7619; 391-5225 (orders)

New Discovery Bks., 299 Jefferson Rd., P.O. Box 480, Parsippany, N.J. 07054-0480 Tel 201-739-8000

New York Public Lib. Astor, Lenox & Tilden Foundations, 5th Ave. & 42nd St., New York, N.Y. 10018 Tel 212-512-0203; refer orders to Publications Office, 8 W. 40th St., 3rd Floor, New York, N.Y. 10018 Tel 212-512-0202

Newmarket Press, 18 E. 48th St., New York, N.Y. 10017 Tel 212-832-3575; 800-669-3903 Fax 212-832-3629; refer orders to Random House Inc., 400 Hahn Rd., Westminster, Md. 21157 Tel 410-848-1900; 800-733-3000 Fax 800-659-2436

North-South Bks., Industriestr. 837, 8625 Gossau, Zurich, Switzerland Tel (01) 9351335 Fax (01) 9351700

Branch offices

U.S.: North-South Bks., 1123 Broadway, Suite 800, New York, N.Y. 10010 Tel 212-463-9736; 800-282-8257 Fax 212-633-1004

Ohio State Univ., 190 N. Oval Mall, Columbus, Ohio 43210 Tel 614-292-6446

Oliver Press Inc. (The), Charlotte Sq., 5707 W. 36th St., Minneapolis, Minn. 55416-2510 Tel 612-926-8981; 800-865-4837 Fax 612-926-8965

Orchard Bks., 95 Madison Ave., 7th Floor, New York, N.Y. 10016 Tel 212-951-2600; 800-621-1115 Fax 212-213-6435

Oryx Press (The), 4041 N. Central Ave., No. 700, Phoenix, Ariz. 85012-3397 Tel 602-265-2651; 800-279-6799 Fax 602-265-6250; 800-279-4663

Overlook Press (The), 149 Wooster St., 4th Floor, New York, N.Y. 10012 Tel 212-477-7162 Fax 212-477-7525; refer orders to 2568 Route 212, Woodstock, N.Y. 12498 Tel 914-679-6838 Fax 914-679-8571

Owen, R.C.: Richard C. Owen Pubs. Inc., P.O. Box 585, Katonah, N.Y. 10536 Tel 914-232-3903; 800-336-5588 Fax 914-232-3977

Oxford Univ. Press, Walton St., Oxford OX2 6DP, Eng. Tel (01865) 56767 Fax (01865) 56646

Branch offices

U.S.: Oxford Univ. Press Inc., 198 Madison Ave., New York, N.Y. 10016-4314 Tel 212-726-6000; 800-334-4249 Fax 212-725-2972; refer orders to 2001 Evans Rd., Cary, N.C. 27513 Tel 919-677-1303; 800-451-7556 Fax 919-677-1303

Pantheon Bks. Inc., 201 E. 50th St., New York, N.Y. 10022 Tel 212-872-8238; 800-638-0600 Fax 212-572-6030; refer orders to Random House Inc., 400 Hahn Rd., Westminster, Md. 21157 Tel 410-848-1900; 800-733-3000 Fax 800-659-2436

Parents' Choice Foundation, P.O. Box 185, Waban, Mass. 02168 Tel 617-965-5913

Parents Mag. Press (The), 685 3rd Ave., New York, N.Y. 10017 Tel 212-878-8700 Fax 212-286-0935; refer orders to Putnam Pub. Group, 390 Murray Hill Parkway, East Rutherford, N.J. 07073

Parnassus Press, P.O. Box 8443, Emeryville, Calif. 94608

Peachtree Pubs. Ltd., 494 Armour Circle N.E., Atlanta, Ga. 30324-4088 Tel 404-876-8761; 800-241-0113 Fax 404-875-2578; 800-875-8909

Pelican Pub. Co. Inc., P.O. Box 3110, Gretna, La. 70054 Tel 504-368-1175; 800-843-1724 (orders only) Fax 504-368-1195

Penguin Bks. See Penguin USA

Penguin USA, 375 Hudson St., New York, N.Y. 10014 Tel 212-366-2000; refer orders to Penguin USA, P.O. Box 120, Bergenfield, N.J. 07621 Tel 201-387-0600; 800-526-0275

Perlman Bks.: Willa Perlman Bks., c.o. HarperCollins Pubs., 10 E. 53rd St., New York, N.Y. 10022-5299 Tel 212-207-7000; 800-331-3761 Fax 212-207-7145; refer orders to 1000 Keystone Ind. Park, Scranton, Pa. 18512 Tel 717-343-4761; 800-982-4377; 800-242-7737 (outside Pa.) Fax 800-822-4090

Phillips: S. G. Phillips Inc., P.O. Box 83, Chatham, N.Y. 12037 Tel 518-392-3068

Philomel Bks., 200 Madison Ave., New York, N.Y. 10016 Tel 212-951-8400; 800-631-8571; refer orders to 390 Murray Hill Parkway, East Rutherford, N.J. 07073

Picture Bk. Studio, 1230 Ave. of the Americas, New York, N.Y. 10020 Tel 212-698-7000; 800-257-5755; refer orders to Simon & Schuster Children's Ordering Dept., 200 Old Tappan Rd., Old Tappan, N.J. 07675 Tel 800-223-2336 (orders) Fax 800-445-6991

Pippin Press, 229 E. 85th St., Gracie Station, P.O. Box 1347, New York, N.Y. 10028 Tel 212-288-4920 Fax 908-225-1562

Platt & Munk Pubs., 200 Madison Ave., New York, N.Y. 10016 Tel 212-951-8700 Fax 212-532-3693; refer orders to 390 Murray Hill Parkway, East Rutherford, N.J. 07073

Plays Inc., 120 Boylston St., Boston, Mass. 02116 Tel 617-423-3157 Fax 617-423-2168

Pocket Bks., Simon & Schuster Bldg., 1230 Ave. of the Americas, New York, N.Y. 10020 Tel 212-698-7000; 800-223-2348 Fax 800-445-6991; refer orders to Simon & Schuster Inc., 200 Old Tappan Rd., Old Tappan, N.J. 07675 Tel 201-767-5937; 800-223-2336

Potter: Clarkson N. Potter Inc. Pubs., 201 E. 50th St., New York, N.Y. 10022 Tel 212-751-2600 Fax 212-572-6192; refer orders to Random House Inc., 400 Hahn Rd., Westminster, Md. 21157 Tel 410-848-1900; 800-733-3000 Fax 800-659-2436

Prentice-Hall Inc., 1 Lake St., Upper Saddle River, N.J. 07428 Tel 201-236-7000; refer orders to Prentice-Hall/Allyn & Bacon, 200 Old Tappan Rd., Old Tappan, N.J. 07675 Tel 800-223-1360 Fax 800-445-6991

Puffin Bks., 27 Wright's Lane, London W8 5TZ, Eng. Tel (0171) 416 3000 Fax (0171) 416 3099; refer orders to Penguin Bks. Ltd., Bath Rd., Harmondsworth, W. Drayton, Middlesex UB7 0DA, Eng. Tel (0181) 899 4000 Fax (0181) 899 4099

Branch offices

U.S.: Puffin Bks., 375 Hudson St., New York, N.Y. 10014-3657 Tel 212-366-2000

Putnam: G. P. Putnam's Sons, 200 Madison Ave., New York, N.Y. 10016 Tel 212-951-8400; 800-631-8571; refer orders to 390 Murray Hill Parkway, East Rutherford, N.J. 07073

Putnam & Grosset Group, 200 Madison Ave., New York, N.Y. 10016 Tel 212-951-8400; 800-631-8571; refer orders to 390 Murray Hill Parkway, East Rutherford, N.J. 07073

R & S Bks., Tegnérgatan 28, Stockholm, Sweden Tel (08) 349960 Fax (08) 344971; refer orders to P.O. Box 45022, 104 30 Stockholm, Sweden

Distributors

U.S.: Farrar, Straus & Giroux

Rabbit Ears Bks., 1230 Ave. of the Americas, New York, N.Y. 10020 Tel 212-698-7000; 800-223-2336 (orders only)

Raintree Steck-Vaughn Pubs., 466 Southern Blvd., Chatham, N.J. 07928 Tel 201-514-1525 Fax 201-514-1612; refer orders to P.O. Box 26105, Austin, Tex. 78755 Tel 800-531-5015

Rand McNally, P.O. Box 7600, Chicago, Ill. 60080 Tel 708-673-9100 Fax 708-673-0813

Random House Inc., 201 E. 50th St., 22nd Floor, New York, N.Y. 10022 Tel 212-751-2600; 800-726-0600; refer orders to 400 Hahn Rd., Westminster, Md. 21157 Tel 410-848-1900; 800-733-3000 Fax 800-659-2436

Reader's Digest Assn. Inc. (The), 260 Madison Ave., New York, N.Y. 10016 Tel 212-850-7007 Fax 212-850-7079; refer orders to Reader's Digest Rd., Pleasantville, N.Y. 10570 Tel 800-431-1246 Fax 914-238-7620

Rizzoli Int. Publs. Inc., 300 Park Ave. S., New York, N.Y. 10010 Tel 212-387-3400; 800-462-2387 Fax 212-387-3535; refer orders to St. Martin's Press Inc., 175 5th Ave., Room 1715, New York, N.Y. 10010 Tel 212-674-5151; 800-221-7945 Fax 212-420-9314

Roberts Rinehart Pubs., 5455 Spine Rd., Mezzanine W., Boulder, Colo. 80301 Tel 303-530-4400; 800-352-1985 Fax 303-530-4488; refer orders to Publishers Group West, P.O. Box 8843, Emeryville, Calif. 94662 Tel 800-788-3123

Runestone Press, 241 1st Ave. N., Minneapolis, Minn. 55401 Tel 612-332-3344; 800-328-4929 Fax 612-332-7615

Sams, 201 W. 103rd St., Indianapolis, Ind. 46290 Tel 317-573-3500; 800-545-5914 Fax 800-876-9371 (orders)

Scarecrow Press Inc., 52 Liberty St., P.O. Box 4167, Metuchen, N.J. 08840 Tel 908-548-8600; 800-462-6420 Fax 908-548-5767

Schocken Bks. Inc., 201 E. 50th St., New York, N.Y. 10022 Tel 212-572-2559; 800-726-0600 Fax 212-572-6030; refer orders to Random House Inc., 400 Hahn Rd., Westminster, Md. 21157 Tel 410-848-1900; 800-733-3000 Fax 800-659-2436

Scholastic Inc., 555 Broadway, New York, N.Y. 10012-3999 Tel 212-343-6100; refer orders to P.O. Box 120, Bergenfield, N.J. 07621 Tel 800-325-6149 (orders only)

Scientific Am. Bks. for Young Readers, 41 Madison Ave., New York, N.Y. 10010 Tel 212-576-9400; refer orders to W. H. Freeman & Co., 4419 W. 1980 S., Salt Lake City, Utah 84104 Tel 801-973-4660; 800-877-5351 Fax 801-977-9712

Scott, Foresman & Co., 1900 E. Lake Ave., Glenview, Ill. 60025 Tel 708-729-3000

Scribner See Simon & Schuster

Scroll Press Inc., 2858 Valerie Ct., Merrick, N.Y. 11566

Seabury Press (The), HarperCollins Pubs., 10 E. 53rd St., New York, N.Y. 10022-5299 Tel 212-207-7000

Sierra Club Bks., 100 Bush St., 13th Floor, San Francisco, Calif. 94103 Tel 415-291-1600 Fax 415-291-1602; refer orders to Random House Inc., 400 Hahn Rd., Westminster, Md. 21157 Tel 410-848-1900; 800-733-3000 Fax 800-659-2436

Sierra Club Bks. for Children, 100 Bush St., 13th Floor, San Francisco, Calif. 94103 Tel 415-291-1619 Fax 415-291-1602; refer orders to Sierra Club Store, 730 Polk St., San Francisco, Calif. 94109 Tel 415-923-5500; 800-935-1056 (credit card orders) Fax 415-776-0350

Silver Burdett Press, 299 Jefferson Rd., P.O. Box 480, Parsippany, N.J. 07054-0480 Tel 201-739-8000

Silver Moon Press, 126 5th Ave., Suite 803, New York, N.Y. 10011 Tel 212-242-6499 Fax 212-242-6799; refer orders to August House, P.O. Box 3223, Little Rock, Ark. 72203-3223 Tel 501-372-5450; 800-284-8784 Fax 501-372-5579

Silver Press, 299 Jefferson Rd., P.O. Box 480, Parsippany, N.J. 07054-0480 Tel 201-739-8000

Simon & Schuster Inc. Pubs., Simon & Schuster Bldg., 1230 Ave. of the Americas, New York, N.Y. 10020 Tel 212-698-7000; 800-223-2348; refer orders to Simon & Schuster, 200 Old Tappan Rd., Old Tappan, N.J. 07675 Tel 800-223-2336 (orders) Fax 800-445-6991

Simon & Schuster Bks. for Young Readers, 1230 Ave. of the Americas, New York, N.Y. 10020 Tel 212-698-7000; 800-257-5755; refer orders to Simon & Schuster Children's Ordering Dept., 200 Old Tappan Rd., Old Tappan, N.J. 07675 Tel 800-223-2336 (orders) Fax 800-445-6991

Smith, P.: Peter Smith Pub., Inc., 5 Lexington Ave., Magnolia, Mass. 01930 Tel 508-525-3562

St. James Press, c.o. Gale Res. Inc., 835 Penobscot Bldg., Detroit, Mich. 48226-4094 Tel 313-961-2242; 800-877-4253 Fax 313-961-6083

St. Martin's Press Inc., 175 5th Ave., Room 1715, New York, N.Y. 10010 Tel 212-674-5151; 800-221-7945 Fax 212-420-9314

Steck-Vaughn See Raintree Steck-Vaughn Pubs.

Stemmer House Pubs. Inc., 2627 Caves Rd., Owings Mills, Md. 21117 Tel 410-363-3690; 800-645-6958 (orders) Fax 410-363-8459

Sterling Pub. Co. Inc., 387 Park Ave. S., New York, N.Y. 10016-8810 Tel 212-532-7160; 800-367-9692 Fax 212-213-2495; 800-542-7567

Stevens, G.: Gareth Stevens Inc., 1555 N. River Center Dr., River Center Bldg., Suite 201, Milwaukee, Wis. 53212 Tel 414-225-0333; 800-341-3569

Stewart, Tabori & Chang Inc., 575 Broadway, 6th Floor, New York, N.Y. 10012 Tel 212-941-2929 Fax 212-941-2982; refer orders to Publisher Resources Inc., 1224 Heil Quaker Blvd., P.O. Box 7001, La Vergne, Tenn. 37086-7001 Tel 615-793-5090; 800-937-5557

Stravon Educ. Press, 845 3rd Ave., New York, N.Y. 10022 Tel 212-371-2880

TAB Bks., P.O. Box 40, Blue Ridge Summit, Pa. 17294-0850 Tel 717-794-2191; 800-233-1128 Fax 717-794-2080

Tambourine Bks., 1350 Ave. of the Americas, New York, N.Y. 10019 Tel 212-261-6500; 800-237-0657 Fax 212-261-6549

Taylor Productions Ltd., 250 W. 24th St., New York, N.Y. 10011 Tel 212-425-3466; refer orders to The Talman Co. Inc., 131 Spring St., Suite 201E-N, New York, N.Y. 10012 Tel 212-431-7175

Teacher Ideas Press, P.O. Box 6633, Englewood, Colo. 80155-6633 Tel 303-770-1200; 800-237-6124 Fax 303-220-8843

Teachers College Press, Teachers College, Columbia Univ., 1234 Amsterdam Ave., New York, N.Y. 10027 Tel 212-678-3929 Fax 212-678-4149; refer orders to P.O. Box 20, Williston, Vt. 05495-0020 Tel 800-488-2665 Fax 802-864-7626

Thames & Hudson Ltd., 30 Bloomsbury St., London WC1B 3QP, Eng. Tel (0171) 636 5488 Fax (0171) 636 1695; refer orders to 44 Clockhouse Rd., Farnborough, Hampshire GU14 7QZ, Eng. Tel (01252) 541 602 Fax (01252) 377 380

Branch offices

U.S.: Thames & Hudson Inc., 500 5th Ave., New York, N.Y. 10110 Tel 212-354-3763 Fax 212-398-1252; refer orders to W. W. Norton & Co. Inc., 500 5th Ave., New York, N.Y. 10110 Tel 212-354-5500; 800-233-4830 (orders) Fax 212-398-1252; 800-458-6515 (orders)

Thomasson-Grant Pub., 1 Morton Dr., Charlottesville, Va. 22903-6806 Tel 804-977-1780; 800-999-1780 Fax 804-977-1696

Ticknor & Fields, 215 Park Ave. S., New York, N.Y. 10003 Tel 212-420-5800; 800-225-3362 Fax 212-420-5855; refer orders to Houghton Mifflin Co., Wayside Rd., Burlington, Mass. 01803 Tel 617-272-1500; 800-225-3362

Ticknor & Fields Bks. for Young Readers, 215 Park Ave. S., New York, N.Y. 10003 Tel 212-420-5800; 800-225-3362 Fax 212-420-5850; refer orders to Wayside Rd., Burlington, Mass. 01803 Tel 617-272-1500; 800-225-3362

Tilbury House, 132 Water St., Gardiner, Me. 04345 Tel 207-582-1899; refer orders to Consortium Bk. Sales & Distr., 1045 Westgate Dr., Suite 90, St. Paul, Minn. 55114-1065 Tel 612-221-9035; 800-283-3572 Fax 612-221-0124

Time Inc., Time & Life Bldg., 1271 Ave. of the Americas, New York, N.Y. 10020 Tel 212-586-1212

Times Bks., 201 E. 50th St., New York, N.Y. 10022 Tel 212-751-2600; 800-726-0600; refer orders to Random House Inc., 400 Hahn Rd., Westminster, Md. 21157 Tel 410-848-1900; 800-733-3000 Fax 800-659-2436

Tundra Bks. Inc., 345 Victoria Ave., Suite 604, Montreal, Que., Can. H3Z 2N2 Tel 514-932-5434 Fax 514-484-2152; refer orders to University of Toronto Press, 5201 Dufferin St., Downsview, Ont., Can. M3H 5T8 Tel 416-667-7791; 800-565-9523 Fax 416-667-7832
Subsidiaries
U.S.: Tundra Bks. of Northern N.Y.

Turner Pub. (Atlanta): Turner Pub. Inc., 1050 Techwood Dr. N.W., Atlanta, Ga. 30318 Tel 404-885-4038 Fax 404-885-4066; refer orders to Andrews & McMeel Inc., 4900 Main St., Kansas City, Mo. 64112 Tel 816-932-6700; 800-826-4216 Fax 816-932-6706

Tuttle: Charles E. Tuttle Co. Inc., 153 Milk St., Boston, Mass. 02109 Tel 617-951-4080 Fax 617-951-4045; refer orders to P.O. Box 410, Rutland, Vt. 05702-0410 Tel 802-773-8930; 800-526-2778 Fax 802-773-6993; 800-329-8885

U.X.L, 835 Penobscot Bldg., Detroit, Mich. 48226-4094 Tel 313-961-2242; 800-877-4253 Fax 313-961-6348

University of Calif. Press, 2120 Berkeley Way, Berkeley, Calif. 94720 Tel 510-642-4247; 800-777-4726 Fax 510-642-7127

University of Chicago Press, 5801 S. Ellis Ave., 4th Floor, Chicago, Ill. 60637 Tel 312-702-7700 Fax 312-702-9756; refer orders to 11030 S. Langley Ave., Chicago, Ill. 60628 Tel 312-568-1550; 800-621-2736 Fax 312-660-2235; 800-621-8476

University of Hawaii Press, 2840 Kolowalu St., Honolulu, Hawaii 96822 Tel 808-956-8694; 956-8255 (orders); 800-956-2840 (orders) Fax 808-988-6052; 800-650-7811 (orders)

University of Ill. Press, 1325 S. Oak St., Champaign, Ill. 61820 Tel 217-244-4689 Fax 217-244-8082; refer orders to P.O. Box 4856, Hampden Post Office, Baltimore, Md. 21211 Tel 800-545-4703 Fax 410-516-6969

Vanguard Press Inc., 424 Madison Ave., New York, N.Y. 10017 Tel 212-753-3906

Viking See Penguin USA

Viking Kestrel See Penguin USA

Viking Penguin See Penguin USA

Walker & Co., 435 Hudson St., New York, N.Y. 10014 Tel 212-727-8300; 800-289-2553 Fax 212-727-0984

Wanderer Bks., Simon & Schuster Bldg., 1230 Ave. of the Americas, New York, N.Y. 10020 Tel 212-245-6400; 800-223-2336

Warne: Frederick Warne & Co. Ltd., 27 Wright's Lane, London W8 5TZ, Eng. Tel (071) 938 2200 Fax (071) 937 8704
Branch offices
U.S.: Warne, 375 Hudson St., New York, N.Y. 10014 Tel 212-366-2000 Fax 212-366-2020; refer orders to Penguin USA, P O Box 999, Dept. 17109, Bergenfield, N.J. 07621 Tel 800-253-6476

Watts: Franklin Watts Inc., 95 Madison Ave., New York, N.Y. 10016 Tel 212-951-2650 Fax 212-689-7803; refer orders to 5450 N. Cumberland Ave., Chicago, Ill. 60656-1484 Tel 800-672-6672 Fax 800-374-4329

Webster's New World, 1633 Broadway, New York, N.Y. 10019 Tel 212-654-3000; refer orders to 201 W. 103rd St., Indianapolis, Ind. 46290 Tel 800-858-7674 Fax 317-871-6728; 800-835-3202

Whitman, A.: Albert Whitman & Co., 6340 Oakton St., Morton Grove, Ill. 60053 Tel 708-581-0033; 800-255-7675 Fax 708-581-0039

Wiley: John Wiley & Sons Inc., 605 3rd Ave., New York, N.Y. 10158-0012 Tel 212-850-6000; 800-225-5945 (orders) Fax 212-850-6088; refer orders to 1 Wiley Dr., Somerset, N.J. 08873-1272 Tel 908-469-4400; 800-879-4539 Fax 908-302-2300

Williamson Pub. Co., P.O. Box 185, Church Hill Rd., Charlotte, Vt. 05445 Tel 802-425-2102; 800-234-8791 Fax 802-425-2199

Wilson, H.W.: The H. W. Wilson Co., 950 University Ave., Bronx, N.Y. 10452 Tel 718-588-8400; 800-367-6770 Fax 718-590-1617

Wordsong, 815 Church St., Honesdale, Pa. 18431 Tel 717-253-1164; 800-949-7777 Fax 717-253-0179

World Almanac, 1 International Blvd., Mahwah, N.J. 07495-0017 Tel 201-529-6900 Fax 201-529-6901

World Assn. of Girl Guides & Girl Scouts, 132 Ebury St., London SW1W 9QQ, Eng.

World Bk. Inc., 525 W. Monroe, 20th Floor, Chicago, Ill. 60661 Tel 312-258-3700; 800-621-8202 Fax 312-258-3950

Young Naturalist Foundation, 59 Front St. E., Toronto, Ont., Can. M5E 1B3

Zoological Soc. of San Diego, P.O. Box 551, San Diego, Calif. 92112